Bud Collins
TOTALTennis
The Ultimate Tennis Encyclopedia

For Billie Jean Moffitt King, Mother Freedom of tennis.
　She's been nurturing the sport with passionate performances on court (and beyond) for so long that its name should probably be changed to Billieball.

And for Anita Ruthling Klaussen, a Champion of cohabitation.
　Her inspiration, perspiration, determination, participation as my loving caretaker keeps me functioning.

—Bud Collins

Acknowledgements

Will anyone suffer hernia from lifting this tome? I hope not. But I do know that I've suffered little in pulling it together because of so many helpful lifts from a variety of contributors and sources. First on my list of thank-you's is, of course, that good old English boy, Major Wingfield, from whose brain this marvelous game arched like a lob onto a patent in London in 1874. You may stop by Kensall Green Cemetery to pay your respects.

Hail, hail—there's a gang here without whom I would feel herniated. Those venerable historian/researcher guys, Frank Phelps and George Alexander have dug for facts so well. Gone to the celestial centre court, Hall of Fame journalists Allison Danzig of the *New York Times*, and Lance Tingay of London's *Daily Telegraph*, are also interred here in their lasting words. So are writers yet extant: Ubiquitous Barry "Orso" Lorge, Steve Flink from *Tennis Week* and CBS Radio, Joe Gergen and Stan Isaacs from *Newsday*, UPI alum Marty Lader, Joel Drucker.

The world has been my oyster in this stew with aid coming from David Studham, librarian extraordinaire of the Melbourne Cricket Club; John Lindsay of Tennis Australia; John Treleven and Nick Imison of the ITF, London; Giovanni Clerici of Mattonaio Italico; David Newman, Randy Walker, Arlen Kantarian of the USTA; Fern Kellmeyer, Vani Vosburgh, Amy Binder, Darrell Fry, Gina Capulong of the WTA; the sharp shark of Ponte Vedra, Greg Sharko, J.J. Carter, Bill Norris, Doug Spreen of the ATP; Mark Young, Mark Stenning, Tony Trabert of the International Hall of Fame; John Barrett of the BBC; Robert Geist, the authoritative Austrian.

Huzzahs also to: Russo Adamo, Neil Amdur, Arthur Ashe, Cugino Basche, Bob Beach, Andrew Blauner, Philippe Bouin, Ron Bookman, Butch Buchholz, Mary Carillo, Rosie Casals, Chris Clarey, Yannick Cochennec, Matt Cronin, Alain Deflassieux, Donald Dell, Lisa Dillman, Bob Dunbar, Bill Dwyre, Dick Ebersol, Judith Elian, Dick Enberg, Elizabeth Erbafina, Ashley Evans, "Hurricane Donna" Fales, Igor Federovsky, John Feinstein, Dee Dee Felich, the Furgalians, Greg Harney, Sandra Harwitt, Julie Hatfield, Gladys and Julius Heldman, Ed Hickey, Phyllis and Zander Hollander, Mike Humphrey, Nagger Ives, Elizabeth and David Kahn, Bob Kelleher, the Killius Kittens (Betsy, Greta, Kristin, Sharon), Harry Kirsch, Danielle Klaussen, Karl H.R. Klaussen, Rob Lacy, Larry Lawrence, C.A. Timothy Leland, Michelino Lupica, C. Gene Mako, Laura and Suzanna Mathews, Geoff Mason, Steve Mayer, Paul Metzler, Pop Merrihew, Murray the Wrench, Roberto Nappo, Ted Nathanson, Archbishop Parsons, Charlie Pasarell, Author Phillips, Warren Pick, S.L. Price, John Roberts, Emily Rooney, Guillermo Salatino, Ronaldo E.Y. Sampson, Jimmy Scalem, Ubaldo Scanagatta, Ken Schanzer, Adam Scharff, Francisco Segura, Fred Sharf, Sam Silverman, Michel Sutter, Bill Talbert, Rooms Tebbutt, Rino Tommasi, David Tratner, Alan Trengove, Candy and Jimmy Van Alen, Vivacious Visser & Stoic Stockton, Hazel Wightman, Tom Winship, R.B.D.H. Wogan.

I'm particularly indebted to Joe and Rose McCauley for their book, *The History of Professional Tennis*. Many thanks. Couldn't have done it without you.

—Bud Collins

Bud Collins
TOTALTennis
The Ultimate Tennis Encyclopedia

SPORT CLASSIC BOOKS

www.sportclassicbooks.com

For information about permission to reproduce selections from this book, please write to:

Permissions
Sport Media Publishing, Inc.,
21 Carlaw Ave.,
Toronto, Ontario, Canada, M4M 2R6
www.sportclassicbooks.com

Cover design: Paul Hodgson / pHd
Front cover photo of Serena Williams: Siggi Bucher
Back cover photo of Pancho Gonzalez: Neil Leifer, The SPORT Collection
Interior design and layout : Paul Hodgson / pHd, Greg Oliver and John Pasternak

ISBN: 0-9731443-4-3

Library of Congress Control Number: 2002116809

Printed in United States of America

Table of Contents

Table of Contents

Martina Navratilova, 2003 At age 46, a 57th Grand Slam title, in mixed doubles with Leander Paes at the Australian Open.

Introduction

Can a mere patch of grass in southwest London be a world of its own? This one is. A playground somberly walled in dull green and yet, surrounded by crowded galleries, it might remind the scribbler, Shakespeare, of his own playhouse, the Globe. Similarly open to the elements, it, too, is the scene of countless dramas—of kings and queens rising and falling.

It is called Centre Court, the planetary heart of a game known as tennis, in the precinct of Wimbledon—a territory often lamentably posing as the rain forest of England. Although Shakespeare pre-dated Wimbledon by centuries, he was acquainted with tennis, even penned a bit making fun of King Henry V in the play of that name.

In a sarcastic "Balls to you!" gesture, the Dauphin of France sends Henry a box of tennis balls, suggesting that the young king is more playboy than warrior. Henry responds by going on the road to break the dauphin's serve and France's nerve at the battle of Agincourt.

Though nothing as perilous as Agincourt takes place at Centre Court, the battles result in an afternoon's triumph or disaster, and become indelible in these pages. Unlike the Bard's, these dramas, played out in all corners of the earth, in one tournament or another, are unscripted. To be or not to be ain't known until the very end.

They can provoke unbearable suspense and passages of high tension, but not tragedy—unless you feel that label can be attached to a moment of elastic betrayal on Centre Court one afternoon in the 1920s. "Zing!" went the snapped waistband string, a prelude to the involuntary descent of the knickers (as that apparel is termed by Brits) belonging to future Hall of Famer Betty Nuthall. Betty, a jolly young thing, kept her chin up anyway, recovered, and would become in 1930 the first Englishwoman to win the U.S. championship.

She was not quite as open, as devil-may-care, on Centre as Melissa Johnson—a pale streak—decades later in the 1996 final. Actually as the overture to the final (contested by champ-to-be Richard Krajicek and MaliVai Washington), when Melissa raced across the green fully unencumbered by attire. The resulting furor probably would have been considered much ado about nothingness by Shakespeare. He might have applauded it as an opening scene he wished he'd thought up, fashioning her as a sort of Godiva of the green.

Years before I'd ever sat at Centre Court, well before I was even aware of its existence, my own courts of dreams lay about 50 yards behind our house in a small Ohio town. Laid out on a bumpy, cracked, dirt flat, four of them, they belonged to the local college, set behind the sandstone gym whose lofty fire escape was my sky box. This was about the same time that something more harmful than knickers—German bombs—fell on Centre Court. The sounds of tennis—my summertime alarm clock—were explosive in their way: the PUH! PUH! PUH! of balls responding to swats, or jangling against wire fences.

It was a nice way to wake up, and I longed to play on those courts. Sometimes I did, but they were usually busy from daylight to dark with grown-ups. Kids squintingly struggled with dusk.

Armed with hand-me-downs—bald, overly-abused balls, and rackets, not infrequently broken-stringed—we slashed and bashed at each other, and felt it was a pretty good game.

My favorite racket, borrowed from older neighbor Edith Reublin, was a wooden sky blue implement entitled, mysteriously, Onwentsia. Was that the name of a famed bygone champ? I coveted Edith's more valued Ellsworth Vines model, bearing the picture of Vines, once world No. 1, on the throat. (Sadly the advent of open-throated rackets has eliminated personalized artwork, visages of such immortals as Jack Kramer, Alice Marble, Little Mo Connolly and Pancho Gonzalez.)

Edith wasn't letting Vines out of her sight. Still, I was happy with Onwentsia, which I learned, long after, was the name of a Chicago tennis club, not a Spanish or Italian Davis Cup hero.

Those courts became a tragedy, at least in my eyes, casualties of war: victims not of bombs, but a patriotic steam shovel. The college, directed by the government to train naval officers during World War II, lacked a swimming pool. Somehow the War Department felt that knowing how to swim was more important to naval officers than a knowledge of tennis. Presto, change-o— the courts were gone, and so was my early tennis career. Hardly a loss to the game.

Not that I lost out entirely. Tennis survived as my lonely passion, played against myself by banging balls at a brick wall of the nearby elementary school. Sure, the wall always won. But, without knowing it, I was hooked, afflicted by a *jones*, an addiction. Maybe we should pin this *jones*, this tennis dependency of mine—and innumerable others—on a Jones called Henry.

Dr. Henry Jones, a 19th century London M.D., may or may not have known much about obstetrics, but shouldn't we blame him for delivering this bouncing baby, baptized Tennis, which turns a healthy 129 in 2003? No, he wasn't the patriarch. That role belonged to a retired British army office, Major Walter Clopton Wingfield, patenting, in 1874, his outdoor variation on the ages-old tennis theme that Shakespeare alluded to in *Henry V*. It was also relished by 'London Fats' himself, King Henry VIII, whose private playroom is yet in use at Hampton Court Palace.

Anyway, Dr. Jones, a founder of the All England Croquet Club in 1870, in the suburb of Wimbledon, fancying himself as an expert on games—he wrote about them for a popular publication called *The Field*—could see there was something to this diversion devised by Major Wingfield. It would go nicely on a croquet lawn. He sold fellow members on the idea of courts, and by 1877 there was enough interest so that he proposed a tournament for men: The Lawn Tennis Championships.

The name is unchanged, although that initial tournament at the club's Worple Road grounds soon became known as just-plain Wimbledon, deferring to the location. As the wicket game took a back seat, the club rearranged its ID as the All England Lawn Tennis & Croquet Club.

Jones may never have written a prescription, but he wrote about tennis, helping to call attention to his tournament. Whether he ever played the game, Dr. Jones was spiritually in tune with a young physician in Boston, Dr. James Dwight. Neither let the practice of medicine interfere with his involvement in tennis.

Doc Dwight, truly the Father of American Tennis, may have been the first to play in America in 1874. If he wasn't the first, this Boston Brahmin was the most enthusiastic. He guided the structuring of the USTA (U.S. Tennis Association) in 1881, competed in the earliest U.S. Championships (winning five doubles titles), presided over the national organization for 21 years, and laid the groundwork for the Davis Cup, launched in 1900.

Though I knew neither Jones nor Dwight, I was acquainted with Dr. Richard Dwight, the son of the Father, like his old man a member of Boston's Longwood Cricket Club. He played into his 90s, and died a very happy man in 1998 because he had—in a way—finally caught up with papa after 103 years, attaining a recognized singles ranking. Doc Dwight the elder was No. 3 in the U.S. in 1888, at 36. In 1991 Doc Dwight the Younger, 88, was No. 1 in New England in the super-seniors, the over-85 category.

"I had to wait a while," he laughed, "but it made me feel good. My father wasn't very impressed by my tennis."

Neither was mine. A man who hadn't touched a racket for years, he beat me handily when I thought myself a hotshot, No. 1 on the high school team.

But he was impressed when the *Boston Globe's* superb editor-in-chief, Tom Winship, hired me away from the rival *Herald* and immediately shipped me to Australia to cover the 1963 Davis Cup challenge round, in Adelaide, a successful invasion by Yanks Chuck McKinley and Dennis Ralston. After a four-year sojourn Down Under, the Cup was spirited back to the U.S. for a brief stay until the Aussies retrieved it in 1964.

Four years after that, a U.S. team spearheaded by Arthur Ashe returned to Adelaide to reclaim the Cup. Ashe, a lieutenant in the U.S. Army, had won the U.S. Amateur and Open titles of 1968. His blackness in a white sport, as well as his championship qualities in several directions, made Arthur a significant story.

"He's a horse you better ride," Winship suggested.

Luckily I did, a wonderful ride across five continents chronicling this humanitarian-with-racket, a rare blend of sensitivity and athleticism. The ride ended too soon, mournfully, at his Richmond, Virginia, graveside in

1993 as whites and blacks joined hands and sang, *We Shall Overcome.*

Arthur was one of those who made the transitional jump in 1968 from one era to the next at the uppermost level: amateurism to 'opens,' eventually shedding amateur status on his release from the Army to become a professional.

Like other professional sports that have succeeded with the public since World War II, tennis has come to be regarded as an entertainment and a business as much as a game. As the 2003 campaign began, the 35th anniversary of the advent of 'opens' (the integration of amateurs and pros with cash payments offered on the basis of performance) more than $150 million was available throughout the world to male and female professionals. The total for that seminal season of prize money was about $400,000.

Grandest financially of the 12 cautiously approved open championships in the new-horizonal year was the U.S. Open at Forest Hills. A $100,000 pot held $14,000 and $6,000 as first prizes for champions Ashe and Virginia Wade respectively. (Arthur, unable to dip into the pot because of his Army-enforced amateur standing, came off with $20-a-day expenses. His final round victim, pro Tom Okker, collected the 14 grand.) By 2002 the purse had sweetened to $16,174,200, the singles first prize (the same for men and women since 1973) amounted to $900,000.

Despite all the gold, this diversion is yet a game that is sometimes raised to an art form—a competitive ballet—by the splendor in movement of such acrobatic zephyrs as Suzanne Lenglen, Henri Cochet, Fred Perry, Maria Bueno, Rod Laver, Ken Rosewall, Evonne Goolagong, Ilie Nastase, Martina Navratilova, John McEnroe, Steffi Graf, Andre Agassi, Martina Hingis, Pete Sampras, the 'Sisters Sledgehammer' (Venus and Serena Williams), Marat Safin, Justine Henin, Lleyton Hewitt and the latest Davis Cup nova, Mikhail Youzhny.

Often it is sublime drama. Never more so than on a chilly, grim October afternoon in Bucharest in 1972 when nationalism and personal pride, strength of character, and moral outlook were all wrapped up in a game of tennis between an American, Stan Smith, and a Romanian, Ion Tiriac, a menacing, Draculan figure right out of the Count D's neighborhood. Even though Smith was the best player in the world that year, he was out of his element. Slipping on the slow, salmon-hued European clay, he was assaulted by a canny, dark-haired grizzly, while a feverish crowd and unfailingly patriotic officials gave him a thumbs-down treatment. Never mind the tennis match, Smith sometimes wondered whether he'd get out of town alive.

At stake was the Davis Cup, that huge silver basin from which world conquerors have swilled victorious champagne since 1900. It is the most difficult bauble to win in tennis, a reward for the global team title, pursued each year by more than 120 countries. In 1972 the United States and Romania were the finalists. The Cup would be decided by the Smith-Tiriac match, and this fact made a boiling kettle of an intimate 7,000-seat wooden stadium that was hastily hammered together for what amounted to a state occasion in Romania. Although Tiriac, a deceptively plodding and unstylish player, wasn't in Smith's league, he lifted himself as high as his native Carpathians with one thought: His tiny homeland, producer of few world-class players besides himself and teammate Ilie Nastase, could score a fantastic victory over the mighty U.S. if he beat Smith.

"I know only one way to play—to win. If I lose," Tiriac said, "then it is nothing. We don't win the Cup."

Ion orchestrated the chanting crowd and deferential line judges into a united front for himself and against Smith. He stalled, he emoted—and he played like a madman, forcing the excruciating match all the way into a fifth set. It seemed a morality play in short pants: the exemplary sportsman Smith, tall and fair-haired, against the scheming Tiriac, bearish and glaring. Somehow Smith held together amid chaos to play to his utmost, too, and win the last set in a run of six games, 4-6, 6-2, 6-4, 2-6, 6-0. Considering the adverse conditions and the magnitude of the prize, Smith's triumph was possibly the most extraordinary in the history of the game. "I concentrated so hard I got a headache," he said.

That was the final, with the Cup at stake. However, Davis Cup, with all its nationalistic overtones, can grip you at any stage, even if it's not your own country enmeshed, and you have no rooting interest.

My heart never beat quicker for tennis than during three rainy May afternoons in Prague, 1971, a seemingly insignificant Cup engagement between the Soviet Union and Czechoslovakia, neither of them contenders.

Insignificant? Not to the tormented folk of Czechoslovakia, under the thumbs of the USSR. Tuned in to TV throughout a tense, capricious weekend, they prayed for their own guys and cursed the white-costumed athletes representing the black-hearted invader whose tanks had echoed across those time-worn streets only three springs before. "Politics!" wailed Jan Kodes, the Czechs' main man, fresh from winning the French Open. "It isn't sport, it's politics, and my head aches from it because people want me to win so bad." Those expectations made Jan tighter than Scarlett O'Hara's corset, and he was beaten by Alex Metreveli, who could feel the hatred directed at him by the jammed-in crowd of 5,000, most of them standing for hours.

Dank silence greeted Metreveli's every point, no matter how brilliantly he might hit the ball. It was eerie. Wild, delighted cheers followed his errors plus anything good Kodes could do. Barbed whistles assailed the Soviets whenever they disputed a line call, many of which were very patriotic (a la Bucharest), in other words against the Soviets, and well worth disputing.

"Yes, we screwed them on some calls," Kodes conceded, "but not as bad as they screwed us last year in Moscow."

Kafkaesque gloom descended after Metreveli beat Kodes. But obscure lefty Frantisek Pala saved the first day with his curlicue spins to defeat Vladimir Korotkov. So-called journalistic objectivity vanished in the drizzle. Sitting and soaking there, I became a Czech, chanting "Doe-tuh-hoe!"—"Come on!"—over and over as a member of the all-encompassing chorus.

Back and forth it went for three sodden days of nerve-quaking play wrapped around rain interruptions, days of hopes dashed and revived, dashed and revived again. "They don't like me much, do they?" Metreveli observed with a wry smile. "Too much politics. I have nothing to do with that. I just do my job: play tennis."

But there was an unexpectedly happy ending. Kodes. Backboned by immense doubles partner Jan Kukal, pulled himself together, and the Czechs won. The hall porter at my hotel was ecstatic. "Tiny Czechoslovakia ... " he held his hands about two inches apart. "Tiny Czechoslovakia ..." and then he spread them a far as possible, "beat giant Soviet Union!"

Momentary bliss.

While Tiriac was chastised outside of Romania for a pragmatic approach to tennis, shunning accepted behavior, he was simply doing the best he could to seize a rare day for his homeland. It was only a game of tennis, but it had assumed a far greater significance for a few hours that afternoon.

The outlook had changed considerably since earlier days at Wimbledon, the 1889 all-comers final, for

instance, when the six-time champ, Willie Renshaw, facing a match point against Harry Barlow, was engaged in a furious exchange—and fell, dropping his racket. Instead of stroking the ball out of Renshaw's reach, Barlow, in the words of the umpire, "elected to toss it amiably back," a soft shot so that Willie had a chance to get up, keep the point going, and won it. Willie saved five other match points, beat Barlow in five sets, and continued to beat his twin brother, Ernest, for a seventh title in the challenge round final.

But those were jolly good English blokes with no cash or computer points at stake. Times change, and the far-reaching significance, and the internationality is a source of much of the appeal of tennis. By this, of course, I mean the established worldwide tournament game to which *Total Tennis* is devoted. The advance of the game since this form of tennis was set forth in London in 1874 by Major Wingfield, has been so complete that all continents are routinely represented in any tournament of consequence. Australians, Asians, Europeans, Africans, and North and South Americans populate a family of tournament players who work their way around the globe on an unending trek. They flit between Melbourne and Munich, Bombay and Buenos Aires, Johannesburg and Jacksonville as casually as suburbanite commuters.

The game may have been restricted to a 78-by-27-foot plot, but it has been is played worldwide on a variety of surfaces. Yet, regardless of how far tennis would stray from grass—to such exotic footing as dried cow dung in India, ant bed in Australia, ersatz grass (Astroturf) in numerous locations, as well as pavement, and plastic carpets for indoor play—the game was once and forever 'lawn tennis' to the Brits, who would rather break their necks than tradition.

Lawn tennis or just-plain-tennis—whatever it is called, however the ball bounces on whichever surface—caught on in the U.S. more widely than anywhere else. Shortly after Wingfield started peddling his game, it reached the U.S. In 1876, Doc Dwight won a baptismal tourney of sorts, a sociable get-together he arranged in the yard of the Appleton estate at Nahant, Massachussets.

However, nobody declared that tennis had landed in America. Or much noticed. For many years afterwards, it was assumed, and written in several histories, that one Mary Outerbridge, of a prominent Staten Island (N.Y.) family, had planted the game in the U.S., on that island across from Manhattan, by bringing a set of tennis equipment home from Bermuda. Feminists may have been dismayed in 1979 by English historian Tom Todd's assertion that it was Dwight—not Outerbridge—who introduced tennis to the States earlier that year. Founding mother or father? Both Outerbridge, longer hailed, and Dwight have their backers.

A century later (1974) an American historian, George Alexander, uncovered evidence of the first recorded play in the U.S. Not in New York or Massachusetts, but—holy half-volleys!—in the wilds of Apache country in the Arizona Territory, also 1874. And a brand new name enters the game's literature: Ella Wilkins Bailey. Was Ella, wife of a U.S. Army officer, the champ of Camp Apache? Unknown. But it has been documented that she played on the court there that year, possibly with her sister, Caroline Wilkins. Fair Ella may or may not have been the first American player. Doc Dwight the Elder and Fred Sears, his cousin, get this editor's nod. But according to the thorough Alexander, Ella Wilkins Bailey is the first for whom a reliable reference has been found.

While some may keen, "Say it ain't so, Doc!" and charge Alexander and Todd with revisionism, Doc Dwight the Younger, ever, gracious, said before his death, "Even my father got mixed up as to the date when he later wrote about it. The main thing is that people did start to play and Mary Outerbridge was important in giving the push in New York. The fact seems to be that both my father and Outerbridge imported sets at about the same time, and nobody can be quite sure who was first."

Although tennis drifted across the country from Staten Island and Nahant and probably Newport, Philadelphia, San Francisco, and New Orleans (site of the New Orleans Tennis Club, the country's first), the power remained in the Northeast. Three decades after Dick Sears began his American championship dynasty in 1881, the American men's championship was still the property of an Ivy League crowd. Exceptions popped up among the women. Best known were Californians Marion Jones, U.S. champ in 1899 and 1902, May Sutton, champ in 1904 (a year prior to her butting into the homebodies' monopoly at Wimbledon), and Hazel Hotchkiss, 1909-11 But the Northeast's early stranglehold had actually been broken by Irishwoman Mabel Cahill (1891-92) and defied by Jones and Myrtle McAteer from Pittsburgh in 1900.

At least, in 1912, the men's U.S. Championships

began to go truly national on the tail of the 'California Comet,' hyper-aggressive Maurice 'Red' McLoughlin, and the general sporting public would soon become aware of tennis. Its evident appeal caused tennis to burst from the cloister of Newport as an amusement of the swells, and in 1915 the U.S. Championships for men moved to the metropolis, New York, and the West Side Tennis Club at Forest Hills. There would be a country-club tinge right up to the present day of heavy money and professionalization, but at Forest Hills tennis gained exposure to larger, more diverse crowds, and a national press.

Once peacetime arrived, following World War I, the press had a tennis hero to hype, and a heroine. Big Bill Tilden, the gangling Philadelphian with a blowtorch serve, and Suzanne Lenglen, a flying Frenchwoman, worked their respective sides of the Atlantic with irresistible flair and shotmaking. Not only were Tilden and Lenglen virtually invincible champions, they were also regal figures, draped in an air of mystery. Theirs was a magnetism that pulled crowds and sold tickets, and tennis became a commercial venture. With Tilden as strong man, the U.S. went on a record rampage of seven straight Davis Cups, and it was necessary to construct a 13,000-seat stadium at Forest Hills to hold the throngs eager to follow Davis Cup engagements and the U.S. Championships. Because of Lenglen, never beaten in singles at Wimbledon, that citadel became too small for all the customers. Thus the All England Lawn Tennis & Croquet Club moved in 1922 to the present Wimbledon grounds where Centre Court accommodated nearly 14,000.

Tennis joined other sports as a business game, but, unfortunately, not as a profession. By 1926 it was apparent that the athletes who sold the tickets deserved to be paid. It was not apparent, however, to those volunteer, usually affluent, officials who controlled the game. For generations past its time, they would keep alive the fiction of 'amateurism' at the game's upper level. Instead of prize money, the subsidy for careerists was 'expenses,' paid beneath the table in proportion to a player's value as a gate attraction. During the 1920s Tilden made more real income out of tennis as an amateur than some of the better pros today. He earned it. But Tilden, a supreme individualist, showed neither gratitude nor obeisance to the amateur authorities and was eventually driven to the wilderness of outright professionalism in 1930, to take his place brilliantly on the treadmill of one-nighters.

Until 1926, the only professionals were instructors, ineligible for customary tournaments. Occasionally they played small tournaments among themselves for pin money. Even though open tennis was discussed wistfully by progressives among players, officials and aficionados, such a sensible arrangement was well in the future.

Amateurs who traveled the world swinging at tennis balls, living and eating well, were called 'tennis bums.' This 'shamateurism' was maintained until 1968. However, those who decided to accept money above the table were considered outlaws traveling under that dirty label, 'professionals.' Forced to scrape for their living outside of the usual framework of private clubs, the pros appeared mainly in public arenas, moving constantly as nomads, folding their canvas court and jaunting to the next night's location.

This way of life began in October 1926 when La Belle Suzanne Lenglen defected from amateurism to roam North America with a troupe that included her nightly foe/pigeon, Mary K. Browne, the U.S. champion of 1912-14, and Vinnie Richards, the American second to Tilden. Their stopovers were regarded as exhibitions, but the pay was all right. Lenglen reportedly collected at least $75,000, a fortune in 1927 dollars, for her four months on the road.

A few months after the debut of the original wandering pros, the first U.S. Pro Championships for men was thrown together at a small club in Manhattan in the summer of 1927 and won by Richards, whose reward was $1,000 from a purse of $2,000. His 1999 successor, at Boston's Longwood Cricket Club, the last champ before the tourney was abandoned, Marat Safin, won $46,000 from a pot of $325,000.

Prior to open tennis, life as a pro meant barnstorming one-nighters. There wasn't enough money to support more than a handful of outlaws. Tournaments that mattered were restricted to amateurs, whose game had structure, continuity, and the attention of the press and sporting public. Interest in amateur sport was high during the 1920s and 1930s, but after World War II that interest shifted to professional sport. While other sports gleamed in television's red eye, tennis languished away from the cameras. Three events maintained an eminence: Wimbledon, Forest Hills, and the Davis Cup finale, which became the postwar preserve of the U.S. and Australia.

As the 1950s dawned, a tidal wave swept from the Antipodes: It was the Aussies, the most dynastic force

ever in tennis. Their muscle lasted for more than two decades, between the Davis Cup seizure by Frank Sedgman & Cohorts in 1950 and the Cup coup of John Newcombe and Rod Laver in 1973. In between were 16 Davis Cups and 14 Wimbledons for the men, two Grand Slams by Rod Laver, and a male record of 28 major titles by Roy Emerson (12 singles, 16 doubles), as well as the rise and fall of Lew Hoad, and the rise and rise of ageless Kenny Rosewall. Australian women were not as pervasive but one of them, Margaret Smith Court, rolled up 62 major titles in singles, doubles and mixed (24-19-19), including a Grand Slam in 1970.

Midway through the 1960s, a period of rising acclaim for sport in general, tennis was sagging at both the amateur and professional levels. The best players were pros, but the best tournaments were amateur. Agitation for open play increased, especially in England, where Wimbledon officials, tiring of exorbitant 'expense' payments to amateurs, sought to present the finest tennis. This was impossible as long as the professional elite—Laver, Rosewall, Pancho Gonzalez, Hoad, Butch Buchholz and Andres Gimeno—were off in limbo.

An impetus for the decisive move toward opens was provided startlingly in 1967 by a man unknown within tennis, Dave Dixon of New Orleans. Buoyed by Texas money supplied by Dallas petrocrat Lamar Hunt, his partner in a wildcat tennis venture, WCT (World Championship Tennis), Dixon signed up amateurs Newcombe, Tony Roche, Roger Taylor, Cliff Drysdale and Nikki Pilic plus pros Buchholz, Pierre Barthes and Dennis Ralston as his WCT Tennis troupe. Another promoter, American ex-Davis Cup captain George MacCall, founder of the NTL (National Tennis League), had enlisted amateur Emerson to blend with pros Laver, Gonzalez, Rosewall, Gimeno, Fred Stolle plus Rosie Casals, Billie Jean King, Ann Jones and Françoise Durr. And so the amateur game was abruptly depleted of its top 10 players.

Aware that Dixon was lurking, Herman David, the Wimbledon chairman, realized that he and Wimbledon must follow their long smoldering desire to open up the game. First, he organized a test run, a three-day, pros-only tournament in August on the august Centre Court. Would the venerated turf wither beneath the feet of out-and-out outlaws (Laver, Rosewall, Gonzalez, Gimeno, Hoad, Stolle, Ralston, Buchholz)? Would the Big W's clientele even show up to watch the banished bad boys jousting for a then-record purse of $35,000?

The temple didn't crumble. It rumbled with applause as starved patrons filled Centre Court the second and third days. David and confreres came as close as All England Clubbies can come to grinning as Laver beat Rosewall in a terrific final, 6-2, 6-2, 12-10. David Gray wrote in *The Guardian*: "Having grown used to margarine, it was good to be reminded of the taste of butter."

There was no turning back. Confident of the British public and press' support, and with the backing of the nation's influential LTA (Lawn Tennis Association), Wimbledon announced that in 1968 it would be open to all players regardless of their status, amateur or pro. When that shot was fired, the U.S., led by enlightened president Bob Kelleher, seconded the revolt, defying the International Tennis Federation. The rest of the world had no choice but to fall into line.

Bournemouth, England, was the scene of the first open, the British Hard Court (meaning clay) Championships in April 1968. Rosewall won the men's title, Wade the women's. Curly-headed Englishman Mark Cox wrote his footnote in sporting history as the first amateur to beat a pro at tennis. Cox, a left-hander, knocked off Pancho Gonzalez and Roy Emerson on successive afternoons to upstage all else on Britain's front pages.

The tennis epidemic to come in the 1970s had been set in motion, along with the venture into high-technology that would make wooden rackets obsolete. Ashe won his U.S. Amateur and Open titles with a split-shaft Head aluminum racket that he called "the snow-shoe." Billie Jean King and Rosie Casals, as well as teenager Jimmy Connors, were waving 'steelies' in the late 1960s. In 1971 Laver crossed the million-dollar mark in prize money after nine years as a pro. But by 1979, 15 other men and three women had followed, making their millions in shorter spans. And in 1977 Argentine's 'Young Bull of the Pampas,' Guillermo Vilas, had a year that would seem a splendid career for most athletes: $800,642.

This was just walking-around money, as the upward-and-onward finances of the '80s and '90s and the first years of the new century would show. In 1990, 19-year-old Pete Sampras carted off a flabbergasting first prize of $2 million for winning the newly-contrived Grand Slam Cup tournament, and wound up the season with men's record winnings of $2,900,057. That mark wouldn't last long. He'd soon be in the $5-million-per-season class. In 1992 an 18-year-old Monica Seles set the female season record, $2,622,352, also perishable as Arantxa Sanchez Vicario was a few dollars shy of $3 million in 1994. Steffi Graf surpassed it in 1996. Ivan Lendl retired in 1994 with the staggering prize-money record of $21,262,417, since hurdled by Sampras ($43,280,489 at the end of 2002), Andre Agassi, Boris Becker and Yevgeny Kafelnikov. Martina Navratilova went out—sort of—at about the same time with $20,337,902, a momentary record representing 22 years of labor, eclipsed by Graf in her 14th professional season. While career millionaires weren't quite a dime a dozen, 294 men and 129 women had earned that appellation by the close of 2002.

At first the boom in prize money benefitted principally the men. As in so many areas of life, the women were left behind. However, guided by brainy Gladys Heldman, publisher of *World Tennis* magazine, and inspired by the liberation-minded firebrand, Billie Jean King, the women divorced themselves from the conventional tournament arrangement they'd shared with the men. Top billing (and top dollars) had always gone to the men. Carrying the banner of Virginia Slims cigarettes, the women crusaded on a separate tour and made good artistically and economically. The Slims tour began haltingly in 1970 and picked up steam in 1971, when Billie Jean won $117,000, the first woman to earn more than 100 grand in prize money. The tour was solid by 1972, when ingenue Chrissie Evert won the first eight-woman playoff at the season's climax. In 1973, the women demanded and got equal prize money at the U.S. Open, one of the few remaining tournaments embracing both men's and women's events.

Television didn't rush to hug tennis when the open era began, although network interest picked up. Two telecasts in particular aided in lifting the game to wide public notice: Rosewall's sensational 4-6, 6-0, 6-3, 6-7 (3-7), 7-6 (7-5), victory over Laver on NBC for the WCT title of 1972 in Dallas; and Billie Jean King's 6-4, 6-3, 6-3, put-down of 55-year-old Bobby Riggs on ABC's bizarre 'Battle of the Sexes' at Houston's Astrodome in 1973.

Tennis began to appear regularly on television, prize money accelerated for the stars, equipment sales and participation accelerated for the hackers. Construction of public courts as well as private clubs increased, particularly in the U.S., where the proliferation of indoor courts was a sporting phenomenon.

Tennis was big business, and the pros, following the example of brethren in other sports, unionized to gain a stronger position in the management of their business. The male ATP (Association of Tennis Pros) and female WTA (Women's Tennis Association) were formed as player guilds, and two new governing bodies were also formed: the International Professional Tennis Councils for men (MIPTC) and women (WIPTC), containing representatives of the unions, the ITF, and the tournament promoters.

Those who thought the war was over when the forces of open tennis triumphed soon realized that strife would become a way of life in tennis. Revolution and evolution continued to change the face of the professional game. Though for a long time the U.S. was the financial base, the stronghold for pro tennis, Europe caught up, and can Asia be far behind?

Interestingly it was another non-tennis figure, Hamilton Jordan, who launched a revolution on behalf of the ATP as Dave Dixon had done in founding WCT. Taking over as chief executive of the ATP in 1988, Jordan, former chief of staff for U.S. President Jimmy Carter, performed a political tour de force in bringing all the men's tourneys (except the four majors) under the umbrella of the ATP Tour in 1990.

This maneuver destroyed the MIPTC and the Grand Prix structure, which had embraced and administered the men's game for almost two decades, and, mercilessly, WCT as well. WCT, which had led the way into professionalization, operated its own circuit until absorbed by the Grand Prix. Nevertheless, WCT continued its annual championship playoff in Dallas, the event that had electrified the game with the $50,000 payoffs to Rosewall for his 1971 and 1972 victories over Laver. But after John McEnroe beat Brad Gilbert in the last of those in 1989, WCT sadly expired. Too, the ATP lost its original focus and function as a players' union, and may be challenged by players who feel they should have more influence in their own lives

As the brainchild of Hall of Famer Jack Kramer, the Grand Prix commenced in 1970, a points scheme linking men's tourneys and leading to a year-end showdown, the Masters, for the tour leaders. Cranked up in 1970 at Tokyo, the Masters had its most successful run at New York's Madison Square Garden, 1977-89, then moving to Germany (Frankfurt, 1990-95, Hannover, 1996-99. Although the Masters continues in format, it was for 10 years (1990-99) re-billed as the ATP World

Championship at Jordan's instigation. Wisely the ATP, under the leadership of Mark Miles, successor to Jordan in 1990, restored the title as the Masters Cup in 2000 at Lisbon. The 2001-02 champ Lleyton Hewitt carted off $1.4 million. The Masters Series of nine prime tournaments (five in Europe, three in the U.S., one in Canada) is the backbone of the ATP Tour.

Feeling threatened by the ATP's increased muscle, the ITF, principally Britain, the U.S., France and Australia, raised extraordinary prize money for their 'Grand Slams'—Wimbledon and the U.S., French and Australian Opens. Furthermore, in 1990, the ITF added to the usual confusion and overcrowded calendar by instituting the $6-million Grand Slam Cup, admitting the top finishers in those four tourneys, as the season's closing event. The obvious attempt was to upstage the ATP Championship by amassing a substantially richer purse. But after 10 years the ITF showed some wisdom by making peace with the ATP to cooperate in one season-ending extravaganza.

Considerably more orderly, at least for a while, the women's tour has been generally easier to follow, underwritten by several sponsors (originally Virginia Slims, then Avon, Colgate, Toyota, back to Slims/Kraft, until 1996, then Corel followed by Sanex). For 21 consecutive years the WTA's season-ending Championships was held at New York's Madison Square Garden. Ill-considered were shifts to Munich in 2001, then Los Angeles in 2002, poorly attended financial disappointments. Since 1990 the WTA, unlike the ATP, has cooperated with the ITF to the extent that the four majors are part of the women's tour.

The U.S. has been a leader in all facets of the game's development, but tennis is truly universal and well received in pro tournament locations in more than 30 countries. Growth continues and change has been constant. Venues are larger, less intimate, and, regrettably, grass and clay playing surfaces have largely given way to hard courts of asphalt base. The U.S. Championship, begun in the grass period from 1881, switched to clay at Forest Hills in 1975. For a while, clay was predominant on the summer circuit. But the paving of Flushing Meadow (eventually, curiously, adding an 's' to become Meadows) led to regrettable conformity and a stony greentopping of America. By 1988, Australia had gone the way of the U.S., forsaking greensward for hard courts at the splendid new center for its Open, Flinders Park (also curiously renamed, now Melbourne Park).

The Grand Slam route, once three-quarters turf, one-quarter clay (at Paris), is now more diverse. But more than 50 percent of professional tournaments are contested on unforgiving, body-unfriendly outdoor and indoor hard surfaces. Injuries are more prevalent.

Whatever the surface and wherever it is played, will the game ever be at peace? Probably not. Particularly with player agents behind the scenes, guiding the greed, and a practically perpetual season, over-cluttered with events. A genuine off-season (October-November-December) and reorganization of the hectic calendar is needed by all concerned to preserve the players' physical and emotnal welfare. But who will have the sense—and guts—to bring about an unselfish ATP-WTA-ITF bonding on behalf of the game?

War and Peace, the old Tolstoy story, could be the tennis theme. Count Leo Tolstoy, by the way, was an avid tennis player. He built a court on his estate at Yasnaya Polyana, one of the first in Russia, and put a tennis scene in his novel *Anna Karenina*. Did poor Anna throw herself in front of a train because she bungled a mixed doubles match with her lover, Vronsky? Stranger things have happened.

At best, tennis does deliciously evoke Kipling's iffy impostors, Triumph and Disaster. Obviously a Borg-McEnroe, Agassi-Sampras, Evert-Navratilova, Graf-Seles epic does—but a first-rounder between nobodies can be just as gripping. Tennis can twist you into knots. But it remains a game, albeit at the professional level one that has been refined and polished, commercialized and subsidized well beyond the 19th-century imagination of the first proclaimed champion, Spencer W. Gore, triumphant at Wimbledon in 1877. The game has flourished and spread across the planet so incessantly that even I, the hopeless lover, am continually, pleasantly, startled. In my sixth decade as a two-way journalist (scribbler/babbler), I must admit that it does beat working for a living. Besides, would anybody else hire me?

Although my Uncle Studley swears that I covered the coming-out of Wimbledon with a quill pen, he's off by a few years. Still, I guess I could give you, treasured reader, a digest of the 129 years of tennis history, and it wouldn't take long:

1874—English gentleman with time on his hands, Major Wingfield, devises and patents the game, makes small change selling sets, and somebody—take your pick of claimants and candidates—starts it off in the U.S.

1877—Wimbledon is launched (first, still foremost),

and even shows a profit of a few pounds.

1881 and 1887—Inaugural U.S. Championships for men, then women.

1900—Harvard rich kid Dwight Davis donates sterling punch bowl for an international team competition, eventually known as Davis Cup. Davis and college pals beat Brits in leadoff finale. Only two countries interested then; more than 120 now.

1905 and 1907—Californian May Sutton and Aussie Norman Brookes, respectively, are first alien winners of Wimbledon, a place no longer safe for the English homebodies.

1919—France's Suzanne Lenglen wins Wimbledon, scandalously, showing thighs and unbeatable strokes. English are so shocked by her flaunting of female assets that the 'new' [present] Wimbledon is built in 1922 to accommodate increasing hordes of offended ticket purchasers.

1920—Big Bill Tilden, arrogant, artistic, all-conquering Philadelphian, dominates the game in the Twenties and makes U.S. tennis-conscious, inspiring construction of Forest Hills Stadium and keeping Davis Cup at home.

1923—Unflappable 'Little Miss Poker Face,' Helen Wills, wins first of seven U.S. titles, succeeds Lenglen as dominatrix, and will win eight Wimbledons from baseline.

1926—Lenglen goes for the dough, signs as first to tour professionally, opening job opportunities in an infant sport.

1927—Four hands are finally better than one: the Four Musketeers—René Lacoste, Henri Cochet, Jean Borotra, Jacques Brugnon—bring down Tilden & Co., carting Davis Cup to France and necessitating the building of Stade Roland Garros in Paris.

1932—English Davis Cupper Bunny Austin liberates male legs by showing up in shorts.

1933—Last known Englishman—as far as many are concerned—to play tennis, Fred Perry, lifts Davis Cup from French and wins Wimbledon from 1934-36 before joining Tilden in the pro ranks.

1938—Don Budge, having retrieved the Davis Cup, wins Australian, French, Wimbledon and U.S. titles, thus achieving the first-ever Grand Slam.

1946—Jack Kramer spearheads the recovery of Davis Cup from Australia. In 1947 he's the first to win Wimbledon in shorts, also captures U.S. and turns pro to swipe that crown from Bobby Riggs.

1950—Frank Sedgman and Ken McGregor heist

Davis Cup from U.S. to launch an Australian dynasty that will make Wimbledon and Forest Hills hostage to such Down Undertakers as Lew Hoad, Ken Rosewall, Rod Laver, Neale Fraser, Roy Emerson, Fred Stolle, John Newcombe, and Tony Roche for a quarter-century.

1953—Maureen 'Little Mo' Connolly, 18, navigates the first female Grand Slam.

1956—New Yorker Althea Gibson, having hurdled the color rampart in 1950, wins the French, becoming the first black to rule a major. She will follow with Wimbledon and U.S. titles in 1957-58.

1961—Billie Jean Moffit, 17, wins Wimbledon doubles with Karen Hantze, the first of B. J.'s record 20 titles at the Big W, six in singles.

1962—Laver, after following Budge and Connolly as the third member of Grand Slam club, turns pro.

1965—Jimmy Van Alen, father of the tie-breaker, shows it off at small Newport, R.I., pro tourney, but it won't be accepted until 1970.

1968—Open tennis dawns. Tennis begins its metamorphosis from a sort-of-amateur sport to a big-business game. But amateur Arthur Ashe stunningly wins the first U.S. Open—the first black male to seize a major—and leads U.S. to Davis Cup success. Back from isolated life as outcast pros, Rosewall at French, Laver at Wimbledon, win the first major opens.

1969—Laver repeats as Grand Slammer, this time as a pro.

1970—Aussie Margaret Smith Court, all-time winner of major titles, 62 (24 in singles), goes Grand Slamming, the fourth member of club.

1971—Schoolgirl Christine Evert, 16, arrives at Forest Hills and coolly goes to semis to launch the Chrissie Craze.

1973—Labor problems. ATP boycotts Wimbledon. Most top men don't play, including Open era champs Laver, Newcombe, Stan Smith. Show goes on but ATP becomes a force. Billie Jean King beats Bobby Riggs in mixed singles schlockathon.

1974—'Lovebirds Double' at Wimbledon. Then affianced Chris Evert and Jimmy Connors triumph and begin cutting long championship swaths. They pay 33-to-1 with London bookies. Bjorn Borg, 18, wins French, and the three of them change the game, guiding the world to two-fisted backhandedness.

1976—High-tech rackets are here to stay, supplanting wood, as Howard Head puts the Prince Classic oversized club into play, drawing initial laughs, but commencing serious alteration of the game.

1977—Borgiastic period is under way at Wimbledon's Centenary celebration as Bjorn wins second of five straight. But the show is stolen by last known Englishwoman—or so it seems—to play tennis. Virginia Wade, 32, accepts championship prize from the other queen in the house, Elizabeth II.

1978—Martina Navratilova beats Evert to win first of record nine Wimbledons, the last in 1990. U.S. Open flees Forest Hills, settling in Flushing.

1979—John McEnroe, 20, wins his first of four U.S. titles, while Tracy Austin, 16, becomes the youngest to rule her country.

1980—Borg holds off McEnroe to win a wowser of a Wimbledon, highlighted by the Battle of 18-16 (fabulous fourth-set tie-breaker). McEnroe will win the 1981 rematch.

1983—Yannick Noah sets off rejoicing across France when he becomes the first citizen in 37 years to win the French men's title.

1984—Ivan Lendl, from two sets back, beats McEnroe for the French title, establishing himself as a major figure who will win three U.S. titles.

1985—Daring volleyer, belly-flopping Boris Becker, 17, becomes the youngest and first unseeded Wimbledon victor.

1988—Steffi Graf, 19, not only becomes the fifth member of the Grand Slam club, but embellishes it with a gold medal as tennis returns to the Olympics. Australian Open bids farewell to grass (and rain-outs), opening a new complex in Melbourne with close-able roof stadium.

1989—Drought-buster Michael Chang, 17, becomes first American man in 34 years to win the French.

1990—Cool summer for the callow: Monica Seles, 16, is the youngest winner of a major in 20th century, taking the French; Pete Sampras, 19, is the youngest U.S. champ.

1993—Seles, stabbed by loony Guenther Parche during match at Hamburg, will lose 26 months of a career already embracing seven major titles. Sampras wins first of seven Wimbledons, and will become Big W's Man of the Century, catching up with Willie Renshaw of the 1880s.

1995—Seles resurfaces to win Toronto and almost beats Graf in a splendid U.S. Open final, but Steffi, with fourth title, becomes only player to hold all four majors at least four times.

1996—Winning a fifth French, seventh Wimbledon, fifth U.S., Steffi eclipses Evert and Navratilova (18), and Helen Wills (19), in major singles. At 21 titles, she's hot on the track of Margaret Court's 24.

1997—Venus rising: 17-year-old Venus Williams, No. 66, unseeded in her first U.S. Open, glides to the final, losing to another 17-year-old, Swiss Martina Hingis, who has already won the Australian and Wimbledon crowns. Aussie revivalist Patrick Rafter ends his island's 24-year dry spell in New York by winning the U.S. Open, and will repeat the following year.

1999—Andre Agassi joins a select society by winning the French, one of five guys capturing all four majors during their careers. The woman he will marry, Steffi Graf, also succeeds in Paris, for a sixth time, closing her career with a 22nd major. Little Sister, Serena Williams, beats Venus to the winner's circle by conquering the U.S. Open at 17, the first African American to take a major since Ashe's Wimbledon of 1975.

2000—Sampras' seventh Wimbledon title is his 13th major, eclipsing the 33-year-old record of Roy Emerson. Spain beats Australia, becoming the 10th country to win the Davis Cup. Venus and Serena collect Olympic gold, Venus winning the singles, following up on her Wimbledon and U.S. titles, and blending with Little Sister in the doubles.

2001—Wimbledon is stunned by Goran Ivanisevic's unique triumph as the lowest-ranked (No. 125), only wild-card champ. Lleyton Hewitt, a 20-year-old Aussie, beats Sampras to win the U.S. and finishes the year as youngest No. 1 man in tennis history.

2002—Jennifer Capriati repeats as Australian Open champ, saving four match points to beat Hingis. But Serena takes over as No. 1 from Venus, grabbing French, Wimbledon and U.S., uniquely beating Big Sister in each final. Sampras concludes a miserable year brilliantly by downing Agassi for the U.S. title, his 14th major. Mikail Youzhny, as a sub, lifts Russia to an exalted position as the 11th country in the Davis Cup Valhalla, winning the fifth match from two sets down over Paul-Henri Mathieu to beat France, 3-2.

2003—Serena keeps cooking—home cooking, burning Venus in the Australian final for Little Sister's fourth successive major title.

Brisk enough? There's much, much more on the following pages. As the opium-loving writer, Thomas DeQuincey, would have said—and I second regarding my own form of dependency—once you've started, it's hard to stop.

How the game started is a delightful tale from Heiner Gillmeister's book, *Tennis: A Cultural History*. It concerns a 12th century French cleric, Pierre, the Abbot of Morimond, who fell deathly ill. His soul was plucked by ball players from Hell, a devilish cast who, with their hands, batted it back and forth across a horridly steaming sulphorous valley. That's as good a theory about the creation of tennis as any. After all, it is a helluva game—with soul.

My hope is that you keep on hackin' as a player, and harkin' to the lore of this marvelous pastime/pleasure/passion.

Bud Collins, Andre Agassi, 1999

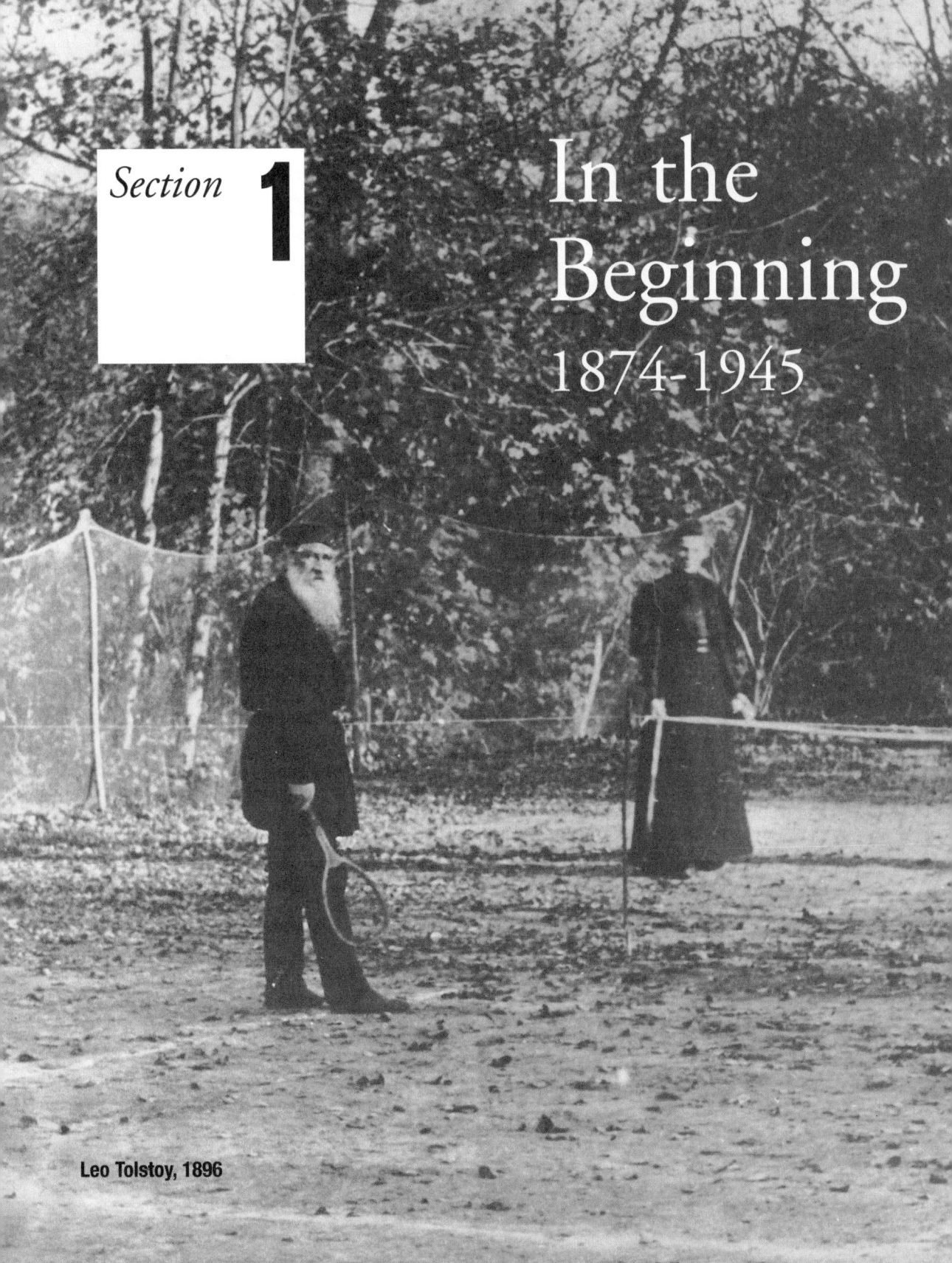

Section 1

In the Beginning
1874-1945

Leo Tolstoy, 1896

Chapter 1

Roots of the Game

Lili de Alvarez, 1928
An early arbiter of court fashion, and later a Comtesse, playing a Wimbledon semi-final.

It had to start somewhere, well before a couple of gents named Gore and Marshall dueled at 25 paces or so on a strip of greensward, batting rubber balls at each other during a London summer afternoon in 1877. That occasion, Spencer Gore carrying the day, was the final of the introductory Wimbledon, recognized as the first tennis tournament. At least the original lawn tennis tournament.

But was it? Sort of. Yes and no.

Yes: It was a public launching of the present-day game with which we're familiar, having played it, seen it in person or on TV, and read about it—a convenient starting date for the innumerable tournaments that since have been played.

No: Tennis, as a game, pre-dates by centuries its patenting by an Englishman in 1874, and the unveiling of his version at Wimbledon three years later. That's the game we know, and what this book is about. But it's the offspring of an ancient sire.

Where does today's game come from? Surely, but mysteriously, from much deeper in history, a descendant of an old sport which evolved, was refined and continues to exist on its own as a separate pastime—played indoors in curiously conformed, concrete-walled courts—known variously as real tennis, royal tennis or court tennis. That game, sequestered in a few private clubs in the United Kingdom, United States, Australia and Europe, dates back to 12th-century France. Or Italy? Or Spain?

Most likely tennis sprang—bounded?—from monastery cloisters in which off-duty monks were channeling their testosterone into batting a ball to and fro, and off the walls. First with their hands—*jeu de paume.* Eventually with rackets that appeared in the 16th century, possibly first in Italy, called *rachette,* to play a game called *gioco di rachette.*

Its precise origins remain shrouded in conjecture, contrasting notions and theories, and lack of documentation despite the diligent delving of historians.

Even the mystery of the name—tennis—and the scoring terms, passed down from real tennis to our game (properly named lawn tennis because it began and prospered on grass) are unsolved. Nevertheless, the good brothers were onto something too good to keep cloistered in their backyards. It spread to commoners in outdoor courts as well as kings with their personal sanctums, evidence of which can be seen in European paintings of long, long ago. At one medieval time, a saying had it: "There are more tennis players in France than drunkards in England."

Terms of engagement? Love? Can you take seriously anything in which love means nothing? Maybe it derives from the French, *l'oeuf:* the old goose or duck egg. However, Heiner Gillmeister in his fascinating tome, *Tennis: A Cultural History,* puts forth a vote for the word *lof.* Gillmeister says it is, "the Dutch or Flemish equivalent of English 'honor.' It looks as if the English expression for a player's failure to score owes its existence to an expression used in the Low Countries, *omme lof spellen*—'to play for the honor'."

The expression 'bagel' for zero would come much later, quite possibly from the lips of Eddie Dibbs, a leading American player during the 1970s and early '80s.

The quartered face of a clock seems the likely source of the game and point scores—15, 30—but why 40 instead of the original 45? Was it a cuckoo clock? It was probably shortened over time, an abbreviation like 5 instead of 15, common among hackers. Nobody really knows. Deuce is the clearest, from the French *a deux.*

'Tennis' itself? There are many theories which American historian George Alexander discusses, and have appeared elsewhere before, but not conclusively. George has his own idea, on 'tens' from the German, different from all the rest, as will be seen.

Lawn tennis reached an early high point of American national prestige during the presidency of Theodore Roosevelt (1901-09), who formed a 'tennis cabinet.' He ordered the White House's first court, clay, built on a site now occupied by the Oval Office. The players, headed by the vigorous president, were drawn from the younger administrators of, or just below, cabinet rank, and from foreign diplomats, led by the French ambassador, J. J. Jusserand. He was small, wiry and quick, and often a match for 'Teddy' himself, the charging hero of San Juan Hill.

The ambassador was a serious player of both real tennis and lawn tennis and a student of the history of those games. Among the studies he undertook was the derivation of the English word 'tennis.' His was not the first search for the origin of the word, nor the last. Then, as now, the usual explanation was that 'tennis' was derived from the French *tendere* meaning 'to hold.' Etymologists rationalized that the server called out *tendere* as a warning to his opponent just prior to serving. At first glance this has an authentic ring, for it carries the approval of scholars of repute. The problem was that it did not make sense to Jusserand.

Jusserand made an extensive study of old French literature and he found much shouting by players—mostly profane—but no one ever seemed to have called out *tendere* or anything like it. Several studies on the subject made before and since the French ambassador have come to the same findings.

In 1878 Julian Marshall, in his monumental *Annals of Tennis,* addresses the matter, and he lists 10 spellings of tennis through the years. But he leaves the decision as to the origin of the word 'tennis' to others, finding no answer that satisfied him.

In *Bailey's* magazine of August 1918, C. E. Thomas offered a slightly more logical explanation. According to him, the derivation is from the French *tenez,* meaning 'take it.' Again a call of warning from the server. No one has come forth with evidence of such ever being done, let alone ever having been the custom.

Tennis Origins and Mysteries, by Malcolm Whitman, one of the pioneer Davis Cuppers, and U.S. champion (1898-1900), devotes a chapter to the subject and covers most of the theories that have been put forth through the years by tennis players with an interest in etymology. Most of these theories have a common root in French words that have 'ten' as the start of words meaning, variously, 'hold,' 'taut,' 'tense,' 'tendon,' and several other similar words.

Two towns, widely separated, one on the Nile River in Egypt, the other in Northern France, having 'Tennis' as their name, are thought to be possible origins of the name. Tennis in France was known for its lace; Tennis in Egypt for its fine long staple cotton. Since balls were often cloth bound (never in the 15th century), some have thought that was connection enough.

Alexander offers a more logical explanation. First, why was a new name for the game necessary when it came to England (some evidence indicates it came earlier to Scotland)? The French name then and now is *jeu de paume* (hand ball). By the time it reached the

British Isles (the date not known with certainty), implements such as battledores, forerunners of rackets, were replacing the hand. Some of the French was retained such as 'deuce' and perhaps 'love,' so no strong aversion to French words existed. This new pastime needed a name to differentiate the game of playing across a net from those played against a wall.

The root stem of 'tens' has given us many words including those such as *tendere,* which is the often-listed parent of 'tennis.' One of the meanings of 'tens' is the 'weaver's shuttle' and other back-and-forth motions. Whitman had previously come across this, but he chose not to pursue it and he dropped it short of the shuttle meaning.

The naming of the game with a descriptive word is more logical than one requiring a tortured explanation. The logic of naming the game after some 'shout' or ball material would have us call golf 'fore' and the games of football 'pigskin' and baseball 'horsehide.' The to-and-fro motion further lent its name to the missile that we know as the shuttlecock in badminton.

While the explanation may satisfy a few, more evidence is needed to support the theory, even though none has been offered to support the usually accepted *tendere.* It is like the unauthenticated, largely wishful, story of Mary Outerbridge introducing the game to the U.S.: Once in place and repeated a few times, it takes on the position of presumed fact. But this is part of the intrigue of tennis.

Although the beginnings of tennis and many other sports and games are unknown and lost in the distant past, the history of modern (lawn) tennis is clearly documented. Its arrival was publicly announced on March 7, 1874, in two papers, the *Court Journal,* read by almost all of the British upper class as well as those who aspired to join, and the *Army & Navy Gazette,* read by the military, which was stationed worldwide—for then the sun truly never set on the vast British Empire.

These notices appeared after the British patent office issued to Major Walter Wingfield provisional letters of patent (No. 685) for 'A Portable Court of Playing Tennis,' dated Feb. 23, 1874. English-speaking sportsmen around the world who read *The Field* of March 21, 1874 were informed in detail of the new game, for it reproduced much of the information about the Major's game of lawn tennis. It contained a short history of tennis, instruction and notes for the "erection of the court," and the six rules of the game.

The game was an immediate success and spread throughout Great Britain and Ireland in a matter of weeks and around the English-speaking world soon thereafter. The equipment to play was sold by the inventor's agents, Messrs. French and Co., 46, Churton Street, London, S.W. The price: Five guineas.

Sales literature noted that "the game is in a painted box, 36 x 12 x 6 inches and contains poles, pegs, and netting for forming the court, 4 tennis bats, by Jeffries and Mallings, a bag of balls, mallet, and brush and the instructive *The Book of the Game."*

The daily sales book for almost a year, July 6, 1874 to June 25, 1875, notes on July 15, 1874 that Major Rowan Hamilton settled his account for tennis sets he purchased in May "for Canada." Sets were bought for India and China. Sets were sold to Russia's royalty and to, of course, the Prince of Wales and many others, including 42 Lords, 44 Ladies and members of Parliament, among them agriculturist Ward Hunt, First Lord of the Admiralty, renowned for his girth which caused a semicircle to be cut from the Admiralty board table.

The records of French and Co. are not the complete list, for many sales went to unnamed parties and wholesale business was done with London retailers and, as so often happens, competing sets were soon on the market despite patent protection.

There were several reasons for this great and widespread success. There was a need for a game that afforded vigorous exercise for both sexes and all ages. That was how Wingfield described his new game. Croquet had been the fad during the 1860s and it inspired the construction of many well-rolled, level courts with close-clipped grass, made possible due to the invention of the lawn mower by Englishman Edwin Budding earlier in the century. The least standard croquet court measured 30 yards by 20 yards. Such courts were ubiquitous and were ready-made for lawn tennis, and "The ground need not even be turf; the only condition is that it must be level."

This was not exactly today's marvelous game, for it was quite simple. It used the scoring of 1, 2, 3, etc. of the game of rackets, but it bore the more refined name 'tennis' rather than 'rackets,' which was associated with taverns and prisons. The game could also be played without buying the set, for items were sold separately. Rackets were 15 shillings, balls were five shillings a dozen, and *The Book of the Game* was six pence. People with rackets of other sports could easily try out the new game.

Wingfield learned, as have most inventors, to their dismay, that rather than receiving the thanks of grateful sportsmen, he was belittled. "Anyone could have invented his game," said numerous skeptics. Others came forth with claims for earlier games. Inventions almost always are based on other inventions, and (lawn) tennis obviously was based on (real/royal/court) tennis. This was acknowledged by Wingfield, as even the title of his patent and the game indicate. The major got another boost 14 years after the fact from another inventor, who also left his name to posterity but didn't profit from it. That was Charles Goodyear, who vulcanized rubber in 1860, leading to the bouncing ball, an innovation seized on by Germans to manufacture thin-walled balls. Wingfield's balls came from Germany.

Outdoor racket, ball and net play goes back to the time of Queen Elizabeth I. Earlier in England and France, a game called long tennis (*longue paume*) was played, and it is still played in France. Other similar games, at best neighborhood games, were without formal rules and they never traveled, soon dying out. The name Harry Gem is associated with such a game. He wrote in *The Field* of Nov. 28, 1874: "He (J.B. Perera) first introduced the game fifteen years ago, and it recently has received the name of Pelota..." After (lawn) tennis arrived, Gem wrote rules for "Pelota," which he sent to *The Field* and to his club, the Leamington Club, which added 'Lawn Tennis' to its name.

Wingfield wrote to Gem in the fall of 1874 that he had worked on the game for a year and a half. After Wingfield's death, an acquaintance wrote that Wingfield's thoughts of a game went back to his service in India. He wrote in *The Book of the Game* that the game was "tested practically at several country houses during the past few months."

Since all five editions of the book are "dedicated to the party assembled at Nantclwyd [in Wales] in December 1873," it has been assumed that was where it was introduced. But there is no evidence of that. The party was a housewarming given by the new owner of the estate Nantclwyd, Major Naylor-Leyland, for his friends in the area. It featured the presentation of two plays and a grand ball. The three-day affair was covered in detail by the *Wrexham Guardian* and makes no mention of lawn tennis or any athletic activity. Wingfield, his host and hostess and a great beauty of the day, Patsy Cornwallis-West, performed in the plays.

It would be reasonable that Onslow Hall, the main estate of his branch of the family, would be one of the test sites. It is more likely a test site than Wingfield's own Rhysnant Hall, which was at that time leased. The one country house that has a written record as a test site is Earnshill in Somerset. In May 1881, Wingfield's first cousin, R. T. Combe of Earnshill, wrote to the *Daily Telegraph,* "It is now some seven or eight years since Major Wingfield first put up a lawn tennis court here."

Several other places have been put forth as being sites of early play but confirming evidence is lacking. The first public exhibition occurred the Saturday following *The Field* announcement of May 4, 1874, which read in part, "It (lawn tennis) may be seen and played next week, on and after the opening of the Princes Cricket Ground, and also at the Polo Club, Lillie-bridge."

In the *Whitehall Review* (Nov. 14, 1896), Wingfield's good friend, Clement Scott, wrote in his column, 'Wheel of Life,' that the exhibition was in 1869. Such is an example of how fallible the human memory is and how important 'the palest ink' is to true history.

The closing of the Haymarket court tennis courts and the outdoor racket courts at taverns in several neighborhoods undoubtedly caused Wingfield to bring forth the new game.

Besides private homes with croquet lawns becoming places to play tennis, it immediately became a game played at public parks and other common lawns and the great clubs. Among the London clubs to take up the sport quickly were M.C.C.—The Marylebone Cricket Club (Lords)—Hurlingham Club and Princes Club, as well as many others throughout the land. A club that waited until 1875 to accept a rival sport was the then five-year-old All England Croquet Club, located off Worple Road in the London suburb, Wimbledon.

Henry Jones, the editor of the Pastimes section of *The Field,* which covered card games, Jones' forte, as well as lawn tennis, was a founder, along with his publisher, John Walsh, of the All England Croquet Club. Jones introduced lawn tennis to the club. He wrote under the *nom de plume* 'Cavendish.' Jones and Walsh were both doctors who had given up the practice of medicine to pursue their greater love, games and sports. Jones earned Wingfield's enmity by presuming to take over his game. It was Jones' nature to assume he had greater knowledge of all matters concerning games, and this included lawn tennis.

To Wingfield, the remarkable success of the game was

evidence of the rightness of it, and that you should not change a winning game. However, in the fall of 1874 he issued a second edition of *The Book of the Game*. There were now twelve rules and a larger court, and it also made more use of the alternate name of *Sphairistike*, Greek for ball games. These changes and complications could be added, for now the game had taken root. By that time some confusion existed, at least on the pages of *The Field*, because Perera's game, pelota, and a rival game, Germains Lawn Tennis, by J. H. Hale, with Jones' help, had been put forth. In reality nothing came of either; they were more complicated with no added redeeming features.

Through the winter, there was continued confusion. John Moyer Heathcote, who with his wife had introduced the Melton cloth-covered ball, wrote to Fitzgerald, secretary of M.C.C., suggesting a meeting of the factions. With the cooperation of Wingfield, the other interested parties agreed to a general meeting with the M.C.C.'s rules committee to establish rules for lawn tennis as they recently had done for real/royal/court tennis. This was done and the rules were announced in *The Field* of May 1875. There were now 25 rules and they appeared in subsequent editions of Wingfield's book.

Before the M.C.C. rules came out on May 2, 1875, Wingfield wrote Fitzgerald that he would execute any legal document "for the public good," canceling "en masse" his rules. A similar letter appeared in *The Field* a week after *The Field* published the M.C.C. rules. With the letter agreeing to the M.C.C. rules, Wingfield withdrew from the tennis scene.

In the spring of 1877 under the leadership of Henry Jones, the All England Club decided to hold a tennis tournament. *The Field* carried the announcement and a call for competitors and the promise "if entries are sufficiently numerous, prizes: Gold Champion Prize and the Silver Prize. Also a Silver Challenge Cup, value 25 guineas..."

The tournament committee worried about infringing on Wingfield's patent. This was unnecessary, for Wingfield had allowed his patent to expire on Feb. 23, 1877, the patent's third anniversary, by not paying the £50 fee to extend the patent seven years. It was public information, being published in the *Official Journal (Patents)*. This was to the game's long-term benefit for it caused new rules to be drawn. These were written by a committee of Jones, Julian Marshall and Charles G. Heathcote. They established much of our present game.

The tournament, the original Wimbledon, was a success. Among 22 entries, Spencer Gore, a rackets player, beat William Marshall, a refugee from real tennis, in the final, 6-1, 6-2, 6-4.

The new rules used tennis scoring and a rectangular court (78 x 27 feet), dropping Wingfield's hourglass shape with baselines wider than the net and tapering to the net posts. Known as Wimbledon—it has been formally entitled The Lawn Tennis Championships from the beginning—the tournament became an annual fixture with Jones as referee. For several years he adjusted the net height and the service line according to the total of points won and lost on service until 1882, when the net heights arrived at today's 3-1/2 feet at the posts and three feet at center with the service line at 21 feet from the net. Regulations then became essentially today's, except for two rules which were troublesome for several years. The changing-of-ends rule went through many alterations until the simple and fair alternating of sides after each odd game of each set was established in 1890. Foot-faulting, a problem even now as serving becomes increasingly dominant, probably should be further addressed in order to ground the leapers and diminish the strong advantage held by powerful, aggressive servers with high-tech rackets.

In the matter of tournament control, two improvements were brought forth. R.B. Bagnal-Wild of Bath in 1883 proposed the present system of having byes in the first round so as to have the number of remaining players be of a power of two. This prevented three players arriving in the semi-finals as happened in the first Wimbledon. Such opening round byes were accepted for the 1885 Championships. The other improvement took longer. In 1883 none other than Charles L. Dodgson, a mathematician who wrote under the name of Lewis Carroll (*Alice in Wonderland*), issued a pamphlet, *Lawn Tennis Tournaments*—"The true method of assigning prizes, with proof of the fallacy of the present method." It was seeding that he envisioned, but he died before it was first permitted in the 1922 tournament.

In 1880 a Northern Lawn Tennis Association (of England) was founded and in 1883 the formation of a Lawn Tennis Association was attempted, but it failed for want of All England Club cooperation. The All England Club became the premier organization in tennis, supplanting the M.C.C. in those matters, and has remained a powerful tennis body, as witness its ability to lead the world to open tennis. The game owes much to the

M.C.C. for its guidance and lending its name and prestige to the infant tennis during its early critical years.

On the courts, tennis made great strides in the 1880s. Progress in the level of play was led by the Renshaw twins. They had grown up with the game and were not handicapped with styles formed for rackets or real tennis. Willie Renshaw won the Wimbledon championships of 1881 through 1886 plus 1889. Ernest won in 1888. Herbert Lawford won in 1887 when Willie, laid up with the first well-known case of tennis elbow, did not defend his title. The Renshaws also dominated the doubles, winning seven of the first 10 titles.

Men's doubles was introduced in 1879, but played at Oxford until 1884, the year ladies' singles made the scene. Ladies' doubles and mixed doubles were added in 1913. The draws were small, only 16 players in 1887 for the men's tournament and six ladies in 1888, the all-time lows. Attendance grew from 200 in 1877 to 3,500 in 1885. This growth of tennis ended in 1890 with interest switching to bicycle activities that were much enhanced by the invention of the modern bicycle. The 1890s were also a time of recession in the business world.

With the cooperation of the A.E.C. (All England Club) the L.T.A. (Lawn Tennis Association) was formed in 1888. It was agreed that the A.E.C. and the L.T.A. would share the funds raised by the Championships. However, the decline in popularity of tennis brought small draws and reduced attendance. The tournament of 1895 was in the red, losing £35. By the turn of the century tennis regained favor and went on to greater crowds and more players.

It was natural that tennis would come quickly to North America for there were close relationships, both social and commercial, with the motherland. British periodicals, including *The Field,* came to many in the U.S. and Canada. The date the first set arrived is not known but its arrival was inevitable. Curiously, the earliest-found record of play is Oct. 8, 1874 in the then-remote Camp Apache, Arizona Territory, north of Tucson.

In Martha Summerhayes's book, *Vanished Arizona,* she reports tennis being played by an Army officer's wife, Ella Wilkins Bailey. Her husband's records confirm the date. The trip to Apache began in San Francisco on Aug. 6, 1874. Based on Major Hamilton's purchase in May 1874, Canada may have had its first taste of the game after he opened his "unpainted box."

Tennis certainly was on the East Coast in the summer of 1874, and who was first is of little importance, for it arrived independently at several places: Boston, Newport, New York and Philadelphia as well as New Orleans and San Francisco. The game did not spread from only one center.

While both Miss Mary Outerbridge of Staten Island, N.Y., and Dr. James Dwight of Boston have their adherents as 'the introducer' of the game to the United States, there is no definite certainty for either. It is certain that neither was trying to be first, and made no claim to that effect. However, leadership of the game in the U.S. clearly fell to Dr. Dwight, who became known rightfully as 'the father of American lawn tennis.'

He may also have been a 'first' player, trying out the game with a cousin, Fred Sears, while summering at seaside Nahant outside of Boston in 1874. They marked out a court in the yard of the Appleton estate, and gave it a try. No date recorded. Regardless, he was associated with almost all important tennis events during the first quarter century of tennis in the U.S. Doc Dwight did, undoubtedly, organize a tournament in 1876. With cousin Fred, he held a formal and handicapped round-robin tournament for 15 entries, Dwight beating Sears in the final. In 1878, the Nahant tournament used the A.E.C. rules. Two years later Doc played in the so-called 'Nationals' at Staten Island Cricket and Baseball Club. Dwight's questioning of the balls used as not being proper was turned aside by the tournament officials by showing the word 'Regulation' marked on each ball.

That unsatisfactory tourney caused the formation of the U.S. National Lawn Tennis Association in 1881. Dwight followed the first president, R.S. Oliver, as president, a position he held for 21 of the association's first 31 years. Under the direction of the new association, the first recognized national tournament was held at Newport and a 19-year-old Harvard student, Dick Sears, a Dwight cousin, was the winner, retaining the title through 1887. The 'other guy' in that original final was an Englishman, William E. Glyn, who was 20 or 21, summered at Newport, and has pretty much been lost in history, not even being accorded celebrity as the first flop, 6-0, 6-3, 6-2. Was he also the first choker?

In the 1881 doubles, Sears and Dwight were surprised losers in the third round to Philadelphia's team of Clarence Clark and Fred Taylor, who went on to win the championship. Sears and Dwight won the doubles five of the next six years. In 1883, following matches between Dwight and Sears versus the winning Clark brothers, Clarence and Joe, the Clarks went off to England. There in an exhibition they lost to the Renshaws 6-4, 8-6, 3-6, 6-1, and a week later the Renshaws won in straight sets.

Later that year, following the U.S. Championships, Dwight went abroad and spent the fall, winter and spring competing against the best English players, including the Renshaws, playing indoors at Maida Vale in London and outdoors at Cannes. In 1885 he lost in the Wimbledon semi-finals to the champion, Herbert Lawford, 6-2, 6-2, 6-3. As the most successful of the first Americans to play Wimbledon, in 1884 (he was joined by Dick Sears and Arthur Rives), Dwight was beaten in the second round of singles by the ambidextrous Herbert Chipp. Chipp had defeated Rives in the first round. Sears, kept out of the singles by injury, then joined Dwight to reach the doubles semi-finals where they lost to the champion Renshaws, 6-0, 6-1, 6-2.

However, Dwight won the Northern England Championship in 1884, the first foreigner to take a title in the game's motherland, and with Willie Renshaw the 1885 Buxton doubles Tournament. During these years he ranked just below the very best of England. He was much respected and through his instructional articles and two books, *Lawn Tennis* in 1886 and *Practical Lawn Tennis* in 1893, did much for the level of play in the U.S. His books were the standard instruction until 1920, when Bill Tilden's *The Art of Lawn Tennis* was published.

Tennis lost ground in the 1890s to both the bicycle and golf, but Dwight saw the game and the USTA through those lean years. It was through his contacts with English players that the Davis Cup was launched in 1900, for which he drew up the rules. This helped restore the game to broad attention.

As the 20th century arrived, tennis had weathered its first recession and came back stronger than ever. It would not be the last time the sport ebbed. By 1900 all the strokes, tactics and strategies had become part of the game. The Renshaws brought the net game; Lawford introduced topspin; and Holcombe Ward and Dwight Davis created the American twist serve (kicker). All these have been improved, but a few, like the reverse twist serve, are no longer used.

Then, as now, most of the play took place on the public courts. This is not to gainsay the importance of the great tennis clubs. In the mid-1880s, Prospect Park in Brooklyn, N.Y., had over 100 clubs using its facilities. Sports clubs have often been targeted as havens of snobs

and bigots. Clubs, as other groups of people, have their share, but they have done much good for tennis and other sports. They established standards of play, deportment and facilities, which elevated the game everywhere. Almost all the greats of the game have started on the public courts, but they refined their games at clubs and colleges.

The year Doc Dwight organized the seminal tournament at Nahant, 1876, was also the year of the founding of the first tennis club in the U.S., the New Orleans Lawn Tennis Club. Founded in 1877, Boston's Longwood Cricket Club, then situated at the corner of Brookline and Longwood Avenues, near the plot where Fenway Park would rise in 1912, adopted lawn tennis in 1878. Longwood is another footnote alluding to the importance of Boston's Sears family in the evolution of the game. The property, a piece of his vast estate called Longwood after the manor in which the exiled Napoleon died on the isle of St. Helena, was rented from David Sears. His nephew, Dick, who won the first seven U.S. championships, was a Napoleon buff. Various other Searses made early marks, including Eleonora Sears, a Hall of Famer, and Evelyn Sears, U.S. champ in 1907.

The inaugural Wimbledon embraced only one event, the men's singles. An entry of 22 was received, and on Monday, July 9, 1877, a fine, sunny day, The Lawn Tennis Championships began. One entrant, C.F. Buller, was absent, so there were only 10 instead of the expected 11 matches. The 11 survivors were reduced to six on Tuesday, then to three on Wednesday. The notion of restricting byes to the first round was still eight years off. On Thursday, William Marshall had a free passage into the final while Spencer W. Gore beat Charles Heathcote. Advantage sets had not been adopted.

The title match was held over until the following Monday. Such delay had been indicated in the prospectus to allow for the Eton-Harrow cricket match at Lords. This was the ultimate sporting event so far as the fashionable London world was concerned, and lawn tennis, itself a fashionable sport, did not dream for many years of coming into conflict with that important fixture. Monday turned out wet, and the final was postponed until Thursday, July 19. That day was also damp, but rather than disappoint 200 spectators, each of whom had paid one shilling (then about 25 cents) to see Wimbledon's baptismal final, Gore and Marshall sportingly agreed to play. Gore came up to the net and volleyed. Whether this was entirely sporting was a matter of some debate, as was his striking the ball before it had crossed the net. He won, 6-1, 6-2, 6-4.

An old Harrovian of 27, Gore had played rackets at school and was a keen cricketer. He didn't think much of the new game. Defending his title the next year, he lost in the challenge round to Frank Hadow, another old Harrovian on leave from coffee planting in Ceylon. Hadow thoughtfully circumvented Gore, the volleyer, by lobbing, a stroke not seen before. For Hadow, one shot—with high shots—at the title was enough. He didn't return until the Jubilee celebration in 1927.

Gore later wrote: "That anyone who has really played well at cricket, [real] tennis, or even rackets, will ever seriously give his attention to lawn tennis, beyond showing himself to be a promising player, is extremely doubtful; for in all probability the monotony of the game as compared with the others would choke him off before he had time to excel at it."

Those were the views of the world's first champion. Gore died in 1906, still an avid cricketer.

Competing in 1878 was a former Cambridge real tennis player, A. T. Myers. He, too, was an innovator, serving overhand. Yet it is obvious that at the time there was more of the vicarage lawn than athleticism about the infant game. In 1879 the Wimbledon champion was in fact a vicar, the Reverend John Hartley, yet another old Harrovian. He kept his title in 1880, and his ability to endlessly return the ball was notorious.

In 1881, the game took on a new dimension. Two wealthy young twins from Cheltenham, in the west of England, initiated a dominance that endured for nearly a decade. They were Willie and Ernest Renshaw. In that year Willie won the first of his seven singles titles at Wimbledon. In the challenge round he beat Hartley, 6-0, 6-1, 6-1, in an extraordinarily brief and devastating 37 minutes. Its brevity is partly explained by the fact that at that time players changed ends only after each set. It is also explained by the difference in style. Hartley was a gentle retriever. Renshaw served hard, volleyed hard, smashed hard and went for fast winners all round. He and Ernest created modern lawn tennis. Crowds flocked to see them play.

In winning six straight titles, a record, Willie had a streak of 12 matches, having to play only the challenge round for titles two through six against the winner of the all-comers final. That system was dropped in 1922. He missed 1887, then won two more matches before succumbing to 'Ghost' Hamilton in the 1888 quarters,

his winning string ending at 14. That was the tourney record for 48 years until countryman Fred Perry, champ in 1934-35-36, broke it with his 15th. Fred went on to establish a record of 21. Thirty-three years passed until that one fell to Aussie Rod Laver, who stretched the record to 31. Laver's mark endured just 11 years, falling to Bjorn Borg, who took it to 41 consecutive match wins.

Ernest Renshaw, overshadowed by his brother Willie, took only one Wimbledon singles title, 1888. But Ernest, who'd allowed the title to slip from the family in losing to Lawford in 1887, might have had another in 1889 if win-happy Willie hadn't made the first extraordinary comeback at the Big W—maybe the most extraordinary—in the all-comers final to beat Harry Barlow, 3-6, 5-7, 8-6, 10-8, 8-6. Willie resurrected himself from 2-5 in the fourth through six match points, and 0-5 in the fifth. Exhilarated by that, Willie beat Ernest in the fratricidal challenge round for his seventh and last title, a total equaled by Pete Sampras 111 years later.

The Scottish Championships in Edinburgh was inaugurated in 1878. The Irish Championships in Dublin, begun in 1879, was notable for initiating a women's singles as well as a mixed doubles event. The women's events, however, were restricted in some degree. While the main part of the tournament was played on courts prepared in Fitzwilliam Square and open to the public, the women were confined to the relative privacy of the Fitzwilliam Club itself. Only members and their guests were permitted the sight of well-turned ankles on display. The game's first woman champion of the world was 14-year-old May Langrishe, beating D. Meldon, 6-2, 0-6, 8-6.

The men's singles champion in the first Irish Championships was Vere 'St. Leger' Goold. In the same year he became finalist in the all-comers' singles at Wimbledon, losing to the gentle Hartley. Many years later Goold wrote a unique, unsavory chapter for himself in the history of the game. Convicted of murder by a French court, he was sent to Devil's Island where he died.

That spurious 'Championship of America,' staged in 1880, began on Sept. 1 on the courts at the Staten Island Cricket and Baseball Club. The prize was a silver cup valued at $100. Rackets scoring was used, with the results turning on the aggregate number of aces. An Englishman, Otway Edward Woodhouse, wrote from Chicago asking if he could enter. A member of the West

Middlesex Club, Ealing, England, he had played that year at Wimbledon and reached the all-comers' final before losing to Lawford. Woodhouse's overhand service was a novelty to American players. With this advantage he reached the final, where he beat a Canadian, J. F. Helmuth, 15-11, 14-15, 15-9, 10-15, victory based on a score of 54 points to 50. It was an unsatisfactory resolution.

In October 1880 a tournament was played at Beacon Park, Boston. The winner was Dick Sears. Real tennis scoring was used. The nonstandardization of the game, both in its equipment and scoring, brought increasing difficulties as it grew. Controversy about the correct way to play lawn tennis highlighted the need for fully accepted regulation. With that in mind, a meeting was arranged at the Fifth Avenue Hotel in New York on May 21, 1881, in the name of three prominent clubs: The Beacon Park Athletic Association of Boston, the Staten Island Cricket and Baseball Club of New York, and the All Philadelphia Lawn Tennis Committee.

Thirty-three clubs were represented, and the U.S. National Lawn Tennis Association, as it was then named, came into being. A constitution was drawn, the rules of the All England Club and the M.C.C. were adopted. R.S. Oliver of the Albany Lawn Tennis Club was elected president, and Clarence Clark secretary-treasurer. A vice president and an executive committee of three were also chosen.

This was the first national association in the world, the doyen of such bodies. Apart from its standardization of the game, where the British example was followed, its other major decision was to inaugurate the National Championships of the United States (hereinafter called the U.S. Championships), embracing men's singles and doubles. The scene would be the Newport Casino at Newport, R.I., probably without equal at that time as the American resort of wealth and fashion.

It began on Aug. 31, 1881, with a singles entry of 26. Except for the final, the best of three sets (not five) was played. Sears, 19 years, 10 months old, won without losing a set. A U.S. champion with a remarkable career, he won seven times in all, playing through in both 1882 and 1883 without losing a set. In 1884 the challenge round was instituted, and in the title match Sears yielded a set for the first time, to Howard Taylor, 6-0, 1-6, 6-0, 6-2. After three further championships, he retired with a singular singles record: Matches played, 18; matches won, 18.

From 1882 through 1887 Sears also won the doubles six times—five with James Dwight and once with Joseph Clark. Sears learned to volley in 1881, the same time that the Renshaw twins were introducing their arts of aggression in England. They did so independently of each other.

In 1884 the Wimbledon meeting was enlarged to include a women's singles and a men's doubles. The doubles cups were passed on from the tournament that had been staged, albeit with failing interest, at Oxford since 1879, and where originally the distance was over the best of seven sets.

The other new Wimbledon event, the women's singles, was staged at the same time. The first winner, from a field of 13 ambitious and progressive-minded young women, was Maud Watson. She was 19 years old, facing in the final her 26-year-old sister, Lilian. They were the daughters of the vicar of Berkswell, a village in the heart of England. Maud won, 6-8, 6-3, 6-3.

The losing semi-finalist to Watson, Blanche Bingley (later Mrs. George Hillyard), became one of the most indefatigable champions of all time. She won the singles six times between 1886 and 1900 and played for the last time in 1913 when she was 49. Before winning at Wimbledon in 1884, Watson beat, in Dublin, the game's first female champion, May Langrishe, the Irish winner of 1879. There was coincidence in the deaths of the two women: Langrishe died in 1939 at a house called 'Hammersmead' in Charmouth, a Devonshire, England seaside resort; seven years later Watson died in the same house.

The women's game, recognized first by the Irish in 1879, made its early efforts in England and Ireland in concert with the men. In the U.S. the women came forward on their own, at least in the beginning. In 1887 the first U.S. Women's Championship, held at the Philadelphia Cricket Club, was an outgrowth of the first (1886) Chestnut Hill Tennis Club Ladies Open. The second 'open' (amateurs nonetheless, but from any club) became the first U.S. Championships when the Wissahickon Inn offered the Wissahickon Cup as the singles prize. Arrangements for the 1886-87 tournaments were conducted by the Chestnut Hill T.C., and play was at the Philadelphia C.C. In 1888 the Cricket Club took over sponsorship of the national championships, and continued until the 1921 move to Forest Hills.

Seven women entered the singles in 1887, all from

the greater Delaware Valley area. The champ, Ellen Hansell, a 6-1, 6-0, victor over Laura Knight, represented Philadelphia's Belmont Cricket Club. The 1888 tourney included New Yorkers Adeline Robinson and the Roosevelt sisters, Ellen and Grace, but was won by another Philadelphian from the Belmont Club, Bertha Townsend.

On Feb. 9, 1889, the USNLTA carried a motion that "its protection be extended to the Lady Lawn Tennis players of the country." Ireland's Mabel Cahill won in 1892 and again one year later. She beat Elisabeth 'Bessie' Moore in 1891. For eight of the next nine years the women played the best of five sets, but only in the all-comers finals and challenge rounds.

The growth of lawn tennis around the world was fast. Clubs were founded in Scotland, Brazil and India in 1875. It was played in Germany in 1876. In 1877 the Fitzwilliam Club was started in Dublin, Ireland, and the Decimal Club in Paris was the first in France. Australia, Sweden, Italy, Hungary and Peru had lawn tennis courts in 1878, and the first tournament in Australia was the Victorian Championship meeting in 1879. Denmark and Switzerland date their beginnings from 1880, Argentina from 1881. The first club in the Netherlands was in 1882; in Jamaica in 1883; and in 1885 in both Greece and Turkey. Lawn tennis came to Lebanon in 1889, to Egypt in 1890 and to Finland in the same year. South Africa's first championship was staged in 1891.

Wealthy Russian landowners were setting up courts in the late 1870s. One of them was the great author, Leo Tolstoy, whose 1878 novel, *Anna Karenina*, includes a tennis scene. An enthusiastic player himself, he was photographed playing as early as 1896 on his court at Yasnaya Polyana. The Lakhta Lawn Tennis Club outside of St. Petersburg was founded in 1888.

In 1879, a prize-money tournament was held at Duke Kinski's castle at Chocen, Bohemia (a sector of the Czech Republic). That year another Bohemian tourney was played on grass at Nove Benatsky involving a thirsty cast: First prize was a barrel of wine. The hungry were involved in the same area in an annual team match between the towns of Zbraslov and Rakovenic: First prize, a gigantic cucumber. Like those remarkable cukes, the game just kept growing.

After the successful intervention of Britain's Otway Woodhouse, in that unofficial American championship of 1880, an Irishman, J.J. Cairnes, was refused entry to the 1881 Championships at Newport. But he was

permitted to play in the Ladies Cup tourney there immediately afterwards, and Cairnes, a semi-finalist in the initial Irish Championships of 1879, won the event easily, beating the newly crowned U.S. champ, Sears, in the final.

In 1889 Ernest Meers, a top British player, was one of the first overseas challengers at Newport. He lost in five sets to Oliver Campbell, 18. The following year Campbell became champion for the first time at the age of 19 years, six months, defeating Henry Slocum. He was the youngest champ for a century, until Sampras, 19 years, one month, in 1990. It was evidently a time that favored youth. One year later, in 1891, Wilfred Baddeley won the men's singles championship at Wimbledon at 19 years, six months, a record lowered by 17-year-old Boris Becker in 1985.

A 'pro tour' of sorts even took brief form in 1889. George Kerr, billed as the Irish professional champ, came to the U.S. to battle Tom Pettit of Boston, the teaching pro at Newport Casino and regarded as the New World's leading professional. They played at Springfield, Mass., Boston and Newport, and Kerr was the victor in three of four matches.

In 1895 what almost amounted to a representative contest between the Americans and the British took the form of a round-robin tournament at the Neighborhood Club, West Newton, Mass. The British players were Ireland's Joshua Pim, the Wimbledon champion of 1893-94, and Harold Mahony, destined to become the champion in 1896. The Americans were Bill Larned, who later became a seven-time U.S. singles champion, Clarence Hobart, Fred Hovey and Malcolm Chace. Pim lost only to Hobart, while Mahony, unbeaten by Americans, lost only to Pim. The first prize went to Pim, the second to Mahony.

The British challenge at Newport in 1897 was formidable, comprising Mahony, Harold Nisbet and Wilberforce Eaves, who was Australian-born but living in England. The British spectators, if there were any among the wealthy and chic who came to the Newport Casino, must have held their heads high. Eaves and Nisbet made it an all-Empire final in the all-comers' singles. Eaves won and challenged Wrenn, but American pride was restored. Wrenn won with difficulty, taking his fourth title. It was his second thwarting of a trans-Atlantic challenge.

For several years Doc Dwight had been trying to stir up the Anglo-American rivalry into a team event instead of individual exercises. In 1900 his hopes reached fruition as his friend, another Harvardian, undergraduate Dwight Davis, put up his famous bauble, the International Lawn Tennis Challenge Trophy, which soon became known as the Davis Cup. Davis had been inspired 12 months earlier by a tennis-playing tour he undertook with Holcombe Ward, Malcolm Whitman and Beals Wright, all keen players in their early 20s. Accompanied by George Wright, a famous baseball player and the father of Beals, they traveled some 8,000 miles, from the Atlantic Coast to the Pacific and up to British Columbia, and were met with friendship and cordial hospitality by fellow tennists along the way. If this sort of competition could generate such good feeling, Davis reasoned (and Dwight agreed), why couldn't it be as worthwhile and rewarding on an international basis.

The USTA accepted Davis' offer and the International Lawn Tennis Challenge Trophy was offered to the world. They had the British primarily in mind and the Brits, despite the Boer War in South Africa, took up the challenge. Davis was named as the U.S. captain for the inaugural. He was then 21 and had reached the all-comers' singles final at Newport in 1899. Whitman, 23, the champion of 1898-99, and Ward, 22, doubles partner of Davis, were the other members, Harvard men all. Their club, Longwood Cricket, at its original Boston site, was selected for the showdown, and the matches were arranged for early August, well before the Newport meeting at the end of the month.

The British team, under the banner of British Isles, comprised playing-Capt. Arthur Gore, Ernest Black, and Herbert Roper Barrett. Gore, 32, with a lot of tennis life in him, had not yet won any of his three Wimbledon singles titles. The Scot, Black, never got as far as the quarters at Wimbledon. Roper Barrett was noted as a player of subtle abilities. It was not the best British team—the preeminent Doherty brothers were unavailable. It was selected not only on playing ability but also on a capacity to spare both the time and the money for the trip.

The British found the courts too soft, the grass too long and the Americans unexpectedly too tough. Barrett would complain that the net "was a disgrace, the balls awful soft and mothery—and when served with the American twist came at you like an animated egg-plum. We never experienced this service before and it quite nonplussed us." The kicking serves, particularly those of

Ward, bounding to the receiver's left, confounded them. But Barrett thought the spectators "impartial" and "the female portion thereof not at all unpleasant to gaze upon."

The first two singles were played simultaneously on side-by-side courts. Whitman beat Gore easily and Davis beat Black. Black and Roper Barrett were helpless the following day against Ward and Davis, losing 6-4, 6-4, 6-4. On the last day, Davis was up, 9-7, 9-9, when rain intervened. The rest of the series was called off, and the U.S. had a 3-0 triumph.

Later, in the U.S. Championships by the sea at Newport, Gore and Black made an effort to retrieve British honor. They clashed in the quarter-finals and Gore won in straight sets only to lose to George Wrenn in the next round. Whitman was still the boss, thrusting back the challenge of Larned, 6-4, 1-6, 6-2, 6-2, to keep his title.

Anglo-American rivalry continued to be the international aspect of tennis for some years. There was no challenge for the Davis Cup in 1901, but in 1902 the British renewed their effort, sending Reggie and Laurie Doherty, the finest British players of the time, with two-time Wimbledon champ Pim. They played against Whitman, Davis and Larned at the Crescent Athletic Club in Brooklyn, N.Y. As in 1900 the two singles were played at the same time on adjacent courts. Fearful of Laurie's fitness, the British played Pim with Reggie Doherty in the singles. An opening afternoon split gave the Brits hope: Wimbledon champ Reggie defeated Larned to offset Whitman's victory over Pim. But when Larned brushed off Pim, 6-3, 6-2, 6-2, and Whitman beat Reggie, 6-1, 7-5, 6-4, the second day, it was all over. The doubles, scheduled to take place on the third day, was to unveil Laurie, well rested, but his and Reggie's expected victory over Davis and Ward was too late.

The classic powers of the Dohertys, which had captivated the crowds at Wimbledon and elsewhere in Britain, were again displayed to American audiences later in the month at Newport. The brothers reached the semi-finals to play one another. Laurie gave a walkover to his elder brother and Reggie went on to beat Whitman in the all-comers final. Although he had beaten Larned in the Davis Cup, Reggie couldn't repeat his success with the U.S. title at stake and fell, 4-6, 6-2, 6-4, 8-6.

The year 1903 was a turning point and the British challenge in the U.S. was as effective as it was formidable. In the Davis Cup, where the British Isles was again the only challenger, the venue was again Longwood in Boston. Reggie and Laurie Doherty, put forward as a two-man side, made a gambling start, giving a match away. Because Reggie was the weaker physically and feeling unwell with a sore right shoulder, he defaulted his opening singles to Larned while Laurie beat Robert Wrenn. Then providence butted in—two days of rain. Reggie felt better and accompanied his brother to doubles victory over the Brothers Wrenn, Robert and George, 7-5, 9-7, 2-6, 6-3.

Thrilling but screwy was the decisive third day when both Dohertys won tight five-set matches, played side by side, that could have gone the other way. Larned's probably should have. In the confusion and tension of spectators, their cheers for one match sometimes interrupted the other as they tried to follow both. Anxiety was high in the stands and among the players as well as the two contests were neck-and-neck in the fifth. But Larned, up 15-40 against Laurie's serve, knocked a winning return and was announced as the leader, 5-4. Hold on. Laurie thought his serve had been a fault, long, and queried umpire Fred Mansfield. The umpire turned to the service linesman and … beheld only an empty chair! That judge had disappeared. As the author of Cup regulations, and referee, Doc Dwight ruled the point replayed. Laurie won the point, the game, and the next two—thus the Cup, 6-4, 3-6, 6-4, 6-8, 7-5. Having paused to monitor the discussion, Reggie proceeded to finish off Wrenn, 6-4, 3-6, 6-3, 6-8, 6-4, and the Cup was to leave its homeland for the first time, 4-1. It stayed away, in London, as the Dohertys backboned their country to a four-year run.

In the 1905 prelims in London, the Souths Seas islanders and the Americans launched what would become the greatest of tennis feuds, fierce yet friendly. The Yanks beat the Australasians, 5-0, the first of 45 clashes (25-20, U.S.) through 2003.

By 1907 the Doherty's had retired and the boys from the Antipodes, Australasia, a two-nation blend in the persons of crafty left-handed Aussie Norman Brookes and strapping, athletic New Zealander Tony Wilding, had arrived. They spirited the Cup way down south and kept it until 1912. They were led by Brookes, 29, the first overseas entrant to win the Wimbledon men's singles. He piloted the Down Undertakers' seizure of their first of 27 Cups. It started with a 3-2 semi-final decision over the U.S. and ended with a 3-2 win over Britain.

In 1912, the Brookes-Rodney Heath ticket couldn't withstand a challenge from Irishman Jim Parke and Charles Dixon, who reclaimed the cup for Britain, 3-2, at Melbourne. But Britain didn't keep it long, losing it to the U.S., 3-2, in 1913. The Americans were back in the swim with the 'Miracle Man,' future U.S. champ Dick Williams. Dick, little more than a year after surviving the doomed *Titanic*, contributed five-for-five singles wins during the longest journey yet to the challenge round: Victories over Australia, 4-1 at Forest Hills, Germany, 5-0 at Nottingham and Canada, 3-0 at Wimbledon.

Nor was the sterling punchbowl to stay long in the States. Brookes and Wilding snatched it back shortly after World War I exploded in August. The Cup went to Melbourne to sit out the war as a flower bowl in Brookes' home until 1920. Both victors went off to war, Wilding to a tragic death, killed in France less than a year later. Americans didn't see the gleaming basin again for six years when the two Bills, Tilden and Johnston, pried it from Brookes & Co. in Auckland.

After snatching the Cup in Boston in 1903, the Dohertys achieved something more in carting off, too, the U.S. Championships at Newport. Once again they were cast as foes in the quarter-finals. This time Laurie was given the walkover. He went on to reach the challenge round, where he relieved Larned of his title. The brothers also retained the doubles title.

Laurie, the first man to take the U.S. singles title overseas, was then 27, perhaps at his peak. Reggie, three years older, won four straight Wimbledon singles, 1897-1900. The more robust Laurie followed with a five-year sequence, 1902-06. Their classic skill became a British legend and their impeccable sportsmanship a byword. In doubles there was only one year between 1897 and 1905 that they missed out on the Wimbledon title.

If 1903 was a momentous year for the U.S. Championships, so was 1905 at Wimbledon. An American woman had entered for the first time in 1900. Marion Jones, then the U.S. champion, got as far as the quarter-finals. Five years later a chubby, robust 18-year-old from California with an intimidating forehand made a memorable appearance. She was May Sutton and she, too, was the U.S. title-holder. As it happened, she was English-born at Plymouth, Devonshire, the daughter of a British naval captain who later took his family to California.

The staunch Sutton penetrated a citadel where the

names of some women were already being spoken of reverently. Most venerated at that time was Lottie Dod, 15-year-old winner in 1887 of the first of her five championships, youngest ever to win a major singles. There was Blanche Hillyard, six-time champion. Dorothea 'Dolly' Douglass (later Mrs. Lambert Chambers) had, when the uninhibited Sutton appeared, already won twice and was on the way to making herself a legend. But Sutton carved through all opposition and had the temerity to stop Douglass from winning for the third time, standing out as the first overseas player to take a Wimbledon championship.

Two years later, all three titles available left the country, another first. Brookes captured the men's singles and took the doubles as well with Wilding. May Sutton, (loser of her title to Dolly Chambers in 1906), regained it in a rematch, 6-1, 6-4. Women's doubles and mixed weren't yet on the card. The Brits would soon have to get used to such thefts.

In the U.S., the championships meeting at Newport settled back into American control after the Doherty sortie of 1903. Outstanding man of the first decade of the century was Larned. A New York stockbroker, he won the U.S. singles for the first time in 1901 over Wright at age 28, and would equal the record of Sears by taking it seven times, the last in 1911 over Maurice McLoughlin as the oldest of champs at 38. He played 73 singles in all and won 61. Big Bill Tilden, the last seven-time winner, did better (69-7). Larned had an unbroken sequence of 11 victories from 1907, when he played through and won, to his success in his last challenge round of 1911.

The popularity of the Newport singles reached unprecedented heights during Larned's career. The entries passed 128 for the first time in 1908 and peaked at 202 in 1911, the last year of the challenge round. McLoughlin, a redheaded 21-year-old known as the 'California Comet,' took over for Larned, beating Wallace Johnson in 1912 and retaining in 1913. McLoughlin's dynamic serving brought a new dimension to the game and so did his background. He was the first public parks player to take a title that had been dominated by club men from wealthy families.

In 1913, the year of McLoughlin's only appearance in England, he was an energetic factor in taking the Davis Cup from the homebodies, and leaving Wimbledon spectators awestruck by his serving—inspiring a new useage: 'Cannonball.' Before record crowds he came

through the all-comers' singles over Aussie Stanley Doust and challenged Wilding, the title-holder since 1910, for the crown. "The history of the match," it was written at the time, "may be succinctly stated by saying that McLoughlin ought to have won the first set and was very near to winning the third. He lost both of them, and the second into the bargain, and so Wilding retained the honors", 8-6, 6-3, 10-8.

Wilding's invincibility at Wimbledon was finally brought to an end in 1914 by his Davis Cup colleague, Brookes, who, at age 36, won his second Wimbledon singles. Not long afterward, they united to carry the Cup away from New York

Three years earlier, in 1911, the West Side Tennis Club had staged its first Davis Cup. The famed, peripatetic club was put together in 1892 by 13 founding members who rented three clay courts on Central Park West between 88th and 89th Streets, Manhattan. By the end of that season there were 43 members, five courts, and the initiation fee was $10, with a yearly subscription of the same amount. A move to a site near Columbia University at 117th Street between Morningside Drive and Amsterdam Avenue occurred in 1902. Six years later another move took the club to 238th Street and Broadway, a site that had room for 12 grass and 15-or-more clay courts. The shift from Manhattan to Forest Hills in Queens was made in 1913.

In 1915 West Side became the grass court host to the U.S. Men's Singles Championship. Williams waved his racket and a farewell to Newport Casino's sod in 1914 by usurping McLoughlin's championship, 6-3, 8-6, 10-8, reversing the outcome of the 1913 final, won by the Comet. The Casino, after 34 years as home of America's most prestigious event, had outlived that purpose, though it remains in the game as a pro tourney site and home of the International Tennis Hall of Fame. The age it represented, of wealth and fashion and leisure, was passing.

In 1921, West Side absorbed the U.S. Women's Champion-ships as well, and New York became the country's tennis capital. Before that the turf of the Philadelphia Cricket Club was the women's battleground. The most consistent champs had been Bessie Moore, four-time victor between 1896 and 1905, and Juliette Atkinson, capturing three between 1895 and 1898. Juliette prevailed in rare, five-set finals to win over Bessie in 1897, and Marion Jones in 1898. The women felt they had the physiques and moxie to play best-of-five finals just like the men, but timidly the USTA soon wimped out on their behalf, settling on best-of-three to much distaff dismay and disagreement.

The champion of 1908, Maud Barger Wallach, took a special place in the roll of winners. A high-society lady who'd taken up the game at 30, she was 38 when she won the title over defender Evelyn Sears (the first left-handed champ). At 45, Maud was still ranked national-ly, No. 5. However, Maud didn't have a chance at keep-ing her crown once a five-foot fireball, University of California student Hazel Hotchkiss, hit Philly. Hazel, who would go on to become known as 'Lady Tennis,' donate the Wightman Cup (as Mrs. George Wightman) for a team competition between the U.S. and Britain, and land in the Hall of Fame, swept Maud away in a tide of volleying, 6-0, 6-1. She recalled pitying her adversary: "Mrs. Barger Wallach didn't have a backhand. She looked 150 to young [22] me."

Hazel tripled that year, adding the doubles and mixed diadems, the first three of her record 45 U.S. adult championships. Ditto 1910 and 1911, a rare and unprecedented triple-triple—all nine U.S. titles in three years—before she settled in as a Boston housewife. Her only precarious singles victory was 1911 over one of the renowned Californian Sutton sisters, Florence. She was followed by yet another Californian triple-tripler Mary K. Browne, seizing all the silver in 1912-13-14.

Next into the winner's circle came the Norwegian-born strongwoman, Molla Bjurstedt, running four of her record eight titles between 1915 and 1918. Wightman grabbed one more singles, and after having a child, in 1919. Then it was Molla again (as Mrs. Franklin Mallory) for three more. Molla, raising the American level in the post-war years, didn't make her record exclu-sively as an American. An Olympian in Stockholm in 1912 she represented Norway, winning the bronze medal in singles on indoor courts.

Tennis was featured as part of the modern Olympic Games from the first in Athens in 1896 to the Paris event of 1924, then restored in 1988. At the pre-war Games, British players predominated except for those at St. Louis in 1904. Only men took part and the gold medallists were exclusively American, Wright taking one for the singles and, with Edgar Leonard, the doubles.

In international administration 1913 was important, the year of the founding of the ILTF (International Lawn Tennis Federation), eventually shortened to the ITF. It was an idea proposed by Philadelphian Duane

Williams, who didn't live to see it come into being. In 1912, he went down with the *Titanic*, from which his championship son, Dick Williams, swam to safety. Prior to this time the world governing body, so far as there had been one, was the LTA (Lawn Tennis Association) of Britain. Its membership included clubs and associations from all around the world. In 1913 the LTA members included the associations of Australasia, Belgium, Bohemia, Ceylon, Chile, Finland, Hungary, Ireland, Jamaica, Mauritius, Netherlands, Norway, the Riviera, Russia, South Africa, Spain and Switzerland, as well as 26 individual clubs from 15 countries.

At the ITF's inaugural meeting in Paris on March 1, 1913, the founding members were Australasia, Austria, Belgium, the British Isles, Denmark, France, Germany, Netherlands, Russia, South Africa, Sweden and Switzerland. No U.S., which was only informally repre-sented, by one of the British delegates, H. Anthony Sabelli, secretary of the LTA. The absence resulted in the Davis Cup organization developing along different lines from the ITF, parallel but separate. (The merger didn't take place until 1978.)

U.S. reluctance to join the ITF was occasioned by the allocation of various 'World Championship' titles. Wimbledon was granted ("in perpetuity") "The World Championships on Grass." There was a 'World Hard Court Championships' (clay), staged in Paris, also a moveable 'World Covered Court Championships.' When these grandiose titles were abolished soon after World War I, the U.S. felt comfortable in joining.

An early winner of the women's singles in the 1914 World's Hard Court Championships in Paris was a promising French schoolgirl, only 15. Also winner of the doubles with American Elizabeth 'Bunny' Ryan, she came from Picardy, and was named Suzanne Lenglen, an all-time great-to-be.

Ryan's name was also to echo reverberatingly. Even before 1914 this Californian had laid the foundation of her career as an assiduous, effective competitor. The women's and mixed doubles at Wimbledon were accept-ed as official championships in 1913, the World title on grass attached to them. In 1914, indefatigable Ryan partnered Agnes Morton to win the women's doubles, the first of her 19 Wimbledon titles, a record that stood until 1979 when Billie Jean King won her 20th.

The Riviera season was by then a well-established feature of the game, reflecting an exclusive atmosphere of fashion, wealth, royalty and internationalism which had become as much a part of tennis in Europe, as exemplified by Newport. Immediately prior to the war, however, it was perhaps Imperial Russia that represented the high point of tennis in its smart social context. British men who played in St. Petersburg in the Russian Championships of 1913 recorded that the ball boys were footmen in ornate uniforms who passed the balls on silver salvers. Ryan was the last women's champion of Imperial Russia, a title she was never able to defend.

Ryan was overshadowed at this time, like all other women, by Mrs. Lambert Chambers, as Dorothea 'Dolly' Douglass had become. Dolly made 13 attempts to win the Wimbledon singles between 1902 and 1920, and was beaten only six times. At the age of 24 she won for the first time, in 1903, over Ethel Thomson. Her seventh success, 1914, over Thomson (who had become Mrs. Dudley Larcombe) set Dolly apart as the precursor of great, near-invincible players. During this period it was still possible to be on top, yet excel at other sports. Dolly was also a champion at badminton and a top field hockey player.

The Davis Cup helped boost tennis internationally. Prior to 1914, when war brought the competition to a temporary halt, there were nine entries: The U.S., British Isles, Belgium, France, Australasia, Austria, Germany, Canada, South Africa. The Australian Championships, staged first in 1905, and won by Rod Heath, would gain recognition as the third.

A notable champion, perhaps the greatest monopolizer of any national title, Miss K. M. Nunneley held the New Zealand title for 13 successive years from 1895. Across the Tasman Sea, Australia didn't hold a women's championship until 1922 when Margaret Mutch 'Mall' Molesworth won the first of her two.

The French, prior to the war, made an impact with men of high caliber, Andre Gobert and Max Decugis most notably. They won the men's doubles at Wimbledon in 1911, but it was not until 1925 that the French Championships was opened to non-citizens, standing forth as the fourth major. A German pair, Heinrich Kleinschroth and Friedrich Rahe, were runners-up for the Wimbledon title in 1913. In 1912 Kleinschroth competed in the U.S. Championships at Newport but did not survive the opening round. The German Championships was an event favored by British players and among the fashionable happenings of the season, staged in Hamburg from 1892.

Canada's first national championships was held two years earlier, in 1890, 12 years after the country's initial tournament on the turf of the Montreal Cricket Club. Like those in the U.S., the first official championships, for men, followed the founding of the Canadian Lawn Tennis Association in Toronto in 1890, with the championships for women launched two years later.

In Europe, war brought a halt to tournament tennis in 1914. Australia kept its championships going for the 1915 season, and a Brit, Gordon Lowe, was the winner, over lefty Horace Rice, 4-6, 6-1, 6-1, 6-4. Rice retaliated in the doubles final, joining with Clairie Todd to beat Lowe and the only one-handed man to grace a major final, a lefty, Bert St. John, 8-6, 6-4, 7-9, 6-3.

Although the American game was affected to a lesser degree by war, the international field dried up. In 1917, after the U.S. had become directly involved in hostilities, there was something of a break. The U.S. Championships was not played as such, but conducted under the heading of 'Patriotic Tournaments,' with proceeds going to wartime charities. Eventually the winners in 1917-18, Lindley Murray and Molla Bjurstedt (the future Mrs. Mallory), were granted full championship status.

In 1918 a tall, somewhat ungainly Philadelphian, William Tatem Tilden II, did well on his third attempt in the U.S. ('Patriotic') singles. Reaching the final, he was handcuffed by the potent left-handed serve of Murray, 6-3, 6-1, 7-5. Murray's aggressiveness had been on display the year before at the expense of figure skating champ Nat Niles from Boston. The juggernaut, Molla, won her sixth and seventh. Tilden did, however, inscribe his name earlier on the U.S. Championship rolls, accompanying Mary K. Browne to the mixed doubles title of 1912, and 15-year-old Vinnie Richards—the youngest male winner of a major—to the doubles title of 1918.

But, making his first significant mark, Tilden was a late developer, 27, at his breakthrough to the singles championships of Wimbledon and the U.S. in 1920. Nevertheless, he was on his way, a principal in 1918, the first of his eight consecutive U.S. finals, six of which he would win. A seventh, in 1929, allowed him to catch up with Sears and Larned. Ultimately, Tilden's career would far surpass theirs, and perhaps that of any other American man.

RECORDS — MATCH WINNING STREAKS, SINGLES

MEN
98—Bill Tilden, 1924-25
92—Don Budge, 1937-38
50—Guillermo Vilas, 1977
55—Roy Emerson, 1955
49—Bjorn Borg, 1978

WOMEN
158—Helen Wills Moody, 1926-33
111—Alice Marble, 1938-40
74—Martina Navratilova, 1984
66—Steffi Graf, 1990
58—Martina Navratilova, 1986-87

Chapter 2

The Golden Age

Fred Perry, 1933
The last Englishman to win Wimbledon, way back in 1936.

It was called 'The Golden Age of Sport.' Hyperbolic, probably, considering the purple language of the sports pages of the past, although there was some truth to it. Sport came on strong in the Roaring Twenties as never before, held high by such highly publicized stars as Babe Ruth in baseball, Jack Dempsey in boxing, Red Grange in football, Bobby Jones in golf, Man o' War in horse racing. Tennis was right up there, too, with players whose names had a broad public impact: Big Bill Tilden, Suzanne Lenglen, Helen Wills Moody, the Gallic 'Four Musketeers': Borotra, Brugnon, Cochet, Lacoste. World War I was over, the trenches silent, and a prosperous period, with more leisure, seemed ripe for games-playing heroes and heroines who could be colored gold.

1919

Oh Suzanne!

Suzanne Lenglen
Elevating hemlines, and the entire women's game.

This was the year of Suzanne Lenglen's arrival on the world tennis stage: She would dominate until she turned pro in 1926. A product of constant drilling by her father, Charles Lenglen, a well-to-do Frenchman, she had style as well as ability and along with contemporary Helen Wills Moody would come to be ranked among the greatest women players of all time.

Lenglen appeared in her first tournament at age 12, and in 1914 won the singles and doubles in the World Hard Court (clay) Championships at 15, so she was not exactly an unknown when she came to Wimbledon upon the resumption of play following World War I. Playing on grass for the first time, Lenglen won the title in a match that is still regarded as one of the greatest Wimbledon women's finals.

Although the stocky Lenglen was no conventional beauty, and never married, she had a captivating allure and numerous love affairs, an appeal that was dynamite at the box office. Her magnetism and invincibility made the original Wimbledon too small, leading to the construction of the 'new' (present) complex in 1922. Her long, Gallic nose and prominent chin were complemented by a fiery disposition, a chic appearance and a dancer's movements. She was 20 and advanced to the challenge round past Phyllis Satterthwaite, 6-1, 6-1, in the all-comers final to face the seven-time champion, Britain's Mrs. Dorothea Douglass Chambers. Chambers had won her first Wimbledon in 1903 and was two months from her 41st birthday.

Lenglen's dress created a sensation. The British had been accustomed to seeing their women in tight-fitting corsets, blouses and layers of petticoats. When Suzanne stepped onto Centre Court in a revealing one-piece dress, with sleeves daringly just above the elbow, her hemline *only* just below the knee, reaction ranged from outrage on the part of many women spectators—some reportedly walked out during her matches, muttering "shocking"—to delight among the men.

But everybody was also impressed by the young Frenchwoman's grace and disciplined shotmaking as she won the title, 10-8, 4-6, 9-7, the 44 games amounting to the longest female final until Margaret Court's 14-12, 11-9 victory over Billie Jean King topped it by two games in 1970.

Future champ Kitty McKane, an eyewitness in the full-house crowd of 8,500 that included King George V and Queen Mary, wrote: "It was a very hot afternoon, and I think Suzanne wanted to quit when she was behind, 4-1, in the second. But her father would have none of it, shaking his umbrella furiously at her, and tossing her sugar cubes soaked with brandy. After losing the second set, she seemed back in control with a 4-1 lead in the third. But Mrs. Chambers, who'd missed out on two set points in the first at 6-5, came back to win five games to 6-5 and 40-15 on her serve, on the verge of her eighth championship with two match points. Suzanne was lucky on the first. Reaching for a lob she hit it barely, on the frame, and the ball hit the net cord, dropping over. But the second she saved with a backhand down the line. She was unstoppable after that."

In the Wimbledon men's championship another golden oldie was involved as the defender, Aussie Norman Brookes, 41, like Dolly Chambers a holdover from 1914, aimed to be the tourney's most elderly monarch, surpassing Arthur Gore, who was younger by two months when he won in 1909 (Brookes had defeated Gore in the 1907 finale, 6-4, 6-2, 6-2). However, another Aussie and a Wimbledon rookie, Gerald Patterson, got in Brookes' way. Known as 'The Catapult' for his huge serve, Patterson advanced to the challenge round by beating Britain's Algernon Kingscote, 6-2, 6-1, 6-3, in the all-comers, and then Brookes, 6-3, 7-5, 6-2. Theirs was the first of 10 totally Aussie title shootouts on Centre Court.

In the 1919 resumption of Davis Cup after a four-year hiatus, Australasia (a combination of Australia and New Zealand) retained the Cup it had won in 1914, beating the British Isles, 4-1. The U.S. did not enter. Patterson was the dominant player, sandwiching singles wins over Arthur Lowe, 6-4, 6-3, 2-6, 6-3, and Kingscote, 6-4, 6-4, 8-6, around a doubles bashing with Brookes of Alfred Beamish and Kingscote, 6-0, 6-0, 6-2. This was the last of six Cups that Brookes, then 42, had a hand in winning. Kingscote, who had won the sole

British point over Jim (J.O.) Anderson, redeemed himself by winning the Australian singles over Eric Pockley, 6-4, 6-0, 6-3.

The U.S. final at Forest Hills between the 1915 champion, 5-foot-8, 120-pound William 'Little Bill' Johnston, and 6-foot-2, William 'Big Bill' Tilden, was billed in *The New York Times* as the battle for the title, 'William the Conqueror.' It was the first of six meetings between the two Bills in the Championships final, and the only one Johnston would win. Tilden had first played in the Championships in 1912 and lost, 6-2, 6-3, 6-4, in the opening round to fellow Philadelphian Wallace Johnson (his victim in the 1921 final). He waited four years before trying again, at age 23, and was a first-round flop again, to a teenager, Harold Throckmorton, 4-6, 6-4, 6-2, 8-6. He finally won a couple of rounds at Forest Hills in 1917 before losing to the champion-to-be, big-serving lefty Lindley Murray, 3-6, 6-4, 6-3, 6-3. At last, at 25 in 1918, Bill was getting it together and made his way to the first of his 10 U.S. finals, losing once more to Murray, 6-3, 6-1, 7-5.

By 1919 he was already being called by some the greatest player of all time—but that designation turned out to be slightly premature. Johnston spotted a weakness in Tilden, a backhand that was totally defensive, hit invariably with underspin. Having beaten Tilden in Chicago for the U.S. Clay Court title, 6-0, 6-1, 4-6, 6-2, Little Bill kept pounding away at the flaw at Forest Hills, winning relatively easily, 6-4, 6-3, 6-3. Johnston's best win was eliminating Wimbledon champ Patterson, 6-2, 3-6, 6-4, 7-5, in the fourth round, prior to derailing 1917-18 champ Murray, ending his 15-match streak in the Championships, 5-7, 6-1, 6-2, 6-4.

1919 CHAMPIONS AND LEADERS

Australian Championships
Men's Singles: Algernon Kingscote
Men's Doubles: Pat O'Hara Wood / Ron Thomas
Wimbledon
Men's Singles: Gerald Patterson
Women's Singles: Suzanne Lenglen
Men's Doubles: Ronald Thomas / Pat O'Hara Wood
Women's Doubles: Suzanne Lenglen / Elizabeth Ryan
Mixed Doubles: Elizabeth Ryan / Randolph Lycett
U.S. Championships
Men's Singles: Bill Johnston
Women's Singles: Hazel Hotchkiss Wightman
Men's Doubles: Norman Brookes / Gerald Patterson
Women's Doubles: Marion Zinderstein / Eleanor Goss
Mixed Doubles: Marion Zinderstein / Vinnie Richards
Year-End Number One
Men: Gerald Patterson
Davis Cup: Australasia

Australia, which presently would play an important—at times domineering—role in the U.S. Championships, had its first titleists in the persons of Brookes and Patterson, winning the doubles at Boston's Longwood Cricket Club over defenders Vinnie Richards and Tilden 8-6, 6-3, 4-6, 4-6, 6-2.

For the women's championship the challenge round was abolished and Mrs. Hazel Hotchkiss Wightman won the title, snapping a four-year reign by Norwegian-American Molla Bjurstedt. Marion Zinderstein eliminated Molla in the semi-finals, 4-6, 6-1, 6-2, ending an 18-match streak, but was beaten 6-1, 6-2, in the all-Bostonian final by Wightman, the first mother to win the title. Wightman's toughest match was the 6-3, 4-6, 6-4, third rounder over Eleanor Goss, a New Yorker who ranked No. 2 for the year behind the champion.

1920

Big Bill Tilden stakes his claim

Bill Tilden
A high-stakes game of possum, followed by the kill, at the U.S. Championships.

William Tatem Tilden II, born in 1893, the son of a Philadelphia wool merchant and prominent civic figure, came of age at 27. He won at Wimbledon and the U.S. Championships at Forest Hills, and helped the United States win the Davis Cup for the first time since 1913.

In the all-comers final at Wimbledon against Japan's sly Zenzo Shimidzu, Tilden fell behind in all three sets, 1-4, 2-4, 2-5, but rallied each time to win, 6-4, 6-4, 13-11. It became the mark of Tilden to put on a show and entertain as well as win. In his remarkable biography, *Big Bill Tilden,* Frank Deford wrote: "Nobody realized it at the time, but it was one of Tilden's amusements, a favor to the crowd, to give lesser opponents a head start." Tilden had whipped Shimidzu, 6-1, 6-1, in a tournament prior to Wimbledon. In the challenge round final, Tilden defeated the defending champion, Australian Gerald Patterson, 2-6, 6-3, 6-2, 6-4. The Associated Press reported that "Tilden in the first set opened with experiments all around the court and then settled down mercilessly to feeding his opponent's backhand, and, as the game progressed, Patterson got worse and worse ... Tilden exploited his famous cut-stroke to his opponent's backhand again and again."

The British marveled at Tilden, acclaimed him the greatest of all time. One observer rhapsodized, "His silhouette as he prepares to serve suggests an Egyptian pharaoh about to administer punishment."

In the U.S. Championships, Tilden beat Bill Johnston in a dramatic five-set final, 6-1, 1-6, 7-5, 5-7, 6-3, that was regarded as the greatest championship battle up to that time. During the match a Navy photographic plane crashed near the club while making passes over Forest Hills and disrupted the match momentarily. The pilot and the photographer were killed. Pandemonium struck. As many spectators noisily departed, rushing toward the accident, umpire Edward Conlin queried the adversaries: "Are you able to continue?" Tilden and Johnston nodded affirmatively, and the crowd settled down.

It was the first of six straight national titles for Tilden, a flamboyant and controversial figure who dominated any match, win or lose. Tilden would not lose an important match until 1926.

In the women's event at Wimbledon, Dorothea Douglass Chambers defeated Americans Molla Bjurstedt Mallory, 6-0, 6-3, and Elizabeth Ryan, 6-2, 6-1, on the way to a return match with Suzanne Lenglen in the challenge round. Lenglen beat Chambers, 6-3, 6-0. Mallory regained the U.S. title, defeating Marion Zinderstein, 6-3, 6-1.

The bullying, bageling Bills, Tilden and Johnston, were emphatic about regaining the Davis Cup: 3-0 over France and 5-0 over Britain, both in England, and 5-0 over Cup-holding Australasia at Auckland, losing just 11 sets in 13 matches. They handled everything, each winning 5-0 in singles, and 3-0 as doubles collaborators.

France was no problem: Johnston over Andre Gobert, 6-3, 8-6, 6-3, Tilden over William Laurent, 4-6, 6-2, 6-1, 6-3, followed by the doubles involving the same guys, 6-2, 6-3, 6-2. Little Bill had to go five to beat Britain's Jim Parke on opening day, 6-4, 6-4, 2-6, 3-6, 6-2, a companion piece to Tilden's 4-6, 6-1, 6-3, 6-1, over Algernon Kingscote. And the Bills needed five to clinch over Parke and Kingscote, 6-4, 4-6, 3-6, 6-4, 7-5.

The wizardly Brookes remained competitive at 43, and made Tilden earn the leadoff match, 10-8, 6-4, 1-6, 6-4, but Johnston overwhelmed Patterson, 6-3, 6-1, 6-1. Brookes and Patterson got rapped together in the wrap-up doubles, 4-6, 6-4, 6-0, 6-4, and the Cup was going home.

1920 OLYMPICS, ANTWERP, BELGIUM

Men's singles: Louis Raymond, South Africa, Gold; Ichiya Kumagae, Japan, Silver; Charles Winslow, South Africa, Bronze
Women's singles: Suzanne Lenglen, France, Gold; Dorothy Holman, Great Britain, Silver; Kitty McKane, Great Britain, Bronze
Men's doubles: Noell Turnbull, South Africa & Max Woosnam, Great Britain, Gold; Seiichiro Kashio & Ichiya Kumagae, Japan, Silver; Max Decugis & Pierre Albarran, France, Bronze
Women's doubles: Kitty McKane & Winifred McNair, Great Britain, Gold; Geraldine Beamish & Dorothy Holman, Great Britain, Silver; Suzanne Lenglen & Elisabeth d'Ayen, France, Bronze
Mixed doubles: Suzanne Lenglen & Max Decugis, France, Gold; Kitty McKane & Max Woosnam, Great Britain, Silver; Ladislav 'Rázny' Zemla & Milada Skrbková, Czechoslovakia, Bronze

1920 CHAMPIONS AND LEADERS

Australian Championships
Men's Singles: Pat O'Hara Wood
Men's Doubles: Pat O'Hara Wood / Ron Thomas
Wimbledon
Men's Singles: Bill Tilden
Women's Singles: Suzanne Lenglen
Men's Doubles: Dick Williams / Chuck Garland
Women's Doubles: Suzanne Lenglen / Elizabeth Ryan
Mixed Doubles: Suzanne Lenglen / Gerald Patterson
U.S. Championships
Men's Singles: Bill Tilden
Women's Singles: Molla Bjurstedt Mallory
Men's Doubles: Bill Johnston / Clarence Griffin
Women's Doubles: Marion Zinderstein / Eleanor Goss
Mixed Doubles: Hazel Hotchkiss Wightman / Wallace Johnson
Year-End Number One
Men: Bill Tilden
Davis Cup: United States

1921

Weeping Lenglen vanquished at last

Molla Mallory
Victory over a defaulting Lenglen brings a sixth U.S. title.

Suzanne Lenglen, who hadn't lost a match to anyone since the end of the war, came to the United States for the first time, and suffered the lone defeat of her life at the top, on a default. It was one of the most stunning results in tennis, and was long talked about and cited whenever Lenglen was discussed.

The position occupied by Lenglen at the time of the great default was described by the eminent tennis writer, Al Laney: "She probably did more for women's tennis than any girl who ever played it. She broke down barriers and created a vogue, reforming tennis dress, substituting acrobatics and something of the art of the ballet where decorum had been the rule. In England and on the Continent, this slim, not very pretty but fascinating French maiden was the most popular performer in sport or out of it on the post-war scene. She became the rage, almost a cult. Even royalty gave her its favor and she partnered King Gustav of Sweden in mixed doubles more than once."

Lenglen was beaten by the defending champion, Molla Mallory, in the second round of the first U.S. Women's Championships at Forest Hills, six years prior to the advent of seeds. Lenglen lost the first set, 6-2, seeming weak and nervous, coughing from time to time, causing some concern to those who had seen her play. Then, when she lost the first point of the second set and double-faulted to trail, 2-6, 0-30, she started weeping. She went to the umpire's chair and, speaking French, said she was too ill to continue. As she and the disappointed Mallory walked off the court, there was a faint hissing sound from the crowd of 8,000, the largest ever to witness a women's match in the United States.

The newspapers reported Lenglen told the umpire that she was unable to breathe and that she coughed throughout the previous night. Others recalled her saying she did not feel like playing and had been listless in a practice session. If she was suffering from menstrual cramps, that was not mentioned because it was then a taboo subject in the public prints. It was also pointed out that she had arrived in the U.S. only four days before her first scheduled match. Her opponent, Eleanor Goss, withdrew, so she did not have a warm-up before her match with Mallory.

Lenglen incurred criticism because she appeared at Forest Hills the next day in good spirits, continuing to attend parties. Despite her signs of physical distress in the match, it was not considered acceptable to default, and there arose speculation about whether Lenglen could accept defeat, something with which she'd had no experience in singles since 1914. For some time the phrase pertaining to her, 'to cough and quit,' was in vogue in New York. In France there were accusations of mistreatment by the Americans and the charge that her first-round opponent had purposely defaulted to help set up Lenglen for defeat.

Mallory went on to win the U.S. Championship, her sixth, with a 4-6, 6-4, 6-2 victory in the final over Mary K. Browne. Lenglen had breezed to her third Wimbledon title with a 6-2, 6-0 victory over American Elizabeth Ryan,

Bill Tilden retained his Wimbledon crown, coming out of a sickbed to defend against South African Brian 'Babe' Norton in the challenge round. Tilden won 4-6, 2-6, 6-1, 6-0, 7-5. It was the third successive five-setter for 21-year-old Norton, who on the way had defeated Frank Hunter, 6-0, 6-3, 5-7, 5-7, 6-2, and in the all-comers final Spaniard Manuel Alonso, 5-7, 4-6, 7-5, 6-3, 6-3. In the quarters the Japanese Zenzo Shimidzu, plus considerable champagne, took their toll on tippling

1921 CHAMPIONS AND LEADERS

Australian Championships
Men's Singles: Rhys Gemmell
Men's Doubles: S. H. Eaton / Rhys Gemmell
Wimbledon
Men's Singles: Bill Tilden
Women's Singles: Suzanne Lenglen
Men's Doubles: Randolph Lycett / Max Woosnam
Women's Doubles: Suzanne Lenglen / Elizabeth Ryan
Mixed Doubles: Elizabeth Ryan / Randolph Lycett
U.S. Championships
Men's Singles: Bill Tilden
Women's Singles: Molla Bjurstedt Mallory
Men's Doubles: Bill Tilden / Vinnie Richards
Women's Doubles: Mary K. Browne / Louise Riddell Williams
Mixed Doubles: Mary K. Browne / Bill Johnston
Year-End Number One
Men: Bill Tilden
Women: Suzanne Lenglen
Davis Cup: United States

Randolph Lycett. Too many refreshing pauses for Lycett, who felt a sip in time might save his spine. Wobbling noticeably in the last stages, he was at least able—barely—to stagger to the distant finish line, the loser, 6-3, 9-11, 3-6, 6-2, 10-8. Alonso had a struggle with Shimidzu before winning 3-6, 7-5, 3-6, 6-4, 8-6.

In the wind-up, after losing the first two sets to Norton, Tilden gave up his normal hard-hitting game, took to chops and slices, and turned the match around. This displeased observers, who booed Tilden despite the remonstrations of the umpire that he was playing quite fairly and within the rules. Norton recovered in the last set, led 5-4 with two match points, but Tilden rallied to hold serve, and prevailed by serving an ace on his own match point. F. P. Adams wrote: "He is an artist, more of an artist than nine-tenths of the artists I know. It is the beauty of the game that Tilden loves; it is the chase always, rather than the quarry."

Still not fully recovered from his illness in England, Tilden registered one of his more difficult and dramatic victories in the 5-0 defense of the Davis Cup over unexpected opposition, Japan, at Germantown Cricket Club in Philadelphia, Big Bill's home club. Mighty mites in straw hats, unorthodox-stroking but quick, 5-foot-6 Shimidzu and Ichiya Kumagae had stunned favored Australasia in the semi-final at Newport, contortedly using the same racket face for forehands and backhands. Johnston opened with a swift 6-2, 6-4, 6-2 win over Kumagae. But the clever retriever, Shimidzu, took the first two sets and was within two points of beating Tilden with a 5-3, 30-15 lead in the third. Groping on a boiling 100-degree afternoon and hobbled by a boil on his foot, Tilden somehow reeled off four games to get through the set. A physician lanced the boil during the intermission, and Bill charged back to win the match, 5-7, 4-6, 7-5, 6-2, 6-1.

Remaining at Germantown for the U.S. Championships, moved there from Forest Hills for a three-year period (1921-23), Tilden through the luck of the unseeded draw faced foremost foe and 1920 finalist Johnston in the fourth round, winning 4-6, 7-5, 6-4, 6-3. He didn't lose another set and one of his victims was Shimidzu, 6-4, 6-4, 6-1. Taking his second straight title in an all-Philadelphia final, he toned down chop-and-slice maestro Wallace Johnson, 6-1, 6-3, 6-1. Johnson had stopped Aussie J.O. Anderson, 6-4, 3-6, 8-6, 6-3.

Rhys Gemmel won an uninspiring Australian Championship over Alf Hedemann, 7-5, 6-1, 6-4.

1922

Lenglen avenges Forest Hills loss

Helen Wills
At Sweet 16, a finalist at the U.S. Championships.

Having outgrown the Worple Road Grounds in the London suburb of Wimbledon it had occupied since 1877, the All England Club moved to its present site in a picturesque hollow at the foot of Church Road near Wimbledon Common, at a construction cost of 140,000 pounds. King George V and Queen Mary attended the opening on June 22 at the new Centre Court holding 9,989 seats, with room for 3,600 standees—a total of 13,589 fans, although it was frequently crammed with more (the previous arena held 8,500). Present-day crowd control laws now limit Centre Court to 13,813 seats with no standing. The royals saw the first match, played by two of their subjects, with Algernon Kingscote beating Leslie Godfree 6-1, 6-3, 6-0.

Portents of the future? Rain fell every day of the tournament, which concluded on the third Wednesday. Showers delayed the debut of architect Stanley Peach's magnificent dodecagon, Centre Court, by an hour. However, with the usual stiffened upper lip of nobility, King George struck a gong thrice at 3:45 p.m. and the Big W was on its frequently wet way into the future, and Centre Court to its destiny as perhaps the planet's most renowned playpen. The first American to tread the hallowed-to-be sod of Centre was a Yale alumnus studying at Oxford, Amos Wilder (younger brother of noted playwright Thornton Wilder), who lost a doubles match with Frank Kingsley to eventual champs J.O. Anderson and Randolph Lycett, 6-2, 2-6, 6-1, 9-7. A first-round loser who would make his name in the game much later as daddy of the tie-breaker, was an American at Cambridge, Jimmy Van Alen, who fell to L.A. Meldon, 6-3, 6-4, 5-7, 6-2

The challenge round was abolished. Bill Tilden did not choose to make the Atlantic crossing to defend his title, won by Australia's Gerald Patterson, whom Tilden had dethroned in 1920. Patterson defeated Great Britain's Lycett (the champagne imbiber of

1921) in the final, 6-3, 6-4, 6-2. An Aussie trail to the final was made when Anderson beat Pat O'Hara Wood in the quarters, 6-3, 6-3, 2-6, 2-6, 6-4, then lost to Patterson, 6-1, 3-6, 7-9, 6-1, 6-3.

Suzanne Lenglen avenged her controversial default to Molla Mallory at Forest Hills the year before when she trounced Mallory in the Wimbledon final, 6-2, 6-0. Lenglen's appeal was such that before her first match, a 6-1, 7-5 decision over Kitty McKane, "a line stretched more than a mile and a half from the underground station to the entrance to the All England Club," wrote Wimbledon official Duncan Macaulay. "People used to call it the 'Leng-len trail a-winding' after the famous World War I song of those days ['a long, long trail . . .']." Lenglen won three Wimbledon titles for the second time, teaming with Aussie Pat O'Hara Wood to win the mixed doubles and with American Elizabeth Ryan in the doubles.

After her loss to Lenglen at Wimbledon, Mallory, 38, returned to Forest Hills to win her seventh U.S. title, defeating 16-year-old Helen Wills in the final, 6-3, 6-1. It was the greatest disparity in ages for any major final.

The meeting between perennial rivals Bill Tilden and Bill Johnston in the U.S. Championships at the Germantown Cricket Club was called 'a match for the Greek gods.' They played for a coveted championship bowl, which each had won twice and which would be retired permanently by any three-time winner. Tilden advanced to the final, beating Wimbledon champion Gerald Patterson, 4-6, 6-4, 6-3, 6-1, while Johnston defeated a promising newcomer, 19-year-old Vinnie Richards, 8-6, 6-2, 6-1. Tilden lost the first two sets to Little Bill, then came back to win the match, 4-6, 3-6, 6-2, 6-3, 6-4. The trophy gained by Tilden had on it the names of such previous winners as William Larned, Lindley Murray, Maurice McLoughlin, Dick Williams

and Johnston.

In the Davis Cup, Australasia advanced past Spain to the challenge round, to be beaten by the United States, 4-1 at Forest Hills. In those days of unusual interest in Davis Cup, something of a stir was created by the loss of the doubles by Tilden and Richards to Patterson and Pat O'Hara Wood, 6-4, 6-0, 6-3. Bill and Vinnie had joined forces for the first time in 1918 to win the U.S. title. But if their reunion was disappointing, Johnston soon destroyed the Aussies' faint hopes with the decisive point, a 6-2, 6-2, 6-1 flattening of Patterson, who had been beaten by Big Bill on the first day, 7-5, 10-8, 6-0.

Patterson also fell in his own national championship to J.O. Anderson, 6-0, 3-6, 3-6, 6-3, 6-2. It was time for an Australian championship for the women, too, the inaugural won by 27-year-old Margaret 'Mall' Mutch Molesworth over Esna Boyd, 6-3, 10-8.

1922 CHAMPIONS AND LEADERS

Australian Championships
Men's Singles: James Anderson
Women's Singles: Mall Molesworth
Men's Doubles: Jack Hawkes / Gerald Patterson
Women's Doubles: Esna Boyd / Marjorie Mountain
Mixed Doubles: Esna Boyd / Jack Hawkes
Wimbledon
Men's Singles: Gerald Patterson
Women's Singles: Suzanne Lenglen
Men's Doubles: James Anderson / Randolph Lycett
Women's Doubles: Suzanne Lenglen / Elizabeth Ryan
Mixed Doubles: Suzanne Lenglen / Pat O'Hara Wood
U.S. Championships
Men's Singles: Bill Tilden
Women's Singles: Molla Bjurstedt Mallory
Men's Doubles: Bill Tilden / Vinnie Richards
Women's Doubles: Marion Zinderstein Jessup / Helen Wills
Mixed Doubles: Molla Bjurstedt Mallory / Bill Tilden
Year-End Number One
Men: Bill Tilden
Women: Suzanne Lenglen
Davis Cup: United States

1923

U.S. blitzes Britain in Hazel's honor

Hazel Hotchkiss Wightman
The grande dame of women's tennis helps inaugurate Forest Hills.

A new stadium was constructed at the West Side Tennis Club grounds in Forest Hills, but the men's U.S. Championships wouldn't return from Philadelphia until 1924. Built at a cost of $250,000, the concrete bowl that would eventually seat 14,000 opened on August 10 with the inauguration of the Wightman Cup matches.

The competition was the brainchild of Hazel Hotchkiss Wightman, a champion in pre–World War I days who would compete until she was past 70, winning the last of her 45 U.S. titles (senior doubles) at the age of 67. She had conceived the idea of a women's competition equivalent to the Davis Cup in 1920 and donated a silver vase. But the idea lay fallow until seized upon by Julian Myrick, a U.S. Tennis Association official, as a way of launching the new Forest Hills stadium.

The competition between Great Britain and the United States consisted of five singles matches and two doubles, and though Wightman hoped to make it an international tournament by bringing in France, that never came to pass. With Wightman as captain, the U.S. team of Molla Mallory, Helen Wills and Eleanor Goss scored a 7-0 sweep, starting with the baptismal match before 5,000 fans who watched Wills beat Kitty McKane, 6-2, 7-5.

Wills won the first of her seven U.S. titles, unseating Mallory, 6-2, 6-1, severing Molla's 22-match streak. Mallory thus had won 40 of 42 matches, beginning with her first title campaign of 1915. Suzanne Lenglen breezed through the Wimbledon field for the fifth straight year, yielding only 11 games in the 12 sets she played, defeating McKane in the final, 6-2, 6-2. She won the doubles again with Elizabeth Ryan.

With Bill Tilden, universally regarded as the kingpin of tennis, absent again from Wimbledon, the Other Bill—Johnston—won for the only time. In straight sets he swept past countryman Vinnie Richards, 6-4, 6-3, 9-7, South African Babe Norton,

6-4, 6-2, 6-4, and then another Yank, Frank Hunter, in a 45-minute final, 6-0, 6-3, 6-1. Johnston's success at Wimbledon would not carry over to the U.S. Championships, where he was crushed by Tilden in the final, 6-4, 6-1, 6-4.

Pat O'Hara Wood won the Australian title, 6-1, 6-1, 6-3, over a marvelous, extraordinary athlete, one-handed Bert St. John, a lefty. A losing finalist in the 1915 doubles, St. John was also a star cricketer and soccer player for Queensland, the lone major finalist crippled by the loss of a hand. Thus, Pat put an O'Hara Wood duo in a select cast of brothers—three sets of them—who've won major singles titles. His older sibling (by a year), Dr. Arthur O'Hara Wood, won the Aussie in 1914 over Gerald Patterson, 6-4, 6-3, 5-7, 6-1, then went off to World War I—and death, when his Royal Air Force

plane was shot down in France a month prior to the Armistice in 1918. Prior to the O'Hara Wood successes, Englishmen Willie (seven times) and Ernest Renshaw (once), and Laurie (five) and Reggie Doherty (four) were Wimbledon champs.

Mall Molesworth retained her Aussie title, again beating Esna Boyd, 6-1, 7-5.

In a Davis Cup field increased to 17 entries from 11, Australasia beat France to challenge the U.S. The U.S. won 4-1 at Forest Hills, although it went into the third day because speedy J.O. Anderson, called 'Greyhound' by his mates, shocked Bill Johnston in the opener, 4-6, 6-2, 2-6, 7-5, 6-2. Tilden tied it briskly over lefty Jack Hawkes, 6-4, 6-2, 6-1, and he and playing captain Dick Williams surged ahead in a suspenseful win over Anderson and Hawkes, 17-15 (the longest set in a Cup finale), 11-13, 2-6, 6-3, 6-2. Johnston then made up for his first-day stumble, and solidified the American hold on the Cup for a fourth successive year by blasting Hawkes, 6-0, 6-2, 6-1.

It is difficult today to appreciate how significant the Davis Cup used to be before open tennis. Prior to 1968 there were no prize-money tournaments, fewer inducements in a schedule that has now grown to world-wide and practically 12-month proportions. Today's players often choose to skip the high-pressure, nationalistic Cup to conserve themselves for chasing big money, and computer points (even though prize money and generous guarantees have become part of the Cup deal). After World War I, an atmosphere of international good fellowship took hold and the Davis Cup acquired tremendous significance, partly because of the U.S. dominance of the competition. It was front-page news then and controversies such as Tilden's threats to quit were looked upon as almost national calamities.

1923 CHAMPIONS AND LEADERS

Australian Championships
Men's Singles: Pat O'Hara Wood
Women's Singles: Mall Molesworth
Men's Doubles: Pat O'Hara Wood / Bert St. John
Women's Doubles: Esna Boyd / Sylvia Lance
Mixed Doubles: Sylvia Lance / Horrie Rice
Wimbledon
Men's Singles: Bill Johnston
Women's Singles: Suzanne Lenglen
Men's Doubles: Leslie Godfree / Randolph Lycett
Women's Doubles: Suzanne Lenglen / Elizabeth Ryan
Mixed Doubles: Elizabeth Ryan / Randolph Lycett
U.S. Championships
Men's Singles: Bill Tilden
Women's Singles: Helen Wills
Men's Doubles: Bill Tilden / Brian Norton
Women's Doubles: Kitty McKane / Phyllis Howkins Covell
Mixed Doubles: Molla Bjurstedt Mallory / Bill Tilden
Year-End Number One
Men: Bill Tilden
Women: Suzanne Lenglen
Davis Cup: United States
Wightman Cup: United States

1924

French Connection begins to sizzle

Jean Borotra
The 'Bounding Basque' ushers in an era of French dominance.

In the latter part of the 1920s, when the French would dominate men's tennis, each of the three great Frenchmen won two Wimbledon singles championships, beginning with the 1924 French final, not yet a major (Only French nationals were accepted) in which 25-year-old Jean Borotra defeated 19-year-old René Lacoste, 6-1, 3-6, 6-1, 3-6, 6-4.

Borotra, the colorful 'Bounding Basque' who wore a beret while playing, and Lacoste, the 'Crocodile,' were two of the Four Musketeers, along with 22-year-old Henri 'The Ballboy of Lyon' Cochet and 29-year-old Jacques 'Toto' Brugnon, who was essentially a doubles specialist. Wimbledon Secretary Duncan Macaulay wrote in *Behind the Scenes* at Wimbledon: "They were all very different in style and temperament, and they sometimes clashed bitterly with one another on the courts. But whenever they felt they were playing for France … they always put France first. Thus it was the combined pressure of Lacoste and Cochet which began to rock the great Bill Tilden on his pedestal, and finally toppled him off it."

Borotra showed at Wimbledon that the French championship, however restricted, was a true indicator of what was to come. Borotra had a rockier time on the grass, but took Wimbledon and Lacoste, 6-1, 3-6, 6-1, 3-6, 6-4 .

Norman Brookes, the 47-year-old Australian immortal who had first played at Wimbledon 20 years before, highlighted early play by upsetting Frank Hunter, finalist the previous year and ranked No. 5 in the world, in the third round, 3-6, 6-3, 6-4, 5-7, 6-3.

Suzanne Lenglen, a five-time winner at Wimbledon weakened by an attack of jaundice earlier in the year, was forced to drop out after winning a quarter-final match over American Elizabeth Ryan in three tough sets, 6-2, 6-8, 6-4. It was the first singles set Lenglen lost—except the great default to Molla Mallory at Forest Hills in 1921—since 1919. Britain's Kitty McKane got a walkover from her in the semi-finals and then defeated Helen Wills in the final, 4-6, 6-4, 6-4, after trailing 1-4 in the second, and facing four set points to trail 1-5. It was Helen's lone loss in 56 Wimbledon matches. Years later, asked what happened—how could iron-minded Helen allow such a lead to disappear?—she was forthright: "Something happened to me that had never happened before. I lost my concentration. But I never let that happen again." Apparently not. She would win her next 50 matches at Wimbledon—the longest streak, male or female, at any major—and a record eight titles, a mark broken by Martina Navratilova's ninth in 1990.

Kitty and Helen had met only a few days earlier in the Wightman Cup at Wimbledon. McKane won, 6-2, 6-2, after beating Molla Mallory, 6-3, 6-3. The British evened the series at 1-1, winning the competition, 6-1. The only U.S. point came on a doubles triumph by Wills and the Cup's namesake, 37-year-old Hazel Hotchkiss Wightman, over McKane and Evelyn Colyer, 2-6, 6-2, 6-4. Eighteen-year-old Wills won her second successive U.S. title, defeating Mallory again, 6-1, 6-3.

Tilden, increasingly at odds with the tennis establishment, sent a letter of resignation to the U.S. Tennis Association, bowing out of the Davis Cup because of a proposed ban on his writing for newspapers about tennis. That was in conflict with amateur rules. The threat of not having Tilden's gate appeal in the Davis Cup competition forced tennis administrators to cave in. Tilden plus Bill Johnston and 21-year-old singles rookie Vinnie Richards swept the Australian team of Gerald Patterson and Pat O'Hara Wood, 5-0, in Tilden's Philly neighborhood, Germantown Cricket Club. Neither Tilden nor Richards lost a set, and the re-issue of the double-valued Bills of 1920 triumphs—Tilden and Johnston co-habiting the court—took care of the sealing point in a fifth straight Cup, 5-7, 6-3, 6-4, 6-1, over O'Hara Wood and Patterson.

Underdog rooters hopeful that Little Bill would break Big Bill's spell over him had reason to believe that Johnston would crash through in the U.S. Championships, the first played in the new West Side Tennis Club Stadium at Forest Hills. Tilden's feud with the USTA and the increased time he was devoting to a hopeful-but-doomed-by-critics theatrical career led to charges that he was out of shape. He came to the final with a desultory five-set victory over Richards, 4-6, 6-2, 8-6, 4-6, 6-4, while Johnston routed Patterson, 6-2, 6-0, 6-0. In the final, however, Tilden crushed Johnston, 6-1, 9-7, 6-2, in a stunning display that tennis savant Al Laney later called "Tilden at his absolute peak, and I have not since seen the like of it." Patterson said: "Tilden is the only player in the world—the rest of us are second-graders."

In Australia, the men's championship was won by J.O. Anderson over Bob Schlesinger, 6-3, 6-4, 3-6, 5-7, 6-3, the second of his three titles. Sylvia Lance was the women's champ. Runner-up Esna Boyd, who was making a bad habit of it, lost her third consecutive final, this time 6-3, 3-6, 8-6.

1924 CHAMPIONS AND LEADERS

Australian Championships
Men's Singles: James Anderson
Women's Singles: Sylvia Lance
Men's Doubles: James Anderson / Norman Brookes
Women's Doubles: Daphne Akhurst / Sylvia Lance
Mixed Doubles: Daphne Akhurst / John Willard
Wimbledon
Men's Singles: Jean Borotra
Women's Singles: Kitty McKane
Men's Doubles: Frank Hunter / Vinnie Richards
Women's Doubles: Hazel Hotchkiss Wightman / Helen Wills
Mixed Doubles: Kitty McKane / Brian Gilbert
U.S. Championships
Men's Singles: Bill Tilden
Women's Singles: Helen Wills
Men's Doubles: Howard Kinsey / Robert Kinsey
Women's Doubles: Hazel Hotchkiss Wightman / Helen Wills
Mixed Doubles: Helen Wills / Vinnie Richards
Year-End Number One
Men: Bill Tilden
Women: Suzanne Lenglen
Davis Cup: United States
Wightman Cup: Great Britain

1924 OLYMPICS, PARIS, FRANCE

Men's singles: Vinnie Richards, United States, Gold; Henri Cochet, France, Silver; Umberto Luigi de Morpurgo, Italy, Bronze
Women's singles: Helen Wills, United States, Gold; Didi Vlasto, France, Silver; Kitty McKane, Great Britain, Bronze
Men's doubles: Frank Hunter & Vinnie Richards, United States, Gold; Jacques Brugnon & Henri Cochet, France, Silver; Jean Borotra & Rene Lacoste, France, Bronze
Women's doubles: Hazel Hotchkiss Wightman & Helen Wills, United States, Gold; Kitty McKane & Phyllis Howkins Covell, Great Britain, Silver; Dorothy Sheperd-Barron & Evelyn Colyer, Great Britain, Bronze
Mixed doubles: Hazel Hotchkiss Wightman & Dick Williams, United States, Gold; Marion Zinderstein Jessup & Vinnie Richards, United States, Silver; Hendrik Timmer & Cornelia Bouman, Netherlands, Bronze

1925

Lenglen, Lacoste a dynamic duo

Bill Tilden (left), Rene Lacoste
One major for Big Bill, two for the 'Crocodile.'

The French dominated Wimbledon as it had never been dominated before, scoring almost a clean sweep of the championships, winning the men's singles and doubles, the mixed doubles and women's singles—and half of the women's doubles.

Suzanne Lenglen, reaching the zenith of her career, lost only five games in sweeping through five opponents. She scored a 6-0, 6-0 semi-final triumph over defending champion Kitty McKane, who had won the title when Lenglen was incapacitated the previous year by jaundice, and defeated another Englishwoman, Joan Fry, in the final, 6-2, 6-0. In fact, in the three rounds prior to the final she double-bageled in succession three of the world's leading women: Elizabeth Ryan, Winifred Ramsey Beamish and McKane. Lenglen combined with American Ryan to win the women's doubles for the sixth time over Katherine Bridge and Mary McIlquam, 6-2, 6-2, and made her third Big W triple crown (the others, 1920, 1922) by winning the mixed doubles with Jean Borotra over Ryan and Umberto de Morpurgo, 6-3, 6-3.

The men's final was a rematch of 1924—this time reversed by 20-year-old René Lacoste, who scored a 6-3, 6-3, 4-6, 8-6 victory over net-rushing Borotra, who was troubled by foot-fault calls. Rene was the greenest Wimbledon champ since 19-year-old Wilfred Baddeley in 1891. In the quarter-final round, Henri Cochet began to gain a Tilden-like reputation for comebacks, losing the first two sets to American John Hennessey, then sweeping the last three to win 7-9, 4-6, 6-1, 6-3, 6-0, before losing to Borotra, 5-7, 8-6, 6-4, 6-1, in their semi-final.

In the first year the French Championships was opened to players from all countries, Lacoste triumphed over Borotra, 7-5, 6-1, 6-4, while Lenglen quickly beat McKane, 6-1, 6-2.

J.O. Anderson won his third Australian title, 11-9, 2-6, 6-2, 6-3, this one over Gerald Patterson, who served 29 aces and 29 double faults. Daphne

Akhurst, for whom the championship cup was eventually named, won the first of her five Australian titles, and Esna Boyd swallowed her fourth successive final-round loss, 1-6, 8-6, 6-4.

Bill Tilden achieved the distinction of winning 57 straight games during the summer. The stage was set for another Big Bill–Little Bill confrontation in the U.S. final at Forest Hills after semi-finals in which Tilden beat Vinnie Richards, 6-8, 6-4, 6-4, 6-1, and Johnston sidelined Dick Williams, 7-5, 6-3, 6-2. Despite an injured shoulder, which prevented him from holding barely half his service games in a long, five-set match, Tilden defeated Johnston, 4-6, 11-9, 6-3, 4-6, 6-3.

Johnston said immediately afterward: "I can't beat him; I can't beat the sonofabitch, I can't beat him." It was the last of Tilden's six straight U.S. titles and the last time

---

1925 CHAMPIONS AND LEADERS

Australian Championships
Men's Singles: James Anderson
Women's Singles: Daphne Akhurst
Men's Doubles: Pat O'Hara Wood / Gerald Patterson
Women's Doubles: Sylvia Lance Harper / Daphne Akhurst
Mixed Doubles: Daphne Akhurst / John Willard
French Championships
Men's Singles: René Lacoste
Women's Singles: Suzanne Lenglen
Men's Doubles: Jean Borotra / René Lacoste
Women's Doubles: Suzanne Lenglen / Didi Vlasto
Mixed Doubles: Suzanne Lenglen / Jacques Brugnon
Wimbledon
Men's Singles: René Lacoste
Women's Singles: Suzanne Lenglen
Men's Doubles: Jean Borotra / René Lacoste
Women's Doubles: Suzanne Lenglen / Elizabeth Ryan
Mixed Doubles: Suzanne Lenglen / Jean Borotra
U.S. Championships
Men's Singles: Bill Tilden
Women's Singles: Helen Wills
Men's Doubles: Dick Williams / Vinnie Richards
Women's Doubles: Mary K. Browne / Helen Wills
Mixed Doubles: Kitty McKane / Jack Hawkes
Year-End Number One
Men: Bill Tilden
Women: Suzanne Lenglen
Davis Cup: United States
Wightman Cup: Great Britain

---

he and Johnston would play for it. Tilden, like most tennis people, admired Johnston greatly, and after Johnston's premature death from tuberculosis in 1946, dedicated his memoirs to Little Bill.

The French made their first breakthrough into the Davis Cup challenge round and lost 5-0 at Philadelphia's Germantown Cricket Club, in what was nonetheless a difficult series for the Cup-holders. Though the Musketeers—Lacoste and Borotra in singles and doubles—were swept by Tilden and Johnston in singles and Dick Williams and Vinnie Richards in doubles, both Frenchmen extended Tilden to five sets. Borotra, leading off, came within two points of shocking Tilden and the U.S. at the outset, serving for victory at 6-5 in the fourth set (and leading 2-0 in the fifth). But Big Bill called on all his wiles to win, 4-6, 6-0, 2-6, 9-7, 6-4. Then Johnston quelled Lacoste, 6-1, 6-1, 6-8, 6-3. On the third day, the outcome was decided by Richards and playing captain Williams, who defeated Borotra and Lacoste, 6-4, 6-4, 6-3. Later, Tilden had to save four match points to beat Lacoste, 3-6, 10-12, 8-6, 7-5, 6-2—65 games, the longest of all the master's 30 Cup singles.

Helen Wills won her third straight U.S. Championship final, defeating Kitty McKane of Great Britain, 3-6, 6-0, 6-2. Wills won both her Wightman Cup matches at Forest Hills, 6-0, 7-5, over Joan Fry and a 6-1, 1-6, 9-7, struggle over McKane. However, it was to no avail as Great Britain won the Cup for the second straight year, 4-3. Dorothea Douglass Chambers was the difference, shortly before her 47th birthday. She won her singles crown over No. 5 American Eleanor Goss, 7-5, 3-6, 6-1, and, yoked to Ermyntrude Harvey, won the doubles, 10-8, 6-1, from antiques Molla Mallory, 41, and May Sutton Bundy, almost 38 and a bygone antagonist of Chambers in the Wimbledon finals of 1905-06-07. That made it 3-3, whereupon McKane and Evelyn Colyer plucked the victory, 6-0, 6-3, over Wills and 34-year-old Mary K. Browne.

1926

Lenglen bests Wills in Riviera showdown

Suzanne Lenglen A match for the ages followed by a dash for the cash.

Suzanne Lenglen and Helen Wills met in springtime on the French Riviera in what would be the only confrontation between the two all-time greats—and one of the most hyped sporting events ever. It was front-page stuff all the way. One writer called it "the most important sporting event of modern times exclusively in the hands of the fair sex"—this almost five decades before Margaret Smith Court and Billie Jean King both met Bobby Riggs.

Wills took off early in the year for a trip to southern

France to participate in invitational tournaments and what some observers regarded as a chance for a showdown with Lenglen. "This girl must be mad," Lenglen told a close friend. "Does she think she can come and beat me on my home court?"

Chaotic and dramatic was the scene as they collided in the final of the normally insignificant Carlton Club tourney at Cannes, which was a magnet for press from around the globe. Ticket scalpers abounded, getting as much as $60, then a princely sum. Carpenters barely completed auxiliary stands before the first serve. Those shut out at the gate commandeered ladders, rooftops and trees for a glimpse of the two goddesses of the game, squaring off in the limited arena crammed with about 3,000 witnesses. Lenglen won, 6-3, 8-6, in 63 minutes, though given a fright, pushed as never before or after, falling apart in tears after Wills erred on a fourth match point.

Confusion took over as Lenglen served at double-match point, 6-5, 40-15, and a spectator called "Out!" though a Wills forehand sped along the line for a winner. Thinking she'd won, Lenglen relaxed, basking in the cheers of compatriots who, prematurely, felt she'd turned back the California invader. However, the no-nonsense Wimbledonian, umpire George Hillyard, restored order after ascertaining that Wills' shot was good. Play

1926 CHAMPIONS AND LEADERS

Australian Championships
Men's Singles: Jack Hawkes
Women's Singles: Daphne Akhurst
Men's Doubles: Jack Hawkes / Gerald Patterson
Women's Doubles: Meryl O'Hara Wood / Esna Boyd
Mixed Doubles: Esna Boyd / Jack Hawkes
French Championships
Men's Singles: Henri Cochet
Women's Singles: Suzanne Lenglen
Men's Doubles: Vinnie Richards / Howard Kinsey
Women's Doubles: Suzanne Lenglen / Didi Vlasto
Mixed Doubles: Suzanne Lenglen / Jacques Brugnon
Wimbledon
Men's Singles: Jean Borotra
Women's Singles: Kitty McKane Godfree
Men's Doubles: Jacques Brugnon / Henri Cochet
Women's Doubles: Mary K. Browne / Elizabeth Ryan
Mixed Doubles: Kitty McKane Godfree / Leslie Godfree
U.S. Championships
Men's Singles: René Lacoste
Women's Singles: Molla Bjurstedt Mallory
Men's Doubles: Dick Williams / Vinnie Richards
Women's Doubles: Elizabeth Ryan / Eleanor Goss
Mixed Doubles: Elizabeth Ryan / Jean Borotra
Year-End Number One
Men: René Lacoste
Women: Suzanne Lenglen
Davis Cup: United States
Wightman Cup: United States

resumed. Frazzled, Lenglen lost serve to 6-6. Then she turned on her greatness again, perhaps for the last time, and seized the remaining two furiously contested games, both going to deuce twice. "She's terrific," lauded Wills. "It was one of my greatest matches."

It was Wimbledon's Jubilee Year, a 50th anniversary celebration presided over by King George V and Queen Mary, bestowing medals on champions. Among the decorated was the elder, the original lob-ster P. Frank Hadow, 71, whose sky balls in 1878 unseated the short-reigned inaugural champ, Spencer Gore of 1877. Also honored was Maud Watson, 61, who started the women's regal line by winning in 1884.

Marring the festivities was the unexpected demise of Lenglen's brilliant amateur career, coming to a sad end amid controversy at Wimbledon when she failed to show up on time for a women's doubles match at which the King and Queen were present. Due to a mix-up after a scheduling change, Lenglen arrived at Centre Court after the Royal Couple had departed. This drew a reprimand and she became hysterical and never quite recovered, though the officials agreed to postpone her match. Meeting hostility from the crowds and the media, Lenglen, with compatriot Didi Vlasto, lost her lone women's doubles match, 3-6, 9-7, 6-2 to the eventual champs, Elizabeth Ryan and Mary K. Browne. It was Suzanne's solitary doubles defeat in 30 such matches at the Big W where her overall record was 90-3 (32-0 in singles, 29-2 in mixed). She won her first two singles, 6-2, 6-3, over Mary K. Browne, the 35-year-old ex-U.S. champ and her foil-to-be on the subsequent pro tour; and 6-2, 6-2, over Mrs. G.J. Dewhurst, She also won a mixed doubles match with Borotra over Miss B.C. Brown and H.I.P. Aitken, 6-3, 6-0, and those were her last matches as an amateur. She withdrew, never to play another amateur tournament.

Signing on as the first touring pro with American promoter Charles C. 'Cash and Carry' Pyle, she went on a North American tour, winning nightly (38-0) over Browne. Unable to entice the Bills, Johnston and Tilden, to turn pro, even with big bills, Pyle settled for the next best American, Vinnie Richards, just 23. He completed the Lenglen troupe with Americans Howard Kinsey and Harvey Snodgrass, Frenchman Paul Feret and Browne, the original cast of barnstorming pros to make their way across the land on one-night stands.

After debuting at New York's Madison Square Garden on October 9, where they drew 13,000 fans and grossed $40,000, they traveled the U.S. and into Canada by train. Lasting four months over the winter of 1926-27, the tour was a success. It was reported that Lenglen was paid a $25,000 bonus beyond her $50,000 guarantee, and that Pyle, who had no interest in tennis as such, made about $80,000 while putting pro tennis into operation, and went off to other interests. Lenglen, barred from the significant tourneys as a pro, retired from competition and did some coaching until her death in 1938.

With Lenglen out the Wimbledon title was won by Great Britain's Kitty McKane Godfree, who beat Lili de Alvarez of Spain, 6-2, 4-6, 6-3, despite lagging 1-3 and a point from 1-4 in the third. The U.S. title, which had been the property of Helen Wills, was opened to others when she was sidelined after an appendectomy. Molla Mallory came back to the winner's circle, seizing the championship for a record eighth time in her record 10th final. Molla was 42, the oldest of all major singles champs. The sentimental favorite of the crowd, she defeated 34-year-old Elizabeth (Bunny) Ryan, 4-6, 6-4, 9-7, after trailing 4-0 in the third set and saving a match point. It was the most elderly of major title bouts.

The six-year reign of Bill Tilden ended in the U.S. Championships when he was eliminated in the quarter-finals by Henri Cochet, 6-8, 6-1, 6-3, 1-6, 8-6. This stopped Tilden's record U.S. run at 42 matches.

In many ways Tilden came to be more popular in defeat than he had been as the kingpin of the sport. Allison Danzig wrote of the Tilden-Cochet match: "The climax of the match, the point at which the gallery broke into the wildest demonstrations, was during the final set when Tilden, trailing at 1-4, rallied to volley Cochet dizzy with one of the most sensational exhibitions he ever gave at the net and pull up to 4-all. Every winning shot of the American was greeted with roars of applause. Tilden, 33, then led, 15-40, on Cochet's serve, but fell back."

Bill Johnston also lost in the same round, to Jean Borotra in five sets, 3-6, 4-6, 6-3, 6-4, 6-4. Borotra advanced to make it the first all-foreigners U.S. final by eliminating Richards, 3-6, 6-4, 4-6, 8-6, 6-2. René Lacoste eliminated Cochet in the semi-finals, patiently getting into the groove, 2-6, 4-6, 6-4, 6-4, 6-3, and then defeated volley specialist Borotra for the title, 6-4, 6-0, 6-4.

It was the first U.S. final since 1917 without Tilden, the first time since 1920 he didn't win, and the first of three years in which Forest Hills and Wimbledon would be swept by the French.

Although Lacoste was ill and unable to defend, a third straight all-French final was the Wimbledon prospect as Borotra eluded a set point in the second while squeezing past Cochet, 2-6, 7-5, 2-6, 6-3, 7-5. Jacques Brugnon held five match points in the fifth set against Howard Kinsey, but the American escaped, 6-4, 4-6, 6-3, 3-6, 9-7, only to fall to Borotra's volleying that overcame his defense and clever lobs. Kinsey lost, 8-6, 6-1, 6-3. He carried on to make a rare 'cripple,' losing the doubles and mixed finals as well, with Vinnie Richards and Mary K. Browne, a last splash before turning pro with the Lenglen tour.

Uncommon attention focused on a men's doubles first-rounder as the left-handed 31-year-old Duke of York (later King George VI) played alongside Louis Grieg. Perhaps it was the aura of the Jubilee that lured the ill-advised Duke. He and Grieg were soundly beaten, 6-1, 6-3, 6-2, by a couple of commoners, old crocks and ex-champs, Herbert Roper Barrett, 52, and Arthur Gore, 58. Was the draw rigged to give His Royal Highness a sporting chance? He looked His Royal Hackerness just the same. Embarrassed, the lone member of the royal family ever to compete thereafter abstained as an entrant. Kitty McKane Godfree and her new husband, Leslie Godfree, became the only married couple to win the mixed, over soon-to-be-pro colleagues Browne and Kinsey, 6-3, 6-4.

A record seventh straight Davis Cup was taken by the U.S., a 4-1 victory over the ever-advancing French at Germantown Cricket Club in Philadelphia. Johnston's and Tilden's respective opening-day sweep of Lacoste, 6-0, 6-4, 0-6, 6-0, and Borotra, 6-2, 6-3, 6-3, plus Richards and playing captain Dick Williams's 6-4, 6-4, 6-2 putdown of Cochet and Brugnon, made the third day meaningless. Except that Tilden, showing signs of wear, was beaten by Lacoste, 4-6, 6-4, 8-6, 8-6. It was Big Bill's first loss in a significant Cup match since 1919, ending his Cup singles streak at 16, a record not broken until 1975.

The French title went to Cochet, 6-2, 6-4, 6-3, over Lacoste, the second all-domestic final after the tournament welcomed 'aliens' in 1925. Lenglen gave Miss Browne a taste of what was coming on their professional head-to-head odyssey, 6-0, 6-2, for her second French championship—the last of her eight major singles. She tripled, as she had in 1925 with the same accomplices, winning the doubles with Julia (Didi) Vlasto and the mixed with Brugnon, to conclude her career with 21 majors: Eight singles, eight doubles, five mixed, all at Wimbledon and the French. Her collection of major triples (five) is a record, probably imperishable. Suzanne had made that agonizing cameo at the U.S. in 1921, and never felt impelled to travel to Australia.

Lefty Jack Hawkes took the Australian without much opposition from Jim Willard, 6-1, 6-3, 6-1, and so did Daphne Akhurst, her second, while the 6-1, 6-3, loser, Esna Boyd set an unenviable majors record: Five finals losses in a row.

Though playing without Helen Wills, the U.S. tied the Wightman Cup competition at 2-2, defeating Great Britain at Wimbledon, 4-3, winning both doubles at the climax and splitting the singles. Kitty Godfree's win over Ryan, 6-1, 5-7, 6-4, made it 3-1 for the home side. But Marion Zinderstain Jessup squeaked past Dorothy Shepherd Barron, 6-1, 5-7, 6-4, and returned to the court with Eleanor Goss for a 6-4, 6-2, win over Barron and last-flinging Dorothea Douglass Chambers, 47. It was 3-3, and longer-in-the-tooth-than-most Ryan, 34, and Browne, 35, grabbed the Cup from Godfrey, 30, and Evelyn Colyer, 24, in a tense decision, 2-6, 6-2, 6-4.

1927

Vive la France! as U.S. loses Cup

Henri Cochet, Jean Borotra, (left), unknown official, Rene Lacoste, Jacques Brugnon Breaking through to win their first of six Davis Cups.

One of the most astounding turnarounds in the history of tennis occurred in the semi-finals at Wimbledon. Bill Tilden at 34 was no longer El Supremo, but he was a legendary figure, imposing and formidable still, seeded second (seedings had just been introduced) only to Lacoste in his first appearance at Wimbledon since winning in 1921. Playing fourth-seeded Henri Cochet, Tilden won the first two sets, reached 5-1, 15-all in the third set and then lost, probably as great a collapse as any outstanding tennis figure would ever experience.

Big Bill had beaten defending champion Cochet in a straight-set semi, 9-7, 6-3, 6-2, at the French. He may have felt he needed to do the same this time, remembering that he'd lost the three-hour Paris final in five sets, 6-4, 4-6, 5-7, 6-3, 11-9, to Lacoste — 61 games, the longest French title match (Tilden held two match points on serve, 9-8, 40-15. Rain was falling, and in three games so was he, double-faulting on match point).

So Tilden went for winners with big forehands, missing three, and Cochet was off on a 17-point binge that lifted him to 5-5, 30-0. Even though Tilden got back in it on a break to 3-2 in the fifth, the inexorable force was with Cochet, roaring to perhaps the most remarkable of Wimbledon championships. His finishing off of Tilden, 2-6, 4-6, 7-5, 6-4, 6-3, was only the appetizer, as it turned out.

Tilden later wrote: "I have heard many interesting, curious, quite inaccurate accounts of what happened. One ingenious explanation was that King Alfonso of Spain arrived at 5-1 in the third set and I decided to let him see some of the match. Ridiculous! I didn't even know he was there. Another was that a group of Hindus hypnotized me. If they did, I didn't know it, but they certainly did a swell job. Personally, I have no satisfactory explanation. All I know is my coordination cracked wide open and I couldn't put a ball in court."

Before ambushing Tilden, Cochet had also come from a 0-2 deficit to beat Bill's doubles partner, Frank Hunter, 3-6, 3-6, 6-2, 6-2, 6-3. But he saved the most exciting for last, overcoming Borotra, who had beaten Lacoste, 6-4, 6-3, 1-6, 1-6, 6-2, in the semis. Henri made it through a minefield of six match points laid by the Bounding Basque at the climax, 4-6, 4-6, 6-3, 6-4, 7-5. He dodged one hazard on his own serve to 3-5, then five more with Borotra trying to serve it out in the next game. From the sixth match point (Borotra missing a volley), Cochet pounced, grabbing 15 of the remaining 18 points. He was the Lazarus of Centre Court.

Wallis Myers, the game's foremost critic, declared Cochet "was favored by the gods." Obviously. Wimbledon secretary Duncan Macaulay wrote: "Cochet

1927 CHAMPIONS AND LEADERS

Australian Championships
Men's Singles: Gerald Patterson
Women's Singles: Esna Boyd
Men's Doubles: Jack Hawkes / Gerald Patterson
Women's Doubles: Meryl O'Hara Wood / Louie Bickerton
Mixed Doubles: Esna Boyd / Jack Hawkes
French Championships
Men's Singles: René Lacoste
Women's Singles: Kea Bouman
Men's Doubles: Henri Cochet / Jacques Brugnon
Women's Doubles: Irene Bowder Peacock / Bobbie Heine
Mixed Doubles: Marguerite Broquedis Bordes / Jean Borotra
Wimbledon
Men's Singles: Henri Cochet
Women's Singles: Helen Wills
Men's Doubles: Frank Hunter / Bill Tilden
Women's Doubles: Helen Wills / Elizabeth Ryan
Mixed Doubles: Elizabeth Ryan / Frank Hunter
U.S. Championships
Men's Singles: René Lacoste
Women's Singles: Helen Wills
Men's Doubles: Bill Tilden / Frank Hunter
Women's Doubles: Kitty McKane Godfree / Ermyntrude Harvey
Mixed Doubles: Eileen Bennett / Henri Cochet
Year-End Number One
Men: René Lacoste
Women: Helen Wills
Davis Cup: France
Wightman Cup: United States

was incredibly cool in a crisis—so much that I sometimes wondered whether he really knew what the score was." Footnote: In the doubles final, Cochet and Jacques Brugnon led Tilden and Frank Hunter, two sets to love, 5-3, 40-15—two match points—on Cochet's serve for the match, only to be stiffed, 1-6, 4-6, 8-6, 6-3, 6-4.

The only people feeling worse than Cochet's singles victims were the members of the tourney committee, tormented by one of the dampest Championships. Rain fell nearly every day, pushing the finish to the third Tuesday.

The 'Crocodile,' Lacoste, won three great matches over Tilden this year to establish his own supremacy in the sport. He won the French, from two match points down, and U.S. Championships in extraordinary finals and also beat Tilden in a crucial Davis Cup match. In the Forest Hills final, Lacoste may have played the best tennis of his life, winning 11-9, 6-3, 11-9.

"It was a match," Allison Danzig wrote, "the like of which will not be seen again soon. On one side of the net stood [Tilden] the perfect tactician and most ruthless stroker the game probably has ever seen, master of every shot and skilled in the necromancy of spin. On the other side was the player who has reduced defense to a mathematical science; who has done more than that, who has developed his defense to the state where it becomes an offense, subconscious in its workings but nonetheless effective in the pressure it brings to bear as the ball is sent back deeper and deeper and into more and more remote territory."

Lacoste, whose career was cut short by ill health and who became famous for conceiving the famed polo shirts bearing the crocodile emblem—thus emancipating male arms from long-sleeved white dress shirts—never played at Forest Hills again.

America's record seven-year reign came to an end in the Davis Cup. France broke through in its third challenge with a 3-2 victory over a U.S. team that included the two men who had brought the Cup to America in 1920: Tilden and Johnston. Lacoste beat the fading Johnston, 6-3, 6-2, 6-2, then Tilden beat Cochet, 6-4, 2-6, 6-2, 8-6, and the Americans took a 2-1 lead on a trying doubles victory by Tilden and Hunter over Borotra and Brugnon, 3-6, 6-3, 6-3, 4-6, 6-0. Tilden could not come through with another victory, losing to Lacoste, 6-3, 4-6, 6-3, 6-2. The Cup got a boat ticket to France when Johnston was beaten by Cochet, 6-4, 4-6, 6-2, 6-4 in a dramatic match.

The overflow crowd of 15,000 at the Germantown Cricket Club was so carried away in loudly pulling for an American victory that, one report said, "it broke all bounds of tennis etiquette and cheered madly both Johnston's winning shots and Cochet's mistakes." Tilden and Lacoste took in the scene calmly, sitting side by side.

With Suzanne Lenglen off in professional ranks, Helen Wills (called Little Miss Poker Face because of her lack of expression on court) assumed complete dominance of the women's ranks at 22. She began a string of four Wimbledon titles with a 6-2, 6-3, victory over Spaniard Lili de Alvarez. Wills won her fifth U.S. Championship, striking down two Hall of Fame-bound teen-agers: 19-year-old Californian Helen Jacobs—soon to be her foremost rival—in a semi-final, 6-0, 6-2, and 16-year-old Betty Nuthall of England, in the final, 6-1, 6-4. Helen had beaten the French champ, Netherlander Kea Bouman, in the quarters, 6-1, 6-2. Charlotte Hosmer Chapin dethroned the energetic 43-year-old defender Molla Mallory, barely, in the quarters, 6-3, 1-6, 6-4.

Lacking Lenglen, the French title went to Bouman over South African Irene Bowder Peacock, 6-2, 6-4.

The United States went ahead in Wightman Cup play, 3-2, beating the British 5-2 at Forest Hills. Wills and Mallory were ruthless. Helen beat Kitty Godfree, 6-1, 6-1, and Joan Fry, 6-2, 6-0; Molla knocked off those two respectively, 6-4, 6-2, and 6-1, 11-9. The donor, Hazel Wightman, 40, won a doubles with Wills over Ermyntrude Harvey and Godfree, 6-4, 4-6, 6-3.

A new concrete horseshoe stadium seating 13,000 at Kooyong in Melbourne, in the style of Forest Hills, was opened for the Australian Championships and remained the focal point of tennis Down Under for six decades until the 1988 unveiling of Flinders (now Melbourne) Park. The title matches were suitably grand. In high 90s heat for more than three hours, Gerald Patterson fought off Jack Hawkes, 3-6, 6-4, 3-6, 18-16, 6-3. He served his way off the ledge of four match points at 12-13, and another at 15-16. Runner-up five straight years, Esna Boyd snapped out of reverse to beat Sylvia Lance, 5-7, 6-1, 6-2.

The first U.S. Pro Championships were played in New York, Vinnie Richards winning $1,000 of the $2,000 pot over Howard Kinsey, 11-9, 6-4, 6-3, at the public courts of the long-since-disappeared Notlek Tennis Club in Manhattan.

1928

Three for Helen, and a Gallic Slam

Helen Wills
Silent, deadly, winning three majors in straight sets.

Controversy raged much of the year between Bill Tilden and the U.S. Tennis Association over his writing newspaper articles about tennis, a violation of amateur rules. Tilden was suspended, missing the interzone Davis Cup defeat of Italy. As the finale with France approached—the first overseas voyage to challenge for the U.S. since 1920—other members of the American team threatened to strike. René Lacoste announced he would not defend his title at Forest Hills. He said: "We would rather lose the Davis Cup than retain it where there may be some excuse in the absence of Tilden."

Having built Stade Roland Garros for the Cup defense (and subsequent French Championships), and needing Tilden's presence to fill the seats, French tennis officials protested the suspension, as did the press and public. To the rescue, U.S. Ambassador Myron T. Herrick defused a potential Franco-American crisis by suggesting to State Department superiors that they lean on the USTA to reinstate Tilden. The USTA diplomatically bowed for the moment, then barring Big Bill again to keep him out of the U.S. Championships.

Then 35, Tilden went out and played what teammate George Lott called his greatest match ever. He defeated Lacoste on clay—the first time that grass hadn't been the surface for the Cup-deciding round—1-6, 6-4, 6-4, 2-6, 6-3. Afterward, Lacoste said: "Two years ago I knew at last how to beat him. Now, he beats me. I never knew how the ball would come off the court; he concealed it so well. I had to wait to see how much it was spinning—and sometimes it didn't spin at all. Is he not the greatest player of all time?"

That victory was not enough. Cochet beat rookie John Hennessey, 5-7, 9-7, 6-3, 6-0 and on the third day he beat Tilden, 6-4, 4-6, 6-2, 6-4, clinching after Jean Borotra and Cochet nipped Frank Hunter and Tilden, 6-4, 6-8, 7-5, 4-6, 6-2. A third day was too much for Big Bill, and France won 4-1, the pick of the

33 nations that started.

French supremacy carried to the major championships where, for the first time, one country's representatives swept all four majors, a 'Gallic Grand Slam.' Cochet won the U.S. and French crowns, carrying his homeland title over Lacoste, 5-7, 6-3, 6-1, 6-3. But Lacoste paid Henri back for his second Wimbledon title.

Borotra turned the Australian Championship into a Vive la France fete. He won the singles, despite almost letting it get away in five sets to a local, Jack Cummings, 6-4, 6-1, 4-6, 5-7, 6-3. The semi hadn't been a snap either, five sets with 19-year-old future champ Jack Crawford, 4-6, 6-3, 1-6, 7-5 (twice two points from defeat at 4-5), 6-4. In fact, the Basque bounded to a triple, taking the doubles with Brugnon over Jim Willard and Gar Moon, 6-2, 4-6, 6-4, 6-4, and the mixed with Daphne Akhurst on a default from defending champions Esna Boyd and Jack Hawkes. Akhurst regained her title, 7-5, 6-2, from Boyd, the extremely experienced loser of finals. It was Akhurst's third title, and Boyd's sixth final-round disappointment, a tournament record for futility.

With Tilden and Lacoste missing from Forest Hills, Cochet won the U.S. title by beating Frank Shields in the semi-final, 6-2, 8-6, 6-4, and Frank Hunter in the final, 4-6, 6-4, 3-6, 7-5, 6-3. It was the third straight victory by a Frenchman there, and it would be the last. Except for Cochet, runner-up in the 1932 U.S. final, there would be no outstanding Frenchman to play in the United States, let alone win, after the retirements of Lacoste and Borotra, until Cedric Pioline lost the 1993 final to Pete Sampras. At Wimbledon, a Lacoste-Cochet final was set up when Lacoste scored a five-set victory over Tilden, 2-6, 6-4, 2-6, 6-4, 6-3 (down a break, 2-1, in the fifth), and Cochet beat countryman Christian Boussus, 11-9, 3-6, 6-2, 6-3. Lacoste won for the second time, 6-1, 4-6, 6-4, 6-2.

Great Britain evened the Wightman Cup series again, 3-3, with a 4-3 victory. Although Helen Wills blew away Phoebe Holcroft Watson, 6-1, 6-2, and Eileen Bennett, 6-3, 6-2, Molla Mallory was past it at 44, losing to Bennett, 6-1, 6-2, and Watson, 2-6, 6-1, 6-2. In a clash of future U.S. champs, American rookie Helen Jacobs, 19, beat 17-year-old Betty Nuthall, 6-3, 6-1. But the Brits swept the doubles: Ermyntrude Harvey and Peggy Saunders over Eleanor Goss and Jacobs, 6-4, 6-1,

climaxing with Bennett and Watson over Penelope Anderson and Wills, 6-2, 6-1.

Wills became the first to hold three majors in one year, and convincingly: 6-1, 6-2 over Bennett at the French; 6-2, 6-3 over Spaniard Lili de Alvarez at Wimbledon; 6-2, 6-1 over Jacobs at the U.S., the second of the intriguing battles of the two Helens from Berkeley. (Wills never journeyed to Australia.) As much was made of Wills' reserved manner as her skills. W. O. McGeehan wrote in the New York *Herald Tribune:* "She is powerful, repressed and imperturbable. She plays her game with a silent, deadly earnestness, concentrated on her work. That, of course, is the way to win games, but it does not please galleries. Of course, there is no reason why an amateur athlete should try to please galleries."

Vinnie Richards, 25, succeeded C. C. Pyle as promoter (continuing as player) of professional matches, importing Karel Kozeluh, a Czech who was being acclaimed as a great player even though he had never played on the amateur circuit. In a head-to-head duel with Richards, Kozeluh proved superior on clay and hardwood, winning a majority of the matches (13-7). But he lost on grass at Forest Hills to Richards in the second U.S. Pro Championships, 8-6, 6-3, 0-6, 6-2.

1928 CHAMPIONS AND LEADERS

Australian Championships
Men's Singles: Jean Borotra
Women's Singles: Daphne Akhurst
Men's Doubles: Jean Borotra / Jacques Brugnon
Women's Doubles: Daphne Akhurst / Esna Boyd
Mixed Doubles: Daphne Akhurst / Jean Borotra
French Championships
Men's Singles: Henri Cochet
Women's Singles: Helen Wills
Men's Doubles: Jean Borotra / Jacques Brugnon
Women's Doubles: Phoebe Holcroft Watson / Eileen Bennett
Mixed Doubles: Eileen Bennett / Henri Cochet
Wimbledon
Men's Singles: René Lacoste
Women's Singles: Helen Wills
Men's Doubles: Jacques Brugnon / Henri Cochet
Women's Doubles: Peggy Saunders / Phoebe Holcroft Watson
Mixed Doubles: Elizabeth Ryan / Pat Spence
U.S. Championships
Men's Singles: Henri Cochet
Women's Singles: Helen Wills
Men's Doubles: George Lott / John Hennessey
Women's Doubles: Hazel Hotchkiss Wightman / Helen Wills
Mixed Doubles: Helen Wills / Jack Hawkes
Year-End Number One
Men: Henri Cochet
Women: Helen Wills
Davis Cup: France
Wightman Cup: Great Britain

1929

Geezers' Gala
goes to Tilden

Henri Cochet A sixth consecutive Wimbledon title for the French men.

In the years the French were dominating Wimbledon and Forest Hills, Tilden was still the most dynamic figure in the sport. René Lacoste wrote: "He seems to exercise a strange fascination over his opponents as well as his spectators. Tilden, even when beaten, always leaves the impression on the public mind that he was superior to the victor."

The French had broken Tilden's six-year dominance at Forest Hills, and now Tilden ended the three-year French reign. He won the U.S. title for the seventh time, coming from behind in the last three matches: 7-5, 2-6, 9-7, 6-2 over Johnny Van Ryn, from 3-5 in the third; 4-6, 6-2, 2-6, 6-4, 6-3, over bullet-serving lefty Johnny Doeg, from a break, 1-2 in the fourth, and a break, 0-1

in the fifth; 3-6, 6-3, 4-6, 6-2, 6-4, over Frank Hunter for his seventh title. This was the Geezers Gala, the 71-year-old final—Hunter, 35, and Tilden, 36, the second-oldest man to wear the U.S. crown. Bill Larned won in 1910 and 1911 at 37 and 38. Only Arthur Gore, 40, over Herbert Roper Barrett, 34, in 1908 at Wimbledon contested a major final with more mileage on the adversaries.

After Lacoste gave way to failing health (he lived to 92 nevertheless) following his French championship, Henri Cochet became the No. 1 Frenchman. He won the last all-French final at Wimbledon, beating Jean Borotra, 6-4, 6-3, 6-4, after defeating Tilden in the semifinals, 6-4, 6-1, 7-5. Great Britain's future great, Fred

Perry, made his Wimbledon debut by losing in the third round to John Olliff, 6-4, 6-2, 2-6, 6-3.

France was extended in winning a third successive Davis Cup over the United States, 3-2 at the wire. Cochet beat Tilden, 6-3, 6-1, 6-2, then Borotra beat American newcomer George Lott, 6-1, 3-6, 6-4, 7-5. In doubles, John Van Ryn and Wilmer Allison kept it alive for the Yanks, flattening Cochet and Borotra, 6-1, 8-6, 6-4, setting up a tie with Tilden's defeat of Borotra, 4-6, 6-1, 6-4, 7-5. Cochet made the difference, defeating 22-year-old Lott, 6-1, 3-6, 6-0, 6-3.

Helen Wills, now Mrs. Frederick Moody, was never more supreme. She swept Wimbledon and Forest Hills for the third straight year and the French Championship for the second, 6-3, 6-4 over Simone Mathieu. In her first of four Wimbledon finals triumphs over Helen Jacobs, she romped, 6-1, 6-2.

At the U.S. Championships, Jacobs was eliminated in the semi-finals by Britain's Phoebe Watson, 6-1, 4-6, 6-4, even though Watson took 12 straight points to 5-3 in the third. Molla Mallory, 45 but yet a force to be reckoned with, made the semis, only to be double-bageled in 21 minutes (8 and 13) by Moody, whom she'd beaten for the title seven years earlier. Then Helen beat Watson, 6-4, 6-2.

South African Billie Tapscott caused an echoing wave of criticism by being the first female player to be seen at Wimbledon without stockings.

Wills led the American team to a 4-3 Wightman Cup victory on the strength of singles superiority. She beat Watson, 6-1, 6-4, and Betty Nuthall, 8-6, 8-6. Jacobs beat Nuthall, 7-5, 8-6, and Edith Cross beat Peggy Saunders Michell, 6-3, 3-6, 6-3. That was sufficient, so the doubles loss of founder Hazel Wightman, 42, and Jacobs to Dorothy Shepherd Barron and Phyllis Howkins Covell, 6-2, 6-1, was of no consequence. The U.S. led in the series, 4-3.

Colin Gregory became the third Brit to win the Australian, beating 1924 finalist Bob Schlesinger, 6-2, 6-2, 5-7, 7-5. Twenty-three years later, Yorkshireman Dr. Gregory, a physician and the team captain, would become the oldest to win a Davis Cup match at 48, when he and Tony Mottram took the doubles in a 3-2 win over Yugoslavia. Daphne Akhurst's title was her fourth, 6-1, 5-7, 6-2 over Louie Bickerton.

In what still was a minor aspect of the sport, the third U.S. Pro Championship went to Czech Karel Kozeluh, who dethroned Vinnie Richards, 6-4, 6-4, 4-6, 4-6, 7-5.

1929 CHAMPIONS AND LEADERS

Australian Championships
Men's Singles: Colin Gregory
Women's Singles: Daphne Akhurst
Men's Doubles: Jack Crawford / Harry Hopman
Women's Doubles: Daphne Akhurst / Louie Bickerton
Mixed Doubles: Daphne Akhurst / Gar Moon
French Championships
Men's Singles: René Lacoste
Women's Singles: Helen Wills
Men's Doubles: René Lacoste / Jean Borotra
Women's Doubles: Lili de Alvarez / Kea Bouman
Mixed Doubles: Eileen Bennett / Henri Cochet
Wimbledon
Men's Singles: Henri Cochet
Women's Singles: Helen Wills
Men's Doubles: Wilmer Allison / John Van Ryn
Women's Doubles: Peggy Saunders Michell / Phoebe Holcroft Watson
Mixed Doubles: Helen Wills / Frank Hunter
U.S. Championships
Men's Singles: Bill Tilden
Women's Singles: Helen Wills Moody
Men's Doubles: George Lott / Johnny Doeg
Women's Doubles: Phoebe Holcroft Watson / Peggy Michell
Mixed Doubles: Betty Nuthall / George Lott
Year-End Number One
Men: Henri Cochet
Women: Helen Wills Moody
Davis Cup: France
Wightman Cup: United States

1930

Call of the pros beckons for Bill

Bill Tilden
A third Wimbledon crown at 37, but a loss to John Doeg in the U.S. final.

Bill Tilden's magnificent career as an amateur came to an end on the last day of the year when he officially announced he was turning professional. He bowed out after one of the most glorious victories of his career. He won his third Wimbledon, becoming at 37 years, five months, the second-oldest man to take the singles title. Arthur Gore won his third straight singles title at 41 in 1909.

Seeded second, Tilden beat an unseeded 25-year-old Texan, Wilmer Allison, 10 years and six days after winning his first Wimbledon over Gerald Patterson. Before defeating Allison, 6-3, 9-7, 6-4, Tilden survived a tough one, 0-6, 6-4, 4-6, 6-0, 7-5 over Borotra, who led 3-1 in the stretch. Allison removed first-seeded Henri Cochet in the quarters, 6-4, 6-4, 6-3, then sidelined fourth-seeded countryman John Doeg, 6-3, 4-6, 8-6, 3-6, 7-5. Doeg would beat Tilden two months later on the way to winning the U.S. title.

Tilden had his most successful European tour, winning the Austrian, Italian and Netherlands titles, losing to Cochet in the French final, 3-6, 8-6, 6-3, 6-1. Previously closed to foreigners, the Italian went international at Milan, and Tilden routinely beat Italian Davis Cupper Umberto de Morpurgo, 6-1, 6-1, 6-2.

Ranked No. 1 in the United States for a record 10th time, Tilden wanted badly to break a tie with Bill Larned and Richard Sears by winning his eighth U.S. title. He made it to the semis where the heavy left arm of 21-year-old Californian Doeg fell on him like an executioner's axe, severing Big Bill from his dream. His powerful serve made Doeg, nephew of a former champion of Wimbledon (1905, 1907) and the U.S. (1904), May Sutton Bundy, a formidable opponent when he had control of his ground game. Eighth seed Doeg whammed 28 aces, 12 in the final set, losing his serve only once in 29 games, to beat Tilden, 10-8, 6-3, 3-6, 12-10. He hit his serve so hard it was reported that he turned the ball into an ellipse—his 'egg ball.' The loss marked the first time Tilden had been beaten by a countryman in a U.S. Championship since Bill Johnston, 11 years earlier. Doeg then beat 19-year-old Frank Shields in the final, 10-8, 1-6, 6-4, 16-14. Shields, seeded 11th, had a set point at 13-14 cancelled by an ace.

Tilden's record in U.S. Championships was 71-7. He had played 78 matches, at least one every year since 1916 (plus one in 1912), except for 1928 when he was suspended. He won 210 and lost 56.

Tilden, who had a long love-hate relationship with crowds that admired his gallant efforts in the face of defeat and his sportsmanship but didn't like some of his showboating, now had no great goals to achieve as an amateur. Frank Deford wrote in his biography of Tilden:

"Frustrated by the reductions of age, appearing more effeminate in his gestures [Tilden would die a lonely, broken figure at 60 after two convictions on morals charges], he became testier, even petty, on the court. Once, on the Riviera in a match of no consequence, the umpire, an Englishman, finally just got up and departed when Tilden kept fussing. Once, at South Orange, New Jersey, he rudely informed the tournament chairman that Big Bill Tilden was not accustomed to competing on grass that had the texture of cow pasture, and had to be coaxed back onto the court."

Earlier in the year, Tilden played in his 11th consecutive and last Davis Cup final round, a 4-1 defeat in Paris as the French kept the Cup for a fourth year. Despite an injured ankle, he came back from a slow start in the opening match, beating Jean Borotra, 2-6, 7-5, 6-4, 7-5. But the U.S. back-up wasn't up to Bill's standard. Cochet beat George Lott, better known as a shrewd doubles player, 6-4, 6-2, 6-2, and linked with another clever doublist, 35-year-old Jacques Brugnon, to give France a 2-1 lead, 6-3, 7-5, 1-6, 6-2, over Johnny Van Ryn and Allison. Borotra applied the finishing touch to Lott, 6-3, 2-6, 6-2, 8-6. It was over as far as the result, and then for Tilden, the Cup stalwart for so long. Cochet was his bye-bye guy, 4-6, 6-3, 6-1, 7-5. Bill went out with a 25-5 Cup singles record.

The year marked the first appearances in the U.S. Top Ten rankings of Sidney Wood, No. 4; Ellsworth Vines, No. 8; and Bitsy Grant, No. 10.

Queen Helen, now Mrs. Helen Wills Moody at 24, won Wimbledon for the fourth straight year without working up much of a sweat in a 6-2, 6-2 final triumph over a perennial, Elizabeth Ryan, 38. Moody and Ryan teamed to win the doubles over Edith Cross and Sarah Palfrey, 6-2, 9-7—Sarah, a future Hall of Famer, was making her Wimbledon debut at 17. Although Moody won the French for a third successive year, beating the other Helen (Jacobs), 6-2, 6-1, she skipped Forest Hills. Britain's 19-year-old Betty Nuthall, finalist to Helen in 1927, won the U.S. title over Anna McCune Harper, 6-1, 6-4. The lone English entry, Betty became the first of her country to triumph in the ex-colony, rising from 2-4 in the second to beat Bostonian Midge Morrill in a semi, 6-8, 6-4, 6-2, and winning the last four games of the final.

Daphne Akhurst won the Australian women's title for

1930 CHAMPIONS AND LEADERS

Australian Championships
Men's Singles: Gar Moon
Women's Singles: Daphne Akhurst
Men's Doubles: Jack Crawford / Harry Hopman
Women's Doubles: Mall Molesworth / Emily Hood
Mixed Doubles: Nell Hall / Harry Hopman
French Championships
Men's Singles: Henri Cochet
Women's Singles: Helen Wills Moody
Men's Doubles: Henri Cochet / Jacques Brugnon
Women's Doubles: Helen Wills Moody / Elizabeth Ryan
Mixed Doubles: Cilly Aussem / Bill Tilden
Wimbledon
Men's Singles: Bill Tilden
Women's Singles: Helen Wills Moody
Men's Doubles: Wilmer Allison / John Van Ryn
Women's Doubles: Helen Wills Moody / Elizabeth Ryan
Mixed Doubles: Elizabeth Ryan / Jack Crawford
U.S. Championships
Men's Singles: Johnny Doeg
Women's Singles: Betty Nuthall
Men's Doubles: George Lott / Johnny Doeg
Women's Doubles: Betty Nuthall / Sarah Palfrey
Mixed Doubles: Edith Cross / Wilmer Allison
Year-End Number One
Men: Henri Cochet
Women: Helen Wills Moody
Davis Cup: France
Wightman Cup: Great Britain

the third straight year in a battle with 1927 finalist Sylvia Lance Harper, 10-8, 2-6, 7-5, the longest of their country's female finals in games played, 38. This was Daphne's fifth title overall, the Australian record until Margaret Smith Court won 11 between 1960 and 1973. And it was the last singles title for the tragic champ, who died in childbirth three years later at 29. As Mrs. Roy Cozens she did win the doubles, teamed with Louie Bickerton in 1931. Gar Moon defeated Harry Hopman for the men's crown, 6-3, 6-1, 6-3. But Harry, who would gain renown as the winningest Davis Cup captain (16 Australian Cups), and coming singles champ Jack Crawford won the doubles for a second straight year, this time over Jack Hawkes and Tim Fitchett, 8-6, 6-1, 2-6, 6-3.

For the fifth time in the eight-year rivalry, Wightman Cup competition ended with the 4-3 score for Great Britain, at home at Wimbledon, to even the series at 4-4. It was no problem for Moody in singles, 6-1, 6-1 over Joan Fry and 7-5, 6-1 over Phoebe Holcroft Watson. But Jacobs, who also beat Fry, 6-0, 6-3, was upset by Watson, 2-6, 6-2, 6-4, and rookie Palfrey lost to Phyllis Mudford, 6-0, 6-2. Doubles superiority saved the Brits: Ermyntrude Harvey and Fry over Edith Cross and Palfrey, 2-6, 6-2, 6-4; Kitty McKane Godfree and Watson over the Helens, Jacobs and Moody, 7-5, 1-6, 6-4.

Women's dress continued to be less cumbersome. Lili de Alvarez was wearing a pagoda-like trouser dress. Eileen Bennett and Betty Nuthall showed up at Wimbledon with open-backed tennis dresses, and necklines continued to drop.

1931

Changing of guard as 19 year olds win

Ellsworth Vines
The boy from Pasadena claims first U.S. title.

Sidney Wood first appeared at Wimbledon as a 15-year-old wearing white knickers on the Centre Court in 1927, the youngest to play in the Championships at that time, losing to René Lacoste, 6-1, 6-3, 6-1. Sidney returned at 19, became the youngest player in the 20th century (until 17-year-old Boris Becker in 1985) to win and the only one ever to win an unplayed Wimbledon final. His opponent, U.S. Davis Cup teammate Frank Shields, withdrew with an ankle injury.

Wood, seeded seventh, advanced to the final, 4-6, 6-2, 6-4, 6-2, over 22-year-old Fred Perry, a fourth-round winner over a promising young German, future three-time finalist Gottfried von Cramm, 7-5, 6-2, 6-4.

Facing top-seeded Jean Borotra, who was fresh from winning the French, Shields managed to take their semi, 7-5, 3-6, 6-4, 6-4, twisting his ankle near the end. Frank was ordered by the U.S. Davis Cup committee to default to teammate Wood in order to recuperate for a Cup semi-final against Britain the following weekend in Paris. There, the winner would challenge France for the Cup. "Frank wanted to play me, and it was an insult to Wimbledon and the public that he didn't," recalled Wood. "But it gives you an idea of the importance of Davis Cup then, and the USTA's tight control of American amateurs. Can you imagine a player today abandoning a Wimbledon final to save himself for Davis Cup? But, as amateurs, we had no say. Frank played well against the Brits, beating Fred Perry, but we lost, 3-2."

Californian Ellsworth Vines, who had been ranked No. 8 in 1930 and hadn't been picked for the Davis Cup team early in the year, came into his own at 19 by winning the U.S. Championship in September. From Pasadena, Vines was a lanky 6-foot-1, weighing only 145 pounds, and with a great cannonball serve. Analyst Julius Heldman wrote: "He had the flattest set of ground strokes ever seen and they were hit so hard, particularly on the forehand, that they could not clear the net by more than a few inches without going out."

Fred Perry scared Vines in the semis by winning the first two sets, but the champ served his way out (4-6, 3-6, 6-4, 6-4, 6-3) and concluded by beating George Lott for the title, 7-9, 6-3, 9-7, 7-5, despite trailing 5-3 in the third and 5-2 in the fourth. Lott, who came from two sets down to outlast Johnny Van Ryn in the quarters, 5-7, 1-6, 6-0, 7-5, 6-1, next knocked out the defender, Johnny Doeg, 7-5, 6-3, 6-0.

At Sydney, uniquely among the majors, a husband and wife took shots at the Australian singles titles. All-timer Jack Crawford made it, the first of his four, 6-4, 6-2, 2-6, 6-1, over Harry Hopman, but Marjorie Cox Crawford couldn't bring in a spouse's double, falling to Coral Buttsworth, 1-6, 6-3, 6-4. Still, the Crawfords won the mixed, to start a three-year run of success as a togetherness-plus couple.

Playing without Bill Tilden, the U.S. failed to appear in the challenge round of the Davis Cup for the first time since 1914. It appeared the Yanks would have a crack at the French in the challenge round when they took a 2-1 lead over Britain in Paris. Johnny Van Ryn and Lott beat George Hughes and Perry, 6-1, 6-3, 4-6, 6-3. Shields, fully recovered from the Wimbledon injury, squared the windy day by beating Perry, 10-8, 6-4, 6-2,

1931 CHAMPIONS AND LEADERS

Australian Championships
Men's Singles: Jack Crawford
Women's Singles: Coral McInnes Buttsworth
Men's Doubles: Charles Donohoe / Ray Dunlop
Women's Doubles: Daphne Akhurst Cozens / Louie Bickerton
Mixed Doubles: Marjorie Cox Crawford / Jack Crawford
French Championships
Men's Singles: Jean Borotra
Women's Singles: Cilly Aussem
Men's Doubles: George Lott / John Van Ryn
Women's Doubles: Eileen Bennett Whittingstall / Betty Nuthall
Mixed Doubles: Betty Nuthall / Pat Spence
Wimbledon
Men's Singles: Sidney Wood
Women's Singles: Cilly Aussem
Men's Doubles: George Lott / John Van Ryn
Women's Doubles: Dorothy Shepherd Barron / Phyllis Mudford
Mixed Doubles: Anna McCune Harper / George Lott
U.S. Championships
Men's Singles: Ellsworth Vines
Women's Singles: Helen Wills Moody
Men's Doubles: Wilmer Allison / John Van Ryn
Women's Doubles: Betty Nuthall / Eileen Bennett Whittingstall
Mixed Doubles: Betty Nuthall / George Lott
Year-End Number One
Men: Henri Cochet
Women: Helen Wills Moody
Davis Cup: France
Wightman Cup: United States

after Wood fell to the weekend's hero, Wilfred 'Bunny' Austin, 2-6, 6-0, 8-6, 7-5. But the Brits roared back, with Perry stopping Wood, 6-3, 8-10, 6-3, 6-3, and Austin shutting down Shields in the decider, 8-6, 6-3, 7-5.

That was almost enough impetus for them to dislodge the Cup from Stade Roland Garros. But the French, triumphant for a fifth consecutive year, had triple-threat master Cochet in the 3-2 finale that went down to an excruciating fifth match. There, Henri outdueled Perry, 6-4, 1-6, 9-7, 6-3. Cochet also beat Austin on the first day, 3-6, 11-9, 6-2, 6-4, and sided with 36-year-old Jacques Brugnon to repel Charles Kingsley and Pat Hughes, 6-1, 5-7, 6-3, 8-6 for the go-ahead point. Perry and Austin both beat Jean Borotra.

With Helen Wills Moody choosing not to play at Wimbledon, it appeared that Helen Jacobs could win, particularly after winning her quarter-final, 6-2, 6-3, over reigning U.S. champ Betty Nuthall. However, Jacobs fell in the semi-finals to Hilde Krahwinkel, 10-8, 0-6, 6-4. In the only all-German Wimbledon final, five-foot Cilly Aussem defeated Krahwinkel, 6-2, 7-5.

Aussem had also won the French by beating Nuthall in the final, 8-6, 6-1. Borotra, loser of the 1925 and 1929 title matches to Rene Lacoste, finally grabbed the trophy in another intramural final, defeating Christian Boussus, 2-6, 6-4, 7-5, 6-4.

Arriving at Forest Hills after missing the 1930 U.S. tourney, and deprived of a major title for the first time in five years (having passed on Wimbledon and the French), Moody rectified that in a hurry. She took her seventh (and last) U.S. title in 35 minutes over Eileen Bennett Whittingstall of England, 6-4, 6-1. By the end of 1931, Moody had gone four years without losing a set at the U.S. Championships.

As the U.S. and Great Britain prepared for the Wightman Cup matches, they were tied at 4-4. The U.S. won 5-2 at Forest Hills, thanks to the two Helens. Each won a pair of singles: Moody over Nuthall, 6-4, 6-2, and Phyllis Mudford, 6-1, 6-4; Jacobs over Nuthall, 8-6, 6-4, and Mudford, 6-4, 6-2. This was the start of a 21-year string of U.S. Cup victories that would not be broken until 1958.

Bill Tilden made his long-awaited debut as a professional in the midst of The Great Depression. As co-promoter of his tour with entrepreneur William O'Brien, Tilden opened against Czech Karel Kozeluh at Madison Square Garden on February 18 before a crowd of 13,000 paying $36,000. Tilden won, 6-4, 6-2, 6-4, then ran off 16 straight victories and went on to beat Kozeluh before big galleries at almost every stop (27-6) of a cross-country tour that grossed $238,000.

Frank Hunter, Bobby Seller and Emmett Pare played subordinate roles on the tour. Other professionals at the time were Hans Nusslein and Roman Najuch of Germany, the three Irish Burke brothers—Albert, Thomas, Edmund—living in France; and Major Rendell of England. At Forest Hills during the summer, the U.S. Pro Championships drew a field of 39, with Tilden trouncing Vinnie Richards, 7-5, 6-2, 6-1, in the final.

1932

Vines triumphs at Wimbledon, U.S.

Bunny Austin
British star introduces short pants to the game at Forest Hills.

Ellsworth Vines became the first man since Bill Tilden in 1921 to win both the Wimbledon and U.S. Championships. Competing in his first Wimbledon at 20, Vines was so impressive that some English reporters were calling him the greatest player of all time.

He defeated Australian Harry Hopman, 7-5, 6-2, 7-5, in the third round and sailed through Australian Jack Crawford, 6-2, 6-1, 6-3, and Britain's Bunny Austin, 6-4, 6-2, 6-0, in the last two rounds. Vines launched 30 aces against Austin, who broke his serve only once. Ellsworth's match point was a service ace and Austin said: "I saw him swing his racket and I heard the ball hit the back canvas. The umpire called game, set and match, so I knew it was all over, but I never saw the ball." The serve was timed at 121 miles per hour. (Pancho Gonzalez's serve was later clocked at 118.)

Crawford, the winner of the Australian Championship by beating Hopman for the second straight year, 4-6, 6-3, 3-6, 6-3, 6-1, had topped Fred Perry in the Wimbledon quarter-final pairing of two future champs, 7-5, 8-6, 2-6, 8-6. An oddity of the tournament was top-seeded Henri Cochet losing in the second round to Brit Ian Collins, 6-2, 8-6, 0-6, 6-3, then entering and winning the All England Plate competition for also-rans eliminated in the first two rounds. He became the first ex-champion to win the Plate.

Americans were so impressed with Vines at Wimbledon that hopes were high the U.S. would win back the Davis Cup after advancing past Germany, 3-2, in the challenge round at Paris. Vines had handled the slow clay of Roland Garros handsomely, beating Daniel Prenn, 6-3, 6-3, 0-6, 6-4, after the ascending 23-year-old Baron Gottfried von Cramm won a tough battle with Frank Shields, 7-5, 5-7, 6-4, 8-6. Reliables Johnny Van Ryn and Wilmer Allison went through Prenn-von Cramm, 6-3, 6-4, 6-1, setting up Vines for the clincher over von Cramm, 3-6, 6-3, 9-7, 6-3, though Elly was two points from losing the third set at 6-7, 30-all.

But then came, the incident called by many 'The Great Cup Robbery.' Vines showed that he was less than invincible in losing to crafty Jean Borotra in the first singles match, 6-4, 6-2, 3-6, 6-4. U.S. captain Bernon Prentice had replaced Shields in the singles with Allison, and when Cochet fought past him, 5-7, 7-5, 7-5, 6-2, to make it 2-0, it looked as if France would win easily. However, a thrilling doubles triumph by Allison and Van Ryn over Cochet and Jacques Brugnon, 6-3, 11-13, 7-5, 4-6, 6-4, tightened the engagement, and set up one of the most controversial episodes in Davis Cup history.

First, the groundskeepers heavily watered the clay at Stade Roland Garros in the hope of slowing the court down to hamper Vines in his final match. The slow court served instead to bother Borotra in the third singles match, against Allison. But Borotra, only days from his 34th birthday and reluctant to join the team, had one last gallant Cup thrust within him. Despite losing the first two sets to Allison, he rode the roars of a chauvinistic jam-packed crowd of 10,000 and volleyed his way back to parity. With gestures he called for their help, and thrice the Bounding Basque bought revival time in the fifth set by changing his flimsy espadrille-style shoes, once during a game.

Still, Allison took a 5-3 lead with serve, 40-15, then advantage—but squandered three match points, one a net cord shot by the Frenchman, the others on over-hit passers. The final blow came at a subsequent match point on Borotra's serve at 4-5. Borotra netted his first serve. The second was long, so long that a relieved Allison, who had performed so well over the three hot days—this his 14th set—hit the ball aside, making no attempt to play it. He moved to the net to shake hands.

"We were cheering," recalled Van Ryn, "thinking it was all tied up at 2-2. Wilmer had won." Or had he? "But then the umpire [Morin] announced, 'Egalite!'— deuce—and we couldn't believe it. The service linesman [Gerrard le Ferrier, thereafter considering himself a notable patriot] had stolen the win. He made no call and indicated the serve was good. The umpire backed him up." That was too much for Wilmer, and he lost the last three games, and 10 of the remaining 12 points, the final score, 1-6, 3-6, 6-4, 6-2, 7-5. "Dwight Davis, who sat next to me, was so mad that he withheld us from attending the official dinner that night," added Van Ryn. "It

was an incredible rebuke to the French from such a great sportsman. I only heard him cuss once, and it was then. He said: 'I'm sorry I ever gave the goddam Cup!'" Most newspaper accounts, including the French, agreed that Borotra's second serve was clearly long.

Fans were left to debate whether Cochet, who won the first two sets and then lost the final match to Vines, 4-6, 0-6, 7-5, 8-6, 6-2, would have been able to pull through if France had needed that point. The 3-2 decision meant a sixth straight Davis Cup for France, but it would be her last until 1991.

Vines, who often wore a white cap, had a curious windmill stroke in which the racket made an almost 360-degree sweep. Starting on high as though he were going to serve, he brought the racket head back almost to the ground and swept up to the ball. He put no spin on it, however, thereby hitting a flat shot with tremendous force that made him unbeatable when he was on.

Opponents came to realize that the way to beat him was to keep the ball in play, hitting him soft stuff until he started making errors. A harbinger was the memorable U.S. semi-final at Forest Hills. Cliff Sutter, the National Intercollegiate champ from Tulane, slowed things down and won the first two sets, and twice came within two points of victory (5-6, deuce in the third set; 5-6, 30-all in the fourth). But Vines persevered in the

1932 CHAMPIONS AND LEADERS

Australian Championships
Men's Singles: Jack Crawford
Women's Singles: Coral McInnes Buttsworth
Men's Doubles: Jack Crawford / Gar Moon
Women's Doubles: Coral McInnes Buttsworth / Marjorie Cox
Mixed Doubles: Marjorie Cox Crawford / Jack Crawford
French Championships
Men's Singles: Henri Cochet
Women's Singles: Helen Wills Moody
Men's Doubles: Henri Cochet / Jacques Brugnon
Women's Doubles: Helen Wills Moody / Elizabeth Ryan
Mixed Doubles: Betty Nuthall / Fred Perry
Wimbledon
Men's Singles: Ellsworth Vines
Women's Singles: Helen Wills Moody
Men's Doubles: Jean Borotra / Jacques Brugnon
Women's Doubles: Doris Metaxa / Josane Sigart
Mixed Doubles: Elizabeth Ryan / Enrique Maier
U.S. Championships
Men's Singles: Ellsworth Vines
Women's Singles: Helen Jacobs
Men's Doubles: Ellsworth Vines / Keith Gledhill
Women's Doubles: Helen Jacobs / Sarah Palfrey
Mixed Doubles: Sarah Palfrey / Fred Perry
Year-End Number One
Men: Ellsworth Vines
Women: Helen Wills Moody
Davis Cup: France
Wightman Cup: United States

exhausting 75-game, 2 1/2-hour struggle, 4-6, 8-10, 12-10, 10-8, 6-1. That left little time for the Cochet-Allison semi, and they were chased by darkness at 2-2. It meant finishing the semi-final the same day as the final, the lone such incident in the Championships history. Beating Allison in the 45-minute fifth set, Cochet—almost 31—was the winner, 6-1, 10-12, 4-6, 6-3, 7-5. He was given about two hours to rest for the final against Vines, who wouldn't be 21 until the end of the month. He complained, justifiably, about having to play again that day, but the U.S. Tennis Association wasn't going to turn away an overflow crowd of 15,000. Henri had a point in saying that American treatment of a foreigner was no better than that received, and bemoaned, by the Americans in the recent Davis Cup contest in Paris. He was plainly weary in a 6-4, 6-4, 6-4 defeat. Twice he was unable to move out of the way in time to avoid being hit by Vines' blinding serve. The last two aces of the match by Vines were so hard that they bounced into the stands. Cochet never returned to Forest Hills.

But Helen Wills Moody did return to Wimbledon after a one-year absence and won her fifth title, losing only 13 games in 12 sets. For the second time in the final she met Helen Jacobs, winning 6-3, 6-1. Moody also won her fourth French Championship, 7-5, 6-1, over long-striving Simone Passemard Mathieu, the native who would absorb a tournament record of six final-round defeats before finally becoming champion in 1938. Jacobs raised English eyebrows at Wimbledon when she played in what now are regarded as Bermuda shorts.

With Moody absent from Forest Hills, Jacobs raised her world ranking to No. 2 (behind Moody) by winning the U.S. title for the first time. She had lost the final in 1928 to Moody, but this time Jacobs beat another Californian, third-seeded Carolin Babcock, 6-2, 6-2.

Future Hall of Famer Alice Marble made her first appearance in the U.S. Top Ten at No. 7.

Henri Cochet notched his fourth French title, the record until Bjorn Borg came along almost five decades later to win a fifth in 1980 before adding a sixth the following year. Cochet turned back the only ambidextrous man to occupy a major final, Italian Giorgio de Stefani, 6-0, 6-4, 4-6, 6-3. Coral McInnes Buttsworth won her second straight Australian title, beating Katherine LeMesurier, 9-7, 6-4, and also won the doubles with Marjorie Cox Crawford. It was a splendid Championships for the Crawfords. Gentleman Jack, as he was called, tripled by adding the men's doubles with Gar Moon and the mixed with wife Marjorie.

Three other married couples have won major mixed titles: Americans Clarence and Augusta Schultz Hobart, the U.S. in 1905; English Leslie and Kitty McKane Godfree, Wimbledon in 1926; Aussies Harry and Nell Hall Hopman, the Australian in 1936-37, 39; and the Crawfords, taking their homeland title in 1931-32-33. But only Jack Crawford had a trifecta year.

The two Helens were almost enough as the U.S. took a 6-4 lead in the Wightman Cup at Wimbledon, 4-3. Moody beat future Wimbledon champ Dorothy Round, 6-2, 6-3, and Eileen Bennett Whittingstall, 6-2, 6-4. Jacobs beat Round, 6-4, 6-3, but lost to Whittingstall, 6-4, 1-6, 6-1. That left it up to Jacobs to revive, accompanying Anne McCune Harper in a decisive doubles over Peggy Saunders Michell and Round, 6-4, 6-1.

Bill Tilden continued to command the thin professional ranks with a mixture of tennis skill and theatrical showmanship. Tilden, Vinnie Richards and Germany's Hans Nusslein were the tour's standouts. Tilden faced Nusslein 100 times, winning 60, and was 12-1 over Richards. But it was Czech Karel Kozeluh who beat Nusslein, 6-2, 6-2, 7-5, for his second U.S. pro title.

1933

Jacobs finally wins, but victory tainted

Jack Crawford (left), with Fred Perry, Jiro Satoh and Ellsworth Vines A pot of tea fuels first man to win three majors in a year.

Although Helen Wills Moody and Suzanne Lenglen are regarded as two of the greatest women players of all time, it's ironic that both are also remembered for matches in which they defaulted and walked off the court at Forest Hills. Lenglen defaulted to Molla Mallory in 1921, and Moody quit in the middle of her U.S. final with Helen Jacobs in 1933.

The two Helens—Moody, almost 28, tall, dark-haired, and coldly methodical, and Jacobs, 25, stocky and outgoing—were natural rivals. Both came from the San Francisco Bay area. Both had the same coach, William 'Pop' Fuller, and the Jacobs family lived in the house where the Wills family had lived. When they met for the second time in a U.S. final (the first was 1928), Moody had long been a practically invulnerable figure. She had won her sixth Wimbledon title that year, over Dorothy Round, 6-4, 6-8, 6-3. She had won seven U.S. titles and never lost to Jacobs after trouncing her, 6-0, 6-0, the first time they collided. Moody beat Jacobs in two Wimbledon finals and the 1928 U.S. final. Jacobs had won the U.S. in 1932 when Moody abstained.

Though Jacobs insisted there was no feud, she wanted badly to beat Moody. She turned to Lenglen, who drilled her in hitting crosscourt so that she would avoid giving Moody the backcourt dominance she liked best. The faster Jacobs was determined to play the net as often as possible.

In the semi-finals, Moody lost her first set in seven years at Forest Hills to Betty Nuthall, 2-6, 6-3, 6-2, while Jacobs beat future Wimbledon champ Dorothy Round, 6-4, 5-7, 6-2. With the title at stake Jacobs took her first set ever from Moody, 8-6. Moody won the second, 6-3, tiring her opponent with drop shots. Given a respite in the intermission, Jacobs broke Moody's service twice for a 3-0 advantage. In his history of tennis, Will Grimsley wrote: "At this point Moody strode to the umpire's chair and put on her sweater. 'I am sorry, my back pains me. I cannot go on,' she said tersely. That was all she said. Wearing a long coat, her familiar eyeshade pulled low, she strode to the dressing room, declining interviews."

It was reported that Jacobs pleaded with her to continue. Jacobs denied this, saying she merely inquired if she would like to rest. Moody said no and walked away without shaking hands. The fans were stunned. The press lambasted her. She was accused of being a poor

1933 CHAMPIONS AND LEADERS

Australian Championships
Men's Singles: Jack Crawford
Women's Singles: Joan Hartigan
Men's Doubles: Keith Gledhill / Ellsworth Vines
Women's Doubles: Mall Molesworth / Emily Hood Westacott
Mixed Doubles: Marjorie Cox Crawford / Jack Crawford
French Championships
Men's Singles: Jack Crawford
Women's Singles: Margaret Scriven
Men's Doubles: Pat Hughes / Fred Perry
Women's Doubles: Simone Passemard Mathieu / Elizabeth Ryan
Mixed Doubles: Margaret Scriven / Jack Crawford
Wimbledon
Men's Singles: Jack Crawford
Women's Singles: Helen Wills Moody
Men's Doubles: Jean Borotra / Jacques Brugnon
Women's Doubles: Simone Passemard Mathieu / Elizabeth Ryan
Mixed Doubles: Hilde Krahwinkel / Gottfried von Cramm
U.S. Championships
Men's Singles: Fred Perry
Women's Singles: Helen Jacobs
Men's Doubles: George Lott / Lester Stoefen
Women's Doubles: Betty Nuthall / Freda James
Mixed Doubles: Elizabeth Ryan / Ellsworth Vines
Year-End Number One
Men: Jack Crawford
Women: Helen Wills Moody
Davis Cup: Britain
Wightman Cup: United States

sport, a quitter, ungracious. Later she said: "I feel that I have spoiled the finish of the U.S. Championships and wish that I had followed the advice of my doctor and returned to California. I still feel I did right in withdrawing because I was on the verge of collapse on the court." The loss was her first since 1926, when Lenglen ended her 27-tournament, 158-match winning streak.

Lining up without Moody (due to her back injury) and Alice Marble (heat exhaustion) in singles, the U.S. still won the Wightman Cup over Britain, 4-3. Jacobs and 20-year-old Sarah Palfrey were the difference at Forest Hills. Helen beat Round, 6-4, 6-2, and Peggy Scriven, 5-7, 6-2, 7-5. Sarah beat Scriven, 6-3, 6-1. A Helen-Sarah combo got the clincher over Mary Heeley and Round, 6-4, 6-2.

But the ordeal of 19-year-old Marble just days before in the compressed tournament at Easthampton, N.Y., kept her out of Cup singles and diminished her at Forest Hills (fourth-round loss to Nuthall in the third set, 6-8, 6-0, 7-5, despite a 5-1 lead and three match points), and may have contributed to her physical collapse and absence from tennis for most of 1934 and 1935. Playing singles and double, semis and finals during one oppressive 104-degree day, Alice played 108 games and wound up suffering sunstroke. In the singles, she beat Midge Gladman Van Ryn, 6-3, 6-8, 6-1, losing the final to Nuthall, 5-7, 6-3, 6-0. In doubles, she and Moody beat Nuthall and Mary Heeley, 6-4, 4-6, 6-1, but lost the final to 41-year-old Elizabeth Ryan and Scriven, 6-2, 9-7. Marble had asked to play only doubles in the three-day event, but was told by U.S. Tennis Association official Julian Myrick that she had to play both to be considered for the Wightman team. "I was heartbroken," she wrote, "when a doctor told me I was too weak to play singles. I'd never been on the team and worked so hard to make it."

The man who almost won something that didn't exist—the Grand Slam—was Aussie Jack Crawford, traveling the world in unprecedented championship style. By the time he reached Forest Hills for the 1933 U.S. Championships, 'Gentleman Jack,' who parted his hair down the middle, had departed from Melbourne, Paris and London with three major titles in his satchel. Nobody had ever done that.

Before Don Budge was to come along and popularize the notion of the Grand Slam—the four majors within a calendar year—Crawford came within a set of achieving that sweep, missing out only at Forest Hills in a five-set loss to Fred Perry.

Wimbledon Secretary Duncan Macaulay wrote in *Behind the Scene at Wimbledon:* "Jack Crawford was one of the most popular champions who ever appeared at Wimbledon. Although he was only 25 when he won the title, he always seemed much older. Perhaps it was the effect of his hairstyle, the sleeves of his cricket shirt buttoned at the wrist [though he was known to roll them up in moments of crisis] and, most of all, the old-fashioned square-headed racquet with which he always played. In a long match he liked to have a pot of tea, complete with milk and sugar, and reserves of hot water, by the umpire's chair, instead of the iced beverages and other revivers favored by the moderns."

English authority Max Robertson wrote in 1974 that if a poll were taken about the best men's singles final at Wimbledon, "the Crawford-Ellsworth Vines match in 1933 would probably head it; certainly it would have to be included in the top six." With 13 aces, Vines ran out 11 service games at love. Crawford played a defensive game against Vines' power, concentrating on Vines' relatively weak backhand. They split the first four sets before Crawford changed tactics, rushing the net. He took Vines' title away, breaking the last game at love, 4-6, 11-9, 6-2, 2-6, 6-4.

The crowd exulted over the first victory by a British Empire player (although Crawford was pressed in the opening round by Spaniard Enrique Maier, 7-5, 6-4, 2-6, 3-6, 6-4) since Gerald Patterson, another Australian, won in 1923. Macaulay wrote: "The cheering of the spectators went on and on, and their enthusiasm was so great there appeared to be a distinct danger that the sacred turf of the Centre Court would be invaded by the multitude."

There were two innovations at Wimbledon. Australian Vivian McGrath showed his two-handed backhand. Brit Bunny Austin, a loser in the quarters to Jiro Satoh, wore shorts for the first time on the Centre Court, having pioneered them at Forest Hills in 1932. Henri Cochet put on a pair, but only for the mixed doubles, and his opponent, Norman Farquharson, rolled up his trousers. The tragic Satoh, who committed suicide the following year, achieved the highest major finish for a Japanese male other than Zenzo Shimizu's appearance in the 1920 all-comers final, losing to Crawford, 6-3, 6-4, 2-6, 6-4, in the semi-finals.

A big disappointment was fourth-seeded Fred Perry, who lost in the second round to South African Farquharson, 7-5, 6-1, 3-6, 4-6, 6-4. Perry finally won his first major title at Forest Hills, when he outlasted Crawford in a grueling match, 6-3, 11-13, 4-6, 6-0, 6-1. Defending champion Vines was staggered in the fourth round, 6-3, 6-3, 6-3, by the dogged retriever 5-foot-4 Bitsy Grant in what was called a Mutt & Jeff match.

The term 'Grand Slam' didn't exist when Crawford began his championship journey by winning his homeland's title for a third time in succession, over Californian Keith Gledhill, 2-6, 7-5, 6-3, 6-2, through rain interruptions on a soggy Melbourne court. An attractive 19-year-old, Joan Hartigan, unseated champ Coral Buttsworth, 6-4, 6-3, the first of her three titles. Crawford shared the marquee with 'The Freak,' his 17-year-old countryman Vivian McGrath, who knocked out favorite Ellsworth Vines, 6-3, 2-6, 8-6, 7-5. McGrath's unconventional two-fisted backhand drives, the first both-handed stroke seen in the upper class, didn't fool Gledhill, who slow-balled the kid out, 6-4, 6-1, 6-1.

Stricken by an asthma attack in France, Crawford recovered in time to wreck Henri Cochet's quest for a fifth title, dethroning the daring half-volleyer, 8-6, 6-1, 6-3. Crawford was the first alien male to win the French. Completing the distress of the locals was the loss by Parisienne Simone Passemard Mathieu, to an unseeded 20-year-old British lefty, Peggy Scriven, 6-2, 4-6, 6-4.

Next for Crawford came Wimbledon. By the time Jack arrived—against his wishes—in New York, he was bushed, anxious to go home after almost five months on the road. Having won 13 straight tournaments, troubled by insomnia and asthma, he wanted to skip the U.S. However, the Australian Association got a $1,500 payment from the USTA guaranteeing his presence and he had no choice. People were beginning to talk of an unprecedented "clean sweep of the Big Four titles," and *New York Times* columnist John Kieran, a bridge player, wrote: "If Crawford wins, it would be something like scoring a grand slam on the courts, doubled and vulnerable."

It looked as though he would, reaching the final losing only two sets, and leading Perry 2-1 in sets at the intermission. But Jack was through, and would win only one more game. While Perry showered and changed, returning to the court refreshed, Crawford, drained, unwisely remained at the court, sitting in wet clothes. Unknown to him, his friend Vinnie Richards had spiked his tea with bourbon as a pick-me-up. It was no help, perhaps a hindrance. But no alibis—there never were from Crawford. And Perry—"I just went mad!"—came on like a firehorse to win eight games on a gallop and his first major, 6-3, 11-13, 4-6, 6-0, 6-1. No sweep or grand slam. Perry's roughest test had been Gledhill in the fourth round, 6-2, 4-6, 1-6, 6-3, 6-3, 4-6. Not for five years would the Grand Slam topic surface again.

After Wimbledon, Perry began his move to greatness. It started in Paris with the heist of the Davis Cup. After he spearheaded Britain's first Cup-seizing triumph since 1912, the front-page headline in London's Daily Express read simply: FRED! The Brits ended France's six-year, 11-victory reign, 3-2, at Stade Roland Garros.

In the first day of the final, Perry stopped Henri Cochet in five, 8-10, 6-4, 8-6, 3-6, 6-1, blotting a set point in the third. Bunny Austin whipped 19-year-old lefty Andre Merlin quickly, 6-3, 6-4, 6-0, and it was 2-0. But the 72-year-old team, Jean Borotra (34) and Jacques Brugnon (38) raced through the doubles past Pat Hughes and Harold Lee, 6-3, 8-6, 6-2, and the third-day crowd of 10,000 was agog as Cochet tied it by outlasting Austin, 5-7, 6-4, 4-6, 6-4, 6-4, coming back from a 1-3 deficit in the fourth and running the last four games of the fifth with irresistible volleying. Perry, dodging two set points in the second, overcame a spirited rookie, Merlin, in the decisive fifth match, 4-6, 8-6, 6-2, 7-5. Merlin was a stroke from a two-set lead over Perry, two set points at 5-4, but the Brit turned Fred-hot. In the decisive fourth, Perry blew a 5-1 lead, but pulled himself together one last time.

Working 13 of a possible 14 singles and six of seven doubles over the Cup run, Perry was 12-1 and 4-2. Austin, the fashion plate (Perry was the only singles player in long trousers), was 13-1 in singles.

The Brits had primed for the final with 4-1 semi-final win over the U.S. It began with Austin stunning Vines, 6-1, 6-1, 6-4. Elly's magic of two years had just about run out. Perry knocked off Allison, 6-1, 7-5, 6-4. Johnny Van Ryn and George Lott, Wimbledon doubles winners in 1931, delayed the Brits for a day, 8-6, 6-4, 6-1, over Hughes and Perry, before Austin shoved aside a highly competitive Allison, 6-2, 7-9, 6-3, 6-4. The Brits had won, but in the meaningless fifth match, with Perry leading Vines, 1-6, 6-0, 4-6, 7-5, 7-6 (40-15), the American fainted and was carried from the court in defeat, an agonizing farewell to Paris.

In the quarter-finals, the Aussies started well, with Crawford beating Austin, 4-6, 6-2, 6-2, 6-3. But teenager Viv McGrath couldn't keep up with Perry, 6-2, 6-4, 6-2, and with Austin in the clincher of the 3-2 decision, 6-4, 7-5, 6-3. In the doubles, Hughes and Perry made the difference over Adrian Quist and Don Turnbull, 7-5, 6-4, 3-6, 6-3.

Bill Tilden's opponent on the pro tour was again Hans Nusslein of Germany. Tilden dominated, though gross receipts dropped from $86,000 to $62,000. Henri Cochet also turned pro and was beaten by Tilden in his debut in Paris, 6-2, 6-4, 6-2. Vinnie Richards won his fourth U.S. Pro title, beating Frank Hunter, 6-3, 6-0, 6-2.

1934

Britannia rules
Centre Court

Fred Perry

"If I live to be 100, I'll never play so well again."

Fred Perry came into his own as the best, capturing Britain's first Wimbledon title since 1909 (Arthur Gore), the year Perry was born. He also became the second man to hold three majors in one year, following up on Jack Crawford's splendid 1933. But just as Fred had dashed Crawford's bid for a 'Grand Slam' at the U.S., his own was cancelled in the French quarters by the forehands-only man, ambidextrous Italian racket-switcher Giorgio de Stefani. Perry's resistance was sapped by spraining his right ankle in the last set, and he fell, 6-2, 1-6, 9-7, 6-2.

Conversely, Crawford was the first to lose three major finals in one year: Australian, French and his seventh straight Wimbledon final (he passed on the U.S.). Perry shattered his three-year grip on the Australian in Sydney, 6-3, 7-5, 6-1, and repeated in the U.S., beating Texan Wilmer Allison, 6-4, 6-3, 1-6, 3-6, 8-6.

In between, Perry collaborated again with Bunny Austin to keep the Davis Cup in London, 4-1 over the U.S.

The Americans' only Cup comeback ever from 0-2 put the quartet of Sidney Wood, Frank Shields, George Lott and Les Stoefen into the challenge round, 3-2, over Australia. Incidentally, the 'Miracle Man,' *Titanic* survivor Dick Williams, was the U.S. captain. Lott and Stoefen won over Crawford and Adrian Quist, 6-4, 6-4, 2-6, 6-4, and then Wood and Shields reversed the singles results: Sidney jolted Crawford, 6-3, 9-7, 4-6, 6-2, and Shields forcefully clinched over 18-year-old Viv McGrath, 6-4, 6-2, 6-4.

However, Lott and Stoefen, the Wimbledon and U.S. champs, beating Harold Lee and George Hughes, 7-5, 6-0, 4-6, 9-7, wasn't enough to divert the British tide. Austin and Perry beat up on Wood and Shields—Perry rebounded to beat Wood, 6-1, 4-6, 5-7, 6-0, 6-3 for a 2-0 lead. Then, Fred met tremendous resistance from Shields in clinching, 6-4, 4-6, 6-2, 15-13, breaking the tall American's serve in the fourth set at 11-10, 15-0.

In his *History of Forest Hills*, Robert Minton wrote: "Perry combined speed with a wristy forehand developed from first playing table tennis, in which he became the world champion. He was an enormous crowd pleaser; handsome enough to be a movie star, and a cocky showman in a white blazer and an unlit pipe, as though he were a lord, and not the son of a Labor Party Member of Parliament. He never ruffled anyone with a display of temper, for he was phlegmatic and won his matches by outlasting his opponents. His physical condition was second to none."

Reporter Ferdinand Kuhn said of Perry's 6-3, 6-0, 7-5, Wimbledon triumph that disenfranchised Crawford: "Perry was always the complete master. He didn't make a half-dozen bad shots in the whole match. He was lithe as a panther, always holding the opponent in check and beating Crawford at his own cool, cautious

1934 CHAMPIONS AND LEADERS

Australian Championships
Men's Singles: Fred Perry
Women's Singles: Joan Hartigan
Men's Doubles: Fred Perry / Pat Hughes
Women's Doubles: Mall Molesworth / Emily Hood Westacott
Mixed Doubles: Joan Hartigan / Gar Moon
French Championships
Men's Singles: Gottfried von Cramm
Women's Singles: Margaret Scriven
Men's Doubles: Jean Borotra / Jacques Brugnon
Women's Doubles: Simone Passemard Mathieu / Elizabeth Ryan
Mixed Doubles: Colette Rosambert / Jean Borotra
Wimbledon
Men's Singles: Fred Perry
Women's Singles: Dorothy Round
Men's Doubles: George Lott / Lester Stoefen
Women's Doubles: Simone Passemard Mathieu / Elizabeth Ryan
Mixed Doubles: Dorothy Round / Ryuki Miki
U.S. Championships
Men's Singles: Fred Perry
Women's Singles: Helen Jacobs
Men's Doubles: George Lott / Lester Stoefen
Women's Doubles: Helen Jacobs / Sarah Palfrey
Mixed Doubles: Helen Jacobs / George Lott
Year-End Number One
Men: Fred Perry
Women: Dorothy Round
Davis Cup: Britain
Wightman Cup: United States

game. Once he performed the amazing feat of capturing 12 games in a row. Perry said: "If I live to be 100, I'll never play so well again."

At the end, with Crawford serving at match point, he hit what looked like an ace, but he was called for a foot fault. He was so shaken by the call that he served into the net, the first time anybody could remember a Wimbledon final ending on a double fault.

Britain's joy was complete when Dorothy Round won the women's title, over Helen Jacobs—flunking on Centre Court for a third time—6-2, 5-7, 6-3. Afterward, to a tumultuous ovation, she and Perry were summoned to the Royal Box to be presented to King George V and Queen Mary. A quarter-century interval had ended. Two British players had won the singles for the first time since 1909 when Arthur Gore was complemented by Dora Boothby's victory over Agnes Morton, 6-4, 4-6, 8-6. It hasn't happened again.

The women's final had come down to a meeting between Round, beaten in the 1933 final by Helen Wills Moody, and Jacobs, loser to Moody in the 1929 and 1932 finals. Playing before the King and Queen, Dorothy was caught up in a scene much like Virginia Wade's Wimbledon Centenary victory in 1977, attended by the Royal Couple's granddaughter, Elizabeth II. Round fought off the invader in a strong third set as Wade would 43 years later.

In the French Open, slick-stroking German nobleman, Baron Gottfried von Cramm, almost 25, made his first big move, taking the title from Crawford, 6-4, 7-9, 3-6, 7-5, 6-3, by erasing a match point at 5-4 in the fourth with a brilliant overhead smash from the baseline. The Baron had semi-final difficulty with both de Stefani's forehands, 3-6, 6-4, 6-1, 3-6, 6-2. Jacobs was unlucky in Paris, too, as English southpaw Peggy Scriven beat her, 7-5, 4-6, 6-1, for the crown.

Another repeater was Joan Hartigan at the Australian, denying a startling bid by the champ of 1922–23, the 40-year-old Mall Molesworth, 6-1, 6-4.

By now shorts and bare legs were much in evidence at Wimbledon. The Prince of Wales said: "I see no reason on earth why any woman should not wear shorts for lawn tennis. They are very comfortable and quite the most practical costume for the game; and I don't think the wearers lose anything in looks."

Elizabeth (Bunny) Ryan, 42, teamed with France's Simone Passemard Mathieu to win the women's doubles crown, 6-3, 6-3, over Dorothy Andrus and Sylvia Jung

Henrotin. It was Bunny's 19th Wimbledon doubles title, 20 years after her first, a record that Billie Jean King would tie, then in 1979 surpass. Ryan won 12 doubles and seven mixed-doubles titles. Wimbledon official Duncan Macaulay offered this insight as to why Ryan, so strong in doubles, never won a major singles championship: "Firstly, her era coincided with that of two superlative singles champions, Suzanne Lenglen and Mrs. Moody; and secondly, Miss Ryan's only stroke on the forehead was a sizzling chop, very effective in doubles—particularly against women—but not so effective in singles as a good flat or topspin drive such as Lenglen or Moody played to perfection."

At Forest Hills, South African Vernon Kirby was the rain-tormented sensation, beating a 19-year-old future great, first-timer Don Budge in the fourth round and then first-seeded American Frank Shields. But Perry cooled him in the semis, 6-2, 4-6, 6-4, 6-2, and steadied at the climax of the final to beat Wilmer Allison, 6-4, 6-3, 3-6, 1-6, 8-6, after a threatening Allison had volleyed away Fred's 5-2 lead in the fifth. Allison was strong in his semi over Wood, 6-3, 6-2, 6-3, after Wood eliminated 18-year-old Frank Parker. Parker would wait a decade to fulfill his callow promise by winning the championship.

Sarah Palfrey Fabyan, almost 22 and playing her seventh U.S. Championships, got to her first final, but Jacobs—winning a third straight—was too tough, 6-1, 6-4. Sarah was still seven years removed from taking that last step. George Lott and Lester Stoefen, team of the year, won the U.S. doubles again, over Allison and Johnny Van Ryn, 6-4, 9-7, 3-6, 6-4, at Longwood in Boston, virtuoso George's fifth title, the 6-foot-4 Stoefen his third partner.

The U.S. increased its Wightman Cup lead to 8-4 with a 5-2 triumph at Wimbledon, powered by Jacobs and Palfrey. They got the necessary points, both beating Dorothy Round and Peggy Scriven. Round lost to Palfrey, 6-3, 3-6, 8-6 and Jacobs, 6-4, 6-4. Scriven lost to Palfrey, 4-6, 6-2, 8-6, and Jacobs, 6-1, 6-1.

The pro tour needed some new blood and got it with the arrival of Ellsworth Vines. With much fanfare before a Madison Square Garden crowd of 14,637, the 23-year-old made his debut against Bill Tilden, 41. The match grossed $30,125 and Tilden won, 8-6, 6-3, 6-2. They went on a tour of 72 cities, grossing $243,000, the most ever for the pros, and Vines beat Tilden, 47 matches to 26. Vines won a match in Los Angeles, 6-0, 21-23, 7-5, 3-6, 6-2. Another memorable match between old adversaries Tilden and Henri Cochet took place at the Garden where 12,663 paid $20,000. Tilden outlasted the 32-year-old Cochet, 7-9, 6-1, 4-6, 6-3, 6-3. Hans Nusslein was a 6-4, 6-2, 1-6, 7-5, victor over Karel Kozeluh in the U.S. Pro final.

1935

Same old ending in tale of two Helens

Helen Jacobs (left), Helen Wills Moody
The 'other Helen' loses, heartbreakingly, again.

Probably no player ever suffered as much frustration against an arch-rival as Helen Jacobs did opposite Helen Wills Moody. The only time Jacobs beat Moody, the victory was less than fully satisfying because Moody quit with back trouble in the 1933 final at Forest Hills. While Jacobs came out on the losing end every other time they played perhaps her toughest setback was the 1935 Wimbledon final.

Moody, seeking her seventh Wimbledon title, had played little the year before and was seeded only fourth. Early in the season she lost a set to Mary Hardwick, even lost a match to English lefty Kay Stammers in the semis at pre-Wimbledon Beckenham, 6-0, 6-4, a tournament won by Dorothy Round, 6-2, 6-0. And in a Wimbledon fourth rounder against an unknown Czech, Slenca Cepkova, she lost the first set and was within a point of trailing 4-1 before rallying to win, 3-6, 6-4, 6-2.

Slender Aussie Joan Hartigan knocked the crown from Round's head in the quarters, 4-6, 6-4, 6-3, only to fall to Moody, 6-3, 6-3. Jacobs, seeded third, beat 1931 runner-up Hilde Krahwinkel Sperling, 6-3, 6-0, but in the final she fell behind 4-0, almost tied at 4-4, then faltered and lost the first set 6-3. Of the second set British authority Max Robertson wrote: "Jacobs' length improved; her favorite forehand chop became as dangerous as a scimitar.

Mrs. Moody tried to come to the net but she was never able to run up and down the court as well as she could cover it from side to side." Jacobs won the second set, 6-3.

Jacobs took a winning 4-2 lead in the third, with one powerful serve knocking the racket from Moody's hand. She then broke Moody's serve to lead 5-2, but Moody broke back to 3-5 in a game where she was facing a match point at 30-40 and Moody flicked a desperation lob with Jacobs at the net. It looked like a simple smash, but a gusty wind caused the ball to sink so swiftly that Jacobs had to drop to her knees to hit it...into the net. That turned the match around. Jacobs went down fighting, serving two aces when trailing 5-6, but losing the match, 6-3, 3-6, 7-5. It was her fourth loss to Moody at Wimbledon, three in a final. Jacobs also lost to Moody in the 1928 U.S. final.

Fred Perry was clearly the cream of the men's sector for the second straight year, even through an injury probably caused him to lose his U.S. title, and Jack Crawford rose up to deprive him of the Australian in a base-lining rematch of the 1934 final, 2-6, 6-4, 6-4, 6-4. However, Fred would always chuckle over his triple-bageling (6-0, 6-0, 6-0) of Giorgio de Stefani in the quarters: "I told Giorgio after he beat me in Paris '34 [possibly costing Fred a Grand Slam] that I wouldn't allow him a game next time, and I meant it." Illness kept Joan Hartigan from going for a third straight Aussie title, and instead two Englishwomen fought for it, Dorothy Round beating Nancy Lyle, 1-6, 6-1, 6-3.

In Paris, Perry exacted his revenge over Crawford, 6-3, 8-6, 6-3, in the semis, ending Jack's run of consecutive major final-round roles at eight. In the title round, Perry bounced 1934 champ Gottfried von Cramm, 6-3, 3-6, 6-1, 6-3, adding the French to his stash and becoming the first to win all four majors. His countrywoman, Peggy Scriven, didn't fare as well. After two straight titles and 14 match wins in a row on the clay, she delighted the locals by losing to Simone Passemard Mathieu in the semis, 8-6, 6-1. But their joy was short-lived as long-legged German-born Danish citizen Sperling followed up on her semi-final elimination of Jacobs (7-5, 6-3) to beat Mathieu for the title, 6-2, 6-1.

At Wimbledon, Perry beat Crawford, 6-2, 3-6, 6-4, 6-4, then trounced von Cramm, the first German male to make the final, 6-2, 6-4, 6-4. Von Cramm had eliminated Don Budge in a semi, 4-6, 6-4, 6-4, 6-2. It was Budge, unseeded, who created the sensation of the tournament by stopping third-seeded Bunny Austin in a quarter-final, 3-6, 10-8, 6-4, 7-5. During that match there was an interruption for Queen Mary to take her seat in the Royal Box. It was written by one British reporter the next day that Budge had waved to the Queen. The story grew that Budge even cried: "Hi, Queenie." Budge took pains in his autobiography to point out that he did not wave, that he did wipe his brow, a reflex gesture. Two years later, though, when Budge was again at Wimbledon and met the Queen, he said she told him: "You know, Mr. Budge, I did not see you a few years ago when you waved to me, but had I, I want you to know that I would have waved back."

The Wimbledon mixed final was marked by the appearance of Mr. and Mrs. Harry Hopman—she the former Nell Hall—of Australia. They had won their own title in 1930, but were beaten in the final by Perry and Dorothy Round, 7-5, 4-6, 6-2.

Budge appeared in the U.S. Davis Cup line-up for the first time and drove the team straight to the challenge round with five straight singles wins, the last two over Henner Henkel, 7-5, 11-9, 6-8, 6-1, and von Cramm, 0-6, 9-7, 8-6, 6-3. The Yanks won, 4-1 at Wimbledon. Wilmer Allison and Johnny Van Ryn rescued five match points in winning the electrifying and pivotal doubles over von Cramm and Kay Lund, 3-6,

1935 CHAMPIONS AND LEADERS

Australian Championships
Men's Singles: Jack Crawford
Women's Singles: Dorothy Round
Men's Doubles: Jack Crawford / Viv McGrath
Women's Doubles: Evelyn Dearman / Nancy Lyle
Mixed Doubles: Louie Bickerton / Christian Boussus
French Championships
Men's Singles: Fred Perry
Women's Singles: Hilde Krahwinkel Sperling
Men's Doubles: Jack Crawford / Adrian Quist
Women's Doubles: Margaret Scriven / Kay Stammers
Mixed Doubles: Lolette Payot / Marcel Bernard
Wimbledon
Men's Singles: Fred Perry
Women's Singles: Helen Wills Moody
Men's Doubles: Jack Crawford / Adrian Quist
Women's Doubles: Freda James / Kay Stammers
Mixed Doubles: Dorothy Round / Fred Perry
U.S. Championships
Men's Singles: Wilmer Allison
Women's Singles: Helen Jacobs
Men's Doubles: Wilmer Allison / John Van Ryn
Women's Doubles: Helen Jacobs / Sarah Palfrey Fabyan
Mixed Doubles: Sarah Palfrey Fabyan / Enrique Maier
Year-End Number One
Men: Fred Perry
Women: Helen Wills Moody
Davis Cup: Britain
Wightman Cup: United States

6-3, 5-7, 9-7, 8-6, to set up attack-minded Allison for the clincher over Henkel, 6-1, 7-5, 11-9.

But the Americans' high spirits and hopes to seize the Cup from the Brits were splintered. Allison missed a huge opportunity in the tense opener against Austin. Serving match game at 4-5, Austin double-faulted to 15-30 as the overflowing crowd of 16,000 in Centre Court groaned. Painful for the invaders was the next point: Allison, charging, netted a routine volley that would have placed him at double match point. Reprieved, Austin ran it out, 6-2, 2-6, 4-6, 6-3, 7-5, and the 5-0 British avalanche to a third straight Cup was underway. Perry sprang on Budge, 6-0, 6-8, 6-3, 6-4, while Allison and Van Ryn couldn't find their usual Cup touch in the clutch, falling to the newly paired Pat Hughes and Charles Tuckey, 6-2, 1-6, 6-8, 6-3, 6-3.

Thirty-year-old Allison would feel a lot better at Forest Hills in his eighth assault on the U.S. title. He had fallen short against Perry in 1934, but this time Perry fell, literally and heavily, on damp grass in the seventh game of their semi. It was discovered that Perry, clutching his back throughout, had damaged a kidney in losing the title he'd won the two previous years, 7-5, 6-3, 6-2. Perry got that far on an oppressive finish against Frank Shields, 6-4, 4-6, 8-6, 6-0, stamping out two set points in the fourth.

Second-seeded Don Budge was felled in the quarters, in unlikely fashion by tiny, pesky go-getter-of-everything, Bitsy Grant, 6-4, 6-4, 5-7, 6-3. Thereupon Sidney Wood stepped over Grant, 6-2, 4-6, 12-10, 6-2, to the final where he was a 40-minute lunch for Allison, 6-2, 6-2, 6-3. A quarter-finalist in 1929 and a semi-finalist in 1932, top-seeded Allison wasn't going to miss. His superb groundies and furious volleying made certain. It was a suitable going-away gift. He would not be seen at Forest Hills again.

For the first time, the women were seen along with the men in the merging of singles Championships, a togetherness continuing to this day. Relentless Jacobs, permitting 30 games and no sets in six starts, won her fourth in a row, equaling the 1915-18 surge of Molla Mallory. In a reprise of the 1934 final, Helen beat Sarah Palfrey Fabyan, 6-2, 6-4, a persistent semi-final victor over Kay Stammers, 9-7, 7-5.

Both women played strong roles in a 4-3 Wightman Cup victory at Forest Hills. Beaten by Stammers, 5-7, 6-1, 9-7 the first day as Britain jumped to a 2-1 lead, Jacobs rebounded to top Dorothy Round, 6-3, 6-2, and join Fabyan (a 6-0, 6-3 winner over Phyllis King) in the decisive doubles triumph, 6-3, 6-2, over Stammers and Freda James.

George Lott and Les Stoefen turned pro, but Tilden, at 42, let Lott know who was in charge. Before a record American crowd of 16,000 at Madison Square Garden the old master gave the 29-year-old rookie a 6-4, 7-5 paddling. Big Bill, though bageled twice, won his second U.S. Pro title, 0-6, 6-1, 6-4, 0-6, 6-4, over Karel Kozeluh.

1936

Eighth major his, Perry moves on

Don Budge (left), Fred Perry Two epic battles, two wins for the departing Englishman.

Fred Perry turned pro late in the year after dominating tennis for four years as few men have. He won three successive Wimbledon titles, three U.S., a French and an Australian, and nine out of 10 Davis Cup challenge round starts.

Perry had laid off for seven months after his kidney injury at Forest Hills, and when he was beaten in the French final by Gottfried von Cramm, 6-0, 6-2, 2-6, 6-2, 6-0—the last set in ten minutes—there was some question whether he could retain his form. At Wimbledon, however, he quickly established that he

would be formidable by sailing through early-round opponents. He beat pesky Bitsy Grant, 6-4, 6-3, 6-1, in the quarters, then in what were his only difficult moments of the tournament, lost the first set to fifth-seeded Don Budge in the semi-finals, before rallying to win, 5-7, 6-4, 6-3, 6-4. He had an easy time in the final—von Cramm ruptured an Achilles tendon in the first set. He continued, limping on a bad leg, and Perry won, 6-1, 6-1, 6-0, the widest margin of victory in a Wimbledon final.

It was the first time since the pre-World War I days

that somebody won three straight Wimbledons and when Bjorn Borg did it in 1978, Perry was there as a radio commentator.

This was the last Wimbledon in which the hosts fared so well, taking four of the five titles. Champions joining Perry were Pat Hughes and Charles Tuckey (men's doubles); Freda James and Kay Stammers (women's doubles); and Perry and Dorothy Round (mixed doubles). Only women's singles was captured by an invader, Helen Jacobs, at last.

So many times the 'other Helen' had come agonizingly close, but on her ninth visit she went all the way in her fifth final, winning 6-2, 4-6, 7-5, over Hilde Krahwinkel Sperling, the French champ. Finishing jitters appeared to get Jacobs after leading 3-1 in the second and third sets. Serving for the championship at 6-5, 40-15, she missed on two match points and slumped to break point. Was it a sour echo of 1935? Nope. She firmed up and took the last three points.

Kept out of the 1935 Australian by illness, Joan Hartigan was back to win her third straight, 6-4, 6-4, over a fresh face, 18-year-old Nancye Wynne, a setter of records Down Under. Nancye won the doubles with Thelma Coyne, a partnership that would ultimately account for 10 homeland titles, the last in 1952. Jack Crawford's sixth straight final was his last, and he lost a close one to a rising shorty, Adrian Quist, 6-2, 6-3, 4-6, 3-6, 9-7.

There was a repeat final at the French and a repeat champion—Sperling, who disappointed the home folks again by beating Simone Mathieu, 6-3, 6-4.

Crawford and Quist combined for Australia to astound the U.S. in merely the Americans' second Davis Cup series of the year, 3-2, at Germantown Cricket Club. This, despite Don Budge's beating both Crawford and Quist. It was, however, the last hurrah for U.S. champ Wilmer Allison—a hoarse one—as one of the more illustrious Cup careers (eight years) ended in two defeats, including the clincher by Crawford, 4-6, 6-3, 4-6, 6-2, 6-2. It had turned on the doubles, a debut together that went awry for Budge and Gene Mako, a great alliance in the making. Quist slithered out of two match points at 4-5, 15-40 in the fourth, initially as Mako bungled a short and simple smash. The Aussies regrouped for a 4-6, 2-6, 6-4, 7-5, 6-4 victory in which they lost but seven points in the last five games.

Not for a dozen years had a team from Down Under ascended to the challenge round. Australia had lost to

the U.S. in 1924. Now the Aussies were back again, 3-2 victors over Germany in the penultimate series at Wimbledon. Von Cramm knocked out Quist altogether on the grim, blustery first day after Crawford had beaten a flu-ridden Henner Henkel (6-2, 6-2, default). Not only did the German ace save three match points at 7-8, 0-40 in the screamer he won on a 10th match point, 4-6, 6-4, 4-6, 6-4, 11-9, but it turned into a TKO because the scrappy Quist twisted an ankle and was finished for the series. From the bench came 21-year-old Viv McGrath. Siding with Crawford for a 6-4, 4-6, 6-4, 6-4 win over Henkel and von Cramm, Viv then clinched it, 6-3, 5-7, 6-4, 6-4, over Henkel.

But the same good old impediments awaited the challenger: The one-two punches of Perry, the good-bye guy in the last four Cup successes, and Austin. They did their first-day stuff for 2-0. Austin scored his first significant win over Crawford, 4-6, 6-3, 6-1, 6-1, before Perry sidestepped a set point while inflating from 5-1 down in the third to beat Quist, 6-1, 4-6, 7-5, 6-2. The Aussies stormed back to take the doubles from Hughes and Tuckey, 6-4, 2-6, 7-5, 10-8, and arrive at 2-2 as Quist stung Austin, 6-4, 3-6, 7-5, 6-2.

What a moment for Perry to stride onto the revered greensward for his Centre Court valedictory before 16,000 patriots. His 52nd and last Cup assignment on

---

1936 CHAMPIONS AND LEADERS

Australian Championships
Men's Singles: Adrian Quist
Women's Singles: Joan Hartigan
Men's Doubles: Adrian Quist / Don Turnbull
Women's Doubles: Thelma Coyne Long / Nancye Wynne
Mixed Doubles: Nell Hall Hopman / Harry Hopman
French Championships
Men's Singles: Gottfried von Cramm
Women's Singles: Hilde Krahwinkel Sperling
Men's Doubles: Jean Borotra / Marcel Bernard
Women's Doubles: Simone Passemard Mathieu / Billie Yorke
Mixed Doubles: Billie Yorke / Marcel Bernard
Wimbledon
Men's Singles: Fred Perry
Women's Singles: Helen Jacobs
Men's Doubles: Pat Hughes / Charles Tuckey
Women's Doubles: Freda James / Kay Stammers
Mixed Doubles: Dorothy Round / Fred Perry
U.S. Championships
Men's Singles: Fred Perry
Women's Singles: Alice Marble
Men's Doubles: Don Budge / Gene Mako
Women's Doubles: Marjorie Gladman Van Ryn / Carolin Babcock
Mixed Doubles: Alice Marble / Gene Mako
Year-End Number One
Men: Fred Perry
Women: Helen Jacobs
Davis Cup: Britain
Wightman Cup: United States

behalf of his country concluded a sixth campaign. He had broken a 2-2 deadlock three years before to wrest the Cup from France. Again he was in a similar cauldron with the Cup at stake. It was what he lived for, and Fred bolted from the starting gate, rushing his long-time foe and friend Crawford off the court, 6-2, 6-3, 6-3. During their four years on top, in Britain's run of 10-0, Perry and Austin had been virtually untouchable in singles with respective marks of 18-1 and 17-3.

Perry and Budge, Wimbledon antagonists, met for a final time in a major setting, the U.S. title bout. It was a classic: Five gripping sets, twice interrupted by downpours, a spiky encounter in which both wore spikes, and future Grand Slammer Budge, 21, clung to two match points on his serve at 5-3 in the fifth. But he lacked the resolve to cash one against fiercely resisting Fred, who won 2-6, 6-2, 1-6, 8-6, 10-8. Point and counter-point they went as Budge, in his first major final, neared the championship again and again, two points away at 7-6 and 8-7, only to be blocked. Every point was a war, but Perry coolly won the last three games, the only man other than Bill Tilden to carry off three titles from Forest Hills. It was Fred's eighth major singles, good for second place all-time then behind Tilden's 10. Budge would play six more major finals, winning them all.

Of the fifth set against Perry, Budge later wrote: "We held serve to 3-2, my favor, and then I got the break for 4-2. Promptly, I permitted Fred to break me back. My serve was a dishrag. However, tired as I was, I was able to break him back again, so I stood at 5-3, serving twice one point away for the Championship of my country against the No. 1 player in the world. All I had to do was hold my serve. I could not. I was so exhausted in reaching up to hit my serve that I felt as if I were leaning on the ball. There was no life in my shots. The stretching and reaching for the serve particularly wore on me. He broke me again—our fourth loss of service in a row— held his own serve at last, and tied the set at 5-all."

Probably the greatest recovery from physical and emotional trauma to date was Alice Marble's to win the U.S. Championship in 1936. Ranked No. 3 in the U.S. for 1933, she collapsed during a match in Paris the following spring and was hospitalized. Cut down by anemia and pleurisy, Alice didn't play competitively for almost two years. But she was rehabilitated by the American summer of '36, and even though she won the Southern California title on concrete in May, the doubting U.S. Tennis Association didn't select her for the Wightman Cup team, and even refused her entries to Eastern grass-circuit tourneys. Marble had to prove herself in practice matches at Forest Hills before she was allowed to play at the height of the season. But her fitness was clear as she won two grass-court events en route to the Championships: The Longwood Bowl in Boston, over Carolyn Roberts, 6-1, 8-6, and Seabright (N.J.), over Carolin Babcock, 6-0, 6-3 in 35 minutes.

Alice, in the month of her 23rd birthday, was ready to puncture the U.S. bubble of Helen Jacobs, who had won four straight and took a 28-match Forest Hills streak into the final. Neither had lost a set, Jacobs relinquishing but 14 games in five matches. But the striking advances made by the 5-foot-8 Marble, who'd become a net-seizing, serve-and-volleyer, were obvious in her surge to a 4-6, 6-3, 6-2 triumph, winning 10 of 11 games from 0-2 down in the second. "The first set was a relief," recalled Marble, who would become the dominant female until she turned pro in 1940. "I was afraid Helen would whitewash me. But I came close, and knew I could beat her."

Even without Marble, the Wightman Cup thrilled Wimbledon with the closest finish ever, right down to 5-5 in the last set of the last doubles. Sarah Palfrey Fabyan was the heroine of the 4-3 U.S. victory, beating lefty Kay Stammers in a critical second-day singles, 6-3, 6-4, after both Stammers and Dorothy Round had stopped Jacobs, 12-10, 6-1, and 6-3, 6-3, respectively. Moreover, Sarah propped Jacobs in the decisive doubles revival, from 1-3 in the third to 1-6, 6-3, 7-5, to disappoint a crowd of 14,000. Carolin Babcock lent strong support to the U.S. cause, beating Rookie Mary Hardwick, 6-4, 4-6, 6-2, and coalescing with rookie Midge Gladman Van Ryn (wife of the Davis Cupper) in a doubles win over Evelyn Dearman and Nancy Lyle, 6-2, 1-5, 6-3.

It was a year of struggle and money-losing tours for the pros. Promoter Bill O'Brien's gimmick was signing on two American women of little appeal. Ethel Burkhardt Arnold beat Jane Sharp—they were Nos. 2 and 13 in the U.S. rankings of 1935—in the usual tour opening at Madison Square Garden. In the Wembley indoor tourney in London, often the best of the pros' infrequent tournaments, Ellsworth Vines won for the third successive year, beating Hans Nusslein, 6-4, 6-4, 6-2. The U.S. Pro, avoided by the leaders, went to Joe Whalen over Charlie Wood, 4-6, 4-6, 6-3, 6-2, 6-3.

1937

Budge hits stride as U.S. retrieves Cup

1937 U.S. Davis Cup Team Sailing toward a date with destiny.

The line of dominant players, which started with Bill Tilden in the 1920s and continued through the French trio of René Lacoste, Henri Cochet and Jean Borotra, then Ellsworth Vines and Fred Perry, continued with the imposing red-headed figure of Don Budge. The 22-year-old American swept Wimbledon and Forest Hills and sailed through the Davis Cup, winning what many rate as the greatest Davis Cup match ever played.

Almost 29 and apparently subsiding, Jack Crawford expected to grace a seventh straight Australian final, and failed because a decidedly bizarre-stroking 18-year-old, John Bromwich, stopped him in the semis. Bromwich was also on his own way to the Hall of Fame, a loping left-hander who served rightie with a loosely strung racket and used a two-handed backhand on the right side. Viv McGrath, at 21, reached his zenith, barely beating Brom for the title, 6-3, 1-6, 6-0, 2-6, 6-1, the first major final in which both competitors employed both-handed backhands. Nancye Wynne, 19, took the first of her six Aussie titles, 6-3, 5-7, 6-4, over Emily Hood Westacott.

With Franco-German tension growing, the home folks didn't much care for the second straight Teutonic double at Roland Garros, especially when Hilde Krahwinkel Sperling (German-born but a Danish citizen through marriage) beat Parisienne Simone Mathieu for a third year in a row, 6-2, 6-4. Sperling's three-peat duplicated Helen Wills' 1928-30 feat, the two of them overtaken by Monica Seles' French reign, 1990-92. Although Gottfried von Cramm didn't defend, his 22-year-old Davis Cup sidekick Henner Henkel came through for the Fatherland, 6-1, 6-4, 6-3, over Bunny Austin.

With Perry moving to professional ranks, it was obvious Great Britain would yield the Davis Cup to the strong challenger that emerged from the semi-final. Budge spearheaded 5-0 U.S. victories over Japan and Australia, beating Aussies Jack Crawford, 6-1, 6-3, 6-2, and John Bromwich, 6-2, 6-3, 5-7, 6-1, on Forest Hills turf. Bitsy Grant opened by out-retrieving Bromwich, 6-2, 7-5, 6-1, and Gene Mako and Budge put it out of reach, 7-5, 6-1, 8-6 over Crawford and McGrath to arrange the Germany showdown.

Before Davis Cup play came Wimbledon. Budge was seeded first, von Cramm second. On his way to the final Budge lost only one set, to teammate Frank Parker in the semi-finals, 2-6, 6-4, 6-4, 6-1, while von Cramm was extended by Crawford, 8-6, 6-3, 12-14, 6-1. Budge then defeated von Cramm, 6-3, 6-4, 6-2. Becoming the first man ever to score a Wimbledon triple, Don added the doubles title with Mako over Pat Hughes and Charles Tuckey, 6-0, 6-4, 6-8, 6-1, and the mixed with Alice Marble over France's Mathieu and Yvon Petra, 6-4, 6-1.

On to the Davis Cup and a match that had implications beyond the tennis court. "War talk was everywhere," Budge recalled. "Hitler was doing everything he could to stir up Germany. The atmosphere was filled with tension although von Cramm was a known anti-Nazi and remained one of the finest gentlemen and most popular players on the circuit."

Two weeks after Budge won Wimbledon, he and teammates Mako, Parker and Grant were back at Centre Court to clash with Germany, and they stayed there, winning on a July Tuesday. They began stripping the Cup from Britain four days later.

Von Cramm took about an hour to beat Bitsy Grant, 6-3, 6-4, 6-2, and Budge less than that to flatten Henkel, 6-2, 6-1, 6-3, and knot the teams at 1-1. Wimbledon doubles champs Budge and Mako won the vital, nip-and-tuck doubles over Henkel and von Cramm, 4-6, 7-5, 8-6, 6-4, even though Henkel served for the second set at 5-4, the Germans had a set point against Budge at 4-5 in the third and led 4-1 in the fourth. How vital it was soon became clear: Henkel, with stronger serve and better volley, ran up big leads in all but the second set

and hung on to topple Grant, 7-5, 2-6, 6-3, 6-4. That set up the decisive match—tantamount to determining the Cup itself—with that dedicated Budge fan, Queen Mary, in the Royal Box.

Just before Budge and von Cramm went onto the court, the Baron was called to the telephone. It was a long-distance call from Adolf Hitler exhorting von Cramm to win for the Fatherland. Budge recalls that "Gottfried came out pale and serious and played as if his life depended on every point." Von Cramm would be imprisoned for anti-Nazi views, and eventually sent to the Russian front as a soldier, seemingly a death sentence. Henkel was killed in that campaign. However, von Cramm performed valiantly and won an Iron Cross.

Von Cramm won the first two sets. Budge rallied, took the next two, then fell behind, 1-4. Then he took desperate measures. Attacking von Cramm's service, going to the net behind his returns, he got the matching break in the seventh game, making the score 3-4, and held service to 4-4. The score went to 5-5, then 6-6. In the 13th game Budge achieved another break. He reached match point five times on his own service only to see von Cramm fight back to the sanctuary of deuce. "The crowd was so quiet I am sure they could hear us breathing," Budge recalled.

"On the sixth match point, there was a prolonged

Australian Championships
Men's Singles: Viv McGrath
Women's Singles: Nancye Wynne
Men's Doubles: Adrian Quist / Don Turnbull
Women's Doubles: Thelma Coyne Long / Nancye Wynne
Mixed Doubles: Nell Hall Hopman / Harry Hopman
French Championships
Men's Singles: Henner Henkel
Women's Singles: Hilde Krahwinkel Sperling
Men's Doubles: Gottfried von Cramm / Henner Henkel
Women's Doubles: Simone Passemard Mathieu / Billie Yorke
Mixed Doubles: Simone Passemard Mathieu / Yvon Petra
Wimbledon
Men's Singles: Don Budge
Women's Singles: Dorothy Round
Men's Doubles: Don Budge / Gene Mako
Women's Doubles: Simone Passemard Mathieu / Billie Yorke
Mixed Doubles: Alice Marble / Don Budge
U.S. Championships
Men's Singles: Don Budge
Women's Singles: Anita Lizana
Men's Doubles: Gottfried von Cramm / Henner Henkel
Women's Doubles: Sarah Palfrey Fabyan / Alice Marble
Mixed Doubles: Sarah Palfrey Fabyan / Don Budge
Year-End Number One
Men: Don Budge
Women: Anita Lizana
Davis Cup: United States
Wightman Cup: United States

rally," Will Grimsley wrote. "Von Cramm sent up a lob. Budge raced back and returned it. Von Cramm then hit a forehand crosscourt. Budge tore after the ball, got his racket on it and took a desperate swing, sprawling to the court. It was a placement – a shot that the fallen Budge didn't see. Game, set, match and the Davis Cup series: 6-8, 5-7, 6-4, 6-2, 8-6. The two-hour, 33-minute match ended at 8:45 p.m. in semi-darkness. The two players went to their dressing rooms, relaxed, dressed and returned more than an hour later to find most of the crowd still on hand, buzzing over the spectacular final."

Because von Cramm was the underdog and the British thought they might have a better chance in a final against the Germans, the crowd slightly favored von Cramm. An oddity was that the Germans were coached by Bill Tilden. It wasn't unusual for a pro in one country to coach another country's Davis Cup team, but it was uncommon for a coach to hold the post when it meant working against his own. At one point, Tilden was so animated in his rooting he infuriated American show-business celebrities Jack Benny, Paul Lukas and columnist Ed Sullivan (a future TV host), who challenged Tilden to a fight. Tilden later told Budge this was the greatest tennis match ever played.

Strictly anti-climactic was the challenge round. Bereft of Perry, Britain could win only the opening match, Bunny Austin's 6-3, 6-2, 7-5 decision over Parker, inserted for Grant. Rookie Charlie Hare, an attack-minded southpaw, kept 11,000 loyalists hopeful of a 2-0 lead for a long while, leading 3-1 and serving for the first set at 5-4. But Budge was unbudgeable, 15-13, 6-1, 6-2, and a 4-1 victory was in the works. Had the Brits, Frank Wilde and Charles Tuckey, cashed a set point against Mako at 9-10 in the fourth, they might have caused some panic in the go-ahead doubles, won by Gene and Don, 6-3, 7-5, 7-9, 12-10. That left it to Parker to apply the finishing touches, which he did smartly, beating Hare, 6-2, 6-4, 6-2. The Cup was headed home after 11 years abroad. As 10,000 fans applauded, who could guess that Parker 11 years later would win both his singles to help the U.S. defeat Australia in the challenge round, the lone man to play singles with Cup-winners before and after World War II?

The Americans returned with the trophy to a ticker-tape parade in New York, and Budge was later greeted with a parade in his hometown, Oakland, receiving a signet ring featuring the city seal flanked by diamonds. At Forest Hills, von Cramm was pushed hard on his way

to the final: Four sets by Don McNeill, and Hal Surface. Those were followed by three full-distance battles: 9-7, 2-6, 2-6, 6-3, 6-3, over troublemaker Grant in the quarters; 0-6, 8-6, 6-8, 6-3, 6-2, over another feisty wind-up doll and future champ, 19-year-old Bobby Riggs, No. 6 in the U.S. rankings.

Von Cramm extended Budge to five sets, yet the American said he felt none of the trauma he found at Wimbledon, which he had won in straight sets. The score this time: 6-1, 7-9, 6-1, 3-6, 6-1. The packed crowd of 14,000 (5,000 were turned away) roared all the way for Budge. He became the first tennis player to win the Sullivan Award, as the outstanding amateur athlete in the U.S.

Despite the victory by Alice Marble over Helen Jacobs at Forest Hills in 1936, Jacobs was seeded first at Wimbledon and Marble fifth. Alice was first, Helen second at the U.S. but seedings and marquee names meant nothing in a curious year for the women at the two biggies. There, the mischief-makers were a couple of hardly-knowns who'd been playing well in England: A chunky, unpronounceable and unrestrainedly hard-hitting Pole, Jadwiga Jedrzejowska, and a subtle mite of a Chilean, 5-footer Anita Lizana. Seventh-seeded Dorothy Round, the champ of 1934, deflated the defender (Jacobs) in the quarters, and Jedrzejowska brought down Marble in the semis. She led Round in their third set, 4-2, but championship experience kept Dorothy calm in her third final, and she won it, 6-2, 2-6, 7-5.

Lizana, a quarter-final loser to Simone Mathieu, 6-3, 6-3, had led Jacobs at the same stage in 1936 (4-2, 30-0 in the third). But re-crossing the Atlantic, petite Anita accomplished an incomprehensible tour de force at the U.S. Championships: One visit only to Forest Hills, one title, no sets lost (in fact merely 28 games in six easy matches). Her quickness and maddening drop shots carried the No. 2 foreign seed well. Around Lizana others fell: Third-seeded ex-finalist Sarah Palfrey Fabyan in a first-round shaker to No. 13 American Dorothy Andrus of New York; a too-casual defending champion Marble in the quarters, to eager 21-year-old Californian Dodo Bundy (daughter of 1904 champ, May Sutton); Jacobs in the semis to Jedrzejowska.

Lizana cooled the blazing forehand of the Pole in winning, 6-4, 6-2, the first all-foreign U.S. final. That completed a shutout of American women at the four majors, making it their most poverty-stricken year since

1918 when Norwegian Molla Mallory won the lone major available in that war year.

International success came in Wightman Cup play—a 6-1 victory over Great Britain, the United States' seventh straight for an 11-4 edge in the series. Marble and Jacobs provided all that was needed: Alice beat Mary Hardwick, 4-6, 6-2, 6-4, and Kay Stammers, 6-3, 6-1; Helen administered similar treatment, 2-6, 6-4, 6-2, and 6-1, 4-6, 6-4, respectively.

Interest in pro tennis was revived with the debut of Fred Perry playing a cross-country tour against Ellsworth Vines, promoted by Frank Hunter, Bill Tilden's old doubles partner, and S. Howard Voshell. Perry opened at Madison Square Garden in fine fashion, defeating Vines, 7-5, 3-6, 6-3, 6-4, before a record crowd of 17,630, paying $58,120, a financial record for the tour. Perry won the first six matches, but Vines finished strongly, winning the series, 32-29. The tour grossed $412,181. Perry, with his guarantee, received the bigger slice, $91,335. Vines got $34,195.

Though Vines was regarded as the 'official' pro champion, Tilden scheduled himself against Perry in the Garden later in the year. Tilden was 44, Perry 28, and though the crowd of 15,132 cheered mightily for the old guy, he was outclassed. He lost in the Garden for the first time, 6-1, 6-3, 4-6, 6-0. Wrote Al Laney: "All they can do is beat him; they cannot ever be his equal." It was estimated Tilden had netted $500,000 (in Depression dollars) since turning pro six years earlier.

The Europeans won the significant pro tournaments: German Hans Nusslein the French over Henri Cochet, 6-2, 8-6, 6-3, and Wembley over Tilden, 6-4, 3-6, 6-3, 2-6, 6-3; Czech Karel Kozeluh, his third U.S. over Texan Bruce Barnes, 6-2, 6-3, 4-6, 4-6, 6-1.

In October, a premature—31 years before its time—and rather plaintive event advertised as the 'first open championship' was held in the West Virginia Hills at the posh Greenbrier resort. Prize money was offered, but no amateurs of note rushed in to test the waters, and the few unknowns who did were suspended by the U.S. Tennis Association. Vines, Tilden and Perry stayed away, too. The event was dominated by the second-line pros, Karel Kozeluh beating Bruce Barnes, 6-2, 6-3, 4-6, 4-6, 6-1, for America's first 'open' title.

1938

Putting $$ on hold, Budge births Slam

Don Budge
Drops only five sets in becoming first player to win all four majors.

At 23, Don Budge had the then-single most successful year of any player in tennis history. He won the four major championships—Australia, France, Wimbledon and the U.S.—a feat that came to be known as the Grand Slam after Budge accomplished it. He also won the triple crown at Wimbledon for the second straight year and helped the U.S. retain the Davis Cup.

Budge had received his first substantial offer to go professional in 1937. He turned it down because he felt indebted to amateur tennis to the extent of helping defend the Davis Cup the U.S. had won in 1937, for the first time since 1926. "The Grand Slam then occurred to me as something of an afterthought," Budge said. He laid his plans carefully, telling only his pal/doubles partner Gene Mako, resolving not to extend himself at any time, so that he shouldn't tire along the way, as Jack Crawford had in 1933 when he won the first three titles before losing in the final at Forest Hills.

Budge started in Australia, after losing frequently in leisurely tune-ups, and swept through the championships, beating John Bromwich, 6-4, 6-1, 6-1, at Adelaide's Memorial Drive in under an hour. Baron Gottfried von Cramm was there, losing to Bromwich in the semis, but shortly afterwards he—Budge's friend—was arrested and thrown into jail, charged with homosexuality but probably imprisoned because of his opposition to Nazi rule. Budge led an unsuccessful athletes' appeal for von Cramm's release.

In the French Championships, though

suffering from diarrhea, Budge had a fairly easy time. He was extended to five sets by a Yugoslav lefty, Franjo Kukuljevic, in the third round. Never behind, Budge said later he didn't feel threatened. Where von Cramm might have been his opponent in the final, he faced 6-foot-4 Czech Roderich Menzel, an outstanding clay-court player. Budge romped, 6-3, 6-2, 6-4, in less than an hour. He recalled the party afterward, at which virtuoso cellist Pablo Casals gave a concert in Budge's honor at Casals' apartment within view of the Eiffel Tower.

At Wimbledon, Budge won without losing a set, yet there was a time in the tournament when he felt panic because he had been having trouble with his backhand. It was his most celebrated weapon, considered by many to have been the greatest backhand of them all. He was undercutting the stroke, and only while watching an older woman member of the All England Club on a side court, hitting with topspin on her backhand, did he realize his error. He won his second successive Wimbledon by sailing past Britain's second-seeded Bunny Austin in the final, 6-1, 6-0, 6-3, then completed another triple with Mako in men's doubles, 6-4, 3-6, 6-4, 8-6, over Germans Henner Henkel and Georg von Metaxa, and with Marble in the mixed, 6-1, 6-4, over Sarah Fabyan and Henkel.

Peppery Californian Bobby Riggs, a Davis Cup rookie, was starting to be noticed as a potential Budge successor. He won the U.S. Clay Court title for a third successive year, beating Gardnar Mulloy, 6-4, 5-7, 4-6, 6-1, 7-5, and was just the challenge-round singles collaborator Budge needed against Australia. Lobbing and passing cleverly, Riggs led off with a 4-6, 6-0, 8-6, 6-1 victory over net-charging Adrian Quist to the delight of 10,000 customers at Philadelphia's Germantown Cricket Club. Budge followed up, 6-2, 6-3, 4-6, 7-5, over Bromwich, who in later years called Budge "the greatest player I've ever seen or played against." Quist and Bromwich kept it alive by beating Budge and Mako, 0-6, 6-3, 6-4, 6-2, giving Don the opportunity to close his Cup career with a clinching crushing of Quist, 8-6, 6-1, 6-2, ending with a 12-match streak.

Budge had been suffering from the flu and lost his voice off and on during the year. But he proceeded to romp through the U.S. Championship with straight-set victories over Welby Van Horn, Bob Kamrath, Charlie Hare, Harry Hopman and Sidney Wood, to reach the final against an astonishing Mako. Gene had become the first unseeded player ever to reach the U.S. final, beating the top foreign seed, Bromwich, 6-1, 7-5, 6-4, in the semis.

To some it looked like a set-up for Budge, but he responded: "Gene was as likely to roll over and play dead for me as peace was to come in our time." Mako did win the second set, only the fifth Budge lost in the four tournaments. Budge then had to explain that he did not intentionally throw a set to his friend, certainly not at Forest Hills with so much at stake: "And I had too much respect and affection for Gene to treat him as if he were an inferior player who could be given a set for his troubles, rather like a condescending pat on the head."

Bromwich and future king Riggs, who would be ranked 3-4 in the world for the year, were the only ones given a chance to jam the Slam. But second-seeded Bobby left early, removed in the fourth round by No. 19 American Gil Hunt, who paced himself with nolo-contendere sets to win. Bromwich fell to Mako, who could not prevent his pal Budge from rolling to the historic Grand Slam, 6-3, 6-8, 6-2, 6-1, before 12,000 witnesses.

Budge, winner of the doubles at Boston's Longwood with Mako over Aussies Bromwich and Quist, 6-3, 6-2, 6-1, and the mixed with Marble over Aussie Thelma Coyne and Bromwich, 6-1, 6-2, thus tripled. He was the first man to do so since Bill Tilden in 1922-23. So did Marble, whose doubles accomplice was Sarah Palfrey

---

1938 CHAMPIONS AND LEADERS

Australian Championships
Men's Singles: Don Budge
Women's Singles: Dorothy Bundy
Men's Doubles: John Bromwich / Adrian Quist
Women's Doubles: Thelma Coyne Long / Nancye Wynne
Mixed Doubles: Margaret Wilson / John Bromwich
French Championships
Men's Singles: Don Budge
Women's Singles: Simone Passemard Mathieu
Men's Doubles: Bernard Destremau / Yvon Petra
Women's Doubles: Simone Passemard Mathieu / Billie Yorke
Mixed Doubles: Simone Passemard Mathieu / Dragutin Mitic
Wimbledon
Men's Singles: Don Budge
Women's Singles: Helen Wills Moody
Men's Doubles: Don Budge / Gene Mako
Women's Doubles: Sarah Palfrey Fabyan / Alice Marble
Mixed Doubles: Alice Marble / Don Budge
U.S. Championships
Men's Singles: Don Budge
Women's Singles: Alice Marble
Men's Doubles: Don Budge / Gene Mako
Women's Doubles: Sarah Palfrey Fabyan / Alice Marble
Mixed Doubles: Alice Marble / Don Budge
Year-End Number One
Men: Don Budge
Women: Helen Wills Moody
Davis Cup: United States
Wightman Cup: United States

Fabyan over Simone Mathieu and Jadwiga Jedrzejowska, 6-8, 6-4, 6-3.

An undefeated season was not to be for Budge, who took a 1937-38 winning streak home to California. The Aussies got him at last. Quist, in the semis of the Pacific Southwest at Los Angeles, 7-5, 6-2, 5-7, 6-3, ended the 92-match, 14-tournament string that dated from a January 1937 loss to Bitsy Grant at Tampa. Then Hopman made Budge's farewell to amateurism a downer, 6-2, 5-7, 6-1, in the quarters of the Pacific Coast. But for two years nobody beat Don when it really mattered. His summary for 1938: Won six of eight tournaments, 43-2 in matches.

Californian Dorothy 'Dodo' Bundy shared some of the hurrahs with Budge in Adelaide as the first American woman to conquer the Australian, beating Aussie Dorothy Stevenson, 6-3, 6-2. Stevenson knocked off three-time champ Joan Hartigan, 6-3, 1-6, 6-1, and future champ Nancye Wynne, 6-3, 6-3. Today, as Mrs. Dodo Bundy Cheney (competing at 86 in 2002), she has far outreached any of her contemporaries, continuing to add to her record number of U.S. senior championships.

Vive la Mathieu! At last, Simone Mathieu heartened her neighbors by winning the French title that eluded her in six other finals, including the immediately previous three to Hilda Krahwinkel Sperling, who didn't enter. Mathieu beat Nelly Adamson Landry, 6-0, 6-3. A left-hander, she was the only Belgian to reach a major final, 6-0, 6-3, until 2001 when Kim Clijsters lost to Jennifer Capriati at the French, and Justine Henin lost to Venus Williams at Wimbledon. Moreover, Simone won the doubles with South African Billie Yorke and mixed with compatriot Yvon Petra, an uncommon triple, a distinction she shares only with Suzanne Lenglen (1925-26) among French at the French.

Aside from Budge's heroics, Wimbledon was marked by a strong women's field, featuring the return after a two-year absence of 32-year-old Helen Wills Moody, who was seeking a record eighth title. Though she had been extended by Kay Stammers in Wightman Cup play and had lost in the semis at Queen's Club, the Wimbledon tune-up, to Hilde Sperling. (Sperling then lost to Jedrzejowska, 6-3, 6-0.) Moody was seeded first. Unseeded Helen Jacobs, closing in on her 30th birthday, knew her way around to uproot the eighth and third seeds, Peggy Scriven and 1937 finalist, Jedrzejowska. She next beat the second, ex-U.S. champ Alice Marble,

spoiling the final everyone wanted: The aging goddess, Moody, against the fresh phenom, Marble. Alas, the final, their fourth at Wimbledon and the last of 11 Helenic confrontations, was a bust. Unfortunately Jacobs, playing so well, had severely strained an Achilles tendon. She came onto the court with it bandaged, struggled to 4-4, then was useless in a 6-4, 6-0, defeat.

Moody, with the 10-1 edge in the celebrated rivalry with the 'other Helen,' shut her major championships book at 19 singles titles, the record until Margaret Smith Court stepped ahead in 1970 on the way to 24. Steffi Graf, who also passed Moody in 1996, wound up with 22, and in 1990 Martina Navratilova pushed ahead of her at Wimbledon with a ninth title. But can anybody possibly surpass Helen's match record of 55-1 at the Big W, the last 50 uninterrupted? An irony of timing was that during the 1938 tournament Suzanne Lenglen, the woman never beaten there (27-0), died from pernicious anemia. She was only 39.

All the female favorites at Forest Hills were imperiled at one time or another. First-seeded Jacobs, four-time champ and never worse than a quarter-finalist since a 1927 debut, was bounced in the third round by a young British lefty, Margot Lumb. Marble, reinstating herself as champ, escaped by hairs two match points—from Fabyan in a volley-rich roller-coaster semi, 5-7, 7-5, 7-5. Marble led 5-1, then trailed 0-4 and 2-5, 15-40 in the second, 1-3 in the third.

Nancye Wynne, the other finalist, scraped through three consecutive three-setters: 8-6, 3-6, 6-1 over Helen Pedersen; 6-4, 5-7, 6-1 over Lumb; 5-7, 6-4, 8-6 over Bundy to become the first Aussie in the title round other than Wilberforce Eaves in 1897 and Jack Crawford in 1933. There wasn't much left, however, and for 22 minutes Marble was Hurricane Alice, winning 6-0, 6-3.

Moody bade good-bye to Wightman Cupping as well as Wimbledon, having been absent since 1932. She scored wins over Peggy Scriven, 6-0, 7-5, and the clincher, 6-2, 3-6, 6-3, over Stammers, her 18th win in 20 singles starts, as the U.S. defeated the Brits, 5-2.

Fred Perry and Ellsworth Vines joined together as co-promoters and foes on the pro tour, won by Vines, 49-35. But Perry won the U.S. Pro title, 6-3, 6-2, 6-4, over Bruce Barnes while Hans Nusslein ruled the European roost, beating Bill Tilden in the Wembley final, 7-5, 3-6, 6-3. 3-6, 6-2, and French Pro final, 6-0, 6-1, 6-2.

1939

On brink of war, a hustler collects big

Bobby Riggs
Ever a gambler, he claimed to leave Wimbledon $108,000 richer.

Grand Slammer Don Budge had gone to the pros, but as the world teetered on the brink of war a cocky and quick little Californian—Bobby Riggs—was ready to take over. And he did just that, showing up in three of the major finals and winning two, Wimbledon and the U.S.

Another Californian, Alice Marble, outdid him by winning those two majors—and everything else she went after to craft an undefeated season: Nine-for-nine in tournaments, 45-0 in matches.

Bobby Riggs' fresh attitude, his willingness to bet on anything, his entire shtick, may have clouded his greatness on court and his resourcefulness in all situations. But foes, especially the better ones, never doubted. He is the only man to play Wimbledon once and win all three titles. He claimed he won $108,000 betting on himself to make the triple.

"I started with 500 bucks," he recalled. "A London bookmaker gave me 3-to-1 odds on the singles, where I was seeded second behind Bunny Austin. I said if I win, let it ride on the doubles so he gave me 6-to-1 on that. I said let's keep going, so he gave me 12-to-1 on the mixed. I had to win the three or lose it all.

"Even though bookmaking was legal there, I was an amateur, and the USTA would have frowned on betting on tennis. I was afraid of what the USTA would do if they knew an amateur had all that money so I was hush-hush about it. I left the dough in a London bank, figuring I'd pick it up after I turned pro. But the war came, so it sat there gathering interest. A nice nest egg when I got out of the Navy. I sure was praying for the British to fight off Hitler and save my money."

Alice Marble also won the singles—6-2, 6-0 over Kay Stammers after double-bageling ex-French champ Heidi Krahwinkel Sperling in the semis—and, with Sarah Palfrey Fabyan, the doubles. But she had no idea how important the mixed was to Bobby. Her triple, hand in hand with a tripling man, was also unique. Sixth-seeded Stammers had knocked off ex-champ, second-seeded Helen Jacobs, then Fabyan in the semis, 7-5, 2-6, 6-3.

When it got down to the last two days of singles, even Riggs must have been edgy. He had a harder time than usual beating sixth-seeded Elwood Cooke for the title from 1-4 down in the second, 2-6, 8-6, 3-6, 6-3, 6-2. Partner Cooke had done him a big favor by removing Austin and fifth-seeded Henner Henkel. In the semis, Bobby beat Yugoslav Ferenc Puncec, 6-2, 6-3, 6-4.

"When I was down 2-1 in sets to Cooke, I thought about my investment," Riggs said. "I think the parlay was a big incentive to my success. We had some close calls in the doubles, but I was too near to let it get away." Probably the toughest was his and Cooke's 6-3, 3-6, 6-8, 6-2, 11-9 quarter-final over Brits Henry Billington and Pat Hughes. They beat two more Brits, Charlie Hare and Frank Wilde, in the final, 6-3, 3-6, 6-3, 9-7. In the mixed Bobby and Alice lost a couple of sets, but finished strong over Brits Nina Brown and Wilde, 9-7, 6-1. Bobby, the ultimate hustler, was rich.

Alice's doubles end of *her* triple, with Fabyan, was a cakewalk over Jacobs and Billie Yorke, 6-1, 6-0.

No Americans went to defend the Australian titles won in 1938 by Budge and Dodo Bundy. John Bromwich, who sandwiched his two titles around the

1939 CHAMPIONS AND LEADERS

Australian Championships
Men's Singles: John Bromwich
Women's Singles: Emily Hood Westacott
Men's Doubles: John Bromwich / Adrian Quist
Women's Doubles: Thelma Coyne Long / Nancye Wynne
Mixed Doubles: Nell Hall Hopman / Harry Hopman
French Championships
Men's Singles: Don NcNeill
Women's Singles: Simone Passemard Mathieu
Men's Doubles: Don McNeill / Charles Harris
Women's Doubles: Simone Passemard Mathieu / Jadwiga Jedrzejowska
Mixed Doubles: Sarah Palfrey Fabyan / Elwood Cooke
Wimbledon
Men's Singles: Bobby Riggs
Women's Singles: Alice Marble
Men's Doubles: Elwood Cooke / Bobby Riggs
Women's Doubles: Sarah Palfrey Fabyan / Alice Marble
Mixed Doubles: Alice Marble / Bobby Riggs
U.S. Championships
Men's Singles: Bobby Riggs
Women's Singles: Alice Marble
Men's Doubles: Adrian Quist / John Bromwich
Women's Doubles: Sarah Palfrey Fabyan / Alice Marble
Mixed Doubles: Alice Marble / Harry Hopman
Year-End Number One
Men: Bobby Riggs
Women: Alice Marble
Davis Cup: Australia
Wightman Cup: United States

war, beat his doubles partner, Adrian Quist, 6-4, 6-1, 6-3. Emily Hood Westacott beat Nell Hall Hopman, 6-1, 6-2, for the other singles, but Nell won the mixed with her spouse, Harry Hopman. Bromwich reversed the 1937 final by defeating Viv McGrath in the semis, while Quist mastered the old master, 30-year-old Jack Crawford. Bromwich and Quist grabbed the second of eight straight doubles titles, 6-4, 7-5, 6-2, over Don Turnbull and Colin Long.

Just 21, a college boy from Kenyon out of Oklahoma, Don McNeill was a scholarly surprise at the French, running 11 games in the final to beat Riggs for the first time, 7-5, 6-0, 6-3. United with another American, Charlie Harris, he also took the doubles, 4-6, 6-4, 6-0, 2-6, 10-8, over the last of the Musketeers, Jacques Brugnon, 44, and Jean Borotra, 40, even though Borotra had four match points on serve at 6-5. Love was blooming in the mixed, won by Cooke and Mrs. Fabyan (later Mrs. Cooke) over Simone Mathieu and Franjo Kukuljevic, 4-6, 6-1, 7-5. Mathieu, in her eighth singles final, retained the title that she'd missed out on six times, holding off the sturdy Pole, Jadwiga Jedrzejowska, 6-3, 8-6. But the two blended to win the doubles.

Minus Budge, the U.S. was still favored to retain the Davis Cup at Philadelphia's Merion Cricket Club. The singles line-up of holdovers from the 1937 and 1938 victories, Riggs and Frank Parker, looked solid against Australia—the first day. Riggs crushed Bromwich, his conqueror of the 1938 challenge round, 6-4, 6-0, 7-5, coming back from 0-4 in the third, and Parker hung on to take Quist, 6-3, 2-6, 6-4, 1-6, 7-5. The 0-2 deficit wasn't the worst of it for the Aussies. Gloom thickened the next day, September 3. As part of the British Empire, they were at war against Germany.

Bromwich recalled: "We didn't know if we'd ever play tennis again. We reckoned we'd have to go into the service almost immediately." They were permitted to remain for the completion of the U.S. summer season. "But we also felt we still had a chance here. Quisty and I were sure we could win the doubles [they'd recently won the U.S. title over teammates Crawford and Hopman, 8-6, 6-1, 6-4], and that we'd play better singles on the third day. We badly wanted to be the first to win as Australia." The last Cup triumph for the Down Under guys had been in 1919 as Australasia.

But 0-2? No country had ever rebounded from 0-2 before (nor since) to win the Cup. The Aussies did. Rookies Joe Hunt, 20, and Jack Kramer, 18 (the youngest American to play a challenge round), both future U.S. champs, were an untried team, and couldn't hold up against the canny Bromwich and dashing Quist, 5-7, 6-2, 7-5, 6-2, despite leading 3-0 in the third. Once they had a sniff of champagne from the Cup, the Aussies went all out to insure a swill. Riggs fought well after falling way behind, but Quist's passing shots brought him down, 6-1, 6-4, 3-6, 6-4. "I made up my mind to hit a thousand balls to Parker's forehand if that's what it took," says Bromwich. He unswervingly concentrated on Frank's right side in long rallies until it collapsed entirely to the dismay of 9,000 fans. Bromwich won the first seven games and the Cup, 6-0, 6-3, 6-1, the most one-sided clinching singles until 1989 when Boris Becker of Germany beat Mats Wilander of Sweden, also in 22 games.

The victory atmosphere was somber, as it had been in 1914 when the Australasian side of Norman Brookes and Tony Wilding lifted the Cup from the U.S. just after the outbreak of World War I. There would again be a long hiatus in Davis Cup, which sat out the war in the Bank of New South Wales at Melbourne.

The Wightman Cup went into storage, too, after a 5-2 U.S. victory sparked by Marble's two singles wins, 6-3, 6-4 over Mary Hardwick, and 3-6, 6-3, 6-4 over Stammers.

A mere footnote, but one boding immense implications, was the initial televising of tennis in the U.S. (it began in 1937 at Wimbledon). Matches at the Rye, N.Y., tournament were covered by NBC primitively, including Riggs' 1-6, 6-4, 6-4, 7-5, victory in the final over Parker. Few sets (with 4-by-3 inch screens) were in use and, according to *American Lawn Tennis* magazine: "When the entire court was shown the figures of the players were so small and far-away-looking that only general movements could be followed; the ball was seldom discernible."

At Forest Hills, Riggs ran into a bright young hope, 19-year-old Californian Welby Van Horn. As the third unseeded finalist (following Frank Shields, 1930, and Gene Mako, 1938), 6-foot-1 Van Horn displayed sharp volleying in running over several seeds including Australian champ Bromwich, 2-6, 4-6, 6-2, 6-4, 8-6. Riggs eliminated Joe Hunt in the semis, 6-1, 6-2, 4-6, 6-1. Van Horn opened the final with two aces, and the supportive crowd roared with approval. Riggs then took charge. The score: 6-4, 6-2, 6-4, and the U.S. had its first short-trousered champ.

Meanwhile, Marble completed one of the most powerful seasons ever enjoyed by a woman. She was threatened by Helen Jacobs, the four-time champion who reached the final by overcoming Stammers, 7-5, 6-0. Bageled in the first set, 6-0, Jacobs won the second 10-8, and took a 3-1 lead in the third before Marble prevailed, 6-0, 8-10, 6-4. Allison Danzig wrote in *The New York Times:* "Here was one of the most dramatic battles that women's tennis had produced in years, fought out for an hour-and-a-half in gusty cross-currents of wind that raised havoc with the strokes, while the gallery of 8,500 roared and screamed its encouragement at Miss Jacobs. The crescendo of the enthusiasm was reached in the final game, a furiously disputed 20-point session in which Miss Jacobs five times came within a stroke of 5-all and twice stood off match point, only to yield finally to Miss Marble's more powerful attacking weapons."

Thus, Marble completed her second U.S. triple in a row, having won the women's doubles with Sarah Palfrey Fabyan for the third straight year (7-5, 8-6 over Freda James Hammersley and Stammers), and then the mixed doubles, not with Riggs, but with the 33-year-old Australian captain Hopman over French champs Fabyan and Cooke, 9-7, 6-1. Riggs' splendid season encompassed nine titles in 13 tournaments, 54 wins in 59 starts.

When Don Budge made his pro debut in Madison Square Garden in January, he was a slight underdog champion Ellsworth Vines. A crowd of 16,725 paid $47,120. Many of them were USTA officials who showed their devotion to Budge for his loyalty in delaying his departure from the amateur ranks in order to defend the Davis Cup. Budge trounced Vines, 6-3, 6-4, 6-2, perhaps because Vines had played only eight matches with Fred Perry in South America that summer.

Later, Budge made a second Garden appearance against Perry, his master as an amateur. Budge won easily, 6-1, 6-3, 6-0. On a tour played mostly in big cities, Budge asserted his superiority, beating Vines, 21-18, and Perry, 18-11. Budge collected more than $100,000, including a $75,000 guarantee, from the $204,503 gross. Vines got $23,000, then deserted tennis for a successful pro golf career. Budge, however, stayed out of the $2,000 U.S. Pro Championships, won in a brilliant three-hour struggle by Vines over Perry, 8-6, 6-8, 6-1, 20-18, at Beverly Hills. Vines took home the magnificent sum of $340.05.

1940

Marble rolls to perfect mark

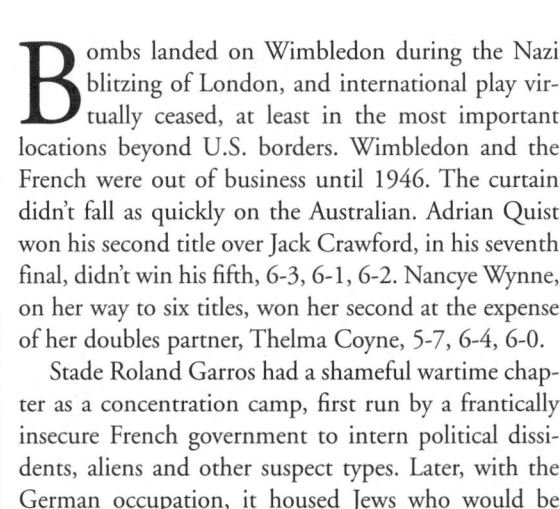

Alice Marble
An 83-0 record leading to a fourth U.S. singles' title.

Bombs landed on Wimbledon during the Nazi blitzing of London, and international play virtually ceased, at least in the most important locations beyond U.S. borders. Wimbledon and the French were out of business until 1946. The curtain didn't fall as quickly on the Australian. Adrian Quist won his second title over Jack Crawford, in his seventh final, didn't win his fifth, 6-3, 6-1, 6-2. Nancye Wynne, on her way to six titles, won her second at the expense of her doubles partner, Thelma Coyne, 5-7, 6-4, 6-0.

Stade Roland Garros had a shameful wartime chapter as a concentration camp, first run by a frantically insecure French government to intern political dissidents, aliens and other suspect types. Later, with the German occupation, it housed Jews who would be shipped east to their doom. Not up to Nazi standards, Roland Garros was returned to the French Federation in 1941. Regardless of an acute shortage of balls and rackets, national tournaments of sorts were held through 1945. Yvon Petra, recovered from his wounds after a stint as a POW, won the men's titles in 1943-44-45, and stayed fit for his successful shot at the first post-war Wimbledon title. In 1943, he beat a re-appeared 41-year-old Musketeer, Henri Cochet, in the final. A friend, ex-French Davis Cupper Robert Abdesselam, says that four-time champ Cochet "felt it important to play during the war, to show himself so that our dispirited youth would know that a Frenchman had been a world champion."

Wimbledon's courts languished untended, used as a civil defense center, with the parking lots tilled and planted as victory gardens—and a home for pigs and chickens. The first bombs struck on October 11, blowing a hole in the Centre Court roof. The club would be damaged from the air three more times during the year.

But the American season went on normally, meaning Alice Marble was omnipotent for another unbeaten year. Not so normal, though, for No. 1

Bobby Riggs, who lost his U.S. Championship (and No. 1 ranking) to Don McNeill, the newly crowned king of the Intercollegiates for Kenyon. McNeill, a 22-year-old Oklahoman, fought one of the great come-from-behind battles against Riggs in a match marked by outstanding sportsmanship. The score: 4-6, 6-8, 6-3, 6-3, 7-5.

McNeill had no fear of Riggs. He'd beaten Bobby a few weeks earlier in the U.S. Clay final, 6-1, 6-4, 7-9, 6-3, and the year before in the French final. But Bobby felt confident on the faster surface, having beaten Don in the U.S. Indoor final, 3-6, 6-1, 6-4, 2-6, 6-2. With the score 4-4 and deuce in the final set, McNeill hit a shot to Riggs' sideline that the linesman first called out. As Riggs turned his back and prepared to serve, the official reversed his call, declaring it good. Riggs did not know of the change until he heard the call, "Advantage McNeill." Allison Danzig wrote: "The defending champion, who rarely questions a decision, turned at the call and then walked back toward the linesman, asking him why he had changed his ruling. The official maintained that the ball was good. Riggs, without quibbling, accepted the costly decision and lost the next point and the game."

Then, in the opening rally of the final game, Riggs had to hit a ball that was falling just over the net and he gingerly endeavored to keep from touching the tape. The umpire instantly announced Riggs' foot touched the net and he lost the point. "At that critical state," Danzig wrote, "it was a bitter pill to swallow, but Riggs took it without arguing. McNeill, however, apparently did not like to win the point that way, even though the ruling

1940 CHAMPIONS

Australian Championships
Men's Singles: Adrian Quist
Women's Singles: Nancye Wynne
Men's Doubles: John Bromwich / Adrian Quist
Women's Doubles: Thelma Coyne Long / Nancye Wynne
Mixed Doubles: Nancye Wynne / Colin Long
U.S. Championships
Men's Singles: Don McNeill
Women's Singles: Alice Marble
Men's Doubles: Jack Kramer / Ted Schroeder
Women's Doubles: Sarah Palfrey Fabyan / Alice Marble
Mixed Doubles: Alice Marble / Bobby Riggs

was correct, and when he knocked Riggs' next service far out of court, the stadium rang with applause."

After losing the first set, McNeill rallied from 1-5 and 15-40 in the second set to tie, saved four set points, went on to take a 6-5 lead, but then dropped the set anyway, 7-9. Down two sets, he still came back, and with the crowd almost completely behind the valiant underdog, he squared the match and then pulled out the final set.

Alice Marble, about to turn 27—and pro—was supreme-plus, charging to her fourth U.S. singles title while never endangered, winning 12 sets, losing only 27 games. This put the finishing touches on her amateur career that had purred uninterruptedly victorious since a Wimbledon semi-final loss to Helen Jacobs in 1938. As in 1939, Alice won nine tournaments, and 45 matches. Moreover, she was 27-0 in doubles, 11-0 in mixed for a stupendous 83-0 record. She left intact a 22-tournament, 111-match streak, second only to Helen Wills Moody's 27—158 leading up to the 1933 U.S. final.

Regal and self-assured in her jaunty white cap, the tallest of U.S. champs at 5-foot-8 until Althea Gibson (5-foot-11) came along, Alice was too strong in the final for the second-seeded Jacobs, 6-2, 6-3, a tame rematch of their 1939 championship encounter. England's Mary Hardwick—after fifth-seeded Sarah Palfrey, 6-1, 6-3, and third-seeded Pauline Betz, 5-7, 6-1, 6-2—harried Jacobs in the semis, 2-6, 6-1, 6-4. Marble, having won a third straight U.S. doubles with Palfrey, over Dodo Bundy and Midge Van Ryn (6-4, 6-3) and the mixed with Riggs over Bundy and Jack Kramer (9-7, 6-1), became a triple-tripler. That put her up there with Hazel Hotchkiss Wightman (1909-10-11) and Mary K. Browne (1912-13-14) in U.S. annals. Marble also tripled at Wimbledon in 1939.

Newlyweds Sarah Palfrey and Elwood Cooke, he a U.S. quarter-finalist, were nationally ranked Nos. 6 and 9 in singles, the second spousal pair to be together in the upper echelon, following Johnny Van Ryn (No. 9 in 1930, No. 4 in 1931) and wife Midge Gladman Van Ryn (Nos. 7 and 8 those years).

Although there was no pro tour, Don Budge remained king, taking his first U.S. Pro title, 6-3, 5-7, 6-4, 6-3, over Fred Perry.

1941

Riggs back on top, Jacobs bows out

Sarah Palfrey Cooke A U.S. champion on lucky 13th try.

Frustration ended at Forest Hills for Sarah Palfrey Cooke and Bobby Riggs. Hers was longer-term. Sarah, who had divorced Marshall Fabyan and married sometimes mixed doubles partner, Elwood Cooke, arrived at the U.S. Championships for a 13th time, seeded second, having done everything but win. A 15-year-old when she first appeared in 1928, she had been seeded every year since 1933, made the final twice (1934 and 1935, losing to Helen Jacobs), the semis (1938), the quarters (1933) and flopped in the first round (1936-37) when seeded second and third.

No woman had waited longer, but her hour at last came. Though the path was strewn with champs past and future, Sarah remained in an offensive frame of mind all the way to beating Pauline Betz, 7-5, 6-2, in the final. She was days from her 29th birthday. Only Maud Barger Wallach, 38 in 1908, and Molla Mallory, 31 in 1915, were older first-time champs. American junior champ Louise Brough, who would rule six years down the road, was a stubborn first-round obstacle (4-6, 6-1,

6-1), as was Sarah's long-time nemesis, Jacobs (6-3, 2-6, 6-1) in the semis. Since she'd delighted her hometown, Boston, by winning the doubles with Margaret Osborne over Dodo Bundy and Betz, 3-6, 6-1, 6-4, and the mixed with Jack Kramer over Betz and Riggs, 4-6, 6-4, 6-4, at Longwood (her home club), Sarah had the triple, joining a select group of 15 U.S. women.

Jacobs' illustrious career at Forest Hills closed after 14 years, four titles, four other finals and 63 match wins, second at the time only to Molla Mallory's 65, although both would be surpassed by Chris Evert (101), Martina Navratilova (89) and Steffi Graf (71).

Riggs, the happy-go-lucky hustler and shrewd strategist, mourned that by losing the 1940 final to Don McNeill he'd wasted a big income year (a $25,000 guaranteed offer to turn pro was withdrawn). Bobby made sure not to flunk Forest Hills this time, making it the year he checked out of amateurism as No. 1. The coup de grace was his 5-7, 6-1, 6-3, 6-3 triumph over Frank Kovacs, his most difficult adversary of the year. Riggs' hardest task was beating Stanford collegian Ted Schroeder in the semis, 6-4, 6-4, 1-6, 9-11, 7-5. Kovacs, a tall, dark and handsome (plus highly talented and entertaining) 21-year-old who sometimes let his showboating get in the way, would earn the No. 2 ranking and turn pro with Riggs. His semi-final victim was McNeill, 6-4, 6-2, 10-8.

Riggs won six tournaments, but was beaten in the final of the U.S. Clay, 6-3, 7-5, 6-8, 4-6, 6-3, by Frank Parker, who also took six titles. Kovacs won four, including a U.S. Indoor triumph over Wayne Sabin, 6-0, 6-4, 6-2. Betz won six, among them the U.S. Clay (over Mary Arnold, 6-3, 6-1) and U.S. Indoor (over Dodo Bundy, 6-1, 10-12, 6-2). Sarah Cooke's six would be her last until 1945—motherhood and life as a Navy wife intervened.

Marble joined the pros and beat Britain's Mary Hardwick, 8-6, 8-6, in their debut at Madison Square Garden. Bill Tilden, 48, came out of semi-retirement to face Don Budge and lost, 6-3, 6-4. The tour was a relative bust, with Budge winning 51 of 58 matches from Tilden. Budge later wrote: "Tilden was still capable of some sustained great play that could occasionally even carry him all the way through a match. Most of the time he could, at his best, hang on for at least a set or two. Despite his age, he was no pushover. The people came out primarily for the show—to see me at my peak, and to see Tilden because they might never have the chance again. Bill could invariably manage to keep things close for a while. It was seldom, however, that he could extend me to the end."

Johnny Faunce did more than extend defending champ Budge in a shook-up U.S. Pro tourney on clay at Chicago, a show stolen by little-known teaching pros. One of them, Faunce, shocked everyone by stopping Budge in the second round, 6-4, 6-1, 6-3. Keith Gledhill ousted third-seeded Tilden, 6-2, 6-3, 6-3. Another pedagogue was the unexpected finalist, Dick Skeen, who had eliminated 1936 champ Joe Whalen, 6-2, 6-4, 6-4, and Faunce, 6-3, 8-6, 2-6, 6-3, before being beaten by Fred Perry, 6-4, 6-8, 6-2, 6-3.

1941 CHAMPIONS

U.S. Championships
Men's Singles: Bobby Riggs
Women's Singles: Sarah Palfrey Cooke
Men's Doubles: Jack Kramer / Ted Schroeder
Women's Doubles: Sarah Palfrey Cooke / Margaret Osborne
Mixed Doubles: Sarah Palfrey Cooke / Jack Kramer

1942

Ball supply dips but show goes on

Pauline Betz
First of three consecutive U.S. titles.

The U.S., stunned by Pearl Harbor, was at war, with all the uncertainties that entailed. But organized sports—particularly baseball and college athletics—were given the go-ahead to continue by the White House, as morale boosters for the home front and troops overseas. The U.S. Tennis Association voted cautiously to hold the U.S. Championships at Forest Hills "as usual, unless..." By that USTA President Holcombe Ward (an original Davis Cupper) meant: "We will gladly eliminate tennis if it interferes with winning the war. But our government doesn't want us to abandon tennis. On the contrary, the Physical Fitness Program sponsored by the government calls for expansion in sports. As long as the government releases moderate amounts of reclaimed rubber for the manufacture of balls, we'll carry on."

Still, numerous tournaments were cancelled for the duration—notably the oldest, Newport, unplayed from 1943 to '45—while others, like the U.S. at Forest Hills, were reduced in time and entrants. It was decided that all five U.S. titles would be bunched in New York, removing the doubles from Boston to cut down on travel, and permit servicemen on short furloughs to play. Men's matches, beginning in 1943, were best-of-three sets until the semis.

Players were advised to use balls longer, because there would be a shortage. Men were called up for service in the armed forces by their draft boards. The women's game was pretty much unaffected and maintained a high standard. "We got more attention at the tournaments with the top men gone," says Pauline Betz Addie. "Transportation could be difficult, but the Eastern grass tournaments were pretty close together, and we'd pool gas rationing coupons, and share cars. We got around." In London, there were no balls to be purchased. Clubs such as Queen's rented them on a per-match basis to members to be used, re-used and overused until disintegrating.

The annual pro tour, Lex Thompson promoter, was

launched December 26, 1941, at Madison Square Garden before 8,000 customers and introduced two headstrong individualists, Bobby Riggs and Frank Kovacs, as neophytes. According to USTA officials, Riggs and Kovacs, ranked 1-2, had deserted amateurism not a moment too soon. They were to be suspended for accepting too much expense money, hardly an uncommon practice. Seeming snakebitten, the tour didn't last long. Wartime travel difficulties and injuries to Kovacs and Fred Perry closed the show April 5, in Palm Springs, the 71st stop.

On opening night of the round-robin barnstorming, Kovacs beat Don Budge, 6-4, 2-6, 6-4, and Riggs beat Perry, 6-3, 4-6, 6-4, 30-15 (default). It ended as Perry fell on his right elbow, suffering an injury that virtually finished his career. At the end Budge had a 15-10 edge on Riggs, a rivalry they would resume on the first postwar tour, and headed the pack with a 52-18 overall record. Riggs was 36-36, Kovacs 25-26, Perry 23-30. All would soon be in military uniforms, but they did reassemble a couple of months later for the U.S. Pro at Forest Hills, where Budge trimmed Riggs, 6-2, 6-2, 6-2.

The first prominent players to enter the service were No. 4 Don McNeill (Navy), the U.S. champ of 1940 and Hal Surface, No. 12 in 1940, and Frank Guernsey, National Intercollegiate champ for Rice in 1938–39, into the Army Air Force.

The U.S. Clay Court tourney in St. Louis was an amusing mess. Heavy rains delayed the wind-up and the final was defaulted in progress—then resumed against 'orders' only to be lost by the supposed victor, through his good sportsmanship. Both finalists, Harris Everett of North Carolina and Seymour Greenberg of Northwestern, were expected immediately in New Orleans for the National Intercollegiate Championships. The train that would get them there on time was leaving at 6 p.m. Locked at 6-6 in the fifth set, Greenberg was ordered by his coach, Paul Bennett, to default so they could catch the train, the college event deemed more important. On the way to the dressing room, Everett, apparently the champ, said to Greenberg: "Aw, to hell with New Orleans. I don't want to win it this way. Let's go back and finish." They did. Greenberg won the next two games and became the genuine champ, 5-7, 7-5, 7-9, 7-5, 8-6. They caught the train the next day, and were excused the tardy arrival.

Neither reached the final. It was a unique Stanford *über alles* production as Ted Schroeder beat teammate

Larry Dee, 6-2, 0-6, 6-2, 6-3. Moreover, Ted, a 21-year-old volleying virtuoso, said so-long to civilian life on a high note. He conquered the U.S. at Forest Hills on his fourth attempt, 8-6, 7-5, 3-6, 4-6, 6-2, over long-suffering Frank Parker, 26 and on his 11th try, and a quarter-finalist as far back as 1934. Parker beat a newcomer from Ecuador, Francisco 'Pancho' Segura, in the semis, 6-1, 6-1, 2-6, 6-2.

It seemed only a logical progression to Schroeder, loser in the third round in 1939, then the quarters and semis. It put him in a class with McNeill, the only men to win the college and U.S. titles the same year. Ted lost a set in the third round to Jimmy Evert, 6-4, 9-11, 6-4, 6-4, a Chicagoan whose future daughter, Chris, would carry off the title 33 years later. Mulloy won the first of his four double titles in the company of Bill Talbert over Sidney Wood and Schroeder, 9-7, 7-5, 6-1. Schroeder also won the mixed with Louise Brough, over Pat Canning Todd and Argentine Alejo Russell, 3-6, 6-1, 6-4.

Nineteen-year-old Californian Louise Brough—winning the grass tests at Easthampton, N.Y. (6-3, 7-5 over Pauline Betz), Philadelphia (Margaret Osborne, 6-4, 10-8), Boston (Osborne, 6-2, 6-1) and Manchester, Mass. (Betz, 6-3, 1-6, 6-3)—came into Forest Hills as the top-seeded favorite. But swift-footed Betz, 23 and the finalist 12 months before, proved a tough cookie under pressure, launching her three-year reign by snapping back to beat Brough for the title, 4-6, 6-1, 6-4. It was tighter in the semis where Pauline quashed a match point with Margaret Osborne leading 5-3 in the third to win, 6-4, 4-6, 7-5. Only 5,148 attended the finals; it seemed that many tennis fans had other things on their minds. A new pairing that would result in a record total of 20 major doubles titles, Brough and Margaret Osborne (later du Pont), took their first, over Betz and Doris Hart, 2-6, 7-5, 6-0.

But tennis did go on elsewhere, including South America and India, and Lt. McNeill, showing up in Buenos Aires as a U.S. Naval attache, won the Argentine title over Andres Hammersley of Chile.

1942 CHAMPIONS

U.S. Championships
Men's Singles: Ted Schroeder
Women's Singles: Pauline Betz
Men's Doubles: Gardnar Mulloy / Bill Talbert
Women's Doubles: Louise Brough / Margaret Osborne
Mixed Doubles: Louise Brough / Ted Schroeder

1943

First—and last— title for Joe Hunt

Pancho Segura
A collegiate title, but a loss in the semis at Forest Hills.

Francisco 'Pancho' Segura, a curious and ebullient character, arrived on the scene from Ecuador in 1941 with a big smile, little English, scrawny bowed legs and a deadly double-fisted forehand. He had the two-handed act all to himself now that Viv McGrath and John Bromwich were in the Australian army. By 1943, Pancho had the depleted tournament circuit practically to himself, too. Shipped to the University of Miami for an education, he was definitely a tennis scholar, winning a record three straight National Intercollegiate titles through 1945. In 1943 his victim was future Wimbledon finalist and U.S. Davis Cupper Tom Brown of California (Berkeley). Segura, 22, had the year's most impressive slate, winning seven of 10 tournaments, 38 of 41 matches, and scorched the grass courts. He took titles at Rye, N.Y. (over Naval Lieutenant Joe Hunt), and Southampton, N.Y. (over Sidney Wood), and moved easily to the semis of the U.S., which had been compressed to six days and 32 entries, 12 of them servicemen on leave.

But two of those excused from duty for a few days were strapping blond Californians of serve-and-volley persuasion: Second-seeded Coast Guard Seaman Jack Kramer, 22, and seventh-seeded Naval Lieutenant Joe Hunt, 24, a tragic figure who had won National Intercollegiate titles for Southern California in doubles (1938) and the singles (1941 over Ted Olewine of Southern California) for the Naval Academy. As kids, they were Davis Cup doubles partners in 1939, losing to Aussies Adrian Quist and Bromwich. Another was Army Air Force Corporal Frank Parker, seeded first ahead of Segura. Bill Talbert, kept out of the service by diabetes, was the lone civilian in the semis, losing to Hunt, 3-6, 6-4, 6-2, 6-4, after Hunt had bulldozed Parker, 8-6, 6-2, 6-3. Though weakened by food poisoning, Kramer hung on to beat Segura, 2-6, 6-4, 7-5, 6-3. However, Kramer was spent after three sets against Hunt, a 6-3, 6-8, 10-8, 6-0 winner. Jack, who served for the third set at 5-4, remembers the bizarre ending: "I hit a forehand long on match point. If I'd kept that ball in court I think I would have been the champ by default." Because as the ball flew beyond him, Hunt crumpled onto the court with leg cramps, probably unable to play another point. Kramer did win the Pacific Southwest, over Segura, 0-6, 6-1, 6-2.

Hunt would not return to Forest Hills. Unable to get leave from sea duty in 1944. he was killed in a plane crash on a training mission in 1945. It happened off Daytona Beach, Fla., when the fighter plane he was piloting plunged into the Atlantic, an accident that was never explained. Playing only four tournaments in 1943, and winning one—La Jolla—Joe was accorded the No. 1 ranking.

Pauline Betz, winner of seven tournaments, completed a national surface triple at Forest Hills, after taking the U.S. Indoor (over Kay Winthrop, 6-4, 6-1) and the U.S. Clay (Nancy Corbett, 6-0, 6-1). Beating Catherine Wolf, 6-0, 6-2, for the Tri-State title in Cincinnati, Pauline scored a golden bagel, winning all 24 first-set points while stroking 18 winners. Lefty Seymour Greenberg won the U.S. Clay over Talbert, 6-1, 4-6, 6-2, 6-3.

Gunning for her second title at Forest Hills, Betz earned it in a rematch struggle of the 1-2 seeds, beating Louise Brough, 6-3, 5-7, 6-3. Doris Hart, the 18-year-old U.S. junior champ—12 years short of winning the big one—took Betz to three sets in the quarters, 9-7, 2-6, 6-1. A first-round loser to seventh-seeded Mary Arnold, 6-1, 6-1, was Gloria Thompson, who had won St. Louis earlier in the summer. She would be back years later with the son she reared to be a great champion, Jimmy Connors.

Keeping the pros alive was the Officers Club of Fort Knox, Ky. As an entertainment treat—free admission—for the post (and the town), the Army played host to the U.S. Pro, building an 11,000-seat temporary stadium with floodlights, and putting up a $2,000 purse. The stands were filled, possibly the event's largest-ever crowd, as Navy Lieutenant Bruce Barnes beat teaching pro John Nogrady, 6-1, 7-9, 7-5, 4-6, 6-3, for the title.

1943 CHAMPIONS

U.S. Championships
Men's Singles: Joseph R. Hunt
Women's Singles: Pauline Betz
Men's Doubles: Jack Kramer / Frank Parker
Women's Doubles: Louise Brough / Margaret Osborne
Mixed Doubles: Margaret Osborne / Bill Talbert

1944

Parker, Betz reign supreme

Frank Parker
One of 15 servicemen in 32-man field at Forest Hills.

Civilians Bill Talbert and Pancho Segura had things pretty much their way during the American season—until Forest Hills, another six-day event with 32 singles entries, 15 of them servicemen on leave. Dauntless Sergeant Frank Parker of the Army Air Force's Muroc (Cal.) base re-appeared to snatch the title he had chased for a dozen years. Seeded fourth, Frank proved the 13th time lucky, despite playing only one preparatory tournament. The longest male chase for the title was over as the dark-haired 28-year-old, wearing dark glasses, brought down third-seeded Talbert for the title, 6-4, 3-6, 6-3, 6-3, before a finals gathering of 8,000.

Talbert wore himself down expelling top seed Segura, 3-6, 6-3, 6-0, 6-8, 6-3, while Parker won his semi over ex-champ, Navy Lieutenant Don McNeill, 6-4, 3-6, 6-2, 6-2. In the second round McNeill beat 46-year-old Gil Hall, who had been discharged from the Army earlier in the year as a veteran of tank warfare, 7-5, 6-4. Hall became unique that week, not only winning a round in the Championship—over Richard Bender, 0-6, 6-3, 6-4—but capturing the concurrent Senior (over-45) title, over William Nassau, Jr., 6-3, 6-2. That made the only man to hold an unusual dual top-10 national ranking: No. 10 among the men and No. 1 among the seniors. He would hold the latter title through 1950.

Even the national junior champ was in the service, too. Air Cadet Bob Falkenburg, 18, of Hollywood, Calif., won the 18s title while on leave, 0-6, 6-4, 6-4, 6-2, over a future Davis Cupper, lefty Bernard 'Tut' Bartzen of San Angelo, Tex. A future Wimbledon champ, Falkenburg won his first major at Forest Hills, the doubles with McNeill, over Segura and Talbert, 7-5, 6-4, 3-6, 6-1. He lost in the singles quarters to Talbert, 6-4, 6-4, 6-3.

A third straight U.S. title for Pauline Betz led the ladies' side as she sprinted through the tournament losing but one set (6-4, 6-8, 6-4, over Virginia

Wolfenden Kovacs in the quarters), and brushing aside 1943 finalist Louise Brough, 6-2, 6-3, in the semis and Margaret Osborne, 6-3, 8-6, in the final. The second set against Osborne was troublesome, Pauline accelerating from 1-4 and dodging a set point at 4-5.

The busiest player was Segura, again National Intercollegiate champ for Miami (over Charles Samson of Notre Dame, 6-0, 6-4, 6-0). He beat Talbert, 9-11, 6-2, 7-5, 2-6, 7-5, to win the U.S. Clay, and altogether bagged six of 10 tournaments while going 36-4 in matches. Talbert won two of nine with a 32-7 record while Parker, who won two of three tournaments and was 13-1, got the No. 1 ranking. Betz won eight tournaments and had a 44-5 match record, but didn't retain the U.S. Clay, losing in the semis 7-5, 6-3 to Dodo Bundy, the champ on a 7-5, 6-4, decision over Mary Arnold. Osborne won three of 11 tournaments and was 33-8, Brough three of 12 with a 30-9 record.

The U.S. Pro tourney became a wartime casualty, but ever-energetic Bill Tilden, 51, kept on the go by playing exhibitions for the troops at military bases all over the country, or benefits for the Red Cross and other charitable causes associated with war relief. Don Budge, in the Army Air Force, beat Coast Guardsman Jack Kramer, 7-5, 7-5, heading a mid-winter fund-raiser at New York's 7th Regiment Armory that sold $2,706,000 in war bonds. Naval couple Elwood and Sarah Palfrey Cooke, out of sight since 1941, made a cameo at the La Jolla tourney, each winning the singles.

The uncle Chris Evert never knew, Jack Evert, one of the four tennis-playing brothers from Chicago, was killed at 22 with the Army in France where a future champ, Art Larsen, was also fighting. Jacque Virgil Hunt, wife of the 1943 champion, Lieutenant Joe Hunt, won the Southern title over Sara Comer, 6-4, 6-2. Refused leave from Naval flight training to compete at Forest Hills, Joe and 1942 champ Ted Schroeder had to settle for a weekend near their base, the Pensacola Labor Day tourney. Playing his last competitive tennis, Joe defeated Ted in the final, 6-3, 7-5.

1944 CHAMPIONS

U.S. Championships
Men's Singles: Frank Parker
Women's Singles: Pauline Betz
Men's Doubles: Don McNeill / Bob Falkenburg
Women's Doubles: Louise Brough / Margaret Osborne
Mixed Doubles: Margaret Osborne / Bill Talbert

1945

A mom and champ, Cooke follows Hazel

Bill Talbert (left), Gardnar Mulloy
Injured in singles final, Talbert persevered to win both U.S. doubles finals.

Peace was clearly on the way, and broke out days before Forest Hills threw open its gates again for a joyful renewal of the U.S. Championships. Attendance was up—35,506, compared to 26,999 for the 1944 tourney and 23,893 for 1943. Sixteen of the male entry list enlarged to 48 were still in uniform but wouldn't be for long. Wimbledon, closed six years, invited the public in June 30 for a U.S. vs. British Empire match between allied armed forces teams. Centre Court had been too badly bombed to be available, but 5,000 witnesses, including Queen Mary, were happy to be back in Court 1. Army seargeants George Lott and Charlie Hare spurred a 4-1 U.S. victory.

Out of the Navy and traveling the American circuit again were Elwood and Sarah Palfrey Cooke, to reclaim Top Ten national rankings last held in 1941, this time No. 1 for her, the champion at Forest Hills, and No. 4 for him, a semifinalist, the highest finish ever for a married couple. An extreme illustration of the manpower shortage was the leniency of tourney officials at the Tri-State in Cincinnati, where the Cookes were permitted to enter the men's doubles as a team. A singular feat, they made it to the final, losing to Bill Talbert and Hal Surface, 6-2, 6-2.

A somber note was the absence of 1943 champion Joe Hunt, the naval pilot killed Feb. 2 in the never-explained plunge of his fighter plane into the Atlantic. Hunt, 26, the highest regarded American player to die in the war, had been expected to shine in the peacetime game.

Army Air Force Sergeant Frank Parker, winner in 1944, was thought to be far out of the picture, stationed on Guam. But his commanding general, Curtis LeMay, had other ideas. He ordered Frank to fly almost 8,000 miles back to the U.S. to defend his title. Parker, 29, had been playing exhibitions with such ex-U.S. champs as Naval Seaman Bobby Riggs and Army Air Force Lieutenant Don Budge for the troops on Pacific Islands. He was fit and ready. Top seeded, Frank cruised to his second title by winning all 13 sets he played, encountering real difficulty only at the outset of the rematch final against Bill Talbert. Frank won his semi, 6-1, 8-6, 7-5, over 1939 Wimbledon finalist Elwood Cooke, who had won the only five-set match of the tournament, in the quarter-final over 1931 Wimbledon champ Sidney Wood, 10-12, 7-5, 6-4, 2-6, 6-0. Subsequently, Parker won the Pacific Southwest over Herbie Flam, 6-2, 6-4, and the Pan American over Ecuador's Pancho Segura, 9-7, 3-6, 6-2, 8-6, at Mexico City. His three-for-three and 16-0 match mark assured him of remaining No. 1.

As civilians, Talbert and Segura—Pancho winner of a third successive Intercollegiate title for the University of Miami, 6-2, 6-2, 6-3, over Frank Mehner of the U.S. Military Academy—were again dominant figures. Bill won eight of 11 tournaments, on a 48-3 record in matches. He beat Segura for the U.S. Clay title, 6-4, 4-6, 6-2, 2-6, 6-2, and took four of five grass-court tests: Southampton over Argentine Alejo Russell; Rye over Segura; Wilmington over Segura; Seabright (N.J.) over Naval Lieutenant Gardnar Mulloy, losing only to Parker at Forest Hills.

In defeating third-seeded Segura, 7-5, 6-3, 6-4, in the semis, second-seeded Talbert wrenched his left knee. Gamely, wearing flannel trousers to hide the strapping, Bill endured an epic afternoon of four matches and 96 games, cheered by 11,556 fans, as he won two titles after bowing to Parker. He held a set point against Parker's serve at 9-10 in the 76-minute first set, 22 games, the longest to that time in a singles final. But that was Talbert's last thrust in the lengthy struggle. Parker's consistency was too much and he won 14-12, 6-1, 6-2.

Returning to the court to complete the doubles final, halted by darkness the previous night at 10-10 in the third, Talbert and Mulloy finished their second title triumph together, 12-10, 8-10, 12-10, 6-2, over Army Seargeant Jack Tuero and Air Cadet Bob Falkenburg. Then it was time for mixed: A semi-final that Talbert and

Margaret Osborne won over Louise Brough and Frank Shields, 6-3, 9-7. It was 6:45 p.m., time for the final. Osborne, who had won the doubles with Brough, was in the third match of her two-title 65-game afternoon. She and Talbert had to play quickly to beat darkness at 7:25, not to mention Hart and Falkenburg, 6-4, 6-4.

Sarah Cooke, a sharp volleyer who won 16 major doubles titles, always wanted to win the U.S. singles and emulate her mentor, Hazel Hotchkiss Wightman and she did just that in 1941. Now, two weeks prior to her 33rd birthday, Sarah wanted to follow Hazel again by winning as a mother. She accomplished this as well, joining an exclusive matronly club whose third member would be Margaret Smith Court in 1973. In a sensational comeback for her last season as an amateur, after almost four years away from the game, Sarah won seven of 13 tournaments and went 43-6 in matches. Her chief rival, defending champion Pauline Betz—they were 1-2 in the rankings—won six of 12 and was 42-6. Sarah beat Pauline for the U.S. Clay title, 8-6, 7-5, and at Forest Hills clipped Pauline's streak of three titles and 19 matches, 3-6, 8-6, 6-4.

"She was a good friend and a thorn in my side," says Pauline, who might well have won a record six straight U.S. crowns but for Sarah, her conqueror in the 1941 and 1945 finals. Sarah led 5-2 in the second, almost let it slip away, then stormed back in the third from a service break to 3-4 to take the last three games. They both turned pro after the season, touring against one another. The 6-3, 6-3 victory Brough and Osborne scored over Betz and Hart was their fourth straight doubles title, breaking the three-straight record (1918-20) of Marion Zinderstein and Eleanor Goss. More would follow.

The pros regrouped to re-establish their U.S. Championships at Rip's Courts in Manhattan after a one-year wartime layoff, and the singles was won by Welby Van Horn over John Nogrady, 6-4, 6-2, 6-2. The doubles was won by the 94-year-old team of Bill Tilden, 52, and Vinnie Richards, 42, over Dick Skeen and Van Horn, 7-5, 6-4, 6-2. Bill and Vinnie had first linked in Boston in 1918 to win the U.S. Doubles.

1945 CHAMPIONS

U.S. Championships
Men's Singles: Frank Parker
Women's Singles: Sarah Palfrey Cooke
Men's Doubles: Gardnar Mulloy / Bill Talbert
Women's Doubles: Louise Brough / Margaret Osborne
Mixed Doubles: Margaret Osborne / Bill Talbert

Bill Tilden, 1929 A dark and complex man, and the game's first larger-than-life star.

Chapter 3

Bill Tilden: King of the Courts

The first half of the 20th century had no player like Bill Tilden, none with his mastery of shots, cannonball serve, loud confidence and flair. Fifty years after being profiled in SPORT *magazine, he remains a tennis immortal.*

SPORT February 1951 By Al Stump

The voice at the Hollywood, California, end of the long-distance line was strained. It said, *"You want to write the story of Bill Tilden—the whole story? Well . . . come on down and see him. But, remember, I'm warning you it'll be tough—very tough."*

"I know that. That's what makes it worth going after."

Pause. Then, slowly, *"Maybe you're right. But do me a favor. I played the circuit with Bill for years. I'm a friend of his. Don't make the story sound like an obituary. Give him that break."*

"Don't worry. It won't be an obituary."

In the year before the Daffy Decade opened, which was 1919, they were cramming into the "cabarets" to beat Prohibition to the punch, a New York Stock Exchange seat sold for a record $110,000, you could roar across a California highway at 35 miles per hour—the fastest legal speed in the country—and somebody slipped Mayor Ole Hanson of Seattle (who ducked) an infernal machine in his morning mail. A Florida scenery-lover had the bright idea of staging something called a bathing beauty contest, Henry Ford slapped a million-dollar libel suit on the Chicago *Tribune,* and the rage of Broadway was a boudoir farce entitled "Up in Mabel's Room." The country was raring back for one wild and wonderful wing-ding.

All but lost in the welter of fast-breaking news was a tennis player who stepped onto the court at Forest Hills that Fall to challenge for the national singles championship. Lank, hawk-faced, and with a heavyweight's shoulders on a flyrod frame, he drew few cheers when he appeared. The crowd knew him well—too well.

He was then 26 years old and no newcomer to the game. As far back as 1916, somebody named Harold Throckmorton had handily bounced the gangling fellow out of the Nationals in the first round. Two years later, R. Lindley Murray, a wild-hitting lefthander with a net attack, had cut him down to size in the title bracket. The customers, still seeking a colorful, rip-snorting clouter in the tradition of the pre-war flash, Maurice McLoughlin, the fabled "California Comet," didn't bother to suppress their yawns.

Facing the big man across the net that gloomy, rain-streaked September afternoon was a frail, jug-eared 118-pounder, a peewee pitted against a giant. Though the little guy, William M. Johnston, had not much of the speed and none of the height, reach, or stroking power of his opponent, he was coolly confident as he crouched at the baseline.

"Ready?"

The giant nodded grimly.

"Little Bill" Johnston then proceeded to turn a match into a marathon. Smashing fierce forehands to the other's erratic backhand, placing lightning thrusts just beyond the reaching racket, Johnston calmly and methodically ran his victim all over the court. He swept the match in three straight sets. It was no contest. The scores were 6-4, 6-4, 6-3.

An hour after the crowd had gone, very few could remember the name of the whipped challenger—William Tatum Tilden II.

It is the supremely ironic touch to the story of Big Bill Tilden, invincible defender of the Davis Cup, flamboyant rebel, a super-showman toasted on four continents, mystery man, and the most fabulous performer his sport has ever known, that it first takes shape with a crushing defeat. Three decades later he stands again in a shadow. The personal tragedy that shrouds the tennis king today is a circumstance well-known to the public. It has caused this country's greatest tennis name to fall into the discard. That name belongs with the elite of the sports world—on a par with Dempsey, Ruth, Thorpe, Jones and Cobb. But, instead, it rarely sees the light of print. The blunt, inescapable fact is that most writers and editors have affixed the period to Tilden's career. You will search in vain through the sports pages to find an account of how the old champion is faring.

Where is he? What is he doing? How does he regard the modern disciples of the game he dominated for so many years. The questions go unanswered.

Yet, on last February 3, over the Associated Press wires, there ticked out the result of the latest in a series of nationwide sportswriter polls to name the top athletes of the half century. The story started: "The greatest tennis player of the past 50 years. Is there any argument?"

Looking far back beyond moral judgments, viewing the issue unemotionally and factually, the AP experts needed only one check of the ballot. The vote was astonishing. Out of a total 393 cast, Babe Ruth led baseball with 253 votes and Bobby Jones held sway over golf with 293. Jesse Owens was the titan of track with 201, and everybody's ring-idol, Jack Dempsey, commanded a smashing 251. But Bill Tilden—well, the jury went overboard.

He got 310 votes, more than any other of the immortals could show! Trailing far behind, with just a scattering of support, were Don Budge, Jack Kramer, Helen Wills, Suzanne Lenglen, Bill Johnston, Fred Perry, and Ellsworth Vines. For one day, at least, the aging net colossus of the Golden Twenties was again the best sports story in America.

"What else could they do?" says Budge, the man generally regarded as the closest approach to Tilden. "Bill is the only genius tennis has produced. He has stunned me so often, left me helpless on the court—many years after he was past his prime—that I'll believe anything they write about him."

Brushing the cobwebs off the records, you can't begin to write it all. Big Bill stuck at the top for an incredible 32 years, from the day in 1913 when he won his first national crown to his last in 1945, when he was a greying but still amazingly agile 53. And the timeless Tilden scored the most stunning clean sweep in any sport. In U.S. singles play, for example, Perry can show three championships and Budge, Vines, and Bobby Riggs two each. Tilden won seven, of which six, from 1920 through 1925, were consecutive. He was the No. 1-ranked player of the land for 10 straight years, from 1920 to 1930, or until he sneezed at his enemies in the United States Lawn Tennis Association and turned professional. No one is close to that record. In eight of the 10 years, Tilden was universally recognized as world's champ. Before going pro, he won 70 American and international titles with the nonchalance of a man shooting fish in a barrel, including the national clay-court singles from 1922 through 1927, the indoor singles in 1920, five national doubles titles, and four each in mixed and indoor doubles.

The gold and silver cups he accumulated represent such a treasure trove that in 1944 he auctioned off two of the lesser baubles at a Philadelphia war-benefit for $75,000. The major awards? Gone, given away to friends and relatives, with the same disdain that he accorded the lawn tennis nabobs. The biggest, most glittering trophy ever cast wouldn't mean ten cents to the lordly W. Tatum Tilden.

He won a few cups abroad, too. Today's athletes who make the overseas rounds a few times and then consider themselves well-traveled should take a look at Tilden's mileage. Recently, one of the top ten American amateurs was dwelling upon his jaunts before impressed listeners at a Los Angeles tennis club. He finished with, "Yes, indeed—I've literally played myself around the world."

An oldtime player, not otherwise friendly to Tilden, ruined the effect by tapping his arm and saying, "Kid, compared to Tilden, you're a stick-in-the-mud. You never got off the dock!"

Roaming anywhere that an opponent had the nerve to stick out his chin and utter a challenge, Tilden covered 750,000 miles in his time—the equivalent of 30 times around the globe! His long, cynical, horse-face, an actor's face combining the dramatic range of John Barrymore, the mobility of Herbert Marshall, and the slight sneer of Basil Rathbone, was as familiar in the Orient and Europe as it was through the British Isles, Australia, New Zealand, and the Middle East. He hit almost every civilized spot on the map—except South

America and South Africa. It's hard to say whether he had a more fanatical following in France, Italy, Austria, Germany, Belgium, or Switzerland—where he met and beat the best—than he had at home.

Where the Davis Cup was concerned, he played with the ferocity of a man defending the Holy Grail. For seven straight years, 1920-26, he led the fight that kept it out of foreign hands. In that stretch, Tilden won a phenomenal 13 straight challenge-round singles matches without a defeat—mowing down such brilliant netsmen as Norman Brookes and Gerald Patterson of Australia, Ichiya Kumagae and Zenzo Shimizu of Japan, and Rene Lacoste and Jean Borotra of France. He was on 11 Davis Cup teams (a record) and scored a hard-to-believe 22 wins in 29 matches played.

The classic crown of all—Wimbledon's—he treated like something you'd shoot for on a public court. Each time he went after the all-England title, which was in 1920-'21 and 1930, he blasted the field with the most spectacular assortment of shots ever to rebound from one racket. He came in like a lion, smashing the tradition that no American could win at Wimbledon. And he left the same way. In '30, they gaped when he met the flashy young Borotra in the semi-finals. He was then 37 years old, unable to carry more than 155 pounds on his six-foot, two-inch frame. After 10 straight years of high-tension competition, if ever a man was over-tennised it was Bill Tilden. Yet he handled Borotra like a baby. In the finals, staid Britons figuratively danced on the seats when he polished off the rising blond whirl-wind from Austin, Texas, Wilmer Allison, in straight sets, 6-3, 9-7, 6-4. After that, Tilden became as much a legend in England as he was in America.

You can't pick any one match, or even one year, out of Big Bill's extended reign and call it his greatest. His span was too wide, his peaks too many and too high, his tennis lives too varied. Consider that when he first sent Little Bill Johnston crashing in 1920 and took over as national champion, the contemporary sports heroes were George Gipp, Charley Paddock, the Original Celtics, and a top-heavy young slugger who had just joined the New York Yankees named Babe Ruth. Two decades later, in 1940, the big names were Tommy Harmon, Joe DiMaggio, Frankie Albert, and Byron Nelson. The storybook stars of the 20's and 30's were just faded ghosts—all but Big Bill, still the best drawing card of his trade.

Maybe, just for a guess—his all-time peak came in his 38th year, in 1931, when he staged his celebrated battle with Vinnie Richards for the world professional title. Richards was 10 years Tilden's junior. He was the game's finest volleyer and the defending champ. The critics had been hammering that Big Bill was far over the hill. For years, they had been warily circling his tall, spare form to see what was holding him up—and getting a tongue-lashing for their temerity.

"Tilden needs new legs," they wrote. "His cannonball serve is gone, his backhand has crumbled, his volley is a hollow shell."

"As usual, the tennis writers are not only incompetent," retorted Tilden, who never hesitated to sink his fangs where they'd hurt most, "but also stupid."

Then he demonstrated. In just 59 minutes, Richards suffered the worst licking of his life. The Forest Hills throng of 6,000 sat stunned as Tilden's sweeping backhand bolts, and that famous serve left the pudgy pride of Yonkers floundering. Once Richards' racket was ripped from his hand as it met the ball. In the final game of the 7-5, 6-2, 6-1 trouncing, Big Bill pounded three service aces across the net.

"Thirty-eight and never better!" gasped Frank Hunter, the Davis Cupper. "He'll still be winning the big ones when the rest of us are making our first payments on wheel-chairs."

Maybe Tilden's best didn't come in those historic middle-year tilts with Henri Cochet, Little Bill, Lacoste, and the rest at all. Maybe it came—fantastic as it sounds—in 1940. That year at Edinburgh, Scotland, Tilden pulled off an unbelievable athletic performance. Touring the British Isles with Budge, Vines, and Les Stoefen, he fell ill and was confined to a hospital for several days with a high fever. He also was suffering from a badly sprained wrist. Dragging himself from sick bay, he insisted on facing the blazing Budge in the featured singles match before a packed house of Scotsmen.

"Let's postpone until you're feeling better, Bill," pleaded Budge. "I'd hate for you to look bad here."

Tilden's piercing eyes bored into the Redhead.

"I'll get the ball back to you," was all he said.

Budge took the court planning to end the slaughter as speedily as possible. An hour later, it was over—and Budge was the one who stood limp and exhausted in defeat. The 24-year-old champion had been raked with such spins and chops as he'd never seen, handcuffed with service bullets he couldn't see, and duped out of position like a raw amateur. *He had been humiliated in straight sets by an ailing man 47 years old!* And Budge, by his own admission, was at the very top of his game that night, playing the strongest tennis of his life.

The older Tilden grew, the tougher he became. Yet one thing didn't change with time. Through all the years, the lean and hungry-looking Philadelphian was the most despised and vilified, the most hated and feared figure who ever stepped onto a court. Fans, officials, linesmen, newspapermen, ball boys, photographers, umpires—he never stopped warring with any of them. A born prima donna, he engaged in more feuds than any 10 players in the game. He was a militant revolutionist to rank with baseball's Ty Cobb or hockey's Eddie Shore, the only man in tennis who could draw the game's hugest crowds and then, more often than not, have these same mobs hooting him and yelling for his opponent to win.

Even today, 21 years after his last national singles triumph, Tilden's hackles rise at the mention of the USLTA. Slouched in a Hollywood hotel easy chair, he said cuttingly, "An assinine, pompous, overstuffed bunch of little men trying to run a big sport. Anything I've said or done to them goes redoubled."

What he did to them was plenty. Time and again he brought the overlords to their knees, made them eat humble pie in public and beg him to save the show. Because, never doubt it, Tilden, the racket renegade, was always the show. Without him, there was no business at the box-office. In 1920, for example, when he returned to the U.S. with the Wimbledon title, he was instructed to enter the Newport Casino tournament. Tilden's answer to Julian Myrick, the ironed "Little Czar" of the USLTA, was a curt, "Sorry, I'm busy."

Here was stark heresy in a day when tennis was never a more tightly dominated society sport. "You'll play or be indefinitely suspended," Myrick told him.

"Then mail my suspension to Philadelphia," Tilden told him. "I'll be there—opening some new public courts."

"Public courts! My God, no!" cried the horrified Myrick. "What about our public?"

"To hell with your public," said Tilden coldly, and was off to Philadelphia.

William the Conqueror went right on dictating to the dictators. Before he was through with them, he had proved that one man could become bigger than tennis itself. The international fireworks he exploded caused

U.S. ambassadors and even a President to crack down on the groggy tennis moguls. He made such a farce of the amateur code that the USLTA had to rewrite it, in deference to Tilden. It was Big Bill who, when asked in the mid-20's why he didn't turn professional, put that classic line in American sports literature: "Why, my dear fellow, I can't afford to."

Other amateurs had surreptitiously cashed in on their reputations in a minor way before Tilden, but it was the king who made the cash-register ring like an alarm bell. In 1924, the USLTA could no longer ignore the fact that its foremost star was waxing fat off self-written syndicated newspaper articles. Yet it dared not push the issue too far. So a Committee of Seven, including three non-partisan sportsmen—George Wharton Pepper, Devereaux Milburn, and Grantland Rice—was named to revise the rules in regard to the player-writer controversy. They amended the code to read that while a player might write analytical criticisms of a tournament in which he was playing, he could not act as a daily reporter covering spot news. This was a sop to Tilden, but it didn't satisfy him. He continued to call his own journalistic shots. In 1928, while the Davis Cup team was warming up for the zone finals against Italy, the USLTA boldly announced his suspension for violating the code in articles filed for the Philadelphia *Ledger* syndicate.

The ensuing uproar almost blew the lid off international tennis. French promoters had been doing a landslide business in advance of the expected United States-France showdown for the Davis Cup. Tilden vs. Borotra and Cochet meant the hugest gate in Gallic history. When the suspension news broke, ticket cancellations poured in so thickly that the promoters stormed the office of Ambassador Myron Herrick of the United States in Paris. "No Tilden, no profits. What can we do?" clamored Pierre Gillou and his confreres.

Herrick could recognize a ticklish diplomatic problem. He told the USLTA to reinstate Tilden. Writing what he pleased for whatever prices he could command, reporter Tilden packed them in at Paris while in New York one critic cried, "American tennis amateurism has been crucified on a cross of gold!"

Two years later, the non-expendable Tilden had them on their knees again. This time a New York feature syndicate reportedly paid him $3,000 for Davis Cup coverage. An attempt to keep him off the Cup team seemed to be succeeding when suddenly the supposedly slipping old warhorse surged back to win at Wimbledon. Now the Cup committee had to have him. Always a master at creating suspense, Big Bill dragged out the negotiations for all that the publicity would bear. Finally, he allowed himself to be persuaded—with the stipulation that the USLTA thereafter keep its long nose out of his literary dealings.

Once, in 1921, he was even summoned to the White House, where a disturbed President Warren Harding, a tennis fan, asked him, "Is it true that you are not returning to Wimbledon to defend your championship?"

"It is, Mr. President."

"May I ask why?"

Tilden was never bashful, even when playing a set with King Gustav of Sweden or cutting up touches with the English peerage. "Because the tennis association is so abominably cheap that it will pay only $1,000 toward my expenses," he told Harding.

The President blew up. "A damned disgrace!" Forty-eight hours later, the USLTA informed its sardonically grinning black sheep that he would go to London in style.

On stage, which was the tennis court, Big Bill was just as full of pyrotechnics. Umpires and linesmen lived in perpetual dread of him. He seldom let an oppor- tunity slip to wag his acid tongue at an official who called a ball out of bounds which Tilden thought was good, or to upbraid one of the "stuffed shirts," in the elevated chairs. When the dignified umpire Samuel Hardy called one against him, Tilden's biting, "You're blind, Sam—you didn't even see that ball!" almost broke up the match. He made a production out of brow-beating linesmen, whom he despised as members of the lowest caste on earth, no matter what their social station in life. He would spin in his tracks and fix them with a baleful glare or throw both skinny arms skyward and cry out, "Ye gods, is there no justice?" With heavy sarcasm, he would stride to the line and point his racket at the exact spot—according to Tilden—where the ball had struck, then inquire in deadly tones, "Would you like to correct your error?"

The best of them often did. He was coercive, demanding, arrogant, a law unto himself. And there wasn't a thing anyone could do about it. When a veteran official withdrew from the court in a huff or scurried out under a barrage of boos, Tilden would stand, arms akimbo, grinning triumphantly, as if saying, "Well, I got rid of that poor fool. Now who's next?"

Nobody was exempt from the plague that gripped a once-genteel pastime, not even P. Schuyler Van Bloem, the Forest Hills national tournament chairman. Once Van Bloem refused to give Tilden permission to wear spiked shoes for a match. With a disdainful snort, Tilden eased himself into a chaise longue on the club veranda. Onlookers were incredulous. A sit-down strike in tennis? In the stands, 10,000 fans began to shout for action.

"This is preposterous!" spluttered a committeeman.

"It certainly is," agreed Tilden. "When will you boobs learn to stop meddling with things you know nothing about?"

Van Bloem tore his hair. The fans threatened to walk out with their refunds and Tilden played—in spikes.

Dramatic critics have panned the actor-playwright Tilden (he wrote and appeared in numerous stage productions) as a particularly redolent slice of ham, but his court histrionics are unequalled. Take the matter of throwing points to even up a bad call against an opponent. Big Bill was always fiercely insistent that the other man get a fair shake. He put the gift-point practice on a mass-production basis. Others might throw a point or two, but Tilden tossed away entire sets! His most epic example of generosity came during the Davis Cup tie with Australia in 1923, against the powerful-slugging Jim Anderson. At set point, Tilden drove a whistling backhander which seemed to hit just beyond the baseline. But the linesman gave the point and set to Tilden. Glowering at the functionary in disgust he proceeded to knock drives far out of the court or bat the ball into the net until the astonished Anderson had won the next set. Then, with everything even again, he returned to whipping the Aussie with his usual deadly attack.

"Playing to the stands!" howled sneering commentators. "That big show-off baboon makes us sick!"

But they learned in time that it was far more than that. Theatrical though he was in everything he did, Bill Tilden was tennis incarnate. The galleries had to come to realize that the game was his life, that he reveled in it. That on that flat surface of grass or clay or concrete, he was an artist creating a masterpiece which no man could be allowed to spoil. One of the shrewdest analyses of Tilden came from Franklin P. Adams, who wrote in 1922: "Ruth and Hornsby, Hagen and Sarazen Dempsey and Leonard are natural one-track champions who let nothing divert them from winning. They are out to slaughter the opposition. But Tilden is an artist. He is more an artist than anything else, the tennis idealist who is more concerned with making a beautiful shot or executing a bit of imaginative strategy than he is in actually winning a point. At a critical moment in a match, he will try a fantastically difficult shot merely for the sheer joy he gets from producing this effect. It is the beauty of the game that Tilden loves—it is the chase always rather than the quarry."

The curious thing was that the fans who disliked Tilden for his overbearing manner and clipped, British-like speech made him their idol. In his savage struggles with Little Bill Johnston, the most popular champion tennis had seen, he always started with the crowd thirsting for his defeat. But, gradually, the hostile house began to swing around to Tilden's side. The impact of his greatness got to them. They sensed his abiding passion for the game, his genius, and they ended up by shouting their heads off for him.

"They damn him today and dote on him tomorrow," summed up Westbrook Pegler, "and damned if I know which emotion is correct."

This complex human, described by Alice Varble as "that strange temperamental man whom nobody really knows," lives today at 5640 Franklin Avenue in Hollywood. He is not far from the swirling neon-brilliant center of the most garish city in the world, but he stays out of the spotlight. His home is an apartment on a quiet street. An interviewer does not see Tilden there, but at such a hotel as the midtown Knickerbocker. You learn early from his friends that the Big Bill whose color-splashed life was once public property has cultivated a deep desire for strict privacy. "Don't ask him about two things—his time served on those morals offenses and his bankroll," they advise you. "Anything else, he'll talk about."

Allegedly, Tilden has gone through a couple of fortunes. Born to wealth of an old, honored Philadelphia family, he earned an estimated $200,000 through his various professional promotions. His recent difficulties and long layoff from major public appearances may have cut into reserves, for Tilden will now play within a few-hundred-mile radius of Los Angeles for the sum of $500. Time was when that wouldn't have paid his expenses.

It is the baffling truth that today, at 57, he can still match strokes with anybody in the world—for one set. In a three-set match, his wonderful legs would give him an even break against the bulk of today's amateurs for whom he has undisguised contempt. "Flam? Cochell? Falkenburg? Nice boys, but not tennis players like we used to breed," he said. "It saddens me to say it, but I can handle any of them."

Last year, Tilden took one set in four from Bobby Riggs. His current protege, 18-year-old Art Anderson, a flashy USC sophomore, has a bare nine-match edge over his old teacher in about 100 matches played.

Rolling up his pants-leg, Tilden said triumphantly, "Does that look like the leg of an old man? See any veins or signs of a breakdown?" There are none. His underpinning is as hard and youthful-looking as any in the national big-time, where 35 is considered a decrepit age.

But the bookings don't come as they used to and Big Bill was delighted last July when invited to play an exhibition at Salt Lake City, where he packed in a capacity crowd. He thought it might be a harbinger of better things ahead. Earlier, he told SPORT in a frank, revealing letter, "I would like to play again if I were welcome ... concerning the Forest Hills tournament last year, I was unofficially informed that my entry would not be accepted, but it was not sent in ... it may be different now ... I have had few if any unpleasant reactions to my playing ... my friends have indeed been my friends, with very few exceptions."

Meanwhile, he throws himself into teaching the game with a fervor that blots out almost all other interests. And Tilden is an intensely intellectual man, author of eight books and a half-dozen plays and a respected authority on classical music. Almost all his waking hours are now spent on the courts of the Charlie Chaplin estate in Beverly Hills or at the Joe Cotten retreat in Santa Monica. His pupils are up-and-comers like Anderson, for whom he predicts a champion's future, an occasional big-timer like Gussie Moran, and the movie colonists—Chaplin, an old friend, Irene Selznick, Jennifer Jones, Evelyn Keyes, Farley Granger, Cotten, and Doris Duke, among others. In 1948, Tilden's comedy-drama "New Shoes" played briefly at the El Patio Theater in Los Angeles. He has since rewritten the play and is looking for a producer.

Meeting the writer at the Knickerbocker, Tilden strode in wearing beat-up tennis shoes, rumpled flannels, and a sweat-stained blue jersey. "Been on court all day," he explained. "That's my schedule—9 o'clock to 7, every day. I've never worked any harder in my life. I play eight to 10 fast sets a day and by 8:30 I'm so bushed I just go home and collapse. But I'm in wonderful condition, which is more than you can say for some of these tea-sippers we have representing us in tennis these days."

Watching him pace a room, nervous energy spilling over, you can believe it. Tilden, in the autumn of life, is still one of the most vital men on earth. The thin face, deeply scorched by many suns, is without the wrinkles of his years. He has only one chin. The high, angular body is still lean and flexible as a buggywhip, every inch an athlete's. Except for thinning wisps of grey hair atop the small, shapely skull, you couldn't estimate his age. At that, he looks closer to 45 than 57. Tilden's speech is an odd mixture of the erudite and the earthy and he fires it at you in fast, interest-catching bursts. "The only thing I fear is being bored," he said. "When the capacity to enjoy life goes, it's time to die."

There's no question that the Old Master somehow has clung to his love for tennis. Only one thing is missing. He'd leap at the chance to be out there before the big stadium crowds again, on center court. Nothing could be more appealing than the chance to organize his own pro circuit and go on tour again. Physically he's still capable. Whether tennis will let him do it is something else again.

Those who know William Tatum Tilden's story only superficially have never given him full credit for becoming the net wizard of the century. Rich men's sons often get that treatment. Born with a silver spoon in his mouth, Tilden is the only scion of aristocracy to become a living American sports legend. The chance of birth handicapped him. If he'd sprung from the shanty side of the tracks, like the Babe, Dempsey and others, the fires of hidden talent banked within him so long might have been touched off far sooner.

As it was, it took him 10 painful, ego-flattening years to hit the top. That story is all but forgotten.

Centuries ago, in England's baronial halls, the name was spelled "Tylden." The modernized version was given the youngest son of William T. and Salina Hey Tilden on February 10, 1893, in the exclusive Germantown district of Philadelphia. The senior Tilden was a distinguished wool-and-hair merchant, long-time president of the Union League, a leader in reform politics and hobnobber with the famous personages of the day. His wife was a brilliant woman of exceptional artistic gifts. The daughter of the noted Heys of Quakertown might

have had a concert career as a pianist. When she died in Bill's late teens, the boy, who worshipped her, was crushed.

Tilden says he grew up amid luxury, "somewhat spoiled and a brat. He has vague memories of playing at the feet of two household guests—Presidents Teddy Roosevelt and William Howard Taft. In the Summers, the Tildens repaired to their Onteora Club home in the Catskills, where the small fry of the wealthy tumbled over private courts from morning to dark.

"My older brother, Herb, was the real tennis star of the family," recounts Bill. "I was just 'Junior Tilden,' the pestiferous punk who got in the older kids' hair. Herb was 13 when I started playing at six and he became the best around Philadelphia. In fact, he could beat Wallace Johnson, the No. 2 man nationally, before he quit to go into business. Whenever I got fatheaded about winning some minor tournament, Herb would march me out to the court and slap my ears down."

At seven, Junior Tilden won the Onteora 15-and-under boys' title, his first. At 12 and 13, he was a ballboy at the Germantown Cricket Club, where the world's leading amateurs could be seen. He grew up chasing balls for such early-day players as Bill Larned, seven times American champion between 1901-11, J.C. Parke of England, Beals Wright, Holcombe Ward, and Norman Brookes, the Australian Davis Cup star. His game became a hodgepodge of the polite, garden-party pat-ball that was still being played in the guise of tennis.

"Nobody wound up and really plastered the ball. Nobody broke out a real sweat. Somehow even then I sensed that this wasn't right," Tilden says now. "It seemed to me that good manners, the well-placed soft shot, and the general air of elegance were okay in their place, but winning was a lot more important."

The explosion that lifted Tilden and tennis out of their rut occurred when he was 17. Along came a carrot-thatched Californian from San Francisco in dirty pants who shocked the effete Easterners right out of their seats. The name was Maurice McLoughlin. A graduate of the public courts, he swung his racket like a flail, raced all over the court, rushed the net with Indian whoops, and hit a powerhouse service that whistled. It was something utterly new. The fascinated Tilden squatted in the stands and watched every move the new national champion made.

McLoughlin flashed but briefly—1909 to 1914—but he planted the seed of the most effective all-court, all-stroke game the ancient pastime has ever known. Strangely, it took shape with such nerve-wracking slowness that time and again Tilden quit tennis in disgust. From his 15th to his 25th year, he was rated only fair, never close to first-class. At times he hit tremendous hot streaks, as in winning the national mixed doubles with Mary K. Browne in 1913. But ordinary club singles players poked his game full of holes and beat him consistently. A faded sports column of 1921 speaks wonderingly of his eventual success:

"He played so unceasingly and with such futility on these same Germantown courts where he now rules as champ that they called him a 'nut' and thought he was 'looney' ... He spent all day with a racket in his hand and those who were then called stars and some who were not stars at all mocked him ... Little did these scoffers suspect that the gangling boy would fill out and return, at length, a prophet with honor in his own country."

The fill-out process started at the University of Pennsylvania, where he managed to make the varsity team, and later as volunteer coach at Germantown Academy. But the death of his mother, father, and brother within a six-year period left him at loose ends. The college-age Tilden is described as extremely nervous, high-strung, moody, and willful. Quitting college in his senior year, he took a reporter's job on the old Philadelphia *Ledger*, covering drama and music. He steeped himself in the arts. Later, he wrote sports under 290-pound Tiny Maxwell, the ex-Penn gridder. He had about decided on a newspaper career when World War I swept him into the Medical Corps. "They kicked me out of the fighting army for flat feet," says Tilden, "which didn't surprise anybody. I'd been pounding the courts for nearly 20 years.

Nobody can say that Big Bill ever lacked guts or that he lucked himself to fame. Something in him wouldn't let him quit what he had started. By 1918 out of the army, the headstrong, fanatical stringbean started to put together the parts of his uncoordinated game. Nobody helped him. It is a fact that Bill Tilden never had a formal tennis lesson in his life. Even as he floundered, he refused to listen to the teachers and theorists. "Keep away from me," he said to them in his teens. "I know as much about this as anybody. What I don't know, I'll find out."

He found out—inch by inch. After Little Bill Johnston, top man of tennis, bounced him around in the 1919 nationals, Tilden retreated to Providence, Rhode Island. He had a job with the Equitable Life Insurance Company, but mostly he stuck to the court and worked endlessly on a weak backhand. Johnston had battered his backhand to death in previous meetings. Tilden forgot the defensive slices he had been using and began to make every backhand a flat, smashing drive. He perfected an assortment of tricky spins and changes of pace. He sweated to develop a real McLoughlin cannonball serve that couldn't be returned. "I spent hours in serving alone, trying to disguise the twist and pace of the ball," he remembers. "I would take a dozen balls and serve them to No. 1 court with one style of delivery. Then I'd cross over and hit them back with another type of service. Next, I'd try the left court from both sides. My next move would be to pick out a certain section of the service court and aim for that until I could put the ball just where wanted it. Finally, I'd strive to put the ball there with tremendous speed."

Shades of Cobb in the sliding pit, of Bobby Jones spending hours in a bunker! Months later, this feverishly determined man could pick off a creeping beetle from across the net. By the Spring of 1920, he was ready to shoot for Wimbledon, the Davis Cup team, Forest Hills—and his deadly little nemesis, Billy Johnston.

The Tilden-Johnston series, stretching over eight years, is one of the sagas of American sport. No more bitter, dramatic tennis matches were ever ought. Fans generally think of Tilden as the complete master, but before 1920 it was the other way around. Little Bill was only five-feet-eight, weighing under 120 most times. But he had a devastating forehand drive and a body chockful of courage. The dead-game, methodical way in which he handled the hulking Big Bill brought him an army of admirers from coast to coast.

"It isn't true, not a bit of it, that we were enemies," swears Tilden. "Billy was one of the most gallant souls I ever knew—the greatest fighting heart tennis ever had. The papers built up a feud that didn't exist and our followers took violent sides. But, hell, I loved the little guy and I know he liked me."

What the public didn't know was that Johnston literally killed himself trying to beat Tilden between 1920-'26. In the end, his health broke and he went to a sanitarium. In 1946, his tennis-weakened heart stopped pumping. Hundreds of messages of consolation flooded in, but the first received by Irene Johnston was a telegram reading simply: "A great sportsman never dies."

It was signed "Bill Tilden."

"Getting that picked me up," said Mrs. Johnston. "Somehow I liked Bill's message being first."

As the 1920 season started, Big Bill trotted out his new weapons. He trimmed wonder-boy Vinnie Richards for the national indoor singles title at New York. Then, named to the Davis Cup team, he invaded England for the first time. In the London Championships, a warm-up for Wimbledon, he got a crack at Little Bill. And Johnston whipped him, 4-6, 6-2, 6-4. When Wimbledon opened, with 128 players in the crack field, few gave the leggy No. 2 American a chance.

Forty-three years of Wimbledon tradition said that no non-British Empire contestant could win on the hallowed centre court. Big Bill was to change a lot of tennis notions, but, typically, he had to start at the very top. In an early round, he caught J. C. Parke, the Irish war hero and former conqueror of Maury McLoughlin, who had eliminated Little Bill. Tilden's mixture of cyclonic serves, controlled spins, soft drop shots, and deadly volleying chased Parke off the court. He bumped out the redoubtable Col. A.R.F. (Algy) Kingscote, the top-dog Englishman, and kept going until he reached the defending champ, Gerald Patterson of Australia.

"Thousands had thought Patterson unbeatable," mourned the London *Times* the next day. "What happened in full view of Their Majesties will rank with such debacles as Hastings Field and Bunker Hill."

That was pretty fancy verbiage for what was no more than a light workout for large William. His crafty brain had picked out a fatal backhand flaw in Patterson's game. For the first set, he deliberately probed it, losing, 2-6. Then he unleashed such a fusillade of cut strokes and chops to the backhand that the Aussie stood pathetically waving his arms for three sets, 6-3, 6-2, 6-4. In the finals, Bill collected another trophy by beating the Japanese star, Zenzo Shimizu.

With Wimbledon under his belt, Tilden teamed with Little Bill to oust France and Britain from the Davis Cup running. In the final doubles match, Little Bill-Big Bill vs. Parke-Kingscote, the full fury of the new Tilden smote the net world for the first time. An eyewitness account described the scene like this:

"The English had won the fifth game of the decisive set when there came the real sensation of the day. Tilden came up grimly and served with blinding speed. Parke, a 10-second man in track, failed to get within two yards of the ball. Probably he never saw it. The next ball by Tilden smashed Kingscote in the body, actually crumpling him up on the court. The third, of hurricane force, left Parke standing helplessly. Not one of these balls had been taken on the receiver's racket! Such a thing had never been seen at Wimbledon before—and the crowd did not know whether to cheer or regard it as a sacrilege."

The home folks didn't know what to make of Big Bill either, when he returned, dripping with honors. He hit the drab, staid, formalized tennis scene like a delayed-action bomb. Putting the frigid focus on quailing umpires, intimidating linesmen, blasting errant ballboys, chatting gaily with the customers one moment and snarling at them the next, he was such a show that the fans couldn't believe that he was true. The USLTA, however, had no doubts. Tilden immediately made it clear that he wrote his own rules. When the tycoons tried to outline a schedule of tune-ups for the upcoming Davis Cup challenge of Australasia, he told them to quit pestering him. For months he gave up tennis altogether and played golf on a Chicago links. The Julian Myrick crowd ground its teeth in helpless rage. "A group of the feeble-minded," was Big Bill's description of the Davis Cup Committee.

Tilden has written in one of his books, "Actually, I am far from arrogant. I am inwardly humble and shy with people ... I am definitely not a social or gregarious being."

You can't prove it by his old associates. "Tilden was the greatest box-office attraction in the game because he never let the spotlight get off him," says Peck Griffin, who was Little Bill's doubles partner for many seasons. "He couldn't walk—he strutted. He was so utterly sold on the Tilden supremacy that it took your breath away. When he barged into a clubhouse or hotel lobby, wearing that weird fuzzy blue sweater or a dirty old polo coat, he looked twice as big as life and the flunkies came running. He operated strictly in the grand manner. I remember once he sent Pola Negri $400 worth of flowers in one bunch. Walter Hagen never had a thing on Bill for impressing the natives. At a party, with the room full of distinguished people, Tilden was always the main event. He'd get up and recite poetry by the hour—everything from Shakespeare to his own material."

Another onetime rival says less kindly, "He was the consummate ham actor. The rest of us prayed that he'd fall down and break a leg."

With his height, length of leg, slim hips, huge shoulders, and deep chest, Tilden's perfect tennis build could have made him one of the sartorial splendors of the day. Instead, he went around looking like an ad for a rummage sale. His famed "blue bearskin" sweater, a wooly monstrosity that he wore into action, shocked Wimbledon. On the street, his idea of a nifty ensemble was a correct white shirt and tie topped off by an old basketball sweatshirt or warm-up jacket. His color extended to all things. At one sitting, he could devour a steak large enough to feed three men. A bridge fiend, he often had to be summoned from the card table to play an important match. Wherever he went, he collected celebrities—John McCormick, King Alfonso of Spain, Mary Garden (his greatest favorite), the Countess of Oxford, Noel Coward, Lily Pons, Doug Fairbanks, Greta Garbo, and hundreds of others. Sportswriters who tried to interview him got a lecture, not on tennis, but on David Belasco's *Pelleas et Melisande* or the works of Alexander Woollcott.

Like Babe Ruth, he always had a big, fast car that he sent rocketing over the highroads. Eventually, in 1946, he cracked up near Wenden, Arizona, and nearly killed himself.

Tilden's dramatic instinct was never sharper than on the court, where he'd experiment until he was far behind, then come up with a late rush to snatch the win in the last instant. Always there had to be the suspenseful build-up followed by a crashing climax.

His matches took strange, unpredictable twists. Against Rene Lacoste in the 1925 Davis Cup challenge round, only one point separated the Frenchman from victory. Tilden smacked a forehand that was sure to go out of bounds by two feet. Lacoste needed only to let the ball go. But in scrambling to get clear he tripped and it hit the sole of his shoe. Tilden, grinning, won the point—and the game, set and match. In another Cup duel with Jean Borotra, Tilden again seemed hopelessly beaten. The "Bounding Basque" was at match point in the fifth set. Tilden netted the crucial ball and the umpire was about to announce Borotra's triumph when Big Bill said, "Hold on."

He walked to the ball, laying in his court, picked it up and handed it to the umpire. It was half-split, a broken ball.

The point had to be replayed and Tilden won it. Then, riding the floodtide of his remarkable fate, he pounded them past the bewildered Borotra for game, set and match.

By turning off the power or turning it on when needed, he kept the fans electrified. Other stars were merciless point-hounds, never wasting a shot and winning by 6-0, 6-0, 6-0 if they could. When Big Bill faced a rising young player, he'd let himself be sucked out of position. As the kid passed him or lobbed over his head, Tilden's cry of "Peach!" rang through the galleries. The delighted kid would never forget the moment and Tilden had another staunch fan.

On the other hand, there was the hotshot who took an opening set from King William. One of the king's admirers offered to bet $500 that his man would win the next set by 6-1. Tilden heard of the wager and immediately lost the first game without trying for the ball. Then, with his backer sweating profusely, he reeled off the next six games so fast that the poor gent across the net looked like Aunt Agnes ineffectually swatting at houseflies.

When his acting flair over-spilled onto Broadway and he trod the boards in "The Kid Himself" and "They All Want Something," he had the USLTA in a cold sweat. The association could never be sure whether Big Bill would be delivering aces or dialogue. During the '25 French-American matches, he played comedy on a New York stage each evening, handling both chores with his usual utter nonchalance. The fact that he was staying up well past midnight didn't appear to affect his tennis at all. He thrived on it. On Saturday, he blithely romped through a two-hour matinee and then rushed to the courts to meet the mighty Borotra in the decisive singles match.

"Tilden fell behind two sets so that he looked badly beaten," Borotra related the incident. "When he returned after 10 minutes rest for the fourth set, he was so pale and drawn that I was sure I had him. Voila! Tilden won without a struggle!"

That night, Thespian Tilden, the iron man, was back before the footlights for an evening show, emoting with all his fervor.

His match with Little Bill Johnston in 1920 sold him to the nation. It stands as one of the most bizarre tennis tangles of all time. Three months after his triumph at Wimbledon, the pair met for the national championship on a gloomy Forest Hills afternoon. Tilden started like a whirlwind, racing through the first set, 6-1. Johnston's smoking forehand narrowed on the target and he polished off Tilden in the second set by the same score. With Big Bill leading, 3-1, in the third set, a press airplane carrying a cameraman and pilot zoomed so low over the stands that the crowd cried out in terror. Tailspinning, the craft crashed just outside the stadium with earthshaking force. Horrified witnesses to the death of two men were about to stampede from the stands.

"I was as badly shaken as anyone and so was Little Bill," describes Tilden. "We stood paralyzed. But umpire Eddie Conlon—and there, kid, was at least *one* bright official—realized in a flash that we must stop the panic. He yelled to us to play and we did. Less than 50 people from a crowd of 10,000 rushed for the gates."

Before the day's fireworks were over, Conlon and referee George Ade were at each other's throats and the whole match seemed washed out by a sudden rainstorm. Ade made a palpably putrid decision against Tilden in the fourth set. Conlon roared protest. Soaked fans headed for the exits. Utter confusion gripped the stadium. Only Tilden and Johnston, their rivalry rising above all else, kept cool.

Slamming screamers, Tilden won the third set, 7-5. Little Bill gallantly squared it by the same score. In a blistering finale, Tilden's sheer power wore down the smaller man, 6-3. Ten years after they called him "that looney kid" at Germantown, he was the champion of America and England.

Little Bill sat sobbing in exhaustion in the clubhouse. "His legs ... his legs," he muttered to his pal, Peck Griffin. "He beat me with those legs." Then his chin came up. "But I'll get him next time," he gritted. "I'll get him—if it kills me!"

At the end of the year, the two Bills sailed for Auckland, New Zealand, to see what they could do about bringing home the Davis Cup. The piled-up publicity made it almost a holy crusade. The Aussies had knocked over the United States for the Cup in 1914 and had held it against Britain in the 1919 renewal. Norman E. Brookes, the fabulous "Wizard of Down Under," and Gerald Patterson were given no less than an even chance to retain the blue-ribbon trophy. Tilden overwhelmed Brookes, the tougher of the two, in four sets. Johnston battered down Patterson in three.

And that, in a nutshell, was the story of American tennis between the years 1920 and 1926. It was the best in the world, maybe the best ever seen. With the two Bills around, the country didn't need anybody else for the longest continuous stretch that one nation has dominated the international field.

Big Bill kept whooping it up. He was so confoundedly invincible, such a prodigious walloper, that they even wanted to change the rules to beat him. A hue and cry went up by ranking players to limit the server to only one ball in big-time match play. Tilden's underspinning ball that traveled like a shell was held to be ruining the game. Tilden fans quashed that by cracking, "Hell, you could give him one ball and a squash paddle and he'd still beat you!"

Not many people know how the lanky spitfire who made every shot look easy suffered to stick on top. In '21, he won the world hard-court championship at Paris over Jean Washer of Belgium while running a high fever and suffering from a severe attack of boils. Crossing to England, Big Bill collapsed. He was packed off to a nursing home. He still had packing in seven of the eruptions and was half doped-up when called from his sickbed to defend his Wimbledon title against Brian I. C. Norton, the South African Olympic Games star. Norton played keep-away with the ailing champ for the first two sets, winning easily, 6-4, 6-2. Unaware of the facts, the huge crowd fell to roasting the limp Tilden.

"Play the game!" they let him have it. "Slacker!" Boos, whistles and catcalls thundered from the stands.

Norton's sense of fair play was outraged. Angrily, he talked back to the customers and let his control waver. Needing only two points to close out the match, he missed by inches on sideline shots. That was all the opening Tilden needed. Somehow reaching down into his immense reserve, he pulled off half a dozen miraculous recoveries that broke Norton's back. After the clinching point in his favor, Big Bill lurched into the clubhouse and collapsed in a dead faint.

"Mister Tennis" went on punishing himself. Back in the U.S., doctors advised a long rest from the competitive strain. Instead he went up against the greatest netman Japan has produced, Zenzo Shimizu, in the Davis Cup challenge round at Forest Hills. The midget with the big head, his loose ducks flopping about his skinny legs, had the big shot right where he wanted him. It was a scorching hot day. Shimizu ran Tilden for miles, winning two of the first three sets. When Tilden dragged himself in for the rest period, he was gasping for air. Shimizu was blandly smiling. The crowd couldn't believe what was happening.

You can't estimate what it cost Tilden in physical torture to make it back to the court and finish the match. Davis Cup Captain Sam Hardy found him standing, fully clothed, under the showers. Hardy feared he would cave in at any moment. "Just dress me in dry clothes," Tilden panted, "and push me out the door."

He made it back. In the fourth set he found one more untapped well of energy and bombarded Shimizu with baffling changes of pace until the heat caught up with the Jap and *he* collapsed. After a leg rubdown, Shimizu made a game attempt to regain control. But Tilden was like a wounded tiger. In five sets, he cut down his victim for his most stirring comeback.

Elements of the USLTA were after Big Bill's scalp as early as 1922. The plot was to trip him on a professionalization charge and heave him out of the amateur ranks. As long as he kept winning, though, it could be only a plot. The break his enemies were waiting for came in October, 1922. Playing an exhibition at Bridgeton, New Jersey, he jammed his racket hand against a poultry-netting backstop. Blood-poisoning set in. His condition quickly became critical, then desperate. Germantown surgeons wanted to remove the hand, or at least the injured middle finger. Tilden shook his head.

"Take off as little of the finger as you have to," he told Dr. William B. Swartley. "Maybe I can still play."

Swartley fought the staphylococcus infection for four months and saved half the finger. Tilden came out of it with his whole future in doubt. Experts claimed that a 4 1/2-fingered player couldn't get by in the big-time— not even Tilden.

"They'd have loved to see me finished," he says now. "So, of course, I had to deny them the satisfaction." Taping the stub, he worked for weeks to perfect a new grip. Each swing sent pain stabbing through his arm, but the king never faltered. In the next year, 1923, all he did was win his third consecutive national singles cup, the U.S., clay court, mixed doubles and doubles titles. And give the USLTA another of his patented jolts.

This time the issue stemmed from a tremendous earthquake in Tokyo, Japan, that killed 143,000 persons. When Zenzo Shimizu in New York asked Big Bill to play a benefit for the quake sufferers, he readily agreed. After a $10,000 advance sale was assured at Jackson Heights, the association cracked down. "No sanction," said officials.

Almost in tears, Shimizu phoned Tilden to break the news. Tilden's description of what he told Julian Myrick is one of the highspots of his colorful book, *My Story— A Champion's Memoirs,* published three years ago. "You'll be barred if you play," Myrick warned him.

"I dare you to bar me!" Tilden erupted. "Try it and I'll spill the whole story to the press. I doubt if the American public will stand for the national champion being barred because he helps the victims of a catastrophe."

When Myrick hastily backed away from that one, it was vivid proof that Big Bill had the whole Lawn Tennis Association on his hip. Two hours after Big Bill called Myrick's bluff, Shimizu had his sanction.

No sporting monarch ever ruled with a heavier hand than Tilden. As the Twenties roared along, opponents cursed his very existence. The press belabored him for making a shambles of the amateur code, then assigned extra men to cover his matches. Officials held indignation meetings. Pro promoters dangled five-figure contracts for him to sign. And John Public, never much of a hand for this society diversion, beat down the gates to see him perform.

Nobody can doubt that Tilden sold tennis to America. The first to master every shot, he was fascinating to watch—a combined ballet dancer and murderous hitter. Playing deep, towering at the baseline, he slugged the cover off the ball, or dropped it just over the net like a feather. It seemed that he would never lose when it really counted. Between 1920 and '25, his grip on the national crown not once wavered. In five of those six years, he had to whip the gamecock Little Bill Johnston in the finals.

By 1926, Big Bill had beaten back three Davis Cup bids by Australasia, one by Japan, and two by France. The first signs of his weariness with it all came in '25 when both Borotra and Lacoste carried him to five bitter sets before he could administer the *coup de grace.* The period of invincibility was slowly running out.

It ended at Forest Hills in '26 when he lost his first championship match in seven years—to Henri Cochet, the most magnificent member of the renowned "Four Musketeers" of France. Cochet toppled the aging king of Forest Hills, who stood up and fought, gamely but hopelessly, despite the physical pain he endured. Bill was suffering from chronic knee-trouble, and it was difficult for him even to hobble around. Doctors had advised him against playing at all. The loss did more to make Bill Tilden an American hero than all his victories. "Bill's star shines brighter than ever before," said *American Lawn Tennis*. "Crippled, suffering agonies of body and mind, he almost plucked victory from certain defeat." And he did. It took a red-hot Cochet five grueling sets to end the Tilden reign.

He had his revenge on the little dancing master from Lyons the next year, outgunning Cochet, 6-4, 2-6, 6-2, 8-6 in the Davis Cup. Sadly, Lacoste rose to fantastic heights to beat both Bills, Cochet edged the worn-out Johnston—and the most prized trophy in international sport was gone at last. Not even Tilden could bring it back.

A lot of observers tell you that the greatest single shot Big Bill ever pulled off came in 1929 at Paris, the year before his amateur career ran out. The 15,000 on hand sounded like 50 million Frenchmen as they roared for their boy, the ice-blooded "Crocodile"—Lacoste. In the crucial fifth set, Tilden played a backhand chop to Lacoste's forehand. Gambling everything that the Musketeer would hit a certain angled volley, Tilden raced to his forehand court. Before he got there, Lacoste hit what looked like an ungettable ball. With a desperate leap, Big Bill got his racket on the ball well outside the net post and between it and the umpire's chair. All he could do was flip it as he went crashing into the concrete court rim and pinwheeled on over into the crowd. Looking back from an upside-down stance, Tilden saw Lacoste standing, shaken, at the net. The ball had cleared the cords and landed out of reach.

A mass shudder went through the crowd. All the fight was knocked out of Lacoste. The Croc blew wide open, double-faulted and Big Bill casually ran out the match.

By now the lanky guy was 37 years old and audibly creaking in the joints. Playing largely on one leg with a sacroiliac that popped in and out, he should have made the 1930 season his worst. Instead it was one of his best. He swept the Riviera tourneys, won the national titles of Italy and Austria, and capped it all with the inspired trouncing of Borotra and young Wilmer Allison for his third Wimbledon coup. Then, when all the dollars they offered couldn't budge him, the perpetual "dramatic artist" (ham, some insist) in Big Bill finally caused him to turn pro.

It was a movie offer from MGM that turned the trick. Earlier, he had spent a season in stock in sundry plays, handled the title role of "Dracula" (perfectly cast, according to the USLTA) for 16 weeks with a road company, and filled a few minor Broadway parts. The chance to let the whole country see Tilden on the silver screen was too tempting. Typically, he rejected a $50,000 pro tennis bid from C. C. ("Bunion Derby") Pyle in 1926, but didn't hesitate to grab the movie contract.

"Anyway, I was sick of the association trying to sink a knife in my back—from behind," comments Tilden.

Parts in two silent pictures and four tennis films for MGM and Warner Brothers constitute the Tilden contribution to cinematic art, but his effect on professional tennis was somewhat more marked. In fact, he made the pro game the big operation it is today. His pro debut in Madison Square Garden on February 18, 1931, against Karel Kozeluh, the Czech "world pro champion," drew nearly 15,000 fans and $36,000. Tilden straight-setted him. They toured the country, with Big Bill as the promotional genius, and cleaned up $238,000, although it was even more one-sided than last season's Kramer-Gonzalez series. Big Bill won 63 of 76 matches with Kozeluh. Goofy sidelights to the tour developed, among them the fact that Jack Curley, the majordomo of the rassling racket, was Tilden's booking agent.

At first, Curley smoothly tried to tie up Tilden in a contract that would have made the grapple man the boss. Tilden glanced through the contract, then pointed a long, bony finger at Curley. "Get this straight," he said in chill tones. "I don't grunt, nor do I groan. In fact, I've been to college and I can read. If you want to be hired as my employee, Curley, we might get together."

Curley saw the light. "You draw up a contract," he said humbly. "I'll sign it."

As the tour turned into a runaway for Tilden, the mat impresario suffered extreme pain. Hell, did *every* match have to be a shooting match?

Tilden nipped that one in the bud. "We don't do business in tennis," he lectured the unhappy Curley. "This is an honest promotion. And I'll fire the first person who tries any funny stuff."

Curley just gave him a hopeless look and walked away.

By 1940, Tilden could look back on a parade of smartly-operated net shows. He grossed $86,000 with Vinnie Richards, $62,000 with Hans Nusslein and Cochet, $243,000 with Ellie Vines and $188,000 with George Lott, Vines, and Stoefen, among other tours. In 1931 and '35 Big Bill beat his younger foes for the world pro belt. At the age of 41 he tackled Vines, then at his peak, before a record 18,000 in the Garden—and polished off the rangy ex-amateur marvel, 8-6, 6-2, 6-2!

He kept on making colorful copy. In '44, he was in Hollywood, coaching movie queens like Tallulah Bankhead, Katharine Hepburn, and Greta Garbo. And he was in the war, as much as a gent topping 50 could be. He organized a tour for British War Relief and another to sell U.S. war bonds (in Philadelphia, alone, a one-day Tilden show sold $4,000,000 worth!), and still another for 200 army, navy, and marine camps. Gussie Moran first exhibited her shapely stems to the national public in these matches, but even Gorgeous Gussie couldn't compete with the Old Master when it came to wowing the patrons. Dressed in Gay Nineties garb, Tilden appeared as "Miss Wilhelmina Shovelshot," a dowager with a swing like a barn door. He brought down the house.

Nobody could understand then, nor does now, how those Tilden legs could last so long. They are unique. Ty Cobb's gam's carried him for 24 big-league seasons. But Ty didn't run nearly as far as Big Bill. Fifty-one years on the court! No wonder that when Bob Hope introduced Tilden to a Los Angeles audience during the war he convulsed them with: "Mr. Tilden comes to you through the courtesy of the Santa Monica Adrenalin Company ..."

Listen to Bobby Riggs in his fascinating "Tennis Is My Racket," published last year, as he speaks of the 1945 Tilden: "Bill came up with the idea of a big professional tournament in Los Angeles ... he not only ran the show like a great pro promoter, but played some unbelievable tennis. In the quarter-finals, he licked Lester Stoefen, 8-6, 6-0. The next day, he cooled off somewhat and lost to Don Budge. But in the third-place playoff, he gave the customers another shock by beating Fred Perry in a tough three-set match. You had to see it to believe it ... don't forget, Bill was a mere 52 years old."

With Budge and Riggs as vice-prexises and Perry as president, the wear-proof oldtimer organized the Professional Players Association in 1946. Big Bill plunged into it up to his ears. His enthusiasm sparked the whole troupe. "As tournament manager, Bill did a job that I'll never cease admiring," goes on Riggs. "He went out and sold the show to various cities, made all the deals, handled the publicity, worked ceaselessly."

Once when Riggs was touring with Budge, the Redhead fell ill in Hershey, Pennsylvania. Tilden, who had just driven 200 miles to watch the matches, came out of the stands to fill in at doubles. The crowd exploded as he came on court with that swinging, step-back- boys-here-comes-the-boss stride. He hadn't played on canvas, under lights, for years. But as always he rose to the occasion. Teamed with Wayne Sabin, he beat Riggs and Johnny Faunce. Later, the promoter offered Tilden a check for his services. He waved it away. In the hall, he whispered to Riggs, "Say, Bobby, how much was that check for?"

"That's Bill," says Riggs. "He probably could have used the money, but he couldn't resist the grand gesture. There was never anything small-time about William T. Tilden."

Right to the last, he kept giving them his magnificent lip. He was last seen—as a champion—by a scant 1,500 fans at Rip's Tennis Courts, New York City, five years ago. The event was the National Pro Tournament. Tilden was playing his old foe, Kozeluh, in the quarter-finals when the Czech, in a burst of temper, tried to default. The Old Master's greying head went back and his lip curled as he stalked to the net. Nobody was going to swipe the show from him. "Are you or are you not," he demanded of Kozeluh, "going to finish this match?"

The browbeaten Kozeluh finished. And the crowd went next to crazy when Old Bill trimmed him in five fast-action sets.

The long haul that started so long ago ended, as it should, when Tilden and the doubles partner of his heyday, Vinnie Richards, won the national pro doubles over the much-younger Welby Van Horn and Dick Skeen. Nobody said much when the king aced Van Horn to clinch the match. A few veterans in the stands shed a nostalgic tear. The rest just sat there marveling. They couldn't know that they we're looking at the big guy for the last time.

After that, suddenly and tragically, the shadows closed in and claimed him. He was arrested in Los Angeles and went to an Honor Farm. When the story broke, the writer was working a metropolitan newspaper night desk. The sports editor came in, picked up the piece of teletype copy, and read it. There was pain on his face. "I've never suppressed a news story in my life," he said. "But don't print this."

There were many others who felt the same way, who remembered that before Big Bill Tilden went into limbo, he put enough records on the books to send the future crop of tennis internationalists running in dizzy circles trying to catch up. That he slashed and stormed and scrapped his way to a pinnacle of immortality from which no man should be allowed to fall. Another 50 years from now, they'll still be shaking their heads over his deeds and saying it couldn't be true. Seven American amateur diadems, three at Wimbledon, eight times the No. 1 player of the world, 13 straight wins in the Davis Cup, and all the other major championships in the field—a record as fantastic as the man who achieved it.

Remember him for that. He was not only the greatest tennis figure that America has produced, but so much the greatest that comparisons are futile. He was Big Bill Tilden, great competitor, swashbuckling pioneer, defender of the Cup, transcendental rebel—the one and the only—and when he bowed out, there was an empty space that never will be filled.

Don Budge, 1938 The first of just five players to achieve the fabled Grand Slam.

Chapter 4

Don Budge: Grand-Slammer of Tennis

Don Budge ruled tennis with his devastating play in 1937 and '38. When this SPORT article ran in 1960, he was still the only holder of a Grand Slam and, for some, that made him the best player ever.

SPORT February 1960 By Will Grimsley

"Playing tennis against Don Budge," says former Wimbledon champion Sidney B. Wood Jr., "was like playing against a concrete wall. There was nothing to attack. There was no weakness. When he was in his prime, no player, past or present, could have beaten him."

Whenever and wherever the clan gathers to debate the relative prowess of the great tennis players, there is always loud and militant support for Budge, the red-haired comet who came out of the West to end a ten-year Davis Cup drought in the United States, to score an unprecedented sweep of the world's amateur championships, and then to rule supreme as a professional until World War II cut into his career.

"Budge was the greatest tennis player of all time, and I think the records prove it," insists Walter Pate, Wall Street attorney, contemporary of Big Bill Tilden, and U.S. Davis Cup captain for 11 years during Budge's heyday. "Tilden had a long and successful career but he was always beatable. You must remember that it was his failure to win matches from Rene Lacoste and Henri Cochet of France that cost us the Davis Cup in 1927, 1928, 1929 and 1930. Budge, on the other hand, never lost an important match when he reached his peak in 1937 and 1938. I think his sweep during this period was one of the great, all-time achievements in sports."

In 1937 Budge won both the Wimbledon and the United States championships. In 1938 he won both of them again and added the French and Australian crowns for the only "Grand Slam" of the world's major titles ever achieved on the tennis court. Winning the four big ones in a single year was a feat that escaped such illustrious predecessors as Little Bill Johnston, Tilden and Ellsworth Vines, and such later stars as Jack Kramer, Pancho Gonzalez, Frank Sedgman and Lew Hoad.

"Athletically speaking, I think this rates even above Bob Jones' 'Grand Slam' in golf," Pate contends. "It's fantastic that a man should be able to go through two years without losing a match of any description. Don dropped a couple of matches on the Pacific Coast late in 1938—to Harry Hopman and Adrian Quist of Australia—but they can hardly be counted. He had already decided to turn pro and he wasn't half trying."

Bobby Riggs, who fought Budge for both amateur and professional honors, calls the redhead "the most devastating and impressive player I have ever seen.

"Tilden often toyed with opponents—he would tease them by letting them get close," Riggs added. "Vines was inconsistent. he was a world-beater one day and a patsy the next. Not Budge. He was not only extremely steady, he was explosive. he could blow you off the court, 6-0, 6-0, 6-0, before you knew it."

What was Budge's distinguishing mark as a champion?

"There wasn't a flaw in his game or temperament," recalls Pate, whom Budge and other Davis Cup players of the time fondly christened "Cap." "Every player I have seen, except Budge, had a soft spot or Achilles heel somewhere in his game. I always felt that there were six strokes which had to be mastered to make the complete tennis player. They are the service, forehand drive, back-hand drive, forehand volley, backhand volley and smash. Budge mastered them all to the extent that he never had to compromise his attack to cover up a weakness. He never had to rush the net. He had such sound ground strokes that he could lie back and go to the net when he pleased. Once there, he was a decisive volleyer and smasher.

"The characteristic of any sports champion is the ability to make hard assignments look easy. Budge did it. His foot work and body control were so perfect he seldom made a jerky motion. He just flowed into his shots. and, you know, in all the matches I've seen him play, I never once saw him fall on the court."

Sidney Wood said he, Frank Shields, Gene Mako, Frankie Parker and other contemporaries of the period often felt that playing against Budge was like playing a different game.

"Don used a tremendously heavy racket," Wood recalled. "It was a bat weighing 16-1/2 ounces. Tilden used a very light racket, about 13-1/2 ounces. Kramer's 15-ounce special always has been considered heavy. But Budge's bat felt like a telephone pole. He wasn't a wristy player and he didn't seem to swing hard, but the ball came back like a rock. He had wonderful rhythm and coordination."

As long as tennis is played, devotees probably will be talking of Budge's backhand, one of the surest and most devastating shots the game has known. While Budge developed strength in all stroking departments—experimenting for years with his forehand—his backhand was his bread-and-butter shot. It was a carry-over from his baseball-playing days as a kid.

He played with rackets belonging to his older brother, Lloyd, and they always were too heavy for him. As a baseball player, Don threw righthanded and batted lefthanded. So he started the backhand racket swing with a two-fisted grip. The left hand was used merely to stabilize and guide the stroke and released itself once the swing got under way. The result was a powerful, whip-like action—not dissimilar from a spring which has been held and then turned loose. Budge learned to unleash this deadly shot almost from any position on the court, and send it down the line or angled cross-court for repeated winners.

Budge did not take to tennis naturally. As a youngster, he liked other games better. He played baseball, football, basketball and hockey. He rode a bicycle, roller skated and liked to dabble with tools. His brother, Lloyd, four years older, kept trying to get Don on a tennis court. Don would hit a few balls, then stroll away to the baseball diamond or hockey field.

"Lloyd always was grabbing me by the collar and seat of the pants and pushing me onto the court," Don says, "but I never really cared for the game then."

Don's father was a good athlete. In his native Scotland, he played soccer for the famous Glasgow Rangers, who performed before crowds of as many as 180,000 people. During a practice match he suffered a serious injury and contracted pneumonia. Later bronchitis set in and the elder Budge was told that if he wished to continue living he had to move to a better climate. So the Scotsman moved to Oakland, Calif., where he met and married a pretty Irish colleen who was to bear him two athletic sons.

The Budges were a family of modest means. The father was manager of a laundry but had to quit the job later because of his poor health. Lloyd loved tennis and worked on his game constantly. Don, a rangy type, won his basketball letter at University High and played football with the neighborhood teams. From the time he was 11 years old until nearly 15, he hardly touched a tennis racket, despite the constant prodding of his brother. His big love was baseball.

Don recalls an interesting incident which happened years later at the well-known Toots Shor's Restaurant in New York. Budge, at this time the professional tennis champion, was having dinner when Joe DiMaggio, then in his prime as the great centerfielder of the New York Yankees, walked over and introduced himself.

"You know something, Don?" Joe asked rhetorically. "I've always envied you. My ambition as a kid was to be a tennis champion."

"That's funny," Don said, "because ever since I can remember, I've thought what a thrill it would be to play center field for the Yankees."

One June night in 1930—Lloyd was 19 and Donald was nearing 15—the older brother began needling the younger at the family dinner table. Lloyd told Don that the California state boys' tennis championship was starting in a week or so, and that if Donald had any gumption he would go out and try to win it. The whole family laughed—except Don.

The next day he went out to the courts and started secret practice. The following day he was back again, and the next day, too. When the tournament came up, he entered. Playing in corduroy pants, he swept to the finals. A pair of starched white ducks were provided for the championship round and young Budge beat Paul Newtown, 6-0, 6-4. Donald had won the first tournament in which he ever had played, and more than that, he had been bitten by the tennis bug.

In 1932 he won the Pacific Coast junior crown, and in 1933 he added the California state junior championship by beating Charlie Hunt, who had crushed his hopes in the two previous finals. In 1933, a stringy, gawky-looking boy of 18, Budge also entered the state senior tournament and won it, beating such players as Edward Chandler, who had held the national intercollegiate title, and Bobby Riggs, who was to become one of his most formidable rivals in both amateur and pro competition.

By this time the red-haired youngster had begun to attract the attention of California tennis enthusiasts, who had seen a steady array of their native sons climb to court greatness. The Northern California Association decided to send Budge to Culver, Ind., to play in the national juniors.

At Culver, Don won his first national title, beating another Californian, Gene Mako of Los Angeles, in the last round. The two became fast friends and later formed a doubles team which was to win two national championships and help win back the Davis Cup.

Mako, a good-looking, blond youngster with a breezy manner, played a big part in loosening up Budge's personality. Free and easy and even a bit prankish among close friends, Don was inclined to be shy and close-mouthed in public. He was very serious. He would cross the street to keep from running into a girl. He had a deep-seated fear of saying or doing the wrong thing. But after a few months with the extrovert Mako, he lost most of his inhibitions.

Budge recalls that he was pretty much of a doubles novice when he first teamed with Mako in the National Clay Court championships in 1933, and Gene quickly put him straight with the terse warning: "I don't care what you do, Don. Just don't miss the ball."

When the two first paired, Mako was the team general. Budge always credited him with a major share of the team's success, although in later years, after Budge had grown to championship stature, Gene was usually blamed by the press and public for most of the setbacks.

Budge was 19 when he first went East in 1934 to play the grass court circuit at Seabright, Longwood, Rye, Newport and finally the Nationals at Forest Hills. En route, he had stopped off in Chicago for the National Clay Court tournament where he beat Frankie Parker in the semi-finals and lost to Bryan (Bitsy) Grant, Atlanta's

"Mighty Atom," in the finals. This, however, was on a heavy, slow surface where the retriever Bitsy was at his best.

The California redhead didn't exactly send whistles tooting and horns blowing on his first appearance in the stuffy, fashionable East where the sport had its American birth. He was far from the dynamic player he became later, and, besides, he was struggling with a cantankerous forehand.

At Seabright, Budge lost in the second round to Henry Prusoff of Seattle. At Longwood, he went down before Berkeley Bell, 6-1, 6-0, 6-0—a humiliating defeat. He fared little better at Rye and Newport. In the Nationals at Forest Hills, he avenged his clay court loss to Bitsy Grant but failing to make a mark in the tournament.

However, the gaunt, long-limbed westerner did not go fully unnoticed. On the sidelines, watching interestedly, was Walter Pate, who later was to become Don's Davis Cup captain and most trusted advisor. "I realized then that this boy had all the makings of a future champion," Pate said later. "I knew his forehand would need correcting but I told friends that this was the fellow who would win back the Davis Cup for us.

"France had been beating our brains out in the Davis Cup competition. When they asked me to be captain, I said I would accept on one condition—that we throw out all the players who had been losing, Tilden and the rest of them, and start with a new team. I figured Budge would be ready in a couple of years or so."

Budge apparently corrected his forehand grip just in time. He had first learned to hit the ball with the eastern grip, which is familiarly known as the "shake hands" grip. It was used by Tilden, Vinnie Richards and most of the leading stars of the period, and Donald learned it from his brother Lloyd. But when Berkeley Bell, George Lott and Gregory Mangin came to the West Coast with their western grips, young Budge was impressed by their top-spin power, and he changed. The western, popularized by Little Bill Johnston and effective for high-bounding balls on the asphalt surface, is a grip that has the palm of the hand back of the racket as if picked up from the floor. It's not good for handling low bounces on soft turf.

After returning home, discouraged with his invasion of the grass court circuit, Don corresponded with Sidney Wood, who advised him to shift back to the eastern grip. Tom Stow, coach of the University of California and

Claremont Country Club, worked all winter with the youngster on revised grips. Then, in the spring of 1935, Pate invited Budge to join the U.S. Davis Cup squad in Mexico. During training, Pate got Budge to use the flat eastern grip. This time the change was permanent, although Don never really mastered the stroke until 1937.

The year 1935 marked Budge's emergence as an international player, although he was a bare 20 years old and his game had not fully matured. One of the preliminary Davis Cup rounds sent the United States against Australia in Philadelphia, and Budge was matched with Jack Crawford, whom he still regards as the finest player Australia has ever produced. At the time Crawford was the world's No. 2 amateur, ranking just back of England's gifted Fred Perry.

After winning the first two sets easily—much to his and everyone's surprise—Budge decided that in order to insure victory he would ease up and try to avoid making errors. Almost before he knew it, Crawford had tied the score at two sets each and was leading 5-3, 30-15, on his own service in the fifth. A couple of lucky breaks and a double-fault enabled Budge to pull out the game and eventually the set, 13-11. The match, played in 105-degree temperature, lasted four hours and ten minutes.

As soon as the final point was won, I developed leg cramps and wouldn't have been able to play another point," Budge recalls. "As I hobbled off the court, I heard a murmur from the crowd. I looked around. Crawford had passed out—cold!"

The victory made possible an overseas trip for the U.S. Davis Cuppers, who were to play at Wimbledon before meeting Germany in the Inter-Zone Final, and if victorious, the British in the Challenge Round.

They say Joseph W. Wear, the overseas team manager, and other members of the American party were biting their fingernails on ship-deck when Budge and Mako, bare-headed and in shirt sleeves, rushed up just before the gangplank was pulled away. They said their had been doing some last-minute shopping for swing records.

Another story was that when the ship reached the other side, Budge was awakened early in the morning by a knock at the door. "Let me see your visa," an official said.

Budge rubbed his eyes, shook off the cobwebs and said, "Oh, you mean my visor. What in the blazes do you want that for?"

"Listen, son," the indignant official said. "I've been in this business twenty years and it's pronounced visa."

"I don't care how long you've been in the business," Budge blurted back. "I've been wearing eyeshades for years, too, and out in California we call 'em visors."

The European campaign provided two other incidents which gave an insight to the perfectly relaxed attitude and naturalness of the gangling tennis player.

Wilmer Allison, senior member of the U.S. squad, recalls the night before the team was to meet Germany, Budge walked down the hotel corridor and saw the light on in Allison's room at 3 a.m.

"Willy, why aren't you asleep?" Budge asked.

"I never sleep before a big match," Allison replied. "How about you—are you restless, too?"

"Naw, I'm just getting a drink of cold water. I've been asleep for hours," Budge said. "I'll get four more hours sleep before breakfast."

English sportswriters reported that when Budge appeared on the center court at Wimbledon for the first time, he waved his racket at the Queen in the royal box. Her Majesty reportedly waved back, to the amusement of the gallery.

Budge has tried to discredit the story, insisting, "I may have been green, but not that green." The Britishers swear it happened.

Budge's first overseas campaign was both successful and disappointing. He scored singles victories in the Inter-Zone over both of Germany's aces—Henner Henkel and Gottfried Von Cramm. He upset Britain's Bunny Austin in the Wimbledon tournament but lost to both Austin and Fred Perry in the Challenge Round. Allison also dropped both of his singles matches, giving the British a 5-0 sweep.

The trip was profitable in other ways. Budge, an astute student of the game and its tactics, spent hours watching the great Perry in action. He particularly was impressed by the Englishman's ability to move quickly to the net behind a forcing shot. Budge took mental note and as a result strengthened another facet of his game.

The tall redhead got off to a bad start in 1936, losing again to the relentless little retriever, Bitsy Grant. However, he rallied to whip both Jack Crawford and Adrian Quist of Australia in the Davis Cup matches at Germantown, Pa., and he scored victories over such players as Bunny Austin, Bobby Riggs and Frank Parker.

In the two big championships in which he played—

Wimbledon and the U.S. Nationals at Forest Hills— Budge was cut down by Perry. The English stylist eliminated Don in four sets in the semi-finals at Wimbledon and won in five sets in the finals at Forest Hills, although Budge had led five games to three in the fifth set.

Budge's collapse after he had the Englishman virtually stashed away in his pocket stunned the gallery. Budge was slender but appeared sinewy and athletically strong. He was only 21 and there appeared no reason, even attacking the net as aggressively as he did, why he should not be able to stand up under a normal five-set match.

Later the cat was let out of the bag. Don and Gene Mako were in the habit of spending their leisure hours listening to records, playing cards and belting thick, rich malted milks. Two days before the final, Budge's stomach became upset. The excessive malteds were blamed.

Still, Perry was the only player able to beat Budge on grass during the 1936 season and Don reaped a measure of revenge when he got the dark-haired Briton on asphalt in the Pacific Southwest tournament later in the summer. Shortly afterward, Perry turned professional, leaving Budge and Germany's Von Cramm to fight it out for the position of No. 1 amateur in the world.

If there was any doubt on whose shoulders the cloak of greatness would rest, it was quickly erased in 1937. Budge, his explosive power reaching its potential, swept through his early Davis Cup tests without the loss of a match. He smashed Japan's Jiro Yamagishi, 6-2, 6-2, 6-4. He won from Australia's Crawford and John Bromwich. He beat Parker and Von Cramm to win his first Wimbledon championship. Then he climaxed his European campaign with an historic victory over Von Cramm in the fifth and deciding match of the Davis Cup Inter-Zone final with Germany at Wimbledon. Many observers rated it the greatest Davis Cup match ever played.

Budge says he can recall the details as if the match had been played yesterday. "War talk was all over," Budge recalls. "Hitler was doing everything he could to stir up Germany. The atmosphere was filled with tension although Von Cramm was a known anti-Nazi and remained one of the finest gentlemen and most popular players on the circuit.

"The two teams had split the first four matches, so the whole works hinged on our final singles. I remember just before we took the court, Von Cramm was called to the telephone. It was a long distance call from Hitler himself exhorting him to win for the Fatherland. He came out, pale and serious, and playing the tennis of his life, he won the first two sets.

"I came back to win the next two sets but Von Cramm shot ahead 4-1 in the fifth. I realized I would lose the match unless I took drastic measures. I made up my mind that if Von Cramm missed his first service I would attack his second service and go to the net behind it. After I'd held service to make it 2-4, I broke him at love for 3-4.

"We held service until the score went to 6-6. Then I broke him again by attacking his second service. Five times I had match point on my service and five times I couldn't make it. Then came the sixth match point and the nervous strain was something fantastic. The crowd was so quiet I was sure they could hear us breathing. My frustration at failing to clinch my many opportunities was mounting.

"Finally, on the sixth match point, we had a long rally in the forecourt. Von Cramm lobbed over my head. I ran back and returned the ball. He hit a forehand cross-court wide to the forehand and came up to the net. I tore after the ball. I was afraid I'd never reach it. I stretched and finally took a desperate swipe at it. As I swung I lost my footing and hit the ground on all fours.

"As I lay on the grass I realized the ball felt pretty good on the racket. I looked up in time to see Von Cramm try to reach it on his right-hand side and miss it. So Cap Pete said he never saw me fall, did he? Well, I fell that time, and it was the most beautiful fall of my life."

An English reporter and tennis authority, Wallace Meyers, kept a detailed chart of the match and came up with some amazing figures. Normally a player is regarded as producing very good tennis if he can score 40 per cent of his points on winners. A 50-50 ratio of placements and errors in a match is figured excellent. In the Budge-Von Cramm match, which Don won, 6-8, 5-7, 6-4, 6-2, 8-6, the German had 105 placements, only 65 errors and 17 service aces. Budge made 55 errors, 115 placements and had 19 aces.

"The match ended around 8:45 at night," Budge said. "It was still light when Gottfried and I went to the dressing room to shower. An hour and a half later we came out to find most of the crowd still there—in semi-darkness—still buzzing about the match. I don't remember that happening in any other match of my career."

Encouraged by this victory, Budge beat Britain's

Charlie Hare and Bunny Austin in the Challenge Round and teamed with Mako to win the doubles. With a singles victory by Frankie Parker, the United States took the series, 4-1, and recaptured the big silver trophy which hadn't been on American shores since 1926. The red-haired, freckle-faced Californian returned home a conquering hero and reaffirmed his position as the best amateur tennis player in the world by winning his own national championship at Forest Hills. He swept into the finals without losing a set and then scored his third straight triumph over Von Cramm.

There was some surprise when Budge, having attained the game's highest pinnacle, declined to turn pro, telling intimates he felt he owed more to the game and that such a move would be selfish. Then followed the spectacular campaign which will be the goal of young tennis players for years to come. Some say it will never be matched.

Budge began the 1938 season by winning the Australian national championship. He took the French title and swept to his second straight Wimbledon crown without the loss of a set. He helped defend the Davis Cup against the Australian challenge at the Germantown, Pa., Cricket Club, beating John Bromwich and Adrian Quist. He lost only one set in retaining his United States crown at Forest Hills—thus completing his famous "Grand Slam" of major amateur titles which remains unparalleled.

In the fall of 1938, Don turned professional. "I don't feel my debt to the tennis association has been squared in full," he said, "but I'm sure they will realize I now have to think of my future.

"For my father and mother I want to buy a nice home in California and get them settled. I want to give them something a little better than they've had, to provide a few more comforts for them. They've made plenty of sacrifices for me."

No rancor could be found among the sternest of the tennis brass when the popular redhead—just 23—made his professional debut against Ellsworth Vines before a crowd of some 16,000 at Madison Square Garden on January 3, 1939. Budge adjusted himself to the strange indoor conditions and won the match. He won the tour from Vines, 21 matches to 18, and then took on his old amateur adversary and nemesis, Fred Perry, winning this series, 18-11.

In 1940, Budge won a tour which included Perry, Bobby Riggs and Frank Kovacs, and in 1941, just before the war broke, he crushed an aging but still brilliant Tilden, 51 matches to seven. Don went into the service with the Air Force, and after five years, returned to the pro circuit. Overweight and overage, he lost a tour to Riggs by the margin of two matches, 23-21. This was a signal for him to quit competition.

There was one tenet that Budge adopted early and followed throughout his career. "When a player arrives at a tournament, one of the first things he does is look at the draw," Don says. "I made up my mind a long time ago never to look at a draw under the premise that if I were good enough to win a tournament I was good enough to beat anyone."

No longer active in competition but still a fine player, the great all-time champion has not lost his love for the game. He is helping fight the war to keep tennis alive and strong.

"Tennis is a marvelous game," he says, "but I think it is the only sport that has not been realistic and progressed with the times. For one thing, we need open competition. Permitting amateurs to play with professionals would give the sport a new spark, new fan appeal.

"I recall during the war when I was the top professional and Jack Kramer was the leading amateur, we played a match for the fourth War Bond drive and sold $4,000,000 worth of bonds in one night. Then there was the Art Larsen benefit a few years ago at the Seventh Regiment Armory in New York. It was announced that both professionals and amateurs would be on the card. The place was a sellout and people were turned away.

"Another matter I feel strongly about is that of court surface. We should adopt a uniform surface for Davis Cup and other international competition. Of the some 40 or more nations who play for the Cup, only three have grass—the United States, Britain and Australia. It's unfair to all the others—the big majority—who must adjust to this strange surface."

A successful businessman in New York, Budge owns a part interest in the midtown Budge-Wood Services, which handles the laundry for the Waldorf-Astoria and many other establishments. He is associated with big brother Lloyd in the Budge Tennis Corp., which builds tennis courts. "You name it and we'll put it down," says Don.

The retired racket wizard and his pretty, brunette wife, Deirdre, have two strapping teen-age sons. Are they future tennis champs? "Not a chance," Budge says wryly. "Like me, they're nuts about baseball."

Coming
of Age
1946-1967

Gussie Moran, 1949
A California gal, aided and
abetted by a prominent couturier,
brings lace panties—and heartfelt gasps—to staid Wimbledon

Section **2**

RECORDS – TOURNAMENTS WON, ONE SEASON, SINGLES

MEN
19—Rod Laver, 1962
18—Rod Laver, 1969
17—Guillermo Vilas, 1977
15—Ivan Lendl, 1982
15—Ilie Nastase, 1973

WOMEN
21—Margaret Smith Court, 1970
18—Margaret Smith Court, 1973
17—Billie Jean King, 1971
16—Chris Evert, 1974-1975
16—Martina Navratilova, 1983

Chapter 5

A Game Divided

Frank Parker (left), Pancho Segura, Jack Kramer, Pancho Gonzalez The Bad Boys of Professional Tennis, circa 1949-50.

World War II was over and international tennis resumed much as before with many of the old names, but also a group of new champions such as Jack Kramer, Pancho Gonzalez and Dinny Pails, bursting from uniform. Unfortunately, despite agitation for a broader outlook, the conservative officials who operated the largely amateur game could not find it in their best self-interest to integrate pros and amateurs into 'open' tennis, emulating golf.

Thus the great divide of the 1930s remained, keeping the game fractured and probably stifling its growth. In this schizophrenic world of big-time tennis, so-called amateurs held sway in the conventional tournaments, anchored by the four majors—the Australian, French, Wimbledon and U.S.—plus the Davis Cup. On the other side, the declared professionals wandered almost anonymously, city to city, continent to continent, a gypsy band on a treadmill of one-nighters plus a few tournaments. They took their money in broad daylight, on the table, but in doing so, reaped minimal attention when compared to the 'shamateurs', who were often paid generous 'expenses' as gate-primers by tournaments or by their national federations, thereby maintaining their eligibility for team events such as the Davis and, later, Federation Cups.

Down Under, a dynasty was forming, with the blossoming Aussies—Frank Sedgman, Lew Hoad, Ken Rosewall, Roy Emerson, Rod Laver et al—placed on sporting goods firms' payroll to maintain their amateur standing as long as possible. But at the same time, burgeoning air travel was making the Australian Championships—and, therefore, the prospect of the elusive Grand Slam—accessible to all, and the game more far flung than ever.

1946

Advantage U.S. as game revives

Margaret Osborne
A French singles crown, one of 36 major titles in career.

The year 1946 was one of reconstruction for international tennis. The French and Wimbledon championships and the Davis Cup had last been played in 1939, the Australian Championships in 1940. The U.S. Championships had continued uninterrupted, although greatly reduced in number of entrants.

Jack Kramer, who had entered the Coast Guard as a seaman and was discharged as a lieutenant after seeing action in the Pacific, returned at the age of 24 to claim the No. 1 U.S. ranking that had been predicted for him since 1942.

It was comparatively easy re-starting championships in countries that had not been ravaged by the war. In Australia, John Bromwich re-established a linkage with the prewar era. He had been the 1939 singles champion and regained the Australian title with a five-set victory over countryman Dinny Pails, 5-7, 6-3, 7-5, 3-6, 6-2. In doubles, it was as if the war had never occurred: Adrian Quist, who had won his national doubles title with Don Turnbull in 1936 and 1937 and with Bromwich in 1938, 1939 and 1940, successfully teamed with Bromwich once again, re-establishing a monopoly that would last through 1950.

In Paris, French tennis fans crowned the first native champion since Henri Cochet in 1932: Left-hander Marcel Bernard. Intending to play only doubles, the 32-year-old Bernard was put in the draw when another player dropped out, and he upset the favorite, Czech Jaroslav

Drobny, 3-6, 2-6, 6-1, 6-4, 6-3. Then he teamed with countryman Yvon Petra to win the doubles.

More startling was Petra's triumph in the singles at Wimbledon, the first Frenchman to win there since Cochet beat Jean Borotra in the all-French final of 1929. (Borotra was refused entry to Wimbledon in 1946 because he had been Minister of Sport in the Vichy government of France, though he was later a Nazi prisoner.)

Kramer, though seeded second, was the favorite, but was done in by a nasty blister on his right hand that had caused him to default at the Queen's Club tune-up tournament the week before. Kramer gave full credit to slick shot-maker Drobny, who beat him in the fourth round, 2-6, 17-15, 6-3, 3-6, 6-3, after Kramer had lost only five games in the three previous rounds despite his ailment.

Pails, 25, was the top seed, but he got lost on the London Underground on his way to Wimbledon for his quarter-final match and arrived late. Unsettled, he lost to the fifth-seeded Petra in four sets, 7-5, 7-5, 6-8, 6-4. Petra—a lanky 6-foot-5 with less than polished strokes—then reached the final by beating San Franciscan Tom Brown, 4-6, 4-6, 6-3, 7-5, 8-6. Petra did not figure to have a chance in the final against Australian Geoff Brown, a player of medium build with a devastating serve and great pace on the rest of his shots, the first to show a two-fisted backhand in a Wimbledon singles final. But Brown made the curious tactical miscalculation of trying to slow-ball during the first two sets. He did win the third and fourth, but by that time was psychologically exhausted, and when he dropped his serve in the opening game of the fifth set, Petra ran out the match, 6-2, 6-4, 7-9, 5-7, 6-4. The Big W had its loftiest champ.

Kramer, playing with his damaged racket hand encased in bandages and a glove, dominated the doubles final, teaming with Tom Brown for a straight-set victory over Geoff Brown and Pails, 6-4, 6-4, 6-2.

There had been some reluctance on the part of the All England Lawn Tennis & Croquet Club to stage the Championships at all in 1946. The club had been heavily damaged by German bombs, and a gaping hole in the Centre Court competitors' stand and adjacent seats had to be cordoned off. The organizing committee did not want to have a tournament if Wimbledon's prewar standards of preeminence could not be maintained. Colonel Duncan Macaulay, who returned as the club's full-time secretary after the war, summarized the obstacles in his book *Behind the Scenes at Wimbledon:*

"The groundsmen were not back from the war, the mowers wouldn't work, the rollers wouldn't roll, nothing would function. We were surrounded by bomb-shelters, improvised buildings and huts of every sort. The back part of the club was covered with broken glass as a result of flying bombs. Britain was under a tight wartime economy and nothing could be obtained without a license or a coupon. There was the difficulty of supplies of balls and rackets and the printing of tickets. Paper was very short. Soap, too, was strictly rationed. Clothes were rationed and tennis flannels and costumes were almost non-existent. And of course, food was rationed, too— and there would be hungry thousands to be fed each day. The club's ration of whiskey was one bottle a month!"

Nevertheless, with customary efficiency and industry, the Championships was staged and again established as a showcase of the tennis world. There was considerable drama on court, both because of the early upsets of the favorites and the uncertainty of form that resulted from the wartime hiatus.

One fact amply demonstrated was the superiority of American women, who put a stranglehold on their side of the game in the immediate postwar years and maintained it through the 1950s, until Australia, Latin America, and Europe again began producing champions in the early 1960s.

Macaulay explained the phenomenon quite logically. "Least upset by the war of all the lawn tennis-playing nations was the United States. Whereas lawn tennis in

1946 THE MAJOR CHAMPIONSHIPS

Australian Championships
Men's Singles: John Bromwich
Women's Singles: Nancye Wynne Bolton
Men's Doubles: John Bromwich / Adrian Quist
Women's Doubles: Joyce Fitch / Mary Bevis
Mixed Doubles: Nancye Wynne Bolton / Colin Long
French Championships
Men's Singles: Marcel Bernard
Women's Singles: Margaret Osborne
Men's Doubles: Marcel Bernard / Yvon Petra
Women's Doubles: Louise Brough / Margaret Osborne
Mixed Doubles: Pauline Betz / Budge Patty
Wimbledon
Men's Singles: Yvon Petra
Women's Singles: Pauline Betz
Men's Doubles: Tom Brown / Jack Kramer
Women's Doubles: Louise Brough / Margaret Osborne
Mixed Doubles: Louise Brough / Tom Brown
U.S. Championships
Men's Singles: Jack Kramer
Women's Singles: Pauline Betz
Men's Doubles: Gardnar Mulloy / Bill Talbert
Women's Doubles: Louise Brough / Margaret Osborne
Mixed Doubles: Margaret Osborne / Bill Talbert

Britain and on the Continent closed down completely during the war and only started up again with many creaks and groans, with ruined courts and grave shortages of equipment, the American lawn tennis courts and clubs remained in being and the U.S. Championships continued all through the war. It was in the sphere of women's tennis that the United States gained such a tremendous advantage during these years."

Few non-Australian women ventured Down Under in those days, so the Australian Championships remained a native affair. Nancye Wynne, the 1940 champ, had become Mrs. Bolton, and continued on top, 6-4, 6-4, over Joyce Fitch. But American women won just about every other title of consequence, setting the pattern for ensuing years.

Margaret Osborne, saving two match points, defeated Pauline Betz, 1-6, 8-6, 7-5, in the French final (Pauline had led 6-5, 40-15, in the second). They teamed with Louise Brough and Doris Hart to rout Great Britain in the resumption of the Wightman Cup at Wimbledon. The Americans did not lose a set in romping, 7-0. None of the four had ever been to England before, but this was the strongest Wightman Cup team assembled to date, and they would all leave their mark.

Betz, an accomplished ground-stroker, lost only 20 games in six matches in winning her sole Wimbledon title, and overcame net-rusher Brough in the final, 6-2, 6-4. Betz had won the U.S. Championship in 1942-43-44, beating Brough the first two years and Osborne the third, but had been runner-up to Sarah Palfrey Cooke in 1945. In her sixth straight year as finalist, a female record, Pauline took her fourth title, 11-9, 6-3, over Hart. Winning her last 27 matches, she etched a marvelous season embellished with eight titles in a dozen tournaments.

Brough and Osborne teamed to win the first of their three French and five Wimbledon doubles titles. The two of them continued their homeland streak as the U.S. Doubles Championships returned to Boston, winning a fifth straight time, 6-1, 6-3, over Pat Canning Todd and Mary Arnold Prentiss,

But the sensation was the 74-game men's final, a third

trophy for Bill Talbert and Gardnar Mulloy, who sidestepped seven match points in the fifth set of the longest title bout, beating Frank Guernsey and Don McNeill, 3-6, 6-4, 2-6, 6-3, 20-18. Seeming beaten several times, the victors clung tough, Mulloy serving out of five match points (6-7, 0-40, and 10-11, 15-40) and Talbert two (13-14, 30-40 and out).

Don Budge and Bobby Riggs, the best players in the world immediately before the war, were antagonists again on the pro circuit. Riggs, who had succeeded Budge as Wimbledon and U.S. champ in 1939 and won the U.S. crown again in 1941, was signed by promoter Jack Harris when he got out of the service. In an abbreviated tour against Budge, Bobby won, 18 matches to 16, lobbing incessantly to take full advantage of Budge's ailing shoulder. He trounced Budge, 6-3, 6-1, 6-1, in the final of the U.S. Pro Championship, which went virtually unnoticed at the West Side Tennis Club.

The tournament that did draw attention at Forest Hills, naturally, was the U.S. Nationals, as America's premier tennis event was called before it became the U.S. Open in 1968. It was here that Jack Kramer finally assumed the crown and top ranking that had been more or less reserved for him, as Hannibal Coons intimated in an article in Collier's in August 1946:

"Six-feet-one, powerfully built and a natural athlete, Jack Kramer has been the logical heir to the American tennis throne since he was fourteen. Successively U.S. Boys' and Interscholastic champion, a Davis Cupper at 18, and three times U.S. Doubles champion, twice with Schroeder and once with Parker, Kramer has for four years been shoved away from the singles title only by the whim of circumstance."

Kramer had re-established himself as a force in the game after his three-year military service by winning the singles (over Frank Parker, 8-6, 6-1, 9-7), the doubles (with Schroeder) and mixed doubles (with Helen Wills Moody Roark) without losing a set at the Southern California Championships at Los Angeles in May. His Wimbledon blisters had extended his reputation as 'the hard-luck kid,' but at Forest Hills there was no stopping him. Kramer had developed his aggressive, hard-hitting game on the concrete courts of the Los Angeles Tennis Club under the watchful eye of the longtime ironhanded developer of Southern California junior talent, Perry T. Jones, and his coach and onetime idol, Ellsworth Vines. Kramer always had a thunderous serve and forehand, and with the formidable backhand he developed

---

1946 CHAMPIONS AND LEADERS

Year-End Number One	**Davis Cup:** United States
Men: Jack Kramer	**Wightman Cup:** United States
Women: Pauline Betz	

on a South American exhibition tour in 1941 also in harness, he ravaged Tom Brown, 9-7, 6-3, 6-0. Brown had beaten defending champ Parker, 6-3, 6-4, 6-8, 3-6, 6-1, and Gar Mulloy, 6-4, 6-2, 6-4.

There was one task left for Kramer in 1946: Recovery of the Davis Cup. He had been an 18-year-old rookie for the U.S. in 1939, playing only doubles with Joe Hunt in a four-set loss to Adrian Quist and John Bromwich as Australia won, 3-2. Now Kramer and his friend Schroeder, 12 days his senior, went to Melbourne's Kooyong in December and socked it to the Aussies, 5-0, the beginning of a four-year U.S. reign.

It was a contentious time for the Yanks. Capt. Walter Pate had tough choices to make with six hungry guys available. Parker and Mulloy thought they should play the doubles. Parker, Mulloy, Schroeder and Brown each thought he should have the other singles job with Kramer. Pate wanted to live-or-die with Schroeder all the way, a two-man lineup. When he announced his singles choices to the team, Audrey Parker, Frank's wife, was livid, saying that Pate had promised her man a singles job. The couple walked out. When Ted delivered in the opener, 3-6, 6-1, 6-2, 0-6, 6-2, over Bromwich, it was a parade that rained on 15,000 faithful jamming the concrete horseshoe. Kramer followed up by confounding Pails, 8-6, 6-2, 9-7, and the two net-swarming buddies wrapped it solidly, 6-2, 7-5, 6-4, over Bromwich and Quist. Audrey declared, "No singles for [the spurned] Frank, no doubles." That ruled out a Mulloy-Parker combination, and Schroeder-Kramer then seemed obvious, the team Pate wanted all along, the U.S. champs of 1941 who would repeat in 1947. Thus, the Cup was liberated from its seven-year wartime internment in Melbourne.

Kramer and Schroeder were the first Davis Cuppers to fly to Australia, then a four-day trip in a propeller-driven aircraft, a converted flying boat that, Schroeder recalls, "was lucky to make 75 mph against headwinds. We thought we'd never get there." The Aussies were sorry they did. Prior to 1946, tennis players had gone to Australia by boat, making the journey in a leisurely month, stopping off and playing exhibitions at ports en route to stay sharp.

1947

Signed and sealed, Kramer delivers

Jack Kramer
"A presence of unutterable awe"—at Wimbledon and beyond.

The tennis world returned to normal in 1947. Of the nine countries (Germany, Italy, Japan, Bulgaria, Finland, Hungary, Romania, Thailand and Libya) that had been expelled from the International Tennis Federation at its first postwar meeting in 1946, four (Italy, Hungary, Finland, and Romania) were readmitted, reflecting a cooling of hatreds that had been kindled by the war. This trend would continue.

If 1946 had marked Jack Kramer's emergence, 1947 verified his greatness. He dominated the amateur game, paving the way for the most significant professional contract of the era. Kramer did not play the Australian or French Championships. But he won the singles and doubles titles of Wimbledon and the U.S.

He also took both his singles as the U.S. defended the Davis Cup with a 4-1 victory over Australia at Forest Hills. Surprisingly Jack and Ted lost the doubles to Colin Long and Bromwich, 6-4, 2-6, 6-2, 6-4, stalling the procession until Ted clinched over a staunchly resisting Pails, 6-3, 8-6, 4-6, 9-11, 10-8. It was a near thing on damp, slick turf, Schroeder saving five set points in the second from 0-40, 5-6, and a match point with a serve-and-volley to reach 7-7 in the decisive fifth. Losing traction and falling frequently, Ted shed his socks and shoes in the second set and became a barefoot boy with a cheeky plan to attack the net incessantly. He then resorted to spikes (which Pails declined) in the sixth game of the fifth set, and went the rest of the way on barbed feet.

Pails and Bromwich were again the finalists in the Australian Championships, but this time Pails reversed the decision of the previous year in another five-setter, 4-6, 6-4, 3-6, 7-5, 8-6, for his only major singles title. Nancye Wynne Bolton beat Nell Hall Hopman, wife of the Australian Davis Cup captain, 6-3, 6-2, for the fourth of her six Australian singles titles. She also teamed with Thelma Long for the sixth of their 11 doubles titles together, re-grasping the championships they had captured from 1936 through 1940 under their maiden names of Wynne and Coyne.

Readmission of Hungary to the ITF permitted unseeded Joszef Asboth, an artistic clay court specialist, back into the international fixtures, and he won the French over South African Eric Sturgess, 8-6, 7-5, 6-4, a slim but accomplished player with superbly accurate ground strokes. Pat Canning Todd, a statuesque and graceful Californian who was largely overshadowed by her American contemporaries, beat Doris Hart for the French women's title, 6-3, 3-6, 6-4.

Hart, a remarkable player who had been stricken with a serious knee infection at age 11 and took up tennis to strengthen her right leg, beat Louise Brough, 2-6, 8-6, 6-4, in the semi-finals at Wimbledon, but had little left for Margaret Osborne in the final and was relegated to being runner-up, 6-2, 6-4. Brough and Osborne had successfully defended their French doubles title, but were dethroned in the Wimbledon final by Hart and Todd, despite holding three match points, 3-6, 6-4, 7-5.

The U.S. Wightman Cup team, a powerhouse—Brough, Osborne, Hart, Todd—goose-egged the Brits again, 7-0, at Forest Hills but did concede a couple of sets in the process. No. 1 Pauline Betz had won her first three tournaments of the year, including the U.S. Indoor over Hart, 6-2, 7-5, and had a 39-match streak going when the U.S. Tennis Association sternly suspended her indefinitely for merely discussing the possibility of turning pro. So she did, to barnstorm with Sarah Palfrey Cooke, with whom she'd split 18 matches as an amateur.

With Betz banished, Brough came through at the U.S., winning the first of her six major singles titles, beating her championship doubles partner, Osborne, 8-6, 4-6, 6-1. But she was fortunate to escape Aussie Bolton in the semis, 4-6, 6-1, 7-5. Bolton held three match points, serving at 5-2, 40-0 in the third, but lost the game. At 5-3 the match was blacked out by nightfall. Unluckily for Bolton, still so close to victory, the two had agreed beforehand to utilize a rule available at the time: To replay any set halted by curfew, which they did the following day. Brough, who had won the doubles

with Osborne at Longwood in Boston (a 5-7, 6-3, 7-5, battle with Hart and Todd) their sixth straight, also seized the mixed with John Bromwich, 6-3, 6-1, over Gussy Moran and Pancho Segura. That packaged a U.S. triple for Louise, last accomplished by Alice Marble in 1940.

Kramer's domination of Wimbledon was so great that ex-player John Olliff, longtime tennis correspondent of London's *Daily Telegraph*, referred to him as "a presence of unutterable awe." In his book *The Romance of Wimbledon,* Olliff recalls: "It became almost boring to watch him mowing down his victims when it was so obvious that nothing short of a physical injury could possibly prevent him from winning. He was an automaton of crushing consistency."

Kramer lost only 37 games in seven matches. In the quarter-finals he beat Geoff Brown, the 1946 runner-up, 6-0, 6-1, 6-3; in the semis, Dinny Pails, 6-1, 3-6, 6-1, 6-0, and in the final, Tom Brown, 6-1, 6-3, 6-2, in just 48 minutes. King George VI and Queen Elizabeth were in the Royal Box, and His Majesty presented the champion's trophy to Kramer, the first titlest in abbreviated costume, shorts, instead of long white flannels. It was the King's first visit to Wimbledon since, as the Duke of York, he had played in the men's doubles in 1926.

Ted Schroeder did not play Wimbledon, but Kramer teamed with Bob Falkenburg—another tall American with a big serve—to win the doubles without losing a set, the final 8-6, 6-3, 6-3, over the Anglo-Aussie alliance

1947 THE MAJOR CHAMPIONSHIPS

Australian Championships
Men's Singles: Dinny Pails
Women's Singles: Nancye Wynne Bolton
Men's Doubles: John Bromwich / Adrian Quist
Women's Doubles: Thelma Coyne Long / Nancye Wynne Bolton
Mixed Doubles: Nancye Wynne Bolton / Colin Long
French Championships
Men's Singles: Joszef Asboth
Women's Singles: Pat Canning Todd
Men's Doubles: Eustace Fannin / Eric Sturgess
Women's Doubles: Louise Brough / Margaret Osborne
Mixed Doubles: Sheila Piercey Summers / Eric Sturgess
Wimbledon
Men's Singles: Jack Kramer
Women's Singles: Margaret Osborne
Men's Doubles: Bob Falkenburg / Jack Kramer
Women's Doubles: Doris Hart / Pat Canning Todd
Mixed Doubles: Louise Brough / John Bromwich
U.S. Championships
Men's Singles: Jack Kramer
Women's Singles: Louise Brough
Men's Doubles: Jack Kramer / Ted Schroeder
Women's Doubles: Louise Brough / Margaret Osborne
Mixed Doubles: Louise Brough / John Bromwich

of Tony Mottram and Billy Sidwell. So on to Forest Hills. Kramer, who had won the U.S. Doubles in Boston — a fourth time, third with Schroeder — was again top-seeded in singles, considered a cinch winner. In fact, he had already signed on Sept. 3, 1947, with promoter Jack Harris to play a tour against Bobby Riggs in 1948. Riggs had beaten Don Budge on a short tour for the second consecutive year, 24 matches to 22 this time, and had edged Budge for the U.S. Pro title, 3-6, 6-3, 10-8, 4-6, 6-3. Kramer was to be the new challenger for pro king Riggs, but the deal—a no-no for an alleged amateur— had to be hushed up until after the U.S. Championships, ending Sept. 14.

Everything went according to plan until, as Kramer recalled in a *Sports Illustrated* article, "I almost blew the whole thing sky high. Here I was, signed and sealed for delivery to Riggs, and I lost the first two sets in the final to Frankie Parker. He was playing his best, but I did my best to help him. I can still remember looking up into the first row of the stadium seats and seeing the top of Jack Harris' bald head because he had it bowed forward in despair." But Kramer pulled himself together, starting the third set with two aces and the first of many winning drop shots. He purged the errors from his game and brought Harris back to life by winning the last three sets easily before a full house of 14,000, 4-6, 2-6, 6-1, 6-0, 6-3.

Allison Danzig, the venerable tennis writer of *The New York Times,* reported on the final: "Not since Sidney Wood tamed the lethal strokes of Ellsworth Vines at Seabright in 1930 with his soft-ball strategy and reduced the Californian to a state of helplessness, has so cleverly designed and executed a plan of battle been in evidence on American turf as Parker employed in this match.

"In the end, the plan failed, as the challenger's strength ebbed and the champion, extricating himself from a morass of errors, loosed the full fury of his attack to win in five sets. But the gallery would long remember the thrill and the chill of those first two sets and also the tense final chapter as the 31-year-old Parker gave his heavily favored and younger opponent the scare of his life."

Kramer exited amateurism on a 41-match streak. He had lost only once during the year, early to Bill Talbert in the Bahamas, taking eight of nine tournaments and going 48-1 in matches, including the U.S. Indoor over Bob Falkenburg, 6-1, 6-2, 6-2. Jack's match loss total after returning to civilian life in 1946: Three.

1947 CHAMPIONS AND LEADERS

Year-End Number One
Men: Jack Kramer
Women: Margaret Osborne duPont

Davis Cup: United States
Wightman Cup: United States

1948

Riggs hustled by young Jack

Pancho Gonzalez
Earns first of two straight U.S. titles at 20, only majors he would win.

Perhaps the most unforgettable event of the tennis year 1948 actually took place on December 26, 1947: Jack Kramer's professional debut against Bobby Riggs at Madison Square Garden as a raging blizzard buffeted New York.

"The city lay paralyzed by the heaviest snowfall in its history," was how esteemed columnist Red Smith recalled the night in *The New York Times* 30 years later. "Yet with taxis, buses, commuter trains and private cars stalled and the subways limping, 15,114 customers found their way into the big barn at Eighth Avenue and 50th Street."

Kramer, the top amateur of 1947, had been signed to face 1946-47 pro champ Riggs on a long tour. Francisco 'Pancho' Segura of Ecuador and Australian Dinny Pails came along as the preliminary attraction—'the donkey act,' in the vernacular of the tour. As was customary, the long and winding road of one-night stands began in the Garden, then the American Mecca of pro tennis.

Riggs won the opener, 6-2, 10-8, 4-6, 6-4, but Kramer gradually got accustomed to the grind of the tour and the style that playing night after night on a lightning-fast canvas court required. He learned to hit a high-kicking second serve to keep the quick and clever Riggs from scooting in behind his return, and to attack constantly, rushing the net on virtually every point and hammering away at Riggs' backhand.

"I began to really get comfortable with this new style around the time our tour reached San Francisco, when we were tied at 13 matches apiece," Kramer reminisced. "I won there, and then we flew to Denver, and Bobby got something started with the stewardess, and that gave me Denver, and then we went into Salt Lake City, where we played on a tremendously slick wood surface. Bobby couldn't handle my serve there, and all of a sudden it was 16-13. And that was it. Now he had to gamble on my serve. He had to take chances or I could get to the net, and he was dead. He was thoroughly demoralized."

By the time the tour worked its way through the hinterlands, a demoralized Riggs was 'tanking' matches. Kramer won 56 of the last 63, finishing with a 69-20 record, the last amateur to overthrow the pro king. Kramer, whose cut of the opening-night receipts at the Garden had been $8,800, earned $89,000. Riggs made $50,000.

Kramer also won the U.S. Pro Championships at Forest Hills. He had a tough match against Welby Van Horn in the quarter-finals, 3-6, 16-14, 4-6, 8-6, 6-4, then beat aging but still formidable Don Budge in the semi-finals, 6-4, 8-10, 3-6, 6-4, 6-0. Al Laney, who covered tennis for 50 years, many of them for the New York *Herald Tribune,* made no secret of his low regard for the pros "because for so many years they have preferred exhibitions to real tournaments," but he begrudgingly put this one on his list of all time memorable matches. The next day Kramer put away Riggs, 14-12, 6-2, 3-6, 6-3, becoming the undisputed ruler of the pros as he had been of the amateurs.

With Kramer out of the amateur ranks, three other Americans took major titles. Parker won the French over Czech lefty Jaroslav Drobny, 6-4, 7-5, 5-7, 8-6. Bob

1948 THE MAJOR CHAMPIONSHIPS

Australian Championships
Men's Singles: Adrian Quist
Women's Singles: Nancye Bolton
Men's Doubles: John Bromwich / Adrian Quist
Women's Doubles: Thelma Coyne Long / Nancye Wynne Bolton
Mixed Doubles: Nancye Wynne Bolton / Colin Long
French Championships
Men's Singles: Frank Parker
Women's Singles: Nelly Adamson Landry
Men's Doubles: Lennart Bergelin / Jaroslav Drobny
Women's Doubles: Doris Hart / Pat Canning Todd
Mixed Doubles: Pat Canning Todd / Jaroslav Drobny
Wimbledon
Men's Singles: Bob Falkenburg
Women's Singles: Louise Brough
Men's Doubles: John Bromwich / Frank Sedgman
Women's Doubles: Louise Brough / Margaret Osborne duPont
Mixed Doubles: Louise Brough / John Bromwich
U.S. Championships
Men's Singles: Pancho Gonzalez
Women's Singles: Margaret Osborne duPont
Men's Doubles: Gardnar Mulloy / Bill Talbert
Women's Doubles: Louise Brough / Margaret Osborne duPont
Mixed Doubles: Louise Brough / Tom Brown

Falkenburg startled Wimbledon by taking the men's singles over John Bromwich. Richard 'Pancho' Gonzalez stormed to the first of his back-to-back U.S. titles, over South African Eric Sturgess.

Adrian Quist, the last pre-war champ, had regained the Australian singles title over doubles partner Bromwich, 6-4, 3-6, 6-3, 2-6, 6-3, but was able to win only one set in the Davis Cup challenge round as Australia fell to the United States, 5-0, at Forest Hills. Parker—denied a singles berth in 1946 and 1947—and Ted Schroeder beat Quist and Billy Sidwell to sweep the four singles matches. The first day disaster for the Aussies: Parker over Sidwell, 6-4, 6-4, 6-4, Schroeder over 35-year-old Quist, 6-3, 4-6, 6-0, 6-0—gave them no chance. But clinching it was still up to the old firm, Bill Talbert, 30, and Gardnar Mulloy, 34, winners of their fourth U.S. Doubles title that year, over Parker and Schroeder, 1-6, 9-7, 6-3, 3-6, 9-7. Bill and Gar beat Sidwell and Colin Long, 8-6, 9-7, 2-6, 7-5, and the Cup stayed home.

Falkenburg, 23, was a 6-foot-3, skinny Californian who dawdled between points, apparently stalling to upset opponents, and threw games or whole sets to grab a breather and pace himself, sometimes actually lying down on the court. He later moved to Rio de Janeiro and played in the Davis Cup for Brazil. Seeded seventh, Falkie beat 20-year-old Aussie Frank Sedgman in the fourth round, 6-1, 6-2, 6-4. In the quarters he won, 6-4, 6-2, 3-6, 6-4, over Swede Lennart Bergelin (conqueror of top-seeded Parker in five sets, 5-7, 7-5, 9-7, 0-6, 10-8). An acrimonious conflict was his semi over Mulloy, 6-4, 6-4, 8-6, who objected to Falkenburg's delays. Then he met Bromwich, 29, in the final.

Lance Tingay, in his book *100 Years of Wimbledon,* described Falkenburg's topsy-turvy 7-5, 0-6, 6-3, 3-6, 7-5, victory: "Bromwich was a much-loved player. Not only did he have a gentle personality but a persuasively gentle game. Craft and skill and guile were his all, never muscle and pace. His racket was lightweight, the grip small and could have been a girl's. With a lefty forehand, he was doubled-fisted on the right. His ability to tease pace-making opponents into defeat by the accuracy of his slow returns was entrancing to watch. Falkenburg, having won the first set, 7-5, palpably threw the second at 6-0. The tactics were legitimate but they hardly endeared him to the crowd. He took the third set, 6-2. Bromwich won the fourth, 6-3. By then the effectiveness of Falkenburg's big serve had declined. And he was missing much with his forehand volley. Bromwich controlled the fifth set decisively, so much so that he led 5-2, 40-15, on his own service. On the two match points Falkenburg played shots that were pure gambles, screaming backhand returns of service. Bromwich had his third match point at advantage and Falkenburg repeated his performance. The Australian, who thought the last of the match point returns was going long, let it pass rather than volley the ball. When it landed as a winner Bromwich 'died' as an effective player. Falkenburg devoured the remaining games. If Bromwich was heartbroken he shared the sentiment with nearly every spectator round the court."

1948 CHAMPIONS AND LEADERS

Year-End Number One
Men: Frank Parker
Women: Margaret Osborne duPont

Davis Cup: United States
Wightman Cup: United States

1949

Lucky, Pancho lead U.S. charge

Gussy Moran "No one in their wildest dreams could have foreseen the furor, the outcry, the sensation..."

Ted Schroeder won the Wimbledon singles on his first and only attempt, and Richard 'Pancho' Gonzalez proved that he was not the 'cheese champion' some had called him. But 1949 will always be remembered as the year of Gertrude 'Gorgeous Gussy' Moran and the lace-trimmed panties that shocked Wimbledon.

Couturier Teddy Tinling, a tennis insider since he umpired matches for Suzanne Lenglen on the Riviera decades earlier, had waged a one-man battle against the unflattering white jersey and skirt that pretty much constituted women's tennis attire. He had experimented with touches of color on the dresses he made for Englishwoman Joy Gannon in 1947, without objection,

but ran into problems in 1948 when Mrs. Hazel Wightman, captain of the U.S. team playing for the Cup she had donated, objected to bits of color on the Tinling frock of British No. 1 Betty Hilton. This resulted in Wimbledon officials issuing an 'all-white' rule.

In 1949, unable to use color as requested by the attractive and sexy Californian Moran out of Santa Monica, Tinling put a half inch of lace trim around her panties, trying to satisfy Gussy's wish for some distinctive adornment. This was probably done innocently, but when the flamboyant Gussy posed for photographers at the pre-Wimbledon garden party at the Hurlingham Club, she caused a sensation. The first time she twirled on Centre Court a tremor went through the staid old arena. "Tennis was then suddenly treated to the spectacle of photographers lying flat on the ground trying to shoot Gussy's panties," Tinling remembered. The "coquettish" undergarment became the subject of Parliamentary debate and photo-stories on front pages around the world.

"No one in their wildest dreams could have foreseen the furor, the outcry, the sensation…" Tinling wrote. "Wimbledon interpreted the lace as an intentional device, a sinister plot by Gussy and myself for the sole purpose of guiding men's eyes to her bottom. At Wimbledon I was told that I had put 'vulgarity and sin' into tennis, and I resigned the Master of Ceremonies job I had held there for 23 years." Fortunately, he continued designing for and dressing most post-war women champions.

The year had begun with Frank Sedgman, age 21, winning his first major title, beating John Bromwich, 6-3, 6-3, 6-2, in the final of the Australian Championships. Bromwich was thus runner-up for the third straight year after winning in 1946, but again captured the doubles with Adrian Quist—it seemed almost a formality by now, their seventh straight. So it was as well for Nancye Wynne Bolton and Thelma Coyne Long in the women's doubles, their eighth out of nine tourneys. But Doris Hart ended Bolton's quest for a fifth consecutive singles title. Her 6-3, 6-4 triumph in the final made Hart the first overseas champion since Californian Dodo Bundy in 1938.

Frank Parker defended his French singles title over the elegant Budge Patty, 6-3, 1-6, 6-1, 6-4, and teamed with Gonzalez to win the doubles. Margaret Osborne duPont recovered the singles title she had won in Paris in 1946, dethroning Nelly Landry, 7-5, 6-2, and teamed with Louise Brough to regain the doubles title they had won in 1946 and 1947.

At Wimbledon, spectators were anxious to see the man Americans called 'Lucky' Schroeder. Though almost 28, he had never played the world's premier championship, but was well known worldwide for his Davis Cup exploits. "Rather stocky, he had a rolling gait which made him look as though he had just got off a horse," remembered Lance Tingay. "Except when he was actually playing he always seemed to have a pipe in his mouth, a corn cob as often as not." Britons found him an intriguing character.

Top-seeded Schroeder lost the first two sets of his first-round match to the dangerous Gardnar Mulloy,

whom he had beaten in the final at Queen's Club just two days earlier, but rescued himself 3-6, 9-11, 6-1, 6-0, 7-5. In the quarters, he was again down two sets to Frank Sedgman, trailed 0-3 in the fifth, and had a match point against him at 4-5. He was called for a foot fault, but coolly followed his second serve to the net and hit a winning volley off the wood. He saved another match point at 5-6, this time with a bold backhand passing shot, and finally pulled out the match, 3-6, 6-8, 6-3, 6-2, 9-7, never having led until the final minutes.

Schroeder continued to live precariously, coming back from two sets to one down against Eric Sturgess in the semi-finals, 3-6, 7-5, 5-7, 6-1, 6-2. In the final, he had his fourth five-setter in seven matches, edging the popular Jaroslav Drobny, 3-6, 6-0, 6-3, 4-6, 6-4, after being within a point of a 0-2 deficit in the final set. 'Lucky' Schroeder, indeed; he was always living on the edge of the ledge.

The women's final came down to a memorable duel between the top two seeds, Louise Brough and duPont. Brough won the first set, 10-8, duPont the second, 6-1, and at 8-all in the third the difference between them was no more than the breadth of a blade of Wimbledon's celebrated grass. Brough served out of a 0-40 predicament like a champion, and then broke for the match and successful defense of her title.

Second-seeded Gonzalez, beaten in the fourth round by Aussie Geoff Brown, 2-6, 6-3, 6-2, 6-1, and Parker added the Wimbledon doubles to the French they had

---

1949 THE MAJOR CHAMPIONSHIPS

Australian Championships
Men's Singles: Frank Sedgman
Women's Singles: Doris Hart
Men's Doubles: John Bromwich / Adrian Quist
Women's Doubles: Thelma Coyne Long / Nancye Wynne Bolton
Mixed Doubles: Doris Hart / Frank Sedgman
French Championships
Men's Singles: Frank Parker
Women's Singles: Margaret Osborne duPont
Men's Doubles: Pancho Gonzalez / Frank Parker
Women's Doubles: Margaret Osborne duPont / Louise Brough
Mixed Doubles: Sheila Piercey Summers / Eric Sturgess
Wimbledon
Men's Singles: Ted Schroeder
Women's Singles: Louise Brough
Men's Doubles: Pancho Gonzalez / Frank Parker
Women's Doubles: Louise Brough / Margaret Osborne duPont
Mixed Doubles: Sheila Piercey Summers / Eric Sturgess
U.S. Championships
Men's Singles: Pancho Gonzalez
Women's Singles: Margaret Osborne duPont
Men's Doubles: John Bromwich / Bill Sidwell
Women's Doubles: Louise Brough / Margaret Osborne duPont
Mixed Doubles: Louise Brough / Eric Strugess

won earlier, over Mulloy and Schroeder, 6-4, 6-4, 6-2, while Brough and duPont joined forces to defend their title over Pat Todd and Moran. The score was 8-6, 7-5—close enough to prevent anyone from quipping that the champs had beaten the lace panties off Gorgeous Gussy.

The American women continued their relentless domination of the Wightman Cup, drubbing Great Britain, 7-0, at Haverford, Pa., riding the singles wins of duPont over Betty Hilton, 6-1, 6-3, and Jean Smith, 6-4, 6-2, and Hart over Smith, 6-3, 6-1, and Hilton, 6-1, 6-3.

Schroeder and Gonzalez gave the U.S. all four singles points as the U.S. men made it four straight victories over Australia in the Davis Cup challenge round at Forest Hills, 4-1. Schroeder was up to his usual five set high-jinks in the opening match, beating Bill Sidwell, 6-1, 5-7, 4-6, 6-2, 6-3, but he put away Sedgman in straight sets, 6-4, 6-3, 6-3, to clinch. Gonzalez made it 2-0 over Sedgman, 8-6, 6-4, 9-7. The Americans lost only the doubles. Sidwell and Bromwich, who also won the 1949 U.S. Doubles at Longwood, beating Bill Talbert and Gar Mulloy, 3-6, 4-6, 10-8, 9-7, 9-7.

There was keen interest in a Schroeder-Gonzalez U.S. Championships showdown at Forest Hills. Because Gonzalez had gone out early to Geoff Brown at Wimbledon, there was speculation that his 1948 U.S. victory had been a fluke. One writer flatly called him a 'cheese champ'—which is one version of how Gonzalez got his nickname, 'Gorgo,' short for 'Gorgonzola.' The other that stuck over the long run was that his colleagues on the pro tour, which consumed his best years, felt he acted like the big cheese (which he did, and was). Gonzalez cared neither for 'Gorgo' nor 'Pancho,' and those close to him used Richard.

Gonzalez was taken to five sets by lefty Art Larsen, 4-6, 6-1, 6-3, 2-6, 6-1, and four by Parker, who let him off the hook in the semis, 3-6, 9-7, 6-3, 6-2. Schroeder was pushed to the limit by Sedgman in the quarters, 6-3, 0-6, 6-4, 6-8, 6-4, and Bill Talbert in the semis, 2-6, 6-4, 4-6, 6-4, 6-4. But finally the men people wanted to see arrived safely in the final.

The old 15,000-seat horseshoe stadium at the West Side Tennis Club was packed and tense as Schroeder and Gonzalez fought to 16-all in the first set. Gonzalez, who was 1-7 against Schroeder, fell behind 0-40, but three big serves got him up to deuce. A net-cord winner gave Schroeder another break point, and Gonzalez lost his serve on a volley that he thought was good. A linesman

called it wide. Schroeder served out the set, then donned spikes on the slippery turf and quickly ran out the second set, 6-2. Gonzalez seethed.

But Pancho always had a knack of channeling his temper, and he turned the rage surging within him to his advantage. Serving and attacking furiously, he achieved one of the great Forest Hills comebacks, 16-18, 2-6, 6-1, 6-2, 6-4, serving 27 aces, 16 of them in the 73-minute first set. Kissing his racket before serving the concluding game, Gonzalez had to smack his way out of a break point, and, on match point could only watch helplessly as Ted passed him with a forehand—that fell barely wide.

duPont, meanwhile, won her second major title of the year, easily, 6-4, 6-1 victory over Hart in the other final, after the sure-thing firm of Brough-duPont rolled to their eighth U.S. Doubles in a row, over Shirley Fry and Hart, 6-4, 10-8. Margaret's pal, Louise, cost her a triple, however, in the mixed final where Brough and Eric Sturgess beat duPont and Bill Talbert, 4-6, 6-3, 7-5.

Jack Harris had quit the promotional game after the successful Kramer-Riggs tour. The new promoter was Riggs, who had won the U.S. Pro title at Forest Hills over Don Budge, 9-7, 3-6, 6-3, 7-5, while Kramer sat out, awaiting a new amateur king.

That was supposed to be Schroeder, who actually had signed after winning Wimbledon but then changed his mind, deciding that his intense constitution was not suited for the nightly grind of the tour. If he had won at Forest Hills, Schroeder undoubtedly would have signed so as not to leave his old friend Kramer in the lurch. Kramer thought that in the back of his mind Schroeder wanted to lose to Gonzalez for that reason.

But in any event, Gonzalez, as two-time U.S. champ, became the only viable alternative, and Riggs signed him for the longest head-to-head tour yet. Frank Parker came along to play Pancho Segura in the prelims. The tour stretched from October 1949 to May 1950, and Kramer clobbered the talented but surly and immature Gonzalez, 96 matches to 27. Both players made $72,000, but the future seemed a dead end for Gonzalez, who was only 21 years old.

1949 CHAMPIONS AND LEADERS

Year-End Number One
Men: Pancho Gonzalez
Women: Margaret Osborne duPont

Davis Cup: United States
Wightman Cup: United States

1950

Althea tennis' Jackie Robinson

Budge Patty Third of four Wimbledon crowns.

The year 1950 was in many ways not only the start of a new decade, but also of a new era in tennis. With Jack Kramer, Pancho Gonzalez, and Frank Parker now pros, the American stranglehold on the international game was loosened. A new crop of Yanks was coming along, led by touch artists Art Larsen and Herbie Flam, the expatriate Californian Budge Patty and the forthright Tony Trabert and Vic Seixas. But Frank Sedgman, Ken McGregor and Mervyn Rose signaled a powerful new line of Australian resistance.

Germany and Japan were readmitted to the International Tennis Federation, indicating that wartime wounds had healed. The Italian Championships was played for the first time since 1935, revived by the energetic promotion of Carlo della Vida, who was intent on building it into one of the international showcases. Despite rains that threatened to flood the sunken Campo Centrale at Rome's Il Foro Italico, the tournament was a success, won by the clay court artist, Jaroslav Drobny, over Bill Talbert, 6-4, 6-3, 7-9, 6-2. Annelies Ullstein Bossi, an Austrian married to an Italian, took the women's prize over Brit Joan Curry, 6-4, 6-4. Not until Raffaela Reggi, 35 years later, did a female holder of an Italian passport win the title.

The self-exiled Czech, Drobny, who traveled on an Egyptian passport until becoming a British citizen in 1959, also won the German championship over enduring 41-year-old Baron Gottfried von Cramm, 6-3,

6-4, 6-4, an event, which had started to rebuild slowly as a Germans-only affair in 1948 and 1949. Von Cramm, the aristocratic and sporting pre-war star, had won both years. The Hamburg and Rome tournaments were destined to rise simultaneously to a stature just below the French Championships as the most important clay court events of Europe.

Sedgman, an athletic serve-and-volleyer with a crunching forehand, defeated McGregor for his second straight Australian singles title, 6-3, 6-4, 4-6, 6-1, while Adrian Quist and John Bromwich won their record eighth doubles title in a tight struggle with Drobny and Eric Sturgess, 6-3, 5-7, 4-6, 6-3, 8-6.

J. Edward 'Budge' Patty, an urbane California native who lived in Paris, won the French over Drobny in a duel of enchanting shot-making, 6-1, 6-2, 3-6, 5-7, 7-5. In his semi Patty needed seven match points to subdue Bill Talbert in a furious marathon, 2-6, 6-4, 4-6, 6-4, 12-10. Drobny, who had crawled through the traps laid by Vic Seixas in the quarters, 7-5, 17-15 (80 minutes for that set), 5-7, 6-4, had a rough semi, too, 6-4, 7-5, 3-6, 12-10, over Eric Sturgess. Patty then became the first player since Don Budge in 1938 to win the Paris-Wimbledon double, beating Frank Sedgman on grass, 6-1, 8-10, 6-2, 6-3, as gracefully as he had overcome Drobny on clay.

Patty was a great stylist, fluent on all his strokes and mesmerizing with the effortlessness of his forehand volley. He was also a painter and patron of the arts. "I have

1950 THE MAJOR CHAMPIONSHIPS

Australian Championships
Men's Singles: Frank Sedgman
Women's Singles: Louise Brough
Men's Doubles: John Bromwich / Adrian Quist
Women's Doubles: Louise Brough / Doris Hart
Mixed Doubles: Doris Hart / Frank Sedgman
French Championships
Men's Singles: Budge Patty
Women's Singles: Doris Hart
Men's Doubles: Bill Talbert / Tony Trabert
Women's Doubles: Doris Hart / Shirley Fry
Mixed Doubles: Barbara Scofield / Enrique Morea
Wimbledon
Men's Singles: Budge Patty
Women's Singles: Louise Brough
Men's Doubles: John Bromwich / Adrian Quist
Women's Doubles: Louise Brough / Margaret Osborne duPont
Mixed Doubles: Louise Brough / Eric Sturgess
U.S. Championships
Men's Singles: Art Larsen
Women's Singles: Margaret Osborne duPont
Men's Doubles: John Bromwich / Frank Sedgman
Women's Doubles: Louise Brough / Margaret Osborne duPont
Mixed Doubles: Margaret Osborne duPont / Ken McGregor

a way to go to catch Rembrandt, but Renoir doesn't stand a chance," he commented once, upon the opening of an exhibition of his canvases in Paris. "He gave the impression," noted journalist Lance Tingay, "of being the most sophisticated champion of all time."

Unsophisticated, flaky, eccentric, and totally original was Art 'Tappy' Larsen, so nicknamed because of his habit, one of many superstitions, of tapping objects from net posts to opponents in ritualistic 'good luck' sequences. Patty was known as a suave playboy who only occasionally trained; Larsen was an eager if unpolished ladies' man who never trained. But he had a great gift for the game, and magnificent touch, as he amply demonstrated in winning the U.S. title over his pal Flam in a lovely match of wits and angles, 6-3, 4-6, 5-7, 6-4, 6-3.

In doubles, Bill Talbert partnered his athletic 19-year-old Cincinnati protégé, Tony Trabert, also a star University of Cincinnati basketball guard, to the French title over Drobny and Sturgess, 6-2, 1-6, 10-8, 6-2. Quist and Bromwich won their only Wimbledon title together, outlasting Geoff Brown and Billy Sidwell, 7-5, 3-6, 6-3, 3-6, 6-2. Bromwich and Sedgman won the U.S. Doubles over four-time champs Talbert and Gardnar Mulloy, 7-5, 8-6, 3-6, 6-1.

Australia, with Harry Hopman returned to the captain's chair that he had occupied in victorious 1939, pried loose the four-year American grip on the Davis Cup with a 4-1 victory in the challenge round at Forest Hills. Sedgman walloped Tom Brown, 6-0, 8-6, 9-7, and surprise starter McGregor ambushed Ted Schroeder, 13-11, 6-3, 6-4, in the opening singles. Next day Sedgman and 31-year-old Bromwich—a holdover from '39—sealed the Aussie triumph by beating Schroeder and Mulloy in the doubles, 4-6, 6-4, 6-2, 4-6, 6-4, and the Cup was traveling south again.

America's women extended their monotonous superiority over Great Britain with another Wightman Cup bagel, 7-0 at Wimbledon, and hoarded all the major titles in singles and doubles. Margaret Osborne duPont and doubles accomplice Louise Brough did the heavy Wightman damage. Both beat Betty Hilton (Margaret, 6-3, 6-4; Louise, 2-6, 6-2, 7-5) and Jean Walker-Smith (Margaret, 6-3, 6-2; Louise, 6-0, 6-0). They also won a doubles over Kay Tuckey and Hilton, 6-2, 6-0.

The Australian final was the first all-American affair, Brough succeeding Doris Hart as champion with a 6-4, 3-6, 6-4 victory over defender Doris. They then teamed to win the doubles, interrupting the long reign of eight-time champions Nancye Bolton and Thelma Long, 6-2, 2-6, 6-3.

Hart won her first French singles, over Pat Todd, 6-4, 4-6, 6-2. Brough and duPont were not only beaten in singles, but the three-time champs lost in the doubles final by Shirley Fry and Hart, 1-6, 7-5, 6-2, despite holding a match point in the second. Italian Annalies Bossi felt lonely in the quarters surrounded by seven Americans. In the semis Todd beat Schofield, 6-2, 6-3.

Brough won her third straight Wimbledon title, beating duPont, 6-1, 3-6, 6-1. Then they shared the same side of the court to grab a fourth doubles championship, avenging the French defeat by beating Fry and Hart, 6-4, 5-7, 6-1. Coupling with Sturgess, Louise completed a triple with the mixed prize, 11-9, 1-6, 6-4, over Todd and Geoff Brown, duplicating her 1948 acquisition. It was her fourth mixed title, with a third collaborator, in five years.

duPont took her third straight U.S. crown, dispatching Hart in the final, 6-3, 6-3, after partnering Brough to their ninth straight doubles success in Boston, 6-2, 6-3, over Fry and Hart. Margaret found an Aussie escort, McGregor, to cement a triple of her own. They won the mixed over Hart and the other Aussie Davis Cup burglar, Sedgman, 6-4, 3-6, 6-3.

An historic breakthrough was the appearance of a future champion and Hall of Famer, 23-year-old Althea Gibson, the first black American to play in the U.S. Championships at Forest Hills. (Athough she had been admitted to the U.S. Indoor in 1949, winning a round, and again, earlier in 1950, to beat Midge Gladman Buck, 6-2, 4-6, 7-5, and reach the final, a 6-0, 6-2, defeat by Nancy Chaffee.) But Forest Hills was the biggie that everybody noticed, and Althea's was a leap of the color bar in tennis every bit as significant as Jackie Robinson's debut with the Brooklyn Dodgers had been three years before. To cement that reality, Gibson nearly toppled the Wimbledon champ, fourth-seeded Louise Brough, in the second round.

Starting off with a prophetic victory over Barbara Knapp, 6-2, 6-2, Gibson overcame nerves and a 1-6 opening set against Brough to seize the second, 6-3. As the sky darkened, Gibson battled to a 7-6 lead in the decisive set. At that moment Brough may have been reprieved: Forest Hills was struck by a thunderstorm so fierce that lightning knocked one of the brooding concrete eagles from the upper rim of the stadium. Resuming the following afternoon, Gibson may have had too much time to think about victory lying within her long reach—four points away. Brough held serve, and won the next two games to escape, 6-1, 3-6, 9-7.

"When lightning put down that eagle," Gibson laughed, "maybe it was an omen times was a-changing. Brough was a little too experienced for me in that situation, but my day would come." And so it did with titles in 1957 and 1958.

A new order was brought to the U.S. Pro Championship as Pancho Segura knocked off Jack Kramer in the semis, 6-4, 8-10, 1-6, 6-4, 6-3, while Frank Kovacs uprooted 1949 champ Bobby Riggs, 6-2, 6-3, 5-7, 7-5. Kovacs broke down with cramps in the final, a 6-4, 1-6, 8-6, 4-4 TKO for Segura. There was no amateur recruit to challenge Kramer for supremacy of the pro game, but Riggs put together a tour with Segura—the swarthy little Ecuadorian with bowed legs, a murderous two-fisted forehand and enormous competitive heart—as the challenger at $1,000 per week salary against 5 percent of the gate. Kramer got 25 percent. Unfortunately, the cunning 'Segoo' simply could not handle Kramer's big serve on fast indoor courts, and the tour was not competitive. Riggs tried to spice it up by signing Gussy Moran to a lucrative contract—$35,000 guaranteed, against 25 percent of profits—to play Pauline Betz. Gussy got tremendous publicity as the glamour girl of the lace pants, but she was not in the same class with Betz, who was overwhelming even after Riggs suggested she try to "carry" her fashionable but outclassed opponent.

The tour was an artistic, competitive, and financial flop. Kramer was still the king, Segura went back to being a prelim boy, Moran tried to make it in showbiz, and Betz, who married noted *Washington Post* sportswriter Bob Addie, became a respected teaching pro in Washington.

1950 CHAMPIONS AND LEADERS

Year-End Number One
Men: Budge Patty
Women: Margaret Osborne duPont

Davis Cup: Australia
Wightman Cup: United States

1951

Australian dynasty gathers steam

Dick Savitt
Seventh U.S. male to win major singles title since war's end.

The new era continued to take shape on the world's tennis courts in 1951. American Dick Savitt surprisingly won the Australian and Wimbledon singles titles, but Frank Sedgman and Ken McGregor helped forge the foundation of a new Australian dynasty, holding onto the Davis Cup and fashioning the only male Grand Slam of doubles. Meanwhile, American women continued their postwar supremacy, but the dominance of Louise Brough, Margaret Osborne duPont, Doris Hart and Shirley Fry was challenged by a stirring new teen-age talent: Maureen Connolly.

Savitt, 24, a rawboned and hulking competitor from Orange, N.J., and Cornell University, sported a big serve, a solid ground game, and an impressive, hard-hit backhand. He was the first American to win the Australian singles—in fact, the first non-Australian finalist—since Don Budge in 1938. He deposed the champ, Sedgman, 2-6, 7-5, 1-6, 6-3, 6-4, and beat McGregor, 6-3, 2-6, 6-3, 6-1. Sedgman and McGregor, in closing down the supremacy of John Bromwich and Adrian Quist—Australian doubles champs eight consecutive times from 1938—kicked off their unique Grand Slam in the stubbornly fought final, 11-9, 2-6, 6-3, 4-6, 6-3.

Like Ted Schroeder two years earlier, sixth-seeded Savitt won Wimbledon on his first attempt. He was aided by Herbie Flam's defeat of top-seeded Sedgman from two sets down in the quarters, 2-6, 1-6, 6-3, 6-4, 7-5, as well as Englishman Tony Mottram's third-round upset of second-seeded Jaroslav Drobny and defending champion Budge Patty's demise in the second round, at the hands of former Tulane star Ham Richardson.

Savitt also had a narrow escape from Flam, whom the BBC's extraordinary radio commentator Max Robertson called "the Paul Newman of tennis players, with hunched and self-deprecating look." Savitt trailed 1-6, 1-5 in the semi-finals before salvaging the second set, 15-13, to turn the match a round. "A couple of points the other way and my whole life might have been different," Savitt mused on the occasion of Wimbledon's Centenary 'parade of champions' in 1977. As it happened, he lost only five games in the third and fourth sets against Flam, 1-6, 15-13, 6-3, 6-2, and then chastened McGregor in the final, 6-4, 6-4, 6-4. Title No. 3 in their circumnavigating Slam was hotly contested, too, but Sedgman and McGregor successfully resisted Jaroslav Drobny and Eric Sturgess, 3-6, 6-2, 6-3, 3-6, 6-3.

Drobny, the crafty left-hander with mournful countenance, spectacles, and a wonderful repertoire of touch and spin to go with his tricky serve, defeated Eric Sturgess, 6-3, 6-3, 6-3, to win the French singles for the first time after being runner-up in 1946, 1948 and 1950. Americans in Paris were in the way of Slam-happy Sedgman and McGregor, but Gar Mulloy and Savitt couldn't derail them in the final, 6-2, 2-6, 9-7, 7-5.

Sedgman, the personification of robust Australian fitness with an unerring forehand volley, atoned for his Wimbledon failure by winning the first of back-to-back U.S. titles. He was the first Australian player to win the U.S., and the first in the final since Jack Crawford lost to Fred Perry in 1933. Sedgman got there in devastating form, ravaging defending champion Art Larsen in the semi-finals, 6-1, 6-2, 6-0, in just 49 minutes, the worst beating ever inflicted on a title-holder. Wrote Allison Danzig in the *New York Times*, "The radiance of the performance turned in by the 23-year-old Sedgman has not often been equaled. With his easy, almost effortless production of stabbing strokes, he pierced the dazed champion's defenses to score at will with a regularity and dispatch that made Larsen's plight almost pitiable."

In the final against seventh-seeded Philadelphian Vic Seixas, Sedgman was nearly as awesome, winning 6-4, 6-1, 6-1. Seixas had played superbly until then, beating McGregor, 4-6, 7-5, 7-5, 6-4; Flam, 1-6, 9-7, 2-6, 6-2, 6-3; then Savitt in the semi-finals, 6-0, 3-6, 6-3, 6-2. Savitt was the top seed, but severely hobbled by an infected left leg, which had to be lanced the day before he faced Seixas.

Sedgman and McGregor's superb cohabitation of a tennis court (Ken on the right) resulted in a tale of two cities finish of their Grand Slam that should have been saluted in lights—except that it all happened in daylight. Rain delayed them after three victories at the usual U.S. Doubles site, Boston's Longwood Cricket Club, and the final was re-scheduled for the following week as part of the carnival of Forest Hills. It was an entirely Aussie gala, Frank and Ken downing the would-be party-poopers, Mervyn Rose and Don Candy, 10-8, 6-4, 4-6, 7-5. Forest Hills was solidly Sedgman since he also won the mixed with Hart over Fry and Rose, 6-3, 6-2.

Savitt had played zone matches against Japan (re-admitted to the Davis Cup, along with Germany, for the first time since the war) and Canada. But Capt. Frank Shields passed him over—angering him and many supporters—for the challenge round in Sydney. Seixas handled lefty Mervyn Rose, 6-3, 6-4, 9-7 and Sedgman beat Ted Schroeder, 6-4, 6-3, 4-6, 6-4 to make it 1-1 on opening day, but the series hinged on the doubles. Schroeder had one of his worst days—"I wanted to cry

1951 THE MAJOR CHAMPIONSHIPS

Australian Championships
Men's Singles: Dick Savitt
Women's Singles: Nancye Bolton
Men's Doubles: Ken McGregor / Frank Sedgman
Women's Doubles: Thelma Coyne Long / Nancye Wynne Bolton
Mixed Doubles: Thelma Coyne Long / George Worthington
French Championships
Men's Singles: Jaroslav Drobny
Women's Singles: Shirley Fry
Men's Doubles: Ken McGregor / Frank Sedgman
Women's Doubles: Doris Hart / Shirley Fry
Mixed Doubles: Doris Hart / Frank Sedgman
Wimbledon
Men's Singles: Dick Savitt
Women's Singles: Doris Hart
Men's Doubles: Ken McGregor / Frank Sedgman
Women's Doubles: Shirley Fry / Doris Hart
Mixed Doubles: Doris Hart / Frank Sedgman
U.S. Championships
Men's Singles: Frank Sedgman
Women's Singles: Maureen Connolly
Men's Doubles: Ken McGregor / Frank Sedgman
Women's Doubles: Shirley Fry / Doris Hart
Mixed Doubles: Doris Hart / Frank Sedgman

for him, he was so bad," recalls old friend Jack Kramer— and he and 21-year-old rookie Tony Trabert were beaten by Sedgman and McGregor, 6-2, 9-7, 6-3. Schroeder did pull himself together after a nervous, sleepless night to beat Rose in a gritty performance, 6-4, 13-11, 7-5. However, Sedgman continued as The Man of the Year, rolling over Seixas in the fifth match, 6-4, 6-2, 6-2, for a 3-2 Australian victory.

U.S. women cruised as expected in a 6-1 Wightman Cup victory over Britain at Longwood as 16-year-old Maureen 'Little Mo' Connolly got her sneakers wet in international competition, and delivered in her only start, 6-1, 6-3, over Kay Tuckey. In the absence of an overseas challenge, Nancye Bolton recaptured the Australian singles title over her partner Thelma Long, 6-1, 7-5, and the two of them took the doubles for the ninth time, 6-2, 6-1, over Mary Hawton and Joyce Fitch.

But Americans again won everything else. Fry, persistent as ever from the backcourt, beat Hart in the French final, 6-3, 3-6, 6-3, but they were together to win the doubles.

Fry got her comeuppance at Wimbledon, where Hart thrashed her, 6-1, 6-0. This was Hart's only singles title at the Big W, where she had been runner-up in 1947 and 1948. She parlayed it into a triple, taking the women's doubles with Fry (starting a three-year rule) over perennials Margaret duPont and Louise Brough, 6-3, 13-11. Her mixed doubles with Sedgman came at the expense of Aussies Bolton and Rose, 7-5, 6-2. What a man's lady. Doris had the first of her five successive mixed triumphs, two with Sedgman and three with Vic Seixas.

After winning the U.S. Doubles at Longwood with Fry over Nancy Chaffee and Pat Todd, 6-4, 6-2, Hart was the top seed at Forest Hills. Everybody thought she was the best in the world, but Doris was given a rude jolt in the semi-finals by the kid, relatively inexperienced 16-year-old Maureen Connolly out of San Diego. Blasting her flawless groundstrokes from both wings,

Connolly overcame a 0-4 deficit to win the first set on a drizzly, miserable day, 6-4. Hart asked several times that the match be halted. It was, but Connolly won the second set the following afternoon, 6-4. In the final, the tenacious and mentally uncompromising fourth-seeded Connolly beat Fry, 6-3, 1-6, 6-4, for the first of three straight championships, becoming the greenest ever U.S. champion until Tracy Austin, a younger 16 in 1979. "I later kidded Maureen that she was lucky to beat me in '51," Hart has said. "But after that she became, unquestionably, the greatest woman player who ever lived."

A distasteful Forest Hills outburst by No. 7 American Earl Cochell brought swift retribution from the U.S. Tennis Association, a demonstration of the arbitrary power national associations held over players prior to the open era and the forming of player unions. Clearly Cochell was out of line in the fourth-rounder, a four-set loss, 4-6, 6-2, 6-1, 6-2, to Gar Mulloy. He acerbically questioned many line calls, erupted in bursts of temper, argued with the umpire and spectators, tried to climb the umpire's chair and grab the microphone to lecture the crowd, and blatantly threw a number of games, batting balls into the stands or playing left-handed (he was right-handed). What really did him in was his abusive verbal attack on the referee, Dr. Ellsworth Davenport, who reprimanded him.

The upshot was that the USTA suspended Cochell for life. Some years later the sentence was lifted, but Cochell, unfairly unranked for 1951, lost perhaps his best years.

It was Little Pancho (Segura) against Big Pancho (Gonzalez) for the U.S. Pro crown, and Segura defended successfully at Forest Hills, 6-3, 6-4, 6-2.

1951 CHAMPIONS AND LEADERS

Year-End Number One
Men: Frank Sedgman
Women: Doris Hart

Davis Cup: Australia
Wightman Cup: United States

1952

Little Mo growing up very quickly

Frank Sedgman
Finalist in 11 of 12 major events, champion of record-tying eight.

Another patch in the nearly complete postwar reconstruction of tennis was put in place in 1952 when the King's Cup, a European team competition for a trophy donated by Swedish monarch and tennis patron Gustav V in 1936, was resumed. But other than Jaroslav Drobny's second straight French title, Europe had little impact on the world tennis stage. Australian men and American women dominated the major championships.

Among the men, it was Frank Sedgman's year all the way. The aggressive, diligent Aussie was in all four of the major finals in singles and doubles, and three in mixed—incredibly 11 of the 12. He bagged eight of them—Singles at Wimbledon and the U.S., all but the U.S. in doubles with Ken McGregor, and, with Doris Hart, all but Australia in the mixed (which he didn't enter). His collection amounted to a one-year record-tying haul of silver, eight major championship trophies. Don Budge had turned a similar trick in 1938.

Sedgman was on the losing end of the first two singles finals, however, beaten by his partner McGregor in the Australian, 7-5, 12-10, 2-6, 6-2, and by the ever-dangerous Drobny on the salmon-colored clay of Paris, 6-2, 6-0, 3-6, 6-3. Together, Frank and

Ken, Grand Slammers of 1951, took their fifth straight doubles major, the Aussie, beating the countrymen against whom they'd completed their Slam, Don Candy and Mervyn Rose, 6-4, 7-5, 6-3. They made it six in a row with the French, a repeat over Americans Dick Savitt and Gar Mulloy, 6-3, 6-4, 6-4.

Sedgman got his revenge on 'Old Drob' in the final at Wimbledon, 4-6, 6-2, 6-3, 6-2, becoming the first Aussie champ there since Jack Crawford in 1933. Two other Aussies, all-timers in the making, embarked on their first overseas tour, and ended up reaching the doubles semi-finals. There would be plenty to hear in the future from Lew Hoad and Ken Rosewall, both 17 years of age.

Drobny took the first set of the final, but Sedgman seized control of the match in a swirling wind on Centre Court when he tuned in his crushing overhead smash. Sedgman, in fact, lost only two sets at Wimbledon, underscoring his superiority. His doubles bandwagon with McGregor continued to roll to a seventh straight major, too fast for Eric Sturgess and Vic Seixas, 6-3, 7-5, 6-4. Doris Hart was his companion in the mixed title, a 4-6, 6-3, 6-4, decision over an Aussie-Argentine yoking of Thelma Long and Enrique Morea. It meant a Wimbledon triple for Sedgman, joining select male company of Don Budge (1937-38) and Bobby Riggs (1939).

At the U.S. Championships, Sedgman rolled impressively to his second straight title. He crunched country-man Mervyn Rose in the semis, 6-3, 6-3, 6-4, and made the final against surprising 37-year-old Gardnar Mulloy look as simple as one-two-three: 6-1, 6-2, 6-3. But he and McGregor had lost out on a second Grand Slam in the U.S. final at Longwood, brought down in a stirring five sets by the Aussie-American coalition of Rose and Seixas, 3-6, 10-8, 10-8, 6-8, 8-6. Still, they had a sensational record—seven straight major titles—and Sedgman had eight since he'd won the 1950 U.S. with John Bromwich. England's Doherty brothers, Laurie and Reggie, had won five straight on two different runs: All Wimbledons, 1897-1901; and U.S. 1902, Wimbledon, 1903, U.S. 1903, Wimbledon 1904-05.

Sedgman also won the Italian, showing Drobny he could handle clay, 7-5, 6-3, 1-6, 6-4.

Adelaide was the scene of Sedgman and McGregor's farewell Davis Cup defense, and they were brutal to the U.S. tourists, Vic Seixas and Tony Trabert, 4-1, dropping only one set that counted in establishing a 3-0 lead. For starters Sedgman beat Seixas, 6-3, 6-4, 6-3, and Ken got rid of Trabert, 11-9, 6-4, 6-1. The finishing doubles went to the peerless pair, 6-3, 6-4, 1-6, 6-3, over Tony and Vic. That was three straight for Capt. Harry Hopman's tribe.

American women again avoided the long journey to Australia, allowing Thelma Long to win her first singles title, 6-2, 6-3, over Helen Angwin, 6-2, 6-3 and team with Nancye Bolton for their 10th doubles title together, 6-1, 6-1, over Allison Baker and Mary Hawton. (Long later won two more.)

But U.S. women were oppressive in the other major championships, as had become their custom. Doris Hart won her second French singles title, reversing the final-round result of a year earlier to beat Shirley Fry, 6-4, 6-4. Fry's semi-final pigeon was Brit Hazel Reddick-Smith, 7-5, 6-4, while Hart beat Dorothy Head Knode, 6-2, 8-6.

Maureen Connolly ascended to the world No.1 ranking at age 17, taking the Wimbledon title away from three-time champ Louise Brough, 7-5, 6-3. Two months later she broke down Hart, 6-3, 7-5, to defend her U.S. crown at Forest Hills. Hart and Fry had taken over from Margaret duPont and Louise Brough as double juggernauts, winning the French, Wimbledon and U.S. without the loss of a set in the finals. They knocked off Brough and Connolly at Wimbledon, 8-6, 6-3, and the U.S., 10-8, 6-4.

Connolly's first appearance at Wimbledon, seeded

1952 THE MAJOR CHAMPIONSHIPS

Australian Championships
Men's Singles: Ken McGregor
Women's Singles: Thelma Long
Men's Doubles: Ken McGregor / Frank Sedgman
Women's Doubles: Thelma Coyne Long / Nancye Wynne Bolton
Mixed Doubles: Thelma Coyne Long / George Worthington
French Championships
Men's Singles: Jaroslav Drobny
Women's Singles: Doris Hart
Men's Doubles: Ken McGregor / Frank Sedgman
Women's Doubles: Doris Hart / Shirley Fry
Mixed Doubles: Doris Hart / Frank Sedgman
Wimbledon
Men's Singles: Frank Sedgman
Women's Singles: Maureen Connolly
Men's Doubles: Ken McGregor / Frank Sedgman
Women's Doubles: Shirley Fry / Doris Hart
Mixed Doubles: Doris Hart / Frank Sedgman
U.S. Championships
Men's Singles: Frank Sedgman
Women's Singles: Maureen Connolly
Men's Doubles: Merv Rose / Vic Seixas
Women's Doubles: Shirley Fry / Doris Hart
Mixed Doubles: Doris Hart / Frank Sedgman

second behind Hart, was a celebrated event. "The pressures under which she played were enormous," noted Lance Tingay. "There was the basic pressure of being expected to win. There was a blaze of publicity because Miss Connolly, for reasons of her skill, her charm and achievement, was 'news' in everything she did. And her guidance went sour at this her first Wimbledon challenge. Her coach—strong-willed, overly protective, and domineering Eleanor 'Teach' Tennant, who had also developed Alice Marble and imbued her with killer psychology—advised Connolly to withdraw because of a mild shoulder strain. Maureen refused and parted company with Tennant forever, removing a stifling weight from her personality."

Connolly lost sets to Englishwomen Susan Partridge, 6-3, 5-7, 7-5, who slow-balled her, giving neither the pace nor angle on which Maureen thrived, and to Long, 5-7, 6-2, 6-0, in the quarter-finals. Partridge, who had won the Italian in an all-Brit final, 6-3, 7-5, over Betty Harrison, proved her toughest foe. Hart was beaten in a long quarter-final, 6-8, 7-5, 6-4, by Pat Todd, leaving Connolly to mow down Fry, 6-4, 6-3, and Brough, 7-5, 6-3, in the final two rounds. Connolly's scythe-like strokes were as deadly as the British had seen or heard; in fact, in three years she never lost a single match in Great Britain.

Great Britain suffered a Wimbledon embarrassment in the Wightman Cup, winning only one set, losing 7-0.

Hart knocked the hyphens out of Jean Quertier-Rinkel, 6-3, 6-3, and Jean Walker-Smith, 7-5, 6-2. Connolly beat both of them, too, but Walker-Smith resisted strongly, 3-6, 6-1, 7-5.

Bobby Riggs had tried to sign Sedgman and McGregor to tour as pros with himself, Pancho Gonzalez and Pancho Segura in 1952, dismissing Jack Kramer by saying he had retired. Riggs struck a deal, but later Gonzalez wanted to change the agreed-upon terms, and Riggs—about to re-marry—got disgusted and left the promoting business.

There was no pro tour in 1952, but Segura startled Gonzalez in the final of the U.S. Pro, 3-6, 6-4, 3-6, 6-4, 6-0, from 3-0 down in the fourth, at Lakewood Park in Cleveland. Afterwards the victor chortled, "Here I am, 30, six years older, and I outlast him." Kramer, who had no intention of retiring, took over as player-promoter, signing Sedgman to a contract ($75,000 guarantee) that was announced right after the Davis Cup challenge round. McGregor also turned pro to face Segura in the prelims on the 1953 tour. Many Australian fans resented their departure.

1952 CHAMPIONS AND LEADERS

Year-End Number One
Men: Frank Sedgman
Women: Maureen Connolly

Davis Cup: Australia
Wightman Cup: United States

1953

Connolly invincible in Grand Slam run

Maureen Connolly (left), Hazel Hotchkiss Wightman
En route to first women's Grand Slam, she finishes the year 61-2.

The year 1953 provided the tennis world with the lovely teen-age days of 'Little Mo' and Ken Rosewall.

The incomparable Maureen Connolly, nicknamed 'Little Mo' by hometown (San Diego) sportswriter Nelson Fisher, because she was as invincible as the World War II battleship *Missouri* ('Big Mo'), steamed to only the game's second Grand Slam. Following in the sneaker steps of another Californian Don Budge 15 years earlier, the 18-year-old swept the Australian, French, Wimbledon and U.S. singles championships. Overall, she won 10 of 12 tournaments and compiled a 61-2 record. This was the crowning year of an abbreviated career that was to end through injury, after just 3-1/2 awesome seasons, in 1954.

Meanwhile, Kenneth Robert Rosewall, also 18 (21 days older than his fellow Australian whiz kid Lew Hoad), took the Australian and French singles titles, the first major accomplishments of a phenomenal career matchless in its longevity. Rosewall would still be going strong a quarter of a century later, nine years after Connolly's death from cancer at age 34. Rosewall, called 'Muscles' by his mates because he had none showing, was the youngest to carry his homeland, a record that yet stands.

Connolly was the first to emulate Don Budge, who took all the 'Big Four' singles titles in 1938 and popularized the feat by calling it the Grand Slam. In doing so, she trampled 22 opponents, losing just one set and a total of 82 games.

'Little Mo' started in Australia, demolishing her partner, Californian Julie Sampson, 6-3, 6-2, before they teamed up to win the doubles over Beryl Penrose and Mary Hawton, 6-4, 6-2. Julie deprived Mo of a triple, ganging up with Aussie Rex Hartwig to beat Connolly and 19-year-old compatriot Hamilton Richardson, 6-4, 6-3.

In the quarter-finals at Paris, Connolly lost that lone set, to Susan Partridge Chatrier, her toughest rival at Wimbledon the year before. By this time Partridge had married France's Philippe Chatrier (future president of the French Federation and the International Tennis Federation). Susan slow-balled again, but Connolly hit her way out of trouble, blasting her ground strokes even harder, deeper, and closer to the lines than usual, prevailing by 3-6, 6-2, 6-2. Then she drubbed two Americans, Dorothy Head Knode, 6-3, 6-3, and Doris Hart in the final, 6-2, 6-4.

Hart was also her final-round opponent at Wimbledon and the U.S. at Forest Hills. "The Wimbledon final was the finest match of the Slam: 8-6, 7-5. The two great players called it the best of their life," noted a silver anniversary tribute to Little Mo's won-drous 1953 record. In the homestretch at Forest Hills, Connolly won driving, as they say at the racetrack, 6-2, 6-3 over Althea Gibson in the quarters; 6-1, 6-1 over Shirley Fry; and 6-2, 6-4 over Hart. During the 22 matches that covered the Slam, Connolly permitted foes an average of three games a match.

In fact, Connolly lost only two matches during the year, to Hart in the final of the Italian, 4-6, 9-7, 6-3, and to Fry, 6-2, 7-5, in the Pacific Southwest at Los Angeles, a tourney Shirley won over Hart, 1-6, 6-3, 6-4. Maureen paid Shirley back in the Pacific Coast final, 9-7, 6-0.

Hart and Fry teamed for the French doubles title, a third successive year, beating Connolly and Sampson, 6-4, 6-3, and did the same at Wimbledon. Only that time Mo, not a standout doubles player because of her distaste for net play, had, with Sampson the negative distinction of not winning a single game. At the time it was the lone 6-0, 6-0, final in the history of major women's doubles. (Margaret Court and Evonne Goolagong equaled the double bagel in winning the 1971 Australian final over Jill Emmerson and Lesley Hunt.) Just before entering the court, Maureen had received a telephone call from her fiancé (and future husband), Olympic equestrian Norman Brinker, telling her he was being sent to the Korean War zone by the U.S. Navy.

Hart and Fry also won the third of their four successive U.S. Doubles titles, but it was a titanic struggle at Longwood to end at 41 matches and nine titles the record major doubles streak of Louise Brough and Margaret duPont, 6-2, 7-9, 9-7. Brough and duPont, abstainers from the 1951 and 1952 Championships, looked safe when they pinched Fry at 2-5 and two match points, but a skillful barrage of lobs undid the perennial champs.

Rosewall, a 5-foot-7, 145-pounder with an angelic face and neither a hair nor a footstep out of place, took the first of his four Australian singles titles, spanning 19 years, by beating left-hander Mervyn Rose, 6-0, 6-3, 6-4. Rosewall beat Vic Seixas, 6-3, 6-4, 1-6, 6-2, in the French final, the first tournament covered by a new magazine, World Tennis, which debuted in June 1953 and would become an influential force in the game. It was edited and published by New Yorker Gladys Heldman. The story under Gardnar Mulloy's by-line described Rosewall as "a young kid with stamina, hard-hitting ground strokes and plenty of confidence."

The Wimbledon and U.S. titles came back into American possession, property of Vic Seixas and Tony Trabert. Seixas, according to Lance Tingay's official his-tory of Wimbledon, was "hardly the prettiest player in the world, for his strokes smacked more of expediency than fluency and polish, but he gave the impression of being prepared to go on attacking forever." In five long sets, Vic edged Hoad in the quarters, 5-7, 6-4, 6-3, 1-6, 9-7, and Rose in the semis, 6-4, 10-12, 9-11, 6-4, 6-3. In the final, he beat unseeded Kurt Nielsen, 9-7, 6-3, the

---

1953 THE MAJOR CHAMPIONSHIPS

Australian Championships
Men's Singles: Ken Rosewall
Women's Singles: Maureen Connolly
Men's Doubles: Lew Hoad / Ken Rosewall
Women's Doubles: Maureen Connolly / Julia Sampson
Mixed Doubles: Julia Sampson / Rex Hartwig
French Championships
Men's Singles: Ken Rosewall
Women's Singles: Maureen Connolly
Men's Doubles: Lew Hoad / Ken Rosewall
Women's Doubles: Doris Hart / Shirley Fry
Mixed Doubles: Doris Hart / Vic Seixas
Wimbledon
Men's Singles: Vic Seixas
Women's Singles: Maureen Connolly
Men's Doubles: Lew Hoad / Ken Rosewall
Women's Doubles: Shirley Fry / Doris Hart
Mixed Doubles: Doris Hart / Vic Seixas
U.S. Championships
Men's Singles: Tony Trabert
Women's Singles: Maureen Connolly
Men's Doubles: Rex Hartwig / Merv Rose
Women's Doubles: Shirley Fry / Doris Hart
Mixed Doubles: Doris Hart / Vic Seixas

Dane whose chopped forehand down the middle of the court had upset top seed Rosewall in the quarters, 7-5, 4-6, 6-8, 6-0, 6-2, bursting whatever dream Kenny might have had of a Grand Slam.

The match of the tournament was the third-round classic in which Jaroslav Drobny defeated his good friend and constant touring companion, Budge Patty, 8-6, 16-18, 3-6, 8-6, 12-10. The Herculean epic began at 5:00 p.m. and ended at nightfall four hours, 23 minutes later, Drobny surviving three match points in the fourth set, three more in the fifth. He won the last two games after the referee's decision at 10-10 was conveyed to a groaning full-house crowd—only enough light remained to play two more games that evening. Those 93 games, played at a consistently high standard, were the most in any Wimbledon singles to that time. But Drobny had torn a muscle in his right leg, and after somehow limping through victories over Australian Rex Hartwig and Swede Sven Davidson, lost to the surprising Nielsen in the semis, 6-4, 6-3, 6-2.

Trabert did in Rosewall, 7-5, 6-3, 6-3, and Seixas beat Hoad, 7-5, 6-4, 6-4, in the U.S. semi-finals at Forest Hills. Then Trabert—serving and volleying consistently and returning superbly whether Seixas charged the net or stayed back—beat the Wimbledon champ for the title, 6-3, 6-2, 6-3, in just one hour. Trabert was less than three months out of the U.S. Navy, but he had trained hard to regain his speed and match fitness, and he leveled Seixas with a vicious onslaught from backcourt and net, off both wings—especially his topspin backhand.

Hoad and Rosewall captured the Australian, French, and Wimbledon doubles titles, each final a totally Aussie production, in order: 9-11, 6-4,10-8, 6-4, over Mervyn Rose and Don Candy in Melbourne; 6-2, 6-1, 6-1 over Rose and Clive Wilderspin in Paris; 6-4, 7-5, 4-6, 7-5, over Rex Hartwig and Rose in London. But they missed out on emulating the 1951 Grand Slam of Frank Sedgman and Ken McGregor on the last leg, the U.S. at Longwood. The quarter-finals were their grassy quicksand, as they were upset by Americans Straight Clark and lefty Hal Burrows, 5-7, 14-12, 18-16, 9-7.

Nevertheless, an Australian flavor remained. Ken and Lew's countrymen, Hartwig and Rose, took the title over popular oldies Bill Talbert, 35, and Gar Mulloy, 38, finalists together for a sixth time, 6-4, 4-6, 6-2, 6-4.

Australia, favored in the Davis Cup challenge round at Melbourne, with their green-but-keen kiddies Hoad and Rosewall just turned 19, nearly threw it away when the team selectors ordered Capt. Harry Hopman to nominate Hartwig and Hoad, both right-court players, as his doubles team. That, strangely, instead of either of the experienced pairs available: Rosewall-Hoad or Hartwig-Rose. The confused Aussie duo lost to Trabert and Seixas, 6-2, 6-4, 6-4.

Hoad had beaten Seixas, 6-4, 6-2, 6-3, and Trabert had stomped Rosewall, 6-3, 6-4, 6-4, the first day. But Australia won from 1-2 down, Hoad beating Trabert, 13-11, 6-3, 2-6, 3-6, 7-5 in the pivotal fourth match, one of the greatest in Davis Cup history. As a crowd of 17,500 huddled in the Kooyong stadium under newspapers to protect themselves from rain, Trabert lost his serve at love at 5-6 in the desperate final set, double faulting to 0-40 and then netting a half volley off a return to his shoe-tops. The next day, Rosewall finished the thriller by defeating Seixas, 6-2, 2-6, 6-3, 6-4. Never before, or since, had a couple of teenagers been responsible for winning the Cup.

Meanwhile Frank Sedgman, the Davis Cup hero of a year earlier, lost a pro tour to Jack Kramer, 54 matches to 41, but earned $102,000, the highest total to date. The tally was closer than it might have been because Kramer was bothered by an arthritic back and was as interested in promoting as playing. Pancho Gonzalez won the U.S. Pro title over Don Budge, 4-6, 6-4, 7-5, 6-2, at Lakewood Park in Cleveland. It was the first of Gonzalez' record eight triumphs in nine years in the event, shakily maintained for the handful of outcast pros.

1953 CHAMPIONS AND LEADERS

Year-End Number One
Men: Tony Trabert
Women: Maureen Connolly

Davis Cup: Australia
Wightman Cup: United States

1954

Triumph, tragedy for Little Mo

Vic Seixas
Finally a U.S. champ on 13th try.

The quotation that hangs above the competitors' entrance to the Centre Court at Wimbledon, and was also adopted for a similar exalted position in the marquee at the Forest Hills stadium, is from the poem *If* by Rudyard Kipling. It says, "If you can meet with triumph and disaster, and treat those two impostors just the same…" The words seldom seemed more appropriate than in 1954, for it was a year of continued triumph and then sudden, unmitigated disaster for Maureen Connolly.

'Little Mo' did not go to Australia to try for another Grand Slam. Experienced Thelma Long, 35, filled the gap, winning her homeland's title a second time, 6-3, 6-4, over Jenny Staley, Lew Hoad's wife-to-be.

But Maureen defended her French title without straining. Her 6-0, 6-1, semi-final win over Italian Sylvia Lazzarino took 26 minutes. In the final she coasted, 6-4, 6-1, over Ginette Bucaille, who had beaten 1948 champ Nelly Adamson, 6-2, 6-4. Connolly also beat Pat Ward, 6-3, 6-0, to take the Italian that had eluded her in 1953. At Wimbledon, Maureen defeated Louise Brough in the final, 6-2, 7-5. Lance Tingay wrote, "The whole event was accounted a trifle dull because of the inevitability of the eventual winner. Miss Connolly, without losing a set, won 73 games and lost but 19."

Little did anyone know that this would be Little Mo's last major title. During the interval between Wimbledon and Forest Hills, she was riding her horse, Colonel Merryboy—a gift from a group of San Diegans after her 1952 Wimbledon triumph—and was struck by a truck. Most people thought she would return in 1955, but in her autobiography Maureen wrote that she knew she was finished: "My right leg was slashed to the bone. All the calf muscles were severed and the fibula broken. Eventually, I got on-court again, but I was aware that I could never play tournament tennis."

It was the shortest of great careers, but few got more done in many more years. During those 3-1/2 years when she was undisputed No. 1, the youngest of five Grand Slammers, she won nine straight majors, a tremendous accomplishment: Australian, 1953; French, 1953-54; Wimbledon, 1952-53-54; U.S. 1951-52-53, on a match record of 50-0. (Her complete record for the majors was 52-2, since she lost in the second round of the U.S. in 1949 and 1950 as a 14- and then 15-year-old.) Moreover, there were the Italian, 1954; Irish, 1952-53; the U.S. Clay, 1953-54 (6-4, 6-4, over Althea Gibson, and, then, 6-3, 6-1, over Doris Hart, her last tournament); plus 7-for-7 in Wightman Cup.

Southpaw Mervyn Rose won his only Australian singles title, over countryman Rex Hartwig, 6-2, 0-6, 6-4, 6-2.

Rugged Tony Trabert—firing like the big guns that adorned the aircraft carrier on which he had served the year before—blasted fellow American, lefty Art Larsen, in the French final, 6-4, 7-5, 6-1. Defending champ Ken Rosewall was plucked from the fourth round by Sven Davidson, 6-3, 3-6, 6-3, 6-3, as was his sidekick, Lew Hoad, by 40-year-old Gar Mulloy, 6-2, 2-6, 7-5, 6-4. But the year ultimately belonged to three players who savored sentimental triumphs that came when they were seemingly a shade past their prime: Jaroslav Drobny, Vic Seixas, and Doris Hart.

Drobny at 34 still had a punishing serve, though not as oppressive as it had been prior to a shoulder injury. He was seeded only 11th in his 11th appearance at Wimbledon, but upset second-seeded Lew Hoad in the quarter-finals, 6-4, 6-3, 6-3, and beat old rival Budge Patty in the semi-finals, 6-2, 6-4, 4-6, 9-7. Ken Rosewall overturned top-seeded Tony Trabert in their semi, 3-6, 6-3, 4-6, 6-1, 6-1. but couldn't get past Drobny in the final, 13-11, 4-6, 6-2, 9-7, in two hours, 37 minutes. Drob became only the second left-handed champion, following Norman Brookes, 1907. No one could have imagined that Rosewall, in the final for the first of four times at age 19, would never win the singles title he coveted most. The galleries loved Drobny, the expansive Czech refugee in dark prescription glasses. "No better final had been seen since Crawford and Vines 21 years before," judged Lance Tingay. "The warmth of Drobny's reception as champion could not have been greater had he been a genial Englishman. In a sense he was, for he had married an Englishwoman and lives in Sussex."

The U.S. triumphs of Vic Seixas and Doris Hart at Forest Hills were just as popular with the American audience. Seixas, 31, and competing for the 13th time, finally won in his third appearance in the final. He stopped the run of Rex Hartwig, 3-6, 6-2, 6-4, 6-4. Rex had upset defending champion Tony Trabert, 6-2, 8-6, 2-6, 6-2, and Rosewall, 6-4, 6-3, 6-4. Hart, runner-up five times in 13 appearances but never champion, at last triumphed, 6-8, 6-1, 8-6 over ex-champ Louise Brough, in her fifth final. Doris vaulted three match points as Brough netted backhand returns, one at 4-5, two more at 5-6.

Seixas, according to Allison Danzig's report in *The New York Times*, "made the most of his equipment and he never lagged in carrying the attack to his opponent. His speed and quickness, the effectiveness of his service, his strong return of service and his staunch volleying all contributed to the victory. Too, he found a vulnerable point in his opponent's game and exploited it by directing his twist service to Hartwig's backhand."

Hart and Seixas built themselves U.S. triples. She started it by winning the doubles with Shirley Fry in Boston for a fourth time, again striking down nine-time champs Margaret duPont and Brough, 6-4, 6-4. He took the same route, registering a Longwood victory with Trabert over Hoad and Rosewall, 3-6, 6-4, 8-6, 6-3.

1954 THE MAJOR CHAMPIONSHIPS

Australian Championships
Men's Singles: Merv Rose
Women's Singles: Thelma Long
Men's Doubles: Rex Hartwig / Merv Rose
Women's Doubles: Mary Bevis Hawton / Beryl Penrose
Mixed Doubles: Thelma Coyne Long / Rex Hartwig
French Championships
Men's Singles: Tony Trabert
Women's Singles: Maureen Connolly
Men's Doubles: Vic Seixas / Tony Trabert
Women's Doubles: Maureen Connolly / Nell Hall Hopman
Mixed Doubles: Maureen Connolly / Lew Hoad
Wimbledon
Men's Singles: Jaroslav Drobny
Women's Singles: Maureen Connolly
Men's Doubles: Rex Hartwig / Merv Rose
Women's Doubles: Louise Brough / Margaret Osborne duPont
Mixed Doubles: Doris Hart / Vic Seixas
U.S. Championships
Men's Singles: Vic Seixas
Women's Singles: Doris Hart
Men's Doubles: Vic Seixas / Tony Trabert
Women's Doubles: Shirley Fry / Doris Hart
Mixed Doubles: Doris Hart / Vic Seixas

Then, after their Forest Hills singles triumphs, Doris and Vic collaborated in the mixed final, over duPont and Rosewall, 4-6, 6-1, 6-1.

Trabert and Seixas, who also beat Hoad and Rosewall for the French, 6-4, 6-2, 6-2, split the majors with Hartwig and Rose. The two Aussies won their own title, over 20-year-old lefty Neale Fraser, and Clive Wilderspin, 6-3, 6-4, 6-2, and Wimbledon over Trabert and Seixas, 6-4, 6-4, 3-6, 6-4.

Connolly showed some doubles skill in Paris, abetting her friend, Nell Hopman (wife of the Aussie Davis Cup captain, Harry Hopman) to win the French over homebodies Maude Galtier and Suzanne Schmitt, 7-5, 4-6, 6-0. The mixed triumph, chaperoned by Lew Hoad, over Jacqueline Patorni and Hartwig, gave Little Mo a triple, 6-4, 6-3.

At Wimbledon Brough and duPont recaptured the title they had won in 1948-49-50, over Fry and Hart, 4-6, 9-7, 6-3, avoiding two match points in the second—their 16th major together.

Connolly, in her last Wightman Cup appearance, led the United States in a 6-0 frolic over Great Britain at Wimbledon, beating Helen Fletcher, 6-1, 6-3, and Anne Shilcock, 6-2, 6-2. Hart topped them both, too, Shilcock, 6-4, 6-1, and, pressed somewhat, Fletcher, 6-1, 6-8, 6-2.

After four straight losses to the Aussies of Capt. Hopman, the U.S., in Capt. Bill Talbert's third of six years at the helm, recovered the Davis Cup on the strokes of Trabert and Seixas, 3-2. This was a disappointment to the record tennis crowds of 25,578 jamming Sydney's White City ground, enlarged with towering auxiliary stands. Seixas, earning his spot because of his Forest Hills form, and Trabert did a flip-flop of 1953. Tony outgunned Hoad, 6-4, 2-6, 12-10, 6-3, and Seixas, previously Rosewall's pigeon, came through for a 2-0 lead, 8-6, 6-8, 6-4, 6-3. Lew, serving a set point at 10-9 in the second, saw it whisked away by Tony's desperate two-handed reflex volley. Tony and Vic finished the job the next day, beating Hoad-Rosewall, 6-2, 4-6, 6-2, 10-8, in the decisive doubles.

Jack Kramer retired as undefeated pro champion and promoted a round-robin tour involving Pancho Gonzalez, Frank Sedgman, Pancho Segura and Don Budge. Gonzalez won it, narrowly defeating Sedgman, and thus gained a previously unheard-of second life in the head-to-head pro tour. He also won the U.S. Pro title over Sedgman, 6-3, 9-7, 3-6, 6-2, indoors at the Cleveland Arena.

1954 CHAMPIONS AND LEADERS

Year-End Number One
Men: Jaroslav Drobny
Women: Maureen Connolly

Davis Cup: United States
Wightman Cup: United States

1955

Only Cup loss mars Tony's year

Tony Trabert
First to win French, Wimbledon and U.S. titles since Budge.

At the midpoint of the postwar decade, 1955, American Tony Trabert established himself as the best player in the world, his Australian rivals snatched back the Davis Cup with a vengeance, and a couple of gallant American women who had left a considerable legacy—Louise Brough and Doris Hart—took their final bows in the world tennis arena.

Ken Rosewall beat Lew Hoad, 9-7, 6-4, 6-4, for his second Australian singles title, but Trabert—the All-American boy from Cincinnati with his ginger crew cut, freckles, and uncompromisingly aggressive game—won the French, Wimbledon and U.S. singles. He might have had a Grand Slam, but never considered it since he lost to Rosewall in the semis of the Australian, 8-6, 6-3, 6-3.

In the Italian Championships, two of the most unorthodox but combative clay-court specialists of Europe—tall and gangly Fausto Gardini ('The Spider') and tiny, gentle Beppe Merlo ('The Little Bird')—met in an all-native final before a raucous Roman crowd. They had their customary epic battle—"We were always like a dog and a cat," Merlo recalls—with Gardini claiming victory, 6-1, 1-6, 3-6, 6-6, as Merlo collapsed with cramps. To make sure his opponent could not recover and win, Gardini counted off one minute while Merlo writhed in pain, then rolled down the net and raised his arms triumphantly.

There were no such histrionics in Paris, where Trabert bulled his way to the French title over Swede Sven Davidson, 2-6, 6-1, 6-4, 6-2. At Wimbledon, Trabert eliminated defending champion Jaroslav Drobny in the quarters, 8-6, 6-1, 6-4, and in the semis, 8-6, 6-2, 6-2, Budge Patty.

In the final Trabert expected to meet Rosewall, but instead came up against 1953 runner-up Kurt Nielsen, who had upset the Australian champ, this time in the semis, 11-9, 6-2, 2-6, 6-4. "Nielsen clearly remembered his success against the Little Master in 1953, when he hit his approach shots down the middle and came to the net, making it difficult for Rosewall to play his favorite passing shots decisively," wrote Max Robertson. "He pursued the same tactics and with the same result; for the second time he had reached the final unseeded—a record which could stand forever." Trabert denied him a more satisfying immortality, however, prevailing 6-3, 7-5, 6-1.

The only real stain on Trabert's record for the year, one of the greatest in history—he won 18 singles and 12 doubles titles—came in late August, in the Davis Cup challenge round at Forest Hills. After Rosewall had beaten Vic Seixas, 6-3, 10-8, 4-6, 6-2, Trabert went down, 4-6, 6-3, 6-3, 8-6, to Hoad in the critical second match. Hoad played with immense power and brilliance.

The next afternoon, Hoad and Rex Hartwig—two years earlier thrown together as first-time doubles partners, with disastrous results—blended beautifully to clinch the Cup with a 12-14, 6-4, 6-3, 3-6, 7-5 victory over Seixas and Trabert that had 12,000 spectators howling with delight through five scintillating sets. The Aussies had their cake and put frosting on it too, running up a 5-0 final margin the next day.

Trabert had the last laugh, though, banishing Rosewall in the U.S. final at Forest Hills, 9-7, 6-3, 6-3. That set him up as the new amateur champ, the fourth man to take at least three of the four majors within a calendar year, following Jack Crawford in 1933, Fred Perry in 1934, and Grand Slammer Don Budge in 1938. Actually, promoter Jack Kramer had signed Hoad and Rosewall as well, to tour with him and Trabert playing a Davis Cup—style format, but the deal fell through. Slazenger, the racket company that Rosewall represented, gave him a bonus, and Jenny Hoad persuaded her husband to make one more grand tour as an amateur. So Trabert's indoctrination into the pros in 1956 wound up taking the more conventional form, a head-to-head tour against the champ, Pancho Gonzalez.

On the women's side, new singles champions were crowned in Australia, where Beryl Penrose defeated

Thelma Long, 6-4, 6-3, and in France, where England's Angela Mortimer, a future Hall of Famer, topped American Dorothy Head Knode, 2-6, 7-5, 10-8.

At Wimbledon, 1948-49-50 champion Louise Brough, seeded second, defeated demonstrative newcomer Darlene Hard in the semis, 6-3, 8-6, reaching the final for the seventh time. Her opponent was ambidextrous (she did not use a backhand, but switched hands on the racket as necessary) Beverly Baker Fleitz, who, serving right-handed, upset top seed Doris Hart, 0-1, 6-3, 6-0, in the semis. Beverly was the only female ambidextrous player to attain a major final, sharing the oddity with Italian Giorgio de Stefani, loser of the French to Henri Cochet in 1932.

"Louise was always prone to tighten up at important points but had a greater breadth of stroke and experience at her command, which just saw her through a keenly fought struggle," reported Max Robertson. "In the sixth game of the second set, for example, it was only after nine deuces and five advantages to Fleitz that Louise wrong-footed her near exhausted opponent with a backhand slice down the line to lead 4-2. This was the turning point and Louise went on to win for the fourth time, 7-5, 8-6."

That was Brough's last of six major singles titles on her way to the Hall of Fame. Hart, also a majestic champion, won her last of six, the U.S. at Forest Hills, site of her narrow and jubilant victory over Brough the year before. This time it was much easier as Hart drubbed

1955 THE MAJOR CHAMPIONSHIPS

Australian Championships
Men's Singles: Ken Rosewall
Women's Singles: Beryl Penrose
Men's Doubles: Vic Seixas / Tony Trabert
Women's Doubles: Mary Bevis Hawton / Beryl Penrose
Mixed Doubles: Thelma Coyne Long / George Worthington
French Championships
Men's Singles: Tony Trabert
Women's Singles: Angela Mortimer
Men's Doubles: Vic Seixas / Tony Trabert
Women's Doubles: Beverly Baker Fleitz / Darlene Hard
Mixed Doubles: Doris Hart / Gordon Forbes
Wimbledon
Men's Singles: Tony Trabert
Women's Singles: Louise Brough
Men's Doubles: Rex Hartwig / Lew Hoad
Women's Doubles: Angela Mortimer / Anne Shilcock
Mixed Doubles: Doris Hart / Vic Seixas
U.S. Championships
Men's Singles: Tony Trabert
Women's Singles: Doris Hart
Men's Doubles: Kosei Kamo / Atsushi Miyagi
Women's Doubles: Louise Brough / Margaret Osborne duPont
Mixed Doubles: Doris Hart / Vic Seixas

Brit Patricia Ward, 6-4, 6-2.

Hart also made her last appearance in the Wightman Cup as the U.S. defeated Great Britain, 6-1, at Westchester Country Club in Rye, N.Y. She had been on the U.S. team since 1946, compiling a record of 13-1 in singles and 8-1 in doubles. Mortimer handed Hart her lone defeat, 6-4, 1-6, 7-5, but she beat Shirley Bloomer, 7-5, 6-3, and other necessary points were provided by Brough (6-0, 6-2 over Mortimer and 6-2, 6-4 over Bloomer) and Knode (6-3, 6-3, over Angela Buxton). At year's end, Doris became a teaching pro.

As for doubles titles in 1955, Brough and Margaret duPont, who had reigned nine successive years between 1942 and 1950, took the U.S. title away from Fry-Hart, 6-3, 1-6, 6-3, starting a new three-year run. Seixas and Trabert won the Australian, over Hoad and Rosewall, 6-3, 6-2, 2-6, 3-6, 6-1, and the French over Italians Nicola Pietrangeli and Orlando Sirola, 6-1, 4-6, 6-2,

6-4. But Hoad and Hartwig, presaging their Davis Cup heroics, won Wimbledon, over mates Neale Fraser and Rosewall, 7-5, 6-4, 6-3. The little-known team of Japanese Davis Cuppers Kosei Kamo and Atsushi Miyagi won the U.S. Doubles, primarily because they were willing to hang around Longwood Cricket Club through Hurricane Diane as most of the favored teams fled Boston. When the lake that Longwood's grass courts became under the assault of fierce downpours finally receded, the tournament ended one week late. The Japanese took their country's only major, triumphing over young unseeded Americans Bill Quillian, 21, and Jerry Moss, 19, in five, 6-2, 6-3, 3-6, 1-6, 6-4.

1955 CHAMPIONS AND LEADERS

Year-End Number One
Men: Tony Trabert
Women: Louise Brough

Davis Cup: Australia
Wightman Cup: United States

1956

Hoad soars to No. 1, Althea takes French

Lew Hoad
Buddy Rosewall thwarts Grand Slam dream.

In 1956, the 21-year-old former 'Whiz Kids' of Australia, Lew Hoad and Ken Rosewall, had clearly grown up into the best amateur tennis players in the world. They smothered the United States in the Davis Cup challenge round, 5-0, for the second straight year, and played each other in three of the four major singles finals. Ultimately, on the last day of Forest Hills, it was Rosewall who prevented his slightly younger countryman from pulling off a Grand Slam.

This was the Diamond Jubilee year of the U.S. Championships, and Rosewall captivated a crowd of 12,000 at the Forest Hills stadium with his 4-6, 6-2, 6-3, 6-3 victory in the first all-foreign final since 1933, when Britain's Fred Perry thwarted Australian Jack Crawford's bid for a Grand Slam. But there was more interest in the trailblazer, "the colored girl," as many referred to Althea Gibson out of Harlem, who powerfully drove to the final in her precinct. Gibson had registered the first major title for a black by winning the French over Brit Angela Mortimer, 6-0, 12-10. She added the doubles with Brit Angela Buxton, 6-8, 8-6, 6-1, over fellow Americans Darlene Hard and Dorothy Knode. Angela was also Althea's partner shortly thereafter in putting the first black on the Wimbledon championship roll, 6-1, 8-6, over Aussies Fay Muller and Daphne Seeney. Earlier Althea had displayed an affinity for continental clay by winning her first important title, the Italian, over Hungarian Suzi Kormoczi, 6-3, 7-5.

The Hoad-Rosewall rivalry reached its

zenith at Forest Hills where, as Allison Danzig wrote in *The New York Times*, "If there were any doubts about the little Australian measuring up to the caliber of a truly great player they were dispelled by his play in the championship. His performance in breaking down the powerful attack and then the will to win over the favored Hoad was even more convincing, considering the breezy conditions, than his wizardry in his unforgettable quarter-final round match against Richard Savitt. Against the powerful, rangy Savitt, Rosewall's ground strokes were the chief instruments of a 6-4, 7-5, 4-6, 8-10, 6-1, victory in a crescendo of lethal driving exchanges seldom equaled on the Forest Hills turf. Yesterday's (final) match between possibly the two most accomplished 21-year-old finalists in the tournament's history was a madcap, lightning-fast duel. The shots were taken out of the air with rapidity and radiance despite a strong wind that played tricks with the ball."

So it had been much of the year, the blond-haired, blue-eyed, muscular, and positively engaging Hoad rousing galleries around the world with his remarkable weight of shot and free-wheeling attack; the immaculate, compact, and quicksilver Rosewall challenging him but constantly rebuffed, until now.

Hoad had beaten Rosewall in the finals of the Australian, 6-4, 3-6, 6-4, 7-5, and Wimbledon, 6-2, 4-6, 7-5, 6-4. He had beaten Sven Davidson in the French final, 6-4, 8-6, 6-3, and won the Italian and German titles on clay as well. Davidson fell before him

1956 THE MAJOR CHAMPIONSHIPS

Australian Championships
Men's Singles: Lew Hoad
Women's Singles: Mary Carter
Men's Doubles: Lew Hoad / Ken Rosewall
Women's Doubles: Mary Bevis Hawton / Thelma Coyne Long
Mixed Doubles: Beryl Penrose / Neale Fraser
French Championships
Men's Singles: Lew Hoad
Women's Singles: Althea Gibson
Men's Doubles: Don Candy / Robert Perry
Women's Doubles: Angela Buxton / Althea Gibson
Mixed Doubles: Thelma Coyne Long / Luis Ayala
Wimbledon
Men's Singles: Lew Hoad
Women's Singles: Shirley Fry
Men's Doubles: Lew Hoad / Ken Rosewall
Women's Doubles: Angela Buxton / Althea Gibson
Mixed Doubles: Shirley Fry / Vic Seixas
U.S. Championships
Men's Singles: Ken Rosewall
Women's Singles: Shirley Fry
Men's Doubles: Lew Hoad / Ken Rosewall
Women's Doubles: Louise Brough / Margaret Osborne duPont
Mixed Doubles: Margaret Osborne duPont / Ken Rosewall

in Rome, 7-5, 6-2, 6-0, and Orlando Sirola in Hamburg, 6-2, 5-7, 6-4, 8-6. But finally Rosewall got him.

Doris Hart, who had climaxed 15 appearances with back-to-back Forest Hills titles in 1954 and 1955, had, like Trabert, turned pro, she to give lessons. In her absence, her old doubles partner, Shirley Fry, took the Wimbledon and Forest Hills singles titles for the first and only time. At Wimbledon, Shirley beat Angela Buxton, 6-3, 6-1, and at Forest Hills, her final victim was Italian and French champion, the New Yorker Gibson. Althea was beaten in her Wimbledon debut by Shirley Fry, 4-6, 6-3, 6-4, in the quarters.

For Fry, 29, it was a glorious journey's end. Begun as a 14-year-old with a first-round look-in at Forest Hills in 1941, the long trip, the quest, was over at destination championship: Shirley's 6-3, 6-4 victory over Gibson completed the most drawn-out of all treks to a U.S. title. It was her 16th sortie, from youngest entrant ever (a record that stood until Kathleen Horvath, a younger 14 in 1979) to one of the oldest champs. She had beaten Althea to win the U.S. Clay, 7-5, 6-1. This time Fry maintained her mastery by attacking the net constantly in the first set, then staying back and thwarting Gibson's attack with deep, accurate ground strokes in the second.

The addition of Buxton, and the improvement of Mortimer made the British Wightman Cup team more competitive than it had been at any time since the war, but the U.S. still prevailed, 5-2, at Wimbledon. Brough and Fry were the mainstays. Louise beat Mortimer, 3-6, 6-4, 7-5, and Buxton, 3-6, 6-3, 6-4. Shirley, beaten by Mortimer, 6-4, 6-3, won over Buxton, 6-2, 6-8. 7-5, and accompanied Brough in a doubles win over Buxton and Mortimer, 6-2, 6-2.

Brough and Margaret duPont continued their unmatched supremacy in the U.S. Doubles, winning their 11th, 6-3, 6-0, over Betty Rosenquest Pratt and Fry.

Hoad and Rosewall, masterful returner Kenny in the right court, took three of the four doubles majors: Australian over Don Candy and Mervyn Rose, 13-11, 10-8, 6-4; Wimbledon over Italians Nicola Pietrangeli and Orlando Sirola, 7-5, 6-2, 6-1; U.S. over Ham Richardson and Vic Seixas, 6-2, 6-2, 3-6, 6-4. They didn't play together at the French where Hoad, in the company of countryman and future Hall of Famer, Ashley Cooper, lost the final to the Aussie-American combine of Candy and Bob Perry, 7-5, 6-3, 6-3

Ken and Lew thoroughly blinded and blanked the U.S., 5-0 in the Davis Cup challenge round at Adelaide. Hoad went through Herbie Flam with ease, 6-2, 6-3, 6-3, and Rosewall had little more trouble with Seixas, 6-1, 6-4, 4-6, 6-1, before the Aussies thumped Seixas and Texan Sammy Giammalva, 1-6, 6-1, 7-5, 6-4, to make sure the third day was merely a workout.

Pro promoter Jack Kramer wanted to sign Hoad, who had won 15 tournaments, but when he vacillated, Kramer went after Rosewall instead, regarding him as the next best attraction to oppose Pancho Gonzalez in 1957. Kramer had started training to play 1955 amateur king Tony Trabert himself in 1956, but was persuaded by Gonzalez's wife, Henrietta, to let Pancho face Trabert on the head-to-head tour. Kramer, now badly afflicted with arthritis, was just as happy to do the promotion and let the strong and hungry Gonzalez play.

Gonzalez, very likely the best player in the world even though few realized it, crushed Trabert, 74 matches to 24. Gonzalez also won the U.S. Pro Championship over Pancho Segura, 21-15, 13-21, 21-14, 22-20 (a ping-pong scoring experiment) indoors at the Cleveland Arena, and beat Frank Sedgman, 4-6, 11-9, 11-9, 9-7, in a match of remarkably high quality at Wembley.

"Wembley, a London suburb of fast-fading respectability, is a shrine of English soccer. In those days its indoor arena was also a shrine of pro tennis," wrote Rex Bellamy in World Tennis more than two decades later. "That night, public transport ceased long before the match did. Stranded spectators did not much mind. They were unlikely to see such a match again."

1956 CHAMPIONS AND LEADERS

Year-End Number One
Men: Lew Hoad
Women: Shirley Fry

Davis Cup: Australia
Wightman Cup: United States

1957

Harlem to Forest Hills, a lifetime's journey

Althea Gibson
Gladiolas, roses and tears on the hallowed Centre Court.

The order that had prevailed in international tennis in the early part of the 1950s was changing rapidly by 1957. A year that began with Lew Hoad and Shirley Fry on top of the world ended with Althea Gibson as the dominant woman and surprising Mal Anderson challenging Ashley Cooper for the top spot among the men.

Any designs Hoad may have on the Grand Slam—he had come within one match in 1956—were shattered quickly. The 'baby bull' was upset in the semi-finals of the Australian singles, 7-5, 3-6, 6-1, 6-4, by a promising young left-hander, Neale Fraser, son of a prominent Labor politician. Cooper, a rather mechanical but solid and determined player who, with Fraser and Anderson, represented the new products off Harry Hopman's Australian Davis Cup assembly line, then won his first major title by beating Fraser in the final, 6-3, 9-11, 6-4, 6-2. Hoad and Fraser took the doubles.

Shortly after the pro tour between Pancho Gonzalez and Ken Rosewall—Gonzalez would win, 50-26—had begun in Australia at the New Year, Hoad had a friend contact promoter Jack Kramer and tell him that he was again interested in turning pro. Kramer was baffled, since Hoad had recently refused his entreaties. Later Kramer figured that Hoad was starting to encounter the back problems that eventually cut short his career, and decided he'd better get his payday while he still could.

Kramer signed Hoad—sending Ted Schroeder to the bank with him to make sure he cashed a $5,000 advance, which would provide proof of a contract if Hoad changed his mind again—but agreed to keep the pact secret until after Wimbledon.

Sven Davidson, the Swedish Davis Cup stalwart who was runner-up the previous two years, won the French singles over Herbie Flam, the last American man in the Paris final for 19 years, 6-3, 6-4, 6-4. Anderson and Cooper were the doubles titleists.

Hoad, whose season had been erratic, made his last amateur tournament a memorable one. At Wimbledon he lost only one set, to fellow Aussie Mervyn Rose in the quarters, 6-4, 4-6, 10-8, 6-3. Then he routed Davidson, the only non-Australian semi-finalist, 6-4, 6-4, 7-5, while Cooper won a tougher semi-final in the other half over Fraser, 1-6, 14-12, 6-3, 8-6. In the final, Hoad was brilliant, humbling Cooper, 6-2, 6-1, 6-2, in a mere 57 minutes. "It was a display of genius and it is to be doubted if such dynamic shot making was sustained with such accuracy before. If Cooper felt he had played badly, he had no chance to do anything else," wrote Lance Tingay. "Hoad was superhuman. It never began to be a contested match."

Gardnar Mulloy, age 43, and Budge Patty, 10 years younger, won their only Wimbledon doubles title—an exciting and sentimental occasion—over top-seeded Fraser and Hoad, 8-10, 6-4, 6-4, 6-4.

Hoad joined the pros, Kramer carefully trying to get him ready for a serious run at Gonzalez the following year. "I used him in a couple of round-robins in the States, and then I made myself into a sparring partner and, with Rosewall and [Pancho] Segura, we took off on an around-the-world tour to get Hoad in shape for Gonzalez," Kramer recalled. "If Hoad could beat Gonzalez, that was my chance to get rid of that tiger. Gonzalez knew what I was doing, too, and he was furious. We played a brutal death march, going to Europe, then across Africa, through India and Southeast Asia, all the way to Manila. I was impressed by how strong Hoad was. He was personally as gentle as a lamb, but on the trip his body could tolerate almost anything."

With Hoad gone, the 20-year-old Cooper was the top seed and heavy favorite to win Forest Hills. But he was upset by Anderson, the first unseeded champion of the U.S. Anderson, a country boy from a remote Queensland cattle station, had lost to Cooper in five of six previous meetings. But in the month before Forest Hills, the thin, quick, dark-haired lad of 22 had become

an entirely different player. Early in the year he had suffered from nervous exhaustion and heat prostration. At Wimbledon he broke a toe. But at Newport, R.I., on the U.S. grass court circuit, he beat U.S. No. 1 Ham Richardson, 6-1, 3-6, 6-0, 6-1, and, in the final, Welshman Mike Davies, 4-6, 6-1, 6-4, 1-6, 6-2, getting a confidence-boosting title under his belt.

At Forest Hills, he clobbered Dick Savitt, who had a cold, 6-4, 6-3, 6-1, then put on a dazzling display of piercing service returns and passing shots to crush Chilean Luis Ayala, 6-1, 6-3, 6-1. In the semi-finals, he overcame Sven Davidson (conqueror of Vic Seixas at Wimbledon) from a 1-2 deficit in sets, 5-7, 6-2, 4-6, 6-3, 6-4.

In his 10-8, 7-5, 6-4 triumph over top-seeded Cooper, Anderson was so good that he inspired rhapsodic prose and superlatives from Allison Danzig in the next day's *The New York Times*: "Anderson's performance ranks with the finest displays of offensive tennis of recent years. His speed of stroke and foot, the inevitability of his volley, his hair-trigger reaction and facileness on the half-volley, the rapidity of his service and passing shots and the adroitness of his return of service, compelling Cooper to volley up, all bore the stamp of a master of the racket. It was offensive tennis all the way, sustained without a letup. The margin of safety on most shots was almost nil. The most difficult shots were taken in stride with the acme of timing, going in or swiftly moving to the side."

1957 THE MAJOR CHAMPIONSHIPS

Australian Championships
Men's Singles: Ashley Cooper
Women's Singles: Shirley Fry
Men's Doubles: Neale Fraser / Lew Hoad
Women's Doubles: Althea Gibson / Shirley Fry
Mixed Doubles: Fay Muller / Mal Anderson
French Championships
Men's Singles: Sven Davidson
Women's Singles: Shirley Bloomer
Men's Doubles: Mal Anderson / Ashley Cooper
Women's Doubles: Shirley Bloomer / Darlene Hard
Mixed Doubles: Vera Puzejova / Jiri Javorsky
Wimbledon
Men's Singles: Lew Hoad
Women's Singles: Althea Gibson
Men's Doubles: Budge Patty / Gardnar Mulloy
Women's Doubles: Althea Gibson / Darlene Hard
Mixed Doubles: Darlene Hard / Merv Rose
U.S. Championships
Men's Singles: Mal Anderson
Women's Singles: Althea Gibson
Men's Doubles: Ashley Cooper / Neale Fraser
Women's Doubles: Louise Brough / Margaret Osborne duPont
Mixed Doubles: Althea Gibson / Kurt Nielsen

Less artistically satisfying, but just as dramatic, was Althea Gibson's 6-3, 6-2 victory in the women's final over Louise Brough. In 1950, when Gibson made history as the first black player admitted to the U.S. Championships, she had gained widespread attention by nearly beating Brough, then the Wimbledon champion, in the second round.

At the start of the year, Shirley Fry captured the Australian, the only one of the major singles titles she had not previously won, over Gibson, 6-3, 6-4. They teamed to win the doubles over Mary Hawton and Fay Muller, 6-2, 6-1. These were Fry's last big titles before retiring to become a housewife and teaching pro in Connecticut.

Englishwoman Shirley Bloomer's victory in the Italian (over Dorothy Head Knode, 1-6, 9-7, 6-2) was overshadowed by the first men's title of the stylish Nicki Pietrangeli over Beppe Merlo, 8-6, 6-2, 6-4. Shirley also, took the French over Knode, 6-1, 6-3, and teamed with Darlene Hard for the doubles crown.

But thereafter Gibson reigned supreme, clobbering Californian Hard, 6-3, 6-2, in the Wimbledon final. Althea won two singles (6-4, 4-6, 6-2, over Bloomer, and 6-4, 6-2, over Christine Truman) and a doubles as the U.S. defeated Great Britain, 6-1, in the Wightman Cup. Althea also won the Wimbledon doubles with Hard, over Aussies Hawton and Thelma Long, 6-1, 6-2. But they lost in the U.S. final, 6-2, 7-5, to Louise Brough and Margaret duPont, who took their last title. It was their third straight and 12th in all, a U.S. record, completing an overall record, their 20th major.

Fifteen years earlier, Gibson had been playing paddle tennis on the streets of Harlem. She had as difficult a path to the pinnacle of tennis as anyone ever did. She had to stare down bigotry as well as formidable opponents. Some tournaments had gone out of existence rather than admit her. But finally, at age 30, she was standing on the stadium court at Forest Hills, already the Wimbledon champion, accepting the trophy that symbolized supremacy in American women's tennis from Vice President Richard Nixon. The cup had white gladiolas and red roses in it, and 'Big Al' had tears in her eyes.

There was one other important piece of silverware at stake in 1957. With Hoad and Rosewall gone, Australia was vulnerable to a U.S. raiding party invading Melbourne for the Davis Cup challenge round. But Anderson edged big-serving Barry MacKay, 6-3, 7-5, 3-6, 7-9, 6-3; Cooper bumped 34-year-old Vic Seixas in a similarly tortuous match, 3-6, 7-5, 6-1, 1-6, 6-3; and Anderson and Mervyn Rose—chosen even though Cooper and Fraser had won the U.S. Doubles—combined to demoralize MacKay and Seixas, 6-4, 6-4, 8-6, in the clincher.

The second-largest Davis Cup crowds, 22,000 a day at Kooyong, witnessed. There were no flowers in the cup, but for the third straight year Aussies drank libations of victory beer from it.

1957 CHAMPIONS AND LEADERS

Year-End Number One
Men: Ashley Cooper
Women: Althea Gibson

Davis Cup: Australia
Wightman Cup: United States

1958

Peru's Olmedo unlikely U.S. hero

Pancho Gonzalez
Bests Lew Hoad 51-36 as pro game ascends, stampede to join ensues.

In 1958, Australians Ashley Cooper, Mal Anderson and Mervyn Rose were the top men in amateur tennis, and American Althea Gibson the outstanding woman. By the end of the year, they had all turned professional, underscoring the rapidly growing distance in quality between the small band of pros who wandered around the world playing one-and two-night stands as unsanctioned outcasts and the amateurs who basked in the limelight of the traditional fixtures.

The previous year the issue of 'open competition' between amateurs and pros was raised formally within the councils of the U.S. Tennis Association for the first time since the 1930s. A special committee report favored open tournaments. This document was promptly tabled since the leadership of the USTA was not nearly as progressive as the committee, but the ferment that ultimately led to the open game a decade later had started, and not only in America.

With Hoad and Rosewall touring professionally with Jack Kramer's World Tennis, Inc., Cooper took over the top amateur ranking by winning the three legs of the Grand Slam played on grass courts: The Australian, Wimbledon and the U.S.

He reversed the result of the 1957 Forest Hills final and took the Australian singles by beating Mal Anderson, 7-5, 6-3, 6-4.

At Wimbledon, loaded with Aussies, second-seeded Anderson injured himself in the quarter-finals, defaulting to Kurt Nielsen at 6-2, 6-3, and Cooper very nearly stumbled in the same round, probably coming within one point of defeat against Bobby Wilson, the pudgy but talented Englishman who delighted British galleries with his deft touch. Wilson had a break point for 6-5 in the fifth set, but Cooper rifled a backhand crosscourt winner within an inch of the sideline, and thereafter fortune favored the bold, 6-4, 6-2, 3-6, 4-6, 7-5. Cooper dominated Rose after losing the first set, 7-9, 6-2, 6-2, 6-3. Then in the final he beat Neale Fraser, 3-6, 6-3, 6-3, 13-11.

Cooper and Fraser were beaten in the doubles final, however, as the title went to an unseeded pair for the second straight year, the strapping Sven Davidson and Ulf Schmidt becoming the first Swedes to have their names inscribed on a Wimbledon championship trophy, 6-4, 6-4, 8-6.

At Forest Hills, Cooper and Anderson advanced to the U.S. final for the second consecutive year. Anderson beat Dick Savitt, 6-1, 3-6, 6-3, 18-16, and Swede Ulf Schmidt, 6-4, 7-5, 6-2. Cooper got there past Vic Seixas, 9-7, 6-2, 3-6, 6-2, and Fraser, 8-6, 6-1, 6-1. But in this championship rematch, Cooper prevailed in the longest final since Gonzalez-Schroeder in 1949, 6-2, 3-6, 4-6, 10-8, 8-6.

Gardnar Mulloy, reporting the match for *World Tennis*, wrote that the final set had "all the drama of a First Night," and suggested that Cooper merited an Oscar for his theatrics. The even-tempered Anderson served for the match at 5-4, but lost his serve at love. At 6-6, 30-15, Cooper apparently twisting an ankle, writhed in pain, hobbled to the sideline, and finally went back out to play after several minutes, to tumultuous applause. He "ran like a deer and served as well or better than he had all afternoon," opined Mulloy, a bit skeptical about the 'injury.' Cooper promptly held serve and then broke Anderson for the match. "Cooper is strong, tenacious, smart, and merciless," wrote Mulloy. "And don't forget his famous one-act play, *The Dying Swan*, a

1958 THE MAJOR CHAMPIONSHIPS

Australian Championships
Men's Singles: Ashley Cooper
Women's Singles: Angela Mortimer
Men's Doubles: Ashley Cooper / Neale Fraser
Women's Doubles: Mary Bevis Hawton / Thelma Coyne Long
Mixed Doubles: Mary Bevis Hawton / Bob Howe
French Championships
Men's Singles: Merv Rose
Women's Singles: Suzi Kormoczi
Men's Doubles: Ashley Cooper / Neale Fraser
Women's Doubles: Rosie Reyes / Yola Ramirez
Mixed Doubles: Shirley Bloomer / Nicola Pietrangeli
Wimbledon
Men's Singles: Ashley Cooper
Women's Singles: Althea Gibson
Men's Doubles: Sven Davidson / Ulf Schmidt
Women's Doubles: Maria Bueno / Althea Gibson
Mixed Doubles: Lorraine Coghlan / Bob Howe
U.S. Championships
Men's Singles: Ashley Cooper
Women's Singles: Althea Gibson
Men's Doubles: Alex Olmedo / Hamilton Richardson
Women's Doubles: Jeanne Arth / Darlene Hard
Mixed Doubles: Margaret Osborne duPont / Neale Fraser

real tear-jerker which clinched the championship for him."

Ham Richardson and Olmedo foreshadowed a U.S. revival in the Davis Cup by winning the U.S. Doubles at Longwood in their first tournament together, beating Sammy Giammalva and Barry MacKay in the final after bumping defenders Cooper and Fraser in a four-set semi, 7-9, 7-5, 6-3, 6-4

Merv Rose, with his tormenting left-handed serve, was the leading Aussie on clay, winning both the Italian and the French, saddening Romans by dethroning Nicola Pietrangeli, 5-7, 8-6, 6-4, 1-6, 6-2, and ripping the Chilean Davis Cupper Luis Ayala in the Paris final, 6-3, 6-4, 6-4. The most astounding match of the tournament was Frenchman Robert Haillet's resurrection in the fourth round to beat ex-champ Budge Patty, 5-7, 7-5, 10-8, 4-6, 7-5, after Patty served at 5-0, 40-0 in the fifth, and had a fourth match point at 5-4. Cooper and Fraser won the doubles, as they had in Australia, but were to advance no farther toward a Grand Slam.

Australia was heavily favored to defend the Davis Cup at the end of the year, but the United States had a potent and somewhat controversial weapon: The sleek, bronze-skinned, personable Alejandro 'Alex' Olmedo, 22, from Arequipa in the snowcapped Peruvian Andes. The nimble 6-foot, 160-pounder was a student at the University of Southern California (National Intercollegiate champ over Stanford's Jack Douglas, 6-3, 3-6, 6-4, 6-1) and a protégé of Perry Jones, czar of tennis in the Southern Cal section. Jones, also U.S. Davis Cup captain, lobbied successfully for Olmedo's inclusion, permissible since Peru did not have a Davis Cup team. 'The Chief,' as he was called because of his regal Incan appearance, had lost a tough five-set semi to Fraser at Forest Hills, 3-6, 6-1, 8-6, 3-6, 6-3. But in the 3-2 Davis Cup victory Olmedo was magnificent.

In the opening singles, before a capacity crowd of 18,000 at the Milton Courts in Brisbane, Olmedo stunned Anderson, 8-6, 2-6, 9-7, 8-6. Cooper beat MacKay, 4-6, 6-3, 6-2, 6-4, to make it 1-1, but on the second day Olmedo teamed with Richardson to outlast Fraser and Anderson, 10-12, 3-6, 16-14, 6-3, 7-5—82 games, a Cup record for final round doubles. Olmedo then capped his bravura performance by clinching the Cup with a 6-3, 4-6, 6-4, 8-6, victory over Cooper. Olmedo was rewarded with the No. 2 U.S. ranking behind Richardson.

No. 1 among the women, in the U.S. and the world,

was clearly the 5-foot-11, 145-pound Gibson, who used her thunderous serve and overhead, long reach and touch on the volley, and hard, flat, deep ground strokes to defend the Wimbledon and U.S singles titles. At Wimbledon she beat a local, Angela Mortimer, in the final, 8-6, 6-2.

Mortimer had won the Australian title over Lorraine Coghlan, 6-3, 6-4. At Forest Hills, Gibson's final victim was Darlene Hard, 3-6, 6-1, 6-2. Gibson teamed with Maria Bueno to win the Wimbledon doubles over Margaret Varner and 40-year-old Margaret duPont, 6-3, 7-5, but they were beaten in the U.S. final by Jeanne Arth and Hard, 2-6, 6-3, 6-4. This was the first of Hard's five consecutive U.S. titles. She won six in all with four partners. Bueno, the enchanting Brazilian, making her first overseas tour at age 18, had won the Italian title, over Aussie Coghlan, 3-6, 6-3, 6-3, and would be a major factor at Wimbledon and Forest Hills.

Gibson lost only four matches during the year, three in the early season (to Beverly Baker Fleitz and Janet Hopps twice), but the one that hurt was to tall Englishwoman Christine Truman in the pivotal match of the Wightman Cup. The British had a fine young team with Truman, Shirley Bloomer (runner-up to Hungarian Suzi Kormoczi, 6-4, 1-6, 6-2, in the French final), and left-hander Ann Haydon, even though Angela Mortimer didn't play. To the glee of the crowd at Wimbledon's Court 1, the British won the Cup for the first time since 1930, 4-3. Truman's 2-6, 6-3, 6-4 upset of Gibson paved the way, and the left-handed Haydon's scrambling 6-3, 5-7, 6-3 triumph over Mimi Arnold was the clincher.

After Forest Hills, Gibson announced her retirement "to pursue a musical career." She needed a source of income. The next year she accepted an offer to turn pro and play pre-game exhibitions at Harlem Globetrotters' basketball games against Karol Fageros, a popular glamour girl noted for her gold lamé panties, but not a player of Gibson's standard. Gibson won the tour with a 114-4 record, and said she made $100,000.

Lew Hoad found pro tennis even more lucrative. Even though he lost his 1958 tour against Gonzalez, 51-36, Hoad made $148,000. Gonzalez, who rallied from a 9-18 deficit after Hoad developed a stiff back in Palm Springs, Cal., made over $100,000.

"That was the last tour to make any real money, though," promoter Kramer later said. It had been a doozy. In Australia at the start of the year, Hoad was awesome, winning eight of 13 matches against a stale and overweight Gonzalez. In San Francisco, on a canvas court indoors, Hoad won, 6-4, 20-18, to inaugurate the U.S. segment of the tour. The next night Gonzalez won in his hometown of Los Angeles, 3-6, 24-22, 6-1. Before a crowd of 15,237 at Madison Square Garden, Gonzalez won the only best-of-five-setter, 7-9, 6-0, 6-4, 6-4.

Then Hoad, strong as an ox and beating Gonzalez in every department—serve, overhead, volley, and ground-strokes—surged to an 18-9 lead. But the bad back got him, and he was never again the factor he had been. Gonzalez won the tour and beat Hoad in the U.S. Pro Championships at the Arena in Cleveland, 3-6, 4-6, 14-12, 6-1, 6-4. Gonzalez was the best in the world, and the next year—Cooper, Anderson, and Rose coming aboard for a round robin—he proved it decisively.

1958 CHAMPIONS AND LEADERS

Year-End Number One
Men: Ashley Cooper
Women: Althea Gibson

Davis Cup: United States
Wightman Cup: Great Britain

1959

Latin beat wafting through majors

Alex Olmedo
Aussie and Wimbledon titles, but no Davis Cup repeat.

T he folly of the uneasy arrangement between amateur officials and pro promoter Jack Kramer during the 'shamateur' days of the late 1950s and early 1960s was apparent in this passage from a 1958 *Sports Illustrated* story on Kramer by Dick Phelan:

"'I look on the amateurs as my farm system' he [Kramer] says flatly, and this has been true particularly in Australia. There he is denounced as a public enemy because his money tempts the best Australian players to abandon their amateur status and thus their eligibility for Davis Cup play. Then when his troupe arrives in Australia the very public that reviled him flocks to his matches and profits mount. This leads the amateur tennis officials, whose own tournaments sometimes follow Kramer's and don't draw nearly so well, to lambaste him afresh. But they let him come back. Their share of his gate receipts helps support the Australian amateurs."

After the heady peak of the Pancho Gonzalez–Lew Hoad tour in 1958, the profits of Kramer's World Tennis, Inc., started to dwindle, despite his personal flair for promotion. Mal Anderson and Ashley Cooper joined the vanquished Hoad and the victorious Gonzalez in a round-robin tour, but the thrill was gone. They did not draw well, nor did similar tours with other personnel. If they had, it might have hastened the willingness of the amateur officials to consider open tennis. With Cooper, Anderson, and Mervyn Rose gone, Alex Olmedo and Neale Fraser ruled the amateur roost, sharing the world stage with the fiery Latin grace of Maria Bueno.

Olmedo, still buoyed by his Herculean accomplishment in the Davis Cup challenge round at the end of 1958, stayed and took the 1959 Australian singles title over southpaw Fraser, 6-1, 6-2, 3-6, 6-3. Rod Laver, starting the climb to greatness, and Bob Mark took the first of their three straight Aussie doubles titles.

Olmedo then returned to the United States and

won the U.S. Indoor at New York, 7-9, 6-3, 6-4, 5-7, 12-10, withstanding 28 aces, over Dick Savitt. Olmedo did not play the Italian Championship, where Luis Ayala prevailed over Fraser, 6-3, 3-6, 6-3, 6-3, or the French, where the great Italian artist Nicola Pietrangeli beat South African Ian Vermaak in the final, 3-6, 6-3, 6-4, 6-1. Pietrangeli and Italian Davis Cup teammate Orlando Sirola won the doubles over the champions of Italy, Fraser and Roy Emerson, 6-3, 6-2, 14-12.

Olmedo's 1958 Davis Cup triumph for the United States elevated him to national hero in his native Peru, and he made a triumphant tour there along with teammate Butch Buchholz, Davis Cup Capt. Perry Jones—and the Cup itself. Olmedo added to his skyrocketing reputation by winning Wimbledon, scoring a double Aussie KO, over Emerson in the semis, 6-4, 6-0, 6-4, and Laver, a left-hander of enormous but as yet unconsolidated talent, in the final, 6-4, 6-3, 6-4. Emerson took the first of his eventual record 16 major men's doubles titles, alongside Fraser, over Laver and Mark, 8-6, 6-3, 14-16, 9-7.

Wimbledon was the peak of Olmedo's year, however. Fraser beat him in the U.S. final at Forest Hills, 6-3, 5-7, 6-2, 6-4, the Chief's serve lacking its customary zip because of a shoulder strain he had suffered in a mixed doubles match the night before. Olmedo had beaten Emerson again, 6-4, 3-6, 6-2, 6-3, and Ron Holmberg, 15-13, 6-4, 3-6, 6-1, to get there after the hot, unseeded Holmberg had eliminated Dick Savitt, 1-6, 6-4, 7-5, 2-6, 9-7, Butch Buchholz, 6-3, 7-5, 8-10, 5-7, 6-3, and Laver, 6-8, 7-5, 6-0, 6-3. Fraser had few problems, beating another lefty, Texan Bernard 'Tut' Bartzen in his semi, 6-3, 6-2, 6-2.

Australia regained the Davis Cup at Forest Hills, 3-2, Olmedo never finding the form to which he had risen the previous December. Fraser beat him again in the opening match, 8-6, 6-8, 6-4, 8-6. Barry MacKay, the hulking 'Ohio Bear' out of Dayton, served mightily in beating Laver, 7-5, 6-4, 6-1, but in the doubles Emerson and Fraser outclassed Olmedo and Butch Buchholz, 7-5, 7-5, 6-4. The Aussies had prevailed in the U.S. Doubles over Alex and Butch by the breadth of their fingernails, 3-6, 6-3, 5-7, 6-4, 7-5, but this time the nails became claws.

Olmedo raised his game to beat Laver, 9-7, 4-6, 10-8, 12-10, to tie the series at 2-all, but Fraser clinched by beating MacKay in a match that was played over two days. They split sets before darkness forced a

postponement, but after a long rain delay, Fraser, returning splendidly, won the last two sets easily for a soggy 8-6, 3-6, 6-2, 6-4 victory.

On the women's side, Mary Carter Reitano won the Australian singles, 6-2, 6-3, over South African Renée Schuurman, who teamed with her countrywoman Sandra Reynolds for the doubles crown. Englishwoman Christine Truman, 18, won both the Italian (over Reynolds, 6-0, 6-1) and French titles, dethroning Hungarian clay-court specialist Suzi Kormoczi in the Paris final, 6-4, 7-5, to become the youngest champ until Steffi Graf, 17, in 1987. Reynolds and Schuurman won the doubles.

Thereafter the season belonged to the incomparably balletic and flamboyant Bueno. Volleying beautifully, playing with breathtaking boldness and panache, the lithe Brazilian became the first South American woman to win the Wimbledon singles, beating Darlene Hard in the final, 6-4, 6-3. Hard did team with Jeanne Arth to add the Wimbledon doubles to the U.S. crown they captured the previous year, and won the mixed with Laver.

Bueno then inspired the galleries at Forest Hills as she had at London, beating the tall and sporting Truman in the final, 6-4, 6-1. Hard and Arth repeated as U.S. Doubles champions at Longwood.

The United States regained the Wightman Cup from Great Britain with a 4-3 victory at the Edgeworth Club in Sewickley, Pa. The British won the final two matches, but only after Hard's 6-3, 6-8, 6-4 victory over Angela

---

1959 THE MAJOR CHAMPIONSHIPS

Australian Championships
Men's Singles: Alex Olmedo
Women's Singles: Mary Carter Reitano
Men's Doubles: Rod Laver / Bob Mark
Women's Doubles: Renee Schuurman / Sandra Reynolds
Mixed Doubles: Sandra Reynolds / Bob Mark
French Championships
Men's Singles: Nicola Pietrangeli
Women's Singles: Christine Truman
Men's Doubles: Orlando Sirola / Nicola Pietrangeli
Women's Doubles: Sandra Reynolds / Renee Schuurman
Mixed Doubles: Yola Ramirez / Billy Knight
Wimbledon
Men's Singles: Alex Olmedo
Women's Singles: Maria Bueno
Men's Doubles: Roy Emerson / Neale Faser
Women's Doubles: Jeanne Arth / Darlene Hard
Mixed Doubles: Darlene Hard / Rod Laver
U.S. Championships
Men's Singles: Neale Fraser
Women's Singles: Maria Bueno
Men's Doubles: Neale Fraser / Roy Emerson
Women's Doubles: Jeanne Arth / Darlene Hard
Mixed Doubles: Margaret Osborne duPont / Neale Fraser

Mortimer, and Beverly Baker Fleitz's 6-4, 6-4 conquest of Truman had given the Americans an unbeatable 4-1 lead.

Gonzalez remained the pro champion. He beat Hoad for the second straight year in the final of the U.S. Pro Championships at Cleveland, 6-4, 6-2, 6-4, after romping in the round-robin tour against Hoad, Cooper, and Anderson. Anderson took the biggie, London, at Wembley, in a tight one with Pancho Segura, 4-6, 6-4, 3-6, 6-3, 8-6.

1959 CHAMPIONS AND LEADERS

Year-End Number One
Men: Neale Fraser
Women: Maria Bueno

Davis Cup: Australia
Wightman Cup: United States

1960

Laver and Smith win first majors

Neale Fraser
Renders Rocket Rod the victim in two of three major finals.

Once again, the start of a new decade was the dawn of a new era in tennis. As 1950 had been, so 1960 was an eventful year.

It began with an Australian Championships that heralded a man and woman who would be king and queen of tennis. Rod Laver skirted a match point at 4-5 in the fourth to beat fellow Aussie left-hander Neale Fraser in an epic final, 5-7, 3-6, 6-3, 8-6, 8-6, the first of his eventual 11 Big Four singles titles. Margaret Smith, who would later become Mrs. Barry Court, beat her countrywoman Jan Lehane, 7-5, 6-2, for the first of seven consecutive Australian titles and 24 major singles titles in all—both records. It was a teen-age final that Smith, 17, and Lehane, 18, would repeat in 1961, unique to the majors until Arantxa Sanchez Vicario, 17, beat Steffi Graf, 19, to win the 1989 French.

It would have been much more of a landmark year but for five votes at the annual general meeting of the International Tennis Federation. By that slim margin, a proposal calling for sanction of between 8 and 13 'open' tournaments in which pros and amateurs would compete together failed to muster the two-thirds majority needed for passage. The proposal had the backing of the U.S., British, French and Australian associations, and the proponents of the 'open' movement were bitterly disappointed when it failed.

Another proposal put forth by the French federation calling for creation of a category of 'registered' players who could capitalize on their skill by bargaining with tournaments for appearance fees higher than the expenses allowed amateurs, was tabled. The U.S. Tennis Association had voted to oppose this resolution on the basis that 'registered player' was just another name for a pro.

Top-seeded Maria Bueno did not reach the semifinals of the Australian singles (cut off in the quarters by Smith, 7-5, 3-6, 6-4) but she teamed with Christine Truman to win the doubles over Smith and Lorraine Coghlan Robinson, 6-2, 5-7, 6-2. That was the first leg of a doubles Grand Slam by Bueno. She went on to win the French, Wimbledon and U.S. titles with American Darlene Hard, losing only one more set along the way, to Karen Hantze and Janet Hopps in the semi-finals at Wimbledon, 3-6, 6-1, 6-4.

Hard won her first major singles title at Paris, struggling through three three-set matches in the early rounds, hanging in over South African Renee Schuurman in the quarters, 5-7, 6-2, 11-9, then whipping Bueno in the semis, 6-3, 6-2, and the quick little Mexican Yola Ramirez in the final, 6-3, 6-4. Ramirez beat South African Sandra Reynolds, 8-10, 6-3, 6-3, in their semi.

One of the luckiest in the tournament's history was an Egyptian woman (a rarity in itself), Betty Abbas: She won one round and found herself in the quarter-finals. Trailing 1958 champ Suzy Kormoczi, 4-5, Abbas was declared winner as the Hungarian sprained an ankle, unable to continue. Her next foe was Aussie Mary Hawton, who sprained an ankle in the warm-up. That

1960 THE MAJOR CHAMPIONSHIPS

Australian Championships
Men's Singles: Rod Laver
Women's Singles: Margaret Smith
Men's Doubles: Rod Laver / Bob Mark
Women's Doubles: Maria Bueno / Christine Truman
Mixed Doubles: Jan Lehane / Trevor Fancutt
French Championships
Men's Singles: Nicola Pietrangeli
Women's Singles: Darlene Hard
Men's Doubles: Roy Emerson / Neale Fraser
Women's Doubles: Maria Bueno / Darlene Hard
Mixed Doubles: Maria Bueno / Bob Howe
Wimbledon
Men's Singles: Neale Fraser
Women's Singles: Maria Bueno
Men's Doubles: Rafael Osuna / Dennis Ralston
Women's Doubles: Maria Bueno / Darlene Hard
Mixed Doubles: Darlene Hard / Rod Laver
U.S. Championships
Men's Singles: Neale Fraser
Women's Singles: Darlene Hard
Men's Doubles: Neale Fraser / Roy Emerson
Women's Doubles: Maria Bueno / Darlene Hard
Mixed Doubles: Margaret Osborne duPont / Neale Fraser

default lifted the Egyptian to the last eight where Ramirez easily beat her, 6-0, 6-4. Leg II in Bueno's doubles Slam was her and Hard's 6-2, 7-5, decision over Brits Pat Ward Hales and Ann Haydon.

Hard also won her first U.S. Singles at Forest Hills, beating Bueno, 6-4, 10-12, 6-4, after the final was postponed nearly a week by Hurricane Donna. She and Bueno had completed leg IV of Maria's Slam at Longwood, over Brits Deidre Catt and Haydon, 6-1, 6-1.

At Wimbledon, where American women had been so dominant for more than a decade after the war, not one of the 10 Americans who entered reached the semifinals. This had not happened since 1925. Hard, the best U.S. hope, lost in the quarter-finals to Reynolds, 6-1, 2-6, 6-1, who reached the final but lost to Bueno, 8-6, 6-0. A year earlier, journalist Lance Tingay had pointed out that the difference between being very good or very bad was, for Bueno, a thin line based on her timing. "Mundane shots did not exist for her," he observed. "It was either caviar or starvation." For the second year in a row it was mostly caviar, and a feast for the spectators. Her Wimbledon performance was good enough to earn Bueno the No.1 world ranking by a shade over Hard. It was also Leg III in Maria's doubles Slam, aided by Hard, over South Africans Reynolds and Schuurman, 6-4, 6-0. Maria missed out on a triple, however, because of Hard, who, accompanied by Laver, took the mixed, 13-11, 3-6, 8-6, over Bueno and Aussie Bob Howe.

Britain won the Wightman Cup for the second time in three years, snatching a 4-3 victory at Wimbledon by winning the final two matches. Hard had given the U.S. a 3-2 lead with a 5-7, 6-2, 6-1 triumph over Ann Haydon, but Mortimer beat Janet Hopps, 6-8, 6-4, 6-1, and Christine Truman paired with Shirley Bloomer Brasher to beat Hopps and Dorothy Head Knode, 6-4, 9-7.

Nicki Pietrangeli defended his French singles title over Luis Ayala, runner-up for the second time in three years, 3-6, 6-3, 6-4, 4-6, 6-3.

The third round was an Aussie disaster, Roy Emerson losing to Italian giant Orlando Sirola, 3-6, 7-5, 8-6, 7-5, and Laver to nifty Spaniard Manolo Santana, 6-1, 4-6, 6-4, 5-7, 6-3. Then mate Neale Fraser, collapsing with leg cramps at the end, was beaten by homeboy Robert Haillet, 6-4, 6-2, 8-10, 3-6, 6-5 (default). Ayala was also second best in Rome, where Barry MacKay served and volleyed on the slow clay, winning the final by a most peculiar score: 7-5, 7-5, 0-6, 0-6, 6-1. MacKay had won the U.S. Indoor on wood in February, 6-2, 2-6, 10-12, 6-1, 6-4, over Dick Savitt, so within four months he took titles on just about the fastest and slowest court surfaces in the world. Roy Emerson and Neale Fraser combined for the French doubles title, over Spaniards Andres Gimeno and Lis Arilla, 6-2, 8-10, 7-5, 6-4, the first of Emmo's six straight, with five partners.

Fraser took over as the No.1 man in the amateur ranks by winning Wimbledon and the U.S. Championship. As with the women, no American man got to the semis at Wimbledon. MacKay was beaten in the quarter-finals by Pietrangeli, 16-14, 6-2, 3-6, 6-4, and Butch Buchholz, 19, led Fraser by 6-4, 3-6, 6-4, 15-15, in the same round and had five match points in the fourth set before being seized with cramps that left him unable to continue. Fraser, 26 and playing for the seventh time, was a sporting and popular champion. His left-handed serve had a wicked kick, and he was a daring and resourceful volleyer. He beat Laver, five years his junior, in the final, 6-4, 3-6, 9-7, 7-5.

A small measure of U.S. pride was saved when the unseeded team of Dennis Ralston, 17, and agile 21-year-old Mexican Rafael Osuna won the men's doubles, the second-youngest team to win Wimbledon. They beat Britons Humphrey Truman and Gerald Oakley in the first round, 6-3, 6-4, 9-11, 5-7, 16-14, and second-seeded Laver and Bob Mark, the Australian champions, 4-6, 10-8, 15-13, 4-6, 11-9, in the semi-final. After that pulsating contest, the final was comparatively easy: 7-5, 6-3, 10-8 over Welshman Mike Davies and Englishman Bobby Wilson.

Laver foreshadowed greatness to come by ripping up the U.S. Eastern grass court circuit, winning four consecutive titles: Pennsylvania Grass over New Yorker Ron Holmberg, 9-7, 8-6, 6-3; Southampton, N.Y. over Holmberg, 12-10, 6-3, 3-6, 2-6, 6-3; Orange, N.J., over Donald Dell, 6-1, 12-10, 6-4; Newport. R.I., over Buchholz, 6-8, 6-1, 6-2. Laver and Mark got revenge on Ralston and Osuna in the semis of the U.S. Doubles at Longwood, 6-2, 8-6, 6-2, but lost the final to Fraser and Emerson, 9-7, 6-2, 6-4.

At Forest Hills, Laver got to the U.S. final by beating Buchholz, who had three match points before again suffering a debilitating attack of cramps and losing, 4-6, 5-7, 6-4, 6-2, 7-5. Fraser beat the precocious Ralston, 11-9, 6-3, 6-2, and then, after sitting around through a week of hurricane rain and wind, slogged to the title over Laver, 6-4, 6-4, 10-8. That closed down Laver's 29-match streak on the green.

For the first time since 1936, the United States failed to reach the challenge round of the Davis Cup, falling to Italy, 3-2 in the inter-zone semi-finals at Perth, Australia, in December.

Italy's first appearance in the challenge round a couple of weeks later was less auspicious, a 4-1 Aussie victory that was over in three matches as Fraser and Laver swept opening day in Sydney: Neale beat Orlando Sirola, 4-6, 6-3, 6-3, 6-3, and Rod went through Nicola Pietrangeli, 8-6, 6-4, 6-3. Fraser and Emerson mopped up the two Italians, 10-8, 5-7, 6-2, 6-4.

This time the Aussies suffered no defections to the pro tour immediately after the Davis Cup, but the Americans did. MacKay and Buchholz, undoubtedly thinking that open tennis was near and wanting a piece of Jack Kramer's checkbook before it arrived, signed to make a tour in 1961 with Lew Hoad, Frank Sedgman, Tony Trabert, Ashley Cooper, Alex Olmedo and the Spaniard Andres Gimeno.

Meanwhile the 1960 tour, won by Pancho Gonzalez over Olmedo, Pancho Segura and Ken Rosewall, was not a financial success. Olmedo, the Wimbledon champ a year before, beat Trabert in the U.S. Pro final, 7-5, 6-4, at Cleveland. But Trabert took London at Wembley over Lew Hoad, 6-8, 6-4, 6-4.

1960 CHAMPIONS AND LEADERS

Year-End Number One
Men: Neale Fraser
Women: Maria Bueno

Davis Cup: Australia
Wightman Cup: Great Britain

1961

Kramer ups ante, ITF buries head

Darlene Hard Above-and-beyond kindness to a friend, then, fittingly, a second U.S. title.

In 1961, the amateur tennis establishment was stunned and smarting from a wholesale raid on its ranks by pro promoter Jack Kramer, who in 1960 signed to contracts several middling players: Spaniard Andres Gimeno, Welshman Mike Davies, Frenchman Robert Haillet and Dane Kurt Nielsen, as well as young Americans Butch Buchholz and Barry MacKay. Kramer tried without success to lure into his fold Australian Neale Fraser, the Wimbledon and Forest Hills champion; Italian Nicki Pietrangeli, champion of France; and Chilean Luis Ayala, runner-up in the 1960

Italian and French Championships.

When a proposal for introducing 'open tournaments' was unexpectedly stymied by just five votes at the 1960 International Tennis Federation annual meeting, there was relatively little official grieving among the member national associations and their officials. However, Kramer's response of taking out his wallet and waving it in front of practically every player of moderate reputation—amateur powers-that-be thought Kramer both irresponsible and reprehensible—started alarm bells sounding. Suddenly the national associations saw their tournaments, and hence their revenues, in grave danger. Kramer became Public Enemy No. 1.

But if his motive was to force the ITF into open competition by his mass signings, as most suspected, he failed. Amateur officials did not like being bullied. A new 'open tournament' proposal was rejected at the 1961 ITF annual meeting at Stockholm. Delegates approved a resolution agreeing "to the principle of an experiment of a limited number of open tournaments," but referred the matter to a committee for another year of study to see how the experiment might be conducted. A U.S.-sponsored 'home rule' resolution, which would have permitted national associations to stage open tournaments at their own discretion, was defeated. The ITF was able to stand up to Kramer because he had been able to sign only two of the previous year's top handful of players: No. 3, MacKay, and No. 5, Buchholz. The amateurs still had Fraser, Rod Laver, Pietrangeli, Roy Emerson and Ayala. But the battle lines had been drawn. Instead of the uneasy coexistence of the past, the amateur associations and Kramer were now at war.

Emerson, a magnificently fit and affable fellow with slick black hair that shone like patent leather and a smile that sparkled with gold fillings, served and volleyed relentlessly to defeat his fellow Queenslander Laver in the Australian final, 1-6, 6-3, 7-5, 6-4. This was the first of six Australian titles in seven years for 'Emmo,' the first of a men's record (at the time) 12 major singles titles in all. Laver and Bob Mark annexed the doubles crown for the third straight year. On the women's side, 'Mighty Margaret' Smith beat Jan Lehane again in the singles final, 6-1, 6-4, and teamed with Mary Carter Reitano for the first of Smith's eight Australian doubles titles.

In Paris, the two greatest European virtuosi of the '60s met in the final. English writer Rex Bellamy was there: "Nicola Pietrangeli, the favorite to win for the third consecutive year, was beaten by the young Manuel 'Manolo' Santana, the first Spaniard to win a major title. The match lasted five sets. Santana and Pietrangeli were like artists at work in a studio exposed to a vast public in the heat of the afternoon. Each in turn played his finest tennis. The flame of Pietrangeli's inspiration eventually died, his brushstrokes overlaid by Santana's flickering finesse. But long before that, these two Latins had established a close rapport with a Latin crowd enjoying a rare blend of sport and aesthetics. At the end there was a tumult of noise. Santana, his nerves strung up to the breaking point, dropped his racket and cried. And

Pietrangeli, disappointed yet instantly responsive to the Spaniard's feelings, went around the net, took Santana in his arms, and patted him on the back like a father comforting a child."

The score was 4-6, 6-1, 3-6, 6-0, 6-2, but bald numbers could hardly convey the emotion of this long afternoon, especially for the toothy Santana. He got to the final by upsetting Emerson, 9-7, 6-2, 6-2, and Laver, 3-6, 6-2, 4-6, 6-4, 6-0. Pietrangeli teased the home folks before beating Gerard Pilet, 6-4, 6-8, 6-3, 6-1, and took out Swede Jan-Erik Lundquist in a semi, 6-4, 6-4, 6-4,

A vivid contrast in style to the gliding and caressing strokes of the singles finalists was provided by Laver and Emerson, who bore in on the net for murderous volleys in winning the doubles over countrymen Bob Howe and Bob Mark, 3-6, 6-1, 6-1, 6-4.

Left-hander Ann Haydon showed the legs, heart, and brain of a clay court stalwart in beating agile volleyer Yola Ramirez, 6-2, 6-1, for the French women's title. Bueno was removed by ex-champ Suzi Kormoczi, 6-3, 6-3. South Africans Renée Schuurman and Sandra Reynolds won the doubles.

Maria Bueno, who had beaten Australian Lesley Turner in the Italian final, 6-4, 6-4, was bedridden in Paris after her quarter-final loss to Kormoczi. Lacking funds to pay for hospital care, she was confined to a tiny hotel chamber for a month, with the rest of the floor quarantined, until she was able to go home to Brazil.

Bueno was thus unable to defend her Wimbledon

1961 THE MAJOR CHAMPIONSHIPS

Australian Championships
Men's Singles: Roy Emerson
Women's Singles: Margaret Smith
Men's Doubles: Rod Laver / Bob Mark
Women's Doubles: Mary Carter Reitano / Margaret Smith
Mixed Doubles: Jan Lehane / Bob Hewitt
French Championships
Men's Singles: Manolo Santana
Women's Singles: Ann Haydon
Men's Doubles: Roy Emerson / Rod Laver
Women's Doubles: Sandra Reynolds / Renee Schuurman
Mixed Doubles: Darlene Hard / Rod Laver
Wimbledon
Men's Singles: Rod Laver
Women's Singles: Angela Mortimer
Men's Doubles: Roy Emerson / Neale Fraser
Women's Doubles: Karen Hantze / Billie Jean Moffitt
Mixed Doubles: Lesley Turner / Fred Stolle
U.S. Championships
Men's Singles: Roy Emerson
Women's Singles: Darlene Hard
Men's Doubles: Chuck McKinley / Dennis Ralston
Women's Doubles: Darlene Hard / Lesley Turner
Mixed Doubles: Margaret Smith / Bob Mark

title. Darlene Hard, her doubles partner and the U.S. champ, also withdrew and generously stayed in Paris to care for her friend. Karen Hantze was the only American to reach the women's quarter-finals. This was the 75th-anniversary Wimbledon, and through the wreckage came seventh and sixth-seeded Angela Mortimer and Christine Truman, opponents in the first all-British women's final since 1914.

The crowd adored Truman, 20, a smiling 6-footer with a big forehand and attacking game, epitomizing all the best British sporting traits, and they moaned when she fell awkwardly on a rain-slicked court in the third set of the final. That tumble cost her the momentum she had built up against the more defensive Mortimer, 29, who, on her 11th try, didn't hesitate to lob and drop-shot in a 4-6, 6-4, 7-5 victory. It had been a long time coming—since the last English champ, Dorothy Round in 1937.

Hantze, age 18, and bouncing, bubbly Billie Jean Moffitt, 17, won the doubles over Aussies Smith and Lehane, 6-3, 6-4. Unseeded, they were the youngest pair ever to seize a Wimbledon crown. Eighteen years later, Billie Jean Moffitt King's 10th doubles title would give her the all-time record for career Wimbledon titles in all events: 20.

Laver, the red-haired Queenslander called 'Rocket,' won the men's title for the first time, over American Chuck McKinley, 6-3, 6-1, 6-4. This was the start of an unprecedented reign: Laver would win 31 singles match-es without a defeat at Wimbledon in five appearances, going to the fourth round in 1970, winning four singles titles plus a BBC-sponsored pro tournament in 1967. In the semis Laver ran over Indian Ramanathan Krishnan, 6-2, 8-6, 6-2, and McKinley tamed the heavy serving of a rare Brit in the last four, Mike Sangster, 6-4, 6-4, 8-6. Top-seeded Neale Fraser, who had lost his title in the round of 16, banished by Englishman Bobby Wilson, 1-6, 6-0, 13-11, 9-7, captured the doubles with Emerson, but then returned home to Australia to tend an ailing knee.

Great Britain had both Wimbledon singles finalists and the French champion on its team, but was startlingly ambushed, 6-1, in the Wightman Cup by a 'mod squad' of eager American juniors. Hantze beat Haydon, 6-1, 6-4, and Truman, 7-9, 6-1, 6-1. Moffitt beat Haydon, 6-4, 6-4, and 18-year-old St. Louis lefty Justina Bricka shocked Mortimer, 10-8, 4-6, 6-3. Hantze-Moffitt clobbered Truman–Deidre Catt, 7-5,

6-2, and the U.S. won the final doubles when Mortimer defaulted with foot cramps. Truman's singles win over Moffitt, 6-3, 6-2, was the only one the shell-shocked English could salvage from the massacre at Chicago's Saddle and Cycle Club.

Texan Bernard 'Tut' Bartzen won his fourth U.S. Clay Court singles since 1954, beating Donald Dell, 6-1, 2-6, 6-2, 6-0. Dell, earlier in the year had gone with doubles partner Mike Franks on a State Department tour of South Africa, the Middle East and the Soviet Union, the first Americans to play in Russia since the 1917 Revolution.

McKinley and Dennis Ralston won the rain-delayed U.S. Doubles over Mexicans Rafe Osuna and Antonio Palafox, 6-3, 6-4, 2-6, 13-11. Hard teamed with Turner for her fourth successive women's doubles title, over the German-Mexican combine of Edda Buding and Yola Ramirez, 6-4, 5-7, 6-0, and was supposed to play with Ralston against Margaret Smith and Bob Mark in the mixed final, at Longwood. But rain postponed the match until Forest Hills, and Ralston was unable to play because he was unfairly suspended by the U.S. Tennis Association for his behavior earlier, in a Davis Cup series against Mexico.

At Forest Hills, spacy, unorthodox Californian Whitney Reed—he never trained, partied all night, but had such a wonderful touch that he earned the No. 1 U.S. ranking—upset second-seeded McKinley, 6-3, 9-7, 3-6, 6-3, in the third round but fell to Osuna, 6-8, 6-3, 6-3, 6-2, in a beguiling battle of touch-shot practitioners. Emerson barely got by the catlike and clever Osuna, 6-3, 6-2, 3-6, 5-7, 9-7, in a rousing semi-final, but then overwhelmed top-seeded Laver in the final, 7-5, 6-3, 6-2, to lay claim to the No. 1 ranking among the amateurs.

Darlene Hard, the only American in the women's quarter-finals, battled past Ramirez, 6-3, 6-1, Smith, 6-4, 3-6, 6-3, and Haydon in the final, 6-3, 6-4, for her second straight U.S. title.

With MacKay and Buchholz professionals, U.S. Davis Cup Capt. David Freed named a 14-man squad that accented youth. The U.S. beat British West Indies and Ecuador, both 5-0, and slipped past Mexico and India, 3-2 on each occasion. Italy again was the barrier to the challenge round and Australia, defeating the U.S. 4-1.

Fausto Gardini refused to go to Australia for the challenge round unless he was assured of a singles berth.

However, he wasn't, and Nicola Pietrangeli and Orlando Sirola couldn't get even one set on the grass at Melbourne until the required three matches had been played: Emerson over Pietrangeli, 8-6, 6-4, 6-0; Laver, over Sirola, 6-1, 6-4, 6-3; Emerson and Fraser over the two, 6-2, 6-3, 6-4, confirming the Aussie defense of the Cup. Final score, 5-0.

Kramer's expanded traveling circus—Pancho Gonzalez, Lew Hoad, Frank Sedgman, Ken Rosewall, Tony Trabert, Ashley Cooper, Alex Olmedo, Andres Gimeno, MacKay and Buchholz as principals, plus the others—did not make enough to cover his vastly increased overhead. Gonzalez beat Sedgman, 6-3, 7-5, in Cleveland for his record eighth and last U.S. Pro title, 6-3, 7-5, and Rosewall won Wembley over Hoad, 6-3, 3-6, 6-2, 6-3. However, the pros were in trouble, and Kramer's grandstanding of the previous autumn had not ultimately helped the cause of open competition.

1961 CHAMPIONS AND LEADERS

Year-End Number One
Men: Rod Laver
Women: Angela Mortimer

Davis Cup: Australia
Wightman Cup: United States

1962

Laver nets Slam, Maggie falls short

Rod Laver
Three of four Slam final wins came at Roy Emerson's expense.

The Australian grip—both hands firmly around the throat of players of any other nationality—was in vogue in 1962, the season of Rod Laver's first Grand Slam and Margaret Smith's inaugural near-Slam.

Laver duplicated Don Budge's supreme feat of 1938, sweeping the singles titles of Australia, France, Great Britain (Wimbledon) and the U.S. He also won the Italian and German titles, not to mention the less prestigious Norwegian, Irish and Swiss, and led Australia to a 5-0 blitz of upstart Mexico in the Davis Cup challenge round. In all, Laver won 19 of 34 tournaments and 134 of 149 matches during his long and incomparably successful year.

Smith (to become better known as Margaret Court after marriage to Barry Court) was staggered in the first round of Wimbledon by the pudgy chatterbox who would grow up to be her archrival, Billie Jean Moffitt (later Billie Jean King) but otherwise won just about everything in sight. Smith's only other loss was to another young American, Carole Caldwell, but 'Mighty Maggie' won 13 of 15 tournaments, including the Australian, French and U.S., and 67 of 69 matches.

Laver, the 'Rockhampton Rocket' from that Queensland town, started his Slam at White City Stadium in Sydney, beating Roy Emerson, 8-6, 0-6, 6-4, 6-4, not that he'd had an easy time making it that far. Laver was particularly harried by Geoff Pares in the third round before prevailing, 10-8, 18-16, 7-9, 7-5. Emerson and Neale Fraser took the doubles.

Laver lived precariously at the French in Paris, the only leg of the Slam on slow clay, going the maximum 15 sets down the stretch. He saved a match point in beating countryman Marty Mulligan in the quarterfinals, 6-4, 3-6, 2-6, 10-8, 6-2. He also went five with Fraser in the semis, 3-6, 6-3, 6-2, 3-6, 7-5, and with Emerson again in the final, 3-6, 2-6, 6-3, 9-7, 6-2. Emerson and Fraser racked up another doubles title.

At Wimbledon, Laver lost only one set to Manolo Santana in a 14-16, 9-7, 6-2, 6-2, quarter-final victory. There were no Americans in the quarters for the first time since 1922, and hardly room for anyone but Australians—six of them—as Yank Frank Froehling fell to Santana,12-10, 6-3, 8-10, 6-3, in the fourth round. The semis were an all-Aussie show: Laver, Mulligan (advanced over Emerson, who had an injured toe), Neale Fraser and his brother John Fraser, a physician by profession, who got an uncommonly lucky draw. Laver beat Neale Fraser, 10-8, 6-1, 7-5, and trampled Mulligan in the final, 6-2, 6-2, 6-1. With Emerson sidelined by the painful toe, defaulting to Mulligan in the quarters, Aussies Bob Hewitt and Fred Stolle won the doubles over two new faces, Yugoslavs Boro Jovanovic and Nikki Pilic, 6-2, 5-7, 6-2, 6-4.

At Forest Hills, Laver lost only one set again en route to the U.S. final—to gangly Froehling, in a 6-3, 13-11, 4-6, 6-3 quarter-final victory. The athletic Emerson was back, but Laver repelled him as he had in Sydney, Rome (6-2, 1-6, 3-6, 6-3, 6-1 in the Italian final) and Paris. Laver hit four fearsome backhand returns to break serve in the first game and dominated the first two sets with his varied backhand, either bashed or chipped, a topspin forehand, and ruthless serving and net play. Emerson, always barreling forward and battling, aroused a crowd of 9,000 by winning the third set, but Laver closed out the match and the Slam, 6-2, 6-4, 5-7, 6-4, and was greeted by original Slammer Budge afterward. They had the male precinct of the ultra-exclusive club to themselves, sharing with only Maureen Connolly.

Astonishingly, there were again no Aussies in the U.S. Doubles final at Longwood, where the 'Mexican Thumping Beans,' collegians Rafe Osuna and Tony Palafox, out-hustled temperamental Americans Chuck McKinley and Dennis Ralston, reversing the previous year's final result, 6-4, 10-12, 1-6, 9-7, 6-3.

Osuna and Palafox had scored a victory of much greater import over Ralston-McKinley earlier in the year, in the pivotal match of Mexico's 3-2 upset of the U.S. in the Davis Cup. Palafox beat Jack Douglas in the rarefied atmosphere of Mexico City, 6-3, 6-1, 3-6, 7-5 after McKinley had disposed of Osuna, 6-2, 7-5, 6-3, in the opener. The doubles point provided the impetus, 8-6, 10-12, 3-6, 6-3, 6-2. The next day Osuna was carried off on the shoulders of jubilant countrymen when he out-nerved Douglas, 9-7, 6-3, 6-8, 3-6, 6-1, for the clinching 3-1 point. This was the first time Mexico had

defeated the U.S. in 15 tries and won the American Zone. Osuna and Palafox lugged their adoring nation all the way to the challenge round: Past Yugoslavia, 4-1, Sweden, 3-2 (Osuna taking the tingling fifth match in Mexico City over Jan-Erik Lundquist, 3-6, 6-4, 6-3, 1-6, 6-3) and India, 4-1 at Madras.

Osuna had gone 5-1 in singles, Palafox 3-2 and they were 4-0 in doubles, all on clay. However the left-handed Laver and Fraser on the swift grass of Brisbane were too steep a proposition, 5-0: Laver slamming Osuna, 6-2, 6-1, 7-5, and Fraser taking Palafox, 7-9, 6-3, 6-4, 11-9. Queensland mates Emerson and Laver settled it over the game Mexicans, 7-5, 6-2, 6-4.

For the third straight year Margaret Smith, 19, drubbed Jan Lehane, 20, in the final of the Australian, 6-0, 6-2, where Jan with her then-rare double-handed backhand removed second-seeded Darlene Hard, 7-5, 6-4, from the quarters.

But Margaret had a much closer French final against another countrywoman, Lesley Turner. Smith had shown she could play on clay too, winning the Italian title, 8-6, 5-7, 6-4, over Maria Bueno, and she prevailed, 6-3, 3-6, 7-5, in Paris, rescuing a match point at 3-5 in the third.

By that time she must have been entertaining thoughts of duplicating the Grand Slam, joining Connolly, who had emulated Budge in 1953. But 18-year-old Billie Jean Moffitt, who had a premonition weeks earlier that she would draw Smith in her opening

---

1962 THE MAJOR CHAMPIONSHIPS

Australian Championships
Men's Singles: Rod Laver
Women's Singles: Margaret Smith
Men's Doubles: Roy Emerson / Neale Fraser
Women's Doubles: Margaret Smith / Robyn Ebbern
Mixed Doubles: Lesley Turner / Fred Stolle
French Championships
Men's Singles: Rod Laver
Women's Singles: Margaret Smith
Men's Doubles: Roy Emerson / Neale Fraser
Women's Doubles: Sandra Reynolds Price / Renee Schuurman
Mixed Doubles: Renee Schuurman / Bob Howe
Wimbledon
Men's Singles: Rod Laver
Women's Singles: Karen Hantze Susman
Men's Doubles: Bob Hewitt / Fred Stolle
Women's Doubles: Billie Jean Moffitt / Karen Hantze Susman
Mixed Doubles: Margaret Osborne duPont / Neale Fraser
U.S. Championships
Men's Singles: Rod Laver
Women's Singles: Margaret Smith
Men's Doubles: Rafael Osuna / Antonio Palafox
Women's Doubles: Darlene Hard / Maria Bueno
Mixed Doubles: Margaret Smith / Fred Stolle

match at Wimbledon, rudely wrecked the dream, 1-6, 6-3, 7-5. It was the first time that the top-seeded female had failed to survive one round. (Steffi Graf would lose to Lori McNeil in 1994, Martina Hingis to Jelena Dokic in 1999, and to Virginia Ruano Pascual in 2001.) Her victory established 'Little Miss Moffitt' as a force to be reckoned with on the Centre Court that already was her favorite stage.

It was eighth-seeded Karen Hantze Susman, with whom Moffitt repeated as doubles champion, taking the singles at age 19 without losing a set, and never in trouble. An outstanding volleyer, Susman was nudged a little in the semis by Ann Jones, 8-6, 6-1, and captured the title with a 6-4, 6-4 victory over unseeded Vera Sukova of Czechoslovakia. A sturdy 31-year-old base-liner, Vera, who would later give birth to two world class players, Helena Sukova and Cyril Suk, had run rampant through a patch of seeds: Sixth, defending champ Angela Mortimer, 1-6, 6-4, 6-3; second, Hard, 6-3, 6-3; third, Maria Bueno, 6-4, 6-3.

Smith was back in form at Forest Hills. With her enormous reach, athleticism, weight of shot and solid arsenal from the backcourt and net alike, she beat Hard in a nerve-wracking match, 9-7, 6-4 to become the first Australian woman to win the U.S. singles. She saved a set point in the 10th game of the first, and benefited from 16 double faults by Hard, who was perplexed by numerous close line calls and burst into prolonged tears in the sixth game of the second set.

Hard beat Christine Truman, 6-2, 6-2, and Haydon, 6-3, 6-8, 6-4, as the U.S. edged Britain, 4-3 in the Wightman Cup at Wimbledon. Capt. Margaret Osborne duPont, 44, teamed up with Margaret Varner to show that she could still win at doubles, 6-3, 2-6, 6-2, over Liz Starkie and Deidre Catt. Susman chipped in a 6-4, 7-5, win over Truman.

While the interest generated by Laver and Smith signaled a banner year for amateur tennis, the pros were struggling. Pancho Gonzalez had retired for the time being, leaving Butch Buchholz to win the U.S. Pro title over Pancho Segura, 6-4, 6-3, 6-4, in Cleveland. Ken Rosewall won at Wembley over Lew Hoad, 6-4, 5-7, 15-13, 7-5.

Jack Kramer had also given up the ghost as promoter. "We had all the best players, but the public didn't want to see them," he recalled. "... There was no acceptance for our players. The conservative and power-ful amateur officials were secure. Among other things, they had succeeded in making me the issue. If you were for pro tennis, you were in favor of handing over all of tennis to Jack Kramer. That was the argument." That is vastly oversimplified, of course. Kramer in many ways had only himself to blame for antagonism. But name-calling aside, the pro game was in sorry shape.

Rosewall was the top dog, but he had little flair for promotion, and the top amateurs no longer were tempted to turn pro and face an uncertain, anonymous future. Under-the-table payments afforded a comfort-able if not lavish lifestyle for the top 'amateurs.' For the second time in the post-war era, there was no pro tour in the United States. Rosewall and Hoad were contemplating retirement. Their only chance at reviving interest, they thought, was to induce Laver to join them, and they pooled resources and personally guaranteed him $125,000 to come aboard for 1963. In the end, he decided he couldn't reject such a generous offer.

1962 CHAMPIONS AND LEADERS

Year-End Number One
Men: Rod Laver
Women: Margaret Smith

Davis Cup: Australia
Wightman Cup: United States

1963

Emmo revs it up, Fed Cup born

Chuck McKinley
Wins only career major, at Wimbledon, without dropping a set.

With Rod Laver out of the amateur ranks, another Australian—the peerlessly fit and universally popular Roy Emerson of rural Blackbutt, Queensland—set his sights on the Grand Slam that Laver had achieved in 1962. Emerson won the first two legs, but was thwarted at Wimbledon as Australian supremacy waned. By the end of the year Latin America had scored a unique double at Forest Hills, and the United States had both recovered the Davis Cup and captured the newly-minted Federation Cup, the women's equivalent.

Politically, it was not a progressive year. With Jack Kramer retired from promoting, amateur officials worldwide felt they had won a battle against some dark specter, and the movement for open competition lagged. In the United States, which had supported the principles of "self-determination" and experimentation with open tournaments, the Old Guard reasserted itself, repudiating far-sighted U.S. Tennis Association president Ed Turville, a supporter of open tennis. The USTA instructed its delegates to the International Tennis Federation to oppose 'opens' and 'home rule.'

Emerson, 26, romped to the Australian title over countryman Ken Fletcher, 6-3, 6-3, 6-1, losing only one set, to Bob Hewitt in the semis, 8-6, 6-4, 3-6, 9-7, while Hewitt and Fred Stolle took the doubles. Margaret Smith systematically disposed of two-fisted backhander Jan Lehane, 6-2, 6-2, for the fourth straight year in the women's final. Margaret, losing no singles sets for the third straight year, tripled. She won the doubles with Rob Ebbern, over Lehane and Lesley Turner, 6-1. 6-3. Moreover she united with Fletcher for a 7-5, 5-7, 6-4, victory over Turner and Fred Stolle. She and Fletch were on their way to a mixed Grand Slam.

Emerson won the French over the first native to reach the men's final since Marcel Bernard's victory in1946, the suave and sporting Pierre Darmon, who in the 1970s would return to Roland Garros as tournament director. The score was 3-6, 6-1, 6-4, 6-4. Darmon had ejected 1961 champ Manolo Santana, 6-3, 4-6, 2-6, 9-7, 6-2, to the rapturous cheers of Parisians in the semis, where Emmo extinguished the torrid serves of Brit Mike Sangster. Emerson then teamed up with Santana for the doubles title,

Leading seed Smith's designs on a singles Slam were scrambled in the quarters 6-3, 8-6, by the steadiness of Vera Sukova, the unseeded Wimbledon finalist of 1962, who was more at home on Parisian clay. The title did remain in Australian hands, however, Turner beating Ann Haydon Jones, 2-6, 6-3, 7-5. Jones teamed with Renée Schuurman for the doubles trophy. Smith and Fletcher did shake a leg for Leg II in pursuit of a mixed Grand Slam, 6-1, 6-2, over Turner and Stolle.

Wimbledon, which had seen five all-Australian men's singles finals in seven years, got its first American male champion (discounting the Peruvian—but U.S. Davis Cupper—Alex Olmedo in 1959) since Tony Trabert in 1955: 22-year-old sparkplug Chuck McKinley, a Missourian attending Trinity University in San Antonio, Tex. He was the first since Trabert to win the title without losing a set, but it was a peculiar year. No seeded men collided.

Emerson, the favorite, ran into Germany's Wilhelm Bungert on a hot day and was beaten in the quarters, 8-6, 3-6, 6-3, 4-6, 6-3. McKinley, a small but athletic man who charged the net like a toy top gone wild, was too sure in his volleying for Bungert, 6-2, 6-4, 8-6, in

1963 THE MAJOR CHAMPIONSHIPS

Australian Championships
Men's Singles: Roy Emerson
Women's Singles: Margaret Smith
Men's Doubles: Bob Hewitt / Fred Stolle
Women's Doubles: Margaret Smith / Robyn Ebbern
Mixed Doubles: Margaret Smith / Ken Fletcher
French Championships
Men's Singles: Roy Emerson
Women's Singles: Lesley Turner
Men's Doubles: Roy Emerson / Manolo Santana
Women's Doubles: Ann Haydon Jones / Renee Schuurman
Mixed Doubles: Margaret Smith / Ken Fletcher
Wimbledon
Men's Singles: Chuck McKinley
Women's Singles: Margaret Smith
Men's Doubles: Rafael Osuna / Antonio Palafox
Women's Doubles: Maria Bueno / Darlene Hard
Mixed Doubles: Margaret Smith / Ken Fletcher
U.S. Championships
Men's Singles: Rafael Osuna
Women's Singles: Maria Bueno
Men's Doubles: Chuck McKinley / Dennis Ralston
Women's Doubles: Robyn Ebbern / Margaret Smith
Mixed Doubles: Margaret Smith / Ken Fletcher

the semis and Fred Stolle in the final, 9-7, 6-1, 6-4, unseeded Stolle having taken care of second-seeded Santana in the semis, 8-6, 6-1, 7-5. This was the first of three straight years as runner-up for the tall, angular Stolle, who never did win the singles. Mexican Davis Cuppers Rafe Osuna and Antonio Palafox became singular as doublists, the lone Latin American team ever to win, beating the French Jean-Claude Barclay and Darmon, 4-6, 6-2, 6-2, 6-2.

Margaret Smith, who had already won four Australian, two Italian, one French and one U.S. titles, became the first Australian woman to carry Wimbledon. In the final, she avenged her first round defeat by Billie Jean Moffitt the previous year, beating the unseeded Californian, 6-3, 6-4, for the title. Billie Jean clipped the wings of the graceful 'São Paulo Swallow,' Maria Bueno, in the quarters, 6-2, 7-5.

Smith never strained, losing but one set, to Rene Schuurman in the quarters, 3-6, 6-0, 6-1. The title was not decided until the start of the third week because of rain, and thus Smith did not get to dance the traditional champions' first foxtrot with McKinley at the Wimbledon Ball. He was perhaps relieved, since he was four inches shorter than Smith. Instead, he guided his wife around the hardwood floor. But Margaret and Ken Fletcher had rhythm, too, winning Leg III of their mixed Grand Slam, 11-9, 6-4, over Hard and Hewitt.

Established as a world championship team event for women, comparable to the Davis Cup, the Federation Cup—two singles and a doubles, all at one site—was inaugurated at Queen's Club in London to celebrate the 50th anniversary of the ITF, attracting 16 entries. The U.S. blanked the Netherlands, Italy, and Great Britain, 3-0, then upset Australia, 2-1 for the Cup. Smith flattened Darlene Hard, 6-3, 6-0, in the opening match, but Billie Jean countered against Turner, 5-7, 6-0, 6-3, and allied with Darlene to take the excruciating doubles from Smith and Turner, 3-6, 13-11, 6-3. Inclement weather drove the final indoors onto swift boards.

The U.S. also beat Britain, 6-1, in the Wightman Cup on clay at the Cleveland Skating Club. Ann Jones beat Hard in the opening match, 6-1, 0-6, 8-6, but Moffitt outlasted Truman, 6-4, 19-17 (the second set a female record for length), to turn things around for teammates Hard, who beat Truman, 6-3, 6-0, and Nancy Richey, 14-12, 6-3, winner over Deidre Catt. Billie Jean also beat Jones, 6-4, 4-6, 6-3.

Richey won the first of her six consecutive U.S. Clay

Court titles, 6-1, 6-1, over Vicky Palmer, and McKinley showed he could be a dirt-kicking dandy, too, stopping his partner and Davis Cup teammate, Dennis Ralston, 6-2, 6-2, 6-4.

For the first time, no American woman made it to the U.S. semi-finals at Forest Hills. Hard, a finalist the previous three years and champion twice, was beaten by Jones in the quarters, 6-4, 6-3, where Richey was bumped out by the champ-to-be, Bueno, 6-3, 6-2. Billie Jean got off in the fourth round, pushed by 5-footer Catt, 2-6, 8-6, 7-5. Even more curious, Australia was shut out of the men's quarter-finals after having had both finalists in six of the previous seven years.

This was a south-of-the-border year, Mexican Rafe Osuna taking the men's singles, and Brazilian Maria Bueno recapturing the women's title she had won in 1959 with a breathtaking display of shot-making in beating Jones, 1-6, 6-2, 9-7, then Smith for the trophy, 7-5, 6-4.

Osuna, a gallery favorite because of his quickness of hand, foot, and smile, ousted Wimbledon champ McKinley in the semis, 6-4, 6-4, 10-8, and unseeded Floridian Frank Froehling III in the final, 7-5, 6-4, 6-2. Froehling, a spare spire of 6-foot-3-1/2 called 'Spider-Man,' had served devastatingly to upset top seed Emerson, 6-4, 4-6, 9-7, 6-2, creep past Bobby Wilson in five, 6-8, 4-6, 6-3, 6-3, 9-7, and bar another Brazilian, Ronnie Barnes, from the final, 6-3, 6-1, 6-4. But Osuna cleverly neutralized Froehling's power with wonderfully conceived and executed tactics, especially lobbed service returns from 10 to 12 feet behind the baseline. Occasionally Osuna would stand in and take Froehling's serve on the rise, chipping the backhand, but more often he lobbed returns to disrupt Froehling's serve-volley rhythm and break down his suspect overhead. In fact nimble Osuna climbed the wall of the stadium to retrieve smashes and float back perfect lobs, frustrating Froehling with his speed around the court, touch and tactical variations.

Bueno was also brilliant, especially in the second set of her victory over Smith. "With the score 1-4 and 0-30 against her, Maria set the gallery wild with the dazzling strokes that stemmed from her racket," wrote Allison Danzig in *The New York Times*. "Her service was never so strong. Her volleys and overhead smashes were the last word, and she hit blazing winners from the backhand and threw up lobs in an overwhelming assault."

One more mixed doubles title for Smith and Fletcher

was enough for them to fill in the last blank for a Grand Slam, 3-6, 8-6, 6-2, over Americans Donna Floyd Fales and lefty Eddie Rubinoff

At Longwood, Hard was not able to snag a sixth straight women's doubles title, as she and Bueno fell in the final to Smith and Robyn Ebbern, 4-6, 10-8, 6-3. McKinley and Ralston met Osuna and Palafox for the third straight year in the men's final, Chuck saving two match points on his serve in recapturing the title, 9-7, 4-6, 5-7, 6-3, 11-9, before a record crowd of 7,000.

That was immediately after they combined to beat Osuna and Palafox, 4-1, in a Davis Cup match at Los Angeles, atoning for the 1962 defeat at Mexico City. Captained by Bob Kelleher and coached by Pancho Gonzalez, the Americans also conquered Iran, Venezuela, Britain and India—all 5-0—to return to the challenge round for the first time in three years, and lift the Cup from Australia at Adelaide, 3-2 on McKinley's dramatic fifth match victory over 19-year-old rookie John Newcombe in four sets.

It had been a long, arduous campaign, mainly on the road, taxing competitively and medically. Ralston nearly lost an eye in an accident in England, McKinley had dysentery in India, Froehling needed his abscessed backside lanced, and McKinley had back spasms. But the squad persevered and took the Cup back from Australia, which had held it in a Melbourne bank vault 11 of the last 13 years. Only Mexico and Venezuela, at Denver, were home series. Ralston took over after McKinley lost the opener to Osuna, 6-2, 3-6, 6-2, 2-6, 6-3, beating Palafox, 6-1, 6-4, 3-6, 6-3, and providing a steady hand in helping overturn the Wimbledon champs, 6-1, 6-3, 8-6, for a 2-1 lead. Facing Osuna, his pal and Southern Cal teammate, the man with whom he had won Wimbledon three years before, Ralston was incisive and relentless, clinching, 6-1, 6-3, 7-5.

Venezuela gets a footnote only because that series unveiled 20-year-old Arthur Ashe on the superfluous third day, the first black man to represent the U.S. It was a quickie, 6-1, 6-1, 6-0, over Orlando Bracamonte. Arthur would be an important cog in the Cups won in 1968-69-70 and 1978.

Five years had passed since the last U.S. Cup heist on

1963 CHAMPIONS AND LEADERS

Year-End Number One	Davis Cup: United States
Men: Rafael Osuna	Federation Cup: United States
Women: Margaret Smith	Wightman Cup: United States

Australian grass. Ralston squandered three match points on serve, but pulled himself together to win the jittery opener over Cup novitiate Newcombe, 6-4, 6-1, 3-6, 4-6, 7-5. McKinley couldn't hold off Emerson, 6-3, 3-6, 7-5, 7-5, but the Americans had a 2-1 lead after a 6-3, 3-6, 11-9, 11-9 defeat of Emerson and Neale Fraser, 30 and bowing out. Emerson flattened Ralston to tie it again, 6-2, 6-3, 3-6, 6-2. With a sellout crowd of 7,500 at Memorial Drive roaring behind him, power-serving Newcombe built a 4-2, 30-0 third-set lead. But the iron-willed teddy bear, McKinley—"this is where I want to be, everything riding on one match"—retaliated with backhand passers and quickness to pinch the Cup, 10-12, 6-2, 9-7, 6-2.

In the pro ranks, Laver was beaten regularly by both Ken Rosewall and Lew Hoad, who had jointly staked him to a $125,000 bankroll in hopes of keeping the fading pro game alive. They succeeded, but barely. Rosewall was supreme, seizing the two biggest tourneys. He beat Lew Hoad at Wembley, 6-4, 6-2, 4-6, 6-3, and Laver in the final of the U.S. Pro Championships at Forest Hills, 6-4, 6-2, 6-2.

1964

Emmo 9, Stolle 1 in three Slam finals

Maria Bueno
Two majors, including a classic Wimbledon finale over Margaret Smith.

As if any additional evidence were necessary to prove the depth of tennis talent in Australia, the Davis Cup went back Down Under for the 11th time in 14 years even though three members of the Aussies squad fled to other countries because of an altercation with the autocratic Lawn Tennis Association of Australia.

Roy Emerson, Fred Stolle, Marty Mulligan, Bob Hewitt and Ken Fletcher were all suspended by the LTAA for the grievous offense of leaving for the overseas tournament circuit earlier than permitted. Emerson and Stolle were reinstated after reaching the Wimbledon final—in time to go about their Davis Cup duties for the homeland.

Emerson beat Stolle in the singles finals of three majors—The Australian, Wimbledon and U.S. Championships— in 1964 but had his notions of a Slam punctured by Nicola Pietrangeli in the French quarter-finals. 'Emmo' and Fred were the core of the raiding party that took the Cup back from the U.S. in Cleveland, the first time a challenge round in the U.S. was played beyond the New York-Philadelphia-Boston triangle, and not on grass. The battleground was clay.

The other three continued to have problems. Mulligan moved to Italy, where he married, became a successful businessman, and played in Davis Cup competition in 1968, nicknamed 'Martino Mulligano' by disapproving Italian journalists. (He had been on the Australian squad but never played, so was eligible to play for Italy when he became a citizen.)

Hewitt married a Johannesburg model and became a mainstay of the South African Davis Cup team, continuing to develop into one of the world's best doubles players. Fletcher took up residence in Hong Kong. It is a measure of the strength of Aussie Capt. Harry Hopman's production line that Australia won the Cup four years in a row, never missing this trio of talented players.

The affable Emerson—strong enough to quaff beer and sing choruses of *Waltzing Matilda* into the wee hours of the morning, then get up early to train and play magnificently athletic tennis—ruled the amateur world in 1964. He won 55 straight singles matches in one stretch, finishing the year with 17 tournament championships and a 109-6 record, including two singles victories in the Davis Cup challenge round.

Emmo won three-quarters of a Slam, derailed only at the French by Pietrangeli, 6-1, 6-3, 6-3. But Nicola fell short of his third title, denied by Manolo Santana, winning his second, 6-3, 6-1, 4-6, 7-5.

Emerson thumped Stolle in all three finals—the Australian, 6-3, 6-4, 6-2, Wimbledon, 6-4, 12-10, 4-6, 6-3, and the U.S., 6-4, 6-1, 6-4. Emmo also took the French doubles, practically an annual acquisition, with Fletcher. Hewitt and Stolle took the Australian and Wimbledon doubles, while Chuck McKinley and Dennis Ralston captured the U.S. title at Longwood for the third time in four years, the first three-timers since Bill Talbert and Gardnar Mulloy (1942, 45-46 and 1948).

1964 THE MAJOR CHAMPIONSHIPS

Australian Championships
Men's Singles: Roy Emerson
Women's Singles: Margaret Smith
Men's Doubles: Bob Hewitt / Fred Stolle
Women's Doubles: Judy Tegart Dalton / Lesley Turner
Mixed Doubles: Margaret Smith / Ken Fletcher
French Championships
Men's Singles: Manolo Santana
Women's Singles: Margaret Smith
Men's Doubles: Roy Emerson / Ken Fletcher
Women's Doubles: Margaret Smith / Lesley Turner
Mixed Doubles: Margaret Smith / Ken Fletcher
Wimbledon
Men's Singles: Roy Emerson
Women's Singles: Maria Bueno
Men's Doubles: Bob Hewitt / Fred Stolle
Women's Doubles: Margaret Smith / Lesley Turner
Mixed Doubles: Lesley Turner / Fred Stolle
U.S. Championships
Men's Singles: Roy Emerson
Women's Singles: Maria Bueno
Men's Doubles: Chuck McKinley / Dennis Ralston
Women's Doubles: Billie Jean Moffitt / Karen Hantze Susman
Mixed Doubles: Margaret Smith / John Newcombe

A preview of America's Davis Cup fate was offered in the most dramatic match of the U.S. Championships, a quarter-final in which Ralston fought back from two sets down against Stolle, saved a match point at 3-5 in the fifth, and hauled himself back to 7-7 before the gripping encounter was halted by darkness. Ralston had two break points at 15-40 as Stolle served the first game of the resumption the next morning, but the lean Aussie with the pained gait and delightful wit held and broke Ralston from 40-15 in the next game for the match.

It was the 25-year-old Stolle's 7-5, 6-3, 3-6, 9-11, 6-4, triumph over Ralston on a clay court at newly built and jam-packed (7,000 a day, at top dollar) Harold T. Clark Stadium in Cleveland that broke America's back in the challenge round. As they had only nine months before, the Americans held a 2-1 lead on Chuck and Denny's squeaky win over Roy and Fred, 6-4, 4-6, 4-6, 6-3, 6-4. (The first day split was achieved by McKinley over Stolle, 6-1, 9-7, 4-6, 6-2, and Emerson retaliating over Ralston, 6-3, 6-4, 6-2.)

On a gray September Sunday, after a long rain delay, they played a majestic match for a national television audience. Ralston saved one match point, serving at 4-5 in the fifth, but Stolle blasted a forehand crosscourt passing shot by him on the next. Emerson wrapped up a 3-2 Australian victory the next afternoon, running like a greyhound and whacking piercing ground strokes and volleys to sear McKinley, 3-6, 6-2, 6-4, 6-4, sending the Davis Cup back to Melbourne.

The French, Italian and German titles, the three biggest on continental clay, all went to Europeans: Manolo Santana beat Nicola Pietrangeli, 6-3, 6-1, 4-6, 7-5, in a rematch of their more memorable meeting in the Parisian final three years earlier; Swede Jan-Erik Lundquist won in Rome over Stolle, 1-6, 7-5, 6-3, 6-1; Wilhelm Bungert took his national title in Hamburg, defeating left-handed compatriot Christian Kuhnke, 0-6, 6-4, 7-5, 6-2.

Among the worldly women of tennis, Margaret Smith had an awesome record, losing only two matches during the year, but those were at Wimbledon and Forest Hills, where Maria Bueno won both titles, and thus took back the No.1 world ranking that illness and Smith had stripped from her.

Smith beat countrywoman Lesley Turner 6-3, 6-2, in the Australian final, a fifth straight title, having beaten up on her usual finalist foil, Jan Lehane, a fifth straight time, though this time in the semis, 6-4, 6-2.

Margaret was 2-1 against Bueno, beating the Brazilian, 5-7, 6-1, 6-2, for the French title. However, Maria's one win over Margaret was the most important—the final at Wimbledon, 6-4, 7-9, 6-3. This was a match of almost unbearable tension, a patchwork of glorious shots and awful ones, and Bueno ultimately controlled her nerves better. Smith seemed more serene beforehand, but her anxiety showed in her usually oppressive serve. She was a little tentative, and double-faulted badly on several key points. "I guess I beat myself. I felt pressure all the way," she said afterward. "It was like beating my head against a wall."

Karen Hantze Susman, the 1962 Wimbledon champion who was back for a fling after temporary retirement for childbirth, troubled Smith in the third round at Wimbledon, 11-9, 6-0, and beat her in the fourth round at Forest Hills, 4-6, 6-4, 6-4. That paved the way for Bueno, who raced through the championship without losing a set. In the final she met surprising ninth-seeded Carole Caldwell Graebner, who had resolutely upset Susman, 6-4, 6-8, 6-3, and, Nancy Richey, 2-6, 9-7, 6-4, Richey was the quarter-final bouncer of Billie Jean Moffitt, 6-4, 6-4. Carole did all this despite suffering from painful second-degree sun-burns of the arms, face and hands. In the final it was not the sun's rays but Bueno who blistered her for the title, 6-1, 6-0, in just 25 minutes.

Bueno thus usurped Smith's throne at the top, even though her record of 82-10 and seven titles was not quite as formidable as Smith's 67-2 and 13 championships. Smith had a 39-match winning streak at one stage.

Lesley Turner blended with Judy Tegart Dalton to win the Australian doubles, and with Smith to win the French and Wimbledon. But Lesley's bid for a Grand Slam, in a last shot alongside Smith, was denied in the final of the U.S. by Susman and Moffitt, 3-6, 6-2, 6-4.

With Darlene Hard, the U.S. No.1 of the past four years, retired to a teaching pro career, the U.S. relinquished the Federation Cup to Australia, 2-1, in the final of a 24-nation assemblage in Philadelphia. Smith beat Moffitt, 6-2, 6-3, and Turner did in No. 1 American Nancy Richey, 7-5, 6-1.

In a 5-2 Wightman Cup triumph for the U.S. at London, Richey and Moffitt won both their singles: Nancy over Deidre Catt, 4-6, 6-4, 7-5, and Ann Haydon Jones, 7-5, 11-9; Billie Jean over Catt, 6-3, 4-6, 6-3, and Jones, 4-6, 6-2, 6-3. Graebner added a victory over Liz Starkie, 6-4, 1-6, 6-3.

Most of the male pros were scattered around the globe, playing the odd exhibition here and there, badly disorganized. Ken Rosewall, the pro king, was observed playing Pancho Segura in a shopping-center parking lot exhibition in Los Angeles.

One who thought this wrong was Ed Hickey of the New England Merchants National Bank in Boston, who convinced his boss to put up $10,000 in sponsorship money to revive the U.S. Pro Championships. John Bottomley, president of the Longwood Cricket Club, threw his support to the project. Jack Kramer was enlisted to contact the far-flung gypsies and put together a short summer tournament circuit with about $80,000 in total prize money. A dozen pros were assembled and Rod Laver won the climactic event at Longwood over Pancho Gonzalez, 4-6, 6-3, 7-5, 6-4, in a rainstorm, a nor'easter that turned the lawn into a quagmire, but didn't diminish their skills. "The show must go on" was the battle cry of those pros, too, demonstrated ably. "We have to play," reasoned Laver, soon headed to the airport, "because we're scheduled in Scotland tomorrow night."

It was a humble renaissance with a $2,200 first prize—"seemed like a million then," said a grateful Laver—but the 37-year-old U.S. Pro, the longest running pro tourney, somehow stayed in business and was to become a fixture at Longwood, as was Laver. He won there four more times. It may not have been straw-berries-and-cream à la Wimbledon, but it was spinach green cash, and the pros were on the rocky road to a comeback.

1964 CHAMPIONS AND LEADERS

Year-End Number One
Men: Roy Emerson
Women: Margaret Smith

Davis Cup: Australia
Federation Cup: Australia
Wightman Cup: United States

1965

The band played *Waltzing Matilda* ... over and over

Roy Emerson
His pair help Aussies win seven of eight singles majors, 17 of 20 overall.

The gloom of a drizzly, gray September afternoon in Forest Hills was pierced by Spanish singing and dancing, and the unmistakable click of castanets filled the old concrete stadium of the West Side Tennis Club. Loud choruses of "*Olé!*" and "*Bravo, Manolo!*" bounced off the clouds. The discreet charm of the bourgeoisie that so long characterized tennis audiences gave way to unabashed Latin celebration as Manolo Santana beat South African Cliff Drysdale in four absorbing sets, 6-2, 7-9, 7-5, 6-1, to become the first Spaniard to win the U.S. singles title.

The balletic and crowd-pleasing Santana, age 28, provided other occasions for rejoicing in 1965, but few places came alive as Forest Hills did when a troupe of entertainers from the Spanish Pavilion at the nearby World's Fair arrived to urge him on with an up-tempo Latin beat. Santana was arguably the No. 1 amateur in the world, winning 10 of 16 tournaments, compiling a 71-7 record, and a 25-match winning streak, longest of the season. He did not enter Wimbledon, devoting his summer instead to Davis Cup preparation and duty on clay.

Such diligence paid off. Ringleader Santana (singles wins over Frank Froehling, Denny Ralston) & Co. lit up the Barcelona sky by bumping off the U.S., 4-1. His gang was on its way to the challenge round at Sydney. An unknown to the Americans, awkward-looking Juan Gisbert, stayed steady from 1-4 in the second set to paralyze Ralston, 3-6, 8-6, 6-1, 6-3, at the outset. A momentous resurgence in the doubles by Santana and Luis Arilla over Ralston and Clark Graebner settled the outcome, 4-6, 3-6, 6-3, 6-4, 11-9, even though Ralston came within two points, serving for it at 5-3, deuce. A break of Graebner in the 19th game, and Arilla's hold set off a bullring-style fiesta, pillows flying from the overjoyed crowd of 5,000, littering the court where the two Spaniards were carried round and round triumphantly by strong-shouldered aficionados.

Not that Spanish music replaced *Waltzing Matilda* as the anthem of the world tennis empire. Australia won the Cup again, for the 14th time since 1950, as Roy Emerson and Fred Stolle gunned down the Spaniards, 4-1, at Sydney.

Australians also captured the Federation Cup, not to mention the other three men's major singles titles, and all four of the women's. Seven for eight ain't bad. Five of those finals were all-Aussie affairs. In doubles Aussies took six for eight, and, mixed, four for four. Aussies grasped seventeen of the 20 premier championships. Never before had one national dominated a tennis year so thoroughly. This was the tennis version of the Holy Roman Empire, and Emerson, Stolle, Smith, Lesley Turner, John Newcombe, Tony Roche et al were holy terrors.

Emerson, winning for a fourth time, out-slugged Stolle, who seemed capable of beating anyone else, from two sets down in the Australian final, 7-9, 2-6, 6-4, 7-5, 6-1. John Newcombe and lefty Tony Roche, the latest in a long line of great Aussie pairs, took their first of a record 12 major doubles titles, in a rip-roaring final over Emmo and Stolle, 3-6, 4-6, 13-11, 6-3, 6-4.

Roche, a ruggedly muscular left-hander with an unerring backhand volley, spoiled Emerson's latest vision of a Grand Slam in the French semi-finals, 6-1, 6-4, 3-6, 6-0. With his chief nemesis out of the way, as well as prickly South African Cliff Drysdale whom Stolle shaded, 6-8, 6-4, 6-1, 4-6, 6-4, Fred prevailed in Paris over Roche, 3-6, 6-0, 6-2, 6-3. It was his first major title after being runner-up in one Australian, two Wimbledons, and one U.S. Championship. Emerson and Stolle took the doubles over more of their blood, Ken Fletcher and Bob Hewitt, 6-8, 6-3, 8-6, 6-2, Emerson's sixth in a row in Paris.

Emerson powered his way through the Wimbledon draw again, a tour de force justifying his top seeding, and made Stolle the bridesmaid for the third consecutive year. This time it was easier than in 1964, 6-2, 6-4, 6-4. Dennis Ralston, seeded fourth, was the U.S. hope after out-volleying another Yank, Marty Riessen, in the quarters, 3-6, 2-6, 6-4, 6-2, 6-2, but was chilled by Emmo, 6-1, 6-2, 7-9, 6-1. Newcombe and Roche won the first of their five Wimbledon doubles titles together, Fletcher and Hewitt sinking again, 7-5, 6-3, 6-4.

Only at Forest Hills, where the U.S. had experienced all-Aussie finals seven of the last nine years, did the Aussie juggernaut falter. None of the men from Down Under made the semis. The Emerson-Stolle monopoly was busted up by Charlie Pasarell, ambushing Stolle in the second round, 6-3, 6-4, 6-2, and Arthur Ashe, who was to gain the No. 2 U.S. ranking behind Dennis Ralston, delivering huge serves and fatal backhands in enough glorious clusters to topple Emerson in the quarters, 13-11, 6-4, 10-12, 6-2. It was Hall of Fame-bound Ashe's initial significant win, but Santana cooled him, 2-6, 6-4, 6-2, 6-4.

Another mischief-maker with his novel—so it seemed at the time—double-fisted backhand, 24-year-old Drysdale revived to dust off the top American, Ralston, saving a match point, 2-6, 3-6, 7-5, 6-3, 8-6, and brought down 1963 champ Rafael Osuna, 6-3, 4-6, 6-4, 6-1. Osuna had lamed unseeded Pasarell's trot in the quarters, 1-6, 6-3, 6-3, 7-5.

Santana vs. Drysdale for the crown that no one from their countries had worn, was thoughtful, much of it from the backcourt, between two intelligent and stylish men. Two-fisted backhands would become common after Chris Evert arrived six years later, but Drysdale's was the first to be seen in a U.S. final. Rain interrupted the match and made the footing slick, but it couldn't dampen Santana's flashy shot-making or the castanets.

Emerson and Stolle were unbeaten in doubles on the U.S. circuit, winning six tournaments and 31 matches, a run climaxed by a 6-4, 10-12, 7-5, 6-4 triumph over

1965 THE MAJOR CHAMPIONSHIPS

Australian Championships
Men's Singles: Roy Emerson
Women's Singles: Margaret Smith
Men's Doubles: John Newcombe / Tony Roche
Women's Doubles: Margaret Smith / Lesley Turner
Mixed Doubles: Robyn Ebbern / Owen Davidson and
  Margaret Smith / John Newcombe (SHARED)
French Championships
Men's Singles: Fred Stolle
Women's Singles: Lesley Turner
Men's Doubles: Roy Emerson / Fred Stolle
Women's Doubles: Margaret Smith / Lesley Turner
Mixed Doubles: Margaret Smith / Ken Fletcher
Wimbledon
Men's Singles: Roy Emerson
Women's Singles: Margaret Smith
Men's Doubles: John Newcombe / Tony Roche
Women's Doubles: Maria Bueno / Billie Jean King
Mixed Doubles: Margaret Smith / Ken Fletcher
U.S. Championships
Men's Singles: Manolo Santana
Women's Singles: Margaret Smith
Men's Doubles: Roy Emerson / Fred Stolle
Women's Doubles: Carole Caldwell Graebner / Nancy Richey
Mixed Doubles: Margaret Smith / Fred Stolle

Pasarell and Frank Froehling in the U.S. final at Longwood.

Emerson won seven of 22 tournaments in singles for an 85-16 record. He was 0-2 against Santana, demolished on clay in the Swedish Championship final, 6-1, 6-1, 6-4, and edged, 2-6, 6-3, 6-3, 15-13, on grass at Sydney in Davis Cup, but the final had been decided by then. A lifelong dream to play for his country in his hometown was fulfilled by Stolle as leadoff man. Reassembling his composure after falling way behind, Fred snapped Santana's 19-match Cup streak, 10-12, 3-6, 6-1, 6-4, 7-5, closing a tense struggle with his 19th ace to reward a cheering throng of 10,000 at White City. That was the blow from which the Spaniards never recovered. Emerson took care of Gisbert quickly, 6-3, 6-2, 6-2, for his 13th Cup singles win without defeat, and the rookies, Newcombe and Roche, put it away, 6-3, 4-6, 7-5, 6-2, over Arilla-Santana. Though meaningless to the result, Santana did hand Emerson his lone Cup defeat on the third day.

Australia beat the United States, 2-1, in the final of the Federation Cup at Kooyong in Melbourne. Lesley Turner beat Carole Graebner, 6-3, 2-6, 6-3, and Margaret Smith stopped Billie Jean Moffitt, 6-4, 8-6.

Smith, 23, won three of the major singles titles in one season for the second time in her still ascendant career. She beat Maria Bueno, who retired with an ankle injury while trailing, 5-7, 6-3, 5-2 in the final set of the Australian final. This was Margaret's sixth straight championship (tying Nancye Wynne Bolton's total between 1937 and 1951), covering a run of 29 successive matches in which she lost just five sets.

She beat Bueno again to win Wimbledon, 6-4, 7-5, and Moffitt to win the U.S., 8-6, 7-5. Only one match kept her from a Grand Slam, the final of the French, lost to Turner, 6-3, 6-4. Turner had clung to Bueno, winning that semi, 2-6, 6-4, 8-6, while Smith, averting two set points in the first eliminated Richey, 7-5, 6-4.

After that, Smith didn't lose another all year, piling up 58 consecutive victories for a season of 103-7, including 18 titles in 25 tournaments.

Bueno, 25, won the Italian, 6-1, 1-6, 6-3, over Nancy Richey, and two other of the 11 tournaments she

entered, finishing 40-8 in a year in which she was hampered by a knee injury that required surgery. She played Forest Hills against the advice of her doctor, losing to Billie Jean in the semis, 6-2, 6-3.

Smith's procession to the title at Forest Hills was impressive: 6-0, 6-0, over lefty Justina Bricka, 6-1, 6-0, over quick and clever Françoise Durr, 6-2, 6-2, over Richey. But Billie Jean battled her, leading 5-3 in both sets of the final, and had two set points in the second. Even though she lost, Moffitt later said this was a turning-point match in her career, adding a great deal to her self-awareness. She knew that the forehand she had gone to Australia to rebuild from scratch the previous year was coming around, complementing her exquisite backhand and volleying, and that she had the ability to rival Smith for No. 1. Billie Jean married Larry King, an attorney, shortly after Forest Hills, and she knew she was coming of age as a player. She had beaten Turner, 6-2, 6-1, to reach the Wimbledon semis where Bueno, though aching, slipped past B.J., 6-4, 5-7, 6-3. The only unseeded outsider in the last four, 6-footer Christine Truman expunged Richey, 6-4, 1-6, 7-5, before falling to Smith, 6-4, 6-0.

Billie Jean was co-ranked No. 1 in the U.S. with Nancy Richey, an unprecedented decision by the U.S. Tennis Association ranking committee. Moffitt had shone on the grass court circuit, which Richey avoided after winning the U.S. Indoor, over Carol Hanks Aucamp, 6-3, 6-2 and U.S. Clay Court over Julie Heldman, 5-7, 6-3, 9-7. The two did not meet.

Unique were the Clay Court finals at Chicago in that each contained a Richey. Nancy's 18-year-old kid brother, Cliff, lost his to Ralston, 6-4, 4-6, 6-4, 6-3. Swede Jan-Erik Lundquist took the U.S. Indoor at Salisbury, Md., over Ralston, 4-6, 13-11, 6-4, 11-9.

Billie Jean and Nancy split their Wightman Cup singles in the 5-2 U.S. victory over Britain at Cleveland. B.J. beat Liz Starkie, 6-3, 6-2, but lost to Ann Jones, 6-2, 6-4. Nancy did likewise, 6-1, 6-0, over Starkie but 6-4, 9-7, to Jones. They got help from Graebner's win over newcomer Virginia Wade, 3-6, 10-8, 6-4, and the doubles: Moffitt-Karen Susman over Jones-Wade, 6-3, 8-6, and Graebner-Richey (the U.S. champs) over Nell Truman-Starkie, 6-1, 6-0.

Richey and Carole Graebner (whose husband, Clark, ranked No. 13 among the U.S. men and would return to the Top Ten the next year) earned the top U.S. ranking in doubles after winning at Longwood, defeating the

---

1965 CHAMPIONS AND LEADERS

Year-End Number One	**Davis Cup:** Australia
Men: Roy Emerson	**Federation Cup:** Australia
Women: Margaret Smith	**Wightman Cup:** United States

defenders Moffitt and Susman in the final, 6-4, 6-4.

Turner teamed with Smith to take the Australian and French. Moffitt captured her third title at Wimbledon with her second partner, Maria Bueno. Smith took three mixed majors, alongside Ken Fletcher at the French and Wimbledon, Stolle at the U.S.

The itinerant pros were still trying to organize. Mike Davies, Butch Buchholz and Barry MacKay were among the driving forces behind the International Professional Tennis Players' Association (IPTPA) formed in 1965, hopeful of forming some structure for the amorphous, struggling outcasts. The U.S. Pro Championships returned to Longwood, Ken Rosewall regaining the title he had won in 1963, and getting paid—albeit modestly, $3,000—this time for beating Rod Laver, 6-4, 6-3, 6-3.

Patrician scoring reformer Jimmy Van Alen of Newport, R.I., whose 'Van Alen Streamlined Scoring System' (VASSS) would become the basis for 'sudden death' tie-breakers in 1970, hosted a pro tournament at famed Newport Casino, where the U.S. Championships had been played from their inauguration in 1881 until 1915. Van Alen put up $10,000 in prize money, on the condition that the pros use his radical VASSS round robin, medal-play format, in which every point counted and each was worth $5. The players were happy to play any way as long as they were paid, though Pancho Segura spoke for most of his colleagues when he disparaged the Van Alen system, saying "It seems half-VASSS to me." Rosewall won over Mal Anderson.

1966

Smith wins 7th Aussie but it's Billie Jean's year

Fred Stolle
No seeding, no problem, as he claims U.S. title.

If variety is indeed the spice of life, 1966 was a flavorful year for international tennis. There were no one-man or one-woman gangs, as the game's major titles got spread around. For the first time since 1948, no player, man or woman, captured more than one of the four major singles crowns.

Fred Stolle, thought to be past his prime at age 27, didn't win a single tournament until August, then came on like the old Australian Mafia. He won the German Championship on clay over Hungarian Istvan Gulyas, 2-6, 7-5, 6-1, 6-2, and took the U.S. title at Forest Hills unseeded, the second to do so, following the 1957 example of countryman Mal Anderson. Peeved at the lack of respect extended to him by the tourney administration, Stolle routed pal/nemesis Roy Emerson in the semi-finals, 6-4, 6-1, 6-1, with an astounding display of power and control, and withstood 21 aces served by the similarly unseeded John Newcombe to win the final, 4-6, 12-10, 6-3, 6-4. Thereafter Stolle won tournaments in California (Pacific Coast on concrete over Charlie Pasarell, 6-4, 2-6, 6-4), and Australia (on grass at Melbourne over Emerson, 6-2, 9-7, 6-3).

He beat both Ramanathan Krishnan, 6-3, 6-2, 6-4 and Jaidip Mukerjea, 7-5, 6-8, 6-3, 5-7, 6-3, as Australia pummeled India, 4-1, in the Davis Cup challenge round. (The lone Aussie loss, delaying champagne celebrations in Melbourne until the third day, was the doubles upset of Newcombe and Tony Roche, 4-6, 7-5, 6-4, 6-4 by Mukerjea and Krishnan. Emerson clinched it by going through Krishnan, 6-0, 6-2, 10-8. (The latter's son, Ramesh Krishnan, would follow in the old man's sneaker steps to a Cup final 21 years later in Sweden, a father-son feat that is theirs alone.) That was the climax of Stolle's amateur career, as he turned pro at the end of the year.

Stolle's Davis Cup accomplice, Emerson, started the year by grabbing their national championship for the fourth consecutive time, a 6-4, 6-8, 6-2, 6-3 extinguishing of Arthur Ashe. The smooth Aussie then went right back on court, accompanied by Stolle, to complete the doubles final over Newcombe and Roche, an 87-game, three-match point-saving victory, 7-9, 3-6, 8-6, 14-12, 12-10, that had stopped for darkness at 7-7 in the fourth the previous evening. That meant Emerson played 128 games within 24 hours. He and Fred went on to post the year's best doubles record, adding the Italian, South African and, over Dennis Ralston and Clark Graebner, 6-4, 6-4, 6-4, the U.S. Championship.

Emerson was perhaps never in better condition or form than at the start of Wimbledon, where he was keen to become the first man to win three successive singles titles since Fred Perry in 1934-35-36. He looked as if he would until fate and his own eagerness intervened during his quarter-final against a compatriot, left-hander Owen Davidson. Richard Evans described what happened in *World Tennis*:

"The first set took Emerson precisely 14 minutes to win 6-1. His first service was going in, his volleys were crisp and accurate, his groundstrokes laden with power and spin. There was no danger in sight unless it lay in the greasy, rain-slicked turf and of this, surely, Emerson was aware. So it surprised many people when he raced for a Davidson drop-volley in the third game of the second set. And it horrified us all when he skidded headlong into the umpire's chair and brought the BBC microphone crashing down on top of him. He was up in a moment, flexing his left shoulder and telling Davidson that he thought he had heard something snap. In fact he had torn the shoulder ligaments—an injury that, in a fatal second, had shattered a dream, ruined weeks of arduous preparation and deprived Wimbledon of its champion." Emmo didn't quit, but was soon thoroughly beaten, 1-6, 6-3, 6-4, 6-4.

Manolo Santana, the clay-court artist who had proved himself a man for all surfaces by winning Forest Hills on grass the previous year, inherited the throne that Emerson abdicated, and he was a popular champion. Grinning and playing extraordinary shots when behind, he beat Aussies in suspenseful struggles: Ken Fletcher, 6-2, 3-6, 8-6, 4-6, 7-5, and then Davidson, 6-2, 4-6, 9-7, 3-6, 7-5, to attain the final. There he repelled Dennis Ralston, who had more firepower but less control, 6-4, 11-9, 6-4.

But Santana had his own problems with injuries during the season. A painful shoulder plagued him as Spain, the 1965 runner-up, went out to Brazil in an early

Davis Cup round, and a bad ankle reduced his Forest Hills' defense to a limp. Nevertheless, he was able to beat Chuck McKinley, 9-7, 9-7, 8-6 and hang in to edge Bowrey, 6-8, 6-2, 8-6, 5-7, 6-4, before losing to Newcombe, 6-3, 6-4, 6-8, 8-6, in the semis.

It was not Santana but Australian lefty Tony Roche who was the 1966 man of the year on clay. He won the Italian, 11-9, 6-1, 6-3 over the aging homeboy Nicola Pietrangeli, 32. Roche then claimed his lone singles major, the French, beating Hungarian roadrunner Gulyas, 6-1, 6-4, 7-5, despite with pain-killing injections in a troublesome ankle, which would thereafter hamper his effectiveness.

So who was the world's No. 1 amateur? Take your pick of the major victors. Stolle won four of 19 tournaments, 70 of 85 matches. Emerson won eight of 16 tournaments, including the rising South African Championship, 6-3, 2-6, 3-6, 6-4, 7-5, over Bob Hewitt and 67 of 78 matches. Santana was 52-16, winning only two of 17 tournaments, but one of those was the biggest, Wimbledon. Roche played the most ambitious schedule, winning 10 of 29 tournaments and 106 of 125 matches.

Ralston, generally considered No. 5 in the world, was top-ranked in the U.S. for the third year in a row, the first man so honored since Don Budge in 1936-37-38, but continued to be frustrated by his failure to win a major singles title. He turned pro with Stolle at the end of the year, leaving Ashe, a lieutenant in the U.S. Army, as heir apparent.

1966 THE MAJOR CHAMPIONSHIPS

Australian Championships
Men's Singles: Roy Emerson
Women's Singles: Margaret Smith
Men's Doubles: Roy Emerson / Fred Stolle
Women's Doubles: Carole Caldwell Graebner / Nancy Richey
Mixed Doubles: Judy Tegart Dalton / Tony Roche
French Championships
Men's Singles: Tony Roche
Women's Singles: Ann Haydon Jones
Men's Doubles: Clark Graebner / Dennis Ralston
Women's Doubles: Margaret Smith / Judy Tegart Dalton
Mixed Doubles: Annette Van Zyl / Frew McMillan
Wimbledon
Men's Singles: Manolo Santana
Women's Singles: Billie Jean King
Men's Doubles: Ken Fletcher / John Newcombe
Women's Doubles: Maria Bueno / Nancy Richey
Mixed Doubles: Margaret Smith / Ken Fletcher
U.S. Championships
Men's Singles: Fred Stolle
Women's Singles: Maria Bueno
Men's Doubles: Roy Emerson / Fred Stolle
Women's Doubles: Maria Bueno / Nancy Richey
Mixed Doubles: Donna Floyd Fales / Owen Davidson

Ralston did have one particularly satisfying doubles triumph, teaming with Clark Graebner to become the first American champions of France since 1955. Their final-round victims, Romanians little known until later, were the hulking Ion Tiriac and his wet-behind-the-ears but gifted protégé, Ilie Nastase, 6-3, 6-3, 6-0. Newcombe, separated from regular partner Roche, won the Wimbledon doubles anyway, with Ken Fletcher, another all-Aussie picnic, 6-3, 6-4, 3-6, 6-3, over Bowrey and Davidson.

It was a dark year for the U.S. in the Davis Cup as Capt. George MacCall's team was bushwhacked, 3-2, by unheralded Brazil at Porto Alegre. Cliff Richey was upset in singles by both Edison Mandarino, 5-7, 6-3, 7-5, 6-3, and lefty Tom Koch, 6-1, 7-5, 6-1, Koch knotting it, 2-2, after Ashe and Ralston had beaten the two Brazilians, 7-5, 6-4, 4-6, 6-2. Mandarino took Ralston in the fifth match, 4-6, 6-4, 4-6, 6-4, 6-1. This was the beginning of Latin laments for Americans, who would lose on dirt south of the border six more times over the next 17 years.

The world's most successful player was the No. 1 woman, Billie Jean King, who won her first Wimbledon singles title at age 23 and spearheaded successful team efforts in the Federation and Wightman Cups. A virus infection diminished her effectiveness later, but Billie Jean won 10 of 16 tournaments and compiled a 57-8 record.

Nancy Richey, co-ranked No. 1 with Billie Jean in 1965, slipped to No. 2 despite reaching the finals of the Australian, French and U.S. singles, and winning six of 14 tournaments, with a 55-9 record. She also won her fourth straight U.S. Clay Court title, beating lefty Stephanie DeFina, 6-2, 6-2, while her brother, Cliff, 19, topped Frank Froehling, 13-11, 6-1, 6-3, to complete a singular family double. Nancy won three of the major doubles titles; the Australian with Carole Graebner over Margaret Smith and Lesley Turner, 6-4, 7-5, and Wimbledon and the U.S. with Maria Bueno, respectively over Smith and Judy Tegart Dalton, 6-3, 4-6, 6-4, and over 17-year-old Rosie Casals and King, 6-3, 6-4.

Margaret Smith won her record seventh consecutive Australian singles title without raising her racket, accepting a final round default from Richey, who injured a knee while beating Kerry Melville, 6-2, 8-6, in the semis. That snapped the tie with Nancye Wynne Bolton, whose half-dozen were registered between 1937 and 1951. Margaret's third consecutive French doubles was with Tegart Dalton over compatriots Fay Toyne and Jill Blackman, 4-6, 6-1, 6-1. But she was increasingly burdened by the pressure and loneliness of big-time tennis competition. Shortly after losing her Wimbledon title in a semi-final defeat by King, 6-3, 6-3, she announced her retirement at age 24 to open a clothing boutique in Perth—the first of several short-lived retirements, as it turned out.

Ann Haydon Jones won her second French singles title, over Richey, 6-3, 6-1.

King, seeded fourth, was magnificently aggressive at Wimbledon. Grass staining her knees on low volleys, she played better than anyone else, as her husband of less than a year sat nervously in the competitors' guest stand. Having dispatched one old rival, top-seeded Smith, in the semis, 6-3, 6-3, she did in another, second-seeded Bueno, in the final, 6-3, 3-6, 6-1, then tossed her racket high in the air and squealed with glee. Bueno, three-time champ, had to battle to get past Jones, 6-3, 9-11, 7-5, and into her fifth final. Billie Jean's toughest on the way was a quarter-final over tall, powerful Annette van Zyl, 1-6, 6-2, 6-4.

King, Julie Heldman and Carole Graebner carried the U.S. to a 3-0 victory over surprise finalist, West Germany, in the Federation Cup on clay at Turin, Italy. Julie beat Helga Niessen, 4-6, 7-5, 6-1, Billie Jean beat Edda Buding, 6-3, 3-6, 6-1, and joined Carole for a mop-up, 6-4, 6-2, over Helga Schultze and Buding.

King, Richey, Mary Ann Eisel and Jane Albert were the Americans in a 4-3 Wightman Cup victory over Great Britain at Wimbledon. Richey and Eisel contributed the decisive point in doubles, over Elizabeth Starkie and Rita Bentley, 6-1, 6-2. Billie Jean won both her singles, 6-2, 6-3, over Virginia Wade, and 5-7, 6-2, 6-3, over Jones, while Richey beat Wade, 2-6, 6-2, 7-5.

Maria Bueno captured her fourth U.S. title, the last of her seven major singles crowns, by beating Richey, 6-3, 6-1, with an all-court display of grace and shot-making magic that completely thwarted Nancy's back-court game. They had teamed for the U.S. doubles title at Longwood, over the new but potent partnership of

1966 CHAMPIONS AND LEADERS

Year-End Number One
Men: Manolo Santana
Women: Billie Jean King

Davis Cup: Australia
Federation Cup: United States
Wightman Cup: United States

King and Casals, 6-3, 6-4. But in the singles final Bueno treated Richey more like a stranger, winning in just 50 minutes. The best match of the tournament had been Bueno's 6-2, 10-12, 6-3 victory over the diminutive, 17-year-old Casals, a feast of dazzling footwork and shot making that captivated a crowd of 14,000. King was jolted in the second round by Aussie 19-year-old Kerry Melville, 6-4, 6-4, who made it to a semi-final defeat by Richey, 6-3, 6-2.

Also noteworthy in 1966 were the longest singles matches on record in top-level competition: Roger Taylor of Britain in 126 games defeated Wieslaw Gasiorek of Poland, 27-29, 31-29, 6-4, on a slick wood surface in a King's Cup match that lasted five hours and 27 minutes, and stretched until the early hours of a bitterly cold Warsaw morning. Perhaps just to show he wasn't out of interminable sets, Taylor, in the same series, was part of the third longest singles set, beating Taddeus Nowicki, 33-31, 6-1. In the female precinct, American Kathy Blake, in a record-length 62 games, outlasted Elena Subirats of Mexico, 12-10, 6-8, 14-12 on grass at the Piping Rock Country Club.

Vigorous Vic Seixas, Hall of Famer-to-be, could talk about a long match, too, his 94-game victory over 22-year-old Aussie Bill Bowrey at the Pennsylvania Grass Championships, 32-34, 6-4, 10-8, in almost four hours. Vic, a month short of his 43rd birthday, lost the next day, 6-3, 6-8, 6-3, to Clark Graebner who won the title over Stan Smith, 6-3, 6-4, 6-3. Vic ranked No. 9, his 13th time in the U.S. Top Ten, which he headed in 1951, 1954 and 1957.

The pros regrouped to revive their U.S. Championship after a one-year layoff, won by Welby Van Horn over John Nogrady, 6-4, 6-2, 6-2.

The pros had decided to cast their fate to small tournament-format events rather than head-to-head tours, as in the past, but the going was still rough. The U.S. Pro at Longwood remained an encouraging beacon, lighting the future, and Rod Laver signaled his takeover from Ken Rosewall as the pro king, beating 'Muscles,' 6-4, 4-6, 6-2, 8-10, 6-3. He had also beaten Rosewall, 6-2, 6-2, 6-3, for his third straight World Pro title at Wembley, a crown that Ken wore in 1957 and 1960 through 1963. But Rosewall was Laver's master for a fourth year in a row at the French Pro, 6-3, 6-2, 14-12, his seventh straight triumph (a record eight in total) in Paris.

1967

Newcombe, King closing monarchs of amateur era

Billie Jean King "Triples" at Wimbledon and U.S., echoing Don Budge and Alice Marble.

By sweeping the singles titles at Wimbledon and Forest Hills, Australian John Newcombe and Californian Billie Jean Moffitt King reigned as the king and queen of amateur tennis in 1967, the last year of the amateur era. By the end of the year two professional troupes—World Championship Tennis (WCT) and the National Tennis League (NTL)—had been formed, prompting Newcombe and a half dozen other leading amateur men to turn pro.

With the blessing of the All England Club and its forceful chairman, Herman David, pros appeared in late summer on Centre Court for an eight-man tourney sponsored and televised by the BBC. The brilliant final, Rod Laver over Ken Rosewall, 6-2, 6-2, 12-10, dwarfed the Newcombe-Bungert Wimbledon final the month before, and was but another factor in whetting the public's appetite for 'open' tennis, and taking the game to the brink of rebellion destined to change forever the old order.

The call to revolution was sounded in December by the Lawn Tennis Association of Britain, spurred by David, who had denounced 'shamateurism' as "a living lie" and urged open competition for some time. When the International Tennis Federation again voted against opens once more at its mid-year annual meeting, David declared, "It seems that we have come to the end of the road constitutionally." He vowed that Wimbledon would continue to be the world's premier tournament, with a field commensurate with that reputation, even if it had to "go it alone" as a pioneer of open competition. Backing him, the LTA took an unconstitutional, revolutionary step by voting overwhelmingly at its December meeting to make British tournaments open in 1968.

The ITF threatened to expel the British from the international organization, but its hand had been forced. A number of compromises later, open tennis became a reality in 1968, though in a much more limited and qualified way than the British had envisioned.

Early in the year, such upheaval did not seem to be in prospect. The U.S. Tennis Association hired Robert Malaga, a successful promoter of the Wightman Cup and Davis Cup in his hometown, Cleveland, as its first full-time executive secretary and signed a product-endorsement agreement with Licensing Corporation of America.

The competitive year began the same way the previous four had, with Roy Emerson winning his native Australian singles title for a record sixth time, over a seven-year span.

Arthur Ashe was his victim in the final for the second straight year, this time in straight sets: 6-4, 6-1, 6-4. Otherwise the triumph was a rough slog for Emmo getting past Tony Roche in the semis, 83 games: 6-3, 4-6, 15-13, 13-15, 6-2. Also for Ashe, beating John Newcombe in 81 games: 12-10, 20-22, 6-3, 6-2. Emmo was unable to defend his doubles crown. Newcombe and Roche, who would go on to win the French and U.S. doubles as well, beat Owen Davidson and Bill Bowrey in a rousing final, 3-6, 6-3, 7-5, 6-8, 8-6.

Nancy Richey, runner-up as Margaret Smith won her seventh consecutive singles title the year before, took advantage of Margaret's temporary retirement to capture the women's title, a 6-1, 6-4, triumph over Lesley Turner. Nancy didn't lose a set, but Turner fought off Françoise Durr, 6-1, 10-8, and 18-year-old Rosie Casals, 4-6, 6-1, 6-4. A 15-year-old newcomer who would be heard from, Evonne Goolagong, won two rounds. Turner and Judy Tegart Dalton captured the doubles.

Turner stung Maria Bueno, 6-3, 6-3, in the Italian final and won the first set of the French final before losing it to Françoise Durr, whose 4-6, 6-3, 6-4, victory was the first by a native woman in Paris since Simone Mathieu in 1939. Durr teamed with Australian Gail Sherriff for the first of five consecutive doubles titles, two with Ann Jones, and two more with Gail Sherriff, who by then had become a French citizen as Mme. Jean

1967 THE MAJOR CHAMPIONSHIPS

Australian Championships
Men's Singles: Roy Emerson
Women's Singles: Nancy Richey
Men's Doubles: John Newcombe / Tony Roche
Women's Doubles: Lesley Turner / Judy Tegart Dalton
Mixed Doubles: Lesley Turner / Owen Davidson
French Championships
Men's Singles: Roy Emerson
Women's Singles: Françoise Durr
Men's Doubles: John Newcombe / Tony Roche
Women's Doubles: Françoise Durr / Gail Sherriff
Mixed Doubles: Billie Jean King / Owen Davidson
Wimbledon
Men's Singles: John Newcombe
Women's Singles: Billie Jean King
Men's Doubles: Bob Hewitt / Frew McMillan
Women's Doubles: Rosie Casals / Billie Jean King
Mixed Doubles: Billie Jean King / Owen Davidson
U.S. Championships
Men's Singles: John Newcombe
Women's Singles: Billie Jean King
Men's Doubles: John Newcombe / Tony Roche
Women's Doubles: Rosie Casals / Billie Jean King
Mixed Doubles: Billie Jean King / Owen Davidson

Baptiste Chanfreau. (Gail would win again in 1976 as Mme. Jean Lovera, with Uruguayan Fiorella Bonicelli.)

Emerson, fit as ever, powered his way to the French men's singles title, dethroning fellow Aussie Tony Roche in the final, 6-1, 6-4, 2-6, 6-2. Roche had to fight off another lefty, Yugoslav Nikki Pilic in the semis, 3-6, 6-3, 6-4, 2-6, 6-4. Emmo lost only two other sets, and galloped past Pierre Darmon in the quarters, 6-0, 6-4, 6-4, then Istvan Gulyas, 6-3, 6-4, 6-2. It was Emmo's 12th major singles title, the male record until Pete Sampras won his 13th at Wimbledon in 2000. Emmo had eclipsed Bill Tilden's 10 by winning the Aussie five months earlier, but nobody, including himself, noticed. Years later, when Sampras was stalking him, Emerson said, "I wasn't aware that there was a record. We didn't think about stuff like that."

Roche had earlier lost his Italian title to transplanted Aussie Marty 'Martino Mulligano' Mulligan, 6-3, 0-6, 6-4, 6-1.

Having cleared the troublesome hurdle of Parisian clay, Emerson set his sights again on the elusive Grand Slam, but his vision was shattered in the fourth round at Wimbledon by tall lefty Pilic, 6-4, 5-7, 6-3, 6-4. Emerson was the favorite after the startling first-round ambush of Manolo Santana by American Charlie Pasarell, 10-8, 6-3, 2-6, 8-6. It was the curtain raiser on Centre Court, the only time a defending male champion and top seed was ever beaten in the first round.

That was the prelude to an upset-filled fortnight. By the quarter-finals, there were no seeded players left in the top half of the draw. The only meeting of seeds came in the quarter-finals, third Newcombe overpowering sixth Ken Fletcher, 6-4, 6-2, 6-4. Two unseeded semi-finalists were lefties—Pilic, 14-12, 8-10, 6-4, 6-2, over Aussie John Cooper (younger brother of 1958 champ Ashley Cooper), and rugged Yorkshireman Roger Taylor, 6-4, 8-6, 6-4, over Aussie lefty Ray Ruffels. So was West German Wilhelm Bungert, 6-4, 4-6, 4-6, 6-1, 6-3, over Brazilian Tom Koch, yet another southpaw.

Bungert depressed the home folks, ever yearning for a champ of their own to succeed Fred Perry (1934-35-36), by erasing Taylor, 6-4, 6-8, 2-6, 6-4, 6-4. But he had nothing left for the final and offered only token, halfhearted resistance as Newcombe claimed the title, 6-3, 6-1, 6-1, after chasing Pilic, 9-7, 4-6, 6-3, 6-4. Bungert's five games equaled the post-war futility of Ashley Cooper's 1957 loss to Lew Hoad, and Mulligan's to Rod Laver in 1962.

In doubles, Newcombe and Roche, reunited and favored to regain the title, fell in the quarters to Englishmen Graham Stilwell and Peter Curtis, 6-4, 4-6, 6-4, 3-6, 8-6. The title went to the freshly minted South African Davis Cup team of Frew McMillan and Bob Hewitt (who, as an Australian, had won twice with Fred Stolle). They drubbed Emerson and Fletcher (the latter the winner in 1966 with Newcombe), 6-2, 6-3, 6-4.

Cumulative attendance for the last amateur Wimbledon exceeded 300,000 for the first time, as 301,896 spectators went through the turnstiles.

Newcombe took the No. 1 world ranking at age 23 by winning eight of 24 tournaments and 83 of 99 matches. A sciatic nerve condition nearly cost him the U.S. Doubles championship, which was decided for the 46th and last time at Longwood Cricket Club, but he and Roche pulled through over Bowrey and Davidson, 6-8, 9-7, 6-3, 6-3. His lower back was still worrying 'Newk' going into the U.S. singles, but he experienced no ill effects in plowing to victory at Forest Hills with the loss of but four sets.

It was Emerson who was plagued first by back problems, then by torn thigh muscles suffered in his quarter-final loss to Clark Graebner. Graebner, one of several players swinging the new steel T-2000 rackets, recently introduced by manufacturer Wilson, crunched 25 aces in his 8-6, 3-6, 19-17, 6-1 victory, and three in a row from 30-40 to end his scintillating 3-6, 3-6, 7-5, 6-4, 7-5 semi-final victory over unseeded Jan Leschly, the clever and sporting left-handed Dane. Newcombe outslugged Graebner, seeking to become the first native champ since 1955, in a serve-and-volley final, 6-4, 6-4, 8-6.

Sharing attention with the winners at Forest Hills were the steel rackets used by women's champ Billie Jean King, fourth rounder Rosie Casals, Graebner and Gene Scott, among others. Wilson's equipment innovation, adapted from a French design pioneered by clothier and ex-champion René Lacoste, was the harbinger of a wave of new racket designs and materials that flooded the market during the next decade. Scott, then a 29-year-old Wall Street lawyer and part-time player who

---

1967 CHAMPIONS AND LEADERS

Year-End Number One
Men: John Newcombe
Women: Billie Jean King

Davis Cup: Australia
Federation Cup: United States
Wightman Cup: United States

would later become the self-styled Renaissance Man of tennis in the '70s, fulfilled many a Walter Mitty fantasy by working mornings in his office and taking the train to Forest Hills, where he reached the semis over Aussie Davidson, 6-3, 8-6, 9-7, before Newcombe jolted him back to reality, 6-4, 6-3, 6-3. Scott predicted that wood rackets would soon be obsolete, but his accurate prophecy did not come to pass immediately.

Woman of the Year in 1967 was Billie Jean Moffitt King, 24, who scored triples—victories in singles, doubles and mixed doubles—at both Wimbledon and the U.S. Only Don Budge in 1938 and Alice Marble in 1939 had also achieved this feat.

Billie Jean and Rosie Casals won all their singles (4-0) in carrying the U.S. to the Federation Cup on clay at Berlin: 3-0 sweeps of Rhodesia, South Africa, West Germany into the final. There it was 2-0 over Great Britain: Billie Jean over Ann Jones, 6-3, 6-4, Rosie over Virginia Wade, 9-7, 8-6.

It was the same story in the Wightman Cup, this time 6-1 over Britain at Cleveland. Billie Jean beat Wade, 6-3, 6-2, and Jones, 6-1, 6-2. Nancy Richey beat Jones, 6-2, 6-2, and took the clinching fourth point grittily over Wade, 3-6, 8-6, 6-2, despite a pulled muscle in her back that pained her through the last six games.

King compiled a 68-5 record during the ranking season and won 10 tournaments. In addition to seizing the Wimbledon and U.S. titles without losing a set, she won the U.S. Indoor, 6-1, 6-0, over left-handed Netherlander Trudy Groenman. She had the season's two longest winning streaks: 23 and 25 matches.

In Johannesburg, beating Bueno for the South African title, 7-5, 5-7, 6-2, she scored another triple (Bueno had a 'cripple', losing all three.) B.J. teamed triumphantly with Casals (her partner in U.S. and Wimbledon doubles victories) to beat Bueno and Judy Tegart Dalton, 4-6, 6-1, 6-3, and with Aussie Owen Davidson (her partner in French, Wimbledon, and U.S. Mixed Doubles Championships), to beat Bueno and Ken Fletcher, 6-1, 6-3. Santana took the men's singles over Leschly, 6-2, 2-6, 4-6, 6-3, 6-4.

Davidson scored a Mixed Grand Slam, having first teamed with Lesley Turner to win the Australian title, over Tegart Dalton and Roche, 9-7, 6-4.

King beat Ann Jones, the tenacious British left-hander, in the Wimbledon final, 6-3, 6-4, and again in the U.S. title match, 11-9, 6-4. At Forest Hills, Jones ignored a pulled hamstring and gallantly fought off nine match points before succumbing. Injuries had influenced the women's singles from the outset, four-time champion Maria Bueno pulling out with tendonitis in the right arm and Nancy Richey with the back ailment sustained in Wightman Cup. Jane 'Peaches' Bartkowicz, a sturdy 18-year-old from Hamtramck, Mich., the first female to ride a two-handed backhand so high, knocked off Casals, 4-6, 6-3, 7-5, before subsiding against Jones, 7-5, 2-6, 6-1, in the quarters. Jones then beat Turner, 6-2, 6-4, and King defeated, by the same score, French champ Françoise Durr. Françoise reached a U.S. high for a Frenchwoman, topping Simone Mathieu's quarterfinal finish in 1938.

Richey earlier won her fifth consecutive U.S. Clay Court title, gunning down Casals, 6-2, 6-3, after little Rosie conquered King in the semis, 6-4, 6-4. Arthur Ashe, whose duties as a lieutenant in the U.S. Army kept him out of Wimbledon and Forest Hills, won the men's version for the only time, beating Marty Riessen, 6-3, 6-1, 7-5. Ashe was ranked No. 2 in the U.S. behind Charlie Pasarell, who beat him twice in three under cover meetings: U.S. Indoor final, 13-11, 6-2, 2-6, 9-7; Richmond Indoor final, in Ashe's hometown, 6-3, 8-6. Arthur beat Charlie for the Philadelphia indoor title, 7-5, 9-7, 6-3. Pasarell won three tournaments, Ashe five.

The U.S. outdoor season survived the longest (147 games) tournament match of all time, in the doubles of the Newport (R.I.) Casino Invitational. Dick Leach and Dick Dell defeated Len Schloss and Tom Mozur, 3-6, 49-47, 22-20. The journey of these Americans consumed six hours and 10 minutes over two days, and undoubtedly provided impetus for the scoring reform championed by Newport's Jimmy Van Alen. Jimmy's 'sudden death' tie-breaker, designed to terminate such monster matches, was finally adopted in 1970.

It was a summer of Social Security number scores that drove not only Van Alen but schedule-making tournament referees wild. Two were played on the lawn of the Meadow Club at Southampton, N.Y. Dick Knight and Mike Sprengelmeyer. Americans, traveled 107 games, Knight winning, 32-30, 3-6, 19-17, in five hours, 30 minutes. Schloss and Mozur, those long-distance guys of Newport, won this time, 90 games, over an Aussie-American alliance of Chris Bovett and Butch Seewagen, 7-5, 48-46. It took South Africans Ray Moore and Cliff Drysdale 105 games to beat the Aussie-Brazilian lineup of Emerson and Ronnie Barnes, 29-31, 8-6, 3-6, 8-6, 6-2, during the U.S. Championships at Longwood. It stands as the U.S. record, tying with the 105-gamer only the year before in which Mexicans Joaquin Loyo-Mayo and Marcelo Lara beat the Mex-Spanish entry, Luis Garcia, and Santana, 10-12, 24-22, 11-9, 3-6, 6-2.

For the third consecutive year under hapless captain George MacCall, the U.S. Davis Cup team was helpless on foreign soil—slow, red clay. The 1967 loss to Ecuador, 3-2, at Guayaquil was the most ignominious of all for Americans, probably the most startling upset in the long history of Davis Cup competition. Ecuador's two players, Pancho Guzman and Miguel Olvera, were barely known internationally.

Cliff Richey, the most comfortable of the Americans on clay, won the first match, beating Guzman, 6-2, 2-6, 8-6, 6-4, and the inconsequential fifth, but the middle three spelled disaster for the Yanks. Olvera, a 26-year-old who had been sidelined by tuberculosis, was a winner, 4-6, 6-4, 6-4, 6-2, over Ashe, whose Cup record (10-0) included two singles wins shortly before in the 4-1 win over Mexico on Mexico City clay. Ecuadorian Capt. Danny Carrera was so thrilled he attempted to leap the net to embrace Olvera, tripped and broke his leg. Still, the 1-1 score did not seem too worrying for the U.S. until the scrambling Olvera and his 21-year-old sidekick Guzman overcame a 0-6, 2-5, deficit and stunned Marty Riessen and Clark Graebner, 0-6, 9-7, 6-4, 4-6, 8-6, setting the stage for a raucous third day. The giddy crowd of 2,200 at the Guayaquil Tennis Club cheered wildly for their sudden heroes and unsettled the Americans with a shower of abuse. Panic gripped MacCall as the slow-balling Guzman withstood two rushes from Ashe and won the decisive match by a score as bizarre as the whole series: 0-6, 6-4, 6-2, 0-6, 6-3.

With the U.S. out, South Africa was expected to reach the challenge round against Australia with Bob Hewitt, Cliff Drysdale and young Ray Moore, three formidable singles players, and Hewitt-McMillan the doubles team of the year. (Their 53-1 record included victories in the Italian, Wimbledon and South African Championships, plus seven other tournaments. Newcombe-Roche won 12 of 19 tournaments, including the Australian, French and U.S.)

But Hewitt broke his ankle in the quarter-final series against India and was unavailable for the semis, in which Spain eliminated South Africa, 3-2. In Australia for the challenge round for the second time in three years, Spain was outclassed again. Emerson took advantage of one of Santana's rare poor matches and won the opener in a rout, 6-4, 6-1, 6-1. Newcombe swamped 18-year-old Cup rookie lefty Manuel Orantes, 6-3, 6-3, 6-2, then teamed with Roche to scald Santana and Orantes, 6-4, 6-4, 6-4, losing only 16 points in 15 service games. The 3-0 lead at Brisbane assured Australia's 15th Cup victory in 18 years.

Emerson, 31, blasted Orantes, 6-1, 6-1, 2-6, 6-4, ending a peerless Davis Cup career in which he was 11-1 in singles, 6-0 in doubles during nine challenge rounds, eight of them won by Australia. Emmo, whose overall Cup record (including zone matches) was 21-2 in singles, 13-2 in doubles, guzzled champagne triumphantly from the sterling tub on eight occasions, more than any other player, and had played the clincher five times, thrice in doubles. Newcombe's last match as an amateur was not as successful. He lost to Santana, making the final score 4-1.

Immediately after the challenge round, Newcombe, Roche, Emerson and Owen Davidson turned pro. Newcombe, Roche, Cliff Drysdale, Roger Taylor and Nikki Pilic signed with New Orleans promoter Dave Dixon, who, bankrolled by Texas oilman Lamar Hunt and his nephew, Al Hill, Jr., had founded World Championship Tennis, Inc. (WCT). Emerson signed with MacCall, who had corralled Rod Laver, Ken Rosewall, Pancho Gonzalez, Andres Gimeno (runner-up to Laver, 4-6, 6-4, 6-3, 7-5, in the U.S. Pro final), Fred Stolle and a few others for his National Tennis League (NTL). Davidson became the pro at the All England Club and Britain's national coach.

The formation of WCT's 'Handsome Eight' barnstorming troupe—seasoned pros Dennis Ralston, Pierre Barthes and Butch Buchholz complementing the five converted amateurs—had an enormous impact on the amateur tennis establishment. In one day, Dixon and his partner Bob Briner, a tennis neophyte who would later become executive director of the ATP (Association of Tennis Professionals), signed Newcombe, Roche, Pilic and Taylor, accounting for three of the 1967 Wimbledon semi-finalists. Ralston had been their first-signed, and they soon added Drysdale, Buchholz and Barthes.

"We had in one fell swoop taken all the stars out of the game. If anyone was ever going to see them again at Wimbledon and Forest Hills, the ITF had to make an accommodation," Briner remembers. "Open tennis came about so fast after that, it was pitiful."

Chapter 6

Althea Gibson, Tennis Pioneer

As a girl she endured poverty in Harlem. As a woman she endured prejudice in tennis. But, as detailed in this reprint from SPORT, Althea Gibson emerged as the consummate world champion.

SPORT April 1963 By Ed Fitzgerald

Althea Gibson, 1960
Tough and uncompromising, qualities befitting tennis' ultimate pioneer.

Althea Gibson used to live in a rundown tenement on Harlem's West 143rd Street, a block that made the one in *West Side Story* look lush. Now she lives in a handsome apartment on Manhattan's Central Park West, and you have to give the doorman your name to get in.

Althea used to think she was eating well when she could, afford a 25-cent hamburger to go with her 15-cent plate of collard greens and rice. Now she eats *filet mignon*, with *sauce bearnaise*.

There was a time when Althea fixed her own hair with a pressing iron and a jar of Dixie Peach Pomade hair grease. Now she patronizes an expensive West Side hairdresser.

As a youngster Althea got her exercise playing paddle tennis in the middle of her Harlem block. Now she plays golf as a member of the predominantly white Englewood Golf Club in New Jersey.

To go, as Althea Gibson has, from the world of poverty to the world of comfort, this rangy, brooding daughter of a Negro sharecropper had to do in tennis what Jackie Robinson did in baseball. She had to be not merely good but sensational simply to get a chance. She had to endure the humiliations Jackie did—more subtle, perhaps, less profane, because tennis prides itself on being a sport of ladies and gentlemen. But the demeanings were just as scarring to this proud girl's sensitive spirit. She had to win the important matches carrying a double load of tension—the kind that grips every athlete competing for a grand prize and the more crushing kind that grips only pioneers. Althea wasn't playing for herself alone, but for all the brown- and black-skinned boys and girls who would follow her through the door—if she could shove it open so firmly that nobody could close it behind her.

Amateur sport, in the hectic years since World War II, has known no more dramatic story than Althea's. Twice Wimbledon champion and twice United States champion, she dominated women's tennis as no one since "Little Mo" Connolly. With her killing serve—delivered with the sweep and power of a man—her slashing net game and her rugged physique. Althea was spectacular to watch. Her role as a pioneer made her an even more interesting figure, and she kept things lively with her own always blunt and often tactless comments.

"The only trouble with Althea," said Sydney Llewellyn, a New York City taxi driver who taught her tennis in his spare time, "is that she doesn't mind hurting people."

Althea denies it, saying, "I say what I think, but I try to be polite. I never went around screaming that the United States Lawn Tennis Association was picking on me when it looked as though they weren't ever going to let me play at Forest Hills. Actually, I think I used to get in more trouble with my own people because I wouldn't crusade enough to suit them. But I'm just not a racially conscious or controversially inclined person, and I don't want to be. I see myself as an individual. I can't help or change my color in any way, so why should I make a big deal out of it? My attitude has always been that I could do more for the Negro by making good, and being accepted because I had made good, than I ever could by popping off. So the Negro press, which likes fireworks, used to call me big-headed, uppity, ungrateful and a few other, things like that."

Other people were also critical of Althea.

"She is rude, uncooperative, assertive and domineering," the English player, Angela Buxton, once said. But Angela later became so friendly with Althea that she shared her London flat during Althea's two winning seasons at Wimbledon.

"I'm not a cold person, underneath," Althea said one night, sipping a pre-dinner martini, "but I know sometimes I appear to be." For a girl who is famous for being difficult to interview, she is very articulate, when she wants to be. "I've always been a loner, suspicious and withdrawn," she says. "I guess I've always been afraid to risk too much by trusting any part of myself with anybody else. You can get hurt pretty bad that way when you're poor, and colored. I guess it all goes back to when

I was a kid."

Althea's childhood was, frankly, brutal. No money, no clothes, only the most primitive kinds of fun, and, worst of all, no hope. She was born on August 25, 1927, in the little South Carolina town of Silver, but her father went to New York to find work a year or so later and her mother followed with the children as soon as there was fare money. They knew there would never be any money for them in South Carolina. "I got a bale and a half of cotton out of my sharecrop the last year we were there," Daniel Gibson, a big, powerful man, remembers. "Cotton was $50 a bale that year, so I got exactly $75 for working all year."

Yet in New York money was still so tight that Althea spent far more of her childhood away from her family than with it. She stayed first with an aunt in New York and then with one in Philadelphia and no matter where she was living, she hated school. Even when she was at home and her father gave her some memorable whalings for truancy, she persistently played hooky. "Me and my friends," she says, shaking her head at her own obstinacy, "used to regard school as a good place to meet and make our plans for what we would do all day."

When she was 12, big for her age, strong and already a neighborhood celebrity because she had won the women's singles paddle tennis championship of New York City, her father decided Althea ought to become a professional boxer. He was serious. He had been reading about women's boxing bouts allowed in some states.

"Daddy thought there might be good money in it," Althea says, "and he wanted to put me in for it. As a matter of fact, I was a pretty fair fighter. Daddy taught me all the moves, and I had a good punch, no kidding. I remember one day he got mad at me for not coming home for a couple of days and when I finally sashayed in, he didn't waste any time going for any strap. He just walked up to me and punched me right in the face and knocked me for a loop. I got right back up and punched him back, as hard as I could, and pretty soon we had a good little fight going, and we weren't fooling around either."

Maybe she didn't hit him hard enough. Mr. Gibson gave up trying to make a boxer of his daughter and concentrated on trying to make a student of her.

A nice, but vain try. Althea somehow graduated from junior high school, but she says, "I don't know how I did it. I think those teachers just made up their minds to pass me on to the next school and let them worry about me." It couldn't have been easy dealing with a street-fighting girl who would spend all day shooting baskets for Cokes at the playground or watching a movie in the afternoon and the stage show at the Apollo at night. After the show at the Apollo, she'd eat a two-cent mickey (potato) roasted in an empty lot, then climb the stairs at home with one eye on the shadowed, landings to make sure nobody jumped her with a knife. Surrounded by her mother and father, her brother Daniel and her sisters Annie and Millie and Lillian, she then went to sleep.

Some nights she didn't go home. She would spend all night riding the subway from one end of the line to the other. In the summer it was cooler on the fan-blown trains than it was on sultry 143rd Street, and in the winter it was warmer.

Inevitably, though, her behavior landed her in a place where society could teach her discipline. She spent a few months in the girls' dormitory of the Society for the Prevention of Cruelty to Children, which she thought was a country club. The hardest work she had to do was to scrub the floor now and then and the food was abundant and good. But the restrictions got on her nerves after a while, and she asked to go home. The authorities agreed, first warning Althea that if she got into any more trouble she would be sent to a girls' correction school. "Which," Althea says wryly, "is polite language for reformatory." That prospect didn't appeal to her, so she decided it was time to work and earn some money.

As a teenager Althea cleaned chickens in a butcher shop, ran deliveries, waited on counters at a Chock Full O' Nuts restaurant, worked as a mail clerk, in a Five-and-Ten, a dressmaking shop and a button factory. During one long stretch between jobs, the City Welfare Department paid her rent for a comfortable room in a private home and supplied her a weekly allowance.

"When I was supposed to be looking for a job," she says, "I was playing basketball and paddle tennis, shooting pool and going to the movies."

It's ironic, that if Althea had cared enough about any job to really work at it, she might never have played tennis. But instead of working she played paddle tennis. And a young musician, Buddy Walker, who was working part-time as a city play-leader, saw her slamming the ball.

Paddle tennis is played on a court marked off much the same as a regular tennis court, except that it is about

half the size. Wooden paddles are used instead of tennis rackets. The balls can be either sponge rubber or tennis balls. When Buddy Walker saw Althea's astonishing skill, it struck him—a tennis fan—that she might play tennis just as well. He bought her a couple of second-hand tennis rackets and soon made a date for her to play a few sets with a friend of his at the Harlem River Tennis Courts.

Juan Serrell, a Negro schoolteacher who was a member of the Cosmopolitan Tennis Club, a private club to which the wealthier Harlem tennis players belonged, saw Althea's workout. He agreed with Walker that she had rare ability and helped provide her with a junior membership in the club and formal instruction by Fred Johnson.

Johnson became the first of a long line of tennis coaches, patrons and officials to try to bend Althea's stubborn will and fiery temperament. They clashed early and often. Althea was willing to take his advice on how to hit a tennis ball but not on how to live her personal life. "I wasn't exactly ready to start studying how to be a fine lady," she says. "I kept wanting to fight my opponent every time I started to lose a match."

Gradually, as she began to feel more comfortable at the club and to study the members covertly, Althea came to feel the mannered customs of the game weren't so silly after all. "I made up my mind that I would go along with the program," she says. "I was learning that you could act like a lady and still beat the living daylights out of the ball."

Althea played in her first tournament in 1942. She was 15, the tournament was the all-Negro American Tennis Association's New York State Open Championship, and she won it. She won the national A.T.A. girls' singles championship in 1944 and '45 and went to the final round of the women's singles its 1946.

The important thing that happened to Althea in that tournament was meeting two tennis-playing doctors from the South, Dr. Robert W. Johnson of Lynchburg, Virginia, and Dr. Hubert A. Eaton of Wilmington, North Carolina. "My two doctors," Althea has affectionately called them ever since. Professionally and financially successful, and alert to any opportunity to encourage Negro participation in tennis, the doctors suggested that Althea devote the next few years to an intensive tennis training program, preferably as a scholarship student in a good Negro college. Obviously Dr. Johnson and Dr. Eaton saw in Althea their dream of a Negro tennis player good enough to break the color line in the major national and international tournaments. To Althea the idea of spending all her time playing tennis was great. But the college part of their proposal stopped her. "I never even went to high school," she said. "How can I go to college?"

The doctors were resourceful. The things they wanted Althea to do couldn't be done by an ignorant girl, no matter how hard she could wallop a tennis ball. So it was arranged that Althea would go to Wilmington for the school year, live with Dr. Eaton and his family, go to high school with the Eaton children and practice her tennis with Dr. Eaton on his backyard court. In the summer she would move to Dr. Johnson's in Lynchburg and, using his home as a base, travel the Negro tournament trail with him.

It was a tremendous opportunity, but it wasn't an easy decision for Althea. She had heard some frightening stories about how it was for colored people down South. "Harlem wasn't heaven," she says, "but at least I knew I could take care of myself there." Fortunately she had made friends that year with boxer Sugar Ray Robinson and his wife, Edna Mae. The Robinsons put an end to her indecision. "You go on down there and do what those people tell you, and you'll never be sorry," Ray told her.

There were times when Althea wondered if she had done the right thing in putting her whole life on the line for the sake of her tennis career. The signs on the Wilmington buses were new to her: "White in front, Colored to the rear."

"It was even worse when I went to the movies," she remembers. "The ushers practically knocked us colored down making sure we got up to the back balcony, which was the only place in the whole theater we were allowed to sit. Actually, I've never really liked to sit in the orchestra. I'll sit in the balcony every time I get the chance. But I never enjoyed a movie all the time I was in the South because I *had* to sit in the balcony."

But her school work progressed well, better than she had dared hope, and her tennis progressed even more. That summer Althea won her first A.T.A. national women's singles title—the first of ten in a row. For whatever it was worth, and Althea knew it wasn't worth much, she was the best Negro woman tennis player in the country.

It was two years later, the summer of 1949, when she first heard the suggestion that she might some day be able to play at Forest Hills. "Althea," Dr. Eaton said to her with elaborate casualness, "how would you feel about playing at Forest Hills next year?"

"He knew how I would feel about it," Althea says. "He knew I would give my right arm to do it. So all I said was, 'Huh, who you kidding?' And he looked like he knew something and said, 'Well, all I can say is, don't think it couldn't happen. Some pretty good people are working on it.'"

It's unlikely those good people, white as well as colored, would have accomplished their goal if it hadn't been for a public outburst in the early summer of 1950 by Alice Marble. Alice wrote an editorial in *American Lawn Tennis* magazine that revealed the undercover Gibson affair. Althea had played in both the Eastern Indoors and the National Indoors the previous winter and had lasted as far as the quarter-finals both times. Graduating from high school in June of 1949 she had accepted a scholarship to Florida A. and M. She had come a long way from the playgrounds of Harlem, but it didn't look as though she were going to be allowed to go any further.

"In order to qualify for the Nationals," Miss Marble quoted a U.S.L.T.A. committeeman, "Miss Gibson must make a strong showing in the major Eastern tournaments to be played between now and the date for the big do at Forest Hills. Most of these major tournaments—Orange, East Hampton, Essex, etc.—are invitational, of course, and if she is not invited to participate, as my committee member freely predicted, then she obviously will be unable to prove anything at all, and it will be the reluctant duty of the committee to reject her entry at Forest Hills. Miss Gibson is over a very cunningly wrought barrel ... If tennis is a game for ladies and gentlemen it's time we acted a little more like gentle people and less like sanctimonious hypocrites."

The first big break-through came when Althea was invited to play in the Eastern Grass Court Championships at South Orange, New Jersey. Althea, painfully over-anxious, defeated Virginia Rise Johnson in the first round and lost to the experienced Helen Pastall Perez in the second. Then she went to the quarter-finals of the National Clay Court Championships at Chicago before losing to Doris Hart. Not long afterward, Harold Lebair, a long-time power in the U.S.L.T.A., passed the word to one of Althea's supporters among the A.T.A. officials that if she applied for a place in the draw at Forest Hills, her entry would be approved. She did apply, and she was swiftly accepted.

Her first National Tournament was an experience Althea will never forget. She won her first-round match and went up against Louise Brough, champion of Wimbledon and former champion of the United States, in the second round. Despite the fact that she appeared to be hopelessly overmatched, it was a glittering opportunity to show what she could do against first-class competition, and Althea took a life-or-death grip on her racket and set out to prove herself. Miss Brough won the first set, 6-1, but Althea laid into the ball with more power and more confidence in the second set and won, 6-3. She was ahead, 7-6, in the third set, and on the verge of a stunning upset, when a thunderstorm struck the stadium. Play had to be suspended until the next day.

"That was the worst thing that could have happened to me," Althea says. "It meant I had to sit around all night thinking about the match, thinking about how much it would mean to me if I won, thinking about how close I had come to beating one of the greatest players in the game and how easy it would be to blow the whole thing. So, naturally, when I went back out there the next day, and we picked up where we had left off, I blew the whole thing."

Still, Althea had forced acceptance of herself as a tournament player of the first rank. She began to play in all of the big events, even in the Good Neighbor tournament at Miami, where she became the first Negro ever to compete in a racially mixed tournament in the Deep South. She went to Wimbledon. "All I got there was experience," she says ruefully. But experience was what she needed. Not that she wasn't disappointed as time went on and she saw herself ranked No. 9 nationally in 1952, No. 7 in 1953, and then dropped to No. 13 in 1954. By then she had a new coach, Sydney Llewellyn.

Althea, two years out of college, champion of nothing but the A.T.A., and getting no younger, was tempted to quit tennis. She actually put in her application for a commission in the Women's Army Corps. But Llewellyn talked her out of it, and then the U.S.L.T.A. boosted her career by sending her on a State Department goodwill tour of Southeastern Asia.

Traveling with Ham Richardson, Bob Perry and Karol Fageros, Althea played the game more intensively than she ever had. She had never had a chance before to play so steadily against such excellent players. Her game improved quickly. In 1956 she won the championship of France, her first major title, and, even though she was beaten in the quarter-finals at Wimbledon, she went to the final round at Forest Hills before losing to Shirley Fry. But she was 29 years old, and if she was ever going to win one of the big ones, it would have to be soon. Plenty of people in tennis predicted she never would. "She's good enough to come close," they said, "but just not quite good enough."

They were wrong. In the eighth year of her campaigning against the best of the white players, Althea finally made it. Tense with the knowledge that Queen Elizabeth was sitting in the royal box at midcourt, Althea won the Wimbledon championship by beating Darlene Hard in straight sets. Then she was led by tournament officials to meet the Queen and accept her trophy. The tough kid from 143rd Street made the deep curtsy she had painstakingly practiced and smiled happily.

"My congratulations," Queen Elizabeth said. "It must have been terribly hot out there."

"Yes, your majesty," Althea said. "I hope it wasn't as hot in your box. At least I was able to stir up a breeze."

It was almost a foregone conclusion then that Althea would also win at Forest Hills, and play on the Wightman Cup team, and win again the next year at Wimbledon and Forest Hills. Althea Gibson was, indisputably, the champion woman tennis player of the world. She recorded an album of torch songs, sang two songs on the Ed Sullivan Show, began to enjoy the fun of playing in tournaments in such exotic spots as Caracas, Ciudad Trujillo and San Juan, and finally took the biggest step of all when she forsook Harlem for Central Park West.

But she couldn't quit. Not Althea. "I'm Althea Gibson, the tennis champion," she wrote in her autobiography, *I Always Wanted To Be Somebody.* "I hope it makes me happy." But already she has embarked on a brand new career. Shooting in the middle 70s after only a few years of serious golf, Althea has set out to win the national women's amateur golf championship. "I plan to work hard on my game and develop it," she says calmly. "I intend to win this thing."

Would you bet against her?

Jack Kramer, 1948 From World War II on, the game's dominant force for change.

Chapter 7

Invincible Jack Kramer

As a tennis player, Jack Kramer had few equals. As a tennis promoter, he had none. He was a dominant force in both arenas, as recounted by SPORT *in this 1965 profile.*

SPORT August 1965 By John M. Ross

At the height of his tennis-playing career, Jack Kramer could throw his arm around a would-be opponent and charm him one day and then utterly, chillingly destroy him on the court 24 hours later. During his later career as a tennis promoter, Jack Kramer was hailed as the game's savior one day and reviled as its very ruination the next. Through it all he turned bad luck into good fortune. Few men have ever wended their way so well through the maze of contradictions.

As a player Kramer ranks with Big Bill Tilden and Don Budge as the greatest in history. To avoid arguments, experts set aside an era for each of them and let it go at that: Kramer's era was 1946-54. He won nearly all the important amateur tournaments and capped this part of his career by teaming with Ted Schroeder in 1948 to recapture the Davis Cup. The cup had been held by Australia since 1939.

In 1948 Kramer began a memorable pro career in which he won 399 matches and lost just 118. On his first tour he annihilated champion Bobby Riggs, 69-20. He was even better against Pancho Gonzalez—98-27. And he closed out his career the way few athletes ever do—in victory. By then Kramer was agonized with an arthritic back condition, but he still was too much for Australia's Golden Boy, Frank Sedgman. Sedgman lost, 54-41, and that was the closest any pro ever came to beating Jack Kramer in a series.

People who came in contact with Kramer off the court saw him one way and his opponents saw him another. This is what tennis authority Allison Danzig wrote in SPORT in December 1948: "Friendly and trustful as a puppy dog, almost naive in his faith in people ... he has nothing but well wishers, and not an enemy or critic anywhere on the entire tennis circuit ... From the time he first came East I have never seen him that he wasn't in the best of spirits and enjoying himself."

And this is how Riggs remembers him: "He was a merciless competitor. Even when he had huge leads in our series, Jack was sore when he lost. He did not take kindly to defeat. He fought from the first match to the last."

That was the big thing about Jack Kramer: You could view him the way you wished, because he gave you two distinct personalities to choose from. You could be mesmerized by his deep-set blue eyes, his sandy, crew-cut hair, his ideal 6-1 physique and his captivating off-court smile. Or you could think of him as a player who didn't know how to compromise and who flung back ready-made alibis in the direction from which they came. In 1946, for example, he lost at Wimbledon to Jaroslav Drobny, the outstanding Czech southpaw. The American press stood by him, blaming the loss on Kramer's badly blistered head. "Nonsense," said Kramer. "The injury didn't beat me. Dronby did."

Since retiring as a player, Kramer has been no less demanding in driving toward new goals. Not surprisingly, there are people in tennis circles who swear by him and many who would like to swear at him. He has campaigned endlessly for open-tennis tournaments—competition between amateurs and pros. Kramer and his followers believe it would help eliminate the hypocrisy of paid amateurism and that the fans would be the real winners because they'd see the best possible tennis. But amateur tennis officials still prefer to indulge the fantasy that their game is simon pure. And they fear, too, that open tennis would reduce their own powers.

As a promoter with a bulging wallet Kramer lured the world's top players to his tour by offering them much more than they ever made as amateurs, and that often took some doing. And he made enemies. In 1959, when Kramer was negotiating with Australia's Ashley Cooper and Mal Anderson, a full-page headline in the tabloid Sydney *Sun* screamed: KRAMER TO BUY CUP TEAM! When he walked the city streets in Australia, people shouted at him: "Go home, Jake!"

Kramer brought top-flight tennis to places both in this country and around the world where it might never otherwise have been seen. His players performed before maharajas of India and the natives of Sudan.

Kramer today is not as active in tennis as he once was. But he admits the game is too much a part of him to ever quit it entirely. And just as much a part of him today as it ever was is his uncompromising attitude, his fighting spirit. He's come too far since the broiling September day in 1947 when he stood on the threshold of a lucrative pro career. What he has obtained today— considerable wealth and stature in addition to the controversies—is what he was seeking that day 18 years ago when Frank Parker threatened to take it away.

That September day, at the U.S. singles championships in Forest Hills, New York, Kramer met Parker for the title. Many people thought Kramer had to win in order to earn a pro contract and embark on a world tour with Riggs. Actually, Kramer knew he was set for the tour win, lose or draw. But Kramer also knew that not many people would come out to see Riggs, the pro champ, play anyone but the best of the amateurs.

The capacity crowd, sitting restlessly on sun-baked, backless benches, saw a startling contrast in styles. Parker was a conservative retriever who relied on his own consistency to draw opponents into errors. Kramer had what was beginning to be called "the big game." It was an all-out offensive. His drives were deep and skimming, his services twisting. He moved in for the kill with murderous, sure-handed volleys and his overhead shots were thundering

Parker's only hope lay in working his slowball tactics to devilish perfection. He began the strategy

immediately, giving his big opponent changes of speed, drop shots, lobs and soft, high floaters. Kramer was quickly thrown off stride and no matter how hard he tried to overcome Parker's annoying style, he couldn't. Jack lost the first set, 6-4.

Now a marked change came over the fans. At the outset they had been more gay than tense, as though they were attending a giant farewell party for Big Jake. But slowly the crowd began to rally to Parker's side. By the start of the second set Parker had the gallery roaring at every point. And there seemed to be no stopping him. Repeatedly he chased Kramer to baseline, disrupting Jack's forecourt attack. Twice Parker broke through his opponent's service and scored a 6-2 second-set victory.

For the third set Big Jake changed his own tactics to match his opponent's. He deliberately began to draw Parker into long rallies, thus steadying his own game and hoping to wear down Parker, who, at 31, was six years Kramer's senior. Jack won the third set, 6-1, and the fourth was no contest. He was back in full command of his power and raked the court with both forehand and backhand. After Parker dropped service twice, he chose to save his waning strength for the fifth and decisive set. Kramer won the fourth, 6-0.

In the final set, Parker won the first game but Kramer took the next three and Parker seemed on the verge of being smothered by fatigue. It was Kramer, 3-2, as he served in the fateful sixth game. He double faulted twice and was down 0-40.

Kramer reached back for all he had to deuce the score, then exploded with a service ace and rocketed a Parker lob off the grass to take a two-game lead. Parker gamely held his service but Kramer swept the next two games for a 6-3 set victory, and, of course, the match, the championship, and the pro jackpot.

Although Jack Kramer's tennis career began mostly by accident, it wasn't surprising that he wound up in some sort of athletic endeavor. His father, David, was a railroad engineer with a strong interest in many sports. Not long after Jack was born (in Las Vegas, Nevada, on August 1, 1921) his father began swamping him with all kinds of baseball equipment.

Jack also played football, and it was that sport, strangely enough, which got him started in tennis. He came home with a bloody nose one day after a sandlot game. That was a little messier but not nearly as painful as the separated ribs he got a short time later. Enough football, said his mother. Tennis anyone? said his father.

Thanks, but no thanks, said Jack.

"Jack, your father always has tried to do so much for you," said Mrs. Kramer. "I think you should do this for him."

"When do we start, Dad?" said Jack.

They started immediately, about the time they moved to San Bernardino, California. Jack, now 13, and his father made a vigorous pair on the courts across the street from their house, but their duels didn't last long. Jack got beaten soundly one day and refused to play an extra set. His father was furious. "I'll never play that kid again," David Kramer stormed to his wife. He did, of course, but by the time they resumed action Jack had surpassed him.

Kramer began taking his tennis racket to school and he played regularly and before long he was so absorbed in the game that he had little time for anything else. He got his first lessons from Dick Skene, a professional, for which he paid $25 down from his own savings and $5 a month. He switched to Perry Jones, however, when Skene wanted him to play one opponent in a tournament and Jones thought he should play someone better.

Jones was one of the most influential men in tennis besides being a fine teacher, and an association with him was Kramer's big break. "He taught me to play by having me practice with some of the best players in the country," recalled Kramer.

Jack developed so quickly that at 15 he beat Alice Marble, then the U.S. and Wimbledon women's champ, in a practice match and he won the national boys' singles title the same year. In 1938, at age 17, he won the national interscholastic crown and decided to try for the national men's title. There, though, progress took a nose dive. He roomed with a delightful screwball named Frankie Kovacs who induced him to try a steady diet of hot dogs and spaghetti. Kramer, stomach sick, was eliminated in an early round. That incident set the pattern for a strange succession of physical jinxes in Kramer's early career.

The next year Jack was invited to practice with the Davis Cup squad. He did so well, that he made the squad at 18, one of the youngest members in history. He teamed with the late Joe Hunt and lost the decisive doubles match to Australians John Bromwich and Adrian Quist.

The next two years Kramer collaborated with fellow Californian Ted Schroeder to win the national men's doubles titles. But Jack was becoming discontented with his reputation. He was irritated that people thought he was fine as a doubles player, but not so hot in singles. So he began to make an effort to get back into top physical shape, which he had neglected.

For nine months before the 1942 U.S., nationals Jack cut out his indiscriminate eating and late hours. He worked long and hard on his weakest strokes. He sharpened his game to its finest point ever and won ten straight tournaments before leaving for the East. Then, on the eve of the nationals, he got appendicitis and had to withdraw from the tournament.

In 1943 Kramer's strange jinx struck again. Playing his old partner, Joe Hunt, for the U.S. title, Jack was struck by ptomaine poisoning he had gotten from some clams the night before. He was barely able to get the ball over the net, but, characteristically, refused to make excuses.

By that time Jack Kramer was Seaman Jack Kramer, U.S. Coast Guard. He had received a furlough to play in the tournament. For the next three years Kramer did little tennis playing. Five landings in the Pacific during World War II kept him more than occupied. He was mustered out in January, 1946 after rising to lt. (j.g.).

Kramer had a difficult time regaining his touch at first. His timing was gone and his stroke felt wrong.

He came around quickly, however, and his comeback was marred only by the blistered hand in his match against Drobny at Wimbledon. The hand was healed by September and Kramer once again went after the elusive national men's singles title. His opponent in the final was Tom Brown, Jr., who had come out of nowhere to knock off Vines and Gardnar Mulloy. But Brown's big game was too similar in style to Kramer's—and not as effective—and Jack whipped him easily. For once, Kramer had overcome his injury jinx and it would be mostly a thing of the past from that point on. His national title also marked the beginning of Kramer's near-invincibility.

In December, in Melbourne, Kramer and Schroeder made short work of the Australians in the Davis Cup match. Schroeder scored an upset over Bromwich, Australia's No. 1 player, and Kramer beat Dinny Pails in straight sets: 8-6, 6-2, 9-7. In the doubles Jack got a measure of revenge for his 1939 defeat by teaming with Schroeder to beat Bromwich and Quist, also in straight sets.

In July, 1947, Kramer went to London, England, to try for the only major amateur title he hadn't yet won: Wimbledon. Kramer's opponent in the final again was Tom Brown. Standing at center court, they bowed to King George, attending his first Wimbledon in 20 years. Then they turned to the match for which they had practiced together and shared each other's nervousness in the locker room. Kramer mercifully disposed of his buddy in 45 minutes in one of the most one-sided matches in Wimbledon history.

By then Kramer had exhausted any serious challenge in the amateur ranks and it was obvious he would soon turn pro. Riggs, with an eye to the box office, began promoting a rivalry with Kramer even before Jack won at Wimbledon. "I can beat Jack Kramer on grass, on clay, on cement, or indoors," said Bobby.

Slightly amused, Kramer had no doubts about his chances against Bobby. "I figure I can beat any defensive tennis player in the world," he said, "and Riggs by his own admission is a defensive player."

Kramer signed his contract with Riggs, because, as he said, "I had been scratching out a meager living in amateur tennis. I also had a side job for $60 a week with a meat-packing company. When I started to catch colds walking in and out of the icebox, I decided that honest work wasn't for me." Then Kramer went out and won better than three of every four matches against Riggs on their nationwide tour. And, just to make it official, he won the national pro singles title from Riggs in June, 1948.

The pro tour was a grueling one but Kramer, amazingly, seemed to thrive on the rugged day-to-day competition. By 1948 he was 27, yet he was still three years from his peak and improving steadily. In 1949 Kramer mauled Pancho Gonzalez, the man who had succeeded him as amateur king. In 1951, after dismantling Pancho Segura, 64-28, Kramer threatened to quit Riggs' tour until "somebody fresh, with color" comes along. In 3-1/2 years Kramer had made a quarter of a million dollars, but he was beginning to sense that the public was tiring of the one-sided routine.

Kramer, however, stayed with Riggs for two more years and then, in 1953, decided to do his own promoting of a series with Sedgman. He easily beat Sedgman and cleared over $100,000.

In 1954, Kramer quit playing entirely and devoted all his time to promoting. Working 18 hours a day at the job, he soon built up a stable of players unrivaled by anyone. The profits rolled in, more from shrewd investments than the tour. Kramer spent just a couple of months in college (Southern California and Rollins), but he seemed to have the knowledge of a Harvard Business School graduate when it came to finances.

Kramer bought considerable stock, a stable of racehorses, a gas well and real estate. With the money he began reaping from various lines of sporting goods and sportswear, he had an income that was climbing over $200,000 a year.

With the money, though, Kramer began getting the headaches—most of them coming from tennis. And much of his tennis troubles, in turn, coming from the temperamental Gonzalez. Kramer had to take Pancho to court (legal, not tennis, court) to prove their contract was valid. Says Jack: "It cost me two things—money for legal fees ($3,500) and Gorgo's (Gonzalez') friendship." Gorgo left the tour for a couple of years.

Kramer tried to do what he honestly felt was best for tennis, in addition to reaping his own profits. He experimented with rule changes, scoring variations and other innovations to make the game more popular.

And his battles went on. He refused to give up his dream of open tennis and continued to expound upon it at every opportunity. "I feel that it will be the salvation of the sport," he said a while back. "Tennis must be brought to the same moral plane as golf, which has amateurs and professionals, but nothing in between. If I had a brain in my head I'd let someone else take this. I've even had to give up my two vices—pro football and horse racing. After all, I have five kids and shouldn't be flying around in the snow. But tennis is too much a part of me to quit, and I'd like to put back into it some of the things it gave me."

Even if Jack Kramer had quit tennis cold in 1954, most of the people who saw him play would have agreed that he had repaid his debt to the sport 100 times over, just through his marvelous play. For eight years he dominated tennis the way it had only been dominated twice before—by Tilden and by Budge. Invincible Jack Kramer had an era all his own.

Chapter 8

Rod Laver, Rocket Man of Tennis

While gunning to complete the first of his two Grand Slams, Rod Laver revealed an off-court shyness that was belied by the bravado exhibited in his play for many more years after this 1962 SPORT profile.

SPORT November 1962 By Dave Anderson

Rod Laver, 1968
From an ant-bed court in Queensland to the pinnacle of the tennis world.

Rod Laver was celebrating with a beer and with a reason. He had just won the 1962 Wimbledon championship and was one tournament victory away from becoming the second tennis player in history to complete what is known as the Grand Slam: winning the Australian, French, Wimbledon and United States amateur titles in the same year. Don Budge, a red-haired American, had done it in 1938 and if Laver, a red-haired Australian, could do it in 1962 it might be worth as much as $100,000 to him in a professional contract. It was cause for celebration and Laver, wearing a tuxedo and a big smile was enjoying himself at the Wimbledon Ball. He was talking ... and talking ... and talking. And Rod Laver talking, at least with strangers within earshot, was the biggest upset of Wimbledon.

"I never knew you talked so much, Rod," a man said.

Laver, suddenly realizing his tongue had loosened, shot the stranger a steel-eyed sidelong glance and stared at the floor. After many moments of uncomfortable silence, Martin Mulligan, who had lost to Laver in the Wimbledon final, spoke up.

"Oh, oh," Mulligan said to the man. "You put Rod back in his shell."

Perhaps no other great athlete of our time lives within himself as much as Rod Laver. Mickey Mantle used to, a decade ago, but the years have matured him into, among other things, a witty after-dinner speaker. Paul Hornung couldn't live within himself if somebody offered him a million dollars to do it. Neither could Arnold Palmer. But Rod (Rocket) Laver, who, at 24, is to tennis what these athletes are to their sports, is different. He tours the world, winning tournament after tournament, as if he were a mechanical man. On the court his freckled face appears to be set in a slightly sneering mask. His expression remains the same if he flicks a cross-court volley for match point or smashes an overhead into the net to lose his serve. Off the court he indulges in quiet activities. He goes to the movies, he listens to his transistor radio, he takes pictures, he drinks an occasional beer with some of the other players.

In many senses Rod's personality is reminiscent of Budge's. When Budge began assaulting the tennis pinnacle, he, too, was withdrawn. Only after he achieved a measure of fame (and spent some time touring with the outgoing Gene Mako) did Don come out of his shell. And even then Don, for a long while, showed personality spark only among close friends. Laver, say his close friends, is the same way.

"Actually," says Fred Stolle, a tennis-touring Australian who has known Laver for years, "Rod isn't in as much of a shell as he used to be. It might seem that way to people who don't know him but with the other players he's a lot looser than he used to be. He's quiet but he likes to have a good time like everybody else. He's a great tennis player but I don't think there's another player who resents his success because Rod has never made a big deal out of himself."

Laver never gloats over a victory. Instead he goes out of his way to console his opponent. He'll say, "Too bad, you played well." Or "you got some bad calls." Or "the court was bad."

Possibly the only time Laver came near crowing over an opponent was after his 6-2, 6-2, 6-1 whipping of Mulligan at Wimbledon in the near-record time of 52 minutes. "I feel," Rod said, "that I played very well." Typical of him, however, this was the understatement of the tennis season.

"I must have done something to make him mad," Mulligan wisecracked. "I never saw him so good."

"Mulligan's only chance," said Australian team manager Alf Chave, "would have been to use a rifle."

In winning the Wimbledon title, recognized as the world championship of amateur tennis, for the second straight year the lefthanded Laver provoked some spirited arguments still going on. Not since Lew Hoad turned pro in 1957, at a record guarantee of $125,000 for 25 months, has an amateur caused so much controversy among tennis people all over the

world. The question: Could Laver dominate pro tennis as he does amateur tennis?

Most experts say he wouldn't have a chance if the king of tennis, Pancho Gonzalez, could be lured out of retirement. The lure would be money, the same lure that is tempting Laver as he awaits what could be his final appearance as an amateur: Australia's Davis Cup defense in December. At Wimbledon, Laver met with Tony Trabert and Frank Sedgman and talked about pro tennis. Trabert, who has replaced Jack Kramer as the pros' contract negotiator, was there as the man with the checkbook. Sedgman, who was Australia's and the world's No. 1 amateur player a decade ago, was there as Laver's boyhood hero. The previous December Kramer had guaranteed Laver $33,600 for a two-year contract. After Wimbledon, with the Grand Slam in sight, Trabert and Sedgman raised the ante to a reported $70,000 for two years and they were willing to go higher. But Laver refused to commit himself. "Let me think about it," he told them. "I won't turn until after the Challenge Round anyway. And I want to make sure I'll be making more money as a professional than as an amateur."

Reading between the words of that last sentence, it would appear that Laver is making about $35,000 a year as an amateur. Appearances, though sometimes deceptive, are sometimes accurate, too. Laver has been able to stash away plenty of "expenses" in his tennis travels. It is no accident, for example, that he remained in Europe after winning Wimbledon the past two summers, thereby avoiding the grass-court circuit in the United States until it was time to play for the prestige title at Forest Hills. In Europe he could command as much as $1,000, and in some cases more, in "expenses" for each tournament. In the U.S., he'd be lucky to get a few hundred and he'd have to fight for that. At Europe's resort tournaments the Wimbledon titles are as good as gold. Literally. "I'd say Laver clears $15,000 to $20,000 under the table every year," says one of his touring companions. "And don't forget. That's all tax-free."

In addition, Rod is on the payroll of Dunlop sporting-goods in Australia (a money-making tie-in that would make a U.S. amateur a pro). Still he would make more in professional tennis. "He's interested," Sedgman said last summer, "but he has been told by some people that pro tennis has had it. I don't believe it but Rod wants to be sure."

Pro tennis, punched in the solar plexus every time the

International Lawn Tennis Federation votes down open tournaments, is no longer a healthy sport in the United States. But it could be revived by a transfusion of talent. Laver would be the best possible new blood. If he and Gonzalez were to play, the matches would most likely draw very well in the U.S. Even without Gonzalez, Laver might be enough to ballyhoo an American tour. In Australia and Europe, where pro tennis flourishes, Laver competing against such old pros as Lew Hoad and Ken Rosewall would assure a sell-out crowd wherever they played. And there seems no doubt Laver would win his share of matches among the pros.

Most important, Laver himself believes he could win. "I think Roy (Emerson) and Neale (Fraser) and myself would win a good part of the time," Laver told some friends even before his Wimbledon triumph. "The pros aren't that bloody good."

Sedgman agrees, at least concerning Laver. "His game has improved so much in the last six months," Sedgman said at Wimbledon, "that I'm sure he would give the top pros a run for their money. His biggest improvement has been in concentration. In the past he often took a couple of sets to get into full swing. In the pros you can't do that and at Wimbledon Rod was attacking from the very first ball and never wavered for an instant."

Even the great Gonzalez, asked not long ago about Laver's future as a pro, conceded:

"For any one match—with me or Rosewall or Hoad or Sedgman, if Frank is in shape—Laver would have as good a chance as we would. But I think—and I'm talking about if I was playing regularly—I think I could beat him on a head-to-head tour of, say 50 matches. I think that Rosewall and Hoad and Sedgman could beat him, too. I'm not so sure about the other pros (Barry MacKay, Earl Buchholz, Alex Olmedo, Ashley Cooper, Mal Anderson et al) because I'm not sure that they're that much better. Laver is a helluva player. And he's got the proper pro temperament. You can tell that from the way he wins just about every tournament every week on every type of surface. You've got to be that way in the pros. You can't let up if you're not playing in a big city or in front of a big crowd. Every match is important. No matter where it is. And no matter who you're playing."

As an amateur Laver has achieved a far greater consistency than either Hoad or Rosewall did in the mid-Fifties. Hoad seldom got steamed up about the insignificant amateur titles. If he fell behind to a second-rater in an early-round match at, for example, Gstaad,

Switzerland or Newport, Rhode Island, he might go through the motions of losing and, with his "expenses" in his pocket, take the rest of the week off. But when it came time for Wimbledon—he won there twice—his eyes gleamed and his game gleamed with them. Rosewall was more consistent in the offbeat tournaments. His problem, however, was that, as a contemporary of Hoad, he never won at Wimbledon. But Rosewall once won the U.S. title, in 1956, to deprive Hoad of a Grand Slam. Hoad had won the Australian, French and Wimbledon championships but faltered on a cold, windy day at Forest Hills.

Laver saw that match. Then 18, he was finished his first world tour. "I remember," Rod said not long ago, "how the wind was swirling in circles inside the stadium and how Lew couldn't toss the ball up as high on his serve as he like to. It bothered him a little and Kenny beat him."

Maybe Rod recalled Hoad's failure when, after Wimbledon, he was repeatedly asked about his chances of a Grand Slam. "It would be nice," he invariably answered," but anything can happen." Roy Emerson, he knew, had beaten him in the Forest Hills final in 1961 but this, everybody was saying, was a different year. Laver's year. The Year of the Left Arm. "Strength can be a beautiful thing," says Gene Scott, one of the most articulate of the amateur tennis tourists. "The statues of Apollo, that type of beauty, with the rippling muscles. But take a good look at Laver's left arm. It's so strong that it's ugly."

After years of hitting thousands upon thousands of tennis shots, Rod's left arm is overdeveloped. "It happens with all tennis players to a certain extent," Scott points out. "I'd say my racket wrist is maybe an inch thicker than the other. But Laver's left wrist is ridiculous. I'll bet it's two to three inches thicker. His whole arm is that way, from the elbow down. His biceps aren't big. He's actually a little guy. About 5-10, 165 pounds. But that left forearm and wrist, that's what he beats you with. That and his pride. When he's behind, he gets tougher. He doesn't like to lose to anybody. Anywhere. Any time."

Another factor in Rod's favor is that he's a lefthander. His success, and that of another lefthander, Neale Fraser, in recent years, have made people forget that lefthanders are rare in tennis. Laver and Fraser, incidentally, are the only two lefties among the outstanding players.

"The advantage for a lefthander," explains Gardnar Mulloy, the old pro of amateur tennis, "is that he's used to playing against righthanders but the righthanders aren't used to a lefthander. They're almost always playing over righthanders. When you're playing a lefthander you've got to make a big adjustment. The ball bounces in the exact opposite direction on each shot. On a serve a lefthander's ball normally will curve to a righthander's backhand instead of his forehand. All the shots are that way. They bounce the other way than what you're used to. As a result it takes time to adjust to that. And by the time you adjust to it, the match can be over. Especially if you're playing Laver."

Laver, however, has a whispered weakness: his forehand volley. "But he's so good with all his other shots," chorus his opponents, "that it's hard to take advantage of it." He has another weakness, too, according to Frank Sedgman, at least in comparison to the pros.

"Rod," Sedgman says, "still has to increase his serving power. At Wimbledon, for example, he rarely served any aces. He was content to put in a well-placed, medium-paced serve and win the point with a volley. In the pros he'll need a stronger serve to keep his opponent off balance and away from the net. But there's not much else I could find fault with in his game. His best features are his backhand return of service and his passing shots—very unusual for a lefthander. And his volleying game is sound and crisp. But he had better work on his serve."

According to Don Budge, the 1938 Grand Slammer, Rod will have to work on his entire game to succeed in the pros.

"Laver is a great amateur, no doubt about that," Budge says. "He has all the shots and he's a fine competitor but I think that he'd get waxed for awhile in the pros. Simply because pro tennis is that much tougher. You must pick your game up one more notch. I don't say that Laver can't do it. In time I should think he would. He seems to be the type who would be eager enough to learn and adjust to it. Bill Tilden used to say that, 'The mark of a champion is the fellow who misses the fewest easy ones.' That's particularly the case in the pros where you must learn to play the percentage shot. Gonzalez got clobbered the first year by Kramer. But he adjusted to the percentage shot. Laver would have to adjust, too, but it takes time."

It is one of those odd quirks of history that Laver was born in the midst of Budge's Grand Slam—on August 9, 1938, at his family's small ranch outside Rockhampton, Queensland, in Australia's cattle country. Besides Rod there are two older brothers and a younger sister.

"My father was a county champion," Rod recalls, "and my two brothers and cousin Len were good players, too. I took up tennis when I was about nine. We belonged to a little tennis club. But it's not like the clubs in the States. Nothing social. Just four courts and a little tennis shed. We had a pro, a man named Charley Hollis, and he was the one who first told me to hit my backhand full, not to chip it, and to use top-spin off both sides. I took a lesson from him once a week. Sort of a clinic lesson. There were 20 or 30 kids in it. I never had a private lesson."

When Rod was 13, his father built a tennis court on their ranch. "An antbed court," Rod says, "out of the dirt from the red-ant hills in Australia. You crush it up fine and spread it on clay and roll it in. They're common in Australia and it's the best dirt surface in the world for a tennis court."

The muscles were beginning to develop in Laver's left arm and so was his tennis reputation around Rockhampton. But unlike Lew Hoad and Ken Rosewall, who were world famous at 17, Laver was never looked upon as a child prodigy. Then one day, when he was 17, his dad drove him 500 miles to a newspaper-sponsored clinic in Brisbane. Harry Hopman, the Australian Davis Cup Captain, was supervising the clinic and he knew Rod was coming. "Charley Hollis," Hopman once said, "had told me about him but I didn't think much about it until I saw the boy hit a few shots. You didn't have to be a genius to know that he was a player." The next year, 1956, Hopman took Laver on a world tour. Then 18, Laver was eligible to play in the U.S. Junior championships and he lugged home all the silverware. He won the singles and shared the doubles with a pick-up partner, Jim Shaffer of St. Petersburg, Florida. "Nobody knew who Rod was before the tournament started," Shaffer recalls, "but everybody knew him when it was over."

Everybody forgot about Laver the next year when he vanished from the circuit. He had to put in his time in the Australian Army. In 1958 he returned and everybody knew him again. Especially Dick Savitt. Dick, a Wimbledon champion, needed a peak performance to survive a scare from Laver in the round of 16 at Forest Hills. Later that year Rod was a non-playing member of the Australian Davis Cup team that was upset by Alex Olmedo's one-man show.

In 1959, after Ashley Cooper and Mal Anderson turned pro, Laver (the Wimbledon runnerup that year to Olmedo) and Neale Fraser suddenly emerged as Davis Cup singles players. Rod lost both his Challenge Round matches, to Barry MacKay and Olmedo, but it resulted in Fraser becoming a national hero in Australia. Fraser won both his matches and teamed with Roy Emerson in the doubles for what Harry Hopman described as "Fraser's Davis Cup." The next year Rod won the Australian championship but was the runnerup again at Wimbledon, this time to Fraser. When Fraser stayed in Europe to play under-the-table tennis, Laver came to the United States with the official Australian touring team and achieved a minor grand slam by winning all four men's singles titles at Merion, Southampton, South Orange and Newport on the Eastern grass-court circuit leading to Forest Hills. "I know Fraser won Wimbledon," Adrian Quist, the Aussie team manager, said in the midst of that streak," but Laver is the better player. He has a better backhand than Fraser, a better forehand, a better volley. But Fraser has a better serve. That's why he won Wimbledon."

Fraser had something else—a whammy on Laver—and beat him in straight sets in the U.S. final. "I'm convinced," Fred Perry, Great Britain's greatest player and the 1936 Wimbledon champion, said that day at Forest Hills, "that Laver has a sort of hero-worship for Fraser and that this works against Laver in his big matches with Fraser."

In 1961 Fraser began to fade. Hobbling on a bad knee that later required surgery, he lost to Great Britain's Bobby Wilson in the fourth round at Wimbledon and Laver won there for the first time, needing only 55 minutes to defeat U.S. Davis Cupper Chuck McKinley in the final. Over the year's tour, though, Roy Emerson challenged him for world superiority. Roy won the Australian title and in the final at Forest Hills beat Laver in straight sets.

This year Laver beat Emerson in four sets for the Australian title. In the final of the Italian tournament, Laver trailed Emerson two sets to one, but rallied to win. In the French tournament at Paris, Laver lost the first two sets to Emerson but came back and won the title. At Wimbledon, Emerson defaulted with a bruised toe in the fourth round and Laver breezed to the championship with the loss of only one set in seven matches.

Laver had been aiming at Wimbledon so much that he took lessons—dancing lessons, not tennis lesson. For weeks before the tournament, Yola Ramirez of Mexico, one of the best dancers on the tennis circuit, taught Laver the fox-trot. At the Wimbledon Ball, the men's champion traditionally begins the party by dancing with the women's champion. The year before Laver had been embarrassed dancing that first one with Great Britain's Angela Mortimer. "I just sort of shuffled around," Rod recalls. "I didn't want to do that again. For the girl's sake as well as mine." This time he danced with Karen Hantze Susman. "I did pretty well," Rod smiles. "Even if I do say so myself."

But Rod's reticence prevents him from being as self-praising about a matter most important to him. He won't come close to saying what everyone else says about his tennis skills.

"Rod Laver," says Frank Sedgman, speaking for the majority, "will go down in tennis history as one of the great players of the world."

204

Pancho Gonzalez, 1955 A career devalued by too many years in the pro game's shadowy reaches, but one of the greatest players of all time.

Chapter 9

The Lone Wolf of Tennis

Pancho Gonzalez was a lonely figure on the 1950s pro tennis tour. As recounted in SPORT, *wounds born of insult and prejudice left him a brooding figure who found little comfort in fame.*

SPORT September 1958 By Dick Schaap

When Richard Alonzo Gonzalez stretches to the top of his toes, whips his right arm high in the air and serves a tennis ball at 112 miles an hour, he is doing more than simply powering the swiftest shot in tennis history. He is swinging at every Southern Californian who ever called a Mexican "Pancho," flailing at every tennis official who ever barred a youngster from a tournament, and whacking at every father who ever ordered his daughter to stop dating the kid from the wrong side of the tracks.

Richard Gonzalez is the greatest tennis player in the world today. He has considerable wealth and prestige, plus an incredible amount of ability—almost everything a man could want. But on his strong right shoulder sits the same chip that marks so many men who have overcome odds not of their own making. It is the chip that has made him the fiercest competitor in tennis, a relentless champion who must prove again and again that in all the world there is no one else so skillful. But it also has had a deeper, more significant effect. It has shaped Gonzalez into the lone wolf of tennis, a dark, brooding figure silhouetted against a rococo backdrop of fame, fortune and talent.

Gonzalez is a loner in the strictest sense of the word. While he was winning the recent pro tennis tour, he did not travel with Lew Hoad, Tony Trabert and Pancho Segura in the spacious station wagons provided by promoter Jack Kramer. He drove alone in his own car, a souped-up Ford Thunderbird, picking his own routes and his own way stations. When the rest of the troupe checked in at one hotel, he generally stayed at another. Usually he ate by himself, away from the bright lights and

the noise. He rarely attended social functions, and, when he did, he seemed to generate electric tension.

Once, the night before the tour made its annual stop in Madison Square Garden, Gonzalez went to a party on New York City's swank East End Avenue. Among the other guests was Gina Lollobridiga, the Italian movie actress who has been described as the most tempting seven syllables since "Come up and see me sometime." At the party, a press photographer suggested, quite logically, that Gina and Pancho pose for a picture together. Gina warmly agreed. Gonzalez seemed somewhat cooler. While the subjects waited, the photographer hurriedly adjusted his camera.

"Come on," Gonzalez snapped. "Let's get this over with."

Gina took a deep breath—and smiled.

The photographer checked his flash attachment.

"What are you waiting for?" Gonzalez demanded.

"Stand a little closer together," the cameraman said. "Would you please smile, Pancho?"

Gonzalez scowled. "Take the damn picture," he said, and then delivered a brief lecture on the social and technological failings of press photographers. A short while later, Gina was still smiling and Gonzalez was still fuming. He left the party.

Yet the same man who verbally dissected the photographer can be genuinely pleasant and cooperative. It is one of the paradoxes of Gonzalez that he deeply wants to be friendly, but he instinctively fears anyone who might hurt or misuse him.

The genial, relaxed Gonzalez appears at strange times. Late one evening this year, he stopped in a restaurant for a light snack. It was after midnight and the match with Hoad, which had ended only 30 minutes earlier, had lasted more than two hours. He was thoroughly exhausted. Blisters seared his feet. He could easily have been curt and irascible.

As he entered the restaurant, Gonzalez spotted five men seated around a table in a corner, all sipping tall glasses of white milk. "What is this," he asked, "the local milk club?" One of the men grinning. "No," he said. "We saw you play tonight and decided it was about time we got in shape."

For the first time all night, Gonzalez cracked a broad smile. He walked over to the milk table, postponing his own meal, and chatted for several minutes about tennis, conditioning and sports in general. When he was finished, he had won five lifelong fans.

His fellow professionals recognize Gonzalez' aloofness and changeability, but, for the most part, they can neither predict nor explain his moods. Even Segura, the little Ecuadorian who is closer to Gonzalez than any other tennis player, admits that he is often puzzled by the champion. "Gorg's a funny guy," Segura says. "He's independent. He likes to be alone. I don't know why."

(The nickname of Gorg, or Gorgo, has stuck with Gonzalez since he won the 1948 U.S. Singles championship and promptly lost half a dozen matches in a row to Ted Schroeder. Tennis write Jim Burchard called Pancho "The Cheese Champ" which inevitably became Gorgonzalez—from Gorgonzola, and Italian cheese—and eventually Gorgo.)

Lew Hoad finds Pancho's outward coolness no easier to handle than his service. "I guess," Hoad says, "that Gorg feels he can't be friendly with a fellow he has to try to beat every night. Maybe that's right. He does rather well, you know."

The only pro who advances a definite theory about Gonzalez is Tony Trabert. "He's got a persecution complex," Trabert insists. "I don't blame him for having had it originally. He was persecuted. Even his nickname was a form of persecution. In California, many prejudiced people call all persons of Mexican descent 'Pancho.' But things have changed since he was a kid. When people call him 'Pancho' now, they say it admiringly. It's time he got over his complex."

But as any psychiatrist will confirm, it is not easy to erase a feeling that has deep roots in childhood and adolescence. The first of Carmen and Manuel Gonzalez' seven children, Richard was born in Los Angeles on May 9, 1928. His father was a house painter and, although the family was never destitute, there was no extra money for luxuries. The Gonzalezes lived in a section of the south side of Los Angeles where a boy was considered an unqualified success if he grew up to become an auto mechanic.

One day, when Richard was seven years old, his father reluctantly gave him permission to cross the street alone and visit South Park, a local playground. The youngster set out on a scooter he had built from two-by-fours and roller skate wheels. When he reached the intersection, he did not stop or look or listen. He barreled into the street just as an automobile was approaching. The driver braked hard, but before the car could stop, its door handle hooked Richard's cheek. The accident left a scar several inches long. Today Pancho scarcely notices it. "Sometimes I forget which side it's on," he says.

But later there were less violent incidents that left more serious scars. Gonzalez suffered one particularly depressing setback when he was 15. By then he was the best tennis player his age in Southern California. An above-average student, he decided his future was not in the classroom. He quit high school to spend all his spare time on the tennis court. As soon as Perry Jones, the czar of Southern California tennis, learned that Gonzalez had left school, he called the boy into his office.

"Richard," Jones began, evenly, "it isn't fair for you to play anybody who goes to school all day while you practice tennis."

"But Mr. Jones," Gonzalez said, "I don't want to go to school any more. I want to play tennis."

Jones paused and leaned forward. "Until you return to school," he said, "I must bar you from all tournaments."

Gonzalez was crushed. He had embraced tennis, and tennis, in turn, had spurned him. Rumors spread that Jones barred Gonzalez because he was Mexican. This was not true, but by repetition, it became a popular theory. Even now, although Pancho concedes that the ban was justified, he still seems to think that somehow he should have been eligible for the junior tournaments.

Not until after four years had elapsed, including 15 months spent swabbing decks in the Navy, was Gonzalez reinstated. Then, suddenly, he received another emotional slap in the face. He had been dating an attractive blonde tennis player from the Los Angeles area. Everyone who saw them agreed that the dark, handsome Gonzalez and the light, beautiful girl made a stunning couple. Everyone, that is, except for her father. He told her to stop seeing Pancho. For a while the girl tried deception. She took her school books, said she was going to the library and, instead, met Pancho. But, finally, the subterfuge proved too burdensome. They stopped dating.

No sensitive adolescent could experience such difficulties without absorbing considerable pain, and Richard Gonzalez was a sensitive boy. His hands were sensitive to the feel of a tennis racket and his mind was sensitive to the stings of an antagonistic society. He reacted naturally; he withdrew into himself.

"I remember Pancho at the first tournament he ever played away from home," says Gussie Moran, the former Wimbledon sensation who is now an entertaining sportscaster. "He was a quiet, shy boy who sat alone in the clubhouse. He had a forlorn look on his face and a chip on his shoulder. When he stepped onto the tennis court, he was someone else. He was a god, patrolling his personal heaven."

Gonzalez, basically, is not much different today. he is a far better tennis player. He has sharpened his strokes to the point of perfection. Yet he still sits by himself in the locker room, his head sunk in his hands, the sweat dripping from his brow.

Until this year, we had seen Gonzalez play as a pro only in big cities where a sizable press corps, an army of tennis stars and the attendant fanfare always acted as a buffer against reality. The best way to understand and appreciate Richard Alonzo Gonzalez, we decided, was to see him on tour in small towns, winning most matches, living alone, traveling alone, eating alone. Late one rainy and foggy afternoon, after a quick stop at the insurance vending machine, we boarded a DC-3 and flew from Newark to join the pro tour in Corning, N.Y.

Corning is an industrial town on the southern tier of upstate New York, nestled near the Finger Lakes. It is known for producing Steuben crystal, the finest glass in the country, and Ted Atkinson, one of the finest jockeys. In Corning everything revolves around the glass works, and there, in a modern gymnasium, Pancho Gonzalez and Lew Hoad played the 67th match of their series.

The picture of Gonzalez in action in unforgettable. For pure artistry, it rates with Musial, coiled and ready to strike; Cousy, flipping a backhanded pass; Snead, at the height of his backswing; and Arcaro, whipping a horse through the stretch. When he serves, Gonzalez strains, rears back and fires. Despite his size, he rushes catlike to the net, defying an opponent to return service. His long, light strides carry him to shots that lesser men never reach. On an overhead slam, he kicks up and follows through with frightening force. His nervous energy is never wasted. It is stacked up into a huge pile until the sheer weight of Pancho's ability falls upon an opponent, startling him at first, then bewildering him and, finally, crushing him.

For 32 games in the first set at Corning, Hoad refused to crack. Then Gonzalez broke service, held his own and won 18-16. He also took the second set, 7-5, and stretched the series to at least five matches, 36-31. After the final point, champion and challenger shook hands perfunctorily, posed for several photographs, and retired to the dressing room.

Hoad entered first, shuffled to his locker in the far corner and sat down. Gonzalez slumped onto a bench five feet away. For fully three minutes, neither said a word. The tension slowly ebbed from their faces. Then Gonzalez spoke. "Give me a towel, will you," he said to Hoad. The taut, hard lines that striped both men's brows began to disappear. Gonzalez drained half a Coke with one swallow. "I was lucky," he said. "I hit two shots that I neversaw. They changed their shirts and socks and walked back to the court for a doubles match. Just as Hoad's right arm swept up for the first serve, Gonzalez dropped his racket loudly to the floor. "Excuse me, Lew," he said, "Did I disturb you?" The doubles served as an escape valve and, throughout the match, Gonzalez clowned openly, hitting balls behind his back and swinging vainly at shots ten feet beyond his reach. On one serve he tossed up three balls and smacked two of them. As the crowd laughed, Pancho relaxed.

Afterward, in the locker room, he stripped off his shoes and socks and poked at the huge callouses beneath the large toe of each foot. "Look at this one," he said. "Full of fluid." A trace of fatigue darkened his face. "This is the toughest sport of all," he said. "Even in pro basketball, they don't play every night. Besides, when they're tired, they get a substitute. We don't. We play even when we're hurt. I've played with a sprained ankle. Lew finished a match one night after colliding with a wall and being knocked unconscious."

Gonzalez showered and put on a pair of slacks and a red polo shirt. Then he turned to me. "I'm going to get something to eat," he said. "Want to come along?" It was a stunning reversal in mood. Only six hours earlier, I had asked Gonzalez if I might ride with him. His answer had been pointed. "No," he had said. "I don't have any room."

As we walked from the locker room, a spectator shouted, "Good exhibition, Pancho." Gonzalez frowned. "It was not an exhibition," he said. "If it had been, it would not have gone on so long."

Outside, in a parking lot behind the glass works, Gonzalez unlocked his Thunderbird. Even in the dark, its yellow body and white top shimmered brightly. He switched on the electric ignition and a modified Cadillac engine roared mightily.

For Gonzalez, there is only one object more fascinating and more challenging than a tennis racket. It is a hot rod. The tennis champion of the world owns four automobiles that are constantly being tuned for drag-strip racing in California. Usually Pancho works as a mechanic, adjusting the steering, changing the gear ratio, pampering the engine. But sometimes he puts on crash helmet and goggles, settles into the driver's seat and hurtles down an old, abandoned air strip at speeds of more than 150 miles an hour.

Gonzalez let the motor idle for several minutes before he slipped into gear. Then he pulled out of the parking lot, turned right, crossed a bridge over the Chemung River and turned right again on Market Street. A few blocks down, he parked at the Athens Restaurant. He walked in and sat down on a stool by the counter. "Give me a rare hamburger steak," he told the waitress, "and a cup of coffee."

Gonzalez leaned forward, resting his elbows on the counter. "When I gain extra weight," he said, "I eat nothing but meat and liquids for a week to ten days. Then I get an awful hunger. It is something you cannot imagine. I see a piece of pie and I want it terribly."

While he ate, Gonzalez said nothing. After a second cup of coffee and a glass of milk, he smoked a cigarette and went out to the Thunderbird. By 1 a.m. he was back in his single room at the Centerway Motel. At 5, he fell asleep. "I replayed the match in my mind," he explained the next day. "I tried to figure out what I did right, why I won. Then I tried to decide how I would play the next match."

The next morning, while Hoad, Trabert and Segura toured the museum at the Corning Glass Works, Gonzalez tried to sleep. At 11:30, a steady, driving rain fell as I walked to the motel to meet Pancho. He was standing outside, conspicuous in his red polo shirt and a yellow sleeveless sweater, bent over the motor of his car.

While the rain drenched him, he changed spark plugs. "You have to have two sets of spark plugs," he said, "one for the city and one for the open road."

For 15 minutes he fastened, checked and adjusted. Then he went into the motel's restaurant and ordered a bowl of Wheaties, two 3-1/2-minute soft-boiled eggs, two cups of coffee and a glass of milk. After breakfast, he returned to the car, checked it once more and packed his clothes and equipment. At 12:15, he climbed into the driver's seat and I got in beside him. We pulled away from the motel on Route 414 and started toward the next town on the tour—Clinton, N.Y., some 160 miles from Corning. Gonzalez began to relax. His hands slipped easily into the ten o'clock and four o'clock positions favored by race drivers. Two miles outside Corning, the motor suddenly sputtered, coughed and died. Despite Pancho's checks and double-checks, we were out of gas.

The road from Corning to Watkins Glen, roughly 30 miles away, is a bumpy one, but after we refueled, Gonzalez cruised along at 60 to 70 miles an hour. It was fast, but not dangerous driving. "I don't open it up," he said. "The T-Bird can do 145 miles an hour if I let it out. It'll go from zero to 115 in 15 seconds." Then, abruptly, we headed into a sharp curve. I braked, involuntarily, where there was no brake. Gonzalez did not even take his foot off the accelerator. We whipped around the bend into a straightaway. "That's how I make up time," he said. "I don't slow down on the curves."

After we passed Watkins Glen, bounced through a long stretch of highway under construction and picked up Route 14, Lake Seneca glimmered in the rain on our right. Gonzalez ignored the scenery and concentrated on the road. "I like to travel alone," he said. "I can leave when I want. I don't have to wait for the others and they don't have to wait for me. When I want to stop and rest, I can."

Water leaked slowly through the windshield on the driver's side. "Is the feud between you and Kramer really bitter?" I asked.

"You're damn right it is," Gonzalez said. "The main reason I don't like Kramer is simple. Money."

He lit a cigarette and continued. "I'm the best player and I deserve the most money. Kramer has me over a barrel now. He's got me under contract till 1960 and I can't do a thing about it. After that we'll see. Some people have suggested that I start my own tour, but that's not my idea. I'll probably stick with this. I want a better deal, though. Somebody's going to get hurt and it's not going to be me."

Under his contract, Gonzalez earns 20 per cent of the gross receipts, an income of close to $75,000 a year. Hoad this year received 25 per cent of the receipts plus a five per cent bonus each night he won. Under a similar setup two years ago, Gonzalez was guaranteed $15,000 and his opponent, Trabert, $75,000.

Before the recent tour, Gonzalez dragged Kramer into court, seeking to have the contract changed. The judge threw out the case. Pancho had no legal complaint, he ruled; the contract was binding. Since then, even when they played gin rummy together at a nickel a point, Gonzalez and Kramer have not spoken. "Pancho hasn't said a social word to me in a year," Kramer says.

Gonzalez passed three cars easily, pulled into the right lane and began to talk about his family. "I've got three boys," he said, "Richard, Michael and Danny. Richard, the oldest, is nine and looks like he's going to be a good tennis player."

He leaned back and rubbed the scar on his left cheek. "My wife Henrietta," he said, "traveled with me in Australia at the beginning of the tour. But when I fell behind, I sent her home. She understands that I can't have any distractions. I don't even like to go to cocktail parties. Most people don't seem to realize that I can't afford to enjoy myself. This is my business. I've got to be the world champion. That's my bargaining point. Ex-champions don't make any money."

We passed Syracuse and the sun threatened to break through the heavy rain clouds. "Pro tennis is a funny game," Gonzalez said. "It's hard not to relax when you get far ahead. That's what Hoad did when he had me, 18-9. That's what I did when I had him, 33-23. He almost caught up and I had to bear down. I had to diet, practice, sleep, train. I'm training harder this year than I ever did before. I'm in the best shape of my life."

A few miles before Utica, we turned onto a side road that led into Clinton. On the outskirts of Clinton, we stopped at a service station. "Change the oil and fill it up," Gonzalez told the attendant. we ran down the road, dodging puddles, to a small restaurant. It was almost 3:30 and Pancho wanted a large meal before the night's matches. he finished off a bowl of soup, a sirloin steak, a lettuce and tomato salad, and a bottle of 7-Up. Then he hesitated. "I'll have a piece of apple pie," he said.

While he ate, Gonzalez read the Utica newspaper. Next to a story announcing the arrival of the tour, there was an AP dispatch praising Jack Kramer for his work in training young Barry MacKay.

"Kramer's always taking the credit," Gonzalez grumbled. "I don't think he played once with the kid. We did all the work."

We hurried back to the service station and, after Pancho supervised the changing of his oil filter and bought a new set of spark plugs, we drove to the Clinton Arena, a barn-like construction that serves as home of the Clinton Comets in the Eastern Hockey League. We got out of the car, walked inside and shivered. It felt cold enough for a hockey game.

Jerry Dashe and Westergard, the tour's equipment managers, were installing the tour's portable canvas tennis court. "When's it going to be ready?" Gonzalez asked. "I want to get some practice."

"Not before five," Westergard called back. "You might as well go out until then."

We went back to the car and drove to a nearby hardware store. Gonzalez bought a set of wrenches, then visited the local Mercury agency. "I want some floor mats for a T-Bird," he said. "Have any?"

The owner picked out two black mats and handed them to Gonzalez. He started to fill out a sales slip. "Could you give me your name, sir?" he said.

"Sure," Pancho answered. "Gonzalez."

"How do you spell that?"

"G-O-N-Z-A-L-E-Z."

"Oh," said the proprietor, "like the tennis player."

"Same guy," said Gonzalez.

"You're Pancho Gonzalez," the owner said, with considerable awe. "I've read about you."

Gonzalez turned his head away, slightly embarrassed. He didn't say a word, took his change and brought the mats out to the car. We returned to the arena, but the court still was not ready. Gonzalez stepped outside and, with his new wrenches, began working on the car. Shortly after five, he went inside, dressed and went on the court for a practice session with Segura. For half an hour, Big Pancho and Little Pancho volleyed back and forth, concentrating on lobs and backhands. Then they went into the locker room. Trabert and Hoad had just arrived. "Hey, Gorg," Trabert said, "what's that big bubble sticking out of the hood on your car?"

"That's an air filter," Gonzalez said, seriously. "I found that particles of dirt were getting into the motor and causing ..."

"Okay, okay," said Trabert. "That's enough. You start

to lose me when you get technical."

Before the preliminary match between Segura and Trabert began, Gonzalez walked outside and climbed into one of the Kramer station wagons. He tried to sleep, but had no success. Spectators, waiting in line for tickets, approached the station wagon and stared at Pancho as though he were the fired unit in a NIKE display. Children banged on the windows and asked for autographs.

Gonzalez gave up and went back into the locker room. In a few minutes, Trabert and Segura came through the door. "How'd it go, Segoo?" Gonzalez asked.

"No good, Gorg," Segura said. "He beat me again. He was really serving the ball tonight."

"How are the lights?"

"Not bad," Segura said. "Sometimes you lose the ball in them."

About 15 minutes before the match time, the lines in Gonzalez' face started to harden again. By the time he ran onto the court, he was wearing his mean face, the one that he reserves for frightening opponents and reporters. But in the first set, Hoad refused to be frightened. His serve boomed across the net and skidded past Gonzalez. His passing shots and net game were superb. He easily polished off the champion, 6-2.

Then Pancho loosened up and, in 40 minutes, swept two sets, 6-3, 6-1, extending his tour lead to six matches. During the last set, Don Westergard, the equipment manager who, in California, had been a mechanic on Gonzalez' cars, mused about Pancho's loneliness.

"I guess it's that Pancho likes things his own way," he said. "Once back home he gave a guy a job to do on one of his cars and the guy didn't do it exactly right. Pancho never went to him again. Then, a couple of weeks ago,

he brought his wife's brother, Danny, on the tour. He asked the kid to do a few easy things like getting the oil changed or buying a pack of cigarettes. The kid fouled things up. Pancho sent him home."

When the match was finished, Gonzalez dressed quickly. The next day's match was scheduled in New Castle, Pa., almost 400 miles away. There was a good deal of driving to be done and not much time for pleasantries. "I'll try to reach at least Buffalo tonight," he said. "Maybe I'll drive all the way." Then he climbed into the Thunderbird, switched on the ignition and, delicately, patiently, let the motor warm up. Alone in the small car, away from the crowds, the dark night enveloping him, Richard Gonzalez looked like a traveling salesman, a Willie Loman without samples. He shifted into reverse, backed out of his parking spot and started off, alone, on a 400-mile trip to a tennis match.

There had been thousands of miles before and there will be thousands of miles later. The end of Gonzalez' reign in tennis is not in sight. What lies ahead?

As knowledgeable an authority as Jack Kramer insists that Pancho will never change. "He doesn't care about being popular," Kramer says. "Look what happened in March. Panch had a helluva month. He came from way behind and passed Hoad. So they hold a poll for the outstanding professional athlete of the month and what happens? Silky Sullivan gets more votes than he does."

But popularity has never been one of Gonzalez' goals. He set out to become the best tennis player in the world and he succeeded. On the tennis court, he is powerful and quick. Off the court, he is a riddle, a man alone against the world. No matter which image survives the pounding of time, one thing remains certain. The forces that worked to produce a great tennis player also created a sensitive man. There can be no separation. The champion and the loner are the same.

Tracy Austin, 1977
In ponytail and pinafore, a U.S. Open quarter-finalist at 14 years, 9 months.

It's Everybody's Game

1968-2002

RECORDS – MATCHES WON, ONE SEASON, SINGLES

MEN
145—Guillermo Vilas, 1977
118—Ilie Nastase, 1973
119—Rod Laver, 1962
113—Ivan Lendl, 1980
107—Ivan Lendl, 1982

WOMEN
112—Billie Jean King, 1971
104—Margaret Smith Court, 1970
102—Margaret Smith Court, 1973
100—Chris Evert, 1974
 90—Martina Navratilova, 1979

Chapter 10

The Open Era

Ken Rosewall, 1972
No one bridged tennis' two great eras quite like the little Aussie.

It took a long time, and many failed attempts, but a wave of sanity finally coursed through the boardrooms of the game in 1967. When the dust settled, the most obvious result—a tremendous surge in the popularity of the game—made everyone wonder anew why it had taken so long.

The fixing-up brought mixing-up—and a brilliant new look and outlook in the sector of the game that most needed repairing, namely highest-level tournament tennis. Since their inception, the four majors—the Australian, French, Wimbledon and U.S. Championships—and the traditional tournament circuit, had belonged solely to the amateurs. Finally, in 1968, they joined hands with their on-court superiors, the outcast minority of professionals, and 'open' tennis was born.

In the 1970s, tennis became truly the 'in' sport of the great middle class, first in the United States, then abroad. In a single decade, the sport threw off and trampled its starched white flannel past and became a favored diversion of the modern leisure class—attired in pastels and playing tiebreaker sets in public parks and clubs. They were equipped with a bewildering variety of gear, from optic yellow, heavy-duty balls to double-strung graphite rackets.

All this was inspired by the advent of the 'opens.' By making tennis at the top level professional, honest, and unabashedly commercial, opens ushered in an era of dramatic growth and development.

For an expanding group of pros, this was boomtime, a veritable bonanza of opportunities. They enjoyed and reaped the benefits of a Brave New World of televised matches and two-fisted backhands, evolution of technique and technology, full-blown tours for women and over-45s, exposure and cash undreamed of even by Wimbledon champions in the pre-open era.

1968

Laver, Ashe excel as open era dawns

Arthur Ashe
Raises level of his game to claim both U.S. amateur and Open titles.

The dawning of 'open competition' some 40 years after the issue was first raised, made 1968 truly a watershed year for tennis.

The British 'revolt' of December 1967 was reinforced by far-seeing U.S. Tennis Association President Bob Kelleher and his orchestration of the association's vote in favor of open tennis at its annual meeting in February. That led to the emergency meeting of the International Tennis Federation at Paris and approval of 12 open tournaments for 1968.

Unfortunately, the hypocrisy and confusion of the 'shamateur' period was not done away with quickly and cleanly. Rather than accept the British proposal that all competitors would be referred to simply as 'players,' abolishing the distinction between amateur and professional, the ITF bowed to heavy pressure from Eastern European countries and their voting allies and effected a compromise that called for four classifications:

1. Amateurs, who would not accept prize money.

2. Teaching professionals, who could compete with amateurs only in open events.

3. 'Contract professionals,' who made their living playing tennis but did not accept the authority of their national associations affiliated to the ITF, signing guaranteed contracts instead with independent promoters.

4. 'Registered players,' who could accept prize money in open tournaments but still obeyed their national associations and retained eligibility for amateur events, including the Davis, Federation, and Wightman Cups.

The prime example of this last strange and short-lived new breed was Dutchman Tom Okker, who won the Italian and South African Championships (not yet prize-money events) and was runner-up to Arthur Ashe in the first U.S. Open at Forest Hills. Okker pocketed $14,000 in first-prize money while Ashe, then a lieutenant in the U.S. Army and a member of the Davis Cup team, had to remain an amateur to maintain his Cup eligibility. The USTA had not adopted the 'registered player' concept so he received only $20 per day expenses.

Other ludicrous examples abounded. Margaret Smith Court, for instance, won and accepted nearly $10,000 in open tournaments in Britain, then came to America and played in the U.S. Amateur in Boston for expenses only, beating old rival Maria Bueno in the final, 6-2, 6-2.

But despite such anomalies of the transition period, great progress had undeniably been made toward a more honest and prosperous international game.

The first open tournament, a month after the concept was approved at the conference table, was the $14,000 British Hard Court Championships. (In Europe, 'hard court' refers to a clay surface, not concrete or similar hard surfaces as the term is used in the U.S.) Staged at the coastal resort of Bournemouth, it was the historic first chapter, and it began damply, coolly on a drizzly, raw Monday, April 22. The 'open era' lurched into being with a minor young Briton, John Clifton, winning the first point but losing his match, 6-2, 6-3, 4-6, 8-6 against Australian pro Owen Davidson—then the British national coach—on the red shale courts of the West Hants Lawn Tennis Club.

The field at Bournemouth was not as distinguished as the historic nature of the occasion warranted. The 'Handsome Eight' of World Championship Tennis were off playing their own tour, leaving the professional portion of the field largely to George MacCall's National Tennis League, plus Davidson and former Chilean Davis Cupper Luis Ayala, then a coach in Puerto Rico, who paid his own way to take part. The top-line amateurs, wary of immediate confrontation with the pros, stayed away. None of the world Top Ten amateurs entered, and Englishman Bobby Wilson was the only amateur seeded. On the women's side, the only four pros at the time— Billie Jean King, Rosemary Casals, Françoise Durr and Ann Haydon Jones, who had just signed contracts with MacCall—were otherwise engaged.

The male pros were expected to dominate the amateur field of Englishmen and a few second-line Australians. But many of the pros were jittery. They knew their reputations were on the line, and the most discerning realized they were ill prepared, given long absence from best-of-five-set matches and exposure to new faces and playing styles.

Pancho Gonzalez particularly recognized the hazards posed by sudden emergence from a small circle of famil-

iar opponents, with its well-established pecking order. It didn't take long for his apprehension to prove justified. In the second round, Mark Cox, a Cambridge-educated, 24-year-old English left-hander ranked only No. 3 in Britain, outlasted Gonzalez, 0-6, 6-2, 4-6, 6-3, 6-3, becoming the first amateur to topple a pro.

Gonzalez, only a month from his 40th birthday, hadn't played a five-set match in four years, but his defeat sent shock waves through the tennis world. Buoyed by his instant celebrity, Cox ousted a two-time Wimbledon champ, rookie pro Roy Emerson the next day, 6-0, 6-1, 7-5, to reach the semi-finals.

Obviously the pros were not invincible—a notion that would be reinforced convincingly throughout the year. But the best of their number, Rod Laver and Ken Rosewall, proved they still inhabited the top echelon. Laver canceled Cox's extravagant run in the semis, 6-4, 6-1, 6-0, and Rosewall—a man for all seasons whose longevity at the top level of international competition is unsurpassed—beat Andres Gimeno, 6-2, 6-1, 6-3, and then Laver, 3-6, 6-2, 6-0, 6-3, in the title match that, because of rain, stretched over two days. Ken, ruling the 32-man draw, collected the initial 'open' paycheck, $2,400, while the loser settled for half.

Attracting almost 30,000 customers during a moist, chilly week at the small club, pioneering Bournemouth

---

1968 THE MAJOR CHAMPIONSHIPS

Australian Championships
Men's Singles: Bill Bowrey
Women's Singles: Billie Jean King
Men's Doubles: Dick Crealy / Allan Stone
Women's Doubles: Karen Krantzcke / Kerry Melville
Mixed Doubles: Billie Jean King / Dick Crealy
French Championships
Men's Singles: Ken Rosewall
Women's Singles: Nancy Richey
Men's Doubles: Ken Rosewall / Fred Stolle
Women's Doubles: Françoise Durr / Ann Haydon Jones
Mixed Doubles: Françoise Durr / Jean Claude Barclay
Wimbledon
Men's Singles: Rod Laver
Women's Singles: Billie Jean King
Men's Doubles: John Newcombe / Tony Roche
Women's Doubles: Rosie Casals / Billie Jean King
Mixed Doubles: Margaret Smith Court / Ken Fletcher
U.S. Championships (Amateur)
Men's Singles: Arthur Ashe
Women's Singles: Margaret Smith Court
Men's Doubles: Bob Lutz / Stan Smith
Women's Doubles: Maria Bueno / Margaret Smith Court
Mixed Doubles: Mary Ann Eisel / Peter Curtis
U.S. Open
Men's Singles: Arthur Ashe
Women's Singles: Virginia Wade
Men's Doubles: Bob Lutz / Stan Smith
Women's Doubles: Maria Bueno / Margaret Smith Court

was deemed a grand success. The British LTA may have opened the new production out-of-town, (a New Haven pre-Broadway try-out?) so that had it bombed Wimbledon could discreetly resume the old ways.

But here was no going back. Virginia Wade, the British No. 1 (No. 8 in the world), would be going forward as a pro, but later in the year. However, as wary as Cox about abdicating amateur status at this mysterious time, she declined the female first prize ($720) for winning that title over Winnie Shaw, 6-4, 6-1. Virginia and kindred cautious amateurs—"Suppose it doesn't work, and we're banned as amateurs, out in the cold?" was the common plaint—got $120 for expenses. Luis Ayala, the pro half of the first integrated heterosexual open team, with Californian Valerie Ziegenfuss as the amateur half, won all of $24 for their semi-final finish in the mixed. Since he got $96 as a second-round singles loser, Luis and Valerie came out even. But could they afford room and board? Welcome to the new land of milk and honey.

Rosewall beat Laver again in the final of the second open, the French Championships, also on clay. As the first of the traditional major/Big Four tournaments to be opened, its field still lacked most of the top American men and Okker, but was considerably stronger than Bournemouth had been.

The French was also memorable because it was played during the general strike and student riots of '68. Paris was a troubled, crippled city, without public transportation or essential services, but record crowds flocked to Stade Roland Garros on the western outskirts of the city—many by bicycle or on foot—because literally nothing else of a sporting nature was happening. Players, many of whom had harrowing true-life adventures getting to Paris, found accommodations within walking distance of the courts.

"Roland Garros was a port in a storm," recalled Rex Bellamy of the *London Times.* "One thought of Drake and his bowls, Nero and his fiddle. In a strife-torn city, the soaring center court blazed with color. People even perched on the scoreboards, which was as high as they could get without a ladder.

"So the fortnight's excitement was two-edged: A rev-

olution on the courts, and a whiff of revolution in the streets ... The first major open was played in the sort of environment that nightmares are made of. But the tennis was often like a dream."

In the quarter-finals, Laver was taken to five sets by the lumbering Romanian Ion Tiriac, 4-6, 4-6, 6-3, 6-3, 6-0, one of numerous protracted struggles that kept the packed galleries gasping appreciatively. Laver then easily handled Gonzalez, 6-3, 6-3, 6-1. But Pancho had enchanted spectators earlier, winning five matches in 19 sets, outlasting Emerson, nine years his junior, in the quarters, 7-5, 6-3, 3-6, 4-6, 6-4, to stand as the oldest ever semi-finalist in Paris. In the final Rosewall again asserted his clay-court mastery at Laver's expense, 6-3, 6-1, 2-6, 6-2—15 years after he'd won the title as a callow amateur of 18. The payoff was $3,000.

The women's singles was also full of surprises. In fourth-round fun for amateurs, Aussie Gail Sherriff (later Gail Chanfreau Lovera) bounced third-seeded defending champ Francoise Durr, 6-3, 6-3, and Mexican Elena Subirats eliminated fourth seeded Rosie Casals, 6-4, 6-3.

Fifth seeded Nancy Richey, a clay-court specialist playing as an amateur—and soon regretting it after having to forego the $1,000 first prize—beat top-seeded Billie Jean King, who always preferred faster and more sure-footed surfaces, in the semi-finals, 2-6, 6-3, 6-4. She won the title over the last of the four women pros, Ann Jones, who had been considered the world's leading dirt-kicking lady, 5-7, 6-4, 6-1

There was more upheaval on the courts, amid the giddy jubilation of a once-in-a-lifetime occasion, at the first open Wimbledon. This was a richly sentimental fortnight, as legendary champions who had been stripped of their All England Club membership upon turning pro were welcomed back to the shrine of the game and again permitted to wear its mauve-and-green colors. Even old-time champions no longer able to compete came back for the festivities surrounding the enactment of a long-held dream. The tournament began with five days of intermittent rain, which held down crowds, but even this couldn't dampen soaring spirits.

Wimbledon, offering a $63,000 pot, was also the first of the open tournaments that every player of consequence entered. The seeding list for the men's singles read like a Who's Who of the present and immediate past: Top-seeded Laver, Rosewall, Andres Gimeno, defending champion John Newcombe, Emerson,

1968 CHAMPIONS AND LEADERS

Top Player Earnings: Men
Rod Laver $70,359
Year-End Number One
Men: Rod Laver
Women: Billie Jean King

Davis Cup: United States
Federation Cup: Australia
Wightman Cup: Great Britain

Manolo Santana, Lew Hoad, Gonzalez, Dennis Ralston, Butch Buchholz, Fred Stolle, Okker, Ashe, Cliff Drysdale, Tony Roche and Nikki Pilic.

There were numerous surprises, none more unsettling to the pros than the third-round defeat of third-seeded Gimeno, the elegant Spaniard who was regarded as just a shade below Laver and Rosewall. That was committed by long-haired, unheralded, 21-year-old South African Ray (Wolfman) Moore, 4-6, 6-3, 7-5, 2-6, 6-2. Hoad, the champ 11 years before, was beaten by Bob Hewitt, 6-3, 9-11, 1-6, 6-3, 6-3, and Gonzalez by Soviet Alex Metreveli, 4-6, 6-4, 6-3, 7-5, in the same round, demonstrating again that the pros were unaccustomed to this Brave New World. Indeed, in the quarter-finals only two old pros—Laver and Buchholz—shared the stage with two relatively recent pros (Ralston and Roche), three amateurs (Clark Graebner, Ashe and Moore) and the lone 'registered player,' Okker.

Second-seeded Rosewall, who had won everything but Wimbledon as an amateur in the '50s, was upset in the riotous fourth round by the tricky left-handed spins of Roche, 9-7, 6-3, 6-2. It was the round in which two ex-champs were banished: Emerson by Okker, 6-3, 9-11, 7-5, 7-5, and defender Newcombe by Ashe, 4-6, 4-6, 6-4, 1-6, 6-3. And a three-time finalist, Stolle by unseeded Graebner, 6-1, 7-5, 7-5. Chesty Graebner, in dark-horn-rimmed spectacles, resembled Clark Kent and called 'Superboy,' had eliminated 1966 champ Santana, 9-7, 6-2, 6-1 in the third round. He went to the semis past upstart Moore, 6-2, 6-0, 9-7. Ashe was also there, 7-9, 9-7, 9-7, 6-2, over Okker, joining Davis Cup teammate Graebner—the last time two amateurs would occupy that echelon.

For a moment or so the prospect of an all-amateur final danced giddily in the delighted minds of anti-open protesters. But Roche, who had beaten Buchholz in the quarters, 3-6, 7-5, 6-4, 6-4, got through two rough sets, scraping by Graebner, 9-7, 8-10, 6-4, 8-6. Laver picked up speed in leveling Ashe, 7-5, 6-2, 6-4. He started his run to a third title by beating Gene Scott, Stan Smith, Marty Riessen and Cox, untroubled until the quarters where Ralston made him go the distance, 4-6, 6-3, 6-1, 4-6, 6-2. The title was his almost immediately in a 59-minute clobbering of Roche, 6-3, 6-4, 6-2, to again command the stage he had made his in 1961 and 1962.

Having artistically made the pros' return to the premier championship of the game triumphant, Laver received $4,800, but said decisively that money had never entered his thoughts. "Wimbledon's first open tournament enabled this fine left-hander to prove his magnificent worth. Wimbledon endorsed his quality," wrote Lance Tingay of London's *Daily Telegraph*. "Equally, Laver endorsed Wimbledon's renewed status as the *de facto* world championship."

The cream also rose in the women's singles. Billie Jean King won her third consecutive singles title and $1,800, equaling a feat last achieved by Maureen Connolly (1952–54). She beat a surprise finalist, seventh-seeded Judy Tegart, 9-7, 7-5. An accomplished doubles player, this affable Australian earned her day in the sun by beating second-seeded Margaret Smith Court in the quarters and third-seeded Nancy Richey in the semis.

King also repeated her doubles triumph of 1967 with Casals, over Durr and Jones, 3-6, 6-4, 7-5 but was unable to defend the mixed doubles title with Owen Davidson for a second consecutive 'triple.' Australians Ken Fletcher (then playing out of Hong Kong) and Court ended their reign in the semis, 6-4, 9-7, and went on to defeat Metreveli and Olga Morozova, the first Soviet players to reach a major final, 6-1, 14-12. Newcombe and Roche beat Rosewall and Stolle in a splendid doubles final made up entirely of Aussie pros, 3-6, 8-6, 5-7, 14-12, 6-3.

One more great 'first open' of 1968 remained: The $100,000 U.S. Open at Forest Hills, richest of the year's events, which was lavishly promoted by Madison Square Garden in the first year of an ultimately uneasy five-year contract with the USTA.

By the end of the summer, observers were no longer startled when amateurs knocked off pros. The biggest upsets were the fourth-round knockouts of the Wimbledon men's singles finalists: A badly off-form top-seeded Laver by Drysdale, 4-6, 6-4, 3-6, 6-1, 6-1, and second-seeded Roche by the clever and rejuvenated Gonzalez, 8-6, 6-4, 6-2.

Gonzalez, a graying grandfather but still the glorious 'Old Wolf,' was the darling of the crowds in the stadium where he had prevailed as a hungry young rebel with a cause in 1948 and 1949. But the speedy 'Flying Dutchman,' Okker, was too fresh for him in the quarters. Gonzalez melted in a broiling sun, 14-16, 6-3, 10-8, 6-3.

Joining Okker in the semis were Rosewall, Ashe and Graebner. Okker was too quick for Rosewall, 8-6, 6-4, 6-8, 6-1 and Ashe was too powerful for Graebner, , 4-6, 8-6, 7-5, 6-2—the match around which author John

McPhee wove his brilliant tome, *Levels of the Game.*

Ashe's flashing fireworks—26 aces, a lightning backhand, and superior volleying—overcame Okker in a superb final, 14-12, 5-7, 6-3, 3-6, 6-3. That was the first five-set final since Ashley Cooper over Mal Anderson a decade earlier, and produced the first native champion since Tony Trabert in 1955. Since Arthur had won the U.S. Amateur final two weeks previously in Boston, he had a record that should stand uniquely forever: The lone amateur to win the U.S. Amateur and Open.

Ashe and Gimeno, an unlikely duo, survived two match points and beat Graebner and Charlie Pasarell, 6-4, 3-6, 4-6, 20-18, 15-13, in the semi-finals of the doubles, the longest match in Forest Hills history to that point (95 games). But they had little left for the final. Stan Smith and Bob Lutz, ascending 21-year-old Californians who had won the U.S. Amateur Doubles over South Africans Hewitt and Moore, 6-4, 6-4, 9-7, two weeks earlier, losing no sets in Boston, took the Open title, 11-9, 6-1, 7-5. They won 11 of 19 tournaments, 57 of 66 matches on the season, to claim the No. 1 U.S. doubles ranking for the first time.

King was unable to defend her title. Like Laver, she was far from peak form and struggled grittily through three sets with South African Maryna Godwin in the quarters, 6-3, 3-6, 6-3, and Bueno in the semis, 3-6, 6-4, 6-2. Sixth-seeded Wade, a 23-year-old Englishwoman of regal bearing recently graduated from Sussex University with a degree in math and physics, stopped Wimbledon finalist Tegart, 6-3, 6-2, and countrywoman Jones, 7-5, 6-1, on the way to beating BJK in the final, 6-4, 6-2. Wade who had worked Bournemouth for an expense check of $120, raked in the $6,000 first prize. Court and Bueno dislodged the defending champs, King and Casals, in the women's doubles finals, 4-6, 9-7, 8-6.

There was only one other open tournament in the U.S., the Pacific Southwest at Los Angeles, and form held truer on concrete, Laver beating Rosewall in the final, 4-6, 6-0, 6-0. Casals beat Bueno for the women's title, 6-4, 6-1.

Despite Laver's Wimbledon triumph and No. 1 world ranking, Ashe, at No. 2, was the Man of the Year in tennis. Winner of 10 tournaments, he earned the No. 1 U.S. ranking for the first time after three straight years at No. 2. The first black male to win a major title, he triumphed at Forest Hills while commuting to his Army duties as a data processing instructor at West Point, N.Y. Ashe won 27 straight matches from the start of the

Pennsylvania Grass Courts, beating Marty Riessen, 6-2, 6-3, 6-3, for the title. His streak continued through the U.S. Amateur, U.S. Open and the Las Vegas Invitational, over Graebner, 9-7, 6-3. It was ended in the semis of the Pacific Southwest by Rosewall, 6-3, 6-2. Also included were singles victories over Juan Gisbert, 6-2, 6-4, 6-2, and Manolo Santana, 11-13, 7-5, 6-3, 13-15, 6-4, in the 4-1 U.S. victory over Spain in the Davis Cup quarter-final. The last, 83 games, the longest Cup singles match for an American to that time, was in a sense meaningless since the U.S. was already ahead, 3-1. Ashe also won the Inter-Service championship over Air Force Pfc. Pasarell.

As cautious about open tennis as some of the players, the USTA closed down a 51-year-old tradition, the U.S. Doubles Championships in Boston, and awarded the pre-Forest Hills week at Longwood over to a U.S. Amateur Championships. The USTA wanted this event to be a continuation of the national tournament that dated to 1881. In the event this two-headed newcomer called the U.S. Open turned out to be a monster, it could be laid away with a minimum of fuss, and the old structure would be in place. Of course the Open only got bigger, better and more profitable, transforming the creaky, penny-pinching USTA into the wealthy bureaucracy it is today.

But during the transitional year of 1968 the Amateur was a significant event, a useful vehicle especially for the U.S. Davis Cup team that a young new captain, Donald Dell, was grooming to take over for the Aussie dynasty that had been riddled by Newcombe, Roche and Emerson's defection to the pros. Curiously, contract pros were ineligible for Davis Cup.

It was at the Amateur, nationally televised on PBS, that Ashe really began to make his name. Top-seeded, he crashed 18 aces and came through an exciting five-set final over unseeded Bob Lutz, 4-6, 6-3, 8-10, 6-0, 6-4. He had launched a singular double, completed at the U.S. Open two Sundays later. Amateur and Open champ. Arthur alone. Though a U.S. Amateur Championships exists today, it is for honest-to-goodness amateurs, people who couldn't get near Flushing Meadows without a ticket.

Ashe and Graebner were the singles players for the U.S. as it recaptured the Davis Cup for the first time since 1963 at Adelaide in December, recording a 4-1 victory over Australia. Imbued with great *esprit de corps* by 29-year-old Dell, the Americans (Ashe, Graebner,

Smith, Lutz and Pasarell) made winning back the Cup into 'a quest.' They lost only three matches, plowing through the West Indies, Mexico, Ecuador, Spain India and Australia.

There were a couple of other notable achievements during this landmark season.

Richey made one of the fantastic comebacks in history, winning 12 straight games (39 of the final 53 points), to beat King, 4-6, 7-5, 6-0, in the semi-finals of the Madison Square Garden International. That was King's last match as an amateur. Within days she and Emerson signed on with George MacCall's short-lived NTL troupe. Richey beat Tegart in one Garden final and Ashe won the other over Emerson.

With King and Casals unavailable in the still-amateur women's team competitions, the U.S. relinquished both the Federation and Wightman Cups. Netherlands beat the U.S. in the Federation semis at Paris, and then Australia snared the Cup, 3-0. At Wimbledon the Truman sisters, Nell and Christine Janes, were socko siblings in the decisive Wightman seventh match, beating Stephanie DeFina and Kathy Harter, 6-3, 2-6, 6-3, to break a U.S. streak of seven years.

The longest match in national championship annals, in terms of playing time and games, took place at Salisbury, Md., when Englishmen Bobby Wilson and Mark Cox defeated Pasarell and Graebner, 26-24, 17-19, 30-28, in a U.S. Indoor doubles quarter-final: Six hours, 20 minutes, 144 games. They then lost to Smith and Lutz, who were then beaten for the title by Tom Koch and Okker, 6-3, 10-12, 8-6. Richey won the singles over Graebner, 6-4, 6-4, 6-4.

King and Casals cleaned up at their version of the U.S. Indoor at Winchester, Mass. Billie Jean stopped Rosie in the singles final, 6-3, 9-7, but they were on the same side in a 6-2, 6-2, prize winner over Eisel and Harter.

1969

Laver, Court superb, Gonzalez a wonder

Rod Laver
A second Slam consolidates hold on No. 1 world ranking.

The second year of open tennis was one of continued progress but lingering confusion on the political front, and towering on-court performances by Rod Laver and Margaret Smith Court.

There were 30 open tournaments around the world and prize money escalated to about $1.3 million. Laver was the leading money winner with $124,000, followed by Tony Roche ($75,045), Tom Okker ($65,451), Roy Emerson ($62,629) and John Newcombe ($52,610).

The Davis Cup and other international team competitions continued to be governed by reactionaries, however, and admitted only players under the jurisdiction of their national associations. This left 'contract pros'—who were paid guarantees and obligated by contract to adhere to the schedule set by independent promoters—on the outs, while players who accepted prize money but remained under the aegis of their national associations were allowed to play. At the end of the year, a proposal to end this silly double standard and include 'contract pros' was rejected by the Davis Cup nations in a 21-19 vote.

The 'registered player' concept, borne of compromise a year earlier, persisted until finally being abolished by a newly elected and more forward-looking International Tennis Federation Committee of Management in July. Still, the public found it difficult to understand who was and who was not a pro. In the United States, those who took prize money but remained under the authority of the U.S. Tennis Association were officially called 'players.' Under the leadership of Capt. Donald Dell, the members of the U.S. Davis Cup team preferred to call themselves 'independent pros,' making it clear that they were competing for prize money.

The USTA leadership would have preferred to keep the U.S. tournament circuit amateur, paying expenses only, except for five open events given ITF sanction (Philadelphia Indoor, Madison Square Garden, U.S.

Open, Pacific Southwest, Howard Hughes Invitational). This would have kept down spiraling overhead costs, a threat to the exclusive clubs, which resisted sponsorship but did not want to lose their traditional events. Dell and the Davis Cup team refused to play in tournaments that offered expenses and guarantees instead of prize money, however, and thus effectively forced a full prize-money circuit into being in the U.S.

Dell led the way by organizing the $25,000 Washington *Star* International in his hometown. It was a prototype tournament in many ways, commercially sponsored and played in a public park for over-the-table prize money rather than under-the-table appearance fees. Other tournaments followed suit, and a new and successful U.S. Summer Circuit began to emerge. In all, 15 U.S. tournaments offered $440,000 in prize money, with the $137,000 U.S. Open again the world's richest event. In 1968, there had been only two prize-money open tournaments in the U.S., the $100,000 U.S. Open and the $30,000 Pacific Southwest.

A few peculiar hybrid events—half-amateur, half-pro—remained. The most obviously unnecessary was the $25,000 National Singles and Doubles at Longwood Cricket Club, which welcomed amateurs and independent pros but excluded the 'contract pros.' Stan Smith beat Bob Lutz, 9-7, 6-3, 6-0, and Court prevailed over Virginia Wade, 4-6, 6-3, 6-0, for the singles titles, but the grandly named tournament was essentially meaningless, except to those cashing checks, and vanished from the scene the next year in a natural sorting-out process.

A U.S. Amateur Championships also was played on clay in Rochester, the telecast of which was interrupted by a sexist act that wouldn't even be contemplated today. Linda Tuero of Metairie, La., and Gwyneth Thomas of Cleveland, hyper-patient, unrepentant baseliners, were contesting the women's final with endless rallies, one point lasting 10-1/2 minutes and 326 strokes. It was too much for referee Ernie Oberlaender. After two hours, 20 minutes, and with no end in sight, he yanked them. He moved them to a court away from the cameras and installed the men's finalists for a match shorter in time, longer in games, won by Butch Seewagen of New York over Zan Guerry of Lookout Mountain, Tenn., 9-7, 6-8, 1-6, 6-2, 6-4.

"What else could I do," the referee was apologetic. "Two fine players, but they got locked into patballing, and neither would give. The crowd and the TV people were getting restless." Linda and Gwyneth actually seemed relieved. "I'm glad they got us off TV," said Tuero, eventually the victor, 4-6, 6-1, 6-2. "I wouldn't have watched it 10 minutes myself."

If the labels put on tournaments and players boggled the public mind, there was no doubt as to who the world's No. 1 players were: Australians Laver and Court, truly dominant.

Laver repeated his 1962 Grand Slam by sweeping the Australian, French, Wimbledon and U.S. titles the first year all four were open.

Laver also won the South African Open over Okker, 6-3, 10-8, 6-3, and finished the season with a 106-16 record and winning 18 of 32 tournaments. He didn't lose a match from the start of Wimbledon in June until the second round of the Pacific Southwest Open in late September, when Ray Moore ended the winning streak at 31 matches, 7-5, 3-6, 6-2. During that stretch, Laver won seven tournaments, including his fourth Wimbledon (where he had not lost since the 1960 final), his second Forest Hills and his fifth U.S. Pro Championship. By the time he got to Los Angeles, Rod just wanted to get 45 minutes farther south to his adopted home of Corona Del Mar, Calif., where his wife, Mary, had just given birth to his son, Rick Rodney.

The most difficult match for Laver of the 26 that

1969 THE MAJOR CHAMPIONSHIPS

Australian Championships
Men's Singles: Rod Laver
Women's Singles: Margaret Smith Court
Men's Doubles: Roy Emerson / Rod Laver
Women's Doubles: Margaret Smith Court / Judy Tegart Dalton
Mixed Doubles: Ann Haydon Jones / Fred Stolle and
  Margaret Smith Court / Marty Riessen (SHARED)

French Open
Men's Singles: Rod Laver
Women's Singles: Margaret Smith Court
Men's Doubles: John Newcombe / Tony Roche
Women's Doubles: Françoise Durr / Ann Haydon Jones
Mixed Doubles: Margaret Smith Court / Marty Riessen

Wimbledon
Men's Singles: Rod Laver
Women's Singles: Ann Haydon Jones
Men's Doubles: John Newcombe / Tony Roche
Women's Doubles: Margaret Smith Court / Judy Tegart
Mixed Doubles: Ann Haydon Jones / Fred Stolle

U.S. Championships (Amateur)
Men's Singles: Stan Smith
Women's Singles: Margaret Smith Court
Men's Doubles: Dick Crealy / Allan Stone
Women's Doubles: Virginia Wade / Margaret Smith Court
Mixed Doubles: Patti Hogan / Paul Sullivan

U.S. Open
Men's Singles: Rod Laver
Women's Singles: Margaret Smith Court
Men's Doubles: Ken Rosewall / Fred Stolle
Women's Doubles: Françoise Durr / Darlene Hard
Mixed Doubles: Margaret Smith Court / Marty Riessen

constituted the Slam came early, in the semi-finals of the Australian. He beat Roche, 7-5, 22-20, 9-11, 1-6, 6-3, enduring more than four hours in the sweltering, 105-degree heat of a Brisbane afternoon. Both players got groggy in the brutal sun, even though they employed an old Aussie trick of putting wet cabbage leaves in their hats to help stay cool. It was so close that it could easily have gone either way, and a controversial line call helped Laver grasp the final set. Having survived, Laver beat Andres Gimeno in the final, 6-3, 6-4, 7-5. Rod had survived an Aussie gauntlet: Emerson in the fourth round, 6-2, 6-4, 3-6, 9-7, Stolle, 6-4, 18-16, 6-4, and Roche. Gimeno traveled a less hazardous route: Butch Buchholz, 6-1, 6-2, 6-2, and Ray Ruffels, 6-2, 11-9, 6-2.

At the French Opoen, Dick Crealy took the first two sets from Laver in a second-rounder, 3-6, 7-9, 6-2, 6-2, 6-4, but the red-haired 'Rocket' accelerated, stopping the increasingly dangerous Stan Smith in the fourth round, 6-4, 6-2, 6-4, Gimeno, 4-6, 6-4, 6-2, 6-4 and Okker, 4-6, 6-0, 6-2, 6-4. Ultimately he played one of his best clay-court matches to beat defender Ken Rosewall in the final, 6-4, 6-3, 6-4, after 'Muscles' had knocked off Roche, 7-5, 6-2, 6-2.

An unheralded Indian named Premjit Lall similarly captured the first two sets in the second round at Wimbledon, but Laver awoke to dispose of him, 3-6, 4-6, 6-3, 6-0, 6-0. Stan Smith took Laver to five sets, 6-4, 6-2, 7-9, 3-6, 6-3, in the fourth round. In the quarters Cliff Drysdale wasn't the impediment he'd been a year before at the U.S. Open, going down, 6-4, 6-2, 6-3. To finish, Rod burst from ambushes to raise the heat and tone down Arthur Ashe in the semis, 2-6, 6-2, 9-7, 6-0, then Newcombe, who had eliminated Roche, 3-6, 6-1, 14-12, 6-4. Despite Newcombe's thoughtful game plan of using lobs and changes of pace instead of the straightforward power for which he was known, Laver prevailed, 6-4, 5-7, 6-4, 6-4.

Then, to complete the Slam, it was on to the U.S. Open. But first the U.S. Pro at Longwood in Boston where Laver, winning for the fifth time, reprised over

Newcombe, 7-5, 6-2, 4-6, 6-1. "How could he do that the week after Wimbledon?" marveled Ashe. But that was Laver in '69, virtually invincible to any physical and mental obstacles.

The climax came at Forest Hills, where Philip Morris and its tennis-minded chairman of the board, Joe Cullman, had infused heavy promotional dollars into the U.S. Open. He brought flamboyant South African promoter Owen Williams in from Johannesburg to run a jazzed-up show and foster corporate patronage. They drew record crowds until the weather turned surly. Rain inundated the already soft and uneven lawns, played havoc with the schedule and pushed the tournament three days past its scheduled conclusion.

Despite the trying conditions and the imminent birth of his son on the West Coast, Laver remained intent. He was taken to five sets only by persistent Dennis Ralston, 6-4, 4-6, 4-6, 6-2, 6-3 in the fourth round. After that Laver disposed of ever-prickly Emerson, 4-6, 8-6, 13-11, 6-4, and defender Ashe, 8-6, 8-3, 14-12. Arthur had brushed aside Rosewall, 8-6, 6-4, 6-3. Roche, in a wowser, denied his mate Newcombe a place in the non-sun final, 3-6, 6-4, 4-6, 6-3, 8-6.

Then they waited through two days of rain as either the Grand Slam or a grand slap hovered. Laver, an old hand at the old ways with the feet, donned spikes in the second set. He became a sure-soled bog runner in climbing over Roche, 7-9, 6-1, 6-3, 6-2, on a gloomy Tuesday before a gathering of only 3,708 fans who sat through rain delays of 90 and 30 minutes.

The weather certainly dampened the occasion, but it was appropriate that Roche—clearly No. 2 in the world, and regarded as Laver's heir apparent until a series of left arm injuries started to plague him the next year—provided the final hurdle. The ruggedly muscular Roche was the only player with a winning record over Laver (5-3) for the year.

Laver uncharacteristically leaped the net in the Fred Perry style of the 1930s—"I don't know why I did that! —and shed a few tears as USTA President Alastair Martin presented him the champion's trophy and check for $16,000, saying, "You're the greatest in the world ... perhaps the greatest we've ever seen."

"I never really think of myself in those terms, but I feel honored that people see fit to say such things about me," said Laver shyly. "Tennis-wise, this year was much tougher than '62. At the time the best players—Ken Rosewall, Lew Hoad, Pancho Gonzalez—were not in the

---

1969 CHAMPIONS AND LEADERS

Top Player Earnings: Men
Rod Laver $124,000
Year-End Number One
Men: Rod Laver
Women: Margaret Smith Court

Davis Cup: United States
Federation Cup: United States
Wightman Cup: United States

amateur ranks. I didn't find out who were the best until I turned pro and had my brains beaten out for six months at the start of 1963."

Now, in the open era, there was no question who was best.

Margaret Smith Court, who had returned to action following a brief retirement (the first of several in her long career), was almost as monopolistic as Laver. She lost only five matches the entire season, winning 19 of 24 tournaments and 98 of 103 matches.

She won the Australian over Billie Jean King, 6-4, 6-1, after trailing Kerry Melville, 3-5, in the final set in the semis, running four games to 3-6, 6-2, 7-5. In the French, Court, covered the last four rounds by beating Pat Pretorius Walkden, 6-4, 6-0; Melville, 9-7, 6-1; defending champ Nancy Richey, 6-3, 4-6, 7-5 and finally Ann Haydon Jones, 6-1, 4-6, 6-3—all splendid clay-court players.

Court's dream of a Grand Slam ended at Wimbledon, however, where Jones beat her in the semi-finals, 10-12, 6-3, 6-2. To the unbridled joy of her British countrymen, the left-handed, 30-year-old Mrs. Philip 'Pip' Jones then won her first Wimbledon title after 14 years of trying, squashing King's bid for a fourth consecutive crown, 3-6, 6-3, 6-2. Billie Jean was shaken by the noisy partisanship of the customarily proper British gallery and what she thought were some dubious line calls, but the British hailed the popular Jones as a conquering heroine.

Injury kept top-seeded Jones out of the U.S. Open, won by second-seeded Court on a loss of no sets. In fact, she lost more than two games in a set only twice in six matches, in beating fellow Aussie Karen Krantzcke in the quarters, 6-0, 9-7, and fifth-seeded defender Wade in the semis, 7-5, 6-0. Sixth-seeded Richey—eschewing her usual baseline game for net-rushing tactics quite foreign to her—helped out by eliminating third-seeded King in the quarters, 6-4, 8-6, but found herself passed repeatedly in the final by some of Court's finest ground-stroking, 6-2, 6-2.

But if Laver and Court clearly reigned supreme, there were other notable heroes, heroines and achievements in 1969.

Phenomenally Pancho Gonzalez, at 41, mowed down in succession four Hall of Famers-to-be—Newcombe, 6-1, 6-2, Rosewall, 6-4, 1-6, 6-3, Smith, 8-6, 7-9, 6-4, and Ashe, 6-0, 6-2, 6-4—to win the $50,000 Howard Hughes Open at Las Vegas, and the $12,500 first prize, second only to the U.S. Open. Gonzalez also won the

Pacific Southwest Open over Cliff Richey, 6-0, 7-5, and had a 2-0 record over Smith, who was ranked No. 1 in the U.S. for the first time. Gonzalez was the top U.S. money-winner with $46,288, and might have returned to the No. 1 spot he occupied in 1948 and 1949 if the USTA had included 'contract pros' in its rankings.

Gonzalez' most dramatic performance, however, came at Wimbledon, where he beat Charlie Pasarell in the first round in the longest match in the history of the oldest and most prestigious of championships. It consumed five hours and 12 minutes and 112 games over two days. Gonzalez lost a marathon first set and virtually threw the second, complaining bitterly that it was too dark to continue play. He was whistled and hooted by the normally genteel Centre Court crowd, but won back all his detractors the next day with a gallant display. Pasarell played well, but Gonzalez was magnificent. In the fifth set he staved off seven match points, twice serving out of 0-40 holes, and won, 22-24, 1-6, 16-14, 6-3, 11-9. Gonzalez lasted until the fourth round, when his protégé, Ashe, beat him, 7-5, 4-6, 6-3, 6-3.

Smith won eight tournaments, including the U.S. Indoor over Egyptian lefty Ismail El Shafei, 6-3, 6-8, 6-4, 6-4, to replace Ashe atop the U.S. rankings. Ashe, bothered by a nagging elbow injury and numerous non-tennis distractions following his big year in 1968, won only two tournaments but had an 83-24 match record and more wins than any other American.

The United States defeated long-shot Romania, 5-0, in the Davis Cup challenge round on a fast asphalt court at Cleveland, painted and polished to make it even slicker, to the home team's benefit. Ashe defeated Ilie Nastase in the opening singles, 6-2, 15-13, 7-5, and Smith escaped the hulking and wily Ion Tiriac, 6-8, 6-3, 5-7, 6-4, 6-4, in the pivotal second match. Smith and Lutz closed out the Romanians, 8-6, 6-1, 11-9.

President Richard M. Nixon, a bowler and golfer who secretly despised tennis, hosted both final-round teams at a White House reception. This was a nice gesture, but the Chief Executive caused a few awkward stares when, as a memento of the occasion, he presented each player with a golf ball. Perhaps these were left over, some speculated, from the golf-happy Eisenhower administration. "I'm a Republican, but I'll never vote for him again," grumbled Richey. "Why he do this? No golf courses in Romania," said a puzzled Tiriac.

Tiny Romania, with the lion-hearted Tiriac and the immensely talented Nastase its only players of international standard, was proud to have gotten past Egypt, Spain, the Soviet Union, India and Great Britain.

Australia failed to reach the final for the first time since 1937—beaten in its first series by Mexico, 3-2, the first opening-round loss ever for Capt. Harry Hopman, and for the Aussies since falling to Italy in 1928. Rafael Osuna, Mexico's popular tennis hero, defeated Bill Bowrey in the decisive fifth match, 6-2, 3-6, 8-6, 6-3, and was hailed triumphantly by his countrymen. This was the engaging Osuna's last hurrah, however. He died tragically shortly thereafter, at age 30, when a private plane carrying him on a business trip crashed into the mountains outside of Monterrey.

In another significant development, the Davis Cup nations voted South Africa and Rhodesia out of the competition for 1970 and 1971 because demonstrations against their racial policies, and the refusal of some nations to play them, made their presence in the draw disruptive.

Nancy Richey was upset in the semi-finals of the U.S. Clay by Gail Sherriff Chanfreau, 6-3, 6-4, ending her tournament record female winning streak at 33 straight matches over seven years. She was trying to become only the second player to win seven consecutive U.S. titles, matching the feat of Richard Sears in the first seven U.S. Men's Championships (1881–87). Chanfreau won that title over Linda Tuero, 6-2, 6-2. Yugoslav Zeljko Franulovic won the other over Ashe, 8-6, 6-3, 6-4. Clark Graebner, uniting with Bill Bowrey in a 6-4, 4-6, 6-4 victory over Aussies Crealy and Allan Stone, had his fifth Clay doubles title, passing Bill Talbert's record set in 1946.

Richey, who retained the No. 1 U.S. women's ranking teamed with Julie Heldman and Jane 'Peaches' Bartkowicz to regain the Federation Cup at Athens and the Wightman Cup at Cleveland. Richey was undefeated in singles (4-0) and Heldman lost only to Court as the U.S. defeated Bulgaria, Italy, Netherlands (each 3-0) and Australia, 2-1, for the world team championship. Heldman, a clever player who nicknamed herself 'Junkball Julie,' set the tone of the 5-2 Wightman Cup victory by upsetting Wade in the opening match, 3-6, 6-1, 8-6, and also beat Winnie Shaw, 6-3, 6-4. Richey

topped Shaw, 8-6, 6-2, and Bartkowicz stopped Christine Truman Janes, 8-6, 6-0.

Ranked No. 2 nationally with eight victories in 20 tournaments and a 67-13 match record, 24-year-old Heldman also became the first American woman to win the Italian Championship since Althea Gibson in 1956, beating three outstanding clay courters—Lesley Turner Bowrey (wife of Bill), 3-6, 6-4, 6-1, Jones, 4-6, 6-4, 6-1, and Kerry Melville, 7-5, 6-3.

One of the most remarkable and crowd-pleasing victories of the year was that of Darlene Hard and Françoise Durr in the U.S. Open doubles. They were a 'pickup' team; Hard, by then a 33-year-old teaching pro, had entered as a lark. Out of tournament condition, she was an embarrassment in losing the first eight games of the final, but seemed suddenly to remember the skills and instincts that had made her the world's premier doubles player, winner of five previous U.S. women's titles. As the crowd loudly cheered their revival, Hard and Durr stunned heavily favored Court and Wade, 0-6, 6-3, 6-4.

Forest Hills had begun with a match of record duration. F. D. Robbins defeated Dick Dell, younger brother of Donald, 22-20, 9-7, 6-8, 8-10, 6-4, the longest in number of singles games—100—in the history of the U.S. Championships. When the tournament ran three days over, the men's doubles finished in a disgraceful shambles, Rosewall and Fred Stolle beating Ralston and Pasarell, 2-6, 7-5, 13-11, 6-3, before a few hundred spectators on a soggy Wednesday. Pasarell-Ralston got defaults from Wimbledon champs Newcombe and Roche in the quarters and Australian Open winners Laver and Emerson in the semis, who were off to other pursuits.

Newcombe-Roche were urged to leave waterlogged New York by their employers, WCT, in order to meet other commitments, a decision that rankled the ITF in its increasingly uneasy dealings with the new pro promoters. After all, it was unseemly for the No. 1 team to walk out on a major. They had repeated at Wimbledon, over Tom Okker–Marty Riessen, 7-5, 11-9, 6-3, and won three other tournaments, including the French (over Emerson and Laver, 4-6, 6-1, 3-6, 6-4, 6-4).

1970

Maggie's Slam finally a reality

Margaret Smith Court
No women's libber, but flawless on the court in winning Grand Slam.

As in 1950 and 1960, the beginning of a new decade also was, in many ways, the start of a new era for tennis. In 1970, the professional game for both men and women fitfully began to assume the structure that would characterize the decade of its most rapid growth.

This was the first year of the men's Grand Prix—a point system under the aegis of the International Tennis Federation, that linked together tournaments, leading to year-end bonus awards for the top finishers in the standings and berths in a new tournament at the end of the year: The Grand Prix Masters.

The brainchild of protean Jack Kramer, the Grand Prix was announced late in 1969 and sponsored by Pepsico. Players earned points, round by round, in the Grand Prix tournaments they entered, and at season's end the top men received cash awards scaled according to their order of finish.

Cliff Richey, for example, collected $25,000 for topping the standings; Arthur Ashe earned $17,000 for placing second; Ken Rosewall $15,000 for coming in third, etc. There were 19 tournaments in the Grand Prix in 1970. The 'bonus pool' totaled $150,000 and another $50,000 was at stake in the six-man Masters.

The underlying intent of the Grand Prix, clearly, was to keep players from signing guaranteed contracts with the professional troupes, World Championship Tennis (WCT) and the struggling National Tennis League (NTL). WCT, which loomed as an ever more formidable rival to the ITF and its 93-member national associations for control of the burgeoning pro game, responded by swiftly signing more players to contracts, then increasing its 'stable' to 30 players by swallowing the NTL in May.

Mike Davies, executive director of WCT, became a member of the ITF scheduling committee, but wariness and distrust between the maneuvering giants continued. It became increasingly difficult for traditional tournaments to count on the participation of the

WCT players because of the 'management fees' demanded by WCT in order to cover their guarantees to the players.

In September, at the U.S. Open, WCT took the wraps off a Grand Prix-style competition of its own, announcing a 'million-dollar circuit' for 1971. The first World Championship of Tennis, for 32 players to be selected by an international press panel, would consist of 20 tournaments with uniform prize money and point standings, leading to a rich, nationally televised playoff with a $50,000 first prize.

This was considered a declaration of war by WCT against the ITF, especially since Davies had never mentioned it to the ITF calendar committee. The battle intensified when, shortly thereafter, WCT announced that it had signed Ashe, Charlie Pasarell and Bob Lutz to five-year contracts in a package deal.

The ITF went ahead and announced an expanded Grand Prix, worth $1.5 million, in 1971, but the battle lines had already been drawn.

The beneficiaries of the infighting, of course, were the players, who found themselves the objects of a giddy bidding war between the ITF, which offered ever-bigger prize money tournaments but no guarantees, and WCT, with its long-term, guaranteed contracts.

Rod Laver did not retain any of the Big Four titles he monopolized in 1969, but still became the first tennis player to crack the $200,000 barrier in winnings.

He collected $201,453, compared to the $157,037 won by Lee Trevino, top earner on the professional golf

circuit. This had heretofore been unimaginable. But prize money was escalating at a rate no one had foreseen—nearly $1 million was up for grabs in U.S. tournaments alone—and three players (Laver, U.S. Open champ Rosewall and Ashe) won more than $100,000.

Growing along with the total purses, however, was the disparity in prize money for men and women. Despite Margaret Smith Court's fulfillment of a long-held ambition—a singles Grand Slam of the Australian, French, Wimbledon and U.S. titles—1970 was for the majority of women players the autumn of their discontent. A group of pioneers, led by the strong-willed Gladys Heldman—a tough, shrewd businesswoman who had founded *World Tennis* magazine in 1953—decided that the women would have to split away from mixed tournaments and form their own tour if they were ever to corner a significant share of the sport's mushrooming riches and publicity. This was a bold step, but the women decided to take it in September, and from a little acorn—a $7,500 renegade tournament for nine women in Houston—there eventually grew a mighty oak, the women's pro tour in the U.S.

The political kettle was boiling, but 1970 was also a spectacularly eventful year on the court. It was made singularly exciting by the advent of the game's first major scoring innovation—tie-breakers—and towering performances by several players, notably Rosewall and Court.

'Mighty Margaret' had twice before (1962, 69) won three of the four major singles titles in a season. In 1970, at age 28, she finally corralled the Grand Slam previously achieved by only one woman—Maureen Connolly in 1953. Court compiled a 104-6 record, winning 21 of 27 tournaments, and had the season's longest winning streak, 39 matches.

But a glitch for Margaret was a small September post-Open tournament at Charlotte, N.C., where she was beaten in the semis by a pony-tailed adolescent whom she would presently face on major battlegrounds: 15-year-old Chris Evert defeated her, 7-6, 7-6. The kid, an amateur in her first final among pros, then lost to Nancy Richey, 6-4, 6-1.

Court lost only three sets during the Slam, none in winning her ninth Australian singles title. She defeated Kerry Melville—one of only four women to beat her during the season—in the final, 6-3, 6-1, and teamed with Judy Tegart Dalton to win the doubles by the same score over Melville and Karen Krantzcke. Rising

1970 THE MAJOR CHAMPIONSHIPS

Australian Open
Men's Singles: Arthur Ashe
Women's Singles: Margaret Smith Court
Men's Doubles: Bob Lutz / Stan Smith
Women's Doubles: Margaret Smith Court / Judy Tegart Dalton
French Open
Men's Singles: Jan Kodes
Women's Singles: Margaret Smith Court
Men's Doubles: Ilie Nastase / Ion Tiriac
Women's Doubles: Gail Sherriff Chanfreau / Françoise Durr
Mixed Doubles: Billie Jean King / Bob Hewitt
Wimbledon
Men's Singles: John Newcombe
Women's Singles: Margaret Smith Court
Men's Doubles: John Newcombe / Tony Roche
Women's Doubles: Rosie Casals / Billie Jean King
Mixed Doubles: Rosie Casals / Ilie Nastase
U.S. Open
Men's Singles: Ken Rosewall
Women's Singles: Margaret Smith Court
Men's Doubles: Pierre Barthes / Nikki Pilic
Women's Doubles: Margaret Smith Court / Judy Tegart Dalton
Mixed Doubles: Margaret Smith Court / Marty Riessen

18-year-old Evonne Goolagong was her quarter-final victim, 6-3, 6-1, and a rare foe she looked up to, 6-foot-2 Krantzcke, in the semis, 6-1, 6-3.

At the French, only rising Russian Olga Morozova pushed Court to three sets, in the second round, 3-6, 8-6, 6-1. Everything else was straight sets: Rosie Casals, 7-5, 6-2, in the quarters, Heldman, 6-0, 6-2, in the semis and finally, 6-2, 6-4, over six-foot German Helga Niessen, who had removed Billie Jean King, 2-6, 8-6, 6-1, in the quarters. Françoise Durr won her fourth consecutive doubles title, alongside Gail Sherriff Chanfreau, over Casals and King, 6-1, 3-6, 6-3.

At Wimbledon, the tall, languid Niessen—not considered a threat on grass courts—took the first set from Court in the quarter-finals, but did not get another game, 6-8, 6-0, 6-0. After Margaret disposed of Casals, 6-4, 6-1, and Billie Jean dumped Durr, 6-3, 7-5, their final was a masterpiece of drama and shotmaking under duress. Both players were hurt. Court had a painfully strained and swollen ankle tightly strapped as she went on court. She had taken a pain-killing injection beforehand. King was hobbling on a deteriorated kneecap, which required surgery immediately after Wimbledon.

Nevertheless, BJK broke service in the first set three times. Each time Court broke back. Their injuries partially dictated the pattern of play, but both players produced magnificent shots under pressure. It was the longest women's final ever at Wimbledon— 46 games— Court finally winning by 14-12, 11-9, in 2-1/2 hours, well after the anesthetic effects of her injection had worn off. King saved three match points with gutsy shots worthy of the contest. "It was a bit like one of those 990-page novels that Trollope and Arnold Bennett used to write," suggested British journalist David Gray, who in 1977 would become general secretary of the ITF. "It started a little slowly, but had so many fascinating twists of character and plot that in the end it became a matter of utter compulsion to see how it all ended."

King took her sixth doubles title, her third with Casals, 6-2, 6-3 over Durr and Virginia Wade. Rosie teamed with Ilie Nastase to win the mixed, over the Soviets, Morozova and Alex Metreveli, 6-3, 4-6, 9-7. Billie Jean was the only player who truly challenged Court, splitting their four matches during the year, but King was still recuperating from her post-Wimbledon surgery.

In her absence, Court completed the Slam, losing only 13 games in mowing down Pam Austin (6-1, 6-0),

Patti Hogan (6-1, 6-1), Pat Faulkner (6-0, 6-2), Helen Gourlay (6-2, 6-2) and Richey (6-1, 6-3 to). Casals, who had out-volleyed Wade, 6-2, 6-7 (4-5) 6-2, in the semi, kept attacking furiously to win the middle set of the final. It was a game but futile effort, 6-2, 2-6, 6-1. "Her arms seemed a mile long," shrugged the diminutive 'Rosebud,' only 5-foot-2 to Court's 5-foot-11. Court also took the doubles, in tandem with Dalton over Casals and Wade, 6-3, 6-4, and the mixed doubles with Marty Riessen, over Dalton and Frew McMillan, 6-4, 6-4, her first U.S., fifth major triple. Don Budge had tripled to complete his Slam, but the doubles was taken previously at Boston. Margaret did it all at one stopover, Forest Hills, She banked $7,500 for the singles and $1,000 each for the doubles.

Court won approximately $50,000 in prize money on the year, about one quarter of what Laver earned for a far less productive season. In most tournaments, the women's share of the prize money was one quarter or less that of the men's. In the Italian Open, for example, King received a mere $600 for beating Heldman, 6-1, 6-3, in the final, while Nastase earned $3,500 for whipping Jan Kodes, 6-3, 1-6, 6-3, 8-6, for the other title.

Court, never a crusader or champion of causes, wanted no part of a 'women's lib' movement in tennis, but King and several others resented the growing inequity in prize-money ratio between men and women. They enlisted strong-willed activist Gladys Heldman as their negotiator and spokeswoman, and focused on the Pacific Southwest Open at Los Angeles— favoring men by an 8-to-1 ratio—as an example of their plight.

Heldman tried to get tournament chairman Jack Kramer to raise the women's purse. He would not. At a highly publicized Forest Hills press conference, a group of nine women declared they would boycott the Los Angeles tournament and play in a $7,500 event in Houston, sponsored by Virginia Slims cigarettes. The U.S. Tennis Association said it would not sanction this rebel event. The women said they would play anyway— and did. After signing token one-dollar contracts with Heldman, the Houston Nine (King, Casals, Heldman, Melville, Dalton, Richey, Kristy Pigeon, Peaches Bartkowicz and Valerie Ziegenfuss) competed in an event that was unexpectedly successful, paving the way for the first Virginia Slims circuit the next year. Casals won over Dalton, 5-7, 6-1, 7-5.

Meanwhile, the major men's singles titles monopolized by Laver in 1969 went to four different players:

Ashe, the runner-up in 1966 and 1967, became the fourth American to win the Australian singles, the first since Dick Savitt 19 years earlier. Laver did not defend, and Dennis Ralston eliminated Newcombe in a 94-game quarter-final (the sixth-longest in history), 19-17, 20-18, 4-6, 6-4. Ashe then took out a worn out Ralston, who begged off in the fourth set, 6-3, 8-10, 6-3, 2-1. The final was straightforward for Arthur, over towering Dick Crealy, 6-4, 9-7, 6-2, while the doubles went to Stan Smith and Lutz over locals John Alexander and Phil Dent, 8-6, 6-3, 6-4, the first Yanks to win since Vic Seixas and Tony Trabert 17 years earlier.

With Laver, Rosewall, and their fellow 'contract pros' out of the French Championships because their bosses couldn't come to a financial accommodation with the French Tennis Federation for their appearance, Czech Kodes, Yugoslav Zeljko Franulovic, American Richey, and Frenchman Georges Goven reached the semi-finals of the richest ($100,000) tournament outside America. Kodes labored against the homeboy, Goven, 2-6, 6-2, 5-7, 6-2, 6-3. Next, playing for the first Czech title since Jaroslav Drobny (by then a defector) in 1954, determined Jan won, 6-2, 6-4, 6-0, over Franulovic, who had rebounded to dodge two match points and deny Richey, 6-4, 4-6, 1-6, 7-5, 7-5. Romanians Nastase and Ion Tiriac took the doubles over Ashe and Pasarell, 6-4, 6-2, 6-3.

At Wimbledon, Laver's record 31-match winning streak (dating back to 1961) in the world's most important tournament, was snapped when he came up badly off-form against English lefty Roger Taylor in the fourth round and tumbled, 4-6, 6-4, 6-2, 6-1. John Newcombe withstood five break points in the fifth set of an excruciating three-hour quarter-final against fellow Aussie Roy Emerson. He won it, 6-1, 5-7, 3-6, 6-2, 11-9, then crushed Spaniard Andres Gimeno, 6-3, 8-6, 6-0 (the Spaniard had beaten Ashe, 7-5, 7-5, 6-2). In the final, Newc, the 1967 champ, beat back Rosewall's third shot at ruling Centre Court, 5-7, 6-3, 6-2, 3-6, 6-1. This was the first five-set final in 21 years, and the 10th all-Aussie men's final in 15 years.

Rosewall had beaten left-handers Tony Roche, 10-8,

6-1, 4-6, 6-2, and Taylor, 6-3, 4-6, 6-2, 6-2, to reach the final 14 years after losing to fellow Aussie 'Whiz Kid' Lew Hoad, but again failed at the last hurdle. Newcombe and Roche teamed for their third consecutive doubles triumph. As the first to achieve this since Reg and Laurie Doherty, the English brothers in 1903-04-05, they won an all-Oz final, over Fred Stolle and Rosewall, 10-8, 6-3, 6-1.

Rosewall, two months shy of his 36th birthday, reigned at Forest Hills, where 14 years earlier he had halted Hoad's Grand Slam bid. It was a wild U.S. Open, the richest in the world with a $176,000 pot. Pastel clothing was permitted in lieu of the traditional 'all white,' and red flags flew every time a set reached 6-6 and went into one of the 'sudden death' best-of-nine-points tie-breakers. Suddenly strange-looking 7-6 scores (seeming typographical errors) were blossoming.

Record crowds totaling 122,996 came out to see all the revolutionary happenings, but Rosewall interjected a reactionary note. After Ralston had achieved one of his career high points, knocking off defending champ and top-seeded Laver in the fourth round, 7-6 (5-3), 7-5, 5-7, 4-6, 6-3, to lead a charge of four Americans into the last eight, third-seeded Rosewall took over. He blasted Stan Smith, 6-2, 6-2, 6-2, and second-seeded Newcombe, 6-3, 6-4, 6-3, before relegating fourth-seeded Roche to the runner-up spot for the second consecutive year, 2-6, 6-4, 7-6 (5-2), 6-3. Rosewall was the oldest champ at Forest Hills since Bill Tillden, 36, won for the seventh and last time in 1929.

The men's doubles event was notable for several reasons. Pancho Gonzalez, the oldest man in the tournament at 42, entered with a then unknown protégé, Jimmy Connors, who at 18 was the youngest guy. They reached the quarters. Nikki Pilic of Yugoslavia and Pierre Barthes of France slew Emerson and Laver in the final, 6-3, 7-6 (5-2), 4-6, 7-6 (5-4), to become the second European team to win the U.S. Doubles, 34 years after Germany's Gottfried von Cramm and Henner Henkel in Boston. The victors won eight of their 15 sets in tie-breakers, the scoring innovation by Jimmy Van Alen that was given its first widespread exposure in the U.S. Pro Championships and U.S. Open.

Players were skeptical, as usual conservative—"It's like rolling dice," said Newcombe—and the best of them presented a petition to tournament director Bill Talnert demanding that the Open not be reduced to a craps shoot by tie-breakers. Talbert laughed them off, saying,

1970 CHAMPIONS AND LEADERS

Top Player Earnings: Men	**Davis Cup:** United States
Rod Laver $201,453	**Federation Cup:** Australia
Year-End Number One	**Wightman Cup:** United States
Men: John Newcombe	**Grand Prix Masters, Tokyo**
Women: Margaret Smith Court	Stan Smith

"Did you ever know a player who bought a ticket?" Agreeing with Talbert, customers, schedule-makers and television producers loved them. So tie-breakers were here to stay—although the more conservative "12-point, but win-by-two" method gradually won favor over nine-point sudden death in professional tournaments.

Although the tie-breaker, springing from Van Alen's pros-only tourney at the Newport (R.I.) Casino in 1965, was approved by the USTA for 1970 use, it didn't get wide exposure until the televised U.S. Pro. In a second rounder Drysdale led Rosewall, 6-4, 6-6. At 4-4 in the breaker it was simultaneous match point for Cliff, set point for Ken, the server. Sudden death. "How strange to play all your life and never be in a situation like this before," said Drysdale, who won the point and the decision.

Two weeks later, during the Pennsylvania Grass Championships in Philadelphia, Tom Gorman, the future U.S. Davis Cup captain, also found himself in the new 'weirdness'—the closest match ever played—against Pakistani Haroon Rahim in the second round. "I'd grown up believing that if you never lost your serve in a match you couldn't lose," said Gorman. "Wrong that day. I didn't lose serve. But neither did Haroon"—the victor by one point, 6-7 (3-5), 7-6 (5-1), 7-6 (5-4). Rahim was four-for-four in breakers until he got the same sort of one-point treatment by Chilean Jaime Fillol, 6-3, 5-7, 7-6 (5-4). Fillol lost the final to Aussie lefty Ray Ruffels, 6-2, 7-6 (5-3), 6-3.

Laver also won the 'Tennis Champions Classic,' a series of head-to-head, winner-take-all challenge matches played in seven cities. He beat Rosewall for the $35,000 top prize at Madison Square Garden, 6-4, 6-3, 6-3.

Nastase underscored his emerging brilliance by winning titles on one of the world's fastest courts—the canvas of the U.S. Indoor at Salisbury, Md., where he escaped a two-set deficit and two match points in the fourth set to beat Richey, 6-8, 3-6, 6-4, 9-7, 6-0—as well as on one of the slowest, the red clay of Foro Italico in Rome. There he beat Kodes for the Italian title, 6-3, 1-6, 6-3, 8-6.

Richey, a scrappy Texan with more tenacity than natural talent, earned the No. 1 U.S. ranking, thereby establishing a unique family achievement. His sister, Nancy, had been the top-ranked U.S woman in 1964-65, '68-69.

Richey won eight of 27 tournaments he played dur-

ing the season, was runner-up in five more and went farther than any other American man at Forest Hills, the semi-finals. His match record for the year was 93-19.

Richey also was the unlikely hero of the lackluster 1970 Davis Cup challenge round. U.S. Capt. Ed Turville agonized over the selection, but finally chose Richey over Smith to face upstart West Germany on a fast asphalt court at Cleveland. Richey, who felt he had been slighted by not being chosen in 1969, responded by clobbering smooth stroking lefty Christian Kuhnke, 6-3, 6-4, 6-2, and former Wimbledon finalist Willy Bungert, 6-4, 6-4, 7-5, to spearhead a 5-0 U.S. victory. Ashe beat Bungert, 6-2, 10-8, 6-2, in the opener. Later he erased Kuhnke, 6-8, 10-12, 9-7, 13-11, 6-4, in the meaningless fifth match, the longest singles—86 games—ever in a Davis Cup final. Smith and Lutz beat Bungert and Kuhnke, 6-3, 7-5, 6-4, becoming the only doubles team to clinch the Cup three straight years.

It was a disappointing final, concluding a tarnished Davis Cup campaign. The exclusion of contract pros, even though all major tournaments were now 'open,' left the Davis Cup a second-rate event.

Australia, denied the services of perhaps its 10 best players, fell pathetically to India, 3-1. Premjit Lall beat Ruffels, 6-2, 6-8, 6-3, 3-6, 14-12, and Crealy, 8-6, 6-2, 6-2. Jai Mukerjea also beat Crealy, 3-6, 6-8, 6-4, 6-3, 6-2, and that was enough for Aussie Capt. Harry Hopman. After 22 years and 16 Cups the most renowned of captains bugged out, moving to the United States to become an outstanding teaching pro.

Future political turmoil within the Cup was also foreshadowed as South Africa was expelled for two years because the apartheid racial policy of its government was considered disruptive to the competition, and Rhodesia withdrew to avoid political problems.

Largely because contract pros were excluded from the Davis Cup, a new competition—grandly misnamed the World Cup—was organized as a charity event in Boston. It put a two-man team of Australian pros, Newcombe and Stolle, against U.S. Davis Cuppers Richey, Smith, Ashe and Clark Graebner for $20,000 in prize money. The Aussies won, 5-2.

West Germany's women also made a global team final and also got bageled in their title bid, 3-0 by Australia. Even though Court abstained, Australia won its fourth Federation Cup at Freiburg, West Germany. Dalton and Krantzcke swept through the competition without losing a match, cinching it as Judy beat Niessen, 4-6, 6-3,

6-3, and Karen beat Helga Schultz Hoesl, 6-2, 6-3. The U.S. lost the Cup in the semis, 2-1 to the Germans. Doubles was the difference, Niessen and Hoesl over Mary Ann Eisel Curtis and Julie Heldman, 7-5, 4-6, 6-0, after Bartkowicz had beaten Hoesl, 6-2, 6-2, and Niessen put away Heldman, 6-0, 8-6.

King was back in the Wightman Cup, beating Wade, 8-6, 6-4, and Jones, 6-4, 6-2, and linking with Bartkowicz for the first time to win the decisive doubles, over Wade and Winnie Shaw, 7-5, 6-8, 6-2. Heldman chipped in a win over Joyce Barclay Williams, 6-3, 6-2, and the outcome was 4-3 for the U.S. at Wimbledon. Wade's singles win over Richey, 6-3, 6-2, had given the British a 3-2 lead.

The season ended with the first Grand Prix Masters tournament, a six-man round-robin in Tokyo. Richey, who topped the Grand Prix point standings, was ill and couldn't participate. Smith and Laver both had 4-1 records in the round-robin, but Smith took the $15,000 first prize because of his head-to-head win over Laver, 4-6, 6-3, 6-4.

The next year, because of the growing strain of the tug-of-war between WCT and the ITF, Smith and Laver would not be playing in the same season-ending playoff tournament. Negotiations throughout the fall of 1970 attempted to develop an accord, and in December WCT and the ITF issued a joint communique pledging that they would "work together toward the development and spectator appeal of the game throughout the world." An agreement in principle for the appearance of WCT contract pros in the 1971 French, Wimbledon, and U.S. Open Championships also was announced, but the cautious harmony turned out to be brief.

1971

King the catalyst for women's tour

John Newcombe A second Wimbledon title, and a year-long battle with Stan Smith for No. 1.

In 1971, both men's and women's professional tennis were split into rival camps. It was an uneasy, acrimonious year politically, but the game prospered.

On court, there were many highlights: John Newcombe's second consecutive Wimbledon triumph, after he trailed U.S. Army Cpl. Stan Smith by two sets to one in the final; Smith's impressive triumph at Forest Hills; the first 'World Championship of Tennis,' in which Ken Rosewall upset Rod Laver in the final; a new women's pro tour, dominated by the indefatigable Billie Jean King; and the emergence of Evonne Goolagong, who won the French Open and Wimbledon at age 19 and Chris Evert, who reached the semi-finals of the U.S. Open at 16.

Rosewall, who in 1970 had captured his second U.S.

Championship 14 years after the first, continued to perform geriatric marvels. He dethroned Arthur Ashe in the Australian Open final, 6-1, 7-5, 6-3, regaining a title he first held in 1953. Flawless all the way, 'Muscles' did not lose a set, and was pushed to only two tie-breakers, canceling ex-champ Roy Emerson in the quarters, 6-4, 6-4, 6-3, then Tom Okker, 6-2, 7-6, 6-4. Rosewall's triumph was made easier by upset losses in the early rounds inflicted upon top-seed Laver, Newcombe and Tony Roche. Newcombe and Roche won the third of their four Australian doubles titles over Marty Riessen and Okker, 6-2, 7-6.

Unfortunately, for much of the season the 34 men under contract to World Championship Tennis and the 'independent pros' who remained under the authority of their national associations played separate tournaments.

WCT's new 'World Championship of Tennis'—a million-dollar series of 20 tournaments in nine countries on four continents—got off to a promising start with the Philadelphia Indoor, where Newcombe beat Laver, 7-6 (7-5), 7-6 (7-1), 6-4, for only the second time in a dozen career meetings.

Meanwhile, the independent pros were playing on an expanding indoor circuit promoted by Bill Riordan under the aegis of the U.S. Tennis Association. The highlight was the U.S. Indoor at Riordan's hometown, Salisbury, Md., where Clark Graebner came from two sets down to upend Romanian Ilie Nastase in the semi-finals (2-6, 1-6, 6-4, 6-2, 6-2), then survived two match points in beating Cliff Richey for the title, 2-6, 7-6 (5-4), 1-6, 7-6 (5-4), 6-0.

The Italian Open at Rome was one of several strange hybrid events, co-promoted by WCT as part of its 20-tournament series, but also open to non-contract pros. This made for a week of exceptional matches and excitement on the red clay of Il Foro Italico. Record crowds and profits were recorded before Laver defeated Czech Jan Kodes in the final, 7-5, 6-3, 6-3.

Only a few of the WCT players entered the French Open. After five months of a grueling travel and playing schedule, Ashe, never a factor on European clay, was the only WCT top name who opted to go to Paris for two weeks of physically demanding best-of-five-set matches in very hot weather. The mass nonappearance of the 'contract pros' infuriated the International Tennis

1971 THE MAJOR CHAMPIONSHIPS

Australian Open
Men's Singles: Ken Rosewall
Women's Singles: Margaret Smith Court
Men's Doubles: John Newcombe / Tony Roche
Women's Doubles: Margaret Smith Court / Evonne Goolagong
French Open
Men's Singles: Jan Kodes
Women's Singles: Evonne Goolagong
Men's Doubles: Arthur Ashe / Marty Riessen
Women's Doubles: Gail Sherriff Chanfreau / Françoise Durr
Mixed Doubles: Françoise Durr / Jean Claude Barclay
Wimbledon
Men's Singles: John Newcombe
Women's Singles: Evonne Goolagong
Men's Doubles: Roy Emerson / Rod Laver
Women's Doubles: Rosie Casals / Billie Jean King
Mixed Doubles: Billie Jean King / Owen Davidson
U.S. Open
Men's Singles: Stan Smith
Women's Singles: Billie Jean King
Men's Doubles: John Newcombe / Roger Taylor
Women's Doubles: Rosie Casals / Judy Tegart Dalton
Mixed Doubles: Billie Jean King / Owen Davidson

Federation and was a major factor in polarizing opposition to WCT.

Meanwhile, the dour but energetically industrious Kodes won his second straight French title, beating the more gifted but less persistent Nastase, 8-6, 6-2, 2-6, 7-5, in an absorbing final. Ashe and Riessen, the top two WCT players entered, won the doubles in a unique Parisian all-American final over Smith and Tom Gorman.

At Wimbledon, No. 1 seed Laver was ambushed by the inspired serving and volleying of Gorman, inviolate on serve, 9-7, 8-6, 6-3, in the quarter-finals. The best match was an enchanting four-hour quarter-final in which Rosewall finally outstroked Richey, 6-8, 5-7, 6-4, 9-7, 7-5, at nightfall. The final between Newcombe and Smith had fewer breathtaking rallies and was dominated by slam-bang points accentuating the serve-volley power of both, but it also became gripping in the end. Smith seemed in control after a seven-game run that took him to 1-0 in the fourth set, but this was his first major final and he got "a little tired mentally." Newcombe was tougher and seized control, ending his 6-3, 5-7, 2-6, 6-4, 6-4 triumph with an ace. In the semis Newc had emphatically avoided the five sets of the 1970 final by putting away Rosewall, 6-1, 6-1, 6-3, while Smith leaned on Gorman, 6-3, 8-6, 6-2.

Emerson, twice a titleist with Neale Fraser (1959 and 1961), partnered Laver to the latter's only Wimbledon doubles title over Ashe and Dennis Ralston, 4-6, 9-7, 6-8, 6-4, 6-4.

The U.S. Open—minus Laver, defending champ Rosewall, and Emerson, who opted to rest—was less than three hours old when Wimbledon champ Newcombe was rudely dismissed by Kodes, 2-6, 7-6 (5-1), 7-6, 6-3. Jan, the French champ, was extremely unhappy about being unseeded even though he said tennis on grass courts was "a joke" that he found totally unfunny. This was the first time in 41 years that a top seed failed to survive his opening match.

But Kodes proved it was no fluke. He came back from two sets down against Pierre Barthes, 2-6, 5-7, 6-4, 6-4, 6-3, and from two sets to one and a service break down in the fourth to beat Ashe in the rain-spattered semi-finals, 7-6 (5-3), 3-6, 4-6, 6-3, 6-4. Kodes also won the first set of the final against Smith, but the 6-foot-4 Californian had learned from his near miss at Wimbledon. Unflinching on the crucial points, he erased the 'bouncing Czech,' 3-6, 6-3, 6-2, 7-6 (5-3).

Smith and Erik van Dillen were even at two sets apiece against Newcombe and Englishman Roger Taylor in the doubles final when darkness closed in. Rather than resume the next day, it was agreed, questionably, and with no precedent, to improvise—a sudden-death tie-breaker would decide the championship. In a cheap abbreviation unique to the men's majors, Newcombe-Taylor won it, 5-3, thus the title, 6-7, 6-3, 7-6 (5-4), 4-6, with a big asterisk.

As the tourney began a 19-year-old Jimmy Connors, registered his initial singles victory, a rousing rebound over 35-year-old ex-Wimbledon champ Alex Olmedo, 2-6, 5-7, 6-4, 7-5, 7-5. Twenty-one years later he would rack up his last, his 98th, a U.S. male record

It was indeed a curious year for men's tennis, climaxed by separate playoffs for the leading 'contract' and independent pros. Laver, Okker, Rosewall, Cliff Drysdale, Ashe, Newcombe, Riessen and Bob Lutz were the top eight men in the WCT standings. They had their playoffs in Houston (two rounds) and Dallas. Rosewall won two magnificent tie-breakers to seize the $50,000—staggering at the time—top prize at Dallas' Memorial Auditorium over Laver as 8,000 watched, 6-4, 1-6, 7-6 (7-3), 7-6 (7-4).

Smith, Nastase, Zeljko Franulovic, Kodes, Richey, Barthes and Gorman were the seven men who made the round-robin Grand Prix Masters at Paris. Smith collected the $25,000 top bonus prize from the season-long point standings, but Nastase went 6-0 in the Masters' unsatisfactory round-robin, including a 5-7, 7-6, 6-3 beating of second place Smith (4-2), who also lost to Kodes, 6-4, 3-6, 6-4. Collecting the tournament's $15,000 top prize, Nastase won the first of his four Masters championships.

At year's end Newcombe and Smith shared Player of the Year honors, but there was no clear-cut No. 1.

The Italian was Laver's biggest title (7-5, 6-3, 6-3, over Kodes), but, at 33, he kept moving busily, winning seven of 26 tournaments, 82 of 100 matches, and was far and away the leading money winner with $292,717, which made him tennis' first career millionaire. His nine-year pro winnings: $1,006,974. His most astounding string came in the second (and last) Tennis Champions Classic, a series of head-to-head, winner-take-all matches in various cities, leading to a four-man playoff in Madison Square Garden. Laver incredibly swept all 13 of his matches against top opponents to win $160,000 in this one event, beating Okker in the final,

6-5, 6-2, 6-1.

Rosewall won seven of 23 tournaments (70 of 86 matches), including the Australian and South African (over Fred Stolle, 6-4, 6-0, 6-4) Opens and his third U.S. Pro Championship, (over Drysdale, 6-4, 6-3, 6-0). He earned $138,371 and would have been unchallenged as 'Old Man of the Year' except for Pancho Gonzalez. Now 43, and a grandfather, the 'Old Wolf' knocked aside like tenpins kiddies Roscoe Tanner, 3-6, 6-1, 6-1, Richey, 7-5, 6-2 and Connors, 3-6, 6-3, 6-3, to win the $10,000 top prize in the Pacific Southwest Open at Los Angeles. Connors had beaten Smith, 3-6, 6-3, 7-5.

Newcombe captured five of 19 tournaments, 53 of 67 matches, and amassed $101,514. Smith, who missed the early season because he was in basic training with the U.S. Army, won six of 19 tournaments and compiled a 70-13 record that included beating Nastase in the opening match and Ion Tiriac in the decisive singles of the 3-2 U.S. Davis Cup challenge round victory over Romania. Smith earned $100,086. Nastase, who finished the season spectacularly, was the top 'independent' earner with $114,000 in winnings.

Relations between the ITF and WCT, strained at the start of the year and aggravated by the French Open, broke down completely at Wimbledon. In a bitter, turbulent press conference, fueled by misunderstanding over several WCT 'points of negotiation' that were falsely interpreted by ITF as 'demands,' both sides admitted that talks aimed at establishing a unified circuit for 1972 had failed miserably.

Two weeks later, at its annual meeting in the northern Italian resort town of Stresa, the ITF voted to ban WCT's 'contract pros' from all tournaments and facilities controlled by the ITF and its 93-member national associations, effective at the start of 1972. After 3-1/2 years of 'open' tournaments, the contract pros were to be made outcasts again.

In November, new ITF president Allan Heyman announced that Commercial Union Assurance, a London-based worldwide insurance group, was taking over sponsorship of the Grand Prix from Pepsico, and expanding the financial commitment to more than $250,000. WCT, meanwhile, said that it would focus its attention on strengthening its own tournament series, which it shifted to a May windup in 1972 for maximum TV exposure in the U.S. In the first week of 1972, Rosewall would win his second consecutive Australian Open. Ironically, this little man who had won the first

Open tournament in 1968 also was going to win the last of the now interrupted Open era to set a longevity record for the majors—19 years between his first and last titles, both Australian, 1953 and 1972. But more would be heard on this clash of factions.

Meanwhile, women's tennis took a dramatically vibrant upturn. A year earlier it seemed to be overshadowed by the men's game and suffering from a dearth of refreshing young talent. But the renegade Virginia Slims of Houston tournament the previous September blossomed into a new women's tour with $309,000 in prize money. King, who energetically promoted the Virginia Slims Circuit—one observer suggested that she "single-handedly talked it into prominence"—won the lioness' share of the rewards: $117,000. She became the first woman athlete to break the $100,000-in-a-year milestone.

Publisher Gladys Heldman was the behind-the-scenes driving force, arranging 14 tournaments with combined prize money of $189,100 for the first four months in 1971, while King was the on court dynamo and chief drumbeater. Trumpeting that she had "my wheels back" after knee surgery in July 1970, Billie Jean won the first five tournaments on the new tour—at San Francisco, her native Long Beach, Milwaukee, Oklahoma City and Chattanooga. She beat Rosemary Casals in the first four finals, then Ann Jones. BJ teamed with Casals to win the doubles at the first seven Slims tournaments.

At Philadelphia—where word came that the USTA had lifted its suspension of the 'rebel' women—Françoise Durr snapped King's singles streak of 22 matches in the semi-finals, 6-2, 5-7, 7-6, and Casals won the tournament, 6-3, 3-6, 6-2. King, who had been ineligible as a 'contract pro' for two years, then recovered the U.S. Indoor title she had held from 1966 through 1968, beating Casals again in the final at Boston, 4-6, 6-2, 6-3. Rosie, so long the whipping girl, got revenge in the tour's disappointing New York stop, 6-4, 6-4, at the shabby old 34th Street Armory. In all, King won eight of

the inaugural 14 tournaments. Jones won the biggest prize ($9,000) at Las Vegas, beating King, 7-5, 6-4.

However, an amateur intruded on the working women on the clay at St. Petersburg, Fla. Knocking off the 'names' she was about to become one herself. Schoolgirl Evert, 16, was the most surprising winner, striking down Durr, 6-0, 7-5, Judy Alvarez, 6-0, 6-2, an ailing King, 6-7, 6-3, default, then, Julie Heldman, 6-1, 6-2, to capture her first of her 157 pro tourney titles. She also won the Southern Championship, 6-1, 6-0, over kid sister, Jeanne Evert, 13, the country's No. 1 in the 14-and-under precinct.

The winter/spring tour—which captured a great deal of media attention, thanks to the clever and energetic promotion of Heldman and King and the emerging fascination with 'women's liberation'—was so successful that the women's tour added five summer tournaments, starting with a $40,000 Virginia Slims International at Houston. King captured the $10,000 first prize there, beating Australian Kerry Melville in the final, 6-4, 4-6, 6-1, and went on to take the $10,000 top bonus in the first women's Grand Prix. King's total of $117,000 in prize money was the highest sum for any American, male or female.

While King & Co. were pioneering under the banner of 'Women's Lob,' Margaret Smith Court and Goolagong dominated the traditional early season. Court beat Jones, 6-8, 6-3, 6-2, and Goolagong walloped Virginia Wade, 6-4, 6-1 as Australia won the 1971 Federation Cup at Perth (actually played the last week in 1970), 3-0 over Great Britain in the final.

The Australian Open was played in March, three months later than usual, and Court beat Goolagong, 2-6, 7-6 (7-0) 7-5, to take her sixth consecutive major singles title (1969 U.S.; 1970 Australian, French Wimbledon and U.S.; 1971 Australian). American Helen Wills Moody, playing the majors irregularly and never traveling to Australia, won 16 straight between 1924 and 1933, while Maureen Connolly won nine straight from 1951 to '54, although, like Helen, she didn't play that many in a row.

Margaret beat Evonne again, 6-3, 6-1, in the final of the South African Open (Goolagong, of one-eighth aboriginal descent, was the first 'non-white' to compete in Johannesburg). They teamed to win the doubles, over locals Brenda Kirk and Laura Roussouw, 6-4, 7-5.

Wade won the Italian Open and King the German, both over Helga Niessen Masthoff in the finals: Virginia,

---

1971 CHAMPIONS AND LEADERS

Top Player Earnings: Men
Rod Laver $292,717
Top Player Earnings: Women
Billie Jean King $117,000
Year-End Number One
Men: John Newcombe
Women: Billie Jean King

Davis Cup: United States
Federation Cup: Australia
Wightman Cup: United States
Grand Prix Masters, Paris
Ilie Nastase
WCT, Dallas
Ken Rosewall

6-4, 6-4; B.J., 6-3, 6-4. But in Paris, Court's major winning streak of 35 matches was surprisingly terminated in the fourth round of the French by Aussie-born French citizen (through marriage) Gail Sherriff Chanfreau, who, bashing her high-rolling topspin forehand, played the match of her life, 6-3, 6-4. She lost in the next round to another Aussie, Helen Gourlay, 6-4, 3-6, 6-3, who went on to beat 1968 titlist Nancy Richey Gunter in the semis, 6-2, 6-3. Nevertheless, the Australian flavor was maintained as carefree 19-year-old Goolagong came through the other half easily over Netherlander Marijke Schaar, 6-4, 6-1, and beat Gourlay in the final, 6-3, 7-5. Evonne was the first since Althea Gibson in 1956 to win the tournament on the first try. Surrounded by Aussies, Parisienne Durr, alongside Chanfreau, won her fifth consecutive doubles title, over Gourlay and Kerry Harris, 6-4, 6-1.

Having won the most prestigious clay-court title, third-seeded Goolagong cemented the No. 1 women's ranking for the year by winning Wimbledon in her second appearance on the grass of the All England Club. The most ethereal of tennis players, graceful, smiling, and free-spirited, she captivated the galleries in dismissing Richey in the quarters, 6-3, 6-2; second-seeded Billie Jean in the semis, 6-4, 6-4; and first-seeded, but nervous, Court in the final, 6-4, 6-1, winning the last six games in a rush.

Couturier Teddy Tinling made Goolagong a special dress for the final, white with a scalloped hem and lilac lining and adornments; his staff worked through the night to get it ready, and sent it to Wimbledon with a 'good luck' message sewn in, and a silver horseshoe. Such was the spirit of the occasion as Evonne became the youngest champion since Karen Susman, 19, in 1962. King and Casals collaborated on their fourth Wimbledon doubles title, over Court and Goolagong, 6-3, 6-2. Court registered a rare 'cripple' in her third final as she and Marty Riessen fell to Billie Jean and Owen Davidson in the mixed, 3-6, 6-2, 15-13. The final set was the longest in any major mixed final.

Despite her triumphs in Paris and London, Goolagong was kept out of the U.S. Open as her coach, Vic Edwards, adhered to his long-range plan of avoiding the U.S. circuit until 1972. Neither Court nor Jones, both of whom were pregnant, entered Forest Hills. But just when it appeared that King would have the stage to herself, Evert emerged as another appealing young rival.

Evert, a 16-year-old high-school student from Fort Lauderdale, Fla., had beaten Court on clay the previous fall and won the Virginia Slims tournament at St. Petersberg on the same surface. But she gained national attention for the first time as the heroine of the 4-3 U.S. Wightman Cup victory over Great Britain on an ultra-slow rubberized court in Cleveland in August. Three months younger than Connolly had been in her first championship year 20 years earlier, Chris crunched Winnie Shaw, 6-0, 6-4, in the opener and a nervous and off-form Wade, 6-1, 6-1, in the decisive sixth match, which clinched victory for the injury-riddled U.S. team that had trailed, 2-1.

Evert then moved on to the Eastern Grass Court Championships at South Orange, N.J., and conquered an international field, winning over Gourlay, 6-4, 6-0. Her only previous tournament on grass had been the U.S. Girls 18 singles, won over Janet Newberry, 6-1, 6-3, two weeks earlier.

At Forest Hills, she immediately became the darling of U.S. Open crowds, the star of the show since three prominent men were missing. Playing every match in the old concrete stadium, she beat German Edda Buding, 6-1, 6-0, then No. 4 American Mary Ann Eisel, 4-6, 7-6 (5-1), 6-1. Mary Ann served for it at 6-5, 40-0, and had six match points, but Chrissie calmly kept belting her groundies in an astounding introduction to her country via TV. Next victims were fifth-seeded Durr, 2-6, 6-2, 6-3; and Aussie Lesley Hunt, 4-6, 6-2, 6-3, Chrissie becoming the youngest semi-finalist, 16 years, 9 months, since Betty Nuthall of England, 16 years, 3-1/2 months in 1927. Eisel, Durr and Hunt all departed in tears, intimidated by the kid's cool backcourt stroking and the wildly partisan crowds cheering for 'Cinderella in Sneakers.'

King had too much of a fast-court arsenal for Evert in the semis and ended her fairy tale, and 22-match winning streak, 6-3, 6-2, before 13,647. Chrissie's initiation to the uppermost level left her with a No. 10 world ranking and the unique dual U.S. ranking of No. 1 junior and No. 3 woman.

BJK wrapped up her second Forest Hills title by beating Casals, 6-4, 7-6 (5-2), sealing the No. 1 U.S. ranking for the fifth time. Her record for the season was 112-13, including victories in 17 out of 31 tournaments.

King's persistent drive to the $100,000 landmark was slowed when she and Casals walked off the court because of a line call dispute at 6-6 in the first set of the final of the Pacific Southwest Open. Were they trying to embarrass promoter Jack Kramer, whose prize money stinginess the previous year had led the foremost women to boycott the tournament? It was one of the strangest episodes in U.S. tournament history and both players were later fined for their 'double default.' BJK finally went over the 100-grand mark at Phoenix, where she again beat Casals, 7-5, 6-1, in the final. BJ celebrated with champagne in the dressing room, and at a news conference in New York the following week received a congratulatory phone call from President Richard Nixon.

The last challenge round was coming up, and the 71-year-old Davis Cup format was about to be scrapped. Therein the Cup-holding country was required to play only once, against the challenger, survivor of the virtually year-long tournament. Feeling that it gave the holder a big edge, choice of home location and surface, the Davis Cup Nations decided that the champion would have to enter the tourney proper in 1972.

As defending captain, Ed Turville infuriated his singles ace of 1970, Cliff Richey, by sportingly deciding that the 1971 windup would be contested on clay, at Charlotte, N.C. Romania, on the backs of Nastase and Tiriac, had come through six matches to reach the ultimate round for a second time. Two years earlier in Cleveland they had been blasted off a lickety-split asphalt court, and Turville felt it would be more entertaining and fairer to stage this one on clay. Richey felt it was treason, giving it away to the dirt-bred Romanians, and he quit the team.

Turville's contention that it would be more exciting was certainly confirmed: A 3-2 U.S. victory minus Richey. Searching for a singles replacement to accompany Smith, he came up with a surprise, 28-year-old Frank Froehling, III, who hadn't been on the team for six years. After Smith beat Nastase, 7-5, 6-3, 6-1, to give the U.S. a 1-0 lead, long-legged, spindly Froehling (called 'Spider-Man' and 'Boy Octopus') had his own surprise for Tiriac: The greatest Cup round comeback for an American in more than a half-century, 3-6, 1-6, 6-1, 6-3, 8-6. That was the critical point for the U.S. since Nastase and Tiriac snuffed Smith and Erik van Dillen in doubles, 7-5, 6-4, 8-6, before Smith clinched over Tiriac, 8-6, 6-3, 6-0. With little more than a forehand, and heart, Froehling survived seven break points, three in the opening game, to take the third set and begin turning it his way. Tiriac fought back from a break down, saved a match point in the fifth to 5-5. Darkness, at 6-6, pushed them to the next day. Froehling broke Tiriac on a second match point with a buzzing forehand, and the U.S. was on its way to a fourth straight Cup.

1972

ITF, WCT make peace, pots grow

Ilie Nastase
A loss in a classic Wimbledon final, then redemption at the U.S. Open.

In 1972, a peace agreement was reached between the International Tennis Federation and World Championship Tennis, reintegrating a men's game that had briefly and regrettably regressed into segregated 'contract pro' and 'independent pro' circuits. But the agreement came too late for the 32 WCT contractees to participate in the French Open or Wimbledon. Stan Smith's triumphs over Ilie Nastase in the Wimbledon final and the Davis Cup gave him the edge over the mercurial Romanian, who won the U.S. Open, for the No. 1 men's ranking. Meanwhile, Billie Jean King swept the French, Wimbledon and U.S. Open titles—she didn't enter the Australian—and again dominated the ascending Virginia Slims circuit, emphatically ruling women's tennis and giving the U.S. dual supremacy in men's and women's tennis for the first time since 1955.

Despite the unsatisfactory separate circuits for men most of the year, prize money kept spiraling, to more than $5 million worldwide. Nastase was the top earner at $176,000, with Smith, property of the U.S. Army, second at $142,300, as probably the highest paid corporal (or any rank) in the world. Four other men (WCT employees Ken Rosewall, Arthur Ashe, John Newcombe and Rod Laver) and one woman, King, collected more than $100,000.

It also was a year of outstanding matches, none finer than the three-hour, 34-minute classic between Rosewall and Laver in the final of the WCT Championships at Dallas in May. Laver was favored to grab the $50,000 plum that had eluded him the previous November, but Rosewall, an enduring marvel at age 38, again stole it. Laver revived himself from 1-4 in the final set, saved a match point with an ace, and had the match on his racket at 5-4 in the 'lingering death' tie-breaker, with two serves to come. He pounded both deep to Rosewall's backhand corner, but the most splendid antique in tennis reached for vintage return winners. Laver failed to return the exhausted

Rosewall's last serve and it was over, 4-6, 6-0, 6-3, 6-7 (3-7), 7-6 (7-5). This had been a duel of torrid, exquisite shotmaking on a 90-degree Mother's Day afternoon, and the sell-out crowd of 9,500 at Moody Coliseum, plus a national television audience of 21-million, was enthralled. Many old hands said it might have been the greatest match of all time, and it was certainly the one that put tennis over as a TV sport in America. It was the closest finish of an important tourney until 1988, when Boris Becker won the Masters final over Ivan Lendl, also a 7-5 fifth-set tie-breaker.

In order to restructure its season for a spring windup, the most advantageous time for U.S. television, WCT counted the last 10 tournaments of 1971 and 10 between January and April 1972 in its point standings. Laver won the Philadelphia opener, rechristened the U.S. Pro Indoor, over Rosewall, 4-6, 6-2, 6-2, 6-2, and four more tournaments to top the point standings heading into the Dallas playoffs. Behind him were Rosewall, Tom Okker, Cliff Drysdale, Marty Riessen, Ashe, Bob Lutz and Newcombe.

Meanwhile, the 'independent pros' were playing the U.S. Tennis Association Indoor Circuit organized by Bill Riordan. Smith played only five of 13 events, but won four in a row, starting with the U.S. Indoor over Nastase, 5-7, 6-2, 6-3, 6-4. Also prominent were rookie pro Jimmy Connors—he dropped out of UCLA after becoming the first freshman to win the National Intercollegiate singles in 1971—and 'Old Wolf' Pancho Gonzalez. At 43, Pancho beat Frenchman Georges

1972 THE MAJOR CHAMPIONSHIPS

Australian Open
Men's Singles: Ken Rosewall
Women's Singles: Virginia Wade
Men's Doubles: Owen Davidson / Ken Rosewall
Women's Doubles: Kerry Harris / Helen Gourlay
French Open
Men's Singles: Andres Gimeno
Women's Singles: Billie Jean King
Men's Doubles: Bob Hewitt / Frew McMillan
Women's Doubles: Billie Jean King / Betty Stove
Mixed Doubles: Evonne Goolagong / Kim Warwick
Wimbledon
Men's Singles: Stan Smith
Women's Singles: Billie Jean King
Men's Doubles: Bob Hewitt / Frew McMillan
Women's Doubles: Billie Jean King / Betty Stove
Mixed Doubles: Rosie Casals / Ilie Nastase
U.S. Open
Men's Singles: Ilie Nastase
Women's Singles: Billie Jean King
Men's Doubles: Cliff Drysdale / Roger Taylor
Women's Doubles: Françoise Durr / Betty Stove
Mixed Doubles: Margaret Smith Court / Marty Riessen

Goven from two sets down, 3-6, 4-6, 6-3, 6-4, 6-2, to win the Des Moines Indoor. He was the oldest male title winner of the open era.

Rosewall had begun the New Year by beating 36-year-old fellow Aussie Mal Anderson, 7-6 (7-2), 6-3, 7-5 in the final of the Australian Open, the last ITF tournament open to WCT pros before the ban voted the previous July went into effect. Rosewall's last Australian championship came 19 years after his first, a unique span between major singles championships, and the final was almost the all-time antique major showdown, totaling 73 years. They topped Bill Tilden, 36, beating Frank Hunter, 35, in the U.S. final of 1929, but not Englishmen Arthur Gore, 40, over Herbert Roper Barrett, 37, in the 1908 Wimbledon championship.

Another Aussie old boy, 35-year-old Roy Emerson, saved a match point and beat Lutz, 4-6, 7-6, 6-3, to give his country the pivotal point in a 6-1 World Cup victory over the U.S. at Hartford, Conn., marked by Laver's first appearance

A contemporary of Laver and Emerson, the elegant Spaniard Andres Gimeno, nearly 35, who had left WCT to return to 'independent pro' status, won his only major singles title, taking the French Open, over surprising ninth-seeded Frenchman Patrick Proisy, 4-6, 6-3, 6-1, 6-1. Gimeno became the event's oldest champ. Proisy had ended top-seeded Jan Kodes' 17-match French winning streak and bid for a third successive title in the quarters and had eliminated fourth seeded Manolo Orantes in the semis. Bob Hewitt and Frew McMillan captured their first French doubles title, over the Chileans Jaime Fillol and Pato Cornejo, 6-3, 8-6, 6-3, 6-1 and within a month would add the Wimbledon crown, over Smith and Erik van Dillen, 6-2, 6-2, 9-7. Orantes extended the Spanish reach to Rome, winning the Italian over Kodes, 4-6, 6-1, 7-5, 6-2.

Smith, 1971 runner-up to the now disenfranchised Newcombe (who went to court to try to break the ITF ban and get a crack at a third straight title), was an overwhelming favorite at Wimbledon. The men's singles was dull until the final—the first ever played on Sunday, after a rain delay—when Smith and Nastase went after each other for five absorbing sets. It was Smith's serve-volley power and forthright resolve against Nastase's incomparable speed, agility and eccentric artistry. The fifth set was electrifying. Smith escaped two break points in the fifth game, which went to seven agonizing deuces, the first with a lunging volley off the wooden frame of his racket. Nastase brushed aside two match points on his serve at 4-5, saved another after having 40-0 at 5-6, then netted an easy, high backhand volley on match point No. 4. A scintillating triumph for Smith: 4-6, 6-3, 6-3, 4-6, 7-5.

It was a tournament dotted with strange-looking 9-8 set scores, signifying Wimbledon's reluctant acceptance of the tie-breaker (called 'tie-break' in that circle). The conservative Brits felt the set to be a better test if, in singles, each party served at least eight games before going to the radical overtime. However, by 1979 the breaker at 6-6 was certified.

Back in America, unseeded Lutz, on a wonderful run that included wins over top-seeded Newcombe and Laver, won the U.S. Pro Championship at Longwood, over 11th-seeded Okker, 6-4, 2-6, 6-1, 6-4, ending a nine-year Australian rule to become the first American champ since Butch Buchholz in 1962.

But it was the U.S. Open that commanded the most attention. Lamar Hunt, the Texas millionaire who bankrolled WCT, and Allan Heyman, the Danish-born English lawyer who was president of the ITF, had been meeting secretly throughout the winter and spring. Prompted by Americans Donald Dell and Jack Kramer, they were seeking a way to reunify the men's game. In April they reached an accord to divide the season into two segments, starting in 1973. WCT would have free reign the first four months of the year, expanding to two groups of 32 players each that would play an 11-tournament series to qualify four men from each group for the May WCT finals in Dallas. During that period, no other tournaments with more than $20,000 would be sanctioned. The last eight months of the year would belong to the ITF for its Grand Prix and Masters.

With this agreement—later modified considerably, under pressure of an antitrust suit by Riordan, who felt he had been sold down the river—the ban of WCT players from the traditional circuit was removed in July, making Forest Hills the year's only big event open to everybody. It turned out to be a wild tournament. Second-seeded Rosewall and eighth-seeded Kodes were beaten in the second round, by Mark Cox and Alex 'Sandy' Mayer, respectively. The third round saw fifth-seeded Newcombe fall to Fred Stolle and seventh-seeded Okker get drilled by Roscoe Tanner. Third-seeded Laver was removed by Cliff Richey in the fourth, while defending champ, first-seeded Smith left courtesy of Ashe in the quarters 7-6 (5-4), 7-5, 6-4, double faulting at match point.

Ashe, Richey and Tom Gorman made the semis three-quarter American for the first time in 21 years, but the lone foreigner, fourth-seeded Nastase, beat Ashe in the final to win the tournament. 'Nasty' incurred the enmity of 14,690 spectators with temper tantrums early in the final but gradually won them over with his shot-making genius. Nasty became the first European since Manolo Santana in 1965, and the first ever from Eastern Europe to triumph on the soft grass at Forest Hills, 3-6, 6-3, 6-7 (1-5), 6-4, 6-3. Roger Taylor, champ with Newcombe the year before, teamed up with Cliff Drysdale to whip Newcombe and Owen Davidson in the doubles final, 6-4, 7-6 (5-3), 6-3.

Smith sealed his No. 1 ranking in the fall, winning the Pacific Southwest Open over Tanner, 6-4, 6-4; Stockholm over Okker, 6-4, 6-3; and the Paris Indoor over Gimeno, 6-2, 6-2, 7-5. He also gave a towering performance in the Davis Cup final at Bucharest.

The Davis Cup Nations had voted in 1971 to do away with the challenge round in which the defending nation sat out and awaited a challenger to plow through zonal competitions. Thus the U.S. had to follow an unprecedented road for a defending champion—five matches, all in the foes' backyards, the last four on dreaded crimson clay. The U.S. lost but one singles match in sprinting past Commonwealth Caribbean, 4-1, Mexico, 5-0 and Chile, 5-0, to the 3-2 semi-final in Spain. It was left to Smith, the Cup stalwart for whom clinching was a specialty, to get the U.S. past Spain and into the final. Feeling more comfortable on European soil, Smith patiently beat Juan Gisbert in the deciding match, 11-9, 10-8, 6-4, ordering the tickets for the final destination. Flabbergastingly, it turned out to be Bucharest, where the home boys were unbeaten for the campaign.

Although the draw for the new Cup format gave the U.S. choice of ground for the final against Romania, the shrewd Ion Tiriac convinced USTA President Robert Colwell that the Romanians were being treated unfairly and should have that privilege since they'd played the 1969 and 1971 challenge rounds in the U.S. The U.S. team, startled and hurt that Colwell would give away the home-court edge, threatened mutiny. Dennis Ralston, ever calm, sold them on being underdogs, beating the other guys at their place.

Romania, with the brilliant Nastase and the menacing Tiriac at home on the red clay of the Progresul Sports

Club, was a heavy favorite. Nastase boasted, "We cannot lose at home"—and his record of 19 straight Cup singles victories and 13 consecutive Romanian triumphs in Bucharest seemed to support his braggadocio. Turgid clay, an adoring and vocal home crowd and notoriously patriotic line judges all favored Nastase and Tiriac.

This was the first Davis Cup finale in Europe in 39 years, and perhaps the greatest international sporting occasion ever in Bucharest, where likenesses of Nastase and Tiriac were everywhere. But the pressure of great expectations worked in reverse. Smith played undoubtedly his finest match on clay, while Nastase was high-strung and erratic as the American took the critical opener, 11-9, 6-2, 6-3. Tiriac, the brooding former ice hockey international who claims kinship with Dracula, used every ploy of gamesmanship, orchestrating the crowd and the linesmen, to come from two sets down and beat Gorman, 4-6, 2-6, 6-4, 6-3, 6-2, in the second match. The doubles, however, was a Romanian disaster.

Once one of the world's premier teams (22-4 in Cup play), Nastase and Tiriac had fallen out as friends, and their incompatibility showed as Smith and van Dillen, playing with skill and élan, humiliated the home team, 6-2, 6-0, 6-3. Tiriac summoned all his wiles and battled fiercely, as though his life depended on it, in the fourth match. Despite numerous pro-Tiriac officiating calls, Smith, knowing he had to hit winners inside the lines, was too good for Ion. He clinched the Cup, 4-6, 6-2, 6-4, 2-6, 6-0, saying he had a headache from concentrating. No Yank abroad in Davis Cup has ever done better.

It had been a wild weekend in Bucharest, made unforgettable by the fervor of the fans, the thievery of the linesmen, the machinations of Tiriac, and extraordinarily heavy security in the aftermath of the Olympic massacre at Munich. (There had been rumors of threats against two Jewish members of the U.S. squad, Harold Solomon and Brian Gottfried.) But in the end, Capt. Ralston's brigade, inspired by Ralston's calm in the caul-dron, could savor the finest victory ever by a U.S. team away from home.

A footnote to the Cup that year was the debut of a 15-year-old for Sweden. Bjorn Borg, a comeback winner over New Zealand's Onny Parun, 4-6, 3-6, 6-3, 6-4, 6-4, during a 4-1 victory, would lead his homeland to the Cup in 1975.

Once again there were separate playoffs for 'contract pros' and 'independents' at the end of the year. WCT scheduled a makeshift 'winter championship' in Rome for the top eight men in a summer-fall circuit that filled the gap before a new two-group format started in 1973. Ashe won the $25,000 first prize, beating Nikki Pilic, 7-6, 6-1, Okker, 6-7 (9-11), 6-3, 6-3, and Lutz, 6-2, 3-6, 6-3, 3-6, 7-6 (7-2).

The Commercial Union Masters was played in Barcelona with the new format—two four-man round-robin groups, with the two players with the best records in each advancing to a 'knockout' semis and final. Gorman had Smith beaten, holding a match point, 7-6, 6-7, 7-5, 5-4, 40-30 in one semi. But Tom, having hurt his back, sportingly defaulted (at 2:35 a.m.) so as not to wreck the final. Nastase, a 6-2, 6-3, 6-2, semi-final victor over Connors, repeated as champion, beating Smith in a rousing final, 6-3, 6-2, 3-6, 2-6, 6-3, pocketing $15,000. But it was his only victory in five meetings on the year with the tall Californian. Gorman was given a sportsmanship bonus of $2,500 for letting the show go on in the final.

One of the most significant developments of 1972 was the formation, at the U.S. Open, of a new players' guild, ATP (Association of Tennis Professionals). Some 50 players paid $400 initial dues, and Washington attorney Donald Dell, a former U.S. Davis Cup captain and personal manager for a number of top players, enlisted Kramer as executive director. The urbane Drysdale was elected president and Dell became the Association's legal counsel. Other players' associations had come and gone in the past, but the ATP was carefully constituted and loomed as a major new force in the pro game's politics and administration.

The politics of women's tennis in 1972 began with conciliation and ended with a new rift.

Early in the year Gladys Heldman, organizer of the rebel women's pro tour the year before, was appointed by the USTA as coordinator of women's tennis and director of the women's tour in a peace effort. Thus empowered, she expanded the winter tour to $302,000 in prize

---

1972 CHAMPIONS AND LEADERS

Top Player Earnings: Men	**Wightman Cup:** United States
Ilie Nastase $176,000	**Grand Prix Masters, Barcelona**
Top Player Earnings: Women	Ilie Nastase
Billie Jean King $119,000	**WCT, Dallas**
Year-End Number One	Ken Rosewall
Men: Stan Smith	**Virginia Slims**
Women: Billie Jean King	**Championships, Boca Raton**
Davis Cup: United States	Chris Evert
Federation Cup: South Africa	

money. But by September the honeymoon was over. Heldman resigned her USTA post amid mutual mistrust and formed the WITF (Women's International Tennis Federation). She took the USTA to court for alleged antitrust violations. Meanwhile, the USTA appointed U.S. Wightman Cup captain, Edy McGoldrick, to form a women's tour in opposition to Heldman's in the winter-spring of 1973.

On the tennis court, there was no question who was boss in 1972. King did not play the Australian Open, but swept the rest of the major singles titles with the loss of only one set, to Virginia Wade in the quarter-finals (6-1, 3-6, 6-3) at Wimbledon. Billie Jean won 10 of 24 tournaments, compiled an 87-13 record, ran away with the women's Grand Prix top prize, and exceeded her prize money landmark of 1971, earning $119,000. Against her greatest career rivals, she was 3-2 over Margaret Smith Court (back on the circuit after the birth of her first child, Daniel) and 4-3 over Nancy Richey Gunter for the year.

Wade won her first major, the Australian, over Evonne Goolagong, 6-4, 6-4. King won her seventh, the French, over Goolagong, 6-3, 6-3, thus joining Doris Hart, Maureen Connolly, Shirley Fry and Court as the only women to have won all four major singles titles. (They would be joined by Chris Evert in 1982, Martina Navratilova in 1983, Steffi Graf in 1988 and Serena Williams in 2003). BJK also dethroned Goolagong, 6-3, 6-3, at Wimbledon after Evonne had thrillingly won her first meeting with debutante Evert in the semis, 4-6, 6-3, 6-4. King had beaten Rosie Casals, 6-2, 6-4.

At the U.S. Open, King beat Wade in the quarters, 6-2, 7-5; Court in the semis, 6-4, 6-4; and, for the title and $10,000, Kerry Melville, 6-3. 7-5. Aussie Kerry had ripped Evert, in the semis, 6-4, 6-2, by skidding clever slices short, low and wide to Chrissie's two-fisted backhand.

Imposing six-foot Dutchwoman Betty Stove was the woman of the year in doubles, teaming with King to win the French (over Brits Winnie Shaw and Christine Truman Janes, 6-1, 6-2) and Wimbledon (over Judy Dalton and Francoise Durr, 6-2, 4-6, 6-3). Then she took up with Durr to seize the U.S., over Court and Wade, 6-3, 1-6, 6-3, the first woman to win all three in a season since Darlene Hard and Maria Bueno in 1960.

Evert, still an amateur at age 17, was the only player with a winning record over King for the year, 3-1,

including a 6-1, 6-0 victory in the final of the Virginia Slims tournament in her hometown of Fort Lauderdale. She also won the richest women's tournament, the inaugural season-ending $100,000 Virginia Slims Championship at Boca Raton, Fla., a climactic gathering of the 'Little Broads,' as Heldman called the Long Way Babies.

Chrissie beat King, 6-4, 6-2, and Melville, 7-5, 6-4, in the final two rounds. But Chrissie couldn't accept the $25,000 first prize. Amateurism was costly, but Colette and Jimmy Evert, her parents, wouldn't let her become a working woman until she had a high school diploma. The millions would come.

Chrissie, 47-7 on the year and winner of four tournaments, spearheaded the 5-2 U.S. Wightman Cup victory over Great Britain at Wimbledon, beating Wade, 6-4, 6-4, and Joyce Williams, 6-2, 6-3, and sharing a doubles win with Patti Hogan over Nell Truman and Shaw, 7-5, 6-4. Soon after Evert beat Court 6-3, 6-3, and Goolagong, 6-1, 6-3 for the only two U.S. victories in a 5-2 loss to Australia in the inaugural Bonne Bell Cup (U.S. vs Australia) at Cleveland. Evert also won her first adult national title—the first of four consecutive U.S. Clay Court singles at Indianapolis—by beating Court in the semis, 6-3, 7-6, and Goolagong in the final, 7-6, 6-1.

The Maureen Connolly Brinker Indoor at Dallas was the first tournament in which both Goolagong and Evert competed, but King delayed their first meeting. She fought off a 1-3, 15-40 deficit and later cramps in the final set to beat Evert in the quarters, 6-7, 6-3, 7-5, and came from behind again to beat Goolagong in the semis, 1-6, 6-4, 6-1. Exhausted, she fell easily to unseeded Gunter in the final, 7-6, 6-1.

The magical first encounter between the two radiant new princesses of women's tennis came, appropriately, in the semis at Wimbledon. It was a majestic match worthy of the occasion, Goolagong winning, 4-6, 6-3, 6-4, after trailing 0-3 in the second and 2-3 (down a break) in the third. Evert promptly won their next two meetings, however, setting the tone for their career rivalry.

The Virginia Slims circuit continued to grow, offering $525,775 in prize purses for 21 tournaments, but the appeal of Evert and Goolagong—they couldn't be enticed by Heldman to side with her in a war against the ITF establishment—made them the cornerstones of the rival USTA circuit in 1973.

1973

Battle of Sexes a romp for Billie Jean

A questionable Centennial was celebrated throughout tennis in 1973. It commemorated the then-accepted, but subsequently disproved, theory of the origin of the modern sport at a shooting party in Wales. Supposedly Major Walter Clopton Wingfield introduced the game he later patented in 1874. Perhaps that misplaced celebration was fitting, considering that 1973 was the game's most peculiar year, one that embraced unprecedented labor strife, a boycott of Wimbledon by most of the foremost guys.

The landmark match of the year did not come in any of the traditional major tournaments. There was nothing traditional at all about the celebrated 'Battle of the Sexes' between 29-year-old Billie Jean King and 55-year-old Bobby Riggs, the self-proclaimed 'King of male chauvinist pigs,' at Houston's Astrodome the night of September 20. But this spectacle—roughly equal parts tennis, carnival, and sociological phenomenon—captured the fancy of America as no pure tennis match ever had. The crowd of 30,472, paying as much as $100 a seat, was the largest ever to witness a tennis match. Some 50 million more watched on prime-time television. The whole gaudy promotion was worth supposedly $3 million, and King collected a $100,000 alleged winner-take-all purse, plus ancillary revenues, for squashing Riggs, 6-4, 6-3, 6-3. He got a big chunk of cash, too.

Riggs, the outspoken hustler who had won Wimbledon and U.S. Championships in 1939, created the bonanza by a challenge proclaiming that women's lib was a farce and that the best of the female tennis pros couldn't even beat him, "an old man with one foot in the grave." He challenged Margaret Smith Court to a winner-take-all challenge match on Mother's Day at a California resort he was plugging in Ramona. She was the ideal victim for his well-perfected 'psych job' and assortment of junk shots, including lobs into the sun at high noon. Margaret

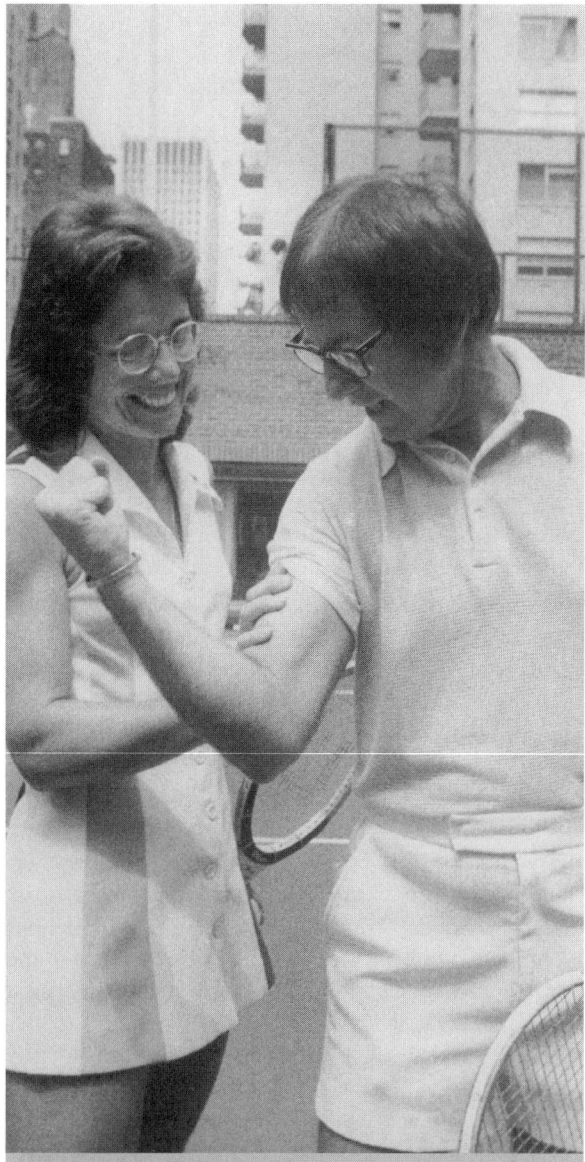

Billie Jean King, Bobby Riggs
Testing Bobby Riggs' biceps before shattering his male chauvinist ego.

choked and Riggs won, 6-2, 6-1. That set the stage for the haranguing challenge against Billie Jean, the leading voice of women's lib in sports. The whole ballyhooed extravaganza was just right for the times, and it became a national media event, front-page news in papers and magazines across the country, even the world. King exulted in her victory, not as a great competitive triumph but as "a culmination" of her years of striving to demonstrate that tennis could be big-league entertainment for the masses, and that women could play.

Tennis was clearly the 'in' sport of the mid-'70s. Sales of tennis equipment, clothing and vacations were burgeoning, and though the pro game remained plagued with disputes—notably a boycott of Wimbledon by the men's Association of Tennis Professionals and an antitrust suit in women's tennis—it continued to grow quickly. Prize money in 1973 rose to nearly $6 million.

World Championship Tennis introduced the new format agreed to in its 1972 accord with the International Lawn Tennis Federation: A January-through-May series with a field of 64 players split into two groups of 32, playing parallel tours of 11, $50,000 tournaments. The top four men of each group (Stan Smith, Rod Laver, Roy Emerson and John Alexander of 'A'; Ken Rosewall, Arthur Ashe, Marty Riessen and Roger Taylor of 'B') went to Dallas for the $100,000 final.

Smith, who had won four consecutive tournaments and six of 11 to top Laver (three victories) in his group, took the $50,000 top prize by beating Ashe, 6-3, 6-3, 4-6, 6-4. Ashe had ended Rosewall's bid for a third straight Dallas title in a five-set semi, 6-4, 6-2, 5-7, 1-6, 6-2, and Smith waylaid Laver, 4-6, 6-4, 7-6, 7-5. For the first time, WCT also conducted a doubles competition, using the same format as singles. Smith and Bob Lutz won the $40,000 first prize in the playoffs at Montreal, beating Riessen and Tom Okker, 6-2, 7-6, 6-0.

Running concurrently with the WCT tour for three months was the U.S. Tennis Association Indoor Circuit of Bill Riordan, who refused to be dealt out by the WCT-International Tennis Federation deal dividing the season, and threatened restraint-of-trade proceedings if forced to limit the prize money in his tournaments. His headliners were Jimmy Connors and Ilie Nastase, both of whom he managed at the time. Connors won six of the eight events he played, including the U.S. Indoor over German Karl Meiler, 3-6, 7-6, 7-6, 6-3.

John Newcombe started the year by winning his first Australian Open title over New Zealander Onny Parun,

6-3, 6-7, 7-5, 6-1. Onny was the first Kiwi in a major final since Harry Parker, loser of the Aussie to Ernest Parker in 1913. Newcombe also shared the doubles with countryman Mal Anderson, over Phil Dent and Alexander, 6-3, 6-4. 7-6. Newcombe won the French doubles, too, with Okker, over Connors and Nastase, 6-1, 3-6, 6-3, 5-7, 6-4, but slumped badly until rededicating himself late in the year, winning the U.S. Open and teaming with Laver to return the Davis Cup to Australia in the first year it was open to 'contract pros.'

On balance, the No. 1 ranking had to go to Nastase, the volatile Romanian (he accumulated fines totaling $11,000) who won 15 of 31 tournaments, 118 of 135 matches, and led the money earning list with $228,750, including a $55,000 bonus for topping the Grand Prix standings. He manhandled Manuel Orantes in the most one-sided Italian Open final, 6-1, 6-1, 6-1; swept through the French Open without losing a set (Niki Pilic was his final victim, 6-3, 6-3, 6-0), and won the Masters for the third straight year, beating Newcombe in the round-robin, 7-5, 6-3, and personal nemesis Okker in the final, 6-3, 7-5, 4-6, 6-3, at Boston.

Defender Andres Gimeno wasn't around long in Paris, pushed from the second round by young Argentine lefty, Guillermo Vilas, 6-2, 5-7, 8-6. Tom Gorman evicted two-time champ Jan Kodes, 6-4, 7-6 (8-6), 4-6, 6-1, to reach the semis where Nastase trimmed him, 6-3, 6-4, 6-1. Adriano Panatta, beaten by Pilic in the semis, 6-4, 6-3, 6-1, had halted the surge of Swedish novitiate, Bjorn Borg, 7-6, 2-6, 7-5, 7-6. The

1973 THE MAJOR CHAMPIONSHIPS

Australian Open
Men's Singles: John Newcombe
Women's Singles: Margaret Smith Court
Men's Doubles: Mal Anderson / John Newcombe
Women's Doubles: Margaret Smith Court / Virginia Wade
French Open
Men's Singles: Ilie Nastase
Women's Singles: Margaret Smith Court
Men's Doubles: John Newcombe / Tom Okker
Women's Doubles: Margaret Smith Court / Virginia Wade
Mixed Doubles: Françoise Durr / Jean Claude Barclay
Wimbledon
Men's Singles: Jan Kodes
Women's Singles: Billie Jean King
Men's Doubles: Jimmy Connors / Ilie Nastase
Women's Doubles: Rosie Casals / Billie Jean King
Mixed Doubles: Billie Jean Moffitt King / Owen Davidson
U.S. Open
Men's Singles: John Newcombe
Women's Singles: Margaret Smith Court
Men's Doubles: Owen Davidson / John Newcombe
Women's Doubles: Margaret Smith Court / Virginia Wade
Mixed Doubles: Billie Jean King / Owen Davidson

cool kid with blond tresses and a blowout mentality, had baselined his way past the experienced Cliff Richey, 6-2, 6-3, Pierre Barthes, 3-6, 6-1, 8-6, and Dick Stockton, 6-7, 7-5, 6-2, 7-6, and would carry off a record six championships by 1981.

Nastase played indifferently at Wimbledon, where he was considered a shoo-in because of the boycott, but was beaten in the fourth round by National Intercollegiate champ Alex 'Sandy' Mayer of Stanford, and at Forest Hills, where Andrew Pattison ambushed him in the second round. But his overall record was the best.

The No. 1 U.S. men's ranking was shared for the only time in history. The ranking committee could not choose between Smith, who won eight of 19 tournaments and 81 of 103 matches but lost his world-beating form after peaking in May, and Connors, who won 10 of 21 tournaments and 81 of 97 matches, sensationally capturing the U.S. Pro and South African, both over Ashe.

Connors, just 20, was the brightest of several ascending youngsters, including Borg and Brian Gottfried (winner of the $30,000 first prize at the ATP's Alan King Classic in Las Vegas, over Ashe, 6-1, 6-3). Connors was the youngest man atop the American rankings since one of his mentors, Pancho Gonzalez, ruled at 20 in 1948, and Smith was the first to be No. 1 four times since Bill Tilden gained the top spot for the 10th time in 1929.

Brimming with confidence after his fine showing on the less-strenuous-than-WCT U.S. Indoor circuit, Connors scattered seeds all over Boston in the U.S. Pro. First he knocked off top-seeded Smith, and went on to whip Ray Moore, sixth-seeded Stockton, fifth-seeded Richey, and second-seeded Ashe.

He saved a match point in beating Smith again at the Pacific Southwest, 3-6, 6-4, 7-6 in the quarters—proceeding to win the title over Okker, 7-5, 7-6—and escaped two match points in beating out Smith, 6-0, 3-6, 7-6 (8-6) for a semi-final berth in the Grand Prix Masters. That gave him a 3-0 record against Stan for the

calendar year. Smith was the only player to reach both the WCT and Masters playoffs.

The already turbulent political waters in tennis were roiled further by formation of a league called World Team Tennis, which planned to start intercity team competition using a unique, Americanized format in 1974. Dennis Murphy, who had helped found the American Basketball Association and the World Hockey Association, envisioned 16 teams with six players apiece (men and women) under contract competing in a May-through-August season.

Jack Kramer and the ATP board came out staunchly opposed to WTT, saying it would harm the long-range players' interest in a healthy worldwide tournament circuit. But even as discussions between the ITF and ATP about team tennis were scheduled, a more immediate problem arose. When ATP member Pilic was suspended by the Yugoslav Tennis Federation for failing to participate in a Davis Cup series in New Zealand, to which he had allegedly committed himself, ATP members objected. They protested that this was precisely the sort of arbitrary disciplinary power by a national association that the formation of players' association was meant to counteract. An ATP threat to withdraw all its 70 members from the French Open if Pilic was barred from the tournament was averted by a delaying tactic, an appeal hearing before the ITF Emergency Committee, which reduced Pilic's suspension from three months to one month.

This did not satisfy the ATP board, which contended that only their own association should have disciplinary authority over players. Many also felt that the one-month suspension, which included Wimbledon, was devised by the ITF to demonstrate its muscle because it believed the players would never support a boycott of the world's premier tournament. Thus 'the Pilic Affair' became a test of the will and organization of the new association. Many ATP leaders felt that if they gave in on this first showdown, they would never be strong, whereas if they held firm and proved to the ITF that even Wimbledon was not sacred, the ATP's unity and power would never be doubted in the future.

After days of tortuous meetings and attempts to find compromises, including the ATP's seeking an injunction in Britain's High Court forcing the All England Club to accept Pilic's entry, ATP members voted to withdraw en masse if Pilic were barred from Wimbledon. Seventy-nine men did withdraw their entries, including 13 of the

---

1973 CHAMPIONS AND LEADERS

Top Player Earnings: Men	**Wightman Cup:** United States
Ilie Nastase $228,750	**Grand Prix Masters, Boston**
Top Player Earnings: Women	Ilie Nastase
Margaret Smith Court $204,400	**WCT, Dallas**
Year-End Number One	Stan Smith
Men: Ilie Nastase	**Virginia Slims**
Women: Margaret Smith Court	**Championships, Boca Raton**
Davis Cup: Australia	Chris Evert
Federation Cup: Australia	

original 16 seeds. Nastase, Englishman Roger Taylor and Australian Ray Keldie were the only members who did not withdraw. (They were later fined by the ATP.)

Amid ferocious English press criticism and bitterness, the tournament was played with a second-rate men's field. The British public, taking up the press crusade that "Wimbledon is bigger than a few spoiled players," turned out in near-record numbers. They made heroes of Nastase, Taylor and such attractive newcomers as Connors and Swedish teenager Borg, who, in long blond locks, became the immediate heartthrob of squealing British schoolgirls.

Borg, destined to become the 'Angelic Assassin' of Centre Court with five straight titles (1976-80), made his debut on that sacred sod memorable for the fact that he and Indian Premjit Lall engaged in the longest singles tie-breaker in a major championship. As it grew and grew and grew like Jack's beanstalk, to a 38th point climax, the scene was punctuated by much laughter from spectators. It was only the beginning of Wimbledon's second year of tie-breaking, and nobody had witnessed such an elongated passage. Borg, Lall and court officials, especially the traveling service line judge, shared the confusion. At last, after Lall had saved seven match points and had six set points himself, it ended at 20-18, and Borg had his first Wimbledon win, 6-3, 6-4, 9-8 (20-18).

Nastase, an overwhelming favorite, was beaten at the end of the first week by constantly attacking Mayer, 6-4, 8-6, 6-8, 6-4. Sandy went on to reach the semi-finals, losing to the Soviet Georgian Alex Metreveli, 6-3, 3-6, 6-3, 6-4. Kodes became the first Czech champ since expatriate Jaroslav Drobny in 1954, beating Metreveli, 6-1, 9-8 (7-5), 6-3, in a predictably uninspiring final.

Left-handed semi-finalist, Yorkshireman Taylor, conqueror of Laver in 1970, was probably the best equipped to win, but the pressure on a homeboy to end the interminable post-Fred Perry drought was fiercer than ever. Not only did the Brits yearn for a champ of their own but they wanted Roger to upstage the boycott. Added pressure of disapproval came from his lodge brothers, whom he didn't join in the walkout. He wasn't quite up to it, falling to Kodes in five, 8-9, 9-7, 5-7, 6-4, 7-5. Kodes' quarter was tight, too, 6-4, 3-6, 4-6, 6-3, 7-5, over tall and stylish Indian 19-year-old Vijay Amritraj, who nearly served-and-volleyed him off the lawn. Connors, beaten by Metreveli, 8-6, 6-2, 5-7, 6-4, paired with Nastase as they clowned their way through five sets to win the doubles title over Australians John Cooper

and ex-champ, 39-year-old Neale Fraser, 3-6, 6-3, 6-4, 8-9 (3-7), 6-1.

Meanwhile, with Wimbledon sacrificed for one year, the U.S. Open became the men's most important competitive test of 1973, luring record attendance, 137,488, and crowds of 15,137 and 15,241 on the last two days.

Defender Nastase, co-seeded No.1 with Smith, squandered a two-set lead and lost to Rhodesian journeyman Pattison in the second round, 6-7, 2-6, 6-3, 6-4, 6-4. Kodes, who resented being downgraded as a 'cheese champion' at Wimbledon, returned serve spectacularly in going all the way to the final, saving a match point at nightfall to outstroke Smith, 7-5, 6-7 (4-5), 1-6, 6-1, 7-5, in the semi-finals. Jan almost repeated his 1971 upset over Newcombe, this time in the final instead of the first round. But the rugged Australian ultimately had too much firepower and won a spectacular finale, 6-4, 1-6, 4-6, 6-2, 6-3. Newcombe and Owen Davidson beat countrymen Laver and Rosewall in the doubles final, 7-5, 2-6, 7-5, 7-5.

Even though they'd been away from Davis Cup for a long time in the wilderness of professionalism, each artifact in Capt. Neale Fraser's 'Antique Show'—Rosewall, 38, Anderson, 38, Laver, 35, Newcombe, 29—made solid contributions in victories over Japan, India, Czechoslovakia and the U.S. that restored the silver tub to Australia. They may have been the greatest quartet assembled for such a purpose, born again, as though they'd been dug up within a time capsule: Laver absent for 10 campaigns, Rosewall 16, Anderson 14, Newcombe five. Laver decided late in autumn to be part of it. He won all six of his matches as an integral figure in the team world championship, his fifth, tacked onto 1959-60-61-62.

The final was in Cleveland and it was quite different from the finals these Aussie relics had known, on grass, in summer sunshine either at Forest Hills or home, Down Under. In the Cup's first indoor final (virtually the rule these days), before disappointing crowds totaling about 10,000 for three days at Cleveland's Public Auditorium, the Aussies smashed the five year U.S. grasp on the Cup, 5-0, a stranglehold that covered a record 17 straight series, dating to 1968.

Newcombe set the mood by beating Smith in the opener, 6-1, 3-6, 6-3, 3-6, 6-4. Artistically, this might well have been the match of the year. Newcombe—an enforced absentee from Davis Cup since 1967—came back from 1-3 and a break point in the fifth set with some sublime play, featuring thoughtful baselining to go with his volleying. Amid volleying fireworks of the second match, Laver beat Gorman, 8-10, 8-6, 6-8, 6-3, 6-1, then surprisingly teamed with Newcombe to pummel Smith and Erik van Dillen in the decisive doubles, 6-1, 6-2, 6-4.

At year's end, the ATP board remained opposed to World Team Tennis and to guaranteed contracts for players—a stance it was forced to reverse the next year, under growing pressure from members who wanted to accept guarantees. WTT named former U.S. Davis Cup captain George MacCall as its commissioner, announced that it would begin operations in May 1974, and signed such prominent players as Newcombe, Rosewall, King and Evonne Goolagong to lucrative contracts.

On the women's side, two separate tours were played in the winter and spring of 1973. The Virginia Slims Circuit of 14 events, starring King and Margaret Smith Court, was conducted under the auspices of the Women's International Tennis Federation (WITF), incorporated as an autonomous body by Gladys Heldman. The USTA—claiming that it had been hoodwinked and double-crossed by Heldman—hastily arranged a circuit of eight tournaments featuring Chris Evert, Goolagong and Virginia Wade.

Noticed by no one but the two players themselves was a first-round match at Akron, a 7-6 (5-4), 6-3, win by Evert (the tournament victor) over a chubby Czech named Martina Navratilova. That initial meeting was merely the first step in the lustrous rivalry that was to run for 80 encounters over 16 years. Evert beat Olga Morozova, 6-3, 6-4, in the final.

In Heldman's suit against the USTA in Federal District Court in New York, Judge Milton Pollack ruled against her, rendering the WITF short-lived. The players who signed with WITF were declared ineligible for the 1973 Commercial Union Grand Prix (won by Evert), but by June an agreement was reached between the USTA and Philip Morris, Inc., parent company of Virginia Slims, for a single women's tour under USTA/ITF auspices starting in September 1973. Part of the compromise was that Heldman would not be involved.

Out of the wreckage of the WITF, a new women players' guild, the WTA (Women's Tennis Association) was formed at Wimbledon. With King as its first president, the WTA worked closely with the USTA's Edy McGoldrick in organizing a strong women's circuit for 1974 and beyond.

It is ironic that, because of Bobby Riggs, 1973 will be remembered as the year of Court's humiliation and King's triumph. In fact, Court was the dominant player of the season winner of the Australian, French, and U.S. Opens (her third year of taking three majors). Bagging, 18 of 25 tournaments, and $204,000 in prize money, the female high, she hadn't been beaten since a loss to Jeanne Evert in Boca Raton the previous fall, a streak of 59. For the calendar year her record was 102-6. She beat King in three of four meetings.

Court started the year by beating Goolagong in the Australian Open final for the third consecutive year, 6-4, 7-5. She then teamed with Wade to win the doubles for the eighth time in 13 years, with her sixth different partner, over two Kerry's—Harris and Melville—neither of whom could carry the other, 6-4, 6-4.

Court was down 3-5, second set, in the final of the French, and two points from defeat, but recovered to beat Evert, 6-7 (5-7), 7-6 (8-6), 6-4. It was her fifth French, topping Helen Wills's title collection (1928-29-30, 32), and would remain the record for a dozen years until the same Evert won a sixth in 1985 (and a seventh a year later). A battle of torrid groundstroking was waged by, Margaret and Chris, the most memorable women's match of the year. Court also won her fourth French doubles title, with Wade, over Françoise Durr and Betty Stove, 6-2, 6-3.

Only Wimbledon prevented Court from recording a second Grand Slam. All eight seeds advanced to the quarter-finals, and the only reversal of form was fourth-seeded Evert's 6-1, 1-6, 6-1 defeat of top-seeded Court in the semis. This was unexpected, as much so as grass-loving Margaret beating clay maven Chrissie in Paris. King, superbly conditioned physically and mentally and operating at a high emotional pitch, beat Goolagong in the volley-happy semi-finals, 6-3, 5-7, 6-3, and blasted Evert in the final, 6-0, 7-5. BJK became the first five-time singles winner since Helen Wills Moody four decades earlier and also teamed with Rosie Casals to win the doubles, over Durr and Stove, 6-1, 4-6, 7-5—B.J.'s ninth, fifth alongside Rosie. Calling on Davidson for a helping left hand, B.J. fashioned her second triple at the Big W, winning a second mixed, 6-3, 6-2, over Mexican Raul Ramirez and Californian Janet Newberry.

At the U.S. Open, the icon, 1971-72 champion, King, fell off her pedestal momentarily. She quit her title defense, walking out while trailing Julie Heldman, 1-4, in the final set of a fourth round match played in exhausting heat and humidity. Heldman complained, her right under the rules, that King was taking far more than the one minute allowed at changeovers. "If you want the match that badly, you can have it," seethed King, who later said she was suffering from a virus that had sapped her strength.

Court beating Wade in two tie-breakers in the quarter-finals, 7-6, 7-6 (5-2), avenged her Wimbledon defeat by Evert, 7-5, 2-6, 6-2, in the semis, and made Goolagong a bridesmaid again in the final, 7-6 (5-2), 5-7, 6-2. For her victory Margaret received $25,000, the same as Newcombe, since the women achieved prize money parity with men in a major championship for the first time. The singles triumph was her record 24th major and last in a Big Four event. Court teamed with Wade for Court's 18th major doubles title, this over Casals and King, 3-6, 6-3, 7-5.

King, despite being hampered by injuries in the early season, won eight of 19 tournaments and 58 of 68 matches. Including her $100,000 triumph over Riggs, she earned $197,000 for the year. In taking the No. 1 U.S. ranking for the seventh time, she equaled a feat previously achieved only by Molla Mallory (between 1915 and 1926) and Moody (between 1923 and 1931).

Evert, having turned pro on her 18th birthday, December 21, 1972, earned $151,352 in her (financial) rookie season. She virtually monopolized the USTA winter tour, winning six of seven tournaments, beating Goolagong in the final of the last three. Evert went on to win 12 of 21 tournaments, 88 of 98 matches, including the Virginia Slims Championship at Boca Raton on clay over her personal nemesis, Nancy Richey Gunter, 6-3, 6-3. Though disappointed to lose three big finals in a row at midseason—the Italian Open to Goolagong, 7-6 (8-6), 6-0, the French to Court, and Wimbledon to King—Chrissie took her first significant international title in the autumn, the South African Open over Goolagong, 6-3, 6-3. Shortly after this tournament, flashing a South African diamond, she announced her engagement to Connors, later called off.

Evert also led the U.S. to a 5-2 victory over a young and, except for Wade, inexperienced British team in the Wightman Cup. As the 50th anniversary of the competition, it was played at Longwood Cricket Club, only yards from the home of Cup donor Hazel Hotchkiss Wightman, who was present and active in the celebrations at age 86. Chrissie beat Wade, 6-4, 6-2, and

Veronica Burton, 6-3, 6-0. Her kid sister, Jeannie, shared a doubles win with Patti Hogan over Lindsey Beaven and Lesley Charles, 6-3, 4-6, 8-6.

Court wasn't available, but Goolagong and Patti Coleman, a five-footer, got the Federation Cup job done for Australia. In the final at Bad Homburg, Germany, Goolagong beat Pat Pretorius Walkden, 6-0, 6-2, and Coleman wore down Brenda Kirk, 10-8, 6-0, in a 3-0 triumph over South Africa. Goolagong's 6-4, 6-3 victory over Evert and Melville's triumph over Heldman, 2-6, 6-1, 6-4, spearheaded an Australian comeback and 6-3 victory over the U.S. in the second Bonne Bell Cup, at Sydney.

Other notable happenings during the year: Casals took the biggest check, $30,000, for winning the new Family Circle Cup at Hilton Head, S.C., the first tourney to offer a purse of $100,000 to the women. Goolagong beat Evert in the final of the Western Championships at Cincinnati, 6-2, 7-5, Chris' last defeat on clay for nearly six years. Evert won her second U.S. Clay Court title the next week over Burton, 6-4, 6-3, beginning an astounding streak on her favorite surface that would stretch to 25 tournaments and 125 matches (including the only three U.S. Opens played on clay) until her defeat by Tracy Austin in the Italian Open semi-finals in May 1979.

Floridian Kathy Kuykendall turned pro at age 16, and then Californian Robin Tenney did her one better, becoming the youngest pro to date at age 15. However, three years later, having been unsuccessful on the tour, she applied for and was granted a return to amateur status in order to play college tennis

Previously denied a visa to South Africa because of his anti-apartheid views and statements, Ashe made an emotional pilgrimage to that country in November, becoming the only 'non-white' male to win a South African title. That was the doubles with Okker over Lew Hoad and Rob Maud, 6-2, 4-6, 6-2, 6-4. Connors was too strong for him in the singles final, 6-4, 7-6, (7-3), 6-3. Evert's title made it a lovebird sweep for the couple. Goolagong had hurdled the color bar on entrants in 1971, followed in 1972 by minor players Wanaro n'Godrella, a black Frenchman from New Caledonia, and Bonnie Logan, a black American. Logan was a first-round loser. But Ashe, playing an exhibition in Soweto, and meeting with political leaders, white and black, was widely covered, making a distinct impact.

1974

Tennis, Jimbo exploding together

Jimmy Connors, Chris Evert
Engagement lasted through Wimbledon, but was history by year's end.

Two young Americans—21-year-old Jimmy Connors and 19-year-old Chris Evert, who had announced their engagement late in 1973 but called it off before getting to the altar the next fall—reigned as the king and queen of tennis in 1974. And as the American game celebrated its centennial, two startling surveys revealed just how popular the game had become in the United States.

The respected A.C. Nielsen Company made its first survey of tennis in 1970, estimating that 10.3 million Americans played occasionally and projecting that the number would increase to 15 million by 1980. A second survey in 1973 indicated that the growth rate was much faster, and fixed the number of players at 20.2 million. A third study, released in September 1974, indicated a staggering 68 percent increase to 33.9 million Americans who said they played tennis 'from time to time,' and a more significant estimate that 23.4 million played at least three times a month.

Almost as surprising as the rate of the participation boom was a Louis Harris survey that indicated a substantial rise in tennis' popularity as a spectator sport. "The number [of sports fans] who say they 'follow' tennis has risen from 17 to 26 percent just in the last year, by far the most dramatic change in American sports preferences," the Harris organization said. This growth was reflected in the tennis industry, as new companies rushed in to offer a dizzying variety of equipment to the burgeoning market, and in the professional game, where prize money continued to skyrocket. Four men and one woman exceeded the $200,000 prize money barrier, which had seemed unattainable just a few years earlier. Connors ($281,309) and Evert ($261,460) led the parade of six-figure earners.

Connors rampaged to the most successful season of any American man since Tony Trabert in 1955, and also became the center of a new political storm in men's tennis.

Connors won 99 out of 103 matches during the year, 15 of 21 tournaments, including the Australian Open, Wimbledon, U.S. Open, U.S. Indoor, U.S. Clay Court and South African Open. He was denied a chance at the Grand Slam when the French Tennis Federation, then led by the strong-willed Philippe Chatrier, barred any player who had signed a contract to compete in the new World Team Tennis league in the U.S., which Europeans viewed as a threat to their summer tournaments.

Thus Connors, who had signed to play some matches with the World Team Tennis Baltimore Banners, and Evonne Goolagong, contracted to the Pittsburgh Triangles, were kept out of the world's premier clay court championship after having won the Australian at the start of the year. Bill Riordan, the maverick Connors' maverick manager, knew there was no way he could sue the French Federation directly, but filed a $40 million antitrust suit against Association of Tennis Professionals officers Jack Kramer and Donald Dell, who had been anti-WTT activists, and Commercial Union Assurance, sponsor of the International Tennis Federation Grand Prix, alleging a conspiracy to monopolize professional tennis and keep Connors (and other WTT players) out of the French.

Few envisioned what a world-beating year it would be for the brash left-hander Connors when he beat Australian Phil Dent, 7-6 (9-7), 6-4, 4-6, 6-3, for the Australian title. His chief rival, John Newcombe, fell in the quarters, 7-6, 6-2, 7-5, to Ross 'Snake' Case, who couldn't slither past Dent, 6-4, 6-1, 2-6, 6-2. Aussies Geoff Masters and Case took the doubles at Kooyong in Melbourne, their first major title, beating countrymen Syd Ball and Bob Giltinan, 6-7, 6-3, 6-4.

Connors dominated Riordan's U.S. Tennis Association Indoor Circuit—played at the same time as an expanded, three-group WCT tour—winning seven of the nine tournaments he played. That included the U.S. Indoor, his second of a record seven such titles, over Frew McMillan, 6-4, 7-5, 6-3.

At Wimbledon, Connors came within two points of defeat at the hands of Dent in the second round, but pulled away to win from 5-6, 0-30 in the fifth set, 5-7, 6-3, 3-6, 6-3, 10-8. He beat defending champ Jan Kodes in five rugged sets, a quarter-final, 3-6, 6-3, 6-3, 6-8, 6-3, and Dick Stockton in a four-set semi, 4-6, 6-2, 6-3, 6-4. Stockton had beaten Ilie Nastase, 4-6, 6-2, 6-3, 9-8. Ageless Ken Rosewall made mincemeat of a couple of considerably younger ex-champs. In the quarters he

tripped his conqueror of the 1970 final, Newcombe, 6-1, 1-6, 6-0, 7-5. Next he sidestepped a match point in the tie-breaker while beating the returned champ of 1972, a 1973 boycotter, Stan Smith, 6-8, 4-6, 9-8 (8-6), 6-1, 6-3. But in the final, unlucky Rosewall's fourth, Connors made him feel twice his 39 years, ravaging 'Muscles,' 6-1, 6-1, 6-4.

Connors' ferocious returns of Rosewall's unintimidating serves kept the old man constantly on the defensive, the young lion always on the attack. Consequently, Connors became the youngest champion since Lew Hoad beat Rosewall at age 22 in the 1956 final. Rosewall, the sentimental choice who had been runner-up in 1954, 56, 70, remains, along with Pancho Gonzalez, Gottfried von Cramm, Fred Stolle and Ivan Lendl 'the greatest players who never won Wimbledon.' Meanwhile, Newcombe captured his sixth doubles title, the fifth with fellow Aussie Tony Roche, over Bob Lutz and Smith, 8-6, 6-4, 6-4.

Connors had a virus that left him doubtful for the last U.S. Open played on grass courts. He lost a great deal of weight, but turned out to be lean and mean as he barreled through the tournament without serious danger, beating Alex Metreveli in the quarters, 3-6, 6-3, 6-4, 6-1 and Roscoe Tanner, 7-6 (5-2), 7-6 (5-2), 6-4, in the semis. Crushing Rosewall again in the final, 6-1, 6-0, 6-1, Jimmy dealt the worst championship beating in U.S. as well as majors history, tying the two games that Willie Renshaw allowed John Hartley in 1881, and Fred Perry permitted Gottfried von Cramm in 1936,

1974 THE MAJOR CHAMPIONSHIPS

Australian Open
Men's Singles: Jimmy Connors
Women's Singles: Evonne Goolagong
Men's Doubles: Ross Case / Geoff Masters
Women's Doubles: Evonne Goolagong / Peggy Michel
French Open
Men's Singles: Bjorn Borg
Women's Singles: Chris Evert
Men's Doubles: Dick Crealy / Onny Parun
Women's Doubles: Chris Evert / Olga Morozova
Mixed Doubles: Martina Navratilova / Ivan Molina
Wimbledon
Men's Singles: Jimmy Connors
Women's Singles: Chris Evert
Men's Doubles: John Newcombe / Tony Roche
Women's Doubles: Evonne Goolagong / Peggy Michel
Mixed Doubles: Billie Jean King / Owen Davidson
U.S. Open
Men's Singles: Jimmy Connors
Women's Singles: Billie Jean King
Men's Doubles: Bob Lutz / Stan Smith
Women's Doubles: Rosie Casals / Billie Jean King
Mixed Doubles: Pam Teeguarden / Geoff Masters

both at Wimbledon. Tanner had beaten both Nastase, 4-6, 6-7, 7-5, 6-4, 6-4, and Smith, 7-6 (5-2), 6-2, 3-6, 6-1. Although Newcombe had beaten Arthur Ashe in a suspenseful quarter-final, 4-6, 6-3, 3-6, 7-6 (5-4), 6-4, Rosewall, two months shy of his 40th birthday, trimmed him, as he had at Wimbledon, 6-7 (3-5), 6-4, 7-6 (5-1), 6-3. Connors became the youngest Forest Hills champion since, ironically, Rosewall in 1956. The doubles title also stayed in America, Smith and Lutz regaining the prize they first won in 1968, beating Chileans Jaime Fillol and Pato Cornejo, 6-3, 6-3.

Connors was the main man, but there were other outstanding performers during the year. Bjorn Borg, the ascending 'Teen Angel' from Sweden, became the youngest player to win the Italian (17) and French (just turned 18) Opens and the U.S. Pro Championship: Over Nastase in Rome, 6-3, 6-4, 6-2; over Manolo Orantes in Paris, reviving, 2-6, 6-7 (1-7), 6-0, 6-1, 6-1; over Tom Okker in Boston, 7-6 (7-3), 6-1, 6-1, a tournament in which he re-inflated from 1-5 down in the fifth set to beat Kodes in an astonishing semi-final, 7-6 (7-3), 6-0, 1-6, 2-6, 7-6 (7-4). Borg won nine tournaments and was runner-up in five more, including the WCT finals at Dallas. There he coolly beat Ashe, 7-5, 6-4, 7-6, and Kodes, 4-6, 6-4, 6-3, 6-2, before running up against Newcombe, 30, who won this one for the older generation, 4-6, 6-3, 6-3, 6-2.

Borg was also runner-up to Connors in the U.S. Clay Court, 5-7, 6-3, 6-4, their only meeting of the year. Bjorn had won their first meeting in the semis of the 1973 Stockholm Open, 6-4, 3-6, 7-6. But now Connors was off on a seven-match run in what would develop into the rivalry of the '70s in the men's game.

Newcombe was the dominant player of the WCT season, winning five of the 11 tournaments in his group (Nastase and Laver won four each in theirs). But the new format of tricolor groups (Red, Blue, Green), each playing 11 tournaments to qualify their two point leaders plus two 'wild cards' for the eight-man Dallas final, was

not very successful. The product was too diluted, difficult to follow, and the zigzagging global travel schedule taxed the players. WCT, which two years before had the inside track in the men's pro game, had over expanded and suffered in prestige in the process.

Bob Hewitt and McMillan won the WCT doubles final at Montreal, sharing $40,000 for beating Newcombe and Owen Davidson in the final, 6-2, 6-7, 6-1, 6-2. A makeshift young Mexican-American doubles team of Raul Ramirez and Brian Gottfried was formed in the spring and immediately proved to be a successful partnership, winning the first of four consecutive Italian doubles titles, 6-3, 6-2, 6-3, over Nastase and Juan Gisbert.

After Wimbledon, another 22-year-old left-hander arose and edged out Connors for the $100,000 top prize in the Commercial Union Grand Prix. Guillermo Vilas of Argentina, who had shown promise of things to come by knocking out defending champ Andres Gimeno at the French Open in 1973, 6-2, 5-7, 8-6, ruled the U.S. summer circuit and won six of his last 15 tournaments.

The attractive and sensitive young Latin, a former law student and part-time poet, also won the Grand Prix Masters at Melbourne, which Connors boycotted. (He claimed a dental problem, but most blamed his suit against sponsor Commercial Union for his absence.) Even though Vilas did not like grass courts, unsuited to his heavy topspin game, he beat Newcombe, 6-4, 7-6, Borg, 7-5, 6-1, and Onny Parun, 7-5, 3-6, 11-9 to win his round-robin group, then Ramirez in the semis, 4-6, 6-3, 6-2, 7-5. Finally he beat Nastase in a brilliant shot-fest, 7-6, 6-2, 3-6, 3-6, 6-4, to claim his biggest title to date.

At season's end, Vilas was not far behind Connors on the money list, having earned $274,327. Newcombe was third with $273,299, Borg fourth with $215,229. Laver won six tournaments, including the U.S. Pro Indoor over Ashe (his 15th consecutive victory over Arthur in 15 years), 6-1, 6-4, 3-6, 6-4, and the rich Alan King Classic in Las Vegas over Marty Riessen, 6-2, 6-2. Temporarily he remained the all-time money winner with a career total of $1,379,454. Connors would catch him soon enough.

Meanwhile, World Team Tennis made its raucous debut in May, offering players a lucrative alternative to tournaments during the summer. Sixteen teams embarked on a schedule of 44 contests each, the format being five one-set matches (men's and women's singles and doubles, plus mixed doubles), with the cumulative games won in all five deciding the outcome.

The Philadelphia Freedoms, with Billie Jean King as player-coach (and with a theme song, *Philadelphia Freedom*, written for her by Elton John) defeated coach Ken Rosewall's Pittsburgh Triangles in the ballyhooed opener at Philadelphia's Spectrum, 31-25. Philadelphia had the best season record, 39-5, but lost the playoffs in two straight to the Denver Racquets, 27-21, 28-24, who promptly moved to Phoenix. No team made money, and the average loss per franchise was estimated to be $300,000. The league was cut down to 12 teams in 1975, and only one came back for the second season with the original owners.

A more traditional team competition, the Davis Cup, continued to be tarnished by political problems and cumbersome scheduling that often left countries playing matches without their best players. Such was the case with both the U.S., ambushed by Colombia, 4-1, at Bogota in January, and Australia, traveling to India undermanned and beaten by the same score. For the first time in the history of the competition, the 74-year-old Cup was decided by default. South Africa became the fifth nation to hold the sterling silver punchbowl when the Indian Government refused to let its team play the final, a protest of South Africa's apartheid racial policies.

Connors declined to play for the U.S. in either the Davis Cup or the World Cup—won by Australia at Hartford, 5-2, with Newcombe spearheading the attack, beating Ashe, 6-2, 5-7, 6-4, and Smith, 6-3, 6-4, and teaming with Roche to beat them in doubles, 6-7, 6-4, 6-4. Laver came aboard to beat Smith, 7-5, 6-3, but his ownership of Ashe ended. Zero-for-15 against the 'Rocket' over a 15-year stretch, Arthur splintered the jinx, 6-3, 6-3.

Evert became the youngest to gain the No. 1 U.S. female ranking since Maureen Connolly reigned supreme in 1951-52-53. Chrissie won 16 tournaments—including Wimbledon, the French, Italian and U.S. Clay Court—and was never beaten before the semi-finals in compiling a 100-7 record in 23 tournaments. Her $261,460 in prize money far outdistanced Margaret Smith Court's record of the previous year. In winning her third straight U.S. Clay, Chrissie savaged the 1969 champ Gail Chanfreau, 6-0, 6-0, rationing five opponents to a total of eight games.

Evert did not have things entirely her own way, even though she compiled a 55-match winning streak in mid-season. Goolagong beat her in four of six meetings, including the finals of the Australian Open and the Virginia Slims Championship at Los Angeles, and the semi-finals of the U.S. Open. King won the Open and took two of three from Evert, including the final of the U.S. Indoor, which BJK captured for the fifth time, 6-3, 3-6, 6-2.

Goolagong played inspired tennis in celebrating the New Year with a 7-6 (7-5), 4-6, 6-0 triumph over Evert at Melbourne, winning her native title for the first time after being runner-up the previous three years. Evonne also paired with American Peggy Michel, her Pittsburgh Triangles teammate and partner in WTT, to win the doubles titles of Australia (over Kerry Harris and Kerry Melville, 7-5, 6-3) and Wimbledon (over Helen Gourlay and Karen Krantzcke, 2-6, 6-4, 6-3).

With Goolagong, King, Melville (who would marry her Boston Lobsters teammate Grover 'Raz' Reid), and most of the other leading women playing WTT during the summer, Evert had the European clay-court season pretty much to herself. She beat Martina Navratilova, the promising young Czech left-hander who had played the USTA women's circuit at age 16 in 1973, in the Italian final, 6-3, 6-3, and Soviet No. 1 Olga Morozova in the French final, 6-1, 6-2. Evert and Morozova won both doubles titles, (over Chanfreau and Katja Ebbinghaus, 6-4, 2-6, 6-1, in Paris).

Evert barely survived her opening match at Wimbledon—squeezed by Lesley Hunt, 8-6, 5-7, 11-9. Their thriller was delayed for several hours by rain, breathtakingly played despite a slippery court, and suspended overnight by darkness at 9-9 in the third set. But Chris went on to complete her 'Old World Triple' by crunching eighth-seeded Morozova in the final, 6-0, 6-4.

Evert did not have to play her two greatest rivals, top-seeded King and Goolagong, because they both came up flat and were stunned in the quarter-finals. Evert got to dance the champions' traditional first foxtrot at the Wimbledon Ball with her fiancé, Connors. The 'lovebird double,' a Connors-Evert parlay, paid bettors 33-to-1 in England's legalized gambling shops.

Evert won 10 consecutive tournaments after losing the U.S. Indoor to King, but her streak ended nerve-wrackingly at 55 matches in the semi-finals at Forest Hills. Goolagong raced to a 6-0, 4-3 lead before rain suspended their match. The next day, Evert pulled level after Goolagong served for the match at 5-4 in the second set, four times reaching deuce. Evonne came within two points of victory twice more when she served at 6-5. Evert broke again, won the tie-breaker, 5-1, but couldn't contend with Goolagong's outstanding volleying in relinquishing the excruciating final set, winning, 6-0, 6-7 (1-5), 6-3.

King avenged her bitter loss of the year before by beating Julie Heldman, 2-6, 6-3, 6-1, in the other semifinal, and toppled Goolagong, 3-6, 6-3, 7-5, in a final of enthralling shotmaking that delighted a Monday sellout crowd of 15,303. Vastly more entertaining than the massacre of the men's final, this volleying masterpiece was alive until the very end. Goolagong broke at love when King served for the match at 5-4, but BJK won eight of the last nine points to seal her fourth singles title. She also collaborated with Rosie Casals for their second U.S. doubles crown, a tight one over Francoise Durr and Betty Stove, 7-6 (5-4), 6-7 (2-5), 6-4. Bulldozers moved into the stadium at the West Side Tennis Club the next day to dig up the grass courts, which were to be replaced with synthetic clay.

Goolagong beat Evert, 7-5, 3-6, 6-4, in the final of the Virginia Slims tournament at Denver and again in the Slims playoff, where she took the richest women's prize to date, $32,000, with a 6-3, 6-4 victory over the 1972-73 champ. That evened their career rivalry at 8-8 over three years.

Melville, who had been runner-up, 6-1, 6-3, to Evert for the $30,000 top prize in the Family Circle Cup in the spring, won the South African Open, her biggest international title, over Australian 17-year-old lefty Dianne Fromholtz, 6-3, 7-5. Fromholtz had eliminated Court, 6-4, 6-4, making a comeback after the birth of her second child.

America's top two players, Evert and King, sat out the Federation, Wightman and Bonne Bell Cups.

Player-captain Heldman rang up a triple, beating both Goolagong, 6-3, 6-1, and Hunt, 6-4, 6-4 in leading the U.S. to a shocking 5-4 victory over Australia in the third Bell Cup, at Cleveland. Julie also blended with lefty Kris Kemmer to take a doubles over Krantzcke and Gourlay, 6-4, 3-6, 6-4. Alas, that concluded the rivalry; the competition was unfortunately abandoned.

Great Britain, psyched by player-captain Virginia Wade's 5-7, 9-7, 6-4 victory over Heldman, sprinted to a 6-1 victory in the Wightman Cup, only their eighth in 46 meetings with the U.S. Glynis Cole also beat Heldman, 6-0, 6-4, and Wade followed up with a 6-1, 6-3, decision over Janet Newberry. Wimbledon was neglected for the first time in the rivalry, this engagement staged at Deeside, Wales. Cup donor Hazel Wightman died at age 87 in December, shortly after the series.

Jeanne Evert, 17, Chrissie's younger sister, ranked No. 9. Two sisters hadn't appeared in the U.S. Top Ten since the California Suttons, Ethel (No. 2) and Florence (No. 3) in 1913. Jeanne and Heldman took the U.S. to the final of the Federation Cup at Naples, Italy, before falling to Australia, 2-1. Goolagong beat Heldman, 6-1, 7-5, for her 13th straight Fed Cup singles without a loss and teamed with Janet Young for the clincher, 7-5, 8-6, over Heldman and Sharon Walsh after Jeanne beat Fromholtz, 2-6, 7-5, 6-4.

Chris Evert was elected to succeed the more activist King as president of the WTA at Wimbledon, where the women threatened to boycott in 1975 unless they received 'equal parity' with the men in prize money, as Evert put it. That was about the only political story in the women's game, however, and it turned out to be no more than a mild tempest in a teapot, solved by teatime.

1975

Ashe reaches top, King takes sixth Wimbledon

Arthur Ashe
Hoists WCT trophy after stirring triumph over Bjorn Borg.

Jimmy Connors joined world leaders as a cover subject for *Time* magazine in 1975, as he beat first Rod Laver and then John Newcombe (avenging a loss in the Australian Open final) in ballyhooed 'Heavyweight Championship of Tennis' challenge matches in Las Vegas.

These extravaganzas—the focal point of a TV sports scandal two years later because of the CBS network's misleading 'winner-take-all' hype—gained high ratings and massive exposure. Connors and his clever, prizefight-style manager Bill Riordan—who were to split bitterly before the end of the year as Connors dropped the controversial antitrust suit he filed in 1974—were the kings of hype. But the ruler of men's tennis was King Arthur Ashe.

At age 32, after nearly 15 years in the big time, Ashe finally fulfilled the promise that had been acclaimed for him in 1968 and gradually abandoned. Seemingly a perennial bridesmaid, loser of 14 of his last 19 final-round matches as the year began, Ashe became the best by dedicating himself to training and positive thinking as never before.

In 29 tournaments he got to 14 finals, winning nine of them, including the two he really set out to win: The WCT final at Dallas (over Bjorn Borg, 3-6, 6-4, 6-4, 6-0), and Wimbledon (over Connors in a four-set stunner). Ashe's $338,337 earnings for the year boosted his total in seven years as a pro to $1,052,202, making him the sport's third million-dollar winner.

Meanwhile, despite Billie Jean King's dramatic sixth Wimbledon singles title, a postwar record, Chris Evert was the indisputable sovereign of women's tennis.

Before celebrating her 21st birthday on Dec. 21, Chrissie defended her Italian and French Open titles, won the first U.S. Open on clay by outgritting archrival Evonne Goolagong, dethroned Goolagong to recapture the Virginia Slims throne, won 16 of 22 tournaments for the year and set an all-time single-season winnings record of $350,977. She didn't lose a match the last six months of the season after succumbing to King in the Wimbledon semis, and was never beaten before the quarter-finals of a tournament.

Ashe was the Man of the Year, but the season began with another self-reclamation project. Newcombe, who was slowed by injuries after winning the WCT title in May 1974, and was to miss Wimbledon and the U.S. Open with new ailments, flogged himself into shape for the Australian Open by doing miles of roadwork and charging countless times up the hill behind his attractive split-level home in the Sydney suburb of Pymble. He struggled to the final (past Geoff Masters, 6-3, 6-7, 6-3, 10-8, and Tony Roche, 6-4, 4-6, 6-4, 2-6, 11-9). But Newc was ready for Connors, serving ferociously to win, 7-5, 3-6, 6-4, 7-5.

Already set before the loss to Newcombe was the first of Connors' challenge matches at Caesar's Palace, the Las Vegas hotel-casino. The opponent was Laver, the Grand Slammer of 1962 and 1969—a 'natural' pairing since they had never played each other. Connors won, 6-4, 6-2, 3-6, 7-5, seizing what was said to be a $100,000 'winner-take-all' purse, but it was widely reported that both players took home big checks from 'ancillary' revenues.

The success of the venture of CBS-TV made a second 'Heavyweight Championship' inevitable, Newcombe being the logical challenger after his popular victory at Melbourne on New Year's Day. Connors won again, 6-3,

1975 THE MAJOR CHAMPIONSHIPS

Australian Open
Men's Singles: John Newcombe
Women's Singles: Evonne Goolagong
Men's Doubles: John Alexander / Phil Dent
Women's Doubles: Evonne Goolagong / Peggy Michel
French Open
Men's Singles: Bjorn Borg
Women's Singles: Chris Evert
Men's Doubles: Brian Gottfried / Raul Ramirez
Women's Doubles: Chris Evert / Martina Navratilova
Mixed Doubles: Fiorella Bonicelli / Thomaz Koch
Wimbledon
Men's Singles: Arthur Ashe
Women's Singles: Billie Jean King
Men's Doubles: Vitas Gerulaitis / Alex Mayer
Women's Doubles: Ann Kiyomura / Kazuko Sawamatsu
Mixed Doubles: Margaret Smith Court / Marty Riessen
U.S. Open
Men's Singles: Manolo Orantes
Women's Singles: Chris Evert
Men's Doubles: Jimmy Connors / Ilie Nastase
Women's Doubles: Margaret Smith Court / Virginia Wade
Mixed Doubles: Rosie Casals / Dick Stockton

4-6, 6-2, 6-2. Connors was said to receive a $250,000 'winner-take-all' purse, but it was later revealed that the match had been structured like a championship prize fight, each player receiving a pre-agreed percentage, win or lose. Connors made $480,000; Newcombe, $280,000.

Although he won these indoor bouts amid the heavyweight hoopla on which he thrived, Connors lost in the finals of the three major championships he had swept the previous year. Newcombe set the example in Australia. Ashe, considered a prohibitive underdog (10-to-1 on the day), came up with a tactical masterpiece at Wimbledon, 6-1, 6-1, 5-7, 6-4. Arthur's friends worried that he'd be embarrassed in the title bout as Ken Rosewall had been 12 months earlier. Their concern was unnecessary. Arthur changed speed and spin smartly, fed junk to Connors' forehand, exposing the vulnerability of that wing to paceless shots, and sliced his serves wide to Connors' backhand, exploiting the slightly limited reach of his two-handed shot.

This was an extraordinary final, the only one between litigants in a lawsuit since President Ashe, along with other officers of the ATP, were named in the $40-million antitrust suit Connors and Riordan had filed against attorney Donald Dell, Jack Kramer and Grand Prix sponsor Commercial Union. There were several other suits and counterclaims associated with this one, but all were quietly settled, out of court and without payment of damages, not long after Ashe's emotion-charged and enormously popular victory.

A bright new event was the Spalding Mixed Doubles Classic at Dallas's Moody Coliseum, scene of the WCT Championship. Betty Stove and Dick Stockton took the title over Rosie Casals and Marty Riessen, 6-7, 6-2, 6-4, 3-6, 6-3.

Ashe was not considered a serious threat at the U.S. Open after the grass courts at the West Side Tennis Club in Forest Hills were dug up immediately after the 1974 tournament, replaced with a synthetic pea-green clay called Har-Tru, which became the predominant surface of the U.S. summer circuit. Sure enough, clay specialist Eddie Dibbs—one of a group of scrappy young Americans coming up to succeed Ashe's generation— beat fourth-seeded Arthur in the fourth round, 6-4, 6-2, 6-3.

Forest Hills, previously dominated by grass-loving Americans and Australians, suddenly became a happy hunting ground for clay-reared Europeans and South

Americans. The most successful was third-seeded Manolo Orantes, the elegant left-hander from Barcelona. In the semi-finals, he revived himself from two sets and 0-2 down, and from 0-5 in the fourth set, saving five match points to beat second-seeded Argentinean left-hander Guillermo Vilas, 4-6, 1-6, 6-2, 7-5, 6-4. That three-hour, 44-minute marathon did not end until 10:40 p.m. on Saturday, the installation of all-weather courts permitting floodlighting and night play for the first time. Orantes didn't get to bed until 3 a.m. because of a plumbing failure in his hotel room. He was assumed to be a lamb going to slaughter in the final against top-seeded Connors, who had hammered Borg in the other semi-final, 7-5, 7-5, 7-5, early the previous afternoon.

But taking his cue from Ashe's strategy at Wimbledon, Orantes slow-balled Connors and cleverly mixed up his game. He drop-shotted and lobbed, chipped and passed, traded ground strokes and sometimes dashed in to take away the forecourt, snaring Connors in his butterfly net.

It was 10 years to the day since Manuel Santana had become the first Spaniard to win at Forest Hills, and again the old concrete stadium was filled with Latin chants and shouts of *"Bravo!"* and *"Ole!"* as 15,669 spectators roared Orantes to an astonishing 6-4, 6-3, 6-3 victory. At the end, he fell to his knees, jubilant, his toothy face the definitive portrait of ecstasy. Why not? His last 24 hours had constituted the most remarkable feat of any player in a major championship since Wimbledon in 1927, when Frenchman Henri Cochet elevated himself from two sets and 1-5 down to beat Bill Tilden in the semi-finals, then from two sets down to overhaul Jean Borotra in the final.

Connors lost his stranglehold on men's tennis, but did not have a bad year by anyone's standards except his own. He entered 19 tournaments and won nine—five of them on Riordan's USLTA Indoor circuit, including the U.S. Indoor over Vitas Gerulaitis, 5-7, 7-5, 6-1, 3-6, 6-0. Connors was runner-up in six others, including the Australian, Wimbledon, and U.S. Open, compiling an 83-10 record, earning well over a half-million dollars with all his 'special' matches. But Ashe was the prize-money leader with $306,712.

Connors also split with Riordan in the fall. He had prospered, financially and competitively, under Riordan's tutelage, but also had become the isolated man of the locker room, despised and openly cold-shouldered by his colleagues. With the divorce from his manager, Connors gradually came in from the cold, re-establishing cordial if never close relations with his fellow players. "I think Jimmy just decided that it wasn't worth going through life hated," said his contemporary, Roscoe Tanner.

Ashe, who had been one of the first to recognize that a deep freeze by his peers would be the most effective way of ending the divisive lawsuits Connors fronted for Riordan, won four of eight tournaments in his group during the WCT season, while Connors was playing the smaller Riordan-organized tour. Laver won four consecutive WCT tournaments and 23 straight matches. But Ashe earned a solid gold tennis ball, valued at $33,333 (188.7 ounces of 24 carat gold—13 pounds but wouldn't bounce), as the top point-winner on the tour. Divided into three groups (Red, Blue and Green) it consisted of 25 tournaments. Arthur won the $50,000 top prize in the eight-man WCT final at Dallas by beating Mark Cox, 1-6, 6-4, 6-4, 7-6, John Alexander, 3-6, 6-1, 6-3, 6-4 and 18-year-old Borg, 3-6, 6-4, 6-4, 6-0.

A man who came close to perfection, Laver was bidding farewell to Dallas, where he'd lost two of these finals, and, at 36 he went out marvelously in a mesmerizing semi-final loss to Borg, a shot-making feast of four hours, 7-6, 3-6, 5-7, 7-6 (7-2), 6-2.

Ashe also played a substantial number of events in the $4-million dollar Commercial Union Grand Prix, which embraced 42 tournaments in 19 countries during its May-through-December calendar, boosting the total prize money available in men's tennis to more than $8 million dollars. Ashe compiled a 16-match winning streak in the fall, winning two tournaments to qualify for the eight-man Grand Prix Masters playoff at Stockholm. He had visions of a unique WCT-Masters double, but was upended in the semis of the Masters by Borg, 6-4, 3-6, 6-2, 6-2, and concluded, "I don't think anybody is strong enough, mentally and physically, to win WCT and the Masters in the same year."

Borg, the unflappable baseliner supreme, was runner-up in both—to Ashe in Dallas and to Ilie Nastase (who came back from a disqualification against Ashe in his opening round-robin match of the Masters) in Stockholm. 'Teen Angel' was in the waning days of his 18th year when he beat Laver at Dallas, perhaps the year's finest match. He had turned 19 by the time he shut down Vilas, 6-2, 6-3, 6-4, for his second consecutive French Open title. Later Borg steamrolled Vilas again, 6-3, 6-4, 6-2, to defend his U.S. Pro crown in

Boston. Borg won five of 23 tournaments on the year, amassed a 78-19 record.

He carried Sweden to its first possession of the Davis Cup, winning all 12 of his singles matches against Poland, West Germany, the Soviet Union, Spain, Chile and, finally, Czechoslovakia at Stockholm. The final was essentially Borg against Jan Kodes, with their seconds, Ove Bengtson, and a combination of Jiri Hrebec and Vladimir Zednik, the fall guys. Borg's record of 16 consecutive Davis Cup singles victories over three years tied the all-time Cup record set by Bill Tilden between 1920 and 1926, and would stretch to his record, 33, by his retirement.

Vilas didn't take any of the big international titles, but won six of 23 tournaments—including Washington and Louisville during a 16-match winning streak early in the U.S. summer circuit—and reached at least the quarter-finals of 21 to seize the $100,000 top prize in the Commercial Union Grand Prix for the second straight year.

Nastase won the Masters for the fourth time in five years, coming back from his disqualification in the opening round-robin match against Ashe. Uncharacteristically furious at Nastase's behavior and stalling, Arthur (ahead, 1-6, 7-5, 4-1) lost his customary cool. He stormed off the court, disqualifying himself. Referee Horst Klosterkemper, declaring that "in my mind I was about to default Nastase" just as Ashe quit, found himself with two losers of the same match. It was ironed out the next day with Ashe announced as the winner. Nevertheless, Nastase, by defeating Orantes, 3-6, 6-4, 6-4, and Italian Adriano Panatta, 7-6, 3-6, 6-0, in his remaining round-robin matches, scraped into the semis. There he beat Vilas, 6-0, 6-3, 6-4, and went on to destroy Borg's rhythm with changes of spins and pace for a 6-2, 6-2, 6-1, championship triumph. This was by far the biggest of Nastase's seven tournament victories for the year. However, he set a dubious achievement record by being defaulted three times, quitting his semi-final match in the Italian Open to ultimate champion Raul Ramirez, and 'tanking' the Canadian Open final to Orantes, 7-6, 6-0, 6-1 after going bonkers over a line call in the first-set tie-breaker.

For this unprofessional conduct, Nastase was fined $8,000 by the newly formed Men's International Professional Tennis Council, a tripartite body made up of three representatives each of the male players, the ITF, and worldwide tournament directors. Nastase's lawyers appealed, and the fine was reduced, but the 'Pro Council' had established itself as an important new administrative and judicial force in the men's game. It was designed to be legislative as well, and became the autonomous governing body of the Grand Prix circuit.

It was a peculiar year in men's doubles. Brian Gottfried and Ramirez were the Team of the Year. They began their reign in the U.S. Pro Indoor at Philadelphia over Stockton and Erik van Dillen, and won the WCT doubles title at Mexico City over Cox and Cliff Drysdale. Gottfried-Ramirez also won a special 'Challenge Match' during the WCT singles finals at Dallas over South African Davis Cuppers Bob Hewitt and Frew McMillan, who had been rudely kicked out of Mexico shortly after their arrival for the doubles playoff—a clumsy power play by the Mexican government to protest the apartheid racial policies of South Africa.

Gottfried-Ramirez also won the French title, over John Alexander-Phil Dent, and the U.S. Pro, over Mike Estep and John Andrews. But they came up flat at the end of the year, failing to win a match in the Masters as a four-team doubles playoff was inaugurated alongside the singles. The doubles was a round-robin affair, which proved to be an unsatisfactory format when three teams tied with identical 2-1 records. Spanish Davis Cuppers Orantes and Juan Gisbert were declared champions on the basis of having the best percentage of games won for their three matches, even though they were beaten head-to-head, 6-0, 6-3, by the spirited new American tandem of Sherwood Stewart and Freddie McNair. (The Masters doubles was changed to a knock-out format in succeeding years.)

The Wimbledon doubles turned into a wildly unpredictable scramble as only one seeded team reached the quarter-finals. Alex 'Sandy' Mayer and Vitas Gerulaitis, who had not blended well earlier in the year, became the first American champions in 18 years (since Budge Patty and Gar Mulloy) with a 7-5, 8-6, 6-4 victory in the final over similarly unseeded Allan Stone of Australia and Colin Dowdeswell of Rhodesia, who had never even met each other until introduced in the tea room the first day of the tournament.

Connors got his only major title of the year by teaming with Nastase to win the U.S. Open doubles over Riessen and Tom Okker, 6-4, 7-6. Connors seldom played doubles thereafter, a trend soon followed by Borg and Vilas as top players began to concentrate singularly on singles.

Connors also ended—only temporarily, as it turned out—his one-man boycott of the U.S. Davis Cup team. Former French, Wimbledon and U.S. champion Tony Trabert replaced Dennis Ralston as the American captain after Raul Ramirez led a 3-2 Mexican ambush of the U.S. at Palm Springs in February 1975, ironically the same weekend that Connors was beating Laver in the first Las Vegas Challenge Match. Ramirez, the best Mexican to play the game other than Rafe Osuna, a quick, resourceful, strong volleyer, was peskier for the U.S. than Pancho Villa. He led two raiding parties within 10 months that eliminated the *norteamericanos*. The notion that Connors' presence alone assured victory in the American Zone was dispelled as Ramirez, an inspired Davis Cup player, led Mexico to another 3-2 upset. This was in the second round of the 1976 competition, actually played December 19-21, 1975. It all came down to the No. 1 players of the two countries in the decisive fifth match, and Ramirez, was as high as the 6,000-foot altitude of Mexico City as he beat Connors, 2-6, 6-3, 6-3, 6-4, in a match suspended overnight by darkness.

The Davis Cup continued to be plagued by political turmoil. Mexico, after eliminating the U.S., refused to play South Africa. Colombia similarly defaulted, putting South Africa—winner of the Cup by default the previous year—into the American Zone final without playing a match. But administrators were momentarily relieved as South African was eliminated by Chile at Santiago, 5-0. But then Chilean No. 1 Jaime Fillol received a death threat from opponents of the military junta in his homeland, forcing massive security precautions for the semi-final in Sweden. The stadium at Baastad was kept almost empty except for thousands of police and troops. Boats patrolled the harbor, aircraft hovered overhead, and huge nets around the stadium protected the players from projectiles hurled by anti-Chile demonstrators. In this unnerving atmosphere, Borg and Birger Anderssen whipped the Chileans, 4-1, to set up their Cup clinching

victory over Czechoslovakia in Stockholm just before Christmas.

The ATP, in a rather clumsy effort to force a consolidation of the Davis Cup into a one or two week showdown at one site, staged a new competition with just such a Federation Cup–style format, calling it the Nations Cup. The American team of Ashe and Tanner defeated Great Britain's Roger Taylor and Buster Mottram, 2-1, in Jamaica, but the competition was not a success. Meanwhile, Laver and 40-year-old Rosewall helped Australia to a 4-3 victory over the U.S. in the World Cup at Hartford, showing that the Aussie dynasty was not entirely dead.

World Team Tennis, despite the huge financial losses of its inaugural season and a ludicrous player draft (numerous showbiz personalities were named by teams in a publicity stunt that made a mockery of the league), surprised many by coming out for a second season. There were 12 teams, four fewer than in 1974, and only one returned with the original ownership, but the league staggered along. Pittsburgh, led by Gerulaitis and Goolagong, beat the San Francisco Bay Area's Golden Gaters in the championship series, 25-26, 28-25, 21-14.

Goolagong started the season by repeating as Australian Open champion, beating Martina Navratilova, 6-3, 6-2, in an emotional final. (Evonne's father had been killed in an auto accident, and Evonne cried on the shoulder of her coach and guardian, Vic Edwards, at the presentation ceremonies.) Goolagong also successfully defended her doubles title with WTT teammate Peggy Michel, over Margaret Smith Court and Russian Olga Morozova , 7-6, 7-6.

Evert cashed the biggest check for women in 'special events'—$50,000 for winning the four-woman L'Eggs World Series over King at Lakeway, Tex., 4-6, 6-3, 7-6. She also won $40,000 for adding her third triumph in the Virginia Slims Championship at Los Angeles, over Navratilova, 6-4, 6-2. Navratilova won the U.S. Indoor at Boston, beating Goolagong in the final, 6-2, 4-6, 6-4. But she lost again to Evert, 7-5, 6-4, in the final of the rich Family Circle Cup at Amelia Island, Fla.

With most of the top women committed to World Team Tennis, Evert and Navratilova were the class of the women's field in the Italian and French Opens. They reached the singles finals of both, Evert winning Rome, 6-1, 6-0, and Paris, 2-6, 6-2, 6-1. Chris and Martina then teamed up to win both the doubles titles.

King, always considering the Centre Court at

Wimbledon her favorite stage, never performed more majestically there than in coming from 0-3 down in the third set to beat Evert in the semi-finals, 2-6, 6-2, 6-3, and burying Goolagong, 6-0, 6-1, in the most lopsided women's final since 1911. BJK's sixth singles title was her 19th in all at Wimbledon, tying the career record of Elizabeth Ryan, who never won the singles but captured 12 doubles and seven mixed crowns between 1914 and 1934. King said this was her last appearance in singles because of a deteriorating knee—"I want to quit on top," she said, "and I can't get much higher than this"—but she eventually returned, in 1977.

The women's doubles champions turned out to be as unlikely as the men's, Kazuko Sawamatsu of Japan and Ann Kiyomura, an American of Japanese ancestry, teaming to upset Françoise Durr and Stove in the final, 7-5, 1-6, 7-5. Court teamed with Riessen for the mixed doubles title over Stove and Allan Stone, 6-3, 2-6, 7-5. Margaret was just about at the end of her tremendous journey of 16 years up a record mountain of 62 major titles. Could anybody ever equal that haul? This mixed was the 61st, and she would close two months later with the 62nd, the U.S. doubles with Virginia Wade. It was 33-year-old Court's 19th doubles, complementing 24 singles and 19 mixed.

Evert won the U.S. Open, dropping only one set. That was in the final, where her 5-7, 6-4, 6-2 victory over Goolagong relegated Evonne to the record books as the only woman to lose three consecutive U.S. singles finals.

More important than tennis was Navratilova's decision, announced at Forest Hills, to defect from her native Czechoslovakia and seek U.S. citizenship. She made the decision after the Czech tennis federation, chiding her for becoming 'too americanized,' initially refused her a visa to compete in the U.S. Open. Navratilova felt she had to follow the lead of the great Czech player Jaroslav Drobny, who defected in 1949, if she were to develop as a tennis player and as a person, but the decision was painful. She knew her action meant that it would be years before she would see her parents and younger sister, Jana, again.

Navratilova (5-0 in singles) and Renata Tomanova (4-1) had led Czechoslovakia past Ireland, 3-0, Netherlands, 2-0, West Germany, 2-1, France, 3-0 and Australia, 3-0 to win the 30-nation Federation Cup at Aix-en-Provence in southern France. The Aussies made the final for the 10th time, but Navratilova ended Goolagong's 16-match unbeaten streak in Cup singles, 6-3, 6-4. Tomanova ambushed Helen Gourlay, 6-4, 6-2, and the Czechs had their first Cup.

Britain also humbled the U.S., 5-2, in the Wightman Cup for the second straight year, its first back-to-back wins since 1924-25. Evert won both her singles, over Wade, 6-3, 7-6 and Glynis Coles, 6-4, 6-1, but that's all the U.S. could get at Cleveland's Public Auditorium. Wade beat Mona Schallau, 6-2, 6-2, as did Coles, 6-3, 7-6. Sue Barker beat Janet Newberry, 6-4, 7-5, and 37-year-old Ann Jones, returning to the fray got a big doubles win with Wade over Anthony and Newberry, 6-2, 6-3.

The most spectacular comeback of the year belonged to Evert, who trailed Nancy Richey Gunter, 6-7, 0-5, 15-40—double match point—in the semi-finals of the U.S. Clay Court at Indianapolis. After that, Chrissie didn't make a mistake in roaring back to win, 6-7, 7-5, 4-2, default. Gunter finally had to quit with cramps. Evert went on to thrash Fromholtz in the final, 6-3, 6-4, for her fourth consecutive Clay crown.

A couple of administrative happenings during 1975 are worthy of note. Over the protests of tournament chairman and director Bill Talbert, the U.S. Open adopted a so-called 12-point tie-breaker (actually best-of-12 but with a margin of two) instead of the best-of-nine-point 'sudden death' that had been in use since 1970. This was a victory for the ATP, whose members preferred the less nerve-wracking 'lingering death.' The change of the surface at Forest Hills permitted night play there for the first time, and a resultant dramatic increase in total attendance, to a record 216,683. This was also the year the U.S. Lawn Tennis Association voted to drop the 'Lawn' from its name, becoming simply the USTA. It was the beginning of a fashion that would, in 1977, see the International Lawn Tennis Federation become the ITF.

1976

Jimbo bests Borg, Chrissie rolls on, Renee comes out

Jimmy Connors
Back on top with 100-12 record, including U.S. Open win over Bjorn Borg.

Jimmy Connors returned to the pinnacle of men's tennis in 1976 and Chris Evert consolidated her stranglehold on the women's game. But the most bizarre and compelling story of the year was the emergence of pro sport's first transsexual.

Richard Raskind, a 41-year-old ophthalmologist, was a good enough player to captain the Yale University varsity in 1954, play at Wimbledon and Forest Hills, and later reach the semi-finals of the U.S. Men's 35-and-over championships in 1972. In August 1975, he had sex reassignment surgery and moved west to Newport Beach, Calif., to start a new life and practice as Dr. Renée Richards.

In July 1976, Dr. Richards—a 6-foot-2 left-hander—entered and won a local women's tournament in La Jolla, Calif. A former acquaintance noticed her resemblance in playing style to Richard Raskind, verified her identity and tipped off a San Diego television sportscaster, who broke the story.

Dr. Richards, who had sought a clean start in California, far from her former wife and four-year-old son in New York, decided to 'go public' and put aside her brilliant career as an eye surgeon in order to play professional tennis.

"I started getting letters, poignant letters from other transsexuals who were considering suicide, whose friends and families won't see them," she explained to *Newsday* reporter Jane Gross. "I realized that this was more than just a tennis thing, my hobby. I could easily give that up. But, if I can do anything for those people, I will. I am in a position to try and make people see that such individuals should be allowed to hold up their heads. I realize this is important from a social standpoint."

The Richards case caused an extraordinary, highly publicized stir in women's tennis. The Women's Tennis Association opposed her eligibility for tournaments, and sided with the USTA in its hasty ruling that women would have to pass an Olympic-style chromosome test before being accepted for women's national championships, including the U.S. Open. Dr. Richards refused to take the test, claiming that it was an unsatisfactory means of determining gender, given the advances of modern medicine.

Many women felt that Dr. Richards would have an unfair competitive advantage because of her size, strength and past experience in competition against men. Others feared that her acceptance would set a bad precedent, paving the way for a younger, stronger trans-sexual to dominate women's tennis in the future. Many WTA members liked Richards personally, admired her courage, but still opposed her acceptance in tournaments.

Dr. Richards, denied admission to the U.S. Open—she took her case to court, and was admitted in 1977 by court order—did play in a pre-Forest Hills tournament at South Orange, N.J. Most WTA members withdrew in protest, but the tournament attracted national television coverage and massive publicity. Richards was beaten in the semi-finals by 17-year-old Lea Antonoplis, 6-7, 6-3, 6-0. Early fears that Dr. Richards would upset the competitive balance of the women's game were unfounded. Richards played several other small tournaments, two in Hawaii, winning at Kauai, at the end of the year over No. 10 American Kathy Kuykendall, 6-1, 6-4, and losing the Kona final to 1962 Wimbledon champ, 35-year-old Karen Hantze Susman, 4-6, 6-4, 6-2.

Along more conventional lines, Connors recaptured the No. 1 world ranking even though he won only one

1976 THE MAJOR CHAMPIONSHIPS

Australian Open
Men's Singles: Mark Edmondson
Women's Singles: Evonne Goolagong Cawley
Men's Doubles: John Newcombe / Tony Roche
Women's Doubles: Evonne Goolagong / Helen Gourlay
French Open
Men's Singles: Adriano Panatta
Women's Singles: Sue Barker
Men's Doubles: Fred McNair / Sherwood Stewart
Women's Doubles: Fiorella Bonicelli / Gail Sherriff Lovera
Mixed Doubles: Ilana Kloss / Kim Warwick
Wimbledon
Men's Singles: Bjorn Borg
Women's Singles: Chris Evert
Men's Doubles: Brian Gottfried / Raul Ramirez
Women's Doubles: Chris Evert / Martina Navratilova
Mixed Doubles: Françoise Durr / Tony Roche
U.S. Open
Men's Singles: Jimmy Connors
Women's Singles: Chris Evert
Men's Doubles: Tom Okker / Marty Riessen
Women's Doubles: Delina Boshoff / Ilana Kloss
Mixed Doubles: Billie Jean King / Phil Dent

major championship, the U.S. Open, in which he edged his major rival, Bjorn Borg, in a superlative final, 6-4, 3-6, 7-6 (11-9), 6-4.

Connors compiled a 100-12 record, winning 13 of 23 tournaments he played. He won the only two WCT events he entered, the two big prize-money events put on by the ATP (American Airlines Games at Palm Springs, over Roscoe Tanner, 6-4, 6-4 and the Alan King Classic at Las Vegas over evergreen 41-year-old Ken Rosewall, 6-1, 6-3) and six of the 10 Commercial Union Grand Prix events he played. He collected $303,335 in prize money, plus more than double that amount in exhibitions—including $500,000 for beating up on Spaniard Manuel Orantes in another 'Heavyweight Championship of Tennis' Challenge Match at Las Vegas. (Orantes, guaranteed more than $250,000 just for showing up, did little more than that, winning three games in three pathetic sets.)

More important in deciding the global game of king-of-the-hill, Connors was 3-0 in head-to-head clashes with Borg. Connors vanquished the young Swede in the U.S. Pro Indoor final at Philadelphia, the semis of the American Airlines Games, and the U.S, Open final.

Otherwise, Borg had an outstanding season, winning seven of 19 tournaments and 63 of 77 matches. He continued his domination of his good friend and sometimes doubles partner, Guillermo Vilas, to win the WCT Final at Dallas, 1-6, 6-1, 7-5, 6-1, in May, 27 days before his 20th birthday. He failed in his bid for a third consecutive French Open title, losing to eventual champ, Italian Adriano Panatta in the quarters. But Bjorn prepared diligently on grass courts and became the third youngest champion in the history of Wimbledon, the first man to sweep through the most prestigious of championships without losing a set since Chuck McKinley in 1963. Borg pulled a muscle in his abdomen in a doubles match the first week, but deadened the pain in his last four singles matches by taking pre-match cortisone injections and spraying his abdomen at changeovers with an aerosol freeze spray. Despite the injury, he never served or smashed more authoritatively than in routing Brian Gottfried, 6-2, 6-2, 7-5; Vilas, 6-3, 6-0, 6-2; Roscoe Tanner 6-4, 9-8 (7-2), 6-4; and Ilie Nastase in the final, 6-4, 6-2, 9-7.

After a seven-week layoff to recuperate—a period during which Sweden relinquished the Davis Cup—Borg extended his winning streak to 19 matches, winning a third consecutive U.S. Pro title, over Harold

Solomon, 6-7 (3-7), 6-4, 6-1, 6-2) and reaching the final of the U.S. Open. That match hinged on a tingling 20 point third-set tie-breaker in which Connors escaped four set points, tilting an epic his way, 6-4, 3-6, 7-6 (11-9), 6-4.

The year began with perhaps the most startling result ever in one of the major championships—21-year-old Australian Mark Edmondson, a burly anonymous serve-and-volleyer recently removed from employment as a janitor and odd-jobs man, won the Australian Open. Lowest ranked ever to capture a major, No. 212, he beat two former champions, 42-year-old Rosewall in the semis, 6-1, 2-6, 6-2, 6-4, and defender John Newcombe, 6-7, 6-3, 7-6, 6-1, the final played in fierce winds and eerie weather of a gathering storm. Edmondson quickly found his level in Paris, losing in the first round of the French to Paraguayan Victor Pecci.

Panatta, handsome and dashing Italian No. 1, won the French during a dazzling 16-match winning streak that established him as the king of European clay for the year. Panatta was superb, dispatching Borg, 6-3, 6-3, 2-6, 7-6 (7-2) in the quarter-finals, Eddie Dibbs in the semis, 6-3, 6-2, 6-4 and the 'Human Grindstone,' Solomon, 6-1, 6-4, 4-6, 7-6 (7-3), in the sweltering final.

At the Italian Open, Panatta withstood 11 match points against Aussie Kim Warwick in the first round, winning, 3-6, 6-4, 7-6, then went on to win the title before his adoring hometown fans in Rome, beating Vilas in the final, 2-6, 7-6 (7-5), 6-2, 7-6 (7-1). He got a big break in the quarters when gutsy little Solomon was beating him, 2-6, 7-5, 5-4 with serve. At 0-15 Panatta lobbed—clearly long—but the line judge signaled the ball to be good in an ordinary display of patriotism. But Solly blew up, losing his temper and the match by walking away.

Arthur Ashe, 1975's No. 1, got off to the best start of his career, winning five of his first six tournaments and 29 of 30 matches. He again topped the WCT point standings, earning a $50,000 bonus, but lost his crown in the first round of the WCT playoffs at Dallas, beaten by Solomon, 7-5, 3-6, 6-1, 6-3, and did little thereafter. His fade was in part attributed to inflammation of a chronic heel injury that required surgery in February 1977.

A pinched nerve in his elbow slowed another of the 1975 heroes, Orantes, but therapy and a switch to a lighter aluminum racket revived him in the autumn. Orantes won five of his last eight tournaments (assembling the year's longest winning streak, 23 matches), reached two other finals and resurrected himself from 1-4 down in the fourth to win a stirring Grand Prix Masters final at Houston over Poland's Wojtek Fibak, the most improved pro of the year, 5-7, 6-2, 0-6, 7-6 (7-1), 6-1.

The Masters concluded five years of Grand Prix sponsorship by the Commercial Union Assurance group, which withdrew because of flagging profits in the insurance business and was replaced by Colgate-Palmolive, which already had undertaken sponsorship of the women's grand prix setup, known as the Colgate International Series. Commercial Union's swan song was soured when Connors decided to pass up the Masters for a third consecutive year (thereby forfeiting the $60,000 he already had earned from the Grand Prix bonus pool for finishing third in the season-long standings). Borg and Nastase chose to play exhibitions in the fall instead of Grand Prix tournaments that could have qualified them for the eight-man Masters.

Mexican Raul Ramirez won only four of 32 tournaments, but he was a tireless and consistent campaigner. His diligence paid off as he earned both the $150,000 prize for topping the Grand Prix singles standings and the $40,000 award for heading the doubles standings, a unique accomplishment. In all, the Grand Prix encompassed 48 tournaments (and produced 23 different winners) in 22 countries, with more than $5 million in prize purses. With the WCT (24 16-man tournaments) and U.S. Indoor circuits added in, more than $9 million was available in men's tournaments worldwide.

The riches available were demonstrated graphically when Nastase collected $180,000 in a single tournament, the WCT-run Avis Challenge Cup, a series of winner-take-all round-robin matches played throughout the winter and spring in Hawaii. Nastase beat Ashe in a five-set final on asphalt, 6-3, 1-6, 6-7, 6-3, 6-1. On the year, Nastase won five of 23 tournaments, compiled a 76-17 record, reached the final at Wimbledon and the semi-finals at Forest Hills, and was the only player with a winning record over Connors (4-1), shutting off Jimmy's four-year hold on the U.S. Indoor, 6-2, 6-3, 7-6. But Connors won the U.S. Clay for a second time, 6-2, 6-4, over Fibak.

In doubles, Newcombe and Tony Roche won their fourth Australian title, over Ross Case and Geoff Masters, 7-6, 6-4. But team-of-the-year honors were shared by Ramirez–Brian Gottfried and Sherwood Stewart–Freddie McNair, who underscored the old axiom that the ordinary singles players can blend extraordinarily in doubles. Stewart-McNair won the French Open, dethroning Gottfried-Ramirez, 7-6 (8-6), 6-3, 6-1, and came back from 1-4 in the fourth set to stun the same team in the Masters doubles final, 6-3, 5-7, 5-7, 6-4, 6-4.

A surprising German-Polish patchwork alliance, Karl Meiler and Fibak won the WCT doubles at Kansas City, hanging tough in five sets, beating Stan Smith and Bob Lutz, 6-3, 2-6, 3-6, 6-3, 6-4, for the title after deposing the defenders, Gotffried-Ramirez, in the semis, 6-4, 6-4, 4-6, 4-6, 6-4.

Gottfried and Ramirez won their third straight Italian title, over Newcombe and Masters, 7-6, 5-7, 6-3, 3-6, 6-3, in a bizarre long-distance, two-continent affair. Completion of the final in Rome was delayed by darkness after the fourth set, and concluded four months later at the Woodlands, outside Houston. At the same event, Gottfried and Ramirez also won the $100,000 ATP Doubles, over Aussies Allan Stone and Phil Dent, 6-1, 6-4, 5-7, 7-6. One stop, two titles. Brian and Raul were so hot they double-bageled Case and Masters, 6-0, 6-0! They had also won Wimbledon, knocking off curiously unseeded Newcombe-Roche (five-time champions) in a tense first rounder—tantamount to a final—7-9, 8-9, 9-7, 6-3, 6-4, and then, in the rousing genuine final, Masters-Case, 3-6, 6-3, 8-6, 2-6, 7-5.

Tom Okker and Marty Riessen took the U.S. Open over long shot Aussies Paul Kronk and Cliff Letcher, 6-4, 6-4.

It was a quiet year politically in men's tennis, aside from the Davis Cup and storms arising from Nastase's tempestuous behavior. The rambunctious Romanian was at his worst in an ugly second-round victory, 7-6 (7-5), 4-6, 7-6 (9-7) over Germany's Hans Pohmann at Forest Hills, saving two match points and winning it on a fifth. Nastase's gamesmanship and outbursts of obscene language, gestures and spitting, along with delays when Pohmann suffered cramps that should have disqualified him, caused this match to get out of control. Nastase, who kept moving to a semi-final defeat by Borg, was eventually fined $1,000, which increased his aggregate disciplinary fines for a 12-month period to more than $3,000 and triggered an automatic 21-day suspension, under provisions of a new Code of Conduct enacted by the Men's International Professional Tennis Council primarily as a reaction to Nastase. (It should have been called the Nastase Code of Conduct.) The suspension was a joke, however, since it applied only to Grand Prix tournaments; Nastase played exhibition tournaments and earned more than $50,000 during the time he was supposed to be disciplined.

In the Davis Cup, Mexico, after upsetting the U.S. in the American Zone, refused to play South Africa for the second consecutive year, and defaulted. When the Davis Cup nations refused to take action against Mexico at its annual meeting, the U.S. led a walkout of the major Cup nations, including France and Great Britain, for 1977. A compromise was worked out within two weeks, however, and these nations returned. The Soviet Union defaulted its semi-final series to Chile in protest of the military junta that had overthrown the socialist regime of Salvador Allende in Santiago in 1973. This was precisely the sort of political disruption that the U.S. was opposing, and a reconstituted Davis Cup Committee of Management threw the USSR out of the 1977 competition.

Italy, runner-up in 1960 and 1961, won the Davis Cup for the first time, beating Chile in Santiago, 4-1, in a final distinguished more by the enthusiasm and sportsmanship of the sellout crowds of 6,500 than by the quality of play. Corrado Barazzutti upset Chilean No. 1 Jaime Fillol at the start, 7-5, 4-6, 7-5, 6-1. Panatta beat game but overmatched Patricio Cornejo, 6-3, 6-1, 6-3, then teamed with Paolo Bertolucci to down Cornejo-Fillol, 3-6, 6-2, 9-7, 6-3, for an unbeatable 3-0 lead as Capt. Nicola Pietrangeli, the star of the final round 1960 and 1961 Italian teams, exulted at courtside. Though the political situation had been tense, Italian leftists opposing the matches, Italians' joy at winning was unrestrained.

Earlier in the year Connors had made his first appearance for the U.S. in the World Cup. The former antagonists, Connor and Ashe, both thrashed Newcombe and Roche in singles, leading Capt. Dennis Ralston's

---

1976 CHAMPIONS AND LEADERS

American squad to a 6-1 victory over declining Australia before sellout crowds of 10,000 in Hartford.

World Team Tennis was more stable in its third season, but even with Evert as a shining new attraction and the respected Butch Buchholz aboard as commissioner, all of the 10 franchises continued to operate in the red. The New York Sets, led by Sandy Mayer, Billie Jean King, Virginia Wade and Phil Dent, captured the league title over the Golden Gaters (San Francisco Bay Area) in the playoff final series, 31-23, 29-31, 31-13. Evert, of the Phoenix Racquets, was the female MVP, her singles winning percentage (.700) the best of any player in WTT.

Evert was unquestionably the queen of tournament tennis as well. She won 75 of 80 matches, 12 of 17 tournaments, including Wimbledon, the U.S. Open and the rich Colgate Inaugural (over Françoise Durr, 6-1, 6-2) at Palm Springs in October. That launched the new Colgate International Series, and was to serve thereafter as its climactic playoff. Its $45,000 top prize was the biggest of the year in women's tennis. It boosted Evert's season winnings to $289,165 and her career winnings to $1,026,604, making her the first woman to earn more than $1 million in prize money. Only four players—Evonne Goolagong (twice), Wade, Martina Navratilova and Dianne Fromholtz—were able to beat Evert during the year.

Goolagong (newly married to Englishman Roger Cawley) started the year by winning her third straight Australian Open title, a 6-2, 6-2 rout of Czechoslovakia's Renata Tomanova, and teaming with Helen Gourlay to defend the doubles titles in a schlocky final over Lesley Turner Bowrey and Tomanova, 8-games-to-1, a so-called 'pro set,' the distance somehow agreed on beforehand.

The lithe Australian was at her best during the January through April Virginia Slims circuit, winning 38 of 40 matches, dropping only 10 sets, and at one point running off 16 consecutive victories without loss of a set. She climaxed her record $133,675 Slims season (en route to a $195,452 year) by beating Evert, 6-3, 5-7, 6-3, in a magnificent match at the Los Angeles Sports Arena, the final of the Virginia Slims championship.

On the season, Evonne won eight of 14 tournaments, 58 of 64 matches. She reached the final of every tournament she played, was 7-0 vs. Wade, 6-0 vs. Rosie Casals, 4-0 over Navratilova and 4-0 over Sue Barker. Evonne had the second-best winning percentage in singles among WTT players, and aside from one-set WTT matches lost to only two players, Evert five times, and King in the Federation Cup at Philadelphia. This was Evonne's most consistent season. But still, as she announced at season's end that she was taking maternity leave, she was overshadowed by Evert.

After losing the Virginia Slims final, Chrissie won her next six tournaments in a dazzling 36-match winning streak, and lost only one more match the rest of the year. Her streak began with her third consecutive triumph in the Family Circle Cup, over Australian Kerry Melville Reid, 6-2, 6-2, at Amelia Island, Fla.

At Wimbledon, where all eight seeds reached the quarter-finals, Evert beat Olga Morozova, 6-3, 6-0, Navratilova, 4-6, 6-3, 6-4, and Goolagong, 6-3, 4-6, 8-6, in a thrilling final that ended Evonne's 25-match streak. This was Evert's first triumph ever over Goolagong on grass. Then Evert and Navratilova took the doubles title over Betty Stove and King, 6-1, 3-6, 7-5.

Evert was at her dominating best on the clay at Forest Hills, winning her second consecutive U.S. Open title with the loss of only 12 games in six matches. (Helen Wills Moody, losing just eight games in six matches in 1929, is the only champion to ever have a more devastating run). Evert stomped Goolagong, 6-3, 6-0, in the most lopsided final since 1964, running the last 10 games. This extended Evert's clay-court winning streak to 21 tournaments and 101 matches, dating to August 1973.

Because of a downpour, unseeded Yugoslav Mima Jausovec could say she battled Evert in the semis for almost seven hours—most of it sitting in the clubhouse after rain halted play at 5-2. Returning under floodlights, Chrissie finished the 69-minute playing-time victory, 6-3, 6-1. On a sentimental journey, 36-year-old Maria Bueno, champion in 1959, 63-64, 66, won two rounds before Casals dismissed her, 7-5, 6-0

A shocker was the first-round dumping of third-seeded Navratilova by No. 8 American Janet Newberry, 1-6, 6-4, 6-3, a low point in Martina's career that left her sobbing beside the court. She wouldn't lose an opening-rounder again in a major until her farewell French in 1994. But it was a tough early-going year for names—fourth, fifth and seventh-seeded Wade, Nancy Richey and Kerry Reid were all bounced in the second round.

Delina 'Linky' Boshoff and Ilana Kloss startlingly won the doubles title over Wade and Morozova, 6-1, 6-4, becoming the first South African women to win a

U.S. title. King and another WTT teammate, Dent, won the mixed doubles over Stove and Frew McMillan, 3-6, 6-2, 7-5.

King came out of her self-imposed singles retirement in the Federation Cup at Philadelphia's Spectrum in August. Colgate assumed sponsorship of this women's team competition, and infused it with prize money for the first time—$130,000 for teams representing 32 nations, $40,000 to the winners. Unfortunately, a political hassle developed when the Soviet Union reneged on a previous promise and led a four-nation walkout (1975 champion Czechoslovakia, Hungary and the Philippines joined the USSR in refusing to play) to protest the inclusion of South African and Rhodesia. The defaulting nations were subsequently fined by the ITF, but they had succeeded in making the draw a shambles.

Billie Jean filled in unexpectedly in singles for Evert, who withdrew with a sore wrist. Playing for the U.S. for the first time since 1967, she teamed with old doubles partner Casals in a two-woman *tour de force*. They sprinted through four 3-0 victories to a meeting with favored Australia in the final. Reid beat Casals, 1-6, 6-3, 7-5, but King found a wellspring of her old inspiration to beat Goolagong, 7-6, 6-4, in a match of exceptionally high standard. King-Casals then toppled Reid-Goolagong, 7-5, 6-3, for the championship.

After rare back-to-back losses in 1974 and 1975, the U.S. regained the Wightman Cup with a 5-2 victory over Great Britain, indoors at London's Crystal Palace. Evert led the way, beating Wade, 6-2, 3-6, 6-3, and then Sue Barker in the decisive match, 2-6, 6-2, 6-2.

In the absence of the leading women, who were contracted to WTT, Barker won the German over Tomanova, 6-3, 6-1, and earned preeminence on European clay by taking the French, also over Tomanova, 6-2, 0-6, 6-2. Jausovec won the Italian, over Lesley Hunt, 6-1, 6-3. Evert put her U.S. Clay title on hold after four victorious years, and tall Kathy May, 20, swung into the void to beat South African Brigitte Cuypers, 6-4, 4-6, 6-2.

A major innovation in equipment was introduced in 1976. New rackets in a dizzying variety of designs and materials—wood, metal, fiberglass, alloys, composites—had been marketed over the previous decade, but the biggest stir since the introduction of Wilson's steel T-2000 in 1967 was created by the Prince racket, with its oversized head. Howard Head, founder of Head Ski and architect of that company's headlong plunge into tennis equipment, joined forces with the manufacturer of Prince ball machines to produce the revolutionary and subsequently imitated new racket, which had much the same balance as conventional rackets but twice the hitting area.

1977

Jimbo, Vilas, Borg battle for No. 1

Guillermo Vilas Fuelled by crowd, out-duels Jimmy Connors in final U.S. Open at Forest Hills.

By any standard, 1977 was a landmark year for tennis. Wimbledon, the oldest of tournaments, celebrated its Centenary. The U.S. Open was played at Forest Hills for the last time. And a technological innovation, the 'double strung' or 'spaghetti' racket, caused such a stir that it was banned from tournament play several months after gaining notoriety, leading to the definition of a racket for the first time in the official rules of the game.

Three men—Bjorn Borg, Guillermo Vilas and Jimmy Connors—waged their own version of the year's hit movie, the science-fiction classic *Star Wars*. They were in a stratospheric super class, a galaxy above anyone else in tennis.

Borg won Wimbledon and had the most solid record, including winning margins against both his rivals. Vilas won the French and U.S. Opens and fashioned the longest winning streak of the 10 years of the open era. Connors won the World Championship of Tennis in Dallas and the Grand Prix Masters, and was runner-up at Wimbledon and Forest Hills. The debate as to who was No. 1 continued right through the Masters, which, because of U.S. television considerations, was moved back by new Grand Prix sponsor Colgate-Palmolive to the first week of January 1978.

There was no similar disagreement as to who was the

ruler of women's tennis. Chris Evert remained the indisputable No. 1, despite Virginia Wade's coronation—after 15 years as the lady-in-waiting—as the queen of Wimbledon.

The celebrations of Wimbledon's Centenary fortnight began with the All England Lawn Tennis and Croquet Club honoring 41 of the 52 living singles champions. A crowd of 14,000 packed Centre Court, and their applause swelled as the Band of the Welsh Guards played *The March of the King* from the opera *Aida,* signaling a wonderfully nostalgic 'Parade of Champions.' The former winners strode out onto the most famous lawn in tennis to receive commemorative medals from the Duke of Kent in a brief, dignified ceremony.

In a touching final gesture, medals were presented to Elizabeth 'Bunny' Ryan, 85, and Jacques 'Toto' Brugnon, 82, 'representing all the doubles champions.' Ryan, winner of 12 women's doubles and seven mixed titles between 1914 and 1934, moved slowly, on walking sticks, but cast them aside to wave to the crowd. Brugnon, winner of Wimbledon doubles titles, twice each with fellow French 'Musketeers' Henri Cochet and Jean Borotra, used a cane and later held the arm of the fourth 'Musketeer,' René Lacoste. Toto died the next

1977 THE MAJOR CHAMPIONSHIPS

Australian Open
Men's Singles (Jan.): Roscoe Tanner
Men's Singles (Dec.): Vitas Gerulaitis
Women's Singles (Jan.): Kerry Melville Reid
Women's Singles (Dec.): Evonne Goolagong Cawley
Men's Doubles (Jan.): Arthur Ashe / Tony Roche
Men's Doubles (Dec.): Ray Ruffels / Allan Stone
Women's Doubles (Dec.): Evonne Goolagong Cawley /
  Helen Gourlay Cawley and Mona Schallau Guerrant /
  Kerry Melville Reid (SHARED - RAINED OUT)
Women's Doubles (Jan.): Dianne Balestrat Fromholtz /
  Helen Gourlay Cawley
French Open
Men's Singles: Guillermo Vilas
Women's Singles: Mima Jausovec
Men's Doubles: Brian Gottfried / Raul Ramirez
Women's Doubles: Regina Marsikova / Pam Teeguarden
Mixed Doubles: Mary Carillo / John McEnroe
Wimbledon
Men's Singles: Bjorn Borg
Women's Singles: Virginia Wade
Men's Doubles: Geoff Masters / Ross Case
Women's Doubles: Helen Gourlay Cawley / JoAnne Russell
Mixed Doubles: Greer Stevens / Bob Hewitt
U.S. Open
Men's Singles: Guillermo Vilas
Women's Singles: Chris Evert
Men's Doubles: Bob Hewitt / Frew McMillan
Women's Doubles: Martina Navratilova / Betty Stove
Mixed Doubles: Betty Stove / Frew McMillan

winter, but for this moment he was ebullient.

The tournament was also richly memorable. Left-hander John McEnroe, 18, of Douglaston, N.Y., became the youngest semi-finalist in Wimbledon's 100 years, the first player ever to come through the qualifying rounds and get that far. He won eight matches in all before Connors brought him back to reality, 6-3, 6-3, 4-6, 6-4. In the other semi-final, Borg defeated the swift and flashy Vitas Gerulaitis, 6-4, 3-6, 6-3, 3-6, 8-6, in breathtaking combat between the charging Lithuanian Lion and the baseline defending Swede. The sustained quality of the shotmaking and drama made this, in the opinion of longtime observers, one of the all-time Centre Court classics.

The final also lived up to a majestic standard. Borg and Connors—destined to be remembered as the archrivals of the '70s—battled each other from the baseline in torrid rallies seldom seen on grass. Connors seemed out of it at 0-4 in the fifth set, but roused himself for one last challenge and came back to 4-4 before a crucial double fault in the ninth game cost him his momentum, his serve and the match, 3-6, 6-2, 6-1, 5-7, 6-4.

In the women's singles, 14-year-old Californian Tracy Austin became one of the youngest players to compete at Wimbledon (Austrian Mita Klima was 13 in 1907). She defeated Ellie Vessies-Appel, 6-3, 6-3, then showed tremendous poise and groundstrokes in losing a Centre Court match to defending champion Evert, 6-1, 6-1. That match, and her first victory ever over Billie Jean King on grass—6-1, 6-2 in the quarter-finals—took an enormous emotional toll on Evert and left her curiously flat for her semi-final against Wade.

'Our Ginny,' as the British affectionately called third seeded Wade, had never prepared better for a tournament, nor felt more self-confident. She hadn't gone beyond the semi-finals in 15 previous Wimbledons, but she kept the pressure on with bold approach shots and magnificent net play to beat Evert, 6-2, 4-6, 6-1. Wade was much more passive in the final against six-foot, 170-pound Betty Stove, the first Dutch finalist at Wimbledon, who had knocked off second-seeded Martina Navratilova in the quarters, 9-8 (8-6), 3-6, 6-1. But Ginny settled down and let her erratic opponent make the mistakes. Wade won nine of the last 10 games and the match, 4-6, 6-3, 6-1.

Wade, the first Englishwoman to win her national title since Ann Jones in 1969, accepted the gold championship plate from Queen Elizabeth II, who was making her first appearance at Wimbledon since 1962 in honor of the Centenary and her own Silver Jubilee celebration. British reserve gave way to an unbridled outpouring of patriotic sentiment. The Duchess of Kent waved excitedly to Wade from the Royal Box, and thousands of delighted Britons broke into a spontaneous, moving chorus of *For She's a Jolly Good Fellow.*

Stove wound up with a 'cripple' as a triple loser of finals—runner-up with Navratilova in the women's doubles to unseeded Floridian JoAnne Russell and Aussie Helen Gourlay Cawley, 6-3, 6-3, and with Frew McMillan in the mixed doubles to South Africans Bob Hewitt and Greer Stevens, 3-6, 7-5, 6-4. In the men's doubles, the first-seeded defending champions Brian Gottfried and Raul Ramirez fell to the Indian-American entry of Sashi Menon and Jim Delaney in the first round, paving the way for an all-Australian final. Ross Case and Geoff Masters, runners-up the previous year, beat John Alexander and Phil Dent in another thriller, 6-3, 6-4, 3-6, 8-9 (4-7), 6-4.

Wimbledon was the highlight of the year. But the most impressive achievement was the winning streak Vilas compiled the last six months of the year. Vilas started the year as runner-up to Roscoe Tanner, the hard-serving left-hander, in the Australian Open, 6-3, 6-3, 6-3. Tanner beat perpetual Ken Rosewall, 42, in the semis, 6-4, 3-6, 6-3, 6-1. Rosewall had avenged his semi-final loss of a year previous by dethroning Mark Edmondson, 6-4, 7-6, 4-6, 6-4. Vilas' semi-final victim, 6-4, 1-6, 6-3, 6-4, was Alexander, who had toppled ex-champ Arthur Ashe, 6-3, 6-4, 4-6, 7-6.

By winning the French Open in the absence of Borg and Connors, Vilas lost only one set in seven matches, and his 6-0, 6-3, 6-0 victory over Gottfried in the drizzly final was the most decisive since the tournament went international in 1925. Thus Guillermo shed his image as 'The Eternal Second'—"they call me that in the Argentine press"— and removed an enormous psychological burden.

Driven by his coach-manager, the hirsute and menacing Romanian Ion Tiriac, Vilas became the fittest and most iron-willed player on the professional circuit. Over his last six months of 1977 he won 13 of 14 tournaments, 80 of 81 matches, including the U.S. Open. His 50-match, July-through-September winning streak was the longest since the advent of open tennis, eclipsing Rod Laver's 31 straight matches of 1969. And he immediately launched another streak of 30.

The record streak ended controversially the first week in October in the final of a tournament at Aix-en-Provence, France, Vilas defaulting angrily after losing the first two sets to Ilie Nastase, who was using the 'spaghetti' racket that had just been barred, effective the following week.

The crowning glory of Vilas' streak was winning the U.S. Open, played at the West Side Tennis Club in the Forest Hills section of New York's borough of Queens for the last time, after 68 years as the Championships site. Clumsy last-ditch efforts by the club's officials to retain the Open could not compensate for their years of foot-dragging on making physical improvements. W. E. 'Slew' Hester of Jackson, Miss., president of the USTA, decided that the neighborhood was too congested, the club management too stubbornly old-fashioned, to accommodate America's premier tournament, which was given 28 hours of television coverage by CBS-TV under a new five-year, $10-million rights contract. Hester set in motion ambitious plans for building a new USTA National Tennis Center in nearby Flushing Meadows Park, site of the 1939-40 and 1964-65 New York World's Fairs.

Vilas helped make 'the last Forest Hills' memorable. He lost only 16 games in five matches up to the semifinals, in which he beat Harold Solomon, 6-2, 7-6 (7-3), 6-2. Connors removed his nemesis of the 1975 final, Manolo Orantes, 6-4, 6-2, 6-3, and then the first Italian ever to get so far, Corrado Barazzutti, 7-5, 6-3, 7-5. In the final, Vilas displayed great physical and mental stamina and a new technical weapon—a fine sliced backhand approach shot—to beat Connors in a match of brutish grace, 2-6, 6-3, 7-6 (7-4), 6-0. The sellout crowd of more than 16,000 cheered for the popular Argentine left-hander against 'the ugly American.' After the last point, many Latins in the crowd spilled into the court, hoisted Vilas to their shoulders and carried him around the old horseshoe stadium like a conquering hero. Connors, furious at both the outcome and the reception given the victor, left in a snit, not bothering to wait for the trophy presentation ceremonies.

Probably the only one leaving Forest Hills feeling worse than Connors was a spectator named James Reilly, suffering a bullet wound during McEnroe's 6-2, 4-6, 6-4, win over Eddie Dibbs, a third-round night match. It was a random shot from outside the stadium, never traced, and Reilly, carted away to hospital in a stretcher, was only mildly scratched in his left thigh. Dibbs and

Mac left the court for a few minutes. The police were wary and nervous for a while because it was the time of the 'Son of Sam' killings that terrorized New York, particularly Queens.

Vilas dominated the Grand Prix point standings, winning the $300,000 prize ear-marked as the top share of the $1.5-million bonus pool put up by Colgate. On the year, Vilas won a record 17 tournaments and $800,642 in prize money—more than he had earned in five previous pro seasons. He played the most ambitious tournament schedule of any of the top men and finished with a 145-14 record, including Davis Cup matches. (With Vilas and Ricardo Cano playing singles, Argentina upset the United States in the American Zone final to reach the Cup semi-finals for the first time.) During his 50-match streak, Vilas won an astonishing 109 of 125 sets. Starting with the French Open, he won 57 consecutive matches on clay.

But even though *World Tennis* magazine declared him No. 1 for the year, most other authorities disagreed and bestowed that mythical honor on Borg, who, top-seeded, defaulted to Dick Stockton, 3-6, 6-4, 1-0, in the fourth round of the U.S. Open with a shoulder injury. The 21-year-old Swede had the best winning percentage for the season—.920, on a record of 81-7. He won 13 of the 20 tournaments he played. Including the Masters—played in 1978, but considered the climax of the 1977 season—Borg was 3-0 over Vilas (two victories in the spring, the third in the semis of the Masters, 6-3, 6-3), and 2-1 over Connors, who beat him in the Masters final, 6-4, 1-6, 6-4, before a crowd of 17,150 at Madison Square Garden.

Connors may have had the season-ending last laugh, but he finished No. 3 after having been the best player in the world in 1974 and 1976, and No. 2 to Arthur Ashe in 1975. Connors won eight of 21 tournaments, 70 of 81 matches. He was in four big finals, winning the WCT playoffs over Stockton, 6-7, 6-1, 6-3, 6-3, and the Masters, losing to Borg at Wimbledon and to Vilas at

Forest Hills. But Connors was 1-2 head-to-head against Borg and 0-2 against Vilas, including a gripping match in the round-robin portion of the Masters, won by Vilas, 6-4, 3-6, 7-5. This spellbinder kept a record tournament crowd of 18,590 riveted to their seats in the Garden until past midnight, 42 minutes into a Friday morning.

While Borg, Vilas, and Connors constituted the ruling triumvirate of men's tennis, there were other noteworthy performers. Spaniard Orantes underwent surgery to repair a pinched nerve in his left elbow in the spring, but came back splendidly to bedazzle Connors, 6-1, 6-3, in the U.S. Clay Court final at Indianapolis and to topple Dibbs, 7-6 (7-3), 7-5, 6-4, in the 50th anniversary U.S. Pro Championships.

Gerulaitis became the first American since Barry MacKay in 1960 to win the Italian on slow clay, beating paisano Tonino Zugarelli, 6-2, 7-6 (7-2), 3-6, 7-6 (7-1) in three hours, 20 minutes. Later Vitas, the boulevardier, demonstrated his versatility by winning the second Australian Open of the calendar year (yes, there were two!) on grass at Melbourne, over Englishman John Lloyd, 6-3, 7-6 (7-1), 5-7, 3-6, 6-2. The tournament was moved up to mid-December so that it could be included in the Grand Prix.

In doubles, South Africans Hewitt, 37, and Frew McMillan, 35, won 13 tournaments, even though separated for four months during the summer because McMillan played World Team Tennis. Their biggest victory came at Forest Hills, where they captured their first U.S. Open doubles title over Gottfried and Ramirez, 6-4, 6-0. Hewitt and McMillan also won the Masters over Stan Smith and Bob Lutz, 7-5, 7-6, 6-3.

Gottfried and Ramirez won the Italian Open doubles for a record fourth consecutive year, over McNair and Stewart, 7-6 (7-2), 6-7 (6-8), 7-5, and recaptured the French Open title, over a Czech-Polish blend of Jan Kodes and Wojtek Fibak, 7-6, 4-6, 6-3, 6-4. Ashe and Tony Roche won the Australian Open, Part I in January, over Americans Erik van Dillen and Charlie Pasarell, 6-4, 6-4. It reverted to an Aussie party in December's Part II, Allan Stone and lefty Ray Ruffels beating Dent and Alexander, 7-6, 7-6. Vijay Amritraj and Stockton made their only doubles victory together count, collecting $40,000 apiece for beating the makeshift pair of Italian Adriano Panatta and Gerulaitis in the WCT doubles finals at Kansas City, 7-6, 7-6, 4-6, 6-3.

The Colgate Grand Prix embraced 76 tournaments, with total prize money of approximately $9 million.

1977 CHAMPIONS AND LEADERS

Top Player Earnings: Men	**Wightman Cup:** United States
Guillermo Vilas $766,065	**Grand Prix Masters, NYC**
Top Player Earnings: Women	Jimmy Connors
Chris Evert $503,134	**WCT, Dallas**
Year-End Number One	Jimmy Connors
Men: Jimmy Connors	**Virginia Slims**
Women: Chris Evert	**Championships, NYC**
Davis Cup: Australia	Chris Evert
Federation Cup: United States	

Worldwide, men's tournaments offered about $12 million, excluding World Team Tennis and exhibition matches. Fifteen players made more than $200,000 in prize money, including Hewitt ($234,184), whose earnings came mostly in doubles. Five players (Vilas, Borg, Ramirez, Smith, and Orantes) crossed the once unimaginable $1-million career earnings mark, increasing the number of tennis millionaires to 13 since Laver first passed the milestone in 1971.

Australia recovered the Davis Cup for the first time since 1973 and tied the U.S. for the most possessions (24). Italy, arriving in Sydney to defend, got a left-handed surprise. Roche, at 32, seemingly well past his prime, had last played for the Cup 10 years before, then only in the clinching doubles with John Newcombe over Spain. But he was Capt. Neale Fraser's ace from deep in the hole for the showdown on White City grass, and justified the long-shot gamble with serve-and-volleying flair to astound Panatta, 6-3, 6-4, 6-4. Alexander took care of Barazzutti, combative though never having won a match on the green, 6-2, 8-6, 4-6, 6-2, and it looked like a romp. However Adriano Panatta and Paolo Bertolucci, jarred Alexander and Dent, 6-4, 6-4, 7-5. It was 2-1. With a goodly number of Italian immigrants in the crowd screaming for him—*"Dai [come on], Adriano!"*—Panatta drove Alexander to the brink of defeat in a difficult swirling wind, but J. A. shoved harder when pushed to wrap up the Cup in five, 6-4, 4-6, 2-6, 8-6, 11-9.

Rosie Casals and Stockton repeated as champions at the third (and last) Spalding Mixed Doubles Classic in Dallas, beating Stove and McMillan, 4-6, 7-6, 6-7, 6-2, 7-6. Despite good attendance and TV exposure, an appealing event was scrapped because players couldn't fit it into their singles-emphasizing schedules.

World Team Tennis completed its fourth season, with the Boston Lobsters topping the East Division, and the Phoenix Racquets the West Division. Ten teams played 44 matches each, and again all operated in the red. The New York Apples, led by King and Sandy Mayer, won the league championship, defeating Phoenix in the final round of the playoffs, 27-22, 28-17.

Evert won three of the four biggest women's tournaments, her fourth Virginia Slims Championship, played at Madison Square Garden, over Englishwoman Sue Barker, 2-6, 6-1, 6-1; her third consecutive U.S. Open, matching a feat last accomplished by Maureen Connolly, 1951-53, and the Colgate Series Championship.

Evert represented the United States for the first time in the Federation Cup, which attracted 42 nations to the grass courts of Devonshire Park in Eastbourne, England, the week before Wimbledon. Chrissie didn't lose a set in singles as the United States romped past Austria, Switzerland, France, South Africa and Australia. Evert defeated Kerry Reid, 7-5, 6-3, and King disposed of Dianne Fromholtz, 6-1, 2-6, 6-2, to clinch the championship.

Evert and King were too much for Britain as the U.S claimed a 39th victory, 7-0, in the 54-year-old Wightman Cup, played on the West Coast for the first time, at Oakland Coliseum. Chrissie opened with a 7-5, 7-6, victory over Wade, and trimmed Barker, 6-1, 6-2. King blistered Barker, 6-1, 6-4, and slipped past Wade, 6-4, 3-6, 8-6, the two of them treating a crowd of 11,317 to a glorious evening.

In all, Evert at age 22 won 11 of 14 tournaments, 70 of 74 matches, and $453,134 in prize money. She was ranked No. 1 in the U.S. for the fourth consecutive year and No. 1 in doubles for the first time, with Casals. Evert won the U.S. Open without losing a set for the second straight year and stretched her remarkable clay-court winning streak to 23 tournaments and 113 matches, dating back to August 1973. Even though Fromholtz surprised her in the round-robin portion of the eight-woman Colgate Series Championships, 7-6 (5-4), 6-4, Evert reached the final and claimed the richest prize in women's tennis, $75,000, by beating King, 6-2, 6-2.

Although Evert was the dominant force, and Wade the sentimental success story, there were other notable achievements in 1977.

Austin, five feet tall and weighing 90 pounds, reached the quarter-finals of the U.S. Open, beating fourth seed Barker, 6-1, 6-4, and Ruzici, 6-3, 7-5 before Stove sent her back to school, 6-2, 6-2. The 14-year-old took enough time off from her eighth-and ninth-grade classes in Rolling Hills, Calif., to play 10 professional tournaments and wound up ranked No. 12 in the world, and No. 4 in the United States—the youngest ever to crack the Top Ten until Jennifer Capriati, a younger 14 in 1990.

Martina Navratilova, starting the season slimmed down and determined to make up for a disappointing 1976, won four of 11 tournaments on the Virginia Slims circuit, beating Evert in the final of the season opener at Washington, D.C., 6-2, 6-3.

Transsexual Renée Richards won her year-long legal

struggle for acceptance in women's tournaments when a New York judge ruled that she could not be barred from the U.S. Open for failing the Olympic chromosome test. The court ruled that medical evidence proved Richards was 'female,' and the USTA and WTA dropped efforts to bar her. She lost in the first round of the Open singles, but reached the doubles final with Californian Betty Ann Grubb Stuart before losing to Navratilova and Stove, 6-1, 7-6. (Stove also won the mixed doubles, with Frew McMillan, over King and Gerulaitis, 6-2, 3-6, 6-3.)

Thereafter, Richards—the lone entrant to use both men's and women's dressing rooms at the U.S. Championships—became a regular competitor on the women's circuit, though several players defaulted against her in protest. Renee lost to Wimbledon champs in her Forest Hills ventures: To Neale Fraser, 6-0, 6-1, 6-1, in 1960, and Wade, 6-1, 6-4 in 1977, both first rounders. She did win a minor tournament, Pensacola, Fla., defeating Evert in the semis (Jeanne Evert, that is), 6-1, 4-6, 6-2, and Caroline Stoll in the final, 6-2, 6-2.

King, recovered from knee surgery the previous November, worked her way back into shape and won three consecutive tournaments and 18 straight matches in the autumn to reach the playoff finale of the $2-million Colgate Series, which carried a $600,000 bonus pool. She was 0-4 on the year against Evert, but 2-0 against WTT teammate Wade, 3-0 against Navratilova, 1-0 against Barker and 4-0 against Stove. King, winning six titles, finished the year with a 53-6 record, ranked No. 2 in the U.S. While the topcats were away, employed in WTT, lesser ladies were at play in Europe: Janet Newberry won the Italian, 6-3, 7-6, (7-5) over Czech Renata Tomanova. Mima Jausovec became the first Yugoslav to win the French, beating Romanian Florenta Mihai, 6-2, 6-7 (5-7), 6-1.

Kerry Reid, at 29, won the two-headed Australian Open for the first time—Part I over fellow Aussie Dianne Fromholtz, 7-5, 6-2. Part II, in December, went to Goolagong, her fourth, over Helen Gourlay Cawley, 6-3, 6-0. Formally it was Mrs. Roger Cawley defeating Mrs. Robert Cawley (the respective English and Australian husbands unrelated). That extended her Aussie streak to 20 match wins. Kept out of the January version because she was pregnant, Goolagong gave birth to her first child—daughter Kelly—in May, and launched a comeback in the fall.

The hottest political controversy of the year con-cerned the rise and fall of the 'double strung' or 'spaghetti' racket, which was actually a radical stringing technique that could be applied to any standard racket frame. There were several versions, but they all used two sets of vertical strings, supported by five or six cross strings threaded through them, and braced with fish line, adhesive tape, rope or other protuberances, including a plastic tubing called 'spaghetti.' While rackets thus strung generally had a very low tension—between 35 and 55 pounds—they were able to generate tremendous power because of a 'trampoline effect,' the ball sinking deep in the double layer of strings and being propelled out. Because the dual layer of strings also moved, they were able to 'brush' the ball, artificially imitating a heavy topspin stroke. Thus, some players were able to hit the ball extremely hard from the backcourt and still keep it in play. The 'spaghetti' racket was all the more maddening to play against because the ball came off it with a dull thud that made it difficult to judge.

The 'double strung' racket was invented in West Germany by a former horticulturist named Werner Fisher, and it created a major scandal in club and national tournaments there as second- and third-line players became champions with it. An adaptation of the racket was first used in a major tournament by Australian lefty Barry Phillips-Moore in the French Open, where he beat Chilean Davis Cupper Pato Cornejo, ranked considerably above him, 6-4, 6-4, 6-0, before losing to fifteenth-seeded Balazs Taroczy. A number of professional players used it in Europe during the summer and it gained further notoriety at the U.S. Open when an obscure American player named Mike Fishbach used his home-made version to trounce Billy Martin, 6-1, 7-5, and 16th-seeded ex-champ Stan Smith, 6-0, 6-2, in the first two rounds. Alarm bells rang but Brit John Feaver quelled the fever for a while, 2-6, 6-4, 6-0.

However, a couple of weeks later, Nastase was beaten, 6-4, 2-6, 6-4, by a French player, Georges Goven, using a 'spaghetti' racket in Paris and swore he would never play against it again. The following week he turned up with one himself and used it to win a tournament at Aix-en-Provence, ending Vilas' long winning streak in the best-of-five set final. Vilas quit after two sets, down 6-1, 7-5, claiming that playing against the exaggerated spin injured his elbow.

The ITF had already acted by that time, however, putting a 'temporary freeze' on use of the double-strung rackets in tournaments, effective Oct. 2. Unfortunately for Vilas that was the day the tournament ended. The ITF based its decision on a report by the University of Brunswick in West Germany, which indicated that every hit with the racket was in fact a 'double hit,' in violation of the rules.

The ITF made its 'ban' permanent the following June by adopting a definition of a racket for the first time: "A racket shall consist of a frame, which may be of any material, weight, size of shape and stringing. The stringing must be uniform and smooth and may be of any material. The strings must be alternately interlaced or bonded where they cross. The distance between the main and/or cross strings shall not be less than one quarter of an inch nor more than one-half inch. If there are attachments they must be used only to prevent wear and tear and must not alter the flight of the ball. They must be uniform with a maximum protrusion of .04 of an inch."

In November, 11 days after his 43rd birthday, Rosewall won Hong Kong, 6-3, 5-7, 6-4, 6-4, over 31-year-old Tom Gorman. He was not quite as old as Pancho Gonzalez, 43, had been in winning DesMoines in 1972. It was Rosewall's 32nd (and last) singles championship of the open era. But, of course, 'Muscles,' or 'The Doomsday Stroking Machine,' won many more during his amateur days. The little Aussie had been a title winner for almost three decades, and he would glide into 1978 to show some kids what it was all about.

1978

McEnroe rising fast but Connors, Borg not done

Bjorn Borg
Narrowest of No. 1's in continuing rivalry with Jimmy Connors.

In 1978, as Wimbledon began its second century and Stade Roland Garros in Paris celebrated its 50th anniversary, the U.S. Open moved to the new U.S. Tennis Association National Tennis Center, the most important new arena for international tennis in half a century.

Bjorn Borg and Jimmy Connors continued their spirited battle of king-of-the-hill in men's tennis, Martina Navratilova and Chris Evert waged a similarly lovely little war for the No. 1 ranking among the women, and several precocious young talents blossomed—19-year-old John McEnroe starting to challenge the top men, and high-school girls Tracy Austin and Pam Shriver asserting themselves in women's tournaments.

Perhaps nothing better symbolized what happened to the once-elitist, white-flanneled sport of tennis in the 1970s than the fact that the U.S. Open, America's premier tournament, moved to a public park, in Flushing Meadow, Queens, N.Y. The National Tennis Center was built, remarkably, in one year on 16 acres of city-owned land in Flushing Meadow Park, adjacent to Shea Stadium.

Relocated to Flushing by drawling, cigar-chomping W. E. 'Slew' Hester, a 66-year-old wildcat oilman from Jackson, Miss., the U.S. Championships was retreating from 97 years in such patrician clubs as Newport (R.I.) Casino, Philadelphia Cricket Club and the West Side Tennis Club. Hester talked like a Southern conservative, but proved in a memorable two-year term to be perhaps the most progressive president in the history of the USTA. Many second-guessed him in September 1977 when, fed up with the reactionary board of governors of the West Side Tennis Club, he announced that the Open would be moved. Few believed the new complex Hester envisioned a couple of miles away could be completed in 12 months, and many considered the project 'Hester's Folly.' But Hester's perseverance and leadership, despite arthritis so severe it was difficult for him to walk, enabled the USTA to cut through bureaucratic red tape, union disputes and cost overruns and get the splendid complex built in time for the 1978 Open.

The National Tennis Center was dedicated on Aug. 30, 1978. Its main arena—Louis Armstrong Stadium, site of the Singer Bowl for the 1964-65 World's Fair and named for the late jazz great who lived nearby—accommodated nearly 20,000 spectators, with barely a bad seat in the house. In addition to the steeply banked, red, white and blue stadium, the complex included a 6,000-seat grandstand, 25 additional lighted outdoor courts, and nine indoor courts, all with the same acrylic asphalt surface that approximates the hard courts most Americans play on. Under a lease agreement between the USTA and the city of New York, the facility is open to the public year-round and is available to the USTA for tournaments and special events 60 days a year, at a modest fee. The USTA, in turn, spent $10 million to renovate and enlarge a stadium that was intended for concerts but had fallen into terrible disrepair.

The result was the most significant new venue for world tennis since the modern All England Club was opened in the London suburb of Wimbledon in 1922 and Stade Roland Garros was dedicated as a civic monument in Paris for the 1928 Davis Cup challenge round.

Roland Garros celebrated its golden anniversary during the 1978 French Open Championships. On balance, this was a dull tournament, but on a day when 32 past champions were honored in gala center-court ceremonies, Borg asserted himself as one of the greatest by winning the most important clay court test for the third time, five days past his 20th birthday. His win came two weeks after he'd won the Italian Open in five difficult sets over Italian Adriano Panatta (Romans saluted Borg with showers of jeers and coins for depriving their matinee idol of victory). He repeated the arduous clay-court 'double' he had first achieved in 1974 by sweeping through seven matches in Paris in 21 straight sets, dropping only 32 games. In the final, he trounced defending champion Guillermo Vilas, 6-1, 6-1, 6-3.

Borg went on to become the first man since Rod Laver in 1962 to sweep the Italian, French and Wimbledon singles—the 'Old World Triple'—in one season. In dominating the grass of Wimbledon as he had the clay in Rome and Paris, Borg also equaled a more important milestone. He became the first man since Englishman Fred Perry in 1934-35-36 to win the

Wimbledon singles three successive years.

Borg routed a rejuvenated Tom Okker, 6-4, 6-4, 6-4, in one semi, while Connors blunted Vitas Gerulaitis, 9-7, 6-2, 6-1 in the other. In a one-sided final, Borg served, volleyed and smashed as never before to win 6-2, 6-2, 6-3. He also displayed a new weapon, a sliced backhand approach shot to Connors' vulnerable forehand, which stayed low on the fast grass. "The way Borg played today," marveled Perry, who hustled down from behind his microphone in the BBC radio commentary booth to congratulate the young Swede on Centre Court, "if he had fallen out of a 45th-story window of a skyscraper, he would have gone straight up."

At the midpoint of the season, it seemed that Borg, with his beefed-up serve, had begun to dominate his grand rivalry with Connors. Despite a loss in the 1977 Grand Prix Masters the first week of the new year, Borg had won five of their last six meetings, giving up only 11 games in six sets, through Wimbledon.

But Connors immediately began to train for another showdown, vowing to "follow that sonofabitch to the ends of the earth" for revenge. He worked on adding oomph to his serve—which deserted him in the Wimbledon final—and shoring up his forehand. Having won 18 straight matches going into the Wimbledon final, he didn't lose another the rest of the summer, winning Grand Prix tournaments at Washington over Eddie Dibbs, Indianapolis (the U.S. Clay Court) over Jose Higueras, and Stowe, Vt., over Tim Gullikson, as he honed his game for the U.S. Open.

1978 THE MAJOR CHAMPIONSHIPS

Australian Open
Men's Singles: Guillermo Vilas
Women's Singles: Chris O'Neil
Men's Doubles: Wojtek Fibak / Kim Warwick
Women's Doubles: Betsy Nagelsen / Renata Tomanova
French Open
Men's Singles: Bjorn Borg
Women's Singles: Virginia Ruzici
Men's Doubles: Gene Mayer / Hank Pfister
Women's Doubles: Mima Jausovec / Virginia Ruzici
Mixed Doubles: Renata Tomanova / Pavel Slozil
Wimbledon
Men's Singles: Bjorn Borg
Women's Singles: Martina Navratilova
Men's Doubles: Bob Hewitt / Frew McMillan
Women's Doubles: Kerry Melville Reid / Wendy Turnbull
Mixed Doubles: Betty Stove / Frew McMillan
U.S. Open
Men's Singles: Jimmy Connors
Women's Singles: Chris Evert
Men's Doubles: Bob Lutz / Stan Smith
Women's Doubles: Billie Jean King / Martina Navratilova
Mixed Doubles: Betty Stove / Frew McMillan

Connors' moment of truth at the Open came in a fourth-round victory over Panatta. Panatta served for the match at 5-4 in the fifth set of this three-hour, 36-minute epic, came within two points of victory at 30-30, and later fended off four match points. Connors got to the fifth with an astounding shot—a backhand down the line on the dead run from 10 feet wide of the court, which he somehow reached and drilled one-handed around the net post for a winner, practically parting net judge Reid Johnson's hair.

Moments later, Connors had the match, 4-6, 6-4, 6-1, 1-6, 7-5, and that, he said later, gave him the impetus to steamroll through the final three rounds without losing a set: over Brian Gottfried, 6-2, 7-6 (7-0), 6-1; McEnroe, 6-2, 6-2, 7-5, and Borg, 6-4, 6-2, 6-2. Never before were Connors' skill, will and churning internal aggression better shown than in the final. He annihilated Borg, who had a blister on the thumb of his racket hand, almost as badly as he had been ravaged at Wimbledon, 6-4, 6-2, 6-2, ending the Swede's 39-match streak.

Connors, the first man since Bill Tilden in the 1920s to reach the singles final five consecutive years, thus became the first man since Perry in 1933-34, 36 to win three U.S. singles titles, and the first American to do so since Tilden. By quirk of history, Connors also gained the singular distinction of having won on grass (1974), clay (1976), and hard court (1978).

The U.S. Open final was the final meeting of the year between Borg and Connors. The last four months of the season belonged to McEnroe, the often-irate left-hander from Douglaston, N.Y., who was the only man other than Ken Rosewall, 19 in 1954, to have reached the semi-finals at both Wimbledon and the U.S. Championships while still a teenager.

After losing to Connors in the Open, McEnroe broke his maiden, winning four Grand Prix singles tournaments, at Hartford over Johan Kriek, San Francisco over

Dick Stockton, Stockholm over Tim Gullikson, and London over Gullikson. He also won seven doubles events, led the U.S. to its first possession of the Davis Cup since 1972 with a spectacular singles debut, and won both the singles and doubles titles at the Colgate Grand Prix Masters at Madison Square Garden the second week in January 1979. His singles record over that stretch was 49-7. McEnroe collected $463,866 in the six months after he turned pro in June following his National Intercollegiate singles title as a Stanford University freshman.

At Stockholm, on a fast tile court, he won his introductory meeting with Borg, 6-3, 6-4. His left-handed serve, sliced low and wide so that it skidded away from Borg's two-fisted backhand, was so effective that McEnroe lost only seven points in 10 service games. It was the first time that Borg, 22, had lost to a younger player.

McEnroe, still virtually unknown, made his Davis Cup debut in doubles in September. He partnered Gottfried to the decisive point in America's 3-2 victory over Chile in the American Zone Final at Santiago, 3-6, 6-3, 8-6, 6-3, over Jaime Fillol and Belus Prajoux. Capt. Tony Trabert used Arthur Ashe and Gerulaitis in singles in the 3-2 semi-final at Goteborg, Sweden, and neither could cope with Borg. But both beat Kjell Johansson. Reliables Stan Smith and Bob Lutz, in a tight one over Ove Bengtsson and Borg, were the margin, 2-6, 6-3, 3-6, 7-5, 6-3.

Following that, McEnroe had his Davis Cup singles coming-out party spectacularly in the final at Rancho Mirage, Calif. He lost his serve only once in demoralizing John Lloyd, 6-1, 6-2, 6-2, in the opening match and Buster Mottram, 6-2, 6-2, 6-1, in the clincher of the 4-1 U.S. victory over Great Britain. Mottram's second match stinging of Gottfried, 4-6, 2-6, 10-8, 6-4, 6-3, cheered the Brits, 41 years after their last presence in the final. But that was a mere speed bump. Smith and Lutz handled David Lloyd and Mark Cox, 6-2, 6-2, 6-3, and left the rest to Mac.

This ended a five-year drought for the numerous gang of Capt. Trabert, and gave the U.S. possession of the trophy symbolizing international team supremacy for a record 25th time. Tony used nine players during the victorious campaign, a record. As for McEnroe's dominance, it should be noted that never before in 67 Davis Cup finals had a player lost as few as 10 games in two singles matches. Bill Tilden in 1924, Jack Kramer in

1978 CHAMPIONS AND LEADERS

Top Player Earnings: Men
Eddie Dibbs $575,273
Top Player Earnings: Women
Chris Evert $454,486
Year-End Number One
Men: Jimmy Connors
Women: Martina Navratilova
Davis Cup: United States
Federation Cup: United States
Wightman Cup: Great Britain

ITF World Champion
Men: Bjorn Borg
Women: Chris Evert Lloyd
Grand Prix Masters, NYC
John McEnroe
WCT, Dallas
Vitas Gerulaitis
Virginia Slims
Championships, Oakland
Martina Navratilova

1946 and Borg in 1975 gave up 12. Mac was the only teenager to spearhead a U.S. Cup triumph with two singles wins, although Michael Chang, at age 18 in 1990, would win one.

McEnroe went into the season-ending Masters playoff AT New York's Madison Square Garden eager for a showdown with Connors, who had beaten him in all four of their career meetings. The Masters, designed to bring together the top eight finishers in the previous year's Grand Prix standings for a $400,000 shootout, had lost much of its luster because Borg and Vilas declined invitations. They had not played the minimum 20 Grand Prix tournaments required to qualify for shares of the $2-million Grand Prix bonus pool, and so turned their backs on the showcase finale. Connors did not qualify for his bonus either, but was coaxed at the 11th hour into defending his title.

The Connors-McEnroe duel was seen as the savior of a disappointing tournament, but it also fizzled because Connors aggravated a blood blister on his foot in the first set of their meeting in the round-robin portion of the tournament, and defaulted while trailing, 7-5, 3-0. McEnroe beat Eddie Dibbs in the semi-finals, 6-1, 6-4, and comebacking 35-year-old Ashe, 6-7 (5-7), 6-3, 7-5, in a scintillating final.

But even if McEnroe was, as Ashe called him, "the best player in the world the last four months of 1978," he was not in the running for Player of the Year honors based on his full-season record of 75-20. The run for the No. 1 ranking was strictly a match race between Borg and Connors.

Tennis magazine's ranking panel voted for Connors, but *World Tennis* and the International Federation—instituting a 'world champion' award—went for Borg. The 'World Champion' title was a new honor to be awarded annually by the International Tennis Federation for men and women. It was intended to establish an official No. 1 player for each calendar year and eliminate the confusion caused by diverse and often contradictory sets of rankings.

Borg was the unanimous choice of the selection committee of three former champions, Fred Perry, Australian Lew Hoad and Californian Don Budge. Their decision was based primarily on his superior record in traditional major events, although Borg also held a 3-2 edge over Connors in head-to-head meetings, including three four-man 'special events.'

Borg's record for the entire season was 88-8, includ-ing a 9-0 singles record in spurring Sweden past Ireland, Yugoslavia, Spain and Hungary to the semi-finals of the Davis Cup. He won 12 titles. Connors, who won 14, was 84-7 overall. He monopolized U.S titles, winning Indoor over Gullikson, plus Clay Court and Open. Following the Wimbledon final, he compiled a 30-match winning streak.

Other notable achievements in 1978:

'Broadway' Gerulaitis, the flamboyant 23-year-old New Yorker, got a default over injured Borg in the semifinals and captured the $100,000 top prize in the eight-man World Championship of Tennis finals at Dallas with an impressive 6-3, 6-2, 6-1 victory over Dibbs. Gerulaitis also collected the $100,000 top prize in WCT's 12-man, $300,000 invitational tournament at Forest Hills in July, beating Ilie Nastase in the final, 6-2, 6-0.

Vilas won eight tournaments, including the German Open over Pole Wojtek Fibak and the Australian Open, which ended Jan. 3, 1979. His 6-4, 6-4, 3-6, 6-3 triumph over unseeded Aussie John Marks was his third major singles title, to go along with his French and U.S. Open crowns of 1977. Amazing four-time champ Rosewall, accorded a seventh-seed at 44, won two rounds in this his 14th (and last) Aussie. Shut out of the titles department for the first time, Rosewall nevertheless would tack up a No. 34 ranking at the end of the year, earning $52,368 in prize money. Not bad for the clever codger.

Ashe, the Wimbledon champion and World No. 1 of 1975, started the year ranked only No. 257 because he had missed almost the entire 1977 season after surgery on a chronic heel ailment. He won three Grand Prix tournaments: San Jose over South African Bernie Mitton, Columbus over Lutz and Los Angeles over Gottfried. He also reached the Masters final and finished the season ranked No. 11.

Bob Hewitt and Frew McMillan won seven doubles titles, including their third at Wimbledon, over Peter Fleming and McEnroe, 6-1, 6-4, 6-2. Okker and Fibak also won seven tournaments, including the WCT finals at Kansas City over Smith and Lutz, for which they split an $80,000 prize. Smith and Lutz captured their third U.S. Open doubles, over Sherwood Stewart and Marty Riessen, 1-6, 7-5, 6-3. McEnroe and Fleming were the hottest team the second half of the season, winning six tournaments between August and December, plus the 1978 Masters over Okker and Fibak early in January, 1979.

On the women's side, the first half of the year belonged to Navratilova, the second half to Evert.

With Evert taking the first three months of the year as a vacation, Navratilova, at age 21, began to fulfill her rich promise. She dominated the Virginia Slims winter circuit—the last under the cigarette company's sponsorship—winning the first seven tournaments and the $150,000 final playoff at Oakland, Calif., over Evonne Goolagong, 7-6, 6-4. That was Navratilova's most important victory to date, an important psychological breakthrough for the expatriate Czech left-hander.

Evert returned to competition in the spring, but Navratilova, supremely fit and confident, beat her in the final of a pre-Wimbledon grass court tournament at Eastbourne, England, coming back from 1-4 in the final set and saving a match point, 6-4, 4-6, 9-7.

They met again in the Wimbledon final, and this time Navratilova came back from 2-4 in the final set, serving magnificently and outsteadying as well as overpowering Evert to win, 2-6, 6-4, 7-5. An Evert volley that beaned her seemed to shake the cobwebs from Martina in the second set as she held serve to 4-2 through two deuces and three break points. Navratilova, whose emotions had regularly overwhelmed her abundant talent, won 12 of the last 13 points. When it was over, Navratilova looked ecstatically toward her friend and manager, Hall of Fame golfer Sandra Haynie, an important stabilizing influence in her life. Martina shed a flood of tears and was puffy-eyed when she received the championship trophy from the Duchess of Kent.

"I don't know if I should cry or scream or laugh. I feel very happy that I won, but at the same time I'm very sad that I can't share this with my family," said Navratilova, who had not seen her parents or her 15-year-old sister, Jana, since defecting to the United States during the 1975 U.S. Open. Her victory, predictably, was all but neglected in the government-controlled media of Czechoslovakia, but her parents watched it on German television by driving to a town near the German border.

Navratilova and Billie Jean King, again foiled in her attempt to win a record-setting 20th career Wimbledon title, were upset in the quarter-finals of the doubles by Mona Schallau Guerrant and Sue Barker. But they did win the U.S. Open title, over Wimbledon champs Kerry Reid and Wendy Turnbull, 7-6 (9-7), 6-4. Australians Reid and Turnbull saved two match points in the tie-breaker to take the Wimbledon crown, a 4-6, 9-8 (12-10), 6-3, thriller over French Open champs Mima Jausovec and Virginia Ruzici. Betty Stove and McMillan won the mixed doubles at Wimbledon, 6-2, 6-2, and Flushing Meadow, 6-3, 7-6, both over King and Ray Ruffels. In a second rounder at Flushing, Mareen Louie and Andy Lucchesi set a mixed doubles tie-breaker record—34 points—in beating Diane Desfor and Horace Reid, 6-2, 6-7, 7-6 (18-16).

Navratilova won her first 37 matches of the year, but the streak finally came to an end in the quarter-finals of the Virginia Slims in Dallas. She was beaten by 15-year-old Californian Austin, 6-3, 2-6, 7-6 (5-4). The tingling match before 10,000 enthralled spectators went down to the final point of a best-of-nine-point tie-breaker, simultaneous match point for both. The tournament produced several startling upsets and three teenaged semi-finalists—Austin, 15-year-old Shriver of Lutherville, Md., and 18-year-old Anne Smith of Dallas. Goolagong, 26, eventually beat Austin in the final, 4-6, 6-0, 6-2. "Someday, that tournament may be looked upon as a landmark, the beginning of a new order," predicted pioneer King.

Those words appeared prophetic as Austin, Shriver and Smith all landed in the U.S. Top Ten for 1978, at Nos. 3-5-8. They appeared to be the vanguard of a wave of promising young women, a notion fortified by the victory of 13-year-old Andrea Jaeger in the 18-and-under division of the prestigious Orange Bowl junior tournament at the end of the year, beating South African Rosalyn Fairbank, 6-1, 6-3.

Austin rose to No. 6 in the world before turning 16 on Dec. 12. She beat Shriver in the finals of the U.S. Girls' 16 and 18 championships, increasing her record total of U.S. junior titles to 27. Tracy turned pro in October, won her first tournament as a professional at Stuttgart, Germany, over Stove, 6-3, 6-3, and won $70,000 within three months.

Shriver, while 0-9 against Austin in their junior careers, one-upped her at the U.S. Open, becoming the youngest finalist in the tournament's history. Seeded 16th, Pam, the six-foot 'Great Whomping Crane,' upset eighth-seeded Reid, an injured Lesley Hunt and first-seed Navratilova, 7-6 (7-5), 7-6 (7-3), in a rain-interrupted semi-final that was arguably the greatest upset in women's major tournament history. Playing nervelessly and aggressively with her Prince (oversized head) racket, Shriver used her serve-and-volley game to extend second-seeded Evert to 7-5, 6-4 before losing an exciting final. But she was the youngest of all U.S. finalists, 16 years, two months, undercutting Maureen Connolly, 1951, by nine months.

Both Austin and Shriver, who remained an amateur, were named to the U.S. Wightman Cup team, which was upset by Great Britain, 4-3, at London's Royal Albert Hall. Evert routed Barker, 6-2, 6-1, and Virginia Wade, 6-0, 6-1, but the British preyed on the inexperience of the American teen-agers. Michele Tyler upset Shriver, 5-7, 6-3, 6-3. Wade (3-6, 7-5, 6-3) and Barker (6-3, 3-6, 6-0) each beat Austin. Wade and Barker teamed up to beat Shriver and Evert, 6-0, 5-7, 6-4, in the decisive doubles match.

Austin also joined Evert and captain King as the U.S. won the Federation Cup for the third straight year, at Melbourne, Australia. The U.S. nipped Australia, 2-1, in the final, Evert and King teaming for the decisive point over Reid and Turnbull, 4-6, 6-1, 6-4.

Evert did not lose a tournament match after the Wimbledon final, winning her last 34 of the year, including three over Navratilova. Evert finished with a 56-3 record, six victories in 10 tournaments, and $443,540 in prize money. She became only the third woman to win the U.S. singles four consecutive years, the first since Helen Jacobs in 1932-35. Evert won the U.S. Open without losing a set for the third consecutive year, an astonishing feat, especially since the surface was changed from clay (on which she had not lost since August 1973) to medium-fast hard courts that were not ideally suited to her backcourt game. She finished the year with a 3-2 record against Navratilova and was voted the ITF 'World Champion' by a panel of three former women champions: Ann Jones, Margaret Smith Court and Margaret Osborne duPont.

Again devalued in the female precinct by the loss of talent to the WTT, the Italian went to Czech Regina Marsikova over Ruzici, 7-5, 7-5, but Virginia turned up the burner to depose Jausovec at the French, 6-2, 6-2. They were the first women of their countries to win those titles.

Tallest major winner of the year was unseeded, ranked No. 111, six-footer Chris O'Neil, who ruled her island by winning the Australian Open. She beat seventh-seeded American, No. 68 Betsy Nagelsen, 6-3, 7-6 (7-4). It was less than a strong field for the $35,000 tourney, and she got help from compatriot Di Evers, who knocked out top-seeded Barker, No. 26, in the quarters.

Nevertheless, 22-year-old serve-and-volleying Chris, with the lone title of her career and $6,000 to show for it, joined countryman Mark Edmondson, the 1976 victor, as the longest shots ever to win a major.

Evert also was voted the Most Valuable Player in World Team Tennis, leading her Los Angeles Strings to their first championship of the intercity league. The Strings beat the Boston Lobsters in the playoff finale, 24-21, 30-20, 26-27, 28-25.

But after five years of financial losses, WTT was shaky as the year ended. Half of the league's 10 teams announced that they were ceasing operations in the fall and, despite some optimistic noises from the commissioner's office in St. Louis, the chances of finding replacements appeared slim. Plans for a seven-week, $1-million women's tournament circuit in Europe in the spring gave Evert, Navratilova and the other women stars of WTT a lucrative alternative. The failure of the league to sign top players for 1979 caused several influential owners to give up the ghost, and the league seemed to unravel quickly after the Boston Lobsters and the New York Apples folded.

Virginia Slims, which had pioneered the promotion of women's tennis since 1971, startlingly departed from the sponsorship scene in April when the WTA board of directors voted not to renew its contract for the winter circuit. The WTA cited "differences in philosophy on the structure of the circuit" for the divorce from the company, which had poured more than $8-million into women's pro tennis over eight years.

Some players thought the termination of the contract was a grave mistake and that no comparable patron of the women's game could be found. But in June it was announced that Avon—the huge cosmetic and costume jewelry firm that had for two years sponsored the 'Futures' satellite circuit—had signed a two-year contract, with additional renewal options, to take over sponsorship of the major circuit as well as the 'Futures.' Avon's $2.2-million annual commitment was to fund 11 'Championship' tournaments with purses between $125,000 and $200,000, leading to a $325,000 singles and doubles championship playoff, and an expanded circuit of $25,000 'Futures' tournaments.

Despite growing pains, sometimes acute, it was obvious that professional tennis was still on the rise as the 1980s approached.

1979

Kids get pushy but Borg, Martina hanging tough

Tracy Austin
Pony-tailed U.S. Open quarter-finalist at 14, champ two years later.

The United Nations designated 1979 as the 'International Year of the Child,' and, in tennis, youth was well served. This was most evident at the U.S. Open, Tracy Austin, 16, became the youngest women's singles champion in the history of America's premier championships, and John McEnroe, 20, reigned as the youngest men's champion since Pancho Gonzalez in 1948.

But while firmly establishing themselves as contenders for the No. 1 world rankings, the 'kids' were not ready to ascend the throne quite yet. The positions of honor in the last year of tennis' remarkable 'growth decade' belonged to 'old-timers:' Martina Navratilova, 22, who won the Avon Championships climaxing the women's indoor circuit and her second consecutive Wimbledon title, and the irrepressible Bjorn Borg, 23, who captured his fourth French Open title and his fourth in a row at Wimbledon, a feat no man had accomplished since before World War I.

Still, it was an exceptional season for the young overachievers, Austin and McEnroe. In addition to her triumph in the Open, Tracy was runner-up to Navratilova in the Avon Championships and snapped Chris Evert Lloyd's six-year, 125-match clay-court winning streak en route to victory in the Italian Open, her first big international title. McEnroe, who had started the year by winning the 1978 Grand Prix Masters, added the World Championship of Tennis title with back-to-back beatings of Jimmy Connors and Borg, and coordinated with Peter Fleming to win the Wimbledon and U.S. Open doubles. They were clearly the best doubles pair in the world.

The rapid ascendance of Austin and McEnroe symbolized a significant change in the old order that had ruled much of the latter part of the decade. Evert and Connors, who had reached the pinnacle of the game in 1974 as the 'Lovebird Double,' young champions engaged to wed, finally did get married. But not to each other. Evert became the bride of British Davis

Cupper John Lloyd. A few weeks earlier, Connors revealed that he was already married, secretly the previous autumn in Japan, to Patti McGuire, a former playmate-of-the-year (*Playboy* magazine version). The couple's first child, Brett David, was born in August.

Meanwhile, though still formidable, neither Evert Lloyd nor Connors was quite the force of before. Their marriages and apparent off-court happiness seemed to coincide with a slight but noticeable decline in their competitive fires.

Evert Lloyd said she was no longer obsessed with the ambition to be the No. 1 player in the world. She did recapture the French Open title in the absence of Navratilova and Austin, but never really resembled her dominant and awesomely consistent form of the prior five years. She failed to reach the semi-finals of the Avon Championships, was runner-up to Navratilova at Wimbledon for the second straight year and succumbed to Austin one hurdle short of an unprecedented fifth consecutive U.S. Open title.

Connors, after being in the finals at Wimbledon four of the five previous years and the U.S. Open five straight times, fell in the semis of each and at the same stage in the WCT playoffs and French Open as well. Moreover, Borg established indisputable superiority in their splendid, long-running rivalry, crushing Connors in straight sets in four meetings on four different surfaces: clay at Boca Raton, Fla., 6-2, 6-3; hard at Las Vegas, 6-3, 6-2; grass at Wimbledon, 6-2, 6-3, 6-2; indoors in Tokyo, 6-2, 6-2.

Connors did defend his titles in both the U.S. Pro Indoor at Philadelphia and the U.S. Indoor at Memphis. In both finals, 6-3, 6-4, 6-1, and 6-4, 5-7, 6-3, respectively he beat Arthur Ashe, who had made an impressive comeback from heel surgery, but shockingly suffered a mild heart attack at age 36 in August. The latter, the U.S. Indoor dating to 1898, is the only national prize to elude Arthur, won for the fifth time by Jimmy.

It was at Moody Coliseum in Dallas, at the end of the winter-spring men's indoor season, that McEnroe gave a convincing glimpse of great things ahead. Appearing in the WCT playoffs for the first time, he beat Australian John Alexander, 6-4, 6-0, 6-2; Connors, 6-1, 6-4, 6-4; and, finally, Borg, 7-5, 4-6, 6-2, 7-6 (7-5). He won the $100,000 first prize with the kind of left-handed serve-and-volley attack—rich in variations of speed and spin, touch and improvisation—not seen since the salad days of Rod Laver.

Navratilova was the prevailing figure on the 12-week, $2.2-million Avon Championship Series, winning four of seven tournaments she played plus the showcase $275,000 finale at Madison Square Garden. In the climactic match, Martina clinched the $100,000 top prize by overcoming her own shaky backhand and Austin's persistent backcourt game, 6-3, 3-6, 6-2.

The most startling development of the Avon Championships, which climaxed a successful first year for the cosmetics firm as heir to Virginia Slims in sponsoring the women's indoor circuit, was the failure of Evert to get through the round-robin portion of the playoffs to the semi-finals. Until 1979, Chrissie had never lost two matches in a row in her professional career. That astounding landmark of consistency was broken when Navratilova beat her in the final of an Avon tournament at Oakland, 7-5, 7-5, and young South African Greer Stevens beat her in the first round at Hollywood, Fla, 6-2, 6-3. In the playoffs at New York, Evert, her mind obviously more on her upcoming wedding than tennis, lost listlessly on successive nights to Austin, 6-3, 6-1, and Dianne Fromholtz, 6-2, 6-3.

Evert did regroup to win her last tournament before her April 17 nuptials, coming from behind to beat Fromholtz (conqueror of Navratilova), 3-6, 6-3, 6-1, for the $100,000 first prize in the four-woman Clairol Crown special event at Carlsbad, Calif. After a two-week honeymoon, Evert Lloyd teamed with Austin, Billie Jean King, and Rosie Casals to give the U.S. its fourth straight victory in the Federation Cup, on clay at Madrid.

1979 THE MAJOR CHAMPIONSHIPS

Australian Open
Men's Singles: Guillermo Vilas
Women's Singles: Barbara Jordan
Men's Doubles: Peter McNamara / Paul McNamee
Women's Doubles: Judy Chaloner / Dianne Evers
French Open
Men's Singles: Bjorn Borg
Women's Singles: Chris Evert Lloyd
Men's Doubles: Gene Mayer / Alex Mayer
Women's Doubles: Betty Stove / Wendy Turnbull
Mixed Doubles: Wendy Turnbull / Bob Hewitt
Wimbledon
Men's Singles: Bjorn Borg
Women's Singles: Martina Navratilova
Men's Doubles: Peter Fleming / John McEnroe
Women's Doubles: Billie Jean King / Martina Navratilova
Mixed Doubles: Greer Stevens / Bob Hewitt
U.S. Open
Men's Singles: John McEnroe
Women's Singles: Tracy Austin
Men's Doubles: John McEnroe / Peter Fleming
Women's Doubles: Betty Stove / Wendy Turnbull
Mixed Doubles: Greer Stevens / Bob Hewitt

Later in the year, an expanded U.S. squad also white-washed Great Britain, 7-0, in the Wightman Cup at Palm Beach, Fla., with a one-two punch of Evert and Austin.

This was the year the WTA embarked on a bold experiment of breaking away from joint events with the men in the leading championships of Europe and playing their own separate tournaments, except in Paris.

Attendance at the new women's-only events was generally disappointing. This was especially true in Rome, where the paid attendance was only about 5,000 for the week, despite the glorious semi-final in which Austin defeated Evert Lloyd, 6-4, 2-6, 7-6 (7-4). The three-point margin in overtime, May 12, marked the end of an illustrious dirt path that stretched almost six years. It was the first time Evert Lloyd had lost a match on a clay court since Aug. 12, 1973, when Evonne Goolagong beat her in the final of the Western Championships at Cincinnati, a fantastic streak covering 25 tournaments and 125 matches. Only eight of those matches stretched to three sets. Evert Lloyd said she was more relieved than stunned when the streak finally ended. Austin was thrilled, and celebrated the next day by beating pudgy West German left-hander Sylvia Hanika—voted the most improved player of the year by the WTA—in the final, 6-4, 1-6, 6-3.

It was a shame that the streak ended before such a sparse and seemingly disinterested audience, however. There were only about 1,500 spectators at Il Foro Italico, compared with a howling sell-out throng of more than 9,000 for the final of the men's Italian Open two weeks later. That was a glorious match, too. Vitas Gerulaitis, the insouciant New Yorker, defeated Guillermo Vilas, 6-7 (4-7), 7-6 (7-0), 6-7 (5-7), 6-4, 6-2, in an enthralling battle of wit and grit begun in the mid-afternoon sunshine and ended in the cool of the evening. In terms of playing time, this is thought to be the longest final ever in big tournament history: Five hours and eight minutes. Title-holding Americans in Rome are rare. Vitas had his second in three years, and 14 years would pass before another Yank had two, Jim Courier, 1992-93.

Interest in the women's matches was also clearly secondary in the French Open at Stade Roland Garros, where the center court was enlarged to 17,000 seats as part of a major renovation targeted at producing a second 'show' arena in 1980. Twelve of the tournament's 14 days were sold out, the French Open having become almost as much of an 'in thing' in Paris as Wimbledon is in London. But only 10,000 spectators turned out on the final Saturday to view the women's singles final. In a terribly tedious match Evert Lloyd ground down erring Wendy Turnbull, 6-2, 6-0. Chrissie, the champion of 1974 and 1975, lost only one set in regaining the title she had abdicated in order to play in World Team Tennis, the American intercity league which was gasping for breath at the end of 1978 and was pronounced officially dead early in 1979 (to be resurrected later).

The men's singles in Paris was expected to produce another duel between Borg and Connors. Jimmy entered the premier clay court championship for the first time since 1973, ending his personal boycott, a reaction to the tourney barring him in 1974 for his WTT affiliation. Instead, it was exciting primarily because of Victor Pecci, a 6-foot-3 Paraguayan with a diamond in his right ear and power in his serve and flamboyant groundies, who arrived ranked No. 30 in the world. Unseeded, he convincingly knocked off three seeds in succession—1976 runner-up Harold Solomon, 1977 champion Vilas and Connors. In the final, Pecci stirred a capacity crowd on a drizzly day by coming back from two sets and 2-5 down to push Borg before bowing, 6-3, 6-1, 6-7 (6-8), 6-4. Gene and Sandy Mayer won the men's doubles over Australians Ross Case and Phil Dent, 6-4, 6-4, 6-4, the first brothers to win a major since the U.S. champs of 1924, fellow Americans Bob and Howard Kinsey. Betty Stove and Wendy Turnbull won the women's doubles over Virginia Wade and Françoise Durr, 2-6, 7-5, 6-4.

McEnroe, who had missed Rome and Paris because of a pulled groin muscle, returned to action and won a Wimbledon tune-up tournament on grass at London's Queen's Club over Pecci, 6-7, 6-1, 6-1, and was simultaneously grilled in the British press for his surly deportment. Dubbed 'Superbrat,' he dominated pre-Wimbledon publicity and was seeded second to Borg, largely because Connors did not reveal until after the draw was made whether he would play or remain at home with his expectant wife.

McEnroe, still bothered by the groin pull, was upset in the fourth round by Tim Gullikson, 6-4, 6-2, 6-4, culminating a first week that was tumultuous for the men (10 of the 16 seeds were beaten in the first five days) and formful for the women. Most observers thought the semi-final between Borg and Connors, who had met in the previous two finals, would be the *de facto* title match, but Borg was in his most devastating form and annihilated his longtime arch rival, 6-2, 6-3, 6-2, in 1:46.

Left-hander Roscoe Tanner, seeded fifth, had been a semi-finalist twice before, and this time came through the wreckage in the other half of the draw, past Gullikson, 6-1, 6-4, 6-7 (3-7), 6-2, and 6-foot-3 American Pat DuPre, 6-3, 7-6 (7-3), 6-3, to reach the final for the first time. Given little chance, Roscoe, the Stanford refugee with the low toss and high velocity serve, attacked at every opportunity. Playing thoughtfully and well, he pushed Borg to the limit in an absorbing final that kept 15,000 spectators and a live television audience in 28 countries spellbound for two hours, 29 minutes.

Half an hour after his 6-7 (4-7), 6-1, 3-6, 6-3, 6-4 win, which made him the first man since New Zealander Tony Wilding in 1910-13 to win the Wimbledon singles four years running, Borg said: "I feel much, much older than when I went on the court. Especially at the end of the match, I have never been so nervous in my whole life ... I almost couldn't hold my racket."

Coupled with Navratilova's 6-4, 6-4 victory over Evert Lloyd in the women's final the previous day, Borg's victory marked the first time that both the men's and women's singles champions had successfully defended their titles since Bill Tilden and Suzanne Lenglen won in 1920 and 1921.

Navratilova was entitled to a first-round bye, but chose instead to play a match in order to enjoy the champion's traditional honor of playing the opening female contest on Centre Court. She had good reason for making this decision: watching her from the competitors' guest box was her mother, whom she had not seen since defecting from Czechoslovakia during the 1975 U.S. Open. Jana Navratilova was granted a two-week tourist visa to visit her daughter in London with the personal approval of Czechoslovak Prime Minister Dr. Lubomir Strougal. "Winning here last year was the greatest moment of my career," a tearful Navratilova said after an unexpectedly tense 4-6, 6-2, 6-1 victory over qualifier Tanya Harford, "but yesterday [the airport reunion with her mother] was one of the greatest moments of my life."

Fighting a cold, Navratilova struggled into the semifinals, losing sets to Stevens, 7-6, 6-7, 6-3 and Fromholtz, 2-6, 6-3, 6-0. But there was no stopping her in the stretch, a 7-5, 6-1, victory over Austin and then Evert Lloyd. Her stepfather, Mirek Navratil and 16-year-old sister, Jana, who were not granted visas, watched the match live on West German television in the border

town of Pilsen, as they had the year before. But this time, instead of ignoring the expatriate's victory, the government-controlled Czech media gave it prominent attention in newspapers and on television.

Navratilova had another thrill in partnering King to the women's doubles title, 5-7, 6-3, 6-2, over Turnbull and Stove. This was King's record 20th Wimbledon title, a 10th doubles to go with six singles and four mixed in the world's most prestigious tournament.

But the occasion was saddened by the death the previous day of 87-year-old Elizabeth 'Bunny' Ryan, with whom King had shared the record since 1975. Miss Ryan, a native Californian who lived in London, was stricken with a heart attack while watching the women's singles final, collapsed in a ladies room at the All England Club and died on the way to a hospital. Winner of 12 doubles and seven mixed doubles titles between 1914 and 1934, but never the singles, Ryan had told friends of a premonition that this would be the year King broke her cherished record. She dreaded the moment, but, happily, never saw it. She died less than 24 hours before being erased from the record book.

Back in the United States, Connors won the U.S. Clay Court singles for the fourth time, beating Vilas in the final, 6-1, 2-6, 6-4. Evert Lloyd—returning after a three-year absence—won her fifth title, over Goolagong, 6-4, 6-3, extending her personal winning streak in the tournament to 26 straight matches.

The U.S. Open was played for the second time at New York's National Tennis Center in Flushing. Amid the cacophony of planes roaring overhead and spectators moving about during play, the youngsters came to the fore. McEnroe's toughest battle came in the second round against Ilie Nastase, no longer the exquisite shotmaker he'd been, but still a tempestuous personality. McEnroe won, 6-4, 4-6, 6-3, 6-2, in a stormy match that could be completed only with great difficulty after the raucous pro-Nastase crowd of 10,000—many of them heavily into their cups at a session that ran past midnight—became a negative influence.

Veteran umpire Frank Hammond, growing flustered, had already hit Nastase earlier in the match with a warning, presently a point penalty for conspicuous stalling. When Hammond justifiably awarded McEnroe a penalty game, raising his lead to 3-1 in the fourth, the customers reacted furiously, showering the court with beer cans and other refuse in protest. Nastase's refusal to play brought referee Mike Blanchard onto the court. Amid the clamor he appealed for a restoration of order, and urged the players to resume. But the noise worsened. As Nastase refused to comply, Blanchard instructed Hammond to "put the clock on him." Hammond had no choice but to invoke correctly the fourth step in the penalty route: default.

That nearly brought the house down. Tourney director Bill Talbert, fearful of a riot, reinstated Nastase and removed Hammond from the chair, replacing him with Blanchard. With that bone thrown to the assemblage, the second-round match was completed in four more games.

McEnroe was at home on the asphalt-based courts less than 15 minutes from his front door in Douglastown, N.Y., though never a favorite with the home crowds because of his incessant pouting and grousing. He won two matches by default, including his quarter-final over injured Eddie Dibbs but stayed sharp playing doubles. In the semi-finals he routed Connors, who was inhibited by back spasms, 6-3, 6-3, 7-5. He won the final with similar ease over Long Island neighbor Gerulaitis, 7-5, 6-3, 6-3.

Gerulaitis had made a magnificent comeback from two sets and a service break down in the semi-finals to beat Tanner, 3-6, 2-6, 7-6 (7-5), 6-3, 6-3. Tanner had served magnificently in upsetting first-seeded Borg in the quarter-finals. Borg hated playing at night, especially against a big server like Tanner, and was thus foiled for the second straight year in his attempt to nail down the third leg of a possible French-Wimbledon-U.S.-Australian Grand Slam.

In the women's singles, seven of the top eight seeds reached the quarter-finals, but third-seeded Austin stopped second-seeded Navratilova in the semis, 7-5, 7-5, and Evert Lloyd in the final, 6-4, 6-3. At 16 years, nine months, the cool Californian became the youngest U.S. champion ever, three days younger than May

Sutton in 1904 and two months younger than Maureen Connolly in 1951. Austin, who had beaten Kathy Jordan and Andrea Jaeger respectively in the first two rounds showed a deft finishing touch in outsteadying Evert Lloyd in 1:33. Chrissie had demolished King in the semis in a 12-game rush, 6-1, 6-0, probably 35-year-old Billie Jean's most painful afternoon in New York.

"I thought the title might intimidate her," said Evert Lloyd, who until a, 4-6, 6-0, 6-2 victory over Sherry Acker in the fourth round had not lost a set in the U.S. Open since the 1975 final and took a 31-match Open streak into the final. "But Tracy was out there like it was just another tennis match."

McEnroe and Fleming won the men's doubles over Stan Smith and Bob Lutz, 6-2, 6-4. The sentimental story, however, was the reunion of Australians Roy Emerson, 42, and Fred Stolle, 40, who had last played together in the U.S. Doubles when it was held in Boston. They were the champions of 1965 and 1966, and added four more victories to reach 15 in a row before Smith and Lutz toppled them in the semi-finals, 7-5, 3-6, 7-5. Stove-Turnbull reversed the result of the Wimbledon final, beating King-Navratilova for the women's doubles title, 7-5, 6-3, while Stevens and Bob Hewitt repeated their Wimbledon victory over Stove and Frew McMillan in the mixed final, 6-3, 7-5.

In the Davis Cup final against Italy, McEnroe and Gerulaitis asserted themselves fast: Mac over Adriano Panatta, 6-2, 6-3, 6-4, Vitas over Corrado Barazzutti, who had to quit with a leg injury, 6-3, 3-2. It was a 5-0 blitz for the U.S., a totally straight-set affair in 14 sets. McEnroe was 8-0 in singles for the campaign (plus 1-0 in doubles). Smith and Lutz, with a 6-4, 12-10, 6-2 decision over Panatta and Paolo Bertolucci, registered their fourth (1968-69-70, '79) Cup-clinching performance, a record eclipsing the 1904-05-06 wins of the British Doherty brothers, Laurie and Reggie. Smith set an individual Cup-clinching record of six, having won the decisive singles in 1971 and 1972. Staged at San Francisco's Civic Auditorium, it was the first final won indoors by the U.S., which would not play another in fresh air.

McEnroe was nearing the end of an open-era season record for dual labor and production: 27 titles overall, surpassing Nastase's 23 (15 singles, 8 doubles) in 1973. Mac won 10 of 22 singles tournaments on 91-13 in matches, 17 of 21 doubles on 84-5.

1979 CHAMPIONS AND LEADERS

Top Player Earnings: Men
Bjorn Borg $1,008,742
Top Player Earnings: Women
Martina Navratilova $618,698
Year-End Number One
Men: Bjorn Borg
Women: Martina Navratilova
Davis Cup: United States
Federation Cup: United States
Wightman Cup: United States

ITF World Champion
Men: Bjorn Borg
Women: Martina Navratilova
Grand Prix Masters, NYC
Bjorn Borg
WCT, Dallas
John McEnroe
Avon Championships, NYC
Martina Navratilova

1980

A match for the ages, and then another one

Bjorn Borg Victory in a sublime, five-set Wimbledon final over John McEnroe.

For such a moment is the grass maintained with tender loving care. For such a moment are the vines trimmed and the roses tended. For such a moment are the stands of the All England Lawn Tennis & Croquet Club retouched every year in a somber shade of green. The moment is everything. It is at the root of all this, beneath the ivy and the proper manners and even the hallowed lawns. Scratch deep enough at Wimbledon and a hundred matches of high drama rise from the earth. They are the foundation of the most significant tennis tournament in the world, the source of the tradition that sets the event apart from all others.

Wimbledon exists for Borg vs. McEnroe, Centre Court, July 5, 1980. The defending champion reeling. His opponent seeking to score the most memorable of upsets. And a huge crowd engrossed in great theatre.

That's Wimbledon at its best, the most marvelous of backdrops for a haunting match, perhaps the most gripping in the history of what club officials call simply The Championships. Bjorn Borg survived the loss of seven match points in the fourth set of the men's final and, finally, the set itself. Then he survived the loss of seven break points in the deciding set before defeating John McEnroe, 1-6, 7-5, 6-3, 6-7 (16-18), 8-6, in a three-hour, 53-minute epic.

At the instant he fell to his knees in that signature ritual of triumph, the man was at the top of his game and at the peak of a career that challenged history for an equal. It marked his fifth consecutive Wimbledon title, following on the heels of a fifth French Open championship, all achieved at the tender age of 24. He would close out the year by winning the Volvo Masters for a second successive year and stand unchallenged as the leading figure in the sport.

But even in his most satisfying season, there were intimations that Borg's grip on tennis was loosening. He had won his last 13 five-set matches when he looked across the net at McEnroe at the start of yet another life-and-death encounter in the final of the U.S. Open. This time he couldn't summon the will to outlast the covetous American on his home terrain.

McEnroe's 7-6 (7-4), 6-1, 6-7 (5-7), 5-7, 6-4 victory, a second consecutive U.S. title, canceled plans for a tennis migration to Australia for what would have been the concluding act of a quest for a men's Grand Slam, last achieved by Rod Laver in 1969. Without that added incentive, Borg and most of his major adversaries bypassed the Christmas season in Melbourne, leaving the Australian Open to lesser mortals. American Brian Teacher, No. 12 and eighth-seeded won the men's title by defeating Aussie Kim Warwick, 7-5, 7-6 (7-4), 6-3. Warwick, ranked No. 22 and 14th seeded, was a shocker, cutting off Guillermo Vilas' run of two titles and 16 matches in the semis, 6-7, 6-4, 6-2, 2-6, 6-4.

Eighteen-year-old Czech Hana Mandlikova, a daring volleyer, seized the first of her three majors, the Australian, with a swift start, 6-0, 7-5, over Queenslander Wendy Turnbull. A 6-4, 7-5, decision over Martina Navratilova followed her toughest match 6-1, 3-6, 6-4 over Virginia Ruzici in the quarters.

1980 THE MAJOR CHAMPIONSHIPS

Australian Open
Men's Singles: Brian Teacher
Women's Singles: Hana Mandlikova
Men's Doubles: Mark Edmondson / Kim Warwick
Women's Doubles: Martina Navratilova / Betsy Nagelsen
French Open
Men's Singles: Bjorn Borg
Women's Singles: Chris Evert Lloyd
Men's Doubles: Victor Amaya / Hank Pfister
Women's Doubles: Kathy Jordan / Anne Smith
Mixed Doubles: Anne Smith / Billy Martin
Wimbledon
Men's Singles: Bjorn Borg
Women's Singles: Evonne Goolagong Cawley
Men's Doubles: Peter McNamara / Paul McNamee
Women's Doubles: Kathy Jordan / Anne Smith
Mixed Doubles: Tracy Austin / John Austin
U.S. Open
Men's Singles: John McEnroe
Women's Singles: Chris Evert
Men's Doubles: Bob Lutz / Stan Smith
Women's Doubles: Billie Jean King / Martina Navratilova
Mixed Doubles: Wendy Turnbull / Marty Riessen

Although overshadowed by the duel of titans on the male side, Chris Evert Lloyd starred in a drama of her own making by dominating the spotlight on the women's tour. Suffering from fatigue, burnout or mid-life crisis—take your pick—she emerged from a three-month sabbatical to capture clay titles at Rome and Paris, reach the final of a Wimbledon which belonged, unexpectedly, to a blithe spirit from the past, Evonne Goolagong Cawley, and reclaim her U.S. Open birthright by overcoming, among others, Tracy Austin, her most recent nemesis.

Austin failed to add a major title to her collection, yet she won a dozen others—including the Avon championship and the Colgate Series championship—and banked more than $600,000 in prize money. Not bad for a high school student.

Also fast-rising, precocious Andrea Jaeger, 15, was a quarter-finalist at Wimbledon and a semi-finalist at Flushing Meadow. Navratilova, suddenly caught in a time warp, had no majors to call her own. She compensated by leading all women in prize money with earnings of $749,250.

Still, it was the men who held the attention of the world, particularly in those instances when Borg and McEnroe shared a major stage. If the Swede added to his legend on the English grass, then the Yank confirmed his mettle by holding his ground on American asphalt. Their two matches formed an exquisite set of mantelpieces that bracketed the summer of 1980.

As the Wimbledon Championships got underway, Borg was in a class of his own. In the French Open, he had ripped with ease through a field that featured 17 of the top 20 players in the world. The man dropped no sets and never more than the seven games he yielded to Vitas Gerulaitis in his 6-4, 6-1, 6-2, grasp of the final. With that victory, he became the only man to win the tournament three years in a row and five times in all.

"For most of us, Paris is a great tournament because of the city, the food, the Continental experience," said Victor Amaya, who won the doubles in the company of Hank Pfister, over Brian Gottfried and Raul Ramirez, 1-6, 6-4, 6-4, 6-3. "But some people don't realize this is the Borg Invitational. They think they can actually win the thing. What a joke!"

At Wimbledon, the Swede was busy establishing the Borg Invitational II. Unlike his experience in previous years, he needed no escape hatches in advancing to the men's final, losing only two sets along the way. Centre

Court belonged to him as it did to no other.

Only McEnroe, jeered at the start of the tournament for intemperate outbursts, stood between Borg and a measure of immortality. Earlier in the week, when he was questioned about his motivation after having won so easily, the Swede said he would like the final "to be 12-10 in the fifth, but only if I know I win." McEnroe came perilously close to meeting that challenge, so much so that Borg actually doubted he would win.

It was in the 34-point fourth-set tie-breaker that a battle for the ages was joined. At 5-4, Borg had only to serve it out for his 35th consecutive triumph on Wimbledon grass. He promptly rolled to a 40-15 advantage, double-match point. But McEnroe saved both points and then broke service. At 6-6, the combatants began a tie-breaker that lasted 22 minutes. It featured five championship points for Borg, seven set points for his opponent. Finally, on the 34th point, with the crowd exhausted from the emotion of the moment, the champion failed to execute a difficult drop volley and the match was tied at two sets apiece.

"I thought mentally he'd get down after that," McEnroe said. "It would've gotten me a little down, but it didn't seem to get to him. He's won it four times. You'd think he might let down and say forget it."

Indeed, Borg did admit to being discouraged at the start of the fifth set. "When I lost those match points, I couldn't believe it," the man conceded. "I was thinking then maybe I will end up losing the match. It is a terrible feeling."

The disappointment lasted two points into the fifth set. Borg fell behind 0-30 on his serve, then dipped deeply into his vast reserve of spirit. He won the next four points to take a 1-0 advantage. From that instant, McEnroe was waging an uphill fight.

Borg would serve 25 more times in the match and win 24 points. He gained his break in the 14th game when, at 15-15, the Swede won the last three points with a return down the line, a volley McEnroe couldn't retrieve and a backhand passing shot. Then he fell to his knees in supplication, as ever, and added an impromptu collapse on the well-worn grass.

"At this rate," McEnroe said, "I don't know when he's ever going to lose here. He hits harder than when I first saw him. He volleys better."

And it was not out of the question then to consider him in the context of Tilden, Budge, Laver. Not with 10 major championships, not with the U.S. Open and a

Grand Slam within his sights. "I want to be remembered as the greatest ever," Borg said.

In the afterglow of that triumph, Borg took a bride, the fair Mariana Simionescu, a Romanian player of modest accomplishment. His warmup for the U.S. Open was jeopardized by a knee injury that caused him to retire in the midst of the Canadian Open final against an ascending star, 20-year-old Ivan Lendl of Czechoslovakia (while ahead, 6-4, 4-5). Earlier in the same tournament, McEnroe twisted an ankle and, ahead 4-3, defaulted to Erik van Dillen in the second round, then was beaten in the first round at Atlanta the following week by John Austin (Tracy's brother), 7-6, 6-4.

Despite hysterical headlines suggesting that neither man might be able to walk—let alone run—on the court at Louis Armstrong Stadium, there was no stopping the two from an appointment in the U.S. Open finale. Their journeys, however, were not without obstacles.

Borg survived a quarter-final scare from Roscoe Tanner, who'd eliminated Borg in the quarters the previous year, and then yielded the first two sets to Johan Kriek in the semi-finals before overwhelming the expatriate South African, 4-6, 4-6, 6-1, 6-1, 6-1. Kriek became the fifth player to take the first two sets of a best-of-five match against Borg and the fifth player to fail to put away the Swede.

Meanwhile, McEnroe had some shaky moments against Lendl in the quarter-finals before rallying for a 4-6, 6-3, 6-2, 7-5 victory. Next up was an amazing semi-final against three-time champion Jimmy Connors that stretched 4:17 as the mutual vitriol flowed. Connors took a 2-1 lead in sets but McEnroe rallied to win the fourth and served for the match at 5-4 in the fifth, only to be broken. Mac finally prevailed in a tie-breaker, 6-4, 5-7, 0-6, 6-3, 7-6 (7-3). Not the ideal preparation for a final against Borg set to start less than 24 hours later.

This was the pairing everyone hoped to see, even McEnroe. "I just want to win the tournament," the defender said on the first day of the two-week event, "but if I knew beforehand that I'd win, I'd rather play Borg in the final. Say 22-20 in the fifth set." When a man noted they play fifth-set tie-breakers at the Open, Mac altered the score. "Okay," he said, "make it 7-0 in the tie-breaker."

As it developed, a decisive tie-breaker wasn't necessary. But that was about all the match lacked. Such was the pressure in what became a battle of survival that McEnroe felt like wilting after Borg squared the score at two sets apiece. "When I lost the fourth set," the 21-year-old American said, "I thought my body was going to fall off."

Neither man played with the artistry that marked the historic match at Wimbledon two months earlier. The record Open crowd of 21,072 appeared not to notice. If it wasn't a classic, it still left people breathless with excitement. McEnroe jousted with the umpires and with a linesman. He slammed a racket against his chair and at one stage he felt so strongly about his game that he handed his weapon to Jack Kramer, seated in a courtside box. Borg served with all the assurance of a waiter in an earthquake. He was reported missing in action during the second set. He kicked one ball over the net after breaking his racket on a serve and it was his best-looking shot in several games.

"I was trying my best," he said, "but I was not playing well. I had no feel for the ball."

And yet somehow the two staggered into an excruciatingly dramatic final scene, stumbling into a cliffhanger finish. The tension was suffocating.

The fatal break occurred in the seventh game of the fifth set after Borg had committed two of his nine uncharacteristic double faults. McEnroe laid claim to the title with a sharp volley at 40-15 of the 10th game, four hours and 13 minutes after the initial serve. He became the first repeat champion since Australian Neale Fraser in 1959-60 and the first Yank to win national honors in consecutive years since Pancho Gonzalez in 1948-49.

They pair met only twice more during the 1980 season, Borg triumphing, 6-3, 6-4, at the Stockholm Open in November and in three tight sets, 6-4, 6-7 (3-7), 7-6 (7-2), in the preliminary round of the Masters.

McEnroe enjoyed a superb year, leading the men in earnings ($972,369) and tournament victories (10). Despite his losses to Borg at Wimbledon and to Connors in the WCT Final before 16,181 at the brand new Reunion Arena in Dallas, he was a legitimate candidate for the top spot in the world when the leading players converged on Madison Square Garden for the Masters. There, he inexplicably lost all three round-robin matches, to Gene Mayer, Jose-Luis Clerc and Borg. Bjorn beat Connors in the semis, 6-4, 6-7 (4-7), 6-3, and Lendl beat Mayer, 6-3, 6-4. The title went to Bjorn, 6-4, 6-2, 6-2, along with the $100,000 top prize and the clear designation as No. 1.

Lendl, who scored a season-high 113 victories in a grueling 142 tournament matches, had his greatest satisfaction in team competition, leading Czechoslovakia to a 4-1 victory over Italy in Prague for its first Davis Cup. Ivan was unbeaten (7-0 in singles, 3-0 in doubles), but it was Tom Smid who sent the home team off to a bright start by bringing down favored Adriano Panatta, 3-6, 3-6, 6-3, 6-4, 6-4, before a howling crowd. Lendl followed, 4-6, 6-1, 6-1, 6-2, over Corrado Barazzutti, and he and Smid persisted to settle it over Panatta and Paolo Bertolucci, 3-6, 6-3, 3-6, 6-3, 6-4.

The Czechoslovaks took a 3-2 semi-final over Argentina at Buenos Aires with Lendl beating Vilas and Clerc. Italy struggled, too, 3-2, over Australia at Rome. Panatta pulled them through by beating Paul McNamee and Peter McNamara in the clincher after a crowd-wowing doubles win with Bertolucci over the Macs. But Prague was the end of the contending line for the Panatta-backboned Italians. The 1976 victors were appearing in their fourth final in five years, but would not place so high again until 1998.

Comebacks marked women's play, the most remarkable being Goolagong's at Wimbledon. Her previous victory on the lawns had occurred nine years earlier as an ethereal teenager. "I just happened to win," she recalled. "I didn't think much of it at the time."

And the thought remained buried as she went on to lose her next seven appearances in a Wimbledon or U.S. final. But neither age, nor her marriage to Roger Cawley and motherhood had dimmed the luster of her strokes and the effortless grace of her movement. She rose to the occasion one last time at 28. Her career had been interrupted several times by injuries and illness but 1980 had been particularly trying. Before she returned to action in June, she hadn't hit a ball for seven weeks.

Goolagong, fourth-seeded, played herself into shape at Wimbledon. She was down a set to Betty Stove, 3-6, 6-2, 6-3, in the third round, and trailed by a set and a break with Mandlikova, 6-7 (6-8), 6-3, 6-1, in the fourth. That experience served her well in the semi-finals

1980 CHAMPIONS AND LEADERS

Top Player Earnings: Men
John McEnroe $972,369
Top Player Earnings: Women
Martina Navratilova $749,250
Year-End Number One
Men: Bjorn Borg
Women: Chris Evert Lloyd
Davis Cup: Czechoslovakia
Federation Cup: United States
Wightman Cup: United States

ITF World Champion
Men: Bjorn Borg
Women: Chris Evert Lloyd
Grand Prix Masters, NYC
Bjorn Borg
WCT, Dallas
Jimmy Connors
Avon Championships, NYC
Tracy Austin

when she faced Austin, who had won 35 of her previous 36 matches. Despite the loss of seven consecutive games, Goolagong rebounded to nip the young American, 6-3, 0-6, 6-4. (Tracy didn't leave empty-handed. She shared the mixed-doubles title with older brother John, becoming the first sister-brother team to win a major.)

Goolagong then upset Evert Lloyd in the final, 6-1, 7-6 (7-4), the only time in the tournament's history that a singles championship has been decided by a tie-breaker. Goolagong became the first mother to claim a Wimbledon singles title since Dorothea Douglass Chambers in 1914. Evert Lloyd had interrupted top-seeded Navratilova's championship progress at two titles and 19 matches in the semis, 4-6, 6-4, 6-2. Martina had beaten 36-year-old Billie Jean King in a quarter-final epic, 7-6 (8-6), 1-6, 10-8, needing nine match points to win a dramatic two-part struggle that began on a cold (48 degree) afternoon, was halted by rain after one set, and concluded the next day.

That Wimbledon defeat represented one of the few setbacks suffered by Evert Lloyd after her return to competitive tennis in time for the European clay circuit. After being beaten by Austin in the opener of the Avon series at Cincinnati, and losing to Navratilova at Chicago, Evert Lloyd had departed the tour in Seattle for what she later called a "leave of absence." Apparently refreshed, she returned and seized her third Italian title in Rome over Ruzici, and then, in the absence of Austin, Navratilova and Goolagong, won her fourth French championship, thrashing 1978 champ Ruzici, 6-0, 6-3, in the final. Evert Lloyd increased her winning streak to 25 matches before losing at Wimbledon to Goolagong.

Chrissie stepped up the pace back in the States, winning a U.S. Clay Court title for the sixth time, over Jaeger (tying Nancy Richey's record) and taking a second Canadian title (a championship her father, Jimmy Evert, had won in 1947), over Ruzici. Evert Lloyd was primed to regain her Open crown and to defeat Austin, the clone who had whipped her five consecutive times. She got her opportunity in the semi-final round.

On the eve of the match, she described herself as a nervous wreck. She told her husband, "I've never wanted a match more." It showed at the start, when she dropped the first four games and the set, 6-4. But the slimmed-down, quicker, hungrier version of the former champion emerged in magnificent fashion thereafter. Forcing Austin into 54 errors in the match, she swept into the final by winning the last two sets convincingly, 6-1, 6-1.

What she called her "most emotional victory" preceded her most satisfying moment of the year. Evert Lloyd had invited her father, he her first teacher, from Florida to witness the semi-final. Papa, preferring to stay far in the background and not engage his nervous system, had never seen his daughter win a major championship in person.

So Evert Lloyd's 5-7, 6-1, 6-1 conquest of 18-year-old Mandlikova—rock-ribbed defense beat daring offense—represented a first of sorts even as it reestablished an old pattern. The ninth-seeded Czech, who had upset her idol, second-seeded Navratilova in a fourth-round volleying showdown, and overcome 15-year-old Jaeger in a battle of prodigies, began strongly against Evert Lloyd. But Hana didn't have the concentration or will to withstand the relentless American. After claiming her fifth Open championship, Evert Lloyd had a 53-5 match record in the tournament.

Nor did she stop there. A month later, she annexed her 100th professional tournament singles title at Deerfield Beach, Fla., over Jaeger, 6-4, 6-1.

Evert Lloyd also enjoyed remarkable success in team play. In the Federation Cup, she (5-0) and teammates won all 15 matches, including a sweep of Australia in the championship round at West Berlin where she beat Diane Fromholtz, 4-6, 6-1, 6-1, and Austin defeated Turnbull, 6-2, 6-3. Capt. Chris concluded a remarkable campaign by leading the U.S. over Britain in the Wightman Cup. She won both singles, over Sue Barker, 6-1, 6-2, and Virginia Wade, in the deciding match, 7-5, 3-6, 7-5. Chrissie teamed with Rosie Casals to win her doubles match over Anne Hobbs and Glynis Coles. It was Evert Lloyd's 23rd overall victory in Wightman play, surpassing Louise Brough's record.

Another Brough standard, one she shared with Nancy Richey for most years ranked among the Top Ten in the U.S. (16), was eclipsed by King, celebrating her 17th year among the elite with a fifth-place finish. Billie Jean, who turned 37 in November, won three singles and 11 doubles titles, including the U.S. championship in partnership with Navratilova, over Pam Shriver and Stove, 7-6 (7-2), 7-5. It was B.J.'s 39th—and last—major title, second then only to Margaret Smith Court's 62. But it was Navratilova's ninth, and she was on her way to eclipsing King, getting her 57th remarkably in 2003, the Aussie mixed with Indian Leander Paes over Eleni Daniilidou and Todd Woodbridge, 6-4, 6-4

1981

Last major for Borg, Mac reaches No. 1

Chris Evert
No. 1 again, but Martina Navratilova's day seemed at hand.

In a land rich in ceremony, men's tennis staged a changing of the guard. Not only did John McEnroe topple Bjorn Borg from his Wimbledon throne in 1981, he replaced Borg as the ruler of his sport. By year's end, the former monarch relinquished all claims to the territories he once commanded.

Borg's decision to reduce his schedule was so drastic that it resulted in virtual retirement from competitive tennis following humbling four-set losses to McEnroe in the finals of both the Wimbledon and the 100th anniversary U.S. Championships. It represented a stunning development in the wake of the Swede's victory at Paris, his sixth French Open title and his 11th major, tying Rod Laver, one behind record-holder Roy Emerson. There would be no others. At 25, the man decided to remove his headband and let down his hair after a decade of single-minded devotion.

He may have been suffering from burnout or come to the realization that he was never going to achieve a U.S. title, let alone the Grand Slam that seemed so close and yet so far. Clearly, the brash McEnroe, three years his junior, had gained sufficient composure and mental toughness to suggest he wasn't going to be easily dislodged.

At Wimbledon, the American had battled with linesmen, umpires, tournament officials and the tabloid press and still exhibited the poise to deprive Borg of a sixth successive title on his own personal lawn. Two months later, McEnroe completed his coup on the hard courts at Flushing Meadow. The defeat was the Swede's fourth in a U.S. Open final and marked him as the most accomplished player never to claim the U.S. championship: Zero for 10 years.

There was no such seismographic activity in the women's ranks. Each of the four major titles was claimed by a different player. Hana Mandlikova won her second major, the French Open, Chris Evert Lloyd excelled at Wimbledon for the third time, Tracy Austin added a second U.S. Open and Martina Navratilova triumphed over a complete women's field in Australia. Chrissie's nine titles, raising her career total to 110, maintained her as world No. 1.

Yet, there wasn't much doubt that Navratilova enjoyed the finest year of the four, and not only for the quality of her tennis. She won 10 tournaments playing singles, a circuit best, and she also combined with Pam Shriver to claim 11 doubles titles, including Wimbledon. Additionally, she was granted U.S. citizenship in midsummer and then, with tears in her eyes, bathed in the sustained applause of the crowd at the National Tennis Center, her National Tennis Center, following a loss to Austin in a brilliant Open final.

If Borg cried following his loss to McEnroe the following day, it was on the inside. For the first time in memory, the well-mannered Swede ignored the protocol of the trophy presentation, spoke not a word to the fans or the media assembled at Flushing Meadow and left the grounds in a huff or, as one timekeeper noted, a minute and a huff. The previous day, while blasting Jimmy Connors in a men's semi-final, he had reportedly been the subject of a telephoned death threat. But for the man who had purchased a luxurious house on Long Island for the express purpose of establishing a home-court advantage at the previously inhospitable playground, it seemed the disappointment of the moment simply overwhelmed him.

That it would be the final picture of Borg at a championship event was perhaps the cruelest twist of fate in a season that had started with such promise at Paris with his 6-1, 4-6, 6-2, 3-6, 6-1 French Open triumph over Ivan Lendl. At the time, it appeared inevitable that the Swede would establish a standard of his own for men's tennis, perhaps before the year was out.

His performance in the French temporarily silenced questions about the man's future. Borg had reported to Paris following an absence from competition of nearly two months, the result of a tender right shoulder. He had played in only three tournaments since January, failing to advance past the second round in two of them, and even he was uncertain of his form.

Still, two weeks of serious practice had left him fit. "I feel strong," he said. "I can be out on the court for a long time if I have to." It wasn't necessary, at least not until the final. The man mowed down his half of the draw until he came to Lendl, who had beaten McEnroe in the quarters and overcome Italian Open champ, Jose-Luis Clerc, in five sets, halting the Argentine's 16 match winning streak. The ascendant Czech answered back twice after Borg took the first and third sets but, in the end, he was worn down by the champion's sheer inexhaustibility.

With a fourth straight French title (and the tournament's record male winning streak, 28 matches), he turned his attention to Wimbledon. A sixth consecutive championship in the London suburb would tie him with Willie Renshaw, who competed before the turn of the century (1881-86) when defenders were treated to a bye into the final. But it was McEnroe who received a greater share of attention—for all the wrong reasons. During his first match, versus Tom Gullikson, McEnroe launched a verbal assault on umpire Ted James ("the pits of the world") and tournament referee Fred Hoyles. The tournament committee actually considered showing him the gate before settling on $1,500 in fines.

McEnroe, labeled 'Superbrat' by the tabloids, grumbled his way into the semi-finals where he again dressed down Hoyles during an interminable victory over unseeded Australian Rod Frawley that was fraught with objections and unprintables. But the real brouhaha began in the interview room after the Yank had vented his spleen on the British tabloid press in the wake of some baiting by a gossip columnist. There followed a dialogue on the nature of journalism among emissaries from various countries and soon an Englishman, Nigel Clark, and an American, Charlie Steiner, were rolling, wrestling, on the floor. It was scored a dead heat, no tiebreaker needed.

Through all the tumult, Borg kept rolling. He over-

1981 THE MAJOR CHAMPIONSHIPS

Australian Open
Men's Singles: Johan Kriek
Women's Singles: Martina Navratilova
Men's Doubles: Mark Edmondson / Kim Warwick
Women's Doubles: Kathy Jordan / Anne Smith
French Open
Men's Singles: Bjorn Borg
Women's Singles: Hana Mandlikova
Men's Doubles: Heinz Gunthardt / Balazs Taroczy
Women's Doubles: Rosalyn Fairbank / Tayna Harford
Mixed Doubles: Andrea Jaeger / Jimmy Arias
Wimbledon
Men's Singles: John McEnroe
Women's Singles: Chris Evert Lloyd
Men's Doubles: Peter Fleming / John McEnroe
Women's Doubles: Martina Navratilova / Pam Shriver
Mixed Doubles: Betty Stove / Frew McMillan
U.S. Open
Men's Singles: John McEnroe
Women's Singles: Tracy Austin
Men's Doubles: Peter Fleming / John McEnroe
Women's Doubles: Anne Smith / Kathy Jordan
Mixed Doubles: Anne Smith / Kevin Curren

came a major challenge from Connors in the semi-finals, rallying from yet another two-set deficit to oust his old adversary, 0-6, 4-6, 6-3, 6-0, 6-4, in a tense match that rivaled any the two had produced for quality and tension, the last Bjorn would win there. "He had to play his best stuff to beat me," Connors said. And it was true.

But even a sharp and determined Borg wasn't enough to hold off a McEnroe who had learned to orchestrate his talents, if not his temper. Uncharacteristically, the defender started fast. Shockingly, he finished second. The American triumphed, 4-6, 7-6 (7-1), 7-6 (7-4), 6-4. The king was dead.

For all practical purposes, Borg lost his title in game 10 of the third set, where he enjoyed four set points for a 2-1 lead. First, McEnroe served out of a 15-40 hole, then overcame two Borg ads in the six-deuce game. He took control of the tie-breaker with two sensational passing shots after Borg served at 3-4. In the fourth set, the one that terminated Borg's Wimbledon male-record winning streak at 41, McEnroe attacked at every opportunity and dominated with his big first serve.

"I was surprised that I served so well," McEnroe said. "I wanted to show that Bjorn's not the only one who can come from behind and win."

The denouement occurred on the Fourth of July in a country not disposed to celebrating revolutions. Attired in blue and white tennis togs and sporting a jaunty red headband—"Stick a feather in his cap and call him McEnroney," telecaster Bud Collins observed—Superbrat closed out an era with a forehand volley winner on his second championship point.

Horrified officials of the All England Club had their revenge. They declined to tender McEnroe an honorary membership, a traditional spoil of victory. Not that the man had any desire to join.

In advance of the U.S. Open, McEnroe whipped Chris Lewis in the final at Cincinnati. Otherwise, the American circuit had been dominated by Clerc, who added four clay-court titles to his dirt demolition of Paraguayan Victor Pecci in Rome: U.S. Pro over Chilean Hans Gildemeister; Washington over countryman Guillermo Vilas; North Conway, N.H., over Vilas; U.S. Clay Court in Indianapolis over Lendl. But the lean Argentine would be no factor on the Open surface.

The Flushing field was reduced to the usual suspects for the semi-finals. McEnroe, who had lost opening sets to the likes of Juan Nunezand and Ramesh Krishnan, lost his cool on several occasions against Vitas Gerulaitis before breaking a racket string against the intrusive CBS courtside microphone. Relieved, he then completed a 5-7, 6-3, 6-2, 4-6, 6-3 triumph. Borg, serving as well as he ever had, wiped out Connors in their semi-final, 6-2, 7-5, 6-4. He had 14 aces plus many unreturnable serves and all of them appeared to occur on the big points.

The victory extended Borg's streak over Connors to 10 matches. Shortly before the match, the switchboard operator at the Tennis Center received a call from a man threatening Borg's life. Additional security guards ringed the stadium court as a precaution but Borg was not informed until after he had vanquished Connors.

As he had at Wimbledon, Borg jumped out in front of McEnroe in the final. But the Yank swept the last three sets to post a 4-6, 6-2, 6-4, 6-3 victory, stamping him as the first man to capture a third successive U.S. singles title since the legendary Bill Tilden strung together six during the Roaring '20s.

Borg's best chance evaporated in the third set when, leading 4-3, he was broken in stunning fashion as McEnroe unleashed four winners, including a pair of spectacular running topspin lobs, to draw even. "I felt I could do anything," the American said. He won eight of the last 11 games. Borg's future flashed before his eyes. It did not include competitive tennis, and his illustrious career was essentially terminated.

One month later, the former No. 1 player in the world said he was taking his first extended vacation from tennis until the following April. Borg also said he would participate in only seven tournaments, a number insufficient for placement in the main draw under the rules of the Men's International Professional Tennis Council. He would have to quality for every Grand Prix tournament he entered, a course he would pursue with apparent disinterest.

Suddenly, the stage was all McEnroe's. Although newly-naturalized U.S. citizen Johan Kriek out of South Africa, whom Mac had defeated in the WCT final at

1981 CHAMPIONS AND LEADERS

Top Player Earnings: Men
John McEnroe $991,000
Top Player Earnings: Women
Martina Navratilova $865,437
Year-End Number One
Men: John McEnroe
Women: Chris Evert Lloyd
Davis Cup: United States
Federation Cup: United States
Wightman Cup: United States

ITF World Champion
Men: John McEnroe
Women: Chris Evert Lloyd
Grand Prix Masters, NYC
Ivan Lendl
WCT, Dallas
John McEnroe
Avon Championships, NYC
Martina Navratilova

Dallas, 6-1, 6-2, 6-4, would emerge from a depleted field to take the Australian title, a 6-2, 7-6 (7-1), 6-7 (1-7), 6-4 victory over Texan Steve Denton. Despite Lendl's first-place finish in the Grand Prix standings and his subsequent triumph over Gerulaitis in the Masters final, McEnroe was the unchallenged leader of the pack.

Not only did the left-hander win nine of 17 singles tournaments, he also teamed with Peter Fleming to win an equal number of doubles titles, including both the championships of Wimbledon, over Stan Smith and Bob Lutz, 6-4, 6-4, 6-4 and the U.S., a default gimme from Heinz Gunthardt and Peter McNamara because Gunthardt was ill.

Additionally, he guided the U.S. to a third Davis Cup, winning seven of eight singles and two doubles, sparkling in the tight windup against Argentina, 3-1, at Cincinnati's Riverfront Coliseum. (In the newly remodeled Davis Cup format, a World Group was established at the top and only 16 countries would be eligible for the Cup. The other nations were to be consigned to zonal warfare below, hoping for promotion the following year). Clerc, with his deadly, rolling topspin backhand, was primed for Cincy, even though the footing was carpet rather than the clay of Argentina's triumph over the U.S. the year before. He whipped Roscoe Tanner, after McEnroe bashed Vilas.

The Argentines then played the doubles of their lives against Fleming and McEnroe, constantly changing tactics in the wild and acrimonious battle—the teams came close to a fistfight at one point—and the Argentines actually moved into winning position late in the fifth set: Match game, Vilas serving at 7-6. Four points away, and with a 2-1 lead, the Argentines could envision taking the Cup home. They came no closer as McEnroe took over, cracking three winners and an awesome backhand return to capsize Vilas. Mac held brilliantly through four deuces and two break points to 8-7, and Vilas averted a match point to 9-9. But McEnroe's net-skimming backhand return tipped Clerc at match point and the four-hour, 11-minute wowser ended, 6-3, 4-6, 6-4, 4-6, 11-9.

Subsequently it was up to the raging Mac. To the roars of 13,327, he fulfilled their pleas, again in a boiling fifth set, 7-5, 5-7, 6-3, 3-6, 6-3. His serves (15 aces) and volleys overcame the tall Latin's groundies. No man had swept the singles at Wimbledon, the U.S. and in the Cup final since Don Budge in 1938, the year of his Grand Slam.

Furthermore, his facility in doubles marked Mac as

the most complete champion since John Newcombe was lending his mustache to a line of tennis gear. Fittingly, the representatives of two generations held an improbable meeting on the stadium court at Flushing Meadow in the doubles semi-finals. Newc, 37, and partner Fred Stolle, 42, both U.S. singles titleists in their halcyon days, had a merry romp through the first four rounds of the draw, in contrast to the grim attitude of Mac and Fleming, finishing their nocturnal third round win over Americans Tony Graham and Bruce Nichols, 3-6, 6-3, 7-6, 4-6, 6-4, at 1:45 the next morning.

Stolle and Newcombe darned near won the title, squeezing Mac and Fleming into a fifth set tie-breaker, losing by a measly four points, their third consecutive encounter of five sets. Their semi was tantamount to a final, which wasn't played because of Gunthardt's illness. The Americans beat the devil-may-care Aussie geezers, 6-2, 6-2, 5-7, 6-7 (2-7), 7-6 (7-3). They won the match but not the crowd, which cheered and laughed as the old Aussies reprised a few vaudeville routines, sometimes sending one man to the other side of the net ostensibly to help their glowering foes. "We always had a fair bit of fun playing doubles in my day," Stolle said.

To Newcombe, who chose not to live his life between the white lines, the current attitude was unfortunate. "I feel sorry for them," he said. "It's a sport. It's a living, too, yes, but they take it over the fringe."

The list of fines for the year indicated just how much court conduct had deteriorated. McEnroe, Gerulaitis and Ilie Nastase all drew 21-day suspensions for exceeding $5,000 in fines. Of the three, Gerulaitis created the biggest stir. In a protest against officiating, he refused to continue playing at 5-5 in the decisive third set of the Melbourne indoor final against McNamara, an offense that earned him a record (at that time) $10,000 penalty.

Tim Mayotte, the husky 21-year-old out of Springfield, Mass., the National Intercollegiate champion for Stanford, made an auspicious professional debut and was honored as Rookie of the Year. He reached the quarter-finals at Wimbledon in only his second tournament as a pro. (In fact he was out of footwear when he arrived, borrowing a pair of Smith's size 13s for his first match.) Tim won 28 of 43 matches in 15 events and finished the year at No. 31.

The march of children into the women's ranks continued with the presence of Kathy Rinaldi at the French Open. In becoming the youngest player to compete in that tournament, the 14-year-old skipped her graduation exercises at St. Joseph's School in Stuart, Fla., and journeyed to Paris where she upset eighth-seeded Dianne Fromholtz and 11th-seeded Anne Smith, before bowing to Mandlikova in the quarters.

Having disposed of the latest princess, Mandlikova went after the queen. Now 19, she sent Evert Lloyd to her second defeat on clay in the last 191 matches, 7-5, 6-4, in the semi-finals. Mandlikova closed out her second major title by stopping Sylvia Hanika, 6-2, 6-4. Hanika, a chunky German lefty, beat Andrea Jaeger, 4-6, 6-1, 6-4, in the semis.

But Jaeger, 15, carried the teen theme to the top with fellow Yank, Jimmy Arias, 16, of Buffalo. They became the youngest of all major doubles champs, taking the mixed, 7-6, 6-4, over the Dutch-American hookup of Betty Stove and Fred McNair.

Mandlikova carried her form onto the grass at Wimbledon, a tournament that lost its defending champion because Evonne Goolagong Cawley interrupted her career to give birth to a second child. That absence was offset by the return of Austin, who missed the first five months of the season with a sciatic nerve condition. In the presence of Rinaldi and Jaeger, Austin, 18, was perceived as a veteran.

Rinaldi became the youngest player to win a match at Wimbledon, a record she would lose in 1990 to Jennifer Capriati, a greener 14 by one day. Averting a third set match point, Kathy beat South African Sue Rollinson in a two hour, 32-minute struggle. But, worn down, she then lost to Swiss qualifier Claudia Pasquale. Jaeger, 16, was upset by Mima Jausovec and an unsteady third-seeded Austin was stunned in the quarters by an overjoyed, almost unbelieving seventh-seeded Shriver, 7-5, 6-4. "Tracy's been beating up on me since I was 11," bubbled Shriver, who was 0-9 against Austin in the juniors, 0-2 as a pro.

The semi-finals matched attackers: Mandlikova (who had double-bageled Wendy Turnbull in the quarters) and Navratilova. Hana, the younger, seeded second despite her ranking of No. 5 on the computer, justified her placement with a 7-5, 4-6, 6-1 victory, winning 11 of the last 13 points in the process. Now all she had to do to claim her third consecutive major title was beat Evert Lloyd, who had moved into a flat just down the road with her husband, John. No small feat that. Evert Lloyd, who had practiced hard in preparation, was peerless once the tournament began. Her 6-3, 6-1 rout of Shriver in the semi-final was typical of her fortnight. So

was the final.

After three consecutive defeats in the championship round, Evert Lloyd took apart a nervous Mandlikova, 6-2, 6-2. "I told myself that if I played Hana at Wimbledon," she said, "I would beat her." And so she did, with relative ease. "Boom-boom-boom…quick-quick-quick!" was the appraisal by Willem Mandlik of his daughter's 61-minute demise.

Not so quick was the 94-hour first-round doubles victory of Americans Chris Dunk and Marty Davis over Aussie brothers Michael and Charlie Fancutt, 7-6, 6-4, 7-6, 7-6, begun on the first Tuesday and played in bits and pieces (because of rain, nightfall and scheduling difficulties) to conclusion four days later, Saturday, on Court 15.

Youth was served on the summer circuit. Most notably at Indianapolis, where 16-year-old Jaeger became the youngest winner of the U.S. Clay Court championship, thrashing the seasoned Romanian, Virginia Ruzici, in the final, 6-1, 6-0. Austin demonstrated she had regained her fitness by outlasting Shriver at San Diego, 6-2, 5-7, 6-2, and then dethroning Evert Lloyd at the Canadian Open, 6-1, 6-4.

For Austin, it was ideal preparation for the U.S. Open, where she breezed through 12 effortless sets to reach the final. The path for the third-seeded Austin was smoothed by Jaeger's second-round collapse against Andrea Leand. One of those rare birds—an amateur!—17-year-old Leand from Brooklandville, Md., was in her first pro tourney and had no ranking. She pulled off one of the largest upsets in U.S. annals over second-seeded Jaeger, 1-6, 7-5, 6-3, and pushed ahead to within two points of the quarters, losing to 11th seeded lefty Barbara Potter.

Form prevailed in the other half of the draw, where Evert Lloyd advanced to her 11th consecutive Open semi-final. Her opponent was Navratilova, who had been frustrated in the tournament since that September day in 1975 when she announced her defection to the U.S. at Forest Hills. After years of complaining about the noise, the constant movement of the crowds and all the other distractions at the Open, Navratilova dispatched Evert Lloyd, 7-5, 4-6, 6-4, in a marvelous and emotional match that was interrupted by beery heckling of Navratilova and a fight between security guards.

That qualified Navratilova for her first U.S final, where she seized the initiative in the first set, 6-1. But the gritty Austin fought back to win the last two sets in tie-breakers, 7-6 (7-4) and 7-6 (7-1), and claim the first major championship decided by an ultimate set breaker. Although Martina double faulted on championship point, ending the longest U.S. final (2:42), the fans' reaction to the loser's efforts thrilled Navratilova as much as anything in her career. Their warm applause interrupted her concession speech on several occasions. She cried from happiness as she turned to all four sides of the court and made a little bow, the kind expected at Wimbledon but seen so rarely in the New World.

A month after the Open, Navratilova snapped Austin's 28-match winning streak with a 6-0, 6-2 victory in the U.S. Indoor final at Minneapolis. Gene Mayer won the male version over Tanner, 6-2, 6-4, in Memphis, where Trey Waltke sabotaged top-seeded McEnroe in the first round. Navratilova also annexed the Avon championship at Madison Square Garden over Jaeger, 6-3, 7-6 (7-3).

Martina won the final major event of the year, overcoming Evert Lloyd, 6-7 (4-7), 6-4, 7-5, in the Australian final. That boosted Martina's singles titles in 1981 to 10 which, combined with the 11 doubles titles she shared with Shriver, enabled her to set a one-season earnings record of $865,437.

Austin rebounded to win the Toyota Series championship that closed out the year at the Meadowlands in East Rutherford, N.J., over Navratilova, 2-6, 6-4, 6-2.

Evert Lloyd ran her singles records in the Wightman Cup and Federation Cup to 20-0 and 23-0, respectively, as the U.S. won all its matches in both competitions, each title won in shutouts of Britain. Tokyo hosted the Federation tourney. Chrissie beat Sue Barker, and Jaeger took Virginia Wade in the 3-0 final. Wade and Barker were the foils also in the 7-0 Wightman romp at Chicago, Evert Lloyd and Austin each beating Wade and Barker.

1982

Jimbo, Chrissie go dancing again

Mats Wilander
At tender 17, a winner over Guillermo Vilas in French Open final.

Normally, a prim-and-proper grand finale would be out of place in such a proletarian celebration as the U.S. Open, staged in a municipally owned complex in a public park. After all, people at the National Tennis Center consider a sweater looped over the shoulders as evening wear. But on this one occasion the tournament of the people, by the people and for the people was worthy of a formal send off.

Something on the order of the Wimbledon Ball would have been appropriate. And for one reason. So Jimmy Connors, men's champion, could have the first dance with Chris Evert Lloyd, the women's champion.

What a picture that would have made. And what a fitting commentary on the state of the sport eight years after they'd reigned as the sweethearts of Centre Court. They had taken divergent paths since 1974 and yet, before the eyes of enthralled spectators and in front of a worldwide television audience, they wound up in the same spot—champions of the New World, Connors at 30 and Evert Lloyd at 27.

They grew up before our eyes. Chrissie, a beribboned semi-finalist at sweet 16, did so with considerably more grace, but Connors got there nonetheless, maturing after his marriage to Patti McGuire and the birth of a son. They had first appeared in the tournament when it was staged at Forest Hills, when the surface was grass, when tennis players dressed only in white.

So Connors' 6-3, 6-2, 4-6, 6-4 victory over Ivan Lendl, which followed by a day Evert Lloyd's 6-3, 6-1 conquest of Hana Mandlikova, was, as much as anything, a triumph of the familiar. And it continued an all-American winning tradition in the singles since the tournament was shifted to Flushing Meadow five years earlier.

It was at the U.S. where Martina Navratilova's quest for a Grand Slam ended prematurely in a quarter-final loss to her doubles partner, Pam Shriver. Evert Lloyd made the most of that opportunity, then defeated Navratilova in the Australian final, 6-3, 2-6, 6-3, to even the score in Big Four tournaments at two apiece. But the naturalized American still reigned as the foremost figure in women's tennis, winning 29 tournaments (15 in singles), earning a record of $1,475,055 and securing the season-closing Toyota Series playoffs, climaxed by a 4-6, 6-1, 6-1 triumph over Evert. Her match record: A phenomenal 90-3 in singles, 70-4 in doubles.

Among the men, Connors stood alone after completing a double that appeared beyond his reach at the age of 30. The irrepressible left-hander prevailed over John McEnroe in the first Wimbledon final of the post-Borg era, then turned back Lendl at Flushing Meadow, while climbing back to the pinnacle from which he had been ousted by Borg and McEnroe.

Mats Wilander, from the first class of Swedish youngsters inspired by Borg, ascended to the French Open title at the tender unseeded age of 17 years, 10 months, becoming the youngest man to annex a major title. Borg was two months older when he won at Paris for the first time in 1974. Wilander, the first non-seed to win since Hungarian Joszef Asboth in 1947, outlasted third-seeded 1977 champion Guillermo Vilas, 1-6, 7-6 (8-6), 6-0, 6-4, in four hours 42 minutes on a sweltering June afternoon. Quick, sturdy and untiring, Wilander had to show his mettle against seasoned seeded pros in reaching the final: 4-6, 7-5, 3-6, 6-4, 6-2, over second Lendl; 6-3, 6-3, 4-6, 6-4, over fifth Vitas Gerulaitis; 7-5, 6-2, 1-6, 7-5, over fourth Jose-Luis Clerc. Top-seeded Connors was expelled by Jose Higueras from the quarters, 6-2, 6-2, 6-2. Before the year was over, Wilander would win four of 20 tournaments, compile a match record of 60-18 and walk off with rookie honors as well as the No. 7 ranking.

In what was a replay of the 1981 Australian Open final, Johan Kriek, a native South African resettled in Florida, routed hard-serving Texan Steve Denton, 6-3, 6-3, 6-2, at Melbourne. Earlier in the year, the man had stripped McEnroe of yet another prize, the U.S. Indoor championship, 6-3, 3-6, 6-4. Mac wasn't nearly as upset by Kriek's other coup, replacing the feisty himself atop the punitive standings: $11,500 to $2,060 in fines.

Lendl continued to outwork—and out-earn—everyone else on the men's tour. Balancing his schedule between the Grand Prix and the more lucrative rival circuit, World Championship Tennis, the lean Czech captured 16 of 24 tournaments he entered, won 107 of 116

matches and overpowered Yannick Noah, Connors and McEnroe to claim a second consecutive Masters title. He also threatened Vilas' open-era record of 50 before Noah terminated his match-winning streak at 44 in February at LaQuinta, Calif.

For all of that, and despite a record one-season haul of $2,028,850 that almost doubled Connors' payoff of $1,173,850, Lendl was denied the No. 1 position by his failure to win a major. He didn't even bother to enter Wimbledon, claiming an allergy to grass while he worked on his golf game back in the States. Nor was he the only defector from the world's most prestigious tournament. No fewer than five of the top 10 males on the ATP computer skipped the event, including the mysterious Borg, and Vilas, whose country was at war with Great Britain over the status of the Falkland Islands.

By then, Borg had become a figure of intrigue. Deciding to play again in the spring but refusing to commit to 10 Grand Prix events, he petitioned the Men's International Professional Tennis Council for a rule change. The nine members, including three player representatives, met in Monaco in conjunction with the Monte Carlo Open, which happened to mark the Swede's debut as a qualifier.

Sir Brian Burnett, chairman of the Wimbledon championships, joined the discussions. He was eager for a compromise that would make it unnecessary for Borg to qualify at Wimbledon. The council was willing. "But," said Arthur Ashe, a council member, "Borg wasn't. For him, it was a matter of principle."

1982 THE MAJOR CHAMPIONSHIPS

Australian Open
Men's Singles: Johan Kriek
Women's Singles: Chris Evert Lloyd
Men's Doubles: John Alexander / John Fitzgerald
Women's Doubles: Martina Navratilova / Pam Shriver
French Open
Men's Singles: Mats Wilander
Women's Singles: Martina Navratilova
Men's Doubles: Sherwood Stewart / Ferdi Taygan
Women's Doubles: Martina Navratilova / Anne Smith
Mixed Doubles: Wendy Turnbull / John Lloyd
Wimbledon
Men's Singles: Jimmy Connors
Women's Singles: Martina Navratilova
Men's Doubles: Peter McNamara / Paul McNamee
Women's Doubles: Martina Navratilova / Pam Shriver
Mixed Doubles: Anne Smith / Kevin Curren
U.S. Open
Men's Singles: Jimmy Connors
Women's Singles: Chris Evert Lloyd
Men's Doubles: Kevin Curren / Steve Denton
Women's Doubles: Rosie Casals / Wendy Turnbull
Mixed Doubles: Anne Smith / Kevin Curren

Standing on principle, Borg, inactive seven months, won his three qualifying matches in April at Monte Carlo, where he made his home. But he performed strangely in the main draw. He prepared to serve from the wrong side of the court in one match. In another, he served underhanded after two double faults. And he whistled during a 6-1, 6-2 loss to Noah in the quarter-finals, after re-launching himself by beating Spaniard Fernando Luna, 6-4, 6-3, and bygone nemesis Adriano Panatta, 6-2, 3-6, 6-4.

Burnett announced the compromise proposal the following week in London. Borg would be accepted for the main draw at Wimbledon if he agreed to play in 10 Grand Prix tournaments before March 31, 1983. Borg, who had taken his principles to Tokyo for a couple of lucrative exhibition matches, declined. He would play according to the dictates of his own schedule, and he would not play qualifying matches at Wimbledon. So much for tradition.

While officials were digesting that news, Borg made a surprise appearance in the qualifying round of the glitzy Alan King-Caesars Palace Classic at Las Vegas two weeks after Monte Carlo. He played like it was a death sentence, squeaking past Victor Amaya before his elimination at the hands of Dick Stockton, 7-6, 1-6, 6-2. In the course of the latter match, the former champion missed a lob and served with an extra ball in his left hand. Borg, observers recalled, clearly, hits his backhand with two hands on the racket. "I don't think he had his heart in the qualifying," Stockton reported.

Following that experience, Borg stated he would play only exhibitions for the remainder of the year but return to the circuit in 1983. Months later, during the Masters, he amended that decision with the announcement he was retiring from competitive tennis.

No wonder it was so much easier to follow the fortunes of the women, especially given the dominant manner in which Navratilova started the season. She was unbeaten in five tournaments on the Avon circuit before the cosmetics company withdrew as winter sponsor, to be replaced by year-round angel Virginia Slims. No sooner had her 27-match winning streak been interrupted by Sylvia Hanika in the Avon finale at Madison Square Garden, then she began a 41-match run that wouldn't be stopped until defeat to Shriver at the U.S. Open in September. Her loss at Flushing Meadow marked the first time all year she had failed to reach a tournament final.

To her immense satisfaction, Navratilova proved as formidable on the clay as she had been on the grass by sweeping both the Family Circle Cup at Hilton Head, S.C., and the French Open. On both occasions, Andrea Jaeger had done the dirty work, eliminating perennial champion Evert Lloyd in the semi-finals. Prior to her meeting with the Illinois high school student, Evert Lloyd not only had won all six previous Family Circle Cups but all 64 sets in which she had participated. Jaeger showed her disrespect with a 6-1, 1-6, 6-2 triumph. A few weeks later, she gave herself a 17th-birthday present by stunning first-seeded Evert Lloyd, favored to win a fifth French title, 6-3, 6-1. Chrissie got to the semis, 6-2, 6-4, past Romanian Lucia Romanov an identical twin. (Sometimes when Lucia and sister Maria were doubles partners, and losing, Lucia, the better of the two, would serve more often if their foes didn't catch on.)

In both tournaments, however, baseline baby Jaeger received her comeuppance from Navratilova. Martina followed a 6-4, 6-2 victory at Hilton Head with a 7-6 (8-6), 6-1 decision at Paris, saving a set point in the tie-breaker. Thus ended the run of the youngest French finalist.

Although Navratilova carried her form onto grass, winning at Eastbourne, over Mandlikova, the major news of the pre-Wimbledon circuit was provided by Billie Jean King. After playing only a few matches in 1981, when she was buffeted by the agonizing, highly publicized palimony lawsuit filed by ex-lover Marilyn Barnett, the 38-year-old Mother Freedom of the women's tour returned with a vengeance. In the Edgbaston Cup at Birmingham, she defeated Rosalyn Fairbank, 6-2, 6-1, for her first tournament singles title in two years and her 66th as a pro. It was a most favorable omen for a Wimbledon desperately in need of an electric charge.

Wimbledon was inundated by so much rain during the first week that the vice chairman of the tournament

1982 CHAMPIONS AND LEADERS

Top Player Earnings: Men	**ITF World Champion**
Ivan Lendl $2,028,850	Men: Jimmy Connors
Top Player Earnings: Women	Women: Martina Navratilova
Martina Navratilova $1,475,055	**Grand Prix Masters, NYC**
Year-End Number One	Ivan Lendl
Men: John McEnroe	**WCT, Dallas**
Women: Martina Navratilova	Ivan Lendl
Davis Cup: United States	**Avon Championships, NYC**
Federation Cup: United States	Sylvia Hanika
Wightman Cup: United States	

was summoned to the interview room to discuss the weather. A subway strike only added to the gloom, flooding streets around the club with traffic. Into this dreary setting stepped a revitalized King and the old tennis shrine fairly glowed with her reflection. On the occasion of her first match, her 100th singles battle at Wimbledon, the club planned to present her with a centennial plate.

Officials didn't announce the ceremony in advance because they feared she would lose to 19-year-old Claudia Pasquale of Switzerland. They also sent her to Court 14, "out in the boondocks" according to King, because her seeding of 12th was based as much on sentiment as recent results. The gift appeared to be the British equivalent of a gold watch: Thanks for your contributions to the game and enjoy your retirement.

But the self-styled Old Lady had other plans. She hammered Pasquale, 6-3, 6-2, saved triple match point against South African Tanya Harford in a remarkable 5-7, 7-6 (7-2), 6-2 third-round triumph and then announced she was a genuine title contender by overcoming third-seeded Tracy Austin, 3-6, 6-4, 6-2, in the quarters, pouncing for a 3-0 lead in the third. St. Billie of the Grassblades hadn't come back to Wimbledon, her favorite haunt, just for a testimonial.

King knew what she wanted when she took a look in the mirror the previous fall. She lifted weights and she ran and she took the first steps back up the ladder, occasionally falling but getting back on her feet and climbing higher. Wimbledon was her goal and she had more than a trinket in mind when she walked onto the grounds.

She wanted the Duke and Duchess of Kent and everyone else who occupied the Royal Box to empty their pockets on the table. This was a holdup. "Unless you win the whole *woiks*" she said, flavoring the All England Club with a dollop of Brooklynese, "it doesn't mean anything."

King's 3-6, 6-4, 6-2 victory over Austin catapulted her into a semi-final against Evert Lloyd, one that was all anyone could have anticipated and more. They presented the tournament with a blast from the past. The younger woman prevailed, but not before King fought off four match points and performed a medley of her greatest shots, perfected over two decades. So small was the edge in Evert Lloyd's 7-6 (7-4), 2-6, 6-3 triumph that the two women split the 30 games and King achieved one more service break.

Meanwhile, Navratilova was cruising through an upset-strewn half of the draw, without the loss of a set, beating German 19-year-old Bettina Bunge, 6-2, 6-2, in the semis. "I really can't believe I've won as easily as I have," she said. "I haven't been tested."

Her test came in the final when she found herself down a break in the third set. A finalist for the sixth consecutive year, Evert Lloyd won the last four games of the second set and broke Navratilova's service in the third game of the third set, stirring uneasy memories of the 1981 U.S. final when the latter unraveled in two tiebreakers against Austin.

"Martina kind of choked that match," Evert Lloyd said. "When she's been in a tough situation in the past, Tracy or I have come out better. But she won this match. She played well under pressure."

Indeed, Navratilova needed mental strength commensurate with her physical talents to beat Evert Lloyd, 6-2, 3-6, 6-2, for her third successive Big Four title, including the Australian Open championship she had claimed in December.

London rains clogged scheduling at tourney's end, forcing the mixed doubles champs, a Texas-South African amalgam of Anne Smith and Kevin Curren, to go four rounds the last day—113 games—winning the title over the Anglo-Aussie team of John Lloyd and Wendy Turnbull, 2-6, 6-3, 7-5.

All went well until the second week of the U.S. Open where top-seeded Navratilova was afflicted by a case of toxoplasmosis, a viral condition transmitted by her cat. She was then was victimized by Shriver, who rallied from a 1-6, 4-5, 15-30 predicament to oust her doubles partner, 7-6 (7-5), 6-2, in the third, shattering the top-seed's 41-match streak. The two women then hugged at the net and both left the court in tears.

Shriver failed to survive the semi-finals, beaten by Mandlikova, who earlier had eliminated defending champ Austin, competing in only her second tournament since Wimbledon. Second-seeded Evert Lloyd received her only real challenge in the quarters from an unlikely source, a 19-year-old former gymnast from Florida, Bonnie Gadusek, dropping one set before sweeping the last 12 games for a 4-6, 6-1, 6-0 triumph. Evert Lloyd then overwhelmed Jaeger, 6-1, 6-2, in the semis and dispatched Mandlikova, 6-3, 6-1, to clinch her sixth Open singles title.

Evert Lloyd continued winning until Navratilova stopped her streak at 31 matches in the final at Brighton, England, in late October. Five weeks later, she reversed the outcome, defeating Navratilova, 6-3, 2-6, 6-3, for her first Australian title. In that instant she became the 10th player of either sex to win all four major singles championships.

The two rivals also teamed for the first time in Federation Cup play as the U.S. stretched its unbeaten streak to 34 rounds en route to its seventh consecutive team championship, 3-0 over Germany. Chrissie beat towering Claudia Kohde-Kilsch, 2-6, 6-1, 6-3, and Martina stopped Bunge, 6-4, 6-4, in the final at Santa Clara, Calif.

Evert Lloyd also captained the American squad to its fourth consecutive Wightman Cup victory over Great Britain, 6-1, winning both her singles and surpassing Helen Wills Moody's U.S. record for most matches entered with 32. Martina abstained, but the captain's wins over Jo Durie, and Sue Barker, plus rookie lefty Barbie Potter's decisions over Barker and Durie were sufficient.

Connors' resurrection salvaged what had been a lackluster Wimbledon among the men. With so many top players absent and with the rain pelting down, the primary topic of conversation was McEnroe's relationship with the All England Club. He complimented officials for their attitude following his opening match but he was not entirely pleased, noting that he had not yet received his trophies from the previous year.

Ted Tinling, the liaison between players and the club, explained that McEnroe had not picked up the silver replicas of the President's Cup, the Challenge Cup and the Renshaw Cup on his way out the door in 1981. Nor had he attended the champion's dinner that night. Tinling said the club considered shipping the silverware to New York but found the insurance prohibitive.

So there they sat until the player's father claimed the prizes later that day. As for membership in the club, which Mac also sought, Tinling said that was another matter entirely. "I explained to Mr. McEnroe," he said, "that it's not an automatic to become a member if you win. It's an elected privilege." Eventually it would all be settled positively.

Unlike the previous year, his advance to the final was virtually free of controversy. He was warned once, for ball abuse, in a second-round victory over Eddie Edwards, and drew a $500 fine for verbal abuse in his 6-3, 6-1, 6-2 semi-final thrashing of Tim Mayotte, the unseeded second-year pro who improved one round on his Wimbledon debut in 1981. Mac's title defense would

be against Connors, who had easily turned aside another surprise semi-finalist, 12th-seeded Mark Edmondson.

It had been eight years since Connors reigned as men's singles champion. He was a whiz kid of 21 when he demolished Ken Rosewall in the '74 final. Only Big Bill Tilden (1921–30) and Evonne Goolagong (1971–80) had gone a longer time between Wimbledon titles.

Brandishing a redesigned serve and hungry for another major championship, Connors outlasted McEnroe, 3-6, 6-3, 6-7 (2-7), 7-6 (7-5), 6-4, in a match that was distinguished more by its length (a Wimbledon final record four hours, 15 minutes) than its brilliance. Despite 13 double faults, Connors grabbed his sixth major title, charging back when it seemed he must lose. McEnroe, with a 2-1 lead in sets, was merely points from victory at 3-2 in the tie-breaker with two serves to come, then 4-3—three points away—after his 17th ace, but Jimmy allowed him no closer. "I'm not a one-timer," he announced, "someone to be forgotten. I've had chances [in finals] three times since then. And I was going to do anything not to let the chance slip by today."

As a special consolation prize, McEnroe was granted the honorary membership denied the previous year. He was so advised between the singles final and doubles final, which he and Peter Fleming lost to Peter McNamara and Paul McNamee of Australia, 6-4, 6-3, 6-4, relinquishing the title they'd won in 1981. "I guess I'm happy," Mac said after being welcomed to the club.

Two months later, in New York, he was separated from his other major singles title. The culprit this time was Lendl, whose serves backed McEnroe almost to the wall in a 6-4, 6-4, 7-6 (8-6) semi-final victory. Connors had a better idea. After dismissing Vilas in the semifinals, he dared Lendl to drive the ball past him. Standing almost contemptuously just behind the baseline, he startled and demoralized the Czech with his returns in a 6-3, 6-2, 4-6, 6-4 triumph that returned the man to the top of the tennis world just when his career appeared to be in eclipse.

"When I won before," Connors said, "everybody thought I would. When I won now, everybody thought I wouldn't. And that's very satisfying." So he was joining the likes of Tilden, Fred Perry, Don Budge, Rod Laver and McEnroe as the only men twice to win Wimbledon and the U.S. in the same year.

Although winning no major individual titles for the first time in four years, McEnroe did lead Capt. Arthur

Ashe's U.S. force to a second consecutive Davis Cup. The 4-1 final over France in Grenoble was notable mainly for McEnroe's 12-10, 1-6, 3-6, 6-2, 6-3 victory over Noah on a clay court built to stop him inside the former Olympic ice rink. Gene Mayer, the first two-way double hander in a Cup final followed up over left-handed rookie Henri Leconte, and McEnroe-Fleming was the crusher of the two Frenchmen, 6-3, 6-4, 9-7.

But even Mac's superb four-hour, 21-minute battle with Noah paled in comparison to his extraordinary 9-7, 6-2, 15-17, 3-6, 8-6 triumph over Wilander in a decisive fifth match of the U.S.-Sweden quarter-final at St. Louis. Time of play: A singles record of six hours, 22 minutes. Mac had beaten Anders Jarryd the first day, but the strong 17-year-old Mats eroded Teltscher in five sets to tie it. Though Mac and Fleming were go-ahead guys over

Hans Simonsson and Jarryd, 6-4, 6-3, 6-0, Jarryd responded to tie it again, beating sub Brian Gottfried, 6-2, 6-2, 6-4.

McEnroe and Teltscher started the 4-1 opening round victory over India at Carlsbad, Calif. John won a volleying faceoff with the stylish Indian Capt. Vijay Amritraj and Eliot took the deft Ramesh Krishnan. Fleming and McEnroe settled it over the Amritraj brothers, Anand and Vijay, 6-3, 6-1, 7-5. In the semi on the greensward of Perth, it was 5-0 over the Aussies in brisk, four-set order: Mac over McNamara; Mayer over Alexander; the Fleming-McEnroe express over their Wimbledon conquerors, McNamee and McNamara, 6-2, 6-2, 3-6, 8-6. For McEnroe it was an unblemished campaign: 8-0 in singles, 4-0 in doubles.

1983

Martina matchless, Connors still has it

Martina Navratilova
But for one May afternoon in Paris, a perfect year.

Considering their backgrounds, their forehands and their achievements, one would not expect to mention them in the same sentence. But on May 28, Martina Navratilova and Kathy Horvath shared a court in Paris. In retrospect, it may have been the most significant match of the year.

Even at the time, it was something special. Navratilova had won her first 36 matches of 1983 before meeting the teenager in the fourth round of the French Open. A former child prodigy, Erika Kathleen Horvath of Hopewell Junction, N.Y., had been runner-up to Chris Evert Lloyd in the German Open the previous week. But nothing prepared her or the tennis world for what happened at Stade Roland Garros.

The unseeded American, a pupil of Harry Hopman, posted a stunning 6-4, 0-6, 6-3 victory. The ramifications of that upset wouldn't be felt for months. Following the defeat, Navratilova won her next 50 matches and swept the field of Wimbledon, the U.S. Open and Australian Open championships. Not only had Horvath denied her the opportunity of achieving a Grand Slam but spoiled what might have been the first perfect campaign in the open era.

Navratilova's domination of the women, marred only by that single loss, and Evert Lloyd's subsequent march to a record-tying fifth French title, was the story of the year in tennis. It overshadowed a mad scramble on the men's circuit as the major championships were divided four ways for the first time in seven years and the race for No. 1 wasn't decided until the Masters in the 13th month of an exhausting season. At the end, the distinction belonged once again to John McEnroe, who boasted a second Wimbledon crown among his seven singles titles.

For breadth of accomplishment, however, Mats Wilander emerged as male Player of the Year. Not only did he win the most matches (82) and singles tournaments (nine) but he went 8-0 in Davis Cup play while leading Sweden to second place behind Australia and he compiled the best record in the major tournaments. He captured the Australian title, was runner-up at the French, reached the quarter-finals at the U.S. and the third round at Wimbledon. He also finished atop the Volvo Grand Prix standings, pocketing a $600,000 bonus which enabled him to finish third in prize money behind Ivan Lendl and McEnroe.

In terms of shock value and fan satisfaction, however, perhaps nothing compared to Yannick Noah's victory in Paris. By turning back defending champ Wilander in the final, the acrobatic athlete from Cameroon became the first French citizen in 37 years to hold the French title. He also became such a celebrity that he found it necessary to flee to little old New York for privacy.

On another national front, Jimmy Connors continued his mastery of the Flushing Meadow hard courts, claiming his fifth U.S. crown while denying Lendl a first Big Four title. The angular Czech also stumbled in the Masters final. He was consoled by checks totaling $1,747,128.

Lendl's earnings exceeded even those of Navratilova. But the $1,456,030 she collected, more than triple the take of Evert Lloyd, was only one indicator of the success she enjoyed. At the very least, it was the most stellar female performance since Margaret Smith Court completed her Grand Slam in 1970. Suzanne Lenglen of France and Americans Helen Wills Moody and Alice Marble had posted unbeaten seasons earlier in the century, but they didn't play in all the major championships or endure the same demanding schedule.

Consider that Navratilova won 16 of the 17 singles events she entered and added 13 doubles championships, including 11 in the company of Pam Shriver. Her greatest satisfaction occurred in New York, where she annexed her first U.S. Open title. That brought to 11 the number of players, male and female, to have won all four of the major championships.

But for the intervention of Horvath, it might have been a season unlike any other. Horvath at 17 was almost four years removed from her greatest moment of fame. An eighth-grader she had advanced through the qualifying rounds to reach the main draw of the 1979 U.S. Open less than a week after her 14th birthday, the youngest ever entered, and received a first-round bye before being ousted, not without a struggle, by sixth-seeded Dianne Fromholtz, 7-6, 6-2.

After two years of consistent progress, Horvath received a setback in 1982 when she was sidelined for four months by a back injury. But she worked her way up to No. 33 on the computer by the spring of 1983, winning Nashville on the satellite circuit over Czech Marcela Skuherska and reaching the semi-finals of the Italian Open. Unseeded at the German Open, Horvath knocked off sixth-seeded Gadusek, 13th Andrea Leand, third Bettina Bunge and second Andrea Jaeger, en- route to the final, where she succumbed to Evert Lloyd, 6-4, 7-6 (7-1).

Understandably, these achievements paled alongside those of Navratilova, who stormed through four tournaments on the Virginia Slims circuit, then overpowered Evert Lloyd, 6-2, 6-0, in the championship finale at New York. Adapting quickly to clay, she won a second consecutive Family Circle Cup at Hilton Head, overcoming Tracy Austin, 5-7, 6-1, 6-0. Limited by injuries to eight tournaments, the luckless Austin appeared in only the one final.

Entering the French, Navratilova appeared unbeatable. She was backstopped by a trainer and motivator (Nancy Lieberman), a regular coach (Mike Estep), a strategist (Renée Richards) and even a nutritionist. 'Team Navratilova' the entourage was called.

Against the biggest arsenal in the game, Horvath marshaled her resolve and an attack strategy that contrasted with her earlier years as a baseline mechanic. "To be in the rankings these days," she said, "you have to be really steady from the baseline but you also have to be able to finish up the point. Against a serve-and-volleyer, when it's close, it's important to get to the net first.

1983 THE MAJOR CHAMPIONSHIPS

Australian Open
Men's Singles: Mats Wilander
Women's Singles: Martina Navratilova
Men's Doubles: Mark Edmondson / Paul McNamee
Women's Doubles: Martina Navratilova / Pam Shriver
French Open
Men's Singles: Yannick Noah
Women's Singles: Chris Evert Lloyd
Men's Doubles: Anders Jarryd / Hans Simonsson
Women's Doubles: Rosalyn Fairbank / Candy Reynolds
Mixed Doubles: Barbara Jordan / Eliot Teltscher
Wimbledon
Men's Singles: John McEnroe
Women's Singles: Martina Navratilova
Men's Doubles: Peter Fleming / John McEnroe
Women's Doubles: Martina Navratilova / Pam Shriver
Mixed Doubles: Wendy Turnbull / John Lloyd
U.S. Open
Men's Singles: Jimmy Connors
Women's Singles: Martina Navratilova
Men's Doubles: Peter Fleming / John McEnroe
Women's Doubles: Pam Shriver / Martina Navratilova
Mixed Doubles: Elizabeth Sayers / John Fitzgerald

They're used to being there, and if you take that away from them, they get shaky."

She did exactly as planned against Navratilova, and the defending champion was as bothered as Horvath had hoped. The youngster kept hitting to Navratilova's backhand and volleying her increasingly weak returns.

Evert Lloyd didn't appear any more pleased than her rival when she heard the score. "All I thought was, 'Damn, I wish I'd been the one to beat her,'" she said.

In six meetings that year, Evert Lloyd failed to do just that but she never got the chance on her best surface. She had to be satisfied with beating Helena Sukova, eighth-seeded Hana Mandlikova, third-seeded Jaeger and Mima Jausovec, 6-1, 6-2 in the last four rounds to clinch her fifth French title, tying Court's record. Jausovec, the 1977 champion, ended Horvath's dream in the quarter-finals, 6-1, 6-1. Another dream was beginning to hatch, though unnoticed, belonging to a 13-year-old German named Steffi Graf. She won, 6-4, 6-1, over Swede Carina Karlsson and lost, 6-0, 7-6, to South African Bev Mould, but it was enough to make her believe she'd win it all one day—and she would, six times, starting four years later.

It didn't take Navratilova long to start on a new streak. She prepared for Wimbledon by routing Wendy Turnbull in the final at Eastbourne, 6-1, 6-1, and was at her devastating best at Wimbledon, where her average match lasted 47 minutes. The field was weakened notably by Evert Lloyd's colossal dismissal in the third round. Suffering from the after-effects of flu, the three-time champion was eliminated by Kathy Jordan, 6-1, 7-6 (7-2). It marked the first time in 35 major tournaments, dating back to 1971, that she had failed to reach the semi-finals.

In her absence, Billie Jean King made another run, 10th-seeded, at the championship at age 39. For the second consecutive year, she won the warmup at Birmingham, over the 1982 National Intercollegiate champ, Stanfordian Alycia Moulton, and then advanced to the round of four with a 7-5, 6-4 triumph over Jordan in the quarter-finals.

The Old Lady, however, was no match for Jaeger in the semis. The 18-year-old, not even half King's age, passed and lobbed her opponent into submission, 6-1, 6-1, to become the youngest women's finalist at Wimbledon since Maureen Connolly in 1952. She had little time or reason to savor the honor. Navratilova, who had crushed unseeded Yvonne Vermaak, a tiny South African in the semi-finals, overwhelmed third-seeded Jaeger, 6-0, 6-3, and proudly accepted the mantle of No. 1 player in the world.

Although no other female player on earth possessed her combination of strength and agility, there remained the faintest of doubts about her composure as she prepared for her final frontier, the U.S. Open. It was the mental edge to which Evert Lloyd clung, even after she fell in the finals to Navratilova at the Virginia Slims of Los Angeles, 6-1, 6-3, and the Canadian Open, 6-4, 4-6, 6-1, in consecutive weeks. The defending champ seemed to be counting upon her rival to fall apart at Flushing Meadow once again.

Certainly, no other threat materialized in the course of the tournament. Navratilova waded through the field with almost as much dispatch as she displayed at Wimbledon. She failed to drop more than four games in any of her first five matches and she continued to limit her court time to under one hour through the semis, where she avenged her 1982 loss to Shriver in businesslike fashion, 6-2, 6-1.

Nor did Evert Lloyd struggle unduly. Her run of straight-set victories included a 6-3, 7-6 (8-6) payback triumph over Jordan in the fourth round. In turning back Jo Durie of Great Britain, 6-4, 6-4, in the semi-finals, she qualified to defend the title she had regained the previous year. If there was any stopping Navratilova, this was the time and, particularly, the place.

But Navratilova had come too far, had worked too hard to trip over her own anxieties. She took charge of the match at the outset, en route to a decisive 6-1, 6-3 victory in 63 minutes. It was the most satisfying victory of her career on her 11th U.S. Open try after one final and four semi-finals. "If I don't win another tournament in my life," she said, "I can still say I've done it all."

With the last jewel in her crown, she silenced criticism of her emotional fortitude. In the second set, Evert Lloyd had rallied briefly for her lone break and then held serve at love for a 3-2 lead. But Navratilova tightened the

---

1983 CHAMPIONS AND LEADERS

Top Player Earnings: Men Ivan Lendl $1,747,128	**Federation Cup:** Czechoslovakia
Top Player Earnings: Women Martina Navratilova $1,456,030	**Wightman Cup:** United States **Grand Prix Masters, NYC**
Year-End Number One Men: John McEnroe Women: Martina Navratilova	John McEnroe **WCT, Dallas** John McEnroe
ITF World Champion Men: John McEnroe Women: Martina Navratilova	**Virginia Slims Championships, NYC** Martina Navratilova
Davis Cup: Australia	

screws, holding her own serve and then breaking Evert Lloyd at love before running out the set. The first-time U.S. champion set a record for fewest games lost in a seven-match tournament (19 of 103).

Navratilova continued to cut a swath through the women's tour all the way to Melbourne. There, in the absence of Evert Lloyd, she was almost undone in the quarters by a soggy lawn and the eighth seed, by another net-seeker, six-footer Durie. The Englishwoman captured the first set before rain postponed the match but Navratilova rallied the following day to win, 4-6, 6-3, 6-4, taking five of the last six games.

She then turned back Shriver and Jordan, completing the campaign with her 50th consecutive victory in her ninth successive tournament final. Sparky 16-year-old Carling Bassett out of Toronto, beat Sharon Walsh, 7-6, 6-4, to make the quarters, a high point in a major for a Canadian, before losing to Shriver, 6-0, 6-1.

Remarkably, Navratilova also teamed with Shriver to retain the doubles title, defeating Turnbull and Anne Hobbs, 6-4, 6-7 (5-7), 6-2—an encore of their championships at Wimbledon, 6-2, 6-2, over Rosie Casals and Turnbull, and the U.S, 6-7 (4-7), 6-1, 6-3, over Ros Fairbank and Candy Reynolds. They had scratched from the French due to a Shriver injury, unable to pursue the Grand Slam that would be theirs in 1984

No female doubles team had won three majors in a season since Court and Virginia Wade 10 years earlier. Their lone defeat, by King and Anne Smith at the Tournament of Champions final in April, 6-3, 1-6, 7-6 (11-9), ended a 40-match streak. So they started another that reached 31 by season's end.

Navratilova also assumed Evert Lloyd's former role as captain and chief assassin of the Wightman Cup team, leading the U.S. to a 6-1 victory over Great Britain at Williamsburg, Va. The captain and Shriver each beat Durie, and Sue Barker.

Neither Martina nor Chrissie were available for the Federation Cup in Zurich, however, and the U.S. was beaten in the semis, 3-0, by champion Czechoslovakia, taking the Cup for a second time. Candy Reynolds gave way to Helena Sukova and Jaeger to Mandlikova, terminating a U.S. streak of seven Cups and 37 series. The one-two punch of unbeaten Mandlikova (5-0) and Sukova (4-1) then took care of West Germany's Bunge and Claudia Kohde-Kilsch in the 3-0 final.

Only two women other than Navratilova won more than two tournaments all year. Evert Lloyd captured six

titles and, aside from her six losses to Navratilova, slipped only twice—to Jordan at Wimbledon and to Lisa Bonder in the first round at Tokyo. Andrea Temesvari won two events besides her Italian Open title: The U.S. Clay Court over Zina Garrison, and Hittfield, Germany, over German Eva Pfaff. And Horvath, the obstacle to perfection at Paris, won the Ginny championship play-off at Honolulu in November over Bassett.

Although the men offered no transcendent figure, they were a lot more competitive from the start of the European season to the finish of a dandy Masters in January, 1984. In a year of new faces, the youngest and freshest belonged to Jimmy Arias, who became the dirt-kicking King of Italy, waving his huge forehand as a scepter in sweeping the country's soil: First, Florence over native Francesco Cancellotti; then the Open in Rome over Spaniard Jose Higueras, at age 18; finally Palermo, as a new 19-year-old, over Argentine Jose-Luis Clerc. A three-year pro who was in the first wave of coach Nick Bollettieri's baseline prodigies, Arias would go on to capture the U.S. Clay Court over Ecuadorian Andres Gomez, skyrocket to No. 6 on the ATP computer and, besieged by injuries, fail to win another tournament in the decade.

Emotionally, no one made a more spectacular jump than Noah, even though he was 23 and had been a steady winner on the tour for five seasons. Until this year, however, he hadn't advanced beyond the quarter-final of a major event. But on the occasion of the 1983 French Open, he was more than a gifted entertainer. He was a champion.

With a running start provided by his victory at the German Open, where he deposed Higueras, sixth-seeded Noah tore through Paris, dropping only one set, that to third-seeded Lendl in the quarter-finals. The fans at Roland Garros were treated to the extraordinary sight of two Frenchmen in the semi-finals after wild card Christophe Roger-Vasselin, No. 230, shocked top-seeded Connors in straight sets, 6-4, 6-4, 7-6 (7-5), the upset of the year and one of the most stunning in French history. The last time two natives had gone so far was 1946: Champion Marcel Bernard and Yvon Petra, Bernard beating Czech Jaroslav Drobny for the title.

Noah easily disposed of his countryman, 6-3, 6-0, 6-0, and then ground down the defending champ, resourceful fifth-seeded Wilander, 6-2, 7-5, 7-6 (7-3). In the quarters Wilander spectacularly evicted second-seeded McEnroe, 1-6, 6-2, 6-4, 6-0—winning the last

11 games, 23 straight points to 1-0, 40-0 (45 of last 57 points)! The last set of the two-hour 12-minute match took 24 minutes

The aftermath wasn't nearly so inspirational. Noah was idled by a 42-day suspension for failing to represent France at the World Team Cup in Dusseldorf and by a knee injury. He played in only four more tournaments, including the U.S. Open where he lost to Arias in a splendid quarter-final match.

But before Flushing Meadow, there was Wimbledon and a new cast of up-and-comers. These included Nduka 'Duke' Odizor of Nigeria and the University of Houston. Serving 14 aces while bouncing fourth-seeded Guillermo Vilas in the first round, he reached the fourth round. Hard-serving Kevin Curren of South Africa dismantled top-seeded Connors, 4-6, 7-6 (7-4), 6-2, 7-6 (8-6), in the fourth round with the help of 33 aces, and went past Tim Mayotte to the semis. There he met Chris Lewis, a dashing Kiwi ranked No. 91, who outlasted Curren in a brilliant five-set semi-final that left the participants applauding each other, 6-7 (3-7), 6-4, 7-6 (7-4), 6-7 (3-7), 8-6.

Lewis became the first unseeded player to reach a Wimbledon final since Willy Bungert in 1967 and the first New Zealander in the championship match since the much-idolized Tony Wilding won four consecutive titles, 1910-1913. There, however, reality struck in the form of McEnroe's impenetrable serving and superb court sense. In three immaculate sets of serve-and-volley tennis, the American won easily, 6-2, 6-2, 6-2, in 85 minutes, to regain the honor he last held in 1981. McEnroe dropped but one set, that to Romanian Florin Segarceanu in the second round.

Californian Trey Waltke, 28, won only his first rounder (over an ex-champ, Stan Smith, 37, injury default), but he lent a nostalgic air to proceedings in long white trousers. Such were universal male apparel for about 60 years until shorts (bravely introduced by Bunny Austin in 1933) took over after World War II. Though it was uncertain who had last appeared in trousers, Yvon Petra in 1946 was the most recent champion.

Two surprise packages at the U.S. Open were a stocky double-hander all the way, Greg Holmes, the National Intercollegiate (Utah) and Pan American Games champ, and skinny 16-year-old Aaron Krickstein from Grosse Pointe, Mich., the country's youngest junior champ. Both made the last 16. Holmes, ranked No. 450,

knocked off an ex-champ, sixth-seeded Vilas. Amateur Krickstein, with no ranking, was, like Arias, a product of Nick Bollettieri's Florida finishing school of two-fisted backhands. In his first major he attracted attention by waylaying a big name, 15th-seeded Vitas Gerulaitis from way behind, 3-6, 3-6, 6-4, 6-3, 6-4.

Krickstein then fell to Noah, who, in turn was eliminated by Aaron's stablemate, Arias, in a five-set match of very good feeling and trick shots. Arias, who had celebrated his 19th birthday three weeks earlier, became the youngest U.S. semi-finalist since 17-year-old Oliver Campbell in 1888. This impressed Lendl not a bit, and he sent the King of Italy home to Bradenton, Fla., 6-4, 6-4, 7-6 (7-4), after chasing Wilander, 6-4, 6-4, 7-6 (7-4).

Awaiting Lendl in the final was Connors, the defending champion. To reach the championship round for a seventh time, third-seeded Connors gave a 6-2, 6-3, 6-2, brush off to slick-volleying Scanlon, who had outnerved and outserved McEnroe in the fourth round, 7-6 (7-2), 7-6 (7-3), 4-6, 6-3. Moving on, Scanlon labored hour after hour well into the following morning to defeat, in a fifth set tie-breaker, the tourney's hypnotic over-achiever, No. 96 Mark Dickson, a Floridian dawdler who routinely bounced the ball 30-or-so times before serving. That inspired a plaintive wall message in red paint in a men's room: I SURVIVED SCANLON-DICKSON—4:14.

Because Connors, just turned 31, was playing with a bone spur on his right little toe, was suffering from diarrhea (he rushed to the men's room late in the second set) and was combating court temperatures in excess of 100 degrees, the time appeared ripe for Lendl. After splitting the first two sets, the Czech expatriate served for the third set at 5-4. The title appeared within his reach. Then, inexplicably, he double-faulted at set point. After that, he said, "I could never recover." In a mysterious meltdown, the man who hadn't lost a set until the final never won another game. Connors whipped through the last nine games to win his fifth U.S. title, 6-3, 6-7 (2-7), 7-5, 6-0. An international statistical panel recently had ruled that some of his early achievements were of an exhibition nature and revised his total of career tournament victories to 99, so Connors re-celebrated his centennial in his favorite setting.

One of those was on the carpet at Memphis, where Jimmy broke a tie with a forgotten rival while winning the U.S. Indoor for a record sixth time. In beating Gene

Mayer, 7-5, 6-0, he renewed a title he first won at Salisbury, Md., a decade before. That sent him ahead of long-departed Wylie Grant from deep in the long-trousered era, a five-time champ, too: 1903-04, 1906, 1908, 1912.

As the season waned, boy Krickstein also found his way into the record book by winning his first pro title. He was 16-years, two months, the youngest to take a professional tournament. It was a long-shot special, wild card Aaron, No. 489, beating No. 189, German Christopher Zipf, 7-6, 6-3, at Tel Aviv. Krickstein, at 15 earlier in the year, became the youngest to play in a pro event, Philadelphia, losing in the first round to Fritz Buehning, 6-2, 6-3.

At the Australian Open, which attracted most of the elite, although Connors bypassed, 19-year-old Wilander knocked off defending champ Kriek, McEnroe and, finally, Lendl, 6-1, 6-4, 6-4, to become the youngest champion Down Under since Ken Rosewall won at 18 in 1953. It was his ninth victory of a season in which 10 players won three or more tour events and 46 men earned at least $100,000 in prize money.

Parity was in the air, and a handful of players had a chance to claim the No. 1 ranking when the Masters got underway at Madison Square Garden. There was only one notable absentee, 1974 champion Vilas, who had been hit with a one-year suspension by the MIPTC for allegedly accepting $60,000 illicit appearance money at Rotterdam. He subsequently lost an appeal and was fined $20,000. Although the suspension was waived in January 1984, he already had been sidelined for six months.

After reversing his fortune against Wilander, 6-2, 6-4, in the semi-final, McEnroe decisively whipped Lendl, 6-3, 6-4, 6-4, for the title and the top ranking. "John deserves to be No. 1," Lendl said. "He had the most consistent year."

For good measure, McEnroe and Peter Fleming, the best doubles team in the world, reprised their Wimbledon and U.S. championship performances by beating the second-best team of Pavel Slozil and Tom Smid, 6-2, 6-2. It was their sixth Masters doubles crown in as many years.

1984

McEnroe, Martina
a dominating duo

John McEnroe
An 82-3 record, the best by a male in the open era.

Rare as it may be for any athlete to be identified as a genius, it's more unlikely still to be branded a tormented genius. But John McEnroe fit the billing, never more than in 1984. En route to the greatest season of his career, he jousted with the furies and toyed with his peers.

But for an occasional slip, it might have been said that the only man capable of beating McEnroe this year was McEnroe himself. Certainly, he had to be credited at least with an assist when he allowed himself to be distracted while holding a two-set lead over Ivan Lendl in the final of the French Open. Lendl went on to win the match for his first major triumph.

Thereafter, McEnroe was magnificent in duplicating his 1981 feat of sweeping Wimbledon and the U.S. Open. He also counted the U.S. Pro Indoor, the WCT championship, the Canadian Open and the season-ending Masters among his 13 tournament victories. In addition to the loss in Paris, he suffered only two more singles defeats, to Vijay Amritraj at Cincinnati, and to Henrik Sundstrom in the Davis Cup final at Goteborg.

McEnroe's 82-3 record produced a .965 winning percentage, highest of the Open era among men. In finishing at the top of the computer rankings for the fourth consecutive year, he enjoyed the most dominant season since Jimmy Connors won the only three major events he entered and compiled a 99-4 mark in 1974. Jimmy was still going strong 10 years after his big year, claiming five titles, reaching the final at Wimbledon and pushing McEnroe to five sets in a brilliant semi-final showdown at Flushing Meadow.

Andres Gomez, the finest player from Ecuador since Pancho Segura, ascended to the Top Ten by winning five tournaments, including the Italian Open over Aaron Krickstein during a dust storm, and the U.S. Clay Court over Hungarian Balazs Taroczy. But the biggest breakthrough occurred among the Swedes. Bjorn Borg's legacy was a nation of nine million swarming with tennis talent. Mats Wilander and four compatriots—Sundstrom, Anders Jarryd, Joakim Nystrom and Stefan Edberg—not only seized the Davis Cup for the first time in nine years but they accounted for 14 tournament victories.

Yet, the only individual to challenge McEnroe for supremacy and attention was Martina Navratilova, who continued her mastery of the women's tour. She won three of the Big Four tournaments and 78 of 80 singles matches, a phenomenal season by any standard but the one she established the previous year. This time Navratilova fell two victories short of a Grand Slam when she was upset by Helena Sukova in the semi-finals of the Australian Open in December. She had suffered her only other loss of the year to Hana Mandlikova 11 months earlier in Oakland. Both women once had served as ballgirls at Navratilova's matches in Czechoslovakia.

In addition to her 13 tournament victories, Martina posted the longest (74 matches) winning streak of the open era and, at the time, the third-longest (54). She also surpassed her great rival, Chris Evert Lloyd, in head-to-head competition by winning all six meetings, with the loss of only one set.

Evert Lloyd did claim the Australian Open title by beating Sukova, thereby extending to 11 years her incredible streak of having won at least one major championship. That was her 132nd professional tournament singles victory, a record for either sex, and increased her total of matches won to 1,003, having nailed her 1,000th over Pascale Paradis of France in the third round.

Manuela Maleeva, a 17-year-old Bulgarian, made the biggest jump among the women. She vaulted from No. 31 to No. 6 in the world rankings by winning four tournaments, among them the rain-plagued Italian Open, where she stunned five-time champion Evert Lloyd, 6-3, 6-3, Manuela's third victory of a strenuous last day in Perugia. She started, 7-6, 4-6, 6-4, over Virginia, Ruzici, followed, 6-2, 6-2, over Carling Bassett, and finished with Evert—67 games. Headed in the opposite direction were Tracy Austin, who played in only one tournament before being sidelined again with a chronic back ailment, and Andrea Jaeger, who withdrew from the tour to enter college after lackluster efforts in six events.

At the Richmond, Va., indoor tournament, a couple of women, Vicki Nelson-Dunbar, 21, of Wooster, Ohio, and Jean Hepner, 25, of Atherton, Calif., had no idea when they went on court for a first rounder that they wouldn't leave for more than six hours. They recorded the longest documented match ever played: Six hours, 31 minutes, won by Nelson-Dunbar, 6-3, 7-6 (13-11). Steadfast, stubborn baseliners, involved in interminable rallies, they devoted 1:47 to the tie-breaker alone, one point of which lasted 29 minutes and 643 strokes.

But the year will belong forever to McEnroe and Navratilova, who never again would stand unchallenged. (Although only 25, McEnroe would not win another major.) The two shared a physical characteristic, left-handedness, and a love for doubles.

McEnroe won seven doubles titles. In six of those tournaments, including Wimbledon and the Masters, he was joined by his steady partner Peter Fleming. Together, they raised their victory total to 52.

According to Fleming, "The best doubles team in the world is John McEnroe and whoever he plays with." As if to prove it, Mac took his 17-year-old brother Patrick, a top junior, to a WCT tournament in Richmond and they routed Kevin Curren and Steve Denton, the 1982 U.S. Open champions, in the final, 7-6 (7-3), 6-2.

Navratilova enjoyed even greater success in doubles, losing one of 61 matches. But with Pam Shriver she was perfection. She and Pam completed the open era's only undefeated season by a team: 11 titles, 53 matches. Pam's personal doubles match record was 59-2. The pair also registered the only Grand Slam by a female doubles team, equaling the 1951 feat of Aussies Frank Sedgman and Ken McGregor. Martina and Pam were 22-0 over

---

1984 THE MAJOR CHAMPIONSHIPS

Australian Open
Men's Singles: Mats Wilander
Women's Singles: Chris Evert Lloyd
Men's Doubles: Mark Edmondson / Sherwood Stewart
Women's Doubles: Martina Navratilova / Pam Shriver
French Open
Men's Singles: Ivan Lendl
Women's Singles: Martina Navratilova
Men's Doubles: Henri Leconte / Yannick Noah
Women's Doubles: Martina Navratilova / Pam Shriver
Mixed Doubles: Anne Smith / Dick Stockton
Wimbledon
Men's Singles: John McEnroe
Women's Singles: Martina Navratilova
Men's Doubles: Peter Fleming / John McEnroe
Women's Doubles: Martina Navratilova / Pam Shriver
Mixed Doubles: Wendy Turnbull / John Lloyd
U.S. Open
Men's Singles: John McEnroe
Women's Singles: Martina Navratilova
Men's Doubles: John Fitzgerald / Tomas Smid
Women's Doubles: Pam Shriver / Martina Navratilova
Mixed Doubles: Manuela Maleeva / Tom Gullikson

that four-way stretch, losing two sets. By beating Sukova and German Claudia Kohde-Kilsch, they added the Australian title to the other three: French over Kohde-Kilsch and Mandlikova; Wimbledon over country-women Anne Smith and Kathy Jordan; and U.S. over the Anglo-Aussie combine of Anne Hobbs and Wendy Turnbull. The Australian was their 52nd career triumph.

Despite the parallel success of the two champions, however, there was a significant distinction in their approach to the sport. Having reshuffled her entourage midway through the 1983 season, Navratilova continued to improve her conditioning under coach Mike Estep and became a disciple of Robert Haas, the nutritionist, whose 'Eat to Win' diet found favor among a number of players.

That led a reporter to inquire of McEnroe, who played doubles in order to avoid tedious practice sessions and whose appetite was ruled by his taste buds, whether he had tried the Haas diet. "No," he smirked, "I prefer the Haagen-Dazs diet."

McEnroe was never better than in 1984, which he began in spectacular fashion. Following his Masters victory, he thrashed Lendl at the U.S. Pro Indoor in Philadelphia, 6-3, 3-6, 6-3, 7-6 (7-3), the Belgian Indoor in Brussels, 6-1, 6-3, the WCT Tournament of Champions at Forest Hills, 6-4, 6-2, and the World Team Cup at Dusseldorf, 6-3, 6-2. He also dismissed Tomas Smid at the Grand Prix de Madrid, 6-0, 6-4, and overwhelmed Connors, 6-1, 6-2, 6-3, at the WCT finals in Dallas. In reaching the championship round of the French Open for the first time, he extended his winning streak to 42 matches, an open-era high for an American man.

Not that his form left him serene. Paris was a struggle from the outset. There, in addition to opponents, Mac battled the usual suspects—courtside photographers, groundskeepers, line judges—as well as the ambience of

the tournament and city itself, of which he had once declared in full voice, "I hate this place."

Top-seeded McEnroe demanded court repairs during a third-round victory over Mel Purcell, drilled two balls into the photographers' pit while beating Jose Higueras and complained so much about calls in a semi-final rout of Connors that the latter offered some free advice while approaching the net. "Shut up," the onetime bad boy yelled. "Grow up. You're a baby."

While the top seed battled his personal demons, Lendl tore through his half of the draw virtually unscathed. He dropped only one set in reaching the final and in the semis blasted the steady Wilander, 6-2, 6-3, 7-5, who had eliminated defending champion Yannick Noah, 7-6 (7-4), 2-6, 3-6, 6-3, 6-3.

For the first two sets of their showdown on clay, McEnroe was completely in charge, granting only 10 points on his serve. He appeared certain to become the first American male since Tony Trabert (1954-55) to win at Roland Garros and given his form and past performances at Wimbledon and the U.S. Open, a Grand Slam was not out of the question. At that critical juncture of history, however, McEnroe snapped. He objected to a television cameraman's headset that was emitting a director's instructions, began grousing at photographers and became the object of hooting and whistling from the crowd.

Meanwhile, Lendl, 0-for-5 in previous Major Championship finals, was ready to shed his reputation for gagging in the majors. He was the stronger down the fifth-set stretch to win 3-6, 2-6, 6-4, 7-5, 7-5, in four hours, eight minutes. "It feels great to finally answer some different questions," the new champion said after becoming only the 14th man in 107 years to overcome a two-set deficit in the final of a Big Four event. An alleged choker no more, Lendl had the first of his eight majors that decorated a great career, after failing in his title bids on this court in 1981, the U.S. in 1982 and 1983 and the Australian in 1983.

McEnroe appeared to have learned his lessons from Paris and a subsequent squall at the Queen's Club in time for Wimbledon. Either that or the uncharacteristically benign weather left him mellow. The defending champ behaved impeccably at the All England Club and he performed brilliantly. Whether the one had anything to do with the other was pure conjecture.

He ceded only one set in the tournament—to Paul McNamee in the first round. 6-4, 6-4, 6-7 (7-9), 6-1—

1984 CHAMPIONS AND LEADERS

Top Player Earnings: Men
John McEnroe $2,026,109
Top Player Earnings: Women
Martina Navratilova $2,173,556
Year-End Number One
Men: John McEnroe
Women: Martina Navratilova
Davis Cup: Sweden
Federation Cup:
Czechoslovakia
Wightman Cup: United States

ITF World Champion
Men: John McEnroe
Women: Martina Navratilova
Grand Prix Masters, NYC
John McEnroe
WCT, Dallas
John McEnroe
Virginia Slims
Championships, NYC
Martina Navratilova

and was mesmerizing in dismissing Connors, 6-1, 6-1, 6-2, in the final. That followed brisk victories over Billy Scanlon, John Sadri and over future champ Pat Cash. Even McEnroe, the perfectionist, allowed that the title bout was "maybe the best match of my life." Connors had beaten Lendl, 6-7 (4-7), 6-3, 7-5, 6-1, to get there.

It had been 46 years since a Wimbledon championship was concluded in such decisive fashion (Don Budge over Bunny Austin, 6-1, 6-0, 6-3). Incredibly McEnroe didn't commit the first of his two unforced errors until the 62-minute mark of Connors' hour-and-a-half ordeal. The champion served 75 percent, with 11 aces, and never permitted Connors a break point in becoming the second American male to win Wimbledon for a third time, following the lead of Bill Tilden, and the first to hold consecutive titles since Budge in 1937 and 1938.

Although this would be the last of 15 major finals for 31-year-old Connors, he had more bullets in his gun, some of them fired at Memphis, where he extended his U.S. Indoor record to seven titles, beating Henri Leconte, 6-3, 4-6, 7-5. Only three American men had won that many U.S. prizes on a particular surface: Dick Sears, Bill Larned and Bill Tilden ruled the foremost U.S. Championship, then played on grass, seven times. Jimmy joined them with his hothouse variety. There were bullets, too, for the U.S. Open, where he fed on the energy of the crowds.

En route to the next duel of American titans, McEnroe suffered his second loss of the year. He was defeated by Indian Amritraj, a budding film star, in the first round at Cincinnati on the day after he wrapped up his first Canadian Open championship with a straight-set conquest of Vitas Gerulaitis. Amritraj, who had slipped to No. 104 in the rankings, had won his first Grand Prix tournament in four years only a month earlier, overcoming Tim Mayotte on the last grass of the U.S., Newport, 3-6, 6-4, 6-4.

Still, there wasn't any question but that McEnroe was poised to dethrone Connors at the U.S. Open. On the Flushing hard courts, McEnroe raced through his first five opponents, including the young Swede who had won an unofficial gold medal (demonstration class) at the Los Angeles Olympics. The 6-1, 6-0, 6-2 rout of Edberg was a barometer of how well he was playing. Meanwhile, Connors, back home on his favorite surface, also won all 15 sets in advancing to the semi-final, including a victory over surprising quarter-finalist, John

(Mr. Chris Evert) Lloyd, 7-5, 6-2, 6-0.

Those who couldn't wait for the showdown of the perennial bad boys had a very long afternoon on Super Saturday at the National Tennis Center. They went on last following a men's 35 match between legends John Newcombe and Stan Smith, the first men's semi-final between Lendl and brash Cash and the women's final between those rivals for the ages, Navratilova and Lloyd. All four matches were carried to the ultimate set and the tennis, which began at 11 a.m., didn't conclude until 11:14 p.m.

Even McEnroe, annoyed that he didn't strike his first ball until 7:28, allowed that, "It had to be the best day (for fans) at the Open ... ever." Certainly, the day's finale qualified as the match of the tournament, if not the year.

After 37 minutes, Connors had equaled the four games he won in the Wimbledon final. Within 90 minutes, he had won a set and broken McEnroe's serve for the fourth time for a 3-1 lead in the third set. In the end only a scant few shots separated the pair, perhaps none more important than a missed forehand by Connors on break point in the seventh game of the final set. Connors finished with 45 winners, to 20 for the winner. But McEnroe's 19 aces pushed him over the top in a magnificent 6-4, 4-6, 7-5, 4-6, 6-3 victory. Both agreed the match was superior to their epic 1980 semi-final.

In the final, Lendl, who barely survived his semi-final over Cash, was no match for a McEnroe at his peak. Eighteen hours after vanquishing Connors, McEnroe routed Lendl, 6-4, 6-3, 6-1, to claim his fourth U.S. title.

The rest of the year wasn't nearly so satisfying for Mac, whose dark side re-emerged while winning the Stockholm Open over Wilander. In the course of a semi-final victory over Jarryd, 1-6, 7-6, 6-2, Mac was fined $2,100 for ball abuse, abuse of an official and unsportsmanlike behavior. The total pushed him over the $7,500 limit, triggering a 21-day suspension.

During his suspension, he injured his left wrist in practice. That caused him to withdraw from the Australian Open, where second-seeded Wilander had a clear path to his second consecutive title, bashing two-time champ Johan Kriek, 6-1, 6-0, 6-2, in the semi-finals, and overcoming Curren in the final, 6-7 (5-7), 6-4, 7-6 (7-3), 6-2.

With Connors at his side, McEnroe was healed in time for the Davis Cup final in Goteborg. On paper, Capt. Arthur Ashe's side was perhaps the strongest of all

U.S. Cup lineups, containing the world Nos. 1 and 2 in singles and No. 1 in doubles. However, it was played not on paper but clay, a surface on which eight of 10 previous U.S. defeats over the last 20 years had occurred. Priced at $30,000, a specially-laid court made of 42 tons of crushed bricks was installed within the Scandinavium. Connors had committed himself to the full year of Cup play for the first time but, distracted by the impending birth of his second child, was as unprepared as McEnroe for the tough Swedes on clay. He hadn't competed in six weeks.

In what was a dark first day for American tennis, both Connors and McEnroe were drubbed and Connors embarrassed himself and his team by incurring a game penalty and adding a $2,000 fine for profane language. Wilander handled Connors easily, 6-1, 6-3, 6-3, but the real surprise occurred in the next match when McEnroe was upset by lanky 20-year-old Henrik Sundstrom, 13-11, 6-4, 6-3.

ITF (International Tennis Federation) management stipulated that Connors apologize for his misbehavior or the entire series would be forfeited to Sweden. Half-heartedly he did, and the show went on. One day later, Jarryd and Edberg applied the finishing strokes to the great doubles team of McEnroe and Fleming. The pair had won 14 Cup matches without defeat but weren't up to the task against the Swedes. The 18-year-old Edberg, with his kicking serve, was particularly effective in the right court in the 7-5, 5-7, 6-2, 7-5 triumph. He became the youngest winning player in a Cup title round.

Although McEnroe's 6-3, 5-7, 6-3 third-day victory over Wilander was mostly cosmetic, it did spare the U.S. the ignominy of a 5-0 shutout and helped to prepare him for the season-ending Masters. Back in New York, McEnroe defeated both Jarryd and Wilander, en route to the final, where he crushed Lendl, 7-5, 6-0, 6-4. That, raised Mac's earnings to $2,026,109. For good measure, he then combined with Fleming to turn back Mark Edmondson and Sherwood Stewart, 6-3, 6-1, for their seventh consecutive Masters doubles title.

In the scarcely shared opinion of the ITF, which ruled in 1982 that a player need only win four consecutive majors to claim a Grand Slam, Navratilova completed the quartet in early June at the French Open. Her reward from the ITF was a $1-million bonus. Still, few were prepared to grant her admission to the select group of those who had won the Big Four in the course of a calendar year—Don Budge, 1938; Maureen Connolly, 1953; Rod Laver, 1962 and 1969, and Margaret Smith Court, 1970.

After Navratilova routed Evert Lloyd, 6-3, 6-1, in Paris, however, few doubted that this would be the year for such a feat. She hadn't lost a match since her first tournament in January. And only Mandlikova, in the semi-finals, took a set off her at Stade Roland Garros.

At Wimbledon, Martina was even more formidable. Her only persistent opposition in England came from the tabloid press, which outdid itself in pursuing Navratilova's relationship with her newest traveling companion, former Texas beauty queen Judy Nelson. On the court, she was tested only in the championship match when Evert Lloyd, who hadn't lost a set either, began with two service breaks for a 3-0 lead. Not to worry. Navratilova stormed back for a 7-6 (7-5), 6-2 victory, handing Evert Lloyd her sixth final-round defeat.

It marked the second consecutive Wimbledon in which Navratilova had failed to drop a set and her third successive title was the first for a female since Billie Jean King's 1966-68 run. As a sidebar, Steffi Graf, who had peeked into the French and Australian Opens in 1983, tried her third major, Wimbledon, and, at 15, showed signs of the 'Fraulein Forehand' she would become, winning three rounds before losing in the quarters to Jo Durie.

The Navratilova pattern continued at Flushing Meadow, which produced one notable sidelight. Gabriela Sabatini, a 14-year, four-month-old Argentine, introduced herself to the world. A future champ, Gaby became the youngest player ever to win a U.S. Open match, 6-3, 3-6, 6-2, over American Paula Smith. Dissatisfied with one, she actually won another, over Kim Schaefer, before losing to Sukova.

Sukova reached the quarter-finals, where she was beaten, 6-3, 6-3, by Navratilova, whom her mother, 1962 Wimbledon finalist Vera Sukova, once had coached back in Czechoslovakia. The top-ranked player in the world marched into the final without the loss of a set, stopping Turnbull in the semis. Ditto her great rival, Evert Lloyd, who had beaten the Torontonian, 14th-seeded Bassett, 6-2, 6-2. Carling's semi-final arrival was the utmost performance for a Canadian in a major.

When Navratilova and Evert Lloyd collided in Louis Armstrong Stadium on Sept. 8, their series stood at 30 victories apiece. Additionally, Navratilova had won 54 consecutive matches, one shy of her opponent's open-era record. With all that and an Open title at stake, Evert

Lloyd played superbly, perhaps the best of any of her nine U.S. finals. Still, it was insufficient. Navratilova rallied for a 4-6, 6-4, 6-4 victory. "It's just not enough to play a good match against her anymore," Evert Lloyd lamented.

With six consecutive majors to Navratilova's credit, the Australian Open appeared a formality. She prepared herself for the grass at Kooyong Stadium by winning a doubles tournament at Brisbane with Shriver (their 78th straight match win together) and the singles at Sydney. At Melbourne, she dropped only one set (to Kathy Rinaldi) in advancing to the semi-finals and then raced through a 6-1 first set against Sukova.

But the 6-foot-2 Sukova, who, at 19, had just notched her first important singles title at Brisbane over Aussie Liz Sayers, broke for 4-2 in the second set and, at 5-5 in the third, achieved the deciding break. Navratilova didn't go down without a fight, saving five match points with a series of admirable forehands before her backhand return sailed over the baseline.

"It hurts but I'm sure I'll get over it," she said after the 1-6, 6-3, 7-5, defeat that terminated her streak at 74

matches and ended the dream of a genuine Grand Slam. Sukova, the ninth-seed, carried the momentum into the final but couldn't sustain it as the steady Evert Lloyd rallied for a 6-7 (4-7), 6-1, 6-3 triumph, her 16th major singles championship.

Earlier, Evert Lloyd, with singles win over Hobbs and Durie, had led the U.S. to its sixth successive Wightman Cup triumph over Britain, 5-2, in London. The Americans rebounded from 1-2 as Evert Lloyd and rookie Alycia Moulton beat Virginia Wade and Amanda Brown, 6-2, 6-2, and Barbie Potter beat Hobbs, 6-1, 6-3.

In the absence of both Evert Lloyd and Navratilova, the U.S. was upended at Sao Paulo, Brazil, by Australia in a Federation Cup semi-final, 2-1, as Liz Sayers and Turnbull took the decisive doubles over Jordan and Smith, 7-6, 6-4. In the final, Australian Anne Minter made it a perfect five-for-five in singles, beating Sukova, 7-5, 7-5, but the Czechs snapped back to their second successive Cup as Mandlikova floored Sayers, 6-1, 6-0, and combined with Sukova, 6-2, 6-2, over Sayers-Turnbull.

1985

Evert Lloyd back on top … for a moment

Boris Becker
Belly-flopping his way to Wimbledon title at 17.

A tention, please. Or, in the native tongue of Boris Becker, *Achtung!* Not only did a new champion appear on the tennis scene in 1985, he also ushered in a new era.

In a year that sparkled with fresh faces, the brightest and most engaging belonged to a 17-year-old son of a West German architect, a teenager either too cool or too naive to know he had no business playing with grown men. At Wimbledon, a tournament that prizes tradition above all else, Becker challenged the past and won.

Never had anyone so young claimed a men's title at The Lawn Tennis Championships. Never had an unseeded player been fitted for a singles crown. Never had a German male ascended to the throne of tennis. Becker changed all of the above in the span of three hours, 18 minutes on one sunlit, summer afternoon.

The youngster, who had won only one previous event on the men's tour (three weeks earlier at Queen's Club in London, over Johan Kriek), climaxed a breathtaking rise to prominence by wearing down eighth-seeded Kevin Curren, 6-3, 6-7 (4-7), 7-6 (7-3), 6-4, in the Wimbledon final. By the end of the season, he had made a spectacular jump in the rankings from No. 65 to No. 6 and become the symbol of change sweeping over the sport.

When Stefan Edberg of Sweden, 22 months older than Becker, dethroned countryman Mats Wilander at the Australian Open, it represented the first time two teen-aged males reigned as champions of the four major tournaments in the same year. Following Wilander's victory in the French Open and Ivan Lendl's breakthrough in the U.S. Open, this also completed a Continental sweep of the major events. Never before had European males held all four majors.

Although Lendl's presence was a familiar one and although he was a relatively old 25, he made a significant contribution to the new order by completing his long and arduous climb to the top of the ATP computer rankings. He posted the biggest triumph of his career by overwhelming John McEnroe, who hadn't lost in four previous U.S. finals, at Flushing Meadow, 7-6 (7-1), 6-3, 6-4. And he solidified his position at the season-ending Masters in January 1986, where he lost no sets en route to his third title in five years.

Newcomers also made an impact on the women's circuits, although none came away with major prizes. In what were portents of the future, 15-year-old Gabriela Sabatini reached the semi-finals of her first French Open and 16-year-old Steffi Graf of West Germany advanced to the final four of the U.S. Open. Additionally, Katerina Maleeva, at 16, two years younger than older sister Manuela, won two tournaments, and Floridian Mary Joe Fernandez became the most callow winner of a U.S. Open match (14 years, eight days), over Italian Laura Garrone, 3-6, 6-1, 6-3.

While Martina Navratilova remained queen of the sport, she yielded two of her dominions. Chris Evert Lloyd unseated her at the French Open and Hana Mandlikova did the honors at the U.S. Open. Navratilova even was separated from her No. 1 ranking by Evert Lloyd after 156 consecutive weeks at the top but she regained her place by the end of the season in which she added the Australian championship to her sixth Wimbledon singles title.

The stranglehold Navratilova and Pam Shriver had on women's doubles competition also was loosened. Their monumental 26-month winning streak, comprising 109 matches and 23 tournaments, ended on Centre Court in the Wimbledon final, where they were beaten by the Aussie-American alliance of Liz Sayers Smylie and Kathy Jordan, 5-7, 6-3, 6-4. They had won a record eight consecutive majors but later surrendered their U.S. title to the 'Twin Towers,' 6-foot-1 Claudia Kohde-Kilsch of West Germany and 6-foot-2 Helena Sukova of Czechoslovakia, 6-7 (5-7), 6-2, 6-3.

Coincidentally, McEnroe and Peter Fleming abdicated after the better part of a decade atop men's doubles. Mac decided to put doubles aside after three tournaments, among them Wimbledon, where they faltered before Aussies Pat Cash and John Fitzgerald, two rounds short of defending their title. Their lone victory, at Houston over Hank Pfister and Ben Testerman, raised their career total to 53 titles. The Wimbledon title went to the Hungarian-Swiss yoking of Balazs Taroczy and Heinz Gunthardt over Cash and Fitzgerald. A first-round win by a Danish-Swedish lineup of Michael

Mortensen and Jan Gunnarsson over an Aussie-Paraguayan pairing of John Frawley and Victor Pecci concluded with the longest of tie-breakers—50 points.

A pair of young Americans quickly filled the vacuum. Ken Flach and Robert Seguso, both 22, inherited the U.S. Davis Cup role from the perennial team, compiled a match record of 62-22 and won eight tournaments, including the U.S. Open over the French Yannick Noah and Henri Leconte, and U.S. Clay Court over the Aussie-Czech blend of Kim Warwick and Pavel Slozil.

But the French pair, Noah and Leconte, hotly disputed the title outcome of Flushing Meadow. Did the French lose by a hair? They thought so: Flach's hair. They accused the Americans of cheating. The play in question came with Seguso serving at 4-6 in the third-set tie-breaker, set point. In a furious exchange Leconte swatted a ball that bounded off the net cord and appeared to touch Flach's abundant Afghan-houndly mane on its way out of court. The French claimed a clear touch, thus the point and set. Seguso indicated agreement by starting to change courts. But Flach said, "It could have, but I'm not sure, so I couldn't make the call. We're pros—it's up to the umpire."

Umpire Zeno Pfau said he didn't see it, so couldn't rule. The French chafed and moaned, saying their foes had violated the sporting code by not calling the point against themselves. The Americans accused the French of the professional sin of giving up after losing the set, as seemed true. It was a $65,000 question (first prize). The result stood. Noah and Leconte went home feeling

1985 THE MAJOR CHAMPIONSHIPS

Australian Open
Men's Singles: Stefan Edberg
Women's Singles: Martina Navratilova
Men's Doubles: Paul Annacone / Christo Van Rensburg
Women's Doubles: Martina Navratilova / Pam Shriver
French Open
Men's Singles: Mats Wilander
Women's Singles: Chris Evert Lloyd
Men's Doubles: Mark Edmondson / Kim Warwick
Women's Doubles: Martina Navratilova / Pam Shriver
Mixed Doubles: Martina Navratilova / Heinz Gunthardt
Wimbledon
Men's Singles: Boris Becker
Women's Singles: Martina Navratilova
Men's Doubles: Heinz Gunthardt / Balazs Taroczy
Women's Doubles: Kathy Jordan / Elizabeth Sayers Smylie
Mixed Doubles: Martina Navratilova / Paul McNamee
U.S. Open
Men's Singles: Ivan Lendl
Women's Singles: Hana Mandlikova
Men's Doubles: Ken Flach / Robert Seguso
Women's Doubles: Claudia Kohde Kilsch / Helena Sukova
Mixed Doubles: Martina Navratilova / Heinz Gunthardt

they'd been clipped.

But there was no arguing that Americans Steve 'Bull' Denton and Richard Matuszewski served like a couple of unshorn Samsons in a hardly noticed first-rounder. It went to No. 482 Matuszewski, a qualifier who hummed 19 aces, 6-7 (8-10), 7-6 (7-4), 6-7 (8-10), 6-4, 6-3. But not before they'd bashed away four hours, 11 minutes, and Denton had set a U.S. record with 39 aces (not to mention 24 double faults). It was a record, too, as the most ace-ridden match (58), a mark that would last a decade.

Nowhere were the changing times better illustrated than at Wimbledon. None of the usual suspects even made it to the last day. Second-seeded Lendl, whose bid for a second successive French title was ended in the final by Wilander, 3-6, 6-4, 6-2, 6-2, was wiped out in the round of 16 by Leconte. Curren, who became a U.S. citizen in March, demolished both top-seeded McEnroe in the quarters and third-seeded Jimmy Connors in the semis.

Bellyflopping Boris, who threw himself at balls with teenage abandon, injured his left ankle in the fourth round against Tim Mayotte and wanted to quit after the fourth set. His manager, Ion Tiriac, dissuaded him. Becker probably should have been defaulted because of the overly long delay in being treated. He resumed thanks only to the sporting forbearance of Mayotte. It was soon obvious that this was a charmed fortnight for the husky redhead. Three of his first six matches were suspended and held over for another day, a circumstance that would unnerve even veteran players.

Not Becker. He responded to every challenge like a man, yet still reacted with the infectious enthusiasm of a boy. In the final, before a capacity crowd that included assorted princes and princesses, the 6-foot-3 man-child answered Curren's serve with a bludgeon of his own— 21 aces to Kevin's 19. He also out-volleyed and out-steadied his 27-year-old opponent from the baseline.

1985 CHAMPIONS AND LEADERS

Top Player Earnings: Men
Ivan Lendl $1,971,074
Top Player Earnings: Women
Martina Navratilova $1,328,829
Year-End Number One
Men: Ivan Lendl
Women: Martina Navratilova
Davis Cup: Sweden
Federation Cup:
Czechoslovakia
Wightman Cup: United States

ITF World Champion
Men: Ivan Lendl
Women: Martina Navratilova
Grand Prix Masters, NYC
Ivan Lendl
WTC, Dallas
Ivan Lendl
Virginia Slims
Championships, NYC
Martina Navratilova

"I should have had the advantage," Curren said. "Being older, being to the semi-finals [1983], being on Centre Court. Maybe he was too young to know about all that stuff."

Or at least too young to rattle. Becker became such a sensation in the early stages of the tournament with his reckless dives—"Usually, he comes off the court with blood on him," observed Tiriac—that the bookmaking chain, Ladbrokes, installed him as a 7-4 favorite after the quarter-finals.

His popularity with the fans was not echoed in the British press, which did not let anyone forget he was a German. Even the respectable broadsheets relentlessly used war analogies in describing the player. In *The Times,* the respected Rex Bellamy duly noted that scheduled television programming in Becker's homeland was interrupted to carry his quarter-final victory over Leconte and added, "How odd it was that Germany should have such a personal interest in a court on which, in 1940, they dropped a bomb."

It's true a bomb did land on the roof of Centre Court in October 1940, destroying 1,200 seats. And no German was permitted to enter the tournament for four years after it was resumed in 1946. (Germans had been banned for nine years after WWI.) Ironically, Becker's shining moment occurred on July 7, the birth date of Baron Gottfried von Cramm. For more than half of the century, the Baron was regarded as one of the finest players never to have won Wimbledon.

The new generation of males wasn't as successful in the cauldron that was Flushing Meadow. Seeded eighth, Becker made 64 unforced errors in bowing to tenth-seeded Joakim Nystrom in four sets in the round of 16, which was where 11th-seeded Edberg came to grief against fourth-seeded Connors. Wilander, an old man of 21, seeded third, did push top-seed McEnroe to five sets in the semi-finals but couldn't put the 26-year-old codger away.

Two other familiar faces turned up in the other semi-final, where second-seeded Lendl romped over Connors, 6-2, 6-3, 7-5. It had been a frustrating season for the 33-year-old campaigner. For the first time in his professional career, Connors failed to win a tournament all year. Yet, he reached the semis of the French, Wimbledon and the U.S., the latter for the twelfth successive year.

For Lendl, the victory also was the continuation of a streak. This was his fourth consecutive final at Flushing

Meadow. Alas, he had lost in all three previous trips. After their Saturday night match, Connors said he didn't expect the man to play well on Sunday. "Because he never has," the gracious loser said.

Certainly, there was little in the early going to indicate otherwise. Lendl was broken in his first service game and failed to get a single point off McEnroe's serve through seven games, creating a 2-5 deficit. But, at set point, the Czech who had moved into a comfortable estate in nearby Greenwich, Conn., hit a crosscourt backhand winner for deuce, held service and then broke McEnroe for the first time. He eventually won a tie-breaker by a stunning 7-1 margin and raced through the next two sets, 6-3, 6-4, for the most satisfying triumph of his career.

"It's the biggest tournament in the world," the first-time titleholder said dryly. "And it is the championship of the country where I enjoy living so much. I have won the Czechoslovakian Open three times, in my native country, but I don't think that is the same."

It was the climax of a superb year for Lendl. He annexed the first of 11 titles by beating Mayotte at the WCT finals in Dallas. In the Tournament of Champions, Lendl prevailed over Mac, 6-3, 6-3, and he also stopped the lefty at Dusseldorf, although a singles victory by Connors over Miloslav Mecir, 6-3, 3-6, 7-5, and a doubles triumph by Flach and Seguso over Lendl and Tom Smid, 6-4, 7-6, lifted the U.S. to a 2-1 victory over Czechoslovakia and the World Team Cup.

Top-seeded in the Australian Open, Lendl appeared to have a clear path to another major title when fourth-seeded Becker was bounced in the first round by No. 188, Dutchman Michiel Schapers, and McEnroe was eliminated in the quarters by massive 6-foot-5 Bobo Zivojinovic of Yugoslavia. But that's when Edberg asserted himself. The teen-ager from Vastervik snapped Lendl's 31-match winning streak, 6-7 (3-7), 7-5, 6-1, 4-6, 9-7 and then overpowered defending champ Wilander, 6-4, 6-3, 6-3, in a rain-delayed final. It marked the first time two Swedes met for a major championship.

Both McEnroe and Lendl argued so incessantly about the slippery condition of the Kooyong courts and other distractions that they surpassed the fine limit, earning 21-day suspensions. Not that either was inclined to play any more in December. For the first time in a while, McEnroe didn't even have Davis Cup commitments.

He had declined to sign a so-called 'behavior guide-line' instigated by the U.S. team's sponsor, Louisiana Pacific, to guarantee there would be no repetition of the ruckus at Goteborg the previous year. Since Connors—the prime instigator—had no intention of returning, the U.S. squad was led by Eliot Teltscher and Aaron Krickstein, who turned 18 just in time for a second-round encounter against West Germany.

That was as far as the Americans went, Germany winning, 3-2, on clay at Hamburg as Becker bashed Krickstein in the decisive fifth match, 6-2, 6-2, 6-1. Boris had beaten Teltscher to lead off, and his lightly regarded companion, Hansjorg Schwaier, supplied the pivotal point by beating Krickstein for a 2-0 lead.

Becker carried the fatherland all the way to the final and nearly upset the Swedes as he defeated both Edberg and Wilander to tie it, 2-2. Not for 21 years, when Roy Emerson beat Chuck McKinley to lift the Cup from the U.S. to Australia, had the fate of the Cup hung on the fifth match. As the sellout crowd of 11,000 rocked Munich's Olympiahalle with stomping and chanting of "MEE-KILE! MEE-KILE!," hulking, 20-year-old Michael Westphal, ranked No. 51, served ace after ace (15) past 19-year-old Edberg to win the first set. But Edberg, No. 5, blunted the German's fury with his own serve-and-volley rhythms, overcame the aces (28) and silenced the home crowd, 3-6, 7-5, 6-4, 6-3, enabling Sweden to become the first European nation to retain the Cup in five decades.

Remarkably, that nation qualified four men for the season-ending Grand Prix Masters, whose field was raised to 16 under the first-time sponsorship of Nabisco. But none of the Swedes was a factor. Edberg lost in the first round to Kriek, Wilander was beaten by Becker in the quarters and Jarryd, who had defeated Nystrom in a first-rounder, was stopped by Becker in the semi-finals. The most resounding loss of all, however, involved McEnroe who, tired and out of sorts, went down in the first round to Brad Gilbert.

In the end, Lendl reverting to the form he had displayed in the U.S. Open, turned back Becker in commanding fashion, 6-2, 7-6 (7-1), 6-3, and raised his earnings to $1,971,074. At last, he was clearly the top male player in the world.

For the first time in what seemed like ages, there actually was some doubt about the identity of the leading woman. The competition wasn't settled until Navratilova beat Mandlikova, her U.S. Open conqueror, in the semi-finals of the Australian Open and then wore down French Open queen Evert Lloyd, 6-2, 4-6, 6-2 in the final at Melbourne. She concluded her season with 12 tournament victories and an 80-5 match record, slightly ahead of Evert Lloyd's 10 titles and an 81-8 mark.

Chrissie also led the U.S. to its seventh consecutive victory over Great Britain in Wightman Cup play, 7-0, at Williamsburg, Va., beating Jo Durie and Annabel Croft. Shriver did likewise over Croft and Durie.

By defeating Navratilova in their thrilling French final, 6-3, 6-7 (4-7), 7-5, Evert Lloyd won the tournament for an unprecedented sixth time and extended to a dozen years her standard for winning at least one of the major titles. It also marked the second time in five months she had overcome her nemesis, the first being at Key Biscayne, Fla., in late January, deadlocking their rivalry at 31-31.

Following that loss in Florida and one to Mandlikova in the U.S. Indoor semis, Navratilova went to an eye doctor. She emerged with spectacles and promptly won 23 consecutive matches (and 46 sets), including the Virginia Slims Championship at Madison Square Garden, beating Sukova, 6-3, 7-5, 6-4. Evert Lloyd interrupted that string at Paris.

"I just hope Chrisie stays around a little bit longer," Navratilova said, "because, quite honestly, she's playing better tennis now than she ever did. It must be nice to know that you can still improve at 30."

Defeat cost Navratilova the honor of being the first player since Margaret Smith Court in 1964 to hold the three French titles simultaneously. She combined with Shriver to win the women's doubles, over Kohde-Kilsch and Sukova, 4-6, 6-2, 6-2, their eighth straight major championship, and with Heinz Gunthardt to win the mixed over Paula Smith and Francisco Gonzalez, 2-6, 6-3, 6-2.

Sabatini had created a great stir at Hilton Head, S.C., in April by beating three Top 10 players (Zina Garrison, Shriver and Manuela Maleeva), en-route to the final. She had a tall order Sunday morning. After completing a rain-delayed quarter with Shriver, then beating Maleeva, the rules said she could put off the final until Monday. But Gaby, the youngest to reach a pro final at that time (14 years, 11 months), insisted on being part of the televised title match. She competed well for a set before losing to Chrissie, 6-4, 6-0.

In Paris, Sabatini, now 15, topspun her way into the semi-finals. Her victims included Ros Fairbank and fourth-seeded Manuela Maleeva. Once again, it took a woman twice her age to stop her. Evert Lloyd.

Sabatini's showing convinced her coach, Pato Apey, that she should enter Wimbledon, where the 'Pearl of the Pampas' became the youngest player ever to be seeded (15th at 15 in a masterstroke of British symmetry). Her presence caused an immediate stir. The tabloids dubbed her 'Gorgeous Gaby' and the special eligibility Commission of the International Tennis Federation called for a "gradual, carefully monitored entry" into pro tennis, restricting the number of events a player can enter before reaching 16. Sabatini won two matches, beating local A.J. Brown and American teen-ager Camille Benjamin.

But the tournament sensation was willowy 24-year-old blonde American Anne White, who showed up—and showed very well—for a first rounder with Shriver in a crowd-attracting body stocking. Her costume satisfied the requirement for white clothing, but its clinging, unconventional nature made the authorities, uncomfortable. Having split sets at dusk, the match was postponed until the following day and No. 93 ranked White was instructed to leave the leotard at home. She returned in a skirt and top, and lost the match. "It was chilly, I wanted to be fully covered," said un-contrite White.

The most surprising of the final eight was No. 154 Molly Van Nostrand, a 20-year-old qualifier from New York who defeated fourth-seeded Manuela Maleeva and was only three games from a semi-final meeting with Navratilova before faltering against Garrison. Kathy Rinaldi, still only 18, made her deepest penetration in a major when she advanced to the semi-finals past sixth-seeded Sukova.

Not that there was ever any doubt but that the women's competition was a two-horse race, but they played the semis anyway: Evert Lloyd over Rinaldi, 6-2, 6-0; Navratilova over Garrison, 6-4, 7-6 (7-3). In a most unusual move, the tournament committee jointly seeded Evert Lloyd and Navratilova No. 1. And their final was almost as close, with Navratilova rallying for a 4-6, 6-3, 6-2 victory.

She became only the third woman in history to win the singles titles four years in a row and the first since Helen Wills Moody in 1930. "This court," Evert decided, "is her court." It also marked Navratilova's sixth triumph in as many Wimbledon finals, equaling the feat of Suzanne Lenglen, the legendary French star of the Roaring '20s.

One of the most affecting moments of the tournament was Virginia Wade's 205th Wimbledon match, her last in the singles draw. 'Our Ginny,' England's last great champion, was beaten by Shriver, 6-2, 5-7, 6-2, in an enthralling third-round match one week shy of her 40th birthday. She left to a standing ovation.

Youth once again was served at the start of the U.S. Open when Fernandez, who had just turned 14, beat towering Sarah Gomer, a 6-foot-3 Brit in the first round, undercutting by four months the Sabatini of 1984 as the greenest to win a match there. But the teenager who wowed the crowds at Flushing Meadow was 11th-seeded Graf. In reaching the semi-finals, she knocked off Manuela Maleeva and, in the match of the tournament, Shriver, 7-6 (7-4), 6-7 (4-7), 7-6 (7-4). It marked the only major match composed entirely of tie-breakers and the longest women's struggle (39 games) since the advent of such overtimes in 1970.

Still, it was a brilliantly attacking Mandlikova who took home the prize. And she did it in remarkable fashion, beating two ex-champs—Evert Lloyd, 4-6, 6-2, 6-3, and Navratilova, 7-6 (7-3), 1-6, 7-6 (7-2). That route hadn't been taken since 1962 when Margaret Smith (Court) won the last two matches over 1959 champ Maria Bueno and defender Darlene Hard. Hana's victory was the first by a European citizen in the U.S. championship. Graf ran out of zip against Martina in the semis, 6-2, 6-3.

The Open title was one of Hana's two great rewards in 1985. The second occurred a month later in Nagoya, Japan, where she won all five of her singles and two deciding doubles in Czechoslovakia's third successive victory in the Federation Cup.

At the Australian Open, order was restored. Navratilova dispensed with Mandlikova, 6-7 (5-7), 6-1, 6-4, en route to another final showdown with Evert Lloyd. It was their 67th meeting and Navratilova's all-out attack won the day, 6-2, 4-6, 6-2, increasing her margin in the rivalry of the age to 35-32

"Martina and I have pushed each other to get better and better," Evert Lloyd said. And they weren't planning to stop anytime soon.

1986

A Prague summer all over the world

Ivan Lendl
Methodical on way to second straight U.S. Open conquest.

They got together on a Sunday in September at a public park. Two men and two women raised in Czechoslovakia met for an afternoon of tennis. Twenty years earlier, when the iron curtain and the sport both were closed, they might have been limited to a game of mixed doubles in Prague but now they gathered as professionals in New York to contest the most important singles championships in the New World. An orchestra should have played the lusty 'New World Symphony' composed by the Czech Anton Dvorak

What an extraordinary development not only for the U.S. Open but for the sport. When Ivan Lendl and Miloslav Mecir followed Martina Navratilova and Helena Sukova onto the stadium court of the National Tennis Center, they raised the profile of a nation whose history had been fragmented and difficult but whose culture was old. Theirs was an unprecedented achievement.

The presence of four finalists born in the same distant land had occurred only four times previously in the history of the major tournaments, twice at Wimbledon and twice at the French Open. Never before had it happened at the U.S. Open and never before had the delegation hailed from Czechoslovakia. Suddenly, the country of 15-million inhabitants ranked as the first nation of tennis.

That Navratilova had received her citizenship papers in the U.S. and that Lendl was an aspiring Connecticut Yankee, or Mecir a Slovak, didn't diminish the impact. All had learned the game, had taken their first steps to prosperity on Czechoslovak clay. And, by virtue of their victories in the third and last major tournament of the year in which there was no Australian Open (a schedule adjustment moved the Aussie to the front of the year from the rear), the expatriates solidified their places at the top of the women's and men's rankings.

Better yet for the land of their youth, Prague

welcomed the first significant international tennis event in Eastern Europe. The Federation Cup attracted teams from 40 nations to brand new Stvanice Stadium where the Czech defenders were denied a fourth successive triumph by the U.S. It so happened that Navratilova won her singles match and paired with Pam Shriver to win the doubles in a 3-0 victory that completed an emotional homecoming for the woman who had defected 11 years earlier.

"The whole experience," she said through tears after a heartwarming reception, "was beyond my wildest dreams."

Aside from the success of its foreign imports, the U.S. endured a desultory year. Chris Evert Lloyd, who won yet another French Open, was the only American-born player to reach the final of a major event, whose number temporarily was reduced to three when the Australian Open was pushed to the front end of the calendar in time for the 1987 season. She also was the only native of either gender to be ranked among the top five players in the game.

Of course, as Navratilova pointed out at Flushing Meadow, if you stress only the country of origin, "... then John McEnroe was born in Germany but he's as red-blooded American as you can get." It's true that McEnroe was born in Wiesbaden, where his father was serving as an officer of the U.S. Air Force. But then McEnroe was not relevant to the discussion, having decided to take a sabbatical for the first six months of the year and having been bounced out of the Open in the very first round by Paul Annacone.

In his absence, Jimmy Connors was the highest-ranked American male, No. 8 on the computer at year's end. But, for a second consecutive season, he failed to win a tournament. Connors didn't even survive the first round at Wimbledon and was a third-round victim at Flushing Meadow.

Once again, the men's tour was dominated by Europeans. Lendl won both the French Open, defeating Mikael Pernfors of Sweden in the final, and the U.S., as well as capturing the Masters. He also reached the final at Wimbledon, only to be stopped one step short of his goal by defending champion Boris Becker. The latter also pressed Lendl at the Masters and rose to No. 2 in the world at the age of 18.

On the women's side, Navratilova continued her reign over Wimbledon by defeating another Czech, Hana Mandlikova. Her only major defeat of the year occurred in Paris, where Evert Lloyd prevailed in a bid for a record seventh singles championship. By the end of 1986, however, it was clear that Steffi Graf was prepared to challenge both women.

'Fraulein Forehand,' as the teenaged German was known, won eight tournaments, two more than Evert, and almost denied Navratilova the U.S. Open title. Graf held three match points, the last in a sensational third-set tie-breaker, in the semi-finals. "I was lucky," Navratilova said. "I was lucky and I was gutsy, too. But anyone could have won."

Two months later, Navratilova again held off Graf at the second Virginia Slims Championships in Madison Square Garden. This represented one of several schedule adjustments that finally brought tennis into line with the calendar. Back in March, Martina had won the first Virginia Slims, the one that purported to be the season-ending event of the 1985 circuit, a 6-2, 6-0, 3-6, 6-1 triumph over Mandlikova. With a victory over Graf, she clinched the designation of No. 1 for 1986.

The men also managed to cram their play into a 12-month season. For the first time since 1976, the Masters was given December dates. Lendl certainly didn't appear rushed. After reaching the final for the seventh consecutive year, he blasted an eager Becker, 6-4, 6-4, 6-4, forestalling the future a while longer.

Perhaps the most far-reaching development of the year occurred at the start. In the wake of a disappointing loss to Brad Gilbert in the first round of the (1985) Masters in January, McEnroe decided to drop off the tour for at least 60 days. His long-standing relationship with actress Tatum O'Neal and impending fatherhood

---

1986 THE MAJOR CHAMPIONSHIPS

Australian Open
Not held
French Open
Men's Singles: Ivan Lendl
Women's Singles: Chris Evert Lloyd
Men's Doubles: John Fitzgerald / Tomas Smid
Women's Doubles: Martina Navratilova / Andrea Temesvari
Mixed Doubles: Kathy Jordan / Ken Flach
Wimbledon
Men's Singles: Boris Becker
Women's Singles: Martina Navratilova
Men's Doubles: Joakim Nystrom / Mats Wilander
Women's Doubles: Martina Navratilova / Pam Shriver
Mixed Doubles: Kathy Jordan / Ken Flach
U.S. Open
Men's Singles: Ivan Lendl
Women's Singles: Martina Navratilova
Men's Doubles: Andres Gomez / Slobodan Zivojinovic
Women's Doubles: Martina Navratilova / Pam Shriver
Mixed Doubles: Raffaella Reggi / Sergio Casal

had become more important than his career.

"My attitude is very bad, very negative," he said. "I'm not happy with my movement ... I shouldn't be playing tennis now ... I'm letting things affect me and I'm embarrassed. As a person I'll learn and grow from what is happening. I hope others do, too. They didn't seem to learn from Borg. Now they see it happening to me."

McEnroe was 26, one year older than Bjorn Borg when the latter walked away from competitive tennis. Like Borg, McEnroe was No. 2 in the world. Unlike the Swede, the American would be back, although not with the same fire.

Meanwhile, Connors sabotaged his own season by walking out of a semi-final match against Lendl in the Lipton International Players championship at Boca Raton, Fla. Lendl was leading, 5-2, in the fifth set when Connors began arguing a linesman's call. He insisted that umpire Jeremy Shales overrule the call and, when that failed, demanded that Shales be removed from the chair.

Eventually, Connors was defaulted. Not only did he lose the match but he was suspended for 70 days, a period that carried through the French Open, where he had been a semi-finalist in each of the two previous years. He was also fined a record $20,000.

With the field at Paris thinned by the abstention of the two top Yanks, Sweden was in position to take over the men's competition. Not only had a Swede won the 1985 edition and six of the previous eight, but representatives of that nation were granted four of the top eight seeds: Mat Wilander (2), Stefan Edberg (5), Joakim Nystrom (6) and Anders Jarryd (7). Yet the only Swede to make it to the quarter-finals and beyond was a total outsider, 10 months a pro, ranked No. 16 at home, No. 27 on the planet.

Mikael Pernfors, out of the village of Hollviksnas, a 22-year-old who had gone the American collegiate route,

made his French Open debut a memorable one. The two-time National Intercollegiate champion (1984-85) from the University of Georgia upset four of the top 11 seeds en route to the final: Edberg (5), Argentine Martin Jaite (11); Becker (3) in the quarters; and, in the semis, shotmaking magician Henri Leconte (8). Defending champ Wilander was stunned, 6-2. 6-3, 6-2, in the second round by Russian Andrei Chesnokov, No. 81 in the world, who advanced to the quarters.

Meanwhile, Lendl thundered through the top half of the draw with the loss of only one set. With the same championship form he had displayed in winning his first Italian Open three weeks earlier, over Spaniard Emilio Sanchez, Lendl dispatched the speedy, scrappy Pernfors, 6-3, 6-2, 6-4.

Some uncertainty was injected into the women's tournament by Mary Joe Fernandez, the Florida teenager making her debut in Paris where she would be a finalist in 1993. Mary Joe, the youngest player ever to win a match at the U.S. Open eight months earlier, overcame two seeds: 14th Andrea Temesvari and fourth Claudia Kohde-Kilsch in advancing to the quarter-finals. There the 14-year-old ranked No. 70, was stopped by sixth-seeded Sukova.

It was also in the quarters that Graf's 23-match winning streak—including titles at the WTA championships over Kohde-Kilsch, the U.S. Clay Court over Gabriela Sabatini, and the German Open over Navratilova—came to an abrupt end. After holding a match point on Mandlikova, Steffi succumbed 2-6, 7-6 (7-3), 6-1. The final was one more reprise of the familiar, Navratilova vs. Evert Lloyd, who had beaten Mandlikova.

The world would never see its like again. Although no one realized it at the moment, it was the last time the two would meet in the championship round of a major. Evert Lloyd, in her penultimate Big Four final, made the most of it with a commanding 2-6, 6-3, 6-3 victory, closing the second set from 0-40, four break points. That raised her total of major singles titles to 18 and extended to 13 years her fantastic longevity record of at least one major conquest.

The cosmetic changes at the 100th edition of Wimbledon included the introduction of yellow tennis balls, the unavailability of McEnroe, who was back in the States changing diapers, and the earliest departure on Connors' record. Connors, the two-time champion and five-time finalist, seeded third, was shown the gate by young Robert Seguso, ranked No. 31 and known as a

1986 CHAMPIONS AND LEADERS

Top Player Earnings: Men
Ivan Lendl $1,987,537
Top Player Earnings: Women
Martina Navratilova $1,905,841
Year-End Number One
Men: Ivan Lendl
Women: Martina Navratilova
ITF World Champion
Men: Ivan Lendl
Women: Martina Navratilova
Davis Cup: Australia
Federation Cup: United States

Wightman Cup: United States
Grand Prix Masters, NYC
Ivan Lendl
WCT, Dallas
Anders Jarryd
Virginia Slims Championships (spring), NYC
Martina Navratilova
Virginia Slims Championships (fall), NYC
Martina Navratilova

doubles specialist, in the first round.

"You don't know what you have until you lose it," said Connors, indicating Wimbledon would miss him more than he would Wimbledon, "and that's what you're feeling toward McEnroe right now." The first-round failures also included eleventh-seeded Kevin Curren, runner-up in 1985, to No. 32 Eric Jelen. John Lloyd also lost, blowing a two set lead to South African Christo Steyn, and immediately retired.

Meanwhile Lloyd's second-seeded wife experienced unaccustomed difficulty of her own. A finalist in seven of the previous eight years, Evert Lloyd struggled through a difficult draw, dropping sets to Pam Casale and, in the quarters, to seventh-seeded Sukova. In the semis, she was eliminated by Mandlikova—nevertheless, Chrissie's 14th semi.

Hana said she was much better prepared for her second Wimbledon final than her first, five years earlier against Evert Lloyd. "I slept very well," she said of her Navratilova eve. "Maybe, as it turned out, too well," she decided afterward.

By contrast, Navratilova was particularly eager for the meeting after rolling unopposed through her first six matches. "I've never, ever been so excited about being in a final," she said. "I couldn't wait to go to sleep so I could get up and play."

Not since the reign of Suzanne Lenglen six decades earlier had a woman won five consecutive singles championships at Wimbledon. And history was no more prepared to stop Martina than was Mandlikova. She finished off the challenger, 7-6 (7-1), 6-3, in 72 minutes. In five years of supremacy, she had dropped only two sets.

Lendl, the top-seeded male, worked harder than any player in the tournament in his effort to secure a Wimbledon title. He struggled past Matt Anger and Tim Mayotte to reach the semis, where he was pushed to the limit again by rocket-serving Serb, 6-foot-6 Slobodan Zivojinovic, 6-2, 6-7 (5-7), 6-3, 6-7 (1-7), 6-4.

His opponent in the final was the defending champ, Becker, as comfortable on the grass as Lendl was wary. Seeded fourth, Becker defeated Laconte in their semi after marching through a bottom half of the draw that was pockmarked by upsets, most notably Mecir's dismissal of second-seeded Edberg and fifth-seeded Wilander's beating by Pat Cash, who entered the tournament as a wild card one month following an appendectomy.

One point illustrated the distinction in the opponents' approach to the grass. In the final game of the third set, Becker serving for the match, but at 15-30, Lendl hit what appeared to be a forehand winner down the line. The German knifed through the air to intercept with a backhand stop volley. Lendl pounced to deliver another hopeful passer, but the ball caught the net cord and crawled over after Becker had landed on his stomach. Without a moment's hesitation, he sprang to his feet and spontaneously chipped a backhand winner crosscourt.

He then pounded two more service winners at Lendl to formalize the 6-4, 6-3, 7-5 victory. No wonder Becker said Wimbledon "feels like my tournament." Lendl, fighting the grass and his allergies and the fans who rallied behind more graceful and flamboyant players, had never felt that.

Two weeks after completion of Wimbledon, the top female players in the world assembled in Czechoslovakia for the most eagerly anticipated Federation Cup in the 24-year history of the event. From start to finish, it was Navratilova's show. Certainly, there was supreme irony in the idea of her leading an American team (with Evert Lloyd, Shriver and Zina Garrison) into Prague. It was shortly after contributing to Czechoslovakia's first Cup victory, in 1975, that she had sought political asylum in the U.S.

For the longest time, her success was not publicized in her native land. Her name did not appear in the Czech press, her matches were not seen on television. Yet, she was welcomed home as a returning heroine. She set out to demonstrate to her long-lost fans what they had missed.

Navratilova played brilliantly, winning every singles and doubles match (4-0 in each) in the course of carrying an unblemished record into her anxiously awaited final-round confrontation with Mandlikova, who made news of her own by marrying a Sydney restaurant owner in Prague's town hall. The U.S. beat China, Spain, West Germany, all 3-3, and Italy, 2-1. The Czechs, Sukova and Mandlikova, were unbeaten, too, in 3-0 wins over Greece, Switzerland, Australia, and 2-1 over Argentina.

The tournament produced one freak accident when an umbrella stand fell on Graf's foot, breaking her big toe. Evert Lloyd was wearing a brace on a balky knee at the start of the event. Following the loss to Cecchini, she removed it, and won her last two matches, against Bettina Bunge of Germany and Sukova, the first point in the final round, leaving Navratilova in position to regain the Cup for the U.S. She did so by beating Mandlikova, 7-5, 6-1. Then she combined with Shriver, a pairing that won all three major doubles events contested in 1986, to defeat Mandlikova and Sukova in doubles, 6-4, 6-2. Martina was cheered loudly. Afterward, she cried tears of happiness.

The journey to her old neighborhood only intensified Navratilova's desire to win another U.S. Open which she now considered her national tournament. The biggest test she would face in New York was administered by Graf after she breezed through the first five rounds. It happened in an epic semi-final match that required two hours and 16 minutes stretched over two days. Navratilova held a 4-1 lead in the first set when rain interrupted play on Friday night and she quickly closed out the set upon its resumption on Saturday.

Thereafter, however, it was a struggle, with both the second and third sets decided by tie-breakers. Graf had two match points in the 10th game of the third set and then a third at 8-7 in the tie-breaker.

"The last time I saved three match points [and won]," Navratilova said after the 6-1, 6-7 (3-7), 7-6 (10-8) victory, "I think I was 10 years old. I know I faced 15 match points once and I lost. Whenever it happened last, I know I was little."

Her great rival, Evert Lloyd, wasn't able to dig so deep against Sukova in their semi-final. The tall Czech hadn't beaten the American in 14 previous meetings but it took her only 70 minutes to dispose of the six-time Open champion, 6-2, 6-4. "Helena, Hana, Steffi, they're not intimidated by Martina or me anymore," said Evert Lloyd, who rested her ailing knee for the remainder of the season, passing up another 7-0 Wightman Cup romp by the U.S. (It was ably handled in London by the lesser lights: Kathy Rinaldi, Jo Durie and Bonnie Gadusek).

Still, Navratilova held the hammer over Sukova, once a ballgirl for Martina back in Prague. In the final that was pushed back until Sunday and staged just before the men's championship, the No. 1 player in the world scored a 6-3, 6-2 victory in 60 minutes. She was presented with her third Open trophy and a check for $210,000, as much as any player had ever won at a single tournament.

The men's competition, even as it wound to a predictable conclusion, was much less orderly. McEnroe and Connors, responsible for seven of the eight previous singles titles, failed to last the first week. In fact, McEnroe, ninth-seeded, didn't make it past sundown on the first day, drilled by Annacone's 25 aces in four sets, 1-6, 6-1, 6-3, 6-3.

To make matters worse, the former king of Queens and partner Peter Fleming arrived six minutes late for their first doubles start and were defaulted. McEnroe's subsequent profane tirade resulted in a $1,000 fine. Weeks later, after Mac's winning three fall tournaments, his intemperate outburst at the Paris Indoor Championships led to a $3,000 fine, pushing him beyond the $7,500 limit and triggering a 42-day suspension that removed whatever slim possibility existed of his qualifying for the Masters.

Those expecting sixth-seeded Connors to ride to the rescue at Flushing Meadow were sadly disappointed. The five-time champion saved six match points but finally lost in three sets to third-year pro, No. 95, Todd Witsken in the third round. It was his earliest exit from his national since 1972. No American reached the semifinals for the first time in two decades.

Fittingly, the mystery man of the Open was a Slovak. The 6-foot-3 Mecir, forever disinterested in appearance but astonishingly quick to the ball, knocked off the second-seeded Wilander, the seventh-seeded Nystrom, and the third-seeded Becker in succession to arrive at the final. He had presented his credentials at Wimbledon, where he reached the quarter-finals, but at Flushing Meadow his performance stunned observers, especially considering how much he professed to dislike New York ("too big") and how much he missed his favorite form of entertainment ("fishing").

"He is maybe the fastest player I've ever played against," Becker said. Indeed, the 22-year-old was called 'Gattone' (Big Cat) by Italians. And his assortment of junkballs and deceptive strokes befuddled some of the best players in the world, especially Swedes, against whom he was 18-3.

But in Lendl he met his match. Lendl, who had dropped only one set, was not mesmerized by the sight of his former countryman. And Mecir, so fluid earlier in the tournament, seemed rooted to the ground, content merely to trade groundies with the steady Lendl. The match produced a lot of yawns in the crowd, which shrank steadily in size over the course of the 6-4, 6-2, 6-0 rout by the two-time champion.

Lendl finished the year with a match record of 74-6 and nine titles, second in the world only to Navratilova's

90-3 mark and 14 championships. In the race to the bank between the two practicing capitalists from Czechoslovakia, Lendl won by a money clip— $1,987,537 to $1,905,841.

Cash flow settled the Davis Cup account in Australia's favor for a 26th time as Patrick Cash flowed through a 6-0 singles and 3-1 doubles campaign. He capped it with a tremendous triple on turf, illuminated by a bounce-back singles victory in his hometown, Melbourne, to strip Sweden of the old silver crock, 3-2. Slow starts and brilliant finishes characterized vicious volleyer Cash's singles wins. He beat the king of Kooyong, Edberg, Aussie Open title-holder, 13-11, 13-11, 6-4 and, after Pernfors beat Paul McNamee to deadlock the first day, Cash teamed with John Fitzgerald

to upset Edberg and Jarryd. With Australia ahead 2-1, Cash met Pernfors and quickly dropped the first two sets. Only once before with the Cup at stake had the decisive match been won from two sets down: Jean Borotra of France over American Wilmer Allison in 1932. But Cash charged relentlessly to what captain Neale Fraser called "Australia's greatest Davis Cup performance"—2-6, 4-6, 6-3, 6-4, 6-3.

Patrick was the clincher, too, in the 3-1 semi-final victory over the U.S., beating Tim Mayotte on opening day, 4-6, 6-1, 6-2, 6-2, and Gilbert, 3-6, 6-2, 6-3, 6-4, on Brisbane sod. Gilbert also lost to McNamee the first day. The chief American problem was the absence of McEnroe, whose accumulated churlish behavior got him ruled off by USTA President Randy Gregson.

1987

Graf No. 1 but Centre Court still Martina's

Steffi Graf
Only two losses were to Navratilova in Wimbledon, U.S. finals.

In a year of mixed blessings for the most relentless campaigners on the world stage, Martina Navratilova and Ivan Lendl added to their collections of major tournament titles by two apiece. But there was a down side for both in 1987. She lost one of her most treasured possessions and he failed once again to win the prize that mattered most.

Navratilova's reign as the No. 1 female practitioner of tennis ended despite victories at Wimbledon and the U.S. Open. The queen was far from dead but, nonetheless, someone else was seated on her throne at the conclusion of the season. Her successor was Steffi Graf, who not only won her first major title at Paris but 75 of the 77 matches in which she participated.

Fortified by triumphs at the French Open and at Flushing Meadow, Lendl continued to hold the top spot in the men's rankings. But he would have traded all his trophies and perhaps thrown in a generous share of his $2,003,656 earnings for the great honor that eluded him for a second successive year. Once more, he lost in the final at Wimbledon. His nemesis was Pat Cash, who had beaten Lendl six months earlier in the last Australian Open played on grass.

But for those two flaws, the Czech native might have joined the list of Grand Slam immortals. As it was, Lendl forged the most victories (25) in the four major tournaments by a male since Rod Laver went 26-0 in his 1969 Grand Slam. Yet he had to stand by and watch forlornly as Cash joyously celebrated the first Wimbledon championship by an Aussie in 16 years with an unprecedented climb through the stands at Centre Court. "It's a miserable feeling," the losing finalist decided.

Before the year was out, Lendl would win eight tournaments, including a third consecutive Masters, for a total of 70. He tied John McEnroe for second place behind Jimmy Connors (105) in the all-time standings. Remarkably, neither American won an event in 1987, although the 35-year-old Connors did reach the semi-final round at both Wimbledon and the U.S. Open and rose to No. 4 on the ATP computer.

The shutout was the first in McEnroe's professional career. Not only was he afflicted by lapses in concentration and an aching back but he contributed to his demise with temper tantrums at the World Team Cup in May and at Flushing Meadow. For walking off the court in Dusseldorf, he defaulted the match to Miroslav Mecir and was fined $10,000. For a profane tirade during a third-round victory over Slobodan Zivojinovic at the U.S. Open he received point and game penalties, fines totaling $17,500 and a two-month suspension.

It was a measure of McEnroe's season that his gamest, most impressive performance came in defeat. In a Davis Cup relegation playoff to determine which nation would be banished to the boondocks (zonal competition) the following year, he played an historic five-set match on behalf of the U.S. against Boris Becker, representing West Germany, in late July. Becker's 4-6, 15-13, 8-10, 6-2, 6-2 victory consumed six hours and 20 minutes, two minutes shy of the Cup singles record set by McEnroe and Mats Wilander in a 1982 quarter-final round match at St. Louis.

Tim Mayotte, whose five tournament victories topped U.S. players, accompanied McEnroe for that U.S. last stand at the Hartford Civic Center. However, the 3-2 defeat appeared sealed when 26-year-old Tim lost the opening match in five sets to No. 68 Eric Jelen. Mac went down and it was 0-2. Ken Flach and Robert Seguso prolonged hope, over Ricki Osterthun and Jelen, as did McEnroe over Jelen. But Becker loomed, a set too good for Mayotte, five sets again, 6-2, 6-3, 5-7, 4-6, 6-2.

The trouble began for the U.S. on that treacherous-for-Yanks footing, clay, in Asuncion, where an intimidating crowd and a revved-up Victor Pecci took the decision and forced the Yanks into the relegation lottery. Coupled with the first-round, 3-2 defeat by Paraguay, the relegation defeat sent the U.S. plunging from the 16-entry World Group to the American Zone for 1988, ineligible to compete for the Cup for the first time. Germany, first round loser to Mexico, stayed with the elite.

Wilander was the strength as the Swedes won a third Davis Cup in four years. He and Anders Jarryd handled the singles in the 5-0 final-round bogging down of upstart India on indoor clay in Goteborg. Nevertheless, the Indians made a nice story, the peerless sportsmen from the subcontinent seeming to be players from another, earlier era. It was a splendid career closer for the Flying Amritraj Brothers—Vijay and Anand—to play a final, even though winning just one set, that together. Thirteen years before, Vijay and Anand lifted India to the same position where they were forced to default to South Africa as their government's anti-apartheid gesture. But in their 16th year of Davis Cup they'd made it again, along with another name in their country's sporting history: Krishnan. This was Ramesh, 26-year-old son of the man—Ramanathan Krishnan—who had carried India to the Cup round in 1966. Never before had a son followed his father to the Cup finals.

American females weren't treated so badly, not with Navratilova still near the top of her form, but there was one jarring note. Chris Evert not only jettisoned her married name following a divorce from John Lloyd but also relinquished her hold on the majors. For the first time since 1974, she failed to win any of the Big Four tournaments. In fact, she wasn't even a finalist.

Furthermore, her performance at Flushing Meadow signaled the beginning of the end of an all-time career. For the first time since her debut at Forest Hills in the era of grass, she failed to reach the semi-finals of the U.S. Open. At least her conqueror was an American, 23-year-old volleyer Lori McNeil, up from a public park in Houston.

By taking Evert's accustomed spot in the final four, McNeil provided a shot in the arm for minorities. Not

1987 THE MAJOR CHAMPIONSHIPS

Australian Open
Men's Singles: Stefan Edberg
Women's Singles: Hana Mandlikova
Men's Doubles: Stefan Edberg / Anders Jarryd
Women's Doubles: Martina Navratilova / Pam Shriver
Mixed Doubles: Zina Garrison / Sherwood Stewart
French Open
Men's Singles: Ivan Lendl
Women's Singles: Steffi Graf
Men's Doubles: Anders Jarryd / Robert Seguso
Women's Doubles: Martina Navratilova / Pam Shriver
Mixed Doubles: Pam Shriver / Emilio Sanchez
Wimbledon
Men's Singles: Pat Cash
Women's Singles: Martina Navratilova
Men's Doubles: Ken Flach / Robert Seguso
Women's Doubles: Claudia Kohde Kilsch / Helena Sukova
Mixed Doubles: Jo Durie / Jeremy Bates
U.S. Open
Men's Singles: Ivan Lendl
Women's Singles: Martina Navratilova
Men's Doubles: Stefan Edberg / Anders Jarryd
Women's Doubles: Martina Navratilova / Pam Shriver
Mixed Doubles: Martina Navratilova / Emilio Sanchez

since Arthur Ashe, in 1972, had a black advanced to a singles semi-final at the Open. Not since Althea Gibson won the tournament in 1958 had a black woman had such an impact. And McNeil did herself proud by pushing Graf to a third set before succumbing, 4-6, 6-2, 6-4.

In the end, of course, it was Navratilova's tournament. Not only did she defeat Graf for the singles title, 7-6 (7-4), 6-1, but she also won the women's doubles with Pam Shriver over Kathy Jordan and Liz Sayers-Smylie, and, after a lunch break, a thrilling mixed title with Spaniard Emilio Sanchez over Betsy Nagelsen and Paul Annacone. Billie Jean King had scored the last triple, at Wimbledon, in 1973. No one had tripled at the U.S. Championships since Margaret Smith Court in 1970.

Still, despite a brilliant Open, reaching the final in all four major singles and winning three majors doubles titles, it was a disappointing season for Navratilova. She won only four of the 12 singles tournaments she entered, fell short of the $1-million mark ($932,102) for the first time since 1981 and faltered in the season-ending Virginia Slims Championships at Madison Square Garden. She never got to contest Graf's claim to No. 1, her 21-match winning streak in the event terminated in straight sets by Gabriela Sabatini.

And yet, Martina and Pam (36-1 in doubles) might have had a Grand Slam to match their 1984 extravaganza. After winning the Australian in an eyeblink, 6-1, 6-0, over Zina Garrison and McNeil, and the French almost as fast, 6-2, 6-1 over Graf and Sabatini, they blipped at the Wimbledon semis, losing to Soviets Larisa Savchenko and Svetlana Parkhomenko 6-2, 6-4. How much sweeter their U.S. title could have been—but three for four majors ain't bad. Nor was the fact that Martina inhabited nine of the 12 major finals altogether, winning six of them.

Graf, whose only two defeats were inflicted by

Navratilova in major finals, overcame Sabatini to win her first Slims title and confirm her place at the top of women's tennis. She also raised her earnings for the year to $1,063,785.

While Evert and Graf bypassed the resurrected Australian Open, staged for the last time on the grass at Kooyong Stadium, Navratilova journeyed Down Under and came away empty, beaten in the final by Hana Mandlikova, 7-5, 7-6 (7-2). That curtailed a 58-match winning streak dating back to the 1986 French Open and sent her into a downward spiral.

Forced to contend with a persistent foot injury and a breakup with coach Mike Estep, she was beaten by Graf in the semis at the International Players Championship (Lipton). "Today," Navratilova said, "she was the best player in the world and she will be until I play her again."

While she waited for the next meeting, Navratilova was overcome by Evert at the Virginia Slims of Houston and routed by Sabatini in the semi-finals of the Italian Open in Rome, where the ladies at long last returned after being relegated to the hinterlands for six years, five at Perugia, 1986 at Taranto. Graf beat Gaby for the title, 7-5, 4-6, 6-0, but was not amused by journalists' satirical references to her nose and didn't return until 1996.

It was in Paris where Navratilova appeared to regain her form, smashing Evert, 6-2, 6-2, in the semi-final and earning another shot at Graf, who had come from 3-5 in the third set against Sabatini to reach the championship round, 6-4, 4-6, 7-5. Again, in a magnificent final, the German lass trailed 3-5 in the third. Again, Graf escaped with a 6-4, 4-6, 8-6 triumph for her first French crown. It ran her string of victories to seven tournaments comprising 39 matches.

Navratilova had to take solace in extending her streak to nine consecutive singles final appearances in major tournaments, a record in the open era. However, Helen Wills Moody and Maureen Connolly, who didn't travel as much, appeared in 22 and nine respectively.

Even the return to blessed English grass didn't reverse her fortunes, at least not instantly. At Eastbourne, where she had tuned her game for Wimbledon by winning each of the five preceding years, she was denied by Helena Sukova. But just when it seemed that her fall was complete, Navratilova dug in her heels at the All England Club. She defeated Evert, 6-2, 5-7, 6-4, in a match worthy of the great rivalry. Yet, it was a sign of the

1987 CHAMPIONS AND LEADERS

Top Player Earnings: Men	**ITF World Champion**
Ivan Lendl $2,003,656	Men: Ivan Lendl
Top Player Earnings: Women	Women: Steffi Graf
Steffi Graf $1,063,785	**Grand Prix Masters, NYC**
Year-End Number One	Ivan Lendl
Men: Ivan Lendl	**WCT, Dallas**
Women: Steffi Graf	Miloslav Mecir
Davis Cup: Sweden	**Virginia Slims**
Federation Cup: W. Germany	**Championships, NYC**
Wightman Cup: United States	Steffi Graf

times that the 73rd meeting of the pair occurred in the semi-final. Theirs had become a warm-up act.

In the other semi, Graf needed merely 51 minutes to bludgeon Shriver. "I can't believe Steffi is only 18 and is so strong," Shriver said. "The ball comes off her racket with unbelievable force."

That force finally was blunted in the final, where Navratilova needed all her athleticism and experience to win, 7-5, 6-3. Not only did it stop Graf's 45-match streak but it gave Navratilova an unprecedented sixth consecutive Wimbledon women's singles championship and her eighth overall, tying the record established by Helen Wills Moody 49 years earlier.

"How many more Wimbledons do you want?" Graf asked. Replied Navratilova: "Nine is my lucky number."

Meanwhile, Graf soared onward. Undefeated, she led West Germany against the U.S. in the final of the Federation Cup at Vancouver, winning all five of her singles and three doubles. Steffi's 6-2, 6-1 rout of Evert offset Shriver's 6-0, 7-6 victory over Claudia Kohde-Kilsch and the two German ladies then rallied from a 1-6, 0-4 deficit to defeat Evert and Shriver in the decisive doubles. Thus did the Fatherland become the fifth nation to own a piece of the Cup.

Two weeks later, after Evert posted a semi-final victory over Navratilova in Los Angeles, Graf dismissed her elder, 6-3, 6-4, in the final and ascended to No. 1.

So shaky was the game of the former Ice Maiden that she even lost to Shriver, in the semi-final round of the Canadian Open. After nine years and 18 unsuccessful attempts, Shriver defeated Evert, 6-4, 6-1, then followed with a 6-4, 6-1 triumph over Garrison for her most significant singles title. She would finish a splendid season with four tournament victories, a match record of 67-13.

Pam also had the honor of captaining the U.S. Wightman Cup team, which beat a British squad for the ninth straight year, by the score of 5-2 at Williamsburg, Va. She beat Jo Durie and Anne Hobbs and got a singles win each out of Garrison and McNeil.

The most touching moment of the U.S. Open didn't occur in the final or even during Evert's quarter-final loss to McNeil. It took place in the round of 16, where McNeil was matched against Garrison, her friend since childhood. Zina and Lori were protégés of John Wilkerson, the coach at McGregor Park's public courts. Garrison and McNeil, whose father, Charlie McNeil once played defensive back for the San Diego Chargers,

were doubles partners and virtually inseparable on the tour. One month older, Garrison had enjoyed the more successful career and had won two of her first three tournaments of 1987, at Sydney over Shriver and Oakland over German Sylvia Hanika. But this was McNeil's moment, her tournament, and she survived two match points and defeated Garrison in a third-set tie-breaker, 7-6 (7-0), 3-6, 7-6 (8-6).

That boosted her into the quarter-finals, where her attacking game wore down Evert, 3-6, 6-2, 6-4, before an agonizing grandstand crowd. Without a clothing company to dress her or endorsements decorating her outfit, McNeil proved she belonged in such surroundings when she jumped on Graf to take the first set of their semi-final. But Graf eventually took control to win 4-6, 6-2, 6-4. Navratilova, who'd won all 12 sets, awaited the German in the final.

The match turned in the tie-breaker when, at 3-3, Graf missed two backhands. Navratilova assumed command and closed out the challenger, 7-6 (7-4), 6-1, in one hour, 17 minutes.

As Navratilova held up the trophy, her fourth U.S. singles prize, both she and Graf were aware that the result wouldn't alter the computer ratings. After convincing victories in the world's two biggest tournaments, Navratilova said, "I'd have to think I have the edge right now." She paused. "Nothing is worse than when people say you're washed up."

She was a long way from that but still she needed to outlast Graf at the Slims Championships if she hoped to reclaim her eminence for the year. Instead, she lost to Sabatini in the quarter-final. Her old rival had an even worse experience as pudgy lefty Hanika beat Evert in the opening round. A new generation made its mark as Graf closed out the season at Madison Square Garden with her 11th title and the designation as best in the game, putting down Sabatini in the best-of-five-set final 4-6, 6-4, 6-0, 6-4.

There would be no change at the top of the men's rankings but that didn't mean the circuit suffered from tired blood. The man who put a charge into the season was Cash, the Australian with the checkered headband, a diamond stud in his ear, a chip on his shoulder and an American temper. He regarded himself as a 'yobbo,' one of the boys.

In his hometown of Melbourne, he became one of the finalists. Starting as the 11th seed, Cash advanced to the title match of the Australian Open by beating third-seeded Yannick Noah and, in the semis, top-seeded Lendl. In the championship match, fourth-seeded Edberg prevailed, 6-3, 6-4, 5-7, 6-3, the first of six t ournament victories that would boost him into second place in the rankings.

Edberg followed with a victory at the U.S. Indoor at Memphis where Connors, a seven-time champion, suffered a knee injury and had to default to Stefan, who led, 6-3, 2-1.

A tournament that one day would become the second-most important in the U.S. found its home in Key Biscayne. Launched by Butch Buchholz as the Lipton International at Delray Beach, Fla., in 1985, it moved to Boca Raton the following year, then farther south, to Key Biscayne's Crandon Park, where the titles went to Mecir over Lendl and Graf over Evert Lloyd.

At the Italian Open, Wilander, warmed up for Paris by beating McEnroe and Argentine Martin Jaite in the last two rounds to win the title. In a fierce battle to avoid elimination in the first round by diminutive Argentine lefty Franco Davin, McEnroe was given relief and rest when the lights failed a couple of times for delays, each of almost a half-hour. Eventually he pulled through, 3-6, 6-2, 6-3. Faulty equipment? Or maybe it was a courtesy to a big ticket seller who had filled Il Foro Italico with 8,000 customers that night? Who can tell?

For McEnroe, his form on the clay was encouraging after a frustrating early season where he reached the finals of the U.S. Pro Indoor at Philadelphia and the WCT final at Dallas, only to lose to Mayotte and Mecir, respectively. But it proved to be an illusion as he staggered in the very first round of the French Open, falling, 4-6, 6-2, 6-4, 6-2, to No. 49 Horacio de la Pena. He flew home with a sore back, not to be seen again until the Davis Cup match with West Germany.

So depressed was the state of American men's tennis that Connors, 34, was the only Yank to reach the quarters in Paris, where he was blown away by Becker. The final, between Lendl and Wilander, was an excruciatingly tiresome, four-hour, 30-minute exchange of ground strokes. The first set alone took 100 minutes. Lendl won 7-5, 6-2, 3-6, 7-6 (7-3) victory.

But it was Wimbledon—one of the wettest—for which Lendl hungered. This looked like it might be the year after Peter Doohan, an Aussie ranked No. 70, stunned Becker, the two-time defending champ, in the second round. In the same round, Lendl survived a stiff five-set challenge from No. 45, Italian Paolo Cane, but

had smoother sailing thereafter. His semi-final defeat of Edberg, 3-6, 6-4, 7-6 (12-10), 6-4, dodging two set points in the tie-breaker, was impressive.

If Lendl's passage was relatively quiet, that was the result of some pyrotechnics in the other half of the draw, most of it caused by that old rabble-rouser, Connors. In the round of 16, the man staged one of the great rallies in the history of tennis by rising from a 1-6, 1-6, 1-4 deficit against Mikael Pernfors to win the last three sets 7-5, 6-4, 6-2. "Phenomenal," Connors decided, "right?" Right.

Then the geezer dodged the thunderbolt serves of Bobo Zivojinovic in a 7-6 (7-5), 7-5, 6-3 quarter-final triumph. It appeared that Jimmy might really have a chance to win a third title. However, he was no match for Cash in the semi-final, losing 6-4, 6-4, 6-1.

That wasn't the only indication the 11th-seeded Aussie was ready to take the biggest step of his career. But grass was his best surface. He was fit after an injury-plagued season and he was a battler. And Cash knew how to play on grass. It was instinctive, the way he covered the net, the way he volleyed. For all his countless hours of practice, Lendl wasn't a natural. He was mechanical. And it showed as the 22-year-old Cash crushed his opponent's spirit, 7-6 (7-5), 6-2, 7-5.

There followed perhaps the most amazing victory celebration in the annals of the proper All England Club. Cash didn't wait to accept the congratulations of the Duke and Duchess of Kent. Instead, he clambered through the crowd massed at one corner of Centre Court and over the ledge to the second level of stands where were gathered his coach, psychologist, sister, father and girlfriend as well as the couple's 14-month-old son, not to mention his London pub mate.

Lendl tuned up for the green slabs of Flushing Meadow by winning at Washington, over Brad Gilbert, reaching the rained-out final at Stratton Mountain against McEnroe and beating Edberg in the Canadian Open. Cash, seeded seventh, continued to celebrate, which helped to explain his first-round loss in the U.S. Open to No. 47, Swede Peter Lundgren. (Later, a knee injury limited Cash to doubles duty as Australia was jolted in Davis Cup competition by India.)

The home team received a nice surprise when Michael Chang, the new U.S. junior champion and the youngest male, 15 years, six months, to compete in the U.S. Championships since Vinnie Richards in 1918, defeated ex-Aussie Davis Cupper, 32-year-old Paul

McNamee in his first match. Nigerian Duke Odizor sent him packing in the second round. Ken Flach, better known for his doubles prowess, penetrated to the fourth round before Wilander beat him. Ken's third-round victory over Mike Cahill climaxed with the lengthiest tie-breaker to date at the Open, 32 points. But and it wasn't long before the American presence was reduced, once again, to McEnroe and Connors.

Mac caused a commotion not with his play but his behavior. He went ballistic, spewing curses at chair umpire Richard Ings and a courtside cameraman while beating Zivojinovic in the third round. Awaiting sentencing, he got to the quarters, where he was overpowered in straight sets by Lendl. The $17,500 fine and suspension he received ended his season.

Once again, Connors was the lone American survivor in the final four but he, too, was set down by Lendl in straight sets. The final, against Wilander, delayed one day by rain, was a replay of the French. Although the quality of tennis was higher, so was the quantity. Lendl's 6-7 (7-9), 6-0, 7-6 (7-4), 6-4 victory lasted a U.S. final record four hours, 47 minutes, a record these two players would break in 1988.

Three weeks after the Open, Lendl was shocked in the semi-finals by Lundgren at San Francisco, ending a 25-match winning streak. Lungren won the title in a totally unseeded final over double-handed-both-ways Californian Jim Pugh, 6-1, 7-5. But Lendl readied himself for the Masters, where he dropped only a set in the round-robin and pounded Wilander, 6-2, 6-3, in the final for a record fifth title, topping Ilie Nastase (1971-'72-'73, '75). Once again, Ivan was No. 1, perhaps with an asterisk that noted "except for Wimbledon."

1988

Steffi scales peak with Golden Slam

Andre Agassi
Gains semi-finals at French and U.S. Opens, and No. 3 world ranking.

Steffi Graf added the Grand Slam to her résumé in 1988, sweeping the championships of Australia, France, Wimbledon and U.S. And Don Budge, the first person to win all four of the world's major tournaments in one season, witnessed each of her conquests. While the West German prodigy expressed mostly relief, the courtly American seemed enormously pleased with Graf's slam-clinching, U.S. Open victory over Gabriela Sabatini.

In welcoming Graf to the most exclusive club in tennis, Budge, who'd accomplished his Grand Slam 50 years earlier, whispered into her ear during the award ceremonies at Flushing Meadow. "He said he knew it all the way," she recalled later. "He said he thinks I'm going to do it a couple more times."

Graf would not achieve a second Grand Slam (of the five persons who have claimed the four major titles within a calendar year, only Rod Laver did so twice) but that in no way diminished what she accomplished in 1988. She lost but two sets in her triumphant march, the first to Martina Navratilova in the Wimbledon final and the second to Sabatini. Budge said he expected Graf to capture the Slam after watching her in Australia. At the Wimbledon Ball, he told her, "Steffi, when you win the Grand Slam, I hope they let me present the trophy."

The U.S. Tennis Association was too conscious of tradition to allow such a radical departure. But Budge was included in the ceremony on the golden anniversary of his achievement. He held one handle of the silver jug while Gordon Jorgensen, the USTA president, held the other. They were surrounded by the Stars and Stripes, the Union Jack, the Tricolor and the Southern Cross.

Clearly, the sport's dominant player in 1988 was a teenaged female who followed in the Grand Slam steps of Maureen Connolly (1953) and Margaret Smith Court (1970). In fact, Graf took a few steps beyond by adding the Olympic title to her collection—call it a Golden Slam.

"There's nothing quite as special as winning a gold medal for your country," she said after her September triumph on a hard court in Seoul, South Korea.

For the first time since 1924, tennis was returned to the Olympics as a medal sport. The acceptance of tennis as a full-fledged medal sport marked a breakthrough—or official breakdown of amateurism—hardly noticed at the time. The ITF got permission from the IOC (International Olympic Committee) to approve the best players available for the Games if nominated by their countries. That meant out-and-out pros. It changed the complexion of the next Games in 1992 at Barcelona, where the NBA 'Dream Team' took basketball gold, and numerous other declared pros took part. Tennis had led the way, for better or worse.

A slam of sorts was registered in men's competition as well. But this was national and not individual. As the result of Mats Wilander's victories at the Australian, French and U.S. championships and Stefan Edberg's ascendancy at Wimbledon, each of the major events was captured by a Swede. There hadn't been a male sweep by citizens of one country since Laver ran the table in 1969.

In a season that would have been lionized if not for Graf's transcendent performance, Wilander also bumped Ivan Lendl from the top spot on the computer. Lendl, slipping from the No. 1 position for the first time in 156 weeks, reached only one Big Four final, at Flushing Meadow. He also surrendered his Masters title, which he had held for three years, to Boris Becker.

Becker, beaten by Edberg in the Wimbledon final, won seven tournaments and also led West Germany to its first Davis Cup, dethroning Sweden, 4-1, at Goteborg. Miloslav Mecir, the enigmatic Czech, took home the Olympic gold medal. He also denied Wilander any chance of a Grand Slam by defeating the Swede in the Wimbledon quarter-finals.

It was another empty year for America's two controversial stars. Neither John McEnroe nor Jimmy Connors advanced beyond the quarters of a major and both sagged in the rankings, Mac to No. 11 and Connors to No. 7. Each won two tournaments, the first for Connors in four years.

Suddenly, however, the future appeared bright for men's tennis in the U.S. Andre Agassi, an 18-year-old graduate of Nick Bollettieri's groundstroke academy who had won his first Grand Prix tournament only the previous November at Itaparica, Brazil, captured six titles,

reached the semi-finals at the French and U.S. Opens and shot from No. 25 to No. 3 in the world standings. Andre also led the 'back from the boonies' march (including a McEnroe cameo) to the American zone title with victories over Peru and Argentina, returning the U.S. to the Davis Cup World Group for 1989. (The U.S. had been relegated in 1987 after losses to Paraguay and Germany).

Two years younger than Agassi, Michael Chang also made great strides. By defeating Johan Kriek to win San Francisco in early October, he became the second-youngest winner of a men's pro tournament at 16 years, seven months (Aaron Krickstein had been 16 years, two months when he triumphed at Israel five years earlier). Chang rose 133 places in the rankings, from No. 163 to No. 30, in his first full season on the circuit.

Graf's monumental accomplishment guaranteed that U.S. women would be denied a major title for the first time since Court's Grand Slam 18 years earlier. Additionally, Navratilova hadn't been blanked in the Big Four since 1980. Still, Martina was a solid No. 2, winning nine tournaments (two fewer than Graf) and amassing a 70-7 record.

But Navratilova reached the final of only one major tournament, Wimbledon. In the first Australian Open played on hard courts in the sparkling new complex at Melbourne's Flinders Park, she was a straight set, semi-final loser to Chris Evert. At the French, she was stunned by 17-year-old Belarussian Natalia Zvereva in the fourth

---

1988 THE MAJOR CHAMPIONSHIPS

Australian Open
Men's Singles: Mats Wilander
Women's Singles: Steffi Graf
Men's Doubles: Rick Leach / Jim Pugh
Women's Doubles: Martina Navratilova / Pam Shriver
Mixed Doubles: Jana Novotna / Jim Pugh

French Open
Men's Singles: Mats Wilander
Women's Singles: Steffi Graf
Men's Doubles: Andres Gomez / Emilio Sanchez
Women's Doubles: Martina Navratilova / Pam Shriver
Mixed Doubles: Lori McNeil / Jorge Lozano

Wimbledon
Men's Singles: Stefan Edberg
Women's Singles: Steffi Graf
Men's Doubles: Ken Flach / Robert Seguso
Women's Doubles: Steffi Graf / Gabriela Sabatini
Mixed Doubles: Zina Garrison / Sherwood Stewart

U.S. Open
Men's Singles: Mats Wilander
Women's Singles: Steffi Graf
Men's Doubles: Sergio Casal / Emilio Sanchez
Women's Doubles: Gigi Fernandez / Robin White
Mixed Doubles: Jana Novotna / Jim Pugh

round. Zina Garrison did the honors in a quarter-final match at Flushing Meadow.

In doubles, Navratilova and Pam Shriver continued their successful amalgam, winning 28 of 30 matches and five championships, including a sixth Australian, over Wendy Turnbull and Evert, and a record-tying fourth French, over Claudia Kohde-Kilsch and Helena Sukova.

Shriver later teamed with Garrison against a Czechoslovakian team of Sukova and Jana Novotna to win an Olympic gold medal for doubles. That equaled the feat of Ken Flach and Robert Seguso, who defeated Spaniards Emilio Sanchez and Sergio Casal.

The first Olympic women's singles champion since Helen Wills in 1924, Graf lost but three matches all year. Sabatini triumphed twice, beating Graf for the first time after 11 consecutive losses to win Boca Raton in March and in a semi-final at Amelia Island one month later, in a tournament won by Navratilova. Shriver applied the final blemish to Graf's record in the semi-finals of the Virginia Slims Championship, which the 18-year-old Sabatini won for her fourth title of the season.

Graf zipped through the Australian without the loss of a set but she was pressed in the final by Evert, who had been sharp in a semi-final victory over Navratilova. For Evert, it was the 34th and last major final of her career. But for tennis the match was an unprecedented, schizophrenic, outdoor-indoor title bout made possible by the new stadium's sliding roof. It was, according to Evert, "the weirdest [final] I ever played."

Rain suspended the match with Graf ahead, 2-1 in the first. Officials decided to close the roof and, after a 91-minute delay, the outdoor tournament resumed indoors. Graf adapted better to the change, racing to a 6-1, 5-1 lead before Evert steadied herself. She won four of the next five games and came within two points of squaring the match before the German prevailed, 6-1, 7-6 (7-1).

1988 CHAMPIONS AND LEADERS

Top Player Earnings: Men
Mats Wilander $1,726,731
Top Player Earnings: Women
Steffi Graf $1,378,128
Year-End Number One
Men: Mats Wilander
Women: Steffi Graf
Davis Cup: Germany
Federation Cup:
Czechoslovakia
Wightman Cup: United States

ITF World Champion
Men: Mats Wilander
Women: Steffi Graf
Grand Prix Masters, NYC
Boris Becker
WCT, Dallas
Boris Becker
Virginia Slims
Championships, NYC
Gabriela Sabatini

Navratilova won five consecutive tournaments and 29 matches in the U.S. before she was again stopped by Evert at Houston in their 77th meeting. But Navratilova would win their last three matches—a Wimbledon semi, and finals in Germany and Chicago—raising her record in the enduring, 80-match rivalry to a concluded 43-37. Their global warfare, concussive but caring, began in Ohio in 1973 and ceased 15 years later in Illinois, touching down in several countries along the way.

Any semblance of competition at the French vanished when third-seeded Evert was dismissed in the third round by future champ, 16-year-old Arantxa Sanchez of Spain, and second-seeded Navratilova was surprised by 13th-seeded Zvereva in the round of 16. Zvereva then upset sixth-seeded Sukova. Next the coltish 17-year-old from Minsk outlasted unseeded Australian Nicole Provis in two hours, six minutes, 6-3, 6-7 (3-7), 7-5 to land in her only major final.

Graf, who had beaten Sabatini in the semi-finals, 6-3, 7-6 (7-3), was brutally efficient against her star-struck opponent. Her 6-0, 6-0, romp lasted only 32 minutes, the most exciting feature of which was an hour rain delay. There hadn't been such a one-sided major tournament championship match since 1911 when Dorothea Chambers rang up two goose eggs over Dora Boothby in an all-English Wimbledon final. Navratilova added another major, keeping the doubles with Shriver, 6-2, 7-5, over Kohde-Kilsch and Sukova.

It was Wimbledon, of course, that loomed as the biggest obstacle to a Steffi Slam. Wimbledon was the seat of Navratilova's power. "Wimbledon is the last thing she's holding onto, the last thing she dominates in women's tennis," Shriver said.

The naturalized American was in position to surpass the record for most singles championships at the All England Club and she prepared in her usual fashion, winning at Eastbourne against Zvereva. But Navratilova was less than commanding once the tournament got underway. She struggled both in the quarter-finals and semi-finals, edging Ros Fairbank and Evert. Indeed, after holding out through three match points in their 78th meeting, Evert picked Graf to win.

Graf appeared jumpy in the first set, serving below her standard and committing a bundle of unforced errors. Navratilova had raced to a 7-5, 2-0 lead and appeared well on her way to another glorious moment. Then Graf broke Navratilova's second service of the second set. Remarkably, the defending champion would not hold service again in the match. Graf allowed Navratilova only one more game and the only delay in a 5-7, 6-2, 6-1 triumph was caused by rain after four games of the third set.

"I hit good volleys," Navratilova reasoned. "I hit good balls that other people wouldn't get to, and then she hits winners. I didn't succumb to pressure today. I succumbed to a better player ... I still played pretty damn well, but she was hitting winners all over the place."

And so ended one phase of Martina's pursuit of Helen Wills Moody, who won a record 50 consecutive matches while capturing eight Wimbledon singles title. Graf snipped Martina's match streak at 47, but the loser would get the ninth title two years down the road.

Graf was only one title away from an achievement that had eluded Navratilova in her prime. She even teamed with Sabatini to win the Wimbledon doubles championship, defeating the Soviet pairing of Zvereva and Larisa Savchenko, who had stopped defending champs Navratilova and Shriver in the third round.

Fittingly, the only genuine competition Graf faced at the U.S. Open was contemporary in nature. Having failed to derail her at Wimbledon, Navratilova lost any opportunity at Flushing Meadow when she was ousted in an exciting quarter-final by Garrison, 6-4, 6-7 (3-7), 7-5. Evert, recently married to former Olympic skier Andy Mill, earned a chance to thwart the Grand Slam but had to withdraw on the day of the semis with a stomach virus that left her so weak she could barely get out of bed.

That left Sabatini, Graf's doubles partner and the person responsible for the '2' in Graf's 61-2 record at that point. Sabatini defeated Garrison in their semi and became the first Argentine to qualify for a major women's final. In the end, although Sabatini did extend 'Fraulein Forehand' to a third set, Graf added the U.S. title to her necklace of jewels with a 6-3, 3-6, 6-1 victory.

After the victory, Graf seemed more relieved than thrilled. She didn't jump for joy or kneel in supplication. Graf merely jogged to the stands to embrace her family and she barely smiled during the award ceremony. "Now I've done it," she said. "There's no more pressure."

In doubles, Navratilova and Shriver were terminated in the semis by Gigi Fernandez and Robin White, who then defeated the U.S.-Canadian alliance of Patty Fendick and Jill Hetherington, 6-4, 6-1, in the final.

Steffi didn't have much time to savor the moment.

The Olympic tournament was scheduled to begin in a week. Naturally, Graf was seeded first. Naturally, she won. In the final, she again bested Sabatini, this time by the definitive score of 6-3, 6-3. A sign of the times: Of the seven Americans representing the U.S. in tennis at Seoul, the only player not to medal was Evert, a third-round victim of Italy's Raffaella Reggi. Tim Mayotte was decorated with silver as the 3-6, 6-2, 6-4, 6-2, final round loser to Czechoslovakia's Mecir.

Neither Evert nor Navratilova survived the quarters at the season-ending Slims Championships in New York. Martina lost to Sukova and Evert lost to Shriver, who then terminated Graf's 46-match winning streak with a 6-3, 7-6 (7-5) decision in the semi-finals. But Sabatini upheld the new order with a 7-5, 6-2, 6-2 victory.

Garrison, the captain, and her pal, Lori McNeil, starred in a 7-0 Wightman Cup victory over a woefully weak British squad that won only one set at London. But McNeil, beaten by Catarina Lindqvist, and Fendick, defeated by Maria Strandlund, were a second-round Federation Cup flop for the U.S., losing 2-1 to Sweden. Sukova was the anchor for a fifth Czechoslovak triumph, 2-1 over the Soviet Union. Both she, beating Zvereva, and Radka Zrubakova, beating Savchenko, went unbeaten in five singles. However, the date and place—December in Melbourne—diminished the quality of participants.

Eleven months earlier in Melbourne, the baptism of Flinders Park (named for Capt. Matthew Flinders of the British Navy, an explorer of those parts near the end of the 18th century) drew 20,836 customers to inspect the complex that sent Australia well ahead of the rest of the tennis world, a very long jump from 61-year-old grass-carpeted Kooyong Stadium. The focal point of the complex was an asphalt-floored, $70-million techno-wonder stadium, with 15,000 seats, air-cooled private boxes and a sliding ceiling that put an end to rainouts.

It was a lively, controversial debut. Curiously, in this he-man land, a 'sheila' (woman) was selected to do the opening honors. Dianne Fromholtz Ballestrat, seeded 14th, was beaten by a totally unknown 23-year-old American qualifier, No. 304 Wendy Wood. The crowd within was anxious for Wood and Ballestrat to move on so they could watch the hometown hero, fourth-seeded, 1987 runner-up Patrick Cash, beat Thomas Muster. Well, not heroic to all. Cash had attracted some barbs for playing in South Africa—winning that country's Open over Brad Gilbert near the end of the 1987 season. On entering the court he was greeted by anti-apartheid banners and shouting protesters. On the changeover after the seventh game, activists pitched two-dozen black tennis balls at Patrick

For the second consecutive year, Cash qualified for the final by beating Lendl, and for the second consecutive year he lost his national championship in five sets to a Swede. In 1987, Cash slipped on the grass against Edberg. This time, on hard courts, he was beaten by Wilander, 6-3, 6-7 (3-7), 3-6, 6-1, 8-6, in what would be remembered as the year's most captivating major final, an all-around battle of extraordinary offense and defense as Wilander's retrieving and lobs finally broke down Cash's volleying. By defeating Edberg and Cash back-to-back, Wilander not only eliminated the two previous finalists but became only the second man to win major titles on three different surfaces—grass, clay, now hard—matching the achievement of Jimmy Connors at the U.S. Open.

Memphis was the launch pad for Agassi, ranked No. 18 after winning his second career tournament, the U.S. Indoor Championship, over Swede Mikael Pernfors. At 17 years, 10 months, he was the youngest player to win the second oldest of U.S. titles. He followed with victories over Jimmy Arias in the U.S. Clay Courtand Slobodan Zivojinovic in the Tournament of Champions at Forest Hills. As a result, he was seeded ninth in the French Open.

Agassi reached the semi-finals, the best American finish in three years, before he was worn down by Wilander. But the Yank who received the best reception was, of all people, McEnroe. He had returned from a seven-month hiatus (and a plunge to No. 25 in world rankings) to defeat Edberg in the final of the Japan Open. In Paris, he wowed the crowd with a reasonable facsimile of his championship form and three straight-

set victories, the last over Chang. But McEnroe was eliminated by Lendl, the defending champ, who in turn was eliminated by unseeded Swede Jonas Svensson. Henri Laconte then beat Svensson to meet Wilander in the final. Wilander missed only two of 74 first serves and committed only nine unforced errors in a 7-5, 6-2, 6-1 rout of the local hero.

Wimbledon was an American wasteland other than in doubles, where Ken Flach and Robert Seguso earned a second consecutive title, over the Aussie-Swede linkup of John Fitzgerald and Anders Jarryd, 6-4, 2-6, 6-4, 7-6 (7-3). Agassi, no fan of grass, went home to Las Vegas after the French. McEnroe should have followed his lead. The man, seeded an unrealistic eighth, won only one match at the All England Club, over Austrian Horst Skoff, before being flattened by No. 64 Masur. Connors, the fifth seed, lasted until the fourth round where he was bounced by hefty-serving German Patrik Kuhnen over two rainy afternoons in the sodden 'Graveyard' (Court 2), where the ball hardly bounced.

Connors, twice champion, winner of more singles here than any other man (81), was understandably peeved to be assigned for interment in that plot at that stage of the tournament and his career. He said he wouldn't return (but of course he did). Any dreams Wilander had of a Grand Slam ended in the quarters, where he lost to Mecir. "My style is not suited to this surface," Wilander said. "If we played three of the four majors on clay, maybe I'd have a chance for the Slam."

One Swede suited for grass was Edberg. He was down two sets to none and 3-3, 0-40 in the third against the crafty Mecir before staging the comeback of his young career, 4-6, 2-6, 6-4, 6-3, 6-4, boosting him into the championship match against Becker. The two-time champion had eliminated Cash and Lendl en-route to another final. Two weeks earlier, Edberg had double-faulted away the final of the Queen's Club tournament to Becker. But this time, Edberg was mentally prepared for the challenge, even after London's dismal weather interrupted play in the first set and delayed completion of the match until Monday. He served well and volleyed impeccably in scoring a 4-6, 7-6 (7-2), 6-4, 6-2 victory that fulfilled the Swede's immense promise. Edberg fell to his knees and then onto his back on match point. "I couldn't think of anything else to do," he said.

Connors bounded back into the picture by beating Andres Gomez, 6-1, 6-4, in 102-degree heat in Washington, his first tournament victory in 45 months,

---

1988 OLYMPICS, SEOUL, SOUTH KOREA

Men's singles: Miloslav Mecir, Czechoslovakia, Gold; Tim Mayotte, United States, Silver; Stefan Edberg, Sweden, Bronze; Brad Gilbert, United States, Bronze
Women's singles: Steffi Graf, Germany, Gold; Gabriela Sabatini, Argentina, Silver; Zina Garrison, United States, Bronze; Manuela Maleeva, Bulgaria, Bronze
Men's doubles: Ken Flach & Robert Seguso, United States, Gold; Sergio Casal & Emilio Sanchez, Spain, Silver; Miloslav Mecir & Milan Srejber, Czechoslovakia, Bronze; Stefan Edberg & Anders Jarryd, Sweden, Bronze
Women's doubles: Zina Garrison & Pam Shriver, United States, Gold; Jana Novotna & Helena Sukova, Czechoslovakia, Silver; Elizabeth Smylie & Wendy Turnbull, Australia, Bronze; Steffi Graf & Claudia Kohde-Kilsch, Germany, Bronze

and rolled into the U.S. Open quarter-finals without much opposition. But there the past was no match for the future as Agassi blasted him, 6-2, 7-6 (8-6), 6-1, securing the No. 1 U.S. ranking for the year, before bowing to Lendl, 7-6 (7-4), 6-1, 3-6, 6-1, the hardy perennial.

McEnroe, seeded a lowly 16th, stumbled in the other half of the draw, falling to Mark Woodforde in the second round. Wilander, the second seed, defeated two more unseeded players, Emilio Sanchez and No. 33 Darren Cahill of Australia, to gain a final berth. Seeking to become the first man to win four consecutive U.S. championships since the era of Bill Tilden, and closing in on Connors' record of 159 weeks at the top of the rankings, Lendl fell one set and three weeks short against his Connecticut neighbor. In the longest Open final on record (four hours, 54 minutes), Wilander won his third major title of the year and moved to the top of the ATP ladder, 6-4, 4-6, 6-3, 5-7, 6-4. "I don't think I've ever felt better," he said.

Earlier in the tournament, he had served as a spokesman for the ATP, the players' association, which announced it was assuming control of the men's tour starting in the 1990 season. Nothing that happened in the last three months of 1988 altered the final standings. Not even Becker's gutsy 5-7, 7-6 (7-5), 3-6, 6-2, 7-6 (7-5) conquest of Lendl in the Masters final. That ended with a whimper, a net-cord dribbler off Boris' racket, equaling the closest finish—two points—of an important final: Ken Rosewall's 7-5 fifth set tie-breaker win over Rod Laver in the 1972 WCT final.

Ironically, neither Wilander nor Edberg, the major champions of the season, could stop Becker and West Germany from wresting away the Davis Cup, 4-1, at Goteborg in the waning days of the year. No fan of clay, Becker nevertheless beat Edberg, 6-3, 6-1, 6-4. But it was No. 79, lefty Charlie Steeb, who truly stunned the home folks by ducking a match point while leading off with a resurgent 8-10, 1-6, 6-2, 6-4, 8-6, triumph over Wilander. That was no left-handed compliment Steeb paid Wilander. Coming back like a bad check for a painful wrap-up, Becker and Eric Jelen banked the Cup by short-changing Edberg and Jarryd, 3-6, 2-6, 7-5, 6-3, 6-2. Wilander's No. 1 ranking (made with three majors and three other titles on a 53-11 mark in 15 tourneys) quickly vanished, like the Cup.

1989

Arantxa stymies Graf as Evert bids adieu

Michael Chang
An unlikely French champion at 17 years, three months of age.

At the end of a memorable decade, the world said hello to Michael Chang and goodbye to Chris Evert. If further proof were needed that a new era was at hand, it was to be found in the disposition of the Major Championships. Only one of the eight singles championships was awarded to a player older than 21.

That individual was Ivan Lendl, the fit Czech expatriate who captured his first Australian Open title at the outset of the season, regained his No. 1 ranking and, at the advanced age of 29, held off a late charge by Boris Becker. The latter added a first U.S. Open crown to his third Wimbledon title and capped an outstanding year by leading West Germany to its second consecutive Davis Cup. However, it was Chang, the 17-year-old American, who provided the most distinctive victory on the men's tour with an improbable triumph at the French Open.

Chang was born in 1972, one year after Evert, then 16, made her sensational debut in the U.S. Open. At 34, Evert decided to make her final tournament appearance in the same event where she first rose to prominence. The last of her major matches was a quarter-final loss to Zina Garrison, 7-6 (7-2), 6-1, at Flushing Meadow. She concluded her career one month later by teaming with Martina Navratilova in the U.S. drive to a Federation Cup title in Tokyo.

As she had the previous year, Steffi Graf dominated the women's tour. At 20, the German lass even surpassed her 1988 record by winning 86 of 88 matches and 14 of 16 tournaments. But the road to an unprecedented second successive Grand Slam was barricaded by 17-year-old by Arantxa Sanchez Vicario, 7-6 (8-6), 3-6, 7-5, in the French final.

Sanchez Vicario became the first Spanish woman to win at Paris, as well as the youngest of any nationality, at 17 years, six months. She had a reputation as a dogged competitor on clay, had risen to No. 10 on the computer before the start of the tournament and was seeded seventh in the event. By comparison, Chang was a nobody.

Well, that's not completely true. He also demonstrated the patience to play forever, a requirement on dirt, had climbed to No. 19 in the rankings and was seeded 15th. Still, who was he to beat the likes of Lendl and Stefan Edberg? Well, he was the youngest male (17 years, three months) to win any of the four majors and he was the first U.S. man to succeed at Roland Garros in 34 years. Not since Tony Trabert defeated Sven Davidson for his second consecutive title in 1955 had an American reigned in Paris.

By the end of the season, no fewer than six Americans held places in the Top Ten, topped by McEnroe's climb to No. 4. For the first time since the advent of the computer in 1973, however, the elite group did not include Connors. The 37-year-old campaigner slipped to No. 11 despite increasing to 109 his record for tournament victories with triumphs at Toulouse (over McEnroe) and Tel Aviv (over Gilad Bloom).

Connors won his first major tournament in 1974 (Australia), the same year Evert made her breakthrough at the French. They were more than contemporaries. Once upon a time, they were engaged to be married. But whereas Evert formally bade farewell to the crowd at Flushing Meadow, Connors vowed to press on even after being eliminated in the same round.

Of course, there was a major difference in the amount of fight left in the player. The 37-year-old Connors forced 19-year-old Andre Agassi, the top-ranked American, to a fifth set before yielding in a men's quarter-final. He never surrendered. "The people were excited," Connors decided. "You know what? I was excited, too."

Damn right, he was planning to continue. But Evert knew she had had enough after her first season without a single tournament victory, let alone a major. She lost three consecutive finals in the spring, to Graf at Boca Raton, to Gabriela Sabatini at Key Biscayne (Lipton) and, finally—did this convince her?—to 15-year-old Monica Seles of Yugoslavia at Houston. Evert did manage to reach the semi-finals at Wimbledon for the 17th time in 18 appearances and she bashed Seles, 6-0, 6-2, in her penultimate match at Flushing Meadow.

Chrissie, the symbol of athletic consistency, finished on a high note, winning all five of her matches in the Federation Cup at Tokyo. Navratilova also was 5-0 as the U.S. won the team championship for the first time since

the great rivals last pooled their talents in 1986 at Prague. They beat Spain, 3-0. Sadly, Evert and Navratilova did not oppose each other at all in 1989 and the record of their meetings remained fixed in history at 43-37 in favor of Navratilova.

Although she retained her No. 2 ranking and won eight of 15 tournaments, Navratilova was frustrated by Graf in the two most significant tournaments she entered. The fraulein needed three sets on both occasions but nonetheless defeated Navratilova in the final at Wimbledon, 6-2, 6-7 (1-7), 6-1, and Flushing Meadow, 3-6, 7-5, 6-1. Graf also turned back Martina in the final of the Virginia Slims Championships, 6-4, 7-5, 2-6, 6-2.

Agassi, continuing to avoid Wimbledon, seemed to have the Italian Open wrapped up in four, but wasted a match point, and folded, losing to the Argentine swatter of explosive groundies, Alberto Mancini, 6-3, 4-6, 2-6, 7-6 (7-2), 6-1. Sanchez Vicario was gaining respect, though losing the women's title to Rome's favorite, Sabatini, 6-2, 5-7, 6-4.

But Arantxa was getting primed for Paris. By the end of the year, she had scrambled from No. 18 to No. 5, one place ahead of Seles. The 15-year-old Yugoslav, operating out of her new home base in Florida, made a stunning professional debut at Washington. She had straight-set wins over Larisa Savchenko, Robin White and Manuela Maleeva, to reach the semi-finals, where an ankle injury forced her to default to Garrison. Then she defeated Evert in the Houston final before pushing Graf in the

1989 THE MAJOR CHAMPIONSHIPS

Australian Open
Men's Singles: Ivan Lendl
Women's Singles: Steffi Graf
Men's Doubles: Rick Leach / Jim Pugh
Women's Doubles: Martina Navratilova / Pam Shriver
Mixed Doubles: Jana Novotna / Jim Pugh
French Open
Men's Singles: Michael Chang
Women's Singles: Arantxa Sanchez Vicario
Men's Doubles: Jim Grabb / Patrick McEnroe
Women's Doubles: Larisa Savchenko / Natalia Zvereva
Mixed Doubles: Manon Bollegraf / Tom Nijssen
Wimbledon
Men's Singles: Boris Becker
Women's Singles: Steffi Graf
Men's Doubles: John Fitzgerald / Anders Jarryd
Women's Doubles: Jana Novotna / Helena Sukova
Mixed Doubles: Jana Novotna / Jim Pugh
U.S. Open
Men's Singles: Boris Becker
Women's Singles: Steffi Graf
Men's Doubles: John McEnroe / Mark Woodforde
Women's Doubles: Hana Mandlikova / Martina Navratilova
Mixed Doubles: Robin White / Shelby Cannon

French Open semi-finals.

Another teenager, Spain's Conchita Martinez, also made inroads, zooming to No. 7 on the WTA computer as a result of three tour victories. And, in a brief promo of coming attractions, 13-year-old Floridian Jennifer Capriati blitzed Clare Wood, 6-0, 6-0, in the course of another 7-0 Wightman Cup wipeout of the Brits at Williamsburg, Va. by the U.S. Still an amateur, Capriati was the youngest participant ever in the event by a full two years.

Not only were the Brits shut out, but—regrettably, dismayingly— so was the 66-year-old Cup itself. It was a TKO. Britain, often an equal in the early years of a special rivalry, could no longer compete realistically. Winning only eight matches while losing the last 11 contests, the Brits had struck a dead end. It was agreed to stop the bleeding, with the hope that someday the United Kingdom would once again produce world class players.

While Graf remained atop the women's rankings, Mats Wilander began a precipitous drop from No. 1 to No. 13 at the Australian Open, one of three major titles he had claimed the previous year. The first-seeded Swede, a three-time champion in the event, stumbled in the second round against No. 51 Ramesh Krishnan of India and never regained his equilibrium. Complaining of shin splints and a loss of motivation, Wilander failed to win a single tournament and reached only one final.

The other Swede with a major title to his credit in 1988 also was shut out. But Edberg was a finalist both at Paris and Wimbledon and he actually climbed the ladder to No. 3 with a strong finish, culminating in a 4-6, 7-6 (8-6), 6-3, 6-1 victory over Becker in the 20th and final edition of the season-ending Grand Prix Masters. He, too, had his problems in Melbourne when he suffered a back injury in the course of a fourth-round victory over Pat Cash and had to withdraw.

With the field thinned, Lendl had a clear shot to one

of the two Big Four titles that had eluded him and he made the most of the opportunity. He blasted 7th-seeded John McEnroe in a quarter-final, overcame 11th-seeded Thomas Muster of Austria in the semis, and then overpowered ninth-seeded Miloslav Mecir in the final, 6-2, 6-2, 6-2.

The women weren't much more competitive after Helena Sukova handed Navratilova a quarter-final defeat and outlasted unseeded Belinda Cordwell of New Zealand in the semis. But Sukova received a 6-4, 6-4 spanking in the final from Graf, who had crushed Sabatini in the semis.

A fiefdom operated by Navratilova and Pam Shriver—that was the women's doubles, which they controlled for the seventh consecutive time, beating a U.S.-Canadian enterprise, Patty Fendick and Jill Hetherington, 3-6, 6-3, 6-2. However, that was the end of their illustrious line of 20 majors (seven Aussie, four French, five Wimbledon, four U.S), launched in 1981. By the end of the year they had parted, and were on opposite sides of the net for the U.S. final, Martina and Hana Mandlikova defeating Pam and Fernandez, 5-7, 6-4, 6-4. Americans Louise Brough and Margaret Osborne duPont had held the record alone for a long time, their 20 made between 1942 and 1957, none in Australia.

It was at Paris that the season took an abrupt turn. After both Evert and Navratilova declined to enter—preferring to devote extra time on preparations for Wimbledon—and Sabatini was upset in the fourth round by Fernandez, a third French title for Graf appeared a mere formality. She ceded a set to Seles in the semi-final, but it was unthinkable that Steffi would lose to a 17-year-old appearing in her first major final.

Not since the 1962 Wimbledon final (Karen Hantze Susman over Vera Sukova) had a woman seeded as low as seventh won a major against a world-class field. But Sanchez Vicario had the spunk, the shots and the determination to stay in a grueling match against a woman primed for her sixth consecutive Big Four title. Their match consumed two hours, 58 minutes, and it was a riveting demonstration of championship tennis.

Sanchez Vicario achieved her upset with an extraordinary comeback from 3-5 in the third set, winning the last four games and 16 of the last 19 points. "This is a great day for me," she said. "This is the tournament I wanted to win all my life."

She had grown up the smallest at 5-foot-5 in a tennis

1989 CHAMPIONS AND LEADERS

Top Player Earnings: Men
Ivan Lendl $2,344,367
Top Player Earnings: Women
Steffi Graf $1,562,905
Year-End Number One
Men: Ivan Lendl
Women: Steffi Graf
Davis Cup: Germany
Federation Cup: United States
Wightman Cup: United States

ITF World Champion
Men: Boris Becker
Women: Steffi Graf
Grand Prix Masters, NYC
Stefan Edberg
WCT, Dallas
John McEnroe
Virginia Slims
Championships, NYC
Steffi Graf

family. Two older brothers, Emilio and Javier, were on the men's tour and an older sister, Marisa, had played for Pepperdine University in California. She was the most competitive of the group.

"Off the court, she is sweet and charming," said her coach, Juan Nunez. "But when she gets on the court, she turns into a lion. What you saw out there was the lion."

Graf appeared pale and sad-eyed after failing to equal Navratilova's streak of six consecutive major titles. "Arantxa is a wonderful girl and she played unbelievable to win," said the German, who suffered cramps in the third set. "But I did nothing at all. It wasn't me out there. It was another person hitting those balls."

It was the second and final loss of the year for Graf, following a three-set defeat by Sabatini in the Amelia Island final. But, for Sanchez Vicario, it was a peerless achievement. At the end of the match, she tossed her racket into the air and collapsed on the red clay. "It is the most joyous moment of my life," she said.

No less remarkable was 15th-seeded Chang's feat. If anything, it may have been more improbable. The 5-foot-8, 135-pounder would have been unseeded if not for the absence of McEnroe and Muster, who suffered a serious knee injury when hit by a drunken driver on the eve of the Lipton final. The son of research chemists who had emigrated from Taiwan, the 17-year-old youngster seemed too small and too inexperienced for such a Herculean task.

But he proved his stamina and his mettle in a fourth-round battle against top-ranked Lendl, whom he trailed two sets to love. Instead of capitulating, he fought through debilitating cramps to oust the No. 1 guy, 4-6, 4-6, 6-3, 6-3, 6-3. He was in such distress late in the fourth set and early in the fifth that he stood at changeovers, munched on bananas, staggered about the court between points and even served underhanded on one occasion, and psyched Lendl into a double fault, ending the four-hour, 39-minute struggle by standing directly behind the service line to receive.

"I've never seen a player show such courage on a tennis court," said Trabert. Chang's coach, Jose Higueras, called it "the most incredible match I've ever seen."

But that only earned him a berth in the quarterfinals. Chang then had to grind out difficult, five-set wins over Ronald Agenor of Haiti and tenacious Russian Andrei Chesnokov to meet Edberg in the final. Realistically, the final should have been the end of the road for Chang. But the youngster stretched the imagi-

nation once more, rallying from one set down and saving 13 straight break points over one stretch. He emerged with a shocking 6-2, 3-6, 4-6, 6-4, 6-2 victory from 0-2 in the fifth. "Whatever happens from now on, good or bad," he said, "this will stay with me for the rest of my life."

Edberg, with three major titles to his credit as well as a superior serve and volley, appeared rattled by his opponent's bottomless reserve. He had 26 break points in the match and converted only six.

"He just keeps coming back," the Swede said. "I have to admire him for it. But you know these young guys. They just hit. They don't have to think."

With his victory, Chang surpassed Wilander (17 years, nine months) as the youngest male winner in Paris and supplanted Becker (17 years, seven months) as the youngest male winner of a major.

"Chang is a little bit different from other young players," said Trabert. "Too many of them aren't patient and willing to play long points. I think it should be a personal point of pride to be a well-rounded player." Michael's patience had lasted through 21 hours, 18 minutes on court in burying the U.S. jinx at Roland Garros, where 532 American guys had been laid to rest in the amber soil between Trabert's and his victory.

If that event offered an unlikely duo of titlists, the next major produced a seemingly inevitable pairing. Becker and Graf had been raised in nearby towns in the southeastern corner of West Germany and had known each other since they were children. "I used to be the worst in the boys and she was the best in the girls," Becker recalled with good humor. "So, when I was maybe nine and she was eight, I would have to hit with her."

Each had grown up to be a Wimbledon champion but not in the same year. In 1989, on the grass of the All England Club, they became the Teutonic Twosome. Even the weather cooperated, in a fashion. Rain pushed back the women's final one day so that Graf and Becker might receive their awards at Centre Court on the same afternoon.

Graf, the defender, had the tougher final. Navratilova was the only foe to take a set from her, but that wasn't enough. Steffi subdued the eight-time champ to gain her own second title, 6-2, 6-7 (1-7), 6-1, finishing in championship form, firing an ace. Graf won 17 of 22 points on her serve in the final set and said she was playing so well. "…I was starting to laugh … I was so loose out there and it showed in my tennis."

Earlier in the tournament, she had toyed with the opposition, including Evert. The latter had defeated Laura Golarsa of Italy to earn one last trip to the Wimbledon semi-finals, her 17th. At least, that gave Evert an opportunity to wave goodbye from Centre Court after her thrashing by Graf, 6-2, 6-1.

In contrast to Graf, Becker had a difficult semi-final. He was thankful for the 76-minute rain delay in the midst of the third set against Lendl, wherein he regained his composure to post a 7-5, 6-7 (2-7), 2-6, 6-4, 6-3 victory. Taking the first set in 22 minutes, he then over-powered Edberg, 6-0, 7-6 (7-1), 6-4, to reverse the result of the previous year's final.

It was Becker's third Wimbledon title but, after two years of disappointment, he seemed to appreciate this one more than the others. "Then it was like a fairy tale," he said of the consecutive championships he won as a teenager. This was real. And the two champions shared the first dance at the Wimbledon Ball.

The U.S. Open lacks such a formal conclusion. Otherwise, the pair could have continued their dance in New York. Graf and Becker each left Flushing Meadow with another major title. They had to work harder than at Wimbledon, and they had to share the spotlight with a departing champion.

Graf was severely tested twice, by Sabatini in the semi-finals, 3-6, 6-4, 6-2, and, once again, by Navratilova in the ultimate match. Navratilova appeared to have the final won on at least a couple of occasions. She was only two games from victory in the second set—confidently waving two fingers at friends in the stands—before double-faulting away a service game. Then she had a break point for a 5-4 lead and squandered that. Seeing the opening, Graf mobilized her gifts and won, 3-6, 7-5, 6-1.

"I was close," said Navratilova, her face streaked with tears. "I was as close as you get."

Becker almost didn't make it out of the second round, where he faced two match points against vagabond Derrick Rostagno in a fourth-set tie-breaker. On the second, his running forehand ticked the net and hopped over the Californian's waiting racket. Becker took that bit of good luck and won the next two points for the set, and the arduous match that had looked lost long before, 1-6, 6-7 (1-7), 6-3, 7-6 (8-6), 6-3.

Connors' 16th trip to the quarters was unrewarded as Agassi made a surprising charge to score his own first

victory in a five-set trial. McEnroe, seeded fourth, didn't get that far, banished from the second round by a qualifier, No. 110 Paul Haarhuis.

"Where are you from?" a reporter asked the anony-mous Dutchman. "Mars," was the smiling reply, and Mac may have believed it. Defending champ Wilander, fifth-seeded, undoubtedly wondered about the prove-nance of his kid conqueror, also in the second round. The 18-year-old's name was Pete Sampras, who in 12 months would illuminate the Meadow, and continue to do so, passing Mac and Wilander, catching up with Connors in the matter of majors—eventually holding the record himself, 14.

Lendl took care of Agassi in one semi and Becker cruised past Aaron Krickstein in the other. In the final, Becker needed three hours and 51 minutes to defeat Lendl, 7-6 (7-2), 1-6, 6-3, 7-6 (7-4). Ivan was appearing in his eighth consecutive final, a Tilden-tying achieve-ment. But after Becker got a full head of serving-and-volleying steam, neither Ivan nor the ghost of Big Bill could stop him. "He just has more power in his game than I do." Lendl said. For Becker, the victory proved he was more than splendor in the grass, that he was able to beat a world-class field somewhere other than Wimbledon. He had filled in the gaps in his game since the summer of '85, firmed his groundstrokes along with his tenacity. Now he was a worthy challenger for the honor of top-ranked men's player on the planet. "If I'm not No. 1," he said, "then I'm quite close to it."

But he couldn't close the narrow gap before year's end, despite his two majors and a 64-8 match record on winning six of 13 tournaments.

Boris' magnificent year had included possibly the most remarkable win—6-7 (4-7), 6-7 (5-7), 7-6 (7-3), 6-3, 6-4, over Agassi in the Davis Cup semis. They had stopped at midnight, returning the next day for the fifth. From a break behind in the last set, 4-3, Boris swooped to take the last three games, and launch the 3-2 victory over the U.S. at Munich. If anything, Boris was even more brutally Beckerian in the final (3-2 over Sweden at Stuttgart for a second straight Cup). He ripped up No. 3 Edberg and the previous year's No. 1 Wilander on a loss of 12 games: Respective 6-2, 6-2, 6-4, and 6-2, 6-0, 6-2, triumphs, probably the worst thrashings dealt such elite men in Cup history. Boris wrapped those around his and Jelen's rock-ribbed, tense victory over Jan Gunnarson and Anders Jarryd, 7-6 (8-6), 6-4, 3-6, 6-7 (4-7), 6-4.

With all his heroics, Becker was still second to Lendl, who won 10 of 17 starts on a 79-7 record with record earnings of $2,334,367. Ivan lost the Masters semi-final to Edberg, who then cut down Becker the following day, 4-6, 7-6 (8-6), 6-3, 6-1.

Still, the U.S. Open was as notable for a dignified exit as for Becker's grand entrance into the circle of champions. Evert made her last stand on the stadium court in the quarter-finals against Garrison, an opponent who had lined up for her autograph 10 years earlier in Houston. In the end, Evert's nerves betrayed her. Twice she served for the first set and was broken both times, 7-6 (7-1), 6-2.

Evert departed with records for most Open victories (101) and most career singles titles (157). Her 5-0 record in the subsequent Federation Cup brought her lifetime record to 1,309-146, an astonishing percentage of .900.

Also fading away was the men's Grand Prix format, a victim of the ATP revolt. For the record, the last GP event in history was the Masters Doubles at the Royal Albert Hall in London on Dec. 10. McEnroe's younger brother, Patrick, teamed with Jim Grabb to beat Wimbledon champions Jarryd and John Fitzgerald in the match that brought down the curtain on two decades of play, Jack Kramer's brainchild, the Grand Prix, 7-5, 7-6 (7-4), 5-7, 6-3.

1990

Wimbledon Final: Martina 9, Helen 8

Stefan Edberg
A second Wimbledon crown, and the No. 1 world ranking.

For the first time in the open era, tennis was just that. The four major singles titles for men and women were divided eight ways. The champions represented seven different nations on three continents and at least two generations.

While Martina Navratilova set a record for the ages, Monica Seles established another for the underaged. Although the gap wasn't quite so large among their male counterparts, Andres Gomez scored a stunning triumph for the 30-and-over crowd in Paris and Pete Sampras became a U.S. Open champion 28 days after celebrating his 19th birthday. Each defeated Andre Agassi for his first major title.

This also was the year in which Stefan Edberg, the Wimbledon champion for a second time, dislodged Australian winner Ivan Lendl from No. 1. Steffi Graf continued at the top of the women's charts but, after losing the French and U.S. finals to Seles and Gabriela Sabatini, respectively, her reign was seriously threatened. And John McEnroe paid for his years of sins against the tennis establishment when he was defaulted in the midst of a major, the Australian.

Astonishing, and then some, was Thomas Muster. Not only was he back in uniform—he was winning, and more impressively than ever, rising to his highest ranking, No. 7. This only months after his career seemed to have been left in a Key Biscayne parking lot where his left knee was wrecked in a collision with a drunken driver. He went at rehab as though it was a major final, and he showed up at the Italian Open, in a wheelchair, vowing he would play at Il Foro Italiano in 1990. True to his word, he returned to take the Italian title. He had actually returned to competition in autumn of 1989, reaching the quarters at Barcelona and semis at Vienna. Eight months after the accident, in January, he won Adelaide and never looked back.

Perhaps the most encouraging development at the start of a new decade was the emergence of Florida teenager Jennifer Capriati, who received $5 million in endorsement contracts before striking her first pulverizing groundstrokes for pay. Making the most widely ballyhooed professional debut in tennis history, 23 days before her 14th birthday at Boca Raton, Fla., she declared perceptively, "The press is out of control!" True enough as reporters and cameras appeared from across the world to record the carnival and the child's initial pro steps, a 7-6 (7-1), 6-1, win over seasoned Mary Lou Piatek Daniels.

True, too, she demonstrated what the fuss was all about, mowing down four more experienced foes before losing a close final to Sabatini. She even had an odd-couple doubles win (first and last pro appearances) with 46-year-old Billie Jean King (6-2, 6-3, over Laura Golarsa and Claudia Porwik) in a tournament that quickly became known as the Virginia Slims of Capriati. Then she became the youngest ever semi-finalist at any of the majors, the French. A fourth-rounder at Wimbledon and the U.S., she plucked her first title at Puerto Rico (over Zina Garrison), had a 42-11 match record and a No. 8 world ranking at season's close.

Another prosperous rookie was the men's tour, managed for the first time by the players themselves, under new executive director Hamilton Jordan, former chief of staff to U.S. President Jimmy Carter. The ATP conducted 75 tournaments on six continents, culminating in season-ending singles and doubles championships. Agassi won the former, defeating Edberg in the final at Frankfurt, and the Franco-Swiss team of Guy Forget and Jakob Hlasek triumphed over Spaniards Sergio Casal and Emilio Sanchez in the latter, staged at Sanctuary Cove, Australia.

Less successful was the Grand Slam Cup, inaugurated by the International Tennis Federation in conjunction with officials of the four majors to combat the muscle of the ATP—the game is never peaceful—and add to the confusing silliness by presenting a second supposedly climactic championship. Entry was based on performance solely in the majors. Although the December event carried a staggering purse of $6 million, many elite pros—including German star Boris Becker—boycotted the competition in Munich because it detracted from the ATP Tour playoffs. Sampras defeated fellow American Brad Gilbert in straight sets for the $2-million first prize.

The U.S. claimed each of the major team championships. Capriati, the Federation Cup rookie, won all five of her singles matches without the loss of a set. But it took a Gigi Fernandez–Garrison doubles operation as

the clincher, 6-4, 6-3, over Larisa Savchenko and Natasha Zvereva, as the U.S. retained the Cup by defeating the Soviet Union, 2-1, in Atlanta.

Agassi and Michael Chang were the stalwarts as the host country took possession of the Davis Cup for the first time in eight years by beating Australia, 3-2. Agassi struggled to beat 6-foot-4 Tasmanian Richard Fromberg and Chang crushed Darren Cahill, setting up Jim Pugh and Rick Leach for the clincher over Pat Cash and John Fitzgerald. It was a bizarre windup to the 29th Cup for the U.S., played indoors in Florida while sun baked the roof of St. Petersburg's Suncoast Dome. And on clay, so often the burial ground for U.S. teams. But the dirt, specially trucked in at a cost of $50,000, was what Capt. Tom Gorman ordered to bog down the best Aussie, Cash, who thus wasn't even selected to oppose the American baseliners. The engagement drew American record Cup crowds, 50,962 in total.

For a topsy-turvy year, 1990 began in conventional fashion. Graf won an eighth major championship in her last nine attempts by outstroking Fernandez, 6-3, 3-6, 6-4, at the Australian Open. The top men turned out in greater numbers at Flinders Park but the final ended in disappointment. Edberg played brilliantly in routing Mats Wilander in the semi-finals, but suffered a torn abdominal muscle in the midst of the third set of his showdown with Lendl and could not continue. Lendl was awarded a 4-6, 7-6 (7-3), 5-2, default, victory and his second consecutive Australian title.

1990 THE MAJOR CHAMPIONSHIPS

Australian Open
Men's Singles: Ivan Lendl
Women's Singles: Steffi Graf
Men's Doubles: Pieter Aldrich / Danie Visser
Women's Doubles: Jana Novotna / Helena Sukova
Mixed Doubles: Natalia Zvereva / Jim Pugh

French Open
Men's Singles: Andres Gomez
Women's Singles: Monica Seles
Men's Doubles: Sergio Casal / Emilio Sanchez
Women's Doubles: Jana Novotna / Helena Sukova
Mixed Doubles: Arantxa Sanchez Vicario / Jorge Lozano

Wimbledon
Men's Singles: Stefan Edberg
Women's Singles: Martina Navratilova
Men's Doubles: Rick Leach / Jim Pugh
Women's Doubles: Jana Novotna / Helena Sukova
Mixed Doubles: Zina Garrison / Rick Leach

U.S. Open
Men's Singles: Pete Sampras
Women's Singles: Gabriela Sabatini
Men's Doubles: Pieter Aldrich / Danie Visser
Women's Doubles: Gigi Fernandez / Martina Navratilova
Mixed Doubles: Elizabeth Sayers Smylie / Todd Woodbridge

At Melbourne, the first of the majors was spiced by the spectacle of McEnroe's banishment. After the testy one received two code violations for racket abuse and intimidation of a linesman during his fourth-round match against Mikael Pernfors, he cursed umpire Gerry Armstrong and referee Ken Farrar. Under the new three-step code of conduct introduced at the start of the season, Mac was automatically disqualified, though in the lead, 1-6, 6-4, 5-7, 4-2.

Despite his history of misbehavior, it marked the man's only default in a major, in fact the only such disqualification from a major event during the open era. McEnroe, who had disqualified himself in 1987 by walking away from a World Team Cup final was fined $6,500. The setback was the first of many in an erratic year that saw him, fourth-seeded, bounced in the first round at Wimbledon by No. 129 Derrick Rostagno, reach the semi-finals of the U.S. Open, post a lone tournament victory and drop from No. 4 to No. 13 in the world rankings.

As it had been the previous year, Paris was the site of two startling results. Considering the form she displayed in routing Navratilova in the Italian Open final and in terminating Graf's 66-match winning streak (second longest of the modern era) in the final of the German Open, Seles' triumph in the French was not a stunning upset. Still, the two-fisted teenager's 7-6 (8-6), 6-4 conquest of Graf suggested a new order in women's tennis.

Before taking on the top-ranked German, second-seeded Seles came close to defeat by Bulgarian Manuela Maleeva in the quarters. Then she eliminated Capriati in a match that was a preview of the future. For Capriati, who had dropped only 20 games in her five previous matches, the 62-minute rout was an educational experience. And her opponent was sure she would be back. "I have the feeling we're going to be playing many, many more times," Seles said.

Monica's current rivalry, however, was with Graf and, suddenly, they appeared to be equals. Although the German still had that booming forehand, her sliced backhand left her vulnerable to Seles, who powers the ball from both sides with both hands. "She hits like she means it," Graf said. Additionally, Graf was bothered by allergies that plague her every spring in Paris and press reports from back home that charged her father with impregnating a German model only slightly older than Steffi. There was a vulnerability about her that no one had sensed since she ascended to the top.

Graf rallied from a 1-4 deficit to force a tie-breaker, where she won the first five points and led, 6-2. One point from the set, however, she dropped the next six, double-faulting on her fourth and final set point. "That's when I knew I had her," Seles said. In her first major final, Monica saved two break points in the ninth game of the second set and then broke Graf in the following game for the biggest victory of her burgeoning career.

At the very least, the victory at Roland Garros made her famous for something other than her grunting on court, her cackle during press interviews and her unruly mane. "I didn't want to go into the history books 20 years from now," she said, "and have people read, 'She was a great grunter, a great giggler and had a lot of hair.'"

Among the missing from Paris were Navratilova and Lendl. Both were consumed with preparations for Wimbledon, a tournament where she would be seeking a record ninth title and he a fulfilling first. Inadvertently, Lendl's decision not to enter the French had a major impact on the results.

Gomez, the man who would become king on the clay, was weighing an offer to serve as a commentator on Ecuadorian television at Paris until he learned that Lendl was bypassing the tournament to practice on grass. The Czech star had eliminated him in four previous French Opens. At 30, the 6-foot-4 left-hander seemed an unlikely semi-finalist, let alone champion. But, given his first chance at a final four in a major event, fourth-seeded Andres bulldozed Muster to earn him a berth opposite the outrageous Agassi, who appeared finally to be living up to his advertising image as the hottest thing on tour.

The youngster from Las Vegas, seeded third, emerged as the favorite in the draw after the Tuesday Massacre, the unprecedented first-round removals of the first and second seeds. Edberg, the finalist of 1989, tumbled to No. 46, Sergi Bruguera (a future champ), and Becker

---

1990 CHAMPIONS AND LEADERS

Top Player Earnings: Men	**Davis Cup:** United States
Pete Sampras $2,900,057	**Federation Cup:** United States
Top Player Earnings: Women	**ATP World Championships,**
Steffi Graf $1,921,853	**Frankfurt**
Year-End Number One	Andre Agassi
Men: Stefan Edberg	**Grand Slam Cup, Munich**
Women: Steffi Graf	Pete Sampras
ITF World Champion	**Virginia Slims**
Men: Ivan Lendl	**Championships, NYC**
Women: Steffi Graf	Monica Seles

lost to a missile-serving lefty (19 aces), No. 51 Goran Ivanisevic. Agassi also gained attention by engaging in a verbal battle with Philippe Chatrier, president of the ITF and the reigning potentate of the tournament. He took one look at Agassi's hot lava (pink) and black tennis ensemble and issued a statement that the French Open would consider requiring predominantly white clothing the following year. Agassi responded by calling the man a "bozo," an insult even in a country that reveres Jerry Lewis.

But the man brought more than bicycle shorts and a matching bandana to the event. He had the talent to whip his 1989 Paris conqueror, Jim Courier, defending champion Chang, and Jonas Svensson en route to what appeared to be a coronation. Gomez was one of the most popular players in the world among his peers but, Agassi pledged, "He's going to be in for a long afternoon because I want it bad."

Surprise. Gomez made relatively short work of the American, 10 years his junior. In the match of his career, he dismissed Agassi, 6-3, 2-6, 6-4, 6-4, claiming the first Big Four title for Ecuador. "I've been coming here for many [11] years," he said, "and I've been dreaming about this day."

At 33, Navratilova was seeking a final sunrise of her own at Wimbledon. Three years without a major victory, she trained diligently under Craig Kardon and her latest coach/motivator, Billie Jean King, for the triumph that would distance her from Helen Wills Moody, the eight-time champion of an earlier era. As it developed, she was virtually unchallenged.

Despite her problems in Paris, Graf still was favored. But from the moment she set foot in London, the German was under siege. If it wasn't the sinus problem that caused her to fly home for treatment during a weekend break, then it was the tabloid press which had a field day with the story of her father and the suddenly notorious Nicole Meissner, whose provocative photos appeared almost daily in the sensational journals.

When they weren't harassing Graf, the arbiters of England's morals were going after the new generation of grunters, Seles in particular. *The Sun* tabloid unveiled a Grunt-o-meter, which allegedly measured the chief offender at 82 decibels—"between a pneumatic drill and a diesel train." As silly as this appeared, the new chairman of the tournament, John Curry, said he would "readily relax the all-white clothes rule if I could just get rid of the grunts."

"Gaby [Sabatini], [Anke] Huber and Jennifer [Capriati] grunt," Seles said. "But probably I'm the loudest. I don't know. I don't even realize I do it until I watch tape of myself on television. I think it's better than it was last year or in the French Open but I can't get rid of it."

Garrison saved officials the trouble of silencing the teenager. Overcoming a match point with a forehand blast, the U.S. veteran rallied to defeat Seles in the quarter-finals. Not only did it halt her opponent's winning streak at six tournaments and 36 matches but it prevented a semi-final showdown between Seles and Graf. Garrison spent years trying unsuccessfully to crack the ranks of the elite when Chris Evert and Navratilova ruled the sport. Then Graf had zoomed past, followed by Seles. The previous fall, after her loss to Navratilova at Flushing Meadow and her marriage to Willard Jackson, she said, "Since I was 16, I felt I would win Wimbledon and the U.S. Open. I still do."

It didn't seem to faze her that her next opponent would be Graf, who had ended Capriati's summer vacation in the fourth round. Although Garrison had beaten Graf only once in six matches—their first meeting when the German was 16—the American was confident. "I've always wanted to play her on the grass," she said.

She made the most of the opportunity in what the normally understated Dan Maskell, who had been telecasting the championships for the BBC since the dawn of time, called an "epic match." In denying Graf entry to a major final after an open era record of 13 consecutive such appearances, Garrison overcame not only the German but her own nerves in a 6-3, 3-6, 6-4 triumph.

To her credit, Graf declined to blame her third loss of the year on either physical or emotional problems, although the ever-vigilant club committee shielded her from elaboration. "I was eager, I was ready," she said. "She didn't make mistakes. She used to make much more errors, unforced errors especially, but she didn't do that today at all." Nevertheless, Graf decided, her conqueror had no chance in the final. "Zina doesn't have the game to beat Martina," she said.

Certainly, there was little in the head-to-head record that suggested a titanic struggle. Of the 28 matches between the two friends, Navratilova had won 27. Moreover, in her 6-3, 6-4 semi-final victory over Sabatini, she had demonstrated she was still near the top of her form. Garrison, who didn't have a clothing deal and was wearing Navratilova's signature line, was compensated on the eve of the championship by a six-figure contract with Reebok. Additionally, her presence in the title match stirred Althea Gibson, the only black woman to win a major, 1958, to fly in from New York.

But no amount of personal or financial support for her opponent was going to stop Navratilova when she was this close to an historic accomplishment. In the match and the tournament that defined her career, Navratilova was more than triumphant. She was regal in a 6-4, 6-1 victory. Martina's virtually flawless solo performance on Centre Court, where nerves can be stretched as taut as racket strings, was one to be preserved in a time capsule. "It was my match to win," Navratilova decided, "and I wasn't afraid of it."

Thus did she surpass Wills Moody, who lost only one of 56 singles matches at Wimbledon in nine tournaments from 1924 through 1933. "Little Miss Poker Face," as Wills was known, won her last Wimbledon final at the age of 32 years, 270 days, making her the oldest female champion since 1914. The 33-year-old Navratilova, 99-9 on the most famous lawns in the world, also took that distinction from Wills. Charlotte Cooper Sterry was 37 as the 1908 champ.

But Zina did get a Wimbledon championship: The mixed doubles with lefty Rick Leach over Aussies Liz Sayers Smylie and Fitzgerald, 7-5, 6-2.

Czechs Jana Novotna and Helena Sukova were moving closer to a Grand Slam when they arrived at Wimbledon. They had already taken the Australian title over Americans Patty Fendick and Fernandez and the French over Soviets Savchenko and Zvereva. But the team to jam a Slam was that of Fernandez and Navratilova. They scissored the Novotna-Sukova 44-match winning string in the final of the U.S. Open—the last of Martina's 31 majors in doubles.

Navratilova was rewarded for her decision to train harder, to bypass Paris for additional practice on the grass. Lendl was not, even after making a greater commitment, journeying to Australia during the winter for seven weeks of training under coach Tony Roche, and (after attending the birth of his first child, Marika) spending six weeks on the grass in England. After playing brilliantly in the traditional warm-up tournament at Queen's Club, blasting McEnroe, 6-2, 6-4, and Becker, 6-3, 6-2, in the last two rounds, he wilted at Wimbledon.

Lendl, top-seeded, used a Czech term to describe his obsession for the only major title he lacked. "Zazrany," he called it. "It means very much into it, almost stubborn." Alas, after weaving fitfully into the semi-finals past no-names, he staggered out of the tournament following a crushing 6-1, 7-6 (7-2), 6-3, semi-final loss to Edberg.

Edberg, third-seeded, earned his third trip to the final, all against second-seeded Becker, who received a scare from 18-year-old hotshot Ivanisevic—his conqueror at the French Open—before advancing. Not since 1894, when homeboy Wilfred Baddeley challenged Ireland's Joshua Pim in their fourth consecutive championship match, had the title contest been an object of such familiarity. This time they produced the longest men's final since Jimmy Connors—sidelined almost the entire 1990 season by a wrist injury that would require surgery—defeated McEnroe in 1982. However, the five-setter wasn't nearly as strained, partly because their similar serve-and-volley styles allowed for no rallies. Edberg won, 6-2, 6-2, 3-6, 3-6, 6-4.

Inspired by the victory, Edberg won his next three tournaments: Los Angeles over Chang; Cincinnati over Gilbert; and Long Island over Ivanisevic. That run of 21 matches took him to the top of the rankings, displacing Lendl on Aug. 13.

Inexplicably, the No. 1 player in the world then lost his first-round match at the U.S. Open to No. 52, lefty Alexander Volkov of the Soviet Union, an all-time opening upset, considering Edberg's top-seeding and Wimbledon title. Lendl also was disappointed, failing to reach the final at Flushing Meadow for the first time since 1981. Sampras beat him in a five-set quarter-final.

Much of the crowd's attention at the Open was diverted by the restoration of the McEnroe legend. Unseeded for the first time since his Open debut 13 years earlier, the former champion went back to his old coach, Tony Palafox, prepared diligently and then won over the fans by beating 10th-seeded Andrei Chesnokov, seventh-seeded Emilio Sanchez and David Wheaton. But he couldn't cope with Sampras' power, the youngster finishing him off in the semis, 6-2, 6-4, 3-6, 6-3, with a 17th ace. "It's been a great run," McEnroe decided.

It was an even more remarkable tournament for 12th-seeded Sampras, the lanky and laid-back Californian who was ranked No. 81 as recently as January, and hadn't won his first pro tournament until February, the U.S. Pro Indoor in Philadelphia. But the best was yet to come—against Agassi. Andre, fourth-seeded, had overcome second-seeded Becker, setting the stage for the first all-American men's final since McEnroe-Gerulaitis, 1979. And Agassi, who had changed to 'electric lime' for this tournament, was nearly undressed in the championship match. Sampras fired 13 more aces, raising his tournament total to a record 100, added 12 service winners and never was broken in demolishing his opponent, 6-4, 6-3, 6-2, in one hour, 42 minutes. "It was a good old-fashioned street mugging," Agassi said.

Sampras was the youngest male player to win America's national championship, supplanting Oliver Campbell, an older 19 one century earlier. Sampras shrugged. "I'm just a normal 19-year-old with an unusual job, doing unusual things," he said.

At 20, Sabatini had been doing unusual things for five years, since her breakthrough season of 1985. But she had reached only one major final (U.S., 1988). However, attacking boldly, she applied the finishing touch to Graf's unhappy post-Australian campaign in the majors. In the final, Gaby bounded off to 4-0, and would win, 6-2, 7-6 (7-5). But not before a torrid back-and-forth windup as Graf nearly pulled herself off the ledge. "I had to win in two," she confessed wearily. Thirteen years after her childhood hero, Guillermo Vilas, ruled Forest Hills, fifth-seeded Sabatini gave Argentina another U.S. champ, the first Latin woman to embrace a major since Brazilian Maria Bueno's 1966 U.S. conquest.

Nevertheless, Steffi retained No. 1 because her pursuer, Seles, was bumped in the third round by No. 82 Linda Ferrando. That was one of two huge first-week upsets. Second-seeded Navratilova was burned by Manuela Maleeva Fragniere in the fourth round.

Graf recovered to win four tournaments in the fall, including two at Sabatini's expense. But Seles served notice of future intentions in November when she became the youngest to win a Virginia Slims championship, defeating Sabatini in a five-set final. It was the first five-set women's match since flowing skirts and corsets were de rigeur and Bessie Moore beat Myrtle McAteer in five sets for the 1901 U.S. title.

1991

Connors makes run to U.S. semis at 39

Monica Seles
Grunting her way to No. 1, despite a Wimbledon sabbatical.

Her talent was undeniable. After she won the three major events she chose to enter, her credentials were impeccable. By the end of the year, only Monica Seles' judgment was considered suspect.

In her third season as a professional, Seles dislodged Steffi Graf as the No. 1 woman in the world and won more money ($2,457,758) than any previous practitioner of tennis, male or female. Not until she had wrapped a ribbon around 1991 by earning a second consecutive Virginia Slims Championship did she turn 18. The teenager pursued and embraced both fame and fortune.

It was the source of the former that the tennis establishment found distasteful, if not embarrassing. A professed admirer of pop singer Madonna and the glamour associated with movie stars, Seles gained a greater share of attention not for her victories at the Australian, French and U.S. Opens but for her mysterious withdrawal from Wimbledon without a suitable explanation. Her subsequent self-imposed exile created a rash of rumors popular in supermarket tabloids.

If her disappearance from public view revealed a fascination for Garbo, her return to tennis at an exhibition event for which she reportedly received a $300,000 appearance fee indicated she also had studied Gabor. On the day of her arrival at the Pathmark Tennis Classic in New Jersey, she posed for photographers with her dog tucked under her arm. Zsa Zsa would have been proud, darling.

In Seles' absence, Graf did manage to regain self-respect by claiming a third Wimbledon title. But the top ranking she had held for an unprecedented 186 weeks slipped away on March 10. The German did regain the No. 1 position for two brief periods during the summer but Seles zoomed back in front after her victory over Martina Navratilova at Flushing Meadow and opened a comfortable margin by winning three late-season tournaments and the Slims Championship, where Graf was upset by Jana Novotna in the quarter-finals.

Graf, in fact, failed to reach the final of any major outside of Wimbledon. She barely held off Gabriela Sabatini for second place. Although Navratilova fell to No. 4 and endured a drawn-out palimony suit brought by former companion Judy Nelson, she surpassed Chris Evert's record of 1,309 tour-match victories and equaled her standard of 157 career singles titles by defeating Seles at Oakland in November. She also advanced to the final of the Slims in New York before falling to the transplanted Yugoslav.

As was the case the previous year, no man won more than one major. Boris Becker won the Australian Open for the first time but was a losing finalist at Wimbledon for the second consecutive year, bowing to countryman Michael Stich in the first all-German title match at the world's most prestigious tournament. Jim Courier became the third young American in three years to win a major event when he defeated Andre Agassi at the French but he was overwhelmed by Stefan Edberg in the final of the U.S. Open.

The last of the Big Four tournaments was energized by the spectacular comeback of Jimmy Connors. After losing all three of his matches the previous year before undergoing surgery on his left wrist, the man was reborn in 1991 when he celebrated his 39th birthday at Flushing Meadow with a sentimental journey to the semi-finals. Over the course of a season in which he also earned standing ovations in Paris and London, Connors rose from No. 936 on the ATP computer to No. 48, a gain of 888 positions.

Courier, a Floridian who turned 21 in mid-August, had the most significant jump of all. With his first major title, the baseline basher in the baseball cap vaulted from No. 25 to No. 3 in the rankings, the highest achievement by an American since John McEnroe in 1985. Mac fell from No. 13 to 28, his lowest finish as a pro, despite gaining his 77th career title. It occurred in Chicago at the expense of his younger brother, 24-year-old Patrick, who rose to No. 36 after he reached the Australian Open semi-finals and achieved his first singles tournament final.

Edberg, who spent much of the year dueling Becker for the top spot, took command at the U.S. Open and became only the fifth player in the era to finish No. 1 for consecutive seasons, joining Connors, Bjorn Borg, McEnroe and Ivan Lendl. He won six of eight finals,

compiled a tour-best 76-17 match record and earned a men's record $2,363,575.

Tendinitis in the knee, however, caused the Swede to withdraw from the ATP championships at Frankfurt. Pete Sampras, whose hangover from his remarkable 1990 success lasted until August, added the season-ending title to three other tour victories in the second half of the season. But Pete finished the year on a down note when he lost both his singles matches in an emotional Davis Cup final won by France at Lyon.

In a bizarre sideshow, Borg attempted a comeback at Monte Carlo 10 years after his last major event. He played with a wooden racket, and lost in the opening round to Jordi Arrese, 6-2, 6-3. After saying he would make an appearance at the French Open, he decided not to ask for a wild card into the main draw and did not appear again for a year.

Seles, born six months before Borg won his first major tournament, emerged as the youngest world champion in history. She began her climb to the top at the Australian Open, where she dropped only 12 games in the first five rounds. She qualified for the final by struggling past Mary Joe Fernandez and, in the final, beat Novotna, 5-7, 6-3, 6-1. Novotna, 10th-seeded, had upset eighth-seeded Zina Garrison, first-seeded Graf and sixth-seeded Arantxa Sanchez Vicario to reach her first major final. For Graf, it was the first time in 17 Big Four appearances she failed to advance to the semi-finals.

Graf's 1,310-day reign as No. 1 ended with her loss

1991 THE MAJOR CHAMPIONSHIPS

Australian Open
Men's Singles: Boris Becker
Women's Singles: Monica Seles
Men's Doubles: Scott Davis / David Pate
Women's Doubles: Patty Fendick / Mary Joe Fernandez
Mixed Doubles: Jo Durie / Jeremy Bates

French Open
Men's Singles: Jim Courier
Women's Singles: Monica Seles
Men's Doubles: John Fitzgerald / Anders Jarryd
Women's Doubles: Gigi Fernandez / Jana Novotna
Mixed Doubles: Helena Sukova / Cyril Suk

Wimbledon
Men's Singles: Michael Stich
Women's Singles: Steffi Graf
Men's Doubles: John Fitzgerald / Anders Jarryd
Women's Doubles: Larisa Savchenko / Natalia Zvereva
Mixed Doubles: Elizabeth Sayers Smylie / John Fitzgerald

U.S. Open
Men's Singles: Stefan Edberg
Women's Singles: Monica Seles
Men's Doubles: John Fitzgerald / Anders Jarryd
Women's Doubles: Pam Shriver / Natalia Zvereva
Mixed Doubles: Manon Bollegraf / Tom Nijssen

to Sabatini in the final at Boca Raton. She did have the satisfaction of defeating Seles at the U.S. Hard Court Championships in San Antonio three weeks later and at Hamburg five weeks after that. But Seles entered the French Open as the top-ranked player and emerged as the clear leader.

Both Graf and Sabatini had the opportunity to move to the top of the ladder with a victory in Paris. But Seles (loser of the Italian Open finale to Sabatini, 6-3, 6-2) defeated Gaby in the semi-finals shortly after Graf (with 44 errors) was humbled by Sanchez Vicario, 6-0, 6-2. The two games were the fewest won by Graf in a complete match since turning pro in October 1982, at the age of 13.

"That hasn't happened in a long, long time," Graf said. "And I hope it's going to be a long, long time until it happens again. I can't remember the last time I played that bad."

Seles, who had dropped only one set in the tournament, defeated Sanchez Vicario in routine fashion, 6-3, 6-4, for her second consecutive French title. It was somewhere between Paris and London, at least in terms of the WTA schedule, that the season took a strange twist.

With the public considering the possibility of a second female Grand Slam in three years, Wimbledon officials were startled to receive a message that Seles had withdrawn from the event "due to an injury caused by a minor accident." There was no additional explanation, no contact with the player herself and the tournament was due to start in three days. Her whereabouts became the hottest topic in tennis.

She was undergoing treatment for a knee injury in Vail, Colo? Or she was having her legs checked in New York? Or she was in hiding at entrepreneur Donald Trump's vast estate in Florida? Maybe it wasn't an injury at all, some tabloids speculated, coming to the conclusion that she was pregnant. Another report had her skipping the grass-court event to preserve her ranking and a

$1-million bonus from the company that manufactured her racket. About the only possibility overlooked was that she had been spirited away by a UFO. Meanwhile, she could not be reached by reporters or agents or the WTA, which levied a $6,000 fine for a late withdrawal.

While she was away, Jennifer Capriati had the time of her life at Wimbledon. The 15-year-old not only became the youngest semi-finalist in tournament history but she did so at the expense of Navratilova. Capriati stunned the most successful singles champion in the annals of the All England Club in the quarter-finals, 6-4, 7-5. It was Navratilova's earliest exit from Wimbledon in 14 years and ended a record streak of nine consecutive finals. Capriati scored her first triumph over a player ranked in the top four and qualified for the semi-finals against Sabatini, where Sabatini won, 6-4, 6-4. Meanwhile, Graf whipped Garrison and Fernandez en route to the final. The championship match was anything but stellar and Graf pulled out a 6-4, 3-6, 8-6 victory, the first extended women's final at Wimbledon since 1976.

The Seles media circus was called to order one week later at Mahwah, New Jersey, where Monica made her first public appearance since her withdrawal from Wimbledon. Sixteen microphones and 13 television cameras were in place as she met the press. The truth, she said, was that she had skipped the most prestigious tournament because of shin splints and the beginning of a stress fracture [left leg]. "People were looking for more exciting answers," she said. "It's so simple, but they were expecting me to say, 'Yes, I'm pregnant.' Or, 'Yes, it's the Yonex contract.' Or, 'Yes, it's some other reason.' I mean, why would I miss Wimbledon? It's the biggest tournament."

The site of her return certainly didn't mollify WTA officials. She chose an exhibition tournament, offering a huge guarantee, over an official tour event the following week in nearby Westchester County, N.Y. For that offense, she was fined $20,000, a penalty paid by the local promoter, John Korff. He also paid the $2,500 fine assessed to Capriati, who defeated Seles in the final of the 16-woman event.

From there, Capriati flew to Nottingham, England, where the U.S. team qualified for the final of the Federation Cup. Despite her singles victory over Conchita Martinez, the Americans lost to Spain, 2-1, as Sanchez Vicario defeated Mary Joe Fernandez and the team of Garrison and Gigi Fernandez was thwarted by the two Spaniards in the doubles.

1991 CHAMPIONS AND LEADERS

Top Player Earnings: Men	**Davis Cup:** France
David Wheaton $2,479,239	**Federation Cup:** Spain
Top Player Earnings: Women	**ATP World Championships,**
Monica Seles $2,457,758	**Frankfurt**
Year-End Number One	Pete Sampras
Men: Stefan Edberg	**Grand Slam Cup, Munich**
Women: Monica Seles	David Wheaton
ITF World Champion	**Virginia Slims**
Men: Stefan Edberg	**Championships, NYC**
Women: Monica Seles	Monica Seles

Returning to the tour at the end of July, Seles was upset by Capriati, 4-6, 6-1, 7-6 (7-2), at San Diego in a match that boasted a pairing of the two youngest finalists in the open era. Two weeks later, Seles beat Kimiko Date, a rising Japanese, to win Los Angeles. Twice in August, however, Graf supplanted Seles at the top of the rankings and the German entered the U.S. Open in the familiar role of No. 1.

It was not to last at this Open, which became the Garden of the Golden Oldies, notable because of 39-year-old semi-finalist Connors and 34-year-old finalist Navratilova. Never had two players in one tournament given so much joy to the geriatric set.

Playing her classic serve-and-volley stuff, the oldest woman in the place had an adventurous excursion, beating Manuela Maleeva Fragniere, Sanchez Vicario and Graf to advance to her eighth U.S. final—and a date with Seles. There was nothing subtle about the other semi, a slugfest of nakedly ferocious, thundering groundies that absorbed the crowd for almost two hours. Mysterious Monica won by the skin of the last four points, stopping Capriati, 6-3, 3-6, 7-6 (7-4).

On the following afternoon, Seles demolished Navratilova, 7-6 (7-1), 6-1, passing her elder at will from either end of the baseline. Navratilova won only 34 points on 76 approaches to the net and committed 26 unforced errors to the champion's five. Seles thus won her third major title of the season in as many attempts. She did not win many new fans, especially after publicly thanking the controversial Trump in post-match ceremonies.

The victory restored her to No. 1, which she held for the remainder of the year. Seles said she didn't regret the decision to withdraw from Wimbledon. "I can't erase it," she said. "But if I were to play Wimbledon, I don't think I could have played the Open [because of the time for recuperation]…there will always be that little emptiness."

Seles finished the season in style, defeating Navratilova at Madison Square Garden in the final of the Slims Championships. Navratilova teamed with her old partner, Pam Shriver, to win the doubles title for the first time in three years, their 10th in this event, over Novotna and Gigi Fernandez.

The men's tour offered surprises as early as the first major tournament, where one of the semi-finalists advised the press, "It's just like you all expected—Edberg, Lendl, Becker and McEnroe." Except that the speaker was Patrick McEnroe and it was the doubles specialist who had advanced to the final four, rather than older brother John. The latter hadn't even made the trip to Australia following his disqualification the previous year.

In his semi, unseeded McEnroe, who had defeated 12th-seeded American Jay Berger, Aussie Mark Woodforde, and Italian Cristiano Caratti, battled Becker for four sets before the German prevailed. Lendl had a tougher time getting to the final, weathering two match points in beating Edberg in five sets. But Lendl couldn't keep the crown, bowing to Becker, 1-6, 6-4, 6-4, 6-4.

Paris belonged to the Americans. For the first time since 1954 (Tony Trabert over Art Larsen) a pair of Yanks made the final. But long before Courier and Agassi walked into Roland Garros to contest the championship, Connors stole the show. A wild-card entry in the only major championship he never won, the 38-year-old Connors eliminated Todd Witsken and outlasted No. 28 Haitian Ronald Agenor. That was his concluding victory in Paris, the 40th, but not quite the conclusion. That was majestic, another crowd-tugging drainer of 3:32. Jimmy won the last point—but ex-champ Michael Chang got the win, 4-6, 7-5, 6-2, 4-6, 0-15 (default). After belting a backhand return winner for the first point of the fifth—"I was ahead, wasn't I?"—Connors surrendered to a man half his age, giving in to a gimpy back and exhaustion.

"I'm sorry," he said to umpire Bruno Rebeuh. "I did all I could. I just can't play anymore. Believe me, if I could … I would."

Certainly, that's what the public believed. The fans accorded him—"JEEM-BO!"—several standing ovations. "To be honest, I felt awful," Connors said after getting an ice massage and an intravenous solution. "I've been run ragged and my back's stiff. But, boy, was it fun. To get a stadium rocking like that is a kick you can't believe."

Agassi, wearing a purple, gray and white outfit that was subdued in comparison to the hot pink ensemble of 1990, advanced to his second consecutive French final by blasting Becker in the semis, 7-5, 6-3, 3-6, 6-1. Courier, four months younger than Agassi, had a more hazardous trip to his first major title match, ousting top-seeded Edberg in the quarter-finals before beating Stich. It marked only the fourth all-American men's final in Paris.

Both players had trained at the Nick Bollettieri

Tennis Academy, but Courier left when he decided Agassi was receiving most of the coach's attention. And Agassi had taken a faster track to the spotlight. But it was Courier who was the more poised in the end, ignoring a couple of rain delays and strong winds and swirling dust in a 3-6, 6-4, 2-6, 6-1, 6-4 victory.

It was Courier's fourth career triumph in as many finals and the $451,660 he pocketed exceeded his total prize money from 1990. He closed with an ace, then flopped backward onto the clay. "There have been lots of happy moments in my life and there will be lots more," the champion said, "but at the moment this is the happiest."

Agassi received greater attention just for showing up at Wimbledon than he did for any of his 1991 results. He hadn't made an appearance at the All England Club since a first-round loss in 1987 to Henri Leconte in under an hour. He said he wasn't ready for the grass and it wasn't clear if officials were ready for a peacock.

And then fifth-seeded Agassi removed the white warmup suit in which he practiced, teasing photographers and spectators alike, to reveal all-white attire without a stripe of color. His only concession to the '90s and his image was the pair of lycra tights that peeked from beneath his white denim shorts. More significantly, after a five-set opening round escape from Canadian Grant Connell, he played reasonably well on the lawns, making the quarters, where he was shot down in five sets by David Wheaton, a 22-year-old American with a big serve.

Unseeded Wheaton, who would cap his season with the $2-million first-place check for beating Chang at the Grand Slam Cup in December, was the only outsider in the semi-finals of a tournament that, in an unprecedented move, opened the gates on the middle Sunday in order to clear a backlog of matches postponed by massive amounts of rain. Tickets were hastily printed after the announcement on Friday and all seats were unreserved, causing a mad dash from the turnstiles. So enthusiastic and unfamiliar with tradition were the fans at Centre Court that they even performed a wave.

Order was restored in time for the final between stick-figure-thin Stich and Becker, who had turned back Wheaton in straight sets. Stich, 6-foot-4, had uprooted defender Edberg, 4-6, 7-6 (7-5), 7-6 (7-5), 7-6 (7-2), the loser having lost serve not once, a curiosity unique to the semi-finals. Tie-breaker maven Stich prevented a fourth straight Becker-Edberg title bout. Strikingly, on this most tie-breakerish day at the Big W, the man who concocted the set-terminating method in 1965 died at Newport, R.I. Jimmy Van Alen was 88. "If he hadn't lived," Edberg said afterwards, not disrespectfully, "Michael and I might still be out there playing."

By winning his match after Edberg lost, Becker climbed to No. 1 in the rankings for the second time in the season. But the added stature did not intimidate Stich. Eleven months younger than Becker, the relatively anonymous German had only one tournament title to his name, Memphis in 1990. He broke his more celebrated compatriot in the first game, slugged 16 aces (for a tournament total of 97) and overwhelmed the three-time champion, 6-4, 7-6 (7-4), 6-4. He would be remembered as the man who beat No. 1 twice in the same tournament.

"It's an incredible feeling," Stich said. To which Becker nodded in agreement. "I know the feeling," the loser said. "He was a nobody, but today he is a star."

Becker held onto the top spot in the rankings until the U.S. Open, where he was upset in the third round by No. 45, Paul Haarhuis. Edberg, who had never reached the final at Flushing Meadow, the major he liked least, made the most of the opportunity. He had straight-set wins over Chang—who'd beaten McEnroe in a four-hour-plus third-rounder that ended at 1:30 a.m.—Javier Sanchez and Lendl to advance to the final against Courier. Courier, who had terminated the 361-day reign of Sampras in the quarters, wasn't off his game against Edberg. But Jim was off the court in 122 minutes because Stefan was in such an oppressive, overpowering serve-and-volleying state, winning, 6-2, 6-4, 6-0. Edberg would often refer to this as "the best match I ever played."

But the star of the tournament was Connors, the wild card with a No. 174 ranking. He owned the crowds in winning five matches, against Patrick McEnroe, Michiel Schapers, 10th-seeded Karel Novacek, Aaron Krickstein and Haarhuis. Connors turned 39 the day he played Krickstein—a first-round winner over No.4 seed Agassi—and had the crowd singing *Happy Birthday* after his melodramatic, four-hour, 41-minute victory, 3-6, 7-6 (10-8), 1-6, 6-3, 7-6 (7-4). Next up was Haarhuis. Some of the 20,000 customers for the nocturnal quarter-final had paid scalpers $500 to get in, and felt they got off cheaply. Jimmy won 4-6, 7-6 (7-3), 6-4, 6-2 to become the second oldest semi-finalist in U.S. history, behind Ken Rosewall, whom he drubbed in the 1974 final on grass at Forest Hills. He was also the only wild card to advance that far. But Connors ran out of miracles against Courier, losing 6-3, 6-3, 6-2, in a match that was coldly efficient and brutally quick.

Courier also reached the final of the ATP World Championship, losing to Sampras. In the doubles event, which reopened South Africa to the men's tour, John Fitzgerald and Anders Jarryd culminated an outstanding year in which they claimed the French, Wimbledon and U.S. Open titles by beating Ken Flach and Robert Seguso at Johannesburg. The Aussie-Swiss coalition beat Americans Scott Davis and David Pata at the U.S., Javier Frana of Argentina and Leonardo Lavalle of Mexico at Wimbledon, and U.S. Davis Cuppers Rick Leach and Jim Pugh at the French.

Still, the historic highlight of the season occurred at Lyon when Capt. Yannick Noah's French team of 'Two Musketeers,' Guy Forget and Leconte—the only pair of lefties to win the Cup—scored a 3-1 victory over the U.S. to return the Davis Cup to France for the first time since 1932. Forget, who enjoyed his finest year as a pro with six singles titles and his first Top Ten ranking (No. 7) defeated Sampras in the clinching match, 7-6 (8-6), 3-6, 6-3, 6-4, after he had combined with Leconte to upset Flach and Seguso in doubles. Leconte, No. 159 and thought to be finished after back surgery four months earlier, also defeated the 20-year-old Sampras, after Agassi had posted a 1-0 U.S. lead by beating Forget.

Victory was followed by an hour-long celebration in which Noah and his latter-day Musketeers were hoisted on jubilant shoulders as a conga line snaked around the court with everybody tearfully singing *La Marseillaise*. One of the celebrants, sharing champagne from the Cup, said he "couldn't wait much longer" for this reprise. He was 93-year-old Jean Borotra, an original of the 'Four Musketeers,' who pried the Cup from the U.S. in 1927 and kept it six years.

1992

Yankees rebound, grab 7 of 8 majors

Jim Courier
Reaching No. 1 the hard way.

In a year in which the U.S. regained the summit of men's tennis, Americans accounted for all but one of the major singles titles. Ironically, the championship that eluded them was the one they prized most, the U.S. Open. Stefan Edberg, the Swede who discovered New York can be a nice place to visit, triumphed at Flushing Meadow for the second consecutive year.

Elsewhere, however, the U.S. reigned supreme. Jim Courier added a second French title to the Australian crown he won five months earlier and finished the season as the No. 1 player in the world, the first Yank to claim that honor since John McEnroe in 1984. Andre Agassi finally annexed his first major at Wimbledon, of all places. And Pete Sampras, a beaten finalist at the U.S. Open, compiled the best match record, 70-18, while gaining No. 3 in the final rankings.

Then, in a classic melding of generations, Courier, Agassi and Sampras combined with McEnroe to reclaim the Davis Cup for the U.S., beating Switzerland in the final. Courier was a loser on opening day to Olympic champ Marc Rosset. But Jim won the clinching singles in an uproarious 3-1 U.S. triumph at Ft. Worth, Tex., a former cow town where hundreds of cowbells, wielded by a good-natured contingent of 1,500 Swiss supporters, clanged incessantly among the crowds of 12,000. Switzerland, never before a factor in the Cup, rode Nos. 35 and 36 Rosset and Jakob Hlasek to the small country's first final, through defending champ France, 3-2, and gave the U.S. a scare before the Americans settled down to win, 6-7 (5-7), 6-7 (7-9), 7-5, 6-1, 6-2.

The male American influence was apparent throughout the entire tour as players from the States accounted for 24 of the 82 singles titles, triple the total of runners-up Spain and Germany. Five U.S. citizens ranked among the Top Ten men, including No. 8 Ivan Lendl, who ended a 14-month drought by winning the Seiko championships in Tokyo three months after receiving his naturalization papers. In all, 43 individuals from 18 countries captured at least one tournament and no player won more than five.

Of the three who shared that distinction—Courier and Sampras were the other two—Boris Becker finished the year on the highest note. The German, shut out of a major final for only the second time in eight years, won the ATP World Championship by defeating Courier, 6-4, 6-3, 7-5, in Frankfurt on his 25th birthday. It marked his third victory in the final eight weeks of the season and raised his ranking to No. 5.

A somber note was Arthur Ashe's revelation in April that he had contracted AIDS through a blood transfusion while undergoing surgery in 1988. Characteristically, he asked not for sympathy, but continued a heavy schedule of obligations in charitable work and TV commentary. He also became active in the fight against AIDS, raising funds for education, research and treatment.

Competition among the women was more one-sided. For the second successive year, Monica Seles captured the Australian, French and U.S. Open titles, won the Virginia Slims Championship, finished atop the WTA rankings and established a record for tennis earnings ($2,622,352). But, in 1992, she was not denied a Grand Slam by an error of omission.

This time she entered Wimbledon and took her case to the final, where she was overwhelmed by Steffi Graf. The German, whose eight victories included a four-tournament winning streak in the fall, demolished Seles, 6-2, 6-1, equaling Martina Navratilova's 6-0, 6-3 conquest of Andrea Jaeger in 1983 as the second most lopsided Wimbledon of the open era. Graf's singles title was her fourth in five years at Wimbledon and her 11th in a major event.

Although Navratilova slipped to No. 5 and failed to reach a Big Four final, she won Chicago over Jana Novotna to break the record for most tournament victories she had shared with Chris Evert at 157. Martina concluded the season with three more titles for a total of 161, the last achieved in Filderstadt, Germany, over Gabriela Sabatini, on her 36th birthday. And the grande dame did reach the last round of the Virginia Slims Championship in New York, where she was drubbed by Seles, 7-5, 6-3, 6-1.

Two months earlier, in a gimmick-ridden send-up of the Battle of the Sexes waged by Billie Jean King and Bobby Riggs 19 years earlier, Navratilova had unraveled in a match against Jimmy Connors at Caesars Palace.

She double-faulted on set point in the first set and lost, 7-5, 6-2, despite getting two serves to her opponent's one and hitting into a court four feet wider. Each player received $500,000 in appearance money and Connors, who had won his first-round match over Jaime Oncins in the U.S. Open on his 40th birthday, earned an extra half-million for his tame victory.

Of greater consequence, 16-year-old Jennifer Capriati picked up a gold medal in the Olympic Games at Barcelona. She did so in dream-like fashion, defeating the defending champion, Graf, in the final. Capriati's 3-6, 6-3, 6-4 victory, the first of her career, lifted her out of the doldrums in a season in which she reportedly balked at the heavy schedule arranged by her father and appeared to lose her zest for tennis.

Three months later, in the semi-finals at Philadelphia, Graf crushed the American teenager, 6-0, 6-1, en route to her fourth consecutive tournament victory, over Arantxa Sanchez Vicario. The German, upset by Lori McNeil in the first round of the Slims showdown, hadn't lost prior to the quarter-finals since 1985. She finished the season ranked No. 2 behind Seles.

Graf was not on hand when Seles took her first major step of the year toward continued domination of women's tennis. She was recuperating from—no kidding—German measles during the Australian Open, where Seles was not taxed. The champion won her second Aussie, 6-2, 6-3, over Mary Joe Fernandez, who had upset Sabatini in the semis.

1992 THE MAJOR CHAMPIONSHIPS

Australian Open
Men's Singles: Jim Courier
Women's Singles: Monica Seles
Men's Doubles: Todd Woodbridge / Mark Woodforde
Women's Doubles: Arantxa Sanchez Vicario / Helena Sukova
Mixed Doubles: Nicole Provis / Mark Woodforde

French Open
Men's Singles: Jim Courier
Women's Singles: Monica Seles
Men's Doubles: Jakob Hlasek / Marc Rosset
Women's Doubles: Gigi Fernandez / Natalia Zvereva
Mixed Doubles: Arantxa Sanchez Vicario / Mark Woodforde

Wimbledon
Men's Singles: Andre Agassi
Women's Singles: Steffi Graf
Men's Doubles: John McEnroe / Michael Stich
Women's Doubles: Gigi Fernandez / Natalia Zvereva
Mixed Doubles: Larisa Savchenko Neiland / Cyril Suk

U.S. Open
Men's Singles: Stefan Edberg
Women's Singles: Monica Seles
Men's Doubles: Jim Grabb / Richey Reneberg
Women's Doubles: Gigi Fernandez / Natalia Zvereva
Mixed Doubles: Nicole Provis / Mark Woodforde

In contrast, the French Open provided some of the finest moments and tightest matches of the year. Merely to qualify for an epic final against Graf, Seles twice had to rally from third-set deficits. The first of her comebacks occurred in the fourth round when she trailed No. 150 Akiko Kijimuta of Japan, 1-4, before running off five consecutive games for a 6-1, 3-6, 6-4 victory. Then, in the semi-finals, she was down 2-4 against the eminently more formidable Sabatini before putting her away, 6-3, 4-6, 6-4.

When it was over, the loser was dumbfounded. "She seemed tired and then suddenly she started hitting the ball very hard," Sabatini said. "I don't know where she got the power."

Graf also passed a critical test in the semi-finals by overcoming Sanchez Vicario, who had demolished the German, 6-0, 6-2, in similar circumstances a year earlier. The result was a final for which the Paris fans were clamoring.

Their match, the first between the two in more than a year, disappointed no one save the loser and her family. And even Graf conceded it was a remarkable experience after saving five championship points in Seles' 6-2, 3-6, 10-8 victory that consumed two hours and 43 minutes. "It definitely was a special match, no doubt about it," Graf said.

On the following day, second-seeded Courier joined Seles, a fellow Florida resident, halfway to a Grand Slam. In the Australian Open final, he avenged the blowout by Edberg in the 1991 U.S. Open four months earlier by beating the Swede, 6-3, 3-6, 6-4, 6-2. He celebrated the victory, which enabled him to leapfrog top-seeded Edberg to No. 1 in the rankings, by jumping into the nearby polluted Yarra River.

Courier displayed a destructive forehand and competitive verve to ascend to No. 1—the first of five changes at the top in 1992—to end nearly a seven-year drought for Americans since McEnroe was toppled from

No. 1 in mid-1985. At 21 years, five months, Courier was the third-youngest male to hold the No. 1 spot, after McEnroe (21 and 15 days) and Bjorn Borg (21 and two months). Yet, his elevation apparently failed to impress Agassi, with whom he had split matches in the two previous French Opens.

Once more, the pairings in Paris pitted the longtime rivals, this time in the semi-finals. Agassi, who had chased Sampras, carried the pre-match buildup by claiming that Courier's game was built on hard work and mental strength because "I don't think he has a lot of natural ability to fall back on." Courier saved his talk for after the match, which he won most convincingly, 6-3, 6-2, 6-2.

"I've been reading about how I don't have much talent," Courier said. "There are many different talents besides hitting a tennis ball. Having guts on the court is a talent; having desire is a talent; having courage to go for a shot when you are love-40 down is a talent. I may not hit the ball as cleanly as anybody out there, but I have got a few talents that are just as good as anybody else's."

Courier's triumph over Agassi pushed his winning streak to 22 matches, which he extended in the final by blasting seventh-seeded Czech, Petr Korda, 7-5, 6-2, 6-1. Unlike the women's final, the men offered little drama. Courier finished off his nervous opponent in one hour, 59 minutes. The normally free-swinging lefty Korda, who had never previously advanced beyond the third round of a Big Four event, had 49 unforced errors and nine double faults.

"I think I played big feet today," he said. "I tell you I was very nervous. My hand is still tight. I couldn't play my game. My body didn't work too much today."

Wimbledon, of course, represented a huge hurdle for Seles and Courier. Hard-hitting baseliners are not at home on grass. Neither had advanced beyond the quarter-finals in previous appearances.

Courier's quest and a 25-match streak came to an abrupt end in the third round when he stumbled against an obscure Russian, the No. 193-ranked Andrei Olhovskiy. That defeat opened the door for McEnroe, a first-round washout at the French who had gained impetus in what he said would be his last Wimbledon. In an engaging four-hour, nine-minute clash of aging ex-champs, No. 30 Mac beat No. 191 Patrick Cash, 6-7 (3-7), 6-4, 6-7 (1-7), 6-3, 6-2. Another old-boy champ saying goodbye, Connors, did it fast in his 20th Big W,

1992 CHAMPIONS AND LEADERS

Top Player Earnings: Men Michael Stich $2,777,411	**Davis Cup:** United States **Federation Cup:** Germany
Top Player Earnings: Women Monica Seles $2,622,352	**ATP World Championships,** **Frankfurt**
Year-End Number One Men: Jim Courier Women: Monica Seles	Boris Becker **Grand Slam Cup, Munich** Michael Stich
ITF World Champion Men: Jim Courier Women: Monica Seles	**Virginia Slims** **Championships, NYC** Monica Seles

a first-round loss to a Mexican lefty, No. 86 Luis Herrera. But Jimmy left behind the male wins record, 84 of 102 matches.

After beating David Wheaton and Olhovskiy, McEnroe won his eighth semi, over ninth-seeded Guy Forget. He had become the talk of London, and a crowd favorite at the tournament where so often he had played the boor. Awaiting him was another surprise. In the midst of a sour season, Agassi had managed to overcome his fear of grass to win five matches, most notably over three-time Wimbledon champ Becker in the quarters. The meeting of the old rebel and the young anarchist was a stunning development, enriched by their growing friendship. After being thrust together on the Davis Cup team, McEnroe and Agassi became occasional dinner companions, frequently practiced against each other, and were doubles sidekicks at the French, winning three matches to a quarter-final defeat.

Indeed, Agassi asked McEnroe for his advice on coping with the Wimbledon grass and the flattered former champion readily agreed. "We hit it off well," McEnroe said. "He's young, he's really inquisitive and he's very, very smart. He asks good questions."

Agassi learned his lessons well. The only help he needed from McEnroe on, fittingly, the Fourth of July, was a reminder to bow to the Duke and Duchess of Kent as he was departing the court after his commanding victory. The shaggy-haired American required only one hour, 51 minutes to cut down McEnroe, 6-4, 6-2, 6-3. Agassi, returning brilliantly, converted all seven break points he held, lost his serve only twice and was in control from the very first game, which McEnroe double-faulted away. McEnroe departed Wimbledon as he greeted it in 1977, a semi-finalist, compiling a 59-11 record for 14 visits.

On the other side of the draw the 'Incendiary I,' Goran Ivanisevic, was a skinny 6-foot-4 Croatian conflagration, the most prolific firer of aces the place had known. Seeded eighth, he had 17 aces in beating German Lars Koslowski, 34 over Mark Woodforde, 22 over Rosset, 27 over Lendl, 33 over Edberg and 36 in a semi-final win over Sampras, a battle of 20-year-old prodigies.

Ironically, maturity may have been Agassi's greatest advantage in the final. He failed to wither when confronted by Ivanisevic's serve, producing 37 more aces for a stunning tournament record total of 206. Andre failed to lose serve until the second game of the fourth set and

appeared much calmer than the easily-distracted Goran. The 22-year-old Yank persevered 6-7 (8-10), 6-4, 6-4, 1-6, 6-4 for his first major title.

At the moment of triumph, Andre, whose past displays had seemed as calculated as his television commercials ("Image is everything"), fell to his knees, sprawled face-first on the turf and appeared genuinely moved. "I've realized my dream of winning a Grand Slam tournament," he said. "To do it here is more than I could ever ask for."

Nor did McEnroe leave the All England Club empty-handed. Fitter and sharper than he had been in years, working with new coach Larry Stefanki, he teamed with Stich, the grass court whiz of 1991, to claim the men's doubles prize. Following the singles championship, unseeded Mac and Michael began a two-day defeating of fourth-seeded Americans Jim Grabb and Richie Reneberg. The match consumed a final-round record five hours and one minute, and was decided by a 36-game fifth set, Wimbledon's longest ultimate set. Stopped by darkness at 9:21 p.m., the fifth set was completed on the third Monday. Resuming at 13-13, it took 10 more games and 34 minutes to complete the result, 5-7, 7-6 (7-5), 3-6, 7-6 (7-5), 19-17. It was the last of McEnroe's 17 major titles, the 10th in doubles.

Seles was a lot more successful than Courier in her assault on the grass but she also endured greater frustration. The complaints about her grunting actually grew in volume and opponents joined in the controversy fueled by the tabloid press. Nathalie Tauziat of France raised the issue before her straight-set dismissal in the quarter-finals and Navratilova did her one better, reporting Seles to umpire Fran McDowell, who called her to the chair for an admonition in the midst of the ladies' semi-final. Seles still prevailed, 6-2, 6-7 (3-7), 6-4.

"It just gets loud and louder," Navratilova said. "You cannot hear the ball being hit... I know she is not doing it on purpose, but she can stop it on purpose."

That's exactly what Seles did in the final. She barely uttered a peep against Graf. Was she psyched out? Whether that was a cause or an effect of her listless performance was a matter for conjecture. The German woman was crisp and dominating from the outset, winning 6-2, 6-1. Although the match lasted 5-1/2 hours, rain delays meant only 58 minutes were devoted to tennis.

"I didn't want to think about it," the loser said of her sudden silence. "I just thought hopefully I can start [not grunting] somewhere, so I started here." Monica was stopped after winning five major singles titles and 41 matches in a row. Including doubles, it was her only loss in seven major finals.

Because she failed to participate in the 1991 Federation Cup, Seles was not eligible for the Olympic tournament. Neither were Navratilova and Sabatini. But Graf, who had helped Germany defeat Spain in the 1992 Federation Cup, arrived for Barcelona clay in pursuit of a second consecutive gold medal. She was one match away from a repeat of Seoul when beaten by Capriati in the final, 6-3, 3-6, 6-4. Capriati bubbled with delight on the medal stand. "I had chills the whole time," the youngster said. "Right now this means more to me than any of the Grand Slams."

The men's competition in intense heat on turgid courts produced bigger surprises. Five of the first six seeds— Courier, Edberg, Sampras, Becker and Chang— were gone by the end of the third round. The man of destiny became the Swiss Rosset, who drove the Spanish crowds to anguish by beating Spaniard Jordi Arrese, the 16th seed, in a five-hour, three minute final, 7-6 (7-2), 6-3, 3-6, 4-6, 8-6.

Becker and Stich combined to win the men's doubles for a unified German team over South Africa's Wayne Ferreira and Piet Norval. Ferreira-Norval were their nation's first medalists since 1960 in Rome. The unrelated Fernandez women, Gigi and Mary Joe, captured the gold medal in doubles for the U.S., beating hometowners Sanchez Vicario and Conchita Martinez.

In retrospect, Gigi Fernandez may have enjoyed the best season of any American woman. In addition to her Olympic honor, she teamed with Belarussian Natalia Zvereva of Minsk to win doubles championships at the French Open, Wimbledon and the U.S. Open. They had no Grand Slam opportunity since each had another partner at the Australian. Joining forces at the French, to

1992 OLYMPICS, BARCELONA, SPAIN

Men's singles: Marc Rosset, Switzerland, Gold; Jordi Arrese, Spain, Silver; Goran Ivanisevic, Croatia, Bronze; Andrei Cherkasov, Unified Team, Bronze
Women's singles: Jennifer Capriati, United States, Gold, Steffi Graf, Germany, Silver; Mary Joe Fernandez, United States, Bronze; Arantxa Sanchez Vicario, Spain, Bronze
Men's doubles: Boris Becker & Michael Stich, Germany, Gold; Wayne Ferreira & Piet Norval, South Africa, Silver; Goran Ivanisevic & Goran Prpic, Croatia, Bronze; Javier Frana & Christian Carlos Miniussi, Argentina, Bronze
Women's doubles: Gigi Fernandez & Mary Joe Fernandez, United States, Gold; Conchita Martinez & Arantxa Sanchez Vicario, Spain, Silver; Natalia Zvereva & Leila Meskhi, Unified Team, Bronze

win over Martinez and Sanchez Vicario, 6-3, 6-2, they would become one of the finest teams in history, amassing 14 majors through 1997.

At Flushing Meadow, Navratilova suffered a shocking second-round defeat administered by No. 17 Magdalena, the third of the three Maleeva sisters on the circuit. One year after she became the oldest woman's major finalist in the open era, she was ousted by a 17-year-old precisely half her age, 6-4, 0-6, 6-3. It marked her earliest exit from the Open since 1976 when she departed in tears following a first-round knockout by Janet Newberry at Forest Hills.

Shocking, too, was Olympic champ Capriati's third-round departure courtesy of petite Cambodian-born Canadian citizen, No. 36 Patricia Hy, 7-5, 6-4. Hy then beat former finalist, 13th- seeded Sukova, 6-1, 7-5, to stand out as the lone Cambodian to go so far, and the second Canadian (Carling Bassett made the quarters in 1984). That was far enough. Seles beat her, 6-1, 6-2. In other quarters, Graf lost to Sanchez Vicario and Sabatini lost to Mary Joe Fernandez, clearing the last major obstacles from Seles' path. She cakewalked to the title without the loss of a set, turning back Fernandez in a semi-final and Sanchez Vicario in the final, 6-3, 6-3.

The men had much greater difficulty settling their differences. They played from here to 'Infiniti,' which happened to be the corporate sponsor of the men's singles. Although all four top seeds reached the semis, it was not without a struggle.

Seldom, if ever, had a champion labored longer for his silver and gold than Edberg. Of the 21 five-set matches recorded, he played three—in a row over Richard Krajicek, Lendl, Chang—that were among the six matches that consumed over four hours. The five hours, 26 minutes epic against Chang, 6-7 (3-7), 7-5, 7-6 (7-3), 5-7, 6-4, was the longest match of either's life, and the longest of all major matches, outdoing the 5:12 two-day Wimbledon siege that Pancho Gonzalez won over Charlie Pasarelli in 1969. Stefan's last four steps to his second title took 19 sets, one under the maximum, a journey such as taken by only one other U.S. champ, Bob Wrenn in 1896. There was no breathing room until Stefan won the final, 6-3, 4-6, 7-6 (7-5), 6-2, in a steadfast performance of only two hours, 52 minutes as Sampras came apart.

Sampras had gunned down top-seeded Courier, 6-1, 3-6, 6-2, 6-2, in the semis, and then went down himself, racing to the bathroom with stomach problems. Had

Pete beaten Edberg, Americans would have possessed all four major championships for the first time since Don Budge did it singlehandedly in 1938. Their last triple was accomplished by Connors (Australian, Wimbledon, U.S.) in 1974.

Edberg lost his place at the top of the computer in the fall and failed a final opportunity at the ATP World Championship when he was eliminated in preliminary round-robin play by losses to Sampras and Becker. Nevertheless, Edberg finished the season as the leader in official earnings, with $2,341,804.

Of course, Stich almost equaled that total in one December weekend. Although he plummeted from the Top 10, the German managed to regain his singles form in time for the Grand Slam Cup in Munich, where he won the first-place prize of $2 million by defeating Chang in the final, 6-2, 6-3, 6-2. Semi-finalist Ivanesevic belted 25 aces while losing to Chang, ending the year with a record 1,017.

The men's season was notable for two other developments. Lendl posted his 1,000th tour victory, second only to Connors, by beating Brett Stevens of New Zealand at the Sydney indoor championships in October, and Borg, 36, failed to capture a set in eight matches of a murky comeback attempt. The legend did, however, win his first tournament of any kind since 1981 when he handled Roscoe Tanner, 6-4, 6-1, at the Advanta Tour of Chicago for players 35 and older.

The 'Woodies,' the Australian duo of Todd Woodbridge and Mark Woodforde won eight doubles titles, including their own, over Americans Kelly Jones and Rick Leach, plus the ATP World Championship in Johannesburg over the Aussie-Swedish hookup of John Fitzgerald and Anders Jarryd.

Among the women, Navratilova pledged to continue playing a full schedule through 1993 but she ended the 12-year doubles partnership with Pam Shriver in order to concentrate on singles. After 79 titles, 20 majors—all four in 1984 for a Grand Slam—plus 10 trips to the winner's circle at the Virginia Slims Championship, they went their separate ways following the season-ending event at Madison Square Garden. The defending champions lost a semi-final to the Spanish-Czech yoking of Sanchez Vicario and Helena Sukova, the eventual champs.

1993

Wimbledon, U.S. Open to Sampras, Graf

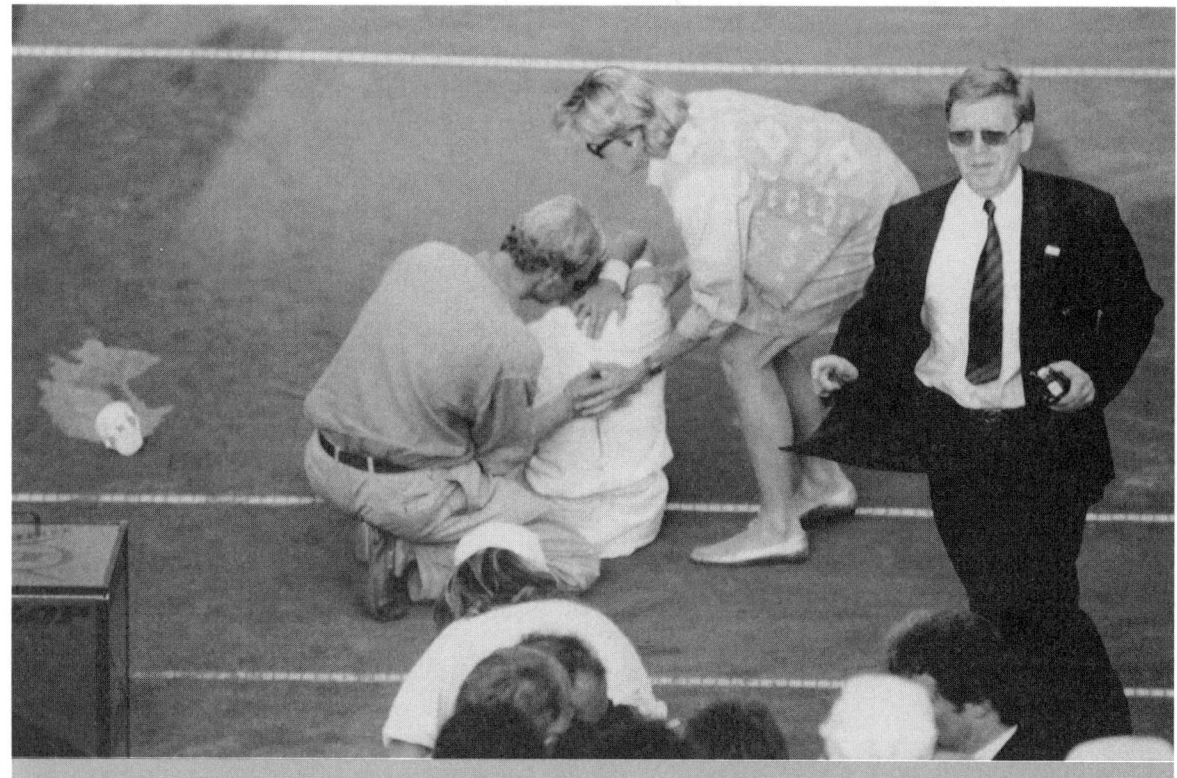

Monica Seles A dark day in Hamburg, and 28 months away from the game.

Seemingly it was just another April afternoon in Hamburg, Germany. Monica Seles found herself engaged in a Citizen Cup quarter-final on the slow red clay against Bulgarian Magdalena Maleeva. The 19-year-old left-hander was sitting at a changeover, holding a 6-4, 4-3 lead, hoping to use this tournament to propel her toward a fourth consecutive French Open championship beginning the following month.

But then, suddenly, a deranged German named Guenther Parche emerged from the stands and stabbed Seles in the back with a nine-inch boning knife. The world No. 1 was carried off the court and rushed to the hospital. The physical harm from this tragic moment was not terribly damaging, but the psychological scars would stay with her for some time to come. She wouldn't return to competition until nearly 28 months later.

The Seles Saga was without question the most significant story of 1993, transcending the sport, reminding everyone that even in the relatively tranquil world of tennis, random acts of violence could take place. The game triumphed on a number of other levels, with a surging Pete Sampras and a stalwart Steffi Graf setting the pace, establishing themselves as the top-ranked players for the year.

Sampras captured the two most prestigious titles,

collecting his first major crown in nearly three years when he won Wimbledon, then concluding a remarkable summer with a second U.S. Open triumph. Graf secured three of the four biggest crowns, sweeping her third French Open, her fifth Wimbledon, and her third U.S. Open. Beyond that, the 22-year-old American and the 24-year-old German were prolific winners across the board on the men's and women's tours.

Sampras was victorious in eight of 23 tournaments, finishing with an impressive 85-16 (.841) match record, posting a 19-match winning streak in the spring. Graf won 10 of 15 tournaments and 76 of 82 matches for an astounding .927 winning percentage. Only once in her last nine tournament appearances was Graf beaten, suffering one other loss in Federation Cup. Graf garnered the season-ending Virginia Slims Championship at New York's Madison Square Garden while Sampras got to the final of the ATP Tour Championships in Frankfurt.

But neither Sampras nor Graf came through in the first of the season's premier events. Jim Courier, the No. 1-ranked player in the world for 1992, successfully defended in the Australian Open final, defeating Stefan Edberg, 6-2, 6-1, 2-6, 7-5, a rematch of the previous year. Courier's crackling backhand returns off Edberg's renowned kick serve were too much for the stylish Swede. Edberg had eliminated Sampras in one semi, while Courier beat Michael Stich in the other. Ex-champs Boris Becker, seeded fourth, and eighth-seeded Ivan Lendl both made early exits.

When Seles collided with Graf in the women's final at Melbourne, it marked the third time in the last four major events that the two superstars had battled in the final. Seles had somehow held back her chief adversary, 6-2, 3-6, 10-8, in the French Open in 1992 but then had been battered, 6-2, 6-1, in the Wimbledon final a month later. Now they had another bruising skirmish under a broiling sun.

Although Seles prevailed, 4-6, 6-3, 6-2, to extend her winning streak to three titles and 21 matches in a row at Flinders Park, the match was much closer than the score reflects. They produced one glorious rally after another, driving their groundstrokes with astonishing pace and precision, exploring every inch of the court, pushing each other to the hilt. It took a top-of-the-line Seles to get through this arduous struggle against an almost defiant Graf. On this occasion, the superior shotmaker beat the better athlete.

When all of the leading players assembled again at the world's premier clay court championship, Courier narrowly failed in his spirited bid to become the first American man ever to capture the French three years in a row. The 22-year-old Floridian played with immense pride and professionalism on a day when his primary weapon—the inside-out forehand—was often betraying him, and in the end the ungainly but wily and unwavering Spaniard Sergi Bruguera was too solid in a 6-4, 2-6, 6-2, 3-6, 6-3 victory. It was Bruguera's first major title and the first major for any Spaniard since Manolo Orantes won at Forest Hills in 1975.

Bruguera, 22, had ousted Sampras in the quarter-finals before dismissing the gifted Russian Andrei Medvedev in a semi-final. A man who had owned Roland Garros for three titles (1984, 86-87), seventh-seeded Lendl was taken out in the opening round of his 52nd major by a French qualifier, No. 297 Stephane Huet.

Graf, meanwhile, was far from the upper level of her game on her worst surface. She was bothered by a nagging foot injury and may have suffered in a strange way from the absence of Seles. But Steffi beat in succession Jennifer Capriati and countrywoman Anke Huber to be severely challenged in the final by fifth-seeded Mary Joe Fernandez, the popular American whom she had beaten in the final of the 1990 Australian Open. That had been a relatively uneventful straight-set skirmish with the issue seldom, if ever, in doubt; this one

---

1993 THE MAJOR CHAMPIONSHIPS

Australian Open
Men's Singles: Jim Courier
Women's Singles: Monica Seles
Men's Doubles: Danie Visser / Laurie Warder
Women's Doubles: Gigi Fernandez / Natalia Zvereva
Mixed Doubles: Arantxa Sanchez Vicario / Todd Woodbridge
French Open
Men's Singles: Sergi Bruguera
Women's Singles: Steffi Graf
Men's Doubles: Luke Jensen / Murphy Jensen
Women's Doubles: Gigi Fernandez / Natalia Zvereva
Mixed Doubles: Eugenia Maniokova / Andrei Olhovskiy
Wimbledon
Men's Singles: Pete Sampras
Women's Singles: Steffi Graf
Men's Doubles: Todd Woodbridge / Mark Woodforde
Women's Doubles: Gigi Fernandez / Natalia Zvereva
Mixed Doubles: Martina Navratilova / Mark Woodforde
U.S. Open
Men's Singles: Pete Sampras
Women's Singles: Steffi Graf
Men's Doubles: Ken Flach / Rick Leach
Women's Doubles: Arantxa Sanchez Vicario / Helena Sukova
Mixed Doubles: Helena Sukova / Todd Woodbridge

was a suspenseful showdown from beginning to end.

The 21-year-old from Miami, who had eliminated Gabriela Sabatini and 1989 French Open titlist Arantxa Sanchez Vicario, had never beaten Graf in 10 previous meetings. Fernandez seized the first set by virtue of her back court play, but lost her edge in the second as Graf gained control of the baseline exchanges and went on to a 4-6, 6-2, 6-4 triumph, winning at Roland Garros for the first time since 1988.

During Capriati's fourth round win over Mary Pierce, Mary's troublesome father, Jim Pierce, was removed from the stands by security guards, who said he was acting "violently," shoving other spectators and shouting at the players. Tournament management withdrew his credentials. It was the start of his being banned from the circuit, eventuating in Mary obtaining a restraining order against him.

On to Wimbledon. Sampras had taken over the No. 1 ranking back in April, but was still searching for his first major prize since the 1990 U.S. Open. A shoulder injury nearly kept him out of the tournament. But, ultimately, Sampras was ready to make his move.

In an all-American final held appropriately on the fourth of July, Sampras stopped a tenacious Courier, 7-6 (7-3), 7-6 (8-6), 3-6, 6-3. Sampras lost his serve only once in four sets. He was clearly the better grass-court player, but was also fortunate. The conclusion was not easy for Sampras. When he served for the match and reached 40-15, he crouched over in obvious pain with abdominal cramps. Courier saved the first match point, but Sampras sealed his title on the second.

"I was more nervous for this match than for any match I have ever played. I wanted that Wimbledon title, and I couldn't sleep the night before," Sampras said.

In the quarter-finals, he had ousted the seventh-seeded defending champion Andre Agassi in a captivating Centre Court skirmish witnessed by Agassi's renowned friend Barbra Streisand, who caused a considerable commotion when she walked into the celebrated cathedral of the sport. Feeding the Las Vegas glitz kid a barrage of soft sliced backhands and moderately paced forehands, robbing Agassi completely of his rhythm, Sampras stormed to a two-sets-to-love lead. But then Agassi blasted his way into the contest with some spectacular returns and stellar passing shots. It took stupendous serving and a cool head to pull Sampras through. Serving for the match at 5-4 in the fifth, he delivered three consecutive aces for 40-0 to firmly settle the issue.

Coming off that emotionally draining victory, Sampras had to deal with three-time former titlist, fourth-seeded Boris Becker in a semi-final. But Sampras didn't lose his serve in a convincing 7-6 (7-5), 6-4, 6-4 win. Third-seeded Courier's semi-final victim was the two-time champ, second-seeded Edberg, 4-6, 6-4, 6-2, 6-4. Surprising himself on the green, Jim got the attention of his mother in the stands, pointed to himself and mouthed, "Who, me?" For the first time since seedings were instituted in 1927, one-through-four made the final four.

The women's final featured Jana Novotna at the peak of her powers right up until the absolute crunch of her contest against the top-seeded Graf. After losing the first set, the 24-year-old Czech demonstrated unequalled completeness in the women's game. She attacked persistently and intelligently to win 10 of the next 12 games, building a 4-1 third-set lead. It seemed certain that eighth-seeded Novotna was going to secure her first major title. But then she fell apart and Graf came back for a 7-6 (8-6), 1-6, 6-4 victory that was surely a fortunate escape as Novotna flagrantly choked.

"The worst part for Novotna is not so much that she lost the final but that she gave it away, and that will be very hard to live with," said Ann Jones, the 1969 Wimbledon champion who called the match for BBC.

It was a lost opportunity of spectacular proportions for Novotna. She had performed with poise defeating Sabatini in the quarters and Martina Navratilova in the semis. For the 16th time in 21 Wimbledon appearances, Navratilova had reached the semi-final round, but she seemed ill at ease and out of sorts throughout her 6-4, 6-4 loss.

When the last major championship of the season, the U.S. Open, took place at Flushing Meadow, the No. 1 world ranking was on the line. It seemed likely that Courier and Sampras would meet in the final to settle the issue. Courier had appeared in the last three major

1993 CHAMPIONS AND LEADERS

Top Player Earnings: Men	**Davis Cup:** Germany
Pete Sampras $4,579,325	**Federation Cup:** Spain
Top Player Earnings: Women	**ATP World Championships,**
Steffi Graf $2,821,337	**Frankfurt**
Year-End Number One	Michael Stich
Men: Pete Sampras	**Grand Slam Cup, Munich**
Women: Steffi Graf	Petr Korda
ITF World Champion	**Virginia Slims**
Men: Pete Sampras	**Championships, NYC**
Women: Steffi Graf	Steffi Graf

finals, while Sampras had clearly picked up steam with his Wimbledon success. But that scenario was spoiled when Courier gave a desultory performance on a dark afternoon against the standout, yet erratic, Frenchman Cedric Pioline.

Pioline, the 15th seed, had never beaten Courier before. Only three weeks earlier in Indianapolis, Courier dispatched Pioline, 6-3, 6-4, on the way to winning that title over Becker. But here in the round of 16, Courier lost his intensity and couldn't find his range off the ground. He went down somewhat tamely, 7-5, 6-7 (4-7), 6-4, 6-4, only moments before rain arrived in the stadium. In every conceivable way, Courier had lost his timing.

Not so Sampras. He was stable and confident despite a wave of upsets surrounding him all through the tournament. In the final, Sampras overwhelmed Pioline, 6-4, 6-4, 6-3, for his second Open crown. He was a class above the 24-year-old Frenchman, serving too severely, returning with more authority and consistency.

Courier, the top seed, was not the only leading player who did not deliver. Joining him in the land of upsets were third-seeded Edberg, the two-time defending champion, who fell in the second-round; and fourth seed Becker, taken apart by Sweden's Magnus Larsson, in the third round. There were so many surprises that former Wimbledon semi-finalist Tim Mayotte could only conclude early in the second week of the event, "I have never, ever, ever seen anything like this here. Never."

The semi-finals included three players of lowly station: Unseeded Wally Masur and 14th and 15th seeds Aleksandr Volkov of Russia and Pioline. You had to search back to 1967 at Forest Hills to uncover a more common U.S. Championship crowd. Diminished to 13th seed, Lendl, once a final round fixture at Flushing, completed his worst season in the majors, one win at Wimbledon. Back pains contributed to his first-round U.S. loss, to Aussie Neil Borwick: 4-6, 6-4, 3-1 (injury default).

The women had some surprises of their own, but nothing to compare with the men. Graf won her third Open and her first since 1989, a 6-3, 6-3 triumph over 13th seed Helena Sukova, the 28-year-old Czech who had lost the 1986 final to Navratilova. Graf was too quick, confident and relaxed. She exploited her topspin backhand passing shot with inordinate success. It was hardly a contest.

Sukova had come from behind to startle her doubles partner, Sanchez Vicario in the semi-finals, toppling the second seed with her shrewd, attacking game plan. Sukova also knocked out the third-seeded Navratilova in the round of 16 with first rate serving-and-volleying. That match called to mind Sukova's upset of Martina in the 1984 Australian Open, preventing Martina from crafting a Grand Slam that year and also ending her open-era record 74 match-winning streak. Graf, meanwhile had trouble getting past Sabatini in the quarters and Manuela Maleeva Fragniere in the semis.

Despite the absence of Becker, Germany captured the Davis Cup with a 4-1 victory over Australia in Dusseldorf. The 1991 Wimbledon champion, Stich, led the charge with victories over Jason Stoltenberg and the icer over Richard Fromberg, 6-4, 6-2, 6-2. A superior accomplishment probably was the least expected, Stich joining Patrik Kuhnen to jar the world's foremost pair, Mark Woodforde and Todd Woodbridge, 7-6 (7-4), 4-6, 6-3, 7-6 (7-4).

Disappointingly, the U.S. had bowed out in the opening round, 4-1 to Australia on grass in Melbourne. This setback came shortly after the U.S. regained the Cup against Switzerland at the close of 1992 with a team of Agassi, Courier, Sampras and John McEnroe. None of those cared to make the trip Down Under, and the hosts virtually wrapped it up the first day before slight gatherings at Kooyong, a crowded bastion during the Aussies' glory days. But Agassi reappeared as the U.S. avoided a free-fall to the nether regions (as in 1987) in the September relegation match, a 5-0 win over the Bahamas at Charlotte, N.C., the last of Capt. Tom Gorman's U.S. record 16 victories.

Spain's accomplished duo of Sanchez Vicario and Conchita Martinez took apart the Australians in the Fed Cup final at Frankfurt, winning, 3-0. Conchita beat Michelle Jaggard-Lai, 6-0, 6-2, and Arantxa beat Nicole Provis, 6-2, 6-3. But Provis produced an astonishing upset in the opening round, a 2-1 win over Germany. Nicole—a semi-finalist at the French Open back in 1988—startled Graf, 6-4, 1-6, 6-1, in the upset of the year among the women. Liz Smylie and Rennae Stubbs won the decisive doubles over Huber and Barbara Rittner, 7-5, 4-6, 6-3.

Meanwhile, the Germans Graf and Stich came through to claim the singles crowns at the season-ending events in New York and Frankfurt. Graf got off to a good start and repelled a challenge from Sanchez Vicario in the Virginia Slims final, prevailing 6-1, 6-4, 3-6, 6-1.

Stich had his most impressive win of the year when he overturned Sampras in the final of the ATP Tour Championships. Serving seven consecutive aces over two service games in the fourth set, Stich surprised the American, 7-6 (7-3), 2-6, 7-6 (9-7), 6-2, to conclude a terrific late-season surge and move past Courier to No. 2 in the year-end rankings.

All in all, it was a captivating year. In 88 ATP Tour events, 45 different champions surfaced. Americans accounted for 27 of those titles, with no other nation coming close to that total. On another statistical note, Sampras' superiority as a server was reflected emphatically in his tour-leading numbers. He served no fewer than 1,011 aces in 94 charted matches, more than 200 beyond the total of anyone else. He held serve 90 percent of the time and won 82 percent of his first serve points.

Meanwhile, the exuberant combination of Gigi Fernandez and Natasha Zvereva came within two matches of a Grand Slam in doubles, a feat realized only by Navratilova and Pam Shriver in 1984. Fernandez-Zvereva took the Australian over the Aussie-American lineup of Liz Sayers Smylie and Shriver; and both the French and Wimbledon over the Latvian-Czech combo, Larisa Savchenko Neiland and Novotna. They climbed all the way to the penultimate round of the U.S. Open only to have their Slam bid halted by Sukova and Sanchez Vicario. Arantxa and Helena took that title, 6-4, 6-2, over the Argentine-South Africa splicing of Gorrochategui and Amanda Coetzer.

The men's doubles majors were divided four ways. The most extraordinary result occurred at the French where the frequently comedic American brothers, unseeded Murphy and ambidextrous Luke Jensen, settled down to beat also unseeded Germans Marc Goellner and David Prinosil. They were the second fraternal victors, following Americans Gene and Sandy Mayer in 1978. Ken Flach, winner of three majors with Robert Seguso, had a new accomplice, lefty Rick Leach, a blending of U.S. Davis Cuppers in taking the homeland title over Czechs Martin Damm and Karel Novacek. The Aussie 'Woodies,' Woodforde and Woodbridge, started their run of success (six titles) at Wimbledon defeating a North American combo, American Pat Galbraith and Canadian Grant Connell. But the Australian title went to South African Danie Visser with homeboy Laurie Warder over the Aussie-Swedish pair of John Fitzgerald and Anders Jarryd.

Bjorn Borg's brief, fruitless comebacks were over. He played three more tourneys, and the closest he came to winning a match was his definite farewell to the big league in a town he was visiting for the first time, Moscow. A match point was yanked away by Aleksandr Volkov, who beat him, 4-6, 6-3, 7-6 (9-7), in the Kremlin Cup's first round.

Ultimately, beyond all of the positive developments in 1993, looking past the traumatic experience of Seles, the tennis world mourned the loss of one of its most remarkable leaders. On February 6, Arthur Ashe died of AIDS complications at 49. A singularly revered statesman and spokesman, unofficial worldwide ambassador for the sport, always a voice of reason and integrity, Ashe left behind a shining legacy.

The winner of the first U.S. Open in 1968, Australian Open titlist two years later, and a dignified Davis Cup player and captain for his country, Ashe had enjoyed the crowning moment of his career in 1975 when he toppled the mighty Jimmy Connors, 6-1, 6-1, 5-7, 6-4, with a strategic masterpiece in the Wimbledon final.

1994

Poignant good-bye for Martina, Lendl

Aranxta Sanchez Vicario
Tenacity to spare, French and U.S. Open wins, and the No. 1 ranking.

As the curtain closed on 1994, two of the greatest players in the history of the game retired simultaneously, taking unparalleled accomplishments with them and leaving with few regrets. Martina Navratilova had planned her departure from singles events nearly a year earlier and realized this would be her final campaign. Ivan Lendl had no intention of quitting, but a nagging back injury forced him to step permanently away from the sport he had dominated with pride and professionalism.

Lendl had little to show for his last year on the ATP Tour. He finished with a mediocre 28-18 match record, reaching only one final in Sydney, losing that to Pete Sampras, sinking to No. 54 in the year-end rankings. In his last match as a professional, he walked off the court in the second round at the U.S. Open, his back causing him too much pain to continue. As Lendl left the stadium that afternoon, no one had a clue he wouldn't return. Defeating Aussie Neil Borwick in the first round, 7-5, 6-2, 6-3, Ivan registered the last of his 1,070 professional singles wins.

But he was 34, his best days clearly behind him. When the year came to an end, he acknowledged that he would no longer compete. He had amassed a career prize-money total of $21,624,417. He had been ranked No. 1 in the world a record 270 weeks in all, including 157 weeks in a row during one stretch, on top at year's end four times (1985, '86, '87, '89). From 1981 through 1992 he was never out of the first five. He had appeared in a Tilden-tying record eight consecutive U.S. finals (1982–89), winning the tournament three times during that span. He had captured three French Opens, two Australian Opens and had twice been a Wimbledon finalist. Altogether, he won 94 singles titles, second to Jimmy Connors' 109 for the open era.

Navratilova lived along the same lines of achievement, but was more of a force in what she said would be her final year. Three months before she turned 38, she reached her 12th Wimbledon singles final, only to fall narrowly short of a 10th title. Nevertheless, she concluded the year at No. 8 in the world, celebrating her 20th consecutive season among the Top Ten. Remarkably, 1994 was the only time in that span that Navratilova failed to finish a year in the Top Five.

She was nine times the Wimbledon singles champion, collecting four U.S. Open titles, three Australian, and two French. She won an open-era record 167 singles titles, was ranked No. 1 in the world for a total of 332 weeks, concluding seven seasons on top of the charts. And in one nearly impeccable stretch, she enjoyed five years on the edge of invincibility, winning 44 of 50 tournaments from 1982 through 1986, taking 254 of 260 matches, and setting a modern record with her 74-match winning streak in 1984. Her career match record was 1,438-212 (.872). Both she and Lendl were headed for the International Tennis Hall of Fame.

And yet, while the departures of Lendl and Navratilova—she would continue to play top-flight doubles and mixed doubles as recently as 2003, winning the Australian mixed that year with Indian Leander Paes—were significant, there were other prominent stories.

In the women's game, the effervescent Arantxa Sanchez Vicario came of age at 23. Heading into the 1994 campaign, she had secured only one of the major championships, at Roland Garros five years earlier. In 1994, the cunning baseliner was the only woman to win

1994 THE MAJOR CHAMPIONSHIPS

Australian Open
Men's Singles: Pete Sampras
Women's Singles: Steffi Graf
Men's Doubles: Jacco Eltingh / Paul Haarhuis
Women's Doubles: Gigi Fernandez / Natalia Zvereva
Mixed Doubles: Larisa Savchenko Neiland / Andrei Olhovskiy
French Open
Men's Singles: Sergi Bruguera
Women's Singles: Arantxa Sanchez Vicario
Men's Doubles: Byron Black / Jonathan Stark
Women's Doubles: Gigi Fernandez / Natalia Zvereva
Mixed Doubles: Kristie Boogert / Menno Oosting
Wimbledon
Men's Singles: Pete Sampras
Women's Singles: Conchita Martinez
Men's Doubles: Todd Woodbridge / Mark Woodforde
Women's Doubles: Gigi Fernandez / Natalia Zvereva
Mixed Doubles: Helena Sukova / Todd Woodbridge
U.S. Open
Men's Singles: Andre Agassi
Women's Singles: Arantxa Sanchez Vicario
Men's Doubles: Jacco Eltingh / Paul Haarhuis
Women's Doubles: Arantxa Sanchez Vicario / Jana Novotna
Mixed Doubles: Elna Reinach / Patrick Galbraith

two majors, capturing a second French Open crown and sealing a first U.S. Open championship.

Although Steffi Graf would remain at No. 1 at year's end, most experts accorded the less talented but incomparably tenacious Spaniard the top ranking, including the ITF. The game's venerable governing body named Sanchez Vicario as their official 'World Champion' for 1994 over Graf, an assessment based on Sanchez Vicario's greater accumulation of Virginia Slims points.

But both the ITF and keen analysts among the media based their belief in Sanchez Vicario's preeminence primarily on her outstanding showing in the majors. Meanwhile, Steffi did seize a fourth consecutive major singles title at the start of the season, gaining a fourth Australian Open championship. But it became a year of unexpected diversity after that, with Sanchez Vicario posting her two big triumphs and her countrywoman Conchita Martinez breaking through at Wimbledon for her only major success.

As was the case with the women, three different men took the top prizes. Pete Sampras won the Australian Open for the first time and won Wimbledon again. Sergi Bruguera held on stubbornly to his French Open title. And then a resurgent Andre Agassi captured the championship of his country, at long last the boss at the U.S. Open.

The season started with the favorites flowing Down Under. Sampras had missed two of the previous three Australian Opens with injuries, and was appearing at Flinders Park for only the fourth time. But the deeply driven American proceeded to register a third major championship in a row, becoming the first man since Rod Laver in the Australian's Grand Slam campaign of 1969 to pull off this hat trick of sorts. Sampras stopped his countryman and golfing buddy Todd Martin in the final, overcoming a cautious start to win comfortably, 7-6 (7-4), 6-4, 6-4.

Graf was close to letter perfect in her 6-0, 6-2 dismantling of Sanchez Vicario in the women's final, driving her formidable forehand with depth and accuracy and serving with overwhelming power and precision. Both the top-seeded German and the second seed from Spain were clear-cut semi-final victors, Graf upending 10th seed Kimiko Date of Japan and Sanchez Vicario dismissing Gabriela Sabatini. Date's final four appearance was the best major finish for a Japanese woman.

When the best players came to Roland Garros for the

French Open, there were many pieces of intrigue spread out across the clay court capital of the world. But above and beyond anyone else, it was Mary Pierce's tournament. The 19-year-old citizen of France, born in Montreal and raised in Florida, blitzed through the draw with ease, hitting her lethal groundstrokes with a velocity seldom, if ever, seen in the women's game.

On her way to a first appearance in a major final, Pierce conceded a mere ten games in six matches. The 12th seed was picking everyone apart meticulously. Even the great Graf couldn't contain her. In a dazzling display in the penultimate round, Pierce toppled the top seed, 6-2, 6-2. In eight service games, Graf was broken a staggering six times, seldom looking so helpless. It was arguably the single most potent performance by a woman all year long, reminiscent in some ways of the absent champ, Monica Seles.

Pierce's remarkable run was suitably noticed by her rivals. As Lindsay Davenport said, "Even Monica couldn't destroy Steffi Graf the way Mary did. It's amazing what Mary has done, great for our game. This is just what we needed, not another Steffi French Open."

But then reality set in for the final. Facing 1989 champion Sanchez Vicario (a semis winner over Martinez), Pierce was forced to sit around all afternoon, waiting for the rain to stop. They finally started at 6:22 p.m., but had to stop when it rained again with Sanchez Vicario serving at 1-2 and a break point down in the first set. When they returned at noon the next day, the pendulum swung decidedly. Pierce self destructed and the Spaniard won, 6-4, 6-4.

As for the men, Sampras saw his 25-match winning streak in majors end at the hands of Courier in the quarter-finals. The week before Roland Garros, Sampras' career-high 29 match-winning streak had come to an end in the World Team Cup against Michael Stich. Despite winning the Italian Open over Boris Becker, Pete didn't seem to believe it was his time to rule on the Parisian clay. Courier, close to the top of his game, defeated Sampras for only the third time in 13 career meetings.

But for the second year in a row, Courier couldn't cope with an imperturbable Bruguera. With the wind blowing fiercely, the defending champion used the adverse conditions to his advantage, while Courier sprayed his groundstrokes dismally out of court. Bruguera won, 6-3, 5-7, 6-3, 6-3, and then handled his unorthodox countryman Alberto Berasategui, 6-3, 7-5,

2-6, 6-1, to keep his French crown.

At Wimbledon, Sampras reaffirmed his status as the best player in the world, losing only a single set in seven matches, setting the record straight with his troublesome adversary Goran Ivanisevic. In 1992, Ivanisevic had stopped Sampras in a four-set semi-final, but this time the American prevailed, 7-6 (7-2), 7-6 (7-5), 6-0, in the final.

Ivanisevic had demoralized Sampras in their 1992 meeting when he released 36 aces over four sets. The towering left-handed Croat came at Sampras with full force again in this battle, banging 16 aces in the first set alone, but Sampras came through in the two tie-breakers and then glided through the third as his opponent surrendered.

The women's Wimbledon was turned upside down on a dark and rainy Tuesday afternoon. Graf was a firm favorite to win her fourth crown in a row, a sixth overall. But she drew the dangerous Lori McNeil in the first round and didn't survive. The 30-year-old from Houston—a U.S. Open semi-finalist to Graf seven years earlier and a first-rate grass court player—produced one of the most significant upsets in the history of the tournament, holding her nerve admirably through two rain delays, to win 7-5, 7-6 (7-5).

Never before in the history of the world's most prestigious tournament had the women's No. 1 seed and defending champion fallen in the first round. And not since the 1984 U.S. Open had Graf made a first-round exit from a major. Graf's startling departure opened up windows everywhere in that half of the draw, and ultimately third-seeded Martinez exploited the opportunity. She crafted an unprecedented run of four consecutive three-set wins to take the title, halting Navratilova with a flock of backhand passers, 6-4, 3-6, 6-3, in the final.

Their 1:59 showdown on a sweltering afternoon was easily the most compelling female major final of the year. It was Martina's 22nd and last appearance as a singles competitor. When it was over, she took some blades of Centre Court grass with her, and then paid proper tribute to the magnificent counter-attacking of her rival. "No one has ever passed me better off the backhand than Conchita did today," she asserted.

Through the end of Wimbledon, Sampras had won eight of his 12 tournaments and was thoroughly dominating the game. But over the summer he hardly competed as tendinitis flared up in his ankle after a Davis Cup loss to Richard Krajicek at Rotterdam. Sampras didn't play a single hard-court tournament on the way to the Open.

That set the stage for an unpredictable tournament. Picked off in the first round were second-seeded Ivanisevic (by No. 68, hulking German, Markus Zoecke) and seventh-seeded ex-champ Becker (by No. 48 Richey Reneberg). In the fourth round, Sampras, the top-seeded champ, came in cold and lost gamely on blistered feet during a scorching afternoon to Peruvian Jaime Yzaga. His defeat made many men believe in their chances, but it was an unseeded American who sensed better than anyone else what was entirely possible.

The 1992 Wimbledon champion, Agassi, was ranked a deceptively low No. 20 in the world because he had started his season in March after wrist surgery the previous December. But, like the last unseeded U.S. victor, Fred Stolle, way back in 1966, Andre had too outstanding a dossier to be considered an upstart. In a record run, Andre knocked out five seeds on his way to the Open crown that eluded him in the 1990 final.

It began with 12th Wayne Ferreira, continued with sixth-seeded Michael Chang, and included 13th Thomas Muster and 9th Martin, setting up a final with Stich, the fourth seed. Stich was appearing in his first major final since his stunning run through Wimbledon three years earlier. But on the Flushing hard courts he couldn't stay with Agassi. Stich's first serve and agility around the net were more than neutralized by Agassi's incomparable return of serve and passing shots in the American's 6-1, 7-6 (7-5), 7-5 triumph.

Cheered on by his actress companion, Brooke Shields, Agassi didn't lose serve, allowing Stich 13 points in 14 service games. Agassi won 69 of 89 points on serve, not because he was hurting Stich severely with his serve, but because he dominated the baseline exchanges. Agassi was utterly in control of the rallies.

The women's final was a stirring clash between Graf and Sanchez Vicario. The two leading players had won one major apiece in 1994. Furthermore, Sanchez Vicario had already stopped Graf twice during the year, in finals at Hamburg and the Canadian Open. Now they were at it again on a hard court and Sanchez Vicario won again, 1-6, 7-6 (7-3), 6-4, in a stirring match that lasted two hours, seven minutes.

Graf raced through a 22-minute first set and, in the second, had a break point for 5-4, and might have served for the title if she hadn't missed a backhand return. But Steffi looked apprehensive—a trainer had come on court to treat her painful back after the ninth game—and Arantxa was accelerating. Even though Graf saved three set points to 5-5, and had a 3-2 lead in the tie-breaker with two serves to come, the bouncy Spaniard closed in a five-point rush. The duo kept breaking each other in the tumultuous third, cheered by 21,045 witnesses. But, holding to 4-3, Steffi couldn't resist the scrambling Arantxa, who hung on to take the rest of the games.

Although the German remained safely ahead of Sanchez Vicario in the race for No. 1, this enormously important match convinced the cognoscenti that Sanchez Vicario was now the best player in the world.

In autumn, the long-awaited professional debut of 14-year-old Venus Williams captivated the public. Having been away from even junior tournaments for three years, the tall and talented African American made her first professional appearance as a wild card in Oakland. She upended Shaun Stafford, 1988 National Intercollegiate champ for Florida, in her first-rounder, 6-3, 6-4, and then bolted to a stunning 6-2, 3-1 lead against Sanchez Vicario. The Spaniard needed all of her renowned guile and match-playing experience to pull through, 2-6, 6-3, 6-0. But Williams had demonstrated that she would be a serious force in the years ahead.

A month earlier, another celebrated coming-out party for a 14-year-old occurred in Zurich. Swiss Martina Hingis (three months younger than Venus and named after Martina Navratilova) was a more familiar figure than Venus, having won international junior titles from age 12. Also a wild card entry in her pro debut, she beat American Intercollegiate champ Patty Fendick before losing to second-seeded Pierce, 6-4, 6-0.

At the end of the season, it was time for Sampras to step forward again and underline his greatness. Having been hobbled by injuries too often in the second half of the year, he won the ATP Tour World Championship in Frankfurt to remain No. 1 for the second straight year.

1994 CHAMPIONS AND LEADERS

Top Player Earnings: Men
Pete Sampras $4,857,812
Top Player Earnings: Women
Arantxa Sanchez Vicario
$2,943,665
Year-End Number One
Men: Pete Sampras
Women: Steffi Graf
ITF World Champion
Men: Pete Sampras
Women: Arantxa Sanchez Vicario

Davis Cup: Sweden
Federation Cup: Spain
ATP World Championships, Frankfurt
Pete Sampras
Grand Slam Cup, Munich
Magnus Larrson
Virginia Slims Championships, New York
Gabriela Sabatini

After overcoming a surging Agassi in a hotly contested semi-final, Sampras reversed a loss to Becker in the round robin by besting the German, 4-6, 6-3, 7-5, 6-4. Sampras had won his 10th tournament of the year, a feat last realized by Lendl in 1989.

That same November week at New York's Madison Square Garden, Sabatini came out of a long slump to capture the Virginia Slims Championship. She crushed Davenport, 6-3, 6-2, 6-4, in the final for her first tournament win since the 1992 Italian Open. The 24-year-old 'Divine Argentine' had opened the week with an emotional 6-4, 6-2 victory over Navratilova in Martina's last singles appearance. It was 'Martina Navratilova Night' in the Garden as a banner bearing her name was hoisted to the rafters.

Meanwhile, there was one more big-money event left for the men, the Grand Slam Cup in Munich, and Sweden's Magnus Larsson took it. The multi-faceted 24-year-old ousted Agassi in the quarter-finals, Martin in the semis and, in the final, singed Sampras, 7-6 (8-6), 4-6, 7-6 (7-5), 6-4.

Larsson, an intimidating 6-foot-5 blond basher, collected $1,500,000, but he would be prouder of his role in helping to bring Sweden its fifth Davis Cup, defeating Russia in the final in Moscow. The Russians were first-time finalists, having astonishingly sabotaged Germany in Hamburg, 4-1. With President Boris Yeltsin in attendance at Moscow's cavernous Olympic Stadium, the home side, led by the brilliant 20-year-old Yevgeny Kafelnikov—who rose from No. 103 to No. 11 within a year—had a wonderful chance. But the Swedes were more composed in the crunch, winning the first three matches in a 4-1 decision. In singles, Edberg defeated lefty Aleksandr Volkov and Larsson beat Kafelnikov, setting up a Cup-clinching doubles win for Jan Apell and Jonas Bjorkman over Kafelnikov and Andrei Olhovskiy

Sweden had defeated the U.S. in a semi-final after rookie Capt. Tom Gullikson called on a worn-out Sampras. Clearly not fit, Sampras barely got through the first day, defeating Larsson, 6-7 (3-7), 6-4, 6-2, 7-6 (7-3), and then defaulted with a calf injury to Edberg after losing the first set. Still, the U.S. led 2-1 when Apell and Bjorkman, the ATP world doubles champs, and 4-0 in Cup play, kept it alive with a 6-4, 6-4, 3-6, 6-2 win over rookies Jared Palmer and Jonathan Stark. Sweden then clinched the victory, 3-2, when Larsson defeated Martin in four sets.

Spain, in the lively persons of Sanchez Vicario and Martinez, ruled the women's world again, beating the U.S. 3-0 in the Federation Cup finale. Neither singles starter came close in the worst of all American beatings (14 games): Davenport lost to Arantxa and Mary Joe Fernandez to Conchita as the Spaniards, enjoying Frankfurt clay, seized their third Cup. As icing, Arantxa and Conchita beat the two Fernandez's, 6-3, 6-4.

1995

Sampras vs. Agassi as good as it gets

Pete Sampras
A loss to Andre Agassi in Melbourne, revenge at Flushing Meadow.

All year long, they went at it in a genuine battle for supremacy. They met in the first major final of the season and again in the last. Their contrasting playing styles and personalities gave the game a spark that had been missing. To be sure, this was a rivalry between two great players devoid of animosity toward each other. But the fact remained that both Pete Sampras and Andre Agassi shared the same goals and knew that more often than not they would need to go through each other to get what they wanted. That meant competing on a very lofty level, which the two Americans emphatically did over and over again.

In the end, it was Sampras who demonstrated beyond a doubt that he was the better big-match player despite losing three of his five skirmishes with his countryman. Agassi had come out of the blocks in style at the Australian Open, overcoming the defending champion Sampras in a hard-fought, four-set final. Sampras retaliated at Indian Wells, Calif. Agassi struck back at The Lipton at Key Biscayne, Fla., and then he subdued Sampras again to take the Canadian Open.

By the time the two best players in the world reached the final of the U.S. Open in September, they were not deceiving themselves in the least. They knew precisely what was at stake, fully recognized the magnitude of the moment. With Sampras having won Wimbledon two months earlier and Agassi boasting a record of decidedly more consistency, this was the closest tennis could come to a heavyweight championship of the world. And when it was over, only Sampras was still standing, a four-set winner over his worthiest rival, and now the holder of the two most prestigious prizes in tennis.

And yet, the year provided drama on other levels. At Wimbledon, the volatile left-handed American Jeff Tarango confronted Germany's Alex Mronz in a third-round match on an outside court. Mronz had won the first set in a tie-break, then fell behind early in the second. Umpire Bruno Rebeuh overruled on a service call which was questioned by Tarango. The crowd came down on Tarango, with some of the fans yelling at him, prompting Tarango to respond: "Shut up!"

Rebeuh gave Tarango a code violation for "audible obscenity," a very questionable decision in light of Tarango's relatively tame comment. Tarango was losing control now, and called Rebeuh "corrupt." The umpire then assessed a point penalty against Tarango, which cost Tarango a game. Tarango asked for a supervisor, who stuck by Rebeuh's decisions. Tarango then walked off the court.

As if that was not extraordinary theater in itself, Tarango's wife, Benedicte, went after Rebeuh, catching up to the umpire near the referee's office and slapping him a couple of times according to an eyewitness.

On to the interview room, where, Tarango disgraced himself even more with a rambling press conference, elaborating on his ludicrous charge of "corruption" against Rebeuh. He was fined $5,000 for walking off the court, $10,000 for his insulting remarks about Rebeuh, and another $500 for his "shut up" stance against the courtside crowd.

But the largely self-inflicted damage was not done. He was suspended from ATP Tour events for two weeks later in the year, and fined $20,000, a figure upheld by the ATP. Furthermore, Tarango was banned from Wimbledon the following year for his actions.

Beyond the Tarango happening and the Sampras-Agassi rivalry, the game welcomed back a superstar, a player of inimitable shotmaking skills, a champion who realized that the time had come for her to put the past behind her and get on with her future. Monica Seles did just that, did it as only she can, and made a remarkable return to tennis.

Still trying to sort out that horrific moment in April 1993 when she had been stabbed in Hamburg, she had taken a long time to recover emotionally. Now she was ready at last, and the 21-year-old made a spectacular return in Toronto. She had been gone almost 28 months but there was scant evidence of that as she resumed her winning ways immediately.

Cracking groundstrokes with her customary authority, moving opponents around at will, competing with unabashed joy, she rolled through the field at the Canadian Open, dropping only 14 games in five matches, routing Gabriela Sabatini, 6-1, 6-1, in the semi-finals, crushing Amanda Coetzer in a lopsided final, 6-0, 6-1. She was nearly as impressive at the U.S. Open and, despite losing a rousing final to Steffi Graf, she remained on top of her game. But tendinitis in her knee and an ankle injury kept her out of action for the rest of the year.

It was a year which began with Mary Pierce delivering on the promise she had made the previous year as runner-up at the French Open. Having trained with dedication in the month leading up to the Australian Open, she was rewarded with her first major title. In seven nearly flawless matches, she did not drop a set; not once was she pushed beyond 6-4. She cut down a cluster of players who had given her serious problems in the past. Fourth-seeded, she halted Germany's Anke Huber in the round of 16, Natasha Zvereva in the quarters, second seed Conchita Martinez in the semi-finals, and then avenged her Roland Garros defeat by Arantxa Sanchez Vicario, toppling the top seed, 6-3, 6-2, in the final.

Mary had come a long way in a few years, enduring the pain of an abusive father, Jim Pierce, who was banned from all tournaments for his unruly behavior. But while she paid tribute to her then coach Nick Bollettieri for her breakthrough triumph in Melbourne, she also gave her father the credit she felt he deserved for the work ethic he instilled for Mary in the early years. As Pierce said after her Australian Open success, "I used to train all day long until the sun went down. My father

---

1995 THE MAJOR CHAMPIONSHIPS

Australian Open
Men's Singles: Andre Agassi
Women's Singles: Mary Pierce
Men's Doubles: Jared Palmer / Richey Reneberg
Women's Doubles: Jana Novotna / Arantxa Sanchez Vicario
Mixed Doubles: Natalia Zvereva / Rick Leach
French Open
Men's Singles: Thomas Muster
Women's Singles: Steffi Graf
Men's Doubles: Jacco Eltingh / Paul Haarhuis
Women's Doubles: Gigi Fernandez / Natalia Zvereva
Mixed Doubles: Larisa Savchenko Neiland / Mark Woodforde
Wimbledon
Men's Singles: Pete Sampras
Women's Singles: Steffi Graf
Men's Doubles: Todd Woodbridge / Mark Woodforde
Women's Doubles: Jana Novotna / Arantxa Sanchez Vicario
Mixed Doubles: Martina Navratilova / Jonathan Stark
U.S. Open
Men's Singles: Pete Sampras
Women's Singles: Steffi Graf
Men's Doubles: Todd Woodbridge / Mark Woodforde
Women's Doubles: Gigi Fernandez / Natalia Zvereva
Mixed Doubles: Meredith McGrath / Matt Lucena

pushed me very hard. In eight years, I probably did the equivalent of 15 years work. But I don't regret it. I have the discipline now, and I am a perfectionist."

Andre Agassi could have spoken almost identical words after the Australian, his second straight major title. He, too, had a father, Mike Agassi, who pushed him to the hilt, and now he was reaping the rewards of his tennis upbringing, not to mention his years of hard work at the Bollettieri boot camp, and strong strategic guidance alongside the brainy Brad Gilbert. Agassi beat Sampras, 4-6, 6-1, 7-6 (8-6), 6-4, in a remarkable final which was settled in the third-set tie-break. As Gilbert would say later, "I felt whoever won that tie-breaker would take control of the match."

For Agassi, who was in his first Australian Open, it was a landmark achievement. For Sampras, it was a stressful time. His coach and close friend Tim Gullikson had collapsed early in the tournament during a practice session, was sent to the hospital for tests, and had to fly home for treatment of a brain tumor before Sampras met Jim Courier in the quarter-finals.

Sampras bested Courier from two sets to love down, 6-7 (4-7), 6-7 (3-7), 6-3, 6-4, 6-3, in a classic, but not before a fan yelled out early in the final set, "Do it for your coach." That jarred the normally imperturbable Sampras, who broke down in tears at a changeover and continued to cry when he went to the opposite side of the court to serve the next game. But he somehow kept serving aces through his tears and got the job done. After Courier, he came from a set down to stop Michael Chang and reach the final, 6-7 (6-8), 6-3, 6-4, 6-4.

By the time the French Open had begun, Sampras himself was more vulnerable on the court than he had been for a long while. He had suffered a crisis of confidence on the European clay-court circuit, losing in the first round at the Italian. Pete's title passed on to Thomas Muster, who beat Sergi Bruguera, 3-6, 7-6 (7-5), 6-2, 6-3. Pete's feet of clay were on display at the French in a first-round loss spread over two days to an obscure Austrian, persistent No. 24 Gilbert Schaller.

Agassi, who had moved past Sampras to No. 1 on the weekly ATP computer in April, was a bigger threat to win on the slow red dirt of Roland Garros. He stormed into the quarter-finals without the loss of a set but then was ushered out of the tournament abruptly by the Russian Yevgeny Kafelnikov, 6-4, 6-3, 7-5. But Kafelnikov was no match for the relentlessly consistent left-handed Austrian, Muster, 6-4, 6-0, 6-4, who moved into his first major final with full conviction. Muster's self-assurance was more than justifiable. He would win 65 of 67 matches on clay over the season, and secure no fewer than 11 titles on that surface.

Six years after his magnificent championship of 1989, 23-year-old Chang, sixth-seeded, was back in the title bout, having brought down two-time champ, Bruguera. Perpetual motion Michael rang up a 5-2 lead that melted as Muster muscled his way through nine straight games, taking over for a 7-5, 6-2, 6-4, triumph.

Graf missed the Australian Open due to a calf injury. Coming into Roland Garros, she was skeptical about her chances as perennial problems with her back persisted. But Graf came to play, played to win, and emerged with an immensely satisfying 16th major title.

In securing a fourth French Open crown, Graf renewed her rivalry with Sanchez Vicario. The defending champion looked likely to hold on to her title when she split the first two sets of the final with Steffi, but Graf produced perhaps the best set of clay-court tennis in her career to prevail, 7-5, 4-6, 6-0. In the final set, a devastating Graf won 24 of 30 points, overwhelming Sanchez Vicario with her piercing shot combinations.

"There were some very difficult weeks for me before I came to this tournament," reflected Graf. "I never really thought I could get to the final. I only had eight or nine days of practice before the tournament and I had been sick. I wasn't sure if that would be enough to get me through."

At Wimbledon, Sampras took another substantial step up the historical ladder of the sport, becoming the first American man ever to win the world's most prestigious tournament three years in a row. A morale-boosting tournament triumph at Queen's Club in London over missile-serving German Marc Goellner eight days before Wimbledon—only the second tournament win for Sampras all year—gave the concussive American just the lift he needed. Sampras was given a

---

1995 CHAMPIONS AND LEADERS

Top Player Earnings: Men
Pete Sampras $5,415,066
Top Player Earnings: Women
Steffi Graf $2,538,620
Year-End Number One
Men: Pete Sampras
Women: Steffi Graf & Monica Seles
Davis Cup: United States
Fed Cup: Spain

ITF World Champion
Men: Pete Sampras
Women: Steffi Graf
ATP World Championships, Frankfurt
Boris Becker
Grand Slam Cup, Munich
Goran Ivanisevic
Corel Championships, NYC
Steffi Graf

demanding test by Goran Ivanisevic in his semi-final as the Croatian left-hander, seeded fourth, served 38 aces, but Sampras' greater stability pulled him through in a five-set victory. In a battle of Wimbledon heroes for the title, Sampras was too good for the three-time champ Boris Becker. In four sets, he was impervious on serve, didn't even face a single break point. Thus, in three Wimbledon finals encompassing eleven sets and a trio of different opponents—Sampras had lost only one service game!

Becker gave himself a considerable boost by taking the first set, in a 7-5 tie-breaker, but was soundly beaten, 6-7 (5-7), 6-2, 6-4, 6-2, as Sampras broke him five times over the next three sets. "In the 1980s," said a sporting Becker after his loss, "Centre Court was my court. But now it belongs to Pete Sampras."

Nevertheless, Becker had brought back those glory days of the '80s in a rousing semi-final comeback over Agassi, the top seed. Agassi was almost beyond belief at the outset, sprinkling the Centre Court with brilliant service returns and passing shots, making the game look impossibly easy in building a 6-2, 4-1, two-service-break lead. But then Becker found his form. When the burly German got back on even terms by seizing the second set, 7-1, in the tie-breaker, Agassi's despondency was almost tangible and Becker completed a 2-6, 7-6 (7-1), 6-4, 7-6 (7-1) triumph.

The men surely had a very good Wimbledon, but in many ways the women upstaged them at the end. Graf and Sanchez Vicario contested a final which will be placed up there among the five best open era title matches. It had already been a bruising and alluring battle when the two towering competitors reached 5-5 in the third. But the 11th game of the final set took the match into another category altogether. They fought ferociously for 20 minutes, through 13 deuces and 32 points. Sanchez Vicario had eight game points before Graf, with lusty forehands, set up her sixth break point and cashed it. Ultimately, Arantxa lost a third straight major tournament final, 4-6, 6-1, 7-5. Perhaps it was the single greatest game in the history of women's tennis at Wimbledon.

As a footnote Martina Navratilova continued to romp on Wimbledon sod. She and Jonathan Stark grabbed the mixed title over Gigi Fernandez and Czech Cyril Suk, 6-4, 6-4. It was the 38-year-old southpaw's 56th major.

As the players moved into the heart of summer no one sizzled more than Agassi. Along the way to Flushing Meadow, Agassi played too well for his own good, capturing four tournament titles in a row: Washington over Stefan Edberg, Canadian Open over Sampras, Cincinnati over Chang, and New Haven over Richard Krajicek. Andre won 20 matches in a row and he thrived in the oppressive heat to become the clear favorite to win the U.S. Open.

But second-seeded Sampras was not unduly worried. The pivotal showdown of the year, this final that everyone had been hoping for, was settled to a very large extent by the final point of the opening set. Agassi was serving at set point—4-5, advantage out—when the two players produced a rally they might not replicate for the rest of their careers. Driving each other from corner to corner, they went for their shots boldly but not recklessly. Finally, Sampras concluded the suspenseful 21-stroke sequence with a perfectly controlled, high-trajectory topspin backhand crosscourt into an empty space. Sampras had the set and it carried him swiftly through the second set. Although Agassi came from a break down to take the third, he could not hold Sampras back in the fourth and Sampras closed out the account, 6-4, 6-3, 4-6, 7-5.

"That was the biggest match of the year for me," he commented, "and one of the biggest in my career. Everything kind of built up to that match the whole year. When I woke up in the morning I thought if I lost, how crushed I would have felt, how great it would be to win. I realized how important it all was to me."

The women, meanwhile, were celebrating a similar conclusion to their Open. Not since January of 1993—Seles over Graf at the Australian Open—had Monica and Steffi met head-to-head. This was a particularly emotional reunion for the two superstars, both vividly recalling that a deranged Guenther Parche, allegedly a fan of Graf's, had interrupted Seles' career for more than two years with a knife stroke.

The two great champions were ready for this confrontation, plainly delighted to be bringing out the best in each other. The first set was as good as it gets, featuring one remarkable baseline rally after another. Graf lost only six points in six service games on her way to a first-set tie-breaker which Seles led, 6-5, serving at set point. Monica was convinced she had served an ace on the center line at this critical point, but it was called fault, a fraction of an inch wide.

Seles was rattled. Then Graf rifled a forehand return

winner off a second serve. Steffi took that sequence, 8-points-to-6, but let her guard down, and Seles struck all of her targets in a 6-0 second set. Graf was down, 0-30, in the first game of the third and break point in the third game, but held on both times. It was her match now as her serve regained velocity and accuracy, and her conviction came back. Seles seemed weary, and her forehand return deteriorated. And so for the seventh time in 11 career meetings—the fourth time in seven at major events—Graf had won, 7-6 (8-6), 0-6, 6-3. But Seles had unmistakably triumphed by even returning to that elite level of the game.

Nobody else welcome (well, almost)—that was the directive from the doubles teams of Gigi Fernandez-Zvereva and Novotna-Sanchez Vicario. They were adversaries in three of the four major finals. Australia and Wimbledon went to Arantxa and Jana. France went to Gigi and Natasha—as did the U.S., but over Rennae Stubbs and Brenda Schultz-McCarthy, the quarter-final conquerors of Arantxa and Jana.

Aussies Mark Woodforde and Todd Woodbridge captured the two biggest of the biggies: Wimbledon for a third straight time, over Americans Rick Leach and Scott Melville, and the U.S. over an American-Aussie connection of Alex O'Brien and Sandon Stolle (son of Hall of Famer Fred Stolle).

In November, the men's and women's season-ending championships needlessly competed against each other again. In Frankfurt, Becker was at his best in a 7-6 (7-3), 6-0, 7-6 (7-5) final-round win over Chang. Chang had ousted Sampras, 6-4, 6-4, in the semi-finals, but Sampras was aware by then that the No. 1 computer ranking for the year already belonged to him. Becker won a close three-set skirmish with Sweden's Thomas Enqvist in his semi-final.

Meanwhile, at Madison Square Garden in New York the same week, Graf managed to conduct one last piece of productive business. She survived an entertaining and fast-paced five sets with countrywoman Anke Huber to win the WTA Tour Championships. With this triumph, she concluded what she acknowledged was her most satisfying year. She waged a more selective campaign, playing fewer matches than any of her other big years, but won the three most important tournaments and four of the top five events. Furthermore, Graf won 47 of 49 matches, won 32 matches in a row and, in one stretch, six consecutive tournaments. It was indeed a very good year.

Sampras, whose Davis Cup singles experiences hadn't been positive, turned that part of his life around by winning all six starts—the last two spectacular—as the U.S. took the Cup in a Cold War-revisited drama over Russia, 3-2, at Moscow. Pete illuminated his greatness within Olympic Stadium, on a clay court that had been trucked in especially to thwart him, by belting his way to the rarest of triples: Having a hand in all the points in a 3-2 (or 3-1) Cup round victory. He is only the tenth member of that club, launched by Henri Cochet of France against Great Britain in 1931.

But it all may have come down to one stroke, the last one Pete hit in his opening salvo, a 3-6, 6-4, 6-3, 6-7 (5-7), 6-4, squeaker over ceaseless retriever Andrei Chesnokov. Sampras was dehydrated and cramping as he and Chesnokov neared the climax. At 5-4, 40-15 in the fifth set, Sampras missed a volley, blowing a first match point. Then came a desperate all-court exchange. Pete going to the net, being pushed back. Stroke after stroke. Pete approached again on a net-skinning forehand, the 22nd stroke, and Chesnokov ran feverishly, overtaking the ball—but couldn't flick it within the court. As he raised his arms in victory, Sampras abruptly collapsed. He was lugged to the dressing room by teammates to be revitalized.

"If my ball is good I don't think Pete can hit another shot ... I win," said Chesnokov. Sampras tended to agree. "I don't know if I could have gone on."

Sampras was back the next day to play doubles. After Kafelnikov beat Courier to make it 1-1, Pete and Todd Martin (returning superbly from the left court) were dynamite in demoralizing Kafelnikov and Andrei Olhovskiy, 7-5, 6-4, 6-3. Pete then turned in a bravura Cup-embracing performance that quickly dampened and muted the crowd of 16,000, beating Kafelnikov, 6-2, 6-4, 7-6 (7-4).

Chesnokov had been the hero of Russia's 3-2 semi-final jolting of Germany, scoring the decisive point in a totally unbelievable four-hour, 18-minute triumph over Michael Stich, 6-4, 1-6, 1-6, 6-3, 14-12. The Russians had set a speed trap for Germany's Becker and Stich by importing clay from Sweden at a cost of $70,000. The expenditure was repeated, the seating enlarged to 16,000, for the American visitors, but there was no dirty trick permitted that time. To further slow the Germans, the hosts had watered the court down to a morass. For that bit of liquid refreshing of the home-court advantage, the Russian federation was fined $25,000 by the International Tennis Federation.

France was the first U.S. victim in the Davis Cup chase, 4-1, indoors at St. Petersburg, Fla. Martin lost to Cedric Pioline, but was charged up to take the clincher from Guy Forget, 6-3, 7-6 (7-3), 7-6 (7-5) after Courier beat Forget and the Palmer-Reneberg unit beat Olivier Delaitre and Forget, 6-4, 3-6, 6-3, 6-4. Italy was easy, 5-0, on clay at Palermo, as Agassi and Sampras came aboard. Martin was the decider again at Las Vegas in a 4-1 semi-final decision over Sweden, subbing for Agassi, who was injured while beating 30-year-old re-tread Mats Wilander the first day. Pete beat Enqvist. It was 2-0, but doubles went Sweden's way, 29-year-old Edberg and Bjorkman over Martin and Stark. So Martin came in for Andre and took Enqvist, 7-5, 7-5, 7-6 (7-2), to book the tickets to Moscow.

Davis Cup-like alterations came to the Federation Cup, the name of which was pointlessly shaved to Fed Cup. A World Group was formed for eight countries to compete for the Cup itself in a Davis Cup-style best-of-five match series, either home or away, over a period of seven months. This replaced the best-of-three match format used since 1963, with all entrants gathering in one location for a week of competition.

The results didn't change in 1995. Those sensational senoritas, Sanchez Vicario and Martinez, won a third straight Cup for Spain, 3-2, over the U.S. in Valencia. Martinez (6-0 for the season) had led off over Chanda Rubin, 7-5, 7-6 (7-3), and clinched the next day in the third match, over Mary Joe Fernandez, 6-3, 6-4. Sanchez Vicario took the second point over Fernandez, 6-3, 6-2, and the Spaniards had won 13 straight series.

1996

U.S. Open win gives Sampras 8th major

Many a performer has felt naked on Centre Court, stripped bare and defenseless by an overpowering opponent. Tony Roche, after losing the 1968 Wimbledon final in under an hour to Rod Laver, lamented, "I just wanted to dig a hole and disappear."

But 23-year-old Englishwoman Melissa Johnson took it a few steps further in a distinctive Centre Court debut. She was a winner, judging from public reaction to her truly letting it all hang out as no champion before. In a final-day dash across the greensward as the Championships' singular streaker, she was perhaps Britain's most notable unclothed athlete since the jockey Godiva.

To the astonishment of Dutchman Richard Krajicek and American MaliVai Washington, a striking Melissa ran past the players and continuously flashed her small white apron, and body, at a stunned Duke and Duchess of Kent in the Royal Box. Moments later, a pair of policemen arrested her and took her to the station, where she was identified as a part-time Wimbledon waitress.

After that, the final proved anticlimactic. Washington lost in straight sets. Asked what role the streaker had played in his performance, the American replied: "I saw these things wobbling around and, jeez, she smiled at me. I was flustered. Three sets later, I was gone: If she'd come back, I might have had more luck."

While that was a rare time of irreverence for a sport sometimes lacking lighter moments, this was a year of serious business for the best players. Boris Becker knew precisely what he wanted to achieve when he commenced his campaign Down Under at Melbourne. Now 28, he was coming off an enviable 1995 and searching for his first major singles title in five years. He realized that goal when he took apart tenacious Michael Chang in the final of the year's first major. Becker sparred successfully with Chang from the base-line, served him off the court and attacked whenever

Richard Krajicek
Hard-serving Dutchman (and streaker) take Wimbledon by surprise.

that avenue was available. With his 6-2, 6-4, 2-6, 6-2 triumph over fifth seed Chang, the fourth seed gathered a sixth major crown over an 11-year span.

For the most part, the tournament was devoid of drama. Before Chang had eliminated Andre Agassi in a semi, Agassi had bounced another ex-champ, Jim Courier. Otherwise, the only surprise was delivered by 19-year-old Australian Mark Philippoussis, a 6-foot-4, 202-pounder, who beat world No. 1 Pete Sampras in the third round.

With Steffi Graf coming off foot surgery and unable to appear at Flinders Park for the second year in a row, Monica Seles was the class of the field. But she was battling a variety of injuries and hurt her shoulder prior to a semi-final showdown with the talented and athletic Chanda Rubin, a 19-year-old African American with an explosive all-court game. Rubin was coming off a 6-4, 2-6, 16-14 quarter-final upset of third-seeded Arantxa Sanchez Vicario, prevailing in three hours, 33 minutes, a tournament record for women. Against Seles, Chanda got within site of an upset before losing 6-7, (1-7), 6-1, 7-5.

But there was no luck involved in the hard-hitting final, a 6-4, 6-1 victory by Seles over German Anke Huber, who was debuting in a major final. Unbeaten in Australia (32-0), Monica had her fourth Open title, ninth major crown. Huber had beaten tireless South African Amanda Coetzer, whose quarter-final prey was 15-year-old Swiss Martina Hingis, making her first impression in a major. Hingis would win it the next three years.

Seles, arriving in Paris for the French Open, had made a questionable professional judgment by moving on from Melbourne to Tokyo the week after the Australian Open, losing, 1-6, 7-6 (7-5), 6-4 in the quarters to steadily improving Iva Majoli, who won the tournament over Sanchez Vicario. Having won in Sydney the week before Melbourne over Lindsay Davenport, Seles' trip to Tokyo represented her fourth consecutive week of competition. That must have exacerbated her shoulder injury, and she didn't return to tournaments until the week before Roland Garros, where she won one match in Madrid before she pulled out to protect her shoulder.

Seles arrived at the French Open still not fully recuperated from her shoulder woes. She struggled through to the quarter-finals and was halted by Jana Novotna. Monica's 25-match winning streak in the

world's most prestigious clay court event came to an end. With Seles gone, and Novotna losing in the semi-finals to her doubles partner Sanchez Vicario, it was time for another Graf–Sanchez Vicario final. This one was even better than the 1995 Wimbledon title match.

It lasted three hours and four minutes—a female French Open final round record—and it was hard and brilliantly fought from beginning to end. Graf took the first set and seemed headed for a straight-set win when she got to 4-1 in the second-set tie-breaker. But then the Spaniard snapped a forehand winner to make it 4-2 and Graf sank into a nervous patch. Four straight unforced errors and a double fault later, she had lost the tie-breaker, 7-points-to-4, and she found herself in a third set she could hardly have relished.

Graf fell behind 2-4 in the third, and Sanchez Vicario twice reached break point for 5-2. Graf held on. But the unwavering Sanchez Vicario served for the match twice at 5-4 and 7-6, only to be denied again. In those two memorable games, Graf did not make a single unforced error. In the end, Graf came through, 6-3, 6-7 (4-7), 10-8. It was a final so stupendous that only Chris Evert's 6-3, 6-7 (4-7), 7-5 triumph over Martina Navratilova in the 1985 final and Seles' 6-2, 3-6, 10-8 title win over Graf in 1992 might be rated above it.

The heart of the men's event at Roland Garros took place long before the final, and the one who took over the spotlight was none other than Sampras. On his way to a first French Open semi-final—he had been in the

1996 THE MAJOR CHAMPIONSHIPS

Australian Open
Men's Singles: Boris Becker
Women's Singles: Monica Seles
Men's Doubles: Stefan Edberg / Petr Korda
Women's Doubles: Chanda Rubin / Arantxa Sanchez Vicario
Mixed Doubles: Larisa Savchenko Neiland / Mark Woodforde
French Open
Men's Singles: Yevgeny Kafelnikov
Women's Singles: Steffi Graf
Men's Doubles: Yevgeny Kafelnikov / Daniel Vacek
Women's Doubles: Lindsay Davenport / Mary Joe Fernandez
Mixed Doubles: Patricia Tarabini / Javier Frana
Wimbledon
Men's Singles: Richard Krajicek
Women's Singles: Steffi Graf
Men's Doubles: Todd Woodbridge / Mark Woodforde
Women's Doubles: Martina Hingis / Helena Sukova
Mixed Doubles: Helena Sukova / Cyril Suk
U.S. Open
Men's Singles: Pete Sampras
Women's Singles: Steffi Graf
Men's Doubles: Todd Woodbridge / Mark Woodforde
Women's Doubles: Natalia Zvereva / Gigi Fernandez
Mixed Doubles: Lisa Raymond / Patrick Galbraith

quarter-finals 1992 through 1994—the world No. 1 survived three bruising five-set skirmishes. He beat 1993–94 titlist Sergi Bruguera in a gruelling second-round contest and then subdued 29-ace serving Todd Martin in the third round. In the quarter-finals, Sampras dropped the first two sets to Courier, but fought back to win his third five-set confrontation of the tournament.

But even with two days off to rest, Pete had passed his physical and emotional limits. His coach, Tim Gullikson, was lost to brain cancer three-and-a-half weeks before, and a mourning Sampras hadn't prepared for Roland Garros as he would have wanted. He had played his way through to the penultimate round with Gullikson at the center of his mind, wanting to win this one for a friend he had cherished and a coach he knew had turned him into a true champion. But with the thermometer soaring to 93 degrees, Sampras wilted in the heat and surrendered to Yevgeny Kafelnikov, 7-6 (7-4), 6-0, 6-2, conceding that "the balloon had burst."

Defending champion Thomas Muster had seemed a safe bet to retain his title. He had won 16 of his last 20 tournaments, 97 of his last 100 matches on clay when he took the court against 1991 Wimbledon champion Michael Stich in the round of 16. But a rejuvenated Stich jarred Muster, 4-6, 6-4, 6-1, 7-6 (7-1). Having endured ankle surgery three months before, Stich had come to Paris hoping only to get a few matches in before Wimbledon. He had considered bypassing the event but was persuaded by his coach Sven Groenveld to play. Dismaying the French patrons, Stich next knocked off Cedric Pioline and, following a straight-set semi-final win over Switzerland's Marc Rosset, Stich found himself in his third major final.

But Kafelnikov stopped Stich 7-6 (7-4), 7-5, 7-6 (7-4), even though Stich led 5-2 in the second, 3-1 in the third. Kafelnikov, the lone Russian to rule a major, doubled his good fortune by taking the doubles title with Czech Daniel Vacek, over the French-Swiss joint venture, Guy Forget and Jakob Hlasek, 6-2, 6-3. The Russian was the first to win both men's titles in Paris since Ken Rosewall (with Fred Stolle) in 1968.

It was not a vintage Wimbledon. The weather during the second week was miserable, rain constantly causing delays during big matches, and the atmosphere dampened for everyone. Nevertheless, the towering Krajicek produced the brightest brand of tennis of his career and thoroughly deserved his major title. The 6-foot-5, 24-year-old Netherlander became the only man from his nation to win one in singles. He was ranked No. 13 but overlooked by the Wimbledon seeding committee. When the seventh-seeded Muster withdrew with an injury, Krajicek was placed in the draw as the next in line, and, after the fact, considered the unorthodox 17th seed by the All England Club. This was way after the world press had correctly anointed Krajicek as the only unseeded winner other than Becker in 1985.

He had a terrific run. He upset 1991 titlist Stich then brought down the mighty Sampras in the quarters. Sampras had won 25 straight matches at Wimbledon but he could not break his unwavering opponent or cope with Krajicek's razor-sharp backhand. Krajicek then ousted Jason Stoltenberg, 7-5, 6-2, 6-1, after the Australian upset fourth seed Goran Ivanisevic in the quarters.

On the opposite half of the draw, Washington upset ninth-seeded Thomas Enqvist in the second round, saved two match points in a five-set quarter-final win over Germany's Alex Radulescu and then stunned countryman and close friend Martin to win their semi-final, 5-7, 6-4, 6-7 (5-7), 6-3, 10-8.

Washington, the first black in the final since Arthur Ashe in 1975, was overwhelmed by Krajicek, 6-3, 6-4, 6-3, in the final, as the Dutchman launched 14 aces to raise his tournament-high total to 147. Washington lost serve in the second game, and never caught up. Even a 68-minute stoppage for rain after one game of the third set couldn't dampen Krajicek's thrust. He lost serve just once, but by then was ahead 4-1 in the third.

The women couldn't reproduce their dazzling moments of a year before. Graf was just too good, too sharp and concentrated, this time around in a rematch of the 1995 final. She moved rapidly to a 6-3, 4-0 lead. Sanchez Vicario was typically combative in fighting her way back to 5-5, taking advantage of two damaging double faults from Graf, serving for the match at 5-4. Had it gone into a third set, Graf could well have been

---

1996 CHAMPIONS AND LEADERS

Top Player Earnings: Men	**ITF World Champion**
Boris Becker $4,313,007	Men: Pete Sampras
Top Player Earnings: Women	Women: Steffi Graf
Steffi Graf $2,664,178	**ATP World Championships,**
Year-End Number One	**Hanover**
Men: Pete Sampras	Pete Sampras
Women: Steffi Graf	**Grand Slam Cup, Munich**
Davis Cup: France	Boris Becker
Fed Cup: United States	**Chase Championships, NYC**
	Steffi Graf

vulnerable, but she raised her game markedly in the next two games, conceding only one more point to close out a 6-3, 7-5 victory for her seventh singles title on Centre Court.

Agassi crashed from his dismal slump by winning the prize he had proclaimed was utmost on his 1996 wish list: The Olympic gold medal on the hard courts of Atlanta's Stone Mountain complex. He did it after numerous escapes before he got the gold by assaulting the Spaniard Bruguera, 6-2, 6-3, 6-1.

Even more impressively, another American won in women's singles. Californian Lindsay Davenport was seeded only ninth but she toppled fifth seed Huber, fourth seed Majoli, seventh seed Mary Joe Fernandez, and third seed Sanchez Vicario, 7-6 (8-6), 6-2, to win gold.

Despite his proud achievement, Agassi was fortunate not to have been thrown out of the Olympics for untoward behavior that included incredibly abusive language directed at complaisant umpires. But he wasn't so lucky a couple of weeks later at encountering ATP officials at Indianapolis who wouldn't stand for that sort of treatment, and disqualified him. Andre was the first prominent player since John McEnroe, at the Australian of 1990, to be ejected. While winning easily against Canadian Daniel Nestor in the second round, he was tossed out after a warning for ball abuse and then a four-letter-word tirade against umpire Dana Loconto. Supervisor Mark Darby, told by Loconto precisely what Agassi had said, showed the gumption to evict one of the game's greatest drawing cards.

Controversy surrounded the U.S. Open before a single ball was struck. The USTA has almost always used the current ATP computer rankings to determine seedings for the last major championship of the season. But this time around, tourney officials chose to make a number of significant departures from the rankings in their projection. They moved Chang past Muster to second in the seedings (reversing their rankings), elevated Agassi from his No. 8 ranking to 6th in the seedings to take into account his recent record, and made a few other suspect changes as well without telling the ATP beforehand.

Kafelnikov, the French Open champion, was furious. He had talked about possibly pulling out of the Open the week before because of an injury. Then he became petulant about the seedings and withdrew. The Russian claimed that his pride had been wounded irreparably by being seeded seventh instead of where he stood in the rankings at No. 4. On top of all of this, the USTA did have to remake the draw after breaking procedure the first time around—and untraditionally in secret—although they defiantly stuck by their seedings.

In the end, order was restored as the unquestionable world No. 1 Sampras secured his only major crown of the season, seventh over the last four years, and eighth altogether, tying him with Jimmy Connors, Ken Rosewall, Ivan Lendl and Fred Perry in the all-time chase, not too far behind Roy Emerson (12), Rod Laver and Bjorn Borg (11), Bill Tilden (10).

Sampras was blazing at the start of his final with Chang, revealing the full range of his fluid talent, breaking down his adversary from the baseline, applying pressure when he needed to, serving with striking assurance. Before Chang knew what had hit him, he was down two sets to love. Sampras fought off a set point, serving at 5-6 in the third and then calmly and confidently completed his mission, 6-1, 6-4, 7-6 (7-3), for a fourth Open crown and an eighth major title.

The seedings had held up well. In the semi-finals, the top-seeded Sampras had defeated fourth-seed Ivanisevic after letting a 6-3, triple-match-point lead slip from his grasp in the tiebreaker. Sampras broke the big left-hander at 3-4 in the fourth, and went unbroken in four sets. Chang obliterated Agassi, 6-3, 6-2, 6-2, cracking 16 aces and not losing his serve. It was his third win in five 1996 meetings with Agassi, his second in a major event.

But none of those matches could compare to Sampras' monumental struggle with 22-year-old Spaniard Alex Corretja in the quarter-finals. In a four-hour, nine-minute confrontation, Sampras trailed two sets to one, struck back to win the fourth. But burdened by extreme dehydration, he vomited near the back of the court at 1-1 in the fifth-set tie-breaker, and was given a code violation warning for taking too much time between points.

As the tie-breaker progressed, it was increasingly apparent that Sampras was in agony. At 6-5, Sampras had a match point but missed a running forehand. He then went down match point at 6-7 and somehow came up with a stunning forehand stretch volley into an open court. Exhausted now, wanting the ordeal to be over, Sampras sent the stadium crowd into a complete frenzy when he hooked an audacious 90 m.p.h. second-serve ace wide to Corretja's forehand in the right court. "How could he do that?" sighed Corretja later. Pete said, "I don't know where it came from, but I knew I didn't want to hit another ball. I don't know if I could have." He didn't have to. Until then No. 31 Corretja had played the match of his life, giving away nothing, in fact outplaying Sampras—even out-acing him with 25. But Pete's second-ball ace seemed to unnerve Alex. The only way the Spaniard could lose was to not put the ball into play—a double fault. As Alex's second serve landed beyond the service line, Sampras was the winner, 7-6 (7-5), 5-7, 5-7, 6-4, 7-6 (9-7). It was the match of the '90s at Flushing Meadow, and easily among the five best in the open era.

For the second year in a row, Graf completed a sweep of the three majors she entered when she repeated her 1994 final-round triumph over Seles, 7-5, 6-4, but this was more thorough. Fraulein Forehand's blasts kept the less fit Seles running from corner to corner, and in vain. Graf, 27, banged 10 aces, lost serve but once, was too unrelentingly skillful in securing her 21st major title, fifth U.S. She had broken from the pack in Paris, leaving Chris Evert and Martina Navratilova behind with 18 majors apiece. At Wimbledon she cruised past Helen Wills Moody's 19, and now Margaret Smith Court's mighty record 24—once seeming Everest—appeared within reach.

But she nearly tripped in the semis over the latest Martina, child Hingis, 15. Cunning Martina II was having a good time, playing and winning more (19 hours, 44 minutes, 12 victories) than anyone else in reaching the semis of singles, doubles and mixed, the first such accomplishment since Martina I tripled in 1987. Her doubles title at Wimbledon (in the company of 31-year-old Helena Sukova, 5-7, 7-5, 6-1, over Larisa Neiland and Meredith McGrath), made Hingis, 15 years, 10 months, the youngest by three days to win a major female title, undercutting Lottie Dod, the 1887 Wimbledon singles champ. After eliminating third-seed-ed 1994 champ Sanchez Vicario and seventh-seeded Novotna, she had her sights on Graf. Only Steffi's stonewalling of five set points in the first set rescued her, 7-5, 6-3. Steffi socked three winners, benefited from two errors on those set points.

Captain Billie Jean King's U.S. team, with a rookie, Seles, on board, pried the Fed Cup away from Spain (a.k.a. Sanchez Vicario and Martinez), 5-0 at Atlantic City. But Mary Joe Fernandez, with a triple, was the lifesaver at the sticky start, 3-2 over Austria at Salzburg. Her wins over Judith Wiesner, 6-3, 7-6 (7-5), and Barbara Paulus, 6-3, 7-6 (7-4), backboned the victory that went down to the last match: Gigi Fernandez and Mary Joe over Wiesner and Petra Schwarz, 6-0, 6-4. Then a line-up of Seles and Davenport overpowered Japan, 5-0, at Nagoya, both beating up Date, the home ace: Lindsay, 6-2, 6-1; Monica, 6-0, 6-2.

Befitting the year's number ones, Sampras and Graf won the climactic playoffs, the ATP World Championship at Hanover, Germany, and WTA (Chase Championships) at New York's Madison Square Garden respectively, though each was pushed to the five-set limit. Beaten by Becker in the round-robin phase, Sampras rebounded to tip Boris in a gripping four-hour final, 3-6, 7-6 (7-5), 7-6 (7-4), 6-7 (11-13), 6-4, breaking serve only once. Muting a Boris chorus of 15,000, Pete had his third ATP, and eighth title for the year (a career 44th), during which he won 65 of 76 matches, and $3,702,919. Graf seemed in trouble as 16-year-old Hingis, the youngest finalist since Andrea Jaeger, 15, in 1981, led her 5-1 in the fourth set. But leg cramps shortly seized the kid, and Steffi came through in the year-ender for a fifth time, 6-3, 4-6, 0-6, 6-4, 6-0, her seventh title of a season in which she won 54 of 58 matches and a female record $2,665,706.

As in 1993, indifference at the top scuttled U.S. hopes of keeping the Davis Cup. Sampras, Agassi and Courier declined invitations to go for another Cup, saying the team event interrupted their schedules. Martin, the only holdover from Moscow '95 willing to show for a quarter-final in Prague, was admirable in the 3-2 defeat to the Czech Republic, securing both points. Todd beat Petr Korda, 6-2, 6-4, 7-5, and Daniel Vacek, 7-6 (7-1), 6-3, 6-1. But in the decisive fifth encounter, Washington, who had lost a tense struggle to Vacek (4-6, 6-3, 6-4, 5-7, 6-4), couldn't hold off Korda, 7-6 (7-1), 6-3, 6-1, and the U.S. was sidelined in the quarters, 3-2, by the Czech Republic in Prague. Korda-Vacek

1996 OLYMPICS, ATLANTA, UNITED STATES

Men's singles: Andre Agassi, United States, Gold; Sergi Bruguera, Spain, Silver; Leander Paes, India, Bronze
Women's singles: Lindsay Davenport, United States, Gold; Arantxa Sanchez Vicario, Spain, Silver; Jana Novotna, Czech Republic, Bronze
Men's doubles: Todd Woodbridge & Mark Woodforde, Australia, Gold; Tim Henman & Neil Broad, Great Britain, Silver; Marc-Kevin Goellner & David Prinosil, Germany, Bronze
Women's doubles: Mary Joe Fernandez & Gigi Fernandez, United States, Gold; Jana Novotna & Helena Sukova, Czechoslovakia, Silver; Martinez & Arantxa Sanchez Vicario, Spain, Bronze

got the go-ahead point from the Patricks, Galbraith and McEnroe, 6-2, 6-3, 6-3.

But perhaps it was poetic that the year of the passing of 92-year-old René Lacoste, the last of France's magnificent Four Musketeers, was capped by an unexpected, nerve-jingling French triumph, 3-2, in the Davis Cup final at Malmo, Sweden. It featured the longest (nine hours, 12 minutes), and possibly the wildest last day in Cup annals. Full-house crowds of 5,600, prepared to hail the farewell appearances of No. 14 Stefan Edberg, were saddened instead by his injury, a twisted right ankle, in losing the opener to No. 21 Pioline, 6-3, 6-4, 6-3. Further grief was theirs two days later as No. 31 Arnaud Boetsch battled uphill to win the closest of all Cup finale fifth matches, the decider, over Edberg's stand-in, No. 64 Nicklas Kulti, 7-6 (7-2), 2-6, 4-6, 7-6 (7-5), 10-8. Boetsch revived from triple-Cup point, 6-7, 0-40 in four hours, 47 minutes. Swede Thomas Enqvist, No. 9, came from way back, too, to tie it, 2-2, by beating Pioline from 2-5 in the fifth, 3-6, 6-7 (8-10), 6-4, 6-4, 9-7, in four hours, 25 minutes. But it turned out that wasn't enough to keep the Cup from the French whose Guillaume Raoux and Guy Forget won the vital doubles over Jonas Bjorkman and Kulti, 6-3, 1-6, 6-3, 6-3.

They must have sensed it was their year after a resurrection from 0-2 in the semi-final at Nantes to beat Italy, 3-2, with Boetsch rehearsing for the decisive victory in the fifth match, beating Andrea Gaudenzi. The U-turn began in doubles, Forget and Raoux blocking Gaudenzi and Diego Nargiso. Pioline tied it over Renzo Furlan, 6-3, 2-6, 6-2, 6-4.

Crowed inspirational captain Yannick Noah, who had led France's 1991 victory over the U.S. "Davis Cup's not about rankings, reputations, or schedules. It's about team, and who will give up things for others, for the team."

1997

Sweet but deadly, 16-year-old Hingis takes three majors

Martina Hingis
Playing a heady game that belied her tender years.

No one in professional tennis achieved more during this memorable season than Switzerland's stylish and precocious Martina Hingis. Before she turned 17 at the end of September, she had appeared in all four major championship tournament finals.

Displaying a strategic acumen far exceeding her years, Hingis won three of those four majors. Across the year, she was victorious in 75 of 80 matches, capturing 12 of 17 tournaments, garnering $3,400,196 to set the prize-money pace among the women. She dominated the game with brain rather than brawn, ruling from the baseline with superb t iming, exemplary ball control, and a deceptive two-handed backhand down the line.

After big hitters Steffi Graf and Monica Seles had controlled the female game for a decade, Hingis brought a refreshingly different style and personality to top-level tennis.

The season began in earnest for Hingis and everyone else Down Under in Melbourne. Martina became the youngest player of the 20th Century (at 16 years, three months, 26 days) to secure a major championship, obliterating 1995 winner Mary Pierce 6-2, 6-2 to claim the Australian Open crown, refusing to concede a set in the entire tournament. No Swiss player had ever captured a major singles championship. Lottie Dod had been two months shy of her 16th birthday when she became the youngest ever to take a major, winning Wimbledon in 1887.

Pete Sampras came through in resolute fashion to capture the men's Australian Open title, upending Spain's surging Carlos Moya, who had toppled defending champion Boris Becker and Michael Chang to reach his first major final. The top seeded Sampras had trailed the imposing Dominik Hrbaty of Croatia 2-4, 15-40 in the fifth set on a stifling afternoon in the round of 16, but swept four games in a row to seal victory. He was pressed into another five set confrontation by Spain's Albert Costa in the quarters, but then accounted for both Thomas Muster and Moya (6-2, 6-3, 6-3) in straight set encounters.

At the next 'Big Four' championship in Paris, the flamboyant Brazilian Gustavo Kuerten made a spectacular run to come away with his first major title. The 20-year-old exploited his magnificent one-handed topspin backhand and upended no fewer than three former champions in the ruling on the slow red clay of Roland Garros. He knocked out 1995 champion Muster in a five-set, third-round showdown after falling behind 3-0 in the final set, prevailed again in five arduous sets against defending champion Yevgeny Kafelnikov in the quarter-finals, and crushed 1993-94 victor Sergi Bruguera of Spain in a straight-set final. Kuerten came into Roland Garros ranked No. 65 in the world; he left with a rapidly rising reputation.

Hingis had hurt her knee in a horse-riding accident less than two months before the French Open. Still struggling to find the top of her game, she managed to make it to the final, but could not contain Iva Majoli, a 19-year-old Croatian with good court sense and stinging ground strokes off both sides. Majoli established herself as the first player from her nation to take one of the majors, upending Hingis in 78 solid minutes, prevailing 6-4, 6-2 without facing a single break point in the match. Martina's 37-match winning streak was over; she was beaten for the first time all year. Hingis had overcome three-time former champion Monica Seles 6-7 (2-7), 7-5, 6-4 in a stirring semi-final.

At Wimbledon, Hingis got back on the winning track. Her victim in the final was Jana Novotna, a superbly crafted grass-court player who was in a class by herself at the net, boasting the best volley off either side in women's tennis. Novotna, the No. 4 seed, attacked skillfully in a devastatingly efficient opening set, but Hingis found her range with impeccable passing shots in a 2-6, 6-3, 6-3 victory.

Sampras, meanwhile, was celebrating one of the great serving fortnights of his career. In sweeping to his fourth Wimbledon tournament win in five years, he held serve in 116 of 118 games. He was hard pressed to defeat the left-handed Petr Korda in a five- set, two-day, round-of-16 collision, but that was his only genuine scare. Korda never broke the American but counter attacked tenaciously in a 6-4, 6-3, 6-7 (8-10), 6-7 (1-7), 6-4 contest stretched over two days. Sampras halted three-time former champion Becker in a four-set quarter-final, and

went on to rout an apprehensive Cedric Pioline 6-4, 6-2, 6-4 in the final, repeating his straight-set triumph over the gifted Frenchman in the 1993 U.S. Open final. Pioline had stopped Michael Stich of Germany in a scintillating five-set semi-final clash. Stich, 28, retired from tennis at the end of the year, having failed yet again at a major after winning Wimbledon in 1991.

When the leading players assembled at Flushing Meadows for the last major of the season, they moved into a brand new 23,000-seat Arthur Ashe Stadium, named after the dignified man who had won the first U.S. Open in 1968. The new theater was not to the liking of most longtime fans, who felt it was marred by two levels of luxury suites and was an impersonal stage that was too large for tennis. Hingis and Sampras were the firm favorites. In the end, she came through to claim the most prestigious hard-court crown, but he did not. Hingis found herself facing Venus Williams in the final, the first African American woman since Althea Gibson at Forest Hills in 1958 to reach a title-round match. Williams, the second unseeded finalist in the championships of her country following Darlene Hard in 1958, was understandably jittery on the big occasion and went down rather tamely 6-0, 6-4. But the 17-year-old ac quitted herself well in the second set, rallying from 1-3 down to reach 4-4, 30-0 before delivering a costly double fault. At No. 66 in the world she was the lowest-ranked woman to reach a major final since Barbara Jordan at the Australian Open in 1979. Hingis,

---

1997 THE MAJOR CHAMPIONSHIPS

Australian Open
Men's Singles: Pete Sampras
Women's Singles: Martina Hingis
Men's Doubles: Todd Woodbridge / Mark Woodforde
Women's Doubles: Martina Hingis / Natalia Zvereva
Mixed Doubles: Manon Bollegraf / Rick Leach
French Open
Men's Singles: Gustavo Kuerten
Women's Singles: Iva Majoli
Men's Doubles: Yevgeny Kafelnikov / Daniel Vacek
Women's Doubles: Gigi Fernandez / Natasha Zvereva
Mixed Doubles: Rika Hiraki / Mahesh Bhupathi
Wimbledon
Men's Singles: Pete Sampras
Women's Singles: Martina Hingis
Men's Doubles: Todd Woodbridge / Mark Woodforde
Women's Doubles: Gigi Fernandez / Natasha Zvereva
Mixed Doubles: Helena Sukova / Cyril Suk
U.S. Open
Men's Singles: Patrick Rafter
Women's Singles: Martina Hingis
Men's Doubles: Yevgeny Kafelnikov / Daniel Vacek
Women's Doubles: Jana Novotna / Lindsay Davenport
Mixed Doubles: Manon Bollegraf / Rick Leach

however, joined a very exclusive club with her triumph, becoming only the seventh woman in history to record three major triumphs in a season, joining Maureen Connolly, Margaret Smith Court, Billie Jean King, Martina Navratilova, Graf and Seles in that category.

The top-seeded Sampras was ousted in a suspenseful, round of 16, Labor Day meeting with Korda. As was the case at Wimbledon, they went the full five sets again. Sampras was up a break in the fifth, serving at 3-1. But a ferociously determined Korda, two points from defeat at 5-6 in ther fifth, struck back boldly to win 6-7 (4-7), 7-5, 7-6 (7-2), 3-6, 7-6 (7-2). Korda retired after losing the first two sets of his quarter-final against Sweden's Jonas Bjorkman, claiming he was hindered by a cold. In the end, a red-hot Patrick Rafter burst into his own and was a worthy champion.

The 24-year-old Australian serve-and-volleyer had won only one tournament over the course of his career, and had lost in five finals across the season. But his heavy kick serve worked wonders on the surface, and he lifted both his game and confidence to unprecedented levels. In the final, the No. 13-seed Rafter defeated unseeded Greg Rusedski of Great Britain in four sets, outplaying the big-serving left-hander in every facet of the game, most notably returning serve with more conviction. Speaking of the five finals he had lost leading up to the Open, Rafter said, "I learned a lot from those experiences about how to handle myself in this final." Rafter had peaked propitiously for his semi-final appointment with No. 2-seed Chang, taking apart the dispirited American in straight sets with an unwavering demonstration of aggression.

Chang was crestfallen when it was over, knowing he would have no better opening to secure a second major title. "All I can say," he lamented, "is that all of these losses hurt. I just hope that my perseverance will pay off one day. When you have these opportunities and don't win, it's frustrating."

Another American who had the misfortune to meet the formidable Rafter was 1994 champion Agassi, who was suffering through a miserable season. Having married actress Brooke Shields in the spring, Agassi did not play any of the other 'Big Four' tournaments. Looking overweight and overanxious, Agassi lost to the hard-charging Rafter in a four-set, round-of-16 collision under the lights. He finished the year with a 12-12 match record, and his ranking plunged to No. 122 in the world.

At the end of the year, Sampras won the season-ending ATP Tour World Championships in Hannover with a straight-set demolition of an outclassed Kafelnikov, while Novotna took the Chase Championships at New York's Madison Square Garden over Pierce.

Of larger significance was this: Sweden won the Davis Cup for the sixth time in 11 final-round appearances, ousting the United States 5-0 at Goteborg. Jonas Bjorkman and Magnus Larsson led the way with victories over Chang and an injured Sampras respectively, and the U.S. could not recover from that disastrous start.

In the Fed Cup final at Den Bosch, France toppled The Netherlands 4-1 with Sandrine Testud taking the decisive match 0-6, 6-3, 6-3 over Miriam Oremans. Making a major contribution to the French cause was none other than the ubiquitous Yannick Noah. Noah had led France into the Davis Cup Final as a player in 1982. He then won the French Open in 1983. He was the Davis Cup captain when France was victorious in 1991 and 1996. And then he led the women to this team triumph, completing a unique range of achievements.

Meanwhile, one of the game's great doubles players decided to retire from tennis. Gigi Fernandez captured her last two major titles during the year, taking the French Open and Wimbledon alongside her longtime partner Natalia Zvereva. Fernandez, 33, left the stage with 17 'Big Four' prizes in her possession, and the knowledge that she was walking away when she was close to the peak of her powers.

1997 CHAMPIONS AND LEADERS

Top Player Earnings: Men
Pete Sampras $6,498,311
Top Player Earnings: Women
Martina Hingis $3,400,196
Year-End Number One
Men: Pete Sampras
Women: Martina Hingis
Davis Cup: Sweden
Fed Cup: France

ITF World Champion
Men: Pete Sampras
Women: Martina Hingis
ATP World Championships, Hanover
Pete Sampras
Grand Slam Cup, Munich
Pete Sampras
Chase Championships, NYC
Jana Novotna

1998

Powerful Lindsay unhinges Hingis

Patrick Rafter
Nearly a first-round victim, then a second straight U.S. Open title.

Some familiar faces won on the stages of conse-quence. Among the women, Martina Hingis defended her Australian Open title, and the effervescent Arantxa Sanchez Vicario ruled at Roland Garros for the third time. In the men's division, Pete Sampras was victorious again at the All England Club, winning Wimbledon for the fifth time in six years, and Patrick Rafter held on safely to his U.S. Open crown with another stellar demonstration of his talent.

But four other players moved beyond themselves to claim their first of the game's preeminent prizes. The left-handed Petr Korda was the victor at the Australian Open. Spain's Carlos Moya took the top honor at Roland Garros. Jana Novotna—twice a beaten finalist in the past—delighted her admirers by capturing the crown at Wimbledon. And Lindsay Davenport produced her best brand of tennis in becoming a worthy United States Open champion.

And so, for the first time since 1990, eight different players had claimed the major championships. Clearly, very little separated the best players in the world. There was no shortage of suspense.

Korda was the first of the surprise winners to stamp his authority at a major championship event. He turned 30 during the fortnight in Melbourne, but his state of mind was considerably younger. Seeded sixth, he went to work purposefully, and lifted his game when it mattered. In the quarter-finals, Korda struck back boldly to topple No. 4 seed Jonas Bjorkman 3-6, 5-7, 6-3, 6-4, 6-2. Buoyed by that gritty triumph, he took apart Karol Kucera in four sets to set up a final-round meeting with Marcelo Rios, a fellow left-hander with similar flair. The No. 9 seed Rios had quietly come through a comfortable draw, and seemed certain to face Korda on even terms. But the enigmatic Chilean failed to deliver on his promise, falling 6-2, 6-2, 6-2 in a lackluster finish. Korda celebrated with his trademark 'scissors kick' dance of delight.

Sampras and Rafter had been seeded first and

second, but they fell short. Rafter went down in the third-round, four-set clash with Alberto Berasategui, the 1994 French Open finalist who then surprised Andre Agassi in the round of 16. Sampras did not drop a set on his way to the quarter-finals, but bowed to an inspired Kucera in a four-set showdown under the lights.

While the men's draw was filled with upsets and startling turnarounds, Hingis refused to let go of her women's crown. The top seed ousted No. 8 seed Conchita Martinez of Spain 6-3, 6-3 in the final. Martinez, looking to win her first major since her triumph at Wimbledon four years earlier, had accounted for No. 2 seed Davenport in a come from behind, three-set semi-final. But the 25-year-old—one of the craftiest match players in the business—was out of her element against a highly charged Hingis, who captured her fourth major in fine fashion.

At Roland Garros, a cavalcade of spirited clay-court players arrived at Roland Garros in search of the world's premier clay court title. But, in the end, it was more like a Spanish Invasion as the capable Moya and the indefatigable Sanchez Vicario swept the singles championships. Moya capped a remarkable event by halting countryman Alex Corretja 6-3, 7-5, 6-3 in the final. His more penetrating forehand and wider range of talent carried him to victory in his second 'Big Four' final. When it was over, Corretja came around to Moya's side of the net and embraced his conqueror.

The women's event came down to the No. 4 seed

1998 THE MAJOR CHAMPIONSHIPS

Australian Open
Men's Singles: Petr Korda
Women's Singles: Martina Hingis
Men's Doubles: Jonas Bjorkman / Jacco Eltingh
Women's Doubles: Martina Hingis / Mirjana Lucic
Mixed Doubles: Venus Williams / Justin Gimelstob
French Open
Men's Singles: Carlos Moya
Women's Singles: Arantxa Sanchez Vicario
Men's Doubles: Jacco Eltingh / Paul Haarhuis
Women's Doubles: Martina Hingis / Jana Novotna
Mixed Doubles: Venus Williams / Justin Gimelstob
Wimbledon
Men's Singles: Pete Sampras
Women's Singles: Jana Novotna
Men's Doubles: Jacco Eltingh / Paul Haarhuis
Women's Doubles: Martina Hingis / Jana Novotna
Mixed Doubles: Serena Williams / Max Mirnyi
U.S. Open
Men's Singles: Patrick Rafter
Women's Singles: Lindsay Davenport
Men's Doubles: Sandon Stolle / Cyril Suk
Women's Doubles: Martina Hingis / Jana Novotna
Mixed Doubles: Serena Williams / Max Mirnyi

Sanchez Vicario against No. 6 Monica Seles in a bruising battle of champions. Seles was seeking a fourth Roland Garros triumph, and was the sentimental favorite. Her father and coach Karolj had died less than two weeks before the start of the tournament. Monica contemplated skipping the event, but chose to participate after weighing every angle of the issue in her mind.

She came agonizingly close to taking the tournament. Against Sanchez Vicario, Monica led 5-3, 30-30 in the opening set but faltered at that critical moment and eventually lost the set in a tiebreak. Seles stormed through the second set, but lost steam in the third. Sanchez Vicario, beaten in 14 of 16 previous head-to-head collisions with Monica, came out on top in this encounter 7-6 (7-5), 0-6, 6-2 to collect a fourth major championship win. In a poignant post-match ceremony, Sanchez Vicario said sportingly, "I'd like to congratulate Monica for getting to the final. I'm sorry I had to beat you. I have so much respect for you. All the players are sorry that your father passed away."

In the semi-finals, Seles was breathtakingly impressive in routing Hingis. Taking full advantage of her sizzling, left-handed, two-fisted strokes off both wings, Seles set the tactical agenda throughout and came away deservedly with a 6-3, 6-2 victory, her first in six career clashes against the Swiss stylist. Sanchez Vicario took her place in the final with a 6-3, 7-6 (7-5) mastering of the No. 2 seed Davenport, who looked out of her element on the slow red clay. The towering Californian held serve only twice in ten service games as her Spanish adversary defended from the backcourt with supreme skill.

To Wimbledon, where Sampras put on one of the most determined stands of his illustrious career. He had won only two of his ten tournaments heading into The Big W. Confronted by the ever-daunting Goran Ivanisevic in the final, Sampras was stretched into his first ever five-set final at a major. In the second set tiebreak, the 26-year-old American was twice a point away from trailing two sets to love. The top seed missed his first serve in both cases, but Ivanisevic drove backhand returns into the net. Sampras climbed out of that dark corner, and prevailed in ther bright sunshine on Centre Court 6-7 (2-7), 7-6 (11-9), 6-4, 3-6, 6-2. From 2-2 in the final set, Sampras collected 16 of the last 19 points to secure his fifth singles championship at Wimbledon, and his 11th Grand Slam tournament title. A despondent Ivanisevic was beaten for the third time in a Wimbledon final, and it was his second defeat against

Sampras in a confrontation for the title. "This is the worst moment of my life," said Ivanisevic. "It hurts the most because this time I had the chance."

Ivanisevic had ousted 1996 champion Richard Krajicek 6-4, 6-3, 5-7, 6-7 (5-7), 15-13 in a tumultuous semi-final. The big left-hander reached double match point at 5-4 in the fourth set, serving an apparent ace. Both players thought the match was over, but a let had been called. Somehow, Krajicek managed to break serve. He took that set in a tiebreak and went up a break in the fifth before faltering. Ivanisevic survived 15-13 in the fifth. Later that afternoon, Sampras beat British No. 1 Tim Henman 6-3, 4-6, 7-5, 6-3 in a spirited grass-court skirmish.

Novotna cast aside all her demons in winning Wimbledon on her 13th attempt. She had wasted a 4-1, two service break lead in the final set against Steffi Graf in the final five years earlier, and had faded after a blazing beginning against Hingis the previous year. Now, in her third final, with everyone wondering how well her nerves would hold up, Novotna stood up ably to the challenge. She was fortunate to be facing Nathalie Tauziat, the No. 16 seed from France and the first woman from her nation to reach the final on Centre Court since Suzanne Lenglen in 1925. Tauziat, 30, had never been beyond the quarter-finals of a major event before.

The No. 3 seed Novotna was the decidedly better grass-court player, winning 6-4, 7-6 (7-2). Novotna trailed 2-0, 40-15 in the first set before taking matters into her own hands. She served for the match at 5-4 in the second set but her normally impeccable forehand volley let her down in that game. Nevertheless, Novotna quickly regained the ascendancy in the tiebreak, and confidently closed it out. "This is a definite dream come true for me," said a jubilant Novotna. "It's really important to always believe in yourself and to have a dream. This is what I have been waiting and working for."

Novotna's best match by far was her 6-4, 6-4 semi-final victory over the top seeded and defending champion Hingis. Martina held a 6-2 career head-to-head edge over Novotna, sweeping the previous four battles they had fought. But the key to the verdict this time was the opening set. Hingis led 3-0, 0-40 but dropped six of the next seven games. The momentum had unmistakably swung, and the top seed could not recover. Meanwhile, in the most stunning development of the tournament, seven-time champion Graf bowed

6-4, 7-5 in the third round against Natalia Zvereva, who then beat Seles on her way to the semi-finals before losing to Tauziat. Graf had not suffered a loss against Zvereva in 17 previous meetings.

At Flushing Meadows, Rafter was hard pressed to survive the opening round, withstanding a barrage of brilliant groundstrokes from the freewheeling and inventive Hicham Arazi, the left-hander from Morocco. Arazi's shot making was magnificent for two sets against the all-out aggression from his Australian adversary, but Rafter staged a stupendous comeback. Boosted by a vocal contingent of Aussie fans enjoying the night session in Ashe Stadium, Rafter rallied valiantly for a 4-6, 4-6, 6-3, 6-3, 6-1 first-round victory. From that juncture on, Rafter was near the top of his game. In the semi-finals, however, he was fortunate to escape again, this time at the hands of the top seeded Sampras.

The American built a two-sets-to-one lead over the defending champion, but was hobbled over the last two sets by a strained left quadruples muscle near the hip. His mobility significantly impaired, Sampras could not stay with the crisp and confident Rafter, who prevailed 6-7 (8-10), 6-4, 2-6, 6-4, 6-3. In the final, matters were much easier for the athletic No. 3 seed, and he crushed countryman Mark Philippoussis 6-3, 3-6, 6-2, 6-0. In four sets, Rafter was made mere five unforced errors. Philippoussis, unseeded but long overdue to be in a big final, had upended No. 5 seed Moya in the penultimate round in four sets.

Sampras avenged his loss to Kucera in Australia with an emphatic straight set quarter-final victory on a chilly evening. Kucera had overcome No. 8 seed Agassi in a two-day, five set match clouded by controversy. The No. 9 seed Kucera had irritated the 1994 champion by frequently letting his high service tosses drop to the ground, waiting until he got the toss precisely where he wanted it before starting the point.

Agassi, exasperated by the constant delays, chose a cheap way to retaliate, imitating his opponent. He deliberately kept letting his own service tosses drop to the ground. Kucera had a commanding two sets to love lead but Agassi took the third and went up a break in the fourth before rain stopped play. The next day, Agassi won the fourth, and led 2-0, 15-40 in the fifth before Kucera revived for a 6-3, 6-3, 6-7 (5-7), 1-6, 6-3 victory.

Davenport had played superb tennis all summer, winning three consecutive events at Stanford, Calif., San Diego, and Los Angeles. In that span, the 22-year-old had toppled an impressive cast of imposing rivals, upending Graf, Venus Williams, Seles, Mary Pierce and Hingis. Although she lost to Graf in the semi-finals at New Haven, Davenport came to New York in the best possible frame of mind. On a balmy afternoon in the final at Flushing Meadows, Davenport struck down the defending champion Hingis 6-3, 7-5.

Davenport overpowered Hingis from the outset, driving her forehand with surprisingly good ball control and depth, blasting her almost impeccable two-handed backhand into the corners with uncanny regularity. The barrage of big strokes Davenport was sending her way overwhelmed Hingis, but Martina made her move in the second set. At 5-4, she served for equality. Had she held there, she might well have won in three sets. But Davenport swept 12 of the next 15 points to close the account in style. In her first final round test at a major event, Davenport passed with flying colors.

Both the No. 3 seed Novotna and No. 5 Venus Williams made it to the semi-finals. Williams stopped No. 4 seed Sanchez Vicario 2-6, 6-1, 6-1 in the quarter-finals, and Novotna accounted for No. 11 Patty Schnyder in straight sets. Schnyder, a left-hander with a deceptive inside-out top-spin forehand, had ousted the five-time champion Graf in the round of 16.

Hingis took the U.S. Open women's doubles title alongside Novotna to complete a sweep of the four majors. Martina had come through at the Australian Open with Mirjana Lucic, joining forces with Novotna for the last three legs of the Grand Slam. Brazil's gifted Maria Bueno had won the Grand Slam in doubles 38 years earlier, also prevailing with two different partners. Martina Navratilova and Pam Shriver had realized that remarkable feat in 1984 with their domination of the premier events establishing themselves as the only female team to record a Grand Slam.

At the tail end of the season, Sampras was on a major mission to attain the No. 1 world ranking on the ATP

computer for a record sixth consecutive year. Jimmy Connors had held the No. 1 ranking for five years in a row (1974-78), but in two of those seasons (1975 and 1977), he had not captured a single major championship. Sampras had taken 10 'Big Four' titles from 1993-98, winning at least one big one in each of those seasons. In any event, he had to work down to the wire to reach his goal, playing six consecutive European indoor events over the autumn in a supreme effort to accumulate ranking points. He would win only four of 22 tournaments he played during the year, but his overall consistency was superior to nearest rivals Rios and Rafter.

At the ATP Tour World Championships in Hannover, Sampras lost an excruciatingly close semi-final contest to Corretja. The Spaniard saved three match points to upset the American 4-6, 6-3, 7-6 (7-3). But by then Pete had clinched the No. 1 spot. Corretja, meanwhile, made another astonishing recovery in the final, overcoming countryman Moya 3-6, 3-6, 7-5, 6-3, 7-5 to capture the most prestigious prize of his career.

At Madison Square Garden in New York, Hingis stopped Davenport in the best-of-five set Chase Championships final 7-5, 6-4, 4-6, 6-2 to garner a fifth singles title for the year. The victory gave Hingis a 7-6 lead in her career series with Lindsay. But Davenport—the winner of six tournaments and the pivotal U.S. Open collision with Hingis—took away the No. 1 world ranking from Hingis despite her end of season setback.

Sweden defeated Italy 4-1 to win the Davis Cup in Milan as Magnus Norman and Magnus Gustafsson clipped Andrea Gaudenzi and Davide Sanguinetti in the opening singles matches. Bjorkman and Nicklas Kulti sealed the triumph for the Swedes with a straight set win over Diego Nargiso and Sanguinetti 7-6 (7-1), 6-1, 6-3.

In the Fed Cup final at Geneva, Spain narrowly moved past Switzerland 3-2. Hingis won both of her singles—defeating Sanchez Vicario and Conchita Martinez—but Martinez managed to stop a determined Schnyder 6-3, 2-6, 9-7 on the last day in a hard fought, three hour, 18-minute tussle. The two nations were locked at 2-2, but Sanchez Vicario and Martinez crushed a depleted Schnyder and Hingis 6-0, 6-2 to finish the task.

Two Americans, Davenport and Sampras, finished the season deservedly on top of the world. But no one dominated the game in either women's or men's tennis, and in many ways the game was better for that.

1998 CHAMPIONS AND LEADERS

Top Player Earnings: Men
Pete Sampras $3,931,497
Top Player Earnings: Women
Martina Hingis $3,175,631
Year-End Number One
Men: Pete Sampras
Women: Lindsay Davenport
ITF World Champion
Men: Pete Sampras
Women: Lindsay Davenport
Davis Cup: Sweden

Fed Cup: Spain
ATP World Championships, Hanover
Alex Corretja
Grand Slam Cup, Munich
Marcelo Rios
Chase Championships, NYC
Martina Hingis
Grand Slam Cup, Munich
Venus Williams

1999

Sampras ties Emmo with 12th major

In every respect, it was a landmark season for the game's most charismatic player. Andre Agassi celebrated the finest campaign of his 14-year professional career. For the first time, he finished a season as the top-ranked player in the world. In another remarkable breakthrough, he won two major titles in a year, a feat he had never realized before. At 29, the confounding American came of age. In an arresting run across the spring and through summer, he captured the French Open and became only the fifth man in history to rule at all four major events. Then he made a strikingly efficient transition from clay to grass, reaching the final at Wimbledon. And he completed his heroics by winning the championship of his country for the second time.

To be sure, Agassi was the Player of the Year. But he did not completely control the climate of the men's game. Pete Sampras stopped his old rival in four of their five head-to-head clashes over the season, including a brilliant and comprehensive victory when they met in the Wimbledon final. Had Sampras not been forced out of the U.S. Open by a herniated disc in his back, he might well have moved to a seventh No. 1 season in a row.

The women had another compelling campaign. For the second straight year, four different females captured major events. Martina Hingis was the victor at the Australian Open, Steffi Graf secured her last career major at Roland Garros, Lindsay Davenport became an exemplary Wimbledon champion, and Serena Williams stepped into the spotlight in New York with an unexpected U.S. Open triumph. All in all, the women more than held their own with the men.

It all began in earnest, of course, at the Australian Open. Russian Yevgeny Kafelnikov—often his own worst enemy in big settings—came away with a second major crown. The 24-year-old was solid and unusually stable over the fortnight Down Under, toppling an apprehensive Thomas Enqvist 4-6, 6-0, 6-3 7-6 (7-1)

Andre Agassi
Finally, at 29, two majors in same year and the No. 1 world ranking.

in the final. The No. 10 seed Kafelnikov took full advantage of an excellent draw, and was forced to confront only one other seeded player—No. 15 Todd Martin, the 1994 finalist—in his seven victories on the Rebound Ace Hard Courts. Sampras, resting after his exhausting 1998 campaign, was not in Melbourne. Said Kafelnikov, "Pete not playing kind of opened up the draw for everybody. A lot of guys thought they could win, even myself."

Another significant surprise was the fourth-round defeat of No. 5 seed Andre Agassi against compatriot Vince Spadea, who was unerring and resourceful from the backcourt in a four-set upset. Agassi would have met Kafelnikov in the penultimate round had he survived; instead; Spadea fell in the quarter-finals against the rapidly rising German Tommy Haas, and Haas was ushered out of the tournament in the semi-finals by Kafelnikov 6-3, 6-4, 7-5.

The No. 2 seed Hingis was at the top of her game once more in Melbourne, winning the event for the third year in a row, dropping only one set along the way. In the final, she was too poised and polished for the sporadically brilliant Amelie Mauresmo of France. Hingis rolled to a 6-2, 6-3 triumph and was rewarded with a fifth major championship. Mauresmo's versatile shot making and her all court prowess was evident all through the contest, but she could not break down her opponent's defenses. Hingis gave almost nothing away while Mauresmo drifted into difficulty frequently with bad shot selection.

1999 THE MAJOR CHAMPIONSHIPS

Australian Open
Men's Singles: Yevgeny Kafelnikov
Women's Singles: Martina Hingis
Men's Doubles: Patrick Rafter / Jonas Bjorkman
Women's Doubles: Martina Hingis / Anna Kournikova
Mixed Doubles: Mariaan de Swardt / David Adams
French Open
Men's Singles: Andre Agassi
Women's Singles: Steffi Graf
Men's Doubles: Mahesh Bhupathi / Leander Paes
Women's Doubles: Venus Williams / Serena Williams
Mixed Doubles: Katarina Srebotnik / Piet Norval
Wimbledon
Men's Singles: Pete Sampras
Women's Singles: Lindsay Davenport
Men's Doubles: Mahesh Bhupathi / Leander Paes
Women's Doubles: Lindsay Davenport / Corina Morariu
Mixed Doubles: Lisa Raymond / Leander Paes
U.S. Open
Men's Singles: Andre Agassi
Women's Singles: Serena Williams
Men's Doubles: Sebastien Lareau / Alex O'Brien
Women's Doubles: Serena Williams / Venus Williams
Mixed Doubles: Ai Sugiyama / Mahesh Bhupathi

Nevertheless, Mauresmo produced a major upset in the semi-finals when she ousted top-seeded Davenport 4-6, 7-5, 7-5 after the American took a 4-2, final set lead. Davenport had been in enviable form during a 6-4, 6-0 rout of No. 5 seed Venus Williams in the quarters, but did not press her advantage against Mauresmo, and paid a substantial price for her lack of conviction.

At the French Open, Agassi came out of one crisis after another. In the second round, he was two points away from a four-set defeat against Frenchman Arnaud Clement, recovering for a five-set win as the Frenchman faded in the final set with cramps. In the round of 16, Agassi was on the ropes against the defending champion Carlos Moya. Moya won the first set and was up two breaks in the second, serving at 4-1. The 29-year-old American worked his way out of that bind and was a four-set victor. And then, in the final, Agassi was obliterated for two sets by an inspired Andrei Medvedev, the unseeded Ukrainian, ranked No. 100 in the world, who had once resided in the top five. Medvedev had been brilliant in the wind, but a rain delay late in the second set was just what Agassi needed to restore himself.

Slowly but surely, Agassi found his range off the ground, and the high-strung Medvedev lost his nerve. Agassi surged back methodically for a 1-6, 2-6, 6-4, 6-3, 6-4 triumph. When it was over, he wept as he turned to greet his coach Brad Gilbert and trainer Gil Reyes in the stands. Then he accepted the trophy from none other than Rod Laver, and nothing could have been more appropriate. Agassi had become the first man since Laver in 1969 to capture all four major championships, and the fifth man in history (Don Budge, Fred Perry, Roy Emerson, and Laver were the others), to record a career sweep of the Grand Slam events. That was no mean feat. He called his improbable Roland Garros triumph "sheer destiny".

The women provided similar drama on the red clay as a highly charged Graf won her first major title in three years and her 22nd overall by battling back mightily to down the top seeded Hingis 4-6,7-5,6-2. Hingis came agonizingly close to winning the only major she had not yet mastered. But her first big mistake occurred when she led 2-0 in the second set. On the first point of the third game, her forehand return was called long. She looked for help from umpire Anne Lasserre, who got out of the chair and conferred with the linesman. Lasserre confirmed that the call was correct. Hingis should have ended her protest right then and there, but a dangerous lapse in judgment cost her dearly. She walked around to Graf's side of the net to check the mark herself, a blatant violation of the rules. Referee Georgina Clark was called out to the court and Hingis was assessed a point penalty following her earlier warning for racket abuse.

The Roland Garros crowd came down hard on the teenager, and turned up the volume of their support for the veteran Graf. But Hingis regrouped. She served for the match at 5-4 in the second set and reached 15-0, standing three points away from a decisive, straight-set victory. But she drove a routine two-handed backhand beyond the baseline for 15-15. Graf broke her at 30 for 5-5, then swept eight of the next nine points to reach one set all.

By the time Graf reached 3-0 in the third set, she had run off six games in a row, and had collected 24 of 29 points in that span. Although Hingis managed to break back for 2-3 in the third and even had a point for 3-3, she was not the same player she had been for nearly two sets. Graf prevailed 4-6, 7-5, 6-2 to garner a fifth French Open crown. The German told the crowd at the post-match ceremony, "I feel French. I've played all over ther world, but I've never had a crowd like this one—ever." Later, Graf added, "This is the biggest win I've ever had for sure. I've had a lot of unexpected ones. But this is by far the most unexpected. I really came into the tournament without belief. This has been incredible."

Little did Graf know then that this would be her last major championship victory. She would reach the final of Wimbledon the following month, and it took a top of the line Davenport to stop her 6-4, 7-5 in the final. Davenport broke the seven-time champion once in each set. Graf squandered three game points in a tense opening game before surrendering her serve. That was enough to carry the Californian through the first set. Then, at 5-5 in the second after a rain delay, she caught Steffi off guard again, breaking at that critical juncture, then serving out the match with brio.

In six previous appearances at the All England Club, Davenport had never advanced beyond the quarter-finals, but she won this time around without the loss of a set in seven matches. Furthermore, she never lost her serve against the imposing Graf, and conceded only five points on her delivery in her last four service games. The No. 3 seed gave perhaps the greatest performance of her career. She struck the ball with admirable pace, depth, and precision, and played the big points better than her revered rival, who waved goodbye to the Centre Court

audience for the final time as a competitor. In her 14 visits to Wimbledon, Steffi had won the world's premier tournament seven times, reaching two additional finals. Moreover, she had triumphed in 22 of 53 career major events, an astonishing success rate of .415. Moreover, she had been beaten only nine times in 31 'Big Four' finals, and had captured 107 tournament titles altogether in her 17 seasons on the tour, a figure surpassed in the open era only by Navratilova (167) and Evert (154).

Meanwhile, Agassi stormed into the men's final on Centre Court with a scintillating, straight-set victory over Rafter. On the other half of the draw, Sampras accounted for Tim Henman in a four-set semi-final for the second straight year. And so the stage was set for the two prodigious Americans to meet for the fourth time in a major final. Sampras held a 2-1 edge heading into this contest. Based on recent form and Agassi's renewed passion and intensity, many insiders believed he would rule on the grass courts at the shrine of the sport for the second time after a seven-year gap.

But too many astute observers overlooked Sampras' propensity to raise his game ineffably for the matches that mattered most to him. The Centre Court was undeniably his home abroad, and he performed in that theater as he did nowhere else. Serving commandingly, backing up his delivery with first volleys of the highest order, returning with unrelenting aggression, he played perhaps the masterpiece match of his career, taking apart his greatest rival 6-3, 6-4, 7-5 to win Wimbledon for the sixth time in seven years. In turn, he had captured the crown three years in a row for the second time. He had surely earned the label, 'Man of the Century' at Wimbledon. And Sampras had secured a 12th Grand Slam tournament singles title, placing him in a tie with Roy Emerson for the men's record.

The key to the outcome was the seventh game of the match. Sampras served at 3-3, 0-40. Agassi stung him three straight times with brilliant, scorching returns. But calmly and purposefully, Sampras served his way stupendously out of that corner, and never looked back. Before Agassi realized what had hit him, Sampras had run out that first set and built a 2-0 second-set lead, sweeping five games in a row. He had soared to another level, and there was no way Agassi could possibly rise with him. Sampras summed it up well: "It was the best tennis I think I've ever played on that court. I think when Andre and I are both playing well, it's the best tennis, maybe ever. He's made me a better player over the years."

Sampras beat Agassi two more times over the summer while winning hard-court events in Los Angeles and Cincinnati. He had won four tournaments in a row by then, and a brief setback in Indianapolis did not alter his status as the heavy favorite to win the U.S. Open. But Sampras hurt himself in practice at The National Tennis Center the day before the tournament. He had to pull out with a herniated disc in his back. Suddenly, irrevocably, Agassi became the main man.

The 1994 Open champion had a comfortable journey to the final, but was given a stern test that afternoon by 6-foot-6 Martin, who was playing the hard court tennis of his life. Martin knew he had to strike relatively quickly in the rallies against the great ground stroker from Las Vegas. And Martin also recognized the importance of serving with authority.

He lost his serve only once in the first three sets, and played two magnificent tiebreaks to build two sets to one lead. With Agassi serving at 4-3 in the fourth, Martin had two break points. Had he converted, he might well have gone on to victory. As it was, Agassi would not acquiesce. He held on, and wore down his debilitated rival 6-4, 6-7 (5-7), 6-7 (2-7), 6-4, 6-2. This three-hour, 23-minute skirmish was the first five-set final at the Open since 1988, when Mats Wilander prevented Ivan Lendl from winning a fourth straight title. In his third consecutive major final, Agassi was too good when it counted. He said, "I don't remember any five setter that I've ever played where I did not lose my serve. I really had to make every point incredibly important. I felt like I was hanging by a thread for most of the match. Todd was really executing in a way that was giving me a lot of problems."

Agassi had come from behind to beat No. 3 seed Kafelnikov in a four-set semi-final, while Martin dispatched unseeded Frenchman Cedric Pioline without the loss of a set. Pioline had brought down two-time

defending champion Patrick Rafter, 4-6, 4-6, 6-3, 7-5, 1-0, ret. The Australian's aching shoulder forced him to surrender. In the quarter-finals, Kafelnikov stopped Richard Krajicek in a fifth-set tie-break, but Krajicek set a record by releasing no fewer than 49 aces in that gripping match.

The women's crown went to none other than No. 7 seed Serena Williams, who became the first African American woman since Althea Gibson at Forest Hills in 1958 to take a major championship. Serena, 17, had an astonishing tournament. In the third round, she was on the brink of defeat against 16-year-old Belgian Kim Clijsters. Clijsters led 5-3 in the final set before Serena blasted her way out of danger by capturing 16 of the last 17 points in a 4-6, 6-2, 7-5 triumph. In the round of 16, Serena rallied from a set down to oust Conchita Martinez. Facing Monica Seles in the quarters, Serena dropped the first set again before recording a 4-6, 6-3, 6-2 victory. Next on her agenda was defending champion Davenport. Serena took that one 6-4, 1-6, 6-4.

And so the stage was set for a final round meeting with the top seeded Hingis, who had won a bruising battle over Venus Williams 6-1, 4-6, 6-3 the day before in the semi-finals. Hingis took too much out of herself in that strenuous showdown, and Serena was just hitting her stride. Williams led 6-3, 5-3, 15-40, double match point against an overwhelmed Hingis, but Martina refused to walk away. She took three games in a row and was two points away from parity at one set all. Hingis led 6-5, 0-30 but Serena rekindled her energy and enthusiasm and came away with a 6-3, 7-6 (7-4), victory in her first major final. As Serena finished off Hingis, big sister Venus watched from the stands, wearing a bittersweet expression. She had been expected to win a big championship before Serena, but the following afternoon the two sisters joined forces to capture the women's doubles title over Chanda Rubin and Sandrine Testud.

At the men's year-end ATP Tour World Championships in Hannover, Sampras put together another superb performance to oust Agassi 6-1, 7-5, 6-4 in the final. Agassi had beaten Sampras in the round robin 6-2, 6-2 during the week, but his formidable rival came through when the chips were down. Coming into Hannover, he had played only one match all fall after missing the U.S. Open, aggravating his back at the indoor event in Paris during a first round win over Francisco Clavet. But, in Hannover, Sampras sparkled

---

1999 CHAMPIONS AND LEADERS

Top Player Earnings: Men	**Davis Cup:** Australia
Agassi, Andre $4,269,265	**Fed Cup:** United States
Top Player Earnings: Women	**ATP World Championships,**
Martina Hingis $3,291,780	**Hannover**
Year-End Number One	Pete Sampras
Men: Andre Agassi	**Grand Slam Cup, Munich**
Women: Martina Hingis	Greg Rusedski
ITF World Champion	**Chase Championships, NYC**
Men: Andre Agassi	Lindsay Davenport
Women: Martina Hingis	**Grand Slam Cup, Munich**
	Serena Williams

again. Meanwhile, in New York, Hingis was beaten 6-4, 6-2 by an inspired Davenport in the final of the Chase Championships. But Hingis, who won seven singles titles and reached the finals in 13 of her 20 events, finished the season at No. 1 in the world for the second time.

At the Fed Cup final at Stanford, Calif., perhaps the finest U.S. team in history assembled. Venus Williams and Davenport took on the singles assignments while Serena Williams joined her sister for the doubles. U.S. captain Billie Jean King had an embarrassment of riches on her side with so much talent surrounding her. Despite her Flushing Meadows brilliance, Serena Williams was not chosen for singles. No matter. Venus won over Elena Likhovtseva 6-3, 6-4 and then Davenport downed Elena Dementieva 6-4, 6-0.

Davenport knocked off Likhovtseva in straight sets, and the Williams sisters prevailed. Venus suffered the lone U.S. loss in an emphatic 4-1 triumph, losing a third set tiebreak to Dementieva.

Australia took the Davis Cup at Nice, upending the host nation France, 3-2. Mark Philippoussis was the hero, winning his opening-day singles over Sebastien Grosjean in straight sets, and clinching the tie with a 6-3, 5-7, 6-1,6-2 over Pioline. Australia seized the Cup for the 27th time, prevailing as the world champion team nation for the first time since 1973. John Newcombe had joined Rod Laver on that occasion to lead the Australians to a 5-0 victory over the U.S. in Cleveland. This time around, Newcombe was the captain, and no less euphoric about the outcome.

2000

Sampras all alone, Venus rising fast

Gustavo Kuerten
An 11th-hour win over Andre Agassi, and No. 1 is his.

When a compelling season came to an end, this much was certain: Brazil's enormously popular Gustavo Kuerten and the strikingly improved Venus Williams were the two players who achieved the most. Kuerten captured the French Open for the second time, and closed his campaign magnificently with a triumph at the elite Tennis Masters Cup in Lisbon, dramatically moving past Russian Marat Safin to finish No. 1 in the world. Venus went to work with more passion and purpose than ever before, sweeping the Wimbledon and U.S. Open titles. Despite securing six singles championships including the gold medal at the Olympic Games, Venus was ranked only third in the world behind Martina Hingis and Lindsay Davenport. But, given the fact that she had won the two biggest tournaments in tennis, Williams was considered the best player in the world by the vast majority of authorities.

To be sure, it was a year when the prestigious prizes were divided among a cluster of leading players. Andre Agassi took the Australian Open for the second time. Safin peaked propitiously at the U.S. Open to collect his first major championship. Most notably, Pete Sampras made history of the highest order, winning Wimbledon to set a record with 13 Grand Slam tournament singles championships. And two top of the line big hitters, Davenport and Mary Pierce, made their presence known by coming through impressively at Grand Slam events.

Hingis had been hoping to seal a fourth singles title in a row in Melbourne at the Australian Open, but an inspired Davenport denied her that opportunity. Raising her record to 3-0 in 'Big Four' finals, Davenport blasted her familiar rival off the court 6-1, 7-5. The American led 5-1 in the second set before the plucky Hingis pressed hard with pride to draw level at 5-5. Undismayed, Davenport took two games in a row for the win.

The pivotal men's match in Melbourne was Agassi's

semi-final with Sampras. Agassi approached that riveting contest with an 11-17 record against his most revered rival; he came away with an exhilarating 6-4, 3-6, 6-7 (0-7), 7-6 (7-5), 6-2 triumph. Sampras was two points away from a four-set win when he led 5-4 on serve in the fourth set tiebreak, but Agassi turned the corner and never looked back, prevailing despite 37 aces from a determined Sampras.

In the final, Agassi ousted defending champion Yevgeny Kafelnikov 3-6, 6-3, 6-2, 6-4 with another dazzling display. It was the sixth major tournament victory for Agassi in his storied career, but he did not take another title of any kind for the rest of the year.

Kuerten stepped up commandingly in the next major, ruling on the slow red clay of Roland Garros. Seeded fifth, the Brazilian overcame Sweden's industrious Magnus Norman 6-2, 6-3, 3-6 7-6 (8-6), but not before the Swede had saved 10 match points in the latter stages of the battle. Kuerten had hung on tenaciously to defeat 1996 champion Kafelnikov in a five-set quarter-final before taking apart the markedly improved Juan Carlos Ferrero of Spain in the penultimate round.

Pierce had finally found the top of her game after a string of disappointing seasons. A finalist at the French Open in 1994 and the winner of the Australian Open in 1995, she had not lived up to those high standards in the ensuing years. But now, at 25, she had reached a new level of maturity. She became the first Frenchwoman since Françoise Durr in 1967 to prevail at Roland Garros.

Seeded sixth, Pierce fought back gamely to oust three-time former titlist Monica Seles 4-6, 6-3, 6-4 in the quarter-finals. In the semi-finals, she removed the top-seeded Hingis 6-4, 5-7, 6-2 in a suspenseful struggle. After those uplifting victories, the final was almost anti-climactic for Pierce. She beat Spain's resourceful Conchita Martinez 6-2, 7-5 to claim her second career major in exemplary fashion. Pierce served at 4-5 in the second set, but ran out the match capably from there.

On the grass at the All England Club, Venus Williams was unbeatable. Not since Althea Gibson 42 years earlier had an African American woman won Wimbledon. Venus came through a difficult draw, holding back a trio of accomplished adversaries—the top seeded Hingis, her sister Serena, and Davenport. The best of those battles was against Hingis. Venus took the first set comfortably, then went up a break at 3-2 in the second. Thereafter, Hingis asserted herself. She broke twice to take the second set. By the time the players were locked at 2-2 in the third, there had been eight consecutive service breaks. Hingis, however, had spent too much of her energy, and Venus picked up her velocity and placement on serve to close out a 6-3, 4-6, 6-4 triumph.

The Venus-Serena semi-final confrontation was only the third ever meeting between sisters at Wimbledon, and the first of the open era. Many among the cognoscenti looked for Serena to beat her older sibling for only the second time in five career head-to-head clashes. She had marched into this battle having lost only 13 games in five matches. She had lost her serve only once in ten sets. She had been breathtakingly effective in all facets of her game. But big sister dominated the day, winning 6-2, 7-6 (7-3).

Serena had a 4-2, second-set lead with three break points at her disposal. Venus hung on tenaciously. In the tiebreak, Serena moved ahead 3-1 but never won another point. A despondent Serena was in tears as she congratulated her sister at the net. Venus put her arm around Serena to console her. But their father and coach, Richard Williams, was not at courtside. He chose to wander through the town of Wimbledon while his daughters competed, claiming it was too painful for him to watch.

When it was over, Serena astutely summed up the match: "I didn't think I played that well today. I missed a lot of shots, especially on my forehand side. Venus brought out her best game against me and I guess I

2000 THE MAJOR CHAMPIONSHIPS

Australian Open
Men's Singles: Andre Agassi
Women's Singles: Lindsay Davenport
Men's Doubles: Rick Leach / Ellis Ferreira
Women's Doubles: Lisa Raymond / Rennae Stubbs
Mixed Doubles: Rennae Stubbs / Jared Palmer

French Open
Men's Singles: Gustavo Kuerten
Women's Singles: Mary Pierce
Men's Doubles: Mark Woodforde / Todd Woodbridge
Women's Doubles: Martina Hingis / Mary Pierce
Mixed Doubles: Mariaan de Swardt / David Adams

Wimbledon
Men's Singles: Pete Sampras
Women's Singles: Venus Williams
Men's Doubles: Todd Woodbridge / Mark Woodforde
Women's Doubles: Venus Williams / Serena Williams
Mixed Doubles: Kimberly Po / Donald Johnson

U.S. Open
Men's Singles: Marat Safin
Women's Singles: Venus Williams
Men's Doubles: Lleyton Hewitt / Max Mirnyi
Women's Doubles: Julie Halard-Decugis / Ai Sugiyama
Mixed Doubles: Arantxa Sanchez Vicario / Jared Palmer

wasn't all that ready. It was my goal to do better in this tournament, but that's okay. I'm only 18. Venus is 20. I have a lot of years ahead of me."

In the final, Venus Williams knocked out the defending champion Davenport 6-3, 7-6 (7-3) in a lackluster showdown. Venus served for the match at 5-4 in the second set, but two double faults and an unprovoked backhand error cost her that game. Nevertheless, she controlled the tiebreak, racing to a 5-1 advantage and moving persuasively to the victory from there.

Venus admitted, "We were both feeling the pressure. I know I was rushing too much on my serve." Davenport was largely in accord, saying, "There were a few points that I'd love to take back, a few things I wish I could have done better. But a lot of that was caused by Venus. She was hitting the ball a lot deeper that I was."

In the men's Centre Court final, Sampras concluded an emotional fortnight with a joyous moment in the twilight. Finishing his 6-7 (10-12), 7-6 (7-5), 6-4, 6-2 final-round triumph over Patrick Rafter at 8:57 p.m. after rain had twice delayed play earlier in the day, the 28-year-old American climbed up into the stands to embrace his mother Georgia and father Sam, who had flown over from California for the title match. They had never seen him win a major title before. Also in the stands was Bridgette Wilson, Pete's fiancé. (They would marry on September 30). As he said later, "Having my parents and future wife there was about as good as it is going to get for me as an athlete."

From the second round on, Sampras played with tendinitis in his left foot and ankle. He managed to win a rugged four set meeting with the dangerous Karol Kucera, and then would not practice in between matches. He took injections before each match to combat the pain, and willed his way on. He had a favorable draw, not meeting a seed until he took on the crafty (No. 12) Rafter, who had beaten second-seeded Agassi in a brilliantly played five-set semi-final. But driven by deep pride and a sense of history, Sampras staged a

spectacular comeback against his worthy Australian rival.

Rafter served with a 4-1 lead in the second set tiebreak, standing three points away from a commanding two sets to love lead. Sampras swept six of the next seven points to get back on level terms at one set all, and refused to look back. Serving with increasing authority, finding the range on his backhand returns, hardly missing a volley, Sampras soared over the last two sets.

He did lost his serve even once in this showdown—the fifth time in seven victorious Wimbledon finals that he had realized that remarkable feat. In turn, Sampras had not been broken in his last 17 sets of the tournament, holding his delivery an incredible 85 times in a row. He had broken the record he shared with Australia's Roy Emerson, capturing a 13th career Grand Slam crown, leading many knowledgeable observers to the conclusion that he was the greatest player of all time.

On to New York, for the U.S. Open. Although Safin had made significant strides over the course of the season—winning Barcelona and Mallorca on clay in the spring, taking the Toronto Tennis Masters Series title over the summer—no one was really prepared for the devastatingly potent tennis he would produce on the hard courts at Flushing Meadows. In the final, he stunned Sampras 6-4, 6-3, 6-3, competing with immense poise in his first major final. It was one of the most comprehensive defeats ever suffered by his illustrious opponent, who was beaten for only the third time in 16 major finals.

Not once did Sampras break Safin's explosive serve and the 20-year-old Russian broke Sampras four times. Pete had lost his delivery the same number of times against his previous six opponents. He simply came up against a madly inspired man who did not fully understand what he was doing. "He reminded me of when I was 19 and won here for the first time, "Sampras said of Safin. "He passed and returned my serve as well as anyone I've seen."

Safin had started off the year with a dismal 5-11 match record, but he was in full flight at the last major the season. He was pushed into arduous five-set showdowns with both the 35-year-old Italian Gianluca Pozzi and the fleet-footed Frenchman Sebastien Grosjean, but the Russian held his ground when it counted.

Sampras, too, was hard pressed to make it to the final. In the quarter-finals, he confronted Richard Krajicek,

2000 CHAMPIONS AND LEADERS

Top Player Earnings: Men	**ITF World Champion**
Gustavo Kuerten $4,701,610	Men: Gustavo Kuerten
Top Player Earnings: Women	Women: Martina Hingis
Martina Hingis $3,457,049	**Tennis Masters Cup, Lisbon**
Year-End Number One	Gustavo Kuerten
Men: Gustavo Kuerten	**Chase Championships, NYC**
Women: Martina Hingis	Martina Hingis
Davis Cup: Spain	
Fed Cup: United States	

the 6-foot-5 Dutchman who had beaten him four of the last five times they had clashed, including a straight-set Wimbledon quarter-final in 1996. Krajicek came at Sampras in full serve-and-volley throttle, taking the first set and moving to 6-2, quadruple set point in the second set tiebreak. In a dazzling sequence, Sampras took six points in a row to reach one set all. He was brimming with conviction thereafter, winning this exhilarating collision 4-6 7-6 (8-6), 6-4, 6-2. He then defeated Lleyton Hewitt in a straight-set semi-final.

Venus Williams demonstrated her grace under pressure in winning the championship of her country for the first time, taking her second straight major in the process. Facing a first-rate Hingis in the semi-finals, Venus trailed 3-5,15-30 in the third set. With an opportunity to reach double match point, Hingis played a cautious overhead down the middle. Venus replied boldly, driving her two-handed backhand down the line for a winner. She had escaped from a precarious position, and proceeded to win four games in a row to come through 4-6, 6-3, 7-5.

In the final against Davenport, Venus was in jeopardy again as the Californian served for a 5-1 first set lead. Venus collected five games in a row to take that set, and took the match 6-4, 7-5.

Only a few weeks after the Open, Venus Williams and Kafelnikov came away with the gold medals at the Olympic Games on the hard courts in Sydney. Venus ousted Russian Elena Dementieva 6-2, 6-4. Joining her sister Serena, she also took the gold medal in the women's doubles, becoming the first player since Helen Wills in 1924 to sweep the singles and doubles. Kafelnikov was surprisingly resilient in a five-set triumph over Germany's Tommy Haas in the men's final, safely coming through that contest 7-6 (7-4), 3-6, 6-2, 4-6, 6-3.

Safin seemed certain to finish the year at No. 1 in the world when he won his seventh tournament of the season at the Tennis Masters Series event indoors at Paris. But Kuerten somehow surpassed him at the last hurdle. The flamboyant Brazilian—flourishing on the slow hard court surface indoors—ousted Sampras in the semi-finals and Agassi in the final to take the Tennis Masters Cup title in Lisbon.

Had he lost to Agassi, Safin would been the year's top player. But Kuerten was magnificent in crushing Agassi 6-4, 6-4, 6-4 with a relentless barrage of sharply angled topspin backhands doing most of the damage. He was

the first South American man ever to finish at No. 1 on the official ATP computer since the inception of the rankings in 1973.

Despite not taking any of the four majors, Hingis finished No. 1 among the women for the third time in four years. Her unfailing consistency kept her at the top. The Swiss backcourt stylist won nine tournaments including the year-end Chase Championships in New York, where she came from behind to oust Seles in a three-set final, raising her record against Monica to 12-2. But, of course, nearly everyone in the know considered Venus Williams the best player since she won the two biggest tournaments.

Spain established itself as the tenth country to win the Davis Cup. In Barcelona, they struck down the Australians 3-1 on red clay. In the tie-clinching triumph, Ferrero stopped Hewitt 6-2, 7-6 (7-5), 4-6 6-4. King Juan Carlos 1 and Queen Sofia cheered on the Spanish men. Spain, beaten in the 1965 and 1967 finals, was too tough for the Australians on the slow surface in front of their vociferous home fans.

The U.S. retained the Fed Cup, with Davenport, Seles, and Jennifer Capriati leading the Americans past Spain 5-0 in the final at Las Vegas. Davenport took apart Conchita Martinez 6-1, 6-2 to give the U.S. an insurmountable 3-0 lead. It had not been a bad year for the U.S. American women had won three of the four majors, and the Fed Cup triumph underlined their supremacy.

Meanwhile, Jim Courier retired from tennis early in the year at 29. The redheaded, industrious, enterprising American won back-to-back French Open titles in 1991-92, and took the Australian Open in 1992-93. Courier reached the finals of the U.S. Open in 1991 and Wimbledon two years later. He played on two victorious U.S. Davis Cup contingents (1992 and 1995). Ranked No. 1 in the world in 1992, he had not finished a campaign among the world's top ten since 1995.

2000 OLYMPICS, SYDNEY, AUSTRALIA

Men's singles: Yevgeny Kafelnikov, Russia, Gold; Tommy Haas, Germany, Silver; Arnaud Di Pasquale, France, Bronze
Women's singles: Venus Williams, United States, Gold; Elena Dementieva, Russia, Silver; Monica Seles, United States, Bronze
Men's doubles: Daniel Nestor & Sebastien Lareau, Canada, Gold; Todd Woodbridge & Mark Woodforde, Australia, Silver; Alex Corretja & Albert Costa, Spain, Bronze
Women's doubles: Venus Williams & Serena Williams, United States, Gold; Kristie Boogert & Miriam Oremans, Netherlands, Silver; Dominique Van Roost & Els Callens, Belgium, Bronze

2001

Aussie rules again as Hewitt reaches World No. 1

S he was indisputably 'Tennis Player of the Year.' Staging one of the most extraordinary comebacks in the modern world of sports, she reached the top of her profession, won two major championships, and captured the hearts of tennis fans across the globe with her unwavering spirit. With her astonishing resurgence, Jennifer Capriati overshadowed almost everyone else with her exploits.

Capriati had endured some tumultuous times on her way to the summit. When she turned pro in 1990 shortly before her 14th birthday, she was expected to move swiftly to the top of her sport. She built an impressive record in her first four years as a pro, finishing each of those seasons among the top ten in the world, reaching the semi-finals of Wimbledon in 1990 and the U.S. Open in 1991, winning the gold medal at the Olympic Games in 1992. Then she fell upon hard times from late 1993 until she returned to the Top 25 in the world in 1996. In that span, she was arrested for drug possession after an earlier shoplifting charge. She had a few more difficult seasons before rising to No. 23 in the world in 1999, then No. 14 in 2000.

So, to be sure, she had planted some promising seeds as she headed into 2001. But not even Capriati herself could have anticipated such a dramatic reversal of fortunes. It all began at the Australian Open in Melbourne. Henrieta Nagyova, a 22-year-old Slovakian, pushed her to 7-5 in the final set in the opening round. In the quarter-finals, Capriati cut down Monica Seles after losing the first set and trailing 4-2 in the second. In the penultimate round, Capriati accounted for defending champion Lindsay Davenport in straight sets. Last, but not least, she upstaged Martina Hingis 6-4, 6-3 to win her first major title. Hingis had won all five of her career meetings with Capriati until then.

When it was over, a beaming Capriati said, "Dreams do come true. If you keep believing in

Jennifer Capriati
"Dreams do come true."

yourself, anything can happen. I'm no longer going to doubt myself in anything." With good reason.

She had taken only one set in her five losses to Hingis. She was appearing in her first major final while Hingis was in her 11th. But Capriati's flat, penetrating groundstrokes were too much for Martina, who was rushed out of points time and again by the American's pace and precision. Hingis rallied from 1-5 to 4-5 in the first set, but Capriati held for the set, and took over from there.

Operating skillfully from the backcourt in the stifling heat Down Under, Andre Agassi crushed Frenchman Arnaud Clement, the energetic counter-puncher who had knocked him out of the U.S. Open in the second round in 2000. This time around, Agassi was in vintage form, coasting to a 6-4, 6-2, 6-2 final-round triumph for his seventh major title.

The real test for the bald-headed American was his semi-final with Patrick Rafter. The first three sets of that encounter were played at an astounding level as the Australian came forward relentlessly, forcing Agassi to keep coming up with impeccable passing shots. The home fans cheered unabashedly for their man as Rafter moved ahead two sets to one, but he was a spent force. Agassi easily resumed his command to win 7-5, 2-6, 6-7 (5-7), 6-2, 6-3.

At Roland Garros, Gustavo Kuerten was the man to beat once more. The Brazilian took the French Open title for the second year in a row and the third time in all, picking apart Spain's Alex Corretja as burdensome winds and light rain gave way to sunshine and calmer conditions. Kuerten stopped Corretja 6-7 (3-7), 7-5, 6-2, 6-0. The 24-year-old cast aside his inhibitions across the last two sets and played with verve and imagination.

Kuerten had nearly suffered a major upset the previous Sunday afternoon against American qualifier Michael Russell, rescuing himself from two sets to love and match point down to prevail in five sets. He went on to dismantle Spain's Juan Carlos Ferrero in a straight-set semi-final.

Agassi, seeded third, was ushered out of the tournament in the quarter-finals by Frenchman Sebastien Grosjean 1-6, 6-1, 6-1, 6-3. After the American had raced through the first set, former President Clinton came into Roland Garros stadium to watch the rest of the match. He was greeted with a rousing round of applause from the crowd. Thereafter, Agassi went sharply into decline, losing his authority and the match. Later,

he unconvincingly claimed he was not aware that Clinton had been present.

Capriati remained on the ascendancy at Roland Garros, winning a gripping final-round confrontation from Kim Clijsters 1-6, 6-4, 12-10 for a second straight major crown.

It was one of the hardest fought and most tightly contested women's major finals of modern times. The Belgian had struck back boldly from a set and 4-2 down to defeat countrywoman Justine Henin 2-6, 7-5, 6-3.

Against Capriati, she exploited her often-brilliant, inside-out forehand and forced the Floridian back on her heels. Clijsters controlled the opening set, then lost a relatively tight second set. The third set hung in the balance until the end. Four times, Capriati was two points away from losing, and yet she kept creating chances for herself as well. After serving to save the match at 4-5 and 5-6 in the third, Capriati tried to serve it out at 7-6. An obstinate Clijsters would not go away. When Capriati took eight points in a row to lead 10-9, she seemed certain to finish the job.

Clijsters broke back again for 10-10, but that was her limit. Capriati closed the account with some timely attacking, and won the longest third set ever in a Roland Garros women's final. "I'm just really happy I pulled it out," she said. "It was such a tough match. I was just fighting to the end because I wanted to win so much. "Clijsters, gracious in defeat, said, "I can't really blame myself that I lost. One of us had to lose, and eventually

---

2001 THE MAJOR CHAMPIONSHIPS

Australian Open
Men's Singles: Andre Agassi
Women's Singles: Jennifer Capriati
Men's Doubles: Jonas Bjorkman / Todd Woodbridge
Women's Doubles: Serena Williams / Venus Williams
Mixed Doubles: Corina Morariu / Ellis Ferreira
French Open
Men's Singles: Gustavo Kuerten
Women's Singles: Jennifer Capriati
Men's Doubles: Mahesh Bhupathi / Leander Paes
Women's Doubles: Virginia Ruano Pascual / Paola Suarez
Mixed Doubles: Virginia Ruano Pascual / Tomas Carbonell
Wimbledon
Men's Singles: Goran Ivanisevic
Women's Singles: Venus Williams
Men's Doubles: Donald Johnson / Jared Palmer
Women's Doubles: Lisa Raymond / Rennae Stubbs
Mixed Doubles: Daniela Hantuchova / Leos Friedl
U.S. Open
Men's Singles: Lleyton Hewitt
Women's Singles: Venus Williams
Men's Doubles: Wayne Black / Kevin Ullyett
Women's Doubles: Rennae Stubbs / Lisa Raymond
Mixed Doubles: Rennae Stubbs / Todd Woodbridge

it had to be me today. She's playing with so much confidence."

That confidence nearly carried Capriati through Wimbledon. Two matches away from a third straight major crown, hoping to become the first woman since Graf in 1988 to win the Grand Slam, she started superbly against Henin in the semi-finals. In 21 minutes, she rolled through the first set. But Henin's exquisite, one-handed topspin backhand was a weapon not to be denied, and the 19-year-old began exploiting the sharp angles off that side, taking Capriati off the court on her two-handed side. The complexion of the match changed irrevocably. Henin succeeded 2-6, 6-4, 6-2.

"Everybody was making such a big deal out of the Grand Slam," said Capriati. "But I'm pretty happy with how the year has gone. Justine was a different player in the last two sets from the beginning. She was going for it—all or nothing—and she was on."

Henin was hard pressed to play at the top of her game in the final against Venus Williams, a 6-2, 6-7 (1-7), 6-1 winner over Davenport in the semi-finals. Venus's big serving and aggression off the ground and on the drive volley propelled her through the first set, but Henin took three games in a row from 3-3 in the second, losing only one point in two service games, breaking Venus in between. But Venus kept attacking at the right times, winning 18 of her 24 net approaches.

She picked up her serving, and swept to a 6-1, 3-6, 6-0 victory—her second championship season in a row on Centre Court. Venus did not gloat; rather, she saluted Henin. "She's really very good. In my first Grand Slam final, I didn't win a set [against Hingis at the 1997 U.S. Open]. Justine is a great player and I want to congratulate her."

The men's final— held a day late due to inclement weather—pitted Goran Ivanisevic against Rafter. Ivanisevic, beaten in his three previous final round appearances at the All England Club, held back his gallant Australian rival 6-3, 3-6, 6-3, 2-6, 9-7 to capture

his first major title at 29. He had lost in the qualifying at the Australian Open at the start of the year, and came into Wimbledon ranked No. 125 in the world. He was granted his request for a wildcard. After suffering with severe shoulder problems for much of the previous year, his days of contending for big titles seemed well behind him.

But the 6-foot-4 Croatian left-hander somehow rekindled his old serving prowess, breaking his own 1992 tournament record of 206 aces by serving 212 against a sterling cast of opponents including Carlos Moya, Andy Roddick, Greg Rusedski, Marat Safin, Tim Henman, and Rafter. When he served at 6-7, 15-30 in the fifth set against Rafter, he was two points away from losing. But he held on for 7-7 and assertively took the last two games to hand Rafter a second straight agonizing final-round defeat on the Centre Court. It was not one of the best-played Wimbledon finals, but it was surely one of the most suspenseful and emotional.

The No. 3 seed Rafter won the highest caliber contest of the fortnight, narrowly escaping defeat against second seeded Agassi. Agassi served for the match at 5-4 in the fifth set and reached 30-15, but Rafter attacked at the propitious moments in that critical game and broke back. He defeated the 31-year-old American 2-6, 6-3, 3-6, 6-2, 8-6. For the second year in a row, he had bested Agassi in the penultimate round of game's biggest tournament.

That battle ended on Friday afternoon. Ivanisevic followed against Henman. Henman built two sets to one lead and they were on serve in the fourth when rain intruded. They returned Saturday, and Ivanisevic regrouped to capture the fourth set. But more rain forced another postponement until Sunday, with Ivanisevic completing a three-day ordeal with a 7-5 6-7 (6-8), 0-6, 7-6 (7-5), 6-3 victory.

Henman had ousted the gifted Roger Federer in the quarter-finals after the 19-year-old Swiss serve-and-volleyer had held back Sampras 7-6 (9-7), 5-7, 6-4, 6-7 (2-7), 7-5 in the round of 16, ending the American's 31-match winning streak at the All England Club. Sampras, the champion for seven of the previous eight years, had two break points at 4-4 in the final set but did not convert.

At the U.S. Open, Sampras was striving to become the first man ever to capture at least one major title for nine consecutive years, and he came remarkably close to realizing that goal. In an unprecedented run, he stopped

2001 CHAMPIONS AND LEADERS

Top Player Earnings: Men
Gustavo Kuerten $4,091,004
Top Player Earnings: Women
Venus Williams $2,662,610
Year-End Number One
Men: Lleyton Hewitt
Women: Lindsay Davenport
Davis Cup: France
Fed Cup: Belgium

ITF World Champion
Men: Lleyton Hewitt
Women: Jennifer Capriati
Tennis Masters Cup, Sydney
Lleyton Hewitt
Sanex Championships, Munich
Serena Williams

the three men who had controlled the tournament since he had won his fourth and last title in 1996. In the round of 16, Sampras took down 1997-98 champion Rafter in four sets to set up a quarter-final appointment with 1994 and 1999 victor Agassi, who had beaten Pete in their last three head-to-head battles.

But in one of the finest matches in the history of the game, Sampras halted Agassi 6-7 (7-9), 7-6 (7-2), 7-6 (7-2), 7-6 (7-5). Neither man broke serve in four scintillating sets under the lights. Agassi had made a mere 19 unforced errors, and still had lost. Before the start of the last tiebreak, the crowd gave both players a well-deserved standing ovation. Finally, Sampras cut down Safin, avenging his loss to the Russian in the 2000 final with an emphatic 6-4, 7-6 (7-5), 6-3 triumph.

By the time Sampras arrived in the final, he had held serve no fewer than 87 straight times since the second round. He seemed ready to run another victory lap. But waiting for him on the last day was none other than Lleyton Hewitt, the Australian with the small frame but large heart. He played surpassingly to defeat Sampras on a windswept afternoon, claiming his first major title with a 7-6 (7-4), 6-1, 6-1 win.

The consistency of Hewitt's service returning was extraordinary; he broke Sampras six times, and produced dazzling passing shots as well. He was much fresher and more highly charged than his 30-year-old adversary. Despite his heroics, Sampras had fallen short. "I'm sure as times goes by," he lamented, "I'll reflect and feel good about what I did here. But only one name gets on the trophy and it's not mine. That's the harsh reality of it."

As for the women, Venus Williams was every bit as convincing in defending her Open title as she had been in ruling again at Wimbledon. In a Saturday night, prime-time final under the lights, she held the upper hand throughout in a 6-2, 6-4 triumph over her sister Serena, her fourth win in five matches against her younger sibling. From 1-2 in the first set, Venus won seven games in a row. Serena found her timing off in this big-hitting battle and led 4-3 on serve in the second. Venus took over from there to win the last three games. She committed 17 fewer unforced errors than Serena, and that made all the difference.

Venus had overcome Capriati 6-4, 6-2 in an uneven semi-final while Serena had peaked in a 6-3, 6-2 drugging of the top-seeded Hingis. The No. 4 seed Venus looked every inch the best player in the world, and the No. 10 seed Serena made it unmistakably clear

that she belonged much closer to the top of her profession.

At the close of the season in Munich, Serena took the Sanex Championships, a much more alluring event when it was played in New York. Davenport, out for two-and-a-half months earlier in the season with a knee injury, hurt it again in a hard fought semi-final victory over Clijsters, then was forced to default the final to Serena. Despite her loss to Venus at the U.S. Open, Serena had finished her season with a flourish.

Meanwhile, the men's Tennis Masters Cup Championships moved to Sydney, where Hewitt firmly established himself as the best player in the world. In the round-robin portion of that event, he stopped Grosjean, Rafter and Agassi. He knocked off Ferrero in the semi-finals, then toppled Grosjean again in the final to end his season in style.

At 20 years, 10 months, he became the youngest ever year-end No. 1 since the inception of the ATP computer rankings. In turn, he was the first Australian man ever to complete a year at No. 1 since the computer was established in 1973.

There were 142 nations contending for the Davis Cup, but the sole survivor was France, a surprising 3-2 winner over Australia in the final on grass in Melbourne. Hewitt was ousted in a five-set thriller on the opening day by the excellent attacking play of Nicolas Escude. Rafter, who went into sabbatical and eventually announced his retirement in early 2003, took care of Grosjean. Then Australian captain John Fitzgerald elected to play Rafter and Hewitt in the doubles, and they lost to Cedric Pioline and Fabrice Santoro. Hewitt got Australia even at 2-2 by erasing Grosjean in straight sets, but Rafter was not fit to play the last singles. He felt his shoulder was too sore for him to play, so the big serving left-hander Wayne Arthurs took his place. The 30-year-old, ranked No. 64 in the world, was taken apart by Escude, 7-6 (7-3), 6-7 (5-7), 6-3, 6-3.

In another sign of their growing stature in the women's game, Clijsters and Henin carried Belgium to a first-ever triumph at the Fed Cup. In the final, they beat Russia 2-1 as Clijsters crushed Dementieva and Henin toppled Nadia Petrova in the singles assignments. While the Williams sisters, Capriati, Davenport and Seles gave the U.S. a presence in the upper echelons no other country could come close to matching, the fact remained that Belgium was surging forward, buoyed by the talent and tenacity of Clijsters and Henin.

2002

Serena takes lead in Williams sister act

Lleyton Hewitt
A worthy successor to Sedgman, Laver, Emerson, Newcombe et al.

In many ways, it was a landmark season in the world of tennis. Serena Williams celebrated more than anyone else, winning eight of 13 tournaments, capturing 56 of 61 matches, securing three of the four major titles. Lleyton Hewitt stood on top of the world for the second straight year, winning Wimbledon for the first time, taking his second straight Tennis Masters Cup title. Veterans Albert Costa of Spain and Thomas Johansson of Sweden came away with their first career major titles and Jennifer Capriati triumphed at the Australian Open for her third major crown.

But perhaps the biggest story of the year was the reemergence of Pete Sampras, who broke an agonizing 33-tournament losing streak by winning the U.S. Open for the fifth time, recording a 14th major triumph in the process. The 31-year-old Sampras became the oldest men's U.S. Open champion since 35-year-old Ken Rosewall took the top honor at Forest Hills in 1970. Moreover, Sampras was the oldest man to rule at any major since Arthur Ashe (five days shy of his 32nd birthday) won Wimbledon in 1975.

To be sure, the soft-spoken yet deeply driven American was the 'Comeback Player of the Year.' In winning at Flushing Meadows for the first time in six years, Sampras emphatically answered the many media critics who insisted he no longer could play at that level. As usual, he spoke eloquently with his racket.

Clearly, no one thought that Johansson would place his name on the winner's trophy Down Under. In 24 previous appearances at the majors, the 26-year-old Swede had never been beyond the quarter-finals. He had finished two years (including 2001) among the top 20 in the world, but did not seem to have the tools to compete at the top of his trade. But the No.-16 seed took full advantage of an excellent draw, and then had the good fortune to meet the enigmatic Marat Safin in the final.

Safin had played his best brand of big-tournament

tennis since his breakthrough victory at the U.S. Open 16 months earlier. He won a high-quality, four-set skirmish from Sampras in the round of 16, and battled back gamely from two sets to one down to topple Tommy Haas in the semi-finals. Seemingly poised to pick off another major, he took the first set from Johansson but slowly came apart at the seams thereafter. Johansson's forehand return was his best feature, and he served progressively better after the opening set. In the end, the Swede prevailed 3-6, 6-4, 6-4, 7-6 (7-4). While Johansson competed with unwavering intensity, Safin surely did not display the fighting attitude he needed for such an important occasion.

Capriati, meanwhile, fought as ferociously as any player could in overcoming three-time former winner Martina Hingis in a gripping final. With temperatures on court measured at 107 degrees Fahrenheit, the 25-year-old American had her back to the wall from the outset. She lost the first set, then trailed 4-0 in the second. Hingis, closing in on her first 'Big Four' championship since the 1999 Australian Open, was exploiting her extraordinary ball control off both sides, moving Capriati craftily around the court, luring Jennifer into mistakes. But Martina had lost the art of closing a deal of this magnitude. She started playing not to lose rather than trying to control her own destiny.

Capriati would not fold. She rallied from 0-4 to 3-4, only to lose her serve again. Hingis served for the match at 5-3 and had a match point. Capriati clipped the line with a backhand crosscourt for a winner. Hingis double faulted at break point down to make it 5-4. Capriati got back to 5-5, but the American double faulted at 5-6, 30-30 to give Martina a second match point; Capriati took it right away by forcing a forehand error from Hingis. Hingis made it to match point for the third time, but Capriati's forehand approach volley provoked a forehand long from Hingis.

On they went to the tiebreak. Hingis saved a set point at 5-6, then reached 7-6 and her fourth match point. She drove a two-hander crosscourt; the shot landed inches long. Capriati took the tie-break 9-7. Both players had left the court for bathroom breaks in the middle of the second set; when it was over, they were granted a ten-minute break before the start of the third. Hingis led 2-1 but, thoroughly debilitated, she never won another game.

Capriati had become the first woman to come back from match point down in a major final since Margaret

Smith [Court] stopped Lesley Turner [Bowrey] in the French Championships final of 1962. "It was really hard to breathe out there," said Capriati. "The air was so thick and hot. But the whole time, even though I was coming from behind, I never thought of myself as being defeated."

Monica Seles went for her first win in seven meetings with Venus Williams, and got it. The No.-8 seed beat the second-seeded Venus 6-7 (4-7), 6-2, 6-3. But Monica could not sustain her sparkling form after a strong start against Hingis, bowing 4-6, 6-1, 6-4 in that semi-final. Capriati accounted for No. 4 seed Kim Clijsters 7-5, 3-6, 6-1 in the other semi-final.

When the next major took place at Roland Garros, the third-seeded Serena crushed 2000 champion Mary Pierce 6-1, 6-1 in the quarters, and then won a pulsating encounter with Capriati in the semi-finals. Capriati took the first set and led 6-5 on serve in the second, but Serena's immense poise under pressure lifted her to a 3-6, 7-6 (7-2), 6-2 victory. In the final, Serena struck down big sister Venus 7-5, 6-3. Venus served for the first set at 5-3 but began that crucial game with a double fault. She proceeded to drop seven games in a row. Serena had more margin for error in the hard-hitting backcourt exchanges, and her second serve was decidedly better than Venus', who lost her serve eight out of 11 times in the match. The bottom line was that Serena was now the better player, and the best in the world.

Speaking of the arduous three years she had endured

2002 THE MAJOR CHAMPIONSHIPS

Australian Open
Men's Singles: Thomas Johansson
Women's Singles: Jennifer Capriati
Men's Doubles: Daniel Nestor / Mark Knowles
Women's Doubles: Martina Hingis / Anna Kournikova
Mixed Doubles: Daniela Hantuchova / Kevin Ullyett
French Open
Men's Singles: Albert Costa
Women's Singles: Serena Williams
Men's Doubles: Paul Haarhuis / Yevgeny Kafelnikov
Women's Doubles: Virginia Ruano Pascual / Paola Suarez
Mixed Doubles: Cara Black / Wayne Black
Wimbledon
Men's Singles: Lleyton Hewitt
Women's Singles: Serena Williams
Men's Doubles: Todd Woodbridge / Jonas Bjorkman
Women's Doubles: Venus Williams / Serena Williams
Mixed Doubles: Elena Likhovtseva / Mahesh Bhupathi
U.S. Open
Men's Singles: Pete Sampras
Women's Singles: Serena Williams
Men's Doubles: Max Mirnyi / Mahesh Bhupathi
Women's Doubles: Paola Suarez / Virginia Ruano Pascual
Mixed Doubles: Lisa Raymond / Mike Bryan

since winning her first major at the U.S. Open of 1999, Serena said, "It was kind of discouraging. I didn't want to be a one hit wonder. I had to get there again. Serena Williams has, in my mind, always been the best tennis player. It was just maybe a lack of results. But in my mind I've always felt that I've been No. 1."

The No. 20 seed Albert Costa claimed the men's crown at Roland Garros with a series of fine wins. He ousted the three time champion Gustavo Kuerten—still rusty after a long layoff for surgery on his groin—in the fourth round, held back Guillermo Canas 6-0 in the fifth set, halted Alex Corretja in a four-set semi-final, and stunned No.11 seed Juan Carlos Ferrero on a bleak afternoon 6-1, 6-0, 4-6, 6-3. Ferrero was a nervous wreck for two sets but made a much better match of it thereafter. He had beaten No. 4 seed Andre Agassi in four sets in the quarters, then clipped No. 3 Safin 6-3, 6-2, 6-4 in the semi-finals. But he put himself in too deep a hole against Costa, who had not won a tournament since 1999.

No major was more tumultuous than Wimbledon. On the third day of the event, three of the big favorites fell in startling second-round upsets. Seven-time champion Sampras, forced to play his match on the infamous Court 2 (better known as the Graveyard of Champions), was beaten by lucky loser George Bastl of Switzerland in five humiliating sets. Safin, the No. 2 seed, went down in four sets against Belgium's Olivier Rochus. And third-seeded Agassi was eliminated in straight sets by the rapidly rising Paradorn Srichaphan of Thailand. Srichaphan put on a shot-making clinic, releasing one blazing winner after another as an astounded Agassi found himself hopelessly out of sync on the Centre Court.

In the end, top-seeded Hewitt restored order. He picked apart Argentina's David Nalbandian 6-1, 6-3, 6-2. The No. 28 seed was thoroughly outclassed in his first major final, but could console himself; he was the first man from his nation ever to reach the final at the All England Club. Along the way, Hewitt had only one

dangerous match. Facing the stylish Dutchman Sjeng Schalken in the fourth round, Hewitt squandered a two-sets-to-love lead before coming through 6-2, 6-2, 6-7 (5-7) 1-6, 7-5.

Serena and Venus Williams always seemed certain to reach the women's final. Serena had moved past her sister to No. 1 in the world, with Venus remaining stationed at No. 2. They had thus fulfilled the prophecy of their father/coach Richard, who had said many years before that his daughters would become the two best players in the world. The siblings marched into the final after never being unduly troubled along the way. Venus, trying to become the first woman since Steffi Graf (1991-93) to win Wimbledon three years running, routed No. 6 seed Justine Henin 6-3, 6-2. Serena handled Frenchwoman Amelie Mauresmo with awesome ease, winning 6-2, 6-1. Mauresmo had given an exquisite display against Capriati, sprinkling the court with spectacular winners off her flowing topspin backhand, attacking cleverly, volleying crisply. Her 6-3, 6-2 upset of the No. 3 seed was encouraging to her band of supporters, but Serena shut her down with unrelenting power and panache.

The final was the best match yet between the two sisters, but once more Serena was superior in every facet of the game, most notably with her second serve and forehand groundstroke. The most telling statistic was this: Serena was on target with 67% of her first serves, winning 73% of those points. Venus finished at 70%, but won only 63% of those points. Serena also had a 10% edge in second-serve points won. Serena made Venus go for higher-percentage first serves, and Venus compromised too much on the speed of her delivery. Her average first serve for the tournament was 109 mph; against Serena, that figure fell to 100 mph.

Nevertheless, Venus battled fiercely. Serena served for the first set at 5-4, and reached 30-0 in that tenth game. Venus came out of that corner with some excellent retrieving and returning, broke back for 5-5, and got into a tiebreak. Serving at 3-4, Venus produced an ill-conceived drop shot off the forehand when she had a short ball she should have punished. Serena easily passed Venus off the backhand to lead 5-3. Serving at 6-4, Serena aced Venus wide to the forehand. Umpire Jane Harvey called a let, but neither player heard her. They proceeded to take their seats at the changeover, and Harvey inexplicably did not interject. Set to Serena.

Venus made another bid to sink her teeth into the

2002 CHAMPIONS AND LEADERS

Top Player Earnings: Men
Lleyton Hewitt $4,619,386
Top Player Earnings: Women
Serena Williams $3,935,668
Year-End Number One
Men: Lleyton Hewitt
Women: Serena Williams
Davis Cup: Russia
Fed Cup: Slovak Republic

ITF World Champion
Men: Lleyton Hewitt
Women: Serena Williams
Tennis Masters Cup,
Shanghai
Lleyton Hewitt
Home Depot Championships,
Los Angeles
Kim Clijsters

match in the second set, breaking back for 3-4. Venus reached 30-30 in her quest to make it back to 4-4, but released a costly double fault. Serena promptly broke her sister, then held at love to close out the 7-6 (7-4), 6-3 victory. Said Serena, "In the beginning of this year, I said, 'I don't care what happens this year, but I want to win Wimbledon.' It was an extra bonus for me to win the French. I couldn't believe I won that. But I really wanted Wimbledon to be a part of history."

A classy Venus said, "To be honest, I think I played well. I played high-percentage tennis. She was just pressing me and hitting a lot of forceful shots. Serena was just tremendous today, but it wasn't like there was a lot between us."

As summer ended and the best in the business came to New York in search of the last major of the year, Sampras played his finest tennis since 1999. Seeded No. 17 at the U.S. Open, his best showing at a major during the 2002 campaign had been a fourth-round appearance in Australia. After Wimbledon, he had re-united with Paul Annacone, his coach from 1995-2001. Over the first half of 2002, he had worked with Tom Gullikson (the twin brother of his late coach Tim and a former Davis Cup captain), and Jose Higueras, the Spanish tactical wizard. But with Annacone back by his side, Sampras was in a comfort zone again.

Despite a difficult hard-court season leading up to Flushing Meadows—he won only three of six matches in the three events he played—Sampras was determined to peak at his country's championships, where he had been a finalist the previous two years. He made good on that goal, and then some. In the third round, he beat 1997 finalist Greg Rusedski in a match contested over two nights as rain badly disrupted the Open program. Rusedski was not a gracious loser.

He said bitterly, "I lost the match. He didn't win it...I'd be surprised if he wins his next match against [Tommy] Haas. To be honest with you, I'd be very surprised. He's a step-and-a-half slow coming to the net. You can get the ball down. He's a great player from the past. You're used to seeing Pete Sampras, 13-time Grand Slam champion. He's not the same player."

Sampras was jovial in his response to Rusedski, but witty as well. "Against him," he retorted, "I don't really need to be a step-and-a-half quicker."

But Sampras responded with alacrity on the court. He took a hard fought four-set contest from the No. 3 seed Haas, and then gave a scintillating account of his all-court talent in a 6-3, 6-2, 6-4 rout of Andy Roddick. It was a signature performance from Sampras, who connected with only 48% of his first serves, but won 26 of 39 second-serve points. More importantly, he was masterful in breaking down Roddick's game, going forward at every opportunity, striking his running forehand cleanly, punching his volleys away with supreme skill. Sampras had lost to the 20-year-old in their only two previous career meetings, but this time around he was not be denied, winning in 90 nearly immaculate minutes. He then held back the unflappable Schalken 7-6 (8-6), 7-6 (7-4), 6-2.

Agassi, meanwhile, was also at the top of his game. He delighted the capacity crowd on Saturday afternoon with a four-set win over the top seeded Hewitt, ending a three-match losing streak against the pugnacious Australian. But it was much more taxing that the score indicates, bruising backcourt battle played over a three-hour span under a hot sun.

That set the stage for the dream final between the icons Sampras and Agassi. Sampras was primed for the occasion. He was devastatingly potent over the first two sets. Pete served 12 aces in the opening set, won 86% of his second-serve points in the second set, and treated Agassi's second serve disdainfully. From 3-3 in the opening set, he won eight of the next ten games. Agassi fought back valiantly to capture the third set. Sampras served at 5-6 to reach a tiebreak and had five game points, but a surging Agassi came up with some trademark scorching returns to get the break as Sampras struggled in vain to get sufficient pace while serving into the wind.

In the fourth set, Sampras served into the wind again in a crucial game at 1-2. It went to seven deuces with Sampras surviving two break points, one of them with a miraculous backhand drop half volley that caught a dumbfounded Agassi in his tracks. At 3-4, Sampras was break point down again, but he kicked his serve high to the Agassi two-hander to elicit a netted return. He held on with an ace, broke Agassi in the following game, and then served out the match with characteristic brio. At 5-4, 30-0, with the wind at his back, Sampras came up with a clutch, second serve ace down the T. It was his 33rd of the match, a personal record for a major final. Two points later, he dispatched a backhand volley into the clear to complete a 6-3, 6-4, 5-7, 6-4 triumph. He had beaten Agassi for the fourth time at the U.S Open without a loss (and the third time in a final), and extended his career edge over his chief rival to 20-14. Sampras now stood at 14-4 in major finals, while Agassi was 7-6.

With his fifth Open triumph in hand—placing him in a tie for the open era record with Jimmy Connors—Sampras climbed into the stands to embrace his wife Bridgette. He was so gratified to be back on top at an elite event that he seriously contemplated retirement for three months before electing to resume his career. Sampras did not compete again in 2002.

Serena and Venus took their expected places for the women's final, their third consecutive championship match at a major. The top seeded Serena had overcome Lindsay Davenport in the semi-finals, recouping from 2-5 down in the second set, saving three set points in the tenth game with typical gusto. Venus had survived two serious skirmishes on her half of the draw. Seeking to become the first woman since Evert (1975-78) to win three or more Opens in a row, Venus struggled inordinately to reach peak form. She had won three tournaments in a row over the summer, but at Flushing Meadows Venus lost her edge.

In the round of 16 against No. 14 seed Chanda Rubin, Venus was break point down at 1-4 in the final set before registering a 6-2, 4-6, 7-5 victory. In the semis, Mauresmo—fresh from her third straight win over Capriati in the quarters—took Venus to 6-3, 5-7, 6-4. Capriati had served for the match against Mauresmo. Mauresmo worried Venus all through their gripping confrontation. In the last game of the match, Williams was down 0-40 but she pulled out of that predicament with a series of scorching deliveries. Against Serena, Venus was error-plagued off the forehand from the outset, and her serve let her down again. Serena broke Venus five times, lost her own delivery only twice, and rolled to victory. Venus led 4-4, 30-0 in the first set but lost six of the next seven games as Serena prevailed 6-4, 6-3. Venus committed 17 more unforced errors than her tidier-hitting sister, and that was the essential difference. Serena, victorious for the fourth time in a major, was now tied with Venus in that category.

Agassi battled on after the Open in search of the No. 1 world ranking, hoping to end a year at the top of the charts for the second time in his career. But when he lost two round-robin matches in a row at Shanghai to Jiri Novak and Ferrero, his chance was gone. With Agassi out of the running for No. 1, Hewitt could have let go of some of his ambition. He refused. The feisty 'Little

Big Man' closed out his second straight Tennis Masters Cup event with a pair of phenomenal victories. In the semi-finals, he beat Roger Federer 7-5, 5-7, 7-5. The next day, he overcame Ferrero after trailing 1-3 in the fifth set, winning that one 7-5, 7-5, 2-6, 2-6, 6-4. He reminded everyone why he deserved his status as the best in the world.

Serena Williams suffered only her fifth defeat of the year in the final of the women's Home Depot [Year-End] Championships in Los Angeles. A resolute Kim Clijsters upended the world No. 1 in straight sets to win the biggest title of her career.

In the Fed Cup final at Gran Canaria, the Slovak Republic toppled Spain 3-1. The tall, rangy Daniela Hantuchova—one of the most improved players in the women's game over the course of the season—won the decisive match over Conchita Martinez in three hours, 21 minutes 6-7 (8-10), 7-5, 6-4. Said the victor, "Even when I lost the first set, I was really happy with the way I was fighting. I would not give up. I am very proud."

Spain's Arantxa Sanchez Vicario, hindered by a leg injury, lost to Janette Husarova 6-0, 6-2. She soon announced her retirement after a long and distinguished career. She would turn 31 at the end of the year, and had been out there on the pro tour for 16 productive years, winning four major singles titles, rising to No. 1 in the world in 1995. She also set Fed Cup records for most matches played (100), most ties (58) and most appearances in the final (10).

As Sanchez Vicario left tennis behind her, Russian Mikhail Youzhny was just beginning what might become a remarkable career. The 20-year-old found himself in a demanding position at the Davis Cup Final indoors in Paris. His nation had never won the Davis Cup before. When the Russians lost to the U.S. in 1995, he was a ballboy. Youzhny was asked to play the fifth and decisive match against France when Yevgeny Kafelnikov begged off. He was down two sets to love against another 20-year-old named Paul-Henri Mathieu. Former Russian President Boris Yeltsin was cheering him on from the stands, but to no avail.

Down a break at 2-1 in the third, Youzhny broke back and won the set, but fell behind again 4-2 in the fourth. In the end, Youzhny, propelled by his marvelously fluent and effective one-handed topspin backhand, came out improbably on top 3-6, 2-6, 6-3, 7-5, 6-4. No one had ever come from two sets to love down in the fifth and decisive match of a Davis Cup final.

Chapter 11

Will The Real Arthur Ashe Please Stand Up?

Arthur Ashe was a former U.S. Open champion but, a year before silencing his critics with a stirring 1975 Wimbledon triumph, SPORT was wondering if he'd ever win again.

SPORT February 1974 By Tony Kornheiser

Arthur Ashe, 1966
Not arrogant enough—or at all.

We took a black boy from Virginia and put a tennis racket into his hands. We sent him to prep school and then to college. He was very carefully taught. He said, "Yes, sir." And, "No, sir." And, "Thank you very much, sir." We held the carrot out to him. The world championship would be his, if he spoke softly, and swung a huge backhand. We watched his progress. We charted his course. We rewarded him with a commission in the Army. And finally, we gave him our blessing.

In 1968, when he was 25 years old, Arthur Ashe won the first U.S. Open championship ever played. The whole world was watching as a black man won at a white man's game.

Since 1968, Ashe has won nothing of major importance.

Something happened. Surely, something happened.

He sat in a leather chair in the players' lounge at Forest Hills, the New York *Times* rolled up in his hand, looking like any junior executive except that he wore a string of beads tied ever so tightly at his neck. A small circle of friends sat by his side.

"They thought I'd be better than I was capable of," Ashe said. "I've had a monkey on my back. I know the public expects me to be a winner. They expect the real Arthur Ashe to surface. They don't understand why he hasn't. Look, I'll probably never know what the hell the real Arthur Ashe is. I never brought out the real me. There are things I feel inhibited doing. I thought one way, and acted another. I wound up doing what was practical. But I'm not apologizing for my lack of guts.

"The way I live my life, I'll probably never become No. 1. At one time there was a need for me to do it. I wasn't afraid of failing. The last three years I gave it my best shot, but the scheduling of tennis worked against me, and anyone else, from becoming No. 1. There, are too many tournaments. . . . So maybe I'll never be as good as Rod Laver, but I ain't too far off.

"You know, there are a couple of ways of looking at it. Me and Laver have more endorsements than any of the others combined. Financially, I've made the most of my productive years to the point that my career is a fantastic success."

Since 1971, Ashe has earned better than $100,000 a year playing tennis. He has a multi-year contract with Head tennis rackets which Donald Dell, Ashe's friend and lawyer, said made him a millionaire with a stroke of a pen. He has had contracts with Coca-Cola, U.S. Banknote and Phillip Morris among other companies. He is a walking portfolio, slicing a hunk of the American Dream Pie.

"I want to tell you a story," he said. "Something that Bill Cosby once told me. He said we have to contain our wealth. We're not allowed to enjoy it, the result of what we have, because fellow blacks come down on us ... None of them are going to do that to me. I worked for it. I earned it. No one is going to tell me how to spend it."

People say that Ashe took the money and ran.

Clark Graebner has known Ashe for a long time, though the two aren't close. They played in a semi-final match at the 1968 Open that later became the subject of John McPhee's definitive book, *Levels of the Game*. Graebner, now a successful stockbroker and part-time tennis player, has his own views on Ashe not becoming No.1.

"The only assumption you can make is that if you haven't made it, you aren't capable of it," Graebner says. "External pressures, business and racial and political commitments, might have kept him from it. But Arthur could have had it any way he wanted it. He did speak out a little, but he took the money. Ultimately he may do more for blacks that way.

"I'm sure Arthur has wasted talent. I'm sure a lot of players have wasted talent. I've wasted talent. If Arthur were white, he would be just another tennis player—

a fine one, but he wouldn't have so many people making such a fuss over him."

The criticism comes in all shapes and colors. Robert Screen, the tennis coach at Hampton Institute who has known Ashe for more than 20 years, thinks Ashe lacks the killer instinct that all champions need. "He can't be a killer," Screen says. "Arthur has fought so long for acceptance that it's impossible for him to look at his opponent as his enemy. He's so talented that when you look at him, you just know he ought to be No. 1. But blacks see him lose to people they know he should be beating and they don't understand why it happens. Blacks don't follow you unless you're top dog."

Richard Russell, a Jamaican who was considered the world's second-best black player for many years, thinks that too much talent is the biggest problem facing Ashe. "It's a contradiction, but Ashe has too much talent and flair to be No. 1," Russell says. "Arthur never had to work like Rod Laver and Ken Rosewall. Arthur was so good, he wasn't hungry. Arthur hates to practice, but work made Laver and Rosewall what they are."

Rosie Casals says Ashe would have been better if he weren't the only black player of world consequence—the lump of coal in the snowbank, as Ashe once described it. "As it was, he wasn't hungry enough," Casals says. "Everything was handed to him. He isn't really black. He's really mostly white. He lives white and he gets paid by whites."

If you had a choice of colors, which one would you choose?

That's what it really comes down to. How black is Arthur Ashe? Don't ask why it matters. It just does. Blacks are tugging at Ashe to be more than tan. Whites are tugging at him to stay a nice predictable gray flannel. And Ashe—a black man who has lived most of his life in a white world—is caught in the middle. Nowhere to run, baby. He is a black tennis player. He runs as an entry.

"Hey, look at me," Ashe said. "I'm black. You think I don't know what I am? . . . I get requests from the black community all the time. I've done too many things for nothing. I've done tons of clinics in Harlem. But who knows about tennis in Harlem? You're not going to get me to say I'm more comfortable in a white world than in a black one. But I've spent most of my life in a white world. It's over ten years since I got on the national rankings, and there still hasn't been another black player.

People tell me it's my fault, that I should have made another player. It takes years to make it, years. Tennis players have to be brought along slowly.

"Tennis has a very low utility in the public schools where black kids go. If you're captain of the basketball team, you can every girl in the school. Our gene pool has things that make us jump further, run faster proportionately. As a race, we excel in those sports accessible in the public school system because those sports are free. In tennis, you gotta take lessons.

"You're asking me if I'm playing it safe by not speaking out on racial issues. Let me tell you this, Anyone can speak out on racial issues in America. That's nothing new. I spoke out on South Africa when nobody else was doing it. Why is everybody after me to speak out on everything? Nobody asks Walt Frazier to speak out on anything. Dammit, Walt has earned his right not to be there, and so have I.

"A few years ago, Rev. Jessie Jackson told me, 'Arthur, you're not arrogant enough.' I told him, 'I'm *not* arrogant.'"

When Ashe was ten years old, a local college student in Virginia introduced him to the late physician, Dr. R. Walter Johnson, who ran a tennis camp designed to train promising young black tennis players for big-time tennis. Johnson believed blacks would be able to infiltrate the tennis world if they played good tennis and displayed the subservient attitude he felt was expected by whites.

Ashe spent summers with Dr. Johnson, learning tennis and the attendant things—like etiquette, grace, bowing and scraping. Ashe was carefully taught to submerge his own personality in favor of the one Dr. Johnson thought was necessary, much like the plan Branch Rickey had for Jackie Robinson. Ashe was picked to be the pioneer in tennis as much for his manner as his ability. The result is a world-class tennis player, and somewhat of an automaton. Computer-chic.

"Dr. Johnson told us no matter what happened, no matter what went against us, we should always show no emotion around whites," Ashe said. "I guess that's why I seem so emotionless on the court. You'll never know how I really feel inside. You'll just see nothing, or you'll see me politely smiling. Then again, the training was so thorough, I may never know what's really going on inside me either."

Ashe is paying the dues now for his malleability. In 1971, he lost at the U.S. Open because he wouldn't ask the referee to stop play even though a slight rain was splattering on the glasses he wore at the time. In 1972, he lost at the Open again, partially because he wouldn't ask the referee to make his final opponent, Ilie Nastase, stop clowning on the court. Both times Ashe made no excuses to the press or public.

He bore his anger internally, and reminded those around him he was taught never to question an umpire's call, never to ask for special favors. Partially because of his lack of emotion, his low profile and his ability to lose gracefully, Ashe has become the white man's black man—the crowd favorite, the highly visible, highly rich token.

But being the white man's black man has caused problems in the other America. Arthur Ashe is also the black man's white man. In the ghetto they call that Uncle Tom.

"Nobody has ever called me that to my face," Ashe said. "If they did, I'd be glad to talk to them face-to-face about it. I'm not a Muhammad Ali. He's not my kind of leader. I'm not a Stokely Carmichael or a Rap Brown. You need people like that, but you don't need two million of them. People who come down on a black personage for acting or saying or doing things that are too safe may be doing it because they think he should be on a soapbox, screaming. On the same hand, these same people criticize companies for not hiring the black man. What the hell do they want? Look, I'm doing things so other people can come after me. I'm opening doors, not closing them."

According to Ashe, in the end it's not how much noise you can make, but how effective you can be. He's picking his spots to put himself out front, and he can stand the traded visibility for effectiveness. He has gambled. And now there is no telling if he's winning or losing.

Robert Screen doesn't blame Ashe for not being more vocal, although he realizes others do hold Ashe accountable. "You can't imagine what a shattering experience it is for a black in tennis," Screen says. "Arthur has lived in a white world for so long, and there are things he just doesn't know about being black. It's so much easier for black basketball players to be vocal—there are zillions of them. I don't know that everything is his responsibility."

Richard Russell, for one, is a great admirer of Ashe. "I admire him tremendously, almost more for his manner than for his tennis," Russell says. "It's a guiding light for black people. They are looking for leaders, and it's nice that someone like Arthur can came through in such a manner that he can be pleasing to all types of ethnic groups and still have such power within his own race."

But Arthur Carrington—a black player who left Dr. Johnson because he felt he could not submerge his own personality to the breaking point that Johnson demanded—is not so enamored of Ashe, the leader. "I admire the hell out of him as a player," Carrington says. "But he's a tennis player, not a leader. I'm more of an Ali fan. Ashe isn't vocal enough for me. He's not trying to identify with blacks. He doesn't show me any courage. There are many clubs I won't play at because of discriminatory policies and I think Arthur shouldn't play there either. He has to publicize these things because he's the only one who the public is listening to. I mean, I understand him. I was there. I understand what it was that he went through, and I believe the man is making his contribution in the ways he can make it. But he's got to stand up taller."

A few months ago Ashe was granted a visa to play in the South African Open (the account of which he went and sold to the highest bidders on two continents). Twice before he had been denied a visa, but this time South Africa—despite its apartheid laws which segregate non-whites from whites—asked Ashe to come and play. The deal was made on Ashe's terms. Otherwise it would not have been made at all.

"I had three conditions that South Africa agreed to," Ashe said. "First, that I could come and go as I pleased and I could say whatever I wanted. Second, I would refuse to play in front of segregated audiences. Third, I would not accept—even for a short time—honorary white status. I didn't come as Arthur Ashe, black man. I came as Arthur Ashe, tennis player, period."

After years of waiting, Ashe had broken a barrier. In the end, it's not how much noise he made, but how effective he was. But even the victory had its price, and Ashe is sensitive—maybe too sensitive.

"Blacks, especially American blacks, will say, 'What the hell is Ashe doing?' But they're just taking potshots at me without knowing what South Africa is all about," Ashe said, before his trip (he lost in the finals). "I've studied the bloody country. I know more about South Africa—for someone who's never been there—than they'll ever know. They're just armchair quarterbacks promoting an all-or-nothing theory on race that doesn't work. They may use words like 'token' or 'tool' when they look at my situation, but when things like this develop, I have to do what I can to make it easier for those who come after me."

A little at a time. A foot in the door. A chance to be heard, not just in one screaming burst, but in steady drops like the waters of conscience. "You used to be a militant," Ashe said, touching me slightly as he spoke, making sure I knew he was calling the shots, letting me see him only as he wanted to be seen. "Now you get a wife and a job with IBM, two cars and your weekends free. You aren't gonna mess with that. That's why there won't be a revolution."

There is a substantial degree of guilt in Ashe as he seeks to do what he can for the black community. Because he has made so much money. Because he has been less black than his birthright demanded. He says he doesn't care if no one ever thanks him for what he does. He says he can go it alone.

To illustrate his self-confidence he told a story an himself. "I went to a basketball game last year," he said. "And I saw Julius Erving play for the first time. I was so wigged out by the things he did on the court, I just had to meet him. So after the game I walked up to him—and this is bold for me—and I said, 'Hi, Julius, I'm Arthur Ashe.' So he reaches down and he shakes my hand and he says, 'Hi. How you doing?' He didn't even know who the hell I was."

Ashe's face becomes a grin. His grin becomes a smile. And the people around him smile with him. But no one knows how much of Ashe is really smiling. And he smiled again because he wanted to keep it that way.

Chapter 12

In Tennis, Four Queens Mean A Full House

Women's tennis exploded into prominence in the early 1970s, due largely to its Four Queens: Billie Jean, Margaret, Chrissie and Evonne. SPORT discovered the women could even push the men into the background.

SPORT December 1972 By Tony Kornheiser

Chris Evert, 1972

The professional women's tennis tour is being financed, largely, by a cigarette company whose slogan insists women have come a long way. There are women who will argue that they haven't come far enough—women with names like Bella and Gloria—but, in tennis, no argument. Women have come almost all the way.

No more begging for an audience of friends and relatives. No more apologies for weak backhands and dainty serves. No more depending on lace panties as the main attraction.

Women's tennis has caught up to men at least in general interest—and the explanation is simple: Little Orphan Annie, Big Momma, Cool Chrissie and The Old Lady.

Their real names are Evonne Goolagong, Margaret Smith Court, Chris Evert and Billie Jean King, and they are four queens who mean a full house everywhere they play.

It's not often that all four get together in a single tournament, but it happened several weeks ago, in the U.S. Open tennis championships at Forest Hills. And when it happened, the men were pushed—tenderly, of course—into the background.

"I suppose I could be the best woman tennis player in the world," said Evonne Goolagong. "But I'm not yet. For me it's more psychological than physical. It's something with me. It's the way I am."

There's not a woman player anywhere who doesn't think Evonne Goolagong has all the physical equipment necessary. Pro tour regular Julie Heldman calls Evonne,

"The fastest lady on wheels. She's just so pretty to watch. But she tends to wander off in the head on the tennis court. Some people have tried to make it a racial thing." Evonne is an aborigine. Her mental lapses have been called "walk-abouts," an aboriginal term.

Evonne has no idea what causes them—other than, "It's the way I am."

At 19, she won Wimbledon, the most prestigious tournament in the world. At 20, she finished second. Now at 21 she came to the Open for the first time, and she was seeded second. Which Billie Jean King called "pathetic."

From the beginning Evonne had no chance of winning. She did not have enough competitive play behind her since Wimbledon. Instead of playing the tournament at Newport, Rhode Island, the week before, Evonne took a holiday on Long Island. Instead of playing tennis, she went sightseeing. Unlike the others, Evonne doesn't have to be No.1.

Evonne Goolagong has to be only what she is—a most beautiful, talented and be-boppy bundle of Little Orphan Annie curls set over a brown sugar face—and what Vic Edwards wants her to be.

Vic Edwards is very special to Evonne. He is her coach and her surrogate father. By agreement with her parents in Australia, he took Evonne as his protegé when she was 14, and he has pulled the strings ever since, all of them. Allegedly, he has demanded money from reporters who wanted to interview Evonne. Allegedly, he has demanded guarantees from promoters who want Evonne to play their tournaments. He has deliberately kept her off the moderately successful women's tour, the Virginia Slims tour, much to the chagrin of the Slimmies who see Evonne's presence as a guarantee of financial respect. Vic Edwards has packaged Evonne, promoted her and all but patented her.

"It makes me mad he doesn't let her play the tour," says tour player Wendy Overton. "She should use her talent and put it on the line. Play for prize money, not guarantees. This is where all the athletes are."

"She's a big girl now," says Julie Heldman. "She'd be better off on her own."

Evonne isn't buying. The Virginia Slims challenge, like all challenges, doesn't mean all that much. Loyalty takes precedence in her life. It always will. "I feel I'm under good management at the moment," she says. "I don't feel like changing at all. Mr. Edwards isn't just a manager. Mr. Edwards is more like a father."

Mr. Edwards? Mr. Edwards.

"Well, you'll have to talk with Mr. Edwards," Evonne says each time a reporter approaches. She is programmed to say that and the words come out like a computer printout. That line is not Evonne. Evonne is easily the most unaffected of all the women tennis players; certainly the most natural. While she was in New York, she relaxed by listening to rock-and-roll on a portable stereo.

"I've been brought into the world the way I am, so I might as well stay the way I am," she says. "I suppose if I wasn't playing tennis, I'd like to own a boutique. As long as there was music in there. I love music. I'd like to be a musician. My brother plays the guitar. I'd like to do that."

If there was pressure on Evonne to win at Forest Hills, she never felt it. She spent most of her practice time on the town, not on the court. She saw the Empire State Building because, "If I was in Paris, wouldn't I see the Eiffel Tower?" She actually said she liked visiting New York, but she wouldn't want to live there. "Too big and too impersonal." She never got to see the Broadway plays she had heard so much about, but she did more than her share of good-timing.

Maybe that was why Evonne Goolagong was the first of the top girls of summer to be eliminated from Forest Hills.

Her first match was breezy. She beat Brenda Kirk of South Africa, 6-2, 6-2, opening up on center court. Her next match was harder. She had to go two tough sets against towering (six-foot-two) Karen Krantzcke of Australia before winning, 6-3, 7-5. Also on center court, and in a slight rain.

Evonne said she needed a match like that to play herself into the tournament. But she needed more than that. She needed a killer instinct of a champion. She didn't, doesn't and won't have it. She is what she is. She said, "I know I'm expected to at least get to the finals, and I have to accept that. But I'm determined not to worry all the time. I just take every day as it comes. Even if I lose, I don't care."

True to her word, Evonne didn't care when she lost in the sixth day of the tournament to Pam Teeguarden, a cute little girl with a cute little lisp. Evonne wasn't ever in the match. The 7-5, 6-1 score was that close mainly on Evonne's reputation. Her motor was not moving, her wheels not turning. But when she came into the interview room after the match, she was smiling like a winner. She did color commentary on the match and eased an embarrassed Miss Teeguarden who wasn't used to all the attention. Evonne was flip and casual as ever. Tomorrow's gonna be, tomorrow's gonna be, tomorrow's gonna be another day.

Evonne Goolagong takes herself less seriously than the media boys drooling all over her Teddy Tinling dresses. "I probably don't push myself enough," she said. "When I won Wimbledon I was the best in the world. Maybe that's taken the excitement out of it."

A few days after she lost, I ran into Evonne in the television lounge of the West Side Tennis Club. She said she'd gotten over her loss quickly enough. She said she just wanted to go home anyway. She said, "All I knew about Forest Hills is that when it was over, I could go back to Australia for a holiday."

Twice in her lifetime Margaret Court has been the undisputed No.1 woman in tennis. Once as Margaret Smith in the mid-Sixties, and once again as Margaret Smith Court in the late-Sixties after coming off a two-year retirement. Now as Margaret Court, mother of an infant son Danny, she's trying for No.1 for a third time.

Very few women have made it back in sports after having a baby. But with only four tournaments worth of competition after a year of inactivity, Margaret Court went into Forest Hills ready to challenge for the title—carrying a set of rackets in one hand and a pacifier in the other.

She traveled with her son and husband Barry, an instantly likeable, Ichabod Crane-like angular man with a prominent nose and his wife's fondness for a cold beer. It was Barry who convinced Margaret that a comeback was morally right. He was sure she could be wife, mother and champion successfully.

It is Barry who keeps Margaret going. "If he weren't here with me, I guess I'd be home," she said, "But this way I feel like I can play for two or three more years. I wanted to come back, too. I was just afraid that with Danny it wouldn't be right."

The decision was made in June. Australia asked her to captain its team in the Bonne Bell Cup in Cleveland. Margaret decided she would captain and play. And go full out as both.

Playing in Newport the week before Forest Hills, Margaret at 30 looked slimmer, prettier and friendlier than ever—almost like an airline hostess in her A-Line dresses. But in traditional whites, her legs gave her away.

Billie Jean King, 1972

Sprinter's legs. Grapefruit calves. And the right side of her body muscularly defined almost like a man's. She played like a man also, and that's the highest compliment the ladies get. She ripped through the tournament, beating Rosemary Casals, Chris Evert and Billie Jean King to win it. A month back into things and Margaret Court was a single step away from the top again.

It was said of her that when she was clearly the best, Margaret Court was so good she made tennis boring. She never had star quality, but she was always the best. Serve, volley, shake hands and shower. "Like a steamroller," Rosie Casals said. She was that way at Newport on the grass. And coming into Forest Hills her No. 5 seeding seemed like a cruel joke played on the higher seeds.

There was only one knock against her. Her nerves.

"Shaky as hell," one tour player said. "She may look good early, but once she gets to a pressure match, she'll fold like an accordion." The knock wasn't falling on deaf ears. The day before the tournament started, Margaret said, "I've got to get tournament tough. I've been winning my early matches easily. But it's the real pressure matches that I haven't had enough of. That's why I'm looking forward to Forest Hills. There won't be that much pressure on me. I'm an outsider now. I haven't been at it long enough to be bored, and I'm just going to give it a good go."

On the second day of the tournament—while Lesley Hunt, a tour player, babysat for Danny, and Barry Court watched from a stadium seat—Margaret Court played front and center and easily beat her best friend, Pat Praetorius. "Playing Pat was more difficult than playing anybody," Margaret said. "I think people thought it was going to be a really good match."

Margaret Court spent 20 minutes in the interview room under the stands at Forest Hills, and that was the only worthwhile quote that came out. There's a good reason why reporters call her Mrs. Court—she holds interviews with graceful diffidence, like a job applicant who really doesn't need the job. She answers all questions and waits for the next one. Margaret Court has never been known as good copy—just as a good tennis player.

Her next three matches were held on outside courts. Only the very curious came to see her beat Janice Metcalf, Barbara Hawcroft and babysitter Lesley Hunt in straight sets, giving up only six games and winning 36. And after every match, the first question put to her was, "What about Billie Jean King? You meet her in the semis? Can you beat her?"

Her answer: "I don't play her next, and I play them one at a time."

Her husband knew better. Barry was always the one to talk to. Up on the clubhouse porch having a brew. Down in the lounge changing a diaper. Barry knew. "She's never been seeded so low," Barry said. "She thinks she can win. Of course Billie Jean is the stopper, isn't she? Margaret's thought about it all right."

To get to Billie Jean, Margaret had to beat Rosie Casals in the quarter-finals. If there was a time for her nerves to act up, this was it. But it was Rosie who folded. Leading in the third set, up a service break, Rosie fell apart and Margaret won the match, 6-4, 4-6, 6-4. Survival made her eligible for Billie Jean. It wasn't the best of draws.

From the start Billie Jean was clearly better. Though the scores were close—6-4, 6-4—Billie Jean won every key point in the match. Twice she had break points, twice she got them. Four times Margaret had break points, four times she failed to get them. The nerves again?

"No, I always like to get a bit nervy out there," Margaret said afterwards. "But I just couldn't concentrate out there. I kept hearing the crowd. I don't usually do that. I just was too loose. I wanted to be tighter. In key point situations, I missed easy shots."

The second one out of the tournament. A shower after her loss to Billie Jean, Margaret Court was busy changing diapers. Barry went to get a couple of beers, and Margaret held Danny close to her and smiled at him. Life goes on, the smile said. Life goes on.

There's an unwritten law in women's tennis promotion where Chris Evert is concerned—when you've got her, flaunt her. Put her on center court, always on center court. Because if you put her anyplace else, you're taking the risk that the fans will tear the place down trying to get a look at her.

Chris Evert is magic, Shirley Temple in sneakers and money in the bank for a tennis tournament.

Years from now there will be Chris Evert trivia contests and it will be important to know that Chris Evert hates her mother's meat loaf, likes McDonald's hamburgers and once had a pet rabbit named Rufus that starved to death when she forgot to feed it. For the moment all ye know and all ye need to know is that Chris Evert is the biggest drawing card in tennis—male or female.

At 17 she is an idol of people three times her age. Cool Chrissie, America's teenage darling, manufactured innocence, approachable—with caution.

"The coolness they talk about is all there," says Julie Heldman. "She's brighter than hell. She's created a good deal of her image. She really knows where it's at."

The image is perfection. Every hair in its proper place. The eyeliner just so. The ribbon matches the dress which matches the panties which match the socks. The smile is there when it ought to be. The frown when it ought to be. And when she plays tennis there is nothing that distracts her—not one thing. It is as if she refuses to lose. And if she does lose, it is never because she is beaten, but because she has run out of games.

Evonne Goolagong, 1974

Margaret Court, 1970

"She's better prepared for every shot than anyone else," says Billie Jean King.

"She's the future of tennis," says Frank Hammond.

"Oh, come on," says Chris Evert. Smirking.

If they aren't quoted, other players are less kind. Chrissie isn't the most popular player in women's tennis among the women. She's made enemies on the Virginia Slims tour by picking her spots to play so carefully that her presence totally obscured the players who'd worked so hard to make the tour go. "Chris Evert the wonder girl," one player said. "This circuit made her, and this circuit can break her."

Ever the diplomat, Chris forgives her critics. "I understand how they feel," she said. "I would have probably felt the same way. But they have to realize I was 16 years old when all this started happening. I was a little girl."

At 17, she is a woman. The giggle is gone from her voice. She is more stockings than bobby-sox. She is at the getting-serious stage, and she knows what's expected of her. "I can't fool around," she said. "I know that. Chris Evert isn't supposed to do those things. I have no intention of getting caught smoking pot or getting pregnant so they can really jump on it."

Chris Evert is being pulled in so many different directions at once. She cannot go anywhere without a reporter or a television camera or an autograph book shoved in her face. She is always in demand. Sometimes at a tournament she hides in the locker room so she can have a free moment. She worries that boys who ask her out do so just because she is Chris Evert, tennis player. One date in Wimbledon with Jimmy Connors and the tennis press was marrying them off. Silly isn't it? "Stupid," she said.

She had hardened by the time she came to Forest Hills. Like the year before, she and her sister Jeannie, who played in the Open for the first time, and their mother Colette stayed at an aunt's house in Larchmont, New York. Unlike the year before, Chrissie Evert wasn't signing as many autographs. She came to Forest Hills as the No. 3 seed, and she had a real chance to make the finals. Her days were filled with practice, her nights filled with sleep.

As always, her matches were on center court. Her first three took maybe two hours total. Laurie Tenney went down, 6-1, 6-1. Marita Redondo went down, 6-1, 6-2. Julie Heldman went down, 6-1, 6-2. No sweat. And while Chris was winning, the top two challengers in her half of the draw, Evonne Goolagong and Nancy Gunter, were being eliminated. Outwardly, Chris said she was sorry the two of them had lost. Inwardly, she was very much relieved.

It was beginning to look as if Chris Evert's magic was really doing a number.

It did in Olga Morozova, the Russian women's champ, in their quarter-final match, the best match of the tournament. Chris lost the first set 3-6. She was losing in the second, and she had to go to the nine-point tiebreak to win in the third set. Chris Evert had to struggle to get to the semis to play Kerry Melville, a 25-year-old Australian with almond-eyes and the nickname Tuppence, "because that's what the girls think my game is worth."

Unbelievably, Chris lost. She lost, 4-6, 2-6, and she wasn't even close. At times it seemed she wasn't even there. And strange things began to happen. Chinks appeared in the armor. The crowd was no longer Chrisophiled, their cheers more polite than cresting. The whumppp of her two-handed backhand appeared more mechanically controlled than before. Chris Evert was so obviously disciplined that people actually whispered she was no fun to see. They used the word, boring.

This was the first time ever that Chris Evert lost when she was supposed to win. Her fame had been built on the big upset; she was always the underdog. But just one match after Billie Jean King ousted Margaret Court—suddenly the third girl of summer had melted away in the heat.

Two days before Christmas, Chris Evert will turn 18 years old and she will announce her professional status.

She will keep the money she wins in tournaments, and she will probably play a great deal in Slims events, drawing the crowds and signing the autographs. But the day she left Forest Hills for her senior year in St. Thomas Aquinas High School in Ft. Lauderdale, Chris Evert left as a mortal. Not just another face, but no longer Cinderella.

Billie Jean King sat and thought about it for a while. I had told her that one of her fellow Slimmies had called her a maniac. A trizophrenic with three separate personalities—calm on court, crazy on court and gentle off court. The description had angered her at first. Then the Billie Jean King smile overflowed her face and she said, "Yeah, I'm a maniac. You can say that about Bobby Fischer, too. But he's winning, right?"

Pleased at her answer, Billie Jean clapped her hands and sat back to wait for the next question.

Winning. That's the name of the game for Billie Jean. Winning. At 28, she is the No. 1 woman in tennis. Before she's done playing the game she may be the all-time No 1. She's won four times at Wimbledon, three times at Forest Hills and last season she won $117,000 playing tennis. She is the Virginia Slims tour. She knows it.

"On the court," says Frank Hammond, "she's an evil, merciless bastard. Totally ruthless. She'll do everything and anything within the rules to win."

She's No.1.

She remembers the feelings starting when she was six. She was Billie Jean Moffitt then. She remembers telling her parents, "I'm going to be a champion one day. But I just don't know in what." When she was 12 she played tennis for the first time, and she remembers the feeling she had the first time she hit the ball. "I knew this was it," she said. "I knew that I would be No. 1 in tennis. I told my parents that afternoon, and I remember that they didn't laugh at me."

The point isn't that she's psychic, but that Billie Jean King likes to believe she's psychic. She likes to believe she's an apostle, spreading the word of women's tennis. She likes to believe the sport would collapse without her. Billie Jean is a monumental egotist about her talents and her role.

We were walking and talking at Forest Hills and she said, "I can't go ten feet without someone coming up to me for something. Everybody wants a freebie." We walked about eight feet when a big kid, one of the beer salesmen, came waddling up to her and said, "Hey Billie, how about a couple of autographs?"

Billie Jean signed, then turned to me and said, "See what I mean?" She tried to sound angry, but her smile gave her away. She loves it—all the attention, all the autographs, all the hassle by the press and all the money. Especially all the money.

It's not that she needs it. She doesn't. It's just that the players measure who's No. 1 by who's making the most. Billie Jean's making the most. There really isn't any question at a big tournament who's going to win. When the money's on the line, Billie Jean is on her game. When she wants it, she's unbeatable.

Tennis is her art. Her passion. Her life. Everything else is secondary. Her husband Larry doesn't travel with her. It's a necessary and workable arrangement because Billie Jean makes it that way. Billie Jean King isn't just frilly underpants. She isn't at all feminine. She's an athlete. She accepts that.

Which is not to say she's not beautiful. She is the most beautiful player of all—bouncy, sweet, lovable. She is a dream person to the press, to whom she never refuses an interview. She is a goddess to children, for whom she never refuses a benefit. She runs and runs and runs at a pace that no one else on the tennis scene could keep up with. She says finally she is getting tired. "When Chris and Margaret join the tour they'll have to do their share of press and television," she said. "I'm certainly not going to keep on doing it. I'm tired." The words come out empty. If you know Billie Jean, you know she will never stop loving the rat race.

She was tired coming into Forest Hills. Tired and moody—and frustrated. Her boycott had dissolved. She had organized the Slims girls to boycott the Open, because the women's first-prize money ($10,000) was so much less than the men's ($25,000). She got all the girls to sign a petition that they wouldn't play, and she sent it to Slims organizer Gladys Heldman to send to Open director Billy Talbert.

But Mrs. Heldman refused. She thought the girls were overreacting. And with the refusal, Billie Jean swallowed hard and agreed to play in the Open.

Though she ran through the tournament without ever losing one set, she ran through it moody. She blasted the prize money every chance she got. "I didn't want to play here this year because of the money," she said. "And I won't play here next year if the money isn't better."

She blasted the poor condition of the grass. She threw tantrums on court. She even blasted Chris Evert. Billie Jean has always turned her public face toward Chris. "Chris is good for tennis," she's always said. "And anything that's good for tennis is good for me." But at Forest Hills, Billie Jean felt Chris' charisma taking over. So she charged that Chris would eventually get all the prize money back that she'd won as an amateur. "She's as much a pro as I am," Billie Jean said. "I know they're keeping the money for her. I know, and I know I'm not supposed to know."

The charge wasn't true. Billie Jean later was sorry for making it. But she's a straight shooter, and she was getting sick and tired of Chris Evert's magic. She wanted to play Chris in the finals very badly. She wanted to beat her. But she had to settle for beating Kerry Melville—easily. Billie Jean didn't try to appear humble when she received the winner's prize. She should have gotten more money.

There is a strong feeling in tennis that it would be nice if Billie Jean King got knocked off her perch. All that ego. All that bitching about money. Billie Jean King makes too many of the tennis fat cats a bit too uncomfortable.

She isn't well liked on the tour. Her good friends are Rosie Casals and Vickie Berner, but to the others she is really only a "Hiya, dear heart," and a quick smile. It's hard to be friendly with all those girls when you're beating them week after week.

But beneath the wire-rimmed glasses, the topspin forehand with its varying speeds and the bulging bank account—there is a most sensitive woman; a most wonderfully unique athlete. In 1971 she had an abortion. And that fact has set her up for a different set of questions than any other athlete ever.

"People automatically assumed I had it because I wanted to win more money," she said. "I don't need any more money. I've made money. I had it because I believe women should have the choice over their futures."

When she told me that, we were sitting on a couch in Newport, the week before Forest Hills. She was aware that Margaret Court—her baby on her lap and her husband at her side—was sitting one seat away. Mrs. Court had been No. 1, gotten pregnant and left the tour. Mrs. King had been No. 1, gotten pregnant and remained No. 1. The irony wasn't lost on Billie Jean King. She looked over.

She lowered her voice.

Jimmy Connors, 1974 "No one to tell him what's right and what's wrong."

Chapter 13

The Self-Destruction of Jimmy Connors

Jimmy Connors was viewed as a beloved curmudgeon by the time his career ended. But at his peak, Connors was anything but loved. As SPORT recounts, the ill will hit a memorable peak at the 1978 U.S. Open.

SPORT January 1978 By Marty Bell

On an unseasonably chilly September Sunday evening, Jimmy Connors scudded around the grainy green stadium court at the West Side Tennis Club in Forest Hills, N.Y., discovering that each of his once-awesome weapons was ineffective against Guillermo Vilas. Connors' ground strokes hit the net and bounced back at him. His approach shots sailed beyond the baseline. His serve landed outside the designated service area. When he did manage an effective shot, he found himself standing helplessly at the net as Vilas returned a passing shot beyond Connors' reach.

The finest American tennis player of his era was being humiliated in the final of his nation's most important championship, the United States Open, by an Argentinian. And the American crowd rejoiced as their countryman died a slow death. They not only cheered Vilas' winners, but also Connors' errors.

"I've never seen anything like this," former American champion Arthur Ashe said as he watched from inside the glass-enclosed press box. "The people out there want blood. They're not gonna stop until they have two ears and a tail."

"I never see this in Europe. Nowhere," said Rumanian Ilie Nastase, who has himself often incited spectator jeers. "Only in America they act like this."

When the match seemed almost over, Connors prolonged his agony. Down two sets to one, five games to love and with triple match point against him, Jimmy fought back to deuce in the sixth game and then to break point. This success inspired Connors to clench his fist and pound his hip—his familiar gestures when he feels in control. But he was not. He double-faulted to again even

the game and curled his lips in anger. Then he hit a forehand volley into the net to give Vilas the advantage and Connors faced another match point.

When Connors slapped a forehand deep to Vilas' forehand—where the American had been attacking all day with only occasional success—Vilas lunged at the ball and managed to return it. But Connors was waiting an arms-length from the net and punched a two-handed volley for what he thought was a winner.

As Jimmy walked back toward the service line, he saw people jumping out of the stands and storming the court. Confused, he turned back to the net and saw Vilas jumping up and down with his fists in the air. Connors stood there with the semi-conscious gaze of a boxer who has been pounded so hard he no longer knows where he is. He could not grasp the fact that it was over. But it was. The line judge had called his forehand—the shot before his "winner"—out. The noise from the crowd had drowned out the call. But Vilas had heard it.

The court was immediately flooded with Americans and Argentinians, who hoisted Vilas on their shoulders and paraded him around the court as though he were a torero who had just killed a raging bull. Connors slithered between the revelers to the chair where his rackets lay. His face was so tight that if it had a seam, it would have split. He bumped into a photographer and took a swing at the man that went as errant as his shots had all day. Standing with his fist and teeth clenched, he shouted, "Who's next?" Then he grabbed his rackets and found his way out of the stadium, muttering, "I'm moving to Monaco to get away from this crap."

As the chant of "Vee-las, Vee-las," filled the cool night

air, Connors walked briskly across the lawn that separates the stadium from the clubhouse. He was surrounded by his entourage—his mother, Gloria, his coach, Pancho Segura, his bodyguard, Doug Henderson, and his go-fer, Lornie Kuhle. At the clubhouse, Connors barked at them, "You wait in the car."

He marched up the steel stairway to the locker room, threw his belongings in a black leather bag, marched down a carpeted stairway and out of the Tudor-style building. With sweat dripping from his white-clad body, Jimmy climbed beside his mother into the front seat of a blue Maverick, and the car disappeared in the dusk. The ceremony to honor the champion and the runner-up as well as the customary conference with the press were still to come. They would go on without the runner-up.

"Running away like that is entirely in character," Ashe said. "I hope you didn't expect anything else from him."

"He's just a screwed up kid," said Bill Riordan, Connors' former manager. "He has no one to tell him what's right and what's wrong and he certainly doesn't know himself."

Connors later said that his abrupt exit was a reaction to the hostile treatment he got from the crowd and their support of Vilas. But he should have expected it. After all, he had spent the past 12 days creating antagonism and inviting humiliation. He had turned this event into a summary of his stormy career by alternately dazzling people with his tennis and offending them with his antics. This dichotomy has always been present in his complex nature. It seems he needs to be unpopular to win, so he systematically puts off everyone until he stands by himself against the world. "When he is at his mean peak," Riordan said, "he is unbeatable. But he has recently had trouble reaching that peak."

In the past, Connors has proved that as long as he wins, he can get away with anything. He tests the American audiences' willingness to ignore abrasive personalities in order to embrace excellence and celebrity. But at Forest Hills, Connors made the one mistake that can turn that fickle audience against him—he did not win.

Jimmy Connors desperately wanted and needed to win at Forest Hills. He came to the tournament in an unusual position for him—seeded second. It was the first time in four years that he was not seeded first in the Open. That distinction was awarded to Bjorn Borg of Sweden who had defeated Connors in a grueling five-set match at Wimbledon in June and moved ahead of the American in the Association of Tennis Professionals computer rankings. (Players are ranked by points based on whom they defeat and how far they advance in tournament play. The tournaments are weighted according to degree of difficulty, the most points being awarded for Wimbledon, the Australian, French and U.S. Opens.)

"He is more obsessed with being No. 1 than any other player," said Bob Lutz, a top doubles player. "Everyone else thinks about winning tournaments, but that is not enough for Connors."

Before he played his first match, Connors affirmed Lutz' comment, telling former-champion-turned-columnist John Newcombe, "I like the view from the top of the mountain. I've been there for three years since I took over from you. We'll sort it out with Bjorn and myself over the next 12 days."

He told another reporter: "It all points to Forest Hills. This is my championship. I own it. I've been building toward it all summer. When I win, I'll be No. 1 in the world."

Connors arrived at the Open on the last day of August with a pain in his back. He claimed he had aggravated the nagging injury during a quarter-final match at the U.S. Pro Championships in Boston the week before Forest Hills. The pain forced him to withdraw from that event (his sixth tournament withdrawal in the past two years) and request a one-day postponement of his first match at the Open. Some players doubted the injury.

"He's arrived at every major tournament in the last three years with some kind of injury," Ashe said. "We expect it from him by now."

"He's gotta be the best injured athlete in the whole world," Vitas Gerulaitis said with a smirk.

When he did play, Jimmy easily defeated Jazjit Singh, 6-2, 6-0, pounding the ball with confidence and abandon from both sides of his body. He quickly postponed the traditional post match press conference for a half-hour so that he could get his back massaged—a routine he would follow throughout the tournament. Finally entering the press tent, Connors slapped his thigh and mumbled, "The crowd's too small. I'm not doing it."

"We've been waiting for you, Jimmy," a reporter said.

"You ain't doing me no favors," Connors said as he sat down.

The first question was, "How's the back?"

"Good enough to play now," Connors said crisply, his lips tight. "I decided to play, so I just go out and play."

"When did you decide to play?" he was asked.

"This morning," he snapped back.

"Are you making any adjustments in your game because of your back?"

"I can't go around changing my game because my back's hurting," he said. "It's like Wimbledon. I don't wait all year for this and then pull out. They're still gonna have to work hard to beat me."

Throughout his tournament press conferences, Connors used his back injury as an offensive weapon to help him reach his mean peak. He waited for the inevitable questions, then threw back answers like darts.

After his third-round win over Zan Guerry, a woman reporter said that she had been told by a friend of Connors that Jimmy went to Boston intending to play a few matches to sharpen his game and then pull out.

"Who told you that?" Connors snapped.

"I can't reveal my source," she said.

"If you think I'm faking," he said, "I feel sorry for you. I wish you could crawl inside my back. . . . No, actually, I wish you were in front of me." He giggled like a naughty boy. "Don't print that," he said.

If the back injury was difficult to detect, the chip on his shoulder was not.

"Can you size up the field?" he was asked at a press conference.

"I don't worry about anybody else," he said. "Let them worry about them. I'll worry about me."

"Who would you like to meet in the final here?" he was asked.

"That's such a stupid question," Connors said. "I don't come here to answer stupid questions."

"Here's another question you might not like," someone said.

"Oh, another asshole," Connors cracked.

The question went unasked.

A writer tried to question him about motivation. "You've won everything there is to win," the writer began, "you've won more money than you could have ever expected—"

"Now hold it," Connors said. "That annoys me. Someone else once said that to me and it annoyed me then. I've worked 22 years to get where I am and I deserve everything I've won."

"But you couldn't have imagined it because there wasn't this much money in the game when you were growing up," the writer argued.

"That doesn't matter," Connors said. "Who says I wouldn't have made it anyway? I didn't have to play tennis. I could have gone into the movies. No, that annoys me. You annoy me."

"We're even," the writer said. "You annoy me, too."

Offended, Connors got up and walked out of the conference.

"All the way back to childhood," Arthur Ashe said, "Jimmy's been brought up with an 'I'll-show-you' attitude."

"I think he's been taught," former tennis great Tony Trabert said, "that the world's against him."

Connors grew up in Belleville, Ill., a blue-collar village across the Mississippi River from St. Louis. "He once told me," said television commentator Bud Collins, "that his grandmother, Bert Thompson, always told him: 'We're from the wrong side of the tracks. Those people at the country clubs in St. Louis don't like us. But we'll show them we're as good as they are. Pull up your socks, Jimmy.'"

When the mop-topped urchin was 17, he, his mother and grandmother left his father James Sr. and brother John behind in Belleville and moved to Los Angeles so that Jimmy could study the game under Pancho Segura. Of the son she left behind, Gloria Connors said, "Jimmy's brother will never be a champion. He has no guts."

It was apparent that Gloria Connors and Bert Thompson intended to use young Jimmy to show the folks across the river that they were their equals.

Segura's temperament made him the perfect accomplice for the matriarchs' scheme. "Segura always thought that we didn't like him because he comes from Ecuador and has an accent," said a rival from Segura's playing days. "He, too, was out to prove he was as good as the rest of us." Through Connors, Segura was able to prolong his own drive to prove something to the world. At Forest Hills, he talked about teaching Jimmy to hit the ball on the rise to get extra power. He was asked why no other coaches teach this since it seems to be such an obvious advantage.

"Because coaches don't have brain to understand," Segura said. "I was only one who play like this and only one who teach like this. The others all stupid. They don't have intuition."

Segura and Gloria Connors taught Jimmy to play and to hate and in 1974, at the age of 22, the boy proved their methods worked. He won the two most prestigious tournaments in the world, Wimbledon and Forest Hills, embarrassing 40-year-old Ken Rosewall in both finals. Overall, Connors won 95 matches that year and lost just four. He dominated his field like ABC dominates the Nielsen ratings.

Connors was then skillfully managed by Bill Riordan of Salisbury, Md., whose background was in prize-fight promoting. Riordan realized that separating his boy from the mass of talented professionals could mean big dollars, so he played on Jimmy's maverick attitude. Connors avoided joining the tennis players' union, the World Championship of Tennis winter circuit and the American Davis Cup team. His individualism antagonized the other players, but paid off financially. Riordan was able to convince CBS to put up half a million dollars each for challenge matches that were called the Heavyweight Championship of Tennis, but should have been called Jimmy Connors Against the World. In his first two such matches, amidst an atmosphere in Las Vegas usually reserved for heavyweight title fights, Connors easily defeated Rod Laver and John Newcombe.

Isolation helped both Connors' bank account and his game. By organizing a National Indoor Circuit to compete with WCT, Riordan surrounded Jimmy with lesser players. It was like a boxing champion putting on traveling exhibitions with his sparring partners. Connors won nearly every week which gave him tremendous confidence. When he did finally face the WCT players in the major tournaments, he presented them with unusual problems.

"In the beginning," said Tony Trabert, who coached Connors in the Davis Cup, "he skipped events where everyone else played. When people did face him for the first time, they had trouble reading his game. I think that had something to do with his early success."

"He plays differently than anyone else," Newcombe said. "He's a lefty with a kick serve and a two-fisted backhand and you don't see any other lefties like that. And he hits a flat ball with incredible pace that takes some getting used to."

Riordan also provided Connors with some personal direction. "Bill was the only strong male influence Jimmy ever had in his life," said one reporter.

"I was the only person who ever told him he *had* to

do something," Riordan said.

"They were a great team," said Bud Collins, "like Cus D'Amato and Floyd Patterson, only better."

The 1975 Wimbledon proved to be a turning point in Connors' career. He went there as the defending champion and didn't lose a set on the way to the final where he met Arthur Ashe, a sly strategist who was able to play away from Connors' unique strengths. He served wide so that Jimmy could not return the ball with power and took pace off the ball so that Jimmy's smashes went awry. Ashe won the match in three straight sets.

"Connors experienced something that happens to all top players," tennis veteran Marty Riessen said. "Someone beats you and then everyone thinks they can. It used to be that people would lose to him 6-2, 6-2 and think it was a triumph. But Ashe changed that. He showed there was an effective strategy that could be used against him and that gave everyone else more confidence."

Connors was bitter after that loss. Ashe said, "His attitude was almost like, 'Goddamn it, I gotta get it back from you.'"

"The first rule of tennis is that you change a losing game," Trabert said. "But Jimmy only plays one way. I can understand that he feels he should be able to return the soft balls he makes errors on. But he doesn't and it kills him."

Connors did continue to win most of the minor events he entered and advanced to the late rounds of the majors. But he developed a reputation for losing the big ones.

Two months after losing to Ashe at Wimbledon, he lost to Manolo Orantes in three straight sets in the final at Forest Hills. Then he joined the Davis Cup squad and lost a crucial match to Raul Ramirez of Mexico. And the following year Roscoe Tanner beat him in three straight sets in the quarter-finals at Wimbledon.

When Connors was at his peak in 1974, he was isolated, feuding with many players, even suing Arthur Ashe. But when he began to lose, it seemed as if he no longer enjoyed being a maverick. He split with Riordan and tried to make the manager the scapegoat for his past reputation. Jimmy played some Davis Cup, some WCT—tried to be one of the guys on the tour. He even gave up some of his annoying on-court antics such as blowing on his hand and bouncing the ball endlessly while his opponent waited for his serve.

"But his good guy image didn't work," said a writer

close to the tour. "People weren't going to forget everything and suddenly accept him for the asking. He has real trouble relating to people. He has lost every friend he ever had. Riordan, Spencer Segura (Pancho's son), Nastase, Gerulaitis—they all used to hang out with him, but you don't see any of them with him anymore. And his mother drove away every girl he was ever involved with. Chris Evert, Susan George, Margie Wallace. Chrissie adored him. She still does. But Gloria always gets in the way."

Nastase said he never had a friendship with Connors: "In Europe friendship means something. Not like in America. In Europe, friends like you no matter. In America peoples know you a little while then walk away and it doesn't matter any more."

After Margie Wallace, the former Miss World, stopped seeing Jimmy, she said, "With the way his mother brought him up, I'm surprised he's not gay."

"He's the loneliest person I've ever seen," one highly-ranked American player said recently.

Connors was still trying to be amiable at the '76 U.S. Open and played a good tournament, giving Vilas only six games in a semi-final rout and defeating Borg convincingly in four sets in the final. But 1977 has been his worst year since he became a top-ranked player. Early in the year he lost to Dick Stockton—who had never previously beaten him—in the INA U.S. Pro Indoor final at Philadelphia. After that match, Connors was informed that his father had died.

"Jimmy's father's death took a lot more out of him than people realize," Riordan said. "He hasn't gotten himself back together mentally. He wasn't close with his father and that's why he's upset. He has regrets about their relationship now."

Connors managed to win his first WCT championship and the Alan King tournament in Las Vegas before his loss to Borg at Wimbledon. But as they arrived at Forest Hills, the other players seemed to feel that when Jimmy is at his best, he can still beat anyone. But he is no longer at his best very often.

"I've never seen him play so many mediocre matches as he did this year at Wimbledon," said Bob Lutz.

"He used to seem to enjoy smashing winners," Roscoe Tanner said, "but now it's like work to him. He's lost some of that hungriness."

"When you're riding the crest like he was," said Vitas Gerulaitis, "you charge the net, you take chances. But when you lose a little, you stop taking chances and your whole game becomes less effective."

Technically, Connors had diversified his game this year. His net play improved and he added a drop shot to his repertoire. But he seemed to have lost his confidence.

"At our level," Brian Gottfried said, "everyone has the strokes. The difference in the players is all mental. The best player has the confidence to hit out and use all his stuff. A power game like Jimmy's is all based on confidence. But because he no longer wins week after week, people come up and ask him what's wrong and that has to affect him. He's very dependent on other people's opinions."

Prior to Forest Hills, Connors had not won any tournament since the WCT championship in mid-May. He had lost to players he used to beat easily and his record against the rest of the top ten was only 9 and 7 in WCT and Grand Prix competition. Even Segura admitted Jimmy's game had dropped off: "You have to work too hard to win. No one win on three shots anymore. You have to run your ass off and it's hard for Jimbo because of all he accomplished. But Borg is the best thing that ever happened to Jimbo. He make Jimbo work to prove he still best. He make Jimbo a mean killer again."

Gloria Connors sat hidden under the steel stairway to the men's locker room at West Side. Her hair was in a bun and her face was like a twist roll. The patio around her was packed like a singles bar on a Friday night, but she did not come to the tournament to socialize: "I just sit here and watch people and get vibrations from them."

When asked about Jimmy's isolation, she said, "It has been difficult for him because he's been independent and he's the only player who has."

"Did you push him too hard?"

"He has the gift and I just gave him the opportunity, I didn't give him to the world. The world wanted him."

The relationship between mother and son has often caused notice. There was a magazine story a few years ago that described a bizarre scene at the Beverly Hills Tennis Club where Jimmy cursed at his mother and directed sexual gestures and insults at her. She just sat by giggling and praising his talent. Others who have been with them have reported similar scenes.

But Connors is quick to defend his mother publicly. After Jimmy lost at Wimbledon in 1976, Riordan said Connors' downfall was caused by the women in his life. Jimmy went on television and said, "No matter what anyone says, I'm not going to tear down my mother. She knows me better than any other woman. She's the only person who understands my needs."

Mrs. Connors became a born-again Christian after her mother died in 1972 and the conversion has apparently softened her. "It all starts with the Lord and ends with the Lord," she said at Forest Hills. "I'm not interested in material gifts."

Though Gloria Connors' religious conversion may have blunted her philosophy, the killer instinct she instilled in her son is still sharp. Through the first ten days of Forest Hills, it appeared that he had regained his mean peak and was no longer concerned with being one of the guys. His only concern was winning.

Hitting the ball hard and deep and rushing the net more consistently than ever, Jimmy pummeled his first three opponents and made his fourth, the talented Tanner, feel as if he were standing under a rock slide.

On the day Connors beat Tanner, Bjorn Borg's injured shoulder caused him to default to Dick Stockton in the third set of their match. When asked his reaction to Borg's withdrawal, Connors played dumb. "Is Borg out?" he asked. "Who beat him?" Then he said, "Why don't you call him up. Maybe he'll finish his match tomorrow."

With Borg out, it seemed as if there was no one around to beat Connors. Though Vilas was riding a long clay-court winning streak and had won the French Open, he still had a reputation for folding in big matches.

The closer Connors got to the U.S. title, the more abrasive he became. He would sit alone with Lornie Kuhle in the middle of the locker room lounge each day and ignore the other players unless they approached him. During press conferences he would run his fingers up and down a microphone pretending he was masturbating. After practicing one day, he walked out onto the clubhouse balcony with only a towel wrapped around his waist. He looked down at the crowd in the patio and announced, "I better get a hard-on to look my best for you people."

These antics were seen by only a few people, but he found ways to antagonize the stadium crowd. On a Thursday night, Connors met Manuel Orantes in a quarter-final match. Connors took the Spaniard's game away from him and won in three sets. In the middle of the last set, the players returned to the court after a break and the crowd cheered loudly for Orantes, begging him to make the match competitive. In defiance, Connors gave the crowd the finger.

"F--- you, too, Jimmy," a woman spectator seated behind him shouted.

Connors walked to the stands and said, "I'll f--- you any time you want to."

After that match, he walked back toward the clubhouse and his mother asked about the incident. Connors reported it and said he got "pissed off" when the lady yelled at him.

Someone said they heard a man shout the same obscenity.

"I'll f--- him any time he wants, too," Connors said.

But as has been his history, Connors' play was so dazzling that the incident was forgiven. Even comedian Alan King, who has never been a Connors fan, went to the locker room to congratulate the winner.

"Look, it's the King," Segura said when he saw the visitor.

"Yeah," Connors said, "there's not many of us left now that Elvis died."

Two days later, in the first set of his semi-final match against Corrado Barrazzuti of Italy, a surprise semi-finalist, Connors lost his head and the crowd. Serving at 3-3 and down an advantage, Connors ended a long rally by smashing a cross-court forehand that the line judge called in. The crowd whistled to protest the call. Before the judge could check the mark and verify his call, Connors scampered to Barrazzuti's side of the court and erased the mark with his sneaker. The crowd was outraged and booed loudly. Play was interrupted. Connors walked back to his side of the court while grinning childishly.

"Mr. Connors, Mr. Connors," umpire Jack Stahr said into the microphone. Jimmy refused to look at him. "You really have no right to do that," Stahr said, "though the ball was in and the score is deuce."

With the crowd against him, Connors played sloppily for the rest of the match, but he was still able to beat Barrazzuti in three sets.

After the match, Connors was humble. "I can't believe I did that," he said. "I bet you'll never see that again. Things just happen off the cuff like that. I surprise myself."

When asked about the umpire's reprimand, his tone became belligerent: "Oh, did he reprimand me? That's like going to the principal's office and getting my hands slapped."

The next day the crowd was solidly behind Vilas from

the outset. Connors is used to playing with crowds against him and even claims to enjoy it. But after Vilas won a tie-breaker in the third set to go ahead two sets to one, Connors seemed to lose his skill. He became tentative and disoriented. He had put too much pressure on himself throughout the tournament and now, with Vilas at the top of his game and the crowd at the height of its hostility, Connors could no longer function—it was as if something snapped in his mind. He lost the last set at love—turning defeat into humiliation—and then made his frantic getaway.

Earlier in the summer, Sandy Mayer, who once played the National Indoor Circuit with Connors, asked Bill Riordan, "How long can anyone win on hate?"

At Forest Hills, Jimmy Connors answered that question.

Martina Navratilova, 1978 "When I retire at 30, I'm just going to escape from all the pressure of winning and being a public figure."

Chapter 14

The Smashing Ms. Navratilova

In 1978, Martina Navratilova won her first of nine Wimbledon singles titles and emerged as the game's No. 1 women's player, Her goal, she told SPORT, *was to become the greatest female player ever.*

SPORT September 1978 By Richard O'Connor

Fifteen minutes before the Boston Lobsters of World Team Tennis would begin practice, Martina Navratilova sat on a courtside folding chair in Boston's Walter Brown Tennis Arena staring at me as if to say: What planet did you descend from?

She was looking that way because I had just asked her if she would spend a few hours talking to me. I had approached this meeting with Martina with some trepidation because the night before a slew of Boston's tennis writers warned me that Martina was no easy interview. "She's like Ted Williams was," said one writer, "she stays very aloof from the press. I don't think I've gotten more than two consecutive sentences out of her in two years." Said another: "Forget it, man. She's too withdrawn, too temperamental. Ask her a question she doesn't like and she's apt to tell you off or walk away. You're better off going home."

Martina's eyes could have frosted my glasses, but she suddenly began to speak. "Listen, I don't want my privacy invaded. Why can't you understand I don't want my life to be public information? You think just because a person is a celebrity you can take up their time and write about them anything you please, don't you?" She picked up a racket and started tapping it forcefully in her hand.

"No, I don't think that," I said, eyeing the racket cautiously. "I'm simply here to find out what's happening with you this year. You've won almost every tournament you've entered."

This season on the Virginia Slims tour, Martina had won a record seven straight tournaments, and her eight overall victories were the most since the circuit was consolidated in 1975. She had also captured the $150,000 Virginia Slims Championship by defeating Evonne Goolagong Cawley 7-6, 6-4. At one point Martina had won every tournament she entered, winning 37 consecutive matches, also a Slims record. And presently, as a member of the Boston Lobsters, she is the No. 1-ranked woman player in World Team Tennis. This winning rampage had made Martina—along with Chris Evert—a heavy favorite to win Wimbledon and the U.S. Open.

Okay then, so what's happened this season to make Martina Navratilova a genuine threat to depose Chris Evert from her accustomed perch atop women's tennis?

Improved attitude, better court concentration and use of a lighter racket were the answers Martina recited to me as if she had answered the question hundreds of times before-which she probably had. She then yawned: It was a gesture which convinced me that the question-and-answer approach wasn't going to produce a scintillating interview. So I closed my notebook and terminated the questioning—at least, for the present.

Martina stood up, put her hands on her hips and began to rotate her upper body in a slow, circular motion. She clenched her teeth and groaned. She was stiff from the previous night's match against the Seattle Cascades in which she defeated Betty Stove in singles and later teamed with Terry Holladay to beat Stove and Marita Redondo in doubles.

Still stretching, she groaned softly, "Oh, God."

"Is it hard for you to get loose after a match?" I asked.

"Yes," she said and continued stretching. A 5-foot-7, solidly built 22-year-old, her present playing weight of

132 pounds is almost 40 pounds less than it was two seasons ago. She has prominent cheekbones and expressive brownish-green eyes. Her thin brown hair fell loosely to the collar of her blue satiny sweatsuit.

"I especially have a hard time with my thighs," she volunteered.

I offered to show her an exercise that might be helpful. I crouched down like a catcher, put my hands through my legs, grabbed my heels and tried to raise my buttocks while keeping my head up and staring straight ahead.

Martina repeated the exercise. "You're right," she said, rising from the squat position. "I can really feel it pulling." Then she smiled. Her smile seemed hesitant, as if there were something in her past that prevented an unrestrained and open expression. "I've got an exercise skiers usually do," she said. Placing her back against a wall, she assumed the posture of someone sitting on a chair. She pushed backward against the wall. "Do this for six or seven minutes and you'll feel it."

Martina looked at me appraisingly. "You're pretty big," she said, referring to my 6-5, 210-pound frame. "Do you play sports?"

"Yes," I said. "Basketball."

"I just started playing that, too," she said. "But my jump shot is erratic. There's a basketball court near my home here in Boston and often I go out and shoot a few. It's a great game."

Martina started asking me questions about basketball—what happened to the 76ers in the playoffs; who was better, David Thompson or Doctor J—and somehow the conversation meandered around to my career: College basketball All-America and briefly a pro. We talked about sacrificing, about single-mindedness of purpose, about the exhilaration of competing. Martina said, "If I weren't a tennis player, I'd be a golfer or a skier or even a baseball player." She pointed to a bruise on her leg. "Got this from playing softball. Obviously I'm not too good. But still I love competing ... and winning. Winning is infectious. When you're winning you push yourself until you start winning again. It's a disease, I guess. There are few things I do—even to playing card games—where I don't feel the need to come out on top. The thrill of winning... is ... just fantastic."

Martina's words were flowing now, yet she still seemed wary because I was, after all, a reporter.

To Martina, reporters generally signify a blight, but this was not always the case. When Martina burst onto the American scene in 1973, she was the darling of the tennis set, a shy, talented 16-year-old whose journey from Czechoslovakia to the U.S. had the overtones of Dorothy spinning from Kansas to Oz.

She soon bought a Mercedes, purchased expensive jewelry and clothes, and indulged in eating orgies at pancake and pizza houses. She gained 30 pounds, but she was colorful copy. "Martina is a girl who upon coming to America found it was love at first bite," wrote one reporter.

Then at Forest Hills in September of 1975, Martina announced she was defecting from Czechoslovakia— escaping from a totalitarian government which she claimed was hindering her tennis career by dictating when and where she could play. Although most defectors are viewed sympathetically, Martina was not. Many reporters accused her of selfish motives. Certainly, Czechoslovakia is not America, but even so, Martina— as a national heroine—lived better than most. Moreover, many press accounts implied she was leaving her homeland simply to live frivolously while her family remained in Czechoslovakia to face the consequences. Whatever, Martina continued to win.

In 1975 she was a finalist in the Australian, French and Italian Opens, a finalist in the Virginia Slims Championship and a semi-finalist at Forest Hills. In 1976, however, her play became sluggish. She was slowed down because she was overweight. Still, paired with Chris Evert at Wimbledon, she captured the doubles title.

Then, barely a month later, came the U.S. Open disaster at Forest Hills. It was the opening round and Martina was a very heavy favorite to defeat her opponent, a virtual unknown named Janet Newberry. After winning the first set 6-1, Martina began to crumble. At four-all in the second set, Newberry assumed control of the match and won the last two sets 6-4, 6-3. It was a shocking upset.

The crowd sat strangely quiet, like mourners at a funeral. There was no applause, no smiles, no whispers—just a transfixed audience staring at Martina who stood paralyzed at the baseline, crying hysterically. Newberry—who later commented, "It was awfully sad; I hope I never see anyone in that condition again"—ran over, put her arms around Martina and escorted her off the court as if assisting an old woman across the street.

Martina was besieged by reporters. They pressed her to admit that her defection in 1975 had culminated in this embarrassing defeat—that by spending foolishly, eating excessively and practicing casually, she had frittered away the talent and drive needed to make a championship tennis player.

But Martina was too overcome to reply to the reporters. She just sat there, a sad, pathetic figure, sobbing uncontrollably. That night a newspaper ran a story about a "washed-up tennis player grown gluttonously fat on American greed and fame and pizza."

The next afternoon Martina defaulted from the doubles competition and announced she was taking a "long needed rest from tennis to evaluate myself and my career."

"At the end of 1974 I was nobody," Martina said at the time. "Then all of a sudden I was No. 2 in the world and seeded No. 2 at Wimbledon when I'd never even been seeded there before. It was too fast. I couldn't handle it. Maybe I should quit."

But she didn't quit, and she returned to play a limited schedule in 1977. Even though her game lacked the brilliance exhibited two years before, she was winning regularly. Yet, whenever she'd lose, invariably a newspaper account would blame her defeat on a less-than-dedicated attitude.

Even her friend and frequent doubles partner, Billie Jean King, criticized her. In an article in the New York *Times* Sunday magazine by Boston columnist and TV announcer Bud Collins, King said: "It would help the women's game if Martina lived up to her potential, and started beating Chris regularly, but I don't know how hard she'll push herself. She likes to enjoy herself. She has a tendency to goof off, get distracted, you know, buying things, not practicing enough."

Yet while Martina's critics condemned her as a capitalist junkie, they overlooked her young age, her lack of a family in America and her beginnings in a communist country where freedom is restricted—where fear is an accepted part of everyday life. In the summer of 1968, when Martina was 11, Russia invaded Czechoslovakia to overthrow what it considered to be the overly liberal government of Alexander Dubcek. Martina was playing in a junior tournament in Pilsen during the invasion and saw the Russian soldiers terrifying townspeople, many of whom were shot senselessly. She sought refuge in a store and hid there until her father found her and, tucking her underneath his coat, drove her on a motorbike 60 miles to their home in Revnice.

Four years later she came to America, became a

tennis phenom, defected and everything changed. She was free, rich and internationally famous. She was also alone, living out of a suitcase.

Contrast this to the early career of Chris Evert whose mother Colette immersed herself in her daughter's life, arranging travel, practice and eating schedules, monitoring dates, spending and curfews, acting as a shield against a demanding press. Chris consequently remained level-headed in the face of success. This same protective pattern is in effect with Tracy Austin and her mother. The young Martina had nobody, but she struggled on, survived her Open disaster and bounced back with an overpowering brand of tennis.

Martina finished stretching, returned to the folding chair and said, "Sure it was hard for me being alone and being on the circuit. Things were so new, so exciting. But all that stuff about my throwing money all over the place was overplayed. Many people resented that I was a Czech foreigner who had made so much money so fast in America. But I earned it and I did what I wanted to do with it. Besides, the jewelry and Mercedes I had before my defection, so what was the big deal?"

Suddenly, a small, black poodle leaped into Martina's lap. She introduced it as Racquet, her constant traveling companion. I shook its paw.

"Last year I bought a home in Dallas," she said, petting Racquet, "and the first day I moved in I found him just I walking around alone . . . homeless. So I took him in. I guess we were two lost souls who had found each other."

"Do you enjoy owning a home?" I asked.

"My home means everything to me," she said. "There's no doubt it's been a key to my success. It's my refuge, the place I go to find strength and peace." Martina almost grinned. "The house was the first thing I owned in America that meant anything to me. Finally I had roots and security. It was what I had been searching for after Forest Hills. You know, the pressure in tennis can get overwhelming at times and you need someplace to hide out. Now I have it."

"Is Racquet your only roommate?"

"No," Martina said. "Sandy lives there, too." Sandy is Sandra Haynie, the professional golfer who won the U.S. Open in 1974. She is Martina's agent and best friend.

"Sandy has had a tremendous influence on me," Martina said. "She doesn't give me advice on tennis but she's encouraged me in other ways, like making me understand the need to be loose, to be calm, not to press or get impatient out on the court. Years ago whenever I got mad or down, I would lose my concentration and perhaps blow the next two or three points. I still lose my temper, of course, but at least I can control my emotions and not have them work against me. I've stopped beating myself."

"I take it then you feel you're playing the best tennis of your career?"

"Perhaps," Martina said. "This year I've beaten Chris two out of the three times we've played Team Tennis and that alone would lead me to say I'm playing my best tennis. But mentally I feel super. Last week I was just about to start a match when the announcer introduced me as the No. 1 female player in the world. That felt super. And I'm working harder than ever to earn that title. Tennis means everything to me. Whether I'm sleeping or eating or drinking I do it with tennis in mind. It's my life's existence." She brought Racquet up to her face and spoke to it affectionately. The dog's tail wiggled.

I remarked that though she may be playing the best tennis of her career it was done while Chris Evert was on a fun-and-sun sabbatical in Florida, and that many people will not consider Martina No. 1 until she does beat Evert in a major tournament instead of a WTT match that goes only one set.

"That is true," Martina said. "I was No. 1 while Chris was away and that is why Wimbledon and Forest Hills are so crucial to me. I want to play Chris and I want to win because even though I've had a great season so far, it will mean almost nothing without winning a major championship. There are a lot of people who don't think I can beat Chris, and I am out to prove them wrong. I want to be the greatest female tennis player."

I smiled and Martina glanced at me as if I had just developed a third eye. "Did I say something funny?" she asked.

"No," I said, "it's just that the Boston writers told me so many unpleasant things about you and yet I find you so ... well ... candid."

Martina shook her head. "I don't know why they say that. What do they want from me?"

"Maybe they want you to talk more about your past," I said.

"But the past is past," she said emphatically. "Besides, there's no way I'm going to do that, and if they don't like it—tough."

"Yeah," I said, "but your recent effort to gain an early American citizenship isn't the past and yet you refuse to talk about that, too." Martina is trying to push a special bill through Congress that will waive the five-year wait required to qualify for citizenship. Thus far her efforts have been in vain, and a few weeks before she had been seen crying as she left a Washington, D.C. courtroom. As it stands now, Martina must wait two more years.

"I don't want to talk about it for many reasons," she said, fidgeting in her chair. "Primarily I don't want to say anything that might hurt my chances of getting my papers. I have people working for me in Texas and, believe me, I want to be an American citizen badly. "

"Don't you miss your family?" I asked. (In Czechoslovakia, Martina is considered a "nonperson." The results of her matches are not carried in the newspapers, and her parents must listen to the Voice of America on radio to find out how she is playing.)

"Of course I do," she said. "I care about them very much and it depresses me greatly at times over what's happened. Listen, I hated leaving my family. But the government control over my career was getting stricter. My family and I decided when I got the opportunity to defect I would. Yes, it's been hard on them, too. My father knows he will never get promoted and my sister is denied playing in certain tennis clubs. But they understand what I did and why I did it. I still talk to them once a month and miss them very much. Perhaps someday ... someday"—she looked forlornly into the distance—"I will return to my family in Czechoslovakia. Then my life will be complete."

A few weeks after my meeting with Martina, I met Sandy Haynie sitting in a courtside seat in Madison Square Garden before a Boston-New York WTT match.

"When I first met Martina," Haynie said with a Texas accent, "I thought, 'My God, what a young talent in need of direction.' She had had a miserable year in 1976, but every athlete goes through a bad year. It makes you appreciate both your talents and your weaknesses. But Martina had never experienced that before and she had trouble coping. So we got together and worked first on her mental attitude, getting her to control her emotions and not let them control her. As an athlete I knew the importance of not getting down on yourself in competition. Martina had a tendency to let things get to her and it would affect her performance. Then we worked on her practice habits and eating habits. Martina lost a tremendous amount of weight, which affected her rhythm and timing. You can work with someone every day and if they don't want success, you can't force it on them. But Martina decided she wanted it and she dedicated herself accordingly."

"Martina had a platoon of advisers previous to you," I said, "yet they didn't seem to draw out her potential as you have."

"Maybe that's because I wasn't a John Doe coming out of the stands," Haynie said. "I was a professional golfer and had been through the rigors of professional sports. On that level it was easy for Martina to relate to me."

"You know," I said, "there seems to be so much more to Martina than ever gets printed."

Sandy smiled at me. "I couldn't agree with you more," she said. "There is her warmth, her sense of humor, her generosity. They never get written about because the press gave Martina such a hard time after her defection that now she has built up a defense. But understand, Martina can't and will not talk about her past or her defection. It wasn't a political decision—it was strictly personal. Remember, her family still lives in Czechoslovakia and whatever she might say could in some way affect their lives."

Back in Boston, Roy Emerson, the Lobsters' coach, called Martina onto the court and for a moment they talked quietly at the net. Then they went to opposite ends of the court. They exchanged ground strokes—slowly at first, but gradually building into a rapid pace. Emerson was sending Martina running all over the court to reach his shots. She dug for every ball. She sprinted back for lobs and raced toward the net for drop shots. She protected the baseline like an angry watchdog, alternating graceful but powerfully hit backhands and forehands. Then she moved to the net and continually punched flawless volleys beyond Emerson's reach. Whenever she mis-hit a ball she looked to the ceiling, cursed and pounded her thigh with her fist.

After a few hours, Emerson shouted to Martina, "Okay, Love, serve up a few hundred balls and you're finished."

A lefty, Martina tossed a ball into the air with her right hand. Her feet drew together, her knees bent, her body seemed to coil back then forward as she whipped her racket into the ball. Her serve, clocked at 91 mph, the fastest in women's tennis, was a blur that landed perfectly in the service court.

As Martina continued practicing her serve, I stopped Emerson and asked about her.

"Martina is in a super frame of mind and in great shape," Emerson said. "She is working the hardest of her life and improving daily. There is no question if she continues to play as she has this year she will leave Evert far behind. Remember, she is still very young."

"You mean mentally or physically?"

"Well, physically Martina is certainly mature," said Emerson. "Mentally she is getting game tough and this has helped her poise on the court. She is not yet a cool customer like Chrissie, but she's coping better. This is going to be her year to win it all."

Martina's problems—her defection, her "psychological breakdown," her junk-food binges—are behind her. Now she has a home—a "refuge" to use her word—in America where she can go and find happiness and friends who care about her. Because of this she is playing the best tennis of her career. More importantly, Martina has finally discovered herself. "I am completely at peace with myself," she said.

A summer sun warmed the asphalt basketball court located behind a luxury high-rise apartment near downtown Boston. Martina Navratilova, wearing her satiny sweat suit, dribbled with her back to the basket. She maneuvered methodically and forcefully—left-right-left-right—like Earl Monroe backing in. Occasionally she glanced over her shoulder while I, towering behind her, my chin almost resting upon her head, was playing her in classic NBA-style defense—hand on her hip, pushing her to impede her forward progress. Her body was firm, incredibly muscular, and she kept advancing. I planted my feet and bumped her with my chest. No reaction. Then quickly she swung to her right, turned and tossed up a jumper. Her form was awkward; the shot was released from her hip. The ball hit the front rim of an eight-foot-high biddy basket and I momentarily bobbled the rebound. It bounced off the asphalt. I reached for it and was about to grab it when, suddenly, Martina charged in, retrieved the ball and scored an easy lay-up. An impish smile flickered briefly across her face. "I told you I was competitive."

My ball. Martina handed it to me and stepped inches away from my chest. She was, basketball coaches would say, "bellying-up"—playing the skin-tight D. I faked and dribbled to my right. Martina crouched, bouncing on the balls of her feet, and made a swipe for a steal. I reverse dribbled, headed toward the basket, went skyward. Martina recovered and, arms outstretched, leaped up to challenge my shot. Luckily, thanks to my Mutt-and-Jeff height advantage over Martina, I barely escaped having my shot rejected into nearby Framingham.

The lead fluctuated back and forth. Martina, who less than an hour earlier had undergone a grueling workout, was inexhaustible. I was in decent shape due to a lifelong love affair with basketball. I continue to play because I savor a good, physical, competitive game. Which, at this moment, Martina, a novice, was providing.

I was ahead 6-5 (seven points was to end the game) when I stopped and fired up a 20-footer. A bad shot. Instinctively I followed for the rebound, elbows flying. But Martina boxed me out and gathered in the ball. She moved outside past the foul line and pivoted. Her face was unsmiling, intense. She went right, stuttered and, with a hesitation move, blew past me and stopped under the goal. She went up—and dunked. She turned and nodded as if to say, "In your face, turkey." I detected a strut in her walk as she bellied-up to guard me for game point.

Slowly, I backed in. Martina leaned against me and bumped me. Her hands were active, flicking like a serpent's tongue after the ball. I maneuvered to the baseline and picked up my dribble. I pumped—made a head

and shoulder fake—and pumped again. Martina went for the fake and left her feet. I waited. She came down. I jumped and shot. Swish!

"Damn," said Martina. "I'll be back for a rematch, but I have to go now."

Walking to her apartment, I asked Martina what she would do after she stopped playing tennis.

She sighed. "When I retire at 30, I'm just going to escape from all the pressure of winning and being a public figure. I'm gonna travel and spend money and ... just go bananas." Then, for the first time since meeting Martina, I saw her unleash a smile without the slightest trace of hesitation.

We reached the entrance to her apartment, shook hands and then I left. I was headed toward my car when suddenly I remembered I had forgotten my sunglasses at the playground.

As I approached the playground a group of young men were whispering, "That's him, that's him."

"Hey," one of the players called, "were you just playing basketball with Martina Navratilova?"

"Yes," I said.

"Man, she was super," said the guy as his cohorts nodded agreement. "Can you imagine some tennis star like Chris Evert shooting baskets in a schoolyard?"

I couldn't.

Chapter 15

A Sister Act That's Tough to Beat

Tennis divas, global icons, cultural standard bearers, Venus and Serena Williams are shaking up the tennis world. The amazing sisters are quickly earning a place among the most important figures in tennis history.

By Joel Drucker

Serena and Venus Williams, 2002

Welcome to 21st century tennis, where in rapid, Internet era speed, the extraordinary has become the familiar so quickly that it's in danger of being taken for granted.

Not once in the 20th century had two siblings met in a Grand Slam singles final. But at the 2003 Australian Open, Serena and Venus Williams met for all the marbles for the fifth time in the last six Slams. In front of a capacity crowd of just over 15,000 at Rod Laver Arena, the sisters staged their first three-set final, Serena scraping out a 7-6, 3-6, 6-4 victory, giving the sisters a combined total of nine Grand Slam singles titles. Serena's completion of the "Serena Slam"—taking four straight—was an incredible accomplishment. Though it was not quite the same as a sweep of all four in a year, it unquestionably validated the sisters' stature atop the tennis world. They'd drawn attention to the sport with the sizzle of an Andre Agassi and the social impact of an Arthur Ashe.

Peers and fans were staggered, not just by the sisters'

on-court prowess, but by their cultural significance. They had emerged from the bullet-laced, gang-ridden parks of south central Los Angeles to become not just wildly-successful athletes, but international icons. Media had chronicled their lives since pre-adolescence, from features on the front page of *The New York Times* to a cover story in *Time* magazine and hundreds more print and broadcast pieces. Each sister was not just physically talented, but intellectually ambitious, speaking with poise and humor about topics ranging far beyond the lines of a tennis court—sometimes with success, sometimes not. With a combined annual income in the $40-million range, with homes in Florida and California, with equipment endorsements and television commercials and public-service campaigns, they remained each other's best friend, practicing together, motivating, encouraging, talking on cell phone and via e-mail when apart. Their insularity set them apart from their rivals, creating odd forms of jealousy, misunderstanding and speculation. Always they conducted themselves with confidence, their rackets making the best case for their place in the red hot center of the popular culture.

"It's the most amazing thing in sports," said Lindsay Davenport, following her 6-3, 7-5 loss to Serena in the semi-finals of the 2002 U.S. Open. "Could you imagine Tiger Woods challenging a sibling to go head-to-head for all the majors?"

One man could.

June 1978. Watching television in his Southern California home, Richard Williams saw a woman named Virginia Ruzici holding a check for 100,000 francs (nearly $22,000). She'd just won the French Open. Richard was staggered by the opportunities tennis offered a young woman. He told the love of his life, a nurse named Oracene Price, that he wanted more daughters. Already the mother of three girls by Richard, Oracene declined. Then she learned a lesson eventually familiar to everyone in tennis: Never underestimate Richard Williams. Courting, cajoling, even hiding her birth control pills, Williams attained his goal. On June 17, 1980, Venus Ebone Starr Williams entered the world, born in Lynwood, California (a suburb of Los Angeles). Serena was born on September 26, 1981 in Saginaw, Michigan. Oracene and Richard were married that same year.

After witnessing Ruzici's triumph, Williams, who'd played basketball, golf and football as a young man in

Shreveport, Louisiana, taught himself to play tennis by studying instructional videos, magazines and television broadcasts. With seven milk crates of tennis balls and a half-dozen rackets, he took the four-year-old Venus to play on the rough-and-tumble public courts of Watts and Compton. The Williams family lived in Compton, a largely African-American city adjacent to Los Angeles that Richard insisted was "a great place to see how tough it is to get by in America." Thus marked the beginning of the Richard Williams Traveling Blarney Show. An entrepreneur, he claimed in the early '90s that he ran a security firm with six employees. A decade later, he'd say his company had a staff of 55. He'd also subsequently say that, "We only lived in Compton because I wanted the girls to get tougher there. We could have afforded to live in nicer parts."

Venus and Serena played at what Richard called "The East Compton Hills Country Club." It was a glass-strewn, poorly-surfaced pair of hardcourts. The girls were taught how to duck should bullets fly near the court. Richard arranged for local gang members to guard the courts during practice sessions.

But Richard was far from provincial. He got to know a few local teaching pros. Paul Cohen, a prominent instructor based in L.A.'s affluent Brentwood area who'd worked with such top pros as John McEnroe, invited the girls to his private court and spent hours drilling them in the fundamentals. The girls were highly-coordinated, fast and eager to hit balls for hours. Venus had run a 5:29 mile at age eight.

Venus began playing Southern California junior tournaments. The temptation here is to think this was a jarring experience: The humble Williams family from Compton coming into contact with tennis' elite, country-club world. The truth was that the bulk of Southern California junior events were played at austere parks, public high schools and state university campuses. Competitors came from many cultural and economic backgrounds.

Venus was an instant success, winning 63 straight matches and becoming Southern California's number one 12-and-under player. Serena followed suit, dominating the 10-and-under division. The two sisters caught the eyes of such tennis notables as Jack Kramer and Dodo Cheney. The bulk of the attention, though, was focused on Venus, who in 1990—at age ten—was featured on the front page of *The New York Times*. Soon after, boxing promoter Don King showed up in

Compton. Playing the Southern California junior championships, the sisters wore shirts with the King Productions logo. But they did not sign up with King, nor with any of the other agents who came knocking. Richard had bigger ideas.

In 1991, in a move that would be debated for years, Richard withdrew the girls from junior competition. He'd claim, "I was sick of all those competitive parents and kids and no one caring about their children's education. I wanted my girls to be smart first. That matters way more than making them tennis players." This was no lip-service comment. Though Richard personally directed much of their schooling, the girls did indeed spend hours solving math problems, reading books and writing papers. These lessons would all surface early in their careers.

Richard also said that by taking them out of competitive events he was following the pattern of Monica Seles, who, at her father's behest, eschewed the results-oriented world of junior tennis throughout her early teens in favor of making herself a better player. Also echoing the pattern of such stars as Seles and Andre Agassi, the Williams family relocated to Florida. Venus and Serena began working with Rick Macci in Delray Beach, Florida and a host of hitting partners. Macci's most prominent student had been Jennifer Capriati. "Six hours a day, six days a week for four years," Macci said about Venus. "There wasn't a day that the girl wouldn't hit 200 serves."

The question during this time was simple: Was Richard Williams protecting his daughters or priming the pump for them? "Any parent who lets their child turn pro at 14 should be shot," Richard said in 1994.

Venus turned 14 that same year. She also turned pro, a move hastened by several changes the Women's Tennis Association had made in its eligibility rules as a safeguard against such burnout cases as Jennifer Capriati and Andrea Jaeger. Had Venus waited, she might well have been forced to play a restricted schedule.

Like many of the high-tech products that were launched in the '90s, Venus was simultaneously hyped and kept under wraps so wisely by Richard that when she was at last unveiled in October 1994, the sound was resounding. Dozens of the world's leading media flocked to Oakland, California for her debut, including *USA Today*, *The New York Times*, *The Boston Globe*, *The Times of London*, *Sports Illustrated*, *Newsweek*, *People* and ESPN. At 14, Venus was already a polished speaker,

giving motivational talks at several Oakland schools. On October 31, the girl Richard called "the Cinderella of the ghetto," played her first pro match, defeating Shaun Stafford in straight sets. In the next round she took a 6-3, 3-1 lead against world number one Arantxa Sanchez Vicario before losing 11 straight games. Asked how the loss compared to previous defeats, Venus noted, "I don't know. I've never lost before." Tennis insiders didn't know whether this comment was cocky or innocent. There was a bluntness to everything this family did that left many feeling off-balance.

Richard compounded the feeling that he was directing more of a performer than an athlete, holding court on everything from education to the history of the American family. As a sidelight, he mentioned that he had another daughter who was even better. Hardly a speck of attention was paid to Serena.

Considering how much time Venus had spent in Macci's laboratory, her strokes were shockingly ill-formed, mostly a mass of long limbs and whipping arm motions. But already her dazzling court coverage was present. Six months later, still having only played one pro tournament, she signed a five-year, $12-million contract with Reebok.

Over the next two years, Venus' appearances were limited. At the end of 1996, her world ranking was 204. She had yet to play a Grand Slam event. Serena, 15 years old at the end of 1996, hadn't played a single pro match.

Throughout the early part of 1997, the sisters remained low on the tennis radar screen. Venus made a disastrous Wimbledon debut, losing to Magdalena Grzybowska in the first round, playing with so little composure that at one point she hit a second serve with a broken string.

Then came a moment where history and an individual collided in vivid, Technicolor glory. The 1997 U.S. Open was the opening year of Arthur Ashe Stadium. It was also the year the great African-American women's champion, Althea Gibson, turned 70. As Venus would remark, "it was time to step up."

All the pieces in her game she'd been assembling began to coalesce. Big serves, running groundstroke winners, attacking forays. It was still a rough, patchy game, but it was also becoming increasingly effective.

But in the semis, versus Rumanian Irina Spirlea, the Cinderella—now not just of the ghetto, but of the U.S. Open—was on the verge of becoming a pumpkin. Spirlea, an accomplished baseliner but also an emotionally mercurial competitor, had attempted to intimidate Williams by bumping into her as they crossed sides on a changeover. Venus would admit she hardly noticed it. The two reached a third-set tiebreak. Spirlea held two match points. Pressed deep into her backhand corner, Williams responded with one of the greatest shots in U.S. Open history—a sizzling up-the-line winner. Minutes later, she'd become the first player to reach the U.S. Open finals in her debut.

It hardly mattered that, once there, Venus lost to Martina Hingis, 6-0, 6-4. Venus and the hundreds of red, white and blue beads in her hair had made a massive splash. Asked how her impact in tennis compared to Tiger Woods' in golf, she said, "He's different from the mainstream, and in tennis I also am. I'm tall. I'm black. Everything's different about me. Just face the facts."

Serena also made a few headlines in 1997. In Chicago, playing her second WTA Tour main draw event, she beat two top ten players, Mary Pierce and Monica Seles. From a ranking of 453 in the world in October, she'd vaulted to 99 by the end of the year.

During these early years, many WTA contemporaries found themselves at odds with the sisters. Neither Venus nor Serena were willing to acknowledge many of their opponents' strengths or achievements. Rumor had it they could barely be bothered to even greet other players in the locker room. Rivals such as Hingis and Lindsay Davenport—each had achieved more than either sister at that point—found this lack of respect grating. In the spirit of such previous parents (Gloria Connors, Peter Graf, Roland Jaeger) who encouraged their progeny to see the world in combative terms, Richard reveled in this climate.

The sisters began 1998 by playing each other in a tournament for the first time. They met in the second round of the Australian Open. Venus won in two uncomfortable sets. She lost in the quarters to Davenport. At that same tournament, in an effort to prove how much they stand out from their peers, the two each played a set versus ATP journeyman Kaarsten Braasch. He beat them easily.

Later that winter, Venus won her first tournament in Oklahoma City. More significantly, she won the prestigious Lipton Championship, the fifth-biggest tournament in the world. Most notable was her semi-final win over Hingis. An example of the rancor between the Williams family and Hingis had come at the previous event in Indian Wells. Hingis had just beaten Venus in

the semis. Venus came into the press conference and repeated her belief that in due time she and Serena would be the number one and two players in the world. Hingis was subsequently asked to comment on Venus' prediction. "She said that again!" exclaimed the Swiss. "I'm tired of hearing that."

Both sisters had painful Wimbledons. Serena, down 7-5, 4-1 to Virginia Ruano Pascual in the third round, defaulted with a foot injury—an ailment that apparently healed fast enough for her to win the mixed doubles with Max Mirnyi. An increasingly mature Venus reached the quarters, only to lose to eventual champion Jana Novotna in a match marred by a massive Venus temper tantrum.

The U.S. Open was only moderately successful, Serena losing in the third round to Spirlea, Venus going out in the semis to Davenport. But the two completed a unique Williams Family Grand Slam. Venus had won the Australian and French mixed with Justin Gimelstob. Serena took Wimbledon and the Open with Mirnyi.

On February 28, 1999, the two became the first sisters in history to win tournaments on the same day, Venus defending her Oklahoma City title, Serena winning in Paris. That whole week the two were e-mailing each other. The geographic disparity was part of Richard's plan to keep the two from playing singles in the same event. Was the motivation financial or emotional? No one could ever tell with Richard Williams.

Two weeks later, Serena won the WTA's Indian Wells event, overcoming a 4-2 third-set deficit to beat Steffi Graf in the finals, 6-3, 3-6, 7-5. On a 16-match winning streak, she arrived in the finals of the Lipton, where this time she met Venus. No fool, Richard had hoped his daughters would meet in this ultra-prestigious event. During the finals—televised on the FOX network—Richard wore a t-shirt that proclaimed "I TOLD YOU SO." In the first all-sisters final since 1884, Venus won 6-1, 4-6, 6-4. Afterwards, each was escorted to different parts of the venue to have their respective photos taken. Along the way, the two were chatting with each other on their cell phones.

Though their subsequent triumphs would make these early wins appear to be mere building blocks towards inevitable domination, in 1999 there was significant doubt about Venus and Serena's long-term prospects. True, each was showing they had the game it took to be a top-level player. But each constantly revealed acres of immaturity—both on and off the court. Serena, arguing over the meaning of the word ghetto with a reporter, stridently declared, "You have my information, I have mine." Venus had cried during tough losses. As competitors, each was prone to erratic play and emotional volatility. Venus had lost in the 1999 Australian quarters to Davenport, a match punctuated by her being penalized when her beads flew on to the court. Serena could become unglued by changes in pace. At the '99 Lipton final, the two had combined for a horrific 107 unforced errors.

Worst of all, Richard shot off his mouth so much he made it easy for the girls' opponents to get extra-motivated. "I think Serena could beat Hingis' butt coming and going," he said in Manhattan Beach the day before the opposite occurred. At least this comment was limited to tennis. Other times, Richard spoke left and right about his desire to see the girls retire, Venus' future as an astronaut, American history, education and more. Though it made him a captivating subject, it also eroded the credibility of his daughters' efforts—which as the decade ended, were in fact becoming quite considerable.

At the 1999 Wimbledon, for example, Venus had played mature, attacking tennis to reach the quarters. Despite losing a tight three-set match to Steffi Graf, she had conducted herself with exceptional poise and professionalism. Amid a cloud of speculation, Serena had defaulted, claiming she had a bad case of the flu.

Then, at the 1999 U.S. Open, Serena turned everything upside-down. Each sister had reached the semis. After Serena scraped through a three-setter over Davenport, the stage was set for an historic all-sisters Slam final. It wasn't to be. Venus, up against Hingis, had fought her way into a third set, but came up miserable, her serve crumbling, her technique failing, Hingis taking the match, 6-1, 4-6, 6-3.

The next day, her younger sister occupying the center stage she thought she would invariably take first, Venus sat in stunned silence, wearing a hooded sweatshirt and looking forlorn. Serena's appetite for the moment was vivid. Playing powerful all-court tennis, punishing Hingis' second serve, she held on for a 6-3, 7-6 victory. It was the first time an African-American woman had won a major singles title since Gibson had won the U.S. Championship in 1958. Later that evening, the sisters won the doubles. A month later, Serena earned her first victory over Venus.

Serena's triumph bolstered their presence as cultural icons. President Clinton had called her from New Zealand with his congratulations hours after the U.S. Open win. In November 1999, the two taped ten episodes of the game show, *Hollywood Squares*. Later they would also appear on *The Simpsons*, co-star in a McDonald's commercial, and make other deals with Avon, Wrigley, Sega, Reebok and Puma. By 2002, *Forbes Magazine* estimated they earned at least $19 million a year annually. At an extremely young age, they had attained financial independence—the concept that, after all, had been the initial attraction of tennis for Richard. But as 2000 dawned, the issue was credibility. Was Serena's Open victory a fluke? Could Venus harness her assets?

The atmosphere only thickened through the first half of 2000. Venus didn't enter a tournament until May. Said Richard, "I would like to see her retire now. I would love to see her do that."

Once again, talk seemed to take priority over action for the family. But then, at Wimbledon, each sister played with extraordinary conviction. Serena reached the semis versus Venus with the loss of but 13 games. Venus had played what to date was the match of her life, beating Hingis in a beguiling three-setter. Venus had been physically in control of virtually every point, but her constant overplaying of the ball led to many errors.

The Serena-Venus semi was typical: Significant, nervous, erratic—and a triumph for Venus, 6-2, 7-6. The most telling moment occurred after their heartfelt handshake. Venus, no doubt excited to have reached her first Slam final in nearly three years, showed none of the emotion that had surfaced throughout her career. Instead, lightly touching her vanquished younger sister, she said, "Let's get out of here." Rumors circled that Richard had demanded Serena throw the match so that Venus could square the major tally. The sisters scarcely took that talk seriously. In many ways, this is where the power of their mother, Oracene, began to assert itself more overtly. It was Oracene who provided the quiet grounding to Richard's bluster. It was Oracene who saw to it that the girls where Jehovah's Witnesses, never issuing a profanity, refusing to indulge in drinking or smoking.

Venus went on to beat Davenport in the finals, 6-3, 7-6. But the triumph was marred by Richard's showmanship. Prancing from his courtside seat, Richard wrote constant messages on a greaseboard: We Love the

Duke and Duchess. The British Fans are the Best in the World. And, most bizarre, It's Venus' Party, and You're Not Invited. Oracene was thousands of miles away, driving back from a visit to her grandmother's grave. Asked by *Sports Illustrated* writer L. Jon Wertheim if she would ever hold up signs like Richard, she crisply responded: "Never. I'm more secure with who I am." There had been rumblings during this time that Richard had beaten her. The sisters never uttered a word about these events. "They're completely loyal to Richard," said ESPN analyst Pam Shriver.

Instead, they focused on tennis, revealing a disarming intelligence rarely seen in tennis. Education had always been vital for the Williams family. "There's no one dumber than a tennis player," Richard had said. For all the puzzling arrogance and insularity the sisters regularly displayed, they were also poised, articulate and literate. At 16, Venus had cogently discussed the likes of Shakespeare and Richard Wright. Serena's favorite author was Maya Angelou, the African-American who had written a series of highly-regarded memoirs. She also confessed to an addiction to shopping on the Internet.

By the time she arrived at the 2000 U.S. Open, Venus had matured considerably. Reflecting on her run to the finals in '97, Venus noted, "I was just a yearling. I didn't know what I was doing basically."

Following a workmanlike three-set quarter-final victory over chip-charging Nathalie Tauziat (Serena had lost in that same round to Davenport), Venus took on Hingis in the semis. If ever there was a moment for a rite of passage, this was it. Though the Wimbledon win had given Venus confidence, the thinking at the Open was that the cagey Hingis would be able to assert herself more on the hardcourts. The memory of Venus' melt-down the previous year was quite vivid.

What the match lacked in quality it made up for in drama. Venus appeared in a daze for much of the match. With Hingis leading 5-3 in the third, Venus kept mouthing the word "unbelievable." As she said afterwards, "It really felt like all of a sudden the match was over."

With Venus serving at 3-5, 15-30, the two engaged in a 29-stroke rally. Hingis came to net, and when Venus threw up a benign lob, it appeared the Swiss would soon have two match points. But a weary Hingis barely hit the overhead, giving Venus the opening to hit another one of the Open's greatest shots—a trademark backhand down-the-line winner. She went on to win 15 of the next 18

points to take the match, 4-6, 6-3, 7-5. Said Hingis, "It's hard to finish her off because she's got so much reach compared to other players."

The final versus Davenport proved to be one of the strangest U.S. Open finals in history. With President Clinton watching (the first sitting president to ever attend the U.S. Open), the capacity crowd was primed for the first All-American final since 1984. But a 90-minute rain delay sapped Arthur Ashe Stadium of energy, compelling the President to leave—and Venus to check out as well. Soon Davenport was serving at 4-1. Venus countered, going on to win five straight games for the set. Then she took the second, 7-5. "Keep it in the family," said Richard Williams moments after the handshake. Though Clinton had left during the rain delay, he called Venus, who cheekily suggested he reduce taxes. She'd indeed come a long way from Compton.

Later that autumn, Venus won the Olympic gold medal. The sisters also won the Olympic doubles. Though Venus' abbreviated schedule left her ranked only third in the world on the WTA Tour's computer, to many she was clearly the year's preeminent player. "She knows how to win, she just knows," said her Fed Cup and Olympics coach, Billie Jean King. "You can't teach that, not really." *Sports Illustrated* named Venus female athlete of the year. A new Reebok contract guaranteed Venus $40 million, at the time the biggest deal in the history of women's sports.

The next year was virtually a carbon copy. One notable deviation occurred at Indian Wells. Well aware of this tournament's significance, Richard had agreed to let both daughters enter it. With the two about to meet in a prime-time, nationally-televised semi-final, Venus pulled out with an injury four minutes prior to the starting time. Despite nursing a sore knee, at no point during the day had she even tipped off a tournament official so that contingency plans could be made. The tournament director only found out through his public address system. Venus could hardly be bothered to apologize to the public. That same week a *National Enquirer* story had hinted that the sisters' 2000 Wimbledon semi-final result had been a fix. Two days later, when Serena took the court for the final, boos cascaded her. A startled Serena began the match poorly, losing the first set before righting herself and taking the title. "Hey, I'm only a kid," she said afterwards. The crowd also booed Richard and Venus when they walked to their courtside seats. More than a week later, Richard would claim he heard several racist comments. But none had been heard or reported that day.

In large part, the issue of fixing matches was a distraction. Who could prove it? As Serena noted, "if it's fixed, how come I've only won once?" What was clear, though, was that the Williams family—at least during this Indian Wells incident—cared little for anyone other than themselves. They had claimed they wanted to be as positive a force in tennis as Tiger Woods had been for golf. Instead, they had let narcissism override sportsmanship, taking their own course with no need to apologize. But they would learn. In 2002, after defaulting at the last minute at the Italian Open, Venus would walk on to the court and make a public apology.

Venus won Wimbledon with nary a peep from Richard. Serena, meanwhile, had suffered two frustrating three-set losses in the quarters of Roland Garros and Wimbledon to a new rival, the resurrected Jennifer Capriati. With Capriati rebounding higher than anyone dared imagine, with Davenport and Hingis still factors, with Belgians Kim Clijsters and Justine Henin rising, it wasn't clear if Serena indeed had the fortitude necessary for big-time success. Certainly she loved the perks of fame: Posing for fashion spreads, spending time with other notables from music and sports, talking about her interests in acting and shopping.

Though the 2001 U.S. Open would vindicate Richard's prediction that his daughters would indeed rule the tennis world, it was their mother, Oracene, who was rapidly emerging as a factor in the sisters' success. "She's the balance, the rock who keeps them solid," said King. By the summer of 2001, Richard was being reduced to a sideshow. Only the most naïve of reporters took his comments seriously. More emphatic was the strength of his daughters' rackets, who on the eve of the Open were featured on the cover of *Time* with the headline, "The Sisters Vs. The World." The world stood little chance. In the semis, Serena and Venus dispatched Hingis and Capriati, respectively. Serena's tight three-set win over Lindsay Davenport in the quarter-final had been a particularly gutty effort.

The all-Williams final was a grand occasion. It had been 117 years since two sisters had met in a major championship final (you mean you don't remember the Watsons?). In another first, it was aired on CBS during primetime, attended by such celebrities as Spike Lee, Diana Ross, Bruce Willis and Robert Redford. Again, the quality disappointed. Venus' 6-2, 6-4 victory fea-

tured excessive errors. Still, the elder sister had joined Steffi Graf and Martina Navratilova as the only women to win both Wimbledon and the U.S. Open in consecutive years. Yet once again, a limited schedule kept her from earning enough ranking points to rise higher than three in the world.

By the end of 2001, Serena was stewing. After winning the WTA's season-ending championship in Munich, she vowed that in 2002 she would make a bigger commitment to tennis. At the time it appeared to be another flip Williams comment.

The revolution the sisters were bringing wasn't just a matter of race or class or attitude. Venus and Serena were doing something rarely seen in an individual sport like tennis: With cell phones and e-mails and practice sessions, they were concurrently bolstering and motivating one another. At the tournaments they'd play together, even when one lost, the vanquished would know another was there to carry the flag for the family. It gave the two a unique form of fortification, a familial link often associated with such tennis nations as Australia, Sweden and Spain (that is, in the men's game). Off-court interests also balanced out the emotionally volatile tennis world. In the brief tennis off-season, Venus began studying fashion design, eventually setting up her own interior design practice. Serena worked on her acting, purchasing a condominium in Los Angeles in 2002. That same year she made her acting debut, playing the role of a kindergarten teacher on ABC's *My Wife and Kids*. Asked about her performance, she noted, "I guess I wasn't that bad."

Their commitment to the African-American community was also significant. As early as 1995, Venus and Serena had conducted clinics for the California Tennis Association for Underprivileged Youths, a longstanding program based in Los Angeles. By 2002, it had become the Venus and Serena Williams Tutorial/Tennis Academy.

But it was their rackets that made the most emphatic sounds in 2002. After a tepid start—Venus lost in the Australian Open quarters to Monica Seles, Serena pulled out with an ankle injury—the sisters began dominating the tour. By the spring, Venus had garnered titles on three continents. Serena was taking even bigger strides, bludgeoning Venus in the semis on the way to winning the near-Slam Key Biscayne event, avenging her losses to Capriati with wins in Scottsdale, Key Biscayne and Rome.

Neither sister had ever done much at the French Open. This time, each charged to the finals, Serena again squeaking by Capriati in the semis, Venus not dropping a set. In the finals, Serena turned the tables, earning a 7-5, 6-3 victory. One of the more memorable moments came during the awards ceremony when Venus joined the ranks of the photographers, bringing her own camera on-court to make sure she snapped shots of Serena hoisting the trophy.

The next month at Wimbledon, the pattern repeated, Serena taking it 7-6, 6-3 in their highest-quality match to date. With Davenport and Hingis felled by injuries, with Capriati and Seles showing signs of combat fatigue, with contenders like Justine Henin, Kim Clijsters and Amelie Mauresmo still on the ascent, the sisters pulled away from the pack. The previous year, their arrival in the U.S. Open final was extraordinary. By the end of 2002, it was business as usual—just another prime-time all-Williams show, played in front of a capacity crowd of 23,164 at Arthur Ashe Stadium. Serena's 6-3, 6-4 win capped an amazing year. She'd reached the top spot on the computer, had won eight of 13 tournaments and more than $3.9 million in prize money.

For Venus, of course, it had been frustrating to lose three straight Slam finals to the same person. At the U.S. Open, she'd been extended in the quarters by Chanda Rubin and in the semis by Mauresmo. Serena was the one who'd improved, bolstering her groundstrokes, adding variety to her game, solidifying her serve. Venus appeared shell-shocked by the strides Serena had made. She had won seven tournaments, but was she getting better? What would her motivation be in 2003? How would she alter her game? Unfortunately for her, despite testing Serena more severely than she had for some time, Australia would see the same result.

It was also clear that each sister had emerged as distinct personalities. First there had been Venus, touted by Richard, exposed to the world. Then, Serena had stolen the spotlight by winning the U.S. Open in 1999. Venus had countered, winning four Grand Slams over a two-year period. "I was tired of not winning," said Serena on the eve of Wimbledon 2002. "It was time for me to start walking the walk and talking the talk." Venus, the older sister, was a protector, pensive, thoughtful, a bit removed in her comments and movements—perhaps in some way like Pete Sampras. Even in the heat of competition, she bore little animus towards her opponents, focusing more on hitting the ball. Serena, younger, the baby of the family, more sassy, had a visceral quality to her, a facile immediacy and flipness that made her a contemporary jock star—more like Andre Agassi. And when a match neared crunchtime, Serena made tennis' one-on-one aspects personal, turning up the grunts and bearing down even harder. "Venus wants to beat you, but doesn't care if you feel the pain or not," said one vanquished opponent. "Serena wants to kill you."

The rise of Venus and Serena had occurred in a fish bowl. Never before had two tennis players gone ostensibly from the sandlot to the major leagues with no stops in between. Their games had matured not in the backcourts of the juniors but on stadium courts all over the world, complete with photographers, TV cameras and probing reporters. Richard Williams had envisioned and orchestrated so much, and he remained involved on and off the court. But Oracene, who divorced Richard in the fall of 2002, reclaiming her maiden name of Price, had also emerged as a factor, providing an anchor amid all the craziness that tennis, fame and money had brought Venus and Serena.

As invariably happens with any rapid ascent, it had not always been particularly humble. In 2001, the ESPN television network had contacted the family to get its cooperation in the production of one of the network's one-hour *SportsCentury* documentaries honoring the two sisters. The initial reaction from the Williams camp: We're not worthy to be in such company as the likes of deceased superstars Jackie Robinson and Arthur Ashe. But when the network persisted, the family countered by demanding separate one-hour programs on each sister. ESPN backed off, producing one program on both—but failing to get any exclusive interviews with anyone from the Williams camp. An opportunity to better acquaint the world with this incredible family had been squandered.

Were the sisters attracting more people to tennis? It was tough to determine. Television networks like CBS, which had carried two prime-time Venus-Serena finals, were reporting higher ratings. But there was no conclusive market research that proved if more people were playing, watching or spending more money on tennis. There was no question, though, that from a publicity standpoint, Venus-Serena was a tremendous story, resonating not just through tennis, but through all of sports and the broader popular culture—not just in America, but throughout the world.

René Lacoste (bottom),
Bill Tilden, 1927
At the top of his game,
the 'Crocodile' prevailed
11-9, 6-3, 11-9 to claim
his second successive
U.S. title at Forest Hills.

The Major
Championships

RECORDS – FASTEST SERVE, SINGLES

MEN
149 mph—Greg Rusedski
    (Indian Wells, 1998)
147 mph—Andy Roddick
    (Indian Wells, 2003)

WOMEN
124 mph—Brenda Schultz-McCarthy
    (Wimbledon, 2001)
122 mph—Venus Williams
    (Australian Open, 2002)

Chapter 16

The Grand Slam Is Born

Don Budge, 1937
Honing his game at Corals Gable, Florida, while plotting strategy for what would become the first Grand Slam.

Don Budge carried a secret plan into the 1938 season. He intended to become the first person to sweep the so-called Big Four titles of tennis—the Australian, French, British and U.S. championships—in the same year.

The closest anyone had come to a sweep had occurred five years earlier, when Australian Jack Crawford won the first three and faced Fred Perry in the final of the U.S. Championships. It was on the eve of the match that the Big Four were christened with the term Grand Slam. "If Crawford beats Perry today," wrote John Kieran of the *New York Times*, a keen bridge player, "it would be something like scoring a Grand Slam on the courts, doubled and vulnerable." As it turned out, Crawford, fatigued after almost five months on the road, came within one set of achieving the first Grand Slam before falling to Perry.

Entering the 1938 season, the last thing Budge wanted was to rekindle excitement about a sweep of the major championships. The only person privy to his ambitious plan was doubles partner Gene Mako. Don't tell anyone, Budge cautioned, or they'll be gunning for me. Budge, an amiable player who, at 6-foot-1, was called a red-haired giant, had won the British/Wimbledon and U.S. titles in 1937 and headed the U.S. team that won the Davis Cup. The temptation to turn professional was great, but he felt compelled to remain an amateur for at least one more year to defend the Davis Cup. It was a gamble. Anything short of another stellar year in 1938 would reduce his box-office appeal when he turned pro. So he was determined to make his final amateur season his finest.

First stop: Australian Open. The journey to Australia lasted 23 days. In the final, Budge needed just 47 minutes to dispatch John Bromwich 6-4, 6-2, 6-1. At Roland Garros, it took 58 minutes for a 6-3, 6-2, 6-4 final sweep of Roderich Menzel. Including his 1937 victories at Wimbledon and the U.S. Open, Budge had now won four consecutive majors, and was half way home in his pursuit of a calendar-year Grand Slam.

He cruised through Wimbledon without dropping a set before demolishing Henry (Bunny) Austin 6-1, 6-0, 6-3 in the final. On Sept. 24, Budge faced his friend Mako in the final of the U.S. Championship at Forest Hills, N.Y. The pair had earlier that summer won the men's doubles at Wimbledon. Budge, 23, completed his Grand Slam bid with a convincing 6-3, 6-8, 6-2, 6-1 victory.

Allison Danzig, a New York Times reporter, praised Budge's "murderous backhand and volcanic service," adding that Budge had achieved "a grand slam that invites comparison with the accomplishment of Bobby Jones in golf."

The feat of winning all four major championships in a calendar year would be known as the Grand Slam of tennis forever after. (Today, Grand Slam is often erroneously used to refer to any one of the four major tournaments. But a player cannot win "one of the Grand Slams." He or she may win a major championship, but only by winning all four of them in a calendar year can they claim a Grand Slam.)

Budge turned professional in 1939, having set the standard by which the greatest players have since been judged. In all the years since, only four others have achieved the Grand Slam: Maureen Connolly (1953), Rod Laver (1962 and 1969), Margaret Smith Court (1970) and Steffi Graf (1988).

Connolly, known as Little Mo, began her Grand Slam by defeating doubles partner Julia Sampson for the Australian title. The teenager from San Diego then met Doris Hart of Coral Gables, Fla. in the final at the next three majors. Hart failed to take a set in any of them, as Connolly won at Roland Garros, at Wimbledon and at the U.S. Championships. She was 18.

Laver, a left-handed Australian who was born a month before Budge's historic 1938 season, is the only other man to win the Grand Slam. And he did it twice, as an amateur in 1962 and as a professional in 1969. In 1962, Laver defeated compatriot and defending champion Roy Emerson for the Australian title, Emerson again for the French title, Marty Mulligan at Wimbledon and Emerson yet again at the U.S.

Seven years later, with the tournaments now open to all players, Laver survived several close calls. The most exhausting was a 90-game semi-final in the Australian Open, won 7-5, 22-20, 9-11, 1-6, 6-3 against countryman Tony Roche. Laver then defeated Andres Gimeno of Spain in an anticlimactic final. Laver followed up by defeating compatriots Ken Rosewall at the French Open and John

Newcombe at Wimbledon, and Roche again at the U.S. Open after dropping the first set in an historic 7-9, 6-1, 6-2, 6-2 match.

By 1970, Australia's Margaret Smith Court had already won 16 major championships, completed a so-called career Grand Slam and won three-quarters of a genuine Grand Slam in three different years (1962, 1965 and 1969). In 1970, she at last won all four in the same year, besting Kerry Melville in the Australian Open, Helga Masthoff Niessen in the French, Billie Jean King at Wimbledon and Rosie Casals at the U.S. Open. The Wimbledon match was a legendary, 46-game showdown, as Court, hobbled by a sprained ankle and in pain, withstood aching-kneed King's assaults for a 14-12, 11-9 victory that remains the longest women's final there at two hours, 28 minutes.

The most recent Grand Slam was achieved in 1988 by German teenager Steffi Graf. At Melbourne, she delivered a forehand volley on match point of the second-set tiebreaker to defeat Chris Evert. At Roland Garros, Graf needed just 32 minutes to administer an unprecedented 6-0, 6-0 spanking of Soviet teenager Natalia Zvereva, who managed only 13 points. At Wimbledon, Graf faced the awesome Martina Navratilova in the final. Down a set and trailing 2-0 in games in the second set, Graf took 12 of the 13 final games for a well-earned 5-7, 6-2, 6-1 victory. At the U.S. Open, Graf completed her Grand Slam by coolly defeating Gabriela Sabatini of Argentina. Weeks later, Graf accomplished a Golden Slam by defeating Sabatini in the Olympic gold-medal game at Seoul, South Korea.

In doubles, Frank Sedgman and Ken McGregor of Australia achieved the first Grand Slam in 1951. Brazil's legendary Maria Bueno matched that feat in 1960, winning the Australian with Christine Truman and the other three with Darlene Hard. Americans Martina Navratilova and Pam Shriver, a peerless doubles pair, won all four tournaments in 1984. In 1998, Martina Hingis of Switzerland paired with Mirjana Lucic to win in Australia, before completing the doubles Slam with Jana Novotna.

In mixed doubles, Australia's Ken Fletcher and Margaret Smith (later Court) put together the first mixed doubles Grand Slam in 1963. Four years later, Owen Davidson, another Australian, won his nation's mixed doubles championship with Lesley Turner before teaming with Billie Jean King to win the other three events.

Several players have won three-quarters of a Grand Slam. But none fell short in quite the manner of Martina Navratilova and Jimmy Connors. In 1974, Connors won in Australia, at Wimbledon and Flushing Meadows but, because he joined the new World Team Tennis League, the French Tennis Federation barred him from Roland Garros. Beginning in 1983, Navratilova won six consecutive major championships without achieving a calendar year Grand Slam. Her streak began at Wimbledon in 1983 and ran through the U.S. Open in 1984. But the Australian was the fourth in 1984, and she missed a Slam by losing in the semis to Helena Sukova, and Chris Evert took the crown. In an ill-advised move the ITF considered her winning four straight over two seasons a Slam, and paid Martina a million dollar bonus for that accomplishment. It wasn't legitimate. But Martina cashed the check anyway, and who can blame her.

Over the past quarter century, a Grand Slam has become more difficult to win. Even if a player is fit enough to combat the travel and the opposition, they must excel on four different playing surfaces: Rebound Ace in Melbourne Park, clay at Roland Garros, grass at Wimbledon and decoturf at Flushing Meadow. Before 1978, there were only grass and clay surfaces.

The Grand Slams

The complete record of all Grand Slams follows:

SINGLES

Don Budge, 1938

Australian, at Memorial Drive, Adelaide: d. Les Hancock, 6-2, 6-3, 6-4; Harold Whillans, 6-1, 6-0, 6-1; Len Schwartz, 6-4, 6-3, 10-8; Adrian Quist, 5-7, 6-4, 6-1, 6-2; John Bromwich, 6-4, 6-2, 6-1.

French at Roland Garros, Paris: d. Antoine Gentien, 6-1, 6-2, 6-4; Ghaus Mohammed, 6-1, 6-1, 5-7, 6-0; Franjo Kukuljevic, 6-2, 8-6, 2-6, 1-6, 6-1; Bernard Destremau, 6-4, 6-3, 6-4; Josip Pallada, 6-2, 6-3, 6-3; Roderich Menzel, 6-3, 6-2, 6-4.

British, at Wimbledon, London: d. Kenneth Gandar Dower, 6-2, 6-3, 6-3; Henry Billington, 7-5, 6-1, 6-1; George Lyttleton Rogers, 6-0, 7-5, 6-1; Ronald Shayes, 6-3, 6-4, 6-1; Franz Cejnar, 6-3, 6-0, 7-5; Ferenc Puncec, 6-2, 6-4, 6-0; Henry "Bunny" Austin, 6-1, 6-0, 6-3.

United States, at Forest Hills, New York: d. Welby Van Horn, 6-0, 6-0, 6-1; Bob Kamrath, 6-3, 7-5, 9-7; Charles Hare, 6-3, 6-4, 6-0; Harry Hopman, 6-3, 6-1, 6-3; Sidney Wood, 6-3, 6-3, 6-3; Gene Mako, 6-3, 6-8, 6-2, 6-1.

Maureen Connolly, 1953

Australian at Kooyong, Melbourne: d. Carmen Boreilli, 6-0, 6-1; Alison Burton Baker, 6-1, 6-0; Pam Southcombe, 6-0, 6-1; Mary Bevis Hawton, 6-2, 6-1; Julie Sampson, 6-3, 6-2.

French, at Roland Garros, Paris: d. Christiane Mercelis, 6-1, 6-3; Raymonde Verber Jones, 6-3, 6-1; Susan Partridge

Chatrier, 3-6, 6-2, 6-2; Dorothy Head Knode, 6-3, 6-3; Doris Hart, 6-2, 6-4.

British, at Wimbledon, London: d. D. Killian, 6-0, 6-0; J. M. Petchell, 6-1, 6-1; Anne Shilcock, 6-0, 6-1; Erika Vollmer, 6-3, 6-0; Shirley Fry, 6-1, 6-1; Doris Hart, 8-6, 7-5.

United States, at Forest Hills, New York: d. Jean Fallot, 6-1, 6-0; Pat Stewart, 6-3, 6-1; Jeanne Arth, 6-1, 6-3; Althea Gibson, 6-2, 6-3; Shirley Fry, 6-1, 6-1; Doris Hart, 6-2, 6-4.

Rod Laver, 1962

Australian, at White City, Sydney: d. Fred Sherriff, 8-6, 6-2, 6-4; Geoff Pares, 10-8, 18-16, 7-9, 7-5; Owen Davidson, 6-4, 9-7, 6-4; Bob Hewitt, 6-1, 4-6, 6-4, 7-5; Roy Emerson, 8-6, 0-6, 6-4, 6-4.

French, at Roland Garros, Paris: d. Michele Pirro, 6-4, 6-0, 6-2; Tony Pickard, 6-2, 9-7, 4-6, 6-1; Sergio Jacobini, 4-6, 6-3, 7-5, 6-1; Marty Mulligan, 6-4, 3-6, 2-6, 10-8, 6-2; Neale Fraser, 3-6, 6-3, 6-2, 7-5; Roy Emerson, 3-6, 2-6, 6-3, 9-7, 6-2.

British, at Wimbledon, London: d. Naresh Kumar, 7-5, 6-1, 6-2; Tony Pickard, 6-1, 6-2, 6-2; Whitney Reed, 6-4, 6-1, 6-4; Pierre Darmon, 6-3, 6-2, 13-11; Manolo Santana, 14-16, 9-7, 6-2, 6-2; Neale Fraser, 10-8, 6-1, 7-5; Marty Mulligan, 6-2, 6-2, 6-1.

United States, at Forest Hills, New York: d. Eleazar Davidman, 6-3, 6-2, 6-3; Eduardo Zuleta, 6-3, 6-3, 6-1; Bodo Nitsche, 9-7, 6-1, 6-1; Antonio Palafox, 6-1, 6-2, 6-2; Frank Froehling, 6-3, 13-11, 4-6, 6-3; Rafe Osuna, 6-1, 6-3, 6-4; Roy Emerson, 6-2, 6-4, 5-7, 6-4.

Rod Laver, 1969

Australian, at Milton Courts, Brisbane: d. Massimo di Domenico, 6-2, 6-2, 6-3; Roy Emerson, 6-2, 6-3, 3-6, 9-7; Fred Stolle, 6-4, 18-16, 6-2; Tony Roche, 7-5, 22-20, 9-11, 1-6, 6-3; Andres Gimeno, 6-3, 6-4, 7-5.

French, at Roland Garros, Paris: d. Koji Watanabe, 6-1, 6-1, 6-1; Dick Crealy, 3-6, 7-9, 6-2, 6-2, 6-4; Pietro Marzano, 6-1, 6-0, 8-6; Stan Smith, 6-4, 6-2, 6-4; Andres Gimeno, 3-6, 6-3, 6-4, 6-3; Tom Okker, 4-6, 6-0, 6-2, 6-4; Ken Rosewall, 6-4, 6-3, 6-4.

British, at Wimbledon, London: d. Nicola Pietrangeli, 6-1, 6-2, 6-2; Premjit Lall, 3-6, 4-6, 6-3, 6-0, 6-0; Jan Leschly, 6-3, 6-3, 6-3; Stan Smith, 6-4, 6-2, 7-9, 3-6, 6-3; Cliff Drysdale, 6-4, 6-2, 6-3; Arthur Ashe, 2-6, 6-2, 9-7, 6-0; John Newcombe, 6-4, 5-7, 6-4, 6-4.

United States, at Forest Hills, New York: d. Luis Garcia, 6-2, 6-4, 6-2; Jaime Pinto-Bravo, 6-4, 7-5, 6-2; Jaime Fillol, 8-6, 6-1, 6-2; Dennis Ralston, 6-4, 4-6, 4-6, 6-2, 6-3; Roy Emerson, 4-6-8-6, 13-11, 6-4; Arthur Ashe, 8-6, 6-3, 14-12; Tony Roche, 7-9, 6-1, 6-2, 6-2.

Margaret Smith Court, 1970

Australian, at White City, Sydney: d. Robyn Ebbern Langsford, 6-0, 6-0, K. Wilkinson, 6-0, 6-1; Evonne Goolagong, 6-3, 6-1; Karen Krantzke, 6-1, 6-3; Kerry Melville, 6-3, 6-1.

French, at Roland Garros, Paris: d. Marijke Jansen Schaar, 6-1, 6-1; Olga Morozova, 3-6, 8-6, 6-1; Lesley Hunt, 6-2, 6-1; Rosie Casals, 7-5, 6-2; Julie Heldman, 6-0, 6-2; Helga Niessen, 6-2, 6-4.

British, at Wimbledon, London: d. Sue Alexander, 6-0, 6-1, Maria Guzman, 6-0, 6-1; Vlasta Vopickova, 6-3, 6-3; Helga Niessen, 6-8, 6-0, 6-0; Rosie Casals, 6-4, 6-1; Billie Jean King, 14-12, 11-9.

United States, at Forest Hills, New York: Pam Austin, 6-1, 6-0; Patti Hogan, 6-1, 6-1; Pat Faulkner, 6-0, 6-2; Helen Gourlay, 6-2, 6-2; Nancy Richey, 6-1, 6-3; Rosie Casals, 6-2, 2-6, 6-1.

Steffi Graf, 1988

Australian, at Flinders Park, Melbourne: d. Amy Jonsson, 6-3, 6-1; Janine Thompson, 6-0, 6-1; Cammy MacGregor, 6-1, 6-2; Catarina Lindqvist, 6-0, 7-5; Hana Mandlikova, 6-2, 6-2; Claudia Kohde Kilsch, 6-2, 6-3; Chris Evert, 6-1, 7-6 (7-3).

French, at Roland Garros, Paris: d. Natalie Guerree, 6-0, 6-4; Ronni Reis, 6-1, 6-0, Susan Sloane, 6-0, 6-1; Nathalie Tauziat, 6-1, 6-3; Bettina Fulco, 6-0, 6-1; Gabriela Sabatini, 6-3, 7-6 (7-3); Natalia Zvereva, 6-0, 6-0.

British, at Wimbledon, London: d. Hu Na, 6-0, 6-0; Karine Quentrec, 6-2, 6-0; Terry Phelps, 6-3, 6-1; Mary Joe Fernandez, 6-2, 6-2; Pascale Paradis, 6-3, 6-1; Pam Shriver, 6-1, 6-2; Martina Navratilova, 5-7, 6-2, 6-1.

United States, at Flushing Meadow, New York: d. Elizabeth Minter 6-1, 6-1; Manon Bollegraf, 6-1, 6-0; Nathalie Herreman, 6-0, 6-1; Patty Fendick, 6-4, 6-2; Katerina Maleeva, 6-3, 6-0; Chris Evert, default (illness); Gabriela Sabatini, 6-3, 3-6, 6-1.

DOUBLES

Frank Sedgman-Ken McGregor, 1951

Australian, at White City, Sydney: d. Don Rocavert-Jim Gilchrist, 6-1, 6-3, 13-11; John Mehaffey-Clive Wilderspin, 6-4, 6-4, 6-3; Merv Rose-Don Candy, 8-6, 6-4, 6-3; Adrian Quist-John Bromwich, 11-9, 2-6, 6-3, 4-6, 6-3.

French, at Roland Garros, Paris: d. Antoine Gentien-Pierre Grandquillot, 6-0, 6-0, 6-0; Umberto "Biddy" Bergamo-Beppe Merlo, 6-2, 7-5, 6-1; Bob Abdesselam-Paul Remy, 6-2, 6-2, 4-6, 6-3; Merv Rose-Ham Richardson, 6-3, 7-5, 6-2; Gardnar Mulloy-Dick Savitt, 6-2, 2-6, 9-7, 7-5.

British, at Wimbledon, London: d. Vladimir Petrovic-Petko Milojkovic, 6-1, 6-1, 6-3; Raymundo Deyro-Gene Garrett, 6-4, 6-4, 6-3; Bernard Destremau-Torsten Johansson, 3-6, 6-3, 6-2, 9-7; Gianni Cucelli-Marcello del Bello, 6-4, 7-5, 16-14; Budge Patty-Ham Richardson, 6-4, 6-2, 6-3; Eric Sturgess-Jaroslav Drobny, 3-6, 6-2, 6-3, 3-6, 6-3.

United States, at Longwood Cricket Club, Boston: d. Harrison Rowbotham-Sumner Rodman, 6-2, 6-3, 6-3; Dave Mesker-Ed Wesely, 6-1, 6-1, 6-1; Earl Cochell-Ham Richardson, default; Budge Patty-Tony Trabert, 6-3, 6-1, 6-4; Don Candy-Merv Rose, 10-8, 4-6, 6-4, 7-5 (final-round match played at Forest Hills, moved from Boston due to heavy rains).

Martina Navratilova-Pam Shriver, 1984

French, at Roland Garros, Paris: d. Heather Crowe-Kim Steinmetz, 6-2, 6-1; Carling Bassett-Andrea Temesvari, 6-4, 6-2; Sandy Collins-Alycia Moulton, 6-2, 6-4; Brenda Remilton-Naoko Sato, 6-2, 6-2; Kathleen Horvath-Virginia Ruzici, 6-0, 7-6; Claudia Kohde Kilsch-Hana Mandlikova, 5-7, 6-3, 6-2.

British, at Wimbledon, London: d. Pam Casale-Lucia Romanov, 6-1, 6-1; Peanut Louie-Heather Ludloff, 6-4, 6-1; Lisa Bonder-Susan Mascarin, 6-0, 6-0; Claudia Kohde Kilsch-Hana Mandlikova, 6-7 (1-7), 6-4, 6-2; Jo Durie-Ann Kiyomura Hayashi, 6-3, 6-3; Kathy Jordan-Anne Smith, 6-3, 6-4.

United States, at Flushing Meadow, New York: d. Jennifer Mundel-Felicia Raschiatore, 6-2, 6-1; Leslie Allen-Kim Shaefer, 6-1, 7-6 (7-4); Catherine Tanvier-Tina Scheuer-Larsen, 6-3, 6-3; Rosalyn Fairbank-Candy Reynolds, 6-3, 6-4; Betsy Nagelsen-Anne White, 6-4, 7-5; Anne Hobbs-Wendy Turnbull, 6-2, 6-4.

Australian, at Kooyong Stadium, Melbourne: d. Rosalyn Fairbank-Candy Reynolds, 7-6, 6-4; Jennifer Mundel-Yvonne Vermaak, 6-2, 6-1; Carling Bassett-Zina Garrison, 6-2, 6-0; Chris Evert Lloyd-Wendy Turnbull, 6-4, 6-3; Claudia Kohde Kilsch-Helena Sukova, 6-3, 6-4.

Maria Bueno (with two partners), 1960

Australian, at Milton Courts, Brisbane: Christine Truman-Bueno d. Val Craig-Hortense Saywell, 6-2, 6-1; Betty Holstein-Sandra Shipton, 6-3, 6-4; Fay Muller-Mary Bevis Hawton, 6-4, 11-9; Margaret Smith-Lorraine Coghlan Robinson, 6-3, 5-7, 6-2.

French, at Roland Garros, Paris: Darlene Hard-Bueno d. Jacqueline Kermina-Pierette Seghers, 6-2, 6-2; Jacqueline Rees Lewis-Jacqueline Morales, 6-2, 6-0; Josette Billaz-Suzanne Le Besnerais, 6-4, 6-4; Mary Bevis Hawton-Jan Lehane, 6-3, 7-5; Pat Ward Hales-Ann Haydon, 6-2, 7-5.

British, at Wimbledon, London: Hard-Bueno d. Myrtle Cheadle-Gem Hoahing, 6-1, 6-2; Pat Hird-Caroline Yates Bell, 6-2, 7-5; Edda Buding-Vera Puzejova, 6-2, 6-3; Karen Hantze-Janet Hopps, 3-6, 6-1, 6-4; Renee Schuurman-Sandra Reynolds, 6-4, 6-0.

United States at Longwood Cricket Club, Boston: Hard-Bueno d. Lorraine Carder-Polly Knowlton, 6-0, 6-2; Linda Vail-Marilyn Montgomery, 6-1, 7-5; Carol Loop-Carole Wright, 6-2, 6-4; Mary Bevis Hawton-Jan Lehane, 8-6, 6-4; Ann Haydon-Deidre Catt, 6-1, 6-1.

Martina Hingis (with two partners), 1998

Australian, at Melbourne Park, Melbourne: Hingis-Lucic d. Saeki Miho-Yoshida Yuka, 6-2, 6-3; Larisa Savchenko Neiland-Anna Kournikova, 7-5, 6-2; Svetlana Krivencheva-Elena Tatarkova, 6-1, 6-3; Manon Bollegraf-Arantxa Sanchez Vicario, 6-1, 6-1; Lisa Raymond-Rennae Stubbs, 4-6, 6-4, 6-1; Lindsay Davenport-Natalia Zvereva, 6-4, 2-6, 6-3.

French, at Roland Garros: Hingis-Novotna d. Ann

Wunderlich-Rika Hiraki, 6-1, 6-0; Shi-Ting Wang-Janet Lee, 6-0, 6-2; Kristine Kunce-Corina Morariu, 6-0, 6-1; Conchita Martinez-Patricia Tarabini, 6-3, 6-2; Sanchez Vicario-Helena Sukova, 7-5, 7-6 (7-2); Davenport-Zvereva, 6-1, 7-6 (7-4).

British, at Wimbledon: Hingis-Novotna d. Surina de Beer-Lindsay Lee-Waters, 6-1, 6-1; Tina Krizan-Katarina Srebotnik, 4-6, 6-1, 6-2; Naoko Kijimuta-Nana Miyagi, 6-3, 6-4; Julie Halard-Decugis-Els Callens, 6-1, 6-4; Raymond-Stubbs, 6-3, 6-2; Davenport-Zvereva, 6-3, 3-6, 8-6.

United States, at Flushing Meadow: Hingis-Novotna d. Elena Wagner-Pavlina Nola, 6-4, 6-2; Karina Habsudova-Tamarine Tanasugarn, 7-6 (7-0), 6-0; Rachel McQuillan-Halard-Decugis, 6-1, 6-0; Barbara Schett-Patty Schnyder, 6-3, 6-4; Raymond-Stubbs, 6-2, 6-2; Davenport-Zvereva, 6-3, 6-3.

MIXED DOUBLES

Margaret Smith Court-Ken Fletcher, 1963

Australian, at Memorial Drive, Adelaide: d. Faye Toyne-Bill Bowrey, 6-2, 6-2; Jill Blackman-Roger Taylor, 6-3, 6-3; Liz Starkie-Mark Cox, 7-5, 5-7, 6-4; Lesley Turner-Fred Stolle, 7-5, 5-7, 6-4.

French, at Roland Garros, Paris: d. Claudine Rouire-Michel Lagard, 6-2, 6-1; Marie Dusapt-Ion Tiriac, 6-0, 6-2; Mary Habicht-Peter Strobl, 6-3, 6-0; Margaret Hunt-Cliff Drysdale, 7-5, 4-6, 6-1; Judy Tegart-Ed Rubinoff, 6-3, 6-1; Lesley Turner-Fred Stolle, 6-1, 6-2.

British, at Wimbledon, London: d. Judy Tegart-Ed Rubinoff, 6-2, 6-2; Judy Alvarez-John Fraser, 6-2, 9-7; Yola Ramirez Ochoa-Alfonso Ochoa, 6-4, 6-4; Renee Schuurman-Wilhelm Bungert, 6-2, 6-1; Ann Jones-Dennis Ralston, 6-1, 7-5; Darlene Hard-Bob Hewitt, 11-9, 6-4.

United States, at Forest Hills, New York: d. Heidi Schildnecht-Peter Scholl, 6-2, 6-3; Jill Rook Mills-Alan Mills, 6-4, 3-6, 6-1; Robyn Ebbern-Owen Davidson, 6-2, 6-2; Billie Jean Moffitt-Donald Dell, 5-7, 8-6, 6-4; Judy Tegart-Ed Rubinoff, 3-6, 8-6, 6-2.

Owen Davidson (with two partners), 1967

Australian, at Memorial Drive, Adelaide: Lesley Turner-Davidson d. Margaret Foster-Brenton Higgins, 6-1, 7-5; Margaret Starr-Paul McPherson, 6-2, 6-4; Jan Lehane O'Neill-Ray Ruffels, 7-5, 6-4; Judy Tegart-Tony Roche, 9-7, 6-4.

French, at Roland Garros, Paris: Billie Jean Moffitt King-Davidson d. Maria Zuleta-Eduardo Zuleta, 6-2, 6-4; Pat Walkden-Colin Stubs, 6-2, 2-6, 6-3; Trudy Groenman-Tom Okker, 6-1, 6-2; Christine Truman-Bob Howe, 6-2, 6-4; Ann Haydon Jones-Ion Tiriac, 6-3, 6-1.

British, at Wimbledon, London: King-Davidson d. Betty Stove-Bob Howe, 6-1, 6-1; Ingrid Lofdahl-Patricio Cornejo, 6-4, 6-1; Mr. and Mrs. John Cottrill, 6-4, 6-1; Annette van Zyl-Frew McMillan, 6-3, 3-6, 6-1; Maria Bueno-Ken Fletcher, 7-5, 6-2.

United States, at Longwood Cricket Club, Boston: King-Davidson d. Joyce Barclay Williams-George Seewagen, Jr., 6-4, 6-4; Donna Floyd Fales-Paul Sullivan, 6-2, 6-2; Mary

Ann Eisel-Peter Curtis, 6-4, 6-3; Kristy Pigeon-Terry Addison, 6-4, 6-4; Rosie Casals-Stan Smith, 6-3, 6-2.

Williams Family Slam, 1998

Australian, at Melbourne Park, Melbourne: Venus-Gimelstob d. Katrina Adams-Ellis Ferreira, 6-3, 7-5; Anna Kournikova-Mark Knowles, 7-5, 6-2; Lisa Raymond-Patrick Galbraith, 7-6 (7-2), 3-6, 6-2; Elena Likhovtseva-Max Mirnyi, 6-2, 6-1; Helena Sukova-Cyril Suk, 6-2, 3-6, 7-6 (7-3).

French, at Roland Garros, Paris: Venus-Gimelstob d. Natalia Medvedeva-Fernon Wibier, 6-1, 6-2; Miriam Oremans-Ellis Ferreira, 6-4, 6-4; Iva Majoli-Todd Martin, 6-0, 7-6 (7-4); Caroline Vis-John-Laffnie De Jager, 6-4, 6-3; Kristine Kunce-Francisco Montana, 6-2, 6-3; Serena Williams-Luis Lobo, 6-4, 6-4.

British, at Wimbledon, London: Serena-Mirnyi d. Catalina Cristea-Geoff Grant, 6-1, 7-6 (11-9); Lindsay Davenport-Brian MacPhie, 4-6, 7-6 (7-4), 6-2; Nathalie Tauziat-Daniel Nestor, 5-7, 6-3, 6-4; Vis-Paul Haarhuis, 4-6, 6-4, 7-5; Mirjana Lucic-Mahesh Bhupathi, 6-4, 6-4.

United States, at Flushing Meadow: Serena-Mirnyi d.Oremans-Nicklas Kulti 6-1, 6-3; Davenport-Jan-Michael Gambill (walkover); Lucic-Bhupathi, 3-6, 7-5, 7-5; Debbie Graham-Sandon Stolle, 6-7 (5-7), 7-6 (7-3), 6-2; Raymond-Galbraith, 6-2, 6-2.

Three-Quarter Slams

Since the inception of the French Open in 1925, 113 individuals and teams have won three of the four major titles in the same calendar year. Here is a complete list of those to complete a Three-Quarter Slam.

MEN'S SINGLES
Jack Crawford, 1933 (Australian, French, Wimbledon)
Fred Perry, 1934 (Australian, Wimbledon, U.S.)
Tony Trabert, 1955 (French, Wimbledon, U.S.)
Lew Hoad, 1956 (Australian, French, Wimbledon)
Ashley Cooper, 1958 (Australian, Wimbledon, U.S.)
Roy Emerson, 1964 (Australian, Wimbledon, U.S.)
Jimmy Connors, 1974 (Australian, Wimbledon, U.S.)
Mats Wilander, 1988 (Australian, French, U.S.)

WOMEN'S SINGLES
Helen Wills Moody, 1928 (French, Wimbledon, U.S.)
Helen Wills Moody, 1929 (French, Wimbledon, U.S.)
Margaret Smith, 1962 (Australian, French, U.S.)
Margaret Smith, 1965 (Australian, Wimbledon, U.S.)
Margaret Smith Court, 1969 (Australian, French, U.S.)
Billie Jean King, 1972 (French, Wimbledon, U.S.)
Margaret Smith Court, 1973 (Australian, French, U.S.)
Martina Navratilova, 1983 (Australian, Wimbledon, U.S.)
Martina Navratilova, 1984 (French, Wimbledon, U.S.)
Steffi Graf, 1989 (Australian, Wimbledon, U.S.)
Monica Seles, 1991 (Australian, French, U.S.)
Monica Seles, 1992 (Australian, French, U.S.)
Steffi Graf, 1993 (French, Wimbledon, U.S.)
Steffi Graf, 1995 (French, Wimbledon, U.S.)

Steffi Graf, 1996 (French, Wimbledon, U.S.)
Martina Hingis, 1997 (Australian, Wimbledon, U.S.)
Serena Williams, 2002 (French, Wimbledon, U.S.)

MEN'S DOUBLES—TEAM

Ken McGregor / Frank Sedgman, 1952 (Australian, French, Wimbledon)
Lew Hoad / Ken Rosewall, 1953 (Australian, French, Wimbledon)
Lew Hoad / Ken Rosewall, 1956 (Australian, Wimbledon, U.S.)
John Newcombe / Tony Roche, 1967 (Australian, French, U.S.)
John Fitzgerald / Anders Jarryd, 1991 (French, Wimbledon, U.S.)

MEN'S DOUBLES—INDIVIDUAL

Jacques Brugnon, 1928 (Australian, French, Wimbledon)
John Van Ryn, 1931 (French, Wimbledon, U.S.)
Jack Crawford, 1935 (Australian, French, Wimbledon)
John Bromwich, 1950 (Australian, Wimbledon, U.S.)
Frank Sedgman, 1952 (Australian, French, Wimbledon)
Ken McGregor, 1952 (Australian, French, Wimbledon)
Ken Rosewall, 1953 (Australian, French, Wimbledon)
Lew Hoad, 1953 (Australian, French, Wimbledon)
Ken Rosewall, 1956 (Australian, Wimbledon, U.S.)
Lew Hoad, 1956 (Australian, Wimbledon, U.S.)
John Newcombe, 1967 (Australian, French, U.S.)
Tony Roche, 1967 (Australian, French, U.S.)
John Newcombe, 1973 (Australian, French, U.S.)
Anders Jarryd, 1987 (Australian, French, U.S.)
Anders Jarryd, 1991 (French, Wimbledon, U.S.)
John Fitzgerald, 1991 (French, Wimbledon, U.S.)
Jacco Eltingh, 1998 (Australian, French, Wimbledon)

WOMEN'S DOUBLES—TEAM

Louise Brough / Margaret Osborne duPont, 1946 (French, Wimbledon, U.S.)
Louise Brough / Margaret Osborne duPont, 1949 (French, Wimbledon, U.S.)
Doris Hart / Shirley Fry, 1951 (French, Wimbledon, U.S.)
Doris Hart / Shirley Fry, 1952 (French, Wimbledon, U.S.)
Doris Hart / Shirley Fry, 1953 (French, Wimbledon, U.S.)
Darlene Hard / Maria Bueno, 1960 (French, Wimbledon, U.S.)
Margaret Smith Court / Virginia Wade, 1973 (Australian, French, U.S.)
Martina Navratilova / Pam Shriver, 1983 (Australian, Wimbledon, U.S.)
Martina Navratilova / Pam Shriver, 1987 (Australian, French, U.S.)
Jana Novotna / Helena Sukova, 1990 (Australian, French, Wimbledon)
Gigi Fernandez / Natalia Zvereva, 1992 (French, Wimbledon, U.S.)
Gigi Fernandez / Natalia Zvereva, 1993 (Australian, French, Wimbledon)
Gigi Fernandez / Natalia Zvereva, 1994 (Australian, French, Wimbledon)
Martina Hingis / Jana Novotna, 1998 (French, Wimbledon, U.S.)

WOMEN'S DOUBLES—INDIVIDUAL

Louise Brough, 1946 (French, Wimbledon, U.S.)
Margaret Osborne duPont, 1946 (French, Wimbledon, U.S.)
Louise Brough, 1949 (French, Wimbledon, U.S.)
Margaret Osborne duPont, 1949 (French, Wimbledon, U.S.)
Louise Brough, 1950 (Australian, Wimbledon, U.S.)
Doris Hart, 1951 (French, Wimbledon, U.S.)
Shirley Fry, 1951 (French, Wimbledon, U.S.)
Doris Hart, 1952 (French, Wimbledon, U.S.)
Shirley Fry, 1952 (French, Wimbledon, U.S.)
Doris Hart, 1953 (French, Wimbledon, U.S.)
Shirley Fry, 1953 (French, Wimbledon, U.S.)
Darlene Hard, 1960 (French, Wimbledon, U.S.)
Lesley Turner, 1964 (Australian, French, Wimbledon)
Nancy Richey, 1966 (Australian, Wimbledon, U.S.)
Betty Stove, 1972 (French, Wimbledon, U.S.)
Margaret Smith Court, 1973 (Australian, French, U.S.)
Virginia Wade, 1973 (Australian, French, U.S.)
Martina Navratilova, 1982 (Australian, French, Wimbledon)
Martina Navratilova, 1983 (Australian, Wimbledon, U.S.)
Pam Shriver, 1983 (Australian, Wimbledon, U.S.)
Martina Navratilova, 1986 (French, Wimbledon, U.S.)
Martina Navratilova, 1987 (Australian, French, U.S.)
Pam Shriver, 1987 (Australian, French, U.S.)
Helena Sukova, 1990 (Australian, French, Wimbledon)
Jana Novotna, 1990 (Australian, French, Wimbledon)
Gigi Fernandez, 1992 (French, Wimbledon, U.S.)
Natalia Zvereva, 1992 (French, Wimbledon, U.S.)
Gigi Fernandez, 1993 (Australian, French, Wimbledon)
Natalia Zvereva, 1993 (Australian, French, Wimbledon)
Gigi Fernandez, 1994 (Australian, French, Wimbledon)
Natalia Zvereva, 1994 (Australian, French, Wimbledon)
Natalia Zvereva, 1997 (Australian, French, Wimbledon)
Jana Novotna, 1998 (French, Wimbledon, U.S.)

MIXED DOUBLES—TEAM

Doris Hart / Frank Sedgman, 1951 (French, Wimbledon, U.S.)
Doris Hart / Frank Sedgman, 1952 (French, Wimbledon, U.S.)
Doris Hart / Vic Seixas, 1953 (French, Wimbledon, U.S.)
Billie Jean King / Owen Davidson, 1967 (French, Wimbledon, U.S.)

MIXED DOUBLES—MEN INDIVIDUAL

Eric Sturgess, 1949 (French, Wimbledon, U.S.)
Frank Sedgman, 1951 (French, Wimbledon, U.S.)
Frank Sedgman, 1952 (French, Wimbledon, U.S.)
Vic Seixas, 1953 (French, Wimbledon, U.S.)
Bob Hewitt, 1979 (French, Wimbledon, U.S.)
Mark Woodforde, 1992 (Australian, French, U.S.)

MIXED DOUBLES—WOMEN INDIVIDUAL

Doris Hart, 1951 (French, Wimbledon, U.S.)
Doris Hart, 1952 (French, Wimbledon, U.S.)
Doris Hart, 1953 (French, Wimbledon, U.S.)
Doris Hart, 1955 (French, Wimbledon, U.S.)
Margaret Smith Court, 1964 (Australian, French, U.S.)
Margaret Smith Court, 1965 (French, Wimbledon, U.S.)
Billie Jean King, 1967 (French, Wimbledon, U.S.)
Martina Navratilova, 1985 (French, Wimbledon, U.S.)

Major Championships – Champions

Men's Singles

Year		Australian	French	Wimbledon	U.S.
2002		Thomas Johansson	Albert Costa	Lleyton Hewitt	Pete Sampras
2001		Andre Agassi	Gustavo Kuerten	Goran Ivanisevic	Lleyton Hewitt
2000		Andre Agassi	Gustavo Kuerten	Pete Sampras	Marat Safin
1999		Yevgeny Kafelnikov	Andre Agassi	Pete Sampras	Andre Agassi
1998		Petr Korda	Carlos Moya	Pete Sampras	Patrick Rafter
1997		Pete Sampras	Gustavo Kuerten	Pete Sampras	Patrick Rafter
1996		Boris Becker	Yevgeny Kafelnikov	Richard Krajicek	Pete Sampras
1995		Andre Agassi	Thomas Muster	Pete Sampras	Pete Sampras
1994		Pete Sampras	Sergi Bruguera	Pete Sampras	Andre Agassi
1993		Jim Courier	Sergi Bruguera	Pete Sampras	Pete Sampras
1992		Jim Courier	Jim Courier	Andre Agassi	Stefan Edberg
1991		Boris Becker	Jim Courier	Michael Stich	Stefan Edberg
1990		Ivan Lendl	Andres Gomez	Stefan Edberg	Pete Sampras
1989		Ivan Lendl	Michael Chang	Boris Becker	Boris Becker
1988		Mats Wilander	Mats Wilander	Stefan Edberg	Mats Wilander
1987		Stefan Edberg	Ivan Lendl	Pat Cash	Ivan Lendl
1986		Not held (date change)	Ivan Lendl	Boris Becker	Ivan Lendl
1985		Stefan Edberg	Mats Wilander	Boris Becker	Ivan Lendl
1984		Mats Wilander	Ivan Lendl	John McEnroe	John McEnroe
1983		Mats Wilander	Yannick Noah	John McEnroe	Jimmy Connors
1982		Johan Kriek	Mats Wilander	Jimmy Connors	Jimmy Connors
1981		Johan Kriek	Bjorn Borg	John McEnroe	John McEnroe
1980		Brian Teacher	Bjorn Borg	Bjorn Borg	John McEnroe
1979		Guillermo Vilas	Bjorn Borg	Bjorn Borg	John McEnroe
1978		Guillermo Vilas	Bjorn Borg	Bjorn Borg	Jimmy Connors
1977	(Jan.)	Roscoe Tanner	Guillermo Vilas	Bjorn Borg	Guillermo Vilas
1977	(Dec.)	Vitas Gerulaitis			
1976		Mark Edmondson	Adriano Panatta	Bjorn Borg	Jimmy Connors
1975		John Newcombe	Bjorn Borg	Arthur Ashe	Manolo Orantes
1974		Jimmy Connors	Bjorn Borg	Jimmy Connors	Jimmy Connors
1973		John Newcombe	Ilie Nastase	Jan Kodes	John Newcombe
1972		Ken Rosewall	Andres Gimeno	Stan Smith	Ilie Nastase
1971		Ken Rosewall	Jan Kodes	John Newcombe	Stan Smith
1970		Arthur Ashe	Jan Kodes	John Newcombe	Ken Rosewall
1969		**Rod Laver**	**Rod Laver**	**Rod Laver**	**Rod Laver**
1968		Bill Bowrey	Ken Rosewall	Rod Laver	Arthur Ashe
1967		Roy Emerson	Roy Emerson	John Newcombe	John Newcombe
1966		Roy Emerson	Tony Roche	Manolo Santana	Fred Stolle
1965		Roy Emerson	Fred Stolle	Roy Emerson	Manolo Santana
1964		Roy Emerson	Manolo Santana	Roy Emerson	Roy Emerson
1963		Roy Emerson	Roy Emerson	Chuck McKinley	Rafael Osuna
1962		**Rod Laver**	**Rod Laver**	**Rod Laver**	**Rod Laver**
1961		Roy Emerson	Manolo Santana	Rod Laver	Roy Emerson
1960		Rod Laver	Nicola Pietrangeli	Neale Fraser	Neale Fraser
1959		Alex Olmedo	Nicola Pietrangeli	Alex Olmedo	Neale Fraser

Year	Australian	French	Wimbledon	U.S.
1958	Ashley Cooper	Merv Rose	Ashley Cooper	Ashley Cooper
1957	Ashley Cooper	Sven Davidson	Lew Hoad	Mal Anderson
1956	Lew Hoad	Lew Hoad	Lew Hoad	Ken Rosewall
1955	Ken Rosewall	Tony Trabert	Tony Trabert	Tony Trabert
1954	Merv Rose	Tony Trabert	Jaroslav Drobny	Vic Seixas
1953	Ken Rosewall	Ken Rosewall	Vic Seixas	Tony Trabert
1952	Ken McGregor	Jaroslav Drobny	Frank Sedgman	Frank Sedgman
1951	Richard Savitt	Jaroslav Drobny	Dick Savitt	Frank Sedgman
1950	Frank Sedgman	Budge Patty	Budge Patty	Art Larsen
1949	Frank Sedgman	Frank Parker	Ted Schroeder	Pancho Gonzalez
1948	Adrian Quist	Frank Parker	Bob Falkenburg	Pancho Gonzalez
1947	Dinny Pails	Joszef Asboth	Jack Kramer	Jack Kramer
1946	John Bromwich	Marcel Bernard	Yvon Petra	Jack Kramer
1945	Not held – WWII	Not held – WWII	Not held – WWII	Frank Parker
1944	Not held – WWII	Not held – WWII	Not held – WWII	Frank Parker
1943	Not held – WWII	Not held – WWII	Not held – WWII	Joseph R. Hunt
1942	Not held – WWII	Not held – WWII	Not held – WWII	Ted Schroeder
1941	Not held – WWII	Not held – WWII	Not held – WWII	Bobby Riggs
1940	Adrian Quist	Not held – WWII	Not held – WWII	Don McNeill
1939	John Bromwich	Don NcNeill	Bobby Riggs	Bobby Riggs
1938	**Don Budge**	**Don Budge**	**Don Budge**	**Don Budge**
1937	Viv McGrath	Henner Henkel	Don Budge	Don Budge
1936	Adrian Quist	Gottfried von Cramm	Fred Perry	Fred Perry
1935	Jack Crawford	Fred Perry	Fred Perry	Wilmer Allison
1934	Fred Perry	Gottfried von Cramm	Fred Perry	Fred Perry
1933	Jack Crawford	Jack Crawford	Jack Crawford	Fred Perry
1932	Jack Crawford	Henri Cochet	Ellsworth Vines	Ellsworth Vines
1931	Jack Crawford	Jean Borotra	Sidney Wood	Ellsworth Vines
1930	Gar Moon	Henri Cochet	Bill Tilden	Johnny Doeg
1929	Colin Gregory	René Lacoste	Henri Cochet	Bill Tilden
1928	Jean Borotra	Henri Cochet	René Lacoste	Henri Cochet
1927	Gerald Patterson	René Lacoste	Henri Cochet	René Lacoste
1926	Jack Hawkes	Henri Cochet	Jean Borotra	René Lacoste
1925	James Anderson	René Lacoste	René Lacoste	Bill Tilden
1924	James Anderson		Jean Borotra	Bill Tilden
1923	Pat O'Hara Wood		Bill Johnston	Bill Tilden
1922	James Anderson		Gerald Patterson	Bill Tilden
1921	Rhys Gemmell		Bill Tilden	Bill Tilden
1920	Pat O'Hara Wood		Bill Tilden	Bill Tilden
1919	Algernon Kingscote		Gerald Patterson	Bill Johnston
1918	Not held – WWI		Not held – WWI	Lindley Murray
1917	Not held – WWI		Not held – WWI	Lindley Murray
1916	Not held – WWI		Not held – WWI	Dick Williams
1915	Gordon Lowe		Not held – WWI	Bill Johnston
1914	Arthur O'Hara Wood		Norman Brookes	Dick Williams
1913	Ernest Parker		Tony Wilding	Maurice McLoughlin
1912	Jim Parke		Tony Wilding	Maurice McLoughlin
1911	Norman Brookes		Tony Wilding	Bill Larned
1910	Rodney Heath		Tony Wilding	Bill Larned
1909	Anthony Wilding		Arthur Gore	Bill Larned

Year	Australian	French	Wimbledon	U.S.
1908	Fred Alexander		Arthur Gore	Bill Larned
1907	Horrie Rice		Norman Brookes	Bill Larned
1906	Anthony Wilding		Laurie Doherty	Bill Clothier
1905	Rodney Heath		Laurie Doherty	Beals Wright
1904			Laurie Doherty	Holcombe Ward
1903			Laurie Doherty	Laurie Doherty
1902			Laurie Doherty	Reggie Doherty
1901			Arthur Gore	Bill Larned
1900			Reggie Doherty	Malcolm Whitman
1899			Reggie Doherty	Malcolm Whitman
1898			Reggie Doherty	Malcolm Whitman
1897			Reggie Doherty	Robert Wrenn
1896			Harold Mahony	Robert Wrenn
1895			Wilfred Baddeley	Fred Hovey
1894			Joshua Pim	Robert Wrenn
1893			Joshua Pim	Robert Wrenn
1892			Wilfred Baddeley	Oliver Campbell
1891			Wilfred Baddeley	Oliver Campbell
1890			Ghost Hamilton	Oliver Campbell
1889			Willie Renshaw	Henry Slocum
1888			Ernest Renshaw	Henry Slocum
1887			Herbert Lawford	Richard Sears
1886			Willie Renshaw	Richard Sears
1885			Willie Renshaw	Richard Sears
1884			Willie Renshaw	Richard Sears
1883			Willie Renshaw	Richard Sears
1882			Willie Renshaw	Richard Sears
1881			Willie Renshaw	Richard Sears
1880			John Hartley	
1879			John Hartley	
1878			Frank Hadow	
1877			Spencer Gore	

Women's Singles

Year	Australian	French	Wimbledon	U.S.
2002	Jennifer Capriati	Serena Williams	Serena Williams	Serena Williams
2001	Jennifer Capriati	Jennifer Capriati	Venus Williams	Venus Williams
2000	Lindsay Davenport	Mary Pierce	Venus Williams	Venus Williams
1999	Martina Hingis	Steffi Graf	Lindsay Davenport	Serena Williams
1998	Martina Hingis	Arantxa Sanchez Vicario	Jana Novotna	Lindsay Davenport
1997	Martina Hingis	Iva Majoli	Martina Hingis	Martina Hingis
1996	Monica Seles	Steffi Graf	Steffi Graf	Steffi Graf
1995	Mary Pierce	Steffi Graf	Steffi Graf	Steffi Graf
1994	Steffi Graf	Arantxa Sanchez Vicario	Conchita Martinez	Arantxa Sanchez Vicario
1993	Monica Seles	Steffi Graf	Steffi Graf	Steffi Graf
1992	Monica Seles	Monica Seles	Steffi Graf	Monica Seles
1991	Monica Seles	Monica Seles	Steffi Graf	Monica Seles
1990	Steffi Graf	Monica Seles	Martina Navratilova	Gabriela Sabatini
1989	Steffi Graf	Arantxa Sanchez Vicario	Steffi Graf	Steffi Graf
1988	**Steffi Graf**	**Steffi Graf**	**Steffi Graf**	**Steffi Graf**

Year		Australian	French	Wimbledon	U.S.
1987		Hana Mandlikova	Steffi Graf	Martina Navratilova	Martina Navratilova
1986		Not held (date change)	Chris Evert Lloyd	Martina Navratilova	Martina Navratilova
1985		Martina Navratilova	Chris Evert Lloyd	Martina Navratilova	Hana Mandlikova
1984		Chris Evert Lloyd	Martina Navratilova	Martina Navratilova	Martina Navratilova
1983		Martina Navratilova	Chris Evert Lloyd	Martina Navratilova	Martina Navratilova
1982		Chris Evert Lloyd	Martina Navratilova	Martina Navratilova	Chris Evert Lloyd
1981		Martina Navratilova	Hana Mandlikova	Chris Evert Lloyd	Tracy Austin
1980		Hana Mandlikova	Chris Evert Lloyd	Evonne Goolagong Cawley	Chris Evert
1979		Barbara Jordan	Chris Evert Lloyd	Martina Navratilova	Tracy Austin
1978		Chris O'Neil	Virginia Ruzici	Martina Navratilova	Chris Evert
1977	(Jan.)	Kerry Melville Reid	Mima Jausovec	Virginia Wade	Chris Evert
1977	(Dec.)	Evonne Goolagong Cawley			
1976		Evonne Goolagong Cawley	Sue Barker	Chris Evert	Chris Evert
1975		Evonne Goolagong	Chris Evert	Billie Jean King	Chris Evert
1974		Evonne Goolagong	Chris Evert	Chris Evert	Billie Jean King
1973		Margaret Smith Court	Margaret Smith Court	Billie Jean King	Margaret Smith Court
1972		Virginia Wade	Billie Jean King	Billie Jean King	Billie Jean King
1971		Margaret Smith Court	Evonne Goolagong	Evonne Goolagong	Billie Jean King
1970		**Margaret Smith Court**	**Margaret Smith Court**	**Margaret Smith Court**	**Margaret Smith Court**
1969		Margaret Smith Court	Margaret Smith Court	Ann Haydon Jones	Margaret Smith Court
1968		Billie Jean King	Nancy Richey	Billie Jean King	Virginia Wade
1967		Nancy Richey	Françoise Durr	Billie Jean King	Billie Jean King
1966		Margaret Smith	Ann Haydon Jones	Billie Jean King	Maria Bueno
1965		Margaret Smith	Lesley Turner	Margaret Smith	Margaret Smith
1964		Margaret Smith	Margaret Smith	Maria Bueno	Maria Bueno
1963		Margaret Smith	Lesley Turner	Margaret Smith	Maria Bueno
1962		Margaret Smith	Margaret Smith	Karen Hantze Susman	Margaret Smith
1961		Margaret Smith	Ann Haydon	Angela Mortimer	Darlene Hard
1960		Margaret Smith	Darlene Hard	Maria Bueno	Darlene Hard
1959		Mary Carter Reitano	Christine Truman	Maria Bueno	Maria Bueno
1958		Angela Mortimer	Suzi Kormoczi	Althea Gibson	Althea Gibson
1957		Shirley Fry	Shirley Bloomer	Althea Gibson	Althea Gibson
1956		Mary Carter	Althea Gibson	Shirley Fry	Shirley Fry
1955		Beryl Penrose	Angela Mortimer	Louise Brough	Doris Hart
1954		Thelma Long	Maureen Connolly	Maureen Connolly	Doris Hart
1953		**Maureen Connolly**	**Maureen Connolly**	**Maureen Connolly**	**Maureen Connolly**
1952		Thelma Long	Doris Hart	Maureen Connolly	Maureen Connolly
1951		Nancye Bolton	Shirley Fry	Doris Hart	Maureen Connolly
1950		Louise Brough	Doris Hart	Louise Brough	Margaret Osborne duPont
1949		Doris Hart	Margaret Osborne duPont	Louise Brough	Margaret Osborne duPont
1948		Nancye Bolton	Nelly Adamson Landry	Louise Brough	Margaret Osborne duPont
1947		Nancye Wynne Bolton	Pat Canning Todd	Margaret Osborne	Louise Brough
1946		Nancye Wynne Bolton	Margaret Osborne	Pauline Betz	Pauline Betz
1945		Not held – WWII	Not held – WWII	Not held – WWII	Sarah Palfrey Cooke
1944		Not held – WWII	Not held – WWII	Not held – WWII	Pauline Betz
1943		Not held – WWII	Not held – WWII	Not held – WWII	Pauline Betz
1942		Not held – WWII	Not held – WWII	Not held – WWII	Pauline Betz
1941		Not held – WWII	Not held – WWII	Not held – WWII	Sarah Palfrey Cooke
1940		Nancye Wynne	Not held – WWII	Not held – WWII	Alice Marble
1939		Emily Hood Westacott	Simone Passemard Mathieu	Alice Marble	Alice Marble

Year	Australian	French	Wimbledon	U.S.
1938	Dorothy Bundy	Simone Passemard Mathieu	Helen Wills Moody	Alice Marble
1937	Nancye Wynne	Hilde Krahwinkel Sperling	Dorothy Round	Anita Lizana
1936	Joan Hartigan	Hilde Krahwinkel Sperling	Helen Jacobs	Alice Marble
1935	Dorothy Round	Hilde Krahwinkel Sperling	Helen Wills Moody	Helen Jacobs
1934	Joan Hartigan	Margaret Scriven	Dorothy Round	Helen Jacobs
1933	Joan Hartigan	Margaret Scriven	Helen Wills Moody	Helen Jacobs
1932	Coral McInnes Buttsworth	Helen Wills Moody	Helen Wills Moody	Helen Jacobs
1931	Coral McInnes Buttsworth	Cilly Aussem	Cilly Aussem	Helen Wills Moody
1930	Daphne Akhurst	Helen Wills Moody	Helen Wills Moody	Betty Nuthall
1929	Daphne Akhurst	Helen Wills	Helen Wills	Helen Wills Moody
1928	Daphne Akhurst	Helen Wills	Helen Wills	Helen Wills
1927	Esna Boyd	Kea Bouman	Helen Wills	Helen Wills
1926	Daphne Akhurst	Suzanne Lenglen	Kitty McKane Godfree	Molla Bjurstedt Mallory
1925	Daphne Akhurst	Suzanne Lenglen	Suzanne Lenglen	Helen Wills
1924	Sylvia Lance		Kitty McKane	Helen Wills
1923	Mall Molesworth		Suzanne Lenglen	Helen Wills
1922	Mall Molesworth		Suzanne Lenglen	Molla Bjurstedt Mallory
1921			Suzanne Lenglen	Molla Bjurstedt Mallory
1920			Suzanne Lenglen	Molla Bjurstedt Mallory
1919			Suzanne Lenglen	Hazel Hotchkiss Wightman
1918			Not held – WWI	Molla Bjurstedt
1917			Not held – WWI	Molla Bjurstedt
1916			Not held – WWI	Molla Bjurstedt
1915			Not held – WWI	Molla Bjurstedt
1914			Dorothea Douglass Chambers	Mary K. Browne
1913			Dorothea Douglass Chambers	Mary K. Browne
1912			Ethel Thomson Larcombe	Mary K. Browne
1911			Dorothea Douglass Chambers	Hazel Hotchkiss
1910			Dorothea Douglass Chambers	Hazel Hotchkiss
1909			Dora Boothby	Hazel Hotchkiss
1908			Charlotte Cooper Sterry	Maud Barger Wallach
1907			May Sutton	Evelyn Sears
1906			Dorothea Douglass	Helen Homans
1905			May Sutton	Elisabeth Moore
1904			Dorothea Douglass	May Sutton
1903			Dorothea Douglass	Elisabeth Moore
1902			Muriel Robb	Marion Jones
1901			Charlotte Cooper Sterry	Elisabeth Moore
1900			Blanche Bingley Hillyard	Myrtle McAteer
1899			Blanche Bingley Hillyard	Marion Jones
1898			Charlotte Cooper	Juliette Atkinson
1897			Blanche Bingley Hillyard	Juliette Atkinson
1896			Charlotte Cooper	Elisabeth Moore
1895			Charlotte Cooper	Juliette Atkinson
1894			Blanche Bingley Hillyard	Helen Hellwig
1893			Charlotte Dod	Aline Terry
1892			Charlotte Dod	Mabel Cahill
1891			Charlotte Dod	Mabel Cahill
1890			Helena Rice	Ellen Roosevelt
1889			Blanche Bingley Hillyard	Bertha Townsend

Year	Australian	French	Wimbledon	U.S.
1888			Charlotte Dod	Bertha Townsend
1887			Charlotte Dod	Ellen Hansell
1886			Blanche Bingley	
1885			Maud Watson	
1884			Maud Watson	

Men's Doubles

Year	Australian	French	Wimbledon	U.S.
2002	Daniel Nestor / Mark Knowles	Paul Haarhuis / Yevgeny Kafelnikov	Todd Woodbridge / Jonas Bjorkman	Max Mirnyi / Mahesh Bhupathi
2001	Jonas Bjorkman / Todd Woodbridge	Mahesh Bhupathi / Leander Paes	Donald Johnson / Jared Palmer	Wayne Black / Kevin Ullyett
2000	Rick Leach / Ellis Ferreira	Mark Woodforde / Todd Woodbridge	Todd Woodbridge / Mark Woodforde	Lleyton Hewitt / Max Mirnyi
1999	Patrick Rafter / Jonas Bjorkman	Mahesh Bhupathi / Leander Paes	Mahesh Bhupathi / Leander Paes	Sebastien Lareau / Alex O'Brien
1998	Jonas Bjorkman / Jacco Eltingh	Jacco Eltingh / Paul Haarhuis	Jacco Eltingh / Paul Haarhuis	Sandon Stolle / Cyril Suk
1997	Todd Woodbridge / Mark Woodforde	Yevgeny Kafelnikov / Daniel Vacek	Todd Woodbridge / Mark Woodforde	Yevgeny Kafelnikov / Daniel Vacek
1996	Stefan Edberg / Petr Korda	Yevgeny Kafelnikov / Daniel Vacek	Todd Woodbridge / Mark Woodforde	Todd Woodbridge / Mark Woodforde
1995	Jared Palmer / Richey Reneberg	Jacco Eltingh / Paul Haarhuis	Todd Woodbridge / Mark Woodforde	Todd Woodbridge / Mark Woodforde
1994	Jacco Eltingh / Paul Haarhuis	Byron Black / Jonathan Stark	Todd Woodbridge / Mark Woodforde	Jacco Eltingh / Paul Haarhuis
1993	Danie Visser / Laurie Warder	Luke Jensen / Murphy Jensen	Todd Woodbridge / Mark Woodforde	Ken Flach / Rick Leach
1992	Todd Woodbridge / Mark Woodforde	Jakob Hlasek / Marc Rosset	John McEnroe / Michael Stich	Jim Grabb / Richey Reneberg
1991	Scott Davis / David Pate	John Fitzgerald / Anders Jarryd	John Fitzgerald / Anders Jarryd	John Fitzgerald / Anders Jarryd
1990	Pieter Aldrich / Danie Visser	Sergio Casal / Emilio Sanchez	Rick Leach / Jim Pugh	Pieter Aldrich / Danie Visser
1989	Rick Leach / Jim Pugh	Jim Grabb / Patrick McEnroe	John Fitzgerald / Anders Jarryd	John McEnroe / Mark Woodforde
1988	Rick Leach / Jim Pugh	Andres Gomez / Emilio Sanchez	Ken Flach / Robert Seguso	Sergio Casal / Emilio Sanchez
1987	Stefan Edberg / Anders Jarryd	Anders Jarryd / Robert Seguso	Ken Flach / Robert Seguso	Stefan Edberg / Anders Jarryd
1986	Not held (date change)	John Fitzgerald / Tomas Smid	Joakim Nystrom / Mats Wilander	Andres Gomez / Slobodan Zivojinovic
1985	Paul Annacone / Christo Van Rensburg	Mark Edmondson / Kim Warwick	Heinz Gunthardt / Balazs Taroczy	Ken Flach / Robert Seguso
1984	Mark Edmondson / Sherwood Stewart	Henri Leconte / Yannick Noah	Peter Fleming / John McEnroe	John Fitzgerald / Tomas Smid
1983	Mark Edmondson / Paul McNamee	Anders Jarryd / Hans Simonsson	Peter Fleming / John McEnroe	Peter Fleming / John McEnroe
1982	John Alexander / John Fitzgerald	Sherwood Stewart / Ferdi Taygan	Peter McNamara / Paul McNamee	Kevin Curren / Steve Denton
1981	Mark Edmondson / Kim Warwick	Heinz Gunthardt / Balazs Taroczy	Peter Fleming / John McEnroe	Peter Fleming / John McEnroe
1980	Mark Edmondson / Kim Warwick	Victor Amaya / Hank Pfister	Peter McNamara / Paul McNamee	Bob Lutz / Stan Smith

Year	Australian	French	Wimbledon	U.S.
1979	Peter McNamara / Paul McNamee	Gene Mayer / Alex Mayer	Peter Fleming / John McEnroe	John McEnroe / Peter Fleming
1978	Wojtek Fibak / Kim Warwick	Gene Mayer / Hank Pfister	Bob Hewitt / Frew McMillan	Bob Lutz / Stan Smith
1977 (Jan.)	Arthur Ashe / Tony Roche	Brian Gottfried / Raul Ramirez	Geoff Masters / Ross Case	Bob Hewitt / Frew McMillan
1977 (Dec.)	Ray Ruffels / Allan Stone			
1976	John Newcombe / Tony Roche	Fred McNair / Sherwood Stewart	Brian Gottfried / Raul Ramirez	Tom Okker / Marty Riessen
1975	John Alexander / Phil Dent	Brian Gottfried / Raul Ramirez	Vitas Gerulaitis / Alex Mayer	Jimmy Connors / Ilie Nastase
1974	Ross Case / Geoff Masters	Dick Crealy / Onny Parun	John Newcombe / Tony Roche	Bob Lutz / Stan Smith
1973	Mal Anderson / John Newcombe	John Newcombe / Tom Okker	Jimmy Connors / Ilie Nastase	Owen Davidson / John Newcombe
1972	Owen Davidson / Ken Rosewall	Bob Hewitt / Frew McMillan	Bob Hewitt / Frew McMillan	Cliff Drysdale / Roger Taylor
1971	John Newcombe / Tony Roche	Arthur Ashe / Marty Riessen	Roy Emerson / Rod Laver	John Newcombe / Roger Taylor
1970	Bob Lutz / Stan Smith	Ilie Nastase / Ion Tiriac	John Newcombe / Tony Roche	Pierre Barthes / Nikki Pilic
1969	Roy Emerson / Rod Laver	John Newcombe / Tony Roche	John Newcombe / Tony Roche	Ken Rosewall / Fred Stolle
1968	Dick Crealy / Allan Stone	Ken Rosewall / Fred Stolle	John Newcombe / Tony Roche	Bob Lutz / Stan Smith
1967	John Newcombe / Tony Roche	John Newcombe / Tony Roche	Bob Hewitt / Frew McMillan	John Newcombe / Tony Roche
1966	Roy Emerson / Fred Stolle	Clark Graebner / Dennis Ralston	Ken Fletcher / John Newcombe	Roy Emerson / Fred Stolle
1965	John Newcombe / Tony Roche	Roy Emerson / Fred Stolle	John Newcombe / Tony Roche	Roy Emerson / Fred Stolle
1964	Bob Hewitt / Fred Stolle	Roy Emerson / Ken Fletcher	Bob Hewitt / Fred Stolle	Chuck McKinley / Dennis Ralston
1963	Bob Hewitt / Fred Stolle	Roy Emerson / Manolo Santana	Rafael Osuna / Antonio Palafox	Chuck McKinley / Dennis Ralston
1962	Roy Emerson / Neale Fraser	Roy Emerson / Neale Fraser	Bob Hewitt / Fred Stolle	Rafael Osuna / Antonio Palafox
1961	Rod Laver / Bob Mark	Roy Emerson / Rod Laver	Roy Emerson / Neale Fraser	Chuck McKinley / Dennis Ralston
1960	Rod Laver / Bob Mark	Roy Emerson / Neale Fraser	Rafael Osuna / Dennis Ralston	Neale Fraser / Roy Emerson
1959	Rod Laver / Bob Mark	Orlando Sirola / Nicola Pietrangeli	Roy Emerson / Neale Faser	Neale Fraser / Roy Emerson
1958	Ashley Cooper / Neale Fraser	Ashley Cooper / Neale Pfister	Sven Davidson / Ulf Schmidt	Alex Olmedo / Hamilton Richardson
1957	Neale Fraser / Lew Hoad	Mal Anderson / Ashley Cooper	Budge Patty / Gardnar Mulloy	Ashley Cooper / Neale Fraser
1956	Lew Hoad / Ken Rosewall	Don Candy / Robert Perry	Lew Hoad / Ken Rosewall	Lew Hoad / Ken Rosewall
1955	Vic Seixas / Tony Trabert	Vic Seixas / Tony Trabert	Rex Hartwig / Lew Hoad	Kosei Kamo / Atsushi Miyagi
1954	Rex Hartwig / Merv Rose	Vic Seixas / Tony Trabert	Rex Hartwig / Merv Rose	Vic Seixas / Tony Trabert
1953	Lew Hoad / Ken Rosewall	Lew Hoad / Ken Rosewall	Lew Hoad / Ken Rosewall	Rex Hartwig / Merv Rose

Year	Australian	French	Wimbledon	U.S.
1952	Ken McGregor / Frank Sedgman	Ken McGregor / Frank Sedgman	Ken McGregor / Frank Sedgman	Merv Rose / Vic Seixas
1951	**Ken McGregor / Frank Sedgman**	**Ken McGregor / Frank Sedgman**	**Ken McGregor / Frank Sedgman**	**Ken McGregor / Frank Sedgman**
1950	John Bromwich / Adrian Quist	Bill Talbert / Tony Trabert	John Bromwich / Adrian Quist	John Bromwich / Frank Sedgman
1949	John Bromwich / Adrian Quist	Pancho Gonzalez / Frank Parker	Pancho Gonzalez / Frank Parker	John Bromwich / Bill Sidwell
1948	John Bromwich / Adrian Quist	Lennart Bergelin / Jaroslav Drobny	John Bromwich / Frank Sedgman	Gardnar Mulloy / Bill Talbert
1947	John Bromwich / Adrian Quist	Eustace Fannin / Eric Sturgess	Bob Falkenburg / Jack Kramer	Jack Kramer / Ted Schroeder
1946	John Bromwich / Adrian Quist	Marcel Bernard / Yvon Petra	Tom Brown / Jack Kramer	Gardnar Mulloy / Bill Talbert
1945	Not held – WWII	Not held – WWII	Not held – WWII	Gardnar Mulloy / Bill Talbert
1944	Not held – WWII	Not held – WWII	Not held – WWII	Don McNeill / Bob Falkenburg
1943	Not held – WWII	Not held – WWII	Not held – WWII	Jack Kramer / Frank Parker
1942	Not held – WWII	Not held – WWII	Not held – WWII	Gardnar Mulloy / Bill Talbert
1941	Not held – WWII	Not held – WWII	Not held – WWII	Jack Kramer / Ted Schroeder
1940	John Bromwich / Adrian Quist	Not held – WWII	Not held – WWII	Jack Kramer / Ted Schroeder
1939	John Bromwich / Adrian Quist	Don McNeill / Charles Harris	Elwood Cooke / Bobby Riggs	Adrian Quist / John Bromwich
1938	John Bromwich / Adrian Quist	Bernard Destremau / Yvon Petra	Don Budge / Gene Mako	Don Budge / Gene Mako
1937	Adrian Quist / Don Turnbull	Gottfried von Cramm / Henner Henkel	Don Budge / Gene Mako	Gottfried von Cramm / Henner Henkel
1936	Adrian Quist / Don Turnbull	Jean Borotra / Marcel Bernard	Pat Hughes / Charles Tuckey	Don Budge / Gene Mako
1935	Jack Crawford / Viv McGrath	Jack Crawford / Adrian Quist	Jack Crawford / Adrian Quist	Wilmer Allison / John Van Ryn
1934	Fred Perry / Pat Hughes	Jean Borotra / Jacques Brugnon	George Lott / Lester Stoefen	George Lott / Lester Stoefen
1933	Keith Gledhill / Ellsworth Vines	Pat Hughes / Fred Perry	Jean Borotra / Jacques Brugnon	George Lott / Lester Stoefen
1932	Jack Crawford / Gar Moon	Henri Cochet / Jacques Brugnon	Jean Borotra / Jacques Brugnon	Ellsworth Vines / Keith Gledhill
1931	Charles Donohoe / Ray Dunlop	George Lott / John Van Ryn	George Lott / John Van Ryn	Wilmer Allison / John Van Ryn
1930	Jack Crawford / Harry Hopman	Henri Cochet / Jacques Brugnon	Wilmer Allison / John Van Ryn	George Lott / Johnny Doeg
1929	Jack Crawford / Harry Hopman	René Lacoste / Jean Borotra	Wilmer Allison / John Van Ryn	George Lott / Johnny Doeg
1928	Jean Borotra / Jacques Brugnon	Jean Borotra / Jacques Brugnon	Jacques Brugnon / Henri Cochet	George Lott / John Hennessey
1927	Jack Hawkes / Gerald Patterson	Henri Cochet / Jacques Brugnon	Frank Hunter / Bill Tilden	Bill Tilden / Frank Hunter
1926	Jack Hawkes / Gerald Patterson	Vinnie Richards / Howard Kinsey	Jacques Brugnon / Henri Cochet	Dick Williams / Vinnie Richards
1925	Pat O'Hara Wood / Gerald Patterson	Jean Borotra / René Lacoste	Jean Borotra / René Lacoste	Dick Williams / Vinnie Richards

Year	Australian	French	Wimbledon	U.S.
1924	James Anderson / Norman Brookes		Frank Hunter / Vinnie Richards	Howard Kinsey / Robert Kinsey
1923	Pat O'Hara Wood / Bert St. John		Leslie Godfree / Randolph Lycett	Bill Tilden / Brian Norton
1922	Jack Hawkes / Gerald Patterson		James Anderson / Randolph Lycett	Bill Tilden / Vinnie Richards
1921	S. H. Eaton / Rhys Gemmell		Randolph Lycett / Max Woosnam	Bill Tilden / Vinnie Richards
1920	Pat O'Hara Wood / Ron Thomas		Dick Williams / Chuck Garland	Bill Johnston / Clarence Griffin
1919	Pat O'Hara Wood / Ron Thomas		Ronald Thomas / Pat O'Hara Wood	Norman Brookes / Gerald Patterson
1918	Not held – WWI		Not held – WWI	Bill Tilden / Vinnie Richards
1917	Not held – WWI		Not held – WWI	Fred Alexander / Harold Throckmorton
1916	Not held – WWI		Not held – WWI	Bill Johnston / Clarence Griffin
1915	Horrie Rice / Clarrie Todd		Not held – WWI	Bill Johnston / Clarence Griffin
1914	Ashley Campbell / Gerald Patterson		Norman Brookes / Tony Wilding	Maurice McLoughlin / Tom Bundy
1913	Alf Hedemann / Ernest Parker		Herbert Roper Barrett / Charles Dixon	Maurice McLoughlin / Tom Bundy
1912	Jim Parke / Charles Dixon		Herbert Roper Barrett / Charles Dixon	Maurice McLoughlin / Tom Bundy
1911	Rodney Heath / Randolph Lycett		Andre Gobert / Max Decugis	Ray Little / Gus Touchard
1910	Ashley Campbell / Horrie Rice		Tony Wilding / Josiah Ritchie	Fred Alexander / Harold Hackett
1909	J. P. Keane / Ernest Parker		Arthur Gore / Herbert Roper Barrett	Fred Alexander / Harold Hackett
1908	Fred Alexander / Alfred Dunlop		Tony Wilding / Josiah Ritchie	Fred Alexander / Harold Hackett
1907	Bill Gregg / Harry Parker		Norman Brookes / Tony Wilding	Fred Alexander / Harold Hackett
1906	Rodney Heath / Tony Wilding		Sidney H. Smith / Frank Riseley	Holcombe Ward / Beals Wright
1905	Randolph Lycett / Tom Tachell		Reggie Doherty / Laurie Doherty	Holcombe Ward / Beals Wright
1904			Reggie Doherty / Laurie Doherty	Holcombe Ward / Beals Wright
1903			Reggie Doherty / Laurie Doherty	Reggie Doherty / Laurie Doherty
1902			Sidney H. Smith / Frank Riseley	Reggie Doherty / Laurie Doherty
1901			Reggie Doherty / Laurie Doherty	Holcombe Ward / Dwight Davis
1900			Reggie Doherty / Laurie Doherty	Holcombe Ward / Dwight Davis
1899			Reggie Doherty / Laurie Doherty	Holcombe Ward / Dwight Davis

Year	Australian	French	Wimbledon	U.S.
1898			Reggie Doherty / Laurie Doherty	Leo Ware / George Sheldon
1897			Reggie Doherty / Laurie Doherty	Leo Ware / George Sheldon
1896			Wilfred Baddeley / Herbert Baddeley	Carr Neel / Sam Neel
1895			Wilfred Baddeley / Herbert Baddeley	Malcolm Chace / Robert Wrenn
1894			Wilfred Baddeley / Herbert Baddeley	Clarence Hobart / Fred Hovey
1893			Joshua Pim / Frank Stoker	Clarence Hobart / Fred Hovey
1892			Ernest Lewis / Harry Barlow	Oliver Campbell / Bob Huntington
1891			Wilfred Baddeley / Herbert Baddeley	Oliver Campbell / Bob Huntington
1890			Joshua Pim / Frank Stoker	Valentine Hall / Clarence Hobart
1889			Willie Renshaw / Ernest Renshaw	Henry Slocum / Howard Taylor
1888			Willie Renshaw / Ernest Renshaw	Oliver Campbell / Valentine Hall
1887			Herbert Wilberforce / Patrick Bowes Lyon	Richard Sears / James Dwight
1886			Willie Renshaw / Ernest Renshaw	Richard Sears / James Dwight
1885			Willie Renshaw / Ernest Renshaw	Richard Sears / Joseph Clark
1884			Willie Renshaw / Ernest Renshaw	Richard Sears / James Dwight
1883				Richard Sears / James Dwight
1882				Richard Sears / James Dwight
1881				Clarence Clark / Fred Taylor

Women's Doubles

Year	Australian	French	Wimbledon	U.S.
2002	Martina Hingis / Anna Kournikova	Virginia Ruano Pascual / Paola Suarez	Venus Williams / Serena Williams	Paola Suarez / Virginia Ruano Pascual
2001	Serena Williams / Venus Williams	Virginia Ruano Pascual / Paola Suarez	Lisa Raymond / Rennae Stubbs	Rennae Stubbs / Lisa Raymond
2000	Lisa Raymond / Rennae Stubbs	Martina Hingis / Mary Pierce	Venus Williams / Serena Williams	Julie Halard-Decugis / Ai Sugiyama
1999	Martina Hingis / Anna Kournikova	Venus Williams / Serena Williams	Lindsay Davenport / Corina Morariu	Serena Williams / Venus Williams
1998	**Martina Hingis /** Mirjana Lucic	**Martina Hingis /** Jana Novotna	**Martina Hingis /** Jana Novotna	**Martina Hingis /** Jana Novotna
1997	Martina Hingis / Natalia Zvereva	Gigi Fernandez / Natasha Zvereva	Gigi Fernandez / Natasha Zvereva	Jana Novotna / Lindsay Davenport
1996	Chanda Rubin / Arantxa Sanchez Vicario	Lindsay Davenport / Mary Joe Fernandez	Martina Hingis / Helena Sukova	Natalia Zvereva / Gigi Fernandez

Year	Australian	French	Wimbledon	U.S.
1995	Jana Novotna / Arantxa Sanchez Vicario	Gigi Fernandez / Natalia Zvereva	Jana Novotna / Arantxa Sanchez Vicario	Gigi Fernandez / Natalia Zvereva
1994	Gigi Fernandez / Natalia Zvereva	Gigi Fernandez / Natalia Zvereva	Gigi Fernandez / Natalia Zvereva	Arantxa Sanchez Vicario / Jana Novotna
1993	Gigi Fernandez / Natalia Zvereva	Gigi Fernandez / Natalia Zvereva	Gigi Fernandez / Natalia Zvereva	Arantxa Sanchez Vicario / Helena Sukova
1992	Arantxa Sanchez Vicario / Helena Sukova	Gigi Fernandez / Natalia Zvereva	Gigi Fernandez / Natalia Zvereva	Gigi Fernandez / Natalia Zvereva
1991	Patty Fendick / Mary Joe Fernandez	Gigi Fernandez / Jana Novotna	Larisa Savchenko / Natalia Zvereva	Pam Shriver / Natalia Zvereva
1990	Jana Novotna / Helena Sukova	Jana Novotna / Helena Sukova	Jana Novotna / Helena Sukova	Gigi Fernandez / Martina Navratilova
1989	Martina Navratilova / Pam Shriver	Larisa Savchenko / Natalia Zvereva	Jana Novotna / Helena Sukova	Hana Mandlikova / Martina Navratilova
1988	Martina Navratilova / Pam Shriver	Martina Navratilova / Pam Shriver	Steffi Graf / Gabriela Sabatini	Gigi Fernandez / Robin White
1987	Martina Navratilova / Pam Shriver	Martina Navratilova / Pam Shriver	Claudia Kohde Kilsch / Helena Sukova	Martina Navratilova / Pam Shriver
1986	Not held (date change)	Martina Navratilova / Andrea Temesvari	Martina Navratilova / Pam Shriver	Martina Navratilova / Pam Shriver
1985	Martina Navratilova / Pam Shriver	Martina Navratilova / Pam Shriver	Kathy Jordan / Elizabeth Sayers Smylie	Claudia Kohde Kilsch / Helena Sukova
1984	**Martina Navratilova / Pam Shriver**	**Martina Navratilova / Pam Shriver**	**Martina Navratilova / Pam Shriver**	**Pam Shriver / Martina Navratilova**
1983	Martina Navratilova / Pam Shriver	Rosalyn Fairbank / Candy Reynolds	Martina Navratilova / Pam Shriver	Pam Shriver / Martina Navratilova
1982	Martina Navratilova / Pam Shriver	Martina Navratilova / Anne Smith	Martina Navratilova / Pam Shriver	Rosie Casals / Wendy Turnbull
1981	Kathy Jordan / Anne Smith	Rosalyn Fairbank / Tayna Harford	Martina Navratilova / Pam Shriver	Anne Smith / Kathy Jordan
1980	Martina Navratilova / Betsy Nagelsen	Kathy Jordan / Anne Smith	Kathy Jordan / Anne Smith	Billie Jean King / Martina Navratilova
1979	Judy Chaloner / Dianne Evers	Betty Stove / Wendy Turnbull	Billie Jean King / Martina Navratilova	Betty Stove / Wendy Turnbull
1978	Betsy Nagelsen / Renata Tomanova	Mima Jausovec / Virginia Ruzici	Kerry Melville Reid / Wendy Turnbull	Billie Jean King / Martina Navratilova
1977 (Jan.)	Dianne Balestrat Fromholtz / Helen Gourlay Cawley	Regina Marsikova / Pam Teeguarden	Helen Gourlay Cawley / JoAnne Russell	Martina Navratilova / Betty Stove
1977 (Dec.)	Evonne Goolagong Cawley / Helen Gourlay Cawley *shared title with* Mona Schallau Guerrant / Kerry Melville Reid			
1976	Evonne Goolagong / Helen Gourlay	Fiorella Bonicelli / Gail Sherriff Lovera	Chris Evert / Martina Navratilova	Delina Boshoff / Ilana Kloss
1975	Evonne Goolagong / Peggy Michel	Chris Evert / Martina Navratilova	Ann Kiyomura / Kazuko Sawamatsu	Margaret Smith Court / Virginia Wade
1974	Evonne Goolagong / Peggy Michel	Chris Evert / Olga Morozova	Evonne Goolagong / Peggy Michel	Rosie Casals / Billie Jean King
1973	Margaret Smith Court / Virginia Wade	Margaret Smith Court / Virginia Wade	Rosie Casals / Billie Jean King	Margaret Smith Court / Virginia Wade
1972	Kerry Harris / Helen Gourlay	Billie Jean King / Betty Stove	Billie Jean King / Betty Stove	Françoise Durr / Betty Stove
1971	Margaret Smith Court / Evonne Goolagong	Gail Sherriff Chanfreau / Françoise Durr	Rosie Casals / Billie Jean King	Rosie Casals / Judy Tegart Dalton
1970	Margaret Smith Court / Judy Tegart Dalton	Gail Sherriff Chanfreau / Françoise Durr	Rosie Casals / Billie Jean King	Margaret Smith Court / Judy Tegart Dalton

Year	Australian	French	Wimbledon	U.S.
1969	Margaret Smith Court / Judy Tegart Dalton	Françoise Durr / Ann Haydon Jones	Margaret Smith Court / Judy Tegart	Françoise Durr / Darlene Hard
1968	Karen Krantzcke / Kerry Melville	Françoise Durr / Ann Haydon Jones	Rosie Casals / Billie Jean King	Maria Bueno / Margaret Smith Court
1967	Lesley Turner / Judy Tegart Dalton	Françoise Durr / Gail Sherriff	Rosie Casals / Billie Jean King	Rosie Casals / Billie Jean King
1966	Carole Caldwell Graebner / Nancy Richey	Margaret Smith / Judy Tegart	Maria Bueno / Nancy Richey	Maria Bueno / Nancy Richey
1965	Margaret Smith / Lesley Turner	Margaret Smith / Lesley Turner	Maria Bueno / Billie Jean King	Carole Caldwell Graebner / Nancy Richey
1964	Judy Tegart Dalton / Lesley Turner	Margaret Smith / Lesley Turner	Margaret Smith / Lesley Turner	Billie Jean Moffitt / Karen Hantze Susman
1963	Margaret Smith / Robyn Ebbern	Ann Haydon Jones / Renee Schuurman	Maria Bueno / Darlene Hard	Robyn Ebbern / Margaret Smith
1962	Margaret Smith / Robyn Ebbern	Sandra Reynolds Price / Renee Schuurman	Billie Jean Moffitt / Karen Hantze	Darlene Hard / Maria Bueno
1961	Mary Carter Reitano / Margaret Smith	Sandra Reynolds / Renee Schuurman	Karen Hantze / Billie Jean Moffitt	Darlene Hard / Lesley Turner
1960	**Maria Bueno /** Christine Truman	**Maria Bueno /** Darlene Hard	**Maria Bueno /** Darlene Hard	**Maria Bueno /** Darlene Hard
1959	Renee Schuurman / Sandra Reynolds	Sandra Reynolds / Renee Schuurman	Jeanne Arth / Darlene Hard	Jeanne Arth / Darlene Hard
1958	Mary Bevis Hawton / Thelma Coyne Long	Rosie Reyes / Yola Ramirez	Maria Bueno / Althea Gibson	Jeanne Arth / Darlene Hard
1957	Althea Gibson / Shirley Fry	Shirley Bloomer / Darlene Hard	Althea Gibson / Darlene Hard	Louise Brough / Margaret Osborne duPont
1956	Mary Bevis Hawton / Thelma Coyne Long	Angela Buxton / Althea Gibson	Angela Buxton / Althea Gibson	Louise Brough / Margaret Osborne duPont
1955	Mary Bevis Hawton / Beryl Penrose	Beverly Baker Fleitz / Darlene Hard	Angela Mortimer / Anne Shilcock	Louise Brough / Margaret Osborne duPont
1954	Mary Bevis Hawton / Beryl Penrose	Maureen Connolly / Nell Hall Hopman	Louise Brough / Margaret Osborne duPont	Shirley Fry / Doris Hart
1953	Maureen Connolly / Julia Sampson	Doris Hart / Shirley Fry	Shirley Fry / Doris Hart	Shirley Fry / Doris Hart
1952	Thelma Coyne Long / Nancye Wynne Bolton	Doris Hart / Shirley Fry	Shirley Fry / Doris Hart	Shirley Fry / Doris Hart
1951	Thelma Coyne Long / Nancye Wynne Bolton	Doris Hart / Shirley Fry	Shirley Fry / Doris Hart	Shirley Fry / Doris Hart
1950	Louise Brough / Doris Hart	Doris Hart / Shirley Fry	Louise Brough / Margaret Osborne duPont	Louise Brough / Margaret Osborne duPont
1949	Thelma Coyne Long / Nancye Wynne Bolton	Margaret Osborne duPont / Louise Brough	Louise Brough / Margaret Osborne duPont	Louise Brough / Margaret Osborne duPont
1948	Thelma Coyne Long / Nancye Wynne Bolton	Doris Hart / Pat Canning Todd	Louise Brough / Margaret Osborne duPont	Louise Brough / Margaret Osborne duPont
1947	Thelma Coyne Long / Nancye Wynne Bolton	Louise Brough / Margaret Osborne	Doris Hart / Pat Canning Todd	Louise Brough / Margaret Osborne
1946	Joyce Fitch / Mary Bevis	Louise Brough / Margaret Osborne	Louise Brough / Margaret Osborne	Louise Brough / Margaret Osborne
1945	Not held – WWII	Not held – WWII	Not held – WWII	Louise Brough / Margaret Osborne
1944	Not held – WWII	Not held – WWII	Not held – WWII	Louise Brough / Margaret Osborne
1943	Not held – WWII	Not held – WWII	Not held – WWII	Louise Brough / Margaret Osborne
1942	Not held – WWII	Not held – WWII	Not held – WWII	Louise Brough / Margaret Osborne

Year	Australian	French	Wimbledon	U.S.
1941	Not held – WWII	Not held – WWII	Not held – WWII	Sarah Palfrey Cooke / Margaret Osborne
1940	Thelma Coyne Long / Nancye Wynne	Not held – WWII	Not held – WWII	Sarah Palfrey Fabyan / Alice Marble
1939	Thelma Coyne Long / Nancye Wynne	Simone Passemard Mathieu / Jadwiga Jedrzejowska	Sarah Palfrey Fabyan / Alice Marble	Sarah Palfrey Fabyan / Alice Marble
1938	Thelma Coyne Long / Nancye Wynne	Simone Passemard Mathieu / Billie Yorke	Sarah Palfrey Fabyan / Alice Marble	Sarah Palfrey Fabyan / Alice Marble
1937	Thelma Coyne Long / Nancye Wynne	Simone Passemard Mathieu / Billie Yorke	Simone Passemard Mathieu / Billie Yorke	Sarah Palfrey Fabyan / Alice Marble
1936	Thelma Coyne Long / Nancye Wynne	Simone Passemard Mathieu / Billie Yorke	Freda James / Kay Stammers	Marjorie Gladman Van Ryn / Carolin Babcock
1935	Evelyn Dearman / Nancy Lyle	Margaret Scriven / Kay Stammers	Freda James / Kay Stammers	Helen Jacobs / Sarah Palfrey Fabyan
1934	Mall Molesworth / Emily Hood Westacott	Simone Passemard Mathieu / Elizabeth Ryan	Simone Passemard Mathieu / Elizabeth Ryan	Helen Jacobs / Sarah Palfrey
1933	Mall Molesworth / Emily Hood Westacott	Simone Passemard Mathieu / Elizabeth Ryan	Simone Passemard Mathieu / Elizabeth Ryan	Betty Nuthall / Freda James
1932	Coral McInnes Buttsworth / Marjorie Cox	Helen Wills Moody / Elizabeth Ryan	Doris Metaxa / Josane Sigart	Helen Jacobs / Sarah Palfrey
1931	Daphne Akhurst Cozens / Louie Bickerton	Eileen Bennett Whittingstall / Betty Nuthall	Dorothy Shepherd Barron / Phyllis Mudford	Betty Nuthall / Eileen Bennett Whittingstall
1930	Mall Molesworth / Emily Hood	Helen Wills Moody / Elizabeth Ryan	Helen Wills Moody / Elizabeth Ryan	Betty Nuthall / Sarah Palfrey
1929	Daphne Akhurst / Louie Bickerton	Lili de Alvarez / Kea Bouman	Peggy Saunders Michell / Phoebe Holcroft Watson	Phoebe Holcroft Watson / Peggy Michell
1928	Daphne Akhurst / Esna Boyd	Phoebe Holcroft Watson / Eileen Bennett	Peggy Saunders / Phoebe Holcroft Watson	Hazel Hotchkiss Wightman / Helen Wills
1927	Meryl O'Hara Wood / Louie Bickerton	Irene Bowder Peacock / Bobbie Heine	Helen Wills / Elizabeth Ryan	Kitty McKane Godfree / Ermyntrude Harvey
1926	Meryl O'Hara Wood / Esna Boyd	Suzanne Lenglen / Didi Vlasto	Mary K. Browne / Elizabeth Ryan	Elizabeth Ryan / Eleanor Goss
1925	Sylvia Lance Harper / Daphne Akhurst	Suzanne Lenglen / Didi Vlasto	Suzanne Lenglen / Elizabeth Ryan	Mary K. Browne / Helen Wills
1924	Daphne Akhurst / Sylvia Lance		Hazel Hotchkiss Wightman / Helen Wills	Hazel Hotchkiss Wightman / Helen Wills
1923	Esna Boyd / Sylvia Lance		Suzanne Lenglen / Elizabeth Ryan	Kitty McKane / Phyllis Howkins Covell
1922	Esna Boyd / Marjorie Mountain		Suzanne Lenglen / Elizabeth Ryan	Marion Zinderstein Jessup / Helen Wills
1921			Suzanne Lenglen / Elizabeth Ryan	Mary K. Browne / Louise Riddell Williams
1920			Suzanne Lenglen / Elizabeth Ryan	Marion Zinderstein / Eleanor Goss
1919			Suzanne Lenglen / Elizabeth Ryan	Marion Zinderstein / Eleanor Goss
1918			Not held – WWI	Marion Zinderstein / Eleanor Goss
1917			Not held – WWI	Molla Bjurstedt / Eleonora Sears
1916			Not held – WWI	Molla Bjurstedt / Eleonora Sears
1915			Not held – WWI	Hazel Hotchkiss Wightman / Eleonora Sears
1914			Agnes Morton / Elizabeth Ryan	Mary K. Browne / Louise Riddell Williams

Year	Australian	French	Wimbledon	U.S.
1913			Winifred Slocock McNair / Dora Boothby	Mary K. Browne / Louise Riddell Williams
1912				Dorothy Green / Mary K. Browne
1911				Hazel Hotchkiss / Eleonora Sears
1910				Hazel Hotchkiss / Edith Rotch
1909				Hazel Hotchkiss / Edith Rotch
1908				Evelyn Sears / Margaret Curtis
1907				Marie Wimer / Carrie Neely
1906				Ann Burdette Coe / Ethel Bliss Platt
1905				Helen Homans / Carrie Neely
1904				May Sutton / Miriam Hall
1903				Elisabeth Moore / Carrie Neely
1902				Juliette Atkinson / Marion Jones
1901				Juliette Atkinson / Myrtle McAteer
1900				Edith Parker / Hallie Champlin
1899				Jane Craven / Myrtle McAteer
1898				Juliette Atkinson / Kathleen Atkinson
1897				Juliette Atkinson / Kathleen Atkinson
1896				Elisabeth Moore / Juliette Atkinson
1895				Helen Hellwig / Juliette Atkinson
1894				Helen Hellwig / Juliette Atkinson
1893				Aline Terry / Harriet Butler
1892				Mabel Cahill / Adeline McKinlay
1891				Mabel Cahill / Emma Leavitt Morgan
1890				Ellen Roosevelt / Grace Roosevelt
1889				Margarette Ballard / Bertha Townsend

Mixed Doubles

Year	Australian	French	Wimbledon	U.S.
2002	Daniela Hantuchova / Kevin Ullyett	Cara Black / Wayne Black	Elena Likhovtseva / Mahesh Bhupathi	Lisa Raymond / Mike Bryan
2001	Corina Morariu / Ellis Ferreira	Virginia Ruano Pascual / Tomas Carbonell	Daniela Hantuchova / Leos Friedl	Rennae Stubbs / Todd Woodbridge
2000	Rennae Stubbs / Jared Palmer	Mariaan de Swardt / David Adams	Kimberly Po / Donald Johnson	Arantxa Sanchez Vicario / Jared Palmer
1999	Mariaan de Swardt / David Adams	Katarina Srebotnik / Piet Norval	Lisa Raymond / Leander Paes	Ai Sugiyama / Mahesh Bhupathi
1998	Venus Williams / Justin Gimelstob	Venus Williams / Justin Gimelstob	Serena Williams / Max Mirnyi	Serena Williams / Max Mirnyi
1997	Manon Bollegraf / Rick Leach	Rika Hiraki / Mahesh Bhupathi	Helena Sukova / Cyril Suk	Manon Bollegraf / Rick Leach
1996	Larisa Savchenko Neiland / Mark Woodforde	Patricia Tarabini / Javier Frana	Helena Sukova / Cyril Suk	Lisa Raymond / Patrick Galbraith
1995	Natalia Zvereva / Rick Leach	Larisa Savchenko Neiland / Todd Woodbridge	Martina Navratilova / Jonathan Stark	Meredith McGrath / Matt Lucena
1994	Larisa Savchenko Neiland / Andrei Olhovskiy	Kristie Boogert / Menno Oosting	Helena Sukova / Todd Woodbridge	Elna Reinach / Patrick Galbraith
1993	Arantxa Sanchez Vicario / Todd Woodbridge	Eugenia Maniokova / Andrei Olhovskiy	Martina Navratilova / Mark Woodforde	Helena Sukova / Todd Woodbridge
1992	Nicole Provis / Mark Woodforde	Arantxa Sanchez Vicario / Mark Woodforde	Larisa Savchenko Neiland / Cyril Suk	Nicole Provis / Mark Woodforde
1991	Jo Durie / Jeremy Bates	Helena Sukova / Cyril Suk	Elizabeth Sayers Smylie / John Fitzgerald	Manon Bollegraf / Tom Nijssen
1990	Natalia Zvereva / Jim Pugh	Arantxa Sanchez Vicario / Jorge Lozano	Zina Garrison / Rick Leach	Elizabeth Sayers Smylie / Todd Woodbridge
1989	Jana Novotna / Jim Pugh	Manon Bollegraf / Tom Nijssen	Jana Novotna / Jim Pugh	Robin White / Shelby Cannon
1988	Jana Novotna / Jim Pugh	Lori McNeil / Jorge Lozano	Zina Garrison / Sherwood Stewart	Jana Novotna / Jim Pugh
1987	Zina Garrison / Sherwood Stewart	Pam Shriver / Emilio Sanchez	Jo Durie / Jeremy Bates	Martina Navratilova / Emilio Sanchez
1986	Not held	Kathy Jordan / Ken Flach	Kathy Jordan / Ken Flach	Raffaella Reggi / Sergio Casal
1985	Not held	Martina Navratilova / Heinz Gunthardt	Martina Navratilova / Paul McNamee	Martina Navratilova / Heinz Gunthardt
1984	Not held	Anne Smith / Dick Stockton	Wendy Turnbull / John Lloyd	Manuela Maleeva / Tom Gullikson
1983	Not held	Barbara Jordan / Eliot Teltscher	Wendy Turnbull / John Lloyd	Elizabeth Sayers / John Fitzgerald
1982	Not held	Wendy Turnbull / John Lloyd	Anne Smith / Kevin Curren	Anne Smith / Kevin Curren
1981	Not held	Andrea Jaeger / Jimmy Arias	Betty Stove / Frew McMillan	Anne Smith / Kevin Curren
1980	Not held	Anne Smith / Billy Martin	Tracy Austin / John Austin	Wendy Turnbull / Marty Riessen
1979	Not held	Wendy Turnbull / Bob Hewitt	Greer Stevens / Bob Hewitt	Greer Stevens / Bob Hewitt
1978	Not held	Renata Tomanova / Pavel Slozil	Betty Stove / Frew McMillan	Betty Stove / Frew McMillan
1977	Not held	Mary Carillo / John McEnroe	Greer Stevens / Bob Hewitt	Betty Stove / Frew McMillan

Year	Australian	French	Wimbledon	U.S.
1976	Not held	Ilana Kloss / Kim Warwick	Françoise Durr / Tony Roche	Billie Jean King / Phil Dent
1975	Not held	Fiorella Bonicelli / Thomaz Koch	Margaret Smith Court / Marty Riessen	Rosie Casals / Dick Stockton
1974	Not held	Martina Navratilova / Ivan Molina	Billie Jean Moffitt King / Owen Davidson	Pam Teeguarden / Geoff Masters
1973	Not held	Françoise Durr / Jean Claude Barclay	Billie Jean Moffitt King / Owen Davidson	Billie Jean King / Owen Davidson
1972	Not held	Evonne Goolagong / Kim Warwick	Rosie Casals / Ilie Nastase	Margaret Smith Court / Marty Riessen
1971	Not held	Françoise Durr / Jean Claude Barclay	Billie Jean Moffitt King / Owen Davidson	Billie Jean King / Owen Davidson
1970	Not held	Billie Jean King / Bob Hewitt	Rosie Casals / Ilie Nastase	Margaret Smith Court / Marty Riessen
1969	Margaret Smith Court / Marty Riessen *shared title with* Ann Haydon Jones / Fred Stolle	Margaret Smith Court / Marty Riessen	Ann Haydon Jones / Fred Stolle	Margaret Smith Court / Marty Riessen
1968	Billie Jean King / Dick Crealy	Françoise Durr / Jean Claude Barclay	Margaret Smith Court / Ken Fletcher	Mary Ann Eisel / Peter Curtis
1967	Lesley Turner / **Owen Davidson**	Billie Jean King / **Owen Davidson**	Billie Jean King / **Owen Davidson**	Billie Jean King / **Owen Davidson**
1966	Judy Tegart / Tony Roche	Annette Van Zyl / Frew McMillan	Margaret Smith / Ken Fletcher	Donna Floyd Fales / Owen Davidson
1965	Robyn Ebbern / Owen Davidson *shared title with* Margaret Smith / John Newcombe	Margaret Smith / Ken Fletcher	Margaret Smith / Ken Fletcher	Margaret Smith / Fred Stolle
1964	Margaret Smith / Ken Fletcher	Margaret Smith / Ken Fletcher	Lesley Turner / Fred Stolle	Margaret Smith / John Newcombe
1963	**Margaret Smith / Ken Fletcher**	**Margaret Smith / Ken Fletcher**	**Margaret Smith / Ken Fletcher**	**Margaret Smith / Ken Fletcher**
1962	Lesley Turner / Fred Stolle	Renee Schuurman / Bob Howe	Margaret Osborne duPont / Neale Fraser	Margaret Smith / Fred Stolle
1961	Jan Lehane / Bob Hewitt	Darlene Hard / Rod Laver	Lesley Turner / Fred Stolle	Margaret Smith / Bob Mark
1960	Jan Lehane / Trevor Fancutt	Maria Bueno / Bob Howe	Darlene Hard / Rod Laver	Margaret Osborne duPont / Neale Fraser
1959	Sandra Reynolds / Bob Mark	Yola Ramirez / Billy Knight	Darlene Hard / Rod Laver	Margaret Osborne duPont / Neale Fraser
1958	Mary Bevis Hawton / Bob Howe	Shirley Bloomer / Nicola Pietrangeli	Lorraine Coghlan / Bob Howe	Margaret Osborne duPont / Neale Fraser
1957	Fay Muller / Mal Anderson	Vera Puzejova / Jiri Javorsky	Darlene Hard / Merv Rose	Althea Gibson / Kurt Nielsen
1956	Beryl Penrose / Neale Fraser	Thelma Coyne Long / Luis Ayala	Shirley Fry / Vic Seixas	Margaret Osborne duPont / Ken Rosewall
1955	Thelma Coyne Long / George Worthington	Darlene Hard / Gordon Forbes	Doris Hart / Vic Seixas	Doris Hart / Vic Seixas
1954	Thelma Coyne Long / Rex Hartwig	Maureen Connolly / Lew Hoad	Doris Hart / Vic Seixas	Doris Hart / Vic Seixas
1953	Julia Sampson / Rex Hartwig	Doris Hart / Vic Seixas	Doris Hart / Vic Seixas	Doris Hart / Vic Seixas
1952	Thelma Coyne Long / George Worthington	Doris Hart / Frank Sedgman	Doris Hart / Frank Sedgman	Doris Hart / Frank Sedgman

Year	Australian	French	Wimbledon	U.S.
1951	Thelma Coyne Long / George Worthington	Doris Hart / Frank Sedgman	Doris Hart / Frank Sedgman	Doris Hart / Frank Sedgman
1950	Doris Hart / Frank Sedgman	Barbara Scofield / Enrique Morea	Louise Brough / Eric Sturgess	Margaret Osborne duPont / Ken McGregor
1949	Doris Hart / Frank Sedgman	Sheila Piercey Summers / Eric Sturgess	Sheila Piercey Summers / Eric Sturgess	Louise Brough / Eric Strugess
1948	Nancye Wynne Bolton / Colin Long	Pat Canning Todd / Jaroslav Drobny	Louise Brough / John Bromwich	Louise Brough / Tom Brown
1947	Nancye Wynne Bolton / Colin Long	Sheila Piercey Summers / Eric Sturgess	Louise Brough / John Bromwich	Louise Brough / John Bromwich
1946	Nancye Wynne Bolton / Colin Long	Pauline Betz / Budge Patty	Louise Brough / Tom Brown	Margaret Osborne / Bill Talbert
1945	Not held – WWII	Not held – WWII	Not held – WWII	Margaret Osborne / Bill Talbert
1944	Not held – WWII	Not held – WWII	Not held – WWII	Margaret Osborne / Bill Talbert
1943	Not held – WWII	Not held – WWII	Not held – WWII	Margaret Osborne / Bill Talbert
1942	Not held – WWII	Not held – WWII	Not held – WWII	Louise Brough / Ted Schroeder
1941	Not held – WWII	Not held – WWII	Not held – WWII	Sarah Palfrey Cooke / Jack Kramer
1940	Nancye Wynne / Colin Long	Not held – WWII	Not held – WWII	Alice Marble / Bobby Riggs
1939	Nell Hall Hopman / Harry Hopman	Sarah Palfrey Fabyan / Elwood Cooke	Alice Marble / Bobby Riggs	Alice Marble / Harry Hopman
1938	Margaret Wilson / John Bromwich	Simone Passemard Mathieu / Dragutin Mitic	Alice Marble / Don Budge	Alice Marble / Don Budge
1937	Nell Hall Hopman / Harry Hopman	Simone Passemard Mathieu / Yvon Petra	Alice Marble / Don Budge	Sarah Palfrey Fabyan / Don Budge
1936	Nell Hall Hopman / Harry Hopman	Billie Yorke / Marcel Bernard	Dorothy Round / Fred Perry	Alice Marble / Gene Mako
1935	Louie Bickerton / Christian Boussus	Lolette Payot / Marcel Bernard	Dorothy Round / Fred Perry	Sarah Palfrey Fabyan / Enrique Maier
1934	Joan Hartigan / Gar Moon	Colette Rosambert / Jean Borotra	Dorothy Round / Ryuki Miki	Helen Jacobs / George Lott
1933	Marjorie Cox Crawford / Jack Crawford	Margaret Scriven / Jack Crawford	Hilde Krahwinkel / Gottfried von Cramm	Elizabeth Ryan / Ellsworth Vines
1932	Marjorie Cox Crawford / Jack Crawford	Betty Nuthall / Fred Perry	Elizabeth Ryan / Enrique Maier	Sarah Palfrey / Fred Perry
1931	Marjorie Cox Crawford / Jack Crawford	Betty Nuthall / Pat Spence	Anna McCune Harper / George Lott	Betty Nuthall / George Lott
1930	Nell Hall / Harry Hopman	Cilly Aussem / Bill Tilden	Elizabeth Ryan / Jack Crawford	Edith Cross / Wilmer Allison
1929	Daphne Akhurst / Gar Moon	Eileen Bennett / Henri Cochet	Helen Wills / Frank Hunter	Betty Nuthall / George Lott
1928	Daphne Akhurst / Jean Borotra	Eileen Bennett / Henri Cochet	Elizabeth Ryan / Pat Spence	Helen Wills / Jack Hawkes
1927	Esna Boyd / Jack Hawkes	Marguerite Broquedis Bordes / Jean Borotra	Elizabeth Ryan / Frank Hunter	Eileen Bennett / Henri Cochet
1926	Esna Boyd / Jack Hawkes	Suzanne Lenglen / Jacques Brugnon	Kitty McKane Godfree / Leslie Godfree	Elizabeth Ryan / Jean Borotra
1925	Daphne Akhurst / John Willard	Suzanne Lenglen / Jacques Brugnon	Suzanne Lenglen / Jean Borotra	Kitty McKane / Jack Hawkes

Year	Australian	French	Wimbledon	U.S.
1924	Daphne Akhurst / John Willard		Kitty McKane / Brian Gilbert	Helen Wills / Vinnie Richards
1923	Sylvia Lance / Horrie Rice		Elizabeth Ryan / Randolph Lycett	Molla Bjurstedt Mallory / Bill Tilden
1922	Esna Boyd / Jack Hawkes		Suzanne Lenglen / Pat O'Hara Wood	Molla Bjurstedt Mallory / Bill Tilden
1921			Elizabeth Ryan / Randolph Lycett	Mary K. Browne / Bill Johnston
1920			Suzanne Lenglen / Gerald Patterson	Hazel Hotchkiss Wightman / Wallace Johnson
1919			Elizabeth Ryan / Randolph Lycett	Marion Zinderstein / Vinnie Richards
1918			Not held – WWI	Hazel Hotchkiss Wightman / Irving Wright
1917			Not held – WWI	Molla Bjurstedt / Irving Wright
1916			Not held – WWI	Eleonora Sears / Willis Davis
1915			Not held – WWI	Hazel Hotchkiss Wightman / Harry Johnson
1914			Ethel Thomson Larcombe / Jim Parke	Mary K. Browne / Bill Tilden
1913			Agnes Daniell Tuckey / Hope Crisp	Mary K. Browne / Bill Tilden
1912				Mary K. Browne / Dick Williams
1911				Hazel Hotchkiss / Wallace Johnson
1910				Hazel Hotchkiss / Joseph Carpenter Jr.
1909				Hazel Hotchkiss / Wallace Johnson
1908				Edith Rotch / Nathaniel Niles
1907				May Sayers / Wallace Johnson
1906				Sarah Coffin / Edward Dewhurst
1905				Augusta Schultz Hobart / Clarence Hobart
1904				Elisabeth Moore / Wylie Grant
1903				Helen Chapman / Harry Allen
1902				Elisabeth Moore / Wylie Grant
1901				Marion Jones / Ray Little
1900				Margaret Hunnewell / Alfred Codman
1899				Elizabeth Rastall / Albert Hoskins

Year	Australian	French	Wimbledon	U.S.
1898				Carrie Neely / Edwin Fischer
1897				Laura Henson / D. L. Magruder
1896				Juliette Atkinson / Edwin Fischer
1895				Juliette Atkinson / Edwin Fischer
1894				Juliette Atkinson / Edwin Fischer
1893				Ellen Roosevelt / Clarence Hobart
1892				Mabel Cahill / Clarence Hobart

All-Time Major Champions – Men

(Through 2003 Australian Open)

NAME	Wins	TOTAL			Australian			French			Wimbledon			U.S.		
		S	D	M	S	D	M	S	D	M	S	D	M	S	D	M
Roy Emerson	28	12	16		6	3		2	6		2	3		2	4	
John Newcombe	25	7	17	1	2	5			3		3	6		2	3	1
Frank Sedgman	22	5	9	8	2	2	2	2	2	2	1	3	2	2	2	2
Bill Tilden	21	10	6	5						1	3	1		7	5	4
Rod Laver	20	11	6	3	3	4		2	1	1	4	1	2	2		
John Bromwich	19	2	13	4	2	8	1				2	2		3	1	
Neale Fraser	19	3	11	5		3	1		3		1	2	1	2	3	3
Fred Stolle	18	2	10	6		3	1	1	2			2	3	1	3	2
Jean Borotra	18	4	9	5	1	1	1	1	5	2	2	3	1			1
Ken Rosewall	18	8	9	1	4	3		2	2			2		2	2	1
Mark Woodforde	18		12	6		2	2		1	2		6	1		3	1
Todd Woodbridge	18		13	5		3	1		1			7	1		2	3
Adrian Quist	17	3	14		3	10			1			2			1	
Jack Crawford	17	6	6	5	4	4	3	1	1	1	1	1	1			
John McEnroe	17	7	9	1						1	3	5		4	4	
Laurie Doherty	16	6	10								5	8		1	2	
Tony Roche	16	1	13	2		5	1	1	2			5	1		1	
Bob Hewitt	15		9	6		2	1		1	2		5	2		1	1
Henri Cochet	15	7	5	3				4	3	2	2	2		1		1
Vic Seixas	15	2	5	8		1			2	1	1		4	1	2	3
Don Budge	14	6	4	4	1			1			2	2	2	2	2	2
Fred Perry	14	8	2	4	1	1		1	1	1	3		2	3		1
Pete Sampras	14	14			2						7			5		
Reggie Doherty	14	4	10								4	8			2	
Dick Sears	13	7	6											7	6	
Lew Hoad	13	4	8	1	1	3		1	1	1	2	3		1		
George Lott	12		8	4					1			2	1		5	3
Jacques Brugnon	12		10	2		1			5	2		4				
Ken Fletcher	12		2	10			2		1	3		1	4			1
Owen Davidson	12		2	10		1	1			1			4		1	4
Willie Renshaw	12	7	5								7	5				
Bjorn Borg	11	11						6			5					
Tony Wilding	11	6	5		2	1					4	4				
Frew McMillan	10		5	5					1	1		3	2		1	2
Gerald Patterson	10	3	6	1	1	5					2		1		1	
Jack Kramer	10	3	6	1							1	2		2	4	1
Jimmy Connors	10	8	2		1						2	1		5	1	
René Lacoste	10	7	3					3	2		2	1		2		
Tony Trabert	10	5	5			1		2	3		1			2	1	
Bill Talbert	9		5	4					1						4	4
Jack Hawkes	9	1	3	5	1	3	3									2
John Fitzgerald	9		7	2		1			2			2	1		2	1
Ken McGregor	9	1	7	1	1	2			2			2			1	1
Rick Leach	9		5	4		3	2					1	1		1	1
Stefan Edberg	9	6	3		2	2					2			2	1	
Vinnie Richards	9		7	2					1			1			5	2

All-Time Major Champions – Women

(Through 2003 Australian Open)

NAME	Wins	TOTAL			Australian Open			French Open			Wimbledon			U.S. Open		
		S	D	M	S	D	M	S	D	M	S	D	M	S	D	M
Margaret Smith Court	62	24	19	19	11	8	2	5	4	4	3	2	5	5	5	8
Martina Navratilova	57	18	31	7	3	8	1	2	7	2	9	7	3	4	9	2
Billie Jean King	39	12	16	11	1		1	1	1	2	6	10	4	4	5	4
Margaret Osborne duPont	37	6	21	10				2	3		1	5	1	3	13	9
Doris Hart	35	6	14	15	1	1	2	2	5	3	1	4	5	2	4	5
Louise Brough	35	6	21	8	1	1			3		4	5	4	1	12	4
Helen Wills Moody	31	19	9	3				4	2		8	3	1	7	4	2
Elizabeth Ryan	26		17	9					4			12	7		1	2
Steffi Graf	23	22	1		4			6			7	1		5		
Pam Shriver	22		21	1		7			4	1		5			5	
Chris Evert	21	18	3		2			7	2		3	1		6		
Darlene Hard	21	3	13	5				1	3	2		4	3	2	6	
Suzanne Lenglen	21	8	8	5				2	2	2	6	6	3			
Nancye Bolton	20	6	10	4	6	10	4									
Natalia Zvereva	20		18	2		3	2		6			5			4	
Maria Bueno	19	7	11	1		1			1	1	3	5		4	4	
Thelma Long	19	2	12	5	2	12	4						1			
Alice Marble	18	5	6	7							1	2	3	4	4	4
Sarah Palfrey Fabyan	18	2	11	5						1		2		2	9	4
Gigi Fernandez	17		17			2			6			4			5	
Hazel Hotchkiss Wightman	17	4	7	6								1		4	6	6
Jana Novotna	17	1	12	4		2	2		3		1	4	1		3	1
Shirley Fry	17	4	12	1	1	1		1	4		1	3	1	1	4	
Arantxa Sanchez Vicario	14	4	6	4		3	1	3		2		1		1	2	1
Daphne Akhurst	14	5	5	4	5	5	4									
Helena Sukova	14		9	5		2			1	1		4	3		2	1
Martina Hingis	14	5	9		3	4			2		1	2		1	1	
Evonne Goolagong	13	7	5	1	4	4		1		1	2	1				
Juliette Atkinson	13	3	7	3										3	7	3
Lesley Turner	13	2	7	4		3	2	2	2			1	2		1	
Mary K. Browne	13	3	6	4								1		3	5	4
Molla Mallory	13	8	2	3										8	2	3
Simone Passemard Mathieu	13	2	9	2				2	6	2		3				
Serena Williams	13	5	6	2		2		1	1		1	2	1	2	1	1
Françoise Durr	12	1	7	4				1	5	3			1		2	
Maureen Connolly	12	9	2	1	1	1		2	1	1	3			3		
Rosie Casals	12		9	3								5	2		4	1
Venus Williams	12	4	5	2		2	1		1	1	2	2		2	1	
Althea Gibson	11	5	5	1		1		1	1		2	3		2		1
Anne Smith	10		5	5		1			2	2		1	1		1	2
Betty Stove	10		6	4					2			1	2		3	2
Betty Nuthall	9	1	4	4					1	2				1	3	2
Helen Jacobs	9	5	3	1							1			4	3	1
Judy Dalton	9		8	1		4	1		1			1			2	
Monica Seles	9	9			4			3						2		
Wendy Turnbull	9		4	5					1	2		1	2		2	1
Bessie Moore	8	4	2	2										4	2	2
Esna Boyd	8	1	4	3	1	4	3									

All-Time Major Champions – Records

(Through 2003 Australian Open)

MEN'S SINGLES – TITLES

	TOTAL		Aus.	Fre.	Wim.	U.S.
Pete Sampras	14	(1990-2002)	2		7	5
Roy Emerson	12	(1961-1967)	6	2	2	2
Bjorn Borg	11	(1974-1981)		6	5	
Rod Laver	11	(1960-1969)	3	2	4	2
Bill Tilden	10	(1920-1930)			3	7
Fred Perry	8	(1933-1936)	1	1	3	3
Ivan Lendl	8	(1984-1990)	2	3		3
Jimmy Connors	8	(1974-1983)	1		2	5
Ken Rosewall	8	(1953-1972)	4	2		2
Andre Agassi	7	(1992-2001)	3	1	1	2
Bill Larned	7	(1901-1911)				7
Dick Sears	7	(1881-1887)				7
Henri Cochet	7	(1926-1932)		4	2	1
John McEnroe	7	(1979-1984)			3	4
John Newcombe	7	(1967-1975)	2		3	2
Mats Wilander	7	(1982-1988)	3	3		1
René Lacoste	7	(1925-1929)		3	2	2
Willie Renshaw	7	(1881-1889)			7	
Boris Becker	6	(1985-1996)	2		3	1
Don Budge	6	(1937-1938)	1	1	2	2
Jack Crawford	6	(1931-1935)	4	1	1	
Laurie Doherty	6	(1902-1906)			5	1
Stefan Edberg	6	(1985-1992)	2		2	2
Tony Wilding	6	(1906-1913)	2		4	
Frank Sedgman	5	(1949-1952)	2		1	2
Tony Trabert	5	(1953-1955)		2	1	2
Ashley Cooper	4	(1957-1958)	2		1	1
Frank Parker	4	(1944-1949)		2		2
Guillermo Vilas	4	(1977-1979)	2	1		1
Jean Borotra	4	(1924-1931)	1	1	2	
Jim Courier	4	(1991-1993)	2	2		
Lew Hoad	4	(1956-1957)	1	1	2	
Manolo Santana	4	(1961-1966)		2	1	1
Reggie Doherty	4	(1897-1900)			4	
Robert Wrenn	4	(1893-1897)				4

MEN'S SINGLES – FINAL APPEARANCES

	TOTAL		Aus.	Fre.	Wim.	U.S.
Ivan Lendl	19	(1981-1991)	4	5	2	8
Pete Sampras	18	(1990-2002)	3		7	8
Rod Laver	17	(1959-1969)	4	3	6	4
Bjorn Borg	16	(1974-1981)		6	6	4
Ken Rosewall	16	(1953-1974)	5	3	4	4
Bill Tilden	15	(1918-1930)		2	3	10
Jimmy Connors	15	(1974-1984)	2		6	7
Roy Emerson	15	(1961-1967)	7	3	2	3
Andre Agassi	13	(1990-2002)	3	3	2	5
Jack Crawford	12	(1931-1940)	7	2	2	1
John McEnroe	11	(1979-1985)		1	5	5
Mats Wilander	11	(1982-1988)	4	5		2
Stefan Edberg	11	(1985-1993)	5	1	3	2
Boris Becker	10	(1985-1996)	2		7	1
Fred Perry	10	(1933-1936)	2	2	3	3
Henri Cochet	10	(1926-1933)		5	3	2
Jean Borotra	10	(1924-1931)	1	3	5	1
John Newcombe	10	(1966-1976)	3		4	3
René Lacoste	10	(1924-1929)		5	3	2
Bill Johnston	9	(1915-1925)			1	8
Arthur Gore	8	(1899-1912)			8	
Bill Larned	8	(1900-1911)				8
Frank Sedgman	8	(1949-1952)	3	1	2	2
Fred Stolle	8	(1963-1966)	2	1	3	2

MEN'S SINGLES – TITLES (continued)

	TOTAL		Aus.	Fre.	Wim.	U.S.
Guillermo Vilas	8	(1975-1982)	3	4		1
Jaroslav Drobny	8	(1946-1954)		5	3	
John Bromwich	8	(1937-1949)	7		1	
Willie Renshaw	8	(1881-1890)			8	

MEN'S SINGLES – FINAL LOSSES

	TOTAL		Aus.	Fre.	Wim.	U.S.
Ivan Lendl	11	(1981-1991)	2	2	2	5
Ken Rosewall	8	(1954-1974)	1	1	4	2
Jimmy Connors	7	(1975-1984)	1		4	2
Andre Agassi	6	(1990-2002)		2	1	3
Bill Johnston	6	(1916-1925)				6
Fred Stolle	6	(1963-1965)	2		3	1
Jack Crawford	6	(1933-1940)	3	1	1	1
Jean Borotra	6	(1925-1929)		2	3	1
John Bromwich	6	(1937-1949)	5		1	
Rod Laver	6	(1959-1968)	1	1	2	2
Arthur Gore	5	(1899-1912)			5	
Bill Tilden	5	(1918-1930)		2		3
Bjorn Borg	5	(1976-1981)			1	4
Gottfried von Cramm	5	(1935-1937)		1	3	1
Herbert Lawford	5	(1880-1888)			5	
Jaroslav Drobny	5	(1946-1952)		3	2	
Stefan Edberg	5	(1989-1993)	3	1	1	
Tony Roche	5	(1965-1970)		2	1	2
Arthur Ashe	4	(1966-1972)	3			1
Boris Becker	4	(1988-1995)			4	
Ernest Renshaw	4	(1882-1889)			4	
Gerald Patterson	4	(1914-1925)	3		1	
Guillermo Vilas	4	(1975-1982)	1	3		
John McEnroe	4	(1980-1985)		1	2	1
Mats Wilander	4	(1983-1987)	1	2		1
Maurice McLoughlin	4	(1911-1915)			1	3
Neale Fraser	4	(1957-1960)	3		1	
Pete Sampras	4	(1992-2001)	1			3

MEN'S SINGLES – SEMI-FINAL APPEARANCES – (1925-2002)

	TOTAL		Aus.	Fre.	Wim.	U.S.
Jimmy Connors	31	(1974-1991)	2	4	11	14
Ivan Lendl	28	(1981-1991)	7	5	7	9
Ken Rosewall	25	(1953-1977)	8	3	6	8
Pete Sampras	23	(1990-2002)	5	1	8	9
Andre Agassi	23	(1988-2002)	5	5	5	8
Jack Crawford	19	(1928-1940)	11	3	4	1
John McEnroe	19	(1977-1992)	1	2	8	8
Roy Emerson	19	(1959-1967)	8	4	3	4
Stefan Edberg	19	(1985-1994)	8	1	6	4
Boris Becker	18	(1985-1996)	2	3	9	4
Rod Laver	18	(1959-1969)	4	4	6	4
Bjorn Borg	17	(1974-1981)		6	6	5
Henri Cochet	16	(1925-1933)		7	6	3
John Newcombe	16	(1965-1976)	6		4	6
Neale Fraser	16	(1956-1962)	6	2	4	4
Jaroslav Drobny	14	(1946-1954)		6	6	2
Jean Borotra	14	(1925-1931)	1	6	6	1
John Bromwich	14	(1937-1954)	9		2	3
Mats Wilander	14	(1982-1990)	5	6		3
Arthur Ashe	13	(1965-1978)	5		3	5
Fred Perry	13	(1931-1936)	2	2	4	5
Tony Roche	13	(1965-1975)	4	4	3	2
Guillermo Vilas	12	(1975-1982)	4	4		4

	TOTAL	Aus.	Fre.	Wim.	U.S.
Bill Tilden	11 (1925-1930)		3	4	4
Fred Stolle	11 (1961-1966)	5	1	3	2
Jim Courier	11 (1991-1995)	3	4	1	3
Eric Sturgess	10 (1947-1952)	1	6	2	1
Frank Parker	10 (1936-1949)		2	1	7
Frank Sedgman	10 (1949-1952)	4	2	2	2
Merv Rose	10 (1952-1958)	4	2	3	1
René Lacoste	10 (1925-1929)		5	3	2
Vic Seixas	10 (1950-1956)	1	1	3	5

WOMEN'S SINGLES – TITLES

	TOTAL	Aus.	Fre.	Wim.	U.S.
Margaret Smith Court	24 (1960-1973)	11	5	3	5
Steffi Graf	22 (1987-1999)	4	6	7	5
Helen Wills Moody	19 (1923-1938)		4	8	7
Chris Evert	18 (1974-1986)	2	7	3	6
Martina Navratilova	18 (1978-1990)	3	2	9	4
Billie Jean King	12 (1966-1975)	1	1	6	4
Maureen Connolly	9 (1951-1954)	1	2	3	3
Monica Seles	9 (1990-1996)	4	3		2
Molla Mallory	8 (1915-1926)				8
Suzanne Lenglen	8 (1919-1926)		2	6	
Dorothea Douglass Chambers	7 (1903-1914)			7	
Evonne Goolagong	7 (1971-1980)	4	1	2	
Maria Bueno	7 (1959-1966)			3	4
Blanche Bingley Hillyard	6 (1886-1900)			6	
Doris Hart	6 (1949-1955)	1	2	1	2
Louise Brough	6 (1947-1955)	1		4	1
Margaret Osborne duPont	6 (1946-1950)		2	1	3
Nancye Bolton	6 (1937-1951)	6			
Alice Marble	5 (1936-1940)			1	4
Althea Gibson	5 (1956-1958)		1	2	2
Charlotte Cooper Sterry	5 (1895-1908)			5	
Daphne Akhurst	5 (1925-1930)	5			
Helen Jacobs	5 (1932-1936)			1	4
Lottie Dod	5 (1887-1893)			5	
Martina Hingis	5 (1997-1999)	3		1	1
Pauline Betz	5 (1942-1946)			1	4
Serena Williams	5 (1999-2002)	1	1	1	2
Arantxa Sanchez Vicario	4 (1989-1998)		3		1
Bessie Moore	4 (1896-1905)				4
Hana Mandlikova	4 (1980-1987)	2	1		1
Hazel Hotchkiss Wightman	4 (1909-1919)				4
Shirley Fry	4 (1951-1957)	1	1	1	1
Venus Williams	4 (2000-2001)			2	2

WOMEN'S SINGLES – FINAL APPEARANCES

	TOTAL	Aus.	Fre.	Wim.	U.S.
Chris Evert	34 (1973-1988)	6	9	10	9
Martina Navratilova	32 (1975-1994)	6	6	12	8
Steffi Graf	31 (1987-1999)	5	9	9	8
Margaret Smith Court	29 (1960-1973)	12	6	5	6
Helen Wills Moody	22 (1922-1938)		4	9	9
Billie Jean King	18 (1963-1975)	2	1	9	6
Doris Hart	18 (1946-1955)	2	5	4	7
Evonne Goolagong	18 (1971-1980)	7	2	5	4
Helen Jacobs	16 (1928-1940)		2	6	8
Louise Brough	14 (1942-1957)	1		7	6
Blanche Bingley Hillyard	13 (1885-1901)			13	
Monica Seles	13 (1990-1998)	4	4	1	4
Arantxa Sanchez Vicario	12 (1989-1998)	2	6	2	2
Maria Bueno	12 (1959-1966)	1	1	5	5
Martina Hingis	12 (1997-2002)	6	2	1	3
Charlotte Cooper Sterry	11 (1895-1912)			11	
Dorothea Douglass Chambers	11 (1903-1920)			11	
Molla Mallory	11 (1915-1926)			1	10
Margaret Osborne duPont	10 (1944-1950)		2	3	5
Ann Haydon	9 (1961-1969)		5	2	2
Maureen Connolly	9 (1951-1954)	1	2	3	3

WOMEN'S SINGLES – FINAL LOSSES

	TOTAL	Aus.	Fre.	Wim.	U.S.
Chris Evert	16 (1973-1988)	4	2	7	3
Martina Navratilova	14 (1975-1994)	3	4	3	4
Doris Hart	12 (1946-1953)	1	3	3	5
Evonne Goolagong	11 (1971-1976)	3	1	3	4
Helen Jacobs	11 (1928-1940)		2	5	4
Steffi Graf	9 (1987-1999)	1	3	2	3
Arantxa Sanchez Vicario	8 (1991-1996)	2	3	2	1
Louise Brough	8 (1942-1957)			3	5
Blanche Bingley Hillyard	7 (1885-1901)			7	
Martina Hingis	7 (1997-2002)	3	2		2
Ann Haydon	6 (1961-1969)		3	1	2
Billie Jean King	6 (1963-1970)	1		3	2
Charlotte Cooper Sterry	6 (1897-1912)			6	
Esna Boyd	6 (1922-1928)	6			
Simone Passemard Mathieu	6 (1929-1937)		6		
Margaret Smith Court	5 (1963-1971)	1	1	2	1
Maria Bueno	5 (1960-1966)	1	1	2	1
Venus Williams	5 (1997-2002)	1	1	1	2
Darlene Hard	4 (1957-1962)			2	2
Dorothea Douglass Chambers	4 (1905-1920)			4	
Hana Mandlikova	4 (1980-1986)			2	2
Helena Sukova	4 (1984-1993)	2			2
Jan Lehane	4 (1960-1963)	4			
Lesley Turner	4 (1962-1967)	2	2		
Margaret Osborne duPont	4 (1944-1950)			2	2
Monica Seles	4 (1992-1998)		1	1	2
Nancy Richey	4 (1966-1969)	1	1		2
Shirley Fry	4 (1948-1952)		2	1	1
Thelma Long	4 (1940-1956)	4			

WOMEN'S SINGLES – SEMI-FINAL APPEARANCES – (1925-2002)

	TOTAL	Aus.	Fre.	Wim.	U.S.
Chris Evert	52 (1971-1989)	6	12	17	17
Martina Navratilova	44 (1975-1994)	9	6	17	12
Steffi Graf	37 (1985-1999)	5	11	10	11
Margaret Smith Court	36 (1960-1975)	12	7	9	8
Billie Jean King	26 (1963-1983)	3	2	14	7
Doris Hart	26 (1943-1955)	2	6	7	11
Louise Brough	25 (1942-1957)	1	3	10	11
Helen Jacobs	24 (1927-1941)		4	8	12
Arantxa Sanchez Vicario	22 (1989-2000)	5	10	3	4
Evonne Goolagong	22 (1971-1980)	7	3	8	4
Ann Haydon	21 (1957-1969)	1	7	8	5
Maria Bueno	20 (1958-1968)	1	5	6	8
Martina Hingis	19 (1996-2002)	6	5	2	6
Gabriela Sabatini	18 (1985-1995)	4	5	4	5
Helen Wills Moody	18 (1925-1938)		4	8	6
Monica Seles	18 (1989-2002)	6	7	1	4
Margaret Osborne duPont	16 (1941-1951)		4	5	7
Simone Passemard Mathieu	15 (1929-1939)		9	6	
Hana Mandlikova	14 (1980-1987)	3	5	3	3
Shirley Fry	14 (1948-1957)	1	4	4	5
Kerry Melville	13 (1966-1977)	8	1	1	3
Lindsay Davenport	13 (1997-2002)	4	1	3	5
Nancy Richey	13 (1964-1971)	2	5	1	5
Nancye Bolton	13 (1936-1952)	11			2
Conchita Martinez	12 (1993-2000)	3	4	3	2
Darlene Hard	12 (1954-1963)		1	4	7

	TOTAL		Aus.	Fre.	Wim.	U.S.
Lesley Turner	**12**	(1962-1969)	4	6	1	1
Venus Williams	**12**	(1997-2002)	2	1	3	6
Hilde Krahwinkel Sperling	**11**	(1931-1939)			5	6
Thelma Long	**11**	(1936-1956)	11			
Jennifer Capriati	**10**	(1990-2002)	3	3	2	2

MEN'S DOUBLES – TITLES – INDIVIDUAL

	TOTAL		Aus.	Fre.	Wim.	U.S.
John Newcombe	**17**	(1965-1976)	5	3	6	3
Roy Emerson	**16**	(1959-1971)	3	6	3	4
Adrian Quist	**14**	(1935-1950)	10	1	2	1
John Bromwich	**13**	(1938-1950)	8		2	3
Todd Woodbridge	**13**	(1992-2002)	3	1	7	2
Tony Roche	**13**	(1965-1977)	5	2	5	1
Mark Woodforde	**12**	(1989-2000)	2	1	6	3
Neale Fraser	**11**	(1957-1962)	3	3	2	3
Fred Stolle	**10**	(1962-1969)	3	2	2	3
Jacques Brugnon	**10**	(1926-1934)	1	5	4	
Laurie Doherty	**10**	(1897-1905)			8	2
Reggie Doherty	**10**	(1897-1905)			8	2
Bob Hewitt	**9**	(1962-1978)	2	1	5	1
Frank Sedgman	**9**	(1948-1952)	2	2	3	2
Jean Borotra	**9**	(1925-1936)	1	5	3	
John McEnroe	**9**	(1979-1992)			5	4
Ken Rosewall	**9**	(1953-1972)	3	2	2	2
Anders Jarryd	**8**	(1983-1991)	1	3	2	2
George Lott	**8**	(1928-1934)		1	2	5
Lew Hoad	**8**	(1953-1957)	3	1	3	1
John Fitzgerald	**7**	(1982-1991)	1	2	2	2
Ken McGregor	**7**	(1951-1952)	2	2	2	1
Peter Fleming	**7**	(1979-1984)			4	3
Vinnie Richards	**7**	(1918-1926)		1	1	5

MEN'S DOUBLES – FINAL APPEARANCES – INDIVIDUAL

	TOTAL		Aus.	Fre.	Wim.	U.S.
Roy Emerson	**28**	(1958-1971)	8	10	5	5
John Newcombe	**21**	(1963-1976)	7	4	6	4
Adrian Quist	**18**	(1933-1951)	12	2	2	2
Neale Fraser	**18**	(1954-1973)	5	4	6	3
Jacques Brugnon	**17**	(1925-1939)	1	9	7	
Ken Rosewall	**17**	(1953-1973)	5	3	5	4
Todd Woodbridge	**17**	(1992-2002)	4	2	8	3
Fred Stolle	**16**	(1961-1970)	6	2	5	3
John Bromwich	**16**	(1937-1951)	10		2	4
Mark Woodforde	**16**	(1989-2000)	3	2	7	4
Tony Roche	**15**	(1964-1977)	6	3	5	1
Frank Sedgman	**14**	(1947-1952)	4	3	3	4
Gardnar Mulloy	**14**	(1940-1957)		2	3	9
Gerald Patterson	**14**	(1914-1932)	7		2	5
Anders Jarryd	**13**	(1983-1993)	2	5	3	3
Bob Hewitt	**13**	(1961-1978)	3	2	7	1
Lew Hoad	**13**	(1953-1957)	4	3	4	2
Reggie Doherty	**13**	(1896-1906)			11	2
Stan Smith	**13**	(1968-1981)	1	2	4	6

MEN'S DOUBLES – FINAL LOSSES – INDIVIDUAL

	TOTAL		Aus.	Fre.	Wim.	U.S.
Roy Emerson	**12**	(1958-1970)	5	4	2	1
Gardnar Mulloy	**9**	(1940-1957)		2	2	5
Gerald Patterson	**8**	(1922-1932)	2		2	4
Ken Rosewall	**8**	(1954-1973)	2	1	3	2
Stan Smith	**8**	(1971-1981)		2	4	2
Jacques Brugnon	**7**	(1925-1939)		4	3	
Ken Fletcher	**7**	(1963-1967)	2	2	3	
Merv Rose	**7**	(1951-1957)	3	2	1	1
Neale Fraser	**7**	(1954-1973)	2	1	4	
Rick Leach	**7**	(1988-2000)	1	1	2	3

	TOTAL		Aus.	Fre.	Wim.	U.S.
Don Candy	**6**	(1951-1959)	4	1		1
Fred Stolle	**6**	(1961-1970)	3		3	
Henri Cochet	**6**	(1925-1931)		4	2	
Jack Crawford	**6**	(1931-1940)	4	1		1
Pat O'Hara Wood	**6**	(1922-1927)	3		1	2
Phil Dent	**6**	(1970-1979)	3	2	1	
Rod Laver	**6**	(1959-1973)		2	1	3

MEN'S DOUBLES – TITLES – TEAM

	TOTAL		Aus.	Fre.	Wim.	U.S.
John Newcombe / Tony Roche	**12**	(1965-1976)	4	2	5	1
Todd Woodbridge / Mark Woodforde	**11**	(1992-2000)	2	1	6	2
Adrian Quist / John Bromwich	**10**	(1938-1950)	8		1	1
Reggie Doherty / Laurie Doherty	**10**	(1897-1905)			8	2
John McEnroe / Peter Fleming	**7**	(1979-1984)			4	3
Ken McGregor / Frank Sedgman	**7**	(1951-1952)	2	2	2	1
Neale Fraser / Roy Emerson	**7**	(1959-1962)	1	2	2	2
Lew Hoad / Ken Rosewall	**6**	(1953-1956)	2	1	2	1
Bob Hewitt / Frew McMillan	**5**	(1967-1978)		1	3	1
Bob Lutz / Stan Smith	**5**	(1968-1980)	1			4
Henri Cochet / Jacques Brugnon	**5**	(1926-1932)		3	2	
Jacco Eltingh / Paul Haarhuis	**5**	(1994-1998)	1	2	1	1
Jean Borotra / Jacques Brugnon	**5**	(1928-1934)	1	2	2	
Richard Sears / James Dwight	**5**	(1882-1887)				5
Willie Renshaw / Ernest Renshaw	**5**	(1884-1889)			5	
Bill Talbert / Gardnar Mulloy	**4**	(1942-1948)				4
Bob Hewitt / Fred Stolle	**4**	(1962-1964)	2		2	
Don Budge / Gene Mako	**4**	(1936-1938)			2	2
Fred Alexander / Harold Hackett	**4**	(1907-1910)				4
John Fitzgerald / Anders Jarryd	**4**	(1989-1991)		1	2	1
Roy Emerson / Fred Stolle	**4**	(1965-1966)	1	1		2
Vic Seixas / Tony Trabert	**4**	(1954-1955)	1	2		1
Wilfred Baddeley / Herbert Baddeley	**4**	(1891-1896)			4	
Wilmer Allison / John Van Ryn	**4**	(1929-1935)			2	2

MEN'S DOUBLES – FINAL APPEARANCES – TEAM

	TOTAL		Aus.	Fre.	Wim.	U.S.
Todd Woodbridge / Mark Woodforde	**15**	(1992-2000)	3	2	7	3
John Newcombe / Tony Roche	**14**	(1964-1976)	5	3	5	1
Adrian Quist / John Bromwich	**12**	(1938-1951)	9		1	2
Reggie Doherty / Laurie Doherty	**12**	(1897-1906)			10	2
Bob Lutz / Stan Smith	**10**	(1968-1981)	1		3	5
Henri Cochet / Jacques Brugnon	**10**	(1925-1932)		6	4	
John McEnroe / Peter Fleming	**10**	(1978-1984)			6	4
Lew Hoad / Ken Rosewall	**9**	(1953-1956)	3	2	2	2
Neale Fraser / Roy Emerson	**9**	(1959-1962)	2	3	2	2
Ken McGregor / Frank Sedgman	**8**	(1951-1952)	2	2	2	2
Wilmer Allison / John Van Ryn	**8**	(1929-1936)			3	5
Brian Gottfried / Raul Ramirez	**7**	(1975-1980)		4	2	1
Don Budge / Gene Mako	**7**	(1935-1938)		1	2	4
Fred Alexander / Harold Hackett	**7**	(1905-1911)				7
Jacco Eltingh / Paul Haarhuis	**7**	(1994-1998)	1	2	2	2
Jean Borotra / Jacques Brugnon	**7**	(1928-1939)	1	3	3	
John Fitzgerald / Anders Jarryd	**7**	(1988-1993)	1	2	3	1

MEN'S DOUBLES – FINAL LOSSES – TEAM

	TOTAL		Aus.	Fre.	Wim.	U.S.
Bob Lutz / Stan Smith	**5**	(1974-1981)		1	3	1
Daniel Nestor / Mark Knowles	**5**	(1995-2002)	1	2	1	1
Don Candy / Merv Rose	**5**	(1951-1957)	3	1		1
Henri Cochet / Jacques Brugnon	**5**	(1925-1931)		3	2	
John Alexander / Phil Dent	**5**	(1970-1977)	3	1	1	
Brian Gottfried / Raul Ramirez	**4**	(1976-1980)		2	1	1
Gerald Patterson / Pat O'Hara Wood	**4**	(1922-1924)	1		1	2
Roy Emerson / Ken Fletcher	**4**	(1964-1967)	1	1	2	
Todd Woodbridge / Mark Woodforde	**4**	(1994-1998)	1	1	1	1
Wilmer Allison / John Van Ryn	**4**	(1932-1936)			1	3
Bill Bowrey / Owen Davidson	**3**	(1966-1967)	1		1	1

	TOTAL		Aus.	Fre.	Wim.	U.S.
Dick Williams / Watson Washburn ...	3	(1921-1924)			1	2
Don Budge / Gene Mako	3	(1935-1938)	1			2
Dwight Davis / Holcombe Ward	3	(1898-1902)			1	2
Eric Sturgess / Jaroslav Drobny ...	3	(1950-1951)	1	1	1	
Fred Alexander / Harold Hackett.....	3	(1905-1911)				3
Geoff Masters / Ross Case	3	(1972-1976)	2		1	
Gerald Patterson / Jack Hawkes	3	(1925-1928)			1	2
Jack Crawford / Viv McGrath	3	(1934-1940)	2	1		
John Fitzgerald / Anders Jarryd	3	(1988-1993)	1	1	1	
John McEnroe / Peter Fleming......	3	(1978-1982)			2	1
Ken Rosewall / Fred Stolle	3	(1968-1970)	1		2	
Lew Hoad / Ken Rosewall	3	(1954-1955)	1	1		1
Paul Kronk / Cliff Letcher	3	(1976-1979)	2			1
Rick Leach / Jim Pugh	3	(1988-1991)		1	1	1
Roy Emerson / Rod Laver	3	(1968-1970)		2		1
Sidney H. Smith / Frank Riseley	3	(1903-1905)			3	
Tom Okker / Marty Riessen	3	(1969-1975)	1		1	1

WOMEN'S DOUBLES – TITLES – INDIVIDUAL

	TOTAL		Aus.	Fre.	Wim.	U.S.
Martina Navratilova	31	(1975-1990)	8	7	7	9
Louise Brough..................	21	(1942-1957)	1	3	5	12
Margaret Osborne duPont	21	(1941-1957)		3	5	13
Pam Shriver	21	(1981-1991)	7	4	5	5
Margaret Smith Court	19	(1961-1975)	8	4	2	5
Natalia Zvereva.................	18	(1992-1997)	3	6	5	4
Elizabeth Ryan	17	(1914-1934)		4	12	1
Gigi Fernandez	17	(1988-1997)	2	6	4	5
Billie Jean King	16	(1961-1980)		1	10	5
Doris Hart	14	(1947-1954)	1	5	4	4
Darlene Hard	13	(1955-1969)		3	4	6
Jana Novotna	12	(1989-1998)	2	3	4	3
Shirley Fry	12	(1950-1957)	1	4	3	4
Thelma Long	12	(1936-1958)	12			
Maria Bueno	11	(1958-1968)	1	1	5	4
Sarah Palfrey Fabyan	11	(1930-1941)			2	9
Nancye Bolton.................	10	(1936-1952)	10			
Helen Wills Moody..............	9	(1922-1932)		2	3	4
Helena Sukova	9	(1985-1996)	2	1	4	2
Martina Hingis	9	(1996-2002)	4	2	2	1
Rosie Casals..................	9	(1967-1982)			5	4
Simone Passemard Mathieu	9	(1933-1939)		6	3	
Judy Dalton	8	(1964-1971)	4	1	1	2
Suzanne Lenglen	8	(1919-1926)		2	6	

WOMEN'S DOUBLES – FINAL APPEARANCES – INDIVIDUAL

	TOTAL		Aus.	Fre.	Wim.	U.S.
Martina Navratilova	36	(1975-1990)	9	7	9	11
Margaret Smith Court	33	(1960-1975)	12	7	6	8
Natalia Zvereva.................	31	(1988-1999)	6	10	9	6
Doris Hart	30	(1942-1955)	2	7	8	13
Billie Jean King	29	(1961-1980)	2	3	12	12
Louise Brough..................	28	(1942-1957)	1	4	8	15
Margaret Osborne duPont	27	(1941-1958)		4	8	15
Pam Shriver	27	(1980-1993)	9	4	6	8
Gigi Fernandez	23	(1988-1997)	4	7	6	6
Jana Novotna	23	(1989-1998)	3	5	8	7
Elizabeth Ryan	21	(1914-1934)		5	13	3
Rosie Casals..................	21	(1966-1983)	1	3	7	10
Shirley Fry	19	(1948-1957)	1	5	5	8
Darlene Hard	18	(1955-1969)	1	5	4	8
Françoise Durr	18	(1965-1979)		8	6	4
Maria Bueno	16	(1958-1968)	1	2	6	7
Thelma Long	16	(1936-1958)	14	1	1	
Sarah Palfrey Fabyan............	15	(1930-1941)		1	4	10
Wendy Turnbull	15	(1978-1988)	2	2	5	6
Betty Stove	14	(1972-1980)		3	6	5
Helena Sukova	14	(1984-1996)	4	3	4	3
Mary Bevis Hawton	14	(1946-1961)	12	1	1	

WOMEN'S DOUBLES – FINAL LOSSES – INDIVIDUAL

	TOTAL		Aus.	Fre.	Wim.	U.S.
Doris Hart....................	16	(1942-1955)	1	2	4	9
Margaret Smith Court	14	(1960-1975)	4	3	4	3
Billie Jean King	13	(1962-1979)	2	2	2	7
Natalia Zvereva................	13	(1988-1999)	3	4	4	2
Rosie Casals..................	12	(1966-1983)	1	3	2	6
Françoise Durr	11	(1965-1979)		3	6	2
Jana Novotna	11	(1990-1996)	1	2	4	4
Wendy Turnbull	11	(1978-1988)	2	1	4	4
Larisa Savchenko Neiland	10	(1988-1996)		3	5	2
Lindsay Davenport..............	9	(1994-2001)	5	2	1	1
Mary Bevis Hawton	9	(1947-1961)	7	1	1	
Betty Stove	8	(1973-1980)		1	5	2
Louise Brough.................	7	(1947-1954)		1	3	3
Pat Todd.....................	7	(1946-1951)		1	2	4
Pauline Betz	7	(1941-1946)		1	1	5
Shirley Fry	7	(1948-1956)		1	2	4
Claudia Kohde Kilsch............	6	(1982-1988)	3	3		
Gigi Fernandez	6	(1991-1997)	2	1	2	1
Helen Jacobs	6	(1931-1939)		1	3	2
Kathy Jordan	6	(1981-1990)		1	4	1
Lesley Turner	6	(1963-1978)	4	1	1	
Margaret Osborne duPont	6	(1947-1958)		1	3	2
Pam Shriver	6	(1980-1993)	2		1	3
Virginia Wade	6	(1969-1979)		1	1	4

WOMEN'S DOUBLES – TITLES – TEAM

	TOTAL		Aus.	Fre.	Wim.	U.S.
Louise Brough / Margaret Osborne duPont	20	(1942-1957)		3	5	12
Martina Navratilova / Pam Shriver ...	20	(1981-1989)	7	4	5	4
Gigi Fernandez / Natalia Zvereva	14	(1992-1997)	2	5	4	3
Doris Hart / Shirley Fry	11	(1950-1954)		4	3	4
Nancye Bolton / Thelma Long	10	(1936-1952)	10			
Billie Jean King / Rosie Casals	7	(1967-1974)			5	2
Sarah Palfrey / Alice Marble........	6	(1937-1940)			2	4
Suzanne Lenglen / Elizabeth Ryan ...	6	(1919-1925)			6	
Darlene Hard / Maria Bueno	5	(1960-1963)		1	2	2
Margaret Smith Court / Judy Dalton ..	5	(1966-1970)	2	1	1	1
Serena Williams / Venus Williams ...	5	(1999-2002)	1	1	2	1
Anne Smith / Kathy Jordan	4	(1980-1981)	1	1	1	1
Helen Wills Moody / Elizabeth Ryan ..	4	(1927-1932)		2	2	
Jana Novotna / Helena Sukova......	4	(1989-1990)	1	1	2	
Margaret Smith Court / Lesley Turner .	4	(1964-1965)	1	2	1	
Margaret Smith Court / Virginia Wade	4	(1973-1975)	1	1		2
Renee Schuurman / Sandra Reynolds.	4	(1959-1962)	1	3		
Simone Passemard Mathieu / Billie Yorke	4	(1936-1938)		3	1	
Simone Passemard Mathieu / Elizabeth Ryan.............	4	(1933-1934)		2	2	

WOMEN'S DOUBLES – FINAL APPEARANCES – TEAM

	TOTAL		Aus.	Fre.	Wim.	U.S.
Louise Brough / Margaret Osborne DuPont	25	(1942-1957)		4	7	14
Martina Navratilova / Pam Shriver ...	23	(1981-1989)	8	4	6	5
Gigi Fernandez / Natalia Zvereva ...	18	(1992-1997)	3	6	5	4
Doris Hart / Shirley Fry	16	(1949-1955)		4	5	7
Billie Jean King / Rosie Casals	14	(1966-1975)	1	2	5	6
Nancye Bolton / Thelma Long	12	(1936-1952)	12			
Anne Smith / Kathy Jordan	8	(1980-1984)	1	2	4	1
Darlene Hard / Maria Bueno	7	(1960-1963)		2	2	3
Arantxa Sanchez Vicario / Jana Novotna	6	(1994-1996)	1	1	2	2
Billie Jean King / Karen Hantze Susman.....	6	(1961-1965)			3	3
Claudia Kohde Kilsch / Helena Sukova	6	(1984-1988)	2	2	1	1
Doris Hart / Pat Canning Todd	6	(1947-1948)		2	2	2
Helen Jacobs / Sarah Palfrey	6	(1932-1936)		1	1	4

	TOTAL		Aus.	Fre.	Wim.	U.S.
Larisa Savchenko Neiland / Natalia Zvereva	6	(1988-1991)		3	3	
Margaret Smith Court / Judy Dalton	6	(1966-1970)	2	1	2	1
Margaret Smith Court / Lesley Turner	6	(1964-1966)	2	2	1	1
Margaret Smith Court / Robyn Ebbern	6	(1962-1964)	3	1	1	1
Margaret Smith Court / Virginia Wade	6	(1969-1975)	1	1		4
Pauline Betz / Doris Hart	6	(1942-1946)		1	1	4
Renee Schuurman / Sandra Reynolds	6	(1959-1962)	1	3	2	
Sarah Palfrey / Alice Marble	6	(1937-1940)			2	4
Suzanne Lenglen / Elizabeth Ryan	6	(1919-1925)			6	

WOMEN'S DOUBLES – FINAL LOSSES – TEAM

	TOTAL		Aus.	Fre.	Wim.	U.S.
Billie Jean King / Rosie Casals	7	(1966-1975)	1	2		4
Pauline Betz / Doris Hart	6	(1942-1946)		1	1	4
Doris Hart / Shirley Fry	5	(1949-1955)			2	3
Jana Novotna / Larisa Savchenko Neiland	5	(1991-1993)		1	2	2
Lindsay Davenport / Natalia Zvereva	5	(1998-1999)	2	1	1	1
Louise Brough / Margaret Osborne duPont	5	(1947-1954)		1	2	2
Anne Smith / Kathy Jordan	4	(1981-1984)		1	3	
Claudia Kohde Kilsch / Helena Sukova	4	(1984-1988)	2	2		
Doris Hart / Pat Canning Todd	4	(1947-1948)		1	1	2
Françoise Durr / Betty Stove	4	(1973-1975)		1	2	1
Gigi Fernandez / Natalia Zvereva	4	(1995-1997)	1	1	1	1
Larisa Savchenko Neiland / Natalia Zvereva	4	(1988-1991)		2	2	
Rosie Casals / Wendy Turnbull	4	(1980-1983)		1	2	1
Arantxa Sanchez Vicario / Jana Novotna	3	(1994-1996)		1	1	1
Billie Jean King / Karen Hantze Susman	3	(1962-1965)			1	2
Evelyn Colyer / Kitty Godfree	3	(1925-1926)		2	1	
Helen Jacobs / Sarah Palfrey	3	(1934-1936)		1	1	1
Margaret Smith Court / Robyn Ebbern	3	(1963-1964)	1	1	1	
Martina Navratilova / Pam Shriver	3	(1981-1985)	1		1	1
Steffi Graf / Gabriela Sabatini	3	(1986-1989)		3		

MIXED DOUBLES – TITLES – MEN

	TOTAL		Aus.	Fre.	Wim.	U.S.
Ken Fletcher	10	(1963-1968)	2	3	4	1
Owen Davidson	10	(1966-1974)	1	1	4	4
Frank Sedgman	8	(1949-1952)	2	2	2	2
Vic Seixas	8	(1953-1956)		1	4	3
Bob Hewitt	6	(1961-1979)	1	2	2	1
Fred Stolle	6	(1961-1969)	1		3	2
Mark Woodforde	6	(1992-1996)	2	2	1	1
Marty Riessen	6	(1969-1980)		1	1	4
Bill Tilden	5	(1913-1930)		1		4
Eric Sturgess	5	(1947-1950)		2	2	1
Frew McMillan	5	(1966-1981)		1	2	2
Harry Hopman	5	(1930-1939)	4			1
Jack Crawford	5	(1930-1933)	3	1	1	
Jack Hawkes	5	(1922-1928)	3			2
Jean Borotra	5	(1925-1934)	1	2	1	1
Jim Pugh	5	(1988-1990)	3		1	1
Neale Fraser	5	(1956-1962)	1		1	3
Todd Woodbridge	5	(1990-2001)	1		1	3

MIXED DOUBLES – FINAL APPEARANCES – MEN

	TOTAL		Aus.	Fre.	Wim.	U.S.
Ken Fletcher	12	(1963-1968)	2	3	6	1
Bill Tilden	11	(1913-1930)		2		9
Frank Sedgman	11	(1948-1952)	2	3	3	3
Fred Stolle	11	(1961-1975)	2	3	3	3
Frew McMillan	11	(1966-1981)		1	4	6
John Bromwich	11	(1938-1954)	6		3	2

	TOTAL		Aus.	Fre.	Wim.	U.S.
Owen Davidson	11	(1966-1974)	1	2	4	4
Todd Woodbridge	11	(1990-2001)	5	1	1	4
Bob Howe	9	(1956-1962)	1	4	3	1
Rick Leach	9	(1989-1999)	4	1	1	3
Cyril Suk	8	(1991-1998)	2	1	4	1
Harry Hopman	8	(1930-1940)	5		2	1
Jack Crawford	8	(1928-1933)	5	1	2	
Mark Woodforde	8	(1992-1996)	2	2	2	2
Marty Riessen	8	(1969-1980)		1	2	5
Vic Seixas	8	(1953-1956)		1	4	3

MIXED DOUBLES – FINAL LOSSES – MEN

	TOTAL		Aus.	Fre.	Wim.	U.S.
John Bromwich	7	(1938-1954)	5		1	1
Bill Tilden	6	(1916-1927)		1		5
Frew McMillan	6	(1970-1980)			2	4
Todd Woodbridge	6	(1992-2000)	4	1		1
Bob Howe	5	(1956-1961)		2	2	1
Fred Stolle	5	(1962-1975)	1	3		1
Rick Leach	5	(1989-1999)	2	1		2
Cyril Suk	4	(1995-1998)	2		1	1
Dennis Ralston	4	(1961-1969)			2	2
John Fitzgerald	4	(1984-1990)			2	2
Merv Rose	4	(1951-1953)		2	1	1
Bill Talbert	3	(1948-1950)		1		2
Bunny Austin	3	(1929-1934)		1	1	1
Ed Rubinoff	3	(1963-1966)				3
Enrique Morea	3	(1952-1955)			3	
Frank Sedgman	3	(1948-1950)		1	1	1
Harry Hopman	3	(1932-1940)	1		2	
Herbert Morris Tilden	3	(1907-1911)				3
Jack Crawford	3	(1928-1930)	2		1	
Jean Claude Barclay	3	(1969-1972)		3		
Lew Hoad	3	(1952-1956)	1			2
Steve Denton	3	(1981-1984)			2	1
Tony Roche	3	(1965-1969)	1		2	

MIXED DOUBLES – TITLES – WOMEN

	TOTAL		Aus.	Fre.	Wim.	U.S.
Margaret Smith Court	19	(1961-1975)	2	4	5	8
Doris Hart	15	(1949-1955)	2	3	5	5
Billie Jean King	11	(1967-1976)	1	2	4	4
Margaret Osborne duPont	10	(1943-1962)			1	9
Elizabeth Ryan	9	(1919-1933)			7	2
Louise Brough	8	(1942-1950)			4	4
Martina Navratilova	8	(1974-1995)	1	2	3	2
Alice Marble	7	(1936-1940)			3	4
Hazel Hotchkiss Wightman	6	(1909-1920)				6
Anne Smith	5	(1980-1984)		2	1	2
Darlene Hard	5	(1955-1961)		2	3	
Helena Sukova	5	(1991-1997)	1	3	1	
Sarah Palfrey Fabyan	5	(1932-1941)		1		4
Suzanne Lenglen	5	(1920-1926)		2	3	
Thelma Long	5	(1951-1956)	4	1		
Wendy Turnbull	5	(1979-1984)		2	2	1

MIXED DOUBLES – FINAL APPEARANCES – WOMEN

	TOTAL		Aus.	Fre.	Wim.	U.S.
Margaret Smith Court	23	(1961-1975)	3	4	7	9
Doris Hart	19	(1945-1955)	2	4	6	7
Billie Jean King	18	(1966-1983)	1	3	7	7
Elizabeth Ryan	14	(1919-1934)		1	10	3
Margaret Osborne duPont	14	(1943-1962)			2	12
Betty Stove	13	(1971-1981)		2	5	6
Martina Navratilova	12	(1974-1995)	2	2	4	4
Darlene Hard	11	(1955-1963)	1	3	4	3
Louise Brough	11	(1942-1955)			6	5
Sarah Palfrey Fabyan	10	(1932-1941)		1	2	7

	TOTAL		Aus.	Fre.	Wim.	U.S.
Thelma Long	10	(1938-1956)	5	2	1	2
Larisa Savchenko Neiland	9	(1992-1999)	3	3	3	
Lesley Turner	9	(1961-1967)	3	3	2	1
Arantxa Sanchez Vicario	8	(1989-2000)	3	3		2
Elizabeth Sayers Smylie	8	(1983-1991)			3	5
Françoise Durr	8	(1968-1976)		6	1	1
Hazel Hotchkiss Wightman	8	(1909-1927)				8
Helena Sukova	8	(1991-1998)	2	1	3	2
Judy Dalton	8	(1963-1970)	2		2	4
Molla Mallory	8	(1915-1924)				8
Nancye Bolton	8	(1938-1951)	5	1	2	

MIXED DOUBLES – FINAL LOSSES – WOMEN

	TOTAL		Aus.	Fre.	Wim.	U.S.
Betty Stove	9	(1971-1981)		2	3	4
Billie Jean King	7	(1966-1983)		1	3	3
Judy Dalton	7	(1963-1970)	1		2	4
Darlene Hard	6	(1956-1963)	1	1	1	3
Maria Bueno	6	(1958-1967)		1	3	2
Elizabeth Ryan	5	(1920-1934)			2	3
Elizabeth Sayers Smylie	5	(1984-1990)			2	3
Larisa Savchenko Neiland	5	(1994-1999)	1	2	2	
Lesley Turner	5	(1962-1964)	1	3		1
Molla Mallory	5	(1915-1924)				5
Sarah Palfrey Fabyan	5	(1933-1939)			2	3
Thelma Long	5	(1938-1952)	1	1	1	2

MIXED DOUBLES – TITLES – TEAM

	TOTAL		Aus.	Fre.	Wim.	U.S.
Margaret Smith Court / Ken Fletcher	10	(1963-1968)	2	3	4	1
Billie Jean King / Owen Davidson	8	(1967-1974)		1	4	3
Doris Hart / Frank Sedgman	8	(1949-1952)	2	2	2	2
Doris Hart / Vic Seixas	7	(1953-1955)		1	3	3
Margaret Smith Court / Marty Riessen	5	(1969-1975)		1	1	3
Betty Stove / Frew McMillan	4	(1977-1981)			2	2
Jana Novotna / Jim Pugh	4	(1988-1989)	2		1	1
Margaret Osborne duPont / Bill Talbert	4	(1943-1946)				4
Margaret Osborne duPont / Neale Fraser	4	(1958-1962)			1	3
Nancye Bolton / Colin Long	4	(1940-1948)	4			
Nell Hall Hopman / Harry Hopman	4	(1930-1939)	4			
Alice Marble / Don Budge	3	(1937-1938)			2	1
Anne Smith / Kevin Curren	3	(1981-1982)			1	2
Darlene Hard / Rod Laver	3	(1959-1961)		1	2	
Eileen Bennett / Henri Cochet	3	(1927-1929)		2		1
Elizabeth Ryan / Randolph Lycett	3	(1919-1923)			3	
Esna Boyd / Jack Hawkes	3	(1922-1927)	3			
Françoise Durr / Jean Claude Barclay	3	(1968-1973)		3		
Greer Stevens / Bob Hewitt	3	(1977-1979)			2	1
Hazel Hotchkiss Wightman / Wallace Johnson	3	(1909-1920)				3
Helena Sukova / Cyril Suk	3	(1991-1997)		1	2	
Juliette Atkinson / Edwin Fischer	3	(1894-1896)				3
Lesley Turner / Fred Stolle	3	(1961-1964)	1		2	
Louise Brough / John Bromwich	3	(1947-1948)			2	1
Marjorie Cox / Jack Crawford	3	(1931-1933)	3			
Sheila Piercey Summers / Eric Sturgess	3	(1947-1949)			2	1
Thelma Coyne Long / George Worthington	3	(1951-1955)	3			
Wendy Turnbull / John Lloyd	3	(1982-1984)		1	2	

MIXED DOUBLES – FINAL APPEARANCES – TEAM

	TOTAL		Aus.	Fre.	Wim.	U.S.
Doris Hart / Frank Sedgman	11	(1948-1952)	2	3	3	3
Margaret Smith Court / Ken Fletcher	11	(1963-1968)	2	3	5	1
Betty Stove / Frew McMillan	9	(1976-1981)			4	5
Billie Jean King / Owen Davidson	9	(1967-1974)		2	4	3
Doris Hart / Vic Seixas	7	(1953-1955)		1	3	3
Lesley Turner / Fred Stolle	7	(1961-1964)	2	3	2	
Margaret Smith Court / Marty Riessen	7	(1969-1975)		1	2	4
Elizabeth Sayers Smylie / John Fitzgerald	6	(1983-1991)			3	3
Françoise Durr / Jean Claude Barclay	6	(1968-1973)		6		
Margaret Osborne duPont / Bill Talbert	6	(1943-1949)				6
Nancye Bolton / Colin Long	6	(1938-1948)	5		1	
Nell Hall Hopman / Harry Hopman	6	(1930-1940)	5		1	
Elizabeth Ryan / Randolph Lycett	5	(1919-1923)			5	
Marjorie Cox / Jack Crawford	5	(1929-1933)	5			
Esna Boyd / Jack Hawkes	4	(1922-1928)	4			
Helena Sukova / Cyril Suk	4	(1991-1998)	1	1	2	
Jana Novotna / Jim Pugh	4	(1988-1989)	2		1	1
Judy Tegart Dalton / Tony Roche	4	(1965-1969)	2		2	
Louise Brough / John Bromwich	4	(1947-1949)			3	1
Margaret Osborne duPont / Neale Fraser	4	(1958-1962)			1	3
Molla Mallory / Bill Tilden	4	(1921-1924)				4
Wendy Turnbull / John Lloyd	4	(1982-1984)		1	3	

MIXED DOUBLES – FINAL LOSSES – TEAM

	TOTAL		Aus.	Fre.	Wim.	U.S.
Betty Stove / Frew McMillan	5	(1976-1980)			2	3
Elizabeth Sayers Smylie / John Fitzgerald	4	(1984-1990)			2	2
Lesley Turner / Fred Stolle	4	(1962-1964)	1	3		
Doris Hart / Frank Sedgman	3	(1948-1950)		1	1	1
Florence Ballin / Bill Tilden	3	(1916-1919)				3
Françoise Durr / Jean Claude Barclay	3	(1969-1972)		3		
Gigi Fernandez / Cyril Suk	3	(1995-1995)	1		1	1
Joyce Fitch / John Bromwich	3	(1946-1949)	3			
Judy Tegart Dalton / Tony Roche	3	(1965-1969)	1		2	
Amy Williams / Mantle Fielding	2	(1895-1896)				2
Arantxa Sanchez Vicario / Todd Woodbridge	2	(1992-2000)	2			
Barbara Potter / Ferdi Taygan	2	(1982-1983)				2
Billie Jean King / Ray Ruffels	2	(1978-1978)			1	1
Darlene Hard / Bob Howe	2	(1956-1957)		1		1
Dorothy Shepherd Barron / Bunny Austin	2	(1931-1934)			1	1
Edna Wildey / Herbert Morris Tilden	2	(1910-1911)				2
Elizabeth Ryan / Randolph Lycett	2	(1920-1922)			2	
Hazel Hotchkiss Wightman / René Lacoste	2	(1926-1927)				2
Helen Wills Moody / Frank Hunter	2	(1928-1929)		2		
Judy Tegart Dalton / Ed Rubinoff	2	(1963-1964)				2
Larisa Savchenko Neiland / Andrei Olhovskiy	2	(1994-1997)			1	1
Lisa Raymond / Patrick Galbraith	2	(1997-1998)		1		1
Louise Hammond / Ray Little	2	(1908-1909)				2
Margaret Osborne duPont / Bill Talbert	2	(1948-1949)				2
Margaret Osborne duPont / Ken Rosewall	2	(1954-1954)			1	1
Margaret Smith Court / Marty Riessen	2	(1971-1973)			1	1
Marjorie Cox / Jack Crawford	2	(1929-1930)	2			
Molla Mallory / Bill Tilden	2	(1921-1924)				2
Nancye Bolton / Colin Long	2	(1938-1947)	1		1	
Natalia Zvereva / Jim Pugh	2	(1990-1991)			1	1
Nell Hall Hopman / Harry Hopman	2	(1935-1940)	1		1	
Nicole Arendt / Luke Jensen	2	(1996-1996)		1	1	
Olga Morozova / Alex Metreveli	2	(1968-1970)			2	
Renee Schuurman / Rod Laver	2	(1959-1959)	1			1
Sarah Palfrey Cooke / Don Budge	2	(1936-1936)			1	1
Sylvie Jung Henrotin / Martin Legeay	2	(1935-1936)		2		
Zina Garrison / Rick Leach	2	(1990-1993)	2			

Chapter 17

Australian Open

Roy Emerson, 1966
En route to his fourth of five straight and, ultimately, a record six
Australian Open titles.

The Australian Open is the Cinderella of the major championships. For much of its first 75 years it was regarded as the lackluster major. It had neither the history of Wimbledon, the romance of Roland Garros, or the stature of Forest Hills. The tournament was primarily a showcase for the top Australians and any foreigners on hand for Davis Cup, or those willing to hop a steamer for more than a fortnight. Only recently has the Australian Open been received as one of the true belles of the ball.

Today, the makeover is complete. About a half-million boisterous spectators buy tickets during the two-week competition, held during school holidays in January. Organizers call it "the Friendly Slam, the People's Slam," said tournament director Paul McNamee, a former Wimbledon doubles champion. More importantly, after resolving issues around venue, date and prize money during the 1980s, the Australian Open has become a staple for most of the game's biggest stars, where men and women are paid equally.

This renaissance is a remarkable turnaround from the state of the Australian event just 20 years ago. Following a golden tennis era from the mid-1950s to mid-'70s, the Open hit a fallow period that nearly saw it fade into irrelevance. The quality of players—and caliber of play—declined. As a result, the Australian Open was unable to keep pace with the sport's upward trend in prize money. Many top players balked at making the long journey, and the tournament's major championship status was in jeopardy. Lesser lights such as Barbara Jordan could steal away with the championship (1979), while Johan Kriek was even a repeat winner (1981, 1982). But an ambitious building project and clever marketing plan by the proud, sport-crazy Aussies resulted in new facilities, additional sponsors and increased purses, rescuing the tournament.

Over its history, the tournament has been held in five different Australian cities and two in New Zealand. But Melbourne became the permanent home in 1972 and in 1988 the event was moved from the traditional grounds of Kooyong Lawn Tennis Club to Flinders Park (later renamed to Melbourne Park), a spectacular 15-acre grounds that features Rod Laver Arena, a 15,000-seat stadium. The ultra-modern facilities, instrumental in reversing the tournament's downward spiral, boast everything a tennis player could wish for with the exception, perhaps, of grass. When the Open moved from Kooyong it left behind the lovely lawns of the private club in favor of a cushioned hard-court surface called Rebound Ace. Composed of polyurethane and synthetic rubber, the surface is slower than the grass of Wimbledon but faster than the clay at Roland Garros. But the biggest difference between the two surfaces is that the synthetic courts fail to absorb heat, as grass does, leaving many players to cope with hot foot and heat exhaustion under the merciless sun of an Australian summer. Courtside temperatures can exceed 104°F (40°C).

The inaugural Australasian Championship, including New Zealand, was held in 1905, just four years after six British colonies had united as the commonwealth of Australia. The tournament became the Australian Championships in 1925, which it remained until the dawning of the Open era led to its name being changed to the Australian Open in 1969. The tournament moved from city to city in the early days. Melbourne has played host on 47 occasions, followed by Sydney (17), Adelaide (14), Brisbane (8), and Perth (3). Two championships were held in New Zealand, at Christchurch in 1906 and Hastings in 1912.

The tournament, once the almost-exclusive preserve of home-grown talent, has not had a native Australian champion since Chris O'Neil won the women's singles in 1978. The last Australian man to win was Mark Edmondson in 1976. Most successful at home were Roy Emerson with six singles between 1961 and 1967 and Margaret Smith Court with 11 between 1960 and 1973. In more recent years, as modern travel made the Australian Open more accessible to European and American players and with ever-increasing prize money, the incentive to head Down Under once a year has never been greater. Athletes from overseas were infrequent participants before 1969. Only eight foreign men won the championship in the years before World War II: Americans Fred Alexander (1908) and Don Budge (1938), Jean Borotra of France in 1928 and British players James Parke (1912), Gordon Lowe (1915), Algernon Kingscote (1919), Colin Gregory (1929) and Fred Perry (1934). The only two non-Aussie women to win before the war were Great Britain's Dorothy Round and American Dorothy Bundy (1938).

The first Australasian Tennis Championship was held in 1905 at the Warehouseman's Cricket Grounds in St. Kilda Road, Melbourne. Rodney Heath triumphed over a 17-man field. The championship moved to Christchurch the next year, the hometown of 22-year-old Tony Wilding, who learned the game while a student at Cambridge and who would, along with Norman Brookes, become the first tennis stars from Australasia (as the combined Australian-New Zealand federation was called). Wilding beat Harry Parker for the 1906 championship and become the first two-time winner in 1909, before starting a streak of four consecutive Wimbledon singles crowns in 1910. Wilding's stature was such that New Zealand was twice awarded the Australasian Championship and, in 1912, the City of Hastings held a tournament devoid of any Australians. Wilding was killed three years later in action on the Western Front at 31.

The tournament barred females as players until 1922. When the doors finally opened to women, four of them—Margaret Molesworth, Sylvia Lance, Daphne Akhurst and Esna Boyd—dominated the event for the next nine years. Molesworth captured the first two titles, followed by Lance and then Akhurst, who won four times in five years. After losing in the final in the first five events, Boyd finally won in 1927.

On the men's side, the most memorable match of that era came in the 1927 final, when defending champion John Hawkes met Gerald Patterson. The match turned into an exhausting affair of 71 games to decide a champion, a tourney record. Patterson outlasted Hawkes 3-6, 6-4, 3-6, 18-16, 6-3, saving four match points at 12-13 and another at 15-16 in the fourth set.

The 1930s ushered in the era of Gentleman Jack Crawford. Beginning in 1931, he made six consecutive appearances in the final, winning four. His losses came in 1934 to the great Fred Perry and in 1936 to Adrian Quist, who would beat Crawford again in the 1940 final. Crawford's seven final appearances stood as a tournament record until equaled by John Bromwich in 1949. In a rare husband-wife occurrence, Crawford's wife, Marjorie Cox Crawford, played in the 1931 women's final, losing to Coral Buttsworth. The Crawfords were certainly compatible on the court—they won the mixed doubles in 1931, 1932 and 1933.

The Championship was not held from 1941 to 1946. In 1948, Quist took a third men's crown, making him the second man to win a major tournament before and after the war, during which he served in the Australian army. Quist holds the men's tournament record of 13 titles, 10 in doubles (eight of them consecutively) from 1938-50, with right-court partner Jack Bromwich. But the first genuine Aussie star of the post-war era emerged in 1949-50, when Frank Sedgman won two consecutive titles, defeating Bromwich in the final both years. Sedgman's 1949 victory became a springboard to 21 major championship titles over four seasons.

Meanwhile, Nancye Wynne Bolton emerged as the first post-war women's star. After losing in the 1936 final as a teenager, when she competed as Nancye Wynne, she won the singles crown in 1937 and 1940. She married George Bolton during the war but the Royal Australian air force sergeant was killed in action in 1942, leaving her a widowed mother of a young daughter. When the tournament resumed in 1946, she rang up three straight wins, giving her four consecutive titles dating back to 1940. Doris Hart ended Bolton's bid for five straight, but she won again in 1951. She ended her career with 20 titles: six singles, 10 doubles (with Thelma Long, nee Coyne), and four mixed (with Colin Long).

One of the most extraordinary champions in tournament history was Ken Rosewall. He arrived in 1953 as a 5-foot-7, 135-pound grocer's son from Sydney and became the youngest men's champion at 18 years, 2 months. He won again in 1955, lost in the final to Lew Hoad in 1956, and turned pro later that season. It would be 16 years before he returned to the final—by then the tournament had become the Australian Open. In 1971 he defeated Arthur Ashe for his third singles title, defending successfully in 1972 to become the oldest men's champion at 37 years, 2 months.

The 1960s are widely regarded as Australia's Golden Age and nowhere was that more evident than at the national championships. Rod Laver, Roy Emerson and Margaret Smith were almost unbeatable at home, combining to win 17 of the 20 men's and women's singles titles, plus 13 doubles, from 1960 to 1969.

Smith was a gangly 18-year-old from the country town of Albury in New South Wales when she became women's champion in 1960, defeating 18-year-old Jan Lehane in the youngest of major-finals. She also defeated Lehane in 1961, 1962 (needing just 14 games for a record 6-0, 6-2 victory) and 1963. Smith then conquered Lesley Turner, Maria Bueno and Nancy Richey (by walkover) to complete an unmatched string of seven consecutive titles. After marrying and temporarily retiring, she returned as Margaret Court to win four more singles titles in the Open Era. Her 11 singles titles seem an unassailable record.

Laver won in 1960, lost in the final to Emerson in 1961 and began a successful Grand Slam in 1962 by defeating Emerson in the final. After that season, Laver turned professional, leaving the stage to Emerson, who took advantage of Laver's absence to win five in a row starting in 1963. His six singles titles lead all men. Only Crawford, Rosewall and Pat O'Hara Wood before him managed as many as four, a level Andre Agassi reached by winning his fourth in 2003. With the advent of the Australian Open, Laver was welcomed back in 1969 and, to the delight of Brisbane's Milton Ground Park patrons, reclaimed the title he had vacated seven years earlier.

In 1971, a toothsome aborigine teenager named Evonne Goolagong made an impressive Open debut. She paired with Court to win the doubles title (a 6-0, 6-0 whitewashing) and then lost to her partner in the women's final. Goolagong, the daughter of an itinerant sheep shearer, won at Roland Garros and Wimbledon later that year but continued for two years as an Australian Open bridesmaid, losing finals in 1972 to Virginia Wade and in 1973 to Court. But the popular Sydney native broke through in grand style in 1974, defeating Chris Evert in the final, then successfully defending her title in 1975 and 1976 and winning a fourth one at the December 1977 Open. She added doubles crowns in each of the four years she won singles.

In 1973, Sydney-born John Newcombe finally managed to win a national singles crown, but a 1975 ill-tempered showdown with Jimmy Connors was more memorable. Prior to the final, Connors took exception to statements by Newcombe. "He should do more talking with his racquet than with his mouth," Connors said. "Every time I reach a final, Newcombe is missing." Newcombe responded with a four-set victory. He was back in the final in 1976, facing unseeded compatriot Mark Edmondson in only the second all-Australian final in 11 years. In one of the great upsets, No. 212 Edmondson —lowest ranked of all major champs—became the first unseeded men's champion. During the trophy presentation, however, he dropped the prize and it broke into pieces on the ground. No Australian man has won since.

The 1980s marked the Europeanization of the Australian Open. For eight consecutive years beginning in 1983, the men's title was won by a player from Europe. Swedes won five times—Mats Wilander thrice and Stefan Edberg twice—while Czech Ivan Lendl also won twice and German Boris Becker once. The European domination was even more pronounced on the women's side, where two wins by Evert were all that prevented European-born players from winning every tournament between 1980 and 1999. Steffi Graf and Monica Seles each won four times, followed by Martina Navratilova (3), Martina Hingis (3) and Hana Mandlikova (2).

Most notable among those wins was Hingis, the Swiss teenager who became the youngest women's champion at 16 years, 3 months, with a straight-sets win over Mary Pierce in 1997. A year earlier, Seles had been a popular champion. Winner of three straight Opens beginning in 1991, she skipped Australia in 1994 and 1995 while recuperating from a stab wound. Her triumph over Anke Huber would be her eighth, and last, major championship.

Among the most memorable non-winners at the Australian Open is John McEnroe. The talented American holds the distinction of being the first player tossed out of the tournament. Facing Mikael Pernfors in a fourth-round match in 1990, McEnroe yelled at a mother comforting a crying baby in the stands and threw his racquet so hard to the ground that it bounced over his head. He was penalized a point for racquet abuse, which prompted a legendary McEnroe tirade. One particularly vile curse was clearly audible to the ticket buyers and those watching on television. The supervisor awarded the match to Pernfors by default, the first such decision in the history of major championship events.

Until recently, the Australian Open was unkind to American men. In the early years of the Open era, Ashe won in 1970, Connors in 1974 and then there was a six-year wait until Brian Teacher in 1980. His victory was followed by a 12-year American drought, before Jim Courier won back to back in 1992 and 1993, launching a 12-year run in which American men won eight times. Pete Sampras took the title in 1994 and 1997, but the most impressive American is Agassi, a four-time winner. He beat Sampras in the 1995 final and has won three of the past four tournaments. In 2003, at age 33, Agassi became the oldest winner since Ken Rosewall's 1972 victory at age 37 by thumping Rainer Schuettler of Germany 6-2, 6-2, 6-1. It was the most one-sided men's final in 77 years.

The new millennium has also been kind to American women. When Lindsay Davenport defeated Hingas in the 2000 final, she became the first U.S.-born champion since Evert in 1974. Jennifer Capriati followed suit by defeating Hingis in both the 2001 and 2002 final. Prior to 2003, neither of the supremely capable Williams sisters, Venus and Serena, had ever reached the finals at Melbourne Park. So, as if to make up for lost time, they both did in 2003. It was their fourth consecutive showdown in a major championship, all won by the younger Serena, who completed her so-called Serena Slam by defeating Venus 7-6 (7-4), 3-6, 6-4.

Finally, one more familiar face enjoyed success at the 2003 Open, as Navratilova teamed with Leander Paes of India for the mixed doubles championship. "This goes beyond any wildest dream," she said. The 57th major championship title of her career made Martina the oldest winner of a major championship event, at 46 years, 3 months.

Australian Open – Champions

Year	Men's Singles	Women's Singles	Men's Doubles	Women's Doubles	Mixed Doubles
2003	Andre Agassi	Serena Williams	Michael Llodra / Fabrice Santoro	Serena Williams / Venus Williams	Martina Navratilova / Leander Paes
2002	Thomas Johansson	Jennifer Capriati	Daniel Nestor / Mark Knowles	Martina Hingis / Anna Kournikova	Daniela Hantuchova / Kevin Ullyett
2001	Andre Agassi	Jennifer Capriati	Jonas Bjorkman / Todd Woodbridge	Serena Williams / Venus Williams	Corina Morariu / Ellis Ferreira
2000	Andre Agassi	Lindsay Davenport	Rick Leach / Ellis Ferreira	Lisa Raymond / Rennae Stubbs	Rennae Stubbs / Jared Palmer
1999	Yevgeny Kafelnikov	Martina Hingis	Patrick Rafter / Jonas Bjorkman	Martina Hingis / Anna Kournikova	Mariaan de Swardt / David Adams
1998	Petr Korda	Martina Hingis	Jonas Bjorkman / Jacco Eltingh	Martina Hingis / Mirjana Lucic	Venus Williams / Justin Gimelstob
1997	Pete Sampras	Martina Hingis	Todd Woodbridge / Mark Woodforde	Martina Hingis / Natalia Zvereva	Manon Bollegraf / Rick Leach
1996	Boris Becker	Monica Seles	Stefan Edberg / Petr Korda	Chanda Rubin / Arantxa Sanchez Vicario	Larisa Savchenko Neiland / Mark Woodforde
1995	Andre Agassi	Mary Pierce	Jared Palmer / Richey Reneberg	Jana Novotna / Arantxa Sanchez Vicario	Natalia Zvereva / Rick Leach
1994	Pete Sampras	Steffi Graf	Jacco Eltingh / Paul Haarhuis	Gigi Fernandez / Natalia Zvereva	Larisa Savchenko Neiland / Andrei Olhovskiy
1993	Jim Courier	Monica Seles	Danie Visser / Laurie Warder	Gigi Fernandez / Natalia Zvereva	Arantxa Sanchez Vicario / Todd Woodbridge
1992	Jim Courier	Monica Seles	Todd Woodbridge / Mark Woodforde	Arantxa Sanchez Vicario / Helena Sukova	Nicole Provis / Mark Woodforde
1991	Boris Becker	Monica Seles	Scott Davis / David Pate	Patty Fendick / Mary Joe Fernandez	Jo Durie / Jeremy Bates
1990	Ivan Lendl	Steffi Graf	Pieter Aldrich / Danie Visser	Jana Novotna / Helena Sukova	Natalia Zvereva / Jim Pugh
1989	Ivan Lendl	Steffi Graf	Rick Leach / Jim Pugh	Martina Navratilova / Pam Shriver	Jana Novotna / Jim Pugh
1988	Mats Wilander	Steffi Graf	Rick Leach / Jim Pugh	Martina Navratilova / Pam Shriver	Jana Novotna / Jim Pugh
1987	Stefan Edberg	Hana Mandlikova	Stefan Edberg / Anders Jarryd	Martina Navratilova / Pam Shriver	Zina Garrison / Sherwood Stewart
1986	Not held – Date change	Not held – Date change	Not held – Date change	Not held – Date change	Not held – Date change
1985	Stefan Edberg	Martina Navratilova	Paul Annacone / Christo Van Rensburg	Martina Navratilova / Pam Shriver	Not held
1984	Mats Wilander	Chris Evert Lloyd	Mark Edmondson / Sherwood Stewart	Martina Navratilova / Pam Shriver	Not held
1983	Mats Wilander	Martina Navratilova	Mark Edmondson / Paul McNamee	Martina Navratilova / Pam Shriver	Not held
1982	Johan Kriek	Chris Evert Lloyd	John Alexander / John Fitzgerald	Martina Navratilova / Pam Shriver	Not held
1981	Johan Kriek	Martina Navratilova	Mark Edmondson / Kim Warwick	Kathy Jordan / Anne Smith	Not held
1980	Brian Teacher	Hana Mandlikova	Mark Edmondson / Kim Warwick	Martina Navratilova / Betsy Nagelsen	Not held
1979	Guillermo Vilas	Barbara Jordan	Peter McNamara / Paul McNamee	Judy Chaloner / Dianne Evers	Not held
1978	Guillermo Vilas	Chris O'Neil	Wojtek Fibak / Kim Warwick	Betsy Nagelsen / Renata Tomanova	Not held
1977*	Roscoe Tanner	Kerry Melville Reid	Arthur Ashe / Tony Roche	Dianne Balestrat Fromholtz / Helen Gourlay Cawley	Not held
1977*	Vitas Gerulaitis	E. Goolagong Cawley	Ray Ruffels / Allan Stone Ray Ruffels / Allan Stone	Evonne Goolagong Cawley / Helen Gourlay Cawley	Not held
1976	Mark Edmondson	E. Goolagong Cawley	John Newcombe / Tony Roche	Evonne Goolagong / Helen Gourlay	Not held
1975	John Newcombe	Evonne Goolagong	John Alexander / Phil Dent	Evonne Goolagong / Peggy Michel	Not held
1974	Jimmy Connors	Evonne Goolagong	Ross Case / Geoff Masters	Evonne Goolagong / Peggy Michel	Not held
1973	John Newcombe	Margaret Smith Court	Mal Anderson / John Newcombe	Margaret Smith Court / Virginia Wade	Not held
1972	Ken Rosewall	Virginia Wade	Owen Davidson / Ken Rosewall	Kerry Harris / Helen Gourlay	Not held
1971	Ken Rosewall	Margaret Smith Court	John Newcombe / Tony Roche	Margaret Smith Court Evonne Goolagong	Not held
1970	Arthur Ashe	Margaret Smith Court	Bob Lutz / Stan Smith	Margaret Smith Court / Judy Tegart Dalton	Not held
1969	Rod Laver	Margaret Smith Court	Roy Emerson / Rod Laver	Margaret Smith Court / Judy Tegart Dalton	Margaret Smith Court / Marty Riessen
1968	Bill Bowrey	Billie Jean King	Dick Crealy / Allan Stone	Karen Krantzcke / Kerry Melville	Billie Jean King / Dick Crealy
1967	Roy Emerson	Nancy Richey	John Newcombe / Tony Roche	Lesley Turner / Judy Tegart Dalton	Lesley Turner / Owen Davidson
1966	Roy Emerson	Margaret Smith	Roy Emerson / Fred Stolle	Carole Caldwell Graebner / Nancy Richey	Judy Tegart / Tony Roche
1965	Roy Emerson	Margaret Smith	John Newcombe / Tony Roche	Margaret Smith / Lesley Turner	Margaret Smith / John Newcombe
1964	Roy Emerson	Margaret Smith	Bob Hewitt / Fred Stolle	Judy Tegart Dalton / Lesley Turner	Margaret Smith / Ken Fletcher
1963	Roy Emerson	Margaret Smith	Bob Hewitt / Fred Stolle	Margaret Smith / Robyn Ebbern	Margaret Smith / Ken Fletcher
1962	Rod Laver	Margaret Smith	Roy Emerson / Neale Fraser	Margaret Smith / Robyn Ebbern	Lesley Turner / Fred Stolle
1961	Roy Emerson	Margaret Smith	Rod Laver / Bob Mark	Mary Carter Reitano / Margaret Smith	Jan Lehane / Bob Hewitt
1960	Rod Laver	Margaret Smith	Rod Laver / Bob Mark	Maria Bueno / Christine Truman	Jan Lehane / Trevor Fancutt
1959	Alex Olmedo	Mary Carter Reitano	Rod Laver / Bob Mark	Renee Schuurman / Sandra Reynolds	Sandra Reynolds / Bob Mark

Year	Men's Singles	Women's Singles	Men's Doubles	Women's Doubles	Mixed Doubles
1958	Ashley Cooper	Angela Mortimer	Ashley Cooper / Neale Fraser	Mary Bevis Hawton / Thelma Coyne Long	Mary Bevis Hawton / Bob Howe
1957	Ashley Cooper	Shirley Fry	Neale Fraser / Lew Hoad	Althea Gibson / Shirley Fry	Fay Muller / Mal Anderson
1956	Lew Hoad	Mary Carter	Lew Hoad / Ken Rosewall	Mary Bevis Hawton / Thelma Coyne Long	Beryl Penrose / Neale Fraser
1955	Ken Rosewall	Beryl Penrose	Vic Seixas / Tony Trabert	Mary Bevis Hawton / Beryl Penrose	Thelma Coyne Long / George Worthington
1954	Merv Rose	Thelma Long	Rex Hartwig / Merv Rose	Mary Bevis Hawton / Beryl Penrose	Thelma Coyne Long / Rex Hartwig
1953	Ken Rosewall	Maureen Connolly	Lew Hoad / Ken Rosewall	Maureen Connolly / Julia Sampson	Julia Sampson / Rex Hartwig
1952	Ken McGregor	Thelma Long	Ken McGregor / Frank Sedgman	Thelma Coyne Long / Nancye Wynne Bolton	Thelma Coyne Long / George Worthington
1951	Richard Savitt	Nancye Bolton	Ken McGregor / Frank Sedgman	Thelma Coyne Long / Nancye Wynne Bolton	Thelma Coyne Long / George Worthington
1950	Frank Sedgman	Louise Brough	John Bromwich / Adrian Quist	Louise Brough / Doris Hart	Doris Hart / Frank Sedgman
1949	Frank Sedgman	Doris Hart	John Bromwich / Adrian Quist	Thelma Coyne Long / Nancye Wynne Bolton	Doris Hart / Frank Sedgman
1948	Adrian Quist	Nancye Bolton	John Bromwich / Adrian Quist	Thelma Coyne Long / Nancye Wynne Bolton	Nancye Wynne Bolton / Colin Long
1947	Dinny Pails	Nancye Wynne Bolton	John Bromwich / Adrian Quist	Thelma Coyne Long / Nancye Wynne Bolton	Nancye Wynne Bolton / Colin Long
1946	John Bromwich	Nancye Wynne Bolton	John Bromwich / Adrian Quist	Joyce Fitch / Mary Bevis	Nancye Wynne Bolton / Colin Long
1941-45		Not held – WW II			
1940	Adrian Quist	Nancye Wynne	John Bromwich / Adrian Quist	Thelma Coyne Long / Nancye Wynne	Nancye Wynne / Colin Long
1939	John Bromwich	Emily Hood Westacott	John Bromwich / Adrian Quist	Thelma Coyne Long / Nancye Wynne	Nell Hall Hopman / Harry Hopman
1938	Don Budge	Dorothy Bundy	John Bromwich / Adrian Quist	Thelma Coyne Long / Nancye Wynne	Margaret Wilson / John Bromwich
1937	Viv McGrath	Nancye Wynne	Adrian Quist / Don Turnbull	Thelma Coyne Long / Nancye Wynne	Nell Hall Hopman / Harry Hopman
1936	Adrian Quist	Joan Hartigan	Adrian Quist / Don Turnbull	Thelma Coyne Long / Nancye Wynne	Nell Hall Hopman / Harry Hopman
1935	Jack Crawford	Dorothy Round	Jack Crawford / Viv McGrath	Evelyn Dearman / Nancy Lyle	Louie Bickerton / Christian Boussus
1934	Fred Perry	Joan Hartigan	Fred Perry / Pat Hughes	Mall Molesworth / Emily Hood Westacott	Joan Hartigan / Gar Moon
1933	Jack Crawford	Joan Hartigan	Keith Gledhill / Ellsworth Vines	Mall Molesworth / Emily Hood Westacott	Marjorie Cox Crawford / Jack Crawford
1932	Jack Crawford	C. McInnes Buttsworth	Jack Crawford / Gar Moon	Coral McInnes Buttsworth / Marjorie Cox	Marjorie Cox Crawford / Jack Crawford
1931	Jack Crawford	C. McInnes Buttsworth	Charles Donohoe / Ray Dunlop	Daphne Akhurst Cozens / Louie Bickerton	Marjorie Cox Crawford / Jack Crawford
1930	Gar Moon	Daphne Akhurst	Jack Crawford / Harry Hopman	Mall Molesworth / Emily Hood	Nell Hall / Harry Hopman
1929	Colin Gregory	Daphne Akhurst	Jack Crawford / Harry Hopman	Daphne Akhurst / Louie Bickerton	Daphne Akhurst / Gar Moon
1928	Jean Borotra	Daphne Akhurst	Jean Borotra / Jacques Brugnon	Daphne Akhurst / Esna Boyd	Daphne Akhurst / Jean Borotra
1927	Gerald Patterson	Esna Boyd	Jack Hawkes / Gerald Patterson	Meryl O'Hara Wood / Louie Bickerton	Esna Boyd / Jack Hawkes
1926	Jack Hawkes	Daphne Akhurst	Jack Hawkes / Gerald Patterson	Meryl O'Hara Wood / Esna Boyd	Esna Boyd / Jack Hawkes
1925	James Anderson	Daphne Akhurst	Pat O'Hara Wood / Gerald Patterson	Sylvia Lance Harper / Daphne Akhurst	Daphne Akhurst / John Willard
1924	James Anderson	Sylvia Lance	James Anderson / Norman Brookes	Daphne Akhurst / Sylvia Lance	Daphne Akhurst / John Willard
1923	Pat O'Hara Wood	Mall Molesworth	Pat O'Hara Wood / Bert St. John	Esna Boyd / Sylvia Lance	Sylvia Lance / Horrie Rice
1922	James Anderson	Mall Molesworth	Jack Hawkes / Gerald Patterson	Esna Boyd / Marjorie Mountain	Esna Boyd / Jack Hawkes
1921	Rhys Gemmell		S. H. Eaton / Rhys Gemmell		
1920	Pat O'Hara Wood		Pat O'Hara Wood / Ron Thomas		
1919	Algernon Kingscote		Pat O'Hara Wood / Ron Thomas		
1916-18		Not held – WW I			
1915	Gordon Lowe		Horrie Rice / Clarrie Todd		
1914	Arthur O'Hara Wood		Ashley Campbell / Gerald Patterson		
1913	Ernest Parker		Alf Hedemann / Ernest Parker		
1912	Jim Parke		Jim Parke / Charles Dixon		
1911	Norman Brookes		Rodney Heath / Randolph Lycett		
1910	Rodney Heath		Ashley Campbell / Horrie Rice		
1909	Anthony Wilding		J. P. Keane / Ernest Parker		
1908	Fred Alexander		Fred Alexander / Alfred Dunlop		
1907	Horrie Rice		Bill Gregg / Harry Parker		
1906	Anthony Wilding		Rodney Heath / Tony Wilding		
1905	Rodney Heath		Randolph Lycett / Tom Tachell		

* Two tournaments were held in 1977, the first, won by Gerulaitis, in January; the second, won by Tanner, in December. The tournament reverted back to January in 1987. No tournament was held in 1986 to accomodate the date change.

Australian Open – Tournament Results

(**Legend: F:** Final; **S:** Semi-final; **Q:** Quarter-final; **Set:** S1, S2, S3, S4, S5)

Men's Singles

Rd	Winner	Defeated	S1	S2	S3	S4	S5
1905 *(Melbourne)*							
F	**Rodney Heath**	**Arthur Curtis**	**4-6**	**6-3**	**6-4**	**6-4**	
S	Rodney Heath	Randolph Lycett	6-3	9-11	6-3	6-1	
S	Arthur Curtis	Alf Dunlop	4-6	11-9	6-3	6-4	
Q	Rodney Heath	H. Turner	6-2	6-1	6-2		
Q	Randolph Lycett	G. W. Wright			(walkover)		
Q	Arthur Curtis	Eric Pockley	3-6	7-5	6-3	6-4	
Q	Alf Dunlop	Reggie Fraser	6-4	6-3	6-2		
1906 *(Christchurch, N.Z.)*							
F	**Anthony Wilding**	**Francis Fisher**	**6-0**	**6-4**	**6-4**		
S	Anthony Wilding	Harry Parker	6-4	7-5	3-6	6-0	
S	Francis Fisher	T. Quill	6-4	3-6	6-2	6-3	
Q	Anthony Wilding	C. C. Cox	6-2	6-2	6-1		
Q	Harry Parker	R. D. Harman	6-1	6-2	6-0		
Q	Francis Fisher	Rodney Heath	2-6	7-5	6-1	5-7	6-2
Q	T. Quill	W. Goss			(walkover)		
1907 *(Brisbane)*							
F	**Horrie Rice**	**Harry Parker**	**6-3**	**6-4**	**6-4**		
S	Horrie Rice	Bill Gregg	6-0	6-2	3-6	6-4	
S	Harry Parker	Eric Pockley	8-6	6-0	2-6	6-3	
S	Horrie Rice	Macauley Turner	4-6	6-1	6-0	6-3	
Q	Bill Gregg	Mr. Turton	6-2	2-6	6-2	2-6	7-5
Q	Harry Parker	V. Rudder	6-1	6-1	6-3		
Q	Eric Pockley	George Wright	8-6	6-2	7-5		
1908 *(Sydney)*							
F	**Fred Alexander**	**Alfred Dunlop**	**3-6**	**3-6**	**6-0**	**6-2**	**6-3**
S	Fred Alexander	Harry Parker	6-3	8-6	1-6	6-0	
S	Alfred Dunlop	Eric Pockley	6-2	6-3	6-2		
S	Fred Alexander	Harry Gibbes	6-2	6-1	6-1		
Q	Harry Parker	Mr. Cupples	6-1	6-3	6-2		
Q	Alfred Dunlop	Stanley Doust	6-3	6-4	4-6	8-6	
Q	Eric Pockley	P. Colquhoum	7-5	1-6	7-5	7-5	
1909 *(Perth)*							
F	**Anthony Wilding**	**Ernest Parker**	**6-1**	**7-5**	**6-2**		
S	Anthony Wilding	R. Kelsey	6-0	6-0	6-1		
S	Ernest Parker	G. O'Dea	6-1	6-2	6-0		
Q	Anthony Wilding	R. Eagle	6-0	6-1	6-0		
Q	R. Kelsey	I. Gibbs	6-4	6-4	2-1		(retired)
Q	Ernest Parker	I. Gaze	6-1	6-0	6-0		
Q	G. O'Dea	L. Crooks	3-6	6-3	6-4	6-3	
1910 *(Adelaide)*							
F	**Rodney Heath**	**Horrie Rice**	**6-4**	**6-3**	**6-2**		
S	Rodney Heath	R. Reid	6-0	6-3	7-5		
S	Horrie Rice	R. Bowen	6-3	6-1	3-6	7-5	
Q	Rodney Heath	Harry Parker	6-2	6-4	9-7		
Q	R. Reid	R. Paxton	6-0	6-3	6-1		
Q	Horrie Rice	Ashley Campbell	6-2	6-2	4-6	6-2	
Q	R. Bowen	H. Hunt	11-9	6-4	6-3		

Rd	Winner	Defeated	S1	S2	S3	S4	S5
1911 *(Melbourne)*							
F	**Norman Brookes**	**Horrie Rice**	**6-1**	**6-2**	**6-3**		
S	Norman Brookes	R. Rolland	7-5	6-3	6-1		
S	Horrie Rice	Arthur O'Hara Wood	7-5	6-3	2-6	6-1	
Q	Norman Brookes	Rodney Heath	4-6	6-4	6-2	6-3	
Q	R. Rolland	F. Down	6-3	6-4	6-3		
Q	Horrie Rice	Ron Thomas	6-1	6-4	6-3		
Q	Arthur O'Hara Wood	S. England	6-1	6-2	6-3		
Rd	Winner	Defeated	S1	S2	S3	S4	S5
1912 *(Hastings, N.Z.)*							
F	**Jim Parke**	**Alfred Beamish**	**3-6**	**6-3**	**1-6**	**6-1**	**7-5**
S	Jim Parke	R. Swanston	6-2	6-2	6-3		
S	Alfred Beamish	H. Brown	6-1	6-1	6-2		
Q	Jim Parke	Geoff Ollivier	6-4	6-1	8-6		
Q	R. Swanston	W. Pearce	6-2	6-1	6-2		
Q	Alfred Beamish	Charles Dixon	4-6	3-6	6-2	7-5	6-1
Q	H. Brown	R. Harman	6-4	6-1	6-3		
1913 *(Perth)*							
F	**Ernest Parker**	**Harry Parker**	**2-6**	**6-1**	**6-3**	**6-2**	
S	Ernest Parker	G. Thomas	6-2	6-2	6-3		
S	Harry Parker	Ron Taylor	6-2	4-6	2-6	6-0	6-1
Q	Ernest Parker	E. Stokes	6-4	6-3	6-2		
Q	G. Thomas	Mr. Kent	3-6	6-3	6-4	6-0	
Q	Harry Parker	A. Hedeman	2-6	6-3	6-1	6-3	
Q	Ron Taylor	A. Leschen	6-4	6-1	6-1		
1914 *(Melbourne)*							
F	**Arthur O'Hara Wood**	**Gerald Patterson**	**6-4**	**6-3**	**5-7**	**6-1**	
S	Arthur O'Hara Wood	Rupert Wertheim	6-3	6-0	3-6	6-4	
S	Gerald Patterson	Rodney Heath	6-3	6-2	6-4		
Q	Arthur O'Hara Wood	C. Buckley	6-4	6-2	6-3		
Q	Rupert Wertheim	Ron Taylor	6-3	6-4	3-6	6-3	
Q	Gerald Patterson	L. Rainey	6-3	6-4	6-2		
Q	Rodney Heath	Ron Thomas	6-1	3-6	6-2	6-3	
1915 *(Brisbane)*							
F	**Gordon Lowe**	**Horrie Rice**	**4-6**	**6-1**	**6-1**	**6-4**	
S	Gordon Lowe	Bert St. John	3-6	6-3	7-5	7-5	
S	Horrie Rice	Clarrie Todd	4-6	2-6	8-6	6-1	7-5
Q	Gordon Lowe	R. Highett	6-3	6-2	6-3		
Q	Bert St. John	R. Goodman	6-3	6-3	6-2		
Q	Clarrie Todd	W. Smith	6-2	6-3	6-2		
Q	Horrie Rice	F. Lendrum	6-3	6-2	6-3		
1916-18 *Not held – WW I*							
1919 *(Sydney)*							
F	**Algernon Kingscote**	**Eric Pockley**	**6-4**	**6-0**	**6-3**		
S	Algernon Kingscote	James Anderson	3-6	7-5	6-4	6-3	
S	Eric Pockley	Arthur Lowe	6-4	6-3	6-1		
Q	Algernon Kingscote	Alfred Beamish			(walkover)		
Q	James Anderson	Henry Marsh	6-1	6-8	6-4	6-3	
Q	Arthur Lowe	Pat O'Hara Wood	6-3	6-2	6-2		
Q	Eric Pockley	L. Darby	6-3	6-4	6-0		

1920 (Adelaide)

Rd	Winner	Defeated	S1	S2	S3	S4	S5
F	**Pat O'Hara Wood**	**Ron Thomas**	6-3	4-6	6-8	6-1	6-3
S	Pat O'Hara Wood	Ron Taylor	6-3	6-1	7-5		
S	Ron Thomas	Horrie Rice	6-4	4-6	6-1	5-7	6-2
Q	Pat O'Hara Wood	B. Utz	6-1	6-1	6-2		
Q	Ron Taylor	A. Scott	3-6	3-6	6-2	6-2	6-3
Q	Horrie Rice	C. Gurner	6-2	6-2	6-2		
Q	Ron Thomas	G. O'Dea	6-0	6-2	6-4		

1921 (Perth)

Rd	Winner	Defeated	S1	S2	S3	S4	S5
F	**Rhys Gemmell**	**Alf Hedemann**	7-5	6-1	6-4		
S	Rhys Gemmell	Mr. Treloar	6-2	6-1	6-3		
S	Alf Hedeman	Mr. McDougall	6-4	3-6	6-1	6-2	
S	Rhys Gemmell	E. Barker	6-0	6-3	6-0		
Q	Mr. Treloar	Mr. Henville	6-3	6-2	6-2		
Q	Mr. McDougall	W. Hayman	2-6	12-10	6-2	6-0	
Q	Alf Hedeman	N. Brearley	6-2	6-1	6-3		

1922 (Sydney)

Rd	Winner	Defeated	S1	S2	S3	S4	S5
F	**James Anderson**	**Gerald Patterson**	6-0	3-6	3-6	6-3	6-2
S	James Anderson	Norman Peach	1-6	6-2	6-2	6-4	
S	Gerald Patterson	Jack Hawkes	8-6	4-6	7-5	3-6	10-8
Q	James Anderson	W. Dive	7-5	6-4	6-3		
Q	Norman Peach	Jack Clemenger	6-1	6-1	9-7		
Q	Jack Hawkes	A. Huthnance		(walkover)			
Q	Gerald Patterson	E. Jones	6-4	5-7	6-1	10-8	

1923 (Brisbane)

Rd	Winner	Defeated	S1	S2	S3	S4	S5
F	**Pat O'Hara Wood**	**Bert St. John**	6-1	6-1	6-3		
S	Pat O'Hara Wood	E. Jordan	6-1	6-1	6-1		
S	Bert St. John	Horrie Rice	9-7	3-6	7-5	6-3	
Q	Pat O'Hara Wood	Mr. Cory	6-0	6-4	6-1		
Q	E. Jordan	L. Oxenham	5-7	3-6	6-3	6-4	7-5
Q	Horrie Rice	C. Ferguson	6-2	6-2	6-2		
Q	Bert St. John	Dudley Bullough	6-4	6-2	6-2		

1924 (Melbourne)

Rd	Winner	Defeated	S1	S2	S3	S4	S5
F	**James Anderson**	**Bob Schlesinger**	6-3	6-4	3-6	5-7	6-3
S	James Anderson	Gar Hone	6-2	6-3	6-2		
S	Bob Schlesinger	Fred Kalms	7-5	8-6	6-0		
Q	James Anderson	Cecil Stuart	8-6	6-1	6-2		
Q	Gar Hone	G. Dickinson	7-5	6-0	6-4		
Q	Fred Kalms	Rupert Wertheim	5-7	5-7	6-1	6-1	8-6
Q	Bob Schlesinger	Ian McInness	5-7	6-3	6-3	9-7	

1925 (Sydney)

Rd	Winner	Defeated	S1	S2	S3	S4	S5
F	**James Anderson**	**Gerald Patterson**	11-9	2-6	6-2	6-3	
S	James Anderson	Pat O'Hara Wood	6-2	6-3	6-3		
S	Gerald Patterson	Bob Schlesinger	6-4	6-4	4-6	6-4	
Q	James Anderson	Gar Hone	6-2	6-0	8-6		
Q	Pat O'Hara Wood	Fred Kalms	6-3	6-2	6-3		
Q	Bob Schlesinger	Norman Peach	6-3	6-2	6-2		
Q	Gerald Patterson	Aubrey Willard	6-0	6-2	9-7		

1926 (Adelaide)

Rd	Winner	Defeated	S1	S2	S3	S4	S5
F	**Jack Hawkes**	**Jim Willard**	6-1	6-3	6-1		
S	Jack Hawkes	James Anderson	6-8	7-5	6-3	6-4	
S	Jim Willard	Bob Schlesinger	3-6	6-3	6-0	6-4	
Q	Jack Hawkes	Gar Hone	4-6	6-0	6-2	6-2	
Q	James Anderson	Pat O'Hara Wood	6-3	6-2	3-6	6-2	
Q	Bob Schlesinger	Norman Peach	6-4	6-1	5-7	6-3	
Q	Jim Willard	E.T. Rowe	6-3	6-1	0-6	6-1	

1927 (Melbourne)

Rd	Winner	Defeated	S1	S2	S3	S4	S5
F	**Gerald Patterson**	**Jack Hawkes**	3-6	6-4	3-6	18-16	6-3
S	Gerald Patterson	Gar Moon	6-3	6-3	9-7		
S	Jack Hawkes	Jim Willard	6-0	4-6	6-2	6-1	
Q	Gerald Patterson	Bob Schlesinger	6-2	6-3	2-6	6-2	
Q	Gar Moon	Jack Crawford	2-6	9-11	8-6	6-3	8-6
Q	Jim Willard	Gordon Lum	6-2	6-0	6-4		
Q	Jack Hawkes	H. Coldham	6-4	6-0	6-1		

1928 (Sydney)

Rd	Winner	Defeated	S1	S2	S3	S4	S5
F	**Jean Borotra**	**Jack Cummings**	6-4	6-1	4-6	5-7	6-3
S	Jean Borotra	Jack Crawford	4-6	6-3	1-6	7-5	6-4
S	Jack Cummings	Bob Schlesinger	6-1	2-6	6-4	8-6	
Q	Jean Borotra	Harry Hopman	6-4	6-4	6-3		
Q	Jack Crawford	Jack Hawkes	6-2	8-6	6-3		
Q	Jack Cummings	Fred Kalms	4-6	2-6	6-3	8-6	6-1
Q	Bob Schlesinger	Gerald Patterson	6-4	7-9	6-4		(retired)

1929 (Adelaide)

Rd	Winner	Defeated	S1	S2	S3	S4	S5
F	**Colin Gregory**	**Bob Schlesinger**	6-2	6-2	5-7	7-5	
S	Colin Gregory	Gar Moon	6-1	7-5	6-2		
S	Bob Schlesinger	Harry Hopman	6-2	6-1	0-6	6-2	
Q	Colin Gregory	E.T. Rowe	6-4	6-2	6-4		
Q	Gar Moon	Bunny Austin	2-6	5-7	6-1	6-2	6-4
Q	Harry Hopman	Pat O'Hara Wood	6-2	11-9	7-5		
Q	Bob Schlesinger	Jack Crawford	6-2	6-3	2-6	6-4	

1930 (Melbourne)

Rd	Winner	Defeated	S1	S2	S3	S4	S5
F	**Gar Moon**	**Harry Hopman**	6-3	6-1	6-3		
S	Gar Moon	Jack Crawford	7-5	6-4	4-6	6-3	
S	Harry Hopman	Jim Willard	6-4	6-2	6-0		
Q	Gar Moon	Jack Cummings	6-4	6-2	6-2		
Q	Jack Crawford	Cliff Sproule	6-3	6-2	6-1		
Q	Jim Willard	Bob Schlesinger	2-6	6-1	10-8	6-2	
Q	Harry Hopman	Jack Clemenger	4-6	6-2	3-6	7-5	6-3

1931 (Sydney)

Rd	Winner	Defeated	S1	S2	S3	S4	S5
F	**Jack Crawford**	**Harry Hopman**	6-4	6-2	2-6	6-1	
S	Jack Crawford	Don Turnbull	6-2	6-2	12-10		
S	Harry Hopman	Jack Cummings	8-6	6-2	6-4		
Q	Jack Crawford	Cliff Sproule	6-0	3-6	6-0	6-3	
Q	Don Turnbull	Gar Moon	9-7	2-6	6-3	4-6	6-2
Q	Jack Cummings	A. Hassett	6-2	6-2	6-4		
Q	Harry Hopman	Aubrey Willard	5-7	6-3	6-4	6-4	

1932 (Adelaide)

Rd	Winner	Defeated	S1	S2	S3	S4	S5
F	**Jack Crawford**	**Harry Hopman**	4-6	6-3	3-6	6-3	6-1
S	Jack Crawford	Cliff Sproule	6-4	2-6	6-2	6-1	
S	Harry Hopman	Jiro Satoh	0-6	6-2	6-3	4-6	6-4
Q	Jack Crawford	Ryosuki Nunoi	3-6	7-5	6-4	6-1	
Q	Cliff Sproule	Jim Willard	6-4	6-2	8-6		
Q	Jiro Satoh	Viv McGrath	6-3	6-3	6-2		
Q	Harry Hopman	Aubrey Willard	12-10	6-3	8-6		

1933 (Melbourne)

Rd	Winner	Defeated	S1	S2	S3	S4	S5
F	**Jack Crawford**	**Keith Gledhill**	2-6	7-5	6-3	6-2	
S	Keith Gledhill	Viv McGrath	6-4	6-1	6-1		
S	Jack Crawford	Wilmer Allison	6-3	3-6	3-6	6-0	6-3
Q	Viv McGrath	Ellsworth Vines	6-3	2-6	8-6	7-5	
Q	Keith Gledhill	Harry Hopman	3-6	2-6	8-6	6-0	6-3
Q	Jack Crawford	Don Turnbull	6-1	6-3	6-2		
Q	Wilmer Allison	Adrian Quist	1-6	3-6	9-7	6-2	6-2

1934 (Sydney)

Rd	Winner	Defeated	S1	S2	S3	S4	S5
F	**Fred Perry**	**Jack Crawford**	6-3	7-5	6-1		
S	Jack Crawford	Adrian Quist	6-4	6-2	6-2		
S	Fred Perry	Viv McGrath	2-6	5-7	6-4	6-4	6-1
Q	Jack Crawford	Harold G.N. Lee	6-2	7-5	3-6	6-2	
Q	Adrian Quist	Gar Moon	6-3	6-3	6-1		
Q	Fred Perry	Harry Hopman	6-3	6-4	6-3		
Q	Viv McGrath	Don Turnbull	6-4	6-3	6-3		

1935 (Melbourne)

Rd	Winner	Defeated	S1	S2	S3	S4	S5
F	**Jack Crawford**	**Fred Perry**	2-6	6-4	6-4	6-4	
S	Fred Perry	Viv McGrath	6-2	6-3	6-1		
S	Jack Crawford	Adrian Quist	6-1	1-6	6-2	3-6	6-3
Q	Fred Perry	Giorgio de Stefani	6-0	6-0	6-0		
Q	Viv McGrath	Don Turnbull	9-7	5-7	6-4	2-6	6-3
Q	Jack Crawford	Gar Moon	6-0	10-8	6-2		
Q	Adrian Quist	Roderick Menzel	6-1	6-3	8-10	1-6	6-1

1936 (Adelaide)

Rd	Winner	Defeated	S1	S2	S3	S4	S5
F	Adrian Quist	Jack Crawford	6-2	6-3	4-6	3-6	9-7
S	Adrian Quist	Harry Hopman	4-6	6-2	10-8	6-3	
S	Jack Crawford	Abe Kay	6-2	9-7	6-2		
Q	Adrian Quist	John Bromwich	6-1	6-4	6-1		
Q	Harry Hopman	Viv McGrath	6-3	0-6	6-3	7-5	
Q	Abe Kay	Don Turnbull	6-3	6-4	3-6	7-5	
Q	Jack Crawford	Gar Moon	6-2	6-3	9-7		

1937 (Sydney)

Rd	Winner	Defeated	S1	S2	S3	S4	S5
F	Viv McGrath	John Bromwich	6-3	1-6	6-0	2-6	6-1
S	John Bromwich	Jack Crawford	6-1	7-9	6-4	8-6	
S	Viv McGrath	Harry Hopman	6-4	6-1	7-5		
Q	Jack Crawford	Leonard Schwartz	6-3	2-6	3-6	6-2	6-3
Q	John Bromwich	Don Turnbull	6-2	6-2	6-0		
Q	Viv McGrath	Abe Kay	6-2	6-2	8-6		
Q	Harry Hopman	Adrian Quist	11-9	3-6	7-5	6-3	

1938 (Adelaide)

Rd	Winner	Defeated	S1	S2	S3	S4	S5
F	Don Budge	John Bromwich	6-4	6-2	6-1		
S	John Bromwich	Gottfried von Cramm	6-3	7-5	6-1		
S	Don Budge	Adrian Quist	6-4	6-2	8-6		
Q	Gottfried Von Cramm	Viv McGrath	6-2	3-6	4-6	7-5	6-0
Q	John Bromwich	Gene Mako	6-4	7-5	6-2		
Q	Don Budge	Leonard Schwartz	6-4	6-3	10-8		
Q	Adrian Quist	George Holland	5-7	6-4	6-1	6-2	

1939 (Melbourne)

Rd	Winner	Defeated	S1	S2	S3	S4	S5
F	John Bromwich	Adrian Quist	6-4	6-1	6-2		
S	John Bromwich	Viv McGrath	6-0	6-3	6-4		
S	Adrian Quist	Jack Crawford	6-1	7-5	6-3		
Q	John Bromwich	Don Turnbull	7-5	6-1	6-0		
Q	Viv McGrath	Harry Hopman	6-1	4-6	6-4	6-3	
Q	Jack Crawford	Jim Gilchrist	4-6	6-4	2-6	6-3	6-4
Q	Adrian Quist	Lionel Brodie	6-3	6-2	6-8	6-3	

1940 (Sydney)

Rd	Winner	Defeated	S1	S2	S3	S4	S5
F	Adrian Quist	Jack Crawford	6-3	6-1	6-2		
S	Jack Crawford	John Bromwich	6-4	6-1	9-7		
S	Adrian Quist	Viv McGrath	6-4	10-8	6-3		
Q	John Bromwich	Dinny Pails	7-5	6-0	6-0		
Q	Jack Crawford	Max Newcombe	6-3	6-0	7-5		
Q	Adrian Quist	Bill Sidwell	6-3	11-13	6-3	6-2	
Q	Viv McGrath	Harry Hopman	6-8	6-1	7-5	6-2	

1941-45   *Not held – WW II*

1946 (Adelaide)

Rd	Winner	Defeated	S1	S2	S3	S4	S5
F	John Bromwich	Dinny Pails	5-7	6-3	7-5	3-6	6-2
S	John Bromwich	Geoff Brown	6-3	6-2	6-1		
S	Dinny Pails	Adrian Quist	6-2	6-4	6-2		
Q	John Bromwich	Jack Harper	6-1	6-2	6-1		
Q	Geoff Brown	Harry Hopman	4-6	6-4	6-3	6-4	
Q	Adrian Quist	Max Bonner	6-0	8-6	3-6	6-2	
Q	Dinny Pails	Lionel Brodie	6-2	6-2	6-0		

1947 (Sydney)

Rd	Winner	Defeated	S1	S2	S3	S4	S5
F	Dinny Pails	John Bromwich	4-6	6-4	3-6	7-5	8-6
S	Dinny Pails	Tom Brown	6-2	6-4	6-1		
S	John Bromwich	Gardnar Mulloy	6-2	6-4	1-6	6-4	
Q	Dinny Pails	Bill Sidwell	6-3	10-8	6-3		
Q	Tom Brown	Adrian Quist	8-6	6-4	5-7	6-2	
Q	John Bromwich	Colin Long	6-2	7-5	4-6	6-0	
Q	Gardnar Mulloy	Lionel Brodie	6-2	6-8	6-2	5-7	6-1

1948 (Melbourne)

Rd	Winner	Defeated	S1	S2	S3	S4	S5
F	Adrian Quist	John Bromwich	6-4	3-6	6-3	2-6	6-3
S	John Bromwich	Geoff Brown	3-6	2-6	6-4	6-4	7-5
S	Adrian Quist	Bill Sidwell	6-1	6-2	1-6	6-3	
Q	John Bromwich	Frank Sedgman	6-2	6-4	6-4		
Q	Geoff Brown	Eddie Moylan	7-5	6-2	2-6	7-5	
Q	Bill Sidwell	Colin Long	6-2	5-7	6-2	6-0	
Q	Adrian Quist	Robert McCarthy	6-3	6-2	6-3		

1949 (Adelaide)

Rd	Winner	Defeated	S1	S2	S3	S4	S5
F	Frank Sedgman	John Bromwich	6-3	6-2	6-2		
S	Frank Sedgman	Bill Sidwell	6-3	6-3	6-2		
S	John Bromwich	Geoff Brown	1-6	6-3	6-3	6-3	
Q	Bill Sidwell	Tom Warhurst	6-3	6-1	4-6	6-4	
Q	Frank Sedgman	Adrian Quist	6-2	4-6	6-4	6-4	
Q	Geoff Brown	George Worthington	6-1	6-3	4-6	6-1	
Q	John Bromwich	Colin Long	6-4	6-4	1-6	6-2	

1950 (Adelaide)

Rd	Winner	Defeated	S1	S2	S3	S4	S5
F	Frank Sedgman	Ken McGregor	6-3	6-4	4-6	6-1	
S	Ken McGregor	Bill Sidwell	7-5	9-7	6-3		
S	Frank Sedgman	Eric Strugess	6-2	6-3	6-8	4-6	6-4
Q	Ken McGregor	George Worthington	6-3	8-6	6-1		
Q	Bill Sidwell	Colin Long	7-5	7-5	7-5		
Q	Frank Sedgman	John Bromwich	5-7	6-3	6-4	6-1	
Q	Eric Strugess	Merv Rose	7-5	6-4	6-1		

1951 (Sydney)

Rd	Winner	Defeated	S1	S2	S3	S4	S5
F	Richard Savitt	Ken McGregor	6-3	2-6	6-3	6-1	
S	Richard Savitt	Frank Sedgman	2-6	7-5	1-6	6-3	6-4
S	Ken McGregor	Art Larsen	11-9	6-2	5-7	6-1	
Q	Frank Sedgman	George Worthington	6-2	7-5	6-0		
Q	Richard Savitt	John Bromwich	6-4	6-3	6-1		
Q	Art Larsen	Merv Rose	6-2	3-6	5-7	6-4	6-2
Q	Ken McGregor	Adrian Quist	8-6	6-2	7-5		

1952 (Adelaide)

Rd	Winner	Defeated	S1	S2	S3	S4	S5
F	Ken McGregor	Frank Sedgman	7-5	12-10	2-6	6-2	
S	Ken McGregor	Dick Savitt	6-4	6-4	3-6	6-4	
S	Frank Sedgman	Merv Rose	6-2	6-4	6-2		
Q	Dick Savitt	Ian Ayre	6-1	6-4	5-7	4-6	6-4
Q	Ken McGregor	Geoff Brown	6-4	6-2	12-10		
Q	Merv Rose	Ken Rosewall	6-4	4-6	5-7	2-6	6-2
Q	Frank Sedgman	Don Candy	7-5	6-1	6-4		

1953 (Melbourne)

Rd	Winner	Defeated	S1	S2	S3	S4	S5
F	Ken Rosewall	Merv Rose	6-0	6-3	6-4		
S	Merv Rose	Ian Ayre	4-6	4-6	6-1	6-4	6-4
S	Ken Rosewall	Vic Seixas	6-3	2-6	7-5	6-4	
Q	Merv Rose	Hamilton Richardson	8-10	6-3	1-6	8-6	
Q	Ian Ayre	Clive Wilderspin	6-4	11-9	1-6	8-6	
Q	Vic Seixas	Geoff Brown	6-4	6-4	7-5		
Q	Ken Rosewall	Straight Clark	6-4	6-4	6-2		

1954 (Sydney)

Rd	Winner	Defeated	S1	S2	S3	S4	S5
F	Merv Rose	Rex Hartwig	6-2	0-6	6-4	6-2	
S	Merv Rose	Ken Rosewall	6-3	6-3	3-6	1-6	7-5
S	Rex Hartwig	John Bromwich	8-6	6-4	9-7		
S	Ken Rosewall	Hamilton Richardson	6-3	6-4	9-7		
Q	Merv Rose	Vic Seixas	8-6	9-7	9-11	6-4	
Q	John Bromwich	George Worthington	3-6	6-3	2-6	6-3	6-1
Q	Rex Hartwig	Ashley Cooper	6-2	6-3	6-4		

1955 (Adelaide)

Rd	Winner	Defeated	S1	S2	S3	S4	S5
F	Ken Rosewall	Lew Hoad	9-7	6-4	6-4		
S	Ken Rosewall	Tony Trabert	8-6	6-3	6-3		
S	Lew Hoad	Rex Hartwig	6-1	6-4	6-4		
Q	Ken Rosewall	Ashley Cooper	6-4	6-2	6-0		
Q	Tony Trabert	Merv Rose	7-5	4-6	6-3	6-1	
Q	Lew Hoad	Vic Seixas	4-6	6-3	6-4	8-6	
Q	Rex Hartwig	Lennart Bergelin	4-6	6-2	4-6	6-4	6-3

Rd	Winner	Defeated	S1	S2	S3	S4	S5
1956 *(Brisbane)*							
F	Lew Hoad	Ken Rosewall	6-4	3-6	6-4	7-5	
S	Lew Hoad	Neale Fraser	6-3	6-2	6-0		
S	Ken Rosewall	Herbie Flam	6-4	6-0	6-2		
Q	Lew Hoad	Merv Rose	3-6	6-1	6-8	6-2	9-7
Q	Neale Fraser	Gilbert Shea	6-2	6-4	6-3		
Q	Herbie Flam	Ashley Cooper	6-8	6-3	6-2	6-3	
Q	Ken Rosewall	Mal Anderson	6-4	6-3	5-7	8-6	
1957 *(Melbourne)*							
F	Ashley Cooper	Neale Fraser	6-3	9-11	6-4	6-2	
S	Neale Fraser	Lew Hoad	7-5	3-6	6-1	6-4	
S	Ashley Cooper	Mal Anderson	6-4	9-7	6-4		
Q	Lew Hoad	Mike Green	4-6	3-6	6-2	6-3	6-3
Q	Neale Fraser	Graham Lovett	6-0	6-1	6-0		
Q	Mal Anderson	Nicola Pietrangeli	9-7	9-7	6-2		
Q	Ashley Cooper	Warren Woodcock	6-2	3-6	6-1	6-4	
1958 *(Sydney)*							
F	Ashley Cooper	Mal Anderson	7-5	6-3	6-4		
S	Ashley Cooper	Neale Fraser	6-3	3-6	10-8	6-3	
S	Mal Anderson	Merv Rose	6-2	5-7	6-4	19-17	
Q	Ashley Cooper	Mike Green	6-1	6-2	4-6	5-7	6-2
Q	Neale Fraser	Roy Emerson	4-6	6-1	6-4	6-3	
Q	Merv Rose	Bob Howe	3-6	4-6	6-1	8-6	6-0
Q	Mal Anderson	Trevor Fancutt	6-3	6-4	5-7	12-10	
1959 *(Adelaide)*							
F	Alex Olmedo	Neale Fraser	6-1	6-2	3-6	6-3	
S	Neale Fraser	Bob Mark	6-4	6-4	6-3		
S	Alex Olmedo	Barry MacKay	3-6	8-6	6-1	3-6	6-3
Q	Neale Fraser	Don Candy	6-2	6-4	4-6	6-4	
Q	Bob Mark	Andres Gimeno	6-4	3-6	7-5	6-4	
Q	Alex Olmedo	Ulf Schmidt	6-4	9-7	3-6	3-6	7-5
Q	Barry MacKay	Roy Emerson	4-6	10-8	6-3	8-6	
1960 *(Brisbane)*							
F	Rod Laver	Neale Fraser	5-7	3-6	6-3	8-6	8-6
S	Neale Fraser	Bob Hewitt	8-6	6-4	11-9		
S	Rod Laver	Roy Emerson	4-6	6-1	9-7	3-6	7-5
Q	Neale Fraser	John Pearce	4-6	7-5	6-3	6-8	6-2
Q	Bob Hewitt	Bob Mark	12-10	6-2	6-1		
Q	Rod Laver	Ken Fletcher	6-3	8-6	4-6	6-4	
Q	Roy Emerson	Marty Mulligan	6-4	6-1			(retired)
1961 *(Melbourne)*							
F	Roy Emerson	Rod Laver	1-6	6-3	7-5	6-4	
S	Rod Laver	Barry Phillips-Moore	6-2	6-2	6-4		
S	Roy Emerson	Fred Stolle	8-6	6-2	7-5		
Q	Rod Laver	Ken Fletcher	6-2	2-4			(retired)
Q	Barry Phillips-Moore	Christian Kuhnke	5-7	6-3	6-2	6-3	
Q	Fred Stolle	Mike Sangster	6-3	6-4	6-3		
Q	Roy Emerson	John Pearce	6-1	6-2	6-3		
1962 *(Sydney)*							
F	Rod Laver	Roy Emerson	8-6	0-6	6-4	6-4	
S	Rod Laver	Bob Hewitt	6-1	4-6	6-4	7-5	
S	Roy Emerson	Neale Fraser	6-4	6-3	6-1		
Q	Rod Laver	Owen Davidson	6-4	9-7	6-4		
Q	Bob Hewitt	Wilhelm Bungert	8-6	6-2	4-6	6-4	
Q	Neale Fraser	Fred Stolle	6-2	4-6	6-2	6-3	
Q	Roy Emerson	John Newcombe	7-9	6-1	6-2	6-2	
1963 *(Adelaide)*							
F	Roy Emerson	Ken Fletcher	6-3	6-3	6-1		
S	Roy Emerson	Bob Hewitt	8-6	6-4	3-6	9-7	
S	Ken Fletcher	Fred Stolle	6-3	6-4	7-5		
Q	Roy Emerson	John Fraser	6-1	7-5	6-2		
Q	Bob Hewitt	John Newcombe	6-3	6-4	5-7	6-4	
Q	Fred Stolle	Owen Davidson	5-7	6-4	6-2	6-2	
Q	Ken Fletcher	Bob Howe	6-4	9-7	6-2		
1964 *(Brisbane)*							
F	Roy Emerson	Fred Stolle	6-3	6-4	6-2		
S	Roy Emerson	Marty Mulligan	6-2	9-7	6-4		
S	Fred Stolle	Ken Fletcher	6-4	3-6	6-3	3-6	6-3
Q	Roy Emerson	Tony Roche	7-5	6-2	6-2		
Q	Marty Mulligan	John Newcombe	3-6	6-4	6-3	6-8	8-6
Q	Ken Fletcher	Mike Sangster	17-15	4-6	6-0	6-1	
Q	Fred Stolle	Owen Davidson	1-6	7-5	6-3	6-2	
1965 *(Melbourne)*							
F	Roy Emerson	Fred Stolle	7-9	2-6	6-4	7-5	6-1
S	Roy Emerson	John Newcombe	7-5	6-4	6-1		
S	Fred Stolle	Tony Roche	6-4	8-6	9-7		
Q	Roy Emerson	Juan Gisbert	6-3	6-3	6-1		
Q	John Newcombe	Bill Bowrey	6-2	4-6	2-6	6-3	6-4
Q	Tony Roche	Pierre Darmon	6-8	6-2	6-3	6-0	
Q	Fred Stolle	Owen Davidson	3-6	6-0	6-3	6-3	
1966 *(Sydney)*							
F	Roy Emerson	Arthur Ashe	6-4	6-8	6-2	6-3	
S	Roy Emerson	John Newcombe	4-6	6-3	6-1	6-2	
S	Arthur Ashe	Fred Stolle	6-4	1-6	6-3	10-8	
Q	Roy Emerson	Bill Bowrey	9-7	4-6	4-6	7-5	9-7
Q	John Newcombe	Clark Graebner	2-6	6-1	6-3	7-5	
Q	Fred Stolle	Lew Gerrard	6-2	7-5	7-5		
Q	Arthur Ashe	Tony Roche	14-12	6-4	6-3		
1967 *(Adelaide)*							
F	Roy Emerson	Arthur Ashe	6-4	6-1	6-4		
S	Roy Emerson	Tony Roche	6-3	4-6	15-13	13-15	6-2
S	Arthur Ashe	John Newcombe	12-10	20-22	6-3	6-2	
Q	Roy Emerson	Bill Bowrey	4-6	6-4	11-9	16-14	
Q	Tony Roche	Cliff Richey	10-8	7-5	4-6	5-7	6-1
Q	John Newcombe	Mark Cox	6-3	7-5	6-4		
Q	Arthur Ashe	Owen Davidson	6-1	6-3	6-2		
1968 *(Melbourne)*							
F	Bill Bowrey	Juan Gisbert	7-5	2-6	9-7	6-4	
S	Bill Bowrey	Barry Phillips-Moore	10-8	6-4	7-5		
S	Juan Gisbert	Ray Ruffels	10-8	3-6	6-2	6-2	
Q	Bill Bowrey	Michael Belkin	16-14	6-3	6-3		
Q	Barry Phillips-Moore	Manolo Orantes	6-1	4-6	6-3	4-6	6-1
Q	Juan Gisbert	Dick Crealy	6-4	10-12	7-5	7-5	
Q	Ray Ruffels	Phil Dent	1-6	6-2	6-1	3-6	6-0
1969 *(Brisbane)*							
F	Rod Laver	Andres Gimeno	6-3	6-4	7-5		
S	Rod Laver	Tony Roche	7-5	22-20	9-11	1-6	6-3
S	Andres Gimeno	Ray Ruffels	6-2	11-9	6-2		
Q	Rod Laver	Fred Stolle	6-4	18-16	6-4		
Q	Tony Roche	John Newcombe	10-8	4-6	6-8	7-5	6-3
Q	Ray Ruffels	Bill Bowrey	9-11	2-6	6-0	6-3	6-4
Q	Andres Gimeno	Butch Buchholz	6-1	6-2	6-2		
1970 *(Sydney)*							
F	Arthur Ashe	Dick Crealy	6-4	9-7	6-2		
S	Dick Crealy	Roger Taylor	6-2	9-11	8-6	3-6	8-6
S	Arthur Ashe	Dennis Ralston	6-3	8-10	6-3	2-1 (retired)	
Q	Roger Taylor	Tony Roche	9-7	7-5	7-5		
Q	Dick Crealy	Tom Okker	6-1	3-6	4-6	7-5	6-3
Q	Arthur Ashe	Ray Ruffels	6-8	6-3	6-4	6-2	
Q	Dennis Ralston	John Newcombe	19-17	20-18	4-6	6-3	
1971 *(Sydney)*							
F	Ken Rosewall	Arthur Ashe	6-1	7-5	6-3		
S	Arthur Ashe	Bob Lutz	6-4	6-4	7-6		
S	Ken Rosewall	Tom Okker	6-2	7-6	6-4		
Q	Bob Lutz	Mark Cox	6-2	6-1	6-2		
Q	Arthur Ashe	Cliff Drysdale	7-6	7-6	2-6	6-2	
Q	Tom Okker	Marty Riessen	6-3	6-3	6-3		
Q	Ken Rosewall	Roy Emerson	6-4	6-4	6-3		

Rd	Winner	Defeated	S1	S2	S3	S4	S5
1972 *(Melbourne)*							
F	**Ken Rosewall**	**Mal Anderson**	7-6(2)	6-3	7-5		
S	Mal Anderson	Alex Metreveli	6-2	7-6	7-6		
S	Ken Rosewall	Allan Stone	7-6	6-1	3-6	7-6	
Q	Mal Anderson	John Newcombe	2-6	6-3	6-4	3-6	9-7
Q	Alex Metreveli	John Cooper	6-7	6-2	6-3	6-4	
Q	Allan Stone	Barry Phillips-Moore	5-7	7-6	7-6	6-3	
Q	Ken Rosewall	Dick Crealy	6-3	6-1	6-3		
1973 *(Melbourne)*							
F	**John Newcombe**	**Onny Parun**	6-3	6-7	7-5	6-1	
S	Onny Parun	Karl Meiler	2-6	6-3	7-5	6-1	
S	John Newcombe	Patrick Proisy	7-6	6-4	6-3		
Q	Karl Meiler	Wanaro N'Godrella	7-6	6-7	6-3	7-6	
Q	Onny Parun	Alex Metreveli	6-4	3-6	6-3	6-7	6-3
Q	Patrick Proisy	John Cooper	6-4	3-6	6-1	7-6	
Q	John Newcombe	Bob Carmichael	6-4	7-5	6-3		
1974 *(Melbourne)*							
F	**Jimmy Connors**	**Phil Dent**	7-6(7)	6-4	4-6	6-3	
S	Phil Dent	Ross Case	6-4	6-1	2-6	6-2	
S	Jimmy Connors	John Alexander	7-6	6-4	6-4		
Q	Ross Case	John Newcombe	7-6	6-2	7-5		
Q	Phil Dent	Colin Dibley	6-4	6-4	6-4		
Q	John Alexander	Bob Giltinan	6-1	5-7	6-1	6-2	
Q	Jimmy Connors	Vladimir Zednik	3-6	7-5	6-3	6-4	
1975 *(Melbourne)*							
F	**John Newcombe**	**Jimmy Connors**	7-5	3-6	6-4	7-6(7)	
S	John Newcombe	Tony Roche	6-4	4-6	6-4	2-6	11-9
S	Jimmy Connors	Dick Crealy	6-4	6-3	6-4		
Q	John Newcombe	Geoff Masters	1-6	6-3	6-7	6-3	10-8
Q	Tony Roche	Alex Metreveli	7-6	3-6	6-4	6-3	
Q	Jimmy Connors	Kim Warwick	6-3	6-1	6-2		
Q	Dick Crealy	John Alexander	6-3	4-6	6-3	7-6	
1976 *(Melbourne)*							
F	**Mark Edmondson**	**John Newcombe**	6-7	6-3	7-6	6-1	
S	Mark Edmondson	Ken Rosewall	6-1	2-6	6-2	6-4	
S	John Newcombe	Ray Ruffels	6-4	6-4	7-6		
Q	Ken Rosewall	Brad Drewett	6-4	3-6	6-2	6-2	
Q	Mark Edmondson	Dick Crealy	7-5	7-6	6-2		
Q	Ray Ruffels	Tony Roche	7-6	2-6	6-7	7-6	6-4
Q	John Newcombe	Ross Case	6-4	6-4	6-1		
1977 (Jan.) *(Melbourne)*							
F	**Roscoe Tanner**	**Guillermo Vilas**	6-3	6-3	6-3		
S	Guillermo Vilas	John Alexander	6-4	1-6	6-3	6-4	
S	Roscoe Tanner	Ken Rosewall	6-4	3-6	6-4	6-1	
Q	Guillermo Vilas	Ross Case	6-4	7-5	1-6	6-3	
Q	John Alexander	Arthur Ashe	6-3	6-4	4-6	7-6	
Q	Ken Rosewall	Mark Edmondson	6-4	7-6	4-6	6-4	
Q	Roscoe Tanner	Phil Dent	6-3	6-4	6-2		
1977 (Dec.) *(Melbourne)*							
F	**Vitas Gerulaitis**	**John Lloyd**	6-3	7-6(1)	5-7	3-6	6-2
S	Vitas Gerulaitis	John Alexander	6-1	6-2	6-4		
S	John Lloyd	Bob Giltinan	6-4	6-2	6-0		
Q	Vitas Gerulaitis	Ray Ruffels	6-7	6-4	6-4	6-2	
Q	John Alexander	Ken Rosewall	7-6	7-6	4-6	6-1	
Q	John Lloyd	John Newcombe	3-6	6-3	7-5	7-5	
Q	Bob Giltinan	Robin Drysdale	6-4	6-4	3-6	7-6	
1978 *(Melbourne)*							
F	**Guillermo Vilas**	**John Marks**	6-4	6-4	3-6	6-3	
S	Guillermo Vilas	Hank Pfister	6-2	6-0	6-4		
S	John Marks	Arthur Ashe	6-4	6-4	2-6	1-6	9-7
Q	Guillermo Vilas	Tony Roche	3-6	6-1	3-6	6-3	6-2
Q	Hank Pfister	Paul Kronk	7-5	6-3	6-3		
Q	Arthur Ashe	Peter Feigl	4-6	6-2	4-6	6-3	6-2
Q	John Marks	John Alexander	6-4	6-4	7-5		
1979 *(Melbourne)*							
F	**Guillermo Vilas**	**John Sadri**	7-6(4)	6-3	6-2		
S	Guillermo Vilas	Victor Amaya	7-5	3-6	7-6	7-6	
S	John Sadri	Colin Dibley	6-4	7-6	6-7	6-4	
Q	Guillermo Vilas	Phil Dent	6-2	3-6	7-6	4-6	6-2
Q	Victor Amaya	Peter Rennert	7-6	6-4	6-4		
Q	John Sadri	Rod Frawley	7-6	6-3	6-7	6-4	
Q	Colin Dibley	Mark Edmondson	3-6	6-4	3-6	7-6	6-4
1980 *(Melbourne)*							
F	**Brian Teacher**	**Kim Warwick**	7-5	7-6(4)	6-3		
S	Kim Warwick	Guillermo Vilas	6-7	6-4	6-2	2-6	6-4
S	Brian Teacher	Peter McNamara	6-7	7-5	6-3	6-4	
Q	Guillermo Vilas	John Sadri	7-5	6-4	2-6	4-6	6-3
Q	Kim Warwick	Bill Scanlon	6-4	6-2	4-6	6-1	
Q	Brian Teacher	Paul McNamee	6-4	4-6	6-0	7-6	
Q	Peter McNamara	Peter Rennert	7-6	5-7	6-2	6-7	6-3
1981 *(Melbourne)*							
F	**Johan Kriek**	**Steve Denton**	6-2	7-6(1)	6-7(1)	6-4	
S	Steve Denton	Hank Pfister	7-6	6-7	6-1	3-6	6-3
S	Johan Kriek	Mark Edmondson	6-0	7-6	7-5		
Q	Hank Pfister	Kim Warwick	6-1	4-6	6-4	6-3	
Q	Steve Denton	Shlomo Glickstein	6-4	3-6	7-6	6-0	
Q	Johan Kriek	Tim Mayotte	7-6	6-3	7-5		
Q	Mark Edmondson	Peter McNamara	7-5	7-6	6-2		
1982 *(Melbourne)*							
F	**Johan Kriek**	**Steve Denton**	6-3	6-3	6-2		
S	Johan Kriek	Paul McNamee	7-6	7-6	4-6	3-6	7-5
S	Steve Denton	Hank Pfister	6-4	4-6	6-3	3-6	7-6
Q	Johan Kriek	Drew Gitlin	6-0	6-4	6-1		
Q	Paul McNamee	Pat Cash	6-4	6-7	6-3	6-4	
Q	Hank Pfister	Brian Teacher	6-1	4-6	6-7	1-6	7-6
Q	Steve Denton	Sammy Giammalva	4-6	6-3	6-3	2-6	6-3
1983 *(Melbourne)*							
F	**Mats Wilander**	**Ivan Lendl**	6-1	6-4	6-4		
S	Ivan Lendl	Tim Mayotte	6-1	7-6	6-3		
S	Mats Wilander	John McEnroe	4-6	6-3	6-4	6-3	
Q	Ivan Lendl	Tomas Smid	7-6	2-6	6-1	6-2	
Q	Tim Mayotte	Eliot Teltscher	6-4	6-2	3-6	7-6	
Q	Mats Wilander	Johan Kriek	6-3	6-4	7-6		
Q	John McEnroe	Wally Masur	6-2	6-1	6-2		
1984 *(Melbourne)*							
F	**Mats Wilander**	**Kevin Curren**	6-7(5)	6-4	7-6(3)	6-2	
S	Kevin Curren	Ben Testerman	2-6	4-6	6-3	6-4	6-4
S	Mats Wilander	Johan Kriek	6-1	6-0	6-2		
Q	Kevin Curren	Scott Davis	7-5	6-2	6-3		
Q	Ben Testerman	Boris Becker	6-4	6-3	6-4		
Q	Johan Kriek	Pat Cash	7-5	6-1	7-6		
Q	Mats Wilander	Stefan Edberg	7-5	6-3	1-6	6-4	
1985 *(Melbourne)*							
F	**Stefan Edberg**	**Mats Wilander**	6-4	6-3	6-3		
S	Stefan Edberg	Ivan Lendl	6-7(3)	7-5	6-1	4-6	9-7
S	Mats Wilander	Slobodan Zivojinovic	7-5	6-1	6-3		
Q	Ivan Lendl	John Lloyd	7-6(5)	6-2	6-1		
Q	Stefan Edberg	Michiel Schapers	6-0	7-5	6-4		
Q	Mats Wilander	Johan Kriek	6-3	7-5	6-2		
Q	Slobodan Zivojinovic	John McEnroe	2-6	6-3	1-6	6-4	6-0
1987 *(Melbourne)*							
F	**Stefan Edberg**	**Pat Cash**	6-3	6-4	3-6	5-7	6-3
S	Pat Cash	Ivan Lendl	7-6	5-7	7-6	6-4	
S	Stefan Edberg	Wally Masur	6-2	6-4	7-6		
Q	Ivan Lendl	Anders Jarryd	7-6	6-1	6-3		
Q	Pat Cash	Yannick Noah	6-4	6-2	2-6	6-0	
Q	Stefan Edberg	Miloslav Mecir	6-1	6-4	6-4		
Q	Wally Masur	Kelly Evernden	6-3	7-5	6-4		

Rd	Winner	Defeated	S1	S2	S3	S4	S5

1988 (Melbourne)

Rd	Winner	Defeated	S1	S2	S3	S4	S5
F	Mats Wilander	Pat Cash	6-3	6-7(3)	3-6	6-1	8-6
S	Pat Cash	Ivan Lendl	6-4	2-6	6-2	4-6	6-2
S	Mats Wilander	Stefan Edberg	6-0	6-7(5)	6-3	3-6	6-1
Q	Ivan Lendl	Todd Witsken	6-2	6-1	7-6(4)		
Q	Pat Cash	Michiel Schapers	6-1	6-4	6-2		
Q	Mats Wilander	Anders Jarryd	7-6	6-2	6-3		
Q	Stefan Edberg	Andrei Chesnokov	4-6	7-6(5)	6-4	6-4	

1989 (Melbourne)

Rd	Winner	Defeated	S1	S2	S3	S4	S5
F	Ivan Lendl	Miloslav Mecir	6-2	6-2	6-2		
S	Miloslav Mecir	Jan Gunnarsson	7-5	6-2	6-2		
S	Ivan Lendl	Thomas Muster	6-2	6-4	5-7	7-5	
Q	Miloslav Mecir	Goran Ivanisevic	7-5	6-0	6-3		
Q	Jan Gunnarsson	Jonas Svensson	6-0	6-3	4-6	6-4	
Q	Thomas Muster	Stefan Edberg		(walkover)			
Q	Ivan Lendl	John McEnroe	7-6(0)	6-2	7-6(2)		

1990 (Melbourne)

Rd	Winner	Defeated	S1	S2	S3	S4	S5
F	Ivan Lendl	Stefan Edberg	4-6	7-6(3)	5-2	(ret. inj.)	
S	Ivan Lendl	Yannick Noah	6-4	6-1	6-2		
S	Stefan Edberg	Mats Wilander	6-1	6-1	6-2		
Q	Ivan Lendl	Andrei Cherkasov	6-3	6-2	6-3		
Q	Yannick Noah	Mikael Pernfors	6-3	7-5	6-2		
Q	Stefan Edberg	David Wheaton	7-5	7-6	3-6	6-2	
Q	Mats Wilander	Boris Becker	6-4	6-4	6-2		

1991 (Melbourne)

Rd	Winner	Defeated	S1	S2	S3	S4	S5
F	Boris Becker	Ivan Lendl	1-6	6-4	6-4	6-4	
S	Ivan Lendl	Stefan Edberg	6-4	5-7	3-6	7-6(3)	6-4
S	Boris Becker	Patrick McEnroe	6-7(2)	6-4	6-1	6-4	
Q	Stefan Edberg	Jaime Yzaga	6-2	6-3	6-2		
Q	Ivan Lendl	Goran Prpic	6-0	7-6(1)	7-6(2)		
Q	Patrick McEnroe	Cristiano Caratti	7-6(2)	6-3	4-6	4-6	6-2
Q	Boris Becker	Guy Forget	6-2	7-6(2)	6-3		

1992 (Melbourne)

Rd	Winner	Defeated	S1	S2	S3	S4	S5
F	Jim Courier	Stefan Edberg	6-3	3-6	6-4	6-2	
S	Stefan Edberg	Wayne Ferreira	7-6(2)	6-1	6-2		
S	Jim Courier	Richard Krajicek		(walkover)			
Q	Stefan Edberg	Ivan Lendl	4-6	7-5	6-1	6-7(5)	6-1
Q	Wayne Ferreira	John McEnroe	6-4	6-4	6-4		
Q	Richard Krajicek	Michael Stich	5-7	7-6(2)	6-7(1)	6-4	6-4
Q	Jim Courier	Amos Mansdorf	6-3	6-2	6-2		

1993 (Melbourne)

Rd	Winner	Defeated	S1	S2	S3	S4	S5
F	Jim Courier	Stefan Edberg	6-2	6-1	2-6	7-5	
S	Jim Courier	Michael Stich	7-6(4)	6-4	6-2		
S	Stefan Edberg	Pete Sampras	7-6(5)	6-3	7-6(3)		
Q	Jim Courier	Petr Korda	6-1	6-0	6-4		
Q	Michael Stich	Guy Forget	6-4	6-4	6-4		
Q	Pete Sampras	Brett Steven	6-3	6-2	6-3		
Q	Stefan Edberg	Christian Bergstrom	6-4	6-4	6-1		

1994 (Melbourne)

Rd	Winner	Defeated	S1	S2	S3	S4	S5
F	Pete Sampras	Todd Martin	7-6(4)	6-4	6-4		
S	Pete Sampras	Jim Courier	6-3	6-4	6-4		
S	Todd Martin	Stefan Edberg	3-6	7-6(7)	7-6(7)	7-6(4)	
Q	Pete Sampras	Magnus Gustafsson	7-6(4)	2-6	6-3	7-6(4)	
Q	Jim Courier	Goran Ivanisevic	7-6(7)	6-4	6-4		
Q	Stefan Edberg	Thomas Muster	6-2	6-3	6-4		
Q	Todd Martin	MaliVai Washington	6-2	7-6(4)	7-6(5)		

1995 (Melbourne)

Rd	Winner	Defeated	S1	S2	S3	S4	S5
F	Andre Agassi	Pete Sampras	4-6	6-1	7-6(6)	6-4	
S	Pete Sampras	Michael Chang	6-7(6)	6-3	6-4	6-4	
S	Andre Agassi	Aaron Krickstein	6-4	6-4	3-0	(retired)	
Q	Pete Sampras	Jim Courier	6-7(4)	6-7(3)	6-3	6-4	6-3
Q	Michael Chang	Andrei Medvedev	7-6(7)	7-5	6-3		
Q	Aaron Krickstein	Jacco Eltingh	7-6(3)	6-4	5-7	6-4	
Q	Andre Agassi	Yevgeny Kafelnikov	6-2	7-5	6-0		

1996 (Melbourne)

Rd	Winner	Defeated	S1	S2	S3	S4	S5
F	Boris Becker	Michael Chang	6-2	6-4	2-6	6-2	
S	Boris Becker	Mark Woodforde	6-4	6-2	6-0		
S	Michael Chang	Andre Agassi	6-1	6-4	7-6(1)		
Q	Mark Woodforde	Thomas Enqvist	6-4	6-4	6-3		
Q	Boris Becker	Yevgeny Kafelnikov	6-4	7-6(9)	6-1		
Q	Michael Chang	Mikael Tillstrom	6-0	6-2	6-4		
Q	Andre Agassi	Jim Courier	6-7(7)	2-6	6-3	6-4	6-2

1997 (Melbourne)

Rd	Winner	Defeated	S1	S2	S3	S4	S5
F	Pete Sampras	Carlos Moya	6-2	6-3	6-3		
S	Pete Sampras	Thomas Muster	6-1	7-6(3)	6-3		
S	Carlos Moya	Michael Chang	7-5	6-2	6-4		
Q	Pete Sampras	Albert Costa	6-3	6-7(5)	6-1	3-6	6-2
Q	Thomas Muster	Goran Ivanisevic	6-4	6-2	6-3		
Q	Carlos Moya	Felix Mantilla	7-5	6-2	6-7(5)	6-2	
Q	Michael Chang	Marcelo Rios	7-5	6-1	6-4		

1998 (Melbourne)

Rd	Winner	Defeated	S1	S2	S3	S4	S5
F	Petr Korda	Marcelo Rios	6-2	6-2	6-2		
S	Petr Korda	Karol Kucera	6-1	6-4	1-6	6-2	
S	Marcelo Rios	Nicolas Escude	6-1	6-3	6-2		
Q	Karol Kucera	Pete Sampras	6-4	6-2	6-7(5)	6-3	
Q	Petr Korda	Jonas Bjorkman	3-6	5-7	6-3	6-4	6-2
Q	Nicolas Escude	Nicolas Kiefer	4-6	3-6	6-4	6-1	6-2
Q	Marcelo Rios	Alberto Berasategui	6-7(6)	6-4	6-4	6-0	

1999 (Melbourne)

Rd	Winner	Defeated	S1	S2	S3	S4	S5
F	Yevgeny Kafelnikov	Thomas Enqvist	4-6	6-0	6-3	7-6(1)	
S	Yevgeny Kafelnikov	Tommy Haas	6-3	6-4	7-5		
S	Thomas Enqvist	Nicolas Lapentti	6-3	7-5	6-1		
Q	Yevgeny Kafelnikov	Todd Martin	6-2	7-6(1)	6-2		
Q	Tommy Haas	Vincent Spadea	7-6(5)	7-5	6-3		
Q	Thomas Enqvist	Marc Rosset	6-3	6-4	6-4		
Q	Nicolas Lapentti	Karol Kucera	7-6(4)	6-7(6)	6-2	0-6	8-6

2000 (Melbourne)

Rd	Winner	Defeated	S1	S2	S3	S4	S5
F	Andre Agassi	Yevgeny Kafelnikov	3-6	6-3	6-2	6-4	
S	Andre Agassi	Pete Sampras	6-4	3-6	6-7(0)	7-6(5)	6-1
S	Yevgeny Kafelnikov	Magnus Norman	6-1	6-2	6-4		
Q	Andre Agassi	Hicham Arazi	6-4	6-4	6-2		
Q	Pete Sampras	Chris Woodruff	7-5	6-3	6-3		
Q	Magnus Norman	Nicolas Kiefer	3-6	6-3	6-1	7-6(4)	
Q	Yevgeny Kafelnikov	Younes El Aynaoui	6-0	6-3	7-6(4)		

2001 (Melbourne)

Rd	Winner	Defeated	S1	S2	S3	S4	S5
F	Andre Agassi	Arnaud Clement	6-4	6-2	6-2		
S	Arnaud Clement	Sebastien Grosjean	5-7	2-6	7-6(4)	7-5	6-2
S	Andre Agassi	Patrick Rafter	7-5	2-6	6-7(5)	6-2	6-3
Q	Arnaud Clement	Yevgeny Kafelnikov	6-4	5-7	7-6(3)	7-6(3)	
Q	Sebastien Grosjean	Carlos Moya	6-1	6-4	6-2		
Q	Andre Agassi	Todd Martin	7-5	6-3	6-4		
Q	Patrick Rafter	Dominik Hrbaty	6-2	6-7(4)	7-5	6-0	

2002 (Melbourne)

Rd	Winner	Defeated	S1	S2	S3	S4	S5
F	Thomas Johansson	Marat Safin	3-6	6-4	6-4	7-6(4)	
S	Marat Safin	Tommy Haas	6-7(5)	7-6(4)	3-6	6-0	6-2
S	Thomas Johansson	Jiri Novak	7-6(5)	0-6	4-6	6-3	6-4
Q	Tommy Haas	Marcelo Rios	7-6(2)	6-4	6-7(2)	7-6(5)	
Q	Marat Safin	Wayne Ferreira	5-2			(retired)	
Q	Jiri Novak	Stefan Koubek	6-2	6-3	6-2		
Q	Thomas Johansson	Jonas Bjorkman	6-0	2-6	6-3	6-4	

2003 (Melbourne)

Rd	Winner	Defeated	S1	S2	S3	S4	S5
F	Andre Agassi	Rainer Schuettler	6-2	6-2	6-1		
S	Rainer Schuettler	Andy Roddick	7-5	2-6	6-3	6-3	
S	Andre Agassi	Wayne Ferreira	6-2	6-2	6-3		
Q	Andy Roddick	Younes El Aynaoui	4-6	7-6(5)	4-6	6-4	21-19
Q	Rainer Schuettler	David Nalbandian	6-3	5-7	6-1	6-0	
Q	Wayne Ferreira	Juan Carlos Ferrero	7-6(4)	7-6(5)	6-1		
Q	Andre Agassi	Sebastien Grosjean	6-3	6-2	6-2		

Women's Singles

Rd	Winner	Defeated	S1	S2	S3
1922 *(Sydney)*					
F	**Mall Molesworth**	**Esna Boyd**	**6-3**	**10-8**	
S	Mall Molesworth	Lorna Utz	6-2	6-3	
S	Esna Boyd	Sylvia Lance	6-4	10-8	
Q	Mall Molesworth	Marjorie Mountain	6-4	6-4	
Q	Lorna Utz	Ms Carr		(walkover)	
Q	Sylvia Lance	Ms Elliott	6-1	6-2	
Q	Esna Boyd	J. Watson	6-3	6-2	
1923 *(Brisbane)*					
F	**Mall Molesworth**	**Esna Boyd**	**6-1**	**7-5**	
S	Mall Molesworth	Sylvia Lance	3-6	6-4	8-6
S	Esna Boyd	Ms Haymen	6-2	6-2	
Q	Mall Molesworth	A. Bell	6-2	6-1	
Q	Sylvia Lance	Ms Roe	6-0	6-4	
Q	Ms Haymen	J. Watson	7-5	8-6	
Q	Esna Boyd	Ms Mitchell	6-1	6-3	
1924 *(Melbourne)*					
F	**Sylvia Lance**	**Esna Boyd**	**6-3**	**3-6**	**6-4**
S	Sylvia Lance	Kathrine Lemesurier	6-2	6-2	
S	Esna Boyd	Daphne Akhurst	6-1	6-4	
Q	Sylvia Lance	Ms Todd	1-6	6-4	6-1
Q	Kathrine Lemesurier	Mall Molesworth	7-9	6-3	8-6
Q	Daphne Akhurst	Ms Mather	6-1	6-4	
Q	Esna Boyd	Ms Simpson	6-1	6-1	
1925 *(Sydney)*					
F	**Daphne Akhurst**	**Esna Boyd**	**1-6**	**8-6**	**6-4**
S	Daphne Akhurst	M. Richardson	6-1	6-1	
S	Esna Boyd	Sylvia Lance Harper	6-2	6-3	
Q	Daphne Akhurst	J. Watson	6-1	6-4	
Q	M. Richardson	P. Meaney	6-4	1-6	6-2
Q	Sylvia Lance Harper	Ms Knoblanche	6-1	6-1	
Q	Esna Boyd	Marjorie Cox	4-6	6-0	9-7
1926 *(Adelaide)*					
F	**Daphne Akhurst**	**Esna Boyd**	**6-1**	**6-3**	
S	Daphne Akhurst	Marjorie Cox	6-1	6-3	
S	Esna Boyd	Sylvia Lance Harper	6-4	3-6	6-3
Q	Daphne Akhurst	Kathrine Lemesurier	7-5	6-2	
Q	Marjorie Cox	M. Richardson	6-2	6-2	
Q	Sylvia Lance Harper	H. Turner	6-1	6-4	
Q	Esna Boyd	Meryl O'Hara Wood	6-1	7-5	
1927 *(Melbourne)*					
F	**Esna Boyd**	**Sylvia Lance Harper**	**5-7**	**6-1**	**6-2**
S	Esna Boyd	Louie Bickerton	6-3	6-1	
S	Sylvia Lance Harper	H. Turner	6-2	6-0	
Q	Esna Boyd	D. Bellamy	6-2	6-3	
Q	Louie Bickerton	Kathrine Lemesurier	6-4	4-6	6-2
Q	H. Turner	Dorothy Weston	6-4	6-0	
Q	Sylvia Lance Harper	Marjorie Cox	1-6	6-3	6-3
1928 *(Sydney)*					
F	**Daphne Akhurst**	**Esna Boyd**	**7-5**	**6-2**	
S	Daphne Akhurst	Meryl O'Hara Wood	6-2	7-5	
S	Esna Boyd	Louie Bickerton	6-2	6-3	
Q	Daphne Akhurst	Dorothy Weston	6-1	6-2	
Q	Meryl O'Hara Wood	Kathrine Lemesurier	1-6	6-4	6-2
Q	Louie Bickerton	P. Meaney	4-6	6-1	6-1
Q	Esna Boyd	Mall Molesworth	7-5	6-2	

Rd	Winner	Defeated	S1	S2	S3
1929 *(Adelaide)*					
F	**Daphne Akhurst**	**Louie Bickerton**	**6-1**	**5-7**	**6-2**
S	Daphne Akhurst	Sylvia Lance Harper	6-3	6-1	
S	Louie Bickerton	Marjorie Cox	6-1	6-3	
Q	Daphne Akhurst	Meryl O'Hara Wood	6-4	6-3	
Q	Sylvia Lance Harper	Mall Molesworth	6-1	6-4	
Q	Marjorie Cox	Emily Hood	6-0	6-1	
Q	Louie Bickerton	Kathrine Lemesurier	6-0	8-6	
1930 *(Melbourne)*					
F	**Daphne Akhurst**	**Sylvia Lance Harper**	**10-8**	**2-6**	**7-5**
S	Daphne Akhurst	Emily Hood	6-0	6-2	
S	Sylvia Lance Harper	Louie Bickerton	6-3	8-6	
Q	Daphne Akhurst	Kathrine Lemesurier	6-1	3-6	6-4
Q	Emily Hood	Marjorie Cox	7-5	6-4	
Q	Louie Bickerton	G. Toyne	6-4	7-5	
Q	Sylvia Lance Harper	Mall Molesworth	6-4	3-6	6-2
1931 *(Sydney)*					
F	**Coral McInnes Buttsworth**	**Marjorie Cox Crawford**	**1-6**	**6-3**	**6-4**
S	Coral McInnes Buttsworth	Sylvia Lance Harper	0-6	6-4	(retired)
S	Marjorie Cox Crawford	Kathrine Lemesurier	3-6	6-2	7-5
Q	Coral McInnes Buttsworth	F. Hoodle-Wrigley	6-1	6-2	
Q	Sylvia Lance Harper	P. Meaney	6-1	6-2	
Q	Kathrine Lemesurier	Louie Bickerton	6-1	6-3	
Q	Marjorie Cox Crawford	Joan Hartigan	6-4	4-6	6-4
1932 *(Adelaide)*					
F	**Coral McInnes Buttsworth**	**Kathrine Lemesurier**	**9-7**	**6-4**	
S	Coral McInnes Buttsworth	Dorothy Weston	6-1	6-1	
S	Kathrine Lemesurier	Emily Hood Westacott	10-8	7-5	
Q	Coral McInnes Buttsworth	Meryl O'Hara Wood	6-1	6-3	
Q	Dorothy Weston	J. Wilson	6-1	6-0	
Q	Emily Hood Westacott	F. Hoodle-Wrigley	6-4	7-5	
Q	Kathrine Lemesurier	Marjorie Cox Crawford	6-2	6-4	
1933 *(Melbourne)*					
F	**Joan Hartigan**	**Coral McInnes Buttsworth**	**6-4**	**6-3**	
S	Joan Hartigan	F. Hoodle-Wrigley	4-6	6-0	6-4
S	Coral McInnes Buttsworth	Emily Hood Westacott	9-7	3-6	6-3
Q	Joan Hartigan	Mall Molesworth	4-6	8-6	9-7
Q	F. Hoodle-Wrigley	E. Bond	3-6	8-6	6-4
Q	Emily Hood Westacott	N. Lewis	6-3	6-4	
Q	Coral McInnes Buttsworth	Nell Hall	6-4	6-2	
1934 *(Sydney)*					
F	**Joan Hartigan**	**Mall Molesworth**	**6-1**	**6-4**	
S	Joan Hartigan	Louie Bickerton	6-1	6-3	
S	Mall Molesworth	Muff Wilson	7-5	6-4	
Q	Joan Hartigan	Ula Valkenburg	6-1	6-4	
Q	Louie Bickerton	Alison Hattersley	6-3	6-1	
Q	Muff Wilson	Emily Hood Westacott	2-6	10-8	6-3
Q	Mall Molesworth	Nell Hall	6-4	6-1	
1935 *(Melbourne)*					
F	**Dorothy Round**	**Nancy Lyle**	**1-6**	**6-1**	**6-3**
S	Dorothy Round	Emily Hood Westacott	6-4	6-2	
S	Nancy Lyle	Nell Hall Hopman	6-1	7-5	
Q	Dorothy Round	May Blick	6-4	6-0	
Q	Emily Hood Westacott	Evelyn Dearman	9-7	7-5	
Q	Nell Hall Hopman	J. Walters	4-6	6-1	6-3
Q	Nancy Lyle	Louie Bickerton	6-2	8-6	
1936 *(Adelaide)*					
F	**Joan Hartigan**	**Nancye Wynne**	**6-4**	**6-4**	
S	Joan Hartigan	May Blick	7-5	6-3	
S	Nancye Wynne	Thelma Coyne Long	1-6	7-5	7-5
Q	Joan Hartigan	G. Griffiths	6-1	6-4	
Q	May Blick	J. Walters	5-7	6-1	6-1
Q	Thelma Coyne Long	Mary Hardcastle	6-2	8-6	
Q	Nancye Wynne	Nell Hall Hopman	3-6	6-3	6-4

Rd	Winner	Defeated	S1	S2	S3
1937 *(Sydney)*					
F	**Nancye Wynne**	**Emily Hood Westacott**	6-3	5-7	6-4
S	Nancye Wynne	Thelma Coyne Long	7-5	4-6	6-4
S	Emily Hood Westacott	Dorothy Stevenson	3-6	8-6	9-7
Q	Nancye Wynne	S. Berryman	6-0	6-1	
Q	Thelma Coyne Long	V. Selwyn	6-1	6-1	
Q	Dorothy Stevenson	Joan Hartigan	4-6	6-3	6-4
Q	Emily Hood Westacott	Margaret Wilson	7-5	8-6	
1938 *(Adelaide)*					
F	**Dorothy Bundy**	**Dorothy Stevenson**	6-3	6-2	
S	Dorothy Bundy	Nell Hall Hopman	6-2	6-3	
S	Dorothy Stevenson	Nancye Wynne	6-3	6-3	
Q	Dorothy Bundy	Mary Hardcastle	6-3	6-4	
Q	Nell Hall Hopman	Thelma Coyne Long	6-4	6-2	
Q	Nancye Wynne	Dorothy Workman	6-4	6-3	
Q	Dorothy Stevenson	Joan Hartigan	6-3	1-6	6-1
1939 *(Melbourne)*					
F	**Emily Hood Westacott**	**Nell Hall Hopman**	6-1	6-2	
S	Emily Hood Westacott	Joan Hartigan	6-2	6-3	
S	Nell Hall Hopman	Thelma Coyne Long	6-3	6-4	
Q	Emily Hood Westacott	C. Coate	6-4	6-2	
Q	Joan Hartigan	S. Berryman	6-1	6-4	
Q	Thelma Coyne Long	May Blick	1-6	6-4	6-1
Q	Nell Hall Hopman	Mary Hardcastle	6-3	6-3	
1940 *(Sydney)*					
F	**Nancye Wynne**	**Thelma Coyne Long**	5-7	6-4	6-0
S	Nancye Wynne	Joan Hartigan	6-0	1-6	6-1
S	Thelma Coyne Long	Nell Hall Hopman	6-4	2-6	6-3
Q	Nancye Wynne	G. O'Halloran	6-0	6-3	
Q	Joan Hartigan	Mary Hardcastle	6-2	6-3	
Q	Nell Hall Hopman	Alison Hattersley	6-3	6-4	
Q	Thelma Coyne Long	C. Coate	6-1	6-3	
1941-45	*Not held – WW II*				
1946 *(Adelaide)*					
F	**Nancye Wynne Bolton**	**Joyce Fitch**	6-4	6-4	
S	Joyce Fitch	Marie Toomey	7-5	6-4	
S	Nancye Wynne Bolton	C. Wilson	6-2	6-1	
Q	Marie Toomey	Nell Hall Hopman	6-2	4-6	6-3
Q	Joyce Fitch	Thelma Long	6-2	6-4	
Q	Nancye Wynne Bolton	D. Whittaker	6-2	6-2	
Q	C. Wilson	Joan Hartigan	6-2	8-6	
1947 *(Sydney)*					
F	**Nancye Wynne Bolton**	**Nell Hall Hopman**	6-3	6-2	
S	Nancye Wynne Bolton	P. Jones	6-2	6-1	
S	Nell Hall Hopman	Thelma Long	6-4	6-1	
Q	Nancye Wynne Bolton	Mary Bevis	6-3	6-1	
Q	P. Jones	Marie Toomey	7-5	2-6	7-5
Q	Thelma Long	J. Wilson	6-2	6-4	
Q	Nell Hall Hopman	Joyce Fitch	6-2	2-6	6-0
1948 *(Melbourne)*					
F	**Nancye Bolton**	**Marie Toomey**	6-3	6-1	
S	Nancye Bolton	Mary Bevis	6-3	6-4	
S	Marie Toomey	Esme Ashford	4-6	7-5	6-4
Q	Nancye Bolton	J. Tuckfield	6-2	6-0	
Q	Mary Bevis	Nell Hall Hopman	7-5	6-4	
Q	Marie Toomey	D. Jenkins	8-6	6-3	
Q	Esme Ashford	Clare Proctor	6-1	6-0	

Rd	Winner	Defeated	S1	S2	S3
1949 *(Adelaide)*					
F	**Doris Hart**	**Nancye Bolton**	6-3	6-4	
S	Doris Hart	R. Baker	6-3	6-1	
S	Nancye Bolton	Thelma Long	6-4	6-2	
Q	Doris Hart	D. Whittaker	3-6	6-3	6-2
Q	R. Baker	Marie Toomey	6-3	1-6	6-3
Q	Thelma Long	M. Newcombe	6-0	6-3	
Q	Nancye Bolton	Mary Bevis Hawton	6-1	6-1	
1950 *(Adelaide)*					
F	**Louise Brough**	**Doris Hart**	6-4	3-6	6-4
S	Louise Brough	Joyce Fitch	6-4	6-4	
S	Doris Hart	Nancye Bolton	6-2	6-3	
Q	Louise Brough	M. Newcombe	6-2	6-2	
Q	Joyce Fitch	Thelma Long	7-5	0-6	6-4
Q	Nancye Bolton	Mary Bevis Hawton	6-0	6-2	
Q	Doris Hart	Nell Hall Hopman	6-0	6-1	
1951 *(Sydney)*					
F	**Nancye Bolton**	**Thelma Long**	6-1	7-5	
S	Nancye Bolton	Esme Ashford	6-1	6-0	
S	Thelma Long	Joyce Fitch	6-8	6-4	6-2
Q	Nancye Bolton	Beryl Penrose	8-6	6-2	
Q	Esme Ashford	Mary Bevis Hawton	6-1	4-6	6-3
Q	Thelma Long	Nell Hall Hopman	6-2	6-1	
Q	Joyce Fitch	Clare Proctor	4-6	6-1	6-3
1952 *(Adelaide)*					
F	**Thelma Long**	**Helen Angwin**	6-2	6-3	
S	Helen Angwin	Nancye Bolton	4-6	6-4	6-4
S	Thelma Long	Mary Bevis Hawton	6-0	7-5	
Q	Nancye Bolton	Alison Baker	6-1	6-1	
Q	Helen Angwin	Beryl Penrose	2-6	6-1	6-2
Q	Mary Bevis Hawton	M. Schultz	6-1	6-3	
Q	Thelma Long	Ann Theile	6-0	4-6	6-2
1953 *(Melbourne)*					
F	**Maureen Connolly**	**Julia Sampson**	6-3	6-2	
S	Maureen Connolly	Mary Bevis Hawton	6-2	6-1	
S	Julia Sampson	D. Fogarty	3-6	6-3	6-4
Q	Mary Bevis Hawton	Fay Muller	6-1	6-2	
Q	Maureen Connolly	Pam Southcombe	6-0	6-1	
Q	Julia Sampson	Ann Theile	6-2	6-2	
Q	D. Fogarty	Jenny Staley	6-4	5-7	6-2
1954 *(Sydney)*					
F	**Thelma Long**	**Jenny Staley**	6-3	6-4	
S	Thelma Long	Mary Carter	6-2	6-3	
S	Jenny Staley	Mary Bevis Hawton	6-1	6-1	
Q	Thelma Long	Nell Hall Hopman	6-0	6-0	
Q	Mary Carter	L. Nichols	7-5	6-4	
Q	Jenny Staley	Hazel Redick-Smith	10-8	5-7	6-3
Q	Mary Bevis Hawton	B. Warby	6-4	6-3	
1955 *(Adelaide)*					
F	**Beryl Penrose**	**Thelma Long**	6-4	6-3	
S	Thelma Long	Mary Carter	6-2	6-1	
S	Beryl Penrose	Jenny Staley	6-4	8-6	
Q	Thelma Long	N. Ellis	6-0	6-3	
Q	Mary Carter	Fay Muller	4-6	6-2	6-3
Q	Jenny Staley	Nell Hall Hopman	6-3	6-0	
Q	Beryl Penrose	Mary Bevis Hawton	6-1	1-6	8-6
1956 *(Brisbane)*					
F	**Mary Carter**	**Thelma Long**	3-6	6-2	9-7
S	Thelma Long	Mary Bevis Hawton	0-6	6-3	9-7
S	Mary Carter	D. Seeney	6-3	7-5	
Q	Mary Bevis Hawton	Lorraine Coghlan	0-6	6-0	6-3
Q	Thelma Long	Fay Muller	7-5	6-1	
Q	D. Seeney	Beryl Penrose	6-2	6-1	
Q	Mary Carter	L. Nichols	6-1	7-5	

Rd	Winner	Defeated	S1	S2	S3

1957 *(Melbourne)*

Rd	Winner	Defeated	S1	S2	S3
F	**Shirley Fry**	**Althea Gibson**	**6-3**	**6-4**	
S	Shirley Fry	Beryl Penrose	6-3	6-4	
S	Althea Gibson	Lorraine Coghlan	7-5	6-3	
Q	Shirley Fry	Mary Bevis Hawton	6-1	9-7	
Q	Beryl Penrose	Jenny Hoad	7-5	6-2	
Q	Lorraine Coghlan	Mary Carter	8-10	6-4	6-1
Q	Althea Gibson	L. Southam	6-1	6-3	

1958 *(Sydney)*

Rd	Winner	Defeated	S1	S2	S3
F	**Angela Mortimer**	**Lorraine Coghlan**	**6-3**	**6-4**	
S	Lorraine Coghlan	Mary Carter	6-1	6-1	
S	Angela Mortimer	Betty Holstein	6-2	6-1	
Q	Lorraine Coghlan	Margaret Rayson	6-3	6-1	
Q	Mary Carter	Bertha Jones	8-6	6-1	
Q	Betty Holstein	Mary Bevis Hawton	7-5	6-8	6-4
Q	Angela Mortimer	Fay Muller	6-1	6-2	

1959 *(Adelaide)*

Rd	Winner	Defeated	S1	S2	S3
F	**Mary Carter Reitano**	**Renee Schuurman**	**6-2**	**6-3**	
S	Renee Schuurman	Mary Bevis Hawton	6-3	6-0	
S	Mary Carter Reitano	Jan Lehane	6-3	6-0	
Q	Renee Schuurman	Lesley Turner	6-2	6-0	
Q	Mary Bevis Hawton	Lorraine Coghlan	6-4	4-6	6-0
Q	Mary Carter Reitano	Beverly Rae	8-6	6-4	
Q	Jan Lehane	Sandra Reynolds	6-3	6-4	

1960 *(Brisbane)*

Rd	Winner	Defeated	S1	S2	S3
F	**Margaret Smith**	**Jan Lehane**	**7-5**	**6-2**	
S	Jan Lehane	Christine Truman	7-5	3-6	7-5
S	Margaret Smith	Mary Carter Reitano	7-5	2-6	6-2
Q	Christine Truman	Fay Muller	6-0	6-0	
Q	Jan Lehane	L. Coghlan Robinson	6-1	6-1	
Q	Mary Carter Reitano	Mary Bevis Hawton	6-2	8-6	
Q	Margaret Smith	Maria Bueno	7-5	3-6	6-4

1961 *(Melbourne)*

Rd	Winner	Defeated	S1	S2	S3
F	**Margaret Smith**	**Jan Lehane**	**6-1**	**6-4**	
S	Margaret Smith	Robyn Ebbern	6-2	6-0	
S	Jan Lehane	Mary Carter Reitano	6-2	4-6	6-1
Q	Margaret Smith	Kaye Dening	6-4	6-3	
Q	Robyn Ebbern	Val Wicks	6-4	6-2	
Q	Mary Carter Reitano	Mary Bevis Hawton	6-4	6-2	
Q	Jan Lehane	L. Coghlan Robinson	6-2	6-2	

1962 *(Sydney)*

Rd	Winner	Defeated	S1	S2	S3
F	**Margaret Smith**	**Jan Lehane**	**6-0**	**6-2**	
S	Margaret Smith	Yola Ramirez	6-2	6-1	
S	Jan Lehane	Mary Carter Reitano	6-2	2-6	6-4
Q	Margaret Smith	Judy Tegart	6-2	7-5	
Q	Yola Ramirez	Norma Marsh	5-7	6-0	6-2
Q	Mary Carter Reitano	Lesley Turner	6-1	1-6	6-2
Q	Jan Lehane	Darlene Hard	7-5	6-4	

1963 *(Adelaide)*

Rd	Winner	Defeated	S1	S2	S3
F	**Margaret Smith**	**Jan Lehane**	**6-2**	**6-2**	
S	Jan Lehane	Lesley Turner	5-7	6-3	6-2
S	Margaret Smith	Robyn Ebbern	6-1	6-3	
Q	Lesley Turner	Elisabeth Starkie	6-2	1-6	6-2
Q	Jan Lehane	Madonna Schacht	6-1	6-4	
Q	Robyn Ebbern	Jill Blackman	6-2	6-4	
Q	Margaret Smith	Rita Bentley	6-1	6-3	

1964 *(Brisbane)*

Rd	Winner	Defeated	S1	S2	S3
F	**Margaret Smith**	**Lesley Turner**	**6-3**	**6-2**	
S	Lesley Turner	Robyn Ebbern	6-3	6-1	
S	Margaret Smith	Jan Lehane	6-4	6-2	
Q	Lesley Turner	Jill Blackman	6-1	6-3	
Q	Robyn Ebbern	Judy Tegart	6-2	6-4	
Q	Jan Lehane	Helen Gourlay	6-2	6-0	
Q	Margaret Smith	Madonna Schacht	4-6	6-1	6-1

1965 *(Melbourne)*

Rd	Winner	Defeated	S1	S2	S3
F	**Margaret Smith**	**Maria Bueno**	**5-7**	**6-3**	**5-2** (retired)
S	Maria Bueno	Annette Van Zyl	6-2	6-3	
S	Margaret Smith	Billie Jean Moffitt	6-1	8-6	
Q	Annette Van Zyl	Lesley Turner	6-3	6-4	
Q	Maria Bueno	Judy Tegart	6-2	6-2	
Q	Billie Jean Moffitt	Kerry Melville	6-1	6-2	
Q	Margaret Smith	Françoise Durr	6-3	6-3	

1966 *(Sydney)*

Rd	Winner	Defeated	S1	S2	S3
F	**Margaret Smith**	**Nancy Richey**	(walkover)		
S	Margaret Smith	Carole Graebner	6-2	6-4	
S	Nancy Richey	Kerry Melville	6-2	8-6	
Q	Margaret Smith	Madonna Schacht	6-1	6-3	
Q	Carole Graebner	Judy Tegart	6-3	6-3	
Q	Kerry Melville	J. Gibson	6-2	3-6	6-4
Q	Nancy Richey	Helen Amos	6-2	6-3	

1967 *(Adelaide)*

Rd	Winner	Defeated	S1	S2	S3
F	**Nancy Richey**	**Lesley Turner**	**6-1**	**6-4**	
S	Lesley Turner	Rosie Casals	4-6	6-1	6-4
S	Nancy Richey	Kerry Melville	6-4	6-1	
Q	Lesley Turner	Françoise Durr	6-1	10-8	
Q	Rosie Casals	Gail Sherriff	6-3	6-3	
Q	Kerry Melville	Judy Tegart	6-1	4-6	10-8
Q	Nancy Richey	L. Coghlan Robinson	6-3	1-0	(retired)

1968 *(Melbourne)*

Rd	Winner	Defeated	S1	S2	S3
F	**Billie Jean King**	**Margaret Smith Court**	**6-1**	**6-2**	
S	Margaret Smith Court	Lesley Turner	6-2	6-3	
S	Billie Jean King	Judy Tegart	4-6	6-1	6-1
S	Lesley Turner	Kathy Harter	3-6	6-2	6-2
Q	Margaret Smith Court	Rosie Casals	6-0	6-2	
Q	Judy Tegart	Karen Krantzcke	4-6	10-8	6-3
Q	Billie Jean King	Astrid Suurbeck	6-1	6-2	

1969 *(Brisbane)*

Rd	Winner	Defeated	S1	S2	S3
F	**Margaret Smith Court**	**Billie Jean King**	**6-4**	**6-1**	
S	Billie Jean King	Ann Haydon Jones	4-6	6-2	6-3
S	Margaret Smith Court	Kerry Melville	3-6	6-2	7-5
Q	Billie Jean King	Karen Krantzcke	11-9	7-5	
Q	Ann Haydon Jones	Lesley Hunt	6-3	6-1	
Q	Kerry Melville	Helen Gourlay	6-3	4-6	6-4
Q	Margaret Smith Court	Rosie Casals	6-4	6-1	

1970 *(Sydney)*

Rd	Winner	Defeated	S1	S2	S3
F	**Margaret Smith Court**	**Kerry Melville**	**6-1**	**6-3**	
S	Kerry Melville	Winnie Shaw	8-6	6-3	
S	Margaret Smith Court	Karen Krantzcke	6-1	6-2	
Q	Margaret Smith Court	Evonne Goolagong	6-3	6-1	
Q	Karen Krantzcke	Judy Tegart Dalton	8-6	11-9	
Q	Kerry Melville	Christina Sandberg	6-0	6-2	
Q	Winnie Shaw	Lesley Hunt	6-4	6-3	

1971 *(Sydney)*

Rd	Winner	Defeated	S1	S2	S3
F	**Margaret Smith Court**	**Evonne Goolagong**	**2-6**	**7-6(0)**	**7-5**
S	Evonne Goolagong	Winnie Shaw	7-6	6-1	
S	Margaret Smith Court	Lesley Hunt	6-0	6-3	
Q	Margaret Smith Court	Helen Gourlay Cawley	6-0	6-4	
Q	Lesley Hunt	Jan O'Neill	6-4	6-4	
Q	Winnie Shaw	Norma Marsh	6-0	7-6	
Q	Evonne Goolagong	Sharon Walsh	6-3	6-4	

Rd	Winner	Defeated	S1	S2	S3
1972	*(Melbourne)*				
F	**Virginia Wade**	**Evonne Goolagong**	**6-4**	**6-4**	
S	Virginia Wade	Kerry Harris	7-6	2-6	6-0
S	Evonne Goolagong	Helen Gourlay	6-2	7-6	
Q	Evonne Goolagong	Barbara Hawcroft	6-1	3-6	6-1
Q	Helen Gourlay Cawley	Olga Morozova	6-2	6-1	
Q	Kerry Harris	Gail Sherriff Chanfreau	6-3	7-6	
Q	Virginia Wade	Patricia Coleman	6-2	6-2	
1973	*(Melbourne)*				
F	**Margaret Smith Court**	**Evonne Goolagong**	**6-4**	**7-5**	
S	Evonne Goolagong	Kazuko Sawamatsu	6-4	6-3	
S	Margaret Smith Court	Kerry Melville	6-1	6-0	
Q	Margaret Smith Court	Karen Krantzcke	6-4	6-3	
Q	Kerry Melville	D. Balestrat Fromholtz	6-1	6-3	
Q	Kazuko Sawamatsu	Virginia Wade	0-6	6-1	6-4
Q	Evonne Goolagong	Kerry Harris	6-4	6-3	
1974	*(Melbourne)*				
F	**Evonne Goolagong**	**Chris Evert**	**7-6(5)**	**4-6**	**6-0**
S	Evonne Goolagong	Kerry Melville	7-6	5-7	6-1
S	Chris Evert	Julie Heldman	6-2	6-3	
Q	Chris Evert	Janet Newberry	6-2	6-4	
Q	Julie Heldman	Lesley Hunt	7-5	6-7	6-2
Q	Kerry Melville	Judy Tegart Dalton	6-3	6-4	
Q	Evonne Goolagong	Karen Krantzcke	4-6	6-3	6-2
1975	*(Melbourne)*				
F	**Evonne Goolagong**	**Martina Navratilova**	**6-3**	**6-2**	
S	Martina Navratilova	Natasha Chmyreva	6-4	6-4	
S	Evonne Goolagong	Sue Barker	6-2	6-4	
Q	Martina Navratilova	Margaret Smith Court	6-4	6-3	
Q	Natasha Chmyreva	Christine Matison	3-6	6-2	7-5
Q	Evonne Goolagong	Kazuko Sawamatsu	6-3	7-5	
Q	Sue Barker	Olga Morozova	6-2	7-6	
1976	*(Melbourne)*				
F	**Evonne Goolagong Cawley**	**Renata Tomanova**	**6-2**	**6-2**	
S	Evonne Goolagong Cawley	Helen Gourlay	6-3	6-3	
S	Renata Tomanova	Elizabeth Ekblom	6-3	6-2	
Q	Evonne Goolagong Cawley	Lesley Turner Bowrey	6-1	7-6	
Q	Helen Gourlay	Heidi Eisterlehner	6-3	6-7	6-2
Q	Renata Tomanova-Roth	Helga Masthoff	4-6	7-5	6-1
Q	Elizabeth Ekblom	Christine Matison	4-6	6-3	6-1
1977 (Jan.)	*(Melbourne)*				
F	**Kerry Melville Reid**	**D. Balestrat Fromholtz**	**7-5**	**6-2**	
S	Kerry Melville Reid	Helen Gourlay	6-2	1-6	6-3
S	D. Balestrat Fromholtz	Karen Krantzcke	7-6(7)	6-4	
Q	D. Balestrat Fromholtz	Jan Wilton	6-3	4-6	6-1
Q	Karen Krantzcke	Naoko Sato	6-3	4-6	6-0
Q	Helen Gourlay	Mary Sawyer	6-1	6-4	
Q	Kerry Melville Reid	Katja Ebbinghaus	6-0	6-4	
1977 (Dec.)	*(Melbourne)*				
F	**Evonne Goolagong Cawley**	**Helen Gourlay Cawley**	**6-3**	**6-0**	
S	Helen Gourlay Cawley	Sue Barker	7-5	6-4	
S	Evonne Goolagong Cawley	Kerry Melville Reid	6-1	6-3	
Q	Evonne Goolagong Cawley	Judy Tegart Dalton	6-3	6-1	
Q	Kerry Melville Reid	Kathy Harter	6-1	7-5	
Q	Helen Gourlay Cawley	Mona Schallau Guerrant	3-6	6-1	6-4
Q	Sue Barker	Rayni Fox	6-3	6-0	
1978	*(Melbourne)*				
F	**Chris O'Neil**	**Betsy Nagelsen**	**6-3**	**7-6(4)**	
S	Chris O'Neil	Diane Evers	6-0	6-3	
S	Betsy Nagelsen	Christine Matison	7-5	6-4	
Q	Diane Evers	Sue Barker	6-2	7-6	
Q	Chris O'Neil	Dorte Ekner	7-5	6-1	
Q	Christine Matison	Mary Sawyer	6-4	6-3	
Q	Betsy Nagelsen	Renata Tomanova	6-4	6-4	

Rd	Winner	Defeated	S1	S2	S3
1979	*(Melbourne)*				
F	**Barbara Jordan**	**Sharon Walsh**	**6-3**	**6-3**	
S	Sharon Walsh	Mary Sawyer	7-6	6-3	
S	Barbara Jordan	Renata Tomanova	5-7	6-3	6-3
Q	Mary Sawyer	Janet Newberry	7-6	6-3	
Q	Sharon Walsh	Michele Gurdal	6-0	6-3	
Q	Renata Tomanova	Cynthia Doerner	6-2	6-1	
Q	Barbara Jordan	Hana Mandlikova	6-2	6-2	
1980	*(Melbourne)*				
F	**Hana Mandlikova**	**Wendy Turnbull**	**6-0**	**7-5**	
S	Wendy Turnbull	Martina Navratilova	6-4	7-5	
S	Hana Mandlikova	Mima Jausovec	6-4	6-1	
Q	Martina Navratilova	Greer Stevens	4-6	6-1	7-6
Q	Wendy Turnbull	Pam Shriver	3-6	6-3	6-2
Q	Hana Mandlikova	Virginia Ruzici	6-1	3-6	6-4
Q	Mima Jausovec	Candy Reynolds	4-6	6-3	6-3
1981	*(Melbourne)*				
F	**Martina Navratilova**	**Chris Evert Lloyd**	**6-7(4)**	**6-4**	**7-5**
S	Chris Evert Lloyd	Wendy Turnbull	6-4	7-6(1)	
S	Martina Navratilova	Pam Shriver	6-3	7-5	
Q	Chris Evert Lloyd	Hana Mandlikova	6-4	7-5	
Q	Wendy Turnbull	Andrea Jaeger	6-3	7-6(10)	
Q	Martina Navratilova	Evonne Goolagong	6-3	6-1	
Q	Pam Shriver	Tracy Austin	7-5	7-6(4)	
1982	*(Melbourne)*				
F	**Chris Evert Lloyd**	**Martina Navratilova**	**6-3**	**2-6**	**6-3**
S	Martina Navratilova	Pam Shriver	6-3	6-4	
S	Chris Evert Lloyd	Andrea Jaeger	6-1	6-0	
Q	Martina Navratilova	Anne Smith	6-2	6-1	
Q	Pam Shriver	Wendy Turnbull	6-7	6-3	6-3
Q	Andrea Jaeger	Eva Pfaff	7-5	6-2	
Q	Chris Evert Lloyd	Billie Jean King	6-2	6-2	
1983	*(Melbourne)*				
F	**Martina Navratilova**	**Kathy Jordan**	**6-2**	**7-6(5)**	
S	Martina Navratilova	Pam Shriver	6-4	6-3	
S	Kathy Jordan	Zina Garrison	7-6	6-1	
Q	Martina Navratilova	Jo Durie	4-6	6-3	6-4
Q	Pam Shriver	Carling Bassett	6-0	6-1	
Q	Zina Garrison	Wendy Turnbull	6-2	7-6	
Q	Kathy Jordan	Sylvia Hanika	7-6	7-5	
1984	*(Melbourne)*				
F	**Chris Evert Lloyd**	**Helena Sukova**	**6-7(4)**	**6-1**	**6-3**
S	Helena Sukova	Martina Navratilova	1-6	6-3	7-5
S	Chris Evert Lloyd	Wendy Turnbull	6-3	6-3	
Q	Martina Navratilova	Barbara Potter	6-3	6-2	
Q	Helena Sukova	Pam Shriver	6-2	6-7	6-1
Q	Wendy Turnbull	Sharon Walsh	7-5	6-2	
Q	Chris Evert Lloyd	Sophie Amiach	6-2	6-1	
1985	*(Melbourne)*				
F	**Martina Navratilova**	**Chris Evert Lloyd**	**6-2**	**4-6**	**6-2**
S	Chris Evert Lloyd	Claudia Kohde Kilsch	6-1	7-6(8)	
S	Martina Navratilova	Hana Mandlikova	6-7(5)	6-1	6-4
Q	Chris Evert Lloyd	Manuela Maleeva	6-3	6-3	
Q	Claudia Kohde Kilsch	Catarina Lindqvist	6-4	6-0	
Q	Hana Mandlikova	Zina Garrison	2-6	6-3	6-3
Q	Martina Navratilova	Helena Sukova	6-2	6-2	
1987	*(Melbourne)*				
F	**Hana Mandlikova**	**Martina Navratilova**	**7-5**	**7-6(2)**	
S	Hana Mandlikova	Claudia Kohde Kilsch	6-1	0-6	6-3
S	Martina Navratilova	Catarina Lindqvist	6-3	6-3	
Q	Claudia Kohde Kilsch	Liz Smylie	7-6	4-6	6-2
Q	Hana Mandlikova	Lori McNeil	6-0	6-0	
Q	Catarina Lindqvist	Pam Shriver	6-3	6-1	
Q	Martina Navratilova	Zina Garrison	6-0	6-3	

Rd	Winner	Defeated	S1	S2	S3
1988 *(Melbourne)*					
F	**Steffi Graf**	**Chris Evert**	**6-1**	**7-6(3)**	
S	Chris Evert	Martina Navratilova	6-2	7-5	
S	Steffi Graf	Claudia Kohde Kilsch	6-2	6-3	
Q	Chris Evert	Claudia Porwik	6-3	6-1	
Q	Martina Navratilova	Helena Sukova	6-4	7-6(3)	
Q	Steffi Graf	Hana Mandlikova	6-2	6-2	
Q	Claudia Kohde Kilsch	Anne Minter	6-2	6-4	
1989 *(Melbourne)*					
F	**Steffi Graf**	**Helena Sukova**	**6-4**	**6-4**	
S	Helena Sukova	Belinda Cordwell	7-6(2)	4-6	6-2
S	Steffi Graf	Gabriela Sabatini	6-3	6-0	
Q	Belinda Cordwell	Catarina Lindqvist	6-2	2-6	6-1
Q	Helena Sukova	Martina Navratilova	6-2	3-6	9-7
Q	Gabriela Sabatini	Zina Garrison Jackson	6-4	2-6	6-4
Q	Steffi Graf	Claudia Kohde Kilsch	6-2	6-3	
1990 *(Melbourne)*					
F	**Steffi Graf**	**Mary Joe Fernandez**	**6-3**	**6-4**	
S	Steffi Graf	Helena Sukova	6-3	3-6	6-4
S	Mary Joe Fernandez	Claudia Porwik	6-2	6-1	
Q	Steffi Graf	Patty Fendick	6-3	7-5	
Q	Helena Sukova	Katerina Maleeva	6-4	6-3	
Q	Mary Joe Fernandez	Zina Garrison	1-6	6-2	8-6
Q	Claudia Porwik	Angelica Gavaldon	6-4	6-3	
1991 *(Melbourne)*					
F	**Monica Seles**	**Jana Novotna**	**5-7**	**6-3**	**6-1**
S	Jana Novotna	Arantxa Sanchez Vicario	6-2	6-4	
S	Monica Seles	Mary Joe Fernandez	6-3	0-6	9-7
Q	Jana Novotna	Steffi Graf	5-7	6-4	8-6
Q	Arantxa Sanchez Vicario	Gabriela Sabatini	6-1	6-3	
Q	Mary Joe Fernandez	Katerina Maleeva	6-3	6-2	
Q	Monica Seles	Anke Huber	6-3	6-1	
1992 *(Melbourne)*					
F	**Monica Seles**	**Mary Joe Fernandez**	**6-2**	**6-3**	
S	Monica Seles	Arantxa Sanchez Vicario	6-2	6-2	
S	Mary Joe Fernandez	Gabriela Sabatini	6-1	6-4	
Q	Monica Seles	Anke Huber	7-5	6-3	
Q	Arantxa Sanchez Vicario	Manuela Maleeva-Fragniere	(walkover)		
Q	Gabriela Sabatini	Jennifer Capriati	6-4	7-6(1)	
Q	Mary Joe Fernandez	Amy Frazier	6-4	7-6(6)	
1993 *(Melbourne)*					
F	**Monica Seles**	**Steffi Graf**	**4-6**	**6-3**	**6-2**
S	Monica Seles	Gabriela Sabatini	6-1	6-2	
S	Steffi Graf	Arantxa Sanchez Vicario	7-5	6-4	
Q	Monica Seles	Julie Halard	6-2	6-7(7)	6-0
Q	Gabriela Sabatini	Mary Pierce	4-6	7-6(12)	6-0
Q	Arantxa Sanchez Vicario	Mary Joe Fernandez	7-5	6-4	
Q	Steffi Graf	Jennifer Capriati	7-5	6-2	
1994 *(Melbourne)*					
F	**Steffi Graf**	**Arantxa Sanchez Vicario**	**6-0**	**6-2**	
S	Steffi Graf	Kimiko Date	6-3	6-3	
S	Arantxa Sanchez Vicario	Gabriela Sabatini	6-1	6-2	
Q	Steffi Graf	Lindsay Davenport	6-3	6-2	
Q	Kimiko Date	Conchita Martinez	6-2	4-6	6-3
Q	Gabriela Sabatini	Jana Novotna	6-3	6-4	
Q	Arantxa Sanchez Vicario	M. Maleeva-Fragniere	7-6(3)	6-4	
1995 *(Melbourne)*					
F	**Mary Pierce**	**Arantxa Sanchez Vicario**	**6-3**	**6-2**	
S	Arantxa Sanchez Vicario	M. Werdel Witmeyer	6-4	6-1	
S	Mary Pierce	Conchita Martinez	6-3	6-1	
Q	Arantxa Sanchez Vicario	Naoko Sawamatsu	6-1	6-3	
Q	Marianne Werdel Witmeyer	Angelica Gavaldon	6-1	6-2	
Q	Mary Pierce	Natasha Zvereva	6-1	6-4	
Q	Conchita Martinez	Lindsay Davenport	6-3	4-6	6-3

Rd	Winner	Defeated	S1	S2	S3
1996 *(Melbourne)*					
F	**Monica Seles**	**Anke Huber**	**6-4**	**6-1**	
S	Monica Seles	Chanda Rubin	6-7(2)	6-1	7-5
S	Anke Huber	Amanda Coetzer	4-6	6-4	6-2
Q	Monica Seles	Iva Majoli	6-1	6-2	
Q	Chanda Rubin	Arantxa Sanchez Vicario	6-4	2-6	16-14
Q	Amanda Coetzer	Martina Hingis	7-5	4-6	6-1
Q	Anke Huber	Conchita Martinez	4-6	6-2	6-1
1997 *(Melbourne)*					
F	**Martina Hingis**	**Mary Pierce**	**6-2**	**6-2**	
S	Mary Pierce	Amanda Coetzer	7-5	6-1	
S	Martina Hingis	Mary Joe Fernandez	6-1	6-3	
Q	Amanda Coetzer	Kimberly Po	6-4	6-1	
Q	Mary Pierce	Sabine Appelmans	1-6	6-4	6-4
Q	Martina Hingis	Irina Spirlea	7-5	6-2	
Q	Mary Joe Fernandez	Dominique Van Roost	7-5	4-0	(retired)
1998 *(Melbourne)*					
F	**Martina Hingis**	**Conchita Martinez**	**6-3**	**6-3**	
S	Martina Hingis	Anke Huber	6-1	2-6	6-1
S	Conchita Martinez	Lindsay Davenport	4-6	6-3	6-3
Q	Martina Hingis	Mary Pierce	6-2	6-3	
Q	Anke Huber	Arantxa Sanchez Vicario	7-6(7)	7-5	
Q	Conchita Martinez	Sandrine Testud	6-3	6-2	
Q	Lindsay Davenport	Venus Williams	1-6	7-5	6-3
1999 *(Melbourne)*					
F	**Martina Hingis**	**Amelie Mauresmo**	**6-2**	**6-3**	
S	Amelie Mauresmo	Lindsay Davenport	4-6	7-5	7-5
S	Martina Hingis	Monica Seles	6-2	6-4	
Q	Lindsay Davenport	Venus Williams	6-4	6-0	
Q	Amelie Mauresmo	Dominique Van Roost	6-3	7-6(3)	
Q	Monica Seles	Steffi Graf	7-5	6-1	
Q	Martina Hingis	Mary Pierce	6-3	6-4	
2000 *(Melbourne)*					
F	**Lindsay Davenport**	**Martina Hingis**	**6-1**	**7-5**	
S	Martina Hingis	Conchita Martinez	6-3	6-2	
S	Lindsay Davenport	Jennifer Capriati	6-2	7-6(4)	
Q	Martina Hingis	Arantxa Sanchez Vicario	6-1	6-1	
Q	Conchita Martinez	Elena Likhovtseva	6-3	4-6	9-7
Q	Jennifer Capriati	Ai Sugiyama	6-0	6-2	
Q	Lindsay Davenport	Julie Halard-Decugis	6-1	6-2	
2001 *(Melbourne)*					
F	**Jennifer Capriati**	**Martina Hingis**	**6-4**	**6-3**	
S	Martina Hingis	Venus Williams	6-1	6-1	
S	Jennifer Capriati	Lindsay Davenport	6-3	6-4	
Q	Martina Hingis	Serena Williams	6-2	3-6	8-6
Q	Venus Williams	Amanda Coetzer	2-6	6-1	8-6
Q	Jennifer Capriati	Monica Seles	5-7	6-4	6-3
Q	Lindsay Davenport	Anna Kournikova	6-4	6-2	
2002 *(Melbourne)*					
F	**Jennifer Capriati**	**Martina Hingis**	**4-6**	**7-6(7)**	**6-2**
S	Jennifer Capriati	Kim Clijsters	7-5	3-6	6-1
S	Martina Hingis	Monica Seles	4-6	6-1	6-4
Q	Jennifer Capriati	Amelie Mauresmo	6-2	6-2	
Q	Kim Clijsters	Justine Henin	6-2	6-3	
Q	Martina Hingis	Adriana Serra Zanetti	6-2	6-3	
Q	Monica Seles	Venus Williams	6-7(4)	6-2	6-3
2003 *(Melbourne)*					
F	**Serena Williams**	**Venus Williams**	**7-6(4)**	**3-6**	**6-4**
S	Serena Williams	Kim Clijsters	4-6	6-3	7-5
S	Venus Williams	Justine Henin-Hardenne	6-3	6-3	
S	Serena Williams	Meghann Shaughnessy	6-2	6-2	
Q	Kim Clijsters	Anastasia Myskina	6-2	6-4	
Q	Justine Henin-Hardenne	Virginia Ruano Pascual	6-2	6-3	
Q	Venus Williams	Daniela Hantuchova	6-4	6-3	

Men's Doubles

Year	Winner	Defeated	S1	S2	S3	S4	S5
1905	Randolph Lycett Tom Tachell	E. T. Barnard B. Spence	11-9	8-6	1-6	4-6	6-1
1906	Rodney Heath Tony Wilding	Harry Parker C. C. Cox	6-2	6-4	6-2		
1907	Bill Gregg Harry Parker	Horrie Rice George Wright	6-2	3-6	6-2	6-2	
1908	Fred Alexander Alfred Dunlop	G. G. Sharp Tony Wilding	6-3	6-2	6-1		
1909	J. P. Keane Ernest Parker	Tom Crooks Tony Wilding	1-6	6-1	6-1	9-7	
1910	Ashley Campbell Horrie Rice	Rodney Heath J. L. O'Dea	6-3	6-3	6-2		
1911	Rodney Heath Randolph Lycett	J. J. Addison Norman Brookes	6-2	7-5	6-0		
1912	Jim Parke Charles Dixon	Alfred Beamish Gordon Lowe	6-4	6-4	6-2		
1913	Alf Hedemann Ernest Parker	Harry Parker Ron Taylor	8-6	4-6	6-4	6-4	
1914	Ashley Campbell Gerald Patterson	Rodney Heath Arthur O'Hara Wood	7-5	3-6	6-3	6-3	
1915	Horrie Rice Clarrie Todd	Gordon Lowe Bert St. John	8-6	6-4	7-9	6-3	
1916-18		Not held – WW I					
1919	Pat O'Hara Wood Ron Thomas	James Anderson Arthur Lowe	7-5	6-1	7-9	3-6	6-3
1920	Pat O'Hara Wood Ron Thomas	Horrie Rice Ron Taylor	6-1	6-0	7-5		
1921	S. H. Eaton Rhys Gemmell	N. Brearley E. Stokes	7-5	6-3	6-3		
1922	Jack Hawkes Gerald Patterson	James Anderson Norman Peach	8-10	6-0	6-0	7-5	
1923	Pat O'Hara Wood Bert St. John	Dudley Bullough Horrie Rice	6-4	6-3	3-6	6-0	
1924	James Anderson Norman Brookes	Gerald Patterson Pat O'Hara Wood	6-2	6-4	6-3		
1925	Pat O'Hara Wood Gerald Patterson	James Anderson Fred Kalms	6-4	8-6	7-5		
1926	Jack Hawkes Gerald Patterson	James Anderson Pat O'Hara Wood	6-1	6-4	6-2		
1927	Jack Hawkes Gerald Patterson	Pat O'Hara Wood Ian McInness	8-6	6-2	6-1		
1928	Jean Borotra Jacques Brugnon	Jim Willard Gar Moon	6-2	4-6	6-4	6-4	
1929	Jack Crawford Harry Hopman	Jack Cummings Gar Moon	6-1	6-8	4-6	6-1	6-3
1930	Jack Crawford Harry Hopman	Jack Hawkes Tim Fitchett	8-6	6-1	2-6	6-3	
1931	Charles Donohoe Ray Dunlop	Jack Crawford Harry Hopman	8-6	6-2	5-7	7-9	6-4
1932	Jack Crawford Gar Moon	Harry Hopman Gerald Patterson	12-10	6-3	4-6	6-4	
1933	Keith Gledhill Ellsworth Vines	Jack Crawford Gar Moon	6-4	10-8	6-2		
1934	Fred Perry Pat Hughes	Adrian Quist Don Turnbull	6-8	6-3	6-4	3-6	6-3
1935	Jack Crawford Viv McGrath	Pat Hughes Fred Perry	6-4	8-6	6-2		
1936	Adrian Quist Don Turnbull	Jack Crawford Viv McGrath	6-8	6-2	6-1	3-6	6-2
1937	Adrian Quist Don Turnbull	John Bromwich Jack Harper	6-2	9-7	1-6	6-8	6-4
1938	John Bromwich Adrian Quist	Gottfried von Cramm Henner Henkel	7-5	6-4	6-0		
1939	John Bromwich Adrian Quist	Don Turnbull Colin Long	6-4	7-5	6-2		
1940	John Bromwich Adrian Quist	Jack Crawford Viv McGrath	6-3	7-5	6-1		
1941-45		Not held – WW II					
1946	John Bromwich Adrian Quist	Max Newcombe Len Schwartz	6-3	6-1	9-7		
1947	John Bromwich Adrian Quist	Frank Sedgman George Worthington	6-1	6-3	6-1		
1948	John Bromwich Adrian Quist	Frank Sedgman Colin Long	1-6	6-8	9-7	6-3	8-6
1949	John Bromwich Adrian Quist	Geoff Brown Bill Sidwell	1-6	7-5	6-2	6-3	
1950	John Bromwich Adrian Quist	Eric Sturgess Jaroslav Drobny	6-3	5-7	4-6	6-3	8-6
1951	Ken McGregor Frank Sedgman	John Bromwich Adrian Quist	11-9	2-6	6-3	4-6	6-3
1952	Ken McGregor Frank Sedgman	Don Candy Merv Rose	6-4	7-5	6-3		
1953	Lew Hoad Ken Rosewall	Don Candy Merv Rose	9-11	6-4	10-8	6-4	
1954	Rex Hartwig Merv Rose	Neale Fraser Clive Wilderspin	6-3	6-4	6-2		
1955	Vic Seixas Tony Trabert	Lew Hoad Ken Rosewall	6-3	6-2	2-6	3-6	6-1
1956	Lew Hoad Ken Rosewall	Don Candy Merv Rose	10-8	13-11	6-4		
1957	Neale Fraser Lew Hoad	Mal Anderson Ashley Cooper	6-3	8-6	6-4		
1958	Ashley Cooper Neale Fraser	Roy Emerson Bob Mark	7-5	6-8	3-6	6-3	7-5
1959	Rod Laver Bob Mark	Don Candy Bob Howe	9-7	6-4	6-2		
1960	Rod Laver Bob Mark	Roy Emerson Neale Fraser	1-6	6-2	6-4	6-4	
1961	Rod Laver Bob Mark	Roy Emerson Marty Mulligan	6-3	7-5	3-6	9-11	6-2
1962	Roy Emerson Neale Fraser	Bob Hewitt Fred Stolle	4-6	4-6	6-1	6-4	11-9
1963	Bob Hewitt Fred Stolle	Ken Fletcher John Newcombe	6-2	3-6	6-3	3-6	6-3
1964	Bob Hewitt Fred Stolle	Roy Emerson Ken Fletcher	6-4	7-5	3-6	4-6	14-12
1965	John Newcombe Tony Roche	Roy Emerson Fred Stolle	3-6	4-6	13-11	6-3	6-4

Year	Winner	Defeated	S1	S2	S3	S4	S5
1966	Roy Emerson Fred Stolle	John Newcombe Tony Roche	7-9	6-3	6-8	14-12	12-10
1967	John Newcombe Tony Roche	Bill Bowrey Owen Davidson	3-6	6-3	7-5	6-8	8-6
1968	Dick Crealy Allan Stone	Terry Addison Ray Keldie	10-8	6-4	6-3		
1969	Roy Emerson Rod Laver	Ken Rosewall Fred Stolle	6-4	6-4	(shortened by agreement)		
1970	Bob Lutz Stan Smith	John Alexander Phil Dent	8-6	6-3	6-4		
1971	John Newcombe Tony Roche	Tom Okker Marty Riessen	6-2	7-6			
1972	Owen Davidson Ken Rosewall	Ross Case Geoff Masters	3-6	7-6	6-2		
1973	Mal Anderson John Newcombe	John Alexander Phil Dent	6-3	6-4	7-6		
1974	Ross Case Geoff Masters	Syd Ball Bob Giltinan	6-7	6-3	6-4		
1975	John Alexander Phil Dent	Bob Carmichael Allan Stone	6-3	7-6			
1976	John Newcombe Tony Roche	Ross Case Geoff Masters	7-6	6-4			
1977 (Jan.)	Arthur Ashe Tony Roche	Charlie Pasarell Erik van Dillen	6-4	6-4			
1977 (Dec.)	Ray Ruffels Allan Stone	John Alexander Phil Dent	7-6	7-6			
1978	Wojtek Fibak Kim Warwick	Paul Kronk Cliff Letcher	7-6	7-5			
1979	Peter McNamara Paul McNamee	Paul Kronk Cliff Letcher	7-6	6-2			
1980	Mark Edmondson Kim Warwick	Peter McNamara Paul McNamee	7-5	6-4			
1981	Mark Edmondson Kim Warwick	Hank Pfister John Sadri	6-3	6-7	6-3		
1982	John Alexander John Fitzgerald	Andy Andrews John Sadri	6-4	7-6			
1983	Mark Edmondson Paul McNamee	Steve Denton Sherwood Stewart	6-3	7-6			
1984	Mark Edmondson Sherwood Stewart	Joakim Nystrom Mats Wilander	6-2	6-2	7-5		
1985	Paul Annacone Christo Van Rensburg	Mark Edmondson Kim Warwick	3-6	7-6	6-4	6-4	
1986	Not held due to change in dates						
1987	Stefan Edberg Anders Jarryd	Peter Doohan Laurie Warder	6-4	6-4	7-6(3)		
1988	Rick Leach Jim Pugh	Jeremy Bates Peter Lundgren	6-3	6-2	6-3		
1989	Rick Leach Jim Pugh	Darren Cahill Mark Kratzmann	6-4	6-4	6-4		
1990	Pieter Aldrich Danie Visser	Grant Connell Glenn Michibata	6-4	4-6	6-1	6-4	
1991	Scott Davis David Pate	Patrick McEnroe David Wheaton	6-7(4)	7-6(8)	6-3	7-5	
1992	Todd Woodbridge Mark Woodforde	Kelly Jones Rick Leach	6-4	6-3	6-4		
1993	Danie Visser Laurie Warder	John Fitzgerald Anders Jarryd	6-4	6-3	6-4		
1994	Jacco Eltingh Paul Haarhuis	Byron Black Jonathan Stark	6-7(3)	6-3	6-4	6-3	
1995	Jared Palmer Richey Reneberg	Mark Knowles Daniel Nestor	6-3	3-6	6-3	6-2	
1996	Stefan Edberg Petr Korda	Alex O'Brien Sebastien Lareau	7-5	7-5	4-6	6-1	
1997	Todd Woodbridge Mark Woodforde	Sebastien Lareau Alex O'Brien	4-6	7-5	7-5	6-3	
1998	Jonas Bjorkman Jacco Eltingh	Todd Woodbridge Mark Woodforde	6-2	5-7	2-6	6-4	6-3
1999	Patrick Rafter Jonas Bjorkman	Leander Paes Mahesh Bhupathi	6-3	4-6	6-4	6-7(10)	6-4
2000	Rick Leach Ellis Ferreira	Andrew Kratzmann Wayne Black	6-4	3-6	6-3	3-6	18-16
2001	Jonas Bjorkman Todd Woodbridge	Byron Black David Prinosil	6-1	5-7	6-4	6-4	
2002	Daniel Nestor Mark Knowles	Michael Llodra Fabrice Santoro	7-6(4)	6-3			
2003	Michael Llodra Fabrice Santoro	Daniel Nestor Mark Knowles	6-4	3-6	6-3		

Women's Doubles

Year	Winner	Defeated	S1	S2	S3
1922	Esna Boyd Marjorie Mountain	Floris St. George Lorna Utz	1-6	6-4	7-5
1923	Esna Boyd Sylvia Lance	Mall Molesworth H. Turner	6-1	6-4	
1924	Daphne Akhurst Sylvia Lance	Kathrine LeMesurier Meryl O'Hara Wood	7-5	6-2	
1925	Sylvia Lance Harper Daphne Akhurst	Esna Boyd Kathrine LeMesurier	6-4	6-3	
1926	Meryl O'Hara Wood Esna Boyd	Daphne Akhurst Marjorie Cox	6-3	6-8	8-6
1927	Meryl O'Hara Wood Louie Bickerton	Esna Boyd Sylvia Lance Harper	6-3	6-3	
1928	Daphne Akhurst Esna Boyd	Kathrine LeMesurier Dorothy Weston	6-3	6-1	
1929	Daphne Akhurst Louie Bickerton	Sylvia Lance Harper Meryl O'Hara Wood	6-2	3-6	6-2
1930	Mall Molesworth Emily Hood	Marjorie Cox Sylvia Lance Harper	6-3	0-6	7-5
1931	D. Akhurst Cozens Louie Bickerton	Nell Lloyd Lorna Utz	6-0	6-4	
1932	C. McInnes Buttsworth Marjorie Cox Crawford	Kathrine LeMesurier Dorothy Weston	6-2	6-2	
1933	Mall Molesworth Emily Hood Westacott	Joan Hartigan Marjorie Gladman Van Ryn	6-3	6-2	
1934	Mall Molesworth Emily Hood Westacott	Joan Hartigan Ula Valkenburg	6-8	6-4	6-4
1935	Evelyn Dearman Nancy Lyle	Louie Bickerton Nell Hall Hopman	6-3	6-4	
1936	Thelma Coyne Long Nancye Wynne	May Blick Katherine Woodward	6-2	6-4	

Year	Winner	Defeated	S1	S2	S3
1937	Thelma Coyne Long / Nancye Wynne	Nell Hall Hopman / Emily Hood Westacott	6-2	6-2	
1938	Thelma Coyne Long / Nancye Wynne	Dorothy Bundy / Dorothy Workman	9-7	6-4	
1939	Thelma Coyne Long / Nancye Wynne	May Hardcastle / Emily Hood Westacott	7-5	6-4	
1940	Thelma Coyne Long / Nancye Wynne	Joan Hartigan / Emily Niemeyer	7-5	6-2	
1941-45	Not held – WW II				
1946	Joyce Fitch / Mary Bevis	Nancye Wynne Bolton / Thelma Coyne Long	9-7	6-4	
1947	Thelma Coyne Long / Nancye Wynne Bolton	Mary Bevis / Joyce Fitch	6-3	6-3	
1948	Thelma Coyne Long / Nancye Wynne Bolton	Mary Bevis / Pat Jones	6-3	6-3	
1949	Thelma Coyne Long / Nancye Wynne Bolton	Doris Hart / Marie Toomey	6-0	6-1	
1950	Louise Brough / Doris Hart	Nancye Wynne Bolton / Thelma Coyne Long	6-2	2-6	6-3
1951	Thelma Coyne Long / Nancye Wynne Bolton	Joyce Fitch / Mary Bevis Hawton	6-2	6-1	
1952	Thelma Coyne Long / Nancye Wynne Bolton	Allison Burton Baker / Mary Bevis Hawton	6-1	6-1	
1953	Maureen Connolly / Julia Sampson	Mary Bevis Hawton / Beryl Penrose	6-4	6-2	
1954	Mary Bevis Hawton / Beryl Penrose	Hazel Redick-Smith / Julia Wipplinger	6-3	8-6	
1955	Mary Bevis Hawton / Beryl Penrose	Nell Hall Hopman / Gwen Thiele	7-5	6-1	
1956	Mary Bevis Hawton / Thelma Coyne Long	Mary Carter / Beryl Penrose	6-2	5-7	9-7
1957	Althea Gibson / Shirley Fry	Mary Bevis Hawton / Fay Muller	6-2	6-1	
1958	Mary Bevis Hawton / Thelma Coyne Long	Lorraine Coghlan / Angela Mortimer	7-5	6-8	6-2
1959	Renee Schuurman / Sandra Reynolds	Lorraine Coghlan / Mary Carter Reitano	7-5	6-4	
1960	Maria Bueno / Christine Truman	L. Coghlan Robinson / Margaret Smith	6-2	5-7	6-2
1961	Mary Carter Reitano / Margaret Smith	Mary Bevis Hawton / Jan Lehane	6-4	3-6	7-5
1962	Margaret Smith / Robyn Ebbern	Darlene Hard / Mary Carter Reitano	6-4	6-4	
1963	Margaret Smith / Robyn Ebbern	Jan Lehane / Lesley Turner	6-1	6-3	
1964	Judy Tegart Dalton / Lesley Turner	Robyn Ebbern / Margaret Smith	6-4	6-4	
1965	Margaret Smith / Lesley Turner	Robyn Ebbern / Billie Jean Moffitt	1-6	6-2	6-3
1966	C. Caldwell Graebner / Nancy Richey	Margaret Smith / Lesley Turner	6-4	7-5	
1967	Lesley Turner / Judy Tegart Dalton	L. Coghlan Robinson / Evelyn Terras	6-0	6-2	
1968	Karen Krantzcke / Kerry Melville	Judy Tegart Dalton / Lesley Turner	6-4	3-6	6-2
1969	Margaret Smith Court / Judy Tegart Dalton	Rosie Casals / Billie Jean King	6-4	6-4	
1970	Margaret Smith Court / Judy Tegart Dalton	Karen Krantzcke / Kerry Melville	6-3	6-1	
1971	Margaret Smith Court / Evonne Goolagong	Jill Emmerson / Lesley Hunt	6-0	6-0	
1972	Kerry Harris / Helen Gourlay	Patricia Coleman / Karen Krantzcke	6-0	6-4	
1973	Margaret Smith Court / Virginia Wade	Kerry Harris / Kerry Melville	6-4	6-4	
1974	Evonne Goolagong / Peggy Michel	Kerry Harris / Kerry Melville	7-5	6-3	
1975	Evonne Goolagong / Peggy Michel	Margaret Smith Court / Olga Morozova	7-6	7-6	
1976	Evonne Goolagong / Helen Gourlay	Lesley Turner Bowrey / Renata Tomanova	8-1	(1 pro set by mutual agreement)	
1977 (Jan.)	D. Balestrat Fromholtz / Helen Gourlay Cawley	Betsy Nagelsen / Kerry Melville Reid	5-7	6-1	7-5
1977 (Dec.)	E. Goolagong Cawley / Helen Gourlay Cawley	Mona Schallau Guerrant / Kerry Melville Reid	(shared title due to rained-out final)		
1978	Betsy Nagelsen / Renata Tomanova	Naoko Sato / Pam Whytcross	7-5	6-2	
1979	Judy Chaloner / Dianne Evers	Leanne Harrison / Marcella Mesker	6-1	3-6	6-0
1980	Martina Navratilova / Betsy Nagelsen	Ann Kiyomura / Candy Reynolds	6-4	6-4	
1981	Kathy Jordan / Anne Smith	Martina Navratilova / Pam Shriver	6-2	7-5	
1982	Martina Navratilova / Pam Shriver	Claudia Kohde Kilsch / Eva Pfaff	6-4	6-2	
1983	Martina Navratilova / Pam Shriver	Anne Hobbs / Wendy Turnbull	6-4	6-7	6-2
1984	Martina Navratilova / Pam Shriver	Claudia Kohde Kilsch / Helena Sukova	6-3	6-4	
1985	Martina Navratilova / Pam Shriver	Claudia Kohde Kilsch / Helena Sukova	6-3	6-4	
1986	Not held due to change in dates				
1987	Martina Navratilova / Pam Shriver	Zina Garrison / Lori McNeil	6-1	6-0	
1988	Martina Navratilova / Pam Shriver	Chris Evert / Wendy Turnbull	6-0	7-5	
1989	Martina Navratilova / Pam Shriver	Patty Fendick / Jill Hetherington	3-6	6-3	6-2
1990	Jana Novotna / Helena Sukova	Patty Fendick / Mary Joe Fernandez	7-6(5)	7-6(6)	
1991	Patty Fendick / Mary Joe Fernandez	Gigi Fernandez / Jana Novotna	7-6(4)	6-1	
1992	A. Sanchez Vicario / Helena Sukova	Mary Joe Fernandez / Zina Garrison	6-4	7-6(3)	
1993	Gigi Fernandez / Natalia Zvereva	Pam Shriver / Elizabeth Sayers Smylie	6-4	6-3	
1994	Gigi Fernandez / Natalia Zvereva	Patty Fendick / Meredith McGrath	6-3	4-6	6-4
1995	Jana Novotna / A. Sanchez Vicario	Gigi Fernandez / Natalia Zvereva	6-3	6-7(3)	6-4
1996	Chanda Rubin / A. Sanchez Vicario	Lindsay Davenport / Mary Joe Fernandez	7-5	2-6	6-4
1997	Martina Hingis / Natalia Zvereva	Lindsay Davenport / Lisa Raymond	6-2	6-2	

Year	Winner	Defeated	S1	S2	S3
1998	Martina Hingis Mirjana Lucic	Lindsay Davenport Natalia Zvereva	6-4	2-6	6-3
1999	Martina Hingis Anna Kournikova	Lindsay Davenport Natalia Zvereva	7-5	6-3	
2000	Lisa Raymond Rennae Stubbs	Martina Hingis Mary Pierce	6-4	5-7	6-4
2001	Serena Williams Venus Williams	Lindsay Davenport Corina Morariu	6-2	2-6	6-4
2002	Martina Hingis Anna Kournikova	Arantxa Sanchez Vicario Daniela Hantuchova	6-2	6-7(4)	6-1
2003	Serena Williams Venus Williams	Virginia Ruano Pascual Paola Suarez	4-6	6-4	6-3

Mixed Doubles

Year	Winner	Defeated	S1	S2	S3
1922	Esna Boyd Jack Hawkes	Lorna Utz H. S. Utz	6-1	6-1	
1923	Sylvia Lance Horrie Rice	Mall Molesworth Bert St. John	2-6	6-4	6-4
1924	Daphne Akhurst John Willard	Esna Boyd Gar Hone	6-3	6-4	
1925	Daphne Akhurst John Willard	Sylvia Lance Harper Bob Schlesinger	6-4	6-4	
1926	Esna Boyd Jack Hawkes	Daphne Akhurst Jim Willard	6-2	6-4	
1927	Esna Boyd Jack Hawkes	Youtha Anthony Jim Willard	6-1	6-3	
1928	Daphne Akhurst Jean Borotra	Esna Boyd Jack Hawkes		default	
1929	Daphne Akhurst Gar Moon	Marjorie Cox Jack Crawford	6-0	7-5	
1930	Nell Hall Harry Hopman	Marjorie Cox Jack Crawford	11-9	3-6	6-3
1931	Marjorie Cox Crawford Jack Crawford	Emily Hood Westacott Aubrey Willard	7-5	6-4	
1932	Marjorie Cox Crawford Jack Crawford	Meryl O'Hara Wood Jiro Satoh	6-8	8-6	6-3
1933	Marjorie Cox Crawford Jack Crawford	M. Gladman Van Ryn Ellsworth Vines	3-6	7-5	13-11
1934	Joan Hartigan Gar Moon	Emily Hood Westacott Ray Dunlop	6-3	6-4	
1935	Louie Bickerton Christian Boussus	Mrs. Bond Vernon Kirby	1-6	6-3	6-3
1936	Nell Hall Hopman Harry Hopman	May Blick Abe Kay	6-2	6-0	
1937	Nell Hall Hopman Harry Hopman	Dorothy Stevenson Don Turnbull	3-6	6-3	6-2
1938	Margaret Wilson John Bromwich	Nancye Wynne Colin Long	6-3	6-2	
1939	Nell Hall Hopman Harry Hopman	Margaret Wilson John Bromwich	6-8	6-2	6-3
1940	Nancye Wynne Colin Long	Nell Hall Hopman Harry Hopman	7-5	2-6	6-4
1941-45		Not held – WW II			
1946	Nancye Wynne Bolton Colin Long	Joyce Fitch John Bromwich	6-0	6-4	
1947	Nancye Wynne Bolton Colin Long	Joyce Fitch John Bromwich	6-3	6-3	
1948	Nancye Wynne Bolton Colin Long	Thelma Coyne Long Bill Sidwell	7-5	4-6	8-6
1949	Doris Hart Frank Sedgman	Joyce Fitch John Bromwich	6-1	5-7	12-10
1950	Doris Hart Frank Sedgman	Joyce Fitch Eric Sturgess	8-6	6-4	
1951	Thelma Coyne Long George Worthington	Clare Proctor Jack May	6-4	3-6	
1952	Thelma Coyne Long George Worthington	Gwen Thiele Tom Warhurst	9-7	7-5	
1953	Julia Sampson Rex Hartwig	Maureen Connolly Hamilton Richardson	6-4	6-3	
1954	Thelma Coyne Long Rex Hartwig	Beryl Penrose John Bromwich	4-6	6-1	6-2
1955	Thelma Coyne Long George Worthington	Jenny Staley Lew Hoad	6-2	6-1	
1956	Beryl Penrose Neale Fraser	Mary Bevis Hawton Roy Emerson	6-2	6-4	
1957	Fay Muller Mal Anderson	J. Langley Billy Knight	7-5	3-6	6-1
1958	Mary Bevis Hawton Bob Howe	Angela Mortimer Peter Newman	9-11	6-1	6-2
1959	Sandra Reynolds Bob Mark	Renee Schuurman Rod Laver	4-6	13-11	6-1
1960	Jan Lehane Trevor Fancutt	Mary Carter Reitano Bob Mark	6-2	7-5	
1961	Jan Lehane Bob Hewitt	Mary Carter Reitano John Pearce	9-7	6-2	
1962	Lesley Turner Fred Stolle	Darlene Hard Roger Taylor	6-3	9-7	
1963	Margaret Smith Ken Fletcher	Lesley Turner Fred Stolle	7-5	5-7	6-4
1964	Margaret Smith Ken Fletcher	Jan Lehane Mike Sangster	6-3	6-2	
1965	Margaret Smith John Newcombe	Robyn Ebbern Owen Davidson	(shared title, final not played)		
1966	Judy Tegart Tony Roche	Robyn Ebbern Bill Bowrey	6-1	6-3	
1967	Lesley Turner Owen Davidson	Judy Tegart Tony Roche	9-7	6-4	
1968	Billie Jean King Dick Crealy	Margaret Smith Court Allan Stone	(walkover)		
1969	Margaret Smith Court Marty Riessen	Ann Haydon Jones Fred Stolle	(shared title, final not played)		
1970-86		Not held			
1987	Zina Garrison Sherwood Stewart	Anne Hobbs Andrew Castle	3-6	7-6(5)	6-3
1988	Jana Novotna Jim Pugh	Martina Navratilova Tim Gullikson	5-7	6-2	6-4
1989	Jana Novotna Jim Pugh	Zina Garrison Sherwood Stewart	6-3	6-4	
1990	Natalia Zvereva Jim Pugh	Zina Garrison Rick Leach	4-6	6-2	6-3
1991	Jo Durie Jeremy Bates	Robin White Scott Davis	2-6	6-4	6-4

Year	Winner	Defeated	S1	S2	S3
1992	Nicole Provis Mark Woodforde	Arantxa Sanchez Vicario Todd Woodbridge	6-3	4-6	11-9
1993	A. Sanchez Vicario Todd Woodbridge	Zina Garrison Jackson Rick Leach	7-5	6-4	
1994	L. Savchenko Neiland Andrei Olhovskiy	Helena Sukova Todd Woodbridge	7-5	6-7(0)	6-2
1995	Natalia Zvereva Rick Leach	Gigi Fernandez Cyril Suk	7-6(4)	6-7(3)	6-4
1996	L. Savchenko Neiland Mark Woodforde	Nicole Arendt Luke Jensen	4-6	7-5	6-0
1997	Manon Bollegraf Rick Leach	L. Savchenko Neiland John-Laffnie de Jager	6-3	6-7(5)	7-5

Year	Winner	Defeated	S1	S2	S3
1998	Venus Williams Justin Gimelstob	Helena Sukova Cyril Suk	6-2	6-1	
1999	Mariaan de Swardt David Adams	Serena Williams Max Mirnyi	6-4	4-6	7-6(5)
2000	Rennae Stubbs Jared Palmer	Arantxa Sanchez Vicario Todd Woodbridge	7-5	7-6(3)	
2001	Corina Morariu Ellis Ferreira	Barbara Schett Joshua Eagle	6-1	6-3	
2002	Daniela Hantuchova Kevin Ullyett	Paolo Suarez Gaston Etlis	6-3	6-2	
2003	Martina Navratilova Leander Paes	Eleni Daniilidou Todd Woodbridge	6-4	7-5	

Australian Open – Records

Australian Slam
(Winner of all 3 events in one year)

MEN

Jack Hawkes, 1926 (with D-Gerald Patterson; M-Esna Boyd)
Jean Borotra, 1928 (with D-Jacques Brugnon; M-Daphne Akhurst)
Jack Crawford, 1932 (with D-Gar Moon; M-Marjorie Cox Crawford)

WOMEN

Daphne Akhurst, 1925 (with D-Sylvia Lance Harper; M-John Willard)
Daphne Akhurst, 1928 (with D-Esna Boyd; M-Jean Borotra)
Daphne Akhurst, 1929 (with D-Louie Bickerton; M-Gar Moon)
Nancye Bolton, 1940 (with D-Thelma Coyne Long; M-Colin Long)
Nancye Bolton, 1947 (with D-Thelma Coyne Long; M-Colin Long)
Nancye Bolton, 1948 (with D-Thelma Coyne Long; M-Colin Long)
Thelma Long, 1952 (with D-Nancy Bolton; M-George Worthington)
Margaret Smith Court, 1963 (with D-Robyn Ebbern; M-Ken Fletcher)

Overall Titles

MOST TITLES ALL TIME – MEN

- 13 Adrian Quist (1936-1950) 3 singles, 10 doubles, 0 mixed.
- 11 Jack Crawford (1929-1935) 4 singles, 4 doubles, 3 mixed.
  John Bromwich (1938-1950) 2 singles, 8 doubles, 1 mixed.
- 9 Roy Emerson (1961-1969) 6 singles, 3 doubles, 0 mixed.
- 7 Jack Hawkes (1922-1927) 1 singles, 3 doubles, 3 mixed.
  John Newcombe (1965-1976) 2 singles, 5 doubles, 0 mixed.
  Ken Rosewall (1953-1972) 4 singles, 3 doubles, 0 mixed.
  Rod Laver (1959-1969) 3 singles, 4 doubles, 4 mixed.
- 6 Frank Sedgman (1949-1952) 2 singles, 2 doubles, 2 mixed.
  Gerald Patterson (1914-1927) 1 singles, 5 doubles, 0 mixed.
  Harry Hopman (1929-1939) 0 singles, 2 doubles, 4 mixed.
  Pat O'Hara Wood (1919-1925) 2 singles, 4 doubles, 0 mixed.
  Tony Roche (1965-1977) 0 singles, 5 doubles, 1 mixed.
- 5 Jim Pugh (1988-1990) 0 singles, 2 doubles, 3 mixed.
  Mark Edmondson (1976-1984) 1 singles, 4 doubles, 0 mixed.
  Rick Leach (1988-2000) 0 singles, 3 doubles, 2 mixed.
- 4 Bob Mark (1959-1961) 0 singles, 3 doubles, 1 mixed.
  Colin Long (1940-1948) 0 singles, 0 doubles, 4 mixed.
  Fred Stolle (1962-1969) 0 singles, 3 doubles, 1 mixed.
  Gar Moon (1929-1934) 1 singles, 1 doubles, 2 mixed.
  Horrie Rice (1907-1923) 1 singles, 2 doubles, 1 mixed.
  James Anderson (1922-1925) 3 singles, 1 doubles, 1 mixed.
  Lew Hoad (1953-1957) 1 singles, 3 doubles, 0 mixed.
  Mark Woodforde (1992-1997) 0 singles, 2 doubles, 2 mixed.
  Neale Fraser (1956-1962) 0 singles, 3 doubles, 1 mixed.
  Rodney Heath (1905-1911) 2 singles, 2 doubles, 0 mixed.
  Stefan Edberg (1985-1996) 2 singles, 2 doubles, 0 mixed.
  Todd Woodbridge (1992-2001) 0 singles, 3 doubles, 1 mixed.
  Andre Agassi (1995-2003) 4 singles, 0 doubles, 0 mixed.

MOST TITLES ALL TIME – WOMEN

- 21 Margaret Smith Court (1960-1973) 11 singles, 8 doubles, 2 mixed.
- 20 Nancye Bolton (1936-1952) 6 singles, 10 doubles, 4 mixed.
- 18 Thelma Long (1936-1958) 2 singles, 12 doubles, 4 mixed.
- 14 Daphne Akhurst (1924-1931) 5 singles, 5 doubles, 4 mixed.
- 12 Martina Navratilova (1980-2003) 3 singles, 8 doubles, 1 mixed.
- 8 Esna Boyd (1922-1928) 3 singles, 4 doubles, 1 mixed.
  Evonne Goolagong (1971-1977) 1 singles, 4 doubles, 3 mixed.
- 7 Martina Hingis (1997-2002) 3 singles, 4 doubles, 0 mixed.
  Pam Shriver (1982-1989) 0 singles, 7 doubles, 0 mixed.
- 6 Mary Bevis Hawton (1946-1958) 0 singles, 5 doubles, 1 mixed.
- 5 Judy Dalton (1964-1970) 0 singles, 4 doubles, 1 mixed.
  Lesley Turner (1962-1967) 0 singles, 3 doubles, 2 mixed.
  Mall Molesworth (1922-1934) 2 singles, 3 doubles, 0 mixed.
  Natalia Zvereva (1990-1997) 0 singles, 3 doubles, 2 mixed.
- 4 Arantxa Sanchez Vicario (1992-1996) 0 singles, 3 doubles, 1 mixed.
  Beryl Penrose (1954-1956) 1 singles, 2 doubles, 1 mixed.
  Doris Hart (1949-1950) 1 singles, 1 doubles, 2 mixed.
  Emily Hood Westacott (1930-1939) 1 singles, 3 doubles, 0 mixed.
  Jana Novotna (1988-1995) 0 singles, 2 doubles, 2 mixed.
  Joan Hartigan (1933-1936) 3 singles, 0 doubles, 1 mixed.
  Louie Bickerton (1927-1935) 0 singles, 3 doubles, 1 mixed.
  Marjorie Cox (1931-1933) 0 singles, 1 doubles, 3 mixed.
  Monica Seles (1991-1996) 4 singles, 0 doubles, 0 mixed.
  Nell Hall Hopman (1930-1939) 0 singles, 0 doubles, 4 mixed.
  Steffi Graf (1988-1994) 4 singles, 0 doubles, 0 mixed.
  Sylvia Lance (1923-1924) 1 singles, 2 doubles, 1 mixed.

Men's Singles

MOST TITLES

- 6 Roy Emerson (1961-1967)
- 4 Andre Agassi (1995-2003)
  Jack Crawford (1931-1935)
  Ken Rosewall (1953-1972)
- 3 Adrian Quist (1936-1948)
  James Anderson (1922-1925)
  Mats Wilander (1983-1988)
  Rod Laver (1960-1969)

MOST FINAL APPEARANCES

- 7 Jack Crawford (1931-1940)
  John Bromwich (1937-1949)
  Roy Emerson (1961-1967)
- 5 Ken Rosewall (1953-1972)
  Stefan Edberg (1985-1993)

MOST FINAL LOSSES

- 5 John Bromwich (1937-1949)
- 3 Arthur Ashe (1966-1971)
  Gerald Patterson (1914-1925)
  Harry Hopman (1930-1932)
  Horrie Rice (1910-1915)
  Jack Crawford (1934-1940)
  Neale Fraser (1957-1960)
  Stefan Edberg (1990-1993)

MOST SEMI-FINAL APPEARANCES
11 Jack Crawford (1928-1940)
9 John Bromwich (1937-1954)
8 Adrian Quist (1934-1948)
Ken Rosewall (1953-1977)
Roy Emerson (1960-1967)
Stefan Edberg (1985-1994)

OLDEST CHAMPION
Ken Rosewall—37 years, 2 months (1972)

YOUNGEST CHAMPION
Ken Rosewall—18 years, 2 months (1953)

TOURNAMENTS PLAYED
20 Jack Crawford (1927-40, 46-48)

MATCHES PLAYED
67 Stefan Edberg (1983-1986)

MATCHES WON
56 Stefan Edberg (1983-1986)

MATCHES WON CONSECUTIVELY
27 Roy Emerson (1963-1969)

MATCH WINNING PERCENTAGE
.836 Stefan Edberg (56 wins, 11 losses) (1983-1986)

Women's Singles

MOST TITLES
11 Margaret Smith Court (1960-1973)
6 Nancye Bolton (1937-1951)
5 Daphne Akhurst (1925-1930)
4 Evonne Goolagong (1974-1977)
Monica Seles (1991-1996)
Steffi Graf (1988-1994)

MOST FINAL APPEARANCES
12 Margaret Smith Court (1960-1973)
8 Nancye Bolton (1936-1951)
7 Esna Boyd (1922-1928)
Evonne Goolagong (1971-1977)

MOST FINAL LOSSES
6 Esna Boyd (1922-1928)
4 Chris Evert (1974-1988)
Jan Lehane (1960-1963)
Thelma Long (1940-1956)
3 Evonne Goolagong (1971-1973)
Martina Hingis (2000-2002)
Martina Navratilova (1975-1987)

MOST SEMI-FINAL APPEARANCES
12 Margaret Smith Court (1960-1973)
11 Nancye Bolton (1936-1952)
Thelma Long (1936-1956)
9 Martina Navratilova (1975-1988)
8 Kerry Melville (1966-1977)
Mary Reitano (1954-1962)

OLDEST CHAMPION
Thelma Long—35 years, 7 months (1954)

YOUNGEST CHAMPION
Martina Hingis—16 years, 4 months (1997)

TOURNAMENTS PLAYED
14 Margaret Smith Court (1959-1975)

MATCHES PLAYED
65 Margaret Smith Court (1959-1975)

MATCHES WON
60 Margaret Smith Court (1959-1975)

MATCHES WON CONSECUTIVELY
38 Margaret Smith Court—1960-68 (1960-1968)

MATCH WINNING PERCENT
.952 Margaret Smith Court (60 wins, 3 losses) (1959-1975)

Men's Doubles

MOST TITLES—TEAM
8 Adrian Quist / John Bromwich (1938-1950)
4 John Newcombe / Tony Roche (1965-1976)
3 Gerald Patterson / Jack Hawkes (1922-1927)
Rod Laver / Bob Mark (1959-1961)

MOST TITLES—INDIVIDUAL
10 Adrian Quist (1936-1950)
8 John Bromwich (1938-1950)
5 Gerald Patterson (1914-1927)
John Newcombe (1965-1976)
Tony Roche (1965-1977)

MOST FINAL APPEARANCES—TEAM
9 Adrian Quist / John Bromwich (1938-1951)
5 John Newcombe / Tony Roche (1965-1976)
4 John Alexander / Phil Dent (1970-1977)

MOST FINAL APPEARANCES—INDIVIDUAL
12 Adrian Quist (1934-1951)
10 John Bromwich (1937-1951)
8 Jack Crawford (1929-1940)
Roy Emerson (1958-1969)

MOST FINAL LOSSES—TEAM
3 Don Candy / Merv Rose (1952-1956)
John Alexander / Phil Dent (1970-1977)
2 Alex O'Brien / Sebastien Lareau (1996-1997)
Daniel Nestor / Mark Knowles (1995-2003)
Geoff Masters / Ross Case (1972-1976)
Jack Crawford / Viv McGrath (1936-1940)
Paul Kronk / Cliff Letcher (1978-1979)

MOST FINAL LOSSES—INDIVIDUAL
5 Roy Emerson (1958-1965)
4 Don Candy (1952-1959)
Jack Crawford (1931-1940)
James Anderson (1919-1926)

OLDEST CHAMPION—MEN
Norman Brookes—46 years, 2 months (1924)

YOUNGEST CHAMPION—Men
Lew Hoad—19 years, 2 months (1953)

Women's Doubles

MOST TITLES—TEAM
10 Nancye Bolton / Thelma Long (1936-1952)
7 Martina Navratilova / Pam Shriver (1982-1989)
3 Mall Molesworth / Emily Westacott (1930-1934)

MOST TITLES—INDIVIDUAL
12 Thelma Long (1936-1958)
10 Nancye Bolton (1936-1952)
8 Margaret Smith Court (1961-1973)
Martina Navratilova (1980-1989)

MOST FINAL APPEARANCES—TEAM
12 Nancye Bolton / Thelma Long (1936-1952)
 8 Martina Navratilova / Pam Shriver (1981-1989)
 3 Gigi Fernandez / Natalia Zvereva (1993-1995)
   Joyce Fitch / Mary Bevis Hawton (1946-1951)
   Judy Dalton / Lesley Turner (1964-1968)
   Mall Molesworth / Emily Westacott (1930-1934)
   Margaret Smith Court / Robyn Ebbern (1962-1964)
   Mary Bevis Hawton / Beryl Penrose (1953-1955)

MOST FINAL APPEARANCES—INDIVIDUAL
14 Thelma Long (1936-1958)
12 Margaret Smith Court (1960-1975)
   Mary Bevis Hawton (1946-1961)
   Nancye Bolton (1936-1952)

MOST FINAL LOSSES—TEAM
 2 Claudia Kohde Kilsch / Helena Sukova (1984-1985)
   Joyce Fitch / Mary Bevis Hawton (1947-1951)
   Kathrine LeMesurier / Dorothy Weston (1928-1932)
   Kerry Harris / Kerry Melville (1973-1974)
   Lindsay Davenport / Natalia Zvereva (1998-1999)
   Nancye Bolton / Thelma Long (1946-1950)

MOST FINAL LOSSES—INDIVIDUAL
 7 Mary Bevis Hawton (1947-1961)
 5 Lindsay Davenport (1996-2001)
 4 Kathrine Lemesurier (1924-1932)
   Kerry Melville (1970-1977)
   Lesley Turner (1963-1976)
   Lorraine Coghlan (1958-1967)
   Margaret Smith Court (1960-1975)

OLDEST CHAMPION
   Thelma Long—37 years, 7 months (1956)

YOUNGEST CHAMPION
   Mirjana Lucic—15 years, 10 months (1998)

Mixed Doubles

MOST TITLES—TEAM
 4 Nancye Bolton / Colin Long (1940-1948)
   Nell Hall / Harry Hopman (1930-1939)
 3 Esna Boyd / Jack Hawkes (1922-1927)
   Marjorie Cox / Jack Crawford (1931-1933)
   Thelma Coyne Long / George Worthington (1951-1955)

MOST TITLES—MEN
 4 Colin Long (1940-1948)
   Harry Hopman (1930-1939)
 3 George Worthington (1951-1955)
   Jack Crawford (1931-1933)
   Jack Hawkes (1922-1927)
   Jim Pugh (1988-1990)

MOST TITLES—WOMEN
 4 Daphne Akhurst (1924-1929)
   Nancye Bolton (1940-1948)
   Nell Hall Hopman (1930-1939)
   Thelma Long (1951-1955)

MOST FINAL APPEARANCES—TEAM
 5 Marjorie Cox / Jack Crawford (1929-1933)
   Nancye Bolton / Colin Long (1938-1948)
   Nell Hall / Harry Hopman (1930-1940)
 4 Esna Boyd / Jack Hawkes (1922-1928)

MOST FINAL APPEARANCES—MEN
 6 John Bromwich (1938-1954)
 5 Colin Long (1938-1948)
   Harry Hopman (1930-1940)
   Jack Crawford (1929-1933)
   Todd Woodbridge (1992-2003)

MOST FINAL APPEARANCES—WOMEN
 5 Daphne Akhurst (1924-1929)
   Esna Boyd (1922-1928)
   Marjorie Cox (1929-1933)
   Nancye Bolton (1938-1948)
   Nell Hall Hopman (1930-1940)
   Thelma Long (1948-1955)

MOST FINAL LOSSES—TEAM
 3 Joyce Fitch / John Bromwich (1946-1949)
 2 Arantxa Sanchez Vicario / Todd Woodbridge (1992-2000)
   Marjorie Cox / Jack Crawford (1929-1930)
   Zina Garrison / Rick Leach (1990-1993)

MOST FINAL LOSSES—MEN
 5 John Bromwich (1939-1954)
 4 Todd Woodbridge (1992-2003)
 2 Cyril Suk (1995-1998)
   Jack Crawford (1929-1930)
   Jim Willard (1926-1927)
   Rick Leach (1990-1993)

MOST FINAL LOSSES—WOMEN
 4 Joyce Fitch (1946-1950)
 3 Zina Garrison (1989-1993)
 2 Arantxa Sanchez Vicario (1992-2000)
   Emily Hood Westacott (1931-1934)
   Esna Boyd (1924-1928)
   Helena Sukova (1994-1998)
   Marjorie Cox (1929-1930)
   Mary Reitano (1960-1961)

OLDEST CHAMPION—MEN
   Sherwood Stewart—40 years, 7 months (1987)

YOUNGEST CHAMPION—MEN
   Tony Roche—20 years, 8 months (1966)

OLDEST CHAMPION—WOMEN
   Martina Navratilova—46 years, 3 months (2003)

YOUNGEST CHAMPION—WOMEN
   Venus Williams—17 years, 7 months (1998)

LONGEST MATCHES, TOTAL GAMES
Men's singles: 93 games – Dennis Ralston d. John Newcombe, 19-17, 20-18, 4-6, 6-4, quarters, 1970
Men's doubles: 94 games – Max Senior / Paul Avery d. Warren Jacques / Cedric Mason, 4-6, 18-16, 7-9, 17-15, 2-0, retired, 1st rd., 1968
Women's singles: 48 games – Chanda Rubin d. Arantxa Sanchez Vicario, 6-4, 2-6, 16-14, quarters, 1996
Women's doubles: 42 games – Linda Gates / Alycia Moulton d. Katerina Maleeva / Manuela Maleeva, 4-6, 6-2, 13-11, 2nd rd., 1985; 42 games, Lise Gregory / Manon Bollegraf d. Elise Burgin / Roslyn Fairbank Nideffer, 5-7, 6-4, 11-9, 3rd rd., 1991
Mixed doubles: 47 games – Jo-Anne Faull / Jason Stoltenberg d. Paula Smith / Mike Bauer, 7-6 (7-5), 4-6, 13-11, 1st rd., 1988

LONGEST MATCHES, PLAYING TIME
Men's singles: 5 hours, 11 minutes – Boris Becker d. Omar Camporese, 7-6 (7-4), 7-6 (7-5), 0-6, 4-6, 14-12, 3rd rd., 1991
Men's doubles: 5 hours, 29 minutes – Pieter Aldrich / Danie Visser d. Scott Davis–Bob Van't Hof, 6-4, 4-6, 7-6 (7-4), 4-6, 23-21 (last set took 2 hours, 53 minutes), quarters, 1990
Women's singles: 3 hours, 33 minutes – Chanda Rubin d. Arantxa Sanchez Vicario, 6-4, 2-6, 16-14, quarters, 1996

LONGEST TIE-BREAKERS
Men's singles: 17-15, third set, Omar Camporese d. Lars Wahlgren, 6-4, 6-2, 7-6 (17-15), 3rd rd., 1992
Women's singles: 15-13, first set, Silke Meier d. Jane Taylor, 7-6 (15-13), 2-6, 6-2, 1st rd., 1995

BIGGEST UPSETS

Men:

1933 - Viv McGrath d. 1st seed Ellsworth Vines (world No. 1), 6-2, 2-6, 8-6, 7-5, QF

1950 - Ken McGregor d. 1st seed Jaroslav Drobny, 11-9, 6-1, 6-3, 2nd rd.

1970 - Mark Cox d. 1st seed Rod Laver, 6-3, 4-6, 6-3, 7-6, 3rd rd.

1976 - Mark Edmondson (No. 212) d. 5th seed Phil Dent, 6-0, 6-4, 4-6, 6-3, 2nd rd.; 1st seed Ken Rosewall, 6-1, 2-6, 6-2, 6-4, SF; 2nd seed John Newcombe, 6-7. 6-3, 7-6, 6-1, F

1978 - John Marks (No. 177) d. 3rd seed Arthur Ashe, 6-4, 6-2, 2-6, 1-6, 9-7, SF (saved 2 MP, 5th)

1980 - 14th seed Kim Warwick d. 1st seed defending champ Guillermo Vilas, 6-7, 6-4, 6-2, 2-6, 6-4, SF

1985 - Slobodan Zivojinovic (No. 66) d. 2nd seed John McEnroe, 2-6, 6-3, 1-6, 6-4, 6-0, QF

1989 - Ramesh Krishnan (No. 40) d. 1st seed defending champ Mats Wilander, 6-3, 6-2, 7-6, 2nd rd.

1993 - Christian Bergstrom (No. 58) d. 8th seed Ivan Lendl, 6-4, 6-4, 2-6, 6-4, 1st rd.

1994 - MaliVai Washington (No. 26) d. 2nd seed Michael Stich, 7-6 (7-4), 6-3, 3-6, 6-2, 1st rd.

1996 - Mark Philippoussis (No. 40) d. 1st seed defending champ Pete Sampras, 6-4, 7-6 (11-9), 7-6 (7-3), 3rd rd.

1997 - Carlos Moya (No. 24) d. 6th seed defending champ Boris Becker, 5-7, 7-6 (7-4), 3-6, 6-1, 6-4, SF

1998 - Karol Kucera (No. 20) d. 1st seed Pete Sampras, 6-4, 6-2, 6-7 (5-7), 6-3, QF. Also Alberto Berasategui (No. 25) d. 2nd seed Patrick Rafter, 6-7 (2-7), 7-6 (9-7), 6-2, 7-6 (7-4), 3rd rd.; (No. 87) Andre Agassi, 3-6, 3-6, 6-2, 6-3, 6-3, 4th rd.

2002 - Albert Martin (No. 39) d. 1st seed Lleyton Hewitt (world No. 1), 1-6, 6-4, 6-4, 7-6 (7-4), 1st rd. Also Julien Boutter (No. 49) d. 2nd seed Gustavo Kuerten, 3-6, 4-6, 7-5, 6-3, 6-3, 1st rd. Also qualifier Alex Kim (No. 234) d. 4th seed Yevgeny Kafelnikov, 6-3, 7-5, 6-3, 2nd rd.

2003 - Younes El Aynaoui (No. 22) d. 1st seed (world No. 1) Lleyton Hewitt,

Women:

1924 - Katherine Lemesurier d. defending champ Margaret "Mall" Mutch Molesworth, 7-9, 3-6, 8-6, QF

1966 - Joan Gibson d. 2nd seed Lesley Turner, 8-6, 6-1, 3rd rd.

1976 - Elisabeth Ekblom d. 2d seed Kerry Melville Reid, 6-4, 6-3, 1st rd.

1979 - Mary Sawyer d. 1st seed Virginia Ruzici, 0-6, 6-2, 6-4, 1st rd.

1980 - Mima Jausovec (No. 20) d. 2nd seed Evonne Goolagong, 6-2, 4-6, 6-4, 2nd rd.

1988 - qualifier Wendy Wood (No. 306) d. 14th seed Dianne Fromholtz Balestrat, 6-2, 4-6, 8-6, 1st rd. (saved 1 MP, 3rd, at 4-5.First stadium match at new Flinders Park)

1997 - 12th seed Amanda Coetzer d. 1st seed Steffi Graf, 6-2, 7-5, 4th rd. Also Dominique Monami Van Roost (No. 43) d. 2nd seed Arantxa Sanchez Vicario, 1-6, 6-4, 8-6, 4th rd. Also Sabine Appelmans (No. 18) d. 3rd seed Conchita Martinez, 2-6, 7-5, 6-1, 4th rd. (all same day)

2003 - Marlene Weingartner (No. 90) d. 3rd seed defending champ Jennifer Capriati, 7-6 (8-6), 6-4, 1st rd. (only 1st rd. defeat of defender)

BEST COMEBACKS

Men:

1960 - 3rd seed Rod Laver d. 1st seed Neale Fraser, 5-7, 3-6, 6-3, 8-6, 8-6, F (saved 1 MP, 4th, at 4-5); 2nd seed Roy Emerson, 4-6, 6-1, 9-7, 3-6, 7-5 (won last 4 games from 3-5)

1985 - 5th seed Stefan Edberg d. Wally Masur (No. 142), 6-7 (4-7, 2-6), 7-6 (7-4), 6-4, 6-2, QF (saved 2 MP, 3rd,at 4-5)

1988 - 5th seed Yannick Noah d. Roger Smith (No. 147), 6-7, 5-7, 6-4, 6-2, 16-14, 1st rd. (saved 2 MP, 5th, at 7-8, 30-40 and ad-out)

2001 - 15th seed Arnaud Clement d. 16th seed Sebastian Grosjean, 5-7, 2-6, 7-6 (7-4), 7-5, 6-2, SF (saved 2 MP)

Women:

1933 - Joan Hartigan d. Margaret "Mall" Mutch Molesworth, 4-6, 8-6, 9-7, QF; Frances Hoddle-Wrigley, 4-6, 6-0, 6-4, SF

1979 - Mary Sawyer d. 1st seed Virginia Ruzici, 0-6, 6-2, 6-4, 1st rd.

1997 - Dominique Monami Van Roost (No. 43) d. 2nd seed Arantxa Sanchez Vicario, 1-6, 6-4, 8-6, 4th rd.

1999 - Amelie Mauresmo (No. 29) d. Corina Morariu, 6-7 (2-7), 7-6 (8-6), 6-2 (saved 2 MP, 2nd, at 5-2)

MATCH POINTS SAVED BY CHAMPION

Men:

1927 - F, Gerald Patterson d. Jack Hawkes, 3-6, 6-4, 3-6, 18-16, 6-3 (saved 5 MP, 4th, 4 at 13-12, 1 at 16-15)

1947 - F, 2nd seed Dinny Pails d. 1st seed John Bromwich, 4-6, 6-4, 3-6, 7-5, 8-6 (saved 1 MP)

1960 - F, 3rd seed Rod Laver d. 1st seed Neale Fraser, 5-7, 3-6, 6-3, 8-6, 8-6 (saved 1 MP, 4th, at 4-5)

1975 - SF, 2nd seed John Newcombe d. 3rd seed Tony Roche, 6-4, 4-6, 6-4, 2-6, 11-9 (saved 3 MP, 5th)

1982 - SF, 1st seed Johan Kriek d. 16th seed Paul McNamee, 7-6, 7-6, 4-6, 3-6, 7-5 (saved 1 MP, 5th)

1985 - QF, 5th seed Stefan Edberg d. Wally Masur (No. 142), 6-7 (4-7), 2-6, 7-6 (7-4), 6-4, 6-2 (saved 2 MP, 3rd, at 4-5)

Women:

1923 - SF, Margaret "Mall" Mutch Molesworth d. Sylvia Lance, 3-6, 6-4, 8-6 (saved 1 MP, 3rd)

1956 - F, 2nd seed Mary Carter d. 5th seed Thelma Coyne Long, 3-6, 6-2, 9-7 (saved 1 MP, 3rd)

1991 - SF, 2nd seed Monica Seles d. 3rd seed Mary Joe Fernandez, 6-3, 0-6, 9-7 (saved 1 MP, 3rd)

2002 - F, 1st seed Jennifer Capriati, d. 3rd seed Martina Hingis, 4-6, 7-6 (7-4), 6-2 (saved 4 MP, 2nd,1 at 5-3, 40-30, 2 at 5-6, 30-40 and ad-out, 1 at 6-7 in tie-breaker)

2003 - SF, 1st seed Serena Williams d. 4th seed Kim Klijsters, 4-6, 6-3, 7-5 (saved 2 MP, 3rd, at 5-2, 40-30 and ad-in)

Chapter 18

French Open

Jacques Brugnon, 1928
Fourth member of France's "Four Musketeers", the courtly doubles specialist won five French doubles titles between 1927 and 1934.

The French Open is the tournament for romantics. How could it be otherwise, staged as it is in Paris in the springtime? But more than just time and place, the French Open rekindles quixotic images of an era when tennis was played at a languorous pace, a time before the serve-and-volley bangers were pounding away at the sublime geometry of the treasured game. Once a year, when the purists gather to romanticize about all of this, the object of their affection becomes red dirt, of all things, because it is the clay of Paris that makes these hearts go all a-flutter.

Clay neutralizes the power servers while advancing those with a complete shot-making repertoire. Clay causes the ball to bounce higher, forcing players to strike at shoulder height, often from meters behind the baseline. On grass and asphalt, points can be shockingly abrupt: service, return, volley. Clay allows the story of a match to unfold like the plot of a good book.

The French Open is memorable for dusty, absorbing, exhausting rallies, as players battle the slippery footing and employ chess-like strategy to win a point. It is, in the words of tennis chronicler Rex Bellamy, "the great but cruel championship," an unforgiving test of physical and mental stamina. Some of the greatest players have failed to win at the French: Bill Tilden, Jimmy Connors, John McEnroe, Pete Sampras, Stefan Edberg, Boris Becker. The terre battue (broken earth) has been kinder to Bjorn Borg, who brought six championships home to Sweden, including four in a row from 1978-81. Chris Evert took seven French championships and her successor, Steffi Graf, claimed six. But even one title was unattainable for Martina Hingis.

Stade Roland Garros stands as a monument to five of France's greatest players—Suzanne Lenglen and the Four Musketeers, Jean Borotra, Henri Cochet, Jacques (Toto) Brugnon and René Lacoste, a quintet that dominated in the 1920s. Their successes provided the impetus for the construction of Roland Garros in 1928, and the new stadium became the permanent home of the national championship, which had become an international event three years earlier.

Today, the site in the Bois de Boulogne near Porte d'Auteuil, has 16 competition courts and another seven for practice. The largest is the 15,059-seat Court Philippe-Chatrier, named for the administrator who was responsible for the recent renaissance of the French Open and for returning tennis to the Olympic Games. Court Suzanne-Lenglen, which seats 10,076 and has an underground irrigation system to control humidity, was built in 1994 as Court A and renamed three years later. A more intimate venue is Court No. 1, a 3,790-seat bowl.

The first French Championship, a one-day event, was held in 1891 at the Stade Français. Entry was restricted to registered players of French clubs and the winner was an English amateur recorded only as H. Briggs. Françoise Masson won the first women's competition, held in 1897, and five of the first seven titles, while Kate Gillou-Fenwick and Jeanne Matthey each claimed four titles in the early years. The most successful man before the Great War was Max Decugis, an eight-time winner.

World War I brought a halt to the tournament until 1920. And instantly, French tennis became the envy of the world, finding in the form of a remarkable woman and four debonair men a deliverance from the deprivations of the war years. Suzanne Lenglen enthralled Parisian crowds. In 1919 she had shocked the upper crust Wimbledon spectators with on-court outfits that exposed her calves and forearms. Parisians, however, adored her, particularly after she was crowned French champion in 1920. By the time she abandoned amateur tennis in 1926, Lenglen had six French titles in seven years to go with her six Wimbledon championships. (Only two of the French, 1925-26, count in modern stats; the others were won before it became an international event.) Her final French championship was done in style—an efficient 6-1, 6-0 carving of the capable Mary K. Browne in just 27 minutes, including an inexplicable crying jag and a shot of brandy between sets. It remains the quickest major championship final ever played.

While Lenglen was a diva among French women, the men had a quartet. They were called the Four Musketeers: beret-wearing Jean Borotra, the Bounding Basque from Biarritz; dashing Henri Cochet, the Ballboy of Lyon; courtly Jacques (Toto) Brugnon, the doubles specialist; and cool Rene Lacoste, the Crocodile, whose brooding eyes revealed no emotion. Among them, the Musketeers captured every singles title but one from 1922 to 1932, including nine in a row.

So great was the appeal of the quartet and "la Lenglen" that organizers decided to make the French Championships an international contest beginning in 1925. To the delight of Paris, the French were magnificent that first year, sweeping all five titles. Lenglen was superb to win singles, team with Didi Vlasto to win doubles and then join Brugnon to win mixed doubles. Lacoste held up the men's honors by winning singles and teaming with Borotra to win doubles.

The 1925 tournament is regarded as the beginning of what became the modern Grand Slam. It was an instant hit, due not only to the success by Lenglen and The Musketeers, but because tennis had become a significant French export by the mid-1920s. The Musketeers gave France a terrific team to challenge for the Davis Cup, which at last was wrested from Bill Tilden and the Americans in 1927. To defend the Cup in 1928, the ecstatic French decided to build a new permanent home for tennis. The national championships had alternated between the Racing Club de France at Croix-Catelan and the Stade Français at Parc de Saint-Cloud, which could barely contain the 5,000 fans who jammed in to watch their French stars. Three Parisian clubs agreed to create a new venue in the south of the Bois de Boulogne on more than seven acres donated by the city. They named the facility for Roland Garros, a former Stade Français member who became a pioneer aviator and war pilot and who received a posthumous Croix de Guerre after he was killed in action.

Before Stade Roland Garros opened, however, Stade Français played host in 1927 to a final match between Lacoste and Tilden that is regarded among the most dramatic in major championship history. The big American had done away with Cochet in straight sets in the semi-finals, but would have a harder time against the Crocodile. The Frenchman took the first set, the American the next two. Lacoste, noted for his sang-froid, took the fourth set. In the decisive fifth, Tilden's serve at 9-8, 40-15 for match point appeared to be an ace, but the line judge ruled it a fault. Lacoste took full advantage of the reprieve for an unforgettable 6-4, 4-6, 5-7, 6-3, 11-9 win.

The magnificent Stade Roland Garros opened in time for the 1928 French Championships. In men's singles, it was an all-French final, with Cochet, the 1926 champion, beating Lacoste, who'd won in 1925 and 1927, in four sets. On the women's side, American Helen Wills won the first of her four French titles. It would take a decade for a French woman to win at Roland Garros.

Meanwhile, The Musketeers moved into Roland

Garros and quickly cemented their reputation, winning the first five championships: Cochet in 1928, 1930 and 1932; Lacoste in 1929; and Borotra in 1931. The men's doubles crown was booty to be shared. The list reads: Lacoste-Borotra (1925), Cochet-Brugnon (1927), Brugnon-Borotra (1928), Borotra-Lacoste (1929), Brugnon-Cochet (1930, 1932), Brugnon-Borotra (1934). Borotra paired with lefty Marcel Bernard to win in 1936.

The era of the Musketeers gave way in mid-decade to a German incursion (in eerie similarity to the world politic of the time) in both men's and women's draws. Baron Gottfried von Cramm and Hilde Sperling combined for five singles titles between 1933 and 1937. The Baron graced the finals three years in a row beginning in 1934, winning twice and losing in 1935 to Fred Perry. Sperling won three in a row from 1935 to 1937, her victim each time Simone Passemard Mathieu, the best French female player since Lenglen.

Mathieu reached the final six times in nine years, losing them all before finally winning in 1938 against compatriot Nelly Adamson Landry. She defended her title the next year against Poland's powerful Jadwiga Jedrzejowska, with whom she would share the doubles championship. A Polish-French partnership on the courts was matched in an alliance in world affairs, as France declared war after Germany invaded Poland in September 1939. International tennis would not grace Roland Garros for the next six years. Instead, the French government used the stadium to house political dissidents and aliens. With the fall of France, it was assigned an even darker purpose.

The grounds on which The Musketeers, von Cramm and Sperling had displayed their artistry became a Nazi prison camp and way station for Jews and others designated for deportation eastward to their doom. Among the prisoners was Arthur Koestler. "At Roland Garros, we called ourselves cave dwellers, about 600 of us who lived beneath the stairways of the stadium," he wrote in his famous novel Darkness at Noon. "We slept on straw, wet straw, because the place leaked. We were so crammed in we felt like sardines. Few of us knew anything about tennis, but when we were allowed to take our walk in the stadium, we could see the names Borotra and Brugnon on the scoreboard. We made jokes about mixed doubles. Indeed, compared to our experiences in the past and the future, Roland Garros was almost an amusement park." The Nazis returned Roland Garos to the French Federation, and five war-time championships were played, of course luring no outsiders.

The return of tennis in 1946 brought a terrific surprise to French fans—a dramatic, come-from-behind victory by one of their own. Marcel Bernard would retire with two doubles and two mixed doubles titles at his national championship, but he is celebrated for the poise he showed in a 3-6, 2-6, 6-1, 6-4, 6-3 triumph against Jaroslav Drobny of Czechoslovakia. Drobny, the son of a tennis club groundskeeper, defected in 1949 from his Communist-ruled homeland and, after losing twice more in the French finals, finally won in 1951 (defeating Eric Sturgess of South Africa) and successfully defended in 1952 against world No. 1 Frank Sedgman of Australia.

For American women, the post-war years brought nine singles titles in eight years, with five different players taking the top prize: Margaret Osborne duPont (1946, 1949), Patricia Todd (1947), Doris Hart (1950, 1952), Shirley Fry (1951) and Maureen Connolly (1953, 1954). But the most significant victory by an American occurred in 1956 when Althea Gibson beat defending champion Angela Mortimer of Britain 6-0, 12-10 to become the first black player to win a major championship. She went on to add two U.S. and two Wimbledon singles titles.

Although hardly noticed at the time, the arrival of air travel in the post-war years had a significant impact on the French Championships; indeed on all of tennis, because it opened up the world to the great players from Australia. Jack Crawford was the only Australian to win a French singles crown before World War II. But, beginning with Ken Rosewall's victory in 1953, Australians claimed 17 men and women's singles titles over the next 20 years. The Aussie success came largely at the expense of America. After Tony Trabert's back-to-back wins in 1954 and 1955, no American man won at Roland Garros for 34 years, while American women won only four times in 20 years after Connolly's 1954 title.

While Australians Lew Hoad (1956) and Mervyn Rose (1958) followed in Rosewall's championship footsteps, the era of Australian dominance really took hold with the arrival of the 1960s. Aussie mastery on the grass courts of Wimbledon might have been anticipated, given their schooling on the fast surfaces Down Under, but their success on clay demonstrated the true breadth of their all-round game. From 1962 to 1973, Australia's men and women won 15 of a possible 22 singles titles at Roland Garros. In 1962 and 1965, the men's and women's finals were all-Aussie affairs, the only times in tournament history one nation provided all four finalists. Margaret Smith Court led the charge with five titles, with female compatriot Lesley Turner Bowrey winning twice and Evonne Goolagong once. But a truer reflection of the depth of Aussie talent came on the men's side, where, from 1962 to 1969, seven titles were spread among five different players: Rod Laver, Roy Emerson, Fred Stolle, Tony Roche and Ken Rosewall. Laver and Emerson were the only two-time winners.

The 1968 tournament was particularly memorable. With the dawn of the Open era, the Roland Garros barriers to professionals were being torn down at the same time that student rioters were building barriers on the streets of Paris. Ground-breaking changes within the sport were occurring upon a city-wide revolutionary stage. But the show went on. The first French Open champions were clay-court specialist amateur Nancy Richey of San Angelo, Texas, and Rosewall, who defeated Laver. A year later, Laver got his revenge against Rosewall in the final, on his way to completing a second Grand Slam.

The two most successful players in French Open history—Bjorn Borg and Chris Evert—both won their first titles in 1974.

Borg, whose outstanding baseline game and heavy topspin made him almost unbeatable at Roland Garros, won six French Open men's titles, a record. His first title came soon after his 18th birthday when he defeated Manuel Orantes in the final to become the youngest-ever men's winner. He defended his title in 1975 and then put together four straight final wins beginning in 1978 (he did not participate in 1977 due to a commitment to World Team Tennis in the United States). During that four-year stretch, Borg built a record 28-match unbeaten streak and, in the finals, knocked off four different opponents: Guillermo Vilas, Victor Pecci, Vitas Gerulaitis and Ivan Lendl. But as quickly as Borg burst onto the scene, he departed, retiring in 1982.

Evert, raised on clay courts in Fort Lauderdale, Fla., graced nine French Open finals, winning a record seven singles titles between 1974 and 1986. Her first appearance in the final was a three-set loss to Court in 1973, but she rebounded a year later to overwhelm Olga Morozova of the Soviet Union, defending her title in 1975 by defeating Martina Navratilova in the final. Over the years, Evert and Navratilova met in four finals, with Evert holding a 3-1 edge, including an unforgettable 6-3, 6-7(4-7), 7-5 nail-biter in 1985.

Navratilova preferred the faster surface at Wimbledon, but did manage two French Open titles, straight-set finals against Andrea Jaegar in 1982 and Evert in 1984. Still, Roland Garros was not particularly kind to her. In a 1987 semi-final, Navratilova beat her nemesis, Evert, 6-2, 6-2, only to confront the 17-year-old German prodigy Steffi Graf in the final. It was a classic match, won by Graf 6-4, 4-6, 8-6 for her first major championship. From 1987 to 1996, Graf appeared in eight finals, winning five times, and beating Spain's Arantxa Sanchez Vicario in three of them. She added a sixth crown in 1999 and shortly thereafter retired. Monica Seles beat Graf in hard-fought finals in 1990 (to become the youngest champion at 16 years, 9 months) and in 1992. Seles, who also won in 1991, was the first woman since Germany's Hilde Sperling in 1937 to win three straight French titles.

During the roaring twenties, the celebrity of Lenglen and the Four Musketeers was parlayed into the establishment of a national institution at Roland Garros. But, with the exception of a 1946 win by unheralded Marcel Bernard, French tennis had little to celebrate in the half century that followed the last of Henri Cochet's singles titles. That changed quite unexpectedly in 1983 when Yannick Noah ended France's 37-year drought. Born in France and raised in Cameroon, Noah was a French citizen when he met the world's No. 1 player, Mats Wilander, in the final. He sparked wild jubilation in the streets and earned a place among French folk heroes with an acrobatic, straight-sets victory. France's Mary Pierce was similarly celebrated when she took the women's title in 2000.

Wilander, a Swede, had arrived at Roland Garros a year earlier, at age 17, to claim the title abdicated by Borg. Over the next six years he battled Lendl for French Open supremacy, with each player taking three titles. In 1989, a 34-year American drought ended when Michael Chang beat Stefan Edberg to become the youngest men's champion at 17 years, 3 months. Fellow American Jim Courier won back-to-back titles in 1991 and 1992, before a trio of Spanish men made their mark on the Parisian clay. Sergi Bruguera ended a 21-year Spanish drought with titles in 1993 and 1994, Carlos Moya won in 1998, and Albert Costa in 2002. Sandwiched among the Spanish conquests was Andre Agassi's French title in 1999, making him only the fifth male to complete a career Grand Slam.

French Open – Champions

Year	Men's Singles	Women's Singles	Men's Doubles	Women's Doubles	Mixed Doubles
2002	Albert Costa	Serena Williams	Paul Haarhuis / Yevgeny Kafelnikov	Virginia Ruano Pascual / Paola Suarez	Cara Black / Wayne Black
2001	Gustavo Kuerten	Jennifer Capriati	Mahesh Bhupathi / Leander Paes	Virginia Ruano Pascual / Paola Suarez	Virginia Ruano Pascual / Tomas Carbonell
2000	Gustavo Kuerten	Mary Pierce	Mark Woodforde / Todd Woodbridge	Martina Hingis / Mary Pierce	Mariaan de Swardt / David Adams
1999	Andre Agassi	Steffi Graf	Mahesh Bhupathi / Leander Paes	Venus Williams / Serena Williams	Katarina Srebotnik / Piet Norval
1998	Carlos Moya	Arantxa Sanchez Vicario	Jacco Eltingh / Paul Haarhuis	Martina Hingis / Jana Novotna	Venus Williams / Justin Gimelstob
1997	Gustavo Kuerten	Iva Majoli	Yevgeny Kafelnikov / Daniel Vacek	Gigi Fernandez / Natasha Zvereva	Rika Hiraki / Mahesh Bhupathi
1996	Yevgeny Kafelnikov	Steffi Graf	Yevgeny Kafelnikov / Daniel Vacek	Lindsay Davenport / Mary Joe Fernandez	Patricia Tarabini / Javier Frana
1995	Thomas Muster	Steffi Graf	Jacco Eltingh / Paul Haarhuis	Gigi Fernandez / Natalia Zvereva	Larisa Savchenko Neiland / Mark Woodforde
1994	Sergi Bruguera	Arantxa Sanchez Vicario	Byron Black / Jonathan Stark	Gigi Fernandez / Natalia Zvereva	Kristie Boogert / Menno Oosting
1993	Sergi Bruguera	Steffi Graf	Luke Jensen / Murphy Jensen	Gigi Fernandez / Natalia Zvereva	Eugenia Maniokova / Andrei Olhovskiy
1992	Jim Courier	Monica Seles	Jakob Hlasek / Marc Rosset	Gigi Fernandez / Natalia Zvereva	Arantxa Sanchez Vicario / Todd Woodbridge
1991	Jim Courier	Monica Seles	John Fitzgerald / Anders Jarryd	Gigi Fernandez / Jana Novotna	Helena Sukova / Cyril Suk
1990	Andres Gomez	Monica Seles	Sergio Casal / Emilio Sanchez	Jana Novotna / Helena Sukova	Arantxa Sanchez Vicario / Jorge Lozano
1989	Michael Chang	Arantxa Sanchez Vicario	Jim Grabb / Patrick McEnroe	Larisa Savchenko / Natalia Zvereva	Manon Bollegraf / Tom Nijssen
1988	Mats Wilander	Steffi Graf	Andres Gomez / Emilio Sanchez	Martina Navratilova / Pam Shriver	Lori McNeil / Jorge Lozano
1987	Ivan Lendl	Steffi Graf	Anders Jarryd / Robert Seguso	Martina Navratilova / Pam Shriver	Pam Shriver / Emilio Sanchez
1986	Ivan Lendl	Chris Evert Lloyd	John Fitzgerald / Tomas Smid	Martina Navratilova / Andrea Temesvari	Kathy Jordan / Ken Flach
1985	Mats Wilander	Chris Evert Lloyd	Mark Edmondson / Kim Warwick	Martina Navratilova / Pam Shriver	Martina Navratilova / Heinz Gunthardt
1984	Ivan Lendl	Martina Navratilova	Henri Leconte / Yannick Noah	Martina Navratilova / Pam Shriver	Anne Smith / Dick Stockton
1983	Yannick Noah	Chris Evert Lloyd	Anders Jarryd / Hans Simonsson	Rosalyn Fairbank / Candy Reynolds	Barbara Jordan / Eliot Teltscher
1982	Mats Wilander	Martina Navratilova	Sherwood Stewart / Ferdi Taygan	Martina Navratilova / Anne Smith	Wendy Turnbull / John Lloyd
1981	Bjorn Borg	Hana Mandlikova	Heinz Gunthardt / Balazs Taroczy	Rosalyn Fairbank / Tayna Harford	Andrea Jaeger / Jimmy Arias
1980	Bjorn Borg	Chris Evert Lloyd	Victor Amaya / Hank Pfister	Kathy Jordan / Anne Smith	Anne Smith / Billy Martin
1979	Bjorn Borg	Chris Evert Lloyd	Gene Mayer / Alex Mayer	Betty Stove / Wendy Turnbull	Wendy Turnbull / Bob Hewitt
1978	Bjorn Borg	Virginia Ruzici	Gene Mayer / Hank Pfister	Mima Jausovec / Virginia Ruzici	Renata Tomanova / Pavel Slozil
1977	Guillermo Vilas	Mima Jausovec	Brian Gottfried / Raul Ramirez	Regina Marsikova / Pam Teeguarden	Mary Carillo / John McEnroe
1976	Adriano Panatta	Sue Barker	Fred McNair / Sherwood Stewart	Fiorella Bonicelli / Gail Sherriff Lovera	Ilana Kloss / Kim Warwick
1975	Bjorn Borg	Chris Evert	Brian Gottfried / Raul Ramirez	Chris Evert / Martina Navratilova	Fiorella Bonicelli / Thomaz Koch
1974	Bjorn Borg	Chris Evert	Dick Crealy / Onny Parun	Chris Evert / Olga Morozova	Martina Navratilova / Ivan Molina
1973	Ilie Nastase	Margaret Smith Court	John Newcombe / Tom Okker	Margaret Smith Court / Virginia Wade	Françoise Durr / Jean Claude Barclay
1972	Andres Gimeno	Billie Jean King	Bob Hewitt / Frew McMillan	Billie Jean King / Betty Stove	Evonne Goolagong / Kim Warwick
1971	Jan Kodes	Evonne Goolagong	Arthur Ashe / Marty Riessen	Gail Sherriff Chanfreau / Françoise Durr	Françoise Durr / Jean Claude Barclay
1970	Jan Kodes	Margaret Smith Court	Ilie Nastase / Ion Tiriac	Gail Sherriff Chanfreau / Françoise Durr	Billie Jean King / Bob Hewitt
1969	Rod Laver	Margaret Smith Court	John Newcombe / Tony Roche	Françoise Durr / Ann Haydon Jones	Margaret Smith Court / Marty Riessen
1968	Ken Rosewall	Nancy Richey	Ken Rosewall / Fred Stolle	Françoise Durr / Ann Haydon Jones	Françoise Durr / Jean Claude Barclay
1967	Roy Emerson	Françoise Durr	John Newcombe / Tony Roche	Françoise Durr / Gail Sherriff	Billie Jean King / Owen Davidson
1966	Tony Roche	Ann Haydon Jones	Clark Graebner / Dennis Ralston	Margaret Smith / Judy Tegart	Annette Van Zyl / Frew McMillan
1965	Fred Stolle	Lesley Turner	Roy Emerson / Fred Stolle	Margaret Smith / Lesley Turner	Margaret Smith / Ken Fletcher
1964	Manolo Santana	Margaret Smith	Roy Emerson / Ken Fletcher	Margaret Smith / Lesley Turner	Margaret Smith / Ken Fletcher
1963	Roy Emerson	Lesley Turner	Roy Emerson / Manolo Santana	Ann Haydon Jones / Renee Schuurman	Margaret Smith / Ken Fletcher
1962	Rod Laver	Margaret Smith	Roy Emerson / Neale Fraser	Sandra Reynolds Price / Renee Schuurman	Renee Schuurman / Bob Howe
1961	Manolo Santana	Ann Haydon	Roy Emerson / Rod Laver	Sandra Reynolds / Renee Schuurman	Darlene Hard / Rod Laver
1960	Nicola Pietrangeli	Darlene Hard	Roy Emerson / Neale Fraser	Maria Bueno / Darlene Hard	Maria Bueno / Bob Howe
1959	Nicola Pietrangeli	Christine Truman	Orlando Sirola / Nicola Pietrangeli	Sandra Reynolds / Renee Schuurman	Yola Ramirez / Billy Knight
1958	Merv Rose	Suzi Kormoczi	Ashley Cooper / Neale Fraser	Rosie Reyes / Yola Ramirez	Shirley Bloomer / Nicola Pietrangeli
1957	Sven Davidson	Shirley Bloomer	Mal Anderson / Ashley Cooper	Shirley Bloomer / Darlene Hard	Vera Puzejova / Jiri Javorsky
1956	Lew Hoad	Althea Gibson	Don Candy / Robert Perry	Angela Buxton / Althea Gibson	Thelma Coyne Long / Luis Ayala
1955	Tony Trabert	Angela Mortimer	Vic Seixas / Tony Trabert	Beverly Baker Fleitz / Darlene Hard	Darlene Hard / Gordon Forbes
1954	Tony Trabert	Maureen Connolly	Vic Seixas / Tony Trabert	Maureen Connolly / Nell Hall Hopman	Maureen Connolly / Lew Hoad
1953	Ken Rosewall	Maureen Connolly	Lew Hoad / Ken Rosewall	Doris Hart / Shirley Fry	Doris Hart / Vic Seixas

Year	Men's Singles	Women's Singles	Men's Doubles	Women's Doubles	Mixed Doubles
1952	Jaroslav Drobny	Doris Hart	Ken McGregor / Frank Sedgman	Doris Hart / Shirley Fry	Doris Hart / Frank Sedgman
1951	Jaroslav Drobny	Shirley Fry	Ken McGregor / Frank Sedgman	Doris Hart / Shirley Fry	Doris Hart / Frank Sedgman
1950	Budge Patty	Doris Hart	Bill Talbert / Tony Trabert	Doris Hart / Shirley Fry	Barbara Scofield / Enrique Morea
1949	Frank Parker	M. Osborne duPont	Pancho Gonzalez / Frank Parker	Margaret Osborne duPont / Louise Brough	Sheila Piercey Summers / Eric Sturgess
1948	Frank Parker	Nelly Adamson Landry	Lennart Bergelin / Jaroslav Drobny	Doris Hart / Pat Canning Todd	Pat Canning Todd / Jaroslav Drobny
1947	Joszef Asboth	Pat Canning Todd	Eustace Fannin / Eric Sturgess	Louise Brough / Margaret Osborne	Sheila Piercey Summers / Eric Sturgess
1946	Marcel Bernard	Margaret Osborne	Marcel Bernard / Yvon Petra	Louise Brough / Margaret Osborne	Pauline Betz / Budge Patty
1940-45		Not held – WW II			
1939	Don NcNeill	S. Passemard Mathieu	Don McNeill / Charles Harris	Simone Passemard Mathieu / Jadwiga Jedrzejowska	Sarah Palfrey Fabyan / Elwood Cooke
1938	Don Budge	S. Passemard Mathieu	Bernard Destremau / Yvon Petra	Simone Passemard Mathieu / Billie Yorke	Simone Passemard Mathieu / Dragutin Mitic
1937	Henner Henkel	H. Krahwinkel Sperling	Gottfried von Cramm / Henner Henkel	Simone Passemard Mathieu / Billie Yorke	Simone Passemard Mathieu / Yvon Petra
1936	Gottfried von Cramm	H. Krahwinkel Sperling	Jean Borotra / Marcel Bernard	Simone Passemard Mathieu / Billie Yorke	Billie Yorke / Marcel Bernard
1935	Fred Perry	H. Krahwinkel Sperling	Jack Crawford / Adrian Quist	Margaret Scriven / Kay Stammers	Lolette Payot / Marcel Bernard
1934	Gottfried von Cramm	Margaret Scriven	Jean Borotra / Jacques Brugnon	Simone Passemard Mathieu / Elizabeth Ryan	Colette Rosambert / Jean Borotra
1933	Jack Crawford	Margaret Scriven	Pat Hughes / Fred Perry	Simone Passemard Mathieu / Elizabeth Ryan	Margaret Scriven / Jack Crawford
1932	Henri Cochet	Helen Wills Moody	Henri Cochet / Jacques Brugnon	Helen Wills Moody / Elizabeth Ryan	Betty Nuthall / Fred Perry
1931	Jean Borotra	Cilly Aussem	George Lott / John Van Ryn	Eileen Bennett Whittingstall / Betty Nuthall	Betty Nuthall / Pat Spence
1930	Henri Cochet	Helen Wills Moody	Henri Cochet / Jacques Brugnon	Helen Wills Moody / Elizabeth Ryan	Cilly Aussem / Bill Tilden
1929	René Lacoste	Helen Wills	René Lacoste / Jean Borotra	Lili de Alvarez / Kea Bouman	Eileen Bennett / Henri Cochet
1928	Henri Cochet	Helen Wills	Jean Borotra / Jacques Brugnon	Phoebe Holcroft Watson / Eileen Bennett	Eileen Bennett / Henri Cochet
1927	René Lacoste	Kea Bouman	Henri Cochet / Jacques Brugnon	Irene Bowder Peacock / Bobbie Heine	Marguerite Broquedis Bordes / Jean Borotra
1926	Henri Cochet	Suzanne Lenglen	Vinnie Richards / Howard Kinsey	Suzanne Lenglen / Didi Vlasto	Suzanne Lenglen / Jacques Brugnon
1925	René Lacoste	Suzanne Lenglen	Jean Borotra / René Lacoste	Suzanne Lenglen / Didi Vlasto	Suzanne Lenglen / Jacques Brugnon

French Open – Tournament Results

(**Legend: F:** Final; **S:** Semi-final; **Q:** Quarter-final; **Set:** S1, S2, S3, S4, S5)

Men's Singles

Rd	Winner	Defeated	S1	S2	S3	S4	S5
1925							
F	**René Lacoste**	**Jean Borotra**	**7-5**	**6-1**	**6-4**		
S	Jean Borotra	Jean Washer	6-2	6-1	6-3		
S	René Lacoste	Sydney Jacob	6-2	6-1	4-6	7-5	
Q	Jean Washer	Henri Cochet	8-6	8-6	6-4		
Q	Jean Borotra	Paul Fret	1-6	6-3	6-3	6-2	
Q	René Lacoste	Eduardo Flaquer	6-4	7-5	6-2		
Q	Sydney Jacob	Andre Gobert	2-6	2-6	6-4	7-5 (retired)	
1926							
F	**Henri Cochet**	**René Lacoste**	**6-2**	**6-4**	**6-3**		
S	René Lacoste	Jean Borotra	8-6	3-6	6-2	6-1	
S	Henri Cochet	Vinnie Richards	6-1	6-4	6-4		
Q	René Lacoste	Nicholai Misu	14-12	6-1	6-1		
Q	Jean Borotra	Howard Kinsey	2-6	6-4	6-1	3-6	7-5
Q	Henri Cochet	Jean Washer	6-4	3-6	7-5	6-4	
Q	Vinnie Richards	Bela von Kehrling	6-1	6-3	6-3		
1927							
F	**René Lacoste**	**Bill Tilden**	**6-4**	**4-6**	**5-7**	**6-3**	**11-9**
S	Bill Tilden	Henri Cochet	9-7	6-3	6-2		
S	René Lacoste	Pat Spence	6-1	6-3	6-2		
Q	Henri Cochet	Otto Froitzheim	6-1	6-1	6-4		
Q	Bill Tilden	Louis Raymond	5-7	6-2	8-6	6-3	
Q	Pat Spence	Antoine Gentien	6-2	3-6	6-4	6-3	
Q	René Lacoste	Jacques Brugnon	6-4	6-4	5-7	6-3	
1928							
F	**Henri Cochet**	**René Lacoste**	**5-7**	**6-3**	**6-1**	**6-3**	
S	Henri Cochet	Jean Borotra	6-3	2-6	7-5	6-4	
S	René Lacoste	Jack Hawkes	6-2	6-4	6-1		
Q	Henri Cochet	Ronaldo Boyd	7-5	6-4	6-2		
Q	Jean Borotra	Christian Boussus	6-1	3-6	7-5	6-3	
Q	Jack Hawkes	Jacques Brugnon	4-6	3-6	6-3	6-3	6-4
Q	René Lacoste	Jack Crawford	6-0	6-1	7-5		
1929							
F	**René Lacoste**	**Jean Borotra**	**6-3**	**2-6**	**6-0**	**2-6**	**8-6**
S	René Lacoste	Bill Tilden	6-1	6-0	5-7	6-3	
S	Jean Borotra	Henri Cochet	6-3	5-7	7-5	6-4	
Q	René Lacoste	Bela von Kehrling	8-6	1-6	6-0	6-3	
Q	Bill Tilden	Umb. de Morpurgo	9-11	3-6	6-1	6-2	8-6
Q	Jean Borotra	Frank Hunter	6-8	10-8	4-6	3-6	6-1
Q	Henri Cochet	Jacques Brugnon	7-5	4-6	6-4	7-5	
1930							
F	**Henri Cochet**	**Bill Tilden**	**3-6**	**8-6**	**6-3**	**6-1**	
S	Bill Tilden	Jean Borotra	2-6	6-2	6-4	4-6	6-3
S	Henri Cochet	Umberto de Morpurgo	7-5	6-1	6-2		
Q	Bill Tilden	Geo. Lyttleton Rogers	6-1	6-1	7-5		
Q	Jean Borotra	Colin Gregory	6-4	6-4	6-3		
Q	Umberto de Morpurgo	Gar Moon	6-2	6-2	4-6	2-6	6-3
Q	Henri Cochet	Harry Hopman	6-1	2-6	6-3	6-3	
1931							
F	**Jean Borotra**	**Christian Boussus**	**2-6**	**6-4**	**7-5**	**6-4**	
S	Christian Boussus	George Hughes	6-1	4-6	6-2	6-3	
S	Jean Borotra	Jiro Satoh	10-8	2-6	5-7	6-1	6-2
Q	George Hughes	George Lott	3-6	4-6	6-2	6-2	6-4
Q	Christian Boussus	Giorgio de Stefani	6-4	6-3	3-6	2-6	9-7
Q	Jiro Satoh	John Van Ryn	8-6	1-6	2-6	6-4	6-3
Q	Jean Borotra	Beni Berthet	6-2	6-3	6-1		
1932							
F	**Henri Cochet**	**Giorgio de Stefani**	**6-0**	**6-4**	**4-6**	**6-3**	
S	Giorgio de Stefani	Roderich Menzel	6-3	2-6	7-5	6-4	
S	Henri Cochet	Marcel Bernard	6-1	6-0	6-4		
Q	Roderich Menzel	Fred Perry	2-6	6-1	1-6	6-3	7-5
Q	Giorgio de Stefani	Harold G.N. Lee	6-3	9-7	6-2		
Q	Marcel Bernard	Geo. Lyttleton Rogers	6-4	6-8	6-4	3-6	6-2
Q	Henri Cochet	Greg Mangin	6-3	7-5	5-7	6-3	
1933							
F	**Jack Crawford**	**Henri Cochet**	**8-6**	**6-1**	**6-3**		
S	Jack Crawford	Jiro Satoh	6-0	6-2	6-2		
S	Henri Cochet	Harold G.N. Lee	9-11	6-3	6-3	6-3	
Q	Jack Crawford	Christian Boussus	6-3	6-3	6-4		
Q	Jiro Satoh	Fred Perry	1-6	7-5	6-4	2-6	6-2
Q	Harold G.N. Lee	Marcel Bernard	10-8	6-4	5-7	6-0	
Q	Henri Cochet	Roderich Menzel	7-5	6-1	6-1		
1934							
F	**Gottfried von Cramm**	**Jack Crawford**	**6-4**	**7-9**	**3-6**	**7-5**	**6-3**
S	Jack Crawford	Christian Boussus	6-3	2-6	7-5	6-4	
S	Gottfried von Cramm	Giorgio de Stefani	3-6	6-4	6-1	3-6	6-2
Q	Jack Crawford	George Hughes	4-6	6-4	6-2	6-3	
Q	Christian Boussus	Bunny Austin	5-7	6-2	6-2	2-6	6-1
Q	Gottfried von Cramm	Roderich Menzel	6-2	6-3	3-6	3-6	6-3
Q	Giorgio de Stefani	Fred Perry	6-2	1-6	9-7	6-2	
1935							
F	**Fred Perry**	**Gottfried von Cramm**	**6-3**	**3-6**	**6-1**	**6-3**	
S	Fred Perry	Jack Crawford	6-3	8-6	6-3		
S	Gottfried von Cramm	Bunny Austin	6-2	5-7	6-1	5-7	6-0
Q	Fred Perry	Christian Boussus	6-1	6-0	6-4		
Q	Jack Crawford	Marcel Bernard	6-3	6-1	6-1		
Q	Bunny Austin	Roderich Menzel	1-6	10-8	2-6	6-4	6-2
Q	Gottfried von Cramm	Viv MacGrath	6-2	6-4	3-6	6-3	
1936							
F	**Gottfried von Cramm**	**Fred Perry**	**6-0**	**2-6**	**6-2**	**2-6**	**6-0**
S	Gottfried von Cramm	Marcel Bernard	7-5	6-1	6-1		
S	Fred Perry	Christian Boussus	6-4	7-5	5-7	6-2	
S	Gottfried von Cramm	Bernard Destremau	6-3	6-1	6-4		
Q	Marcel Bernard	Bunny Austin	4-6	1-0		(retired)	
Q	Christian Boussus	Andre Merlin	1-6	6-3	7-5	1-6	6-1
Q	Fred Perry	Boris Maneff	9-7	6-3	4-6	6-3	
1937							
F	**Henner Henkel**	**Bunny Austin**	**6-1**	**6-4**	**6-3**		
S	Henner Henkel	Bernard Destremau	6-1	6-4	6-3		
S	Bunny Austin	Christian Boussus	7-5	6-2	1-6	6-3	
Q	Bernard Destremau	Charles Hare	11-9	4-6	7-9	7-5	7-5
Q	Henner Henkel	George Hughes	6-3	6-4	6-2		
Q	Christian Boussus	Franz Cejnar	6-2	6-2	6-1		
Q	Bunny Austin	Yvon Petra	6-4	6-2	6-1		

Rd	Winner	Defeated	S1	S2	S3	S4	S5
1938							
F	**Don Budge**	**Roderich Menzel**	6-3	6-2	6-4		
S	Roderich Menzel	Franjo Puncec	6-4	6-4	6-4		
S	Don Budge	Josip Pallada	6-2	6-3	6-3		
Q	Franjo Puncec	Franz Cejnar	3-6	6-3	6-2	6-3	
Q	Roderich Menzel	Dragutin Mitic	6-0	6-0	6-1		
Q	Josip Pallada	Christian Boussus	6-1	3-6	4-6	6-1	6-2
Q	Don Budge	Bernard Destremau	6-4	6-3	6-4		
1939							
F	**Don NcNeill**	**Bobby Riggs**	7-5	6-0	6-3		
S	Don NcNeill	Elwood Cooke	6-2	7-5	7-9	6-2	
S	Bobby Riggs	Otto Szigeti	6-3	6-0	6-4		
Q	Don NcNeill	Franjo Puncec	6-4	1-6	6-3	6-1	
Q	Elwood Cooke	Henry Billington	6-4	6-4	6-1		
Q	Otto Szigeti	Christian Boussus	7-5	1-6	2-6	7-5	6-4
Q	Bobby Riggs	Clock Tloczynski	6-2	2-6	8-6	7-5	
1940-45	*Not held – WW II*						
1946							
F	**Marcel Bernard**	**Jaroslav Drobny**	3-6	2-6	6-1	6-4	6-3
S	Jaroslav Drobny	Tom Brown	7-5	3-6	6-4	5-7	6-2
S	Marcel Bernard	Yvon Petra	5-7	6-2	6-3	5-7	6-2
Q	Tom Brown	Pierre Pellizza	6-2	6-2	6-2		
Q	Jaroslav Drobny	Dragutin Mitic	6-2	7-5	6-8	8-6	
Q	Marcel Bernard	Budge Patty	2-6	6-2	6-1	4-6	7-5
Q	Yvon Petra	Ferdinand Vrba	2-6	6-0	6-4	6-2	
1947							
F	**Joszef Asboth**	**Eric Sturgess**	8-6	7-5	6-4		
S	Joszef Asboth	Tom Brown	6-2	6-2	6-1		
S	Eric Sturgess	Marcel Bernard	3-6	2-6	6-3	8-6	6-3
Q	Joszef Asboth	Yvon Petra	4-6	6-3	6-2	6-1	
Q	Tom Brown	Pierre Pellizza	7-5	6-1	6-2		
Q	Eric Sturgess	Adam Stolpa	6-4	6-3	6-2		
Q	Marcel Bernard	Gianni Cucelli	6-4	6-2	0-6	3-6	6-4
1948							
F	**Frank Parker**	**Jaroslav Drobny**	6-4	7-5	5-7	8-6	
S	Jaroslav Drobny	Budge Patty	2-6	6-3	4-6	6-4	6-3
S	Frank Parker	Eric Sturgess	6-2	6-2	6-1		
Q	Budge Patty	Marcello Del Bello	7-5	9-7	1-0	(retired)	
Q	Jaroslav Drobny	Lennart Bergelin	6-2	6-1	6-4		
Q	Eric Sturgess	Marcel Bernard	6-3	6-2	9-7		
Q	Frank Parker	Gianni Cucelli	6-1	6-2	6-1		
1949							
F	**Frank Parker**	**Budge Patty**	6-3	1-6	6-1	6-4	
S	Budge Patty	Pancho Gonzalez	6-4	6-3	3-6	6-3	
S	Frank Parker	Eric Sturgess	6-2	6-1	6-4		
Q	Pancho Gonzalez	Marcel Bernard	6-1	7-5	5-7	6-1	
Q	Budge Patty	Gianni Cucelli	7-5	10-12	6-3	8-6	
Q	Eric Sturgess	Robert Abdesselam	6-1	6-4	6-2		
Q	Frank Parker	Dragutin Mitic	6-0	6-2	6-4		
1950							
F	**Budge Patty**	**Jaroslav Drobny**	6-1	6-2	3-6	5-7	7-5
S	Budge Patty	Tony Trabert	2-6	6-4	6-4	12-10	
S	Jaroslav Drobny	Eric Sturgess	6-4	7-5	3-6	12-10	
Q	Budge Patty	Irving Dorfman	0-6	6-1	3-6	6-1	11-9
Q	Tony Trabert	John Bromwich	6-2	6-2	6-3		
Q	Eric Sturgess	Art Larsen	4-6	6-3	6-2	6-4	
Q	Jaroslav Drobny	Vic Seixas	7-5	17-15	5-7	6-4	

Rd	Winner	Defeated	S1	S2	S3	S4	S5
1951							
F	**Jaroslav Drobny**	**Eric Sturgess**	6-3	6-3	6-3		
S	Jaroslav Drobny	Frank Sedgman	6-0	6-3	6-1		
S	Eric Sturgess	Ken McGregor	10-8	7-9	8-6	5-7	9-7
Q	Frank Sedgman	Straight Clark	6-4	6-4	6-3		
Q	Jaroslav Drobny	Dick Savitt	1-6	6-8	6-4	8-6	6-3
Q	Eric Sturgess	Merv Rose	11-9	4-6	6-3	6-3	
Q	Ken McGregor	Lennart Bergelin	9-7	9-7	6-1		
1952							
F	**Jaroslav Drobny**	**Frank Sedgman**	6-2	6-0	3-6	6-4	
S	Frank Sedgman	Eric Sturgess	7-5	6-2	8-6		
S	Jaroslav Drobny	Ken McGregor	6-3	6-0	4-6	6-3	
Q	Frank Sedgman	Budge Patty	6-4	6-2	6-2		
Q	Eric Sturgess	Dick Savitt	6-2	6-8	4-6	8-6	6-3
Q	Ken McGregor	Felicisimo Ampon	6-1	6-1	6-2		
Q	Jaroslav Drobny	Gardnar Mulloy	6-1	6-2	6-2		
1953							
F	**Ken Rosewall**	**Vic Seixas**	6-3	6-4	1-6	6-2	
S	Ken Rosewall	Enrique Morea	2-6	6-2	6-4	0-6	6-2
S	Vic Seixas	Jaroslav Drobny	6-3	6-2	3-6	6-3	
Q	Enrique Morea	Gardnar Mulloy	6-8	6-3	8-6	6-3	
Q	Ken Rosewall	Felicisimo Ampon	6-2	6-1	6-1		
Q	Vic Seixas	Lew Hoad	6-3	6-3	6-4		
Q	Jaroslav Drobny	Fausto Gardini	6-3	6-1	1-6	6-4	
1954							
F	**Tony Trabert**	**Art Larsen**	6-4	7-5	6-1		
S	Tony Trabert	Budge Patty	6-1	7-5	6-4		
S	Art Larsen	Enrique Morea	6-4	6-3	6-4		
Q	Tony Trabert	Merv Rose	7-5	4-6	6-4	6-2	
Q	Budge Patty	Sven Davidson	6-4	6-0	6-4		
Q	Art Larsen	Vic Seixas	6-4	1-6	8-6	6-1	
Q	Enrique Morea	Gardnar Mulloy	6-3	6-4	6-1		
1955							
F	**Tony Trabert**	**Sven Davidson**	2-6	6-1	6-4	6-2	
S	Sven Davidson	Beppo Merlo	6-3	6-3	6-2		
S	Tony Trabert	Hamilton Richardson	6-1	2-2		(retired)	
Q	Beppo Merlo	Vic Seixas	12-10	6-3	6-3		
Q	Sven Davidson	Budge Patty	7-5	10-8	6-0		
Q	Hamilton Richardson	Herbie Flam	6-3	4-6	6-1	6-3	
Q	Tony Trabert	Merv Rose	6-2	3-6	6-3	6-0	
1956							
F	**Lew Hoad**	**Sven Davidson**	6-4	8-6	6-3		
S	Sven Davidson	Ashley Cooper	6-2	9-7	5-7	6-3	
S	Lew Hoad	Beppo Merlo	6-4	7-5	6-4		
Q	Ashley Cooper	Jackie Brichant	6-4	8-6	2-6	6-3	
Q	Sven Davidson	Herbie Flam	6-2	6-4	7-5		
Q	Beppo Merlo	Paul Rmy	4-6	6-2	2-6	6-4	10-8
Q	Lew Hoad	Nicola Pietrangeli	6-1	6-3	6-0		
1957							
F	**Sven Davidson**	**Herbie Flam**	6-3	6-4	6-4		
S	Sven Davidson	Ashley Cooper	6-4	2-6	2-6	6-2	6-3
S	Herbie Flam	Merv Rose	4-6	6-4	4-6	6-2	7-5
Q	Ashley Cooper	Neale Fraser	0-6	8-6	7-5	4-6	6-3
Q	Sven Davidson	Jackie Brichant	6-2	6-2	4-6	6-2	
Q	Merv Rose	Robert Haillet		(walkover)			
Q	Herbie Flam	Philippe Washer	5-7	6-4	4-6	4-6	6-4
1958							
F	**Merv Rose**	**Luis Ayala**	6-3	6-4	6-4		
S	Merv Rose	Jackie Brichant	10-8	6-1	6-3		
S	Luis Ayala	Ashley Cooper	9-11	4-6	6-4	6-2	7-5
Q	Jackie Brichant	Neale Fraser	5-7	5-7	7-5	6-0	6-3
Q	Merv Rose	Pierre Darmon	6-4	8-10	6-3	6-1	
Q	Luis Ayala	Robert Haillet	6-0	7-5	6-4		
Q	Ashley Cooper	Beppo Merlo	7-9	6-2	7-9	6-3	6-2

Rd	Winner	Defeated	S1	S2	S3	S4	S5

1959

Rd	Winner	Defeated	S1	S2	S3	S4	S5
F	**Nicola Pietrangeli**	**Ian Vermaak**	**3-6**	**6-3**	**6-4**	**6-1**	
S	Nicola Pietrangeli	Neale Fraser	7-5	6-3	7-5		
S	Ian Vermaak	Luis Ayala	6-2	6-1	6-4		
Q	Neale Fraser	Marty Mulligan	6-4	8-6	6-1		
Q	Nicola Pietrangeli	Billy Knight	6-1	6-2	6-1		
Q	Ian Vermaak	Jackie Brichant	4-6	2-5	6-4	6-3	6-4
Q	Luis Ayala	Roy Emerson	1-6	6-4	6-4	6-3	

1960

Rd	Winner	Defeated	S1	S2	S3	S4	S5
F	**Nicola Pietrangeli**	**Luis Ayala**	**3-6**	**6-3**	**6-4**	**4-6**	**6-3**
S	Nicola Pietrangeli	Robert Haillet	6-4	7-5	7-5		
S	Luis Ayala	Orlando Sirola	6-4	6-0	6-2		
Q	Robert Haillet	Neale Fraser	6-4	6-2	8-10	3-6	6-5
							(default)
Q	Nicola Pietrangeli	Andres Gimeno	6-3	6-1	3-6	6-2	
Q	Luis Ayala	Manolo Santana	6-1	7-5	6-2		
Q	Orlando Sirola	Barry MacKay	6-3	15-13	6-4		

1961

Rd	Winner	Defeated	S1	S2	S3	S4	S5
F	**Manolo Santana**	**Nicola Pietrangeli**	**4-6**	**6-1**	**3-6**	**6-0**	**6-2**
S	Manolo Santana	Rod Laver	3-6	6-2	4-6	6-4	6-0
S	Nicola Pietrangeli	Jan-Erik Lundquist	6-4	6-4	6-4		
Q	Rod Laver	Ronald Holmberg	6-4	6-0	3-6	6-3	
Q	Manolo Santana	Roy Emerson	9-7	6-2	6-2		
Q	Jan-Erik Lundquist	Carlos Fernandes	6-4	6-4	6-3		
Q	Nicola Pietrangeli	Gerard Pilet	6-3	6-8	6-3	6-1	

1962

Rd	Winner	Defeated	S1	S2	S3	S4	S5
F	**Rod Laver**	**Roy Emerson**	**3-6**	**2-6**	**6-3**	**9-7**	**6-2**
S	Roy Emerson	Manolo Santana	6-4	3-6	6-1	2-6	6-3
S	Rod Laver	Neale Fraser	3-6	6-3	6-2	3-6	7-5
Q	Roy Emerson	Ramanathan Krishnan	4-6	6-1	3-6	6-2	6-0
Q	Manolo Santana	Pierre Darmon	6-4	6-2	6-3		
Q	Neale Fraser	Nicola Pietrangeli	4-6	6-3	11-9	6-1	
Q	Rod Laver	Marty Mulligan	6-4	3-6	2-6	10-8	6-2

1963

Rd	Winner	Defeated	S1	S2	S3	S4	S5
F	**Roy Emerson**	**Pierre Darmon**	**3-6**	**6-1**	**6-4**	**6-4**	
S	Pierre Darmon	Manolo Santana	6-3	4-6	2-6	9-7	6-2
S	Roy Emerson	Mike Sangster	8-6	6-3	6-4		
Q	Manolo Santana	Jean Claude Barclay	1-6	6-2	6-0	2-6	6-3
Q	Pierre Darmon	Bobby Wilson	6-3	6-4	6-3		
Q	Mike Sangster	Ken Fletcher	8-6	6-3	6-8	6-3	
Q	Roy Emerson	Nicola Pietrangeli	6-8	4-6	6-1	6-3	6-4

1964

Rd	Winner	Defeated	S1	S2	S3	S4	S5
F	**Manolo Santana**	**Nicola Pietrangeli**	**6-3**	**6-1**	**4-6**	**7-5**	
S	Manolo Santana	Pierre Darmon	8-6	6-4	3-6	2-6	6-4
S	Nicola Pietrangeli	Jan-Erik Lundquist	4-6	6-3	6-4	6-4	
Q	Pierre Darmon	Eugene Scott	6-3	6-2	6-0		
Q	Manolo Santana	Ronnie Barnes	6-4	6-3	6-3		
Q	Jan-Erik Lundquist	Cliff Drysdale	6-4	6-4	3-6	6-1	
Q	Nicola Pietrangeli	Roy Emerson	6-1	6-3	6-3		

1965

Rd	Winner	Defeated	S1	S2	S3	S4	S5
F	**Fred Stolle**	**Tony Roche**	**3-6**	**6-0**	**6-2**	**6-3**	
S	Tony Roche	Roy Emerson	6-1	6-4	3-6	6-0	
S	Fred Stolle	Cliff Drysdale	6-8	6-4	6-1	4-6	6-4
S	Roy Emerson	Pierre Barthes	6-4	6-4	6-4		
Q	Tony Roche	Ingo Buding	6-4	4-6	7-5	0-6	6-3
Q	Fred Stolle	John Newcombe	6-1	7-5	11-9		
Q	Cliff Drysdale	Toomas Leius			(walkover)		

1966

Rd	Winner	Defeated	S1	S2	S3	S4	S5
F	**Tony Roche**	**Istvan Gulyas**	**6-1**	**6-4**	**7-5**		
S	Tony Roche	Franois Jauffret	6-3	6-4	6-4		
S	Istvan Gulyas	Cliff Drysdale	6-4	2-6	7-9	6-2	6-3
Q	Franois Jauffret	Roy Emerson	1-6	6-3	6-4	4-6	6-4
Q	Tony Roche	Alex Metreveli	5-7	6-3	6-1	7-5	
Q	Istvan Gulyas	Ken Fletcher	7-5	6-2	6-3		
Q	Cliff Drysdale	Fred Stolle	1-6	6-4	6-2	11-9	

1967

Rd	Winner	Defeated	S1	S2	S3	S4	S5
F	**Roy Emerson**	**Tony Roche**	**6-1**	**6-4**	**2-6**	**6-2**	
S	Tony Roche	Nikki Pilic	3-6	6-3	6-4	2-6	6-4
S	Roy Emerson	Istvan Gulyas	6-3	6-4	6-2		
Q	Tony Roche	Cliff Drysdale	2-6	2-6	6-3	6-2	6-4
Q	Nikki Pilic	Tom Okker	6-3	11-9	6-2		
Q	Istvan Gulyas	Owen Davidson	5-7	6-3	6-3	6-0	
Q	Roy Emerson	Pierre Darmon	6-0	6-4	6-4		

1968

Rd	Winner	Defeated	S1	S2	S3	S4	S5
F	**Ken Rosewall**	**Rod Laver**	**6-3**	**6-1**	**2-6**	**6-2**	
S	Rod Laver	Pancho Gonzalez	6-3	6-3	6-1		
S	Ken Rosewall	Andres Gimeno	3-6	6-3	7-5	3-6	6-3
Q	Rod Laver	Ion Tiriac	4-6	4-6	6-3	6-3	6-0
Q	Pancho Gonzalez	Roy Emerson	7-5	6-3	3-6	4-6	6-4
Q	Andres Gimeno	Boro Jovanovic	6-4	6-0	6-2		
Q	Ken Rosewall	Thomaz Koch	8-6	6-2	3-6	6-3	

1969

Rd	Winner	Defeated	S1	S2	S3	S4	S5
F	**Rod Laver**	**Ken Rosewall**	**6-4**	**6-3**	**6-4**		
S	Rod Laver	Tom Okker	4-6	6-0	6-2	6-4	
S	Ken Rosewall	Tony Roche	7-5	6-2	6-2		
Q	Rod Laver	Andres Gimeno	3-6	6-2	6-4	6-4	
Q	Tom Okker	John Newcombe	5-7	6-2	4-6	6-2	6-2
Q	Tony Roche	Zeljko Franulovic	4-6	7-5	6-0	4-6	6-1
Q	Ken Rosewall	Fred Stolle	12-10	4-6	7-5	6-2	

1970

Rd	Winner	Defeated	S1	S2	S3	S4	S5
F	**Jan Kodes**	**Zeljko Franulovic**	**6-2**	**6-4**	**6-0**		
S	Zeljko Franulovic	Cliff Richey	6-4	4-6	1-6	7-5	7-5
S	Jan Kodes	Georges Goven	2-6	6-2	5-7	6-2	6-3
Q	Cliff Richey	Ilie Nastase	7-5	9-7	4-6	6-3	
Q	Zeljko Franulovic	Arthur Ashe	6-3	3-6	10-8	4-6	6-3
Q	Georges Goven	Franois Jauffret	8-6	6-8	6-2	6-1	
Q	Jan Kodes	Marty Mulligan	6-1	6-3	7-5		

1971

Rd	Winner	Defeated	S1	S2	S3	S4	S5
F	**Jan Kodes**	**Ilie Nastase**	**8-6**	**6-2**	**2-6**	**7-5**	
S	Jan Kodes	Zeljko Franulovic	6-4	6-2	7-5		
S	Ilie Nastase	Frank Froehling III	6-0	2-6	6-4	6-3	
Q	Jan Kodes	Patrick Proisy	6-4	8-6	1-6	6-1	
Q	Zeljko Franulovic	Istvan Gulyas	6-3	6-2	4-6	6-2	
Q	Ilie Nastase	Stan Smith	6-1	6-3	3-6	6-4	
Q	Frank Froehling III	Arthur Ashe	6-4	4-6	6-3	3-6	8-6

1972

Rd	Winner	Defeated	S1	S2	S3	S4	S5
F	**Andres Gimeno**	**Patrick Proisy**	**4-6**	**6-3**	**6-1**	**6-1**	
S	Patrick Proisy	Manolo Orantes	6-3	7-5	6-2		
S	Andres Gimeno	Alex Metreveli	4-6	6-3	6-1	2-6	6-3
Q	Patrick Proisy	Jan Kodes	6-4	6-2	6-4		
Q	Manolo Orantes	Harold Solomon	6-4	5-7	6-3	6-2	
Q	Andres Gimeno	Stan Smith	6-1	7-9	6-0	7-5	
Q	Alex Metreveli	Adriano Panatta	8-6	7-9	6-3	6-3	

1973

Rd	Winner	Defeated	S1	S2	S3	S4	S5
F	**Ilie Nastase**	**Nikki Pilic**	**6-3**	**6-3**	**6-0**		
S	Nikki Pilic	Adriano Panatta	6-4	6-3	6-2		
S	Ilie Nastase	Tom Gorman	6-3	6-4	6-1		
Q	Adriano Panatta	Tom Okker	6-3	5-7	6-3	6-4	
Q	Nikki Pilic	Paolo Bertolucci	6-3	6-4	3-6	6-4	
Q	Tom Gorman	Jan Kodes	6-4	7-6(6)	4-6	6-1	
Q	Ilie Nastase	Roger Taylor	6-0	6-2	7-6(7)		

1974

Rd	Winner	Defeated	S1	S2	S3	S4	S5
F	Bjorn Borg	Manolo Orantes	2-6	6-7(1)	6-0	6-1	6-1
S	Bjorn Borg	Harold Solomon	6-4	2-6	6-2	6-1	
S	Manolo Orantes	Franois Jauffret	6-2	6-4	6-4		
Q	Harold Solomon	Ilie Nastase	6-4	6-4	0-6	3-6	6-4
Q	Bjorn Borg	Raul Ramirez	6-2	5-7	4-6	6-2	6-3
Q	Manolo Orantes	Patricio Cornejo	6-3	6-3	6-1		
Q	Franois Jauffret	Han Jurgen Pohmann	7-6	6-3	6-2		

1975

Rd	Winner	Defeated	S1	S2	S3	S4	S5
F	Bjorn Borg	Guillermo Vilas	6-2	6-3	6-4		
S	Bjorn Borg	Adriano Panatta	6-4	1-6	7-5	6-4	
S	Guillermo Vilas	Eddie Dibbs	6-1	6-4	1-6	6-1	
Q	Bjorn Borg	Harold Solomon	6-1	7-5	6-4		
Q	Adriano Panatta	John Andrews	6-4	5-7	7-6	6-2	
Q	Guillermo Vilas	Onny Parun	6-2	6-2	7-6		
Q	Eddie Dibbs	Raul Ramirez	4-6	7-6	6-1	5-7	6-4

1976

Rd	Winner	Defeated	S1	S2	S3	S4	S5
F	Adriano Panatta	Harold Solomon	6-1	6-4	4-6	7-6(3)	
S	Adriano Panatta	Eddie Dibbs	6-3	6-2	6-4		
S	Harold Solomon	Raul Ramirez	6-7(5)	6-0	4-6	6-4	6-4
Q	Adriano Panatta	Bjorn Borg	6-3	6-3	2-6	7-6(2)	
Q	Eddie Dibbs	Manolo Orantes	6-3	3-6	6-3	6-3	
Q	Raul Ramirez	Balazs Taroczy	4-6	7-6(7)	2-6	6-1	7-5
Q	Harold Solomon	Guillermo Vilas	6-1	0-6	4-6	6-4	6-4

1977

Rd	Winner	Defeated	S1	S2	S3	S4	S5
F	Guillermo Vilas	Brian Gottfried	6-0	6-3	6-0		
S	Brian Gottfried	Phil Dent	7-5	6-3	7-5		
S	Guillermo Vilas	Raul Ramirez	6-2	6-0	6-3		
Q	Brian Gottfried	Ilie Nastase	4-6	3-6	6-2	6-2	6-3
Q	Phil Dent	Jose Higueras	6-1	6-3	3-6	6-7	6-3
Q	Guillermo Vilas	Wojtek Fibak	6-4	6-0	6-4		
Q	Raul Ramirez	Adriano Panatta	7-6(6)	6-3	7-5		

1978

Rd	Winner	Defeated	S1	S2	S3	S4	S5
F	Bjorn Borg	Guillermo Vilas	6-1	6-1	6-3		
S	Bjorn Borg	Corrado Barazzutti	6-0	6-1	6-0		
S	Guillermo Vilas	Dick Stockton	6-3	6-3	6-2		
Q	Bjorn Borg	Raul Ramirez	6-3	6-3	6-4		
Q	Corrado Barazzutti	Eddie Dibbs	6-2	7-6(7)	6-1		
Q	Dick Stockton	Manolo Orantes	7-5	6-1	6-3		
Q	Guillermo Vilas	Hans Gildemeister	6-4	2-6	6-1	3-6	6-3

1979

Rd	Winner	Defeated	S1	S2	S3	S4	S5
F	Bjorn Borg	Victor Pecci	6-3	6-1	6-7(6)	6-4	
S	Bjorn Borg	Vitas Gerulaitis	6-2	6-1	6-0		
S	Victor Pecci	Jimmy Connors	7-5	6-4	5-7	6-3	
Q	Bjorn Borg	Hans Gildemeister	6-4	6-1	7-5		
Q	Vitas Gerulaitis	Jose Higueras	6-1	3-6	6-4	6-4	
Q	Victor Pecci	Guillermo Vilas	6-0	6-2	7-5		
Q	Jimmy Connors	Eddie Dibbs	6-2	2-6	6-4	6-2	

1980

Rd	Winner	Defeated	S1	S2	S3	S4	S5
F	Bjorn Borg	Vitas Gerulaitis	6-4	6-1	6-2		
S	Bjorn Borg	Harold Solomon	6-2	6-2	6-0		
S	Vitas Gerulaitis	Jimmy Connors	6-1	3-6	6-7(3)	6-2	6-4
Q	Bjorn Borg	Corrado Barazzutti	6-0	6-3	6-3		
Q	Harold Solomon	Guillermo Vilas	1-6	6-4	7-6	7-5	
Q	Jimmy Connors	Hans Gildemeister	6-4	6-0	6-0		
Q	Vitas Gerulaitis	Wojtek Fibak	6-3	5-7	6-4	3-6	6-3

1981

Rd	Winner	Defeated	S1	S2	S3	S4	S5
F	Bjorn Borg	Ivan Lendl	6-1	4-6	6-2	3-6	6-1
S	Bjorn Borg	Victor Pecci	6-4	6-4	7-5		
S	Ivan Lendl	Jose-Luis Clerc	3-6	6-4	4-6	7-6	6-2
Q	Bjorn Borg	Balazs Taroczy	6-3	6-3	6-2		
Q	Victor Pecci	Yannick Noah	3-6	6-4	6-4	6-4	
Q	Ivan Lendl	John McEnroe	6-4	6-4	7-5		
Q	Jose-Luis Clerc	Jimmy Connors	4-6	6-2	4-6	7-5	6-0

1982

Rd	Winner	Defeated	S1	S2	S3	S4	S5
F	Mats Wilander	Guillermo Vilas	1-6	7-6(6)	6-0	6-4	
S	Guillermo Vilas	Jose Higueras	6-1	6-3	7-6(3)		
S	Mats Wilander	Jose-Luis Clerc	7-5	6-2	1-6	7-5	
Q	Jose Higueras	Jimmy Connors	6-2	6-2	6-2		
Q	Guillermo Vilas	Yannick Noah	7-6	6-3	6-4		
Q	Jose-Luis Clerc	Peter McNamara	6-2	6-2	6-2		
Q	Mats Wilander	Vitas Gerulaitis	6-3	6-3	4-6	6-4	

1983

Rd	Winner	Defeated	S1	S2	S3	S4	S5
F	Yannick Noah	Mats Wilander	6-2	7-5	7-6(3)		
S	Yannick Noah	Chris. Roger-Vasselin	6-3	6-0	6-0		
S	Mats Wilander	Jose Higueras	7-5	6-7(4)	6-3	6-0	
Q	Chris. Roger-Vasselin	Jimmy Connors	6-4	6-4	7-6(5)		
Q	Yannick Noah	Ivan Lendl	7-6(5)	6-2	5-7	6-0	
Q	Jose Higueras	Guillermo Vilas	6-2	6-7(1)	6-1	4-6	6-1
Q	Mats Wilander	John McEnroe	1-6	6-2	6-4	6-0	

1984

Rd	Winner	Defeated	S1	S2	S3	S4	S5
F	Ivan Lendl	John McEnroe	3-6	2-6	6-4	7-5	7-5
S	John McEnroe	Jimmy Connors	7-5	6-1	6-2		
S	Ivan Lendl	Mats Wilander	6-3	6-3	7-5		
S	John McEnroe	Jimmy Arias	6-3	6-4	6-4		
Q	Jimmy Connors	Henrik Sundstrom	7-6(4)	6-1	6-4		
Q	Mats Wilander	Yannick Noah	7-6(4)	2-6	3-6	6-3	6-3
Q	Ivan Lendl	Andres Gomez	6-3	6-7	6-4	6-3	

1985

Rd	Winner	Defeated	S1	S2	S3	S4	S5
F	Mats Wilander	Ivan Lendl	3-6	6-4	6-2	6-2	
S	Mats Wilander	John McEnroe	6-1	7-5	7-5		
S	Ivan Lendl	Jimmy Connors	6-2	6-3	6-1		
Q	John McEnroe	Joakim Nystrom	6-7(1)	6-2	6-2	3-6	7-5
Q	Mats Wilander	Henri Leconte	6-4	7-6(5)	6-7(4)	7-5	
Q	Jimmy Connors	Stefan Edberg	6-4	6-3	7-6(2)		
Q	Ivan Lendl	Martin Jaite	6-4	6-2	6-4		

1986

Rd	Winner	Defeated	S1	S2	S3	S4	S5
F	Ivan Lendl	Mikael Pernfors	6-3	6-2	6-4		
S	Ivan Lendl	Johan Kriek	6-2	6-1	6-0		
S	Mikael Pernfors	Henri Leconte	2-6	7-5	7-6(4)	6-3	
Q	Ivan Lendl	Andres Gomez	6-7(4)	7-6(3)	6-0	6-0	
Q	Johan Kriek	Guillermo Vilas	3-6	7-6(6)	7-6(5)	7-6	
Q	Mikael Pernfors	Boris Becker	2-6	6-4	6-2	6-0	
Q	Henri Leconte	Andrei Chesnokov	6-3	6-4	6-3		

1987

Rd	Winner	Defeated	S1	S2	S3	S4	S5
F	Ivan Lendl	Mats Wilander	7-5	6-2	3-6	7-6(3)	
S	Ivan Lendl	Miloslav Mecir	6-3	6-3	7-6(4)		
S	Mats Wilander	Boris Becker	6-4	6-1	6-2		
Q	Ivan Lendl	Andres Gomez	5-7	6-4	6-1	6-1	
Q	Miloslav Mecir	Karel Novacek	7-6(4)	6-1	6-2		
Q	Mats Wilander	Yannick Noah	6-4	6-3	6-2		
Q	Boris Becker	Jimmy Connors	6-3	6-3	7-5		

1988

Rd	Winner	Defeated	S1	S2	S3	S4	S5
F	Mats Wilander	Henri Leconte	7-5	6-2	6-1		
S	Henri Leconte	Jonas Svensson	7-6(3)	6-2	6-3		
S	Mats Wilander	Andre Agassi	4-6	6-2	7-5	5-7	6-0
S	Jonas Svensson	Ivan Lendl	7-6(5)	7-5	6-2		
Q	Henri Leconte	Andrei Chesnokov	6-3	6-2	7-6(4)		
Q	Mats Wilander	Emilio Sanchez	6-7(5)	7-6(3)	6-3	6-4	
Q	Andre Agassi	G. Perez-Roldan	6-2	6-2	6-4		

1989

Rd	Winner	Defeated	S1	S2	S3	S4	S5
F	Michael Chang	Stefan Edberg	6-1	3-6	4-6	6-4	6-2
S	Michael Chang	Andrei Chesnokov	6-1	5-7	7-6(4)	7-5	
S	Stefan Edberg	Boris Becker	6-3	6-4	5-7	3-6	6-2
Q	Michael Chang	Ronald Agenor	6-4	2-6	6-4	7-6	
Q	Andrei Chesnokov	Mats Wilander	6-4	6-0	7-5		
Q	Stefan Edberg	Alberto Mancini	6-1	6-3	7-6(5)		
Q	Boris Becker	Jay Berger	6-3	6-4	6-1		

Rd	Winner	Defeated	S1	S2	S3	S4	S5
1990							
F	**Andres Gomez**	**Andre Agassi**	6-3	2-6	6-4	6-4	
S	Andre Agassi	Jonas Svensson	6-1	6-4	3-6	6-3	
S	Andres Gomez	Thomas Muster	7-5	6-1	7-5		
Q	Jonas Svensson	Henri Leconte	3-6	7-5	6-3	6-4	
Q	Andre Agassi	Michael Chang	6-2	6-1	4-6	6-2	
Q	Andres Gomez	Thierry Champion	6-3	6-3	6-4		
Q	Thomas Muster	Goran Ivanisevic	6-2	4-6	6-4	6-3	
1991							
F	**Jim Courier**	**Andre Agassi**	3-6	6-4	2-6	6-1	6-4
S	Jim Courier	Michael Stich	6-2	6-7(8)	6-2	6-4	
S	Andre Agassi	Boris Becker	7-5	6-3	3-6	6-1	
Q	Jim Courier	Stefan Edberg	6-4	2-6	6-3	6-4	
Q	Michael Stich	Franco Davin	6-4	6-4	6-4		
Q	Andre Agassi	Jakob Hlasek	6-3	6-1	6-1		
Q	Boris Becker	Michael Chang	6-4	6-4	6-2		
1992							
F	**Jim Courier**	**Petr Korda**	7-5	6-2	6-1		
S	Jim Courier	Andre Agassi	6-3	6-2	6-2		
S	Petr Korda	Henri Leconte	6-2	7-6(4)	6-3		
Q	Jim Courier	Goran Ivanisevic	6-2	6-1	2-6	7-5	
Q	Andre Agassi	Pete Sampras	7-6(6)	6-2	6-1		
Q	Henri Leconte	Nicklas Kulti	6-7(8)	3-6	6-3	6-3	6-3
Q	Petr Korda	Andrei Cherkasov	6-4	6-7(3)	6-2	6-4	
1993							
F	**Sergi Bruguera**	**Jim Courier**	6-4	2-6	6-2	3-6	6-3
S	Sergi Bruguera	Andrei Medvedev	6-0	6-4	6-2		
S	Jim Courier	Richard Krajicek	6-1	6-7(2)	7-5	6-2	
Q	Sergi Bruguera	Pete Sampras	6-3	4-6	6-1	6-4	
Q	Andrei Medvedev	Stefan Edberg	6-0	6-7(3)	7-5	6-4	
Q	Richard Krajicek	Karel Novacek	3-6	6-3	3-6	6-3	6-4
Q	Jim Courier	Goran Prpic	6-1	4-6	6-0	7-5	
1994							
F	**Sergi Bruguera**	**Alberto Berasategui**	6-3	7-5	2-6	6-1	
S	Sergi Bruguera	Jim Courier	6-3	5-7	6-3	6-3	
S	Alberto Berasategui	Magnus Larsson	6-3	6-4	6-1		
Q	Jim Courier	Pete Sampras	6-4	5-7	6-4	6-4	
Q	Sergi Bruguera	Andrei Medvedev	6-3	6-2	7-5		
Q	Alberto Berasategui	Goran Ivanisevic	6-4	6-3	6-3		
Q	Magnus Larsson	Hendrik Dreekmann	3-6	6-7(1)	7-6(3)	6-0	6-1
1995							
F	**Thomas Muster**	**Michael Chang**	7-5	6-2	6-4		
S	Thomas Muster	Yevgeny Kafelnikov	6-4	6-0	6-4		
S	Michael Chang	Sergi Bruguera	6-4	7-6(5)	7-6 (0)		
Q	Yevgeny Kafelnikov	Andre Agassi	6-4	6-3	7-5		
Q	Thomas Muster	Albert Costa	6-2	3-6	6-7(6)	7-5	6-2
Q	Michael Chang	Adrian Voinea	7-5	6-0	6-1		
Q	Sergi Bruguera	Renzo Furlan	6-2	7-5	6-2		
1996							
F	**Yevgeny Kafelnikov**	**Michael Stich**	7-6(4)	7-5	7-6(4)		
S	Yevgeny Kafelnikov	Pete Sampras	7-6(4)	6-0	6-2		
S	Michael Stich	Marc Rosset	6-3	6-4	6-2		
Q	Pete Sampras	Jim Courier	6-7(4)	4-6	6-4	6-4	6-4
Q	Yevgeny Kafelnikov	Richard Krajicek	6-3	6-4	6-7(4)	6-2	
Q	Marc Rosset	Bernd Karbacher	4-6	4-6	6-3	7-5	6-0
Q	Michael Stich	Cedric Pioline	4-6	6-4	6-3	6-2	
1997							
F	**Gustavo Kuerten**	**Sergi Bruguera**	6-3	6-4	6-2		
S	Sergi Bruguera	Patrick Rafter	6-7(6)	6-1	7-5	7-6(1)	
S	Gustavo Kuerten	Filip Dewulf	6-1	6-4	7-6(4)		
Q	Filip Dewulf	Magnus Norman	6-2	6-7(2)	6-4	6-3	
Q	Gustavo Kuerten	Yevgeny Kafelnikov	6-2	5-7	2-6	6-0	6-4
Q	Patrick Rafter	Galo Blanco	6-3	7-6(3)	6-3		
Q	Sergi Bruguera	Hicham Arazi	4-6	6-3	6-2	6-2	
1998							
F	**Carlos Moya**	**Alex Corretja**	6-3	7-5	6-3		
S	Carlos Moya	Felix Mantilla	5-7	6-2	6-4	6-2	
S	Alex Corretja	Cedric Pioline	6-3	6-4	6-2		
Q	Felix Mantilla	Thomas Muster	6-4	6-2	4-6	6-3	
Q	Carlos Moya	Marcelo Rios	6-1	2-6	6-2	6-4	
Q	Alex Corretja	Filip Dewulf	7-5	6-4	6-3		
Q	Cedric Pioline	Hicham Arazi	3-6	6-2	7-6(6)	4-6	6-3
1999							
F	**Andre Agassi**	**Andrei Medvedev**	1-6	2-6	6-4	6-3	6-4
S	Andre Agassi	Dominik Hrbaty	6-4	7-6(6)	3-6	6-4	
S	Andrei Medvedev	Fernando Meligeni	7-5	3-6	6-4	7-6(6)	
Q	Dominik Hrbaty	Marcelo Rios	7-6(4)	6-2	6-7(6)	6-3	
Q	Andre Agassi	Marcelo Filippini	6-2	6-2	6-0		
Q	Fernando Meligeni	Alex Corretja	6-2	6-2	6-0		
Q	Andrei Medvedev	Gustavo Kuerten	7-5	6-4	6-4		
2000							
F	**Gustavo Kuerten**	**Magnus Norman**	6-2	6-3	2-6	7-6(6)	
S	Magnus Norman	Franco Squillari	6-1	6-4	6-3		
S	Gustavo Kuerten	Juan Carlos Ferrero	7-5	4-6	2-6	6-4	6-3
Q	Franco Squillari	Albert Costa	6-4	6-4	2-6	6-4	
Q	Magnus Norman	Marat Safin	6-4	6-3	4-6	7-5	
Q	Gustavo Kuerten	Yevgeny Kafelnikov	6-3	3-6	4-6	6-4	6-2
Q	Juan Carlos Ferrero	Alex Corretja	6-4	6-4	6-2		
2001							
F	**Gustavo Kuerten**	**Alex Corretja**	6-7(3)	7-5	6-2	6-0	
S	Gustavo Kuerten	Juan Carlos Ferrero	6-4	6-4	6-3		
S	Alex Corretja	Sebastien Grosjean	7-6(2)	6-4	6-4		
Q	Gustavo Kuerten	Yevgeny Kafelnikov	6-1	3-6	7-6(3)	6-4	
Q	Juan Carlos Ferrero	Lleyton Hewitt	6-4	6-2	6-1		
Q	Sebastien Grosjean	Andre Agassi	1-6	6-1	6-1	6-3	
Q	Alex Corretja	Roger Federer	7-5	6-1	7-5		
2002							
F	**Albert Costa**	**Juan Carlos Ferrero**	6-1	6-0	4-6	6-3	
S	Albert Costa	Alex Corretja	6-3	6-4	3-6	6-3	
S	Juan Carlos Ferrero	Marat Safin	6-3	6-2	6-4		
Q	Albert Costa	Guillermo Canas	7-5	3-6	6-7(3)	6-4	6-0
Q	Alex Corretja	Andrei Pavel	7-6(5)	7-5	7-5		
Q	Juan Carlos Ferrero	Andre Agassi	6-3	5-7	7-5	6-3	
Q	Marat Safin	Sebastien Grosjean	6-3	6-2	6-2		

Women's Singles

Rd	Winner	Defeated	S1	S2	S3
1925					
F	**Suzanne Lenglen**	**Kitty McKane**	6-1	6-2	
S	Suzanne Lenglen	Helen Contostavlos	6-2	6-0	
S	Kitty McKane	Didi Vlasto	6-2	6-2	
Q	Suzanne Lenglen	Evelyn Colyer	6-0	6-2	
Q	Helen Contostavlos	Simone Passemard Mathieu	7-5	6-3	
Q	Kitty McKane	Marguerite Billout	6-0	10-8	
Q	Didi Vlasto	Mlle Desclercs	6-1	6-2	
1926					
F	**Suzanne Lenglen**	**Mary K. Browne**	6-1	6-0	
S	Suzanne Lenglen	Joan Fry	6-2	6-1	
S	Mary K. Browne	Kea Bouman	8-6	6-2	
Q	Suzanne Lenglen	Simone Passemard Mathieu	6-0	6-0	
Q	Joan Fry	Elizabeth Ryan	7-5	3-6	11-9
Q	Mary K. Browne	Kitty McKane Godfree	7-5	6-0	
Q	Kea Bouman	Helen Contostavlos	6-2	7-9	8-6

1927

Rd	Winner	Defeated	S1	S2	S3
F	**Kea Bouman**	**Irene Bowder Peacock**	6-2	6-4	
S	Kea Bouman	Bobbie Heine	5-7	6-1	6-3
S	Irene Bowder Peacock	Eileen Bennett	5-7	6-4	9-7
Q	Bobbie Heine	Lili de Alvarez	3-6	7-5	7-5
Q	Kea Bouman	Ilse Friedleben	6-2	6-0	
Q	Irene Bowder Peacock	Cilly Aussem	4-6	6-2	6-4
Q	Eileen Bennett	Marguerite Broquedis Bordes	4-6	6-2	6-2

1928

Rd	Winner	Defeated	S1	S2	S3
F	**Helen Wills**	**Eileen Bennett**	6-1	6-2	
S	Helen Wills	Cristobel H. Hardie	6-1	6-1	
S	Eileen Bennett	Kea Bouman	6-2	8-6	
Q	Helen Wills	Rollin Couquerque	6-2	6-0	
Q	Cristobel H. Hardie	Daphne Akhurst	10-8	6-2	
Q	Kea Bouman	Mme Vaussard	6-0	6-0	
Q	Eileen Bennett	Penelope Anderson	6-3	7-9	7-5

1929

Rd	Winner	Defeated	S1	S2	S3
F	**Helen Wills**	**Simone Passemard Mathieu**	6-3	6-4	
S	Simone Passemard Mathieu	Cilly Aussem	8-6	2-6	6-2
S	Helen Wills	Eileen Bennett	6-2	7-5	
Q	Cilly Aussem	Bobbie Heine	5-7	6-3	6-4
Q	Simone Passemard Mathieu	Phoebe Holcroft Watson	4-6	6-3	6-1
Q	Eileen Bennett	Alida Neave	7-5	6-1	
Q	Helen Wills	Sylvia Lafaurie	6-4	6-1	

1930

Rd	Winner	Defeated	S1	S2	S3
F	**Helen Wills Moody**	**Helen Jacobs**	6-2	6-1	
S	Helen Jacobs	Lili de Alvarez	6-1	6-0	
S	Helen Wills Moody	Cilly Aussem	6-2	6-1	
Q	Helen Jacobs	Phoebe Holcroft Watson	5-7	6-3	6-1
Q	Lili de Alvarez	Simone Passemard Mathieu	6-3	7-5	
Q	Cilly Aussem	Elizabeth Ryan	4-6	6-1	6-0
Q	Helen Wills Moody	Mlle Rost	6-0	6-1	

1931

Rd	Winner	Defeated	S1	S2	S3
F	**Cilly Aussem**	**Betty Nuthall**	8-6	6-1	
S	Betty Nuthall	Hilde Krahwinkel	6-1	6-2	
S	Cilly Aussem	Lili de Alvarez	6-0	7-5	
Q	Hilde Krahwinkel	Simone Passemard Mathieu	6-4	6-3	
Q	Betty Nuthall	Helen Jacobs	6-3	6-2	
Q	Lili de Alvarez	Elizabeth Ryan	5-7	6-3	6-4
Q	Cilly Aussem	Lucia Valerio	8-6	6-2	

1932

Rd	Winner	Defeated	S1	S2	S3
F	**Helen Wills Moody**	**Simone Passemard Mathieu**	7-5	6-1	
S	Simone Passemard Mathieu	Betty Nuthall	6-2	6-4	
S	Helen Wills Moody	Hilde Krahwinkel	6-3	10-8	
Q	Betty Nuthall	Cilly Aussem	5-7	6-4	(retired)
Q	Simone Passemard Mathieu	Helen Jacobs	6-4	6-4	
Q	Hilde Krahwinkel	Eileen Bennett Whittingstall	6-3	6-3	
Q	Helen Wills Moody	Lolette Payot	6-2	7-5	

1933

Rd	Winner	Defeated	S1	S2	S3
F	**Margaret Scriven**	**S. Passemard Mathieu**	6-2	4-6	6-4
S	Simone Passemard Mathieu	Helen Jacobs	8-6	6-3	
S	Margaret Scriven	Betty Nuthall	6-2	4-6	6-3
Q	Helen Jacobs	Jacqueline Goldschmidt	1-6	6-1	6-3
Q	Simone Passemard Mathieu	Eileen Bennett Whittingstall	6-2	6-0	
Q	Margaret Scriven	Mary Heeley	6-2	6-4	
Q	Betty Nuthall	Dorothy Andrus Burke	6-3	6-1	

1934

Rd	Winner	Defeated	S1	S2	S3
F	**Margaret Scriven**	**Helen Jacobs**	7-5	4-6	6-1
S	Margaret Scriven	Cilly Aussem	7-5	6-3	
S	Helen Jacobs	Simone Passemard Mathieu	6-2	6-2	
Q	Margaret Scriven	Nancy Lyle	6-1	6-1	
Q	Cilly Aussem	Kay Stammers	6-4	6-2	
Q	Simone Passemard Mathieu	Lucia Valerio	6-3	6-2	
Q	Helen Jacobs	Lolette Payot	6-3	1-6	8-6

1935

Rd	Winner	Defeated	S1	S2	S3
F	**Hilde Krahwinkel Sperling**	**Simone Passemard Mathieu**	6-2	6-1	
S	Hilde Krahwinkel Sperling	Helen Jacobs	7-5	6-3	
S	Simone Passemard Mathieu	Margaret Scriven	8-6	6-1	
Q	Helen Jacobs	Sylvie Jung Henrotin	6-4	6-2	
Q	Hilde Krahwinkel Sperling	Simone Iribarne	6-2	6-2	
Q	Simone Passemard Mathieu	Lolette Payot	7-5	6-4	
Q	Margaret Scriven	Rollin Couquerque	6-0	6-3	

1936

Rd	Winner	Defeated	S1	S2	S3
F	**Hilde Krahwinkel Sperling**	**Simone Passemard Mathieu**	6-3	6-4	
S	Simone Passemard Mathieu	Marie Luise Horn	6-4	6-4	
S	Hilde Krahwinkel Sperling	Lili de Alvarez	6-2	6-1	
Q	Simone Passemard Mathieu	Nelly Adamson	6-0	6-2	
Q	Marie Luise Horn	Simone Gorodnitchenko	6-1	6-4	
Q	Lili de Alvarez	Simone Iribarne	6-4	6-2	
Q	Hilde Krahwinkel Sperling	Sylvie Jung Henrotin	6-3	6-0	

1937

Rd	Winner	Defeated	S1	S2	S3
F	**Hilde Krahwinkel Sperling**	**Simone Passemard Mathieu**	6-2	6-4	
S	Simone Passemard Mathieu	Jadwiga Jedrzejowska	7-5	7-5	
S	Hilde Krahwinkel Sperling	Lili de Alvarez	6-1	6-1	
Q	Simone Passemard Mathieu	Marie Luise Horn	11-9	7-5	
Q	Jadwiga Jedrzejowska	Helen Jacobs	6-3	6-4	
Q	Lili de Alvarez	Margaret Scriven	6-2	1-6	6-2
Q	Hilde Krahwinkel Sperling	Sylvie Jung Henrotin	6-4	6-1	

1938

Rd	Winner	Defeated	S1	S2	S3
F	**Simone Passemard Mathieu**	**Nelly Adamson Landry**	6-0	6-3	
S	Nelly Adamson Landry	Rollin Couquerque	6-2	6-4	
S	Simone Passemard Mathieu	Arlette Halff	6-1	6-1	
Q	Rollin Couquerque	Jacqueline Goldschmidt	6-2	6-1	
Q	Nelly Adamson Landry	Sylvie Jung Henrotin	6-2	6-2	
Q	Arlette Halff	Suzanne Pannetier	2-6	6-4	6-3
Q	Simone Passemard Mathieu	Dorothy Stevenson	6-4	6-0	

1939

Rd	Winner	Defeated	S1	S2	S3
F	**Simone Passemard Mathieu**	**Jadwiga Jedrzejowska**	6-3	8-6	
S	Jadwiga Jedrzejowska	M. Lebailly	6-3	2-6	6-3
S	Simone Passemard Mathieu	Suzanne Pannetier	6-2	6-2	
Q	M. Lebailly	Sarah Palfrey Fabyan	6-1	6-1	
Q	Jadwiga Jedrzejowska	Arlette Halff	4-6	6-2	6-4
Q	Suzanne Pannetier	Mary Hardwick	7-5	6-4	
Q	Simone Passemard Mathieu	Alice Weiwers	6-3	6-3	

1940-45   *Not held – WW II*

1946

Rd	Winner	Defeated	S1	S2	S3
F	**Margaret Osborne**	**Pauline Betz**	1-6	8-6	7-5
S	Margaret Osborne	Louise Brough	7-5	6-3	
S	Pauline Betz	Dorothy Bundy	6-3	6-4	
Q	Margaret Osborne	Alice Weiwers	6-3	6-2	
Q	Louise Brough	Doris Hart	6-4	4-6	6-4
Q	Dorothy Bundy	Nelly Adamson Landry	6-4	5-7	6-4
Q	Pauline Betz	Betty Hilton	6-4	6-0	

1947

Rd	Winner	Defeated	S1	S2	S3
F	**Pat Canning Todd**	**Doris Hart**	6-3	3-6	6-4
S	Doris Hart	Louise Brough	6-2	7-5	
S	Pat Canning Todd	Margaret Osborne	2-6	6-3	6-4
Q	Doris Hart	Magda Rurac	6-3	6-4	
Q	Louise Brough	Sheila Piercey Summers	6-1	6-0	
Q	Pat Canning Todd	L. Manfredi	6-1	6-4	
Q	Margaret Osborne	Suzi Kormoczi	6-0	6-3	

Rd	Winner	Defeated	S1	S2	S3
1948					
F	**Nelly Adamson Landry**	**Shirley Fry**	**6-2**	**0-6**	**6-0**
S	Nelly Adamson Landry	Pat Canning Todd	(walk-over)		
S	Shirley Fry	Doris Hart	6-3	4-6	11-9
Q	Pat Canning Todd	Annelies Ullstein Bossi	(walk-over)		
Q	Nelly Adamson Landry	Mary Arnold Prentiss	6-4	6-3	
Q	Shirley Fry	Maria Weiss	6-3	7-5	
Q	Doris Hart	Helen Pedersen Rihbany	6-3	6-3	
1949					
F	**Margaret Osborne duPont**	**Nelly Adamson Landry**	**7-5**	**6-2**	
S	Nelly Adamson Landry	Annelies Ullstein Bossi	6-3	6-0	
S	Margaret Osborne duPont	Sheila Piercey Summers	6-3	6-3	
Q	Annelies Ullstein Bossi	Joan Curry	6-3	4-6	6-3
Q	Nelly Adamson Landry	Helen Pedersen Rihbany	7-9	6-3	6-3
Q	Sheila Piercey Summers	Anne-Marie Simon Seghers	6-3	6-1	
Q	Margaret Osborne duPont	Jean Quertier	6-4	6-2	
1950					
F	**Doris Hart**	**Pat Canning Todd**	**6-4**	**4-6**	**6-2**
S	Doris Hart	Louise Brough	6-2	6-3	
S	Pat Canning Todd	Barbara Scofield	6-2	6-3	
S	Louise Brough	Betty Rosenquest	6-2	6-2	
Q	Doris Hart	Annelies Ullstein Bossi	6-4	6-2	
Q	Pat Canning Todd	Shirley Fry	6-3	6-3	
Q	Barbara Scofield	Margaret Osborne duPont	3-6	6-0	6-2
1951					
F	**Shirley Fry**	**Doris Hart**	**6-3**	**3-6**	**6-3**
S	Shirley Fry	Margaret Osborne duPont	6-2	9-7	
S	Doris Hart	Jean Walker Smith	6-2	6-1	
Q	Margaret Osborne duPont	Nelly Adamson	8-6	1-6	6-1
Q	Shirley Fry	Thelma Long	12-10	6-1	
Q	Jean Walker Smith	Beverly Baker	3-6	6-4	6-1
Q	Doris Hart	Arlette de Cazalet	6-0	6-4	
1952					
F	**Doris Hart**	**Shirley Fry**	**6-4**	**6-4**	
S	Doris Hart	Dorothy Head	6-2	8-6	
S	Shirley Fry	Hazel Redick-Smith	7-5	6-4	
Q	Doris Hart	Julia Wipplinger	8-6	6-4	
Q	Dorothy Head	Joy Gannon Mottram	6-3	4-6	7-5
Q	Hazel Redick-Smith	Maria Weiss	6-3	6-1	
Q	Shirley Fry	Joan Curry	4-6	6-0	6-3
1953					
F	**Maureen Connolly**	**Doris Hart**	**6-2**	**6-4**	
S	Doris Hart	Shirley Fry	8-6	6-4	
S	Maureen Connolly	Dorothy Head Knode	6-3	6-3	
Q	Doris Hart	Jean Quertier-Rinkel	6-3	6-3	
Q	Shirley Fry	Nelly Adamson	6-1	4-6	6-0
Q	Dorothy Head Knode	Ginette Bucaille	6-3	6-0	
Q	Maureen Connolly	Susan Partridge Chatrier	3-6	6-2	6-2
1954					
F	**Maureen Connolly**	**Ginette Bucaille**	**6-4**	**6-1**	
S	Ginette Bucaille	Nelly Adamson	6-2	6-4	
S	Maureen Connolly	Silvana Lazzarino	6-0	6-1	
Q	Nelly Adamson	Dorothy Levine	6-1	6-2	
Q	Ginette Bucaille	Josette Amouretti	6-1	6-1	
Q	Silvana Lazzarino	Anne-Marie Simon Seghers	6-3	6-3	
Q	Maureen Connolly	Angela Buxton	6-1	6-0	
1955					
F	**Angela Mortimer**	**Dorothy Head Knode**	**2-6**	**7-5**	**10-8**
S	Angela Mortimer	Heather Brewer	6-1	6-1	
S	Dorothy Head Knode	Beverly Baker Fleitz	6-2	6-3	
Q	Angela Mortimer	Erika Vollmer	6-3	6-4	
Q	Heather Brewer	Beryl Penrose	7-5	6-8	6-3
Q	Dorothy Head Knode	Shirley Bloomer	6-3	6-3	
Q	Beverly Baker Fleitz	Ginette Bucaille	6-1	6-1	

Rd	Winner	Defeated	S1	S2	S3
1956					
F	**Althea Gibson**	**Angela Mortimer**	**6-0**	**12-10**	
S	Althea Gibson	Angela Buxton	2-6	6-0	6-4
S	Angela Mortimer	Suzi Kormoczi	6-4	6-3	
Q	Angela Buxton	Edda Buding	8-6	6-2	
Q	Althea Gibson	Shirley Bloomer	6-2	6-1	
Q	Suzi Kormoczi	Ingo Buding	6-1	6-1	
Q	Angela Mortimer	Jenny Hoad	6-0	4-6	7-5
1957					
F	**Shirley Bloomer**	**Dorothy Head Knode**	**6-1**	**6-3**	
S	Dorothy Head Knode	Ann Haydon	6-4	10-8	
S	Shirley Bloomer	Vera Puzejova	6-4	2-6	6-4
Q	Dorothy Head Knode	Heather Brewer	6-1	9-7	
Q	Ann Haydon	Christine Mercelis	6-2	6-1	
Q	Vera Puzejova	Darlene Hard	6-3	5-7	8-6
Q	Shirley Bloomer	Suzi Kormoczi	6-1	6-1	
1958					
F	**Suzi Kormoczi**	**Shirley Bloomer**	**6-4**	**1-6**	**6-2**
S	Suzi Kormoczi	Heather Segal	6-1	6-0	
S	Shirley Bloomer	Maria Bueno	2-6	6-1	6-2
Q	Heather Segal	Christine Truman	6-2	6-1	
Q	Suzi Kormoczi	Ann Haydon	6-3	6-4	
Q	Maria Bueno	Dorothy Head Knode	6-2	8-6	
Q	Shirley Bloomer	Rosie Reyes	5-7	6-4	6-2
1959					
F	**Christine Truman**	**Suzi Kormoczi**	**6-4**	**7-5**	
S	Christine Truman	Sandra Reynolds	4-6	8-6	6-2
S	Suzi Kormoczi	Rosie Reyes	6-3	6-0	
Q	Christine Truman	Paule Courteix	6-1	8-6	
Q	Sandra Reynolds	Maria Bueno	2-6	6-4	6-2
Q	Rosie Reyes	Mary Carter Reitano	4-6	6-1	6-4
Q	Suzi Kormoczi	Vera Puzejova	6-3	6-4	
1960					
F	**Darlene Hard**	**Yola Ramirez**	**6-3**	**6-4**	
S	Darlene Hard	Maria Bueno	6-3	6-2	
S	Yola Ramirez	Sandra Reynolds	8-10	6-3	6-3
Q	Maria Bueno	Jan Lehane	6-1	2-6	6-3
Q	Darlene Hard	Renee Schuurman	5-7	6-2	11-9
Q	Sandra Reynolds	Vera Puzejova	7-5	6-2	
Q	Yola Ramirez	Betsy Abbas	6-0	6-4	
1961					
F	**Ann Haydon**	**Yola Ramirez**	**6-2**	**6-1**	
S	Ann Haydon	Suzi Kormoczi	3-6	6-1	6-3
S	Yola Ramirez	Edda Buding	6-4	4-6	6-3
Q	Suzi Kormoczi	Maria Bueno	6-3	6-3	
Q	Ann Haydon	Margaret Smith	7-5	12-10	
Q	Yola Ramirez	Christine Truman	10-8	7-5	
Q	Edda Buding	Pili Barril	3-6	6-4	6-2
1962					
F	**Margaret Smith**	**Lesley Turner**	**6-3**	**3-6**	**7-5**
S	Margaret Smith	Renee Schuurman	8-6	6-3	
S	Lesley Turner	Ann Haydon	6-4	5-7	6-3
Q	Margaret Smith	Edda Buding	6-2	6-4	
Q	Renee Schuurman	Donna Floyd	6-3	6-1	
Q	Lesley Turner	Sandra Reynolds Price	8-6	6-3	
Q	Ann Haydon	Jan Lehane	6-4	6-1	
1963					
F	**Lesley Turner**	**Ann Haydon Jones**	**2-6**	**6-3**	**7-5**
S	Lesley Turner	Christine Truman	11-9	6-2	
S	Ann Haydon Jones	Vera Sukova	6-0	6-1	
Q	Lesley Turner	Jill Blackman	6-4	6-4	
Q	Christine Truman	Robyn Ebbern	6-0	6-2	
Q	Ann Haydon Jones	Jan Lehane	6-0	6-0	
Q	Vera Sukova	Margaret Smith	6-3	8-6	

Rd	Winner	Defeated	S1	S2	S3
1964					
F	**Margaret Smith**	**Maria Bueno**	**5-7**	**6-1**	**6-2**
S	Maria Bueno	Lesley Turner	3-6	6-2	6-0
S	Margaret Smith	Helga Schultze	6-3	4-6	6-2
Q	Maria Bueno	Karen Hantze Susman	6-4	6-0	
Q	Lesley Turner	Christine Truman	6-1	6-3	
Q	Helga Schultze	Jan Lehane	6-2	6-3	
Q	Margaret Smith	Vera Sukova	6-1	6-1	
1965					
F	**Lesley Turner**	**Margaret Smith**	**6-3**	**6-4**	
S	Lesley Turner	Maria Bueno	2-6	6-4	8-6
S	Margaret Smith	Nancy Richey	7-5	6-4	
S	Maria Bueno	Annette Van Zyl	6-4	6-3	
Q	Lesley Turner	Ann Haydon Jones		(default)	
Q	Nancy Richey	Françoise Durr	8-6	9-7	
Q	Margaret Smith	Norma Baylon	6-3	6-1	
1966					
F	**Ann Haydon Jones**	**Nancy Richey**	**6-3**	**6-1**	
S	Ann Haydon Jones	Maria Bueno	4-6	8-6	6-3
S	Nancy Richey	Margaret Smith	6-1	6-3	
Q	Maria Bueno	Françoise Durr	3-6	6-4	6-4
Q	Ann Haydon Jones	Helga Schultze	6-4	6-4	
Q	Nancy Richey	Annette Van Zyl	3-6	6-3	6-2
Q	Margaret Smith	Julie Heldman	6-2	6-2	
1967					
F	**Françoise Durr**	**Lesley Turner**	**4-6**	**6-3**	**6-4**
S	Françoise Durr	Kerry Melville	8-6	6-3	
S	Lesley Turner	Annette Van Zyl	6-1	6-4	
Q	Kerry Melville	Ann Haydon Jones	0-6	6-4	8-6
Q	Françoise Durr	Maria Bueno	5-7	6-1	6-4
Q	Lesley Turner	Helga Schultze	7-5	6-2	
Q	Annette Van Zyl	Billie Jean King	6-2	5-7	6-4
1968					
F	**Nancy Richey**	**Ann Haydon Jones**	**5-7**	**6-4**	**6-1**
S	Nancy Richey	Billie Jean King	2-6	6-3	6-4
S	Ann Haydon Jones	Annette Du Plooy	7-5	6-3	
Q	Ann Haydon Jones	Vlasta Vopickova	6-2	6-1	
Q	Annette Du Plooy	Gail Sherriff Chanfreau	8-6	6-3	
Q	Nancy Richey	Elena Subirats	6-1	6-0	
Q	Billie Jean King	Maria Bueno	6-4	6-4	
1969					
F	**Margaret Smith Court**	**Ann Haydon Jones**	**6-1**	**4-6**	**6-3**
S	Margaret Smith Court	Nancy Richey	6-3	4-6	7-5
S	Ann Haydon Jones	Lesley Turner Bowrey	6-1	6-2	
Q	Margaret Smith Court	Kerry Melville	9-7	6-1	
Q	Nancy Richey	Julie Heldman	6-3	9-7	
Q	Ann Haydon Jones	Rosie Casals	6-2	6-0	
Q	Lesley Turner Bowrey	Billie Jean King	6-3	6-3	
1970					
F	**Margaret Smith Court**	**Helga Niessen-Masthoff**	**6-2**	**6-4**	
S	Margaret Smith Court	Julie Heldman	6-0	6-2	
S	Helga Niessen-Masthoff	Karen Krantzcke	6-3	6-1	
Q	Margaret Smith Court	Rosie Casals	7-5	6-2	
Q	Julie Heldman	Vlasta Vopickova	6-1	6-3	
Q	Karen Krantzcke	Virginia Wade	6-2	1-6	6-3
Q	Helga Niessen-Masthoff	Billie Jean King	2-6	8-6	6-1
1971					
F	**Evonne Goolagong**	**Helen Gourlay**	**6-3**	**7-5**	
S	Helen Gourlay	Nancy Richey Gunter	6-2	6-3	
S	Evonne Goolagong	Marijke Schaar	6-4	6-1	
Q	Helen Gourlay	Gail Sherriff Chanfreau	6-4	3-6	6-3
Q	Nancy Richey Gunter	Lesley Turner Bowrey	6-2	6-4	
Q	Evonne Goolagong	Françoise Durr	6-3	6-0	
Q	Marijke Schaar	Linda Tuero	6-2	6-3	

Rd	Winner	Defeated	S1	S2	S3
1972					
F	**Billie Jean King**	**Evonne Goolagong**	**6-3**	**6-3**	
S	Billie Jean King	Helga Niessen-Masthoff	6-4	6-4	
S	Evonne Goolagong	Françoise Durr	9-7	6-4	
Q	Helga Niessen-Masthoff	Katja Ebbinghaus	6-3	8-6	
Q	Billie Jean King	Virginia Wade	6-1	6-3	
Q	Françoise Durr	Olga Morozova	4-6	6-3	6-2
Q	Evonne Goolagong	Corinne Molesworth	6-2	6-2	
1973					
F	**Margaret Smith Court**	**Chris Evert**	**6-7(5)**	**7-6(6)**	**6-4**
S	Margaret Smith Court	Evonne Goolagong	6-3	7-6	
S	Chris Evert	Françoise Durr	6-1	6-0	
Q	Margaret Smith Court	Katja Ebbinghaus	6-2	6-3	
Q	Evonne Goolagong	Martina Navratilova	7-6(3)	6-4	
Q	Françoise Durr	Odile De Roubin	6-0	1-6	6-1
Q	Chris Evert	Helga Niessen-Masthoff	6-3	6-3	
1974					
F	**Chris Evert**	**Olga Morozova**	**6-1**	**6-2**	
S	Olga Morozova	Raquel Giscafre	6-3	6-2	
S	Chris Evert	Helga Niessen-Masthoff	7-5	6-4	
Q	Raquel Giscafre	Katja Ebbinghaus	7-5	6-7	6-3
Q	Olga Morozova	Marie Pinterova	6-3	6-2	
Q	Helga Niessen-Masthoff	Martina Navratilova	7-6	6-3	
Q	Chris Evert	Julie Heldman	6-0	7-5	
1975					
F	**Chris Evert**	**Martina Navratilova**	**2-6**	**6-2**	**6-1**
S	Chris Evert	Olga Morozova	6-4	6-0	
S	Martina Navratilova	Janet Newberry	6-2	6-3	
Q	Chris Evert	Kazuko Sawamatsu	6-2	6-2	
Q	Olga Morozova	Raquel Giscafre	7-5	6-7	6-0
Q	Janet Newberry	Eva Szabo	6-1	6-2	
Q	Martina Navratilova	Donna Ganz	6-1	6-1	
1976					
F	**Sue Barker**	**Renata Tomanova**	**6-2**	**0-6**	**6-2**
S	Renata Tomanova	Florenta Mihai	7-5	7-6	
S	Sue Barker	Virginia Ruzici	6-3	1-6	6-2
Q	Renata Tomanova	Helga Niessen-Masthoff	6-2	6-4	
Q	Florenta Mihai	Kathy Kuykendall	6-2	0-6	6-1
Q	Virginia Ruzici	Miroslava Holubova	6-1	6-3	
Q	Sue Barker	Regina Marsikova	4-6	6-2	8-6
1977					
F	**Mima Jausovec**	**Florenta Mihai**	**6-2**	**6-7(5)**	**6-1**
S	Florenta Mihai	Janet Newberry	7-6	6-3	
S	Mima Jausovec	Regina Marsikova	6-1	3-6	6-3
Q	Janet Newberry	Kathy May	6-4	5-7	6-2
Q	Florenta Mihai	Linky Boshoff	6-3	4-6	7-5
Q	Regina Marsikova	Renata Tomanova	7-6	6-7	6-3
Q	Mima Jausovec	Pam Teeguarden	7-5	6-4	
1978					
F	**Virginia Ruzici**	**Mima Jausovec**	**6-2**	**6-2**	
S	Virginia Ruzici	Brigitte Simon	6-3	6-0	
S	Mima Jausovec	Regina Marsikova	6-3	6-4	
Q	Brigitte Simon	Miroslava Bendlova	6-3	6-3	
Q	Virginia Ruzici	Fiorella Bonicelli	6-7	6-4	8-6
Q	Regina Marsikova	Helga Niessen-Masthoff	6-3	6-3	
Q	Mima Jausovec	Kathy May	6-4	6-2	
1979					
F	**Chris Evert Lloyd**	**Wendy Turnbull**	**6-2**	**6-0**	
S	Chris Evert Lloyd	Dianne Balestrat Fromholtz	6-1	6-3	
S	Wendy Turnbull	Regina Marsikova	6-4	6-3	
Q	Chris Evert Lloyd	Ruta Gerulaitis	6-0	6-4	
Q	Dianne Balestrat Fromholtz	Virginia Ruzici	6-0	6-4	
Q	Wendy Turnbull	Hana Mandlikova	6-3	6-3	
Q	Regina Marsikova	Renata Tomanova	6-1	6-1	

Rd	Winner	Defeated	S1	S2	S3
1980					
F	**Chris Evert Lloyd**	**Virginia Ruzici**	**6-0**	**6-3**	
S	Virginia Ruzici	Dianne Balestrat Fromholtz	7-6	6-1	
S	Chris Evert Lloyd	Hana Mandlikova	6-7	6-2	6-2
Q	Virginia Ruzici	Wendy Turnbull	6-2	6-0	
Q	Dianne Balestrat Fromholtz	Billie Jean King	6-1	6-4	
Q	Hana Mandlikova	Ivanna Madruga	6-2	6-3	
Q	Chris Evert Lloyd	Kathy Jordan	6-2	6-0	
1981					
F	**Hana Mandlikova**	**Sylvia Hanika**	**6-2**	**6-4**	
S	Sylvia Hanika	Andrea Jaeger	4-6	6-1	6-4
S	Hana Mandlikova	Chris Evert Lloyd	7-5	6-4	
Q	Sylvia Hanika	Martina Navratilova	6-2	6-4	
Q	Andrea Jaeger	Mima Jausovec	4-6	6-2	6-0
Q	Hana Mandlikova	Kathy Rinaldi	6-1	6-3	
Q	Chris Evert Lloyd	Virginia Ruzici	6-4	6-4	
1982					
F	**Martina Navratilova**	**Andrea Jaeger**	**7-6(6)**	**6-1**	
S	Andrea Jaeger	Chris Evert Lloyd	6-3	6-1	
S	Martina Navratilova	Hana Mandlikova	6-0	6-2	
Q	Hana Mandlikova	Tracy Austin	7-6	6-7	6-2
Q	Martina Navratilova	Zina Garrison	6-3	6-2	
Q	Andrea Jaeger	Virginia Ruzici	6-1	6-0	
Q	Chris Evert Lloyd	Lucia Romanov	6-2	6-4	
1983					
F	**Chris Evert Lloyd**	**Mima Jausovec**	**6-1**	**6-2**	
S	Mima Jausovec	Jo Durie	3-6	7-5	6-2
S	Chris Evert	Andrea Jaeger	6-3	6-1	
Q	Andrea Jaeger	Gretchen Rush	6-2	6-2	
Q	Chris Evert	Hana Mandlikova	4-6	6-3	6-2
Q	Mima Jausovec	Kathy Horvath	6-1	6-1	
Q	Jo Durie	Tracy Austin	6-1	4-6	6-0
1984					
F	**Martina Navratilova**	**Chris Evert Lloyd**	**6-3**	**6-1**	
S	Chris Evert Lloyd	Camille Benjamin	6-0	6-0	
S	Martina Navratilova	Hana Mandlikova	3-6	6-2	6-2
Q	Hana Mandlikova	Melissa Brown	6-1	6-4	
Q	Martina Navratilova	Kathy Horvath	6-4	6-2	
Q	Chris Evert Lloyd	Carling Bassett	4-6	6-1	6-0
Q	Camille Benjamin	Lisa Bonder	7-6(3)	5-7	6-3
1985					
F	**Chris Evert Lloyd**	**Martina Navratilova**	**6-3**	**6-7(4)**	**7-5**
S	Martina Navratilova	Claudia Kohde Kilsch	6-4	6-4	
S	Chris Evert Lloyd	Gabriela Sabatini	6-4	6-1	
Q	Martina Navratilova	Sandra Cecchini	6-2	6-2	
Q	Claudia Kohde Kilsch	Hana Mandlikova	6-4	6-4	
Q	Gabriela Sabatini	Manuela Maleeva	6-3	1-6	6-1
Q	Chris Evert Lloyd	Terry Phelps	6-4	6-0	
1986					
F	**Chris Evert Lloyd**	**Martina Navratilova**	**2-6**	**6-3**	**6-3**
S	Chris Evert Lloyd	Hana Mandlikova	6-1	6-1	
S	Martina Navratilova	Helena Sukova	4-6	7-6(4)	6-2
Q	Helena Sukova	Mary Joe Fernandez	6-2	6-4	
Q	Martina Navratilova	Kathy Rinaldi	7-5	6-4	
Q	Hana Mandlikova	Steffi Graf	2-6	7-6(3)	6-1
Q	Chris Evert Lloyd	Carling Bassett	5-7	6-2	6-1
1987					
F	**Steffi Graf**	**Martina Navratilova**	**6-4**	**4-6**	**8-6**
S	Martina Navratilova	Chris Evert	6-2	6-2	
S	Steffi Graf	Gabriela Sabatini	6-4	4-6	7-5
Q	Martina Navratilova	Claudia Kohde Kilsch	6-1	6-2	
Q	Chris Evert	Raffaella Reggi	6-2	6-2	
Q	Gabriela Sabatini	Arantxa Sanchez Vicario	6-4	6-0	
Q	Steffi Graf	Manuela Maleeva	6-4	6-1	
1988					
F	**Steffi Graf**	**Natalia Zvereva**	**6-0**	**6-0**	
S	Steffi Graf	Gabriela Sabatini	6-3	7-6(3)	
S	Natalia Zvereva	Nicole Provis	6-3	6-7(3)	7-5
Q	Steffi Graf	Bettina Fulco	6-0	6-1	
Q	Gabriela Sabatini	Helen Kelesi	4-6	6-1	6-3
Q	Nicole Provis	Arantxa Sanchez Vicario	7-5	3-6	6-4
Q	Natalia Zvereva	Helena Sukova	6-2	6-3	
1989					
F	**Arantxa Sanchez Vicario**	**Steffi Graf**	**7-6(6)**	**3-6**	**7-5**
S	Steffi Graf	Monica Seles	6-3	3-6	6-3
S	Arantxa Sanchez Vicario	Mary Joe Fernandez	6-2	6-2	
Q	Steffi Graf	Conchita Martinez	6-0	6-4	
Q	Monica Seles	Manuela Maleeva	6-3	7-5	
Q	Arantxa Sanchez Vicario	Jana Novotna	6-2	6-2	
Q	Mary Joe Fernandez	Helen Kelesi	6-2	7-5	
1990					
F	**Monica Seles**	**Steffi Graf**	**7-6(6)**	**6-4**	
S	Steffi Graf	Jana Novotna	6-1	6-2	
S	Monica Seles	Jennifer Capriati	6-2	6-2	
Q	Steffi Graf	Conchita Martinez	6-1	6-3	
Q	Jana Novotna	Katerina Maleeva	4-6	6-2	6-4
Q	Jennifer Capriati	Mary Joe Fernandez	6-2	6-4	
Q	Monica Seles	Manuela Maleeva-Fragniere	3-6	6-1	7-5
1991					
F	**Monica Seles**	**Arantxa Sanchez Vicario**	**6-3**	**6-4**	
S	Monica Seles	Gabriela Sabatini	7-5	6-1	
S	Arantxa Sanchez Vicario	Steffi Graf	6-0	6-2	
Q	Monica Seles	Conchita Martinez	6-0	7-5	
Q	Gabriela Sabatini	Jana Novotna	5-7	7-6(10)	6-0
Q	Arantxa Sanchez Vicario	Mary Joe Fernandez	6-3	6-2	
Q	Steffi Graf	Nathalie Tauziat	6-3	6-2	
1992					
F	**Monica Seles**	**Steffi Graf**	**6-2**	**3-6**	**10-8**
S	Monica Seles	Gabriela Sabatini	6-3	4-6	6-4
S	Steffi Graf	Arantxa Sanchez Vicario	0-6	6-2	6-2
Q	Monica Seles	Jennifer Capriati	6-2	6-2	
Q	Gabriela Sabatini	Conchita Martinez	3-6	6-3	6-2
Q	Arantxa Sanchez Vicario	Manon Bollegraf	6-2	6-3	
Q	Steffi Graf	Natasha Zvereva	6-3	6-7(4)	6-3
1993					
F	**Steffi Graf**	**Mary Joe Fernandez**	**4-6**	**6-2**	**6-4**
S	Steffi Graf	Anke Huber	6-1	6-1	
S	Mary Joe Fernandez	Arantxa Sanchez Vicario	6-2	6-2	
Q	Steffi Graf	Jennifer Capriati	6-3	7-5	
Q	Anke Huber	Conchita Martinez	6-7(2)	6-4	6-4
Q	Mary Joe Fernandez	Gabriela Sabatini	1-6	7-6(4)	10-8
Q	Arantxa Sanchez Vicario	Jana Novotna	6-2	7-5	
1994					
F	**Arantxa Sanchez Vicario**	**Mary Pierce**	**6-4**	**6-4**	
S	Mary Pierce	Steffi Graf	6-2	6-2	
S	Arantxa Sanchez Vicario	Conchita Martinez	6-3	6-1	
Q	Steffi Graf	Ines Gorrochategui	6-4	6-1	
Q	Mary Pierce	Petra Ritter	6-0	6-2	
Q	Conchita Martinez	Sabine Hack	2-6	6-0	6-2
Q	Arantxa Sanchez Vicario	Julie Halard	6-1	7-6(6)	
1995					
F	**Steffi Graf**	**Arantxa Sanchez Vicario**	**7-5**	**4-6**	**6-0**
S	Arantxa Sanchez Vicario	Kimiko Date	7-5	6-3	
S	Steffi Graf	Conchita Martinez	6-3	6-7(5)	6-3
Q	Arantxa Sanchez Vicario	Chanda Rubin	6-3	6-1	
Q	Kimiko Date	Iva Majoli	7-5	6-1	
Q	Conchita Martinez	Virginia Ruano Pascual	6-0	6-4	
Q	Steffi Graf	Gabriela Sabatini	6-1	6-0	

Rd	Winner	Defeated	S1	S2	S3
1996					
F	**Steffi Graf**	**Arantxa Sanchez Vicario**	**6-3**	**6-7(4)**	**10-8**
S	Steffi Graf	Conchita Martinez	6-3	6-1	
S	Arantxa Sanchez Vicario	Jana Novotna	6-3	7-5	
Q	Steffi Graf	Iva Majoli	6-3	6-1	
Q	Conchita Martinez	Lindsay Davenport	6-1	6-3	
Q	Arantxa Sanchez Vicario	Karina Habsudova	6-2	6-7(4)	10-8
Q	Jana Novotna	Monica Seles	7-6(7)	6-3	
1997					
F	**Iva Majoli**	**Martina Hingis**	**6-4**	**6-2**	
S	Martina Hingis	Monica Seles	6-7(2)	7-5	6-4
S	Iva Majoli	Amanda Coetzer	6-3	4-6	7-5
Q	Martina Hingis	Arantxa Sanchez Vicario	6-2	6-2	
Q	Monica Seles	Mary Joe Fernandez	3-6	6-2	7-5
Q	Iva Majoli	Ruxandra Dragomir	6-3	5-7	6-2
Q	Amanda Coetzer	Steffi Graf	6-1	6-4	
1998					
F	**Arantxa Sanchez Vicario**	**Monica Seles**	**7-6(5)**	**0-6**	**6-2**
S	Arantxa Sanchez Vicario	Lindsay Davenport	6-3	7-6(5)	
S	Monica Seles	Martina Hingis	6-3	6-2	
Q	Martina Hingis	Venus Williams	6-3	6-4	
Q	Monica Seles	Jana Novotna	4-6	6-3	6-3
Q	Arantxa Sanchez Vicario	Patty Schnyder	6-2	6-7(5)	6-0
Q	Lindsay Davenport	Iva Majoli	6-1	5-7	6-3
1999					
F	**Steffi Graf**	**Martina Hingis**	**4-6**	**7-5**	**6-2**
S	Steffi Graf	Monica Seles	6-7(2)	6-3	6-4
S	Martina Hingis	Arantxa Sanchez Vicario	6-3	6-2	
Q	Martina Hingis	Barbara Schwartz	6-2	6-2	
Q	Arantxa Sanchez Vicario	Sylvia Plischke	6-2	6-4	
Q	Monica Seles	Conchita Martinez	6-1	6-4	
Q	Steffi Graf	Lindsay Davenport	6-1	6-7(5)	6-3
2000					
F	**Mary Pierce**	**Conchita Martinez**	**6-2**	**7-5**	
S	Mary Pierce	Martina Hingis	6-4	5-7	6-2
S	Conchita Martinez	Arantxa Sanchez Vicario	6-1	6-2	
Q	Martina Hingis	Chanda Rubin	6-1	6-3	
Q	Mary Pierce	Monica Seles	4-6	6-3	6-4
Q	Arantxa Sanchez Vicario	Venus Williams	6-0	1-6	6-2
Q	Conchita Martinez	Marta Marrero	7-6(5)	6-1	
2001					
F	**Jennifer Capriati**	**Kim Clijsters**	**1-6**	**6-4**	**12-10**
S	Jennifer Capriati	Martina Hingis	6-4	6-3	
S	Kim Clijsters	Justine Henin	2-6	7-5	6-3
Q	Martina Hingis	Francesca Schiavone	6-1	6-4	
Q	Jennifer Capriati	Serena Williams	6-2	5-7	6-2
Q	Kim Clijsters	Petra Mandula	6-1	6-3	
Q	Justine Henin	Lina Krasnoroutskaya	6-1	6-2	
2002					
F	**Serena Williams**	**Venus Williams**	**7-5**	**6-3**	
S	Serena Williams	Jennifer Capriati	3-6	7-6(2)	6-2
S	Venus Williams	Clarisa Fernandez	6-1	6-4	
Q	Jennifer Capriati	Jelena Dokic	6-4	4-6	6-1
Q	Serena Williams	Mary Pierce	6-1	6-1	
Q	Clarisa Fernandez	Paola Suarez	2-6	7-6(5)	6-1
Q	Venus Williams	Monica Seles	6-4	6-3	

Men's Doubles

Year	Winner	Defeated	S1	S2	S3	S4	S5
1925	Jean Borotra René Lacoste	Henri Cochet Jacques Brugnon	7-5	4-6	6-3	2-6	6-3
1926	Vinnie Richards Howard Kinsey	Henri Cochet Jacques Brugnon	6-4	6-1	4-6	6-4	
1927	Henri Cochet Jacques Brugnon	Jean Borotra René Lacoste	2-6	6-2	6-0	1-6	6-4
1928	Jean Borotra Jacques Brugnon	Henri Cochet Ren de Buzelet	6-4	3-6	6-2	3-6	6-4
1929	René Lacoste Jean Borotra	Henri Cochet Jacques Brugnon	6-3	3-6	6-3	3-6	8-6
1930	Henri Cochet Jacques Brugnon	Harry Hopman Jim Willard	6-3	9-7	6-3		
1931	George Lott John Van Ryn	Vernon Kirby Norman Farquharson	6-4	6-3	6-4		
1932	Henri Cochet Jacques Brugnon	Christian Boussus Marcel Bernard	6-4	3-6	7-5	6-3	
1933	Pat Hughes Fred Perry	Adrian Quist Viv McGrath	6-2	6-4	2-6	7-5	
1934	Jean Borotra Jacques Brugnon	Jack Crawford Viv McGrath	11-9	6-3	2-6	4-6	9-7
1935	Jack Crawford Adrian Quist	Viv McGrath Don Turnbull	6-1	6-4	6-2		
1936	Jean Borotra Marcel Bernard	Charles Tuckey Pat Hughes	6-2	3-6	9-7	6-1	
1937	Gottfried von Cramm Henner Henkel	Norman Farquharson Vernon Kirby	6-4	7-5	3-6	6-1	
1938	Bernard Destremau Yvon Petra	Don Budge Gene Mako	3-6	6-3	9-7	6-1	
1939	Don McNeill Charles Harris	Jean Borotra Jacques Brugnon	4-6	6-4	6-0	2-6	10-8
1940-45		Not held – WW II					
1946	Marcel Bernard Yvon Petra	Enrique Morea Pancho Segura	7-5	6-3	0-6	1-6	10-8
1947	Eustace Fannin Eric Sturgess	Tom Brown Billy Sidwell	6-4	4-6	6-4	6-3	
1948	Lennart Bergelin Jaroslav Drobny	Harry Hopman Frank Sedgman	8-6	6-1	12-10		
1949	Pancho Gonzalez Frank Parker	Eustace Fannin Eric Sturgess	6-3	8-6	5-7	6-3	
1950	Bill Talbert Tony Trabert	Jaroslav Drobny Eric Sturgess	6-2	1-6	10-8	6-2	
1951	Ken McGregor Frank Sedgman	Gardnar Mulloy Dick Savitt	6-2	2-6	9-7	7-5	
1952	Ken McGregor Frank Sedgman	Gardnar Mulloy Dick Savitt	6-3	6-4	6-4		
1953	Lew Hoad Ken Rosewall	Mervyn Rose Clive Wilderspin	6-2	6-1	6-1		
1954	Vic Seixas Tony Trabert	Lew Hoad Ken Rosewall	6-4	6-2	6-1		
1955	Vic Seixas Tony Trabert	Nicola Pietrangeli Orlando Sirola	6-1	4-6	6-2	6-4	
1956	Don Candy Robert Perry	Ashley Cooper Lew Hoad	7-5	6-3	6-3		

Year	Winner	Defeated	S1	S2	S3	S4	S5
1957	Mal Anderson Ashley Cooper	Don Candy Mervyn Rose	6-3	6-0	6-3		
1958	Ashley Cooper Neale Fraser	Bob Howe Abe Segal	3-6	8-6	6-3	7-5	
1959	Orlando Sirola Nicola Pietrangeli	Roy Emerson Neale Fraser	6-3	6-2	14-12		
1960	Roy Emerson Neale Fraser	Jose-Luis Arilla Andres Gimeno	6-2	8-10	7-5	6-4	
1961	Roy Emerson Rod Laver	Bob Howe Bob Mark	3-6	6-1	6-1	6-4	
1962	Roy Emerson Neale Fraser	Wilhelm Bungert Christian Kuhnke	6-3	6-4	7-5		
1963	Roy Emerson Manuel Santana	Gordon Forbes Abe Segal	6-2	6-4	6-4		
1964	Roy Emerson Ken Fletcher	John Newcombe Tony Roche	7-5	6-3	3-6	7-5	
1965	Roy Emerson Fred Stolle	Ken Fletcher Bob Hewitt	6-8	6-3	8-6	6-2	
1966	Clark Graebner Dennis Ralston	Ilie Nastase Ion Tiriac	6-3	6-3	6-0		
1967	John Newcombe Tony Roche	Roy Emerson Ken Fletcher	6-3	9-7	12-10		
1968	Ken Rosewall Fred Stolle	Roy Emerson Rod Laver	6-3	6-4	6-3		
1969	John Newcombe Tony Roche	Roy Emerson Rod Laver	4-6	6-1	3-6	6-4	6-4
1970	Ilie Nastase Ion Tiriac	Arthur Ashe Charles Pasarell	6-2	6-4	6-3		
1971	Arthur Ashe Marty Riessen	Tom Gorman Stan Smith	6-8	4-6	6-3	6-4	11-9
1972	Bob Hewitt Frew McMillan	Patricio Cornejo Jaime Fillol	6-3	8-6	3-6	6-1	
1973	John Newcombe Tom Okker	Jimmy Connors Ilie Nastase	6-1	3-6	6-3	5-7	6-4
1974	Dick Crealy Onny Parun	Stan Smith Bob Lutz	6-3	6-2	3-6	5-7	6-1
1975	Brian Gottfried Raul Ramirez	John Alexander Phil Dent	6-2	2-6	6-2	6-4	
1976	Fred McNair Sherwood Stewart	Brian Gottfried Raul Ramirez	7-6(6)	6-3	6-1		
1977	Brian Gottfried Raul Ramirez	Wojtek Fibak Jan Kodes	7-6	4-6	6-3	6-4	
1978	Gene Mayer Hank Pfister	Jose Higueras Manuel Orantes	6-3	6-2	6-2		
1979	Gene Mayer Alex Mayer	Ross Case Phil Dent	6-4	6-4	6-4		
1980	Victor Amaya Hank Pfister	Brian Gottfried Raul Ramirez	1-6	6-4	6-4	6-3	
1981	Heinz Gunthardt Balazs Taroczy	Terry Moor Eliot Teltscher	6-2	7-6	6-3		
1982	Sherwood Stewart Ferdi Taygan	Hans Gildemeister Belus Prajoux	7-5	6-3	1-1	(retired)	
1983	Anders Jarryd Hans Simonsson	Mark Edmondson Sherwood Stewart	7-6(4)	6-4	6-2		
1984	Henri Leconte Yannick Noah	Pavel Slozil Tomas Smid	6-4	2-6	3-6	6-3	6-2

Year	Winner	Defeated	S1	S2	S3	S4	S5
1985	Mark Edmondson Kim Warwick	Schlomo Glickstein Hans Simonsson	6-3	6-4	6-7	6-3	
1986	John Fitzgerald Tomas Smid	Stefan Edberg Anders Jarryd	6-3	4-6	6-3	6-7(4)	14-12
1987	Anders Jarryd Robert Seguso	Guy Forget Yannick Noah	6-7	6-7	6-3	6-4	6-2
1988	Andres Gomez Emilio Sanchez	John Fitzgerald Anders Jarryd	6-3	6-7(8)	6-4	6-3	
1989	Jim Grabb Patrick McEnroe	Mansour Bahrami Eric Winogradsky	6-4	2-6	6-4	7-6(5)	
1990	Sergio Casal Emilio Sanchez	Goran Ivanisevic Petr Korda	7-5	6-3			
1991	John Fitzgerald Anders Jarryd	Rick Leach Jim Pugh	6-0	7-6(2)			
1992	Jakob Hlasek Marc Rosset	David Adams Andrei Olhovskiy	7-6(4)	6-7(3)	7-5		
1993	Luke Jensen Murphy Jensen	Marc Goellner David Prinosil	6-4	6-7(4)	6-4		
1994	Byron Black Jonathan Stark	Jan Apell Jonas Bjorkman	6-4	7-6(5)			
1995	Jacco Eltingh Paul Haarhuis	Nicklas Kulti Magnus Larsson	6-7(3)	6-4	6-1		
1996	Yevgeny Kafelnikov Daniel Vacek	Guy Forget Jakob Hlasek	6-2	6-3			
1997	Yevgeny Kafelnikov Daniel Vacek	Mark Woodforde Todd Woodbridge	7-6(12)	4-6	6-3		
1998	Jacco Eltingh Paul Haarhuis	Daniel Nestor Mark Knowles	6-3	3-6	6-3		
1999	Mahesh Bhupathi Leander Paes	Goran Ivanisevic Jeff Tarango	6-2	7-5			
2000	Mark Woodforde Todd Woodbridge	Paul Haarhuis Sandon Stolle	7-6	6-4			
2001	Mahesh Bhupathi Leander Paes	Petr Pala Pavel Vizner	7-6	6-3			
2002	Paul Haarhuis Yevgeny Kafelnikov	Mark Knowles Daniel Nestor	7-5	6-4			

Women's Doubles

Year	Winner	Defeated	S1	S2	S3
1925	Suzanne Lenglen Didi Vlasto	Evelyn Colyer Kitty McKane	6-1	9-11	6-2
1926	Suzanne Lenglen Didi Vlasto	Evelyn Colyer Kitty McKane Godfree	6-1	6-1	
1927	Irene Bowder Peacock Bobbie Heine	Peggy Saunders Phoebe Holcroft Watson	6-2	6-1	
1928	Phoebe Holcroft Watson Eileen Bennett	Suzanne Deve Sylvia Lafaurie	6-0	6-2	
1929	Lili de Alvarez Kea Bouman	Bobbie Heine Alida Neave	7-5	6-3	
1930	Helen Wills Moody Elizabeth Ryan	Simone Barbier Simone Passemard Mathieu	6-3	6-1	
1931	Eileen Bennett Whittingstall Betty Nuthall	Cilly Aussem Elizabeth Ryan	9-7	6-2	
1932	Helen Wills Moody Elizabeth Ryan	Betty Nuthall Eileen Bennett Whittingstall	6-1	6-3	

Year	Winner	Defeated	S1	S2	S3
1933	Simone Passemard Mathieu / Elizabeth Ryan	Sylvie Jung Henrotin / Colette Rosambert	6-1	6-3	
1934	Simone Passemard Mathieu / Elizabeth Ryan	Helen Jacobs / Sarah Palfrey	3-6	6-4	6-2
1935	Margaret Scriven / Kay Stammers	Ida Adamoff / Hilde Krahwinkel Sperling	6-4	6-0	
1936	Simone Passemard Mathieu / Billie Yorke	Susan Noel / Jadwiga Jedrzejowska	2-6	6-4	6-4
1937	Simone Passemard Mathieu / Billie Yorke	Dorothy Andrus / Sylvie Jung Henrotin	3-6	6-2	6-2
1938	Simone Passemard Mathieu / Billie Yorke	Arlette Halff / Nelly Adamson Landry	6-3	6-3	
1939	Simone Passemard Mathieu / Jadwiga Jedrzejowska	Alice Florian / Hella Kovac	7-5	7-5	
1940-45		Not held – WW II			
1946	Louise Brough / Margaret Osborne	Pauline Betz / Doris Hart	6-4	0-6	6-1
1947	Louise Brough / Margaret Osborne	Doris Hart / Pat Canning Todd	7-5	6-2	
1948	Doris Hart / Pat Canning Todd	Shirley Fry / Mary Arnold Prentiss	6-4	6-2	
1949	Margaret Osborne duPont / Louise Brough	Joy Gannon / Betty Hilton	7-5	6-1	
1950	Doris Hart / Shirley Fry	Louise Brough / Margaret Osborne duPont	1-6	7-5	6-2
1951	Doris Hart / Shirley Fry	Beryl Bartlett / Barbara Scofield	10-8	6-3	
1952	Doris Hart / Shirley Fry	Hazel Redick-Smith / Julie Wipplinger	7-5	6-1	
1953	Doris Hart / Shirley Fry	Maureen Connolly / Julia Sampson	6-4	6-3	
1954	Maureen Connolly / Nell Hall Hopman	Maude Galtier / Suzanne Schmitt	7-5	4-6	6-0
1955	Beverly Baker Fleitz / Darlene Hard	Shirley Bloomer / Pat Ward	7-5	6-8	13-11
1956	Angela Buxton / Althea Gibson	Darlene Hard / Dorothy Head Knode	6-8	8-6	6-1
1957	Shirley Bloomer / Darlene Hard	Yola Ramirez / Rosie Reyes	7-5	4-6	7-5
1958	Rosie Reyes / Yola Ramirez	Mary Bevis Hawton / Thelma Coyne Long	6-4	7-5	
1959	Sandra Reynolds / Renee Schuurman	Yola Ramirez / Rosie Reyes	2-6	6-0	6-1
1960	Maria Bueno / Darlene Hard	Pat Ward Hales / Ann Haydon	6-2	7-5	
1961	Sandra Reynolds / Renee Schuurman	Maria Bueno / Darlene Hard	(walkover)		
1962	Sandra Reynolds Price / Renee Schuurman	Justina Bricka / Margaret Smith	6-4	6-4	
1963	Ann Haydon Jones / Renee Schuurman	Robyn Ebbern / Margaret Smith	7-5	6-4	
1964	Margaret Smith / Lesley Turner	Norma Baylon / Helga Schultze	6-3	6-1	
1965	Margaret Smith / Lesley Turner	Françoise Durr / Jeanine Lieffrig	6-3	6-1	
1966	Margaret Smith / Judy Tegart	Jill Blackman / Fay Toyne	4-6	6-1	6-1
1967	Françoise Durr / Gail Sherriff	Annette Van Zyl / Pat Walkden	6-2	6-2	
1968	Françoise Durr / Ann Haydon Jones	Rosie Casals / Billie Jean King	7-5	4-6	6-4
1969	Françoise Durr / Ann Haydon Jones	Margaret Smith / Nancy Richey	6-0	4-6	7-5
1970	Gail Sherriff Chanfreau / Françoise Durr	Rosie Casals / Billie Jean King	6-1	3-6	6-3
1971	Gail Sherriff Chanfreau / Françoise Durr	Helen Gourlay / Kerry Harris	6-4	6-1	
1972	Billie Jean King / Betty Stove	Winnie Shaw / Christine Truman Janes	6-1	6-2	
1973	Margaret Smith Court / Virginia Wade	Françoise Durr / Betty Stove	6-2	6-3	
1974	Chris Evert / Olga Morozova	Gail Sherriff Chanfreau / Katja Ebbinghaus	6-4	2-6	6-1
1975	Chris Evert / Martina Navratilova	Julie Anthony / Olga Morozova	6-3	6-2	
1976	Fiorella Bonicelli / Gail Sherriff Lovera	Kathy Harter / Helga Niessen-Masthoff	6-4	1-6	6-3
1977	Regina Marsikova / Pam Teeguarden	Rayni Fox / Helen Gourlay	5-7	6-4	6-2
1978	Mima Jausovec / Virginia Ruzici	Lesley Turner Bowrey / Gail Sherriff Lovera	5-7	6-4	8-6
1979	Betty Stove / Wendy Turnbull	Françoise Durr / Virginia Wade	3-6	7-5	6-4
1980	Kathy Jordan / Anne Smith	Ivanna Madruga / Adriana Villagran	6-1	6-0	
1981	Rosalyn Fairbank / Tayna Harford	Candy Reynolds / Paula Smith	6-1	6-3	
1982	Martina Navratilova / Anne Smith	Rosie Casals / Wendy Turnbull	6-3	6-4	
1983	Rosalyn Fairbank / Candy Reynolds	Kathy Jordan / Anne Smith	5-7	7-5	6-2
1984	Martina Navratilova / Pam Shriver	Claudia Kohde Kilsch / Hana Mandlikova	5-7	6-3	6-2
1985	Martina Navratilova / Pam Shriver	Claudia Kohde Kilsch / Helena Sukova	4-6	6-2	6-2
1986	Martina Navratilova / Andrea Temesvari	Steffi Graf / Gabriela Sabatini	6-1	6-2	
1987	Martina Navratilova / Pam Shriver	Steffi Graf / Gabriela Sabatini	6-2	6-1	
1988	Martina Navratilova / Pam Shriver	Claudia Kohde Kilsch / Helena Sukova	6-2	7-5	
1989	Larisa Savchenko / Natalia Zvereva	Steffi Graf / Gabriela Sabatini	6-4	6-4	
1990	Jana Novotna / Helena Sukova	Larisa Savchenko / Natalia Zvereva	6-4	7-5	
1991	Gigi Fernandez / Jana Novotna	Larisa Savchenko / Natalia Zvereva	6-4	6-0	
1992	Gigi Fernandez / Natalia Zvereva	Conchita Martinez / Arantxa Sanchez Vicario	6-3	6-2	
1993	Gigi Fernandez / Natalia Zvereva	Larisa Savchenko Neiland / Jana Novotna	6-3	7-5	
1994	Gigi Fernandez / Natalia Zvereva	Lindsay Davenport / Lisa Raymond	6-2	6-2	

Year	Winner	Defeated	S1	S2	S3
1995	Gigi Fernandez / Natalia Zvereva	Jana Novotna / Arantxa Sanchez Vicario	6-7(6)	6-4	7-5
1996	Lindsay Davenport / Mary Joe Fernandez	Gigi Fernandez / Natalia Zvereva	6-2	6-1	
1997	Gigi Fernandez / Natasha Zvereva	Mary Joe Fernandez / Lisa Raymond	6-2	6-3	
1998	Martina Hingis / Jana Novotna	Lindsay Davenport / Natasha Zvereva	6-1	7-6(4)	
1999	Venus Williams / Serena Williams	Martina Hingis / Anna Kournikova	6-3	6-7(2)	8-6
2000	Martina Hingis / Mary Pierce	Virginia Ruano Pascual / Paola Suarez	6-2	6-4	
2001	Virginia Ruano Pascual / Paola Suarez	Jelena Dokic / Conchita Martinez	6-2	6-1	
2002	Virginia Ruano Pascual / Paola Suarez	Lisa Raymond / Rennae Stubbs	6-4	6-2	

Mixed Doubles

Year	Winner	Defeated	S1	S2	S3
1925	Suzanne Lenglen / Jacques Brugnon	Didi Vlasto / Henri Cochet	6-2	6-2	
1926	Suzanne Lenglen / Jacques Brugnon	Suzanne LeBesnerais / Jean Borotra	6-4	6-3	
1927	Marg. Broquedis Bordes / Jean Borotra	Lili de Alvarez / Bill Tilden	6-4	2-6	6-2
1928	Eileen Bennett / Henri Cochet	Helen Wills / Frank Hunter	3-6	6-3	6-3
1929	Eileen Bennett / Henri Cochet	Helen Wills / Frank Hunter	6-3	6-2	
1930	Cilly Aussem / Bill Tilden	Eileen Bennett Whittingstall / Henri Cochet	6-4	6-4	
1931	Betty Nuthall / Pat Spence	Dorothy Shepherd Barron / Bunny Austin	6-3	5-7	6-3
1932	Betty Nuthall / Fred Perry	Helen Wills Moody / Sidney Wood	6-4	6-2	
1933	Margaret Scriven / Jack Crawford	Betty Nuthall / Fred Perry	6-2	6-3	
1934	Colette Rosambert / Jean Borotra	Elizabeth Ryan / Adrian Quist	6-2	6-4	
1935	Lolette Payot / Marcel Bernard	Sylvie Jung Henrotin / Martin Legeay	4-6	6-2	6-4
1936	Billie Yorke / Marcel Bernard	Sylvie Jung Henrotin / Martin Legeay	7-5	6-8	6-3
1937	Simone Passemard Mathieu / Yvon Petra	Marie Luise Horn / Roland Journu	7-5	7-5	
1938	Simone Passemard Mathieu / Dragutin Mitic	Nancye Wynne / Christian Boussus	2-6	6-3	6-4
1939	Sarah Palfrey Fabyan / Elwood Cooke	Simone Passemard Mathieu / Franjo Kukuljevic	4-6	6-1	7-5
1940-45		Not held – WW II			
1946	Pauline Betz / Budge Patty	Dorothy Bundy / Tom Brown	7-5	9-7	
1947	Sheila Piercey Summers / Eric Sturgess	Jadwiga Jedrzejowska / Christian Caralulis	6-0	6-0	
1948	Pat Canning Todd / Jaroslav Drobny	Doris Hart / Frank Sedgman	6-3	3-6	6-3

Year	Winner	Defeated	S1	S2	S3
1949	Sheila Piercey Summers / Eric Sturgess	Jean Quertier / Gerry Oakley	6-1	6-1	
1950	Barbara Scofield / Enrique Morea	Pat Canning Todd / Bill Talbert	(walkover)		
1951	Doris Hart / Frank Sedgman	Thelma Coyne Long / Merv Rose	7-5	6-2	
1952	Doris Hart / Frank Sedgman	Shirley Fry / Eric Sturgess	6-8	6-3	6-3
1953	Doris Hart / Vic Seixas	Maureen Connolly / Merv Rose	4-6	6-4	6-0
1954	Maureen Connolly / Lew Hoad	Jacqueline Patorni / Rex Hartwig	6-4	6-3	
1955	Darlene Hard / Gordon Forbes	Jenny Staley / Luis Ayala	5-7	6-1	6-2
1956	Thelma Coyne Long / Luis Ayala	Doris Hart / Bob Howe	4-6	6-4	6-1
1957	Vera Puzejova / Jiri Javorsky	Edda Buding / Luis Ayala	6-3	6-4	
1958	Shirley Bloomer / Nicola Pietrangeli	Lorraine Coghlan / Bob Howe	6-8	6-2	
1959	Yola Ramirez / Billy Knight	Renee Schuurman / Rod Laver	6-4	6-4	
1960	Maria Bueno / Bob Howe	Ann Haydon / Roy Emerson	1-6	6-1	6-2
1961	Darlene Hard / Rod Laver	Vera Puzejova / Jiri Javorsky	6-0	2-6	6-3
1962	Renee Schuurman / Bob Howe	Lesley Turner / Fred Stolle	3-6	6-4	6-4
1963	Margaret Smith / Ken Fletcher	Lesley Turner / Fred Stolle	6-1	6-2	
1964	Margaret Smith / Ken Fletcher	Lesley Turner / Fred Stolle	6-3	4-6	8-6
1965	Margaret Smith / Ken Fletcher	Maria Bueno / John Newcombe	6-4	6-4	
1966	Annette Van Zyl / Frew McMillan	Ann Haydon Jones / Clark Graebner	1-6	6-3	6-2
1967	Billie Jean King / Owen Davidson	Ann Haydon Jones / Ion Tiriac	6-3	6-1	
1968	Françoise Durr / Jean Claude Barclay	Billie Jean King / Owen Davidson	6-1	6-4	
1969	Margaret Smith Court / Marty Riessen	Françoise Durr / Jean Claude Barclay	6-3	6-2	
1970	Billie Jean King / Bob Hewitt	Françoise Durr / Jean Claude Barclay	3-6	6-4	6-2
1971	Françoise Durr / Jean Claude Barclay	Winnie Shaw / Tomas Lejus	6-2	6-4	
1972	Evonne Goolagong / Kim Warwick	Françoise Durr / Jean Claude Barclay	6-2	6-4	
1973	Françoise Durr / Jean Claude Barclay	Betty Stove / Patrice Dominguez	6-1	6-4	
1974	Martina Navratilova / Ivan Molina	Rosie Reyes Darmon / Marcelo Lara	6-3	6-3	
1975	Fiorella Bonicelli / Thomaz Koch	Pam Teeguarden / Jaime Fillol	6-4	7-6	
1976	Ilana Kloss / Kim Warwick	Delina Boshoff / Colin Dowdeswell	5-7	7-6	6-2

Year	Winner	Defeated	S1	S2	S3	Year	Winner	Defeated	S1	S2	S3
1977	Mary Carillo John McEnroe	Florenta Mihai Ivan Molina	7-6	6-3		**1990**	Arantxa Sanchez Vicario Jorge Lozano	Nicole Provis Danie Visser	7-6(5)	7-6(8)	
1978	Renata Tomanova Pavel Slozil	Virginia Ruzici Patrice Dominguez	7-6		(retired)	**1991**	Helena Sukova Cyril Suk	Caroline Vis Paul Haarhuis	3-6	6-4	6-1
1979	Wendy Turnbull Bob Hewitt	Virginia Ruzici Ion Tiriac	6-3	2-6	6-3	**1992**	Arantxa Sanchez Vicario Todd Woodbridge	Lori McNeil Bryan Shelton	6-2	6-3	
1980	Anne Smith Billy Martin	Renata Tomanova Stanislav Birner	2-6	6-4	8-6	**1993**	Eugenia Maniokova Andrei Olhovskiy	Elna Reinach Danie Visser	6-2	4-6	6-4
1981	Andrea Jaeger Jimmy Arias	Betty Stove Fred McNair	7-6	6-4		**1994**	Kristie Boogert Menno Oosting	Larisa Savchenko Neiland Andrei Olhovskiy	7-5	3-6	7-5
1982	Wendy Turnbull John Lloyd	Claudia Monteiro Cassio Motta	6-2	7-6		**1995**	Larisa Savchenko Neiland Mark Woodforde	Jill Hetherington John-Laffnie de Jager	7-6(8)	7-6(4)	
1983	Barbara Jordan Eliot Teltscher	Lesley Allen Charles Strode	6-2	6-3		**1996**	Patricia Tarabini Javier Frana	Nicole Arendt Luke Jensen	6-2	6-2	
1984	Anne Smith Dick Stockton	Anne Minter Laurie Warder	6-2	6-4		**1997**	Rika Hiraki Mahesh Bhupathi	Lisa Raymond Patrick Galbraith	6-4	6-1	
1985	Martina Navratilova Heinz Gunthardt	Paula Smith Francisco Gonzalez	2-6	6-3	6-2	**1998**	Venus Williams Justin Gimelstob	Serena Williams Luis Lobo	6-4	6-4	
1986	Kathy Jordan Ken Flach	Rosalyn Fairbank Mark Edmondson	3-6	7-6(3)	6-3	**1999**	Katarina Srebotnik Piet Norval	Larisa Savchenko Neiland Rick Leach	6-3	3-6	6-3
1987	Pam Shriver Emilio Sanchez	Lori McNeil Sherwood Stewart	6-3	7-6(4)		**2000**	Mariaan de Swardt David Adams	Rennae Stubbs Todd Woodbridge	6-3	3-6	6-3
1988	Lori McNeil Jorge Lozano	Brenda Schultz Michiel Schapers	7-5	6-2		**2001**	Virginia Ruano Pascual Tomas Carbonell	Paola Suarez Jaime Oncins	7-5	6-3	
1989	Manon Bollegraf Tom Nijssen	Arantxa Sanchez Vicario Horacio de la Pena	6-3	6-7(3)	6-2	**2002**	Cara Black Wayne Black	Elena Bovina Mark Knowles	6-3	6-3	

The Grand Slammers

Opposite page: Maureen Connolly, a mere 18 when she captured all four majors—the Australian, French, Wimbledon and U.S. championships—in 1953

Top left: Rod Laver, the only double Slammer, in 1962 and 1969

Lower left: Steffi Graf, the club's most recent member, in 1988

Lower right: Margaret Smith Court, who Slammed in 1970 on her way to a record 24 singles and 62 overall (including doubles and mixed doubles) major titles

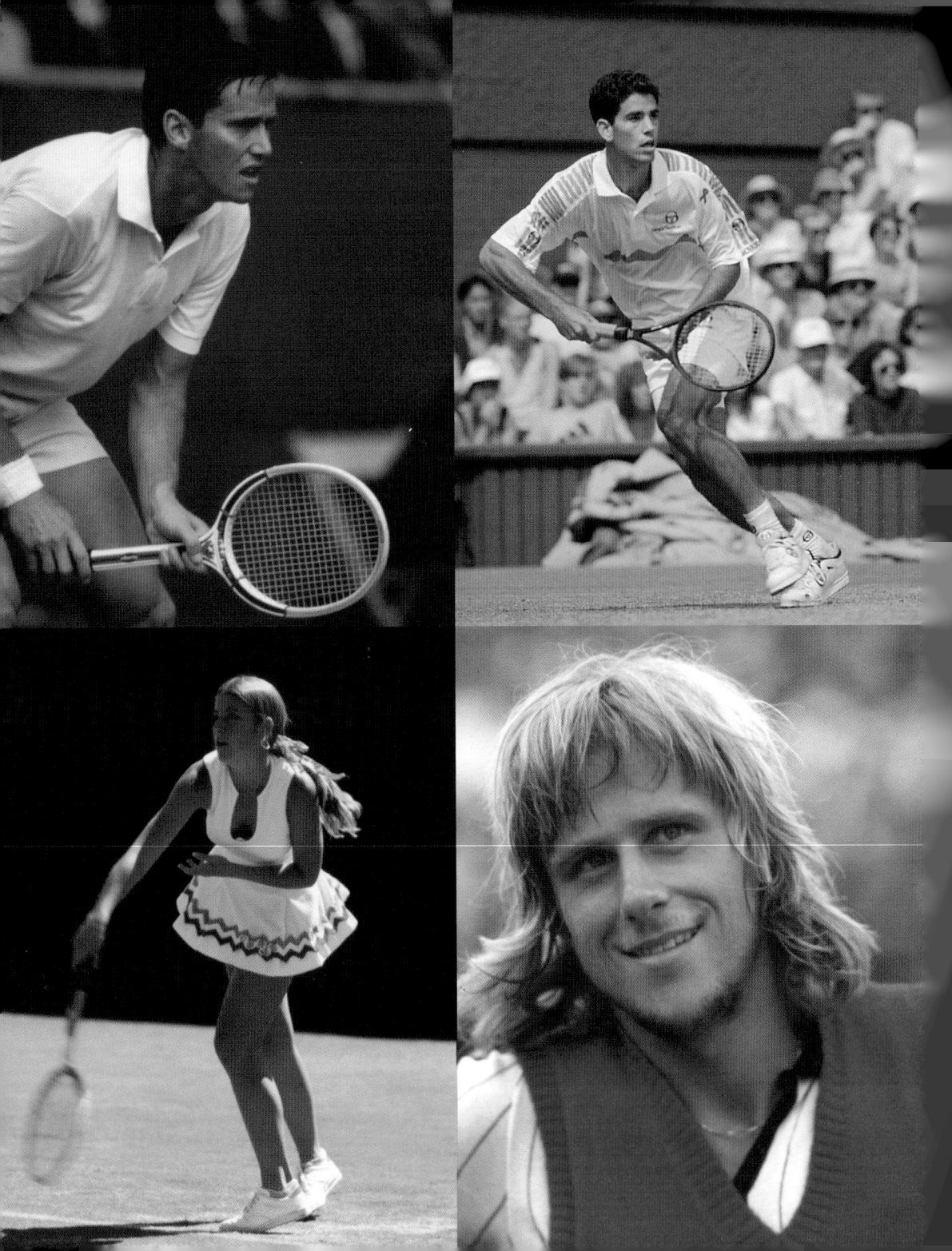

The Greats

Opposite page, clockwise from top left: Roy Emerson, owner of 12 major singles titles; Pete Sampras, who eclipsed Emmo's record and now has 14; Bjorn Borg, winner of 11 majors, including five straight Wimbledons; Chris Evert, 18 times a major singles champ

Top left: Martina Navratilova, Wimbledon singles champ an incredible nine times, among 18 singles and 57 overall majors

Lower left: Billie Jean King, winner of 20 Wimbledon titles, six in singles, among 39 overall majors

The Pioneers

Top left: Arthur Ashe, the first black man to win a major, the U.S. Open in 1968

Top right: Richard 'Pancho' Gonzalez, a mercurial figure and perhaps the greatest player ever

Lower left: Jack Kramer, who practically invented pro tennis

Far right: Althea Gibson, the first black woman to win a major, the French in 1956

The Golden Girls

Opposite page: Margaret Osborne duPont, 37 overall major titles, 31 in doubles and mixed doubles—including a record 20 with Louise Brough—between 1941 and 1962

Top right: Louise Brough, 35 majors, 29 in doubles and mixed doubles—20 as duPont's alter-ego

Lower right: Doris Hart, 35 majors, 29 in doubles and mixed doubles

The Golden Guys

Opposite page: (Seated) Jack Kramer, Pancho Segura, Lew Hoad, Richard 'Pancho' Gonzalez, Frank Sedgman, Ken Rosewall; *(standing)* Ashley Cooper, Mal Anderson, Mervyn Rose, Tony Trabert, soaking up rays at the West Side Tennis Club during a stop on the pro tour of 1959

Top left: Budge Patty, matinee idol and 1950 Wimbledon champ

Top right: Vic Seixas, entrant in 28 U.S. Championships, the most by anyone in any major

Lower left: Bobby Riggs, a charmer of the ladies long before he met Billie Jean

The Leading Men

Opposite page: Jimmy Connors, five U.S. Open titles among eight major singles titles, ranked No. 1 in world five years in a row, 1974-1978

Left: John McEnroe, seven major singles crowns, ranked No. 1 four straight years, 1981-1984

Lower left: Ken Rosewall winner of eight major singles titles, owner of Top 10 world rankings 23 years apart (1952 and 1975)

Lower right: John Newcombe, seven major singles titles, ranked No. 1 in world three times

The Modern Warriors

Previous page: Venus Williams, four singles majors by 21, only to be eclipsed by sister Serena's five by the same age

Top left: Lleyton Hewitt, first Aussie to reach No. 1 in 30 years

Top right: Jennifer Capriati, three major singles titles since storied comeback

Lower left: Lindsay Davenport, two majors, twice a No. 1

French Open – Records

French Slam
(Winner of all 3 events in one year)

MEN

WOMEN

Suzanne Lenglen (with D-Didi Vlasto; M-Jacques Brugnon) (1925)

Suzanne Lenglen (with D-Didi Vlasto; M-Jacques Brugnon) (1926)

Simone Passemard Mathieu (with D-Billie Yorke; M-Dragutin Mitic (1938)

Doris Hart (with D-Shirley Frye; M-Frank Sedgman) (1952)

Maureen Connolly (with D-Nell Hall Hopman; M- Lew Hoad) (1954)

Margaret Smith (with D-Lesley Turner; M- Ken Fletcher) (1964)

Overall Titles

MOST TITLES ALL TIME MEN
9 Henri Cochet (1926-1932) 4 singles, 3 doubles, 2 mixed.
8 Jean Borotra (1925-1936) 1 singles, 5 doubles, 2 mixed.
   Roy Emerson (1960-1967) 2 singles, 6 doubles, 0 mixed.
7 Jacques Brugnon (1925-1934) 0 singles, 5 doubles, 2 mixed.
6 Bjorn Borg (1974-1981) 6 singles, 0 doubles, 0 mixed.
5 Marcel Bernard (1935-1946) 1 singles, 2 doubles, 2 mixed.
   René Lacoste (1925-1929) 3 singles, 2 doubles, 0 mixed.
   Tony Trabert (1950-1955) 2 singles, 3 doubles, 0 mixed.
4 Frank Sedgman (1951-1952) 0 singles, 2 doubles, 2 mixed.
   Jaroslav Drobny (1948-1952) 2 singles, 1 doubles, 1 mixed.
   Ken Fletcher (1963-1965) 0 singles, 1 doubles, 3 mixed.
   Ken Rosewall (1953-1968) 2 singles, 2 doubles, 0 mixed.
   Nicola Pietrangeli (1958-1960) 2 singles, 1 doubles, 1 mixed.
   Rod Laver (1961-1969) 2 singles, 1 doubles, 1 mixed.
   Yevgeny Kafelnikov (1996-2002) 1 singles, 3 doubles, 0 mixed.
3 Anders Jarryd (1983-1991) 0 singles, 3 doubles, 0 mixed.
   Bob Hewitt (1970-1979) 0 singles, 1 doubles, 2 mixed.
   Emilio Sanchez (1987-1990) 0 singles, 2 doubles, 1 mixed.
   Eric Sturgess (1947-1949) 0 singles, 1 doubles, 2 mixed.
   Frank Parker (1948-1949) 2 singles, 1 doubles, 0 mixed.
   Fred Perry (1932-1935) 1 singles, 1 doubles, 1 mixed.
   Fred Stolle (1965-1968) 1 singles, 2 doubles, 0 mixed.
   Gottfried von Cramm (1934-1937) 2 singles, 1 doubles, 0 mixed.
   Gustavo Kuerten (1997-2001) 3 singles, 0 doubles, 0 mixed.
   Ivan Lendl (1984-1987) 3 singles, 0 doubles, 0 mixed.
   Jack Crawford (1933-1935) 1 singles, 1 doubles, 1 mixed.
   Jean Claude Barclay (1968-1973) 0 singles, 0 doubles, 3 mixed.
   John Newcombe (1967-1973) 0 singles, 3 doubles, 0 mixed.
   Kim Warwick (1972-1985) 0 singles, 1 doubles, 2 mixed.
   Lew Hoad (1953-1956) 1 singles, 1 doubles, 1 mixed.
   Mahesh Bhupathi (1997-2001) 0 singles, 2 doubles, 1 mixed.
   Manolo Santana (1961-1964) 2 singles, 1 doubles, 0 mixed.
   Mark Woodforde (1992-2000) 0 singles, 1 doubles, 2 mixed.
   Mats Wilander (1982-1988) 3 singles, 0 doubles, 0 mixed.
   Neale Fraser (1958-1962) 0 singles, 3 doubles, 0 mixed.
   Paul Haarhuis (1995-2002) 0 singles, 3 doubles, 0 mixed.
   Tony Roche (1966-1969) 1 singles, 2 doubles, 0 mixed.
   Vic Seixas (1953-1955) 0 singles, 2 doubles, 1 mixed.
   Yvon Petra (1937-1946) 0 singles, 2 doubles, 1 mixed.

MOST TITLES ALL TIME WOMEN
13 Margaret Smith Court (1962-1973) 5 singles, 4 doubles, 4 mixed.
11 Martina Navratilova (1974-1988) 2 singles, 7 doubles, 2 mixed.
10 Doris Hart (1948-1955) 2 singles, 5 doubles, 3 mixed.
    Simone Passemard Mathieu (1933-1939) 2 singles, 6 doubles, 2 mixed.
9 Chris Evert (1974-1986) 7 singles, 2 doubles, 0 mixed.
   Françoise Durr (1967-1973) 1 singles, 5 doubles, 3 mixed.
6 Darlene Hard (1955-1961) 1 singles, 3 doubles, 2 mixed.
   Gigi Fernandez (1991-1997) 0 singles, 6 doubles, 0 mixed.
   Helen Wills Moody (1928-1932) 4 singles, 2 doubles, 0 mixed.
   Natalia Zvereva (1989-1997) 0 singles, 6 doubles, 0 mixed.
   Steffi Graf (1987-1999) 6 singles, 0 doubles, 0 mixed.
   Suzanne Lenglen (1925-1926) 2 singles, 2 doubles, 2 mixed.
5 Ann Haydon (1961-1969) 2 singles, 3 doubles, 0 mixed.
   Arantxa Sanchez Vicario (1989-1998) 3 singles, 0 doubles, 2 mixed.
   Margaret Osborne duPont (1946-1949) 2 singles, 3 doubles, 0 mixed.
   Pam Shriver (1984-1988) 0 singles, 4 doubles, 1 mixed.
   Renee Schuurman (1959-1963) 0 singles, 4 doubles, 1 mixed.
   Shirley Fry (1950-1953) 1 singles, 4 doubles, 0 mixed.
4 Anne Smith (1980-1984) 0 singles, 2 doubles, 2 mixed.
   Billie Jean King (1967-1972) 1 singles, 1 doubles, 2 mixed.
   Billie Yorke (1936-1938) 0 singles, 3 doubles, 1 mixed.
   Eileen Bennett (1928-1931) 0 singles, 2 doubles, 2 mixed.
   Elizabeth Ryan (1930-1934) 0 singles, 4 doubles, 0 mixed.
   Gail Sherriff (1967-1976) 0 singles, 4 doubles, 0 mixed.
   Lesley Turner (1963-1965) 2 singles, 2 doubles, 0 mixed.
   Margaret Scriven (1933-1935) 2 singles, 1 doubles, 1 mixed.
   Maureen Connolly (1953-1954) 2 singles, 1 doubles, 1 mixed.

Men's Singles

MOST TITLES
6 Bjorn Borg (1974-1981)
4 Henri Cochet (1926-1932)
3 Gustavo Kuerten (1997-2001)
   Ivan Lendl (1984-1987)
   René Lacoste (1925-1929)
   Mats Wilander (1982-1988)
2 Jaroslav Drobny (1951-1952)
   Frank Parker (1948-1949)
   Gottfried von Cramm (1934-1936)
   Jan Kodes (1970-1971)
   Jim Courier (1991-1992)
   Ken Rosewall (1953-1968)
   Manolo Santana (1961-1964)
   Roy Emerson (1963-1967)
   Tony Trabert (1954-1955)
   Nicola Pietrangeli (1959-1960)
   Rod Laver (1962-1969)
   Sergi Bruguera (1993-1994)

MOST FINAL APPEARANCES
6 Bjorn Borg (1974-1981)
5 René Lacoste (1925-1929)
   Mats Wilander (1982-1988)
   Ivan Lendl (1981-1987)
   Henri Cochet (1926-1933)
   Jaroslav Drobny (1946-1952)
4 Nicola Pietrangeli (1959-1964)
   Guillermo Vilas (1975-1982)

MOST FINAL LOSSES
3   Jaroslav Drobny (1946-1950)
    Guillermo Vilas (1975-1982)
2   Alex Corretja (1998-2001)
    Andre Agassi (1990-1991)
    Bill Tilden (1927-1930)
    Eric Sturgess (1947-1951)
    Ivan Lendl (1981-1985)
    Jean Borotra (1925-1929)
    Luis Ayala (1958-1960)
    Mats Wilander (1983-1987)
    Nicola Pietrangeli (1961-1964)
    Tony Roche (1965-1967)
    René Lacoste (1926-1928)
    Sven Davidson (1955-1956)

MOST SEMI-FINAL APPEARANCES
7   Henri Cochet (1926-1933)
6   Jean Borotra (1925-1931)
    Bjorn Borg (1974-1981)
    Eric Sturgess (1947-1952)
    Jaroslav Drobny (1946-1953)
    Mats Wilander (1982-1988)
5   Ivan Lendl (1981-1987)
    Andre Agassi (1988-1999)
    René Lacoste (1925-1929)

OLDEST CHAMPION
Andres Gimeno—34 years, 10 months (1972)

YOUNGEST CHAMPION
Michael Chang—17 years, 4 months (1989)

TOURNAMENTS PLAYED
20 Francois Jauffret—1961-80

MATCHES PLAYED
75 Guillermo Vilas—1972-89

MATCHES WON
58 Guillermo Vilas—1972-89

MATCHES WON CONSECUTIVELY
28 Bjorn Borg—1978-81

MATCH WINNING PERCENTAGE
.961 Bjorn Borg—1973-76 (49-2)

Women's Singles

MOST WINS
7   Chris Evert (1974-1986)
6   Steffi Graf (1987-1999)
5   Margaret Smith Court (1962-1973)
4   Helen Wills Moody (1928-1932)
3   Arantxa Sanchez Vicario (1989-1998)
    Hilde Krahwinkel Sperling (1935-1937)
    Monica Seles (1990-1992)

MOST FINAL APPEARANCES
9   Chris Evert (1973-1986)
    Steffi Graf (1987-1999)
8   Simone Passemard Mathieu (1929-1939)
6   Arantxa Sanchez Vicario (1989-1998)
    Margaret Smith Court (1962-1973)
    Martina Navratilova (1975-1987)
5   Ann Haydon (1961-1969)
    Doris Hart (1947-1953)

MOST FINAL LOSSES
6   Simone Passemard Mathieu (1929-1937)
4   Martina Navratilova (1975-1987)
3   Ann Haydon (1963-1969)
    Arantxa Sanchez Vicario (1991-1996)
    Doris Hart (1947-1953)
    Steffi Graf (1989-1992)

MOST SEMI-FINAL APPEARANCES
12 Chris Evert (1973-1987)
11 Steffi Graf (1987-1999)
10 Arantxa Sanchez Vicario (1989-2000)
9   Simone Passemard Mathieu (1929-1939)
7   Ann Haydon (1957-1969)
    Monica Seles (1989-1999)
    Margaret Smith Court (1962-1973)

OLDEST CHAMPION
Suzi Kormoczi—33 years, 9 months (1958)

YOUNGEST CHAMPION
Monica Seles—16 years, 6 months (1990)

TOURNAMENTS PLAYED
19 Andree Varin—1932-64
    Anne-Marie Simon—1937-66

MATCHES PLAYED
97 Steffi Graf—1983-99

MATCHES WON
87 Steffi Graf

MATCHES WON CONSECUTIVELY
29 Chris Evert—1974-1981

MATCH WINNING PERCENT
1.000 Helen Wills Moody—1928-30 (20-0)
.923 Chris Evert—1973-88 (72-6)

Men's Doubles

MOST TITLES—TEAM
3   Henri Cochet / Jacques Brugnon (1927-1932)
2   Brian Gottfried / Raul Ramirez (1975-1977)
    Leander Paes / Mahesh Bhupathi (1999-2001)
    Vic Seixas / Tony Trabert (1954-1955)
    Jean Borotra / Jacques Brugnon (1928-1934)
    Yevgeny Kafelnikov / Daniel Vacek (1996-1997)
    Jean Borotra / René Lacoste (1925-1929)
    Ken McGregor / Frank Sedgman (1951-1952)
    Neale Fraser / Roy Emerson (1960-1962)
    Jacco Eltingh / Paul Haarhuis (1995-1998)
    John Newcombe / Tony Roche (1967-1969)

MOST TITLES—INDIVIDUAL
6   Roy Emerson (1960-1965)
5   Jacques Brugnon (1927-1934)
    Jean Borotra (1925-1936)
3   Paul Haarhuis (1995-2002)
    John Newcombe (1967-1973)
    Neale Fraser (1958-1962)
    Henri Cochet (1927-1932)
    Tony Trabert (1950-1955)
    Yevgeny Kafelnikov (1996-2002)
    Anders Jarryd (1983-1991)

MOST FINAL APPEARANCES—TEAM
6 Henri Cochet / Jacques Brugnon (1925-1932)
4 Brian Gottfried / Raul Ramirez (1975-1980)
3 Neale Fraser / Roy Emerson (1959-1962)
  Jean Borotra / Jacques Brugnon (1928-1939)
  John Newcombe / Tony Roche (1964-1969)
  Jean Borotra / René Lacoste (1925-1929)
  Roy Emerson / Rod Laver (1961-1969)

MOST FINAL APPEARANCES—INDIVIDUAL
10 Roy Emerson (1959-1969)
9 Jacques Brugnon (1925-1939)
7 Jean Borotra (1925-1939)
  Henri Cochet (1925-1932)
5 Anders Jarryd (1983-1991)

MOST FINAL LOSSES—TEAM
3 Henri Cochet / Jacques Brugnon (1925-1929)
2 Daniel Nestor / Mark Knowles (1998-2002)
  Roy Emerson / Rod Laver (1968-1969)
  Gardnar Mulloy / Dick Savitt (1951-1952)
  Brian Gottfried / Raul Ramirez (1976-1980)

MOST FINAL LOSSES—INDIVIDUAL
4 Henri Cochet (1925-1929)
  Roy Emerson (1959-1969)
  Jacques Brugnon (1925-1939)
3 Viv McGrath (1933-1935)

OLDEST CHAMPION—MEN
Jacques Brugnon—39 years (1934)

YOUNGEST CHAMPION—Men
Lew Hoad—18 years, 7 months (1953)

Women's Doubles

MOST TITLES—TEAM
5 Gigi Fernandez / Natalia Zvereva (1992-1997)
4 Doris Hart / Shirley Fry (1950-1953)
  Martina Navratilova / Pam Shriver (1984-1988)
3 Renee Schuurman / Sandra Reynolds (1959-1962)
  Louise Brough / Margaret Osborne duPont (1946-1949)
  Simone Passemard Mathieu / Billie Yorke (1936-1938)

MOST TITLES—INDIVIDUAL
7 Martina Navratilova (1975-1988)
6 Simone Passemard Mathieu (1933-1939)
  Natalia Zvereva (1989-1997)
  Gigi Fernandez (1991-1997)
5 Doris Hart (1948-1953)
  Françoise Durr (1967-1971)

MOST FINAL APPEARANCES—TEAM
6 Gigi Fernandez / Natalia Zvereva (1992-1997)
4 Martina Navratilova / Pam Shriver (1984-1988)
  Doris Hart / Shirley Fry (1950-1953)
  Louise Brough / Margaret Osborne duPont (1946-1950)

MOST FINAL APPEARANCES—INDIVIDUAL
10 Natalia Zvereva (1989-1998)
8 Françoise Durr (1965-1979)
7 Martina Navratilova (1975-1988)
  Doris Hart (1946-1953)
  Gigi Fernandez (1991-1997)
  Margaret Smith Court (1962-1973)
  Simone Passemard Mathieu (1930-1939)

MOST FINAL LOSSES—TEAM
3 Steffi Graf / Gabriela Sabatini (1986-1989)
2 Rosie Reyes / Yola Ramirez (1957-1959)
  Evelyn Colyer / Kitty Godfree (1925-1926)
  Claudia Kohde Kilsch / Helena Sukova (1985-1988)
  Billie Jean King / Rosie Casals (1968-1970)
  Larisa Savchenko / Natalia Zvereva (1990-1991)

MOST FINAL LOSSES—INDIVIDUAL
4 Natalia Zvereva (1990-1998)
3 Françoise Durr (1965-1979)
  Gabriela Sabatini (1986-1989)
  Margaret Smith Court (1962-1969)
  Lisa Raymond (1994-2002)
  Rosie Casals (1968-1982)
  Claudia Kohde Kilsch (1984-1988)
  Steffi Graf (1986-1989)

OLDEST CHAMPION
Elizabeth Ryan—42 years, 3 months (1934)

YOUNGEST CHAMPION
Martina Hingis—17 years, 4 months (1998)

Mixed Doubles

MOST TITLES—TEAM
3 Françoise Durr / Jean Claude Barclay (1968-1973)
  Margaret Smith Court / Ken Fletcher (1963-1965)
2 Suzanne Lenglen / Jacques Brugnon (1925-1926)
  Doris Hart / Frank Sedgman (1951-1952)
  Sheila Piercey Summers / Eric Sturgess (1947-1949)
  Eileen Bennett / Henri Cochet (1928-1929)

MOST TITLES—MEN
3 Jean Claude Barclay (1968-1973)
  Ken Fletcher (1963-1965)
2 Bob Hewitt (1970-1979)
  Bob Howe (1960-1962)
  Eric Sturgess (1947-1949)
  Frank Sedgman (1951-1952)
  Henri Cochet (1928-1929)
  Jacques Brugnon (1925-1926)
  Jean Borotra (1927-1934)
  Jorge Lozano (1988-1990)
  Kim Warwick (1972-1976)
  Marcel Bernard (1935-1936)
  Mark Woodforde (1992-1995)

MOST TITLES—WOMEN
4 Margaret Smith Court (1963-1969)
3 Doris Hart (1951-1953)
  Françoise Durr (1968-1973)

MOST FINAL APPEARANCES—TEAM
6 Françoise Durr / Jean Claude Barclay (1968-1973)
3 Margaret Smith Court / Ken Fletcher (1963-1965)
  Doris Hart / Frank Sedgman (1948-1952)
  Lesley Turner / Fred Stolle (1962-1964)

MOST FINAL APPEARANCES—MEN
6 Jean Claude Barclay (1968-1973)
4 Henri Cochet (1925-1930)
  Bob Howe (1956-1962)

MOST FINAL APPEARANCES—WOMEN
6 Doris Hart (1948-1956)
  Françoise Durr (1968-1973)
4 Margaret Smith Court (1963-1969)

MOST FINAL LOSSES—TEAM

3 Françoise Durr / Jean Claude Barclay (1969-1972)
   Lesley Turner / Fred Stolle (1962-1964)
2 Helen Wills Moody / Frank Hunter (1928-1929)
   Sylvie Jung Henrotin / Martin Legeay (1935-1936)

MOST FINAL LOSSES—MEN

3 Fred Stolle (1962-1964)
   Jean Claude Barclay (1969-1972)
2 Danie Visser (1990-1993)
   Ion Tiriac (1967-1979)
   Henri Cochet (1925-1930)
   Luis Ayala (1955-1957)
   Frank Hunter (1928-1929)
   Martin Legeay (1935-1936)
   Merv Rose (1951-1953)
   Patrice Dominguez (1973-1978)
   Bob Howe (1956-1958)

MOST FINAL LOSSES—WOMEN

3 Lesley Turner (1962-1964)
   Françoise Durr (1969-1972)
   Helen Wills Moody (1928-1932)
   Ann Haydon (1960-1967)

OLDEST CHAMPION—MEN

Bob Hewitt—39 years, 5 months (1979)

YOUNGEST CHAMPION—MEN

Jimmy Arias—16 years, 8 months (1981)

OLDEST CHAMPION—WOMEN

Thelma Long Coyne—38 years (1956)

YOUNGEST CHAMPION—WOMEN

Andrea Jaegar—15 years, 11 months (1981)

LONGEST MATCHES, TOTAL GAMES

Men's singles: 76 games – Eric Sturgess d. Ken McGregor, 10-8, 7-9, 8-6, 5-7, 9-7, semis, 1951
Men's doubles: 81 games – Gordon Forbes / Russell Seymour d. Merv Rose / George Worthington, 11-13, 6-1, 7-5, 4-6, 15-13, 2nd rd., 1952
Women's singles: 56 games – Kerry Melville (Reid) d. Pam Teeguarden, 9-7, 4-6, 16-14, 3rd rd., 1972
Women's doubles: 50 games – Beverly Baker Fleitz / Darlene Hard d. Shirley Bloomer (Brasher) / Pat Ward (Hales), 7-5, 6-8, 13-11, final, 1955
Mixed doubles: 48 games – Rosie Reyes Darmon / Bob Howe d. Marina Tshuvirina / Teimuraz Kakulia, 5-7, 10-8, 10-8, 1st rd., 1972. 48 games, Lucia Bassi / Francisco Contreras d. Edda Buding / Ingo Buding, 10-12, 9-7, 6-4, 2nd rd., 1960

LONGEST MATCHES, PLAYING TIME

Men's singles: 5 hours, 2 minutes – Ronald Agenor d. David Prinosil, 6-7 (4-7), 6-7 (2-7), 6-3, 6-4, 14-12, 2nd rd., 1994
Women's singles: 4 hours, 7 minutes – Virginia Buisson d. Noelle van Lottum, 6-7 (3-7), 7-5, 6-2, 1st rd., 1996

LONGEST TIE-BREAKERS

Men's singles: 16-14, second set - Wayne Arthurs d. Andy Roddick, 4-6, 7-6 (16-14), 4-6, 7-5, 6-3, 1st rd., 2002
Women's singles: 16-14, first set – Nathalie Dechy d. Stephanie Foretz, 6-7 (14-16), 7-6 (7-1), 6-1, 1st rd., 1999

BIGGEST UPSETS

Men:

1946 - Marcel Bernard d. Jaroslav Drobny, 3-6, 2-6, 6-1, 6-4, 6-3, F, 1st unseeded champ

1979 - Victor Pecci (No. 30) d. 6th seed Harold Solomon, 6-1, 6-4, 6-3, 4th rd.; d. 3rd seed Guillermo Vilas, 6-0, 6-2, 7-5, QF; d. 2nd seed Jimmy Connors, 7-5, 6-4, 5-7, 6-3, SF

1982 - Mats Wilander (No. 30) d. 2nd seeded Ivan Lendl, 4-6, 7-5, 3-6, 6-4, 6-2, QF; d. 3rd seed Guillermo Vilas, 1-6, 7-6 (8-6), 6-0, 6-4, F, 2nd unseeded champ, following Bernard, 1946.Also 14th seed Jose Higueras d. 1st seed Jimmy Connors, 6-2, 6-2, 6-2, QF

1983 - wild card Christophe Roger-Vasselin (No. 230) d. 1st seed Jimmy Connors, 6-4, 6-4, 7-6 (7-5), QF

1986 - Andrei Chesnokov (No. 81) d. 2d seed defending champ Mats Wilander, 6-2, 6-3, 6-2, 3rd rd.

1989 - 15th seed Michael Chang d. 1st seed 3-time champ Ivan Lendl, 4-6, 4-6, 6-3, 6-3, 6-3, 4th rd., ending Lendl's 28 match win streak; d. 3rd seed Stefan Edberg, 6-1, 3-6, 4-6, 6-4, 6-2, F

1990 - Sergi Bruguera (No. 46) d. 1st seed Stefan Edberg, 6-4, 6-2, 6-1, 1st rd. and Goran Ivanisevic (No. 51) d. 2nd seed Boris Becker, 5-7, 6-4, 7-5, 6-2, 1st round (same day, only time 1-2 seeds defeated 1st rd.)

1993 - wild card Stephane Huet (No. 297) d. 7th seed Ivan Lendl, 3-6, 7-5, 6-0, 7-6 (7-2), 1st rd., 1st match in a major

1996 - Chris Woodruff (No. 72) d. 3rd seed Andre Agassi, 4-6, 6-4, 6-7 (7-9), 6-3, 6-2, 2nd rd.

1997 - Gustavo Kuerten (No. 66), 3rd unseeded champ, d. 3 ex-champs: 5th seed Thomas Muster, 6-7 (3-7), 6-1, 6-3, 3-6, 6-4, 3rd rd.; 3rd seed Yevgeny Kafelnikov, 6-2, 5-7, 2-6, 6-0, 6-4, QF; 16th seed Sergi Bruguera, 6-3, 6-4, 6-2, F

1998 - qualifier Marat Safin (No. 118) d. Andre Agassi (No. 20), 5-7, 7-5, 6-2, 3-6, 6-2, 1st rd.; d.. 8th seed defending champ Gustavo Kuerten, 3-6, 7-6 (7-5), 3-6, 6-1, 6-4, 2nd rd. Also qualifier Mariano Zabaleta (No. 213) d. 2nd seed Petr Korda, 6-0, 6-2, 3-6, 4-6, 6-3, 1st rd.

2002 - 15th seed Guillermo Canas d. 1st seed Lleyton Hewitt, 6-7 (1-7), 7-6 (15-13), 6-4, 6-3, QF, 4:13

*Astoundingly inept and unfortunate on the clay of Roland Garros, Pete Sampras (24-13 in Paris), has suffered more defeats considered upsets than any other player, unable to win two matches only once since a SF finish in 1996: 1997 - 1st seed, beaten by No. 65 Magnus Norman, 6-2, 6-4, 2-6, 6-4, 3rd rd.; 1998 - 1st seed, beaten by No. 98 Ramon Delgado, 7-6 (8-6) 6-3, 6-4, 2nd rd.; 1999 - 2nd seed, beaten by No. 100 Andrei Medvedev, 7-5, 1-6, 6-4, 6-3, 2nd rd.; 2000 - 2nd seed, beaten by No. 17 Mark Philippoussis, 4-6, 7-5, 7-6 (7-4), 4-6, 8-6, 1st rd.; 2001 - 5th seed, beaten by No. 76 Galo Blanco, 7-6 (7-4), 6-3, 6-2, 2nd rd.; 2002 - 12th seed, beaten by No. 69 Andreas Gaudenzi, 3-6, 6-4, 6-2, 7-6 (7-3), 1st rd.

Women:

1971 - Gail Sheriff Chanfreau d. 1st seed defending champ Margaret Smith Court, 6-3, 6-4, 3rd rd.

1972 - Nathalie Fuchs d. 2d seed Virginia Wade, 7-5, 6-4, 2nd rd.

1981 - 4th seed Hana Mandlikova d. 1st seed defending champ Chris Evert, 7-5, 6-4, SF, ends Evert's 29 match win streak

1983 - Kathy Horvath (No. 33) d. 1st seed defending champ Martina Navratilova, 6-4, 0-6, 6-3, 4th rd. (Navratilova's only defeat of year, ending her 39 match win streak)

1988 - 13th seed Natasha Zvereva d. 2nd seed Martina Navratilova, 6-3, 6-7 (3-7), 7-5, SF. Also Arantxa Sanchez Vicario (No. 22) d. 3rd seed 7-time champ Chris Evert, 6-3, 7-6 (7-4). (Evert's 78th, last match in Paris)

1989 - 7th seed Arantxa Sanchez Vicario d. 1st seed defending champ Steffi Graf, 7-6 (8-6), 3-6, 7-5, F

1990 - Mercedes Paz (No. 71) d. 3rd-seed defending champ Arantxa Sanchez Vicario, 7-5, 3-6, 6-1, 2nd rd.

1994 - 12th seed Mary Pierce d. 1st seed defending champ Steffi Graf, 6-2, 6-2, QF

1997 - Nicole Arendt (No. 87) d. 4th seed Jana Novotna, 3-6, 6-4, 6-4, 3rd rd. (Arendt came in 1-3 in matches for year)

1999 - qualifier Barbara Schwartz (No. 124) d. 5th seed Venus Williams, 2-6, 7-6 (9-7), 6-3, 4th rd. (saved 3 MP, 2nd, at 5-6, 0-40)

2002 - qualifier Anika Kapros (No. 179) d. 5th seed Justine Henin, 4-6, 6-1, 6-0, 1st rd. Also Clarisa Fernanandez (No. 87) d. 4th seed Kim Clijsters, 6-4, 6-0, 3rd rd.

BEST COMEBACKS

Men:

1930 - Jean Borotra d. Yoshiro Ohta, 3-6, 3-6, 6-4, 6-1, 9-7, 3rd round (saved 2 MP, 5th, 1 at 3-5, 1 at 5-4)

1958 - Robert Haillet d. Budge Patty, 5-7, 7-5, 10-8, 4-6, 7-5, 4th rd. (from 5-0, 40-0, 5th, saved 4 MP: 3 to 1-5, 1 at 5-4)

1984 - 2nd seed Ivan Lendl d. 1st seed John McEnroe, 3-6, 2-6, 6-4, 7-5, 7-5, F (down 0-2, 3rd, 2 breaks, 4th, 2-1 and 3-2. Time 4:08, ended McEnroe's 42 match win streak)

1986 - 8th seed Henri Leconte d. Cassio Motta, 1-6, 3-6, 7-6 (12-10), 6-0, 6-0, 3rd rd. (saved 2 MP in tie-breaker).Also 12th seed Guillermo Vilas d. Guy Forget, 6-2, 3-6, 4-6, 6-1, 8-6, 4th rd. (saved 1 MP, 5th, at 4-5, Time 4:15)

1990 - Milan Srejber d. David Wheaton, 3-6, 5-7, 6-3, 7-6 (7-4), 6-3, 1st rd. (saved 2 MP, 4th, at 5-6, 4)

1991 - Aaron Krickstein (No. 49) d. Eduardo Masso (No. 109), 6-7 (3-7), 6-4, 2-6, 6-4, 7-5, 1st rd. (saved 2 MP, 5th, at 4-5). Also, 2nd seed Boris Becker d. Todd Woodbridge (No. 40), 5-7, 1-6, 6-4, 6-4, 6-4, 2nd rd. (from 2-4, 4th, held serve to 5-4, 4th, 5 deuces, 2 break points; Time 4:29). Also 6th seed Pete Sampras d. Thomas Muster (No. 64), 4-6, 4-6, 6-4, 6-1, 6-4, 1st rd. (served match game from 0-40; lost 2nd rd. to No. 76 Thierry Champion, 6-3, 6-1, 6-1)

1994 - Magnus Larsson (No. 46) d. Hendrik Dreekmann (No. 89), 3-6, 6-7 (1-7), 7-6 (7-3), 6-0, 6-1, QF (saved 6 MP, 3rd: 2 at 4-5, 4 at 5-6, 3:03). Also Ronald Agenor (No. 31) d. David Prinosil (No. 119), 6-7 (4-7), 6-7 (2-7), 6-3. 6-4, 14-12, 2nd rd (Time 5:02, 2 days; Agenor served for victory 5 times, won on 4th MP)

Women:

1926 - Simone Passemard Mathieu d. Marion Zinderstein Jessup, 2-6, 9-7, 6-0, 2nd rd. (saved 8 MP, 2nd)

1991 - 3rd seed Gabriela Sabatini d. 6th seed Jana Novotna, 5-7, 7-6 (12-10), 6-0, QF (from 2-5, 2nd, saved 2 MP in tie-breaker)

1993 - 5th seed Mary Joe Fernandez d. 3rd seed Gabriela Sabatini, 1-6, 7-6 (7-4), 10-8, QF (from 5-1, 40-30, 2nd, saved 4 MP: 1 to 2-5, 3 at 5-3, 40-15 and ad-in. Sabatini served again for victory at 7-6, 3rd, fought off 4 MP herself. Time 3:34).Also 1st seed Steffi Graf d. Fernandez, 4-6, 6-2, 6-4, F.(Mary Joe led 2-0, 3rd with 2 break points, broke to lead 4-3, 30-15)

1994 - qualifier Karin Kschwendt (No. 143) d. wild card Angelique Olivier (No. 242), 5-7, 6-4, 9-7, 1st rd. (saved 6 MP from 0-5, 3rd: 1 at 0-5, 4 at 2-5 from 0-40, 1 at 5-3; won last 9 points, Time 3:20)

1995 - Chanda Rubin (No. 53) d. 5th seed Jana Novotna, 7-6 (10-8), 4-6, 8-6, 3rd rd. (from 0-5, 0-40, 3rd, saved 9 MP: 5 to 1-5, 1 to 5-2, 3 to 5-5; also saved 2 SP in tie-breaker).Also wild card Virginia Buisson (No. 198) d. wild card Noelle van Lottum (No. 161), 6-7 (3-7), 7-5, 6-2, 1st rd. (saved 3 MP, 2nd, at 2-5, 0-40, 4:07, longest French match)

1997 - Lisa Raymond d. Maggie Maleeva, 4-6, 7-5, 6-3 (saved 3 MP, 2nd, at 5-4)

1999 - 6th seed Steffi Graf d. 1st seed Martina Hingis, 4-6, 7-5, 6-2, F (Hingis served for match, 2nd,3 points from victory at 5-4, 15-0, 15-15)

MATCH POINTS SAVED BY CHAMPION

Men:

1927 - F, Rene Lacoste d. Bill Tilden, 6-4, 4-6, 5-7, 6-3, 11-9 (saved 2 MP, 5th, at 9-8, 40-15)

1934 - F, Gottfried von Cramm, 6-4, 7-9, 3-6, 7-5, 6-3 (saved 1 MP, 4th at 5-4 with overhead smash from baseline)

1962 - QF, Rod Laver d. Marty Mulligan, 6-4, 2-6, 3-6, 10-8, 6-2 (saved 1 MP, 4th, at 4-5, 30-40 with serve-and-volley, 2nd serve)

1976 - 1st rd, 5th seed Adriano Panatta d. Pavel Hutka, 2-6, 6-2, 6-2, 0-6, 12-10 (saved 1 MP, 5th, with lunging volley)

2001 - 4th rd., 1st seed Gustavo Kuerten d. qualifier Michael Russell (No. 135), 3-6, 4-6, 7-6 (7-3), 6-3, 6-1 (saved 1 MP, 3rd, at 5-3, ad-in, with forehand winner on 25th stroke)

Women:

1946 - F, 2nd seed Margaret Osborne duPont d. 1st seed Pauline Betz, 1-6, 8-6. 7-5 (saved 2 MP, 2nd, at 5-6)

1962 - F, Margaret Smith (Court) d. Lesley Turner (Bowrey), 6-3, 3-6, 7-5 (saved 1 MP, 3rd, at 3-5)

Chapter 19   Wimbledon

Bjorn Borg, 1980
How sweet it was after besting John McEnroe for his record fifth straight Wimbledon crown.

It is considered the championships of Great Britain, is officially called the Lawn Tennis Championships but is known the world over by a single word: Wimbledon. Since its simple beginning in 1877 it has matured into an international tennis extravaganza with annual attendance surpassing 450,000, plus millions of television viewers worldwide.

A Wimbledon champion's trophy is regarded as the ultimate medal of tennis achievement. Wimbledon continues to resist overt commercialism in favor of a tight hold on its cherished tradition. Of the four major championships, only Wimbledon is still played on grass, and has been organized since its inception by the All England Lawn Tennis and Croquet Club, initially at the Worple Road ground and moving in 1922 to its present location at Church Rd.

Wimbledon began in 1877 as an amateur event for men only. Back then, the All England Club's primary sport was croquet. But as tennis began to overtake that more genteel sport in the 1870s it was decided to give tennis its own championship. The inaugural tournament comprised 22 entries in men's singles and was won by Spencer Gore in a final that was postponed 10 days by rain, completed in 48 minutes and watched by 200 people. Ladies singles was not added until 1884, attracting just 13 entries, with Maud Watson emerging as champion. That same year, men's doubles was added.

The popularity of Wimbledon grew rapidly and by the mid-1880s the tournament was attracting large crowds, due largely to its first star attractions, British twins Ernest and William Renshaw. The twins won a total of 13 Wimbledon titles in singles and doubles between 1881 and 1889, years known as the 'Renshaw Rush' because the era marked a golden growth of British tennis. William claimed six consecutive singles titles from 1881, a tournament winning streak that has never been matched. William then won a seventh singles title in 1889, a feat that remained unequaled for 111 years until Pete Sampras won his seventh singles crown in 2000.

(From 1878 to 1921 the tournament was conducted by a challenge-round system. An all-comers tournament was conducted to select a player who would square off against the defending champion. It was therefore easier to win consecutive championships because the defending champion had only to play one match to retain the title.)

Wimbledon's ascendance as an international event began around the turn of the century. Its first non-British champion was crowned in 1905, when American May Sutton defeated two-time defending champion Dorothea Douglass. Douglass regained the title in 1906 but lost to Sutton in 1907, a significant year in Wimbledon history because, when Australian Norman Brookes won the men's event, the tournament had produced overseas champions in both men's and ladies singles for the first time. Only two British men, Arthur Gore and Fred Perry, have won Wimbledon since Brookes broke the British hold on the title.

Wimbledon was suspended during World War I and when it resumed in 1919 it was graced by a fresh wave of champions. Brightest among these roaring twenties stars was a Parisian female who shocked the staid tennis community with her eccentric behavior and provocative attire. Suzanne Lenglen spurned heavy, ankle-length dresses in favor of a skirt cut just below the knee. She was also known to find strength between sets with a sip of brandy. In 1926 she caused a Wimbledon furor when, due to a misunderstanding, she arrived late on court as King George and Queen Mary waited in the Royal Box. On the court, Lenglen is remembered for sweeping both the singles and doubles (with Elizabeth Ryan) titles for five consecutive years from 1919. She swept both events again in 1925 and added three mixed doubles titles to finish her Wimbledon career with 15 titles.

But Lenglen's reign as the all-time Wimbledon queen was short lived. Beginning in 1927, American sensation Helen Wills Moody won four consecutive Wimbledon singles titles and, with a power game well suited for grass, she would win eight singles titles in 12 years, a tournament record, surpassed in 1990 by Martina Navratolova.

On the men's side, Bill Tilden won the singles title the first two times he entered Wimbledon, 1920 and 1921, and then, in his final year as an amateur, won again in 1930 at age 37. But he's also remembered for causing an uproar in 1928 when he filed press reports from Wimbledon, in violation of the amateur rules, which led to his suspension from the U.S. Championships later that year. The 1920s, however, are best remembered as the decade when France conquered Wimbledon.

Beginning with Lenglen, France had a singles champion in every year of the decade. The end of Lenglen's reign coincided with the arrival of the "Four Musketeers" —René Lacoste, Jean Borotra, Henri Cochet and Jacques Brugnon. For six consecutive years beginning in 1924, Lacoste, Borotra or Cochet won the Wimbledon singles title, with each claiming two victories. Further, with the exception of 1926, every men's final between 1924 and 1929 was contested between two of the Frenchmen.

By 1920 the tournament had outgrown its home on Worple Road and land was purchased on Church Road to build a new facility. The new grounds opened in 1922, ushering in the stadium era in tennis. Centre court was designed to hold 14,000 people and within 10 years, as the game continued to grow and Wimbledon's reputation as a major event was cemented, total attendance at the tournament had surpassed 200,000.

Wimbledon's continuing popularity in the 1930s was abetted by what is regarded as the golden era for British tennis. Coming on the heels of French domination in the 1920s, the British regained a measure of pride by claiming 11 titles beginning in the mid-30s. The resurgence was led by Fred Perry, who won three successive singles titles from 1934, and by Dorothy Round, singles winner in 1934 and 1937. But the decade closed with the Americans on top. Don Budge won singles in 1937, and Budge and Wills Moody took the titles in 1938. In 1939, Bobby Riggs and Alice Marble swept the tournament. After winning in singles and doubles, they teamed to win the mixed doubles, marking the third time in Wimbledon history anyone had won three titles in a single year.

During the Second World War, when Wimbledon was suspended, the grounds were used for fire and ambulance services, Home Guard support and a decontamination unit. Centre Court was struck by a bomb in October 1940, destroying 1,200 seats. It would not be until 1949 that the grounds were fully restored, although the tournament resumed in 1946 more or less where it had left off in 1939—with American players dominating.

On the women's side, Americans won 13 consecutive singles titles from 1946, led by the Hall of Fame trio of Louise Brough, Maureen Connolly and Althea Gibson. Brough, Wimbledon's first post-war star, appeared in 21 of the 31 finals from 1946 to 1950, winning 13 titles, including four singles crowns and, in 1950, a rare triple. By 1951, Brough had been passed by Connolly as the top U.S. player. Little Mo, as she was called, won her first Wimbledon singles title in 1952 at age 17, and defended the title in 1953 (when she won the Grand Slam) and 1954. She seemed poised to challenge Lenglen's five consecutive Wimbledon titles but her career was ended by a traffic accident in 1954. History was made in 1956 when Gibson became the first black player to win a Wimbledon title by teaming with Britain's Angela Buxton in doubles. She followed up with singles crowns in 1957 and 1958.

In men's competition, the post-war years produced an array of outstanding Wimbledon champions—including such Hall of Famers as Jack Kramer, Ted Schroeder and Tony Trabert—but no player dominated in singles competition. In fact, the singles crown was won by 10 different players from 1946 to 1955, the only time in Wimbledon history that a decade produced 10 different champions.

By the mid 1950s, advances in air travel made Wimbledon more attractive to overseas players. And no nation took greater advantage of air travel than the Australians. From 1956 to 1971, Australians won 13 of 16 titles in men's singles and four more in women's. Multiple winners included: Lew Hoad, who won back-to-back titles in 1956 and 1957; Rod Laver, who won back to back in 1961 and 1962 and again in 1968 and 1969; Roy Emerson, who won back to back in 1964 and 1965; and John Newcombe who won in 1967, and then again in 1970 and 1971. On the women's side, Margaret Smith Court became the first Australian woman to win the event, taking singles titles in 1963, 1965, 1970, and Yvonne Goolagong won twice (1971 and 1980). Laver's story was particularly remarkable. He turned pro in 1962 and, after Wimbledon opened its doors to professionals in 1968, he returned to Centre Court to win two more titles. Starting in 1959, Laver reached the Wimbledon final in six consecutive tournaments he entered, matching a tournament record, and by winning in four consecutive attempts he became the first man since World War I to win four straight. He then made it to the fourth round in 1970 to set a Wimbledon record of 31 consecutive match victories.

An irony of Wimbledon's history is that a tournament so nourished by tradition would become the first to welcome professionals. By the 1950s, many so-called amateur tennis players (or "shamateurs", as they were known) were making handsome livings from under-the-table payments. Wimbledon officials, weary of this apparent hypocrisy, first proposed in 1959 that its doors be open to all players. But the International Tennis Federation and various tennis associations refused to budge. It wasn't until 1967 that the governing bodies relented and, in 1968 at Wimbledon,

the second "open" major championship was held following the French.

The Open Era brought even greater prosperity to Wimbledon and, indeed, to all of tennis. Fans welcomed the return of professionals such as Laver, Pancho Gonzales, who last played at Wimbledon in 1949, Pancho Segura, Lew Hoad and Ken Rosewall. In 1969, they were delighted that Britain's Ann Haydon Jones defeated three-time defending champion Billie Jean King in the women's singles final. Billie Jean regained her title in 1972, successfully defended in 1973 (when she also won the doubles and mixed doubles titles) and won her sixth singles crown in 1975. She had arrived in Wimbledon as 17-year-old Billie Jean Moffit and ended a 23-year Wimbledon career with a record 20 titles (six singles, 10 doubles, four mixed), playing a then record 265 matches to secure a place in Wimbledon lore.

The one blemish of those early Open-era years came in 1973 when the tournament was boycotted by 79 members of the Association of Tennis Professionals. The men walked when Wimbledon decided to honor a suspension to Nikki Pilic handed down by the Yugoslavian Lawn Tennis Association over a Davis Cup dispute between Pilic and his federation. Thirteen of the original 16 men's seeds withdrew, but the action was not joined by non-ATP members Jimmy Connors and teen sensation Bjorn Borg, plus top seed Ilie Nastase (who claimed he was forced by the Romanian Federation to compete). After the ATP failed in an attempt to obtain an injunction to force Pilic's entry into the tournament, the event proceeded without incident and was won by Czechoslovak Jan Kodes. In addition to the walkout, 1973 is memorable because it introduced the world to "Borgomania." Borg was besieged by adoring young women wherever he went.

As Wimbledon prepared for its centenary, two players destined to join the ranks of the greatest champions in the tournament history were beginning to make their marks. Navratilova won her first Wimbledon title (mixed doubles) in 1975, while Borg won his first (men's singles) in 1976 without loss of a set to become the youngest men's champion (20 years, one month) in the modern era (although Boris Becker lowered the record to 17 years, eight months in 1985).

Borg arrived at Wimbledon with a baseline game that seemed better suited for the slower courts of the French Open. But he would go on to win five consecutive singles titles before losing in to John McEnroe in the 1981 final. Along the way he won 41 consecutive matches to smash

Laver's men's Wimbledon record of 31. The fifth title, won in a 1-6, 7-5, 6-3, 6-7 (16-18), 8-6 final against McEnroe, is recognized as one of the greatest matches in Wimbledon history.

Navratilova would win a total of 19 titles over 20 years at Wimbledon, including nine singles titles to eclipse the record set in 1938 by Helen Wills Moody. She won six consecutive singles titles from 1982, a tournament record, during which she won 47 consecutive matches. She exited Wimbledon after 22 years holding records for consecutive finals (nine), matches (289), single wins (119), double wins (85), overall wins (249). Navratilova's success during those years came largely at the expense of a darling of the Wimbledon crowd, Chris Evert. Prior to Navratilova's explosion onto the scene, Evert had won three singles titles, but lost all five times she faced Navratilova in the final between 1978 and 1985.

Borg retired from tennis at age 25, leaving the Wimbledon stage to his fiercest rival, McEnroe. McEnroe made his Wimbledon debut as an 18-year-old amateur and stunned the tennis world by posting the then best-ever result by a Wimbledon qualifier, losing to Connors in the semi-final. After losing to Borg in the thrilling 1980 final, McEnroe won Wimbledon in 1981, lost to Connors in the 1982 final (Connors' second singles title at Wimbledon) and rebounded to win in 1983 and 1984. His straight-set demolition of Connors in 1984 is regarded as a technical masterpiece. McEnroe also added four doubles titles with Peter Fleming. But McEnroe will be as much remembered at Wimbledon for his fiery outbursts as his superb shotmaking. The press called him Superbrat or Supermac, depending on his behavior. He was booed in 1980 as he entered Centre Court for the final against Borg, which put him in a class with Connors, who was booed in 1977 because he boycotted a parade of former champions to celebrate Wimbledon's centenary.

If McEnroe's Wimbledon initiation was considered amazing, then the debut of Becker was nothing short of phenomenal. The hard-hitting German burst upon the scene in 1985 as a 17-year-old unknown and proceeded to the final, where he upset Kevin Curren to become Wimbledon's first unseeded champion, its youngest champion and Germany's first champion. Becker returned at 18 to defend his title, defeating the world's top-ranked player, Ivan Lendl, in the final. Over a seven-year span, Becker appeared in six Wimbledon finals, winning three.

Overnight Becker had become the most successful player in German tennis history but, almost as quickly, was eclipsed by a female compatriot whose speed and power made her a natural at Wimbledon. Steffi Graf is regarded among the greatest Wimbledon champions of all time. After losing to Navratilova in the 1987 final, Graf, on her way to a Grand Slam, won her first Wimbeldon by defeating Navratilova in the 1988 final. Between them, Graf and Navratilova would win an amazing 16 of 19 Wimbledon singles titles between 1978 and 1996. Graf's contribution was seven titles over the nine years, including a memorable 1993 victory over Jana Novotna that left the Czechoslovak crying on the shoulder of the Duchess of Kent. Coinciding with Graf's final title in 1996, Martina Hingas of Switzerland made history by winning the doubles crown (with Helena Sukova) to become the youngest ever Wimbledon champion at 15 years, 282 days. Hingas returned in 1987 to become the youngest singles champion since 15-year-old Lottie Dod in 1887.

On the men's side, the 1990s belonged to Pete Sampras. After failing to get past the second round in his first three appearances at Wimbledon, Sampras' outstanding serve-and-volley game came to the fore in 1993. After defeating Andre Agassi and Becker in earlier rounds, Sampras beat the then world number one, Jim Courier in the final for his first title. He successfully defended in 1994 and 1995 and, beginning in 1997 won four more singles crowns in succession to give him seven career Wimbledon singles titles, tying him atop the all-time men's list with Willie Renshaw. Sampras' attempt in 2001 at a record eighth title was snapped by a fourth-round loss to Roger Federer of Switzerland, only his second loss at Wimbledon in nine years. The event was won that year by unseeded Goran Ivanisevic, who became the first wildcard to win the men's singles.

As the 20th century came to a close, the Williams sisters, Venus and Serena, emerged as the new queens of Wimbledon. Venus was first to arrive, winning consecutive championships in 2000 and 2001, becoming the first African American since Althea Gibson in 1958 to win the women's title. The 2001 final had pitted Venus against Serena in the second all-sister final in Wimbledon history. The sisters met again in the 2002 final, but this time Serena, younger by 15 months, won to give the sisters a three-years singles winning streak.

Wimbledon – Champions

Year	Men's Singles	Women's Singles	Men's Doubles	Women's Doubles	Mixed Doubles
2002	Lleyton Hewitt	Serena Williams	Todd Woodbridge / Jonas Bjorkman	Venus Williams / Serena Williams	Elena Likhovtseva / Mahesh Bhupathi
2001	Goran Ivanisevic	Venus Williams	Donald Johnson / Jared Palmer	Lisa Raymond / Rennae Stubbs	Daniela Hantuchova / Leos Friedl
2000	Pete Sampras	Venus Williams	Todd Woodbridge / Mark Woodforde	Venus Williams / Serena Williams	Kimberly Po / Donald Johnson
1999	Pete Sampras	Lindsay Davenport	Mahesh Bhupathi / Leander Paes	Lindsay Davenport / Corina Morariu	Lisa Raymond / Leander Paes
1998	Pete Sampras	Jana Novotna	Jacco Eltingh / Paul Haarhuis	Martina Hingis / Jana Novotna	Serena Williams / Max Mirnyi
1997	Pete Sampras	Martina Hingis	Todd Woodbridge / Mark Woodforde	Gigi Fernandez / Natasha Zvereva	Helena Sukova / Cyril Suk
1996	Richard Krajicek	Steffi Graf	Todd Woodbridge / Mark Woodforde	Martina Hingis / Helena Sukova	Helena Sukova / Cyril Suk
1995	Pete Sampras	Steffi Graf	Todd Woodbridge / Mark Woodforde	Jana Novotna / Arantxa Sanchez Vicario	Martina Navratilova / Jonathan Stark
1994	Pete Sampras	Conchita Martinez	Todd Woodbridge / Mark Woodforde	Gigi Fernandez / Natalia Zvereva	Helena Sukova / Todd Woodbridge
1993	Pete Sampras	Steffi Graf	Todd Woodbridge / Mark Woodforde	Gigi Fernandez / Natalia Zvereva	Martina Navratilova / Mark Woodforde
1992	Andre Agassi	Steffi Graf	John McEnroe / Michael Stich	Gigi Fernandez / Natalia Zvereva	Larisa Savchenko Neiland / Cyril Suk
1991	Michael Stich	Steffi Graf	John Fitzgerald / Anders Jarryd	Larisa Savchenko / Natalia Zvereva	Elizabeth Sayers Smylie / John Fitzgerald
1990	Stefan Edberg	Martina Navratilova	Rick Leach / Jim Pugh	Jana Novotna / Helena Sukova	Zina Garrison / Rick Leach
1989	Boris Becker	Steffi Graf	John Fitzgerald / Anders Jarryd	Jana Novotna / Helena Sukova	Jana Novotna / Jim Pugh
1988	Stefan Edberg	Steffi Graf	Ken Flach / Robert Seguso	Steffi Graf / Gabriela Sabatini	Zina Garrison / Sherwood Stewart
1987	Pat Cash	Martina Navratilova	Ken Flach / Robert Seguso	Claudia Kohde Kilsch / Helena Sukova	Jo Durie / Jeremy Bates
1986	Boris Becker	Martina Navratilova	Joakim Nystrom / Mats Wilander	Martina Navratilova / Pam Shriver	Kathy Jordan / Ken Flach
1985	Boris Becker	Martina Navratilova	Heinz Gunthardt / Balazs Taroczy	Kathy Jordan / Elizabeth Sayers Smylie	Martina Navratilova / Paul McNamee
1984	John McEnroe	Martina Navratilova	Peter Fleming / John McEnroe	Martina Navratilova / Pam Shriver	Wendy Turnbull / John Lloyd
1983	John McEnroe	Martina Navratilova	Peter Fleming / John McEnroe	Martina Navratilova / Pam Shriver	Wendy Turnbull / John Lloyd
1982	Jimmy Connors	Martina Navratilova	Peter McNamara / Paul McNamee	Martina Navratilova / Pam Shriver	Anne Smith / Kevin Curren
1981	John McEnroe	Chris Evert Lloyd	Peter Fleming / John McEnroe	Martina Navratilova / Pam Shriver	Betty Stove / Frew McMillan
1980	Bjorn Borg	E. Goolagong Cawley	Peter McNamara / Paul McNamee	Kathy Jordan / Anne Smith	Tracy Austin / John Austin
1979	Bjorn Borg	Martina Navratilova	Peter Fleming / John McEnroe	Billie Jean King / Martina Navratilova	Greer Stevens / Bob Hewitt
1978	Bjorn Borg	Martina Navratilova	Bob Hewitt / Frew McMillan	Kerry Melville Reid / Wendy Turnbull	Betty Stove / Frew McMillan
1977	Bjorn Borg	Virginia Wade	Geoff Masters / Ross Case	Helen Gourlay Cawley / JoAnne Russell	Greer Stevens / Bob Hewitt
1976	Bjorn Borg	Chris Evert	Brian Gottfried / Raul Ramirez	Chris Evert / Martina Navratilova	Françoise Durr / Tony Roche
1975	Arthur Ashe	Billie Jean King	Vitas Gerulaitis / Alex Mayer	Ann Kiyomura / Kazuko Sawamatsu	Margaret Smith Court / Marty Riessen
1974	Jimmy Connors	Chris Evert	John Newcombe / Tony Roche	Evonne Goolagong / Peggy Michel	Billie Jean Moffitt King / Owen Davidson
1973	Jan Kodes	Billie Jean King	Jimmy Connors / Ilie Nastase	Rosie Casals / Billie Jean King	Billie Jean Moffitt King / Owen Davidson
1972	Stan Smith	Billie Jean King	Bob Hewitt / Frew McMillan	Billie Jean King / Betty Stove	Rosie Casals / Ilie Nastase
1971	John Newcombe	Evonne Goolagong	Roy Emerson / Rod Laver	Rosie Casals / Billie Jean King	Billie Jean Moffitt King / Owen Davidson
1970	John Newcombe	Margaret Smith Court	John Newcombe / Tony Roche	Rosie Casals / Billie Jean King	Rosie Casals / Ilie Nastase
1969	Rod Laver	Ann Haydon Jones	John Newcombe / Tony Roche	Margaret Smith Court / Judy Tegart	Ann Haydon Jones / Fred Stolle
1968	Rod Laver	Billie Jean King	John Newcombe / Tony Roche	Rosie Casals / Billie Jean King	Margaret Smith Court / Ken Fletcher
1967	John Newcombe	Billie Jean King	Bob Hewitt / Frew McMillan	Rosie Casals / Billie Jean King	Billie Jean Moffitt King / Owen Davidson
1966	Manolo Santana	Billie Jean King	Ken Fletcher / John Newcombe	Maria Bueno / Nancy Richey	Margaret Smith / Ken Fletcher
1965	Roy Emerson	Margaret Smith	John Newcombe / Tony Roche	Maria Bueno / Billie Jean Moffitt	Margaret Smith / Ken Fletcher
1964	Roy Emerson	Maria Bueno	Bob Hewitt / Fred Stolle	Margaret Smith / Lesley Turner	Lesley Turner / Fred Stolle
1963	Chuck McKinley	Margaret Smith	Rafael Osuna / Antonio Palafox	Maria Bueno / Darlene Hard	Margaret Smith / Ken Fletcher
1962	Rod Laver	Karen Hantze Susman	Bob Hewitt / Fred Stolle	Billie Jean Moffitt / Karen Hantze Susman	Margaret Osborne duPont / Neale Fraser
1961	Rod Laver	Angela Mortimer	Roy Emerson / Neale Fraser	Karen Hantze / Billie Jean Moffitt	Lesley Turner / Fred Stolle
1960	Neale Fraser	Maria Bueno	Rafael Osuna / Dennis Ralston	Maria Bueno / Darlene Hard	Darlene Hard / Rod Laver
1959	Alejandro Olmedo	Maria Bueno	Roy Emerson / Neale Faser	Jeanne Arth / Darlene Hard	Darlene Hard / Rod Laver
1958	Ashley Cooper	Althea Gibson	Sven Davidson / Ulf Schmidt	Maria Bueno / Althea Gibson	Lorraine Coghlan / Bob Howe
1957	Lew Hoad	Althea Gibson	Budge Patty / Gardnar Mulloy	Althea Gibson / Darlene Hard	Darlene Hard / Merv Rose
1956	Lew Hoad	Shirley Fry	Lew Hoad / Ken Rosewall	Angela Buxton / Althea Gibson	Shirley Fry / Vic Seixas
1955	Tony Trabert	Louise Brough	Rex Hartwig / Lew Hoad	Angela Mortimer / Anne Shilcock	Doris Hart / Vic Seixas
1954	Jaroslav Drobny	Maureen Connolly	Rex Hartwig / Merv Rose	Louise Brough / Margaret Osborne duPont	Doris Hart / Vic Seixas
1953	Vic Seixas	Maureen Connolly	Lew Hoad / Ken Rosewall	Shirley Fry / Doris Hart	Doris Hart / Vic Seixas
1952	Frank Sedgman	Maureen Connolly	Ken McGregor / Frank Sedgman	Shirley Fry / Doris Hart	Doris Hart / Frank Sedgman

Year	Men's Singles	Women's Singles	Men's Doubles	Women's Doubles	Mixed Doubles
1951	Dick Savitt	Doris Hart	Ken McGregor / Frank Sedgman	Shirley Fry / Doris Hart	Doris Hart / Frank Sedgman
1950	Budge Patty	Louise Brough	John Bromwich / Adrian Quist	Louise Brough / Margaret Osborne duPont	Louise Brough / Eric Sturgess
1949	Ted Schroeder	Louise Brough	Pancho Gonzalez / Frank Parker	Louise Brough / Margaret Osborne duPont	Sheila Piercey Summers / Eric Sturgess
1948	Bob Falkenburg	Louise Brough	John Bromwich / Frank Sedgman	Louise Brough / Margaret Osborne duPont	Louise Brough / John Bromwich
1947	Jack Kramer	Margaret Osborne	Bob Falkenburg / Jack Kramer	Doris Hart / Pat Canning Todd	Louise Brough / John Bromwich
1946	Yvon Petra	Pauline Betz	Tom Brown / Jack Kramer	Louise Brough / Margaret Osborne	Louise Brough / Tom Brown
1940-45		Not held – WW II			
1939	Bobby Riggs	Alice Marble	Elwood Cooke / Bobby Riggs	Sarah Palfrey Fabyan / Alice Marble	Alice Marble / Bobby Riggs
1938	Don Budge	Helen Wills Moody	Don Budge / Gene Mako	Sarah Palfrey Fabyan / Alice Marble	Alice Marble / Don Budge
1937	Don Budge	Dorothy Round	Don Budge / Gene Mako	Simone Passemard Mathieu / Billie Yorke	Alice Marble / Don Budge
1936	Fred Perry	Helen Jacobs	Pat Hughes / Charles Tuckey	Freda James / Kay Stammers	Dorothy Round / Fred Perry
1935	Fred Perry	Helen Wills Moody	Jack Crawford / Adrian Quist	Freda James / Kay Stammers	Dorothy Round / Fred Perry
1934	Fred Perry	Dorothy Round	George Lott / Lester Stoefen	Simone Passemard Mathieu / Elizabeth Ryan	Dorothy Round / Ryuki Miki
1933	Jack Crawford	Helen Wills Moody	Jean Borotra / Jacques Brugnon	Simone Passemard Mathieu / Elizabeth Ryan	Hilde Krahwinkel / Gottfried von Cramm
1932	Ellsworth Vines	Helen Wills Moody	Jean Borotra / Jacques Brugnon	Doris Metaxa / Josane Sigart	Elizabeth Ryan / Enrique Maier
1931	Sidney Wood	Cilly Aussem	George Lott / John Van Ryn	Dorothy Shepherd Barron / Phyllis Mudford	Anna McCune Harper / George Lott
1930	Bill Tilden	Helen Wills Moody	Wilmer Allison / John Van Ryn	Helen Wills Moody / Elizabeth Ryan	Elizabeth Ryan / Jack Crawford
1929	Henri Cochet	Helen Wills	Wilmer Allison / John Van Ryn	Peggy Saunders Michell / Phoebe Holcroft Watson	Helen Wills / Frank Hunter
1928	René Lacoste	Helen Wills	Jacques Brugnon / Henri Cochet	Peggy Saunders / Phoebe Holcroft Watson	Elizabeth Ryan / Pat Spence
1927	Henri Cochet	Helen Wills	Frank Hunter / Bill Tilden	Helen Wills / Elizabeth Ryan	Elizabeth Ryan / Frank Hunter
1926	Jean Borotra	Kitty McKane Godfree	Jacques Brugnon / Henri Cochet	Mary K. Browne / Elizabeth Ryan	Kitty McKane Godfree / Leslie Godfree
1925	René Lacoste	Suzanne Lenglen	Jean Borotra / René Lacoste	Suzanne Lenglen / Elizabeth Ryan	Suzanne Lenglen / Jean Borotra
1924	Jean Borotra	Kitty McKane	Frank Hunter / Vinnie Richards	Hazel Hotchkiss Wightman / Helen Wills	Kitty McKane / Brian Gilbert
1923	Bill Johnston	Suzanne Lenglen	Leslie Godfree / Randolph Lycett	Suzanne Lenglen / Elizabeth Ryan	Elizabeth Ryan / Randolph Lycett
1922	Gerald Patterson	Suzanne Lenglen	James Anderson / Randolph Lycett	Suzanne Lenglen / Elizabeth Ryan	Suzanne Lenglen / Pat O'Hara Wood
1921	Bill Tilden	Suzanne Lenglen	Randolph Lycett / Max Woosnam	Suzanne Lenglen / Elizabeth Ryan	Elizabeth Ryan / Randolph Lycett
1920	Bill Tilden	Suzanne Lenglen	Dick Williams / Chuck Garland	Suzanne Lenglen / Elizabeth Ryan	Suzanne Lenglen / Gerald Patterson
1919	Gerald Patterson	Suzanne Lenglen	Ronald Thomas / Pat O'Hara Wood	Suzanne Lenglen / Elizabeth Ryan	Elizabeth Ryan / Randolph Lycett
1915-18		Not held – WW I			
1914	Norman Brookes	D. Douglass Chambers	Norman Brookes / Tony Wilding	Agnes Morton / Elizabeth Ryan	Ethel Thomson Larcombe / Jim Parke
1913	Tony Wilding	D. Douglass Chambers	Herbert Roper Barrett / Charles Dixon	Winifred Slocock McNair / Dora Boothby	Agnes Daniell Tuckey / Hope Crisp
1912	Tony Wilding	E. Thomson Larcombe	Herbert Roper Barrett / Charles Dixon		
1911	Tony Wilding	D. Douglass Chambers	Andre Gobert / Max Decugis		
1910	Tony Wilding	D. Douglass Chambers	Tony Wilding / Josiah Ritchie		
1909	Arthur Gore	Dora Boothby	Arthur Gore / Herbert Roper Barrett		
1908	Arthur Gore	Charlotte Cooper Sterry	Tony Wilding / Josiah Ritchie		
1907	Norman Brookes	May Sutton	Norman Brookes / Tony Wilding		
1906	Laurie Doherty	Dorothea Douglass	Sidney H. Smith / Frank Riseley		
1905	Laurie Doherty	May Sutton	Reggie Doherty / Laurie Doherty		
1904	Laurie Doherty	Dorothea Douglass	Reggie Doherty / Laurie Doherty		
1903	Laurie Doherty	Dorothea Douglass	Reggie Doherty / Laurie Doherty		
1902	Laurie Doherty	Muriel Robb	Sidney H. Smith / Frank Riseley		
1901	Arthur Gore	Charlotte Cooper Sterry	Reggie Doherty / Laurie Doherty		
1900	Reggie Doherty	Blanche Bingley Hillyard	Reggie Doherty / Laurie Doherty		
1899	Reggie Doherty	Blanche Bingley Hillyard	Reggie Doherty / Laurie Doherty		
1898	Reggie Doherty	Charlotte Cooper	Reggie Doherty / Laurie Doherty		
1897	Reggie Doherty	Blanche Bingley Hillyard	Reggie Doherty / Laurie Doherty		
1896	Harold Mahony	Charlotte Cooper	Wilfred Baddeley / Herbert Baddeley		
1895	Wilfred Baddeley	Charlotte Cooper	Wilfred Baddeley / Herbert Baddeley		
1894	Joshua Pim	Blanche Bingley Hillyard	Wilfred Baddeley / Herbert Baddeley		
1893	Joshua Pim	Charlotte Dod	Joshua Pim / Frank Stoker		

Year	Men's Singles	Women's Singles	Men's Doubles	Women's Doubles	Mixed Doubles
1892	Wilfred Baddeley	Charlotte Dod	Ernest Lewis / Harry Barlow		
1891	Wilfred Baddeley	Charlotte Dod	Wilfred Baddeley / Herbert Baddeley		
1890	Ghost Hamilton	Helena Rice	Joshua Pim / Frank Stoker		
1889	Willie Renshaw	Blanche Bingley Hillyard	Willie Renshaw / Ernest Renshaw		
1888	Ernest Renshaw	Charlotte Dod	Willie Renshaw / Ernest Renshaw		
1887	Herbert Lawford	Charlotte Dod	Herbert Wilberforce / Patrick Bowes Lyon		
1886	Willie Renshaw	Blanche Bingley	Willie Renshaw / Ernest Renshaw		
1885	Willie Renshaw	Maud Watson	Willie Renshaw / Ernest Renshaw		
1884	Willie Renshaw	Maud Watson	Willie Renshaw / Ernest Renshaw		
1883	Willie Renshaw				
1882	Willie Renshaw				
1881	Willie Renshaw				
1880	John Hartley				
1879	John Hartley				
1878	Frank Hadow				
1877	Spencer Gore				

Wimbledon – Tournament Results

(**Legend: F:** Final; **S:** Semi-final; **Q:** Quarter-final; **Ch:** Challenge Round; **Set:** S1, S2, S3, S4, S5)

Men's Singles

1877

Rd	Winner	Defeated	S1	S2	S3	S4	S5
F	**Spencer Gore**	**William Marshall**	**6-1**	**6-2**	**6-4**		
S	Spencer Gore	C.G. Heathcote	6-2	6-5	6-2		
S	William Marshall		(bye)				
Q	Spencer Gore	F.N. Langham	6-3	6-2	5-6	6-1	
Q	C.G. Heathcote	Julian Marshall	6-3	6-3	6-5		
Q	William Marshall	L. Robert Erskine	6-5	5-6	6-4	6-1	

1878

Rd	Winner	Defeated	S1	S2	S3	S4	S5
Ch	**Frank Hadow**	**Spencer Gore**	**7-5**	**6-1**	**9-7**		
F	Frank Hadow	L. Robert Erskine	6-4	6-4	6-4		
S	L. Robert Erskine	Herbert Lawford	6-3	6-1	6-3		
S	Frank Hadow		(bye)				
Q	L. Robert Erskine	C.G. Hamilton	6-4	3-6	6-1	3-6	6-5
Q	Herbert Lawford		(bye)				
Q	Frank Hadow	Arthur T. Myers	6-0	6-4	6-3		

1879

Rd	Winner	Defeated	S1	S2	S3	S4	S5
Ch	**John Hartley**	**Frank Hadow**			(walkover)		
F	John Hartley	Vere "St. Leger" Goold	6-2	6-4	6-2		
S	John Hartley	C.F. Parr	2-6	6-0	6-1	6-1	
S	Vere "St. Leger" Goold		(bye)				
Q	John Hartley	C.G. Heathcote	6-4	6-3	6-3		
Q	C.F. Parr	C.D. Barry	6-2	6-5	6-4		
Q	Vere "St. Leger" Goold	G.E. Tabor	6-2	6-5	5-6	6-3	

1880

Rd	Winner	Defeated	S1	S2	S3	S4	S5
Ch	**John Hartley**	**Herbert Lawford**	**6-3**	**6-2**	**2-6**	**6-3**	
F	Herbert Lawford	Otway E. Woodhouse	6-5	6-4	6-0		
S	Otway E. Woodhouse	Geo. A. Montgomerie	6-4	2-6	6-3	5-6	6-1
S	Herbert Lawford	G.M. Butterworth	6-2	6-3	6-3		
Q	Otway E. Woodhouse	Ernest Renshaw	6-3	6-3	3-6	6-0	
Q	Geo. A. Montgomerie	H.C. Jenkins	6-3	5-6	6-2	2-6	6-3
Q	Herbert Lawford	W.H. 'd'Esterre'	6-0	6-3	6-1		
Q	G.M. Butterworth	R.R. Farrer	1-6	6-1	6-4	6-5	

1881

Rd	Winner	Defeated	S1	S2	S3	S4	S5
Ch	**Willie Renshaw**	**John Hartley**	**6-0**	**6-1**	**6-1**		
F	Willie Renshaw	Richard T. Richardson	6-4	6-2	6-3		
S	Willie Renshaw	Herbert Lawford	1-6	6-3	6-2	5-6	6-3
S	Richard T. Richardson		(bye)				
Q	Willie Renshaw	Otway E. Woodhouse	4-6	6-4	6-0	6-3	
Q	Herbert Lawford	G.S. Murray-Hill	6-1	6-1	6-0		
Q	Richard T. Richardson	W.H. Darby	6-0	6-4	6-1		

1882

Rd	Winner	Defeated	S1	S2	S3	S4	S5
Ch	**Willie Renshaw**	**Ernest Renshaw**	**6-1**	**2-6**	**4-6**	**6-2**	**6-2**
F	Ernest Renshaw	Richard T. Richardson	6-5	6-3	2-6	6-3	
S	Ernest Renshaw	Herbert Lawford	6-4	4-6	6-2	3-6	6-0
S	Richard T. Richardson	Frank R. Benson	6-1	6-2	6-1		
Q	Ernest Renshaw	Humphrey Berkeley	6-5	6-1	6-4		
Q	Herbert Lawford	Herbert Wilberforce	6-2	6-5	6-5		
Q	Richard T. Richardson	Otway E. Woodhouse	6-1	6-0	6-2		
Q	Frank R. Benson		(bye)				

1883

Rd	Winner	Defeated	S1	S2	S3	S4	S5
Ch	**Willie Renshaw**	**Ernest Renshaw**	**2-6**	**6-3**	**6-3**	**4-6**	**6-3**
F	Ernest Renshaw	Donald Stewart	0-6	6-3	6-0	6-2	
S	Donald Stewart	William C. Taylor	6-0	6-1	6-3		
S	Ernest Renshaw		(bye)				
Q	Donald Stewart	Herbert Wilberforce	6-5	3-6	5-6	6-5	6-4
Q	William C. Taylor	M. Constable	6-3	6-5	5-6	4-6	6-3
Q	Ernest Renshaw	Charles W. Grinstead	6-4	6-3	6-3		

1884

Rd	Winner	Defeated	S1	S2	S3	S4	S5
Ch	**Willie Renshaw**	**Herbert Lawford**	**6-0**	**6-4**	**9-7**		
F	Herbert Lawford	Charles W. Grinstead	7-5	2-6	6-2	9-7	
S	Charles W. Grinstead	Ernest Renshaw	2-6	6-4	6-2	6-3	
S	Herbert Lawford	Herbert Chipp	7-5	6-4	6-4		
Q	Ernest Renshaw	Wilfred Milne	6-3	6-3	7-5		
Q	Charles W. Grinstead	Ernest Browne de Sylly	5-7	4-6	7-5	6-4	6-1
Q	Herbert Chipp	William C. Taylor	10-8	6-1	6-4		
Q	Herbert Lawford		(bye)				

1885

Rd	Winner	Defeated	S1	S2	S3	S4	S5
Ch	**Willie Renshaw**	**Herbert Lawford**	**7-5**	**6-2**	**4-6**	**7-5**	
F	Herbert Lawford	Ernest Renshaw	5-7	6-1	0-6	6-2	6-4
S	Ernest Renshaw	Ernest Browne de Sylly	6-4	8-6	2-6	5-7	6-4
S	Herbert Lawford	James Dwight	6-2	6-2	6-3		
Q	Ernest Renshaw	Herbert Chipp	6-4	7-5			
Q	Ernest Browne de Sylly	M.G. McNamara	6-1	7-5	6-2		
Q	James Dwight	Arthur J. Stanley	6-3	6-3	6-4		
Q	Herbert Lawford	Patrick Bowes Lyon	6-2	7-5	6-3		

1886

Rd	Winner	Defeated	S1	S2	S3	S4	S5
Ch	**Willie Renshaw**	**Herbert Lawford**	**6-0**	**5-7**	**6-3**	**6-4**	
F	Herbert Lawford	Ernest Lewis	6-2	6-3	2-6	4-6	6-4
S	Herbert Lawford	T.R. Garvey	6-3	6-2	6-0		
S	Ernest Lewis	Herbert Wilberforce	3-6	6-2	1-6	6-1	6-3
Q	Herbert Lawford	Ghost Hamilton	8-6	6-1	8-6		
Q	T.R. Garvey	William C. Taylor	8-6	6-4	2-6	6-3	
Q	Ernest Lewis	Ernest Renshaw	4-6	5-7	6-4	6-1	6-0
Q	Herbert Wilberforce	C.H.A. Ross	3-6	2-6	6-4	6-2	6-4

1887

Rd	Winner	Defeated	S1	S2	S3	S4	S5
Ch	**Herbert Lawford**	**Willie Renshaw**	(walk-over)				
F	Herbert Lawford	Ernest Renshaw	1-6	6-3	3-6	6-4	6-4
S	Herbert Lawford	Harry Grove	4-6	6-3	7-5	7-5	
S	Ernest Renshaw	Charles Lacy Sweet			(walkover)		
Q	Harry Grove	Patrick Bowes Lyon	6-3	6-2	10-8		
Q	Herbert Lawford	Oswald Milne	7-5	6-0	6-3		
Q	Ernest Renshaw	Ernest Lewis	7-5	6-2	6-4		
Q	Charles Lacy Sweet	Wilfred Milne	6-3	6-1	6-3		

1888

Rd	Winner	Defeated	S1	S2	S3	S4	S5
Ch	**Ernest Renshaw**	**Herbert Lawford**	**6-3**	**7-5**	**6-0**		
F	Ernest Renshaw	Ernest Lewis	7-9	6-1	8-6	6-4	
S	Ernest Renshaw	Ghost Hamilton	7-5	7-5	5-7	6-3	
S	Ernest Lewis	William C. Taylor	9-7	6-4	6-4		
Q	Ernest Renshaw	Herbert Wilberforce	4-6	6-3	7-5	4-6	6-0
Q	Ghost Hamilton	Willie Renshaw	5-7	7-5	6-4	6-2	
Q	Ernest Lewis	Harry S. Scrivener	7-5	6-3	6-1		
Q	William C. Taylor	F.L. Rawson	6-4	6-0	4-6	4-6	6-1

Rd	Winner	Defeated	S1	S2	S3	S4	S5
1889							
Ch	**Willie Renshaw**	**Ernest Renshaw**	6-4	6-1	3-6	6-0	
F	Willie Renshaw	Harry Barlow	3-6	5-7	8-6	10-8	8-6
S	Harry Barlow	Ghost Hamilton	3-6	6-3	2-6	6-3	6-3
S	Willie Renshaw	Herbert Lawford	7-5	5-7	6-3	6-2	
Q	Ghost Hamilton	Ernest Lewis	4-6	7-5	6-3	5-7	6-4
Q	Harry Barlow	George Hillyard	7-5	6-2	6-4		
Q	Willie Renshaw	Manliffe Goodbody	7-5	6-4	6-4		
Q	Herbert Lawford	A.G. Ziffo	6-2	6-2	6-0		
1890							
Ch	**Ghost Hamilton**	**Willie Renshaw**	6-8	6-2	3-6	6-1	6-1
F	Ghost Hamilton	Harry Barlow	2-6	6-4	6-4	4-6	7-5
S	Ghost Hamilton	Joshua Pim	0-6	6-4	6-4	6-2	
S	Harry Barlow	Ernest Lewis	7-5	6-4	4-6	7-5	
Q	Joshua Pim	Harry S. Scrivener	6-3	12-10	6-0		
Q	Ghost Hamilton	Wilfred Baddeley	6-3	6-0	6-1		
Q	Ernest Lewis	Dean Miller	6-3	6-1	6-1		
Q	Harry Barlow	D.Grainger Chaytor	8-10	6-4	2-6	6-1	6-1
1891							
Ch	**Wilfred Baddeley**	**Ghost Hamilton**			(walkover)		
F	Wilfred Baddeley	Joshua Pim	6-4	1-6	7-5	6-0	
S	Wilfred Baddeley	Ernest Renshaw	6-0	6-1	6-1		
S	Joshua Pim	Harold Mahony	6-4	6-0	6-2		
Q	Ernest Renshaw	Harry Grove	6-3	7-5	6-2		
Q	Wilfred Baddeley	Edward J. Avory	6-0	6-1	4-6	6-2	
Q	Harold Mahony	H.A.B. Chapman	6-2	6-0	6-1		
Q	Joshua Pim	Harry Barlow	5-7	0-6	6-2	6-3	7-5
1892							
Ch	**Wilfred Baddeley**	**Joshua Pim**	4-6	6-3	6-3	6-2	
F	Joshua Pim	Ernest Lewis	2-6	5-7	9-7	6-3	6-2
S	Ernest Lewis	H.A.B. Chapman	2-6	6-3	6-1	6-2	
S	Joshua Pim	Harold Mahony	6-1	12-10	2-6	6-2	
Q	Ernest Lewis	Wilberforce Eaves	7-5	6-2	6-2		
Q	H.A.B. Chapman	Reginald Gamble	6-4	6-0	6-1		
Q	Harold Mahony	Arthur Gore	4-6	6-2	6-3	6-4	
Q	Joshua Pim	Harry Barlow	3-6	9-7	6-2	7-5	
1893							
Ch	**Joshua Pim**	**Wilfred Baddeley**	3-6	6-1	6-3	6-2	
F	Joshua Pim	Harold Mahony	9-7	6-3	6-0		
S	Joshua Pim	Harry Barlow	9-7	6-2	6-3		
S	Harold Mahony	Archdale Palmer	3-6	6-3	6-3	6-1	
Q	Harry Barlow	Arthur W. Hallward	7-9	6-2	10-8	6-8	6-1
Q	Joshua Pim	Manliffe Goodbody	8-6	6-3	3-6	6-1	
Q	Harold Mahony	Wilberforce Eaves	10-8	11-9	6-0		
Q	Archdale Palmer	Neville Durlacher	6-3	6-4	7-5		
1894							
Ch	**Joshua Pim**	**Wilfred Baddeley**	10-8	6-2	8-6		
F	Wilfred Baddeley	Ernest Lewis	6-0	6-1	6-0		
S	Wilfred Baddeley	Tom Chaytor			(walkover)		
S	Ernest Lewis	Herbert Baddeley	2-6	7-5	6-3	1-6	7-5
Q	Wilfred Baddeley	John F. Talmage	6-2	6-1	6-3		
Q	Tom Chaytor	Ernest G. Meers	1-6	6-1	6-8	8-6	6-4
Q	Ernest Lewis	Geo. Mieville Simond	6-2	6-3	6-2		
Q	Herbert Baddeley	Harry Barlow	0-6	6-3	4-6	6-1	6-1
1895							
Ch	**Wilfred Baddeley**	**Joshua Pim (walkover)**					
F	Wilfred Baddeley	Wilberforce Eaves	4-6	2-6	8-6	6-2	6-3
S	Wilfred Baddeley	Herbert Baddeley			(walkover)		
S	Wilberforce Eaves	Ernest G. Meers	6-3	7-9	9-11	6-4	6-1
Q	Wilfred Baddeley	Harry Barlow	6-1	6-4	8-6		
Q	Herbert Baddeley	Reggie Doherty	6-4	6-2	6-4		
Q	Ernest G. Meers	J.M. Flavelle	6-1	6-2	6-1		
Q	Wilberforce Eaves	Geo. Mieville Simond	6-4	6-2	7-5		
1896							
Ch	**Harold Mahony**	**Wilfred Baddeley**	6-2	6-8	5-7	8-6	6-3
F	Harold Mahony	Wilberforce Eaves	6-2	6-2	11-9		
S	Harold Mahony	Harold Nisbet	6-4	2-6	8-6	4-6	6-3
S	Wilberforce Eaves	Herbert Baddeley	6-4	6-3	6-4		
Q	Harold Mahony	Frank Riseley	7-5	5-7	7-5	6-3	
Q	Harold Nisbet	Geo. Mieville Simond	2-6	6-4	6-4	1-6	6-3
Q	Wilberforce Eaves	Clem Cazalet	7-5	6-3	6-0		
Q	Herbert Baddeley	Bill Larned	3-6	3-6	6-4	6-4	6-3
1897							
Ch	**Reggie Doherty**	**Harold Mahony**	6-4	6-4	6-3		
F	Reggie Doherty	Wilberforce Eaves	6-3	7-5	2-0		(retired)
S	Wilberforce Eaves	Sidney H. Smith	6-2	5-7	1-6	6-2	6-1
S	Reggie Doherty	Wilfred Baddeley	6-3	6-0	6-3		
Q	Sidney H. Smith	George Hillyard	3-6	6-4	6-2	6-4	
Q	Wilberforce Eaves	T. George P. Greville	6-1	6-2	8-10	6-0	
Q	Wilfred Baddeley	Laurie Doherty	6-4	6-2	6-2		
Q	Reggie Doherty	Frank Riseley			(walkover)		
1898							
Ch	**Reggie Doherty**	**Laurie Doherty**	6-3	6-3	2-6	5-7	6-1
F	Laurie Doherty	Harold Mahony	6-1	6-2	4-6	2-6	14-12
S	Laurie Doherty	Clarence Hobart	6-1	6-4	6-3		
S	Harold Mahony	Arthur Gore	6-2	3-6	4-6	6-2	6-4
Q	Clarence Hobart	Josiah Ritchie	6-2	3-6	6-3	6-2	
Q	Laurie Doherty	J.M. Fiavelle	6-2	6-3	3-6	6-0	
Q	Arthur Gore	Sidney H. Smith	4-6	6-0	4-6	6-3	7-5
Q	Harold Mahony	Geo. Mieville Simond	6-2	6-4	6-4		
1899							
Ch	**Reggie Doherty**	**Arthur Gore**	1-6	4-6	6-3	6-3	6-3
F	Arthur Gore	Sidney H. Smith	3-6	6-1	6-2	6-4	
S	Arthur Gore	Harold Mahony	4-6	3-6	7-5	6-1	
S	Sidney H. Smith	Herbert Roper Barrett	2-6	11-9	4-6	8-6	8-6
Q	Arthur Gore	P.G. Pearson	6-3	6-2	9-7		
Q	Harold Mahony	T. George P. Greville	6-3	9-7	2-6	10-8	
Q	Sidney H. Smith	Harold Nisbet	6-3	7-5	6-4		
Q	Herbert Roper Barrett	Clarence Hobart	8-6	7-5	6-4		
1900							
Ch	**Reggie Doherty**	**Sidney H. Smith**	6-8	6-3	6-1	6-2	
F	Sidney H. Smith	Arthur Gore	6-4	4-6	6-2	6-1	
S	Arthur Gore	Laurie Doherty	4-6	8-6	8-6	6-1	
S	Sidney H. Smith	Harold Nisbet	6-0	6-1	6-1		
Q	Arthur Gore	Frederick J.G. Plaskitt	6-3	6-2	6-0		
Q	Laurie Doherty	Robert McNair	6-2	6-2	6-4		
Q	Sidney H. Smith	Herbert Roper Barrett	6-1	4-6	7-5	6-2	
Q	Harold Nisbet	Fred W. Payn	6-2	6-8	6-4	3-6	6-2
1901							
Ch	**Arthur Gore**	**Reggie Doherty**	4-6	7-5	6-4	6-4	
F	Arthur Gore	Charles Dixon	6-4	6-0	6-3		
S	Charles Dixon	Harold Mahony	6-3	6-4	11-9		
S	Arthur Gore	Herbert Roper Barrett	8-6	6-1	7-5		
Q	Harold Mahony	Robert McNair	6-3	3-6	6-3		
Q	Charles Dixon	Geo. Mieville Simond	6-4	7-5	1-6	6-3	
Q	Herbert Roper Barrett	Sidney H. Smith	7-5	6-4	8-6		
Q	Arthur Gore	George Hillyard	6-1	2-6	4-6	8-6	6-2
1902							
Ch	**Laurie Doherty**	**Arthur Gore**	6-4	6-3	3-6	6-0	
F	Laurie Doherty	Josiah Ritchie	8-6	6-3	7-5		
S	Josiah Ritchie	Sidney H. Smith	6-4	4-6	6-4	6-4	
S	Laurie Doherty	Harold Mahony	4-6	4-6	8-6	2-0	(retired)
Q	Josiah Ritchie	Alfred Ernest Crawley	6-2	6-1	2-6	6-3	
Q	Sidney H. Smith	Herbert Roper Barrett	6-3	6-4	6-3		
Q	Laurie Doherty	T. George P. Greville	6-1	4-6	6-3	7-5	
Q	Harold Mahony	Fred W. Payn	6-2	6-2	6-4		

1903

Rd	Winner	Defeated	S1	S2	S3	S4	S5
Ch	**Laurie Doherty**	**Frank Riseley**	**7-5**	**6-3**	**6-0**		
F	Frank Riseley	Josiah Ritchie	1-6	6-3	8-6	13-11	
S	Frank Riseley	Sidney H. Smith	7-5	6-3	7-9	1-6	9-7
S	Josiah Ritchie	George Caridia	6-1	6-0	4-6	6-1	
Q	Frank Riseley	George Hillyard	6-1	6-4	6-4		
Q	Sidney H. Smith	Henry Pollard	6-2	6-3	6-1		
Q	George Caridia	E.S. Salmon	6-3	6-4	6-2		
Q	Josiah Ritchie	Ernest S. Wills	6-1	6-2	6-2		

1904

Rd	Winner	Defeated	S1	S2	S3	S4	S5
Ch	**Laurie Doherty**	**Frank Riseley**	**6-1**	**7-5**	**8-6**		
F	Frank Riseley	Josiah Ritchie	6-0	6-1	6-2		
S	Frank Riseley	Sidney H. Smith	7-5	5-7	8-6	5-7 (retired)	
S	Josiah Ritchie	Paul de Borman	6-3	6-1	6-1		
Q	Frank Riseley	Arthur Gore	3-6	6-1	3-6	6-4	6-3
Q	Sidney H. Smith	George Caridia	7-5	8-6	6-3		
Q	Josiah Ritchie	W. Lemaire de Warzee	6-1	8-6	6-4		
Q	Paul de Borman	Robert McNair	6-0	6-4	6-4		

1905

Rd	Winner	Defeated	S1	S2	S3	S4	S5
Ch	**Laurie Doherty**	**Norman Brookes**	**8-6**	**6-2**	**6-4**		
F	Norman Brookes	Sidney H. Smith	1-6	6-4	6-1	1-6	7-5
S	Norman Brookes	Arthur Gore	6-3	9-7	6-2		
S	Sidney H. Smith	Josiah Ritchie	6-0	3-6	6-4	4-6	6-1
Q	Arthur Gore	Tony Wilding	8-6	6-2	6-2		
Q	Norman Brookes	Frank Riseley	6-3	6-2	6-4		
Q	Sidney H. Smith	Bill Larned	6-2	6-4	6-4		
Q	Josiah Ritchie	Arthur K. Cronin	6-0	6-2	6-0		

1906

Rd	Winner	Defeated	S1	S2	S3	S4	S5
Ch	**Laurie Doherty**	**Frank Riseley**	**6-4**	**4-6**	**6-2**	**6-3**	
F	Frank Riseley	Arthur Gore	6-3	6-3	6-4		
S	Arthur Gore	Tony Wilding	9-7	6-1	8-6		
S	Frank Riseley	Sidney H. Smith	8-6	2-6	6-2	6-4	
Q	Tony Wilding	Josiah Ritchie	6-4	6-1	4-6	3-6	6-2
Q	Arthur Gore	Alfred Ernest Crawley	6-0	6-1	8-6		
Q	Frank Riseley	Ray Little	6-3	6-1	6-4		
Q	Sidney H. Smith	Clem Cazalet	6-2	4-6	7-5	(retired)	

1907

Rd	Winner	Defeated	S1	S2	S3	S4	S5
Ch	**Norman Brookes**	**Laurie Doherty**			(walkover)		
F	Norman Brookes	Arthur Gore	6-4	6-2	6-2		
S	Arthur Gore	Wilberforce Eaves	9-7	7-5	6-2		
S	Norman Brookes	Josiah Ritchie	6-0	6-1	6-4		
Q	Arthur Gore	A.R. Sawyer	6-0	6-3	6-0		
Q	Wilberforce Eaves	Leonard H. Escombe	6-0	4-6	6-3	1-6	6-3
Q	Norman Brookes	Sydney H. Adams	6-1	6-3	6-3		
Q	Josiah Ritchie	Oscar Kreuzer	6-4	6-1	6-2		

1908

Rd	Winner	Defeated	S1	S2	S3	S4	S5
Ch	**Arthur Gore**	**Norman Brookes**			(walkover)		
F	Arthur Gore	Herbert Roper Barrett	6-3	6-2	4-6	3-6	6-4
S	Arthur Gore	Robert B. Powell	10-8	6-4	6-2		
S	Herbert Roper Barrett	Josiah Ritchie	6-3	6-1	3-6	6-1	
Q	Robert B. Powell	W. Lemaire de Warzee	6-4	8-6	6-4		
Q	Arthur Gore	Charles Dixon	10-8	6-3	3-6	6-0	
Q	Josiah Ritchie	Alfred Ernest Crawley	6-1	6-3	6-2		
Q	Herbert Roper Barrett	Tony Wilding	2-6	6-4	6-4	6-0	

1909

Rd	Winner	Defeated	S1	S2	S3	S4	S5
Ch	**Arthur Gore**	**Josiah Ritchie**	**6-8**	**1-6**	**6-2**	**6-2**	**6-2**
F	Josiah Ritchie	Herbert Roper Barrett	6-2	6-3	4-6	6-4	
S	Josiah Ritchie	Theo. Mavrogordato	3-6	6-3	6-3	6-2	
S	Herbert Roper Barrett	Friedrich Rahe	6-4	6-2	6-8	7-5	
Q	Theo. Mavrogordato	George Caridia	6-1	9-7	2-6	4-6	6-4
Q	Josiah Ritchie	Charles Dixon	8-10	6-1	6-1	6-4	
Q	Herbert Roper Barrett	Leonard H. Escombe	4-6	7-5	11-9	(retired)	
Q	Friedrich Rahe	Gordon Lowe	12-10	6-0	6-4		

1910

Rd	Winner	Defeated	S1	S2	S3	S4	S5
Ch	**Tony Wilding**	**Arthur Gore**	**6-4**	**7-5**	**4-6**	**6-2**	
F	Tony Wilding	Beals Wright	4-6	4-6	6-3	6-2	6-3
S	Tony Wilding	Cecil Parke	7-5	6-1	6-2		
S	Beals Wright	Arthur Lowe	6-3	3-6	6-4	6-4	
Q	Cecil Parke	Alfred Beamish	8-6	5-7	6-4	6-3	
Q	Tony Wilding	Otto Froitzheim	6-1	6-1	6-2		
Q	Arthur Lowe	Stanley Doust	6-3	6-3	2-6	6-4	
Q	Beals Wright	Robert B. Powell	6-3	6-1	6-1		

1911

Rd	Winner	Defeated	S1	S2	S3	S4	S5
Ch	**Tony Wilding**	**H. Roper Barrett**	**6-4**	**4-6**	**2-6**	**6-2** (ret'd)	
F	Herbert Roper Barrett	Charles Dixon	5-7	4-6	6-4	6-3	6-1
S	Charles Dixon	Max Decugis	6-2	5-7	6-2	6-3	
S	Herbert Roper Barrett	Gordon Lowe	6-2	6-3	6-2		
Q	Max Decugis	Rodney Heath	10-8	6-4	7-5		
Q	Charles Dixon	George A. Thomas	6-4	5-7	8-6	6-3	
Q	Herbert Roper Barrett	Alfred Beamish	6-1	1-6	6-4	6-3	
Q	Gordon Lowe	Friedrich Rahe	5-7	6-3	6-2	9-7	

1912

Rd	Winner	Defeated	S1	S2	S3	S4	S5
Ch	**Tony Wilding**	**Arthur Gore**	**6-4**	**6-4**	**4-6**	**6-4**	
F	Arthur Gore	Andre Gobert	9-7	2-6	7-5	6-1	
S	Andre Gobert	Max Decugis	6-3	6-3	1-6	4-6	6-4
S	Arthur Gore	Alfred Beamish	6-2	0-6	11-9	6-4	
Q	Andre Gobert	Friedrich Rahe	6-1	6-2	7-5		
Q	Max Decugis	Herbert Roper Barrett	6-3	7-5	4-6	6-4	
Q	Alfred Beamish	James Zimmerman	6-4	6-3	6-1		
Q	Arthur Gore	Robert B. Powell	6-3	6-2	4-6	6-2	

1913

Rd	Winner	Defeated	S1	S2	S3	S4	S5
Ch	**Tony Wilding**	**Maurice McLoughlin**	**8-6**	**6-3**	**10-8**		
F	Maurice McLoughlin	Stanley Doust	6-3	6-4	7-5		
S	Maurice McLoughlin	Cecil Parke	6-4	7-5	6-4		
S	Stanley Doust	Oscar Kreuzer	6-3	6-2	6-3		
Q	Maurice McLoughlin	W.A. Ingram	6-1	6-2	6-4		
Q	Cecil Parke	R. Douglas Watson	6-4	6-1	6-4		
Q	Oscar Kreuzer	Kenneth Powell	6-4	6-1	5-7	6-0	
Q	Stanley Doust	Hope Crisp	7-5	6-3	3-6	11-9	

1914

Rd	Winner	Defeated	S1	S2	S3	S4	S5
Ch	**Norman Brookes**	**Tony Wilding**	**6-4**	**6-4**	**7-5**		
F	Norman Brookes	Otto Froitzheim	6-2	6-1	5-7	4-6	8-6
S	Otto Froitzheim	Theo. Mavrogordato	6-3	6-2	7-5		
S	Norman Brookes	Alfred Beamish	6-0	6-3	6-2		
Q	Otto Froitzheim	Cecil Parke	5-7	6-2	9-7	6-2	
Q	Theo. Mavrogordato	Maurice Germot	8-3	2-6	6-4	6-1	
Q	Alfred Beamish	Percival Davson	6-4	6-2	6-1		
Q	Norman Brookes	Arthur Gore	7-5	6-1	6-2		

1915-18   *Not held – WW I*

1919

Rd	Winner	Defeated	S1	S2	S3	S4	S5
Ch	**Gerald Patterson**	**Norman Brookes**	**6-3**	**7-5**	**6-2**		
F	Gerald Patterson	Algie Kingscote	6-2	6-1	6-3		
S	Gerald Patterson	Josiah Ritchie	6-1	7-5	1-6	6-3	
S	Algie Kingscote	Chuck Garland	6-1	6-4	2-6	5-7	6-4
Q	Josiah Ritchie	Charles Dixon	4-6	6-4	6-3	6-3	
Q	Gerald Patterson	Andre Gobert	10-8	6-3	6-2		
Q	Algie Kingscote	Pat O'Hara Wood	6-4	3-6	6-3	1-6	6-4
Q	Chuck Garland	Ronald Thomas	6-4	6-0	6-1		

1920

Rd	Winner	Defeated	S1	S2	S3	S4	S5
Ch	**Bill Tilden**	**Gerald Patterson**	**2-6**	**6-3**	**6-2**	**6-4**	
F	Bill Tilden	Zenzo Shimizu	6-4	6-4	13-11		
S	Zenzo Shimizu	Theo. Mavrogordato	3-6	6-4	6-0	6-2	
S	Bill Tilden	Chuck Garland	6-4	8-6	6-2		
Q	Theo. Mavrogordato	Dick Williams	6-3	4-6	9-7	7-5	
Q	Zenzo Shimizu	Neville Willford	6-0	6-1	6-2		
Q	Bill Tilden	Randolph Lycett	7-5	4-6	6-4	7-5	
Q	Chuck Garland	Cecil Blackbeard	4-6	6-1	6-3	6-1	

Rd	Winner	Defeated	S1	S2	S3	S4	S5

1921

Rd	Winner	Defeated	S1	S2	S3	S4	S5
Ch	**Bill Tilden**	**Brian Norton**	**4-6**	**2-6**	**6-1**	**6-0**	**7-5**
F	Brian Norton	Manuel Alonso	5-7	4-6	7-5	6-3	6-3
S	Manuel Alonso	Zenzo Shimidzu	3-6	7-5	3-6	6-3	8-6
S	Brian Norton	Frank Hunter	6-0	6-3	5-7	5-7	6-2
Q	Zenzo Shimidzu	Randolph Lycett	6-3	9-11	3-6	6-2	10-8
Q	Manuel Alonso	Algie Kingscote	6-1	6-3	2-6	6-2	
Q	Frank Hunter	Cecil Campbell	6-2	7-5	3-6	6-4	
Q	Brian Norton	Henry Mayes	4-6	6-2	6-2	6-2	

1922

Rd	Winner	Defeated	S1	S2	S3	S4	S5
F	**Gerald Patterson**	**Randolph Lycett**	**6-3**	**6-4**	**6-2**		
S	Randolph Lycett	Brian Gilbert	8-6	9-7	6-3		
S	Gerald Patterson	James Anderson	3-6	7-9	6-1	6-3	
Q	Randolph Lycett	Percival Davson	2-6	6-1	6-4	8-6	
Q	Brian Gilbert	Theo. Mavrogordato	6-4	3-6	6-3	3-6	6-2
Q	James Anderson	Pat O'Hara Wood	6-3	6-3	2-6	2-6	6-4
Q	Gerald Patterson	Cecil Campbell	7-9	6-3	6-2	6-1	

1923

Rd	Winner	Defeated	S1	S2	S3	S4	S5
F	**Bill Johnston**	**Frank Hunter**	**6-0**	**6-3**	**6-1**		
S	Frank Hunter	Gordon Lowe	6-3	7-5	6-4		
S	Bill Johnston	Brian Norton	6-4	6-2	6-4		
Q	Gordon Lowe	D.M. Evans	6-2	8-6	7-5		
Q	Frank Hunter	Manuel de Gomar	3-6	4-6	6-1	6-3	6-2
Q	Bill Johnston	Cecil Campbell	6-1	5-7	6-2	6-2	
Q	Brian Norton	Max Woosnam	7-5	6-3	6-2		

1924

Rd	Winner	Defeated	S1	S2	S3	S4	S5
F	**Jean Borotra**	**René Lacoste**	**6-1**	**3-6**	**6-1**	**3-6**	**6-4**
S	Jean Borotra	Louis Raymond	6-2	6-4	7-5		
S	René Lacoste	Dick Williams	6-1	3-6	6-2	6-3	
Q	Jean Borotra	Vinnie Richards	6-4	4-6	6-0	6-3	
Q	Louis Raymond	Watson Washburn	6-0	7-5	17-15		
Q	René Lacoste	Jean Washer	6-1	5-7	6-4	6-2	
Q	Dick Williams	Algie Kingscote	5-7	6-4	6-3	6-4	

1925

Rd	Winner	Defeated	S1	S2	S3	S4	S5
F	**René Lacoste**	**Jean Borotra**	**6-3**	**6-3**	**4-6**	**8-6**	
S	René Lacoste	James Anderson	6-4	7-5	6-1		
S	Jean Borotra	Henri Cochet	5-7	8-6	6-4	6-1	
Q	James Anderson	Hector Fisher	6-1	6-1	6-4		
Q	René Lacoste	Sydney Jacob	6-3	6-8	6-0	6-4	
Q	Henri Cochet	John Hennessey	7-9	4-6	6-1	6-3	6-0
Q	Jean Borotra	Lewis Barclay	6-3	5-7	6-3	6-3	

1926

Rd	Winner	Defeated	S1	S2	S3	S4	S5
F	**Jean Borotra**	**Howard Kinsey**	**8-6**	**6-1**	**6-3**		
S	Howard Kinsey	Jacques Brugnon	6-4	4-6	6-3	3-6	9-7
S	Jean Borotra	Henri Cochet	2-6	7-5	2-6	6-3	7-5
Q	Jacques Brugnon	Charles Kingsley	6-2	4-6	6-2	4-6	6-4
Q	Howard Kinsey	Pat Spence	6-3	6-3	3-6	6-3	
Q	Henri Cochet	Colin Gregory	3-6	6-4	6-2	4-6	6-3
Q	Jean Borotra	Jan Kozeluh	6-4	4-6	9-7	6-1	

1927

Rd	Winner	Defeated	S1	S2	S3	S4	S5
F	**Henri Cochet**	**Jean Borotra**	**4-6**	**4-6**	**6-3**	**6-4**	**7-5**
S	Henri Cochet	Bill Tilden	2-6	4-6	7-5	6-4	6-3
S	Jean Borotra	René Lacoste	6-4	6-3	1-6	1-6	6-2
Q	Bill Tilden	Jacques Brugnon	6-3	6-1	3-6	7-5	
Q	Henri Cochet	Frank Hunter	3-6	3-6	6-2	6-2	6-3
Q	René Lacoste	Jan Kozeluh	6-4	6-3	6-4		
Q	Jean Borotra	Henk Timmer	6-1	3-6	6-3	6-0	

1928

Rd	Winner	Defeated	S1	S2	S3	S4	S5
F	**René Lacoste**	**Henri Cochet**	**6-1**	**4-6**	**6-4**	**6-2**	
S	Henri Cochet	Christian Boussus	11-9	3-6	6-2	6-3	
S	René Lacoste	Bill Tilden	2-6	6-4	2-6	6-4	6-3
Q	Henri Cochet	John Hennessey	6-4	6-1	5-7	6-3	
Q	Christian Boussus	Jacques Brugnon	12-10	10-8	6-2		
Q	René Lacoste	Umberto de Morpurgo	6-2	6-3	6-4		
Q	Bill Tilden	Jean Borotra	8-6	3-6	6-3	6-2	

1929

Rd	Winner	Defeated	S1	S2	S3	S4	S5
F	**Henri Cochet**	**Jean Borotra**	**6-4**	**6-3**	**6-4**		
S	Henri Cochet	Bill Tilden	6-4	6-1	7-5		
S	Jean Borotra	Bunny Austin	6-1	10-8	5-7	6-1	
Q	Henri Cochet	Henk Timmer	6-4	7-5	6-2		
Q	Bill Tilden	P. Landry	6-4	2-6	6-3	7-5	
Q	Jean Borotra	George Lott	6-3	6-3	6-4		
Q	Bunny Austin	Bela von Kehrling	6-2	8-6	6-3		

1930

Rd	Winner	Defeated	S1	S2	S3	S4	S5
F	**Bill Tilden**	**Wilmer Allison**	**6-3**	**9-7**	**6-4**		
S	Wilmer Allison	Johnny Doeg	6-3	4-6	8-6	3-6	7-5
S	Bill Tilden	Jean Borotra	0-6	6-4	4-6	6-0	7-5
Q	Wilmer Allison	Henri Cochet	6-4	6-4	6-3		
Q	Johnny Doeg	Gregory Mangin	6-3	1-6	6-3	6-4	
Q	Bill Tilden	Colin Gregory	6-1	6-2	6-3		
Q	Jean Borotra	George Lott	2-6	6-3	6-4	6-4	

1931

Rd	Winner	Defeated	S1	S2	S3	S4	S5
F	**Sidney Wood**	**Francis Shields**		(walkover)			
S	Sidney Wood	Fred Perry	4-6	6-2	6-4	6-2	
S	Francis Shields	Jean Borotra	7-5	3-6	6-4	6-4	
Q	Sidney Wood	George Hughes	4-6	6-4	6-3	6-1	
Q	Fred Perry	John Van Ryn	6-4	8-6	7-5		
Q	Jean Borotra	Jiro Satoh	6-2	6-3	4-6	6-4	
Q	Francis Shields	Bunny Austin	6-3	2-6	5-7	7-5	6-1

1932

Rd	Winner	Defeated	S1	S2	S3	S4	S5
F	**Ellsworth Vines**	**Bunny Austin**	**6-4**	**6-2**	**6-0**		
S	Ellsworth Vines	Jack Crawford	6-2	6-1	6-3		
S	Bunny Austin	Jiro Satoh	7-5	6-2	6-1		
Q	Ellsworth Vines	Enrique Maier	6-2	6-3	6-2		
Q	Jack Crawford	Fred Perry	7-5	8-6	2-6	8-6	
Q	Bunny Austin	Francis Shields	6-1	9-7	5-7	6-1	
Q	Jiro Satoh	Sidney Wood	7-5	7-5	2-6	6-4	

1933

Rd	Winner	Defeated	S1	S2	S3	S4	S5
F	**Jack Crawford**	**Ellsworth Vines**	**4-6**	**11-9**	**6-2**	**2-6**	**6-4**
S	Ellsworth Vines	Henri Cochet	6-2	8-6	3-6	6-1	
S	Jack Crawford	Jiro Satoh	6-3	6-4	2-6	6-4	
Q	Ellsworth Vines	Roderich Menzel	6-2	6-4	3-6	6-3	
Q	Henri Cochet	Lester Stoefen	3-6	6-4	6-3	6-1	
Q	Jiro Satoh	Bunny Austin	7-5	6-3	2-6	2-6	6-2
Q	Jack Crawford	George Hughes	6-1	6-1	7-5		

1934

Rd	Winner	Defeated	S1	S2	S3	S4	S5
F	**Fred Perry**	**Jack Crawford**	**6-3**	**6-0**	**7-5**		
S	Jack Crawford	Francis Shields	2-6	4-6	6-4	6-3	6-4
S	Fred Perry	Sidney Wood	3-6	3-6	7-5	5-7	6-3
Q	Jack Crawford	Lester Stoefen	7-5	2-6	7-5	6-0	
Q	Francis Shields	Bunny Austin	4-6	2-6	7-5	6-3	7-5
Q	Fred Perry	George Lott	6-4	2-6	7-5	10-8	
Q	Sidney Wood	Vernon Kirby	6-1	6-4	3-6	6-0	

1935

Rd	Winner	Defeated	S1	S2	S3	S4	S5
F	**Fred Perry**	**Gottfried von Cramm**	**6-2**	**6-4**	**6-4**		
S	Fred Perry	Jack Crawford	6-2	3-6	6-4	6-4	
S	Gottfried von Cramm	Don Budge	4-6	6-4	6-3	6-2	
Q	Fred Perry	Roderich Menzel	9-7	6-1	6-1		
Q	Jack Crawford	Sidney Wood	6-4	6-3	6-8	5-7	6-1
Q	Don Budge	Bunny Austin	3-6	10-8	6-4	7-5	
Q	Gottfried von Cramm	Viv MacGrath	6-4	6-2	4-6	6-1	

Rd	Winner	Defeated	S1	S2	S3	S4	S5
1936							
F	**Fred Perry**	**Gottfried von Cramm 6-1**	**6-1**	**6-0**			
S	Fred Perry	Don Budge	5-7	6-4	6-3	6-4	
S	Gottfried von Cramm	Bunny Austin	8-6	6-3	2-6	6-3	
Q	Fred Perry	Bryan Grant Jr.	6-4	6-3	6-1		
Q	Don Budge	Adrian Quist	6-2	6-4	6-4		
Q	Bunny Austin	Wilmer Allison	6-1	6-4	7-5		
Q	Gottfried von Cramm	Jack Crawford	6-1	7-5	6-4		
1937							
F	**Don Budge**	**Gottfried von Cramm 6-3**	**6-4**	**6-2**			
S	Gottfried von Cramm	Bunny Austin	8-6	6-3	12-14	6-1	
S	Don Budge	Frank Parker	2-6	6-4	6-4	6-1	
Q	Gottfried von Cramm	Jack Crawford	6-3	8-6	3-6	2-6	6-2
Q	Bunny Austin	Bryan Grant Jr.	6-1	7-5	6-4		
Q	Frank Parker	Henner Henkel	6-3	7-5	4-6	4-6	6-2
Q	Don Budge	Viv MacGrath	6-3	6-1	6-4		
1938							
F	**Don Budge**	**Bunny Austin**	**6-1**	**6-0**	**6-3**		
S	Bunny Austin	Henner Henkel	6-2	6-4	6-0		
S	Don Budge	Franjo Puncec	6-2	6-1	6-4		
Q	Bunny Austin	Max S. Ellmer	6-2	6-1	6-2		
Q	Henner Henkel	Ladislav Hecht	7-5	6-1	6-2		
Q	Franjo Puncec	Donald MacPhail	6-2	6-1	6-1		
Q	Don Budge	Franz Cejnar	6-3	6-0	7-5		
1939							
F	**Bobby Riggs**	**Elwood Cooke**	**2-6**	**8-6**	**3-6**	**6-3**	**6-2**
S	Elwood Cooke	Henner Henkel	6-3	4-6	6-4	6-4	
S	Bobby Riggs	Franjo Puncec	6-2	6-3	6-4		
Q	Elwood Cooke	Bunny Austin	6-3	6-0	6-1		
Q	Henner Henkel	Franjo Kukuljevic	6-1	6-3	6-2		
Q	Franjo Puncec	M. Eugene Smith	6-0	6-2	6-2		
Q	Bobby Riggs	Ghaus Mohammed	6-2	6-2	6-2		
1940-45	*Not held – WW II*						
1946							
F	**Yvon Petra**	**Geoff Brown**	**6-2**	**6-4**	**7-9**	**5-7**	**6-4**
S	Yvon Petra	Tom Brown Jr.	4-6	4-6	6-3	7-5	8-6
S	Geoff Brown	Jaroslav Drobny	6-4	7-5	6-2		
Q	Yvon Petra	Dinny Pails	7-5	7-5	6-8	6-4	
Q	Tom Brown Jr.	Franjo Puncec	6-2	8-6	6-4		
Q	Geoff Brown	Lennart Bergelin	13-11	11-9	6-4		
Q	Jaroslav Drobny	Pierre Pellizza	6-4	6-4	6-4		
1947							
F	**Jack Kramer**	**Tom Brown Jr.**	**6-1**	**6-3**	**6-2**		
S	Tom Brown Jr.	Budge Patty	6-3	6-3	6-3		
S	Jack Kramer	Dinny Pails	6-1	3-6	6-1	6-0	
Q	Budge Patty	Jaroslav Drobny	3-6	6-4	7-9	6-2	6-3
Q	Tom Brown Jr.	Yvon Petra	7-5	6-2	6-4		
Q	Dinny Pails	Bob Falkenburg	4-6	4-6	6-3	6-0	6-2
Q	Jack Kramer	Geoff Brown	6-0	6-1	6-3		
1948							
F	**Bob Falkenburg**	**John Bromwich**	**7-5**	**0-6**	**6-2**	**3-6**	**7-5**
S	Bob Falkenburg	Gardnar Mulloy	6-4	6-4	8-6		
S	John Bromwich	Jozsef Asboth	6-3	14-12	6-2		
Q	Gardnar Mulloy	Tony Mottram	6-2	1-6	7-5	6-1	
Q	Bob Falkenburg	Lennart Bergelin	6-4	6-2	3-6	6-4	
Q	John Bromwich	Budge Patty	6-4	7-5	6-1		
Q	Jozsef Asboth	Tom Brown Jr.	4-6	6-3	4-6	6-1	6-1

Rd	Winner	Defeated	S1	S2	S3	S4	S5
1949							
F	**Ted Schroeder**	**Jaroslav Drobny**	**3-6**	**6-0**	**6-3**	**4-6**	**6-4**
S	Jaroslav Drobny	John Bromwich	6-1	6-3	6-2		
S	Ted Schroeder	Eric Sturgess	3-6	7-5	5-7	6-1	6-2
Q	Jaroslav Drobny	Geoff Brown	2-6	7-5	1-6	6-2	6-4
Q	John Bromwich	Bob Falkenburg	3-6	9-11	6-0	6-0	6-4
Q	Eric Sturgess	Frank Parker	3-6	6-4	3-6	6-1	6-3
Q	Ted Schroeder	Frank Sedgman	3-6	6-8	6-3	6-2	9-7
1950							
F	**Budge Patty**	**Frank Sedgman**	**6-1**	**8-10**	**6-2**	**6-3**	
S	Frank Sedgman	Jaroslav Drobny	3-6	3-6	6-3	7-5	6-2
S	Budge Patty	Vic Seixas	6-3	5-7	6-2	7-5	
Q	Frank Sedgman	Art Larsen	8-10	5-7	7-5	6-3	7-5
Q	Jaroslav Drobny	Gardnar Mulloy	6-3	6-4	6-4		
Q	Vic Seixas	Eric Sturgess	9-7	6-8	3-6	6-2	7-5
Q	Budge Patty	Tony Trabert	3-6	6-4	6-2	6-3	
1951							
F	**Dick Savitt**	**Ken McGregor**	**6-4**	**6-4**	**6-4**		
S	Dick Savitt	Herbie Flam	1-6	15-13	6-3	6-2	
S	Ken McGregor	Eric Sturgess	6-4	3-6	6-3	7-5	
Q	Herbie Flam	Frank Sedgman	2-6	1-6	6-3	6-4	7-5
Q	Dick Savitt	Art Larsen	6-1	6-4	6-4		
Q	Ken McGregor	Armando Vieira	6-2	6-0	6-3		
Q	Eric Sturgess	Lennart Bergelin	6-0	4-6	5-7	6-2	6-4
1952							
F	**Frank Sedgman**	**Jaroslav Drobny**	**4-6**	**6-2**	**6-3**	**6-2**	
S	Frank Sedgman	Merv Rose	6-4	6-4	7-5		
S	Jaroslav Drobny	Herbie Flam	6-2	6-4	0-6	8-10	6-4
Q	Frank Sedgman	Eric Sturgess	7-5	6-1	6-0		
Q	Merv Rose	Dick Savitt	6-4	3-6	6-4	4-6	6-2
Q	Herbie Flam	Vic Seixas	6-4	3-6	6-3	7-5	
Q	Jaroslav Drobny	Ken McGregor	6-0	3-6	2-6	7-5	7-5
1953							
F	**Vic Seixas**	**Kurt Nielsen**	**9-7**	**6-3**	**6-4**		
S	Vic Seixas	Merv Rose	6-4	10-12	9-11	6-4	6-3
S	Kurt Nielsen	Jaroslav Drobny	6-4	6-3	6-2		
Q	Vic Seixas	Lew Hoad	5-7	6-4	6-3	1-6	9-7
Q	Merv Rose	Art Larsen	6-3	6-3	16-14		
Q	Jaroslav Drobny	Sven Davidson	7-5	6-4	6-0		
Q	Kurt Nielsen	Ken Rosewall	7-5	4-6	6-8	6-0	6-2
1954							
F	**Jaroslav Drobny**	**Ken Rosewall**	**13-11**	**4-6**	**6-2**	**9-7**	
S	Jaroslav Drobny	Budge Patty	6-2	6-4	4-6	9-7	
S	Ken Rosewall	Tony Trabert	3-6	6-3	4-6	6-1	6-1
Q	Jaroslav Drobny	Lew Hoad	6-4	6-3	6-3		
Q	Budge Patty	Vic Seixas	7-5	4-6	6-3	6-2	
Q	Ken Rosewall	Rex Hartwig	6-3	3-6	3-6	6-3	6-1
Q	Tony Trabert	Merv Rose	6-2	6-2	7-5		
1955							
F	**Tony Trabert**	**Kurt Nielsen**	**6-3**	**7-5**	**6-1**		
S	Kurt Nielsen	Ken Rosewall	11-9	6-2	2-6	6-4	
S	Tony Trabert	Budge Patty	8-6	6-2	6-2		
Q	Ken Rosewall	Sven Davidson	6-4	6-1	6-2		
Q	Kurt Nielsen	Nicola Pietrangeli	1-6	6-3	5-7	6-2	7-5
Q	Budge Patty	Lew Hoad	6-4	6-4	6-4		
Q	Tony Trabert	Jaroslav Drobny	8-6	6-1	6-4		
1956							
F	**Lew Hoad**	**Ken Rosewall**	**6-2**	**4-6**	**7-5**	**6-4**	
S	Lew Hoad	Hamilton Richardson	3-6	6-4	6-2	6-4	
S	Ken Rosewall	Vic Seixas	6-3	3-6	6-8	6-3	7-5
Q	Lew Hoad	Mal Anderson	4-6	6-1	6-1	13-11	
Q	Hamilton Richardson	Neale Fraser	6-3	9-11	7-5	6-4	
Q	Vic Seixas	Allen Morris	13-11	6-0	6-3		
Q	Ken Rosewall	Ulf Schmidt	6-1	6-3	6-2		

Rd	Winner	Defeated	S1	S2	S3	S4	S5
1957							
F	**Lew Hoad**	**Ashley Cooper**	**6-2**	**6-1**	**6-2**		
S	Ashley Cooper	Neale Fraser	1-6	14-12	6-3	8-6	
S	Lew Hoad	Sven Davidson	6-4	6-4	7-5		
Q	Ashley Cooper	Herbie Flam	6-3	7-5	6-1		
Q	Neale Fraser	Ulf Schmidt	1-6	6-4	6-8	6-4	6-4
Q	Sven Davidson	Vic Seixas	5-7	6-4	6-4	6-4	
Q	Lew Hoad	Merv Rose	6-4	4-6	10-8	6-3	
1958							
F	**Ashley Cooper**	**Neale Fraser**	**3-6**	**6-3**	**6-4**	**13-11**	
S	Neale Fraser	Kurt Nielsen	6-4	6-4	17-19	6-4	
S	Ashley Cooper	Merv Rose	7-9	6-2	6-2	6-3	
Q	Kurt Nielsen	Mal Anderson	6-2	6-3		(retired)	
Q	Neale Fraser	Sven Davidson	6-4	6-8	6-2	3-6	8-6
Q	Merv Rose	Barry MacKay	6-2	6-4	6-4		
Q	Ashley Cooper	Bobby Wilson	6-4	6-2	3-6	4-6	7-5
1959							
F	**Alejandro Olmedo**	**Rod Laver**	**6-4**	**6-3**	**6-4**		
S	Rod Laver	Barry MacKay	11-13	11-9	10-8	7-9	6-3
S	Alejandro Olmedo	Roy Emerson	6-4	6-0	6-4		
Q	Barry MacKay	Neale Fraser	5-7	10-8	0-6	6-3	6-1
Q	Rod Laver	Jean-Claude Molinari	6-3	6-3	6-0		
Q	Roy Emerson	Bobby Wilson	6-3	6-4	6-2		
Q	Alejandro Olmedo	Luis Ayala	7-5	3-6	6-3	6-3	
1960							
F	**Neale Fraser**	**Rod Laver**	**6-4**	**3-6**	**9-7**	**7-5**	
S	Rod Laver	Nicola Pietrangeli	4-6	6-3	8-10	6-2	6-4
S	Neale Fraser	Ramanathan Krishnan	6-3	6-2	6-2		
Q	Nicola Pietrangeli	Barry MacKay	16-14	6-2	3-6	6-4	
Q	Rod Laver	Roy Emerson	6-4	5-7	6-4	6-4	
Q	Ramanathan Krishnan	Luis Ayala	7-5	10-8	6-2		
Q	Neale Fraser	Earl Buchholtz Jr.	4-6	6-3	4-6	15-15 (retired)	
1961							
F	**Rod Laver**	**Chuck McKinley**	**6-3**	**6-1**	**6-4**		
S	Rod Laver	Ramanathan Krishnan	6-2	8-6	6-2		
S	Chuck McKinley	Mike Sangster	6-4	6-4	8-6		
Q	Rod Laver	Luis Ayala	6-1	6-3	6-2		
Q	Ramanathan Krishnan	Roy Emerson	6-1	6-4	6-4		
Q	Chuck McKinley	Iyo Pimentel	6-2	6-2	6-4		
Q	Mike Sangster	Bobby Wilson	6-4	6-4	4-6	6-4	
1962							
F	**Rod Laver**	**Marty Mulligan**	**6-2**	**6-2**	**6-1**		
S	Rod Laver	Neale Fraser	10-8	6-1	7-5		
S	Marty Mulligan	John Fraser	6-3	6-2	6-2		
Q	Rod Laver	Manolo Santana	14-16	9-7	6-2	6-2	
Q	Neale Fraser	Rafael Osuna	6-3	6-1	4-6	4-6	6-2
Q	John Fraser	Ken Fletcher	1-6	7-9	6-4	6-1	6-2
Q	Marty Mulligan	Bob Hewitt	6-8	6-4	6-3	6-4	
1963							
F	**Chuck McKinley**	**Fred Stolle**	**9-7**	**6-1**	**6-4**		
S	Chuck McKinley	Wilhelm Bungert	6-2	6-4	8-6		
S	Fred Stolle	Manolo Santana	8-6	6-1	7-5		
Q	Wilhelm Bungert	Roy Emerson	8-6	3-6	6-3	4-6	6-3
Q	Chuck McKinley	Bobby Wilson	8-6	6-4	6-2		
Q	Fred Stolle	Frank Froehling III	9-7	7-5	6-4		
Q	Manolo Santana	Christian Kuhnke	6-3	6-4	6-4		
1964							
F	**Roy Emerson**	**Fred Stolle**	**6-4**	**12-10**	**4-6**	**6-3**	
S	Roy Emerson	Wilhelm Bungert	6-3	15-13	6-0		
S	Fred Stolle	Chuck McKinley	4-6	10-8	9-7	6-4	
Q	Roy Emerson	Bob Hewitt	6-1	6-4	6-4		
Q	Wilhelm Bungert	Rafael Osuna	6-4	6-2	6-3		
Q	Fred Stolle	Christian Kuhnke	6-3	7-5	6-3		
Q	Chuck McKinley	Abe Segal	6-3	6-3	4-6	6-4	

Rd	Winner	Defeated	S1	S2	S3	S4	S5
1965							
F	**Roy Emerson**	**Fred Stolle**	**6-2**	**6-4**	**6-4**		
S	Roy Emerson	Dennis Ralston	6-1	6-2	7-9	6-1	
S	Fred Stolle	Cliff Drysdale	6-3	6-4	7-5		
Q	Roy Emerson	Keith Diepraam	4-6	6-3	6-1	6-1	
Q	Dennis Ralston	Marty Riessen	3-6	2-6	6-4	6-2	6-2
Q	Cliff Drysdale	Allen Fox	4-6	6-2	7-5	7-5	
Q	Fred Stolle	Rafael Osuna	11-13	6-3	6-1	6-2	
1966							
F	**Manolo Santana**	**Dennis Ralston**	**6-4**	**11-9**	**6-4**		
S	Manolo Santana	Owen Davidson	6-2	4-6	9-7	3-6	7-5
S	Dennis Ralston	Cliff Drysdale	6-8	8-6	3-6	7-5	6-3
Q	Owen Davidson	Roy Emerson	1-6	6-3	6-4	6-4	
Q	Manolo Santana	Ken Fletcher	6-2	3-6	8-6	4-6	7-5
Q	Dennis Ralston	Bob Hewitt	7-5	6-2	11-9		
Q	Cliff Drysdale	Anthony Roche	9-7	6-2	6-2		
1967							
F	**John Newcombe**	**Wilhelm Bungert**	**6-3**	**6-1**	**6-1**		
S	Wilhelm Bungert	Roger Taylor	6-4	6-8	2-6	6-4	6-4
S	John Newcombe	Nikki Pilic	9-7	4-6	6-3	6-4	
Q	Wilhelm Bungert	Thomaz Koch	6-4	4-6	4-6	6-1	6-3
Q	Roger Taylor	Ray Ruffels	6-4	8-6	6-4		
Q	John Newcombe	Ken Fletcher	6-4	6-2	6-4		
Q	Nikki Pilic	John Cooper	14-12	8-10	6-4	6-2	
1968							
F	**Rod Laver**	**Tony Roche**	**6-3**	**6-4**	**6-2**		
S	Rod Laver	Arthur Ashe	7-5	6-2	6-4		
S	Tony Roche	Clark Graebner	9-7	8-10	6-4	8-6	
Q	Rod Laver	Dennis Ralston	4-6	6-4	6-1	4-6	6-2
Q	Arthur Ashe	Tom Okker	7-9	9-7	9-7	6-2	
Q	Clark Graebner	Raymond Moore	6-2	6-0	9-7		
Q	Tony Roche	Butch Buchholz	3-6	7-5	6-4	6-4	
1969							
F	**Rod Laver**	**John Newcombe**	**6-4**	**5-7**	**6-4**	**6-4**	
S	Rod Laver	Arthur Ashe	2-6	6-2	9-7	6-0	
S	John Newcombe	Tony Roche	3-6	6-1	14-12	6-4	
Q	Rod Laver	Cliff Drysdale	6-4	6-2	6-3		
Q	Arthur Ashe	Bob Lutz	6-4	6-2	4-6	7-5	
Q	John Newcombe	Tom Okker	8-6	3-6	6-1	7-5	
Q	Tony Roche	Clark Graebner	4-6	4-6	6-3	6-4	11-9
1970							
F	**John Newcombe**	**Ken Rosewall**	**5-7**	**6-3**	**6-3**	**3-6**	**6-1**
S	Ken Rosewall	Roger Taylor	6-3	4-6	6-3	6-3	
S	John Newcombe	Andres Gimeno	6-3	8-6	6-0		
Q	Roger Taylor	Clark Graebner	6-3	11-9	12-10		
Q	Ken Rosewall	Tony Roche	10-8	6-1	4-6	6-2	
Q	Andres Gimeno	Bob Carmichael	6-1	6-2	6-4		
Q	John Newcombe	Roy Emerson	6-1	5-7	3-6	6-2	11-9
1971							
F	**John Newcombe**	**Stan Smith**	**6-3**	**5-7**	**2-6**	**6-4**	**6-4**
S	Stan Smith	Tom Gorman	6-3	8-6	6-2		
S	John Newcombe	Ken Rosewall	6-1	6-1	6-3		
Q	Tom Gorman	Rod Laver	9-7	8-6	6-3		
Q	Stan Smith	Onny Parun	8-6	6-3	6-4		
Q	Ken Rosewall	Cliff Richey	6-8	5-7	6-4	9-7	7-5
Q	John Newcombe	Colin Dibley	6-1	6-2	6-3		
1972							
F	**Stan Smith**	**Ilie Nastase**	**4-6**	**6-3**	**6-3**	**4-6**	**7-5**
S	Stan Smith	Jan Kodes	3-6	6-4	6-1	7-5	
S	Ilie Nastase	Manolo Orantes	6-3	6-4	6-4		
Q	Stan Smith	Alex Metreveli	6-2	8-6	6-2		
Q	Jan Kodes	Onny Parun	6-2	6-3	6-4		
Q	Manolo Orantes	Colin Dibley	6-2	6-0	6-2		
Q	Ilie Nastase	Jimmy Connors	6-4	6-4	6-1		

Rd	Winner	Defeated	S1	S2	S3	S4	S5
1973							
F	**Jan Kodes**	**Alex Metreveli**	6-1	9-8(5)	6-3		
S	Alex Metreveli	Sandy Mayer	6-3	3-6	6-3	6-4	
S	Jan Kodes	Roger Taylor	8-9	9-7	5-7	6-4	7-5
Q	Sandy Mayer	Jurgen Fassbender	3-6	4-6	6-3	6-4	6-4
Q	Alex Metreveli	Jimmy Connors	8-6	6-2	5-7	6-4	
Q	Roger Taylor	Bjorn Borg	6-1	6-8	3-6	6-3	7-5
Q	Jan Kodes	Vijay Amritraj	6-4	3-6	4-6	6-3	7-5
1974							
F	**Jimmy Connors**	**Ken Rosewall**	6-1	6-1	6-4		
S	Ken Rosewall	Stan Smith	6-8	4-6	9-8(6)	6-1	6-3
S	Jimmy Connors	Dick Stockton	4-6	6-2	6-3	6-4	
Q	Ken Rosewall	John Newcombe	6-1	1-6	6-0	7-5	
Q	Stan Smith	Ismail El Shafei	9-8(2)	7-5	6-8	7-5	
Q	Jimmy Connors	Jan Kodes	3-6	6-3	6-3	6-8	6-3
Q	Dick Stockton	Alex Metreveli	6-4	7-5	6-1		
1975							
F	**Arthur Ashe**	**Jimmy Connors**	6-1	6-1	5-7	6-4	
S	Jimmy Connors	Roscoe Tanner	6-4	6-1	6-4		
S	Arthur Ashe	Tony Roche	5-7	6-4	7-5	8-9(4)	6-4
Q	Jimmy Connors	Raul Ramirez	6-4	8-6	6-2		
Q	Roscoe Tanner	Guillermo Vilas	6-4	5-7	6-8	6-2	6-2
Q	Arthur Ashe	Bjorn Borg	2-6	6-4	8-6	6-1	
Q	Tony Roche	Tom Okker	2-6	9-8(11)	2-6	6-4	6-2
1976							
F	**Bjorn Borg**	**Ilie Nastase**	6-4	6-2	9-7		
S	Ilie Nastase	Raul Ramirez	6-2	9-7	6-3		
S	Bjorn Borg	Roscoe Tanner	6-4	9-8(2)	6-4		
Q	Raul Ramirez	Vitas Gerulaitis	4-6	6-4	6-2	6-4	
Q	Ilie Nastase	Charlie Pasarell	6-4	6-2	6-3		
Q	Bjorn Borg	Guillermo Vilas	6-3	6-0	6-2		
Q	Roscoe Tanner	Jimmy Connors	6-4	6-2	8-6		
1977							
F	**Bjorn Borg**	**Jimmy Connors**	3-6	6-2	6-1	5-7	6-4
S	Jimmy Connors	John McEnroe	6-3	6-3	4-6	6-4	
S	Bjorn Borg	Vitas Gerulaitis	6-4	3-6	6-3	3-6	8-6
Q	Jimmy Connors	Byron Bertram	6-4	3-6	6-4	6-2	
Q	John McEnroe	Phil Dent	6-4	8-9(7)	4-6	6-3	6-4
Q	Bjorn Borg	Ilie Nastase	6-0	8-6	6-3		
Q	Vitas Gerulaitis	Billy Martin	6-2	8-9	6-2	6-2	
1978							
F	**Bjorn Borg**	**Jimmy Connors**	6-2	6-2	6-3		
S	Bjorn Borg	Tom Okker	6-4	6-4	6-4		
S	Jimmy Connors	Vitas Gerulaitis	9-7	6-2	6-1		
Q	Bjorn Borg	Sandy Mayer	7-5	6-4	6-4		
Q	Tom Okker	Ilie Nastase	7-5	6-1	2-6	6-3	
Q	Vitas Gerulaitis	Brian Gottfried	7-5	4-6	9-7	6-2	
Q	Jimmy Connors	Raul Ramirez	6-4	6-4	6-2		
1979							
F	**Bjorn Borg**	**Roscoe Tanner**	6-7(4)	6-1	3-6	6-3	6-4
S	Bjorn Borg	Jimmy Connors	6-2	6-3	6-2		
S	Roscoe Tanner	Pat Dupre	6-3	7-6(3)	6-3		
Q	Bjorn Borg	Tom Okker	6-2	6-1	6-3		
Q	Jimmy Connors	Bill Scanlon	6-3	4-6	7-6(1)	6-4	
Q	Pat Dupre	Adriano Panatta	3-6	6-4	6-7(3)	6-4	6-3
Q	Roscoe Tanner	Tim Gullikson	6-1	6-4	6-7(3)	6-2	
1980							
F	**Bjorn Borg**	**John McEnroe**	1-6	7-5	6-3	6-7(16)	8-6
S	Bjorn Borg	Brian Gottfried	6-2	4-6	6-2	6-0	
S	John McEnroe	Jimmy Connors	6-3	3-6	6-3	6-4	
Q	Bjorn Borg	Gene Mayer	7-5	6-3	7-5		
Q	Brian Gottfried	Wojtek Fibak	6-4	7-6	6-2		
Q	Jimmy Connors	Roscoe Tanner	1-6	6-2	4-6	6-2	6-2
Q	John McEnroe	Peter Fleming	6-3	6-2	6-2		

Rd	Winner	Defeated	S1	S2	S3	S4	S5
1981							
F	**John McEnroe**	**Bjorn Borg**	4-6	7-6(1)	7-6(4)	6-4	
S	Bjorn Borg	Jimmy Connors	0-6	4-6	6-3	6-0	6-4
S	John McEnroe	Rod Frawley	7-6(2)	6-4	7-5		
Q	Bjorn Borg	Peter McNamara	7-6(2)	6-2	6-3		
Q	Jimmy Connors	Vijay Amritraj	2-6	5-7	6-4	6-3	6-2
Q	Rod Frawley	Tim Mayotte	4-6	7-6(5)	7-6(4)	6-3	
Q	John McEnroe	Johan Kriek	6-1	7-5	6-1		
1982							
F	**Jimmy Connors**	**John McEnroe**	3-6	6-3	6-7(2)	7-6(5)	6-4
S	John McEnroe	Tim Mayotte	6-3	6-1	6-2		
S	Jimmy Connors	Mark Edmondson	6-4	6-3	6-1		
Q	John McEnroe	Johan Kriek	4-6	6-2	7-5	6-3	
Q	Tim Mayotte	Brian Teacher	6-7	7-6	7-5	3-6	6-1
Q	Mark Edmondson	Vitas Gerulaitis	7-6	3-6	6-4	6-3	
Q	Jimmy Connors	Gene Mayer	6-1	6-2	7-6		
1983							
F	**John McEnroe**	**Chris Lewis**	6-2	6-2	6-2		
S	Chris Lewis	Kevin Curren	6-7(3)	6-4	7-6(4)	6-7(3)	8-6
S	John McEnroe	Ivan Lendl	7-6(5)	6-4	6-4		
Q	Kevin Curren	Tim Mayotte	4-6	7-6(4)	6-2	7-6(6)	
Q	Chris Lewis	Mel Purcell	6-7	6-0	6-4	7-6	
Q	Ivan Lendl	Roscoe Tanner	7-5	7-6(3)	6-3		
Q	John McEnroe	Sandy Mayer	6-3	7-5	6-0		
1984							
F	**John McEnroe**	**Jimmy Connors**	6-1	6-1	6-2		
S	John McEnroe	Pat Cash	6-3	7-6(5)	6-4		
S	Jimmy Connors	Ivan Lendl	6-7(4)	6-3	7-5	6-1	
Q	John McEnroe	John Sadri	6-3	6-3	6-1		
Q	Pat Cash	Andres Gomez	6-4	6-4	6-7	7-6	
Q	Jimmy Connors	Paul Annacone	6-2	6-4	6-2		
Q	Ivan Lendl	Tomas Smid	6-1	7-6	6-3		
1985							
F	**Boris Becker**	**Kevin Curren**	6-3	6-7(4)	7-6(3)	6-4	
S	Kevin Curren	Jimmy Connors	6-2	6-2	6-1		
S	Boris Becker	Anders Jarryd	2-6	7-6(3)	6-3	6-3	
Q	Kevin Curren	John McEnroe	6-2	6-2	6-4		
Q	Jimmy Connors	Ricardo Acuna	6-1	7-6(3)	6-2		
Q	Anders Jarryd	Heinz Gunthardt	6-4	6-3	6-2		
Q	Boris Becker	Henri Leconte	7-6(7)	3-6	6-3	6-4	
1986							
F	**Boris Becker**	**Ivan Lendl**	6-4	6-3	7-5		
S	Ivan Lendl	Slobodan Zivojinovic	6-2	6-7(5)	6-3	6-7(1)	6-4
S	Boris Becker	Henri Leconte	6-2	6-4	6-7(4)	6-3	
Q	Ivan Lendl	Tim Mayotte	6-4	4-6	6-4	3-6	9-7
Q	Slobodan Zivojinovic	Ramesh Krishnan	6-2	7-6(4)	4-6	6-3	
Q	Boris Becker	Miloslav Mecir	6-4	6-2	7-6(5)		
Q	Henri Leconte	Pat Cash	4-6	7-6(7)	7-6(5)	6-3	
1987							
F	**Pat Cash**	**Ivan Lendl**	7-6(5)	6-2	7-5		
S	Pat Cash	Jimmy Connors	6-4	6-4	6-1		
S	Ivan Lendl	Stefan Edberg	3-6	6-4	7-6(8)	6-4	
Q	Jimmy Connors	Slobodan Zivojinovic	7-6(5)	7-5	6-3		
Q	Pat Cash	Mats Wilander	6-3	7-5	6-4		
Q	Stefan Edberg	Anders Jarryd	4-6	6-4	6-1	6-3	
Q	Ivan Lendl	Henri Leconte	7-6(5)	6-3	7-6(6)		
1988							
F	**Stefan Edberg**	**Boris Becker**	4-6	7-6(2)	6-4	6-2	
S	Boris Becker	Ivan Lendl	6-4	6-3	6-7(8)	6-4	
S	Stefan Edberg	Miloslav Mecir	4-6	2-6	6-4	6-3	6-4
Q	Ivan Lendl	Tim Mayotte	7-6(2)	7-6(1)	6-3		
Q	Boris Becker	Pat Cash	6-4	6-3	6-4		
Q	Stefan Edberg	Patrik Kuhnen	6-3	4-6	6-1	7-6(2)	
Q	Miloslav Mecir	Mats Wilander	6-3	6-1	6-3		

Men's Singles

Rd	Winner	Defeated	S1	S2	S3	S4	S5
1989							
F	**Boris Becker**	**Stefan Edberg**	**6-0**	**7-6(1)**	**6-4**		
S	Boris Becker	Ivan Lendl	7-5	6-7(2)	2-6	6-4	6-3
S	Stefan Edberg	John McEnroe	7-5	7-6(2)	7-6(5)		
Q	Ivan Lendl	Dan Goldie	7-6(8)	7-6(4)	6-0		
Q	Boris Becker	Paul Chamberlin	6-1	6-2	6-0		
Q	John McEnroe	Mats Wilander	7-6(6)	3-6	6-3	6-4	
Q	Stefan Edberg	Tim Mayotte	7-6(2)	7-6(12)	6-3		
1990							
F	**Stefan Edberg**	**Boris Becker**	**6-2**	**6-2**	**3-6**	**3-6**	**6-4**
S	Stefan Edberg	Ivan Lendl	6-1	7-6(2)	6-3		
S	Boris Becker	Goran Ivanisevic	4-6	7-6(4)	6-0	7-6(5)	
Q	Ivan Lendl	Brad Pearce	6-4	6-4	5-7	6-4	
Q	Stefan Edberg	Christian Bergstrom	6-3	6-2	6-4		
Q	Goran Ivanisevic	Kevin Curren	4-6	6-4	6-4	6-7(8)	6-3
Q	Boris Becker	Brad Gilbert	6-4	6-4	6-1		
1991							
F	**Michael Stich**	**Boris Becker**	**6-4**	**7-6(4)**	**6-4**		
S	Michael Stich	Stefan Edberg	4-6	7-6(5)	7-6(5)	7-6(2)	
S	Boris Becker	David Wheaton	6-4	7-6(4)	7-5		
Q	Stefan Edberg	Thierry Champion	6-3	6-2	7-5		
Q	Michael Stich	Jim Courier	6-3	7-6(2)	6-2		
Q	David Wheaton	Andre Agassi	6-2	0-6	3-6	7-6(3)	6-2
Q	Boris Becker	Guy Forget	6-7(5)	7-6(3)	6-2	7-6(7)	
1992							
F	**Andre Agassi**	**Goran Ivanisevic**	**6-7(8)**	**6-4**	**6-4**	**1-6**	**6-4**
S	Andre Agassi	John McEnroe	6-4	6-2	6-3		
S	Goran Ivanisevic	Pete Sampras	6-7(4)	7-6(5)	6-4	6-2	
Q	John McEnroe	Guy Forget	6-2	7-6(9)	6-3		
Q	Andre Agassi	Boris Becker	4-6	6-2	6-2	4-6	6-3
Q	Pete Sampras	Michael Stich	6-3	6-2	6-4		
Q	Goran Ivanisevic	Stefan Edberg	6-7(8)	7-5	6-1	3-6	6-3
1993							
F	**Pete Sampras**	**Jim Courier**	**7-6(3)**	**7-6(6)**	**3-6**	**6-3**	
S	Pete Sampras	Boris Becker	7-6(5)	6-4	6-4		
S	Jim Courier	Stefan Edberg	4-6	6-4	6-2	6-4	
Q	Pete Sampras	Andre Agassi	6-2	6-2	3-6	3-6	6-4
Q	Boris Becker	Michael Stich	7-5	6-7(5)	6-7(5)	6-2	6-4
Q	Jim Courier	Todd Martin	6-2	7-6(5)	6-3		
Q	Stefan Edberg	Cedric Pioline	7-5	7-5	6-3		
1994							
F	**Pete Sampras**	**Goran Ivanisevic**	**7-6(2)**	**7-6(5)**	**6-0**		
S	Pete Sampras	Todd Martin	6-4	6-4	3-6	6-3	
S	Goran Ivanisevic	Boris Becker	6-2	7-6(6)	6-4		
Q	Pete Sampras	Michael Chang	6-4	6-1	6-3		
Q	Todd Martin	Wayne Ferreira	6-3	6-2	3-6	5-7	7-5
Q	Goran Ivanisevic	Guy Forget	7-6(3)	7-6(3)	6-4		
Q	Boris Becker	Christian Bergstrom	7-6(5)	6-4	6-3		
1995							
F	**Pete Sampras**	**Boris Becker**	**6-7(5)**	**6-2**	**6-4**	**6-2**	
S	Boris Becker	Andre Agassi	2-6	7-6(1)	6-4	7-6(1)	
S	Pete Sampras	Goran Ivanisevic	7-6(7)	4-6	6-3	4-6	6-3
Q	Andre Agassi	Jacco Eltingh	6-2	6-3	6-4		
Q	Boris Becker	Cedric Pioline	6-3	6-1	6-7(6)	6-7(10)	9-7
Q	Goran Ivanisevic	Yevgeny Kafelnikov	7-5	7-6(11)	6-3		
Q	Pete Sampras	Shuzo Matsuoka	6-7(5)	6-3	6-4	6-2	
1996							
F	**Richard Krajicek**	**MaliVai Washington**	**6-3**	**6-4**	**6-3**		
S	Richard Krajicek	Jason Stoltenberg	7-5	6-2	6-1		
S	MaliVai Washington	Todd Martin	5-7	6-4	6-7(6)	6-3	10-8
Q	Richard Krajicek	Pete Sampras	7-5	7-6(3)	6-4		
Q	Jason Stoltenberg	Goran Ivanisevic	6-3	7-6(3)	6-7(3)	7-6(3)	
Q	Todd Martin	Tim Henman	7-6(5)	7-6(2)	6-4		
Q	MaliVai Washington	Alex Radulescu	6-7(5)	7-6(1)	5-7	7-6(3)	6-4

Rd	Winner	Defeated	S1	S2	S3	S4	S5
1997							
F	**Pete Sampras**	**Cedric Pioline**	**6-4**	**6-2**	**6-4**		
S	Pete Sampras	Todd Woodbridge	6-2	6-1	7-6(3)		
S	Cedric Pioline	Michael Stich	6-7(2)	6-2	6-1	5-7	6-4
Q	Pete Sampras	Boris Becker	6-1	6-7(5)	6-1	6-4	
Q	Todd Woodbridge	Nicolas Kiefer	7-6(7)	2-6	6-0	6-4	
Q	Michael Stich	Tim Henman	6-3	6-2	6-4		
Q	Cedric Pioline	Greg Rusedski	6-4	4-6	6-4	6-3	
1998							
F	**Pete Sampras**	**Goran Ivanisevic**	**6-7(2)**	**7-6(9)**	**6-4**	**3-6**	**6-2**
S	Pete Sampras	Tim Henman	6-3	4-6	7-5	6-3	
S	Goran Ivanisevic	Richard Krajicek	6-3	6-4	5-7	6-7(5)	15-13
Q	Pete Sampras	Mark Philippoussis	7-6(5)	6-4	6-4		
Q	Tim Henman	Petr Korda	6-3	6-4	6-2		
Q	Goran Ivanisevic	Jan Siemerink	7-6(10)	7-6(5)	7-6(6)		
Q	Richard Krajicek	Davide Sanguinetti	6-2	6-3	6-4		
1999							
F	**Pete Sampras**	**Andre Agassi**	**6-3**	**6-4**	**7-5**		
S	Pete Sampras	Tim Henman	3-6	6-4	6-3	6-4	
S	Andre Agassi	Patrick Rafter	7-5	7-6(5)	6-2		
Q	Pete Sampras	Mark Philippoussis	4-6	2-1		(retired)	
Q	Tim Henman	Cedric Pioline	6-4	6-2	4-6	6-3	
Q	Andre Agassi	Gustavo Kuerten	6-3	6-4	6-4		
Q	Patrick Rafter	Todd Martin	6-3	6-7(5)	7-6(5)	7-6(3)	
2000							
F	**Pete Sampras**	**Patrick Rafter**	**6-7(10)**	**7-6(5)**	**6-4**	**6-2**	
S	Pete Sampras	Vladimir Voltchkov	7-6(4)	6-2	6-4		
S	Patrick Rafter	Andre Agassi	7-5	4-6	7-5	4-6	6-3
Q	Pete Sampras	Jan-Michael Gambill	6-4	6-7(4)	6-4	6-4	
Q	Vladimir Voltchkov	Byron Black	7-6(2)	7-6(2)	6-4		
Q	Patrick Rafter	Alexander Popp	6-3	6-2	7-6(1)		
Q	Andre Agassi	Mark Philippoussis	7-6(4)	6-3	6-4		
2001							
F	**Goran Ivanisevic**	**Patrick Rafter**	**6-3**	**3-6**	**6-3**	**2-6**	**9-7**
S	Goran Ivanisevic	Tim Henman	7-5	6-7(6)	0-6	7-6(5)	6-3
S	Patrick Rafter	Andre Agassi	2-6	6-3	3-6	6-2	8-6
Q	Tim Henman	Roger Federer	7-5	7-6(6)	2-6	7-6(6)	
Q	Goran Ivanisevic	Marat Safin	7-6(2)	7-5	3-6	7-6(3)	
Q	Patrick Rafter	Thomas Enqvist	6-1	6-3	7-6(5)		
Q	Andre Agassi	Nicolas Escude	6-7(3)	6-3	6-4	6-2	
2002							
F	**Lleyton Hewitt**	**David Nalbandian**	**6-1**	**6-3**	**6-2**		
S	Lleyton Hewitt	Tim Henman	7-5	6-1	7-5		
S	David Nalbandian	Xavier Malisse	7-6(2)	6-1	1-6	2-6	6-2
Q	Lleyton Hewitt	Sjeng Schalken	6-2	6-2	6-7(5)	1-6	7-5
Q	Tim Henman	Andre Sa	6-3	5-7	6-4	6-3	
Q	Xavier Malisse	Richard Krajicek	6-1	4-6	6-2	3-6	9-7
Q	David Nalbandian	Nicolas Lapentti	6-4	6-4	4-6	4-6	6-4

Women's Singles

Rd	Winner	Defeated	S1	S2	S3
1884					
F	**Maud Watson**	**Lilian Watson**	**6-8**	**6-3**	**6-3**
S	Maud Watson	Blanche Bingley	3-6	6-4	6-2
S	Lillian Watson	M. Leslie	7-5	5-7	6-3
Q	Maud Watson	B.E. Williams	7-5	6-0	
Q	Blanche Bingley	F.M. Winckworth	6-0	6-8	6-3
Q	Lillian Watson	Mrs. G. J. Cooper	7-5	5-7	6-3
Q	M. Leslie		(bye)		

Rd	Winner	Defeated	S1	S2	S3
1885					
F	**Maud Watson**	**Blanche Bingley**	**6-1**	**7-5**	
S	Blanche Bingley	E. Gurney	6-1	6-2	
S	Maud Watson	E.F. Hudson	6-0	6-1	
Q	Blanche Bingley	Mrs. Dransfield	(walkover)		
Q	E. Gurney	J. Meikle	7-5	6-4	
Q	E.F. Hudson	Miss Bryan	6-3	6-0	
Q	Maud Watson	May Langrishe	6-0	6-2	
1886					
Ch	**Blanche Bingley**	**Maud Watson**	**6-3**	**6-3**	
F	Blanche Bingley	A. Tabor	6-2	6-0	
S	A. Tabor	Edith Maud Shackle	6-4	7-5	
S	Blanche Bingley	Lillian Watson	6-3	8-6	
Q	Edith Maud Shackle	J. Mackenzie	6-3	6-4	
Q	A. Tabor	F.M. Pearson	6-1	6-2	
Q	Blanche Bingley	J. Shackle	6-2	6-1	
Q	Lillian Watson	A.M. Chambers	6-3	6-3	
1887					
Ch	**Charlotte Dod**	**Blanche Bingley Hillyard**	**6-2**	**6-0**	
F	Charlotte Dod	Edith Mary Cole	6-2	6-3	
S	Charlotte Dod	B. James	6-1	6-1	
S	Edith Mary Cole	J. Shackle	6-4	6-1	
Q	Charlotte Dod		(bye)		
Q	B. James	Edith Maud Shackle	8-6	6-2	
Q	Edith Mary Cole		(bye)		
Q	J. Shackle		(bye)		
1888					
Ch	**Charlotte Dod**	**Blanche Bingley Hillyard**	**6-3**	**6-3**	
F	Blanche Bingley Hillyard	Miss Howes	6-1	6-2	
S	Miss Howes	Miss D. Patterson	6-4	6-2	
S	Blanche Bingley Hillyard	Miss Phillimore	(walkover)		
Q	Miss Howes		(bye)		
Q	Miss D. Patterson	B.E. Williams	6-0	6-3	
Q	Blanche Bingley Hillyard	Miss Canning	6-2	6-2	
Q	Miss Phillimore		(bye)		
1889					
Ch	**Blanche Bingley Hillyard**	**Charlotte Dod**	(walkover)		
F	Blanche Bingley Hillyard	Helena Rice	4-6	8-6	6-4
S	Helena Rice	M. Jacks	6-2	6-0	
S	Blanche Bingley Hillyard	Bertha Steedman	8-6	6-1	
Q	Helena Rice		(bye)		
Q	M. Jacks	Mary Steedman	6-4	6-2	
Q	Blanche Bingley Hillyard	Annie Elizabeth Rice	6-3	6-0	
Q	Bertha Steedman		(bye)		
1890					
Ch	**Helena Rice**	**Blanche Bingley Hillyard**	(walkover)		
F	Helena Rice	M. Jacks	6-4	6-1	
S	M. Jacks	Edith Mary Cole	6-4	7-5	
S	Helena Rice	Mary Steedman	7-5	6-2	
1891					
Ch	**Charlotte Dod**	**Helena Rice**	(walkover)		
F	Charlotte Dod	Blanche Bingley Hillyard	6-2	6-1	
S	Charlotte Dod	Bertha Steedman	6-3	6-1	
S	Blanche Bingley Hillyard	May Langrishe	6-4	6-1	
Q	Charlotte Dod	Mrs. Parsons	6-0	6-0	
Q	Bertha Steedman	Helen Jackson	6-2	6-2	
Q	May Langrishe	M. Jacks	11-9	6-3	
Q	Blanche Bingley Hillyard	P. Legh	6-3	6-2	
1892					
Ch	**Charlotte Dod**	**Blanche Bingley Hillyard**	**6-1**	**6-1**	
F	Blanche Bingley Hillyard	Edith Maud Shackle	6-1	6-4	
S	Edith Maud Shackle	Bertha Steedman	6-4	6-3	
S	Blanche Bingley Hillyard	Mrs. C. Martin	1-6	6-3	9-7
Q	Bertha Steedman	Miss Barefoot	6-0	6-1	
Q	Edith Maud Shackle	Helen Jackson	6-3	6-4	
Q	Blanche Bingley Hillyard	Mrs. G.A. Draffen	6-2	6-2	
Q	Mrs. C. Martin		(bye)		
1893					
Ch	**Charlotte Dod**	**Blanche Bingley Hillyard**	**6-8**	**6-1**	**6-4**
F	Blanche Bingley Hillyard	Edith Maud Shackle	6-3	6-2	
S	Edith Maud Shackle	Edith Austin	6-0	6-2	
S	Blanche Bingley Hillyard	Charlotte Cooper	6-3	6-1	
Q	Edith Austin	S. Robins	6-2	6-1	
Q	Edith Maud Shackle	P. Legh	10-8	6-1	
Q	Charlotte Cooper	Henrietta Horncastle	6-4	6-1	
Q	Blanche Bingley Hillyard		(bye)		
1894					
Ch	**Blanche Bingley Hillyard**	**Charlotte Dod**	(walkover)		
F	Blanche Bingley Hillyard	Edith Austin	6-1	6-1	
S	Blanche Bingley Hillyard	Miss Bryan	6-1	6-1	
S	Edith Austin	S. Robins	6-1	6-1	
Q	Blanche Bingley Hillyard	Chatterton Clarke	6-1	6-0	
Q	Miss Bryan	Mrs. G.A. Draffen	6-3	7-5	
Q	Edith Austin	Charlotte Cooper	6-1	3-6	6-3
Q	S. Robins	Mrs. Edwardes	6-2	6-1	
1895					
Ch	**Charlotte Cooper**	**Blanche Bingley Hillyard**	(walkover)		
F	Charlotte Cooper	Helen Jackson	7-5	8-6	
S	Helen Jackson	Alice Simpson Pickering	6-4	3-6	8-6
S	Charlotte Cooper	Mrs. G.A. Draffen	6-2	6-8	6-1
Q	Alice Simpson Pickering	Edith Maud Shackle	3-6	6-3	6-3
Q	Helen Jackson	Miss Bernard	6-0	6-2	
Q	Charlotte Cooper	L.H. Patterson	6-3	9-11	6-2
Q	Mrs. G.A. Draffen	Henrietta Horncastle	6-2	6-0	
1896					
Ch	**Charlotte Cooper**	**Alice Simpson Pickering**	**6-2**	**6-3**	
F	Alice Simpson Pickering	Edith Austin	4-6	6-3	6-3
S	Edith Austin	Henrietta Horncastle	(walkover)		
S	Alice Simpson Pickering	Mrs. G.A. Draffen	6-3	7-5	
Q	Henrietta Horncastle		(bye)		
Q	Edith Austin	L.H. Patterson	6-4	6-1	
Q	Alice Simpson Pickering	Miss 'Hungerford'	6-1	6-0	
Q	Mrs. G.A. Draffen		(bye)		
1897					
Ch	**Blanche Bingley Hillyard**	**Charlotte Cooper**	**5-7**	**7-5**	**6-2**
F	Blanche Bingley Hillyard	Alice Simpson Pickering	6-2	7-5	
S	Blanche Bingley Hillyard	Henrietta Horncastle	(walkover)		
S	Alice Simpson Pickering	Ruth Dyes	6-4	4-6	6-1
Q	Blanche Bingley Hillyard	Edith Austin	6-0	6-1	
Q	Henrietta Horncastle	E.M. Thyme	12-10	6-4	
Q	Ruth Dyes	E.J. Bromfield	6-0	6-3	
Q	Alice Simpson Pickering		(bye)		
1898					
Ch	**Charlotte Cooper**	**Blanche Bingley Hillyard**	(walkover)		
F	Charlotte Cooper	Louisa Martin	6-4	6-4	
S	Louisa Martin	P. Legh	(walkover)		
S	Charlotte Cooper	Edith Austin	6-4	6-1	
Q	P. Legh	C. Morgan	6-0	6-1	
Q	Louisa Martin	E.R. Morgan	6-2	6-0	
Q	Edith Austin	Ruth Dyes	4-6	6-3	6-4
Q	Charlotte Cooper	Bertha Steedman	4-6	6-3	6-4

Rd	Winner	Defeated	S1	S2	S3
1899					
Ch	**Blanche Bingley Hillyard**	**Charlotte Cooper**	**6-2**	**6-3**	
F	Blanche Bingley Hillyard	Ruth Durlacher	7-5	6-8	6-1
S	Ruth Durlacher	Bertha Steedman	6-4	6-2	
S	Blanche Bingley Hillyard	Beryl Tulloch	6-3	3-6	6-2
Q	Ruth Durlacher	Muriel Robb	6-1	5-7	6-3
Q	Bertha Steedman	H.A. Kirby	4-6	6-2	6-2
Q	Blanche Bingley Hillyard	Edith Austin	8-6	6-4	
Q	Beryl Tulloch	E.J. Bromfield	3-6	6-2	6-1
1900					
Ch	**Blanche Bingley Hillyard**	**Charlotte Cooper**	**4-6**	**6-4**	**6-4**
F	Charlotte Cooper	Louisa Martin	8-6	5-7	6-1
S	Charlotte Cooper	Edith Greville	6-1	6-2	
S	Louisa Martin	Ellen Evered	6-0	6-2	
Q	Charlotte Cooper	Muriel Robb	6-3	9-7	
Q	Edith Greville	Beryl Tulloch	7-5	6-0	
Q	Ellen Evered	Marion Jones	7-5	6-2	
Q	Louisa Martin	Dorothea Douglass	6-4	6-3	
1901					
Ch	**Charlotte Cooper Sterry**	**Blanche Bingley Hillyard**	**6-2**	**6-2**	
F	Charlotte Cooper Sterry	Louisa Martin	6-3	6-4	
S	Louisa Martin	Agnes Morton	7-5	6-2	
S	Charlotte Cooper Sterry	Miss Adams	6-1	6-1	
Q	Louisa Martin	Edith Greville	4-6	6-3	6-4
Q	Agnes Morton	Alice Simpson Pickering	6-3	7-5	
Q	Charlotte Cooper Sterry	Muriel Robb	6-0	6-0	
Q	Miss Adams	Miss Hughes D'Eath	6-1	6-0	
1902					
Ch	**Muriel Robb**	**Charlotte Cooper Sterry**	**7-5**	**6-1**	
F	Muriel Robb	Agnes Morton	7-5	6-4	
S	Muriel Robb	Dorothea Douglass	6-4	2-6	9-7
S	Agnes Morton	Edith Greville	7-5	6-4	
Q	Muriel Robb	Hilda Lane	6-1	7-5	
Q	Dorothea Douglass	Ruth Durlacher	6-2	10-8	
Q	Agnes Morton	Winifred Longhurst	6-3	6-4	
Q	Edith Greville	Bertha Steedman	6-1	3-6	6-2
1903					
Ch	**Dorothea Douglass**	**Muriel Robb**		**(walkover)**	
F	Dorothea Douglass	Ethel Thomson	4-6	6-4	6-2
S	Dorothea Douglass	Towpie Lowther	6-4	6-2	
S	Ethel Thomson	Angela Greene	6-3	6-1	
Q	Towpie Lowther	Agnes Morton	6-1	6-0	
Q	Dorothea Douglass	Getrude Houselander	6-2	6-0	
Q	Ethel Thomson	Constance M. Wilson	6-4	8-6	
Q	Angela Greene	E.J. Bromfield	6-0	4-6	6-3
1904					
Ch	**Dorothea Douglass**	**Charlotte Cooper Sterry**	**6-0**	**6-3**	
F	Charlotte Cooper Sterry	Agnes Morton	6-3	6-3	
S	Charlotte Cooper Sterry	Angela Greene	6-2	6-1	
S	Agnes Morton	Constance M. Wilson	3-6	6-4	8-6
Q	Charlotte Cooper Sterry	Edith Greville	8-6	9-7	
Q	Angela Greene	Ruth Winch	6-4	6-4	
Q	Agnes Morton	Winifred Longhurst	6-1	6-4	
Q	Constance M. Wilson	E.L. Bosworth	6-3	6-4	
1905					
Ch	**May Sutton**	**Dorothea Douglass**	**6-3**	**6-4**	
F	May Sutton	Constance M. Wilson	6-3	8-6	
S	May Sutton	Agnes Morton	6-4	6-0	
S	Constance M. Wilson	Blanche Bingley Hillyard	7-5	9-11	6-2
Q	Agnes Morton	Mrs. H.I. Harper	6-2	6-4	
Q	May Sutton	Ethel Thomson	8-6	6-1	
Q	Blanche Bingley Hillyard	Dora Boothby	6-3	6-2	
Q	Constance M. Wilson	B.M. Holder	6-2	6-0	
1906					
Ch	**Dorothea Douglass**	**May Sutton**	**6-3**	**9-7**	
F	Dorothea Douglass	Charlotte Cooper Sterry	6-2	6-2	
S	Dorothea Douglass	Beryl Tulloch	6-2	6-2	
S	Charlotte Cooper Sterry	Towpie Lowther	4-6	8-6	6-4
Q	Dorothea Douglass	Winifred Longhurst	6-4	6-3	
Q	Beryl Tulloch	Blanche Bingley Hillyard	6-3	6-1	
Q	Charlotte Cooper Sterry	Violet Pickney	6-4	6-2	
Q	Towpie Lowther	Gladys Eastlake Smith	6-3	6-3	
1907					
Ch	**May Sutton**	**D. Douglass Chambers**	**6-1**	**6-4**	
F	May Sutton	Constance M. Wilson	6-4	6-2	
S	May Sutton	E.L. Bosworth	6-2	6-2	
S	Constance M. Wilson	Blanche Bingley Hillyard	6-3	6-2	
Q	E.L. Bosworth	M.E. Brown	6-1	6-2	
Q	May Sutton	Constance Meyer	6-0	6-3	
Q	Constance M. Wilson	Angela Greene	6-2	9-7	
Q	Blanche Bingley Hillyard	Edith G. Johnson	6-2	6-3	
1908					
Ch	**Charlotte Cooper Sterry**	**May Sutton**		**(walkover)**	
F	Charlotte Cooper Sterry	Agnes Morton	6-4	6-4	
S	Charlotte Cooper Sterry	Dora Boothby	6-2	6-4	
S	Agnes Morton	Gladys Lamplough	6-3	6-4	
Q	Dora Boothby	Violet Pickney	6-1	6-4	
Q	Charlotte Cooper Sterry	Dorothea Douglass Chambers	6-3	7-5	
Q	Agnes Morton	Beryl Tulloch	7-5	6-1	
Q	Gladys Lamplough	Agnes Daniell Tuckey	6-3	6-1	
1909					
Ch	**Dora Boothby**	**Charlotte Cooper Sterry**		**(walkover)**	
F	Dora Boothby	Agnes Morton	6-4	4-6	8-6
S	Agnes Morton	Aurea Edgington	6-0	6-4	
S	Dora Boothby	Maud Garfitt	6-2	6-1	
Q	Aurea Edgington	Madeline O'Neill	7-5	6-4	
Q	Agnes Morton	Edith G. Johnson	6-0	6-3	
Q	Maud Garfitt	Mabel Parton	6-3	6-4	
Q	Dora Boothby	Francis Helen Aitchison	6-4	3-0	(retired)
1910					
Ch	**D. Douglass Chambers**	**Dora Boothby**	**6-2**	**6-2**	
F	Dorothea Douglass Chambers	Edith G. Johnson	6-4	6-2	
S	Edith G. Johnson	Gladys Lamplough	1-6	6-0	6-3
S	Dorothea Douglass Chambers	Winifred Slocock McNair	6-1	6-0	
Q	Gladys Lamplough	Sophie Castenschiold	7-9	6-4	6-3
Q	Edith G. Johnson	Mabel Parton	7-5	6-4	
Q	Dorothea Douglass Chambers	Francis Helen Aitchison	6-2	6-1	
Q	Winifred Slocock McNair	Aurea Edgington	2-6	6-3	6-3
1911					
Ch	**Dorothea Douglass Chambers**	**Dora Boothby**	**6-0**	**6-0**	
F	Dora Boothby	Edith Hannam	6-2	7-5	
S	Edith Hannam	Francis Helen Aitchison	6-3	6-8	7-5
S	Dora Boothby	Mabel Parton	6-3	6-4	
Q	Edith Hannam	Mildred Coles	6-4	4-6	7-5
Q	Francis Helen Aitchison	Marie Hazel	6-0	6-3	
Q	Dora Boothby	Aurea Edgington	6-2	6-4	
Q	Mabel Parton	Dorothy Holman	6-0	8-6	
1912					
Ch	**Ethel Thomson Larcombe**	**D. Douglass Chambers**		**(walkover)**	
F	Ethel Thomson Larcombe	Charlotte Cooper Sterry	6-3	6-1	
S	Charlotte Cooper Sterry	Dorothy Holman	6-3	4-6	7-5
S	Ethel Thomson Larcombe	Blanche Bingley Hillyard	6-1	6-0	
Q	Charlotte Cooper Sterry	Winifred Longhurst	6-1	6-3	
Q	Dorothy Holman	Agnes Morton	7-5	6-2	
Q	Ethel Thomson Larcombe	Winifred Slocock McNair	6-2	5-7	6-0
Q	Blanche Bingley Hillyard	Elizabeth Ryan	3-6	8-6	6-3

Rd	Winner	Defeated	S1	S2	S3
1913					
Ch	**D. Douglass Chambers**	**Ethel Thomson Larcombe**	(walkover)		
F	Dorothea Douglass Chambers	Winifred Slocock McNair	6-0	6-4	
S	Winifred Slocock McNair	Dorothy Holman	2-6	6-2	7-5
S	Dorothea Douglass Chambers	Francis Helen Aitchison	6-2	6-3	
Q	Winifred Slocock McNair	Charlotte Cooper Sterry	0-6	6-4	9-7
Q	Dorothy Holman	Phyllis Satterthwaite	6-4	6-1	
Q	Dorothea Douglass Chambers	Mildred Coles	6-1	6-0	
Q	Francis Helen Aitchison	Madeline O'Neill	6-2	6-0	
1914					
Ch	**D. Douglass Chambers**	**Ethel Thomson Larcombe**	7-5	6-4	
F	Ethel Thomson Larcombe	Elizabeth Ryan	6-3	6-2	
S	Ethel Thomson Larcombe	Aurea Edgington	6-4	6-3	
S	Elizabeth Ryan	Francis Helen Aitchison	6-4	6-3	
Q	Aurea Edgington	Doris Covell Craddock	6-1	6-3	
Q	Ethel Thomson Larcombe	Agnes Daniell Tuckey	(walkover)		
Q	Francis Helen Aitchison	B. Leader	6-2	6-0	
Q	Elizabeth Ryan	Betty Crundall Punnett	6-0	6-3	

1915-18   *Not held – WW I*

Rd	Winner	Defeated	S1	S2	S3
1919					
Ch	**Suzanne Lenglen**	**D. Douglass Chambers**	10-8	4-6	9-7
F	Suzanne Lenglen	Phyllis Satterthwaite	6-1	6-1	
S	Phyllis Satterthwaite	Geraldine Ramsey Beamish	6-4	10-8	
S	Suzanne Lenglen	Elizabeth Ryan	6-4	7-5	
Q	Geraldine Ramsey Beamish	Aurea Edgington	6-8	6-3	6-2
Q	Phyllis Satterthwaite	Ruth Winch	6-3	6-4	
Q	Suzanne Lenglen	Kitty McKane	6-0	6-1	
Q	Elizabeth Ryan	Mabel Parton	6-2	6-3	
1920					
Ch	**Suzanne Lenglen**	**D. Douglass Chambers**	6-3	6-0	
F	Dorothea Douglass Chambers	Elizabeth Ryan	6-2	6-1	
S	Elizabeth Ryan	Mabel Parton	6-4	6-2	
S	Dorothea Douglass Chambers	Molla Bjurstedt Mallory	6-0	6-3	
Q	Elizabeth Ryan	Violet Pickney	(walk-over)		
Q	Mabel Parton	Phyllis Satterthwaite	6-4	6-4	
Q	Molla Bjurstedt Mallory	Helen Leisk	6-3	6-1	
Q	Dorothea Douglass Chambers	Winifred Slocock McNair	3-6	6-0	6-2
1921					
Ch	**Suzanne Lenglen**	**Elizabeth Ryan**	6-2	6-0	
F	Elizabeth Ryan	Phyllis Satterthwaite	6-1	6-0	
S	Phyllis Satterthwaite	Mabel Clayton	8-6	6-2	
S	Elizabeth Ryan	Irene Bowder Peacock	8-6	6-4	
Q	Mabel Clayton	Dorothy Shepherd	6-3	6-2	
Q	Phyllis Satterthwaite	Phyllis Howkins	6-1	6-8	6-1
Q	Elizabeth Ryan	Winifred Slocock McNair	7-5	2-6	6-4
Q	Irene Bowder Peacock	Molla Bjurstedt Mallory	0-6	6-4	6-4
1922					
F	**Suzanne Lenglen**	**Molla Bjurstedt Mallory**	6-2	6-0	
S	Suzanne Lenglen	Irene Bowder Peacock	6-4	6-1	
S	Molla Bjurstedt Mallory	Geraldine Ramsey Beamish	6-2	6-2	
Q	Suzanne Lenglen	Elizabeth Ryan	6-1	8-6	
Q	Irene Bowder Peacock	Peggy Dransfield	6-2	6-2	
Q	Geraldine Ramsey Beamish	Mrs. I.F.L. Elliot	8-6	6-1	
Q	Molla Bjurstedt Mallory	Aurea Edgington	6-2	6-4	
1923					
F	**Suzanne Lenglen**	**Kitty McKane**	6-2	6-2	
S	Suzanne Lenglen	Geraldine Ramsey Beamish	6-0	6-0	
S	Kitty McKane	Elizabeth Ryan	1-6	6-2	6-4
Q	Suzanne Lenglen	Marie Hazel	6-2	6-1	
Q	Geraldine Ramsey Beamish	Molla Bjurstedt Mallory	4-6	7-5	6-4
Q	Kitty McKane	Eleanor Goss	6-2	6-2	
Q	Elizabeth Ryan	Eleanor Florence Rose	6-0	6-0	

Rd	Winner	Defeated	S1	S2	S3
1924					
F	**Kitty McKane**	**Helen Wills**	4-6	6-4	6-4
S	Helen Wills	Phyllis Satterthwaite	6-2	6-1	
S	Kitty McKane	Suzanne Lenglen	(walkover)		
Q	Phyllis Satterthwaite	Dorothy Shepherd Barron	6-4	10-8	
Q	Helen Wills	Mrs. J.S. Colegate	6-1	6-0	
Q	Kitty McKane	Marion Zinderstein Jessup	6-1	6-3	
Q	Suzanne Lenglen	Elizabeth Ryan	6-2	6-8	6-4
1925					
F	**Suzanne Lenglen**	**Joan Fry**	6-2	6-0	
S	Suzanne Lenglen	Kitty McKane	6-0	6-0	
S	Joan Fry	Marguerite Billout	6-2	4-6	6-3
Q	Kitty McKane	Esna Boyd	6-1	6-1	
Q	Suzanne Lenglen	Geraldine Ramsey Beamish	6-0	6-0	
Q	Joan Fry	Daphne Akhurst	2-6	6-4	6-3
Q	Marguerite Billout	Mary Hart McIlquham	6-3	6-3	
1926					
F	**Kitty McKane Godfree**	**Lili de Alvarez**	6-2	4-6	6-3
S	Lili de Alvarez	Molla Bjurstedt Mallory	6-2	6-2	
S	Kitty McKane Godfree	Didi Vlasto	6-4	6-0	
Q	Lili de Alvarez	Claire Beckingham	6-2	6-2	
Q	Molla Bjurstedt Mallory	Kea Bouman	3-6	7-5	6-3
Q	Didi Vlasto	Helen Contostavlos	6-3	6-3	
Q	Kitty McKane Godfree	C. Tyrrell	6-2	6-0	
1927					
F	**Helen Wills**	**Lili de Alvarez**	6-2	6-4	
S	Lili de Alvarez	Elizabeth Ryan	2-6	6-0	6-4
S	Helen Wills	Joan Fry	6-3	6-1	
Q	Elizabeth Ryan	Kitty McKane Godfree	3-6	6-4	6-4
Q	Lili de Alvarez	Phoebe Holcroft Watson	6-3	3-6	8-6
Q	Helen Wills	Irene Bowder Peacock	6-3	6-1	
Q	Joan Fry	Betty Nuthall	1-6	6-3	6-4
1928					
F	**Helen Wills**	**Lili de Alvarez**	6-2	6-3	
S	Helen Wills	Elizabeth Ryan	6-1	6-1	
S	Lili de Alvarez	Daphne Akhurst	6-3	6-0	
Q	Helen Wills	Phoebe Holcroft Watson	6-3	6-0	
Q	Elizabeth Ryan	Helene Nicolopoulo	6-1	4-6	6-2
Q	Lili de Alvarez	Cilly Aussem	7-5	6-3	
Q	Daphne Akhurst	Eileen Bennett	2-6	6-3	6-2
1929					
F	**Helen Wills**	**Helen Jacobs**	6-1	6-2	
S	Helen Wills	Elsie Goldsack	6-2	6-4	
S	Helen Jacobs	Joan Ridley	6-2	6-2	
Q	Helen Wills	Bobbie Heine	6-2	6-4	
Q	Elsie Goldsack	Billie Tapscott	6-3	6-3	
Q	Helen Jacobs	Mary Hart McIlquham	6-1	6-0	
Q	Joan Ridley	May Sutton Bundy	6-3	6-2	
1930					
F	**Helen Wills Moody**	**Elizabeth Ryan**	6-2	6-2	
S	Helen Wills Moody	Simone Passemard Mathieu	6-3	6-2	
S	Elizabeth Ryan	Cilly Aussem	6-3	0-6	4-4 (retired)
Q	Helen Wills Moody	Phyllis Mudford	6-1	6-2	
Q	Simone Passemard Mathieu	Joan Ridley	6-2	6-1	
Q	Elizabeth Ryan	Betty Nuthall	6-2	2-6	6-0
Q	Cilly Aussem	Helen Jacobs	6-2	6-1	

Rd	Winner	Defeated	S1	S2	S3

1931

F	**Cilly Aussem**	**Hilde Krahwinkel**	**6-2**	**7-5**	
S	Cilly Aussem	Simone Passemard Mathieu	6-0	2-6	6-3
S	Hilde Krahwinkel	Helen Jacobs	10-8	0-6	6-4
Q	Cilly Aussem	Lolette Payot	2-6	6-2	6-1
Q	Simone Passemard Mathieu	Margaret Scriven	1-6	6-2	7-5
Q	Helen Jacobs	Betty Nuthall	6-2	6-3	
Q	Hilde Krahwinkel	Dorothy Round	7-5	6-3	

1932

F	**Helen Wills Moody**	**Helen Jacobs**	**6-3**	**6-1**	
S	Helen Wills Moody	Mary Heeley	6-2	6-0	
S	Helen Jacobs	Simone Passemard Mathieu	7-5	6-1	
Q	Helen Wills Moody	Dorothy Round	6-0	6-1	
Q	Mary Heeley	Eileen Bennett Whittingstall	6-4	6-0	
Q	Helen Jacobs	Hilde Krahwinkel	6-2	6-4	
Q	Simone Passemard Mathieu	Betty Nuthall	6-0	6-3	

1933

F	**Helen Wills Moody**	**Dorothy Round**	**6-4**	**6-8**	**6-3**
S	Dorothy Round	Helen Jacobs	4-6	6-4	6-2
S	Helen Wills Moody	Hilde Krahwinkel	6-4	6-3	
Q	Dorothy Round	Lucia Valerio	6-3	6-2	
Q	Helen Jacobs	Simone Passemard Mathieu	6-1	1-6	6-2
Q	Hilde Krahwinkel	Margaret Scriven	6-4	3-6	6-1
Q	Helen Wills Moody	Lolette Payot	6-4	6-1	

1934

F	**Dorothy Round**	**Helen Jacobs**	**6-2**	**5-7**	**6-3**
S	Dorothy Round	Simone Passemard Mathieu	6-4	5-7	6-2
S	Helen Jacobs	Joan Hartigan	6-2	6-2	
Q	Dorothy Round	Lolette Payot	6-4	6-2	
Q	Simone Passemard Mathieu	Sarah Palfrey	6-3	6-8	6-2
Q	Helen Jacobs	Cilly Aussem	6-0	6-2	
Q	Joan Hartigan	Margaret Scriven	3-6	6-3	6-1

1935

F	**Helen Wills Moody**	**Helen Jacobs**	**6-3**	**3-6**	**7-5**
S	Helen Wills Moody	Joan Hartigan	6-3	6-3	
S	Helen Jacobs	Hilde Krahwinkel Sperling	6-3	6-0	
Q	Joan Hartigan	Dorothy Round	4-6	6-4	6-3
Q	Helen Wills Moody	Simone Passemard Mathieu	6-3	6-0	
Q	Helen Jacobs	Jadwiga Jedrzejowska	6-1	9-7	
Q	Hilde Krahwinkel Sperling	Kay Stammers	7-5	7-5	

1936

F	**Helen Jacobs**	**Hilde Krahwinkel Sperling**	**6-2**	**4-6**	**7-5**
S	Helen Jacobs	Jadwiga Jedrzejowska	6-4	6-2	
S	Hilde Krahwinkel Sperling	Simone Passemard Mathieu	6-3	6-2	
Q	Helen Jacobs	Anita Lizana	6-2	1-6	6-4
Q	Jadwiga Jedrzejowska	Kay Stammers	6-2	6-3	
Q	Simone Passemard Mathieu	Marie Luise Horn	7-5	6-3	
Q	Hilde Krahwinkel Sperling	Dorothy Round	6-3	8-6	

1937

F	**Dorothy Round**	**Jadwiga Jedrzejowska**	**6-2**	**2-6**	**7-5**
S	Jadwiga Jedrzejowska	Alice Marble	8-6	6-2	
S	Dorothy Round	Simone Passemard Mathieu	6-4	6-0	
Q	Alice Marble	Hilde Krahwinkel Sperling	7-5	2-6	6-3
Q	Jadwiga Jedrzejowska	Margaret Scriven	6-1	6-2	
Q	Simone Passemard Mathieu	Anita Lizana	6-3	6-3	
Q	Dorothy Round	Helen Jacobs	6-4	6-2	

1938

F	**Helen Wills Moody**	**Helen Jacobs**	**6-4**	**6-0**	
S	Helen Jacobs	Alice Marble	6-4	6-4	
S	Helen Wills Moody	Hilde Krahwinkel Sperling	12-10	6-4	
Q	Alice Marble	Simone Passemard Mathieu	6-2	6-3	
Q	Helen Jacobs	Jadwiga Jedrzejowska	6-2	6-3	
Q	Hilde Krahwinkel Sperling	Sarah Palfrey Fabyan	4-6	6-4	6-4
Q	Helen Wills Moody	Kay Stammers	6-2	6-1	

1939

F	**Alice Marble**	**Kay Stammers**	**6-2**	**6-0**	
S	Kay Stammers	Sarah Palfrey Fabyan	7-5	2-6	6-3
S	Alice Marble	Hilde Krahwinkel Sperling	6-0	6-0	
Q	Kay Stammers	Helen Jacobs	6-2	6-2	
Q	Sarah Palfrey Fabyan	Simone Passemard Mathieu	6-4	6-2	
Q	Hilde Krahwinkel Sperling	Mary Hardwick	6-4	6-0	
Q	Alice Marble	Jadwiga Jedrzejowska	6-1	6-4	

1940-45   Not held – WW II

1946

F	**Pauline Betz**	**Louise Brough**	**6-2**	**6-4**	
S	Pauline Betz	Dorothy Bundy	6-2	6-3	
S	Louise Brough	Margaret Osborne	8-6	7-5	
Q	Pauline Betz	Joan Curry	6-0	6-3	
Q	Dorothy Bundy	Kay Stammers Menzies	4-6	6-1	6-3
Q	Louise Brough	Jean Bostock	6-1	6-2	
Q	Margaret Osborne	Doris Hart	5-7	6-4	6-4

1947

F	**Margaret Osborne**	**Doris Hart**	**6-2**	**6-4**	
S	Doris Hart	Louise Brough	2-6	8-6	6-4
S	Margaret Osborne	Sheila Piercey Summers	6-1	6-2	
Q	Louise Brough	Nancye Wynne Bolton	6-2	6-3	
Q	Doris Hart	Jean Bostock	4-6	6-1	6-2
Q	Sheila Piercey Summers	Pat Canning Todd	7-5	6-4	
Q	Margaret Osborne	Kay Stammers Menzies	6-2	6-4	

1948

F	**Louise Brough**	**Doris Hart**	**6-3**	**8-6**	
S	Doris Hart	Margaret Osborne duPont	6-4	2-6	6-3
S	Louise Brough	Pat Canning Todd	6-3	7-5	
Q	Margaret Osborne duPont	Jean Bostock	7-5	6-3	
Q	Doris Hart	Nelly Adamson Landry	6-0	6-2	
Q	Pat Canning Todd	Jean Quertier	6-2	6-4	
Q	Louise Brough	Shirley Fry	3-1		(retired)

1949

F	**Louise Brough**	**Margaret Osborne duPont**	**10-8**	**1-6**	**10-8**
S	Louise Brough	Pat Canning Todd	6-3	6-0	
S	Margaret Osborne duPont	Helen Pedersen Rihbany	6-2	6-2	
Q	Louise Brough	Molly Lincoln Blair	6-2	6-3	
Q	Pat Canning Todd	Jean Walker Smith	3-6	6-4	6-3
Q	Helen Pedersen Rihbany	Peggy Dawson-Scott	7-5	7-5	
Q	Margaret Osborne duPont	Betty Hilton	6-1	6-3	

1950

F	**Louise Brough**	**Margaret Osborne duPont**	**6-1**	**3-6**	**6-1**
S	Louise Brough	Doris Hart	6-4	6-3	
S	Margaret Osborne duPont	Pat Canning Todd	8-6	4-6	8-6
S	Louise Brough	Shirley Fry	2-6	6-3	6-0
Q	Doris Hart	Barbara Scofield	6-1	6-1	
Q	Pat Canning Todd	Betty Harrison	6-2	6-2	
Q	Margaret Osborne duPont	Gussy Moran	6-4	6-4	

1951

F	**Doris Hart**	**Shirley Fry**	**6-1**	**6-0**	
S	Doris Hart	Beverly Baker	6-3	6-1	
S	Shirley Fry	Louise Brough	6-4	6-2	
Q	Beverly Baker	Margaret Osborne duPont	6-1	4-6	6-3
Q	Doris Hart	Nancy Chaffee	6-3	6-3	
Q	Shirley Fry	Jean Walker Smith	8-6	6-4	
Q	Louise Brough	Kay Tuckey	5-7	6-1	6-3

Rd	Winner	Defeated	S1	S2	S3
1952					
F	**Maureen Connolly**	**Louise Brough**	**7-5**	**6-3**	
S	Maureen Connolly	Shirley Fry	6-4	6-3	
S	Louise Brough	Pat Canning Todd	6-3	3-6	6-1
Q	Maureen Connolly	Thelma Long	5-7	2-6	6-0
Q	Shirley Fry	Jean Walker Smith	6-3	6-3	
Q	Louise Brough	Jean Quertier-Rinkel	6-1	9-7	
Q	Pat Canning Todd	Doris Hart	6-8	7-5	6-4
1953					
F	**Maureen Connolly**	**Doris Hart**	**8-6**	**7-5**	
S	Doris Hart	Dorothy Head Knode	6-2	6-2	
S	Maureen Connolly	Shirley Fry	6-1	6-1	
Q	Doris Hart	Suzi Kormoczi	7-5	7-5	
Q	Dorothy Head Knode	Angela Mortimer	6-4	6-3	
Q	Shirley Fry	Julia Sampson	6-4	6-2	
Q	Maureen Connolly	Erika Vollmer	6-3	6-0	
1954					
F	**Maureen Connolly**	**Louise Brough**	**6-2**	**7-5**	
S	Louise Brough	Doris Hart	2-6	6-3	6-3
S	Maureen Connolly	Betty Rosenquest Pratt	6-1	6-1	
Q	Doris Hart	Helen Fletcher	6-1	6-3	
Q	Louise Brough	Angela Mortimer	6-1	6-3	
Q	Betty Rosenquest Pratt	Shirley Fry	6-4	9-11	6-3
Q	Maureen Connolly	Margaret Osborne duPont	6-1	6-1	
1955					
F	**Louise Brough**	**Beverly Baker Fleitz**	**7-5**	**8-6**	
S	Beverly Baker Fleitz	Doris Hart	6-3	6-0	
S	Louise Brough	Darlene Hard	6-3	8-6	
Q	Doris Hart	Dorothy Head Knode	6-4	6-3	
Q	Beverly Baker Fleitz	Angela Buxton	6-2	6-2	
Q	Darlene Hard	Suzi Kormoczi	6-2	6-3	
Q	Louise Brough	Beryl Penrose	6-2	6-0	
1956					
F	**Shirley Fry**	**Angela Buxton**	**6-3**	**6-1**	
S	Angela Buxton	Pat Ward	6-1	6-4	
S	Shirley Fry	Louise Brough	6-4	4-6	6-3
Q	Angela Buxton	Beverly Baker Fleitz		(walkover)	
Q	Pat Ward	Angela Mortimer	6-3	6-0	
Q	Shirley Fry	Althea Gibson	4-6	6-3	6-4
Q	Louise Brough	Shirley Bloomer	5-7	6-1	6-3
1957					
F	**Althea Gibson**	**Darlene Hard**	**6-3**	**6-2**	
S	Darlene Hard	Dorothy Head Knode	6-2	6-3	
S	Althea Gibson	Christine Truman	6-1	6-1	
Q	Darlene Hard	Louise Brough	6-2	6-2	
Q	Dorothy Head Knode	Rosie Reyes	6-4	6-0	
Q	Christine Truman	Betty Rosenquest Pratt	9-7	5-7	6-4
Q	Althea Gibson	Sandra Reynolds	6-3	6-4	
1958					
F	**Althea Gibson**	**Angela Mortimer**	**8-6**	**6-2**	
S	Angela Mortimer	Suzi Kormoczi	6-0	6-1	
S	Althea Gibson	Ann Haydon	6-2	6-0	
Q	Suzi Kormoczi	Mimi Arnold	6-1	5-7	8-6
Q	Angela Mortimer	Margaret Osborne duPont	4-6	6-3	10-8
Q	Ann Haydon	Maria Bueno	6-3	7-5	
Q	Althea Gibson	Shirley Bloomer	6-3	6-8	6-2
1959					
F	**Maria Bueno**	**Darlene Hard**	**6-4**	**6-3**	
S	Darlene Hard	Sandra Reynolds	6-4	6-4	
S	Maria Bueno	Sally Moore	6-2	6-4	
Q	Sandra Reynolds	Angela Mortimer	7-5	8-6	
Q	Darlene Hard	Ann Haydon	1-6	6-4	7-5
Q	Maria Bueno	Edda Buding	6-3	6-3	
Q	Sally Moore	Yola Ramirez	6-3	6-2	

Rd	Winner	Defeated	S1	S2	S3
1960					
F	**Maria Bueno**	**Sandra Reynolds**	**8-6**	**6-0**	
S	Maria Bueno	Christine Truman	6-0	5-7	6-1
S	Sandra Reynolds	Ann Haydon	6-3	2-6	6-4
Q	Maria Bueno	Angela Mortimer	6-1	6-1	
Q	Christine Truman	Karen Hantze	4-6	6-4	6-4
Q	Ann Haydon	Renee Schuurman	7-5	1-6	6-2
Q	Sandra Reynolds	Darlene Hard	6-1	2-6	6-1
1961					
F	**Angela Mortimer**	**Christine Truman**	**4-6**	**6-4**	**7-5**
S	Christine Truman	Renee Schuurman	6-4	6-4	
S	Angela Mortimer	Sandra Reynolds	11-9	6-3	
Q	Christine Truman	Margaret Smith	3-6	6-3	9-7
Q	Renee Schuurman	Karen Hantze	6-4	2-6	7-5
Q	Angela Mortimer	Vera Sukova	6-3	6-4	
Q	Sandra Reynolds	Yola Ramirez	4-6	6-3	6-0
1962					
F	**Karen Hantze Susman**	**Vera Sukova**	**6-4**	**6-4**	
S	Karen Hantze Susman	Ann Haydon	8-6	6-1	
S	Vera Sukova	Maria Bueno	6-4	6-3	
Q	Ann Haydon	Billie Jean Moffitt	6-3	6-1	
Q	Karen Hantze Susman	Renee Schuurman	6-4	6-4	
Q	Maria Bueno	Lesley Turner	2-6	6-4	6-2
Q	Vera Sukova	Darlene Hard	6-4	6-3	
1963					
F	**Margaret Smith**	**Billie Jean Moffitt**	**6-3**	**6-4**	
S	Margaret Smith	Darlene Hard	6-3	6-3	
S	Billie Jean Moffitt	Ann Haydon Jones	6-4	6-4	
Q	Margaret Smith	Renee Schuurman	3-6	6-0	6-1
Q	Darlene Hard	Jan Lehane	6-1	1-2	(retired)
Q	Ann Haydon Jones	Donna Floyd Fales	6-4	6-1	
Q	Billie Jean Moffitt	Maria Bueno	6-2	7-5	
1964					
F	**Maria Bueno**	**Margaret Smith**	**6-4**	**7-9**	**6-3**
S	Margaret Smith	Billie Jean Moffitt	6-3	6-4	
S	Maria Bueno	Lesley Turner	3-6	6-4	6-4
Q	Margaret Smith	Norma Baylon	6-0	2-0	(retired)
Q	Billie Jean Moffitt	Ann Haydon Jones	6-3	6-3	
Q	Lesley Turner	Nancy Richey	6-3	6-4	
Q	Maria Bueno	Robyn Ebbern	6-4	6-1	
1965					
F	**Margaret Smith**	**Maria Bueno**	**6-4**	**7-5**	
S	Maria Bueno	Billie Jean Moffitt	6-4	5-7	6-3
S	Margaret Smith	Christine Truman	6-4	6-0	
Q	Maria Bueno	Jane Albert	6-2	6-2	
Q	Billie Jean Moffitt	Lesley Turner	6-2	6-1	
Q	Christine Truman	Nancy Richey	6-4	1-6	7-5
Q	Margaret Smith	Justina Bricka	6-3	6-0	
1966					
F	**Billie Jean King**	**Maria Bueno**	**6-3**	**3-6**	**6-1**
S	Billie Jean King	Margaret Smith	6-3	6-3	
S	Maria Bueno	Ann Haydon Jones	6-3	9-11	7-5
Q	Margaret Smith	Trudy Groenman	6-0	6-3	
Q	Billie Jean King	Annette Van Zyl	1-6	6-2	6-4
Q	Ann Haydon Jones	Nancy Richey	4-6	6-1	6-1
Q	Maria Bueno	Françoise Durr	6-4	6-3	
1967					
F	**Billie Jean King**	**Ann Haydon Jones**	**6-3**	**6-4**	
S	Billie Jean King	Kathy Harter	6-0	6-3	
S	Ann Haydon Jones	Rosie Casals	2-6	6-3	7-5
Q	Billie Jean King	Virginia Wade	7-5	6-2	
Q	Kathy Harter	Lesley Turner	7-5	1-6	6-2
Q	Ann Haydon Jones	Mary Ann Eisel	6-2	4-6	7-5
Q	Rosie Casals	Judy Tegart	7-5	6-4	

Rd	Winner	Defeated	S1	S2	S3
1968					
F	**Billie Jean King**	**Judy Tegart**	**9-7**	**7-5**	
S	Judy Tegart	Nancy Richey	6-3	6-1	
S	Billie Jean King	Ann Haydon Jones	4-6	7-5	6-2
Q	Judy Tegart	Margaret Smith Court	4-6	8-6	6-1
Q	Nancy Richey	Maria Bueno	6-4	6-2	
Q	Ann Haydon Jones	Françoise Durr	6-2	6-2	
Q	Billie Jean King	Lesley Turner Bowrey	6-3	6-4	
1969					
F	**Ann Haydon Jones**	**Billie Jean King**	**3-6**	**6-3**	**6-2**
S	Ann Haydon Jones	Margaret Smith Court	10-12	6-3	6-2
S	Billie Jean King	Rosie Casals	6-1	6-0	
Q	Rosie Casals	Lesley Turner Bowrey	3-6	9-7	7-5
Q	Billie Jean King	Judy Tegart	4-6	7-5	8-6
Q	Ann Haydon Jones	Nancy Richey	6-2	7-5	
Q	Margaret Smith Court	Julie Heldman	4-6	6-3	6-3
1970					
F	**Margaret Smith Court**	**Billie Jean King**	**14-12**	**11-9**	
S	Billie Jean King	Françoise Durr	6-3	7-5	
S	Margaret Smith Court	Rosie Casals	6-4	6-1	
Q	Françoise Durr	Cecilia Martinez	6-0	6-4	
Q	Billie Jean King	Karen Krantzcke	3-6	6-3	6-2
Q	Rosie Casals	Winnie Shaw	6-2	6-0	
Q	Margaret Smith Court	Helga Masthoff	6-8	6-0	6-0
1971					
F	**Evonne Goolagong**	**Margaret Smith Court**	**6-4**	**6-1**	
S	Evonne Goolagong	Billie Jean King	6-4	6-4	
S	Margaret Smith Court	Judy Tegart Dalton	4-6	6-1	6-0
Q	Margaret Smith Court	Winnie Shaw	6-2	6-1	
Q	Judy Tegart Dalton	Kerry Melville	6-2	3-6	6-3
Q	Evonne Goolagong	Nancy Richey Gunter	6-3	6-2	
Q	Billie Jean King	Françoise Durr	2-6	6-2	6-2
1972					
F	**Billie Jean King**	**Evonne Goolagong**	**6-3**	**6-3**	
S	Billie Jean King	Rosie Casals	6-2	6-4	
S	Evonne Goolagong	Chris Evert	4-6	6-3	6-4
Q	Chris Evert	Patti Hogan	6-2	4-6	6-1
Q	Evonne Goolagong	Françoise Durr	8-6	7-5	
Q	Rosie Casals	Nancy Richey Gunter	3-6	6-4	6-0
Q	Billie Jean King	Virginia Wade	6-1	3-6	6-3
1973					
F	**Billie Jean King**	**Chris Evert**	**6-0**	**7-5**	
S	Chris Evert	Margaret Smith Court	6-1	1-6	6-1
S	Billie Jean King	Evonne Goolagong	6-3	5-7	6-3
Q	Margaret Smith Court	Olga Morozova	4-6	6-4	6-1
Q	Chris Evert	Rosie Casals	6-2	4-6	6-2
Q	Evonne Goolagong	Virginia Wade	6-3	6-3	
Q	Billie Jean King	Kerry Melville	9-8(5)	8-6	
1974					
F	**Chris Evert**	**Olga Morozova**	**6-0**	**6-4**	
S	Olga Morozova	Virginia Wade	1-6	7-5	6-4
S	Chris Evert	Kerry Melville	6-2	6-3	
Q	Olga Morozova	Billie Jean King	7-5	6-2	
Q	Virginia Wade	Linky Boshoff	6-3	6-2	
Q	Kerry Melville	Evonne Goolagong	9-7	1-6	6-2
Q	Chris Evert	Helga Masthoff	6-4	6-2	
1975					
F	**Billie Jean King**	**Evonne Goolagong Cawley 6-0**		**6-1**	
S	Evonne Goolagong Cawley	Margaret Smith Court	6-4	6-4	
S	Billie Jean King	Chris Evert	2-6	6-2	6-3
Q	Chris Evert	Betty Stove	5-7	7-5	6-0
Q	Billie Jean King	Olga Morozova	6-3	6-3	
Q	Evonne Goolagong Cawley	Virginia Wade	5-7	6-3	9-7
Q	Margaret Smith Court	Martina Navratilova	6-3	6-4	
1976					
F	**Chris Evert**	**Evonne Goolagong Cawley 6-3**		**4-6**	**8-6**
S	Evonne Goolagong Cawley	Virginia Wade	6-1	6-2	
S	Chris Evert	Martina Navratilova	6-3	4-6	6-4
Q	Chris Evert	Olga Morozova	6-3	6-0	
Q	Martina Navratilova	Sue Barker	6-3	3-6	7-5
Q	Virginia Wade	Kerry Melville Reid	6-4	6-2	
Q	Evonne Goolagong Cawley	Rosie Casals	7-5	6-3	
1977					
F	**Virginia Wade**	**Betty Stove**	**4-6**	**6-3**	**6-1**
S	Betty Stove	Sue Barker	6-4	2-6	6-4
S	Virginia Wade	Chris Evert	6-2	4-6	6-1
Q	Chris Evert	Billie Jean King	6-1	6-2	
Q	Virginia Wade	Rosie Casals	7-5	6-2	
Q	Sue Barker	Kerry Melville Reid	6-3	6-4	
Q	Betty Stove	Martina Navratilova	9-8(6)	3-6	6-1
1978					
F	**Martina Navratilova**	**Chris Evert**	**2-6**	**6-4**	**7-5**
S	Martina Navratilova	Evonne Goolagong Cawley	2-6	6-4	6-4
S	Chris Evert	Virginia Wade	8-6	6-2	
Q	Chris Evert	Billie Jean King	6-3	3-6	6-2
Q	Virginia Wade	Mima Jausovec	6-0	6-4	
Q	Evonne Goolagong Cawley	Virginia Ruzici	7-5	6-3	
Q	Martina Navratilova	Marise Kruger	6-2	6-4	
1979					
F	**Martina Navratilova**	**Chris Evert Lloyd**	**6-4**	**6-4**	
S	Chris Evert Lloyd	Evonne Goolagong Cawley	6-3	6-2	
S	Martina Navratilova	Tracy Austin	7-5	6-1	
Q	Tracy Austin	Billie Jean King	6-4	6-7(5)	6-2
Q	Evonne Goolagong Cawley	Virginia Wade	6-4	6-0	
Q	Chris Evert Lloyd	Wendy Turnbull	6-3	6-4	
Q	Martina Navratilova	Dianne Balestrat Fromholtz	2-6	6-3	6-0
1980					
F	**Evonne Goolagong Cawley**	**Chris Evert Lloyd**	**6-1**	**7-6(4)**	
S	Evonne Goolagong Cawley	Tracy Austin	6-3	0-6	6-4
S	Chris Evert Lloyd	Martina Navratilova	4-6	6-4	6-2
Q	Martina Navratilova	Billie Jean King	7-6(6)	1-6	10-8
Q	Evonne Goolagong Cawley	Wendy Turnbull	6-3	6-2	
Q	Chris Evert Lloyd	Andrea Jaeger	6-1	6-1	
Q	Tracy Austin	Greer Stevens	6-3	6-3	
1981					
F	**Chris Evert Lloyd**	**Hana Mandlikova**	**6-2**	**6-2**	
S	Hana Mandlikova	Martina Navratilova	7-5	4-6	6-1
S	Chris Evert Lloyd	Pam Shriver	6-3	6-1	
Q	Chris Evert Lloyd	Mima Jausovec	6-2	6-2	
Q	Pam Shriver	Tracy Austin	7-5	6-4	
Q	Martina Navratilova	Virginia Ruzici	6-2	6-3	
Q	Hana Mandlikova	Wendy Turnbull	6-0	6-0	
1982					
F	**Martina Navratilova**	**Chris Evert Lloyd**	**6-1**	**3-6**	**6-2**
S	Chris Evert Lloyd	Billie Jean King	7-6(4)	2-6	6-3
S	Martina Navratilova	Bettina Bunge	6-2	6-2	
Q	Martina Navratilova	JoAnne Russell	6-3	6-4	
Q	Bettina Bunge	Anne Smith	6-3	2-6	6-0
Q	Billie Jean King	Tracy Austin	3-6	6-4	6-2
Q	Chris Evert Lloyd	Barbara Potter	6-2	6-1	
1983					
F	**Martina Navratilova**	**Andrea Jaeger**	**6-0**	**6-3**	
S	Andrea Jaeger	Billie Jean King	6-1	6-1	
S	Martina Navratilova	Yvonne Vermaak	6-1	6-1	
Q	Martina Navratilova	Jennifer Mundel	6-3	6-1	
Q	Yvonne Vermaak	Virginia Wade	6-3	2-6	6-2
Q	Andrea Jaeger	Barbara Potter	6-4	6-1	
Q	Billie Jean King	Kathy Jordan	7-5	6-4	

Rd	Winner	Defeated	S1	S2	S3
1984					
F	**Martina Navratilova**	**Chris Evert Lloyd**	**7-6(5)**	**6-2**	
S	Chris Evert Lloyd	Hana Mandlikova	6-1	6-2	
S	Martina Navratilova	Kathy Jordan	6-3	6-4	
Q	Martina Navratilova	Manuela Maleeva	6-3	6-2	
Q	Kathy Jordan	Pam Shriver	2-6	6-3	6-4
Q	Hana Mandlikova	Jo Durie	6-1	6-4	
Q	Chris Evert Lloyd	Carina Karlsson	6-2	6-2	
1985					
F	**Martina Navratilova**	**Chris Evert Lloyd**	**4-6**	**6-3**	**6-2**
S	Martina Navratilova	Zina Garrison	6-4	7-6(3)	
S	Chris Evert Lloyd	Kathy Rinaldi	6-2	6-0	
Q	Chris Evert Lloyd	Barbara Potter	6-2	6-1	
Q	Kathy Rinaldi	Helena Sukova	6-1	1-6	6-1
Q	Zina Garrison	Molly Van Nostrand	2-6	6-3	6-0
Q	Martina Navratilova	Pam Shriver	7-5(5)	6-3	
1986					
F	**Martina Navratilova**	**Hana Mandlikova**	**7-6(1)**	**6-3**	
S	Hana Mandlikova	Chris Evert Lloyd	7-6(5)	7-5	
S	Martina Navratilova	Gabriela Sabatini	6-2	6-2	
Q	Martina Navratilova	Bettina Bunge	6-1	6-3	
Q	Gabriela Sabatini	Catarina Lindqvist	6-2	6-3	
Q	Hana Mandlikova	Lori McNeil	6-7(4)	6-0	6-2
Q	Chris Evert Lloyd	Helena Sukova	7-6(8)	4-6	6-4
1987					
F	**Martina Navratilova**	**Steffi Graf**	**7-5**	**6-3**	
S	Martina Navratilova	Chris Evert	6-2	5-7	6-4
S	Steffi Graf	Pam Shriver	6-0	6-2	
Q	Martina Navratilova	Dianne Balestrat	6-2	6-1	
Q	Chris Evert	Claudia Kohde Kilsch	6-1	6-3	
Q	Pam Shriver	Helena Sukova	4-6	7-6(1)	10-8
Q	Steffi Graf	Gabriela Sabatini	4-6	6-1	6-1
1988					
F	**Steffi Graf**	**Martina Navratilova**	**5-7**	**6-2**	**6-1**
S	Steffi Graf	Pam Shriver	6-1	6-2	
S	Martina Navratilova	Chris Evert	6-1	4-6	7-5
Q	Steffi Graf	Pascale Paradis	6-3	6-1	
Q	Pam Shriver	Zina Garrison	6-4	6-4	
Q	Chris Evert	Helena Sukova	6-3	7-6(4)	
Q	Martina Navratilova	Rosalyn Fairbank	4-6	6-4	7-5
1989					
F	**Steffi Graf**	**Martina Navratilova**	**6-2**	**6-7(1)**	**6-1**
S	Steffi Graf	Chris Evert	6-2	6-1	
S	Martina Navratilova	Catarina Lindqvist	7-6(5)	6-2	
Q	Steffi Graf	Arantxa Sanchez Vicario	7-5	6-1	
Q	Chris Evert	Laura Golarsa	6-3	2-6	7-5
Q	Catarina Lindqvist	Rosalyn Fairbank	7-5	7-5	
Q	Martina Navratilova	Gretchen Rush Magers	6-1	6-2	
1990					
F	**Martina Navratilova**	**Zina Garrison**	**6-4**	**6-1**	
S	Zina Garrison	Steffi Graf	6-3	3-6	6-4
S	Martina Navratilova	Gabriela Sabatini	6-3	6-4	
Q	Steffi Graf	Jana Novotna	7-5	6-2	
Q	Zina Garrison	Monica Seles	3-6	6-3	9-7
Q	Gabriela Sabatini	Natasha Zvereva	6-2	2-6	8-6
Q	Martina Navratilova	Katerina Maleeva	6-1	6-1	
1991					
F	**Steffi Graf**	**Gabriela Sabatini**	**6-4**	**3-6**	**8-6**
S	Steffi Graf	Mary Joe Fernandez	6-2	6-4	
S	Gabriela Sabatini	Jennifer Capriati	6-4	6-4	
Q	Steffi Graf	Zina Garrison	6-1	6-3	
Q	Mary Joe Fernandez	Arantxa Sanchez Vicario	6-2	7-5	
Q	Jennifer Capriati	Martina Navratilova	6-4	7-5	
Q	Gabriela Sabatini	Laura Gildemeister	6-2	6-1	
1992					
F	**Steffi Graf**	**Monica Seles**	**6-2**	**6-1**	
S	Monica Seles	Martina Navratilova	6-2	6-7(3)	6-4
S	Steffi Graf	Gabriela Sabatini	6-3	6-3	
Q	Monica Seles	Nathalie Tauziat	6-1	6-3	
Q	Martina Navratilova	Katerina Maleeva	6-3	7-6(2)	
Q	Gabriela Sabatini	Jennifer Capriati	6-1	3-6	6-3
Q	Steffi Graf	Natasha Zvereva	6-3	6-1	
1993					
F	**Steffi Graf**	**Jana Novotna**	**7-6(6)**	**1-6**	**6-4**
S	Steffi Graf	Conchita Martinez	7-6 (0)	6-3	
S	Jana Novotna	Martina Navratilova	6-4	6-4	
Q	Steffi Graf	Jennifer Capriati	7-6(3)	6-1	
Q	Conchita Martinez	Helena Sukova	6-1	6-4	
Q	Jana Novotna	Gabriela Sabatini	6-4	6-3	
Q	Martina Navratilova	Natasha Zvereva	6-3	6-1	
1994					
F	**Conchita Martinez**	**Martina Navratilova**	**6-4**	**3-6**	**6-3**
S	Conchita Martinez	Lori McNeil	3-6	6-3	10-8
S	Martina Navratilova	Gigi Fernandez	6-4	7-6(6)	
Q	Lori McNeil	Larisa Savchenko Neiland	6-3	6-4	
Q	Conchita Martinez	Lindsay Davenport	6-2	6-7(4)	6-3
Q	Martina Navratilova	Jana Novotna	5-7	6-0	6-1
Q	Gigi Fernandez	Zina Garrison Jackson	6-4	6-4	
1995					
F	**Steffi Graf**	**Arantxa Sanchez Vicario**	**4-6**	**6-1**	**7-5**
S	Steffi Graf	Jana Novotna	5-7	6-4	6-2
S	Arantxa Sanchez Vicario	Conchita Martinez	6-3	6-7(5)	6-1
Q	Steffi Graf	Mary Joe Fernandez	6-3	6-0	
Q	Jana Novotna	Kimiko Date	6-2	6-3	
Q	Conchita Martinez	Gabriela Sabatini	7-5	7-6(5)	
Q	Arantxa Sanchez Vicario	Brenda Schultz-McCarthy	6-4	7-6(4)	
1996					
F	**Steffi Graf**	**Arantxa Sanchez Vicario**	**6-3**	**7-5**	
S	Steffi Graf	Kimiko Date	6-2	2-6	6-3
S	Arantxa Sanchez Vicario	Meredith McGrath	6-2	6-1	
Q	Steffi Graf	Jana Novotna	6-3	6-2	
Q	Kimiko Date	Mary Pierce	3-6	6-3	6-1
Q	Arantxa Sanchez Vicario	Judith Wiesner	6-4	6-0	
Q	Meredith McGrath	Mary Joe Fernandez	6-3	6-1	
1997					
F	**Martina Hingis**	**Jana Novotna**	**2-6**	**6-3**	**6-3**
S	Martina Hingis	Anna Kournikova	6-3	6-2	
S	Jana Novotna	Arantxa Sanchez Vicario	6-4	6-2	
S	Martina Hingis	Denisa Chladkova	6-3	6-2	
Q	Anna Kournikova	Iva Majoli	7-6(1)	6-4	
Q	Jana Novotna	Yayuk Basuki	6-3	6-3	
Q	Arantxa Sanchez Vicario	Nathalie Tauziat	6-2	7-5	
1998					
F	**Jana Novotna**	**Nathalie Tauziat**	**6-4**	**7-6(2)**	
S	Jana Novotna	Martina Hingis	6-4	6-4	
S	Nathalie Tauziat	Natasha Zvereva	1-6	7-6(1)	6-3
Q	Martina Hingis	Arantxa Sanchez Vicario	6-3	3-6	6-3
Q	Jana Novotna	Venus Williams	7-5	7-6(2)	
Q	Natasha Zvereva	Monica Seles	7-6(4)	6-2	
Q	Nathalie Tauziat	Lindsay Davenport	6-3	6-3	
1999					
F	**Lindsay Davenport**	**Steffi Graf**	**6-4**	**7-5**	
S	Lindsay Davenport	Alexandra Stevenson	6-1	6-1	
S	Steffi Graf	Mirjana Lucic	6-7(3)	6-4	6-3
Q	Alexandra Stevenson	Jelena Dokic	6-3	1-6	6-3
Q	Lindsay Davenport	Jana Novotna	6-3	6-4	
Q	Mirjana Lucic	Nathalie Tauziat	4-6	6-4	7-5
Q	Steffi Graf	Venus Williams	6-2	3-6	6-4

Rd	Winner	Defeated	S1	S2	S3

2000

Rd	Winner	Defeated	S1	S2	S3
F	**Venus Williams**	**Lindsay Davenport**	**6-3**	**7-6(3)**	
S	Venus Williams	Serena Williams	6-2	7-6(3)	
S	Lindsay Davenport	Jelena Dokic	6-4	6-2	
Q	Venus Williams	Martina Hingis	6-3	4-6	6-4
Q	Serena Williams	Lisa Raymond	6-2	6-0	
Q	Jelena Dokic	Magui Serna	6-3	6-2	
Q	Lindsay Davenport	Monica Seles	6-7(4)	6-4	6-0

2001

Rd	Winner	Defeated	S1	S2	S3
F	**Venus Williams**	**Justine Henin**	**6-1**	**3-6**	**6-0**
S	Justine Henin	Jennifer Capriati	2-6	6-4	6-2
S	Venus Williams	Lindsay Davenport	6-2	6-7(1)	6-1
Q	Justine Henin	Conchita Martinez	6-1	6-0	
Q	Jennifer Capriati	Serena Williams	6-7(4)	7-5	6-3
Q	Lindsay Davenport	Kim Clijsters	6-1	6-2	
Q	Venus Williams	Nathalie Tauziat	7-5	7-1	

2002

Rd	Winner	Defeated	S1	S2	S3
F	**Serena Williams**	**Venus Williams**	**7-6(4)**	**6-3**	
S	Venus Williams	Justine Henin	6-3	6-2	
S	Serena Williams	Amelie Mauresmo	6-2	6-1	
Q	Venus Williams	Elena Likhovtseva	6-2	6-0	
Q	Justine Henin	Monica Seles	7-5	7-6(4)	
Q	Amelie Mauresmo	Jennifer Capriati	6-3	6-2	
Q	Serena Williams	Daniela Hantuchova	6-3	6-2	

Men's Doubles

Year	Winner	Defeated	S1	S2	S3	S4	S5
1884	Willie Renshaw Ernest Renshaw	Ernest Lewis Edward Williams	6-3	6-1	1-6	6-4	
1885	Willie Renshaw Ernest Renshaw	Claude Farrar Arthur Stanley	6-3	6-3	10-8		
				(challenge round instituted)			
1886	Willie Renshaw Ernest Renshaw	Claude Farrar Arthur Stanley	6-3	6-3	4-6	7-5	
1887	Herbert Wilberforce Patrick Bowes Lyon	James Crisp Barratt Smith	7-5	6-3	6-2		
1888	Willie Renshaw Ernest Renshaw	Herbert Wilberforce Patrick Bowes Lyon	2-6	1-6	6-3	6-4	6-3
1889	Willie Renshaw Ernest Renshaw	Ernest Lewis George Hillyard	6-4	6-4	3-6	0-6	6-1
1890	Joshua Pim Frank Stoker	Ernest Lewis George Hillyard	6-0	7-5	6-4		
1891	Wilfred Baddeley Herbert Baddeley	Joshua Pim Frank Stoker	6-1	6-3	1-6	6-2	
1892	Ernest Lewis Harry Barlow	Wilfred Baddeley Herbert Baddeley	4-6	6-2	8-6	6-4	
1893	Joshua Pim Frank Stoker	Ernest Lewis Harry Barlow	4-6	6-3	6-1	2-6	6-0
1894	Wilfred Baddeley Herbert Baddeley	Harry Barlow Charles Martin	5-7	7-5	4-6	6-3	8-6
1895	Wilfred Baddeley Herbert Baddeley	Ernest Lewis Wilberforce Eaves	8-6	5-7	6-4	6-3	
1896	Wilfred Baddeley Herbert Baddeley	Reggie Doherty Harold Nisbet	1-6	3-6	6-4	6-2	6-1
1897	Reggie Doherty Laurie Doherty	Wilfred Baddeley Herbert Baddeley	6-4	4-6	8-6	6-4	
1898	Reggie Doherty Laurie Doherty	Harold Nisbet Clarence Hobart	6-4	6-4	6-2		

Year	Winner	Defeated	S1	S2	S3	S4	S5
1899	Reggie Doherty Laurie Doherty	Harold Nisbet Clarence Hobart	7-5	6-0	6-2		
1900	Reggie Doherty Laurie Doherty	Herbert Roper Barrett Harold Nisbet	9-7	7-5	4-6	3-6	6-3
1901	Reggie Doherty Laurie Doherty	Dwight Davis Holcombe Ward	4-6	6-2	6-3	9-7	
1902	Sidney H. Smith Frank Riseley	Reggie Doherty Laurie Doherty	4-6	8-6	6-3	4-6	11-9
1903	Reggie Doherty Laurie Doherty	Sidney H. Smith Frank Risely	6-4	6-4	6-4		
1904	Reggie Doherty Laurie Doherty	Sidney H. Smith Frank Riseley	6-1	6-2	6-4		
1905	Reggie Doherty Laurie Doherty	Sidney H. Smith Frank Riseley	6-2	6-4	6-8	6-3	
1906	Sidney H. Smith Frank Riseley	Reggie Doherty Laurie Doherty	6-8	6-4	5-7	6-3	6-3
1907	Norman Brookes Tony Wilding	Beals Wright Karl Behr	6-4	6-4	6-2		
1908	Tony Wilding Josiah Ritchie	Arthur Gore Herbert Roper Barrett	6-1	6-2	1-6	1-6	9-7
1909	Arthur Gore Herbert Roper Barrett	Stanley Doust Harry Parker	6-2	6-1	6-4		
1910	Tony Wilding Josiah Ritchie	Arthur Gore Herbert Roper Barrett	6-1	6-1	6-2		
1911	Andre Gobert Max Decugis	Tony Wilding Josiah Ritchie	9-7	5-7	6-3	2-6	6-2
1912	Herbert Roper Barrett Charles Dixon	Andre Gobert Max Decugis	3-6	6-3	6-4	7-5	
1913	Herbert Roper Barrett Charles Dixon	Friedrich Rahe Heinrich Kleinschroth	6-2	6-4	4-6	6-2	
1914	Norman Brookes Tony Wilding	Herbert Roper Barrett Charles Dixon	6-1	6-1	5-7	8-6	
1915-18		Not held – WW I					
1919	Ronald Thomas Pat O'Hara Wood	Randolph Lycett Rodney Heath	6-4	6-2	4-6	6-2	
1920	Dick Williams Chuck Garland	Algie Kingscote Jim Parke	4-6	6-4	7-5	6-2	
1921	Randolph Lycett Max Woosnam	Arthur Lowe Frank Lowe	6-3	6-0	7-5		
1922	James Anderson Randolph Lycett	Gerald Patterson Pat O'Hara Wood	3-6	7-9	6-4	6-3	11-9
1923	Leslie Godfree Randolph Lycett	Manuel de Gomar Eduardo Flaquer	6-3	6-4	3-6	6-3	
1924	Frank Hunter Vinnie Richards	Dick Williams Watson Washburn	6-3	3-6	8-10	8-6	6-3
1925	Jean Borotra René Lacoste	John Hennessey Ray Casey	6-4	11-9	4-6	1-6	6-3
1926	Jacques Brugnon Henri Cochet	Howard Kinsey Vinnie Richards	7-5	4-6	6-3	6-2	
1927	Frank Hunter Bill Tilden	Jacques Brugnon Henri Cochet	1-6	4-6	8-6	6-3	6-4
1928	Jacques Brugnon Henri Cochet	Gerald Patterson Jack Hawkes	13-11	6-4	6-4		
1929	Wilmer Allison John Van Ryn	Colin Gregory Ian Collins	6-4	5-7	6-3	10-12	6-4

Year	Winner	Defeated	S1	S2	S3	S4	S5
1930	Wilmer Allison / John Van Ryn	Johnny Doeg / George Lott	6-3	6-3	6-2		
1931	George Lott / John Van Ryn	Jacques Brugnon / Henri Cochet	6-2	10-8	9-11	3-6	6-3
1932	Jean Borotra / Jacques Brugnon	Fred Perry / Pat Hughes	6-0	4-6	3-6	7-5	7-5
1933	Jean Borotra / Jacques Brugnon	Ryosuki Nunoi / Jiro Satoh	4-6	6-3	6-3	7-5	
1934	George Lott / Lester Stoefen	Jean Borotra / Jacques Brugnon	6-2	6-3	6-4		
1935	Jack Crawford / Adrian Quist	Wilmer Allison / John Van Ryn	6-3	5-7	6-2	5-7	7-5
1936	Pat Hughes / Charles Tuckey	Charles Hare / Frank Wilde	6-4	3-6	7-9	6-1	6-4
1937	Don Budge / Gene Mako	Pat Hughes / Charles Tuckey	6-0	6-4	6-8	6-1	
1938	Don Budge / Gene Mako	Henner Henkel / Georg von Metaxa	6-4	3-6	6-3	8-6	
1939	Elwood Cooke / Bobby Riggs	Charles Hare / Frank Wilde	6-3	3-6	6-3	9-7	
1940-45		Not held – WW II					
1946	Tom Brown / Jack Kramer	Geoff Brown / Dinny Pails	6-4	6-4	6-2		
1947	Bob Falkenburg / Jack Kramer	Tony Mottram / Bill Sidwell	8-6	6-3	6-3		
1948	John Bromwich / Frank Sedgman	Tom Brown / Gardnar Mulloy	5-7	7-5	7-5	9-7	
1949	Pancho Gonzalez / Frank Parker	Gardnar Mulloy / Ted Schroeder	6-4	6-4	6-2		
1950	John Bromwich / Adrian Quist	Geoff Brown / Bill Sidwell	7-5	3-6	6-3	3-6	6-2
1951	Ken McGregor / Frank Sedgman	Jaroslav Drobny / Eric Sturgess	3-6	6-2	6-3	3-6	6-3
1952	Ken McGregor / Frank Sedgman	Vic Seixas / Eric Sturgess	6-3	7-5	6-4		
1953	Lew Hoad / Ken Rosewall	Rex Hartwig / Merv Rose	6-4	7-5	4-6	7-5	
1954	Rex Hartwig / Merv Rose	Vic Seixas / Tony Trabert	6-4	6-4	3-6	6-4	
1955	Rex Hartwig / Lew Hoad	Neale Fraser / Ken Rosewall	7-5	6-4	6-3		
1956	Lew Hoad / Ken Rosewall	Nicola Pietrangeli / Orlando Sirola	7-5	6-2	6-1		
1957	Budge Patty / Gardnar Mulloy	Neale Fraser / Lew Hoad	8-10	6-4	6-4	6-4	
1958	Sven Davidson / Ulf Schmidt	Ashley Cooper / Neale Fraser	6-4	6-4	8-6		
1959	Roy Emerson / Neale Faser	Rod Laver / Bob Mark	8-6	6-3	14-16	9-7	
1960	Rafael Osuna / Dennis Ralston	Mike Davies / Bobby Wilson	7-5	6-3	10-8		
1961	Roy Emerson / Neale Fraser	Bob Hewitt / Fred Stolle	6-4	6-8	6-4	6-8	8-6
1962	Bob Hewitt / Fred Stolle	Boro Jovanovic / Nikki Pilic	6-2	5-7	6-2	6-4	
1963	Rafael Osuna / Antonio Palafox	Jean Claude Barclay / Pierre Darmon	4-6	6-2	6-2	6-2	
1964	Bob Hewitt / Fred Stolle	Roy Emerson / Ken Fletcher	7-5	11-9	6-4		
1965	John Newcombe / Tony Roche	Ken Fletcher / Bob Hewitt	7-5	6-3	6-4		
1966	Ken Fletcher / John Newcombe	Bill Bowrey / Owen Davidson	6-3	6-4	3-6	6-3	
1967	Bob Hewitt / Frew McMillan	Roy Emerson / Ken Fletcher	6-2	6-3	6-4		
1968	John Newcombe / Tony Roche	Ken Rosewall / Fred Stolle	3-6	8-6	5-7	14-12	6-3
1969	John Newcombe / Tony Roche	Tom Okker / Marty Riessen	7-5	11-9	6-3		
1970	John Newcombe / Tony Roche	Ken Rosewall / Fred Stolle	10-8	6-3	6-1		
1971	Roy Emerson / Rod Laver	Arthur Ashe / Dennis Ralston	4-6	9-7	6-8	6-4	6-4
1972	Bob Hewitt / Frew McMillan	Stan Smith / Eric van Dillen	6-2	6-2	9-7		
1973	Jimmy Connors / Ilie Nastase	John Cooper / Neale Fraser	3-6	6-3	6-4	8-9(3)	6-1
1974	John Newcombe / Tony Roche	Bob Lutz / Stan Smith	8-6	6-4	6-4		
1975	Vitas Gerulaitis / Alex Mayer	Colin Dowdeswell / Allan Stone	7-5	8-6	6-4		
1976	Brian Gottfried / Raul Ramirez	Ross Case / Geoff Masters	3-6	6-3	8-6	2-6	7-5
1977	Geoff Masters / Ross Case	John Alexander / Phil Dent	6-3	6-4	3-6	8-9(4)	6-4
1978	Bob Hewitt / Frew McMillan	Peter Fleming / John McEnroe	6-1	6-4	6-2		
1979	Peter Fleming / John McEnroe	Brian Gottfried / Raul Ramirez	4-6	6-4	6-2	6-2	
1980	Peter McNamara / Paul McNamee	Bob Lutz / Stan Smith	7-6(5)	6-3	6-7(4)	6-4	
1981	Peter Fleming / John McEnroe	Bob Lutz / Stan Smith	6-4	6-4	6-4		
1982	Peter McNamara / Paul McNamee	Peter Fleming / John McEnroe	6-3	6-2			
1983	Peter Fleming / John McEnroe	Tim Gullikson / Tom Gullikson	6-4	6-3	6-4		
1984	Peter Fleming / John McEnroe	Pat Cash / Paul McNamee	6-2	5-7	6-2	3-6	6-3
1985	Heinz Gunthardt / Balazs Taroczy	Pat Cash / John Fitzgerald	6-4	6-3	4-6	6-3	
1986	Joakim Nystrom / Mats Wilander	Gary Donnelly / Peter Fleming	7-6(4)	6-3	6-3		
1987	Ken Flach / Robert Seguso	Sergio Casal / Emilio Sanchez	3-6	6-7(6)	7-6(3)	6-1	6-4
1988	Ken Flach / Robert Seguso	John Fitzgerald / Anders Jarryd	6-4	2-6	6-4	7-6(3)	
1989	John Fitzgerald / Anders Jarryd	Rick Leach / Jim Pugh	3-6	7-6(4)	6-4	7-6(4)	
1990	Rick Leach / Jim Pugh	Pieter Aldrich / Danie Visser	7-6(5)	7-6(4)	7-6(5)		

Year	Winner	Defeated	S1	S2	S3	S4	S5
1991	John Fitzgerald Anders Jarryd	Javier Frana Leonardo Lavalle	6-3	6-4	6-7(7)	6-1	
1992	John McEnroe Michael Stich	Jim Grabb Richey Reneberg	5-7	7-6(5)	3-6	7-6(5)	19-17
1993	Todd Woodbridge Mark Woodforde	Grant Connell Patrick Galbraith	7-5	6-3	7-6(4)		
1994	Todd Woodbridge Mark Woodforde	Grant Connell Patrick Galbraith	7-6(3)	6-3	6-1		
1995	Todd Woodbridge Mark Woodforde	Rick Leach Scott Melville	7-5	7-6(8)	7-6(5)		
1996	Todd Woodbridge Mark Woodforde	Byron Black Grant Connell	4-6	6-1	6-3	6-2	
1997	Todd Woodbridge Mark Woodforde	Jacco Eltingh Paul Haarhuis	7-6(4)	7-6(7)	5-7	6-3	
1998	Jacco Eltingh Paul Haarhuis	Todd Woodbridge Mark Woodforde	2-6	6-4	7-6(3)	5-7	10-8
1999	Mahesh Bhupathi Leander Paes	Paul Haarhuis Jared Palmer	6-7(10)	6-3	6-4	7-6(4)	
2000	Todd Woodbridge Mark Woodforde	Paul Haarhuis Sandon Stolle	6-3	6-4	6-1		
2001	Donald Johnson Jared Palmer	Jiri Novak David Rikl	6-4	4-6	6-3	7-6(6)	
2002	Todd Woodbridge Jonas Bjorkman	Daniel Nestor Mark Knowles	6-1	6-2	6-7(7)	7-5	

Women's Doubles

Year	Winner	Defeated	S1	S2	S3
1913	Winifred Slocock McNair Dora Boothby	Charlotte Cooper Sterry Dorothea Douglass Chambers	4-6	2-4	retired
1914	Agnes Morton Elizabeth Ryan	Edith Boucher Hannam Ethel Thomson Larcombe	6-1	6-3	
1915-18		Not held – WW I			
1919	Suzanne Lenglen Elizabeth Ryan	Ethel Thomson Larcombe Dorothea Douglass Chambers	4-6	7-5	6-3
1920	Suzanne Lenglen Elizabeth Ryan	Ethel Thomson Larcombe Dorothea Douglass Chambers	6-4	6-0	
1921	Suzanne Lenglen Elizabeth Ryan	Geraldine Ramsey Beamish Irene Bowder Peacock	6-1	6-2	
1922	Suzanne Lenglen Elizabeth Ryan	Kitty McKane Margaret McKane Stocks	6-0	6-4	
1923	Suzanne Lenglen Elizabeth Ryan	Joan Austin Evelyn Colyer	6-3	6-1	
1924	Hazel Hotchkiss Wightman Helen Wills	Phyllis Howkins Covell Kitty McKane	6-4	6-4	
1925	Suzanne Lenglen Elizabeth Ryan	Kathleen Lidderdale Bridge Mary Hart McIlquham	6-2	6-2	
1926	Mary K. Browne Elizabeth Ryan	Kitty McKane Godfree Evelyn Colyer	6-1	6-1	
1927	Helen Wills Elizabeth Ryan	Bobbie Heine Irene Bowder Peacock	6-3	6-2	
1928	Peggy Saunders Phoebe Holcroft Watson	Eileen Bennett Ermyntrude Harvey	6-2	6-3	
1929	Peggy Saunders Michell Phoebe Holcroft Watson	Phyllis Howkins Covell Dorothy Shepherd Barron	6-4	8-6	

Year	Winner	Defeated	S1	S2	S3
1930	Helen Wills Moody Elizabeth Ryan	Edith Cross Sarah Palfrey	6-2	9-7	
1931	Dorothy Shepherd Barron Phyllis Mudford	Doris Metaxa Josane Sigart	3-6	6-3	6-4
1932	Doris Metaxa Josane Sigart	Helen Jacobs Elizabeth Ryan	6-4	6-3	
1933	Simone Passemard Mathieu Elizabeth Ryan	Freda James Billie Yorke	6-2	9-11	6-4
1934	Simone Passemard Mathieu Elizabeth Ryan	Dorothy Andrus Sylvie Jung Henrotin	6-3	6-3	
1935	Freda James Kay Stammers	Simone Passemard Mathieu Hilde Krahwinkel Sperling	6-1	6-4	
1936	Freda James Kay Stammers	Sarah Palfrey Fabyan Helen Jacobs	6-2	6-1	
1937	Simone Passemard Mathieu Billie Yorke	Phyllis Mudford King Elsie Goldsack Pittman	6-3	6-3	
1938	Sarah Palfrey Fabyan Alice Marble	Simone Passemard Mathieu Billie Yorke	6-2	6-3	
1939	Sarah Palfrey Fabyan Alice Marble	Helen Jacobs Billie Yorke	6-1	6-0	
1940-45		Not held – WW II			
1946	Louise Brough Margaret Osborne	Pauline Betz Doris Hart	6-3	2-6	6-3
1947	Doris Hart Pat Canning Todd	Louise Brough Margaret Osborne	3-6	6-4	7-5
1948	Louise Brough Margaret Osborne duPont	Doris Hart Pat Canning Todd	6-3	3-6	6-3
1949	Louise Brough Margaret Osborne duPont	Gussy Moran Pat Canning Todd	8-6	7-5	
1950	Louise Brough Margaret Osborne duPont	Shirley Fry Doris Hart	6-4	5-7	6-1
1951	Shirley Fry Doris Hart	Louise Brough Margaret Osborne duPont	6-3	13-11	
1952	Shirley Fry Doris Hart	Louise Brough Maureen Connolly	8-6	6-3	
1953	Shirley Fry Doris Hart	Maureen Connolly Julia Sampson	6-0	6-0	
1954	Louise Brough Margaret Osborne duPont	Shirley Fry Doris Hart	4-6	9-7	6-3
1955	Angela Mortimer Anne Shilcock	Shirley Bloomer Pat Ward	7-5	6-1	
1956	Angela Buxton Althea Gibson	Fay Muller Daphne Seeney	6-1	8-6	
1957	Althea Gibson Darlene Hard	Mary Bevis Hawton Thelma Coyne Long	6-1	6-2	
1958	Maria Bueno Althea Gibson	Margaret Osborne duPont Margaret Varner	6-3	7-5	
1959	Jeanne Arth Darlene Hard	Beverly Baker Fleitz Christine Truman	2-6	6-2	6-3
1960	Maria Bueno Darlene Hard	Sandra Reynolds Renee Schuurman	6-4	6-0	
1961	Karen Hantze Billie Jean Moffitt	Jan Lehane Margaret Smith	6-3	6-4	
1962	Billie Jean Moffitt Karen Hantze Susman	Sandra Reynolds Price Renee Schuurman	5-7	6-3	7-5
1963	Maria Bueno Darlene Hard	Robyn Ebbern Margaret Smith	8-6	9-7	

Year	Winner	Defeated	S1	S2	S3
1964	Margaret Smith Lesley Turner	Billie Jean Moffitt Karen Hantze Susman	7-5	6-2	
1965	Maria Bueno Billie Jean Moffitt	Françoise Durr Jeanine Lieffrig	6-2	7-5	
1966	Maria Bueno Nancy Richey	Margaret Smith Judy Tegart	6-3	4-6	6-4
1967	Rosie Casals Billie Jean King	Maria Bueno Nancy Richey	9-11	6-4	6-2
1968	Rosie Casals Billie Jean King	Françoise Durr Ann Haydon Jones	3-6	6-4	7-5
1969	Margaret Smith Court Judy Tegart	Patti Hogan Peggy Michel	9-7	6-2	
1970	Rosie Casals Billie Jean King	Françoise Durr Virginia Wade	6-2	6-3	
1971	Rosie Casals Billie Jean King	Margaret Smith Court Evonne Goolagong	6-3	6-2	
1972	Billie Jean King Betty Stove	Judy Tegart Dalton Françoise Durr	6-2	4-6	6-3
1973	Rosie Casals Billie Jean King	Françoise Durr Betty Stove	6-1	4-6	7-5
1974	Evonne Goolagong Peggy Michel	Helen Gourlay Karen Krantzcke	2-6	6-4	6-3
1975	Ann Kiyomura Kazuko Sawamatsu	Françoise Durr Betty Stove	7-5	1-6	7-5
1976	Chris Evert Martina Navratilova	Billie Jean King Betty Stove	6-1	3-6	7-5
1977	Helen Gourlay Cawley JoAnne Russell	Martina Navratilova Betty Stove	6-3	6-3	
1978	Kerry Melville Reid Wendy Turnbull	Mima Jausovec Virginia Ruzici	4-6	9-8(10)	6-3
1979	Billie Jean King Martina Navratilova	Betty Stove Wendy Turnbull	5-7	6-3	6-2
1980	Kathy Jordan Anne Smith	Rosie Casals Wendy Turnbull	4-6	7-5	6-1
1981	Martina Navratilova Pam Shriver	Kathy Jordan Anne Smith	6-3	7-6(6)	
1982	Martina Navratilova Pam Shriver	Kathy Jordan Anne Smith	6-4	6-1	
1983	Martina Navratilova Pam Shriver	Rosie Casals Wendy Turnbull	6-2	6-2	
1984	Martina Navratilova Pam Shriver	Kathy Jordan Anne Smith	6-3	6-4	
1985	Kathy Jordan Elizabeth Sayers Smylie	Martina Navratilova Pam Shriver	5-7	6-3	6-4
1986	Martina Navratilova Pam Shriver	Hana Mandlikova Wendy Turnbull	6-1	6-3	
1987	Claudia Kohde Kilsch Helena Sukova	Betsy Nagelsen Elizabeth Sayers Smylie	7-5	7-5	
1988	Steffi Graf Gabriela Sabatini	Larisa Savchenko Natalia Zvereva	6-3	1-6	12-10
1989	Jana Novotna Helena Sukova	Larisa Savchenko Natalia Zvereva	6-1	6-2	
1990	Jana Novotna Helena Sukova	Kathy Jordan Elizabeth Sayers Smylie	6-3	6-4	
1991	Larisa Savchenko Natalia Zvereva	Gigi Fernandez Jana Novotna	6-4	3-6	6-4

Year	Winner	Defeated	S1	S2	S3
1992	Gigi Fernandez Natalia Zvereva	Jana Novotna Larisa Savchenko Neiland	6-4	6-1	
1993	Gigi Fernandez Natalia Zvereva	Jana Novotna Larisa Savchenko Neiland	6-4	6-7(4)	6-4
1994	Gigi Fernandez Natalia Zvereva	Jana Novotna Arantxa Sanchez Vicario	6-4	6-1	
1995	Jana Novotna Arantxa Sanchez Vicario	Gigi Fernandez Natasha Zvereva	5-7	7-5	6-4
1996	Martina Hingis Helena Sukova	Meredith McGrath Larisa Savchenko Neiland	5-7	7-5	6-1
1997	Gigi Fernandez Natasha Zvereva	Nicole Arendt Manon Bollegraf	7-6(4)	6-4	
1998	Martina Hingis Jana Novotna	Lindsay Davenport Natasha Zvereva	6-3	3-6	8-6
1999	Lindsay Davenport Corina Morariu	Mariaan de Swardt Elena Tatarkova	6-4	6-4	
2000	Venus Williams Serena Williams	Ai Sugiyama Julie Halard-Decugis	6-3	6-2	
2001	Lisa Raymond Rennae Stubbs	Kim Clijsters Ai Sugiyama	6-4	6-3	
2002	Venus Williams Serena Williams	Paola Suarez Virginia Ruano Pascual	6-2	7-5	

Mixed Doubles

Year	Winner	Defeated	S1	S2	S3
1913	Agnes Daniell Tuckey Hope Crisp	Ethel Thomson Larcombe Jim Parke	3-6	5-3	retired
1914	Ethel Thomson Larcombe Jim Parke	Marguerite Broquedis Tony Wilding	4-6	6-4	6-2
1915-18	Not held – WW I				
1919	Elizabeth Ryan Randolph Lycett	Dorothea Douglass Chambers Albert Prebble	6-0	6-0	
1920	Suzanne Lenglen Gerald Patterson	Elizabeth Ryan Randolph Lycett	7-5	6-3	
1921	Elizabeth Ryan Randolph Lycett	Phyllis Howkins Max Woosnam	6-3	6-1	
1922	Suzanne Lenglen Pat O'Hara Wood	Elizabeth Ryan Randolph Lycett	6-4	6-3	
1923	Elizabeth Ryan Randolph Lycett	Dorothy Shepherd Barron Lewis Deane	6-4	7-5	
1924	Kitty McKane Brian Gilbert	Dorothy Shepherd Barron Leslie Godfree	6-3	3-6	6-3
1925	Suzanne Lenglen Jean Borotra	Elizabeth Ryan Umberto de Morpurgo	6-3	6-3	
1926	Kitty McKane Godfree Leslie Godfree	Mary K. Browne Howard Kinsey	6-3	6-4	
1927	Elizabeth Ryan Frank Hunter	Kitty McKane Godfree Leslie Godfree	8-6	6-0	
1928	Elizabeth Ryan Pat Spence	Daphne Akhurst Jack Crawford	7-5	6-4	
1929	Helen Wills Frank Hunter	Joan Fry Ian Collins	6-1	6-4	
1930	Elizabeth Ryan Jack Crawford	Hilde Krahwinkel Daniel Prenn	6-1	6-3	
1931	Anna McCune Harper George Lott	Joan Ridley Ian Collins	6-3	1-6	6-1

Year	Winner	Defeated	S1	S2	S3
1932	Elizabeth Ryan / Enrique Maier	Josane Sigart / Harry Hopman	7-5	6-2	
1933	Hilde Krahwinkel / Gottfried von Cramm	Mary Heeley / Norman Farquharson	7-5	8-6	
1934	Dorothy Round / Ryuki Miki	Dorothy Shepherd Barron / Bunny Austin	3-6	6-4	6-0
1935	Dorothy Round / Fred Perry	Nell Hall Hopman / Harry Hopman	7-5	4-6	6-2
1936	Dorothy Round / Fred Perry	Sarah Palfrey Fabyan / Don Budge	7-9	7-5	6-4
1937	Alice Marble / Don Budge	Simone Passemard Mathieu / Yvon Petra	6-4	6-1	
1938	Alice Marble / Don Budge	Sarah Palfrey Fabyan / Henner Henkel	6-1	6-4	
1939	Alice Marble / Bobby Riggs	Nina Brown / Frank Wilde	9-7	6-1	
1940-45		Not held – WW II			
1946	Louise Brough / Tom Brown	Dorothy Bundy / Geoff Brown	6-4	6-4	
1947	Louise Brough / John Bromwich	Nancye Wynne Bolton / Colin Long	1-6	6-4	6-2
1948	Louise Brough / John Bromwich	Doris Hart / Frank Sedgman	6-2	3-6	6-3
1949	Sheila Piercey Summers / Eric Sturgess	Louise Brough / John Bromwich	9-7	9-11	7-5
1950	Louise Brough / Eric Sturgess	Pat Canning Todd / Geoff Brown	11-9	1-6	6-4
1951	Doris Hart / Frank Sedgman	Nancye Wynne Bolton / Merv Rose	7-5	6-2	
1952	Doris Hart / Frank Sedgman	Thelma Coyne Long / Enrique Morea	4-6	6-3	6-4
1953	Doris Hart / Vic Seixas	Shirley Fry / Enrique Morea	9-7	7-5	
1954	Doris Hart / Vic Seixas	Margaret Osborne duPont / Ken Rosewall	5-7	6-4	6-3
1955	Doris Hart / Vic Seixas	Louise Brough / Enrique Morea	8-6	2-6	6-3
1956	Shirley Fry / Vic Seixas	Althea Gibson / Gardnar Mulloy	2-6	6-2	7-5
1957	Darlene Hard / Merv Rose	Althea Gibson / Neale Fraser	6-4	7-5	
1958	Lorraine Coghlan / Bob Howe	Althea Gibson / Kurt Nielsen	6-3	13-11	
1959	Darlene Hard / Rod Laver	Maria Bueno / Neale Fraser	6-4	6-3	
1960	Darlene Hard / Rod Laver	Maria Bueno / Bob Howe	13-11	3-6	8-6
1961	Lesley Turner / Fred Stolle	Edda Buding / Bob Howe	11-9	6-2	
1962	Margaret Osborne duPont / Neale Fraser	Ann Haydon / Dennis Ralston	2-6	6-3	13-11
1963	Margaret Smith / Ken Fletcher	Darlene Hard / Bob Hewitt	11-9	6-4	
1964	Lesley Turner / Fred Stolle	Margaret Smith / Ken Fletcher	6-4	6-4	
1965	Margaret Smith / Ken Fletcher	Judy Tegart / Tony Roche	12-10	6-3	
1966	Margaret Smith / Ken Fletcher	Billie Jean Moffitt King / Dennis Ralston	4-6	6-3	6-3
1967	Billie Jean Moffitt King / Owen Davidson	Maria Bueno / Ken Fletcher	7-5	6-2	
1968	Margaret Smith Court / Ken Fletcher	Olga Morozova / Alex Metreveli	6-1	14-12	
1969	Ann Haydon Jones / Fred Stolle	Judy Tegart / Tony Roche	6-3	6-2	
1970	Rosie Casals / Ilie Nastase	Olga Morozova / Alex Metreveli	6-3	4-6	9-7
1971	Billie Jean Moffitt King / Owen Davidson	Margaret Smith Court / Marty Riessen	3-6	6-2	15-13
1972	Rosie Casals / Ilie Nastase	Evonne Goolagong / Kim Warwick	6-4	6-4	
1973	Billie Jean Moffitt King / Owen Davidson	Janet Newberry / Raul Ramirez	6-3	6-2	
1974	Billie Jean Moffitt King / Owen Davidson	Lesley Charles / Mark Farrell	6-3	9-7	
1975	Margaret Smith Court / Marty Riessen	Betty Stove / Allan Stone	6-4	7-5	
1976	Françoise Durr / Tony Roche	Rosie Casals / Dick Stockton	6-3	2-6	7-5
1977	Greer Stevens / Bob Hewitt	Betty Stove / Frew McMillan	3-6	7-5	6-4
1978	Betty Stove / Frew McMillan	Billie Jean Moffitt King / Ray Ruffels	6-2	6-2	
1979	Greer Stevens / Bob Hewitt	Betty Stove / Frew McMillan	7-5	7-6(7)	
1980	Tracy Austin / John Austin	Dianne Balestrat Fromholtz / Mark Edmondson	4-6	7-6(6)	6-3
1981	Betty Stove / Frew McMillan	Tracy Austin / John Austin	4-6	7-6(2)	6-3
1982	Anne Smith / Kevin Curren	Wendy Turnbull / John Lloyd	2-6	6-3	7-5
1983	Wendy Turnbull / John Lloyd	Billie Jean Moffitt King / Steve Denton	6-7(5)	7-6(5)	7-5
1984	Wendy Turnbull / John Lloyd	Kathy Jordan / Steve Denton	6-3	6-3	
1985	Martina Navratilova / Paul McNamee	Elizabeth Sayers Smylie / John Fitzgerald	7-5	4-6	6-2
1986	Kathy Jordan / Ken Flach	Martina Navratilova / Heinz Gunthardt	6-3	7-6(7)	
1987	Jo Durie / Jeremy Bates	Nicole Provis / Darren Cahill	7-6(10)	6-3	
1988	Zina Garrison / Sherwood Stewart	Gretchen Rush Magers / Kelly Jones	6-1	7-6(3)	
1989	Jana Novotna / Jim Pugh	Jenny Byrne / Mark Kratzmann	6-4	5-7	6-4
1990	Zina Garrison / Rick Leach	Elizabeth Sayers Smylie / John Fitzgerald	7-5	6-2	
1991	Elizabeth Sayers Smylie / John Fitzgerald	Natalia Zvereva / Jim Pugh	7-6(4)	6-2	
1992	Larisa Savchenko Neiland / Cyril Suk	Miriam Oremans / Jacco Eltingh	7-6(2)	6-2	
1993	Martina Navratilova / Mark Woodforde	Manon Bollegraf / Tom Nijssen	6-3	6-4	

Year	Winner	Defeated	S1	S2	S3
1994	Helena Sukova Todd Woodbridge	Lori McNeil Todd Jason Middleton	3-6	7-5	6-3
1995	Martina Navratilova Jonathan Stark	Gigi Fernandez Cyril Suk	6-4	6-4	
1996	Helena Sukova Cyril Suk	Larisa Savchenko Neiland Mark Woodforde	1-6	6-3	6-2
1997	Helena Sukova Cyril Suk	Larisa Savchenko Neiland Andrei Olhovskiy	4-6	6-3	6-4
1998	Serena Williams Max Mirnyi	Mirjana Lucic Mahesh Bhupathi	6-4	6-4	
1999	Lisa Raymond Leander Paes	Anna Kournikova Jonas Bjorkman	6-4	3-6	6-3
2000	Kimberly Po Donald Johnson	Kim Clijsters Lleyton Hewitt	6-4	7-6(3)	
2001	Daniela Hantuchova Leos Friedl	Liezel Huber Mike Bryan	4-6	6-3	6-2
2002	Elena Likhovtseva Mahesh Bhupathi	Daniela Hantuchova Kevin Ullyett	6-2	1-6	6-1

Wimbledon – Records

Wimbledon Slam
(Winner of all 3 events in one year)

MEN

Don Budge (with D-Gene Mako; M-Alice Marble) (1937)
Don Budge (with D-Gene Mako; M-Alice Marble) (1938)
Bobby Riggs (with D-Elwood Cooke; M-Alice Marble) (1939)
Frank Sedgman (with D-Ken McGregor; M-Doris Hart) (1952)

WOMEN

Suzanne Lenglen (with D-Elizabeth Ryan; M-Gerald Patterson) (1920)
Suzanne Lenglen (with D-Elizabeth Ryan; M-Pat O'Hara Wood) (1922)
Suzanne Lenglen (with D-Elizabeth Ryan; M-Jean Borotra) (1925)
Alice Marble (with D-Sarah Palfrey Fabyan; M-Bobby Riggs) (1939)
Louise Brough (with D-Margaret Osborne duPont; M-John Bromwich) (1948)
Louise Brough (with D-Margaret Osborne duPont; M-Eric Sturgess) (1950)
Doris Hart (with D-Shirley Fry; M-Frank Sedgman) (1951)
Billie Jean King (with D-Rosie Casals; Owen Davidson) (1967)
Billie Jean King (with D-Rosie Casals; Owen Davidson) (1973)

Overall Titles

MOST TITLES ALL TIME MEN
13 Laurie Doherty (1897-1906) 5 singles, 8 doubles, 0 mixed.
12 Reggie Doherty (1897-1905) 4 singles, 8 doubles, 0 mixed.
   Willie Renshaw (1881-1889) 7 singles, 5 doubles, 0 mixed.
9 John Newcombe (1965-1974) 3 singles, 6 doubles, 0 mixed.
8 John McEnroe (1979-1992) 3 singles, 5 doubles, 0 mixed.
   Todd Woodbridge (1993-2002) 0 singles, 7 doubles, 1 mixed.
   Tony Wilding (1907-1914) 4 singles, 4 doubles, 0 mixed.
7 Bob Hewitt (1962-1979) 0 singles, 5 doubles, 2 mixed.
   Mark Woodforde (1993-2000) 0 singles, 6 doubles, 1 mixed.
   Pete Sampras (1993-2000) 7 singles, 0 doubles, 0 mixed.
   Rod Laver (1959-1971) 4 singles, 1 doubles, 2 mixed.
   Wilfred Baddeley (1891-1896) 3 singles, 4 doubles, 0 mixed.
6 Don Budge (1937-1938) 2 singles, 2 doubles, 2 mixed.
   Ernest Renshaw (1884-1889) 1 singles, 5 doubles, 0 mixed.
   Frank Sedgman (1948-1952) 1 singles, 3 doubles, 2 mixed.
   Jean Borotra (1924-1933) 2 singles, 3 doubles, 1 mixed.
   Randolph Lycett (1919-1923) 0 singles, 3 doubles, 3 mixed.
   Tony Roche (1965-1976) 0 singles, 5 doubles, 1 mixed.
5 Bjorn Borg (1976-1980) 5 singles, 0 doubles, 0 mixed.
   Fred Perry (1934-1936) 3 singles, 0 doubles, 2 mixed.
   Fred Stolle (1961-1969) 0 singles, 2 doubles, 3 mixed.
   Frew McMillan (1967-1981) 0 singles, 3 doubles, 2 mixed.
   Ken Fletcher (1963-1968) 0 singles, 1 doubles, 4 mixed.
   Lew Hoad (1953-1957) 2 singles, 3 doubles, 0 mixed.
   Roy Emerson (1959-1971) 2 singles, 3 doubles, 0 mixed.
   Vic Seixas (1953-1956) 1 singles, 0 doubles, 4 mixed.

MOST TITLES ALL TIME WOMEN
20 Billie Jean King (1961-1979) 6 singles, 10 doubles, 4 mixed.
19 Elizabeth Ryan (1914-1934) 0 singles, 12 doubles, 7 mixed.
   Martina Navratilova (1976-1995) 9 singles, 7 doubles, 3 mixed.
15 Suzanne Lenglen (1919-1925) 6 singles, 6 doubles, 3 mixed.
13 Louise Brough (1946-1955) 4 singles, 5 doubles, 4 mixed.
12 Helen Wills Moody (1924-1938) 8 singles, 3 doubles, 1 mixed.
10 Doris Hart (1947-1955) 1 singles, 4 doubles, 5 mixed.
   Margaret Smith Court (1963-1975) 3 singles, 2 doubles, 5 mixed.
8 Maria Bueno (1958-1966) 3 singles, 5 doubles, 0 mixed.
   Steffi Graf (1988-1996) 7 singles, 1 doubles, 0 mixed.
7 Darlene Hard (1957-1963) 0 singles, 4 doubles, 3 mixed.
   Dorothea Douglass Chambers (1903-1914) 7 singles, 0 doubles, 0 mixed.
   Helena Sukova (1987-1997) 0 singles, 4 doubles, 3 mixed.
   Margaret Osborne duPont (1946-1962) 1 singles, 5 doubles, 1 mixed.
   Rosie Casals (1967-1973) 0 singles, 5 doubles, 2 mixed.
6 Alice Marble (1937-1939) 1 singles, 2 doubles, 3 mixed.
   Blanche Bingley Hillyard (1886-1900) 6 singles, 0 doubles, 0 mixed.
   Jana Novotna (1989-1998) 1 singles, 4 doubles, 1 mixed.
5 Althea Gibson (1956-1958) 2 singles, 3 doubles, 0 mixed.
   Charlotte Cooper Sterry (1895-1908) 5 singles, 0 doubles, 0 mixed.
   Dorothy Round (1934-1937) 2 singles, 0 doubles, 3 mixed.
   Lottie Dod (1887-1893) 5 singles, 0 doubles, 0 mixed.
   Natalia Zvereva (1991-1997) 0 singles, 5 doubles, 0 mixed.
   Pam Shriver (1981-1986) 0 singles, 5 doubles, 0 mixed.
   Shirley Fry (1951-1956) 1 singles, 3 doubles, 1 mixed.

Men's Singles

MOST TITLES OVERALL
7 Willie Renshaw (1881-1889)
   Pete Sampras (1993-2000)
5 Bjorn Borg (1976-1980)
   Laurie Doherty (1902-1906)
4 Rod Laver (1961-1969)
   Tony Wilding (1910-1913)
   Reggie Doherty (1897-1900)
3 Wilfred Baddeley (1891-1895)
   Arthur Gore (1901-1909)
   Bill Tilden (1920-1930)
   Boris Becker (1985-1989)
   Fred Perry (1934-1936)
   John Newcombe (1967-1971)
   John McEnroe (1981-1984)

MOST CHALLENGE ROUND APPEARANCES (1878-1921)
9 Willie Renshaw (1881-1890)
7 Arthur Wentworth Gore (1899-1912)

MOST CHALLENGE ROUND VICTORIES (1878-1921)
7 Willie Renshaw (1881-1886, 1889)
5 Laurie Doherty (1902-06)
4 Reggie Doherty (1897-1900)
   Tony Wilding (1910-13)

MOST CHALLENGE ROUND LOSSES (1878-1921)
5 Herbert Lawford (1880, 84-86, 88)
4 Arthur Gore (1899, 1902, 10, 12)
3 Ernest Renshaw (1882-83, 87)
   Will Baddeley (1893-94, 96)
   Frank Risely (1903-04, 06)
   Norman Brookes (1905, 08, 19)

MOST TITLES (1922 to 2002)

- 7 Pete Sampras (1993-2000)
- 5 Bjorn Borg (1976-1980)
- 4 Rod Laver (1961-1969)
- 3 John Newcombe (1967-1971)
  Fred Perry (1934-1936)
  John McEnroe (1981-1984)
  Boris Becker (1985-1989)
- 2 Henri Cochet (1927-1929)
  Jean Borotra (1924-1926)
  René Lacoste (1925-1928)
  Lew Hoad (1956-1957)
  Roy Emerson (1964-1965)
  Don Budge (1937-1938)
  Stefan Edberg (1988-1990)
  Jimmy Connors (1974-1982)

MOST FINAL APPEARANCES (1922 to 2002)

- 7 Boris Becker (1985-1995)
  Pete Sampras (1993-2000)
- 6 Jimmy Connors (1974-1984)
  Bjorn Borg (1976-1981)
  Rod Laver (1959-1969)
- 5 Jean Borotra (1924-1929)
  John McEnroe (1980-1984)
- 4 Goran Ivanisevic (1992-2001)
  Ken Rosewall (1954-1974)
  John Newcombe (1967-1971)

MOST FINAL LOSSES (1922-2002)

- 4 Boris Becker (1988-1995)
  Jimmy Connors (1975-1984)
  Ken Rosewall (1954-1974)
- 3 Jean Borotra (1925-1929)
  Fred Stolle (1963-1965)
  Goran Ivanisevic (1992-1998)
  Gottfried von Cramm (1935-1937)

MOST SEMI-FINAL APPEARANCES (1922-2002)

- 11 Jimmy Connors (1974-1987)
- 9 Boris Becker (1985-1995)
- 8 John McEnroe (1977-1992)
  Pete Sampras (1992-2000)
- 7 Ivan Lendl (1983-1990)
  Jean Borotra (1924-1931)
- 6 Ken Rosewall (1954-1974)
  Rod Laver (1959-1969)
  Goran Ivanisevic (1990-2001)
  Jaroslav Drobny (1946-1954)
  Stefan Edberg (1987-1993)
  Bjorn Borg (1976-1981)
  Henri Cochet (1925-1933)

YOUNGEST CHAMPION

Boris Becker—17 years, 227 days (1985)

OLDEST CHAMPION

Arthur Gore—41 years, 182 days (1909)

TOURNAMENTS PLAYED

30 Arthur Gore (1888-1922)

MATCHES PLAYED

102 Jimmy Connors (1972-92)

MATCHES WON

84 Jimmy Connors (1972-92)

MATCHES WON CONSECUTIVELY

41 Bjorn Borg (1976-81)

MATCH WINNING PERCENTAGE

.927 Bjorn Borg (51-4) (1973-81)

Women's Singles

MOST TITLES OVERALL

- 9 Martina Navratilova (1978-1990)
- 8 Helen Wills Moody (1927-1938)
- 7 Dorothea Douglass Lambert Chambers (1903-1914)
  Steffi Graf (1988-1996)
- 6 Blanche Bingley Hillyard (1886-1900)
  Suzanne Lenglen (1919-1925)
  Billie Jean King (1966-1975)
- 5 Lottie Dod (1887-1893)
  Charlotte Cooper Sterry (1895-1908)
- 4 Louise Brough (1948-1955)
- 3 Chris Evert (1974-1981)
  Maria Bueno (1959-1964)
  Maureen Connolly (1952-1954)
  Margaret Smith Court (1963-1970)

MOST CHALLENGE ROUND APPEARANCES (1884-1921)

- 12 Blanche Bingley Hilliard (1886-89, 92-95, 97, 99-01)
- 11 Dorothea Douglass Chambers (1903-07, 10-11, 13-14, 19-20)
- 10 Charlotte Cooper Sterry (1895-1902, 04, 08)

MOST CHALLENGE ROUND VICTORIES (1884-1921)

- 7 Dorothea Douglass Chambers (1903-04, 06, 10-11, 13-14)
- 6 Blanche Bingley (1886, 89 94, 97, 99-00,)
- 5 Lottie Dod (1887-88, 91-93)
  Charlotte Cooper Sterry (1895-96, 98, 1901, 08)

MOST CHALLENGE ROUND LOSSES (1884-1921)

- 5 Blanche Bingley Hilliard (87-88, 92-93, 1901)
  Charlotte Cooper Sterry (1897, 99-1900, 02, 04)
- 4 Dorothea Douglass Chambers (1905, 07, 19, 20)

MOST TITLES (1922 to present)

- 9 Martina Navratilova (1978-1990)
- 8 Helen Wills Moody (1927-1938)
- 7 Steffi Graf (1988-1996)
- 6 Billie Jean King (1966-1975)
- 4 Louise Brough (1948-1955)
- 3 Margaret Smith Court (1963-1970)
  Chris Evert (1974-1981)
  Maureen Connolly (1952-1954)
  Suzanne Lenglen (1922-1925)
  Maria Bueno (1959-1964)

MOST FINAL APPEARANCES (1922 to 2002)

- 12 Martina Navratilova (1978-1994)
- 10 Chris Evert (1973-1985)
- 9 Helen Wills Moody (1924-1938)
  Steffi Graf (1987-1999)
  Billie Jean King (1963-1975)
- 7 Louise Brough (1946-1955)
- 6 Helen Jacobs (1929-1938)
- 5 Maria Bueno (1959-1966)
  Evonne Goolagong (1971-1980)
  Margaret Smith Court (1963-1971)

MOST FINAL LOSSES (1922 to 2002)

- 7 Chris Evert (1973-1985)
- 5 Helen Jacobs (1929-1938)
- 3 Louise Brough (1946-1954)
  Evonne Goolagong (1972-1976)
  Doris Hart (1947-1953)
  Lili de Alvarez (1926-1928)
  Billie Jean King (1963-1970)
  Martina Navratilova (1988-1994)

MOST SEMI-FINAL APPEARANCES (1922 to 2002)
- 17 Chris Evert (1972-1989)
- Martina Navratilova (1976-1994)
- 14 Billie Jean King (1963-1983)
- 10 Steffi Graf (1987-1999)
- Louise Brough (1946-1956)
- 9 Helen Wills Moody (1924-1938)
- Margaret Smith Court (1963-1975)
- 8 Evonne Goolagong (1971-1980)
- Ann Haydon (1958-1969)
- Helen Jacobs (1929-1938)

OLDEST CHAMPION
Charlotte Cooper Sterry—37 years, 282 days (1908)

YOUNGEST CHAMPION
Charlotte Dod—15 years, 285 days (1887)

TOURNAMENTS PLAYED
- 24 Blanche Bingley Hillyard (1884-1913)
- Virginia Wade (1962-1985)

MATCHES PLAYED
- 132 Martina Navratilova (1973-2002)

MATCHES WON
- 119 Martina Navratilova (1973-2002)

MATCHES WON CONSECUTIVELY
- 50 Helen Wills Moody (1927-1930)

MATCH WINNING PERCENTAGE
- 1.000 Suzanne Lengelen (28-0) (1919-1923)
- .982 Helen Wills Moody (55-1) (1924-1938)

Men's Doubles

MOST TITLES—TEAM
- 8 Reggie Doherty / Laurie Doherty (1897-1905)
- 6 Todd Woodbridge / Mark Woodforde (1993-2000)
- 5 Willie Renshaw / Ernest Renshaw (1884-1889)
- John Newcombe / Tony Roche (1965-1974)
- 4 Wilfred Baddeley / Herbert Baddeley (1891-1896)
- John McEnroe / Peter Fleming (1979-1984)
- 3 Bob Hewitt / Frew McMillan (1967-1978)

MOST TITLES—INDIVIDUAL
- 8 Laurie Doherty (1897-1905)
- Reggie Doherty (1897-1905)
- 7 Todd Woodbridge (1993-2002)
- 6 John Newcombe (1965-1974)
- Mark Woodforde (1993-2000)
- 5 Bob Hewitt (1962-1978)
- Ernest Renshaw (1884-1889)
- John McEnroe (1979-1992)
- Tony Roche (1965-1974)
- Willie Renshaw (1884-1889)

MOST FINAL APPEARANCES—INDIVIDUAL
- 11 Reggie Doherty (1896-1906)
- 10 Laurie Doherty (1897-1906)
- 8 Todd Woodbridge (1993-2002)
- 7 Herbert Roper Barrett (1900-1914)
- Mark Woodforde (1993-2000)
- Jacques Brugnon (1926-1934)
- Peter Fleming (1978-1986)
- Bob Hewitt (1961-1978)
- John McEnroe (1978-1992)

MOST FINAL APPEARANCES—TEAM
- 10 Reggie Doherty / Laurie Doherty (1897-1906)
- 7 Todd Woodbridge / Mark Woodforde (1993-2000)
- 6 Wilfred Baddeley / Herbert Baddeley (1891-1897)
- John McEnroe / Peter Fleming (1978-1984)
- 5 Willie Renshaw / Ernest Renshaw (1884-1889)
- John Newcombe / Tony Roche (1965-1974)
- Sidney H. Smith / Frank Riseley (1902-1906)
- 4 Henri Cochet / Jacques Brugnon (1926-1931)

MOST FINAL LOSSES—TEAM
- 3 Bob Lutz / Stan Smith (1974-1981)
- Sidney H. Smith / Frank Riseley (1903-1905)
- 2 John McEnroe / Peter Fleming (1978-1982)
- Charles Hare / Frank Wilde (1936-1939)
- Reggie Doherty / Laurie Doherty (1902-1906)
- Ken Rosewall / Fred Stolle (1968-1970)
- Claude Farrar / Arthur Stanley (1885-1886)
- Grant Connell / Patrick Galbraith (1993-1994)
- Roy Emerson / Ken Fletcher (1964-1967)
- Harold Nisbet / Clarence Hobart (1898-1899)
- Arthur Gore / Herbert Roper Barrett (1908-1910)
- Henri Cochet / Jacques Brugnon (1927-1931)
- Ernest Lewis / George Hillyard (1889-1890)
- Wilfred Baddeley / Herbert Baddeley (1892-1897)

MOST FINAL LOSSES—INDIVIDUAL
- 5 Ernest Lewis (1884-1895)
- 4 Stan Smith (1972-1981)
- Herbert Roper Barrett (1900-1914)
- Neale Fraser (1955-1973)
- Harold Nisbet (1896-1900)

OLDEST CHAMPION
Gardnar Mulloy—43 years, 226 days (1957)

YOUNGEST CHAMPION
Dennis Ralston—17 years, 341 days (1960)

Women's Doubles

MOST TITLES—TEAM
- 6 Suzanne Lenglen / Elizabeth Ryan (1919-1925)
- 5 Billie Jean King / Rosie Casals (1967-1973)
- Martina Navratilova / Pam Shriver (1981-1986)
- Louise Brough / Margaret Osborne duPont (1946-1954)
- 4 Gigi Fernandez / Natalia Zvereva (1992-1997)
- 3 Doris Hart / Shirley Fry (1951-1953)

MOST TITLES—INDIVIDUAL
- 12 Elizabeth Ryan (1914-1934)
- 10 Billie Jean King (1961-1979)
- 7 Martina Navratilova (1976-1986)
- 6 Suzanne Lenglen (1919-1925)
- 5 Margaret Osborne duPont (1946-1954)
- Louise Brough (1946-1954)
- Maria Bueno (1958-1966)
- Natalia Zvereva (1991-1997)
- Pam Shriver (1981-1986)
- Rosie Casals (1967-1973)

MOST FINAL APPEARANCES—INDIVIDUAL
- 13 Elizabeth Ryan (1914-1934)
- 12 Billie Jean King (1961-1979)
- 9 Natalia Zvereva (1988-1998)
- Martina Navratilova (1976-1986)
- 8 Jana Novotna (1989-1998)
- Louise Brough (1946-1954)
- Margaret Osborne duPont (1946-1958)
- Doris Hart (1946-1954)

MOST FINAL APPEARANCES—TEAM
7　Louise Brough / Margaret Osborne duPont (1946-1954)
6　Suzanne Lenglen / Elizabeth Ryan (1919-1925)
　　Martina Navratilova / Pam Shriver (1981-1986)
5　Billie Jean King / Rosie Casals (1967-1973)
　　Doris Hart / Shirley Fry (1950-1954)
　　Gigi Fernandez / Natalia Zvereva (1992-1997)
4　Anne Smith / Kathy Jordan (1980-1984)

MOST FINAL LOSSES—TEAM
3　Anne Smith / Kathy Jordan (1981-1984)
2　Françoise Durr / Betty Stove (1973-1975)
　　Rosie Casals / Wendy Turnbull (1980-1983)
　　Renee Schuurman / Sandra Reynolds (1960-1962)
　　Louise Brough / Margaret Osborne duPont (1947-1951)
　　Jana Novotna / Larisa Savchenko Neiland (1992-1993)
　　Dorothea Douglass Lambert Chambers / Ethel Thomson
　　　　Larcombe (1919-1920)
　　Larisa Savchenko Neiland / Natalia Zvereva (1988-1989)
　　Doris Hart / Shirley Fry (1950-1954)

MOST FINAL LOSSES—INDIVIDUAL
6　Françoise Durr (1965-1975)
5　Larisa Savchenko Neiland (1988-1996)
　　Betty Stove (1973-1979)
4　Jana Novotna (1991-1994)
　　Wendy Turnbull (1979-1986)
　　Kathy Jordan (1981-1990)
　　Natalia Zvereva (1988-1998)
　　Doris Hart (1946-1954)
　　Margaret Smith Court (1961-1971)

OLDEST CHAMPION
Elizabeth Ryan—42 years, 152 days (1934)

YOUNGEST CHAMPION
Martina Hingis—15 years, 282 days (1996)

Mixed Doubles

MOST TITLES—TEAM
4　Margaret Smith Court / Ken Fletcher (1963-1968)
　　Billie Jean King / Owen Davidson (1967-1974)
3　Elizabeth Ryan / Randolph Lycett (1919-1923)
　　Doris Hart / Vic Seixas (1953-1955)

MOST TITLES—MEN
4　Vic Seixas (1953-1956)
　　Owen Davidson (1967-1974)
　　Ken Fletcher (1963-1968)
3　Fred Stolle (1961-1969)
　　Randolph Lycett (1919-1923)
　　Cyril Suk (1992-1997)

MOST TITLES—WOMEN
7　Elizabeth Ryan (1919-1932)
5　Margaret Smith Court (1963-1975)
　　Doris Hart (1951-1955)
4　Billie Jean King (1967-1974)
　　Louise Brough (1946-1950)

MOST FINAL APPEARANCES—MEN
6　Ken Fletcher (1963-1968)
5　Randolph Lycett (1919-1923)
4　Frew McMillan (1977-1981)
　　Vic Seixas (1953-1956)
　　Owen Davidson (1967-1974)
　　Cyril Suk (1992-1997)

MOST FINAL APPEARANCES—WOMEN
10　Elizabeth Ryan (1919-1932)
7　Margaret Smith Court (1963-1975)
　　Billie Jean King (1966-1983)
6　Louise Brough (1946-1955)
　　Doris Hart (1948-1955)
5　Betty Stove (1975-1981)

MOST FINAL APPEARANCES—TEAM
5　Elizabeth Ryan / Randolph Lycett (1919-1923)
　　Margaret Smith Court / Ken Fletcher (1963-1968)
4　Betty Stove / Frew McMillan (1977-1981)
　　Billie Jean King / Owen Davidson (1967-1974)

MOST FINAL LOSSES—TEAM
2　Olga Morozova / Alex Metreveli (1968-1970)
　　Judy Tegart Dalton / Tony Roche (1965-1969)
　　Elizabeth Ryan / Randolph Lycett (1920-1922)
　　Elizabeth Sayers Smylie / John Fitzgerald (1985-1990)
　　Betty Stove / Frew McMillan (1977-1979)

MOST FINAL LOSSES—MEN
3　Enrique Morea (1952-1955)
2　Neale Fraser (1957-1959)
　　Leslie Godfree (1924-1927)
　　Geoff Brown (1946-1950)
　　Harry Hopman (1932-1935)
　　John Fitzgerald (1985-1990)
　　Dennis Ralston (1962-1966)
　　Frew McMillan (1977-1979)
　　Ken Fletcher (1964-1967)
　　Randolph Lycett (1920-1922)
　　Ian Collins (1929-1931)
　　Bob Howe (1960-1961)
　　Steve Denton (1983-1984)
　　Tony Roche (1965-1969)
　　Alex Metreveli (1968-1970)

MOST FINAL LOSSES—WOMEN
3　Elizabeth Ryan (1920-1925)
　　Althea Gibson (1956-1958)
　　Betty Stove (1975-1979)
　　Billie Jean King (1966-1983)
　　Maria Bueno (1959-1967)
　　Dorothy Shepherd Barron (1923-1934)

OLDEST CHAMPION—MEN
Sherwood Stewart—42 years, 28 days (1998)

YOUNGEST CHAMPION—MEN
Rod Laver—20 years, 328 days (1959)

OLDEST CHAMPION—WOMEN
Margaret Osborne duPont—44 years, 125 days (1962)

YOUNGEST CHAMPION—WOMEN
Serena Williams—16 years, 282 days (1998)

Miscellaneous Records

LONGEST MATCHES, TOTAL GAMES

Men's singles: 112 games – Richard "Pancho" Gonzalez d. Charlie Pasarell 22-24, 1-6, 16-14, 6-3, 11-9, 1st rd., 1969

Men's doubles: 98 games – Nikki Pilic / Gene Scott d. Cliff Richey / Torben Ulrich 19-21, 12-10, 6-4, 4-6, 9-7, 1st rd., 1966

Women's singles: 58 games – Chanda Rubin d. Patricia Hy-Boulais, 7-6 (7-4), 6-7 (5-7), 17-15, 2nd rd., 1996

Women's doubles: 50 games – Martina Hingis / Arantxa Sanchez Vicario d. Chanda Rubin / Brenda Schultz-McCarthy, 7-6 (14-12), 6-7 (6-8), 13-11, 3rd rd., 1997 (3 hours, 9 minutes)

Mixed doubles: 77 games – Brenda Schultz (McCarthy) / Michiel Schapers d. Andrea Temesvari / Tom Nijssen 6-3, 5-7, 29-27, 1st rd., 1991

LONGEST MATCHES, PLAYING TIME

Men:

5 hours, 28 minutes – Greg Holmes d. Todd Witsken, 5-7, 6-4, 7-6 (7-5), 4-6, 14-12, 2nd rd., 1989 (played over 3 days)

5 hours, 12 minutes – "Pancho" Gonzalez d. Charlie Pasarell, 22-24, 1-6, 16-14, 6-3, 11-9 (played over 2 days)

5 hours, 5 minutes – Mark Philippoussis d. Sjeng Schalken, 4-6, 6-3, 6-7 (7-9), 7-6 (7-4), 20-18, 3rd rd., 2000 (1 day)

Women:

3 hours, 45 minutes – Chanda Rubin d. Patricia Hy-Boulais, 7-6 (7-4), 6-7 (5-7), 17-15. 2nd rd., 1996

LONGEST TIE-BREAKERS

Men's singles: 20-18, third set, Bjorn Borg d. Premjit Lall, 6-3, 6-4, 9-8 (20-18), 1st rd., 1973. Doug Flach (qualifier ranked No. 281 in the world) defeated 3rd-seeded Andre Agassi, 2-6, 7-6 (7-1), 6-4, 7-6 (7-4), 1996.

Women's singles: 15-13, second set, Virginia Wade d. Jo Durie, 3-6, 7-6 (15-13), 6-2. 1st rd., 1982

BIGGEST UPSETS

Men:

1932 - non-seed Ian Collins d. 1st seed Henry Cochet, 6-2, 8-6, 0-6, 6-3, 2nd rd.

1946 - non-seed Jaroslav Drobny d. 2nd seed Jack Kramer, 2-6, 17-15, 6-3, 3-6, 6-3, 4th rd.

1967 - non-seed Charlie Pasarell d. 1st seed defending champ Manolo Santana, 10-8, 6-3, 2-6, 8-6 (only 1st rd. defeat of 1st seed defender)

1970 - 16th seed Roger Taylor d. 1st seed defending champ Rod Laver, 4-6, 6-4, 6-2, 6-1, 4th rd., ends Laver's 31 match streak at Wimbledon

1971 - non-seed Tom Gorman d. 1st seed Rod Laver, 9-7, 8-6, 6-3, 4th rd.

1973 - non-seed Alex Mayer d. 1st seed Ilie Nastase, 6-4, 8-6, 6-8, 6-4, 4th rd.

1975 - 6th seed Arthur Ashe d. 1st seed defending champ Jimmy Connors, 6-1, 6-1, 5-7, 6-4, F

1979 - 15th seed Tim Gullikson d. 2nd seed John McEnroe, 6-6, 6-2, 6-4, 4th rd.

1983 - 12th seed Kevin Curren d. 1st seed defending champ Jimmy Connors, 6-3, 6-7 (6-8), 6-3, 7-6 (7-4), 4th rd.

1985 - 15th seed Boris Becker d. 7th seed Joakim Nystrom, 3-6, 7-6 (7-5), 6-1, 4-6, 9-7, 3rd rd.; 16th seed Tim Mayotte, 6-3, 4-6, 6-7 (7-9), 7-6 (7-5), 6-2, 4th rd.; 5th seed Anders Jarryd, 2-6, 7-6 (7-3), 6-3, 6-3, SF; 8th seed Kevin Curren, 6-3, 6-7 (4-7), 7-6 (7-3), 6-4, F. Also Curren d. 1st seed John McEnroe, 6-2, 6-2, 6-4, QF; 3rd seed Jimmy Connors, 6-2, 6-2, 6-1, SF

1987 - Peter Doohan (No. 70) d. 1st seed defending champ Boris Becker, 7-6 (7-4), 2-6, 6-2, 6-4, 2nd rd.

1990 - Derrick Rostagno (No. 129) d. 4th seed John McEnroe, 7-5, 6-4, 6-4, 1st rd.

1992 - qualifier Andrei Olhovskiy (No. 193) d. 1st seed Jim Courier, 6-4, 4-6, 6-4, 6-4, 3rd round

1994 - qualifier Bryan Shelton d. 2nd seed Michael Stich, 6-3, 7-5, 1-6, 6-7 (7-9), 6-2, 1st rd.

1995 - lucky loser Dick Norman (No. 178) d. 13th seed Stefan Edberg, 6-3, 6-4, 6-4, 2nd rd.

1996 - unseeded Richard Krajicek d. 1st seed defending champ Pete Sampras, 7-5, 7-6 (7-3), 6-4, QF, ends Sampras' 25 match Wimbledon streak. Also qualifier Doug Flach (No. 281) d. 3rd seed Andre Agassi, 2-6, 7-6 (7-1), 6-4, 7-6 (8-6), 1st rd.

2000 - qualifier Olivier Rochus (No. 179) d. 3rd seed Magnus Norman, 6-4, 2-6, 6-4, 6-7 (4-7), 6-1, 2nd rd.

2001 - 15th seed Roger Federer d. 1st seed defending champ Pete Sampras, 7-6 (9-7), 5-7, 6-4, 6-7 (2-7), 7-5, 4th rd., ends Sampras' 31 match Wimbledon streak. Also wild card Goran Ivanisevic (No. 125) d. 4th seed Marat Safin, 7-6 (7-2), 7-5, 3-6, 7-6 (7-3), QF; 6th seed Tim Henman, 7-5, 6-7 (6-8), 0-6, 7-6 (7-5), 6-3, SF; 3rd seed Patrick Rafter, 6-3, 3-6, 6-3, 2-6, 9-7, F

2002 - lucky loser George Bastl (No. 145) d. 6th seed Pete Sampras, 6-3, 6-2, 4-6, 3-6, 6-4, 2nd rd. Also Olivier Rochus (No. 84) d. 2nd seed Marat Safin, 6-2, 6-4, 3-6, 7-6 (7-1), 2nd rd. Also Paradorn Schrichaphan (No. 67) d. 3rd seed Andre Agassi, 6-4, 7-6 (7-5), 6-2, 2nd rd. (all same day)

Women:

1927 - non-seed Betty Nuthall d. 6th seed Molla Mallory, 2-6, 6-2, 6-0, 3rd rd.

1928 - non-seed Helene Contostavlos Nicolopoulo d. 5th seed Kea Bouman, 12-10, 8-6, 3rd rd.

1929 - non-seed Mary Hart McIlquham d. 2nd seed Lily de Alvarez, 1928 finalist, 6-4, 4-6, 6-2, 4th rd.

1959 - non-seed Yola Ramirez d. 1st seed Christine Truman, 6-3, 6-2, QF

1962 - non-seed No. 3 U.S. Billie Jean King d. 1st seed Margaret Court, 1-6, 6-3, 7-5, 2nd rd. (1st defeat for 1st seed in 1st match). Also non-seed Vera Sukova d. 6th seed defending champ Angela Mortimer, 1-6, 6-4, 6-3, 4th rd.; 2nd seed Darlene Hard, 6-4, 6-3, QF; 3rd seed Maria Bueno, 6-4, 6-3, SF

1974 - 8th seed Olga Morozova d. 1st seed defending champ Billie Jean King, 7-5, 6-2, QF

1983 - non-seed Kathy Jordan d. 2nd seed Chris Evert, 6-1, 7-6 (7-2), 3rd rd. (only time Evert failed to make SF)

1985 - non-seed Liz Sayers Smylie d. 3rd seed Hana Mandlikova, 6-1, 7-6 (7-5), 3rd rd. Also qualifier Molly Van Nostrand (No. 154) d. 4th seed Manuela Maleeva, 7-5, 6-4

1990 - 5th seed Zina Garrison d. 3rd seed Monica Seles, 3-6, 6-3, 9-7, QF; 1st seed defending champ Steffi Graf, 6-3, 3-6, 6-4, SF

1991 - 9th seed Jennifer Capriati d. 3rd seed defending champ Martina Navratilova, 6-4, 7-5, QF

1994 - Lori McNeill (No. 22) d. 1st seed defending champ Steffi Graf, 7-5, 7-6 (7-5), 1st rd. (only 1st rd. defeat of1st seed defender)

1996 - non-seed Katarina Studenikova (No. 59) d. 2nd seed Monica Seles, 7-5, 7-6, 6-2

1997 - non-seed Anna Kournikova (No. 43) d. 4th seed Iva Majoli, 7-6 (7-1), 6-4, QF. Also non-seed Denisa Chladkova (No. 89) d. 5th seed Lindsay Davenport, 7-5, 6-2, 2nd rd.

1998 - non-seed Natasha Zvereva (No. 22) d. 4th seed Steffi Graf, 6-4, 7-5, 3rd rd.; 6th seed Monica Seles, 7-6 (7-4), 6-2; QF

1999 - qualifier Jelena Dokic (No. 129) d. 1st seed Martina Hingis, 6-2, 6-0.Also non-seed Mirjana Lucic d. 8th seed Nathalie Tauziat, 4-6, 6-4, 7-5, QF

2001 - Non-seed Virginia Ruano Pascual (No. 83) d. 1st seed Martina Hingis, 6-4, 6-2, 1st rd.

BEST COMEBACKS

Men:

1927 - All-time champion comebacker: 4th seed Henri Cochet d. non-seed U.S. No. 2 Frank Hunter, 3-6, 2-6, 6-2, 6-2, 6-3, QF; 2nd seed Bill Tilden, 3-6, 4-6, 7-5, 6-4, 6-3, SF (won 17 straight points from 1-5, 15-all to 5-5, 30-0, 3rd, and down a break down, 3-2, 5th); 3rd seed defending champ Jean Borotra, 4-6, 4-6, 6-3, 6-4, 7-5, F (saved 6 MP, 5th, 1 at 2-5, 5 at 5-3).

1953 - 4th seed Jaroslav Drobny d. non-seed Budge Patty, 8-6, 16-18, 3-6, 8-6, 12-10, 3rd rd., 4:20 (saved 6 MP, 3 in 4th, 3 in 5th)

1969 - "Pancho" Gonzalez d. Charlie Pasarell, 22-24, 1-6, 16-14, 6-3, 11-9, 1st rd. (saved 7 MP, 5th, twice serving out of 0-40 to 4-4 and 6-6, won last 11 points).

1974 - 9th seed Ken Rosewall d. 4th seed Stan Smith, 6-8, 4-6, 9-8 (8-6), 6-1, 6-3, SF (saved 1 MP, 5-6 in tie-breaker)

1987 - 7th seed Jimmy Connors d. Mikail Pernfors, 1-6, 1-6, 7-5, 6-4, 6-2, 4th rd. (from 1-4, 3rd, 0-2, 4th)

1988 - 3rd seed Stefan Edberg d. 9th seed Miloslav Mecir, 4-6, 2-6, 6-4, 6-3, 6-4, SF (from 3-3, 0-40, 3rd; 3-3, 4 break points, 4 deuces, 4th; 3-1 down, 5th). Also qualifier Ricardo Acuna d. David Pate, 3-6, 5-7, 7-6, 7-6 (7-1), 6-4 (saved 4 MP, 4th)

1996 - non-seed MaliVai Washington (No. 20) d. Alex Radulescu (No. 91), 6-7 (5-7), 7-6 (7-1), 5-7, 7-6 (7-3), 6-4, QF (saved 2 MP, serving at 5-6, 15-40, 4th); 13th seed Todd Martin, 5-7, 6-4, 6-7 (6-8), 6-3, 10-8 (from 2-0 and 5-1 down, 5th, 2 points from defeat 4 times: 5-4, 30-15 and 30-all, 6-7, 15-30 and 30-all)

2000 - 2nd seed Andre Agassi d. Todd Martin, 6-4, 2-6, 7-6 (7-3), 2-6, 10-8, 2nd rd. (from 5-2 down, 5th, saved 2 MP at 4-5)

Women:

1889 - Blanche Bingley Hillyard d. Helena Rice, 4-6, 8-6, 6-4, F (saved 3 MP, 2nd, at 3-5)

1924 - Kitty McKane d. Helen Wills, 4-6, 6-4, 6-4, F (from 1-4 and 4 break points, 2nd, 3-3, 3rd)

1958 - Angela Mortimer d. Margaret Osborne duPont, 4-6, 6-3, 10-8, QF

1966 - Helga Schultz d. Jeanine Lieffrig, 4-6, 11-9, 12-10, 1st rd. (saved 11 MP)

1975 - 3rd seed Billie Jean King d. 1st seed Chris Evert, 2-6, 6-2, 6-3, SF (from 0-3, 2 break points, 3rd)

1977 - Maria Bueno d. Janet Newberry, 1-6, 8-6, 8-6, 2nd rd. (saved 1 MP at 6-5, 3rd)

1978 - 14th seed Sue Barker d. Pam Shriver, 2-6, 8-6, 7-5, 3rd rd. (from 0-3, 3-5, 3rd; saved 3 MP, 3rd, 1 at 5-3, 2 at 5-6)

1980 - 5th seed Billie Jean King d. Pam Shriver, 5-7, 7-6 (7-5), 10-8, 4th rd. (saved 1 MP, 2d, at 5-4; behind 4-2, 3rd)

1982 - 12th seed Billie Jean King d. Tanya Harford, 5-7, 7-6 (7-5), 6-3, 3rd rd. (saved 3 MP, 2nd, at 4-5, 0-40). Also JoAnne Russell (No. 32) d. 8th seed Mima Jausovec, 6-7 (2-7), 6-3, 7-5 (saved 2 MP, 3rd).Also Virginia Wade d. Jo Durie, 3-6, 7-6 (15-13), 6-2, 1st rd. (saved 4 MP in tie-breaker)

1983 - Virginia Wade d. Eva Pfaff, 3-6, 7-6 (7-5), 7-5, 4th rd. (saved MP at 4-5, 3rd). Also 10th seed Billie Jean King d. Beth Herr, 6-7 (4-7), 6-2, 8-6, 2nd rd.

1987 - 5th seed Pam Shriver d. 16th seed Sylvia Hanika, 6-7 (4-7), 7-5, 10-8, 4th rd. (saved 2 MP, 3rd, at 5-6.2:33). Also Shriver d. 4th seed Helena Sukova, 4-6, 7-6 (7-1), 10-8, QF (saved 1 MP, 3rd, at 6-7.)

1989 - Gretchen Rush Magers d. 8th seed Pam Shriver, 2-6, 6-2, 12-10, 4th rd.

1990 - 5th seed Zina Garrison d. 3rd seed Monica Seles, 3-6, 6-3, 9-7, QF (saved MP at 6-7, 3rd, with forehand winner)

1991 - Brenda Schultz d. Elena Brioukhovets, 5-7, 6-4, 7-5, 3rd rd. (saved 2 MP at 3-5, 3rd)

1995 - Chanda Rubin d. Patricia Hy-Boulais 7-6 (7-4), 6-7 (5-7), 17-15, 2nd rd. (broke Hy-Boulais when she served to win at 10-9, 13-12, 15-14. Time, 3:45)

1998 - 16th seed Nathalie Tauziat d. Natasha Zvereva (No. 22), 1-6, 7-6 (7-1), 6-3, SF (3 points from defeat, 2nd, at 5-6, 15-15)

MATCH POINTS SAVES BY SINGLES CHAMPION

Men:

1889 - F, Willie Renshaw d. Harry Barlow, 3-6, 5-7, 8-6, 10-8, 8-6. Saved 6 MP, 4th: 2 at 2-5, 2 at 3-5, 2 at 6-7

1895 - F, Wilfred Baddeley d. Wilberforce Eaves, 4-6, 2-6, 8-6, 6-2, 6-3. Saved 1 MP, 3rd, at 5-6

1901 - QF, Arthur Gore d. George Hillyard, 6-1, 2-6, 4-6, 8-6, 6-2. Saved 2 MP, 4th, at 4-5

1921 - F, Bill Tilden d. Brian "Babe" Norton, 4-6, 2-6, 6-1, 6-0, 7-5. Saved 2 MP, 5th, at 4-5

1927 - F, 4th seed Henri Cochet d. 3rd seed Jean Borotra, 4-6, 4-6, 6-3, 6-4, 7-5. Saved 6 MP, 5th, 1 at 2-3, 5 at 5-3

1948 - F, 7th seed Bob Falkenburg d. 2nd seed John Bromwich, 7-5, 0-6, 6-2, 3-6, 7-5. Saved 3 MP, 5th, at 3-5

1949 - QF, 1st seed Ted Schroeder d. 8th seed Frank Sedgman, 3-6, 6-8, 6-3, 6-2, 9-7.Saved 2 MP, 5th, 1 at 4-5, 1 at 5-6

1960 - QF, 1st seed Neale Fraser d. 8th seed Butch Buchholz, 4-6, 6-3, 4-6, 15-15, retired, cramps. Saved 5 MP, 4th, 1 at 4-5, 2 at 5-6, 2 at 13-14

Women:

1889 - F, Blanche Bingley Hillyard d. Helena Rice, 4-6, 8-6, 6-4. Saved 3 MP, 2nd, at 3-5

1919 - F, Suzanne Lenglen d. Dorothea Douglass Chambers, 10-8, 4-6, 9-7. Saved 2 MP, 3rd, at 5-6

1935 - F, 4th seed Helen Wills Moody d. 3rd seed Helen Jacobs, 6-3, 3-6, 7-5. Saved 1 MP, 3rd, at 3-5

1935 - F, 4th seed Helen Wills Moody d. 3rd seed Helen Jacobs, 6-3, 3-6, 7-5. Saved 1 MP, 3rd, at 3-5.

Chapter 20

U.S. Open

Althea Gibson, 1958
Riding her thunderous serve to a second straight U.S. title, she would retire "to pursue a musical career"—and pro tennis—months later.

There has always been something particularly grand about the fourth, and final, major championship on the calendar. Initiated in 1881 under the grandiose name of U.S. National Lawn Tennis Association Championship, it initially served as extravagant entertainment for millionaires summering in Rhode Island. Today, the U.S. Open is the longest-running uninterrupted show in tennis and is noted less for its well-heeled patrons than for its status as the sport's richest tournament—and the one with the best tennis played after midnight anywhere in the world.

Although four years younger than Wimbledon, the U.S. tournament was the only major championship conducted during the two World Wars. (In 1917-18 National Patriotic Tournaments were held that were eventually recognized as official championships.) It will celebrate its 125th anniversary in 2006. The first tournament had 26 amateurs (men only) and turned a profit of $4.32. Today the tournament is open to men and women, professionals and amateurs, and generates profits in the tens of millions. From a prize pool of $100,000 at the first professional event in 1968, prize money has grown to more than $16-million. The tournament had separate beginnings for men and women. The first Championships, for men only, was staged at the Newport Casino in 1881 and was held there through 1914. In 1915 the men's singles tournament and doubles finals (the finalists emerging from sectional tournaments) moved to the West Side Tennis Club, Forest Hills, New York. In 1917, the men's doubles championship, conducted as a separate tournament, was installed at the Longwood Cricket Club, Boston, and remained there through 1967, with two exceptions, 1934 at Germantown Cricket Club, Philadelphia, and 1942 through 1945 at Forest Hills. The men's singles departed briefly from Forest Hills for a three-year stay at Germantown Cricket, 1921 through 1923, and thereafter was staged at West Side's newly constructed Stadium.

The women's championships in singles and doubles began in 1887 at the Philadelphia Cricket Club (but the

1887-88 doubles were not considered championship events) and remained there through 1920 along with the mixed doubles, begun in 1892. In 1921 the women's singles and doubles moved to Forest Hills, but as an event prior to and separate from the men's championship, while the mixed doubles moved to Longwood to be played concurrently with the men's doubles.

In 1935 the men's and women's singles championships were united at Forest Hills while the women's doubles moved to Longwood as part of the U.S. Doubles with men's and mixed events. During World War II all five events—men's and women's singles and doubles and mixed-were consolidated at Forest Hills. In 1946 the men and women's doubles returned to Longwood but the mixed remained at West Side until 1967, when it also returned to Longwood. Finally in 1968, all the events were combined for the first U.S. Open at Forest Hills. The tournament moved to Queens in 1978 and has been held ever since at the USTA (United States Tennis Association) National Tennis Center, a facility in a park called Flushing Meadows that boasts 45 courts, including 23,000-seat Arthur Ashe Stadium. It all began at The Casino in Newport, Rhode Island, a private club built for the Gilded Age aristocracy of Newport. For 30 years, high-society politely cheered a succession of champions that hailed largely from Ivy League schools. Richard Sears, a 19-year-old Harvard student from a moneyed Boston family, won the first seven singles titles and six of the first seven doubles crowns. (Defending a title was much easier in the early days because the reigning champion earned automatic entry into a one-match final against the survivor of an all-comers tournament.) On the women's side, 17-year-old hometown lass Ellen Hansell won the inaugural event in 1887. In 1890 sisters Ellen and Grace Roosevelt teamed to win the doubles, a feat matched by Juliette and Kathleen Atkinson in 1897-98, and by sisters Venus and Serena Williams in 1999.

Before the challenge-round format was eliminated for men in 1912 (1919 for women) Bill Larned would equal Sears' record of seven singles titles, the last coming in 1911 when he was 38 years, 8 months, 3 days. He remains the oldest men's champion. His final victory came against a player called the California Comet, Maurice (Red) McLoughlin. He had burst upon the scene with fellow Californian Hazel Hotchkiss in 1909 and introduced a revolutionary attacking style to the traditional eastern game. Over the ensuing years, McLoughlin and Hotchkiss would win a combined 19 titles. Of those, Hotchkiss won

14, including an unprecedented three-year run when she won nine finals—sweeping singles, doubles and mixed doubles in each of 1909, 1910 and 1911.

When Hotchkiss took time off to have a family, another hard-hitting Californian, Mary K. Browne, stepped up to record her own triple-triple, sweeping all nine titles from 1912 to 1914. Browne was succeeded by a 31-year-old Norwegian immigrant named Anna (Molla) Bjurstedt, the tournament's greatest singles champion. Beginning in 1915, Bjurstedt, a bronze medallist at the 1912 Olympics, won seven singles titles in eight years. She added an eighth in 1926, when, playing under her married name, Molla Mallory, she was 42 years old. She still holds records for most singles titles and oldest champion. On the men's side, a tall righthander out of Philadelphia named Bill Tilden was making a mark of his own. After losing in the final in 1918 and 1919, Tilden peeled off six consecutive singles titles from 1920 to 1925 (he would add a seventh in 1929). Five of those victories came against Bill Johnston. Beginning in 1920, Tilden registered a 42-match undefeated streak at Forest Hills. His career record at the U.S. was 71-7 (a winning percentage of .910), including 16 titles.

Henri Cochet ended Tilden's six-year singles streak in 1926 as France's famous tennis Musketeers invaded Forest Hills. Cochet eliminated Tilden in a memorable quarter-final (6-8, 6-1, 6-3, 1-6, 8-6). But it was Cochet's countrymen, René Lacoste and Jean Borotra, who advanced to the final (the first all-foreign final in tournament history), with Lacoste winning handily. Tilden was back in the final in 1927, but lost to Lacoste. It was Cochet's turn to win in 1928, giving France three consecutive titles, before Tilden returned the title to America in 1929.

The 1930s were a time for revolving champions—and for the introduction of the phrase Grand Slam to the lexicon of tennis. Prior to 1933, the notion of one player winning the Australian, French, Wimbledon and U.S. Championships in a calendar year seemed remote. But when Australian Jack Crawford arrived at Forest Hills in 1933 with the first three titles already won, the possibility of a sweep, the so-called "Grand Slam," became quite real. Crawford landed in the U.S. with 13 consecutive tournament victories and advanced rather easily to the final against England's Fred Perry. Crawford led in sets 2-1 at the intermission and then ran out of gas, winning just one game after the break. Perry would defend the title in 1934 and win again in 1936. No Englishman has won since.

A Grand Slam remained elusive until 1938, when

23-year-old American Don Budge completed the most successful season the sport had ever seen by adding the U.S. title to earlier victories at Wimbledon, Roland Garros and Australia. He romped to the final and beat his doubles partner, Gene Mako, the first unseeded player ever to reach the final at Forest Hills, 6-3, 6-8, 6-2, 6-1. Budge then turned professional, a typical outcome among male players of the era. Subsequent champions lured by the promise of lucre included Bobby Riggs (1939, 1941), Jack Kramer (1946-47), and Pancho Gonzales (1948-49).

Among women, Helen Wills was even more dominant than Tilden, building a 45-match unbeaten streak from 1927-33. She took seven titles in nine years, the last in 1931 as Helen Wills Moody. Her career mark was an astounding 50-2, the last of those defeats coming in a controversial 1933 final against Helen Jacobs when she retired at 0-3 in the third set, claiming back pain. Her unexpected exit triggered considerable criticism, including the charge that she was a quitter and poor sport.

Jacobs was an eight-time U.S. finalist between 1928 and 1940, winning four consecutive titles from 1932. She was succeeded by a string of outstanding women who won in bunches: Alice Marble (1936, 1938, 1939, 1940), Pauline Betz (1942, 1943, 1944, 1946), Margaret Osborne duPont (1948, 1949, 1950), and Maureen Connolly (1951, 1952, 1953). Connolly, among the most popular players in championship history, was just 16 when she took her first title, the youngest U.S. champ ever until Tracy Austin in 1979. In 1953 she defeated Doris Hart in the final to become the first woman to win a Grand Slam.

The U.S. Championships were a segregated event until Althea Gibson, at age 23, broke the color barrier in 1950. On Aug. 28, she made her historic debut by defeating Barbara Knapp, 6-2, 6-2, before being eliminated in the next round. (Dr. Reginald Weir was the first African-American male entered in the Championship, making his debut on Aug. 29, 1952.) It would take seven years, but Gibson eventually became the first black player to win at Forest Hills. In the 1957 final, she won 6-3, 6-2 against Louise Brough, and then successfully defended her title in 1958.

While less historic than Gibson's arrival, the 1950s marked a watershed in men's play due to a brilliant crop of Australians. It began with wins by Frank Sedgman in 1951 and 1952 and then exploded beginning in 1956. Over the next 12 years, 10 titles were won by eight different Aussies—Ken Rosewall, Mal Anderson, Ashley Cooper, Neale Fraser, Roy Emerson, Rod Laver, Fred Stolle and John Newcombe. Fraser (1959, 1960) and Emerson (1961, 1964) were the only two-time winners. With the advent of Open tennis in 1968, Rosewall returned as a professional to win again in 1970 (he remains the oldest male winner in the Open era at 35 years, 10 months, 7 days). Both Laver victories, in 1962 and 1969, completed Grand Slams. Not to be outdone at Forest Hills, Australian Margaret Smith Court won five women's titles in eight years from 1968 to 1973, finishing a Grand Slam in 1970.

In 1968, the tournament welcomed professionals and was renamed the U.S. Open. But the USTA decided to maintain a second tournament to crown an amateur national champion (the twin-tournament format was abandoned after the 1969 season). And so the ground was laid for Arthur Ashe to write a little history. Ashe, a lieutenant in the U.S Army, won the amateur crown at Longwood in Boston and was fifth seeded for the inaugural Open the next week at Forest Hills. Facing Tom Okker of the Netherlands in a thrilling final, Ashe blasted 26 aces to win a roller-coaster battle, 14-12, 5-7, 6-3, 3-6, 6-3. Ashe became the first black male to win a major championship and the only male to win both the U.S. amateur and Open titles in the same year.

The 1970s brought innovation: the 1970 introduction of tie-breakers for a major championship (between 1970 and 1974 the system was "sudden death," best-of-nine points rather than the current best-of-12, but with a margin of two); the adoption of equal prize money for men and women (1973); the replacement of grass at Forest Hills with a green clay called Har-Tru, and the first night match under floodlights (1975); the change in venues to Flushing Meadows (1978). There was also a changing of the guard as Aussie dominance gave way to a new wave of American stars, most notably Jimmy Connors and John McEnroe in men's play, and Chris Evert and Tracy Austin in women's.

First, though, Billie Jean King, who won a singles title in 1967 but watched Court take the first three Open crowns, ran up victories in 1971, 1973 and 1974 to solidify her place among the great U.S. champions. King was also a force off the court. Her relentless campaign for equality factored into the bold move by the USTA in 1973 to give women an equal share of the purse.

The final U.S. Open played on grass, in 1974, launched a decade in which Connors would appear in seven finals, winning five times. Having celebrated his 22nd birthday a week earlier, Connors crushed Rosewall, 39, in the final. He needed just 78 minutes to complete the most one-sided men's final ever, 6-1, 6-0, 6-1. Connors defeated Bjorn Borg in an exhilarating 1976 final and hammered Borg again two years later, when Connors became the first man since Tilden to appear in five consecutive finals. In addition, with the tournament shifting to Flushing Meadows in 1978, Connors became the only player to have won on three different surfaces—grass, clay and hard court. His 98 match wins are the most among men.

Connors would win again in 1982 and 1983, beating Ivan Lendl in both finals, but the intervening years belonged to McEnroe. Reared on nearby Long Island, McEnroe's first U.S. title came in 1979, at age 20, when he beat Vitas Gerulaitis to become the youngest winner in 31 years. Loud and vulgar, he was an unpopular champion. But he successfully defended in 1980 and 1981, both times beating Borg, who was 0-for-4 in Open finals. His final win came over Lendl in 1984, ending an era in which McEnroe and Connors won nine of 11 titles.

Like Connors, the unflappable Evert made a smooth transition when the USTA changed venues. A master on clay, Evert had won the final three titles at Forest Hills and then won the inaugural event on the hard courts of Flushing Meadows to become the first woman in 43 years to win four consecutive titles. But hopes for an unprecedented fifth title were dashed in the 1979 final by Austin, who, at 16 years, 8 months, 28 days, became the youngest champion ever. Evert won in 1980, Austin in 1981 and Evert added her final title in 1982. Her 101 match victories are a tournament record.

If the 1970s were the era of Connors and Evert, the 1980s belonged to two Czechoslovak players who would later become American citizens. Ivan Lendl appeared in eight consecutive finals from 1982, matching Tilden's streak in the 1920s. But two losses to Connors and one to McEnroe in his first three finals left Lendl to explain an inability to win the big match. He finally silenced critics by reeling off three consecutive wins, defeating McEnroe (1985), Miloslav Mecir (1986) and Mats Wilander (1987). Meanwhile, the peerless Martina Navratilova appeared in eight finals between 1981 and 1991, winning

four times (she also added nine doubles titles). The record book would have shown an unprecedented five-straight wins for Navratilova if not for a virtuoso performance by Hana Mandlikova in 1985. After eliminating Evert, the young Czech defeated Navratilova in a close final to become the first female European citizen to win the U.S. championship.

Between Evert in 1982 and American Lindsay Davenport in 1998, no U.S.-born woman won the national championship. Navratilova passed the crown to Germany's Steffi Graf, a five-time winner. Yugoslav Monica Seles won twice, while Argentinean Gabriela Sabatini, Spaniard Arantxa Sanchez Vicario and Swiss Martina Hingis each won once. But the arrival of the Williams sisters, Venus and Serena, tipped the balance back towards the U.S., beginning with Serena's unexpected win in 1998. Seeded seventh, she upset No. 1 seed Hingis to become the first African American woman since Gibson in 1958 to win a major championship. Serena failed to get past the quarters in 2000, but Venus kept the title in the family, defeating 1998 champion Davenport in the final. In the first all-sister final in tournament history, Venus successfully defended in 2001, but Serena turned the tables by defeating Venus in the 2002 final, giving the sisters four consecutive titles.

On the men's side, Pete Sampras emerged as the 1990s man of the decade. He burst upon the scene in 1990 when, seeded 12th, he knocked off former champs McEnroe and Lendl on way to a straight-set final thrashing of Andre Agassi. At 19 years, 28 days, Sampras was the youngest champion in tournament history. Agassi would earn two titles (1994 and 1999), but lose twice more to Sampras in finals, including the 2002 event that was, perhaps, Sampras' finest hour. Reminiscent of 1990, Sampras, seeded 17th and mired in a 33-tournament losing streak, was given little chance. But he called upon past brilliance to win his fifth title, equaling Connors' Open era record and, at 31, becoming the oldest men's champion since 35-year-old Ken Rosewall in 1970.

U.S. Open – Champions

Year	Men's Singles	Women's Singles	Men's Doubles	Women's Doubles	Mixed Doubles
2002	Pete Sampras	Serena Williams	Max Mirnyi / Mahesh Bhupathi	Paola Suarez / Virginia Ruano Pascual	Lisa Raymond / Mike Bryan
2001	Lleyton Hewitt	Venus Williams	Wayne Black / Kevin Ullyett	Rennae Stubbs / Lisa Raymond	Rennae Stubbs / Todd Woodbridge
2000	Marat Safin	Venus Williams	Lleyton Hewitt / Max Mirnyi	Julie Halard-Decugis / Ai Sugiyama	Arantxa Sanchez Vicario / Jared Palmer
1999	Andre Agassi	Serena Williams	Sebastien Lareau / Alex O'Brien	Serena Williams / Venus Williams	Ai Sugiyama / Mahesh Bhupathi
1998	Patrick Rafter	Lindsay Davenport	Sandon Stolle / Cyril Suk	Martina Hingis / Jana Novotna	Serena Williams / Max Mirnyi
1997	Patrick Rafter	Martina Hingis	Yevgeny Kafelnikov / Daniel Vacek	Jana Novotna / Lindsay Davenport	Manon Bollegraf / Rick Leach
1996	Pete Sampras	Steffi Graf	Todd Woodbridge / Mark Woodforde	Natalia Zvereva / Gigi Fernandez	Lisa Raymond / Patrick Galbraith
1995	Pete Sampras	Steffi Graf	Todd Woodbridge / Mark Woodforde	Gigi Fernandez / Natalia Zvereva	Meredith McGrath / Matt Lucena
1994	Andre Agassi	Arantxa Sanchez Vicario	Jacco Eltingh / Paul Haarhuis	Arantxa Sanchez Vicario / Jana Novotna	Elna Reinach / Patrick Galbraith
1993	Pete Sampras	Steffi Graf	Ken Flach / Rick Leach	Arantxa Sanchez Vicario / Helena Sukova	Helena Sukova / Todd Woodbridge
1992	Stefan Edberg	Monica Seles	Jim Grabb / Richey Reneberg	Gigi Fernandez / Natalia Zvereva	Nicole Provis / Mark Woodforde
1991	Stefan Edberg	Monica Seles	John Fitzgerald / Anders Jarryd	Pam Shriver / Natalia Zvereva	Manon Bollegraf / Tom Nijssen
1990	Pete Sampras	Gabriela Sabatini	Pieter Aldrich / Danie Visser	Gigi Fernandez / Martina Navratilova	Elizabeth Sayers Smylie / Todd Woodbridge
1989	Boris Becker	Steffi Graf	John McEnroe / Mark Woodforde	Hana Mandlikova / Martina Navratilova	Robin White / Shelby Cannon
1988	Mats Wilander	Steffi Graf	Sergio Casal / Emilio Sanchez	Gigi Fernandez / Robin White	Jana Novotna / Jim Pugh
1987	Ivan Lendl	Martina Navratilova	Stefan Edberg / Anders Jarryd	Martina Navratilova / Pam Shriver	Martina Navratilova / Emilio Sanchez
1986	Ivan Lendl	Martina Navratilova	Andres Gomez / Slobodan Zivojinovic	Martina Navratilova / Pam Shriver	Raffaella Reggi / Sergio Casal
1985	Ivan Lendl	Hana Mandlikova	Ken Flach / Robert Seguso	Claudia Kohde Kilsch / Helena Sukova	Martina Navratilova / Heinz Gunthardt
1984	John McEnroe	Martina Navratilova	John Fitzgerald / Tomas Smid	Pam Shriver / Martina Navratilova	Manuela Maleeva / Tom Gullikson
1983	Jimmy Connors	Martina Navratilova	Peter Fleming / John McEnroe	Pam Shriver / Martina Navratilova	Elizabeth Sayers / John Fitzgerald
1982	Jimmy Connors	Chris Evert Lloyd	Kevin Curren / Steve Denton	Rosie Casals / Wendy Turnbull	Anne Smith / Kevin Curren
1981	John McEnroe	Tracy Austin	Peter Fleming / John McEnroe	Anne Smith / Kathy Jordan	Anne Smith / Kevin Curren
1980	John McEnroe	Chris Evert	Bob Lutz / Stan Smith	Billie Jean King / Martina Navratilova	Wendy Turnbull / Marty Riessen
1979	John McEnroe	Tracy Austin	John McEnroe / Peter Fleming	Betty Stove / Wendy Turnbull	Greer Stevens / Bob Hewitt
1978	Jimmy Connors	Chris Evert	Bob Lutz / Stan Smith	Billie Jean King / Martina Navratilova	Betty Stove / Frew McMillan
1977	Guillermo Vilas	Chris Evert	Bob Hewitt / Frew McMillan	Martina Navratilova / Betty Stove	Betty Stove / Frew McMillan
1976	Jimmy Connors	Chris Evert	Tom Okker / Marty Riessen	Delina Boshoff / Ilana Kloss	Billie Jean King / Phil Dent
1975	Manolo Orantes	Chris Evert	Jimmy Connors / Ilie Nastase	Margaret Smith Court / Virginia Wade	Rosie Casals / Dick Stockton
1974	Jimmy Connors	Billie Jean King	Bob Lutz / Stan Smith	Rosie Casals / Billie Jean King	Pam Teeguarden / Geoff Masters
1973	John Newcombe	Margaret Smith Court	Owen Davidson / John Newcombe	Margaret Smith Court / Virginia Wade	Billie Jean King / Owen Davidson
1972	Ilie Nastase	Billie Jean King	Cliff Drysdale / Roger Taylor	Françoise Durr / Betty Stove	Margaret Smith Court / Marty Riessen
1971	Stan Smith	Billie Jean King	John Newcombe / Roger Taylor	Rosie Casals / Judy Tegart Dalton	Billie Jean King / Owen Davidson
1970	Ken Rosewall	Margaret Smith Court	Pierre Barthes / Nikki Pilic	Margaret Smith Court / Judy Tegart Dalton	Margaret Smith Court / Marty Riessen
1969	Rod Laver	Margaret Smith Court	Ken Rosewall / Fred Stolle	Françoise Durr / Darlene Hard	Margaret Smith Court / Marty Riessen
1969*	Stan Smith	Margaret Smith Court	Dick Crealy / Allan Stone	Virginia Wade / Margaret Smith Court	Patti Hogan / Paul Sullivan
1968	Arthur Ashe	Virginia Wade	Bob Lutz / Stan Smith	Maria Bueno / Margaret Smith Court	
1968*	Arthur Ashe	Margaret Smith Court	Bob Lutz / Stan Smith	Maria Bueno / Margaret Smith Court	Mary Ann Eisel / Peter Curtis
1967	John Newcombe	Billie Jean King	John Newcombe / Tony Roche	Rosie Casals / Billie Jean King	Billie Jean King / Owen Davidson
1966	Fred Stolle	Maria Bueno	Roy Emerson / Fred Stolle	Maria Bueno / Nancy Richey	Donna Floyd Fales / Owen Davidson
1965	Manolo Santana	Margaret Smith	Roy Emerson / Fred Stolle	Carole Caldwell Graebner / Nancy Richey	Margaret Smith / Fred Stolle
1964	Roy Emerson	Maria Bueno	Chuck McKinley / Dennis Ralston	Billie Jean Moffitt / Karen Hantze Susman	Margaret Smith / John Newcombe
1963	Rafael Osuna	Maria Bueno	Chuck McKinley / Dennis Ralston	Robyn Ebbern / Margaret Smith	Margaret Smith / Ken Fletcher
1962	Rod Laver	Margaret Smith	Rafael Osuna / Antonio Palafox	Darlene Hard / Maria Bueno	Margaret Smith / Fred Stolle
1961	Roy Emerson	Darlene Hard	Chuck McKinley / Dennis Ralston	Darlene Hard / Lesley Turner	Margaret Smith / Bob Mark
1960	Neale Fraser	Darlene Hard	Neale Fraser / Roy Emerson	Maria Bueno / Darlene Hard	Margaret Osborne duPont / Neale Fraser
1959	Neale Fraser	Maria Bueno	Neale Fraser / Roy Emerson	Jeanne Arth / Darlene Hard	Margaret Osborne duPont / Neale Fraser
1958	Ashley Cooper	Althea Gibson	Alex Olmedo / Hamilton Richardson	Jeanne Arth / Darlene Hard	Margaret Osborne duPont / Neale Fraser
1957	Mal Anderson	Althea Gibson	Ashley Cooper / Neale Fraser	Louise Brough / Margaret Osborne duPont	Althea Gibson / Kurt Nielsen
1956	Ken Rosewall	Shirley Fry	Lew Hoad / Ken Rosewall	Louise Brough / Margaret Osborne duPont	Margaret Osborne duPont / Ken Rosewall

Year	Men's Singles	Women's Singles	Men's Doubles	Women's Doubles	Mixed Doubles
1955	Tony Trabert	Doris Hart	Kosei Kamo / Atsushi Miyagi	Louise Brough / Margaret Osborne duPont	Doris Hart / Vic Seixas
1954	Vic Seixas	Doris Hart	Vic Seixas / Tony Trabert	Shirley Fry / Doris Hart	Doris Hart / Vic Seixas
1953	Tony Trabert	Maureen Connolly	Rex Hartwig / Merv Rose	Shirley Fry / Doris Hart	Doris Hart / Vic Seixas
1952	Frank Sedgman	Maureen Connolly	Merv Rose / Vic Seixas	Shirley Fry / Doris Hart	Doris Hart / Frank Sedgman
1951	Frank Sedgman	Maureen Connolly	Ken McGregor / Frank Sedgman	Shirley Fry / Doris Hart	Doris Hart / Frank Sedgman
1950	Art Larsen	M. Osborne duPont	John Bromwich / Frank Sedgman	Louise Brough / Margaret Osborne duPont	Margaret Osborne duPont / Ken McGregor
1949	Pancho Gonzalez	M. Osborne duPont	John Bromwich / Bill Sidwell	Louise Brough / Margaret Osborne duPont	Louise Brough / Eric Strugess
1948	Pancho Gonzalez	M. Osborne duPont	Gardnar Mulloy / Bill Talbert	Louise Brough / Margaret Osborne duPont	Louise Brough / Tom Brown
1947	Jack Kramer	Louise Brough	Jack Kramer / Ted Schroeder	Louise Brough / Margaret Osborne	Louise Brough / John Bromwich
1946	Jack Kramer	Pauline Betz	Gardnar Mulloy / Bill Talbert	Louise Brough / Margaret Osborne	Margaret Osborne / Bill Talbert
1945	Frank Parker	Sarah Palfrey Cooke	Gardnar Mulloy / Bill Talbert	Louise Brough / Margaret Osborne	Margaret Osborne / Bill Talbert
1944	Frank Parker	Pauline Betz	Don McNeill / Bob Falkenburg	Louise Brough / Margaret Osborne	Margaret Osborne / Bill Talbert
1943	Joseph R. Hunt	Pauline Betz	Jack Kramer / Frank Parker	Louise Brough / Margaret Osborne	Margaret Osborne / Bill Talbert
1942	Ted Schroeder	Pauline Betz	Gardnar Mulloy / Bill Talbert	Louise Brough / Margaret Osborne	Louise Brough / Ted Schroeder
1941	Bobby Riggs	Sarah Palfrey Cooke	Jack Kramer / Ted Schroeder	Sarah Palfrey Fabyan Cooke / Margaret Osborne	Sarah Palfrey Fabyan Cooke / Jack Kramer
1940	Don McNeill	Alice Marble	Jack Kramer / Ted Schroeder	Sarah Palfrey Fabyan / Alice Marble	Alice Marble / Bobby Riggs
1939	Bobby Riggs	Alice Marble	Adrian Quist / John Bromwich	Sarah Palfrey Fabyan / Alice Marble	Alice Marble / Harry Hopman
1938	Don Budge	Alice Marble	Don Budge / Gene Mako	Sarah Palfrey Fabyan / Alice Marble	Alice Marble / Don Budge
1937	Don Budge	Anita Lizana	Gottfried von Cramm / Henner Henkel	Sarah Palfrey Fabyan / Alice Marble	Sarah Palfrey Fabyan / Don Budge
1936	Fred Perry	Alice Marble	Don Budge / Gene Mako	Marjorie Gladman Van Ryn / Carolin Babcock	Alice Marble / Gene Mako
1935	Wilmer Allison	Helen Jacobs	Wilmer Allison / John Van Ryn	Helen Jacobs / Sarah Palfrey Fabyan	Sarah Palfrey Fabyan / Enrique Maier
1934	Fred Perry	Helen Jacobs	George Lott / Lester Stoefen	Helen Jacobs / Sarah Palfrey	Helen Jacobs / George Lott
1933	Fred Perry	Helen Jacobs	George Lott / Lester Stoefen	Betty Nuthall / Freda James	Elizabeth Ryan / Ellsworth Vines
1932	Ellsworth Vines	Helen Jacobs	Ellsworth Vines / Keith Gledhill	Helen Jacobs / Sarah Palfrey	Sarah Palfrey / Fred Perry
1931	Ellsworth Vines	Helen Wills Moody	Wilmer Allison / John Van Ryn	Betty Nuthall / Eileen Bennett Whittingstall	Betty Nuthall / George Lott
1930	Johnny Doeg	Betty Nuthall	George Lott / Johnny Doeg	Betty Nuthall / Sarah Palfrey	Edith Cross / Wilmer Allison
1929	Bill Tilden	Helen Wills Moody	George Lott / Johnny Doeg	Phoebe Holcroft Watson / Peggy Michell	Betty Nuthall / George Lott
1928	Henri Cochet	Helen Wills	George Lott / John Hennessey	Hazel Hotchkiss Wightman / Helen Wills	Helen Wills / Jack Hawkes
1927	René Lacoste	Helen Wills	Bill Tilden / Frank Hunter	Kitty McKane Godfree / Ermyntrude Harvey	Eileen Bennett / Henri Cochet
1926	René Lacoste	Molla Bjurstedt Mallory	Dick Williams / Vinnie Richards	Elizabeth Ryan / Eleanor Goss	Elizabeth Ryan / Jean Borotra
1925	Bill Tilden	Helen Wills	Dick Williams / Vinnie Richards	Mary K. Browne / Helen Wills	Kitty McKane / Jack Hawkes
1924	Bill Tilden	Helen Wills	Howard Kinsey / Robert Kinsey	Hazel Hotchkiss Wightman / Helen Wills	Helen Wills / Vinnie Richards
1923	Bill Tilden	Helen Wills	Bill Tilden / Brian Norton	Kitty McKane / Phyllis Howkins Covell	Molla Bjurstedt Mallory / Bill Tilden
1922	Bill Tilden	Molla Bjurstedt Mallory	Bill Tilden / Vinnie Richards	Marion Zinderstein Jessup / Helen Wills	Molla Bjurstedt Mallory / Bill Tilden
1921	Bill Tilden	Molla Bjurstedt Mallory	Bill Tilden / Vinnie Richards	Mary K. Browne / Louise Riddell Williams	Mary K. Browne / Bill Johnston
1920	Bill Tilden	Molla Bjurstedt Mallory	Bill Johnston / Clarence Griffin	Marion Zinderstein / Eleanor Goss	Hazel Hotchkiss Wightman / Wallace Johnson
1919	Bill Johnston	H. Hotchkiss Wightman	Norman Brookes / Gerald Patterson	Marion Zinderstein / Eleanor Goss	Marion Zinderstein / Vinnie Richards
1918	Lindley Murray	Molla Bjurstedt	Bill Tilden / Vinnie Richards	Marion Zinderstein / Eleanor Goss	Hazel Hotchkiss Wightman / Irving Wright
1917	Lindley Murray	Molla Bjurstedt	Fred Alexander / Harold Throckmorton	Molla Bjurstedt / Eleonora Sears	Molla Bjurstedt / Irving Wright
1916	Dick Williams	Molla Bjurstedt	Bill Johnston / Clarence Griffin	Molla Bjurstedt / Eleonora Sears	Eleonora Sears / Willis Davis
1915	Bill Johnston	Molla Bjurstedt	Bill Johnston / Clarence Griffin	Hazel Hotchkiss Wightman / Eleonora Sears	Hazel Hotchkiss Wightman / Harry Johnson
1914	Dick Williams	Mary K. Browne	Maurice McLoughlin / Tom Bundy	Mary K. Browne / Louise Riddell Williams	Mary K. Browne / Bill Tilden
1913	Maurice McLoughlin	Mary K. Browne	Maurice McLoughlin / Tom Bundy	Mary K. Browne / Louise Riddell Williams	Mary K. Browne / Bill Tilden
1912	Maurice McLoughlin	Mary K. Browne	Maurice McLoughlin / Tom Bundy	Dorothy Green / Mary K. Browne	Mary K. Browne / Dick Williams
1911	Bill Larned	Hazel Hotchkiss	Ray Little / Gus Touchard	Hazel Hotchkiss / Eleonora Sears	Hazel Hotchkiss / Wallace Johnson
1910	Bill Larned	Hazel Hotchkiss	Fred Alexander / Harold Hackett	Hazel Hotchkiss / Edith Rotch	Hazel Hotchkiss / Joseph Carpenter Jr.
1909	Bill Larned	Hazel Hotchkiss	Fred Alexander / Harold Hackett	Hazel Hotchkiss / Edith Rotch	Hazel Hotchkiss / Wallace Johnson
1908	Bill Larned	Maud Barger Wallach	Fred Alexander / Harold Hackett	Evelyn Sears / Margaret Curtis	Edith Rotch / Nathaniel Niles
1907	Bill Larned	Evelyn Sears	Fred Alexander / Harold Hackett	Marie Wimer / Carrie Neely	May Sayers / Wallace Johnson
1906	Bill Clothier	Helen Homans	Holcombe Ward / Beals Wright	Ann Burdette Coe / Ethel Bliss Platt	Sarah Coffin / Edward Dewhurst

Year	Men's Singles	Women's Singles	Men's Doubles	Women's Doubles	Mixed Doubles
1905	Beals Wright	Elisabeth Moore	Holcombe Ward / Beals Wright	Helen Homans / Carrie Neely	Augusta Schultz Hobart / Clarence Hobart
1904	Holcombe Ward	May Sutton	Holcombe Ward / Beals Wright	May Sutton / Miriam Hall	Elisabeth Moore / Wylie Grant
1903	Laurie Doherty	Elisabeth Moore	Reggie Doherty / Laurie Doherty	Elisabeth Moore / Carrie Neely	Helen Chapman / Harry Allen
1902	Reggie Doherty	Marion Jones	Reggie Doherty / Laurie Doherty	Juliette Atkinson / Marion Jones	Elisabeth Moore / Wylie Grant
1901	Bill Larned	Elisabeth Moore	Holcombe Ward / Dwight Davis	Juliette Atkinson / Myrtle McAteer	Marion Jones / Ray Little
1900	Malcolm Whitman	Myrtle McAteer	Holcombe Ward / Dwight Davis	Edith Parker / Hallie Champlin	Margaret Hunnewell / Alfred Codman
1899	Malcolm Whitman	Marion Jones	Holcombe Ward / Dwight Davis	Jane Craven / Myrtle McAteer	Elizabeth Rastall / Albert Hoskins
1898	Malcolm Whitman	Juliette Atkinson	Leo Ware / George Sheldon	Juliette Atkinson / Kathleen Atkinson	Carrie Neely / Edwin Fischer
1897	Robert Wrenn	Juliette Atkinson	Leo Ware / George Sheldon	Juliette Atkinson / Kathleen Atkinson	Laura Henson / D. L. Magruder
1896	Robert Wrenn	Elisabeth Moore	Carr Neel / Sam Neel	Elisabeth Moore / Juliette Atkinson	Juliette Atkinson / Edwin Fischer
1895	Fred Hovey	Juliette Atkinson	Malcolm Chace / Robert Wrenn	Helen Hellwig / Juliette Atkinson	Juliette Atkinson / Edwin Fischer
1894	Robert Wrenn	Helen Hellwig	Clarence Hobart / Fred Hovey	Helen Hellwig / Juliette Atkinson	Juliette Atkinson / Edwin Fischer
1893	Robert Wrenn	Aline Terry	Clarence Hobart / Fred Hovey	Aline Terry / Harriet Butler	Ellen Roosevelt / Clarence Hobart
1892	Oliver Campbell	Mabel Cahill	Oliver Campbell / Bob Huntington	Mabel Cahill / Adeline McKinlay	Mabel Cahill / Clarence Hobart
1891	Oliver Campbell	Mabel Cahill	Oliver Campbell / Bob Huntington	Mabel Cahill / Emma Leavitt Morgan	
1890	Oliver Campbell	Ellen Roosevelt	Valentine Hall / Clarence Hobart	Ellen Roosevelt / Grace Roosevelt	
1889	Henry Slocum	Bertha Townsend	Henry Slocum / Howard Taylor	Margarette Ballard / Bertha Townsend	
1888	Henry Slocum	Bertha Townsend	Oliver Campbell / Valentine Hall		
1887	Richard Sears	Ellen Hansell	Richard Sears / James Dwight		
1886	Richard Sears		Richard Sears / James Dwight		
1885	Richard Sears		Richard Sears / Joseph Clark		
1884	Richard Sears		Richard Sears / James Dwight		
1883	Richard Sears		Richard Sears / James Dwight		
1882	Richard Sears		Richard Sears / James Dwight		
1881	Richard Sears		Clarence Clark / Fred Taylor		

U.S. Open – Tournament Results

(**Legend: F:** Final; **S:** Semi-final; **Q:** Quarter-final; **Ch:** Challenge Round; **Set:** S1, S2, S3, S4, S5)

Men's Singles

Rd	Winner	Defeated	S1	S2	S3	S4	S5
1881							
F	**Richard Sears**	**William Glyn**	6-0	6-3	6-2		
S	Richard Sears	Edward Gray	6-3	6-0			
S	William Glyn	Robert Gould Shaw	6-2	6-2			
Q	Richard Sears	Crawford Nightingale	6-3	6-5			
Q	Edward Gray				(bye)		
Q	William Glyn	William Gammell, Jr.	6-4	4-6	6-4		
Q	Robert Gould Shaw	Mr. Kessler	6-1	6-2			
1882							
F	**Richard Sears**	**Clarence Clark**	6-1	6-4	6-0		
S	Richard Sears				(bye)		
S	Clarence Clark	Edward Gray	6-2	6-2			
Q	Richard Sears	James Rankine	6-0	6-4			
Q	Clarence Clark	James Dwight			(default)		
Q	Edward Gray				(bye)		
1883							
F	**Richard Sears**	**James Dwight**	6-2	6-0	9-7		
S	Richard Sears	Foxhall Keane	6-0	6-0			
S	James Dwight	Richard Conover	6-4	6-3			
Q	Richard Sears	H. Willing Hare Powell	4-6	6-0			
Q	Foxhall Keane	G. Mathewson Smith	6-3	6-4			
Q	James Dwight	Godfrey Brinley	6-2	6-3			
Q	Richard Conover				(bye)		
1884							
Ch	**Richard Sears**	**Howard Taylor**	6-0	1-6	6-0	6-2	
F	Howard Taylor	William V.S. Thorne	6-4	4-6	6-1	6-4	
S	Howard Taylor	Percy Knapp	6-2	2-6	6-1		
S	William V.S. Thorne	Clarence Clark	2-6	6-2	6-3		
Q	Percy Knapp	Livingston Beeckman	6-1	6-2			
Q	Howard Taylor	Alex. Van Rensselaer	6-4	6-1			
Q	William V.S. Thorne	George Richards			(default)		
Q	Clarence Clark	A.C. Galt	6-2	6-2			
1885							
Ch	**Richard Sears**	**Godfrey Brinley**	6-3	4-6	6-0	6-3	
F	Godfrey Brinley	Percy Knapp	6-3	6-3	3-6	6-4	
S	Percy Knapp	Joseph Clark	6-4	6-3			
S	Godfrey Brinley	Walter Berry	3-6	9-7	6-1		
Q	Joseph Clark	Alex Moffat	7-6	1-6	6-3		
Q	Percy Knapp	Howard Taylor	4-6	10-8	6-2		
Q	Godfrey Brinley	Charles Belmont Davis	6-2	6-1			
Q	Walter Berry	Foxhall Keane	6-2	6-1			
1886							
Ch	**Richard Sears**	**Livingston Beeckman**	4-6	6-1	6-3	6-4	
F	Livingston Beeckman	Howard Taylor	2-6	6-3	6-4	6-2	
S	Howard Taylor	Joseph Clark	6-5	6-2	6-3		
S	Livingston Beeckman	Charles Chase	6-4	6-0	6-2		
Q	Joseph Clark	Henry Slocum	1-6	6-5	6-5	6-2	
Q	Howard Taylor	Quincy A.Shaw	6-3	6-5	6-5		
Q	Livingston Beeckman	Fred Mansfield	6-4	3-6	6-0	6-3	
Q	Charles Chase	Morgan G. Post	6-0	6-2	6-4		
1887							
Ch	**Richard Sears**	**Henry Slocum**	6-1	6-3	6-2		
F	Henry Slocum	Howard Taylor	12-10	7-5	6-4		
S	Henry Slocum	Joseph Clark	6-8	6-4	6-3	6-2	
S	Howard Taylor	William L. Thatcher	6-3	6-1	6-1		
Q	Joseph Clark	Fred Mansfield	3-6	6-2	6-8	6-1	6-4
Q	Henry Slocum	George Fearing	6-1	7-5	6-2		
Q	Howard Taylor	Philip Sears	6-1	1-6	6-3	6-1	
Q	William L. Thatcher	Godfrey Brinley	6-4	8-6	3-6	6-4	
1888							
Ch	**Henry Slocum**	**Richard Sears**			(default)		
F	Henry Slocum	Howard Taylor	6-4	6-1	6-0		
S	Henry Slocum	Oliver Campbell	6-2	6-3	6-4		
S	Howard Taylor	Philip Sears	5-7	6-4	6-2	6-2	
Q	Henry Slocum	James Dwight	4-6	6-3	6-0	6-2	
Q	Oliver Campbell	A. Empie Wright	4-6	6-3	1-6	8-6	6-2
Q	Philip Sears	John Ryerson	8-6	6-0	6-4		
Q	Howard Taylor	Arthur L. Williston	6-2	6-3	7-5		
1889							
Ch	**Henry Slocum**	**Quincy A.Shaw**	6-3	6-1	4-6	6-2	
F	Quincy A.Shaw	Oliver Campbell	1-6	6-4	6-3	6-4	
S	Quincy A.Shaw	Percy Knapp	4-6	6-1	6-4	6-4	
S	Oliver Campbell	Ernest G. Meers	5-7	6-1	5-7		6-2
Q	Quincy A.Shaw	Charles Chase	6-4	6-4	4-6	6-3	
Q	Percy Knapp	Dean Miller	6-4	6-3	6-2		
Q	Ernest G. Meers	Fred Mansfield	6-1	6-2	6-2		
Q	Oliver Campbell	Joseph Clark	10-12	7-5	6-3	6-3	
1890							
Ch	**Oliver Campbell**	**Henry Slocum**	6-2	4-6	6-3	6-1	
F	Oliver Campbell	Percy Knapp	8-6	0-6	6-2	6-3	
S	Percy Knapp	Clarence Hobart	10-8	7-5	6-2		
S	Oliver Campbell	Bob Huntington	3-6	6-2	5-7	6-2	6-1
Q	Clarence Hobart	Valentine Hall	6-4	6-3	5-7	3-6	6-3
Q	Percy Knapp	Charles Chase	6-2	6-8	6-3	6-3	
Q	Oliver Campbell	John Ryerson	6-1	7-5	6-3		
Q	Bob Huntington	George W. Lee	5-7	6-1	6-1	6-1	
1891							
Ch	**Oliver Campbell**	**Clarence Hobart**	2-6	7-5	7-9	6-1	6-2
F	Clarence Hobart	Fred Hovey	6-4	3-6	6-4	6-8	6-0
S	Clarence Hobart	Valentine Hall	6-2	6-4	6-2		
S	Fred Hovey	Marmaduke Smith	6-4	6-2	3-6	1-6	6-4
Q	Clarence Hobart	Edward Hall	3-6	6-4	11-9	6-4	
Q	Valentine Hall	Charles Lee	6-4	6-4	0-6	6-0	
Q	Fred Hovey	Allison W. Post	4-6	6-4	6-3	6-0	2-6
Q	Marmaduke Smith	Joseph Clark	6-1	6-0	6-4		
1892							
Ch	**Oliver Campbell**	**Fred Hovey**	7-5	3-6	6-3	7-5	
F	Fred Hovey	Bill Larned	6-0	6-2	7-5		
S	Fred Hovey	Robert Wrenn	6-4	7-5	6-3		
S	Bill Larned	Edward Hall	2-6	6-0	6-4	1-6	8-6
Q	Robert Wrenn	Mantle Fielding	6-1	4-6	9-7	6-0	
Q	Fred Hovey	Richard Stevens	6-1	6-4	6-0		
Q	Edward Hall	Samuel Chase	1-6	6-3	4-6	6-2	6-3
Q	Bill Larned	Valentine Hall	6-4	6-3	7-5		

Rd	Winner	Defeated	S1	S2	S3	S4	S5
1893							
Ch	**Robert Wrenn**	**Oliver Campbell**			(default)		
F	Robert Wrenn	Fred Hovey	6-4	3-6	6-4	6-4	
S	Robert Wrenn	Samuel Chase	8-6	6-1	6-2		
S	Fred Hovey	Clarence Hobart	7-5	6-0	6-3		
Q	Robert Wrenn	Richard Stevens	6-1	6-2	2-6	6-2	
Q	Samuel Chase	Duncan Candler	6-3	6-4	6-2		
Q	Clarence Hobart	Bill Larned	6-3	6-4	3-6	5-7	6-2
Q	Fred Hovey	Valentine Hall	6-2	5-7	8-6	6-2	
1894							
Ch	**Robert Wrenn**	**Manliffe Goodbody**	**6-8**	**6-1**	**6-4**	**6-4**	
F	Manliffe Goodbody	Bill Larned	4-6	6-1	3-6	7-5	6-2
S	Manliffe Goodbody	J.B. Read	3-6	6-0	6-0	6-1	
S	Bill Larned	Malcolm Chace	6-4	6-2	8-6		
Q	J.B. Read	Samuel G. Thomson	6-3	6-1	6-2		
Q	Manliffe Goodbody	Clarence Hobart	6-2	6-2	2-6	3-6	8-6
Q	Bill Larned	Richard Stevens	6-2	4-6	6-3	8-6	
Q	Malcolm Chace	Charles E. Sands	7-5	6-2	7-5		
1895							
Ch	**Fred Hovey**	**Robert Wrenn**	**6-3**	**6-2**	**6-4**		
F	Fred Hovey	Bill Larned	6-1	9-7	6-4		
S	Fred Hovey	Carr Neel	6-4	6-4	6-4		
S	Bill Larned	John Howland	7-5	8-6	6-1		
Q	Fred Hovey	Charles Hinckley	6-1	6-2	7-5		
Q	Carr Neel	Malcolm Chace	6-4	6-1	6-4		
Q	John Howland	Clarence Budlong	6-3	2-6	6-4	6-3	
Q	Bill Larned	Arthur Foote	6-3	6-4	3-6	6-1	
1896							
Ch	**Robert Wrenn**	**Fred Hovey**	**7-5**	**3-6**	**6-0**	**1-6**	**6-1**
F	Robert Wrenn	Bill Larned	4-6	3-6	6-4	6-4	6-3
S	Robert Wrenn	Carr Neel	2-6	14-12	4-6	6-4	6-1
S	Bill Larned	Edwin Fischer	6-1	6-2	6-1		
Q	Carr Neel	Richard Stevens	6-4	6-0	7-9	9-7	
Q	Robert Wrenn	George Wrenn	2-6	9-7	7-5	9-7	
Q	Bill Larned	Malcolm Whitman	6-4	6-1	6-2		
Q	Edwin Fischer	George Sheldon	6-4	7-5	2-6	8-6	
1897							
Ch	**Robert Wrenn**	**Wilberforce Eaves**	**4-6**	**8-6**	**6-3**	**2-6**	**6-2**
F	Wilberforce Eaves	Harold Nisbet	7-5	6-3	6-2		
S	Harold Nisbet	Bill Larned	3-6	2-6	9-7	6-4	6-4
S	Wilberforce Eaves	Leo Ware	6-0	6-2	6-4		
Q	Harold Nisbet	Malcolm Whitman	8-6	4-6	6-4	3-6	7-5
Q	Bill Larned	Edwin Fischer	6-4	6-1	6-3		
Q	Wilberforce Eaves	Parmly Paret	6-4	6-1	3-6	6-3	
Q	Leo Ware	Holcombe Ward	6-3	6-4	6-4		
1898							
Ch	**Malcolm Whitman**	**Robert Wrenn**			(default)		
F	Malcolm Whitman	Dwight Davis	3-6	6-2	6-2	6-1	
S	Dwight Davis	William Bond	6-1	11-13	6-4	6-3	
S	Malcolm Whitman	Leo Ware	6-2	6-0	6-2		
Q	William Bond	Holcombe Ward	6-3	6-3	6-4		
Q	Dwight Davis	Richard Stevens	8-6	6-4	7-5		
Q	Leo Ware	George W. Lee	6-2	6-3	6-4		
Q	Malcolm Whitman	Clarence Budlong	11-9	4-6	4-6	6-2	8-6
1899							
Ch	**Malcolm Whitman**	**Parmly Paret**	**6-1**	**6-2**	**3-6**	**7-5**	
F	Parmly Paret	Dwight Davis	7-5	8-10	6-3	2-6	6-4
S	Parmly Paret	Leo Ware	7-5	6-2	6-4		
S	Dwight Davis	Kreigh Collins	6-4	6-1	8-6		
Q	Leo Ware	Holcombe Ward	3-6	6-4	9-11	6-2	6-4
Q	Parmly Paret	Bob Huntington	3-6	6-3	4-6	6-4	6-0
Q	Dwight Davis	William Bond	6-4	6-4	1-6	6-4	
Q	Kreigh Collins	George Wrenn	8-6	4-6	4-6	6-4	6-3

Rd	Winner	Defeated	S1	S2	S3	S4	S5
1900							
Ch	**Malcolm Whitman**	**Bill Larned**	**6-4**	**1-6**	**6-2**	**6-2**	
F	Bill Larned	George Wrenn	6-3	6-2	6-2		
S	Bill Larned	Beals Wright	11-9	8-6	1-6	6-3	
S	George Wrenn	Arthur Gore	9-7	1-6	0-6	6-2	6-2
Q	Beals Wright	Dwight Davis	4-6	4-6	8-6	6-3	6-2
Q	Bill Larned	Malcolm Chace	6-1	6-1	4-6	6-0	
Q	Arthur Gore	Ernest D. Black	6-0	7-5	6-0		
Q	George Wrenn	Robert Wrenn	6-4	6-1	6-4		
1901							
Ch	**Bill Larned**	**Malcolm Whitman**			(default)		
F	Bill Larned	Beals Wright	6-2	6-8	6-4	6-4	
S	Bill Larned	Leo Ware	6-3	6-2	6-2		
S	Beals Wright	Ray Little	7-5	2-6	6-1	6-2	
Q	Leo Ware	Edgar Leonard	6-2	6-2	6-1		
Q	Bill Larned	Edward Larned			(default)		
Q	Ray Little	Bill Clothier	6-3	10-8	1-6	6-1	
Q	Beals Wright	Clarence Hobart	6-3	8-6	6-4		
1902							
Ch	**Bill Larned**	**Reggie Doherty**	**4-6**	**6-2**	**6-4**	**8-6**	
F	Reggie Doherty	Malcolm Whitman	6-1	3-6	6-3	6-0	
S	Malcolm Whitman	Bob Huntington	10-8	4-6	6-1	6-2	
S	Reggie Doherty	Laurie Doherty			(default)		
Q	Bob Huntington	Ray Little	8-6	6-2	6-2		
Q	Malcolm Whitman	Kreigh Collins	6-0	6-1	6-4		
Q	Laurie Doherty	Leo Ware	6-3	6-2	6-2		
Q	Reggie Doherty	L.H. Waldner			(default)		
1903							
Ch	**Laurie Doherty**	**Bill Larned**	**6-0**	**6-3**	**10-8**		
F	Laurie Doherty	Bill Clothier	6-3	6-2	6-3		
S	Laurie Doherty	Richard Carleton	6-2	6-0	6-0		
S	Bill Clothier	Edward Larned	6-3	6-1	6-2		
Q	Richard Carleton	R.C. Seaver	6-3	6-2	6-1		
Q	Laurie Doherty	Reggie Doherty			(default)		
Q	Edward Larned	Bob Huntington	6-0	4-6	6-0	6-3	
Q	Bill Clothier	Harry Allen	6-3	6-1	6-2		
1904							
Ch	**Holcombe Ward**	**Laurie Doherty**			(default)		
F	Holcombe Ward	Bill Clothier	10-8	6-4	9-7		
S	Bill Clothier	Bill Larned	6-4	3-6	2-6	6-2	6-3
S	Holcombe Ward	Edgar Leonard	6-3	6-4	6-4		
Q	Bill Larned	Beals Wright	6-1	6-0	6-3		
Q	Bill Clothier	Alphonzo Bell	6-3	7-5	6-3		
Q	Holcombe Ward	Fred Alexander	6-4	9-7	7-5		
Q	Edgar Leonard	Nathaniel Niles	6-0	6-1	6-1		
1905							
Ch	**Beals Wright**	**Holcombe Ward**	**6-2**	**6-1**	**11-9**		
F	Beals Wright	Clarence Hobart	6-4	6-1	6-3		
S	Clarence Hobart	Kreigh Collins	4-6	6-4	7-9	6-4	6-4
S	Beals Wright	Bill Larned	4-6	6-3	6-2	6-2	
Q	Kreigh Collins	Jed Jones	7-5	5-7	6-3	6-1	
Q	Clarence Hobart	Richard Stevens	2-6	6-4	6-2	6-4	
Q	Beals Wright	Bill Clothier	9-7	6-2	6-2		
Q	Bill Larned	Karl Behr	6-2	6-1	6-1		
1906							
Ch	**Bill Clothier**	**Beals Wright**	**6-3**	**6-0**	**6-4**		
F	Bill Clothier	Karl Behr	6-2	6-4	6-2		
S	Bill Clothier	Jed Jones	6-3	6-3	6-3		
S	Karl Behr	Ray Little	2-6	6-2	6-8	11-9	6-4
Q	Jed Jones	Edgar Leonard	6-2	6-3	6-1		
Q	Bill Clothier	Fred Alexander	8-6	6-2	4-6	1-6	7-5
Q	Karl Behr	Bob LeRoy	1-6	6-4	6-3	6-3	
Q	Ray Little	Harold Hackett	6-2	2-1			(default)

Rd	Winner	Defeated	S1	S2	S3	S4	S5
1907							
Ch	**Bill Larned**	**Bill Clothier**			(default)		
F	Bill Larned	Bob LeRoy	6-2	6-2	6-4		
S	Bill Larned	Clarence Hobart	6-2	6-1			
S	Bob LeRoy	Henry J. Mollenhauer	4-6	6-4	1-6	8-6	6-0
Q	Bill Larned	H. LaVerne Westfall	6-4	6-1	6-0		
Q	Clarence Hobart	Wallace Johnson	6-4	6-3	5-7	5-7	6-2
Q	Henry J. Mollenhauer	Leroy Russ	6-4	11-9	5-7	6-4	
Q	Bob LeRoy	Richard Palmer	6-0	6-2	6-2		
1908							
Ch	**Bill Larned**	**Beals Wright**	**6-1**	**6-2**	**8-6**		
F	Beals Wright	Fred Alexander	6-3	6-3	6-3		
S	Fred Alexander	Bill Clothier	7-5	7-5	6-3		
S	Beals Wright	Nat Emerson	6-2	6-4	5-7	6-3	
Q	Fred Alexander	Frank Sulloway	6-1	6-3	6-1		
Q	Bill Clothier	Gus Touchard	6-1	8-6	6-0		
Q	Nat Emerson	Jed Jones	6-8	10-8	6-1	2-6	9-7
Q	Beals Wright	"Henry Torrance, Jr."	6-3	6-1	6-3		
1909							
Ch	**Bill Larned**	**Bill Clothier**	**6-1**	**6-2**	**5-7**	**1-6**	**6-1**
F	Bill Clothier	Maurice McLoughlin	7-5	6-4	9-11	6-3	
S	Bill Clothier	Tom Bundy	6-3	6-3	6-8	7-5	
S	Maurice McLoughlin	Gus Touchard	6-3	4-6	7-5	6-2	
Q	Bill Clothier	Edward H. Whitney	6-1	7-5	6-4		
Q	Tom Bundy	William B. Cragin Jr.	6-1	7-5	6-2		
Q	Maurice McLoughlin	Richard Palmer	7-5	6-4	6-2		
Q	Gus Touchard	Fred C. Inman	6-4	4-6	4-6	8-6	6-2
1910							
Ch	**Bill Larned**	**Tom Bundy**	**6-1**	**5-7**	**6-0**	**6-8**	**6-1**
F	Tom Bundy	Beals Wright	6-8	6-3	6-2	10-8	
S	Beals Wright	Edward H. Whitney	4-6	7-5	4-6	6-2	7-5
S	Tom Bundy	Fred Colston	6-8	6-1	6-3	6-3	
Q	Edward H. Whitney	Charles S. Cutting	6-2	6-3	7-5		
Q	Beals Wright	Maurice McLoughlin	6-3	6-3	6-2		
Q	Fred Colston	Dean Mathey	6-4	8-6	6-4		
Q	Tom Bundy	William B. Cragin Jr.	4-6	6-4	6-3	6-2	
1911							
Ch	**Bill Larned**	**Maurice McLoughlin**	**6-4**	**6-4**	**6-2**		
F	Maurice McLoughlin	Beals Wright	6-4	4-6	7-5	6-3	
S	Maurice McLoughlin	Gus Touchard	6-2	6-4	6-3		
S	Beals Wright	Tom Bundy	6-4	6-3	6-1		
Q	Gus Touchard	Carlton Gardner	6-3	6-4	7-5		
Q	Maurice McLoughlin	Watson Washburn	6-1	6-2	6-4		
Q	Beals Wright	Nathaniel Niles	6-8	1-6	6-3	10-8	7-5
Q	Tom Bundy	Jed Jones	6-3	8-6	6-3		
1912							
F	**Maurice McLoughlin**	**Wallace Johnson**	**3-6**	**2-6**	**6-2**	**6-4**	**6-2**
S	Maurice McLoughlin	Bill Clothier	8-6	6-2	3-6	6-4	
S	Wallace Johnson	Karl Behr	4-6	6-0	6-3	6-2	
Q	Maurice McLoughlin	Dick Williams	6-4	5-7	6-4	3-6	6-3
Q	Bill Clothier	Ray Little	7-5	6-0	6-1		
Q	Karl Behr	George Church	6-2	6-2	6-0		
Q	Wallace Johnson	Watson Washburn	8-6	6-2	3-6	6-3	
1913							
F	**Maurice McLoughlin**	**Dick Williams**	**6-4**	**5-7**	**6-3**	**6-1**	
S	Dick Williams	Nathaniel Niles	6-4	7-5	3-6	6-1	
S	Maurice McLoughlin	Wallace Johnson	6-0	7-5	6-1		
Q	Nathaniel Niles	Leonard Beekman	6-0	9-7	6-2		
Q	Dick Williams	Watson Washburn	6-1	7-5	6-3		
Q	Wallace Johnson	John Strachan	2-6	6-2	6-2	6-4	
Q	Maurice McLoughlin	Bill Clothier	6-3	7-5	6-4		

Rd	Winner	Defeated	S1	S2	S3	S4	S5
1914							
F	**Dick Williams**	**Maurice McLoughlin**	**6-3**	**8-6**	**10-8**		
S	Dick Williams	Elia Fottrell	6-4	6-3	6-2		
S	Maurice McLoughlin	Bill Clothier	6-4	6-4	6-3		
Q	Elia Fottrell	Gus Touchard	6-1	6-1	6-2		
Q	Dick Williams	Karl Behr	6-1	6-2	7-5		
Q	Bill Clothier	Watson Washburn	6-2	9-7	6-1		
Q	Maurice McLoughlin	Clarence Griffin	6-1	6-4	3-6	8-6	
1915							
F	**Bill Johnston**	**Maurice McLoughlin**	**1-6**	**6-0**	**7-5**	**10-8**	
S	Bill Johnston	Dick Williams	5-7	6-4	5-7	6-2	6-2
S	Maurice McLoughlin	Theodore Pell	6-2	6-0	7-5		
Q	Bill Johnston	Clarence Griffin	6-2	6-1	6-8	5-7	6-1
Q	Dick Williams	William Rand III	8-6	7-5	6-1		
Q	Maurice McLoughlin	Frank Hunter	6-2	6-4	6-0		
Q	Theodore Pell	Irving Wright	6-3	6-1	6-1		
1916							
F	**Dick Williams**	**Bill Johnston**	**4-6**	**6-4**	**0-6**	**6-2**	**6-4**
S	Dick Williams	Clarence Griffin	6-3	6-3	6-3		
S	Bill Johnston	Lindley Murray	6-2	6-3	6-1		
Q	Clarence Griffin	Wallace Johnson	6-4	6-2	6-2		
Q	Dick Williams	Douglas Watters	3-6	6-1	6-1	6-2	
Q	Bill Johnston	Watson Washburn	6-2	6-2	7-5		
Q	Lindley Murray	George Church	3-6	4-6	6-2	6-4	6-4
1917							
F	**Lindley Murray**	**Nathaniel Niles**	**5-7**	**8-6**	**6-3**	**6-3**	
S	Lindley Murray	John Strachan	4-6	6-3	6-3	6-1	
S	Nathaniel Niles	Dick Williams	6-2	4-6	6-4	6-3	
Q	Lindley Murray	Craig Biddle	4-6	6-1	6-4	4-6	6-2
Q	John Strachan	Chuck Garland	6-1	2-6	6-2	6-3	
Q	Nathaniel Niles	Clarence Griffin	6-1	6-3	6-0		
Q	Dick Williams	Harold Throckmorton	4-6	6-3	7-5		
1918							
F	**Lindley Murray**	**Bill Tilden**	**6-3**	**6-1**	**7-5**		
S	Lindley Murray	S. Howard Voshell	6-4	6-3	8-6		
S	Bill Tilden	Ichiya Kumagae	6-2	6-2	6-0		
Q	S. Howard Voshell	Craig Biddle	6-2	6-3	9-7		
Q	Lindley Murray	Nathaniel Niles	7-5	6-4	2-6	7-5	
Q	Ichiya Kumagae	Lyle Mahan	4-6	6-3	6-0	6-1	
Q	Bill Tilden	Walter Merrill Hall	3-6	6-1	5-7	7-5	6-1
1919							
F	**Bill Johnston**	**Bill Tilden**	**6-4**	**6-4**	**6-3**		
S	Bill Johnston	Wallace Johnson	2-6	6-1	6-3	6-3	
S	Bill Tilden	Dick Williams	6-1	7-5	6-3		
Q	Bill Johnston	Lindley Murray	5-7	6-1	6-2	6-4	
Q	Wallace Johnson	Walter Merrill Hall	6-4	6-0	6-2		
Q	Bill Tilden	Norman Brookes	1-6	6-4	7-5	6-3	
Q	Dick Williams	Maurice McLoughlin	6-0	6-3	6-2		
1920							
F	**Bill Tilden**	**Bill Johnston**	**6-1**	**1-6**	**7-5**	**5-7**	**6-3**
S	Bill Johnston	G.Colket Caner	6-3	4-6	8-6	6-4	
S	Bill Tilden	Wallace Johnson	14-12	6-4	6-4		
Q	G.Colket Caner	Irving Wright	6-3	6-4	6-2		
Q	Bill Johnston	Watson Washburn	6-4	6-4	7-5		
Q	Wallace Johnson	Clarence Griffin	6-1	6-3	2-6	6-4	
Q	Bill Tilden	Walter Wesbrook	6-3	8-6	6-1		
1921							
F	**Bill Tilden**	**Wallace Johnson**	**6-1**	**6-3**	**6-1**		
S	Wallace Johnson	James Anderson	6-4	3-6	8-6	6-3	
S	Bill Tilden	Willis Davis	10-8	6-2	6-1		
Q	Wallace Johnson	Craig Biddle	6-0	6-3	6-4		
Q	James Anderson	Frank Hunter	6-1	6-3	6-4		
Q	Bill Tilden	Gordon Lowe	6-4	6-3	6-4		
Q	Willis Davis	Robert Kinsey	6-3	4-6	6-4	1-6	6-4

1922

Rd	Winner	Defeated	S1	S2	S3	S4	S5
F	Bill Tilden	Bill Johnston	4-6	3-6	6-2	6-3	6-4
S	Bill Johnston	Vinnie Richards	8-6	6-2	6-1		
S	Bill Tilden	Gerald Patterson	4-6	6-4	6-3	6-1	
Q	Bill Johnston	Manuel Alonso	6-0	6-2	7-5		
Q	Vinnie Richards	James Anderson	6-4	6-2	7-5		
Q	Bill Tilden	Zenzo Shimidzu	6-2	6-3	6-1		
Q	Gerald Patterson	Dick Williams	6-3	6-3	6-4		

1923

Rd	Winner	Defeated	S1	S2	S3	S4	S5
F	Bill Tilden	Bill Johnston	6-4	6-1	6-4		
S	Bill Tilden	Brian Norton	6-3	7-5	6-2		
S	Bill Johnston	Frank Hunter	6-4	6-2	7-5		
Q	Bill Tilden	Manuel Alonso	6-0	6-2	6-2		
Q	Brian Norton	Dick Williams	1-6	6-3	6-4	3-6	6-4
Q	Bill Johnston	Frank T. Anderson	8-6	6-1	7-5		
Q	Frank Hunter	Robert Kinsey	6-2	6-4	8-6		

1924

Rd	Winner	Defeated	S1	S2	S3	S4	S5
F	Bill Tilden	Bill Johnston	6-1	9-7	6-2		
S	Bill Tilden	Vinnie Richards	4-6	6-2	8-6	4-6	6-4
S	Bill Johnston	Gerald Patterson	6-2	6-0	6-0		
Q	Bill Tilden	Howard Kinsey	6-3	6-4	3-6	6-2	
Q	Vinnie Richards	Wallace Johnson	6-1	6-4	11-9		
Q	Bill Johnston	René Lacoste	6-3	6-3	6-3		
Q	Gerald Patterson	George Lott	6-1	6-4	6-3		

1925

Rd	Winner	Defeated	S1	S2	S3	S4	S5
F	Bill Tilden	Bill Johnston	4-6	11-9	6-3	4-6	6-3
S	Bill Johnston	Dick Williams	7-5	6-3	6-2		
S	Bill Tilden	Vinnie Richards	6-8	6-4	6-4	6-1	
Q	Bill Johnston	Manuel Alonso	6-3	6-8	6-1	6-2	
Q	Dick Williams	Howard Kinsey	7-5	6-4	6-3		
Q	Bill Tilden	Wallace Johnson	6-4	6-0	6-4		
Q	Vinnie Richards	René Lacoste	6-4	6-4	6-3		

1926

Rd	Winner	Defeated	S1	S2	S3	S4	S5
F	René Lacoste	Jean Borotra	6-4	6-0	6-4		
S	René Lacoste	Henri Cochet	2-6	4-6	6-4	6-4	6-3
S	Jean Borotra	Vinnie Richards	3-6	6-4	4-6	8-6	6-2
Q	Henri Cochet	Bill Tilden	6-8	6-1	6-3	1-6	8-6
Q	René Lacoste	Dick Williams	6-0	6-3	8-6		
Q	Vinnie Richards	Jacques Brugnon	6-2	6-1	6-2		
Q	Jean Borotra	Bill Johnston	3-6	4-6	6-3	6-4	6-4

1927

Rd	Winner	Defeated	S1	S2	S3	S4	S5
F	René Lacoste	Bill Tilden	11-9	6-3	11-9		
S	Bill Tilden	Frank Hunter	14-12	6-1	4-6	9-7	
S	René Lacoste	Bill Johnston	6-2	2-6	6-4	6-4	
Q	Bill Tilden	Jean Borotra	6-1	3-6	10-8	6-1	
Q	Frank Hunter	John Hennessey	4-6	5-7	6-0	6-3	6-4
Q	Bill Johnston	Jacques Brugnon	3-6	6-2	6-4	6-4	
Q	René Lacoste	Manuel Alonso	6-8	6-4	6-1	6-2	

1928

Rd	Winner	Defeated	S1	S2	S3	S4	S5
F	Henri Cochet	Frank Hunter	4-6	6-4	3-6	7-5	6-3
S	Frank Hunter	George Lott	6-8	6-4	6-3	6-4	
S	Henri Cochet	Francis Shields	6-2	8-6	6-4		
Q	George Lott	Johnny Doeg	6-2	6-2	7-5		
Q	Frank Hunter	Jack Crawford	7-5	3-6	6-3	6-4	
Q	Francis Shields	Jacques Brugnon	7-5	6-1	6-0		
Q	Henri Cochet	Gregory Mangin	4-6	6-3	6-1	6-2	

1929

Rd	Winner	Defeated	S1	S2	S3	S4	S5
F	Bill Tilden	Frank Hunter	3-6	6-3	4-6	6-2	6-4
S	Bill Tilden	Johnny Doeg	4-6	6-2	2-6	6-4	6-3
S	Frank Hunter	Fritz Mercur	6-4	6-8	6-4	6-3	
Q	Bill Tilden	John Van Ryn	7-5	2-6	9-7	6-2	
Q	Johnny Doeg	Bunny Austin	6-4	6-4	6-3		
Q	Fritz Mercur	Wilmer Allison	8-6	10-8	6-4		
Q	Frank Hunter	R.Norris Williams II	6-0	6-3	6-4		

1930

Rd	Winner	Defeated	S1	S2	S3	S4	S5
F	Johnny Doeg	Francis Shields	10-8	1-6	6-4	16-14	
S	Francis Shields	Sidney Wood	6-2	6-3	4-6	6-3	
S	Johnny Doeg	Bill Tilden	10-8	6-3	3-6	12-10	
Q	Francis Shields	Gregory Mangin	3-6	6-8	6-2	6-1	6-1
Q	Sidney Wood	Clifford Sutter	6-4	6-3	2-6	7-5	
Q	Bill Tilden	John Van Ryn	4-6	6-2	6-4	6-4	
Q	Johnny Doeg	Frank Hunter	11-13	6-4	3-6	6-2	6-4

1931

Rd	Winner	Defeated	S1	S2	S3	S4	S5
F	Ellsworth Vines	George Lott	7-9	6-3	9-7	7-5	
S	Ellsworth Vines	Fred Perry	4-6	3-6	6-4	6-4	6-3
S	George Lott	Johnny Doeg	7-5	6-3	6-0		
Q	Ellsworth Vines	Berkeley Bell	6-1	6-4	8-6		
Q	Fred Perry	Frank Bowden	6-2	6-3	6-4		
Q	Johnny Doeg	Francis Shields	6-2	11-9	4-6	8-6	
Q	George Lott	John Van Ryn	5-7	1-6	6-0	7-5	6-1

1932

Rd	Winner	Defeated	S1	S2	S3	S4	S5
F	Ellsworth Vines	Henri Cochet	6-4	6-4	6-4		
S	Ellsworth Vines	Clifford Sutter	4-6	8-10	12-10	10-8	6-1
S	Henri Cochet	Wilmer Allison	6-1	10-12	4-6	6-3	7-5
Q	Ellsworth Vines	Lester Stoefen	6-3	7-5	6-4		
Q	Clifford Sutter	George Lott	10-8	6-0	6-0		
Q	Wilmer Allison	Sidney Wood	5-7	6-3	6-2	6-4	
Q	Henri Cochet	Francis Shields	4-6	6-3	6-4	6-0	

1933

Rd	Winner	Defeated	S1	S2	S3	S4	S5
F	Fred Perry	Jack Crawford	6-3	11-13	4-6	6-0	6-1
S	Fred Perry	Lester Stoefen	6-3	6-2	6-2		
S	Jack Crawford	Francis Shields	7-5	6-4	6-3		
Q	Lester Stoefen	Bryan Grant Jr.	8-6	6-4	3-6	7-5	
Q	Fred Perry	Adrian Quist	6-4	6-4	6-0		
Q	Francis Shields	Gregory Mangin	6-4	4-6	6-3		
Q	Jack Crawford	Clifford Sutter	6-3	6-4	6-4		

1934

Rd	Winner	Defeated	S1	S2	S3	S4	S5
F	Fred Perry	Wilmer Allison	6-4	6-3	3-6	1-6	8-6
S	Fred Perry	Vernon Kirby	6-2	2-6	6-4	6-2	
S	Wilmer Allison	Sidney Wood	8-6	6-2	6-3		
Q	Vernon Kirby	Francis Shields	4-6	6-4	6-4	6-3	
Q	Fred Perry	Clifford Sutter	6-3	6-0	6-2		
Q	Wilmer Allison	Lester Stoefen	8-6	4-6	11-9	6-8	6-3
Q	Sidney Wood	Frank Parker	6-4	6-4	7-5		

1935

Rd	Winner	Defeated	S1	S2	S3	S4	S5
F	Wilmer Allison	Sidney Wood	6-2	6-2	6-3		
S	Sidney Wood	Bryan Grant Jr.	6-2	4-6	12-10	6-2	
S	Wilmer Allison	Fred Perry	7-5	6-3	6-3		
Q	Bryan Grant Jr.	Don Budge	6-4	6-4	5-7	6-3	
Q	Sidney Wood	Gregory Mangin	3-6	6-1	6-1	6-2	
Q	Wilmer Allison	Enrique Maier	6-2	6-4	6-4		
Q	Fred Perry	Francis Shields	6-4	4-6	8-6	6-0	

1936

Rd	Winner	Defeated	S1	S2	S3	S4	S5
F	Fred Perry	Don Budge	2-6	6-2	8-6	1-6	10-8
S	Fred Perry	Bryan Grant Jr.	6-4	3-6	7-5	6-2	
S	Don Budge	Frank Parker	6-4	6-3	6-3		
Q	Bryan Grant Jr.	John Van Ryn	3-6	8-6	6-0	6-3	
Q	Fred Perry	Henry Culley	6-3	6-2	6-1		
Q	Don Budge	John McDiarmid	6-4	6-3	6-2		
Q	Frank Parker	Gregory Mangin	10-12	6-0	4-6	6-1	6-3

1937

Rd	Winner	Defeated	S1	S2	S3	S4	S5
F	Don Budge	G. von Cramm	6-1	7-9	6-1	3-6	6-1
S	Don Budge	Frank Parker	6-2	6-1	6-3		
S	Gottfried von Cramm	Bobby Riggs	0-6	8-6	6-8	6-3	6-2
Q	Don Budge	Joseph R. Hunt	6-1	6-2	6-4		
Q	Frank Parker	John Van Ryn	6-2	12-10	6-2		
Q	Bobby Riggs	Charles Hare	4-6	1-6	6-3	6-0	7-5
Q	Gottfried von Cramm	Bryan Grant Jr.	9-7	2-6	2-6	6-3	6-3

1938

Rd	Winner	Defeated	S1	S2	S3	S4	S5
F	Don Budge	Gene Mako	6-3	6-8	6-2	6-1	
S	Don Budge	Sidney Wood	6-3	6-3	6-3		
S	Gene Mako	John Bromwich	6-3	7-5	6-4		
Q	Don Budge	Harry Hopman	6-3	6-1	6-3		
Q	Sidney Wood	Bryan Grant Jr.	6-2	6-3	6-2		
Q	Gene Mako	Gilbert A. Hunt Jr.	7-5	1-6	8-6	6-0	
Q	John Bromwich	Joseph R. Hunt	6-1	9-11	6-3	6-4	

1939

Rd	Winner	Defeated	S1	S2	S3	S4	S5
F	Bobby Riggs	Welby Van Horn	6-4	6-2	6-4		
S	Bobby Riggs	Joseph R. Hunt	6-1	6-2	4-6	6-1	
S	Welby Van Horn	John Bromwich	2-6	4-6	6-2	6-4	8-6
Q	Bobby Riggs	Harry Hopman	6-1	10-8	6-3		
Q	Joseph R. Hunt	Don McNeill	15-13	8-10	4-6	6-2	
Q	John Bromwich	Gilbert A. Hunt Jr.	6-3	6-4	6-1		
Q	Welby Van Horn	Wayne Sabin	4-6	2-6	6-4	7-5	6-3

1940

Rd	Winner	Defeated	S1	S2	S3	S4	S5
F	Don McNeill	Bobby Riggs	4-6	6-8	6-3	6-3	7-5
S	Don McNeill	Jack Kramer	6-1	5-7	6-4	6-3	
S	Bobby Riggs	Joseph R. Hunt	4-6	6-3	5-7	6-3	6-4
Q	Don McNeill	Elwood Cooke	9-7	6-8	6-4	6-3	
Q	Jack Kramer	Frank Parker	1-6	6-1	3-6	6-3	6-1
Q	Bobby Riggs	Ted Schroeder	6-1	5-7	6-3	6-4	
Q	Joseph R. Hunt	Frank Kovacs	6-4	6-1	6-4		

1941

Rd	Winner	Defeated	S1	S2	S3	S4	S5
F	Bobby Riggs	Frank Kovacs	5-7	6-1	6-3	6-3	
S	Frank Kovacs	Don McNeill	6-4	6-2	10-8		
S	Bobby Riggs	Ted Schroeder	6-4	6-4	1-6	9-11	7-5
Q	Frank Kovacs	Jack Kramer	6-4	7-5	7-5		
Q	Don McNeill	Wayne Sabin	6-3	7-5	3-6	6-3	
Q	Bobby Riggs	Frank Parker	6-4	6-3	4-6	6-2	
Q	Ted Schroeder	Bryan Grant Jr.	6-8	6-1	6-2	6-3	

1942

Rd	Winner	Defeated	S1	S2	S3	S4	S5
F	Ted Schroeder	Frank Parker	8-6	7-5	3-6	4-6	6-2
S	Frank Parker	Pancho Segura	6-1	6-1	2-6	6-2	
S	Ted Schroeder	Gardnar Mulloy	9-7	6-3	6-4		
Q	Frank Parker	Seymour Greenburg	6-0	6-0	6-4		
Q	Pancho Segura	Bill Talbert	6-4	3-6	6-2	6-4	
Q	Ted Schroeder	Alejo Russell	6-3	6-8	6-3	7-5	
Q	Gardnar Mulloy	George Richards	6-2	8-6	7-5		

1943

Rd	Winner	Defeated	S1	S2	S3	S4	S5
F	Joseph R. Hunt	Jack Kramer	6-3	6-8	10-8	6-0	
S	Jack Kramer	Pancho Segura	2-6	6-4	7-5	6-3	
S	Joseph R. Hunt	Bill Talbert	3-6	6-4	6-2	6-4	
Q	Pancho Segura	Seymour Greenburg	6-2	6-4	6-1		
Q	Jack Kramer	Jack Tuero	6-1	6-2	6-4		
Q	Joseph R. Hunt	Frank Parker	8-6	6-2	6-3		
Q	Bill Talbert	Elwood Cooke	6-1	4-6	8-6	6-4	

1944

Rd	Winner	Defeated	S1	S2	S3	S4	S5
F	Frank Parker	Bill Talbert	6-4	3-6	6-3	6-3	
S	Bill Talbert	Pancho Segura	3-6	6-3	6-0	6-8	6-3
S	Frank Parker	Don McNeill	6-4	3-6	6-2	6-2	
Q	Pancho Segura	Alexander H. Carver	6-0	6-3	6-4		
Q	Bill Talbert	Bob Falkenburg	6-4	6-4	6-3		
Q	Don McNeill	Seymour Greenburg	6-3	4-6	3-6	6-1	8-6
Q	Frank Parker	Charles Oliver	6-2	6-4	6-1		

1945

Rd	Winner	Defeated	S1	S2	S3	S4	S5
F	Frank Parker	Bill Talbert	14-12	6-1	6-2		
S	Frank Parker	Elwood Cooke	6-4	8-6	7-5		
S	Bill Talbert	Pancho Segura	7-5	6-3	6-4		
Q	Frank Parker	Seymour Greenburg	6-2	6-3	6-2		
Q	Elwood Cooke	Sidney Wood	10-12	7-5	6-4	2-6	6-0
Q	Bill Talbert	Alejo Russell	6-1	6-2	9-7		
Q	Pancho Segura	Bob Falkenburg	6-2	4-6	6-1	6-1	

1946

Rd	Winner	Defeated	S1	S2	S3	S4	S5
F	Jack Kramer	Tom Brown Jr.	9-7	6-3	6-0		
S	Jack Kramer	Bob Falkenburg	6-0	6-4	6-4		
S	Tom Brown Jr.	Gardnar Mulloy	6-4	6-2	6-4		
Q	Jack Kramer	Don McNeill	6-3	6-2	1-6	6-2	
Q	Bob Falkenburg	Bill Talbert	3-6	6-1	2-6	6-2	7-5
Q	Tom Brown Jr.	Frank Parker	6-3	6-4	6-8	3-6	6-1
Q	Gardnar Mulloy	Pancho Segura	4-6	6-4	12-10	6-3	

1947

Rd	Winner	Defeated	S1	S2	S3	S4	S5
F	Jack Kramer	Frank Parker	4-6	2-6	6-1	6-0	6-3
S	Jack Kramer	Jaroslav Drobny	3-6	6-3	6-0	6-1	
S	Frank Parker	John Bromwich	6-3	4-6	6-3	6-8	8-6
Q	Jack Kramer	Bob Falkenburg	6-2	7-5	6-1		
Q	Jaroslav Drobny	Tom Brown Jr.	7-5	6-3	6-4		
Q	Frank Parker	Pancho Segura	6-3	11-9	6-4		
Q	John Bromwich	Gardnar Mulloy	7-5	6-1	6-1		

1948

Rd	Winner	Defeated	S1	S2	S3	S4	S5
F	Pancho Gonzalez	Eric Sturgess	6-2	6-3	14-12		
S	Pancho Gonzalez	Jaroslav Drobny	8-10	11-9	6-0	6-3	
S	Eric Sturgess	Herbie Flam	9-7	6-3	6-2		
Q	Pancho Gonzalez	Frank Parker	8-6	2-6	7-5	6-3	
Q	Jaroslav Drobny	Bob Falkenburg	8-6	6-1	6-3		
Q	Eric Sturgess	Earl Cochell	6-2	8-6	3-6	5-7	6-3
Q	Herbie Flam	Harry Likas Jr.	2-6	6-4	6-1	6-0	

1949

Rd	Winner	Defeated	S1	S2	S3	S4	S5
F	Pancho Gonzalez	Ted Schroeder	16-18	2-6	6-1	6-2	6-4
S	Pancho Gonzalez	Frank Parker	3-6	9-7	6-3	6-2	
S	Ted Schroeder	Bill Talbert	2-6	6-4	4-6	6-4	6-4
Q	Pancho Gonzalez	Art Larsen	4-6	6-1	6-3	2-6	6-1
Q	Frank Parker	Gardnar Mulloy	6-4	6-2	6-4		
Q	Ted Schroeder	Frank Sedgman	6-3	0-6	6-4	6-8	6-4
Q	Bill Talbert	Jaroslav Drobny	6-4	6-2	6-2		

1950

Rd	Winner	Defeated	S1	S2	S3	S4	S5
F	Art Larsen	Herbie Flam	6-3	4-6	5-7	6-4	6-3
S	Herbie Flam	Gardnar Mulloy	2-6	6-2	9-11	6-3	
S	Art Larsen	Dick Savitt	6-2	10-8	7-9	6-2	
Q	Herbie Flam	Bill Talbert	9-7	6-4	6-3		
Q	Gardnar Mulloy	Earl Cochell	6-3	7-5	6-2		
Q	Dick Savitt	Sidney Schwartz	8-6	6-2	2-6	6-3	
Q	Art Larsen	Tom Brown Jr.	6-3	2-6	6-1	6-4	

1951

Rd	Winner	Defeated	S1	S2	S3	S4	S5
F	Frank Sedgman	Vic Seixas	6-4	6-1	6-1		
S	Vic Seixas	Dick Savitt	6-0	3-6	6-3	6-2	
S	Frank Sedgman	Art Larsen	6-1	6-2	6-0		
Q	Dick Savitt	Budge Patty	6-3	1-6	4-6	6-1	6-4
Q	Vic Seixas	Herbie Flam	1-6	9-7	2-6	6-2	6-3
Q	Art Larsen	Gardnar Mulloy	6-8	6-1	6-2	6-4	
Q	Frank Sedgman	Tony Trabert	3-6	6-2	7-5	3-6	6-3

1952

Rd	Winner	Defeated	S1	S2	S3	S4	S5
F	Frank Sedgman	Gardnar Mulloy	6-1	6-2	6-3		
S	Gardnar Mulloy	Hamilton Richardson	10-8	6-0	8-6		
S	Frank Sedgman	Merv Rose	6-3	6-3	6-4		
Q	Gardnar Mulloy	Ken Rosewall	6-4	3-6	4-6	7-5	7-5
Q	Hamilton Richardson	Straight Clark	6-8	11-9	5-7	8-6	6-4
Q	Merv Rose	Dick Savitt	6-3	8-6	8-6		
Q	Frank Sedgman	Lew Hoad	6-2	6-1	6-3		

1953

Rd	Winner	Defeated	S1	S2	S3	S4	S5
F	Tony Trabert	Vic Seixas	6-3	6-2	6-3		
S	Tony Trabert	Ken Rosewall	7-5	6-3	6-3		
S	Vic Seixas	Lew Hoad	7-5	6-4	6-4		
Q	Tony Trabert	Budge Patty	6-4	6-4	6-2		
Q	Ken Rosewall	Sven Davidson	6-0	8-10	2-6	6-0	11-9
Q	Vic Seixas	Kurt Nielsen	6-3	7-9	8-6	6-4	
Q	Lew Hoad	Gardnar Mulloy	6-4	6-2	11-9		

Rd	Winner	Defeated	S1	S2	S3	S4	S5
1954							
F	**Vic Seixas**	**Rex Hartwig**	**3-6**	**6-2**	**6-4**	**6-4**	
S	Rex Hartwig	Ken Rosewall	6-4	6-3	6-4		
S	Vic Seixas	Hamilton Richardson	6-3	12-14	8-6	6-2	
Q	Rex Hartwig	Tony Trabert	6-2	8-6	2-6	6-2	
Q	Ken Rosewall	Art Larsen	9-7	4-6	4-6	6-3	6-4
Q	Vic Seixas	Tom Brown Jr.	6-4	6-2	6-2		
Q	Hamilton Richardson	Lew Hoad	6-4	7-5	11-13	4-6	6-3
1955							
F	**Tony Trabert**	**Ken Rosewall**	**9-7**	**6-3**	**6-3**		
S	Ken Rosewall	Vic Seixas	6-4	6-4	7-5		
S	Tony Trabert	Lew Hoad	6-4	6-2	6-1		
Q	Vic Seixas	Bernard Bartzen	6-3	6-1	13-11		
Q	Ken Rosewall	Hamilton Richardson	6-4	9-7	2-6	6-3	
Q	Tony Trabert	Herbie Flam	6-2	6-3	6-4		
Q	Lew Hoad	Sammy Giammalva	6-3	6-2	5-7	6-3	
1956							
F	**Ken Rosewall**	**Lew Hoad**	**4-6**	**6-2**	**6-3**	**6-3**	
S	Ken Rosewall	Vic Seixas	10-8	6-0	6-3		
S	Lew Hoad	Neale Fraser	15-13	6-2	6-4		
Q	Ken Rosewall	Dick Savitt	6-4	7-5	4-6	8-10	6-1
Q	Vic Seixas	Ashley Cooper	9-7	3-6	9-7	10-12	6-4
Q	Lew Hoad	Roy Emerson	8-6	6-3	7-5		
Q	Neale Fraser	Hamilton Richardson	3-6	6-3	6-2	6-4	
1957							
F	**Mal Anderson**	**Ashley Cooper**	**10-8**	**7-5**	**6-4**		
S	Ashley Cooper	Herbie Flam	6-1	7-5	6-4		
S	Mal Anderson	Sven Davidson	5-7	6-2	4-6	6-3	6-4
Q	Ashley Cooper	Budge Patty	6-2	6-3	6-1		
Q	Herbie Flam	Vic Seixas	6-4	3-6	6-4	4-6	6-1
Q	Mal Anderson	Luis Ayala	6-1	6-3	6-1		
Q	Sven Davidson	Cliff Mayne	3-6	6-3	7-5	6-4	
1958							
F	**Ashley Cooper**	**Mal Anderson**	**6-2**	**3-6**	**4-6**	**10-8**	**8-6**
S	Ashley Cooper	Neale Fraser	8-6	8-6	6-1		
S	Mal Anderson	Ulf Schmidt	6-4	7-5	6-2		
Q	Ashley Cooper	Vic Seixas	9-7	6-2	3-6	6-2	
Q	Neale Fraser	Alejandro Olmedo	3-6	6-1	8-6	3-6	6-3
Q	Mal Anderson	Dick Savitt	18-16	6-1	3-6	6-3	
Q	Ulf Schmidt	Herbie Flam	7-5	8-6	8-6		
1959							
F	**Neale Fraser**	**Alejandro Olmedo**	**6-3**	**5-7**	**6-2**	**6-4**	
S	Neale Fraser	Bernard Bartzen	6-3	6-2	6-2		
S	Alejandro Olmedo	Ronald Holmberg	15-13	6-4	3-6	6-1	
Q	Neale Fraser	Luis Ayala	6-3	6-4	6-4		
Q	Bernard Bartzen	Barry MacKay	6-3	6-4	6-4		
Q	Alejandro Olmedo	Roy Emerson	6-4	3-6	6-2	6-3	
Q	Ronald Holmberg	Rod Laver	6-8	7-5	6-0	6-3	
1960							
F	**Neale Fraser**	**Rod Laver**	**6-4**	**6-4**	**9-7**		
S	Rod Laver	Earl Buchholtz Jr.	4-6	5-7	6-4	6-2	7-5
S	Neale Fraser	Dennis Ralston	11-9	6-3	6-2		
Q	Rod Laver	Bobby Wilson	9-7	6-1	6-3		
Q	Earl Buchholtz Jr.	Hamilton Richardson	3-6	6-3	6-4	6-4	
Q	Neale Fraser	Chuck McKinley	6-2	6-4	6-2		
Q	Dennis Ralston	Bob Mark	1-6	6-3	6-3	6-2	
1961							
F	**Roy Emerson**	**Rod Laver**	**7-5**	**6-3**	**6-2**		
S	Rod Laver	Mike Sangster	13-11	7-5	6-4		
S	Roy Emerson	Rafael Osuna	6-3	6-2	3-6	5-7	9-7
Q	Rod Laver	Donald Dell	6-4	7-9	6-3	6-4	
Q	Mike Sangster	Jon Douglas	6-4	7-5	6-1		
Q	Rafael Osuna	Whitney Reed	6-8	6-3	6-3	6-2	
Q	Roy Emerson	Ron Holmberg	6-4	6-2	7-5		
1962							
F	**Rod Laver**	**Roy Emerson**	**6-2**	**6-4**	**5-7**	**6-4**	
S	Rod Laver	Rafael Osuna	6-1	6-3	6-4		
S	Roy Emerson	Chuck McKinley	4-6	6-4	6-3	6-2	
Q	Rod Laver	Frank Froehling III	6-3	13-11	4-6	6-3	
Q	Rafael Osuna	Gordon Forbes	6-4	6-4	7-5		
Q	Roy Emerson	Andy Lloyd	6-1	6-1	6-3		
Q	Chuck McKinley	Hamilton Richardson	6-2	6-2	6-8	6-4	
1963							
F	**Rafael Osuna**	**Frank Froehling III**	**7-5**	**6-4**	**6-2**		
S	Rafael Osuna	Chuck McKinley	6-4	6-4	10-8		
S	Frank Froehling III	Ronald Barnes	6-3	6-1	6-4		
Q	Chuck McKinley	Thomaz Koch	6-4	4-6	4-6	8-6	6-4
Q	Rafael Osuna	Marty Riessen	3-6	9-7	6-3	6-3	
Q	Ronald Barnes	Dennis Ralston	6-4	7-5	6-3		
Q	Frank Froehling III	Bobby Wilson	6-8	4-6	6-3	6-3	9-7
1964							
F	**Roy Emerson**	**Fred Stolle**	**6-4**	**6-1**	**6-4**		
S	Roy Emerson	Chuck McKinley	7-5	11-9	6-4		
S	Fred Stolle	Rafael Osuna	6-3	8-6	6-3		
Q	Roy Emerson	Anthony Roche	13-11	8-6	6-2		
Q	Chuck McKinley	Roger Taylor	13-11	9-7	6-1		
Q	Rafael Osuna	Mike Sangster	3-6	9-7	12-10	6-3	
Q	Fred Stolle	Dennis Ralston	6-2	6-3	4-6	3-6	9-7
1965							
F	**Manolo Santana**	**Cliff Drysdale**	**6-2**	**7-9**	**7-5**	**6-1**	
S	Manolo Santana	Arthur Ashe	2-6	6-4	6-2	6-4	
S	Cliff Drysdale	Rafael Osuna	6-3	4-6	6-4	6-1	
Q	Arthur Ashe	Roy Emerson	13-11	6-4	10-12	6-2	
Q	Manolo Santana	Antonio Palafox	6-3	9-7	6-1		
Q	Cliff Drysdale	Dennis Ralston	2-6	3-6	7-5	6-3	8-6
Q	Rafael Osuna	Charlie Pasarell	1-6	6-3	6-3	7-5	
1966							
F	**Fred Stolle**	**John Newcombe**	**4-6**	**12-10**	**6-3**	**6-4**	
S	John Newcombe	Manolo Santana	6-3	6-4	6-8	8-6	
S	Fred Stolle	Roy Emerson	6-4	6-1	6-1		
Q	Manolo Santana	Bill Bowrey	6-8	6-2	8-6	5-7	6-4
Q	John Newcombe	Mark Cox	3-6	6-1	3-6	6-2	6-1
Q	Fred Stolle	Clark Graebner	6-3	6-4	6-2		
Q	Roy Emerson	Owen Davidson	10-12	6-4	6-3	6-2	
1967							
F	**John Newcombe**	**Clark Graebner**	**6-4**	**6-4**	**8-6**		
S	John Newcombe	Eugene Scott	6-4	6-3	6-3		
S	Clark Graebner	Jan Leschly	3-6	3-6	7-5	6-4	7-5
Q	John Newcombe	Bob Hewitt	4-6	6-0	7-5	6-3	
Q	Eugene Scott	Owen Davidson	6-3	8-6	9-7		
Q	Jan Leschly	Ronald Barnes	7-9	6-4	2-6	6-3	8-6
Q	Clark Graebner	Roy Emerson	8-6	3-6	19-17	6-1	
1968							
F	**Arthur Ashe**	**Tom Okker**	**14-12**	**5-7**	**6-3**	**3-6**	**6-3**
S	Arthur Ashe	Clark Graebner	4-6	8-6	7-5	6-2	
S	Tom Okker	Ken Rosewall	8-6	6-4	6-8	6-1	
Q	Arthur Ashe	Cliff Drysdale	8-10	6-3	9-7	6-4	
Q	Clark Graebner	John Newcombe	5-7	11-9	6-1	6-4	
Q	Ken Rosewall	Dennis Ralston	6-2	6-2	6-3		
Q	Tom Okker	Pancho Gonzalez	14-16	6-3	10-8	6-3	
1968 – amateur							
F	**Arthur Ashe**	**Bob Lutz**	**4-6**	**6-3**	**8-10**	**6-0**	**6-4**
S	Arthur Ashe	Jim McManus	6-4	6-2	14-16	6-3	
S	Bob Lutz	Clark Graebner	6-4	7-5	6-4		
Q	Arthur Ashe	Alan Stone	3-6	7-5	9-7	6-3	
Q	Jim McManus	Patricio Cornejo	6-2	6-3	6-2		
Q	Bob Lutz	Bob Hewitt	9-7	1-6	6-3	6-2	
Q	Clark Graebner	Joaquin Loyo-Mayo	6-1	6-4	6-3		

Rd	Winner	Defeated	S1	S2	S3	S4	S5
1969							
F	**Rod Laver**	**Tony Roche**	**7-9**	**6-1**	**6-2**	**6-2**	
S	Rod Laver	Arthur Ashe	8-6	6-3	14-12		
S	Tony Roche	John Newcombe	3-6	6-4	4-6	6-3	8-6
Q	Rod Laver	Roy Emerson	4-6	8-6	13-11	6-4	
Q	Arthur Ashe	Ken Rosewall	8-6	6-3	6-4		
Q	Tony Roche	Butch Buchholz	6-1	9-7	5-7	6-0	
Q	John Newcombe	Fred Stolle	7-9	3-6	6-1	6-4	13-11
1969 – amateur							
F	**Stan Smith**	**Bob Lutz**	**9-7**	**6-3**	**6-1**		
S	Bob Lutz	Arthur Ashe	6-4	4-6	10-8	6-8	6-4
S	Stan Smith	Charlie Pasarell	4-6	2-6	6-2	8-6	15-13
Q	Arthur Ashe	Allan Stone	3-6	6-3	6-8	8-6	6-4
Q	Bob Lutz	R. Barth	6-3	3-6	10-8	6-2	
Q	Charlie Pasarell	Clark Graebner	8-6	3-6	3-6	6-2	6-4
Q	Stan Smith	Ray Ruffels	3-6	6-3	6-2	3-6	12-10
1970							
F	**Ken Rosewall**	**Tony Roche**	**2-6**	**6-4**	**7-6(2)**	**6-3**	
S	Tony Roche	Cliff Richey	6-2	7-6(3)	6-1		
S	Ken Rosewall	John Newcombe	6-3	6-4	6-3		
Q	Cliff Richey	Dennis Ralston	7-6	6-3	6-4		
Q	Tony Roche	Brian Fairlie	6-3	7-5	7-6		
Q	Ken Rosewall	Stan Smith	6-2	6-2	6-2		
Q	John Newcombe	Arthur Ashe	6-1	7-6(4)	5-7	7-6(2)	
1971							
F	**Stan Smith**	**Jan Kodes**	**3-6**	**6-3**	**6-2**	**7-6(3)**	
S	Jan Kodes	Arthur Ashe	7-6(3)	3-6	4-6	6-3	6-4
S	Stan Smith	Tom Okker	7-6(4)	6-3	3-6	2-6	6-3
Q	Jan Kodes	Frank Froehling III	6-0	7-6	6-3		
Q	Arthur Ashe	Jim Osborne	6-1	6-2	7-6		
Q	Tom Okker	Clark Graebner	6-2	6-3	6-4		
Q	Stan Smith	Marty Riessen	7-6(4)	6-2	7-6(1)		
1972							
F	**Ilie Nastase**	**Arthur Ashe**	**3-6**	**6-3**	**6-7(5)**	**6-4**	**6-3**
S	Arthur Ashe	Cliff Richey	6-1	6-4	7-6(4)		
S	Ilie Nastase	Tom Gorman	4-6	7-6(4)	6-2	6-1	
Q	Arthur Ashe	Stan Smith	7-6	6-4	7-5		
Q	Cliff Richey	Frew McMillan	3-6	6-1	6-4	6-2	
Q	Ilie Nastase	Fred Stolle	6-4	3-6	6-3	6-2	
Q	Tom Gorman	Roscoe Tanner	7-6	5-7	7-6	5-7	6-4
1973							
F	**John Newcombe**	**Jan Kodes**	**6-4**	**1-6**	**4-6**	**6-2**	**6-3**
S	Jan Kodes	Stan Smith	7-5	6-7(4)	1-6	6-1	7-5
S	John Newcombe	Ken Rosewall	6-4	7-6(3)	6-3		
Q	Stan Smith	Onny Parun	6-3	6-3	6-2		
Q	Jan Kodes	Nikki Pilic	6-2	4-6	6-1	3-6	7-5
Q	Ken Rosewall	Vijay Amritraj	6-4	6-3	6-3		
Q	John Newcombe	Jimmy Connors	6-4	7-6(4)	7-6(4)		
1974							
F	**Jimmy Connors**	**Ken Rosewall**	**6-1**	**6-0**	**6-1**		
S	Jimmy Connors	Roscoe Tanner	7-6(2)	7-6(2)	6-4		
S	Ken Rosewall	John Newcombe	6-7(3)	6-4	7-6(1)	6-3	
Q	Jimmy Connors	Alex Metreveli	3-6	6-1	6-4	6-1	
Q	Roscoe Tanner	Stan Smith	7-6 (2)	6-2	3-6	6-1	
Q	Ken Rosewall	Vijay Amritraj	2-6	6-3	6-3	6-2	
Q	John Newcombe	Arthur Ashe	4-6	6-3	3-6	7-6(0)	6-4

Rd	Winner	Defeated	S1	S2	S3	S4	S5
1975							
F	**Manolo Orantes**	**Jimmy Connors**	**6-4**	**6-3**	**6-3**		
S	Jimmy Connors	Bjorn Borg	7-5	7-5	7-5		
S	Manolo Orantes	Guillermo Vilas	4-6	1-6	6-2	7-5	6-4
Q	Jimmy Connors	Andrew Pattison	6-2	6-1	6-2		
Q	Bjorn Borg	Eddie Dibbs	6-4	7-6	4-6	7-6	
Q	Manolo Orantes	Ilie Nastase	6-2	6-4	3-6	6-3	
Q	Guillermo Vilas	Jaime Fillol	6-4	6-0	6-1		
1976							
F	**Jimmy Connors**	**Bjorn Borg**	**6-4**	**3-6**	**7-6(9)**	**6-4**	
S	Jimmy Connors	Guillermo Vilas	6-4	6-2	6-1		
S	Bjorn Borg	Ilie Nastase	6-3	6-3	6-4		
Q	Jimmy Connors	Jan Kodes	7-5	6-3	6-1		
Q	Guillermo Vilas	Eddie Dibbs	6-1	2-6	7-6(5)	7-6(2)	
Q	Bjorn Borg	Manolo Orantes	4-6	6-0	6-2	5-7	6-4
Q	Ilie Nastase	Dick Stockton	4-6	6-4	6-2	6-3	
1977							
F	**Guillermo Vilas**	**Jimmy Connors**	**2-6**	**6-3**	**7-6(4)**	**6-0**	
S	Guillermo Vilas	Harold Solomon	6-2	7-6	6-2		
S	Jimmy Connors	Corrado Barazzutti	7-5	6-3	7-5		
Q	Harold Solomon	Dick Stockton	6-4	6-4	6-2		
Q	Guillermo Vilas	Raymond Moore	6-1	6-1	6-0		
Q	Corrado Barazzutti	Brian Gottfried	6-2	6-1	6-2		
Q	Jimmy Connors	Manolo Orantes	6-2	6-4	6-3		
1978							
F	**Jimmy Connors**	**Bjorn Borg**	**6-4**	**6-2**	**6-2**		
S	Bjorn Borg	Vitas Gerulaitis	6-3	6-2	7-6(3)		
S	Jimmy Connors	John McEnroe	6-2	6-2	7-5		
Q	Bjorn Borg	Raul Ramirez	6-7	6-4	6-4	6-0	
Q	Vitas Gerulaitis	Johan Kriek	6-2	6-1	6-2		
Q	John McEnroe	Butch Walts	6-1	6-2	7-6(4)		
Q	Jimmy Connors	Brian Gottfried	6-2	7-6 (0)	6-1		
1979							
F	**John McEnroe**	**Vitas Gerulaitis**	**7-5**	**6-3**	**6-3**		
S	Vitas Gerulaitis	Roscoe Tanner	3-6	2-6	7-6(5)	6-3	6-3
S	John McEnroe	Jimmy Connors	6-3	6-3	7-5		
Q	Roscoe Tanner	Bjorn Borg	6-2	4-6	6-2	7-6(2)	
Q	Vitas Gerulaitis	Johan Kriek	5-7	6-3	6-4	6-3	
Q	John McEnroe	Eddie Dibbs	2-1			(retired)	
Q	Jimmy Connors	Pat Dupre	6-2	6-1	6-1		
1980							
F	**John McEnroe**	**Bjorn Borg**	**7-6(4)**	**6-1**	**6-7(5)**	**5-7**	**6-4**
S	Bjorn Borg	Johan Kriek	4-6	4-6	6-1	6-1	6-1
S	John McEnroe	Jimmy Connors	6-4	5-7	0-6	6-3	7-6(3)
Q	Bjorn Borg	Roscoe Tanner	6-4	3-6	4-6	7-5	6-3
Q	Johan Kriek	Wojtek Fibak	4-6	6-2	3-6	6-1	7-6
Q	Jimmy Connors	Eliot Teltscher	6-1	3-6	6-3	6-0	
Q	John McEnroe	Ivan Lendl	4-6	6-3	6-2	7-5	
1981							
F	**John McEnroe**	**Bjorn Borg**	**4-6**	**6-2**	**6-4**	**6-3**	
S	John McEnroe	Vitas Gerulaitis	5-7	6-3	6-2	4-6	6-3
S	Bjorn Borg	Jimmy Connors	6-2	7-5	6-4		
Q	John McEnroe	Ramesh Krishnan	6-7	7-6	6-4	6-2	
Q	Vitas Gerulaitis	Bruce Man Son Hing	6-4	6-2	4-6	6-1	
Q	Jimmy Connors	Eliot Teltscher	6-3	6-1	6-2		
Q	Bjorn Borg	Roscoe Tanner	7-6(4)	6-3	6-7(4)	7-6(7)	
1982							
F	**Jimmy Connors**	**Ivan Lendl**	**6-3**	**6-2**	**4-6**	**6-4**	
S	Ivan Lendl	John McEnroe	6-4	6-4	7-6(6)		
S	Jimmy Connors	Guillermo Vilas	6-1	3-6	6-2	6-3	
Q	John McEnroe	Gene Mayer	4-6	7-6(4)	6-3	4-6	6-1
Q	Ivan Lendl	Kim Warwick	6-4	6-3	6-1		
Q	Guillermo Vilas	Tom Gullikson	6-2	6-1	6-3		
Q	Jimmy Connors	Rodney Harmon	6-1	6-3	6-4		

Rd	Winner	Defeated	S1	S2	S3	S4	S5
1983							
F	**Jimmy Connors**	**Ivan Lendl**	**6-3**	**6-7(2)**	**7-5**	**6-0**	
S	Jimmy Connors	Bill Scanlon	6-2	6-3	6-2		
S	Ivan Lendl	Jimmy Arias	6-2	7-6(3)	6-1		
Q	Bill Scanlon	Mark Dickson	3-6	4-6	4-6	6-3	7-6(4)
Q	Jimmy Connors	Eliot Teltscher	7-6 (0)	6-2	6-2		
Q	Jimmy Arias	Yannick Noah	7-6(4)	4-6	6-3	1-6	7-5
Q	Ivan Lendl	Mats Wilander	6-4	6-4	7-6(4)		
1984							
F	**John McEnroe**	**Ivan Lendl**	**6-3**	**6-4**	**6-1**		
S	John McEnroe	Jimmy Connors	6-4	4-6	7-5	4-6	6-3
S	Ivan Lendl	Pat Cash	3-6	6-3	6-4	6-7(5)	7-6(4)
Q	John McEnroe	Gene Mayer	7-5	6-3	6-4		
Q	Jimmy Connors	John Lloyd	7-5	6-2	6-0		
Q	Pat Cash	Mats Wilander	7-6	6-4	2-6	6-3	
Q	Ivan Lendl	Andres Gomez	6-4	6-4	6-1		
1985							
F	**Ivan Lendl**	**John McEnroe**	**7-6(1)**	**6-3**	**6-4**		
S	John McEnroe	Mats Wilander	3-6	6-4	4-6	6-3	6-3
S	Ivan Lendl	Jimmy Connors	6-2	6-3	7-5		
Q	John McEnroe	Joakim Nystrom	6-1	6-0	7-5		
Q	Mats Wilander	Anders Jarryd	2-6	6-2	5-0	(retired)	
Q	Jimmy Connors	Heinz Gunthardt	6-2	6-2	6-4		
Q	Ivan Lendl	Yannick Noah	6-2	6-2	6-4		
1986							
F	**Ivan Lendl**	**Miloslav Mecir**	**6-4**	**6-2**	**6-0**		
S	Ivan Lendl	Stefan Edberg	7-6(6)	6-2	6-3		
S	Miloslav Mecir	Boris Becker	4-6	6-3	6-4	3-6	6-3
Q	Ivan Lendl	Henri Leconte	7-6	6-1	1-6	6-1	
Q	Stefan Edberg	Tim Wilkison	6-3	6-3	6-3		
Q	Boris Becker	Milan Srejber	6-3	6-2	6-1		
Q	Miloslav Mecir	Joakim Nystrom	6-4	6-2	3-6	6-2	
1987							
F	**Ivan Lendl**	**Mats Wilander**	**6-7(7)**	**6-0**	**7-6(4)**	**6-4**	
S	Ivan Lendl	Jimmy Connors	6-4	6-2	6-2		
S	Mats Wilander	Stefan Edberg	6-4	3-6	6-3	6-4	
Q	Ivan Lendl	John McEnroe	6-3	6-3	6-4		
Q	Jimmy Connors	Brad Gilbert	4-6	6-3	6-4	6-0	
Q	Mats Wilander	Miloslav Mecir	6-3	6-7	6-4	7-6	
Q	Stefan Edberg	Ramesh Krishnan	6-2	6-2	6-2		
1988							
F	**Mats Wilander**	**Ivan Lendl**	**6-4**	**4-6**	**6-3**	**5-7**	**6-4**
S	Ivan Lendl	Andre Agassi	4-6	6-2	6-3	6-4	
S	Mats Wilander	Darren Cahill	6-4	6-4	6-2		
Q	Ivan Lendl	Derrick Rostagno	6-2	6-2	6-0		
Q	Andre Agassi	Jimmy Connors	6-2	7-6(6)	6-1		
Q	Darren Cahill	Aaron Krickstein	6-2	5-7	7-6(2)	5-7	6-3
Q	Mats Wilander	Emilio Sanchez	3-6	7-6(3)	6-0	6-4	
1989							
F	**Boris Becker**	**Ivan Lendl**	**7-6(2)**	**1-6**	**6-3**	**7-6(4)**	
S	Ivan Lendl	Andre Agassi	7-6(4)	6-1	3-6	6-1	
S	Boris Becker	Aaron Krickstein	6-4	6-3	6-4		
Q	Ivan Lendl	Tim Mayotte	6-4	6-0	6-1		
Q	Andre Agassi	Jimmy Connors	6-1	4-6	0-6	6-3	6-4
Q	Aaron Krickstein	Jay Berger	3-6	6-4	6-2	1-0 (retired)	
Q	Boris Becker	Yannick Noah	6-3	6-3	6-2		
1990							
F	**Pete Sampras**	**Andre Agassi**	**6-4**	**6-3**	**6-2**		
S	Pete Sampras	John McEnroe	6-2	6-4	3-6	6-3	
S	Andre Agassi	Boris Becker	6-7(10)	6-3	6-2	6-3	
Q	John McEnroe	David Wheaton	6-1	6-4	6-4		
Q	Pete Sampras	Ivan Lendl	6-4	7-6(4)	3-6	4-6	6-2
Q	Andre Agassi	Andrei Cherkasov	6-2	6-2	6-3		
Q	Boris Becker	Aaron Krickstein	3-6	6-3	6-2	6-3	
1991							
F	**Stefan Edberg**	**Jim Courier**	**6-2**	**6-4**	**6-0**		
S	Jim Courier	Jimmy Connors	6-3	6-3	6-2		
S	Stefan Edberg	Ivan Lendl	6-3	6-3	6-4		
Q	Jimmy Connors	Paul Haarhuis	4-6	7-6(3)	6-4	6-2	
Q	Jim Courier	Pete Sampras	6-2	7-6(4)	7-6(5)		
Q	Ivan Lendl	Michael Stich	6-3	3-6	4-6	7-6(5)	6-1
Q	Stefan Edberg	Javier Sanchez	6-3	6-2	6-3		
1992							
F	**Stefan Edberg**	**Pete Sampras**	**3-6**	**6-4**	**7-6(5)**	**6-2**	
S	Pete Sampras	Jim Courier	6-1	3-6	6-2	6-2	
S	Stefan Edberg	Michael Chang	6-7(3)	7-5	7-6(3)	5-7	6-4
Q	Jim Courier	Andre Agassi	6-3	6-7(6)	6-1	6-4	
Q	Pete Sampras	Alexander Volkov	6-4	6-1	6-0		
Q	Michael Chang	Wayne Ferreira	7-5	2-6	6-3	6-7(4)	6-1
Q	Stefan Edberg	Ivan Lendl	6-3	6-3	3-6	5-7	7-6(3)
1993							
F	**Pete Sampras**	**Cedric Pioline**	**6-4**	**6-4**	**6-3**		
S	Cedric Pioline	Wally Masur	6-1	6-7(3)	7-6(2)	6-1	
S	Pete Sampras	Alexander Volkov	6-4	6-3	6-2		
Q	Cedric Pioline	Andrei Medvedev	6-3	6-1	3-6	6-2	
Q	Wally Masur	Magnus Larsson	6-2	7-5	7-5		
Q	Alexander Volkov	Thomas Muster	7-6(6)	6-3	3-6	2-6	7-5
Q	Pete Sampras	Michael Chang	6-7 (0)	7-6(2)	6-1	6-1	
1994							
F	**Andre Agassi**	**Michael Stich**	**6-1**	**7-6(5)**	**7-5**		
S	Michael Stich	Karel Novacek	7-5	6-3	7-6(4)		
S	Andre Agassi	Todd Martin	6-3	4-6	6-2	6-3	
Q	Karel Novacek	Jaime Yzaga	6-2	6-7(7)	6-1	5-7	6-3
Q	Michael Stich	Jonas Bjorkman	6-4	6-4	6-7(7)	6-4	
Q	Andre Agassi	Thomas Muster	7-6(5)	6-3	6-0		
Q	Todd Martin	Bernd Karbacher	6-4	7-6(5)	4-6	6-4	
1995							
F	**Pete Sampras**	**Andre Agassi**	**6-4**	**6-3**	**4-6**	**7-5**	
S	Andre Agassi	Boris Becker	7-6(4)	7-6(2)	4-6	6-4	
S	Pete Sampras	Jim Courier	7-5	4-6	6-4	7-5	
Q	Andre Agassi	Petr Korda	6-4	6-2	1-6	7-5	
Q	Boris Becker	Patrick McEnroe	6-4	7-6(2)	6-7(3)	7-6(6)	
Q	Jim Courier	Michael Chang	7-6(5)	7-6(3)	7-5		
Q	Pete Sampras	Byron Black	7-6(3)	6-4	6-0		
1996							
F	**Pete Sampras**	**Michael Chang**	**6-1**	**6-4**	**7-6(3)**		
S	Pete Sampras	Goran Ivanisevic	6-3	6-4	6-7(9)	6-3	
S	Michael Chang	Andre Agassi	6-3	6-2	6-2		
Q	Pete Sampras	Alex Corretja	7-6(5)	5-7	5-7	6-4	7-6(7)
Q	Goran Ivanisevic	Stefan Edberg	6-3	6-4	7-6(9)		
Q	Andre Agassi	Thomas Muster	6-2	7-5	4-6	6-2	
Q	Michael Chang	Javier Sanchez	7-5	6-3	6-7(2)	6-3	
1997							
F	**Patrick Rafter**	**Greg Rusedski**	**6-3**	**6-2**	**4-6**	**7-5**	
S	Greg Rusedski	Jonas Bjorkman	6-1	3-6	3-6	6-3	7-5
S	Patrick Rafter	Michael Chang	6-3	6-3	6-4		
Q	Jonas Bjorkman	Petr Korda	7-6(3)	6-2	1-0	retired	
Q	Greg Rusedski	Richard Krajicek	7-5	7-6(5)	7-6(6)		
Q	Patrick Rafter	Magnus Larsson	7-6(4)	6-4	6-2		
Q	Michael Chang	Marcelo Rios	7-5	6-2	4-6	4-6	6-3
1998							
F	**Patrick Rafter**	**Mark Philippoussis**	**6-3**	**3-6**	**6-2**	**6-0**	
S	Patrick Rafter	Pete Sampras	6-7(8)	6-4	2-6	6-4	6-3
S	Mark Philippoussis	Carlos Moya	6-1	6-4	5-7	6-4	
Q	Pete Sampras	Karol Kucera	6-3	7-5	6-4		
Q	Patrick Rafter	Jonas Bjorkman	6-2	6-3	7-5		
Q	Mark Philippoussis	Thomas Johansson	4-6	6-3	6-7(3)	6-3	7-6(10)
Q	Carlos Moya	Magnus Larsson	6-4	6-3	6-3		

Rd	Winner	Defeated	S1	S2	S3	S4	S5

1999

Rd	Winner	Defeated	S1	S2	S3	S4	S5
F	**Andre Agassi**	**Todd Martin**	6-4	6-7(5)	6-7(2)	6-3	6-2
S	Todd Martin	Cedric Pioline	6-4	6-1	6-2		
S	Andre Agassi	Yevgeny Kafelnikov	1-6	6-3	6-3	6-3	
Q	Todd Martin	Slava Dosedel	6-3	5-7	6-4	6-4	
Q	Cedric Pioline	Gustavo Kuerten	4-6	7-6(6)	7-6(14)	7-6(8)	
Q	Yevgeny Kafelnikov	Richard Krajicek	7-6 (0)	7-6(4)	3-6	1-6	7-6(5)
Q	Andre Agassi	Nicolas Escude	7-6(3)	6-3	6-4		

2000

Rd	Winner	Defeated	S1	S2	S3	S4	S5
F	**Marat Safin**	**Pete Sampras**	6-4	6-3	6-3		
S	Pete Sampras	Lleyton Hewitt	7-6(7)	6-4	7-6(5)		
S	Marat Safin	Todd Martin	6-3	7-6(4)	7-6(1)		
Q	Lleyton Hewitt	Arnaud Clement	6-2	6-4	6-3		
Q	Pete Sampras	Richard Krajicek	4-6	7-6(6)	6-4	6-2	
Q	Marat Safin	Nicolas Kiefer	7-5	4-6	7-6(5)	6-3	
Q	Todd Martin	Thomas Johansson	6-4	6-4	3-6	7-5	

2001

Rd	Winner	Defeated	S1	S2	S3	S4	S5
F	**Lleyton Hewitt**	**Pete Sampras**	7-6(4)	6-1	6-1		
S	Lleyton Hewitt	Yevgeny Kafelnikov	6-1	6-2	6-1		
S	Pete Sampras	Marat Safin	6-3	7-6(5)	6-3		
Q	Yevgeny Kafelnikov	Gustavo Kuerten	6-4	6-0	6-3		
Q	Lleyton Hewitt	Andy Roddick	6-7(5)	6-3	6-4	3-6	6-4
Q	Marat Safin	Mariano Zabaleta	6-4	6-4	6-2		
Q	Pete Sampras	Andre Agassi	6-7(7)	7-6(2)	7-6(2)	7-6(5)	

2002

Rd	Winner	Defeated	S1	S2	S3	S4	S5
F	**Pete Sampras**	**Andre Agassi**	6-3	6-4	5-7	6-4	
S	Andre Agassi	Lleyton Hewitt	6-4	7-6(5)	6-7(1)	6-2	
S	Pete Sampras	Sjeng Schalken	7-6(6)	7-6(4)	6-2		
Q	Lleyton Hewitt	Younes El Aynaoui	6-1	7-6(6)	4-6	6-2	
Q	Andre Agassi	Max Mirnyi	6-7(5)	6-3	7-5	6-3	
Q	Pete Sampras	Andy Roddick	6-3	6-2	6-4		
Q	Sjeng Schalken	Fernando Gonzalez	6-7(5)	6-3	6-3	6-7(5)	7-6(2)

Women's Singles

Rd	Winner	Defeated	S1	S2	S3	S4	S5

1887

Rd	Winner	Defeated	S1	S2	S3	S4	S5
F	**Ellen Hansell**	**Laura Knight**	6-1	6-0			
S	Ellen Hansell	Helen Day Harris	2-6	6-4	6-4		
S	Laura Knight	Alice Janney	6-0	6-1			
Q	Ellen Hansell	Jessie Harding	6-1	6-0			
Q	Helen Day Harris	Louise Alderdice	6-3	6-5			
Q	Laura Knight	Ruth Cott	6-0	6-3			
Q	Alice Janney				(bye)		

1888

Rd	Winner	Defeated	S1	S2	S3	S4	S5
Ch	**Bertha Townsend**	**Ellen Hansell**	6-3	6-5			
F	Bertha Townsend	Marion Wright	6-2	6-2			
S	Marion Wright				(bye)		
S	Bertha Townsend	Adeline Robinson	1-6	6-5	6-3		
Q	Marion Wright	Violet Ward	6-0	6-5			
Q	Bertha Townsend				(bye)		
Q	Adeline Robinson	Ellen Roosevelt	6-4	3-6	6-3		

1889

Rd	Winner	Defeated	S1	S2	S3	S4	S5
Ch	**Bertha Townsend**	**Lida Voorhees**	7-5	6-2			
F	Lida Voorhees	Helen Day Harris	6-5	2-6	6-3		
S	Lida Voorhees	Grace Roosevelt	6-1	4-6	6-5		
S	Helen Day Harris	D.F. Butterfield	6-1	6-3			
Q	Grace Roosevelt	Marion Wright			(default)		
Q	Lida Voorhees	Laura Knight	6-1	6-2			
Q	Helen Day Harris	Rebecca H. Lycett	6-1	6-1			
Q	D.F. Butterfield	Anna C. Smith	6-3	6-1			

1890

Rd	Winner	Defeated	S1	S2	S3	S4	S5
Ch	**Ellen Roosevelt**	**Bertha Townsend**	6-2	6-2			
F	Ellen Roosevelt	Lida Voorhees	6-3	6-1			
S	Ellen Roosevelt	Mabel Cahill	2-6	6-5	3-2	(retired)	
S	Lida Voorhees	Margaretha Ballard	6-4	3-6	6-5		
Q	Ellen Roosevelt	D.F. Butterfield	6-0	6-0			
Q	Mabel Cahill	Rebecca H. Lycett	6-1	6-1			
Q	Lida Voorhees	F.K. Gregory	6-1	3-6	6-1		
Q	Margarette Ballard	S. Day	6-2	6-1			

1891

Rd	Winner	Defeated	S1	S2	S3	S4	S5
Ch	**Mabel Cahill**	**Ellen Roosevelt**	6-4	6-1	4-6	6-3	
F	Mabel Cahill	Grace Roosevelt	6-3	7-5			
S	Mabel Cahill	Lida Voorhees	6-1	6-0			
S	Grace Roosevelt	Adelaide Clarkson	6-1	6-1			
Q	Mabel Cahill	Annabella Wistar	6-5	6-4			
Q	Lida Voorhees	Amy Williams	4-6	6-3	6-3		
Q	Adelaide Clarkson	Emma Leavitt Morgan	6-2	6-5			
Q	Grace Roosevelt	Helen Day Harris	3-6	6-3	6-4		

1892

Rd	Winner	Defeated	S1	S2	S3	S4	S5
Ch	**Mabel Cahill**	**Elisabeth Moore**	5-7	6-3	6-4	4-6	6-2
F	Elisabeth Moore	Helen Day Harris	5-7	6-1	6-1		
S	Elisabeth Moore	Annabella Wistar			(default)		
S	Helen Day Harris	Augusta Schultz	6-2	8-6			
Q	Elisabeth Moore	Elizabeth Slevin	6-0	6-0			
Q	Annabella Wistar	Harriet Butler	6-4	2-6	8-6		
Q	Helen Day Harris	Hattie Beaumont	6-2	4-6	6-2		
Q	Augusta Schultz	Josephine White	6-1	6-1			

1893

Rd	Winner	Defeated	S1	S2	S3	S4	S5
Ch	**Aline Terry**	**Mabel Cahill**			(default)		
F	Aline Terry	Augusta Schultz	6-1	6-3			
S	Augusta Schultz	Miss Underhill	6-2	3-6	6-0		
S	Aline Terry	Elisabeth Moore	6-3	4-6	6-4		
Q	Miss Underhill	Miss Bent	4-6	6-4	9-7		
Q	Augusta Schultz	Annabella Wistar	6-3	6-1			
Q	Elisabeth Moore	Helen Hellwig	7-5	1-6	6-4		
Q	Aline Terry	Hattie Beaumont	6-2	6-0			

1894

Rd	Winner	Defeated	S1	S2	S3	S4	S5
Ch	**Helen Hellwig**	**Aline Terry**	7-5	3-6	6-0	3-6	6-3
F	Helen Hellwig	B. Townsend Toulmin	6-2	7-5	6-4		
S	Helen Hellwig	Ethel Bankson	6-2	6-1			
S	B. Townsend Toulmin	Juliette Atkinson	4-6	6-5	6-4		
Q	Ethel Bankson	Hattie Beaumont	6-1	6-0			
Q	Helen Hellwig	Amy Williams	6-2	6-2			
Q	B. Townsend Toulmin	Mrs. Clement Beecroft	6-1	6-0			
Q	Juliette Atkinson	Elizabeth Slevin	6-1	6-1			

1895

Rd	Winner	Defeated	S1	S2	S3	S4	S5
Ch	**Juliette Atkinson**	**Helen Hellwig**	6-4	6-2	6-1		
F	Juliette Atkinson	Elisabeth Moore	6-3	7-5	3-6	6-0	
S	Elisabeth Moore	B. Townsend Toulmin	6-4	6-4			
S	Juliette Atkinson	Kathleen Atkinson	6-1	6-4			
Q	Elisabeth Moore	Grace Booth	6-0	6-2			
Q	B. Townsend Toulmin	Elizabeth Taylor	6-0	6-2			
Q	Kathleen Atkinson	Mary Warren	6-3	6-2			
Q	Juliette Atkinson	Amy Williams	6-0	6-4			

1896

Rd	Winner	Defeated	S1	S2	S3	S4	S5
Ch	**Elisabeth Moore**	**Juliette Atkinson**	6-4	4-6	6-2	6-2	
F	Elisabeth Moore	Annabella Wistar	6-3	7-5	6-0		
S	Elisabeth Moore	Gertrude Kimball	6-3	6-1			
S	Annabella Wistar	Edith Rotch	6-4	6-2			
Q	Elisabeth Moore	Amy Williams	6-4	6-5			
Q	Gertrude Kimball	Kathleen Atkinson	6-5	6-1			
Q	Annabella Wistar	Grace Booth	6-2	6-1			
Q	Edith Rotch	Helen Booth	6-3	6-2			

1897

Rd	Winner	Defeated	S1	S2	S3	S4	S5
Ch	**Juliette Atkinson**	**Elisabeth Moore**	**6-3**	**6-3**	**4-6**	**3-6**	**6-3**
F	Juliette Atkinson	Edith Kenderline	6-2	6-4	6-0		
S	Juliette Atkinson	Kathleen Atkinson	6-1	6-3			
S	Edith Kenderline	Carrie Neely	7-5	2-6	6-1		
Q	Juliette Atkinson	Maud Banks	6-1	4-6	6-1		
Q	Kathleen Atkinson	Hattie Beaumont	6-4	6-0			
Q	Edith Kenderline	Ellen Ketcham	6-2	4-6	8-6		
Q	Carrie Neely	Mrs. Frank Edwards	6-2	6-1			

1898

Rd	Winner	Defeated	S1	S2	S3	S4	S5
Ch	**Juliette Atkinson**	**Marion Jones**	**6-3**	**5-7**	**6-4**	**2-6**	**7-5**
F	Marion Jones	Helen Crump	6-4	7-5	6-4		
S	Marion Jones	Carrie Neely	6-0	6-2			
S	Helen Crump	Marie Wimer	6-3	2-6	10-8		
Q	Marion Jones	Kathleen Atkinson	6-4	6-3			
Q	Carrie Neely	Helen Chapman	6-3	6-2			
Q	Helen Crump	Maud Banks	6-1	6-3			
Q	Marie Wimer	Elizabeth Rastall	6-1	6-0			

1899

Rd	Winner	Defeated	S1	S2	S3	S4	S5
Ch	**Marion Jones**	**Juliette Atkinson**			(default)		
F	Marion Jones	Maud Banks	6-1	6-1	7-5		
S	Maud Banks	Carrie Neely	6-3	4-6	6-1		
S	Marion Jones	Jane Craven	6-1	6-0			
Q	Maud Banks	Myrtle McAteer	3-6	7-5	7-5		
Q	Carrie Neely	Georgina Jones	6-0	6-2			
Q	Marion Jones	Hallie Champlin	6-1	6-2			
Q	Jane Craven	Edith Parker	7-5	3-6	6-1		

1900

Rd	Winner	Defeated	S1	S2	S3	S4	S5
Ch	**Myrtle McAteer**	**Marion Jones**			(default)		
F	Myrtle McAteer	Edith Parker	6-2	6-0	6-0		
S	Edith Parker	Dorothea Morris	6-0	6-2			
S	Myrtle McAteer	Maud Banks	6-4	7-5			
Q	Dorothea Morris	Huldah J. Steel	6-2	4-6	7-5		
Q	Edith Parker	Hallie Champlin	8-6	6-2			
Q	Myrtle McAteer	Marie Wimer	6-3	6-3			
Q	Maud Banks	Margaret Hunnewell	6-3	3-6	6-3		

1901

Rd	Winner	Defeated	S1	S2	S3	S4	S5
Ch	**Elisabeth Moore**	**Myrtle McAteer**	**6-4**	**3-6**	**7-5**	**2-6**	**6-2**
F	Elisabeth Moore	Marion Jones	4-6	1-6	9-7	9-7	6-3
S	Elisabeth Moore	Juliette Atkinson	6-2	9-7			
S	Marion Jones	Emma Warren	6-1	6-2			
Q	Juliette Atkinson	Helen Huey	6-2	6-4			
Q	Elisabeth Moore	Carrie Neely	6-1	7-5			
Q	Marion Jones	Helen Dillingham			(default)		
Q	Emma Warren	Georgina Jones	7-5	6-4			

USLTA adopts 3-set format

1902

Rd	Winner	Defeated	S1	S2	S3
Ch	**Marion Jones**	**Elisabeth Moore**	**6-1**	**1-0(default)**	
F	Marion Jones	Carrie Neely	8-6	6-4	
S	Carrie Neely	Juliette Atkinson	8-6	3-6	6-2
S	Marion Jones	Helen Chapman	6-1	6-0	
Q	Carrie Neely	Nona Closterman	6-2	6-0	
Q	Juliette Atkinson	Clara T. Chase	6-1	6-3	
Q	Marion Jones	Marie Wimer	6-4	6-0	
Q	Helen Chapman	Mrs. M.R. Fielding	6-4	3-6	7-5

1903

Rd	Winner	Defeated	S1	S2	S3
Ch	**Elisabeth Moore**	**Marion Jones**	**7-5**	**8-6**	
F	Elisabeth Moore	Carrie Neely	6-2	6-4	
S	Elisabeth Moore	Marjorie Oberteuffer	6-0	6-0	
S	Carrie Neely	Helen Chapman	6-0	6-1	
Q	Elisabeth Moore	Miriam Hall	6-1	6-3	
Q	Marjorie Oberteuffer	Gertrude Fetterman	6-2	6-3	
Q	Helen Chapman	Corrine Mock	6-1	8-6	
Q	Carrie Neely	Clara T. Chase	6-0	6-1	

1904

Rd	Winner	Defeated	S1	S2	S3
Ch	**May Sutton**	**Elisabeth Moore**	**6-1**	**6-2**	
F	May Sutton	Helen Homans	6-1	6-1	
S	Helen Homans	Miriam Hall	6-4	6-3	
S	May Sutton	Sarah Coffin	6-1	6-0	
Q	Helen Homans	Carrie Neely	7-5	11-9	
Q	Miriam Hall	Marie Wimer	6-3	6-2	
Q	Sarah Coffin	Clara T. Chase	6-3	6-2	
Q	May Sutton	Frances Stotesbury	6-1	6-0	

1905

Rd	Winner	Defeated	S1	S2	S3
Ch	**Elisabeth Moore**	**May Sutton**			(default)
F	Elisabeth Moore	Helen Homans	6-4	5-7	6-1
S	Elisabeth Moore	Margaret LeRoy	6-1	6-3	
S	Helen Homans	Mary Coates	6-1	6-0	
Q	Margaret LeRoy	Clara T. Chase	6-3	6-8	6-1
Q	Elisabeth Moore	Carrie Neely	4-6	6-1	6-2
Q	Mary Coates	Evelyn V. Howell	6-2	7-5	
Q	Helen Homans	Mrs. C. Wainwright			(default)

1906

Rd	Winner	Defeated	S1	S2	S3
Ch	**Helen Homans**	**Elisabeth Moore**			(default)
F	Helen Homans	Maud Barger Wallach	6-4	6-3	
S	Helen Homans	Edith Rotch	6-2	6-3	
S	Maud Barger Wallach	Bertha Townsend Toulmin	6-2	6-3	
Q	Edith Rotch	Clover Boldt	6-1	4-6	6-0
Q	Helen Homans	Rachel Harlan	4-6	6-4	6-4
Q	Bertha Townsend Toulmin	Gertrude Fetterman	6-1	6-2	
Q	Maud Barger Wallach	Annetta G. McCall	6-1	6-0	

1907

Rd	Winner	Defeated	S1	S2	S3
F	**Evelyn Sears**	**Carrie Neely**	**6-3**	**6-2**	
S	Evelyn Sears	Mrs. George L. Chapman	6-2	6-1	
S	Carrie Neely	Helen Pouch	8-6	7-5	
Q	Evelyn Sears	Elizabeth G. Ostheimer	6-1	6-1	
Q	Mrs. George L. Chapman	Phyllis Green	6-2	6-0	
Q	Helen Pouch	Emily Scott	6-4	6-2	
Q	Carrie Neely	Rachel Harlan	2-6	6-4	6-3

1908

Rd	Winner	Defeated	S1	S2	S3
Ch	**Maud Barger Wallach**	**Evelyn Sears**	**6-3**	**1-6**	**6-3**
F	Maud Barger Wallach	Marie Wagner	4-6	6-1	6-3
S	Maud Barger Wallach	Edith Rotch	6-2	6-4	
S	Marie Wagner	M. Johnson	7-5	6-2	
Q	Edith Rotch	Helen Pouch	2-6	7-5	6-1
Q	Maud Barger Wallach	Matilda Borda	6-3	6-2	
Q	M. Johnson	Eleanor Cohen	8-6	6-2	
Q	Marie Wagner	Carrie Neely	6-4	4-6	7-5

1909

Rd	Winner	Defeated	S1	S2	S3
Ch	**Hazel Hotchkiss**	**Maud Barger Wallach**	**6-0**	**6-1**	
F	Hazel Hotchkiss	Louise Hammond	6-8	6-1	6-4
S	Hazel Hotchkiss	Edith Rotch	6-2	7-5	
S	Louise Hammond	Lois Moyes	6-0	6-2	
Q	Hazel Hotchkiss	Emily Scott	6-3	6-0	
Q	Edith Rotch	Alice Day	6-1	6-0	
Q	Louise Hammond	Gwendolyn Rees	6-4	6-1	
Q	Lois Moyes	Margaret Roberts	6-1	8-6	

Rd	Winner	Defeated	S1	S2	S3
1910					
Ch	**Hazel Hotchkiss**	**Louise Hammond**	**6-4**	**6-2**	
F	Louise Hammond	Adelaide Browning	6-2	6-4	
S	Louise Hammond	Edith Rotch	7-5	6-2	
S	Adelaide Browning	Edna Wildey	6-1	6-4	
Q	Louise Hammond	Carrie Neely	6-1	8-6	
Q	Edith Rotch	Constance Evans Sullivan	6-2	6-4	
Q	Edna Wildey	Lois Moyes	6-3	6-4	
Q	Adelaide Browning	Dorothy Green	3-6	6-3	6-2
1911					
Ch	**Hazel Hotchkiss**	**Florence Sutton**	**8-10**	**6-1**	**9-7**
F	Florence Sutton	Eleonora Sears	6-2	6-1	
S	Eleonora Sears	Mrs. G. Warren	6-1	6-3	
S	Florence Sutton	Adelaide Browning	6-3	6-2	
Q	Eleonora Sears	Mrs. Wallinston Hardy	6-2	6-2	
Q	Mrs. G. Warren	Edith Handy	3-6	6-2	6-3
Q	Florence Sutton	Edna Wildey	6-1	6-3	
Q	Adelaide Browning	Marie Wagner	6-3	3-6	6-2
1912					
F	**Mary K. Browne**	**Eleonora Sears**	**6-4**	**6-2**	
S	Mary K. Browne	Adelaide Browning	6-4	3-6	9-7
S	Eleonora Sears	Mary Merrick	5-7	6-0	6-2
Q	Adelaide Browning	Mrs. Frederick Schmitz	6-1	10-8	
Q	Mary K. Browne	Marion Fenno	6-0	6-4	
Q	Eleonora Sears	Helen D. Alexander	6-2	6-2	
Q	Mary Merrick	Effie Wheeler		(default)	
1913					
Ch	**Mary K. Browne**	**Dorothy Green**	**6-2**	**7-5**	
F	Dorothy Green	Edna Wildey	6-3	6-4	
S	Edna Wildey	Mrs. H.J.D. Paul	6-1	6-2	
S	Dorothy Green	Louise Riddell Williams	7-5	6-3	
Q	Edna Wildey	Marion Cresswell	6-0	6-2	
Q	Mrs. H.J.D. Paul	Flora Brown Harvey	2-6	6-3	7-5
Q	Dorothy Green	Mrs. Robert Herold	6-4	6-2	
Q	Louise Riddell Williams	Helen D. Alexander	6-0	4-6	6-2
1914					
Ch	**Mary K. Browne**	**Marie Wagner**	**6-2**	**1-6**	**6-1**
F	Marie Wagner	Clare Cassel	6-1	7-5	
S	Marie Wagner	Louise Hammond Raymond	6-4	6-4	
S	Clare Cassel	Isabel Pendleton	6-2	6-1	
Q	Marie Wagner	Carrie Neely	6-2	6-3	
Q	Louise Hammond Raymond	Constance Evans Sullivan	4-6	6-2	6-1
Q	Isabel Pendleton	Margarette Myers	6-2	6-1	
Q	Clare Cassel	Ann W. Sheafe	4-6	6-4	6-1
1915					
Ch					
F	**Molla Bjurstedt**	**Hazel Hotchkiss Wightman**	**4-6**	**6-2**	**6-0**
S	Molla Bjurstedt	Martha Guthrie	3-6	6-2	6-2
S	Hazel Hotchkiss Wightman	Eliza M. Fox	6-1	6-4	
Q	Molla Bjurstedt	Ann W. Sheafe	10-8	6-2	
Q	Martha Guthrie	Marion Vanderhoef	7-5	6-0	
Q	Eliza M. Fox	Alice Cunningham	6-2	6-1	
Q	Hazel Hotchkiss Wightman	Eleonora Sears	6-3	5-7	6-2
1916					
Ch	**Molla Bjurstedt**	**Louise Hammond Raymond**	**6-0**	**6-1**	
F	Louise Hammond Raymond	Eleonora Sears	6-3	6-4	
S	Louise Hammond Raymond	Evelyn Sears	6-2	6-1	
S	Eleonora Sears	Susanne White	6-2	6-3	
Q	Evelyn Sears	Alice Patterson	6-3	6-2	
Q	Louise Hammond Raymond	Maud Barger Wallach	6-1	6-3	
Q	Eleonora Sears	Phyllis Walsh	6-3	6-3	
Q	Susanne White	Mrs. J.R. Hall	4-6	8-6	7-5
1917					
Ch					
F	**Molla Bjurstedt**	**Marion Vanderhoef**	**4-6**	**6-0**	**6-2**
S	Marion Vanderhoef	Eleonora Sears	8-6	6-3	
S	Molla Bjurstedt	Flora Brown Harvey	4-6	6-0	6-0
Q	Marion Vanderhoef	Susanne White	3-6	6-2	6-2
Q	Eleonora Sears	Mrs. Knud Dahl	6-2	6-4	
Q	Molla Bjurstedt	Phyllis Walsh	6-4	6-1	
Q	Flora Brown Harvey	Teresa Wood	1-6	6-4	7-5
1918					
Ch	**Molla Bjurstedt**	**Eleanor Goss**	**6-4**	**6-3**	
F	Eleanor Goss	Helene Pollak	6-2	7-5	
S	Helene Pollak	Clare Cassel	6-3	6-0	
S	Eleanor Goss	Helen Ledoux	6-3	6-4	
Q	Helene Pollak	Dorothy Walker	6-1	6-0	
Q	Clare Cassel	Eleonora Sears	6-2	6-4	
Q	Helen Ledoux	Barbara F. Hooker	6-4	6-1	
Q	Eleanor Goss	Emily Stokes Weaver	6-2	6-4	
1919					
F	**Hazel Hotchkiss Wightman**	**Marion Zinderstein**	**6-1**	**6-2**	
S	Hazel Hotchkiss Wightman	Flora Brown Harvey	6-2	6-2	
S	Marion Zinderstein	Molla Bjurstedt	4-6	6-1	6-2
Q	Hazel Hotchkiss Wightman	Anne B. Townsend	6-0	6-1	
Q	Flora Brown Harvey	Leslie Bancroft	6-2	4-6	6-4
Q	Molla Bjurstedt	Marie Wagner	6-2	6-8	6-4
Q	Marion Zinderstein	Clare Cassel	6-3	6-1	
1920					
F	**Molla Bjurstedt Mallory**	**Marion Zinderstein**	**6-3**	**6-1**	
S	Molla Bjurstedt Mallory	Helene Pollak	6-2	6-3	
S	Marion Zinderstein	Eleanor Goss	6-3	6-4	
Q	Helene Pollak	Edith Sigourney	6-3	8-6	
Q	Molla Bjurstedt Mallory	Eleanor Tennant	6-2	2-6	6-3
Q	Eleanor Goss	Martha Niles	6-4	6-2	
Q	Marion Zinderstein	Leslie Bancroft	6-4	6-2	
1921					
F	**Molla Bjurstedt Mallory**	**Mary K. Browne**	**4-6**	**6-4**	**6-2**
S	Mary K. Browne	Patricia Butlin Hitchins	6-3	6-0	
S	Molla Bjurstedt Mallory	May Sutton Bundy	8-6	6-2	
Q	Patricia Butlin Hitchins	Adelaide Browning Greene	8-6	6-2	
Q	Mary K. Browne	Ann Sheafe Cole	6-1	6-2	
Q	Molla Bjurstedt Mallory	Helene Pollak Falk	6-2	6-1	
Q	May Sutton Bundy	Helen Gilleaudeau	6-1	6-2	
1922					
F	**Molla Bjurstedt Mallory**	**Helen Wills**	**6-3**	**6-1**	
S	Helen Wills	May Sutton Bundy	6-4	6-3	
S	Molla Bjurstedt Mallory	Leslie Bancroft	6-0	6-4	
Q	May Sutton Bundy	Martha Bayard	12-10	4-6	6-0
Q	Helen Wills	Marion Zinderstein Jessup	2-6	6-4	6-2
Q	Molla Bjurstedt Mallory	Edith Sigourney	6-0	6-1	
Q	Leslie Bancroft	Clare Cassel	8-6	6-3	
1923					
F	**Helen Wills**	**Molla Bjurstedt Mallory**	**6-2**	**6-1**	
S	Helen Wills	Eleanor Goss	6-4	6-0	
S	Molla Bjurstedt Mallory	Mabel Clayton	6-4	6-2	
Q	Helen Wills	Kitty McKane	2-6	6-2	7-5
Q	Eleanor Goss	Phyllis Howkins Covell	6-1	2-6	8-6
Q	Molla Bjurstedt Mallory	Helen Hooker	6-3	6-1	
Q	Mabel Clayton	Leslie Bancroft	6-1	6-2	

Rd	Winner	Defeated	S1	S2	S3
1924					
F	**Helen Wills**	**Molla Bjurstedt Mallory**	**6-1**	**6-3**	
S	Molla Bjurstedt Mallory	Eleanor Goss	6-3	6-4	
S	Helen Wills	Mary K. Browne	6-4	4-6	6-3
Q	Molla Bjurstedt Mallory	Edna Hauselt Roeser	6-1	6-0	
Q	Eleanor Goss	Martha Bayard	8-6	6-4	
Q	Helen Wills	Marion Zinderstein Jessup	6-3	6-3	
Q	Mary K. Browne	Mayme MacDonald	6-2	5-7	6-4
1925					
F	**Helen Wills**	**Kitty McKane**	**3-6**	**6-0**	**6-2**
S	Kitty McKane	Molla Bjurstedt Mallory	4-6	7-5	8-6
S	Helen Wills	Eleanor Goss	3-6	6-0	6-2
Q	Kitty McKane	Elizabeth Ryan	3-6	7-5	6-2
Q	Molla Bjurstedt Mallory	Penelope Anderson	6-2	6-1	
Q	Helen Wills	Joan Fry	4-6	6-0	6-3
Q	Eleanor Goss	Dorothea Douglass Chambers	6-2	11-9	
1926					
F	**Molla Bjurstedt Mallory**	**Elizabeth Ryan**	**4-6**	**6-4**	**9-7**
S	Elizabeth Ryan	Mary K. Browne	6-1	6-3	
S	Molla Bjurstedt Mallory	Martha Bayard	6-3	6-3	
Q	Elizabeth Ryan	Eleanor Goss	3-6	6-0	
Q	Mary K. Browne	Penelope Anderson	7-5	6-1	
Q	Martha Bayard	Margaret Blake	6-4	6-2	
Q	Molla Bjurstedt Mallory	Charlotte Hosmer Chapin	7-5	6-0	
1927					
F	**Helen Wills**	**Betty Nuthall**	**6-1**	**6-4**	
S	Helen Wills	Helen Jacobs	6-0	6-2	
S	Betty Nuthall	Charlotte Hosmer Chapin	6-1	4-6	6-3
Q	Helen Wills	Kea Bouman	6-1	6-2	
Q	Helen Jacobs	Edna Hauselt Roeser	6-8	8-6	6-2
Q	Charlotte Hosmer Chapin	Molla Bjurstedt Mallory	6-3	1-6	6-4
Q	Betty Nuthall	Eleanor Goss	4-6	7-5	6-2
1928					
F	**Helen Wills**	**Helen Jacobs**	**6-2**	**6-1**	
S	Helen Wills	Edith Cross	6-0	6-1	
S	Helen Jacobs	Molla Bjurstedt Mallory	6-2	7-5	
Q	Helen Wills	Charlotte Hosmer Chapin	6-2	6-4	
Q	Edith Cross	Hazel Hotchkiss Wightman	6-3	6-4	
Q	Molla Bjurstedt Mallory	Marjorie Morrill	6-2	3-6	6-3
Q	Helen Jacobs	Penelope Anderson	6-4	6-1	
1929					
F	**Helen Wills Moody**	**Phoebe Holcroft Watson**	**6-4**	**6-2**	
S	Helen Wills Moody	Molla Bjurstedt Mallory	6-0	6-0	
S	Phoebe Holcroft Watson	Helen Jacobs	6-1	3-6	6-4
Q	Helen Wills Moody	Peggy Michell	6-0	6-1	
Q	Molla Bjurstedt Mallory	Betty Nuthall	6-3	6-3	
Q	Helen Jacobs	Mary Greef	6-2	6-2	
Q	Phoebe Holcroft Watson	Edith Cross	2-6	6-1	6-3
1930					
F	**Betty Nuthall**	**Anna McCune Harper**	**6-1**	**6-4**	
S	Betty Nuthall	Marjorie Morrill	6-8	6-4	6-2
S	Anna McCune Harper	Maud Rosenbaum Levi	6-2	6-3	
Q	Marjorie Morrill	Ethel Burkhardt	4-6	6-3	6-2
Q	Betty Nuthall	Dorothy Weisel	6-1	6-1	
Q	Anna McCune Harper	Mary Greef	3-6	6-1	6-4
Q	Maud Rosenbaum Levi	Penelope Anderson	4-6	6-4	7-5
1931					
F	**Helen Wills Moody**	**Eileen Bennett Whittingstall**	**6-4**	**6-1**	
S	Helen Wills Moody	Phyllis Mudford	6-2	6-4	
S	Eileen Bennett Whittingstall	Betty Nuthall	6-2	3-6	6-4
Q	Helen Wills Moody	Dorothy Weisel	6-1	6-2	
Q	Phyllis Mudford	Anna McCune Harper	4-6	6-3	6-2
Q	Eileen Bennett Whittingstall	Helen Jacobs	3-6	6-3	8-6
Q	Betty Nuthall	Dorothy Shepherd Barron	6-2	6-1	
1932					
F	**Helen Jacobs**	**Carolin Babcock**	**6-2**	**6-2**	
S	Helen Jacobs	Elsie Goldsack Pittman	6-2	6-3	
S	Carolin Babcock	Joan Ridley	4-6	7-5	6-3
Q	Helen Jacobs	Marjorie Gladman Van Ryn	3-6	6-3	6-1
Q	Elsie Goldsack Pittman	Mary Greef	6-3	6-2	
Q	Carolin Babcock	Anna McCune Harper	6-3	7-5	
Q	Joan Ridley	Marjorie Morrill Painter	3-6	8-6	6-4
1933					
F	**Helen Jacobs**	**Helen Wills Moody**	**8-6**	**3-6**	**3-0 (default)**
S	Helen Wills Moody	Betty Nuthall	2-6	6-3	6-2
S	Helen Jacobs	Dorothy Round	6-4	5-7	6-2
Q	Helen Wills Moody	Mary Heeley	6-0	6-2	
Q	Betty Nuthall	Alice Marble	6-8	6-0	6-2
Q	Helen Jacobs	Josephine Cruickshank	11-9	6-4	
Q	Dorothy Round	Sarah Palfrey	6-4	9-7	
1934					
F	**Helen Jacobs**	**Sarah Palfrey**	**6-1**	**6-4**	
S	Sarah Palfrey	Dorothy Andrus	6-3	6-4	
S	Helen Jacobs	Carolin Babcock	7-5	6-0	
Q	Sarah Palfrey	Freda James	6-3	3-6	6-1
Q	Dorothy Andrus	Maud Rosenbaum Levi	6-1	6-4	
Q	Helen Jacobs	Elizabeth Ryan	6-0	6-1	
Q	Carolin Babcock	Kay Stammers	6-3	2-6	6-4
1935					
F	**Helen Jacobs**	**Sarah Palfrey Fabyan**	**6-2**	**6-4**	
S	Helen Jacobs	Phyllis Mudford King	6-4	6-3	
S	Sarah Palfrey Fabyan	Kay Stammers	9-7	7-5	
Q	Helen Jacobs	Nancy Lyle	6-0	6-4	
Q	Phyllis Mudford King	Marjorie Gladman Van Ryn	6-2	6-0	
Q	Sarah Palfrey Fabyan	Freda James	7-5	5-7	6-4
Q	Kay Stammers	Eunice Earle Dean	5-7	6-3	6-2
1936					
F	**Alice Marble**	**Helen Jacobs**	**4-6**	**6-3**	**6-2**
S	Helen Jacobs	Kay Stammers	6-4	6-3	
S	Alice Marble	Helen Pedersen	6-1	6-1	
Q	Helen Jacobs	Gussie Raegener	6-1	6-0	
Q	Kay Stammers	Marjorie Gladman Van Ryn	7-5	3-6	6-4
Q	Helen Pedersen	Dorothy Bundy	6-3	3-6	6-4
Q	Alice Marble	Gracyn Wheeler	6-2	11-9	
1937					
F	**Anita Lizana**	**Jadwiga Jedrzejowska**	**6-4**	**6-2**	
S	Jadwiga Jedrzejowska	Helen Jacobs	6-4	6-4	
S	Anita Lizana	Dorothy Bundy	6-2	6-3	
Q	Helen Jacobs	Kay Stammers	7-5	6-3	
Q	Jadwiga Jedrzejowska	Mary Hardwick	6-4	6-2	
Q	Dorothy Bundy	Alice Marble	1-6	7-5	6-1
Q	Anita Lizana	Marjorie Gladman Van Ryn	6-1	6-1	
1938					
F	**Alice Marble**	**Nancye Wynne**	**6-0**	**6-3**	
S	Nancye Wynne	Dorothy Bundy	5-7	6-3	8-6
S	Alice Marble	Sarah Palfrey Fabyan	5-7	7-5	7-5
Q	Nancye Wynne	Margot Lumb	6-4	5-7	6-1
Q	Dorothy Bundy	Simone Passemard Mathieu	6-3	3-6	6-0
Q	Alice Marble	Kay Stammers	6-8	6-3	6-0
Q	Sarah Palfrey Fabyan	Jadwiga Jedrzejowska	6-1	6-4	

Rd	Winner	Defeated	S1	S2	S3
1939					
F	**Alice Marble**	**Helen Jacobs**	**6-0**	**8-10**	**6-4**
S	Helen Jacobs	Kay Stammers	7-5	6-0	
S	Alice Marble	Virginia Wolfenden	6-0	6-1	
Q	Helen Jacobs	Valerie Scott	2-6	6-2	6-3
Q	Kay Stammers	Sarah Palfrey Fabyan	1-6	6-3	6-3
Q	Alice Marble	Mary Hardwick	6-3	6-8	6-2
Q	Virginia Wolfenden	Dorothy Bundy	2-6	6-1	6-1
1940					
F	**Alice Marble**	**Helen Jacobs**	**6-2**	**6-3**	
S	Helen Jacobs	Mary Hardwick	2-6	6-1	6-4
S	Alice Marble	Valerie Scott	6-3	6-3	
Q	Helen Jacobs	Virginia Wolfenden	3-6	6-4	6-1
Q	Mary Hardwick	Pauline Betz	5-7	6-1	6-2
Q	Alice Marble	Helen Bernhard	6-3	6-3	
Q	Valerie Scott	Dorothy Bundy	3-6	6-4	6-3
1941					
F	**Sarah Palfrey Cooke**	**Pauline Betz**	**7-5**	**6-2**	
S	Sarah Palfrey Cooke	Helen Jacobs	6-3	2-6	6-1
S	Pauline Betz	Margaret Osborne	6-4	6-3	
Q	Sarah Palfrey Cooke	Hope Knowles	6-4	7-5	
Q	Helen Jacobs	Dorothy Bundy	6-3	11-9	
Q	Pauline Betz	Barbara Krase	6-2	6-2	
Q	Margaret Osborne	Helen Bernhard	6-3	6-1	
1942					
F	**Pauline Betz**	**Louise Brough**	**4-6**	**6-1**	**6-4**
S	Pauline Betz	Margaret Osborne	6-4	4-6	7-5
S	Louise Brough	Helen Bernhard	5-7	6-4	6-2
Q	Pauline Betz	Shirley Fry	6-2	6-0	
Q	Margaret Osborne	Doris Hart	7-5	6-0	
Q	Louise Brough	Mary Arnold	3-6	6-4	6-3
Q	Helen Bernhard	Helen Pedersen Rihbany	6-0	6-4	
1943					
F	**Pauline Betz**	**Louise Brough**	**6-3**	**5-7**	**6-3**
S	Pauline Betz	Doris Hart	9-7	2-6	6-1
S	Louise Brough	Dorothy Bundy	6-4	7-5	
Q	Pauline Betz	Dorothy Head	6-0	6-1	
Q	Doris Hart	Sarah Palfrey Cooke	6-1	6-3	
Q	Louise Brough	Mary Arnold	3-6	6-3	7-5
Q	Dorothy Bundy	Margaret Osborne	6-3	3-6	7-5
1944					
F	**Pauline Betz**	**Margaret Osborne**	**6-3**	**8-6**	
S	Pauline Betz	Louise Brough	6-2	6-3	
S	Margaret Osborne	Dorothy Bundy	4-6	6-4	6-0
Q	Pauline Betz	Virginia Kovacs	6-4	6-8	6-4
Q	Louise Brough	Mary Arnold	3-6	6-3	8-6
Q	Margaret Osborne	Shirley Fry	6-3	6-1	
Q	Dorothy Bundy	Doris Hart	5-7	8-6	6-4
1945					
F	**Sarah Palfrey Cooke**	**Pauline Betz**	**3-6**	**8-6**	**6-4**
S	Sarah Palfrey Cooke	Louise Brough	6-3	6-4	
S	Pauline Betz	Doris Hart	6-3	6-2	
Q	Sarah Palfrey Cooke	Dorothy Bundy	6-3	6-4	
Q	Louise Brough	Pat Todd	6-2	6-4	
Q	Pauline Betz	Mary Arnold	0-6	6-4	6-4
Q	Doris Hart	Margaret Osborne	6-2	6-3	
1946					
F	**Pauline Betz**	**Doris Hart**	**11-9**	**6-3**	
S	Pauline Betz	Pat Todd	6-2	6-3	
S	Doris Hart	Mary Arnold Prentiss	6-3	6-3	
Q	Pauline Betz	Gussy Moran	6-1	3-6	6-2
Q	Pat Todd	Louise Brough	6-2	6-2	
Q	Doris Hart	Margaret Osborne	6-4	5-7	7-5
Q	Mary Arnold Prentiss	Dorothy Head	6-2	6-1	

Rd	Winner	Defeated	S1	S2	S3
1947					
F	**Louise Brough**	**Margaret Osborne duPont**	**8-6**	**4-6**	**6-1**
S	Louise Brough	Nancye Wynne Bolton	4-6	6-4	7-5
S	Margaret Osborne duPont	Doris Hart	7-5	7-5	
Q	Louise Brough	Dorothy Head	6-8	6-2	6-0
Q	Nancye Wynne Bolton	Pat Todd	6-4	6-1	
Q	Margaret Osborne duPont	Magda Rurac	6-4	6-4	
Q	Doris Hart	Barbara Krase	8-6	6-2	
1948					
F	**Margaret Osborne duPont**	**Louise Brough**	**4-6**	**6-4**	**15-13**
S	Margaret Osborne duPont	Gussy Moran	10-8	6-4	
S	Louise Brough	Pat Todd	6-3	6-3	
Q	Gussy Moran	Doris Hart	6-4	6-4	
Q	Margaret Osborne duPont	Beverly Baker	1-6	6-2	6-0
Q	Louise Brough	Virginia Kovacs	6-3	6-2	
Q	Pat Todd	Madge Vosters	6-3	6-1	
1949					
F	**Margaret Osborne duPont**	**Doris Hart**	**6-4**	**6-1**	
S	Doris Hart	Louise Brough	7-5	6-1	
S	Margaret Osborne duPont	Betty Hilton	6-2	6-3	
Q	Louise Brough	Beverly Baker	6-1	2-6	6-2
Q	Doris Hart	Barbara Scofield	6-2	6-0	
Q	Margaret Osborne duPont	Pat Todd	6-3	10-8	
Q	Betty Hilton	Helen Perez	6-4	4-6	6-3
1950					
F	**Margaret Osborne duPont**	**Doris Hart**	**6-3**	**6-3**	
S	Margaret Osborne duPont	Nancy Chaffee	6-1	1-6	6-0
S	Doris Hart	Beverly Baker	6-4	6-1	
Q	Margaret Osborne duPont	Pat Todd	6-3	6-4	
Q	Nancy Chaffee	Barbara Scofield	6-2	6-2	
Q	Doris Hart	Shirley Fry	6-4	6-4	
Q	Beverly Baker	Betty Rosenquest	6-2	9-7	
1951					
F	**Maureen Connolly**	**Shirley Fry**	**6-3**	**1-6**	**6-4**
S	Shirley Fry	Jean Walker Smith	2-6	6-2	6-1
S	Maureen Connolly	Doris Hart	6-4	6-4	
Q	Shirley Fry	Kay Tuckey	9-7	3-6	6-2
Q	Jean Walker Smith	Magda Rurac	6-2	6-3	
Q	Doris Hart	Nancy Chaffee	6-2	6-4	
Q	Maureen Connolly	Jean Quertier	6-3	6-3	
1952					
F	**Maureen Connolly**	**Doris Hart**	**6-3**	**7-5**	
S	Doris Hart	Louise Brough	9-7	8-6	
S	Maureen Connolly	Shirley Fry	4-6	6-4	6-1
Q	Doris Hart	Angela Mortimer	6-3	6-2	
Q	Louise Brough	Thelma Long	6-4	6-2	
Q	Maureen Connolly	Nancy Kiner	6-3	6-0	
Q	Shirley Fry	Baba Lewis	6-3	6-0	
1953					
F	**Maureen Connolly**	**Doris Hart**	**6-2**	**6-4**	
S	Maureen Connolly	Shirley Fry	6-1	6-1	
S	Doris Hart	Louise Brough	6-2	6-4	
Q	Maureen Connolly	Althea Gibson	6-2	6-3	
Q	Shirley Fry	Margaret Osborne duPont	8-6	7-5	
Q	Doris Hart	Jean Quertier-Rinkel	6-1	6-0	
Q	Louise Brough	Helen Perez	8-6	6-3	
1954					
F	**Doris Hart**	**Louise Brough**	**6-8**	**6-1**	**8-6**
S	Louise Brough	Darlene Hard	6-2	6-3	
S	Doris Hart	Shirley Fry	6-2	6-0	
Q	Louise Brough	Betty Rosenquest Pratt	6-2	6-3	
Q	Darlene Hard	Dennis Bradshaw	6-3	5-7	6-2
Q	Doris Hart	Lois Felix	6-1	6-1	
Q	Shirley Fry	Beverly Baker Fleitz	(default)		

Rd	Winner	Defeated	S1	S2	S3
1955					
F	**Doris Hart**	**Pat Ward**	**6-4**	**6-2**	
S	Doris Hart	Dorothy Head Knode	6-1	6-1	
S	Pat Ward	Barbara Breit	6-1	6-2	
Q	Doris Hart	Nancy Kiner	6-4	6-4	
Q	Dorothy Head Knode	Shirley Fry	9-7	8-6	
Q	Pat Ward	Belmar Gunderson	9-7	6-0	
Q	Barbara Breit	Beverly Baker Fleitz	8-6	4-6	6-0
1956					
F	**Shirley Fry**	**Althea Gibson**	**6-3**	**6-4**	
S	Shirley Fry	Shirley Bloomer	6-4	6-4	
S	Althea Gibson	Betty Rosenquest Pratt	6-1	10-8	
Q	Shirley Fry	Margaret Osborne duPont	6-2	4-6	6-2
Q	Shirley Bloomer	Louise Brough	6-3	6-3	
Q	Althea Gibson	Darlene Hard	9-7	6-1	
Q	Betty Rosenquest Pratt	Dorothy Head Knode	4-6	6-0	6-2
1957					
F	**Althea Gibson**	**Louise Brough**	**6-3**	**6-2**	
S	Althea Gibson	Dorothy Head Knode	6-2	6-2	
S	Louise Brough	Darlene Hard	6-2	6-4	
Q	Althea Gibson	Mary Bevis Hawton	6-2	6-2	
Q	Dorothy Head Knode	Lois Felix	6-2	6-1	
Q	Louise Brough	Ann Haydon	7-5	6-1	
Q	Darlene Hard	Shirley Bloomer	6-0	6-1	
1958					
F	**Althea Gibson**	**Darlene Hard**	**3-6**	**6-1**	**6-2**
S	Althea Gibson	Beverly Baker Fleitz	6-4	6-2	
S	Darlene Hard	Jeanne Arth	7-5	6-2	
Q	Althea Gibson	Christine Truman	11-9	6-1	
Q	Beverly Baker Fleitz	Maria Bueno	6-1	6-2	
Q	Jeanne Arth	Dorothy Head Knode	6-3	6-2	
Q	Darlene Hard	Sally Moore	6-4	6-3	
1959					
F	**Maria Bueno**	**Christine Truman**	**6-1**	**6-4**	
S	Christine Truman	Ann Haydon	6-2	6-3	
S	Maria Bueno	Darlene Hard	6-2	6-4	
Q	Ann Haydon	Sandra Reynolds	6-3	6-2	
Q	Christine Truman	Dorothy Head Knode	6-1	6-2	
Q	Maria Bueno	Louise Clapp	6-3	6-2	
Q	Darlene Hard	Karen Hantze	5-7	9-7	6-3
1960					
F	**Darlene Hard**	**Maria Bueno**	**6-4**	**10-12**	**6-4**
S	Maria Bueno	Christine Truman	6-3	9-7	
S	Darlene Hard	Donna Floyd	6-1	7-5	
Q	Maria Bueno	Nancy Richey	6-2	6-4	
Q	Christine Truman	Bernice Vukovich	6-3	6-3	
Q	Donna Floyd	Ann Haydon	3-6	6-2	9-7
Q	Darlene Hard	Jan Lehane	6-2	6-1	
1961					
F	**Darlene Hard**	**Ann Haydon**	**6-3**	**6-4**	
S	Darlene Hard	Margaret Smith	6-4	4-6	6-3
S	Ann Haydon	Angela Mortimer	6-4	6-2	
Q	Darlene Hard	Yola Ramirez	6-3	6-1	
Q	Margaret Smith	Christine Truman	8-10	6-4	6-3
Q	Angela Mortimer	Lesley Turner	6-3	6-4	
Q	Ann Haydon	Jan Lehane	6-4	5-7	6-2
1962					
F	**Margaret Smith**	**Darlene Hard**	**9-7**	**6-4**	
S	Margaret Smith	Maria Bueno	6-8	6-3	6-4
S	Darlene Hard	Victoria Palmer	6-2	6-3	
Q	Margaret Smith	Sandra Price	6-3	6-3	
Q	Maria Bueno	Donna Floyd	6-1	6-3	
Q	Victoria Palmer	Gwyneth Thomas	6-4	2-6	6-2
Q	Darlene Hard	Vera Sukova	6-2	6-1	

Rd	Winner	Defeated	S1	S2	S3
1963					
F	**Maria Bueno**	**Margaret Smith**	**7-5**	**6-4**	
S	Margaret Smith	Deidre Catt	6-2	6-0	
S	Maria Bueno	Ann Haydon Jones	1-6	6-2	9-7
S	Margaret Smith	Christine Truman	3-6	6-2	6-2
Q	Deidre Catt	Yola Ramirez Ochoa		(default)	
Q	Maria Bueno	Nancy Richey	6-3	6-2	
Q	Ann Haydon Jones	Darlene Hard	6-4	6-3	
1964					
F	**Maria Bueno**	**Carole Caldwell Graebner**	**6-1**	**6-0**	
S	Carole Caldwell Graebner	Nancy Richey	2-6	9-7	6-4
S	Maria Bueno	Carol Hanks	6-4	6-0	
Q	Carole Caldwell Graebner	Karen Hantze Susman	6-4	6-8	6-3
Q	Nancy Richey	Billie Jean Moffitt	6-4	6-4	
Q	Carol Hanks	Ann Haydon Jones	7-5	2-6	8-6
Q	Maria Bueno	Robyn Ebbern	6-4	6-1	
1965					
F	**Margaret Smith**	**Billie Jean Moffitt**	**8-6**	**7-5**	
S	Margaret Smith	Nancy Richey	6-2	6-2	
S	Billie Jean Moffitt	Maria Bueno	6-2	6-3	
Q	Margaret Smith	Françoise Durr	6-1	6-0	
Q	Nancy Richey	Norma Baylon	6-4	7-5	
Q	Billie Jean Moffitt	Ann Haydon Jones	16-14	6-2	
Q	Maria Bueno	Carole Caldwell Graebner	8-6	1-6	9-7
1966					
F	**Maria Bueno**	**Nancy Richey**	**6-3**	**6-1**	
S	Maria Bueno	Rosie Casals	6-2	10-12	6-3
S	Nancy Richey	Kerry Melville	6-3	6-2	
S	Maria Bueno	Norma Baylon	6-0	6-1	
Q	Rosie Casals	Françoise Durr	6-4	6-4	
Q	Nancy Richey	Virginia Wade	6-3	6-1	
Q	Kerry Melville	Madonna Schacht	6-1	6-2	
1967					
F	**Billie Jean King**	**Ann Haydon Jones**	**11-9**	**6-4**	
S	Billie Jean King	Françoise Durr	6-2	6-4	
S	Ann Haydon Jones	Lesley Turner	6-2	6-4	
Q	Billie Jean King	Annette Van Zyl	6-1	6-4	
Q	Françoise Durr	Valerie Ziegenfuss	6-0	6-3	
Q	Lesley Turner	Rita Bentley	6-1	6-2	
Q	Ann Haydon Jones	Peaches Bartkowicz	7-5	2-6	6-1
1968					
F	**Virginia Wade**	**Billie Jean King**	**6-4**	**6-2**	
S	Virginia Wade	Ann Haydon Jones	7-5	6-1	
S	Billie Jean King	Maria Bueno	3-6	6-4	6-2
Q	Virginia Wade	Judy Tegart Dalton	6-3	6-2	
Q	Ann Haydon Jones	Peaches Bartkowicz	10-8	6-3	
Q	Maria Bueno	Margaret Smith Court	7-5	2-6	6-3
Q	Billie Jean King	Maryna Godwin	6-3	3-6	6-3
1968 – amateur					
F	**Margaret Smith Court**	**Maria Bueno**	**6-2**	**6-2**	
S	Maria Bueno	Virginia Wade	4-6	7-5	6-2
S	Margaret Smith Court	Cecilia Martinez	6-3	6-4	
Q	Maria Bueno	Mary Ann Eisel	9-7	6-2	
Q	Virginia Wade	Kathy Harter	6-3	6-3	
Q	Cecilia Martinez	Linda Tuero	6-2	8-6	
Q	Margaret Smith Court	Victoria Rogers	6-1	6-2	
1969					
F	**Margaret Smith Court**	**Nancy Richey**	**6-2**	**6-2**	
S	Nancy Richey	Rosie Casals	7-5	6-3	
S	Margaret Smith Court	Virginia Wade	7-5	6-0	
Q	Rosie Casals	Peaches Bartkowicz	6-2	6-2	
Q	Nancy Richey	Billie Jean King	6-4	8-6	
Q	Virginia Wade	Julie Heldman	6-4	6-3	
Q	Margaret Smith Court	Karen Krantzcke	6-0	9-7	

Rd	Winner	Defeated	S1	S2	S3
1969 – amateur					
F	**Margaret Smith Court**	**Virginia Wade**	**4-6**	**6-3**	**6-0**
S	Virginia Wade	Mary Ann Eisel Curtis	10-8	6-8	6-3
S	Margaret Smith Court	Kerry Melville	6-2	6-2	
Q	Mary Ann Eisel Curtis	Karen Krantzcke	3-6	6-3	6-4
Q	Virginia Wade	Betty Ann Grubb	6-0	6-2	
Q	Kerry Melville	Christine Truman Janes	8-6	7-5	
Q	Margaret Smith Court	Gail Williams	6-1	6-1	
1970					
F	**Margaret Smith Court**	**Rosie Casals**	**6-2**	**2-6**	**6-1**
S	Rosie Casals	Virginia Wade	6-2	6-7(4)	6-2
S	Margaret Smith Court	Nancy Richey	6-1	6-3	
Q	Virginia Wade	Françoise Durr	5-7	6-4	6-0
Q	Rosie Casals	Kerry Melville	6-4	4-6	6-4
Q	Margaret Smith Court	Helen Gourlay Cawley	6-2	6-2	
Q	Nancy Richey	Lesley Hunt	6-4	6-4	
1971					
F	**Billie Jean King**	**Rosie Casals**	**6-4**	**7-6(2)**	
S	Rosie Casals	Kerry Melville	6-4	6-3	
S	Billie Jean King	Chris Evert	6-3	6-2	
Q	Chris Evert	Lesley Hunt	4-6	6-2	6-3
Q	Billie Jean King	Laura DuPont	6-3	7-5	
Q	Kerry Melville	Judy Tegart Dalton	6-3	7-5	
Q	Rosie Casals	Gail Williams	6-4	2-6	6-4
1972					
F	**Billie Jean King**	**Kerry Melville**	**6-3**	**7-5**	
S	Billie Jean King	Margaret Smith Court	6-4	6-4	
S	Kerry Melville	Chris Evert	6-4	6-2	
Q	Billie Jean King	Virginia Wade	6-2	7-5	
Q	Margaret Smith Court	Rosie Casals	6-4	4-6	6-4
Q	Chris Evert	Olga Morozova	3-6	6-3	7-6(1)
Q	Kerry Melville	Pam Teeguarden	6-0	6-2	
1973					
F	**Margaret Smith Court**	**Evonne Goolagong**	**7-6(2)**	**5-7**	**6-2**
S	Evonne Goolagong	Helga Masthoff	6-1	4-6	6-4
S	Margaret Smith Court	Chris Evert	7-5	2-6	6-2
Q	Helga Masthoff	Julie Heldman	6-3	6-3	
Q	Evonne Goolagong	Kerry Melville	6-3	7-5	
Q	Chris Evert	Rosie Casals	6-1	7-5	
Q	Margaret Smith Court	Virginia Wade	7-6	7-6(2)	
1974					
F	**Billie Jean King**	**Evonne Goolagong**	**3-6**	**6-3**	**7-5**
S	Evonne Goolagong	Chris Evert	6-0	6-7(3)	6-3
S	Billie Jean King	Julie Heldman	2-6	6-3	6-1
Q	Julie Heldman	Nancy Richey Gunter	7-5	7-6	
Q	Billie Jean King	Rosie Casals	6-1	7-6	
Q	Evonne Goolagong	Kerry Melville	6-4	7-5	
Q	Chris Evert	Lesley Hunt	7-6(4)	6-3	
1975					
F	**Chris Evert**	**Evonne Goolagong**	**5-7**	**6-4**	**6-2**
S	Evonne Goolagong	Virginia Wade	7-5	6-1	
S	Chris Evert	Martina Navratilova	6-4	6-4	
Q	Evonne Goolagong	Kazuko Sawamatsu	7-6	7-5	
Q	Virginia Wade	Katja Ebbinghaus	6-3	6-0	
Q	Martina Navratilova	Margaret Smith Court	6-2	6-4	
Q	Chris Evert	Kerry Melville Reid	6-2	6-1	
1976					
F	**Chris Evert**	**Evonne Goolagong**	**6-3**	**6-0**	
S	Evonne Goolagong	Dianne Balestrat Fromholtz	7-6(5)	6-0	
S	Chris Evert	Mima Jausovec	6-3	6-1	
Q	Mima Jausovec	Virginia Ruzici	6-2	6-1	
Q	Chris Evert	Natasha Chmyreva	6-1	6-2	
Q	Evonne Goolagong	Rosie Casals	6-1	6-2	
Q	Dianne Balestrat Fromholtz	Zenda Liess	6-1	6-3	

Rd	Winner	Defeated	S1	S2	S3
1977					
F	**Chris Evert**	**Wendy Turnbull**	**7-6(3)**	**6-2**	
S	Wendy Turnbull	Martina Navratilova	2-6	7-5	6-4
S	Chris Evert	Betty Stove	6-3	7-5	
Q	Betty Stove	Tracy Austin	6-2	6-2	
Q	Martina Navratilova	Mima Jausovec	6-4	6-1	
Q	Wendy Turnbull	Virginia Wade	6-2	6-1	
Q	Chris Evert	Billie Jean King	6-2	6-0	
1978					
F	**Chris Evert**	**Pam Shriver**	**7-5**	**6-4**	
S	Chris Evert	Wendy Turnbull	6-3	6-0	
S	Pam Shriver	Martina Navratilova	7-6(5)	7-6(3)	
Q	Wendy Turnbull	Kathy May	3-6	7-6	6-3
Q	Chris Evert	Tracy Austin	7-5	6-1	
Q	Pam Shriver	Lesley Hunt	6-2	6-0	
Q	Martina Navratilova	Virginia Ruzici	6-3	6-2	
1979					
F	**Tracy Austin**	**Chris Evert Lloyd**	**6-4**	**6-3**	
S	Tracy Austin	Martina Navratilova	7-5	7-5	
S	Chris Evert Lloyd	Billie Jean King	6-1	6-0	
Q	Billie Jean King	Virginia Wade	6-3	7-6	
Q	Chris Evert Lloyd	Evonne Goolagong	7-5	6-2	
Q	Tracy Austin	Sylvia Hanika	6-1	6-1	
Q	Martina Navratilova	Kerry Melville Reid	6-4	6-1	
1980					
F	**Chris Evert**	**Hana Mandlikova**	**5-7**	**6-1**	**6-1**
S	Hana Mandlikova	Andrea Jaeger	6-1	3-6	7-6
S	Chris Evert Lloyd	Tracy Austin	4-6	6-1	6-1
Q	Hana Mandlikova	Barbara Hallquist	6-2	6-2	
Q	Andrea Jaeger	Ivanna Madruga	6-1	6-3	
Q	Chris Evert Lloyd	Mima Jausovec	7-6	6-2	
Q	Tracy Austin	Pam Shriver	6-2	6-3	
1981					
F	**Tracy Austin**	**Martina Navratilova**	**1-6**	**7-6(4)**	**7-6(1)**
S	Tracy Austin	Barbara Potter	6-1	6-3	
S	Martina Navratilova	Chris Evert	7-5	4-6	6-4
Q	Tracy Austin	Sylvia Hanika	6-4	6-3	
Q	Barbara Potter	Barbara Gerken	7-5	7-5	
Q	Martina Navratilova	Anne Smith	7-5	6-4	
Q	Chris Evert Lloyd	Hana Mandlikova	6-1	6-3	
1982					
F	**Chris Evert Lloyd**	**Hana Mandlikova**	**6-3**	**6-1**	
S	Hana Mandlikova	Pam Shriver	6-4	2-6	6-2
S	Chris Evert Lloyd	Andrea Jaeger	6-1	6-2	
Q	Pam Shriver	Martina Navratilova	1-6	7-6(5)	6-2
Q	Hana Mandlikova	Tracy Austin	4-6	6-4	6-4
Q	Andrea Jaeger	Gretchen Rush	3-6	6-1	6-0
Q	Chris Evert Lloyd	Bonnie Gadusek	4-6	6-1	6-0
1983					
F	**Martina Navratilova**	**Chris Evert Lloyd**	**6-1**	**6-3**	
S	Chris Evert Lloyd	Jo Durie	6-4	6-4	
S	Martina Navratilova	Pam Shriver	6-2	6-1	
Q	Pam Shriver	Andrea Jaeger	7-6	6-3	
Q	Chris Evert Lloyd	Hana Mandlikova	6-4	6-3	
Q	Jo Durie	Ivanna Madruga-Osses	6-2	6-2	
Q	Martina Navratilova	Sylvia Hanika	6-0	6-3	
1984					
F	**Martina Navratilova**	**Chris Evert Lloyd**	**4-6**	**6-4**	**6-4**
S	Chris Evert Lloyd	Carling Bassett	6-2	6-2	
S	Martina Navratilova	Wendy Turnbull	6-4	6-1	
S	Chris Evert Lloyd	Sylvia Hanika	6-2	6-3	
Q	Carling Bassett	Hana Mandlikova	6-4	6-3	
Q	Wendy Turnbull	Pam Shriver	2-6	6-3	6-3
Q	Martina Navratilova	Helena Sukova	6-3	6-3	

Rd	Winner	Defeated	S1	S2	S3
1985					
F	**Hana Mandlikova**	**Martina Navratilova**	7-6(3)	1-6	7-6(2)
S	Hana Mandlikova	Chris Evert Lloyd	4-6	6-2	6-3
S	Martina Navratilova	Steffi Graf	6-2	6-3	
Q	Hana Mandlikova	Helena Sukova	7-6	7-5	
Q	Chris Evert Lloyd	Claudia Kohde Kilsch	6-3	6-3	
Q	Martina Navratilova	Zina Garrison	6-2	6-3	
Q	Steffi Graf	Pam Shriver	7-6(4)	6-7(4)	7-6(4)
1986					
F	**Martina Navratilova**	**Helena Sukova**	6-3	6-2	
S	Helena Sukova	Chris Evert Lloyd	6-2	6-4	
S	Martina Navratilova	Steffi Graf	6-1	6-7(3)	7-6(8)
Q	Chris Evert Lloyd	Manuela Maleeva	6-2	6-3	
Q	Helena Sukova	Wendy Turnbull	6-4	6-0	
Q	Steffi Graf	Bonnie Gadusek	6-3	6-1	
Q	Martina Navratilova	Pam Shriver	6-2	6-4	
1987					
F	**Martina Navratilova**	**Steffi Graf**	7-6(4)	6-1	
S	Martina Navratilova	Helena Sukova	6-2	6-2	
S	Steffi Graf	Lori McNeil	4-6	6-2	6-4
Q	Martina Navratilova	Gabriela Sabatini	7-5	6-3	
Q	Helena Sukova	Claudia Kohde Kilsch	6-1	6-3	
Q	Lori McNeil	Chris Evert	3-6	6-2	6-4
Q	Steffi Graf	Pam Shriver	6-4	6-3	
1988					
F	**Steffi Graf**	**Gabriela Sabatini**	6-3	3-6	6-1
S	Steffi Graf	Chris Evert		(walkover)	
S	Gabriela Sabatini	Zina Garrison	6-4	7-5	
Q	Steffi Graf	Katerina Maleeva	6-3	6-0	
Q	Chris Evert	Manuela Maleeva	3-6	6-4	6-2
Q	Gabriela Sabatini	Larisa Savchenko	4-6	6-4	6-1
Q	Zina Garrison	Martina Navratilova	6-4	6-7(3)	7-5
1989					
F	**Steffi Graf**	**Martina Navratilova**	3-6	7-5	6-1
S	Steffi Graf	Gabriela Sabatini	3-6	6-4	6-2
S	Martina Navratilova	Zina Garrison	7-6(4)	6-2	
Q	Steffi Graf	Helena Sukova	6-1	6-1	
Q	Gabriela Sabatini	Arantxa Sanchez Vicario	3-6	6-4	6-1
Q	Zina Garrison	Chris Evert	7-6(1)	6-2	
Q	Martina Navratilova	Manuela Maleeva	6-0	6-0	
1990					
F	**Gabriela Sabatini**	**Steffi Graf**	6-2	7-6(4)	
S	Steffi Graf	Arantxa Sanchez Vicario	6-1	6-2	
S	Gabriela Sabatini	Mary Joe Fernandez	7-5	5-7	6-3
Q	Steffi Graf	Jana Novotna	6-3	6-1	
Q	Arantxa Sanchez Vicario	Zina Garrison	6-2	6-2	
Q	Gabriela Sabatini	Leila Meskhi	7-6(5)	6-4	
Q	Mary Joe Fernandez	Manuela Maleeva-Fragniere	6-2	2-6	6-1
1991					
F	**Monica Seles**	**Martina Navratilova**	7-6(1)	6-1	
S	Martina Navratilova	Steffi Graf	7-6(2)	6-7(6)	6-4
S	Monica Seles	Jennifer Capriati	6-3	3-6	7-6(3)
Q	Steffi Graf	Conchita Martinez	6-1	6-3	
Q	Martina Navratilova	Arantxa Sanchez Vicario	6-7(6)	7-6(5)	6-2
Q	Jennifer Capriati	Gabriela Sabatini	6-3	7-6(1)	
Q	Monica Seles	Gigi Fernandez	6-1	6-2	
1992					
F	**Monica Seles**	**Arantxa Sanchez Vicario**	6-3	6-3	
S	Monica Seles	Mary Joe Fernandez	6-3	6-2	
S	Arantxa Sanchez Vicario	Manuela Maleeva-Fragniere	6-2	6-1	
Q	Monica Seles	Patricia Hy	6-1	6-2	
Q	Mary Joe Fernandez	Gabriela Sabatini	6-2	1-6	6-4
Q	Manuela Maleeva-Fragniere	Magdalena Maleeva	6-2	5-3	(retired)
Q	Arantxa Sanchez Vicario	Steffi Graf	7-6(5)	6-3	
1993					
F	**Steffi Graf**	**Helena Sukova**	6-3	6-3	
S	Steffi Graf	Manuela Maleeva-Fragniere	4-6	6-1	6-0
S	Helena Sukova	Arantxa Sanchez Vicario	6-7(7)	7-5	6-2
Q	Steffi Graf	Gabriela Sabatini	6-2	5-7	6-1
Q	Manuela Maleeva-Fragniere	Kimiko Date	7-5	7-5	
Q	Helena Sukova	Katerina Maleeva	6-4	6-7(3)	6-3
Q	Arantxa Sanchez Vicario	Natasha Zvereva	3-0		(retired)
1994					
F	**Arantxa Sanchez Vicario**	**Steffi Graf**	1-6	7-6(3)	6-4
S	Steffi Graf	Jana Novotna	6-3	7-5	
S	Arantxa Sanchez Vicario	Gabriela Sabatini	6-1	7-6(6)	
Q	Steffi Graf	Amanda Coetzer	6-0	6-2	
Q	Jana Novotna	Mary Pierce	6-4	6-0	
Q	Gabriela Sabatini	Gigi Fernandez	6-2	7-5	
Q	Arantxa Sanchez Vicario	Kimiko Date	6-3	6-0	
1995					
F	**Steffi Graf**	**Monica Seles**	7-6(6)	0-6	6-3
S	Steffi Graf	Gabriela Sabatini	6-4	7-6(5)	
S	Monica Seles	Conchita Martinez	6-2	6-2	
Q	Steffi Graf	Amy Frazier	6-2	6-3	
Q	Gabriela Sabatini	Mary Joe Fernandez	6-1	6-3	
Q	Conchita Martinez	Brenda Schultz McCarthy	3-6	7-6(3)	6-2
Q	Monica Seles	Jana Novotna	7-6(5)	6-2	
1996					
F	**Steffi Graf**	**Monica Seles**	7-5	6-4	
S	Steffi Graf	Martina Hingis	7-5	6-3	
S	Monica Seles	Conchita Martinez	6-4	6-3	
Q	Steffi Graf	Judith Wiesner	7-5	6-3	
Q	Martina Hingis	Jana Novotna	7-6(1)	6-4	
Q	Conchita Martinez	Linda Wild	7-6(6)	6-0	
Q	Monica Seles	Amanda Coetzer	6-0	6-3	
1997					
F	**Martina Hingis**	**Venus Williams**	6-0	6-4	
S	Martina Hingis	Lindsay Davenport	6-2	6-4	
S	Venus Williams	Irina Spirlea	7-6(5)	4-6	7-6(7)
Q	Martina Hingis	Arantxa Sanchez Vicario	6-3	6-2	
Q	Lindsay Davenport	Jana Novotna	6-2	4-6	7-6(5)
Q	Venus Williams	Sandrine Testud	7-5	7-5	
Q	Irina Spirlea	Monica Seles	6-7(5)	7-6(8)	6-3
1998					
F	**Lindsay Davenport**	**Martina Hingis**	6-3	7-5	
S	Martina Hingis	Jana Novotna	3-6	6-1	6-4
S	Lindsay Davenport	Venus Williams	6-4	6-4	
Q	Martina Hingis	Monica Seles	6-4	6-4	
Q	Jana Novotna	Patty Schnyder	6-2	6-3	
Q	Venus Williams	Arantxa Sanchez Vicario	2-6	6-1	6-1
Q	Lindsay Davenport	Amanda Coetzer	6-0	6-4	
1999					
F	**Serena Williams**	**Martina Hingis**	6-3	7-6(4)	
S	Martina Hingis	Venus Williams	6-1	4-6	6-3
S	Serena Williams	Lindsay Davenport	6-4	1-6	6-4
Q	Martina Hingis	Anke Huber	6-2	6-0	
Q	Venus Williams	Barbara Schett	6-4	6-3	
Q	Serena Williams	Monica Seles	4-6	6-3	6-2
Q	Lindsay Davenport	Mary Pierce	6-2	6-3	7-5
2000					
F	**Venus Wiliams**	**Lindsay Davenport**	6-4	7-5	
S	Venus Williams	Martina Hingis	4-6	6-3	7-5
S	Lindsay Davenport	Elena Dementieva	6-2	7-6(5)	
Q	Martina Hingis	Monica Seles	6-0	7-5	
Q	Venus Wiliams	Nathalie Tauziat	6-4	1-6	6-1
Q	Elena Dementieva	Anke Huber	6-1	3-6	6-3
Q	Lindsay Davenport	Serena Williams	6-4	6-2	

Rd	Winner	Defeated	S1	S2	S3
2001					
F	**Venus Williams**	**Serena Williams**	**6-2**	**6-4**	
S	Serena Williams	Martina Hingis	6-3	6-2	
S	Venus Williams	Jennifer Capriati	6-4	6-2	
Q	Martina Hingis	Daja Bedanova	6-2	6-0	
Q	Serena Williams	Lindsay Davenport	6-3	6-7(7)	7-5
Q	Venus Williams	Kim Clijsters	6-3	6-1	
Q	Jennifer Capriati	Amelie Mauresmo	6-3	6-4	
2002					
F	**Serena Williams**	**Venus Williams**	**6-4**	**6-3**	
S	Serena Williams	Lindsay Davenport	6-3	7-5	
S	Venus Williams	Amelie Mauresmo	6-3	5-7	6-4
Q	Serena Williams	Daniela Hantuchova	6-2	6-2	
Q	Lindsay Davenport	Elena Bovina	3-6	6-0	6-2
Q	Amelie Mauresmo	Jennifer Capriati	4-6	7-6(5)	6-3
Q	Venus Williams	Monica Seles	6-2	6-3	

Men's Doubles

Year	Winner	Defeated	S1	S2	S3	S4	S5
1881	Clarence Clark / Fred Taylor	Alex. Van Rensselaer / Arthur Newbold	6-5	6-4	6-5		
1882	Richard Sears / James Dwight	Crawford Nightingale / George Smith	6-2	6-4	6-4		
1883	Richard Sears / James Dwight	Alex. Van Rensselaer / Arthur Newbold	6-0	6-2	6-2		
1884	Richard Sears / James Dwight	Alex. Van Rensselaer / Walter Berry	6-4	6-1	8-10	6-4	
1885	Richard Sears / Joseph Clark	Henry Slocum / Percy Knapp	6-3	6-0	6-2		
1886	Richard Sears / James Dwight	Howard Taylor / Godfrey Brinley	7-5	5-7	7-5	6-4	
1887	Richard Sears / James Dwight	Howard Taylor / Henry Slocum	6-4	3-6	2-6	6-3	6-3
1888	Oliver Campbell / Valentine Hall	Clarence Hobart / Edward MacMullen	6-4	6-2	6-4		
1889	Henry Slocum / Howard Taylor	Valentine Hall / Oliver Campbell	14-12	10-8	6-4		
1890	Valentine Hall / Clarence Hobart	John Carver / John Ryerson	6-3	4-6	6-2	2-6	6-3
1891	Oliver Campbell / Bob Huntington	Valentine Hall / Clarence Hobart	6-3	6-4	8-6		
1892	Oliver Campbell / Bob Huntington	Valentine Hall / Edward Hall	6-4	6-2	4-6	6-3	
1893	Clarence Hobart / Fred Hovey	Oliver Campbell / Bob Huntington	6-4	6-4	4-6	6-2	
1894	Clarence Hobart / Fred Hovey	Carr Neel / Sam Neel	6-3	8-6	6-1		
1895	Malcolm Chace / Robert Wrenn	Clarence Hobart / Fred Hovey	7-5	6-1	8-6		
1896	Carr Neel / Sam Neel	Robert Wrenn / Malcolm Chace	6-3	1-6	6-1	3-6	6-1
1897	Leo Ware / George Sheldon	Harold Mahony / Harold Nisbet	11-13	6-2	9-7	1-6	6-1
1898	Leo Ware / George Sheldon	Holcombe Ward / Dwight Davis	1-6	7-5	6-4	4-6	7-5
1899	Holcombe Ward / Dwight Davis	Leo Ware / George Sheldon	6-4	6-4	6-3		

Year	Winner	Defeated	S1	S2	S3	S4	S5
1900	Holcombe Ward / Dwight Davis	Fred Alexander / Ray Little	6-4	9-7	12-10		
1901	Holcombe Ward / Dwight Davis	Leo Ware / Beals Wright	6-3	9-7	6-1		
1902	Reggie Doherty / Laurie Doherty	Holcombe Ward / Dwight Davis	11-9	12-10	6-4		
1903	Reggie Doherty / Laurie Doherty	Kreigh Collins / Harry Waidner	7-5	6-3	6-3		
1904	Holcombe Ward / Beals Wright	Kreigh Collins / Ray Little	1-6	6-2	3-6	6-4	6-1
1905	Holcombe Ward / Beals Wright	Fred Alexander / Harold Hackett	6-2	6-1	6-3		
1906	Holcombe Ward / Beals Wright	Fred Alexander / Harold Hackett	6-3	3-6	6-3	6-3	
1907	Fred Alexander / Harold Hackett	Nat Thornton / Wylie Grant	6-2	6-1	6-1		
1908	Fred Alexander / Harold Hackett	Ray Little / Beals Wright	6-1	7-5	6-2		
1909	Fred Alexander / Harold Hackett	Maurice McLoughlin / George Janes	6-4	6-4	6-0		
1910	Fred Alexander / Harold Hackett	Tom Bundy / Trowbridge Hendrick	6-1	8-6	6-3		
1911	Ray Little / Gus Touchard	Fred Alexander / Harold Hackett	7-5	13-15	6-2	6-4	
1912	Maurice McLoughlin / Tom Bundy	Ray Little / Gus Touchard	3-6	6-2	6-1	7-5	
1913	Maurice McLoughlin / Tom Bundy	John Strachan / Clarence Griffin	6-4	7-5	6-1		
1914	Maurice McLoughlin / Tom Bundy	George Church / Dean Mathey	6-4	6-2	6-4		
1915	Bill Johnston / Clarence Griffin	Maurice McLoughlin / Tom Bundy	2-6	6-3	6-4	3-6	6-3
1916	Bill Johnston / Clarence Griffin	Maurice McLoughlin / Ward Dawson	6-4	6-3	5-7	6-3	
1917	Fred Alexander / Harold Throckmorton	Harry Johnson / Irving Wright	11-9	6-4	6-4		
1918	Bill Tilden / Vinnie Richards	Fred Alexander / Beals Wright	6-3	6-4	3-6	2-6	6-2
1919	Norman Brookes / Gerald Patterson	Bill Tilden / Vinnie Richards	8-6	6-3	4-6	4-6	6-2
1920	Bill Johnston / Clarence Griffin	Willis Davis / Roland Roberts	6-2	6-2	6-3		
1921	Bill Tilden / Vinnie Richards	Dick Williams / Watson Washburn	13-11	12-10	6-1		
1922	Bill Tilden / Vinnie Richards	Gerald Patterson / Pat O'Hara Wood	4-6	6-1	6-3	6-4	
1923	Bill Tilden / Brian Norton	Dick Williams / Watson Washburn	3-6	6-2	6-3	5-7	6-2
1924	Howard Kinsey / Robert Kinsey	Gerald Patterson / Pat O'Hara Wood	7-5	5-7	7-9	6-3	6-4
1925	Dick Williams / Vinnie Richards	Gerald Patterson / Jack Hawkes	6-2	8-10	6-4	11-9	
1926	Dick Williams / Vinnie Richards	Bill Tilden / Al Chapin	6-4	6-8	11-9	6-3	
1927	Bill Tilden / Frank Hunter	Bill Johnston / Dick Williams	10-8	6-3	6-3		

Year	Winner	Defeated	S1	S2	S3	S4	S5
1928	George Lott / John Hennessey	Gerald Patterson / Jack Hawkes	6-2	6-1	6-2		
1929	George Lott / Johnny Doeg	Berkeley Bell / Lewis White	10-8	16-14	6-1		
1930	George Lott / Johnny Doeg	John Van Ryn / Wilmer Allison	8-6	6-3	4-6	13-15	6-4
1931	Wilmer Allison / John Van Ryn	Greg Mangin / Berkeley Bell	6-4	8-6	6-3		
1932	Ellsworth Vines / Keith Gledhill	Wilmer Allison / John Van Ryn	6-4	6-3	6-2		
1933	George Lott / Lester Stoefen	Frank Shields / Frank Parker	11-13	9-7	9-7	6-3	
1934	George Lott / Lester Stoefen	Wilmer Allison / John Van Ryn	6-4	9-7	3-6	6-4	
1935	Wilmer Allison / John Van Ryn	Don Budge / Gene Mako	6-4	6-2	3-6	2-6	6-1
1936	Don Budge / Gene Mako	Wilmer Allison / John Van Ryn	6-4	6-2	6-4		
1937	Gottfried von Cramm / Henner Henkel	Don Budge / Gene Mako	6-4	7-5	6-4		
1938	Don Budge / Gene Mako	Adrian Quist / John Bromwich	6-3	6-2	6-1		
1939	Adrian Quist / John Bromwich	Jack Crawford / Harry Hopman	8-6	6-1	6-4		
1940	Jack Kramer / Ted Schroeder	Gardnar Mulloy / Henry Prusoff	6-4	8-6	9-7		
1941	Jack Kramer / Ted Schroeder	Wayne Sabin / Gardnar Mulloy	9-7	6-4	6-2		
1942	Gardnar Mulloy / Bill Talbert	Ted Schroeder / Sidney Wood	9-7	7-5	6-1		
1943	Jack Kramer / Frank Parker	Bill Talbert / David Freeman	6-2	6-4	6-4		
1944	Don McNeill / Bob Falkenburg	Bill Talbert / Pancho Segura	7-5	6-4	3-6	6-1	
1945	Gardnar Mulloy / Bill Talbert	Bob Falkenburg / Jack Tuero	12-10	8-10	12-10	6-2	
1946	Gardnar Mulloy / Bill Talbert	Don McNeill / Frank Guernsey	3-6	6-4	2-6	6-3	20-18
1947	Jack Kramer / Ted Schroeder	Bill Talbert / Bill Sidwell	6-4	7-5	6-3		
1948	Gardnar Mulloy / Bill Talbert	Frank Parker / Ted Schroeder	1-6	9-7	6-3	3-6	9-7
1949	John Bromwich / Bill Sidwell	Frank Sedgman / George Worthington	6-4	6-0	6-1		
1950	John Bromwich / Frank Sedgman	Bill Talbert / Gardnar Mulloy	7-5	8-6	3-6	6-1	
1951	Ken McGregor / Frank Sedgman	Don Candy / Merv Rose	10-8	6-4	4-6	7-5	
1952	Merv Rose / Vic Seixas	Ken McGregor / Frank Sedgman	3-6	10-8	10-8	6-8	8-6
1953	Rex Hartwig / Merv Rose	Gardnar Mulloy / Bill Talbert	6-4	4-6	6-2	6-4	
1954	Vic Seixas / Tony Trabert	Lew Hoad / Ken Rosewall	3-6	6-4	8-6	6-3	
1955	Kosei Kamo / Atsushi Miyagi	Gerald Moss / Bill Quillian	6-2	6-3	3-6	1-6	6-4
1956	Lew Hoad / Ken Rosewall	Hamilton Richardson / Vic Seixas	6-2	6-2	3-6	6-4	
1957	Ashley Cooper / Neale Fraser	Gardnar Mulloy / Budge Patty	4-6	6-3	9-7	6-3	
1958	Alex Olmedo / Hamilton Richardson	Sammy Giammalva / Barry MacKay	3-6	6-3	6-4	6-4	
1959	Neale Fraser / Roy Emerson	Alex Olmedo / Butch Buchholz	3-6	6-3	5-7	6-4	7-5
1960	Neale Fraser / Roy Emerson	Rod Laver / Bob Mark	9-7	6-2	6-4		
1961	Chuck McKinley / Dennis Ralston	Rafael Osuna / Antonio Palafox	6-3	6-4	2-6	13-11	
1962	Rafael Osuna / Antonio Palafox	Chuck McKinley / Dennis Ralston	6-4	10-12	1-6	9-7	6-3
1963	Chuck McKinley / Dennis Ralston	Rafael Osuna / Antonio Palafox	9-7	4-6	5-7	6-3	11-9
1964	Chuck McKinley / Dennis Ralston	Graham Stilwell / Mike Sangster	6-3	6-2	6-4		
1965	Roy Emerson / Fred Stolle	Frank Froehling III / Charlie Pasarell	6-4	10-12	7-5	6-3	
1966	Roy Emerson / Fred Stolle	Clark Graebner / Dennis Ralston	6-4	6-4	6-4		
1967	John Newcombe / Tony Roche	Bill Bowrey / Owen Davidson	6-8	9-7	6-3	6-3	
1968*	Bob Lutz / Stan Smith	Bob Hewitt / Raymond Moore	6-4	6-4	9-7		
1968	Bob Lutz / Stan Smith	Arthur Ashe / Andres Gimeno	11-9	6-1	7-5		
1969*	Dick Crealy / Allan Stone	Bill Bowrey / Charlie Pasarell	9-11	6-3	7-5		
1969	Ken Rosewall / Fred Stolle	Charlie Pasarell / Dennis Ralston	2-6	7-5	13-11	6-3	
1970	Pierre Barthes / Nikki Pilic	Roy Emerson / Rod Laver	6-3	7-6(4)	4-6	7-6(2)	
1971†	John Newcombe / Roger Taylor	Stan Smith / Erik van Dillen	6-7	6-3	7-6(4)	4-6	5-3
1972	Cliff Drysdale / Roger Taylor	Owen Davidson / John Newcombe	6-4	7-6(3)	6-3		
1973	Owen Davidson / John Newcombe	Rod Laver / Ken Rosewall	7-5	2-6	7-5	7-5	
1974	Bob Lutz / Stan Smith	Patricio Cornejo / Jaime Fillol	6-3	6-3			
1975	Jimmy Connors / Ilie Nastase	Tom Okker / Marty Riessen	6-4	7-6			
1976	Tom Okker / Marty Riessen	Paul Kronk / Cliff Letcher	6-4	6-4			
1977	Bob Hewitt / Frew McMillan	Brian Gottfried / Raul Ramirez	6-4	6-0			
1978	Bob Lutz / Stan Smith	Marty Riessen / Sherwood Stewart	1-6	7-5	6-3		
1979	John McEnroe / Peter Fleming	Bob Lutz / Stan Smith	6-2	6-4			

*   Denotes amateur tournament. In 1968 and 1969 the USTA conducted both Amateur and Open Championships. Thereafter there was only the Open as principal championships.

Year	Winner	Defeated	S1	S2	S3	S4	S5
1980	Bob Lutz / Stan Smith	Peter Fleming / John McEnroe	7-5	3-6	6-1	3-6	6-3
1981	Peter Fleming / John McEnroe	Heinz Gunthardt / Peter McNamara	(walkover)				
1982	Kevin Curren / Steve Denton	Victor Amaya / Hank Pfister	6-2	6-7(4)	5-7	6-2	6-4
1983	Peter Fleming / John McEnroe	Fritz Buehning / Van Winitsky	6-3	6-4	6-2		
1984	John Fitzgerald / Tomas Smid	Stefan Edberg / Anders Jarryd	7-6	6-3	6-3		
1985	Ken Flach / Robert Seguso	Henri Leconte / Yannick Noah	6-7(5)	7-6(1)	7-6(6)	6-0	
1986	Andres Gomez / Slobodan Zivojinovic	Joakim Nystrom / Mats Wilander	4-6	6-3	6-3	4-6	6-3
1987	Stefan Edberg / Anders Jarryd	Ken Flach / Robert Seguso	7-6(1)	6-2	4-6	5-7	7-6(2)
1988	Sergio Casal / Emilio Sanchez	Rick Leach / Jim Pugh	(walkover)				
1989	John McEnroe / Mark Woodforde	Ken Flach / Robert Seguso	6-4	4-6	6-3	6-3	
1990	Pieter Aldrich / Danie Visser	Paul Annacone / David Wheaton	6-2	7-6(3)	6-2		
1991	John Fitzgerald / Anders Jarryd	Scott Davis / David Pate	6-3	3-6	6-3	6-3	
1992	Jim Grabb / Richey Reneberg	Kelly Jones / Rick Leach	3-6	7-6(2)	6-3	6-3	
1993	Ken Flach / Rick Leach	Martin Damm / Karel Novacek	6-7(3)	6-4	6-2		
1994	Jacco Eltingh / Paul Haarhuis	Todd Woodbridge / Mark Woodforde	6-3	7-6(1)			
1995	Todd Woodbridge / Mark Woodforde	Alex O'Brien / Sandon Stolle	6-3	6-3			
1996	Todd Woodbridge / Mark Woodforde	Paul Haarhuis / Jacco Eltingh	4-6	7-6(5)	7-6(2)		
1997	Yevgeny Kafelnikov / Daniel Vacek	Jonas Bjorkman / Nicklas Kulti	7-6(8)	6-3			
1998	Sandon Stolle / Cyril Suk	Mark Knowles / Daniel Nestor	4-6	7-6	6-2		
1999	Sebastien Lareau / Alex O'Brien	Mahesh Bhupathi / Leander Paes	7-6(7)	6-4			
2000	Lleyton Hewitt / Max Mirnyi	Rick Leach / Ellis Ferreira	6-4	5-7	7-6		
2001	Wayne Black / Kevin Ullyett	Donald Johnson / Jared Palmer	7-6	2-6	6-3		
2002	Max Mirnyi / Mahesh Bhupathi	Jiri Novak / Radek Stepanek	6-3	3-6	6-4		

Women's Doubles

Year	Winner	Defeated	S1	S2	S3	S4	S5
1889	Margarette Ballard / Bertha Townsend	Marion Wright / Laura Knight	6-0	6-2			
1890	Ellen Roosevelt / Grace Roosevelt	Bertha Townsend / Margarette Ballard	6-1	6-2			
1891	Mabel Cahill / Emma Leavitt Morgan	Grace Roosevelt / Ellen Roosevelt	2-6	8-6	6-4		

Year	Winner	Defeated	S1	S2	S3	S4	S5
1892	Mabel Cahill / Adeline McKinlay	Helen Day Harris / Amy Williams	6-1	6-3			
1893	Aline Terry / Harriet Butler	Augusta Schultz / Ms Stone	6-4	6-3			
1894	Helen Hellwig / Juliette Atkinson	Annabella Wistar / Amy Williams	6-4	8-6	6-2		
1895	Helen Hellwig / Juliette Atkinson	Elisabeth Moore / Amy Williams	6-2	6-2	12-10		
1896	Elisabeth Moore / Juliette Atkinson	Annabella Wistar / Amy Williams	6-3	9-7			
1897	Juliette Atkinson / Kathleen Atkinson	Mrs. Frank Edwards / Elizabeth Rastall	6-2	6-1	6-1		
1898	Juliette Atkinson / Kathleen Atkinson	Marie Wimer / Carrie Neely	6-1	2-6	4-6	6-1	6-2
1899	Jane Craven / Myrtle McAteer	Maud Banks / Elizabeth Rastall	6-1	6-1	7-5		
1900	Edith Parker / Hallie Champlin	Marie Wimer / Myrtle McAteer	9-7	6-2	6-2		
1901	Juliette Atkinson / Myrtle McAteer	Marion Jones / Elisabeth Moore	default				

USLTA adopts 3-set format

Year	Winner	Defeated	S1	S2	S3
1902	Juliette Atkinson / Marion Jones	Maud Banks / Nona Closterman	6-2	7-5	
1903	Elisabeth Moore / Carrie Neely	Miriam Hall / Marion Jones	4-6	6-1	6-1
1904	May Sutton / Miriam Hall	Elisabeth Moore / Carrie Neely	3-6	6-3	6-3
1905	Helen Homans / Carrie Neely	Marjorie Oberteuffer / Virginia Maule	6-0	6-1	
1906	Ann Burdette Coe / Ethel Bliss Platt	Helen Homans / Clover Boldt	6-4	6-4	
1907	Marie Wimer / Carrie Neely	Edna Wildey / Natalie Wildey	6-1	2-6	6-4
1908	Evelyn Sears / Margaret Curtis	Carrie Neely / Marion Steever	6-3	5-7	9-7
1909	Hazel Hotchkiss / Edith Rotch	Dorothy Green / Lois Moyes	6-1	6-1	
1910	Hazel Hotchkiss / Edith Rotch	Adelaide Browning / Edna Wildey	6-4	6-4	
1911	Hazel Hotchkiss / Eleonora Sears	Dorothy Green / Florence Sutton	6-4	4-6	6-2
1912	Dorothy Green / Mary K. Browne	Maud Barger Wallach / Mrs. Frederick Schmitz	6-2	5-7	6-0
1913	Mary K. Browne / Louise Riddell Williams	Dorothy Green / Edna Wildey	12-10	2-6	6-3
1914	Mary K. Browne / Louise Riddell Williams	Louise Hammond Raymond / Edna Wildey	8-6	6-2	
1915	Hazel Hotchkiss Wightman / Eleonora Sears	Helen Homans McLean / Mrs. George L. Chapman	10-8	6-2	
1916	Molla Bjurstedt / Eleonora Sears	Louise Hammond Raymond / Edna Wildey	4-6	6-2	10-8
1917	Molla Bjurstedt / Eleonora Sears	Phyllis Walsh / Grace Moore LeRoy	6-2	6-4	

Year	Winner	Defeated	S1	S2	S3	Year	Winner	Defeated	S1	S2	S3
1918	Marion Zinderstein Eleanor Goss	Molla Bjurstedt Mrs. Johan Rogge	7-5	8-6		1946	Louise Brough Margaret Osborne	Pat Canning Todd Mary Arnold Prentiss	6-1	6-3	
1919	Marion Zinderstein Eleanor Goss	Eleonora Sears Hazel Hotchkiss Wightman	10-8	9-7		1947	Louise Brough Margaret Osborne	Pat Canning Todd Doris Hart	5-7	6-3	7-5
1920	Marion Zinderstein Eleanor Goss	Eleanor Tennant Helen Baker	13-11	4-6	6-3	1948	Louise Brough Margaret Osborne duPont	Pat Canning Todd Doris Hart	6-4	8-10	6-1
1921	Mary K. Browne Louise Riddell Williams	Helen Gilleaudeau Aletta Bailey Morris	6-3	6-2		1949	Louise Brough Margaret Osborne duPont	Doris Hart Shirley Fry	6-4	10-8	
1922	Marion Zinderstein Jessup Helen Wills	Edith Sigourney Molla Bjurstedt Mallory	6-4	7-9	6-3	1950	Louise Brough Margaret Osborne duPont	Doris Hart Shirley Fry	6-2	6-3	
1923	Kitty McKane Phyllis Howkins Covell	Hazel Hotchkiss Wightman Eleanor Goss	2-6	6-2	6-1	1951	Shirley Fry Doris Hart	Nancy Chaffee Pat Canning Todd	6-4	6-2	
1924	Hazel Hotchkiss Wightman Helen Wills	Eleanor Goss Marion Zinderstein Jessup	6-4	6-3		1952	Shirley Fry Doris Hart	Louise Brough Maureen Connolly	10-8	6-4	
1925	Mary K. Browne Helen Wills	May Sutton Bundy Elizabeth Ryan	6-4	6-3		1953	Shirley Fry Doris Hart	Louise Brough Margaret Osborne duPont	6-2	7-9	9-7
1926	Elizabeth Ryan Eleanor Goss	Mary K. Browne Charlotte Hosmer Chapin	3-6	6-4	12-10	1954	Shirley Fry Doris Hart	Louise Brough Margaret Osborne duPont	6-4	6-4	
1927	Kitty McKane Godfree Ermyntrude Harvey	Betty Nuthall Joan Fry	6-1	4-6	6-4	1955	Louise Brough Margaret Osborne duPont	Doris Hart Shirley Fry	6-3	1-6	6-3
1928	Hazel Hotchkiss Wightman Helen Wills	Edith Cross Anna McCune Harper	6-2	6-2		1956	Louise Brough Margaret Osborne duPont	Betty Rosenquest Pratt Shirley Fry	6-3	6-0	
1929	Phoebe Holcroft Watson Peggy Michell	Phyllis Howkins Covell Dorothy Shepherd Barron	2-6	6-3	6-4	1957	Louise Brough Margaret Osborne duPont	Althea Gibson Darlene Hard	6-2	7-5	
1930	Betty Nuthall Sarah Palfrey	Edith Cross Anna McCune Harper	3-6	6-3	7-5	1958	Jeanne Arth Darlene Hard	Althea Gibson Maria Bueno	2-6	6-3	6-4
1931	Betty Nuthall Eileen Bennett Whittingstall	Helen Jacobs Dorothy Round	6-2	6-4		1959	Jeanne Arth Darlene Hard	Maria Bueno Sally Moore	6-2	6-3	
1932	Helen Jacobs Sarah Palfrey	Marjorie Morrill Painter Alice Marble	8-6	6-1		1960	Maria Bueno Darlene Hard	Ann Haydon Deidre Catt	6-1	6-1	
1933	Betty Nuthall Freda James	Helen Wills Moody Elizabeth Ryan	(default)			1961	Darlene Hard Lesley Turner	Edda Buding Yola Ramirez	6-4	5-7	6-0
1934	Helen Jacobs Sarah Palfrey	Carolin Babcock Dorothy Andrus	4-6	6-3	6-4	1962	Darlene Hard Maria Bueno	Karen Hantze Susman Billie Jean Moffitt	4-6	6-3	6-2
1935	Helen Jacobs Sarah Palfrey Fabyan	Carolin Babcock Dorothy Andrus	6-4	6-2		1963	Robyn Ebbern Margaret Smith	Darlene Hard Maria Bueno	4-6	10-8	6-3
1936	Marjorie Gladman Van Ryn Carolin Babcock	Helen Jacobs Sarah Palfrey Fabyan	9-7	2-6	6-4	1964	Billie Jean Moffitt Karen Hantze Susman	Margaret Smith Lesley Turner	3-6	6-2	6-4
1937	Sarah Palfrey Fabyan Alice Marble	Marjorie Gladman Van Ryn Carolin Babcock	7-5	6-4		1965	Carole Caldwell Graebner Nancy Richey	Billie Jean Moffitt Karen Hantze Susman	6-4	6-4	
1938	Sarah Palfrey Fabyan Alice Marble	Simone Passemard Mathieu Jadwiga Jedrzejowska	6-8	6-4	6-3	1966	Maria Bueno Nancy Richey	Billie Jean King Rosie Casals	6-3	6-4	
1939	Sarah Palfrey Fabyan Alice Marble	Kay Stammers Freda James Hammersley	7-5	8-6		1967	Rosie Casals Billie Jean King	Mary Ann Eisel Donna Floyd Fales	4-6	6-3	6-4
1940	Sarah Palfrey Fabyan Alice Marble	Dorothy Bundy Marjorie Gladman Van Ryn	6-4	6-3		1968*	Maria Bueno Margaret Smith Court	Virginia Wade Joyce Barclay Williams	6-3	7-5	
1941	Sarah Palfrey Fabyan Cooke Margaret Osborne	Dorothy Bundy Pauline Betz	3-6	6-1	6-4	1968	Maria Bueno Margaret Smith Court	Billie Jean King Rosie Casals	4-6	9-7	8-6
1942	Louise Brough Margaret Osborne	Pauline Betz Doris Hart	2-6	7-5	6-0	1969*	Virginia Wade Margaret Smith Court	Mary Ann Eisel Curtis Valerie Ziegenfuss	6-1	6-3	
1943	Louise Brough Margaret Osborne	Pauline Betz Doris Hart	6-4	6-3		1969	Françoise Durr Darlene Hard	Margaret Smith Court Virginia Wade	0-6	6-4	6-4
1944	Louise Brough Margaret Osborne	Pauline Betz Doris Hart	4-6	6-4	6-3	1970	Margaret Smith Court Judy Tegart Dalton	Rosie Casals Virginia Wade	6-3	6-4	
1945	Louise Brough Margaret Osborne	Pauline Betz Doris Hart	6-3	6-3							

* Denotes amateur tournament. In 1968 and 1969 the USTA conducted both Amateur and Open Championships. Thereafter there was only the Open as principal championships.

Year	Winner	Defeated	S1	S2	S3
1971	Rosie Casals Judy Tegart Dalton	Gail Sherriff Chanfreau Françoise Durr	6-3	6-3	
1972	Françoise Durr Betty Stove	Margaret Smith Court Virginia Wade	6-3	1-6	6-3
1973	Margaret Smith Court Virginia Wade	Billie Jean King Rosie Casals	3-6	6-3	7-5
1974	Rosie Casals Billie Jean King	Françoise Durr Betty Stove	7-6(4)	6-7 (2)	6-4
1975	Margaret Smith Court Virginia Wade	Billie Jean King Rosie Casals	7-5	2-6	7-6(5)
1976	Delina Boshoff Ilana Kloss	Olga Morozova Virginia Wade	6-1	6-4	
1977	Martina Navratilova Betty Stove	Renee Richards Betty Ann Grubb Stuart	6-1	7-6	
1978	Billie Jean King Martina Navratilova	Kerry Melville Reid Wendy Turnbull	7-6(7)	6-4	
1979	Betty Stove Wendy Turnbull	Billie Jean King Martina Navratilova	7-5	6-3	
1980	Billie Jean King Martina Navratilova	Pam Shriver Betty Stove	7-6(2)	7-5	
1981	Anne Smith Kathy Jordan	Rosie Casals Wendy Turnbull	6-3	6-3	
1982	Rosie Casals Wendy Turnbull	Sharon Walsh Barbara Potter	6-4	6-4	
1983	Pam Shriver Martina Navratilova	Rosalyn Fairbank Candy Reynolds	6-7(4)	6-1	6-3
1984	Pam Shriver Martina Navratilova	Anne Hobbs Wendy Turnbull	6-2	6-4	
1985	Claudia Kohde Kilsch Helena Sukova	Martina Navratilova Pam Shriver	6-7	6-2	6-3
1986	Martina Navratilova Pam Shriver	Hana Mandlikova Wendy Turnbull	6-4	3-6	6-3
1987	Martina Navratilova Pam Shriver	Kathy Jordan Elizabeth Sayers Smylie	5-7	6-4	6-2
1988	Gigi Fernandez Robin White	Patty Fendick Jill Hetherington	6-4	6-1	
1989	Hana Mandlikova Martina Navratilova	Mary Joe Fernandez Pam Shriver	5-7	6-4	6-4
1990	Gigi Fernandez Martina Navratilova	Jana Novotna Helena Sukova	6-2	6-4	
1991	Pam Shriver Natalia Zvereva	Jana Novotna Larisa Savchenko	6-4	4-6	7-6(5)
1992	Gigi Fernandez Natalia Zvereva	Jana Novotna Larisa Savchenko Neiland	7-6(4)	6-1	
1993	Arantxa Sanchez Vicario Helena Sukova	Amanda Coetzer Ines Gorrochategui	6-4	6-2	
1994	Arantxa Sanchez Vicario Jana Novotna	Katerina Maleeva Robin White	6-3	6-3	
1995	Gigi Fernandez Natalia Zvereva	Brenda Schultz-McCarthy Rennae Stubbs	7-5	6-3	
1996	Natalia Zvereva Gigi Fernandez	Jana Novotna Arantxa Sanchez Vicario	1-6	6-1	6-4
1997	Jana Novotna Lindsay Davenport	Gigi Fernandez Natasha Zvereva	6-3	6-4	
1998	Martina Hingis Jana Novotna	Lindsay Davenport Natasha Zvereva	6-3	6-3	

Year	Winner	Defeated	S1	S2	S3
1999	Serena Williams Venus Williams	Chanda Rubin Sandrine Testud	4-6	6-1	6-4
2000	Julie Halard-Decugis Ai Sugiyama	Cara Black Elena Likhovtseva	6-0	1-6	6-1
2001	Rennae Stubbs Lisa Raymond	Kimberly Po-Messerli Nathalie Tauziat	6-2	5-7	7-5
2002	Paola Suarez Virginia Ruano Pascual	Elena Dementieva Janette Husarova	6-2	6-1	

Mixed Doubles

Year	Winner	Defeated	S1	S2	S3	S4	S5
1892	Mabel Cahill Clarence Hobart	Elisabeth Moore Rod Beach	5-7	6-1	6-4		
1893	Ellen Roosevelt Clarence Hobart	Ethel Bankson Robert Willson Jr.	6-1	4-6	10-8	6-1	
1894	Juliette Atkinson Edwin Fischer	Mrs. McFadden Gustav Remack Jr.	6-3	6-2	6-1		
1895	Juliette Atkinson Edwin Fischer	Amy Williams Mantle Fielding	4-6	8-6	6-2		
1896	Juliette Atkinson Edwin Fischer	Amy Williams Mantle Fielding	6-2	6-3	6-3		
1897	Laura Henson D. L. Magruder	Maud Banks B. L. C. Griffiths	6-4	6-3	7-5		
1898	Carrie Neely Edwin Fischer	Helen Chapman J. A. Hill	6-2	6-4	8-6		
1899	Elizabeth Rastall Albert Hoskins	Jennie Craven James Gardner	6-4	6-0			(default)
1900	Margaret Hunnewell Alfred Codman	T. Shaw George Atkinson	11-9	6-3	6-1		
1901	Marion Jones Ray Little	Myrtle McAteer Clyde Stevens	6-4	6-4	7-5		

USLTA adopts 3-set format

Year	Winner	Defeated	S1	S2	S3
1902	Elisabeth Moore Wylie Grant	Elizabeth Rastall Albert Hoskins	6-2	6-1	
1903	Helen Chapman Harry Allen	Carrie Neely W. H. Rowland	6-4	7-5	
1904	Elisabeth Moore Wylie Grant	May Sutton Trevanion Dallas	6-2	6-1	
1905	Augusta Schultz Hobart Clarence Hobart	Elisabeth Moore Edward Dewhurst	6-2	6-4	
1906	Sarah Coffin Edward Dewhurst	Margaret Johnson Wallace Johnson	6-3	7-5	
1907	May Sayers Wallace Johnson	Natalie Wildey Herbert Morris Tilden	6-1	7-5	
1908	Edith Rotch Nathaniel Niles	Louise Hammond Ray Little	6-4	4-6	6-4
1909	Hazel Hotchkiss Wallace Johnson	Louise Hammond Ray Little	6-2	6-0	
1910	Hazel Hotchkiss Joseph Carpenter Jr.	Edna Wildey Herbert Morris Tilden	6-2	6-2	
1911	Hazel Hotchkiss Wallace Johnson	Edna Wildey Herbert Morris Tilden	6-4	6-4	

Year	Winner	Defeated	S1	S2	S3
1912	Mary K. Browne / Dick Williams	Eleonora Sears / Bill Clothier	6-4	2-6	11-9
1913	Mary K. Browne / Bill Tilden	Dorothy Green / C. S. Rogers	7-5	7-5	
1914	Mary K. Browne / Bill Tilden	Margarette Myers / J. R. Rowland	6-1	6-4	

Year	Winner	Defeated	S1	S2	S3
1915	Hazel Hotchkiss Wightman / Harry Johnson	Molla Bjurstedt / Irving Wright	6-0	6-1	
1916	Eleonora Sears / Willis Davis	Florence Ballin / Bill Tilden	6-4	7-5	
1917	Molla Bjurstedt / Irving Wright	Florence Ballin / Bill Tilden	10-12	6-1	6-3
1918	Hazel Hotchkiss Wightman / Irving Wright	Molla Bjurstedt / Fred Alexander	6-2	6-4	
1919	Marion Zinderstein / Vinnie Richards	Florence Ballin / Bill Tilden	2-6	11-9	6-2
1920	Hazel Hotchkiss Wightman / Wallace Johnson	Molla Bjurstedt Mallory / Craig Biddle	6-4	6-3	
1921	Mary K. Browne / Bill Johnston	Molla Bjurstedt Mallory / Bill Tilden	3-6	6-4	6-3
1922	Molla Bjurstedt Mallory / Bill Tilden	Helen Wills / Howard Kinsey	6-4	6-3	
1923	Molla Bjurstedt Mallory / Bill Tilden	Kitty McKane / Jack Hawkes	6-3	2-6	10-8
1924	Helen Wills / Vinnie Richards	Molla Bjurstedt Mallory / Bill Tilden	6-8	7-5	6-0
1925	Kitty McKane / Jack Hawkes	Ermyntrude Harvey / Vinnie Richards	6-2	6-4	
1926	Elizabeth Ryan / Jean Borotra	Hazel Hotchkiss Wightman / René Lacoste	6-4	7-5	
1927	Eileen Bennett / Henri Cochet	Hazel Hotchkiss Wightman / René Lacoste	6-2	0-6	6-2
1928	Helen Wills / Jack Hawkes	Edith Cross / Gar Moon	6-1	6-3	
1929	Betty Nuthall / George Lott	Phyllis Howkins Covell / Bunny Austin	6-3	6-3	
1930	Edith Cross / Wilmer Allison	Marjorie Morrill / Frank Shields	6-4	6-4	
1931	Betty Nuthall / George Lott	Anna McCune Harper / Wilmer Allison	6-3	6-3	
1932	Sarah Palfrey / Fred Perry	Helen Jacobs / Ellsworth Vines	6-3	7-5	
1933	Elizabeth Ryan / Ellsworth Vines	Sarah Palfrey / George Lott	11-9	6-1	
1934	Helen Jacobs / George Lott	Elizabeth Ryan / Lester Stoefen	4-6	13-11	6-2
1935	Sarah Palfrey Fabyan / Enrique Maier	Kay Stammers / Roderich Menzel	6-3	3-6	6-4
1936	Alice Marble / Gene Mako	Sarah Palfrey Fabyan / Don Budge	6-3	6-2	
1937	Sarah Palfrey Fabyan / Don Budge	Sylvie Jung Henrotin / Yvon Petra	6-2	8-10	6-0
1938	Alice Marble / Don Budge	Thelma Coyne Long / John Bromwich	6-1	6-2	
1939	Alice Marble / Harry Hopman	Sarah Palfrey Fabyan / Elwood Cooke	9-7	6-1	

Year	Winner	Defeated	S1	S2	S3
1940	Alice Marble / Bobby Riggs	Dorothy Bundy / Jack Kramer	9-7	6-1	
1941	Sarah Palfrey Fabyan Cooke / Jack Kramer	Pauline Betz / Bobby Riggs	4-6	6-4	6-4
1942	Louise Brough / Ted Schroeder	Pat Canning Todd / Alejo Russell	3-6	6-1	6-4

Year	Winner	Defeated	S1	S2	S3
1943	Margaret Osborne / Bill Talbert	Pauline Betz / Pancho Segura	10-8	6-4	
1944	Margaret Osborne / Bill Talbert	Dorothy Bundy / Don McNeill	6-2	6-3	
1945	Margaret Osborne / Bill Talbert	Doris Hart / Bob Falkenburg	6-4	6-4	
1946	Margaret Osborne / Bill Talbert	Louise Brough / Robert Kimbrell	6-3	6-4	
1947	Louise Brough / John Bromwich	Gussy Moran / Pancho Segura	6-3	6-1	
1948	Louise Brough / Tom Brown	Margaret Osborne duPont / Bill Talbert	6-4	6-4	
1949	Louise Brough / Eric Strugess	Margaret Osborne duPont / Bill Talbert	4-6	6-3	7-5
1950	Margaret Osborne duPont / Ken McGregor	Doris Hart / Frank Sedgman	6-4	3-6	6-3
1951	Doris Hart / Frank Sedgman	Shirley Fry / Merv Rose	6-3	6-2	
1952	Doris Hart / Frank Sedgman	Thelma Coyne Long / Lew Hoad	6-3	7-5	
1953	Doris Hart / Vic Seixas	Julia Sampson / Rex Hartwig	6-2	4-6	6-4
1954	Doris Hart / Vic Seixas	Margaret Osborne duPont / Ken Rosewall	4-6	6-1	6-1
1955	Doris Hart / Vic Seixas	Shirley Fry / Gardnar Mulloy	7-5	5-7	6-2
1956	Margaret Osborne duPont / Ken Rosewall	Darlene Hard / Lew Hoad	9-7	6-1	
1957	Althea Gibson / Kurt Nielsen	Darlene Hard / Bob Howe	6-3	9-7	
1958	Margaret Osborne duPont / Neale Fraser	Maria Bueno / Alex Olmedo	6-4	3-6	9-7
1959	Margaret Osborne duPont / Neale Fraser	Janet Hopps / Bob Mark	7-5	13-15	6-2
1960	Margaret Osborne duPont / Neale Fraser	Maria Bueno / Antonio Palafox	6-3	6-2	
1961	Margaret Smith / Bob Mark	Darlene Hard (default—Ralston under suspension) / Dennis Ralston			
1962	Margaret Smith / Fred Stolle	Lesley Turner / Frank Froehling III	7-5	6-2	
1963	Margaret Smith / Ken Fletcher	Judy Tegart / Ed Rubinoff	3-6	8-6	6-2
1964	Margaret Smith / John Newcombe	Judy Tegart / Ed Rubinoff	10-8	4-6	6-3
1965	Margaret Smith / Fred Stolle	Judy Tegart / Frank Froehling III	6-2	6-2	
1966	Donna Floyd Fales / Owen Davidson	Carol Hanks Aucamp / Ed Rubinoff	6-1	6-3	
1967	Billie Jean King / Owen Davidson	Rosie Casals / Stan Smith	6-3	6-2	

Year	Winner	Defeated	S1	S2	S3
1968	Mary Ann Eisel / Peter Curtis	Tory Ann Fretz / Robert Perry	6-4	7-5	
1969	Margaret Smith Court / Marty Riessen	Françoise Durr / Dennis Ralston	7-5	6-3	
1970	Margaret Smith Court / Marty Riessen	Judy Tegart Dalton / Frew McMillan	6-4	6-4	
1971	Billie Jean King / Owen Davidson	Betty Stove / Rob Maud	6-3	7-5	
1972	Margaret Smith Court / Marty Riessen	Rosie Casals / Ilie Nastase	6-3	7-5	
1973	Billie Jean King / Owen Davidson	Margaret Smith Court / Marty Riessen	6-3	3-6	7-6
1974	Pam Teeguarden / Geoff Masters	Chris Evert / Jimmy Connors	6-1	7-6	
1975	Rosie Casals / Dick Stockton	Billie Jean King / Fred Stolle	6-3	7-6	
1976	Billie Jean King / Phil Dent	Betty Stove / Frew McMillan	3-6	6-2	7-5
1977	Betty Stove / Frew McMillan	Billie Jean King / Vitas Gerulaitis	6-2	3-6	6-3
1978	Betty Stove / Frew McMillan	Billie Jean King / Ray Ruffels	6-3	7-6	
1979	Greer Stevens / Bob Hewitt	Betty Stove / Frew McMillan	6-3	7-5	
1980	Wendy Turnbull / Marty Riessen	Betty Stove / Frew McMillan	7-5	6-2	
1981	Anne Smith / Kevin Curren	JoAnne Russell / Steve Denton	6-4	7-6(4)	
1982	Anne Smith / Kevin Curren	Barbara Potter / Ferdi Taygan	6-7	7-6(4)	7-6(5)
1983	Elizabeth Sayers / John Fitzgerald	Barbara Potter / Ferdi Taygan	3-6	6-3	6-4
1984	Manuela Maleeva / Tom Gullikson	Elizabeth Sayers / John Fitzgerald	2-6	7-5	6-4
1985	Martina Navratilova / Heinz Gunthardt	Elizabeth Sayers Smylie / John Fitzgerald	6-3	6-4	
1986	Raffaella Reggi / Sergio Casal	Martina Navratilova / Peter Fleming	6-4	6-4	
1987	Martina Navratilova / Emilio Sanchez	Betsy Nagelsen / Paul Annacone	6-4	6-7(6)	7-6(12)
1988	Jana Novotna / Jim Pugh	Elizabeth Sayers Smylie / Patrick McEnroe	7-5	6-3	
1989	Robin White / Shelby Cannon	Meredith McGrath / Rick Leach	3-6	6-2	7-5
1990	Elizabeth Sayers Smylie / Todd Woodbridge	Natalia Zvereva / Jim Pugh	6-4	6-2	
1991	Manon Bollegraf / Tom Nijssen	Arantxa Sanchez Vicario / Emilio Sanchez	6-2	7-6(2)	
1992	Nicole Provis / Mark Woodforde	Helena Sukova / Tom Nijssen	4-6	6-3	6-3
1993	Helena Sukova / Todd Woodbridge	Martina Navratilova / Mark Woodforde	6-3	7-6(6)	
1994	Elna Reinach / Patrick Galbraith	Jana Novotna / Todd Woodbridge	6-2	6-4	
1995	Meredith McGrath / Matt Lucena	Gigi Fernandez / Cyril Suk	6-4	6-4	
1996	Lisa Raymond / Patrick Galbraith	Manon Bollegraf / Rick Leach	7-6(6)	7-6(4)	
1997	Manon Bollegraf / Rick Leach	Mercedes Paz / Pablo Albano	3-6	7-5	7-6(3)
1998	Serena Williams / Max Mirnyi	Lisa Raymond / Patrick Galbraith	6-2	6-2	
1999	Ai Sugiyama / Mahesh Bhupathi	Kimberly Po / Donald Johnson	6-4	6-4	
2000	Arantxa Sanchez Vicario / Jared Palmer	Anna Kournikova / Max Mirnyi	6-4	6-3	
2001	Rennae Stubbs / Todd Woodbridge	Lisa Raymond / Leander Paes	6-4	5-7	(9)
2002	Lisa Raymond / Mike Bryan	Katarina Srebotnik / Bob Bryan	7-6(9)	7-6(1)	

U.S. Open – Records

U.S. Slam
(Winner of all 3 events in one year)

MEN
Bill Tilden (with D-Vinnie Richards; M-Molla Bjurstedt Mallory) (1922)
Bill Tilden (with D-Brian Norton; M-Molla Bjurstedt Mallory) (1923)
Don Budge (with D-Gene Mako: M-Alice Marble); (1938)
Frank Sedgman (with D-Ken McGregor; M-Doris Hart) (1951)
Vic Seixas (with D-Tony Trabert: M-Doris Hart) (1954)
Ken Rosewall (with D-Lew Hoad; M-Margaret Osborne Dupont) (1956)
Neale Fraser (with D-Roy Emerson; M-Margaret Osborne Dupont) (1959)
Neale Fraser (with D-Roy Emerson; M-Margaret Osborne Dupont) (1960)

WOMEN
Mabel Cahill (with D-Adeline McKinlay; M-Clarence Hobart) (1892)
Juliette Atkinson (with D-Helen Hellwig; M-Edwin Fisher) (1895)
Hazel Hotchkiss Wightman (with D-Edith Rotch; M-Wallace Johnson) (1909)
Hazel Hotchkiss Wightman (with D-Edith Rotch; M-Joseph Carpenter) (1910)
Hazel Hotchkiss Wightman (with D-Eleonora Sears; M-Wallace Johnson) (1911)
Mary K. Browne (with D-Dorothy Green; M-Dick Williams) (1912)
Mary K. Browne (with D-Louise Riddell Williams; M-Bill Tilden) (1913)
Mary K. Browne (with D-Louise Riddell Williams; M-Bill Tilden) (1914)
Molla Mallory (with D-Eleonora Sears; Irving Wright) (1917)
Helen Wills Moody (with D-Hazel Hotchkiss Wightman; M-Vinnie Richards) (1924)
Helen Wills Moody (with D-Hazel Hotchkiss Wightman; M-Jack Hawkes (1928)
Helen Jacobs (with D-Helen Jacobs; M-George Lott) (1934)
Alice Marble (with D-Sarah Palfrey Fabyan; M-Don Budge) (1938)
Alice Marble (with D-Sarah Palfrey Fabyan; M-Harry Hopman) (1939)
Alice Marble (with D-Sarah Palfrey Fabyan; M-Bobby Riggs) (1940)
Sarah Palfrey Fabyan (with D-Margaret Osborne Dupont: M-Jack Kramer) (1941)
Louise Brough (with D-Margaret Osborne Dupont: M-John Bromwich) (1947)
Margaret Osborne duPont (with D-Louise Brough; M-Ken McGregor) (1950)
Doris Hart (with D- Shirely Fry; M-Vic Seixas) (1954)
Billie Jean King (with D-Rosie Casals; M-Owen Davidson) (1967)
Margaret Smith Court (with D-Judy Tegart; M-Marty Riessen) (1970)
Martina Navratilova '(with D-Pam Shriver; M-Emilio Sanchez) (1987)

Overall Titles

MOST TITLES ALL TIME MEN
16 Bill Tilden (1913-1929) 7 singles, 5 doubles, 4 mixed.
13 Dick Sears (1881-1887) 7 singles, 6 doubles, 0 mixed.
8 Bill Talbert (1942-1948) 0 singles, 4 doubles, 4 mixed.
   George Lott (1928-1934) 0 singles, 5 doubles, 3 mixed.
   John McEnroe (1979-1989) 4 singles, 4 doubles, 0 mixed.
   Neale Fraser (1957-1960) 2 singles, 3 doubles, 4 mixed.
7 Bill Larned (1901-1911) 7 singles, 0 doubles, 0 mixed.
   Holcombe Ward (1899-1906) 1 singles, 6 doubles, 0 mixed.
   Jack Kramer (1940-1947) 2 singles, 4 doubles, 1 mixed.
   Vinnie Richards (1918-1926) 0 singles, 5 doubles, 2 mixed.
6 Bill Johnston (1915-1921) 2 singles, 3 doubles, 1 mixed.
   Clarence Hobart (1890-1905) 0 singles, 3 doubles, 3 mixed.
   Don Budge (1936-1938) 2 singles, 2 doubles, 2 mixed.
   Frank Sedgman (1950-1952) 2 singles, 2 doubles, 2 mixed.
   Fred Stolle (1962-1969) 1 singles, 3 doubles, 2 mixed.
   Jimmy Connors (1974-1983) 5 singles, 1 doubles, 0 mixed.
   John Newcombe (1964-1973) 2 singles, 3 doubles, 1 mixed.
   Oliver Campbell (1888-1892) 3 singles, 3 doubles, 0 mixed.
   Roy Emerson (1959-1966) 2 singles, 4 doubles, 0 mixed.
   Vic Seixas (1952-1955) 1 singles, 2 doubles, 3 mixed.
5 Dick Williams (1912-1926) 2 singles, 2 doubles, 1 mixed.
   Fred Alexander (1907-1917) 0 singles, 5 doubles, 0 mixed.
   James Dwight (1882-1887) 0 singles, 5 doubles, 0 mixed.
   Ken Rosewall (1956-1970) 2 singles, 2 doubles, 1 mixed.
   Marty Riessen (1969-1980) 0 singles, 1 doubles, 4 mixed.
   Maurice McLoughlin (1912-1914) 2 singles, 3 doubles, 0 mixed.
   Owen Davidson (1966-1973) 0 singles, 1 doubles, 4 mixed.
   Pete Sampras (1990-2002) 5 singles, 0 doubles, 0 mixed.
   Robert Wrenn (1893-1897) 4 singles, 1 doubles, 0 mixed.
   Stan Smith (1968-1980) 1 singles, 4 doubles, 0 mixed.
   Ted Schroeder (1940-1947) 1 singles, 3 doubles, 1 mixed.
   Todd Woodbridge (1990-2001) 0 singles, 2 doubles, 3 mixed.

MOST TITLES ALL TIME WOMEN

- 25 Margaret Osborne duPont (1941-1960) 3 singles, 13 doubles, 9 mixed.
- 18 Margaret Smith Court (1961-1975) 5 singles, 5 doubles, 8 mixed.
- 17 Louise Brough (1942-1957) 1 singles, 12 doubles, 4 mixed.
- 16 Hazel Hotchkiss Wightman (1909-1928) 4 singles, 6 doubles, 6 mixed.
- 15 Martina Navratilova (1977-1990) 4 singles, 9 doubles, 2 mixed.
  Sarah Palfrey Fabyan (1930-1945) 2 singles, 9 doubles, 4 mixed.
- 13 Billie Jean King (1964-1980) 4 singles, 5 doubles, 4 mixed.
  Helen Wills Moody (1922-1931) 7 singles, 4 doubles, 2 mixed.
  Juliette Atkinson (1894-1902) 3 singles, 7 doubles, 3 mixed.
  Molla Mallory (1915-1926) 8 singles, 2 doubles, 3 mixed.
- 12 Alice Marble (1936-1940) 4 singles, 4 doubles, 4 mixed.
  Mary K. Browne (1912-1925) 3 singles, 5 doubles, 4 mixed.
- 11 Doris Hart (1951-1955) 2 singles, 4 doubles, 5 mixed.
- 8 Bessie Moore (1896-1905) 4 singles, 2 doubles, 2 mixed.
  Darlene Hard (1958-1969) 2 singles, 6 doubles, 0 mixed.
  Helen Jacobs (1932-1935) 4 singles, 3 doubles, 1 mixed.
  Maria Bueno (1959-1968) 4 singles, 4 doubles, 0 mixed.
- 6 Betty Nuthall (1929-1933) 1 singles, 3 doubles, 2 mixed.
  Chris Evert (1975-1982) 6 singles, 0 doubles, 0 mixed.
- 5 Betty Stove (1972-1979) 0 singles, 3 doubles, 2 mixed.
  Eleonora Sears (1911-1917) 0 singles, 4 doubles, 1 mixed.
  Gigi Fernandez (1988-1996) 0 singles, 5 doubles, 0 mixed.
  Mabel Cahill (1891-1892) 2 singles, 2 doubles, 1 mixed.
  Marion Zinderstein Jessup (1918-1922) 0 singles, 4 doubles, 1 mixed.
  Pam Shriver (1983-1991) 0 singles, 5 doubles, 0 mixed.
  Rosie Casals (1967-1982) 0 singles, 4 doubles, 1 mixed.
  Shirley Fry (1951-1956) 1 singles, 4 doubles, 0 mixed.
  Steffi Graf (1988-1996) 5 singles, 0 doubles, 0 mixed.

Men's Singles

MOST WINS

- 7 Bill Larned (1901-1911)
  Bill Tilden (1920-1929)
  Dick Sears (1881-1887)
- 5 Jimmy Connors (1974-1983)
  Pete Sampras (1990-2002)
- 4 John McEnroe (1979-1984)
  Robert Wrenn (1893-1897)

MOST CHALLENGE ROUND APPEARANCES (1884-1911)

- 9 Bill Larned (7-2) (1900-03, 07-11)
- 5 Robert Wrenn (4-1) (1893-97)
- 4 Richard Sears (4-0) (1884-87)

MOST CHALLENGE ROUND VICTORIES (1884-1911)

- 7 Bill Larned (1901-02, 07-11)
- 4 Robert Wrenn (1893-94, 96-97)
  Richard Sears (1884-87)

MOST CHALLENGE ROUND LOSSES (1884-1911)

- 2 Henry Slocum (1887, 90)
  Fred Harvey (1892, 96)
  Bill Larned (1900, 03)
  Beals Wright (1906, 1908)

MOST TITLES (1912-2002)

- 7 Bill Tilden (1920-1929)
- 5 Pete Sampras (1990-2002)
  Jimmy Connors (1974-1983)
- 4 John McEnroe (1979-1984)
- 3 Dick Sears (1881-1883)
  Ivan Lendl (1985-1987)
  Fred Perry (1933-1936)

MOST FINAL APPEARANCES (1912-2002)

- 10 Bill Tilden (1918-1929)
- 8 Pete Sampras (1990-2002)
  Ivan Lendl (1982-1989)
  Bill Johnston (1915-1925)
- 7 Jimmy Connors (1974-1983)
- 5 Andre Agassi (1990-2002)
  John McEnroe (1979-1985)

MOST FINAL LOSSES (1912-2002)

- 6 Bill Johnston (1916-1925)
- 5 Ivan Lendl (1982-1989)
- 4 Bjorn Borg (1976-1981)
- 3 Pete Sampras (1992-2001)
  Bill Tilden (1918-1927)
  Andre Agassi (1990-2002)

MOST SEMI-FINAL APPEARANCES

- 14 Jimmy Connors (1974-1991)
- 11 Bill Tilden (1918-1930)
- 9 Pete Sampras (1990-2002)
  Ivan Lendl (1982-1991)
  Bill Johnston (1915-1927)
- 8 John McEnroe (1978-1990)
  Andre Agassi (1988-2002)
  Ken Rosewall (1953-1974)

YOUNGEST CHAMPION

Pete Sampras—19 years, 1 month (1990)

OLDEST CHAMPION

Bill Larned—38 years, 8 months (1911)

TOURNAMENTS PLAYED

28 Vic Seixas—1940-43, 1946-69

MATCHES PLAYED

115 Jimmy Connors—1970-89, 1991-92

MATCHES WON

98 Jimmy Connors—1970-89, 1991-92

MATCHES WON CONSECUTIVELY

42 Bill Tilden—1920-1926

MATCH WINNING PERCENTAGE

1.000 Dick Sears—1881-87 (18-0)
.910 Bill Tilden—1916-27, 1929-30 (71-7)

Women's Singles

MOST WINS

- 8 Molla Mallory (1915-1926)
- 7 Helen Wills Moody (1923-1931)
- 6 Chris Evert (1975-1982)
- 5 Margaret Smith Court (1962-1973)
  Steffi Graf (1988-1996)
- 4 Hazel Hotchkiss Wightman (1909-1919)
  Billie Jean King (1967-1974)
  Pauline Betz (1942-1946)
  Helen Jacobs (1932-1935)
  Martina Navratilova (1983-1987)
  Maria Bueno (1959-1966)
  Alice Marble (1936-1940)
  Bessie Moore (1896-1905)

MOST CHALLENGE ROUND APPEARANCES (1887-1918)

- 8 Elizabeth Moore (4-4) (1892, 96-97, 1901-06)
- 4 Marion Jones (2-2) (1898-99, 1902-03)

MOST CHALLENGE ROUND VICTORIES (1887-1918)

- 4 Elisabeth Moore (1896, 1901, 03, 05)
- 3 Juliet Atkinson (1895, 97-97)
  Hazel Hotchkiss (1909-11)

MOST CHALLENGE ROUND LOSSES (1887-1918)
- 4 Elizabeth Moore (1892, 97, 1902, 04)
- 2 Louise Hammond Raymond (1910, 16)

MOST TITLES (1919-2002)
- 7 Helen Wills Moody (1923-1931)
- 6 Chris Evert (1975-1982)
- 5 Steffi Graf (1988-1996)
  Margaret Smith Court (1962-1973)
- 4 Martina Navratilova (1983-1987)
  Billie Jean King (1967-1974)
  Helen Jacobs (1932-1935)
  Alice Marble (1936-1940)
  Maria Bueno (1959-1966)
  Molla Mallory (1920-1926)
  Pauline Betz (1942-1946)

MOST FINAL APPEARANCES (1919-2002)
- 9 Chris Evert (1975-1984)
  Helen Wills Moody (1922-1933)
- 8 Steffi Graf (1987-1996)
  Helen Jacobs (1928-1940)
  Martina Navratilova (1981-1991)
- 7 Doris Hart (1946-1955)
- 6 Billie Jean King (1965-1974)
  Molla Mallory (1920-1926)
  Margaret Smith Court (1962-1973)
  Louise Brough (1942-1957)
  Pauline Betz (1941-1946)

MOST FINAL LOSSES (1919-2002)
- 5 Doris Hart (1946-1953)
  Louise Brough (1942-1957)
- 4 Martina Navratilova (1981-1991)
  Helen Jacobs (1928-1940)
  Evonne Goolagong (1973-1976)
- 3 Steffi Graf (1987-1994)
  Chris Evert (1979-1984)

MOST SEMI-FINAL APPEARANCES
- 17 Chris Evert (1971-1988)
- 12 Helen Jacobs (1927-1941)
  Martina Navratilova (1975-1991)
- 11 Doris Hart (1943-1955)
  Louise Brough (1942-1957)
  Steffi Graf (1985-1996)
- 9 Helen Wills Moody (1922-1933)
  Molla Mallory (1920-1929)

OLDEST CHAMPION
Molla Bjurstedt Mallory—42 years, 5 months (1926)

YOUNGEST CHAMPION
Tracy Austin—16 years, 9 months (1978)

TOURNAMENTS PLAYED
- 21 Martina Navratilova—1973-93

MATCHES PLAYED
- 113 Chris Evert—1971-89

MATCHES WON
- 101 Chris Evert—1971-89

MATCHES WON CONSECUTIVELY
- 46 Helen Wills Moody—1923-25

MATCH WINNING PERCENTAGE
- .962 Helen Wills Moody—1922-25, 27-29, 31, 33 (51-2)

Men's Doubles

MOST TITLES—TEAM
- 5 Richard Sears / James Dwight (1882-1887)
- 4 Bob Lutz / Stan Smith (1968-1980)
  Fred Alexander / Harold Hackett (1907-1910)
  Bill Talbert / Gardnar Mulloy (1942-1948)

MOST TITLES—INDIVIDUAL
- 6 Dick Sears (1882-1887)
  Holcombe Ward (1899-1906)
- 5 James Dwight (1882-1887)
  George Lott (1928-1934)
  Vinnie Richards (1918-1926)
  Bill Tilden (1918-1927)
  Fred Alexander (1907-1917)

MOST FINAL APPEARANCES—TEAM
- 7 Fred Alexander / Harold Hackett (1905-1911)
- 6 Bill Talbert / Gardnar Mulloy (1942-1953)
- 5 Wilmer Allison / John Van Ryn (1931-1936)
  Richard Sears / James Dwight (1882-1887)
  Dwight Davis / Holcombe Ward (1898-1902)
  Bob Lutz / Stan Smith (1968-1980)

MOST FINAL APPEARANCES—INDIVIDUAL
- 10 Fred Alexander (1900-1918)
- 9 Bill Talbert (1942-1953)
  Gardnar Mulloy (1940-1957)
- 8 Holcombe Ward (1898-1906)
- 7 Harold Hackett (1905-1911)
  Bill Tilden (1918-1927)

MOST FINAL LOSSES—TEAM
- 3 Wilmer Allison / John Van Ryn (1932-1936)
  Fred Alexander / Harold Hackett (1905-1911)
- 2 Dick Williams / Watson Washburn (1921-1923)
  Gerald Patterson / Pat O'Hara Wood (1922-1924)
  Gerald Patterson / Jack Hawkes (1925-1928)
  Ken Flach / Robert Seguso (1987-1989)
  Dwight Davis / Holcombe Ward (1898-1902)
  Don Budge / Gene Mako (1935-1937)
  Rafael Osuna / Antonio Palafox (1961-1963)
  Bill Talbert / Gardnar Mulloy (1950-1953)
  Alexander Van Rensselaer / Arthur Newbold (1881-1883)

MOST FINAL LOSSES—INDIVIDUAL
- 5 Gardnar Mulloy (1940-1957)
  Fred Alexander (1900-1918)
  Bill Talbert (1943-1953)
- 4 Wilmer Allison (1930-1936)
  Ray Little (1900-1912)
  John Van Ryn (1930-1936)
  Gerald Patterson (1922-1928)

OLDEST CHAMPION
Bob Hewitt—37 years, 8 months (1977)

YOUNGEST CHAMPION
Vinnie Richards—15 years, 4 months (1918)

Women's Doubles

MOST TITLES—TEAM
- 12 Louise Brough / Margaret Osborne duPont (1942-1957)
- 4 Sarah Palfrey / Alice Marble (1937-1940)
  Martina Navratilova / Pam Shriver (1983-1987)
  Doris Hart / Shirley Fry (1951-1954)
- 3 Gigi Fernandez / Natalia Zvereva (1992-1996)
  Helen Jacobs / Sarah Palfrey (1932-1935)
  Mary K. Browne / Louise Riddell Williams (1913-1921)
  Eleanor Goss / Marion Zinderstein (1918-1920)

MOST TITLES—INDIVIDUAL
- 13 Margaret Osborne duPont (1941-1957)
- 12 Louise Brough (1942-1957)
- 9 Martina Navratilova (1977-1990)
   Sarah Palfrey Fabyan (1930-1941)
- 7 Juliette Atkinson (1894-1902)
- 6 Hazel Hotchkiss Wightman (1909-1928)
   Darlene Hard (1958-1969)

MOST FINAL APPEARANCES—TEAM
- 14 Louise Brough / Margaret Osborne duPont (1942-1957)
- 7 Doris Hart / Shirley Fry (1949-1955)
- 6 Billie Jean King / Rosie Casals (1966-1975)
- 5 Martina Navratilova / Pam Shriver (1983-1987)
- 4 Helen Jacobs / Sarah Palfrey (1932-1936)
   Margaret Smith Court / Virginia Wade (1969-1975)
   Sarah Palfrey / Alice Marble (1937-1940)
   Gigi Fernandez / Natalia Zvereva (1992-1997)
   Eleanor Goss / Marion Zinderstein (1918-1924)
   Pauline Betz / Doris Hart (1942-1945)

MOST FINAL APPEARANCES—INDIVIDUAL
- 15 Louise Brough (1942-1957)
   Margaret Osborne duPont (1941-1957)
- 13 Doris Hart (1942-1955)
- 12 Billie Jean King (1962-1980)
- 11 Martina Navratilova (1977-1990)
- 10 Rosie Casals (1966-1982)
   Sarah Palfrey Fabyan (1930-1941)

MOST FINAL LOSSES—TEAM
- 4 Billie Jean King / Rosie Casals (1966-1975)
   Pauline Betz / Doris Hart (1942-1945)
- 3 Doris Hart / Shirley Fry (1949-1955)
- 2 Edith Cross / Anna McCune Harper (1928-1930)
   Margaret Smith Court / Virginia Wade (1969-1972)
   Doris Hart / Pat Canning Todd (1947-1948)
   Louise Hammond Raymond / Edna Wildey (1914-1916)
   Carolin Babcock / Dorothy Andrus (1934-1935)
   Louise Brough / Margaret Osborne duPont (1953-1954)
   Billie Jean King / Karen Hantze Susman (1962-1965)
   Annabella Wistar / Amy Williams (1894-1896)
   Jana Novotna / Larisa Savchenko (1991-1992)

MOST FINAL LOSSES—INDIVIDUAL
- 9 Doris Hart (1942-1955)
- 7 Billie Jean King (1962-1979)
- 6 Rosie Casals (1966-1981)
- 5 Pauline Betz (1941-1945)
   Edna Wildey (1907-1916)

OLDEST CHAMPION
   Hazel Hotchkiss Wightman—41 years, 8 months (1928)

YOUNGEST CHAMPION
   May Sutton—17 ytears, 11 months (1904)

Mixed Doubles

MOST TITLES—TEAM
- 4 Margaret Osborne duPont / Bill Talbert (1943-1946)
- 3 Margaret Smith Court / Marty Riessen (1969-1972)
   Hazel Hotchkiss Wightman / Wallace Johnson (1909-1920)
   Margaret Osborne duPont / Neale Fraser (1958-1960)
   Juliette Atkinson / Edwin Fischer (1894-1896)
   Doris Hart / Vic Seixas (1953-1955)
   Billie Jean King / Owen Davidson (1967-1973)

MOST TITLES—MEN
- 4 Marty Riessen (1969-1980)
   Wallace Johnson (1907-1920)
   Owen Davidson (1966-1973)
   Bill Talbert (1943-1946)
   Bill Tilden (1913-1923)
   Edwin Fischer (1894-1898)

MOST TITLES—WOMEN
- 9 Margaret Osborne duPont (1943-1960)
- 8 Margaret Smith Court (1961-1972)
- 6 Hazel Hotchkiss Wightman (1909-1920)
- 5 Doris Hart (1951-1955)

MOST FINAL APPEARANCES—TEAM
- 6 Margaret Osborne duPont / Bill Talbert (1943-1949)
- 5 Betty Stove / Frew McMillan (1976-1980)
- 4 Molla Mallory / Bill Tilden (1921-1924)
   Margaret Smith Court / Marty Riessen (1969-1973)

MOST FINAL APPEARANCES—MEN
- 9 Bill Tilden (1913-1924)
- 6 Bill Talbert (1943-1949)
   Frew McMillan (1970-1980)
- 5 Wallace Johnson (1906-1920)
   Marty Riessen (1969-1980)

MOST FINAL APPEARANCES—WOMEN
- 12 Margaret Osborne duPont (1943-1960)
- 9 Margaret Smith Court (1961-1973)
- 8 Molla Mallory (1915-1924)
   Hazel Hotchkiss Wightman (1909-1927)

MOST FINAL LOSSES—TEAM
- 3 Betty Stove / Frew McMillan (1976-1980)
   Florence Ballin / Bill Tilden (1916-1919)
- 2 Louise Hammond / Ray Little (1908-1909)
   Margaret Osborne duPont / Bill Talbert (1948-1949)
   Edna Wildey / Herbert Morris Tilden (1910-1911)
   Hazel Hotchkiss Wightman / René Lacoste (1926-1927)
   Molla Mallory / Bill Tilden (1921-1924)
   Elizabeth Sayers Smylie / John Fitzgerald (1984-1985)
   Barbara Potter / Ferdi Taygan (1982-1983)
   Judy Tegart Dalton / Ed Rubinoff (1963-1964)
   Amy Williams / Mantle Fielding (1895-1896)

MOST FINAL LOSSES—MEN
- 5 Bill Tilden (1916-1924)
- 4 Frew McMillan (1970-1980)
- 3 Ed Rubinoff (1963-1966)
   Herbert Morris Tilden (1907-1911)

MOST FINAL LOSSES—WOMEN
- 5 Molla Mallory (1915-1924)
- 4 Judy Dalton (1963-1970)
   Betty Stove (1971-1980)

OLDEST CHAMPION—MEN
   Bob Hewitt—39 years, 8 months (1979)

YOUNGEST CHAMPION—MEN
   Vinnie Richards—16 years, 3 months (1919)

OLDEST CHAMPION—WOMEN
   Mararet Osborn du Pont—42 years, 5 months (1960)

YOUNGEST CHAMPION—WOMEN
   Manuela Maleeva Fragniere—17 years, 7 months (1984)

LONGEST MATCHES, TOTAL GAMES

Men's singles: 100 games – F. D. Robbins d. Dick Dell 22-20, 9-7, 6-8, 8-10, 6-4, 1st rd., 1969

Men's doubles: 105 games – Marcelo Lara / Joaquin Loyo-Mayo d. Luis Garcia / Manuel Santana 10-12, 24-22, 11-9, 3-6, 6-2, 3rd rd., 1966. 105 games, Cliff Drysdale / Ray Moore d. Ronnie Barnes / Roy Emerson 29-31, 8-6, 3-6, 8-6, 6-2, quarters, 1967

Women's singles: 51 games – Juliette Atkinson d. Marion Jones 6-3, 5-7, 6-4, 2-6, 7-5. Challenge round, 1898

Women's doubles: 48 games – Mrs. George L. Chapman / Marion Chapman (mother-daughter) d. Dorothy Green Briggs / Corinne Stanton Henry 10-8, 6-8, 9-7, 1st rd., 1922

Mixed doubles: 71 games – Margaret Osborne duPont / Bill Talbert d. Gertrude "Gussy" Moran / Bob Falkenburg 27-25, 5-7, 6-1, semis, 1948

LONGEST MATCH, PLAYING TIME

Men's singles: 5 hours 26 minutes – Stefan Edberg d. Michael Chang 6-7 (3-7), 7-5, 7-6, (7-3), 5-7, 6-4, semis, 1992

Women's singles: 2 hours 47 minutes – Steffi Graf d. Pam Shriver, 7-6 (7-4), 6-7 (4-7), 7-6 (7-4), QF, 1985

LONGEST TIE-BREAKERS

Men's singles: 20-18, third set, Goran Ivanisevic d. Daniel Nestor, 6-4, 7-6 (7-5), 7-6 (20-18), 1st rd., 1993

Women's singles: 13-11, second set, Hana Mandlikova d. Nathalie Herreman, 6-3, 6-7 (11-13), 6-2, 2nd rd., 1987

BIGGEST UPSETS

Men:

1928 - non-seed U.S. No. 12 George King d. 1st seed John Hennessey, 7-5, 6-4, 6-4, 1st rd.

1933 - non-seed U.S. No. 13 Bitsy Grant d. 1st seed defending champ Ellsworth Vines, 6-2, 6-3, 6-3, 4th rd.

1939 - unranked Welby Van Horn d. 3rd foreign seed John Bromwich, 2-6, 4-6, 6-2, 6-4, 8-6, SF

1957 - non-seed Mal Anderson d. 2nd seed Dick Savitt, 6-4, 6-3, 6-1; 4th rd.; 3rd seed Sven Davidson, 5-7, 6-2, 4-6, 6-3, 6-4, SF; and 1st seed Ashley Cooper, 10-8, 7-5, 6-4, to win title.

1968 - 16th seed Cliff Drysdale d. 1st seed Rod Laver, 4-6, 6-4, 3-6, 6-1, 6-1, 4th rd.

1970 - 19th seed Dennis Ralston d. 1st seed defending champ Rod Laver, 7-6 (5-3), 7-5, 5-7, 4-6, 6-3, 4th rd.

1973 - unranked Andy Pattison d. 2nd seed defending champ Ilie Nastase, 6-7, 2-6, 6-3, 6-3, 6-4, 2nd rd.

1983 - 16th seed Bill Scanlon d. 1st seed John McEnroe, 7-6 (7-2), 7-6 (7-3), 4-6, 6-3, 4th rd.

1986 - Todd Witsken (No. 95) d. 6th seed Jimmy Connors, 6-2, 6-4, 7-5, 3rd rd. Paul Annacone (No. 43) d. 9th seed John McEnroe, 1-6, 6-1, 6-3, 6-3, 1st rd.

1989 - qualifier Paul Haarhuis (No. 116) d. 4th seed John McEnroe, 6-4, 4-6, 6-3, 7-5, 2nd rd. Pete Sampras d. 5th seed defending champ Mats Wilander, 5-7, 6-3, 1-6, 6-1, 6-4, 2nd rd. (both same day).

1990 - Aleksandr Volkov (No. 52) d. 1st seed Stefan Edberg (Wimbledon champ), 6-3, 7-6 (7-1), 7-2, 1st rd.

1991 - Paul Haarhuis (No. 45) d. 1st seed Boris Becker, 6-2, 6-3, 6-4, 3rd rd.

1994 - Jaime Yzaga (No. 23) d. 1st seed defending champ Pete Sampras, 3-6, 6-3, 4-6, 7-6, (7-4), 7-5, 4th rd.

1997 - 15th seed Petr Korda d. 1st seed defending champ Pete Sampras, 6-7 (4-7), 7-5, 7-6 (7-2), 3-6, 7-6 (7-3)

1998 - qualifier Bernd Karbacher (No. 155) d. 4th seed Petr Korda, 2-6, 6-3, 6-2, 6-1, 1st rd.

1999 - Cedric Pioline (No. 26) d. 4th seed defending champion Patrick Rafter, 4-6, 4-6, 6-3, 7-5, 1-0, retired (right shoulder injury)

2000 - Arnaud Clement (No. 37) d. 1st seed defending champ Andre Agassi, 6-3, 6-2, 6-4. Wayne Arthurs (No. 102) d. 2nd seed Gustavo Kuerten, 4-6, 6-3, 7-6 (7-4), 7-6 (7-1), 1st rd.

Women:

1971 - Chris Evert (unranked amateur) d. U.S. No. 3 Mary Ann Eisel, 4-6, 7-6 (5-1), 6-1, 2nd rd., saved 6 MP

1973 - non-seed U.S. No. 8 Julie Heldman d. 1st seeded defending champ Billie Jean King, 3-6, 6-4, 4-2, retired, fatigued, 3rd rd.

1978 - 16th seeded Pam Shriver d. 1st seed Martina Navratilova (Wimbledon champ), 7-6 (7-5), 7-6 (7-3), SF

1979 - qualifier Julie Harrington (No. 109) d. 14th seed Pam Shriver (1978 finalist), 6-2, 6-1, 1st rd.

1981 - Andrea Leand (unranked amateur, 1st open tourney) d. 2nd seed Andrea Jaeger, 1-6, 7-5, 6-3, 2nd rd.

1982 - Susan Mascarin (unranked amateur) d. 12th seed Billie Jean King, 6-3, 6-2, 1st rd.

1988 - qualifier Kim Steinmetz (No. 183) d. 8th seed Natasha Zvereva, 4-6, 6-3, 6-4, 1st rd.

1992 - Maggie Maleeva (No. 17) d. 3rd seed Martina Navratilova (1991 finalist), 6-4, 0-6, 6-3, 2nd rd.

1994 - Mana Endo (No. 44) d. 6th seed Lindsay Davenport, 6-3, 7-6 (7-1), 4th rd.

1997 - Venus Williams (No. 66) d. 11th seed Irina Spirlea, 7-6 (7-5), 4-6, 7-6 (9-7), SF, saved 2 MP

2001 - Daja Bedanova (No. 37) d. 7th seeded Monica Seles, 7-5, 4-6, 6-3, 4th rd.

BEST COMEBACKS

Men:

1932 - 1sr seed defending champ Ellsworth Vines d. U.S. No. 6 Cliff Sutter, 4-6, 8-10, 12-10, 10-8, 6-1, 4th rd. (twice 2 points from defeat, 3rd, 5-6, deuce, 4th, 5-6, 30-all)

1939 - unranked Welby Van Horn d. 3rd foreign seed John Bromwich, 2-6, 4-6, 6-2, 6-4, 8-6, SF

1946 - Amado Sanchez d. Charles Sampson, 5-7, 3-6, 9-7, 9-7, 7-5, 1st rd. Saved 2 MP: at 1 6-5, 3rd set, 1 at 4-5, 5th set after trailing 1-4.

1960 - Rod Laver d. Butch Buchholz, 4-6, 5-7, 6-4, 6-2, 7-5, SF. Saved 3 MP

1975 - Manolo Orantes d. Guillermo Vilas, 4-6, 1-6, 6-2, 7-5, 64, SF, from 0-2, 3rd. Saved 5 MP, 4th: 3 at 0-5, 2 at 5-1.

1979 - Vitas Gerulaitis d. Roscoe Tanner, 3-6, 2-6, 7-6 (7-5), 6-3, 6-3, SF, down a break in 3rd set, and 2 points from defeat

1989 - Boris Becker d. Derrick Rostagno, 1-6, 6-7 (1-7), 6-3, 7-6 (8-6), 6-3, 2nd rd. Saved 2 MP from 6-4 in tie-breaker

1991 - wild card Jimmy Connors (No. 174) d. Aaron Krickstein (No. x), 3-6, 7-6(10-8), 1-6, 6-3, 7-6 (7-4), 4th rd. (saved 2 SP, in tie-breaker, came from 2-5, 5th, twice 2 points from defeat, deuce, 5-3; 4:41, Connors 39th birthday. Krickstein d. 4th seed Andre Agassi, 7-5, 7-6 (7-4), 6-2, 1st rd.)

1993 - Wally Masur d. Jamie Morgan, 3-6, 4-6, 6-3, 6-4, 7-5, 4th rd., from 0-5, 5th set. Saved 1 MP at 5-1, won 25 of last 28 points from there.

1999 - Todd Martin d. Greg Rusedski, 5-7, 0-6, 7-6 (7-3), 6-4, 6-4, 4th rd. Rusedski served for match, 5-4, 3rd set, led 4-1, 5th set, whereupon Martin won 18 straight points to 5-4, 30-0, 20 of last 21 points

1998 - 3rd seed defending champ Patrick Rafter d. Hicham Arazi (No. 44), 1st rd., continued to title, held to 4-3, 3rd set from 15-40. Carlos Moya d. Michael Chang, 3-6, 1-6, 7-6 (7-5), 6-4, 6-3. Saved 3 MP at 4-5, 3rd set

Women:

1926 - Molla Mallory d. Elizabeth Ryan, 4-6, 6-4, 9-7, F. From 0-4, 3rd set, saved 1 MP at 6-7

1933 - Betty Nuthall d. Alice Marble, 8-10, 6-0, 7-5, QF. Saved 3 MP from 5-1, 40-15, ad-in down.

1971 - Chris Evert d. Mary Ann Eisel, 4-6, 7-6 (5-1), 6-1, 2nd rd. Saved 6 MP, Eisel serving at 6-5, 40-0 and 3 ads-in.

1983 - Barbie Bramblett d. Kathy Horton, 2-6, 7-6 (7-3), 6-3, qualifying. Saved 16 MP, from 0-5, 0-40, 2nd set.

1998 - Mary Jo Fernandez d. Alexandra Fusai, 6-3, 4-6, 7-6 (12-10). Saved 6 MP: 2 at 5-6, 15-40, 4 in tie-breaker.

BEST OPEN FINISHES BY AMATEURS

1968 - Arthur Ashe, won title
1981 - Barbara Gerken, QF
1982 - Gretchen Rush, Rodney Harmon, QF

MATCH POINTS SAVED BY SINGLES CHAMPION

Men:

1906 - QF, Bill Clothier d. Fred Alexander, 8-6, 6-2, 4-6, 1-6, 7-5. 3 MP at 2-5, 0-40, 5th set
1936 - F, Fred Perry d. Don Budge, 2-6, 6-2, 8-6, 1-6, 10-8. 2 MP at 4-5, 5th set
1975 - SF, Manolo Orantes d. Guillermo Vilas, 4-6, 1-6, 6-2, 7-5, 6-4. 5 MP, 3 at 0-5, 2 at 5-1, 4th set
1989 - 2nd rd., Boris Becker d. Derrick Rostagno, 1-6, 6-7 (1-7), 6-3, 7-6 (8-6), 6-3. 2 MP at 4-6, 4th set tie-breaker
1996 - Pete Sampras d. Alex Corretja, 7-6 (7-5), 5-7, 5-7, 6-4, 7-6 (9-7), QF. 1 MP in tie-breaker, 5th set, 6-7

Women:

1901 - F, Elisabeth Moore d. Myrtle McAteer, 6-4, 3-6, 7-5, 2-6, 6-2. 1 MP 3rd set
1911 - F, Hazel Hotchkiss (Wightman) d. Florence Sutton, 8-10, 6-1, 9-7, 1 MP, 6-5, 40-30, 3rd set, saved with overhead smash.
    1926 - F, Molla Mallory d. Elizabeth Ryan, 4-6, 6-4, 9-7. 1 MP at 6-7, 3rd set
1938 - SF, Alice Marble d. Sarah Palfrey Fabyan, 5-7, 7-5, 7-5. 2 MP at 2-5, 3rd set
1942 - SF, Pauline Betz d. Margaret Osborne, 6-4, 4-6, 7-5. 2 MP at 5-3, 3rd set
1947 - SF, Louise Brough d. Nancye Wynne Bolton, 4-6, 6-4, 7-5. 3 MP at 5-2, 40-0, 3rd set
1948 - F, Margaret Osborne duPont d. Louise Brough, 4-6, 6-4, 15-13. 1 MP at 5-6, 3rd set
1954 - F, Doris Hart d. Louise Brough, 6-8, 6-1, 8-6. 3 MP, 3rd set
1986 - SF, Martina Navratilova d. Steffi Graf, 6-1, 6-7, 7-6 (10-8), 3 MP: 2 at 4-5, ads-out; 1 in tie-breaker, at 8-7

DAVIS CUP 1956 CHALLENGE ROUND

AUSTRALIA 3 U.S.A. 0

PREVIOUS SETS

	GAMES	POINTS
K. ROSEWALL (AUST)	4	15
V		
S. GIAMMALVA (USA)	5	30

International
Play

Section 5

Ken Rosewall, 1956
Flawless in 5-0 challenge round win over U.S.,
Rosewall beat Sammy Giammalva here and
was 17-2 in Davis Cup singles over his career.

RECORDS – MATCH WINNING PERCENT, ONE SEASON, SINGLES

MEN
.987—Bill Tilden, 1925 (78-1)
.965—John McEnroe, 1984 (82-3)

WOMEN
1.000—Alice Marble, 1939 (45-0)
.981—Martina Navratilova, 1983 (86-1)

(minimum 25 matches)

Chapter 21

The Davis Cup

Ted Schroeder, Frank Parker, non-playing captain Alrick H. Man Jr., Gardnar Mulloy, Bill Talbert, 1948
The U.S. team overwhelmed Australia 5-0 at Forest Hills.

Dwight Filley Davis hailed from a family of wealthy merchants from St. Louis. He graduated from Harvard University before embarking on a distinguished career, including decoration as a war hero and stints as secretary of war under President Calvin Coolidge and as civilian governor-general of the Philippines.

His achievements in public service were over-shadowed by a single purchase he made as a young man, as Davis himself learned during a visit to the Chamber of Deputies in Paris many years later, in 1932. Davis was initially seated behind a pillar. As recounted in Nancy Kriplen's biography, a companion appealed for a better seat. Didn't they realize this man had been recently ruler of the Philippines? A French official was unmoved. But he was also once in Coolidge's cabinet, the companion added. The official shrugged. You don't understand, the companion pressed on, this man Davis is the Davis of *la coupe Davis*. He was promptly moved to the front row.

Davis (1879-1945) was called the Harvard Cyclone in his student days. He won an intercollegiate singles championship and thoroughly enjoyed team competition against other schools. In the wake of an 1899 tennis junket to the west coast with Harvardians Holcombe Ward and Malcolm Whitman, with whom he would stand as the first U.S. team, plus Beals Wright, Davis, struck by the hospitality and comradeship, felt that spirit could be kindled internationally with a tennis competition. The idea sprang forth—a cup materialized that would inspire generations of male tennis players around the world.

In 1900, he commissioned a trophy from Shreve, Crump & Low Co. of Boston, which assigned the task to the William B. Durgin Company of Concord, N.H. Rowland Rhodes, an English-born designer, crafted a stunning bowl of 217 troy ounces of silver, the top edge scalloped with primroses and acanthus leaves. The 13-inch-tall cup had an 18-inch bowl. Not bad for "About $1,000," according to an official of Shreves, suggesting that it would cost some $200,000 to duplicate today. Since the names of players of both final-round teams are engraved on the trophy (first on the bowl, then on an accompanying tray, now on silver tablets attached to two subsequently added circular bases), a search for more space is unending.

The prize, officially entitled as the International Lawn Tennis Challenge Trophy has long been known simply as the Davis Cup. It is the oldest, most prestigious and most cherished of tennis trophies, even if Davis' friends teasingly referred to the Cup as 'Dwight's pot.'

Through 2002, the Davis Cup had been presented 91 times since first contested in 1900, with a hiatus in 1901 and 1910, and twice suspended by world wars. The United States has the most championships at 31, followed by Australia with 27. Britain and France have nine each. (Australia's first six Cups were claimed by Australasia in an antipodean partnership with New Zealand, while a team representing the British Isles took four of their nine Cups.) Other victorious nations include Sweden (seven titles) and Germany (three), while single championships have been won by South Africa, Italy, Czechoslovakia, Spain, and Russia, in a thrilling comeback against France in 2002.

The prestigious competition has attracted the greatest names in tennis history, from the Doherty brothers and Norman Brookes, to the French Musketeers and the double Bills (Tilden and Johnston), to the modern era where surnames alone are needed to appreciate tennis mastery from the likes of Newcombe and Ashe and McEnroe and Edberg and Agassi.

The first Davis Cup was a challenge by the Americans to representatives of the British Isles. Until 1922, the Cup holders played the winners of an open, all-comers' draw. The first two zones were created in 1923 (European and American) with an Eastern Zone added in the 1950s. Europe split into A and B sections in 1966, and the American Zone was divided into north and south sections the following year.

The elimination of the challenge round in 1972 ended the domination of the four powers of Davis Cup play (the U.S., Britain, Australia, France). No longer was the champion guaranteed a spot in the finals at home.

As of 2003, a total of 142 nations take part in the competition, although the winner will come from among the 16 members of the World Group. A system of relegation and promotion determines the composition of the World Group each year.

Dr. James Dwight, mentor of Davis, devised a best-of-five format still in use more than a century later. Each three-day series consists of five matches, with two singles on the opening day, followed the next day by a doubles match, with reverse singles held on the final day.

The inaugural tournament began on Aug. 8, 1900, on the grass at Davis' club, Longwood Cricket Club in Boston, where Davis, ranked No. 2 in the U.S. at the time, and fellow Harvard graduates Holcombe Ward (ranked No. 9) and Malcolm Whitman (ranked No. 1) easily handled Arthur Gore, Herbert Roper Barrett and Ernest Black, representing the British Isles. The U.S. built a 3-0 lead before thunderstorms washed out the final day of play.

As Cup holders, the Americans were to play host to the 1901 competition. However, no competition was held as the British were unable to raise a team.

In 1902, the brothers Laurie and Reggie Doherty joined with Dr. Joshua Pim to challenge the Americans in Brooklyn, N.Y. The visitors built a 2-1 lead after winning the doubles against Ward and Davis, who thus ended his playing career for the Cup that bears his name. Bill Larned took his singles match against Pim, while Whitman defeated Reggie Doherty 6-1, 7-5, 6-4 to retain the Cup.

The Doherty brothers would have their revenge the next year in Boston, taking the Cup four matches to one. In 1904, Belgium and France signed on for the challenge, with Belgium beating France for the right to challenge Britain. The United States was unable to raise a team to cross the Atlantic in 1904 and the British retained the Cup with a 5-0 drubbing of the Belgians, which managed to win only a single set.

The British Isles team similarly humiliated the U.S. team in 1906 and 1907. Led by Laurie Doherty, whose doubles partner was his brother Reggie, the British scored two more consecutive 5-0 whitewashes.

The first Davis Cup dynasty ended after four Cups when the Australasian duo of Norman Brookes and Tony Wilding upset the defenders 3-2, the decisive match, the fourth, Brookes' 6-2, 6-0, 6-3 deconstruction of Roper Barrett.

Brookes, who was later knighted, was part of six Cup-winning teams. His wife, the future Dame Mabel, usually placed the Cup on a dining-room sideboard, the bowl filled with loose-petalled red peonies to lessen the gaudiness of the shiny silverware.

Wilding, a Cambridge-educated lawyer from New Zealand, joined Brookes on three of those teams, including the 1914 side. He was a captain in the armored car division of the Royal Marines when killed in action on the Western Front on May 9, 1915, a Wimbledon and Davis Cup champion dead at age 31.

The U.S. regained its hold on the Cup in 1920 when Big Bill Tilden and Little Bill Johnston traveled to Auckland, New Zealand, to administer a 5-0 beating on Australasia. The pair held the Davis Cup for seven consecutive years, aided in some series by Vincent Richards and Dick Williams.

After two defeats in Philadelphia, a quartet of Frenchman known as the Four Musketeers at last won the Cup in 1927. Rene Lacoste's ability to limit the damage done by Tilden's relentless attack was the key to a 6-3, 4-6, 6-3, 6-2 victory in the decisive fourth match.

A new stadium, named Roland Garros for a French aviation pioneer, was built for the defense of the Cup. The Musketeers—the speedy Henri Cochet, doubles specialist Jacques 'Toto' Brugnon, the flamboyant, beret-wearing Jean Borotra, and Lacoste, the Crocodile, the symbol that still adorns clothing that bears his name — were masters of the clay at their new stadium. France defended the Cup against five more challenges (one British, four American) before Britain's Fred Perry and Henry (Bunny) Austin ended their reverie 3-2 in 1933. The Frenchmen took their conquerors and the Davis Cup on a tour of Parisian nightspots that evening, though Perry, the son of a Labour member of parliament, was more teetotaler than bon vivant.

The British put together a modest four-year streak and faced an American team led by Don Budge in the 1937 final. The Americans narrowly escaped elimination at the hands of Germany in an Interzone final played at Wimbledon. Gottfried von Cramm seemed certain to gain a berth in the challenge round as he led Budge 4-1 in the fifth set of the deciding singles match. The American battled back, however, and von Cramm saved four match points before Budge smacked a forehand winner on the run. The 6-8, 5-7, 6-4, 6-2, 8-6 drama is remembered as a classic. A week later, Budge led the Americans to their first Davis Cup in a decade with a victory over Britain, whose hippity-hop singles players were Bunny Austin and Charlie Hare.

Budge won the second of the four Cups he contested in 1938, while Adrian Quist and John Bromwich ended a 20-year drought by bringing the Cup to Australia in 1939.

From 1946 until 1959, only Australia and the United States appeared in the challenge round. The Australians took eight of those head-to-head showdowns, while the Americans had six.

One of the more remarkable contests occurred in the fourth match of the 1953 final. With the U.S. leading 2-1, Lew Hoad of Australia needed 62 games to overcome Tony Trabert of the U.S. 13-11, 6-3, 2-6, 3-6, 7-5 in an epic struggle played in rain in Melbourne. Ken Rosewall then defeated Vic Seixas for the Cup.

These were the golden years of Australian tennis, as Harry Hopman, a notoriously strict disciplinarian, guided the likes of Hoad, Newcombe, Ken Rosewall, Neale Fraser, Rod Laver, Roy Emerson and Tony Roche to 15 Davis Cup victories in 18 years. Emerson belonged to a Cup-winning team a record eight times.

In 23 consecutive challenge-round appearances, the Australians also frustrated Italy, Mexico, Spain and India.

After demolishing Spain in the 1967 final, during which the Spanish failed to win a single set until after Australia clinched with a 3-0 lead, the entire Aussie team turned professional.

The Davis Cup was slower than the rest of the tennis world to embrace professionals. The competition was confined to amateurs until 1969, when certain pros, those with ties to their national federations, became eligible. In 1973 it finally became a truly open event, with all players welcome, and the Aussies won with perhaps the strongest team ever, a group of pros who had been absent from the Davis Cup scene for years—Laver, Rosewall, Newcombe and Mal Anderson.

South Africa claimed the Cup in 1974 in a walkover, as the Indian government refused to let its team play as a protest against the racist policies of the South African government. South Africa's presence in the tournament was a source of debate throughout the decade.

In 1975, Bjorn Borg was the key to Sweden's triumph over Czechoslovakia at Stockholm in the first all-European final since 1933.

Italy made the first of four finals appearances in five years in 1976, coming away with a 4-1 victory over Chile for the nation's only Cup success. The Italian captain was Nicola Pietrangeli, the most prolific Davis Cup player of all time, having set records in a playing career lasting from 1954 to 1972 for most matches played (164), most singles played (110), most singles won (78), most doubles played (54), and most doubles won (42).

The most successful American in Davis Cup play, a woolly-haired wild man by the name of John McEnroe, played in his first final in 1978, defeating Britain's John Lloyd and Buster Mottram. The Cup was the first of five he would hoist (1978, '79, '81, '82 and '92), as he established U.S. Davis Cup records for singles victories on a 41-8 record.

The most notorious of those defeats was a straight-sets loss courtesy of Henrik Sundstrom in 1984, as Sweden won its second Cup. McEnroe and teammate Jimmy Connors' appalling behavior—"ugly Americans" was a common phrase in headlines—put them at odds with USTA leadership. They refused to sign a behavior agreement and were not asked to play the next year. Connors would not return but McEnroe did in 1987.

Sweden, with Mats Wilander and Stefan Edberg, would win two more Cups in the next three years. Boris Becker earned the second of two consecutive Davis Cups with a convincing 6-2, 6-0, 6-2 dismantling of Wilander in 1989.

Two of the more dramatic Davis Cup finals have occurred in recent years. In 1996, the Cup was settled after a nine-hour marathon of compelling tennis, as France and Sweden dueled to the last shot. France nursed a 2-1 lead on the final day, having taken the doubles match. Sweden's Thomas Enqvist evened the matches at 2-2 by surviving a five-set battle with Cedric Pioline. The decider match would be handled by Arnaud Boetsch, while Sweden's hopes rested on Nicklas Kulti, a stand-in for Edberg, who had twisted his ankle. Kulti was ranked 32 spots lower than the Frenchman, yet offered a spirited challenge to the delight of Swedish partisans in Malmo. Boetsch finally ended the day's exhausting drama by saving three Cup points at 6-7, 0-40, completing a 7-6 (7-2), 2-6, 4-6, 7-6 (7-5), 10-8 epic, the first time in 96 years that the Cup was decided in the fifth set of the fifth match.

It would only take another six years before another nail-biting thriller was recorded. France led two matches to one heading into the third day of the 2002 final against Russia. Marat Safin kept Russia's hopes alive by dispatching Sebastien Grosjean 6-3, 6-2, 7-6 (13-11). The Russians shocked observers by replacing Yevgeny Kafelnikov with 20-year-old Mikhail Youzhny to face Paul-Henri Mathieu. The Russian quickly dropped the first two sets, before finding his game, thanks in part to an unconventional one-handed backhander with which he began making winners. Mathieu was within two points of victory in the fourth set with Youzhny serving at 4-5 and deuce, but the Russian kept his head and forced a fifth set. The 3-6, 2-6, 6-3, 7-5, 6-4 victory for Youzhny was the greatest Davis Cup comeback in 38 years. The Russian entourage swarmed the court to toss their young hero in the air.

"He's a Russian man," was coach Shamil Tarpishchev's succinct summation. "He knows how to fight."

DAVIS CUP CHAMPIONS

CHALLENGE ROUNDS
1900
United States d. British Isles 3-0 (Boston)
Malcolm Whitman d. Arthur Gore 6-1, 6-3, 6-2
Dwight Davis d. Ernest Black 4-6, 6-2, 6-4, 6-4
Holcombe Ward–Dwight Davis d. Ernest Black–
  Herbert Roper Barrett 6-4, 6-4, 6-4
Malcolm Whitman vs. Ernest Black (not played)
Dwight Davis vs. Arthur Gore 9-7, 9-9 (unfinished)
1901 Not held
1902
United States d. British Isles 3-2 (Brooklyn, N.Y.)
Reggie Doherty (B) d. Bill Larned 2-6, 3-6, 6-3, 6-4, 6-4
Malcolm Whitman (US) d. Joshua Pim 6-1, 6-1, 1-6, 6-0
Bill Larned d. Joshua Pim 6-3, 6-2, 6-3
Malcolm Whitman d. Reggie Doherty 6-1, 7-5, 6-4
Reggie Doherty–Laurie Doherty d. Holcombe Ward–
  Dwight Davis 3-6, 10-8, 6-3, 6-4

1903
British Isles d. United States 4-1 (Boston)
Laurie Doherty (B) d. Robert Wrenn 6-0, 6-3, 6-4
Bill Larned (US) d. Reggie Doherty (walkover, injury)
Reggie Doherty–Laurie Doherty d. Robert Wrenn–George Wrenn
7-5, 9-7, 2-6, 6-3
Laurie Doherty d. Bill Larned 6-3, 6-8, 6-0, 2-6, 7-5
Reggie Doherty d. Robert Wrenn 6-4, 3-6, 6-3, 6-8, 6-4

1904
British Isles d. Belgium 5-0 (Wimbledon)
Laurie Doherty d. Paul de Borman 6-4, 6-1, 6-1
Frank Riseley d. Willie Lemaire de Warzee 6-1, 6-4, 6-2
Reggie Doherty–Laurie Doherty d. Paul de Borman–
Willie Lemaire de Warzee 6-0, 6-1, 6-3
Laurie Doherty d. Willie Lemaire de Warzee (walkover)
Frank Riseley d. Paul de Borman 4-6, 6-2, 8-6, 7-5

1905
British Isles d. United States 5-0 (Wimbledon)
Laurie Doherty d. Holcombe Ward 7-9, 4-6, 6-1, 6-2, 6-0
Sidney Smith d. Bill Larned 6-4, 6-4, 5-7, 6-4
Reggie Doherty–Laurie Doherty d. Holcombe Ward–Beals Wright
8-10, 6-2, 6-2, 4-6, 8-6
Sidney Smith d. Bill Clothier 4-6, 6-1, 6-4, 6-3
Laurie Doherty d. Bill Larned 6-4, 2-6, 6-8, 6-4, 6-2

1906
British Isles d. United States 5-0 (Wimbledon)
Sidney Smith d. Raymond Little 6-4, 6-4, 6-1
Laurie Doherty d. Holcombe Ward 6-2, 8-6, 6-3
Reggie Doherty–Laurie Doherty d. Holcombe Ward–Raymond Little
3-6, 11-9, 9-7, 6-1
Sidney Smith d. Holcombe Ward 6-1, 6-0, 6-4
Laurie Doherty d. Raymond Little 3-6, 6-3, 6-8, 6-1, 6-3

1907
Australasia d. British Isles 3-2 (Wimbledon)
Norman Brookes (A) d. Arthur Gore 7-5, 6-1, 7-5
Tony Wilding (A) d. Herbert Roper Barrett 1-6, 6-4, 6-3, 7-5
Arthur Gore–Herbert Roper Barrett d. Norman Brookes–
Tony Wilding 3-6, 4-6, 7-5, 6-2, 13-11
Norman Brookes d. Herbert Roper Barrett 6-2, 6-0, 6-3
Arthur Gore d. Tony Wilding 3-6, 6-3, 7-5, 6-2

1908
Australasia d. United States 3-2 (Melbourne)
Norman Brookes (A) d. Fred Alexander 5-7, 9-7, 6-2, 4-6, 6-3
Beals Wright (US) d. Tony Wilding 3-6, 7-5, 6-3, 6-1
Norman Brookes–Tony Wilding d. Beals Wright–Fred Alexander
6-4, 6-2, 5-7, 1-6, 6-4
Beals Wright d. Norman Brookes 0-6, 3-6, 7-5, 6-2, 12-10
Tony Wilding d. Fred Alexander 6-3, 6-4, 6-1

1909
Australasia d. United States 5-0 (Sydney)
Norman Brookes d. Maurice McLoughlin 6-2, 6-2, 6-4
Tony Wilding d. Melville Long 6-2, 7-5, 6-1
Norman Brookes–Tony Wilding d. Maurice McLoughlin–
Melville Long 12-10, 9-7, 6-3
Norman Brookes d. Melville Long 6-4, 7-5, 8-6
Tony Wilding d. Maurice McLoughlin 3-6, 8-6, 6-2, 6-3

1910 No competition

1911
Australasia d. United States 5-0 (Christchurch, New Zealand)
Norman Brookes d. Beals Wright 6-4, 2-6, 6-3, 6-3
Rod Heath d. Bill Larned 2-6, 6-1, 7-5, 6-2
Norman Brookes–Alfred Dunlop d. Beals Wright–
Maurice McLoughlin 6-4, 5-7, 7-5, 6-4
Norman Brookes d. Maurice McLoughlin 6-4, 3-6, 4-6, 6-3, 6-4
Rod Heath d. Beals Wright (walkover)

1912
British Isles d. Australasia 3-2 (Melbourne)
James Parke (B) d. Norman Brookes 8-6, 6-3, 5-7, 6-2
Charles Dixon (B) d. Rod Heath 5-7, 6-4, 6-4, 6-4
Norman Brookes–Alfred Dunlop d. Cecil Parke–Alfred Beamish
6-4, 6-1, 7-5
James Parke d. Rod Heath 6-2, 6-4, 6-4
Norman Brookes d. Charles Dixon 6-2, 6-4, 6-4

1913
United States d. British Isles 3-2 (Wimbledon)
James Parke (B) d. Maurice McLoughlin 8-10, 7-5, 6-4, 1-6, 7-5
Dick Williams (US) d. Charles Dixon 8-6, 3-6, 6-2, 1-6, 7-5
Harold Hackett–Maurice McLoughlin d. Herbert Roper
Barrett–Charles Dixon 5-7, 6-1, 2-6, 7-5, 6-4
Maurice McLoughlin d. Charles Dixon 8-6, 6-3, 6-2
James Parke d. Dick Williams 6-2, 5-7, 5-7, 6-4, 6-2

1914
Australasia d. United States 3-2 (Forest Hills)
Tony Wilding (A) d. Dick Williams 7-5, 6-2, 6-3
Maurice McLoughlin (US) d. Norman Brookes 17-15, 6-3, 6-3
Norman Brookes–Tony Wilding d. Maurice McLoughlin–Tom Bundy
6-3, 8-6, 9-7
Norman Brookes d. Dick Williams 6-1, 6-2, 8-10, 6-3
Maurice McLoughlin d. Tony Wilding 6-2, 6-3, 2-6, 6-2

1915-18 Not held, World War I
1919
Australasia d. British Isles 4-1 (Sydney)
Gerald Patterson (A) d. Arthur Lowe 6-4, 6-3, 2-6, 6-3
Algernon Kingscote (B) d. Jim Anderson 6-7, 6-3, 6-3
Norman Brookes–Gerald Patterson d. Algernon Kingscote–
Alfred Beamish 6-0, 6-0, 6-2
Gerald Patterson d. Algernon Kingscote 6-4, 6-4, 8-6
Jim Anderson d. Arthur Lowe 6-4, 5-7, 6-3, 4-6, 12-10

1920
United States d. Australasia 5-0 (Auckland)
Bill Tilden d. Norman Brookes 10-8, 6-4, 1-6, 6-4
Bill Johnston d. Gerald Patterson 6-3, 6-1, 6-1
Bill Tilden–Bill Johnston d. Norman Brookes–Gerald Patterson
4-6, 6-4, 6-2, 6-3
Bill Tilden d. Gerald Patterson 5-7, 6-2, 6-3, 6-3
Bill Johnston d. Norman Brookes 5-7, 7-5, 6-3, 6-3

1921
United States d. Japan 5-0 (Forest Hills)
Bill Johnston d. Ichiya Kumagae 6-2, 6-4, 6-2
Bill Tilden d. Zenzo Shimidzu 5-7, 4-6, 7-5, 6-2, 6-1
Dick Williams–Watson Washburn d. Zenzo Shimidzu–
Ichiya Kumagae 6-2, 7-5, 4-6, 7-5
Bill Tilden d. Ichiya Kumagae 9-7, 6-4, 6-1
Bill Johnston d. Zenzo Shimidzu 6-3, 5-7, 6-2, 6-4

1922
United States d. Australasia 4-1 (Forest Hills)
Bill Tilden (US) d. Gerald Patterson 7-5, 10-8, 6-0
Bill Johnston (US) d. Jim Anderson 6-1, 6-2, 6-3
Gerald Patterson–Pat O'Hara Wood d. Bill Tilden–Vinnie Richards
6-3, 6-0, 6-4
Bill Johnston d. Gerald Patterson 6-2, 6-2, 6-1
Bill Tilden d. Jim Anderson 6-4, 5-7, 3-6, 6-4, 6-2

1923
United States d. Australia 4-1 (Forest Hills)
Jim Anderson (A) d. Bill Johnston 4-6, 6-2, 2-6, 7-5, 6-2
Bill Tilden (US) d. John Hawkes 6-4, 6-2, 6-1
Bill Tilden–Dick Williams d. Jim Anderson–John Hawkes
17-15, 11-13, 2-6, 6-3, 6-2
Bill Johnston d. John Hawkes 6-0, 6-2, 6-1
Bill Tilden d. Jim Anderson 6-2, 6-3, 1-6, 7-5

1924
United States d. Australia 5-0 (Philadelphia)
Bill Tilden d. Gerald Patterson 6-4, 6-2, 6-2
Vincent Richards d. Pat O'Hara Wood 6-3, 6-2, 6-4
Bill Tilden–Bill Johnston d. Gerald Patterson–Pat O'Hara Wood
  5-7, 6-3, 6-4, 6-1
Bill Tilden d. Pat O'Hara Wood 6-2, 6-1, 6-1
Vincent Richards d. Gerald Patterson 6-3, 7-5, 6-4

1925
United States d. France 5-0 (Philadelphia)
Bill Tilden d. Jean Borotra 4-6, 6-0, 2-6, 9-7, 6-4
Bill Johnston d. René Lacoste 6-1, 6-1, 6-8, 6-3
Vincent Richards–Dick Williams d. René Lacoste–Jean Borotra
  6-4, 6-4, 6-3
Bill Tilden d. René Lacoste 3-6, 10-12, 8-6, 7-5, 6-2
Bill Johnston d. Jean Borotra 6-1, 6-4, 6-0

1926
United States d. France 4-1 (Philadelphia)
Bill Johnston (US) d. René Lacoste 6-0, 6-4, 0-6, 6-0
Bill Tilden (US) d. Jean Borotra 6-2, 6-3, 6-3
Dick Williams–Vincent Richards (US) d. Henri Cochet–
  Jacques Brugnon 6-4, 6-4, 6-2
Bill Johnston d. Jean Borotra 8-6, 6-4, 9-7
René Lacoste d. Bill Tilden 4-6, 6-4, 8-6, 8-6

1927
France d. United States 3-2 (Philadelphia)
René Lacoste (F) d. Bill Johnston 6-3, 6-2, 6-2
Bill Tilden (US) d. Henri Cochet 6-4, 2-6, 6-2, 8-6
Bill Tilden–Frank Hunter d. Jean Borotra–Jacques Brugnon
  3-6, 6-3, 6-3, 4-6, 6-0
René Lacoste d. Bill Tilden 6-3, 4-6, 6-3, 6-2
Henri Cochet d. Bill Johnston 6-4, 4-6, 6-2, 6-4

1928
France d. United States 4-1 (Paris)
Bill Tilden (US) d. René Lacoste 1-6, 6-4, 6-4, 2-6, 6-3
Henri Cochet (F) d. John Hennessey 5-7, 9-7, 6-3, 6-0
Henri Cochet–Jean Borotra d. Bill Tilden–Frank Hunter
  6-4, 6-8, 7-5, 4-6, 6-2
Henri Cochet d. Bill Tilden 9-7, 8-6, 6-4
René Lacoste d. John Hennessey 4-6, 6-1, 7-5, 6-3

1929
France d. United States 3-2 (Paris)
Jean Borotra (F) d. George Lott 6-1, 3-6, 6-4, 7-5
Henri Cochet (F) d. Bill Tilden 6-3, 6-1, 6-2
John Van Ryn–Wilmer Allison d. Henri Cochet–Jean Borotra
  6-1, 8-6, 6-4
Bill Tilden d. Jean Borotra 4-6, 6-1, 6-4, 7-5
Henri Cochet d. George Lott 6-1, 3-6, 6-0, 6-3

1930
France d. United States 4-1 (Paris)
Bill Tilden (US) d. Jean Borotra 2-6, 7-5, 6-4, 7-5
Henri Cochet (F) d. George Lott 6-4, 6-2, 6-2
Henri Cochet–Jacques Brugnon d. Wilmer Allison–John Van Ryn
  6-3, 7-5, 1-6, 6-2
Jean Borotra d. George Lott 5-7, 6-3, 2-6, 6-2, 8-6
Henri Cochet d. Bill Tilden 4-6, 6-3, 6-1, 7-5

1931
France d. Great Britain 3-2 (Paris)
Henri Cochet (F) d. Bunny Austin 3-6, 11-9, 6-2, 6-4
Fred Perry (B) d. Jean Borotra 4-6, 10-8, 6-0, 4-6, 6-4
Henri Cochet–Jacques Brugnon d. Pat Hughes–Charles Kingsley
  6-1, 5-7, 6-3, 8-6
Bunny Austin d. Jean Borotra 7-5, 6-3, 3-6, 7-5
Henri Cochet d. Fred Perry 6-4, 1-6, 9-7, 6-3

1932
France d. United States 3-2 (Paris)
Jean Borotra (F) d. Ellsworth Vines 6-4, 6-2, 3-6, 6-4
Henri Cochet (F) d. Wilmer Allison 5-7, 7-5, 7-5, 6-2
Wilmer Allison–John Van Ryn d. Henri Cochet–Jacques Brugnon
  6-3, 11-13, 7-5, 6-4, 6-4
Jean Borotra d. Wilmer Allison 1-6, 3-6, 6-4, 6-2, 7-5
Ellsworth Vines d. Henri Cochet 4-6, 0-6, 7-5, 8-6, 6-2

1933
Great Britain d. France 3-2 (Paris)
Bunny Austin (GB) d. Andre Merlin 6-3, 6-4, 6-0
Fred Perry (GB) d. Henri Cochet 8-10, 6-4, 8-6, 3-6, 6-1
Jean Borotra–Jacques Brugnon (F) d. Pat Hughes–Harold Lee
  6-3, 8-6, 6-2
Henri Cochet d. Bunny Austin 5-7, 6-4, 4-6, 6-4, 6-4
Fred Perry d. Andre Merlin 4-6, 8-6, 6-2, 7-5

1934
Great Britain d. United States 4-1 (Wimbledon)
Bunny Austin (GB) d. Frank Shields 6-4, 6-4, 6-1
Fred Perry (GB) d. Sidney Wood 6-1, 4-6, 5-7, 6-0, 6-3
George Lott–Lester Stoefen (US) d. Pat Hughes–Harold Lee
  7-5, 6-0, 4-6, 9-7
Fred Perry d. Frank Shields 6-4, 4-6, 6-2, 15-13
Bunny Austin d. Sidney Wood 6-4, 6-0, 6-8, 6-3

1935
Great Britain d. United States 5-0 (Wimbledon)
Bunny Austin d. Wilmer Allison 6-2, 2-6, 4-6, 6-3, 7-5
Fred Perry d. Don Budge 6-0, 6-8, 6-3, 6-4
Pat Hughes–Charles Tuckey d. Wilmer Allison–John Van Ryn
  6-2, 1-6, 6-8, 6-3, 6-3
Bunny Austin d. Don Budge 6-2, 6-4, 6-8, 7-5
Fred Perry d. Wilmer Allison 4-6, 6-4, 7-5, 6-3

1936
Great Britain d. Australia 3-2 (Wimbledon)
Bunny Austin (B) d. Jack Crawford 4-6, 6-3, 6-1, 6-1
Fred Perry (B) d. Adrian Quist 6-1, 4-6, 7-5, 6-2
Jack Crawford–Adrian Quist d. Pat Hughes–Charles Tuckey
  6-4, 2-6, 7-5, 10-8
Adrian Quist d. Bunny Austin 6-4, 3-6, 7-5, 6-2
Fred Perry d. Jack Crawford 6-2, 6-2, 6-3

1937
United States d. Great Britain 4-1 (Wimbledon)
Bunny Austin (GB) d. Frank Parker 6-3, 6-2, 7-5
Don Budge (US) d. Charlie Hare 15-13, 6-1, 6-2
Don Budge–Gene Mako d. Charles Tuckey–Frank Wilde
  6-3, 7-5, 7-9, 12-10
Frank Parker d. Charlie Hare 6-2, 6-4, 6-2
Don Budge d. Bunny Austin 8-6, 3-6, 6-4, 6-3

1938
United States d. Australia 3-2 (Philadelphia)
Bobby Riggs (US) d. Adrian Quist 4-6, 6-0, 8-6, 6-1
Don Budge (US) d. John Bromwich 6-2, 6-3, 4-6, 7-5
Adrian Quist–John Bromwich d. Don Budge–Gene Mako
  0-6, 6-3, 6-4, 6-2
Don Budge d. Adrian Quist 8-6, 6-1, 6-2
John Bromwich d. Bobby Riggs 6-4, 4-6, 6-0, 6-2

1939
Australia d. United States 3-2 (Haverford, Pa.)
Bobby Riggs (US) d. John Bromwich 6-4, 6-0, 7-5
Frank Parker (US) d. Adrian Quist 6-3, 2-6, 6-4, 1-6, 7-5
Adrian Quist–John Bromwich d. Jack Kramer–Joe Hunt
  5-7, 6-2, 7-5, 6-2
Adrian Quist d. Bobby Riggs 6-1, 6-4, 3-6, 3-6, 6-4
John Bromwich d. Frank Parker 6-0, 6-3, 6-1

1940-45 Not held, World War II

1946

United States d. Australia 5-0 (Melbourne)
Ted Schroeder d. John Bromwich 3-6, 6-1, 6-2, 0-6, 6-3
Jack Kramer d. Dinny Pails 8-6, 6-2, 9-7
Jack Kramer–Ted Schroeder d. John Bromwich–Adrian Quist
  6-2, 7-5, 6-4
Gardnar Mulloy d. Dinny Pails 6-3, 6-3, 6-4
Jack Kramer d. John Bromwich 8-6, 6-4, 6-4

1947

United States d. Australia 4-1 (Forest Hills)
Jack Kramer (US) d. Dinny Pails 6-2, 6-1, 6-2
Ted Schroeder (US) d. John Bromwich 6-4, 5-7, 6-3, 6-4
John Bromwich–Colin Long d. Jack Kramer–Ted Schroeder
  6-4, 2-6, 6-2, 6-4
Ted Schroeder d. Dinny Pails 6-3, 8-6, 4-6, 9-11, 10-8
Jack Kramer d. John Bromwich 6-3, 6-2, 6-2

1948

United States d. Australia 5-0 (Forest Hills)
Frank Parker d. Bill Sidwell 6-4, 6-4, 6-4
Ted Schroeder d. Adrian Quist 6-3, 4-6, 6-0, 6-0
Bill Talbert–Gardnar Mulloy d. Bill Sidwell–Colin Long
  8-6, 9-7, 2-6, 7-5
Ted Schroeder d. Bill Sidwell 6-2, 6-1, 6-1
Frank Parker d. Adrian Quist 6-2, 6-2, 6-3

1949

United States d. Australia 4-1 (Forest Hills)
Ted Schroeder (US) d. Bill Sidwell 6-1, 5-7, 4-6, 6-2, 6-3
Pancho Gonzalez (US) d. Frank Sedgman 8-6, 6-4, 9-7
Bill Sidwell–John Bromwich d. Bill Talbert–Gardnar Mulloy
  3-6, 4-6, 10-8, 9-7, 9-7
Ted Schroeder d. Frank Sedgman 6-4, 6-3, 6-3
Pancho Gonzalez d. Bill Sidwell 6-1, 6-3, 6-3

1950

Australia d. United States 4-1 (Forest Hills)
Frank Sedgman (A) d. Tom Brown 6-0, 8-6, 9-7
Ken McGregor (A) d. Ted Schroeder 13-11, 6-3, 6-4
Frank Sedgman–John Bromwich d. Ted Schroeder–Gardnar Mulloy
  4-6, 6-4, 6-2, 4-6, 6-4
Frank Sedgman d. Ted Schroeder 6-2, 6-2, 6-2
Tom Brown d. Ken McGregor 9-11, 8-10, 11-9, 6-1, 6-4

1951

Australia d. United States 3-2 (Sydney)
Vic Seixas (US) d. Mervyn Rose 6-3, 6-4, 9-7
Frank Sedgman (A) d. Ted Schroeder 6-4, 6-3, 4-6, 6-4
Ken McGregor–Frank Sedgman d. Ted Schroeder–Tony Trabert
  6-2, 9-7, 6-3
Ted Schroeder d. Mervyn Rose 6-4, 13-11, 7-5
Frank Sedgman d. Vic Seixas 6-4, 6-2, 6-2

1952

Australia d. United States 4-1 (Adelaide)
Frank Sedgman (A) d. Vic Seixas 6-3, 6-4, 6-3
Ken McGregor (A) d. Tony Trabert 11-9, 6-4, 6-1
Ken McGregor–Frank Sedgman d. Vic Seixas–Tony Trabert
  6-3, 6-4, 1-6, 6-3
Frank Sedgman d. Tony Trabert 7-5, 6-4, 10-8
Vic Seixas d. Ken McGregor 6-3, 8-6, 6-8, 6-3

1953

Australia d. United States 3-2 (Melbourne)
Lew Hoad (A) d. Vic Seixas 6-4, 6-2, 6-3
Tony Trabert (US) d. Ken Rosewall 6-3, 6-4, 6-4
Vic Seixas–Tony Trabert d. Rex Hartwig–Lew Hoad 6-2, 6-4, 6-4
Lew Hoad d. Tony Trabert 13-11, 6-3, 2-6, 3-6, 7-5
Ken Rosewall d. Vic Seixas 6-2, 2-6, 6-3, 6-4

1954

United States d. Australia 3-2 (Sydney)
Tony Trabert (US) d. Lew Hoad 6-4, 2-6, 12-10, 6-3
Vic Seixas (US) d. Ken Rosewall 8-6, 6-8, 6-4, 6-3
Vic Seixas–Tony Trabert d. Lew Hoad–Ken Rosewall
  6-2, 4-6, 6-2, 10-8
Ken Rosewall d. Tony Trabert 9-7, 7-5, 6-3
Rex Hartwig d. Vic Seixas 4-6, 6-3, 6-2, 6-3

1955

Australia d. United States 5-0 (Forest Hills)
Ken Rosewall d. Vic Seixas 6-3, 10-8, 4-6, 6-2
Lew Hoad d. Tony Trabert 4-6, 6-3, 6-3, 8-6
Lew Hoad–Rex Hartwig d. Tony Trabert–Vic Seixas
  12-14, 6-4, 6-3, 3-6, 7-5
Lew Hoad d. Vic Seixas 7-9, 6-1, 6-4, 6-4
Ken Rosewall d. Ham Richardson 6-4, 3-6, 6-1, 6-4

1956

Australia d. United States 5-0 (Adelaide)
Lew Hoad d. Herbie Flam 6-2, 6-3, 6-3
Ken Rosewall d. Vic Seixas 6-1, 6-4, 4-6, 6-1
Lew Hoad–Ken Rosewall d. Sammy Giammalva–Vic Seixas
  1-6, 6-1, 7-5, 6-4
Ken Rosewall d. Sammy Giammalva 4-6, 6-1, 8-6, 7-5
Lew Hoad d. Vic Seixas 6-2, 7-5, 6-3

1957

Australia d. United States 3-2 (Melbourne)
Mal Anderson (A) d. Barry MacKay 6-3, 7-5, 3-6, 7-9, 6-3
Ashley Cooper (A) d. Vic Seixas 3-6, 7-5, 6-1, 1-6, 6-3
Mal Anderson–Mervyn Rose d. Barry MacKay–Vic Seixas
  6-4, 6-4, 8-6
Vic Seixas d. Mal Anderson 6-3, 4-6, 6-3, 0-6, 13-11
Barry MacKay d. Ashley Cooper 6-4, 1-6, 4-6, 6-4, 6-3

1958

United States d. Australia 3-2 (Brisbane)
Alex Olmedo (US) d. Mal Anderson 8-6, 2-6, 9-7, 8-6
Ashley Cooper (A) d. Barry MacKay 4-6, 6-3, 6-2, 6-4
Alex Olmedo–Ham Richardson d. Mal Anderson–Neale Fraser
  10-12, 3-6, 16-14, 6-3, 7-5
Alex Olmedo d. Ashley Cooper 6-3, 4-6, 6-4, 8-6
Mal Anderson d. Barry MacKay 7-5, 13-11, 11-9

1959

Australia d. United States 3-2 (Forest Hills)
Neale Fraser (A) d. Alex Olmedo 8-6, 6-8, 6-4, 8-6
Barry MacKay (US) d. Rod Laver 7-5, 6-4, 6-1
Neale Fraser–Roy Emerson d. Alex Olmedo–Butch Buchholz
  7-5, 7-5, 6-4
Alex Olmedo d. Rod Laver 9-7, 4-6, 10-8, 12-10
Neale Fraser d. Barry MacKay 8-6, 3-6, 6-2, 6-4

1960

Australia d. Italy 4-1 (Sydney)
Neale Fraser (A) d. Orlando Sirola 4-6, 6-3, 6-3, 6-3
Rod Laver (A) d. Nicola Pietrangeli 8-6, 6-4, 6-3
Neale Fraser–Roy Emerson d. Nicola Pietrangeli–Orlando Sirola
  10-8, 5-7, 6-2, 6-4
Rod Laver d. Orlando Sirola 9-7, 6-2, 6-3
Nicola Pietrangeli d. Neale Fraser 11-9, 6-3, 1-6, 6-2

1961

Australia d. Italy 5-0 (Melbourne)
Roy Emerson d. Nicola Pietrangeli 8-6, 6-4, 6-0
Rod Laver d. Orlando Sirola 6-1, 6-4, 6-3
Neale Fraser–Roy Emerson d. Nicola Pietrangeli–Orlando Sirola
  6-2, 6-3, 6-4
Rod Laver d. Nicola Pietrangeli 6-3, 3-6, 4-6, 6-3, 8-6
Roy Emerson d. Orlando Sirola 6-3, 6-3, 4-6, 6-2

1962
Australia d. Mexico 5-0 (Brisbane)
Rod Laver d. Rafael Osuna 6-2, 6-1, 7-5
Neale Fraser d. Tony Palafox 7-9, 6-3, 6-4, 11-9
Roy Emerson–Rod Laver d. Rafael Osuna–Tony Palafox 7-5, 6-2, 6-4
Neale Fraser d. Rafael Osuna 3-6, 11-9, 6-1, 3-6, 6-4
Rod Laver d. Tony Palafox 6-1, 4-6, 6-4, 8-6

1963
United States d. Australia 3-2 (Adelaide)
Dennis Ralston (US) d. John Newcombe 6-4, 6-1, 3-6, 4-6, 7-5
Roy Emerson (A) d. Chuck McKinley 6-3, 3-6, 7-5, 7-5
Chuck McKinley–Dennis Ralston d. Roy Emerson–Neale Fraser
  6-3, 4-6, 11-9, 11-9
Roy Emerson d. Dennis Ralston 6-2, 6-3, 3-6, 6-2
Chuck McKinley d. John Newcombe 10-12, 6-2, 9-7, 6-2

1964
Australia d. United States 3-2 (Cleveland)
Chuck McKinley (US) d. Fred Stolle 6-1, 9-7, 4-6, 6-2
Roy Emerson (A) d. Dennis Ralston 6-3, 6-1, 6-2
Chuck McKinley–Dennis Ralston d. Roy Emerson–Fred Stolle
  6-4, 4-6, 4-6, 6-3, 6-4
Fred Stolle d. Dennis Ralston 7-5, 6-3, 3-6, 9-11, 6-4
Roy Emerson d. Chuck McKinley 3-6, 6-2, 6-4, 6-4

1965
Australia d. Spain 4-1 (Sydney)
Fred Stolle (A) d. Manuel Santana 10-12, 3-6, 6-1, 6-4, 7-5
Roy Emerson (A) d. Juan Gisbert 6-3, 6-2, 6-2
John Newcombe–Tony Roche d. Jose Luis Arilla–Manuel Santana
  6-3, 4-6, 7-5, 6-2
Manuel Santana d. Roy Emerson 2-6, 6-3, 6-4, 15-13
Fred Stolle d. Juan Gisbert 6-2, 6-4, 8-6

1966
Australia d. India 4-1 (Melbourne)
Fred Stolle (A) d. Ramanathan Krishnan 6-3, 6-2, 6-4
Roy Emerson (A) d. Jaidip Mukerjea 7-5, 6-4, 6-2
Ramanathan Krishnan–Jaidip Mukerjea d. John Newcombe–
  Tony Roche 4-6, 7-5, 6-4, 6-4
Roy Emerson d. Ramanathan Krishnan 6-0, 6-2, 10-8
Fred Stolle d. Jaidip Mukerjea 7-5, 6-8, 6-3, 5-7, 6-3

1967
Australia d. Spain 4-1 (Brisbane)
Roy Emerson (A) d. Manuel Santana 6-4, 6-1, 6-1
John Newcombe (A) d. Manuel Orantes 6-3, 6-3, 6-2
John Newcombe–Tony Roche d. Manuel Santana–Manuel Orantes
  6-4, 6-4, 6-4
Manuel Santana d. John Newcombe 7-5, 6-4, 6-2
Roy Emerson d. Manuel Orantes 6-1, 6-1, 2-6, 6-4

1968
United States d. Australia 4-1 (Adelaide)
Clark Graebner (US) d. Bill Bowrey 8-10, 6-4, 8-6, 3-6, 6-1
Arthur Ashe (US) d. Ray Ruffels 8-6, 7-5, 6-3, 6-3
Bob Lutz–Stan Smith d. John Alexander–Ray Ruffels 6-4, 6-4, 6-2
Clark Graebner d. Ray Ruffels 3-6, 8-6, 2-6, 6-3, 6-1
Bill Bowrey d. Arthur Ashe 2-6, 6-3, 11-9, 8-6

1969
United States d. Romania 5-0 (Cleveland)
Arthur Ashe d. Ilie Nastase 6-2, 15-13, 7-5
Stan Smith d. Ion Tiriac 6-8, 6-3, 5-7, 6-4, 6-4
Bob Lutz–Stan Smith d. Ilie Nastase–Ion Tiriac 8-6, 6-1, 11-9
Stan Smith d. Ilie Nastase 4-6, 4-6, 6-4, 6-1, 11-9
Arthur Ashe d. Ion Tiriac 6-3, 8-6, 3-6, 4-0 (default)

1970
United States d. Germany 5-0 (Cleveland)
Arthur Ashe d. Wilhelm Bungert 6-2, 10-8, 6-2
Cliff Richey d. Christian Kuhnke 6-3, 6-4, 6-2
Bob Lutz–Stan Smith d. Christian Kuhnke–Wilhelm Bungert
  6-3, 7-5, 6-4
Cliff Richey d. Wilhelm Bungert 6-4, 6-4, 7-5
Arthur Ashe d. Christian Kuhnke 6-8, 10-12, 9-7, 13-11, 6-4

1971
United States d. Romania 3-2 (Charlotte, N.C.)
Stan Smith (US) d. Ilie Nastase 7-5, 6-3, 6-1
Frank Froehling (US) d. Ion Tiriac 3-6, 1-6, 6-1, 6-3, 8-6
Ilie Nastase–Ion Tiriac d. Stan Smith–Erik van Dillen 7-5, 6-4, 8-6
Stan Smith d. Ion Tiriac 8-6, 6-3, 6-0
Ilie Nastase d. Frank Froehling 6-3, 6-1, 4-6, 6-4

FINAL ROUNDS
1972
United States d. Romania 3-2 (Bucharest)
Stan Smith (US) d. Ilie Nastase 11-9, 6-2, 6-3
Ion Tiriac (R) d. Tom Gorman 4-6, 2-6, 6-4, 6-3, 6-2
Stan Smith–Erik van Dillen d. Ilie Nastase–Ion Tiriac 6-2, 6-0, 6-3
Stan Smith d. Ion Tiriac 4-6, 6-2, 6-4, 2-6, 6-0
Ilie Nastase d. Tom Gorman 6-1, 6-2, 5-7, 10-8

1973 *(First Open Davis Cup)*
Australia d. United States 5-0 (Cleveland)
John Newcombe d. Stan Smith 6-1, 3-6, 6-3, 3-6, 6-4
Rod Laver d. Tom Gorman 8-10, 8-6, 6-8, 6-3, 6-1
John Newcombe–Rod Laver d. Erik van Dillen–Stan Smith
  6-1, 6-2, 6-4
John Newcombe d. Tom Gorman 6-2, 6-1, 6-3
Rod Laver d. Stan Smith 6-3, 6-4, 3-6, 6-2

1974
South Africa d. India (default—Indian government ordered team not
to play, a protest against the South African government's policy of
apartheid. The South African team was Bob Hewitt, Frew McMillan,
Ray Moore, and Rob Maud. The Indian team was Vijay Amritraj,
Anand Amritraj, Jasjit Singh, and Sashi Menon.)

1975
Sweden d. Czechoslovakia 3-2 (Stockholm)
Bjorn Borg (S) d. Jiri Hrebec 6-1, 6-3, 6-0
Jan Kodes (C) d. Ove Bengtson 4-6, 6-2, 7-5, 6-4
Bjorn Borg–Ove Bengtson d. Jan Kodes–Vladimir Zednik
  6-4, 6-4, 6-4
Bjorn Borg d. Jan Kodes 6-4, 6-2, 6-2
Jiri Hrebec d. Ove Bengtson 1-6, 6-3, 6-1, 6-4

1976
Italy d. Chile 4-1 (Santiago)
Corrado Barazzutti (I) d. Jaime Fillol 7-5, 4-6, 7-5, 6-1
Adriano Panatta (I) d. Patricio Cornejo 6-3, 6-1, 6-3
Adriano Panatta–Paolo Bertolucci d. Patricio Cornejo–
  Jaime Fillol 3-6, 6-2, 9-7, 6-3
Adriano Panatta d. Jaime Fillol 8-6, 6-4, 3-6, 10-8
Belus Prajoux (C) d Antonio Zugarelli 6-4, 6-4, 6-2

1977
Australia d. Italy 3-1 (Sydney)
Tony Roche (A) d. Adriano Panatta 6-3, 6-4, 6-4
John Alexander (A) d. Corrado Barazzutti 6-4, 8-6, 4-6, 6-2
Adriano Panatta–Paolo Bertolucci d. John Alexander–Phil Dent
  6-4, 6-4, 7-5
John Alexander d. Adriano Panatta 6-4, 4-6, 2-6, 8-6, 11-9
Tony Roche vs. Corrado Barazzutti 12-12 (unfinished)

1978
United States d. Great Britain 4-1 (Rancho Mirage, Cal.)
John McEnroe (US) d. John Lloyd 6-1, 6-2, 6-2
Buster Mottram (GB) d. Brian Gottfried 4-6, 2-6, 10-8, 6-4, 6-3
Stan Smith–Bob Lutz (US) d. David Lloyd–Mark Cox 6-2, 6-2, 6-3
John McEnroe d. Buster Mottram 6-2, 6-2, 6-1
Brian Gottfried d. John Lloyd 6-1, 6-2, 6-4

1979
United States d. Italy 5-0 (San Francisco)
Vitas Gerulaitis d. Corrado Barazzutti 6-3, 3-2 (default, injury)
John McEnroe d. Adriano Panatta 6-2, 6-3, 6-4
Stan Smith–Bob Lutz d. Paolo Bertolucci–Adriano Panatta
  6-4, 12-10, 6-2
John McEnroe d. Antonio Zugarelli 6-4, 6-3, 6-1
Vitas Gerulaitis d. Adriano Panatta 6-1, 6-3, 6-3

1980
Czechoslovakia d. Italy 4-1 (Prague)
Tomas Smid (C) d. Adriano Panatta 3-6, 3-6, 6-3, 6-4, 6-4
Ivan Lendl (C) d. Corrado Barazzutti 4-6, 6-1, 6-1, 6-2
Ivan Lendl–Tomas Smid d. Paolo Bertolucci–Adriano Panatta
   3-6, 6-3, 3-6, 6-3, 6-4
Corrado Barazzutti d. Tomas Smid 3-6, 6-3, 6-2
Ivan Lendl d. Gianni Ocleppo 6-3, 6-3

WORLD GROUP: FINAL ROUND
1981
United States d. Argentina 3-1 (Cincinnati)
John McEnroe (US) d. Guillermo Vilas 6-3, 6-2, 6-2
Jose-Luis Clerc (A) d. Roscoe Tanner 7-5, 6-3, 8-6
Peter Fleming–John McEnroe d. Jose-Luis Clerc–Guillermo Vilas
   6-3, 4-6, 6-4, 4-6, 11-9
John McEnroe d. Jose-Luis Clerc 7-5, 5-7, 6-3, 3-6, 6-3
Roscoe Tanner vs. Guillermo Vilas (suspended at 11-10, first set)
SF: United States 5, Australia 0
SF: Argentina 5, Great Britain 0
QF: Argentina 3, Romania 2
QF: Great Britain 4, New Zealand 1
QF: Australia 3, Sweden 1
QF: United States 4, Czechoslovakia 1
1982
United States d. France 4-1 (Grenoble)
John McEnroe (US) d. Yannick Noah 12-10, 1-6, 3-6, 6-2, 6-3
Gene Mayer (US) d. Henri Leconte 6-2, 6-2, 7-9, 6-4
Peter Fleming–John McEnroe d. Henri Leconte–Yannick Noah
   6-3, 6-4, 9-7
Yannick Noah d. Gene Mayer 6-1, 6-0
John McEnroe d. Henri Leconte 6-2, 6-3
SF: United States 5, Australia 0
SF: France 3, New Zealand 2
QF: United States 3, Sweden 2
QF: Australia 4, Chile 1
QF: New Zealand 3, Italy 2
QF: France 3, Czechoslovakia 2
1983
Australia d. Sweden 3-2 (Melbourne)
Mats Wilander (S) d. Pat Cash 6-3, 4-6, 9-7, 6-3
John Fitzgerald (A) d. Joakim Nystrom 6-4, 6-2, 4-6, 6-4
Mark Edmondson–Paul McNamee (A) d. Anders Jarryd–
   Hans Simonsson 6-4, 6-4, 6-2
Pat Cash d. Joakim Nystrom 6-4, 6-1, 6-1
Mats Wilander d. John Fitzgerald 6-8, 6-0, 6-1
SF: Australia 4, France 1
SF: Sweden 4, Argentina 1
QF: France 3, Paraguay 2
QF: Australia 5, Romania 0
QF: Sweden 3, New Zealand 2
QF: Argentina 5, Italy 0
1984
Sweden d. United States 4-1 (Goteborg, Sweden)
Mats Wilander (S) d. Jimmy Connors 6-1, 6-3, 6-3
Henrik Sundstrom (S) d. John McEnroe 13-11, 6-4, 6-3
Stefan Edberg–Anders Jarryd d. Peter Fleming–John McEnroe
   7-5, 5-7, 6-2, 7-5
John McEnroe d. Mats Wilander 6-3, 5-7, 6-3
Henrik Sundstrom d. Jimmy Arias 3-6, 8-6, 6-3
SF: United States 4, Australia 1
SF: Sweden 5, Czechoslovakia 0
QF: Australia 5, Italy 0
QF: United States 5, Argentina 0
QF: Czechoslovakia 3, France 2
QF: Sweden 4, Paraguay 1

1985
Sweden d. Germany F.R. 3-2 (Munich)
Mats Wilander (S) d. Michael Westphal 6-3, 6-4, 10-8
Boris Becker (G) d. Stefan Edberg 6-3, 3-6, 7-5, 8-6
Joakim Nystrom–Mats Wilander d. Boris Becker–Andreas Maurer
   6-4, 6-2, 6-1.
Boris Becker d. Mats Wilander 6-3, 2-6, 6-3, 6-3
Stefan Edberg d. Michael Westphal 3-6, 7-5, 6-4, 6-3
SF: Germany F.R. 5, Czechoslovakia 0
SF: Sweden 5, Australia 0
QF: Germany F.R. 3, United States 2
QF: Czechoslovakia 5, Ecuador 0
QF: Australia 3, Paraguay 2
QF: Sweden 4, India 1
1986
Australia d. Sweden 3-2 (Melbourne)
Pat Cash (A) d. Stefan Edberg 13-11, 13-11, 6-4
Mikael Pernfors (S) d. Paul McNamee 6-3, 6-1, 6-3
Pat Cash–John Fitzgerald d. Stefan Edberg–Anders Jarryd
   6-3, 6-4, 4-6, 6-1
Pat Cash d. Mikael Pernfors 2-6, 4-6, 6-3, 6-4, 6-3
Stefan Edberg d. Paul McNamee 10-8, 6-4
SF: Australia 3, United States 1
SF: Sweden 4, Czechoslovakia 1
QF: United States 4, Mexico 1
QF: Australia 4, Great Britain 1
QF: Czechoslovakia 5, Yugoslavia 0
QF: Sweden 5, Italy 0
1987
Sweden d. India 5-0 (Goteborg, Sweden)
Mats Wilander d. Ramesh Krishnan 6-4, 6-1, 6-3
Anders Jarryd d. Vijay Amritraj 6-3, 6-3, 6-1
Joakim Nystrom–Mats Wilander d. Anand Amritraj–Vijay Amritraj
   6-3, 3-6, 6-1, 6-2
Anders Jarryd d. Ramesh Krishnan 6-4, 6-3
Mats Wilander d. Vijay Amritraj 6-2, 6-0
SF: Sweden 3, Spain 2
SF: India 3, Australia 2
QF: Sweden 4, France 1
QF: Spain 3, Paraguay 2
QF: India 4, Israel 0
QF: Australia 4, Mexico 1
1988
Germany d. Sweden 4-1 (Goteborg, Sweden)
Carl-Uwe Steeb (G) d. Mats Wilander 8-10, 1-6, 6-2, 6-4, 8-6
Boris Becker (G) d. Stefan Edberg 6-3, 6-1, 6-4
Boris Becker–Eric Jelen d. Stefan Edberg–Anders Jarryd
   3-6, 2-6, 7-5, 6-3, 6-2
Stefan Edberg d. Carl-Uwe Steeb 6-4 8-6
Patrick Kuhnen (G) d. Kent Carlsson (walkover)
SF: Sweden 4, France 1
SF: Germany F.R. 5, Yugoslavia 0
QF: Sweden 3, Czechoslovakia 2
QF: France 5, Australia 0
QF: Germany F.R. 5, Denmark 0
QF: Yugoslavia 4, Italy 1
1989 *(*First use of tie-breaker in Davis Cup)*
Germany d. Sweden 3-2 (Stuttgart, Germany)
Mats Wilander (S) d. Carl-Uwe Steeb 5-7, 7-6 (7-0), 6-7 (4-7), 6-2, 6-3
Boris Becker (G) d. Stefan Edberg 6-2, 6-2, 6-4
Boris Becker–Eric Jelen d. Jan Gunnarson–Anders Jarryd
   7-6 (8-6), 6-4, 3-6, 6-7 (4-7), 6-4
Boris Becker d. Mats Wilander 6-2, 6-0, 6-2
Stefan Edberg d. Carl-Uwe Steeb 6-2, 6-4
SF: Sweden 4, Yugoslavia 1
SF: Germany F.R. 3, United States 2
QF: Sweden 3, Austria 2
QF: Yugoslavia 4, Spain 1
QF: United States 5, France 0
QF: Germany F.R. 3, Czechoslovakia 2

1990
United States d. Australia 3-2 (St. Petersburg, Fla.)
Andre Agassi (US) d. Richard Fromberg 4-6, 6-2, 4-6, 6-2, 6-4
Michael Chang (US) d. Darren Cahill 6-2, 7-6 (7-4), 6-0
Rick Leach–Jim Pugh (US) d. Pat Cash–John Fitzgerald
  6-4, 6-2, 3-6, 7-6 (7-2)
Darren Cahill d. Andre Agassi 6-4, 4-6 (retired)
Richard Fromberg d. Michael Chang 7-5, 2-6, 6-3
SF: Australia 5, Argentina 0
SF: United States 3, Austria 2
QF: Argentina 3, Germany 2
QF: Australia 3, New Zealand 2
QF: United States 4, Czechoslovakia 1
QF: Austria 5, Italy 0

1991
France d. United States 3-1 (Lyon)
Andre Agassi (US) d. Guy Forget 6-7 (7-9), 6-2, 6-1, 6-2
Henri Leconte (F) d. Pete Sampras 6-4, 7-5, 6-4
Guy Forget–Henri Leconte d. Ken Flach–Robert Seguso
  6-1, 6-4, 4-6, 6-2
Guy Forget d. Pete Sampras 7-6 (8-6), 3-6, 6-3, 6-4
Henri Leconte vs. Andre Agassi (not played)
SF: United States 3, Germany 2
SF: France 5, Yugoslavia 0
QF: United States 4, Spain 1
QF: Germany 5, Argentina 0
QF: Yugoslavia 4, Czechoslovakia 1
QF: France 3, Australia 2

1992
United States d. Switzerland 3-1 (Fort Worth, Tex.)
Andre Agassi (US) d. Jakob Hlasek 6-1, 6-2, 6-2
Marc Rosset (S) d. Jim Courier 6-3, 6-7 (9-11), 3-6, 6-4, 6-4
John McEnroe–Pete Sampras d. Jakob Hlasek–Marc Rosset
  6-7 (5-7), 6-7 (7-9), 7-5, 6-1, 6-2
Jim Courier d. Jakob Hlasek 6-3, 3-6, 6-3, 6-4
Andre Agassi vs. Marc Rosset (not played)
SF: Switzerland 5, Brazil 0
SF: United States 4, Sweden 1
QF: Switzerland 3, France 2
QF: Brazil 3, Italy 1
QF: Sweden 5, Australia 0
QF: United States 3, Czechoslovakia

1993
Germany d. Australia 4-1 (Dusseldorf)
Michael Stich (G) d. Jason Stoltenberg 6-7 (2-7), 6-3, 6-1, 4-6, 6-3
Richard Fromberg (A) d. Marc Goellner 3-6, 5-7, 7-6 (10-8), 6-2, 9-7
Michael Stich–Patrick Kuhnen d. Todd Woodbridge–Mark Woodforde
  7-6 (7-4), 4-6, 6-3, 7-6 (7-4)
Michael Stich d. Richard Fromberg 6-4, 6-2, 6-2
Marc Goellner d. Jason Stoltenberg 6-1, 6-7 (2-7), 7-6 (7-3)
SF: Australia 5, India 0
SF: Germany 5, Sweden 0
QF: Australia 3, Italy 2
QF: India 3, France 2
QF: Sweden 4, Netherlands 1
QF: Germany 4, Czech Republic 1

1994
Sweden d. Russia 4-1 (Moscow)
Stefan Edberg (S) d. Alexander Volkov 6-4, 6-2, 6-7 (2-7), 0-6, 8-6
Magnus Larsson (S) d. Yevgeny Kafelnikov 6-0, 6-2, 3-6, 2-6, 6-3
Jan Apell–Jonas Bjorkman d. Yevgeny Kafelnikov–Andrei Olhovskiy
  6-7 (4-7), 6-2, 6-3, 1-6, 8-6
Yevgeny Kafelnikov d. Stefan Edberg 4-6, 6-4, 6-0
Magnus Larsson d. Alexander Volkov 7-6 (7-4), 6-4
SF: Sweden 3, United States 2
SF: Russia 4, Germany 1
QF: United States 3, Netherlands 2
QF: Sweden 3, France 2
QF: Russia 3, Czech Republic 2
QF: Germany 3, Spain 2

1995
United States d. Russia 3-2 (Moscow)
Pete Sampras (US) d. Andrei Chesnokov 3-6, 6-4, 6-3, 6-7 (5-7), 6-4
Yevgeny Kafelnikov (R) d. Jim Courier 7-6 (7-1), 7-5, 6-3
Pete Sampras–Todd Martin d. Yevgeny Kafelnikov–Andrei Olhovskiy
  7-5, 6-4, 6-3
Pete Sampras d. Yevgeny Kafelnikov 6-2, 6-4, 7-6 (7-4)
Andrei Chesnokov d. Jim Courier 6-7 (1-7), 7-5, 6-0
SF: United States 4, Sweden 1
SF: Russia 3, Germany 2
QF: United States 5, Italy 0
QF: Russia 4, South Africa 1
QF: Germany 4, Netherlands 1

1996
France d. Sweden 3-2 (Malmo, Sweden)
Cedric Pioline (F) d. Stefan Edberg 6-3, 6-4, 6-3
Thomas Enqvist (S) d. Arnaud Boetsch 6-4, 6-3, 7-6 (7-2)
Guy Forget–Guillaume Raoux (F) d. Jonas Bjorkman–Nicklas Kulti
  6-3, 1-6, 6-3, 6-3
Thomas Enqvist d. Cedric Pioline 3-6, 6-7 (8-10), 6-4, 6-4, 9-7
Arnaud Boetsch d. Nicklas Kulti 7-6 (7-2), 2-6, 4-6, 7-6 (7-5), 10-8
SF: France 3, Italy 2
SF: Sweden 4, Czech Republic 1
QF: Italy 4, South Africa 1
QF: France 5, Germany 0
QF: Sweden 5, India 0
QF: Czech Republic 3, United States 0

1997
Sweden 5, United States 0 (Gotenburg, Sweden)
Jonas Bjorkman d. Michael Chang 7-5, 1-6, 6-3, 6-3
Magnus Larsson d. Pete Sampras 3-6, 7-6 (7-1), 2-1 retired
Jonas Bjorkman–Nicklas Kulti d. Todd Martin-Jonathan Stark
  6-4, 6-4, 6-4
Jonas Bjorkman d. Jonathan Stark 6-1, 6-1
Magnus Larsson d. Michael Chang 7-6 (7-4), 6-7 (6-8), 6-4
SF: United States 4, Australia 1
SF: Sweden 4, Italy 1
QF: United States 4, Netherlands 1
QF: Australia 5, Czech Republic 0
QF: Italy 4, Spain 1
QF: Sweden 3, South Africa 2

1998
Sweden 4, Italy 1 (Milan)
Magnus Norman (S) d. Andrea Gaudenzi 6-7, 7-6, 4-6, 6-3, 6-6, retired
Magnus Gustafsson (S) d. Davide Sanguinetti 6-1, 6-4, 6-0
Jonas Bjorkman–Nicklas Kulti d. Davide Sanguinetti-Diego Nargiso
  7-6 (7-1), 6-1, 6-3
Magnus Gustafsson d. Gianluca Pozzi 6-4, 6-2
Diego Nargiso d. Magnus Norman 6-2, 6-3
SF: Sweden 4, Spain 1
SF: Italy 4, United States 1
QF: Sweden 3, Germany 2
QF: Spain 4, Switzerland 1
QF: Italy 5, Zimbabwe 0
QF: United States 4, Belgium 1

1999
Australia b. France 3-2 (Nice)
Mark Philippoussis (A) d. Sebastien Grosjean 6-4, 6-2, 6-4
Cedric Pioline (F) d. Lleyton Hewitt 7-6 (9-7) 7-6 (8-6), 7-5
Mark Woodforde-Todd Woodbridge (A) d. Olivier Delaitre-
  Fabrice Santoro 2-6, 7-5, 6-2, 6-2
Mark Philippoussis d. Cedric Pioline 6-3, 5-7, 6-1, 6-2
Sebastien Grosjean d. Lleyton Hewitt 6-4, 6-3
SF: Australia 4, Russia 1
SF: France 4, Belgium 1
QF: Russia 3, Slovakia 2
QF: Australia 4, United States 1
QF: France 3, Brazil 2
QF: Belgium 3, Switzerland 2

2000
Spain 3, Australia 1 (Barcelona)
Lleyton Hewitt (A) d. Albert Costa 3-6, 6-1, 2-6, 6-4, 6-4
Juan Carlos Ferrero (S) d. Patrick Rafter
  6-7 (4-7), 7-6 (7-2), 6-2, 3-1, retired
Joan Balcells-Alex Corretja (S) d. Mark Woodforde-Sandon Stolle
  6-4, 6-4, 6-4
Juan Carlos Ferrero d. Lleyton Hewitt 6-2, 7-6 (7-5), 4-6, 6-4
Albert Costa vs. Patrick Rafter, canceled
SF: Spain 5, United States 0
SF: Australia 5, Brazil 0
QF: United States 3, Czech Republic 2
QF: Spain 4, Russia 1
QF: Brazil 3, Slovakia 2
QF: Australia 3, Germany 2

2001
France d. Australia 3-2 (Melbourne)
Nicolas Escude (F) d. Lleyton Hewitt 4-6, 6-3, 3-6, 6-3, 6-4
Patrick Rafter (A) d. Sebastien Grosjean 6-3, 7-6 (7-6), 7-5
Cedric Pioline-Fabrice Santoro d. Lleyton Hewitt-Patrick Rafter
  2-6, 6-3, 7-6 (7-5), 6-1
Lleyton Hewitt d. Sebastien Grosjean 6-3, 6-2, 6-3
Nicolas Escude d. Wayne Arthurs 7-6 (7-3), 6-7 (5-7), 6-3, 6-3
SF: Australia 4, Sweden 1
SF: France 3, Netherlands 2
QF: Australia 3, Brazil 1
QF: Sweden 4, Russia 1
QF: France 3, Switzerland 2
QF: Netherlands 4, Germany 1

2002
Russia d. France 3-2 (Paris)
Marat Safin (R) d. Paul-Henri Mathieu 6-4, 3-6, 6-1, 6-4
Sebastien Grosjean (F) d. Yevgeny Kafelnikov 7-6 (3), 6-3, 6-0
Fabrice Santoro-Nicolas Escude d. Yevgeny Kafelnikov-Marat Safin
  6-3, 3-6, 5-7, 6-3, 6-4
Marat Safin d. Sebastien Grosjean 6-3, 6-2, 7-6 (11)
Mikhail Youzhny (R) d. Paul-Henri Mathieu 3-6, 2-6, 6-3, 7-5, 6-4.
SF: France 3, United States 2
SF: Russia 3, Argentina 2
QF: France 3, Czech Republic 2
QF: United States 3, Spain 1
QF: Russia 4, Sweden 1
QF: Argentina 3, Croatia 2

ALL-TIME DAVIS CUP RECORDS

NATION

MOST TITLES
	Wins	Years
USA	31	1900, 1902, 1913, 1920-26, 1937-38, 1946-49, 1954, 1958, 1963, 1968-72, 1978-79, 1981-82, 1990, 1992, 1995
Australia	27	1907-09, 1911, 1914, 1919, 1939, 1950-53, 1955-57, 1959-62, 1964-67, 1973, 1977, 1983, 1986, 1999
France	9	1927-32, 1991, 1996, 2001
Great Britain	9	1903-06, 1912, 1933-36
Sweden	7	1975, 1984-85, 1987, 1994, 1997, 1998
Germany	3	1988-89, 1993
Czechoslovakia	1	1980
Italy	1	1976
Russia	1	2002
South Africa	1	1974
Spain	1	2000

MOST MATCHES WON
	W-L	Yrs.played	First Yr
U.S.A.	194 - 57	88	1900
AUSTRALIA	162 - 56	83	1905
ITALY	142 - 72	72	1922
FRANCE	141 - 74	83	1904
SWEDEN	136 - 62	69	1925
GREAT BRITAIN	132 - 81	91	1900
GERMANY	127 - 64	67	1913
CZECH REPUBLIC	103 - 67	69	1921
INDIA	97 - 64	66	1921
SPAIN	96 - 65	67	1921
JAPAN	86 - 69	68	1921
YUGOSLAVIA	83 - 66	68	1927
BELGIUM	77 - 78	80	1904
DENMARK	73 - 75	74	1921
BRAZIL	72 - 53	54	1932

MOST FINAL APPEARANCES
	Total	W-L
USA	59	31 - 28
Australia	46	27 - 19
Great Britain	17	9 - 8
France	15	9 - 6
Sweden	12	7 - 5
Italy	7	1 - 6
Germany	5	3 - 2
Spain	3	1 - 2
India	3	0 - 3
Romania	3	0 - 3
Czechoslovakia	2	1 - 1
Russia	3	1 - 2
South Africa	1	1 - 0
Chile	1	0 - 1
Argentina	1	0 - 1
Belgium	1	0 - 1
Japan	1	0 - 1
Mexico	1	0 - 1
Switzerland	1	0 - 1

INDIVIDUAL

MOST SERIES PLAYED
	Total	W-L
PIETRANGELI, Nicola (ITA)	66	120 - 44
NASTASE, Ilie (ROM)	52	109 - 37
ABDUL-AAL, Esam (BRN)	51	70 - 24
VICINI, Domenico (SMR)	47	36 - 35
AL MEGAYEL, Badar (KSA)	46	52 - 38
SANTANA, Manuel (ESP)	46	92 - 28
SIROLA, Orlando (ITA)	46	57 - 33
AL KHULAIFI, Nasser-Ghanim (QAT)	45	24 - 47
KOCH, Tomas (BRA)	44	74 - 44
BUNGERT, Wilhelm (GER)	43	67 - 36
KRISHNAN, Ramanathan (IND)	43	69 - 28
MANDARINO, Jose-Edison (BRA)	43	68 - 41
MUKERJEA, Jaidip (IND)	43	62 - 35
TIRIAC, Ion (ROM)	43	70 - 39
BRICHANT, Jacques (BEL)	42	71 - 49
GANDONOU, Alphonse (BEN)	42	22 - 43

MOST MATCHES PLAYED

	Total	W-L
PIETRANGELI, Nicola (ITA)	164	66
NASTASE, Ilie (ROM)	146	52
SANTANA, Manuel (ESP)	120	46
BRICHANT, Jacques (BEL)	120	42
TIRIAC, Ion (ROM)	119	43
KOCH, Tomas (BRA)	118	44
MANDARINO, Jose-Edison (BRA)	109	43
KRISHNAN, Ramanathan (IND)	107	43
METREVELI, Alex (RUS)	105	38
BUNGERT, Wilhelm (GER)	103	43
SCHMIDT, Ulf (SWE)	102	38
WASHER, Philippe (BEL)	102	39
VON CRAMM, Gottfried (GER)	101	37
PANATTA, Adriano (ITA)	100	38
TAROCZY, Balazs (HUN)	95	33
KODES, Jan (TCH)	95	39

MOST WINS, OVERALL

	Total	Ties
PIETRANGELI, Nicola (ITA)	120 - 44	66
NASTASE, Ilie (ROM)	109 - 37	52
SANTANA, Manuel (ESP)	92 - 28	46
VON CRAMM, Gottfried (GER)	82 - 19	37
METREVELI, Alex (RUS)	80 - 25	38
TAROCZY, Balazs (HUN)	76 - 19	33
KOCH, Tomas (BRA)	74 - 44	44
BRICHANT, Jacques (BEL)	71 - 49	42
ABDUL-AAL, Esam (BRN)	70 - 24	51
TIRIAC, Ion (ROM)	70 - 39	43
KRISHNAN, Ramanathan (IND)	69 - 28	43
MANDARINO, Jose-Edison (BRA)	68 - 41	43
BUNGERT, Wilhelm (GER)	67 - 36	43
SCHMIDT, Ulf (SWE)	66 - 36	38
WASHER, Philippe (BEL)	66 - 36	39

MOST WINS, SINGLES

	W-L	Ties
PIETRANGELI, Nicola (ITA)	78 - 32	66
NASTASE, Ilie (ROM)	74 - 22	52
SANTANA, Manuel (ESP)	69 - 17	46
VON CRAMM, Gottfried (GER)	58 - 10	37
METREVELI, Alex (RUS)	56 - 14	38
BUNGERT, Wilhelm (GER)	53 - 27	43
BRICHANT, Jacques (BEL)	52 - 27	42
TAROCZY, Balazs (HUN)	50 - 12	33
KRISHNAN, Ramanathan (IND)	50 - 19	43
ABDUL-AAL, Esam (BRN)	47 - 11	51
LUNDQUIST, Jan-Erik (SWE)	47 - 16	35
MENZEL, Roderich (GER)	47 - 13	35
KOCH, Tomas (BRA)	46 - 32	44
WASHER, Philippe (BEL)	46 - 18	39
VILAS, Guillermo (ARG)	45 - 10	29

MOST WINS, DOUBLES

	W-L	Ties
PIETRANGELI, Nicola (ITA)	42 - 12	66
NASTASE, Ilie (ROM)	35 - 15	52
SIROLA, Orlando (ITA)	35 - 8	46
TIRIAC, Ion (ROM)	30 - 11	43
KOCH, Tomas (BRA)	28 - 12	44
MANDARINO, Jose-Edison (BRA)	27 - 10	43
PANATTA, Adriano (ITA)	27 - 10	38
TAROCZY, Balazs (HUN)	26 - 7	33
WILSON, Bobby (GBR)	25 - 8	34
LALL, Premjit (IND)	24 - 12	41
LIKHACHEV, Sergei (URS)	24 - 9	33
METREVELI, Alex (RUS)	24 - 11	38
VON CRAMM, Gottfried (GER)	24 - 9	37
ABDUL-AAL, Esam (BRN)	23 - 13	51
DAVIDSON, Sven (SWE)	23 - 9	36

MOST WINS, DOUBLES TEAM

	W-L	Ties	Yrs
PIETRANGELI, Nicola / SIROLA, Orlando (ITA)	34 - 8	42	9
NASTASE, Ilie / TIRIAC, Ion (ROM)	27 - 7	34	10
KOCH, Tomas / MANDARINO, Jose-Edison (BRA)	23 - 9	32	10
BERTOLUCCI, Paolo / PANATTA, Adriano (ITA)	22 - 8	30	11
CUCELLI, Giovanni / DEL BELLO, Marcello (ITA)	19 - 5	24	7
LIKHACHEV, Sergei / METREVELI, Alex (RUS)	18 - 7	25	7
SZOKE, Peter / TAROCZY, Balazs (HUN)	17 - 2	19	8
AMRITRAJ, Anand / AMRITRAJ, Vijay (IND)	17 - 9	26	15
HEWITT, Bob / MC MILLAN, Frew (RSA)	16 - 1	17	5
LUNDQUIST, Jan-Erik / SCHMIDT, Ulf (SWE)	16 - 8	24	6
BRICHANT, Jacques / WASHER, Philippe (BEL)	16 - 14	30	11
ARILLA, Jose-Luis / SANTANA, Manuel (ESP)	15 - 7	22	7
FLEMING, Peter / MCENROE, John (USA)	14 - 1	15	6
WOODBRIDGE, Todd / WOODFORDE, Mark (AUS)	14 - 2	16	7
ALLISON, Wilmer / VAN RYN, John (USA)	14 - 2	16	5
CASAL, Sergio / SANCHEZ, Emilio (ESP)	14 - 7	21	11
LALL, Premjit / MUKERJEA, Jaidip (IND)	14 - 9	23	9

MOST APPEARANCES, FINAL

Finals	W-L	
TILDEN, Bill	11	21 - 7
EMERSON, Roy	9	15 - 3
BOROTRA, Jean	9	7 - 2
BROOKES, Norman	8	15 - 7
COCHET, Henri	8	14 - 6
JOHNSTON, William	8	13 - 3
SMITH, Stan	8	12 - 4
EDBERG, Stefan	7	6 - 8
SEIXAS, Vic	7	6 - 1
MCENROE, John	6	12 - 2
WILANDER, Mats	6	9 - 4
SCHROEDER, Ted	6	9 - 6
FRASER, Neale	6	8 - 3
AUSTIN, Bunny	6	8 - 4
BROMWICH, John	6	7 - 7
WILLIAMS, Norris	6	5 - 3
BRUGNON, Jacques	6	3 - 3
JARRYD, Anders	6	3 - 4
DOHERTY, Laurence	5	12 - 0
LAVER, Rod	5	10 - 2
PERRY, Fred	5	9 - 1
DOHERTY, Reggie	5	7 - 1
NEWCOMBE, John	5	6 - 4
LUTZ, Bob	5	5 - 0
QUIST, Adrian	5	5 - 7
TRABERT, Tony	5	4 - 8
HUGHES, Patrick	5	1 - 4

YOUNGEST PLAYERS

	Age	Year
Kenny Banzer (LIE)	14 yrs, 5 days	2000
Hadi Badri (UAE)	14 yrs, 42 days	1995
Franklyn Emmanuel (SRI)	14 yrs, 54 days	2002
Omar Bahrouzyan (UAE)	14 yrs, 63 days	1996
Sree Roy (BAN)	14 yrs, 99 days	2002

OLDEST PLAYERS

	Age	Year
Yaka-Garonfin Koptigan (TOG)	59 yrs, 147 days	2001
Claude Butlin (MEX)	50 yrs, 105 days	1927
Rene Rozic (MON)	50 yrs, 87 days	1969
Torben Ulrich (DEN)	48 yrs, 349 days	1978
Jean Borotra (FRA)	48 yrs, 306 days	1947

MISCELLANEOUS RECORDS

Most Cup-winning years: 8, Roy Emerson, Australia, 1959-67
Most years played: 21, Torben Ulrich, Denmark, 1948-68, 1978
Most singles played: 110, Nicola Pietrangeli, Italy; 96, Ilie Nastase, Romania; 86, Manuel Santana, Spain
Most doubles played: 54, Nicola Pietrangeli, Italy; 50, Ilie Nastase, Romania; 43, Orlando Sirola, Italy
Most consecutive singles wins: 33, Bjorn Borg, Sweden, 1973–79
Longest singles: 100 games, Harry Fritz, Canada, d. Jorge Andrew, Venezuela, 16-14, 11-9, 9-11, 4-6, 11-9. American Zone, 2nd rd., Caracas, 1982.
Longest doubles: 122 games, Stan Smith and Erik van Dillen, U.S., d. Jaime Fillol and Patricio Cornejo, Chile, 7-9, 37-39, 8-6, 6-1, 6-3; zone match, Little Rock, Ark., 1973
Best record in challenge round and/or finals: 7-0 in singles, 5-0 in doubles, Laurie Doherty, Britain, 1902–06
Most Cups won as captain: 16, Harry Hopman, Australia, 1938–67
Oldest winner: Colin Gregory, Britain, 1952, 48 years, 295 days, vs. Yugoslavia, with Tony Mottram, d. Stevan Laszlo–Josip Pallada, 6-4, 1-6, 9-11, 6-2, 6-2
Most series won: 194, United States
Most consecutive series won: 17, U.S., 1968-1973

BIGGEST UPSETS

1921: Ichiya Kumagae, Japan, d. Jack Hawkes, Australia, 3-6, 2-6, 8-6, 6-2, 6-3, Newport, R.I. Gave Japan 2-0 lead in 4-1 upset.
1932: Jean Borotra, France, d. Ellsworth Vines, U.S., 6-4, 6-2, 3-6, 6-4, challenge round, Paris. Defeat of No. 1, Wimbledon, U.S. champ, gave France 1-0 lead in 3-2, victory.
1939: Adrian Quist, Australia, d. Bobby Riggs, U.S., 6-1, 6-4, 3-6, 3-6, 6-4, challenge round, Philadelphia. Defeat of No. 1, Wimbledon, U.S. champ, tied score 2-2 in all-time comeback from 0-2 to 3-2 Aussie victory.
1950: Ken McGregor, Australia, d. Ted Schroeder, U.S., 13-11, 6-3, 6-4, challenge round, New York. Gave Aussies 2-0 lead in 4-1 upset.
1953: Lew Hoad, Australia, d. Tony Trabert, 13-11, 6-3, 2-6, 3-6, 7-5, final, Melbourne. Defeat of U.S. champ tied score 2-2 in 3-2 Aussie victory.

1967: Pancho Guzman, Ecuador, d. Arthur Ashe, U.S., 0-6, 6-4, 7-5, 0-6, 6-3, Guayaquil. Gave Ecuador decisive 3-1 lead in 3-2 victory, sealing biggest upset in U.S. history
1974: Jairo Velasco, Colombia, d. Harold Solomon, U.S., 6-1, 3-6, 4-6, 6-3, 7-5, Bogota. Gave Colombia 1-0 lead in 4-1 upset.
1984: Henrik Sundstrom (No. 7) Sweden, d. John McEnroe (No. 1), 13-11, 6-4, 6-3, final, Goteborg. Gave Sweden 2-0 lead in 4-1 upset.
1987: Hugo Chapacu (No. 282), Paraguay, d. Jimmy Arias (No. 54) U.S., 6-4, 6-1, 5-7, 3-6, 9-7, from 1-5, saving 3 match points in 5th. Tied score 2-2 in 3-2 upset.
1991: Henri Leconte (No. 159), France d. Pete Sampras (No. 6), U.S., 6-4, 7-5, 6-4, final, Lyon. Tied score 1-1 in 3-1 French victory.
1992: Daniel Nestor (No. 238), Canada, d. Stefan Edberg (No. 1), Sweden, 4-6, 6-3, 1-6, 6-3, 6-4. Gave Canada 2-0 lead in 3-2 defeat. Nestor lost clincher to Magnus Gustafson, 6-4, 2-6, 3-6, 7-5, 6-4
2001: Nicolas Escude (No. 27), France, d. Lleyton Hewitt (No. 1), Australia, 4-6, 6-3, 3-6, 6-3, 6-4, final, Melbourne. Gave France 1-0 lead in 3-2 upset. Escude also won clincher over Wayne Arthurs, 7-6 (7-3), 6-7 (5-7), 6-3, 6-3.

BEST COMEBACKS

1930: Wilmer Allison d. Giorgio deStefani, Italy, 4-6. 7-9, 6-4, 8-6, 10-8, from 2-4, 4th, 1-5, 5th, saving 18 match points. Gave U.S. 1-0 lead in 4-1 victory.
1932: Jean Borotra, France, d. Wilmer Allison, U.S., 1-6, 3-6, 6-4, 6-2, 7-5, challenge round, Paris (saved 3 MP, 5th, 5-3, 40-15, and 4-5, 30-40). Made score 3-1, clinching 3-2 French victory.
1960: Barry MacKay U.S. d. Nicola Pietrangeli, Italy, 8-6, 3-6, 8-10, 8-6, 13-11, from 5-3 down, 5th, saving 8 match points. Gave U.S. 2-0 lead in 3-2 defeat by Italy.
1965: Fred Stolle, Australia, d. Manolo Santana, Spain, 10-12, 3-6, 6-1, 6-4, 7-5, final, Sydney. Gave Aussies 1-0 lead in 4-1 victory.
1986: Pat Cash, Australia, d. Mikail Pernfors, Sweden, 2-6, 4-6, 6-3, 6-4, 6-3, final, Melbourne. Clinching match, making score 3-1 in 3-2 victory.
1971: Frank Froehling, U.S., d. Ion Tiriac, Romania, 3-6, 1-6, 6-1, 6-3, 8-6, final, Charlote, N.C. Saved 7 vital break points in 5th, missed on 2 MP, but came back strong next day after match suspended at 6-6, 5th. Gave U.S. 2-0 lead in 4-1 victory.
1987: Hugo Chapacu (No. 282), Paraguay, d. Jimmy Arias (No. 54) U.S., 6-4, 6-1, 5-7, 3-6, 9-7, from 1-5, saving 3 match points in 5th. Tied score 2-2 in 3-2 upset.
1994: Stefan Edberg, Sweden, d. Aleksandr Volkov, 6-4, 6-2, 6-7, 0-6, 9-7, final, Moscow. (Saved 1 MP, 5th, 5-4, ad-in; trailed 3-5). Gave Sweden 1-0 lead in 4-1 victory.
1995: Andrei Chesnokov, Russia, d. Michael Stich, Germany, 6-4, 1-6, 1-6, 6-3, 14-12. Stich, serving at 7-6, 5th, held 9 match points. Clinched 3-2 Russian semi-final victory.
1996 - Arnaud Boetsch, France, d. Nicklas Kulti, Sweden, 7-6 (7-2), 2-6, 4-6, 7-6 (7-5), 10-8, final, Malmo, Sweden. Clinched Cup, 3-2 (Saved 3 Cup points, 5th, 6-7, 0-40, won 4 of last 5 games.)
2002 - Mikhail Youzhny, Russia, d. Paul-Henri Mathieu, 3-6, 2-6, 6-3, 7-5, 6-4, final, Paris. Clinched Cup, 3-2; 2 points from defeat, 5th, at 4-5, deuce.

Chapter 22

The Fed Cup

Captain Billie Jean King, coach Zina Garrison, Meghann Shaughnessy, Lisa Raymond, Lindsay Davenport, Monica Seles
The U.S. defeats Israel 5-0 in Fed Cup quarter-final play, July 2002, in Springfield, Missouri.

As the Davis Cup is to men, so the Fed Cup is to women.

The Fed Cup marks its 40th anniversary in 2003, as 94 nations will compete to become the women's world team champions. Only 16 will qualify in the World Group and, in November, one will be presented the large silver bowl that gives the competition its name.

The Fed Cup—the name was given a questionable post-modern contraction from the original Federation Cup for marketing reasons in 1995—had a humble launch in 1963. Organizers at the International Tennis Federation, celebrating its 50th anniversary that year, were uncertain about participation, so scheduled the event for London the week before Wimbledon to ensure the top players would compete.

Over the years, the competition has become ever more stiff. The greatest names of women's tennis in the past half-century have contested the Cup: Margaret Smith Court, Billie Jean King, Virginia Wade, Evonne Goolagong, Chris Evert, Pam Shriver, Steffi Graf, Monica Seles, Venus and Serena Williams, and, of course, Martina Navratilova, who helped win the Cup for her native Czechoslovakia before doing the same three times for her adopted homeland of the United States.

A handful of accomplishments stand out. Court would win all 20 of the singles matches in her Fed Cup career and would lead Australia to four titles, while Evert belonged to eight winning American teams. Wade played in more than 100 matches for Britain in a Cup career lasting from 1967 to 1983. Spain's dynamic duo of Conchita Martinez and Arantxa Sanchez Vicario played in their 10th final in 2002, a Fed Cup record.

Only nine nations have ever won the Cup. The United States has celebrated 17 championships, including the first in 1963, followed by Australia with seven, Spain and Czechoslovakia with five, and Germany with two. Four nations have a single title to their credit: South Africa (1972), France (1997), Belgium (2001) and the Slovak Republic (2002).

Britain has been a runner-up five times, most recently in 1981. Australia, once a powerhouse on the women's world stage, has not been to the final since losing 3-0 to Spain in 1993. The Aussies have suffered 10 losses in the finals, while the Americans have had nine and the Spanish five.

Until 1995, the Fed Cup was a weeklong knockout event with a championship series consisting of three matches: two singles and a doubles. One nation winning both singles matches made for a dead doubles, meaning the outcome had already been decided. The format was then switched to a Davis Cup-style, best-of-five schedule, with two singles on the first day followed by reverse singles and a deciding doubles on the following day. If necessary, a doubles match determines the champion.

Following its uncertain early history, the Fed Cup has become a significant event in women's tennis. The championship also brings the top names in tennis to nations other than the hosts of the four majors.

The original concept for the Fed Cup can be traced back to 1919, when Hazel Hotchkiss Wightman, a perennial U.S. champion, developed the notion of a broad women's team competition. When this idea seemed impractical, she settled on the notion of an annual match between the U.S. and Great Britain, and thus the Wightman Cup was born in 1923. Then, in 1962, Nell Hopman, wife of the legendary Australian Davis Cup Captain Harry Hopman, worked with Mary Hardwick Hare, a British resident of the U.S., to persuade the ITF that Wightman's original notion was an idea whose time had come.

The new prize was a response to the rise of Australian players as a challenge to traditional powers Britain and the United States. (The venerable Wightman Cup would continue to be contested through 1989.) The Fed Cup also provided a needed forum for international competition for women similar to the Davis Cup for men.

The inaugural Fed Cup tournament was held on the grass courts at Queen's Club, London, in June 1963, although rain pushed the final indoors. Only 16 nations competed and they had to pay their own way; the tournament had no sponsor and offered no prize money. The U.S., represented by Darlene Hard and Billie Jean Moffitt (later King), advanced to the final by overcoming Italy, the Netherlands and Britain. Margaret Smith (later Court) and Lesley Turner led Australia to victories over Belgium, Hungary and South Africa.

Smith continued her dominance in singles, beating Hard in straight sets, while Moffitt defeated Turner after losing the first set. The four women offered a thrilling doubles showdown, won 6-3, 11-13, 6-3 by the Americans.

The 1968 tournament in Paris was held during the upheaval of student protests, although the only team of 23 to withdraw was neighboring West Germany. The Americans were eliminated by an unseeded Dutch team which promptly lost to Australia's Court and Kerry Melville.

The federation had awarded the 1972 Fed Cup to South Africa, which coincidentally was barred from competition by Davis Cup organizers for its continued policy of racial apartheid. Eastern European countries under Communist rule did not take part in the tournament. The home team upset Britain with a doubles victory before a rabidly partisan crowd at Ellis Park, Johannesburg.

Czechoslovakia unveiled a strikingly poised and talented team at Aix-en-Provence, France, in 1975. Renata Tomanova, 21, and Martina Navratilova, 18, defeated Ireland, the Netherlands and West Germany before stifling the host nation 3-0 to advance to face the Australians in the final on outdoor clay courts. Evonne Goolagong and Helen Gourlay had needed an 11-9, 6-1 victory in the doubles against Julie Heldman and Janet Newberry of the U.S. to win their semi-final 2-1. Tomanova handled Helen Cawley Gourlay 6-4, 6-2, while Navratilova was similarly impressive in clinching the Cup with a 6-3, 6-4 victory over Goolagong Cawley, ending the latter's 16-match unbeaten streak. The Czech pair took the doubles for good measure.

Navratilova had been squabbling with the Czech tennis federation, which had declared her to be "too Americanized" and initially refused her permission to travel to the U.S. Open. Once there, she defected and declared her intention to seek American citizenship. In the ensuing years, Navratilova would help her new country win three more Cups.

The defending champion Czechoslovaks pulled out of the 1976 Cup, joining Hungary and the Philippines in a boycott led by the Soviet Union to protest the inclusion of Rhodesia and South Africa, which were led by white-supremacist governments.

The Cup was played indoors at the Spectrum in Philadelphia in a year during which the U.S. was celebrating its bicentennial. A sponsor, Colgate Group, offered prize money for the first time, with $40,000 promised the winners.

Chris Evert had to withdraw with a sore wrist. King, representing the U.S. for the first time in eight years, was a formidable replacement, pairing with Rosie Casals for a quartet of 3-0 victories before upsetting Australia 2-1 in the final. Casals lost to Kerry Melville Reid, King beat Goolagong, and then the Americans managed a doubles win in straight sets for the Cup.

The triumph ended a seven-year drought and heralded a brilliant era for American women, who would roll up seven consecutive championships. The Australians, having just lost the final to the Czechs and the Americans, would continue to lose in the finals for the next four years, an unfortunate streak of futility for their talented players.

British fans had high hopes for their team of Virginia Wade and Sue Barker, ranked in the world's Top 5, when the Fed Cup moved to the grass courts of Devonshire Park in Eastbourne, England, in 1977. But the Brits were toppled by Australia's Reid and Dianne Fromholtz in the semi-final.

Evert, making her first appearance for the U.S. in Fed Cup play, did not disappoint. She won every singles set against opponents from Austria, Switzerland, France and South Africa, before defeating Reid 7-5, 6-3. King clinched the Cup with a 6-1, 2-6, 6-2 win over Fromholtz. A victory in the dead doubles was little consolation for the Australians.

Disappointment would continue for the Australians on their home turf in Melbourne in 1978, as Evert and King recovered from a first-set loss to Reid and Wendy Turnbull in the deciding doubles contest to reclaim the Cup with a 4-6, 6-1, 6-4 victory.

The United States would not be pushed by the Australians to a deciding doubles match in 1979 (in Madrid on clay) or 1980 (in Berlin on clay), as Evert and Tracy Austin each won their singles matches in both years.

The Fed Cup was held in Asia for the first time in 1981, in homage to a new sponsor, NEC, a Japanese computer and communications company. The sponsor was new, the location (Tokyo) was new, one of the finalists was new (Britain beat Australia in the semis), but the result was the same—another victory for the Americans, with Andrea Jaeger beating Wade and Evert disposing of Barker. (Casals and Kathy Jordan even won the meaningless doubles in straight sets.) The Americans would run the string to seven in 1982 at Santa Clara, Calif., as Evert aided Navratilova's first Fed Cup win as a new American citizen.

The American streak ended when those two were unavailable for the 1983 showdown in Zurich, Switzerland. Czechoslovakia's Helena Sukova and Hana Mandlikova defeated West Germany for the Cup. The Czech pair defeated Australia the following year, and were joined by compatriots Andrea Holikova and Regina Marsikova in beating the U.S. in 1985.

The Americans had their revenge when the Fed Cup moved to Prague the following year, the first time the event was held in a Communist country. It also marked Navratilova's first return to her homeland since defecting 11 years earlier.

Evert's streak of 30 consecutive singles victories in Cup play ended with a 3-6, 6-4, 6-3 quarter-final loss to Sandra Cecchini of Italy, but the American team persevered to advance to a much-anticipated final against the host nation.

Evert outlasted Sukova, 7-5, 7-6, setting the stage for Navratilova to win the Cup, which she did by overcoming Mandlikova, 7-5, 6-1.

The Fed Cup came to the Hollyburn Country Club in West Vancouver in 1987, the first time the tournament was held in Canada. Steffi Graf trounced Evert 6-1, 6-1 in the final after teammate Claudia Kohde-Kilsch had lost the opening singles rubber to Pam Shriver. In the deciding doubles, the Germans trailed 1-6, 0-4 before staging one of the most dramatic comebacks in Fed Cup history, taking Germany's first Cup, 1-6, 7-5, 6-4.

Two years later, Spain's Conchita Martinez and Arantxa Sanchez Vicario made their first appearance in a final, losing to Evert, Navratilova and Shriver and Zina Garrison in doubles.

The Spaniards returned to the final in 1991, taking the Cup with a three-set doubles victory over Garrison and Gigi Fernandez.

Martinez and Sanchez Vicario fell to Graf and the Germans the following year before running off a string of three successive victories, over Australia (1993) and the United States (1994, 1995). Monica Seles and Lindsay Davenport returned the Cup to America in 1996. Davenport was also part of winning American teams over Russia in 1999 (with Venus and Serena Williams) and Spain 2000 (with Seles, Jennifer Capriati and Lisa Raymond).

The U.S. withdrew from the 2001 tournament, citing security risks following the attacks of Sept. 11. The final, reduced to a best-of-three, ended in rapid-fire straight sets, as Belgium's Justine Henin demolished Nadia Petrova 6-0, 6-3 in 50 minutes before Kim Clijsters humiliated Elena Dementieva 6-0, 6-4 in 49 minutes, as lopsided a victory as ever enjoyed at the Fed Cup.

The 2002 Cup went to the Slovak Republic over Spain, as Daniela Hantuchova won both her singles matches and Janette Husarova upended Sanchez Vicario, 6-0, 6-2, in the decisive fourth rubber

FED CUP CHAMPIONS

1963
United States d. Australia 2-1 (London)
Margaret Smith (A) d. Darlene Hard 6-3, 6-0
Billie Jean Moffitt (US) d. Lesley Turner 5-7, 6-0, 6-3
Darlene Hard–Billie Jean Moffitt d. Margaret Smith–Lesley Turner 3-6, 13-11, 6-3

1964
Australia d. United States 2-1 (Philadelphia)
Margaret Smith (A) d. Billie Jean Moffitt 6-2, 6-3
Lesley Turner (A) d. Nancy Richey 7-5, 6-1
Billie Jean Moffitt–Karen Susman (US) d. Margaret Smith–Lesley Turner 4-6, 7-5, 6-1

1965
Australia d. United States 2-1 (Melbourne)
Lesley Turner (A) d. Carole Caldwell Graebner 6-3, 2-6, 6-3
Margaret Smith (A) d. Billie Jean Moffitt 6-4, 8-6
Billie Jean Moffitt–Carole Caldwell Graebner (US) d. Margaret Smith–Judy Tegart 7-5, 4-6, 6-4

1966
United States d. Germany 3-0 (Turin)
Julie Heldman d. Helga Niessen 4-6, 7-5, 6-1
Billie Jean King d. Edda Buding 6-3, 3-6, 6-1
Carole Caldwell Graebner–Billie Jean King d. Helga Schultze–Edda Buding 6-4, 6-2

1967
United States d. Great Britain 2-0 (Berlin)
Rosie Casals d. Virginia Wade 9-7, 8-6
Billie Jean King d. Ann Jones 6-3, 6-4
Doubles match called at set-all

1968
Australia d. Netherlands 3-0 (Paris)
Kerry Melville d. Marijke Jansen 4-6, 7-5, 6-3
Margaret Smith Court d. Astrid Suurbeek 6-1, 6-3
Margaret Smith Court–Kerry Melville d. Astrid Suurbeek–Lidy Venneboer 6-3, 6-8, 7-5

1969
United States d. Australia 2-1 (Athens)
Nancy Richey (US) d. Kerry Melville 6-4, 6-3
Margaret Smith Court (A) d. Julie Heldman 6-1, 8-6
Peaches Bartkowicz–Nancy Richey d. Margaret Smith Court–Judy Tegart 6-4, 6-4

1970
Australia d. Germany 3-0 (Freiburg, West Germany)
Karen Krantzcke d. Helga Schultze Hoesl 6-2, 6-3
Judy Tegart Dalton d. Helga Niessen 4-6, 6-3, 6-3
Karen Krantzcke–Judy Dalton d. Helga Hoesl–Helga Niessen 6-2, 7-5

1971
Australia d. Great Britain 3-0 (Perth, Australia)
Margaret Smith Court d. Ann Haydon Jones 6-8, 6-3, 6-2
Evonne Goolagong d. Virginia Wade 6-4, 6-1
Margaret Smith Court–Lesley Hunt d. Virginia Wade–Winnie Shaw 6-4, 6-4

1972
South Africa d. Great Britain 2-1 (Johannesburg)
Virginia Wade (GB) d. Pat Walkden Pretorius 6-3, 6-2
Brenda Kirk (SA) d. Winnie Shaw 4-6, 7-5, 6-0
Brenda Kirk–Pat Pretorius d. Winnie Shaw–Virginia Wade 6-1, 7-5

1973
Australia d. South Africa 3-0 (Bad Homburg, West Germany)
Evonne Goolagong d. Pat Walkden Pretorius 6-0, 6-2
Patti Coleman d. Brenda Kirk 10-8, 6-0
Evonne Goolagong–Janet Young d. Brenda Kirk–Pat Pretorius 6-1, 6-2

1974
Australia d. United States 2-1 (Naples, Italy)
Evonne Goolagong (A) d. Julie Heldman 6-1, 7-5
Jeanne Evert (US) d. Dianne Fromholtz 2-6, 7-5, 6-4
Evonne Goolagong–Janet Young d. Julie Heldman–Sharon Walsh 7-5, 8-6

1975
Czechoslovakia d. Australia 3-0 (Aix-en-Provence, France)
Martina Navratilova d. Evonne Goolagong 6-3, 6-4
Renata Tomanova d. Helen Gourlay 6-4, 6-2
Martina Navratilova–Renata Tomanova d. Dianne Fromholtz–Helen Gourlay 6-3, 6-1

1976
United States d. Australia 2-1 (Philadelphia)
Kerry Melville Reid (A) d. Rosie Casals 1-6, 6-3, 7-5
Billie Jean King (US) d. Evonne Goolagong 7-6 (7-4), 6-4
Billie Jean King–Rosie Casals d. Evonne Goolagong–Kerry Melville Reid 7-5, 6-3

1977
United States d. Australia 2-1 (Eastbourne, England)
Billie Jean King (US) d. Dianne Fromholtz 6-1, 2-6, 6-2
Chris Evert (US) d. Kerry Melville Reid 7-5, 6-3
Kerry Melville Reid–Wendy Turnbull (A) d. Chris Evert–Rosie Casals 6-3, 6-3

1978
United States d. Australia 2-1 (Melbourne)
Kerry Melville Reid (A) d. Tracy Austin 6-3, 6-3
Chris Evert (US) d. Wendy Turnbull 3-6, 6-1, 6-1
Chris Evert–Billie Jean King d. Wendy Turnbull–Kerry Melville Reid 4-6, 6-1, 6-4

1979
United States d. Australia 3-0 (Madrid)
Tracy Austin d. Kerry Melville Reid 6-3, 6-0
Chris Evert Lloyd d. Dianne Fromholtz 2-6, 6-3, 8-6
Billie Jean King–Rosie Casals d. Wendy Turnbull–
  Kerry Melville Reid 3-6, 6-3, 8-6

1980
United States d. Australia 3-0 (Berlin)
Chris Evert Lloyd d. Dianne Fromholtz 4-6, 6-1, 6-1
Tracy Austin d. Wendy Turnbull 6-2, 6-3
Rosie Casals–Kathy Jordan d. Dianne Fromholtz–Susan Leo
  2-6 6-4, 6-4

1981
United States d. Great Britain 3-0 (Tokyo)
Chris Evert Lloyd d. Sue Barker 6-2, 6-1
Andrea Jaeger d. Virginia Wade 6-3, 6-1
Kathy Jordan–Rosie Casals d. Sue Barker–Virginia Wade 6-4, 7-5

1982
United States d. Germany 3-0 (Santa Clara, Calif.)
Chris Evert Lloyd d. Claudia Kohde-Kilsch 2-6, 6-1, 6-3
Martina Navratilova d. Bettina Bunge 6-4, 6-4
Martina Navratilova–Chris Evert Lloyd d. Claudia Kohde-Kilsch–
  Bettina Bunge 3-6, 6-1, 6-2

1983
Czechoslovakia d. Germany 2-1 (Zurich, Switzerland)
Helena Sukova (C) d. Claudia Kohde-Kilsch 6-4, 2-6, 6-2
Hana Mandlikova (C) d. Bettina Bunge 6-2, 3-0 ret.
Claudia Kohde Kilsch–Eva Pfaff d. Iva Budarova–
  Marcela Skuherska 3-6 6-2, 6-1

1984
Czechoslovakia d. Australia 2-1 (Sao Paulo, Brazil)
Anne Minter (A) d. Helena Sukova 7-5, 7-5
Hana Mandikova (C) d. Elizabeth Sayers 6-1, 6-0
Hana Mandikova–Helena Sukova d. Elizabeth Sayers–
  Wendy Turnbull 6-2, 6-2

1985
Czechoslovakia d. United States 2-1 (Nagoya, Japan)
Hana Mandlikova (C) d. Kathy Jordan 7-5, 6-1
Helena Sukova (C) d. Elise Burgin 6-3, 6-7, 6-4
Elise Burgin–Sharon Walsh d. Regina Marsikova–Andrea Holikova
  6-2, 6-3

1986
United States d. Czechoslovakia 3-0 (Prague, Czechoslovakia)
Chris Evert Lloyd d. Helena Sukova 7-5, 7-6 (7-5)
Martina Navratilova d. Hana Mandlikova 7-5, 6-1
Martina Navratilova–Pam Shriver d. Hana Mandlikova–
  Helena Sukova 6-4, 6-2

1987
Germany d. United States 2-1 (West Vancouver, British Columbia)
Pam Shriver (US) d. Claudia Kohde-Kilsch 6-0, 7-6 (7-5)
Steffi Graf (G) d. Chris Evert 6-2, 6-1
Steffi Graf–Claudia Kohde-Kilsch d. Chris Evert–Pam Shriver
  1-6, 7-5 6-4

1988
Czechoslovakia d. U.S.S.R. 2-1 (Melbourne)
Radka Zrubakova (C) d. Larisa Savchenko 6-1, 7-6 (7-2)
Helena Sukova (C) d. Natalia Zvereva 6-3, 6-4
Larisa Savchenko–Natalia Zvereva d. Jana Novotna–
  Jana Pospisilova 7-6 (7-5), 7-5

1989
United States d. Spain 3-0 (Tokyo)
Chris Evert d. Conchita Martinez 6-3, 6-2
Martina Navratilova d. Arantxa Sanchez Vicario 0-6, 6-3, 6-4
Zina Garrison–Pam Shriver d. Conchita Martinez–
  Arantxa Sanchez Vicario 7-5, 6-1

1990
United States d. U.S.S.R. 2-1 (Atlanta)
Jennifer Capriati (US) d. Leila Meskhi 7-6 (13-11), 6-2
Natalia Zvereva (USSR) d. Zina Garrison 6-3, 7-5
Zina Garrison–Gigi Fernandez d. Natalia Zvereva–
  Larisa Savchenko 6-4, 6-3

1991
Spain d. United States 2-1 (Nottingham, England)
Jennifer Capriati (US) d. Conchita Martinez 4-6, 7-6 (7-3), 6-1
Arantxa Sanchez Vicario (S) d. Mary Joe Fernandez 6-3, 6-4
Conchita Martinez–Arantxa Sanchez Vicario d. Gigi Fernandez–
  Zina Garrison 3-6, 6-1, 6-1

1992
Germany d. Spain 2-1 (Frankfurt)
Steffi Graf (G) d. Arantxa Sanchez Vicario 6-4, 6-2
Anke Huber (G) d. Conchita Martinez 6-3, 6-7 (1-7), 6-1
Arantxa Sanchez Vicario–Conchita Martinez (S) d. Anke Huber–
  Barbara Rittner 6-1, 6-2

1993
Spain d. Australia 3-0 (Frankfurt)
Conchita Martinez d. Michelle Jaggard-Lai 6-0, 6-2
Arantxa Sanchez Vicario d. Nicole Provis 6-2, 6-3
Conchita Martinez–Arantxa Sanchez Vicario d. Liz Sayers Smylie–
  Rennae Stubbs 3-6, 6-1, 6-3

1994
Spain d. United States 3-0 (Frankfurt)
Conchita Martinez d. Mary Joe Fernandez 6-2, 6-2
Arantxa Sanchez Vicario d. Lindsay Davenport 6-2, 6-1
Conchita Martinez–Arantxa Sanchez Vicario d. Gigi Fernandez–
  Mary Joe Fernandez 6-3, 6-4

1995
Spain d. United States 3-2 (Valencia)
Conchita Martinez (S) d. Chanda Rubin 7-5, 7-6 (7-3)
Arantxa Sanchez Vicario (S) d. Mary Joe Fernandez 6-3, 6-2
Conchita Martinez d. Mary Joe Fernandez 6-3, 6-4
Chanda Rubin d. Arantxa Sanchez Vicario 1-6, 6-4, 6-4
Lindsay Davenport–Gigi Fernandez (US) d. Virginia Ruano Pascual–
  Maria Antonia Sanchez Lorenzo 6-3, 7-6 (7-3)

1996
United States d. Spain 5-0 (Atlantic City)
Monica Seles d. Conchita Martinez 6-2, 6-4
Lindsay Davenport d. Arantxa Sanchez Vicario 7-5, 6-1
Monica Seles d. Arantxa Sanchez Vicario 3-6, 6-3, 6-1
Lindsay Davenport d. Gala Leon Garcia 7-5, 6-2
Mary Joe Fernandez–Lindsay Davenport d. Gala Leon Garcia–
  Virginia Ruano Pascual 6-1, 6-4

1997
France d. Netherlands 4-1 (Den Bosch, Netherlands)
Sandrine Testud (F) d. Brenda Schultz-McCarthy 6-4, 4-6, 6-3
Mary Pierce (F) d. Miriam Oremans 6-4 6-1
Brenda Schultz-McCarthy d. Mary Pierce 4-6, 6-3, 6-4
Sandrine Testud d. Miriam Oremans 0-6, 6-3, 6-3
Alexandra Fusai–Nathalie Tauziat (F) d. Manon Bollegraf–
  Caroline Vis 6-3, 6-4

1998
Spain d. Switzerland 3-2 (Geneva)
Arantxa Sanchez Vicario (Sp) d. Patty Schnyder 6-2, 3-6, 6-2
Martina Hingis (Sw) d. Conchita Martinez 6-4, 6-4
Martina Hingis d. Arantxa Sanchez Vicario 7-6 (7-5), 6-3
Conchita Martinez d. Patty Schnyder 6-3, 2-6, 9-7
Conchita Martinez–Arantxa Sanchez Vicario d. Martina Hingis–
  Patty Schnyder 6-0, 6-2

1999
United States d. Russia 4-1 (Stanford, Calif.)
Venus Williams (US) d. Elena Likhovtseva (R) 6-3, 6-4
Lindsay Davenport (US) d. Elena Dementieva (R) 6-4, 6-0
Lindsay Davenport d. Elena Likhovtseva 6-4, 6-4
Elena Dementieva d. Venus Williams 1-6, 6-3, 7-6
Serena Williams–Venus Williams d. Elena Dementieva–
　Elena Makarova 6-2, 6-1

2000
United States d. Spain 5-0 (Las Vegas)
Monica Seles d. Conchita Martinez (S) 6-2, 6-3
Lindsay Davenport d. Arantxa Sanchez Vicario (S) 6-2, 1-6, 6-3
Lindsay Davenport d. Conchita Martinez 6-1, 6-2
Jennifer Capriati d. Arantxa Sanchez Vicario 6-1, 1-0, retired
Jennifer Capriati–Lisa Raymond d. Virginia Ruano-Pascual–
　Magui Serna (S) 4-6, 6-4, 6-2

2001
Belgium d. Russia 2-1 (Madrid, Spain)
Justine Henin (B) d. Nadia Petrova 6-0, 6-3
Kim Clijsters (B) d. Elena Dementieva 6-0, 6-4
Nadia Petrova–Elena Likhovtseva d. Els Callens–Laurence Courtois
　7-5, 7-6 (7-2)

2002
Slovak Republic d. Spain 3-1 (Maspalomas, Canary Islands)
Conchita Martinez (Sp) d. Janette Husarova 6-4, 7-6 (8-6)
Daniela Hantuchova (Sl) d. Magui Serna 6-2, 6-1
Daniela Hantuchova d. Conchita Martinez 6-7 (8-10), 7-5, 6-4
Janette Husarova d. Arantxa Sanchez Vicario 6-0, 6-2
Virginia Ruano Pascual–Magui Serna vs. Janette Husarova–
　Daniela Hantuchova, canceled

FEDERATION CUP RECORDS

NATION

MOST TITLES

	Total	Years
USA	17	1963, 1966-67, 1969, 1976-82, 1986, 1989-90, 1996, 1999, 2000
Australia	7	1964-65, 1968, 1970-71, 1973-74
Czechoslovakia	5	1975, 1983-85, 1988
Spain	5	1991, 1993, 1994, 1995, 1998
Germany	2	1987, 1992
Belgium	1	2001
France	1	1997
South Africa	1	1972
Slovak Republic	1	2002

MOST TIES WON

	Total	Yrs played
U.S.A.	128 - 22	39
AUSTRALIA	103 -37	40
GREAT BRITAIN	92 - 48	40
CZECH REPUBLIC	77 - 28	32
GERMANY	76 - 39	38
NETHERLANDS	76 - 49	39
FRANCE	68 - 44	40
KOREA, REP.	66 - 46	28
RUSSIA	64 - 30	26
SPAIN	62 - 36	31
CANADA	59 - 53	39
JAPAN	59 - 47	35
ARGENTINA	58 - 41	34
BELGIUM	56 - 54	38
INDONESIA	56 - 51	33

MOST FINAL APPEARANCES

	Total	Record
USA	25	17 - 8
Australia	17	7 - 10
Spain	10	5 - 5
Czechoslovakia	6	5 - 1
Germany	6	2 - 4
Great Britain	4	0 - 4
Russia	4	0 - 4
South Africa	2	1 - 1
Netherlands	2	0 - 2
Belgium	1	1 - 0
France	1	1 - 0
Slovak Republic	1	1 - 0
Switzerland	1	0 - 1

INDIVIDUAL

MOST TIES PLAYED

	Total	W-L
SANCHEZ VICARIO, Arantxa (ESP)	58	72 - 28
WADE, Virginia (GBR)	57	66 - 33
BASUKI, Yayuk (INA)	55	58 - 28
NEILAND, Larisa (LAT)	55	65 - 22
SUKOVA, Helena (CZE)	54	57 - 16
ZVEREVA, Natalia (BLR)	54	59 - 21
MARTINEZ, Conchita (ESP)	51	64 - 23
SCHAERER, Larissa (PAR)	51	57 - 31
WANG, Shi-Ting (TPE)	49	51 - 25
MANDLIKOVA, Hana (AUS)	45	49 - 12
SMASHNOVA, Anna (ISR)	45	29 - 20
TURNBULL, Wendy (AUS)	45	46 -16
ANGGARKUSUMA, Suzanna (INA)	42	34 - 30
EVERT, Chris (USA)	42	57 - 4
NILAND, Gina (IRL)	42	34 - 19

MOST MATCHES PLAYED

	Total	Ties
SANCHEZ VICARIO, Arantxa (ESP)	100	58
WADE, Virginia (GBR)	99	57
SCHAERER, Larissa (PAR)	88	51
NEILAND, Larisa (LAT)	87	55
MARTINEZ, Conchita (ESP)	87	51
BASUKI, Yayuk (INA)	86	55
ZVEREVA, Natalia (BLR)	80	54
WANG, Shi-Ting (TPE)	76	49
SUKOVA, Helena (CZE)	73	54
CABEZAS, Paula (CHI)	70	39
WIESNER, Judith (AUT)	66	40
MONTESINO, Yoany (CUB)	63	38
TURNBULL, Wendy (AUS)	62	45
KRIZAN, Tina (SLO)	62	37
EVERT, Chris (USA)	61	42
MANDLIKOVA, Hana (AUS)	61	45
REID, Kerry (AUS)	61	36

MOST WINS, OVERALL

	Total	Ties
SANCHEZ VICARIO, Arantxa (ESP)	72 - 28	58
WADE, Virginia (GBR)	66 - 33	57
NEILAND, Larisa (LAT)	65 - 22	55
MARTINEZ, Conchita (ESP)	64 - 23	51
ZVEREVA, Natalia (BLR)	59 - 21	54
BASUKI, Yayuk (INA)	58 - 28	55
EVERT, Chris (USA)	57 - 4	42
SCHAERER, Larissa (PAR)	57 - 31	51
SUKOVA, Helena (CZE)	57 -16	54
KING, Billie Jean (USA)	52 - 4	36
WANG, Shi-Ting (TPE)	51 - 25	49
CABEZAS, Paula (CHI)	49 - 21	39
MANDLIKOVA, Hana (AUS)	49 - 12	45
TURNBULL, Wendy (AUS)	46 - 16	45
STOVE, Betty (NED)	45 - 15	33

MOST WINS, SINGLES

	W-L	Ties
SANCHEZ VICARIO, Arantxa (ESP)	50 - 22	58
SUKOVA, Helena (CZE)	45 - 11	54
MARTINEZ, Conchita (ESP)	44 - 18	51
EVERT, Chris (USA)	40 - 2	42
WADE, Virginia (GBR)	36 - 20	57
SCHAERER, Larissa (PAR)	35 - 17	51
ZVEREVA, Natalia (BLR)	35 - 16	54
MANDLIKOVA, Hana (AUS)	34 - 6	45
WANG, Shi-Ting (TPE)	33 - 12	49
BASUKI, Yayuk (INA)	29 - 21	55
NEILAND, Larisa (LAT)	29 - 15	55
SMASHNOVA, Anna (ISR)	28 - 18	45
WIESNER, Judith (AUT)	28 - 16	40
CABEZAS, Paula (CHI)	26 - 14	39
KING, Billie Jean (USA)	26 - 3	36

MOST WINS, DOUBLES

	W-L	Ties
NEILAND, Larisa (LAT)	36 - 7	55
WADE, Virginia (GBR)	30 - 13	57
BASUKI, Yayuk (INA)	29 - 7	55
TURNBULL, Wendy (AUS)	29 - 8	45
KING, Billie Jean (USA)	26 - 1	36
CASALS, Rosie (USA)	26 - 1	29
ZVEREVA, Natalia (BLR)	24 - 5	54
CABEZAS, Paula (CHI)	23 - 7	39
STOVE, Betty (NED)	23 - 10	33
SANCHEZ VICARIO, Arantxa (ESP)	22 - 6	58
SCHAERER, Larissa (PAR)	22 - 14	51
MONTESINO, Yoany (CUB)	22 - 8	38
KRIZAN, Tina (SLO)	22 - 13	37
DURIE, Jo (GBR)	22 - 5	36
MARTINEZ, Conchita (ESP)	20 - 5	51
ANGGARKUSUMA, Suzanna (INA)	20 - 9	42

MOST WINS, DOUBLES TEAM

	W-L	Ties	Yrs
MARTINEZ, Conchita / SANCHEZ VICARIO, Arantxa (ESP)	18-3	21	10
ANGGARKUSUMA, Suzanna / BASUKI, Yayuk (INA)	15-3	18	9
CABEZAS, Paula / CASTRO, Barbara (CHI)	15-5	20	5
BARKER, Sue / WADE, Virginia (GBR)	13-3	16	7
NEILAND, Larisa / ZVEREVA, Natalia (RUS)	12-1	13	4
DURIE, Jo / HOBBS, Anne (GBR)	12-2	14	6
CORDOVA, Yamile / MONTESINO, Yoany (CUB)	12-5	15	6
KIM, Il-Soon / LEE, Jeong-Myung (KOR)	12-5	17	5
REID, Kerry / TURNBULL, Wendy (AUS)	11-4	15	3
SEQUERA, Milagros / VENTO-KABCHI, Maria (VEN)	11-5	16	4
GURDAL, Michele / VAN HAVER, Monique (BEL)	11-9	20	9
CASALS, Rosie / KING, Billie Jean (USA)	10-0	12	4
CASALS, Rosie / JORDAN, Kathy (USA)	10-0	10	2
FERNANDEZ, Gigi / GARRISON-JACKSON, Zina (USA)	10-1	11	3
AKSIT-OAL, Ismet-Duygu / GULTEKIN, Gulberk (TUR)	10-5	15	7
DELHEES-JAUCH, Petra / JOLISSAINT, Christiane (SUI)	10-6	16	5

MOST APPEARANCES, FINAL

	Total	W-L
MARTINEZ, Conchita	10	11 - 9
SANCHEZ VICARIO, Arantxa	10	10 - 10
KING, Billie Jean	9	12 - 2
EVERT, Chris	9	10 - 3
COURT, Margaret	6	8 - 4
CASALS, Rosie	6	5 - 2
REID, Kerry	6	5 - 6
DAVENPORT, Lindsay	5	7 - 1
CAWLEY, Evonne	5	5 - 3
SUKOVA, Helena	5	4 - 3
TURNBULL, Wendy	5	1 - 5
BALESTRAT, Dianne	5	0 - 6
NAVRATILOVA, Martina	4	7 - 0
MANDLIKOVA, Hana	4	4 - 2
FERNANDEZ, Gigi	4	2 - 2
FERNANDEZ, Mary-Joe	4	1 - 5
WADE, Virginia	4	1 - 6
RUANO PASCUAL, Virginia	4	0 - 3

MISCELLANEOUS RECORDS

Most Cup-winning years: 7, Billie Jean Moffitt King, U.S., 1963, 66-67, 76-79

Most singles played: 72, Arantxa Sanchez Vicario, Spain 1986-2002

Most doubles played: 43, Virginia Wade, Great Britain, 1967-83; Larisa Savchenko Neiland, USSR and Latvia, 1983-91, 1992-2000

Most consecutive singles won: 29, Chris Evert, 1977-82, 86

Longest singles match: 54 games, Victoria Baldovinos, Spain, d. Judith Connor, New Zealand, 6-4, 11-13, 11-9, 1974; Nathalie Tauziat, France, d. Naoko Sawamatsu, Japan, 7-5, 4-6, 17-15, 1997

Longest doubles match: 51 games, Margaret Smith Court-Kerry Melville Reid, Australia, d. Winnie Shaw-Virginia Wade, Great Britain, 9-7, 3-6, 14-12, 1968

Most Cups won as captain: 4, Vicki Berner, U.S., 1977-80; Miguel Margets, Spain, 1993-95, 98; Billie Jean King, U.S., 1976, 96, 99-2000

Most team series played: 58, Arantxa Sanchez Vicario, Spain, 1986-2002

Most series won: 128, United States

Most consecutive series won: 38, U.S. (1976-1983)

Chapter 23

The Olympics

Steffi Graf, 1988
A Grand Slam and an Olympic gold, all in the same brilliant year.

The final point won and game, set, match and Olympic gold medal his, a triumphant Yevgeny Kafelnikov sent his racquet spiraling into the crowd at Homebush in Sydney, Australia, one warm afternoon in the fall of 2000. He then took a victory lap wrapped in the Russian flag.

"I knew I would regret it the rest of my life if I did not win," the young Russian proclaimed after defeating Tommy Haas of Germany in a three-hour show of severe hitting, 7-6, 3-6, 6-2, 4-6, 6-3. The uncharacteristically flamboyant display by the native of the Black Sea holiday port of Sochi was all the more surprising considering Kafelnikov had declared earlier in 2000 that he had little interest in competing in the Olympics. Once you find yourself in the midst of them, the Olympic Games can have that sort of creeping effect on an otherwise world-weary athlete.

In men's doubles at the Sydney Games, Canadians Sebastien Lareau and Daniel Nestor scored a shocking upset over defending champions—and hometown favorites—Mark Woodforde and Todd Woodbridge. Canada's first medal in tennis ruined the retirement act of the Woodies, one of the most successful doubles partnerships of all time.

Venus Williams of the United States needed just 58 minutes to dispose of an overmatched Elena Dementieva of Russia, 6-2, 6-4. She then joined her sister Serena to overwhelm Kristie Boogert and Miriam Oremans to claim the women's doubles gold with a 6-1, 6-1 victory. The Netherlands press was harsh on the Dutch pair, criticizing them for treating the Olympics like a Club Med retreat.

If indeed the Dutch pair was guilty of such an approach, they were not alone. Tennis fits somewhat uneasily into the Olympic family. Though some dream of the Olympic tournament joining the four majors to comprise a 'Golden Slam,' many still have the impression that millionaire players treat the Games as little more than a noisy vacation. Too many top players have skipped out and too many have noted the lack of a payday, or of rankings points.

Tennis was one of the original sports of the first modern Games in 1896. The definition of a professional, squabbles over the rulebook, and a clash of dates with Wimbledon cost the sport a place in the Games after 1924 and tennis was only re-instituted after years of lobbying by International Tennis Federation president Philippe Chatrier. In 1968 and 1984, tennis was a non-medal demonstration sport.

Tennis was the breakthrough sport for professionals entering the Games in 1988, setting the stage for the U.S. basketball 'Dream Team' in 1992. Juan Antonio Samaranch, the International Olympic Committe president—a tennis fan—wanted the best in the event when the sport returned, and the IOC left it to members to nominate their top players. Miloslav Mecir, a Slovak representing Czechoslovakia, who was a fine but not outstanding player, became the first men's gold medal winner in 64 years by coming from behind against Stefan Edberg in the semi-finals before knocking off Tim Mayotte of the U.S. Steffi Graf, 19, who had completed her Grand Slam by winning the U.S. Open only a week before the Olympics opened, became the first woman gold medallist in tennis since Helen Wills won as an 18-year-old sensation back in 1924.

Since 1988, Olympic medals have been awarded in four events: men's and women's singles and men's and women's doubles. The other recent gold medallists in singles have been Marc Rosset of Switzerland (1992), and Americans Agassi (1996), Jennifer Capriati (1992) and Lindsay Davenport (1996).

The return of tennis did not include a mixed doubles competition, which was last won in 1924 by American golden oldies Hazel Hotchkiss Wightman, 37, and Richard Norris Williams, 33. In fact, Americans won all five gold medals before tennis took its long Olympic hiatus—Vinnie Richards; Wills; reigning Wimbledon champions Richards and Frank Hunter in doubles; and Wightman and Wills in women's doubles.

The American domination at Paris in 1924 was not typical for early Olympic tennis. Britain claimed 16 gold, 13 silver, and 16 bronze from 1896 to 1924. Kitty McKane took five of those medals.

Other female stars of the early years included Suzanne Lenglen of France, who won two golds (singles, mixed doubles) and a bronze (doubles) in 1920, and Wills (later Wills Moody) who claimed victories in the singles and doubles in 1924.

In 1908 and 1912, separate competitions were held for indoor and outdoor play.

Tennis players were among the first 19 women to compete at the Olympics in Paris in 1900. Charlotte Cooper, nicknamed Chattie, had three of what would be five Wimbledon titles to her credit when she became the first female Olympic gold medallist by defeating Helene Prevost of France 6-1, 6-4.

The first men's gold medal was won by John Pius Boland, a Dublin-born student at Christ's College, Oxford, who attended the inaugural 1896 Games in Athens as a spectator. In Greece to join in an archaeological dig, he was encouraged to enter the tennis tournament as the 13th competitor. On April 11, he defeated Dionysios Kasdaglis of Greece 6-3, 6-1. On that same day, Boland joined Fredrich 'Fritz' Traun of Germany in defeating the unlucky Kasdaglis and Greek partner Demetrios Petrokokkinos of Greece 5-7, 6-4, 6-1. Boland, who went on to a remarkable career as a barrister, member of Parliament, and advocate of independence for his Irish homeland, had been a last-minute replacement for Traun's sick partner.

OLYMPIC GAME RESULTS

1896, Athens
Men's Singles—John Pius Boland, Great Britain-Ireland d. Dionysius Kasdaglis, Greece, 7-5, 6-4, 6-1. Bronze—Momcsillo Topavicza, Hungary; K. Paspatos, Greece
Men's Doubles—John Pius Boland, Great Britain-Ireland & Fritz Traun, Germany d. Dionysius Kasdaglis & Demetrios Petrokokkinos, Greece, 6-2, 6-4. Bronze—Edwin Flack & George Robertson, Australia-Great Britain

1900, Paris
Men's Singles—Laurie Doherty, Great Britain d. Harold Segerson Mahony, Great Britain-Ireland, 6-4, 6-2, 6-3. Bronze—Reggie Doherty, Great Britain; A.B.J. Norris, Great Britain
Women's Singles—Charlotte Cooper, Great Britain d. Helene Prevost, France, 6-1, 6-4. Bronze—Marion Jones, United States
Men's Doubles—Reggie Doherty & Laurie Doherty, Great Britain d. Basil de Garmendia, United States & Max Decugis, France, 6-1, 6-1, 6-0. Bronze—Andre Prevost & G. De La Chapelle, France; Harold Mahony & A.B.J. Norris, Ireland-Great Britain
Mixed Doubles—Charlotte Cooper & Reggie Doherty, Great Britain d. Helene Prevost, France & Harold Segerson Mahony, Ireland, 6-2, 6-4. Bronze—Archibald Warden, Great Britain & Hedwiga Rosenbaumová, Bohemia; Laurie Doherty, Great Britain & Marion Jones, United States

1904, St. Louis
Men's Singles—Beals Wright, United States d. Robert LeRoy, United States, 6-4, 6-4. Bronze—Alonzo Bell, United States; Edgar Leonard, United States
Men's Doubles—Edgar Welch Leonard & Beals Wright, United States d. Alphonzo Bell & Robert LeRoy, United States, 6-4, 6-4, 6-2. Bronze—Joseph Wear & Allen West, United States; Clarence Gamble & Arthur Wear, United States

1908, London

Men's Singles—Josiah Ritchie, Great Britain d. Otto Froitzheim, Germany, 7-5, 6-3, 6-4. Bronze—Wilberforce Eaves, Great Britain
Women's Singles—Dorothea Douglass Chambers, Great Britain d. Dora Boothby, Great Britain, 6-1, 7-5. Bronze—Joan Winch, Great Britain
Men's Doubles—George Hillyard & Reggie Doherty, Great Britain d. Josiah Ritchie & James Parke, Great Britain-Ireland, 9-7, 7-5, 9-7. Bronze—Charles Cazalet & Charles Dixon, Great Britain

1908, London (Indoor)

Men's Singles—Arthur Gore, Great Britain d. George Caridia, Great Britain, 6-3, 7-5, 6-4. Bronze—Josiah Ritchie, Great Britain
Women's Singles—Gladys Eastlake-Smith, Great Britain d. Angela Greene, Great Britain, 6-2, 4-6, 6-0. Bronze—Martha Adlerstrahle, Sweden
Men's Doubles—Arthur Gore & Herbert Roper Barrett, Great Britain d. George Mieville Simond & George Caridia, Great Britain, 6-2, 2-6, 6-3, 6-3. Bronze—Gunnar Setterwall & Wollmar Bostrom, Sweden

1912, Stockholm

Men's Singles—Charles Winslow, South Africa d. Harold Kitson, South Africa, 7-5, 4-6, 10-8, 8-6. Bronze—Oscar Kreuzer, Germany
Women's Singles—Marguerite Broquedis, France d. Dora Koring, Germany, 4-6, 6-3, 6-4. Bronze—Molla Bjurstedt, Norway
Men's Doubles—Charles Winslow & Harold Kitson, South Africa d. Felix Pipes & Arthur Zborzil, Austria, 4-6, 6-1, 6-2, 6-2. Bronze—Albert Canet & Marc Meny De Marangue, France
Mixed Doubles—Dora Koring & Heinrich Schomburg, Germany d. Sigrid Fick & Gunnar Setterwall, Sweden, 6-4, 6-0. Bronze—Albert Canet & Marguerite Broquedis, France

1912, Stockholm (Indoor)

Men's Singles—Andre Gobert, France d. Charles Dixon, Great Britain, 8-6, 6-4, 6-4. Bronze—Tony Wilding, New Zealand
Women's Singles—Edith Hannam, Great Britain d. Sofia Castenschiold, Denmark, 6-4, 6-3. Bronze—Mabel Parton, Great Britain
Men's Doubles—Andre Gobert & Maurice Germot, France d. Gunnar Setterwall & Carl Kempe, Sweden, 14-12, 6-2, 6-4. Bronze—Charles Dixon & Alfred Beamish, Great Britain
Mixed Doubles—Edith Hannam & Charles Dixon, Great Britain d. Helen Aitchison & Herbert Roper Barrett, Great Britain, 6-4, 3-6, 6-2. Bronze—Gunnar Setterwall & Sigrid Fick, Sweden

1920, Antwerp

Men's Singles—Louis Raymond, South Africa d. Ichiya Kumagae, Japan, 5-7, 6-4, 7-5, 6-4. Bronze—Charles Winslow, South Africa
Women's Singles—Suzanne Lenglen, France d. Dorothy Holman, Great Britain, 6-3, 6-0. Bronze—Kitty McKane, Great Britain
Men's Doubles—Noell Turnbull, South Africa & Max Woosnam, Great Britain d. Seiichiro Kashio & Ichiya Kumagae, Japan, 6-2, 5-7, 7-5, 7-5. Bronze—Max Decugis & Pierre Albarran, France
Women's Doubles—Kitty McKane–Winifred McNair, Great Britain d. Geraldine Beamish & Dorothy Holman, Great Britain, 8-6, 6-4. Bronze—Suzanne Lenglen & Elisabeth d'Ayen, France
Mixed Doubles—Suzanne Lenglen & Max Decugis, France d. Kitty McKane & Max Woosnam, Great Britain, 6-4, 6-2. Bronze—Ladislav Zemla & Milada Skrbková, Czechoslovakia

1924, Paris

Men's Singles—Vinnie Richards, United States d. Henri Cochet, France, 6-4, 6-4, 5-7, 4-6, 6-2. Bronze—Umberto Luigi de Morpurgo, Italy
Women's Singles—Helen Wills, United States d. Didi Vlasto, France, 6-2, 6-2. Bronze—Kitty McKane, Great Britain
Men's Doubles—Frank Hunter & Vinnie Richards, United States d. Jacques Brugnon & Henri Cochet, France, 4-6, 6-2, 6-3, 2-6, 6-3. Bronze—Jean Borotra & Rene Lacoste, France
Women's Doubles—Hazel Hotchkiss Wightman & Helen Wills, United States d. Kitty McKane & Phyllis Howkins Covell, Great Britain, 7-5, 8-6. Bronze—Dorothy Sheperd-Barron & Evelyn Colyer, Great Britain
Mixed Doubles—Hazel Hotchkiss Wightman & Dick Williams, United States d. Marion Zinderstein Jessup & Vinnie Richards, United States, 6-2, 6-3. Bronze—Hendrik Timmer & Cornelia Bouman, Netherlands

1988, Seoul

Men's Singles—Miloslav Mecir, Czechoslovakia d. Tim Mayotte, United States, 3-6, 6-2, 6-4, 6-2. Stefan Edberg, Sweden; Brad Gilbert, United States
Women's Singles—Steffi Graf, Germany d. Gabriela Sabatini, Argentina, 6-3, 6-3. Bronze—Zina Garrison, United States; Manuela Maleeva, Bulgaria
Men's Doubles—Ken Flach & Robert Seguso, United States d. Sergio Casal & Emilio Sanchez, Spain, 6-3, 6-4, 6-7 (5-7), 6-7 (1-7), 9-7. Bronze—Miloslav Mecir & Milan Srejber, Czechoslovakia; Stefan Edberg & Anders Jarryd, Sweden
Women's Doubles—Zina Garrison & Pam Shriver, United States d. Jana Novotna & Helena Sukova, Czechoslovakia, 4-6, 6-2, 10-8. Bronze—Elizabeth Smylie & Wendy Turnboll, Australia; Bronze—Steffi Graf & Claudia Kohde-Kilsch, Germany

1992, Barcelona

Men's Singles—Marc Rosset, Switzerland d. Jordi Arrese, Spain, 7-6 (7-2), 6-4, 3-6, 4-6, 8-6. Bronze—Goran Ivanisevic, Croatia; Andrei Cherkasov, Unified Team
Women's Singles—Jennifer Capriati, United States d. Steffi Graf, Germany, 3-6, 6-3, 6-4. Bronze—Mary Joe Fernandez, United States; Arantxa Sanchez Vicario, Spain
Men's Doubles—Boris Becker & Michael Stich, Germany d. Wayne Ferreira & Piet Norval, South Africa, 7-6 (7-5), 4-6, 7-6 (7-5), 6-3. Bronze—Goran Ivanisevic & Goran Prpic, Croatia; Javier Frana & Christian Carlos Miniussi, Argentina
Women's Doubles—Gigi Fernandez & Mary Joe Fernandez, United States d. Conchita Martinez & Arantxa Sanchez Vicario, Spain, 7-5, 2-6, 6-2. Bronze—Natalia Zvereva & Leila Meskhi, Unified Team

1996, Atlanta

Men's Singles—Andre Agassi, United States d. Sergi Bruguera, Spain, 6-2, 6-3, 6-1. Bronze—Leander Paes, India d. Fernando Meligeni, Brazil, 3-6, 6-2, 6-4
Women's Singles—Lindsay Davenport, United States d. Arantxa Sanchez Vicario, Spain, 7-6 (8-6), 6-2. Bronze—Jana Novotna, Czech Republic d. Mary Joe Fernandez, United States, 7-6 (8-6), 6-4
Men's Doubles—Todd Woodbridge & Mark Woodforde, Australia d. Tim Henman & Neil Broad, Great Britain, 6-4, 6-4, 6-2. Bronze—Marc-Kevin Goellner & David Prinosil, Germany d. Jacco Eltingh & Paul Haarhuis, Netherlands, 6-2, 7-5
Women's Doubles—Mary Joe Fernandez & Gigi Fernandez, United States d. Jana Novotna & Helena Sukova, Czechoslovakia, 7-6 (8-6), 6-4. Bronze—Conchita Martinez & Arantxa Sanchez Vicario, Spain d. Manon Bollegraf & Brenda Schultz-McCarthy, Netherlands, 6-1, 6-3

2000, Sydney

Men's Singles—Yevgeny Kafelnikov, Russia d. Tommy Haas, Germany, 7-6 (7-4), 3-6, 6-2, 4-6, 6-3. Bronze—Arnaud Di Pasquale, France d. Roger Federer, Switzerland, 7-6 (7-5), 6-7 (7-9), 6-3
Women's Singles—Venus Williams, United States d. Elena Dementieva, Russia, 6-2, 6-4. Bronze—Monica Seles, United States d. Jelena Dokic, Australia, 6-1, 6-4
Men's Doubles—Daniel Nestor & Sebastien Lareau d. Todd Woodbridge & Mark Woodforde, Australia, 5-7, 6-3, 6-4, 7-6 (7-2). Bronze—Alex Corretja & Albert Costa, Spain d. David Adams & John-Laffnie de Jager, South Africa, 2-6, 6-4, 6-3.
Women's Doubles—Venus Williams & Serena Williams, United States d. Kristie Boogert & Miriam Oremans, Netherlands, 6-1, 6-1. Bronze—Dominique Van Roost & Els Callens, Belgium d. Olga Barabanschikova & Natalia Zvereva, Belarus, 4-6, 6-4, 6-1

As a demonstration Sport

1968

Men's Singles—Manuel Santana, Spain
Men's Doubles—Rafael Osuna & Vicente Zarazua, Mexico
Women's Singles—Helga Niessen, West Germany
Women's Doubles—Edda Buding & Helga Niessen, West Germany
Mixed Doubles—Herb Fitzgibbon & Julie Heldman, United States

1984 (21-and-under)

Men's Singles—Stefan Edberg, Sweden, Gold; Francisco Maciel, Mexico, Silver; James Arias, United States & Paola Cane, Italy, Bronze
Women's Singles—Steffi Graf, West Germany, Gold; Sabrina Goles, Yugoslavia, Silver; Raffaela Reggi, Italy & Catherine Tanvier, France, Bronze

Chapter 24

The Wightman Cup

Helen Wills Moody, 1930

The pause that refreshes wasn't enough to wrest the Wightman Cup, as the U.S. fell 4-3 to Britain at Wimbledon.

Hoping to stimulate international interest in women's tennis as the Davis Cup did in men's, Hazel Hotchkiss Wightman, an all-time champion from Boston, donated a sterling vase to the U.S. Tennis Association as a prize for such a team competition. It was decided to invite Great Britain to challenge for the prize in 1923 to open the new Forest Hills Stadium at the West Side Tennis Club in New York. With Mrs. Wightman as player-captain, the U.S. won the inaugural, 7-0. The rivalry was rewarding to both countries and initially developed into a close competition, an annual match between the two with the prize soon known as the Wightman Cup. The matches were played in even years in Britain and in odd years in the U.S.

Interrupted only by World War II, the series became dominated by the U.S., which mounted a 50-10 record through 1989, when it was mutually agreed to suspend what was no longer a competition.

WIGHTMAN CUP CHAMPIONS

1923
United States d. Great Britain 7-0 (Forest Hills)
Helen Wills d. Kitty McKane 6-2, 0-6, 7-5
Molla Bjurstedt Mallory d. M. H. Davey Clayton 6-1, 8-6
Eleanor Goss d. Geraldine Beamish 6-2, 0-6, 7-5
Helen Wills d. M. H. Davey Clayton 6-2, 6-3
Molla Bjurstedt Mallory d. Kitty McKane 6-2, 6-3
Hazel Hotchkiss Wightman–Eleanor Goss d. Kitty McKane–
    Phyllis Howkins Covell 10-8, 5-7, 6-4
Molla Bjurstedt Mallory–Helen Wills Moody d. Geraldine Beamish–
    M. H. Clayton 6-3, 6-2

1924
Great Britain d. United States 6-1 (Wimbledon)
Phyllis Howkins Covell (GB) d. Helen Wills 6-2, 6-4
Kitty McKane (GB) d. Molla Bjurstedt Mallory 6-3, 6-3
Kitty McKane d. Helen Wills 6-2, 6-2
Phyllis Howkins Covell d. Molla Bjurstedt Mallory 6-2, 5-7, 6-3
Geraldine Beamish (GB) d. Eleanor Goss 6-1, 8-10, 6-3
Phyllis Howkins Covell–Dorothy Shepherd Barron d.
    Marion Zinderstein Jessup–Eleanor Goss 6-2, 6-2
Hazel Hotchkiss Wightman–Helen Wills d. Kitty McKane–
    Evelyn Colyer 2-6, 6-2, 6-4

1925

Great Britain d. United States 4-3 (Forest Hills)
Kitty McKane (GB) d. Molla Bjurstedt Mallory 6-4, 5-7, 6-0
Helen Wills (US) d. Joan Fry 6-0, 7-5
Dorothea Douglass Chambers (GB) d. Eleanor Goss 7-5, 3-6, 6-1
Helen Wills (US) d. Kitty McKane 6-1, 1-6, 9-7
Molla Bjurstedt Mallory d. Joan Fry 6-3, 6-0
Dorothea Douglass Chambers–Ermyntrude Harvey d.
  Molla Bjurstedt Mallory–May Sutton Bundy 10-8, 6-1
Kitty McKane–Evelyn Colyer d. Helen Wills–Mary K. Browne 6-0, 6-3

1926

United States d. Great Britain 4-3 (Wimbledon)
Elizabeth Ryan d. Joan Fry (GB) 6-1, 6-3
Kitty McKane Godfree (GB) d. Mary K. Browne 6-1, 7-5
Joan Fry d. Mary K. Browne 3-6, 6-0, 6-4
Kitty McKane Godfree (GB) d. Elizabeth Ryan 6-1, 5-7, 6-4
Marion Zinderstein Jessup d. Dorothy Shepherd Barron 6-1, 5-7, 6-4
Marion Zinderstein Jessup–Eleanor Goss d.
  Dorothea Douglass Chambers–Dorothy Shepherd Barron 6-4, 6-2
Mary K. Browne–Elizabeth Ryan d. Kitty McKane Godfree–
  Evelyn Colyer 2-6, 6-2, 6-4

1927

United States d. Great Britain 5-2 (Forest Hills)
Helen Wills (US) d. Joan Fry 6-2, 6-0
Molla Bjurstedt Mallory (US) d. Kitty McKane Godfree 6-4, 6-2
Betty Nuthall (GB) d. Helen Jacobs 6-3, 2-6, 6-1
Helen Wills d. Kitty McKane Godfree 6-1, 6-1
Molla Bjurstedt Mallory d. Joan Fry 6-2, 11-9
Gwendolyn Sterry–Betty Hill (GB) d. Eleanor Goss–
  Charlotte Hosmer Chapin 5-7, 7-5, 7-5
Helen Wills–Hazel Hotchkiss Wightman d. Kitty McKane Godfree–
  Ermyntrude Harvey 6-4, 4-6, 6-3

1928

Great Britain d. United States 4-3 (Wimbledon)
Helen Wills (US) d. Phoebe Holcroft Watson 6-1, 6-2
Eileen Bennett (GB) d. Molla Bjurstedt Mallory 6-1, 6-3
Helen Wills d. Eileen Bennett 6-3, 6-2
Phoebe Holcroft Watson d. Molla Bjurstedt Mallory 2-6, 6-1, 6-2
Helen Jacobs (US) d. Betty Nuthall 6-3, 6-1
Ermyntrude Harvey–Peggy Saunders d. Eleanor Goss–Helen Jacobs
  6-4, 6-1
Eileen Bennett–Phoebe Holcroft Watson d. Helen Wills–
  Penelope Anderson 6-2, 6-1

1929

United States d. Great Britain 4-3 (Forest Hills)
Helen Wills (US) d. Phoebe Holcroft Watson 6-1, 6-4
Helen Jacobs (US) d. Betty Nuthall 7-5, 8-6
Phoebe Holcroft Watson d. Helen Jacobs 6-3, 6-2
Edith Cross (US) d. Peggy Michell 6-3, 3-6, 6-3
Helen Wills d. Betty Nuthall 8-6, 8-6
Phoebe Watson–Peggy Michell d. Helen Wills–Edith Cross 6-4, 6-1
Phyllis Howkins Covell–Dorothy Shepherd Barron d. Helen Jacobs–
  Hazel Hotchkiss Wightman 6-2, 6-1

1930

Great Britain d. United States 4-3 (Wimbledon)
Helen Wills Moody (US) d. Joan Fry 6-1, 6-1
Phoebe Holcroft Watson (GB) d. Helen Jacobs 2-6, 6-2, 6-4
Helen Wills Moody d. Phoebe Watson 7-5, 6-1
Helen Jacobs d. Joan Fry 6-0, 6-3
Phyllis Mudford (GB) d. Sarah Palfrey 6-0, 6-2
Joan Fry–Ermyntrude Harvey d. Sarah Palfrey–Edith Cross
  2-6, 6-2, 6-4
Phoebe Holcroft Watson–Kitty McKane Godfree d. Helen Jacobs–
  Helen Wills Moody 7-5, 1-6, 6-4

1931

United States d. Great Britain 5-2 (Forest Hills, N.Y.)
Helen Wills Moody (US) d. Betty Nuthall 6-4, 6-2
Anna McCune Harper (US) d. Dorothy Round 6-3, 4-6, 9-7
Helen Jacobs (US) d. Phyllis Mudford 6-4, 6-2
Helen Wills Moody d. Phyllis Mudford 6-1, 6-4
Helen Jacobs d. Betty Nuthall 8-6, 6-4
Phyllis Mudford–Dorothy Shepherd Barron d. Sarah Palfrey–
  Hazel Hotchkiss Wightman 6-4, 10-8
Betty Nuthall–Eileen Bennett Whittingstall d. Helen Moody–
  Anna Harper 8-6, 5-7, 6-3

1932

United States d. Great Britain 4-3 (Wimbledon)
Helen Jacobs (US) d. Dorothy Round 6-4, 6-3
Helen Wills Moody (US) d. Eileen Bennett Whittingstall 6-2, 6-4
Helen Wills Moody d. Dorothy Round 6-2, 6-3
Eileen Bennett Whittingstall d. Helen Jacobs 6-4, 2-6, 6-1
Phyllis Mudford King (GB) d. Anna McCune Harper 3-6, 6-3, 6-1
Anna McCune Harper–Helen Jacobs d. Peggy Saunders Michell–
  Dorothy Round 6-4, 6-1
Eileen Bennett Whittingstall–Betty Nuthall d. Helen Wills Moody–
  Sarah Palfrey 6-3, 1-6, 10-8

1933

United States d. Great Britain 4-3 (Forest Hills)
Helen Jacobs (US) d. Dorothy Round 6-4, 6-2
Sarah Palfrey (US) d. Margaret Scriven 6-3, 6-1
Betty Nuthall (US) d. Carolin Babcock 1-6, 6-1, 6-3
Dorothy Round d. Sarah Palfrey 6-4, 10-8
Helen Jacobs d. Margaret Scriven 5-7, 6-2, 7-5
Helen Jacobs–Sarah Palfrey d. Dorothy Round–Mary Heeley 6-4, 6-2
Betty Nuthall–Freda James d. Marjorie Gladman Van Ryn–
  Alice Marble 7-5, 6-2

1934

United States d. Great Britain 5-2 (Wimbledon)
Sarah Palfrey (US) d. Dorothy Round 6-3, 3-6, 8-6
Helen Jacobs (US) d. Margaret Scriven 6-1, 6-1
Helen Jacobs d. Dorothy Round 6-4, 6-4
Sarah Palfrey d. Margaret Scriven 4-6, 6-2, 8-6
Betty Nuthall (GB) d. Carolin Babcock 5-7, 6-3, 6-4
Nancy Lyle–Evelyn Dearman d. Carolin Babcock–
  Josephine Cruickshank 7-5, 7-5
Helen Jacobs–Sarah Palfrey d. Kitty McKane Godfree–
  Betty Nuthall 5-7, 6-3, 6-2

1935

United States d. Great Britain 4-3 (Forest Hills)
Kay Stammers (GB) d. Helen Jacobs 5-7, 6-1, 9-7
Dorothy Round (GB) d. Ethel Burkhardt Arnold 6-0, 6-3
Sarah Palfrey Fabyan (US) d. Phyllis Mudford King 6-0, 6-3
Helen Jacobs d. Dorothy Round 6-3, 6-2
Ethel Burkhardt Arnold d. Kay Stammers 6-2, 1-6, 6-3
Helen Jacobs–Sarah Palfrey Fabyan d. Kay Stammers–
  Freda James 6-3, 6-2
Nancy Lyle–Evelyn Dearman (GB) d. Dorothy Andrus–
  Carolin Babcock 3-6, 6-4, 6-1

1936

United States d. Great Britain 4-3 (Wimbledon)
Kay Stammers (GB) d. Helen Jacobs 12-10, 6-1
Dorothy Round (GB) d. Sarah Palfrey Fabyan 6-3, 6-4
Sarah Palfrey Fabyan d. Kay Stammers 6-3, 6-4
Dorothy Round (GB) d. Helen Jacobs 6-3, 6-3
Carolin Babcock (US) d. Mary Hardwick 6-4, 4-6, 6-2
Carolin Babcock–Marjorie Gladman Van Ryn d. Evelyn Dearman–
  Nancy Lyle 6-2, 1-6, 6-3
Helen Jacobs–Sarah Palfrey Fabyan d. Kay Stammers–
  Freda James 1-6, 6-3, 7-5

1937
United States d. Great Britain 6-1 (Forest Hills)
Alice Marble (US) d. Mary Hardwick 4-6, 6-2, 6-4
Helen Jacobs (US) d. Kay Stammers 6-1, 4-6, 6-4
Helen Jacobs d. Mary Hardwick 2-6, 6-4, 6-2
Alice Marble d. Kay Stammers 6-3, 6-1
Sarah Palfrey Fabyan (US) d. Margot Lumb 6-3, 6-1
Alice Marble–Sarah Palfrey Fabyan d. Evelyn Dearman–
   Joan Ingram 6-3, 6-2
Kay Stammers–Freda James d. Marjorie Gladman Van Ryn–
   Dorothy Bundy 6-3, 10-8

1938
United States d. Great Britain 5-2 (Wimbledon)
Kay Stammers (GB) d. Alice Marble 3-6, 7-5, 6-3
Helen Wills Moody (US) d. Margaret Scriven 6-0, 7-5
Sarah Palfrey Fabyan (US) d. Margot Lumb 5-7, 6-2, 6-3
Alice Marble d. Margaret Scriven 6-3, 3-6, 6-0
Helen Wills Moody d. Kay Stammers 6-2, 3-6, 6-3
Alice Marble–Sarah Palfrey Fabyan d. Margot Lumb–Freda James
   6-4, 6-2
Evelyn Dearman–Joan Ingram d. Helen Wills Moody–Dorothy Bundy
   6-2, 7-5

1939
United States d. Great Britain 5-2 (Forest Hills)
Alice Marble (US) d. Mary Hardwick 6-3, 6-4
Kay Stammers (GB) d. Helen Jacobs 6-2, 1-6, 6-3
Valerie Scott (GB) d. Sarah Palfrey Fabyan 6-3, 6-4
Alice Marble d. Kay Stammers 3-6, 6-3, 6-4
Helen Jacobs d. Mary Hardwick 6-2, 6-2
Dorothy Bundy–Mary Arnold (US) d. Betty Nuthall–Nina Brown
   6-3, 6-1
Alice Marble–Sarah Palfrey Fabyan d. Kay Stammers–
   Freda James Hammersley 7-5, 6-2

1940-45 Not held, World War II

1946
United States d. Great Britain 7-0 (Wimbledon)
Pauline Betz d. Jean Bostock 6-2, 6-4
Margaret Osborne d. Jean Bostock 6-1, 6-4
Margaret Osborne d. Kay Stammers Menzies 6-3, 6-2
Louise Brough d. Joan Curry 8-6, 6-3
Pauline Betz d. Kay Stammers Menzies 6-4, 6-4
Margaret Osborne–Louise Brough d. Jean Bostock–Mary Halford
   6-2, 6-1
Pauline Betz–Doris Hart d. Betty Passingham–Molly Lincoln 6-1, 6-3

1947
United States d. Great Britain 7-0 (Forest Hills)
Margaret Osborne d. Jean Bostock 6-4, 2-6, 6-2
Louise Brough d. Kay Stammers Menzies 6-4, 6-2
Doris Hart d. Betty Hilton 4-6, 6-3, 7-5
Louise Brough d. Jean Bostock 6-4, 6-4
Margaret Osborne d. Kay Stammers Menzies 7-5, 6-2
Doris Hart–Pat Canning Todd d. Joy Gannon–Jean Quertier 6-1, 6-2
Margaret Osborne–Louise Brough d. Jean Bostock–Betty Hilton
   6-1, 6-4

1948
United States d. Great Britain 6-1 (Wimbledon)
Margaret Osborne duPont (US) d. Jean Bostock 6-4, 8-6
Louise Brough (US) d. Betty Hilton 6-1, 6-1
Margaret Osborne DuPont d. Betty Hilton 6-3, 6-4
Louise Brough d. Jean Bostock 6-2, 4-6, 7-5
Doris Hart (US) d. Joy Gannon 6-1, 6-4
Louise Brough–Margaret Osborne DuPont d. Kay Stammers
   Menzies–Betty Hilton 6-2, 6-2
Jean Bostock–Molly Lincoln Blair d. Doris Hart–Pat Canning Todd
   6-3, 6-4

1949
United States d. Great Britain 7-0 (Haverford, Pa.)
Doris Hart d. Jean Walker Smith 6-3, 6-1
Margaret Osborne duPont d. Betty Hilton 6-1, 6-3
Doris Hart d. Betty Hilton 6-1, 6-3
Margaret Osborne duPont d. Jean Smith 6-4, 6-2
Beverly Baker d. Jean Quertier 6-4, 7-5
Doris Hart–Shirley Fry d. Jean Quertier–Molly Lincoln Blair 6-1, 6-2
Gussy Moran–Pat Canning Todd d. Betty Hilton–Kay Tuckey 6-4, 8-6

1950
United States d. Great Britain 7-0 (Wimbledon)
Margaret Osborne duPont d. Betty Hilton 6-3, 6-4
Doris Hart d. Joan Curry 6-2, 6-4
Louise Brough d. Betty Hilton 2-6, 6-2, 7-5
Margaret Osborne duPont d. Jean Walker-Smith 6-3, 6-2
Louse Brough d. Jean Smith 6-0, 6-0
Pat Canning Todd–Doris Hart d. Jean Walker-Smith–Jean Quertier
   6-2, 6-3
Louise Brough–Margaret Osborne duPont d. Betty Hilton–
   Kay Tuckey 6-2, 6-0

1951
United States d. Great Britain 6-1 (Chestnut Hill, Mass.)
Doris Hart (US) d. Jean Quertier 6-4, 6-4
Shirley Fry (US) d. Jean Walker-Smith 6-1, 6-4
Maureen Connolly (US) d. Kay Tuckey 6-1, 6-3
Doris Hart d. Jean Walker-Smith 6-4, 2-6, 7-5
Jean Quertier d. Shirley Fry 6-3, 8-6
Pat Canning Todd–Nancy Chaffee (US) d. Pat Ward–
   Joy Gannon Mottram 7-5, 6-2
Shirley Fry–Doris Hart d. Jean Quertier–Kay Tuckey 6-3, 6-3

1952
United States d. Great Britain 7-0 (Wimbledon)
Doris Hart d. Jean Quertier-Rinkel 6-3, 6-3
Maureen Connolly d. Jean Walker-Smith 3-6, 6-1, 7-5
Doris Hart d. Jean Walker-Smith 7-5, 6-2
Maureen Connolly d. Jean Quertier-Rinkel 9-7, 6-2
Shirley Fry d. Susan Partridge 6-0, 8-6
Shirley Fry–Doris Hart d. Helen Fletcher–Jean Quertier-Rinkel 8-6, 6-4
Louise Brough–Maureen Connolly d. Joy Gannon Mottram–
   Pat Ward 6-0, 6-3

1953
United States d. Great Britain 7-0 (Rye, N.Y.)
Maureen Connolly d. Angela Mortimer 6-1, 6-1
Doris Hart d. Helen Fletcher 6-4, 7-5
Shirley Fry d. Jean Quertier-Rinkel 6-2, 6-4
Maureen Connolly d. Helen Fletcher 6-1, 6-1
Doris Hart d. Angela Mortimer 6-1, 6-1
Maureen Connolly–Louise Brough d. Angela Mortimer–
   Anne Shilcock 6-2, 6-3
Doris Hart–Shirley Fry d. Jean Quertier-Rinkel–Helen Fletcher
   6-2, 6-1

1954
United States d. Great Britain 6-0 (Wimbledon)
Maureen Connolly d. Helen Fletcher 6-1, 6-3
Doris Hart d. Anne Shilcock 6-4, 6-1
Doris Hart d. Helen Fletcher 6-1, 6-8, 6-2
Louise Brough d. Angela Buxton 8-6, 6-2
Maureen Connolly d. Anne Shilcock 6-2, 6-2
Louise Brough–Margaret Osborne duPont d. Angela Buxton–
   Pat Hird 2-6, 6-4, 7-5
Helen Fletcher–Anne Shilcock vs. Shirley Fry–Doris Hart (not played)

1955
United States d. Great Britain 6-1 (Rye, N.Y.)
Angela Mortimer (GB) d. Doris Hart 6-4, 1-6, 7-5
Louise Brough (US) d. Shirley Bloomer 6-2, 6-4
Louise Brough d. Angela Mortimer 6-0, 6-2
Dorothy Head Knode (US) d. Angela Buxton 6-3, 6-3
Doris Hart d. Shirley Bloomer 7-5, 6-3
Louise Brough–Margaret Osborne duPont d. Shirley Bloomer–
   Pat Ward 6-3, 6-3
Doris Hart–Shirley Fry d. Angela Mortimer–Angela Buxton
   3-6, 6-2, 7-5

1956
United States d. Great Britain 5-2 (Wimbledon)
Louise Brough (US) d. Angela Mortimer 3-6, 6-4, 7-5
Shirley Fry (US) d. Angela Buxton 6-2, 6-8, 7-5
Louise Brough d. Angela Buxton 3-6, 6-3, 6-4
Shirley Bloomer (GB) d. Dorothy Head Knode 6-4, 6-4
Angela Mortimer d. Shirley Fry 6-4, 6-4
Dorothy Knode–Beverly Baker Fleitz d. Shirley Bloomer–Pat Ward
   6-1, 6-4
Louise Brough–Shirley Fry d. Angela Buxton–Angela Mortimer
   6-2, 6-2

1957
United States d. Great Britain 6-1 (Sewickley, Pa.)
Althea Gibson (US) d. Shirley Bloomer 6-4, 4-6, 6-2
Dorothy Head Knode (US) d. Christine Truman 6-2, 11-9
Ann Haydon (GB) d. Darlene Hard 6-3, 3-6, 6-4
Dorothy Head Knode d. Shirley Bloomer 5-7, 6-1, 6-2
Althea Gibson d. Christine Truman 6-4, 6-2
Althea Gibson–Darlene Hard d. Shirley Bloomer–Sheila Armstrong
   6-3, 6-4
Louise Brough–Margaret Osborne duPont (US) d. Anne Shilcock–
   Ann Haydon 6-4, 6-1

1958
Great Britain d. United States 4-3 (Wimbledon)
Althea Gibson (US) d. Shirley Bloomer 6-3, 6-4
Christine Truman (GB) d. Dorothy Head Knode 6-4, 6-4
Dorothy Head Knode d. Shirley Bloomer 6-4, 6-2
Christine Truman d. Althea Gibson 2-6, 6-3, 6-4
Ann Haydon (GB) d. Mimi Arnold 6-3, 5-7, 6-3
Christine Truman–Shirley Bloomer d. Karol Fageros–Dorothy Knode
   6-2, 6-3
Althea Gibson–Janet Hopps d. Anne Shilcock–Pat Ward 6-4, 3-6, 6-3

1959
United States d. Great Britain 4-3 (Sewickley, Pa.)
Beverly Baker Fleitz (US) d. Angela Mortimer 6-2, 6-1
Christine Truman (GB) d. Darlene Hard 6-4, 2-6, 6-3
Darlene Hard d. Angela Mortimer 6-3, 6-8, 6-4
Beverly Baker Fleitz d. Christine Truman 6-4, 6-4
Ann Haydon (GB) d. Sally Moore 6-1, 6-1
Darlene Hard–Jeanne Arth d. Shirley Bloomer Brasher–
   Christine Truman 9-7, 9-7
Ann Haydon–Angela Mortimer d. Janet Hopps–Sally Moore 6-2, 6-4

1960
Great Britain d. United States 4-3 (Wimbledon)
Ann Haydon (GB) d. Karen Hantze 2-6, 11-9, 6-1
Darlene Hard (US) d. Christine Truman 4-6, 6-3, 6-4
Darlene Hard d. Ann Haydon 5-7, 6-2, 6-1
Christine Truman d. Karen Hantze 7-5, 6-3
Angela Mortimer (GB) d. Janet Hopps 6-8, 6-4, 6-1
Karen Hantze–Darlene Hard d. Ann Haydon–Angela Mortimer 6-0, 6-0
Christine Truman–Shirley Bloomer Brasher d. Janet Hopps–
   Dorothy Head Knode 6-4, 9-7

1961
United States d. Great Britain 6-1 (Chicago)
Karen Hantze (US) d. Christine Truman 7-9, 6-1, 6-1
Billie Jean Moffitt (US) d. Ann Haydon 6-4, 6-4
Karen Hantze d. Ann Haydon 6-1, 6-4
Christine Truman d. Billie Jean Moffitt 6-3, 6-2
Justina Bricka (US) d. Angela Mortimer 10-8, 4-6, 6-3
Karen Hantze–Billie Jean Moffitt d. Christine Truman–Deidre Catt
   7-5, 6-2
Margaret Osborne duPont–Margaret Varner d. Angela Mortimer–
   Ann Haydon (default)

1962
United States d. Great Britain 4-3 (Wimbledon)
Darlene Hard (US) d. Christine Truman 6-2, 6-2
Ann Haydon (GB) d. Karen Hantze Susman 10-8, 7-5
Deidre Catt (GB) d. Nancy Richey 6-1, 7-5
Darlene Hard d. Ann Haydon 6-3, 6-8, 6-4
Karen Susman d. Christine Truman 6-4, 7-5
Margaret Osborne duPont–Margaret Varner d. Deidre Catt–
   Elizabeth Starkie 6-3, 2-6, 6-2
Christine Truman–Ann Haydon d. Darlene Hard–Billie Jean Moffitt
   6-4, 6-3

1963
United States d. Great Britain 6-1 (Cleveland)
Ann Haydon Jones (GB) d. Darlene Hard 6-1, 0-6, 8-6
Billie Jean Moffitt (US) d. Christine Truman 6-4, 19-17
Nancy Richey (US) d. Deidre Catt 14-12, 6-3
Darlene Hard d. Christine Truman 6-3, 6-0
Billie Jean Moffitt d. Ann Jones 6-4, 4-6, 6-3
Darlene Hard–Billie Jean Moffitt d. Christine Truman–Ann Jones
   4-6, 7-5, 6-2
Nancy Richey–Donna Floyd Fales d. Deidre Catt–Elizabeth Starkie
   6-4, 6-8, 6-2

1964
United States d. Great Britain 5-2 (Wimbledon)
Nancy Richey (US) d. Deidre Catt 4-6, 6-4, 7-5
Billie Jean Moffitt d. Ann Haydon Jones 4-6, 6-2, 6-3
Carole Caldwell (US) d. Elizabeth Starkie 6-4, 1-6, 6-3
Nancy Richey d. Ann Jones 7-5, 11-9
Billie Jean Moffitt d. Deidre Catt 6-3, 4-6, 6-3
Deidre Catt–Ann Jones d. Carole Caldwell–Billie Jean Moffitt
   6-3, 4-6, 6-0
Angela Mortimer–Elizabeth Starkie d. Nancy Richey–
   Donna Floyd Fales 2-6, 6-3, 6-4

1965
United States d. Great Britain 5-2 (Cleveland)
Ann Haydon Jones (GB) d. Billie Jean Moffitt 6-2, 6-4
Nancy Richey (US) d. Elizabeth Starkie 6-1, 6-0
Carole Graebner (US) d. Virginia Wade 3-6, 10-8, 6-4
Billie Jean Moffitt d. Elizabeth Starkie 6-3, 6-2
Ann Haydon Jones d. Nancy Richey 6-4, 9-7
Carole Graebner–Nancy Richey d. Nell Truman–Elizabeth Starkie
   6-1, 6-0
Billie Jean Moffitt–Karen Hantze Susman d. Ann Jones–
   Virginia Wade 6-3, 8-6

1966
United States d. Great Britain 4-3 (Wimbledon)
Ann Haydon Jones (GB) d. Nancy Richey 2-6, 6-4, 6-3
Billie Jean King (US) d. Virginia Wade 6-2, 6-3
Winnie Shaw (GB) d. Mary Ann Eisel 6-3, 6-3
Nancy Richey d. Virginia Wade 2-6, 6-2, 7-5
Billie Jean King d. Ann Jones 5-7, 6-2, 6-3
Ann Jones–Virginia Wade d. Billie Jean King–Jane Albert 7-5, 6-2
Nancy Richey–Mary Ann Eisel d. Rita Bentley–Elizabeth Starkie
   6-1, 6-2

1967
United States d. Great Britain 6-1 (Cleveland)
Billie Jean King (US) d. Virginia Wade 6-3, 6-2
Nancy Richey (US) d. Ann Haydon Jones 6-2, 6-2
Christine Truman (GB) d. Rosie Casals 3-6, 7-5, 6-1
Nancy Richey d. Virginia Wade 3-6, 8-6, 6-2
Billie Jean King d. Ann Haydon Jones 6-1, 6-2
Rosie Casals–Billie Jean King d. Ann Jones–Virginia Wade 10-8, 6-4
Mary Ann Eisel–Carole Graebner (US) d. Joyce Barclay Williams–
   Winnie Shaw 8-6, 12-10

1968
Great Britain d. United States 4-3 (Wimbledon)
Nancy Richey (US) d. Christine Truman Janes 6-1, 8-6
Virginia Wade (GB) d. Mary Ann Eisel 6-0, 6-1
Peaches Bartkowicz (US) d. Winnie Shaw 7-5, 3-6, 6-4
Mary Ann Eisel d. Christine Truman Janes 6-4, 6-3
Virginia Wade d. Nancy Richey 6-4, 2-6, 6-3
Virginia Wade–Winnie Shaw d. Nancy Richey–Mary Ann Eisel
   5-7, 6-4, 6-3
Nell Truman– Christine Truman Janes d. Stephanie DeFina–
   Kathy Harter 6-3, 2-6, 6-3

1969
United States d. Great Britain 5-2 (Cleveland)
Julie Heldman (US) d. Virginia Wade 3-6, 6-1, 8-6
Nancy Richey (US) d. Winnie Shaw 8-6, 6-2
Peaches Bartkowicz (US) d. Christine Truman Janes 8-6, 6-0
Christine Truman Janes–Nell Truman (GB) d. Mary Ann Eisel Curtis–
   Valerie Ziegenfuss 6-1, 3-6, 6-4
Virginia Wade d. Nancy Richey 6-3, 2-6, 6-4
Julie Heldman d. Winnie Shaw 6-3, 6-4
Julie Heldman–Peaches Bartkowicz d. Winnie Shaw–Virginia Wade
   6-4, 6-2

1970
United States d. Great Britain 4-3 (Wimbledon)
Billie Jean King (US) d. Virginia Wade 8-6, 6-4
Ann Haydon Jones (GB) d. Nancy Richey 6-3, 6-3
Julie Heldman (US) d. Joyce Williams 6-3, 6-2
Virginia Wade d. Nancy Richey 6-3, 6-2
Billie Jean King d. Ann Haydon Jones 6-4, 6-2
Ann Haydon Jones–Joyce Williams d. Julie Heldman–
   Mary Ann Eisel Curtis 6-3, 6-2
Billie Jean King–Peaches Bartkowitz d. Virginia Wade–Winnie Shaw
   7-5, 6-8, 6-2

1971
United States d. Great Britain 4-3 (Cleveland)
Chris Evert (US) d. Winnie Shaw 6-0, 6-4
Virginia Wade (GB) d. Julie Heldman 7-5, 7-5
Joyce Barclay Williams (GB) d. Kristy Pigeon 7-5, 3-6, 6-4
Mary Ann Eisel Curtis–Valerie Ziegenfuss (US) d. Nell Truman–
   Christine Truman Janes 6-1, 6-4
Valerie Ziegenfuss d. Winnie Shaw 6-4, 4-6, 6-3
Chris Evert d. Virginia Wade 6-1, 6-1
Virginia Wade–Joyce Williams d. Carole Graebner–Chris Evert
   10-8, 4-6, 6-1

1972
United States d. Great Britain 5-2 (Wimbledon)
Joyce Barclay Williams (GB) d. Wendy Overton 6-3, 3-6, 6-3
Chris Evert (US) d. Virginia Wade 6-4, 6-4
Chris Evert–Patti Hogan d. Winnie Shaw–Nell Truman 7-5, 6-4
Patti Hogan d. Corinne Molesworth 6-8, 6-4, 6-2
Chris Evert d. Joyce Williams 6-2, 6-3
Virginia Wade d. Wendy Overton 8-6, 7-5
Valerie Ziegenfuss–Wendy Overton d. Virginia Wade–Joyce Willams
   6-3, 6-3

1973
United States d. Great Britain 5-2 (Brookline, Mass.)
Chris Evert (US) d. Virginia Wade 6-4, 6-2
Patti Hogan (US) d. Veronica Burton 6-4, 6-3
Linda Tuero (US) d. Glynis Coles 7-5, 6-2
Virginia Wade–Glynis Coles d. Chris Evert–Marita Redondo 6-3, 6-4
Chris Evert d. Veronica Burton 6-3, 6-0
Virginia Wade d. Patti Hogan 6-2, 6-2
Patti Hogan–Jeanne Evert d. Lindsey Beaven–Lesley Charles
   6-3, 4-6, 8-6

1974
Great Britain d. United States 6-1, (Queensferry, North Wales)
Virginia Wade (GB) d. Julie Heldman 5-7, 9-7, 6-4
Glynis Coles (GB) d. Janet Newberry 4-6, 6-1, 6-3
Sue Barker (GB) d. Jeanne Evert 4-6, 6-4, 6-1
Lesley Charles–Sue Barker d. Janet Newberry–Betsy Nagelsen
   4-6, 6-2, 6-1
Glynis Cole d. Julie Heldman 6-0, 6-4
Virginia Wade d. Janet Newberry 6-1, 6-3
Julie Heldman–Mona Schallau d. Virginia Wade–Glynis Coles 7-5, 6-4

1975
Great Britain d. United States 5-2 (Cleveland)
Virginia Wade (GB) d. Mona Schallau 6-2, 6-2
Chris Evert (US) d. Glynis Coles 6-4, 6-1
Sue Barker (GB) d. Janet Newberry 6-4, 7-5
Virginia Wade–Ann Haydon Jones d. Janet Newberry–Julie Anthony
   6-2, 6-3
Chris Evert d. Virginia Wade 6-3, 7-6
Glynis Coles d. Mona Schallau 6-3, 7-6
Glynis Coles–Sue Barker d. Chris Evert–Mona Schallau 7-5, 6-4

1976
United States d. Great Britain 5-2 (Wimbledon)
Chris Evert (US) d. Virginia Wade 6-2, 3-6, 6-3
Sue Barker (GB) d. Rosie Casals 1-6, 6-3, 6-2,
Terry Holladay (US) d. Glynis Coles 3-6, 6-1, 6-4
Chris Evert–Rosie Casals d. Virginia Wade–Sue Barker 6-0, 5-7, 6-1
Virginia Wade (GB) d. Rosie Casals 3-6, 9-7, ret.
Chris Evert d. Sue Barker 2-6, 6-2, 6-2
Ann Kiyomura–Mona Schallau Guerrant (US) d. Sue Mappin–
   Lesley Charles 6-2, 6-2

1977
United States d. Great Britain 7-0 (Oakland)
Chris Evert d. Virginia Wade 7-5, 7-6
Billie Jean King d. Sue Barker 6-1, 6-4
Rosie Casals d. Michele Tyler 6-2, 3-6, 6-4
Billie Jean King–JoAnne Russell d. Sue Mappin–Lesley Charles
   6-0, 6-1
Billie Jean King d. Virginia Wade 6-4, 3-6, 8-6
Chris Evert d. Sue Barker 6-1, 6-2
Chris Evert–Rosie Casals d. Virginia Wade–Sue Barker 6-2, 6-4

1978
Great Britain d. United States 4-3 (London)
Chris Evert (US) d. Sue Barker 6-2, 6-1
Michele Tyler (GB) d. Pam Shriver 5-7, 6-3, 6-3
Virginia Wade (GB) d. Tracy Austin 3-6, 7-5, 6-3
Billie Jean King–Tracy Austin d. Sue Mappin–Anne Hobbs
   6-2, 4-6, 6-2
Chris Evert d. Virginia Wade 6-0, 6-1
Sue Barker d. Tracy Austin 6-3, 3-6, 6-0
Virginia Wade–Sue Barker d. Chris Evert–Pam Shriver 6-0, 5-7, 6-4

1979
United States d. Great Britain 7-0 (Palm Beach, Fla.)
Chris Evert Lloyd d. Sue Barker 7-5, 6-2
Kathy Jordan d. Anne Hobbs 6-4, 6-7, 6-2
Tracy Austin d. Virginia Wade 6-1, 6-4
Tracy Austin–Ann Kiyomura d. Jo Durie–Debbie Jevans 6-3, 6-1
Tracy Austin d. Sue Barker 6-4, 6-2
Chris Evert Lloyd d. Virginia Wade 6-1, 6-1
Chris Evert Lloyd–Rosie Casals d. Virginia Wade–Sue Barker 6-0, 6-1

1980
United States d. Great Britain 5-2 (London)
Chris Evert Lloyd (US) d. Sue Barker 6-1 6-2
Anne Hobbs (GB) d. Kathy Jordan 4-6, 6-4, 6-1
Andrea Jaeger (US) d. Virginia Wade 3-6, 6-3, 6-2
Rosie Casals–Chris Evert Lloyd d. Glynis Coles–Anne Hobbs 6-3, 6-3
Chris Evert Lloyd d. Virginia Wade 7-5, 3-6, 7-5
Sue Barker d. Andrea Jaeger 5-7, 6-3, 6-3
Kathy Jordan–Anne Smith d. Sue Barker–Virginia Wade 6-4, 7-5

1981
United States d. Great Britain 7-0 (Chicago)
Tracy Austin d. Sue Barker 7-5, 6-3
Andrea Jaeger d. Anne Hobbs 6-0, 6-0
Chris Evert Lloyd d. Virginia Wade 6-1, 6-3
Andrea Jaeger–Pam Shriver d. Anne Hobbs–Jo Durie 6-1, 6-3
Tracy Austin d. Virginia Wade 6-3, 6-1
Chris Evert Lloyd d. Sue Barker 6-3, 6-0
Chris Evert Lloyd–Rosie Casals d. Glynis Coles–Virginia Wade 6-3, 6-3

1982
United States d. Great Britain 6-1 (London)
Barbara Potter (US) d. Sue Barker 6-2, 6-2
Anne Smith (US) d. Virginia Wade 3-6, 7-5, 6-3
Chris Evert Lloyd (US) d. Jo Durie 6-2, 6-2
Jo Durie–Anne Hobbs d. Rosie Casals–Anne Smith 6-3, 2-6, 6-2
Barbara Potter d. Jo Durie 5-7, 7-6, 6-2
Chris Evert Lloyd d. Sue Barker 6-4, 6-3
Barbara Potter–Sharon Walsh d. Sue Barker–Virginia Wade 2-6, 6-4, 6-4

1983
United States d. Great Britain 6-1 (Williamsburg, Va.)
Martina Navratilova (US) d. Sue Barker 6-2, 6-0
Kathy Rinaldi (US) d. Virginia Wade 6-2, 6-2
Pam Shriver (US) d. Jo Durie 6-3, 6-2
Sue Barker–Virginia Wade d. Candy Reynolds–Paula Smith 7-5, 3-6, 6-1
Pam Shriver d. Sue Barker 6-0, 6-1
Martina Navratilova d. Jo Durie 6-3, 6-3
Martina Navratilova–Pam Shriver d. Annabel Croft–Jo Durie 6-2, 6-1

1984
United States d. Great Britain 5-2 (London)
Chris Evert Lloyd (US) d. Anne Hobbs 6-2, 6-2
Annabel Croft (GB) d. Alycia Moulton 6-1, 5-7, 6-4
Jo Durie (GB) d. Barbara Potter 6-3, 7-6
Chris Evert Lloyd–Alycia Moulton d. Virginia Wade–Amanda Brown 6-2, 6-2
Barbara Potter d. Anne Hobbs 6-1, 6-3
Chris Evert Lloyd d. Jo Durie 7-6, 6-1
Barbara Potter–Sharon Walsh d. Jo Durie–Anne Hobbs 7-6, 4-6, 9-7

1985
United States d. Great Britain 7-0 (Williamsburg, Va.)
Chris Evert Lloyd d. Jo Durie 6-2, 6-3
Kathy Rinaldi d. Anne Hobbs 7-5, 7-5
Pam Shriver d. Annabel Croft 6-0, 6-0
Betsy Nagelsen–Anne White d. Annabel Croft–Virginia Wade 6-4, 6-1
Pam Shriver d. Jo Durie 6-4, 6-4
Chris Evert Lloyd d. Annabel Croft 6-3, 6-0
Chris Evert Lloyd–Pam Shriver d. Jo Durie–Anne Hobbs 6-3, 6-7, 6-2

1986
United States d. Great Britain 7-0 (London)
Kathy Rinaldi d. Sara Gomer 6-3, 7-6
Stephanie Rehe d. Annabel Croft 6-3, 6-1
Bonnie Gadusek d. Jo Durie 6-2, 6-4
Bonnie Gadusek–Kathy Rinaldi d. Annabel Croft–Sara Gomer 6-3, 5-7, 6-3
Bonnie Gadusek d. Anne Hobbs 2-6, 6-4, 6-4
Kathy Rinaldi d. Jo Durie 6-4, 6-2
Elise Burgin–Anne White d. Jo Durie–Anne Hobbs 7-6, 6-3

1987
United States d. Great Britain 5-2 (Williamsburg, Va.)
Zina Garrison (US) d. Anne Hobbs 7-5, 6-2
Lori McNeil (US) d. Sara Gomer 6-2, 6-1
Pam Shriver (US) d. Jo Durie 6-1, 7-5
Gigi Fernandez–Robin White d. Sara Gomer–Clare Wood 6-4, 6-1
Pam Shriver d. Anne Hobbs 6-4, 6-3
Jo Durie d. Zina Garrison 7-6, 6-3
Jo Durie–Anne Hobbs d. Zina Garrison–Lori McNeil 0-6, 6-4, 7-5

1988
United States d. Great Britain 7-0 (London)
Zina Garrison d. Jo Durie 6-2, 6-4
Patty Fendick d. Monique Javer 6-2, 6-1
Lori McNeil d. Sara Gomer 6-7, 6-4, 6-4
Lori McNeil–Betsy Nagelsen d. Sara Gomer–Julie Salmon 6-3, 6-2
Zina Garrison d. Claire Wood 6-3, 6-2
Lori McNeil d. Jo Durie 6-1, 6-2
Gigi Fernandez–Zina Garrison d. Jo Durie–Clare Wood 6-1, 6-3

1989
United States d. Great Britain 7-0 (Williamsburg, Va.)
Lori McNeil d. Jo Durie 7-5, 6-1
Jennifer Capriati d. Clare Wood 6-0, 6-0
Mary Joe Fernandez d. Sara Gomer 6-1, 6-2
Mary Joe Fernandez–Betsy Nagelsen d. Sara Gomer–Clare Wood 6-2 7-6
Lori McNeil d. Sara Gomer 6-4, 6-2
Mary Joe Fernandez d. Jo Durie 6-1, 7-5
Patty Fendick–Lori McNeil d. Jo Durie–Anne Hobbs 6-3, 6-3

WIGHTMAN CUP RECORDS

INDIVIDUAL

Most Cup-winning years: 12—Chris Evert, U.S., 1971–73, 76-82, 84-85; 11—Helen Jacobs, U.S., 1927–39
Most years played: 21—Virginia Wade, Britain, 1965–85
Most singles played: 35—Virginia Wade, Britain
Most singles won: 26—Chris Evert, U.S.
Most doubles played: 20—Virginia Wade, Britain
Most doubles won: 10—Louise Brough, U.S., 1946–57
Most singles and doubles together: 55—Virginia Wade, Britain
Most singles and doubles won together: 34—Chris Evert, U.S.
Most consecutive singles won: 26—Chris Evert, U.S.
Best winning percentage, 15 or more wins, singles and doubles altogether: 1.000—Chris Evert, U.S., 26 wins, 0 losses.
Best winning percentage, doubles, 5 or more wins: 1.000—Louise Brough, U.S., 10 wins, 0 losses
Best doubles team record: 7-0—Margaret Osborne duPont and Louise Brough, U.S., 1946–57
Longest singles: 46 games—Billie Jean Moffitt King, U.S., d. Christine Truman, 19-17, 6-4, 1963
Longest doubles: 40 games—Hazel Hotchkiss Wightman and Eleanor Goss, U.S., d. Kitty McKane and Phyllis Howkins Covell, 10-8, 5-7, 6-4, 1923
Most Cups won by captain: 12—Hazel Hotchkiss Wightman, 1923–48

Lindsay Davenport, 2002
Ranked No. 1 in 1998 and
2001, she led the late '90s
renaissance of U.S. women.

Biographies

RECORDS – TOURNAMENTS WON, CAREER, SINGLES

MEN
109—Jimmy Connors, 1970-89
 94—Ivan Lendl, 1980-94
 77—John McEnroe, 1978-92
 62—Bjorn Borg, 1974-81
 62—Guillermo Vilas, 1973-86

WOMEN
167—Martina Navratilova, 1973-94
157—Chris Evert, 1970-89
102—Steffi Graf, 1982-96
 79—Margaret Smith Court, 1968-77
 67—Billie Jean King, 1968-83

Chapter 25

Notable players

Pam Shriver, 1988
A loss in her only Virigina Slims final, to Gabriela Sabatini.

Shakespeare once wrote that all the world's a stage, and all the men and women merely players. The great bard could have been writing about tennis, where drama, tragedy and, on occasion, comedy are staged by talented casts of nomadic performers. Throughout its history, tennis has been shaped by the artists whose individual styles and personalities give life to the grand game. And, like any well-rounded cast, the athletes have come in all manner of size and disposition.

The subjects on the following pages have all been winners, but we like to think they each brought more to the game than a steely resolve to win. They have been selected both for their enormous accomplishments, but also because this group has defined tennis through the ages. There are the pure champions like Margaret Smith Court and Bill Tilden, but also characters like Bobby Riggs and Ilie Nastase; crusaders like Billie Jean King and Jack Kramer; bad boys like Jimmy Connors and John McEnroe; girl-next-door types like Maureen Connolly and Chris Evert; freedom seekers like Martina Navratilova and Ivan Lendl; pioneers like Arthur Ashe and Althea Gibson; trend-setters like Suzanne Lenglen and Andre Agassi—and many more who have served with distinction over the past century.

ANDRE AGASSI
United States (1970–)

A player of irresistible flair, appeal and shotmaking ability, since appearing on the professional landscape as a 16-year-old in 1986, Andre Kirk Agassi, was the first Nevadan to make an impact on the game. And what a tremendous impact, although it took longer than expected for him to make the predicted leap to his first major championship, Wimbledon, 1992—and even longer to re-dedicate himself to his profession so that he was solidly established at the heights. At age 33 he was playing better than ever, winning his fourth Australian championship, his eighth major.

Despite a seemingly disastrous slump during which he plummeted to No. 141 in 1997, and finished the year at No. 122, Andre rebounded sensationally to rise to No. 6 in 1998—a record turn-around—and nail down five of his majors. The piece de resistance was his French triumph in 1999, evicting the defender Carlos Moya in the fourth round and finishing in a dazzling recovery over Russian Andrei Medvedev. The win catapulted Agassi into the select company of Fred Perry, Don Budge, Rod Laver and Roy Emerson as only the fifth man to own all four majors.

Andre's first title major, Wimbledon, came after he'd failed, as the favorite, to beat Pete Sampras for the U.S. Open title in 1990, and Andres Gomez and Jim Courier for the French in 1990 and 1991. After a quick, unhappy thrashing by Henri Leconte at Wimbledon in 1987, Agassi had assiduously avoided the grass until 1991, a successful reappearance ending in a quarter-final loss to David Wheaton. Realizing the greensward wasn't that forbidding, he returned a year later to take it all, his twelfth seeding making him among Wimbledon's lowest regarded champions at the starting gate. "This was not the one people looked for me to win," he said correctly, after his buzzing groundies outdid the missile attack of 36-ace-serving Goran Ivanisevic in the final, 6-7 (8-10), 6-4, 6-4, 1-6, 6-4.

Ranked low again in 1994, No. 20, he became only the third non-seed to win the U.S., taking it on his ninth shot, over Michael Stich, joining Mal Anderson (1957) and Fred Stolle (1966) in the exclusive unseeded club. He had also made excuses for skipping the long trip to Australia, yet won it on his first try, 1995, spectacularly over Sampras, the defender.

Following his French title, Andre won his second

U.S. title—and fifth major—in a five-set battle with Todd Martin in 1999. He then won the 2000 Aussie over Yevgeny Kafelnikov after being two points from defeat in a fourth-set, semi-final tie-breaker against Sampras. His third and fourth Aussie titles were both in straight-set finals, over Frenchman Arnaud Clement in 2001 and German Rainer Schuettler in 2003. (He missed 2002 with a wrist injury.)

A brilliant shotmaker and thoughtful attacker from the baseline who takes the ball so early that he seems to be playing ping-pong, Agassi needed time to sort out whether being a commercial success was enough. As the most widely marketed player of all-time—'image is everything' was one of his sales pitches—he has made more millions off the court than on it. Fortunately, he decided to utilize his gifts to attract as much attention by winning. Never has there been such a controversial figure so broadly associated with the game, thanks to TV commercials. His ever-changing hairstyle, brightly hued attire, and such items as black shoes, and denim shorts, considered garish by traditionalists, lured countless buyers as hip or avant-garde. His engagement to actress Brooke Shields (granddaughter of Hall of Famer Frank Shields), whom he married on April 19, 1997, didn't hurt Andre's visibility that transcends the sports page. That marriage was short-lived, but he made another high-profile pairing when he wed Steffi Graf in 2001 (they have a son, Jaden Gil, b. Oct. 26, 2001).

But beneath the peacock and the pop idol is a tennis player whose timing, anticipation, coordination and determination enable him to deliver withering, top-spinning barrages with flicks of the wrist. "When Andre's on, forget it," says Sampras. "He does practically everything better than anybody else."

Agassi was born April 29, 1970, in Las Vegas, and lives there, although he was farmed out to Nick Bollettieri's Tennis Academy at Brandenton, Fla., at age 13. His father, Mike Agassi, an Iranian immigrant and naturalized U.S. citizen, was a strict taskmaster who was determined that Andre would be a top tennis player. Papa pushed the kid from cradle onward, then gave the prodigy over to surrogate father Bollettieri. An Olympic boxer for Iran in 1952, Mike fell for tennis and taught Andre "the new game, based on the way a fighter throws punches, plus a two-handed backhand for added power." A right-hander, Andre is 5-foot-11, 170 pounds.

It all worked, and led Andre to his own Olympics, 1996 in Atlanta, where he made off with the gold medal by thumping Spaniard Sergi Bruguera in 78 minutes. Again, it had taken him an inordinate amount of time to put his act together. He had declined taking part in 1988 and 1992.

By lifting the Australian crown from Sampras in 1995, Agassi also took Pete's No. 1 jersey, and they dueled throughout the year for the top. But Pete ended Andre's excellent summer streak of four tournaments and 26 matches with a four-set, final-round defeat to regain his U.S. Open title and top ranking. That loss seemed to deflate Agassi, and 1996—other than the Olympics—was a downer, his worst in the majors: Ghastly first- and second-round losses respectively at Wimbledon (No. 186 Doug Flach) and the French (No. 73 Chris Woodruff), and desultory semi-final losses to Michael Chang at the Australian and the U.S.

His was an uneven course through the first 11 years, up one year, down another (four first-round losses at the U.S. Open for instance), but the sheer firepower within makes him a threat to blast anybody off any court at any time. A world top ten 14 times between 1988 and 2002, Agassi was No 1 for 30 weeks in 1995, two weeks in '96 and 52 weeks in 1999-2000.

Bollettieri, feeling Andre didn't work hard enough, severed their decade-long relationship in 1993, but he won six majors with Brad Gilbert as coach. Plunging to No. 24, his lowest adult ranking then, after losing the first round of the 1993 U.S. Open to No. 61 Thomas Enqvist, he required surgery to repair a damaged wrist— "I thought my career was over." But he came back strong. Aussie Darren Cahill became his coach in 2002, and his fitness guru, fellow Las Vegan Gil Reyes, has overseen Andre's superb physical condition.

In 1988, as one of the youngest U.S. Davis Cup rookies, he won all his singles on Latin clay (historic trouble ground for gringos) at Peru and Argentina to spearhead his fallen nation's recovery from the perdition of relegation. He became a valuable hand in the Cup triumphs of 1990, 1992 and 1995 with a 22-4 record, but played sporadically thereafter. Registering four singles wins in 3-2 decisions over Zimbabwe and the Czech Republic in 2000, he bowed out after 10 years of Cupping and a 30-5 singles record, second among Americans only to John McEnroe's 41 singles wins.

Andre made his first splash at Stratton Mountain, Vt., in 1987, beating Wimbledon champion Pat Cash on the way to the semis. Shortly thereafter he took his first title, Itaparica (Brazil), over Luiz Mattar. His most

productive season was 1995: Seven titles on 73-9 in matches, but two of his five titles in 1999 were the French and U.S. During a 17-year pro career, through 2002, has won 54 singles (of 80 finals), one doubles titles and $25,658,496, second only to Sampras's $43,280,489. His career singles W-L is 738-231 (.762)

In establishing the Andre Agassi Charitable Foundation, he has shown responsibility and concern, donating millions to such worthy projects as building the Agassi College Preparatory Academy and Agassi Boys and Girls Club in the troubled sector, West Las Vegas.

MAJOR TITLES (8)–*Australian singles, 1995, 2000, 2002, 2003; French singles, 1999; Wimbledon singles, 1992; U.S. singles, 1994, 1999.* **OTHER U.S. TITLES** (2)–*Indoor singles, 1988; Clay Court singles, 1988.* **DAVIS CUP**–*1988, 1989, 1990, 1991, 1992, 1995, 1998, 2000; record: 22-4 in singles.* **SINGLES RECORD IN THE MAJORS**–*Australian (12-1), French (31-9), Wimbledon (23-6), U.S. (38-10).*

FRED ALEXANDER
United States (1880–1969)
Hall of Fame 1961

As the first foreigner to win the Australian titles, Frederick Beasley Alexander beat Alf Dunlop in 1908 and joined with native Dunlop to take the doubles, too. That year he and Beals Wright were the U.S. Davis Cup team in an unsuccessful attempt to pry the Cup away from Australasia (Norman Brookes and Tony Wilding), 3-2 in Melbourne. He lost a tough opener to Brookes, 6-3 in the fifth, and the decisive match to Wilding in three. Right-handed, a New Yorker and Princeton man, he won the U.S. Intercollegiate singles (1901) and doubles (1900).

He ranked six times in the U.S. Top Ten between 1904 and 1918, the last, at 38, his highest, No. 3 in 1908. He was Harold Hackett's partner in a standout doubles team, U.S. finalists a record seven straight times, beginning in 1905, winning in 1907, 1908, 1909 and 1910. In 1917, at 37, he won a fifth U.S. title, shepherding 19-year-old Harold Throckmorton to the doubles championship. Lean and lanky, a smooth stroker, he was born in New York Aug. 14, 1880, and died in Beverly Hills, Calif., March 3, 1969. Inducted into the Hall of Fame in 1961.

MAJOR TITLES (7)–*Australian singles, 1908; Australian doubles, 1908; U.S. doubles, 1907, 1908, 1909, 1910, 1917.* **OTHER U.S. TITLES** (8)–*Indoor doubles, 1906, 1907, 1908, with Harold Hackett; 1911, 1912, with Theodore Pell; 1917, with William Rosenbaum; Intercollegiate singles, 1901; Intercollegiate doubles, 1900, with Raymond Little.* **DAVIS CUP**–*1908; record: 0-2 in singles, 1-1 in doubles.* **SINGLES RECORD IN THE MAJORS**–*Australian (4-0), U.S. (27-12).*

WILMER ALLISON

United States (1904–1977)
Hall of Fame 1963

Although the firm of Allison & Van Ryn was synonymous with doubles excellence, Texan Wilmer Lawson Allison, who played the left court, had several singles triumphs at the top of the game. Foremost, he won the U.S. Championship in 1935 when, at age 30, he shot through not only 23-year-old ex-Wimbledon champ Sidney Wood, 6-2, 6-2, 6-3, in one of the most lopsided finals, but 1933, 1934 and 1936 champ Fred Perry in the semis, 7-5, 6-3, 6-3. That ended a Forest Hills streak of 18 matches for Perry, and eased some of Allison's pain of losing the 1934 final to Fred, 8-6 in the fifth.

As a Davis Cupper, primarily in doubles, he and Johnny Van Ryn—U.S. champs in 1931 and 1935 and Wimbledon champs in 1929 and 1930—won 14 of 16 Cup doubles between 1929 and 1936, the best record by a U.S. team until Peter Fleming and John McEnroe's 14-1. Their 24 team matches (tied with Stan Smith and Vic Seixas) are second only to McEnroe's 30 in U.S. annals. They beat the topnotch French teams in Cup finales in Paris (Jean Borotra-Henri Cochet in 1929, Cochet-Jacques Brugnon in 1932) but could do no more than prolong successful French defenses.

A 5-foot-11, 155-pound right-hander, Allison experienced two extraordinary Cup singles matches in Paris in 1931 and 1932. Opening the 4-1 semi-final victory over Italy he made an all-time comeback to beat ambidextrous Giorgio de Stefani, 4-6, 7-9, 6-4, 8-6, 10-8. Allison squandered four set points of his own in the second, but the most exciting was to come; from 2-5 down in the fourth he saved two match points, and in the last set, from 1-5 down, 16 more.

The following year, with France ahead, 2-1, and the Cup at stake, he lost a controversial match to Borotra, 1-6, 3-6, 6-4, 6-2, 7-5, after the Frenchman saved four match points in the fifth set. On the fourth, at 4-5 advantage out, Borotra apparently double-faulted by a considerable margin. But the local linesman made no call, and it was a point against Allison, who was on his way to the net to shake hands.

Objective Al Laney wrote for the consumption of U.S. readers: "The U.S. has won the Cup, but the trophy remains in France. A linesman [Gerard de Ferrier] kept Allison from his just victory." Ellsworth Vines beat Cochet in the fifth match, to make the score 3-2, France,

but nobody can know how that match would have gone had it been decisive.

Allison played 44 singles and doubles Cup matches, third for the U.S. behind McEnroe (69) and Seixas (55), and won 32. Allison, who had also been a U.S. semi-finalist in 1932, did not defend his title, withdrawing from the scene after losing a 1936 quarter-final to Bunny Austin, 6-1, 6-4, 7-5, at Wimbledon, where he'd lost the 1930 final to Bill Tilden, Big Bill's last major title. He had been in the U.S. Top Ten from 1928, eight straight years, No. 1 in 1934 and 1935, and the World Top Ten five times between 1930 and 1935, No. 4 in 1932 and 1935. He was born Dec. 8, 1904, in San Antonio, and won the U.S. Intercollegiate title for his alma mater, Texas, in 1927.

During World War II he was a colonel in the U.S. Army Air Force. He entered the Hall of Fame in 1963, and died April 20, 1977, in Austin, Tex.

MAJOR TITLES (6)–*U.S. singles, 1935; Wimbledon doubles, 1929, 1930; U.S. doubles, 1931, 35; U.S. mixed, 1930.* **OTHER U.S. TITLE**–*Intercollegiate singles, 1927.* **DAVIS CUP**–*1928, 1929, 1930, 1931, 1932, 1933, 1935, 1936; record: 18-10 in singles, 14-2 in doubles.* **SINGLES RECORD IN THE MAJORS**–*Wimbledon (16-5), U.S. (27-8).*

MANUEL ALONSO

Spain (1895–1984)
Hall of Fame 1977

As the first Spanish male of international stature, Manolo Alonso de Areyzaga made his country's best showing at Wimbledon and the U.S. Championships before Manolo Santana won them in 1966 and 1965, respectively. He beat Zenzo Shimidzu in a terrific battle, 3-6, 7-5, 3-6, 6-4, 8-6, to reach the Wimbledon all-comers final of 1921, where he lost to Babe Norton in another tense struggle, 5-7, 4-6, 7-5, 6-3, 6-3. A U.S. resident for several years during the 1920s, he was a U.S. Championships quarter-final ist in 1922, 1923, 1925 and 1927 and was ranked in the U.S. Top Ten in 1925, 1926 and 1927, No. 2 in 1926. He was also in the World Top Ten three years, 1925, 1926 and 1927, No. 5 the last year.

A dark-haired 5-foot-9, 145-pound right-hander, he played Davis Cup for Spain. He was born Nov. 12, 1895, in San Sebastian and died Oct. 11, 1984, in Madrid. He entered the Hall of Fame in 1977.

DAVIS CUP–*1921, 1922, 1924, 1925, 1931, 1936; record: 11-7 in singles, 3-4 in doubles.* **SINGLES RECORD IN THE MAJORS**–*Wimbledon (8-3), U.S. (20-10).*

MAL ANDERSON

Australia (1935–)
Hall of Fame 2000

They called him 'Country' and 'Cowboy.' He came from a remote, vast territory of cattle, kangaroos, kookaburas—and home-made tennis courts of ant bed. Knock over a few crimson ant hills, something like fireplugs, spread the grit in a rectangle, roll and line, and—presto: You've got the kind of court that rural Queensland lads like Malcolm James Anderson grew up on.

Mal Anderson, 22, was as unknown to Americans as his home turf, a cattle station [ranch] at Burnside, when he showed up at Forest Hills for the third time in 1957 and became the first unseeded guy to win the U.S. championship, beating a fellow Aussie and future Davis Cup teammate, first-seeded Ashley Cooper, 10-8, 7-5, 6-4. He was the forerunner of the four Queenslanders emerging from what's sometimes called 'never-never land' (so far from anything) who conquered the U.S., followed by Roy Emerson (1961, 64), Rod Laver (1962, 69) and Patrick Rafter (1997-98). And, in a two-part career he could yet be seen on the international circuit at age 38.

Lean as a rail at 6-foot-1, dark hair slicked back, he was attack all the way, quick and sure of volley, fast around the court, a worthy successor to compatriots Frank Sedgman (1951-52) and Ken Rosewall (1956). Prior to the U.S., his 1957 season had not gone well: Heat prostration, later a broken toe at Wimbledon. But a win over No. 1 American Ham Richardson in the Newport final, the second title of his career, got him in fine fettle for the drive across the Forest Hills greensward. He beat the 1-2-3 seeds—No. 2 Dick Savitt, No. 1 Chilean Luis Ayala,, and in his toughest, No. 3 Swede Sven Davidson in a comeback, to enter the final. There his slick backhand, quickness and anticipation zapped Cooper, who had lost the Wimbedon final to Lew Hoad. His was a unique U.S. achievement—from first-round loser to champ 12 months later—until Swede Stefan Edberg pulled it off in 1991.

Anderson's menacing 1957 form continued through victories at home, Adelaide and Melbourne, and the successful post-Christmas Davis Cup defense, 3-2, over the U.S. at Melbourne. Hoad and Rosewall had fled to the pros, and the pressure was on leadoff man Mal. Few have made a more solid final-round debut: He cut down huge-serving Barry MacKay in five sets and the next day (after Cooper had beaten Vic Seixas), accompanied Mervyn Rose for the coup de grace: 6-4, 6-4, 8-6, over MacKay and Seixas.

Although he won six tournaments in 1958, repeating at Newport, Anderson couldn't win the Australian championship (beaten in the final by Cooper, 7-5, 6-3, 6-4) or retain the U.S. title. He came very close, losing a five-set final to Cooper.

The Davis Cup was a disappointment, too, a 3-2 loss to the U.S., especially since the final was in Queensland, the Milton Grounds at Brisbane. Peruvian Alex Olmedo, a U.S. resident, outgunned Anderson in a tight one, 8-6, 2-6, 9-7, 8-6, and would beat Cooper in the third-day clincher. Heart-breaking was the doubles, Anderson and Cup rookie Neale Fraser overtaken by Olmedo and Richardson, 10-12, 3-6, 16-14, 6-3, 7-5.

Those defeats reduced his value to pro promoter Jack Kramer, but Mal signed for a $22,000 guarantee over two years, and exceeded it. As a rookie in 1959 Mal won the most important of the pro championships, Wembley in London, beating Pancho Segura in five sets. He barnstormed for a while, retired, then reappeared in 1969, at 34, attaching Part II to his resume with the advent of opens, adding the last five of his 21 career singles titles. Fourteen years after first gracing the Australian final, he made it again in 1972, losing to Rosewall. A year later, at 38, he took the Aussie doubles in the company of John Newcombe over Phil Dent and John Alexander. He played Davis Cup for two more years, winning 10 singles, and was a contributing member of possibly the greatest of all Davis Cup teams—Capt. Neale Fraser's winning Antique Show: Rod Laver, 35, Ken Rosewall, 39, Newcombe, 29, and Anderson. Born March 5, 1935, at home in Burnside (18 miles from the nearest pub at Theodore), he grew up on a 6,000-acre property with 1,000 head of cattle. Mal spent a lot of time on horseback doing the work of a ringer (cowboy). "Fell off a few times, too," he laughs. He was sent to school in Rockhampton and was tutored at tennis by Charlie Hollis, Laver's coach. Entering the International Hall in 2000, he was named to the Australian Tennis Hall of Fame in 2001.

MAJOR TITLES (4)–*U.S. singles, 1957; Australian doubles, 1973; French doubles, 1957; Australian mixed, 1957.* **DAVIS CUP**–*1957, 1958, 1973; record: 11-3 in singles, 2-3 in doubles.* **SINGLES RECORD IN THE MAJORS**–*Australian (16-8), French (1-1), Wimbledon (13-5), U.S. (16-4).*

ARTHUR ASHE

United States (1943–1993)
Hall of Fame 1985

A singular figure in the game's history as the first black male to win a major singles titles—the first three in fact—Arthur Robert Ashe, Jr., also set a record in 1968 that is most unlikely to be equaled: He won both the U.S. Amateur and Open championships, the first time such a double was possible. No one has come remotely close since.

That first season of the open era was a whirlwind year for him, then 1st Lt. Ashe of the U.S. Army. In order to maintain Davis Cup eligibility and gain time away from duty for important tournaments, Ashe was required to maintain his amateur status. Determining that the traditional (and previously amateur) U.S. Singles Championships at Forest Hills would become the inaugural U.S. Open in 1968, the USTA designated Longwood Cricket Club in Boston as the site for a U.S. Amateur tournament. Seeded first in Boston, Ashe came through to the title by surging past teammate Bob Lutz in the exciting final, 4-6, 6-3, 8-10, 6-0, 6-4.

However, with pros introduced to Forest Hills, Ashe was a lightly regarded fifth seed. Nevertheless, at 25, he came of age as an internationalist. Unflappable over the New York fortnight, he served-and-volleyed splendidly. In the final he clocked 26 aces, returned with precision, and held his cool in a five-set final-round victory over pro Tom Okker.

An amateur would never do so well again. As the last remaining pro, Okker got the $14,000 first prize while Ashe was happy to settle for $20 daily expenses for his historic triumph, the first major for an African American since Althea Gibson's Forest Hills triumph a decade before. Ashe's victory also boosted American morale by ending the U.S. male championship drought that dated back 13 years to Tony Trabert's 1955 win.

That year Ashe was also a Davis Cup drought-buster, spearheading the U.S. drive to the sterling tub last won five years before. He won 11 straight singles (the most in one campaign for an American) in the drive to retrieve the Cup from Australia in Adelaide. In the finale he started slowly but beat lefty Ray Ruffels on opening day for a 2-0 lead. After the Cup was clinched by Lutz and Stan Smith in doubles, he finally gave way, losing to Bill Bowrey in a meaningless third-day match. The season closed with Ashe winner of 10 of 22 tournaments on a 72-10 match record.

He would win both his singles in 1969 as the U.S. successfully defended the Cup, 5-0, against Romania. He beat Ilie Nastase on the first day. Next came West Germany, 5-0, at Cleveland in 1970, and his first-day win over Willy Bungert. In the latter his third-day defeat of Christian Kuhnke, 6-8, 10-12, 9-7, 13-11, 6-4, was the longest match (86 games) in a Cup-deciding round. Eight years later he reappeared for a vital cameo that led to another Cup for the U.S. His singles victory over Kjell Johansson was the clincher over Sweden, 3-2, in the semi-final at Goteborg.

Ashe put in 10 years of Davis Cup, topped for the U.S. only by John McEnroe's 12 and Bill Tilden and Stan Smith's 11 each, and won 27 singles, third to McEnroe's 41 and Andre Agassi's 30. He returned in 1981 as captain for five years, piloting the victors of 1981 and 1982.

Ashe was born July 10, 1943, in Richmond, Va., where he grew up. Since racial segregation was the law at that time, he could not play in the usual junior tournaments. With the aid of the concerned Lynchburg, Va., physician, Dr. Walter Johnson (who had also befriended and helped Althea Gibson), Ashe finished high school in St. Louis, where he could get the necessary tennis competition.

In 1961, after Dr. Johnson's lobbying got him into the previously segregated U.S. Interscholastic tourney, Ashe won it for Sumner High. Four years later, leading man of his alma mater's varsity (University of California at Los Angeles), he won the U.S. Intercollegiate singles.

Although Ashe was a man of strong character, poised and able to overcome racial blocks, it took him a while to harness his power, groove his groundstrokes and become a thoughtful player, comfortable on all surfaces. He won 35 amateur singles tournaments. As one whose career overflowed the amateur and open eras, he followed the 1968 breakthrough with 11 sterling years as a professional that netted 33 singles titles including the 1970 Australian and the gloriously unexpected Wimbledon, 1975.

In 1975, days before his 32nd birthday, seeded sixth, he was a longer shot than he had been seven years earlier at Forest Hills. Defending champ Jimmy Connors, seemingly inviolable, was a 10-to-1 favorite in the final, but Ashe was too slick and cerebral in one of the momentous upsets, 6-1, 6-1, 5-7, 6-4. Changing pace and spin cleverly, startling Connors with a sliced serve wide to the two-fisted backhand, Ashe out-foxed the man a decade his junior.

This was the centerpiece of Ashe's preeminent year, a heavy-duty season when he won nine of 29 tourneys on a 108-23 match record and wound up No. 1 in the U.S., No. 4 in the world. He reached No. 2 in 1976. Improving with age, he unfortunately was grounded prematurely, and permanently, by a heart attack in July 1979. In 1992 he revealed that he'd contracted AIDS through a 1988 blood transfusion.

For nine years he was in the world top ten. He was one of the founders of the ATP in 1972, served as president and had been a reasoned, intelligent spokesman for the game, serving on numerous corporate boards and received several honorary degrees.

A long-time protester of apartheid in South Africa, he was, after several refusals, granted a visa to visit that country in 1973, and became the first black to win a title there, the doubles (with Okker) in the South African Open, over Lew Hoad and Rob Maud, after losing the singles final to Connors. "You have shown our black youth that they can compete with whites and win," poet Don Mattera lauded him.

He was gratified to return again after the overturning of apartheid and meet with president Nelson Mandela (who identified himself as "an Ashe fan"). Ashe lent himself, his name and his money to various enlightened causes. He was arrested not long before his death in a protest against what he regarded as cruel U.S. policies toward Haitian refugees. His principal cause was fostering and furthering education for needy kids, and he was the guiding light in the Safe Passage Foundation for that purpose. He was also a warrior in the fight against AIDS. A tennis player who went well beyond the game, Arthur upheld the qualities that distinguished him as a champion: He showed that it was possible to compete ferociously while maintaining personal honor and sportsmanship. Having entered the Hall of Fame in 1985, he died Feb. 6, 1993, leaving his wife, Jeanne, and 6-year-old daughter, Camera. He was posthumously awarded the Presidential Medal of Freedom by President Clinton.

MAJOR TITLES (5)–*Australian singles, 1970; Wimbledon singles, 1975; U.S. singles, 1968; Australian doubles, 1977; French doubles, 1971.* **OTHER U.S. TITLES** (8)–*Amateur singles, 1968; Clay Court singles, 1967; Hard Court singles, 1963; Intercollegiate singles, 1965; Indoor doubles, 1967, with Charles Pasarell; 1970, with Stan Smith; Clay Court doubles, 1970, with Clark Graebner; Intercollegiate doubles, 1965, with Ian Crookenden.* **DAVIS CUP (As player)**–*1963, 1965,*

1966, 1967, 1968, 1969, 1970, 1975, 1977, 1978; record: 27-5 in singles, 1-1 in doubles; **(As captain)**–*1981, 1982, 1983, 1984, 1985; record: 13-3, 2 Cups.* **SINGLES RECORD IN THE MAJORS**–*Australian (25-5), French (25-8), Wimbledon (35-11), U.S. (53-17).*

JULIETTE ATKINSON
United States (1873–1944)
Hall of Fame 1974

Juliette Paxton Atkinson, a right-handed 5-footer who lived in Brooklyn, N.Y., was prominent in singles for four years at the U.S. Championships, a finalist, 1895-98, winning the title thrice: 1895, 1897 and 1898. She did not defend in 1899, defaulting the challenge round to Californian Marion Jones, who gave her a terrific struggle for the 1898 title, 6-3, 5-7, 6-4, 2-6, 7-5–one of the longest matches in terms of games (51) ever played by women. But she did continue to compete through 1902.

She won the U.S. doubles seven times with five different partners between 1894 and 1902. She had five in a row with three partners (1894-98), the last two with her younger sister, Kathleen. Other than the Roosevelts, Ellen and Grace in 1900, they were the only sisters to win the title. They were the first sisters to face one another in the Championships, Juliette winning semifinals in 1895, 6-1, 6-4, and 1897, 6-1, 6-3. She was born April 15, 1873, in Rahway, N.J., died Jan. 12, 1944, in Lawrenceville, Ill., and entered the Hall of Fame in 1974.

MAJOR TITLES (13)–*U.S. singles, 1895, 1897, 1898; U.S. doubles, 1894, 1895, 1896, 1897, 1898, 1901, 1902; U.S. mixed, 1894, 1895, 1896.* **SINGLES RECORD IN THE MAJORS**–*U.S. (14-4).*

BUNNY AUSTIN
Great Britain (1906–2000)
Hall of Fame 1997

Short on fabric, long on Davis Cup exploits, the genial English gentleman Henry Wilfred 'Bunny' Austin was amused that baring his knees "may have made me more famous than helping win the Cup for Britain." Liberating male legs by bravely introducing shorts to the upper level of the game would seem his finest contribution to many. But Bunny was a marvelous player—a world top ten inhabitant 11 consecutive years, No. 2 in 1931 and 1938—without whom the Brits would never have relished their four years of greatest glory: 1933-36.

Fred Perry, of course, was the point man with his three Wimbledon championships (1934-35-36), the derby thoroughbred. "And I was known as the old cab horse," Austin laughed. But a very reliable one when the business at hand was Davis Cup. He played nine years longer than Fred, playing more series (24 to 20) and winning more singles (36 to 34). He was all the more remarkable in that he soldiered on through periods of a recurring mysterious, weakening illness that wasn't diagnosed until his playing career was over. "It was called Gilbert's Syndrome, a periodic liver misfunction that was discovered, and treated, when I was in the U.S. Army during World War II," Austin said shortly before his death in 2000.

A two-year Cup drought ended for Britain, an original in the competition, during a hot July, 1933, weekend in Paris. Bunny, 26, led off by beating Henri Merlin and Perry, 24, finished it over Merlin as French rule of six years collapsed beneath the Anglo assault, 3-2. "That had been my goal since I joined the team in '29," Austin said. "It was a time of great celebration when we arrived home. It was a long campaign [seven series in all], and there was nothing like playing for your country. Especially in our three successful defenses at Wimbledon." Bunny went 13-1 during the Cup-seizing season, losing only when he tired in five sets against Henri Cochet, in the final.

"I think I played best in our 1934 defense against the U.S. [4-1] when I beat Frank Shields the first day and Sidney Wood on the third day." The next year, 5-0, over the U.S., he rallied to beat Wilmer Allison in five sets to to start, then the rising Don Budge in four.

In the 1936 defense against Australia, 3-2, he led off beating Jack Crawford but lost to Adrian Quist. But that was the last Cup for Britain. Perry's defection to the pros left the home side in need. Bunny made a bold, hopeful beginning against the conquering Americans, beating Frank Parker, but Budge came on too strongly as the U.S. carried off the prize, 4-1.

Bunny said he had a dream of playing Wimbledon when he was four. That dream materialized in 1928, and he proceeded to the fourth round. He was one of the most consistent of Wimbledon players, never worse than the round of 16 over 13 years, a semi-finalist in 1929, '36 and '37, and a quarter-finalist five other times. His worst major was a third-round finish at the U.S. in 1928.

Twice he reached the Wimbledon championship round, but was overwhelmed by a couple of No. 1's, Ellsworth Vines in 1932 and Don Budge in '38. He was also a losing finalist at the French in 1937, beaten by German Henner Henkel, No. 3 that year.

Stylish in everything he did, Bunny, a slim, handsome 5-foot-10, a graduate of Repton School and Cambridge University, was a tennis court vision with fluid, classic strokes. "He seemed to have stepped out of a tennis textbook," said Perry. He had long harbored the desire to play in shorts, not as a rebel but a practical man. "I wore them as a schoolboy soccer player, and knew the value in running. There was an awful lot of weight in flannels between the knees and shoes, so I decided to cut it out. I had a pair made for the U.S. Championships in '32 at Forest Hills. When I left the hotel with a polo coat covering my tennis kit a kindly bellman, seeing my shins and thinking to save me from embarrassment said, 'Haven't you forgotten something, Mr. Austin? Your trousers?' The American officials didn't like it, but surprisingly, when I wore them at Wimbledon in '33 nothing was said." However, acceptance was slow, and no male champ was crowned naked-kneed at the Big W until Jack Kramer in 1947. Bunny was also a racket innovator, unveiling a split-shaft open-throat model in 1936, a common look today, but in wood then. His older sister, Joan Austin, Wimbledon doubles finalist in 1923, was sartorially daring, too, earlier, the first to appear minus stockings on Centre Court in 1931. They were the leggy bare pair.

Born Aug. 20, 1906, he died on his 94th birthday, pleased that he had been on Centre Court for a last time amid an assemblage of tennis notables the previous month.

DAVIS CUP–*1929, 1930, 1931, 1932, 1933, 1934, 1935, 1936, 1937; record: 36-12 in singles.* **SINGLES RECORD IN THE MAJORS**–*French (12-4), Wimbledon (56-13), U.S. (9-3).*

TRACY AUSTIN
United States (1962–)
Hall of Fame 1992

One of the game's prodigies, Tracy Ann Austin was meteoric, an iron-willed girl whose blaze was glorious though fleeting. A variety of injuries cut short what had promised to be one of the great careers. At 14 her junior career was practically a memory.

She had won the U.S. 12s title at 10 in 1972, and added 21 more age-group titles. Arriving at Forest Hills in 1977, an unseeded amateur, she was already the youngest winner of a pro tournament, Portland (Ore.), earlier in the year. Sensationally, she made her way to the last eight of the U.S. Open by beating fourth-seeded 1976 French champ Sue Barker, 6-1, 6-4, and Virginia Ruzici, who would win the French in 1978, 6-3, 7-5. Wimbledon finalist Betty Stove stopped her there, 6-2, 6-2, but the 5-foot, 90-pound Tracy, in ponytail and pinafore, was the youngest of all major quarter-finalists—until Jennifer Capriati, a younger 14, was a French semi-finalist in 1990.

Her performance earned no dollars, but she did get a congratulatory phone call from the First Hacker, President Jimmy Carter.

Two years later, 1979, at 16 years, 9 months, Tracy not only dethroned four-time champ Chris Evert, 6-4, 6-3, at Flushing Meadow but undercut Maureen Connolly (1951) as the youngest U.S. champ by a couple of months. Earlier that year she severed Evert's 125-match clay-court winning streak in the semis of the Italian, 6-4, 2-6, 7-6 (7-4), then won the title, her first important prize, over lefty Sylvia Hanika, 6-4, 1-6, 6-3.

She won the U.S. again in 1981 in a thrilling tie-breaker finish over Martina Navratilova, 1-6, 7-6 (7-4), 7-6 (7-1). That year she won seven other tourneys and had a 58-7 match record, and in 1980 12 titles on 68-7. Having made her Wimbledon debut in 1977 (a third-round loss to Evert, 6-1, 6-0), she was a semi-finalist in 1979 and 1980, losing to the champs, Navratilova, 6-4, 6-7 (5-7), 6-2, and Evonne Goolagong, 6-3, 0-6, 6-4.

But back maladies began to impair her effectiveness and sideline her for long stretches. San Diego, 1982, was the last of Austin's 29 pro titles. By 1983, before her 21st birthday, she was virtually finished. She has tried comebacks, as recently as 1994, in two tournaments, the Australian and French Opens, but that was it. In Melbourne, however, she became the only post-induction Hall of Famer to win a major singles match, beating Elna Reinach, 6-1, 7-5, then losing to Sabine Hack, 6-1, 5-7, 6-2. In Paris, ranked No. 78, she lost to Marketa Kochta, 6-0, 6-1, and called it quits, posting a career record of 29 singles titles and 13 other finals of 122 tournaments on 348-87 (.800) in matches. She won four doubles titles. A near-fatal auto accident in 1989 was another discouraging factor. A resolute 5-foot-4 ground-stroker, right-handed with a two-fisted backhand, she had immense patience and fortitude, and deadly passing shots. Few errors marred her performances.

Evert, who reclaimed her U.S. title in the 1980 final, recalls, "Tracy's mental strength was scary. She had no weaknesses, she was obsessive about winning." By 1977

Austin was No. 4 in the U.S. rankings, the greenest to stand so high until Capriati's No. 3 in 1990. She continued in that elite group through 1983, No. 1 in 1980. Five straight years, from 1978, she was in the World Top Ten, No. 2 in 1980 and 1981. Briefly in 1980 she was No. 1 on the WTA computer, breaking the Evert/Navratilova stranglehold of nearly six years. She had tremendous battles with those two. At the close of 1981 she won the Toyota Championship at East Rutherford, N.J., by beating Chris (6-1, 6-2) and Martina (2-6, 6-4, 6-2) in succession, the first of only three to accomplish that back-to-back double, preceding Hana Mandlikova and Steffi Graf.

Turning pro in October 1978, she won $1,966,487 in career prize money. She played on three winning Federation Cup teams (1978, 1979 and 1980) for the U.S., and two Wightman Cup winners (1979, 1981). Tracy was born into a tennis family Dec. 12, 1962, in Palos Verdes, Calif., and grew up in Rolling Hills. Her older sister and brothers—Pam, Jeff and John—played the pro circuit, and she and John won the Wimbledon mixed in 1980, the only brother-sister pairing to do so. She entered the Hall of Fame in 1992, married Scott Holt in 1994, has a child, and works frequently as a TV tennis commentator.

MAJOR TITLES (3)–*U.S. singles, 1979, 81; Wimbledon mixed, 1980.* **FEDERATION CUP**–*1978, 1979, 1980; record: 13-1 in singles.* **WIGHTMAN CUP**–*1978, 1979, 1981; record: 4-2 in singles, 2-0 in doubles.* **SINGLES RECORD IN THE MAJORS**–*Australian (3-2), French (7-3), Wimbledon (21-6), U.S. (31-4).*

BORIS BECKER

Germany (1968–)
Hall of Fame 2003

A redheaded phenomenon, Boris Becker illuminated 1985 and 1986 with his Wimbledon triumphs at the improbable ages of 17 and 18.

The records came tumbling down in 1985 when the unseeded German teenager beat eighth-seeded Kevin Curren, 6-3, 6-7 (4-7), 7-6 (7-3), 6-4, in the final. He was the first German champ, first non-seed to win— Boris was ranked No. 20—and the youngest male ever to win a major at 17 years, 7 months. (Michael Chang, at 17 years, 3 months, lowered that four years later in winning the French.) Richard Krajicek in 1996 and Goran Ivanisevic in 2001 followed his unseeded route.

A big man (6-foot-3, 180) playing a big, carefree game of booming serves, heavy forehand, penetrating volleys and diving saves, he was an immediate crowd favorite. Despite his youth, he showed sensitivity in rejecting an early, obvious nickname, 'Boom Boom,' considering it "too warlike."

For Germany, never better than a 1970 finalist in the quest for the Davis Cup, Becker was an instant hero. Almost alone he carried his country to the 1985 final in Munich and beat both Stefan Edberg, 6-3, 3-6, 7-5, 8-6, and Mats Wilander, 6-3, 2-6, 6-3, 6-3, in the 3-2 loss to Sweden. Three years later he lifted the Fatherland to the long longed-for Cup in a 4-1 victory over the Swedes in Goteborg. Boris pummeled his final round conqueror at Wimbledon, Edberg, 6-3, 6-1, 6-4, then paired with Eric Jelen for the exciting clinching doubles win over Edberg and Anders Jarryd. In 1989 he won both his singles, defeating Wilander and Edberg, plus the doubles again with Jelen, at Stuttgart as Germany kept the Cup, 3-2, over Sweden.

By the close of the 1992 season he had won 21 straight Cup singles, and had lost only two of 34 starts, both to Sergio Casal of Spain. He didn't play in 1993-94, but in 1995 extended the streak to 22, second longest in Cup history (to Bjorn Borg's 33), before losing to the Netherlands' Paul Haarhuis.

Becker beat Ivan Lendl, 6-4, 6-3, 7-5, in 1986 for his second Wimbledon title, and Edberg just as swiftly in 1989 for a third, 6-0, 7-6 (7-1), 6-4, developing the feeling that Centre Court was his special haunt. He and Edberg also contested the 1988 and 1990 finals, Edberg winning both times. They were the first men in almost a century, since Wilfred Baddeley and Joshua Pim split four finals, 1891-94, to monopolize the final for at least three successive years. In the only all-German male final on Centre Court, Michael Stich upset him in 1991, 6-4, 7-6 (7-4), 6-4. He and Stich collaborated the following year for Olympic gold, defeating South Africans Wayne Ferreira and Piet Norval, one of Boris's 15 doubles titles.

It took him four years to work his way back to a seventh Wimbledon final. To get there required one of his more brilliant Centre Court performances, beating favored Andre Agassi from a set and 1-4 (two breaks) down. But he couldn't solve Pete Sampras' serve in the title match, losing 6-7 (5-7), 6-2, 6-4, 6-2. Becker's Wimbledon farewell, a fourth-round loss to Patrick Rafter in 1999, finished his match record at 71-12.

By 1996 it seemed that his days of winning majors were past. He was 28, had a wife, Barbara, and a young son. But he arrived in Melbourne fit and eager, (inspired by Barbara's plea, "I never saw you win a big one") and captured his sixth, the Australian, with a blistering attack on Chang, 6-2, 6-4, 2-6, 6-2.

He started out as an unlikely pauper, an 18-to-1 shot on the path to that first Wimbledon title. He might not have gotten past the fourth round if not for the good nature of Tim Mayotte, who waited patiently while Becker, trailing in the match, received treatment for a twisted ankle. Becker wanted to quit, but his manager, Ion Tiriac, talked him out of it, and Mayotte sportingly permitted Boris more than a usual break to recover. Becker won in five sets. Next, Swede Joakim Nystrom had served for the match twice in the third round. Henri Leconte was close to a two-set lead in the quarters, and another Swede, Jarryd, held a set and a set point in the second set of the semis. Didn't matter. Boris wore a halo.

Boris Franz Becker, a right-hander, was born Nov. 22, 1967, in the small town of Leiman, Germany, and grew up there, not far from Bruhl, where the other German wunderkind, Steffi Graf, was raised. The two sometimes practiced together. A promising junior, he dropped out of high school to become a pro. An atypical European player, he prefers faster surfaces to his native clay. His best finishes at the French were semi-finals in 1989 and '91, and the quarters in 1986. Of his 49 singles titles (in 77 finals), ranking ninth in the open era, none was on dirt.

At the conclusion of 1988, he squashed Ivan Lendl's bid for a sixth Masters title by the narrowest possible of final-round margins—two points—on a net-cord dribbler that won the fifth-set tie-breaker, 7-5. His marvelous 1989 season, during which he won six of 13 tournaments on a 64-8 match record, included his fourth major, the U.S. Open in a 7-6 (7-2), 1-6, 6-3, 7-6 (7-4) victory over No. 1-ranked Ivan Lendl. It was the lone major male final to conclude in a tie-breaker.

His fifth major (the third over Lendl) was the Australian at the outset of 1991, giving him the No. 1 ranking momentarily. During his 16 years as a pro he was in the world Top Ten 11 times, three times at No. 2 (1986, 1989, 1990). He won $25,080,956, third in prize money standings behind Sampras and Andre Agassi. He was selected to enter the International Tennis Hall of Fame in 2003.

MAJOR TITLES (6)–*Australian singles, 1991, 1996; Wimbledon singles, 1985, 1986, 1989; U.S. singles, 1989.* **DAVIS CUP**–*1985, 1986, 1987, 1988, 1989, 1991, 1992, 1995; record: 38-3 in singles, 16-9 in doubles.* **SINGLES RECORD IN THE MAJORS**–*Australian (29-9), French (26-9), Wimbledon (71-12), U.S. (37-10).*

KARL BEHR

United States (1885–1949)
Hall of Fame 1969

A Yale man, Karl Howell Behr won the U.S. Intercollegiate doubles in 1904, and played on the 1907 U.S. Davis Cup team. Behr, a 5-foot-9-1/2-inch, 155-pound survivor of the *Titanic* sinking in 1912, forever considered himself a lucky man. But he didn't have much good fortune in his lone Cup assignment, with Beals Wright, against Australasia, a 3-2 defeat at Wimbledon in 1907. He lost a toughie to Tony Wilding the first day, 1-6, 6-3, 3-6, 7-5, 6-3, dropping the last four games, and the clincher to Norman Brookes, 4-6, 6-4, 6-1, 6-2. But he and Wright did prolong it to the third day with a stirring doubles victory over Wimbledon champs Brookes-Wilding, 3-6, 12-10, 4-6, 6-2, 6-3. Brookes and Wilding proceeded to take the Cup from Britain, 3-2. Playing Wimbledon that year, Behr made one of the better American showings of that early time, reaching the fourth round where he gave the champ, Brooks, a stiff fight, 6-4, 6-2, 2-6, 3-6, 6-1.

He ranked in the U.S. Top Ten seven times between 1906 and 1915, No. 3 in 1907, and again in 1914 when he beat future champ Lindley Murray, 3-6, 6-2, 7-5, 3-6, 8-6, to reach the quarters in the U.S Championships at Newport. There he lost to the champion-to-be, Dick Williams, 6-2, 6-2, 7-5, in a battle of *Titanic* alumni. In 1906, ranked No. 11, Behr had jolted an all-time champ, No. 3 Bill Larned, in the second round, 6-4, 6-4, 7-5, and fought past No. 9 Raymond Little, 2-6, 6-2, 6-8, 11-9, 6-4, to the final of the all-comers, where Bill Clothier, en route to the championship, stopped him, 6-2, 6-4, 6-2. He was a semi-finalist in 1912, losing to Wallace Johnson, 4-6, 6-0, 6-3, 6-2.

Behr, a right-hander, was born May 30, 1885, in Brooklyn, N.Y., and died Oct. 15, 1949, in New York. He entered the Hall of Fame in 1969.

U.S. TITLE–*Intercollegiate doubles, 1904, with George Bodman.* **DAVIS CUP**–*1907; record: 0-2 in singles, 1-0 in doubles.* **SINGLES RECORD IN THE MAJORS**–*Wimbledon (3-1), U.S. (31-13).*

PAULINE BETZ

United States (1919–)
Hall of Fame 1965

Many believe Pauline May Betz Addie was the finest of the immediate post-World War II players of the U.S., even though her career was cut short in her prime by a controversial ruling by the USTA. She won her fourth U.S. title in 1946 over Doris Hart, 11-9, 6-3. However, in 1947 she was declared a professional for merely exploring the possibilities of making a pro tour.

There was no pro tennis as such for women at the time, but she did make two tours of one-night stands against Sarah Palfrey Cooke in 1947, and Gussy Moran in 1951, dominating both opponents. Then she became a teaching professional and married sportswriter Bob Addie.

Born Aug. 6, 1919, in Dayton, Ohio, she grew up lean in Los Angeles, and became noted for her extreme speed and mobility. Although she could get to the net quickly and volley with sureness, she preferred to run down balls and pass the net-rushers, particularly with a penetrating backhand.

World War II deprived her of the chance for much international play, but she won Wimbledon the only time she entered, in 1946, without losing a set. Her closest match, not close at all, was the 6-2, 6-4 final over Louise Brough. In Betz's only Wightman Cup series against Britain, in 1946, she helped the U.S. win by taking both her singles matches and her doubles.

Betz, World No. 1 in 1946, first entered the U.S. Top Ten, at No. 8 in 1939, and stayed in that select group for seven more years, standing at No. 1 in 1942-43-44, '46, the years she won the U.S. Championship in singles at Forest Hills, No. 2 in 1941, '45, and No. 3 in 1940.

She closed out her amateur career in 1946 by winning eight of 12 tournaments, and her last 27 matches. That was the fourth of her most productive campaigns that netted seven titles in 1943, eight in 1944, six in 1945. In 1943 she emphasized her superbly rounded game by making a U.S. triple, with Indoor and Clay Court singles titles preceding Forest Hills success. Beating Catherine Wolf, 6-0, 6-2, to win the Tri-State of 1943, Pauline scored an almost unheard of 'golden set,' relinquishing no points in the first set.

Top-seeded Louise Brough was the 4-6, 6-1, 6-4, victim in her first triumph at Forest Hills, but the semi was tougher, 6-4, 4-6, 7-5, over Margaret Osborne (duPont), from match point down at 3-5. She beat Brough again in 1943, 6-3, 5-7, 6-3, and Osborne in 1944, 6-3, 8-6.

Two other years, 1941 and 1945, she was runner-up to Sarah Cooke, thus setting a U.S. record of six straight years in the final, tied by Chris Evert, 1975-80. In playing Forest Hills eight times, she won 33 of 37 matches.

She captured 19 U.S. titles on various surfaces,

including the Clay Court singles in 1941, '43 and the Indoor singles in 1939, '41, '43, '47. Twice she scored triples at the Indoor Championships, winning the singles, doubles and mixed doubles in 1941 and 1943, a feat equaled only by Billie Jean King in 1966 and 1968.

Tennis historian Jerome Scheuer called her "the fastest woman on foot ever to play the game."

She was selected for the International Tennis Hall of Fame in 1965.

MAJOR TITLES (6)–*Wimbledon singles, 1946; U.S. singles, 1942, 1943, 1944, 1946; French mixed, 1946.* OTHER U.S. TITLES (15)–*Indoor singles, 1939, 1941, 1943, 1947; Indoor doubles, 1941, with Dorothy Bundy; 1943, with Hazel Hotchkiss Wightman; Indoor mixed, 1939, with Wayne Sabin; 1940, with Bobby Riggs; 1941, 1943, with Al Stitt; Clay Court singles, 1941, 1943; Clay Court doubles, 1943, with Nancy Corbett; 1944, 1945, with Doris Hart.* WIGHTMAN CUP–*1946; record: 2-0 in singles, 1-0 in doubles.* SINGLES RECORD IN THE MAJORS–*French (4-1), Wimbledon (6-0), U.S. (33-4).*

BJORN BORG

Sweden (1956–)
Hall of Fame 1987

Before he was 21, Bjorn Rune Borg had registered feats that would set him apart as one of the game's greats—and before he was 26, the headbanded, golden-locked Swede was through. No male career of the modern era has been so brief and bright.

Tennis is filled with instances of precocious achievements and championships, but none is quite as impressive as those of the seemingly emotionless Borg. Just before his 18th birthday he was the youngest winner of the Italian Championship, and two weeks later he was the youngest winner of the French Championship (a record lowered by Mats Wilander, 17, in 1982, and subsequently by Michael Chang, a younger 17 in 1989). Eighteen months later, at 19, he climaxed a Davis Cup-record winning streak of 19 singles by lifting Sweden to the 1975 Cup for the first time in a 3-2 final-round victory over Czechoslovakia. His Cup singles streak of 33 was intact at his retirement, still a record.

Although Lew Hoad and Ken Rosewall were a few months younger in 1953 when they won the Davis Cup for Australia, both were beaten during the final round. But Borg won both his singles in straight sets, over Jiri Hrebec and the clincher over Jan Kodes, after teaming with Ove Bengtson for the doubles win. Borg's Davis Cup debut at 16 in 1972, as one of the youngest ever in that competition, was phenomenal: A five-set win over seasoned pro Onny Parun of New Zealand. Borg was also the youngest winner of the oldest professional championship, the U.S. Pro, whose singles he took in 1974 at 18 over Tom Okker (and, subsequently, 1975 and 1976). Aaron Krickstein, 16, lowered that record in 1984.

A player of great strength and endurance, he had a distinctive and unorthodox style and appearance, bow-legged, yet very fast. His muscular shoulders and well-developed torso gave him the strength to lash at the ball with heavy topspin on both forehand and backhand. A right-hander, he used a two-handed backhand, adapted from the slap shot in hockey, a game he favored as a child. By the time he was 13 he was beating the best of Sweden's under-18 players and Davis Cup captain Lennart Bergelin cautioned against anyone trying to change Borg's rough-looking, jerky strokes. They were effective. Through 1977 he had never lost to a player younger than himself.

Born June 6, 1956, in Sodertalje, Sweden, where he grew up, Bjorn was fascinated by a tennis racket his father had won as a prize in a ping-pong tournament. His father gave him the racket and that was the start.

Borg preferred to battle from the baseline, trading groundstrokes tirelessly in long rallies, retrieving and waiting patiently to outlast his opponent. Volleying, with his Western grip forehand and two-fisted backhand, was troublesome, and his serve was not impressive at first. He didn't do much on grass until 1976, when he was determined to win Wimbledon, and did so after devoting himself to two weeks of solid practice on serve-and-volley tactics. He won the most important tournament without loss of a set, beating favored Ilie Nastase in the final, 6-4, 6-2, 9-7. Borg was the youngest champion of the modern era at 20 years, one month, (until Boris Becker, 17, won in 1985). Borg repeated in 1977, although the tournament was more demanding. His thrilling five-set victories over Americans Vitas Gerulaitis in the semi-finals, and Jimmy Connors in the final were considered two of the best ever played at Wimbledon. By that time Borg had more confidence and proficiency in his volleying. Borg repeated over Connors in 1978, overpoweringly, 6-2, 6-2, 6-3, becoming the first to win three successive years since Fred Perry (1934-36). He made it four in a row with a five-set triumph over American Roscoe Tanner in the 1979 final, thus becoming the first player since Tony Wilding (1910-13) to win four straight years.

His fifth straight Wimbledon championship, in 1980, climaxed with an all-time great final, a 1-6, 7-5, 6-

3, 6-7 (16-18), 8-6 triumph over John McEnroe. During one of the most electrifying passages in tennis history, the 34-point tie-breaker, Borg was stymied on five match points and saved six set points before giving way. But his famous resolve brought him through in the brilliantly battled fifth.

Borg was now flirting with the ancient Wimbledon record of six straight titles. That was the much less demanding feat of Willie Renshaw (1881-86), who, in the era of the challenge-round format, needed to play only one match to win each of his last five titles. Thus his match winning streak was only 13.

While winning 1980, Borg also surpassed Rod Laver's Wimbledon male match winning-streak record of 31. Bjorn built that to his own record 41 (Helen Wills Moody won 50 straight between 1927 and 1938) by reaching the 1981 final. There he was finally dethroned by McEnroe, 4-6, 7-6 (7-1), 7-6 (7-4), 6-4.

When he won his male record sixth French title in 1981, with another record, his 28th straight match win, over Ivan Lendl, it seemed that Borg, then 25, would surely surpass Roy Emerson's male record of 12 major singles titles (subsequently surpassed by Pete Sampras, 14). Borg had 11. But he would not win another, remaining tied with Laver.

His left-handed nemesis, McEnroe, followed up on Wimbledon by beating Borg in a second successive U.S. Open final to take over the No. 1 ranking that the Swede had held in 1979 and 1980. That defeat, 4-6, 6-2, 6-4, 6-3, effectively ended Borg's career. He won only two more matches, reaching the quarters of Monte Carlo in 1982. Shortly after that he retired, having won 62 singles (of 88 finals) and four pro career doubles titles, including the Masters of 1979-80, and $3,655,751. He was inducted into the Hall of Fame in 1987.

Nevertheless, he did try comebacks in 1991, 1992 and 1993, all unsuccessful. The balletic footwork and marvelous anticipation couldn't be coaxed to return with him, even though others had stayed afloat and earning at 35. He lost eight first-rounders in 1992, three in 1993. Bjorn's parting shot, in Moscow's Kremlin Cup, was as close as he got, holding a match point in a farewell tie-breaker while losing to Aleksandr Volkov, 4-6, 6-3, 7-6 (9-7). Thereafter he confined himself to senior events, renewing his rivalry with Connors, against whom he had been 10-7. He was 7-7 lifetime against McEnroe.

The U.S. Open was his particular jinx. He failed to win in 10 tries, losing four finals, 1976 and 1978 to Connors, and 1980 and 1981 to McEnroe. Thrice (1978-79-80) he was halfway to a Grand Slam after victories at the French and Wimbledon only to falter at the three-quarter pole at Flushing Meadow. His career singles win-loss record was 606-123 (.831).

MAJOR TITLES (11)–*French singles, 1974, 1975, 1978, 1979, 1980, 1981; Wimbledon singles, 1976, 1977, 1978, 1979, 1980.* **DAVIS CUP**–*1972, 1973, 1974, 1975, 1978, 1979, 1980; record: 37-3 in singles, 8-8 in doubles.* **SINGLES RECORD IN THE MAJORS**–*Australian (1-1), French (49-2), Wimbledon (51-4), U.S. (40-10).*

JEAN BOROTRA

France (1898–1994)
Hall of Fame 1976

In many ways, Jean Robert Borotra fit the image of the cosmopolitan Frenchman: A spectacular, debonair personality, a gallant kissing ladies' fingertips, a host of elegant parties aboard the *Ile de France* or at his fashionable residence in Paris.

Borotra, a right-hander (6-foot-1, 160), was spectacular, too, on the tennis court in the 1920s and early '30s. He won Wimbledon in 1924 and 1926 and was runner-up in 1925 and 1927. He won the championship of France in 1924 and 1931 and the Australian title in 1928. And he was a demon in international play, one of the Four Musketeers who in 1927 broke the U.S. grip on the Davis Cup and brought it to France for the first time.

Born on Aug. 13, 1898, at Arbonne, Basque Pyrenees country near Biarritz, France, he first attracted wide attention when he played in the 1921 covered-court championship in Paris. Standing out with a dramatic, aggressive style of play—and with the blue beret he always wore—Borotra became known as the 'Bounding Basque from Biarritz.' His energy on the court was limitless, marked by headlong assaults and dashes for the net, both on his service and return of service, then a stampede back to retrieve lobs. No player could start faster or dash so madly. His service was not a cannonball, but it was not to be trifled with. His backhand return of service and backhand volley were vividly individual, thrusts for the kill.

Borotra was named to France's Davis Cup team in 1922, and in 1923 he assembled with René Lacoste, Henri Cochet, and Jacques Brugnon, a great doubles player, to form the Four Musketeers. Not only did the French win their first Cup in 1927, but they also held it for five years thereafter.

In the 1932 challenge round, Borotra reached heights of inspiration against the U.S. He defeated Ellsworth Vines, the winner of Wimbledon and the U.S. Championship that year. On the final day, Borotra lost the first two sets to Wilmer Allison, and with the Texan holding a fourth match point in the fifth set, Borotra's second serve appeared to be out. Allison ran forward for the handshake, thinking he had won, but the linesman insisted the serve was good and play resumed. Borotra pulled out the victory and France retained the Cup.

With his dazzling performances, Borotra was popular everywhere. This included the Seventh Regiment Armory in New York, where he was in his element on the fast board courts and four times won the U.S. Indoor Championship. He was not rated quite the player that Cochet and Lacoste were, but Borotra's celebrity endured and the legs that ran like fury kept him active in tennis into his 70s as a competitor in the senior division at Wimbledon. He was among the champions honored at the 1977 Wimbledon Centenary a year after he was enshrined with the three other Musketeers in the Hall of Fame.

He was ranked in the World top ten nine straight years from 1924, No. 2 in 1926. He entered the Hall of Fame in 1976 and died July 17, 1994.

MAJOR TITLES *(16)–Australian singles, 1928; French singles, 1931; Wimbledon singles, 1924, 1926; Australian doubles, 1928; French doubles, 1925, 1928, 1929, 1934, 1936; Wimbledon doubles, 1925, 1932, 1933; Australian mixed, 1928; French mixed, 1927, 1934; Wimbledon mixed, 1925; U.S. mixed, 1926.* **DAVIS CUP**–*1922, 1923, 1924, 1925, 1926, 1927, 1928, 1929, 1930, 1931, 1932, 1933, 1934, 1935, 1936, 1937, 1947; record: 19-12 in singles, 17-6 in doubles.* **SINGLES RECORD IN THE MAJORS**–*Australian (5-0), French (30-6), Wimbledon (55-10), U.S. (13-6).*

JOHN BROMWICH

Australia (1918–1999)
Hall of Fame 1984

Elected to the Hall of Fame in 1984 as one-half of the great Australian doubles team of Bromwich and Quist, John Edward Bromwich missed winning Wimbledon by the narrowest of margins. In the 1948 final Bob Falkenburg escaped him at three match-point junctures, from 3-5, 15-40, then advantage out, in the fifth set, won by the Californian, 7-5. But Bromwich did win two major singles, the Australian in 1939 and 1946, and was a three-time U.S. semi-finalist, 1938, 1939, 1947. He lost the last one to the only other U.S. semi-finalist playing before and after World War II, Frank Parker.

A loping, big-jawed man, 5-foot-10-1/2, 152 pounds, with an unruly shock of blond hair, Bromwich was one of the most curious stylists in the game's history. A natural left-hander, he nevertheless served right-handed, stroked with two hands on his right side and one, the left, on his left side. Using an extremely loosely-strung racket, he had superb touch and chipped his returns maddeningly on his foes' shoetops. "People called my racket an onion bag," he laughs, "and complained they couldn't hear me hit the ball. But at least they didn't see me serve with both hands, which I did as a young player, sort of like chopping wood." He was an attacker, his volleys well placed, and his competitive fire ever burning high.

World War II interrupted the strong partnership of himself—the right court player—and Adrian Quist, but they won their native Australian title eight straight times, a team record for majors, and gave up the title only after a tremendous final-round struggle, 6-3 in the fifth against youngsters Frank Sedgman and Ken McGregor in 1951. Bromwich was 33, Quist 38. The two of them scored a singular triumph as the Australian Davis Cup team in 1939, rebounding from 0-2 down against the Cup-holding U.S. in Philadelphia to win. They began turning it around with a 5-7, 6-2, 7-5, 6-2 doubles victory over Joe Hunt and Jack Kramer, and Bromwich clinched in the decisive fifth match, 6-0, 6-3, 6-1, over Parker.

Ted Schroeder recalls, "Jack and Joe were up a set and a break, but after that Brom played the most phenomenal 2-1/2 sets of doubles I've ever seen." Bromwich was described by journalist friend Jim Russell as "so tight-fisted with a point he made Scrooge seem a philanthropist," and Schroeder seconds it: "You had to win the point from Brom; he never gave one away."

Bromwich smiles at that cordially, and remembers, "in '39 our tennis association was too poor to send us to the French and Wimbledon. But there was no doubt we'd get to the U.S. to challenge for the Cup. We were sure we'd win because we'd only lost 3-2 the year before, and their great Don Budge had turned pro. Three weeks by boat to California, then train to Philadelphia. War had been declared just before the matches began so everything was up in the air. We were surprised to be down 0-2, and didn't have much confidence, even after the doubles. But Quisty was back again at his best to beat Bobby Riggs in five, and it was up to me against Parker. Our coach, Fred Perry, told me if I hit one ball to

Frankie's forehand to hit 5,000. That's all I did. They tell me the first point lasted two minutes, the first game 13, and his forehand came apart. Very satisfying because we wanted to be the first to win the Cup as Australia after the Australasia years.

"But more thrilling to me was to come back 11 years later, to Forest Hills, and be part of our next winner, at 31. The Yanks had been thrashing us after the war, and I wasn't surprised when Hop [captain Harry Hopman] went with the youngsters, Sedgman and McGregor, in the singles. I thought he'd play them all the way, but he said he wanted my experience with Sedg in the doubles, and we took the Cup by beating Schroeder and Gar Mulloy in five. A nice way for me to go out"—winning his 20th of 21 Cup doubles. Ranked in the world Top Ten on both sides of the war—he, Quist and Parker were the only ones of such longevity—Brom made the list in 1938, 1939, 1946, 1947 and 1948, coming back splendidly after army service in which he was wounded and contracted malaria in the New Guinea campaign.

Born Nov. 14, 1918, in Kogarah, New South Wales, he lived at Point Lonsdale, outside of Melbourne, with his wife Zend until his death in Geelong, Oct. 21, 1999.

MAJOR TITLES *(19)–Australian singles, 1939, 1946; Australian doubles, 1938, 1939, 1940, 1946, 1947, 1948, 1949, 1950; Wimbledon doubles, 1948, 1950; U.S. doubles, 1939, 1949, 1950; Australian mixed, 1938; Wimbledon mixed, 1947, 1948; U.S. mixed, 1947.* **DAVIS CUP**–*1937, 1938, 1939, 1946, 1947, 1949, 1950; record: 19-11 in singles, 20-1 in doubles.* **SINGLES RECORD IN THE MAJORS**–*Australian (39-9), French (4-1), Wimbledon (19-5), U.S. (16-5).* **MAJOR TITLES WITH QUIST** *(10)–Australian doubles, 1938, 1939, 1940, 1946, 1947, 1948, 1949, 1950; Wimbledon doubles, 1950; U.S. doubles, 1939.* **DAVIS CUP**–*1938, 1939, 1946; record: 9-1 in doubles.*

NORMAN BROOKES

Australia (1877–1968)
Hall of Fame 1977

They called him the Wizard. A figure of heroic stature, Sir Norman Everard Brookes was renowned both as a player—for many years Australia's best—and as an administrator. He was 5-foot-11, 150 pounds, had a sallow complexion and pale blue eyes, austere in bearing, rather taciturn, a man of strength and character to command respect and win honors.

And win honors he did. Born Nov. 14, 1877, in Melbourne, Australia, he became in 1907 the first male from overseas to win the championship at Wimbledon, having lost the 1905 final to Laurie Doherty. He won Wimbledon again in 1914 and was runner-up in 1919

after returning from World War I. Long ranked as the best of left-handed players, the first to win Wimbledon, he was a member of nine Australasian Davis Cup teams between 1905 and 1920 and played in eight challenge rounds.

World rankings were instituted after his best days, but he was in the Top Ten in 1913-14, 1919, and 1920, the last at 43.

He was an exponent of the serve-and-volley game, the 'big game' that was supposed to have originated after World War II. Brookes played that type of game in 1914, but he had more than a serve and volley. He had ground strokes adequate to hold his own from the back of the court. Because his serve was so big an asset—flat, slice, twist, even reverse twist—and he volleyed so much, his methods were characterized as unorthodox when he was in his prime. He often used the same side of the racket for forehand and backhand.

In 1907 Brookes' decisive 6-2, 6-0, 6-3 win over Roper Barrett settled Australasia's 3-2 victory at Wimbledon to break Britain's four-year hold on the Davis Cup and take the prize Down Under for the first time. It stayed there until a British reprisal in 1912, Brookes going 5-1 in singles and 3-0 in doubles as his side beat the U.S. three times. Even though he, 36, lost the memorable first-day match to 24-year-old Maurice McLoughlin, 17-15, 6-3, 6-3, in 1914, the Aussies spirited the Cup away, 3-2, as he clinched, 6-1, 6-2, 8-10, 6-3, over Dick Williams. Five years later, at age 41, he won the doubles with Gerald Patterson as the Aussies beat Britain, 4-1, the oldest to play with a Cup winner. A year after that, his Cup swan song, he gave Big Bill Tilden a furious battle, 10-8, 6-4, 1-6, 6-4, as the Americans retrieved the sterling bowl.

Returning to Wimbledon in 1914, his first appearance since winning seven years before, Brookes again demonstrated his all-around strength in a severe all-comers final test (6-2, 6-1, 5-7, 4-6, 8-6, over German Otton Froitzheim) preparatory to wresting the title from his close friend and teammate, Tony Wilding, 6-4, 6-4, 7-5, with a display of faultless ground strokes. Brookes' durability was demonstrated again in 1924 at Wimbledon when, at 46, he ousted World No. 5 Frank Hunter, finalist in 1923 and 17 years his junior.

But five war years passed, and in his next go at Wimbledon, as the defending champ he couldn't hold off Patterson in the challenge round, 6-3, 7-5, 6-2. However, that summer the two of them went to America to win the U.S. Doubles over Tilden and Vinnie Richards, 8-6, 6-3, 4-6, 4-6, 6-2, the first of many Aussies to cart off American titles. He gave incoming champ Tilden—who called him "the greatest tennis brain"—a fright in the singles quarters, 1-6, 6-4, 7-5, 6-3. Brookes, who had won his first major, Wimbledon, 1907, took his last in 1924, the Aussie doubles with James Anderson. He was in his 47th year, the elder of all major champions.

The honors didn't stop for the man who seemed to command them. In 1926, he was named president of the Lawn Tennis Association of Australia, a post he held until 1955. He was decorated with the French Legion of Honor for his services in World War I as a captain in the British Army and, in 1939, he was knighted.

He died Sept. 28, 1968, in Melbourne and entered the Hall of Fame in 1977.

MAJOR TITLES *(7)–Australian singles, 1911; Wimbledon singles, 1907, 1914; Australian doubles, 1924; Wimbledon doubles, 1907, 1914; U.S. doubles, 1919.* **DAVIS CUP**–*1905, 1907, 1908, 1909, 1911, 1912, 1914, 1919, 1920; record: 18-7 in singles, 10-4 in doubles.* **SINGLES RECORD IN THE MAJORS**–*Australian (5-0), Wimbledon (25-2), U.S. (4-2).*

LOUISE BROUGH

United States (1923–)
Hall of Fame 1967

One of the great volleyers in history was Althea Louise Brough, whose handiwork at the net earned her 13 titles at Wimbledon alone, in singles, doubles and mixed, including a rare triple—championships in each—in 1950. Of the foremost U.S. females only Chris Evert (19 times) and Billie Jean King (18) lasted longer in the U.S. Top Ten. Brough was there 16 times between 1941 and 1957, No. 1 in 1947. She made the World top ten 12 times between 1946 and 1957, including No. 1 in 1955, five times No. 2 and four times No. 3.

Brough was born March 11, 1923, in Oklahoma City, Okla., but grew up in Southern California, where she came to prominence as a junior, winning the U.S. 18-and-under title in 1940-41. "I had to attack; I didn't feel very comfortable on defense," she said.

Wimbledon was not held during World War II, but when the tournament reopened in 1946 Brough was ready to play a dominant role for a decade in the leading tournament, and is recalled as one of the most overwhelming players to compete there. In the first postwar visit she appeared in every final and just missed out on a triple, losing the singles to Pauline Betz, 6-2, 6-4. But the right-handed Brough won the doubles with Margaret duPont and the mixed with Tom Brown. During the Brough decade a Wimbledon final without her was unusual. Between 1946 and 1955, she won her way into 21 of the 30 finals, taking the singles in 1948 over Doris Hart, 6-3, 8-6; 1949 over doubles partner Margaret Osborne duPont, in a wowser, 10-8, 1-6, 10-8; 1950 over duPont, 6-1, 3-6, 6-1; and 1955 over Beverly Baker Fleitz, 7-5, 8-6. She also won the doubles five times from 1946-1954 with duPont, and the mixed four times, in 1946 with Tom Brown, in 1947 and 1948 with John Bromwich and in 1950 with Eric Sturgess.

Although she won the U.S. Singles Championship at Forest Hills only in 1947, over duPont, 8-6, 4-6, 6-1, she was a finalist on five other occasions. Doubles was the stage for her utmost success in the U.S., allied with duPont in possibly the finest female team ever, certainly the most victorious in major events. They won 20 Big Four titles together (12 U.S., 5 Wimbledon, 3 French), a record total equaled by Martina Navratilova and Pam Shriver in 1989.

Included in their record dozen U.S. titles was the longest championship run in any of the Big Four Events–nine straight doubles between 1942 and 1950. (Max Decugis and Maurice Germot won the French doubles 10 straight times between 1906 and 1920, but competition then was restricted to French citizens.) Brough and duPont did not enter the U.S. doubles in 1951 and 1952, but they returned to increase their record match winning streak to 41 before narrowly losing the 1953 final to Doris Hart and Shirley Fry. As a team in the U.S. doubles they won 12 of 14 times entered and 58 of 60 matches, losing but five sets.

Altogether, Brough won 35 of the major titles in singles, doubles and mixed doubles to rank fifth on the all-time list behind Margaret Court (62), Martina Navratilova (57), Billie Jean King (39) and Margaret duPont (37). Brough won the Australian singles in 1950 over Doris Hart, 6-4, 3-6, 6-4. Her various U.S. titles amounted to 18, and she was inducted into the Hall of Fame in 1967.

A willowy blonde, 5-foot-7-1/2, she was quiet and diffident but the killer in the left court when at play alongside duPont. Despite their close friendship and partnership, they were keen rivals in singles, and Brough's most difficult Wimbledon triumphs were the three-set wins over duPont in 1949 and 1950.

After retiring from the amateur circuit she married

Dr. A. T. Clapp, and later occasionally played in senior (over 40) tournaments, winning the U.S. Hard Court Doubles in that category in 1971 and 1975 with Barbara Green Weigandt.

MAJOR TITLES *(35)–Australian singles, 1950; Wimbledon singles, 1948, 1949, 1950, 1955; U.S. singles, 1947; Australian doubles, 1950; French doubles, 1946, 1947, 1949; Wimbledon doubles, 1946, 1948, 1949, 1950, 1954; U.S. doubles, 1942, 1943, 1944, 1945, 1946, 1947, 1948, 1949, 1950, 1955, 1956, 1957; Wimbledon mixed, 1946, 1947, 1948, 1950; U.S. mixed, 1942, 1947, 1948, 1949.* **OTHER U.S. TITLE**–*Hard Court doubles, 1948, with duPont.* **WIGHTMAN CUP**–*1946, 1947, 1948, 1949, 1950, 1952, 1953, 1954, 1955, 1956, 1957; record: 12-0 in singles, 10-0 in doubles.* **SINGLES RECORD IN THE MAJORS**–*Australian (5-0), French (10-4), Wimbledon (56-7), U.S. (57-17).*

MARY K. BROWNE

United States (1891–1971)
Hall of Fame 1957

As the first American female professional, Mary Kendall Browne left a splendid amateur record behind in 1926 to join promoter C. C. Pyle's original troupe of touring pros. (France's great Suzanne Lenglen was the centerpiece. Others: Vinnie Richards, Howard Kinsey, Harvey Snodgrass and Paul Feret.) During the winter of 1926-27, well past her prime, 35, she played one-night stands across North America as 'the opponent' against the invincible Lenglen, losing all 38 matches.

A 5-foot-2 right-hander and staunch volleyer, Browne was born June 3, 1891, in Ventura County, Calif., and came East to dominate the U.S. Championships at Philadelphia, scoring triples—singles, doubles, mixed titles—in 1912, 1913 and 1914. Only Hazel Hotchkiss Wightman, the previous three years, and Alice Marble (1938, 1939 and 1940) swept the field as thoroughly.

She was unique for an American woman in transferring her talent to golf, spectacularly in 1924. Shortly after making the U.S. semis at Forest Hills, losing to Helen Wills in three sets, she entered the U.S. Women's Golf Championships and beat the legendary Glenna Collett Vare to reach the final. There she lost the title to Dorothy Campbell Hurd.

In one of the most demanding days in tennis annals, Mary played 82 games while winning the 1912 singles, doubles and mixed finals all in the same afternoon, much of it in a downpour. "The rain was coming down in torrents, and still we went on," she later recalled, "our rackets mushy and our clothes soaked." She beat Eleo Sears, 6-4, 6-2, in the all-comers singles to become champion since Wightman didn't defend the title. With Dorothy Green she won the doubles, 6-2, 5-7, 6-0, over Maud Barger Wallach and Mrs. Frederick Schmitz. And, with Dick Williams, she won the soggy mixed, 6-4, 2-6, 11-9, over Evelyn Sears and Bill Clothier.

Mary ranked No. 1 in the U.S. in 1913 and 1914, the first two years of the Top Ten, returning to the select group at No. 2 in 1921 and 1924, and No. 6 in 1925. In 1926 she had a world ranking of No. 6, the USTA declining to give her a high ranking that she'd earned because she turned pro. She was later married to Kenneth Kenneth-Smith. Browne, remaining a fine golfer in her 70s, capable of shooting close to her age, died Aug. 19, 1971, in Laguna Hills, Calif. She was elected to the Hall of Fame in 1957.

MAJOR TITLES *(13)–U.S. singles, 1912, 1913, 1914; Wimbledon doubles, 1926; U.S. doubles, 1912, 1913, 1914, 1921, 1925; U.S. mixed, 1912, 1913, 1914, 1921.* **OTHER U.S. TITLES** *(3)–Indoor doubles, 1926, with Elizabeth Ryan; Clay Court singles, 1914; Clay Court doubles, 1914, with Louise Riddell Williams.* **WIGHTMAN CUP**–*1925, 1926; record: 0-2 in singles, 1-1 in doubles.* **SINGLES RECORD IN THE MAJORS**–*French (4-1), Wimbledon (0-1), U.S. (22-4).*

JACQUES BRUGNON

France (1895–1978)
Hall of Fame 1976

Jacques 'Toto' Brugnon was the elder of France's celebrated Four Musketeers who won the Davis Cup in 1927 from the U.S., and kept it six years. He preceded the other three—Jean Borotra, Henri Cochet, René Lacoste—as an internationalist, playing first on the Cup team in 1921. A master at doubles, he won Wimbledon four times, 1926 and 1928 with Cochet and 1932 and 1933 with Borotra, and appeared in three other finals. He won the French five times, three with Cochet, two with Borotra, and the Australian with Borotra, plus two French mixed for a dozen major titles.

Although doubles expertise overshadowed his singles, the small (5-foot-6-1/2, 139 pounds), neatly mustachioed and courtly Toto had many fine moments alone. He was ranked world Nos. 10 and 9 in 1926 and 1927, golden years for the French: They were 40 percent of the Top Ten, his fellow Musketeers occupying places in the first four, Lacoste at No. 1. In his greatest singles moment, his clever volleying took him to the Wimbledon semis of 1926 and five times a match point away from joining Borotra in the championship round. American Bob Kinsey got away from him, though, 6-4, 4-6, 6-3, 3-6, 9-7, slipping from 4-5, 15-40, and 5-6,

15-40 and out in the last set. Wallis Myers, the connoisseur, wrote: "Brugnon is a player of rare stroke variety and delicacy of touch." He was a quarter-finalist in 1927, and stands fourth among all male Wimbledonians in wins with 129: 37-19 in singles, 69-16 in doubles, 23-16 in mixed.

His Davis Cup career ran 11 years, and he had a hand in four of the Cup triumphs as a right-handed left-court player. For a time he was a teaching professional in California. He was born May 11, 1895, in Paris, and died there March 20, 1978. He entered the Hall of Fame in 1976.

MAJOR TITLES *(12)–Australian doubles, 1928; French doubles, 1927, 1928, 1930, 1932, 1934; Wimbledon doubles, 1926, 1928, 1932, 1933; French mixed, 1925, 1926.* **DAVIS CUP***–1921, 1923, 1924, 1925, 1926, 1927, 1930, 1931, 1932, 1933, 1934; record: 4-2 in singles, 22-9 in doubles.* **SINGLES RECORD IN THE MAJORS***–Australian (1-1), French (21-13), Wimbledon (37-19), U.S. (12-11).*

DON BUDGE

United States (1915–2000)
Hall of Fame 1964

In sheer achievement, John Donald Budge accomplished what nobody before 1938 had been able to do—he won the Grand Slam of tennis, capturing the championships of Australia, France, Wimbledon and the United States in the same year. People were suddenly speaking of Budge in the same breath with the already immortal Bill Tilden.

Born June 13, 1915, in Oakland, Calif., Budge had been less interested in tennis than in baseball, basketball and football while growing up in the California city, where his Scottish-born father, a former soccer player, had settled.

When the 6-foot-1, 160-pound right-hander turned to tennis, his strapping size enabled him to play a game of maximum power. His service was battering, his backhand considered perhaps the finest the game has known, his net play emphatic, his overhead drastic. Quick and rhythmic, he was truly the all-around player and, what is more, was temperamentally suited for the game. Affable and easygoing, he could not be shaken from the objective of winning with the utmost application of hitting power.

The red-haired young giant was a favorite wherever he played, and he moved quickly up the tennis ladder. At the age of 19, he was far enough advanced to be named to the Davis Cup team. The next year, 1936, he lost at Wimbledon and Forest Hills to Fred Perry, the world's No.1 amateur, but beat Perry in the Pacific Southwest tournament.

In 1937 Perry turned pro and Budge became the world's No. 1. He won at Wimbledon and Forest Hills and led the U.S. to its first Davis Cup in 11 years, 4-1 over Britain. The most brilliant act therein was his famous revival in the fifth set of the fifth match against Germany in the person of the stylish Baron Gottfried von Cramm to win the inter-zone final at neutral Wimbledon. He had already beaten Henner Henkel and won the doubles with Gene Mako over Henkel–von Cramm, so, with the score knotted, 2-2, up came the decisive test, another of his classic jousts with von Cramm. Not only was Budge far back, by two sets, but he had to rise from 1-4 in the fifth to win on a sixth match point, 6-8, 5-7, 6-4, 6-2, 8-6, and tip the series to the U.S., 3-2.

After that, the challenge round against Britain, also at Wimbledon, was relatively easy, though Don had to beat lefty Charlie Hare in a rugged first set, and take him, 15-13, 6-1, 6-2, to offset Frank Parker's leadoff loss to Bunny Austin. Budge and Mako won the doubles, and Don beat Austin on the third day, his 18th successive singles win on his seeming home turf. Culminating a fantastic year, Budge received the Sullivan Award as America's top amateur athlete, the first tennis player to be so honored.

The high regard in which Budge was held by fellow players, spectators and officials was reflected by the loyalty he demonstrated in 1937. He was a big attraction for pro tennis but decided against leaving the amateur ranks for another year. The United States had the Davis Cup and he decided that, in return for all tennis had done for him, he must help in the defense of the Cup for at least another year.

So he turned down the professional offers, aware that poor fortunes in 1938 could hurt, if not end, his earning power as a pro. As it turned out, 1938 would be his most glorious year. He defeated John Bromwich, 6-4, 6-2, 6-1, in the Australian final, losing only one set in the entire tournament. In the French championship he beat Roderich Menzel of Czechoslovakia in the final, 6-3, 6-2, 6-4, and yielded three sets in the tournament. At Wimbledon he did not lose a single set, beating Bunny Austin of Britain, 6-1, 6-0, 6-3, for the title, and at Forest Hills he gave up but one set—to Gene Mako in the final—in winning the U.S. crown, 6-3, 6-8, 6-2, 6-1.

Budge had won the Grand Slam and was the toast of the tennis world. After helping the U.S. retain the Davis Cup over Australia, beating Adrian Quist and Bromwich, and after four years in the World Top Ten (No. 1 in 1937 and 1938) and five years in the U.S. Top Ten, he left the amateur ranks. He did so with the blessing of the USTA president, Holcombe Ward, and the Davis Cup captain, Walter L. Pate, who wished him well in his pro career.

He made his professional debut at Madison Square Garden in New York early in 1939 and, before a crowd of 16,725, defeated Ellsworth Vines, 6-3, 6-4, 6-2. On tour, Budge defeated Vines, 21 matches to 18, and also defeated Perry, 18-11. On tour with the 47-year-old Tilden, Budge beat him, 51-7.

Before entering the Air Force in 1942, Budge won two U.S. Pro titles at Forest Hills—1940 over Perry and 1942 over Bobby Riggs. A shoulder injury suffered in military training reduced his post-war effectiveness, and he lost the pro tour hegemony to challenger Riggs in a close journey of one-nighters, 24-22. Still, he battled to the U.S. Pro tourney finals of 1946, '47, '49, and '53, losing the first three to Riggs and the last to 25-year-old Pancho Gonzalez, 13 years his junior, and left little doubt as to his greatness. "I consider him," said Bill Tilden, "the finest player 365 days a year who ever lived."

He was elected to the Hall of Fame in 1964. He died Jan. 26, 2000 at Poughkeepsie, N.Y.

MAJOR TITLES (14)–*Australian singles, 1938; French singles, 1938; Wimbledon singles, 1937, 1938; U.S. singles, 1937, 1938; Wimbledon doubles, 1937, 1938; U.S. doubles, 1936, 1938; Wimbledon mixed, 1937, 1938; U.S. mixed, 1937, 1938.* **OTHER U.S. TITLES**–*Clay Court doubles, 1934, with Gene Mako; Pro singles, 1940, 1942; Pro doubles, 1940, 1941, with Fred Perry; 1942, 1947, with Bobby Riggs; 1949, with Frank Kovacs; 1953, with Richard (Pancho) Gonzalez.* **DAVIS CUP**–*1935, 1936, 1937, 1938; record: 19-2 in singles, 6-2 in doubles.* **SINGLES RECORD IN THE MAJORS**–*Australian (5-0), French (6-0), Wimbledon (24-2), U.S. (23-3).*

MARIA BUENO

Brazil (1939–)
Hall of Fame 1964

Maria Esther Andion Bueno came swirling out of Brazil as a teenager to quickly establish herself as one of the world's most graceful and proficient athletes, a delight to watch and dangerous to deal with since she had a wide repertoire of shots and the skill and grace to deliver them constantly.

As the 'São Paulo Swallow,' she was slim, 5-foot-7 and quick, swooping to the net to conquer with piercing volleys. She was a blend of power and touch, a woman of superb movement and rhythms. Stylishly gowned by the tennis couturier, Ted Tinling, she was the frilly treasure of Wimbledon's Centre Court, where she was at her best and won eight titles—three in singles (1959, 1960 and 1964), and five in doubles.

Grass was her favorite surface, suiting her attacking nature. Born Oct. 11, 1939, in São Paulo, she was clearly the best female player to come from Latin America, and was ranked in the Top Ten from 1958 to 1968, including No. 1 in 1959 and 1960, plus No. 2 four times. In her regal choreography, the versatile right-hander was one of a triumvirate of women—including Frenchwoman Suzanne Lenglen and Australian Evonne Goolagong—whose fluidity and artistry set them apart.

She was agreeable, but reserved, a private person who underwent a number of physical career-harming agonies, without complaint. Her best days were as an amateur. By the time open tennis and prize money dawned in 1968 she was hobbled by a variety of arm and leg injuries. After a long retirement, she felt sufficiently well to try the pro tour in 1975, and returned to Wimbledon for a spiritual triumph in 1976 after a hiatus of seven years. There were glimpses of the wondrous Maria as she won three rounds, and most spectators were gratified to see her again. "In her day she was so marvelous to watch," said Billie Jean King, an old rival and doubles accomplice, after defeating Maria at Wimbledon in 1977. "But it was painful to play her today. I wanted to remember her as she was."

Bueno seemed undismayed to be a loser. "I have always loved tennis, and still enjoy playing. I've had my glory," she said. She crashed through to a first major singles triumph by defeating another aggressor, Darlene Hard, 6-4, 6-3, in the 1959 Wimbledon final. Two months later, in a rare teenage final at Forest Hills, Maria, 18, beat the British 6-footer Christine Truman, 19, for the U.S. title, 6-1, 6-4. That was her first of four U.S. singles prizes. She winged to the heights in the finals of 1963 and 1964, taking a shot-making feast from Margaret Smith (Court), 7-5, 6-4, to wow the gallery, and the following year stunning the spectators by destroying Carole Caldwell Graebner, 6-1, 6-0. At Wimbledon in 1964 she and Margaret staged another rouser of volleying violence for the title that went to Maria, 6-4, 7-9, 6-3. She won her last major singles final, the U.S. of 1966, over Nancy Richey, 6-3, 6-1, but was beaten in her last important final, the U.S. Amateur of 1968, by Margaret, 6-2, 6-2.

At 18, in the company of Althea Gibson, Maria won her first Wimbledon prize, the doubles of 1958. In all she won 19 major titles in singles, doubles and mixed, including the U.S. Singles at Forest Hills in 1959, 1963-64, 1966. She and American Darlene Hard were one of the best teams, taking the Wimbledon title twice (1960, 1963) and the U.S. twice (1960, 1962). Maria's skill at doubles was such that she won her 12 majors with six partners, and in 1960 scored one of three doubles Grand Slams, with two partners: Christine Truman in the Australian, Hard in the French, Wimbledon and U.S. She won the Japan Open in 1974, her lone pro title in singles, to complement 62 as an amateur, making her an unusual champ who won titles in three decades.

MAJOR TITLES *(18)–Wimbledon singles, 1959, 1960, 1964; U.S. singles, 1959, 1963, 1964, 1966; Australian doubles, 1960; French doubles, 1960; Wimbledon doubles, 1958, 1960, 1963, 1965; U.S. doubles, 1960, 1962, 1966, 1968; French mixed, 1960.* **FEDERATION CUP**–*1965; record: 1-0 in singles, 0-1 in doubles.* **SINGLES RECORD IN THE MAJORS**–*Australian (6-2), French (33-10), Wimbledon (50-9), U.S. (48-7).*

MABEL CAHILL
Ireland (1863–19??)
Hall of Fame 1976

Little is known of Mabel Esmonde Cahill except that, as an Irish citizen, she was the first foreigner to win one of the major championships. That was the U.S. singles of 1891 when she got even with Ellen Roosevelt, who had defeated her in the all-comers final of 1890 and gone on to win the title. In 1891, Cahill, a right-hander, decimated the Roosevelts, beating Ellen's sister, Grace, in the all-comers final, 6-3, 7-5, and then Ellen in the challenge round, 6-4, 6-1, 4-6, 6-3. She retained the title by defeating Bessie Moore in the 1892 challenge round, 5-7, 6-3, 6-4, 4-6, 6-2. That year she also won the mixed doubles with Clarence Hobart.

But she declined to return to Philadelphia for the 1893 Championships, defaulting her title to Aline Terry in the challenge round. During her residence in the U.S. she belonged to the New York Tennis Club. She was born April 2, 1863, in Ballyragget, County Kilkenny, Ireland. No details of her death, believed to have occurred in Ireland in 1904 or 1905, have been found. She was named to the Hall of Fame in 1976.

MAJOR TITLES *(5)–U.S. singles, 1891, 1892; U.S. doubles 1891, 1892; U.S. mixed, 1892.* **SINGLES RECORD IN THE MAJORS**–*U.S. (6-1).*

OLIVER CAMPBELL
United States (1871–1953)
Hall of Fame 1955

For a century Oliver Samuel Campbell had the distinction of being the youngest to win the U.S. singles title. He did it as a 19-year-old Columbia student in 1890. (Pete Sampras, a younger 19, became the youngest when he won the title in 1990.)

Four years earlier, Campbell, at 15 years, 5 months, had lost in the opening round at Newport to the man he would dethrone four years later, Henry Slocum. Oliver was the youngest entry until 1918 when Vinnie Richards undercut him by a month.

After his first exposure to Newport, Campbell determined to transform himself from a baseliner into a net-storming volleyer. "I ran to the net behind every service until the day I retired," he later recalled. It paid off in a U.S. doubles title (his first of three) in the company of Valentine Hall in 1888, with whom he'd won the Intercollegiate doubles that year for Columbia.

Campbell, a 5-foot-11-1/2 right-hander, lost to Slocum again in the 1888 semis, and to lefty Quincy Shaw in the 1889 all-comers final. In 1890 he outbattled Bob Huntington, 3-6, 6-2, 5-7, 6-2, 6-1, in the semis, and Percy Knapp, 8-6, 0-6, 6-2, 6-3, in the all-comers final. Stronger physically, he kept rushing the net, and at last beat Slocum, deposing the champ, 6-2, 4-6, 6-3, 6-1.

Campbell endured another struggle in the challenge round of 1891, 2-6, 7-5, 7-9, 6-1, 6-2, over Clarence Hobart. He made it three straight, 7-5, 3-6, 6-3, 7-5, over Fred Hovey in 1892, and retired, leaving the 1893 title to Bob Wrenn by default. In 1888 he made the U.S. Top Ten for the first of five straight years, No. 1 in 1890, 1891 and 1892. He was born Feb. 25, 1871, in New York, and died July 11, 1953, in Campellton, Canada. He entered the Hall of Fame in 1955.

MAJOR TITLES *(6)–U.S. single's, 1890, 1891, 1892; U.S. doubles, 1888, 1891, 1892.* **OTHER U.S. TITLES** *(2)–Intercollegiate doubles, 1888, with Valentine Hall; 1889, with Empie Wright.* **SINGLES RECORD IN THE MAJORS**–*U.S. (16-3).*

ROSIE CASALS
United States (1940–)
Hall of Fame 1996

Citizen Kane, who wasn't much fun, had his mysterious 'Rosebud.' There was, however, no mystery about the Rosebud of tennis, Citizen Casals. She just wanted to be the best ever. Inch-for-inch she was—and the fun flowed in all directions from this diminutive dynamo who took such joy from playing, and passed it along to grateful witnesses.

Tiny package, explosive contents. Tennis was no waiting game at the baseline for 62-inch Rosemary 'Rosie/Rosebud' Casals. She went for the jugular fast, a serve-and-volleying acrobat whose incredible arsenal of strokes and tankful of competitive verve were necessities merely to stay alive among the sisterhood that established female professional tennis during the 1970s.

"I'm out there with (5-foot-11 Margaret 'The Arm') Court," recalls San Franciscan Casals, "with those arms and legs that stretch forever, and I had to make my shots count right away."

They counted and counted and counted during a 15-year career in the stratosphere, 12 times in the World Top Ten (1966-77), No. 3 in 1970. So much so that she was elevated to the Hall in 1996.

Billie Jean King and protégé Rosie Casals ... names that went together like wine and roses. No finer female combo illuminated doubles. But all the while their influence as pioneering pros ran deeper than the five Wimbledon and two U.S. titles together. Although Rosie, the riveting volleyer, is the smallest modern in the tennis valhalla, she and Billie Jean were giants in launching the long march of the 'Long Way Babies' as the Virginia Slims circuit began to take shape in 1970.

With another Hall of Famer, Gladys Heldman, publisher of *World Tennis* magazine, as behind-the-scenes organizer and encourager, B.J. and Rosie were the ringleaders on court, close friends, doubles partners, frequent final-round foes, super saleswomen for the emerging tour. They were perfect role players, feisty but good-humored kids off the public courts who believed women had a destiny in professional sport. A born (Sept. 16, 1948) and bred San Franciscan, right-handed Rosie started at Golden Gate Park.

"Those early Slims days were an exciting time, and a little scary, too, although I laugh looking back at 1970," Rosie says. "Even though open tennis came in in 1968, the men got most of the money and publicity. The tournaments were still like the amateur days, men and women together. We knew we had to break away, go on our own. That first Slims tournament, '70 in Houston, the USTA didn't like our rebel ways and threatened to suspend us Americans if we played. They did, and for a while we wondered if that was the end of tennis for us. Of course it wasn't."

A full Slims tour commenced in 1971 and King and Casals "played our little bahoolas off"—Billie Jean's words. That year Rosie played a record 32 tournaments in singles, 31 in doubles, amounting to 205 matches while Billie Jean was in the same neighborhood with 36-21-210. More than 200 matches in a season? Steffi Graf played as many as 117 only once.

Different times. "We had to play much more than they do today because the money was slight." Rosie offers her soulful gamine's smile, and shrugs when you mention her unapproachable record of playing 685 singles and doubles tournaments. "If you won both the singles and doubles it was worth only a couple of thousand bucks. You couldn't afford to default with an injury. And we were paying all our own expenses, not getting free hotel and per diem like the stars now. But I'm glad for them. We were trying to pave the way.

"I got $3,750 when I lost the U.S. Open final to Court, the last victim in her Grand Slam. Not even close to what a first-round loser got in '96. [$10,000]. But it didn't matter. We thought we were rich, and there was a great feeling of family, of being together to make the tour work, provide the future for the game."

A distant relative of the cello virtuoso, Pablo Casals, the Rosebud improvised brilliant cadenzas on her strings. For sheer shotmaking sorcery, plus merrymaking on one side of the net, the amalgam of Casals and Ilie Nastase, winning the Wimbledon mixed in 1970 and 1972, may never be equalled. "I had to take care of him, mother him a little when he went crazy," she says.

Doubles was her shtick, 56 of the titles with King. But Rosie was a singles contender at all the majors, and beat King and clay maven Nancy Richey in succession to win the first big bucks tourney, the Family Circle Cup, worth $30,000 to her, in 1973. She won 11 singles, 112 pro doubles titles, the latter second only to Martina Navratilova's 162, collecting the last as a 41-year-old, "for old times' sake," in Oakland in 1988 alongside Martina. Her prize money, $1,364,955. Casals was a quarter-finalist or better in all the majors–Australian semi-final, 1967; French quarter-final, 1969 and 1970; Wimbledon semi-final, 1967, 1969, 1970, 1972; U.S. final, 1970, 1971, semi-final, 1969.

Dashing dressmaker, Hall of Famer Ted Tinling, adored her, gowning Rosie in spangles, sequins, a variety of color combinations. At Wimbledon '72 they caused a stir when his purple-squiggled dress—with Casals in it—was evicted. "It was predominantly white, complying with the rules," she says, "but the purple designs upset the referee. He ordered me off the court to change. I loved to get their goat and enjoyed the whole scene.

"It became a famous dress and beat me to the Hall of Fame to be displayed some time ago." But Citizen Casals has caught up with her notorious frock, and a Rosebud now blooms in Newport.

MAJOR TITLES *(12) (all doubles)–Wimbledon, 1967, 1968, 1970, 1971, 1973; U.S. 1967, 1971, 1974, 1982; Wimbledon mixed, 1970, 1972; U.S. mixed, 1975.* **OTHER U.S. TITLES** *(8)–Hard Court singles, 1965. Indoor doubles, 1966, 1968, 1975 with Billie Jean King, 1976 with Françoise Durr; Hard Court doubles, 1966 with King; Clay Court doubles, 1970 with Gail Chanfreau; Hard Court mixed, 1966 with Ian Crookenden.* **FEDERATION CUP**–*1967, 1976, 1977, 1978, 1979, 1980, 1981, helped U.S. win all seven (8-1 in singles, 27-1 in doubles).* **WIGHTMAN CUP**–*1967, 1976, 1977, 1978, 1979, 1980, 1981, helped U.S. win all seven (1-3 in singles, 6-1 in doubles).* **SINGLES RECORD IN THE MAJORS**–*Australian (9-5), French (10-7), Wimbledon (48-18), U.S. (47-21).*

MALCOLM CHACE
United States (1875–1955)
Hall of Fame 1961

A Rhode Islander born in Valley Falls on March 12, 1875, beanpole Malcolm Greene Chace, 6-foot-1, 150 pounds, made his first mark in the game by winning the U.S. Interscholastic title in 1892 for University Grammar in Providence. In 1893 (for Brown) and 1894 and 1895 (for Yale), he became the only three-straight winner of both the U.S. Intercollegiate singles and doubles titles, the only man to win both for two different colleges. He was a semi-finalist at the U.S. Championships in 1894, losing to Bill Larned and won the doubles title in 1895 with Robert Wrenn. Right-handed, he ranked in the U.S. Top Ten four times, beginning in 1892, No. 3 in 1895. He died July 16, 1955 in Yarmouth, Mass., and was named to the Hall of Fame in 1961.

MAJOR TITLE *(1)–U.S. doubles, 1895.* **OTHER U.S. TITLES** *(6)–Intercollegiate singles, 1893, 1894, 1895; Intercollegiate doubles, 1893, with Clarence Budlong; 1894, 1895, with Arthur Foote.* **SINGLES RECORD IN THE MAJORS**–*U.S. (16-9).*

DOROTHEA CHAMBERS
Great Britain (1878–1960)
Hall of Fame 1981

What a clash of eras and customs it was in the Wimbledon final of 1919 when the sturdily conformed, long-skirted 40-year-old matron, Dorothea Katherine

Douglass Chambers, seven times champion between 1903 and 1914, faced the slim new kid half her age, audacious, skimpily dressed (for the time) Suzanne Lenglen. They battled through the longest final up to that time, 44 games, Mrs. Robert Chambers narrowly missing two match points in the third set of the 10-8, 4-6, 9-7 decision, the first of six titles for Lenglen, never beaten at Wimbledon.

With King George V, Queen Mary, and the Princess Royal in the committee box, one of the finest matches to be played at Wimbledon, by men or women, was enacted. Against the all-court game of Lenglen, the right-handed Chambers delighted the gallery with superb resistance. She drove with such power and length from both forehand and backhand, passed so accurately, put up lobs so irretrievable, and had so much touch on her drop shot that her young opponent was showing signs of physical distress and found herself in danger of losing.

After two sets, the match was even and Lenglen was sipping brandy to ease her peril. In the third set, trailing, 4-1, Chambers put on a remarkable comeback and seemed to have the victory in hand at 6-5, 40-15, on her service at double match point. But, just as remarkably, Lenglen rallied and pulled out the match, 10-8, 4-6, 9-7. Both players were so exhausted that when asked to come to the Royal Box, they said they were physically unable to do so. It had been an epic struggle between the past and the future in tennis.

Despite the interruption of World War I, Chambers was in 11 Wimbledon singles finals—third behind Blanche Hillyard's 13 and Martina Navratilova's 12—the last in 1920 when she lost again to Lenglen, and, at 41, was the oldest female finalist. Continuing to play the Big W through 1927, she played 115 matches in all there: 32-8 in singles, 29-11 in doubles, 24-11 in mixed. Dolly, as some called her, won two of her Wimbledons after the birth of her first child, two more after the birth of her second.

As Britain's Wightman Cup captain in 1925, at 46, she helped her side win, 4-3, at Forest Hills by beating 30-year-old Eleanor Goss, 7-5, 3-6, 6-1. She also captained the team in 1926. She was born Sept. 3, 1878, in Ealing, England and died in 1960. She entered the Hall of Fame in 1981.

MAJOR TITLES *(7)–Wimbledon singles, 1903, 1904, 1906, 1910, 1911, 1913, 1914.* **WIGHTMAN CUP**–*1925, 1926; record: 1-1 in doubles.* **SINGLES RECORD IN THE MAJORS**–*Wimbledon (32-8), U.S. (3-1).*

CLARENCE CLARK

United States (1859–1937)
Hall of Fame 1983

A member of a distinguished Philadelphia family, Clarence Monroe Clark had the distinction of winning the first U.S. doubles title at Newport in 1881. He and Fred Taylor beat Alexander van Rensselaer and Arthur Newbold, 6-5, 6-4, 6-5. Earlier they eliminated the favorites, Dick Sears and James Dwight. The next year at Newport he made it to the singles final, losing to Sears, the original champ, 6-1, 6-4, 6-0. His brother, Joe Clark (named to the Hall of Fame in 1955), won the first Intercollegiate title for Harvard in 1883.

Joe and Clarence tested foreign waters for America, journeying to England in 1883, playing and losing two doubles matches against the dominant Renshaw twins, Willie and Ernest. Clarence was the first secretary of the newly formed USTA in 1881 and was, along with Dwight and Eugenius Outerbridge, a guiding light in the organization's establishment. He was born Aug. 27, 1859, in Germantown, Pa., died there June 29, 1937, and was named to the Hall of Fame in 1983.

MAJOR TITLE *(1)–U.S. doubles, 1881.* **SINGLES RECORD IN THE MAJORS**–*U.S. (7-2).*

JOE CLARK

United States (1861–1956)
Hall of Fame 1955

Two years after the first U.S. Championships at Newport, the Intercollegiate Championships was established in 1883 and won by Joseph Sill Clark of Harvard in both singles and doubles. Clark, a senior, was the Harvard champ that year, feeling justifiably proud of himself because he won the title over classmate Dick Sears, who happened to be the U.S. champion.

The first Intercollegiates, which Sears did not enter, was played on the grounds of a mental hospital in Hartford, and Clark recalled that some of the patients served as ball boys. Clark, a right-hander, was a Philadelphian, brother of Clarence Clark, who won the first U.S. doubles title with Fred Taylor. Together he and his brother were a formidable doubles team. They played in England in 1883 after beating the reigning U.S. champs, Sears and Dr. James Dwight, in matches in Boston and New York. They represented the U.S. against the foremost English pair, the Renshaw brothers, Ernest and Willie, in a series for the world championship. The

Renshaws won the two matches played, losing one set in the first.

In 1885 Joe Clark joined Sears to win the U.S. doubles, 6-3, 6-0, 6-2, over Henry Slocum and Percy Knapp. Joe was a singles semi-finalist in 1885, 1886 and 1887, and brother Clarence lost the 1882 final to Sears. Joe ranked in the U.S. Top Ten five straight years from 1885, No. 4 in 1888. He was born Nov. 30, 1861, in Germantown, Pa., entered the Hall of Fame in 1955, and died April 14, 1956. He was president of the USTA, 1889-91.

MAJOR TITLE *(1)–U.S. doubles, 1885.* **OTHER U.S. TITLES** *(2)–Intercollegiate singles, 1883; Intercollegiate doubles, 1883, with Howard Taylor.* **SINGLES RECORD IN THE MAJORS**–*U.S. (18-11).*

BILL CLOTHIER

United States (1881–1962)
Hall of Fame 1956

Another Harvard man to win the Intercollegiate championship (1902) in the early days, William Jackson Clothier was the U.S. champ four years later, ranking No. 1 in the U.S. Clothier, a right-handed net rusher, said that "he never played better" than in the 1906 Championships, gaining confidence from his quarter-final victory over Fred Alexander, 8-6, 6-2, 4-6, 1-6, 7-5, in which he came from triple match point (2-5, 0-40) to race through the last five games. He took the title from Beals Wright in the challenge round, 6-3, 6-0, 6-4.

He lost the U.S. final to Holcombe Ward in 1904 and, in a five-set battle, to Bill Larned in 1909. He held a Top Ten ranking for 11 years between 1901 and 1914. In 1905 he beat two French champions, Max Decugis, 6-3, 6-4, 6-4, and Maurice Germot, 6-3, 5-7, 6-1, 6-3, in the first U.S. Davis Cup engagement abroad, a 5-0 victory over France at Queen's Club in London. Although he wasn't chosen for the next tie against Australasia or the final against Britain, Clothier, a powerful, aggressive 6-foot-2, 170-pounder, caught the attention of scribe Wallace Myers in a good Wimbledon showing. It was a fourth-round loss to future champ Tony Wilding, 5-7, 1-6, 8-6, 7-5, 10-8, in 3-1/2 hours on Centre Court. Bill led 5-2, 40-15 with two match points in the third. "Both men were such splendid specimens of youth and vigor, such hard hitters, such gallant fighters," Myers wrote. He and his son, William Clothier II, won two U.S. Father and Son doubles titles in 1935 and 1936.

He was born in Philadelphia Sept. 27, 1881, and died there Sept. 4, 1962. He was inducted into the Hall of Fame in 1956.

MAJOR TITLE *(1)–U.S. singles, 1906.* **OTHER U.S. TITLES** *(2)–Intercollegiate singles, 1902; Intercollegiate doubles, 1902, with Edward Leonard.* **DAVIS CUP**–*1905 and 1909; record: 4-1 in singles.* **SINGLES RECORD IN THE MAJORS**–*Wimbledon (2-1), U.S. (57-18).*

HENRI COCHET

France (1901–1987)
Hall of Fame 1976

It could be said that Henri Jean Cochet had as pronounced a gift for playing tennis as anyone who attained world supremacy. A racket in his hand became a wand of magic, doing the impossible, most often in a position on the court considered untenable, and doing it with nonchalant ease and fluency. He took the ball early, volleys and half-volleys rippling off the strings. His overheads invariably scored, though his service seemingly was innocuous.

He developed his skills early in Lyon, France, where he was born Dec. 14, 1901, and where his father was secretary of the tennis club. Henri worked at the club as a ball boy and practiced with his friends and sister when nobody was using the courts. In 1921 he went to Paris where he and Jean Borotra, both unknowns, reached the final of the covered-court championship. Cochet was the winner.

The next year, he and Borotra played on the Davis Cup team, and in 1923 they joined with René Lacoste and Jacques Brugnon in the origin of the Four Musketeers. Cochet won 10 successive Davis Cup challenge-round matches from the time the Musketeers wrested the Cup from the U.S. in 1927.

A sensitivity of touch and timing, resulting in moderately hit strokes of genius, accounted for the success the little Frenchman (5-foot-6, 145 pounds) had in turning back the forceful hitters of the 1920s and early '30s. Following a stunning victory over Bill Tilden in the quarter-finals of the 1926 U.S. Championships, ending Tilden's six-year sway, and a triumph over William Johnston in the 1927 challenge round, the right-handed Cochet established himself in 1928 as the world's foremost player. Winner of the U.S. and French Championships that year, and runner-up at Wimbledon, he became more of a national hero than ever as he scored three victories in the Cup challenge round.

With Lacoste's retirement from international play in 1929, Cochet was France's indispensable man. He led his country to victory over the United States in the challenge round in 1929, 1930 and 1932, and over the British in 1931.

'The Ballboy of Lyon,' as he was called, was champion of France five times (four times after it was opened to non-French citizens in 1925), and won two Wimbledons (1927, 1929) and one U.S. (1928). Probably justifiably he felt unfairly treated in trying for a second U.S. in 1932. Darkness shut down his semi-final win over Wilmer Allison at 2-2 in sets. He had to complete that victory, 7-5, the following day, and then, after two hours rest, contest the final in which the weary Frenchman was no match for a fresh Ellsworth Vines, 6-4, 6-4, 6-4.

But for three matches as he closed out his 1927 Wimbledon championship, fourth seeded, he was a singular Henri Houdini. No one has concluded a major in such spectacular escapes, and all from Hall of Famers. Down two sets, he beat Frank Hunter in the quarters, 3-6, 3-6, 6-2, 6-2, 6-4. Trailing the great second-seeded Tilden, three points from defeat at 1-5, 15-all in the third, he reeled off 17 straight points, also survived a service break to 3-2 in the fifth and won the last four games to seize their semi, 3-6, 4-6, 7-5, 6-4, 6-3. For an encore magnifique in the final, he lagged again and had to repel six match points to beat third-seeded Borotra, 4-6, 4-6, 6-3, 6-4, 7-5: Hurdling a match point at 2-5, and five more with Borotra serving at 5-3!

He ranked No. 1 from 1928 through 1931 and was in the World Top Ten 10 times between 1922 and 1933. After France lost the Davis Cup to Great Britain in 1933, Cochet turned professional. He did not have much of a career as a pro, however, and after the war, in 1945, one of the most naturally gifted tennis players in history received reinstatement as an amateur, a role in which he had once ruled the tennis world, and continued playing well. Elected to the Hall of Fame in 1976, he died April 1, 1987, in St. Germain-en-Laye, France.

MAJOR TITLES *(15)–French singles, 1926, 1928, 1930, 1932; Wimbledon singles, 1927, 1929; U.S. singles, 1928; French doubles, 1927, 1930, 1932; Wimbledon doubles, 1926, 1928; French mixed, 1928, 1929; U.S. mixed, 1927.* **DAVIS CUP**–*1922, 1923, 1924, 1926, 1927, 1928, 1929, 1930, 1931, 1932, 1933; record: 34-8 in singles, 10-6 in doubles.* **SINGLES RECORD IN THE MAJORS**–*French (38-4), Wimbledon (43-8), U.S. (15-3).*

MAUREEN CONNOLLY

United States (1934–1969)
Hall of Fame 1968

A too-brief flash on the tennis scene was that of Maureen Catherine Connolly, but it was of brilliant incandescence; she may have been the finest of all female players.

Nicknamed 'Little Mo' for her big-gunning, unerring groundstrokes (it was an allusion to 'Big Mo,' the U.S. battleship *Missouri*), she was devastating from the baseline, and seldom needed to go to the net. A small and compact right-hander (5-foot-4, 120 pounds), she won her nine major singles championships as a teenager: Three successive Wimbledons, 1952-54, and U.S. Championships at Forest Hills, 1951-53. At 16 years, 11 months, she was the youngest U.S. champ ever until Tracy Austin won in 1979 at 16 years, nine months. In addition, Connolly won three other American titles and held the No. 1 U.S. rankings, 1951-53. She was undisputed World No. 1, 1952-1954. Connolly was born Sept. 17, 1934, in San Diego, Calif., and grew up there. She was a pupil of Eleanor 'Teach' Tennant, an instructor who had guided a previous world champ, Alice Marble. Connolly first came East in 1949 to win the U.S. junior title and repeated in 1950. She entered Forest Hills both years, losing in the second round. But she would soon have the world under her right thumb while still technically a junior, not yet 19, an obstreperous intruder overthrowing the established order of older women. Her third time around at the U.S. biggie, seeded fourth, she ran six games from 1-4 down in the first set while beating top-seeded 26-year-old Doris Hart, 6-4, 6-4, in a semi halted by rain after the first game of the second, and resumed the following day. A day after that completion, Maureen was given a harder time by second-seeded 24-year-old Shirley Fry, but her long-range shelling was decisive, 6-3, 1-6, 6-4.

A cheerful and sporting competitor, she crushed the opposition, never losing an important match, only occasionally losing a set. She helped the U.S. beat Britain in the Wightman Cup matches of 1951-54, winning all seven of her singles.

Fifteen years after Don Budge scored the first Grand Slam, Connolly traveled the same route in 1953, winning all the major singles championships (Australian, French, Wimbledon, U.S.) within a calendar year to achieve the first female Slam. She lost only one set in doing so. Following the Aussie triumph over doubles partner and fellow Californian, Julie Sampson, 6-3, 6-2, Maureen had to get past Hart thrice: 6-2, 6-4, at the French, 8-6, 7-5, at Wimbledon, 6-2, 6-4, in the home stretch. That season she won 10 of 12 tournaments on a 61-2 match record. By winning the three French titles in 1954—singles, doubles with Aussie Nell Hopman, her mentor after splitting from Tennant, mixed with Lew Hoad—she became the fourth of five players to score a triple in Paris.

Nobody has measured up to her perfect record in the majors after early U.S. defeats in 1949-50. She sailed through nine successive majors (three U.S., three Wimbledons, two French, one Australian), unbeaten in 50 matches. The closest to that were four other greats who won six straight: Budge, 1937-38; Margaret Court, 1969-70, Martina Navratilova, 1983-84; Steffi Graf, 1995-96. Helen Wills Moody, who played irregularly, won 15 straight majors between 1924 and 1933.

In 1954 her playing career ended with heartbreaking suddenness, aborted by an unusual traffic accident, not long after she won her last titles, the U.S. Clay singles. While riding her horse, Col. Merryboy, a gift from San Diego admirers, she was struck by a truck, severely injuring a leg. "I knew immediately I'd never play again," she said. By then she was Mrs. Norman Brinker, wife of a U.S. Olympic equestrian. She recovered sufficiently to give tennis instruction, and helped a number of players with their games, but she died at 34 in 1969 of cancer.

She was inducted into the Hall of Fame in 1968 and is memorialized by the Maureen Connolly Brinker Cup, an international team competition between the U.S. and Britain for girls under 21.

"Whenever a great player comes along you have to ask, 'could she have beaten Maureen?'" That was the standard of Lance Tingay, the Hall of Fame tennis correspondent of the *Daily Telegraph* of London. "In every case the answer is, I think not."

MAJOR TITLES (12)–*Australian singles, 1953; French singles, 1953, 1954; Wimbledon singles, 1952, 1953, 1954; U.S. singles, 1951, 1952, 1953; Australian doubles, 1953; French doubles, 1954; French mixed, 1954.* **OTHER U.S. TITLES** (3)–*Clay Court singles, 1953, 1954; Clay Court doubles, 1954, with Doris Hart.* **WIGHTMAN CUP**–*1951, 1952, 1953, 1954; record: 7-0 in singles, 2-0 in doubles.* **SINGLES RECORD IN THE MAJORS**–*Australian (5-0), French (10-0), Wimbledon (18-0), U.S. (19-2).*

JIMMY CONNORS

United States (1952–)
Hall of Fame 1998

A marvel of longevity and self-motivation, he is (as one-time agent Bill Riordan boasted) "the one and only James Scott Connors."

Fiery of temperament and shotmaking, this lefty with a two-fisted backhand pounded foes for more than two professional decades in rip-roaring baseline style, a ragdoll throwing himself into his groundies with utter gusto. Often controversial, he fought verbally with opponents, officials and the crowd.

Considered a feisty wiseguy in his earlier days, he eventually became a respected elder. The championships, honors and prize money piled up, but not as high as his zeal as he continued to compete forcefully against much younger men into his 41st year and through the 1992 season when he roused galleries in Paris, London and New York and compiled a 17-15 match record, ending the season with a remarkable No. 83 ranking.

Turning pro in 1972, Jimmy won his first title that year at Jacksonville, Fla., and continued at a prodigious pace, arriving at his 109th—a male record—in 1989 by winning Israel. He attained 54 other finals, and played more tournaments (401) and won more matches (1,337-285, a .824 mark), than any other male pro, and, in fact, never announced his retirement. He also won 19 doubles titles, two of them majors: Wimbledon, 1973, and the U.S., 1975, both with Ilie Nastase. Having lost a first-rounder at Atlanta in 1996, he was the only player who had been on the ATP computer since its inception in 1973, latest ranking a not-too-shabby No. 1,304 at age 44, having been World No. 1 five straight years, 1974-78, an open era record until surpassed by Sampras' six, 1993-98.

His specialty has been the U.S. Open (five championships), where he was singular in winning on all three surfaces: Grass (1974) and clay (1976) at Forest Hills, and hard (1978, 1982, 1983) at Flushing Meadow.

He also won Wimbledon twice (1974 and 1982) and the Australian (1974) for a total of 8 singles majors, tied with Andre Agassi and behind only to Sampras (14) and Bill Tilden (10) among American men, and even with Fred Perry, Ken Rosewall, Ivan Lendl, Stefan Edberg, Mats Wilander on the all-time roll.

Perhaps 1991 was the most extraordinary year of his progression toward a Hall of Fame berth in 1998. His career had seemed ended. Troubled by a deteriorated left wrist, he had played (and lost) only three matches in 1990, dropping to No. 936 in the rankings. However, surgery restored him, and he came back smoking, playing 14 tournaments and climaxing with a phenomenal semi-final finish (his fourteenth) at the U.S. Open.

His first- and second-round victories as a Wimbledon wild card raised his tournament male record to 84 match wins. Wild-carded again at Flushing, because of a No. 174 ranking, Jimmy exploded by beating Patrick McEnroe from two sets down as well as Michael Schapers and tenth-seeded Karel Novacek, then celebrated his 39th birthday in a tumultuous victory over Aaron Krickstein, soaring from 2-5 in the fifth set to win in a stirring tie-breaker, 3-6, 7-5 (10-8), 1-6, 6-3, 7-6 (7-4). Then he beat Paul Haarhuis from a set and a break down, 4-6, 7-6, 6-4, 6-2, but was outgunned at last by Jim Courier, 6-3, 6-3, 6-2. He was the oldest semifinalist since 39-year-old Rosewall lost the title match to none other than James himself 17 years before. Although Stefan Edberg won the title, it was Connors' Open in the public eye.

Ever a sensational celebrator of his own birthday (he won 10 of 11 matches on that day at the U.S. Open), Jimmy took the cake—literally, delivered on court—in 1992 on his 40th by beating Jaime Oncins, 6-1, 6-2, 6-3, notching a tournament-record 98th match win.

He was raised to be a tennis player by his mother, a teaching pro named Gloria Thompson Connors, and 'Two Mom,' grandmother Bertha Thompson. Connors grew up in Belleville, Ill., across the Mississippi from St. Louis. Although he was always smaller than his contemporaries on his way up the ladder, he made up for that through determination and grit. He played in his first U.S. Championship, the U.S. boys' 11-and-under of 1961, when he was only eight. He was born Sept. 2, 1952, in East St. Louis, Ill., and claimed to have begun playing when he was two. "My mother rolled balls to me, and I swung at them. I held the racket with both hands because that was the only way I could lift it."

Connors, who grew to 5-foot-10, 155 pounds, became known as a maverick when he refused to join the ATP (Association of Tennis Pros) in 1972, the then-new union embracing most male professionals, and avoided the mainstream of pro tennis to play in and dominate a series of smaller tournaments organized by Bill Riordan, his manager, a clever promoter.

In 1974 he and Riordan began bringing lawsuits,

eventually amounting to $10 million, against the ATP and its president, Arthur Ashe, for allegedly restricting his freedom in the game. It stemmed from Connors' banning from the French Open in 1974 after he had signed a contract to play WTT (World Team Tennis) for Baltimore. Connors had sought to enter the French, the only major championship he did not win that year, but because the ATP and the French administration opposed WTT—it conflicted with their tournament—the entries of WTT players were refused. The 1975 Wimbledon final, then, was unique, a duel between opponents in a lawsuit. Ashe won, and shortly thereafter Connors dropped the suits, and parted with Riordan.

Deprived unfairly by the French of a chance for a second leg on what might have been a Grand Slam, Connors nevertheless enjoyed in 1974 one of the finest seasons ever, the best by an American since Tony Trabert's 1955. Connors lost only four matches in 20 tournaments, while winning 99.

Among the 14 tournaments he won—a record for American male pros—were the Australian, Wimbledon, South African, U.S. at Forest Hills, U.S. Clay Court and U.S. Indoor. He was clearly No. 1, a status he enjoyed from July 1974, for 159 straight weeks and was there a total of 263 weeks, second only to Ivan Lendl's 269.

Although he trailed his foremost rivals head-to-head—Bjorn Borg, 7-10; John McEnroe, 13-20; Lendl, 13-22—he had great moments at their expense. He saved four set points to win a thrilling and vital 11-9 third-set tie-breaker while beating Borg in the 1976 U.S. final at Forest Hills, 6-4, 3-6, 7-6 (11-9), 6-4, and stunned the Swede (his conqueror at Wimbledon) to take the inaugural Flushing Meadow final in 1978, 6-4, 6-2, 6-2. Three points from defeat in the fourth-set tie-breaker, he startled McEnroe to win Wimbledon in five sets in 1982, 3-6, 6-3, 6-7 (2-7), 7-6 (7-5), 6-4, bridging a gap of eight years between titles there. Jimmy's incredible service returning jolted Lendl in the 1982 and 1983 U.S. Open finals, 6-3, 6-2, 4-6, 6-4, and 6-3, 6-7 (2-7), 7-5, 6-0.

By winning the U.S. Indoor singles three straight years (1973-75) he tied a record set by Gus Touchard (1913-15). He made this his most successful tourney, adding wins in 1978, '79, '83 '84 for a record total of seven. At the U.S. Clay Court in 1974, '76, '78, '79, his four titles were the most since Frank Parker's five between 1933 and 1947.

Connors seemed to delight in keeping the public off-balance. He annoyed numerous tennis fans in the U.S. with his sometimes vulgar on-court behavior, and his refusal to play Davis Cup (except briefly during the 1976, '81, '84 seasons). He was booed at Wimbledon—a rare show of disapproval there—for snubbing the Parade of Champions on the first day of the Centenary in 1977.

After irritating sponsors and tennis officials by shunning the climactic Masters for three years, Connors entered and won the 1977 event over Borg, 6-4, 1-6, 6-4 having qualified by finishing among the top eight in the worldwide Grand Prix series.

His two crushing final-round victories over Ken Rosewall in 1974 (6-1, 6-1, 6-4 at Wimbledon, and 6-1, 6-0, 6-1, at Forest Hills) made Connors seem invincible. His manager, Riordan, proclaimed Jimmy "heavyweight champion of tennis," and arranged a series of challenges over three years at Las Vegas and Puerto Rico in which Connors retained his 'title' by defeating Rod Laver, John Newcombe, Manolo Orantes and Ilie Nastase. Connors grossed over a million dollars from television rights for those four exhibitions.

Beginning in 1974, Connors played in five successive U.S. finals, the first man to do so since Bill Tilden, who was in eight between 1918 and 1925. He was the first since Fred Perry (1933-34, '36) to win the U.S. title three years. Connors was jolted in the finals by Spanish-speaking lefties Manolo Orantes in 1975, 6-4, 6-3, 6-3, and by Guillermo Vilas, 2-6, 6-3, 7-6 (7-4), 6-0, in 1977, striking the last ball, an error, in championship play in Forest Hills Stadium.

Jimmy went to college one year at the University of California at Los Angeles, where he won the National Intercollegiate Singles in 1971 and attained All-American status.

It was in 1973 that he made his first big splash by winning the U.S. Pro Singles, his first significant title, at 20, toppling Ashe, the favorite, in five-set final, 6-3, 4-6, 6-4, 3-6. 6-2. Ashe said, "I've played them all, and I never saw anybody hit the ball so hard for so long as Jimmy did." That year Connors was ranked co-No. 1 in the U.S. with Stan Smith, but was No. 1 alone seven other years (1974, '76-'77-'78, '82, '86-'87), and in the U.S. Top Ten a record 20 times. During his 21-year pro career he was in the World Top Ten a record 16 times, 11 other than his No. 1's: No. 3, 1973, '80-'81, '83; No. 2, 1979, '82, '84; No. 4, 1985, '87; No. 8, 1986; No. 7, 1988. His prize money amounted to $8,641,040. Jimmy, married with two children, lived on profitably for several years as the mainstay of an 'over 35' senior tour. Although it had various sponsors, it was generally known as the 'Connors Circuit.'

MAJOR TITLES *(10)–Australian singles, 1974; Wimbledon singles, 1974, 1982; U.S. singles, 1974, 1976, 1978, 1982, 1983; Wimbledon doubles, 1973; U.S. doubles, 1975.* **OTHER U.S. TITLES** *(15)–Indoor singles, 1973, 1974, 1975, 1978, 1979, 1983, 1984; Clay Court singles, 1974, 1976, 1978, 1979; Indoor doubles, 1974, with Frew McMillan; 1975, with Ilie Nastase; Clay Court doubles, 1974, with Nastase; Pro singles, 1973.* **DAVIS CUP**–*1976, 1981, 1984; record: 10-3 in singles.* **SINGLES RECORD IN THE MAJORS**–*Australian (11-1), French (40-13), Wimbledon (84-18), U.S. (98-17).*

ASHLEY COOPER
Australia (1936–)
Hall of Fame 1991

Among the seemingly endless platoon of Aussies who were to dominate the world after Frank Sedgman showed them how, handsome, dark-haired Ashley John Cooper was the third of their number to win Wimbledon (1958) and the fourth to capture the U.S. the same year. Because he turned pro shortly after those successes, the right-handed Ash's career in the public eye was brief though very productive. His last two amateur years, 1957 and 1958, could compare well to anyone's: Six finals and four championship out of eight major starts, and two semis at the French, the only ones he didn't win.

An athletic 5-foot-10, he was of an attacking mindset, like the others of his tribe, a thorough, smooth, if not spectacular, stroker in attaining his goals at the net. He also won the Australian championship in 1958, one of only 10 men to grab three majors in one year. But whatever hopes he had for a Grand Slam were dashed in Paris by Luis Ayala, 9-11, 4-6, 6-4, 6-2, 7-5. Still, he had one of the finest years with a 25-1 match record in the majors.

Cooper, who had lost the 1957 Wimbledon final to Lew Hoad, was upset in the U.S. final by unseeded Mal Anderson, but they got together three months later to successfully defend the Davis Cup against the U.S., 3-2. Despite an ankle injury incurred during their final at Forest Hills in 1958, Cooper regrouped and came from behind to beat Anderson, 6-2, 3-6, 4-6, 10-8, 8-6. Cooper spent three years, 1956-58, in the World Top Ten, No. 1 the last two years. He was born Sept. 15, 1936, in Melbourne, and entered the Hall of Fame in 1991.

MAJOR TITLES *(8)–Australian singles, 1957, 1958; Wimbledon singles, 1958; U.S. singles, 1958; Australian doubles, 1958; French*

doubles, 1957, 1958; U.S. doubles, 1957.* **DAVIS CUP**–*1957, 1958; record: 2-2 in singles.* **SINGLES RECORD IN THE MAJORS**–*Australian (16-3), French (13-3), Wimbledon (19-4), U.S. (20-4).*

JACK CRAWFORD
Australia (1908–1991)
Hall of Fame 1979

Few players so completely won the gallery as did John Herbert Crawford, called by one commentator the "most popular Wimbledon winner in history."

Indeed, Crawford, a right-hander, was an exemplary sportsman, as well as a handsome figure on the court (6-foot-1, 168 pounds) in his long, white flannels and long-sleeved shirt. And he moved easily, gracefully, over the turf with his flat-topped racket, a model of early vintage. He was in the World Top Ten six times, 1932-37, No. 1 in 1933.

Crawford, born March 22, 1908, in Albury, Australia, was a masterful player from the back of the court, driving the ball with length and pinpoint control with seemingly little strain. He played the classical game of solid, fluent strokes, and he played it so well that he came within one set of completing a Grand Slam five years before Don Budge accomplished the feat of winning the four major championships in one year.

Crawford's bid came in 1933, a year after he won 16 tournaments, starting with a victory over American Keith Gledhill, 2-6, 7-5, 6-3, 6-2, in the Australian final. Next Crawford won the French Championship, beating Henri Cochet for the title. At Wimbledon came a legendary final against Ellsworth Vines that Crawford won.

Crawford, a 5-to-1 short-ender with London bookies, twice held from 0-40 in the critical second set, and came to the wire breaking Vines at love with four winners, abruptly surging to the net in the last two games. Al Laney wrote: "For superlative play on both sides, the blending of stroke and strategy, the unrelenting speed of serve and considered counterstroke, I cannot remember another to place above it."

So a reluctant, fatigued Crawford moved on to Forest Hills and the U.S. Championships with an opportunity to complete the ultimate sweep. After defeating Frank Shields in the semi-finals, Crawford faced Fred Perry as the last obstacle in his path. Crawford lost the first set, but then won the next two and was one set away from a Slam. But his strength faded, owing in part to the asthma and insomnia he had at the time. Perry went on to victory in the next two sets, dashing Crawford's hopes, 6-3, 11-13, 4-6, 6-0, 6-1.

Still, the gallery loved this man—'Gentleman Jack,' they called him—from Down Under. He won the championship of his country four times, and he did it all his way, seemingly never hurried, his every move appearing effortless, his serve belonging in a picture book. Jack Crawford was one of the greats of his time while playing tennis in the style of a gentleman of the old school.

Like most Aussies he got immense pleasure from Davis Cup, selected first in 1928, and was proud of being a member of the victorious 1939 team although he didn't play. Jack led the team to a 3-2 upset of the U.S. in Philadelphia as he beat Wilmer Allison in the decider, 4-6, 6-3, 4-6, 6-2, 6-2. A victory over Germany, with him winning both singles, put the first Down Under entry as Australia (no longer Australasia) into the Cup round since 1924, but Britain resisted, 3-2, as Jack was beaten by long-time rival, Perry, in the fifth match, 6-2, 6-3, 6-3.

When he beat Perry to win the 1935 Australian, Jack was taking part in his tenth straight major final (he didn't enter the U.S. in 1934), extraordinary consistency. Rod Laver would equal it when he got to the Wimbledon final in 1968 (Wimbledon, U.S. finalist, 1961, a Grand Slam in 1962, plus French of 1968, following his banishment as a pro). Bill Tilden was in 10 straight (1918-26), but his forays included only U.S. and Wimbledon. Crawford's seventh Aussie singles final, a record later tied by Roy Emerson, was lost in 1940 to Adrian Quist, but, at 32, he did knock off defending champ John Bromwich in the semis.

He took delight in winning three straight Aussie mixed titles with his wife, Marjorie Cox Crawford (1931-33). They were a unique wedded couple in appearing in major finals simultaneously in 1931, he winning, she losing the Australian.

He entered the Hall of Fame in 1979, and died Sept. 10, 1991, in Sydney.

MAJOR TITLES *(17)–Australian singles, 1931, 1932, 1933, 1935; French singles, 1933; Wimbledon singles, 1933; Australian doubles, 1929, 1930, 1932, 1935; French doubles, 1935; Wimbledon doubles, 1935; Australian mixed, 1931, 1932, 1933; French mixed, 1933; Wimbledon mixed, 1930.* **DAVIS CUP**–*1928, 1930, 1932, 1933, 1934, 1935, 1936, 1937; record: 23-16 in singles, 13-5 in doubles.* **SINGLES RECORD IN THE MAJORS**–*Australian (52-15), French (19-4), Wimbledon (36-8), U.S. (10-4).*

LINDSAY DAVENPORT
United States (1976–)

With three major championship singles titles, an Olympic gold medal and two year-end No. 1 world rankings, Lindsay Davenport restored pride to American woman's tennis following a fallow period that accompanied the end of the Chris Evert era.

In 1998 Davenport became the first U.S.-born woman since Evert in 1982 to win the U.S. Open singles title, and the first since Evert in 1985 to be ranked No. 1. The following year, Davenport ended an 18-year drought for U.S.-born women at Wimbledon, and in 2000 ended a similar drought at the Australian Open. From 1997 to 2001, she retained a top-three ranking, twice earning the year-end No. 1 spot, and her 37 tournament victories lead all American-born women in the post-Evert era.

Born in Palos Verdes, Calif., on June 8, 1976, she was a shy, gangly teenager, so self-conscious about her height that she would drop her shoulders and hunch over whenever possible. Unlike many of her tennis contemporaries, Davenport was never a child prodigy or teen sensation. When she transferred schools midway through high school, her new classmates only learned Lindsay was a tennis player when newspapers carried stories about her beating Gabriela Sabatini.

At 6-foot-2-1/2 and a trimmed-down 175 pounds, Davenport is blessed with a massive serve and can follow up with a bewildering choice of penetrating ground strokes. She was named the WTA Tour player of the year in 1998 and '99, and is regarded among the most respected and liked players on tour.

Her first of six major championship titles (three singles, three doubles) came at Roland Garros in 1996 when she won doubles with Mary Joe Fernandez. At the Atlanta Olympics later that summer, Davenport struck gold by defeating a quartet of Top 10 players: Anke Huber of Germany, Iva Majoli of Croatia, Fernandez, and Arantxa Sanchez Vicario of Spain.

The biggest victory of her career came before partisan crowds at the Arthur Ashe Stadium at the U.S. Open in 1998. Davenport overpowered world No. 1 Martina Hingis 6-3, 7-5 in the final. Ten months later at Wimbledon, Davenport overcame seven-time champion Steffi Graf to become only the third American-born woman of the Open era to take the singles title at the Championships. She also teamed with Corina Morariu to win doubles. Her other doubles crowns came at the 1997 U.S. Open in 1997, teaming with Jana Novotna.

The Californian reached the finals of three major championships in 2000, ending Hingis's streak of three titles at the Australian Open before losing to Venus Williams at both Wimbledon and the U.S. Open. (Back spasms led to a first-round upset at Roland Garros, the tournament she still needs to win to complete a career Grand Slam.)

Knee surgery in November 2001 forced Davenport to miss much of the 2002 season. She played in only nine events and, for the first time since 1992, failed to win a tournament as she dropped to No. 12 in the year-end rankings.

When Davenport earned the No. 1 computer ranking on Oct. 12, 1998, she ended an 80-week reign by Hingis. She also became the first U.S.-born woman in 14 years to hold the top spot and was the third U.S. native to ascend to No. 1 in the computer rankings after Evert and Tracy Austin (Serena Williams has since joined the elite group). Davenport held the top spot five times and finished as No. 1 in 1998 and 2001.

In addition to her 1996 gold medal, Davenport competed in the 2000 Games, and has represented the U.S. nine times in Fed Cup. She went undefeated in Fed Cup play in 1999 and 2000, leading the United States to a pair of championships.

MAJOR TITLES *(6)–Australian singles, 2000; Wimbledon singles, 1999; U.S. singles, 1998; French doubles, 1996; Wimbledon doubles 1999; U.S. doubles, 1997.* **FED CUP**–*1993, 1994, 1995, 1996, 1997, 1998, 1999, 2000, 2002; record: 23-2 in singles, 5-0 in doubles.* **SINGLES RECORD IN THE MAJORS**–*Australian (41-9), French (21-8), Wimbledon (33-8), U.S. (42-11).*

DWIGHT DAVIS
United States (1879–1945)
Hall of Fame 1956

A left-handed, big-serving Harvardian who won the Intercollegiate title in 1899, 6-foot, 190-pound Dwight Filley Davis ranked in the U.S. Top Ten four times between 1898 and 1901, No. 2 in 1899 and 1900. But he is best known for launching in 1900 the great worldwide team competition that bears his name: Davis Cup. He intended for it to be called the International Lawn Tennis Challenge Trophy when he purchased the silver bowl at the Boston jeweler, Shreve, Crump & Low. His fellow members at Longwood Cricket Club, where the inaugural was staged in 1900, jocularly referred to it as 'Dwight's pot.' Soon, just-plain 'Davis Cup' was the accepted handle.

The original U.S. team was a Harvard production, Davis captaining, he and schoolmates Malcolm Whitman and Holcombe Ward playing a 3-0 victory over the British Isle. Davis was a member of President Coolidge's cabinet as Secretary of War, and also served his country as governor-general of the Philippines. He was born in St. Louis July 5, 1879, and died Nov. 28, 1945, in Washington, D.C. He was inducted into the Hall of Fame in 1956.

MAJOR TITLES *(3)–U.S. doubles, 1899, 1900, 1901.* **OTHER U.S. TITLES** *(2)–Intercollegiate singles, 1899; Intercollegiate doubles, 1899, with Holcombe Ward.* **DAVIS CUP**–*1900, 1902; record: 1-0 in singles, 1-1 in doubles.* **SINGLES RECORD IN THE MAJORS**–*U.S. (16-7).*

LOTTIE DOD
Great Britain (1871–1960)
Hall of Fame 1983

Tall and athletic, Charlotte 'Lottie' Dod became the youngest of major champions at 15 years, 10 months by winning Wimbledon in 1887, knocking off the defending champion, Blanche Bingley, 6-2, 6-0, in the challenge round. She played four other years, never lost—in 10 matches she dropped one set—though her championship foe, each time, now Mrs. Hillyard, did give her a tough match, 6-8, 6-1, 6-4, in the 1893 final. She also won the Irish title in 1887, was exceptional at ice skating, archery (an Olympic silver medalist in 1908), field hockey and golf. She represented Britain in international hockey in 1889 and 1890 and won the British Ladies Golf Championship in 1904 at Troon, defeating May Hezlet in the final, 1-up. She won 10 of 12 matches at Wimbledon. Born Sept. 24, 1871, in Lower Bebington, England, she died June 27, 1960, in Sway, England. She entered the Hall of Fame in 1983.

MAJOR TITLES *(5)–Wimbledon singles, 1887, 1888, 1891, 1892, 1893.* **SINGLES RECORD IN THE MAJORS**–*Wimbledon (10-2).*

JOHNNY DOEG
United States (1908–1978)
Hall of Fame 1962

As the fourth left-handed U.S. champ (following Bob Wrenn, Beals Wright, Lindley Murray), sixth-seeded John Thomas Godfray Hope Doeg hit the title jackpot in 1930. As a collateral exploit, he exploded 28 aces in the semis to thwart top-seeded Bill Tilden's fervent bid for a record eighth title, 10-8, 6-3, 3-6, 12-10. That was

Big Bill's Forest Hills farewell. But there was more to Doeg's championship than that. His was a strenuous serve-and-volleying rush to the prize, a determination to keep pressure on foes with incessant in-your-face forays to the net. Quite different from his baselining Aunt May (Sutton), who'd won the women's title 26 years before.

But at 6-foot-1, 170 pounds, 21-year-old blond Doeg could keep the pounding going. He lost seven sets in six matches, two to ex-Harvard football All-American Barry Wood at the outset, and two more in the quarters to Frank Hunter, 11-13, 6-4, 3-6, 6-2, 6-4. He got past the last-hurrahing 37-year-old Tilden, the Wimbledon champ (Doeg had lost there in the semis to Wilmer Allison), and was fiercely opposed by eleventh-seeded 19-year-old Frank Shields. Refusing to bend in the record-length closing set of a major singles final, Doeg won, 10-8, 1-6, 6-4, 16-14. An ace cancelled Shields' set point at 13-14. The title won him the No. 1 U.S. ranking, No. 4 in the world, up from No. 7 in 1929. His brilliant serving, speed and spin, made him a feared foe for five years as he ranked in the U.S. Top Ten between 1927 and 1931.

Doeg and George Lott were Wimbledon doubles finalists in 1930 and won the U.S. titles of 1929 and 1930. He was the U.S. junior champ in 1926, the first of eight males to make the transition from the 18s to the adult championship. Johnny was born in Guayamas, Sonora, Mexico, Dec. 7, 1908, and grew up in California. He was a son of a Southern California champ, the former Violet Sutton.

He entered the Hall of Fame in 1962 and died April 27, 1978, in Redding, Calif.

MAJOR TITLES (3)–*U.S. singles, 1930; U.S. doubles, 1929, 1930.* **DAVIS CUP**–*1930; record: 1-0 in singles.* **SINGLES RECORD IN THE MAJORS**–*Wimbledon (5-1), U.S. (19-5).*

LAURIE DOHERTY

Great Britain (1875–1919)
Hall of Fame 1980

Laurie, or 'Little Do,' born Hugh Laurence Doherty, was the shorter, at 5-foot-10, younger, and probably better, of the Cambridge (Trinity College)-educated Doherty brothers who illuminated the tennis skies in their native England and at Wimbledon at the turn of the century. Although Laurie lost the 1898 Wimbledon final to Reggie, 6-1, in the fifth, he won the title five straight times, beginning in 1902.

The brothers carried Britain to its first four Davis Cups, beginning in 1903, by taking it from the U.S., 4-1, in Boston after falling short, 3-2, the previous year in Brooklyn. He never lost a Cup match, winning seven singles and five doubles.

The Dohertys, who parted their dark wavy hair in the middle, also devised the more aggressive doubles formation of parting the pair, with the receiver's partner at the net, to be joined by the receiver.

As the first serious foreign contenders for the U.S. singles crown, the brothers failed in 1902 at Newport. Laurie sportingly defaulted to Reggie rather than face him in the semis, whereupon Reggie beat Malcolm Whitman in the all-comers final, 6-1, 3-6, 6-3, 6-0, but lost the challenge round to the defender, Bill Larned, 4-6, 6-2, 6-4, 8-6.

But in 1903, after Reggie returned the default courtesy to his brother in the quarters, Laurie became the initial alien male champ of the U.S., beating Bill Clothier in the all-comers, 6-3, 6-2, 6-3, and unseating Larned, 6-0, 6-3, 10-8. The Brothers D took the U.S. doubles both years, and had been gold medalists in the 1900 Olympics, winning the doubles, and Laurie taking the singles as well. Laurie was born in London, Oct. 8, 1875, and died Aug. 21, 1919, in Broadstairs, England. He accompanied his brother into the Hall of Fame in 1980.

MAJOR TITLES (16)–*Wimbledon singles, 1902, 1903, 1904, 1905, 1906; U.S. singles, 1903; Wimbledon doubles, 1897, 1898, 1899, 1900, 1901, 1903, 1904, 1905; U.S. doubles, 1902, 1903.* **DAVIS CUP**–*1902, 1903, 1904, 1905, 1906; record: 7-0 in singles, 5-0 in doubles.* **SINGLES RECORD IN THE MAJORS**–*Wimbledon (21-6), U.S. (12-0).*

REGGIE DOHERTY

Great Britain (1872–1910)
Hall of Fame 1980

The appealing and dominant Doherty brothers, Reggie and Laurie, Cambridge (Trinity College) men, enhanced the popularity of tennis and Wimbledon in their homeland, England, at the turn of the century, and were the backbone of Britain's first four Davis Cup triumphs, 1903-06. Reginald Frank Doherty, the older and known as 'Big Do,' at 6-foot-1, only 140 pounds, was frequently ill with digestive problems, and wasn't considered as good as Laurie, but did win four straight Wimbledons (1897-1900), beating his sibling in the 1898 final, 6-1 in the fifth.

Contesting a record 10 straight doubles finals together (1897-1906), they won a record eight, losing only in 1896 to the Baddeley brothers, Herbert and

Wilfred, and in 1902 and 1906 to Syd Smith and Frank Riseley. Reggie, who played the left court with his brother, was in 11 straight, losing with Harold Nesbit in 1897. They won all five Davis Cup doubles together, clinching the 1904, 1905 and 1906 Cups. Reggie was born Oct. 14, 1872, in London and died Dec. 29, 1910. They entered the Hall of Fame together in 1980.

MAJOR TITLES (14)–*Wimbledon singles, 1897, 1898, 1899, 1900; U.S. doubles, 1902, 1903; Wimbledon doubles, 1897, 1898, 1899, 1900, 1901, 1903, 1904, 1905.* DAVIS CUP–*1902, 1903, 1904, 1905, 1906; record: 2-1 in singles, 5-0 in doubles.* SINGLES RECORD IN THE MAJORS–*Wimbledon (9-5), U.S. (7-1).*

JAROSLAV DROBNY

Czechoslovakia/Egypt/Great Britain (1921–2001)
Hall of Fame 1983

Nobody at Wimbledon paid any attention to a 16-year-old left-hander from Czechoslovakia who lost a lively first-rounder to an Argentine, Alejo Russell, 10-8, 6-4, 7-9, 6-3. His country was in the news, threatened by the Nazi dictator, Adolf Hitler. It was 1938, war was imminent. Jaroslav Drobny would get one more crack at the Big W, winning a couple of rounds in 1939, briefly noticed because he played two tough sets against top-seeded Bunny Austin before defaulting with an arm injury. Then he vanished into the cloud of World War II in his conquered homeland, wondering if he would ever play a big tournament again.

"We were just trying to stay alive. The torch of freedom with the Allies gave us hope," he said. Luckily he avoided deportation to Germany as a forced laborer, and was able to play hockey throughout the war, his best sport then. "Food was short, but we got along."

But he did take up tennis seriously again, seven years later, fashioning a magnificent 15-year amateur career that contained, despite so much time lost to the war, an amazing 133 singles titles—from Algeria to Knokke-le-Zoute—and membership in the world Top Ten for 10 successive years from 1946, No. 1 in 1954, No. 2 in 1952, No. 3 in 1946, 51. In 1946 Drobny returned to Wimbledon for the postwar reopening. Rusty from little play during the war, expecting nothing from himself, he beat the world's best, Jack Kramer, 2-6, 17-15, 6-3, 3-6, 6-3, in the fourth round, got to the semis and was hailed as a national hero at home, suddenly a name in the game in which he would become an all-timer.

At the time he was a remarkable two-sport world-class athlete: Hockey in winter, tennis the rest of the time. So good was Drob as a forward on the ice that he

played a leading role in Czechoslovakia's winning the world amateur championship in 1947 (he scored three goals in the final game against the U.S.), and gaining silver at the 1948 Olympics. By 1949, though, tennis had become his life. It was the year Drobny made the decision to leave his homeland that had become a police-state Communist satellite in 1948, defecting with Davis Cup teammate Vladimir Cernik during a Swiss tournament at Gstaad. Twice the two of them had carried their country to the cup semis, losses to Australia in 1947 and 1948. Drob won one of the exceptional matches in the latter, beating (fellow Hall of Famer-to-be) Adrian Quist on grass in Boston from match point down, 6-8, 3-6, 18-16, 6-3, 7-5.

A hockey injury gravely affected his eyesight, and he wore prescription dark glasses on court for the remainder of a long tennis career that included 17 Wimbledons, where his deft touch and agreeable nature made him a great favorite.

Drobny was born Oct. 12, 1921, in Prague and resided there until 1949, son of the groundskeeper at Prague's premier tennis on the island of Stvanice. "It was fortunate for me," he said, "because we lived at the club and I grew up in the game, ballboying, watching good players, starting out myself at age five. And we flooded the courts in winter to play hockey." During the war he won the championship of the Nazi-occupied protectorate of Bohemia and Moravia, 1940-44, then the Czechoslovak title five straight times, 1945-49 before defecting. He solidified his 1946 Wimbledon reputation by reaching the final of the first postwar French (played after Wimbledon that year), losing to Marcel Bernard in five sets.

Paris was a happy hunting ground for portly Drob, a clever court manager and user of a full arsenal of varied speeds, spins, angles, lobs and drop shots. Good stuff on continental clay, but his fast and sliced serve and penetrating volleys made him a menace on fast courts as well. Five times he graced the French final, losing again in 1948 to Frank Parker and in 1950 to Budge Patty before crashing the winner's circle resoundingly. He beat Eric Sturgess in 1951 and, in 1952, disarmed the world No. 1, Frank Sedgman, 6-2, 6-0, 3-6, 6-4. Rome, too, was his territory as he won the Italian over Bill Talbert in 1950, Gianni Cucelli in 1951 and Lew Hoad in 1953, losing the 1952 final to Sedgman.

Though Drob, 32, was written off by 1954, 11 was his lucky number. Seeded eleventh, on his eleventh try, he came through, beating Patty in a semi, and outmaneuvering a 19-year-old named Ken Rosewall for the title he most wanted, 13-11, 4-6, 6-2, 9-7, in 2 hours, 37 minutes, the longest final at that time. Drob was the Big W's remotest-chance success at that time, although nonseeds Boris Becker (1985), Richard Krajicek (1996), Goran Ivanisevic (2001), eleventh-seed Pat Cash (1987) and twelfth-seed Andre Agassi (1992) were to join his long-shot club. He was dethroned by the next champ, Tony Trabert, in the 1955 quarters. Traveling on Egyptian papers then, he became a British citizen in 1959, and lived in London with his wife, the former Rita Anderson, one-time English player. Drobny was tapped for the Hall of Fame in 1983, and died Sept. 13, 2001.

MAJOR TITLES *(5)–French singles, 1951, 1952; Wimbledon singles 1954; French doubles, 1948, French mixed, 1948.* **DAVIS CUP**–*1946, 1947, 1948, 1949; record: 24-4 in singles, 13-2 in doubles.* **SINGLES RECORD IN THE MAJORS**–*Australian (0-1), French (47-13), Wimbledon (50-16), U.S. (15-5).*

JAMES DWIGHT

United States (1852–1917)
Hall of Fame 1955

Hailed deservedly as the 'Father of American Tennis,' Doc Dwight, a Bostonian and graduate of Harvard and Harvard Medical, may have introduced the game to the U.S., playing with his cousin, Fred Sears, at Nahant, Mass., in 1874. It arrived from England at several locations that year. He did organize and win the initial 1876 tournament, a sociable competition at Nahant.

More importantly he was a driving force behind the organization of the USTA (then the U.S. National Lawn Tennis Association) in 1881, and its first National Championship that year at the Newport Casino, as well as the first Davis Cup match (1900) between the U.S. and the British Isles at his Boston club, Longwood Cricket Club.

As a player, right-handed and short (about 5-foot-5), he was more adept at doubles, sharing five U.S. titles with his protégé, Dick Sears, who defeated him in the 1883 singles final. He was No. 2 in 1885 and 1886, the first years of U.S. rankings, and No. 3 in 1888. He, Sears and A. L. Rives were the American pioneers at Wimbledon in 1884, Dwight the only one to win a round. He beat F. J. Ridgeway, 6-2, 6-1, 6-1, the first U.S. victory, a small one at the Big W. Doc fought gamely against ambidextrous Herbert Chipp, who had removed Rives, but fell to nothing but forehands, 6-1,

2-6, 6-3, 2-6, 7-5. Though Dwight and Sears reached the doubles semis, the U.S. champs were no match for the dynamic, ruling Renshaw twins, Willie and Ernest, 6-0, 6-1, 6-2. Dwight returned the following year, making greater strides, to the semis where future champ Herbert Lawford topspun him out, 6-2, 6-2, 6-3.

Shepherding the USTA through its formative years, he was president 21 years, 1882-84 and 1894-1911. He entered the Hall of Fame in 1955. Born in Paris July 14, 1852, he died July 13, 1917 in Mattapoisett, Mass. His son, Dr. Richard Dwight, a retired Paris physician, continued to compete, in super-senior events for the over-85s until his death.

MAJOR TITLES *(5)–U.S. doubles, 1882, 1883, 1884, 1886, 1887.* **SINGLES RECORD IN THE MAJORS**–*Wimbledon (4-2), U.S. (8-3).*

STEFAN EDBERG

Sweden (1966–)

A stylistic misfit among the Swedish legion that rose in Bjorn Borg's sneakersteps and image, Stefan Edberg has ever been an extraordinarily graceful attacker. A serve-and-volleyer, he has done superbly with only one hand propelling his backhand.

Clay, on which he was reared, hasn't been his favorite surface, although he nearly beat Michael Chang in a five-set French final in 1989.

A splendid junior career led to great expectations, which he fulfilled with six major singles—two each, Australian (1985, '87), Wimbledon (1988, '90), U.S. (1991, '92). In 1983 he became the lone achiever of a junior Grand Slam, winning the Australian, French, Wimbledon and U.S. 18-and-under singles.

Making his Davis Cup bow in 1984, at 18, he was the youngest to play for a Cup winner (until Chang, a slightly younger 18 in 1990). Edberg performed a consequential one-day role in Sweden's startling upending of the U.S. in the final at Goteborg. He and Anders Jarryd clinched the 4-1 victory by stunning Peter Fleming and John McEnroe, unbeaten in 14 previous Cup starts, 7-5, 5-7, 6-2, 7-5. In successfully defending the Cup the following year in Munich, a 3-2 victory over Germany, Edberg won it at the wire, a thrilling, rebounding fifth-match decision over Michael Westphal. Though he didn't play in the 1987 final, he had an earlier hand in winning that Cup.

A brilliant end-of-the-line backhand seized victory from Aleksandr Volkov at match point down in the fifth set as the 1994 Cup final began in Moscow. Turning that upside down for a 6-4, 6-2, 6-7 (2-7), 0-6, 8-6 win, Stefan set the tone in a 4-1 triumph, Sweden's fifth Cup. Having slipped below the standard he set for himself, he announced that the 1996 season would be his valedictory. Stefan had a good year, beating Chang at the French, playing all four to stretch his participation record to 54 straight major championship appearances at the U.S. Open, where he knocked off Wimbledon champ Richard Krajicek and made the quarters (a 25th time at that stage).

Edberg, a slim 6-foot-2 blond right hander, was born in the seaside town of Vastervik, Sweden, Jan. 19, 1966, and was reared there. He lives in London with his Swedish wife, Annette. He had a hammering serve, as well as a difficult kicker and a raking backhand, and he is one of the finest of all volleyers. His groundstrokes improved continuously throughout his career. Outwardly unemotional, he dispelled doubts about his competitiveness by winning Wimbledon in 1988. He charged from two sets down to beat Miloslav Mecir in the semis, 4-6, 2-6, 6-4, 6-3, 6-4, and a set down to overcome favored Boris Becker, 4-6, 7-6 (7-2), 6-4, 6-2, for the title.

His rivalry with Becker was a highlight of the '80s and '90s. At the close his career, Becker was in the lead, 25-10.

Beating the 1983-84 champ, countryman Mats Wilander, in the final, 6-4, 6-4, 6-3, Stefan took the Australian in 1985, his first major. He repeated two years later, the last man to win it on grass, 6-3, 6-4, 3-6, 5-7, 6-3 over Pat Cash.

Flushing Meadow was almost the mystery to him that it had been for Borg (no titles in 10 tries). But on his ninth, Edberg came through for the U.S. crown in one of the most devastating final round performances, 6-2, 6-4, 6-0, over Jim Courier, holding serve throughout. Edberg, a first-round loser the year before (to Volkov) was the second in the tournament's history to spring from such ignominy to the title. Mal Anderson did so in 1957. Edberg refused to relinquish the title, beating Pete Sampras in the 1992 final. In the semis he overcame Chang, 6-7 (3-7), 7-5, 7-6 (7-3), 5-7, 6-4, the longest-lasting major match—5 hours, 26 minutes. Edberg's last major final (his tenth) was the Australian of 1993, when he lost to Courier. During 14 professional seasons he was in the World Top Ten 10 times, including No. 1 in 1990 and '91, also: No. 5, 1985-86, 88, 93; No. 2, 1987, 92;

No. 3, 1989; No. 7, 1994.

Edberg represented Sweden in the 1988 and 1992 Olympics, winning a bronze in singles in the former.

Fittingly, he closed his career in Sweden in the 1996 Davis Cup final against France, to the cheering of countrymen at Malmo. However, he went out in defeat, slowed by ankle injury while losing to Cedric Pioline and couldn't play the third day of the 3-2 loss. Stefan's career achievements: Won 41 singles, 18 doubles pro titles and $20,630,941 in prize money. He had an 806-270 (.749) singles mark.

MAJOR TITLES (8)–*Australian singles, 1985, 1987; Wimbledon singles, 1988, 1990; U.S. singles, 1991, 1992, Australian doubles, 1987; U.S. doubles, 1987.* **DAVIS CUP**–*1984, 1985, 1986, 1987, 1988, 1989, 1990, 1991, 1992, 1993, 1994, 1995, 1996; record: 34-14 in singles, 12-8 in doubles, 6 finals, 4 Cups.* **SINGLES RECORD IN THE MAJORS**–*Australian (56-11), French (30-13), Wimbledon (49-12), U.S. (39-11).*

ROY EMERSON
Australia (1936–)
Hall of Fame 1982

In the grand days for Australia of domination of the tennis world, nobody played as large a role as the country boy out of tiny Blackbutt in Queensland, Roy Stanley 'Emmo' Emerson.

Emerson, a slim, quick, athletic farm kid who strengthened his wrists for tennis by milking innumerable cows on his father's property, played on eight winning Davis Cup teams between 1959 and 1967, a record. He won 28 of the major singles and doubles championships, a lofty male record. His dozen singles were six Australian (1961, '63-'64-'65-'66-'67), two each French, (1963, '67), Wimbledon (1964-65), U.S. (1961, '64). That was a record, created over seven years that he held for 33 years, without knowing it until writers noticed that he was being stalked by Pete Sampras. Sampras broke it with a thirteenth, Wimbledon 2000, and was congratulated by Emerson, who had eclipsed Bill Tilden's standard of 10 (set between 1920 and 1930), unaware, at winning his last Australian in 1967, that he was the new record holder. "Nobody paid attention to that sort of thing then, or kept track," he laughs. "We just played."

His accomplishments as a right-court doubles player who could make anybody look good amounted to 16 Big Four titles (6 French, 4 U.S., 3 each Wimbledon, Australian) with five different partners, the last in 1971 at Wimbledon with his old Queensland pal, Rod Laver.

His best-known alliance was with Aussie left-hander Neale Fraser, with whom he won Wimbledon in 1959 and 1961, the U.S. title in 1959-60 and the doubles of the Davis Cup triumphs of 1959-60-61.

Known as 'Emmo' to his wide circle of friends, he was a rollicking, gregarious six-foot right-hander with patent leather black hair and a golden smile (enhanced by dental fillings) who could lead the partying and singing without jeopardizing his high standards of play. Fitness was his hallmark. He trained hard and was always ready for strenuous matches and tournaments. Although primarily a serve-and-volleyer, he could adapt to the rigors of slow courts. He won the French singles in 1963 over Pierre Darmon and 1967, by lifting the crown from the head of teammate Tony Roche. He also led the 3-2 Davis Cup victory over the U.S. on clay in Cleveland in 1964. That year he was unbeaten in eight Davis Cup singles as the Aussies regained the Cup. Emmo had a singles winning streak of 55 matches, during that summer and autumn, second longest in male history to Don Budge's 92 (1937-38). Establishing himself as World No. 1, he won 17 tournaments and 109 of 115 matches. The only prize to elude him in that majestic year of triumphs in three of the majors was a Grand Slam.

Fate may have intervened to cost him a third straight Wimbledon in 1966 when he was heavily favored. Winning a 4th rounder against Owen Davidson, he skidded chasing a short ball, crashed into the umpire's stand, damaging a shoulder, and was unable to do much but finish the match. His Australian hegemony began in 1961 when he beat Laver for the title, 1-6, 6-3, 7-5, 6-4. Laver took it back the following year as part of his Grand Slam, but after that for five years it was all-Emmo, for an Aussie male record six singles titles, the toughest reversing himself from two sets down to overcome Fred Stolle in the 1965 final. He beat Arthur Ashe in the last two in 1966 and in 1967. His Wimbledon wins were both over Stolle, in 1964 and in 1965. He beat Stolle again in the U.S. final of 1964.

Ever high spirited and capable of firing up his teammates, Emerson also took part in two Australian victories in the World Cup, a since disbanded annual competition against the U.S. He exemplified the Aussie code of sportsmanship and competitiveness, stating it as, "You should never complain about an injury. We believe that if you play, then you aren't injured, and that's that."

Emerson was born Nov. 3, 1936, in Blackbutt, a crossroads where people make a living in cattle and timber (the blackbutt is a variety of eucalyptus). His family moved to Brisbane, where he could get better competition and coaching, when his tennis talent became evident.

After resisting several offers, he turned pro in 1968 just before open tennis began, and was still competing in 1978 as player-coach of the Boston Lobsters in World Team Tennis, directing them to the semi-finals of the league playoffs. Of all Australia's Davis Cup luminaries under Capt. Harry Hopman, Emerson made the best record, vital in winning eight Cups, high for any participant, playing the decisive match in either singles or doubles six times. He won 21 of 23 singles, but never lost when it counted, and 13 of 15 doubles.

Beginning in 1959, he was in the World Top Ten 9 straight times, No. 1 in 1964-65. Also: No. 7, 1959; No. 6, 1960; No. 2, 1961-62, '67; No. 3, 1964, '66.

Emerson was elevated to the Hall of Fame in 1982 after a career that bridged the amateur and open eras and was credited with three pro titles in singles and 30 in doubles, and $400,000 in prize money. Overall, amateur and pro, he was one of the few centurions with 106 singles titles. His son, Antony, was All-American in tennis at the University of Southern California and played the pro tour briefly. They won the U.S. Hard Court Father-and-Son title in 1978.

MAJOR TITLES (28)–*Australian singles, 1961, 1963, 1964, 1965, 1966, 1967; French singles, 1963, 1967; Wimbledon singles, 1964, 1965; U.S. singles, 1961, 1964; Australian doubles, 1962, 1966, 1969; French doubles, 1960, 1961, 1962, 1963, 1964, 1965; Wimbledon doubles, 1959, 1961, 1971; U.S. doubles, 1959, 1960, 1965, 1966.* **DAVIS CUP**–*1959, 1960, 1961, 1962, 1963, 1964, 1965, 1966, 1967; record: 21-2 in singles, 13-2 in doubles.* **SINGLES RECORD IN THE MAJORS**–*Australian (47-8), French (43-10), Wimbledon (60-14), U.S. (59-14).*

CHRIS EVERT
United States (1954–)
Hall of Fame 1995

In 1970, at a small, insignificant tournament in North Carolina, 15-year-old Christine Marie Evert gave notice to the world that a dynamo was on the way up. Chrissie defeated Margaret Court, 7-6, 7-6, who had recently completed her singles Grand Slam and was the No. 1 player of the world.

A year later in the U.S. Open at Forest Hills, Evert reconfirmed by marching resolutely to the semi-finals, at 16 years, eight months, 20 days, the youngest at that time to reach that stage. Before losing to Billie Jean

King, 6-3, 6-2, the eventual champion, schoolgirl Evert bowled over a succession of seasoned pros, mostly in come-from-behind thrillers that raised tears on the defeated older players and cheers in the Forest Hills stadium that Chrissie filled day after day. They went down in a row: Edna Buding, Mary Ann Eisel, fifth-seeded Françoise Durr and Lesley Hunt. Against Eisel, the No. 4 American, Evert wowed the first national TV audience to behold her by stonewalling when Eisel served for the match at 6-5, 40-0. Undaunted, the kid made six match points melt with bold shotmaking.

Although essentially a slow-court baseline specialist, raised on clay in Fort Lauderdale, Fla., where she was born Dec. 21, 1954, right-handed Evert showed that booming groundstrokes could succeed on the fast Forest Hills, Wimbledon and Australian grass. She was the Little Ice Maiden, a pony-tailed kid, deadpan, with metronomic strokes that seldom missed. Her two-handed backhand, a powerful drive, stimulated a generation of newcomers to copy her, even though her father, teaching pro Jimmy Evert, advised against it. "I didn't teach the two-hander to her," said her father, who had won the Canadian singles in 1947. "She started that way because she was too small and weak to swing the backhand with one hand. I hoped she'd change—but how can I argue with this success?"

It was such a success that by the time she completed a 20-year career in 1989 she had won $8,896,195 in prize money and a record 157 pro singles titles on a 1,309-146 won-lost record. That's an .8996 winning average, highest in pro history.

Martina Navratilova would overtake her in singles titles in 1992. Evert also was runner-up for 72 singles titles, which meant she made it to 76 percent of the finals of 303 tournaments entered.

After turning pro in 1973, she was the first to reach $1 million in career prize money, in 1976.

Her major singles titles numbered 21—six behind Margaret Court, three behind Steffi Graf, one behind Helen Wills Moody, tied with Navratilova. Chris won at least one major singles for 13 consecutive years, a record. She started in Paris in 1974, beating Olga Morozova for the title, and ended in 1986 at the French where she was the all-time champ with seven championships on a 72-6 match record. Her other singles majors: Australian, 1982, 84; Wimbledon, 1974, 76, 81; U.S., 1975-76-77-78, 80, 82. Her last final, age 34, was the Australian, 1988, a stiffly resisting 6-1, 7-6 (7-3) defeat by 18-year-

old Steffi Graf, launching the German's Grand Slam. Chris almost tied a longevity record of Helen Wills Moody, 16 years between major final appearances (1922-38). Her span was 15, but she was playing year after year while Moody was sporadic. Evert, while still an amateur, won the first pro tournament she entered, St. Petersburg, Fla., in 1971.

By winning the U.S. title a fourth consecutive time in 1978 she was the first to do so since Helen Jacobs' run of 1932-35. Between 1973 and 1979 she won 125 consecutive matches on clay, including 24 tournaments. The streak came to an end in the semi-finals of the Italian Open in Rome when she lost, 6-4, 2-6, 7-6 (7-4), to Tracy Austin.

Her introduction to Evonne Goolagong was the 1972 Wimbledon semi-final, an exciting three-set struggle won by Goolagong, 4-6, 6-3, 6-4, the defending champion. That was the start of one of the two most compelling female rivalries of the open era, one in which Evert held a 21-12 edge. The other, perhaps the most renowned in the game's history, was Chris' friendly feud with Martina Navratilova. From 1973 through 1988 it stretched, 80 matches. Evert won the first meeting in Akron, Ohio, 7-6 (5-4), 6-3, and took a big early lead, but Navratilova overtook her, and came out ahead, 43-37, winning nine of 13 of their major final engagements.

During the open era, the Virginia Slims circuit and its championship became prominent in women's tennis. Evert won the first of her four Slims championships in 1972 at 17. In choosing to preserve her amateur status until her 18th birthday that year, she disdained more than $50,000 in prize money, including the $25,000 Slims award for beating Kerry Reid, 7-5, 6-4.

Once she entered tennis for a living, she was a thorough exemplary professional in her relations with colleagues, press and public, and perennially a hard but sporting competitor. Fairly soon she lost her status as the darling little girl. Her style was based on flawless barrages from the backcourt, and her constant winning seemed monotonous to many. Nevertheless she was a smart player, able to maneuver a foe cleverly, scoring decisively with a well-disguised drop shot. She was also a better volleyer than given credit for, after overcoming an early distaste for the net. "I realize that a lot of fans think my game is boring, and they want to see me lose, or at least for somebody to give me a good fight all the time. But this is the game I played to win," she said. "Losing hurts me. I was always determined to be the best."

A lithe 5-foot-6, 125 pounds, she was in the World Top Ten 19 years, including five times No. 1 (1975-76-77, '80-'81) and seven times No. 2 (1978-79, '82-'83-'84-'85-'86). A paragon of consistency, she entered 57 of the major tourneys, won 18, and was at least a semifinalist 53 times.

As one of five tennis-playing Evert children, she was clearly the star, but her sister, Jeanne, three years younger, was also a pro.

In 1974 Jeanne ranked No. 9 in the U.S. and they were the first sisters to be ranked in the Top Ten since Florence (No. 3) and Ethel Sutton (No. 2) in 1913. Chris and Jeanne were teammates on the victorious U.S. Wightman Cup team of 1973, the only sisters to play together in the series against Britain.

Her final-round surges past Goolagong for a first U.S. Open crown in 1975 and to the Wimbledon title of 1976 are well remembered. But her most satisfying victories were probably the last majors, the French final upsets of Navratilova in 1985 and, at age 33, in 1986.

Her farewell to Flushing Meadow was the defeat by Zina Garrison, leaving her with a record 101 match wins in that event. She closed her career by winning all five singles matches as the U.S. won the Federation Cup in 1989. It was her ninth year and eighth Cup-winning team. She was undefeated in Wightman Cup singles (26-0), helping the U.S. win 11 Cups in the 13 years she played, captaining the team 1980-82, '85-'86.

Evert was the first player to win more than 1,000 singles matches as well as 150 tournaments, the only one other than Court and King to win more than 100 matches in a season, which she did during a mammoth 1974 when she won 16 of 24 tournaments on a 103-7 record. Her 55-match winning streak in 1974 (ended at the U.S. Open by Goolagong) was an open-era record until eclipsed by Navratilova's 74 in 1984. She also had streaks of 34 wins in a row in 1978, and 31 in 1979. Chris was on the 1988 Olympic team, but didn't medal, beaten by Italian Raffaela Reggi.

Three seasons of World Team Tennis included 1976-77 with Phoenix and 1978 with champion Los Angeles. Her eight-year marriage to English player John Lloyd ended in divorce. She then married ex-Olympic skier Andy Mill, with whom she has three sons.

MAJOR TITLES (21)–*Australian singles, 1982, 1984; French singles, 1974, 1975, 1979, 1980, 1983, 1985, 1986; Wimbledon singles, 1974, 1976, 1981; U.S. singles, 1975, 1976, 1977, 1978, 1980, 1982; French doubles, 1974, 1975; Wimbledon doubles, 1976.* **OTHER U.S.**

TITLES (6)–*Clay Court singles, 1972, 1973, 1974, 1975, 1979, 1980.* **FEDERATION CUP**–*1977, 1978, 1979, 1980, 1981, 1982, 1986, 1987, 1989; record: 40-2 in singles, 17-2 in doubles.* **WIGHTMAN CUP (As player)**–*1971, 1972, 1973, 1975, 1976, 1977, 1978, 1979, 1980, 1981, 1982, 1984, 1985; record: 26-0 in singles, 8-4 in doubles;* **(As captain)**–*1980, 1981, 1982, 1985, 1986; record: 5-0, 5 Cups.* **SINGLES RECORD IN THE MAJORS**–*Australian (30-4), French (72-6), Wimbledon (96-15), U.S. (101-12).*

BOB FALKENBURG

United States/Brazil (1926–)
Hall of Fame 1974

A gangling, dark-haired 6-foot-3 right-hander, Robert Falkenburg came from a tennis family. He and brother Tom won the U.S. Interscholastic title for Los Angeles Fairfax High in 1942, the same year Bob won the singles. Both played in the U.S. Championships at Forest Hills, as did sister Jinx. But Bob, seventh-seeded, made the family's name with a sensational Wimbledon triumph in 1948, eluding three match points while defeating second-seeded John Bromwich, 7-5, 0-6, 6-2, 3-6, 7-5. Bromwich served at 5-3, 40-15 and advantage. Falkenburg responded boldly with backhand passing returns. The last appeared futile. Brom made no attempt to play it, and the crowd gasped as the ball unexpectedly landed just inside the baseline.

He and Jack Kramer won the doubles the year before, and in 1944, at 18, he won the U.S. doubles with Don McNeill, one few teenagers to hold that title.

A slam-bang, big-serving net-charger, he attended the University of Southern California, winning the U.S. Intercollegiate title in 1946. He was an early success, his career short. He won the U.S. junior title in 1942 and 1943, the second year while in the U.S. Army Air Force. He was one of the youngest to make his entry into the U.S. Top Ten, 17 in 1943 at No. 7. He was there four more times through 1948, No. 5 the last year. He was No. 7 in the world rankings that year.

A semi-finalist at the U.S. Championships in 1946 and a quarter-finalist in 1947, he lost both times to the champ, Kramer. He was also a quarter-finalist in 1948.

Bromwich had his revenge as Falkenburg defended the Wimbledon title in 1949, taking their quarter-final, 3-6, 9-11, 6-0, 6-0, 6-4. Falkenburg did not endear himself to customers by his practice of tanking sets and sprawling on the court to rest.

Marrying a Brazilian and becoming a resident, Bob played Davis Cup for Brazil. He was born Jan. 29, 1926, in Brooklyn, N.Y., and entered the Hall of Fame in 1974.

MAJOR TITLES *(3)–Wimbledon singles, 1948; Wimbledon doubles, 1947; U.S. doubles, 1944.* **OTHER U.S. TITLE**–*Indoor doubles, 1947, with Jack Kramer.* **DAVIS CUP**–*Brazil 1954, 1955; record: 2-4 in singles, 1-3 in doubles.* **SINGLES RECORD IN THE MAJORS**–*Wimbledon (17-3), U.S. (18-8).*

NEALE FRASER

Australia (1933–)
Hall of Fame 1984

A serve-bombing lefty whose onerous delivery was flat, sliced and kicked, Neale Fraser backed it up with tough volleying and was a marvelous competitor. Solidly built and athletic at 6-foot-1, he was especially overpowering on fast surfaces. Although he won Wimbledon in 1960 and the U.S. title in 1959 and 1960, Fraser found team play—doubles and Davis Cup—nearest his heart. As one of eight men to win all four majors in doubles, Fraser took three each Australian, French and U.S. and two Wimbledon with three different partners: Ashley Cooper, Lew Hoad, Roy Emerson.

His toughest match of the 1960 Wimbledon championship was won literally over the dead-weary body of Butch Buchholz. But before the frustrated American keeled over with cramps in their quarter-final, Fraser had to dodge five match points in the 30-game fourth set. It ended with winner Fraser on the short end in games, 4-6, 6-3, 4-6, 15-15.

His most successful alliance was with Emerson for eight majors. Losing only one singles, he was a mainstay for four Cup-winning Australia sides, starting in 1959 at Forest Hills. Then he won both his singles, and, with Emerson, the doubles in heisting the punchbowl from the U.S., 3-2. On opening day he beat Wimbledon champ Alex Olmedo. In the decisive fifth match, he beat Barry MacKay, 8-6, 3-6, 6-2, 6-4, in a tense duel interrupted by rain and carried over to the following day.

His love for Davis Cup showed when he succeeded legendary Harry Hopman as non-playing captain in 1970, and held the job for a record 23 years, piloting four winners: 1973, 1977, 1983 and 1986, and a record 49 series victories. He lost the 1990 final to the U.S. He was No. 1 in the world in 1959 and 1960 and in the Top Ten every year between 1956 and 1962. Although he retired in 1963, he played a cameo at Wimbledon 10 years later as doubles finalist (to Jimmy Connors and Ilie Nastase) with John Cooper, younger brother of Ashley Cooper, with whom he'd won the U.S. doubles in 1957. A brother, Dr. John Fraser, a physician, was also a fine

doubles player, a Wimbledon semi-finalist with Rod Laver, as was Neale with Emerson in 1962. Neale was born Oct. 3, 1933, in Melbourne, where he lives, and entered the Hall of Fame in 1984.

MAJOR TITLES *(19)–Wimbledon singles, 1960; U.S. singles, 1959, 1960; Australian doubles, 1957, 1958, 1962; French doubles, 1958, 1960, 1962; Wimbledon doubles, 1959, 1961; U.S. doubles, 1957, 1959, 1960; Australian mixed, 1956; Wimbledon mixed, 1962; U.S. mixed, 1958, 1959, 1960.* **DAVIS CUP (As player)**–*1958, 1959, 1960, 1961, 1962, 1963; record: 11-1 in singles, 7-2 in doubles;* **(As captain)**–*197-92; record: 49-19; 4 Cups, 1973, 1977, 1983, 1986.* **SINGLES RECORD IN THE MAJORS**–*Australian (25-10), French (18-5), Wimbledon (38-13), U.S. (32-5).*

SHIRLEY FRY

United States (1927–)
Hall of Fame 1970

One of the elite 13 men and women to win each of the major championships in singles, Shirley June Fry Irvin is also one of only five to win them all in doubles as well. The French was the first to fall to her, in 1951, over her good friend and double partner, Doris Hart; the Australian the last, in 1957, over Althea Gibson. After that she retired to become Mrs. Karl Irvin and live in Hartford, Conn., and raise a family and teach the game.

In 1956 she won Wimbledon over Angela Buxton and—on the 16th and last try—the U.S., beating Shirley Bloomer in the semis, and Gibson for the title. A right-hander, born on June 30, 1927, and raised in Akron, Ohio, she was in 1941 the youngest ever to play in the U.S. Championships until slightly younger 14-year-olds Kathy Horvath (1979) and Mary Joe Fernandez (1985). In a less nervous era in America, her parents sent her to tournaments alone on buses.

As a 15-year-old in 1942, she became, unseeded, the Championships' youngest quarter-finalist. She lost the 1951 final to Maureen Connolly, 6-3, 1-6, 6-4—whom hardly anybody beat—but came through five years later, outsteadying Gibson. She had a solid groundstroking game, but showed her volleying skills in doubles alongside Hart. They were the only team to win four straight French (1950–53). They won three straight Wimbledons (1951-53) and four straight U.S. (1951-54).

In their hard-fought 1953 final-round U.S. victory in Boston, 6-2, 7-9, 9-7, despite two match points held by perennial champs, Louise Brough and Margaret Osborne duPont, Shirley and Doris terminated the Brough-duPont record streaks of nine straight titles

(1942–50) and 41 matches. Their own streak, until losing the 1955 final to Brough-duPont, was 20 matches.

Shirley, 5-foot-5, 125 pounds, ranked in the U.S. Top Ten 13 straight years (1944-56), No. 1 in 1956, and made the World Top Ten nine times between 1946 and 1956, No. 1 the last year. She played Wightman Cup for the U.S. six times, never on a loser, winning 10 of her 12 matches. She entered the Hall of Fame in 1970.

MAJOR TITLES *(17)–Australian singles, 1957; French singles, 1951; Wimbledon singles, 1956; U.S. singles, 1956; Australian doubles, 1957; French doubles, 1950, 1951, 1952, 1953; Wimbledon doubles, 1951, 1952, 1953; U.s. doubles, 1951, 1952, 1953, 1954. Wimbledon mixed, 1957.* **OTHER U.S. TITLES** *(4)–Clay Court singles, 1956; Clay Court doubles, 1946, with Mary Arnold Prentiss; 1950, with Doris Hart; 1956, with Dorothy Head Knode.* **WIGHTMAN CUP**–*1949, 1951, 1952, 1953, 1955, 1956; record: 4-2 in singles, 6-0 in doubles.* **SINGLES RECORD IN THE MAJORS**–*Australian (5-0), French (23-4), Wimbledon (34-7), U.S. (38-14).*

CHUCK GARLAND

United States (1898–1971)
Hall of Fame 1969

A Yale man who won the U.S. Intercollegiate doubles in 1919, Charles Stedman Garland joined a Harvardian, Dick Williams, the following year to beat Algernon Kingscote and James Parke, 4-6, 6-4, 7-5, 6-2, and become the first Americans to win the doubles at Wimbledon.

Ranked three times in the U.S. Top Ten, 1918, 1919 and 1920 (No. 8 each time), he was selected for the Hall of Fame in 1969 as much for his service to the USTA as committeeman as player. One of his duties was captaining the 1927 Davis Cup team. Garland, a 5-foot-7-1/2 right-hander, was born Oct. 29, 1898, in Pittsburgh. He later lived in Baltimore and died there Jan. 28, 1971.

MAJOR TITLE *(1)–Wimbledon doubles, 1920.* **OTHER U.S. TITLES** *(4)–Intercollegiate singles, 1919; Intercollegiate doubles, 1919, with Ken Hawkes; Clay Court doubles, 1917, 1918, with Sam Hardy.* **SINGLES RECORD IN THE MAJORS**–*Wimbledon (12-3), U.S. (10-7).*

ALTHEA GIBSON

United States (1927–)
Hall of Fame 1971

No player overcame more obstacles to become a champion than Althea Gibson, the first black to win at Wimbledon and Forest Hills.

Her entry in the U.S. Championships of 1950 at Forest Hills was historic: The first appearance of an African American in that event. It took seven more years for Gibson to work her way to the championship there, in 1957. Tennis was pretty much a segregated sport in the U.S. until the American Tennis Association, the governing body for black tournaments, prevailed on the U.S. Tennis Association to permit the ATA female champion, Gibson, to enter Forest Hills. Two years earlier, in 1948, Dr. Reginald Weir, a New York physician, was the first black permitted in a USTA championship, playing in the U.S. Indoor event.

Three years after Jackie Robinson had integrated major league baseball, playing for the Brooklyn Dodgers, Althea's first appearance at Forest Hills was not only a notable occasion, it was nearly a moment of staggering triumph. Making her historic debut in a 6-2, 6-2, win over Barbara Knapp, she encountered in the second round third-seeded Louise Brough, the reigning Wimbledon champion, and came within one game of winning. Recovering from nerves, Althea led, 1-6, 6-3, 7-6, when providence intervened: A thunderstorm struck Forest Hills, curtailing the match until the following day, when Brough reaffirmed her eminence by winning three straight games.

During the violent storm, a bolt of lightning had toppled one of the concrete guardian eagles from the upper reaches of the stadium. "It may have been an omen that times were changing," Althea recalled.

Born Aug. 25, 1927, in Silver, S.C., Gibson, a right-hander, grew up in Harlem. Her family was poor, but she was fortunate in coming to the attention of Dr. Walter Johnson, a Lynchburg, Va., physician who was active in the black tennis community. He became her patron, as he would later be for Arthur Ashe. Through Dr. Johnson, Gibson received better instruction and competition, and contacts were set up with the USTA to inject her into the recognized tennis scene. Ex-champs Alice Marble and Sarah Palfrey Cooke were leading voices favoring Althea's inclusion, Marble writing a strong it's-about-time editorial in influential *American Lawn Tennis Magazine.*

Tall (5-foot-11), strong, and extremely athletic, she would have come to prominence earlier but for segregation. She was 23 when she first played at Forest Hills, 30 when she won her first of two successive U.S. Championships, in 1957, finally beating Brough. She repeated in 1958 over Darlene Hard. In her first U.S. final, she was beaten by Shirley Fry in 1956. During the two years she won Wimbledon, 1957 over Hard and 1958 over Angela Mortimer, she was World No. 1, No. 2

in 1956, and of course U.S. No. 1 as well, 1957-58.

She was never completely at ease in amateur tennis for she realized that, despite her success, she was still unwelcome at some clubs where important tournaments were played. A mark of general acceptance, however, was her 1957 selection to represent the U.S. on the Wightman Cup team against Britain. She played two years, 3-1 in singles, 2-2 in doubles.

Gibson was a big hitter with an awesome serve. She liked to attack, but developed consistency at the baseline eventually, and made her major breakthrough—the first for a black—by winning the French of 1956, overcoming the turgid clay of Roland Garros and the steady Englishwoman, Mortimer, 6-0, 12-10. That year she also tamed the clay of Il Foro Italico, winning the Italian over the stubborn Hungarian, Suzy Kormoczi.

Crossing the Channel, she allied herself with Englishwoman, Angela Buxton, to win the Wimbledon doubles over Aussies Fay Muller and Daphne Seeney and the Big W had its pioneering black champ.

In all, Gibson won 11 major titles in singles and doubles. After six years of trying at Forest Hills, she seemed ready to win in 1956, reaching the heavily publicized final, but appeared overanxious and lost to the more controlled and experienced Shirley Fry, the Wimbledon champ in her second U.S. title match. A year later Gibson was solidly in control, beating Darlene Hard to take Wimbledon, and would at last rule her own country at Brough's expense.

After winning the U.S. a second time in 1958, Althea turned pro. She played a series of head-to-head matches in 1960 against Floridian Karol Fageros, who had been ranked No. 8 in the U.S. Their tour was played in conjunction with the Harlem Globetrotters, the matches staged on basketball courts prior to Trotter games. Gibson won 114 of 118 matches. She said she earned over $100,000 in one year as her share of the gate, but there was no professional game in tennis for women then, and she turned to the pro golf tour for a few years. She showed an aptitude for that game, but was too late in starting.

Althea tried to play a few pro tennis events after open tennis began in 1968, but by then she was too old. She was married briefly to W. A. Darben, and worked as a tennis teaching pro after ceasing competition. She was inducted into the Hall of Fame in 1971.

MAJOR TITLES *(11)–French singles, 1956; Wimbledon singles, 1957, 1958; U.S. singles, 1957, 1958; Australian doubles, 1957; French*

doubles, 1956; Wimbledon doubles, 1956, 1957, 1958; U.S. mixed, 1957. **OTHER U.S. TITLES** *(2)–Clay Court singles, 1957; Clay Court doubles, 1957, with Darlene Hard.* **WIGHTMAN CUP**–*1957, 1958; record: 3-1 in singles, 2-0 in doubles.* **SINGLES RECORD IN THE MAJORS**–*Australian (4-1), French (6-0), Wimbledon (16-1), U.S. (27-7).*

KITTY GODFREE
Great Britain (1896–1992)
Hall of Fame 1978

Kathleen McKane Godfree, a sturdy, good-natured competitor, may have been the best female player Britain has produced. In winning Wimbledon for the first time in 1924, she charged back from 1-4 in the second set to hand Helen Wills her lone defeat in nine visits to the Big W, 4-6, 6-4, 6-4. She also beat Wills in the British Wightman Cup victory that year at Wimbledon. Who else could boast of royal-flushing 'Little Miss Poker Face' twice in a season?

Kitty won Wimbledon again two years later over Lili de Alvarez. Thus Kitty and Dorothy Round (1934, '37) were the only Brits to win twice since World War I. She was one of a select group to play more than 100 matches (146) at Wimbledon, 19th on the list: 38-11 in singles, 33-12 in doubles, 40-12 in mixed between 1919 and 1934.

In 1923 Kitty had reached her third Wimbledon final but lost to Suzanne Lenglen, 6-2, 6-2. In the U.S. Championships that year, Kitty offered a dangerous quarter-final challenge to Wills, coming from 2-5 to 5-all in the third set before losing, 2-6, 6-2, 7-5. In 1925 she pushed Wills in the final of the U.S. Championships, losing 3-6, 6-0, 6-2, after eliminating Molla Mallory and Elizabeth Ryan.

She was a member of the British team that played the United States for the Wightman Cup in the inaugural matches in 1923 in the Forest Hills stadium. She lost to Wills and Mallory, both members of the host team. But the following year, in the first of these international team competitions held in Britain, Kitty beat Mallory as well as Wills, and the home team won by a surprising margin of 6-1. Then in 1925 the British won again, 4-3, with Kitty defeating Mallory and losing to Wills. In 1926 she beat both Mary K. Browne and Ryan, but the British lost, 4-3, at Wimbledon despite Kitty's heroics.

Speedy, smart and a fighter with an all-around game, she was her country's most successful Olympian, gathering five medals in the 1920 and 1924 Games. In 1920 she won a gold in the doubles with Winifred McNair, a silver in mixed doubles with Max Woosnam and a bronze in singles. Four years later, a silver in doubles with Phyllis Covell and a bronze in singles. Active throughout her long life, she was a 92-year-old spectator at the 1988 Games in Seoul, and approved the entry of professionals, saying, "It's a sign of the times if you want the best in the Olympics."

Kitty and her husband, Leslie Godfree, were the only married couple to win the Wimbledon mixed, in 1926. In 1922 she and Margaret McKane Stocks were the only sisters to contest a Wimbledon doubles final, losing to Lenglen and Ryan. She was in the World Top Ten 1925, 1926, and 1927, No. 2 in 1926.

She was among the champions of the past who received Centenary medallions on Wimbledon's Centre Court in 1977 and was inducted into the Hall of Fame in 1978. Born May 7, 1896, in London, she died there at the age of 96, June 19, 1992.

MAJOR TITLES (7)–*Wimbledon singles, 1924, 1926; U.S. doubles, 1923, 1927; U.S. mixed, 1925; Wimbledon mixed, 1924, 1926.* WIGHTMAN CUP–*1923, 1924, 1925, 1926, 1927, 1930, 1934; record: 5-5 in singles, 2-5 in doubles.* SINGLES RECORD IN THE MAJORS–*French (6-2), Wimbledon (38-11), U.S. (7-2).*

PANCHO GONZALEZ

United States (1928–1995)
Hall of Fame 1968

Very much his own man, a loner and an acerbic competitor, Richard Alonzo 'Pancho' Gonzalez was probably as good as anyone who ever played the game, if not better. Most of his great tennis was played beyond wide public attention, on the nearly secret pro tour amid a small band of gypsies of whom he was the ticket-selling mainstay.

His rages against opponents, officials, photographers, newsmen and even spectators were frequently spectacular—but they only served to intensify his own play, and didn't disturb his concentration, as fits of temper do most others. Pancho got mad and played better. "We hoped he wouldn't get upset; it just made him tougher," said Rod Laver. "Later when he got older, he would get into arguments to stall for time and rest, and we had to be careful that it didn't put us off our games."

Gonzalez, a right-hander, born May 9, 1928, in Los Angeles, was always out of the tennis mainstream, a fact that seemed to goad him to play harder. Because he came from a Chicano family, he was never acceptable in the supposedly proper upper circles of his city's tennis establishment. And because he was a truant he wasn't permitted to play in Southern California junior tournaments. Once he got out of the Navy in 1946 there was no preventing him from mixing in the game, and beating everyone. He had a marvelously pure and effortless service action that delivered thunderbolts, and he grew up as an attacker on fast West Coast concrete.

Although not regarded as anything more than promising on his second trip East in 1948, he was at age 20 ready to win the big one, the U.S. Championship at Forest Hills. Ranked 17th nationally at the time, and seeded eighth, he served and volleyed his way to the final, where he beat South African Eric Sturgess with ease, 6-2, 6-3, 14-12. The following year Gonzalez met the favorite, a Southern California antagonist, top-seeded Ted Schroeder. It was one of the most gripping finals. Schroeder won the first two sets as expected, but they were demanding and exhausting, 18-16, 6-2, and after that Gonzalez rolled up the next three, 6-1, 6-2, 6-4, for the title. In 1949 Pancho also helped the U.S. hold the Davis Cup against Australia, then went for the money, turning pro to tour against the monarch, Jack Kramer. Gonzalez was too green for Kramer, losing, 96-27, and he faded from view for several agonizing years.

When Kramer retired, Gonzalez won a tour over Don Budge, Pancho Segura and Frank Sedgman in 1954 to determine Jack's successor, and stood himself as Emperor Pancho, proud and imperious, for a long while, through the challenges of Tony Trabert, Ken Rosewall, Lew Hoad, Ashley Cooper, Mal Anderson, Alex Olmedo and Segura. For a decade Gonzalez and pro tennis were synonymous. A promoter couldn't hope to rally crowds unless Pancho was on the bill. During his reign Pancho won the U.S. Pro singles a record eight times of 11 finals between 1951 and 1964, and Wembley in London, considered the world pro championship, 4 times of 5 finals between 1950 and 1956.

By the time Rosewall and Laver were reaching their zeniths during the mid- and late-1960s, the aging Gonzalez hung on as a dangerous foe, still capable of defeating all. In 1964, his last serious bid for his ninth U.S. Pro title, he lost the final to Laver in four hard sets on grass in a rainstorm. Yet there was still much more glory ahead. In 1968, at 40, he beat the defending champion, 31-year-old Roy Emerson, to attain the semis of the first major open, the French, to be beaten by Laver. Three months later, at the initial U.S. Open, he toppled second-seeded Tony Roche (the 23-year-old Wimbledon finalist) to make the quarters, where he defeated Tom

Okker. A year later, this grandfather (literally) electrified Wimbledon by overcoming Charlie Pasarell in the tournament's longest match, 112 games, a first-rounder that consumed five hours, 12 minutes, a major tourney record that stood until 1992, eclipsed by 14 minutes by Stefan Edberg over Michael Chang at the U.S. Open.

The marathon with Pasarell began one afternoon and concluded on the next after darkness intervened. In winning, 22-24, 1-6, 16-14, 6-3, 11-9, Gonzalez saved seven match points in the 5th set.

Later that year, he beat John Newcombe, Rosewall, Stan Smith and Arthur Ashe in succession to win $12,500, second-highest prize of the year, and the title at a rich tournament at Las Vegas. Early in 1970, in the opener of a series of $10,000 winner-take-all challenge matches leading to a grand final, he toppled Laver. The Aussie, just off his second Grand Slam year (and the eventual winner of this tournament), was clearly No. 1 in the world, but Pancho warmed a crowd of 14,761 at New York's Madison Square Garden with a 7-5, 3-6, 2-6, 6-3, 6-2 victory.

Three months before his 44th birthday, in 1972, he was the oldest to record a tournament title in the open era, winning Des Moines (Iowa) over 24-year-old French Davis Cupper Georges Goven. That year he was No. 9 in the U.S., the oldest to rank so high, and equaled Vic Seixas' Top Ten longevity span of 24 years. As for the World Top Ten, he is alone in that he was a member in 1948-49 and again in 1968-69, ranking No. 1 in 1949, No. 6 in 1969.

In 1968, though still active, he was named to the Hall of Fame and he was a consistent winner on the Grand Masters tour for the over-45 champs beginning in 1973. Although his high-speed serve, so effortlessly delivered, was a trademark, Gonzalez, a 6-foot-2, 180-pounder, was a splendid athlete and tactician who excelled at defense, too. "My legs, retrieving, lobs and change-of-pace service returns meant as much or more to me than my power," he said. "But people overlooked that because of the reputation of my serve." He won $911,078 between 1950 and 1972, and crossed the million mark as a Grand Master. Altogether as amateur and pro he won 74 singles title. He was married six times, the last to a good player, Rita Agassi, sister of another all-timer, Andre Agassi, by whom he had a son. Not a bad tennis bloodline for the young man, Skylar Gonzalez. Gonzalez died July 3, 1995, of cancer in Las Vegas, where he had been a teaching pro for some time.

MAJOR TITLES *(4)–U.S. singles, 1948, 1949; French doubles, 1949; Wimbledon doubles, 1949.* **OTHER U.S. TITLES** *(17)–Indoor singles, 1949; Clay Court singles, 1948, 1949; Indoor mixed, 1949, with Gussy Moran; Pro singles, 1953, 1954, 1955, 1956, 1957, 1958, 1959, 1961; Pro doubles, 1953, with Don Budge; 1954, 1958, with Pancho Segura; 1957, with Ken Rosewall; 1969, with Rod Laver.* **DAVIS CUP**–*1949; record: 2-0 in singles.* **SINGLES RECORD IN THE MAJORS**–*Australian (2-1), French (9-2), Wimbledon (10-5), U.S. (23-7).*

EVONNE GOOLAGONG
Australia (1951–)
Hall of Fame 1988

The most improbable of a long line of champions from Down Under, Evonne Fay Goolagong Cawley is the only native Australian, an Aborigine, to become a tennis internationalist. Born July 31, 1951, in Griffith, New South Wales, she grew up to a lissome 5-foot-6, in near poverty. As one of eight children of an itinerant sheep-shearer, Ken Goolagong, and his wife, Melinda, she spent her formative years in the small country town of Barellan in wheat and sheep territory west of Sydney. Her father, long-armed and limber, knew nothing of tennis. It's unlikely that she would have left Barellan if a kindly resident, Bill Kurtzman, hadn't seen her peering through the fence at the local courts and encouraged her to play.

She was a natural, a free-flowing right-hander blessed with speed, lightning reflexes and a carefree temperament. Tipped off to this by two of his assistants, Vic Edwards, proprietor of a tennis school in Sydney, journeyed upcountry to take a look. He immediately spotted the talent that would eventually result in two Wimbledon, one French and four Australian championships and a 1988 posting to the Hall of Fame.

Edwards convinced her parents to allow Evonne to move to Sydney and live in his household, where he could coach her. This she did in 1967 at age 13, becoming one of the family and an early doubles partner of Edwards' daughter, Patricia. Her rise was swift. On her second world tour, in 1971, Goolagong, just before turning 20, beat countrywoman Helen Gourlay to win the French. A month later, in her last act as a teenager, seeded third, she stunned the defending champion, her girlhood idol, Margaret Court, in the Wimbledon final.

Called 'Sunshine Supergirl' in London, she captivated crowds wherever she played with her graceful movement and gracious manner. Three more times she got to the final, losing to Billie Jean King in 1972 and 1975, and Chris Evert in 1976. However, a unique success was to be hers: Victory again at the end of a nine-year gap, in 1980—her last tournament triumph. Evonne, seeded fourth, made a spirited run through 1977 runner-up Betty Stove, ninth-seeded Hana Mandlikova, sixth-seeded Wendy Turnbull, second-seeded U.S. champ Tracy Austin, and in the final, third-seeded Evert, 6-1, 7-6 (7-1), the only Wimbledon singles title to end in a tie-breaker.

By then she had married Englishman Roger Cawley and had the first of their two children. Thus she was the first mother to win since Dorothea Douglass Chambers 66 years before. At Wimbledon, Evonne was 49-9 in singles, 21-7 in doubles and 19-8 in mixed.

Her exciting rivalry with Evert—the volleyer against the baseliner—began at the top, the 1972 Wimbledon semis, won by Evonne. Overall Evert led 21-12, but in the majors her edge was only 5-4, Chris winning three of their five finals. Goolagong took their initial championship encounter, the 1974 Australian. She beat Martina Navratilova to repeat in the Australian in 1975.

Although she won the U.S. Indoor in 1973 over Virginia Wade, she couldn't quite make it at the Open, the only woman to lose the final four successive years, 1973-1976, at Forest Hills, falling to Court, King, then twice to Evert.

For a decade, Evonne, refreshing as a zephyr, illuminated the World Top Ten: No. 1 in 1971 and No. 2 in 1974. She won the season-climaxing Virginia Slims title in 1974 and 1976, both over Evert. She retired after the 1983 season, with pro career totals of 43 singles and nine doubles titles, and $1,399,431 in prize money.

A seven-year mainstay of Australia's Federation Cup team, she led the way to Cups in 1971, '73-'74, and finals in 1975-76. She has held government posts in Aboriginal affairs, and was named to the Australian Tennis Hall of Fame in 1994.

MAJOR TITLES (13)–*Australian singles, 1974, 1975, 1976, 1977; French singles, 1971; Wimbledon singles, 1971, 1980; Australian doubles, 1971, 1974, 1975, 1976; Wimbledon doubles, 1974; French mixed, 1972.* **FEDERATION CUP**–*1971, 1972, 1973, 1974, 1975, 1976, 1982; record: 21-3 in singles, 11-2 in doubles.* **SINGLES RECORD IN THE MAJORS**–*Australian (39-9), French (16-3), Wimbledon (49-9), U.S. (26-6).*

STEFFI GRAF
Germany (1969–)

It was a grand moment for 16-year-old Stephanie Maria Graf: Her first pro tournament victory victimized an all-timer, Chris Evert, in the final of the 1986 Family Circle Cup at Hilton Head, S.C.

A trim blonde, 5-foot-9, she was precocious and powerfully athletic, out of the small German town of Bruhl, and she would attain heights unimaginable before 1988. That year she registered the sixth Grand Slam (third female) and topped it off with a gold medal at Seoul as tennis returned to the Olympics after a 64-year absence. It was a quintessential quintuple for 'Fraulein Forehand,' a right-handed proprietor of that feared weapon.

Before it was over in August of 1999, her majestic career was stocked with 22 major singles titles (seven Wimbledon, six French, five U.S., four Australian), starting with a 1987 French triumph over Martina Navratilova. Although she didn't quite reach Margaret Court's record stash of 24 singles, Steffi is the only player, male or female, to win each of the majors more than four times. Finishing with tennis she took up with Andre Agassi for a championship marriage Oct. 22, 2001 (14 majors ahead of him), and gave birth to their son, Jaden Gil, Oct. 26, 2001.

Born June 14, 1969, in Neckarau, Germany, she became one of the fastest of all female players, a nimble retriever who prefered the baseline but volleyed ably. She ran and played speedily, hardly pausing, impatient to win the next point.

Steffi had her sights on being the greatest ever anywhere, and she may well have been. Despite a variety of injuries and family crises, she continued to pile up major triumphs, passing Martina Navratilova and Chris Evert (18 singles each) and even Helen Wills Moody (19). Moreover, she had her 22nd, a wild 4-6, 7-5, 6-2, putdown of 18-year-old Martina Hingis, in the 1999 French final, days from her 30th birthday. Court finished collecting at 31, Moody at 32, Navratilova at 33, Evert at 31. Altogether, Steffi, a pro from age 13, won 107 singles, 11 doubles career titles, $21,895,277. Her singles W-L was 902-115.

After she'd stunned Evert (the eight-time champ) at Hilton Head in 1986, Steffi began to roll up titles at an incredible pace: 11 in 1987 and 1988, 14 in 1989, 10 in 1990. Days before her 18th birthday she grabbed her first major, the 1987 French. But it was in Paris three years later that she stumbled while strongly bidding for Navratilova's open-era record (74) for consecutive match victories. Steffi was stopped at 66 in the final by Monica Seles. She also had streaks of 46, 45 and 44.

As a pro she has won matches at an .887 clip (Evert was .899, Navratilova .878). By mid-1987 she deposed

Navratilova at No. 1, and hung on to the top spot for four years (a record 186 weeks) until displaced in 1991 by Seles. She took over the penthouse again in 1993, traded it on and off with Sanchez Vicario in 1995, shared it with the returned Seles until having it all alone again at the close of 1996, and was No. 3 when she quit, shortly after losing her last (31st) major final, Wimbledon, to Lindsay Davenport.

Steel-willed and industrious, she displayed full-speed-ahead-damn-the-slings-and-arrows character in the face of daunting physical injuries and emotional trials. Probably no great champion has played hurt so often. She was kept from the Australian in 1995 by a calf injury, and in 1996 by foot surgery. Might she have had two more Grand Slams otherwise? Back and knee problems were constant, the left knee sidelining her during the 1996 Olympics. When would-be assassin Guenther Parche removed Seles from the picture (and the No. 1 spot) with his knife in 1993, Steffi bore the anguish when Parche said he did it to restore Steffi to the top.

Peter Graf, who raised her specifically for tennis, turning her pro in October 1982 to support the family, has been a prized target of the tabloids for his waywardness. The father's most serious scandal was his arrest and imprisonment in 1995 on the charge of income tax evasion of millions of dollars in managing her fortune. He was convicted and sentenced to a jail term in January 1997. Nevertheless, she remained loyal to him, and steadfast in her pursuit of victory, though cutting down her schedule to 11 tournaments in 1995 and 1996.

Graf said she missed the challenge of Seles, who beat for the Australian title in 1993, shortly before the assault by Parche. She welcomed Monica's return to the U.S. Open of 1995. In a highly-charged final, Steffi won, 7-6 (8-6), 0-6, 6-3, and one year later won the rematch even more impressively with quickness and battering forehands, 7-5, 6-4.

But the gems of those two years were Wimbledon '95 and the French '96 because of what it took to throttle the passionate opposition of Arantxa Sanchez Vicario in the finals. Perhaps the greatest single game ever was the 11th of their third set on Centre Court: A spellbinding 20-minute passage of 32 points—13 deuces—until Steffi punched through Arantxa's serve to 6-5, and won, 4-6, 6-1, 7-5. Twice the Spaniard served for victory at Roland Garros, at 5-4 and 7-6 in the third. Again, Steffi just wouldn't let her have it, 6-3, 6-7 (4-7), 10-8, in 3 hours, 3 minutes.

Centre Court was Steffi's rumpus room as much as Martina's. Steffi ran off with the 1988 and 1989 finals at Martina's expense, thus halting Navratilova's run of six straight years on top and 47 consecutive match wins, three short of Moody's Wimbledon record.

In the 1993 Wimbledon final, Steffi kept her poise when it appeared she would lose to Jana Novotna, taking the last five games and her fifth title, 7-6 (8-6), 1-6, 6-4.

On the other side of the coin the following year, Steffi added to Wimbledon history through defeat, the only top-seeded woman to fall in the first round—to Lori McNeil, 7-5, 7-6 (7-5). It was her lone failure to attain at least the quarters in 45 majors since making the semis of the U.S. in 1985 (31 of which she was in the final, and, of course, won 22).

Her Grand Slam year amounted to 11 singles titles in 14 tournaments on a 73-3 match record. In navigating the Australian, French, Wimbledon and U.S. finals, she beat Evert, Natalia Zvereva, Navratilova and Gabriela Sabatini. Then she beat Sabatini for the 1988 Olympic crown, but relinquished it to Jennifer Capriati in 1992 at Barcelona.

Almost as impressive was 1989 with 14 wins in 16 tournaments on a 86-2 match record, and 1993, winning 10 of 15 tournaments on 76-6. Four times she won the season-closing WTA (née Virginia Slims) Championship at Madison Square Garden, 1987, '89, '93, '95. Her swath of reaching 20 consecutive finals through the German Open of 1994 was second in that consistency to Navratilova's 23, 1983-84.

She led Germany to the 1987 and 1992 Federation Cups in which her singles record was 19-2. The ITF named her World Champion seven times, 1987-88-89-90, 93, 95-96. After losing her first pro match to Tracy Austin (the only one she played in 1982), she became a winner (21-15) in 1983, registering at No. 98 on the computer. She was World No. 1, eight times (1987-88-89-90, '93-'94-'95-'96), No. 2 twice (1991-92) and among the Top 10 three other times.

MAJOR TITLES *(22)–Australian singles, 1988, 1989, 1990, 1994; French singles, 1987, 1988, 1993, 1995, 1996, 1999; Wimbledon, 1988, 1989, 1991, 1992, 1993, 1995, 1996; U.S. singles, 1988, 1989, 1993, 1995, 1996; Wimbledon doubles, 1988.* **FEDERATION CUP**–*1986, 1987, 1989, 1991, 1992, 1993, 1996; record: 19-2 in singles, 8-1 in doubles.* **SINGLES RECORD IN THE MAJORS**–*Australian (40-4), French (73-9), Wimbledon (66-5), U.S. (70-8).*

BITSY GRANT

United States (1910–1986)

Hall of Fame 1972

A scrappy little guy, 5-foot-4, 120-pound Bryan Morel 'Bitsy' Grant was the smallest American man to attain championship stature. A right-handed retriever supreme, he was able to beat such heavy-hitting greats as Don Budge and Ellsworth Vines even on grass. Between 1930 and 1941 he was ranked nine times in the U.S. Top Ten, No. 3 in 1935 and 1936. In 1936 and 1937 he was in the World Top Ten, Nos. 8 and 6, respectively.

Reared on the clay of his native Georgia, he won the U.S. title on that surface thrice (1930, 1934, 1935) but he had his moments on the grass at Forest Hills, reaching the U.S. semis in 1935 by beating second-seeded Budge, 6-4, 6-4, 5-7, 6-3, and in 1936, losing to eventual champion, Fred Perry, 6-4, 3-6, 7-5, 6-2. He was a quarter-finalist in 1937, losing to Gottfried von Cramm, 9-7, 2-6, 2-6, 6-3, 6-3, and reached the same round a year later.

He played Davis Cup 1935, 1936 and 1937, helping the U.S. regain the prize in 1937 after a 10-year slump. He continued to compete as a senior, winning 19 U.S. singles titles on the four surfaces: Grass Court—45s (1956 and 1957), 55s (1965, 1966, 1967 and 1968); Indoor—55s (1966); Clay Court—45s (1959, 1960, 1961 and 1963), 55s (1965, 1966, 1967, 1968 and 1969), 65s (1976 and 1977); Hard Court—65s (1976).

He was born in Atlanta, Dec. 25, 1910, and died there June 5, 1986. Named for him, the Bitsy Grant Tennis Center in his hometown is one of the finest public court complexes. He entered the Hall of Fame in 1972.

U.S. TITLES (4)–*Clay Court singles, 1930, 1934, 1935; Clay Court doubles, 1932, with George Lott.* **DAVIS CUP**–*1935, 1936, 1937; record: 8-2 in singles.* **SINGLES RECORD IN THE MAJORS**–*Wimbledon (8-2), U.S. (35-15).*

CLARENCE GRIFFIN

United States (1888–1973)

Hall of Fame 1970

Clarence James 'Peck' Griffin ranked in the U.S. Top Ten three times (1915, 1916, 1920), No. 6 the last two, but made his mark in doubles alongside fellow Californian Bill Johnston. They won the U.S. title thrice, 1915, 1916 and 1920. He was also in the 1913 final with John Strachan. He and Strachan won the U.S. Clay Court title that year, and in 1914 Griffin reached

his singles apogee in a comeback beating of Elia Fottrell, 3-6, 6-8, 8-6, 6-0, 6-2, for the Clay Court singles crown. That was the all-comers final.

Defender Strachan, unable to be in Cincinnati, defaulted the challenge round to Griffin. He was a 5-foot-7 right-hander, born Jan. 19, 1888, in San Francisco, and died March 28, 1973, in Santa Barbara Calif. He entered the Hall of Fame in 1970. His nephew is the well-known entertainer Merv Griffin.

MAJOR TITLES (3)–*U.S. doubles, 1915, 1916, 1920.* **OTHER U.S. TITLES** (2)–*Clay Court singles, 1914; Clay Court doubles, 1913, with John Strachan.* **SINGLES RECORD IN THE MAJORS**–*U.S. (18-9).*

HAROLD HACKETT

United States (1878–1937)

Hall of Fame 1961

A New Yorker, Harold Humphrey Hackett was best known as the partner of Fred Alexander in one of the most successful doubles teams. The 5-foot-9 Hackett was the softer, more deceptive stroker of the two. Beginning in 1905 they were U.S. finalists a record seven successive years, winning in 1907, 1908, 1909 and 1910. A Yale man, and right-handed, he was born July 12, 1878, in Hingham, Mass. He and Alexander won the U.S. Indoor doubles thrice (1906-08), and he completed a sweep of the surface titles available then by taking the Clay doubles in 1912 with Walter Hall.

The following year, 1913, he was player-captain of the U.S. Davis Cup team that broke a decade drought by seizing the Cup in a 3-2 beating of Britain. He and Maurice McLoughlin won the vital go-ahead point over H. Roper Barrett and Charles Dixon, 6-4 in the fifth. He was ranked in the U.S. Top Ten twice, 1902 and 1906, No. 7 in 1906 when he was a U.S. quarter-finalist. He was inducted into the Hall of Fame in 1961. He died in New York Nov. 20, 1937.

MAJOR TITLES (4)–*U.S. doubles, 1907, 1908, 1909, 1910.* **OTHER U.S. TITLES** (5)–*Indoor doubles, 1906, 1907, 1908, 1909, with Fred Alexander; Clay Court doubles, 1912, with Walter Hall.* **DAVIS CUP**–*1908, 1909, 1913; record: 5-1 in doubles.* **SINGLES RECORD IN THE MAJORS**–*U.S. (3-2).*

ELLEN HANSELL

United States (1869–1937)

Hall of Fame 1965

The original U.S. female champion, Ellen Forde Hansell Allerdice was a Philadelphian who won the title in 1887, in her hometown, not long before her 18th birthday. She beat Laura Knight, 6-1, 6-0, at the Philadelphia Cricket Club, but lost the title the following year to Bertha Townsend, and wasn't a factor again. A right-hander, she served sidearm, as, she said, did most of the women in that inaugural.

Forty-four years later, she recalled that she had been an anemic child, who showed some "enthusiasm and aptitude" for tennis. Her mother was advised by the family doctor to take Ellen out of school and put her on a court daily to build herself up. She remembered her mother making her tennis dresses of red plaid gingham: "A red felt hat topped the tight-collared and be-corseted body. I also wore a blazer of red and blue stripes ... we did now and then grip our overdraped, voluminous skirts with our left hand to give us a bit more limb freedom when dashing to make a swift, snappy stroke, every bit as well placed as today, but lacking the force and great physical strength of the modern girl. Is it possible for you to envision the gallery? A loving, but openly prejudiced crowd standing within two feet of the court lines, calling out hurrahs of applause plus groans of disappointment, and some suggestive criticism, such as: 'Run to the net.' 'Place it to her left.' 'Don't dare lose this game.'"

She was born Sept, 18, 1869, in Philadelphia, and died, Mrs. Taylor Allderdice, May 11, 1937, in Pittsburgh. Induction into the Hall of Fame came in 1965.

MAJOR TITLE *(1)–U.S. singles, 1887.* **SINGLES RECORD IN THE MAJORS**–*U.S. (3-1).*

DARLENE HARD

United States (1936–)
Hall of Fame 1973

An all-out attacking Californian with a splendid serve, volley and overhead, Darlene Ruth Hard nevertheless won the French singles on slow clay (1960) as well as the U.S. title on grass at Forest Hills (1960, 1961), and was a Wimbledon finalist twice (1957, 1959). A stocky blonde right-hander, 5-foot-5, 140 pounds, she was born Jan. 6, 1936, in Los Angeles and attended Pomona, for whom she won the U.S. Intercollegiate title in 1958.

She played with considerable zest, inspiring a variety of doubles partners, winning the U.S. title five straight years (1958-62) and again in 1969 with four different accomplices, the French twice with different partners and four Wimbledons with three different partners. The

1969 win with Françoise Durr—a last-minute, one-time amalgamation—may have been her most sensational in that Darlene, no longer competing, looked so out of place in the final. But after a disastrous start, losing the first eight games, she recalled the old moves as they beat Margaret Court and Virginia Wade, 0-6, 6-3, 6-4.

Between 1954 and 1963 she ranked in the U.S. Top Ten 10 times, No. 1 four straight years (1960-63), and in the World Top Ten nine times, No. 2 in 1960 and 1961. She was a standout Wightman and Federation Cup player.

As the grande dame of the original U.S. Fed Cup team, squiring 19-year-olds Billie Jean Moffitt (King) and Carole Caldwell (Graebner), Darlene, 27, led the way to 1963 victory. A blend of all-time doubles champs, present and future, she and B. J. won the Cup decider over Aussies Smith (Court) and Lesley Turner, 3-6, 13-11, 6-3, on a fast, slick, wooden court inside Queen's Club, London. She totaled 22 major titles in singles, doubles and mixed (3-13-5).

Inducted into the Hall of Fame in 1973, she married Richard Waggoner in 1977.

MAJOR TITLES *(21)–French singles, 1960; U.S. singles, 1960, 1961; French doubles, 1955, 1957, 1960; Wimbledon doubles, 1957, 1959, 1960, 1963; U.S. doubles, 1958, 1959, 1960, 1961, 1962, 1969; French mixed, 1955, 1961; Wimbledon mixed, 1957, 1959, 1960.* **OTHER U.S. TITLES** *(7)–Clay Court doubles, 1957, with Althea Gibson; 1960, with Billie Jean Moffitt King; 1962, with Sue Behlmar; 1963, with Maria Bueno; Hard Court singles, 1963; Hard Court doubles, 1963, with Paulette Verzin; Intercollegiate singles, 1958.* **FEDERATION CUP**–*1963; record: 3-1 in singles, 3-0 in doubles.* **WIGHTMAN CUP**–*1957, 1959, 1960, 1962, 1963; record: 6-3 in singles, 4-1 in doubles.* **SINGLES RECORD IN THE MAJORS**–*French (14-4), Wimbledon (29-7), U.S. (43-9).*

DORIS HART

United States (1925–)
Hall of Fame 1969

As a child Doris Jane Hart was certainly not a candidate for sports immortality. She was stricken by a serious knee infection later erroneously publicized as polio, and faced the prospect of being crippled for life. She began to play tennis at age six as therapy, and recovered so successfully that, despite bowed legs, she became one of the all-time champions.

"One of the first newspaper stories on me described me as having recovered from polio," she once said. "It was a good story that just caught on. But it wasn't so."

Her total of 35 major championships in singles, doubles and mixed ties her with Louise Brough, behind only

Margaret Court (62), Martina Navratilova (57), Billie Jean King (39) and Margaret duPont (37). Hart and Court are the only players in history, male or female, to win all 12 of the major titles at least once, and she is one of 13 to win all four singles within her career.

For 14 successive years between 1942 and 1955 she was ranked in the U.S. Top Ten, standing at No. 1 in 1954-55.

Possibly her finest tournament was Wimbledon of 1951, when she scored a triple—championships in singles, doubles, and mixed—and lost only one set, that in the mixed. After handing her good friend and partner, Shirley Fry, one of the worst beatings in the tournament's history (6-1, 6-0), Doris united with Shirley for the doubles title, over rivals Brough and duPont, 6-3, 13-11, then annexed the mixed with Frank Sedgman. Doris won the mixed the following year with Sedgman, and the next three years with Vic Seixas, a Wimbledon record of five straight years.

After being a runner-up at Forest Hills for the U.S. Singles Championship four times, Hart finally was rewarded on her fifteenth try at the title. She beat Brough in a thriller, 6-8, 6-1, 8-6, in the 1954 title match, averting three match points. She retained that title, 6-4, 6-2, over Englishwoman Pat Ward, then retired to become a teaching pro.

Born June 20, 1925, in St. Louis, Hart, a right-hander, grew up in Coral Gables, Fla. She was an intelligent and solid all-around player whose strokes were crisp and stylish. She moved very well, despite the early handicap of her legs, and had an excellent disposition. She was effective at the net, or in the backcourt, as attested by her championships in the French singles of 1950, over Pat Canning Todd and 1952, over defender Fry, who had beaten her in the 1951 final. Doris also won the U.S. Clay Court singles in 1950 over Fry.

During her first of two ventures to Australia, 1949, a rare American there that year, she started seizing major singles, the first of six, snipping the three-year string of Nancye Bolton and won the mixed with Sedgman over Joyce Fitch and John Bromwich. She lost her title to Brough the following year.

She and Shirley were one of the outstanding pairs in history, with 11 majors, standing behind the record 20 of Brough-duPont and Martina Navratilova-Pam Shriver, and the 14 of Gigi Fernandez and Natalia Zvereva. They won the French a record four straight from 1950, losing only one set in all the finals that while

deposing long-time antagonists Brough and duPont in 1950. (Fernandez and Zvereva tied the four-straight record as 1992-95 champs.) Hart and Fry also won three Wimbledons in a row, beginning in 1951. In the 1953 U.S. final they ended the record streak of Brough and duPont at nine championships and 41 matches in a furious 6-2, 7-9, 9-7 struggle. In turn their own streak of four championships and 20 matches was stopped in the 1955 final by Brough and duPont.

During a decade of U.S. supremacy over Britain (1946–55) in the Wightman Cup, Hart won all 14 of her singles and eight of nine doubles. She captained the winning U.S. team in 1970.

Her U.S. championships on various surfaces amounted to 22 singles and doubles. In 1969 she was enshrined in the Hall of Fame. Beginning in 1946 she was in the World Top Ten 10 successive years, No. 1 in 1951, otherwise: No. 4, 1946; No. 3, 1947-48-49-50; No. 2, 1952-53-54-55.

MAJOR TITLES *(35)–Australian singles, 1949; French singles, 1950, 1952; Wimbledon singles, 1951; U.S. singles, 1954, 1955; Australian doubles, 1950; French doubles, 1948, 1950, 1951, 1952, 1953; Wimbledon doubles, 1947, 1951, 1952, 1953; U.S. doubles, 1951, 1952, 1953, 1954; Australian mixed, 1949, 1950; French mixed, 1951, 1952, 1953; Wimbledon mixed, 1951, 1952, 1953, 1954, 1955; U.S. mixed, 1951, 1952, 1953, 1954, 1955.* **OTHER U.S. TITLES** *(11)–Clay Court singles, 1950; Hard Court singles, 1949; Indoor doubles, 1947, 1948, with Barbara Schofield; Hard Court Mixed, 1949, with Eric Sturgess; Clay Court doubles, 1944, 1945, with Pauline Betz; 1950, with Shirley Fry; 1954, with Maureen Connolly; Indoor mixed, 1947, 1948, with Bill Talbert.* **WIGHTMAN CUP**–*1946, 1947, 1948, 1949, 1950, 1951, 1952, 1953, 1954, 1955; record: 14-0 in singles, 8-1 in doubles.* **SINGLES RECORD IN THE MAJORS**–*Australian (8-1), French (28-5), Wimbledon (43-8), U.S. (57-13).*

BOB HEWITT

Australia/South Africa (1940–)
Hall of Fame 1992

Tapped for the Hall of Fame in 1992 in harness with his partner, Frew McMillan, Robert Anthony John Hewitt was the right-court player in the alignment of Hewitt and McMillan. They combined for five major championships and were one of the shrewdest, strongest of all teams, men whose prowess spanned the amateur and open eras. In 1974 they were central to South Africa's winning the Davis Cup, the fifth member of the exclusive club, and first newcomer since France in 1927.

Hewitt was a born and bred Aussie, beginning life Jan. 12, 1940, in Dubbo, New South Wales. He became one of a tribe that terrorized the tennis world, and first came to attention winning the Wimbledon doubles in 1962 and 1964 with compatriot Fred Stolle. But love broke up that potent alliance. Hewitt fell for a South African lass named Delaille, and moved to Johannesburg to wed. Since he hadn't played Davis Cup for Australia, he was eligible, as a resident, to compete for South Africa.

In 1966 he and McMillan were put together as teammates, and they stayed together for much of the next 15 years to win Wimbledon thrice (1967, 1972, 1978), the French (1972), the U.S. (1977) plus 60 other titles. Hewitt, bald, bearded and sometimes volatile on court, was a blocky 6-footer with surprisingly delicate touch, an accurate and seldom failing returner.

He was the better singles player, taking seven pro titles in singles, along with 65 in doubles, the latter total placing him sixth on the all-time winners' list. He was a Wimbledon quarter-finalist in 1964 and 1966, won the U.S. Clay Court singles, and three other singles tourneys in 1972 and was ranked No. 6 in the world in 1967. Hewitt had six major mixed titles, too, one of five to win all four. He won three (Wimbledon, 1977-79, U.S., 1979) with Greer Stevens. His career prize money amounted to more than $1 million.

MAJOR TITLES (15)–*Australian doubles, 1963, 1964; French doubles, 1972; Wimbledon doubles, 1962, 1964, 1967, 1972, 1978; U.S. doubles, 1977; Australian mixed, 1961; French mixed, 1970, 1979; Wimbledon mixed, 1977, 1979; U.S. mixed, 1979.* **DAVIS CUP**–*1967, 1968, 1969, 1974, 1978; record: 22-3 in singles, 16-1 in doubles.* **SINGLES RECORD IN THE MAJORS**–*Australian (12-7), French (21-14), Wimbledon (34-19), U.S. (13-9).* **MAJOR TITLES WITH MCMILLAN** (5)–*French doubles, 1972; Wimbledon doubles, 1967, 1972, 1978; U.S. doubles, 1977.* **DAVIS CUP**–*1967, 1968, 1969, 1974, 1978; record: 16-1 in doubles.*

LLEYTON HEWITT
Australia (1981–)

Lleyton Hewitt is a screaming, fist-pumping, chest-thumping firebrand on court. "C'mon, Balboa!" he yells at himself, finding inspiration in his obsession with the movie *Rocky* about an underdog boxer. At 5-foot-11, he is a racquet-thin 150 pounds. The leanness is deceptive, for he grew up playing breakneck Aussie Rules Football and hurls his body with abandon at shots others would let pass. Such intensity made him the youngest men's No. 1 since computer rankings began in 1973.

Hewitt has won two major championship singles titles—the 2001 U.S. Open in 2001 and 2002 Wimbledon—as well as the U.S. doubles in 2000 with Max Mirnyi. He has also won 17 other ATP tournaments since turning pro in 1998 at age 16. He was the year-end No. 1 in 2001 and 2002.

The Australian's passing shots and, especially, his return of serve, are strengths. Hewitt himself is enamored with his topspin lob. Critics of Hewitt—and he has many—suggest he lacks the tools to become a dominant player, missing a booming serve, a killer return or a crushing groundstroke. All he does is win. Pat Rafter, his compatriot, called Hewitt a "little mongrel" for his refusal to be beaten. He has also been called an "undersized, overcharged kid," a "racquet-wielding Energizer Bunny," and "Bart Simpson with a Yonex."

For his part, Hewitt has called Australian fans "stupid"; called a chair umpire a "spastic"; made an insensitive remark about an African-American linesman; dismissed his coach in controversial fashion; and had a long public spat with the Association of Tennis Professionals after being fined $103,000 for refusing to do a television interview. But his romance with Belgium's level-headed Kim Clijsters, whom he calls a calming influence, would indicate that opposites do indeed attract.

Hewitt was born in Adelaide on Feb. 24, 1981. His father Glynn played Australian Rules Football for Richmond and his mother Cherilyn was a former professional netballer. Neither sport is for the faint-hearted. Their son learned tennis on the family's grass courts and they took him to his first Australian Open as a spectator at age five.

Hewitt qualified for the Australian Open in January, 1997, a month before his 16th birthday, the youngest qualifier in the tournament's 95 years. He debuted that month on the ATP Rankings at No. 797. Four years later, at 20 years, nine months, he would be the youngest No. 1 ever (surpassing Jimmy Connors, 22 years, three months).

His precocious talent was displayed at age 16 when he captured his hometown title at Adelaide. The five men he beat had a combined total of 1,108 career victories; Hewitt had none until then. He became the lowest-ranked player, at No. 550, to win in tour history. He wore his ball cap backwards at the tournament and has done so ever since, a trademark that contributes to his bratty reputation. (Another trademark, a long blond ponytail, has since been hacked off.)

In 1999, Hewitt won his first clay-court title (Delray Beach) in his only victory in four finals appearances. He made his Davis Cup debut in July against the United States, winning two singles rubbers. Russia's Yevgeny

Kafelnikov promised to administer a "tennis lesson" to the brash upstart in their World Group semi-final. Instead, the Russian was humbled in straight sets. Against France, Hewitt lost both his singles rubbers in an Australian victory. He led his nation to two more finals, losing to Spain (2000) and France (2001).

Hewitt won four titles in 2000, the first teenager to win that many since Pete Sampras a decade earlier. He got his first major championship title, a doubles crown, at the U.S. Open with Max (The Beast) Mirnyi, which made Hewitt the youngest male, at 19 years, 6 months, to win a Slam doubles in the Open era.

At Flushing Meadows the following year, he defeated Kafelnikov in the semis and Sampras in the final in straight sets to claim his first singles major championship. Hewitt won five other tournaments in 2001, including the year-end Tennis Masters Cup, and topped the ATP Rankings.

Some thought him a caretaker in the top spot until a more skilled player arrived to succeed the likes of Sampras and Agassi. But not only did he hold the ranking, he added a second major championship and defended his title at the Tennis Masters Cup. He dropped only two sets at Wimbledon as he demolished surprise finalist David Nalbandian of Argentina (6-1, 6-3, 6-2) to become the first Australian in 15 years to win at Wimbledon.

MAJOR TITLES *(3)–Wimbledon singles, 2002; U.S. singles, 2001; U.S. doubles, 2000.* **DAVIS CUP**–*1999, 2000, 2001, 2002; record: 18-5 singles, 8-1 in doubles.* **SINGLES RECORD IN THE MAJORS**–*Australian (8-1), French (28-5), Wimbledon (43-8), U.S. (57-13).*

MARTINA HINGIS
Slovakia/Switzerland (1980–)

In a sport renowned for its child prodigies, few have been as prodigious as Switzerland's Martina Hingis. Martina II (she was named for Martina Navratilova), turned pro at 14 and by the time she was 16-1/2 had become the youngest World No. 1 in the game's history.

She reached the top ranking in 1997, a season in which Martina sparkled. She reached the singles final of all four major championships, winning three (Australia, Wimbledon and U.S.), while becoming the youngest person in the 20th century (16 years, three months) to win a major singles title, defeating Mary Pierce in Melbourne. Martina had opened that season with 37 straight wins, tying Navratilova for the second best start ever (behind Steffi Graf, 1987), and ended the year with 12 titles and a decade-best .938 winning percentage.

Over the next 4-1/2 years, Hingis would retain the No. 1 ranking for all but 28 weeks, a total of 209 weeks overall. She'd also increase her major titles to 14 (five singles, nine doubles), while in 1998, becoming the fourth woman to achieve a doubles grand slam. She won Australia with Mirjani Lukic and then teamed with Jana Novotna to take the French, Wimbledon and U.S. titles. She had kicked off her major championship career in 1996 by teaming with Helena Sukova to win Wimbledon doubles, becoming the youngest Wimbledon champion ever (15 years, 282 days).

Hingis was born Sept. 30, 1980 in Kosice, Slovakia, and moved to Switzerland at age eight. Coached by her mother, Melanie Molitor, she rapidly climbed the junior tennis ranks. At age 12 she became the youngest junior winner at Roland Garros and added the record for youngest doubles winner the next year. She also broke the age record at Wimbledon, winning the junior crown in 1994 at 13 years, 276 days.

She made her WTA debut in 1994, beating Patty Fendick before losing in the second round to World No. 5 Mary Pierce. It took her just 2-1/2 years to crack the Top 10 and she was No. 4 by the end of 1996, a year in which she'd won her first tour event and made it to the U.S. semi-finals.

In addition to her three-quarters slam in 1997, Martina won Australia in 1998 and 1999. Her final major title came with Anna Kournikova in the 2002 Australian doubles.

At 5-foot-7, 130 pounds, Hingis' primary attribute was her extraordinary poise. She was a thoughtful right-hand (two-handed backhand) strokemaker who won singles events just about everywhere except on the clay at Roland Garros.

Recurring ankle problems caused her to announce her retirement in February 2003. She'd undergone surgery on her right ankle in October 2001 and on the left ankle seven months later. In between, she'd reached the final of the 2002 Australian Open for a sixth time, losing to Jennifer Capriati. She ended the year ranked No. 10 and was convinced she'd never reclaim the top spot. "When you have been world number one for four years you cannot content yourself with less," she said. "I don't want people to feel sorry for me—I have a great life. Even without competition, I am happy."

Hingis retired with 76 tour wins (including 36 doubles), a career W-L record of 471-100 (.825 winning percent) and prize money of $18,344,660. She also had an 18-2 singles record in Fed Cup play.

MAJOR TITLES (14)–*Australian singles, 1997, 1998, 1999; Wimbledon singles, 1997; U.S. singles, 1997; Australian doubles, 1997, 1998, 1999, 2002; French doubles, 1998, 2000; Wimbledon doubles, 1996, 1998 U.S. doubles, 1998.* FEDERATION CUP–*1995, 1996, 1997, 1998; record: 18-2 in singles, 8-2 in doubles.* SINGLES RECORD IN THE MAJORS–*Australian (44-5), French (31-7), Wimbledon (19-6), U.S. (40-7).*

LEW HOAD

Australia (1934–1994)

Hall of Fame 1980

During his quarter-century career as a professional, Pancho Gonzalez faced a vast array of first-rate players, and the one he considered the most devastating was Lewis Alan Hoad. "When Lew's game was at its peak nobody could touch him," said Gonzalez, who cited Hoad as his toughest foe during his years of the pro tours, mainly head-to-head one-night-stands.

Hoad, who turned pro in 1957, after winning his second successive Wimbledon singles, was one rookie who seemed able to dethrone Gonzalez as the pro king. They were just about even when Hoad's troublesome back gave way during the winter of 1958. Gonzalez won the tour, 51-36, but felt threatened all the way, and trailed at one point, 18-9 as Lew won six straight. It was Pancho's closest brush with defeat after taking over leadership in 1954.

Hoad, a strapping 5-foot-8, 175-pounder with a gorilla chest and iron wrists, may have been the strongest man to play tennis in the world class. He blistered the ball and became impatient with rallying, preferring to hit for winners. It was a flamboyant style, and made for some bad errors when he wasn't in tune. But when his power was focused along with his concentration, Hoad came on like a tidal wave. He was strong enough to use topspin as an offensive drive. He was assault-minded, but had enough control to win the French title on slow clay in 1956, over Swede Sven Davidson.

Born Nov. 23, 1934, 21 days after Ken Rosewall, in the same city, Sydney, the right-handed Hoad was bracketed with Rosewall throughout his amateur days. Although entirely different in stature, style, and personality, the two were called Australia's tennis twins, the prodigies who drew attention as teenagers and were rivals and teammates through 1956. Hoad was stronger, but less patient and consistent, more easygoing. His back problems cut his career short in the mid-1960s while

Rosewall, whose style was less taxing, kept on going into the next decade.

His countrymen fondly remember Hoad's Davis Cup triumph of 1953 over Tony Trabert on a rainy Melbourne afternoon. At 19, he and Rosewall had been selected to defend the Cup. The U.S. led, 2-1, in the finale and seemed about to clinch the Cup when the more experienced Trabert, already the U.S. champion, caught up at two sets all. Hoad hung on to win, however, 13-11, 6-3, 3-6, 2-6, 7-5, and Rosewall beat Vic Seixas the following day to save the Cup, 3-2.

Although they lost it to the Americans the next year, Hoad and Rosewall were awesome in 1955, retaking the prize from the Yanks, 5-0. Hoad beat Wimbledon champ Trabert the first day and got the clincher with Rex Hartwig over Trabert and Seixas. The twins defended the Cup from the U.S. for the last time together in 1956, 5-0, winning everything. Lew wiped out Herbie Flam on opening day and united with Kenny a last time to decide it, over Sammy Giammalva and Seixas.

Their first major titles were bagged in 1953, when Lew and Ken were allied to win the Australian, French, and Wimbledon doubles. They missed out on a Grand Slam on the last leg, the U.S. at Longwood in Boston, in a quarter-final upset by unseeded Americans Straight Clark and Hal Burrows. But, taking 19 of 20 matches, he (in the left court) and Ken were the only male team other than countrymen Frank Sedgman and Ken McGregor (1951-52) and John Newcombe and Tony Roche (1967) to win three of the four in one year. Lew won 13 major titles in singles and doubles, and in 1956 appeared on his way to winning all four (Australian, French, Wimbledon and U.S.) singles within one calendar year, thus achieving a rare Grand Slam. However, after Hoad was three quarters of the way there, Rosewall spoiled the Slam with a 4-6, 6-2, 6-2, 6-3, triumph. In his last significant tournament appearance in 1973, Lew reached the final of the South African doubles with Rob Maud, losing to Arthur Ashe and Tom Okker.

Despite losing out on a Grand Slam, his 1956 season was a luminous hard-working campaign that netted 32 titles: 15 victories in 26 singles tourneys on a 95-11 match record, 17 victories in 23 doubles starts on 79-5. He had planned to turn pro after that but decided to go for the Slam again. That dream was drilled almost immediately in the semis of the Australian by Neale Fraser. Though Lew resolutely and smashingly did repeat at Wimbledon on the loss of one set, blasting Ashley

Cooper in the final—his 42nd singles title—he felt it was time to cash in. He accepted an offer from promoter Jack Kramer and began preparing for Gonzalez. For five straight years, he was in the World Top Ten, No. 1 in 1956.

Hoad (five attempts) and Bjorn Borg (10) are probably the two greatest players not to win the U.S. Championship. Lew married another player, countrywoman Jenny Staley (finalist in the 1954 Australian singles. He died July 3, 1994, in Fuengirola, Spain, where he and Jenny operated a tennis resort.

MAJOR TITLES *(13)–Australian singles, 1956; French singles, 1956; Wimbledon singles, 1956, 1957; Australian doubles, 1953, 1956, 1957; French doubles, 1953; Wimbledon doubles, 1953, 1955, 1956; U.S. doubles, 1956; French mixed, 1954.* **DAVIS CUP**–*1953, 1954, 1955, 1956; record: 10-2 in singles, 7-2 in doubles.* **SINGLES RECORD IN THE MAJORS**–*Australian (15-5), French (17-5), Wimbledon (32-7), U.S. (21-5).*

HARRY HOPMAN

Australia (1906–1985)
Hall of Fame 1978

A fine player, particularly in doubles, at which he won seven major titles, Henry Christian Hopman made his name as the most successful of all Davis Cup captains, piloting Australia to 16 Cups between 1939 and 1967. His was the era of perhaps the greatest Cup players of all, the Hall of Fame Aussies from Frank Sedgman through Lew Hoad, Ken Rosewall, Ashley Cooper, Mervyn Rose, Rex Hartwig, Mal Anderson, Neale Fraser, Roy Emerson, Rod Laver, John Newcombe, Fred Stolle, Tony Roche.

Emphasizing super fitness, he drove and inspired them, and built pride in their underpopulated country's beating up on the rest of the world. The first of his 22 teams, 1938, reached the challenge round final, losing to the U.S. But he was back with the same pair, Adrian Quist and Jack Bromwich, to win a singular victory over the U.S. in 1939, from 0-2 down after the first day in Philadelphia.

Hop concentrated on his job as a newspaperman after World War II. But after the Aussies lost the Cup to the U.S. in 1946, and three more finales through 1949, there was a clamor for him to return to the captain's chair. With two youngsters, Sedgman and Ken McGregor, he won the Cup in New York in 1950, and the Down Under-takers were in business for a glorious near-quarter-century. His teams compiled a 38-6 record.

As a player—a trim 5-foot-7, 133 pounds—he won the Australian doubles with Jack Crawford in 1929 and 1930 and four mixed titles with his first wife, the former Nell Hall, a record for married couples. In singles his high point was the U.S. Championships of 1938 when he beat fifth-seeded Elwood Cooke, 6-2, 4-6, 6-4, 10-8, and future U.S. and French champ Don McNeill, 6-4, 6-3, 7-5, to reach the quarters, where he was an historic footnote in Don Budge's original Grand Slam, 6-3, 6-1, 6-3.

Following his last Davis Cup match as captain, a loss to Mexico at Mexico City in 1969, he emigrated to the U.S. to become a highly successful teaching pro, counseling such champions-to-be as Vitas Gerulaitis and John McEnroe at the Port Washington (N.Y.) Tennis Academy. He later opened his own Hopman Tennis Academy with his wife, Lucy, at Largo, Fla. Hop was born Aug. 12, 1906, in Sydney and died Dec. 27, 1985, in Largo, Fla. He entered the Hall of Fame in 1978.

MAJOR TITLES *(7)–Australian doubles, 1929, 1930; U.S. mixed, 1939; Australian mixed, 1930, 1936, 1937, 1939.* **DAVIS CUP (As player)**–*1928, 1930, 1932; record: 4-5 in singles, 4-3 in doubles.* **(As captain)**–*1938, 1939, 1950, 1951, 1952, 1953, 1954, 1955, 1956, 1957, 1958, 1959, 1960, 1961, 1962, 1963, 1964, 1965, 1966, 1967, 1968, 1969; record: 38-6, 16 Cups.* **SINGLES RECORD IN THE MAJORS**–*Australian (34-16), French (8-6), Wimbledon (15-9), U.S. (9-6).*

FRED HOVEY

United States (1868–1945)
Hall of Fame 1974

Frederick Howard Hovey, a Bostonian and Harvardian, won the U.S. Intercollegiate singles in 1890 and 1891 as well as the doubles with Bob Wrenn the second year. Four years later he, a 5-foot-8, 170-pound right-hander, beat lefty Wrenn, 6-3, 6-2, 6-4, to end his fellow Bostonian's two-year reign at the U.S. Championships. Wrenn returned the favor the next year, 1896, 6-1 in the fifth set of the challenge round.

Between 1890 and 1896 he was in the U.S. Top Ten seven times, No. 1 in 1895. In 1893 he and Clarence Hobart, twice U.S. champs in doubles, won the championship of the World Columbian Exposition at Chicago. He was born Oct. 7, 1868, in Newton Centre, Mass., and died Oct. 18, 1945, in Miami Beach, Fla. He entered the Hall of Fame in 1974.

MAJOR TITLES *(3)–U.S. singles, 1895; U.S. doubles, 1893, 1894.* **OTHER U.S. TITLES** *(3)–Intercollegiate singles, 1890, 1891; Intercollegiate doubles, 1891, with Robert Wrenn.* **SINGLES RECORD IN THE MAJORS**–*U.S. (25-5).*

JOE HUNT

United States (1919–1945)

Hall of Fame 1966

Nobody knows for certain what went wrong when Lt. Joe Hunt sent his Navy fighter plane into its last dive. Pilot error? Mechanical failure? There were rumors of both, but the Atlantic swallowed forever all evidence of the Grumman Hellcat—along with the 1943 U.S. champion.

Fifteen days short of his 26th birthday, Joseph Raphael Hunt of the U.S. Navy was a victim of World War II, killed Feb. 2, 1945, during a routine training mission off Daytona Beach, Fla. The accident, with his training nearly complete, was never explained. Thus Hunt was the shortest-lived of Hall of Famers, ranked No. 1 for his U.S. title-winning performance, but unable the following year, 1944, to get leave from duty to defend the title.

A sturdy, handsome blond Los Angeleno, 6-feet, 165 pounds, he came from a wealthy tennis family. His father, Reuben, won the Southern championship in 1906, and his older sister Marianne in 1934, and brother Charles in 1945, ranked No. 20 nationally. His wife, Jacque Virgil, had been the No. 1 Southern California junior and played Forest Hills in 1943, too.

"He was a strong guy, big serve and volley, and took to grass, coming from the Southern California concrete," says fellow Hall of Famer, Pancho Segura. "Everybody though he'd be the big man, along with Jack Kramer, after the war."

Joe was alone in his progression to the top, the only man to win the U.S. junior 15s and 18s, the Intercollegiate singles (for the Naval Academy) and then the U.S. Championship. In a bizarre finish to his title triumph over Southern California buddy and rival, Kramer (6-3, 6-8, 10-8, 6-0), Hunt, on leave from the Atlantic fleet, won the title, so to speak, lying down. He collapsed to the turf with leg cramps as Kramer's last shot flew out of court, and might not have been able to play another point. The humid 90-degree afternoon got to him in the unique all-military final. Seaman Kramer was also on leave, from the Coast Guard. It was the last important tennis tournament for Joe, who had to report back to his destroyer. However, a year later, at Pensacola, Fla., he did win a local Labor Day event over a fellow flight trainee, 1942 U.S. champ Ted Schroeder.

In 1938 at Southern Cal (doubles) and 1941 at the Naval Academy (singles), Hunt was the only player other than Malcolm Chace (Brown and Yale, 1893, 1894, 1895), to win U.S. Intercollegiate titles for two different schools. Husky and athletic, Hunt also played football at Navy. He, 20, and Kramer, 18, were the second youngest Davis Cup doubles pair for the U.S., losing in 1939 at Philadelphia to Australians John Bromwich and Adrian Quist, the first domino in the only final-round 3-2 loss from a 2-0 lead.

One of the youngest to make the U.S. Top Ten at 17 in 1936, he was a Forest Hills quarter-finalist in 1937 and 1938, semi-finalist in 1939 and 1940, losing both times to Bobby Riggs. Born Feb. 17, 1919 in San Francisco, he was inducted into the Hall of Fame in 1966.

MAJOR TITLE *(1)–U.S. singles, 1943.* **OTHER U.S. TITLES** *(3)–Intercollegiate singles, 1941; Clay Court doubles, 1938, with Lew Wetherell; Intercollegiate doubles, 1938, with Wetherell.* **DAVIS CUP**–*1939; record: 0-1 in doubles.* **SINGLES RECORD IN THE MAJORS**–*U.S. (21-4).*

FRANK HUNTER

United States (1894–1981)

Hall of Fame 1961

As one of the earlier touring pros, Francis Townsend Hunter joined the nomad ranks in 1931 after a distinguished amateur career. A right-handed New Yorker, he was born there June 28, 1894. He played extremely well for his country, taking a 1924 Olympic gold medal in doubles alongside Vinnie Richards, and helping build a 2-1 lead in the losing Davis Cup 1927 finale, yoked to Bill Tilden in a five-set win over France's Jacques Brugnon and Jean Borotra.

He came close, as finalist, to the U.S. title twice in succession: 1928 final, 6-3 in the fifth to Henri Cochet, and 1929, 6-4 in the fifth to Tilden. He also lost the 1923 Wimbledon final to Bill Johnston. And he was one of those unlucky three victims in a row who built two-set leads over 1927 champ Cochet, Hunter in the quarter-finals, preceding Tilden and Borotra. But he won the Wimbledon doubles twice, 1924 with Olympic sidekick Richards and 1927 with Tilden.

His greatest singles success was under cover at New York's Seventh Regiment Armory, winning the U.S. Indoor titles of 1922 over Frank Anderson, 6-4, 1-6, 7-5, 6-2, and 1930 over Julius Seligson, 6-3, 6-2, 6-3. He lost the finals of 1923 and 1924 to Richards, and 1929 to Jean Borotra, and won the doubles in 1923 and 1924 with Richards and 1929 with Tilden. Hunter, a fine volleyer, stressed power in forehand and serve, putting his 5-11, 180-pound frame into those strokes. He ranked in the U.S. Top Ten five times between 1922 and 1929, No. 2 in 1927, 1928, 1929, and in the World Top Ten, 1923, 1927, 1928 and 1929, No. 4 in 1928. He was named to the Hall of Fame in 1961 and died Dec. 2, 1981, in Palm Beach, Fla.

MAJOR TITLES *(5)–U.S. doubles, 1927; Wimbledon doubles, 1924, 1927; Wimbledon mixed, 1927, 1928, 1929.* **OTHER U.S. TITLES** *(5)–Indoor singles, 1922, 1930; Indoor doubles, 1923, 1924, with Vinnie Richards; 1929, with Bill Tilden.* **DAVIS CUP**–*1927, 1928, 1929; record: 3-1 in singles, 1-1 in doubles.* **SINGLES RECORD IN THE MAJORS**–*French (7-3), Wimbledon (18-6), U.S. (38-13).*

HELEN JACOBS

United States (1908–1997)
Hall of Fame 1962

Helen Hull Jacobs had the misfortune to be a contemporary of Helen Wills Moody. Four times in the battle of Helens in the final round at Wimbledon, Jacobs lost. She also lost to her arch-rival at Forest Hills in the 1928 U.S. final.

On top of all those defeats to Helen the First, Jacobs was beaten in the 1934 Wimbledon final by Dorothy Round of Britain, and three times she was turned back in a U.S. final by Alice Marble (1936, 1939, 1940).

Particularly bitter for her to take was a defeat in the 1935 Wimbledon final. Moody that season was struggling, and in the final round Jacobs led at match point, 5-3. Victory seemed at hand when Wills threw up a lob that barely got to the net, and Jacobs waited to smash it for the final point. But a wind current caught the ball and Jacobs, off balance, hit it into the net. Moody rallied and went on to her seventh Wimbledon title. At the time, Jacobs had none.

In spite of so much adversity, Jacobs, a 5-foot-6, 145-pound right-hander, born Aug. 6, 1908, in Globe, Ariz., was as stout of heart as any champion. A U.S. finalist eight times over a stretch of a dozen years (1928-40), Jacobs won four straight, 1932–35, ringing up a 28-match winning streak until dropping a hard-fought 1936 final to her Forest Hills nemesis, Alice Marble. Only Helen Wills (46) and Chris Evert (31) had longer U.S. streaks, but she and Evert were the only victors four straight years.

In 1932 at Forest Hills she caused a sartorial furor, introducing shorts to the female tournament. At last in 1936 she took the victor's silver at Wimbledon, beating Hilda Krahwinkel Sperling, 6-2, 4-6, 7-5. Twice she made it to the French final, but fell to the other Helen in 1930 and lefty Peggy Scriven in 1934.

Jacobs' unflagging courage and iron will to win, was her biggest assets. She had little of the power that Moody applied, and Jacobs' forehand stroke was so unsatisfactory that she forsook it for a sliced cut at the ball, not too effective either to stand off a full-blooded drive or to repel a volleyer. Her backhand, while not severe, was steadfast, reliable against any amount of pressure, and she won heavily with it.

It was at the net where she was most effective. She was not as conclusive with her volley or her smash as Marble, but she was a determined, skilled foe at close quarters, and her fighting traits counted most, whatever her position on the court. Even when afflicted with injuries, she refused to be discouraged. Her admirable qualities, including sportsmanship and great self-reliance, had a strong appeal for tennis galleries.

A feud was built up in publications between the two Helens that Jacobs said never existed. Moody was pictured as resenting Jacobs following in her footsteps. Both played at the Berkeley (Calif.) Tennis Club, had the same coach, William 'Pop' Fuller, won national junior championships two years in a row and attended the University of California. The Jacobs' family lived in the Wills' former home. The two Helens did not see each other except in connection with tennis.

Jacobs, after eight losses to Moody, finally got the victory she was after in the 1933 U.S. Championships, although even then it was not a complete one. She won the first set against Moody, 8-6, and lost the second, 6-3. When the score went to 3-0 in Jacobs' favor in the third set, Moody walked to the umpire's stand, informed the official that because of pain in her back she was unable to continue, and conceded the match. Jacobs had dealt Moody her first big defeat since 1926. It would be Jacobs' lone win in an 11-match rivalry.

She was ranked in the World Top Ten 12 straight times from 1928, including No. 1 in 1936, and served in the Navy in World War II.

She was elected to the Hall of Fame in 1962 and died June 2, 1997 in East Hampton, N.Y.

MAJOR TITLES *(10)–Wimbledon singles, 1936; U.S. singles, 1932, 1933, 1934, 1935; U.S. doubles, 1932, 1933, 1934,1935; U.S. mixed, 1934.* **WIGHTMAN CUP**–*1927, 1928, 1929, 1930, 1931, 1932, 1933, 1934, 1935, 1936, 1937, 1939; record: 14-7 in singles, 5-4 in doubles.* **SINGLES RECORD IN THE MAJORS**–*French (21-7), Wimbledon (55-11), U.S. (64-11).*

BILL JOHNSTON

United States (1894–1946)
Hall of Fame 1958

William M. Johnston's name is inevitably associated with Bill Tilden's. Tilden was 'Big Bill' (6-foot-2) and Johnston 'Little Bill' (5-foot-8-1/2) and they were the twin terrors who turned back the Australasians, French and Japanese in the Davis Cup challenge round from 1920 through 1926, a seven-year span of invincibility unequaled in those international team matches.

Big Bill and Little Bill were teammates and they were also rivals. It was Johnston's bad luck that his career was contemporaneous with the player many regard as the greatest ever. Otherwise Johnston might have won the U.S. Championships most of the years it fell to Tilden, from 1920 to 1925. As it was, Little Bill won it twice, in 1915 and in 1919, defeating Maurice McLoughlin the first time and Tilden in the 1919 final. Johnston was runner-up six times, and in five of those years it was Tilden who beat him in the final.

Until the French began to catch up to Big Bill and Little Bill in 1926, Johnston had been winning his Davis Cup matches with the loss of few sets. In seven challenge rounds, he won 11 of 14 matches in singles. He lost only once until 1927, when his age and his health began to tell. He ranked in the World Top Ten eight straight years from 1919 and in the U.S. Top Ten 12 times between 1913 and 1926, No. 1 in 1915 and in 1919.

The topspin forehand drive he hammered with the western grip was one of the most famous and effective shots in tennis history. No other player executed it as well as he did, taking the ball shoulder high and leaping off the ground on his follow-through. He was also one of the best volleyers the game has known, despite meeting the ball near the service line, where he stationed himself because of his shortness. He used the same face of the racket for backhand and forehand.

A right-hander, Johnston was born Nov. 2, 1894, in San Francisco and developed many of his skills on public parks courts. His whole game was aggressive and he played to win on the merit of his strokes rather than on the opponent's errors. Though he did not have a big serve, overhead he was secure and angled his smash effectively. He had as much fight as anyone who was ever champion, and many times when he came off the court, dripping with perspiration after a prolonged struggle, he was five to eight pounds below his usual weight of 125.

Such was the case in his U.S. final with Tilden in 1922 at the Germantown Cricket Club in Philadelphia in which Johnston won the first two sets and led by 3-0 in the fourth. It seemed that every spectator in the stands was cheering for Johnston, the favorite of galleries virtually every time he went on the court. Both he and Tilden had two legs on the challenge trophy, and Little Bill had his heart set on retiring it for his permanent keeping in this match. It was a crushing disappointment when he lost in five sets.

Following the 1927 season, Johnston retired from competition. His health had not been robust from the time he served in the Navy in World War I. He died May 1, 1946, and 12 years later was enshrined in the Hall of Fame. Little Bill had made a big name in tennis.

MAJOR TITLES (7)–*Wimbledon singles, 1923; U.S. singles, 1915, 1919; U.S. doubles, 1915, 1916, 1920; U.S. mixed, 1921.* OTHER U.S. TITLES–*Clay Court singles, 1919, 1920; Clay Court doubles, 1919, with Sam Hardy.* DAVIS CUP–*1920, 1921, 1922, 1923, 1924, 1925, 1926, 1927; record: 14-3 in singles, 4-0 in doubles.* SINGLES RECORD IN THE MAJORS–*Wimbledon (8-1), U.S. (59-11).*

ANN HAYDON JONES

Great Britain (1930–)
Hall of Fame 1985

The first left-handed woman to win Wimbledon, Adrianne Shirley Haydon Jones had to cool a rampaging Billie Jean King to do it in the 1969 final, 3-6, 6-3, 6-2. King had won three straight times and 24 straight matches. Before that, Ann had shown her all-around value and steadiness by winning the French in 1961 and 1966. She could attack or stay back, and had a compact service motion with little windup. In 1967, despite a leg injury that hobbled her, she pushed King hard (11-9, 6-4) in the U.S. final, gamely extricating herself from nine set points before losing the first, and two match points at the end.

A buxom blonde, 5-foot-7, 135 pounds, Ann was always a stalwart in playing for her country in Federation and Wightman Cups. In 1975, at 37, after she'd stopped touring, she set aside motherhood for a weekend to play a small but important doubles role in Britain's 5-2 Wightman triumph at Cleveland's Public Auditorium. She and Virginia Wade beat Julie Anthony and Janet Newberry, 6-2, 3-6, 7-6. Deciding to go for dollars, she, King, Françoise Durr and Rosie Casals became the first professional female touring troupe, signing with George MacCall, promoter of the National Tennis League, in 1968.

Jones was born Oct. 7, 1938, in Birmingham, England, to parents who were outstanding table tennis players. She followed in their paddling steps as a five-time finalist for various world championship titles. But she was to make her name in tennis after winning the British junior championships of 1954 and 1955, moving on to place in the World Top Ten every year between 1957 and 1970 (except for 1964), No. 2 in 1967 and 1969.

Her Wimbledon triumph was a gem of persistence—Ann won on her fourteenth try—and, fourth-seeded, beat the fifth, first and second seeds in the stretch to do so: Nancy Richey, 6-2, 7-5; Margaret Court, 10-12, 6-3, 6-2; and King. Jones played 157 matches at Wimbledon: 57-13 in singles, 33-15 in doubles, 29-10 in mixed. She married P. F. Jones in 1962 and entered the Hall of Fame in 1985.

MAJOR TITLES *(7)–French singles, 1961, 1966; Wimbledon singles, 1969; French doubles, 1963, 1968, 1969; Wimbledon mixed, 1969.* **FEDERATION CUP**–*1963, 1964, 1965, 1966, 1967, 1971; record: 11-8 in singles, 13-7 in doubles.* **WIGHTMAN CUP**–*1957, 1958, 1959, 1960, 1961, 1962, 1963, 1964, 1965, 1966, 1967, 1970, 1975; record: 10-11 in singles, 6-5 in doubles.* **SINGLES RECORD IN THE MAJORS**–*Australian (3-3), French (46-9), Wimbledon (57-13), U.S. (36-10).*

BILLIE JEAN KING

United States (1943–)
Hall of Fame 1987

The fireman's daughter, Billie Jean Moffitt King, began blazing through the tennis world in 1960 when she first appeared in the U.S. women's rankings at No. 4. She was 17. For more than four decades she has continued as a glowing force in the game—the all-time Wimbledon champion, frequently the foremost player, a crusader in building the female professional game (enhancing the game as a whole), remaining relevant to sport today, an inspiration to millions.

Born Nov. 22, 1943, in Long Beach, Calif., Billie Jean, a 5-foot-4-1/2, 130-pound right-hander, was named for her father, Bill Moffitt, a Long Beach fireman and an enthusiastic athlete, though not a tennis player. Her brother, Randy Moffitt, became a pitcher for the San Francisco Giants. She developed on the public courts of Long Beach and first gained international recognition in 1961 by joining 18-year-old Karen Hantze for a surprising triumph in the Wimbledon women's doubles over Aussies Margaret Smith (Court) and Jan Lehane. Unseeded, they were the youngest team

to win it. That was the first of 20 Wimbledon championships, making King the record winner at the most prestigious tourney. Centre Court was her magic garden from the first time she saw it in 1961.

In 1979 she got the 20th at her 19th Wimbledon, the doubles, in the company of Martina Navratilova (over Betty Stove and Wendy Turnbull). She won her last major, the U.S. doubles, in 1980, beside Martina, over Pam Shriver and Stove.

Elizabeth Ryan's 19 Wimbledon titles (between 1914 and 1934) were all in doubles and mixed doubles. King won six singles, 10 doubles, and four mixed between 1961 and 1979, and in 1979 lengthened another Wimbledon record by appearing in her 27th final, the doubles. Ryan was in 24 finals. Of all the men and women to compete at Wimbledon only Navratilova played more matches (279) than King's 265, of which B.J. was 95-15 in singles, 74-12 in doubles, 55-14 in mixed. She won 12 singles titles at major championships (one Australian, one French, six Wimbledon and four U.S.).

In her initial singles major, Wimbledon, 1966, she beat three-time champ Maria Bueno. She followed up by beating Ann Jones in 1967 and Judy Tegart (Dalton) in the first open Wimbledon, 1968. In 1967 she took her first U.S. singles over Jones, but the most rousing of the four was 1974, a pyrotechnical performance from two assault-minded dolls, over Goolagong, 3-6, 6-3, 7-5. Probably her most memorable Wimbledon match was a loss, the record 46-game 1970 final to Court, 14-12. 11-9. Neither let up in attacking, even though both were playing hurt.

Billie Jean's has been a career of firsts. In 1968 she was the first woman of the open era to sign a pro contract to tour in a female tournament group, with Rosie Casals, Françoise Durr and Jones as the women's auxiliary of the NTL (National Tennis League), which also included six men. (A few women before King had turned pro to make head-to-head barnstorming tours.)

In 1971 B.J. was the first woman athlete over the 100-grand hurdle, winning $117,000. During that memorable season she played 31 tournaments in singles, winning 17, and 26 in doubles, winning a record 21. She had a match mark of 112-13 in singles, a record number of wins, and 80-5 in doubles. Overall it added up to 38 titles on 192 match wins, both records. Imagine how many millions such a campaign would be worth today.

In 1973 Billie Jean engaged in a 'Battle of the Sexes'

challenge match, defeating 55-year-old ex-Wimbledon champ Bobby Riggs, 6-4, 6-3, 6-3, in a heavily publicized and nationally televised extravaganza that captured the nation's fancy and drew a record tennis crowd, 30,472, to Houston's Astrodome.

In 1974 she became the first woman to coach a professional team containing men when she served as player-coach of the Philadelphia Freedoms of World Team Tennis, a league she and her husband, Larry King, helped establish. As a tribute to her, Elton John composed and recorded *Philadelphia Freedom*. Traded to the New York Apples, she led that team to WTT titles in 1976-77 as a player.

Ten years after Riggs, B.J. was to establish a geriatric mark herself, winning Birmingham (England) over Alycia Moulton. At 39 years, five months she was the oldest woman to take a pro singles title.

An aggressive, emotional player, Billie Jean specialized in serve-and-volley tactics, aided by quickness and a highly competitive nature. She overcame several knee operations to continue as a winner into her 40th year. As a big-match player she was unsurpassed, excelling in team situations when she represented the U.S. In nine years on the Federation Cup team, she helped the U.S. gain the final each time, and take seven Cups by winning 51 of her 55 singles and doubles. In the Wightman Cup against Britain she played on only one losing side in 10 years, winning 21 of her 26 singles and doubles.

Outspoken on behalf of women's rights, in and out of sports—tennis in particular—she was possibly the most influential player in popularizing professional tennis in the United States. She worked tirelessly to promote the Virginia Slims tour during the early 1970s when the women realized they must separate from the men to achieve recognition and significant prize money on their own. With the financial backing of Virginia Slims, the organizational acumen of Gladys Heldman and the salesmanship and winning verve of King, the women pros built an extremely profitable circuit.

Only two women, Margaret Smith Court (62) and Navratilova (57) won more majors than King's 39 in singles, doubles and mixed. In regard to U.S. titles on all surfaces (grass, clay, hard court, indoor), King is second at 31 behind Hazel Hotchkiss Wightman's 34. But Billie Jean is the only woman to win on all four, equalling Tony Trabert, the lone man. King and Casals were the only doubles team to win U.S. titles on all four surfaces. She won seven of her major doubles with Casals, her most frequent and successful partner.

Between 1963 and 1980, Billie Jean was in the World Top Ten 18 times, including five times as No. 1 (1966, '67, '68, '71, '74) and four times as No. 2 (1970, '73, '75, '77). She held her last World ranking, No. 13, at age 40 in 1983.

She greatly aided Owen Davidson in making his mixed doubles Grand Slam in 1967 with two partners. King and Davidson won the French, Wimbledon and U.S. after he took the Australian with Lesley Turner. She scored three major triples, winning the singles, doubles and mixed at Wimbledon in 1967 and 1973, and at the U.S. in 1967, and won the longest singles set played by women (36 games) in a 1963 Wightman Cup win over Christine Truman, 6-4, 19-17.

Billie Jean's grand swan song occurred at 39 in 1983 at Wimbledon, a semi-final finish (her fourteenth), losing to 18-year-old Andrea Jaeger, 6-1, 6-1. Seven years later she played a cameo role in the Boca Raton, Fla., tourney, winning a doubles match with 13-year-old pro rookie Jennifer Capriati.

In a career encompassing the amateur and open eras, she won 67 pro and 37 amateur career singles titles. She reached 38 other pro finals and had 677-149 singles W-L record as a pro. Her prize money: $1,966,487.

Divorce ended her marriage. A founder and ex-president of the WTA, B.J. remains active in World Team Tennis as an officer, formerly commissioner. She returned to her USTA roots in 1995 as captain of the Federation Cup team, having been player-captain in 1965 (a loss) and 1976 (a win). She guided the U.S. team to three Cups (1996, 1999, and 2000). As U.S. women's Olympic coach, she mentored Lindsay Davenport, Gigi Fernandez and Mary Joe Fernandez to gold medals in 1996, as well as Venus and Serena Williams to golds, and Monica Seles to a bronze in 2000.

MAJOR TITLES *(39)–Australian singles, 1968; French singles, 1972; Wimbledon singles, 1966, 1967, 1968, 1972, 1973, 1975; U.S. singles, 1967, 1971, 1972, 1974; French doubles, 1972; Wimbledon doubles, 1961, 1962, 1965, 1967, 1968, 1970, 1971, 1972, 1973, 1979; U.S. doubles, 1964, 1967, 1974, 1977, 1980; Australian mixed, 1968; French mixed, 1967, 1970; Wimbledon mixed, 1967, 1971, 1973, 1974; U.S. mixed, 1967, 1971, 1973, 1976.* **OTHER U.S. TITLES** *(18)–Indoor singles, 1966, 1967, 1968, 1971, 1974; Clay Court singles, 1971; Hard Court singles, 1966; Indoor doubles, 1966, 1968, 1971, 1975, with Rosie Casals; 1979, with Martina Navratilova; 1983, with Sharon Walsh; Clay Court doubles, 1960, with Darlene Hard; 1971, with Judy Tegart Dalton; Hard Court doubles, 1966, with Casals; Indoor mixed, 1966, 1967, with Paul Sullivan.* **FEDERATION**

CUP (As player)–*1963, 1964, 1965, 1966, 1967, 1976, 1977, 1978, 1979; record 25-4 in singles, 27-0 in doubles;* (As captain)–*1965, 1976, 1995, 1996; record: 12-2, 2 Cups.* WIGHTMAN CUP–*1961, 1962, 1963, 1964, 1965, 1966, 1967, 1970, 1977, 1978; record: 14-2 in singles, 7-3 in doubles.* SINGLES RECORD IN THE MAJORS–*Australian (17-4), French (21-6), Wimbledon (95-15), U.S. (58-14).*

JAN KODES

Czechoslovakia (1945–)
Hall of Fame 1990

Determination marked the grim-faced Jan Kodes, who clawed and battled to many a victory, though seemingly exhausted. As a sportsman he was even more a hero to many of his countrymen for his refusal to leave the repressed country as Jaroslav Drobny, Martina Navratilova and Ivan Lendl had done. Thus they shared more fully in his major triumphs: Wimbledon of 1973, and the French of 1970 and 1971.

A compact, muscular 5-foot-9 right-hander, Kodes was a standout and dogged groundstroker. He volleyed well, too, but was disdainful of grass even though he signalled his ability there in 1971 by knocking top-seeded John Newcombe out of the U.S. Open in the first round, 2-6, 7-6 (5-1), 7-6 (5-1), 6-3. Nothing like that had happened since 1930 when Berkeley Bell grounded top foreign-seed Jean Borotra in the opening round.

Pushing upward and onward, all the while moaning about "this joke tennis, this grass," Jan, beaten in the first round at Wimbledon, next escaped Pierre Barthes, 2-6, 5-7, 6-4, 6-4, 6-4, who served at 4-3, 40-30 in the fifth. In the semis he startled third-seeded Arthur Ashe, 7-6 (5-3), 3-6, 4-6, 6-3, 6-4, to become an unseeded U.S. finalist. He didn't break in tie-breakers (four-for-four) until the last one finished his astonishing journey: Stan Smith beat him in the final, 3-6, 6-3, 6-2, 7-6 (5-3). Two years later he was the Wimbledon champ, defeating Alex Metreveli in straight sets, and fought Newcombe in a brilliant five-set U.S. final, losing the last set, 6-3.

Kodes, seventh-seeded, easily beat Zeljko Franulovic, 6-2, 6-4, 6-0, to win the French in 1970, countered the artistry of Ilie Nastase, 8-6, 6-2, 2-6, 7-5, the following year, but fell to Patrick Proisy, 6-4, 6-2, 6-4, in the 1972 quarters, ending a 17-match run at Roland Garros.

As a devoted Davis Cupper, he played 15 years and 39 series for Czechoslovakia beginning in 1966, and was among the top 20 players in matches played (95) and won (60): 39-20 in singles, 21-15 in doubles. He led the team to the 1975 Cup round, a 3-2 defeat by Sweden at Stockholm, and played a cameo doubles role along the

way in 1980 as he realized a dream—the Cup for Czechoslovakia, Lendl-powered.

Besides his three majors he won six pro titles in singles, 17 in doubles, and accumulated $693,197 in career prize money. Jan was in the World Top Ten in 1971 and 1973, No. 5 in the former. Born March 1, 1945, in Prague, he has served as his country's national coach and Davis Cup captain, and entered the Hall of Fame in 1990.

MAJOR TITLES (3)–*French singles, 1970, 1971; Wimbledon singles, 1973.* DAVIS CUP–*1966, 1967, 1968, 1969, 1970, 1971, 1972, 1973, 1974, 1975, 1976, 1977, 1978, 1979, 1980; record: 39-20 in singles, 21-15 in doubles.* SINGLES RECORD IN THE MAJORS–*French (43-13), Wimbledon (19-14), U.S. (27-9).*

ANNA KOURNIKOVA

Russia (1981–)

Despite zero wins in singles events on the WTA Tour and consistent early exits from major championships, Anna Kournikova is one of the most popular athletes on the planet. The statuesque star is a one-woman industry of pin-ups, posters and product pitches. *People* magazine placed her on its 50 Most Beautiful List, while *FHM* magazine named her sexiest woman of the year in 2002. She is the most popular attraction on the Web and her name was given to a notorious computer virus that banished countless Internet surfers to cyberia.

The sports pages, not to mention gossip columns, are filled with stories about her (rumored/ secret/ broken) marriage(s) to hockey's Sergei Fedorov and/or Pavel Bure. Her most reprinted quotation is an immodest: "I'm beautiful, famous and gorgeous." The most photographed woman in tennis history is celebrated far more for her curves than her serves.

Born in Moscow on June 7, 1981, Kournikova says her parents sold a television to buy her a tennis racquet at age 5. Her early promise won her a coveted spot at the Spartak tennis club. She later was sent to the Nick Bollettieri Tennis Academy in Bradenton, Fla.

Her WTA Tour debut came in her hometown in 1995. At age 14 in 1996, she won a singles rubber against Anna-Karin Svensson of Sweden to become the youngest player credited with a Fed Cup victory.

In her first appearance at Wimbledon, in 1997, she went to the semi-finals, the best debut since Chris Evert in 1972. But that precociousness was never matched by her subsequent performances. Incredibly, Kournikova, once ranked as high as the world No. 8, has yet to win a single tournament on her own.

In doubles, Kournikova and Martina Hingis shared Australian Open honors in 1999 and 2002. She also has 16 doubles titles on the tour, the first with Monica Seles at the Princess Cup in Tokyo in 1998.

In 2002, she was eliminated in the first round of all four Grand Slam tournaments.

MAJOR TITLES (2)–*Australian doubles 1999, 2002.* FED CUP–*1996, 1997, 2000; record: 2-5 in singles, 10-2 in doubles.* SINGLES RECORD IN THE MAJORS– *Australian (4-6), French (29-4), Wimbledon (6-4), U.S. (14-6).*

JACK KRAMER

United States (1921–)
Hall of Fame 1968

The impact of John Albert 'Jake' Kramer on tennis has been fourfold: As great player, exceptional promoter, thoughtful innovator and astute television commentator.

Kramer, born Aug. 1, 1921, in Las Vegas, Nev., grew up in the Los Angeles area. He achieved international notice in 1939 as a teenager when he was selected to play doubles, alongside Joe Hunt, for the U.S. in the Davis Cup finale against Australia. At 18, Kramer was the youngest to play in the Cup title round, although John Alexander of Australia lowered the record to 17 by playing in 1968.

Kramer and Hunt were the golden boys out of Southern California, their careers intertwined. Joe beat Jake, at Forest Hills in 1939, where they were both losing semi-finalists the following year. Both were to go to sea during World War II, Jake in the Coast Guard, Joe in the Navy, and to receive leaves to play again in the U.S. Championships of 1943, where they collided in the final. Hunt won, barely, sprawling on the court with cramps as Kramer's last shot flew long. Kramer, who'd had a bout with food poisoning, laughed later, "If I could've kept that ball in play I might have been a champ on a default." Hunt was killed 17 months afterwards in a military plane crash.

Because of the war Jake had to wait three years to return to Forest Hills. Then he rose to prominence as a splendid champion, so dominant that he was voted fifth on a list of all-time greats selected by a panel of expert tennis journalists in 1969. The powerful right-hander was the leading practitioner of the 'big game,' rushing to the net constantly behind his serve, and frequently attacking on return of serve. His serve took opponents off the court, setting them up for the volley, as did his crushing forehand.

A blistered racket hand probably decided his gruelling fourth-round defeat by cunning lefty Jaroslav Drobny, and prevented Jake from winning the first postwar Wimbledon. But he came back awesomely in 1947, the first to win in shorts, making short work of everybody. Whipping doubles partner Tom Brown in 48 minutes, 6-1, 6-3, 6-2, he lost merely 37 games in seven matches, the most lopsided run to the championship.

Brown had been his 1946 U.S. final-round victim, another one-sided excursion for Jake, a crew-cut blond whose goal was to reclaim the Davis Cup that he and Hunt failed to clinch in 1939. In December he and good buddy Ted Schroeder—the U.S. doubles champs of 1940—were members of a highly talented team that captain Walter Pate took to Australia for the challenge round. Every man—those two plus Brown, Frank Parker, Gardnar Mulloy, Bill Talbert—thought he should play. Pate picked Ted and Jake to do it all, controversial until the pals paralyzed the favored Aussies on opening day. Schroeder won in five over John Bromwich and Kramer nailed Dinny Pails. Together they grabbed the Cup by flattening the team that had beaten Hunt and Kramer in '39: Bromwich and Adrian Quist, 6-2, 7-5, 6-4.

The following summer, Jake and Ted repelled the Australian challenge for the Cup at Forest Hills. Then Kramer closed out his amateur career memorably by overhauling Parker in the U.S. final. Kramer lost the first two sets, and was in danger of losing out on a lucrative professional contract as well as his championship. Counterpunching, he won, 4-6, 2-6, 6-1, 6-0, 6-3, and set off in pursuit of Bobby Riggs, the reigning pro champ. Kramer, who had lost only two matches in 1946, dropped but one (to Talbert) in 1947, winning eight of nine tournaments on 48-1, closing his amateur life with a 41-match rush, and 18 singles titles.

Kramer knocked Riggs off the summit by winning their odyssey of one-nighters throughout the U.S., which was the test of professional supremacy of that day. Their opener was a phenomenon: New York was buried by a blizzard that brought the city to a stop, yet 15,114 customers made it on foot to the old Madison Square Garden on Dec. 27, 1947, to watch Riggs win. But Bobby couldn't keep it up. Kramer won the tour, 69-20, and stayed in action while Riggs took over as the promoter and signed Pancho Gonzalez to challenge Kramer. Nobody was up to Kramer then. He bruised the rookie Gonzalez 96-27 on the longest of the tours. Kramer made $85,000 against Riggs as his percentage, and $72,000 against Gonzalez.

In 1952 Kramer assumed the position of promoter himself, the boss of pro tennis, a role he would hold for over a decade, well past his playing days. Kramer's last tour as a principal was against the first man he recruited, Frank Sedgman, the Aussie who was tops among amateurs. Kramer won, 54-41. An arthritic back led to his retirement as a player, but he kept the tour going, resurrecting one of his victims, Gonzalez, who became the strongman.

One of the shrewdest operators in tennis, Kramer was looked to for advice when the open era began in 1968. He devised the Grand Prix for the men's game, a series of tournaments leading to a Masters Championship for the top eight finishers, and a bonus pool to be shared by more than a score of the leading players. The Grand Prix, incorporating the most attractive tournaments around the world, functioned from 1970 until 1990, when the ATP Tour took over the structure. In 1972 he was instrumental in forming the ATP (Association of Tennis Pros), the male players' union, and was its first executive director. His role as leader of the ATP's principled boycott of Wimbledon in 1973 made him unpopular in Britain for a time. Nevertheless, it was a landmark act, assuring the players of the right to control their own destiny after being in thrall to national associations until then. Later he served on the Men's International Professional Tennis Council, the worldwide governing board.

For more than 20 years Kramer served as a perceptive analyst on tennis telecasts in many countries, notably for the British Broadcasting Corporation at Wimbledon and for all the American networks at Forest Hills, and at other events, second to none. He ranked in the U.S. Top Ten five times between 1940 and 1947, No. 1 in the U.S. and the world in 1946 and 1947. Kramer won the U.S. Pro title in 1948 over the defender, Riggs, and the world pro title in 1949 over Riggs.

Kramer, winner of 13 U.S. singles and doubles titles, was named to the Hall of Fame in 1968. His son, Bob Kramer, continues the family's tennis interests as director of the Los Angeles ATP tourney.

MAJOR TITLES (10)–*Wimbledon singles, 1947; U.S. Singles, 1946, 1947; Wimbledon doubles, 1946, 1947; U.S. doubles, 1940, 1941, 1943, 1947; U.S. mixed, 1941.* **OTHER U.S. TITLES** (6)–*Indoor singles, 1947; Pro singles, 1948; Pro doubles, 1948, 1955, with Pancho Segura; Indoor doubles, 1947, with Bob Falkenburg; Clay Court doubles, 1941, with Ted Schroeder.* **DAVIS CUP**–*1939, 1946,* *1947; record: 6-0 in singles, 1-2 in doubles.* **SINGLES RECORD IN THE MAJORS**–*Wimbledon (10-1), U.S. (24-5).*

GUSTAVO KUERTEN
Brazil (1976–)

Gustavo Kuerten is the King of Clay. The Brazilian star has conquered Roland Garros three times—in 1997, 2000 and 2001, and is one of only five players since 1950 to win all four important clay-court titles, the French, Hamburg, Monte Carlo and Rome.

Following his 2001 win, Brazil issued a postage stamp featuring Kuerten (called Guga in his homeland) with the Eiffel Tower in the background. Kuerten's unruly black curls, toothy smile and outlandishly colored clothes have made him an icon among Brazilian teenagers. Born on Sept. 10, 1976, in Florianopolis in the southern state of Santa Catarina, the 6-foot-3, 167-pound Kuerten is the first South American to reach a No. 1 ranking and the biggest tennis star at home since Maria Bueno won three Wimbledon and four U.S. singles championships between 1959 and 1966.

Guga would rather surf than play on turf. He skipped grass tournaments for a second consecutive year in 2002, even squabbling with Wimbledon officials about their seeding structure. His game has always been suited to clay. His place in Brazilian sporting history was assured in 1997 when he defeated three former champions— Thomas Muster, Yevgeny Kafelnikov and Sergi Bruguera—on his way to claiming the French Open title. Just 20 years old, he was ranked a lowly No. 66 in the world.

He took his second title in 2000, besting Magnus Norman in the final. Kuerten won four other titles that year, including the season-ending Tennis Masters Cup in Sydney, where he got past Pete Sampras in the semifinals and Andre Agassi in the final 6-4, 6-4, 6-4. That put him at the top of the ATP Rankings, ending an eight-year reign by Americans.

Kuerten defended his crown at Roland Garros in 2001, becoming only the fourth player in the Open Era with three or more French titles, joining Bjorn Borg (6), Ivan Lendl (3) and Mats Wilander (3). Roland Garros was one of six tournaments he won that year, five of them on clay. But he suffered from injuries all season, especially with problems to his hip. After getting as far as the quarter-finals of the U.S. Open, he dropped 11 of his next 12 matches.

He lost the coveted No. 1 ranking to Lleyton Hewitt

of Australia by bowing out early at the Tennis Masters Cup. Some consolation could be found in leading the ATP in prize money for a second consecutive season.

Arthroscopic surgery was performed on his right hip in Nashville, Tenn., on Feb. 26, 2002. Kuerten returned to the European clay-court circuit just two months later. The warm-ups were not enough to get him match ready for a fourth title at Roland Garros, where a 17-match winning streak was ended by eventual winner Albert Costa in the fourth round. A rare bright spot in a season that saw Kuerten drop from the top 10 for the first time since 1998 was winning his 17th career title at Bahia, his first championship on home soil. He also led Brazil back into the Davis Cup World Group by beating Canada.

MAJOR TITLES (3)–French singles 1997, 2000, 2001. **DAVIS CUP**–1996, 1997, 1998, 1999, 2000, 2001, 2002; record: 16-18 in singles, 10-3 in doubles. **SINGLES RECORD IN THE MAJORS**–Australian (4-6), French (29-4), Wimbledon (6-4), U.S. 14-6.

RENÉ LACOSTE

France (1904–1996)
Hall of Fame 1976

He was not particularly athletic in build or in his movements, and as a reserved and rather shy youth he seemed to be more fitted for the world of education, law or medicine than for athletic achievement. But Jean René Lacoste, known as the Crocodile, would win Wimbledon and the U.S. twice, the French thrice and become a member of the Four Musketeers, the scourges of the tennis world in the 1920s. He was in the World Top Ten six straight years from 1924, No. 1 in 1926-27.

Lacoste was a self-made champion, a player who won world renown through sheer hard work and devoted application rather than through the benefit of natural talent. Born in Paris, July 2, 1904, he did not go onto a court until he was 15 years old, while on a trip with his father to England. His development after that was slow.

His father, a wealthy manufacturer of automobiles, agreed to his son's devoting himself to tennis, but with the understanding that he must set himself the task of becoming a world champion and achieve his goal within five years or drop it.

In his determination to excel, Lacoste trained faithfully and read and observed everything, even keeping a notebook on the strengths and weaknesses of his contemporaries. He became a master of the backcourt game, choosing to maintain a length of inexorable pressure to exact the error or the opening for the finishing shot, and repelling the volleyer with passing shots and lobs.

In recognition of his growing success, he was selected in 1923 as the fourth Musketeer to blend with Jean Borotra, Jacques Brugnon and Henri Cochet in the alliance that would bring France the Davis Cup, and the following year he was in his first major final, Wimbledon, only to lose to Borotra. But in 1925 he came back to win the Big W in a four-set rematch, and took it for a second time in 1928 over Cochet. Also in 1925 Lacoste won the French, over Borotra, whom he also beat in a memorable rainy 1929 final.

As the French drew closer to the Cup, losing the challenge round to the U.S., 4-1, in 1926, Lacoste made the breakthrough for team morale, beating Tilden, 4-6, 6-4, 8-6, 8-6, Big Bill's first Cup loss after 16 wins. The year 1927 was momentous, enclosing three victories over Tilden: In the French final, in the challenge-round-squaring triumph as the French grabbed the Cup, and in the U.S. final.

Perhaps the U.S. was the most stirring, where the efficiency of his backcourt game thwarted the great one. The 34-year-old Tilden attacked for close to two hours and volleyed far more than was his custom, but despite efforts that brought him to the point of exhaustion, he could not win a set. The sphinx-like Lacoste, 22, kept the ball going back the full length of the court with the inevitability of fate and hardly an inexcusable error. The score of the fabulous match was 11-9, 6-3, 11-9, enabling Lacoste to retain the U.S. title he had won the previous year against Borotra.

In 1928 Lacoste lost the opener in the Davis Cup to Tilden and it marked the Frenchman's last appearance in international team matches, owing to his health. After winning the French title in 1929, he withdrew from competition, having more than fulfilled the goal he once never seemed suited for—that of a tennis champion.

He captained the victorious French Davis Cup teams of 1931-32. Ever seeking to improve playing conditions, he designed the first shirts specifically for tennis, the short-sleeved cotton polo so common now, and put his familiar trademark, a crocodile, on the breast, starting the flood of apparel logos. Lacoste also developed the split-shaft steel racket that appeared in 1967 as the Wilson T2000, used for years by Jimmy Connors.

His wife, Simone Thion de la Chaume, was a French amateur golf champion, and his daughter, Catherine Lacoste, won the U.S. Open golf title in 1967. He died Oct. 12, 1996, in St. Jean-de-Luz, France.

MAJOR TITLES *(10)–French singles, 1925, 1927, 1929; U.S. singles, 1926, 1927; Wimbledon singles, 1925, 1928; French doubles, 1925, 1929; Wimbledon doubles, 1925.* **DAVIS CUP**–*1923, 1924, 1925, 1926, 1927, 1928; record: 32-8 in singles, 8-3 in doubles.* **SINGLES RECORD IN THE MAJORS**–*French (29-3), Wimbledon (28-5), U.S. (19-3).*

BILL LARNED

United States (1872–1926)
Hall of Fame 1956

One of the Big Three of the U.S. men's championship, William Augustus Larned won seven times, as did Dick Sears before him and Bill Tilden after. Like Tilden, he was a late achiever, 28 years old when, after failing in the final before Malcolm Whitman the previous year, he won the title in 1901 for a first time, over Beals Wright. His last, ending a five-year run, in 1911, made him the oldest male singles champ, 38.

He began playing the Championships in 1891 and in 19 years, through 1911, fell short of the semis only twice, making a 61-12 match record. He was ranked in the U.S. Top Ten 19 times, starting with No. 6 in 1892, and probably would have been there 20 straight years if he hadn't missed the 1898 season serving with the Rough Riders in the Spanish-American War. Nineteen years was a record for eight decades until topped by Jimmy Connors.

Bill, a strong-armed 5-foot-11, 170-pounder, was No. 1 eight times, tied by Connors, topped by Tilden's 10. Three of those years his younger brother, Edward Larned, was also in the Top Ten, No. 6 in 1903. He was a member of five Davis Cup teams, in 1902 a Cup winner. He was a powerful groundstroker with an oppressive topspinning right-handed forehand.

Bill was born Dec. 30, 1872, in Summit, N.J., and attended Cornell, for whom he won the Intercollegiate title in 1892. He committed suicide on Dec. 16, 1926, in New York. He was inducted into the Hall of Fame in 1956.

MAJOR TITLES *(7)–U.S. singles, 1901, 1902, 1907, 1908, 1909, 1910, 1911.* **OTHER U.S. TITLE**–*Intercollegiate singles, 1892.* **DAVIS CUP**–*1902, 1903, 1905, 1908, 1909, 1911; record: 9-5 in singles.* **SINGLES RECORD IN THE MAJORS**–*Wimbledon (5-2), U.S. (61-12).*

ART LARSEN

United States (1925–)
Hall of Fame 1969

A sleek left-hander with splendid touch, Arthur David 'Tappy' Larsen in 1950 was the first southpaw champion of the U.S. in the post-World War II era, the first since Johnny Doeg two decades before. He battled fellow Californian, Herbie Flam, in a long-shot final—they were seeded fifth and second, respectively—to win at Forest Hills, 6-3, 4-6, 5-7, 6-4, 6-3.

A European-combat veteran of the U.S. Army in World War II, the 5-foot-10, 150-pound Larsen was delayed in his start in big-time tennis, making the U.S. Top Ten the first of eight successive times at No. 6 in 1949, at age 24. He was No. 1 in 1950, and ranked in the World Top Ten thrice, 1950, 1951, 1954, No. 3 the first year.

By adding the U.S. Clay and Hard Court (1952) and Indoor (1953) titles to this Forest Hills prize he became the first man to take the championships on the four surfaces. Only he and Tony Trabert have done so. Losing the French to Trabert in 1954, he was only the ninth of 15 American men to attain that final. Larsen was born April 17, 1925, in Hayward, Calif., and entered the Hall of Fame in 1969.

MAJOR TITLE *(1)–U.S. singles, 1950.* **OTHER U.S. TITLES** *(8)–Indoor singles, 1953; Clay Court singles, 1952; Hard Court singles, 1950, 1952; Indoor doubles, 1953, with Kurt Nielsen; Clay Court doubles, 1950, with Herb Flam; 1952, with Grant Golden; Hard Court doubles, 1952, with Tom Brown.* **DAVIS CUP**–*1951, 1952; record: 4-0 in singles.* **SINGLES RECORD IN THE MAJORS**–*French (16-4), Wimbledon (20-7), U.S. (31-8).*

ROD LAVER

Australia (1938–)
Hall of Fame 1981

Rod Laver was so scrawny and sickly as a child in the Australian bush that no one could guess he would become a left-handed whirlwind who would conquer the tennis world and be known as possibly the greatest player ever.

A little more than a month before Don Budge completed the first Grand Slam, Rodney George 'Rocket' Laver was born Aug. 9, 1938, at Rockhampton, Queensland, Australia. Despite lack of size and early infirmities, Laver grew strong and tough on his father's cattle property and emulated Budge by making the second male Grand Slam in 1962 as an amateur—then became the only double Grand Slammer seven years later by taking the major singles (Australian, French, Wimbledon, U.S.) as a pro.

Few champions have been as devastating and dominant as Laver was as amateur and pro during the 1960s. An incessant attacker, he was nevertheless a complete player who glowed in the backcourt and at the net. Laver's 5-foot-8-1/2, 145-pound body seemed to dangle from a massive left arm that belonged to a gorilla, an arm with which he bludgeoned the ball and was able to impart ferocious topspin. Although others had used top-spin, Laver may have inspired a wave of heavy-hitting topspin practitioners of the 1970s such as Bjorn Borg and Guillermo Vilas. The stroke became basic after Laver.

As a teenager he was sarcastically nicknamed 'Rocket' by Australian Davis Cup Capt. Harry Hopman. "He was anything but a Rocket," Hopman recalled. "But Rod was willing to work harder than the rest, and it was soon apparent to me that he had more talent than any other of our fine Australian players."

His initial international triumph came during his first trip abroad in 1956, when he won the U.S. Junior Championship at 17. Four years later he was ready to take his place among the world's best when he won the Australian singles, snapping back to beat another lefty, Neale Fraser and, with Bob Mark, the doubles for a second time. He was runner-up to Alex Olmedo for the Wimbledon championship, that would presently be his four times. The Australian victories were the first of Laver's 20 major titles in singles, doubles and mixed, placing him fifth among all-time male winners behind Roy Emerson (28), John Newcombe (25), Frank Sedgman (22) and Bill Tilden (21). Jean Borotra also won 20. His 11 singles (equaled by Bjorn Borg) were second to Emerson's long-standing record of 12, later eclipsed by Pete Sampras' 14.

The losing Wimbledon finals of 1959-60 were but a prelude to an incredible run of success in that tournament. He was a finalist six straight times he entered, winning in 1961 over Chuck McKinley and 1962, over Marty Mulligan. After a five-year absence as an outcast professional, he returned to the fanfare of opens to win again in 1968, over Tony Roche, and in 1969, over Newcombe. While winning Wimbledon in four straight appearances (the only man since World War I to win four prior to Borg) and proceeding to the fourth round in 1970, Laver set a male tournament record of 31 consecutive match wins, ended by his loss to Roger Taylor (passed in 1980 by Borg, who lengthened the record to 41).

The year 1969 was Laver's finest, perhaps the best experienced by any player, as he won an open-era record 17 singles tournaments (tied by Guillermo Vilas in 1977) of 32 played on a 106-16 match record. In 1962 he won 19 of 34 on 134-15. Unlike his Grand Slam year of 1962 as an amateur, he was playing in tournaments that were open to all, amateur and pro, and this Slam was all the more impressive.

After his second year running as the No. 1 amateur, 1962, and helping Australia win a fourth successive Davis Cup, Laver turned pro, his appearance saving the sagging professional game, a stimulus to keeping it breathing until opens arrived in 1968. It was a life of one-nighters, but Pancho Gonzalez was no longer supreme. Kenny Rosewall was at the top and gave Laver numerous beatings as their long, illustrious rivalry began. Rosewall beat Laver to win the U.S. Pro singles in 1963, but the next year Laver defeated Rosewall, then eight-time champ Gonzalez, to win the first of his five crowns, four of them in a row beginning in 1966. He had a streak of 19 wins in the U.S. Pro until losing the 1970 final to Roche.

When open tennis dawned in 1968, Laver was ready to resume where he'd left off at the traditional tournaments, whipping Roche in less than an hour to take the first open Wimbledon.

In 1971 Laver won $292,717 in tournament prize money (a season record that stood until Arthur Ashe won $338,337 in 1975), enabling him to become the first tennis player to make a million dollars on the court. Until the last days of 1978, when he was playing few tournaments, Laver was still the all-time leading money-winner with $1,564,213. Jimmy Connors then surpassed him, along with numerous others.

In 1973 all professionals were at last permitted to play Davis Cup, and Laver, 35, honed himself for one last effort, after 11 years away. He was brilliant, teaming with Newcombe to end a five-year U.S. reign, 5-0. Laver beat Tom Gorman in five sets on the first day and paired with Newcombe for a crushing doubles victory over Stan Smith and Erik van Dillen that clinched the Cup, Laver's fifth. Of all the marvelous Aussie Davis Cup performers he was the only one never to play in a losing series, 11 of them, compiling 16-4 and 4-0 marks in singles and doubles.

He was also a factor in winning three World Cups (1972, '74-'75) for Australia in the since disbanded team competition against the U.S. In 1976, as his tournament career was winding down, Laver signed with San Diego in World Team Tennis and was named the league's Rookie of the Year at age 38.

During a 23-year career that spanned the amateur and open eras, he won 47 pro titles in singles and was runner-up 21 times. Overall, amateur and pro, he was the all-time leader with 184 singles titles, and was elevated to the International Tennis Hall of Fame in 1981, and the Australian Tennis Hall of Fame in 1993. In 2001 the principal stadium of Melbourne Park, scene of the Australian Open, was named Rod Laver Arena. Despite spending five of his prime years in the unranked wilderness of the pros, he was among the World Top Ten 12 times, 1959-1962, and 1968-75 (the last at age 37). He was No. 2 four times, 1961, '62, '68, '69.

Suffering a massive stroke that might have killed him in 1998, he rehabilitated with the same drive that made him a champion, and today continues normally, playing tennis and golf with friends.

MAJOR TITLES (20)–*Australian singles, 1960, 1962, 1969; French singles, 1962, 1969; Wimbledon singles, 1961, 1962, 1968, 1969; U.S. singles, 1962, 1969; Australian doubles, 1959, 1960, 1961, 1969; French doubles, 1961; Wimbledon doubles, 1971; French mixed, 1961; Wimbledon mixed, 1959, 1960.* **DAVIS CUP**–*1959, 1960, 1961, 1962, 1973; record: 16-4 in singles, 4-0 in doubles.* **SINGLES RECORD IN THE MAJORS**–*Australian (21-6), French (25-6), Wimbledon (50-7), U.S. (44-10).*

IVAN LENDL

Czechoslovakia/United States (1960–)
Hall of Fame 2001

Although he'd been a prodigious winner for four years, it was not until the French final of 1984 that Ivan Lendl began to really stake his claim to greatness. Then, from two sets down to the year's leading player, John McEnroe, Lendl battled back to win in five sets, seizing the first of his eight major singles (of 17 finals). He won two other French (1986-87), two Australian (1989, '90), and three U.S. (1985, '86, '87).

Until 1984, at 24, his competitive zeal in big finals had been questioned, particularly after his U.S. Open finals losses to Jimmy Connors of 1982-83. But Lendl dispelled all that, and won in 1985 over McEnroe, in 1986 over Miroslav Mecir and 1987 over Mats Wilander. Ivan's two other French titles were banged out in 1986 and 1987 over Swedes Mikail Pernfors and Wilander. In Australia, after falling in the 1983 final to Wilander, he bounced back to win in 1989 over Mecir and 1990 over Edberg in an injury default.

His 1985 U.S. Open conquest of McEnroe hoisted him past the New Yorker to No. 1 in the world, a position he held until losing the Open in 1988 to Wilander—156 straight weeks, three short of Jimmy Connors's open era record. He returned to No. 1 for 1989 and spent a record total 269 weeks at the peak during 13 seasons in the Top Ten between 1980 and 1992.

Lendl's Flushing Meadow time has been spectacular: Appearing in eight successive finals (from 1982), he equalled the record of Big Bill Tilden (1918-25). His loss of the 1988 final to Wilander halted a 27-match winning streak in the U.S. championship, second only to Tilden's string of 42 between 1920 and the quarters of 1926.

Born March 7, 1960, at Ostrava, Czechoslovakia, and reared there, he has an excellent tennis bloodline. His mother, Olga Lendlova, was a Top Ten player in their homeland, ranking as high as No. 2. His father, Jiri Lendl, also was a fine player, ranking as high as No. 15, and who, in 1990, became president of the Czechoslovak Tennis Federation.

Unlike countrywoman Martina Navratilova, he did not announce his defection, but left no doubt when he settled in the U.S. in 1984, and declined to play further Davis Cup after 1985. In 1992, he became a U.S. citizen.

In 1980 Lendl, unbeaten in seven singles and three doubles, led Czechoslovakia to its lone Davis Cup. Before an uproarious final round crowd in Prague, he anchored the 4-1 triumph over Italy. He won both his singles on the first day and, with Tom Smid, clinched with a stirring doubles decision over Adriano Panatta and Paolo Bertolucci.

A 6-foot-2, 175-pound, right-handed paragon of hard work and fitness, he amassed stunning numbers campaigning tirelessly between 1980 and 1983, when he won 36 of 101 tournaments. He played 32 in 1980, winning three on a 113-29 match record, and won 15 of 23 in 1982 on 107-9. He won 11 of 17 in 1985 on 84-7. His last big production year was 1989: 10 of 17 on 79-7. His 92nd pro singles title in 1992 left him second only to Connors' 109 in the open era. In 1982 he put together the third longest winning streak of the open era, 44 straight matches, six shy of Guillermo Vilas' 1977 record. A basher from the baseline, relying on strength and heavy topspin, Lendl wasn't particularly stylish but got the job done with an intimidating will and appetite for victory. His anticipation and speed afoot were often overlooked.

Ivan's pursuit of the one prize beyond him, Wimbledon, was Jobian. He played 14 times at the Big W but, strain and try as he did to become a serve-

and-volleyer, and as close as he came—final-round losses to Boris Becker in 1986 and Pat Cash in 1987—grass was his no-no. That may be unfair to say about a man who batted .774 there, was also thrice a semi-finalist, but he joined Ken Rosewall and Pancho Gonzalez as the greatest never to win the Big W.

An aching back didn't help as, seeded seventh, he lost his last attempt, in 1993, to Arnaud Boetsch in the second round. The damaged back caused him to default in the third set of his second-rounder against Bernd Karbacher at the 1994 U.S. Open. He would not play again, and announced his retirement shortly after that at age 34, ranked No. 30. His last title, Tokyo (indoor) in 1993, was a 6-4, 6-4 win over Todd Martin, and his last final, Sydney 1994, was a loss to Pete Sampras.

Lendl's was a hefty pro career of 17 years: 94 singles titles, six doubles titles, and a 1,279-274 singles W-L record (.805), topped only by Connors. He was the all-time prize money champ with $21,282,417 when he quit. An avid golfer, he lives in Connecticut.

MAJOR TITLES (8)–*Australian singles, 1989, 1990; French singles, 1984, 1986, 1987; U.S. singles, 1985, 1986, 1987.* OTHER U.S. TITLES–*Clay Court singles, 1985; Pro singles, 1992, 1993, 1994.* DAVIS CUP–*1978, 1979, 1980, 1981, 1982, 1983, 1984, 1985; record: 18-11 in singles, 4-4 in doubles.* SINGLES RECORD IN THE MAJORS–*Australian (48-10), French (53-12), Wimbledon (48-14), U.S. (73-13).*

SUZANNE LENGLEN

France (1899–1938)
Hall of Fame 1978

In the days of ground-length tennis dresses, Suzanne Rachel Flore Lenglen played at Wimbledon with her dress cut just above the calf. She wept openly during matches, pouted and sipped brandy between sets. Some called her shocking and indecent, but she was merely ahead of her time, and she brought France the greatest global sports renown it had ever known.

Right-hander Lenglen was No. 1 in 1925-26, the first years of world rankings. She won Wimbledon every year but one from 1919 through 1925, the exception being 1924, when illness led to her withdrawal after the fourth round. Her 1919 title match, at the age of 20, with 40-year-old Dorothea Douglass Chambers is one of the hallmarks of tennis history.

Chambers, the seven-time champion, was swathed in stays, petticoats, high-necked shirtwaist, and a long skirt that swept the court. The young Lenglen was in her revealing dress that shocked the British at the sight of ankles and forearms. After the second set, Lenglen took some comfort from her brandy and won, 10-8, 4-6, 9-7, in a dramatic confrontation, rescuing two match points.

After her victory, Lenglen became easily the greatest drawing card tennis had known, and she was one of those who made it a major box-office attraction. Along with a magnetic personality, grace and style, she was the best woman player the world had seen.

Lenglen, born May 24, 1899, in Paris, played an all-court game such as few had excelled at. She moved with rare grace, unencumbered by the tight layers of garments others wore. She had extraordinary accuracy with her classical, rhythmic ground strokes. For hours daily her father, Charles Lenglen, had her direct the ball at a handkerchief he moved from spot to spot. Her control was so unfailing that she thought it shameful to hit the ball into the net or beyond the line. In addition, she had so keen a sense of anticipation that she invariably was in the right position to meet her opponent's shot.

Her 1926 match against Helen Wills in a tournament at Cannes, France, caused a sensation. Tickets brought unheard-of wealth to scalpers, and the roofs and windows of apartments and hotels overlooking the court were crowded with fans. Lenglen, on the verge of collapse during the tense match, but saved by smelling salts and brandy, defeated the 20-year-old Wills, 6-3, 8-6.

Lenglen's career was not free of setbacks, however. In the 1921 U.S. Championships, having lost the first set badly to Molla Mallory, Lenglen walked weeping and coughing to the umpire and said she could not continue, defaulting the match. She made up for it the next year at Wimbledon by defeating Mallory, 6-2, 6-0, in the final and did not lose another match for the remainder of her amateur career.

In the 1926 Wimbledon, Lenglen had a terrifying ordeal. She kept Queen Mary waiting in the Royal Box for her appearance when, owing to a misunderstanding or a failure of communications, Lenglen did not have the correct information about the time she was to be on court. The ghastly error was too much. She fainted and Wimbledon saw her no more as a competitor. She withdrew from the tournament, and that year went on a tour for money in the United States under the management of C. C. Pyle, winning all 38 matches against Mary K. Browne. It marked the start of professional tennis as a playing career.

At the age of 39, Lenglen died of pernicious anemia, July 4, 1938, in Paris. She was elected to the Hall of

Fame in 1978. There was speculation that her health had been undermined by her long hours of practice as a young girl. But she had brought the glamour of the stage and the ballet to the court, and queues formed at tennis clubs where before there had been indifference. She had emancipated the female player from layers of starched clothing and set the short-hair style as well. During her career she won 81 singles titles (seven without the loss of a game!), 73 doubles and 8 mixed. She had brought the game of tennis into a new era.

MAJOR TITLES (21)–*French singles, 1925, 1926; Wimbledon singles, 1919, 1920, 1921, 1922, 1923, 1925; French doubles, 1925, 1926; Wimbledon doubles, 1919, 1920, 1921, 1922, 1923, 1925; French mixed, 1925, 1926; Wimbledon mixed, 1920, 1922, 1925.* **SINGLES RECORD IN THE MAJORS**–*French (10-0), Wimbledon (32-0), U.S. (0-1).*

GEORGE LOTT
United States (1906–1991)
Hall of Fame 1964

A good baseball player at the University of Chicago, George Martin Lott, Jr., made his name principally in doubles, where, a slick tactician and volleyer, he could make any partner look good. He won the U.S. title five times with three different accomplices: John Hennessey, 1928; Johnny Doeg, 1929 and 1930; Les Stoefen, 1933 and 1934. He joined the touring pros in 1934.

He was a U.S. Davis Cup stalwart between 1928 and 1934, going undefeated in 11 doubles matches. He ranked in the U.S. Top Ten nine times between 1924 and 1934, No. 2 in 1931 when he lost the final at Forest Hills to Ellie Vines, keeping it close with his clever use of spin, 7-9, 6-3, 9-7, 7-5. George, a right-hander, came from way back to disappoint Johnny Van Ryn—his Wimbledon-winning comrade that year—in the quarters, 5-7, 0-6, 6-1, 7-5, 6-1, then unseat the defender, Johnny Doeg, 7-5, 6-3, 6-0. He also won the Wimbledon doubles with Stoefen in 1934. A 160-pound 6-footer, George beat dashing dirt-kicker Bitsy Grant in a five-set struggle for the 1932 U.S. Clay Court title, 3-6, 6-2, 3-6, 6-3, 6-3, and had his ultimate clay opportunities in Paris as a singles starter for the U.S. in the Davis Cup finales of 1929 and 1930. The Frenchmen were just too tough at home. Henri Cochet beat him in the decisive fifth match in 1929, 6-1, 3-6, 6-0, 6-3, and Jean Borotra scored the painful clincher in 1930, 5-7, 6-3, 2-6, 6-2, 8-6.

He was born Oct. 16, 1906, in Springfield Ill., and died Dec. 2, 1991, in Chicago, where he was still active as varsity coach of Loyola University. He was inducted into the Hall of Fame in 1964.

MAJOR TITLES (12)–*French doubles, 1931; Wimbledon doubles, 1931, 1934; U.S. doubles, 1928, 1929, 1930, 1933, 1934; Wimbledon mixed, 1931; U.S. mixed, 1929, 1931, 1934.* **OTHER U.S. TITLES**–*Clay Court singles, 1932; Indoor doubles, 1932, with John Van Ryn; 1934, with Lester Stoefen; Clay Court doubles, 1932, with Bitsy Grant; Pro doubles, 1935, with Stoefen; 1937, with Vinnie Richards.* **DAVIS CUP**–*1928, 1929, 1930, 1931, 1933, 1934; record: 7-4 in singles, 11-0 in doubles.* **SINGLES RECORD IN THE MAJORS**–*French (4-1), Wimbledon (16-5), U.S. (24-10).*

GENE MAKO
Hungary/United States (1916–)
Hall of Fame 1973

Though brief, the career of Hungarian-born Constantine Gene Mako was one of the most remarkable in that he achieved his foremost results after sustaining a devastating and painful right-shoulder injury that would have finished most men as competitors. As a teenager he had one of the most powerful serves, but he injured himself by overdoing it. This was compounded by a 1936 tumble in London that finished the job of wrecking his right (playing) shoulder, and kept him out of Wimbledon that year.

"I continued only because my friend and doubles partner, Don Budge, asked me to do so," Mako says. "I told him I'd be serving like a little old lady and would have to shovel the ball around, but it was okay with him."

Despite the sometimes puny appearance of his strokes, 6-foot, 170-pound Mako, in the right court alongside Budge, was a canny playmaker, a man who knew the angles and where to put the ball—and competed fiercely—as they became one of the greatest teams. They won Wimbledon in 1937 and 1938, and were in four successive U.S. finals from 1935, triumphing in 1936 and 1938.

A formidable singles player as well, he performed on four Davis Cup teams (two winners), seizing the go-ahead point with Budge in the 1937 lifting of the Cup from Britain, 4-1, to end a 10-year U.S. dry spell. They beat Charles Tuckey and Frank Wilde, 6-3, 7-5, 7-9, 12-10. Just as vital was their go-ahead win in the previous round, a 3-2 thriller over Germany—a 4-6, 7-5, 8-6, 6-4 squeeze past Henner Henkel and Gottfried von Cramm.

Mako was in the U.S. Top Ten in 1937 and 1938, No. 3 the second year, and No. 9 in the world ranking of 1938. That year he was the last obstacle between Budge and the original Grand Slam in the U.S. final at Forest Hills. Unseeded, Mako dashed to his only major singles final on victories over sixth-seed Frank Kovacs and the third and first foreign seeds, Franjo Puncec and John Bromwich. He resisted Budge well, holding off the inevitable for four sets, 6-3, 6-8, 6-2, 6-1. Mako had one of the four sets Budge lost during the Slam.

Gene had a brief fling at pro tennis while serving in the Navy during World War II, winning the U.S. Pro doubles in 1943 with Bruce Barnes. Upon discharge, he made another sort of sporting name on the West Coast as a semi-pro basketball player. Born in Budapest Jan. 24, 1916, he moved with his family to Buenos Aires, then to Los Angeles when he was seven. There he remained, winning the intercollegiate singles and doubles for Southern California in 1934. Today he's a gregarious art dealer. He entered the Hall of Fame in 1973.

MAJOR TITLES (5)–*Wimbledon doubles, 1937, 1938; U.S. doubles, 1936, 1938; U.S. mixed, 1936.* **OTHER U.S. TITLES** (6)–*Clay Court doubles, 1933, with Jack Tidball; 1934, with Don Budge; 1939, with Frank Parker; Pro doubles, 1943, with Bruce Barnes; Intercollegiate singles, 1934; Intercollegiate doubles, 1934, with Philip Castlen.* **DAVIS CUP**–*1935, 1936, 1937, 1938; record: 0-1 in singles, 6-2 in doubles.* **SINGLES RECORD IN THE MAJORS**–*Australian (2-1), French (0-1), Wimbledon (7-2), U.S. (18-8).*

MOLLA MALLORY

Norway/United States (1884–1959)
Hall of Fame 1958

Anna Margarethe 'Molla' Bjurstedt Mallory had less in the way of stroke equipment than most players who have become tennis champions. But the sturdy, Norwegian-born woman, the daughter of an army officer, had the heart and pride of a gladiator, could run with limitless endurance, and was a fierce competitor. She won the U.S. Championship a record eight times and she administered the only post-World War I defeat that Suzanne Lenglen suffered as an amateur.

It was her match with Lenglen in the second round of the U.S. Championship at Forest Hills in 1921 that won Mallory her greatest celebrity. She won the first set, 6-2, playing with a fury that took her opponent by surprise, running down balls interminably to wear out the French girl in long rallies, and hitting her mighty topspin forehand down the line for blazing winners. Lenglen, the Wimbledon queen, out of breath from running, coughing and weeping, walked to the umpire's stand after two points of the second set and informed the official that

she was ill and could not continue. This was as sensational a reversal as ever recorded on the courts.

Mallory, a right-hander, whose game was developed in Oslo, Norway, where she was born March 6, 1884, came to the United States as Molla Bjurstedt in 1915 and won the U.S. Championship in 1915, 1916, 1917, 1918, 1920, 1921, 1922 and in 1926 at age 42, as the elder among all major singles champions.

She was a player of the old school. She held that a woman could not sustain a volleying attack in a long match and she put her reliance on her baseline game. That game amounted to a forehand attack and an omnivorous defense that wore down her opponents. She took the ball on the rise and drove it from corner to corner to keep her rival on the constant run and destroy her control. The quick return made her passing shots all the more effective.

In her first U.S. Championship final—in 1915, against Hazel Hotchkiss Wightman, who had won the title three times—Mallory yielded only the first set, after which Wightman began to tire and could not get to the volleying position, and won, 4-6, 6-2, 6-0.

Eleanor Goss in the 1918 final and Marion Zinderstein in the 1920 final were strong volleyers, like Mrs. Wightman, but neither could win a set against the Norwegian native.

Mallory yielded her title to Helen Wills in 1923 after defeating her in the 1922 final, and lost to her again in 1924. In 1926 Mallory hit one of the heights of her career when she came back from 0-4 in the third set of the final against Elizabeth Ryan and saved a match point in winning her eighth championship. Never had a gallery at Forest Hills in the years of her triumphs cheered her on as it did in this remarkable rally.

Mallory reached the final at Wimbledon in 1922 and lost to Lenglen, 6-2, 6-0. Mallory was twice a semi-finalist at Wimbledon, and she played on the Wightman Cup team in 1923, 1924, 1925, 1927 and 1928.

Although she had won an Olympic bronze in singles for Norway in 1912 at Stockholm, and was the champion of her homeland, Molla was relatively unknown when she arrived in New York as Miss Bjurstedt to begin work as a masseuse in 1915. She entered the U.S. Indoor Championships that year unheralded and beat defending champ Marie Wagner, the first of five singles titles on the boards. Having thus made something of a name, she went outdoors to enlarge on it on Philadelphia turf by beginning her record collection of eight U.S. titles, winning the fifth as Mrs. Franklin Mallory in 1920. In 15 years at Forest Hills her worst finish was a quarter-final in 1927 at age 43!

She was in the World Top Ten in 1925, 1926 and 1927, its first three years, and the U.S. Top Ten 13 times between 1915 and 1928, No. 1 in 1915, 1916, 1918 through 1922, and 1926. She bade farewell to the U.S. Champion-ships as a 45-year-old semi-finalist in 1929. She entered the Hall of Fame in 1958 and died Nov. 22, 1959, in Stockholm.

MAJOR TITLES *(13)–U.S. singles, 1915, 1916, 1917, 1918, 1920, 1921, 1922, 1926; U.S. doubles, 1916, 1917; U.S. mixed, 1917, 1922, 1923.* **OTHER U.S. TITLES**–*Indoor singles, 1915, 1916, 1918, 1921, 1922; Indoor doubles, 1916, with Marie Wagner; Indoor mixed, 1921, 1922, with Bill Tilden; Clay Court singles, 1915, 1916; Clay Court mixed, 1916, with George Church.* **WIGHTMAN CUP**–*1923, 1925, 1927, 1928; record: 5-5 in singles, 1-1 in doubles.* **SINGLES RECORD IN THE MAJORS**–*French (1-1), Wimbledon (19-9), U.S. (67-7).*

HANA MANDLIKOVA

Czechoslovakia (1962–)
Hall of Fame 1994

Just possibly there are more appealing places to flop on your back than a grimy, steaming strip of asphalt in New York. But you won't convince Hana Mandlikova. It was her place in the furtive sun, and the bumpy landing she made, after whirling to bat a last spectacular volley, was a splendidly happy one. Hana gazed at the smoggy sky, and it seemed heaven as a deluge of applause and cheers from 21,169 captivated witnesses burst on her. The pavement of Flushing Meadow "didn't feel too bad. It felt nice," laughs Mandlikova, who arose from the floor as champion.

That was 1985. Seldom has the U.S. Open been illuminated by such a display of shotmaking fireworks. Hana's victim was Martina Navratilova at her zenith, 7-6 (7-3), 1-6, 7-6 (7-2). Like Martina, whom she'd admired while growing up in Prague (where she was born Feb. 19, 1962), Hana was a magnificent athlete who felt the only thing better than attacking was attacking more.

As the star of the 40th Hall of Fame class, 1994, Hana is the third Czech, following Jaroslav Drobny and Jan Kodes. Her relatively early retirement at 28 concluded a professional career that commenced in 1978 and closed in 1990 after she had accumulated 27 singles, 15 pro doubles titles and $3,340,959 in prize money. At singles Hana was 567-195 in matches (.783); at doubles 253-104. She left ranked No. 14, having graced the World Top Ten seven times, 1980-82, 1984-87, No. 3 in 1984 and 1985. Her time was emblazoned by the irresistible crescendos of winning four majors–two Australian (1980, 1987), a French (1981) and her crown jewel U.S. Open. She had four other shots, finals of Wimbledon, 1981, 1986 and the U.S., 1980, 1982.

Her speed and jock genes came from her papa. Willem Mandlik, an Olympic 100-meter finalist for Czechoslovakia in 1956 and 1960, uttered a profound one-sentence summary of his nervous kid's one-sided defeat by Evert, 6-2, 6-2, in the 1981 Wimbledon final: "Boom-boom-boom ... miss-miss-miss ... quick-quick-quick!"

Leggy and limber, a 5-foot-8 right-hander coltish in her movement, she was as high-strung as a thoroughbred, living for flamboyant cavalry charges: "Too impatient to stay on the baseline, on clay—even though I was raised on it—or anything," Hana smiles. "Jan Kodes was my first hero. I grew up watching him. I was a ballgirl for Martina [Navratilova] when I was 12, and she was a motivation for me. We played the same way—and I wanted to be good enough to beat her some day."

And she did, spoiling several big occasions for Martina. Even though she was 7-30 in their rivalry, Hana won four of 10 major meetings, beating her elder at Wimbledon, twice at the U.S., once at the Australian. The last, the 1987 final, 7-5, 7-6 (7-2), ended Navratilova's 58-match winning streak. Three years earlier, winning Oakland, Hana snipped another of Martina's strings at 54. They got together to win the U.S. doubles in 1989. "Nice memories," she says, balancing them with the terror, the "terrible memory of the Soviet tanks coming into Prague [1968]. I was only six, but I understood. It was not nice to see my country invaded. But the political conditions proved a motivation for me and others—to improve, to be so good we could get out to travel abroad."

Billie Jean King says, "Hana could reach highs beyond any of us—inexplicable lows, too. She had incredibly broad shotmaking ability, but trouble sustaining her best. Maybe because she couldn't resist going for the most spectacular shots." She came at foes in a red-bandana'd rush like Geronimo in sneakers. So it was that September afternoon of '85 when she knocked off Chris Evert and Navratilova in succession for the U.S. title, a singular twin-killing of those two all-timers, first time in a major, although Steffi Graf did it at Wimbledon. Like her father, Hana represented her country proudly, back-boning three successive Czechoslovak Federation Cup triumphs, 1983-85.

MAJOR TITLES *(5)–Australian singles, 1980, 1987; French singles, 1981; U.S. singles, 1985; U.S. doubles, 1989.* FEDERATION CUP–*1978, 1979, 1980, 1981, 1982, 1983, 1984, 1985, 1986, 1987; record: 34-6 singles, 15-6 doubles.* SINGLES RECORD IN THE MAJORS–*Australian (29-8), French (39-11), Wimbledon (34-11), U.S. (41-10).*

ALICE MARBLE

United States (1913–1990)
Hall of Fame 1964

One of the most attractive players to grace the courts, Alice Marble was deceptive. Her blonde loveliness and her trim athletic but feminine figure belied the fact that she played tennis in the late 1930s in a masculine manner that more closely approximated the game of Don Budge or Ellsworth Vines than it did the game of any woman.

There had been women before her who could volley and hit overheads—Suzanne Lenglen and Helen Wills Moody among them—but none played the 'big game,' the game of the big serve-and-volley, as it was to be called years later, as their standard method of attack the way Marble did regularly. No woman had a stronger service. Her first serve was as severe as any, and she delivered the taxing American twist serve as few women have been able to do. She followed it to the net for emphatic volleys or the strongest kind of overhead smash.

A right-hander pressing the attack without a letup, she could win from the back of the court as well as at the net. Her groundstrokes, made with a short backswing and taking the ball on the rise, were not overpowering, and her forehand was not always steadfast against the many fine backcourt players of her day, in part because of her daring in playing for winners. But in the aggressive all-court game she played, with her speed and agility and with her skill in the use of the drop shot, they served to carry her to four U.S. titles and to the Wimbledon Championship. World War II brought about French, Wimbledon and Australian tournament suspension or she might have added appreciably to her major conquests.

Her dominance is evidenced by her record of invincibility in 1939 and 1940. She did not lose a match of consequence either year. In winning her fourth U.S. title in 1940, she did not yield a set. She was voted by sportswriters the Woman Athlete of the Year in 1939 and 1940.

She was in the World Top Ten in 1933, 1936, 1937, 1938 and 1939, No. 1 the last year, and in the U.S. Top Ten those years, plus 1932 and 1940, No. 1 from 1936 through 1940.

Second-seeded at Wimbledon in 1938, but jolted in the semis by unseeded Helen Jacobs, Alice then embarked invulnerably on one of the greatest passages in the game's history. She won the remaining 18 tournaments and 111 matches of her amateur tenure, posting nine tourney titles and 45-0 match marks in 1939 and 1940. The streak was second only to Helen Wills Moody's 27 titles, 158-match procession to the 1933 U.S. final. Thus, for her last three years of amateurism she won 23 of 24 tournaments, 120 of 122 matches.

Born Sept. 28, 1913, on a farm in Plumas County, Calif., she was a product of the public courts of San Francisco's Golden Gate Park, a natural athlete who worked out with the minor league baseball players of the local Seals (including Joe DiMaggio) when she was their 13-year-old mascot. Marble made perhaps the most remarkable recovery from illness and obscurity in the game's annals to become the very best of her time.

Her soaring career—in 1933 she was No. 10 in the world, a U.S. quarter-finalist—seemed over by her 20th birthday, and she vanished from the scene for almost two years. In a weekend tourney at Easthampton, N.Y., that year she had to play singles and doubles semi-finals and finals on the last day (108 games!) in 100-degree heat. The result was sunstroke, keeping her from Wightman Cup singles, weakening her for the remainder of the season. The following spring, during team matches in Paris, Alice collapsed and was hospitalized. Cut down by anemia and pleurisy, frustrated and depressed by misdiagnosis of tuberculosis and the medical judgment that she must forget tennis, she didn't recover her health fully until 1936 when, startlingly, she won the first of her four U.S. titles, deposing Helen Jacobs, 4-6, 6-3, 6-2.

She began to play again in 1935 in California, and changed to the eastern grip. When in 1936 Marble returned to the East, officials of the USTA were fearful that she might jeopardize her health permanently if she resumed serious competition. But she was determined, and with the help of her coach, Eleanor Tennant, she undertook to re-establish herself and get back to the top.

At Forest Hills she came up against Jacobs in the U.S. final. Jacobs had held the title four years in a row, but Marble won, attaining the No. 1 ranking. In 1937 she lost in the quarter-finals but again was ranked No. 1, and she held the top spot in 1938, 1939 and 1940, winning the U.S. crown all three years and winning all three titles at Wimbledon in 1939. In four years of Wightman Cup play she lost but one match in each singles and doubles.

An aging Bill Tilden, 48, and Don Budge, 25, at the top of his game, headlined the 1941 pro tour that opened at Madison Square Garden, along with Alice Marble and Mary Hardwick. Budge won, 51-7, and Marble was 72-3 in the head-to-head series of matches.

In her 1991 autobiography, *Courting Danger*, Alice wrote that she decided to turn pro at the end of 1940 because, "What's left for me? I'm champion ... and may as well make the most of it." She got a $75,000 guarantee from L. B. Icely, the president of Wilson, who bankrolled the tour. This, she said, despite a $100,000 offer from the wealthy tennis fan Will duPont (who later married Margaret Osborne) to not turn pro because he enjoyed watching her on the Eastern grass circuit. During World War II she played exhibitions at military installations across the U.S., and revealed in her book that she was sent as a government agent to Switzerland in 1945 to spy on Nazis before the war ended.

She entered the Hall of Fame in 1964, and died Dec. 13, 1990, in Palm Springs, Calif.

MAJOR TITLES (18)–*Wimbledon singles, 1939; U.S. singles, 1936, 1938, 1939, 1940; Wimbledon doubles, 1938, 1939; U.S. doubles, 1937, 1938, 1939, 1940; Wimbledon mixed, 1937, 1938, 1939; U.S. mixed, 1936, 1937, 1938, 1940.* **OTHER U.S. TITLES**–*Clay Court singles, 1940; Clay Court doubles, 1940, with Mary Arnold.* **WIGHTMAN CUP**–*1933, 1937, 1938, 1939; record: 5-1 in singles, 3-1 in doubles.* **SINGLES RECORD IN THE MAJORS**–*Wimbledon (14-2), U.S. (31-4).*

JOHN MCENROE

United States (1959–)
Hall of Fame 1999

Right from the start, in his 1977 introduction to pro tennis, John Patrick McEnroe, Jr., was a hit.

An 18-year-old amateur (he would not turn pro until winning the National Intercollegiate singles as a Stanford freshman in 1978), McEnroe made his first splash in Paris, a boy edging into man's territory. He won his first of 17 major titles there, the French mixed with childhood pal, Mary Carillo, over the Romanian-Colombian combine of Florenta Mihai and Ivan Molina.

Soon after, electrifying Wimbledon, he went through the qualifying tourney and all the way to the semis, losing to Jimmy Connors. It was a major tourney record for a qualifier (equaled by Belarussian Vladimir Voltchkov in 2000). It was also a record for an amateur in the open

era. Immediately Mac was a player to reckon with.

Born Feb. 16, 1959, in Wiesbaden, Germany, where his father was stationed with the U.S. Air Force, he grew up in the Long Island suburb of Douglaston, N.Y. A 5-foot-11, 170-pound left-hander, McEnroe stands as perhaps the most skilled—and controversial—of all players. Brilliant in doubles and singles, he was distinguished by shotmaking artistry, competitive fire and a volatile temper. The last led to heavy fines, suspensions and, at the 1990 Australian Open, an extraordinary fourth-round disqualification for showering abusive language on court officials.

A magnificent volleyer with a feathery touch, he was an attacker whose fast court style netted four U.S. Open and three Wimbledon singles. He had the baselining strength to do well on clay at the French. He might have won that at his zenith, but in the 1984 final he led Ivan Lendl, 2-0 in sets, only to be distracted by temperamental outbursts, and was beaten, 3-6, 2-6, 6-4, 7-5, 7-5.

He revived American interest in the Davis Cup that had been shunned by Connors and other leading countrymen, saying, "My mother made me promise her I'd always play for my country if I was asked." Right from the start, as a 19-year-old rookie in 1978, he gave Capt. Tony Trabert's team a lift, and gave the U.S. the Cup that had belonged to other countries since 1973. In the championship round against Britain at Rancho Mirage, Calif., he evinced none of the jitters so common to many other greats making debuts in the nationalistic setting. Mac was a miser, rationing John Lloyd (6-1, 6-2, 6-2) and Buster Mottram (6-2, 6-2, 6-1) to 10 games. Nobody had been stingier in a final. He was the most callow American to do so well in the Cup round, although Lew Hoad, a younger 19 by eight months for victorious Australia, also took both his singles in 1953, and American Michael Chang, 18, won one singles in the winning 1990 final. Aussie Lleyton Hewitt, also older than Hoad at 19, split his singles in the triumphant 2000 final.

McEnroe continued as a mainstay in helping the U.S. win four more Cups (1979, '81-'82, '92), and set numerous U.S. records: Years played (12), series (30), singles wins (41), singles and doubles wins altogether (59). A workhorse, he played both singles and doubles in 13 series, and he and Peter Fleming won 14 of 15 Cup doubles together.

An epic performance was his record-time six-hour-22 minute, five-set victory over Mats Wilander in St. Louis, clinching a 1982 quarter-final, 3-2, win over Sweden. He and German Boris Becker nearly topped that, using six hours, 21 minutes for Boris' 1987 Cup relegation victory at Hartford. Another thriller was Mac's five-set win over Jose-Luis Clerc of Argentina to send the Cup to the U.S. in the 1981 final at Cincinnati.

McEnroe was named U.S. captain in 1999 and served one year, 2000, quitting after three series (3-2 wins over Zimbabwe and the Czech Republic, a 5-0 loss to Spain), and was replaced by his younger brother, Patrick McEnroe.

At 20, John won the U.S. title for the first time over fellow New Yorker Vitas Gerulaitis, the youngest winner since Pancho Gonzalez, also 20, 31 years before. He repeated in dramatic battles with Bjorn Borg in 1980 and 1981. Borg retired shortly thereafter. McEnroe won for the last time in 1984, over Lendl. But he was defeated in the Flushing Meadow rematch 12 months later, relinquishing to Lendl the World No. 1 ranking McEnroe had held for four years.

His most celebrated result may have been a loss, the 1980 Wimbledon final called by many the greatest of all. Beaten, 1-6, 7-5, 6-3, 6-7 (16-18), 8-6, McEnroe nervelessly staved off five match points during the monumental fourth-set tie-breaker to fight Borg to the fifth-set wire. A year later he cut down Borg on Centre Court, 4-6, 7-6 (7-1), 7-6 (7-4), 6-4, ending Bjorn's incredible five-year, 41-match Wimbledon run.

McEnroe won again in 1983, a quickie with unseeded New Zealander Chris Lewis and in 1984, reaching the pinnacle of his virtuosity, a virtually flawless wipeout of Connors, 6-1, 6-2, 6-2. There were many ups and downs at Wimbledon, where McEnroe came close to being tossed out prior to his initial championship, 1981, following a second-round flareup while beating Tom Gullikson. It was the infamous scene of labeling the umpire, Ted James, "pits of the world," and calling the referee every name but Fred Hoyles (which was his name). He went out in grand manner in 1992. Unseeded at No. 30, 33-year-old Mac wound up where he'd begun 15 years before: The semis, on a stirring knockout of ninth-seeded Guy Forget. He'd already beaten 16th-seeded David Wheaton in three, and won a rousing four-hour, nine-minute 'battle of champions' over Pat Cash. But champ-to-be Andre Agassi was too much for him in the goodbye singles, 6-4, 6-2, 6-3.

Yet there was more, and Mac's fading presence would be stretched triumphantly over two days and Wimbledon's longest closing act on the third Monday: His fifth doubles title, this time without old collaborator Peter Fleming, but with a stranger who did just fine, Michael Stich. Two points from defeat in the fourth-set tie-breaker, tied at darkness, 13-13, the German-American combine came through over Richey Renneberg and Jim Grabb, 5-7, 7-6 (7-5), 3-6, 7-6 (7-5), 19-17, a record-length final, five hours, one minute. Eight years had passed since his last title. "It was a great atmosphere [Court 1 was packed with 6,500 Mac fans], a great way to go out," Mac said.

Three intense rivalries stand out during his career. He had the edge on Connors (31-20), but not Lendl (15-21), and was even with Borg (7-7). Except for the French Open lapse against Lendl, he was unbeatable in 1984, winning 13 of 15 singles tournaments on an 82-3 record. Other big seasons were 1979 (10 titles on a 94-12 record), 1980 (10 titles on 88-18). In 1979 he set an open-era record with 27 overall tournament victories, 17 in doubles, winning a record total of 177 matches. He won the season-climaxing Masters singles thrice, 1978, '83-'84, and is the all-time overall open era leader with 154 tournament victories: A 77-77 singles-doubles split. He is third in singles titles behind Connors's 109 and Lendl's 92, second in doubles behind Tom Okker's 78. His career singles W-L record is 849-184.

Ten years a member of the World Top Ten, he was four times No. 1 (1981-84).

Brother, Patrick McEnroe, younger by seven years (b. July 1, 1966), followed him as a standout pro, winning the French doubles (with Grabb) in 1989, ranking as high as No. 28 in 1995. In 1991 they met in the Chicago final, the second such clash of brothers (Emilio Sanchez defeated Javier Sanchez in the 1987 Madrid final). John won, 3-6, 6-2, 6-4. His prize money for 15 years as a pro was $12,539,827. He has three children by ex-wife Tatum O'Neal, two by wife Patty Smythe, continues to play senior events and has made a successful career as a TV commentator on tennis.

MAJOR TITLES (17)–*Wimbledon singles, 1981, 1983, 1984; U.S. singles, 1979, 1980, 1981, 1984; Wimbledon doubles, 1979, 1981, 1983, 1984, 1992; U.S. doubles, 1979, 1981, 1983, 1984; French mixed, 1977.* **OTHER U.S. TITLES** (4)–*Indoor singles, 1980; Hard Court singles, 1989; Indoor doubles, 1980, with Brian Gottfried; Clay Court doubles, 1979, with Gene Mayer.* **DAVIS CUP**–*1978, 1979, 1980, 1981, 1982, 1983, 1984, 1987, 1988, 1989, 1991, 1992; record: 41-8 in singles, in 18-2 in doubles.* **SINGLES RECORD IN THE MAJORS**–*Australian (18-5), French (25-10), Wimbledon (59-11), U.S. (65-12).*

KEN MCGREGOR

Australia (1929–)
Hall of Fame 1999

"It was a surprise to me, the Yanks—and everybody else," smiles Kenneth Bruce McGregor, recounting the 1950 weekend when Australia began taking over the tennis world. He was the unexpected, relatively inexperienced taker, selected for a singles role by Capt. Harry Hopman in an effort to halt a U.S. Davis Cup landslide in the challenge-round final on the lawn of Forest Hills in New York.

The Americans had heisted the Cup from Australia, 5-0, at Melbourne in 1946, as McGregor, a 17-year-old more interested in football [Australian rules], listened at home in Adelaide to the sad tidings on the radio. U.S. victories over challenging Australia in 1947-48-49 compounded the distress Down Under, and the Yanks were favored again.

"It was assumed that John Bromwich would get the other singles job with my doubles partner, Frank Sedgman," Ken says. "But Hopman picked me, and used Brom with Frank in the doubles."

That arrangement worked splendidly in a 4-1 triumph. McGregor, a late blossomer with only three previous Cup singles in routine preliminary rounds that year on his resume, could feel his country on his back, wondering about Hop's judgment. But he responded handsomely, beating an Aussie nemesis, Ted Schroeder, in the second match. Schroeder had been 7-0 since 1946 against the Aussies. "The first set was tense, but after that I was very confident. Sedg took some of the pressure away by beating Tom Brown in the first match." Sedgman and Bromwich clinched in the doubles over Schroeder and Gar Mulloy.

It was the start of the Aussie reign of terror: 15 Cups in 18 years, and McGregor had a fine right hand in the first three. He (in the right court) and Sedgman, one of the greatest doubles combos, went together like gin and vermouth, Butch Cassidy and the Sundance Kid. They crafted the lone male Grand Slam in 1951, and that year beat Schroeder and Tony Trabert, the pivotal point in the Aussies' successful defense, 3-2. By narrowly winning the 1951 Aussie they shut down the procession of eight consecutive titles by the revered amalgam of Bromwich and Adrian Quist.

Ken was back in the singles lineup the next year, a treat for his fellow citizens at Memorial Drive in Adelaide, as he beat Trabert and collaborated with Sedgman in the doubles over Trabert and Vic Seixas that made it 3-0 in the 4-1 victory. That was the end of a brief, resplendent amateur career. He and Sedgman joined the gypsies, the barnstorming pros. Ken played the warmup act against Pancho Segura preceding the feature—Sedgman trying vainly to unseat the king of the hill, Jack Kramer. The first year (a 71-25 beating by the seasoned Segura) was a rude introduction. "Ken was a big-occasion player, not suited to the night-after-night pro grind, mostly at different venues," said historian Joe McCauley.

"I hated to leave Davis Cup," Ken recalls, "but the money [from promoter Jack Kramer] was too good to turn down. We were getting 25 shillings a day as amateurs, and I had a guarantee of about $60,000 for three years."

At 6-3, 180 pounds, a quick, agile and aggressive serve-and-volleyer, McGregor may have been the most athletic of the Australian mob. His sights were on football, but his father, once a pro footballer, thought him too light and guided him toward tennis, saying, "If you don't make the Davis Cup in three years you can go back to footy." Hopman liked his devotion to fitness, and brought him along well. Hall of Famer Ellsworth Vines commented, "Ken was difficult to pass because of his prehensile reach, and he had the most extraordinary overhead of all time."

On the scene barely four years, he won three singles titles and was in the World Top Ten three times: No. 8, 1950; No. 7, 1951; No. 3, 1952. He lost the 1950 Australian final (to Sedgman) and 1951 (to Dick Savitt) before winning in 1952 over Sedgman. He also lost so Savitt in the 1951 Wimbledon final.

Born June 2, 1929, at Adelaide, he was elevated to the International Hall in 1999, and named to the Australian Tennis Hall of Fame in 2000.

MAJOR TITLES (9)–*Australian singles, 1952; Australian doubles, 1951, 1952; French doubles, 1951, 1952; Wimbledon doubles, 1951, 1952; U.S. doubles, 1951; U.S. mixed doubles, 1950.* **DAVIS CUP**–*1950, 1951, 1952; record: 4-3 in singles, 2-0 in doubles.* **SINGLES RECORD IN THE MAJORS**–*Australian (14-4), French (11-3), Wimbledon (13-3), U.S. (3-3).*

CHUCK MCKINLEY

United States (1941–1986)
Hall of Fame 1986

Bubbling with energy and grit, Charles Robert McKinley, Jr., was a tough little guy who hustled every minute and died tragically of a brain tumor shortly after learning, in 1986, that he had been named to the Hall of Fame. But he had achieved his utmost tennis goals, both in 1963—winning Wimbledon, and leading the U.S. to the Davis Cup with a 3-2 victory over the holder, Australia, at Adelaide.

A stubby, chesty, 5-foot-9 Missourian, he learned to play at a St. Louis YMCA, where he was already proficient at table tennis. He was a crowd-wowing player, hurling himself about the court, leaping for smashes at which he was expert since so many opponents tried to lob him. Although favored to win the U.S. Intercollegiate title in 1963 for Trinity in San Antonio, Chuck obtained permission from the college president to go for the larger prize, Wimbledon, and, seeded fourth, came through without losing a set or—luck of the draw—without facing a seeded opponent. He beat Fred Stolle in the final, 9-7, 6-1, 6-4, showing that despite limited stature he could serve and volley with anyone.

Curiously, seeded eighth, he had opposed no other seeds in making his first Wimbledon splash in 1961, until losing the final to second-seeded Rod Laver in straight sets. As the defender in 1964, he was paid back by Stolle in a four-set semi, 4-6, 10-8, 9-7, 6-4. As the left-court player, he blended splendidly with Dennis Ralston in three U.S. doubles championships, 1961, 1963 and 1964. They beat Mexico's Rafe Osuna and Tonio Palafox the first two times, McKinley serving out of two match points in the exciting 11-9 fifth set in 1963.

During the long Cup campaign of 1963 he won six of eight singles, all four doubles matches with Ralston. The Cup round was McKinley's tour de force although he lost to Roy Emerson the first day. He and Ralston got the go-ahead point over Emerson and Neale Fraser, but after Ralston lost to Emerson on the third day it "was up to me. That's the way I wanted it, the Cup riding on one match."

It was a rare position for an American. None had (or has since) come through in the Cup-deciding fifth match. McKinley did, despite being down a service break in the fourth to the thunder-serving Aussie rookie John Newcombe, 10-12, 6-2, 9-7, 6-2, as the Memorial Drive stadium rocked with patriotic fervor for Newc. The following year, however, in Cleveland, McKinley couldn't repeat, losing the decisive fifth to Emerson, 3-6, 6-2, 6-4, 6-4, as Australia regained the Cup, 3-2.

More intent on getting a college degree and

establishing himself in business, McKinley resisted professional offers, and his career was relatively brief without a great deal of international play. He was ranked seven successive years in the U.S. Top Ten from 1960, No. 1 in 1962 and 1963, and four times in the World Top Ten from 1961, No. 2 in 1963. The U.S. title eluded him, although he was a semi-finalist three straight years, 1962-64, losing to champs Osuna in 1963, 6-4, 6-4, 10-8, and Emerson in 1962, 4-6, 6-4, 6-3, 6-2, and in 1964, 6-4, 11-9, 6-4. He was born Jan. 5, 1941, in St. Louis, and died Aug. 10, 1986, in Dallas.

MAJOR TITLES (4)–*Wimbledon singles, 1963; U.S. doubles, 1961, 1963, 1964.* OTHER U.S. TITLES (9)–*Indoor singles, 1962, 1964; Clay Court singles, 1962, 1963; Indoor doubles, 1962, with Rod Laver; 1963, 1965, with Dennis Ralston; Clay Court doubles, 1961, 1964, with Ralston.* DAVIS CUP–*1960, 1961, 1962, 1963, 1964, 1965; record: 16-6 in singles, 13-3 in doubles.* SINGLES RECORD IN THE MAJORS–*Wimbledon (20-4), U.S. (34-13).*

MAURICE McLOUGHLIN
United States (1890–1957)
Hall of Fame 1957

He came out of out the West with a cannonball service, spectacular volleys and overhead smashes. He created great excitement in the East and abroad at Wimbledon with the violence of his attack. And more than anything else, Maurice Evans 'Red' McLoughlin, known as the California Comet, opened the eyes of the public to tennis as a demanding game of speed, endurance and skill.

Tennis at the turn of the century was a moderately paced game contested from the back of the court. But McLoughlin, a right-hander, carried this attack forward, projecting the cannonball serve and rushing in behind it to meet the return near the net with a cataclysmic overhead or a masterful volley. The volley was not new to the game (it had been used in the first Championship in 1881), but it had not nearly been the finishing stroke that Red Mac made it.

Born Jan. 7, 1890, in Carson City, Nev., McLoughlin polished his game on the public parks courts of northern California, and this in itself was a departure in the direction of democratizing the game. Most of the top-ranking players had developed their games on the turf of exclusive clubs in the East or their own private family courts.

At 19, he had developed sufficiently to be named to the Davis Cup team to play alongside another San Francisco teenager, Melville Long, 18, against Australasia in the 1909 challenge round. They were whitewashed but Red absorbed valuable international seasoning. He enlivened five straight U.S. finals, starting in 1911, winning 1912 and 1913 battles over Wallace Johnson and Dick Williams, losing his title to Williams in the Championships' farewell to Newport. At the Forest Hills inaugural, an all-San Francisco clash, he was beaten by the rising Bill Johnston, 1-6, 6-0, 7-5, 10-8.

His one venture to England, 1913, was an artistic success as the U.S. regained the Davis Cup, and he helped draw unprecedented large crowds to Wimbledon, where he won the all-comers over Aussie Stanley Doust. In the challenge round he fought defending champ Tony Wilding all the way, but missed a set point at 5-4, 40-30, and was beaten, 8-6, 6-3, 10-8. Then came the Cup tests, shutouts of Germany and Canada, and a 1-1 first day split against Cup-holding Britain. That evolved to a 3-2 U.S. victory as McLoughlin partnered Harold Hackett to a five-set win over Roper Barrett and Charles Dixon. It set up Red for the finisher over Dixon, 8-6, 6-3, 6-2.

McLoughlin reached his peak the next year in the Davis Cup final, even though the Cup was lost. The matching of McLoughlin and Norman Brookes of Australasia brought forth tennis that was a revelation to the thousands who attended. The match was character-ized as "never been equaled." McLoughlin won, 17-15, 6-3, 6-3. The matches attracted 14,000 people daily, and McLoughlin was given much of the credit for the large crowds.

After the Davis Cup success, the 1915 *Tennis Guide* said, "In McLoughlin America undoubtedly has the greatest tennis player of all time." Yet he never again attained that form. Absent from the East for several years, he returned after Army duty in World War I and was hardly recognizable. He had lost his cannonball and his punch. Gone was his whirlwind speed. After he was defeated by Dick Williams decisively in the 1919 quar-ters, he left the tennis scene for golf, where he soon was shooting in the low 70s. His tennis career had come to a premature end. Some said he was burned out from his violent exertions on the court.

On Dec. 10, 1957—the year of his entry into the Hall of Fame—the Comet died. But in the short time that he had lighted the tennis firmament, as no one before him, he had started the sport on its way to becoming a popular game for Americans. He ranked No. 1 in 1914 and was in the U.S. Top Ten seven straight years from 1909, No. 1 in 1912, 1913 and 1914.

MAJOR TITLES (5)–*U.S. singles, 1912, 1913; U.S. doubles, 1912, 1913, 1914.* **DAVIS CUP**–*1909, 1911, 1913, 1914; record: 9-4 in singles, 3-4 in doubles.* **SINGLES RECORD IN THE MAJORS**–*Wimbledon (7-1), U.S. (49-9).*

FREW MCMILLAN

South Africa (1942–)
Hall of Fame 1992

Side by side again entering the Hall of Fame in 1992, Frew Donald McMillan was reunited with his one-time collaborator on the team of Hewitt and McMillan. The unorthodox McMillan—stroking with two hands on both sides in the left court—and Bob Hewitt were a dynamite blend, winning five major titles (three Wimbledons) and driving South Africa to the 1974 Davis Cup.

Love was the prime ingredient in bringing them together in 1966. It was Hewitt's romance with his South African wife-to-be that moved the Australian westward to Johannesburg. When he became eligible to play for his new land, Hewitt was yoked to McMillan in 1966, and they were an immediate hit. They won their first start together late that year, and didn't lose until the quarters of the French the following year, a 45-match streak.

In 1967 they won Wimbledon, and repeated in 1972 and 1978. A springy 6-foot-1, the slim McMillan was born in Springs, South Africa, May 20, 1942, and grew up there.

"We were touch and thrust," he says of the combina-tion that was so winning over a 15-year period. "Right from the start each of us knew what the other would do. Bob had wonderful returning touch from the first court." McMillan, a right-hander, handled the racket like a cricket bat and could slug or chip. Distinctive beneath a tiny white cap that partially covered his shining dark hair, Frew was the first player of inter-national prominence of two-way, two-fisted swinging.

A straight-set Wimbledon quarter-final win over five-time champs John Newcombe and Tony Roche en route to the 1978 title showed them at their very best. They continued lethally through the final, 6-1, 6-4, 6-2, over Peter Fleming and John McEnroe. Spanning the ama-teur and open eras, they added 60 titles to their five majors. McMillan's individual total of pro doubles titles was 74, third on the all-time list behind Tom Okker (78) and McEnroe (77). Frew won two pro singles titles. He also had five major mixed titles, two Wimbledons and two U.S. with Betty Stove, for a career total of 10 majors.

MAJOR TITLES *(10)–French doubles, 1972; Wimbledon doubles, 1967, 1972, 1978; U.S. doubles, 1977; French mixed, 1966; Wimbledon mixed, 1979, 1981; U.S. mixed, 1977, 1978.* **DAVIS CUP**–*1965, 1966, 1967, 1968, 1969, 1973, 1974, 1975, 1976, 1977, 1978; record: 2-0 in singles, 23-5 in doubles.* **SINGLES RECORD IN THE MAJORS**–*Australian (0-1), French (8-10), Wimbledon (9-17), U.S. (12-10).* **MAJOR TITLES WITH HEWITT** *(5)–French doubles, 1972; Wimbledon doubles, 1967, 1972, 1978; U.S. doubles, 1977.* **DAVIS CUP**–*1967, 1968, 1969, 1974, 1978; record: 16-1 in doubles.*

DON MCNEILL

United States (1918–1996)
Hall of Fame 1965

It was a long way to Paris from Oklahoma, but a tennis court in one place was the same as one in another to a college boy named William Donald McNeill, who became the second American man to win the French title. Doing so in 1939 by beating favorite Bobby Riggs—the year's No. 1—7-5, 6-0, 6-3, Don served notice that he would be a thorn in the little hustler's side and intentions.

Though McNeill may have lost his best years to World War II, in which he served as a U.S. Naval intelligence officer, he stands as one of only four Americans to win on the grass at Forest Hills, the U.S. title (1940), and on the clay at Roland Garros, succeeding Don Budge, and preceding Frank Parker and Tony Trabert.

McNeill, a nimble 5-foot-10, 155 pounds, out of Oklahoma City, with a very sharp backhand, had gone to Europe on a lark. He returned to move unseeded to the U.S. quarterfinals, and give sixth-seeded Joe Hunt a scare, 6-4, 15-13, 8-10, 4-6, 6-2, in three-plus hours spread over two days. Don felt he could win it one day, and that day wasn't far off. Back to college he went, to graduate and win the Intercollegiate title for tiny Kenyon (Ohio) in 1940, then sting Riggs twice. If beating him in the U.S. Clay final, 6-1, 6-4, 7-9, 6-3, wasn't enough, he then completely wrecked defender Bobby's pro plans at Forest Hills. After taking Jack Kramer in the semis, Don staged a counterattack to seize the U.S. final, 4-6, 6-8, 6-3, 6-3, 7-5. McNeill was the third of five players in the championship round to rebound from two sets down. The victory completed an unusual coupling of headgear: Wearing the college and national crowns in the same year, he would have only one such equal, Ted Schroeder in 1942.

His versatility shows in a record that includes the U.S. Clay Court title of 1940, and as the only man to win the U.S. Indoor before and after the war: As a 19-year-old collegian in 1938 over Frank Bowden, 9-7, 3-6, 6-4, 7-5, and in 1950 over Fred Kovaleski, 11-9, 4-6, 6-2, 6-2. Not to mention numerous doubles prizes. Especially the French of '39 when he and Charlie Harris flinched not at two of the grand old Musketeers, and beat Jacques Brugnon and Jean Borotra for the title, 4-6, 6-4, 6-0, 2-6, 10-8, even though Borotra had four match points on serve at 6-5. McNeill was the first of only two American men to ring up a double in Paris. Tony Trabert emulated by winning both titles in 1954 and 1955.

He ranked in the U.S. Top Ten six times between 1937 and 1946, No. 1 in 1940, World No. 7 in 1939. On leave from the Navy, he won the U.S. doubles in 1944 with Bob Falkenburg.

"I thought I won it again," he laughed. "Several times that afternoon in Boston." He means the titanic U.S. doubles final of 1946 at Longwood. Don and Frank Guernsey had seven match points in the fifth set, but couldn't sway the champs, Bill Talbert and Gardnar Mulloy, 3-6, 6-4, 2-6, 6-3, 20-18. McNeill, born April 30, 1918, at Chickasha, Okla., spent most of his post-college life in New York as an advertising executive, and died Nov. 28, 1996, at Vero Beach, Fla. He was named to the Hall of Fame in 1965.

MAJOR TITLES *(4)–French singles, 1939; U.S. singles, 1940; French doubles, 1939; U.S. doubles, 1944.* **OTHER U.S. TITLES** *(9)–Indoor singles, 1938, 1950; Clay Court singles, 1940; Intercollegiate singles, 1940; Indoor doubles, 1941, 1946, with Frank Guernsey; 1949, 1950, 1951, with Bill Talbert.* **SINGLES RECORD IN THE MAJORS**–*French (6-0), Wimbledon (1-1), U.S. (27-9).*

HELEN WILLS MOODY

United States (1905–1998)
Hall of Fame 1959

It scarcely seems possible that two players of the transcendent ability of Helen Newington Wills Moody Roark and Suzanne Lenglen could have been contemporaries. They were ranked for close to half a century as the two best female tennis players of all time. Their records are unmatched and hardly have been approached.

While indeed contemporaries, they were rivals in only one match, played in 1926 and won by Lenglen, 6-3, 8-6, at Cannes, France. Lenglen, not yet 27, was at the crest of her game, with six Wimbledon championships in her possession. Wills' game at 20 had not quite attained full maturity, though she had been in the

Wimbledon final of 1924, and would win eight times. Their rivalry was limited to the single meeting, for later that same year Wills was stricken with appendicitis and Lenglen turned pro.

It would be difficult to imagine two players of more different personalities and types of game. Between 1919 and 1938 Wills won 52 of 92 tournaments on a 398-35-match record, a .919 average, and had a 158-match winning streak (27 tournaments to the 1933 U.S. final, the only time she lost to Helen Jacobs in 11 meetings).

Quiet, reserved, and never changing expression, Wills, known as Little Miss Poker Face, played with unruffled poise and never exhibited the style, flair or emotional outbursts that Lenglen did. From her first appearance in the East in 1921, when she was national junior champion, Wills' typical garb on the court was a white sailor suit, white eyeshade and white shoes and stockings.

The game she played right-handed was one of sheer power, which she had developed in practice against men on the West Coast. From both forehand and backhand she hammered the ball almost the full length of the court regularly, and the speed, pace and depth of her drives, in conjunction with her tactical moves, sufficed to subdue her opponents. She could hit winners as spectacularly from the baseline on the backhand as on the forehand.

She went to the net occasionally, not nearly as often as Lenglen, and Wills was sound in her volleying and decisive overhead with her smash. Her slice service, breaking wide and pulling the receiver beyond the alley, was as good as any female player has commanded.

Her footwork was not so good. She did not move with the grace and quickness of Lenglen, and opponents fared best against her by using the drop shot or changes of length to draw her forward and send her running back. Anchored to the baseline, she could run any opponent into the ground. Because of her sense of anticipation, she seemed to be in the right spot, and it was not often that she appeared to be hurried in her stroking.

She was born Oct. 6, 1905, in Centreville, Calif., and the facts of her invincibility are stark. She won the Wimbledon title a record eight times (surpassed by Martina Navratilova's nine in 1990) in nine tries, her only loss coming in her first appearance, in 1924. From 1927 to 1932 she did not lose a set in singles anywhere. She won seven U.S., five Wimbledon and four French titles without loss of a set until Dorothy Round of Britain extended her to 6-4, 6-8, 6-3 in the 1933 Wimbledon final.

In Wightman Cup play from 1923 to 1938, she won 18 singles matches and lost two, both in 1924. She won the Olympic singles and doubles in Paris in 1924. When she scored her first Wimbledon victory, in 1927, she was the first American woman to be crowned there since May Sutton in 1905.

Two of her three most remarkable matches were her meeting with Lenglen in 1926 and her default because of back pain to rival Helen Jacobs when trailing 0-3 in the third set of the 1933 U.S. Championships. The third remarkable match was in the 1935 Wimbledon final in which Jacobs led, 5-2, in the third set and stood at match point, only to see the-then Mrs. Moody rally and add one more victory to her astounding record.

In 1928 she became the first player to win three majors in the same year—French, Wimbledon and U.S.—and the first American to rule at Stade Roland Garros, where she was unbeaten while winning four titles. Her total of 19 major singles titles was the record for 32 years, until Margaret Smith Court (24) passed her in 1970. But her success was the most phenomenal ever, considering that she won 19 of 22 entered, winning 126 of 129 matches (.977), never worse than finalist.

She became Mrs. Aidan Roark in 1939 and was inducted into the Hall of Fame in 1969. She died Jan. 1, 1998 in Carmel, Calif.

MAJOR TITLES *(31)–French singles, 1928, 1929, 1930, 1932; Wimbledon singles, 1927, 1928, 1929, 1930, 1932, 1933, 1935, 1938; U.S. singles, 1923, 1924, 1925, 1927, 1928, 1929, 1931; French doubles, 1930, 1932; Wimbledon doubles, 1924, 1927, 1930; U.S. doubles, 1922, 1924, 1925, 1928; Wimbledon mixed, 1929; U.S. mixed, 1924, 1928.* **WIGHTMAN CUP**–*1923, 1924, 1925, 1927, 1928, 1929, 1930, 1931, 1932, 1938; record: 18-2 in singles, 3-7 in doubles.* **SINGLES RECORD IN THE MAJORS**–*French (20-0), Wimbledon (55-1), U.S. (51-2).*

BESSIE MOORE

United States (1876–1959)
Hall of Fame 1971

Elisabeth Holmes Moore, a New Yorker, was a young champ, winning the first of her U.S. titles at 20 in 1896. But four years before, she was in the final, losing the first five-set match played by women, 5-7, 6-3, 6-4, 4-6, 6-2, to Ireland's Mabel Cahill. She was the youngest U.S. finalist at 16 until Pam Shriver, a younger 16 in 1978.

Winning four singles titles (1896, 1901, 1903, 1905), she was in four other finals, and though she was eligible for a fifth in 1906 (as the 1905 champ), she did not choose to play in the challenge round, defaulting the title to Helen Homans, the all-comers victor. Her U.S. total of eight finals was later surpassed by Molla Mallory's 10 and Helen Wills Moody and Chris Evert's nine. Her longevity spread between the finals of 1892 and 1905 is also a U.S. record.

In 1901, she beat Marion Jones in the all-comers final, 4-6, 1-6, 9-7, 9-7, 6-3 (58 games, the longest of all major women's finals), then ousted defender Myrtle McAteer in the challenge round, 6-4, 3-6, 7-5, 2-6, 6-2, to become the lone woman to play five-set matches on successive days.

The 105 games alarmed the men who ran the USTA. They decreed best-of-three-set finals thereafter. Moore and the other women hadn't complained about five-set matches and she said they felt "dissatisfied" by the decision and patronized by the male establishment. Moore, a right-hander, was born March 5, 1876, in Brooklyn, N.Y., and died Jan. 22, 1959, in Starke, Fla. She was elected to the Hall of Fame in 1971.

MAJOR TITLES *(8)–U.S. singles, 1896, 1901, 1903, 1905; U.S. doubles, 1896, 1903; U.S. mixed, 1902, 1904.* **OTHER U.S. TITLES** *(3)–Indoor singles, 1907; Indoor doubles, 1908, with Helen Pouch; 1909, with Erna Marcus.* **SINGLES RECORD IN THE MAJORS**–*U.S. (25-6).*

ANGELA MORTIMER
Great Britain (1932–)
Hall of Fame 1993

Turning a physical impairment to her advantage, Florence Angela Margaret Mortimer Barrett capped an excellent career with a rebounding, unexpected Wimbledon triumph in 1961. She was 29 and partially deaf.

"I could hear the applause of the crowd, but not much else," she recalled. "I think it helped me concentrate, shutting out distractions. When I hear players say they have to hear the ball, I smile. I couldn't."

Much applause stirred Centre Court the afternoon the 5-foot-6 Mortimer, seventh seed, overcame the crowd favorite, 6-foot and sixth-seeded 20-year-old Christine Truman, 4-6, 6-4, 7-5. It was the first all-English finale in 47 years.

Born April 21, 1932, at Plymouth, Mortimer didn't start playing tennis until she was 15. But her resolve, speed and intelligence combined to produce a strong all-around game, with emphasis on groundstrokes, particularly a battering forehand.

Mortimer lost the Wimbledon final to Althea Gibson in 1958 and was a quarter-finalist in 1953, 1954, 1956,

1959 and 1960. She won the French in 1955 and Australian in 1958, and the Wimbledon doubles in 1955.

She played Wightman Cup six years, helping Britain win, 4-3, in 1960 with a critical victory over Janet Hopps, 6-8, 6-4, 6-1, and captained the team seven years (1964-70), piloting the 1968 victory. She was in the World Top Ten, 1953-62, Nos. 1, 4 and 4 in 1961, 1955 and 1956, respectively.

Following the 1961 season, in which she was a U.S. semi-finalist, losing to Ann Haydon (Jones), 6-4, 6-2, she underwent a stapedectomy, improving her hearing significantly. But she was never again the player of her Wimbledon glory. Angela was a Wimbledon centurion, playing more than 100 matches, 35-18 in doubles, 5-6 in mixed.

She is married to John Edward Barrett, former British Davis Cup player and captain. They live in England.

MAJOR TITLES *(4)–Australian singles, 1958; French singles, 1955; Wimbledon singles, 1961; Wimbledon doubles, 1955.* **WIGHTMAN CUP**–*1953, 1955, 1956, 1959, 1960, 1961; record: 3-7 in singles, 1-4 in doubles.* **SINGLES RECORD IN THE MAJORS**–*Australian (5-0), French (9-2), Wimbledon (36-11), U.S. (10-5).*

GARDNAR MULLOY
United States (1913–)
Hall of Fame 1972

An eternal beacon in the game, Gardnar Putnam Mulloy held his first U.S. national ranking in 1936 (No. 11 in men's doubles) and his most recent merely 60 years later, in 1996: No. 1 in 80s singles and doubles as a slim 6-footer with all his hair and wiles, bereft of maybe a step or two, seemingly fit as ever, he continues to play effortlessly. He is a man with a complete game, whose volleys and smashes lit up the left court as he and Bill Talbert became one of the finest teams.

They won the U.S. title four times (1942, 1945, 1946, 1948), and were finalists in 1950 and 1953. Probably the one they remember best almost got away seven times. That was the overblown 1946 final of 74 games as the tourney returned to Longwood after a wartime stay at Forest Hills, where Bill and Gar won their first two. In the record fifth set for any major, they just said no to seven match points while beating Don McNeill and Frank Guernsey, 3-6, 6-4, 2-6, 6-3, 20-18. Their six final-round appearances are one short of Fred Alexander and Harold Hackett's team record. He and Talbert won the clinching point in the 1948 Davis Cup victory over Australia at Forest Hills, beating Billy

Sidwell and Colin Long. Gar was on the team six other years, helping also to win the Cups of 1946 and 1949, and was a winning player-captain in two zone matches, 1952 and 1953. Playing on the 1957 team at 43, he was the oldest U.S. Cupper.

Ranking in the U.S. Top Ten 14 times between 1939 and 1954, he was No. 1 in 1952, when he was U.S. finalist at Forest Hills, losing to 24-year-old Frank Sedgman. At 38, Mulloy was the oldest to attain that eminence, five weeks older than 38-year-old Bill Larned in 1911. He ranked in the World Top Ten thrice: 1946, 1949 and 1952, No. 7 the last year. His most startling triumph may have been the Wimbledon doubles in 1957, at 43, joined with Budge Patty, 33. Unseeded, they became the oldest championship team of the post-World War I era by stunning the top-seeded Lew Hoad, 22, and Neale Fraser, 23, 8-10, 6-4, 6-4, 6-4.

A right-hander, he was born Nov. 22, 1913, in Washington, D.C., but has been a lifelong Miamian, a graduate of the University of Miami and its law school, organizer-coach-leading player of its first tennis team. His first U.S. Championships were the Father and Son doubles with his father, Robin Mulloy, in 1939, 1941 and 1942, but they have continued to flow from his rackets unceasingly for more than a half-century. Campaigning among the seniors since he won the singles at the Grass Court 45s in 1960, he has racked up 52 U.S. titles in singles through the age groups and 47 in doubles including the Grass 45s of 1963, 1964, 1965 and 1967 with his old sidekick, Talbert. In 1995 and 1996, he won four 80s singles, two grass, one indoor and one hard court.

Serving in the U.S. Navy in World War II, he commanded a landing craft in North African and European invasions. He entered the Hall of Fame in 1972.

MAJOR TITLES *(5)–Wimbledon doubles, 1957; U.S. doubles, 1942, 1945, 1946, 1948.* **OTHER U.S. TITLE**–*Clay Court doubles, 1946, with Bill Talbert.* **DAVIS CUP**–*1946, 1948, 1949, 1950, 1952, 1953, 1957; record: 3-0 in singles, 8-3 in doubles.* **SINGLES RECORD IN THE MAJORS**–*Australian (3-1), French (13-4), Wimbledon (31-18), U.S. (51-20).*

LINDLEY MURRAY

United States (1892–1970)
Hall of Fame 1958

A big-serving 6-foot-2 lefty out of California, Robert Lindley Murray was born Nov. 3, 1892, in San Francisco. He had a brief, bright run in the U.S. Championships, losing in the 1916 semis to Bill Johnston, 6-2, 6-3, 6-1, and taking the title in 1917 (over Nat Niles) and 1918 (over Bill Tilden).

He was ranked No. 1 in the U.S. in 1918, No. 4 in 1916 and 1919. A chemical engineer who graduated from Stanford, he was working on explosives production during World War I and had no intention of entering the 1917 Championships, billed as a "patriotic" tournament to raise money for the Red Cross. His employer, Elon Hooker of Hooker Chemical, talked Murray into it and he had an explosive tourney—the only one he played that summer.

"My strong points were a vicious serve, a quick dash to the net and the ability to volley decisively anything that came near me," he said.

His serve was lightning on the boards of the Seventh Regiment Armory in New York as Lindley won the 1916 U.S. Indoor over Alrick Man, 6-2, 6-2, 9-7.

He settled in the Buffalo area and died Jan. 17, 1970, in Lewiston Heights, N.Y. He was named to the Hall of Fame in 1958.

MAJOR TITLES *(2)–U.S. singles, 1917, 1918.* **OTHER U.S. TITLE**–*Indoor singles, 1916.* **SINGLES RECORD IN THE MAJORS**–*U.S. (21-3).*

ILIE NASTASE

Romania (1946–)
Hall of Fame 1991

No player in history has been more gifted or mystifying than the Bucharest Buffoon, Ilie Nastase, noted both for his sorcery with the racket and his bizarre, even objectionable behavior. He was an entertainer second to none, amusing spectators with his antics and mimicry, also infuriating them with gaucheries and walkouts.

Despite a fragile nervous system and erratic temperament, Nastase—a slender 6-footer, quick, leggy and athletic—could do everything, and when his concentration held together he was an artist creating with great originality and panache. His record in the season-closing Masters was spectacular. He won four times, 1971-73, '75, and was finalist to Guillermo Vilas in five sets in 1974.

Born July 19, 1946, in Bucharest, he was the greatest of his country, the first Romanian of international prominence. Largely through his play that small country rose to the Davis Cup final on three occasions, 1969, '71-'72, losing each time to the U.S. At the end of 1985 after playing Davis Cup since 1966, Nastase ranked second behind Italian Nicola Pietrangeli among the busiest players in Cup history, the only men to have won more than 100 matches. Nastase, 11 wins behind, captured 109: 74-22 in singles, 35-15 in doubles for 52 series.

Romania was favored to lift the Cup from the U.S. in the 1972 finale on the friendly slow clay of Nastase's hometown. However, his nervousness combined with an inspired performance by Stan Smith added up to an 11-9, 6-2, 6-3 victory for the American in the crucial opening singles, and the U.S. kept the Cup, 3-2. Nastase's foremost disappointment occurred three months prior, when Smith narrowly defeated him in the Wimbledon final, 4-6, 6-3, 6-3, 4-6, 7-5, one of the most exciting championship matches there. Nastase was in another Wimbledon singles final in 1976, but was beaten easily by Bjorn Borg.

Nastase, a right-hander, first came to attention in 1966 when he and his first mentor, countryman Ion Tiriac, reached the final of the French doubles, losing to Clark Graebner and Dennis Ralston.

Romania was a nowhere nation in Davis Cup until Nastase came along to link with the hulking, Draculan ice hockey luminary, Tiriac. The country had entered sporadically since first joining in 1922, winning only one series before 1959. That year Tiriac, from Count Dracula's Transylvanian neighborhood, spurred a couple of wins. Still, Romania had won but nine prior to the 1969 Ilie-Ion splurge of five victories that carried them to the semis against Britain, a 3-2 victory at Wimbledon. There the irrepressible duo, then unknown, flabbergasted everybody, themselves included—"we can't play on this grass," said Tiriac after beating Mark Cox on opening day. It took a fifth match victory by Nastase over Cox to propel them into the final against the U.S. in Cleveland. Another foreign surface, asphalt, plus Arthur Ashe and Stan Smith ended the unfamiliar joyride, 5-0. But they became very familiar figures, getting to the final in the U.S. again in 1971, and getting closer, 3-2. However, it was Ilie's failure against Smith in the opening match (7-5, 6-3, 6-1) that made the difference, as it was a year later in Bucharest.

By 1970 Nastase began to assert himself. He won the Italian singles over French Open champ Jan Kodes and jolted Cliff Richey in the U.S. Indoor final.

Following his Davis Cup and Wimbledon heartaches of 1972, Nastase had the immeasurable consolation of winning the U.S. Open at Forest Hills from a seeming losing position, down 2-4 in the fourth set and a service break to open the fifth against Ashe. The score: 3-6, 6-3,

6-7 (1-5), 6-4, 6-3. It was his only major grass-court singles prize.

His finest season was 1973, when he was regarded as No. 1 in the world after winning the most one-sided Italian final, 6-1, 6-1, 6-1, over Manolo Orantes, the French, over Nikola Pilic, 6-3, 6-3, 6-0, and 13 other titles, plus downing Tom Okker in the Masters final, 6-3, 7-5, 4-6, 6-3. That season he won 15 of 31 tourneys on a 118-17 match record, also eight doubles for an overall total of 23, tying Rod Laver's open-era record (17 singles, 6 doubles), broken by John McEnroe's 27 in 1979.

Though he provoked controversy, and his career was marred by fines, disqualifications, and suspensions, Nastase was good-natured, likeable and friendly offcourt. He had a sense of humor in his on-court shenanigans, but frequently did not know when to stop and lost control of himself. "I am a little crazy," he said, "but I try to be a good boy." His comrade, Tiriac, amicably put it this way: "His brain is like a bird in a cage."

He was expert at putting the ball just beyond an opponent's reach, and applying discomfiting spin. He lobbed and retrieved splendidly, in his prime possibly the fastest player of all, and he could play either baseline or serve-and-volley. In 1976 he was the first European to exceed $1 million in career prize money, and had a career total of $2,076,761. Nastase played World Team Tennis for Hawaii in 1976 and Los Angeles in 1977-78, leading L.A. to the league title in 1978 as player-coach.

Eight times between 1970 and 1977 he was ranked in the World Top Ten, No. 1, in 1973, the year he won the French and Italian back-to-back, an unusual coupling.

In a career begun in the amateur era and continued in the open era, he was one of five players to win more than 100 pro titles in singles (57) and doubles (51). He was inducted into the Hall of Fame in 1991. Ilie lives in New York with his American wife, Alexandra. He has been Romanian Davis Cup captain and president of the Romanian Tennis Federation. He reaped considerable international attention again by running for mayor of Bucharest in 1996, but he was defeated. "Probably a very good thing for him and Bucharest," chuckled Tiriac.

MAJOR TITLES *(7)–French singles, 1973; U.S. singles, 1972; French doubles, 1970; Wimbledon doubles, 1973; U.S. doubles, 1975; Wimbledon mixed, 1970, 1972.* **DAVIS CUP**–*1966, 1967, 1968, 1969, 1970, 1971, 1972, 1973, 1974, 1975, 1976, 1977, 1979, 1980, 1982, 1983, 1984, 1985; record: 74-22 in singles, 35-15 in doubles.* **SINGLES RECORD IN THE MAJORS**–*Australian (0-1), French (33-13), Wimbledon (35-15), U.S. (29-14).*

MARTINA NAVRATILOVA

Czechoslovakia/United States (1956–)
Hall of Fame 2000

As the game's most prolific winner of the open era—probably ever—Martina Navratilova, the puissant left-hander, continues to add to her record totals, getting on with her tennis life indefinitely. Yet a presence in doubles, she won the Wimbledon mixed in 1995 with Jonathan Stark, and, incredibly, buoyantly, the Australian mixed with Leander Paes as the 2003 season commenced, her 57th major.

Marvelous Martina may have retired from singles at the 1994 year-end WTA Championships at Madison Square Garden, an opening-round defeat by Gabriela Sabatini, 6-4, 6-2, as thousands cheered and wept, saying goodbye and thanks for the memories. After all she had done so much in New York, winning that prime championship eight times in singles (five times runner-up), 10 times in doubles, plus four singles and 11 doubles titles across the East River at the U.S. Open. But, as it has turned out, that wasn't enough to slake her thirst for the game. Her Melbourne win made her, at 46-years-three months, the—shall we say?—most mature personage to grab a major, slightly longer in the tooth than the local boy, Norman Brookes, who was 46 years, two months in winning the 1924 Australian doubles.

Nobody, ever, has such a glittering trove of numbers. As a pro since 1973, she played the most singles tournaments (383) and matches (1,653), and won the most titles (168) and matches (1,440) with a W-L mark of 1,440-213. She won more prize money, $20,527,874, than all but Ivan Lendl and Pete Sampras.

Her doubles feats, attesting to a grandeur of completeness, were also sparkling: Second most tournaments (274), most matches played (1,111), most titles (162) and matches won (989), with a won-lost mark of 989-122. Including mixed doubles (27 tournaments played, eight titles and a 94-19 W-L record), she holds records for most titles (337) and matches won (2,521, against just 353 losses). Thus she batted .872 in singles, .890 in doubles, .832 in mixed—.877 for everything. It means she won 48.6 percent of all the tournaments she entered. Whew!

In the matter of major titles, her starburst of 57 (18 singles, 31 doubles, seven mixed) didn't quite reach Margaret Court's stratospheric 62 (24-19-19). Despite her record 19 Wimbledon titles (including a record nine

in singles), she's still a step behind Billie Jean King's overall record of 20 (6-10-4), Martina holding 9-7-3. She was inducted into the International Tennis Hall of Fame in 2000.

Arguably the greatest player of all time, Martina was born on Oct. 18, 1956, in Prague, Czechoslovakia, and became a U.S. citizen in 1981, after defecting six years earlier. She was raised by her mother, Jana, and stepfather, Mirek Navratil, whose name she took.

Despite her upbringing on slow clay in the small town of Revnice, outside of Prague, she has always been a tornado-like attacker, a net-rusher. She attracted notice at 16 in Paris, the French Open of 1973, by serving-and-volleying a clay specialist, and former champ, fifth-seeded Nancy Richey, to defeat, reaching the quarters unseeded.

Her lustrous 16-year rivalry with Chris Evert was launched that year in Akron, Ohio, an indoor defeat. "She was overweight, but eager and gifted," Evert remembered. "It was a close match (7-6, 6-3). Even though I'd never heard of her, and couldn't pronounce or spell her name, I could tell she'd be trouble. Especially if she got in shape."

She was trouble, and eventually the 5-foot-7-1/2, 140-pound Navratilova made extreme fitness her trademark in overcoming Evert, who became her good friend. Although Evert led in the rivalry, 21-4, at the high point of her dominance, Navratilova won their last encounter, Chicago, in 1988, to wind up with a 43-37 edge. Three years later, also in Chicago, Martina scaled Evert's seemingly unattainable record of 157 pro singles tournament victories. By beating Jana Novotna from two match points down she nailed victory No. 158, and kept going. She had unknowingly begun to stalk Evert at home with her initial title, Pilsen, in 1973.

Her proudest times were spent in the game's temple, Centre Court, Wimbledon, where she became the all-time singles champ by defeating Zina Garrison in 1990, her ninth championship. The record of eight had been achieved more than a half-century before when Helen Wills Moody beat Helen Jacobs in 1938.

Navratilova began her run at Moody by beating top-seeded Evert in the 1978 final. She repeated over Evert, but was deterred, momentarily, in the 1980 and 1981 semis by Evert and Hana Mandlikova. Rebounding, she reeled off championships in six successive years, snapping Suzanne Lenglen's mark of five straight (1919-23). Driving to the 1988 final, she had rolled up 47 straight match wins, three short of Moody's Wimbledon record streak. But Martina was stopped by the Grand Slammer of that year, Steffi Graf.

Graf beat her for the title in 1989, too, but, when Graf lost to Garrison in the 1990 semis, Martina triumphed again in her eleventh final. There would be one last Centre Court singles final, the twelfth, in 1994. The Big M left some lofty records at the Big W for her 22 years besides the titles: Most consecutive finals (nine), most matches (279), singles wins (119), doubles wins (80), overall wins (243). She was 119-13 in singles, 80-14 in doubles, 44-9 in mixed.

Navratilova also won four U.S., three Australian and two French singles. The Australian: 1981, over Evert; 1983, over Kathy Jordan; 1985, over Evert. The French: 1982, over Andrea Jaeger; 1984, over Evert. Winning the U.S. was her most frustrating trial. Not until her eleventh try, in 1983 (having lost the 1981 final in a tiebreaker to Tracy Austin) did Navratilova make it: 6-1, 6-3, over Evert. She duplicated the next year over Evert, in a high quality struggle, adding 1986 over Helena Sukova and 1987 over Graf. In 1991, almost 35, she was the tourney's oldest losing finalist since 40-year-old Molla Mallory in 1924, bowing to Monica Seles, 7-6 (7-1), 7-1.

Only one prize, a singles Grand Slam, eluded her— barely in 1983 and 1984. Although 1983 was her most overpowering season (16 victories in 17 tournaments on an 86-1 match record), it was 1984 (13 victories in 15 tourneys on 78-2) when the Slam seemed certain. With three of the titles in her satchel, she reached the semis of the last that year, the Australian, on a pro record 74-match winning streak. However, Sukova, who had ball-girled for her in Prague years before, intervened, 1-6, 6-3, 7-5, snapping her streak of six consecutive major titles. After that Martina took off on a 54-match streak, severed by Hana Mandlikova. Mandlikova also snipped her second longest streak, 56, in the 1987 Australian final.

Navratilova did, however, register a doubles Grand Slam with Pam Shriver in 1984. Perhaps the greatest of all teams, Navratilova-Shriver won 20 majors (equaling the record total of Louise Brough and Margaret duPont, 1942-57). The Navratilova-Shriver combine produced 79 tournament victories, including 10 season-climaxing Virginia Slims titles, and a record 109-match winning streak between 1983 and a 1985 loss in the Wimbledon final to Liz Smylie and Kathy Jordan, 5-7, 6-3, 6-4.

From 1985 to 1987, she was in the final of all 11 majors (Australian not held in 1986), winning six, a sin-

gular feat until Steffi Graf played in 12 straight between 1987 and 1990, winning 10. In 1987 she made a rare triple at the U.S. Open (singles, doubles, mixed), the third of the open era.

Phenomenally, for almost two decades, 1975-91, Navratilova was no worse than No. 4 in the World Top Ten, seven times attaining No. 1 (1978-79, '82-'83-'84-'85-'86). Returning to the top in 1982, she embarked on a record run of 156 weeks into 1987, until supplanted by Graf, who broke the record with 186 straight weeks.

Martina moved to the United States in 1975 after learning that sports federation authorities in the communist Czechoslovak government reportedly planned to curtail her travel because they disapproved of what was called her increasing 'Americanization.' "I knew I had to defect," she said. She announced her intention of becoming a U.S. citizen at the U.S. Open of 1975. For years after she was considered a 'non-person,' her results never printed or announced in Czechoslovakia.

Returning to her homeland in triumph (and to the government's discomfort) as a U.S. citizen in 1986, she led her adopted country's team to a Federation Cup victory, as she had done for Czechoslovakia 11 years before. Playing for the U.S., she was peerless, unbeaten, winning the decisive singles over Mandlikova and helped win two other Federation Cups, 1982 and 1989, as well as one Wightman Cup, 1983.

Navratilova credits one of her coaches, pro basketball luminary Nancy Lieberman, of "turning my career around in 1981. Even though I'd won two Wimbledons, she sternly lectured me that I was wasting my talent, needed to work harder than ever, give tennis total commitment. Thanks to her burning me I did."

Oakland was her last tour stop prior to the Garden in 1994, and Martina's last final on her own. She lost narrowly and gamely to Arantxa Sanchez Vicario, 1-6, 7-6 (7-5), 7-6 (7-3). "It would have been nice to have said goodbye to the tour with a win," she sighed after the two-hour, 23-minute test. As it developed, she didn't say goodbye, only see-ya in a bit. She dabbled in doubles for three tourneys in 1995, got her Wimbledon mixed title, reappeared in 2000, and found out she could keep up with the kids, and then some. With Natalia Zvereva in 2002, she resumed adding to her record, winning Madrid over Sanchez Vicario and Rossano Neffa-de los Rios. For a lark she entered one more singles tournament, Eastbourne. Astoundingly she beat No. 25 Tatiana Panova, then nearly upset Daniela Hantuchova. "What's that lady doing charging the net?" the kids wondered, thinking they'd seen the ghost of championships past.

Another of her coaches, Renée Richards, had it right at the Hall of Fame induction, calling her "Martina the Magnificent."

MAJOR TITLES *(57)–Australian singles, 1981, 1983, 1985; French singles, 1982, 1984; Wimbledon singles, 1978, 1979, 1982, 1983, 1984, 1985, 1986, 1987, 1990; U.S. singles, 1983, 1984, 1986, 1987; Australian doubles, 1980, 1982, 1983, 1984, 1985, 1987, 1988, 1989; Australian mixed, 2003; French doubles, 1975, 1982, 1984, 1985, 1986, 1987, 1988; Wimbledon doubles, 1976, 1979, 1981, 1982, 1983, 1984, 1986; U.S. doubles, 1977, 1978, 1980, 1983, 1984, 1986, 1987, 1989, 1990; French mixed, 1974, 1985; Wimbledon mixed, 1985, 1993, 1995; U.S. mixed, 1985, 1987.* **OTHER U.S. TITLES** *(8)–Indoor singles, 1975, 1981, 1984, 1986; Indoor doubles, 1979, with Billie Jean King; 1981, 1984, 1985, with Pam Shriver.* **FEDERATION CUP**–*1975, 1982, 1986, 1989; record: 20-0 in singles, 16-0 in doubles.* **WIGHTMAN CUP**–*1983; record: 2-0 in singles, 1-0 in doubles.* **SINGLES RECORD IN THE MAJORS**–*Australian (46-7), French (52-10), Wimbledon (119-13), U.S. (89-17).*

JOHN NEWCOMBE

Australia (1944–)
Hall of Fame 1986

When good mates John Newcombe and Tony Roche, a potent Australian pair, won the Wimbledon doubles of 1965, it was the start not only of an extraordinary string of major titles for Newcombe but also for the two of them as a unit.

Two years earlier, Newcombe, at 19, attracted international attention as one of the youngest Aussies ever to play Davis Cup. He was selected for the finale to play singles against the U.S. Though beaten by both Dennis Ralston and Chuck McKinley during a 3-2 U.S. victory, Newcombe served notice that he was a player to reckon with when he pushed Wimbledon champion McKinley to four hard sets in the decisive fifth match.

Newcombe and the left-handed Roche, one of the great doubles teams in history, won five Wimbledons together (1965, '68, '69, '70, '74) a modern record until countrymen Mark Woodforde and Todd Woodbridge edged ahead of them with six. (The English Doherty brothers won eight between 1897 and 1905, and the English Renshaw brothers won seven between 1880 and 1889.) Newcombe and Roche also won the U.S. in 1967, the French in 1967, '69, and the Australian in 1965, '67, '71, '76, standing as one of only five teams— all Australians—to win all the Big Four titles during a career and leading all teams with 12 majors.

It was in singles, though, that Newcombe made his

name. He and Rod Laver are the only players to win the men's singles at Forest Hills and Wimbledon as amateurs and pros. Newcombe, the last amateur champion at Wimbledon beat Willy Bungert in 1967 and repeated in 1970 over Ken Rosewall, and 1971 over Stan Smith.

In all Newcombe, a 6-foot, 170-pound right-hander, won 25 major titles in singles, doubles, and mixed doubles to stand second behind Roy Emerson (28) in the list of all-time male championships.

John David Newcombe was born May 23, 1944, in Sydney, and was more interested in other sports as a youngster. Not until he was 17 did a career in tennis appeal to him. But he was powerful, athletic and extremely competitive, and Australian Davis Cup Capt. Harry Hopman was glad when Newcombe turned his full attention to tennis. Newcombe helped Hopman win four Cups, 1964-67. He then returned to Cup play in 1973 for Capt. Neale Fraser when all pros were reinstated, joining perhaps the strongest team ever, alongside Laver, Ken Rosewall and Mal Anderson. In the finale that year Newcombe and Laver were overpowering. Both beat Stan Smith and Tom Gorman in singles, and teamed in crushing Smith and Erik van Dillen, 6-1, 6-2, 6-4, in the doubles during a 5-0 Australian victory that ended five-year possession of the Cup by the U.S. Newc's leadoff taming of Smith, 6-1, 3-6, 6-3, 3-6, 6-4, set the tone, and he and Laver took it out of reach.

Newcombe also played in the World Cup in 1970, the inaugural of the since disbanded team match between the Aussies and the U.S., and helped win five of those Cups for his country.

Newcombe's serve, forehand and volleying were the backbone of his attacking game, which was at its best on grass. His heavy serve was possibly the best of his era. Grass was the setting for his foremost singles wins, the three Wimbledons plus two U.S. Championships at Forest Hills in 1967 and 1973, a tight victory over Jan Kodes. "You're only as good as your second serve and first volley," was the motto of this intelligent, fun-loving Aussie, and he lived up to it.

Newcombe regretted missing successive Wimbledons of 1972 and 1973 when he felt he might have added to his string. In 1972 he was a member of the World Championship Tennis pro troupe that was banned because of the quarrels between its leader, Lamar Hunt, and the ITF. In 1973, Newcombe was a member of the players union, ATP, which unselfishly boycotted Wimbledon in another dispute with the ITF. The following year he stretched his Wimbledon match win streak to 18 before losing to Rosewall in the quarter-finals. That year Newcombe won the World Championship Tennis singles over an adolescent Bjorn Borg.

Newcombe felt, "I'm at my best in a five-set match, especially if I get behind. My adrenaline starts pumping." This was evident in two of his outstanding triumphs, both over Stan Smith, a strong rival for world supremacy in the early 1970s, in the 1971 Wimbledon final and the 1973 Davis Cup finale, rating the latter as his finest performance.

In 1967 he was the No. 1 amateur in the world and, in 1970 and 1971, No. 1 of all. He was one of the first to sign a contract to play World Team Tennis (with Houston) in 1974, his presence helping give the new league credibility, although he played just that one season. His best pro season was 1971, when he won five of 19 singles tourneys on a 53-14 match record.

He totaled 73 pro titles, 32 in singles, 41 in doubles, and won $1,062,408. Overall, amateur and pro, he won 66 singles titles. Newcombe was named to the Hall of Fame, along with Roche, in 1986. He is married to former German player Angelika Pfannenburg and was appointed Australian Davis Cup captain in 1995, winning the 2000 Cup over Spain.

MAJOR TITLES (25)–Australian singles, 1973, 1975; Wimbledon singles, 1967, 1970, 1971; U.S. singles, 1967, 1973; Australian doubles, 1965, 1967, 1971, 1973, 1976; French doubles, 1967, 1969, 1973; Wimbledon doubles, 1965, 1966, 1968, 1969, 1970, 1974; U.S. doubles, 1967, 1971, 1973; U.S. mixed, 1964. **DAVIS CUP**–1963, 1964, 1965, 1966, 1967, 1973, 1975, 1976; record: 16-7 in singles, 9-2 in doubles. **SINGLES RECORD IN THE MAJORS**–Australian (45-14), French (17-9), Wimbledon (45-11), U.S. (45-9).

BETTY NUTHALL

Great Britain (1911–1983)
Hall of Fame 1983

Until Betty Kay Nuthall came along from England, no one in the 20th century had taken the women's championship out of the U.S. It was a far less widespread and organized game when Irishwoman Mabel Cahill won at Philadelphia in 1891–92. In 1927, the 16-year-old Nuthall, a prodigy who had won the British Hard Court title in the spring (a quarter-finalist there at 14), was not only threatening a long-lived American monopoly at Forest Hills but a record of Bessie Moore, the 16-year-old finalist to Cahill in 1892.

Still serving underhanded, as she had all her life—a habit she would soon change—Betty might have been the youngest of all U.S. champs. But Helen Wills took care of that in the U.S. final, 6-1, 6-4. Nevertheless, Nuthall, exactly the same age, to the day, as Moore had been, shared the 'youngest finalist' record with her until Pam Shriver, a younger 16, displaced them in 1978.

Three years later, 1930, and still a teenager, Nuthall did get the U.S. title, beating in succession the second and first seeds, Midge Morrill and Mrs. Anna McCune Harper. Defending the title, she reached the 1931 semis, losing to Wightman Cup teammate Eileen Bennett Whitingstall. Nuthall again was a semi-finalist in 1933, startling onlookers by pushing the champ, Helen Wills Moody, 2-6, 6-3, 6-2. As the youngest to play for Britain when she joined the team in 1927, she was a Wightman Cupper eight years, beating the redoubtable Helen Jacobs in her debut.

She had a fine French in 1931, beating Jacobs before having to contend with the Germans who would clash for the Wimbledon title weeks later. Betty beat Hilde Krahwinkel in the semis to prevent a preview of Wimbledon's all-German final, but lost the title match to the tiny woman who ruled Paris and London, 5-footer Cilly Aussem. But she took the doubles with Whitingstall.

The main strength of Betty's game was her forehand. Holding the racket out with extended right arm, she used it as a flail, and hit with great power. Speed was the essence of her game; there was no temporizing. She hit with length and discernment, and was resourceful and wise in tactics.

Born May 23, 1911, in Surbiton, Surrey, she took up the game at seven with her father's guidance. She accomplished little in 1928 after her success the previous year, which included beating reigning U.S. champion Molla Mallory at Wimbledon to gain the quarters. It was not until she was bypassed for the Wightman Cup team in 1930 that she decided to take matters into her own hands and campaign alone. Packing her trunk, and accompanied by her brother, Jimmy (the English junior champ), she sailed for the U.S., and her perseverance, initiative and faith in herself were rewarded. This time, serving overhand, she came through, the only Brit to rule Forest Hills until Virginia Wade in 1968, thus establishing herself as one of her country's most distinguished performers, ranking in the World Top Ten five times between 1927 and 1933.

Selected for the Hall of Fame in 1977, she died

Nov. 8, 1983, in New York, where she had been a resident, as Mrs. Franklin Shoemaker.

MAJOR TITLES *(9)–U.S. singles, 1930; French doubles, 1931; U.S. doubles, 1930, 1931, 1933; French mixed, 1931, 1932; U.S. mixed, 1929, 1931.* **WIGHTMAN CUP**–*1927, 1928, 1929, 1931, 1932, 1933, 1934, 1939; record: 3-5 in singles, 3-2 in doubles.* **SINGLES RECORD IN THE MAJORS**–*French (13-5), Wimbledon (27-13), U.S. (24-6).*

ALEX OLMEDO

Peru/United States (1936–)
Hall of Fame 1987

Alejandro Olmedo, called 'Chief' at the University of Southern California because of his regal bearing at 6-foot-1 and his Incan features, was an aggressive volleyer who constantly sought the net. He fared best on the quickest terrain: Concrete (U.S. Intercollegiate titles in singles and doubles for USC in 1956 and 1958); boards (U.S. Indoor titlist in 1959 over Dick Savitt, 7-9, 6-3, 6-4, 5-7, 12-10) and grass (Wimbledon and Australian chieftain in 1959). His was a quick but huge splash that covered two years.

Born March 24, 1936, in Arequipa, Peru, he picked up the game in his homeland as an extremely agile athlete. But it was refined when he came to USC where he was thrust into the limelight—and controversy—by one of his patrons, Southern California tennis czar Perry Jones. Jones, the U.S. Davis Cup captain in 1958 and 1959, saw in Olmedo the chance for victory after three lean years. Lobbying successfully for Olmedo's inclusion on the basis that the Peruvian was a U.S. resident whose own country had no team, Jones installed him for the semi-final victory over Italy on grass at Perth. Alex won his debut over Nicola Pietrangeli, 5-7, 10-8, 6-0, 6-1. This launched a storm of press criticism over the U.S. using a non-citizen for the only time. Another hassle developed at the Cup round when the No. 1 American, Ham Richardson, was benched in singles in favor of Olmedo. But Jones' policy worked. Olmedo anchored the 3-2 victory over the Aussies at Brisbane with two singles victories and by joining his U.S. championship partner, Richardson, in an epic 82-game doubles win over Mal Anderson and Neale Fraser, 10-12, 3-6, 16-14, 6-3, 7-5. Alex led off by beating Anderson, 8-6, 2-6, 9-7, 8-6, and clinched over Wimbledon champ Ashley Cooper, 6-3, 4-6, 6-4, 8-6.

A half-year later Wimbledon belonged to Olmedo, 6-4, 3-6, 9-7, 7-5, over Rod Laver. Although he beat Laver again in the Cup round the following month, the U.S. lost the Cup to Australia, 3-2, at Forest Hills. Fraser, his conqueror in that series, also beat him for the U.S. title, 6-3, 5-7, 6-2, 6-4. In 1960 Olmedo turned pro and joined the nomads on their odyssey of one-night stands. His brief mention in the rankings were in 1958, No. 2 in the U.S.; 1959, No. 1 in the U.S., No. 2 in the world. His daughter, Amy Olmedo, won the U.S. Public Parks Championship for 12s in 1975. He entered the Hall of Fame in 1987, and became a U.S. citizen in 1999.

MAJOR TITLES *(2)–Wimbledon singles, 1959; Australian singles, 1959.* **OTHER U.S. TITLES** *(11)–Indoor singles, 1959; Pro singles, 1960; Pro doubles, 1960, with Ashley Cooper; Indoor doubles, 1959, with Barry MacKay; Clay Court doubles, 1956, with Francisco Contreras; Hard Court singles, 1956; Hard Court doubles, 1957, with Mike Franks; Intercollegiate singles, 1956, 1958; Intercollegiate doubles, 1956, with Contreras; 1958, with Ed Atkinson.* **DAVIS CUP**–*1958, 1959; record: 5-1 in singles, 2-1 in doubles.* **SINGLES RECORD IN THE MAJORS**–*Australian (5-0), French (0-2), Wimbledon (10-3), U.S. (15-9).*

MARGARET OSBORNE DUPONT

United States (1918–)
Hall of Fame 1967

One of the most cerebral players, Margaret Evelyn Osborne duPont was a collector of major championships topped only by Margaret Court (62), Martina Navratilova (57) and Billie Jean King (39). In two decades duPont accumulated 37 championships in singles, doubles and mixed, although never entering the Australian.

Peerless at doubles, she was the canny 5-foot-5-1/2, 145-pound, right-court player, superbly complementing Louise Brough in the most successful team prior to Navratilova and Pam Shriver. Together they won a record 20 major titles: 12 U.S., 5 Wimbledon, 3 French, a mark tied by Navratilova and Shriver in 1989. She won the U.S. doubles first with Sarah Palfrey Fabyan (later Cooke) in 1941, and the next time with Brough in a record streak that ran from 1942 through 1950. Their match win streak of 41 ended in the 1951 final, a 6-2, 7-9, 9-7 defeat by Shirley Fry and Doris Hart. As a team in the U.S. Championships, Brough and duPont won 12 of the 14 times they entered and 58 of 60 matches. DuPont, a right-hander, was the playmaker, utilizing a devilish forehand chop and a variety of other spins that kept the ball low. She lobbed and volleyed excellently, and set up her volley with an effective serve.

Although 31 of her major titles were doubles and mixed doubles, she was just as tough in singles, winning the U.S. thrice in five visits to the final, Wimbledon one-for-three and the French two-for-two. Her rivalry with Brough was as close as their friendship and partnership. They split two of the more spectacular finals at the two top championships. Brough won the 1949 Wimbledon final, 10-8, 1-6, 10-8, and duPont the 1948 Forest Hills, ducking a match point, 4-6, 6-4, 15-13— 48 games, the longest female final played there.

She also won the U.S. in 1949, over Doris Hart, and again in 1950 over Hart; Wimbledon in 1947, over Hart, 6-2, 6-4; the French in 1946 over Pauline Betz, 1-6, 8-6, 7-5, despite two match points, and in 1949, over Nelly Adamson Landry. In the U.S. Mixed Doubles Championship she set a record by winning nine times: 1943-46 with Bill Talbert; 1950 with Ken McGregor; 1956 with Ken Rosewall; and 1958-60 with Neale Fraser. In the 1948 semi-final she and Talbert won the longest mixed doubles played until 1991, 71 games, over Gussy Moran and Bob Falkenburg, 27-25, 5-7, 6-1. Forty-three years later, Brenda Schultz and Michael Schapers exceeded that in a 77-game Wimbledon win over Andrea Temesvari and Tom Nijssen.

Born March 4, 1918, in Joseph, Ore., Margaret grew up in San Francisco. She made her initial appearance in the U.S. Top Ten in 1938 at No. 7 and set a longevity record for U.S. females, ranking No. 5 two decades later at age 40 in 1958. Over the 20 years, she was ranked in the U.S. Top Ten 14 times, No. 1 1948-50. Between 1946 and 1957 she was in the World Top Ten nine times, including three years as No. 1 (1947-50).

She married William duPont in 1947 and later interrupted her career to give birth to a son. She was one of the few women to win a major title after childbirth.

Hers was one of the finest Wightman Cup records. In nine years of the British-U.S. series, she was unbeaten in 10 singles and nine doubles, and did not play on a losing side between 1946 and 1962. She also captained the U.S. team nine times, presiding over eight victories.

In 1967 she was inducted into the Hall of Fame.

MAJOR TITLES (37)–*French singles, 1946, 1949; Wimbledon singles, 1947; U.S. singles, 1948, 1949, 1950; French doubles, 1946, 1947, 1949; Wimbledon doubles, 1946, 1948, 1949, 1950, 1954; U.S. doubles, 1941, 1942, 1943, 1944, 1945, 1946, 1947, 1948, 1949, 1950, 1955, 1956, 1957; Wimbledon mixed, 1962; U.S. mixed, 1943, 1944, 1945, 1946, 1950, 1956, 1958, 1959, 1960.* **OTHER U.S. TITLES** (2)–*Hard Court doubles, 1948, with Louise Brough, Hard Court mixed, 1948 with Tom Brown.* **WIGHTMAN CUP**–*1946, 1947, 1948, 1949, 1950, 1954, 1955, 1957, 1961, 1962; record: 10-0 in singles, 9-0 in doubles.* **SINGLES RECORD IN THE MAJORS**–*French (14-2), Wimbledon (34-8), U.S. (54-14).*

RAFE OSUNA
Mexico (1938–1969)
Hall of Fame 1979

Mexico's greatest player, Rafael Herrera Osuna, died tragically in an air crash near Monterey, June 6, 1969— shortly after one of his brightest performances. He had spearheaded Mexico's lone Davis Cup triumph over Australia, 3-2, in Mexico City by winning both his singles (the exciting fifth-match clincher over Bill Bowrey, 6-2, 3-6, 8-6, 6-3) as well as the doubles with Vicente Zarazua over John Alexander and Phil Dent. Ironically it was not only his last match, but the last appearance in the Australian captain's chair of the man whose side he defeated, legendary Harry Hopman.

Long the anchor of Mexico's team, the super-quick and clever 5-foot-10 Osuna, was the better known half of an extraordinary combine. He and Antonio Palafox showed what two good men could do for their country in 1962, taking Mexico past the U.S. for the first time, 3-2; Yugoslavia, 4-1; Sweden, 3-2; India, 5-0, all the way to the finale at Brisbane, where they lost to Cup-holding Australia, 5-0.

During that campaign en route to Australia, Osuna was 5-1 in singles, and with Palafox, 4-0 in doubles. Twice he came through in emotional and decisive fifth sets of fifth matches, beating Jack Douglas of the U.S. at the wire, 9-7, 6-3, 6-8, 3-6, 6-1, and Jan-Erik Lundquist of Sweden, likewise, 3-6, 6-4, 6-3, 1-6, 6-3, both at Mexico City.

Twice he won the doubles at Wimbledon, his country's only triumphs there, 1960 and 1963. The first time, at 21, with his University of Southern California pal and partner, Dennis Ralston, 17, they were unseeded, and the second-youngest champs, beating Mike Davies and Bobby Wilson, 7-5, 6-3, 10-8. In 1963 he and Palafox beat Pierre Darmon and Jean Claude Barclay. The two of them had a terrific series with Ralston and Chuck McKinley in three straight U.S. finals, 1961-63, the Mexicans winning in 1962 and holding fifth-set match points in 1963.

Ubiquitous on court, confusing to foes, ever seeking the net, he reached a zenith in singles by winning the U.S. title at Forest Hills in 1963, bewildering huge-serving Frank Froehling III, 7-5, 6-4, 6-2, with lobs, chips, angles, flying volleys and footspeed. Slouching, unimposing until his feet and hands whirred in action, he had a beguiling smile and a court manner that endeared him to galleries. At Southern Cal, where he was an All-American, he won the U.S. Intercollegiate singles in 1962 and was the first player since World War I to take the doubles three times: 1961 and 1962 with Ramsey Earnhart, 1963 with Ralston. Osuna was in the World Top Ten thrice, 1962-64, No. 1 in 1963. He was born Sept. 15, 1938, in Mexico City and he made it into the Hall of Fame in 1979.

MAJOR TITLES (4)–*U.S. singles, 1963; U.S. doubles, 1962; Wimbledon doubles, 1960, 1963.* DAVIS CUP–*1958, 1960, 1961, 1962, 1963, 1964, 1965, 1966, 1967, 1968, 1969; record: 23-13 in singles, 14-8 in doubles.* SINGLES RECORD IN THE MAJORS–*French (2-2), Wimbledon (17-6), U.S. (34-7).*

SARAH PALFREY COOKE

United States (1912–1996)
Hall of Fame 1963

If any player may be said to have been the sweetheart of tennis, as Mary Pickford was of the movies, her name was Sarah Palfrey. Twice U.S. champion, Sarah Hammond Palfrey Fabyan Cooke Danzig was twice a runner-up for the title to Helen Jacobs, nine times U.S. doubles champion, and twice doubles champion at Wimbledon, and she was an international attraction on both sides of the Atlantic and west to the Pacific.

Born Sept. 18, 1912, in Sharon, Mass., she was a carefully reared girl of upper-register Boston and a protégé of Hazel Hotchkiss Wightman. The galleries loved her radiant smile and her unfailing graciousness in triumph and defeat alike, and they marveled at the cleverness and dispatch she used in the volleying position and at the execution of her sweeping backhand. She was one of the most accomplished performers around the net, thanks in part to the instruction of Wightman, a pioneer in introducing the volley as a major component of the women's game. A slip of a girl (5-foot-4, 116 pounds), Sarah was remarkable in the way she stood up to the more powerful hitters.

Sarah was so prized as a doubles partner in the 1930s and 1940s that she had the pick of the best. Seven times in Wightman Cup play she teamed with Jacobs, three times with Alice Marble, and once with Helen Wills Moody. But prestige comes from superiority in singles play, and in this the artful right-hander ranked no fewer than 13 times in the U.S. Top Ten. She was No. 1, No. 2 or No. 3 seven times. She was in the World Top Ten six times between 1933 and 1939.

A 14-year-old Sarah made her Forest Hills debut in 1927 (doubles and mixed), but not until her thirteenth campaign in 1941 did she win. She joyfully recalled her initial trip abroad, so different from the casual jet-jaunting of today: "It was 1930, and I was 17. My mother and a sister went with me aboard the liner *Scythia*. We dressed for dinner and danced away every night."

Unable to defend her 1941 U.S. singles title because of pregnancy and wartime family commitments to her husband, naval officer Elwood Cooke (1939 Wimbledon finalist to Bobby Riggs), Sarah made an extraordinary comeback to the Forest Hills scene in 1945 to win again, this time as a mother on the verge of her 33rd birthday. She mirrored her idol Wightman in this, too, becoming only the second to win the U.S. after bearing a child.

"She was a thorn for me," says four-time champ Pauline Betz Addie, recalling that but for Sarah she might well have run a record six straight championships. Pauline was in six successive finals, but Sarah won in 1941, 7-5, 6-2, and in a 1945 thriller, 3-6, 8-6, 6-4. "That 1945 final was the best I played, but still Sarah beat me with her volleying." She won the last three games from a service break behind.

An oddity was Sarah's appearance on a male championship honor roll. Because of the wartime manpower crisis, she and husband Elwood were permitted to enter the men's doubles of the Tri-State Championships in Cincinnati. They went to the final, losing to Hal Surface and Hall of Famer Bill Talbert.

A brood of tennis prodigies were the five Palfrey sisters, each of whom won at least one U.S. junior title, but Sarah was the one to achieve international renown. After her playing career, she was a successful business executive (as Mrs. Jerry Danzig in New York), and wrote on tennis in books and magazines.

Along with Alice Marble she lobbied the USTA to remove the color bar and allow future Hall of Famer Althea Gibson to play at the upper level amid whites in 1950. "She was calmly persuasive, had clout as an ex-champ, and got Althea into the U.S. Championships in 1950," says Gladys Heldman, founder of the women's pro tour. She was voted into the Hall of Fame in 1963, and died Feb. 27, 1996, in New York.

MAJOR TITLES (18)–*U.S. singles, 1941, 1945; Wimbledon doubles, 1938, 1939; U.S. doubles, 1930, 1932, 1934, 1935, 1937, 1938, 1939, 1940, 1941; French mixed, 1939; U.S. mixed, 1932, 1935, 1937, 1941.* OTHER U.S. TITLES–*Clay Court singles, 1945; Indoor singles, 1940; Indoor doubles, 1928, 1929, 1930, 1931, 1933, with Hazel Hotchkiss Wightman; Indoor mixed, 1931, with Larry Rice; 1933, with G. Holmes Perkins; Clay Court mixed, 1945, with Elwood Cooke.*

WIGHTMAN CUP–*1930, 1931, 1932, 1933, 1934, 1935, 1936, 1937, 1938, 1939; record: 7-4 in singles, 7-2 in doubles.* **SINGLES RECORD IN THE MAJORS**–*French (2-2), Wimbledon (16-6), U.S. (41-14).*

FRANK PARKER

United States (1916–1997)
Hall of Fame 1966

Frank Andrew Parker, a marvelous groundstroker, particularly on the backhand side, was a paragon of durability, ranking in the U.S. Top Ten 17 straight years (1933-49), a male record until Jimmy Connors surpassed it in 1988. One of the youngest to rank with the elite, 17 in 1933, he was No. 1 in 1944 and 1945, and the oldest ever to play in the U.S. Championships, 52 in 1968.

He entered in 1968 for fun, this man who had teamed with Don Budge and Gene Mako to win the Davis Cup for the U.S. in 1937, saying he wanted to be part of yet another era, the 'open.' He lost his first match to eventual champion, Arthur Ashe, 6-3, 6-2, 6-2, thus completing a championship career that began with a third-round defeat by fourth-seeded George Lott, 6-1, 6-4, 4-6, 6-2, at Forest Hills in 1932. In between, as Sgt. Parker, Frankie won the U.S. title on his thirteenth try in 1944, again in 1945, both while on leave from the U.S. Army Air Force during World War II. He beat civilian Bill Talbert both times. A 6-3, 6-4, 6-8, 3-6, 6-1 quarter-final defeat in 1946 by Tom Brown busted his dream of winning three straight. But he nearly jolted Jack Kramer by winning the first two sets of their 1947 final. After the 1949 Forest Hills, his 19th, ending in a semis loss, 3-6, 9-7, 6-3, 6-2, to champ Pancho Gonzalez, Frankie turned pro to tour with Kramer, Gonzalez and Pancho Segura.

Grass or clay? Didn't matter to 5-foot-8-1/2, 145-pound Frank, at home anywhere, the third of only four American men able to win on the greensward of Forest Hills and the heavy salmon-toned soil of Roland Garros. In 1948 and 1949 at the French he followed Don Budge and Don McNeill, and preceded Tony Trabert. But his sure-fire groundies looked especially good in the U.S. Clay Court championship that he won five times between 1933 and 1947. His 24-match streak was ended in the 1949 final by Gonzalez, 6-1, 3-6, 8-6, 6-3. Parker built the streak on titles in 1941 (over Bobby Riggs, 6-3, 7-5, 6-8, 4-6, 6-3), 1946 (over Talbert, 6-4, 6-4, 6-2), 1947 (over Ted Schroeder, 8-6, 6-2, 6-4). Although he and Gonzalez were known primarily for singles, they

played a brief but forceful duet on both sides of the English Channel in '49, winning the French and Wimbledon doubles.

Frank won 12 of 14 Davis Cup matches. In 1948 he won both singles in the successful defense against Australia. Coupled with his singles win while the U.S. heisted the Cup from Britain in 1937, this made him the only man to help win the Cup with singles victories at either end of World War II. He was ranked in the World Top Ten six times between 1937 and 1949, No. 1 in 1948. Born in Milwaukee Jan. 31, 1916, he was christened Franciszek Andrzej Paikowski. He entered the Hall of Fame in 1966, and died July 24, 1997 at San Diego.

MAJOR TITLES (6)–*French singles, 1948, 1949; U.S. singles, 1944, 1945; Wimbledon doubles, 1949; French doubles, 1949.* **OTHER U.S. TITLES** (7)–*Clay Court singles, 1933, 1939, 1941, 1946, 1947; Clay Court doubles, 1939, with Gene Mako; Indoor doubles, 1937, with Greg Mangin.* **DAVIS CUP**–*1937, 1939, 1946, 1948; record: 12-2 in singles.* **SINGLES RECORD IN THE MAJORS**–*French (12-1), Wimbledon (12-3), U.S. (60-18).*

GERALD PATTERSON

Australia (1895–1967)
Hall of Fame 1989

A strapping 6-footer, Gerald Leighton Patterson followed Norman Brookes as Australia's second international tennis star. A heroic Military Cross winner with the Australian army in World War I, he played the game with daring, too, charging the net behind an explosive serve, both flat and twisting. His exemplary smash, stiff volleying and good forehand rewarded him with two Wimbledon championships.

An all-or-nothing outlook never was displayed more glaringly than in his Australian championship victory in 1927. Beating lefty Jack Hawkes, 6-3 in the fifth, he blasted 29 aces and 29 doubles faults. In 1919 Patterson took the Wimbledon title from Brookes, who had to wait five years, through World War I, to defend in the challenge round. Patterson lost it to Bill Tilden in 1920, but with Tilden failing to defend in 1922, he helped christen the 'new' (present) site by defeating Randolph Lycett easily. It was over so fast (6-3, 6-4, 6-2) that no fat lady had a chance to sing. But the world's most famous singer was in the debuting Centre Court, beaming, if not screaming, for her Gerald. That was Dame Nellie Melba, the great Australian diva, Patterson's aunt and No. 1 fan. Patterson was known as the 'Human Catapult' at home for his brutal serve, and there were tales that some of his aces were so forceful they bounded into the grandstand.

He spurred Australia to the Davis Cup finales of 1922 and 1924, and helped win the only point against the U.S. at Forest Hills, joining Pat O'Hara Wood for a doubles victory over Tilden and Vinnie Richards in 1922. In 1925 he was considerably ahead of his time, using for a while a steel racket strung with wire. His best U.S. showings were semi-final finishes at Forest Hills, losing to Tilden in 1922, 4-6, 6-4, 6-3, 6-1, and Bill Johnston, 6-2, 6-0. 6-0, in 1924. He did better against Johnston when Bill won the 1919 title, losing 7-5 in the fifth, a fourth-rounder. But that summer in Boston, Patterson and Norman Brookes made the first dent in the U.S. that would become a canyon: Aussies taking one of the Yanks' championships, the doubles, as they beat Tilden and Richards in five.

Five Aussie doubles titles were his between 1914 and 1927, three with Hawkes. He was among the World Top Ten six times between 1919 and 1925, No. 1 in 1919. Patterson was born Dec. 17, 1895, in Melbourne, and died there June 13, 1967. He was voted into the Hall of Fame in 1989.

MAJOR TITLES (9)–*Australian singles, 1927; Wimbledon singles, 1919, 1922; Australian doubles, 1922, 1925, 1926, 1927; U.S. doubles, 1919; Wimbledon mixed, 1920.* **DAVIS CUP**–*1919, 1920, 1922, 1924, 1925, 1928; record: 21-10 in singles, 11-4 in doubles.* **SINGLES RECORD IN THE MAJORS**–*Australian (19-4), French (2-1), Wimbledon (17-2), U.S. (10-3).*

BUDGE PATTY

United States (1924–)
Hall of Fame 1977

A rare combination for an American male was 'Budge' Patty's French-Wimbledon double of 1950. Only Don Budge in 1938 and Tony Trabert in 1955 achieved such a double.

John Edward Patty was born Feb. 11, 1924, at Ft. Smith, Ark., and grew up in Los Angeles, the tennis vineyard of his youth. He says a brother gave him the nickname 'Budge' because "I was so lazy he said I wouldn't budge." It stuck, but he budged gracefully on a tennis court, and graciously in his bearing otherwise, a trim cosmopolitan fellow of 6-foot-1 who preferred to live in Europe after serving there with the U.S. Army in World War II. His smooth groundstroking game played well on the Continent's clay. He won the Italian in 1954. But he was a sharp volleyer, too, a fine doubles player. Seeded fifth, Patty beat second-seeded Bill Talbert in the quarters and top-seeded Frank Sedgman for his 1950 Wimbledon title, 6-1, 8-10, 6-2, 6-3.

At Paris the same year he overcame lefty Jaroslav Drobny for the title, 6-1, 6-2, 3-6, 5-7, 7-5. Defending in 1951, he was upset by Ham Richardson in the second round at Wimbledon, and by Lennart Bergelin in the fourth round at Paris. Probably his two most renowned matches, both at Wimbledon, were a singles defeat and a doubles victory. In the third round of 1953, despite six match points, he fell to Drobny at dusk in a 93-game, four-hour-20-minute classic, 8-6, 16-18, 3-6, 8-6, 12-10. Four years later, he, 33, and Gar Mulloy, 43—unseeded—were the oldest team of the post-World War I era to win at the Big W, beating top-seeded Lew Hoad, 22, and Neale Fraser, 23, 8-10, 6-4, 6-4, 6-4.

They reached the title round of the U.S. Championships that year, the oldest finalists there, losing to Fraser and Ashley Cooper. Patty is also remembered in Paris for an incredible defeat, a 1958 fourth-rounder in which Robert Haillet revived from 5-0, 40-0 down, Patty serving, in the fifth set, to win, 5-7, 7-5, 10-8, 4-6, 7-5, saving four match points. Seldom appearing in the U.S., Patty was a quarter-finalist in the 1951 Championships, losing to Dick Savitt, 6-4 in the fifth, and played Davis Cup briefly, to get his only U.S. Top Ten ranking, No. 10. But he was ranked seven times in the World Top Ten between 1947 and 1957, No. 1 in 1950. He entered the Hall of Fame in 1977.

Over his 15-year amateur career, Patty won 76 singles titles.

MAJOR TITLES (4)–*French singles, 1950; Wimbledon singles, 1950; Wimbledon doubles, 1957; French mixed, 1946.* **OTHER U.S. TITLES** (2)–*Indoor doubles, 1952, with Bill Talbert; Indoor mixed, 1950, with Nancy Chaffee.* **DAVIS CUP**–*1951; record: 1-0 in singles, 1-0 in doubles.* **SINGLES RECORD IN THE MAJORS**–*French (44-14), Wimbledon (44-14), U.S. (16-6).*

TEDDY PELL

United States (1879–1967)
Hall of Fame 1966

Theodore Roosevelt Pell made his mark inside, winning the U.S. Indoor singles in 1907, 1909 and 1911, and the doubles four times between 1905 and 1912. A right-hander, he had a particularly strong backhand, and was ranked in the U.S. Top Ten five times between 1910 and 1918, No. 5 in 1913 and 1915. Pell, a slender 6-foot New Yorker, did have a good time outdoors in 1915, though, in a run to the U.S. semis at Newport, beating two fellow Hall-of-Famers-to-be in straight sets, Watson Washburn and Beals Wright, on the way. But the 'Comet' fell on him, Maurice McLoughlin, 6-2, 6-0, 7-5.

Born in New York, May 12, 1879, he died Aug. 18, 1967, in Sands Point, N.Y. He was elected to the Hall of Fame in 1966.

U.S. TITLES *(7)–Indoor singles, 1907, 1909, 1911; Indoor doubles, 1905, with H.F. Allen; 1909, with Wylie Grant; 1911, 1912, with Fred Alexander.* **SINGLES RECORD IN THE MAJORS**–*U.S. (21-13).*

FRED PERRY

Great Britain (1909–1995)
Hall of Fame 1975

It was the technique of one particular stroke that made Fred Perry into a world champion—and considered the best tennis player Great Britain has produced.

The knack of making the stroke baffled the promising Briton for so long that he was on the verge of giving up in despair. He had been advised that to get very far he would have to learn to take the ball early on his continental forehand, the racket making impact instantly as the ball rose from the court.

For months he could not master the timing. Then suddenly, like riding a bicycle, it came to him and he was on his way—on his way to the net on a running forehand, going forward with the swing of the racket to gain good volleying position if the drive did not win outright. And on his way to three Wimbledon Championships, three U.S. Championships, an Australian, a French and a lucrative pro career.

Born May 18, 1909, in Stockport, England, the right-handed Frederick John Perry did not take up tennis until he was 18 years old. But he had good coaching and took to the game quickly, for he had been playing table tennis for years and winning tournaments and international recognition.

Perry developed an undercut backhand that came off with surprising pace. He hit the ball smartly with good length and regularity on the service, was sharp and sound with his smash, perfect in his footwork and timing, and volleyed with dispatch. None of his strokes was overpowering, but his attack was impetuous and relentless, ever challenging, and he ran like a deer in retrieving.

He was the completely equipped and efficient adversary, jaunty, a bit cocky in his breezy self-assurance, with gallery appeal. He could be sarcastic and some thought him egotistical, but it was a pose and he had an ever-ready grin. He cut a handsome figure with his regular features, raven black hair, and physique that was perfection for the game. Once he developed the stroke that had eluded him, he was virtually unstoppable.

In 1933 Perry led the British Isles to a 4-1 wn over the U.S. in the inter-zone final and to the glorious 3-2 victory over France that brought the Davis Cup back to Britain after a wait of 21 years. As Stade Roland Garros boiled with patriotic fervor, a seventh straight Cup in the balance for the home side, Fred icily erased a set point in the second to take the last match from rookie Andre Merlin. It was the climax of the greatest individual season for a Cup winner: 12-1 in singles, 4-2 in doubles.

Britain retained the Cup through 1936 as Perry won every singles match he played in the four challenge rounds. England had not produced a Wimbledon singles champion for a quarter-century, but Perry took care of that, too. He won three straight Wimbledon finals without loss of a set, defeating Jack Crawford in 1934 and Gottfried von Cramm in 1935 and 1936.

At Forest Hills in 1933 he was the stopper in five sets as Crawford reached the U.S. final with an unprecedented Grand Slam within reach. The next year Fred might have had the first Slam himself but for a quarter-final defeat at the French by Giorgio de Stefani.

Perry, a 6-footer, was also impressive elsewhere, winning the U.S. Championship in 1933, 1934 and 1936, an assault interrupted only in 1935, when he suffered a painful kidney injury and lost in the semi-finals to Wilmer Allison. In 1934 he won the Australian Championship and in 1935 the French Championship, the first and one of only five men to take all four majors. His total is eight, behind only Pete Sampras (14), Roy Emerson (12), Rod Laver and Bjorn Borg (11), Bill Tilden (10), and even with Ken Rosewall, Jimmy Connors, Ivan Lendl and Andre Agassi among the men.

When Perry joined the pro tour, he drew huge crowds to see him play Ellsworth Vines and Tilden. Perry won the U.S. Pro Championship in both 1938 and 1941.

After his playing career, he became associated with the manufacture of tennis clothes, was a tennis correspondent for a London newspaper and took part in radio and television coverage of tennis. He was elected to the Hall of Fame in 1975 and died Feb. 2, 1995, in Melbourne. He ranked in the World Top Ten from 1931 through 1936, No. 1 the last three years.

MAJOR TITLES *(14)–Australian singles, 1934; French singles, 1935; Wimbledon singles, 1934, 1935, 1936; U.S. singles, 1933, 1934, 1936; Australian doubles, 1934; French doubles, 1933; French mixed, 1932; Wimbledon mixed, 1935, 1936; U.S. mixed, 1932.* **DAVIS CUP**–*1931, 1932, 1933, 1934, 1935, 1936; record: 34-4 in singles, 11-3 in doubles.* **SINGLES RECORD IN THE MAJORS**–*Australian (7-1), French (22-5), Wimbledon (35-5), U.S. (34-4).*

NICKY PIETRANGELI

Italy (1933–)
Hall of Fame 1986

Nicola 'Nicky' Pietrangeli was Signor Davis Cup. That team competition seemed Nicky's private preserve, although he won his only Cup from the sidelines as Italy's non-playing captain in 1976. Before that, as a smooth touch operator, winner of the French (1957 over Ian Vermaak and 1960 over Luis Ayala), he had made his name synonymous with Italy. He did it in Davis Cup by playing (164) and winning (120) more matches than anyone before or since during a Cup career that reached from 1954 through 1972. In 66 ties for his country he was 78-32 in singles, 42-12 in doubles.

Twice he carried Italy all the way to the Cup round, 1960 and 1961, but on alien grass in Australia, and during the reign of Aussie powerhouses, he and 6-foot-7 accomplice Orlando Sirola were unable to come closer to the Cup than a good look. Still, to get there in 1960 they pulled off one of Italy's greatest victories, 3-2 from 0-2, over the U.S. in the semi-final at Perth. Despite their discomfort on grass, Pietrangeli—he had squandered eight match points in losing to Barry MacKay, 8-6, 3-6, 8-10, 8-6, 13-11—and Sirola, perhaps the finest doubles team developed in post-World War II Europe, struck back to beat Chuck McKinley and Butch Buchholz, 3-6, 10-8, 6-4, 13-11, seemingly only to prolong their distress. But Pietrangeli stopped Buchholz, 6-1, 6-2, 6-8, 3-6, 6-4, and Sirola clinched, 9-7, 6-3, 8-6, over MacKay.

Pietrangeli was too much for the U.S. to overcome in the following year's semi at Rome as he beat both Whitney Reed and Jack Douglas, teamed with Sirola again triumphantly in a 4-1 victory. But in the two finales, only Pietrangeli's third-day win over Neale Fraser could be salvaged as Australia won, 5-0 and 4-1.

Solidly built, possessing exceptional instincts for the game and anticipation, 5-foot-11 Nicky was an all-around performer who moved with grace and purpose. He was in four French finals, losing to Manolo Santana in 1961 and 1964, and four Italian. His best showing away from compatible clay was a 1960 Wimbledon semi-final which he lost to Laver, 6-4 in the fifth. His was a career of the amateur era during which he won 53 singles titles and was in the World Top Ten five times between 1957 and 1964, No. 3 in 1959 and 1960. Retired from the court, he captained Italy to the Cup round twice, defeating Chile in 1976 but losing to

Australia in 1977. A right-hander, born Sept. 11, 1933, in Tunis, he is a bon vivant, ever popular with fans and colleagues. He and Sirola were the biggest winners of Cup doubles teams, 34-8.

He entered the Hall of Fame in 1986.

MAJOR TITLES *(4)–French singles, 1959, 1960; French doubles, 1959; French mixed, 1958.* **DAVIS CUP**–*1954, 1955, 1956, 1957, 1958, 1959, 1960, 1961, 1962, 1963, 1964, 1965, 1966, 1967, 1968, 1969, 1971, 1972; record 78-32 in singles, 42-12 in doubles.* **SINGLES RECORD IN THE MAJORS**–*Australian (2-1), French (46-12), Wimbledon (29-18), U.S. (5-3).*

ADRIAN QUIST

Australia (1913–1991)
Hall of Fame 1984

Elected to the Hall of Fame in 1984 as the left-court half of the great Australian doubles team of John Bromwich and Quist, Adrian Karl Quist also won three major singles, the Australian, 1936, 1940 and 1948. Quist was the only man to win a major before and after World War II, in which he served in the Australian army.

He was also the only man to win a Wimbledon title before and after, doubles with Jack Crawford in 1935, and with Brom in 1950. It seemed fitting that the two old comrades who wreaked so much damage together should meet in the last Aussie singles final with a pre-war flavor, 1948, before the kids led by Frank Sedgman took over. And that it should go to the wire on a sweltering afternoon at Kooyong. Quisty scraped and scraped to hold onto serve to 3-3 in the fifth, then won the last three games from Brom.

His 13 Australian titles are high for that tournament, and he holds major doubles records: Most titles in one tournament, 10, and most with one partner, eight, alongside Jack Bromwich. They won those eight successively, also a record, between 1938 and 1950. Quist also won in 1936 and 1937 with Don Turnbull for a personal 10-straight, also a record.

He and Brom registered a unique triumph in lifting the Davis Cup from the U.S. in 1939. Losing their singles the first day in Philadelphia (Quist to Frank Parker, 7-5 in the fifth), they began the unparalleled comeback by beating Jack Kramer and Joe Hunt in a four-set doubles, even though they lost the first set and trailed 1-3 in the third. Hunt led 3-2, 30-15 on serve in the third when the turnabout began. Quist, a short (5-foot-6-1/2), bouncy right-hander with an all-court game and telling volleys, then hung on after losing the third and fourth sets to beat Wimbledon champ Bobby Riggs,

6-1, 6-4, 3-6, 3-6, 6-4, even though Riggs saved a match point at 5-2 and reached 4-5. Bromwich beat Frank Parker in a groundstroking duel to ice it in the fifth match.

Quist and Bromwich won the U.S. doubles, too, in 1939, and, well beyond expectations, took their lone Wimbledon crown together in 1950, beating Billy Sidwell and Geoff Brown, 6-2 in the fifth. Quisty was within a month of his 37th birthday, Brom 31. Having won the French title with Jack Crawford in 1935, Quist—holder of 17 majors altogether—was one of 11 to win all four in doubles. Quist first appeared in the World Top Ten in 1936 at No. 4, No. 6 in 1938 and No. 3 in 1939. He was born Aug. 4, 1913, in Medindia, South Australia, and died Nov. 17, 1991, in Sydney.

MAJOR TITLES *(17)–Australian singles, 1936, 1940, 1948; Australian doubles, 1936, 1937, 1938, 1939, 1940, 1946, 1947, 1948, 1949, 1950; French doubles, 1935; Wimbledon doubles, 1935, 1950; U.S. doubles, 1939.* **DAVIS CUP**–*1933, 1934, 1935, 1936, 1937, 1938, 1939, 1946, 1948; record: 24-10 in singles, 19-3 in doubles.* **SINGLES RECORD IN THE MAJORS**–*Australian (42-12), French (8-4), Wimbledon (15-6), U.S. (11-4).* **MAJOR TITLES WITH BROMWICH** *(10)–Australian doubles, 1938, 1939, 1940, 1946, 1947, 1948, 1949, 1950; Wimbledon doubles, 1950; U.S. doubles, 1939.* **DAVIS CUP**–*1938, 1939, 1946; record: 9-1 in doubles.*

PATRICK RAFTER

Australia (1971–)

Patrick Rafter sat out the 2002 season to recover from stress fracture injuries in his right arm before coming to a decision Australian fans expected but hoped would not yet come. The beloved player known by his compatriots simply as 'Our Pat' retired in January 2003.

"I will have regrets that the Wimbledon and Davis Cup trophies are not in my cupboard," he said, "but that's sport, you win some and you lose some."

Rafter's victories included 11 singles and 10 doubles championships, most notably back-to-back U.S. Open singles titles in 1997 and 1998. In July 1999 he became the first Australian since John Newcombe in 1974 to hold the world No. 1 ranking. He was a two-time runner-up at Wimbledon.

A humble man known for a gracious manner on the court and a gentlemanly demeanor at all times, Rafter carried the hopes of his tennis-mad land for a decade. Nine times he contested the Australian Open and nine times he came away empty-handed, only once reaching the semi-finals, in 2001. He also failed to win a Davis Cup for his homeland.

What would be the final match of his career came during the opening day of the Cup final in Melbourne in 2001, when he defeated Sebastien Grosjean of France before having to retire from the competition with a shoulder injury. He could only watch from the sidelines as France took the decisive singles rubber to win the Davis Cup, 3-2. Rafter's career record in Davis Cup play was 21-11 (18-10 singles, 3-1 doubles).

Rafter was born on Dec. 28, 1971, the seventh of nine children. He grew up in Mount Isa, a mining town in the Queensland outback. Small for his age and forced to play older and larger children due to his late-December birth date, young Patrick soon won notice for his athleticism and exceptionally quick hands at the net. He turned pro at age 19 in 1991 and enjoyed a breakthrough season two years later, notably defeating Wayne Ferreira and No. 1 Pete Sampras at a tournament in Indianapolis, before losing in the semis to Boris Becker.

His best years were 1997 and 1998, when U.S. Open victories catapulted him to No. 2 and No. 4 in ATP year-end rankings, leaving him the first Aussie in 24 years to have back-to-back years in the top five. His wins at the U.S. Open came against Greg Rusedski in '97 and countryman Mark Philippoussis in '98 and made him the first Aussie to win consecutive U.S. Opens since Neale Fraser in 1959-60.

In 2000 he defeated Andre Agassi in an epic five-set Wimbledon semi-final before losing in four sets to Pete Sampras. The next year, Rafter again prevailed over Agassi in a grueling five-set semi, this time facing Goran Ivanisevic in the final. Their match was held the day after the official end of The Championships, a 'People's Monday' for which fanatics queued overnight to get tickets. In one of the most dramatic finals in All England history, Ivanisevic, a wild-card entry, won 9-7 in the longest championship fifth set in Wimbledon history.

In a sport with its share of outrageous egos, Rafter was liked for his charm and respected for his politeness. It was his habit to say, "Sorry, mate," when he had to catch his service toss. Named Australian of the Year in 2002, he was a dream client for sports marketers and is expected to have a public profile long after the end of his professional career.

MAJOR TITLES *(3)–U.S. singles, 1997, 1998; Australian doubles, 1999.* **DAVIS CUP**–*1994, 1995, 1997, 1998, 1999, 2000, 2001; record: 18-10 in singles, 3-1 in doubles.* **SINGLES RECORDS IN THE MAJORS**– *Australian (15-9), French (12-8), Wimbledon (29-9), U.S. (20-7).*

DENNY RALSTON

United States (1942–)
Hall of Fame 1987

Robert Dennis Ralston was one of those rare men who was a Davis Cup winner both as player and captain. He was considered a stormy figure early in his career although his actions seem tame in comparison with numerous who came after, and he has made a name as an outstanding educator and influence while varsity tennis coach at Southern Methodist University.

It was as a doubles player, in the right court alongside Chuck McKinley, that he made his strongest showing. They won the U.S. title thrice (1961, 1963, 1964) and were in the final in 1962.

Wimbledon and the tennis public first heard from him in 1960. As a 17-year-old joined with his University of Southern California teammate, 21-year-old Rafe Osuna, he took the doubles prize. Unseeded, they were the second-youngest to win at the Big W, 7-5, 6-3, 10-8, over Mike Davies and Bobby Wilson. He suffered many frustrations as a Davis Cup player, but it all came together for him and McKinley as they pried the punch-bowl away from Australia, 3-2, at Adelaide in 1963.

During an arduous campaign he won six of seven singles and all five doubles, four with McKinley. He led off in a difficult win over rookie John Newcombe, firming up when all seemed lost, 6-4, 6-1, 3-6, 4-6, 7-5, and teamed with McKinley for the go-ahead doubles point. After he lost to Roy Emerson, McKinley clinched against Newcombe. They lost the Cup to the Aussies the following year, 3-2, though winning the doubles—he and McKinley were 8-2 in Cup doubles.

Between 1968 and 1971 he served as coach of winning U.S. teams, and in 1972 he became captain for a four-year term. His coolness and calming manner in the face of an uproarious crowd and patriotic local line judges in Bucharest was a highlight of the 1972 Cup victory over Romania.

A slim 6-footer, Ralston was a stylish stroker with a piercing backhand, a fine server and excellent volleyer who was in the U.S. Top Ten for seven straight years from 1960. He was the first to be No. 1 three straight years (1963-65) since Don Budge (1936-38). His career spanned the amateur and open eras and he made the World Top Ten in both: 1963, 1964, 1965, 1966 and 1968, No. 5 in 1966 when he lost the Wimbledon final to Manolo Santana.

He had one pro singles title, five in doubles. Denny was an unseeded U.S. semi-finalist in 1960, losing to the champ, Neale Fraser. But his best Forest Hills moment was a 7-6 (5-3), 7-5, 5-7, 4-6, 6-3 triumph in 1970 over No. 1 Rod Laver, the defender, to reach the quarters, where he lost to Cliff Richey. He and his dad, Bob Ralston, won the U.S. Father and Son title in 1964. He was born July 27, 1942, in Bakersfield, Calif. He entered the Hall of Fame in 1987 and now is tennis director at the Broadmoor resort at Colorado Springs, Colo. He was the first of three men to have won U.S. doubles titles on the four surfaces (grass, clay, indoor, hard), followed by Stan Smith and Bob Lutz.

MAJOR TITLES (5)–*French doubles, 1966; U.S. doubles, 1961, 1963, 1964; Wimbledon doubles, 1960.* **OTHER U.S. TITLES** (13)–*Indoor singles, 1963; Clay Court singles, 1964, 1965; Hard Court singles, 1964, 1965; Indoor doubles, 1963, 1965, with Chuck McKinley; Clay Court doubles, 1961, 1964, with McKinley; 1966, with Clark Graebner; Hard Court doubles, 1964, with Bill Bond; 1965, with Tom Edlefsen; Pro doubles, 1967, with Ken Rosewall.* **DAVIS CUP (As player)**–*1960, 1961, 1962, 1963, 1964, 1965, 1966; record: 14-5 in singles, 11-4 in doubles;* **(As captain)**–*1972, 1973, 1974, 1975; record: 9-3, 1 Cup.* **SINGLES RECORD IN THE MAJORS**–*Australian (4-2), French (5-2), Wimbledon (29-13), U.S. (31-13).*

ERNEST RENSHAW

Great Britain (1861–1899)
Hall of Fame 1983

James Ernest Renshaw was the older of the fabled English Renshaw twins by 15 minutes, and he was a half-inch taller at 5-foot-10-1/2. He wasn't, however, as successful in amassing singles titles as brother Willie. The two of them ushered in an attacking era and together were an a awesome pair at doubles, winning Wimbledon seven times between 1880 and 1889, a record surpassed by one by the Doherty brothers, Laurie and Reggie.

Ernest, who made the singles title round five times, won in 1888, and might have done better if his brother hadn't been in the way, losing the prize to Willie three times, 1882, 1883 and 1889, and to Herbert Lawford in 1887. Like the Dohertys, the Renshaws were miserable playing against one another. A right-hander, Ernest was born Jan. 3, 1861, in Leamington, England, and died Sept. 2, 1899, in Twyford, England. He entered the Hall of Fame in 1983.

MAJOR TITLES (6)–*Wimbledon singles, 1888; Wimbledon doubles, 1884, 1885, 1886, 1888, 1889.* **SINGLES RECORD IN THE MAJORS**–*Wimbledon (32-10).*

WILLIE RENSHAW

Great Britain (1861–1904)
Hall of Fame 1983

Bjorn Borg said in 1981, "Yes, I know who Mr. Willie Renshaw was." Few others did. Borg, who had won five straight Wimbledons, was trying to overtake that bygone luminary, but couldn't make it. Nobody has. Not only did William Charles Renshaw, a forceful right-handed aggressor, win an unequaled six straight Wimbledons from 1881, wresting the title from John Hartley, 6-0, 6-2, 6-1, but he added a record seventh title in 1889, defeating older (by 15 minutes) brother, Ernest Renshaw, in the title round, 6-4, 6-1, 3-6, 6-0.

In the all-comers final against Harry Barlow, Willie made an all-time recovery. He ducked six match points in the fourth set, trailing 5-2, and came back from 0-5 in the fifth to win, 3-6, 5-7, 8-6, 10-8, 8-6.

England's Renshaw twins (Ernest was also right-handed) were rivals and accomplices. Willie stopped Ernest for the Wimbledon title on three occasions, but five times between 1884 and 1889 they combined for the doubles championship, a record later topped by the Doherty brothers, Laurie and Reggie. The offense-minded Renshaws played doubles as never before, rushing the net and volleying more frequently and effectively than their predecessors, helped by the lowering of the net to its present three feet in 1882.

Willie, noted particularly for his serve and overhead smash, was a third-round loser to O. E. Woodhouse in his Wimbledon debut, 1880. He lost only twice after that, to nemesis Willoughby Hamilton in the 1888 quarters, and again in the 1890 challenge round, 6-8, 6-2, 3-6, 6-1, 6-1.

He won 22 of 25 Wimbledon matches in singles, and had a 14-match streak from 1881 to the 1888 defeat by Hamilton, having declined to defend in 1887 because of an elbow injury. That mark wasn't broken until after the challenge round system was abandoned and Fred Perry recorded a fifteenth straight match win in the first round of his 1936 title.

The Renshaws seemed to be the first to take the game really seriously, playing a full English summer schedule, and then competing on the Riviera during the winter, building a court at Cannes in 1880. Willie was born Jan. 3, 1861, in Leamington, England, and died Aug. 12, 1904, in Swanage, England. He entered the Hall of Fame in 1983.

MAJOR TITLES (12)–*Wimbledon singles, 1881, 1882, 1883, 1884, 1885, 1886, 1889; Wimbledon doubles, 1884, 1885, 1886, 1888, 1889.* **SINGLES RECORD IN THE MAJORS**–*Wimbledon (22-3).*

VINNIE RICHARDS

United States (1903–1959)
Hall of Fame 1959

Vincent Richards was the boy wonder of his day, and hasn't lost that luster: The youngest male to win any of the major championships. A volleying master all his life, he was 15 when Big Bill Tilden, on the verge of greatness, selected the kid as partner in the U.S. doubles championships of 1918 at Longwood Cricket Club in Boston. They marched through the field, and Vinnie must have felt as though he were in the geriatric ward.

He and Tilden, 25, beat a couple of 38-year-old ex-champs, Fred Alexander and Beals Wright, for the title, 6-3, 6-4, 3-6, 2-6, 6-2. They won twice more in 1921 and 1922, beating Davis Cup teammates Dick Williams and Watty Washburn, then the Australian Cup pair, Gerald Patterson and Pat O'Hara Wood. Fittingly, the last national title Richards and Tilden won was a vale-dictory together, the U.S. Pro doubles 27 years after, in 1945, over Welby Van Horn and Dick Skeen, 7-5, 6-4, 6-2.

Richards was a pro pioneer, signing on with promoter C. C. Pyle as leading man of the original pro-fessional touring troupe in 1926. His mates barnstorm-ing North America during the winter of 1926-27 were the star attraction, Suzanne Lenglen and Paul Feret of France, and fellow Americans Mary K. Browne, Howard Kinsey and Harvey Snodgrass.

It was tough to break into the Davis Cup lineup in singles with Bill Johnston and Tilden around. But Vinnie got his chance in 1924, and beat both Patterson and O'Hara Wood in straight sets during the 5-0 victory over Australia. That year he won two Olympic golds (singles, doubles) and a silver (mixed). He was on four Cup-winning teams, losing only a doubles with Tilden in 1922. In 1918 Richards was also the youngest ever to play or win a match in the U.S. singles, and he steadily advanced toward the top, a 19-year-old semi-finalist in 1922, losing to Johnston, 8-6, 6-2, 6-1. He was back in the semis in 1924, losing to the champ, Tilden, 4-6, 6-2, 8-6, 4-6, 6-4, repeating the next year but falling to Big Bill, 6-8, 6-4, 6-4, 6-1. In 1926 he was generally acknowledged as the best American, losing to

Jean Borotra in the semis, 3-6, 6-4, 4-6, 8-6, 6-2, while Tilden lost in the quarters to Henri Cochet.

Many felt that 5-foot-10 Richards, who had refined his game well beyond his teenage volleying skills, deserved the No. 1 U.S. ranking. Instead, because he turned pro, the USTA unfairly awarded him no ranking for that year when he was No. 6 in the world rankings. He had been in the U.S. and World Top Ten five straight years from 1921, No. 2 in both in 1924.

Once the initial Pyle tour was disbanded, he was active in trying to find other opportunities for the fledgling professionals, no longer welcome at the traditional events. Vinnie, who championed the pros during those difficult years, even after his playing days were over, helped organize the first U.S. Pro Championships in New York in 1927, an event that continues as the longest-running pro tournament. The purse was $2,000. Richards beat Kinsey, 11-9, 6-4, 6-3, for that title and a first prize of $1,000, and was its singles victor three more times. Born March 20, 1903, and raised in Yonkers, N.Y., he died Sept. 28, 1959, in New York, shortly after entering the Hall of Fame.

MAJOR TITLES (9)–French doubles, 1926; Wimbledon doubles, 1924; U.S. doubles, 1918, 1921, 1922, 1925, 1926; U.S mixed, 1919, 1924. Other U.S titles (20)–Indoor singles, 1919, 1923, 1924; Indoor doubles, 1919, 1920, with Bill Tilden; 1921, with Howard Voshell; 1923, 1924, with Frank Hunter; Clay Court doubles, 1920, with Roland Roberts; Pro singles, 1927, 1928, 1930, 1933; Pro doubles, 1929, with Karel Kozeluh; 1930, 1931, with Howard Kinsey; 1933, with Charles Wood; 1937, with George Lott; 1938, with Fred Perry, 1945, with Bill Tilden. **DAVIS CUP**–1922, 1924, 1925, 1926; record: 2-0 in singles, 2-1 in doubles. **SINGLES RECORD IN THE MAJORS**–Wimbledon (8-3), U.S. (26-9).

BOBBY RIGGS

United States (1918–1995)
Hall of Fame 1967

Though he had little of the power of Don Budge and Jack Kramer, and though his physique was hardly comparable to that of these six-footers, right-hander Bobby Riggs was one of the smartest, most calculating and resourceful court strategists tennis has seen, particularly in his defensive circumventions. He had a temperament that was unruffled in all circumstances and he hung in the fight without showing a trace of discouragement other than a slight shake of the head. He won the championship at Wimbledon and twice at Forest Hills.

Budge, with his vast power, usually had to work his hardest to turn back the little Californian, whose forte was to subdue the fury of the big hitters. Riggs had both the brains and the shots to quell the cannonaders, particularly the drop shot from both forehand and backhand, and a lob matched by few in the way he masked it and his control of its length. Most often Budge required four sets, if not five, to win when they were amateurs. When they met as pros, Riggs won his full share.

Born Feb. 25, 1918, in Los Angeles, Robert Larimore Riggs first began to make tennis progress at the age of 12, when Dr. Esther Bartosh saw him hitting balls and took over his instruction. In 1934, at 16, he beat Frank Shields, a finalist at Wimbledon and Forest Hills. Two years later Riggs was ranked No. 4 in the country, and he was second to Budge in 1937 and 1938.

Riggs had his best record—the best in the world—in 1939, racking up a triple at Wimbledon the only time he played there, adding the U.S. while winning nine of 13 tournaments and 54-5 in matches. He said he "scraped up every dime I could find" to bet on himself with a London bookmaker to win the three Wimbledon titles, and came off with $108,000.

After yielding his U.S. title to Don McNeill in the 1940 final, he regained it in 1941, beating Frank Kovacs, a spectacular shotmaker. His career as an amateur soon ended. Riggs was in demand on the pro circuit.

In 1942 he competed in the U.S. Pro Championships and lost in the final to Budge. But the next time they met was after World War II, in 1946, and this time Riggs beat Budge in the U.S. Pro final at Forest Hills. They went on tour and Riggs won 24 matches to 22 for Budge. Again in 1947 they met in the final of the Pro Championships and Riggs won in five long sets. Late in the year Kramer made his pro debut at Madison Square Garden in New York and Riggs beat him before a crowd of 15,114 who had plowed through 25 inches of snow in a blizzard. However, Kramer won the tour, 69-20.

After losing to Kramer in the final of the U.S. Pro at Forest Hills and regaining the title in 1949 against Budge, Riggs began to taper off as a player and tried his hand as a promoter when Gussy Moran and Pauline Betz made their debuts as pros in 1950. Years later, in 1973, after fading into virtual obscurity as a senior player who would make a bet on the drop of a hat, Riggs was back, taking on first Margaret Smith Court and then Billie Jean King in mixed singles matches that gave tennis much publicity. He defeated Court, but King made him look like Humpty Dumpty, 6-4, 6-4, 6-3, before a record tennis crowd of 30,472, at Houston's Astrodome. Few things ever fazed Riggs, though, or made him unhappy. And nothing ever made him forget his good manners and sportsmanship in the years when he was playing serious tennis.

He made the World Top Ten in 1937, 1938 and 1939, No. 1 the last year, and the U.S. Top Ten, 1936 through 1941, and was named to the Hall of Fame in 1967 and died Oct. 25, 1995, in Leucadia, Calif.

MAJOR TITLES (6)–*Wimbledon singles, 1939; U.S. singles, 1939, 1941; Wimbledon doubles, 1939; Wimbledon mixed, 1939; U.S. mixed, 1940;* **OTHER U.S. TITLES**–*Indoor singles, 1940; Clay Court singles, 1936, 1937, 1938; Indoor doubles, 1940, with Elwood Cooke; Clay Court doubles, 1936, with Wayne Sabin; Indoor mixed, 1940, with Pauline Betz; Pro singles, 1946, 1947, 1949; Pro doubles, 1942, 1947, with Don Budge.* **DAVIS CUP**–*1938, 1939; record: 2-2 in singles.* **SINGLES RECORD IN THE MAJORS**–*French (5-1), Wimbledon (7-0), U.S. (27-4).*

TONY ROCHE
Australia (1945–)
Hall of Fame 1986

With most of a glorious career behind him, it was extremely satisfying for the rugged, self-effacing Anthony Dalton Roche to make his biggest hit for Australia at 31 as a Davis Cup retread in 1977. In 1965 and 1967, alongside John Newcombe, he'd won the Cup-clinching doubles, both years against Spain. Ten years later he was recalled for singles duty before his friends and neighbors in Sydney, and came through.

In a stunning opening-day victory, he turned back Adriano Panatta (6-3, 6-4, 6-4), who had led Italy to the 1976 Cup. That set the tone for a 3-1 Australian victory. His yoking with Newcombe (Roche in the left court) was one of the all-time teams. They won Wimbledon five times (1965, 1968, 1969, 1970, 1974), the best showing of any 20th-century male pair until Mark Woodforde and Todd Woodbridge won a sixth in 1997. Roche, with his wicked left-handed serve and magnificent volleying, took 13 major doubles, 12 with Newcombe, setting a team record. They were among only five male teams to win all four majors.

But Tony, broad-shouldered and barrel-chested, had the groundstrokes to succeed on clay, winning the difficult Continental double in 1966, the Italian and French singles. Paradoxically he lost three major finals on his best surface, grass, and to older countrymen whom he'd idolized: Wimbledon, 1968, and the U.S., 1969, to Rod Laver; U.S., 1970, to Ken Rosewall.

Shoulder and elbow trouble curtailed a career that spanned the amateur and open eras, but he was in the

World Top Ten in both, six straight years from 1965. No. 2 in 1969, and won 12 pro titles in singles, 27 in doubles. In 1968 he turned pro, signing with World Championship Tennis as one of the so-called 'Handsome Eight' along with other rookies Newcombe, Cliff Drysdale, Nikki Pilic and Roger Taylor. His prize money amounted to $529,199. He was a player-coach for Phoenix and Boston in World Team Tennis, and has tutored several pros including Ivan Lendl. Roche was a country boy, born in the New South Wales hamlet of Tarcutta on May 17, 1945, a son of the local butcher. He entered the Hall of Fame, along with Newcombe, appropriately, in 1986.

MAJOR TITLES (16)–*French singles, 1966; Australian doubles, 1965, 1967, 1971, 1976, 1977; French doubles, 1967, 1969; Wimbledon doubles, 1965, 1968, 1969, 1970, 1974; U.S. doubles, 1967; Australian mixed, 1966; Wimbledon mixed, 1976.* **DAVIS CUP**–*1964, 1965, 1966, 1967, 1974, 1975, 1976, 1977, 1978; record; 7-3 in singles, 7-2 in doubles.* **SINGLES RECORD IN THE MAJORS**–*Australian (33-13), French (23-5), Wimbledon (32-13), U.S. (25-8).*

ELLEN ROOSEVELT
United States (1868–1954)
Hall of Fame 1975

The Roosevelt sisters, Ellen, 20, and Grace, 21, first played in the U.S. Championships in 1888, and two years later both were champions. Ellen Crosby Roosevelt won the 1890 singles over defending champ Bertha Townsend in the challenge round, 6-2, 6-2, and joined with Grace for the doubles championship, 6-1, 6-2, over Townsend and Margarette Ballard.

The Roosevelts, who were born and raised in Hyde Park, N.Y., and were first cousins of U.S. President Franklin D. Roosevelt, were the first sisters to win a major title. They were emulated only by Juliette and Kathleen Atkinson at the U.S. of 1897 and 1898. In 1891, however, the Roosevelts were done in by an Irishwoman, Mabel Cahill. Cahill beat Grace, 6-3, 7-5, in the final of the all-comers, then deposed Ellen, 6-4, 6-1, 4-6, 6-3, in the challenge round. In the doubles Cahill and Mrs. Emma Leavitt Morgan unseated the sisters, 2-6, 8-6, 6-4.

The only Roosevelt reappearance in the Championships was Ellen's mixed-doubles title with Clarence Hobart in 1893. The Roosevelts, reared on a private court at home, may have been the first to be prodded by a tennis parent. Recalled original champ Ellen Hansell: "Their father [John Roosevelt] coached and treated them as if they were a pair of show ponies. We silly, non-serious-minded players giggled at their early-to-bed and careful food habits."

Ellen, a right-hander, was born in August 1868 and died in Hyde Park, Sept. 26, 1954. She entered the Hall of Fame in 1975. Also a right-hander, Grace Walton Roosevelt, who became Mrs. Appleton Clark, was born June 3, 1867, in Hyde Park and died there Nov. 29, 1945.

MAJOR TITLES *(3)–U.S. singles, 1890; U.S. doubles, 1890; U.S. mixed, 1893.* **SINGLES RECORD IN THE MAJORS–***U.S. (5-2).*

MERV ROSE

Australia (1930–)
Hall of Fame 2001

Mervyn Gordon 'Rosie' Rose saw some kids playing tennis in his hometown, Coffs Harbour, New South Wales, liked what he saw, borrowed a pair of sneakers and a racket and won a junior tournament. From that impulsive, humble start grew a man who would seize major singles titles on clay and grass, help his country win two Davis Cups and land in the Hall in 2001.

An Aussie who went his own way, often to the consternation of tennis officials, he had a carefree nature and a good sense of humor to go along with a mean left-handed serve and "rhythmic game," said Fred Perry. Groundstrokes weren't his forte but blended with the serve and accurate volleying they brought him the French title of 1958 over a clay court stalwart, Chilean Luis Ayala. Four years earlier his serve-and-volleying had outdone that of compatriot Rex Hartwig in the Australian final. Rose lost the 1953 Australian final to Ken Rosewall.

He had taken to clay by winning the German title in 1957, but perhaps a day 'Rosie' will remember more than most occurred in May of 1958 when he entered Rome's Il Foro Italico to face the all-time home hero Nicola Pietrangeli for the Italian title. It was the tennis version of Christians at the mercy of lions in the Colosseum. Romans, not very hospitable toward a stranger trying to deprive one of their own, must have wished they could round up some lions to sic on the defiant 6-foot Aussie. They growled and raged themselves, urging Nicola to win for a second straight year. But Rose refused to bend to the virulent chorus or the vibrant Pietrangeli, and won, 5-7, 8-6, 6-4, 1-6, 6-2, with an ultimate set surge. The beer, even if it wasn't good old Aussie beer, tasted mighty good afterwards, the new champ said.

Practically every Aussie lad wants to grow up to have a hand in winning the Davis Cup, and having a swig of beer (or champagne) from it. Rose got his final-round chance twice, but the second time, 1957, six years after the first, was better because he was on the court when the 3-2 victory over the U.S. was cinched. In Melbourne's storied Kooyong Stadium, he and Mal Anderson pounded Vic Seixas and Barry MacKay, 6-4, 6-4, 8-6, to give the natives an insurmountable 3-0 lead. While it was a team effort in 1951 at Sydney's White City, Rose, 21, suffered two losses as Australia beat the U.S., 3-2. Seixas beat him in the opener, followed by 30-year-old Ted Schroeder, in his last Cup hurrah, tying the series. Frank Sedgman took 'Rosie' off the hook by beating Seixas.

Five of his seven majors were in doubles, all on grass. His most formidable partner was farm boy Hartwig, with whom he won the Australian and Wimbledon in 1954 and the U.S. in 1953. In 1952 at Longwood he united with Davis Cup foe Seixas to stop the Aussie juggernaut, Ken McGregor and Sedgman's run at a second successive Grand Slam. Ken and Frank, winners of seven straight majors, were cut down in a massive U.S. final of 73 games, 3-6, 10-8, 10-8, 6-8, 8-6. It was particularly satisfying to Rose because he had lost the Grand Slamming U.S. final 12 months before with another Aussie, Don Candy. Rose also won the Wimbledon mixed of 1957 with American Darlene Hard.

Seven years he was among the World Top Ten, as high as No. 3 in 1958. His other 27 singles titles, 12 in 1957, eight in 1958, were racked up on four continents at such way stations as Brisbane, Cuba, Panama, Baranquilla, Dallas and Naples.

He turned pro in 1959 for a brief fling at barnstorming during which he "learned more about tennis from Pancho Gonzalez, Lew Hoad, Ken Rosewall and the rest than I'd ever known." He then became, and continues, as an astute, successful coach. Billie Jean King credits him with reforming her forehand and advancing her game substantially. Rose, born Jan. 23, 1930, at Coff Harbour, where he resides, was named to the Australian Tennis Hall of Fame in 2002.

MAJOR TITLES *(7)–Australian singles, 1954; French singles, 1958; Australian doubles, 1954; Wimbledon doubles, 1954; U.S. doubles, 1952, 1953; Wimbledon mixed doubles, 1957.* **DAVIS CUP–***1951, 1957: 0-2 in singles, 1-0 in doubles.* **SINGLES RECORD IN THE MAJORS–***Australian (24-8), French (28-7), Wimbledon (26-8), U.S. (12-4).*

KEN ROSEWALL

Australia (1934–)
Hall of Fame 1980

As the Doomsday Stroking Machine, the remarkable Kenneth Robert 'Muscles' Rosewall was a factor in three decades of tennis, winning his first major titles, the Australian and French singles in 1953 as a teen-ager, and continuing as a tournament winner past his 43rd birthday. Probably nobody played better longer. He was yet a tough foe into 1978. At the close of the 1977 season, he was still ranked as one of the top players in the game, No. 12, on the ATP computer, having won two of 24 tournaments on a 44-23 match record.

"It's something I enjoy and find I still do well," was his simple explanation of his prowess in 1977, "but I never imagined myself playing so long when I turned pro in 1957."

The son of a Sydney, Australia, grocer, Rosewall was born in that city Nov. 2, 1934, and grew up there. A natural left-hander, he was taught to play right-handed by his father, Robert Rosewall, and developed a peerless backhand. Some felt his size (5-foot-7, 135 pounds) would impede him, but it was never a problem. He moved quickly, with magnificent anticipation and perfect balance, and never suffered a serious injury. Though his serve wasn't formidable, he placed it well, and backed it up with superb volleying. Rosewall was at home on any surface, and at the baseline or the net. He had an even temperament, was shy and reticent, but good-natured.

Although Rosewall, the little guy, always seemed overshadowed by a rival, first Lew Hoad, then Pancho Gonzalez and Rod Laver, he outlasted them all, and had the last competitive word. Even when Laver was acknowledged as the best in the world, Rosewall could bother him, and twice shocked Rod in the rich World Championship Tennis finals in Dallas (1971 and 1972), snatching the $50,000 first prize from the favorite's grasp. The latter match, thought by many to be the greatest ever played—a 3-1/2 hour struggle watched by millions on TV—went to Rosewall, 4-6, 6-0, 6-3, 6-7 (3-7), 7-6, (7-5), when he stroked two magnificent backhand returns to escape a seemingly untenable position in the decisive tie-breaker (down 5-points-to-4) and win by two points, It was the closest finish of an important championship until Boris Becker beat Ivan Lendl, also 7-5, in a fifth-set tie-breaker, for the 1988 Masters title.

Rosewall and Hoad, born only 21 days apart, Ken the elder, were linked as teammates and adversariess almost from their first days on court. In 1952 as 17-year-olds they made an immediate impact on their first overseas tour, both reaching the quarter-finals of the U.S. Championships at Forest Hills, Ken beating the No. 1 American, Vic Seixas, 3-6, 6-2, 7-5, 5-7, 6-3. Later the following year (having won the Wimbledon doubles together), shortly after their 19th birthdays, they became the youngest Davis Cup defenders, collaborating for Australia to repel the U.S. challenge in the finale. Rosewall beat Seixas in the decisive last match to ensure a 3-2 victory.

Though Hoad was considerably stronger physically than Rosewall, who had been given the sardonic nickname 'Muscles' by his mates, Ken always managed to keep up with (and often surpass) him in the early days. Hoad beat Rosewall in the 1956 Wimbledon final, but his bid for a Grand Slam was spoiled when Rosewall knocked him off in the U.S. final at Forest Hills.

Linked in doubles as well as the public mind, Ken and Lew might well have made a Grand Slam together in 1953, but came up three wins short. After taking the Australian, French and Wimbledon, they had a bad day in Boston, dropping a close U.S. quarter-final decision to unseeded Americans Hal Burrows and Straight Clark, 5-7, 14-12, 18-16, 9-7. But they (Kenny unerring of return from the right court) grabbed that title in 1956, standing as one of five teams to win all four, apparently an Aussie specialty. Frank Sedgman and Ken McGregor preceded them, followed by Roy Emerson and Neale Fraser, John Newcombe and Tony Roche and Mark Woodforde and Todd Woodbridge.

After helping Australia win the Davis Cup twice more, both 5-0 over the U.S. in 1955 and 1956, winning all four singles and a doubles seemingly effortlessly, Rosewall turned pro to take on the professional king, Pancho Gonzalez. Gonzalez stayed on top, winning their head-to-head tour, 50-26, but it was apparent that Rosewall belonged at the uppermost level. Thus began one of the longest professional careers, certainly the most distinguished in regard to significant victories over so lengthy a span. Rosewall won the first of his three U.S. Pro singles titles over Laver in 1963, the second by beating in succession, Gonzalez, then and Laver in 1965, and the third over Cliff Drysdale in 1971.

That was one of the three championships that the pros held dearest during their days as outcasts prior to opens. The others were the French Pro, won by Rosewall eight times, including seven in a row (1960-66), and Wembley in London, won five times by Rosewall between 1957 and 1968. Memorable battles were the five-set, 1963 French Pro final over Laver and the 1962 Wembley final over Hoad. Ken's sparkling rivalry with Laver stretched over 111 encounters, Rod ahead, 62-49 (6-4 in the open era). He was 59-101 against Gonzalez and 45-25 over Hoad.

Rosewall holds several longevity records. Fourteen years after his 1956 Forest Hills triumph over Hoad, he beat the favored Tony Roche, 10 years his junior, to win the U.S. Championship again. Eighteen years after that final—having beaten favored John Newcombe, 6-7 (3-5), 7-6 (5-1), 6-3—he was crushed in the 1974 windup by Jimmy Connors. Twenty years after appearing in the first of four Wimbledon finals, he lost the 1974 final to Connors. The only big one Rosewall missed out on was Wimbledon singles, but he won the doubles twice. Nineteen years after his first major title, the Australian, over Mervyn Rose, he won it again, in 1972, over Mal Anderson. He also made it to the semis in 1976 and 1977—24 years after the first time! Twenty years after his first Davis Cup appearance, he returned to help Australia win once again in 1973, and played his last cup match in 1975, having been in on four Australian Davis Cups and three World Cups in the since-disbanded team match against the U.S.

Altogether, Rosewall won 18 major titles in singles, doubles and mixed, the sixth-highest male total. In 1974, he served as player-coach of the Pittsburgh Triangles of World Team Tennis. He was the second tennis player to cross one million dollars in prize money, following Laver, and had a career total of $1,600,300.

Like Laver, Gonzalez and Hoad, and a few others, he had one of those rare careers spanning the amateur era, pro one-night stand years and the open era. His victories were innumerable, but in the last section, begun at age 33, he won 50 titles, 32 in singles, 18 in doubles. The first of those was the baptismal 'Open,' the British Hard Court singles at Bournemouth in April 1968; the second, the initial major open, the French, a month later—both over Laver. His last pro triumph, Hong Kong in 1977 over 30-year-old Tom Gorman, was recorded two weeks after his 43rd birthday, making him the second oldest (just shy of Gonzalez) to win an open-era title.

Still going, like some super battery, gray but the same in frame and slick of backhand, Ken is just warming up for the super senior wars.

Rosewall was named to the International Tennis Hall of Fame in 1980, and the Australian Tennis Hall of Fame in 1995.

MAJOR TITLES *(18)–Australian singles, 1953, 1955, 1971, 1972; French singles, 1953, 1968; U.S. singles, 1956, 1970; Australian doubles, 1953, 1956, 1972; French doubles, 1953, 1968; Wimbledon doubles, 1953, 1956; U.S. doubles, 1956, 1969; U.S. mixed, 1956.* **DAVIS CUP**–*1953, 1954, 1955, 1956, 1973, 1975; record: 17-2 in singles, 2-1 in doubles.* **SINGLES RECORD IN THE MAJORS**– *Australian (45-10), French (24-3), Wimbledon (47-11), U.S. (57-10).*

DOROTHY ROUND

Great Britain (1908–1982)
Hall of Fame 1986

Dorothy Edith Round Little was the leading British female player at the time Helen Wills Moody ruled the courts in the 1930s. Round distinguished herself on several counts, among them that she was the only British player besides Kitty McKane Godfree to win Wimbledon twice since World War I, and she was in 1935 the only woman from overseas to win the Australian Championship.

Born July 13, 1908, in Dudley, Worcestershire, England, she developed a right-handed groundstroke game of power and precision and volleying ability equaled by few. She won the Wimbledon crown in 1934 and repeated in 1937. Her play at the net was a factor in her victory over Helen Jacobs in the 1934 final. In the 1937 final, she defeated the strong Polish woman, Jadwiga Jedrzejowska, overcoming a 1-4 deficit in the final set.

To get to the Wimbledon final of 1937, Round defeated Jacobs and Simone Mathieu, France's leading player. Round appeared to rise to her best form when confronted by Jacobs or Moody. In 1933 Round got to the final at Wimbledon and gave Moody one of the most challenging fights of her career, yielding at 6-4, 6-8, 6-3. That same year in the U.S. Championships, she lost to Jacobs in the semi-finals.

Round was not as successful, however, in Wightman Cup matches as in tournaments for the championship of England, U.S. and Australia.

She was a member of the British team from 1931 to 1936. She lost to Jacobs four times before defeating the American in 1936, in her final appearance in the international team matches, 6-3, 6-3. Round (Mrs. Douglas Little in 1937) probably relished that victory particularly, for it was the year Jacobs finally achieved her ambition of winning Wimbledon.

She was in the World Top Ten from 1933 through 1937, No. 1 in 1934, and was named to the Hall of Fame in 1986. She died Nov. 12, 1982, in Kidderminster, England.

MAJOR TITLES *(6)–Australian singles, 1935; Wimbledon singles, 1934, 1937. Wimbledon mixed, 1934, 1935, 1936.* WIGHTMAN CUP*–1931, 1932, 1933, 1934, 1935, 1936; record: 4-7 in singles, 0-2 in doubles.* SINGLES RECORD IN THE MAJORS*–Australian (4-0), Wimbledon (35-9), U.S. (6-2).*

ELIZABETH RYAN

United States (1892–1979)
Hall of Fame 1972

Elizabeth Montague 'Bunny' Ryan, a magnificent doubles player who long held the major tournament record for total championships—19 at Wimbledon between 1914 and 1934—dearly wished to win a major in singles. But she missed out in three finals, losing to Suzanne Lenglen (1921) and Helen Mills Moody (1930) at Wimbledon, and coming closest in 1926, a heart-breaker at the U.S.

In the most elderly of major finals, Ryan, 34, led Molla Mallory, 42, 4-0 in the third, and had a match point in the thirteenth game only to fall, 4-6, 6-4, 9-7, at Forest Hills.

It may be that she was a bit too stout (at 5-foot-5-1/2, 145 pounds) and slow of foot to equal her doubles success on the singles court. Still, with superb anticipation and tactics, she won numerous singles titles, including the last played in Imperial Russia in 1914. "I got the last train out as the war [World War I] descended," she later recalled.

Her 12 Wimbledon doubles titles (and 13 finals) are the tourney records, as are five straight with Lenglen (1919-23), plus 1925, and six straight doubles titles (1914-23; no play World War I, 1915-18). She won a record seven mixed (of a record 10 finals) with five different partners, three with Randolph Lycett. She and Lenglen never lost (31-0) at the Big W.

Yet standing is Ryan's Wimbledon doubles record of 50 straight match victories from 1914 to the 1928 final. She first played Wimbledon in 1912, reaching the quarters in singles, and was to set a championship longevity record: 20 years between first and last titles (1914-34). Only Billie Jean King (224) and Martina Navratilova (293) won more matches at Wimbledon, where Ryan was 190-28: 47-15 in singles, 73-4 in doubles, 70-9 in mixed.

Ryan, a right-hander with a severe chop, volley and drop shot, was born Feb. 5, 1892, in Anaheim, Calif., and while she played for her native land in the 1926 Wightman Cup, she spent most of her life as a London resident. She did work as a teaching pro for a time in the U.S. Intensely protective of her Wimbledon record of 19 titles (of 25 finals), she was uncomfortable sharing it with King when Billie Jean tied her by winning the singles in 1975. She was undoubtedly pleased not to see herself eclipsed.

Ryan collapsed and died July 8, 1979, at her beloved Wimbledon, the day before King got No. 20 by winning the doubles with Navratilova. Twice she played enough in the U.S. to make the Top Ten rankings, No. 2 in 1925 and 1926. She was in the World Top Ten five times between 1924 and 1930, No. 3 in 1927. She entered the Hall of Fame in 1972.

MAJOR TITLES *(26)–French doubles, 1930, 1932, 1933, 1934; Wimbledon doubles, 1914, 1919, 1920, 1921, 1922, 1923, 1925, 1926, 1927, 1930, 1933, 1934; U.S. doubles, 1926; Wimbledon mixed, 1919, 1921, 1923, 1927, 1928, 1930, 1932; U.S. mixed, 1926, 1933.* WIGHTMAN CUP*–1926; record: 1-1 in singles, 1-0 in doubles.* SINGLES RECORD IN THE MAJORS*–French (8-3), Wimbledon (47-15), U.S. (10-3).*

PETE SAMPRAS

United States (1971–)

It just happened. He couldn't explain it or understand it. "I didn't know what I was doing. I was just a new kid. Everything I did worked," Pete Sampras would say later, discussing his Flushing Meadow triumph of 1990 that anointed him as the youngest of all U.S. champions at 19 years, one month.

He knows what he's doing now, doing it as 'Silky' Sampras, smoothly, uniquely, gliding along a path of greatness in an outwardly unconcerned and effortless manner while mounting a planned and concerted assault on the citadels of the past. Pete knows his tennis history, and was consciously pursuing the man on the spire, Aussie Roy Emerson, who seized 12 major singles championships between 1961 and 1967, the men's record (six Australian, two each French, Wimbledon, U.S.).

Pete razed Emerson's 33-year-old citadel by beating another Queensland country boy, Patrick Rafter, for a thirteenth major at Wimbledon 2000. New century, new record. But in the shadows of dusk that day he also caught up with a ghost, Willie Renshaw. Willie had won seven Wimbledons between 1881 and 1889, and this was the seventh for Pete. Emerson sent his congratulations after being eclipsed, laughing that he hadn't even known of holding a record until Sampras began stalking him, and the press picked up on it.

Pete raised his own stronghold higher at 14 by winning the U.S. Open of 2002, even though he was lurching through his worst year, and a spell dryer than the Sahara—33 tournaments without a title. At Wimbledon, where he'd won his last four titles consecutively, and strung together 29 straight match wins, Pete lost in the second round to a stranger, No. 145 George Bastl. At Paris, No. 69 Andrea Gaudenzi booted him from the opening round. He even lost on grass, with a two-set lead, in a Davis Cup match at Houston to turf-wary Spaniard Alex Corretja. Never had he been so down and disregarded.

Yet Pete, ranked and seeded 17th, was inspired at Flushing Meadow, the scene of his 1989 breakthrough. Then he'd knocked off defending champion Mats Wilander in the second round. But after suffering final-round defeats by 20-year-olds Marat Safin in 2000 and Lleyton Hewitt in 2001, Pete was somehow ready to claim his fifth U.S. title, defeating lifetime rival Andre Agassi in the final, 6-3, 6-4, 5-7, 6-4.

It had been a while since Pete had ruled the U.S. Squelching the perpetual motion of Michael Chang in the all-Californian Open final of 1996, he had boosted his majors total to eight. He had passed John McEnroe, Wilander, John Newcombe, René Lacoste, Henri Cochet, and Renshaw; and stood even with Ivan Lendl, Jimmy Connors, Ken Rosewall and Fred Perry. Now he was within sight of Emerson, Bjorn Borg and Rod Laver's 11, Bill Tilden's 10. Moreover, except for Borg, he was younger than any of them had been at the eighth, and Borg was finished at 25. At that age Pete felt he was just flexing his muscles.

Impressive flexing, although he had an off Wimbledon in 1996, losing in the quarters to the new champ Richard Krajicek. Pete was, after all, shooting for his fourth in a row, and had won 25 straight where only Borg (41) and Laver (31) had longer streaks. He would still close out his ninth professional campaign as No. 1 for a fourth consecutive year. At 6-foot-1, 175 pounds, with a full head of dark hair, the lanky Greek-blooded high school drop-out from Palos Verdes, Calif., was handling his affluence and standing modestly and well. "It's not a good year unless I win two majors. They're what count," he said.

But he was happy to salvage 1996 with one, consid-

ering the year's heartaches with the death of his coach and best friend, Tim Gullikson, of a brain tumor, which had been discovered at the Australian Open of 1995. Though unprepared for the French, which followed Gullikson's funeral, he made his finest showing in Paris, the one major that has befuddled him, falling in the semis to the champ Yevgeny Kafelnikov. That was after exciting, draining five-set wins over ex-champs Sergi Bruguera and Jim Courier, as well as Todd Martin.

Born Aug. 1, 1971, in Washington, D.C., the right-hander grew up in Southern California. His older sister, Stella Sampras, played professionally and now coaches the women's varsity of her alma mater, UCLA. Brother Gus operates the Scottsdale, Ariz., tourney. Pete's tennis life was changed at 14 by a pediatrician (and moonlighting tennis pedagogue), Dr. Pete Fisher. Fisher, feeling that Pete's two-handed backhand and baselining were childish, preached volleying, a free-flowing traditional backhand and reverence for the greats of yesteryear in performance and behavior, Rod Laver and Ken Rosewall. As Pete grew, so did his vaunted serve, and everything fell into place. Later it was Gullikson, Pete says, "who helped me to grow up, compete, focus, learn to play on grass. I owe so much to him."

Rookie pro Pete was out of his first U.S. Open, 1988, almost before it opened, beaten by Jaime Yzaga, 6-7, 6-7, 6-4, 7-5, 6-2, in the first round. But he got a foot-note in 1989, deposing the champ, Wilander, reaching the fourth round. The next year he was golden, if "unconscious." A long shot, seeded twelfth and ranked No. 81 when the season commenced, he went through in a spray of aces (100) on a loss of four sets. He showed his mettle by taking out ex-champs Lendl and McEnroe back-to-back. Pete demonstrated authenticity, the fact that he was unstoppable, by coolly sealing off canny third-seeded Lendl's counterattack in the quarters, 6-4, 7-6 (7-3), 3-6, 4-6, 6-2, embellishing with 26 aces. "He just kicked my ass," was Andre Agassi's terse summation of unbreakable Pete's 106-minute final-round caper, 6-4, 6-3, 6-2. Up jumped the name of Oliver Campbell, dead man dispossessed. He had held the record as youngest champ, 19 years, six months. Pete outgreened him by five months.

A few months later Pete made a bigger financial splash, collecting a record $2 million for winning the inaugural Grand Slam Cup in Munich over Brad Gilbert. Uncomfortable with all the attention brought by these deeds, and rocketing to No. 5 in the rankings, he actually seemed relieved to have the U.S. title lifted from him in the 1991 quarters by Courier. But he matured, accepted the responsibilities and challenges of life at the top, and became a solid World No. 1 in 1993, repelling all-would-be usurpers for six straight years, topping Jimmy Connors's open era record of five in a row (1974-78). Nothing as imposing had been seen for almost three-quarters of a century, since Big Bill Tilden's No. 1 parade of six years (1920-25) in the precomputer days. Though Agassi took it away momentarily by beating Pete in the 1995 Australian Open, Sampras struck back in the U.S. final eight months later, dispiriting Andre, 6-4, 6-3, 4-6, 7-5. Their hot rivalry stood at 20-14 for Pete at the close of 2002. Other than the six No. 1's, Pete's 12-year World Top Ten residency: No. 5, 1990; No. 6, 1991; No. 3, 1992, 1999, 2000; No. 10, 2001; and No. 13 in 2002.

Davis Cup was not altogether happy for Pete, especially his jitters-wracked debut in the 1991 final. A raucous, nationalistic French crowd in Lyon unnerved him, and Henri Leconte and Guy Forget pummeled him to defeats, Guy in the clincher that gave the French an unexpected Cup, 3-1. He played a winning right-court doubles part (alongside McEnroe) in the 3-1 Cup victory over Switzerland in 1992.

In the 1995 final at Moscow, on a clay court spread especially to spread-eagle him within Olympic Stadium, Pete responded by taking charge in the 3-2 victory over Russia in as glorious a weekend triple as performed by any American abroad. First was a five-set out-grinding of dirt maven Andrei Chesnokov, immediately after which Pete keeled over, exhausted. Then came a nifty duet with Todd Martin in the 7-5, 6-4, 6-3, go-ahead flooring of Andrei Olhovskiy and Kafelnikov. Finally a definitive curtain-lowering riddling of Kafelnikov in a shower of aces (16) and forehand winners (19). All his extraordinary qualities were on display: The grit and stubbornness underlying fluid groundies, thundering serves, casual yet deadly volleys and racing forehands.

It all appears so relaxed and glissando, although his head still slumps in adverse moments. Beneath the calm facade lurk certain physical and emotional frailties, a hereditary blood problem called thalyssemia. This was evident when he collapsed the instant the Chesnokov ordeal ended, and the memorable 1996 evening at Flushing when he lost his lunch but not his title. Ill and vomiting in the conclusive fifth-set tie-breaker of his defining quarter-final win over Alex Corretja, Pete wormed his way out of a match point with a lunging volley. Staggering, he hooked a 90 mph second-serve ace—"I don't know where it came from ... I was out of it"—to give himself match point at 8-7. Whereupon, "not wanting to hit another ball," he didn't have to. Corretja lost the only way Pete could win—a double fault. Kismet.

"Ah, but that's sweet Pete," says longtime friend and rival, Courier. "Just when you think he's dying, that's when he kills you."

At the close of 2002, he had won 64 of 265 singles tournaments, losing 24 finals. He'd also won two doubles titles. In the majors, he won 14 of 18 finals. His singles W-L record stands at an impressive 762-222 (.776), 203-39 in the majors (.839). Winning more prize money than anyone else, $43,280,489, he set the single-season record, $6,498,311, in 1997. His most productive season was 1994, winning 10 of 18 singles tournaments on 77-12. In the 1992 Olympics he was beaten in the third round by Russian Andrei Cherkasov.

Regardless of how long the game is played he will forever be the Big Man of the Big W.

MAJOR TITLES (14)–*Australian singles, 1994, 1997; Wimbledon singles, 1993, 1994, 1995; 1997, 1998, 1999, 2000; U.S. singles, 1990, 1993, 1995, 1996, 2002.* **OTHER U.S. TITLES** (2)–*Hard Court singles, 1991, 1992.* **DAVIS CUP**–*1991, 1992, 1994, 1995, 1997, 1999, 2000, 2002; record, 15-8 in singles, 4-1 in doubles.* **SINGLES RECORD IN THE MAJORS**–*Australian (45-9), French (24-13), Wimbledon (63-7), U.S. (71-9).*

ARANTXA SANCHEZ VICARIO
Spain (1971–)

Buzzing and flitting the width and breadth of arenas across the planet, the Barcelona Bumblebee—Arantxa Sanchez Vicario—was unceasing in determined pursuit of tennis balls, none seeming too distant to be retrieved in some manner and returned again and again to demoralize opponents. This went on most of her life, more than half of it as a professional, with no reduction in her zest or desire to win.

Long after the glamorous Lili de Alvarez of Madrid enhanced the 1926-27-28 Wimbledon finals, industrious little Sanchez-Vicario, a 5-foot-6, 130-pound right-hander, revived female tennis in their country. It happened on a June afternoon in Paris, 1989, as 17-year-old Arantxa faced defeat in the French final. Seeded seventh, she had done very well to get that far on her third try. She had come to attention the year before by chasing the all-time champ out of town: Chris Evert's last stand,

6-3, 7-6 (7-4). But now Steffi Graf, winner of five consecutive majors, was across the net and serving for the title at 5-4 in the third. Whereupon the intransigent Catalan went into overdrive, punching topspin forehands and two-fisted backhand drives relentlessly, relinquishing only two points and winning, 7-6 (8-6), 3-6, 7-5. Not only the first Spanish woman to take a major, she was the youngest French champ, until Monica Seles weighed in at 16 the following year.

She would become one of 14 women to appear in the finals of all four majors, winning the French again over Mary Pierce in 1994 and Seles in 1998. In 1994, she took the U.S. crown from Graf in a tumultuous 1-6, 7-6 (7-3), 6-4, decision and was named the ITF's World Champion. She lost Wimbledon and French finals to Graf in 1995 and 1996, the Australian to Pierce in 1995.

Perhaps her finest matches were heart-stopping defeats by Graf as they goaded each other to the heights at Wimbledon 1995 and French 1996. Arantxa served for victory at 5-4 and 7-6 in a shotmaking extravaganza in Paris, losing, 6-3, 6-7 (4-7), 10-8 in three hours, three minutes. On Centre Court they waged a game of games, the 11th of the third set. On it went for 20 minutes and 13 deuces. Serving, Arantxa had eight game points, but couldn't make it, 4-6, 6-1, 7-5, losing the last six points.

Aranzazu Isabel Maria 'Arantxa' Sanchez was born Dec. 18, 1971, in Barcelona. The last of a historic tennis-playing Sanchez brood of four, she was a surprise to her non-tennis parents, Emilio and the former Marisa Vicario, whose name Arantxa attached as a tribute, adding it in 1998. Arantxa is also the subject of a family tale. After the births of Marisa (a varsity player at Pepperdine in Santa Monica, Calif.) and Emilio and Javier (both successful pros and Spanish Davis Cuppers), Mama Marisa was told she could have no more children. However, three years later, not long after taking the kids on a roller-coaster ride, she became pregnant. Now she has a special place in her heart for that shake-and-rolling rattler at the Tibidabo amusement park overlooking the city. The babe's given name, Aranzazu, is that of a Basque saint.

A woman of sunny nature, Arantxa presented a rather severe look at play, her flowing black hair tightly headbanded above a contentious countenance that conveys her outlook: Surrender never. Ever a hustler on short, spirited legs, she never got enough tennis. Strictly a baseliner at first, she constantly improved her volleying to become one of the finer doubles players. She liked the

dual load of singles and doubles, carrying it better than anyone else, usually leading woman in matches played and won. She was one of the few centurions with 100 titles—29 singles, 67 doubles, four mixed, 14 of them majors: Four singles, six doubles, four mixed. Her career singles W-L for 329 tournaments: 759-295 (.720); doubles W-L for 298 tournaments: 667-216 (.755).

Arantxa represented Spain handsomely in three Olympics and 16 years of Federation Cup. In 1992 at Barcelona, with her king, Juan Carlos, spectating she won a bronze in singles, silver in doubles with Conchita Martinez. In 1996, she took silver in singles, losing the final to Lindsay Davenport and bronze again, with Martinez in doubles. She and Conchita, the most successful one-two punch in the competition's history wrapped up the Federation Cup five times, 1991, 1993-94-95 and 1998, and attained five other finals, 1989, 1992, 1996, 2000 and 2002. Arantxa holds the records for most years played (16), series (58), total matches (100), wins (72), singles wins (50). She was 18-3 in doubles with Conchita. As a pro 17 years, 1985-2002 (starting at 13 years, six months), she was in the World Top Ten 11 times (No. 1 for brief intervals during 1995): No. 5, 1989, 1991; No. 7, 1990; No. 4, 1992, 1998; No. 2, 1993-94, 1996; No. 3, 1995; No. 9, 1997, 2000, retiring at No. 53 in 2002. Her career prize money is $16, 917,312.

She was a little lady giving the game a big buzz.

MAJOR TITLES (14)–*French singles, 1989, 1994, 1998; U.S. singles, 1994; Australian doubles, 1992, 1995, 1996; Wimbledon doubles, 1995; U.S. doubles, 1993, 1994; Australian mixed, 1993; French mixed, 1990, 1992; U.S. mixed, 2000.* **FEDERATION CUP**–*1986, 1987, 1988, 1989, 1990, 1991, 1992, 1993, 1994, 1995, 1996, 1997, 1998, 1999, 2000, 2001, 2002; record: 50-22 in singles, 22-6 in doubles.* **SINGLES RECORD IN THE MAJORS**–*Australian (41-11), French (72-13), Wimbledon (41-15), U.S. (56-15).*

MANOLO SANTANA

Spain (1938–)
Hall of Fame 1984

One of the masters of legerdemain, Manuel Martinez 'Manolo' Santana was the first post-World War II European to gain universal respect because of his ease not only on Continental clay, but the way he took to grass. As well as his winning the most difficult clay event, the French singles in 1961 and 1964, both over Nicola Pietrangeli, he also captured the greensward gems, Wimbledon of 1966 and the U.S. Championship of 1965 at Forest Hills. In doing so, the engaging Spaniard was the first European champ at Forest Hills since Frenchman Henri Cochet in 1928.

"He was a magician on clay," says Rod Laver. "Manolo could hit the most incredible angles, drive you crazy with topspin lobs or drop shots. And he improved his volleying so that he was dangerous on grass, too. He toyed with me a couple of times in Europe, letting me know I had a lot to learn about clay."

In 1965 Santana became a national hero in Spain and was decorated by the country's leader, Francisco Franco, with the coveted Medal of Isabella, qualifying for the title *Ilustrissimo*. That year Santana spearheaded the 4-1 upset of the U.S. at Barcelona during the Davis Cup campaign and led Spain all the way to the finale for the first time. Although the Spaniards were turned back in Australia, 4-1, Santana gave Roy Emerson his only defeat in 12 title-round singles. Two years later he drove Spain to the finale again, salvaging the only point in a 4-1 defeat by beating John Newcombe.

Only Pietrangeli (164 singles and doubles in 46 series) and Romanian Ilie Nastase played more Davis Cup than Santana. Manolo worked 120 singles (69-17) and doubles (23-11) in 46 series between 1958 and 1973. He set Cup records by winning 13 singles matches in 1967 (equalled by Nastase in 1971), and also by winning 17 singles and doubles in 1965 and 1967 (topped by Nastase's 18 in 1971).

Born May 10, 1938, in Madrid, he worked as a ball boy at a local club and picked up the game. He was very appealing, a slender 5-foot-11 right-hander, who frequently flashed his warm, toothy smile at play and was an admirable sportsman. His racket control was phenomenal, enabling him to hit with touch and power. He had great flair, the ability to improvise and to inspire himself and his partners and teammates. Never losing heart in the doubles of the 1965 Davis Cup against the U.S., he rallied partner Luis Arilla as they stormed back to beat Dennis Ralston and Clark Graebner, 4-6, 3-6, 6-3, 6-4, 11-9, in an emotional battle that clinched the decision. Cushions showered down on the two Spaniards as they were carried about the stadium court of the Real Club de Tenis in the manner of bullfighters. Santana and Arilla wept with joy at the most tremendous victory in Spanish tennis annals. Manolo had given the home side a 2-0 lead by beating Frank Froehling, after Juan Gisbert upset Ralston.

Less than a month later a similarly jubilant celebration was staged at Forest Hills after Santana jolted Cliff Drysdale in the U.S. final. A troupe of dancers from the World's Fair's Spanish Pavilion toted him from stadium to clubhouse, whereupon they serenaded him.

The following year was Santana's at Wimbledon, where he beat Ralston in the final and enthralled the gallery with his point and counterpoint thrusts. But 12 months later, beaten by Charlie Pasarell, he made an historic footnote as the lone top-seeded defending champion to lose in Wimbledon's first round.

Beginning in 1961, Santana was in the World Top Ten seven years, No. 1 in 1966. His career was virtually over when the open era arrived, but he did elate his countrymen by winning Barcelona in 1970, his last singles victory, plus three pro doubles titles. Overall as amateur and pro he won 72 singles titles.

Santana came out of retirement briefly in 1973 to play his last season of Davis Cup, and again in 1974 to act as player-coach for New York in the new World Team Tennis League. He was named to the Hall of Fame in 1984, the second Spaniard, following Manuel Alonso, 1977. His successes spurred the rapid development of tennis in Spain, where the sport was not much noticed prior to 1965, but is booming today. His protégé was Manuel Orantes, called Manolito (Little Manolo), who won the U.S. Championship at Forest Hills a decade after his own, beating Jimmy Connors though the surface had by then been transformed to clay.

He spent time as Spain's Davis Cup captain, and has long been a friend to aspiring young players. But despite Spain's important current standing in tennis today, none of its fine players has yet measured up to his four major singles. Call him the Godfather of the Groundstrokes.

MAJOR TITLES (5)–*French singles, 1961, 1964; Wimbledon singles, 1966; U.S. singles, 1965; French doubles, 1963.* **DAVIS CUP**–*1958, 1959, 1960, 1961, 1962, 1963, 1964, 1965, 1966, 1967, 1968, 1969, 1970, 1973; record: 69-17 in singles, 23-11 in doubles.* **SINGLES RECORD IN THE MAJORS**–*French (33-6), Wimbledon (22-9), U.S. (25-7).*

DICK SAVITT

United States (1927–)
Hall of Fame 1976

Only four American men have won the Australian and Wimbledon titles in one year, Richard 'Dick' Savitt was the second in 1951 (following Don Budge, 1938, and preceding Jimmy Connors, 1974, and Pete Sampras, 1977). He beat Ken McGregor in both, four sets in the Aussie's lair and straight sets at Wimbledon.

Any hopes he had of a Grand Slam were squelched by

champ Jaroslav Drobny, 1-6, 6-8, 6-4, 8-6, 6-3, in a quarter-final of the French. Defending his Aussie title, Savitt was beaten in the 1952 semis by McGregor, 6-4, 6-4, 3-6, 6-4, and at Wimbledon by Mervyn Rose in a quarter-final, 6-4, 3-6, 6-4, 4-6, 6-2. In the U.S. Championships he was a semi-finalist in 1950, losing to the champ, Art Larsen, 6-2, 10-8, 7-9, 6-2; a semi-finalist in 1951, losing to Vic Seixas, 6-0, 3-6, 6-3, 6-2; and a quarter-finalist in 1952, 1956 and 1958. In 1956 he lost a stirring baseline slugfest to the champ, Ken Rosewall, 6-4, 7-5, 4-6, 8-10, 6-1.

A large, broad-shouldered, dark-haired right-hander, 6-foot-3, 180 pounds, he was a powerful groundstroker and stubborn competitor. Sav was a king of the Seventh Regiment Armory, a boards runner, in his Manhattan neighborhood, winning the U.S. Indoor thrice. He deposed Bill Talbert in 1952, 6-2, 6-3, 6-4, beat Budge Patty in 1958, 6-1, 6-2, 3-6, 12-10, and, at 34 (no longer ranked), knocked off No. 1 American Whitney Reed, 6-2, 11-9, 6-3, in 1961. But the best remembered of his five finals was a rousing joust lost to world No. 1 Alex Olmedo, 7-9, 6-3, 6-4, 5-7, 12-10, in 1959. He ranked six times in the U.S. Top Ten between 1950 and 1959, No. 2 in 1951, and four times in the World Top Ten between 1951 and 1957, No. 2 in 1951.

A Cornell graduate, Dick was born March 4, 1927, in Bayonne, N.J. In 1981 he and his son, Robert, won the U.S. Father and Son doubles title. He was elected to the Hall of Fame in 1976.

MAJOR TITLES (2)–*Australian singles, 1951; Wimbledon singles, 1951.* **OTHER U.S. TITLES** (3)–*Indoor singles, 1952, 1958, 1961.* **DAVIS CUP**–*1951; record: 3-0 in singles.* **SINGLES RECORD IN THE MAJORS**–*Australian (8-1), French (8-2), Wimbledon (11-1), U.S. (29-12).*

TED SCHROEDER

United States (1921–)
Hall of Fame 1966

Emulating Don McNeill in 1940, Frederick Rudolph 'Ted' Schroeder of Stanford became in 1942 only the second player to win the U.S. Intercollegiate and the U.S. singles in the same year. A standout big-situation competitor—especially in Davis Cup—volleying wizard Schroeder, along with his pal, Jack Kramer, recovered the Cup for the U.S. in 1946 after it had spent seven years in Australia during World War II.

Their teammates, Gar Mulloy and Frank Parker, weren't happy when captain Walter Pate selected attack-minded Kramer and Schroeder to play all the way

against the favored Aussies in Melbourne. But Schroeder led off by stopping John Bromwich, 3-6, 6-1, 6-2, 0-6, 6-3, and the 5-0 sweep was on. A daring right-hander, Ted helped the U.S. keep the Cup in 1947-48-49 by winning both his singles against Australia each year.

But he was beaten by both Frank Sedgman and Ken McGregor as the Aussies lifted the Cup in 1950, and though he tied the 1951 finale at Sydney at 2-2 by beating Mervyn Rose, the U.S. was tipped, 3-2, and he retired. A part-time player, taking vacations from business to compete, Ted rose to his peak in 1949 when he won Wimbledon the only time he entered. That year Ted not only captured the title with his daring volleying, but he also captivated London with his personality as an outgoing, straightforward Yank smoking a corn-cob pipe. He was known admiringly as 'Lucky Ted' for his five-set escapes, four of them, starting with an old antagonist, Gar Mulloy in the first round, 3-6, 9-11, 6-1, 6-0, 7-5, and ending with Jaroslav Drobny in the final, 3-6, 6-0, 6-3, 4-6, 6-4. The last three went the distance—the only such run other than Henri Cochet's in 1927—and he appeared truly lost in the quarters against Sedgman, 3-6, 6-8, 6-3, 6-2, 9-7. Sedg held two match points against serve, one each at 4-5 and 5-6. Ted wriggled free with serve-and-volley—but on a second serve (having foot-faulted on the first), the volley off the frame! The second was a backhand passer. He was also behind Eric Sturgess in the semis, 3-6, 7-5, 5-7, 6-1, 6-2. Ted's 29 sets and four five-set matches outdid any other champ in that respect.

Seven years after winning Forest Hills, he reappeared in the U.S. final and seemed the winner after taking the first two sets from Pancho Gonzalez, but faded, 16-18, 2-6, 6-1, 6-2, 6-4. He and Kramer formed one of the great doubles teams, winning the U.S. title thrice, 1940, 1941 and 1947. He refused several offers to join Kramer as a pro. A Californian, he was born July 20, 1921, in Newark, N.J., and was ranked in the U.S. Top Ten nine times between 1940 and 1951, No. 1 in 1942. He was in the World Top Ten six straight times from 1946, No. 2 the first four years. He served in the U.S. Naval Air Force in World War II and entered the Hall of Fame in 1966. His son, John Schroeder, was an accomplished professional golfer.

MAJOR TITLES (6)–*Wimbledon singles, 1949; U.S. singles, 1942; U.S. doubles, 1940, 1941, 1947; U.S. mixed, 1942.* **OTHER U.S. TITLES** (9)–*Intercollegiate singles, 1942; Intercollegiate doubles, 1942, with Larry Dee; Hard Court singles, 1948, 1949, 1951; Clay Court* *doubles, 1941, with Jack Kramer; 1947, with Jack Tuero; Hard Court doubles, 1948, with Vic Seixas; 1949, with Eric Sturgess.* **DAVIS CUP**–*1946, 1947, 1948, 1949, 1950, 1951; record: 11-3 in singles, 2-3 in doubles.* **SINGLES RECORD IN THE MAJORS**–*Wimbledon (7-0), U.S. (20-4).*

ELEO SEARS

United States (1881–1968)
Hall of Fame 1968

Eleonora Randolph Sears, though of a proper Bostonian background, was noted for her athleticism and vigor. She was an equestrian, golfer and determined walker (frequently striding the 40 miles between her Boston home and Providence, R.I.), and maintained a trim, healthful figure into old age.

The right-handed Eleo was from a tennis-playing family. Her father, Fred Sears, was one of the first (if not the first) to play tennis in the U.S., with Dr. James Dwight in 1874. Her uncle, Dick Sears, was the original U.S. champion.

Eleo made it to the U.S. singles final in 1912, losing to Mary K. Browne, and won four U.S. doubles, two with Hazel Hotchkiss Wightman (1911 and 1915) and two with Molla Bjurstedt Mallory (1916 and 1917), as well as the mixed with Willis Davis (1916). She ranked in the U.S. Top Ten twice, 1914 and 1916, No. 6 in the first year. She was born Sept. 28, 1881, in Boston, died March 16, 1968, in Palm Beach, Fla., and entered the Hall of Fame in 1968.

MAJOR TITLES *(5)–U.S. doubles, 1911, 1915, 1916, 1917; U.S. mixed, 1916.* **SINGLES RECORD IN THE MAJORS**–*Wimbledon (0-2), U.S. (27-14).*

DICK SEARS

United States (1861–1943)
Hall of Fame 1955

Never beaten in the U.S. Championships, the original singles champ, Richard Dudley Sears, won his first of seven titles in 1881 while still a Harvard ('83) student. As one of 24 entries he, a Bostonian, ventured onto the lawn of the Newport (R.I.) Casino in knickerbockers, long wool socks, a necktie and cap, and wielding a slightly lopsided racket (similar to those for court tennis) that weighed 16 ounces.

Beating first-round opponent Powell, 6-0, 6-2, Dick was off on an 18-match streak that would carry him through the Championships of 1887, after which he retired from the game. Not until the challenge round format was abandoned and 1920-21 champion Bill

Tilden beat Zenzo Shimidzu, 6-2, 6-3, 6-1, to reach the 1922 semis (and register a 19th successive win in the Championships), was Sears' record eclipsed.

Sears later recalled the Championships' launching in 1881: "The nets were four-feet at the posts and three-feet at center. This led to a scheme of attack by playing, whenever possible, across court to avoid lifting drives over the highest part of the net at the sidelines. This method just suited me. I had taken up a mild form of volleying, and all I had to do was to tap the balls, as they came over, first to one side and then to the other, running my opponent all over the court."

A few of the players served underhand, though not the right-handed Sears. In the final, his fifth match, he beat William Glyn, an Englishman who regularly summered at Newport, 6-0, 6-3, 6-2. During his first three championships Sears lost no sets, concluding the 1883 tournament with a 6-2, 6-0, 9-7 victory over his mentor, and second cousin, James Dwight.

In that year the 5-foot-9, 150-pound Sears began to hit a topspin forehand that he'd seen used in England by the originator, Herbert Lawford. Since the challenge round was instituted in 1884 he had to play but one match, against the victor in the all-comers tournament, to retain the title the last four years. Then he lost one set each to Howard Taylor in 1884, Godfrey Brinley in 1885 and Livingston Beeckman in 1886.

Those last four years he used a prized racket given to him in England by the all-time Wimbledon champ, Willie Renshaw, and won four singles and doubles titles with it. He and Dwight won the doubles five times together, and he won once with Joseph Clark, 1885. Sears was the first of the 19-year-olds to conquer the U.S., slightly older than Oliver Campbell in 1890, and the very youngest, Pete Sampras, in 1990. He was No. 1 in the U.S. 1885, 1886 and 1887, the first years of national rankings. Scion of a prominent Boston family, he was born there Oct. 16, 1861, and died there April 8, 1943. His older brother, Fred, played with Dwight, possibly the first tennis in the U.S., in 1874, and a younger brother, Philip, was in the U.S. Top Ten five years. A cousin, Eleo Sears, is also in the Hall of Fame. After giving up lawn tennis, Sears won the U.S. Court Tennis singles title in 1892. He served as USTA president in 1887 and 1888 and was elected to the Hall of Fame in 1955.

MAJOR TITLES *(13)–U.S. singles, 1881, 1882, 1883, 1884, 1885, 1886, 1887; U.S. doubles, 1882, 1883, 1884, 1885, 1886, 1887.* **SINGLES RECORD IN THE MAJORS**–*U.S. (18-0).*

FRANK SEDGMAN
Australia (1927–)
Hall of Fame 1979

The beginning of the most oppressive—yet jolly—dynasty in tennis history was in the strokes of Frank Allan Sedgman, the Australian savior of 1950. He wasn't around long, but he got an awful lot done in a hurry.

Australia was drooping in the Davis Cup after World War II, losing four successive finales to the U.S. Then, in 1950, 22-year-old Sedgman—loser of both his final round singles the previous year—startled crowds at Forest Hills and the favored U.S. team by leading the Cup-snatching gang of Capt. Harry Hopman. Australia, winner of a total of two matches in the four previous beatings, got one right away as Sedgman pounced on Tom Brown, 6-0, 8-6, 9-7. Newcomer Ken McGregor beat Ted Schroeder, and Sedgman returned to the court with 31-year-old John Bromwich to ice it over Gardnar Mulloy and Schroeder. "At last," enthused Bromwich. The Aussies had the Cup, which Brom had helped win 11 years before during Hopman's first tenure.

Sedg's third-day crunching of Schroeder, a holdover from the 1946 victors, put him in the company of an original, Norman Brookes. Brookes, who spurred the first Cup-taking by the lads from Down Under in 1907, was the most recent Aussie to win three matches in a final. That was in 1911.

The next year was considerably harder, the defense at Sydney, but tripling Sedgman made sure the Cup remained in Australia, 3-2. He beat Schroeder on opening day but Mervyn Rose lost to Vic Seixas. Linked to McGregor in a 6-2, 9-7, 6-3, win over Tony Trabert and Schroeder, Sedg paced a 2-1 lead. But Rose lost again to Schroeder, and it was up to Sedgman. It didn't take long to see he was the master of the situation, beating Seixas, 6-4, 6-2, 6-2. A year later, 1952, virtually the same story at Adelaide—three points for Sedgman, Australia beats the U.S., 4-1. Australia was mad about Sedgman for good reason: Three years, three Cups, 9-for-9 in matches, playing the clincher every year.

Those Cup successes were the start of Capt. Hopman's second stewardship under which Australia won the Davis trophy 15 times between 1950 and 1967, a reign admirable not only for the quality of the tennis but the sportsmanship and jocular nature of the Aussie oppressors.

There was more for Sedgman, the complete three-way player: Singles, doubles and mixed. In 1951, beating Seixas, he became the first of 13 Aussie men to win U.S. singles championships (18 titles in all), and repeated the following year over Mulloy. For three years (1950-51-52) he was the king, with few slips. He first made a rumbling serve-and-volleying noise in 1949 by beating the venerable Bromwich for the Australian title, securing a Davis Cup position and finishing No. 4 in the world. Then he posted three supreme years without male equal. Of the 36 events at the four majors, he was in 23 of the finals, winning 19 titles: Four singles (Australian 1950, U.S. 1951-52, Wimbledon 1952); eight doubles (Australian 1951-52, French 1951-52, Wimbledon 1951-52, U.S. 1950-51); seven mixed (Australian 1950, French 1951-52, Wimbledon 1951-52, U.S. 1951-52). In 1952 he was in 11 of the 12 finals, and got the title he most wanted: Wimbledon over crafty lefty Jaroslav Drobny, 4-6, 6-2, 3-6, 6-2. A very busy, energetic guy, indeed. Only the French singles eluded him, in the 1952 final lost to Drobny, 6-2, 6-0, 3-6, 6-4—but Frank beat him for the Italian title the same spring.

Sedgman, an athletic 5-foot-11, 170-pound right-hander, born Oct. 29, 1927, in Mont Albert, Victoria, Australia, was such an acquisitive winner of major titles during the briefest of stretches, 1949-53, that he stands third among all-time male champions with 22 major victories in singles, doubles and mixed doubles, three behind John Newcombe, six behind Roy Emerson.

In 1951 Sedgman and McGregor scored the only Grand Slam in men's doubles by winning all the majors within a calendar year. They came oh-so-close to Slamming again the following year, going all the way to the U.S. final, where it took another Aussie, Merv Rose, allied with Yank Seixas, to barely beat them. As it was, Frank and Ken won seven straight major doubles, a male record, and Sedg had eight in a row, having taken the U.S. with John Bromwich in 1950. In his last season as an amateur, Sedgman was the last man to make a rare Wimbledon triple, adding the doubles (with McGregor) and mixed (with Doris Hart) to his singles conquest.

Speed, brilliant volleying and a heavy forehand were his chief assets, plus a fighting—though good-natured—spirit.

Jack Kramer, proprietor of the professional tour and its foremost player, enticed Sedgman to become his challenger in 1953, and they played the customary head-to-head tour between the amateur-king-turned-pro-rookie and the incumbent. Kramer stayed on top, 54-41.

However, Sedgman's share of the gate was $102,000. He was the first male player to earn more than 100 grand in a season.

Sedgman continued to barnstorm with the pros into the 1960s. He was finalist to Pancho Gonzalez for the U.S. Pro singles championship in 1954 and won the U.S. Pro doubles with Andres Gimeno in 1961. Twice he won the pros' highest regarded championship, Wembley, at London—1953 over Gonzalez and 1958 over Tony Trabert. Keeping himself superbly fit, he was able to launch a second professional career in 1974 when promoter Al Bunis formed the Grand Masters tour for ex-champs over 45. Sedgman won the Grand Masters championship in a season's-end playoff among the top eight players in 1975, 1977 and 1978, and, in this second phase of professionalism, won more than $250,000 over six seasons.

He made the World Top Ten in 1949 (No. 4) and reached No. 1 in 1951 and 1952. Altogether he won 36 amateur and pro singles titles, was named to the International Tennis Hall of Fame in 1979, and the Australian Tennis Hall of Fame in 1996. He lives in Melbourne with his wife, Jean, and is an owner of race horses of whom he says, "They eat too much."

MAJOR TITLES (22)–*Australian singles, 1949, 1950; Wimbledon singles, 1952; U.S. singles, 1951, 1952; Australian doubles, 1951, 1952; French doubles, 1951, 1952; Wimbledon doubles, 1948, 1951, 1952; U.S. doubles, 1950, 1951; Australian mixed, 1949, 1950; French mixed, 1951, 1952; Wimbledon mixed, 1951, 1952; U.S. mixed, 1951, 1952.* **DAVIS CUP**–*1949, 1950, 1951, 1952; record: 16-3 in singles, 9-0 in doubles.* **SINGLES RECORD IN THE MAJORS**–*Australian (19-5), French (13-4), Wimbledon (26-6), U.S. (20-3).*

PANCHO SEGURA

Ecuador (1921–)
Hall of Fame 1984

A curious sight was Francisco Olegario 'Pancho' Segura when he appeared on the North American scene in 1941, a mite who began to make a big impression with jarring strokes and jovial personality despite seeming physical limitations. He had won his native Ecuadorian title at 17 in 1938 along with various other Latin American titles, and presently was on his way to big-time tennis in the U.S., riding a tennis scholarship at the University of Miami where his coach was Gardnar Mulloy, his Hall of Fame colleague-to-be. "Mulloy saved me. I didn't have any money, and spoke no English, but he helped 'em with everything," Segura recalls.

A big smile and a yen for the battle offset what appeared, at first appraisal, to be disadvantages: An unorthodox two-fisted forehand, flimsy-looking bowed legs and a 5-foot-6 frame. Yet his footwork was admirable. He was quick, nimble, extremely effective. By 1942 he had a No. 4 U.S. ranking, and would be the ever-welcome centerpiece at depleted homefront tournaments during World War II, his status as an alien keeping him out of uniform. Over the 1943-45 period he was the big winner, grabbing 15 of 30 tournaments (7 of 10 in 1943) and 107 of 122 matches. He could never realize his dream of conquering the U.S. at Forest Hills, coming as close as the semis, 1942-45, and the quarters in 1946-47.

Segura was born June 20, 1921, in Guayaquil, Ecuador and was raised there. A childhood attack of rickets deformed his legs but his will was strong, and he drove himself to play tennis well, even though he was so weak at first that he had to grip the racket with both hands. A right-hander, he was likely the first to utilize a two-fisted forehand.

At Miami he won the National Intercollegiate singles in 1943-44-45, the only man since Malcolm Chace to take three straight—for Brown in 1893, and Yale in 1894-95. Pancho won the U.S. Indoor title of 1946 and the U.S. Clay Court of 1944, and was a member of the U.S. Top Ten six times.

But his best days were ahead of him, as a professional. After settling in the U.S., he left the amateurs in 1947, signing on to play mostly the secondary matches on the strung-out world-wide tour of one-nighters. Unfortunately for Segura, he was out of the limelight once he became a professional. While he lost to Aussie Dinny Pails, 41-31 at their end of his first tour (Jack Kramer and Pancho Gonzalez the headliners), he would overcome Frank Parker, and Ken McGregor in their series. Sharpening his strokes and tactics and becoming one of the great players, he received little recognition. Kramer and Gonzalez were the stars, but Segura was making his mark in a small circle as a shrewd strategist, a cunning lobber, and a killer with that (then) strange forehand.

And Pancho was becoming dangerous for anybody. He prizes a 6-4, 8-10, 1-6, 6-4, 6-3, victory over world-best Kramer in the semis of the U.S. Pro of 1950, a tourney he won over Frank Kovacs, forcing Kovacs to surrender with cramps. That earned Segura a tour against Kramer the following year, but Jack was still too strong, 64-28. Nevertheless, short Pancho was long on endurance. Again he won the U.S. Pro in 1951-52, both times over Gonzalez, seven years his junior. He then lost the final to Gonzalez, 1955-56-57, as well as the final of the pros' biggie, Wembley at London, to Gonzalez in 1951. There he made the final three more times, 1957, 1959-60, losing to 25-year-old Ken Rosewall in 1960. Segura was 39, and seven years later he beat Rosewall during a tournament at Binghamton, N.Y. At 41 he lost his last U.S. Pro final, to Butch Buchholz, 6-4, 6-3, 6-4, in 1962. Pancho also won the U.S. Pro doubles with Kramer in 1948 and 1995, and Gonzalez in 1958.

He toured for more than two decades and stands as one of the prominent figures in the history of the pros' days in the wilderness, prior to opens. Hardy and good-natured, Segura was a favorite with crowds. He could always smile and crack a joke, yet was thoroughly professional and a constant competitor. He never made big money. Open tennis arrived too late for him, but he entered the doubles of the first open Wimbledon in 1968 with Alex Olmedo, and in the second round they won the longest doubles match of Wimbledon's open era, 94 games, over Abe Segal and Gordon Forbes, 32-30, 5-7, 6-4, 6-4. The 62-game set was the longest ever at Wimbledon.

When his playing career ended he became a one of the best teaching pros, settling in Southern California, and making his mark as one of the sharpest minds in the game. He was instrumental in Jimmy Connors' development, and was elected to the Hall of Fame in 1984.

U.S. TITLES (14)–*Intercollegiate singles, 1943, 1944, 1945; Indoor singles, 1946; Clay Court singles, 1944; Pro singles, 1950, 1951, 1952; Clay Court doubles, 1944, 1945 with Bill Talbert; Pro doubles, 1948, 1955 with Jack Kramer; 1954, 1958 with Pancho Gonzalez.* **SINGLES RECORD IN THE MAJORS**–*French (2-1), Wimbledon (2-2), U.S. (21-7).*

VIC SEIXAS

United States (1923–)
Hall of Fame 1971

When Vic Seixas played—and won—the fifth-longest singles match in tennis history, he was 42. That was in 1966, when Vic went 94 games to beat a 22-year-old Australian Davis Cup player, Bill Bowrey, 32-34, 6-4, 10-8, during the Pennsylvania Grass Championships at Philadelphia. It took nearly four hours.

Elias Victor Seixas, Jr., born Aug 30, 1923, in Philadelphia, played the U.S. Championships at Forest Hills a record 28 times between 1940 and 1969, winning the singles in 1954 over Rex Hartwig, 3-6, 6-4,

6-4, 6-4. He played more Davis Cup matches than any other American, until John McEnroe, winning 38 of 55 singles and doubles encounters during his seven years on the team between 1951 and 1957. Thirteen times he was ranked in the Top Ten in the U.S. between 1942 and 1966, setting an American longevity record of a 24-year span between his first and last entries (later equaled by Pancho Gonzalez, 1948-72).

In 1953, when Seixas won the Wimbledon singles over Kurt Nielsen, 9-7, 6-3, 6-4, and led the U.S. to the Davis Cup final, he was considered No. 3 in the amateur world, his high point.

Although he helped the U.S. attain the finale every year he played Davis Cup, the team could win only once, the high spot of 1954 when he and Tony Trabert were victorious. After Trabert opened with a win over Lew Hoad, Seixas followed with a stunning 8-6, 6-8, 6-4, 6-3 triumph over his nemesis, Ken Rosewall. That put the U.S. ahead, 2-0, on the first day, and Seixas and Trabert clinched the Cup the following day with a doubles victory over Hoad and Rex Hartwig, 6-2, 4-6, 6-2, 10-8, before a record outdoor crowd of 25,578 at Sydney.

Seixas won 15 major titles in singles, doubles and mixed, setting a Wimbledon record by winning the mixed four successive years, 1953, 1954, 1955 with Doris Hart, and 1956 with Shirley Fry.

Among his 13 U.S. titles were the Clay Court singles in 1953 and 1957, the Hard Court doubles (with Ted Schroeder) in 1948, and the Indoor doubles (with Trabert) in 1955, making Seixas one of three men to win national titles on all four surfaces. In 1971 he was named to the Hall of Fame.

The 6-foot-1, 180-pound, right-handed Seixas was an attacker who won more on determination and conditioning than on outstanding form. His volleying was exceptional, and he had an excellent match temperament, but a thrashing topspin forehand and sliced backhand were utilitarian. His career was interrupted for three years by World War II, during which he served as a pilot in the U.S. Army Air Force. He graduated from the University of North Carolina. Seixas was one of the few extraordinary amateurs who did not join the pro tour, winning 56 singles titles. Eventually, though, after the age of 50, he did become a pro to compete on the Grand Masters circuit.

MAJOR TITLES (15)–*Wimbledon singles, 1953; U.S. singles, 1954; French doubles, 1954, 1955; U.S. doubles, 1952, 1954; Australian doubles, 1955; French mixed, 1953; Wimbledon mixed, 1953,*

1954, 1955, 1956; U.S. mixed, 1953, 1954, 1955. **OTHER U.S. TITLES** *(7)–Clay Court singles, 1953, 1957; Clay Court doubles, 1949, with Sam Match; 1954, with Tony Trabert; Hard Court doubles, 1948, with Ted Schroeder; Indoor doubles, 1955, with Trabert; 1956 with Sam Giammalva.* **DAVIS CUP (As player)**–*1951, 1952, 1953, 1954, 1955, 1956, 1957; record: 24-12 in singles, 14-5 in doubles;* **(As captain)**–*1952, 1957, 1964; record: 3-2.* **SINGLES RECORD IN THE MAJORS**–*Australian (4-2), French (17-4), Wimbledon (31-8), U.S. (74-26).*

MONICA SELES
Yugoslavia/United States (1973–)

How could anybody stop her? An all-time prodigy, a unique No. 1 with her double-barrelled fusillades—both hands on both sides—Monica Seles was a 19-year-old tearing up tennis until that fateful day in Hamburg, April 30, 1993. An allegedly demented German spectator, Guenther Parche, stopped her, struck her down with a knife in the back as she sat beside the court on a changeover.

The quarter-final match against Maggie Maleeva ended at that abrupt moment, and so did tennis for a kid who seemed destined to be the greatest of all. She had won eight majors (three French, three Australian, two U.S.). After taking the U.S. of 1992 over Arantxa Sanchez Vicario, 6-3, 6-3, she was the youngest ever to hold seven of them (18 years, eight months), undercutting Maureen Connolly by three months. (Curiously, Connolly, who wound up with nine, had been cut off, too, as a teenager, in a traffic accident.) Breaking Steffi Graf's four-year hold on the No. 1 ranking in 1991, Seles had held off Steffi in her last major appearance, to win the Australian, 4-6, 6-3, 6-2.

But putative assassin Parche intervened, claiming he knifed Seles to restore Graf to preeminence, a story the Seles family doubted. It was 28 months before Monica was seen on court again. The psychological damage had been more severe than the physical. She, like everybody else—except, apparently, the judge in Parche's trial and re-trial—wondered why he was not incarcerated. "He's still out there walking the streets," she worried.

Attempting to put it behind her, Monica re-emerged in August 1995, beating Martina Navratilova in an exhibition at Atlantic City, content with the co-No. 1 ranking with Graf granted her by the WTA. Then acting as though nothing had changed, she was back in business. Electrifyingly so. Opponents at the Canadian Open in Toronto acted as though they were seeing a ghost. They were—a ghost of championships past as she marched to

the title on a loss of no sets, 12 games in five matches, ripping Amanda Coetzer in the final, 6-0, 6-1.

On to Flushing Meadow, where she'd won 14 straight matches. The opposition continued to melt until the final, where Graf ended the streak at 20, fitter in the third set, 7-6 (8-6), 0-6, 6-3. At 6-5 in the tie-breaker Monica groused at a call of fault on her bid—a fraction wide—for a set-point ace. She lost her composure momentarily, and may have missed the title by a smidgen of an inch.

Her return to Australia, where she'd never been beaten, was triumphant. She won Sydney from match point down over Lindsay Davenport, 4-6, 7-6 (9-7), 6-3, then the Open (Graf was absent) over Anke Huber, 6-4, 6-1, a ninth major. However, after that the 1996 season didn't go as well as she and her fans had hoped. Knee and shoulder injuries were bothersome. Her conditioning was suspect; she pulled out of several tourneys. Though she did win three more tournaments and help the U.S. regain the Federation Cup, there was disappointment at the French and Wimbledon. Jana Novotna clipped her Paris streak of 25 in the quarters. More painful perhaps was losing the last four games and a second-rounder at the Big W to an unknown Slovak, No. 59 Katerina Studenikova. "I'm playing too defensively, not attacking the ball the way I used to," Monica said accurately. She was a finalist again at the U.S. Open but was pushed around by a charged-up Graf whose superior quickness showed, 7-5, 6-4.

Seles, a left-hander who has grown to nearly six feet, was born Dec. 2, 1973, of Serbo-Hungarian parentage, at Novy Sad in what was then Yugoslavia. Getting her started, her father, Karolj Seles, a professional cartoonist and keen student of the game, drew faces on the balls for her to hit. He and her mother, Esther, felt her future lay in the U.S. They moved to Nick Bollettieri's Tennis Academy at Brandenton, Fla., in 1986 when Monica was 12, and headmaster Nick oversaw her early development. Papa took over the coaching again at their Sarasota residence until his death in 1998. Monica became a U.S. citizen in 1995.

Monica sounded the alarm in 1989 as a 15-year-old by spoiling the last final of Chris Evert's illustrious career in Houston, 3-6, 6-1, 6-4. "She's the next," exulted an overwhelmed witness, historian Ted Tinling. Soon after, 'Moanin' Monica' took her bubbly grimacing-and-grunting act to Roland Garros to show Parisians noisy tennis nouvelle: Rip-roaring groundies, bludgeoned from anywhere in a baseball switch-hitting style (the backhand cross-handed). She constantly went for winners, seemingly off-balance and out-of-position but buoyed by excellent footwork and anticipation. Graf barely escaped in the semis. But she wouldn't a year later, in the final, 7-6 (8-6), 6-4. Seles became a major player. She bounded into the World Top Ten in 1989, No. 6, and has been there ever since, 13 years, (except for non-ranked 1994): No. 2, 1990; No. 1, 1991-92; No. 8, 1993; co-No. 1, 1995; co-No. 2, 1996; No. 5, 1997; No. 6, 1998; No. 4, 1999-2000; No. 10, 2001; No. 7, 2002.

For 2-1/2 years Monica was nearly invincible as the titles piled up and her ball-impacting shriek—"Uhh-eee!"—was heard across the globe. She charmed the public with girlish élan and mystified people by vanishing before Wimbledon in 1991 and then resurfacing to win the U.S. Open. She may have been psyched out of a 1992 Grand Slam when complaints about the grunting from Wimbledon victims Nathalie Tauziat and Martina Navratilova (leading to a warning from the referee) muted her in the final, where she was destroyed by Graf, 6-2, 6-1. Still, she was the first to win three majors in successive years since Margaret Court (three and four, 1969-70), a feat equaled by Graf in 1995-96. Among her souvenirs was the 1991 U.S. final, when, 17, she defeated Navratilova, 34, a singular generation gapper. Her brightest seasons of 10 singles titles each were 1991 (winning 74 of 80 matches) and 1992 (70 of 75).

At the close of 2002, after 11 pro seasons, and portions of two others, she had played 177 tournaments and won 53 singles titles with a 585-115 W-L record (.836); 179-29 in the majors (.861). She has also won four doubles titles and $14,615,549. She won a singles bronze at the 2000 Olympics.

An exemplary figure who has coped well with much adversity, including several injuries, she is not the player she might have been, yet is clearly, constantly upbeat, saying, "Tennis will never end for me because I love it so much. When my professional career if over I will continue to play all my life." Monica has put an indelible signature on the game with her style, persona and championships, a woman doubtless on a journey to the Hall of Fame.

MAJOR TITLES (9)–*Australian singles, 1991, 1992, 1993, 1996; French singles, 1990, 1991, 1992; U.S. singles, 1991, 1992.* **OTHER U.S. TITLES** (1)–*Hard Court singles, 1990.* **FEDERATION CUP**–*1996, 1998, 1999, 2000, 2002; record: 15-2 in singles, 2-0 in doubles.* **SINGLES RECORD IN THE MAJORS**–*Australian (42-3), French (54-7), Wimbledon (30-9), U.S. (53-10. Federation Cup).*

FRANK SHIELDS

United States (1909–1975)
Hall of Fame 1964

A dashing, handsome performer who spent some time in Hollywood in bit movie roles, unseeded Francis Xavier Shields was the only Wimbledon finalist to lose without going onto the court. Frank defaulted the 1931 final to Sidney Wood beforehand, sidelined by an ankle injury suffered in the semis when he beat Jean Borotra, the 1924 and 1926 champ, 7-5, 3-6, 6-4, 6-4.

The 6-foot-3 right-hander was a came-close guy. Eleventh-seeded, in his first major final, the U.S. of 1930, he had a shot at Johnny Doeg, but couldn't connect on a set point against Doeg's rugged lefty serve at 13-14 in the deciding set and lost, 10-8, 1-6, 6-4, 16-14. In 1928, an 18-year-old seventh seed, he got to the U.S. semis, losing to the champ, Henri Cochet, 6-2, 8-6, 6-4, and again, second-seeded in 1933, falling to the top foreign-seeded Wimbledon champ Jack Crawford, 7-5, 6-4, 6-3. A year later at Wimbledon, he came closer but couldn't hold Crawford down, 2-6, 4-6, 6-4, 6-3, 6-4. Between 1928 and 1945 he was ranked eight times in the U.S. Top Ten, No. 1 in 1933, No. 2 in 1930. He was a U.S. Davis Cupper in 1931, 1932 and 1934, winning 19 of 25 matches, and was non-playing captain in 1951 when the team won four series, then lost the finale in Australia, 3-2. In 1934 he sent the U.S. into the finale (a 4-1 loss to Britain) by winning the decisive fifth match, 6-4, 6-2, 6-4, over Viv McGrath to clinch a 3-2 victory over Australia at Wimbledon. It was the only time the U.S. came back from 0-2 to win a Cup tie.

Shields was born in New York Nov. 18, 1909, and died there Aug. 19, 1975. Movie and television actress Brooke Shields is his granddaughter. He was inducted into the Hall of Fame in 1964.

DAVIS CUP–*1931, 1932, 1934; record: 16-6 in singles, 3-0 in doubles.* **SINGLES RECORD IN THE MAJORS**–*French (2-1), Wimbledon (14-3), U.S. (37-23).*

PAM SHRIVER

United States (1962–)
Hall of Fame 2002

Few have made as spectacular a debut in a major championship as 16-year-old Pamela Howard Shriver at the U.S. Open in 1978. A tall schoolgirl amateur with a big racket, big ambition, she had no inhibition about charging the net and bringing down such as the

Wimbledon champion, Martina Navratilova. She was the first to go to the final in her first U.S. since the champ of 1937, Chilean Anita Lizana.

Presently Pam and Martina—voracious volleyers—would join forces to inscribe the greatest doubles numbers in the history of the female game: A Grand Slam in 1984, 20 major championships, a 109-match winning streak, 79 titles together.

Everything was new in 1978. The Flushing Meadow complex, hard courts, the oversized Prince racket in her right hand and the 6-foot kid with short curly hair and dimples who was called the 'Great Whomping Crane.'

Ten years before, Arthur Ashe had been the lone amateur to win the Open. Pam, 16th seeded, the greenest ever to attain the title round (five months younger than 1979 champ Tracy Austin), came within one victory of equaling him, after beating top-seeded Navratilova in the semis, a mammoth upset. However, Chris Evert fought off her fast-forward forays in the final, 7-5, 6-4. Lustrous as her 20-year career was, containing 21 singles and 94 doubles titles (one of five women winning more than 100 overall), a position in the World Top Ten nine times and an Olympic gold medal, Pam never made it to the singles final of a major again.

But she was no stranger to the winners' circle in the highest doubles neighborhoods. Besides the 20 with Navratilova she won two other majors: The U.S. with Natalia Zvereva in 1991 and the French mixed with Emilio Sanchez in 1987. She and Martina also won the season-ending championship at Madison Square Garden a record 10 times between 1981 and 1991.

An effervescent personality, sharp-witted, Pam was in her element at press conferences as well as on the court, and now makes her mark as a tennis TV commentator. Not an exceptional athlete—"I ran like a duck"—she made up for that with smarts and heart. A preppy in Lutherville, Md., she had her sights on college "with no thought to playing tennis for a living." But one of the old Aussie gang, teaching pro Don Candy, giving her lessons, saw the future when she was 14, and counseled her and her parents to be prepared for everyone's life to change. He was convinced, "She'll make it as a career."

So she did. "After that first Open everything moved so fast. I turned pro in '79. No college plans," she recalls. "I was out in the tough working women's world. I'm glad, but it took a while for me to catch up with myself, to handle the attention, the publicity, travel and injuries."

It was a "startling" phone call from Navratilova in 1980 that would propel her upward among the game's goddesses. "She asked me to be her doubles partner. I couldn't believe it."

They went together like ice cream and cake, Pam in the right court (though occasionally they switched). Their 20 majors between 1981 and 1989 caught up with Margaret Osborne duPont and Louise Brough's record total amassed between 1942 and 1957. First was Wimbledon, 1981, over Anne Smith and Kathy Jordan, where they also ruled in 1982-83-84, 1986. The remainder: Australian, 1982-83-84-85, (no tourney in 1986), 1987-88-89; French, 1984-85, 1987-88; U.S., 1983-84, 1986-87. They lost two finals, both in 1985, the U.S. and Wimbledon, to Kathy Jordan and Liz Sayers Smylie, 5-7, 6-3, 6-4, concluding their 109 match procession that included 22 wins during their 1984 Slam. Within the streak they won eight successive majors.

Pam, whose career W-L record in singles was 625-270, treasures most the two wins over Navratilova at the U.S. (1978, 1982, 7-6, 6-2), and victories over Chris Evert in the Canadian Open semis of 1987, and Steffi Graf at Madison Square Garden in the season-ending Virginia Slims Championships of 1988. "I was 0-18 against Chrissie before that win, and I beat Zina Garrison in the final, my biggest title, at the Garden, where I also beat Evert. I was never more focused. It was Steffi's Grand Slam and gold medal year." But she fell to Gabriela Sabatini in the final, 7-5, 6-2, 6-2.

Probably her most emotional triumph was the Olympic gold medal final in Seoul, allied with Garrison in a tremendous battle with Czechs Helena Sukova and Jana Novotna. Winning 4-6, 6-2, 10-8, Pam and Zina clung to each other weeping elatedly.

She was in the World Top Ten from 1980 to 1989, reaching No. 4 three times (1983, 1984, 1985) and had career winning of won $5,460,566. Her career doubles W-L record was 622-122. Born July 4, 1962, at Baltimore, she is married to Australian actor (a James Bond portrayer), George Lazenby, and was raised to the Hall in 2002. She was delighted to return to Newport's Casino where she won two of her singles titles and one doubles on the historic lawn.

MAJOR TITLES *(21)–Australian doubles, 1982, 1983, 1984, 1985, 1987, 1988, 1989; French doubles, 1984, 1985, 1987, 1989; Wimbledon doubles, 1981, 1982, 1983, 1984, 1986; U.S. doubles, 1983, 1984, 1986, 1987, 1991.* **FED CUP**–*1986, 1987, 1989, 1992; record: 4-0 in singles, 14-1 in doubles.* **SINGLES RECORD IN THE MAJORS**–*Australian(31-16), French (2-2), Wimbledon (40-16), U.S. (44-18).*

HENRY SLOCUM

United States (1862–1949)
Hall of Fame 1955

A football and tennis player at Yale, Henry Warner Slocum played in the first Intercollegiate Championships, in 1883, as partner of the great footballer, Walter Camp. He took time out from his New York law practice to refine his tennis (to the disapproval of his father), and on his fourth try at the U.S. title in Newport, 1887, he beat Howard Taylor, 12-10, 7-5, 6-4, in the all-comers final, only to become Dick Sears' last championship victim in the challenge round, 6-1, 6-3, 6-2.

But in 1888 he trained harder, and the players showed, he said, "more than the usual keenness" because Sears had announced he wouldn't defend. In the all-comers final, to decide the championship, Slocum, a 5-foot-10, 150-pound right-hander, was sharper against the quick 5-foot-4 Taylor, and became the second champion of the U.S., 6-4, 6-1, 6-0. He successfully defended in 1889 over lefty Quincy Shaw, 6-3, 6-1, 4-6, 6-2.

That year he and Taylor beat Valentine Hall and Oliver Campbell for the doubles crown, 6-1, 6-3, 6-2. It was Slocum's third time in the doubles final. He lost in 1885 with Percy Knapp and 1887 with Ollie Taylor. But Slocum, 28, was overtaken by collegian Campbell, 19, in the 1890 challenge round, 6-2, 4-6, 6-3, 6-1.

Slocum had realized his tennis ambitions, and immersed himself in law. But he returned to Newport for an 1892 cameo, registering one of the Championships' rare triple bagels—6-0, 6-0, 6-0, over W. N. Ryerson. He was back again 11 years later to play nine times between 1903 and 1913 when he made his last appearance, at 51, beating future World War I flying hero and Massachusetts Congressman Larry Curtis, 6-3, 6-2, 6-3, and losing to future finalist (1921), 24-year-old Wallace Johnson, 6-1, 6-3, 6-3. For his U.S. career, covering 29 years (1884-1913), the remarkably durable Slocum had a 26-14 singles record. In the 1888 quarters, he gave the godfather, James Dwight, 36, his last singles defeat, 4-6, 6-3, 6-0, 6-2. Five straight years, from 1886, he was in the U.S. Top Ten, No. 1 in 1888 and 1889. Slocum was born May 28, 1862, died Jan. 22, 1949, and entered the Hall of Fame in 1955. He was president of the USTA, 1892-93.

MAJOR TITLES *(3)–U.S. singles, 1888, 1889; U.S. doubles, 1889.* **SINGLES RECORD IN THE MAJORS**–*U.S. (26-14).*

STAN SMITH

United States (1946–)
Hall of Fame 1987

One of the great Davis Cup competitors, Stan Smith added the U.S. (1971) and Wimbledon (1972) titles to his laurels, and, with Bob Lutz, was part of one of the preeminent doubles teams. Smith, who overcame teenage awkwardness to become a feared 6-foot-3 foe with crashing serves and volleys, may have hit his zenith on alien clay. That was in Bucharest in 1972 as the U.S. won a fifth consecutive Cup, and he supplied the clinching victory—the insuperable third point—for a fifth time. That's a Davis Cup record to which he added in 1979, with Lutz, in the 5-0 victory over Italy at San Francisco.

Stan was in at the finish of seven Cup victories, tying him with Bill Tilden for a U.S. high. And he had a smaller share of an eighth Cup, in 1981, when he and Lutz took a doubles over Ivan Lendl and Tom Smid—the Cup adieu for Stan and Bob, at Flushing Meadow—in the win over Czechoslovakia en route to the final.

A notable sportsman, he had to "concentrate so hard I got a headache," he said after the three-day ordeal at the hands of a loud partisan crowd and overly patriotic line judges in Bucharest. It was an extended, rocky campaign during which Smith won seven of eight singles and, with Erik van Dillen, all five doubles. Stan scored the clinching point in each of five matches and nailed down two of the most dramatic singles victories ever by an American in the finale. Romania, loser to the U.S. in the 1969 and 1971 showdowns, appeared the favorite on home earth, but Smith shocked Ilie Nastase on the slow court to lead off, and then out-battled the sly, combative Ion Tiriac in a tense five-set struggle.

Knowing that he had to hit outright winners well away from the lines to make sure of the points, Smith did just that to storm through a last-set bagel and send the U.S. safely ahead, 3-1, in the 3-2 victory.

Born Dec. 14, 1946, in Pasadena, Calif., he grew up there and was an All-American at the University of Southern California, where he won the U.S. Intercollegiate singles (1968) and, with Lutz, doubles in 1967 and 1968.

During an 11-year Davis Cup career that began in 1968, embracing 24 engagements, he was on the winning side 22 times, and 16 times provided the clinching point: Three times in singles, 13 times in doubles (nine with Lutz, four with van Dillen). He and Lutz won 13 of 14 Cup matches together. As the U.S. ran up a record Cup streak of 17 victories from 1968 to the finale of 1973, Smith was involved in 14, the clincher in 12.

His 1972 Wimbledon triumph over Nastase, 4-6, 6-3, 6-3, 4-6, 7-5, was one of the outstanding finals, and his 1971 defeat of Jan Kodes at Forest Hills, 3-6, 6-3, 6-2, 7-6 (5-3), was the first U.S. final to conclude in a tie-breaker. Smith and Lutz won the U.S. doubles four times, the Australian once. In a career spanning the amateur and open eras, he was one of five centurions, winning at least 100 pro titles overall in singles and doubles. Stan hit the century with 39 singles, 61 doubles, and made $1,774,881 in career prize money. Eleven times between 1967 and 1980 he was in the U.S. Top Ten, No. 1 four years, 1969, 1971, 1972 and 1973. Six straight times from 1970 he was in the World Top Ten, No. 1 in 1972.

Stan entered the Hall of Fame in 1987. He served in the U.S. Army.

MAJOR TITLES *(7)–Wimbledon singles, 1972; U.S. singles, 1971; Australian doubles, 1970; U.S. doubles, 1968, 1974, 1978, 1980.* **OTHER U.S. TITLES** *(15)–Indoor singles, 1972; Indoor doubles, 1966, 1969 with Bob Lutz; 1970, with Arthur Ashe; Clay Court doubles, 1968, with Lutz; Hard Court singles, 1966, 1967, 1968; Hard Court doubles, 1966, with Lutz; Pro doubles, 1973, with Erik van Dillen; 1974, 1977, with Bob Lutz; Intercollegiate singles, 1968; Intercollegiate doubles, 1967, 1968 with Lutz.* **DAVIS CUP**–*1968, 1969, 1970, 1971, 1972, 1973, 1975, 1977, 1979, 1981; record; 15-5 in singles, 20-3 in doubles.* **SINGLES RECORD IN THE MAJORS**–*Australian (5-3), French (23-9), Wimbledon (45-17), U.S. (39-19).*

MARGARET SMITH COURT

Australia (1942–)
Hall of Fame 1979

For sheer strength of performance and accomplishment there has never been a tennis player to match Margaret Smith Court. As the most prolific winner of major championships, she rolled up 62 titles in singles, doubles and mixed doubles between 1960 and 1975, and took the Australian, French, Wimbledon and U.S. singles all within 1970 for the second female Grand Slam. She is the only player to achieve a Slam in doubles as well as in singles; Margaret and fellow Aussie Ken Fletcher won the four titles in mixed in 1963.

Her closest rivals statistically are not close: Martina Navratilova with 57 majors, and Roy Emerson heading the men with 28. Court has 24 alone in singles, two ahead of Steffi Graf.

From the country town of Albury in New South Wales, where she was born July 16, 1942, Margaret was one of the first Australian notables to be developed outside of the principal cities. Tall and gangling, nearly six feet, she worked hard in the gym and on the road, as well as on-court, to attain coordination and marshal her prodigious strength. She was self-made through determination and training. Her power and incredible reach ("I call her The Arm," said rival Billie Jean King) first paid off and called international attention to her when she won the Australian singles at 18 in 1960, 7-5, 6-2, over countrywoman Jan Lehane. It was the first of her record 11 conquests of her homeland, the first seven in a row.

In 1961 she traveled abroad for the first time and played in her first Wimbledon final, the doubles that she and Lehane lost to Karen Hantze and a budding star, Billie Jean Moffitt (King).

Margaret was to win three Wimbledon, five French, and seven U.S. singles championships, and the greatest of those victories was probably the 1970 Wimbledon final. In considerable pain with a sprained ankle, she held off Billie Jean, 14-12, 11-9, in possibly the finest of female finals there, and certainly the longest in point of games, 46 (two more than the Suzanne Lenglen-Dorothea Chambers record in 1919).

She retired briefly upon marrying Barry Court in 1967, but was soon back on the trail of championships. Margaret was remarkable in that she continued to win major titles, such as the U.S. in 1973, after the birth of her first of three children, and was still competing at age 34 in 1977. She was shy, soft-spoken. Late in her career, she became a lay minister.

Court was primarily an attacker, basing her game on a heavy serve and volley, and relying on athleticism and endurance. She could conquer with ground strokes, though, as she demonstrated in stopping clay court terror Chris Evert in the splendid French final of 1973, 6-7 (5-7), 7-6 (8-6), 6-4. Sometimes Court fell prey to nerves, as in her 1971 Wimbledon final defeat by the crowd's favorite, Evonne Goolagong; or the bizarre televised challenge by 55-year-old Bobby Riggs in 1973, which she lost implausibly and badly. She couldn't reach the inspirational heights of her chief foe, King, but held a lifetime edge over Billie Jean, 22-10.

Her Grand Slam year, 1970, makes those of Maureen Connolly, 1953 (12 tournaments), and Steffi Graf, 1988 (14 tournaments), seem almost leisurely. Court won 21 of 27 tournaments on a 104-6 match record, earning $14,800 for the four titles while Graf's prize money take for the four was $877,724. Connolly was an amateur, and certainly several of Court's best years were as such during an 18-year career. As an amateur she had such years as 1962 (winning 13 of 15 tournaments on a 67-2 match record) and 1964 (13 of 16 on 67-2, including a 39-match winning streak).

She won 79 pro singles titles, had her last sensational season in 1973, winning 18 of 25 tourneys on 102-6, among them the Australian, French and U.S. Altogether, amateur and pro, she won a whopping 194 singles titles, almost beyond imagination. Representing Australia six times in the worldwide Federation Cup team competition, she played in the first in 1963 (a final-round defeat by the U.S.) and spearheaded Cup victories in 1964-65, 1968, 1971, and was undefeated in 22 singles.

Tapped for the Hall of Fame in 1979, Court was born a left-hander. She was transformed to a right-handed player (like two other Famers, Maureen Connolly and Ken Rosewall), as frequently happened in that era. She had the best two-season run in history, 1969-70, with seven majors, missing out only at Wimbledon, 1969, where she lost in the semis to champion Ann Jones, 10-12, 6-3, 6-2. That defeat, as well as a first-round loss at Wimbledon to King in 1962, a final-round loss to Lesley Turner at the French in 1965, and a semi-final loss at Wimbledon to Evert in 1973—her only major losses those years—may have cost her four additional Grand Slams.

She scored triples (singles, doubles, mixed titles) at the Australian in 1963, Wimbledon and the U.S. in 1970. She won her first major, Australian singles, in 1960 and last, U.S. doubles, in 1975, and between 1961 and 1975 was in the World Top Ten 13 times, No. 1 seven times: 1962-63-64-65, 1969-70), 1973), two behind Helen Wills Moody's record. Her career, overlapping the amateur and open eras, yielded $550,000 in prize money.

MAJOR TITLES (62)–*Australian singles, 1960, 1961, 1962, 1963, 1964, 1965, 1966, 1969, 1970, 1971, 1973; French singles, 1962, 1964, 1969, 1970, 1973; Wimbledon singles, 1963, 1965, 1970; U.S. singles, 1962, 1965, 1969, 1970, 1973; Australian doubles, 1961, 1962, 1963, 1965, 1969, 1970, 1971, 1973; French doubles, 1964, 1965, 1966, 1973; Wimbledon doubles, 1964, 1969; U.S. doubles, 1963, 1968, 1970, 1973, 1975; Australian mixed, 1963, 1964; French mixed, 1963, 1964, 1965, 1969; Wimbledon mixed, 1963, 1965, 1966, 1968, 1975; U.S. mixed, 1961, 1962, 1963, 1964, 1965, 1969, 1970, 1972.* **FEDERATION CUP**–*1963, 1964, 1965, 1968, 1969, 1971; record: 22-0 in singles, 15-5 in doubles.* **SINGLES RECORD IN THE MAJORS**–*Australian (60-3), French (20-1), Wimbledon (51-9), U.S. (51-6).*

FRED STOLLE
Australia (1938–)
Hall of Fame 1985

A loose-limbed, slender 6-foot-3 blond, Frederick Sydney Stolle had his Wimbledon singles frustrations, but overflowed with success everywhere else as one of the overpowering phalanx of Aussies in the 1960s and 1970s. Known as 'Fiery Fred' or 'Fiery' to his teammates for his outspoken competitiveness, he became also known as the 'Old Hacker' at the U.S. Championships of 1966. A proven grass-court player for some time, member of winning Australian Davis Cup teams, and thrice Wimbledon runner-up (1963, 1964, 1965), he was outraged on arriving at Forest Hills, fresh from winning the German title, to find himself unseeded.

"I guess they think I'm just an old hacker," said he, almost 28. Then he proceeded to win the title, the second unseeded man to do so, over unseeded John Newcombe, chortling, "Well, I guess the Old Hacker can still play a bit."

He had won the French in 1965, showing that he could be patient at the baseline, too, although his strengths were a high-velocity serve, stinging volleys and a splendid backhand. These paid off in his 16 major doubles titles. He is one of 11 men to win all four majors, and had his greatest success with Bob Hewitt (two Wimbledons, two Australian), Roy Emerson (two U.S. and an Australian), Ken Rosewall (a U.S. and French).

As a member of three victorious Australian Davis Cup teams, 1964, 1965 and 1966, he scored his most memorable win the first year in the Cup round at Cleveland, 7-5, 6-3, 3-6, 9-11, 6-4, over Dennis Ralston. Down a break in the fifth, with his side trailing the U.S. 2-1, Stolle pulled it out so that Emerson could win the Cup-lifting clincher over Chuck McKinley. Perhaps his lead-off win in the following year's Cup finale meant more since it came in his hometown, Sydney, and he had to dig himself from a very deep hole to beat the Spanish ace, Manolo Santana, 10-12, 3-6, 6-1, 6-4, 7-5, to send the Aussies on their way.

His career spanned the amateur and open eras, and he was in the World Top Ten four years, starting with 1963, No. 2 in 1964 and 1966. He turned pro in 1967, and as a pro won two singles and 13 doubles titles, and about $500,000 in career prize money. He had a last U.S. fling in 1972, at 33, beating 5th and 11th seeds Newcombe and Cliff Drysdale to gain the quarters, where he lost to the champ, Ilie Nastase, 6-4, 3-6, 6-3, 6-2.

Born Oct. 8, 1938, in Hornsby, New South Wales, Fred has worked as a teaching pro, was player-coach of the title-winning New York Apples of World Team Tennis in 1976 and 1977, and of Australia 10 times (5-5) in the since disbanded World Cup against the U.S., 1970-79. His son, Sandon, is a touring pro, and has played the major championships. For some time Fred has been a successful television commentator on tennis. He entered the Hall of Fame in 1985.

Fred won 31 amateur singles titles.

MAJOR TITLES (18)–*French singles, 1965; U.S. singles, 1966; Australian doubles, 1963, 1964, 1966; French doubles, 1965, 1968; Wimbledon doubles, 1962, 1964; U.S. doubles, 1965, 1966, 1969; Australian mixed, 1962; U.S. mixed, 1962, 1965; Wimbledon mixed, 1961, 1964, 1969.* **DAVIS CUP**–*1964, 1965, 1966; record: 10-2 in singles, 3-1 in doubles.* **SINGLES RECORD IN THE MAJORS**–*Australian (21-9), French (25-8), Wimbledon (31-12), U.S. (25-9).*

MAY SUTTON BUNDY

United States (1886–1975)
Hall of Fame 1956

Although May Godfray Sutton was, as a U.S. citizen, the first outsider from beyond the British Isles—and first American—to win Wimbledon, she had a distinct English connection. Born in Plymouth Sept. 25, 1886, daughter of a British Naval captain, Adolphus Sutton, she moved with the family at age six to a ranch outside of Pasadena, Calif. Her father built a concrete tennis court, the starting point for herself and three of her four sisters to become outstanding players. Capt. Sutton was one of the greatest tennis sires: May won Wimbledon; grandchildren Dorothy Bundy (Cheney, daughter of May) won the Australian in 1938, John Doeg (son of Violet) won the U.S. in 1930; great grandson Brian Cheney had a U.S. national ranking and played the U.S. and Wimbledon. The saying in Southern California was "It takes a Sutton to beat a Sutton" because four of them—May, Violet, Florence, Ethel—dominated that section for almost a generation through 1915.

May, a husky 5-foot-4-1/2, 140-pound, highly competitive right-hander with a powerful topspin forehand, was the best known of them, with her U.S. title of 1904, 6-1, 6-2, over defending Bessie Moore, and her two Wimbledon titles over Dorothea Douglass, in 1905 and 1907. She took the title from the Englishwoman, 6-3, 6-4, lost in the following year, and subdued Dorothea (who'd become Mrs. Lambert Chambers), 6-1, 6-4, as the two contested three successive finals. She shocked English crowds at first by rolling up her sleeves to bare her elbows, and wearing a shorter skirt than most, showing ankles.

In 1912 she married Tom Bundy, a top player who won three U.S. doubles titles (1912, 1913, 1914) with Maurice McLoughlin. Their daughter, Australian champ Dorothy Cheney, ranked as high as No. 6 in the world in 1946. Now in her 80s, she continues to win a record number of U.S. senior titles. May had her best days before U.S. rankings for women were established in 1913. But her groundstrokes were formidable enough when she made a comeback in 1921 to earn her the No. 4 ranking at age 35. That made her the third of the sisters to rank in the U.S. Top Ten—a record. Ethel was No. 2 in 1913; Florence 3, 2 and 4 in 1913, 1914 and 1915, respectively. Moreover May played Wightman Cup for the U.S. four years later and ranked No. 5 in 1928 at 42. She entered the Hall of Fame in 1956, and died Oct. 4, 1975, in Santa Monica, Calif.

MAJOR TITLES (4)–*Wimbledon singles, 1905, 1907; U.S. singles, 1904; U.S. doubles, 1904.* **OTHER U.S. TITLES** (2)–*Clay Court singles, 1912; Clay Court mixed, 1912, with Fred Harris.* **WIGHTMAN CUP**–*1925; record: 0-1 in doubles.* **SINGLES RECORD IN THE MAJORS**–*Wimbledon (14-1), U.S. (10-2).*

BILL TALBERT

United States (1918–1999)
Hall of Fame 1967

Adapting intelligently and inspiringly to life as a diabetic at a time when a quiet, unstrenuous regimen was prescribed, William Franklin Talbert became a champion. Urbane, immaculately groomed, he represented the game handsomely not only as a winning player but a Davis Cup captain and thoughtful administrator as director of the U.S. Open. Thwarted twice in U.S. singles finals, 1944 and 1945, by Frank Parker, the 5-foot-11 right-handed Talbert made his best showing in doubles in the right court alongside Gardnar Mulloy.

They were in the U.S. final six times, one short of Fred Alexander and Harold Hackett's team record, winning four, 1942, 1945, 1946 and 1948. The 1946 title was the prickliest and most noteworthy, a 74-game drama with Frank Guernsey and Don McNeill, 3-6, 6-4, 2-6, 6-3, 20-18, the longest windup set for any major final. It seemed ended numerous times, but Talbert and Mulloy kept shunning match points. Five of them came and went against Mulloy's serve (6-7, 0-40 and 10-11, 15-40). But the sixth at 13-14, 30-40 caused a great furor. Talbert, serving, sent back Guersey's return crosscourt with an angled backhand volley that looked wide to many. Guernsey and McNeill rejoiced, shaking hands. "It didn't look good for us," Talbert remembers. "But there was no call. The sidelinesman was signaling my shot was good. Barely touched the line, I guess." Play resumed. After losing a point, Talbert saved match point seven with a good serve that Guernsey netted. The next match point, 10 games later, settled it for the comebackers, and the closest of all U.S. finals was over. "There'll never be another one like that because of tie-breakers," says Talbert. He was the most instrumental in the acceptance of the elongated-set-dooming innovation at the Open in 1970, the first of his 10 years in charge. The other majors followed his lead.

Bill himself was in the U.S. doubles final nine times.

He and Mulloy won the clinching point in the Davis Cup victory over Australia in 1948 at Forest Hills, defeating Billy Sidwell and Colin Long. He was on the team six years, winning nine of 10 matches, and captained it to the victory over Australia in 1954, as well as the full seasons of 1955, 1956 and 1957 and portions of 1952 and 1953, compiling a 13-4 record.

A stylish groundstroker and excellent volleyer and tactician, he ranked in the U.S. Top Ten 13 times between 1941 and 1954, No. 2 in 1944 and 1945. He was in the World Top Ten in 1949 and 1950, No. 3 the first year. An Ohioan, born Sept. 4, 1918, in Cincinnati, he grew up there, moving to New York during his playing career. He and Margaret Osborne duPont won the U.S. mixed a record four straight years, 1943-46.

With Bruce Old, Talbert wrote definitive books, *The Game of Singles in Tennis* and *The Game of Doubles in Tennis*. He also wrote an autobiography, *Playing for Life* and a history of the U.S. men's singles championships, *Tennis Observed*. He was involved in the financial printing business for many years, and entered the Hall of Fame in 1967. He died Feb. 28, 1999 in New York City.

MAJOR TITLES *(9)–French doubles, 1950; U.S. doubles, 1942, 1945, 1946, 1948; U.S. mixed, 1943, 1944, 1945, 1946:* **OTHER U.S. TITLES** *(14)–Indoor singles, 1948, 1951; Clay Court singles, 1945; Indoor doubles, 1949, 1950, 1951, with Don McNeill; 1952, with Budge Patty; 1954, with Tony Trabert; Clay Court doubles, 1942, with Bill Reedy; 1944, 1945, with Pancho Segura; 1946, with Gardnar Mulloy; Indoor mixed, 1947, 1948, with Doris Hart.* **DAVIS CUP (As player)**–*1946, 1948, 1949, 1951, 1952, 1953; record: 2-0 in singles, 7-1 in doubles.* **(As captain)**–*1952, 1953, 1954, 1955, 1956, 1957; record: 13-4.* **SINGLES RECORD IN THE MAJORS**–*Australian o(1-1), French (5-1), Wimbledon (4-1), U.S. (46-17).*

BILL TILDEN
United States (1893–1953)
Hall of Fame 1959

If a player's value is measured by the dominance and influence he exercises over a sport, then William Tatem 'Big Bill' Tilden II could be considered the greatest player in the history of tennis.

From 1920 through 1926, he dominated the game as has no player before or since. During those years he was invincible in the United States, won Wimbledon both times he competed there, and captured 13 successive singles matches in the Davis Cup challenge round against the best players from Australia, France and Japan.

As an amateur (1912-30) he won 138 of 192 tournaments, lost 28 finals and had a 907-62 match record—a phenomenal .936 average.

His last major triumph, the Wimbledon singles of 1930, gave him a total of 10 majors, standing as the male high until topped by Roy Emerson (12) in 1967, and later Rod Laver and Bjorn Borg (11), and Pete Sampras (14). He missed another by two match points he held against René Lacoste in the 1927 French final. Bill won the U.S. mixed with Mary K. Browne in 1913–14, but had been beaten in the first round of the 1912 singles at Newport by fellow Philadelphian Wallace Johnson (whom he would defeat in the 1921 final). He didn't feel sure enough of his game to try again until 1916, in New York. He was 23, a first-round loser to a kid named Harold Throckmorton. Ignominious, tardy starts in an illustrious career that would contain seven U.S. titles and 69 match victories (a record 42 straight between 1920 and 1926).

By 1918, a war-riddled year, he got to the final, blown away by a bullet-serving Lindley Murray, 6-3, 6-1, 7-5. But he'd be back: Seven more finals in a row. In 1918 Big Bill's electrifying rivalry with Little Bill Johnston began—six U.S. finals in seven years, more than any other two men skirmished for a major. After losing to Little Bill in 1919, Tilden, disgusted with his puny defensive backhand, hid out all winter at the indoor court of a friend, J. D. E. Jones, in Providence, retooling. He emerged with a brand new, fearsome, multifaceted backhand and complete game, and was ready to conquer the world. He did not lose to Little Bill again in a U.S. final, and held an 11-6 edge in their rivalry. His concentration could be awesome, as during a two-tournament stretch in 1925 when he won 57 straight games at Glen Cove, N.Y., and Providence. Trailing Alfred Chapin, one of few to hold a win over him, 3-4 in the final, he ran it out, 6-4, 6-0, 6-0. Staying in tune on the next stop he won three straight 6-0, 6-0 matches, then 6-0, 6-1. Another 6-1 set made it 75 of 77 games.

When he first won Wimbledon, in 1920, he was 27 years old, an advanced age for a champion. But he had a long and influential career, and at the age of 52, in 1945, he was still able to push the 27-year-old Bobby Riggs to the limit in a professional match.

Tilden, a 6-foot-2 right-hander, born Feb. 10, 1893, in Philadelphia, had the ideal tennis build, 6-foot-2, 155 pounds, with thin shanks and big shoulders. He had speed and nimbleness, coordination and perfect balance. He also had marked endurance, despite smoking cigarettes incessantly when not playing. In stroke equipment, he had the weapons to launch an overpowering assault and the resources to defend and confound through a variety of spins and pace when the opponent was impervious to sheer power.

Nobody had a more devastating service than Tilden's cannonball, or a more challenging second serve than his kicking American twist. No player had a stronger combination of forehand and backhand drives, supplemented by a forehand chop and backhand slice. Tilden's mixture of shots was a revelation in his first appearance at Wimbledon. Gerald Patterson of Australia, the defending champion, found his backcourt untenable and was passed over and over when he went to the net behind his powerful service.

The backcourt was where Tilden played tennis. He was no advocate of the 'big game,' the big serve and rush for the net for the instant volley coup. He relished playing tennis as a game of chess, matching wits as well as physical powers. The drop shot, at which he was particularly adroit, and the lob were among his disconcerting weapons.

His knowledge and mastery of spin has hardly ever been exceeded, as evidenced not only on the court but also in his *Match Play and the Spin of the Ball,* a classic written more than half a century ago. Yes, Tilden was a writer, too, but he longed to be an actor above anything else. Unsuccessful in his efforts to the point of sinking most of his family wealth, his tennis earnings and his writing royalties into the theater, he was happiest when playing on the heartstrings of a tennis gallery.

Intelligent and opinionated, he was a man of strong likes and dislikes. He had highly successful friends, both men and women, who were devoted to him, and there were others who disliked him and considered him arrogant and inconsiderate of officials and ball boys who served at his matches. He was constantly wrangling with officers and committeemen of the USTA on Davis Cup policy and enforcement of the amateur rule, and in 1928 he was on the front pages of the American press when he was removed as captain and star player of the Davis Cup team, charged with violating the amateur rule with his press accounts of the Wimbledon Championships, in which he was competing. So angry were the French over the loss of the star member of the cast for the Davis Cup challenge round—the first ever held on French soil— that the American ambassador, Myron T. Herrick, interceded for the sake of good relations between the countries, and Tilden was restored to the team.

When Tilden, in the opening match, beat René Lacoste, the French gallery suffered agony and cursed themselves for insisting that '*Teel-den*' be restored to the team. It all ended happily for them, however, as the French won the other four matches and kept the Davis Cup. On Tilden's return home, he was brought up on the charges of violating the rule at Wimbledon. He was found guilty and was suspended from playing in the U.S. Championships that year.

Eligible for the U.S. title again in 1929, after the lifting of his suspension, he won it for the seventh time, defeating his doubles partner, Frank Hunter. In 1930 he won Wimbledon for the third time, at the age of 37. After the U.S. Championships, in which he was beaten in the semis by John Doeg, he notified the USTA of his intention to make a series of motion pictures for profit, thus disqualifying him for further play as an amateur. He was in the World Top Ten from 1919 through 1930, No. 1 a record six times (1920-25)—equaled by Pete Sampras in 1993—and in the U.S. Top Ten 12 straight years from 1918, No. 1 a record 10 times (1920-29). He was named to the Hall of Fame in 1959.

In 1931 he entered upon a professional playing career, joining Vinnie Richards, Hans Nusslein and Roman Najuch of Germany and Karel Kozeluh of Czechoslovakia. Tilden's name revived pro tennis, which had languished since its inception in 1926 when Suzanne Lenglen went on tour. His joining the pros paved the way for Ellsworth Vines, Fred Perry and Don Budge to leave the amateur ranks and play for big prize money. Tilden won his pro debut against Kozeluh, 6-4, 6-2, 6-4, before 13,000 fans in Madison Square Garden.

Joining promoter Bill O'Brien, Tilden toured the country in 1932 and 1933, but the Depression was on and new blood was needed. Vines furnished it. Tilden and O'Brien signed him on, and in 1934 Tilden defeated Vines in the younger man's pro debut, 8-6, 6-3, 6-2, before a turnaway crowd of 16,200 at Madison Square Garden. That year Tilden and Vines went on the first of the great tennis tours, won by Vines, 47-26.

The tours grew in the 1930s and 1940s, and Tilden remained an attraction even though he was approaching the age of 50. For years he traveled across the country, driving by day and sometimes all night and then going on a court a few hours after arriving. At times, when he was managing his tour, he had to help set the stage for the matches.

Tragically, his activity and fortunes dwindled after his conviction on a morals charge and imprisonment in 1947, and again in 1949 for parole violation (both terms less than a year). He died of a heart attack under pitiful circumstances, alone and with few resources, on June 5, 1953, in Los Angeles. His bag was packed for a trip to Cleveland to play in the U.S. Pro Championships when perhaps the greatest tennis player of them all was found dead in his room.

MAJOR TITLES (21)–*Wimbledon singles, 1920, 1921, 1930; U.S. singles, 1920, 1921, 1922, 1923, 1924, 1925, 1929; Wimbledon doubles, 1927; U.S. doubles, 1918, 1921, 1922, 1923, 1927; French mixed, 1930; U.S. mixed, 1913, 1914, 1922, 1923.* **OTHER U.S. TITLES**–*Indoor singles, 1920; Indoor doubles, 1919, 1920, with Vinnie Richards; 1926, with Frank Anderson; 1929, with Frank Hunter; Indoor mixed, 1921, 1922, with Molla Mallory, 1924, with Hazel Hotchkiss Wightman; Clay Court singles, 1918, 1922, 1923, 1924, 1925, 1926, 1927; Pro singles, 1931, 1935; Pro doubles, 1932, with Bruce Barnes; 1945, with Vinnie Richards.* **DAVIS CUP**–*1920, 1921, 1922, 1923, 1924, 1925, 1926, 1927, 1928, 1929, 1930; record: 25-5 singles, 9-2 in doubles.* **SINGLES RECORD IN THE MAJORS**–*French (14-3), Wimbledon (30-3), U.S. (69-7).*

BERTHA TOWNSEND

United States (1869–1909)
Hall of Fame 1974

A Philadelphia-born right-hander, Bertha Louise Townsend appeared in the Championships in her hometown five times. She won in 1888, unseating original champ, Ellen Hansell, in the challenge round, 6-3, 6-5. She fought off the challenge of Lida Vorhees, 7-5, 6-3, to become the first repeating female champ, but then fell to Ellen Roosevelt, 6-2, 6-2, in the 1890 challenge round.

She reappeared, married, in 1894, to reach the final of the all-comers, losing 6-2, 7-5 to Helen Hellwig, who became champion. The following year she was a semi-finalist, and that ended her career with an 8-3 U.S. singles record.

She was born March 7, 1869, died May 12, 1909, in Haverford, Pa. as Mrs. Harry Toulmin, and was inducted into the Hall of Fame in 1974.

MAJOR TITLES (2)–*U.S. singles, 1888, 1889.* **SINGLES RECORD IN THE MAJORS**–*U.S. (8-3).*

TONY TRABERT

United States (1930–)
Hall of Fame 1970

One of the finest seasons ever achieved was the 1955 of Tony Trabert, who won three of the Big Four singles titles—Wimbledon, French, and U.S.—to earn acclaim as the No. 1 amateur of that year. Only two other men, Don Budge (1938) and Rod Laver (1962 and 1969), en route to their Grand Slams, have won those three uppermost championships within a calendar year.

Moreover, Trabert also won the U.S. Indoor and U.S. Clay Court titles, adding them to the pre-eminent American championships on grass at Forest Hills.

For that year, probably the most productive ever by an American man—30 titles—he won 18 of 23 singles tourneys on a 106-7 match record. Included was a winning streak of 36 matches. He also won 12 doubles titles (with Vic Seixas).

An exceptional athlete, Marion Anthony Trabert was born Aug. 16, 1930, in Cincinnati, where he grew up. He was a standout basketball player at the University of Cincinnati, for which he also won the U.S. Intercollegiate singles title in 1951.

The French Championships has traditionally been the most difficult battleground for American men. Trabert won five titles in Paris, the singles in 1954 and 1955. It was 34 years before another American, Michael Chang, won in 1989. Trabert also won the doubles in 1950 (with Bill Talbert) and in 1954 and 1955 (with Vic Seixas). Only a defeat by Ken Rosewall (the eventual champ) in the semi-finals of the Australian Championships ruined Trabert's chance at a Grand Slam in 1955.

For five years Trabert was a mainstay of the U.S. Davis Cup team, along with Seixas. In each of those years the U.S. reached the challenge round finale, and Trabert's best-remembered match may have been a defeat, a tremendous struggle against Lew Hoad on a rainy afternoon in 1953 at Melbourne. Hoad won out, 7-5, in the fifth, and Australia kept the Cup. However,

Trabert and Seixas returned to Australia a year later, where Trabert beat Hoad on the opening day in singles and he and Seixas won the doubles over Hoad and Rex Hartwig in a 3-2 triumph, the only U.S. seizure of the Cup from the Aussies during an eight-year stretch.

Though an attacker with a powerful backhand and strong volley, the competitive right-hander also had exceptional groundstrokes. In winning the U.S. singles at Forest Hills twice, 1953 and 1955, and Wimbledon, 1955, he did not lose a set, a rare feat.

Amassing 13 U.S. titles in singles and doubles, he was one of two Americans (the other was Art Larsen) to win singles championships on all four surfaces: Grass at Forest Hills, indoor, clay court and hard court.

Following the custom of the time, Trabert, as the top amateur, signed on with the professionals to challenge the ruler, Pancho Gonzalez, on a head-to-head tour in 1956. Gonzalez won, 74-27. Trabert was runner-up to Alex Olmedo for the U.S. Pro singles title in 1960, having won the doubles with Hartwig in 1956.

When his playing career ended, Trabert worked as a teaching pro and as a television commentator on tennis. In 1976 he returned to the Davis Cup scene as the U.S. captain, leading the Cup-winning teams of 1978 and 1979.

He had four years in the U.S. and World Top Ten, 1951, 1953, 1954 and 1955, No. 1 in each in 1953 and 1955, before turning pro. His amateur career was interrupted by service in the U.S. Navy. He was named to the Hall of Fame in 1970.

MAJOR TITLES (10)–French singles, 1954, 1955; Wimbledon singles, 1955; U.S. singles, 1953, 1955; Australian doubles, 1955; French doubles, 1950, 1954, 1955; U.S. doubles, 1954. OTHER U.S. TITLES (13)–Intercollegiate singles, 1951; Indoor singles, 1955; Clay Court singles, 1951, 1955; Hard Court singles, 1953; Indoor doubles, 1954, with Bill Talbert; 1955, with Vic Seixas; Clay Court doubles, 1951, 1955, with Hamilton Richardson; 1954, with Seixas; Hard Court doubles, 1950, 1953, with Tom Brown; Pro doubles, 1956, with Rex Hartwig. DAVIS CUP (As player)–1951, 1952, 1953, 1954, 1955; record: 16-5 in singles, 11-3 in doubles; (As captain)–1953, 1976, 1977, 1978, 1979, 1980; Record: 14-3, 2 Cups. SINGLES RECORD IN THE MAJORS–Australian (4-2), French (18-2), Wimbledon (13-2), U.S. (23-5).

LESLEY TURNER BOWREY

Australia (1942–)
Hall of Fame 1997

Although, as an Australian, Lesley Rosemary Turner Bowrey knew her way around extremely well on native grass courts, she achieved her foremost feats far from home, in Paris. Dealing with a surface very foreign to Aussies, she showed superior movement, grit and groundstrokes to triumph twice on clay in the French singles at Stade Roland Garros, 1963 and 1965. She would have owned a trifecta had she cashed a match point against Margaret Smith (Court) in the 1962 final, losing, 6-3, 3-6, 7-5. The next year Lesley won, bouncing back against twice-champ, English lefty Ann Haydon Jones, 2-6, 6-3, 7-5. Two years later she repeated, this time over countrywoman Smith, who was by then No. 1. Her fourth time in the final, 1967, was a close call, loss to homebody Françoise Durr. "At least I made the French happy," she says, knowing they hadn't enjoyed one of their own as champion in 38 years (Simone Passemard Mathieu).

On her first trip abroad, an 18-year-old in the spring of 1961, Turner discovered her affinity for continental earth, going to the Italian final, a 6-4, 6-4, defeat by No. 1 Maria Bueno. She and compatriot Jan Lehane won the doubles, an accomplishment she equaled in 1964 with Smith, and 1967 with Rosie Casals. Rome, too, had become a gleeful hunting ground. After losing two more finals, to Smith in 1963 and 1964, Lesley got back at both her conquerors, beating Bueno for the 1967 title, and Margaret (now Mrs. Court) for the crown in 1968. Her five finals were the tourney record until Chris Evert's sixth and seventh, 1982 and 1984.

She was unable to win her homeland's title in singles, falling in the 1964 final to Smith and in the final of 1967 to American Nancy Richey. In 1967 Lesley hooked up with Aussie Bill Bowrey to win the Italian mixed over Durr and Frew McMillan. It was such a good lineup that they decided to make it permanent, marrying the next year. As a wedding present she won the Italian singles for him, and he reciprocated by winning the Australian singles for her. They stand as the only married couples to win important national titles in the same year. Despite her baseline preference, Lesley was a sharp volleyer, winning 11 of her 13 major championships in doubles. She led off unexpectedly during that initial round-the-world tour with a U.S. title as the pickup partner of American Darlene Hard in Boston. Freshly turned 19, Lesley, having injured her right wrist in a bathtub fall, didn't expect to play. Neither did Hard, the defender, because her usual partner, Bueno, was ill. But they got together and went all the way, beating the Mexican-German alliance of Yola Ramirez and Edda Buding.

Majors in doubles followed at the Australian, 1964 and 1967 (with Judy Tegart Dalton), 1965 (with Smith); French, 1964 and 1965 (with Smith); Wimbledon, 1964 (with Smith); Australian mixed, 1962 (with Fred Stolle) and 1967 (with Owen Davidson); Wimbledon mixed, 1961 and 1964 (with Stolle). She jump-started Davidson's mixed Grand Slam that he completed with Billie Jean King. She was a regular in the World Top Ten for six years, No. 2 in 1963.

A petite, good-natured but very determined (5-foot-4, 117-pound) right-hander out of Sydney, where she was born Aug. 16, 1942, Lesley played a strong role in Australia's Federation Cup victories in 1964 and 1965 and reaching the final of 1963. Playing four years and 13 series she was 7-3 in singles, 6-3 in doubles. Tapped for the Hall in 1997, she has long been one of Australia's leading coaches. She was named to the Australian Tennis Hall of Fame in 1998. Consistent in the majors, she was a finalist in four, and quarter-finalist or better in 21 of 30 majors she entered.

"A marvelous doubles partner," lauds Stolle. "But here's the odd, funny fact. In 1961, the first year we won the Wimbledon mixed, we were beaten in our local club's tournament."

MAJOR TITLES *(13)–French singles, 1963, 1965; Australian doubles, 1964, 1965, 1967; French doubles, 1964, 1965; Wimbledon doubles, 1964; U.S. doubles, 1961; Australian mixed, 1962, 1967; Wimbledon mixed, 1961, 1964.* **SINGLES RECORD IN THE MAJORS**–*Australian (25-9), French (34-6), Wimbledon (29-9), U.S. (11-4).* **FEDERATION CUP**–*1963, 1964, 1965, 1967; record: 7-3 in singles, 6-3 in doubles.*

JOHNNY VAN RYN

United States (1905–1999)
Hall of Fame 1963

Allison and Van Ryn were a headline combination during their bright career between 1929 and 1936 as one of the most formidable U.S. Davis Cup partnerships. Wilmer Allison and John William Van Ryn, Jr. won 14 of 16 Cup matches together, the best for Americans until Peter Fleming and John McEnroe's 14-1.

Their 24 team ties (tied with Stan Smith and Vic Seixas) are second only to McEnroe's 30 in U.S. annals. Van Ryn's 24 doubles matches and 22 wins are highs for the U.S. They beat the splendid French teams in Parisian Cup finales (Henri Cochet-Jean Borotra in 1929, Cochet-Jacques Brugnon in 1932), but could do no more than stave off France's successful defenses. A Princeton man (class of '28), Van Ryn, right-handed,

superb at the net, and returning from the right court, won the U.S. Intercollegiate doubles in 1927.

Allison and Van Ryn were in the U.S. final six times, one behind Fred Alexander and Harold Hackett's record, winning in 1931 and 1935. They also won Wimbledon in 1929, 1930 and "should've won again in '35," says the engaging Van Ryn, recalling the splendid mixture of himself and Allison, as choice as gin and vermouth. "We had a match point in the fifth set of the final against Jack Crawford and Adrian Quist. They put up a fluky little lob. My ball. Easy. But for some reason I hesitated in starting for it. Wilmer noticed, and decided he'd better take it—and missed the shot. My fault. All those years together," he smiles, "and we mess up a simple play." Van Ryn, 5-foot-10, 155 pounds, a fluid, well-rounded strokesman, remembers, "My best Wimbledon in singles was '31. I beat (fourth-seeded) Christian Boussus, got to the quarters."

In 1931 Van Ryn teamed with George Lott to win the French and Wimbledon, the only American to win the latter three successive times. He ranked in the U.S. Top Ten six times between 1927 and 1932, No. 4 in 1931 when he was a five-set quarter-final loser at Forest Hills to George Lott. He was also a quarter-finalist in 1929 and 1930, losing to Bill Tilden each time in four sets, and 1936 and 1937. In 1929 and 1931 he was in the World Top Ten. He was born June 30, 1905, in Newport News, Va., grew up in Orange, N.J. He was once married to Marjorie Gladman, also an excellent doubles player, and in 1930 and 1931 they were the first of four married couples to be ranked together in the U.S. singles Top Ten, he Nos. 9 and 4, she 7 and 8. Van Ryn was taken into the Hall of Fame in 1963, and died Aug. 7, 1999.

MAJOR TITLES *(6)–French doubles, 1931; Wimbledon doubles, 1929, 1930, 1931; U.S. doubles, 1931, 1935.* **OTHER U.S. TITLES** *(2)–Indoor doubles, 1932, with George Lott; Intercollegiate doubles, 1927, with Kenneth Appel.* **DAVIS CUP**–*1929, 1930, 1931, 1932, 1933, 1934, 1935, 1936; record: 7-1 in singles, 22-2 in doubles.* **SINGLES RECORD IN THE MAJORS**–*Australian (1-1), French (4-1), Wimbledon (13-6), U.S. (29-15).*

GUILLERMO VILAS

Argentina (1952–)
Hall of Fame 1991

Seldom has a player found such empathy beyond his own borders as did Guillermo Vilas, the 'Young Bull of the Pampas,' during his pro career. As the foremost Latin American male, he is the only Argentine to be tapped for the Hall of Fame (1991), and the first to win major titles (four of them).

The burly 5-foot-11, 175-pound left-hander captivated audiences everywhere with his sportsmanship and sensitivity of a poet—which he is. An appealing headbanded figure of the 1970s and early 1980s, his chestnut hair flowing below his shoulders, Vilas was the epitome of strength and fitness, endurance and patience on court, outlasting opponents from the baseline with his high-rolling top-spinning strokes—hour after hour, a destructive metronome.

His 1977 was a monumental year in the game's history: He won 17 of 33 tournaments (tying Rod Laver's record) on a record of 145 match wins against 14 losses. Among his souvenirs were an open-era winning streak record of 50 matches and the French and U.S. titles. His streak, begun after Wimbledon, was stopped at Aix-en-Provence in September by Ilie Nastase, who used one of the controversial 'spaghetti' rackets that produced weird strokes and bounces. Vilas quit in disgust; such rackets were shortly banned.

Although he reveled in the backcourt, Vilas startled Jimmy Connors with volleying forays that turned the U.S. Open his way, and set off a wild celebration after he'd won the last championship match in the 54-year-old Forest Hills Stadium, 2-6, 6-3, 7-6 (7-4), 6-0. Joyous fans carried him on victory laps within the concrete arena, as though he were a triumphant bullfighter.

Though grass seemed anathema to the clay-loving Villas, he did win the Australian twice (1978 and 1979) and the Masters of 1974 at the same place, Melbourne's Kooyong. Perhaps he wasn't a serve-volley smoothie, but his Australian Open record is excellent: Two titles plus a final-round loss to Roscoe Tanner in 1977, and a 16-match streak to a semis loss to Kim Warwick in 1980, 6-7, 6-4, 6-2, 2-6, 6-4.

As Argentina's foremost Davis Cupper he took great satisfaction in bulwarking three American Zone wins over the U.S. (1977, 1980, 1983). Vilas won all six of his singles on the Buenos Aires loam, including victories over John McEnroe the last two years. In 1981 he led Argentina to the Cup round, a narrow 3-1 defeat by the U.S. in Cincinnati where, in the fifth set, Guillermo actually served for an improbable doubles victory at 7-6, and an unrealized 2-1 lead (with Jose-Luis Clerc) against McEnroe and Peter Fleming. Vilas and Clerc were hardly a team, or doubles players; McEnroe and Fleming were the best. But the match, lost 6-3, 4-6, 6-4, 4-6,

11-9, showed Guillermo's heart and desire on behalf of his homeland.

He was in four French finals, but couldn't get past the Swedes, losing to Bjorn Borg in 1975 and 1978 and, wearing down before 17-year-old Mats Wilander in 1982. It was his last major final in a career that landed him in fifth place among the all-time pro winners headed by Connors: 62 singles titles, even with Borg. His career prize money amounted to $4,904,922. It was in Paris, 1973, that he first gained notice, removing defending champ Andres Gimeno from the French in the second round, 6-2, 5-7, 8-6.

Beginning in 1974 he graced the World Top Ten for nine straight years, No. 2 in 1977. He was born Aug. 17, 1952, in Mar del Plata, Argentina, where he grew up.

MAJOR TITLES (4)–*Australian singles, 1978, 1979; French singles, 1977; U.S. singles, 1977.* **DAVIS CUP**–*1970, 1971, 1972, 1973, 1975, 1976, 1977, 1978, 1979, 1980, 1981, 1982, 1983, 1984; record: 45-10 in singles, 12-14 in doubles.* **SINGLES RECORD IN THE MAJORS**–*Australian (23-3), French (56-17), Wimbledon (15-11), U.S. (43-14).*

ELLSWORTH VINES
United States (1911–1994)
Hall of Fame 1962

One night in 1930, an 18-year-old lad sat in a rocking chair on the porch of the Peninsula Inn in Seabright, N.J., looking out to sea and thinking that his tennis dreams were shattered. "I guess I'm just a flash in the pan like they say," said Henry Ellsworth Vines, Jr.

Weeks earlier, they had been calling him another California Comet, a lanky youth with the kick of a mule in his cannonball service that terrorized the Eastern grass-court circuit. Vines, a right-hander born Sept. 29, 1911 in Los Angeles, ambled along mournfully like slow molasses when he wasn't in hot pursuit of a tennis ball. On the court he was devastating, wherefore came the comparisons to the original California Comet, Maurice McLoughlin.

The Southern California champ and a cornstalk at 6-foot-2, 143 pounds, Vines had easily disposed of two of the better Americans, Frank Hunter and Frank Shields, at Seabright. However, he lost the final to Sidney Wood, unable to cope with Wood's seemingly innocuous game of moderate strokes, and some were saying the new Comet had burned out. It looked that way at Forest Hills, where George Lytleton Rogers beat him in the third round from two sets down. But Elly went home, won the Pacific Southwest, practiced all winter and spring against slow-ball strategy and came back east in 1931 to take the U.S. title over George Lott, winning the last two sets after trailing 5-3 in the third and 5-2 in the fourth.

His 1932 was a splendid campaign—the Wimbledon title and another U.S. in 59 minutes over Henri Cochet, after recovering in a semi-final in which he was two points from losing to Cliff Sutter. As a Davis Cup rookie Vines was 9-1, driving the U.S. to the challenge round, a 3-2 loss to France. He won four of eight tournaments, was 46-5 in matches, and ranked No. 1 in the world.

He played amateur tennis on the grass circuit only four years, 1930 through 1933, making the World Top Ten the last three of those years, and the U.S. Top Ten the first three. In 1932 and 1933, he was No. 1. In those four years Vines established at Forest Hills and Wimbledon that he had one of the best serves, if not the fastest serve ever turned loose, with almost no spin. He also had as fast and as risky a forehand as ever seen, a murderous overhead, and a skill in the volleying position to compare with the best.

Moreover, his disposition and temperament were foolproof. Where others might explode over a line call, Vines would slowly turn his head and grin at the linesman. He was a gambler on the court. He hit his forehand flat, with all his whizzing might, and closer to the net and the lines than anyone dared. At his best, he was equal to beating any player, but his margin of safety was so thin that on days when he did not have the feel and touch, his errors could be ruinous.

Wimbledon crowds marveled at the devastating fury of his attack in his straight-sets victory over Bunny Austin in the 1932 final, which ended with his 30th service ace. The ball catapulted by Austin so fast that the Briton said he did not know whether it went by on his left or his right. Don Budge marvels: "Thirty aces in 12 serving games! Considering it was against one of the finest players of the era, and a Wimbledon final, it could be the greatest serving demonstration ever."

But 1933 was a comedown. In one magnificent Wimbledon final, Elly lost his title to Jack Crawford, failing to cash numerous break points in the second set, losing it 11-9. Both Austin and Fred Perry beat him as the U.S. lost the Davis Cup semi-final in Paris, a prelude to Britain's seizing the Cup from France, and so did the mite, Bitsy Grant, in the fourth round at Forest Hills. Disgusted, Vines could not wait to cut the gut from his rackets and leave for home, his tennis career as an amateur soon to end.

He signed a professional contract to go on tour with Bill Tilden and lost their opening match, 8-6, 6-3, 6-2, before 16,200 fans at Madison Square Garden. But Vines ultimately carved a 47-26 edge in matches with the aging Tilden. One match in the Garden between Vines and Perry drew 17,630 spectators. He was the No. 1 pro through 1937, winning the Wembley World Pro title over Tilden (1935) and Hans Nusslein (1934, 1936).

Near the end of the decade, Vines' interest in tennis waned. He turned to golf and became the best golfer of top tennis players. For years he was a teaching pro, one good enough to reach the semi-finals of the 1951 PGA Championship.

He was enshrined in the Hall of Fame in 1962, and died March 17, 1994. In 1977 he attended the Wimbledon Centenary as one of the former champions receiving commemorative medals. He had turned out to be much, much more than a flash in the pan.

MAJOR TITLES *(6)–Wimbledon singles, 1932; U.S. singles, 1931, 1932; Australian doubles, 1933; U.S. doubles, 1932; U.S. mixed, 1933.* **OTHER U.S. TITLES**–*Clay Court singles, 1931; Clay Court doubles, 1931, with Keith Gledhill; Pro singles, 1939.* **DAVIS CUP**–*1932, 1933; record: 13-3 in singles.* **SINGLES RECORD IN THE MAJORS**– *Australian (2-1), Wimbledon (13-1), U.S. (16-2).*

BARON GOTTFRIED VON CRAMM

Germany (1909–1976)
Hall of Fame 1977

If any player was the prince charming of tennis, he was Gottfried von Cramm, a baron of the German nobility, six feet tall with blond hair, green eyes and a magnetism that, in the words of Don Budge, "made him dominate any scene he was part of." The most accomplished tennis player Germany had known, von Cramm must be one of the finest players never to have won Wimbledon—he was runner-up three years in a row, to Fred Perry in 1935 and 1936, and to Budge in 1937.

Von Cramm, known as The Baron, was also runner-up to Budge in 1937 for the U.S. Championship and again to Budge in what has been termed the greatest Davis Cup match ever played, the fifth and deciding one in the 1937 semi-final. Budge came from 1-4 and had match point five times before he hit the final shot (8-6), racing across the court beyond the alley, and he lay sprawled on the ground as the umpire declared the United States to be winner.

Said The Baron as he stood at the net waiting for Budge to pick himself up: "Don, this was absolutely the finest match I have ever played in my life. I'm very happy I could have played it against you, whom I like so much. Congratulations." The next moment, their arms were around each other.

Von Cramm, a right-hander, was born July 7, 1909, at Nettlingen, Hanover, Germany. He was noted for his endurance and tenacity. In recalling their thrilling Cup match, Budge related how he put four of his best first serves in play, in succession, and all four came back as von Cramm winners.

Few have endured what he did in taking the first of his two French titles in 1934. Five-set matches were the rule and he fought through four of them (of six), and snatched a match point away from Jack Crawford to win the final. Two years later another five-setter was his ticket to victory over the No. 1 Fred Perry, starting and ending with astounding set scores of 6-0. But Perry beat him in 1935 and 1936, as Budge did in 1937 so von Cramm lost three straight Wimbledon finals, a record for frustration he shares with Herbert Lawford (1884-86) and Fred Stolle (1963-65). He won six German titles, 1932-35, and two more—remarkably—after the war, the last at age 40.

But that wasn't the last that aficionados heard of The Baron. He had always loved representing the Fatherland in Davis Cup, was saddened by the Nazi takeover, and elated when the tennis community welcomed back a democratic Germany in 1951. He played three Davis Cups, leading Germany in 1951 to four wins and the final of the European zone with a 9-1 singles record, beating men half his age such as Dane Kurt Nielsen, a future Wimbledon runner-up. In 1953, at 44, he returned to Paris to say adieu in defeat by France, registering the last of his 58 Cup singles wins over Paul Remy, 30. He was a Cup centurion, one of only 14 who played more than 100 matches (111). His most productive year was 1935: 11-1 in singles, 4-1 in doubles. In 1937, the year he came so close to winning it, he was 7-2 in singles, 4-1 in doubles.

Popular everywhere he went, von Cramm delighted Americans in 1937 as a U.S. champ and runner-up finalist to Budge at Forest Hills and doubles victor with Henner Henkel over Budge and Gene Mako in Boston. It was the same story in Australia 1938 when the two Germans were doubles runners-up to John Bromwich and Adrian Quist.

Von Cramm, at the height of his career when Hitler was preparing for Germany to launch World War II, declined to speak for Nazism and was imprisoned by the Gestapo in 1938. After the war, during which he was a hero on the Russian front, he had a successful business career and was an administrator in tennis, serving as president of Lawn Tennis Club Rot-Weiss in Berlin. The Baron died in an automobile crash near Cairo, Egypt, Nov. 8, 1976, and a year later was enshrined in the Hall of Fame.

MAJOR TITLES (5)–*French singles, 1934, 1936; French doubles, 1937; U.S. doubles, 1937; Wimbledon mixed, 1933.* **DAVIS CUP**–*1932, 1933, 1934, 1935, 1936, 1937, 1951, 1952, 1953; record: 58-10 in singles, 24-11 in doubles.* **SINGLES RECORD IN THE MAJORS**–*Australian (3-1), French (18-1), Wimbledon (26-7), U.S. (5-1).*

VIRGINIA WADE
Great Britain (1945–)
Hall of Fame 1989

If ever a player achieved high drama by winning Wimbledon, it was 'Our Ginny,' as her compatriots throughout the United Kingdom called her. It was 1977, Sarah Virginia Wade's 17th try, and the year of the magnificent Wimbledon Centenary. Moreover Queen Elizabeth appeared for the first time in a quarter-century to present the women's prize. Ginny had set the stage by deposing 1976 champ Chris Evert in the semis, 6-2, 4-6, 6-1.

Attacking incessantly, heedless of whatever mistakes she made, Wade finished strongly to beat Betty Stove for the title, 4-6, 6-3, 6-1, nine days short of her 32nd birthday. An extraordinary jubilant Centre Court crowd of more than 14,000, unaccustomed to homegrown success, became a chorus in singing *For She's a Jolly Good Fellow!* A tennis queen was saluted by her Queen.

Dark-haired Wade was slender (5-foot-8) and nimble, of elegant bearing. She had the longest and, considering the highly competitive age in which she sparkled, the most fruitful career of any Englishwoman. Her career spanned the amateur and open eras, and in 1968 she scored two notable firsts. As an amateur she won the inaugural open, the British Hard Court at Bournemouth, turning down the $720 first prize, and five months later, as a pro, she captured the initial U.S. Open (and $6,000), upending the favored defender and Wimbledon champ, Billie Jean King, 6-4, 6-2.

As a pro she won 55 singles titles, seventh among the all-time leaders, and amassed $1,542,278 in career prize money. She won the Australian title in 1972, only the third Brit to do so, following Dorothy Round (1935) and Angela Mortimer (1958). With her severely sliced backhand approach and splendid volleying, right-handed Ginny was a natural on grass. But she showed her clay mettle in winning the Italian in 1971. She added doubles majors at the Australian, French and U.S., all with Margaret Court.

She continued to play Wimbledon through 1987—a record 26 years in all—getting as far as a semi-final defeat by Evert, 8-6, 6-2, in her 1978 defense, and the quarters in 1979 and 1983, when ranked No. 63. She is fifth among all players in matches played there (212): 64-23 in singles, 53-24 in doubles, 24-24 in mixed. She entered the World Top Ten in 1967 and was there 13 straight years, No. 2 in 1968. She set records for participation in Federation Cup (18 years) and ties (57). She has played (99) and won (66) the most matches. She is tied for third in most singles won (36), and, for Britain, years of Wightman Cup play (21 years) and total wins (12-23 in singles, 7-14 in doubles).

She was born July 10, 1945 in Bournemouth, England, learned to play tennis in South Africa, where she grew up, and was inducted into the Hall of Fame in 1989. She lives in New York.

MAJOR TITLES (7)–*Australian singles, 1972; Wimbledon singles, 1977; U.S. singles. 1967; Australian doubles, 1973; French doubles, 1973; U.S. doubles, 1973, 1975.* **FEDERATION CUP**–*1967, 1968, 1969, 1970, 1971, 1972, 1973, 1974, 1975, 1976, 1977, 1978, 1979, 1980, 1981, 1982, 1983; record: 36-20 in singles, 30-13 in doubles.* **WIGHTMAN CUP**–*1965, 1966, 1967, 1968, 1969, 1970, 1971, 1972, 1973, 1974, 1975, 1976, 1977, 1978, 1979, 1980, 1981, 1982, 1983, 1984, 1985; record: 12-23 in singles, 7-14 in doubles.* **SINGLES RECORD IN THE MAJORS**–*Australian (10-4), French (16-13), Wimbledon (64-23), U.S. (49-19).*

MARIE WAGNER

United States (1883–1975)
Hall of Fame 1969

Queen of the boards, Marie Wagner, a New Yorker, was the scourge of Manhattan's Seventh Regiment Armory where she won the U.S. Indoor singles a record six times (1908, 1909, 1911, 1913, 1914, 1917), and the doubles four times. She was also singles finalist in 1915 to Molla Mallory. Her best outdoor showing was as the 1914 U.S. finalist to Mary K. Browne, losing, 6-2, 1-6, 6-1.

She ranked No. 6 in 1913 when the U.S. Top Ten was established, and was in that select group every year

through 1920—No. 3 in 1914—as well as 1922 when she was No. 9 at age 39. A right-hander, she was born Feb. 2, 1883, in Freeport, N.Y., and died April 1, 1975. She entered the Hall of Fame in 1969.

U.S. TITLES (10)–*Indoor singles, 1908, 1909, 1911, 1913, 1914, 1917; Indoor doubles, 1910, 1913 with Clara Kutroff; 1916, with Molla Bjurstedt; 1917, with Margaret Taylor.* **SINGLES RECORD IN THE MAJORS**–*U.S. (17-7).*

MAUD BARGER WALLACH

United States (1870–1954)
Hall of Fame 1958

A late-in-life tennis success, Maud Barger Wallach— "I started to play at about 30"—became the oldest major champion in 1908. She was 38 when she toppled the defending U.S. champ, lefty Evelyn Sears, 6-3, 1-6, 6-3, in the challenge round, after having beaten Marie Wagner, 4-6, 6-1, 6-3, in the all-comers. Molla Mallory, winning in 1926 at 42, took away her old-age record.

In her first shot at the title, 1906, Maud lost the final to Helen Homans, 6-4, 6-3. Hazel Hotchkiss Wightman, who took the crown from her in the 1909 challenge round, recalled that Mrs. Richard Wallach had a good forehand "but not much of backhand. I concentrated on it until I was well ahead"—winning, 6-1, 6-0.

Maud was a New Yorker, a right-hander, born there June 15, 1870. She was a familiar summer figure at Newport, R.I., generally playing beneath a distinctive wide-brimmed straw hat. "Mine was not a great career," she recalled, "but a long and happy one."

At 46 she made the U.S. quarter-finals of 1916 (losing to runner-up Louise Raymond, 6-1, 6-3) and ranked No. 10, the oldest to do so well in the tournament and the rankings. National rankings for women weren't instituted until 1913, then largely because of her lobbying. But she was No. 5 in 1915. After dying in Baltimore, April 2, 1954, she was buried at Newport, not far from her beloved Casino, and was placed there eternally on her 1958 induction into the Hall of Fame.

MAJOR TITLE–*U.S. singles, 1908.* **SINGLES RECORD IN THE MAJORS**–*U.S. (16-6).*

HOLCOMBE WARD

United States (1878–1967)
Hall of Fame 1956

One of the originals, the Harvard Three forming the first U.S. Davis Cup team, Holcombe Ward is also credited with originating the American twist serve which bedeviled the British invaders as the Cup was put into play in 1900. He accompanied donor Dwight Davis—his partner in two subsequent U.S. doubles championships—to the clinching doubles win in the 3-0 victory over the British Isles.

The 5-foot-9, 135-pound right-hander played for the Cup-winners again in 1902, and the losers, to the Brits in 1905 and 1906. At Harvard, Ward partnered Davis to the Intercollegiate doubles title in 1899, and broke through as U.S. singles champ in 1904, over Bill Clothier, 10-8, 6-4, 9-7. That year he was ranked No. 1, the acme of his seven years in his country's Top Ten. In 1922 Ward and Davis reunited to win the U.S. Seniors 45s doubles title. He served as president of the USTA between 1937 and 1947.

A New Yorker, he was born there Nov. 23, 1878, and died Jan. 23, 1967, in Red Bank, N.J. He was inducted into the Hall of Fame in 1956.

MAJOR TITLES (7)–*U.S. singles, 1904; U.S. doubles, 1899, 1900, 1901, 1904, 1905, 1906.* **OTHER U.S. TITLES** (2)–*Indoor singles, 1901; Intercollegiate doubles, 1899, with Dwight Davis.* **DAVIS CUP**–*1900, 1902, 1905, 1906; record: 3-4 in singles, 4-3 in doubles.* **SINGLES RECORD IN THE MAJORS**–*Wimbledon (0-1), U.S. (19-8).*

WATTY WASHBURN

United States (1894–1973)
Hall of Fame 1965

A New Yorker and a Harvard man, Watson McLean Washburn had a hand in the U.S. record run of seven Davis Cups that began in 1920. Watty played in the first defense, at Forest Hills in 1921, where he and Dick Williams won the Cup-clinching match over Japan's Zenzo Shimidzu and Ichiya Kumagae, 6-2, 7-5, 4-6, 7-5.

A 6-foot right-hander who won the U.S. Intercollegiate doubles while at Harvard in 1913, Washburn served in the U.S. Army in World War I. He ranked seven times in the U.S. Top Ten between 1914 and 1922, No. 5 in 1921, and continued to play extremely well into his 50s, winning the U.S. 45s singles in 1940 and the doubles in that category thrice, 1940, 1942, 1944.

He was born June 13, 1894, in New York, was a committeeman for the USTA, and died in New York, Dec. 2, 1973. An uncle of Hall of Famer Sidney Wood, he was inducted into the Hall of Fame in 1965.

U.S. TITLES (2)–*Indoor doubles, 1915, with Gus Touchard; Intercollegiate doubles, 1913, with Joe Armstrong.* **DAVIS CUP**–*1921; record: 1-0 in doubles.* **SINGLES RECORD IN THE MAJORS**–*Wimbledon (7-4), U.S. (38-24).*

MAL WHITMAN

United States (1877–1932)
Hall of Fame 1955

One of the Harvard Three, the original U.S. Davis Cup team, Malcolm Douglass Whitman shared leadoff honors with Cup donor Dwight Davis in the initial U.S. vs. British Isles clash in 1900. Playing on side-by-side courts at their club, Boston's Longwood Cricket Club, Whitman beat Arthur Gore, 6-1, 6-3, 6-2, while Davis beat Ernest Black, 4-6, 6-2, 6-4, 6-4. Next day, Holcombe Ward joined Davis for a 6-4, 6-4, 6-4 win over Herbert Roper Barrett and Black to defeat the British Isles, 3-0.

A quarter-finalist in the 1896 and 1897 U.S. Championships, Whitman came through at Newport in 1898 with the first of his three straight championships. In the all-comers title match he beat Davis, 3-6, 6-3, 6-2, 6-1, and was crowned champion because 1897 victor Bob Wrenn, off to the Spanish-American War, didn't defend in the challenge round.

After another successful defense in 1899, Whitman had to first win a fight with his father, who wanted him to concentrate on law school (Harvard) and put away his racket. The son won, and that enabled him to put down challenger Bill Larned, 6-4, 1-6, 6-2, 6-2, for his third crown. Whitman had a weirdly bounding reverse twist serve (a stroke no longer seen) and was a sharp volleyer.

He didn't defend in 1901 but returned for a 1902 cameo "to represent my country," helping turn back the British invaders once more, and he reached the U.S. all-comers final, only to be stung by Reggie Doherty, 6-1, 3-6, 6-3, 6-0.

In the Davis Cup he won both his matches (over Joshua Pim, 6-1, 6-1, 1-6, 6-0, and over Reggie Doherty, 6-1, 7-5, 6-4) and the U.S. kept the Cup, 3-2.

Whitman, a handsome 6-foot-2 right-hander, was through, after posting an unbeaten Cup record and a 19-3 U.S. match record at Newport. He was in the U.S. Top Ten six times from 1896, No. 1 1898, 1899, 1900, and No. 2 in 1902. Ever absorbed by the game's history, he wrote *Tennis Origins and Mysteries,* published in 1931. Born March 15, 1877, in New York, he committed suicide there Dec. 28, 1932. He was named to the Hall of Fame in 1955.

MAJOR TITLES (3)–*U.S. singles, 1898, 1899, 1900.* **OTHER U.S. TITLES** (3)–*Intercollegiate singles, 1896; Intercollegiate doubles, 1897, 1898 with Leo Ware.* **DAVIS CUP**–*1900, 1902; record: 3-0 in singles.* **SINGLES RECORD IN THE MAJORS**–*U.S. (19-3).*

HAZEL HOTCHKISS WIGHTMAN

United States (1886–1974)
Hall of Fame 1956

'Lady Tennis,' as she came to be known, remembered herself as a shy, somewhat awed and fascinated college girl when she arrived at the Philadelphia Cricket Club in 1909 for the U.S. Championships. A Californian, Hazel Virginia Hotchkiss hadn't played on grass, but with her attacking style and rock-ribbed volleying—she was the first woman to rely so heavily on the volley—22-year-old Hazel, a right-hander, scythed through the field to lift the title effortlessly (6-0, 6-1) from 39-year-old Maud Barger Wallach in the challenge round, and won the doubles and mixed as well.

Losing only one set (in the all-comers final over Louise Hammond), she was the first of three triple-triple winners in U.S. annals. Repeating singles, doubles and mixed titles in 1910-11, Hazel was emulated by Mary K. Browne (1912-13-14) and Alice Marble (1938-39-40).

Hazel had no trouble with Hammond in the 1910 challenge round, but an old West Coast rival, May Sutton—champion in 1904—pushed her hard in 1911, 8-10, 6-4, 9-7. In 1910, at Seattle, she blitzed a Miss Huiskamp in the only recorded 'golden match,' 6-0, 6-0, outscoring poor Huiskamp 48-points-to-zero.

Marrying Bostonian George Wightman in 1912, she didn't defend. But, responding to a challenge from her father—to win after becoming a mother, a U.S. first—she reappeared in 1915 to lose the singles final to Molla Mallory, and win the doubles and mixed. But papa's wish came true for the spunky 125-pound 5-footer in another comeback, 1919. At 32, she won her fourth singles title. She lost only one set, beating Marion Zinderstein, 6-1, 6-2, in the final, and reaching the doubles final. Thereafter her long-lived and unapproached success (U.S. adult titles between 1909 and 1943) was confined to doubles, at which she was one of the supremes.

Hazel, devoted to the game in all aspects, generously instructed innumerable players, at no charge, throughout her life, and was able to win important titles with two of her protégés who would join her in the Hall of Fame: Wimbledon, U.S. and Olympic doubles with Helen Wills in 1924; U.S. Indoor doubles with Sarah Palfrey 1928 through 1931. Her second Olympic gold in 1924 came in the mixed with Dick Williams.

She envisioned a team tournament for women similar to the Davis Cup, and offered a silver vase as prize. In 1923 British women were the strongest apart from Americans, and Julian Myrick of the USTA decided that a U.S.-Britain competition would be in order for the Wightman Cup. The event, with Hazel captaining and playing for a winning U.S. side, opened the newly constructed stadium at Forest Hills. A treasured series, it lasted through 1989, disbanded unfortunately with the Brits no longer able to offer competition.

The last of Hazel's record 34 U.S. adult titles was recorded in 1943 as she, 56, and Pauline Betz, 23, won the Indoor doubles over Lillian Lopaus and Judy Atterbury, 7-5, 6-1. Though short, she anticipated and moved extremely well and competed fiercely though undemonstrably. She perfected her volleying early, hitting the ball against the family home in Berkeley, where she grew up and graduated from the University of California. She refused to let the ball bounce because the yard was so uneven. She used to play against her four brothers and then the proud and spiky Sutton sisters, outlasting them by recording 11 U.S. senior (over 40) doubles titles between 1940 and 1954, the last at age 67.

As the Bostonian Mrs. Wightman, she was in the U.S. Top Ten in 1915, 1918 and 1919, No. 1 the last. She was born Dec. 20, 1886, in Healdsburg, Calif., and died Dec. 5, 1974, in Chestnut Hill, Mass. She entered the Hall of Fame in 1956.

MAJOR TITLES *(17)–U.S. singles, 1909, 1910, 1911, 1919; Wimbledon doubles, 1924; U.S. doubles, 1909, 1910, 1911, 1915, 1924, 1928; U.S. mixed, 1909, 1910, 1911, 1915, 1918, 1920.* **OTHER U.S. TITLES** *(18)–Indoor singles, 1919, 1927; Indoor doubles, 1919, 1921, 1924, 1927, with Marion Zinderstein Jessup; 1928, 1929, 1930, 1931, 1933, with Sarah Palfrey; 1943, with Pauline Betz; Indoor mixed, 1923, with Burnham Dell; 1924, with Bill Tilden; 1926, 1927, with G. Peabody Gardner, Jr.; 1928, with Henry Johnson; Clay mixed, 1915, with Harry Johnson.* **WIGHTMAN CUP**–*1923, 1924, 1927, 1929, 1931; record: 3-2 in doubles.* **SINGLES RECORD IN THE MAJORS**–*Wimbledon (2-1), U.S. (22-4).*

MATS WILANDER

Sweden (1964–)

No sooner had Swedes grieved the retirement of Bjorn Borg, and wistfully wished for his sixth French title in 1981, than an unheralded young countryman conquered Paris the following year. Unseeded 17-year-old Mats Arne Olof Wilander, a rugged 6-footer who beat powerful one-time champ Guillermo Vilas at his own baseline game, became the youngest of French champs. It was the first of seven singles majors for Wilander over a seven-year stretch when he competed at the top of the game, reaching No. 1 in 1988.

Although Michael Chang, a younger 17 in 1989, usurped his male precocity record for the majors, Wilander won the French again in 1985 (dethroning Ivan Lendl, 6-2 in the fourth) and 1988, and the Australian, on grass, in 1983 and 1984.

But it was 1988, an all-time season, that stands as his masterpiece. He won three majors, starting with a magnificent five-set Australian final-round victory over hometown hero Patrick Cash in Melbourne's newly opened Flinders Park. It was the Aussie Open's first year on hard courts, and victory meant that Mats was only the second man (emulating Jimmy Connors) to win majors on grass, clay and hard.

While he won the French without much trouble, his dreams of a Grand Slam were pierced by Miloslav Mecir in the Wimbledon quarters. An arduous U.S. backcourt duel with Lendl, who'd beaten him for the title in 1987, lasted over four hours before at last Wilander showed more offensive initiative to win. As the first winner of three majors in a year since Connors in 1974, he completed 1988 with six victories in 15 tournaments, with a 53-11 record, and personal prize money of $1,726,731.

But after that, having attained the No. 1 ranking, his motivation seemed to disappear. He was through as a factor, and by 1991 he was retired. His last of 33 career titles was at Itaparica (Brazil) in 1990, yet in some ways Wilander outdid Borg. Bjorn never won three majors in a year, and he led Sweden to but one Davis Cup. Mats won three. Stunning Connors in straight sets on opening day in Goteborg in 1984, Wilander launched Sweden to a 4-1 upset of the U.S., he backboned a 3-2 win over Germany in 1985 in Munich, and a 5-0 win over India in 1987 in Goteborg.

In 1991, he had dropped to No. 157. However, he felt the urge to play again in 1993, and came back to do moderately well, climbing to No. 45 in 1995 and earning about $500,000. He was even selected as a starter for the Davis Cup semi-final against the U.S. in 1995, losing to Andre Agassi and Pete Sampras.

Speedy afoot and an unrelenting competitor through 1988, he was at first a pure top-spinning, grind-it-out baseliner, a right-hander with a two-fisted backhand. But Mats developed attacking skills and a good volley, winning the Wimbledon doubles in 1986 with Joakim Nystrom.

Two memorable matches were Davis Cup losses, the longest and third-longest played: Six hours and 32 minutes against John McEnroe in 1982; six hours and four minutes against Horst Skoff of Austria in 1989. His career figures: 33 wins in 220 tournaments; a 524-164 match record, and earnings of $7,976,256.

He was born Aug. 22, 1964, in Vaxjo, Sweden, and grew up there. Today, he lives with his wife, Sonya, in Greenwich, Conn.

MAJOR TITLES *(8)–Australian singles, 1983, 1984, 1988; French singles, 1982, 1985, 1988; U.S. singles, 1988; Wimbledon doubles, 1986.* **DAVIS CUP**–*1981, 1982, 1983, 1984, 1985, 1986, 1987, 1988, 1989, 1990; record: 36-14 in singles, 7-2 in doubles.* **SINGLES RECORD IN THE MAJORS**–*Australian (36-7), French (47-9), Wimbledon (25-10), U.S. (36-11).*

TONY WILDING
New Zealand (1883–1915)
Hall of Fame 1978

The British idolized Tony Wilding. He was a superb figure of a man, his sportsmanship was exemplary, and, besides, he learned his tennis at Cambridge University.

Anthony Frederick Wilding, born Oct. 31, 1883, in Christchurch, New Zealand, stood with Norman Brookes as two of the game's foremost players for nearly a decade. On his sixth try, 1910, Tony won Wimbledon, unseating Arthur Gore in the challenge round, and he kept the title through 1913. In that challenge round, he beat Maurice McLoughlin, the formidable California Comet. "He was in prime physical condition," wrote distinguished British tennis authority A. Wallis Myers. "All his best fighting instincts were aroused, his tactics were as sound as his strokes and he won a great victory, the greatest of his career, in three sets."

Wilding, a 6-foot-2, 185-pound right-hander, lost his title to Brookes in 1914 and joined with the Australian 'Wizard' to win the Davis Cup back from the U.S. that same year. Wilding's triumph over Dick Williams on the first day was a shock. Williams was one of the most daring and brilliant shotmakers in history, but Wilding played almost unerringly and won in just 29 games.

He played the classic game that was in vogue. His drives were the strength of his attack and his defense was outstanding. He could hit with immense pace and overspin, but when prudence and judgment dictated security of stroke rather than speed, as against a player of Williams' daring, Wilding could temper his drives and play faultlessly from the baseline.

Wilding made his debut on the Australasian Davis Cup team at the age of 21 in 1905. After winning the second Australian Championship in 1906 over a fellow New Zealander, lefty Francis Fisher, his Antipodean partnership with Brookes took off. They stripped the Davis Cup from Britain at Wimbledon in 1907, and while hard-pressed they kept the trophy the next year at Melbourne, turning back the U.S., with Wilding taking the decisive point over Fred Alexander. Then they spanked the U.S. 5-0 in 1909. Tony was absent as Australia lost the 1911-12 showdowns, and his reappearance in 1914 invasion marked his farewell to tennis.

Following their victory at Forest Hills, he and Brookes went to war. Wilding never came back. At the age of 31, on May 9, 1915, he was killed in action at Neuve Chapelle, France. He had been No. 3 in the world in 1914, and was named to the Hall of Fame in 1978.

MAJOR TITLES (11)–*Australian singles, 1906, 1909; Wimbledon singles, 1910, 1911, 1912, 1913; Australian doubles, 1906; Wimbledon doubles, 1907, 1908, 1910, 1914.* **DAVIS CUP**–*1905, 1906, 1907, 1908, 1909, 1914; record: 15-6 in singles, 6-3 in doubles.* **SINGLES RECORD IN THE MAJORS**–*Australian (10-0), Wimbledon (23-6).*

DICK WILLIAMS

United States (1891–1968)
Hall of Fame 1957

Richard Norris Williams II survived the sinking of the *Titanic* and after that harrowing experience, tennis must have seemed easy, for he became one of the outstanding players of his time, a risk-taking shotmaker. Born of American parents in Geneva, Switzerland on January 29, 1891, he left for the U.S. in 1912 aboard the *S.S. Titanic,* which struck an iceberg and sank.

At the insistence of his father, who went down with the ship, Dick dived from the deck at the last possible moment, swam to a half-submerged lifeboat and clung there in near-freezing water for six hours. When rescued, a ship's doctor advised amputation of the frozen-stiff, seemingly useless legs, common treatment at the time. Fortunately, Williams refused, and only months later he was in the quarters of the U.S. Championships, losing in four to champion Maurice McLoughlin.

He lived until age 77, and for that the tennis world was always grateful.

Williams, a 5-foot-11 right-hander, learned to play in Switzerland, using the continental grip and hitting his groundstrokes with underspin. He developed his game as a Harvard undergrad, winning the Intercollegiate championship in 1913 and 1915. During his career he won 42 singles, 51 doubles and 13 mixed titles.

In 1913, he was runner-up at Newport but he won the next year over McLoughlin, 6-3, 8-6, 10-8, a stirring final before a large crowd on the new championship court at the Casino. Throughout the match Williams maintained a terrific pace and marvelous control, averting the loss of the final set several times with bursts of speed and master strokes that thwarted even so aggressive and courageous a foe as the California Comet. In 1916, he won the U.S. title again, this time over Little Bill Johnston, and attained No. 1 ranking.

Beginning in 1913, he played on five winning Davis Cup teams. After wartime combat service in France with the Army, a decorated hero (a French Croix de Guerre among his medals), Dick captained six Cup winners, 1921-26, plus the team of 1934. He was a victorious doubles player in four of those years, a volleyer whose doubles titles were numerous, including Wimbledon in 1920 with Chuck Garland. He laughed about his 1924 Olympic gold medal in mixed doubles alongside Hazel Wightman: "I had a sprained ankle and suggested to her that we default. Not on your life with her. She told me to stay at the net, and she'd do the running. It worked [over Marion Jessup and Vinnie Richards] even though I was 34 and she 37." He continued playing the U.S. Championships (21 in all, the fifth-highest total) through 1935 when he won a round at 44. He won 65 of 84 U.S. matches, tied for fifth with John McEnroe.

Williams had a daring style of play, taking every possible ball on the rise, when not in volleying position, with hair-trigger timing. Always he hit boldly, sharply for the winner, and that included serving for the winner on both the first and second ball. He did not know what it was to temporize. On occasion, his errors caused by his gutsy tactics might bring defeat to opponents of inferior ability. But it was the commonly held opinion that Williams, on his best days, when he had the feel and touch and his breathtaking strokes were flashing on the lines, was unbeatable against any and all. Once, he won a set over Bill Tilden in five minutes!

He made the World Top Ten in 1913-14, 1919, 1920, 1921, 1922, 1923 and 1925, was No. 4 in 1923, No. 5 in 1925, and was in the U.S. Top Ten 12 times between 1912 and 1925, No. 1 in 1916. In 1957, he was elevated to the Hall of Fame. He died June 2, 1968, in Bryn Mawr, Pa.

MAJOR TITLES (6)–*U.S. singles, 1914, 1916; Wimbledon doubles, 1920; U.S. doubles, 1925, 1926; U.S. mixed, 1912.* **OTHER U.S. TITLES**–*Clay Court singles, 1912, 1915; Intercollegiate singles, 1913, 1915; Intercollegiate doubles, 1914, 1915 with Dick Harte.* **DAVIS CUP**–*1913, 1914, 1921, 1923, 1925, 1926; record: 6-3 in singles, 4-0 in doubles.* **SINGLES RECORD IN THE MAJORS**–*Wimbledon (10-3), U.S. (65-19).*

SERENA WILLIAMS
United States (1981–)

Serena Williams ended 2002 as the best tennis player in her family, which made her the best women's player on the planet. She opened 2003 by completing a 'Serena Slam,' winning the Australian Open, her thirteenth major title, making it four straight major titles. Each time, she defeated her older sister, Venus, in the final.

Serena Williams' campaign that year was one for the ages. She triumphed at the French, Wimbledon and the U.S., missing a calendar Grand Slam when a twisted ankle kept her out of the Australian Open. She led the WTA Tour by taking eight of 13 tournaments (and was twice a runner-up), taking 56 of 61 matches for a .918 winning percentage. The computer ranked her No. 1 on July 8 and she held the top spot for the rest of the year.

In one season, she went from being a successful and promising athlete to a dominating one. By winning the 2003 Australian Open, she became only the fifth woman to hold all four major titles simultaneously.

She attributed her success to maturity and a more relaxed outlook. On the court, she showed an ever-improving talent at constructing points to go with her all-court coverage and power. Her 53 aces at the U.S. Open were twice as many as any other woman.

Born on Sept. 26, 1981, in Saginaw, Mich., Serena was a sister to Lyndrea, Isha, Yetunde and Venus and the fifth daughter born to a man with dreams of creating a tennis champion. Her father, Richard, trained his two youngest on the uneven Compton public courts in a hard-scrabble section of Los Angeles.

Serena played her first professional match in Quebec City shortly after her 14th birthday. She joined Venus, who is 15 months and nine days older, on the WTA Tour in 1997. An early sign of Serena's skill came that year when, while ranked 304th, she beat world No. 7 Mary Pierce and No. 4 Monica Seles in Chicago.

In 1998, Serena won her first major championship title by teaming with Max Mirnya in mixed doubles at Wimbledon and the U.S. Open. Her sister and Justin Gimelstob completed the family's mixed doubles Grand Slam by winning the Australian and French Opens.

Her first pro singles title came at the Paris Indoors tournament on Feb. 28, 1999, a day on which Venus won half a world away at Oklahoma City. It was the first of five championships that year, none as dramatic as victory in the U.S. Open, where she defeated Martina

Hingis in the final to join Althea Gibson as the only African-American women with a major championship. The Williams sisters also took the U.S. Open doubles title, following up on their win at the French Open.

A string of injuries in 1999 and 2000 slowed Serena's progress, although she teamed with Venus in 2000 to win doubles at Wimbledon and at the Sydney Olympics. The sisters completed their career doubles Grand Slam at the Australian Open in 2001, becoming only the fifth team in tennis history to win all four titles. Later that year, they met for the first time in a major championship singles final, the U.S. Open. Venus, the defending champion, won in straight sets and, after the final point, she put her arm around her little sister and said: "We still love each other, right?"

In 2002, the younger Williams, at 5-foot-10, 145 pounds, showed her gregarious and feisty personality in her appearance on and off the court. She dyed her hair blond and wore striking outfits, notably a black cat suit at Flushing Meadows. She made cameos in sitcoms and rap videos, and became a marketing icon, joining Venus in commercials and appearing solo on toothpaste boxes.

Her eight titles in 2002 included a trio of major championships, beating Venus in straight sets at Roland Garros, at Wimbledon and at the U.S. Open. After taking the Australian Open 4-6, 6-3, 7-5 in January 2003, Serena had a 5-4 edge over her sister in major titles.

MAJOR TITLES (13)–*Australian singles, 2003; French singles, 2002; Wimbledon singles, 2002; U.S. singles, 1999, 2002; Australian doubles, 2001, 2003; French doubles, 1999; Wimbledon doubles, 2000, 2002; U.S. doubles, 1999; Wimbledon mixed, 1998; U.S. mixed, 1998.* **FED CUP**–*1999; record: 2-0 in singles, 1-0 in doubles.* **SINGLES RECORD IN THE MAJORS**–*Australian (17-4), French (16-3), Wimbledon (18-3), U.S. (26-3).*

VENUS WILLIAMS
United States (1980–)

The elder of the amazing Williams sisters, Venus, is a two-time winner of both Wimbledon and the U.S. Open. Unlike Serena, she has also won a singles gold medal at the Olympics. She entered 2003 ranked No. 2 behind little sister, but in February 2002, Venus became the first African American in the history of the WTA computer rankings to become world No. 1. She held the top spot on three separate occasions that year.

Venus has 12 major titles. In addition to her four major singles titles, Venus has teamed with Serena to win six doubles (including a career slam in doubles), as well as two mixed doubles. She also has an Olympic gold medal, won at the 2000 Sydney Games.

At 6-foot-1, 160 pounds, Venus plays an overpowering game. She mixes a thundering serve with penetrating groundstrokes and attacking net play. Entering 2003, she had 37 tournament wins, including nine in doubles, plus $11.9 million in career earnings and endorsement contracts worth tens of millions.

She was born Venus Ebony Starr Williams on June 17, 1980, in Lynnwood, Calif. Fifteen months later, Serena was born, and a budding tennis father had what he would later call his "ghetto Cinderellas." Unable to send his daughters to a hothouse tennis academy, Richard Williams trained them according to his own regimen—even if it meant a flat tennis ball on an uneven, glass-strewn public court in Compton, a notoriously tough section of Los Angeles. According to legend, the first lesson the girls learned was to stay low when the local gangs were engaging in gunplay.

A gangly teenager, Venus turned professional as a 14-year-old in 1994. Her breakthrough season came in 1997 when she made the final of the U.S. Open by twice saving match point in the semi-finals. Williams, age 17, was the first unseeded woman finalist at the U.S. Open since 1958. She lost in two sets (and 16 games) to 16-year-old 'Swiss Miss' Martina Hingis.

Venus won her first pro singles title at Oklahoma in 1998, and won $1.77 million that year. On match point in the quarter-finals of the Italian Open against Mary Pierce, Venus delivered a 127-mph ace, the fastest serve ever recorded on the WTA Tour. That year also brought her first two major titles, in mixed doubles with Justin Gimelstob at the Australian and French Opens. Serena finish off the 'family slam' in mixed doubles by winning Wimbledon and the U.S. Open with Max Mirnyi.

Both sisters won tournaments on Feb. 28, 1999—Venus at Oklahoma City and Serena at Paris Indoors. It was the first time sisters had won simultaneous events. Venus then beat Serena at Miami. They teamed to win the 1999 U.S. Open doubles title, but then the unexpected happened. It had always been speculated Venus would claim the family's first major singles title, but after she was eliminated in the quarters, Serena advanced to defeat Hingis. A distraught Venus buried her face in her jacket at the presentation ceremony.

A four-month respite as Venus recovered from tendinitis in both wrists at the start of the 2000 season was an unpromising beginning to what became her most successful season. At Wimbledon, she defeated Hingis,

her sister and, in the final, defending champion Lindsay Davenport to claim her first major singles title. She took the doubles with her sister for good measure, and then won the U.S. Open singles, followed by Olympic gold medals in singles and doubles.

The Williams sisters won the doubles in Australia in 2001, becoming only the fifth pair to complete a career Grand Slam. After defending her Wimbledon title, Venus held her U.S. title against Serena in the final, the first time sisters had met in a major final since 1884.

After dominating Serena for years, Venus lost to her little sister in four straight major finals, including the 2003 Australian Open.

Introverted, Venus is regarded as the family polymath, and has shown greater interest in life away from tennis, including an interior-design firm she opened near the mansion she shares with her sister in Palm Beach Garden, Fla. She also designs women's leather apparel.

MAJOR TITLES (12)–*Wimbledon singles, 2000, 2001; U.S. singles, 2000, 2001; Australian doubles, 2001, 2003; French doubles, 1999; Wimbledon doubles, 2000, 2002; U.S. doubles, 1999; Australian mixed, 1998; French mixed, 1998.* **FED CUP**–*1999; record: 3-1 in singles, 2-0 in doubles.* **SINGLES RECORD IN THE MAJORS**–*Australian (23-5), French (18-6), Wimbledon (28-4), U.S. (35-4).*

SIDNEY WOOD

United States (1911–)
Hall of Fame 1964

Playing in knickerbockers against the great Frenchman, René Lacoste, 15-year-old Sidney Burr Beardsley Wood was the youngest male Wimbledon entrant ever in 1927. Four years later he became the second-youngest champion of Centre Court, and without stepping onto the hallowed sod. Frank Shields, with an injured ankle, withdrew, marking the only time Wimbledon has had a defaulted final.

Wood, a sickly child afflicted with tuberculosis, was born Nov. 1, 1911, at Black Rock, Conn. A 5-foot-9-1/2 right-hander, he never reached the Wimbledon final again, although he did get to play a major final, losing the U.S. to Wilmer Allison in 1935, 6-2, 6-2, 6-3. A slim, nimble blond, he ranked in the U.S. Top Ten 10 times between 1930 and 1945, No. 2 in 1934, and was in the World Top Ten five times between 1931 and 1938, No. 5 in 1938, No. 6 in 1931.

He was a Davis Cupper in 1931 and 1934, and in the latter year was part of the most astounding U.S. comeback, from 0-2 against Australia in London. Having lost to Viv McGraw, Wood was heartened by George Lott and Les Stoefen's holding action doubles victory over Adrian Quist and Jack Crawford, and he knocked off Jack Crawford, 6-3, 9-7, 4-6, 4-6, 6-2, to open the third day and tie the score at 2-2. Then Shields beat McGrath, and the U.S. entered the finals, losing, 4-1, to Britain. There, on opening day, Wood battled the Cup-holder's main man, Fred Perry, losing 6-1, 4-6, 5-7, 6-0, 6-3, and also lost to Bunny Austin on the third day.

An inventive man, he continued in 2002, at age 91, working on his inventions, one of which was a plastic carpet (Supreme Court), long used for indoor tourneys. He was inducted into the Hall of Fame in 1964.

MAJOR TITLE–*Wimbledon singles, 1931.* **DAVIS CUP**–*1931, 1934; record: 5-6 in singles, 3-0 in doubles.* **SINGLES RECORD IN THE MAJORS**–*French (2-1), Wimbledon (21-5), U.S. (42-25).*

BOB WRENN

United States (1873–1925)
Hall of Fame 1955

A four-time U.S. singles champ, Robert Duffield Wrenn won the last of those titles in 1897 before serving in Cuba with Teddy Roosevelt's Rough Riders in the Spanish-American War. One of Bob's comrades in arms was future champion Bill Larned. Unfortunately Wrenn contracted yellow fever during that campaign and never regained pre-war form.

He came from a prominent Chicago family of s everal fine athletes, and became a topflight football, baseball and tennis player at Harvard. Noted for swiftness and court coverage, a defensive star featuring devilish lobs, he was the first left-hander to win the U.S. singles. He beat Fred Hovey for the 1893 title, 7-5, 3-6, 6-3, 7-5, and kept it by repelling Manliffe Goodbody in the 1894 challenge round.

Hovey took it from him easily in 1895. But Bob wrested it back, 7-5, 3-6, 6-0, 1-6, 6-1, in the 1896 challenge round, and fended off the first Aussie to chase a U.S. title, Wilberforce Eaves, 4-6, 8-6, 6-3, 2-6, 6-2, in the 1897 challenge round. War service prevented him from defending in 1898. He did team with his right-handed younger brother, George Wrenn, as the U.S. Davis Cup doubles pair in 1903 when they lost to the British Dohertys, Laurie and Reggie, 7-5, 9-7, 2-6, 6-3, the only instance of brothers clashing for the Cup.

They were the only brothers to play together for the U.S., and to rank concurrently in the U.S. Top Ten: Bob was No. 1 in 1893, 1894, 1896 and 1897, No. 8 in 1892 and 1900; George four times No. 6 during his five years

up there between 1896 and 1900. Another brother, Everts, ranked No. 18 in 1896. In Bob's last thrust for the U.S. singles title he was beaten by George in a 1900 quarter-final, 6-4, 6-1, 6-4, the only such brotherly battle at the U.S. until the Spanish Sanchez brothers met in 1992, Emilio beating Javier, 6-4 in the fifth.

After leaving Harvard, Bob became a stockbroker in New York, and was president of the USTA from 1912 through 1915. Born Sept. 20, 1873, in Highland Park, Ill., he died in New York Nov. 12, 1925, and was named to the Hall of Fame in 1955.

MAJOR TITLES *(5)–U.S. singles, 1893, 1894, 1896, 1897; U.S. doubles, 1895.* **OTHER U.S. TITLES** *(1)–Intercollegiate doubles, 1892, with F. B. Winslow.* **DAVIS CUP**–*1903; record: 0-2 in singles, 0-1 in doubles.* **SINGLES RECORD IN THE MAJORS**–*U.S. (20-3).*

BEALS WRIGHT

United States (1879–1961)
Hall of Fame 1956

Before the turn of the century, Beals Coleman Wright was a national champion, winning the Interscholastic singles for Boston's Hopkinson School in 1898 at 18, and repeating in 1899 when he made his first of 11 entries in the U.S. Top Ten at No. 8. In 1900 his brother, Irving, won the Interscholastic for the same school.

In 1905, dethroning Holcombe Ward, he was the second lefty to win the U.S. singles, following Bob Wrenn. He had to beat the future champ, Bill Clothier, 9-7, 6-2, 6-2, and an ex-champ, Bill Larned, 4-6, 6-3, 6-2, 6-2, plus Clarence Hobart, to reach the challenge round to topple Ward, 6-2, 6-1, 11-9.

His biggest year was 1905. It included one of his three U.S. doubles titles (with Ward), and Davis Cup victories over Australian greats Tony Wilding, 6-3, 6-2, 6-4, and Norman Brookes, 12-10, 5-7, 12-10, 6-4, that sent the U.S. into a losing Cup round against Britain. In 1908 he beat those two again, even more stunning victories since it was the Davis Cup finale at Melbourne, their home turf. But it wasn't enough in a 3-2 defeat. He was born Dec. 19, 1879, in Boston, lived in Brookline, Mass., and died Aug. 23, 1961, in Alton, Ill. He was inducted into the Hall of Fame in 1956.

Wright won the Canadian singles thrice, 1902-04, and brother Irving won it in 1906.

MAJOR TITLES *(4)–U.S. singles, 1905; U.S. doubles, 1904, 1905, 1906.* **DAVIS CUP**–*1905, 1907, 1908, 1911; record: 6-4 in singles, 3-3 in doubles.* **SINGLES RECORD IN THE MAJORS**–*Wimbledon (6-2), U.S. (47-11).*

Chapter 26

They Also Serve

Tom Okker, 1975
The Flying Dutchman's 100-plus overall pro titles put him in the top five men all-time.

Although a substantial number of the game's all-time elite are to be found in the preceeding biography chapter, numerous others during 126 years of tournament tennis have made distinctive/unusual marks and contributions. A select number may be found here—such as the eventually unlovable 'St. Leger' Goold. Some players may be said to have gotten away with murder, but he is the only Wimbledon finalist to be convicted of same.

Abbreviations used: LH, left-hander; RH, right-hander; B., born; D., died. Denoting tournament finish: RD., round; QF, quarter-final; SF, semi-final; F, final; MP, match points.

AKHURST, DAPHNE: Daphne Jessie Akhurst Cozens, Australian RH, country's first prolific champ, first female to make World Top Ten (No. 3, 1928), though had short career and life. B. April 22, 1903, d. Jan. 9, 1933, in childbirth. Between 1925 and 1931, won 14 majors, all Australian: five singles (1925-26, 28-29-30), five doubles, four mixed. Last doubles, 1931, won as Mrs. Roy Cozens. Made Wimbledon SF 1928, QF, 1925; French QF 1928. Women's singles championship trophy at Aussie Open named for her.

ALVAREZ, LILI DE: Spain's most accomplished female until Arantxa Sanchez Vicario, the chic Lili de Alvarez, later Comtesse de la Valdene, was World No. 2, 1927-28; No. 3, 1926, No. 8, 1930-31. RH, b. May 9, 1905, Rome. Delighted photographers, spectators in avant garde outfits such as culottes, 1931, at Wimbledon. Lost Wimbledon F to Kitty McKane, 1926; to Helen Wills, 1928. Made French SF 1930-31, QF, 1927. Won French doubles, 1929. Tripled at Italian, 1930, winning singles, doubles, mixed. Lived in Madrid, d. there July 8, 1998.

AMPON, FELICISIMO: Felicisimo Hermoso Ampon, speedy, popular miniature, 4-foot-11, 100 pounds, smallest world-class man. Philippines' finest,

RH, b. Oct. 27, 1920, Manila. Splendid retriever, made mark at French: QF 1952 (beat Tony Trabert), 1953 (beat Budge Patty). Incredible Davis Cup career over 29-year span (played 16; 36 series)—from Philippines' initial team, 1939, to farewell victory, age 47, 1968. Led team to 22-16 record, was 34-26, singles, 6-9 doubles. Nadir: 6-0, 6-0, 6-0, Cup beating by Frank Parker, U.S., 1946. Won 16 post-World War II singles titles.

AMRITRAJ, VIJAY; ANAND; ASHOK: Three rangy, RH brothers, pros, from India with attacking styles, all born and raised in Madras (now Chennai). Vijay and Anand played Davis Cup together 15 years, led India to two title rounds, 1974 and 1987. All live in Los Angeles.

Vijay Amritraj, b., Dec. 14, 1953, graceful 6-3, superb volleyer, Best World rank, No. 20, 1980. Won 16 singles, 13 doubles career pro titles, $1,325,833. Winning Bretton Woods, N.H., 1973, saved three match points each vs. Humphrey Hose, Rod Laver, two more in F over Jimmy Connors. Made QF Wimbledon, U.S., 1973 (beating 2nd seed Laver in latter). Davis Cup: 1970-88, 27-18 singles, 18-10 doubles. A top tennis telecaster.

Anand Amritraj, 6-1, b. March 20, 1952. Best World rank, No. 87, 1974. Won 13 pro career doubles titles, eight with Vijay, $331,698. Davis Cup 1968-88, 12-15 singles, 21-14 doubles.

Ashok Amritraj, 6-1, b. Feb 22, 1957. Best World rank, No. 206, 1976.

ANDERSON, J. O.: Australian Davis Cupper, 6-3 RH James Outram 'Greyhound' Anderson, always known as J.O. B. Sept. 17, 1895, Enfield, d. July 19, 1960, Sydney. World Top Ten: No. 6, 1921; No. 5. 1922; No. 3, 1923-24. Swift afoot, with husky, damaging forehand, poking 'upside-down' backhand (using same racket face as forehand). Won Australian singles, 1922, 24-25; doubles, 1924. Davis Cup: 1919-25, 20-7 singles, 8-1 doubles. Led Aussies to F, 1922-23 gave Bill Johnston, U.S., first Cup defeat, 1923.

ATKINSON, KATHLEEN: Kathleen Gill Atkinson, American RH b. Nov. 5, 1875, d. April 30, 1957, Maplewood, N.J. Won 7 U.S. doubles, 1897-98, with Hall of Fame sister Juliette. In first instance of sisters clashing in U.S. Championships, Juliette beat Kathleen in 1895 SF, 6-1, 6-4, again in 1897 SF, 6-1, 6-3. More than a century later, Manuela beat Maggie in Maleeva

sisters meeting, U.S. QF. 1992. Williams sisters (Venus, Serena) were adversaries in 2001-02 U.S. F.

ASBOTH, JOSZEF: Probably Hungary's finest player, Joszef Asboth was clever performer on clay, won French, 1947. Made Wimbledon SF, 1948. B. Sept. 18, 1917, Szombathely. Davis Cup: 1938-1957; 18-12 singles, 6-5 doubles. World Top Ten: No. 8, 1947-48. Turned teaching pro, 1958. Won 10 post-World War II amateur singles titles.

AUSSEM, CILLY: Until Steffi Graf, Cilly Aussem was Germany's most successful woman. Tiny 5-foot RH baseliner. Won French, Wimbledon, 1931 (latter over Hilde Krahwinkel, only all-German female final). Made Wimbledon SF, 1930; French SF, 1929-30, 34. Won French mixed, 1930. World Top Ten: No. 7, 1928, No. 2, 1930-31. B. Jan. 4, 1909, Cologne; d., as Countess F. M. della Corte Brae, March 22, 1963, Portofino, Italy.

AUSTIN, JOAN: Joan Winifred Austin. B. Jan. 23, 1903, London; d. Apr. 2, 1998, Horley, England. Lost Wimbledon doubles F, 1923. Younger brother, Hall of Famer Henry Wilfred 'Bunny' Austin (1906-2000), introduced shorts internationally, 1932, liberating male legs, made singles F Wimbledon, 1932, 38; French, 1937. Joan, a liberator herself, first to play on Centre Court without stockings, 1931. Only sister-brother to make major finals. One of her four marriages was to Randolph Lycett, winner Wimbledon doubles, 1921-22-23.

AUSTIN, TRACY; PAM; JOHN; JEFF: Exraordinary California siblings, all played professionally.

Tracy, an all-timer, inducted International Tennis Hall of Fame, 1992. She and John first sister-brother team to win major mixed, Wimbledon, 1980. Later Helena Sukova-Cyril Suk won French, 1991, Wimbledon, 1996. Cara Black-Wayne Black won French, 2002. *See Chapter 25 for full biography.*

Pamela Jeanne Austin, b. March 12, 1950, Waltham, Mass., RH, 6-1. Played 5 years. Won Ecuador Open, 1972. With Jeff, member Denver Racquets, World Team Tennis champs, 1974. Won Pac8 Doubles for University California Los Angeles, 1968; U.S. Amateur doubles with Margie Cooper, 1969; U.S. Amateur Hard Court doubles with Tam O'Shaughnessy, 1969.

William Jeffrey Austin, b. July 5, 1951, Waltham, Mass., RH, 5-11, 160. All-American 1972-73, UCLA. Best world ranking: No. 52, 1973.

John Reed Austin, b. July 31, 1957, Torrance, Calif., RH. 6-3, 180. All-American 1977-78, UCLA, helped win National Intercollegiate team title, 1976. Won NCAA doubles, 1978, with Bruce Nichols. Best World ranking: No. 97, 1978. Lost F, Columbus, to Brian Teacher, 1983.

A fifth sibling, Douglas Edward Austin, b. Feb. 16, 1954, was varsity regular at California State Long Beach.

AYALA, LUIS: Chile's most successful male prior to Marcelo Rios in 1990s. A stocky RH, best on clay. B. Sept. 18, 1932, Santiago. Won Italian, 1959; lost F 1960. Lost. French F, 1958, 60. made SF 1959. Won French mixed, 1956. Made Wimbledon QF, 1959, 61; U.S. QF, 1957, 59. Davis Cup: 1952-57; 27-6 singles, 10-8 doubles. Captained team to F, 1976, lost to Italy. Turned pro, 1961. World Top Ten: No. 5, 1958; No. 6, 1959; No. 7, 1960-61. Won 42 amateur singles titles.

BADDELEY, HERBERT; WILFRED: English twins, Herbert and Wilfred Baddeley, RH, b. Jan. 11, 1872, Bromley. Made names at Wimbledon. In 1891 Wilfred, 19 years, 5 months, youngest singles champ for almost a century, until Boris Becker, 17, 1985. Wilfred made F six straight years, winning also 1892, 95. Linked as doubles team, twins made F seven straight years from 1891, winning 1891, 94-95-96. In 1895 beat English Doherty brothers for the title, lost it in a reversal, 1897—only sets of twins to square off for major title. Wilfred d. Jan. 24, 1929, Menton, France; Herbert d. July 20, 1931, Cannes, France.

BARKER, SUE: One of last two Brits to make a major impression (along with Virginia Wade), 5-5 blonde Susan Dorothy Barker Tankard, with forceful RH forehand, won French singles, 1976. Had three key singles wins in last British Wightman Cup victories over U.S., 1974, 1975, 1978 (over Jeanne Evert, Janet Newberry, Tracy Austin). Made Wimbledon SF 1977, QF, 1976; Australian SF 1977, QF 1978. Won 15 pro singles titles, $878,701. World Top Ten: No. 5, 1976-77, No. 10, 1979. Federation Cup, 1975-82, 15-8 singles, 16-6 doubles; Wightman Cup, 1974-83, 5-13 singles, 4-5 doubles. B. April 19, 1956, Paignton, England. Now a leading BBC telecaster.

ROPER BARRETT, HERBERT: Herbert Roper Barrett, English RH, b. Nov. 24, 1873, Upton. An original Davis Cupper with losing British, 1900. Also played 1907, 12-13-14; 0-2 singles, 4-4 doubles.

Captained Cup winners of 1933-1936. Had good long run, won Wimbledon doubles, 1909, 12-13. In 1922, age 48, with Arthur Gore, 54, won historic 1st round over Duke of York (future King George VI) and Louis Grieg, only appearance of royalty on court. D. July 27, 1943, Horsham.

BERNARD, MARCEL: French LH, Marcel Bernard had no intention of winning French, 1946. He was 32, rusty, planned to play only doubles, but said OK when they wanted to put him in the draw—startling everyone, including himself, by making F, beating favored Jaroslav Drobny, 5 sets. Also won doubles with Yvon Petra, 11 years after first French titles, 1935-36 mixed. Davis Cup: 12 years, 1935-56; 13-8 singles, 16-5 doubles. World Top Ten: No. 5, 1946. B. May 18, 1914, La Madeleine, France, d. April 29, 1994.

BLACK, CARA; BYRON; WAYNE: Extraordinary siblings, unique African world class trio, each representing homeland, Zimbabwe, stalwartly, Byron, Wayne in Davis Cup, Cara (wishing Zimbabwe had another female, thus a Federation Cup team). Short, quick, clever. Brothers 10-5 as partners, Cup doubles. Sire, Don Black, fine amateur 1950s, made 3rd rd. Wimbledon, 1953, 56; won Monte Carlo, Cannes, 1954.

Cara Cavell Black, b. Feb. 17, 1979, Harare, like brothers, grew up barefoot on grass courts in family backyard. A 5-5 RH with two-handed backhand, turned pro 1998. World No. 1 junior 1997, winning Wimbledon, U.S. Open juniors. Won 1 singles, 10 doubles (7 in 2001) pro titles, $1,533,808 through 2002; career singles W-L 242-153. Won French mixed with brother Wayne, 2002 (second brother-sister to win, following Helena Sukova-Cyril Suk, 1991). Lost U.S. doubles F 2000 with Elena Likhovtseva. Best singles major: French 4th rd., 2001. Best World singles ranking: No, 43, 2000.

Byron Hamish Black, 5-8 RH with two-handed forehand, backhand, b. Oct. 6, 1969, Harare, had splendid college career University Southern California. All-American 4 times doubles, 3 times singles, a factor in USC winning National Intercollegiate title 1991. Turned pro 1991, retired 2002. Won 2 singles, 22 doubles pro career titles, $5,146,894 through 2002. Made QF U.S., 1995. Won French doubles 1994 with Jonathan Stark. Lost Australian doubles F, 1994 with Stark; 2001 with David Prinosil. Lost Wimbledon doubles F 1996 with Grant Connell. Best World singles ranking: No. 28, 1998. Davis Cup: 1987-2002, 39-20 singles, 17-8 doubles. Huge Cup upset: Brothers beat home team Australia, 3-2, 1st rd., grass, Mildura, 1998—Byron d. U.S. champ Pat Rafter, 3-6, 6-3, 6-2, 7-6 (7-0), Jason Stoltenberg, 6-3, 6-3, 6-3, 6-4; Wayne d. Mark Woodforde, 6-3, 7-5, 6-7 (6-8), 6-2.

Wayne Hamilton Black, 5-7 RH with two-handed backhand, b. Nov. 14, 1973, Harare. Excellent college career University Southern California. All-American 2 times singles, doubles, lost National Intercollegiate F 1994 to Mark Merklein, Florida. Turned pro 1994, having most success in doubles. Won 13 career pro titles, $2,152,775; career doubles W-L 206-137. Best World singles ranking, No. 95, 1998. Won U.S. doubles with Kevin Ullyett, 2001; French mixed with sister Cara, 2002. Lost Australian doubles F with Andrew Kratzman, 2000. Davis Cup, since 1992, 23-18 singles, 17-6 doubles.

BLOOMER, SHIRLEY: Quick, agile Shirley Juliet Bloomer Brasher, English RH won French 1957 over Dorothy Head Knode, lost title, F 1958, to Suzi Kormoczi. Lost F Wimbledon doubles 1955 with Pat Ward to Angela Mortimer-Anne Shilcock. Made French QF 1955-56; Wimbledon QF, 1956, 58; U.S. SF 1956, QF 1957. World Top Ten: No. 7, 1956, No. 3, 1957, No. 5, 1958. Wightman Cup: 1955-60; 1-6 singles, 2-4 doubles (won 2 Cups). Married, 1959, world-class distance runner Christopher Brasher (Olympic steeplechase gold medalist, 1956). B. June 13, 1934, Grimsby, Lincolnshire, England.

BOLLETTIERI, NICK: Most renowned coach, effervescent Nicholas James Bollettieri, b. July 31, 1931, Pelham, N.Y. Runs assembly line for champs, Bollettieri Sports Academy, Bradenton, Fla. Ex-U.S. Army paratrooper, graduate of Spring Hill (Ala.) College, became teaching pro, 1958. Among pupils to make World Top Ten: Andre Agassi, Jimmy Arias, Carling Bassett, Jim Courier, Aaron Krickstein, Monica Seles, Mary Pierce, Iva Majoli, Tommy Haas.

BOLTON, NANCYE: Nancye Hazel Meredith Wynne Bolton, RH Australian, career extended around World War II. B. June 10, 1916, Melbourne. Prodigious winner of Australian titles (record 20 until topped by Margaret Court—6 singles, 10 doubles, 4 mixed). Tall, big hitter. First Aussie woman in U.S. F, lost to Alice

Marble, 1938. Won first Aussie title, 1936, last, 1952, both doubles. Won Aussie record 10 doubles (left court) with Thelma Coyne Long. First Aussie singles title 1937. Beat Long for singles title, 1940, again for title, 1951. Member Australian Tennis Hall of Fame. Made Wimbledon QF 1947; U.S. SF, 1947 (lost to champ Louise Brough after holding 3 MP on serve at 5-2, 40-0, in 3rd). Lost Australian F, 1936, 49; SF 1938,50,52; QF 1939. World Top Ten: No. 10, 1938; No. 4, 1947-48-49. D. Nov. 9, 2001, Melbourne.

BOOTHBY, DORA: Penelope Dora Harvey Boothby, later Mrs. A.C. Geen, a leading English player of her day. Won Wimbledon singles, 1909, doubles, 1913. But poor Dora, twice singles finalist (1910-11), only double-bagel victim, losing 1911 title to Dorothea Douglass Chambers, 6-0, 6-0—two weeks after Chambers double-bageled her at Beckenham. RH, b. Aug. 2, 1881, Finchley, d. Feb. 22, 1970, London.

BOUMAN, KEA: Only Netherlander to win major women's singles, RH Katerina Cornelia 'Kea' Bouman took French, 1927, also French doubles, 1929, Olympic bronze (mixed with Henk Timmer), 1924. Lauded by Bill Tilden as "very strong with good serve, hard forehand, excellent footwork." B. Nov. 23, 1903, Almeto, quit to marry Swiss oarsman Alexander Tiedemann, 1931. World Top Ten: No. 9 1927; No. 8, 1928. D. Nov. 17, 1998.

BOWREY, BILL: Australian RH husband of Hall of Famer Lesley Turner Bowrey. They scored singularly year of marriage, 1968, he winning Australian singles, she Italian. Only husband-wife to hold major singles (she won French, 1963, 65) until Steffi Graf married Andre Agassi 2001. William Walter 'Tex' Bowrey, b. Dec. 25, 1943, Sydney. Made Australian QF, 1965, 1967; U.S. QF, 1966. Made doubles F Australian, 1967; Wimbledon, 1966; U.S. 1967. Davis Cup: 1968-69; 2-2 singles, lost F, 1968.

BOYD, ESNA: Try, try again and again did Aussie RH Esna Flora Boyd—does the sixth time never fail? Lost first five Australian singles F, 1922-26, at last won, 1927, 5-7, 6-1, 6-2, over Sylvia Harper, then lapsed to second place again, 1928, setting Aussie record for most F lost. Did better in Australian doubles, won 1922-23, 28, lost F 1925-26-27. Even better in mixed with southpaw Jack Hawkes, winning 1922, 26-27, losing F 1928, for a total of 7 Aussie crowns. Won Scottish singles, 1931. Relied on strong flat forehand. B. 1901, Melbourne, d., Mrs. Angus Robertson, 1962.

BRUGUERA, SERGI: Big, strong (6-2, 170), fast, ungainly Spanish RH (2-handed backhand) baseliner. Won French singles, 1993-94. Made F 1997, SF 1995, with heavy, murderous topspin. World Top Ten: No. 4, 1993-94; No. 8, 1997. Olympic silver medal, 1996. Davis Cup: 1990-96; 11-9 singles, 2-1 doubles. Turned pro 1988. Won 14 singles, 3 doubles pro titles, $11,632,199. B. Jan. 16, 1971, Barcelona.

BUCHHOLZ, BUTCH: Man-about-every-phase of the game, Earl Henry 'Butch' Buchholz, Jr., willowy 6-2 RH out of St. Louis was World Top Ten: No. 5, 1960. U.S. Top Ten: No. 3, 1960; No. 9, 1958; No. 6, 1959; No. 10, 1970. Davis Cup, 1959-60, 3-1 singles, 3-2 doubles; lost F 1959. Barnstorming pro. 1961-67. (U.S. Pro champ, 1962). Commissioner World Team Tennis, 1976-78, Executive Director ATP, 1981-82. Founder-operator of prime attraction Lipton Championships (now NASDAQ-100), since 1985, Key Biscayne, Fla. Had volley, has vision, uncommon tennis leader. B. Sept. 16, 1940, St. Louis. Right-hand man at Lipton was brother Clifford Buchholz (U.S. No. 18, 1966).

BUNDY, DOROTHY: Dorothy May 'Dodo' Bundy Cheney, the most enduring champ, flowing uninterrupted from teens into superiority as super-senior. Californian RH, b. Sept. 1, 1916, Los Angeles, grew up Santa Monica. Won Australian singles, 1938, made U.S. Top Ten 10 times:1936-37-38-39-40-41, 43-44-45-46 (No. 3, 1937-38, 41). Keeps winning. First U.S. title, 1941, Indoor doubles with Pauline Betz. Most recently 10 singles, doubles titles in the 85s category during 2001-02. At end of 2002, held record total 316 U.S. Senior titles from 40s age group on up (45, 50, 55, 60, 65, 70, 75, 80, 85), beginning 1957. Won Hard Court 40s singles 13 straight, 1957-69. Achieved 29 U.S. Senior Grand Slams (Grass, Clay, Indoor, Hard singles/doubles within calendar year). Singles Slams: 5 in 70s, 1986-87-88-89, 92; 3 in 75s, 1993-94-95; 3 in 80s, 1997-98-99; 1 in 85s, 2002. Great genes: mother, Hall of Famer May Sutton Bundy, won Wimbledon, 1905, 07, U.S., 1904; father, Tom Bundy, won U.S. doubles, 1912-14. No end in sight for this grand lady.

BUTTSWORTH, CORAL: Briefly at the heights, Coral A. 'Corrie' McInnes Buttsworth came out of Taree, New South Wales to win Australian singles, 1931-32, relinquishing title in 1933 F. Also won doubles, 1932. B., Taree. Married Cecil Buttsworth, 1920.

CAPRIATI, JENNIFER: Jennifer Marie Capriati, American prodigy, RH (two-fisted backhand), b. March 29, 1976, New York, grew up in Florida. Won 3 major singles: Australian 2001-02, French 2001. Saved 4 MP to beat Martina Hingis, Australian F, 2002, most in major women's F. Only defending Australian champ to lose 1st rd. following year, 2003 to Marlene Weingartner. Attracted great attention as youngest pro finalist, making debut at 13 years, 11 months, Boca Raton, Fla., 1990, losing F to Gabriela Sabatini. Made numerous 'youngest' marks: Federation Cupper (and winner), 1990; Wightman Cupper (and winner), 1989; Wimbledon SF, 1991. Six times in U.S. Top Three: No. 3, 1990, 2002; No. 2, 1991-92-93. Also No. 6, 1996, 2000, No. 7 1999. Six times World Top Ten: No. 8, 1990, No. 6 1991; No. 7 1992; No. 9 1993; No. 2 2001; No. 3 2002. Olympic gold medalist, singles, 1992, deposed Steffi Graf in F. Powerful 5-9 ground-stroker, dethroned two major champs, 1991—Martina Navratilova, Wimbledon; Sabatini, U.S. Disenchantment with tennis, personal problems removed her 1994-95. Tried comebacks but slipped to No. 101, 1998. Grittily turned career around, up to Australian SF and No. 14, 2000. Also made Australian QF 1992-93; French SF 2002, QF 1992-93; Wimbledon SF 1991, 2001, QF 1992-93, 2002; U.S. SF 1991, 2001, QF 2002. Won 13 singles, 1 doubles career pro titles, $6,974,563 through 2002. Lost 14 singles F. Singles W-L, 359-146. Federation Cup, 1990-91, 96, 2000: 10-3 singles, 1-1 doubles, 13 series, 2 Cups. Wightman Cup, 1989: 1-0 singles, 1 Cup.

CARILLO, MARY: Mary Jean Carillo, LH, b. March 15, 1957, New York. Played women's tour, collaborated with John McEnroe, his first major title, French mixed, 1977. Best known as sportscaster, foremost tennis, ESPN, CBS, NBC, HBO, refreshingly informative, uninhibited style. Ex-husband, Bill Bowden, teaching pro; 2 children.

CASH, PAT: Powerful Aussie RH (6-0, 185), career shortened by injuries. Strong server, excellent volleyer, Patrick Hart Cash hit high points: won Wimbledon singles 1987; led Davis Cup victories, 1983, 86, and to F 1990. Lost sensational Australian F, 1987-88, to Stefan Edberg, Mats Wilander. Won Cup clinchers over

Sweden both years; in 1986, beat Edberg and, stirringly from 0-2 in sets, Mikael Pernfors, called "best Aussie Cup performance" by Capt. Neale Fraser. Davis Cup: 1983-90; 23-7 singles, 8-3 doubles. World Top Ten: No. 8 1984, No. 7 1987. B. May 27, 1965, Melbourne. Turned pro 1982. Won 7 singles, 11 doubles career pro titles.

CHANG, MICHAEL: Diminutive (5-7), tenacious Michael Chang, RH American (two-handed backhand). Tireless retriever. B. Feb. 22, 1972, Hoboken, N.J., of Chinese-American parentage, reared in Southern California. Electrified French, 1989, as youngest major male champ, 17, first American victor since 1955 (Tony Trabert). Beat favorite No. 1 Ivan Lendl from 2-sets down 4th rd. and cramping, 4-6, 4-6, 6-3, 6-3, 6-3, in 4:39; Stefan Edberg in 5-set F. Lost longest major match (5:26) to Edberg, SF, U.S., 1992. Youngest, 18, to help U.S. win Davis Cup, 1990; beat Aussie Darren Cahill in F. In SF that year (3-2 over Austria at Vienna), won extraordinary deciding match from 2-sets down over Horst Skoff. Turned pro 1988. Won 34 singles career pro titles, $19,070,332 through 2002. Lost 24 singles F, including Australian, U.S. 1996, French 1995. Career singles W-L, 660-302. World Top Ten 7 times: No. 5, 1989, 95; No. 6, 1992, 94; No. 8, 1993; No. 2, 1996; No. 3, 1997. Made Australian SF 1995, French QF 1990-91; U.S. SF 1992, 97, QF 1993, 95. Davis Cup: 1989-90, 96-97; 8-4 singles. Coached by brother, Carl Chang, who played for U. of California, Berkeley.

COCHELL, EARL: Earl Cochell, RH American, created stir at U.S., Forest Hills, 1951, behaving erratically, disruptively, verbally assaulted referee Ellsworth Davenport, other court officials, while losing 4th rd. to Gardnar Mulloy. USTA reacted by banning him for life, unprecedented penalty. Ban later rescinded but had ended exceptional career of Top Ten amateur. Made U.S. Top Ten four times: No. 9, 1947; No. 6, 1948; No 7 1949-50. Not ranked again though 1951 play warranted another Top Ten spot. A Californian, won 11 amateur singles titles, National Intercollegiate doubles, University Southern California (with Hugh Stewart), 1951. B. May 18, 1922, Sacramento.

COSTA, ALBERT: A happy hunting ground for Spaniards, Roland Garros came under the rule of unseeded, No. 22 Albert Costa in 2002, the fifth of his country to seize the French championship, Spain's 7th,

dating back to Manolo Santana, 1961, 64. It was a 3rd all-Spanish F as he beat 11th seeded Juan Carlos Ferrero. B. June 25, 1975, Lerida, Spain, stocky 5-11 Costa never better previously in a major than French QF, 1995. Quick, tireless, he turned pro 1993, won 12 career pro singles titles (all clay), $6,367,250 through 2002; career singles W-L 326-210. Davis Cup: 4 years since 1996, had a strong hand in Spain's Cup triumph, 2000; 8-5 singles, 0-1 doubles. World Top Ten: No. 8, 2002 (from No. 40, 2001).

COURIER, JIM: James Spencer Courier, ruggedly built 6-1 RH American with two-handed backhand, from Dade City, Fla. Parlayed ferocious groundstrokes to French titles, 1991-92; Australian titles, 1992-93; Made F French, Wimbledon, 1993; U.S. 1991. Made Australian SF, 1994, QF 1995-96; French SF 1994; U.S. SF 1995. B. Aug. 17, 1970, Sanford, Fla. Helped U.S. win Davis Cup, 1992, 95. U.S. Top Ten: No. 1, 1991-92; No. 2. 1993; No. 4, 1994-95; No. 6, 1996; No. 3, 1997; No. 8, 1998; No. 5, 1999. World Top Ten: No. 1, 1992; No. 2, 1991; No. 3, 1993; No. 8, 1995. Won 23 singles, 13 doubles pro career titles (5 singles titles, 25-match win streak, 1992), $14,033,132. Davis Cup: 1991-92, 95, 99. 16-10 singles, 1-0 doubles. U.S. was 13-1 with him in lineup. Thrice he won decisive 5th match, a U.S. record: 1994 over Jacco Eltingh, Netherlands; 1998 over Marat Safin, Russia; 1999 over Greg Rusendski, Britain. Turned pro 1988. Davis Cup coach, 2002-03.

COX, MARK: English LH, Cambridge grad, Mark Cox has niche as first amateur to beat a pro in open competition. Defeated Pancho Gonzalez, Roy Emerson successive April afternoons, gained SF, British Hard Court Championships, Bournemouth 1968, inaugural open. B. July 5, 1943, Leicester. Davis Cup 1967-69, 1973, 1978-79, helped Britain reach F, 1978, 15-6 singles, 8-6 doubles.

DALTON, JUDY: Judith Anne Marshall Tegart Dalton, Australian RH, b. Dec. 12, 1937, Melbourne. Tall, sturdy, excellent doubles player, won all majors (8): Australian, 1964, 67, 69-70; French, 1966; Wimbledon, 1969; U.S., 1970-71; five with Margaret Court. Made Australian QF 1970, 74, 77; Wimbledon F, 1968; SF, 1971; U.S. QF. 1968, 71 Federation Cup, 1965-67, 69-70 (won 1965, 70). Singles 6-1 doubles 12-3. World Top Ten: No. 10. 1967; No. 7, 1968; No. 9, 1971.

DATE, KIMIKO: Most successful modern-day Japanese, quick 5-4 Kimiko 'Kid Butterfly' Date with flat groundies (two-handed backhand), excellent anticipation, natural LH transformed to RH. Surprisingly retired at 26, 1996, ranked World No. 9 (No. 9, 1994; No. 4, 1995). Best win, saved 2 match points over Steffi Graf, 7-6 (9-7), 3-6, 12-10, Federation Cup, 1996, led Japan to SF. Made SF Australian, 1994, French, 1995, Wimbledon, 1996; QF, U.S., 1993-94. B. Sept. 28, 1970, Kyoto. Federation Cup, 1989-96, 9-5 singles, 4-3 doubles. Turned pro 1988, won 7 career pro singles titles, $1,974,253.

DAVIDSON, OWEN: Owen Keir Davidson, LH Australian ladies man: mixed doubles ace. B. Oct. 4, 1943, Melbourne. Mixed Grand Slam, 1967, with Lesley Turner (Australian), Billie Jean King other three. Won eight major mixed—Aussie, 1967; French, 1967; Wimbledon, 1967, 71, 73; U.S., 1967, 71, 73—plus two doubles: U.S., with John Newcombe, 1973; Australian, with Ken Rosewall, 1972. Made Wimbledon singles SF, 1966; U.S. QF, 1967. Rookie pro, 1968, as British national coach. Played, won very first 'open' match, beating amateur John Clifton, inaugural open, British Hard Court, Bournemouth.

DAVIDSON, SVEN: Most prominent Swede prior to Bjorn Borg was Sven Viktor Davidson, RH b. July 13, 1928, Boras, Sweden. First Swede to win majors: French singles, 1957, after losing 1955-56 F; Wimbledon doubles, 1958, with Ulf Schmidt. World Top Ten: No. 7, 1953; No. 10, 1954-55, 58; No. 5, 1956; No. 3, 1957. Davis Cup: 1950-1961; 39-14 singles, 23-9 doubles.

DMITRIEVA, ANNA: Russian pioneer, Anna Vladimirovna Dmitrieva was first Soviet permitted to play abroad, lost F Wimbledon junior 1956. LH, b. Dec. 16, 1940, Moscow, 5-4, 126. Won Soviet title, 1960, 64, also Algerian (over Françoise Durr), 1964, Czechoslovak, Hungarian, 1961 and 1962. Now outstanding Russian broadcaster. Federation Cup, 1968, 1-1 singles.

DRYSDALE, CLIFF: Eric Clifford Drysdale, best South African male, RH (with two-handed backhand). B. May 26, 1941, Nelspruit, Transvaal. Slim 6-2, deceptive groundstroker, good volleyer. First to use double-handed stroke in U.S. F, 1965, lost to Manolo Santana. Second South African to make major F, following Eric

Sturgess, U.S., 1948. Won a doubles major, U.S. 1972, with Roger Taylor. Career spanned amateur, open eras. Made French, Wimbledon, SF, 1965-66. Became pro, 1968, with WCT 'Handsome Eight.' Made Australian QF, 1971; U.S. QF, 1968 (beat favorite Rod Laver). Davis Cup: 1962-67, 1974; 30-12 singles, 3-2 doubles, helped South Africa win Cup, 1974. Became U.S. citizen. Won 5 singles, 7 doubles career pro titles; 28 amateur singles titles. World Top Ten six times: No. 4, 1965; No. 9, 1966; No. 10, 1967; No. 9, 1968-69, 71. Now noted TV tennis commentator.

EAVES, WILBERFORCE: An Aussie who got around, Dr. Wilberforce Vaughan Eaves first of his country to play for major titles abroad. Excellent volleyer. Lost Wimbledon F 1895, despite holding 1 match point, to Wilfred Baddeley (his lob fell inches long). Lost U.S. F 1897 to Bob Wrenn, 5 sets. (Also lost Wimbledon all-comers F 1896, 1897 to eventual champs Harold Mahony, Reggie Doherty.) Lost Wimbledon doubles F 1895 with Ernest Lewis. Had 13-6 Wimbledon singles record. Lived in London, won singles bronze medal for Britain 1908 Olympics. Won Irish title 1895, Welsh 1897, Scottish 1901. Served British army as physician in Boer War. B. Dec. 10, 1867, Melbourne, d. Feb. 2, 1920, London.

EDMONDSON, MARK: Mark Ronald 'Eddo' Edmondson, husky 6-1 Aussie RH, longest-shot winner of men's major, Australian, 1976. B. June 28, 1954, Gosford. From obscurity (supported himself as janitor), unseeded, ranked No. 212, won homeland title. Beat all-timers, 2-1 seeds, Ken Rosewall, SF, John Newcombe, F. Thereafter, fine career. Made Australian SF, 1981; QF, 1977, 79; Wimbledon SF, 1982. Serve-and-volleyer, best at doubles: won French, 1985, Australian, 1980-81. Davis Cup: 1977-85; 11-7 singles, 8-3 doubles, helped win 1983 Cup (4-0 doubles, 2-0 singles). Won 6 singles, 35 career doubles pro titles, $1,449,486. Best World rank, No. 20, 1981.

FERNANDEZ, GIGI: Great U.S. doubles performer, acrobatic volleyer (left court), RH beauty Beatriz Cristina 'Gigi' Fernandez won 17 majors, 14 with Natalia Zvereva—2 Australian (1993-94), 5 French (1992-93-94-95, 97), 4 Wimbledon (1992-93-94, 97) 3 U.S (1992, 95-96)—second all-time team total). Other 3 majors: French, 1991, with Jana Novotna; U.S., 1988, with Robin White; 1990, with Martina Navratilova.

Also two Olympic golds, 1992, 1996, with Mary Joe Fernandez (no relation). She and Zvereva barely missed Grand Slams, 1993, lost SF, U.S., to Arantxa Sanchez Vicario-Helena Sukova, 1-6, 6-3, 6-4, ending 40-match major streak, and 1994, lost SF, U.S., to Katerina Maleeva-Robin White, 7-6 (7-2), 1-6, 6-3. Made Wimbledon singles SF, 1994. Best World singles ranking, No. 22, 1991. B. Feb. 22, 1964, San Juan, Puerto Rico. All-American, Clemson, 1983. Federation Cup, 1988, 90-91-92, 94-95-96; 3-1 singles, 20-2 doubles (won 1990, 1996 Cups). Wightman Cup, 1987-88; 2-0 doubles (won 2 Cups). Turned pro 1983. Won 3 singles, 67 doubles career pro titles, $4,681,906. Career W-L singles 270-232; doubles 664-184.

FIBAK, WOJTEK: Best Polish man, Wojtek Fibak, RH, b. Aug. 30, 1952, Poznan. Trained as lawyer. Late starter, first Polish pro, 22, despite opposition of Polish Federation, solid 13-year career. Davis Cup: 1972-92; 19-5 singles, 9-7 doubles. Agile 6-footer, superb volleyer, best at doubles, won 15 singles, 48 doubles career pro titles; was in 34 other doubles F, made $2,725,133. Lost Masters F, 1976. Made French QF, 1977, 80; Wimbledon, U.S. QF, 1980. Best World rank, No. 13, 1977. Only Pole to win major: Australian doubles, 1978.

FLEITZ, BEVERLY: Unique among female major finalists: no backhand. Ambidextrous. (A male ambi, Giorgio de Stefani of Italy, lost the French F to Henri Cochet, 1932.) American RH Beverly Joyce Baker Beckett Fleitz hit forehands both sides, No. 1 American, 1959. Lost Wimbledon F, 1955, to Louise Brough. Lost Wimbledon doubles F with Christine Truman to Jeane Arth-Darlene Hard, 1959. Made French SF 1955, QF 1951; Wimbledon SF 1951, QF 1956; U.S. SF 1950, QF 1948-49, 1954-55, 58. World Top Ten: No. 7, 1950, No. 8, 1951; No. 3, 1954-55, 58; No. 4, 1959. Other U.S. Top Ten: No. 5, 1948, 55; No. 8, 1949; No. 4, 1950; No. 6, 1951; No. 3, 1954; No. 2, 1958. Wightman Cup: 1949, 56, 59; 3-0 singles, 1-0 doubles (won 3 Cups). B. March 13, 1930, Providence, R.I.

GARRISON, ZINA: Zina Lynna Garrison, American RH from Houston Public parks, won 1988 Olympic gold (doubles with Pam Shriver), bronze (singles). Gave Chris Evert her last defeat, QF U.S., 1989. First black woman in major F, Wimbledon, 1990 (as Mrs. Willard Jackson), since Althea Gibson won there, 1958. Lost first

pro F between two blacks, Largo, Fla., 1988, to childhood pal, Lori McNeil. Aggressive, quick, fine volleyer. B. Nov. 16, 1963, Houston. Made U.S. SF, 1988-89; QF, 1987, 90; Wimbledon SF, 1985, QF, 1985, 91. World Top Ten: No. 10, 1983, 90; No. 9, 1984, 87-88; No. 8, 1985; No. 4, 1989. Turned pro 1982. Federation Cup: 1984-94; 7-4 singles, 15-1 doubles (2 Cups, 1989-90). Wightman Cup: 1987-88; 3-1 singles, 1-1 doubles (2 Cups, captain, 1988). Won 14 pro singles, 20 doubles career pro titles, $4,587,816. Operates youth tennis program, Houston. Coach U.S. Olympic, 2000, Federation Cup, 2002-03, teams. Also a USTA national coach.

GEMMEL, RICE: Rice Thomas Hopkins Gemmel, b. 1896, Caulfield, Victoria, was the man of the year 1921 at Australian. A fleeting presence he beat Alf Hedemann for the singles title, collaborated with S.H. Eaton for the doubles prize. Not heard from again, and so uncelebrated that he's listed as Rhys (not Rice) in some record books.

GERULAITIS, VITAS: Vitas Kevin Gerulaitis, the 'Lithuanian Lion,' with flowing golden mane, was a lean and speedy 6-foot, RH. A determined attacker, only American male to win Italian twice, 1977, 79. Lost French F, 1980. Made SF or better all majors. Won Australian, 1977. Stunning comeback U.S. SF, 1979, beat Roscoe Tanner from two sets and service break down; lost F to John McEnroe, first all-American U.S. male F since Tony Trabert over Vic Seixas, 1953. That season won four of 22 tournaments on 75-21 match record. Davis Cup: 1977-80; 11-3 singles (1979, 5-1 for Cup winner, including incredible SF escape from Mark Edmondson at Australia, down triple match point at 7-8, 0-40 in 3rd to win, 6-8, 14-16, 10-8, 6-3, 6-3). Lost sensational 1977 5-set Wimbledon SF, Bjorn Borg, 8-6, 5th. Made French SF 1979; QF 1982. Wimbledon QF, 1976, 82; U.S. SF, 1978, 81. Won Wimbledon doubles, 1975. Lost Masters F, 1979, 81. Won 27 singles, 9 doubles career pro titles, $2,778,748. World Top Ten 6 times: No. 4, 1977, 79; No. 5, 1978, 82; No. 9, 1980-81. B. July 26, 1954, Brooklyn, N.Y., d. Sept. 17, 1994. Father, Vitas, champion of native Lithuania. Sister, Ruta, was on women's pro tour, No. 31, 1980; French QF, 1979.

GIMENO, ANDRES: Spanish RH, Andres Gimeno, oldest male winner French, 34, 1972. Best years as touring pro, from 1960, prior to open era. Graceful, slender

6-2, solid groundstrokes, good serve, competent volley. B. Aug. 3, 1937, Barcelona. Won 7 singles, 4 doubles career pro titles. Lost Australian F, 1969, QF, 1959. Made French SF, 1968; QF, 1969; Wimbledon SF, 1970. Davis Cup: 1958-60, 1972-73; 18-5 singles, 5-5 doubles, led team to SF, 1972. World Top Ten: No. 10, 1969-70, 72.

GOMEZ, ANDRES: Lone Ecuadoran to win major, French 1990, 6-4 LH Andres 'Gogo' Gomez beat favored Andre Agassi. Also made QF French, 1984, 86-87; Wimbledon, U.S. 1984. Heavy server, sharp volleyer, smart user of spin, all-arounder. Won 21 singles, 34 doubles (French 1988) pro career titles, $4,385,040. Retired 1993. B. Feb. 27, 1960, Guayaquil. Davis Cup: 1979-93; 31-12 singles, 20-15 doubles. World Top Ten: No. 5, 1984; No. 10, 1986

GORE, ARTHUR: An original Davis Cupper, Arthur William Charles Gore (unrelated to first champ, Spencer Gore), lost to Malcolm Whitman as Cup play got under way at Boston in 1900, and captained the British team. English RH, became Wimbledon's most enduring player, thrice singles victor (1901, 08-09). Oldest major male champ, 1909, 41-years-7 months. First entered 1888, continued in singles through 1922, age 54 (oldest such), doubles through 1927, totaling 156 matches over record 35 years. Was very productive singles player (64-26), second to Jimmy Connors (84-17). B. Jan. 2, 1868, Lyndhurst, d. Dec. 1, 1928, London. Davis Cup: 3 years, 2-3 singles, 1-0 doubles.

GORE, SPENCER: Spencer William Gore, English RH, b. March 10, 1850, Wimbledon; d. April 19, 1906, Ramsgate, England. Game's original champ, Wimbledon, 1877, as opportunistic volleyer. Lost F, 1878, walked away. Ex-rackets champ, not overly taken by tennis, thought the game boring.

GOTTFRIED, BRIAN: Brian Edward Gottfried, hard-working, energetic 6-foot RH. Sound groundstrokes, preferred serve-and-volley. B. Jan. 27, 1952, Baltimore, raised in Florida, All-American, Trinity (Tex.) U., 1971-72, lost F National Intercollegiate singles, doubles, 1972. Davis Cup: 1976-82 (with 1978 winner); 6-7 singles, 1-0 doubles. QF or better all majors but Aussie, lost F French, 1977, to Guillermo Vilas. Heavy-duty 1977: won 5 of 27 tournaments, 108-23 record. U.S. Top Ten, 10 times: No. 2, 1977; No. 3, 1978; No. 5, 1976; No. 6, 1975, 80; No. 8, 1981; No. 9, 1973;

No. 10, 1972, 82-83. World Top Ten: No. 10, 1976; No. 5, 1977; No. 7, 1978. With Raul Ramirez won 39 doubles, including Wimbledon, 1976; French, 1975, 77; Italian, 1974-75-76-77. Won 25 singles, 54 doubles pro titles, $2,782,514.

GOOLD, ST. LEGER: Vere Thomas 'St. Leger' Goold, Irish RH, Wimbledon finalist, 1879. Personal finale: death in prison, was most ignominious for a champ. Won native (Irish) championship, 1879, skilled volleyer. Played as 'St. Leger' (pseudonyms not uncommon at time). Lost F, Wimbledon, to John Hartley before crowd of 1,100. In 1907, with French wife, Violet Girodin, convicted in French court of murdering Emma Levin, given life sentence. D. Sept. 8, 1909, Devils Island, French Guiana. B. Oct. 2, 1853, Waterford.

GRAEBNER, CAROLE; CLARK: American couple, RH Carole and Clark Graebner, only husband-wife to rank World Top Ten, play major F while married. Fourth couple ranked U.S. Top Ten same years, following Sarah Palfrey and Elwood Cooke (1940, 45), Marjorie 'Midge' Gladman and John Van Ryn (1930-31), Virginia Wolfenden and Frank Kovacs (1941). Teammates, Cleveland, World Team Tennis, 1974. However, during divorce proceedings Clark, player-coach, traded her to Pittsburgh for Laura DuPont, a unique divestiture.

Carole Caldwell Graebner, b. June 24, 1943, Pittsburgh, grew up in Southern California. Baseliner, good volleyer. Lost U.S. F, 1964, to Maria Bueno, 6-1, 6-0 (equaling worst such beating, original F, 1884, Ellen Hansell over Laura Knight). Won U.S. doubles, 1965. World Top Ten: No. 4, 1964; No. 9, 1965. U.S. Top Ten: No. 9, 1961; No. 4, 1962-63; No. 3, 1964-65; No. 6, 1967. Federation Cup: 1963-66; 2-1 singles, 9-1 doubles (with winner, 1963, 66). Wightman Cup: 1963-64-65, 67, 71; 2-0 singles, 2-2 doubles (all 5 Cups).

Clark Edward Graebner, b. Nov. 4, 1943, Cleveland, grew up there, graduate Northwestern U. Strong, 6-2, serve-and-volleyer. Lost U.S. F, 1967; SF, 1968. Made Wimbledon SF, 1968. World Top Ten: No. 8, 1967; No. 7, 1968. U.S. Top Ten: No. 9, 1964; No. 3 1966, 71; No. 4, 1967, 69-70; No. 2, 1968; No. 8, 1972. Davis Cup: 1965-68; 9-2 singles; 5-2 doubles (with 1968 winner). Won singles, U.S. Indoor, 1971; Clay, 1966. French doubles, 1966.

GREGORY, COLIN: Covering remarkable spread of almost three decades, Davis Cup career of Dr. John

Colin Gregory, English physician, concluded in triumph. He, playing captain, oldest to win Cup match: 48 years, 295 days, with Tony Mottram, beat Josip Pallada-Stevan Laszlo, Yugoslavia, 6-4, 1-6, 9-11, 6-2, 6-2, 1952, Belgrade, making the difference in Brits' 3-2 win. Good-humored Yorkshire RH, b. July 28, 1903, Beverly, took a major 23 years before, Australian singles, 1929. Same year lost Wimbledon doubles F. Davis Cup: 1926-52; 13-9 singles, 8-1 doubles. D. Sept. 10, 1959, Wimbledon.

GULLIKSON, TIM; TOM: Identical twins, RH Timothy Ernest, LH Thomas Robert Gullikson, b. Sept. 8, 1951, LaCrosse, Wis., Tom elder by minutes. Graduates, Northern Illinois U. Lost Wimbledon F, 1983, third twins in major F, following English Wimbledonians Renshaws (1884-85-86, 88-89) and Baddeleys (1891, 94-95-96). Sturdy, 5-11, 185, attackers, won 10 pro doubles titles together. Tim, best World rank No. 18, 1978, won 4 singles, 16 doubles pro career titles, $1,120,570. Tom, best World rank, No. 56, 1981, won 1 singles, 12 doubles pro career titles, $889,042. Each won at U.S. original site, Newport: Tim, 1977, Tom, 1985. Tim, d. May 3, 1996, Wheaton, Ill. Coached Pete Sampras to six majors. Tom, U.S. Davis Cup captain, 1994-98, record 13-4 (won Cup, 1995).

HADOW, FRANK: Patrick Francis Hadow, English RH, b. Jan. 24, 1855, Regents Park; d. June 29, 1946, Bridgwater. Loftiest Wimbledon champ: introduced the lob to thwart, bring down volleyer Spencer Gore, defender, second Wimbledon F, 1878. Lost no sets in tourney, played on holiday from his coffee plantation in Ceylon. Didn't return to defend, may never have played again.

HAMILTON, GHOST: Pale, frail-looking Irishman haunted Willie Renshaw by giving him only loss in Wimbledon F, 1890, depriving Willie of eighth title, RH Willoughby James 'Ghost' Hamilton from County Kildare made brief mark. Illness (blood poisoning) prevented him from defending. B. Dec. 8, 1864, Monasterevan, County Kildare, Ireland, d. Sept. 27, 1943, Dublin.

HARPER, SYLVIA: Single life may have been better for Sylvia Lance Harper's singles game. She won the Australian title over Esna Boyd in 1924, and the doubles as well at age 28, with Daphne Akhurst. But after

becoming Mrs. Harper she lost the final twice, to Boyd in 1927 and Akhurst in 1929. She did win the doubles again, as Mrs. Harper in 1925, repeating with Akhurst. An older man suited her in 1923 as she won the mixed with 51-year-old Horrie Rice. B. Oct. 1895 at Canterbury, New South Wales.

HARTIGAN, JOAN: An international trail-blazer for Aussie women, tall RH Joan Marcia Hartigan reached World Top Ten: No. 8, 1934; No. 9, 1935, when she reached Wimbledon SF (lost to Helen Jacobs, 1934, champ Helen Moody, 1935, after beating defender Dorothy Round). B. 1912, Sydney, d. there Aug. 31, 2000. Rode puissant forehand from baseline to Australian singles titles, 1934-35, 37. Made Aussie QF, 1937-38, 46; SF, 1939-40. Also won mixed, 1937. Won Scottish singles 1934. Used 'upside-down' backhand (same racket face as forehand) Married Hugh Bathurst, 1947.

HARTLEY, JOHN: English clergyman, only such to win major, Wimbledon singles 1879-80. Rev. John Thorneycroft Hartley, RH, Oxford grad, extremely steady, unerring, but overwhelmed in 1881 F as Willie Renshaw launched 6-title run. B. Jan. 9, 1849, Tong, England, d. Aug. 21, 1935, Knaresborough, England.

HAWKES, JACK: Unpredictable LH Australian with good twist serve and volley. John Bailey Hawkes won Aussie title 1926, also doubles (left court) with Gerald Patterson, 1922, 26-27. Had 7 match points but lost 1927 F to Patterson. They lost Wimbledon F 1928. World No. 10, 1928. Davis Cup: 1921-23; 6-7 singles, 5-2 doubles. B. June 7, 1899, Geelong, Australia, d. there, May 31, 1990.

HEATH, ROD: Wilfrid Rodney Heath, first Australian male champ, RH, won at 21 in hometown, Melbourne, 1905, conquering field of 17 at Warehousemen's Cricket Ground, beating Dr. Arthur H. Curtis's volleying with forehand drives. Won again, 1910. Davis Cup: 1911-1912 (won Cup, 1911); 1-2 singles. After aviation duty, World War I, lost Wimbledon doubles F, 1919, with Randolph Lycett, his SF victim in 1905 Aussie. B. June 15, 1884, Melbourne, d. there Oct. 6, 1936.

HELLWIG, HELEN: Helen Rebecca Hellwig, RH out of Brooklyn, was sixth to win U.S. women's title, 1894, at 20, deposing Aline Terry, 5 sets. She and Juliette Atkinson first team to repeat in women's doubles, 1894-

1895. Reappeared 12 years later, made SF, 1907, QF, 1908, as Mrs. William Pouch. Last played 1916 at 42, had 14-8 U.S. singles record. B. March 1874, Brooklyn, d. Nov. 26, 1960, New York.

HENIN-HARDENE, JUSTINE: Won three WTA tournaments in 2001 to climb from 48th position to seventh in the WTA year-end rankings. Reached 2001 French SF and Wimbledon F (vs. Venus Williams). Helped Belgium defeat Russia in Fed Cup final. In 2002, had best-ever finish in year-end rankings, No. 5, after reaching Wimbledon SF and Australian QF. Employs a topspin backhand John McEnroe calls best in the game. B. Liege, Belgium, June 1, 1982. At age 15, became youngest ever winner of Belgian National Championships, and won French Open junior title. Fifth WTA player to win first professional tournament, Antwerp, 1999, at age 16. Six career tour titles: 2002, German Open, Linz; 2001, Gold Coast, Canberra, Hertogenbosch, Antwerp, 1999. With Kim Clijsters, led Belgium to 2001 Fed Cup championship over Russia. Married Pierre-Yves Hardenne, Nov. 16, 2002.

HENKEL, HENNER: The younger of Germany's splendid pre-World War II one-two punch, RH 6-foot Heinrich Ernst Otto 'Henner' Henkel was dead at 27, a soldier killed on Stalingrad front, Jan 13, 1943. He and Gottfried von Cramm nearly won Davis Cup, 1937, 3-2 SF loss to U.S. That year they were World Nos. 3 and 2, won French and U.S. doubles, and Henkel won French singles. He was also No. 9, 1936; No. 6, 1939. Davis Cup: 1935-39; 33-13 singles, 16-4 doubles (team also made SF, 1935-36, 38). Made Wimbledon SF, 1938-39; QF, 1938. B. Oct. 9, 1915, Posen, Germany.

HENMAN, TIM: Versatile, all-round player, solid on all surfaces. Strong serve-and-volleyer, has nine ATP tour wins. Year-end top 10 four times between 1998-2002, reached No. 5, July 1999. B. Oxford, England, Sept. 6, 1974. 6-foot-1, 170 pounds. British No. 1 who generates incredible hype at each Wimbledon. Wimbledon SF 1998, 1999, 2001, 2002, but lost each time to eventual champion (Pete Sampras twice, Goran Ivanisevic, Lleyton Hewitt). Was the first Brit to reach Wimbledon SF since Roger Taylor, 1973. Came within two points of reaching final in 2001. Grandfather, Henry Billington, first competed at Wimbledon in 1948, while great-grandmother, Ellen Stawell Brown, was the first woman to serve overhand, in 1901. Won doubles silver medal

with Neil Broad at 1996 Olympics (vs. Todd Woodbridge, Mark Woodforde). Davis Cup 1995-2002, 30-11 career record (22-6 in singles). Wife, Lucy, is a top cancer surgeon in Britain.

HILLYARD, BLANCHE BINGLEY: Hardy, enthusiastic Englishwoman, Blanche Bingley Hillyard played in the first female Wimbledon, 1884, was still around 29 years later, 1913, her last of 17 at age 49. Between 1885 and 1901, played a majors record 13 F. She won 6, had a record 14-year spread from first, 1886, to last, 1900, at 36, second-oldest female champ. Her 7 F lost are also a record for majors. A RH, b. Nov. 3, 1863, Greenford, Middlesex, d. Aug. 6, 1946, Pulborough, Sussex. At Wimbledon, 48-18 in singles. Best comeback in major F, 1889, beat Lena Rice, 4-6, 8-6, 6-4, from 3-5, 3 match points 2nd set, until Jennifer Capriati saved 4 MP beating Martina Hingis, Australian F 2002. Also won three Irish, two German titles. Her 1912 victim, rookie Bun Ryan, made Hall of Fame.

HOMANS, HELEN: Helen Homans, a New Yorker, started as U.S. champ in doubles, 1905, losing singles F. Turned it around 1906, winning singles, losing doubles. B. 1878 or 1879, d., as Mrs. McLean, March 29, 1949, age 70, Bronxville, N.Y. Brother, Shep Homans, better known athlete, All-American in football, fullback, Princeton, 1890-91.

IVANISEVIC, GORAN: Spidery yet powerful Croatian, Goran Simun Ivanisevic, 6-5 LH (with two-handed backhand). Huge server, streaky, strong strokes. Appealingly jocular. B. Sept. 13, 1971, Split. Only Croat to win Wimbledon, 2001, a thriller, 9-7 in 5th over Pat Rafter. Serving tournament record 213 aces unique champ—unseeded wild card ranked No. 125, having lost 3 previous F: 1992, to Andre Agassi; 1994, 98 to Pete Sampras. First Croat male in major F since fellow townsman, Nikki Pilic, French, 1973. Served 206 aces, Wimbledon 1992 (37 vs Agassi). Holds season ace record, 1,477, 1996. Won Olympic bronzes, singles, doubles (with Goran Prpic), 1992. Made Wimbledon SF, 1990; French QF, 1990, 92, 94; Australian QF, 1989, 94; U.S. SF, 1996. World Top Ten: No. 9, 1990; No. 4, 1992, 96; No. 7, 1993; No. 5, 1994; No. 10, 1995. Won 22 singles 9 doubles career pro titles, $19,748,638 through 2002; career singles W-L 595-320. Davis Cup, 8 years since 1993, 20-6 singles, 12-5 doubles.

JAEGER, ANDREA: Peppery, meteoric 5-3, 105-pound blonde prodigy, Andrea Jaeger was one of youngest ranked in World Top Ten: No. 5 at age 15, 1980. Also No. 6, 1981; No. 3, 1982; No. 4, 1983; then virtually finished by injuries like contemporary rival of similar style, Tracy Austin. Fast, competitive, hard-hitting RH (two-handed backhand), baseliner, youngest champ U.S. Clay Court singles, 1981. Lost two major F to Martina Navratilova: French, 1982 (defeated Chris Evert, SF), Wimbledon, 1983 (defeated Billie Jean King, SF). Both 16, she and Jimmy Arias won French mixed, 1981 (youngest team to win major doubles). Made SF, Australian, 1982; QF, 1981; SF French, 1981, 83; QF Wimbledon, 1980; SF U.S., 1980, 82; QF, 1983. Federation Cup, 2 years (1981 winner), 8-1 singles. Wightman Cup, 1980-81 (both winners), 2-1 singles, 1-0 doubles. B. June 4, 1965, Chicago, raised Lincolnshire, Ill. Won 14 pro singles titles, $1,379,066. Admirably selfless adult, she fundraises, operates Silver Lining Ranch for terminally ill kids, Aspen, Colorado.

JAUSOVEC, MIMA: Continental clay was the ballroom for nimble, fleet-footed little Mima Jausovec. Winning French, 1977, Italian, 1976, and German, 1978, titles she stands as the best Slovenian. B. July 20, 1956, Maribor, Yugoslavia (now Slovenia), she also won all three in doubles, 1978, linked to Virginia Ruzizci; they lost Wimbledon F to Kerry Reid-Wendy Turnbull. A factor at all majors, she lost 2 French F, deposed by Ruzici, 1978, beaten by Chris Evert, 1983. Made SF Australian, 1980; QF French, 1981; Wimbledon, 1978, 81; SF U.S., 1976; QF 1977, 80. Well-rounded, 5-foot-4 Mima was fine volleyer, also a good skier, growing up in mountainous Maribor. Won 5 singles, 6 doubles pro career titles, $933,926; career singles W-L 351-248. Federation Cup, Yugoslavia, 1973, 75-76, 78-79-80, 84. 7-8 singles, 3-3 doubles. Best World ranking: No. 11, 1977.

JEDRZEJOWSKA, JADWIGA: Jadwiga 'JaJa' Jedrzejowska, best Polish woman, mouthful for umpires, handful for foes. RH, b. Oct. 15, 1912, Krakow; d. Feb. 28, 1980, Katowice. Married Alfred Gallert, 1947. Only Pole in major singles F. Wimbledon, 1937 (beat Alice Marble, lost F to Dorothy Round, 7-5, 3rd, led, 4-1); U.S., 1937, lost first all-foreign F to Anita Lizana, Chile. Won French doubles with Simone Mathieu, 1939. Husky, good-natured baseliner with battering forehand. World Top Ten: No. 6, 1936, 38; No. 3, 1937; No. 7, 1939.

JOHANSSON, TOM: One of the more startling champs, 5-11 RH Thomas Johansson was fifth Swede to win a major, Australian, 2002. Never beyond 3d. rd. in seven previous tries, never in Top Ten, came in at No. 18 but beat favored No. 2 Marat Safin. Made U.S. QF, 1998, 2000. Quick, has all-round game. Best world rank, No, 14, 2002. Won 7 pro career singles titles, $4,339,844; career singles W-L 227-185. Davis Cup, 4 years from 1998, 8-5 singles, 0-2 doubles. B. March 24, 1975, Linkoping, Sweden. Turned pro 1994.

JOHNSON, WALTER: As the imposing patron of Althea Gibson and Arthur Ashe, Dr. Robert Walter 'Whirlwind' Johnson, Lynchburg, Va., physician, was strong influence in breaking color line in American tennis. Guided early phases of their careers and other black players, overseeing Gibson's entry into U.S. Tennis Association events in 1950, thus ending tennis segregation. B. April 16, 1899, Norfolk, Va. Graduate Lincoln (Pa.) University (named Negro All-American football running back dubbed 'Whirlwind'), and Meharry (Tenn.) Medical School. Developed passion for tennis as intern at Prairie View (Tex.) Hospital. Later won six American Tennis Association mixed doubles titles with Gibson. Selected for Virginia Sports Hall of Fame, 1972. D. June 28, 1971, Lynchburg.

JONES, HENRY: Games playing appealed more than medicine to Dr. Henry Jones, English physician who operated only as a sports scribbler for the *Field* (pen name 'Cavendish'). Smitten by lawn tennis, he proposed its introduction at All England Club, helped organize the original Wimbledon, 1877, ran the show as referee. B. Nov. 2, 1831, London, d. Feb. 10, 1899.

JONES, MARION: Making the long journey East, pioneering petite Marion Jones, 5-2, led the charge from the most productive tennis vineyard: California. At 19, beating Maud Banks, 1899, was the first of 30 U.S. champs (16 women, 14 men) to spring from that state. Lost 1898 U.S. F to lucky Juliette Atkinson despite holding MP in 5th—lost on a fluke when Atkinson shot hit stray ball in Jones's court whereupon Juliette took over. Won again 1902 (by default) over Bessie Moore, who fainted in 2nd set. Lost U.S. F, 1903, to Moore. Had 17-3 singles record in 5 U.S. Championships. Won U.S. doubles 1902 with Juliette Atkinson. Lost U.S. doubles F, 1901, with Moore; 1903, with Miriam Hall. Won U.S. mixed 1901 with Raymond Little. Also won 17 other titles within U.S. (10 singles, including Southern California, 1894-95-96-97-98; 7 doubles). First U.S. woman to play abroad, made Wimbledon QF 1900. Marion, younger sister Georgina, first Americans to play play Olympic tennis, Paris, 1900, Marion losing SF to champ Charlotte Cooper. Father, John Percival Jones, wealthy proprietor Comstock Lode, was U.S. senator from Nevada, 30 years. Marion, b. Nov. 2, 1879, Gold Hill, Nevada, married Robert David Farquar Sept. 29, 1903, d. March 14, 1965, West Hollywood, Calif.

JORDAN, BARBARA; KATHY: American sisters, Barbara and Kathy Jordan out of King of Prussia, Pa. RH, All-Americans, Stanford, then winners major titles. Only sisters in major singles F (both at Australian) since Maud and Lillian Watson clashed for first Wimbledon title, 1884, and before Williams sisters, Venus and Serena, began their title showdowns at U.S., 2001. Kathy higher rated.

Barbara Jordan, b. April 2, 1957, Milwaukee. Smooth-stroking serve-and-volleyer. Long-shot winner of Australian, 1979 (unseeded, ranked No. 68). Only American champ there 1970s, beat favorite Hana Mandlikova (1980, 87 champ), and Sharon Walsh, won $10,000, high in $135,534 career. Only pro singles title; won two doubles, plus major mixed, French, 1983 with Eliot Teltscher. Best World rank, No. 37, 1980.

Kathryn 'KJ' Jordan, b. Dec. 3, 1959, Bryn Mawr, Pa. Willowy, 5-8, attacker, awkward-looking but effective stroker, extreme Western forehand, excellent volleyer. Won National Intercollegiate singles, doubles, 1979 (with Alycia Moulton), then turned pro. Lost F, Australian, 1983, to Martina Navratilova. Made QF French, 1980; SF Wimbledon, 1984 (beating Chris Evert, 3rd rd., first of two times in 19 years Evert failed to make SF). Won all major doubles: Australian, U.S., 1981; French, 1980; Wimbledon, 1980, 85, latter with Liz Smylie, ending Navratilova-Pam Shriver 109-match streak. Won 1 singles, 39 doubles (of 71 F) career pro titles, $1,592,111, plus Wimbledon mixed. 1986. As rookie, minor circuit, won San Antonio, 1979, through pre-qualifying, qualifying, main draw—13 wins, a record. Federation Cup: 1980-85, 6-3 singles, 17-1 doubles (with 1980-81 winners). Wightman Cup: 1979-80; 1-1 singles, 1-0 doubles (both winners). Best World rank, No. 10, 1984; No. 11, 1979; No. 13, 1980.

KAFELNIKOV, YEVGENY: Smooth, confident RH (two-handed backhand), Yevgeny Alexandrevic Kafelnikov of Sochi only Russian to win major singles: French, 1996, over Michael Stich; Australian, 1999, over Thomas Enqvist. Best of that area since Soviet (Georgian) Alex Metreveli (Wimbledon F, 1973, World No. 9, 1974). World Top Ten: No. 6, 1995; No. 3, 1996; No. 5, 1997, 2000; No. 2, 1999; No. 4, 2001. Was No. 1 briefly during 1999. B. Feb. 18, 1974, Sochi, 6-3 blond, prefers baseline, though sharp volleyer. Rare singles-doubles combiner today, also won French doubles, 1996 (with Daniel Vacek): first to score major double since Ken Rosewall, Australian, 1972, and at French since Rosewall, 1968. Lost F Australian, 2000. Made QF Australian, 1995-96; SF French, 1995; QF 1997, 2000-01; QF Wimbledon, 1995; SF U.S., 1999, 2001. Won Olympic singles gold, 2000. Davis Cup: 1993-2002; 31-14 singles, 12-11 doubles, led homeland to F, 1994-1995, won Cup 2002. Turned pro 1992, won 26 singles, 25 doubles pro career titles, $23,202,345 through 2002. Career singles W-L 580-280.

KINGSCOTE, ALGIE: Algernon Robert Fitzhardinge 'Algie' Kingscote, World War I hero, English RH, journeyed Down Under in 1919 to play in Britain's losing Davis Cup cause, but won Australian singles. Made Wimbledon SF, 1919; QF, 1920-21 (lost in 5 to champ Bill Tilden, 1920). Sound all-around. World Top Ten: No. 3, 1920; No. 5, 1919. Davis Cup: 1914, 1924; 7-6 singles, 2-2 doubles. B. 1888, India.

KORDA, PETR: Gifted skinny Czech LH Petr Korda. 6-3. 160, won Australian, 1998, over Marcelo Rios; lost French F, 1992, to Jim Courier. Turned pro 1987. Won Australian doubles, 1996, with Stefan Edberg; lost F French, 1990, with Goran Ivanicevic. Electrifying, though erratic, all-court shotmaker; knocked Pete Sampras off U.S. throne, 1996, 4th rd. B. Jan. 23, 1968, Prague. World Top Ten: No. 9, 1991; No. 7, 1992 (as high as No. 2, Feb., 1998). Made QF Australian, 1993; Wimbledon, 1998; U.S., 1995, 97. Won 10 singles, 10 doubles pro career titles, $10,448,450; career singles W-L 410-248, Davis Cup, 10 years from 1988, 18-9 singles, 11-4 doubles. Ended career in controversy. Suspended after testing positive for anabolic steroid nandralone at Wimbledon, 1998, forfeited $94,529 QF prize money. ITF officials believed 'unintentional,' but he lost appeal, July 1999, and retired. Wife, Czech Regina Rajchrtova, played WTA Tour; best World ranking No. 39, 1991.

KORMOCZI, SUZI: Hungary's best woman, Suzi Kormoczi was persistent baseliner, patient pursuing success, rose to World No. 2. RH, b. Aug. 25, 1924, Budapest. First entered French, 1947, won 1958, oldest champ, almost 34. Oldest champ Italian, 1960. Lost French, 1959 F, to Christine Truman. Made SF French, 1956, 61; SF Wimbledon, 1958. World Top Ten 7 times: No. 7, 1953, 61; No. 10, 1955; No. 5, 1956, 60; No. 2, 1958; No. 8, 1959.

KRAJICEK, RICHARD: A fabulous 1996 fortnight was his: Wimbledon's second unseeded champ, Richard Peter Stanislav Krajicek, Netherlands' only winner of a men's major. Gangling 6-5 RH, he ranked No. 13 coming in, had a case to dissent to non-seed but let his racket be his bombastic mouthpiece, especially with serve, backhand. Romped on loss of one set, ended No. 1 Pete Sampras' 25-match Big W streak, QF. Took F from Mal Washington fast, lone major F. B. Dec. 6, 1971, Rotterdam, parents defected from Czechoslovakia. Made SF Australian, 1992; SF French, 1993; QF, 1996; QF Wimbledon, 2002; QF U.S., 1999-2000. Davis Cup: 1991-95; 4-6 singles, 1-0 doubles. World Top Ten: No. 7, 1996; No. 10, 1998-99. Won 17 singles, 3 doubles career pro titles, $9,977,484 through 2002. Career singles W-L 400-209.

KRIEK, JOHAN: Swift, compact, fine volleying 5-8 RH, Johan Christian Kriek reached peak on Down Under grass, won Australian, 1981-82, made SF, 1984, QF, 1983, 85. South African farm boy by birth, April 5, 1958, Pongola. Became U.S. citizen, 1982. Made SF French, 1986; QF Wimbledon, 1982; SF U.S., 1980; QF, 1978-79. Won 14 pro career singles titles (including South African, 1983, U.S. Indoor over John McEnroe, 1982), 8 doubles, $2,381,844. Best World Rank, No. 12, 1981; No. 13, 1982, 84.

KRISHNAN, RAMANATHAN; RAMESH: Father, son, Ramanathan and Ramesh Krishnan, possibly India's best. Unique, both helping homeland to Davis Cup finales, reaching QF, Wimbledon. RH, clever, deceptive. Born, raised in Madras (now Chennai).

Ramanathan Krishnan, b. April 11, 1932, Madras, World Top Ten: No. 9, 1959, 62; No, 8, 1960; No. 6 in 1961. Davis Cup: 18 years, 1953-69, 1976; 50-20 singles, 19-9 doubles; led India to finale, 1966. Made SF Wimbledon, 1960-61.

Ramesh Krishnan, b. June 5, 1961, Madras, pro since 1976, best World rank, No. 24 in 1980. Made QF, Wimbledon, 1986; U.S., 1981, 87. Davis Cup: 11 years between 1978 and 1992; 23-19 singles, 6-2 doubles (won 5 of 8 singles, leading India to 1987 F). Won 8 singles, 1 doubles career pro titles, $1,235,548.

LANDRY, NELLY: A decade after losing French F 1938 to Simone Passemard Mathieu, French LH Nelly Jeanne Adamson Landry hurdled World War II to win in 1948 at age 31 over Shirley Fry. B. Dec. 28, 1916, of Belgian parentage in London. Became French citizen, 1937, marrying French player Paul Landry. Two children. Diminutive 5-foot-3 but excelled as attacker, volleyer. Lost title, 1949 French F, to Margaret Osborne duPont. Lost 1939 French doubles F with Arlette Halff to Adeline York-Mathieu. Made French SF 1954, QF, 1936, 46, 51, 53; Wimbledon QF 1948. World Top Ten: No. 7, 1946; No. 10, 1948.

LANGRISHE, MAY: Mary Isabella Langrishe, original female champ—and youngest, 14, to win national title. Won her own, Irish, 1879, the inaugural, at Dublin's Fitzwilliam Club, first to welcome women. RH, b. Dec. 31, 1864, Ireland. Beat D. Meldon, 6-2, 0-6, 8-6, to rule field of seven. Also won first female doubles title, Northern Championship, Manchester, England, 1882, with older sister. D. Jan. 24, 1939.

LARCOMBE, ETHEL: English RH Ethel Warneford Thomson Larcombe jolted Charlotte Cooper Sterry's hopes of 7th Wimbledon title, beat her in 1912 F. Played at both ends of World War I, losing Wimbledon singles, doubles F, 1914, doubles F, 1919-20. In Wimbledon mixed F, 1913, leading with Jim Parke, was hit in eye by shot, unable to continue, defaulted title to Agnes Tuckey-Hope Crisp. Won Irish, 1912, Scottish, 1910, titles. Fine athlete, won All England badminton singles 1900-01, 03-04,06; doubles 1902,04, 06, mixed 1903, 06. Married Dudley Larcombe, 1906. B. June 8, 1879, Islington, d. Aug. 11, 1965, Budleigh Salterton. Became teaching pro, 1922.

LAWFORD, HERBERT: Herbert Fortescue Lawford, English RH innovator, Wimbledon champ, 1887. Introduced topspin—known as 'Lawford Stroke'—around 1880, first of his six years in title round. Renshaw twins were his nemeses. Lost F 1884-85-86 to Willie, 1888 to Ernest whom he beat in 1887. B. May 15, 1851, Bayswater; d. April 20, 1925, Dess, Scotland.

LIZANA, ANITA: Chilean RH Anita Lizana, a significant blip—played U.S. Championships once, 1937, and won, over Pole Jadwiga Jedrzejowska, first all-foreign F. First Latin American to win a major, and be No. 1 prior to Brazilian Maria Bueno, 1959. B. 1915, Santiago, married Ronald Ellis, settled in England. Made Wimbledon QF, 1936 (led champ Helen Jacobs, 4-2, 30-0 in 3rd) and 1937. Short, quick, solid groundstroker with good passing shots, drop shot, admirable footwork. World Top Ten: No. 1, 1937; No. 8, 1936.

LONG, THELMA: Thelma Dorothy Coyne Long, sturdy Australian RH, b. Oct. 14, 1918, Sydney. Had one of longest careers, stretching over 22 years as significant winner. Fine volleyer, won first of record 12 Australian doubles, 1936 (with Nancye Wynne Bolton, her partner in 10 of them), last, 1958. Also won singles, 1952, 54, mixed 1951-51, 54-55 times. French mixed, 1956, with Luis Ayana gave her total of 19 major titles. Lost Australian F, 1940, 51, 55-56. Made SF, 1947, 49. World Top Ten: No. 7, 1952. Named to Australian Tennis Hall of Fame, 2002.

MAIN, LORNE: Lorne Garnet Main was inadvertent father of rare two-way, two-handed style, both forehand and backhand. Foremost proponent today, Monica Seles. "Seemed natural to me as a boy since I was a baseball switch-hitter." Canadian RH, 5-8, 145, b. July 9, 1930, Vancouver. No. 1, Canada, 1951-54. Biggest title, Monte Carlo, 1954. Davis Cup, 1949-55, 10-11 singles, 4-3 doubles.

LOWE, GORDON; ARTHUR: Sir Francis Gordon Lowe, English RH, won last pre-World War I Australian, 1915. B. June 21, 1884, Edgbaston, Cambridge grad, d. May 17, 1972, London. Davis Cup: 1921-25; 8-6 singles.

Brother Arthur Holden Lowe, RH b. Jan. 29, 1886, Edgbaston, Oxford grad, d. Oct. 22, 1958, London. Also British Davis Cup: 1911-19; 0-5 singles. Both World Top Ten, 1914: Arthur No. 7, Gordon No. 8. At ages 37 and 35, became fourth of five sets of brothers in Wimbledon doubles F, lost, 1921.

MAHONY, HAROLD: Tall, quick-tempered RH Irishman Harold Segerson Mahony won Wimbledon, 1896, unseating Wilfred Baddeley, a fleeting success before Doherty brothers took over. B. Feb. 13, 1867, Edinburgh, d. June 27, 1904, Caragh Hill, Ireland.

MAJOLI, IVA: Croatian baseliner Iva Majoli, 9th seeded, won French 1997 at 19 over No. 1 Martina Hingis, depriving her (winner other 3 majors) of Grand Slam. RH with two-handed backhand. Turned pro 1991, won 8 singles, 1 doubles pro career titles, $4,258,381 through 2002; career singles W-L 301-199. Made Australian QF 1996; French QF 1996, 98; Wimbledon QF 1997. Federation Cup: 9 years from 1993, 15-12 singles, 5-5 doubles. World Top 10: No. 9, 1995; No. 6, 1997; No. 7, 1996. B. Aug. 12, 1977, Zagreb.

MALEEVA, MANUELA; KATERINA; MAGDALENA: Internationally most exceptional trio of sisters ever, clearly greatest in Bulgaria annals. All three—baselining RH with two-handed backhands, born and brought up in Sofia—played for Bulgaria in Federation Cup, Olympics, made World Top Ten. Mother, Yulia Berberian, champion of Bulgaria nine years; father, Gyorgy Maleev, Olympic basketball player, 1956. Unique accomplishments, until Williams sisters, Venus and Serena, came along—Katerina, Manuela in World Top Ten together, 1990, have been in QF every major, together at French, 1990, were only sisters to do so. Manuela's 1992 U.S. QF win over Maggie (winner over Martina Navratilova) first such sisterly encounter since 1897 champ Juliette Atkinson beat sibling, Kathleen, SF. Manuela, Katerina in 1988 U.S. QF, first sisters there since Atkinsons. Manuela in U.S. QF five times, 1990 by beating Navratilova.

Manuela Maleeva Fragniere, 5-8, b. Feb. 14, 1967, Sofia. Won rain-delayed Italian, 1984, three wins last day, F over Chris Evert. Won Olympic bronze, singles, 1988. Married Swiss tennis coach François Fragniere, 1987, became citizen, played Federation Cup, 1992 Olympics for Switzerland. Through 1994 retirement won 19 singles, 5 doubles career pro titles, $3,034,945. World Top Ten 9 times: No. 6, 1984, 88; No. 7, 1975; No. 8, 1986-87; No. 9, 1989-90, 92; No. 10, 1991. Federation Cup, 1984-87, 1989, 1991-92, 21-5 singles, 7-10 doubles.

Katerina Maleeva, 5-6, b. May 7, 1969, Sofia. Won Japan Open, 1987. Through 1996 had 12 singles, 5 doubles pro titles, $1,936,887. World Top Ten: No. 6, 1990. Federation Cup, 1984-89, 1991-95, 20-9 singles, 9-13 doubles.

Magdalena 'Maggie' Maleeva, 5-7, b. April 1, 1975, Sofia. Won first pro title, San Marino, 1992. Won 9 singles, 2 doubles career pro titles, $3,207,217 through

2002; career singles W-L 368-224. World Top Ten: No. 6, 1995. Federation Cup, 1991-95, 7-2 singles, 3-3 doubles.

MARTINEZ, CONCHITA: Only Spanish woman to win Wimbledon, 1994, thwarted Martina Navratilova's bid for 10th title in F with topspinning groundies, backhand passers. Quick, 5-7 RH, top-notch performer all majors, losing Australian F, 1998, to Martina Hingis; French F, 2000, to Mary Pierce. Made SF Australian, 1995, 2000; QF, 1994, 96; SF French, 1994-95-6; QF 1989-90-91-92-93, 99; SF Wimbledon, 1993, 95; QF 2001; SF U.S., 1995-96; QF, 1991. Won record three straight Italian, 1994-96. Best year, 1995. Won six singles titles. With Arantxa Sanchez Vicario, made Spain dominant in Federation Cup, played 1988-96, won 5 Cups (1991, 1993-94-95, 98); 36-7 singles, 15-5 doubles. Olympic silver, 1992, bronze, 1996 (doubles with Sanchez Vicario). B. April 16, 1972, Monzon, Spain. Turned pro 1988. World Top Ten 9 times: No. 7, 1989; No. 9, 1991; No. 8, 1992; No, 4, 1993; No. 3, 1994; No. 2, 1995; No. 5, 1996, 2000; No. 8, 1998. Won 32 singles, 10 doubles career pro titles, $10,117,481 through 2002. Career singles W-L 660-240.

MATHIEU, SIMONE PASSEMARD: Following Suzanne Lenglen, Simone Passemard Mathieu was best French woman prior to World War II. B. Jan. 11, 1908, Neuilly-sur-Seine. Was a heroine in the Resistance during the war, d. Jan. 7, 1980, Paris. Married Rene Mathieu, 1925. Steady, accurate, strong topspin backhand, maintained consistently high level. Won French, 1938-39, after losing F, 1932-33, 36-37. Made SF Wimbledon, 1930-31-32, 34, 36-37; QF, 1933, 35, 38-39; QF U.S., 1938. Won 9 major doubles—Wimbledon, 1933-34, 37; French, 1933-34, 36-37-38-39, her 6th French record until Martina Navratilova's 7th, 1987. Also French mixed, 1937-38. Her 13 majors are second only to Lenglen's 21 Among French women. World Top Ten 11 straight years: No. 6, 1929, 33-34; No. 5, 1930, 36-37-38-39; No. 7, 1931; No. 3, 1932; No. 8, 1935.

MAYER, SANDY; GENE: American brothers, Sandy and Gene Mayer, RH, winners of major doubles, one together (French, 1979, only brothers to do so). First brothers to win major since Bob and Howard Kinsey, U.S., 1924. Also only brothers to rank together U.S. Top Ten, 1983 (Gene higher, 4-8), World Top Fifteen, 1981

(Gene higher, 7-14), and make Wimbledon QF open era. Family pro title total: 25 singles, 40 doubles titles. Stanford grads, All-Americans.

Alexander 'Sandy' Mayer, b. April 5, 1952, Flushing, N.Y., sleek 5-10 attacker, excellent volleyer, won National Intercollegiate singles, 1973, doubles, 1972 (with Roscoe Tanner), 1973 (with Jim Delaney). Made Wimbledon SF, 1973 (rookie pro beat top seed Ilie Nastase, 4th rd., huge upset); QF, 1978, 83. Won Wimbledon doubles, 1975. Best World rank, No. 14, 1981. Won 11 singles, 24 doubles pro titles, $1,057,783. Rare amateur to win open title, Birmingham (Ala.) over pro Charlie Owens, 1973.

Eugene Mayer, b. April 11, 1956, New York, slender 6-footer, unorthodox style: both-handed backhand, forehand. Solid groundstroker, good volleyer. Davis Cup: 1982-83; helped win 1982 (3-1, singles). Made QF Wimbledon, 1980, 82; QF U.S., 1982. World Top Ten: No. 4, 1980 (won 5 titles); No. 7, 1981; No. 8, 1982; No. 10, 1983. Won 14 singles, 16 doubles pro titles, $1,381,562.

McATEER, MYRTLE: Myrtle McAteer from Pittsburgh was in three U.S. women's F, winning singles, 1900, doubles, 1899, 1901. Lost F doubles, 1900, mixed 1901. After losing singles title in 5-set battle with Bessie Moore, 1901, didn't play again. No details known on b. or d. U.S. singles record (5-1).

McGRATH, VIV: Vivian 'Viv' McGrath, pronounced 'McGraw,' Australian original: RH, introduced two-handed backhand to international game (although at Wimbledon 1911, a native, Harold Bache, used two hands on his backhand in a 1st rd. loss). McGrath's was considered strongest pre-war shot among Aussies. B. Feb. 17, 1916, Mudgee; d. 1978, Buradee. Called 'Wonder Boy' at 16, beat World No. 1 Ellie Vines, QF, Australian, 1933. Won homeland title, 1937, over another rising double-hander, John Bromwich. Won Australian doubles, 1935 Made SF, Australian, 1934-35, 39-40; QF, 1932, 36, 38; QF Wimbledon, 1935, 37. Youngest Aussie Davis Cupper, 17, 1933, Played through 37, 11-12 singles, 1-2 doubles (4-4 singles, 1933, as team lost European Zone F, 3-2, at Britain, eventual Cup winner). World Top Ten: No. 8, 1935; No. 10, 1936. Unable to regain form after army service, World War II.

MECIR, MILOSLAV: Slovak RH (two-handed backhand) Miloslav 'Gattone' Mecir (Big Cat), 6-3, 180, was Czechoslovakia's best, 1985-89. Quick, clever, deceptively mixed speeds, spins, angles. Took Olympic gold, singles, 1988. Davis Cup: 1983-89; 18-8 singles, 5-1 doubles. Lost F U.S., 1986; Australian, 1989, both to Ivan Lendl. Made QF Australian, 1987; SF French, 1987; SF Wimbledon. 1988; QF U.S., 1987. Turned pro 1982. B. May 19, 1964, Bojnice, Czechoslovakia, career ended 1991 by back problems. Won 10 singles, 9 doubles career pro titles, $2,632,538.

METREVELI, ALEXANDER: Foremost Soviet man, Alexander Metreveli gained prominence open era, beating Pancho Gonzalez, Wimbledon, 1968. Georgian RH, b. Feb. 11, 1944, Tblisi. Atypical Soviet, serve-and-volleyer, poised 5-10. Only USSR male in major F, until Yevgeny Kafelnikov (French 1996, Australian, 1999). Lost Wimbledon F 1973. Also, with Olga Morozova, lost F Wimbledon mixed, 1968, 70. In career overlapping amateur, open eras, QF or better all majors. Davis Cup standout, 14 years, spanning 1963 to 1980, one of select few to have played 100 matches or more (56-14, singles; 24-11, doubles). Best World rank, No. 13, 1974. Won eight singles, two doubles pro titles.

MOLESWORTH, MALL: Margaret 'Mall' Mutch Molesworth, first Australian women's champ. RH, b. 1894, Brisbane; d. July 9, 1985. Might have exceeded two singles, 1922-23; three doubles, 1930, 33-34, had Championships welcomed women prior to 1922, Sydney. Won first title at 27, with complete game, feared serve. Lost doubles F, 1923, Remained factor for some time: lost singles F, age 40, 1934 to Joan Hartigan. Won 29 other singles titles throughout the country, the last in 1935, age 41; also 16 other doubles and 9 mixed.

MOON, GAR: "New star is born—it's a Moon!" declared an Aussie newspaper when Edgar Moon, Queensland RH, beat 1922 Wimbledon champ Gerald Patterson, 1st rd. Australian, 1926. He won title, 1930, over Harry Hopman, beating future champ Jack Crawford, SF. Won Aussie doubles with Crawford, 1932. Strong groundies, all-round game. Davis Cup, 1930, 4-0 in singles. B. Dec. 3, 1904, Forest Hill, Australia, d. May 26, 1976.

MOROZOVA, OLGA: Preeminent Soviet woman, Olga Morozova, RH, b. Feb. 22, 1949, Moscow. Unusual Soviet, preferred serve-and-volley. Quick, athletic, 5-7. Only USSR female in Wimbledon singles F, 1974. Lost to Chris Evert, beat defender Billie Jean King, QF. Made QF or better all majors. Won 31 singles, 10 doubles career pro titles. World Top Ten: No. 10, 1972; No. 8, 1974; No. 7, 1975. First Soviet winner of a U.S. title—Indoor doubles, 1973, with compatriot Marina Kroshina. Federation Cup, 1968, 1978-80; 8-3 singles, 4-1 doubles.

MOTTRAM, TONY; JOY; BUSTER; LINDA: Internationalist English family: father, Tony; mother, Joy; son, Buster; daughter, Linda. All RH.

Anthony John Mottram, b. June 8, 1920, Coventry. Davis Cup: 1947-1955; 25-13 singles, 11-7 doubles. Made QF Wimbledon 1948; lost doubles F, 1947. Best Brit immediate post-war.

Joy Gannon Mottram, b. March 21, 1928, Enfield. Wightman Cup: 1947-52, 0-1 singles, 0-3 doubles. Won German, 1954. Made Wimbledon 3rd rd., 1946-47, 49; QF French, 1952.

Christopher John 'Buster' Mottram, b. April 25, 1955, Kingston, lanky 6-3, free-swinging big hitter. Made Wimbledon 4th rd., 1982; French 4th rd., 1977. Davis Cup: 1975-83; 27-8 singles, 4-2 doubles (high point, 1978, led Britain to first Davis Cup finale since 1937, 8-2 singles, 1-0 doubles, beat Brian Gottfried for lone Brit point in F). Won two singles, five doubles pro titles, about $500,000. Best World rank, No. 19, 1982.

Linda Mottram, b. May 17, 1957, Wimbledon. Played Wimbledon 6 straight years from 1974, lost 3rd rd., 1975. Won German Indoor, 1976.

MOYA, CARLOS: Powerful groundstroking Spaniard (6-3, 185) Carlos Moya won French 1998 over compatriot Alex Corretja, held No. 1 ranking 2 weeks 1999. RH with two-handed backhand. Turned pro 1995, won 11 singles pro titles, $8,376,152 through 2002; career singles W-L 323-182. Lost Australian F, 1997 to Pete Sampras; made QF 2001. Lost F Masters 1998 to Corretja; SF 2002. Davis Cup: 5 years from 1996, 10-6 singles. World Top 10: No. 7, 1997; No. 6, 1998, No. 5, 2002. B. Aug. 27, 1976, Palma de Mallorca, Spain.

MUSTER, THOMAS: Muscular 'Moo Man,' bellowing bovine noises as he belted at the baseline, Austrian Thomas Muster, 5-11 LH, seemed indestructible in body and spirit. Sovereign of the soil, strongman of the '90s on clay, won French singles, 1995, Italian, 1990, 95-96. Astoundingly rehabbed left knee, which had been wrecked in 1989 auto accident, to reappear as a winner in 1990, rack up 37 of 42 career singles titles, 1990-96. Huge year, 1995: won 12 titles on 86-18 (40 straight on clay), saved match points in five wins (beat Boris Becker, Monte Carlo F, from 2 sets, 2 match points down). On dirt won 40 titles of 45 F), 422-126 in matches (.770). World Top Ten 5 times: No. 7, 1990; No, 9, 1993, 97; No. 3, 1995; No. 5, 1996 (No. 1 for 6 weeks during 1996). Davis Cup: 1984-96; 33-7 singles, 9-9 doubles, nearly beat U.S. single-handed, 1990 SF (3-2). Made SF Australian, 1989, QF, 1984; SF French, 1990; QF U.S. 1993-94, 96. Won 44 singles, 1 doubles pro career titles, $12,224.210; career singles W-L 622-271. B. Oct. 2, 1967, Liebnitz.

NA, HU: When she defected to the U.S. in 1982, she became the first Chinese pro. Slim, 5-8, RH, a serve-and-volleyer. B. April 16, 1963, Chengdu, No. 1 Peoples Republic. Federation Cup: 1981-82; 1-0 singles, 1-2 doubles. Best World rank, No. 58 in 1987. High point, five wins at Wimbledon, 1985—qualifying and making 3rd rd. Won one pro title, doubles, $213,220. Became U.S. citizen, 1989.

NOAH, YANNICK: Yannick Simone Camille Noah, b. May 18, 1960, Sedan, France. Foremost Frenchman in accomplishment, popularity since Four Musketeers. Attained all-time renown with countrymen winning French, 1983 (over Mats Wilander), first male title for Frenchman since Marcel Bernard, 1946. Imposing physical specimen, 6-4, 190, RH. Davis Cup hero: 1978-90; 26-15 singles, 13-7 doubles. Led French (6-2, singles; 2-2 doubles) to first Cup F in 49 years, 1982, lost to U.S. As non-playing captain directed France to first Cup in 59 years, 3-1 over U.S., 1991; also 1996, 3-2 over Sweden; also to Federation Cup, 1997, over Netherlands. Son of Cameroonian father, French mother, discovered in Yaounde, Cameroon, 1971, recommended to French Federation for development by touring Arthur Ashe. Appealing net-rushing gambler, leaping volleyer, big server. World Top Ten 6 times: No. 9, 1982; No. 5, 1983; No. 10, 1984; No. 7, 1985; No. 4, 1986; No. 8, 1987. Made SF Australian, 1990; QF, 1987; QF French, 1981-82, 84, 87; QF U.S., 1982, 84, 89. Won Palm Springs, 1982, ending Ivan Lendl's 44-match streak. Won French doubles, 1984. Over 12 years won 23 singles, 16 doubles career pro titles, $3,440,390; career singles W-L. 474-209.

NOVOTNA, JANA: An attacker, brilliant serve-and-volleyer, 5-10 RH Czech Jana Novotna, b. Oct. 2, 1968, Brno, Czech Republic. Distinguished herself as an athletic all-rounder over 14-year pro career, persisted through 44 majors before winning on 45th singles try, Wimbledon 1998 at 29, over Nathalie Tauziat. Lost Wimbledon F 1993 to Steffi Graf (from 4-1, 40-30 lead in 3rd); F 1997 to Martina Hingis (6-3 in 3rd). Became first since Doris Hart (1951) to win after losing F twice. Won 16 doubles majors: Australian 1990 (with Helena Sukova), 95 (with Arantxa Sanchez Vicario); French 1990 (with Sukova), 91 (with Gigi Fernandez), 98 (with Hingis); Wimbledon 1989-90 (with Sukova), 95 (with Sanchez Vicario), 98 (with Hingis); U.S. 1994 (with Sanchez Vicario), 97 (with Lindsay Davenport), 98 (with Hingis); Australian mixed, 1988-89 (with Jim Pugh), Wimbledon, 1988 (with Pugh), U.S. 1987 (with Pugh). Won 1,268 singles and doubles matches, and 24 singles, 77 doubles career pro titles, $11,249,134; career W-L, singles 571-225, doubles 697-152. Besides 3 Wimbledon F made SF, 1995; QF, 1990, 94, 96, 99. Lost Australian F 1991, to Monica Seles, QF 1994. Made French SF 1990, 96; QF 1989, 91, 93, 98; U.S, SF, 1994, 98; QF 1990, 95-96-97. Olympic medals: 1988, silver, doubles (with Sukova); 1996, bronze, singles, silver, doubles (with Sukova). World Top Ten 7 times: No. 7, 1991; No. 10, 1992; No. 6, 1993; No. 4, 1994, 96; No.2, 1997; No. 3, 1998. Won year-end WTA championship, 1997. Federation Cup: 1987-93, 95-98 (won Cup 1988), 22-7 singles, 11-5 doubles. Retired 1999.

NUSSLEIN, HANS: Extraordinary German Hans 'Hanne' Nusslein, perhaps best until Boris Becker, was largely unnoticed as pro trouper, no amateur background. Finest years 1930s. Beat Bill Tilden numerous times, won World Pro title, 1933, 36-37-38, U.S. Pro, 1934, French Pro, 1937-38. Excellent groundstrokes. RH, b. March 31, 1910, Nuremberg, d. June 28, 1991, Altenkirchen.

O'HARA WOOD, ARTHUR; PAT: Australian brothers, Arthur and Pat O'Hara Wood, RH, both winners Australian singles title, only brothers to do so. First brothers to win majors since English Wimbledon champs Dohertys—Laurie (1902-03-04-05-06), Reggie (1897-98-99-00).

Dr. Arthur Holroyd O'Hara Wood, b. 1890, Melbourne, d. Oct. 4 or 6, 1918, with Royal Air Force,

World War I, shot down over St. Quentin, France. Melbourne physician with all-round game. Defeated future Hall of Famer Gerald Patterson, 1914 F, then went to war.

Patrick O'Hara Wood also served, Aussie army, survived to win Australian twice, 1920, 23, plus four Aussie doubles, Wimbledon doubles and, with Suzanne Lenglen, mixed, 1922. Short, quick, consistent, effortless strokemaker. Davis Cup: 1922, 1924; 9-5 singles, 8-1 doubles, helped Australia gain F both years. B. April 30, 1891. Melbourne; d. there, Dec. 3, 1961. World Top Ten: No. 7, 1922. Wife, Meryl Waxman O'Hara Wood, won Australian doubles, 1926, 27.

OKKER, TOM: Flying Dutchman Tom Samuel Okker, Netherlands' finest male before Wimbledon champ Richard Krajicek. RH, b. Feb. 22, 1944, Amsterdam. Slight (5-9, 145), speedy, excellent volleyer, one of five men to win more than 100 pro titles (30 singles, record 78 doubles). Lost F first U.S. Open, 1968, to amateur Arthur Ashe, taking $14,000 first prize. Made SF all majors: Australian, U.S., 1971; French, 1969; Wimbledon, 1978. Made doubles F all majors, won French, 1973, with John Newcombe; U.S., 1976, with Marty Riessen. World Top Ten 5 times: No. 5, 1968-69; No. 6, 1970; No. 8, 1971-72; No. 7, 1973, Davis Cup: 1964-81; 10-13 singles, 5-7 doubles.

O'NEIL, CHRIS: Tall Aussie, 6-footer Christine Merle O'Neil, RH, was longest shot to win women's major, Australian, 1978. Unseeded, ranked No. 111, she went through weak field, beat No. 68 Betsy Nagelsen in F, 6-3, 7-6 (7-4), on Melbourne grass, winning $6,000. Only pro title. B. March 19, 1956, Newcastle, serve-and-volleyer. Highest World rank, No. 80, 1978. Now a teaching pro.

ORANTES, MANOLO: Manuel 'Manolo' Orantes, stocky, prestidigitating, gracious Spanish LH, master of spin and placement. Won U.S., 1975, sensationally, beating ex-champ Ilie Nastase, 2-1 seeds Guillermo Vilas, defender Jimmy Connors, in succession. Great SF comeback over Vilas: 4-6, 1-6, 6-2, 7-5, 6-4, from 0-5, three match points, then 5-1, two match points 4th. B. Feb. 6, 1949, Granada. Davis Cup: 1967-80; 39-19 singles, 21-8 doubles, helped Spain to finale, 1967. Career, 16 years, spanned amateur, open eras. Won 32 singles, 24 doubles career pro titles, including Masters, 1976, U.S. Pro, 1977-78, $1,338,601. World Top Ten: No. 5,

1975; No. 4, 1976; No. 7, 1977.

PAILS, DINNY: First of Aussie post-war-developed champs, RH Denis Robert Pails, b. March 4, 1921, at Nottingham, England, won Australian, 1947; lost F 1946. Made SF Wimbledon, 1947; QF, 1946. Davis Cup: 1946-47; 3-5 singles. Turned pro with Jack Kramer, 1947. World No. 6, 1947.

PALFREY, POLLY; LEE; MIANNE; SARAH; JOEY: Five remarkable Bostonians, Palfrey sisters—Joey, Lee, Mianne, Polly, Sarah—all won U.S. junior titles. Sarah won 18 majors, made the Hall of Fame. All RH, b. in Boston, except Sarah, born in Sharon, Mass.

Margaret Germaine 'Polly' Palfrey Woodrow, b. Oct. 7, 1906. Won 1 junior: 18 doubles, 1924, with Fanny Curtis.

Elizabeth Howland 'Lee' Palfrey Fullerton, b. Jan. 14, 1909; d. Jan. 5, 1987. Won 1 junior: 18 Indoor doubles, 1926, with Midge Morrill.

Sarah Hammond Palfrey Fabyan Cooke Danzig, b. Sept. 18, 1912, d. Feb. 27, 1996. Won 13 juniors: 18 singles, 1928-29-1930; 18 doubles, 1926, 28-29, with Mianne; 18 Indoor singles, 1927-28, 30; 18 Indoor doubles, 1927-28-29, with Mianne, 1930, with Joey. *See Chapter 25 for full biography.*

Mary Ann 'Mianne' Palfrey Dexter, b. March 6, 1911, d. Nov. 2, 1993. Won 7 juniors: 18 Indoor singles, 1929; 18 doubles, 1926, 28-29, with Sarah; 18 Indoor doubles, 1927-28-29, with Sarah. Also won adult U.S. Indoor singles, 1930.

Joanna 'Joey' Oakes Palfrey Brown, b. Jan. 30, 1915, d. Jan. 25, 2002. Won 1 junior: 18 Indoor doubles, 1930, with Sarah.

PANATTA, ADRIANO: Best Italian open era, Adriano Panatta, RH, b. July 9, 1950, Rome. Slick 6-foot god at Il Foro Italico, Rome, responding winningly to feverish chants, "AD-REE-ANNO!" Strong serve, whipping forehand, called 'Portiere' (Goaltender) for brilliant volleying saves. Spectacular 1976: Won Italian, French, 45-15 match record, led Italy to lone Davis Cup (10-1 singles; 5-1 doubles). Also to F, 1977, 79-1980. Cup record: 1970-83; 37-26 singles; 27-10 doubles, one of 14 to play 100 matches. Match point escapes in big titles, 1976: 11, vs. Kim Warwick, Italian. Best World rank, No. 7, 1976. Won 10 singles, 18 doubles pro career titles, $776,187. Younger brother, Claudio

Panatta (b. Feb. 2, 1960, Rome) played Davis Cup, pro tour.

PARKE, JIM: Sturdy, speedy Irish RH James Cecil Parke, the man of 1912 Australian season, won singles title, backboned Davis Cup upset to lift the Cup for Britain. Stunned Norman Brookes, Rod Heath in F. Beat U.S. champs Maurice McLoughlin, Dick Williams in losing Cup defense, 1913. World Top Ten: No. 4, 1913; No. 6, 1914. Also rugby international for Ireland, 1913-18. B. July 26, 1881, Clones County, Ireland, d. Feb. 27, 1946, Llandudno, Wales. Davis Cup: 1908-13, 8-7 singles, 0-5 doubles.

PARKER, ERNEST: Three champions of Australia were killed in World War I. Two of them met for the 1909 title, Ernest Frederick Parker, a Perth attorney, losing to New Zealander Tony Wilding. But four years later Parker, 30, beat another New Zealander, 40-year-old Harry Parker (no relation) for the title. As he had in 1909, Ernest also won the doubles. Almost five years after that, an artilleryman in the Australian army, he was killed by an enemy shell in France, May 3, 1918. B. Nov. 5, 1883, Perth, he was outstanding, too, at cricket and golf, though slightly built. Ironically turned down twice by the army for weak eyesight, he was finally allowed to join. He played the Championships only twice.

PENROSE, BERYL: Made brief mark, 1955. Won Australian (upset Thelma Long, 6-4, 6-3), German titles. Made QF Wimbledon, ranked World No. 8. Tall, slender RH, b. 1930, Sydney.

PETRA, YVON: Yvon François Marie Petra, French RH, at 6-5 tallest winner major singles, Wimbledon, 1946, a surprise, rising above 5th seed to beat 3rd Geoff Brown. B. March 8, 1916, Cholon, Indochina, d. Sept. 12, 1984, Paris. Won French doubles twice, 1938, 46. Davis Cup: 1937-39, 1946-47; 11-3 singles, 4-4 doubles, led France to SF, 1946. French army, wounded, POW in World War II. Turned pro, 1948. Strong server, last man to win a major, Wimbledon, in long trousers. World rank, No. 4, 1946.

PIERCE, MARY: Riding a dynamite forehand, 5-11 Mary Caroline Pierce, Franco-America RH with two-handed backhand powered her way to Australian, 1995, and French, 2000, titles. B. Jan. 15, 1975, at Montreal, Canada, reared in Florida, daughter of a French mother, American father, she holds three passports, and cast her

lot with France, whom she led to the Federation Cup, 1997. First female citizen to win French title since Hall of Famer Françoise Durr, 1967. Turned pro 1989 at 14-2, youngest until Jennifer Capriati at 13-11 in 1990. Junoesque blonde glamorized return of the tennis dress. Coached by overbearing father, Jim Pierce, until she obtained restraining order, 1993. Won 15 singles, 9 doubles career pro titles, $6,451,861 through 2002; career singles W-L 408-181. Also made F Australian, 1997, lost to Martina Hingis; QF, 1993, 98-99. Lost F French, 1994 to Arantxa Sanchez Vicario (deposing champ Steffi Graf in SF). Made QF Wimbledon, 1996; U.S., 1994, 99. World Top Ten 5 times: No. 5, 1994-95, 99; No. 7, 1997-98, 2000. Federation Cup, 7 years from 1990; 11-8 singles, 2-2 doubles.

PILIC, NIKKI: Nikola 'Nikki' Pilic, slim 6-3 Croat, LH, from Split, former- Yugoslavia's best of post-war (until another Split lefty, Goran Ivanisevic). Country's first pro athlete, 1968, with WCT 'Handsome Eight.' Cause of famous Wimbledon boycott, 1973: most ATP colleagues walked out, protesting Wimbledon honoring his unfair suspension by Yugoslav Federation. Solidarity on Pilic's behalf established year-old union. B. Aug. 27, 1939, Split. Big serve, forehand. Lost French F to Ilie Nastase, 1973 (second oldest finalist). Made QF, 1967; SF Wimbledon, 1967; QF U.S., 1973. Won U.S. doubles with Pierre Barthes, 1970. Best World rank, No. 7, 1967. Davis Cup: 11 years 1961-77; 27-12 singles, 11-12 doubles. Won 4 singles, 7 doubles career pro titles. Became German citizen, captained Davis Cup team, winner 1988-89, 93. Now captains Croatia.

PIM, JOSHUA: His cup runneth over with Wimbledon titles—singles, 1893-94, doubles, 1890, 93. Ireland's Dr. Joshua Pim, mustachioed physician with daring netside manner, delighted in difficult volleys, flamboyant shotmaking. Four-year rivalry with Wilfred Baddeley resulted in two F lost, 1891-92, then the titles. After that, retirement to medicine, with a brief losing comeback in a Davis Cup F weekend for Britain in Boston, 1902. B. May 20, 1869, Bray, Ireland, d. April 15, 1942, Dublin.

RAHIM, HAROON: Foremost player of Pakistan, Haroon Rahim, RH, b. Nov. 12, 1949, Lahore, one of 14 children. Quick, fine volleying All-American, National Intercollegiate doubles champ (with Jeff Borowiak), UCLA, 1971. For years youngest ever Davis

Cupper, 15 years, 109 days, 1965 against South Vietnam (beat Vo Van Bay, 6-1 in 5th). Several greener lads, all insignificant otherwise, have lowered the mark since 1990, the youngest being Kenny Banzer, Liechtenstein, 14-years-5 days in 2002 against Algeria. Haroon beat Tom Gorman in closest match ever, 6-7 (3-5), 7-6 (5-1), 7-6 (5-4), Pennsylvania Grass, 1970. Won one singles, six doubles pro titles. Best World rank, No. 49, 1976.

RAMIREZ, RAUL: Raul Carlos Ramirez, Mexico's premier player open era, got tennis education in U.S. All-American, University Southern Caliofrnia, combined with Brian Gottfried in superb doubles team (39 titles). RH, b. June 20, 1953, Ensenada. Quick 6-footer, improviser fond of attack, splendid volleyer. Davis Cup: 1971-82; 22-8 singles, 14-5 doubles. Thorn in U.S. side: Won four singles, two doubles in two 3-2 Cup wins, 1975-76. Beat Roscoe Tanner, Jimmy Connors, respective decisive matches. QF or better all majors but Aussie. Won Italian, 1975 (beat defender Bjorn Borg, Ilie Nastase, Manolo Orantes). World Top Ten: No. 5, 1976; No. 8, 1977-78. Won 17 singles, 62 doubles pro career titles, $2,213,671.

REDL, HANS: Austrian Hans Redl, RH (subsequently only-hander) of extraordinary grit. B. Jan. 19, 1914, Vienna, d. May 26, 1976. Davis Cup, Austria, 1937, then Germany, 1938-39, when his country was annexed. Lost left arm, World War II, fighting with German army in Russia. Amazingly resumed play at upper level, Davis Cup, Austria, 1948-55. Cup record: 2-2 singles with both arms; 3-10 singles, 3-8 doubles, with one arm. Made 4th rd. Wimbledon, 1947. Because of him, rules amended to allow one-armed players to make service toss with racket.

REID, KERRY: Among very best Aussies, Kerry Anne Meville Reid won homeland singles, Jan.-1977, her 11th try. Lost F, 1970 (to Margaret Court), U.S. F, 1972 (to Billie Jean King). All-rounder with strong forehand, volley, World Top Ten 12 times: No. 5, 1971; No. 10, 1966, 75, 77; No. 9, 1967; No. 7, 1969, 73-74; No. 8, 1970, 72, 76, 78; Made SF all majors: Australian, 1966-67,69, 73-74, Dec.-1977; French, 1967; Wimbledon, 1974; U.S., 1966, 74. Met American husband Grover 'Raz' Reid as teammates on Boston Lobsters, WTT, married 1975. Won 10 singles, 10 doubles (Australian, Dec.-1977; Wimbledon, 1978) pro titles, $750,000. An original 'Long Way Baby' of women's pro tour, 1970.

Federation Cup: 1967-79, 20-4 singles, 17-6 doubles (won one Cup, 1968, made 4 F, 1969, 76-77-78). B. Aug. 7, 1947, Mosman, Australia, lives in U.S.

REITANO, MARY: Tiniest Australian champ, 5-2 RH Mary Carter Reitano won under maiden name (1956), married (1959). Saved match point over Thelma Long, 3-6, 6-2, 9-7, in 1956 F; beat all-timer Margaret Court, 16, 2nd rd., 1959, last defeat for Court in nationals until 1968. B. Nov. 29, 1934, Sydney, had solid all-court game.

RICE, HORRIE: Longest-running Australian, LH Horace M. Rice, played first interstate match for New South Wales at 22, 1894, last at 53, 1925. Won Australian singles at 35, 1907, over Harry Parker lost F 1910-11, 15, to Rod Heath, Norman Brookes, Gordon Lowe respectively. Made SF, 1920, 23, last at age 51. Won doubles, 1915 with Clarrie Todd. Davis Cup rookie at 39, 1913, 0-2 singles. Eager retriever, distinctive in white knickers, long black sox. Sliced serve, strong backhand, hit with same face of racket as forehand, a stroke described admiringly by Tony Wilding: "Peculiar, one of his own; for ugliness and effectiveness combined I have never seen anything to approach it." B. Sept. 5, 1873.

RICE, LENA: With luck Irish woman Helena Bertha Grace 'Lena' Rice might have been second woman to win successive Wimbledons. Served at 5-3, 40-15 and advantage, 3 match points, 2nd set, but lost 1889 F to Blanche Bingley Hillyard, 4-6, 8-6, 6-4. Did win, 1890. RH, b. June 21, 1866, Newinn; d. there, June 21, 1907.

RICHARDS, RENÉE: American LH, 6-1, ophthalmological surgeon, b. Richard Raskind, Aug. 19, 1934, New York. Graduate Yale, Rochester Medical. Unique: Played U.S. as amateur male (1955-56-57, 60), pro female (1977-81). Lost F U.S. doubles, 1977, with Bettyann Stuart to Martina Navratilova-Betty Stove. Strong server, clever tactician. Following 1975 sex change surgery, sought to play women's pro tour, faced opposition, resorted to courts of law to gain entry. New York Supreme Court ruling, August 1977, cleared way to enter WTA, USTA events. Age 43, lost 1st rd., U.S., 1977, to Wimbledon champ Virginia Wade. Made 3rd rd., 1979, lost to Chris Evert. Reasonable pro career, five years, winning one singles title. Returned to medicine. Best World rank, No. 22, 1977.

RICHEY, NANCY; CLIFF: American brother and sister, Nancy (*See Appendix A for full biography*) and Cliff Richey, RH, out of San Angelo, Tex. Attained highest standing for such a family pair. Unique: Both held No. 1 U.S., rank, she 1964-65, 68-69; he, 1970. Both won U.S. Clay Court singles, 1966, played Davis/Federation/Wightman Cup. Careers spanned amateur, open eras.

George Clifford Richey, Jr., b. Dec. 31, 1946, San Angelo, Tex. Quick, stocky (5-7, 170), scrappy, hard worker, strong groundstroker, good volleyer. Led U.S. to 1970 Davis Cup over West Germany; also played 1966-67, 10-3 singles. Biggest season, 1970, won eight titles (including U.S. Clay), 93-19 record, made SF, French, US; World rank, No. 7. Took U.S. No. 1 rank by narrowest margin: 1-point victory. His beating No. 2 Stan Smith in 5-4 5th set tie-breaker, Pacific Coast SF decided order of rank.

ROBB, MURIEL: An intruding champ, 1902 Wimbledon, English RH Muriel Evelyn Robb interrupted title monopolies of Charlotte Sterry, Blanche Hillyard and Dorothea Douglass Chambers, beating Sterry in two-part F. She had to work harder than most, 4 sets. A downpour halted F at 1 set apiece, and it was decided to play the whole thing over again the next day, Robb winning, 7-5, 6-1. B. May 13, 1878, Newcastle-upon-Tyne, she had brief British celebrity—winning Welsh, 1899, Irish, Scottish titles, 1901—and briefest life of any champ. Less than five years after Wimbledon triumph she was dead, age 28, Feb. 12, 1907, town of her birth.

RODDICK, ANDY: Heralded as natural heir to Andre Agassi and Pete Sampras. Talented, brash 6-foot RH American plays a power game. Serve clocked at 144 mph at Wimbledon, second fastest recorded serve in ATP history. In rookie pro season, 2002, at age 19, became first teenager since Sampras in 1990 to win three tournaments (Atlanta, U.S. Clay Court Championships, Washington). Added two more wins (U.S. Clay Court Championships vs. Sampras; Memphis) in 2002 to place No. 10 in year-end rankings, youngest American since Michael Chang in 1992 to achieve top 10. Reached U.S. QF 2001, 2002, losing to eventual champion each time (Leyton Hewitt, Sampras). B. Aug. 30, 1982, Omaha, Neb. Six-time world junior champion. Turned pro, 2000. Attacks the net with ferocity and not afraid to attempt dangerous shots even with a match on the line.

Nicknamed A-Rod.

His 7-0 record in Davis Cup is best Cup start for an American player since Agassi, 1988-89.

RUZICI, VIRGINIA: Romania's standout woman, Virginia Ruzici, b. Jan. 31, 1955, Cimpa-Turzil, grew up in Bucharest. Lissome, 5-8, RH, baseliner with lusty forehand. Won French singles (over Mima Jausovec), doubles, 1978. Won U.S. Clay, 1982. Federation Cup. Over 13-year career won 14 singles, 8 doubles pro career titles, $1,184,228. Best World rank: No. 11, 1980; No. 12, 1978, 82. Federation Cup, 1973-77, 80-81, 83; 12-6 singles, 8-4 doubles. Made QF Australian, 1980 SF French, 1976, 80; QF, 1979, 81-82; QF Wimbledon, 1978, 81; QF U.S., 1976, 78.

SABATINI, GABRIELA: Argentina's Gabriela Sabatini, RH, finest Latin American female since Maria Bueno. Tall, 5-9, dark-haired beauty, the 'Divine Argentine.' Powerful topspin, groundstroker, showed attacking qualities to win U.S., 1990, over defender Steffi Graf, reach Wimbledon F, 1991; U.S. F, 1988 (both lost to Graf). B. May 16, 1970, Buenos Aires, lives in Florida, where she spent formative years. Won Olympic silver, singles, 1988, runner-up to Graf. First impact at 14: Three-match day at rain-compressed Hilton Head, 1985, beat Pam Shriver, Manuela Maleeva, lost F to Chris Evert. Won Italian, 1988-89, 91-92. Painful loss to Graf, Wimbledon F, 1991, led 3rd set, 6-5, 30-15. Made SF Australian, 1992, QF, 1991; SF French, 1985, 87, 89, 91-92; SF Wimbledon, 1986, 90, 92, QF 1987; SF U.S., 1989; QF, 1987, 91-92. World Top Ten: No. 10, 1986; No. 6, 1987; No. 4, 1988; No. 3, 1989. 91-92; No. 5, 1990, 93; No. 7, 1994-95. Made F of 3 season-ending championships, beating Pam Shriver, 1988; Lindsay Davenport, 1994; lost mammoth F to Monica Seles, 1990, 5 sets, 3:47. Retired after 1996. Won 27 singles, 14 doubles pro career titles, $8,185,849.

SAFIN, MARAT: Big, blazing, bumptious, and sometimes bumbling, excessive in everything he does, 6-4, 200 pound Marat Safin is a good-natured bundle of immense talent waiting to be tamed. Nobody can stop him when he fires on all cylinders, as Pete Sampras learned, swept away, 6-4, 6-3, 6-3, in 2000 U.S. F. Marat, 20 then, lone Russian to win the title, appeared to have No. 1 wrapped up that year (won 7 titles), but unraveled at Masters, finished No. 2 behind Guga

Kuerten. Blends speed, touch, power; however, moodiness can transform him to headless horseman. Fined $2,500 for not trying, 1st rd. loss to Grant Stafford, first major, 2000, Australian. A champion racket-smasher, he turned it all around, seeded 6th at Flushing. Turned pro 1996. First splash: Beat Andre Agassi, 1st rd., Kuerten 2nd rd. French, 1998, made 4th rd. B. Jan. 27, 1980, Moscow of tennis-teaching parentage. Mother, Rausa Islanova, coached him age 6-to-13, sent him to Valencia, Spain to live under tutelage Rafael Mensua. Sister Dinara Safina (b. April 17, 1986) also world class, ranked No. 68, 2002. Davis Cup, 1998-to-date, 11-10 singles, 6-3 doubles. Mainstay as Russia won first Cup, 2002. Beat France, 3-2, F. He was 6-1 singles, 2-2 doubles; won decisive singles over Michel Kratochvil, Switzerland, David Nalbandian, Argentina; beat Paul-Henri Mathieu, Sebastian Grosjean in F. Lost F Australian, 2002, to Tom Johansson. Made SF French, 2002, QF, 2000; QF Wimbledon, 2001; SF U.S., 2001. Won 11 singles, 1 doubles pro career titles, $8,402,773 through 2002; career singles W L 230-131. World Top Ten: No. 2, 2000; No. 3, 2002 (No. 11, 2001).

SANCHEZ, ARANTXA; EMILIO; JAVIER: Probably most accomplished family combination ever at uppermost level: Arantxa Sanchez Vicario (*See Chapter 25 for full biography*) and her brothers, Emilio and Javier, all RH from Barcelona, represented Spain, Davis/Federation Cup, Emilio in Olympics.

Emilio Sanchez, quick, smooth-stroking 5-10, b. May 29, 1965, Madrid. Won Italian, 1991. Excellent at doubles. With Sergio Casal won U.S., 1988; Italian and French, 1990; Olympic silver medal, 1988. Won two major mixed, 1987—French with Pam Shriver, U.S. with Martina Navratilova. Davis Cup: 1984-95; 18-14 singles, 14-9 doubles. Made QF U.S., 1988. Through 1996 had 15 singles, 50 doubles pro titles (44 with Casal, 3 with brother Javier), $5,303,210. Best World rank, No. 8, 1990.

Javier Sanchez, speedy, 5-10, b. Feb. 1, 1968, Pamplona. Consistent winner singles, doubles. Made QF U.S. 1991, 96. Davis Cup: 1987-89; 3-2 singles. Through 1996 had 4 singles, 20 doubles (3 with brother Emilio) career titles, $3,455,007. Best World rank, No. 23, 1994.

JIRO SATOH: Highest ranking Japanese ever—yet tragic. World No. 3, 1933, also No. 9, 1931, 5-5 RH Jiro Satoh killed himself at age 26, having thrice led Japan to Cup SF. B. Jan. 5, 1908, Tokyo, all-rounder, nifty touch. Adept on clay, grass: Made SF French, 1931, 33; SF Wimbledon, 1933, QF, 1931; SF Australian, 1932. Lost Wimbledon doubles F, 1933. Had wins over Hall of Famers Jack Crawford, Fred Perry, Elly Vines. Despondent over 3-2 loss to Australia, 1933, feeling pressure of leading team—"I would have been unable to help..." said suicide note—he leaped from shipboard into Strait of Malacca, April 5, 1934, on the way to Cup opener in England. Davis Cup: 1931-33; 14-4 singles, 8-2 doubles.

SAWAMATSU, KAZUKO; JUNKO: Sisters, Kazuko and Junko Sawamatsu, RH (with two-handed backhands), first Japanese women to make mark on pro tour. Federation Cup together, 1970-71. Kazuko first Japanese woman to win major, Wimbledon doubles, 1975.

Kazuko Sawamatsu, sturdy 5-7, b. Jan. 5, 1951, Nishinomiya. Solid groundstroker, won 3 career pro singles titles (Japan Open, 1968, 72, 75). Made SF Australian, 1973 (beat Virginia Wade); QF French, 1975; Won Japanese National, 1967, 72; Wimbledon, French Junior, 1969. In one-time unseeded partnership with Japanese-American Ann Kiyomura, won Wimbledon, 1975; made QF, 1970, with Junko.

Junko Sawamatsu, b. April 10, 1948, Nishinomiya. Made Australian QF, 1973. Daughter, Naoko Sawamatsu (RH with two-handed backhand, b. March 23, 1973, Nishinomiya), was on WTA tour 10 years, made QF Australian, 1995, won 4 singles pro career titles, $1,107,264. Best World rank, No. 17, 1995.

SCOTT, GENE: Protean New York RH Eugene Lytton Scott, 6-1, 165, made U.S. Top Ten: 1962-64, 67-68; best, No. 4, 1963. Unseeded, reached U.S. SF, 1967. Davis Cup: 1963-65; 3-0 singles, 1-0 doubles. Varsity letterman—hockey, soccer, tennis, track—at Yale ('60). Virginia Law ('65). Practiced law. Founder-publisher-columnist *Tennis Week* magazine, 1974 to date. Founder Kremlin Cup, Moscow (ATP Tour), 1990. B. Dec. 27, 1937, New York. TV commentator with Howard Cosell, Rosie Casals for King-Riggs extravaganza, 1973.

SCRIVEN, PEGGY: First of five LH to win French, England's Margaret Croft 'Peggy' Scriven was 20, beat Simone Passemard Mathieu in 1933 F. Repeated in 1934 over Helen Jacobs. Made SF 1935— a Paris winning streak of 14 matches—QF 1936; Wimbledon QF 1931,

33-34, 37. Won French doubles 1935 with Kay Stammers. World Top Ten: No. 5, 1933-34, No. 10, 1935. Wightman Cup: 1933-34; 0-4 singles. B. Aug 17, 1912, Leeds, Yorkshire, England, d. Jan. 25, 2001 as Mrs. F. H. Vivian, Haslemere, Surrey, England.

SEARS, EVELYN: Evelyn Georgianna Sears of Waltham, Mass., Longwood Cricket Club member, first LH to win U.S. titles, singles 1907, doubles 1908. Didn't venture to Philadelphia until '07, won impressively at 32, losing no sets, 17 games in 5 matches. Lost challenge round, 1908. Tried again, 1916, made SF. Good bloodline, cousin of initial U.S. champ, Richard Sears. B. March 9, 1875, Waltham, d. there, Nov. 10, 1966.

SHIMIDZU, ZENZO: Zenzo 'Shimmy' Shimidzu, first Japanese of note, attained highest male level. B. March 25, 1891, Tokyo; d. April 12, 1977, Amagaski City, Japan. Self-taught, 5-6, quick-footed, unorthodox RH. Weird stroker, heavy topspin; same face of racket, forehand, backhand, yet effective on grass. Lost Wimbledon F (all-comers), 1920, to champ Bill Tilden; SF, 1921, to Manuel Alonso. In Japan's Davis Cup debut year, 1921, he, with Ichiya Kumagae (b. Sept. 10, 1891; d. Aug. 16, 1968), upset Australia in SF, took country to Cup zenith, the challenge round vs. defender, U.S., Forest Hills. Astoundingly Shimidzu came within two points, 3rd set, of beating Tilden, losing, 5-7, 4-6, 7-5, 6-2, 6-1. Davis Cup: 1921-25; 9-8 singles, 3-5 doubles. World Top Ten: No. 9, 1920; No. 4. 1921. Working in the U.S., the pair had Top Ten U.S. rankings: Shimidzu (No. 7, 1922), Kumagae (No. 5, 1916; No. 6, 1918, No. 3, 1919; No, 4, 1920; No, 7, 1921).

SIROLA, ORLANDO: Gaunt, towering Italian RH Orlando Sirola, tallest (6-6) to play in Davis Cup F (1960-61), major F (won French doubles, 1959, lost Wimbledon, 1956, both with Nicola Pietrangeli) until 6-6 Todd Martin was in Cup F, 1995, lost Australian F, 1994, U.S. final, 1999. B. April 30, 1928, Fiume, d. Nov. 13, 1995, Bologna. Self-taught, late starter, 1950. Huge serve, overhead, good volleyer, streaky. Joined Cup team, 1953, aligned with Pietrangeli, 1955, playing, winning as pair most doubles in Cup history (34-8) through 1963. Among most active Cuppers: 22-25 singles, 35-8 doubles. High point, 1960 Cup SF, 3-2 comeback from 0-2 over U.S.: won pivotal doubles, 13-11, 4th, over Butch Buchholz-Chuck McKinley,

decider in singles over Barry MacKay, 9-7, 6-3, 8-6.

SPERLING, HILDE: Tall, slim RH Hilde Krahwinkel Sperling was strong presence for decade, World Top Ten 10 straight years: No. 10, 1930; No. 6, 1931; No. 5, 1932; No. 4, 1933, 35, 37-38-39; No. 3, 1934; No. 2, 1936. Won three straight French, 1935-37, tying Helen Moody's 1928-30 run, equalled by Monica Seles, 1990-92. Lost only all-German female Wimbledon F to Cilly Aussem, 1931, also F to Helen Jacobs, 1936. B. March 26, 1908, Essen, Germany, became Danish citizen (marrying Svend Sperling, 1933), d. March 7, 1981, Halsingborg, Sweden.

STERRY, CHARLOTTE: English RH Charlotte Reinagle Cooper Sterry, consistent factor at Wimbledon over extraordinary period of 18 years and two centuries with 5 singles title. During record run of 8 straight F (1895-92), she won 4 (1895-96, 98, 1901), lost 3 (1897, 99-1900) as Miss Cooper. As Mrs. Rex Sterry won 2 (1901-08), lost 3 (1902, 04, 1912), last at age 41. Lost doubles F 1913. Her record was eclipsed in 1990: Martina Navratilova appeared in 9th straight final. Won Olympic singles, 1900, first woman gold medalist any sport. Won Scottish, 1895, Irish, 1895, 98, titles. B. Sept. 22, 1870, Ealing; d. Oct. 10, 1966, Helensburgh, Scotland.

STICH, MICHAEL: Spindly 6-4 RH, fluid stroker, attacker with big serve, Michael Stich dethroned countryman Boris Becker, Wimbledon, 1991, only all-German male F. Also made QF, 1993. Lost F U.S. 1994 to Andre Agassi, French, 1996, to Yevgeny Kafelnikov; SF French, 1991. Davis Cup: 1990-95; 21-9 singles, 14-2 doubles. Led Germany to 1993 Cup, 4-1 over Australia with rare triple with series alive: won both singles over Jason Stoltenberg and clincher over Richard Fromberg plus doubles with Patrik Kuhnen. World Top Ten: No. 4, 1991; No. 2, 1993; No. 9, 1994. Turned pro 1988. Won 18 singles, 13 doubles pro career titles, $12,628,890; career singles W-L 385-176. B. Oct. 18, 1968, Pinneberg, Germany.

ST. JOHN, BERT: Remarkable one-handed athlete at upper level of Australian sport, LH Queenslander Cecil Bertram Vernon St. John is only man thus impaired to reach major tennis finals. At 44, oldest Australian singles finalist, lost, 1923, to Pat O'Hara Wood. Earlier, 1915, lost doubles F with Gordon Lowe to Horrie Rice-Clairie Todd. Also made SF, 1915. Exceptional at cricket, football. B. 1879, d. Sept. 19, 1932.

STOVE, BETTY: Netherlands' Betty Flippina Stove, 6-foot RH, her country's foremost woman. Powerful server, fine volleyer, erratic. Only female Hollander in Wimbledon F, 1977 (lost to Virginia Wade), and country's foremost holder major titles (10)—U.S. doubles, 1972, with Françoise Durr; 1977, with Martina Navratilova; 1979, with Wendy Turnbull; Wimbledon, French doubles, 1972, with Billie Jean King, 1979, with Wendy Turnbull; Wimbledon mixed, 1978, 81, with Frew McMillan; U.S. mixed 1977-78, with McMillan. Rarity: Lost all 3 Wimbledon F, 1977. Made QF Wimbledon, 1975; SF U.S., 1977. B. June 24, 1945, Rotterdam. Federation Cup: 1966–76; 20-4 singles, 20-8 doubles. World Top Ten: No. 7, 1976-77, No. 9, 1978.

SUK/SUKOVA, VERA; HELENA; CYRIL: Great name in Czechoslovak game. Mother, Vera; son, Cyril; daughter, Helena, all RH major champions. Played for country in Federation and Davis Cup. Only mother, daughter in major singles F, World Top Ten. Father, Cyril Suk, was president Czechoslovak Federation.

Vera Puzejova Sukova, b. June 13, 1931, Uherske Hradiste; d. May 13, 1982, Prague. Married Suk, 1961. Unimpressive serve, strokes, but strong, persistent, competitive. Stolid baseliner, fine passing shots: Made SF French, 1957, losing to champ Shirley Bloomer, 6-4, 3rd; QF, 1959-60, 63-64. Unseeded, had stunning Wimbledon, 1962, beat 6th, 2nd, 3rd seeds—defender Angela Mortimer, Darlene Hard, ex-champ Maria Bueno—lost F to Karen Susman. Also QF, U.S., 1962. World Top Ten: No. 6, 1957; No. 5, 1962; No. 10, 1963. Was Czechoslovak national coach, early tutor of Martina Navratilova.

Helena Sukova, b. Feb. 23, 1965, Prague. At 6-2 tallest ever female player of consequence, until 6-3 Lindsay Davenport won Olympic gold, 1996. Standout serve-and-volleyer, possessing sound groundies. Lost F Australian, 1984 to Chris Evert; 1989, to Steffi Graf; U.S., 1986, to Martina Navratilova (beat Evert in SF). Ended Navratilova's pro record 74-match streak and Grand Slam bid, SF, Australian, 1984, 1-6, 6-3, 7-5. Made French SF, 1986; QF, 1988; Wimbledon QF, 1985, 88; U.S. SF, 1987; QF, 1984-85, 89. World Top Ten: No. 7, 1984, 87; No. 9, 1985; No. 5, 1986; No, 8, 1988-89. Superior at doubles, won 14 majors: Australian, 1990, 92; French, 1990; Wimbledon, 1987, 89-90, 96 (last with half-her-age Martina Hingis, 15);

U.S., 1985, 93; French mixed, 1991, with Suk (only brother-sister to win); Wimbledon, 1994; U.S., 1993 (both with Todd Woodbridge); Wimbledon, 1996-97 (with Cyril). Missed Grand Slam with Jana Novotna, 1990, lost U.S. F to Martina Navratilova-Gigi Fernandez, 6-2, 6-4. Federation Cup all-timer, 1981-96, 42-11 singles, 12-5 doubles (with four winners, 1983-85, 1988). Through 2002 won 10 singles, 67 doubles pro titles, $11,249,134. Olympic silver, doubles, 1988, 1996, with Novotna.

Cyril Suk, b. Jan. 19, 1967, Prague. Quick, clever, 5-11. Singles (best World rank, No. 184, 1988) overshadowed by doubles expertise. Davis Cup: 1992-96; 6-3 doubles. Won 26 career pro doubles titles, $2,941,015; career doubles W-L 488-412. Won 6 majors: U.S. doubles with Sandon Stolle, 1998; with Helena French mixed, 1991; Wimbledon mixed, 1996-97; U.S. mixed, 1993 (only sister-brother to win French, U.S.); Wimbledon mixed, 1992, with Larisa Savchenko Neiland.

SUSMAN, KAREN: Lovely, free-flowing, 5-7 brilliant RH serve-and-volleyer out of Chula Vista, Calif., Karen Janice Hantze was 1961 unseeded surprise champ at Wimbledon, 18, alongside Billie Jean Moffitt (King), 17: youngest doubles winners. Again surprising, 1962, as Mrs. Rod Susman seeded 8th, won singles, repeated with BJ in doubles. Didn't defend, gave birth to daughter. She and King also won U.S. doubles, 1964. Made Wimbledon QF, 1961; U.S. QF, 1959, 64. World Top Ten: No. 10, 1961, No. 4, 1962, No. 8, 1964. U.S. Top Ten: No. 6, 1959; No. 2, 1960-61-62; No. 4, 1964. Wightman Cup, 1960-62, 1965, 3-3 singles, 3-0 doubles (won 3 Cups). Federation Cup, 1964: 4-0 doubles. Won 13 amateur singles titles. B. Dec. 11, 1942, San Diego.

TAPSCOTT, BILLIE: South African Ruth Daphne 'Billie' Tapscott, b. May 31, 1903, Kimberly; d. 1970. Emancipated female legs, shocked Wimbledon, 1927, appearing without stockings. "It's just the way we do it at home." With bared gams, made QF, probably inspired Joan Austin Lycett, first bold peeler of hose for Centre Court match, 1931, as stockings went way of corsets. RH, won South African singles, 1930. Married South African player Collin John James Robbins, 1930.

TEACHER, BRIAN: Long-armed lightning server from San Diego, 6-3-1/2 RH Brian David Teacher seized his monumental prize, Australian singles, 1980, on cruise control, lost 3 sets, beat homeboy Kim Warwick quick in F. Made QF Australian, Wimbledon, 1982. UCLA grad, 4 years All-American. Best World Rank, No. 12, 1980; No. 16, 1981. Won 8 singles, 17 doubles pro career titles, $1,426,244. B. Dec. 23, 1954, San Diego.

TERRY, ALINE: Mystery woman of U.S. Championships. Came from Princeton, N.J., becoming fifth to win singles, doubles titles, 1893. Lost both, 1894, singles in 5-set challenge round struggle with Helen Hellwig. Never heard from again. Age unknown, no details b. or d. Called "lithe, feline, leaped at balls like a tiger" by champ Juliette Atkinson.

TIRIAC, ION: First prominent Romanian of open era, Ion Ioan Tiriac, b. May 9, 1939, Brasov. Hulking, glowering, ungainly 6-foot RH, excellent athlete, fierce competitor, played Olympic ice hockey prior late start in tennis. Career, almost two decades, spanned amateur, open era. Shrewd polyglot, tactician: "I am best tennis player who cannot play tennis." Davis Cup: 1959-77; led way for protégé Ilie Nastase. Together carried Romania to three F, all lost to U.S.: 1969, 71-72. Sixth in all-time Cup matches played, 109 (40-28, singles: 30-11, doubles). Highest World rank No. 72, 1974 (best years were pre-computer). Won 2 singles, 27 doubles career pro titles. Entrepreneur in variety of businesses, has a hand in tennis operating tournaments, managed champs Guillermo Vilas, Boris Becker.

TODD, PAT: Mary Patricia Canning Todd, 5-8 California RH, says she "got by on a backhand and guts," made fine immediate post-war record. Won French singles, 1947, over Doris Hart. Lost F, 1950, played despite blood poisoning, 3 sets to Hart, then hospitalized. World Top Ten: No. 5 1946, 50-51; No. 4, 1947, 49; No. 6, 1948; 52, No. 7. 1952. Made SF French, 1948; SF Wimbledon, 1948-49-50, 52; QF, 1947; SF U.S. 1946, 48, QF, 1945, 1947,49-50. Only winner over Mo Connolly 3 times, 1952. Won French doubles, mixed, 1948. Might have had triple, defaulted SF to champ-to-be Nelly Landry, France: referee unfairly advanced starting time to 'now' while she ate lunch. Wightman Cup, 1947-51, 4-1 doubles (won Cup every year). B. July 22, 1922, San Francisco.

TRUMAN, CHRIS: Darling of homeland fans from teenage years onward, English 6-foot blonde RH

Christine Clara Truman won 1959 French singles at 18, youngest until Steffi Graf, 1987. Lost U.S. F 1959 to Maria Bueno. Chris had won compatriots' hearts beating Althea Gibson, Dorothy Knode, winning doubles, 1958 Wightman Cup victory over U.S., 4-3. She, as Mrs. Gerry Janes, and sister, Nell Truman, won decisive doubles in 4-3 win, 1968. World Top Ten: No. 9, 1957; No. 6. 1958; No. 2, 1959; No. 4, 1960; No. 7, 1961, 65. Heartbreaker: 1961 Wimbledon F loss to Angela Mortimer, 4-6, 6-4, 7-5; made SF, 1957, 60, 65, was 34-14 there. Federation Cup, 1963, 1965, 1968, 6-3 singles, 2-2 doubles. Wightman Cup, 1957-71, 6-12 singles, 5-4 doubles (won 3 Cups). B. Feb. 16, 1941, Loughton, England.

TURNBULL, WENDY: All-time Aussie Wendy May 'Rabbit'1 Turnbull, 5-3 RH was noted for speed, exceptional volley. Only woman of her country other than Margaret Court and Evonne Goolagong to make three major singles F: Lost Australian, 1980, to Hana Mandlikova; French, 1979, to Chris Evert; U.S., 1977, to Evert. Won 9 major doubles: French, 1979; Wimbledon, 1978; U.S., 1979, 82. Plus five mixed: French, 1979, 82; Wimbledon, 1983-84; U.S., 1980; 4 with John Lloyd, U.S. with Marty Riessen. Upset No. 2 Martina Navratilova, U.S. SF, 1977. Made SF Australian, 1981, 84; QF, 1980-81, QF French, 1980; QF Wimbledon, 1979-80-81; SF U.S., 1978, 84; QF, 1986. World Top Ten: No. 9, 1977; No. 7, 1978-79; No. 8, 1980-81, 83; No. 5, 1982, 84. Federation Cup, 1977—88, most Aussie wins, 17-8 singles, 29-8 doubles (lost 4 F). Won 7 singles, 10 doubles career pro titles, $2,769,024. B. Nov. 25, 1952, Brisbane. Olympic bronze, 1988, doubles with Liz Smylie.

ULRICH, EINER; TORBEN; JORGEN: Davis Cup workhorses for Denmark. Father, Einer, two sons, Torben and Jorgen Ulrich, all b. in Copenhagen, played 218 Cup matches between 1924 and 1978.

Einer Ulrich, RH, b. May 6, 1896. Davis Cup: 1924-38; 23-23 singles, 16-12 doubles.

Torben Ulrich, free-spirited, bearded LH, b. Oct. 4, 1928; family's most prominent, strong serve, delicate touch. Career spanned amateur, open eras. Made 4th rd. French, 1959; 3rd rd., U.S., 1969, at 40. Davis Cup: 1948-61, 1964-68, 1978; one of few in over 100 matches; 31-35 singles, 15-21 doubles. Fourth oldest of all Cuppers, 48 years, 11 months, last match, 1978.

Jorgen Ulrich, RH. b. Aug. 21, 1935. Davis Cup:

1955, 1958-71; 18-18 singles, 8-10 doubles—3-3 with Torben.

WASHINGTON, MAL; MASHISKA; MASHONA; MICHEALA:

Exceptional siblings from Swartz Creek, Mich., all RH (two-handed backhands), two currently on pro tour, coached by father, William Washington.

MaliVai Onyeaka, b. June 20, 1969, Glen Cove, N.Y., sinewy 5-11, well-rounded game. First black U.S. Davis Cupper since Arthur Ashe, 1993, 96-97 (3-2 singles). Wrecked left knee beating Gustavo Kuerten in Cup victory at Brazil, 1997, led to 1999 retirement. Unseeded, made Wimbledon F, 1996, lost to Richard Krajicek; incredible SF comeback from 1-5 in the 5th over Todd Martin, 5-7, 6-4, 6-7 (6-8), 6-3, 10-8. Made Australian QF, 1994; Olympic QF, 1996. Best World rank, No. 13, 1992. All-American, University of Michigan, 1987-88. Won 4 career pro singles titles, $3,239,865; career singles W-L 254-184.

Mashiska Isabelita, b. Dec. 19, 1974, Flint, Mich., 5-11. All-American, Michigan State, 1994. Best World ranking: No. 290, 1999. Won $125,234 through 2002.

Mashona Lakuta, b. May 31, 1976, Flint, Mich. Won U.S. 18 Indoor singles, 1992. Best World ranking: No. 113, 2002. Turned pro 1995. Won $312,413. Career singles W-L 214-189.

Micheala Bharati, b. Jan. 27, 1966, Carbondale, Ill. Played one year as pro. World ranking No. 81, 1984. Won $30,525.

WATSON, MAUD:

First lady of Wimbledon, Englishwoman Maud Edith Eleanor Watson, 19, won intramural battle, becoming pioneer among major champs. Beat sister, Lillian Mary Watson, 26, as Wimbledon introduced female tourney (13 entered), 1884. Also won Irish, 1884-85; Welsh, 1887. RH, b. Oct. 9, 1864, Harrow; d. June 6, 1946, Charmouth. Lillian b. Sept. 17, 1857, Harrow; d. May 27, 1918, Berkswell, England.

WEIR, REGINALD:

Racial pioneer, New York physician, Dr. Reginald S. Weir, overcame early discrimination to win U.S. titles. Though Althea Gibson received much attention entering U.S. at Forest Hills, 1950, RH Weir was first black to play national championship sanctioned by USTA: U.S. Indoor, 1948, New York, 7th Regt. Armory. Also first to win U.S. title, Senior (over 45) Indoor singles, 1956-57, 59 (doubles, 1961-62), at 7th Regt., gratifying turnaround where he'd been refused entry U.S. Junior Indoor, 1929. Beat Ed Tarangioli, 5-7, 6-3, 6-1, first title. B. 1911; d. Aug. 21, 1987, Fairlawn, N.J.

WESTACOTT, EMILY:

Unorthodox Queenslander, using same racket face for backhand and forehand, RH Emily Jane Lucy Harding Hood Westacott was baseline banger patiently, but exuberantly, pursuing Australian title. After QF finishes 1932-33-34, SF 1935, lost F to Nancye Wynne 1937. Then went all the way 1939 over Nell Hall Hopman. Won Aussie doubles 1933-34 with Mall Molesworth, lost F 1937 with Hopman, 1939 with May Hardcastle. B. May 6, 1910, Brisbane, married Clyde Westacott Aug. 20, 1930; d. Oct. 9, 1980.

THE WOODIES: MARK WOODFORDE, TODD WOODBRIDGE:

Todd Andrew Woodbridge, b. April 2, 1971, Sydney; Mark Raymond Woodforde (left court), b. Sept. 23, 1965, Adelaide: Extraordinary Aussie doubles team, best of post-John Newcombe-Tony Roche, John McEnroe-Peter Fleming eras. Won 11 majors together (1 behind record holders Newcombe-Roche). Won 6 Wimbledon, 2000, and 5 straight (1993-97), longest run there since Doherty brothers' 5 (1897-1901); record 35 match streak stopped by Jacco Eltingh-Paul Haarhuis, 1998 F. Majors also won: Australian, 1992, 97; French, 2001; U.S., 1995-96. Also won World Doubles, 1992, 96. Altogether they won 61 pro titles as partners. Davis Cup together, 1993-96, 14-2.

Woodforde, slim 6-2, LH redhead. Turned pro 1984. Retired 2001. Made SF Australian, 1996. Won 16 major doubles, 11 with Woodbridge, U.S. with John McEnroe, 1989; U.S., Australian mixed, 1992 (with Nicole Provis); Wimbledon mixed, 1993 (with Martina Navratilova); French mixed, 1995 (with Larisa Savchenko Neiland). Won 6 other pro career doubles without Woodbridge (personal total 67), 4 singles titles (best World rank, No. 27, 1996), $8,324,401. Davis Cup, 10 years from 1988: 4-10 singles, 17-5 doubles.

Woodbridge, 5-10, RH. Won 20 major doubles, 11 with Woodforde; Australian with Jonas Bjorkman, 2001; French with Bjorkman, 2002; Wimbledon with Bjorkman, 2002; Australian mixed with Arantxa Sanchez Vicario, 1993; French mixed with Sanchez Vicario, 1992; Wimbledon mixed with Helena Sukova, 1994; U.S. mixed with Liz Smylie, 1990; with Sukova, 1993; with Rennae Stubbs, 2001. Won 13 other pro career doubles without Woodforde (personal total 74),

2 singles titles (best World rank, No. 34, 1995), $8,688,899 through 2002. Davis Cup: 11 years from 1991, 3-2 singles, 19-6 doubles.

ZVEREVA, NATALIA: Mother Freedom of Soviet tennis, demanded full prize money, 1989, at a time country's players received meager subsidy from federation out of money they won. Risky business then, earned public disapproval—but got her way, benefitting colleagues. Nimble, sharp volleying RH Belarussian, leggy 5-8, b. April 16, 1971, Minsk. Often referred to as Natasha. Upset No. 2 Martina Navratilova 4th rd. but nervously lost only major F, French, 1988, fast, 6-0, 6-0, to Steffi Graf. Made QF Australian, 1995; French, 1992; Wimbledon, 1990, 92-93, SF 1998 (beat Graf, first time 19 tries en-route); QF U.S., 1993. Two-way toiler, won 1,148 matches, singles and doubles. Became doubles great (right court), won 20 majors, 14 with Gigi Fernandez—2 Australian (1993-94); 5 French (1992-93-94-95, 97); 4 Wimbledon (1992-93-94, 97); 3 U.S. (1992, 95-96)—second all-time team total. They narrowly missed Grand Slams, 1993, lost SF, U.S., to Arantxa Sanchez Vicario-Helena Sukova, 1-6, 6-3, 6-4, ending 40-match major streak, and 1994, lost SF, U.S., to Katerina Maleeva-Robin White, 7-6 (7-2), 1-6, 6-3. First Soviet to win major, French with Larisa Savchenko (Neiland), 1989. Other 3 doubles majors: Australian, 1997, with Martina Hingis; Wimbledon, 1991, with Neiland; U.S. with Pam Shriver, 1991. Also Australian mixed, 1995, with Rick Leach; 1990, with Jim Pugh. World Top Ten: No. 7, 1988; No, 10, 1994. Federation Cup (USSR/Belarus), 1986-96, 23-11 singles, 18-4 doubles. Made Olympics, QF, 1988, 3rd rd., 1992, won doubles bronze with Leila Meskhi, 1992, also played 1996, 2000. Turned pro, 1988. Won 4 singles 82 doubles career pro titles, $7,792,503; career singles W-L 434-252; career doubles W-L 714-170 through 2002.

Section **7**

The Registers

Helen Wills Moody
On the verge of winning her eighth Wimbledon title, a record which Martina Navratilova would eclipse 52 years later.

RECORDS – PRIZE MONEY, CAREER

MEN		WOMEN	
Pete Sampras	$43,280,489	Steffi Graf	$21,895,277
Andre Agassi	$26,923,233	Martina Navratilova	$20,613,751
Boris Becker	$25,080,956	Martina Hingis	$18,344,660
Yevgeny Kafelnikov	$23,457,273	Arantxa Sanchez Vicario	$16,917,312
Ivan Lendl	$21,262,417	Lindsay Davenport	$15,530,827

Chapter 27

Uncovering History

During the reign of William the Conqueror in the eleventh century, detailed information about the landowners of England and their assets was gathered and recorded in what were called "Domesday Books." Much of what we know about early England comes from those books. Sports have their own Domesday books, encyclopedias that provide a complete accounting of their subject's history.

The book you now hold in your hands is an attempt to provide the most complete and exhaustive history of tennis ever published. Unlike such team sports as baseball and football, however, tennis lacks a substantial foundation on which to build. The first baseball encyclopedia, for example, was published in 1951. It contained a record of every player and manager who had appeared in a Major League game. In the years that followed, additional research added to the body of knowledge, and subsequent encyclopedias became more and more exhaustive in their coverage.

Tennis has not benefited from that kind of intensive effort. Part of the problem is inherent with tennis itself. Team sports such as baseball are well organized, with schedules and results recorded by league offices, and their complete records have been preserved for more than a century. Tennis tournaments were independent events, with no central organizing body existing for most of the early years. While the appeal of tennis was certainly widespread, competition tended to be fairly regional. For many decades, only American born players competed in the U.S. Open. This was not the result of any exclusionary policy, merely a reflection of the practical limitations of travel, particularly in the days before commercial aviation.

Today, the men and women's professional tours are well covered by the media, and the tours themselves publish detailed records each year. Various international governing bodies and the major tournaments themselves do the same things, providing us an exhaustive account of modern players and a statistical account of their competitions.

Unfortunately, that record becomes less complete as we go back in time. While the four major championship events are fairly well documented in their entirety, most other tennis tournaments of the amateur era are not. In many cases, future research may help us build a more accurate record of tennis in those years. In other cases, there are things that we will simply never know. In the 19th century, for example, draw sheets for the major championships show many phantom names. Some are players who appeared in just one tournament, and about whom we know nothing beyond the scores of their matches—not their full name, not their birth date, not their place of residence. In some instances, players entered using fictitious names, such as "Mr. T. Ennis" or "Mr. N. Other." Early records list women by their married name (e.g., Mrs. Alan Harris), which also hampers researchers.

It is hoped that these gaps in the historical record might be viewed as an opportunity for future research, and that the information published hear might serve as a good starting point for what may some day become a truly complete statistical record of tennis.

Criteria for Selection

The player Register that follows offers what may be the most detailed attempt to capture the statistical record of tennis. It contains the singles tournament statistics for close to 400 of the game's best players. To be included here, the players had to meet at least one of the following criteria as of January 1, 2003:

- Selected as a member of the International Tennis Hall of Fame
- Winner of a major championship singles event
- Runner-up in a major championship singles event after 1967
- Ranked in the year-end top-ten after 1967

The Register records results from singles tournaments only. It is divided into two sections, one for Amateur Era players (those whose competitive careers ended before

1968) and Open Era players (those whose careers ended in 1968 or later). Each player's entry begins with biographical information: name, date and place of birth, height and weight, and whether they played left or right handed. If they played professionally, the year they turned pro is listed, along with the career earnings on the ATP or WTA tours. The highest ranking a player attained in their career is also listed (for Open Era players, the highest overall ranking may be different than the year-end ranking in cases where a player achieved a high ranking in mid year but was unable to hold it through year end).

The biographical information precedes a year-by-year record of each player's career. It includes their year-end rankings, a summary of their tournament play in singles events, followed by their singles match record in major championship events and, for Open Era players, the Olympics. Match records for men include Davis Cup results while the women's records include Fed Cup results (called Federation Cup until 1995).

For Open Era players, a more detailed breakdown of match play is included, beginning in 1968 but adding even more detail after 1976. A player's overall match record is supplemented by two different breakouts. Records are broken down by surface (clay, grass, hard court, or carpet) and venue (indoor and outdoor).

The sections that follow describe some of this data in more detail.

Major Championship events

For each major championship event in which a player competed, the Register reflects the last round to which they advanced. An entry of "1rd" (2rd, etc.) indicates that the player failed to advance past the first round. (Players were normally eliminated by a defeat, but on occasion fell victim to injury or other events that caused their exit. The Register makes no distinction between losses and these extenuating circumstances). An entry of "PRE" indicates that the player lost in a preliminary (or qualifying) round prior to the tournament proper. The number of rounds in each major championship event varied during the early years of tennis. In the women's singles at Wimbledon in 1887, the third round was the final match. In other years, the third round was the group of 32—not even the halfway point.

Elimination in the round of eight or beyond is designated differently: "QF" for quarter-finals; "SF" for semi-finals, and "F" for the final round. The winner is designated with a "W".

The Challenge Round

In the early years of Wimbledon and the U.S. Open, the tournament structure featured a challenge round. Under that format, the reigning champion waited until the rest of the field had narrowed to one, and then this "All Comers" winner would challenge the defending champion to determine the new champion. This format was used at Wimbledon through 1921, and at the U.S. Open through 1911 (with the women continuing until 1919). Under this system, a player might need to win five or six matches to initially win the title, but only one match a year later to defend it. On occasion, the reigning champion did not defend their title, but usually they did.

In years when the challenge round was employed at major championship singles events, there could be three finalists: The All Comers winner, the player he or she defeated in the All Comers tournament, and the defending champion. The winner of the challenge round match is noted with either "WC" (winner as challenger) or "WD" (winner as title holder). If the All-Comers winner lost in the challenge round, the designation is "AC". If the defending champion loses in the challenge round, the designation is "CR". The loser of the All Comers final is noted with an "F".

The Olympics

Tennis was played at the Olympics from 1896-1924. Men's competition thrived immediately, but there was a small field for women's events in the early years. No more than eight female players entered in any year before 1920; twice there were as few as five. In 1908 and 1912, there were separate events (and separate medals) for indoor and outdoor tennis.

Olympic tennis was eventually discontinued because of concerns over creeping professionalism, as well as fears that the Games might overshadow Wimbledon as the sport's premier event. In 1912, for example, the Olympics drew a disappointingly small field because the Games occurred the same week as Wimbledon.

Tennis returned to the Olympics as an exhibition sport in 1984. That year featured a 21-and under singles event for which no medals were awarded. It became a medal event four years later. In 1988 and 1992, two bronze medals were awarded. In 1996, a bronze medal round was introduced in which the two semi-final losers met to determine third place. This bronze medal format had been utilized during the first incarnation of Olympic Tennis. In the Register, gold medallists are designated with "W", silver medallists with "F" (having lost in the Olympic finals) and bronze medallists receive either "SF" (in years when two bronze medals were awarded) or "SFB" (in years when a bronze medal round was played).

Davis Cup/Fed Cup

Since 1900, teams of men representing their home countries have competed for the Davis Cup. The format of the tournament has varied slightly over time, but typically an entrant would play two matches in a series, with one team advancing and the other being eliminated. The women play a similar tournament, which began in 1963. Originally called the Federation Cup, it is now known simply as the Fed Cup.

The Register records a player's match records for any appearances in these team competitions. Because it is the team, not the individual, that wins each round, no tournament wins or finals appearances are credited for Davis Cup or Fed Cup play. The Register also includes the country that each player represented. Emigration and changing borders have resulted in a handful of players having represented more than one country.

Professional Tours

In what was largely an amateur sport, some players were openly professional as early as the mid 1920s. The men and women who opted to accept prize money were stripped of their amateur status and competed in loosely organized tournaments and barnstorming tours. Promoters organized these events (rather than international sanctioning bodies), and the focus was on profit rather than winners and losers. There simply are no records for most of these events, and so it is unlikely that we'll ever have a robust record of professional play during the amateur era.

The advent of professional tennis brought with it a number of organizing bodies. When the major championship tournaments first included professionals in 1968, there was sufficient incentive for professional players to organize. The two most notable organizations are the Association of Tennis Professionals (ATP), formed in 1972, and Women's Tennis Association (WTA), which began in 1974. As these central authorities matured over time, record keeping was vastly improved. As a result, since 1976

we're able to present a relatively complete record of all professional tennis tournaments.

Tournaments played under the auspices of the ATP and WTA tours are well documented. Unfortunately, the record is incomplete for professional events played prior to the formation of these tours and for non-tour events in the early years of their existence. Detailed match statistics are not available for all of the events from defunct tours such as World Team Tennis, the Grand Prix, the Virginia Slims Circuit, and World Championship Tennis. For the period from 1968-1976, the register presents a complete record of tournament wins, but our match statistics are not complete. We have included match statistics for all Grand Slam tournaments and a handful of other non-ATP and non-WTA pro events for which we have detailed statistics. For many of these events, however, we know who won but don't know the scores of the matches played or the results of the early rounds. Future research may help us fill in these gaps, but this data hasn't yet been compiled. Therefore, for players who competed in professional events prior to, or during the early years of, the ATP and WTA, you'll find that the match totals presented here may be lower than generally accepted career totals

Rankings and Earnings

An entire book could be written on the subject of tennis rankings, and it is certainly a frequent subject of debate among tennis fans. Many different sets of rankings exist. Some are purely subjective, while others are based on mathematical formulae so complex that computers must perform the compilation.

The Register relies on two principal sources for rankings. Computer rankings, compiled weekly by the ATP (since 1973) and WTA (since 1975) are used for professional era players. Prior to that, we use the year-end rankings published by respected journalists. They are: From London's *Daily Telegraph*, Wallis Myers (1913-1938), John Olliff (1939-51), and Lance Tingay (1952-1967), and from the Boston Globe, Bud Collins (1968-1974). The journalists ranked the top ten players at the end of each year: 1913-1972 for men and 1921 plus 1925-1974 for women.

While each of the professional tours has changed their ranking method over time, the one constant has been that the rankings are updated after each tournament. Thus, a player's ranking can change each week. The Register notes the ranking each player held at the end of the calendar year.

For Open Era players, we also note the highest ranking they achieved during the course of a year. Often, a player reaches a ranking during the year that is higher than what they achieve at the end of a calendar year. Carlos Moya earned the number one ranking after a victory at Indian Hills in March of 1999. Two weeks later, he dropped from the top spot, and in August he suffered a back injury that shortened his season. At the end of 1999, Moya had dropped to number 24 in the rankings. Even though Moya held the number one ranking during the year, he has never ranked that high in the year-end rankings.

For professional-era players, career earnings are included. These are the official totals published by the ATP and WTA, and may not include winnings from non-tour events. No accurate records exist for the earnings of professional players during the amateur era, so that information is not included in this register.

The statistics in the Player Register appear under the following abbreviated headings:

Amateur Era

Year:	Year of play
Rk:	Year-end ranking
TP:	Tournaments Played
TW:	Tournaments Won
TF:	Tournament Finals
Aus:	Australian Championships
Fre:	French Championships
Wim:	Wimbledon
US:	U.S. Championships
Oly:	Olympic Games
DC:	Davis Cup
FC:	Federation Cup
PRE:	Preliminary round
WC:	Challenge Round winner – as challenger
WD:	Challenge Round winner – as defending champion
AC:	Challenge Round loser – as All Comers champion
CR:	Challenge Round loser – as defending champion
F:	Loser in all-comers final

SF:	Loser in semi-final
QF:	Loser in quarter-final
1rd:	Loser in first round
2rd:	Loser in second round
3rd:	Loser in third round
4rd:	Loser in fourth round

Open Era

Year:	Year of play
Rk:	Year-end ranking
TP:	Tournaments Played
TW:	Tournaments Won
TF:	Tournament Finals
GS:	Matches won-lost, major championships
Aus:	Australian Open
Fre:	French Open
Wim:	Wimbledon
US:	U.S. Open
Oly:	Olympic Games
DC:	Davis Cup
FC:	Fed Cup
MW:	Matches won
ML:	Matches lost
Pct:	Winning percentage
CL:	Clay
GR:	Grass
HD:	Hard court
CP:	Carpet
IN:	Indoors
OD:	Outdoors
W:	Tournament winner
F:	Loser in final
SF:	Loser in semi-final
SFB:	Olympic bronze medallist
QF:	Loser in quarter-final
1rd:	Loser in first round
2rd:	Loser in second round
3rd:	Loser in third round
4rd:	Loser in fourth round

— *Sean Lahman*

Chapter 28

Amateur Era Register

(Register Abbreviations – see page 796)

- **ADAMSON, Nelly**   see **LANDRY, Nelly,** page 809

- **ADDIE, Pauline**   see **BETZ, Pauline,** page 799

- **AKHURST, Daphne**   Daphne Jessie Akhurst Cozens

Female. Born: Apr. 22, 1903. Australia.
Died: Jan. 9, 1933. Height: –. Weight: –. Plays: right.
Status: Amateur. Highest Ranking: 3 (Dec. 1928).

Year	Rk	TP	TW	TF	Aus	Fre	Wim	US	FC
1924	....	1	0	0	SF	....	....	....	....
1925	....	2	1	0	W	....	QF	....	....
1926	....	1	1	0	W	....	....	....	....
1928	3	3	1	0	W	QF	SF	....	....
1929	....	1	1	0	W	....	....	....	....
1930	....	1	1	0	W	....	....	....	....
TOTALS		**9**	**5**	**0**	....	....	....	....	....

Competed as Daphne Akhurst until 1931. Doubles Titles: Aus (5).

- **ALEXANDER, Fred**   Frederick Beasley Alexander

Male. Born: Aug. 14, 1880. Seabright, NJ, United States.
Died: Mar. 3, 1969. Height: –. Weight: –. Plays: right.
Status: Amateur. Highest Ranking: –. HOF: 1961

Year	Rk	TP	TW	TF	Aus	Fre	Wim	US	DC
1906	....	1	0	0	....	....	....	QF	....
1908	....	2	1	1	W	....	....	F	0-2
1915	....	1	0	0	....	....	....	4rd	....
1916	....	1	0	0	....	....	....	2rd	....
1917	....	1	0	0	....	....	....	2rd	....
1918	....	1	0	0	....	....	....	3rd	....
1919	....	1	0	0	....	....	....	1rd	....
1920	....	1	0	0	....	....	....	3rd	....
1921	....	1	0	0	....	....	....	4rd	....
1922	....	1	0	0	....	....	....	3rd	....
TOTALS		**11**	**1**	**1**	....	....	....	....	....

Doubles Titles: Aus (1), US (5).

- **ALEXANDER, John**   see page 825

- **ALLISON, Wilmer**   Wilmer Lawson Allison

Male. Born: Dec. 8, 1904. San Antonio, TX, United States.
Died: Apr. 20, 1977. Height: 5' 11". Weight: 155 lbs. Plays: right.
Status: Amateur. Highest Ranking: 4 (Dec. 1932). HOF: 1963

Year	Rk	TP	TW	TF	Aus	Fre	Wim	US	DC
1927	....	1	0	0	....	....	....	1rd	....
1928	....	1	0	0	....	....	....	2rd	1-0
1929	....	1	0	0	....	....	....	QF	2-0
1930	6	2	0	1	....	....	F	4rd	3-1

Year	Rk	TP	TW	TF	Aus	Fre	Wim	US	DC
1931	....	1	0	0	....	....	....	2rd	2-0
1932	4	1	0	0	....	....	....	SF	4-2
1933	....	2	0	0	SF	....	....	4rd	5-2
1934	5	1	0	1	....	....	....	F	....
1935	4	2	1	0	....	....	1rd	W	1-3
1936	7	1	0	0	....	....	QF	....	0-2
TOTALS		**13**	**1**	**2**	....	....	....	....	....

Doubles Titles: US (1)

- **ALONSO, Manuel**   Manolo Alonso de Areyzaga

Male. Born: Nov. 12, 1895. San Sebastian, Spain.
Died: Oct. 11, 1984. Height: 5' 9". Weight: 145 lbs. Plays: right.
Status: Amateur. Highest Ranking: 5 (Dec. 1927). HOF: 1977

Year	Rk	TP	TW	TF	Aus	Fre	Wim	US	DC
1921	8	1	0	1	....	....	F	....	1-1
1922	....	2	0	0	....	....	2rd	QF	3-1
1923	8	1	0	0	....	....	....	2rd	....
1924	10	2	0	0	....	....	2rd	2rd	2-0
1925	8	1	0	0	....	....	....	QF	5-1
1926	8	1	0	0	....	....	....	3rd	....
1927	5	1	0	0	....	....	....	QF	....
1928	....	1	0	0	....	....	....	1rd	....
1931	0	0	0	0	....	....	....	....	0-2
1932	....	1	0	0	....	....	....	3rd	....
1933	....	1	0	0	....	....	....	3rd	....
1934	....	1	0	0	....	....	....	2rd	....
1935	....	1	0	0	....	....	....	4rd	....
1936	....	1	0	0	....	....	....	2rd	0-2
TOTALS		**15**	**0**	**1**	....	....	....	....	....

- **ANDERSON, James**   James Outram "Greyhound" Anderson

Male. Born: Sept. 17, 1895. Enfield, Great Britain.
Died: July 19, 1960. Height: –. Weight: –. Plays: right.
Status: Amateur. Highest Ranking: 3 (Dec. 1923).

Year	Rk	TP	TW	TF	Aus	Fre	Wim	US	DC
1915	....	1	0	0	....	....	....	1rd	....
1916	....	1	0	0	....	....	....	2rd	....
1918	....	1	0	0	....	....	....	PRE	....
1919	....	1	0	0	SF	....	....	....	....
1920	....	1	0	0	....	....	....	1rd	1-1
1921	6	1	0	0	....	....	....	SF	6-2
1922	5	2	1	0	W	....	....	QF	4-2
1923	3	1	0	0	....	....	....	1rd	6-1
1924	3	1	1	0	W	....	....	....	....
1925	....	3	1	0	W	....	SF	3rd	3-1
1926	....	1	0	0	SF	....	....	....	....
TOTALS		**14**	**3**	**0**	....	....	....	....	....

Represented Australia in the Davis Cup (1920-1925)

• ANDERSON, Mal   see page 826

• ASBOTH, Joszef   Joszef Asboth

Male. Born: Sept. 18, 1927. Szombathely, Hungary.
Height: –. Weight: –. Plays: –.
Status: Turned Pro 1958. Highest Ranking: 8 (Dec. 1948).

Year	Rk	TP	TW	TF	Aus	Fre	Wim	US	DC
1939	....	1	0	0	....	3rd	....	....	3-1
1947	9	2	1	0	....	W	3rd	....	....
1948	8	2	0	0	....	2rd	SF	....	5-1
1949	....	1	0	0	....	....	3rd	....	6-0
1951	....	1	0	0	....	....	4rd	....	....
1952	....	0	0	0	....	....	....	....	0-2
1953	....	1	0	0	....	....	1rd	....	0-2
1954	....	1	0	0	....	3rd	....	....	4-2
1955	....	1	0	0	....	1rd	....	....	0-2
1956	....	1	0	0	....	3rd	....	....	....
1957	....	1	0	0	....	2rd	....	....	0-2
TOTALS		**12**	**1**	**0**	....	....	....	....	....

• ASHE, Arthur   see page 826

• ATKINSON, Juliette   Juliette Paxton Atkinson

Female. Born: Apr. 15, 1873. Rahway, NJ, United States.
Died: Jan. 12, 1944. Height: 5'. Weight: –. Plays: right.
Status: Amateur. Highest Ranking: –. HOF: 1974

Year	Rk	TP	TW	TF	Aus	Fre	Wim	US	FC
1894	....	1	0	0	....	....	....	SF	....
1895	....	1	1	0	....	....	....	WC	....
1896	....	1	0	1	....	....	....	CR	....
1897	....	1	1	0	....	....	....	WC	....
1898	....	1	1	0	....	....	....	WD	....
1901	....	1	0	0	....	....	....	SF	....
1902	....	1	0	0	....	....	....	SF	....
TOTALS		**7**	**3**	**1**	....	....	....	....	....

Doubles Titles: US (7)

• AUSSEM, Cilly   Cilly Aussem

Female. Born: Jan. 4, 1909. Cologne, Germany.
Died: Mar. 22, 1963. Height: 5'. Weight: –. Plays: right.
Status: Amateur. Highest Ranking: 2 (Dec. 1930).

Year	Rk	TP	TW	TF	Aus	Fre	Wim	US	FC
1927	....	2	0	0	....	QF	2rd	....	....
1928	7	2	0	0	....	3rd	QF	....	....
1929	....	2	0	0	....	SF	4rd	....	....
1930	2	2	0	0	....	QF	SF	....	....
1931	2	2	2	0	....	W	W	....	....
1932	....	2	0	0	....	QF	1rd	....	....
1933	....	1	0	0	....	2rd	....	....	....
1934	9	2	0	0	....	SF	QF	....	....
TOTALS		**15**	**2**	**0**	....	....	....	....	....

• AUSTIN, Bunny   Wilfred "Bunny" Austin

Male. Born: Aug. 26, 1906. London, Great Britain.
Height: –. Weight: –. Plays: right.
Status: Amateur. Highest Ranking: 2 (Dec. 1931). HOF: 1997

Year	Rk	TP	TW	TF	Aus	Fre	Wim	US	DC
1926	....	1	0	0	....	....	4rd	....	....
1928	7	2	0	0	....	....	4rd	3rd	....
1929	9	3	0	0	....	2rd	SF	QF	5-3
1930	10	1	0	0	....	....	4rd	....	1-1
1931	2	2	0	0	....	3rd	QF	....	12-2
1932	9	2	0	1	....	....	F	4rd	0-2
1933	4	1	0	0	....	....	QF	....	10-2
1934	4	2	0	0	....	QF	QF	....	2-0

Year	Rk	TP	TW	TF	Aus	Fre	Wim	US	DC
1935	5	2	0	0	....	SF	QF	....	2-0
1936	5	2	0	0	....	QF	SF	....	1-1
1937	4	2	0	1	....	F	SF	....	1-1
1938	2	1	0	1	....	....	F	....	....
1939	....	1	0	0	....	....	QF	....	....
TOTALS		**22**	**0**	**3**	....	....	....	....	....

Doubles Titles: Wim (3)

• BADDELEY, Wilfred   Wilfred Baddeley

Male. Born: Jan. 11, 1872. Bromley, Great Britain.
Died: Jan. 30, 1929. Height: –. Weight: –. Plays: right.
Status: Amateur. Highest Ranking: –.

Year	Rk	TP	TW	TF	Aus	Fre	Wim	US	DC
1890	....	1	0	0	....	....	QF	....	....
1891	....	1	1	0	....	....	WC	....	....
1892	....	1	1	0	....	....	WD	....	....
1893	....	1	0	1	....	....	CR	....	....
1894	....	1	0	1	....	....	AC	....	....
1895	....	1	1	0	....	....	WC	....	....
1896	....	1	0	1	....	....	CR	....	....
1897	....	1	0	0	....	....	SF	....	....
TOTALS		**8**	**3**	**3**	....	....	....	....	....

• BARGER WALLACH, Maud   Maud Barger Wallach

Female. Born: June 15, 1870. New York, NY, United States.
Died: Apr. 2, 1954. Height: –. Weight: –. Plays: right.
Status: Amateur. Highest Ranking: –. HOF: 1958

Year	Rk	TP	TW	TF	Aus	Fre	Wim	US	FC
1907	....	1	0	0	....	....	....	3rd	....
1908	....	1	1	0	....	....	....	WC	....
1909	....	1	0	1	....	....	....	CR	....
1910	....	1	0	0	....	....	....	PR	....
1912	....	1	0	0	....	....	....	2rd	....
1915	....	1	0	0	....	....	....	3rd	....
1916	....	1	0	0	....	....	....	QF	....
1925	....	1	0	0	....	....	....	1rd	....
1926	....	1	0	0	....	....	....	1rd	....
1931	....	1	0	0	....	1rd	....	....	....
TOTALS		**10**	**1**	**1**	....	....	....	....	....

• BEHR, Karl   Karl Howell Behr

Male. Born: May 30, 1885. Brooklyn, NY, United States.
Died: Oct. 15, 1949. Height: 5' 9". Weight: 155 lbs. Plays: right.
Status: Amateur. Highest Ranking: –. HOF: 1969

Year	Rk	TP	TW	TF	Aus	Fre	Wim	US	DC
1903	....	1	0	0	....	....	....	1rd	....
1904	....	1	0	0	....	....	....	4rd	....
1905	....	1	0	0	....	....	....	QF	....
1906	....	1	0	1	....	....	....	F	....
1907	....	2	0	0	....	....	4rd	1rd	0-2
1909	....	1	0	0	....	....	....	4rd	....
1911	....	1	0	0	....	....	....	3rd	....
1912	....	1	0	0	....	....	....	SF	....
1913	....	1	0	0	....	....	....	2rd	....
1914	....	1	0	0	....	....	....	QF	....
1915	....	1	0	0	....	....	....	4rd	....
1916	....	1	0	0	....	....	....	4rd	....
1917	....	1	0	0	....	....	....	2rd	....
1919	....	1	0	0	....	....	....	1rd	....
TOTALS		**15**	**0**	**1**	....	....	....	....	....

• BERNARD, Marcel   Marcel Bernard

Male. Born: May 18, 1914. La Madeleine, France.
Died: Apr. 29, 1994. Height: –. Weight: –. Plays: left.
Status: Amateur. Highest Ranking: 5 (Dec. 1946).

Year	Rk	TP	TW	TF	Aus	Fre	Wim	US	DC
1931	....	2	0	0	....	3rd	....	2rd	....
1932	....	2	0	0	....	SF	....	3rd	....
1933	....	1	0	0	....	QF	....	....	....
1934	....	1	0	0	....	3rd	....	....	....
1935	....	2	0	0	....	QF	1rd	....	....
1936	....	1	0	0	....	SF	....	....	....
1937	....	2	0	0	....	3rd	3rd	....	1-0
1946	5	1	1	0	....	W	....	....	1-1
1947	....	0	0	0	....	....	....	....	3-2
1948	....	1	0	0	....	QF	....	....	2-2
1949	....	1	0	0	....	QF	....	....	5-2
1950	....	0	0	0	....	...	....	....	1-1
1951	....	1	0	1	....	F	....	....	....
1952	....	1	0	0	....	2rd	....	....	....
1953	....	1	0	0	....	3rd	....	....	....
1956	....	1	0	0	....	3rd	....	....	....
TOTALS		**18**	**1**	**1**	....	....	....	....	....

Doubles Titles: Fre (2)

• BETZ, Pauline   Pauline May Betz Addie

Female. Born: Aug. 6, 1919. Dayton, OH, United States.
Height: –. Weight: –. Plays: right.
Status: Turned Pro 1947. Highest Ranking: 1 (Dec. 1946). HOF: 1965

Year	Rk	TP	TW	TF	Aus	Fre	Wim	US	FC
1939	....	1	0	0	....	....	....	1rd	....
1940	....	1	0	0	....	....	....	QF	....
1941	....	1	0	1	....	....	....	F	....
1942	....	1	1	0	....	....	....	W	....
1943	....	1	1	0	....	....	....	W	....
1944	....	1	1	0	....	....	....	W	....
1945	....	1	0	1	....	....	....	F	....
1946	1	3	2	1	....	F	W	W	....
TOTALS		**10**	**5**	**3**	....	....	....	....	....

Held number one world ranking 1 time during amateur era. Declared a professional in 1947 by USTA.

• BINGLEY HILLYARD, Blanche   Blanche Bingley Hillyard

Female. Born: Nov. 3, 1863. Greenford, Great Britain.
Died: Aug. 6, 1946. Height: –. Weight: –. Plays: right.
Status: Amateur. Highest Ranking: –.

Year	Rk	TP	TW	TF	Aus	Fre	Wim	US	FC
1885	....	1	0	0	....	....	SF	....	....
1886	....	1	1	0	....	....	WC	....	....
1887	....	1	0	1	....	....	CR	....	....
1888	....	1	0	1	....	....	AC	....	....
1889	....	1	1	0	....	....	WC	....	....
1890	....	1	0	0	....	....	SF	....	....
1891	....	1	0	1	....	....	F	....	....
1892	....	1	0	1	....	....	AC	....	....
1893	....	1	0	1	....	....	AC	....	....
1894	....	1	1	0	....	....	WC	....	....
1897	....	1	1	0	....	....	WC	....	....
1899	....	1	1	0	....	....	WC	....	....
1900	....	1	1	0	....	....	WD	....	....
1901	....	1	0	1	....	....	CR	....	....
1902	....	1	0	0	....	....	2rd	....	....
1904	....	1	0	0	....	....	3rd	....	....
1905	....	1	0	0	....	....	SF	....	....
1906	....	1	0	0	....	....	QF	....	....
1907	....	1	0	0	....	....	SF	....	....

Year	Rk	TP	TW	TF	Aus	Fre	Wim	US	FC
1908	....	1	0	0	....	....	2rd	....	....
1909	....	1	0	0	....	....	2rd	....	....
1912	....	1	0	0	....	....	SF	....	....
1913	....	1	0	0	....	....	2rd	....	....
TOTALS		**23**	**6**	**6**	....	....	....	....	....

Competed as Blanche Bingley until 1886

• BJURSTEDT, Molla   see **MALLORY, Molla,** page 811

• BLOOMER, Shirley   see page 829

• BOLTON, Nancye   Nancye Meredith Wynne Bolton

Female. Born: June 10, 1916. Melbourne, Australia.
Height: –. Weight: –. Plays: right.
Status: Amateur. Highest Ranking: 4 (Dec. 1947).

Year	Rk	TP	TW	TF	Aus	Fre	Wim	US	FC
1936	....	1	0	1	F	....	....	....	....
1937	....	1	0	0	W	....	....	....	....
1938	10	4	0	1	SF	3rd	4rd	F	....
1940	....	1	1	0	W	....	....	....	....
1946	....	1	1	0	W	....	....	....	....
1947	4	3	1	0	W	....	QF	SF	....
1948	4	1	1	0	W	....	....	....	....
1949	4	1	0	1	F	....	....	....	....
1950	....	1	0	0	SF	....	....	....	....
1951	....	2	1	0	W	....	3rd	....	....
1952	....	1	0	0	SF	....	....	....	....
TOTALS		**17**	**5**	**3**	....	....	....	....	....

Competed as Nancye Wynne until 1940. Doubles Titles: Aus (10).

• BOOTHBY, Penelope   Penelope Dora Harvey Boothby

Female. Born: Aug. 2, 1881. Finchley, Great Britain.
Died: Feb. 22, 1970. Height: –. Weight: –. Plays: right.
Status: Amateur. Highest Ranking: –.

Year	Rk	TP	TW	TF	Aus	Fre	Wim	US	FC
1904	....	1	0	0	....	....	2rd	....	....
1905	....	1	0	0	....	....	QF	....	....
1906	....	1	0	0	....	....	1rd	....	....
1907	....	1	0	0	....	....	1rd	....	....
1908	....	2	0	1	....	....	SF	....	....
1909	....	2	1	0	....	....	WC	1rd	....
1910	....	2	0	1	....	....	CR	QF	....
1911	....	2	0	1	....	....	AC	PR	....
1912	....	2	0	0	....	....	3rd	2rd	....
1913	....	2	0	1	....	....	2rd	AC	....
1914	....	1	0	0	....	....	3rd	....	....
1917	....	1	0	0	....	....	....	2rd	....
TOTALS		**18**	**1**	**4**	....	....	....	....	....

Won Silver in the 1908 Olympics

• BOROTRA, Jean   Jean Robert Borotra

Male. Born: Aug. 13, 1898. Arbonne, France.
Died: July 17, 1994. Height: 6' 1". Weight: 160 lbs. Plays: right.
Status: Amateur. Highest Ranking: 2 (Dec. 1926). HOF: 1976

Year	Rk	TP	TW	TF	Aus	Fre	Wim	US	DC
1922	....	1	0	0	....	....	3rd	....	2-0
1923	....	1	0	0	....	....	5rd	....	1-1
1924	6	3	1	0	....	....	W	3rd	0-2
1925	6	3	0	1	....	F	F	3rd	7-3
1926	2	3	1	1	....	SF	W	F	2-2
1927	4	3	0	1	....	3rd	F	QF	3-0
1928	5	4	1	0	W	SF	QF	3rd	....
1929	3	2	0	1	....	F	F	....	1-1

Year	Rk	TP	TW	TF	Aus	Fre	Wim	US	DC
1930	3	3	0	0	....	SF	SF	1rd	1-1
1931	7	2	1	0	....	W	SF	....	0-2
1932	3	1	0	0	....	....	4rd	....	....
1935	....	2	0	0	....	1rd	2rd	....	....
1936	....	1	0	0	....	....	1rd	....	....
TOTALS		**29**	**4**	**4**	....	....	....	....	....

Doubles Titles: Aus (1), Fre (5), Wim (3)

• BOUMAN, Kea Katerina Cornelia "Kea" Bouman

Female. Born: Nov. 23, 1903. Almeto, Netherlands.
Height: –. Weight: –. Plays: right.
Status: Amateur. Highest Ranking: 8 (Dec. 1928).

Year	Rk	TP	TW	TF	Aus	Fre	Wim	US	FC
1923	....	1	0	0	....	....	2rd	....	....
1924	....	1	0	0	....	....	1rd	....	....
1925	....	1	0	0	....	....	2rd	....	....
1926	....	2	0	0	....	SF	QF	....	....
1927	9	3	1	0	....	W	4rd	QF	....
1928	8	2	0	0	....	SF	3rd	....	....
1929	....	2	0	0	....	1rd	3rd	....	....
TOTALS		**12**	**1**	**0**	....	....	....	....	....

• BOWREY, Bill see page 830

• BOWREY, Lesley see TURNER, Lesley, page 893

• BOYD, Esna Esna Boyd

Female. Born: 1901. Melbourne, Australia.
Died: 1962. Height: –. Weight: –. Plays: right.
Status: Amateur. Highest Ranking: 10 (Dec. 1928).

Year	Rk	TP	TW	TF	Aus	Fre	Wim	US	FC
1922	....	1	0	1	F	....	....	....	....
1923	....	1	0	1	F	....	....	....	....
1924	....	1	0	1	F	....	....	....	....
1925	....	1	0	1	F	....	....	....	....
1926	....	1	0	1	F	....	....	....	....
1927	....	1	1	0	W	....	....	....	....
1928	10	2	0	1	F	3rd	....	....	....
TOTALS		**8**	**1**	**6**	....	....	....	....	....

• BROMWICH, John John Edward Bromwich

Male. Born: Nov. 14, 1918. Kogarah, Australia.
Height: 5' 10". Weight: 150 lbs. Plays: left.
Status: Amateur. Highest Ranking: 2 (Dec. 1939). HOF: 1984

Year	Rk	TP	TW	TF	Aus	Fre	Wim	US	DC
1936	....	1	0	0	QF	....	....	....	....
1937	....	2	0	1	F	....	3rd	....	1-2
1938	3	2	0	1	F	....	....	SF	4-2
1939	2	2	1	0	W	....	....	SF	8-2
1940	....	1	0	0	SF	....	....	....	....
1946	6	1	1	0	W	....	....	....	0-2
1947	4	3	0	1	F	....	4rd	SF	2-2
1948	4	3	0	2	F	1rd	F	....	....
1949	....	3	0	1	F	....	SF	3rd	2-0
1950	....	4	0	0	QF	QF	4rd	3rd	2-1
1951	....	1	0	0	QF	....	....	....	....
1954	....	1	0	0	SF	....	....	....	....
TOTALS		**24**	**2**	**6**	....	....	....	....	....

Doubles Titles: Aust (8), Wim (2), US (3)

• BROOKES, Norman Sir Norman Everard Brookes

Male. Born: Nov. 14, 1877. Melbourne, Australia.
Died: Sept. 28, 1968. Height: 5' 11". Weight: 150 lbs. Plays: left.
Status: Amateur. Highest Ranking: 2 (Dec. 1913). HOF: 1977

Year	Rk	TP	TW	TF	Aus	Fre	Wim	US	DC
1905	....	1	0	1	....	....	AC	....	2-2
1907	....	1	1	0	....	....	WC	....	4-0
1908	....	1	0	1	....	....	CR	....	1-1
1909	....	0	0	0	....	....	....	....	2-0
1911	....	1	1	0	W	....	....	....	....
1912	....	0	0	0	....	....	....	....	3-1
1914	2	1	1	0	....	....	WC	....	6-1
1919	5	2	0	1	....	....	CR	QF	....
1920	6	0	0	0	....	....	....	....	0-2
1924	....	2	0	0	....	....	4rd	2rd	....
1928	....	1	0	0	....	1rd	....	....	....
TOTALS		**10**	**3**	**3**	....	....	....	....	....

Doubles Titles: Aus (1), Wim (2), US (1)

• BROUGH, Louise Althea Louise Brough Clapp

Female. Born: Mar. 11, 1923. Oklahoma City, OK, United States.
Height: 5' 7". Weight: –. Plays: right.
Status: Amateur. Highest Ranking: 1 (Dec. 1955). HOF: 1967

Year	Rk	TP	TW	TF	Aus	Fre	Wim	US	FC
1939	....	1	0	0	....	....	....	1rd	....
1940	....	1	0	0	....	....	....	1rd	....
1941	....	1	0	0	....	....	....	2rd	....
1942	....	1	0	1	....	....	....	F	....
1943	....	1	0	1	....	....	....	F	....
1944	....	1	0	0	....	....	....	SF	....
1945	....	1	0	0	....	....	....	SF	....
1946	3	3	0	1	....	SF	F	QF	....
1947	2	3	1	0	....	SF	SF	W	....
1948	2	2	1	1	....	....	W	F	....
1949	2	3	1	0	....	3rd	W	SF	....
1950	2	4	1	1	W	SF	F	3rd	....
1951	7	1	0	0	....	....	SF	....	....
1952	3	2	0	1	....	....	F	SF	....
1953	3	1	0	0	....	....	....	SF	....
1954	4	2	0	2	....	....	F	F	....
1955	1	2	1	0	....	....	W	3rd	....
1956	3	2	0	0	....	....	SF	QF	....
1957	4	2	0	1	....	....	QF	F	....
TOTALS		**34**	**5**	**9**	....	....	....	....	....

Held number one world ranking 1 time during amateur era. Doubles Titles: Aus (1), Fre (3), Wim (5), US (12).

• BROWNE, Mary K. Mary Kendall Browne

Female. Born: June 3, 1891. Ventura County, CA, United States.
Died: Aug. 19, 1971. Height: 5' 2". Weight: –. Plays: right.
Status: Turned Pro 1926. Highest Ranking: 3 (Dec. 1921). HOF: 1957

Year	Rk	TP	TW	TF	Aus	Fre	Wim	US	FC
1912	....	1	1	0	....	....	....	WC	....
1913	....	1	1	0	....	....	....	WD	....
1914	....	1	1	0	....	....	....	WD	....
1921	3	1	0	1	....	....	....	F	....
1924	....	1	0	0	....	....	....	SF	....
1926	6	3	0	1	....	F	1rd	SF	....
TOTALS		**8**	**3**	**2**	....	....	....	....	....

Doubles Titles: Wim (1), US (5)

• BROWNING, Françoise see DURR, Françoise, page 839

• BRUGNON, Jacques
Jacques "Toto" Brugnon

Male. Born: May 11, 1895. Paris, France.
Died: Mar. 20, 1978. Height: 5' 6". Weight: 140 lbs. Plays: right.
Status: Amateur. Highest Ranking: 9 (Dec. 1927). HOF: 1976

Year	Rk	TP	TW	TF	Aus	Fre	Wim	US	DC
1920	....	1	0	0	....	....	4rd	....	....
1921	....	0	0	0	....	....	....	....	0-1
1922	....	1	0	0	....	....	4rd	....	....
1923	....	2	0	0	....	....	4rd	3rd	0-1
1924	....	2	0	0	....	....	3rd	2rd	....
1925	....	3	0	0	....	3rd	4rd	2rd	....
1926	10	3	0	0	....	2rd	SF	4rd	2-0
1927	9	3	0	0	....	QF	QF	QF	2-0
1928	....	3	0	0	....	QF	QF	QF	....
1929	....	2	0	0	....	QF	3rd	....	....
1930	....	2	0	0	....	2rd	2rd	....	....
1931	....	2	0	0	....	....	3rd	2rd	....
1932	....	2	0	0	....	4rd	1rd	....	....
1933	....	2	0	0	....	3rd	2rd	....	....
1934	....	2	0	0	....	2rd	2rd	....	....
1935	....	3	0	0	....	2rd	1rd	1rd	....
1936	....	3	0	0	....	1rd	2rd	3rd	....
1937	....	3	0	0	....	3rd	2rd	1rd	....
1938	....	3	0	0	....	2rd	1rd	1rd	....
1939	....	3	0	0	....	2rd	4rd	1rd	....
1948	....	1	0	0	....	1rd	....	....	....
TOTALS		**46**	**0**	**0**	....	....	....	....	....

Doubles Titles: Aus (1), Fre (5), Wim (4)

• BUDGE, Don
John Donald Budge

Male. Born: June 13, 1915. Oakland, CA, United States.
Height: 6' 1". Weight: 160 lbs. Plays: right.
Status: Turned Pro 1939. Highest Ranking: 1 (Dec. 1937). HOF: 1964

Year	Rk	TP	TW	TF	Aus	Fre	Wim	US	DC
1934	....	1	0	0	....	....	....	4rd	....
1935	6	2	0	0	....	....	SF	QF	5-2
1936	3	2	0	1	....	....	SF	F	4-0
1937	1	2	1	0	....	....	W	W	8-0
1938	1	4	1	0	W	W	W	W	2-0
TOTALS		**11**	**2**	**1**	....	....	....	....	....

Held number one world ranking 2 times during amateur era. Doubles Titles: Wim (2), US (2).

• BUENO, Maria
see page 830

• BUNDY, Dorothy
Dorothy May "Dodo" Bundy Cheney

Female. Born: Sept. 1, 1916. Los Angeles, CA, United States.
Height: –. Weight: –. Plays: right.
Status: Amateur. Highest Ranking: 6 (Dec. 1946).

Year	Rk	TP	TW	TF	Aus	Fre	Wim	US	FC
1936	....	1	0	0	....	....	....	4rd	....
1937	10	1	0	0	....	....	....	SF	....
1938	....	3	1	0	W	....	4rd	SF	....
1939	....	1	0	0	....	....	....	QF	....
1940	....	1	0	0	....	....	....	QF	....
1941	....	1	0	0	....	....	....	QF	....
1943	....	1	0	0	....	....	....	SF	....
1944	....	1	0	0	....	....	....	SF	....
1945	....	1	0	0	....	....	....	QF	....
1946	6	3	0	0	....	SF	SF	1rd	....
1948	....	1	0	0	....	....	....	2rd	....
1955	....	1	0	0	....	....	....	3rd	....
1959	....	1	0	0	....	....	....	1rd	....
TOTALS		**17**	**1**	**0**	....	....	....	....	....

• BUNDY, May
see SUTTON BUNDY, May, page 819

• BUTTSWORTH, Coral
Coral Buttsworth

Female. Born: Sydney, Australia.
Height: –. Weight: –. Plays: right.
Status: Amateur. Highest Ranking: –.

Year	Rk	TP	TW	TF	Aus	Fre	Wim	US	FC
1931	....	1	1	0	W	....	....	....	....
1932	....	1	1	0	W	....	....	....	....
1933	....	1	0	1	F	....	....	....	....
TOTALS		**3**	**2**	**1**	....	....	....	....	....

• CAHILL, Mabel
Mabel Esmonde Cahill

Female. Born: Apr. 2, 1863. Ballyragget, Ireland.
Died: 1904 or 1905. Height: –. Weight: –. Plays: right.
Status: Amateur. Highest Ranking: –. HOF: 1976

Year	Rk	TP	TW	TF	Aus	Fre	Wim	US	FC
1890	....	1	0	0	....	....	....	SF	....
1891	....	1	1	0	....	....	....	WC	....
1892	....	1	1	0	....	....	....	WD	....
TOTALS		**3**	**2**	**0**	....	....	....	....	....

Doubles Titles: US (2)

• CAMPBELL, Oliver
Oliver Samuel Campbell

Male. Born: Feb. 25, 1871. Brooklyn, NY, United States.
Died: July 11, 1953. Height: 5' 11". Weight: –. Plays: right.
Status: Amateur. Highest Ranking: –. HOF: 1955

Year	Rk	TP	TW	TF	Aus	Fre	Wim	US	DC
1886	....	1	0	0	....	....	....	1rd	....
1887	....	1	0	0	....	....	....	PRE	....
1888	....	1	0	0	....	....	....	SF	....
1889	....	1	0	1	....	....	....	F	....
1890	....	1	1	0	....	....	....	WC	....
1891	....	1	1	0	....	....	....	WD	....
1892	....	2	1	0	....	....	2rd	WD	....
TOTALS		**8**	**3**	**1**	....	....	....	....	....

Doubles Titles: US (3)

• CASALS, Rosie
see page 831

• CAWLEY, Evonne
see GOOLAGONG, Evonne, page 846

• CHACE, Malcolm
Malcolm Greene Chace

Male. Born: Mar. 12, 1875. Valley Falls, RI, United States.
Died: July 16, 1955. Height: 6' 1". Weight: 150 lbs. Plays: right.
Status: Amateur. Highest Ranking: –. HOF: 1961

Year	Rk	TP	TW	TF	Aus	Fre	Wim	US	DC
1892	....	1	0	0	....	....	....	1rd	....
1893	....	1	0	0	....	....	....	1rd	....
1894	....	1	0	0	....	....	....	SF	....
1897	....	1	0	0	....	....	....	PRE	....
1899	....	1	0	0	....	....	....	1rd	....
1900	....	1	0	0	....	....	....	QF	....
1904	....	1	0	0	....	....	....	2rd	....
1905	....	1	0	0	....	....	....	1rd	....
1907	....	1	0	0	....	....	....	3rd	....
1908	....	1	0	0	....	....	....	2rd	....
1910	....	1	0	0	....	....	....	4rd	....
1911	....	1	0	0	....	....	....	PRE	....
TOTALS		**12**	**0**	**0**	....	....	....	....	....

Doubles Titles: US (1)

• CHAMBERS, Dorothea

Dorothea Katherine Douglass Lambert Chambers

Female. Born: Sept. 3, 1878. Ealing, Great Britain.
Died: 1960. Height: –. Weight: –. Plays: right.
Status: Amateur. Highest Ranking: 7 (Dec. 1925). HOF: 1981

Year	Rk	TP	TW	TF	Aus	Fre	Wim	US	FC
1900	....	1	0	0	....	....	QF	....	....
1902	....	1	0	0	....	....	SF	....	....
1903	....	1	1	0	....	....	WC	....	....
1904	....	1	1	0	....	....	WD	....	....
1905	....	1	0	1	....	....	CR	....	....
1906	....	1	1	0	....	....	WC	....	....
1907	....	1	0	1	....	....	CR	....	....
1908	....	2	1	0	....	....	QF	....	....
1910	....	1	1	0	....	....	WC	....	....
1911	....	1	1	0	....	....	WD	....	....
1913	....	1	1	0	....	....	WC	....	....
1914	....	1	1	0	....	....	WD	....	....
1919	....	1	0	1	....	....	CR	....	....
1920	....	1	0	1	....	....	AC	....	....
1925	7	1	0	0	....	....	....	QF	....
TOTALS		**16**	**8**	**4**	....	....	....	....	....

Competed as Dorothea Douglass until 1907. Won Gold in the 1908 Olympics.

• CLARK, Clarence

Clarence Monroe Clark

Male. Born: Aug. 27, 1859. Germantown, PA, United States.
Died: June 29, 1937. Height: –. Weight: –. Plays: right.
Status: Amateur. Highest Ranking: –. HOF: 1983

Year	Rk	TP	TW	TF	Aus	Fre	Wim	US	DC
1882	....	1	0	1	....	....	....	F	....
1884	....	1	0	0	....	....	....	SF	....
1885	....	1	0	0	....	....	....	PRE	....
TOTALS		**3**	**0**	**1**	....	....	....	....	....

Doubles Titles: US (1)

• CLARK, Joe

Joseph Sill Clark

Male. Born: Nov. 30, 1861. Germantown, PA, United States.
Died: Apr. 14, 1956. Height: –. Weight: –. Plays: right.
Status: Amateur. Highest Ranking: –. HOF: 1955

Year	Rk	TP	TW	TF	Aus	Fre	Wim	US	DC
1882	....	1	0	0	....	....	....	3rd	....
1884	....	2	0	0	....	....	1rd	2rd	....
1885	....	1	0	0	....	....	....	SF	....
1886	....	1	0	0	....	....	....	SF	....
1887	....	1	0	0	....	....	....	SF	....
1888	....	1	0	0	....	....	....	2rd	....
1889	....	1	0	0	....	....	....	QF	....
1890	....	1	0	0	....	....	....	2rd	....
1891	....	1	0	0	....	....	....	QF	....
1892	....	1	0	0	....	....	....	1rd	....
1893	....	1	0	0	....	....	....	1rd	....
TOTALS		**12**	**0**	**0**	....	....	....	....	....

• CLOTHIER, Bill

William Jackson Clothier

Male. Born: Sept. 27, 1881. Philadelphia, PA, United States.
Died: Sept. 4, 1962. Height: –. Weight: –. Plays: right.
Status: Amateur. Highest Ranking: –. HOF: 1956

Year	Rk	TP	TW	TF	Aus	Fre	Wim	US	DC
1896	....	1	0	0	....	....	....	PRE	....
1897	....	1	0	0	....	....	....	PRE	....
1898	....	1	0	0	....	....	....	1rd	....
1899	....	1	0	0	....	....	....	PRE	....
1900	....	1	0	0	....	....	....	2rd	....
1901	....	1	0	0	....	....	....	QF	....

Year	Rk	TP	TW	TF	Aus	Fre	Wim	US	DC
1902	....	1	0	0	....	....	....	4rd	....
1903	....	1	0	1	....	....	....	F	....
1904	....	1	0	1	....	....	....	F	....
1905	....	2	0	0	....	....	4rd	QF	2-1
1906	....	1	1	0	....	....	....	W	....
1908	....	1	0	0	....	....	....	SF	....
1909	....	1	0	1	....	....	....	AC	2-0
1911	....	1	0	0	....	....	....	PRE	....
1912	....	1	0	0	....	....	....	SF	....
1913	....	1	0	0	....	....	....	QF	....
1914	....	1	0	0	....	....	....	SF	....
1916	....	1	0	0	....	....	....	4rd	....
TOTALS		**19**	**1**	**3**	....	....	....	....	....

• COCHET, Henri

Henri Jean Cochet

Male. Born: Dec. 14, 1901. Lyon, France.
Died: Apr. 1, 1987. Height: –. Weight: –. Plays: right.
Status: Turned Pro 1933. Highest Ranking: 1 (Dec. 1928). HOF: 1976

Year	Rk	TP	TW	TF	Aus	Fre	Wim	US	DC
1922	6	1	0	0	....	....	4rd	....	2-1
1923	10	0	0	0	....	....	....	....	5-1
1924	9	1	0	1	....	....	....	....	5-1
1925	....	2	0	0	....	QF	SF	....	....
1926	3	3	1	0	....	W	SF	SF	7-1
1927	3	3	1	0	....	SF	W	3rd	5-2
1928	1	3	2	1	....	W	F	W	2-0
1929	1	2	1	0	....	SF	W	....	2-0
1930	1	1	0	0	....	....	QF	....	1-0
1931	1	1	0	0	....	....	1rd	....	2-0
1932	2	3	1	1	....	W	2rd	F	1-1
1933	6	2	0	1	....	F	SF	....	1-1
TOTALS		**22**	**6**	**4**	....	....	....	....	....

Held number one world ranking 4 times during amateur era. Won Silver in the 1924 Olympics. Doubles Titles: Aus (1), Fre (1).

• CONNOLLY, Maureen

Maureen Catherine "Little Mo" Connolly Brinker

Female. Born: Sept. 17, 1934. San Diego, CA, United States.
Height: 5' 4". Weight: 120 lbs. Plays: right.
Status: Amateur. Highest Ranking: 1 (Dec. 1952). HOF: 1968

Year	Rk	TP	TW	TF	Aus	Fre	Wim	US	FC
1949	....	1	0	0	....	....	....	2rd	....
1950	....	1	0	0	....	....	....	2rd	....
1951	2	1	1	0	....	....	....	W	....
1952	1	2	2	0	....	....	W	W	....
1953	1	4	4	0	W	W	W	W	....
1954	1	2	2	0	....	W	W	....	....
TOTALS		**11**	**9**	**0**	....	....	....	....	....

Held number one world ranking 3 times during amateur era. Career ended by auto accident in 1954. Doubles Titles: Aus (1), Fre (1).

• **COOKE, Sarah**   see **PALFREY COOKE, Sarah**, page 814

• **COOPER, Ashley**   see page 834

• **COOPER, Charlotte**   see **STERRY, Charlotte**, page 819

• **COURT, Margaret**   see **SMITH COURT, Margaret**, page 888

• **COYNE, Thelma**   see **LONG, Thelma**, page 810

• **COZENS, Daphne**   see **AKHURST, Daphne**, page 797

• CRAWFORD, Jack
John Herbert Crawford

Male. Born: Mar. 22, 1908. Albury, Australia.
Died: Sept. 10, 1991. Height: 6' 1". Weight: 170 lbs. Plays: right.
Status: Amateur. Highest Ranking: 1 (Dec. 1933). HOF: 1979

Year	Rk	TP	TW	TF	Aus	Fre	Wim	US	DC
1927	....	1	0	0	QF	....	....	....	....
1928	....	4	0	0	SF	QF	4rd	QF	0-1
1929	....	1	0	0	QF	....	....	....	....
1930	....	3	0	0	SF	1rd	3rd	....	6-2
1931	....	1	1	0	W	....	....	....	....
1932	10	1	1	0	W	....	....	....	1-2
1933	1	4	3	1	W	W	W	F	6-1
1934	2	3	0	3	F	F	F	....	4-3
1935	2	3	1	0	W	SF	SF	....	3-2
1936	6	2	0	1	F	....	QF	....	3-3
1937	7	2	0	0	SF	....	QF	....	0-2
1939	....	2	0	0	SF	....	....	3rd	....
1940	....	1	0	1	F	....	....	....	....
1947	....	1	0	0	....	....	....	1rd	....
TOTALS		**29**	**6**	**6**	....	....	....	....	....

Held number one world ranking 1 time during amateur era. Doubles Titles: Wim (1), Aus (4), Fre (1).

• CREALY, Dick   see page 835

• DALTON, Judy   see page 836

• DAVIDSON, Sven
Sven Viktor Davidson

Male. Born: July 13, 1928. Boras, Sweden.
Height: –. Weight: –. Plays: right.
Status: Amateur. Highest Ranking: 3 (Dec. 1957).

Year	Rk	TP	TW	TF	Aus	Fre	Wim	US	DC
1949	....	1	0	0	....	1rd	....	....	....
1950	....	3	0	0	....	4rd	1rd	2rd	4-0
1951	....	2	0	0	....	3rd	2rd	....	8-2
1952	....	0	0	0	....	....	....	....	2-1
1953	9	3	0	0	....	4rd	QF	QF	3-1
1954	10	3	0	0	....	QF	4rd	4rd	8-2
1955	10	3	0	1	4rd	F	QF	....	4-3
1956	5	2	0	1	....	F	2rd	....	4-2
1957	3	3	1	0	....	W	SF	SF	3-1
1958	10	1	0	0	....	....	QF	....	2-1
1959	....	1	0	0	....	....	3rd	....	....
1960	....	0	0	0	....	....	....	....	1-1
1963	....	1	0	0	....	4rd	....	....	....
1964	....	1	0	0	....	2rd	....	....	....
1967	....	1	0	0	....	QF	....	....	....
TOTALS		**25**	**1**	**2**	....	....	....	....	....

Doubles Titles: Wim (1)

• DAVIS, Dwight
Dwight Filey Davis

Male. Born: July 5, 1879. Philadelphia, PA, United States.
Died: Nov. 28, 1945. Height: 6'. Weight: 190 lbs. Plays: left.
Status: Amateur. Highest Ranking: –. HOF: 1956

Year	Rk	TP	TW	TF	Aus	Fre	Wim	US	DC
1896	....	1	0	0	....	....	....	1rd	....
1897	....	1	0	0	....	....	....	1rd	....
1898	....	1	0	1	....	....	....	F	....
1899	....	1	0	1	....	....	....	F	....
1900	....	1	0	0	....	....	....	QF	1-0
1901	....	1	0	0	....	....	....	3rd	....
1902	....	1	0	0	....	....	....	3rd	....
TOTALS		**7**	**0**	**2**	....	....	....	....	....

Doubles Titles: US (3)

• DOD, Lottie
Charlotte "Lottie" Dod

Female. Born: Sept. 24, 1871. Lower Bebington, Great Britain.
Died: June 27, 1960. Height: –. Weight: –. Plays: right.
Status: Amateur. Highest Ranking: –. HOF: 1983

Year	Rk	TP	TW	TF	Aus	Fre	Wim	US	FC
1887	....	1	1	0	....	....	WC	....	....
1888	....	1	1	0	....	....	WD	....	....
1889	....	1	0	1	....	....	CR	....	....
1891	....	1	1	0	....	....	WC	....	....
1892	....	1	1	0	....	....	WD	....	....
1893	....	1	1	0	....	....	WD	....	....
1920	....	1	0	0	....	....	....	....	....
TOTALS		**7**	**5**	**1**	....	....	....	....	....

• DOEG, Johnny
John Thomas Godfray Hope Doeg

Male. Born: Dec. 7, 1908. Guayamas, Mexico.
Died: Apr. 27, 1978. Height: 6' 1". Weight: 170 lbs. Plays: left.
Status: Amateur. Highest Ranking: 4 (Dec. 1930). HOF: 1962

Year	Rk	TP	TW	TF	Aus	Fre	Wim	US	DC
1927	....	1	0	0	....	....	....	1rd	....
1928	....	1	0	0	....	....	....	QF	....
1929	7	1	0	0	....	....	....	SF	....
1930	4	2	1	0	....	....	SF	W	6-0
1931	....	1	0	0	....	....	....	SF	....
1939	....	1	0	0	....	....	....	3rd	....
1940	....	1	0	0	....	....	....	2rd	....
TOTALS		**8**	**1**	**0**	....	....	....	....	....

Represented the United States in the Davis Cup (1930). Doubles Titles: US (2).

• DOHERTY, Laurie
Hugh Lawrence "Little Do" Doherty

Male. Born: Oct. 8, 1875. London, Great Britain.
Died: Aug. 21, 1919. Height: 5' 10". Weight: –. Plays: right.
Status: Amateur. Highest Ranking: –. HOF: 1980

Year	Rk	TP	TW	TF	Aus	Fre	Wim	US	DC
1897	....	1	0	0	....	....	QF	....	....
1898	....	1	0	1	....	....	AC	....	....
1900	....	2	1	0	....	....	SF	....	....
1901	....	1	0	0	....	....	3rd	....	....
1902	....	2	1	0	....	....	WC	SF	....
1903	....	2	2	0	....	....	WD	WC	2-0
1904	....	1	1	0	....	....	WD	....	1-0
1905	....	1	1	0	....	....	WD	....	2-0
1906	....	1	1	0	....	....	WD	....	2-0
TOTALS		**12**	**7**	**1**	....	....	....	....	....

Won Gold in the 1900 Olympics. Doubles Titles: Wim (8), US (2).

• DOHERTY, Reggie
Reginald Frank Doherty

Male. Born: Oct. 14, 1872. London, Great Britain.
Died: Dec. 29, 1910. Height: –. Weight: –. Plays: right.
Status: Amateur. Highest Ranking: –. HOF: 1980

Year	Rk	TP	TW	TF	Aus	Fre	Wim	US	DC
1894	....	1	0	0	....	....	1rd	....	....
1895	....	1	0	0	....	....	QF	....	....
1896	....	1	0	0	....	....	1rd	....	....
1897	....	1	1	0	....	....	WC	....	....
1898	....	1	1	0	....	....	WD	....	....
1899	....	1	1	0	....	....	WD	....	....
1900	....	2	1	0	....	....	WD	....	....
1901	....	1	0	1	....	....	CR	....	....
1902	....	2	0	1	....	....	1rd	AC	1-1

Year	Rk	TP	TW	TF	Aus	Fre	Wim	US	DC
1903	....	1	0	0	....	....	....	QF	1-1
1904	....	1	0	0	....	....	1rd	....	....
1905	....	1	0	0	....	....	1rd	....	....
TOTALS		**14**	**4**	**2**	....	....	....	....	....

Won Bronze in the 1900 Olympics. Doubles Titles: Wim (8), US (2).

• DOUGLASS LAMBERT, Dorothea
see CHAMBERS, Dorothea, page 802

• DROBNY, Jaroslav   Jaroslav Drobny
Male. Born: Oct. 12, 1921. Prague, Czech Republic.
Height: –. Weight: –. Plays: left.
Status: Amateur. Highest Ranking: 1 (Dec. 1954). HOF: 1983

Year	Rk	TP	TW	TF	Aus	Fre	Wim	US	DC
1938	....	1	0	0	....	....	1rd	....	....
1939	....	1	0	0	....	....	3rd	....	....
1946	3	2	0	1	....	F	QF	....	1-1
1947	5	2	0	0	....	....	QF	SF	10-1
1948	5	3	0	1	....	F	2rd	SF	8-1
1949	7	2	0	1	....	....	F	QF	5-1
1950	4	4	0	1	4rd	F	SF	3rd	....
1951	3	2	1	0	....	W	3rd	....	....
1952	2	2	1	1	....	W	F	....	....
1953	4	2	0	0	....	SF	SF	....	....
1954	1	2	1	0	....	4rd	W	....	....
1955	9	1	0	0	....	....	QF	....	....
1956	....	2	0	0	....	4rd	1rd	....	....
1957	....	2	0	0	....	2rd	2rd	....	....
1958	....	2	0	0	....	3rd	4rd	....	....
1959	....	2	0	0	....	4rd	1rd	....	....
1960	....	2	0	0	....	2rd	1rd	....	....
1962	....	1	0	0	....	1rd	....	....	....
1963	....	1	0	0	....	3rd	....	....	....
1964	....	2	0	0	....	2rd	....	1rd	....
1965	....	1	0	0	....	1rd	....	....	....
TOTALS		**39**	**3**	**5**	....	....	....	....	....

Held number one world ranking 1 time during amateur era. Doubles Titles: Fre (1).

• DRYSDALE, Cliff   see page 838

• DUPONT, Margaret
see OSBORNE DUPONT, Margaret, page 814

• DURR, Françoise   see page 839

• DWIGHT, James   James "Doc" Dwight
Male. Born: July 14, 1852. Paris, France.
Died: July 13, 1917. Height: 5' 5". Weight: –. Plays: right.
Status: Amateur. Highest Ranking: –. HOF: 1955

Year	Rk	TP	TW	TF	Aus	Fre	Wim	US	DC
1882	....	1	0	0	....	....	....	QF	....
1883	....	1	0	1	....	....	....	F	....
1884	....	2	0	0	....	....	2rd	1rd	....
1885	....	1	0	0	....	....	SF	....	....
1886	....	1	0	0	....	....	....	1rd	....
1888	....	1	0	0	....	....	....	QF	....
TOTALS		**7**	**0**	**1**	....	....	....	....	....

Doubles Titles: US (5).

• EMERSON, Roy   see page 840

• FABYAN, Sarah   see PALFREY COOKE, Sarah, page 814

• FALKENBURG, Bob   Robert Falkenburg
Male. Born: Jan. 29, 1926. Brooklyn, NY, United States.
Height: 6' 3". Weight: –. Plays: right.
Status: Amateur. Highest Ranking: 7 (Dec. 1948). HOF: 1974

Year	Rk	TP	TW	TF	Aus	Fre	Wim	US	DC
1942	....	1	0	0	....	....	....	2rd	....
1943	....	1	0	0	....	....	....	2rd	....
1944	....	1	0	0	....	....	....	QF	....
1945	....	1	0	0	....	....	....	QF	....
1946	....	1	0	0	....	....	....	SF	....
1947	....	2	0	0	....	....	QF	QF	....
1948	7	2	1	0	....	....	W	QF	....
1949	....	1	0	0	....	....	QF	....	....
1954	....	2	0	0	....	4rd	3rd	....	1-2
1955	....	1	0	0	....	....	....	2rd	1-2
TOTALS		**13**	**1**	**0**	....	....	....	....	....

Represented Brazil in the Davis Cup (1954). Doubles Titles: US (1)

• FRANULOVIC, Zeijko   see page 843

• FRASER, Neale   see page 843

• FRY, Shirley   Shirley June Fry Irvin
Female. Born: June 30, 1927. Akron, OH, United States.
Height: 5' 5". Weight: 125 lbs. Plays: right.
Status: Amateur. Highest Ranking: 1 (Dec. 1956). HOF: 1970

Year	Rk	TP	TW	TF	Aus	Fre	Wim	US	FC
1941	....	1	0	0	....	....	....	1rd	....
1942	....	1	0	0	....	....	....	QF	....
1943	....	1	0	0	....	....	....	1rd	....
1944	....	1	0	0	....	....	....	QF	....
1945	....	1	0	0	....	....	....	1rd	....
1946	9	1	0	0	....	....	....	1rd	....
1947	....	1	0	0	....	....	....	3rd	....
1948	8	3	0	1	....	F	QF	3rd	....
1949	....	2	0	0	....	....	4rd	3rd	....
1950	8	3	0	0	....	QF	QF	QF	....
1951	3	3	1	2	....	W	F	F	....
1952	4	3	0	1	....	F	SF	SF	....
1953	4	3	0	0	....	SF	SF	SF	....
1954	6	2	0	0	....	....	QF	SF	....
1955	10	1	0	0	....	....	....	QF	....
1956	1	2	2	0	....	....	W	W	....
1957	....	1	0	0	W	....	....	....	....
TOTALS		**30**	**4**	**4**	....	....	....	....	....

Held number one world ranking 1 time during amateur era. Doubles Titles: Aus (1), Fre (4), Wim (3), US (4).

• GARLAND, Chuck   Charles Stedman Garland
Male. Born: Oct. 29, 1898. Pittsburgh, PA, United States.
Died: Jan. 28, 1971. Height: 5' 7". Weight: –. Plays: right.
Status: Amateur. Highest Ranking: –. HOF: 1969

Year	Rk	TP	TW	TF	Aus	Fre	Wim	US	DC
1915	....	1	0	0	....	....	....	2rd	....
1916	....	1	0	0	....	....	....	1rd	....
1917	....	1	0	0	....	....	....	4rd	....
1919	....	1	0	0	....	....	....	4rd	....
1920	....	1	0	0	....	....	....	4rd	....
1921	....	1	0	0	....	....	....	1rd	....
1923	....	1	0	0	....	....	....	1rd	....

Year	Rk	TP	TW	TF	Aus	Fre	Wim	US	DC
1926	....	1	0	0	....	....	....	1rd	....
1928	....	1	0	0	....	....	....	1rd	....
TOTALS		**9**	**0**	**0**	....	....	....	....	....

Doubles Titles: Wim (1)

• GEMMELL, Rhys　　　　　　　　Rhys Gemmell

Male. Born: Australia.
Height: –. Weight: –. Plays: right.
Status: Turned Pro 1927. Highest Ranking: –.

Year	Rk	TP	TW	TF	Aus	Fre	Wim	US	DC
1921	....	1	1	0	W	....	....	....	....
TOTALS		**1**	**1**	**0**	....	....	....	....	....

• GIBSON, Althea　　　　　　　　Althea Gibson Darben

Female. Born: Aug. 25, 1927. Silver, SC, United States.
Height: 5' 11". Weight: –. Plays: right.
Status: Amateur. Highest Ranking: 1 (Dec. 1957). HOF: 1971

Year	Rk	TP	TW	TF	Aus	Fre	Wim	US	FC
1950	....	1	0	0	....	....	....	2rd	....
1951	....	2	0	0	....	....	3rd	3rd	....
1952	....	1	0	0	....	....	....	3rd	....
1953	....	1	0	0	....	....	....	QF	....
1954	....	1	0	0	....	....	....	1rd	....
1955	....	1	0	0	....	....	....	3rd	....
1956	2	3	1	1	....	W	QF	F	....
1957	1	3	2	1	F	....	W	W	....
1958	1	2	2	0	....	....	W	W	....
TOTALS		**15**	**5**	**2**	....	....	....	....	....

Held number one world ranking 2 times during amateur era. Doubles Titles: Aus (1), Fre (1), Wim (3).

• GIMENO, Andres　　see page 845

• GODFREE, Kitty　　　Kathleen "Kitty" McKane Godfree

Female. Born: May 7, 1896. London, Great Britain.
Died: June 19, 1992. Height: –. Weight: –. Plays: right.
Status: Amateur. Highest Ranking: 2 (Dec. 1926). HOF: 1978

Year	Rk	TP	TW	TF	Aus	Fre	Wim	US	FC
1919	....	1	0	0	....	....	QF	....	....
1920	....	2	0	0	....	....	QF	....	....
1921	5	2	0	0	....	....	2rd	1rd	....
1922	....	2	0	0	....	....	2rd	2rd	....
1923	....	2	0	1	....	....	F	QF	....
1924	....	2	1	0	....	....	W	....	....
1925	3	2	0	1	....	....	SF	F	....
1926	2	3	1	0	....	QF	W	1rd	....
1927	5	2	0	0	....	....	QF	1rd	....
1933	....	1	0	0	....	....	2rd	....	....
1934	....	1	0	0	....	....	3rd	....	....
TOTALS		**20**	**2**	**2**	....	....	....	....	....

Competed as Kitty McKane until 1925. Won Bronze in the 1920 and 1924 Olympics. Doubles Titles: US (2).

• GONZALEZ, Pancho　　see page 846

• GOOLAGONG, Evonne　　see page 846

• GORE, Arthur　　　　　　Arthur William Charles Gore

Male. Born: Jan. 2, 1868. Lyndhurst, Great Britain.
Died: Dec. 1, 1928. Height: –. Weight: –. Plays: right.
Status: Amateur. Highest Ranking: –.

Year	Rk	TP	TW	TF	Aus	Fre	Wim	US	DC
1888	....	1	0	0	....	....	2rd	....	....
1889	....	1	0	0	....	....	1rd	....	....
1890	....	1	0	0	....	....	1rd	....	....
1891	....	1	0	0	....	....	2rd	....	....
1892	....	1	0	0	....	....	QF	....	....
1893	....	1	0	0	....	....	2rd	....	....
1894	....	1	0	0	....	....	1rd	....	....
1895	....	1	0	0	....	....	2rd	....	....
1896	....	1	0	0	....	....	1rd	....	....
1897	....	1	0	0	....	....	3rd	....	....
1898	....	1	0	0	....	....	SF	....	....
1899	....	1	0	1	....	....	AC	....	....
1900	....	2	1	1	....	....	F	SF	0-1
1901	....	1	0	0	....	....	WC	....	....
1902	....	1	0	1	....	....	CR	....	....
1903	....	1	0	0	....	....	2rd	....	....
1904	....	1	0	0	....	....	QF	....	....
1905	....	1	0	0	....	....	SF	....	....
1906	....	1	0	1	....	....	F	....	....
1907	....	1	0	1	....	....	F	....	1-1
1908	....	2	2	0	....	....	WC	....	....
1909	....	1	1	0	....	....	WD	....	....
1910	....	1	0	1	....	....	CR	....	....
1911	....	1	0	0	....	....	4rd	....	....
1912	....	1	0	1	....	....	AC	....	1-1
1913	....	1	0	0	....	....	4rd	....	....
1914	....	1	0	0	....	....	QF	....	....
1919	....	1	0	0	....	....	1rd	....	....
1920	....	1	0	0	....	....	2rd	....	....
1921	....	1	0	0	....	....	1rd	....	....
1922	....	1	0	0	....	....	1rd	....	....
TOTALS		**33**	**4**	**7**	....	....	....	....	....

Won Gold in the 1908 Olympics. Doubles Titles: Wim (1).

• GORE, Spencer　　　　　　Spencer William Gorre

Male. Born: Mar. 10, 1850. Wimbledon, Great Britain.
Died: Apr. 19, 1906. Height: –. Weight: –. Plays: right.
Status: Amateur. Highest Ranking: –.

Year	Rk	TP	TW	TF	Aus	Fre	Wim	US	DC
1877	....	1	1	0	....	....	W	....	....
1878	....	1	0	1	....	....	CR	....	....
TOTALS		**2**	**1**	**1**	....	....	....	....	....

• GOURLAY, Helen　　see page 847

• GRAEBNER, Clark　　see page 847

• GRANT, Bitsy　　　　　Bryan Morel "Bitsy" Grant

Male. Born: Dec. 25, 1910. Atlanta, GA, United States.
Died: June 5, 1986. Height: 5' 4". Weight: 120 lbs. Plays: right.
Status: Amateur. Highest Ranking: 6 (Dec. 1937). HOF: 1972

Year	Rk	TP	TW	TF	Aus	Fre	Wim	US	DC
1930	....	1	0	0	....	....	....	3rd	....
1931	....	1	0	0	....	....	....	4rd	....
1933	....	1	0	0	....	....	....	QF	....
1934	....	1	0	0	....	....	....	3rd	....
1935	....	1	0	0	....	....	....	SF	4-0
1936	8	1	0	0	....	....	....	SF	2-0
1937	6	1	0	0	....	....	....	QF	2-2
1938	....	1	0	0	....	....	....	QF	....
1939	....	1	0	0	....	....	....	4rd	....

Year	Rk	TP	TW	TF	Aus	Fre	Wim	US	DC
1940	....	1	0	0	....	....	....	4rd	....
1941	....	1	0	0	....	....	....	4rd	....
1943	....	1	0	0	....	....	....	2rd	....
1946	....	1	0	0	....	....	....	3rd	....
1947	....	1	0	0	....	....	....	1rd	....
TOTALS		**14**	**0**	**0**	....	....	....	....	....

• GREGORY, John
Dr. John Colin Gregory

Male. Born: July 28, 1903. Yorkshire, Great Britain.
Died: Sept. 10, 1959. Height: –. Weight: –. Plays: right.
Status: Amateur. Highest Ranking: –.

Year	Rk	TP	TW	TF	Aus	Fre	Wim	US	DC
1926	....	1	0	0	....	3rd	....	....	2-2
1927	....	0	0	0	....	....	....	....	1-1
1928	....	2	0	0	....	2rd	....	1rd	6-2
1929	....	2	0	0	W	3rd	....	....	4-2
1930	....	1	0	0	....	QF	....	....	0-2
TOTALS		**6**	**0**	**0**	....	....	....	....	....

Doubles Titles: US (3)

• GRIFFIN, Clarence
Clarence James "Peck" Griffin

Male. Born: Jan. 19, 1888. Santa Barbara, CA, United States.
Height: 5' 7". Weight: –. Plays: right.
Status: Amateur. Highest Ranking: –. HOF: 1970

Year	Rk	TP	TW	TF	Aus	Fre	Wim	US	DC
1913	....	1	0	0	....	....	....	1rd	....
1916	....	1	0	0	....	....	....	SF	....
1917	....	1	0	0	....	....	....	4rd	....
1919	....	2	0	0	....	....	2rd	2rd	....
1920	....	1	0	0	....	....	....	QF	....
1923	....	1	0	0	....	....	....	1rd	....
1924	....	1	0	0	....	....	....	1rd	....
1927	....	1	0	0	....	....	....	3rd	....
1931	....	1	0	0	....	....	....	3rd	....
TOTALS		**10**	**0**	**0**	....	....	....	....	....

• HACKETT, Harold
Harold Humphrey Hackett

Male. Born: July 12, 1878. Hingham, MA, United States.
Died: Nov. 20, 1937. Height: 5' 9". Weight: –. Plays: right.
Status: Amateur. Highest Ranking: –. HOF: 1961

Year	Rk	TP	TW	TF	Aus	Fre	Wim	US	DC
1898	....	1	0	0	....	....	....	2rd	....
1900	....	1	0	0	....	....	....	2rd	....
TOTALS		**2**	**0**	**0**	....	....	....	....	....

Doubles Titles: US (4)

• HADOW, Frank
Patrick Francis Hadow

Male. Born: Jan. 24, 1855. Regents Park, Great Britain.
Died: June 29, 1946. Height: –. Weight: –. Plays: right.
Status: Amateur. Highest Ranking: –.

Year	Rk	TP	TW	TF	Aus	Fre	Wim	US	DC
1878	....	1	0	0	....	....	WC	....	....
TOTALS		**1**	**0**	**0**	....	....	....	....	....

• HAMILTON, Ghost
Willoughby James "Ghost" Hamilton

Male. Born: Dec. 8, 1864. Monasterevan, Ireland.
Died: Sept. 27, 1943. Height: –. Weight: –. Plays: right.
Status: Amateur. Highest Ranking: –.

Year	Rk	TP	TW	TF	Aus	Fre	Wim	US	DC
1890	....	1	0	0	....	....	WC	....	....
TOTALS		**1**	**0**	**0**	....	....	....	....	....

• HANSELL, Ellen
Helen Forde Hansell Allerdice

Female. Born: Sept. 18, 1869. Philadelphia, PA, United States.
Died: May 11, 1937. Height: –. Weight: –. Plays: right.
Status: Amateur. Highest Ranking: –. HOF: 1965

Year	Rk	TP	TW	TF	Aus	Fre	Wim	US	FC
1884	....	1	0	0	....	....	QF	....	....
1887	....	1	0	0	....	....	....	W	....
1888	....	1	0	1	....	....	....	CR	....
TOTALS		**3**	**0**	**1**	....	....	....	....	....

• HANTZE, Karen
see SUSMAN, Karen, page 891

• HARD, Darlene
Darlene Ruth Hard Waggoner

Female. Born: Jan. 6, 1936. Los Angeles, CA, United States.
Height: 5' 5". Weight: 140 lbs. Plays: right.
Status: Amateur. Highest Ranking: 2 (Dec. 1957). HOF: 1973

Year	Rk	TP	TW	TF	Aus	Fre	Wim	US	FC
1953	....	1	0	0	....	....	....	2rd	....
1954	....	1	0	0	....	....	....	SF	....
1955	7	3	0	0	....	2rd	SF	3rd	....
1956	10	3	0	0	....	3rd	3rd	QF	....
1957	2	3	0	1	....	QF	F	SF	....
1958	4	1	0	1	....	....	....	F	....
1959	3	2	0	1	....	F	SF	....	....
1960	2	3	2	0	....	W	QF	W	....
1961	2	2	1	0	....	4rd	....	W	....
1962	3	3	0	1	QF	....	QF	F	....
1963	6	3	0	0	....	2rd	SF	QF	3-1
TOTALS		**25**	**3**	**4**	....	....	....	....	**3-1**

Doubles Titles: Fre (3), Wim (4), US (6)

• HART, Doris
Doris Jane Hart

Female. Born: June 20, 1925. St. Louis, MO, United States.
Height: –. Weight: –. Plays: right.
Status: Amateur. Highest Ranking: 1 (Dec. 1951). HOF: 1969

Year	Rk	TP	TW	TF	Aus	Fre	Wim	US	FC
1940	....	1	0	0	....	....	....	2rd	....
1941	....	1	0	0	....	....	....	1rd	....
1942	....	1	0	0	....	....	....	QF	....
1943	....	1	0	0	....	....	....	SF	....
1944	....	1	0	0	....	....	....	QF	....
1945	....	1	0	0	....	....	....	SF	....
1946	4	3	0	1	....	QF	QF	F	....
1947	3	3	0	2	....	F	F	SF	....
1948	3	3	0	1	....	SF	F	QF	....
1949	3	2	1	1	W	....	....	F	....
1950	3	4	1	2	F	W	SF	F	....
1951	1	3	1	1	....	F	W	SF	....
1952	2	3	1	1	....	W	QF	F	....
1953	2	3	0	3	....	F	F	F	....
1954	2	2	1	0	....	....	SF	W	....
1955	2	2	1	0	....	....	SF	W	....
TOTALS		**34**	**6**	**12**	....	....	....	....	....

Held number one world ranking 1 time during amateur era. Doubles Titles: Aus (1), Fre (5), Wim (4), US (4).

• HARTIGAN, Joan
Joan Hartigan

Female. Born: 1912. Sydney, Australia.
Height: –. Weight: –. Plays: right.
Status: Amateur. Highest Ranking: 8 (Dec. 1934).

Year	Rk	TP	TW	TF	Aus	Fre	Wim	US	FC
1931	....	1	0	0	QF	....	....	....	....
1933	....	1	1	0	W	....	....	....	....
1934	8	3	1	0	W	3rd	SF	....	....
1935	9	1	0	0	....	....	SF	....	....

Year	Rk	TP	TW	TF	Aus	Fre	Wim	US	FC
1936	....	1	1	0	W	....	....	....	....
1937	....	1	0	0	QF	....	....	....	....
1938	....	2	0	0	QF	....	2rd	....	....
1939	....	1	0	0	SF	....	....	....	....
1940	....	1	0	0	SF	....	....	....	....
1946	....	1	0	0	QF	....	....	....	....
1947	....	2	0	0	4rd	....	3rd	....	....
1949	....	1	0	0	....	....	1rd	....	....
TOTALS		**16**	**3**	**0**	....	....	....	....	....

• HARTLEY, John
Rev. John Thorneycroft Hartley

Male. Born: Jan. 9, 1849. Tong, Great Britain.
Died: Aug. 21, 1935. Height: –. Weight: –. Plays: right.
Status: Amateur. Highest Ranking: –.

Year	Rk	TP	TW	TF	Aus	Fre	Wim	US	DC
1879	....	1	1	0	....	....	WC	....	....
1880	....	1	1	0	....	....	WD	....	....
1883	....	1	0	0	....	....	2rd	....	....
TOTALS		**3**	**2**	**0**	....	....	....	....	....

• HAWKES, Jack
John Baily Hawkes

Male. Born: June 7, 1889. Geelong, Australia.
Died: May 31, 1990. Height: –. Weight: –. Plays: left.
Status: Amateur. Highest Ranking: 10 (Dec. 1928).

Year	Rk	TP	TW	TF	Aus	Fre	Wim	US	DC
1921	....	1	0	0	....	....	....	3rd	1-4
1922	....	1	0	0	SF	....	....	....	....
1923	....	1	0	0	....	....	....	1rd	4-3
1925	....	0	0	0	....	....	....	....	1-0
1926	....	1	1	0	W	....	....	....	....
1927	....	1	0	1	F	....	....	....	....
1928	10	3	0	0	QF	SF	2rd	....	....
TOTALS		**8**	**1**	**1**	....	....	....	....	....

Doubles Titles: Aus (3)

• HAYDON, Ann   see page 849

• HEATH, Rod
Wilfrid Rodney Heath

Male. Born: June 15, 1884. Melbourne, Australia.
Died: Oct. 6, 1936. Height: –. Weight: –. Plays: right.
Status: Amateur. Highest Ranking: –.

Year	Rk	TP	TW	TF	Aus	Fre	Wim	US	DC
1905	....	1	1	0	W	....	....	....	....
1906	....	1	0	0	QF	....	....	....	....
1910	....	1	1	0	W	....	....	....	....
1911	....	2	0	0	QF	....	QF	....	....
1912	....	0	0	0	....	....	....	....	1-2
1914	....	1	0	0	SF	....	....	....	....
1919	....	1	0	0	....	....	4rd	....	....
1925	....	2	0	0	....	1rd	1rd	....	....
TOTALS		**9**	**2**	**0**	....	....	....	....	....

• HELDMAN, Julie   see page 849

• HELLWIG, Helen
Helen Rebecca Hellwig Pouch

Female. Born: 1874. Brooklyn, NY, United States.
Died: Nov. 26, 1960. Height: –. Weight: –. Plays: right.
Status: Amateur. Highest Ranking: –.

Year	Rk	TP	TW	TF	Aus	Fre	Wim	US	FC
1893	....	1	0	0	....	....	....	QF	....
1894	....	1	1	0	....	....	....	WC	....
1895	....	1	0	1	....	....	....	CR	....
1907	....	1	0	0	....	....	....	QF	....
1908	....	1	0	0	....	....	....	QF	....
1909	....	1	0	0	....	....	....	2rd	....
1910	....	1	0	0	....	....	....	2rd	....
1912	....	1	0	0	....	....	....	2rd	....
1916	....	1	0	0	....	....	....	2rd	....
TOTALS		**9**	**1**	**1**	....	....	....	....	....

Competed as Helen Hellwig until 1907. Doubles Titles: US (2).

• HENKEL, Henner
Henner Ernst Otto Henkel

Male. Born: Oct. 9, 1915. Posen, Germany.
Height: 6'. Weight: –. Plays: right.
Status: Amateur. Highest Ranking: 3 (Dec. 1937).

Year	Rk	TP	TW	TF	Aus	Fre	Wim	US	DC
1934	....	1	0	0	....	....	2rd	....	4-0
1935	....	2	0	0	....	3rd	1rd	....	4-4
1936	9	2	0	0	....	3rd	1rd	....	9-2
1937	3	3	1	0	W	QF	1rd	....	6-2
1938	....	1	0	0	....	....	SF	....	4-3
1939	6	2	0	0	....	....	SF	1rd	6-2
TOTALS		**11**	**1**	**0**	....	....	....	....	....

• HEWITT, Bob   see page 850

• HILLYARD, Blanche
see BINGLEY HILLYARD, Blanche, page 799

• HOAD, Lew   see page 852

• HOMANS, Helen
Helen Homans McLean

Female. Born: 1878 or 1879. New York, NY, United States.
Died: Mar. 29, 1949. Height: –. Weight: –. Plays: right.
Status: Amateur. Highest Ranking: –.

Year	Rk	TP	TW	TF	Aus	Fre	Wim	US	FC
1904	....	1	0	1	....	....	....	F	....
1905	....	1	0	1	....	....	....	F	....
1906	....	1	1	0	....	....	....	WC	....
TOTALS		**3**	**1**	**2**	....	....	....	....	....

Doubles Titles: US (1)

• HOPMAN, Harry
Henry Christian Hopman

Male. Born: Aug. 12, 1906. Glebe, Australia.
Died: Dec. 27, 1985. Height: 5' 7". Weight: 135 lbs. Plays: right.
Status: Amateur. Highest Ranking: –. HOF: 1978

Year	Rk	TP	TW	TF	Aus	Fre	Wim	US	DC
1928	....	4	0	0	QF	1rd	2rd	1rd	0-1
1929	....	1	0	0	SF	....	....	....	....
1930	....	3	0	1	F	QF	3rd	....	2-2
1931	....	1	0	1	F	....	....	....	....
1932	....	2	0	1	F	....	3rd	....	2-2
1933	....	1	0	0	QF	....	....	....	....
1934	....	3	0	0	QF	4rd	4rd	....	....
1935	....	2	0	0	....	4rd	4rd	....	....
1936	....	1	0	0	SF	....	....	....	....
1937	....	1	0	0	SF	....	....	....	....
1938	....	1	0	0	....	....	....	QF	....
1939	....	2	0	1	QF	....	....	QF	....
1940	....	1	0	0	QF	....	....	....	....
1946	....	3	0	0	QF	....	2rd	2rd	....
1947	....	1	0	0	3rd	....	....	....	....
1948	....	4	0	0	3rd	2rd	2rd	2rd	....
1949	....	1	0	0	4rd	....	....	....	....
1950	....	4	0	0	4rd	2rd	3rd	2rd	....
1951	....	1	0	0	4rd	....	....	....	....

Year	Rk	TP	TW	TF	Aus	Fre	Wim	US	DC
1952	....	2	0	0	....	1rd	1rd	....	....
1953	....	1	0	0	....	2rd	....	....	....
TOTALS		**40**	**0**	**4**	....	....	....	....	....

• HOTCHKISS WIGHTMAN, Hazel   Hazel Virginia Hotchkiss Wightman

Female. Born: Dec. 20, 1886. Healdsburg, CA, United States.
Died: Dec. 5, 1974. Height: –. Weight: –. Plays: right.
Status: Amateur. Highest Ranking: –. HOF: 1957

Year	Rk	TP	TW	TF	Aus	Fre	Wim	US	FC
1909	....	1	1	0	....	....	....	WC	....
1910	....	1	1	0	....	....	....	WD	....
1911	....	1	1	0	....	....	....	WD	....
1915	....	1	0	1	....	....	....	F	....
1919	....	1	1	0	....	....	....	W	....
1924	....	1	0	0	....	....	3rd		....
1926	....	1	0	0	....	....	....	3rd	....
1927	....	1	0	0	....	....	....	1rd	....
1928	....	1	0	0	....	....	....	QF	....
TOTALS		**9**	**4**	**1**	....	....	....	....	....

Competed as Hazel Hotchkiss until 1912. Doubles Titles: Wim (1), US (6).

• HOVEY, Fred   Frederick Howard Hovey

Male. Born: Oct. 7, 1868. Newton Centre, MA, United States.
Died: Oct. 18, 1945. Height: 5' 8". Weight: 170 lbs. Plays: right.
Status: Amateur. Highest Ranking: –. HOF: 1974

Year	Rk	TP	TW	TF	Aus	Fre	Wim	US	DC
1890	....	1	0	0	....	....	....	1rd	....
1891	....	1	0	1	....	....	....	F	....
1892	....	1	0	1	....	....	....	AC	....
1893	....	1	0	1	....	....	....	F	....
1894	....	1	0	0	....	....	....	2rd	....
1895	....	1	1	0	....	....	....	WC	....
1896	....	1	0	1	....	....	....	CR	....
TOTALS		**7**	**1**	**4**	....	....	....	....	....

Doubles Titles: US (2)

• HUNT, Joe   Joseph Raphael Hunt

Male. Born: Feb. 17, 1919. San Francisco, CA, United States.
Died: Feb. 2, 1944. Height: 6'. Weight: 165 lbs. Plays: right.
Status: Amateur. Highest Ranking: 10 (Dec. 1939). HOF: 1966

Year	Rk	TP	TW	TF	Aus	Fre	Wim	US	DC
1936	....	1	0	0	....	....	....	3rd	....
1938	....	2	0	0	....	....	1rd	QF	....
1939	10	1	0	0	....	....	....	SF	....
1940	....	1	0	0	....	....	....	SF	....
1943	....	1	1	0	....	....	....	W	....
TOTALS		**6**	**1**	**0**	....	....	....	....	....

• HUNT, Lesley   see page 852

• HUNTER, Frank   Francis Townsend Hunter

Male. Born: June 28, 1894. New York, NY, United States.
Died: Dec. 2, 1981. Height: –. Weight: –. Plays: right.
Status: Amateur. Highest Ranking: 4 (Dec. 1928). HOF: 1961

Year	Rk	TP	TW	TF	Aus	Fre	Wim	US	DC
1915	....	1	0	0	....	....	....	QF	....
1916	....	1	0	0	....	....	....	2rd	....
1920	....	1	0	0	....	....	....	1rd	....
1921	....	2	0	0	....	....	SF	QF	....
1922	....	1	0	0	....	....	....	4rd	....
1923	5	1	0	1	....	....	F	....	....
1924	....	2	0	0	....	....	3rd	3rd	....
1925	....	1	0	0	....	....	....	2rd	....

Year	Rk	TP	TW	TF	Aus	Fre	Wim	US	DC
1926	....	1	0	0	....	....	....	3rd	....
1927	6	3	0	0	....	2rd	QF	SF	....
1928	4	3	0	1	....	3rd	1rd	F	1-1
1929	5	3	0	1	....	QF	2rd	F	2-0
1930	....	1	0	0	....	....	....	QF	....
TOTALS		**21**	**0**	**3**	....	....	....	....	....

Doubles Titles: Wim (2), US (1)

• JACOBS, Helen   Helen Hull Jacobs

Female. Born: Aug. 9, 1908. Globe, AZ, United States.
Height: 5' 6". Weight: 145 lbs. Plays: right.
Status: Amateur. Highest Ranking: 1 (Dec. 1936). HOF: 1962

Year	Rk	TP	TW	TF	Aus	Fre	Wim	US	FC
1927	....	1	0	0	....	....	....	SF	....
1928	9	2	0	1	....	....	3rd	F	....
1929	3	2	0	1	....	....	F	SF	....
1930	6	2	0	1	....	F	QF	....	....
1931	2	2	0	0	....	QF	....	QF	....
1932	2	3	1	1	....	QF	F	W	....
1933	2	3	1	0	....	SF	SF	W	....
1934	2	3	1	2	....	F	F	W	....
1935	2	3	1	1	....	SF	F	W	....
1936	1	2	1	1	....	....	W	F	....
1937	6	3	0	0	....	QF	QF	SF	....
1938	2	2	0	1	....	....	F	3rd	....
1939	3	2	0	1	....	....	QF	F	....
1940	....	1	0	0	....	....	....	F	....
1941	....	1	0	0	....	....	....	SF	....
TOTALS		**32**	**5**	**11**	....	....	....	....	....

Held number one world ranking 1 time during amateur era. Doubles Titles: US (3).

• JOHNSTON, Bill   William M. "Little Bill" Johnston

Male. Born: Nov. 2, 1894. San Francisco, CA, United States.
Died: May 1, 1946. Height: 5' 8". Weight: 125 lbs. Plays: right.
Status: Amateur. Highest Ranking: 1 (Dec. 1919). HOF: 1958

Year	Rk	TP	TW	TF	Aus	Fre	Wim	US	DC
1913	....	1	0	0	....	....	....	3rd	....
1914	....	1	0	0	....	....	....	2rd	....
1915	....	1	1	0	....	....	....	W	....
1916	....	1	0	1	....	....	....	F	....
1919	1	1	1	0	....	....	....	W	....
1920	2	2	0	1	....	....	2rd	F	5-0
1921	2	1	0	0	....	....	....	4rd	2-0
1922	2	1	0	1	....	....	....	F	2-0
1923	2	2	1	1	....	....	W	F	1-1
1924	4	1	0	1	....	....	....	F	....
1925	2	1	0	1	....	....	....	F	2-0
1926	4	1	0	0	....	....	....	4rd	2-0
1927	....	1	0	0	....	....	....	SF	0-2
TOTALS		**15**	**3**	**6**	....	....	....	....	....

Held number one world ranking 1 time during amateur era. Doubles Titles: US (3).

• JONES, Anne   see HAYDON, Anne, page 849

• JONES, Marion   Marion Jones

Female. Born: .
Height: –. Weight: –. Plays: –.
Status: Amateur. Highest Ranking: –.

Year	Rk	TP	TW	TF	Aus	Fre	Wim	US	FC
1898	....	1	0	1	....	....	....	AC	....
1899	....	1	1	0	....	....	....	WC	....

Year	Rk	TP	TW	TF	Aus	Fre	Wim	US	FC
1900	....	2	0	0	....	....	QF	....	....
1901	....	1	0	1	....	....	....	F	....
1902	....	1	1	0	....	....	....	WC	....
1903	....	1	0	1	....	....	....	CR	....
TOTALS		7	2	3	....	....	....	....	....

Won Bronze in the 1900 Olympics. Doubles Titles: US (1).

• KING, Billie Jean   see page 855

• KINGSCOTE, Algie   Algernon Robert Fitzhardinage "Algie" Kingscote

Male. Born: Dec. 3, 1888. India.
Height: –. Weight: –. Plays: right.
Status: Amateur. Highest Ranking: 3 (Dec. 1920).

Year	Rk	TP	TW	TF	Aus	Fre	Wim	US	DC
1914	....	1	0	0	....	....	2rd	....	....
1919	6	2	1	1	W	....	F	....	4-0
1920	3	1	0	0	....	....	4rd	....	1-3
1921	....	1	0	0	....	....	QF	....	....
1922	9	1	0	0	....	....	4rd	....	1-1
1924	....	1	0	0	....	....	QF	....	1-3
1927	....	1	0	0	....	....	2rd	....	....
TOTALS		8	1	1	....	....	....	....	....

Represented Great Britian in the Davis Cup (1919-1924)

• KODES, Jan   see page 856

• KORMOCZI, Suzi   Suzi Kormoczi

Female. Born: Aug. 25, 1924. Budapest, Hungary.
Height: –. Weight: –. Plays: right.
Status: Amateur. Highest Ranking: 2 (Dec. 1958).

Year	Rk	TP	TW	TF	Aus	Fre	Wim	US	FC
1947	....	2	0	0	....	QF	1rd	....	....
1948	....	2	0	0	....	2rd	4rd	....	....
1951	....	1	0	0	....	....	3rd	....	....
1953	7	1	0	0	....	....	QF	....	....
1955	10	2	0	0	....	1rd	QF	....	....
1956	5	2	0	0	....	SF	4rd	....	....
1957	....	2	0	0	....	QF	2rd	....	....
1958	2	2	1	0	....	W	SF	....	....
1959	8	1	0	1	....	F	....	....	....
1960	5	2	0	0	....	3rd	2rd	....	....
1961	8	2	0	0	....	QF	4rd	....	....
1962	....	2	0	0	....	4rd	2rd	....	....
1963	....	3	0	0	....	1rd	2rd	2rd	1-1
1964	....	2	0	0	....	3rd	1rd	....	....
TOTALS		26	1	1	....	....	....	....	1-1

• KRAMER, Jack   John Albert "Jake" Kramer

Male. Born: Aug. 1, 1921. Las Vegas, NV, United States.
Height: 6'. Weight: –. Plays: right.
Status: Turned Pro 1947. Highest Ranking: 1 (Dec. 1946). HOF: 1968

Year	Rk	TP	TW	TF	Aus	Fre	Wim	US	DC
1938	....	1	0	0	....	....	....	2rd	....
1939	....	1	0	0	....	....	....	2rd	....
1940	....	1	0	0	....	....	....	SF	....
1941	....	1	0	0	....	....	....	4rd	....
1943	....	1	0	1	....	....	....	F	....
1946	1	2	1	0	....	....	4rd	W	4-0
1947	1	2	2	0	....	....	W	W	2-0
TOTALS		9	3	1	....	....	....	....	....

Held number one world ranking 2 times during amateur era. Doubles Titles: Wim (2), US (4).

• LACOSTE, Rene   Jean Rene Lacoste

Male. Born: July 2, 1904. Paris, France.
Died: Aug. 12, 1996. Height: –. Weight: –. Plays: –.
Status: Amateur. Highest Ranking: 1 (Dec. 1926). HOF: 1976

Year	Rk	TP	TW	TF	Aus	Fre	Wim	US	DC
1922	....	1	0	0	....	....	1rd	....	....
1923	....	2	0	0	....	....	5rd	2rd	3-2
1924	5	3	0	1	....	....	F	QF	9-0
1925	4	3	2	0	....	W	W	QF	6-3
1926	1	3	1	1	....	F	1rd	W	5-2
1927	1	3	2	0	....	W	SF	W	8-0
1928	2	2	1	1	....	F	W	....	1-1
1929	2	1	1	0	....	W	....	....	....
1930	....	1	1	0	....	W	....	....	....
1932	....	1	0	0	....	4rd	....	....	....
TOTALS		20	8	3	....	....	....	....	....

Held number one world ranking 2 times during amateur era. Doubles Titles: Fre (2), Wim (1).

• LANCE, Sylvia   Sylvia Lance Harper

Female. Born: Australia.
Height: –. Weight: –. Plays: right.
Status: Amateur. Highest Ranking: –.

Year	Rk	TP	TW	TF	Aus	Fre	Wim	US	FC
1922	....	1	0	0	SF	....	....	....	....
1923	....	1	0	0	SF	....	....	....	....
1924	....	1	1	0	W	....	....	....	....
1925	....	1	0	0	SF	....	....	....	....
1926	....	1	0	0	SF	....	....	....	....
1927	....	1	0	1	F	....	....	....	....
1929	....	1	0	0	SF	....	....	....	....
1930	....	1	0	1	F	....	....	....	....
1931	....	1	0	0	SF	....	....	....	....
TOTALS		9	1	2	....	....	....	....	....

Doubles Titles: Aus (1).

• LANDRY, Nelly   Nelly Adamson Landry

Female. Born: 12/?/1916. Tilbury, Great Britain.
Height: –. Weight: –. Plays: –.
Status: Amateur. Highest Ranking: –.

Year	Rk	TP	TW	TF	Aus	Fre	Wim	US	FC
1933	....	1	0	0	....	....	1rd	....	....
1934	....	2	0	0	....	2rd	2rd	....	....
1935	....	2	0	0	....	3rd	2rd	....	....
1936	....	2	0	0	....	QF	4rd	....	....
1938	....	1	0	1	....	F	....	....	....
1946	....	2	0	0	....	QF	2rd	....	....
1948	....	3	1	0	....	W	QF	3rd	....
1949	....	2	0	1	....	F	3rd	....	....
1951	....	1	0	0	....	QF	....	....	....
1952	....	2	0	0	....	....	4rd	1rd	....
1953	....	2	0	0	....	QF	4rd	....	....
1954	....	2	0	0	....	SF	2rd	....	....
TOTALS		22	1	2	....	....	....	....	....

• LARCOMBE, Ethel   Ethel Warneford Thomson Larcombe

Female. Born: June 8, 1879. Islington, Great Britain.
Died: Aug. 11, 1965. Height: –. Weight: –. Plays: right.
Status: Amateur. Highest Ranking: –.

Year	Rk	TP	TW	TF	Aus	Fre	Wim	US	FC
1902	....	1	0	0	....	....	1rd	....	....
1903	....	1	0	1	....	....	F	....	....
1904	....	1	0	0	....	....	3rd	....	....
1905	....	1	0	0	....	....	QF	....	....
1906	....	1	0	0	....	....	2rd	....	....

Year	Rk	TP	TW	TF	Aus	Fre	Wim	US	FC
1912	....	1	1	0	....	....	WC	....	....
1914	....	1	0	1	....	....	AC	....	....
1919	....	1	0	0	....	....	2rd	....	....
TOTALS		8	1	2	....	....	....	....	....

• LARNED, Bill
William Augustus Larned

Male. Born: Dec. 30, 1872. Summit, NJ, United States.
Died: Dec. 16, 1926. Height: 5' 11". Weight: 170 lbs. Plays: right.
Status: Amateur. Highest Ranking: –. HOF: 1956

Year	Rk	TP	TW	TF	Aus	Fre	Wim	US	DC
1891	....	1	0	0	....	....	....	3rd	....
1892	....	1	0	1	....	....	....	F	....
1893	....	1	0	0	....	....	....	QF	....
1894	....	1	0	1	....	....	....	F	....
1895	....	1	0	1	....	....	....	F	....
1896	....	2	0	1	....	....	QF	F	....
1897	....	1	0	0	....	....	....	SF	....
1899	....	1	0	0	....	....	....	1rd	....
1900	....	1	0	1	....	....	....	AC	....
1901	....	1	1	0	....	....	....	WC	....
1902	....	1	1	0	....	....	....	WD	1-1
1903	....	1	0	1	....	....	....	CR	0-1
1904	....	1	0	0	....	....	....	SF	....
1905	....	2	0	0	....	....	QF	SF	2-2
1906	....	1	0	0	....	....	....	2rd	....
1907	....	1	1	0	....	....	....	WC	....
1908	....	1	1	0	....	....	....	WD	2-0
1909	....	1	1	0	....	....	....	WD	2-0
1910	....	1	1	0	....	....	....	WD	....
1911	....	1	1	0	....	....	....	WD	2-0
1912	....	0	0	0	....	....	....	....	0-1
1913	....	1	0	0	....	....	....	1rd	....
1914	....	1	0	0	....	....	....	1rd	....
1921	....	1	0	0	....	....	....	1rd	....
TOTALS		25	7	6	....	....	....	....	....

• LARSEN, Art
Arthur David "Tappy" Larsen

Male. Born: Apr. 17, 1925. Hayward, CA, United States.
Height: 5' 10". Weight: 150 lbs. Plays: left.
Status: Amateur. Highest Ranking: 3 (Dec. 1950). HOF: 1956

Year	Rk	TP	TW	TF	Aus	Fre	Wim	US	DC
1948	....	1	0	0	....	....	....	4rd	....
1949	....	1	0	0	....	....	....	QF	....
1950	3	3	0	0	....	QF	QF	W	....
1951	9	3	0	0	SF	....	QF	SF	2-0
1952	....	2	0	0	....	....	1rd	4rd	2-0
1953	....	2	0	0	....	....	QF	4rd	....
1954	9	3	0	0	....	SF	3rd	QF	....
1955	....	3	0	0	....	4rd	4rd	4rd	....
1956	....	3	0	0	....	4rd	4rd	3rd	....
TOTALS		21	0	0	....	....	....	....	....

• LAVER, Rod   see page 859

• LAWFORD, Herbert
Herbert Fortescue Lawford

Male. Born: May 15, 1851. Bayswater, Great Britain.
Died: Apr. 20, 1925. Height: –. Weight: –. Plays: right.
Status: Amateur. Highest Ranking: –.

Year	Rk	TP	TW	TF	Aus	Fre	Wim	US	DC
1878	....	1	0	0	....	....	SF	....	....
1879	....	1	0	0	....	....	1rd	....	....
1880	....	1	0	1	....	....	AC	....	....
1881	....	1	0	0	....	....	SF	....	....
1882	....	1	0	0	....	....	SF	....	....

Year	Rk	TP	TW	TF	Aus	Fre	Wim	US	DC
1883	....	1	0	0	....	....	1rd	....	....
1884	....	1	0	1	....	....	AC	....	....
1885	....	1	0	1	....	....	AC	....	....
1886	....	1	0	1	....	....	AC	....	....
1887	....	1	1	0	....	....	WC	....	....
1888	....	1	0	0	....	....	CR	....	....
1889	....	1	0	0	....	....	SF	....	....
1890	....	1	0	0	....	....	2rd	....	....
TOTALS		13	1	4	....	....	....	....	....

• LENGLEN, Suzanne
Suzanne Rachel Flore Lenglen

Female. Born: May 24, 1899. Paris, France.
Died: July 4, 1938. Height: –. Weight: –. Plays: right.
Status: Turned Pro 1926. Highest Ranking: 1 (Dec. 1921). HOF: 1978

Year	Rk	TP	TW	TF	Aus	Fre	Wim	US	FC
1919	....	1	1	0	....	....	WC	....	....
1920	....	2	2	0	....	....	WD	....	....
1921	1	2	1	0	....	....	WD	2rd	....
1922	....	1	1	0	....	....	W	....	....
1923	....	1	1	0	....	....	W	....	....
1924	....	1	0	0	....	....	SF	....	....
1925	1	2	2	0	....	W	W	....	....
1926	1	2	1	0	....	W	3rd	....	....
TOTALS		12	9	0	....	....	....	....	....

Held number one world ranking 3 times during amateur era. Won Gold in the 1920 Olympics. Doubles Titles: Fre (2), Wim (6).

• LITTLE, Dorothy   see ROUND, Dorothy, page 817

• LIZANA, Anita
Anita Lizana Ellis

Female. Born: 1915. Santiago, Chile.
Height: –. Weight: –. Plays: right.
Status: Amateur. Highest Ranking: 1 (Dec. 1937).

Year	Rk	TP	TW	TF	Aus	Fre	Wim	US	FC
1935	....	2	0	0	....	3rd	3rd	....	....
1936	8	1	0	0	....	....	QF	....	....
1937	1	2	1	0	....	....	QF	W	....
1938	....	1	0	0	....	....	2rd	....	....
TOTALS		6	1	0	....	....	....	....	....

Held number one world ranking 1 time during amateur era.

• LONG, Thelma
Thelma Dorothy Coyne Long

Female. Born: Aug. 14, 1918. Sydney, Australia.
Height: –. Weight: –. Plays: right.
Status: Amateur. Highest Ranking: 7 (Dec. 1952).

Year	Rk	TP	TW	TF	Aus	Fre	Wim	US	FC
1936	....	1	0	0	SF	....	....	....	....
1937	....	1	0	0	SF	....	....	....	....
1938	....	4	0	0	QF	2rd	3rd	3rd	....
1939	....	1	0	0	SF	....	....	....	....
1940	....	1	0	1	F	....	....	....	....
1946	....	1	0	0	QF	....	....	....	....
1947	....	1	0	0	SF	....	....	....	....
1948	....	1	0	0	4rd	....	....	....	....
1949	....	2	0	0	SF	....	4rd	....	....
1950	....	2	0	0	QF	....	3rd	....	....
1951	....	2	0	1	F	QF	....	....	....
1952	7	3	1	0	W	....	QF	QF	....
1953	....	1	0	0	....	....	....	3rd	....
1954	10	1	1	0	W	....	....	....	....
1955	....	1	0	1	F	....	....	....	....
1956	....	3	0	1	F	3rd	1rd	....	....
1957	....	1	0	0	....	....	1rd	....	....

Year	Rk	TP	TW	TF	Aus	Fre	Wim	US	FC
1958	....	4	0	0	4rd	3rd	4rd	2rd	....
1959	....	1	0	0	3rd	....	....	....	....
TOTALS		32	2	4	....	....	....	....	....

Competed as Thelma Long until 1946. Doubles Titles: Aus (12).

• LOTT, George   George Martin Lott, Jr.

Male. Born: Oct. 16, 1906. Springfield, IL, United States.
Died: Dec. 2, 1991. Height: 6'. Weight: 160 lbs. Plays: right.
Status: Amateur. Highest Ranking: 6 (Dec. 1928). HOF: 1964

Year	Rk	TP	TW	TF	Aus	Fre	Wim	US	DC
1924	....	1	0	0	....	....	....	QF	....
1925	....	1	0	0	....	....	....	3rd	....
1926	....	1	0	0	....	....	....	2rd	....
1927	7	1	0	0	....	....	....	1rd	....
1928	6	1	0	0	....	....	....	SF	2-0
1929	6	1	0	0	....	....	....	3rd	1-2
1930	7	1	0	0	....	....	....	2rd	4-2
1931	8	2	0	1	....	QF	....	F	....
1932	....	1	0	0	....	....	....	QF	....
1933	....	1	0	0	....	....	....	3rd	....
1934	....	1	0	0	....	....	....	3rd	....
TOTALS		12	0	1	....	....	....	....	....

Doubles Titles: Fre (1), Wim (2), US (5).

• LOWE, Gordon   Francis Gordon Lowe

Male. Born: June 21, 1884. Edgbaston, Great Britain.
Height: –. Weight: –. Plays: right.
Status: Amateur. Highest Ranking: 8 (Dec. 1914).

Year	Rk	TP	TW	TF	Aus	Fre	Wim	US	DC
1906	....	1	0	0	....	....	3rd	....	....
1907	....	1	0	0	....	....	3rd	....	....
1908	....	1	0	0	....	....	2rd	....	....
1909	....	1	0	0	....	....	QF	....	....
1910	....	1	0	0	....	....	3rd	....	....
1911	....	1	0	0	....	....	SF	....	....
1912	....	2	0	0	....	....	4rd	....	....
1913	....	1	0	0	....	....	2rd	....	....
1914	8	1	0	0	....	....	3rd	....	....
1915	....	1	1	0	W	....	....	....	....
1920	....	2	0	0	....	....	2rd	....	....
1921	....	2	0	0	....	....	3rd	QF	2-2
1922	....	1	0	0	....	....	3rd	....	2-0
1923	....	1	0	0	....	....	SF	....	....
1924	....	1	0	0	....	....	3rd	....	....
1925	....	1	0	0	....	....	4rd	....	2-0
1926	....	1	0	0	....	....	3rd	....	....
TOTALS		20	1	0	....	....	....	....	....

• LUTZ, Bob   see page 861

• MAHONY, Harold   Harold Segerson Mahony

Male. Born: Feb. 13, 1867. Edinburgh, Ireland.
Died: June 27, 1904. Height: –. Weight: –. Plays: right.
Status: Amateur. Highest Ranking: –.

Year	Rk	TP	TW	TF	Aus	Fre	Wim	US	DC
1890	....	1	0	0	....	....	1rd	....	....
1891	....	1	0	0	....	....	SF	....	....
1892	....	1	0	0	....	....	SF	....	....
1893	....	1	0	1	....	....	F	....	....
1894	....	1	0	0	....	....	2rd	....	....
1896	....	1	1	0	....	....	WC	....	....
1897	....	1	0	1	....	....	CR	....	....
1898	....	1	0	1	....	....	F	....	....
1899	....	1	0	0	....	....	SF	....	....
1900	....	2	0	1	....	....	2rd	....	....
1901	....	1	0	0	....	....	SF	....	....
1902	....	1	0	0	....	....	SF	....	....
1903	....	1	0	0	....	....	3rd	....	....
1904	....	1	0	0	....	....	3rd	....	....
1905	....	1	0	0	....	....	2rd	....	....
TOTALS		16	1	4	....	....	....	....	....

Won Silver in the 1900 Olympics

• MAKO, Gene   Constantine Gene Mako

Male. Born: Jan. 24, 1916. Budapest, Hungary.
Height: 6'. Weight: 170 lbs. Plays: right.
Status: Turned Pro 1943. Highest Ranking: 9 (Dec. 1938). HOF: 1973

Year	Rk	TP	TW	TF	Aus	Fre	Wim	US	DC
1933	....	1	0	0	....	....	....	3rd	....
1934	....	1	0	0	....	....	....	3rd	....
1935	....	1	0	0	....	....	4rd	....	0-1
1936	....	2	0	0	....	....	2rd	4rd	....
1937	....	2	0	0	....	....	4rd	2rd	....
1938	9	3	0	1	QF	....	4rd	F	....
1939	....	1	0	0	....	....	....	2rd	....
1941	....	1	0	0	....	....	....	3rd	....
TOTALS		12	0	1	....	....	....	....	....

Represented the United States in the Davis Cup (1935). Doubles Titles: Wim (2), US (2).

• MALLORY, Molla   Anna Margarethe "Molla" Bjurstedt Mallory

Female. Born: Mar. 6, 1884. Oslo, Norway.
Died: Nov. 22, 1959. Height: –. Weight: –. Plays: right.
Status: Amateur. Highest Ranking: 2 (Dec. 1921). HOF: 1958

Year	Rk	TP	TW	TF	Aus	Fre	Wim	US	FC
1909	....	1	0	0	....	....	2rd	....	....
1912	....	1	0	0	....	....	....	....	....
1915	....	1	1	0	....	....	....	WC	....
1916	....	1	1	0	....	....	....	WD	....
1917	....	1	1	0	....	....	....	WD	....
1918	....	1	1	0	....	....	....	W	....
1919	....	1	0	0	....	....	....	SF	....
1920	....	2	1	0	....	....	SF	W	....
1921	2	2	1	0	....	....	QF	W	....
1922	....	1	1	0	....	....	....	W	....
1923	....	2	0	1	....	....	QF	F	....
1924	....	3	0	1	....	....	2rd	F	....
1925	5	1	0	0	....	....	....	SF	....
1926	4	2	1	0	....	....	SF	W	....
1927	4	2	0	0	....	....	3rd	QF	....
1928	....	2	0	0	....	2rd	....	SF	....
1929	....	2	0	0	....	....	3rd	SF	....
TOTALS		26	8	2	....	....	....	....	....

Competed as Molla Bjurstedt until 1919. Won Bronze in the 1912 Olympics. Doubles Titles: US (2).

• MARBLE, Alice   Alice Marble

Female. Born: Sept. 28, 1913. Plumas County, CA, United States.
Died: Dec. 13, 1990. Height: –. Weight: –. Plays: right.
Status: Turned Pro 1941. Highest Ranking: 1 (Dec. 1939). HOF: 1964

Year	Rk	TP	TW	TF	Aus	Fre	Wim	US	FC
1931	....	1	0	0	....	....	....	1rd	....
1932	....	1	0	0	....	....	....	3rd	....
1933	10	1	0	0	....	....	....	QF	....
1934	....	1	0	0	....	2rd	....	....	....
1936	4	1	1	0	....	....	....	W	....

Year	Rk	TP	TW	TF	Aus	Fre	Wim	US	FC
1937	7	2	0	0	....	....	SF	QF	....
1938	3	2	1	0	....	....	SF	W	....
1939	1	2	2	0	....	....	W	W	....
1940	....	1	1	0	....	....	....	W	....
TOTALS		**12**	**5**	**0**	....	....	....	....	....

Held number one world ranking 1 time during amateur era. Doubles Titles: Wim (2), US (4).

• MATHIEU, Simone
see PASSEMARD MATHIEU, Simone, page 815

• MCATEER, Myrtle
Myrtle McAteer

Female. Born: .
Height: –. Weight: –. Plays: –.
Status: Amateur. Highest Ranking: –.

Year	Rk	TP	TW	TF	Aus	Fre	Wim	US	FC
1899	....	1	0	0	....	....	....	QF	....
1900	....	1	1	0	....	....	....	WC	....
1901	....	1	0	1	....	....	....	CR	....
TOTALS		**3**	**1**	**1**	....	....	....	....	....

• MCGRATH, Viv
Vivian McGrath

Male. Born: Feb. 17, 1916. Mudgee, Australia.
Height: –. Weight: –. Plays: right.
Status: Amateur. Highest Ranking: 8 (Dec. 1935).

Year	Rk	TP	TW	TF	Aus	Fre	Wim	US	DC
1932	....	1	0	0	QF	....	....	....	....
1933	....	4	0	0	SF	2rd	3rd	4rd	4-4
1934	....	3	0	0	SF	4rd	1rd	....	4-4
1935	8	3	0	0	SF	QF	QF	....	1-4
1936	10	2	0	0	QF	....	4rd	....	1-0
1937	....	2	1	0	W	....	QF	....	1-0
1938	....	1	0	0	QF	....	....	....	....
1939	....	1	0	0	SF	....	....	....	....
1940	....	1	0	0	SF	....	....	....	....
TOTALS		**18**	**1**	**0**	....	....	....	....	....

• MCGREGOR, Ken
Kenneth Bruce McGregor

Male. Born: June 2, 1929. Adelaide, Australia.
Height: 6' 3". Weight: 180 lbs. Plays: right.
Status: Turned Pro 1953. Highest Ranking: 3 (Dec. 1952). HOF: 1999

Year	Rk	TP	TW	TF	Aus	Fre	Wim	US	DC
1948	....	1	0	0	3rd	....	....	....	....
1949	....	1	0	0	4rd	....	....	....	....
1950	8	4	0	1	F	4rd	4rd	1rd	3-2
1951	7	4	0	1	F	SF	F	4rd	....
1952	3	4	1	0	W	SF	QF	1rd	1-1
TOTALS		**14**	**1**	**2**	....	....	....	....	....

Doubles Titles: Aus (2), Fre (2), Wim (2), US (1).

• MCKANE, Kitty
see GODFREE, Kitty, page 805

• MCKINLEY, Chuck
see page 865

• MCLOUGHLIN, Maurice
Maurice "Red" McLoughlin

Male. Born: Jan. 7, 1890. Carson City, NV, United States.
Died: Dec. 10, 1957. Height: –. Weight: –. Plays: right.
Status: Amateur. Highest Ranking: 1 (Dec. 1914). HOF: 1957

Year	Rk	TP	TW	TF	Aus	Fre	Wim	US	DC
1909	....	1	0	0	....	....	....	2rd	....
1910	....	1	0	0	....	....	....	QF	....
1911	....	1	0	1	....	....	....	AC	....
1912	....	1	1	0	....	....	....	W	....

Year	Rk	TP	TW	TF	Aus	Fre	Wim	US	DC
1913	2	2	1	1	....	....	AC	W	....
1914	1	1	0	1	....	....	....	F	....
1915	....	1	0	1	....	....	....	F	....
1916	....	1	0	0	....	....	....	4rd	....
1919	....	1	0	0	....	....	....	QF	....
TOTALS		**10**	**2**	**4**	....	....	....	....	....

Held number one world ranking 1 time during amateur era. Doubles Titles: US (3).

• MCMILLAN, Frew
see page 865

• MCNEILL, Don
William Donald McNeil

Male. Born: Apr. 30, 1918. Chicksha, OK, United States.
Died: Nov. 25, 1996. Height: 5' 10". Weight: 155 lbs. Plays: right.
Status: Amateur. Highest Ranking: 7 (Dec. 1939). HOF: 1965

Year	Rk	TP	TW	TF	Aus	Fre	Wim	US	DC
1938	....	1	0	0	....	....	....	4rd	....
1939	7	3	1	0	....	W	2rd	QF	....
1940	....	1	1	0	....	....	....	W	....
1941	....	1	0	0	....	....	....	QF	....
1944	....	1	0	0	....	....	....	SF	....
1946	....	1	0	0	....	....	....	QF	....
1950	....	1	0	0	....	....	....	2rd	....
1952	....	1	0	0	....	....	....	1rd	....
TOTALS		**10**	**2**	**0**	....	....	....	....	....

Doubles Titles: Fre (1), US (1).

• MELVILLE, Kerry
see REID, Kerry, page 880

• METREVELI, Alexander
see page 867

• MOFFITT, Billie Jean
see KING, Billie Jean, page 855

• MOLESWORTH, Mall
Margaret "Mall" Mutch Molesworth

Female. Born: 1894. Brisbane, Australia.
Died: July 9, 1985. Height: –. Weight: –. Plays: right.
Status: Amateur. Highest Ranking: –.

Year	Rk	TP	TW	TF	Aus	Fre	Wim	US	FC
1922	....	1	1	0	W	....	....	....	....
1923	....	1	1	0	W	....	....	....	....
1924	....	1	0	0	QF	....	....	....	....
1928	....	1	0	0	QF	....	....	....	....
1929	....	1	0	0	QF	....	....	....	....
1930	....	1	0	0	QF	....	....	....	....
1933	....	1	0	0	QF	....	....	....	....
1934	....	3	0	1	F	3rd	1rd	....	....
TOTALS		**10**	**2**	**1**	....	....	....	....	....

Doubles Titles: Aus (3)

• MOODY, Helen
see WILLS MOODY, Helen, page 822

• MOON, Gar
Edgar Moon

Male. Born: Dec. 3, 1904. Forest Hill, Australia.
Died: May 26, 1976. Height: –. Weight: –. Plays: right.
Status: Amateur. Highest Ranking: –.

Year	Rk	TP	TW	TF	Aus	Fre	Wim	US	DC
1927	....	1	0	0	SF	....	....	....	....
1928	....	2	0	0	....	....	4rd	1rd	....
1929	....	1	0	0	SF	....	....	....	....
1930	....	3	1	0	W	QF	1rd	....	4-0
1931	....	1	0	0	QF	....	....	....	....
1934	....	1	0	0	QF	....	....	....	....

Year	Rk	TP	TW	TF	Aus	Fre	Wim	US	DC
1935	....	1	0	0	QF	....	....	....	....
1936	....	1	0	0	QF	....	....	....	....
TOTALS		**11**	**1**	**0**	....	....	....	....	....

Doubles Titles: Aus (1)

• MOORE, Bessie
Elizabeth "Bessie" Holmes Moore

Female. Born: Mar. 5, 1876. Brooklyn, NY, United States.
Died: Jan. 22, 1959. Height: –. Weight: –. Plays: right.
Status: Amateur. Highest Ranking: –. HOF: 1971

Year	Rk	TP	TW	TF	Aus	Fre	Wim	US	FC
1892	....	1	0	1	....	....	....	AC	....
1893	....	1	0	0	....	....	....	SF	....
1895	....	1	0	1	....	....	....	F	....
1896	....	1	1	0	....	....	....	WC	....
1897	....	1	0	1	....	....	....	CR	....
1901	....	1	1	0	....	....	....	WC	....
1902	....	1	0	1	....	....	....	CR	....
1903	....	1	1	0	....	....	....	WC	....
1904	....	1	0	1	....	....	....	CR	....
1905	....	1	1	0	....	....	....	WC	....
TOTALS		**10**	**4**	**5**	....	....	....	....	....

• MOROZOVA, Olga
see page 867

• MORTIMER, Angela
Florence Angela Margaret Mortimer Barrett

Female. Born: Apr. 21, 1932. Plymouth, Great Britain.
Height: 5' 6". Weight: –. Plays: –.
Status: Amateur. Highest Ranking: 1 (Dec. 1961). HOF: 1993

Year	Rk	TP	TW	TF	Aus	Fre	Wim	US	FC
1951	....	1	0	0	....	....	2rd	....	....
1952	....	2	0	0	....	....	3rd	QF	....
1953	8	3	0	0	....	3rd	QF	3rd	....
1954	9	1	0	0	....	....	QF	....	....
1955	4	2	1	0	....	W	2rd	....	....
1956	4	2	0	1	....	F	QF	....	....
1957	....	1	0	0	....	....	3rd	....	....
1958	7	2	1	1	W	....	F	....	....
1959	6	2	0	0	....	....	QF	2rd	....
1960	7	1	0	0	....	....	QF	....	....
1961	1	2	1	0	....	....	W	SF	....
1962	10	1	0	0	....	....	4rd	....	....
TOTALS		**20**	**3**	**2**	....	....	....	....	....

Held number one world ranking 1 time during amateur era. Doubles Titles: Wim (1).

• MULLOY, Gardnar
Gardnar Putnam Mulloy

Male. Born: Nov. 22, 1913. Washington, DC, United States.
Height: 6'. Weight: –. Plays: right.
Status: Amateur. Highest Ranking: 7 (Dec. 1952). HOF: 1972

Year	Rk	TP	TW	TF	Aus	Fre	Wim	US	DC
1936	....	1	0	0	....	....	....	2rd	....
1937	....	1	0	0	....	....	....	2rd	....
1938	....	1	0	0	....	....	....	3rd	....
1939	....	1	0	0	....	....	....	4rd	....
1940	....	1	0	0	....	....	....	1rd	....
1941	....	1	0	0	....	....	....	3rd	....
1942	....	1	0	0	....	....	....	QF	....
1945	....	1	0	0	....	....	....	2rd	....
1946	8	1	0	0	....	....	....	SF	1-1
1947	10	2	0	0	SF	....	....	QF	....
1948	....	2	0	0	....	....	SF	4rd	....
1949	9	2	0	0	....	....	1rd	QF	....
1950	....	2	0	0	....	....	QF	SF	....
1951	....	3	0	0	....	3rd	3rd	QF	....

Year	Rk	TP	TW	TF	Aus	Fre	Wim	US	DC
1952	7	3	0	1	....	QF	4rd	F	....
1953	....	3	0	0	....	QF	4rd	QF	1-0
1954	....	3	0	0	....	QF	4rd	4rd	....
1955	....	2	0	0	....	....	1rd	2rd	....
1956	....	2	0	0	....	....	1rd	2rd	....
1957	....	2	0	0	....	....	3rd	2rd	....
1958	....	2	0	0	....	....	4rd	1rd	....
1959	....	2	0	0	....	....	4rd	2rd	....
1960	....	1	0	0	....	....	3rd	....	....
1961	....	2	0	0	....	1rd	2rd	....	....
1962	....	1	0	0	....	....	1rd	....	....
1963	....	1	0	0	....	....	1rd	....	....
1965	....	1	0	0	....	....	2rd	....	....
1966	....	1	0	0	....	....	1rd	....	....
TOTALS		**46**	**0**	**1**	....	....	....	....	....

Doubles Titles: Wim (1), US (4)

• MURRAY, Lindley
Robert Lindley Murray

Male. Born: Nov. 3, 1892. San Francisco, CA, United States.
Died: Jan. 17, 1970. Height: 6' 2". Weight: –. Plays: left.
Status: Amateur. Highest Ranking: –. HOF: 1958

Year	Rk	TP	TW	TF	Aus	Fre	Wim	US	DC
1916	....	1	0	0	....	....	....	SF	....
1917	....	1	1	0	....	....	....	W	....
1918	....	1	1	0	....	....	....	W	....
1919	....	1	0	0	....	....	....	QF	....
TOTALS		**4**	**2**	**0**	....	....	....	....	....

• NASTASE, Ilie
see page 869

• NEWCOMBE, John
see page 870

• NIESSEN, Helga
see page 870

• NUTHALL, Betty
Betty Kay Nuthall Shoemaker

Female. Born: May 23, 1911. Surbiton, Great Britain.
Died: Nov. 8, 1983. Height: –. Weight: –. Plays: right.
Status: Amateur. Highest Ranking: 4 (Dec. 1929). HOF: 1977

Year	Rk	TP	TW	TF	Aus	Fre	Wim	US	FC
1926	....	1	0	0	....	....	2rd	....	....
1927	....	2	0	1	....	....	QF	F	....
1928	....	2	0	0	....	2rd	1rd	....	....
1929	4	2	0	0	....	....	3rd	QF	....
1930	9	2	1	0	....	....	QF	W	....
1931	5	2	0	1	....	F	....	SF	....
1932	....	2	0	0	....	SF	QF	....	....
1933	8	3	0	0	....	SF	4rd	SF	....
1934	....	3	0	0	....	3rd	1rd	2rd	....
1936	....	1	0	0	....	....	2rd	....	....
1937	....	1	0	0	....	....	4rd	....	....
1938	....	1	0	0	....	....	4rd	....	....
1939	....	2	0	0	....	....	1rd	3rd	....
1946	....	1	0	0	....	....	4rd	....	....
TOTALS		**25**	**1**	**2**	....	....	....	....	....

Doubles Titles: Fre (1), US (3)

• O'HARA WOOD, Arthur   Dr. Arthur Holroyd O'Hara Wood

Male. Born: 1890. Melbourne, Australia.
Died: Oct. 6, 1918. Height: –. Weight: –. Plays: right.
Status: Amateur. Highest Ranking: –.

Year	Rk	TP	TW	TF	Aus	Fre	Wim	US	DC
1911	....	1	0	0	SF	....	....	....	....
1914	....	1	1	0	W	....	....	....	....
TOTALS		**2**	**1**	**0**	....	....	....	....	....

• O'HARA WOOD, Pat   Patrick O'Hara Wood

Male. Born: Apr. 30, 1891. Melbourne, Australia.
Died: Dec. 3, 1961. Height: –. Weight: –. Plays: right.
Status: Amateur. Highest Ranking: 7 (Dec. 1922).

Year	Rk	TP	TW	TF	Aus	Fre	Wim	US	DC
1919	....	2	0	0	QF	....	QF	....	....
1920	....	1	1	0	W	....	....	....	....
1922	7	2	0	0	....	....	QF	4rd	....
1923	....	1	1	0	W	....	....	....	....
1924	....	1	0	0	....	....	....	3rd	....
1925	....	1	0	0	SF	....	....	....	....
1926	....	1	0	0	QF	....	....	....	....
1929	....	1	0	0	QF	....	....	....	....
TOTALS		**10**	**2**	**0**	....	....	....	....	....

Doubles Titles: Aus (4), Wim (1)

• OKKER, Tom   see page 872

• OLMEDO, Alex   see page 873

• ORANTES, Manolo   see page 873

• OSBORNE DUPONT, Margaret   Margaret Evelyn Osborne duPont

Female. Born: Mar. 4, 1918. Joseph, OR, United States.
Height: 5' 5". Weight: 145 lbs. Plays: right.
Status: Amateur. Highest Ranking: 1 (Dec. 1947). HOF: 1967

Year	Rk	TP	TW	TF	Aus	Fre	Wim	US	FC
1936	....	1	0	0	....	....	....	2rd	....
1938	....	1	0	0	....	....	....	2rd	....
1940	....	1	0	0	....	....	....	3rd	....
1941	....	1	0	0	....	....	....	SF	....
1942	....	1	0	0	....	....	....	SF	....
1943	....	1	0	0	....	....	....	QF	....
1944	....	1	0	1	....	....	....	F	....
1945	....	1	0	0	....	....	....	QF	....
1946	2	3	1	0	....	W	SF	QF	....
1947	1	3	1	1	....	SF	W	F	....
1948	1	2	1	0	....	....	SF	W	....
1949	1	3	2	1	....	W	F	W	....
1950	1	3	2	0	....	QF	W	W	....
1951	....	2	0	0	....	SF	QF	....	....
1953	5	1	0	0	....	....	....	QF	....
1954	5	2	0	0	....	....	QF	3rd	....
1956	10	1	0	0	....	....	....	QF	....
1958	....	2	0	0	....	....	QF	3rd	....
1960	....	1	0	0	....	....	....	1rd	....
1962	....	1	0	0	....	....	1rd	....	....
TOTALS		**32**	**7**	**3**	....	....	....	....	....

Held number one world ranking 4 times during amateur era. Competed as Margaret Osborne until 1947. Doubles Titles: Fre (2), Wim (5), US (13).

• OSUNA, Rafe   see page 874

• PAILS, Dinny   Denis Robert Pails

Male. Born: Mar. 4, 1921. Nottingham, Great Britain.
Height: –. Weight: –. Plays: right.
Status: Turned Pro 1947. Highest Ranking: –.

Year	Rk	TP	TW	TF	Aus	Fre	Wim	US	DC
1940	....	1	0	0	QF	....	....	....	....
1946	....	2	0	1	F	....	QF	....	0-2
1947	....	3	1	0	W	....	SF	4rd	3-3
TOTALS		**6**	**1**	**1**	....	....	....	....	....

Represented Australia in the Davis Cup (1946-1947)

• PALFREY COOKE, Sarah

    Sarah Hammond Palfrey Fabyan Cooke Danzig

Female. Born: Sept. 18, 1912. Sharon, MA, United States.
Died: Feb. 27, 1996. Height: 5' 4". Weight: 115 lbs. Plays: right.
Status: Turned Pro 1947. Highest Ranking: 4 (Dec. 1934). HOF: 1963

Year	Rk	TP	TW	TF	Aus	Fre	Wim	US	FC
1928	....	1	0	0	....	....	....	1rd	....
1929	....	1	0	0	....	....	....	3rd	....
1930	....	2	0	0	....	....	2rd	3rd	....
1931	....	1	0	0	....	....	....	3rd	....
1932	....	2	0	0	....	....	4rd	2rd	....
1933	7	1	0	0	....	....	....	QF	....
1934	4	3	0	1	....	3rd	QF	F	....
1935	5	1	0	1	....	....	....	F	....
1936	9	1	0	0	....	....	....	1rd	....
1937	....	1	0	0	....	....	....	1rd	....
1938	7	2	0	0	....	....	QF	SF	....
1939	6	2	0	0	....	....	SF	QF	....
1940	....	1	0	0	....	....	....	3rd	....
1941	....	1	1	0	....	....	....	W	....
1943	....	1	0	0	....	....	....	QF	....
1945	....	1	1	0	....	....	....	W	....
TOTALS		**22**	**2**	**2**	....	....	....	....	....

Competed as Sarah Palfrey Fabyan until 1941. Doubles Titles: Wim (2), US (9).

• PARKE, Jim   James Cecil Parke

Male. Born: July 26, 1881. Clones County, Ireland.
Died: Feb. 27, 1946. Height: –. Weight: –. Plays: right.
Status: Amateur. Highest Ranking: 4 (Dec. 1913).

Year	Rk	TP	TW	TF	Aus	Fre	Wim	US	DC
1908	....	0	0	0	....	....	....	....	0-2
1909	....	1	0	0	....	....	2rd	....	0-2
1910	....	1	0	0	....	....	SF	....	....
1911	....	1	0	0	....	....	1rd	....	....
1912	....	2	1	0	W	....	3rd	....	2-0
1913	4	1	0	0	....	....	SF	....	2-0
1914	6	1	0	0	....	....	QF	....	4-0
1920	4	1	0	0	....	....	3rd	....	0-2
TOTALS		**8**	**1**	**0**	....	....	....	....	....

Represented Great Britian in the Davis Cup (1908-1920)

• PARKER, Ernie   Ernie Parker

Male. Born: Australia.
Died: May 2, 1918. Height: –. Weight: –. Plays: right.
Status: Amateur. Highest Ranking: –.

Year	Rk	TP	TW	TF	Aus	Fre	Wim	US	DC
1909	....	1	0	1	F	....	....	....	....
1913	....	1	1	0	W	....	....	....	....
TOTALS		**2**	**1**	**1**	....	....	....	....	....

• PARKER, Frank   see page 874

• PARUN, Onny see page 875

• PASSEMARD MATHIEU, Simone
Simone Passemard Mathieu

Female. Born: Jan. 11, 1908. Neuilly-sur-Seine, France.
Died: Jan. 7, 1980. Height: –. Weight: –. Plays: right.
Status: Amateur. Highest Ranking: 3 (Dec. 1931).

Year	Rk	TP	TW	TF	Aus	Fre	Wim	US	FC
1925	....	1	0	0	....	QF	....	....	....
1926	....	1	0	0	....	QF	....	....	....
1927	....	2	0	0	....	3rd	2rd	....	....
1929	6	2	0	0	....	SF	3rd	....	....
1930	5	2	0	0	....	QF	SF	....	....
1931	3	2	0	0	....	QF	SF	....	....
1932	3	2	0	1	....	F	SF	....	....
1933	6	2	0	1	....	F	QF	....	....
1934	6	2	0	0	....	SF	SF	....	....
1935	8	2	0	1	....	F	QF	....	....
1936	5	2	0	1	....	F	QF	....	....
1937	5	2	0	1	....	F	QF	....	....
1938	5	3	1	0	....	W	QF	QF	....
1939	5	3	1	0	....	W	QF	1rd	....
1946	....	1	0	0	....	....	1rd	....	....
TOTALS		**29**	**2**	**5**	....	....	....	....	....

Competed as Simone Passemard until 1925. Doubles Titles: Wim (3), Fre (6).

• PATTERSON, Gerald
Gerald Leighton Patterson

Male. Born: Dec. 17, 1895. Melbourne, Australia.
Died: June 13, 1967. Height: 6'. Weight: –. Plays: right.
Status: Amateur. Highest Ranking: 1 (Dec. 1919). HOF: 1989

Year	Rk	TP	TW	TF	Aus	Fre	Wim	US	DC
1914	....	1	0	1	F	....	....	....	....
1919	1	2	1	0	....	....	WC	4rd	....
1920	10	1	0	1	....	....	CR	....	2-2
1922	3	3	1	1	F	....	W	SF	7-2
1924	8	1	0	0	....	....	....	SF	7-3
1925	7	1	0	1	F	....	....	....	4-2
1927	....	1	1	0	W	....	....	....	....
1928	....	3	0	0	QF	3rd	4rd	....	1-1
TOTALS		**13**	**3**	**4**	....	....	....	....	....

Held number one world ranking 1 time during amateur era. Doubles Titles: Aus (4), US (1).

• PATTY, Budge
John Edward "Budge" Patty

Male. Born: Feb. 11, 1924. Fort Smith, AK, United States.
Height: 6' 1". Weight: –. Plays: right.
Status: Amateur. Highest Ranking: 1 (Dec. 1950). HOF: 1977

Year	Rk	TP	TW	TF	Aus	Fre	Wim	US	DC
1941	....	1	0	0	....	....	....	2rd	....
1946	....	2	0	0	....	QF	....	4rd	....
1947	8	2	0	0	....	4rd	SF	....	....
1948	....	3	0	0	....	SF	QF	3rd	....
1949	8	2	0	1	....	F	3rd	....	....
1950	1	3	2	0	....	W	W	1rd	....
1951	....	3	0	0	....	4rd	2rd	QF	1-0
1952	....	2	0	0	....	QF	4rd	....	....
1953	8	3	0	0	....	4rd	3rd	QF	....
1954	8	2	0	0	....	SF	SF	....	....
1955	6	2	0	0	....	QF	SF	....	....
1956	10	2	0	0	....	4rd	2rd	....	....
1957	8	3	0	0	....	4rd	4rd	QF	....
1958	....	3	0	0	....	3rd	4rd	1rd	....
1959	....	2	0	0	....	3rd	1rd	....	....
1960	....	2	0	0	....	2rd	1rd	....	....
TOTALS		**37**	**2**	**1**	....	....	....	....	....

Held number one world ranking 1 time during amateur era. Doubles Titles: Wim (1).

• PELL, Teddy
Theodore Roosevelt Pell

Male. Born: May 12, 1879. New York, NY, United States.
Died: Aug. 18, 1967. Height: 6'. Weight: –. Plays: right.
Status: Amateur. Highest Ranking: –. HOF: 1966

Year	Rk	TP	TW	TF	Aus	Fre	Wim	US	DC
1902	....	1	0	0	....	....	....	2rd	....
1907	....	1	0	0	....	....	....	1rd	....
1908	....	1	0	0	....	....	....	2rd	....
1909	....	1	0	0	....	....	....	4rd	....
1911	....	1	0	0	....	....	....	1rd	....
1914	....	1	0	0	....	....	....	4rd	....
1915	....	1	0	0	....	....	....	SF	....
1916	....	1	0	0	....	....	....	3rd	....
1917	....	1	0	0	....	....	....	2rd	....
1918	....	1	0	0	....	....	....	2rd	....
1919	....	1	0	0	....	....	....	4rd	....
1920	....	1	0	0	....	....	....	1rd	....
1924	....	1	0	0	....	....	....	2rd	....
TOTALS		**13**	**0**	**0**	....	....	....	....	....

• PENROSE, Beryl
Beryl Penrose Collier

Female. Born: Dec. 22, 1930. Sydney, Australia.
Height: –. Weight: –. Plays: right.
Status: Amateur. Highest Ranking: 8 (Dec. 1955).

Year	Rk	TP	TW	TF	Aus	Fre	Wim	US	FC
1950	....	1	0	0	3rd	....	....	....	....
1951	....	2	0	0	QF	....	2rd	....	....
1952	....	3	0	0	QF	3rd	3rd	....	....
1953	....	1	0	0	QF	....	....	....	....
1954	....	1	0	0	3rd	....	....	....	....
1955	8	3	1	0	W	QF	QF	....	....
1956	....	1	0	0	QF	....	....	....	....
1957	....	1	0	0	SF	....	....	....	....
TOTALS		**13**	**1**	**0**	....	....	....	....	....

Doubles Titles: Aus (2), Fre (2), Wim (2), US (1)

• PERRY, Fred
Frederick John Perry

Male. Born: May 18, 1909. Stockport, Great Britain.
Died: Feb. 2, 1995. Height: –. Weight: –. Plays: right.
Status: Turned Pro 1938. Highest Ranking: 1 (Dec. 1934). HOF: 1975

Year	Rk	TP	TW	TF	Aus	Fre	Wim	US	DC
1929	....	1	0	0	....	....	3rd	....	....
1930	....	2	0	0	....	....	4rd	4rd	....
1931	4	3	0	0	....	4rd	SF	SF	7-2
1932	7	3	0	0	....	QF	QF	4rd	5-1
1933	2	3	1	0	....	QF	2rd	W	12-1
1934	1	4	3	0	W	QF	W	W	2-0
1935	1	4	2	1	F	W	W	SF	2-0
1936	1	3	2	1	....	F	W	W	2-0
TOTALS		**23**	**8**	**2**	....	....	....	....	....

Held number one world ranking 3 times during amateur era. Doubles Titles: Aus (1), Fre (1).

• PETRA, Yvon
Yvon Francois Marie Petra

Male. Born: Mar. 8, 1916. Cholon, Viet Nam.
Height: 6' 5". Weight: –. Plays: right.
Status: Amateur. Highest Ranking: 4 (Dec. 1946).

Year	Rk	TP	TW	TF	Aus	Fre	Wim	US	DC
1936	....	2	0	0	....	1rd	....	4rd	....
1937	....	3	0	0	....	QF	1rd	4rd	1-0
1938	....	2	0	0	....	1rd	....	4rd	5-1
1939	....	3	0	0	....	....	....	....	0-1
1946	4	1	0	0	....	QF	W	2rd	5-1
1947	....	2	0	0	....	QF	4rd	....	....
TOTALS		**13**	**0**	**0**	....	....	....	....	....

Represented France in the Davis Cup (1937-1946)

• PIETRANGELI, Nicky   see page 877

• PILIC, Nikki   see page 877

• PIM, Joshua
Dr. Joshua Pim

Male. Born: May 20, 1869. Bray, Ireland.
Died: May 25, 1942. Height: –. Weight: –. Plays: –.
Status: Amateur. Highest Ranking: –.

Year	Rk	TP	TW	TF	Aus	Fre	Wim	US	DC
1890	....	1	0	0	....	....	SF	....	....
1891	....	1	0	1	....	....	F	....	....
1892	....	1	0	1	....	....	AC	....	....
1893	....	1	1	0	....	....	WC	....	....
1894	....	1	1	0	....	....	WD	....	....
1902	....	1	0	0	....	....	....	4rd	0-2
TOTALS		**6**	**2**	**2**	....	....	....	....	....

Represented Great Britian in the Davis Cup (1902)

• QUIST, Adrian
Adrian Karl Quist

Male. Born: Aug. 14, 1913. Medindia, Australia.
Died: Nov. 17, 1991. Height: –. Weight: –. Plays: –.
Status: Amateur. Highest Ranking: 3 (Dec. 1939). HOF: 1984

Year	Rk	TP	TW	TF	Aus	Fre	Wim	US	DC
1933	....	4	0	0	QF	2rd	2rd	QF	1-0
1934	....	3	0	0	SF	3rd	4rd	....	....
1935	....	3	0	0	SF	4rd	3rd	....	....
1936	4	2	1	0	W	....	QF	....	2-3
1937	....	1	0	0	QF	....	....	....	2-0
1938	6	2	0	0	SF	....	....	4rd	6-2
1939	3	2	0	1	F	....	....	4rd	9-1
1940	....	1	1	0	W	....	....	....	....
1946	....	1	0	0	SF	....	....	....	....
1947	....	1	0	0	QF	....	....	....	....
1948	10	2	1	0	W	....	....	4rd	4-4
1949	....	1	0	0	QF	....	....	....	....
1950	....	2	0	0	....	3rd	4rd	....	....
1951	....	1	0	0	QF	....	....	....	....
1952	....	1	0	0	4rd	....	....	....	....
1953	....	1	0	0	4rd	....	....	....	....
1955	....	1	0	0	....	....	3rd	....	....
TOTALS		**29**	**3**	**1**	....	....	....	....	....

Doubles Titles: Aus (10), Wim (1), Fre (2), US (1)

• RALSTON, Denny   see page 879

• REID, Kerry   see page 880

• REITANO, Mary
Mary Carter Reitano

Female. Born: Nov. 29, 1934. Sydney, Australia.
Height: 5' 2". Weight: –. Plays: right.
Status: Amateur. Highest Ranking: –.

Year	Rk	TP	TW	TF	Aus	Fre	Wim	US	FC
1954	....	1	0	0	SF	....	....	....	....
1955	....	2	0	0	SF	....	4rd	....	....
1956	....	1	1	0	W	....	....	....	....
1957	....	1	0	0	QF	....	....	....	....
1958	....	2	0	0	SF	....	2rd	....	....
1959	....	3	1	0	W	QF	3rd	....	....
1960	....	1	0	0	SF	....	....	....	....
1961	....	3	0	0	SF	4rd	2rd	....	....
1962	....	1	0	0	SF	....	....	....	....
TOTALS		**15**	**2**	**0**	....	....	....	....	....

• RENSHAW, Ernest
James Ernest Renshaw

Male. Born: Jan. 3, 1861. Leamington, Great Britain.
Died: Sept. 2, 1899. Height: 5' 10". Weight: –. Plays: right.
Status: Amateur. Highest Ranking: –. HOF: 1983

Year	Rk	TP	TW	TF	Aus	Fre	Wim	US	DC
1879	....	1	0	0	....	....	1rd	....	....
1881	....	1	0	0	....	....	3rd	....	....
1882	....	1	0	1	....	....	AC	....	....
1883	....	1	0	1	....	....	AC	....	....
1884	....	1	0	0	....	....	SF	....	....
1885	....	1	0	1	....	....	F	....	....
1886	....	1	0	0	....	....	QF	....	....
1887	....	1	0	1	....	....	F	....	....
1888	....	1	1	0	....	....	WC	....	....
1889	....	1	0	1	....	....	CR	....	....
1890	....	1	0	0	....	....	1rd	....	....
1891	....	1	0	0	....	....	SF	....	....
1893	....	1	0	0	....	....	2rd	....	....
TOTALS		**13**	**1**	**5**	....	....	....	....	....

• RENSHAW, Willie
William Charles Renshaw

Male. Born: Jan. 3, 1861. Leamington, Great Britain.
Died: Aug. 12, 1904. Height: 5' 10". Weight: –. Plays: right.
Status: Amateur. Highest Ranking: –. HOF: 1983

Year	Rk	TP	TW	TF	Aus	Fre	Wim	US	DC
1879	....	1	0	0	....	....	1rd	....	....
1880	....	1	0	0	....	....	3rd	....	....
1881	....	1	1	0	....	....	WC	....	....
1882	....	1	1	0	....	....	WD	....	....
1883	....	1	1	0	....	....	WD	....	....
1884	....	1	1	0	....	....	WD	....	....
1885	....	1	1	0	....	....	WD	....	....
1886	....	1	1	0	....	....	WD	....	....
1888	....	1	0	0	....	....	QF	....	....
1889	....	1	1	0	....	....	WC	....	....
1890	....	1	0	1	....	....	CR	....	....
1893	....	1	0	0	....	....	1rd	....	....
TOTALS		**12**	**7**	**1**	....	....	....	....	....

• RICE, Horrie
Horace M. Rice

Male. Born: Sept. 5, 1873. Australia.
Height: –. Weight: –. Plays: left.
Status: Amateur. Highest Ranking: –.

Year	Rk	TP	TW	TF	Aus	Fre	Wim	US	DC
1907	....	1	1	0	W	....	....	....	....
1910	....	1	0	0	F	....	....	....	....

Year	Rk	TP	TW	TF	Aus	Fre	Wim	US	DC
1911	....	1	0	1	F	....	....	....	....
1913	....	1	0	0	....	....	2rd	....	0-2
1915	....	1	0	1	F	....	....	....	....
1920	....	1	0	0	SF	....	....	....	....
1923	....	1	0	0	SF	....	....	....	....
TOTALS		**7**	**1**	**2**	....	....	....	....	....

Doubles Titles: Aus (1)

• RICE, Lena

Helena Bertha Grace "Lena" Rice

Female. Born: June 21, 1866. Newinn, Ireland.
Died: June 21, 1907. Height: –. Weight: –. Plays: right.
Status: Amateur. Highest Ranking: –.

Year	Rk	TP	TW	TF	Aus	Fre	Wim	US	FC
1889	....	1	0	1	....	....	F	....	....
1890	....	1	1	0	....	....	WC	....	....
TOTALS		**2**	**1**	**1**	....	....	....	....	....

• RICHARDS, Vinnie

Vincent Richards

Male. Born: Mar. 20, 1903. Yonkers, NY, United States.
Died: Sept. 28, 1959. Height: 5' 10". Weight: –. Plays: right.
Status: Turned Pro 1926. Highest Ranking: 2 (Dec. 1924). HOF: 1961

Year	Rk	TP	TW	TF	Aus	Fre	Wim	US	DC
1918	....	1	0	0	....	....	....	3rd	....
1919	....	1	0	0	....	....	....	2rd	....
1920	....	1	0	0	....	....	....	4rd	....
1921	3	1	0	0	....	....	....	3rd	....
1922	4	1	0	0	....	....	....	SF	....
1923	6	2	0	0	....	....	5rd	3rd	....
1924	2	3	1	0	....	....	QF	SF	2-0
1925	3	1	0	0	....	....	....	SF	....
1926	6	3	0	0	....	SF	2rd	SF	....
TOTALS		**14**	**1**	**0**	....	....	....	....	....

Won Gold in the 1924 Olympics. Doubles Titles: Fre (2), Wim (2), US (5).

• RICHEY, Nancy   see page 880

• RIGGS, Bobby

Robert Larimore Riggs

Male. Born: Feb. 25, 1918. Los Angeles, CA, United States.
Died: Oct. 10, 1995. Height: –. Weight: –. Plays: right.
Status: Turned Pro 1942. Highest Ranking: 1 (Dec. 1939). HOF: 1967

Year	Rk	TP	TW	TF	Aus	Fre	Wim	US	DC
1936	....	1	0	0	....	....	....	4rd	....
1937	5	1	0	0	....	....	....	SF	....
1938	4	1	0	0	....	....	....	4rd	1-1
1939	1	3	2	1	....	F	W	W	1-1
1940	....	1	0	1	....	....	....	F	....
1941	....	1	1	0	....	....	....	W	....
TOTALS		**8**	**3**	**2**	....	....	....	....	....

Held number one world ranking 1 time during amateur era. Doubles Titles: Wim (1).

• ROBB, Muriel

Muriel Robb

Female. Born: May 13, 1878. Newcastle upon Tyne, Great Britain.
Died: Feb. 12, 1907. Height: –. Weight: –. Plays: right.
Status: Amateur. Highest Ranking: –.

Year	Rk	TP	TW	TF	Aus	Fre	Wim	US	FC
1899	....	1	0	0	....	....	QF	....	....
1900	....	1	0	0	....	....	QF	....	....
1901	....	1	0	0	....	....	QF	....	....
1902	....	1	1	0	....	....	WC	....	....
TOTALS		**4**	**1**	**0**	....	....	....	....	....

• ROCHE, Tony   see page 881

• ROOSEVELT, Ellen

Ellen Crosby Roosevelt Crosby

Female. Born: 8/?/1868. Hyde Park, NY, United States.
Died: Sept. 26, 1954. Height: –. Weight: –. Plays: right.
Status: Amateur. Highest Ranking: –. HOF: 1975

Year	Rk	TP	TW	TF	Aus	Fre	Wim	US	FC
1888	....	1	0	0	....	....	....	QF	....
1890	....	1	1	0	....	....	....	WC	....
1891	....	1	0	1	....	....	....	CR	....
TOTALS		**3**	**1**	**1**	....	....	....	....	....

Doubles Titles: US (1)

• ROSE, Merv   see page 881

• ROSEWALL, Ken   see page 882

• ROUND, Dorothy

Dorothy Edith Round Little

Female. Born: July 13, 1908. Dudley, Great Britain.
Died: Nov. 12, 1982. Height: –. Weight: –. Plays: right.
Status: Amateur. Highest Ranking: 1 (Dec. 1934). HOF: 1986

Year	Rk	TP	TW	TF	Aus	Fre	Wim	US	FC
1928	....	1	0	0	....	....	1rd	....	....
1929	....	1	0	0	....	....	2rd	....	....
1930	....	1	0	0	....	....	3rd	....	....
1931	....	1	0	0	....	....	....	3rd	....
1932	....	1	0	0	....	....	QF	....	....
1933	3	2	0	1	....	....	F	SF	....
1934	1	1	1	0	....	....	W	....	....
1935	6	2	1	0	W	....	QF	....	....
1936	3	1	0	0	....	....	QF	....	....
1937	2	1	1	0	....	....	W	....	....
1939	....	1	0	0	....	....	4rd	....	....
TOTALS		**13**	**3**	**1**	....	....	....	....	....

Held number one world ranking 1 time during amateur era. Competed as Dorothy Round until 1937.

• RYAN, Elizabeth

Elizabeth Montague "Bunny" Ryan

Female. Born: Feb. 5, 1892. Anaheim, CA, United States.
Died: July 8, 1979. Height: 5' 5". Weight: 145 lbs. Plays: right.
Status: Amateur. Highest Ranking: 4 (Dec. 1921). HOF: 1972

Year	Rk	TP	TW	TF	Aus	Fre	Wim	US	FC
1912	....	1	0	0	....	....	QF	....	....
1913	....	1	0	0	....	....	1rd	....	....
1914	....	1	0	1	....	....	F	....	....
1919	....	1	0	0	....	....	SF	....	....
1920	....	1	0	1	....	....	F	....	....
1921	4	1	0	1	....	....	AC	....	....
1922	....	1	0	0	....	....	QF	....	....
1923	....	1	0	0	....	....	SF	....	....
1924	....	1	0	0	....	....	QF	....	....
1925	4	2	0	0	....	....	2rd	QF	....
1926	5	3	0	1	....	QF	3rd	F	....
1927	3	1	0	0	....	....	SF	....	....
1928	6	1	0	0	....	....	SF	....	....
1929	....	1	0	0	....	....	3rd	....	....
1930	4	2	0	1	....	QF	F	....	....
1931	....	1	0	0	....	QF	....	....	....
1932	....	2	0	0	....	1rd	1rd	....	....
1933	....	1	0	0	....	....	1rd	....	....
1934	....	2	0	0	....	....	1rd	QF	....
TOTALS		**25**	**0**	**5**	....	....	....	....	....

Doubles Titles: Fre (4), Wim (12), US (1)

• SANTANA, Manolo   see page 885

• SAVITT, Dick

Richard Savitt

Male. Born: Mar. 4, 1927. Bayonne, NJ, United States.
Height: 6' 3". Weight: 180 lbs. Plays: right.
Status: Amateur. Highest Ranking: 2 (Dec. 1951). HOF: 1976

Year	Rk	TP	TW	TF	Aus	Fre	Wim	US	DC
1946	....	1	0	0	....	....	....	3rd	....
1947	....	1	0	0	....	....	....	2rd	....
1948	....	1	0	0	....	....	....	3rd	....
1950	....	1	0	0	....	....	....	SF	....
1951	2	4	2	0	W	QF	W	SF	3-0
1952	9	3	0	0	SF	....	QF	QF	....
1956	8	1	0	0	....	....	....	QF	....
1957	10	1	0	0	....	....	....	4rd	....
1958	....	1	0	0	....	....	....	QF	....
1959	....	1	0	0	....	....	....	3rd	....
TOTALS		**15**	**2**	**0**	....	....	....	....	....

• SCHROEDER, Ted

Frederick Randolph "Ted" Schroeder

Male. Born: July 20, 1921. Newark, NY, United States.
Height: –. Weight: –. Plays: –.
Status: Amateur. Highest Ranking: 2 (Dec. 1946). HOF: 1966

Year	Rk	TP	TW	TF	Aus	Fre	Wim	US	DC
1939	....	1	0	0	....	....	....	3rd	....
1940	....	1	0	0	....	....	....	QF	....
1941	....	1	0	0	....	....	....	QF	....
1942	....	1	1	0	....	....	....	W	....
1946	2	0	0	0	....	....	....	....	2-0
1947	2	0	0	0	....	....	....	....	2-0
1948	2	0	0	0	....	....	....	....	2-0
1949	2	2	1	1	....	....	W	F	2-0
1950	6	0	0	0	....	....	....	....	0-2
1951	6	0	0	0	....	....	....	....	3-1
TOTALS		**6**	**2**	**1**	....	....	....	....	....

Doubles Titles: US (3)

• SCRIVEN, Margaret

Peggy Scriven Croft

Female. Born: Aug. 18, 1912. Leeds, Great Britain.
Height: –. Weight: –. Plays: left.
Status: Amateur. Highest Ranking: 5 (Dec. 1933).

Year	Rk	TP	TW	TF	Aus	Fre	Wim	US	FC
1930	....	1	0	0	....	....	S	....	....
1931	....	1	0	0	....	....	QF	....	....
1932	....	1	0	0	....	....	2rd	....	....
1933	5	3	1	0	....	W	QF	1rd	....
1934	5	2	1	0	....	W	QF	....	....
1935	10	2	0	0	....	SF	3rd	....	....
1936	....	1	0	0	....	2rd	....	....	....
1937	....	2	0	0	....	QF	QF	....	....
1938	....	1	0	0	....	....	4rd	....	....
1939	....	1	0	0	....	....	4rd	....	....
TOTALS		**15**	**2**	**0**	....	....	....	....	....

• SEARS, Dick

Richard Dudley Sears

Male. Born: Aug. 16, 1861. Boston, MA, United States.
Died: Apr. 8, 1943. Height: 5' 9". Weight: 150 lbs. Plays: right.
Status: Amateur. Highest Ranking: –. HOF: 1955

Year	Rk	TP	TW	TF	Aus	Fre	Wim	US	DC
1881	....	1	1	0	....	....	....	W	....
1882	....	1	1	0	....	....	....	W	....
1883	....	1	1	0	....	....	....	W	....
1884	....	1	1	0	....	....	....	WD	....
1885	....	1	1	0	....	....	....	WD	....

Year	Rk	TP	TW	TF	Aus	Fre	Wim	US	DC
1886	....	1	1	0	....	....	....	WD	....
1887	....	1	1	0	....	....	....	WD	....
TOTALS		**7**	**7**	**0**	....	....	....	....	....

• SEARS, Eleo

Eleonora Randolph Sears

Female. Born: Sept. 28, 1881. Boston, MA, United States.
Died: Mar. 16, 1968. Height: –. Weight: –. Plays: right.
Status: Amateur. Highest Ranking: –. HOF: 1968

Year	Rk	TP	TW	TF	Aus	Fre	Wim	US	FC
1911	....	1	0	1	....	....	....	F	....
1912	....	1	0	1	....	....	....	F	....
1915	....	1	0	0	....	....	....	QF	....
1916	....	1	0	1	....	....	....	F	....
1917	....	1	0	0	....	....	....	SF	....
1918	....	1	0	0	....	....	....	QF	....
1919	....	1	0	0	....	....	....	3rd	....
1921	....	1	0	0	....	....	....	2rd	....
1922	....	1	0	0	....	....	1rd	....	....
1923	....	2	0	0	....	....	2rd	1rd	....
1924	....	2	0	0	....	....	1rd	3rd	....
1925	....	1	0	0	....	....	1rd	....	....
1926	....	1	0	0	....	....	....	2rd	....
1928	....	1	0	0	....	....	....	2rd	....
1929	....	1	0	0	....	....	....	1rd	....
TOTALS		**17**	**0**	**3**	....	....	....	....	....

• SEARS, Evelyn

Evelyn Georgianna Sears

Female. Born: Mar. 9, 1875. Waltham, MA, United States.
Died: Nov. 10, 1966. Height: –. Weight: –. Plays: left.
Status: Amateur. Highest Ranking: –.

Year	Rk	TP	TW	TF	Aus	Fre	Wim	US	FC
1907	....	1	1	0	....	....	....	WC	....
1908	....	1	0	1	....	....	....	CR	....
1916	....	1	0	0	....	....	....	SF	....
TOTALS		**3**	**1**	**1**	....	....	....	....	....

• SEDGMAN, Frank   see page 885

• SEGURA, Pancho   see page 886

• SEIXAS, Vic   see page 886

• SHIELDS, Frank

Francis Xavier Shields

Male. Born: Nov. 18, 1909. New York, NY, United States.
Died: Aug. 19, 1975. Height: 6' 3". Weight: –. Plays: right.
Status: Amateur. Highest Ranking: 5 (Dec. 1930). HOF: 1964

Year	Rk	TP	TW	TF	Aus	Fre	Wim	US	DC
1926	....	1	0	0	....	....	....	1rd	....
1927	....	1	0	0	....	....	....	1rd	....
1928	....	1	0	0	....	....	....	SF	....
1929	....	1	0	0	....	....	....	3rd	....
1930	5	1	0	1	....	....	....	F	....
1931	5	2	0	1	....	....	F	QF	7-1
1932	....	2	0	0	....	....	QF	QF	5-2
1933	7	2	0	0	....	4rd	....	SF	....
1934	8	2	0	0	....	....	SF	QF	4-3
1935	7	1	0	0	....	....	....	QF	....
1938	....	1	0	0	....	....	....	3rd	....
1939	....	1	0	0	....	....	....	2rd	....
1940	....	1	0	0	....	....	....	1rd	....
1941	....	1	0	0	....	....	....	1rd	....
1945	....	1	0	0	....	....	....	2rd	....
1947	....	1	0	0	....	....	....	2rd	....
1948	....	1	0	0	....	....	....	2rd	....

Year	Rk	TP	TW	TF	Aus	Fre	Wim	US	DC
1949	....	1	0	0	....	....	....	2rd	....
1950	....	1	0	0	....	....	....	1rd	....
1951	....	1	0	0	....	....	....	2rd	....
1952	....	1	0	0	....	....	....	1rd	....
1953	....	1	0	0	....	....	....	1rd	....
1954	....	1	0	0	....	....	....	2rd	....
TOTALS		**27**	**0**	**2**	....	....	....	....	....

• SLOCUM, Henry   Henry Warner Slocum

Male. Born: May 28, 1862. United States.
Died: Jan. 22, 1949. Height: 5' 10". Weight: 150 lbs. Plays: right.
Status: Amateur. Highest Ranking: –. HOF: 1955

Year	Rk	TP	TW	TF	Aus	Fre	Wim	US	DC
1884	....	1	0	0	....	....	....	2rd	....
1885	....	1	0	0	....	....	....	1rd	....
1886	....	1	0	0	....	....	....	QF	....
1887	....	1	0	1	....	....	....	AC	....
1888	....	2	1	0	....	....	SF	WC	....
1889	....	2	1	0	....	....	SF	WD	....
1890	....	1	0	1	....	....	....	CR	....
1892	....	1	0	0	....	....	....	2rd	....
1903	....	1	0	0	....	....	....	2rd	....
1905	....	1	0	0	....	....	....	3rd	....
1906	....	1	0	0	....	....	....	1rd	....
1907	....	1	0	0	....	....	....	1rd	....
1908	....	1	0	0	....	....	....	2rd	....
1909	....	1	0	0	....	....	....	1rd	....
1910	....	1	0	0	....	....	....	3rd	....
1911	....	1	0	0	....	....	....	3rd	....
1912	....	1	0	0	....	....	....	4rd	....
1913	....	1	0	0	....	....	....	2rd	....
TOTALS		**20**	**2**	**2**	....	....	....	....	....

• SMITH, Stan   see page 887

• SMITH COURT, Margaret   see page 888

• SPERLING, Hilde   Hilde Kranwinkel Sperling

Female. Born: Mar. 26, 1908. Essen, Germany.
Died: Mar. 7, 1981. Height: –. Weight: –. Plays: right.
Status: Amateur. Highest Ranking: 2 (Dec. 1936).

Year	Rk	TP	TW	TF	Aus	Fre	Wim	US	FC
1928	....	1	0	0	....	....	2rd	....	....
1930	10	2	0	0	....	3rd	2rd	....	....
1931	5	1	0	0	....	SF	....	....	....
1932	5	2	0	0	....	SF	QF	....	....
1933	4	2	0	0	....	2rd	SF	....	....
1934	3	1	0	0	....	....	4rd	....	....
1935	4	2	1	0	....	W	SF	....	....
1936	2	2	1	1	....	W	F	....	....
1937	4	2	1	0	....	W	QF	....	....
1938	4	1	0	0	....	....	SF	....	....
1939	4	1	0	0	....	....	SF	....	....
TOTALS		**17**	**3**	**1**	....	....	....	....	....

• STERRY, Charlotte   Charlotte Reinagle Cooper Sterry

Female. Born: Sept. 22, 1870. Ealing, Great Britain.
Died: Oct. 10, 1966. Height: –. Weight: –. Plays: right.
Status: Amateur. Highest Ranking: –.

Year	Rk	TP	TW	TF	Aus	Fre	Wim	US	FC
1893	....	1	0	0	....	....	SF	....	....
1894	....	1	0	0	....	....	QF	....	....
1895	....	1	1	0	....	....	WC	....	....
1896	....	1	1	0	....	....	WD	....	....
1897	....	1	0	1	....	....	CR	....	....
1898	....	1	1	0	....	....	WC	....	....
1899	....	1	0	1	....	....	CR	....	....
1900	....	2	1	1	....	....	AC	....	....
1901	....	1	1	0	....	....	WC	....	....
1902	....	1	0	1	....	....	CR	....	....
1904	....	1	0	1	....	....	AC	....	....
1906	....	1	0	1	....	....	F	....	....
1907	....	1	0	0	....	....	1rd	....	....
1908	....	1	1	0	....	....	WC	....	....
1910	....	1	0	0	....	....	2rd	....	....
1911	....	1	0	0	....	....	2rd	....	....
1912	....	1	0	1	....	....	F	....	....
1913	....	1	0	0	....	....	QF	....	....
1914	....	1	0	0	....	....	3rd	....	....
1919	....	1	0	0	....	....	3rd	....	....
1927	....	1	0	0	....	....	....	3rd	....
TOTALS		**22**	**6**	**7**	....	....	....	....	....

Competed as Charlotte Cooper until 1901. Won Gold in the 1900 Olympics

• STOCKTON, Dick   see page 889

• STOLLE, Fred   see page 889

• STOVE, Betty   see page 890

• STURGESS, Eric   Eric Sturgess

Male. Born: May 10, 1920. Johannesburg, South Africa.
Height: –. Weight: –. Plays: right.
Status: Amateur. Highest Ranking: 6 (Dec. 1948).

Year	Rk	TP	TW	TF	Aus	Fre	Wim	US	DC
1947	....	1	0	1	....	F	....	F	5-1
1948	6	2	0	1	....	SF	....	F	3-1
1949	6	2	0	0	....	SF	....	3rd	3-1
1950	10	2	0	0	SF	SF	....	....	....
1951	....	1	0	1	....	F	....	....	2-0
1952	8	1	0	0	....	SF	....	....	....
TOTALS		**9**	**0**	**3**	....	....	....	....	....

• SUSMAN, Karen   see page 891

• SUTTON BUNDY, May   May Godfray Sutton Bundy

Female. Born: Sept. 25, 1886. Plymouth, Great Britain.
Died: Oct. 4, 1975. Height: 5' 4". Weight: 140 lbs. Plays: right.
Status: Amateur. Highest Ranking: 6 (Dec. 1921). HOF: 1956

Year	Rk	TP	TW	TF	Aus	Fre	Wim	US	FC
1904	....	1	1	0	....	....	....	WC	....
1905	....	1	1	0	....	....	WC	....	....
1906	....	1	0	1	....	....	CR	....	....
1907	....	1	1	0	....	....	WC	....	....
1911	....	1	0	1	....	....	....	AC	....
1921	6	1	0	0	....	....	....	SF	....
1922	....	1	0	0	....	....	....	SF	....
1925	....	1	0	0	....	....	....	3rd	....
1928	....	1	0	0	....	....	....	3rd	....
1929	....	1	0	0	....	....	....	3rd	....
TOTALS		**10**	**3**	**2**	....	....	....	....	....

Competed as May Sutton until 1912. Doubles Titles: US (1).

• TALBERT, Bill
William Franklin Talbert

Male. Born: Sept. 4, 1918. Cincinnati, OH, United States.
Height: 5' 11". Weight: –. Plays: right.
Status: Amateur. Highest Ranking: 3 (Dec. 1949). HOF: 1967

Year	Rk	TP	TW	TF	Aus	Fre	Wim	US	DC
1938	....	1	0	0	....	....	....	2rd	....
1939	....	1	0	0	....	....	....	4rd	....
1940	....	1	0	0	....	....	....	3rd	....
1941	....	1	0	0	....	....	....	2rd	....
1942	....	1	0	0	....	....	....	4rd	....
1943	....	1	0	0	....	....	....	SF	....
1944	....	1	0	0	....	....	....	SF	....
1945	....	1	0	1	....	....	....	F	....
1946	....	1	0	0	....	....	....	QF	2-0
1947	....	2	0	0	4rd	....	....	1rd	....
1948	....	1	0	0	....	....	....	4rd	....
1949	3	1	0	0	....	....	....	SF	....
1950	9	3	0	0	....	SF	QF	QF	....
1951	....	1	0	0	....	....	....	4rd	....
1952	....	1	0	0	....	....	....	4rd	....
1953	....	1	0	0	....	....	....	4rd	....
1954	....	2	0	0	3rd	....	....	4rd	....
TOTALS		**21**	**0**	**1**	....	....	....	....	....

Doubles Titles: Fre (1), US (4)

• TEGART, Judy
see **DALTON, Judy,** page 836

• TERRY, Aline
Aline Terry

Female. Born: Princeton, NJ, United States.
Height: –. Weight: –. Plays: –.
Status: Amateur. Highest Ranking: –.

Year	Rk	TP	TW	TF	Aus	Fre	Wim	US	FC
1893	....	1	1	0	....	....	....	WC	....
1894	....	1	0	1	....	....	....	CR	....
TOTALS		**2**	**1**	**1**	....	....	....	....	....

Doubles Titles: US (1)

• TILDEN, Bill
William Tatem "Big Bill" Tilden

Male. Born: Feb. 10, 1893. Philadelphia, PA, United States.
Died: June 5, 1953. Height: 6' 2". Weight: 155 lbs. Plays: right.
Status: Turned Pro 1931. Highest Ranking: 1 (Dec. 1920). HOF: 1959

Year	Rk	TP	TW	TF	Aus	Fre	Wim	US	DC
1912	....	1	0	0	....	....	....	1rd	....
1916	....	1	0	0	....	....	....	1rd	....
1917	....	1	0	0	....	....	....	3rd	....
1918	....	1	0	1	....	....	....	F	....
1919	4	1	0	1	....	....	....	F	....
1920	1	2	2	0	....	....	WC	W	5-0
1921	1	2	2	0	....	....	WD	W	2-0
1922	1	1	1	0	....	....	....	W	2-0
1923	1	1	1	0	....	....	....	W	2-0
1924	1	1	1	0	....	....	....	W	2-0
1925	1	1	1	0	....	....	....	W	2-0
1926	5	1	0	0	....	....	....	QF	1-1
1927	2	3	0	2	....	F	SF	F	1-1
1928	3	1	0	0	....	....	SF	....	4-1
1929	4	3	1	0	....	SF	SF	W	3-1
1930	2	3	1	0	....	F	W	SF	1-1
TOTALS		**24**	**10**	**4**	....	....	....	....	....

Held number one world ranking 6 times during amateur era. Doubles Titles: Wim (1), US (5).

• TODD, Pat
Mary Patricia Canning Todd

Female. Born: July 22, 1922. San Francisco, CA, United States.
Height: 5' 8". Weight: –. Plays: right.
Status: Amateur. Highest Ranking: 4 (Dec. 1950).

Year	Rk	TP	TW	TF	Aus	Fre	Wim	US	FC
1938	....	1	0	0	....	....	....	1rd	....
1939	....	1	0	0	....	....	....	1rd	....
1940	....	1	0	0	....	....	....	3rd	....
1941	....	1	0	0	....	....	....	3rd	....
1942	....	1	0	0	....	....	....	2rd	....
1944	....	1	0	0	....	....	....	2rd	....
1945	....	1	0	0	....	....	....	QF	....
1946	5	3	0	0	....	3rd	3rd	SF	....
1947	5	3	1	0	....	W	QF	QF	....
1948	5	3	0	0	....	SF	SF	SF	....
1949	5	2	0	0	....	....	SF	QF	....
1950	4	3	0	1	....	F	SF	QF	....
1951	9	1	0	0	....	....	....	3rd	....
1952	5	1	0	0	....	....	SF	....	....
1957	....	1	0	0	....	....	....	3rd	....
TOTALS		**24**	**1**	**1**	....	....	....	....	....

Doubles Titles: Fre (1)

• TOWNSEND, Bertha
Bertha Louise Townsend Toulmin

Female. Born: Mar. 7, 1869. Haverford, PA, United States.
Died: May 12, 1909. Height: –. Weight: –.
Status: Amateur. Highest Ranking: –. HOF: 1974

Year	Rk	TP	TW	TF	Aus	Fre	Wim	US	FC
1888	....	1	1	0	....	....	....	WC	....
1889	....	1	1	0	....	....	....	WD	....
1890	....	1	0	1	....	....	....	CR	....
1894	....	1	0	1	....	....	....	F	....
1895	....	1	0	0	....	....	....	SF	....
1906	....	1	0	0	....	....	....	SF	....
TOTALS		**6**	**2**	**2**	....	....	....	....	....

• TRABERT, Tony
Marion Anthony Trabert

Male. Born: Aug. 16, 1930. Cincinnati, OH, United States.
Height: 6' 1". Weight: 180 lbs. Plays: right.
Status: Turned Pro 1956. Highest Ranking: 1 (Dec. 1953). HOF: 1970

Year	Rk	TP	TW	TF	Aus	Fre	Wim	US	DC
1948	....	1	0	0	....	....	....	3rd	....
1949	....	1	0	0	....	....	....	2rd	....
1950	....	3	0	0	....	4rd	2rd	1rd	....
1951	5	1	0	0	....	....	....	QF	4-0
1952	....	1	0	0	....	4rd	....	....	2-2
1953	1	1	1	0	....	....	....	W	5-1
1954	2	4	1	0	4rd	W	SF	QF	5-2
1955	1	4	3	0	SF	W	W	W	....
TOTALS		**16**	**5**	**0**	....	....	....	....	....

Held number one world ranking 2 times during amateur era. Doubles Titles: Aus (1), Fre (3), US (1).

• TRUMAN, Chris
Christine Clara Truman

Female. Born: Feb. 16, 1941. Loughton, Great Britain.
Height: 6'. Weight: –. Plays: right.
Status: Amateur. Highest Ranking: 2 (Dec. 1959).

Year	Rk	TP	TW	TF	Aus	Fre	Wim	US	FC
1957	9	3	0	0	....	1rd	SF	3rd	....
1958	6	3	0	0	....	QF	4rd	QF	....
1959	2	2	1	0	....	W	4rd	....	....
1960	4	3	0	0	SF	....	SF	SF	....
1961	7	3	0	1	....	QF	F	QF	....
1962	....	2	0	0	....	4rd	3rd	....	....
1963	....	4	0	0	3rd	SF	4rd	QF	....

Year	Rk	TP	TW	TF	Aus	Fre	Wim	US	FC
1964	....	2	0	0	....	QF	2rd	....	....
1965	7	2	0	0	4rd	....	SF	....	....
1966	....	1	0	0	....	....	2rd	....	....
1967	....	2	0	0	....	3rd	2rd	....	....
TOTALS		**27**	**1**	**1**	....	....	....	....	....

• TURNER, Lesley   see page 893

• VAN RYN, Johnny   John William Van Ryn

Male. Born: June 30, 1905. Newport News, VA, United States.
Height: 5' 10". Weight: 155 lbs. Plays: right.
Status: Amateur. Highest Ranking: 8 (Dec. 1929). HOF: 1963

Year	Rk	TP	TW	TF	Aus	Fre	Wim	US	DC
1923	....	1	0	0	....	....	2rd	....	....
1924	....	1	0	0	....	....	....	1rd	....
1925	....	1	0	0	....	....	....	1rd	....
1926	....	1	0	0	....	....	....	1rd	....
1927	....	1	0	0	....	....	....	3rd	....
1928	....	1	0	0	....	....	....	3rd	....
1929	8	2	0	0	....	....	2rd	QF	4-1
1930	....	2	0	0	....	....	3rd	QF	2-0
1931	10	3	0	0	....	QF	QF	QF	....
1932	....	2	0	0	....	....	3rd	4rd	1-0
1933	....	1	0	0	....	....	....	2rd	....
1935	....	2	0	0	....	....	3rd	4rd	....
1936	....	2	0	0	....	....	3rd	QF	....
1937	....	1	0	0	....	....	....	QF	....
TOTALS		**21**	**0**	**0**	....	....	....	....	....

Doubles Titles: Fre (1), Wim (3), US (2)

• VINES, Ellsworth   Henry Ellsworth Vines, Jr.

Male. Born: Sept. 29, 1911. Los Angeles, CA, United States.
Died: Mar. 17, 1994. Height: 6' 2". Weight: 145 lbs. Plays: right.
Status: Turned Pro 1934. Highest Ranking: 1 (Dec. 1932). HOF: 1962

Year	Rk	TP	TW	TF	Aus	Fre	Wim	US	DC
1930	....	1	0	0	....	....	....	3rd	....
1931	3	1	1	0	....	....	....	W	....
1932	1	2	2	0	....	....	W	W	9-1
1933	5	3	0	1	QF	....	F	4rd	4-2
TOTALS		**7**	**3**	**1**	....	....	....	....	....

Held number one world ranking 1 time during amateur era. Doubles
Titles: Aus (1), US (1).

• VON CRAMM, Gottfried   Baron Gottfried von Cramm

Male. Born: July 7, 1909. Nettlingen, Germany.
Died: Nov. 8, 1976. Height: 6'. Weight: –. Plays: right.
Status: Amateur. Highest Ranking: 2 (Dec. 1936). HOF: 1977

Year	Rk	TP	TW	TF	Aus	Fre	Wim	US	DC
1931	....	2	0	0	....	4rd	4rd	....	....
1932	8	2	0	0	....	2rd	2rd	....	9-3
1933	9	1	0	0	....	....	3rd	....	9-1
1934	3	2	1	0	....	W	4rd	....	6-0
1935	3	2	0	2	....	F	F	....	7-1
1936	2	2	1	1	....	W	F	....	8-1
1937	2	2	0	2	....	....	F	F	7-1
1938	....	1	0	0	SF	....	....	....	....
1951	....	1	0	0	....	....	1rd	....	8-1
1952	....	1	0	0	....	1rd	....	....	1-1
1953	....	0	0	0	....	....	....	....	3-1
TOTALS		**16**	**2**	**5**	....	....	....	....	....

Doubles Titles: Fre (1), US (1)

• WADE, Virginia   see page 894

• WAGNER, Marie   Marie Wagner

Female. Born: Feb. 2, 1883. Freeport, NY, United States.
Died: Apr. 1, 1975. Height: –. Weight: –. Plays: –.
Status: Amateur. Highest Ranking: –. HOF: 1969

Year	Rk	TP	TW	TF	Aus	Fre	Wim	US	FC
1907	....	1	0	1	....	....	....	3rd	....
1908	....	1	0	1	....	....	....	F	....
1909	....	1	0	0	....	....	....	2rd	....
1911	....	1	0	0	....	....	....	QF	....
1914	....	1	0	1	....	....	....	AC	....
1919	....	1	0	0	....	....	....	QF	....
1921	....	1	0	0	....	....	....	1rd	....
TOTALS		**7**	**0**	**2**	....	....	....	....	....

• WARD, Holcombe   Holcombe Ward

Male. Born: Nov. 23, 1878. New York, NY, United States.
Died: Jan. 23, 1967. Height: 5' 9". Weight: 135 lbs. Plays: right.
Status: Amateur. Highest Ranking: –. HOF: 1956

Year	Rk	TP	TW	TF	Aus	Fre	Wim	US	DC
1896	....	1	0	0	....	....	....	2rd	....
1897	....	1	0	0	....	....	....	QF	....
1898	....	1	0	0	....	....	....	QF	....
1899	....	1	0	0	....	....	....	QF	....
1900	....	1	0	0	....	....	....	3rd	....
1901	....	1	0	0	....	....	....	2rd	....
1902	....	1	0	0	....	....	....	3rd	....
1903	....	1	0	0	....	....	....	4rd	....
1904	....	1	1	0	....	....	....	WC	....
1905	....	2	0	1	....	....	1rd	CR	2-1
1906	....	0	0	0	....	....	....	....	1-3
1917	....	1	0	0	....	....	....	3rd	....
TOTALS		**12**	**1**	**1**	....	....	....	....	....

Doubles Titles: US (6)

• WASHBURN, Watty   Watson McLean Washburn

Male. Born: June 13, 1894. New York, NY, United States.
Died: Dec. 2, 1973. Height: 6'. Weight: –. Plays: right.
Status: Amateur. Highest Ranking: –. HOF: 1965

Year	Rk	TP	TW	TF	Aus	Fre	Wim	US	DC
1911	....	1	0	0	....	....	....	QF	....
1912	....	1	0	0	....	....	....	QF	....
1913	....	1	0	0	....	....	....	QF	....
1914	....	1	0	0	....	....	....	4rd	....
1915	....	1	0	0	....	....	....	3rd	....
1916	....	1	0	0	....	....	....	QF	....
1917	....	1	0	0	....	....	....	3rd	....
1919	....	1	0	0	....	....	....	3rd	....
1920	....	1	0	0	....	....	....	QF	....
1921	....	1	0	0	....	....	....	2rd	....
1922	....	1	0	0	....	....	....	4rd	....
1923	....	1	0	0	....	....	....	1rd	....
1924	....	1	0	0	....	....	....	4rd	....
1925	....	1	0	0	....	....	....	1rd	....
1926	....	1	0	0	....	....	....	2rd	....
1927	....	1	0	0	....	....	....	2rd	....
1928	....	1	0	0	....	....	....	1rd	....
1929	....	1	0	0	....	....	....	1rd	....
1930	....	1	0	0	....	....	....	2rd	....
1931	....	1	0	0	....	....	1rd	....	....
1933	....	1	0	0	....	....	....	1rd	....
1934	....	1	0	0	....	....	....	2rd	....
1935	....	1	0	0	....	....	....	1rd	....
1936	....	1	0	0	....	....	....	1rd	....
1937	....	1	0	0	....	....	....	1rd	....
TOTALS		**25**	**0**	**0**	....	....	....	....	....

• WATSON, Maud
Maud Edith Eleanor Watson

Female. Born: Oct. 9, 1864. Harrow, Great Britain.
Died: May 27, 1918. Height: –. Weight: –. Plays: right.
Status: Amateur. Highest Ranking: –.

Year	Rk	TP	TW	TF	Aus	Fre	Wim	US	FC
1885	....	1	1	0	....	....	W	....	....
1886	....	1	0	1	....	....	CR	....	....
TOTALS		**2**	**1**	**1**	....	....	....	....	....

• WESTACOTT, Emily
Emily Hood Westacott

Female. Born: Australia.
Height: –. Weight: –. Plays: right.
Status: Amateur. Highest Ranking: –.

Year	Rk	TP	TW	TF	Aus	Fre	Wim	US	FC
1929	....	1	0	0	QF	....	....	....	....
1930	....	1	0	0	SF	....	....	....	....
1932	....	1	0	0	SF	....	....	....	....
1933	....	1	0	0	SF	....	....	....	....
1934	....	1	0	0	QF	....	....	....	....
1935	....	1	0	0	SF	....	....	....	....
1937	....	1	0	1	F	....	....	....	....
1939	....	1	1	0	W	....	....	....	....
TOTALS		**8**	**1**	**1**	....	....	....	....	....

• WHITMAN, Mal
Malcolm Douglass Whitman

Male. Born: Mar. 15, 1877. New York, NY, United States.
Died: Dec. 28, 1932. Height: 6' 2". Weight: –. Plays: right.
Status: Amateur. Highest Ranking: –. HOF: 1955

Year	Rk	TP	TW	TF	Aus	Fre	Wim	US	DC
1896	....	1	0	0	....	....	....	QF	....
1897	....	1	0	0	....	....	....	QF	....
1898	....	1	1	0	....	....	....	WC	....
1899	....	1	1	0	....	....	....	WD	....
1900	....	1	1	0	....	....	....	WD	1-0
1902	....	0	0	0	....	....	....	....	2-0
1917	....	1	0	0	....	....	....	1rd	....
TOTALS		**6**	**3**	**0**	....	....	....	....	....

• WIGHTMAN, Hazel
see **HOTCHKISS WIGHTMAN, Hazel,** page 808

• WILDING, Tony
Anthony Frederick Wilding

Male. Born: Oct. 31, 1883. Christchurch, New Zealand.
Died: May 9, 1915. Height: 6' 2". Weight: 185 lbs. Plays: right.
Status: Amateur. Highest Ranking: 1 (Dec. 1913). HOF: 1978

Year	Rk	TP	TW	TF	Aus	Fre	Wim	US	DC
1904	....	1	0	0	....	....	2rd	....	....
1905	....	1	0	0	....	....	QF	....	2-2
1906	....	2	1	0	W	....	SF	....	2-0
1907	....	1	0	0	....	....	2rd	....	2-2
1908	....	1	0	0	....	....	QF	....	1-1
1909	....	1	1	0	W	....	....	....	2-0
1910	....	1	1	0	....	....	WC	....	....
1911	....	1	1	0	....	....	WD	....	....
1912	....	2	1	0	....	....	WD	....	....
1913	1	1	1	0	....	....	WD	....	....
1914	2	2	0	1	....	....	CR	1rd	6-1
TOTALS		**14**	**6**	**1**	....	....	....	....	....

Held number one world ranking 1 time during amateur era. Won Bronze in the 1912 Olympics. Represented Australia in the Davis Cup (1905-1914). Doubles Titles: Aus (1), Wim (4).

• WILLIAMS, Dick
Richard Norris Williams II

Male. Born: Jan. 29, 1891. Geneva, Sweden.
Died: June 2, 1968. Height: –. Weight: –. Plays: right.
Status: Amateur. Highest Ranking: 4 (Dec. 1923). HOF: 1957

Year	Rk	TP	TW	TF	Aus	Fre	Wim	US	DC
1912	....	1	0	0	....	....	....	QF	....
1913	5	2	0	1	....	....	4rd	F	....
1914	5	1	1	0	....	....	....	W	....
1915	....	1	0	0	....	....	....	SF	....
1916	....	1	1	0	....	....	....	W	....
1917	....	1	0	0	....	....	....	SF	....
1919	7	1	0	0	....	....	....	SF	....
1920	7	2	0	0	....	....	QF	4rd	....
1921	9	2	0	0	....	....	3rd	4rd	....
1923	4	1	0	0	....	....	....	QF	....
1924	....	2	0	0	....	....	SF	2rd	....
1925	5	1	0	0	....	....	....	SF	....
1926	....	1	0	0	....	....	....	QF	....
1927	....	1	0	0	....	....	....	1rd	....
1928	....	1	0	0	....	....	....	1rd	....
1929	....	1	0	0	....	....	....	QF	....
1930	....	1	0	0	....	....	....	4rd	....
1933	....	1	0	0	....	....	....	2rd	....
1935	....	1	0	0	....	....	....	2rd	....
TOTALS		**23**	**2**	**1**	....	....	....	....	....

Doubles Titles: Wim (1), US (2)

• WILLS MOODY, Helen
Helen Newington Wills Moody Roark

Female. Born: Oct. 6, 1905. Centreville, CA, United States.
Died: Jan. 1, 1998. Height: –. Weight: –. Plays: right.
Status: Amateur. Highest Ranking: 1 (Dec. 1927). HOF: 1959

Year	Rk	TP	TW	TF	Aus	Fre	Wim	US	FC
1922	....	1	0	0	....	....	....	F	....
1923	....	1	1	0	....	....	....	W	....
1924	....	3	2	1	....	....	F	W	....
1925	2	1	1	0	....	....	....	W	....
1926	....	2	0	0	....	2rd	1rd	....	....
1927	1	2	2	0	....	....	W	W	....
1928	1	3	3	0	....	W	W	W	....
1929	1	3	3	0	....	W	W	W	....
1930	1	3	3	0	....	W	W	W	....
1931	1	1	1	0	....	....	....	W	....
1932	1	2	2	0	....	W	W	....	....
1933	1	2	1	1	....	....	W	F	....
1935	1	1	1	0	....	....	W	....	....
1938	1	1	1	0	....	....	W	....	....
TOTALS		**26**	**21**	**3**	....	....	....	....	....

Held number one world ranking 9 times during amateur era. Competed as Helen Wills until 1929. Won Gold in the 1924 Olympics. Doubles Titles: Fre (2), Wim (3), US (4).

• WOOD, Sidney
Sidney Burr Beardsley Wood

Male. Born: Nov. 1, 1911. Black Rock, CT, United States.
Height: 5' 9". Weight: –. Plays: right.
Status: Amateur. Highest Ranking: 5 (Dec. 1958). HOF: 1964

Year	Rk	TP	TW	TF	Aus	Fre	Wim	US	DC
1927	....	3	0	0	....	1rd	1rd	1rd	....
1928	....	3	0	0	....	2rd	3rd	1rd	....
1930	....	1	0	0	....	....	....	SF	....
1931	6	2	1	0	....	....	W	3rd	2-3
1932	....	3	0	0	....	3rd	QF	QF	....
1933	8	1	0	0	....	....	....	4rd	....
1934	6	2	0	0	....	....	SF	SF	3-3
1935	10	2	0	1	....	....	QF	F	....
1936	....	1	0	0	....	....	....	4rd	....
1938	5	1	0	0	....	....	....	SF	....

Year	Rk	TP	TW	TF	Aus	Fre	Wim	US	DC
1939	....	1	0	0	....	....	....	2rd	....
1940	....	1	0	0	....	....	....	3rd	....
1941	....	1	0	0	....	....	....	1rd	....
1942	....	1	0	0	....	....	....	3rd	....
1943	....	1	0	0	....	....	....	1rd	....
1944	....	1	0	0	....	....	....	1rd	....
1945	....	1	0	0	....	....	....	QF	....
1946	....	1	0	0	....	....	....	1rd	....
1947	....	1	0	0	....	....	....	1rd	....
1948	....	1	0	0	....	....	....	3rd	....
1949	....	1	0	0	....	....	....	1rd	....
1951	....	1	0	0	....	....	....	1rd	....
1952	....	1	0	0	....	....	....	2rd	....
1953	....	1	0	0	....	....	....	2rd	....
1954	....	1	0	0	....	....	....	1rd	....
1956	....	1	0	0	....	....	....	1rd	....
TOTALS		**35**	**1**	**1**	....	....	....	....	....

• WRENN, Bob

Robert Duffield Wren

Male. Born: Sept. 20, 1873. Highland Park, IL, United States.
Died: Nov. 12, 1925. Height: –. Weight: –. Plays: left.
Status: Amateur. Highest Ranking: –. HOF: 1955

Year	Rk	TP	TW	TF	Aus	Fre	Wim	US	DC
1892	....	1	0	0	....	....	....	SF	....
1893	....	1	1	0	....	....	....	WC	....
1894	....	1	1	0	....	....	....	WD	....
1895	....	1	0	1	....	....	....	CR	....
1896	....	1	1	0	....	....	....	WC	....
1897	....	1	1	0	....	....	....	WD	....
1900	....	1	0	0	....	....	....	QF	....
1903	....	0	0	0	....	....	....	....	0-2
TOTALS		**7**	**4**	**1**	....	....	....	....	....

Doubles Titles: US (1)

• WRIGHT, Beals

Beals Coleman Wright

Male. Born: Dec. 19, 1879. Boston, MA, United States.
Died: Aug. 23, 1961. Height: –. Weight: –. Plays: left.
Status: Amateur. Highest Ranking: –. HOF: 1956

Year	Rk	TP	TW	TF	Aus	Fre	Wim	US	DC
1897	....	1	0	0	....	....	....	2rd	....
1898	....	1	0	0	....	....	....	1rd	....
1899	....	1	0	0	....	....	....	2rd	....
1900	....	1	0	0	....	....	....	SF	....
1901	....	1	0	1	....	....	....	F	....
1902	....	1	0	0	....	....	....	4rd	....
1903	....	1	0	0	....	....	....	1rd	....
1904	....	2	1	0	....	....	....	QF	....
1905	....	2	1	0	....	....	4rd	WC	2-0
1907	....	2	0	0	....	....	1rd	1rd	1-1
1908	....	1	0	1	....	....	....	AC	3-1
1910	....	2	0	2	....	....	F	F	....
1911	....	1	0	1	....	....	....	F	....
1912	....	1	0	0	....	....	....	1rd	0-1
1918	....	1	0	0	....	....	....	3rd	....
TOTALS		**19**	**2**	**5**	....	....	....	....	....

Won Gold in the 1904 Olympics. Doubles Titles: US (3).

• WYNNE, Nancye

see **BOLTON, Nancye,** page 799

Chapter 29

Open Era Register

(Register Abbreviations – see page 796)

• AGASSI, Andre

Andre Kirk Agassi

Male. Born: Apr. 29, 1970. Las Vegas, NV, United States. Height: 5' 11". Weight: 175 lbs. Plays: right.
Status: Turned Pro 1986. Earnings: $25,658,496. Highest Ranking: 1 (Apr. 1995).

Year	Rk	TP	TW	TF	GS	Aus	Fre	Wim	US	DC	Oly	MW	ML	Pct	CL	GR	HD	CP	IN	OD
1986	91	6	0	0	0-1	....	....	....	1rd	....	....	5	6	.455	0-0	0-0	4-5	1-1	1-1	4-5
1987	25	18	1	1	1-3	....	2rd	1rd	1rd	....	....	26	17	.605	5-5	0-1	21-10	0-1	3-3	23-14
1988	3	17	6	1	10-2	....	SF	....	SF	3-0	....	63	11	.851	29-3	0-0	33-6	1-2	6-2	57-9
1989	7	20	1	1	7-2	....	3rd	....	SF	4-2	....	41	19	.683	13-4	0-0	20-6	8-9	9-10	32-9
1990	4	16	4	3	12-2	....	F	....	F	2-2	....	45	12	.789	9-4	0-0	26-5	10-3	11-4	34-8
1991	10	19	2	1	10-3	....	F	QF	1rd	3-0	....	39	17	.696	10-4	4-1	17-7	8-5	12-6	27-11
1992	9	18	3	0	16-2	....	SF	W	QF	7-0	....	42	15	.737	15-4	7-1	19-7	1-4	5-5	37-10
1993	24	13	2	0	4-2	....	....	QF	1rd	1-0	....	33	11	.750	2-1	4-2	27-8	0-0	7-1	26-10
1994	2	19	5	1	11-2	....	2rd	4rd	W	....	....	52	14	.788	4-4	3-1	29-6	16-3	16-3	36-11
1995	2	16	7	4	22-3	W	QF	SF	F	2-0	....	73	9	.890	11-3	5-1	53-3	4-2	9-2	64-7
1996	8	17	3	1	11-4	SF	2rd	1rd	SF	....	W	38	14	.731	2-2	0-1	34-7	2-4	6-6	32-8
1997	122	12	0	0	3-1	....	....	....	4rd	....	....	12	12	.500	1-1	0-0	11-10	0-1	3-3	9-9
1998	6	23	5	5	7-4	4rd	1rd	2rd	4rd	2-1	....	68	18	.791	5-3	1-1	47-10	15-4	20-5	48-13
1999	1	19	5	3	23-2	4rd	W	F	W	....	....	63	14	.818	9-2	6-1	41-9	7-2	15-5	48-9
2000	6	16	1	2	14-3	W	2rd	SF	2rd	4-0	....	40	15	.727	4-3	6-2	25-9	5-1	12-3	28-12
2001	3	19	4	1	20-3	W	QF	SF	QF	....	....	45	15	.750	5-4	5-1	35-10	0-0	5-4	40-11
2002	2	17	5	2	11-3	....	QF	2rd	F	....	....	53	12	.815	13-2	1-1	36-7	3-2	11-5	42-7
TOTALS		**285**	**54**	**26**	**182-42**	....	....	....	....	**28-5**		**738**	**231**	**.762**	**137-49**	**42-14**	**478-125**	**81-44**	**151-68**	**587-163**

Held number one tour ranking 4 times for a total of 87 weeks. Last ranked number one in 2000.

• ALEXANDER, John

John Alexander

Male. Born: July 4, 1951. Sydney, Australia. Height: 6' 3". Weight: 180 lbs. Plays: right.
Status: Turned Pro 1968. Earnings: $1,214,079. Highest Ranking: 8 (Dec. 1975).

Year	Rk	TP	TW	TF	GS	Aus	Fre	Wim	US	DC	Oly	MW	ML	Pct	CL	GR	HD	CP	IN	OD
1967	....	1	0	0	....	2rd	....	....	....	....	....	....	....	....	....	....	....	....	....	....
1968	....	2	0	0	2-2	....	3rd	2rd	....	....	....	2	2	.500	1-1	1-1	0-0	0-0	0-0	2-2
1969	....	4	0	0	5-4	2rd	1rd	4rd	2rd	....	....	5	4	.556	0-1	5-3	0-0	0-0	0-0	5-4
1970	....	3	0	1	2-3	3rd	1rd	2rd	....	1-0	....	2	3	.400	0-1	2-2	0-0	0-0	0-0	2-3
1971	....	6	0	3	5-4	1rd	2rd	2rd	4rd	....	....	6	6	.500	1-2	4-3	0-0	1-1	1-1	5-5
1972	....	5	0	1	2-2	3rd	....	....	2rd	....	....	4	5	.444	0-0	2-2	2-3	0-0	0-1	4-4
1973	29	11	0	2	3-3	2rd	1rd	....	4rd	....	....	11	11	.500	2-3	3-3	4-3	2-2	2-2	9-9
1974	28	7	0	1	6-3	SF	....	2rd	3rd	2-0	....	13	7	.650	5-2	6-3	2-1	0-1	0-1	13-6
1975	8	10	2	2	7-4	QF	4rd	2rd	2rd	0-1	....	16	8	.667	7-3	5-3	3-1	1-1	1-1	15-7
1976	47	10	0	0	2-2	....	....	1rd	3rd	2-0	....	10	10	.500	2-2	0-1	3-2	5-5	5-5	5-5
1977	19	15	1	1	10-4	SF/SF	....	2rd	2rd	6-1	....	25	14	.641	6-3	13-5	2-2	4-4	4-4	21-10
1978	22	21	0	3	9-4	QF	4rd	4rd	1rd	3-1	....	37	21	.638	15-6	17-5	2-5	3-5	3-6	34-15
1979	22	24	1	3	3-3	1rd	....	3rd	2rd	3-3	....	33	23	.589	17-6	3-5	6-5	7-7	7-7	26-16
1980	111	15	0	0	0-1	1rd	....	....	....	0-1	....	11	15	.423	4-4	1-3	4-5	2-3	3-5	8-10
1981	61	21	0	0	2-3	3rd	....	1rd	1rd	....	....	23	21	.523	8-6	7-5	7-9	1-1	2-2	21-19
1982	31	25	2	1	4-4	4rd	1rd	2rd	1rd	0-2	....	38	23	.623	10-7	16-5	6-5	6-6	8-7	30-16
1983	67	27	1	1	5-3	2rd	4rd	2rd	....	....	....	24	26	.480	11-9	2-7	7-5	4-5	6-7	18-19
1984	141	24	0	0	1-3	2rd	2rd	1rd	....	....	....	12	24	.333	4-8	3-7	4-6	1-3	1-4	11-20
1985	405	6	0	0	0-1	1rd	....	....	....	....	....	0	6	.000	0-1	0-2	0-0	0-0	0-0	0-5
TOTALS		**237**	**7**	**19**	**68-53**	....	....	....	....	**17-9**	....	**272**	**229**	**.543**	**93-65**	**90-65**	**52-55**	**37-44**	**43-54**	**229-175**

Doubles Titles: Wim (2)

• ANDERSON, Mal   Malcolm James "Cowboy" Anderson

Male. Born: Mar. 3, 1935. Theodore, Australia. Height: –. Weight: –. Plays: right.
Status: Turned Pro 1959. Earnings: –. Highest Ranking: 2 (Dec. 1957). HOF: 2000

Year	Rk	TP	TW	TF	GS	Aus	Fre	Wim	US	DC	Oly	MW	ML	Pct	CL	GR	HD	CP	IN	OD
1954	....	1	0	0	....	3rd	....	....	....	....	....	....	....	....	....	....	....	....	....	....
1955	....	2	0	0	....	4rd	....	1rd	....	....	....	....	....	....	....	....	....	....	....	....
1956	....	3	0	0	....	QF	....	QF	1rd	....	....	....	....	....	....	....	....	....	....	....
1957	2	3	1	0	....	SF	....	4rd	W	1-1	....	....	....	....	....	....	....	....	....	....
1958	9	3	0	2	....	F	....	QF	F	1-1	....	....	....	....	....	....	....	....	....	....
1962	....	1	0	0	....	2rd	....	....	....	....	....	....	....	....	....	....	....	....	....	....
1968	....	1	0	0	1-1	....	....	....	3rd	....	....	1	1	.500	0-0	1-1	0-0	0-0	0-0	1-1
1969	....	2	0	0	4-2	3rd	....	3rd	....	....	....	4	2	.667	0-0	4-2	0-0	0-0	0-0	4-2
1970	....	1	0	0	0-1	1rd	....	....	....	....	....	0	1	.000	0-0	0-1	0-0	0-0	0-0	0-1
1971	....	1	0	0	1-1	2rd	....	....	....	....	....	1	1	.500	0-0	1-1	0-0	0-0	0-0	1-1
1972	....	3	0	0	5-2	F	....	....	3rd	....	....	5	3	.625	0-0	5-2	0-1	0-0	0-1	5-2
1973	....	1	0	0	0-1	....	....	....	....	....	....	0	1	.000	0-0	0-1	0-0	0-0	0-0	0-1
1974	....	1	0	0	0-0	....	....	....	....	....	....	0	1	.000	0-0	0-0	0-1	0-0	0-0	0-1
1976	....	2	0	0	2-1	3rd	....	....	....	....	....	2	2	.500	0-0	2-1	0-1	0-0	0-0	2-2
1977	....	1	0	0	0-1	/1rd	....	....	....	....	....	0	1	.000	0-0	0-1	0-0	0-0	0-0	0-1
1978	....	1	0	0	0-0	....	....	....	....	....	....	1	1	.500	0-0	1-1	0-0	0-0	0-0	1-1
1979	....	1	0	0	0-0	....	....	....	....	....	....	0	1	.000	0-0	0-1	0-0	0-0	0-0	0-1
1981	....	1	0	0	0-0	....	....	....	....	....	....	1	1	.500	0-0	1-1	0-0	0-0	0-0	1-1
TOTALS		**29**	**1**	**2**	**13-10**	....	....	....	....	**2-2**		**15**	**16**	**.484**	**0-0**	**15-13**	**0-3**	**0-0**	**0-1**	**15-15**

Doubles Titles: Aus (1), Fre (1)

• ARIAS, Jimmy   Jimmy Arias

Male. Born: Aug. 16, 1964. Buffalo, NY, United States. Height: 5' 9". Weight: 155 lbs. Plays: right.
Status: Turned Pro 1980. Earnings: $1,834,140. Highest Ranking: 6 (Dec. 1983).

Year	Rk	TP	TW	TF	GS	Aus	Fre	Wim	US	DC	Oly	MW	ML	Pct	CL	GR	HD	CP	IN	OD
1980	272	5	0	0	1-1	....	....	....	2rd	....	....	3	5	.375	0-2	0-0	3-3	0-0	0-0	3-5
1981	81	10	0	0	2-2	....	2rd	....	2rd	....	....	10	10	.500	5-5	0-0	5-4	0-1	0-1	10-9
1982	20	18	1	2	4-2	....	3rd	....	3rd	....	....	30	17	.638	22-9	0-0	3-4	5-4	5-4	25-13
1983	6	19	4	2	8-2	....	4rd	....	SF	....	....	45	15	.750	36-9	0-0	8-2	1-4	1-4	44-11
1984	14	22	0	0	8-3	....	QF	4rd	2rd	0-1	....	41	22	.651	20-10	3-1	12-7	6-4	6-6	35-16
1985	21	21	0	3	2-3	....	1rd	1rd	3rd	....	....	32	21	.604	7-6	0-1	24-9	1-5	1-6	31-15
1986	48	20	0	0	0-1	....	....	....	1rd	1-1	....	19	20	.487	11-7	0-0	8-11	0-2	0-2	19-18
1987	34	20	0	1	3-3	....	4rd	1rd	1rd	0-2	....	22	20	.524	13-10	0-1	9-8	0-1	2-3	20-17
1988	106	14	0	1	0-2	....	1rd	....	1rd	....	....	7	14	.333	6-7	0-0	1-7	0-0	0-0	7-14
1989	92	17	0	0	2-2	....	3rd	....	1rd	....	....	17	17	.500	6-7	0-0	11-9	0-1	3-2	14-15
1990	60	26	0	1	2-3	1rd	2rd	....	2rd	....	....	24	26	.480	7-9	0-0	14-13	3-4	5-6	19-20
1991	63	19	0	1	4-3	3rd	2rd	....	2rd	....	....	23	19	.548	9-6	0-0	14-13	0-0	0-1	23-18
1992	192	8	0	0	0-1	1rd	....	....	....	....	....	4	8	.333	0-2	0-0	4-6	0-0	0-1	4-7
1993	183	4	0	0	0-0	....	....	....	....	....	....	5	4	.556	1-2	0-0	4-2	0-0	1-1	4-3
1994	....	4	0	0	0-0	....	....	....	....	....	....	3	4	.429	1-2	0-0	2-2	0-0	0-0	3-4
1998	711	1	0	0	0-0	....	....	....	....	....	....	1	1	.500	0-0	0-0	1-1	0-0	0-0	1-1
TOTALS		**228**	**5**	**11**	**36-28**	....	....	....	....	**1-4**		**286**	**223**	**.562**	**144-93**	**3-3**	**123-101**	**16-26**	**24-37**	**262-186**

• ASHE, Arthur   Arthur Robert Ashe, Jr.

Male. Born: July 10, 1943. Richmond, VA, United States. Died: Feb. 6, 1993. Height: 6' 1". Weight: 160 lbs. Plays: right.
Status: Turned Pro 1968. Earnings: $1,584,909. Highest Ranking: 2 (Dec. 1968). HOF: 1985

Year	Rk	TP	TW	TF	GS	Aus	Fre	Wim	US	DC	Oly	MW	ML	Pct	CL	GR	HD	CP	IN	OD
1959	....	1	0	0	....	....	....	....	1rd	....	....	....	....	....	....	....	....	....	....	....
1960	....	1	0	0	....	....	....	....	2rd	....	....	....	....	....	....	....	....	....	....	....
1961	....	1	0	0	....	....	....	....	2rd	....	....	....	....	....	....	....	....	....	....	....
1962	....	1	0	0	....	....	....	....	2rd	....	....	....	....	....	....	....	....	....	....	....
1963	....	2	0	0	....	....	....	3rd	3rd	1-0	....	....	....	....	....	....	....	....	....	....
1964	....	2	0	0	....	....	....	4rd	4rd	....	....	....	....	....	....	....	....	....	....	....
1965	10	2	0	0	....	....	....	4rd	SF	4-0	....	....	....	....	....	....	....	....	....	....
1966	7	2	0	1	....	F	....	....	3rd	2-0	....	....	....	....	....	....	....	....	....	....
1967	9	1	0	1	....	F	....	....	....	2-2	....	....	....	....	....	....	....	....	....	....
1968	2	3	1	0	11-1	....	....	SF	W	11-1	....	12	2	.857	0-0	12-2	0-0	0-0	0-0	12-2
1969	8	5	0	1	13-3	....	4rd	SF	SF	2-0	....	17	5	.773	5-2	10-2	2-1	0-1	0-1	17-4
1970	9	10	5	0	15-3	W	4rd	4rd	QF	2-0	....	21	5	.808	4-1	11-2	3-1	3-2	3-2	18-3
1971	6	9	2	5	15-4	F	QF	3rd	SF	....	....	22	7	.759	7-2	11-3	0-0	4-2	4-2	18-5
1972	5	8	4	2	6-1	....	....	....	F	....	....	9	4	.692	0-0	6-1	2-2	1-1	1-1	8-3

Year	Rk	TP	TW	TF	GS	Aus	Fre	Wim	US	DC	Oly	MW	ML	Pct	CL	GR	HD	CP	IN	OD
1973	10	11	2	7	5-2	....	4rd	....	3rd	....	....	19	9	.679	4-2	3-2	7-3	5-2	6-3	13-6
1974	7	12	4	6	9-3	....	4rd	3rd	QF	1-0	....	26	8	.765	3-1	7-3	11-2	5-2	11-2	15-6
1975	4	14	8	2	10-1	....	....	W	4rd	....	....	29	6	.829	4-2	10-1	6-3	9-1	15-2	14-4
1976	12	20	5	3	7-3	....	4rd	4rd	2rd	1-1	....	50	15	.769	16-7	3-2	6-2	25-4	25-4	25-11
1977	130	1	0	0	3-1	QF/	....	....	....	....	....	3	1	.750	0-0	3-1	0-0	0-0	0-0	3-1
1978	13	24	2	1	10-4	SF	4rd	1rd	4rd	1-1	....	56	22	.718	18-5	11-5	10-5	17-7	21-9	35-13
1979	7	13	0	2	2-2	....	3rd	1rd	....	....	....	28	13	.683	5-5	4-2	0-1	19-5	19-5	9-8
TOTALS		**143**	**33**	**34**	**106-28**	....	....	....	....	**27-5**		**292**	**97**	**.751**	**66-27**	**91-26**	**47-20**	**88-27**	**105-31**	**187-66**

Doubles Titles: Aus (1), Fre (1)

• AUSTIN, Tracy   Tracy Ann Austin Holt

Female. Born: Dec. 12, 1962. Palos Verdes Peninsula, CA, United States. Height: 5' 5". Weight: 120 lbs. Plays: right.
Status: Turned Pro 1978. Earnings: $2,092,380. Highest Ranking: 1 (Apr. 1980). HOF: 1992

Year	Rk	TP	TW	TF	GS	Aus	Fre	Wim	US	FC	Oly	MW	ML	Pct	CL	GR	HD	CP	IN	OD
1977	12	8	0	0	5-2	....	....	3rd	QF	....	....	11	8	.579	6-3	1-1	2-1	2-3	2-3	9-5
1978	6	15	2	2	7-2	....	....	4rd	QF	4-1	....	43	13	.768	3-1	11-4	15-5	14-3	14-3	29-10
1979	3	19	8	3	11-1	....	....	SF	W	4-0	....	74	11	.871	14-0	8-1	26-4	26-6	31-6	43-5
1980	2	19	11	5	10-2	....	....	SF	SF	5-0	....	86	8	.915	13-1	11-1	23-2	39-4	44-4	42-4
1981	2	15	8	1	13-2	QF	....	QF	W	....	....	55	7	.887	2-1	12-2	26-1	15-3	24-4	31-3
1982	4	12	1	2	10-3	....	QF	QF	QF	....	....	35	11	.761	3-1	6-3	15-3	11-4	17-6	18-5
1983	9	8	0	1	4-1	....	QF	....	....	....	....	24	8	.750	8-2	4-1	0-0	12-5	12-5	12-3
1984	....	2	0	0	0-0	....	....	....	....	....	....	2	2	.500	0-0	0-0	0-0	2-2	2-2	0-0
1989	....	2	0	0	0-0	....	....	....	....	....	....	0	2	.000	0-1	0-0	0-1	0-0	0-0	0-2
1993	115	6	0	0	0-0	....	....	....	....	....	....	6	6	.500	0-0	0-0	5-4	1-2	1-2	5-4
1994	....	8	0	0	1-2	2rd	1rd	....	....	....	....	5	8	.385	2-3	0-1	3-4	0-0	1-1	4-7
TOTALS		**114**	**30**	**14**	**61-15**	....	....	....	....	**13-1**		**341**	**84**	**.802**	**51-13**	**53-14**	**115-25**	**122-32**	**148-36**	**193-48**

Held number one tour ranking 2 times for a total of 22 weeks. Last ranked number one in 1980.

• BALESTRAT, Dianne   see **FROMHOTLZ, Dianne**, page 843

• BARAZZUTTI, Corrado   Corrado Barazzutti

Male. Born: Feb. 19, 1953. Udine, Italy. Height: 5' 10". Weight: 155 lbs. Plays: right.
Status: Turned Pro 1971. Earnings: $775,783. Highest Ranking: 10 (Dec. 1978).

Year	Rk	TP	TW	TF	GS	Aus	Fre	Wim	US	DC	Oly	MW	ML	Pct	CL	GR	HD	CP	IN	OD
1971	....	2	0	0	0-1	....	1rd	....	....	....	....	0	2	.000	0-2	0-0	0-0	0-0	0-0	0-2
1972	....	3	0	0	0-1	....	....	1rd	....	3-1	....	1	3	.250	1-1	0-1	0-0	0-0	0-1	1-2
1973	....	5	0	0	2-3	....	3rd	1rd	1rd	3-1	....	3	5	.375	2-2	0-2	1-1	0-0	1-1	2-4
1974	56	2	0	0	2-1	....	3rd	....	....	1-1	....	3	2	.600	3-2	0-0	0-0	0-0	0-0	3-2
1975	40	4	0	1	2-2	....	3rd	1rd	....	1-1	....	3	4	.429	3-3	0-1	0-0	0-0	0-0	3-4
1976	22	9	1	2	4-2	....	4rd	....	2rd	5-1	....	18	8	.692	18-8	0-0	0-0	0-0	1-2	18-8
1977	11	11	3	1	5-2	....	1rd	....	SF	4-3	....	11	8	.579	10-5	0-1	0-0	1-2	1-2	10-6
1978	10	25	0	2	6-2	....	SF	....	2rd	1-1	....	51	25	.671	37-13	0-0	10-5	4-7	9-10	42-15
1979	33	22	0	2	2-2	....	3rd	1rd	....	9-2	....	37	22	.627	24-11	0-1	9-4	4-6	10-8	27-14
1980	24	19	1	0	5-2	....	QF	2rd	....	5-3	....	34	18	.654	28-13	1-1	1-1	4-3	5-4	29-14
1981	53	19	0	0	0-1	....	1rd	....	....	2-2	....	19	19	.500	15-17	0-0	0-0	4-2	4-2	15-17
1982	113	24	0	0	0-1	....	1rd	....	....	2-2	....	22	24	.478	10-15	0-0	4-3	8-6	12-9	10-15
1983	54	16	0	0	0-0	....	....	....	....	2-2	....	18	16	.529	17-13	0-0	1-2	0-1	1-3	17-13
1984	....	8	0	0	1-1	....	2rd	....	....	1-1	....	6	8	.429	5-6	0-0	0-0	1-2	1-2	5-6
TOTALS		**169**	**5**	**8**	**29-21**	....	....	....	....	**39-21**		**226**	**164**	**.579**	**173-111**	**1-7**	**26-17**	**26-29**	**44-42**	**182-122**

• BARKER, Sue   Sue Barker

Female. Born: Apr. 19, 1956. Paignton, Great Britain. Height: 5' 5". Weight: 115 lbs. Plays: right.
Status: Turned Pro 1976. Earnings: $878,701. Highest Ranking: 4 (Mar. 1977).

Year	Rk	TP	TW	TF	GS	Aus	Fre	Wim	US	FC	Oly	MW	ML	Pct	CL	GR	HD	CP	IN	OD
1973	....	2	1	1	1-1	....	....	2rd	....	....	....	1	1	.500	0-0	1-1	0-0	0-0	0-0	1-1
1974	....	5	3	0	2-2	3rd	....	1rd	....	....	....	2	2	.500	0-0	2-2	0-0	0-0	0-0	2-2
1975	....	8	1	2	8-4	SF	3rd	3rd	2rd	1-1	....	9	6	.600	4-3	5-2	0-1	0-0	0-1	9-5
1976	7	8	3	2	13-3	QF	....	4rd	....	2-1	....	16	5	.762	8-1	5-2	0-1	3-1	3-1	13-4
1977	5	23	2	7	9-3	/SF	....	SF	3rd	3-1	....	46	16	.742	2-1	13-5	5-2	26-8	26-8	20-8
1978	26	15	0	0	5-2	QF	....	4rd	....	1-1	....	13	15	.464	0-0	6-4	0-2	7-9	7-9	6-6
1979	10	26	4	5	1-3	....	2rd	1rd	2rd	2-1	....	35	22	.614	4-3	11-4	8-6	12-9	12-9	23-13
1980	16	17	0	2	2-2	3rd	....	2rd	....	2-1	....	28	17	.622	3-2	9-5	2-2	14-8	14-8	14-9
1981	14	20	1	0	5-4	3rd	1rd	3rd	2rd	3-1	....	31	19	.620	7-4	9-5	6-4	9-6	9-6	22-13

Year	Rk	TP	TW	TF	GS	Aus	Fre	Wim	US	FC	Oly	MW	ML	Pct	CL	GR	HD	CP	IN	OD
1982	62	20	0	0	0-2	1rd	....	1rd	....	1-1	....	12	20	.375	4-3	3-6	2-3	3-8	3-8	9-12
1983	57	16	0	0	0-1	....	....	1rd	....	....	....	15	16	.484	2-4	3-3	7-5	3-4	3-4	12-12
1984	....	14	0	0	1-3	....	1rd	2rd	1rd	....	....	2	14	.125	0-4	2-4	0-5	0-1	0-3	2-11
TOTALS		**174**	**15**	**19**	**47-30**	....	....	....	....	**15-8**	....	**210**	**153**	**.579**	**34-25**	**69-43**	**30-31**	**77-54**	**77-57**	**133-96**

• BECKER, Boris   Boris Becker

Male. Born: Nov. 22, 1967. Leimen, Germany. Height: 6' 3". Weight: 185 lbs. Plays: right.
Status: Turned Pro 1984. Earnings: $25,080,956. Highest Ranking: 1 (Jan. 1991).

Year	Rk	TP	TW	TF	GS	Aus	Fre	Wim	US	DC	Oly	MW	ML	Pct	CL	GR	HD	CP	IN	OD
1983	563	1	0	0	0-0	....	....	....	....	....	....	0	1	.000	0-0	0-0	0-0	0-1	0-1	0-0
1984	65	11	0	0	6-2	QF	....	3rd	....	....	....	11	11	.500	2-3	6-3	1-3	2-2	3-5	8-6
1985	6	22	3	2	11-3	2rd	2rd	W	4rd	7-1	....	57	19	.750	11-5	13-1	12-3	21-10	21-10	36-9
1986	2	19	6	3	16-2	....	QF	W	SF	4-0	....	69	13	.841	12-4	10-1	24-4	23-4	28-4	41-9
1987	5	18	3	1	11-4	4rd	SF	2rd	4rd	3-1	....	53	15	.779	10-4	9-2	22-5	12-4	15-5	38-10
1988	4	16	7	1	10-3	....	4rd	F	2rd	6-0	....	56	9	.862	7-4	12-1	17-2	20-2	26-2	30-7
1989	2	13	5	2	22-2	4rd	SF	W	W	7-0	....	64	8	.889	15-3	7-1	15-3	27-2	27-2	37-6
1990	2	20	5	5	15-4	QF	1rd	F	SF	....	....	71	15	.826	10-5	10-2	25-5	26-3	31-3	40-12
1991	3	14	2	3	20-3	W	SF	F	3rd	4-0	....	50	12	.806	10-3	6-1	17-5	17-3	17-3	33-9
1992	5	20	5	0	9-3	3rd	....	QF	4rd	2-0	3rd	52	15	.776	7-5	4-2	17-4	24-4	31-5	21-10
1993	11	22	2	1	9-4	1rd	2rd	SF	4rd	....	....	41	20	.672	5-6	7-2	13-6	16-6	16-7	25-13
1994	3	21	4	3	5-2	....	....	SF	1rd	....	....	49	17	.742	4-2	5-2	19-6	21-7	25-8	24-9
1995	5	20	2	4	13-4	1rd	3rd	F	SF	3-1	....	54	18	.750	7-4	9-2	15-6	23-6	29-7	25-11
1996	6	19	5	1	9-1	W	....	3rd	....	....	....	42	14	.750	5-5	7-1	9-3	21-5	22-6	20-8
1997	63	11	0	0	4-2	1rd	....	QF	....	2-0	....	19	11	.633	4-3	7-2	4-3	4-3	5-4	14-7
1998	69	10	0	1	0-0	....	....	....	....	....	....	15	10	.600	10-4	0-1	3-2	2-3	3-4	12-6
1999	131	6	0	1	3-1	....	....	4rd	....	....	....	10	6	.625	1-1	4-2	5-3	0-0	0-0	10-6
TOTALS		**263**	**49**	**28**	**163-40**	....	....	....	....	**38-3**	....	**713**	**214**	**.769**	**120-61**	**116-26**	**218-63**	**259-65**	**299-76**	**414-138**

Held number one tour ranking 2 times for a total of 12 weeks. Last ranked number one in 1991.

• BERASATEGUI, Alberto   Alberto Berasategui

Male. Born: June 28, 1973. Bilbao, Spain. Height: 5' 8". Weight: 145 lbs. Plays: right.
Status: Turned Pro 1991. Earnings: $4,676,187. Highest Ranking: 8 (Dec. 1994).

Year	Rk	TP	TW	TF	GS	Aus	Fre	Wim	US	DC	Oly	MW	ML	Pct	CL	GR	HD	CP	IN	OD
1992	115	11	0	0	0-1	....	1rd	....	....	....	....	8	11	.421	5-7	0-0	3-4	0-0	0-0	8-11
1993	36	20	1	3	2-2	....	2rd	....	2rd	1-0	....	28	19	.596	26-17	0-0	2-2	0-0	0-0	28-19
1994	8	33	7	2	6-2	....	F	....	1rd	1-0	....	65	26	.714	63-15	0-0	1-3	1-8	1-8	64-18
1995	33	32	1	1	2-1	....	3rd	....	....	0-2	....	36	31	.537	27-20	0-1	7-7	2-3	2-3	34-28
1996	19	29	3	0	3-2	....	3rd	....	2rd	....	....	46	26	.639	37-17	0-0	6-5	3-4	3-4	43-22
1997	26	28	1	1	2-3	3rd	1rd	....	1rd	....	....	40	27	.597	32-15	0-0	7-9	1-3	1-4	39-23
1998	21	25	1	1	7-3	QF	4rd	....	1rd	....	....	32	24	.571	25-15	0-0	7-9	0-0	0-0	32-24
1999	61	20	0	1	3-2	1rd	4rd	....	....	....	....	20	20	.500	20-15	0-0	0-5	0-0	0-0	20-20
2000	153	14	0	0	0-3	1rd	1rd	1rd	....	....	....	4	14	.222	3-8	0-1	1-5	0-0	0-0	4-14
2001	737	1	0	0	0-0	....	....	....	....	....	....	0	1	.000	0-1	0-0	0-0	0-0	0-0	0-1
TOTALS		**213**	**14**	**9**	**25-19**	....	....	....	....	**2-2**	....	**279**	**199**	**.584**	**238-130**	**0-2**	**34-49**	**7-18**	**7-19**	**272-180**

• BERGER, Jay   Jay Berger

Male. Born: Nov. 26, 1966. Fort Dix, NJ, United States. Height: 5' 11". Weight: 165 lbs. Plays: right.
Status: Turned Pro 1985. Earnings: $992,136. Highest Ranking: 10 (Dec. 1989).

Year	Rk	TP	TW	TF	GS	Aus	Fre	Wim	US	DC	Oly	MW	ML	Pct	CL	GR	HD	CP	IN	OD
1985	250	2	0	0	3-1	....	....	....	4rd	....	....	3	2	.600	0-1	0-0	3-1	0-0	0-0	3-2
1986	82	4	1	0	1-1	....	....	....	2rd	....	....	7	3	.700	6-1	0-0	1-2	0-0	0-0	7-3
1987	47	19	0	1	3-2	....	3rd	....	2rd	....	....	28	19	.596	14-9	0-0	13-9	1-1	1-1	27-18
1988	34	17	1	0	3-3	....	2rd	2rd	2rd	1-0	....	29	16	.644	8-5	1-1	20-9	0-1	0-2	29-14
1989	10	20	1	2	8-2	....	QF	....	QF	....	....	40	19	.678	14-4	0-0	22-12	4-3	4-4	36-15
1990	18	18	0	1	3-2	....	1rd	....	4rd	1-0	....	32	18	.640	9-8	0-0	19-7	4-3	4-3	28-15
1991	....	3	0	0	2-1	3rd	....	....	....	....	....	2	3	.400	0-0	0-0	2-2	0-1	0-1	2-2
TOTALS		**83**	**3**	**4**	**23-12**	....	....	....	....	**2-0**	....	**141**	**80**	**.638**	**51-28**	**1-1**	**80-42**	**9-9**	**9-11**	**132-69**

• BJORKMAN, Jonas　　　　Jonas Lars Bjorkman

Male. Born: Mar. 23, 1972. Vaxjo, Sweden. Height: 6'. Weight: 180 lbs. Plays: right.
Status: Turned Pro 1991. Earnings: $9,114,985. Highest Ranking: 4 (Nov. 1997).

Year	Rk	TP	TW	TF	GS	Aus	Fre	Wim	US	DC	Oly	MW	ML	Pct	CL	GR	HD	CP	IN	OD
1991	691	1	0	0	0-0	....	....	....	....	....	....	0	1	.000	0-1	0-0	0-0	0-0	0-0	0-1
1992	331	1	0	0	0-0	....	....	....	....	....	....	0	1	.000	0-0	0-0	0-0	0-1	0-1	0-0
1993	95	8	0	0	1-1	....	....	....	2rd	....	....	6	8	.429	0-1	0-1	3-2	3-4	5-5	1-3
1994	50	26	0	0	10-4	2rd	3rd	4rd	QF	....	....	31	26	.544	3-2	5-3	17-14	6-7	6-8	25-18
1995	30	28	0	0	5-4	3rd	1rd	2rd	3rd	1-1	....	35	28	.556	4-5	2-3	23-14	6-6	8-8	27-20
1996	69	25	0	0	8-4	4rd	4rd	1rd	3rd	2-0	1rd	25	25	.500	6-4	5-3	13-16	1-2	2-5	23-20
1997	4	29	3	2	9-4	4rd	2rd	1rd	SF	5-1	....	71	26	.732	6-5	6-3	45-13	14-5	25-9	46-17
1998	24	28	1	0	10-4	QF	1rd	3rd	QF	3-1	....	38	27	.585	3-6	8-2	19-14	8-5	9-7	29-20
1999	74	23	0	0	3-4	1rd	1rd	2rd	3rd	....	....	24	23	.511	2-3	4-3	18-16	0-1	3-3	21-20
2000	44	25	0	0	6-4	3rd	1rd	4rd	2rd	....	....	30	25	.545	1-3	8-3	15-16	6-3	10-7	20-18
2001	60	26	0	0	3-4	1rd	1rd	3rd	2rd	0-2	....	23	26	.469	1-4	5-3	15-18	2-1	3-5	20-21
2002	48	24	1	0	4-4	QF	1rd	1rd	1rd	0-1	....	21	23	.477	0-6	5-2	13-12	3-3	4-5	17-18
TOTALS		**244**	**5**	**3**	**59-37**	....	....	....	....	**11-6**		**304**	**239**	**.560**	**26-40**	**48-26**	**181-135**	**49-38**	**75-63**	**229-176**

• BLOOMER, Shirley　　　　Shirley Bloomer Brasher

Female. Born: June 13, 1934. Grimsby, Great Britain. Height: –. Weight: –. Plays: –.
Status: Amateur. Earnings: –. Highest Ranking: 3 (Dec. 1957).

Year	Rk	TP	TW	TF	GS	Aus	Fre	Wim	US	FC	Oly	MW	ML	Pct	CL	GR	HD	CP	IN	OD
1952	....	1	0	0	....	....	....	1rd	....	....	....	....	....	....	....	....	....	....	....	....
1953	....	1	0	0	....	....	....	3rd	....	....	....	....	....	....	....	....	....	....	....	....
1954	....	1	0	0	....	....	3rd	....	....	....	....	....	....	....	....	....	....	....	....	....
1955	....	3	0	0	....	....	QF	4rd	3rd	....	....	....	....	....	....	....	....	....	....	....
1956	7	3	0	0	....	....	QF	QF	SF	....	....	....	....	....	....	....	....	....	....	....
1957	3	3	1	0	....	....	W	4rd	QF	....	....	....	....	....	....	....	....	....	....	....
1958	5	2	0	1	....	....	F	QF	....	....	....	....	....	....	....	....	....	....	....	....
1959	....	2	0	0	....	....	QF	....	3rd	....	....	....	....	....	....	....	....	....	....	....
1960	....	1	0	0	....	....	....	3rd	....	....	....	....	....	....	....	....	....	....	....	....
1961	....	1	0	0	....	....	....	2rd	....	....	....	....	....	....	....	....	....	....	....	....
1963	....	1	0	0	....	....	....	2rd	....	....	....	....	....	....	....	....	....	....	....	....
1966	....	1	0	0	....	....	....	4rd	....	....	....	....	....	....	....	....	....	....	....	....
1968	....	1	0	0	1-1	....	....	4rd	....	....	....	1	1	.500	0-0	1-1	0-0	0-0	0-0	1-1
1969	....	1	0	0	1-1	....	....	2rd	....	....	....	1	1	.500	0-0	1-1	0-0	0-0	0-0	1-1
1970	....	1	0	0	1-1	....	....	3rd	....	....	....	1	1	.500	0-0	1-1	0-0	0-0	0-0	1-1
TOTALS		**23**	**1**	**1**	**3-3**	....	....	....	....	....		**3**	**3**	**.500**	**0-0**	**3-3**	**0-0**	**0-0**	**0-0**	**3-3**

Doubles Titles: Fre (1)

• BORG, Bjorn　　　　Bjorn Rune Borg

Male. Born: June 6, 1956. Sodertalje, Sweden. Height: 5' 11". Weight: 160 lbs. Plays: right.
Status: Turned Pro 1972. Earnings: $3,655,751. Highest Ranking: 1 (Aug. 1977). HOF: 1987

Year	Rk	TP	TW	TF	GS	Aus	Fre	Wim	US	DC	Oly	MW	ML	Pct	CL	GR	HD	CP	IN	OD
1972	....	2	0	0	0-0	....	....	....	....	2-2	....	1	2	.333	0-0	0-0	1-1	0-1	1-2	0-0
1973	18	6	0	5	10-3	....	4rd	QF	4rd	3-1	....	18	6	.750	3-1	7-2	4-2	4-1	8-2	10-4
1974	3	15	7	5	11-3	3rd	W	3rd	2rd	6-0	....	24	8	.750	13-0	5-6	4-1	2-1	6-2	18-6
1975	3	13	5	4	16-2	....	W	QF	SF	12-0	....	32	8	.800	17-3	4-1	7-3	4-1	11-4	21-4
1976	2	16	6	2	17-2	....	QF	W	F	....	....	49	10	.831	16-3	7-1	7-3	19-4	22-5	27-5
1977	3	14	10	2	10-1	....	....	W	4rd	....	....	32	4	.889	7-1	7-1	9-1	9-2	14-2	18-2
1978	2	13	9	1	20-1	....	W	W	F	9-0	....	52	4	.929	18-0	7-1	10-2	17-2	21-3	31-1
1979	1	19	13	1	18-1	....	W	W	QF	3-0	....	74	6	.925	23-1	7-1	17-2	27-3	29-3	45-3
1980	1	15	9	3	20-1	....	W	W	F	2-0	....	60	6	.909	20-1	7-1	20-3	13-2	17-3	43-3
1981	4	9	3	3	19-2	....	W	F	F	....	....	35	6	.854	17-1	6-1	6-1	6-3	6-3	29-3
1982	262	1	0	0	0-0	....	....	....	....	....	....	2	1	.667	2-1	0-0	0-0	0-0	0-0	2-1
1983	285	1	0	0	0-0	....	....	....	....	....	....	1	1	.500	1-1	0-0	0-0	0-0	0-0	1-1
1984	....	1	0	0	0-0	....	....	....	....	....	....	0	1	.000	0-1	0-0	0-0	0-0	0-0	0-1
1991	....	1	0	0	0-0	....	....	....	....	....	....	0	1	.000	0-1	0-0	0-0	0-0	0-1	0-0
1992	....	8	0	0	0-0	....	....	....	....	....	....	0	8	.000	0-4	0-0	0-4	0-0	0-2	0-6
1993	....	3	0	0	0-0	....	....	....	....	....	....	0	3	.000	0-0	0-0	0-1	0-2	0-3	0-0
TOTALS		**137**	**62**	**26**	**141-16**	....	....	....	....	**37-3**	....	**380**	**75**	**.835**	**137-19**	**57-15**	**85-24**	**101-22**	**135-34**	**245-41**

Held number one tour ranking 6 times for a total of 109 weeks. Last ranked number one in 1981.

• BOWREY, Bill   William Bowrey

Male. Born: Dec. 25, 1943. Sydney, Australia. Height: –. Weight: –. Plays: right.
Status: Amateur. Earnings: –. Highest Ranking: –.

Year	Rk	TP	TW	TF	GS	Aus	Fre	Wim	US	DC	Oly	MW	ML	Pct	CL	GR	HD	CP	IN	OD
1962	....	2	0	0	....	3rd	....	2rd	....	....	....	....	....	....	....	....	....	....	....	....
1963	....	1	0	0	....	3rd	....	....	....	....	....	....	....	....	....	....	....	....	....	....
1964	....	4	0	0	....	4rd	2rd	1rd	4rd	....	....	....	....	....	....	....	....	....	....	....
1965	....	3	0	0	....	QF	3rd	1rd	....	....	....	....	....	....	....	....	....	....	....	....
1966	....	4	0	0	....	QF	1rd	4rd	QF	....	....	....	....	....	....	....	....	....	....	....
1967	....	4	0	0	....	QF	2rd	3rd	4rd	....	....	....	....	....	....	....	....	....	....	....
1968	....	3	1	0	5-1	W	....	2rd	....	1-1	....	6	2	.750	0-0	6-2	0-0	0-0	0-0	6-2
1969	....	4	0	0	8-4	QF	2rd	3rd	3rd	1-1	....	8	4	.667	1-1	7-3	0-0	0-0	0-0	8-4
1970	....	3	0	0	3-3	3rd	....	2rd	3rd	....	....	3	3	.500	0-0	3-3	0-0	0-0	0-0	3-3
1971	....	7	0	0	4-4	1rd	3rd	1rd	3rd	....	....	4	7	.364	2-3	2-3	0-0	0-1	0-1	4-6
1972	....	1	0	0	0-0	....	....	....	....	....	....	0	1	.000	0-0	0-0	0-1	0-0	0-0	0-1
1973	....	1	0	0	0-1	1rd	....	....	....	....	....	0	1	.000	0-0	0-1	0-0	0-0	0-0	0-1
1975	....	1	0	0	0-1	1rd	....	....	....	....	....	0	1	.000	0-0	0-1	0-0	0-0	0-0	0-1
TOTALS		**38**	**1**	**0**	**20-14**	....	....	....	....	**2-2**	....	**21**	**19**	**.525**	**3-4**	**18-13**	**0-1**	**0-1**	**0-1**	**21-18**

• BOWREY, Lesley   see TURNER, Lesley, page 893

• BROWNING, Françoise   see DURR, Françoise, page 839

• BRUGUERA, Sergi   Sergi Bruguera

Male. Born: Jan. 16, 1971. Barcelona, Spain. Height: 6' 2". Weight: 170 lbs. Plays: right.
Status: Turned Pro 1988. Earnings: $11,632,199. Highest Ranking: 3 (Aug. 1994).

Year	Rk	TP	TW	TF	GS	Aus	Fre	Wim	US	DC	Oly	MW	ML	Pct	CL	GR	HD	CP	IN	OD
1988	333	1	0	0	0-0	....	....	....	....	....	....	0	1	.000	0-1	0-0	0-0	0-0	0-0	0-1
1989	26	13	0	0	3-3	....	4rd	1rd	1rd	....	....	23	13	.639	23-11	0-1	0-1	0-0	0-0	23-13
1990	28	28	0	2	4-4	2rd	2rd	2rd	2rd	1-3	....	36	28	.563	23-17	1-1	7-7	5-3	5-3	31-25
1991	11	25	3	2	2-3	1rd	2rd	....	2rd	2-0	....	51	22	.699	38-9	0-0	7-8	6-5	7-6	44-16
1992	16	25	3	3	1-2	....	1rd	....	2rd	0-2	2rd	46	22	.676	39-10	0-0	5-4	2-8	3-9	43-13
1993	4	30	5	4	10-2	4rd	W	....	1rd	2-2	....	65	25	.722	44-9	0-0	13-7	8-9	9-10	56-15
1994	4	28	3	3	13-2	....	W	4rd	4rd	3-1	....	66	25	.725	35-6	4-2	13-8	14-9	14-9	52-16
1995	13	19	0	1	6-2	....	SF	....	2rd	3-1	....	40	19	.678	26-9	0-0	10-5	4-5	5-6	35-13
1996	81	21	0	1	3-2	....	2rd	....	3rd	....	F	26	21	.553	12-9	0-0	14-8	0-4	3-6	23-15
1997	8	28	0	4	11-3	3rd	F	....	4rd	....	....	49	28	.636	20-8	0-0	19-11	10-9	10-11	39-17
1998	135	27	0	0	1-3	1rd	1rd	....	2rd	....	....	12	27	.308	7-15	0-0	3-9	2-3	2-3	10-24
1999	372	1	0	0	0-0	....	....	....	....	....	....	0	1	.000	0-1	0-0	0-0	0-0	0-1
2000	85	15	0	1	0-1	....	1rd	....	....	....	....	17	15	.531	14-13	0-0	3-2	0-0	0-0	17-15
2001	108	21	0	0	1-4	1rd	2rd	1rd	1rd	....	....	15	21	.417	14-14	0-1	0-5	1-1	1-1	14-20
2002	290	3	0	0	0-0	....	....	....	....	....	....	1	3	.250	1-3	0-0	0-0	0-0	0-0	1-3
TOTALS		**285**	**14**	**21**	**55-31**	....	....	....	....	**11-9**	....	**447**	**271**	**.623**	**296-135**	**5-5**	**94-75**	**52-56**	**59-64**	**388-207**

• BUENO, Maria   Maria Esther Andion Bueno

Female. Born: Oct. 11, 1939. Sao Paolo, Brazil. Height: 5' 7". Weight: 125 lbs. Plays: right.
Status: Turned Pro 1974. Earnings: –. Highest Ranking: 1 (Dec. 1959). HOF: 1964

Year	Rk	TP	TW	TF	GS	Aus	Fre	Wim	US	FC	Oly	MW	ML	Pct	CL	GR	HD	CP	IN	OD
1957	....	1	0	0	....	....	1rd	....	....	....	....	....	....	....	....	....	....	....	....	....
1958	9	3	0	0	....	....	SF	QF	QF	....	....	....	....	....	....	....	....	....	....	....
1959	1	3	2	0	....	....	QF	W	W	....	....	....	....	....	....	....	....	....	....	....
1960	1	4	1	1	....	QF	SF	W	F	....	....	....	....	....	....	....	....	....	....	....
1961	....	1	0	0	....	QF	....	....	....	....	....	....	....	....	....	....	....	....	....	....
1962	2	2	0	0	....	....	SF	SF	....	....	....	....	....	....	....	....	....	....	....	....
1963	3	2	1	0	....	....	QF	W	....	....	....	....	....	....	....	....	....	....	....	....
1964	2	3	2	1	....	....	F	W	W	....	....	....	....	....	....	....	....	....	....	....
1965	2	4	0	2	....	F	SF	F	SF	1-0	....	....	....	....	....	....	....	....	....	....
1966	3	3	1	1	....	....	SF	F	W	....	....	....	....	....	....	....	....	....	....	....
1967	5	3	0	0	8-3	....	QF	4rd	2rd	0-0	....	8	3	.727	4-1	3-1	1-1	0-0	0-0	8-3
1968	....	5	2	1	10-3	....	QF	QF	SF	....	....	10	3	.769	3-1	7-2	0-0	0-0	0-0	10-3
1975	....	2	1	0	0-0	....	....	....	....	....	....	0	1	.000	0-0	0-0	0-1	0-0	0-1	0-0
1976	....	4	0	0	4-3	....	1rd	4rd	3rd	0-1	....	4	4	.500	1-2	3-1	0-0	0-1	0-1	4-3
1977	....	5	0	1	1-2	....	....	3rd	2rd	1-1	....	3	5	.375	1-2	2-2	0-0	0-1	0-1	3-4
TOTALS		**45**	**10**	**7**	**23-11**	....	....	....	....	**2-2**	....	**25**	**16**	**.610**	**9-6**	**15-6**	**1-2**	**0-2**	**0-3**	**25-13**

Held number one world ranking 2 times during amateur era. Doubles Titles: Aus (1), Fre (1), Wim (5), US (5).

• BUNGE, Bettina   Bettina Bunge

Female. Born: June 13, 1963. Adilswil, Sweden. Height: 5' 8". Weight: 125 lbs. Plays: right.
Status: Turned Pro 1979. Earnings: $1,126,424. Highest Ranking: 6 (Mar. 1983).

Year	Rk	TP	TW	TF	GS	Aus	Fre	Wim	US	FC	Oly	MW	ML	Pct	CL	GR	HD	CP	IN	OD
1978	105	2	0	0	2-1	....	....	....	3rd	....	....	2	2	.500	0-0	0-0	2-2	0-0	0-0	2-2
1979	32	16	0	1	3-3	....	3rd	2rd	1rd	....	....	10	16	.385	3-4	4-4	2-5	1-3	2-4	8-12
1980	19	23	0	1	6-4	1rd	3rd	3rd	3rd	4-0	....	35	23	.603	10-3	9-6	9-6	7-8	11-10	24-13
1981	9	23	0	2	8-4	3rd	4rd	2rd	3rd	3-0	....	50	23	.685	6-2	8-4	14-6	22-11	22-11	28-12
1982	9	23	3	1	6-3	....	2rd	SF	3rd	4-1	....	39	20	.661	9-5	7-2	10-5	13-8	13-10	26-10
1983	7	13	1	0	1-2	....	2rd	1rd	....	4-1	....	30	12	.714	14-5	3-2	0-0	13-5	13-5	17-7
1984	21	21	0	0	7-4	2rd	3rd	3rd	3rd	....	....	28	21	.571	2-4	12-6	8-4	6-7	8-8	20-13
1985	23	17	0	0	4-4	1rd	3rd	3rd	1rd	....	....	25	17	.595	8-4	5-4	9-5	3-4	3-4	22-13
1986	13	21	0	0	6-3	....	2rd	QF	2rd	1-1	....	35	21	.625	9-6	5-2	6-5	13-8	16-9	19-12
1987	15	18	0	1	5-2	....	....	3rd	4rd	....	....	32	18	.640	6-4	4-3	15-6	7-5	8-6	24-12
1989	71	4	0	0	0-0	....	....	....	....	....	....	7	4	.636	0-0	0-0	5-1	2-3	4-3	3-1
TOTALS		**181**	**4**	**6**	**48-30**	....	....	....	....	**16-3**	....	**293**	**177**	**.623**	**67-37**	**57-33**	**80-45**	**89-62**	**100-70**	**193-107**

Represented Germany in the Federation Cup (1980-1986)

• CAPRIATI, Jennifer   Jennifer Marie Capriati

Female. Born: Mar. 29, 1976. New York, NY, United States. Height: 5' 5". Weight: 135 lbs. Plays: right.
Status: Turned Pro 1990. Earnings: $6,974,563. Highest Ranking: 1 (Oct. 2001).

Year	Rk	TP	TW	TF	GS	Aus	Fre	Wim	US	FC	Oly	MW	ML	Pct	CL	GR	HD	CP	IN	OD
1990	8	12	1	2	11-3	....	SF	4rd	4rd	5-0	....	42	11	.792	13-3	4-2	23-4	2-2	2-2	40-9
1991	6	14	2	1	13-3	....	4rd	SF	SF	4-1	....	42	12	.778	9-4	5-1	23-4	5-3	5-3	37-9
1992	7	13	2	0	14-4	QF	QF	QF	3rd	....	W	35	11	.761	14-4	4-1	14-3	3-3	3-3	32-8
1993	9	12	1	1	12-4	QF	QF	QF	1rd	....	....	29	11	.725	12-6	4-1	13-4	0-0	0-0	29-11
1994	....	1	0	0	0-0	....	....	....	....	....	....	0	1	.000	0-0	0-0	0-0	0-1	0-1	0-0
1996	24	11	0	0	0-2	....	1rd	....	1rd	0-2	....	16	11	.593	0-3	0-0	10-6	6-2	9-4	7-7
1997	66	11	0	0	0-2	1rd	....	1rd	1rd	....	....	10	11	.476	3-2	0-0	7-7	0-2	2-4	8-7
1998	101	12	0	0	1-2	....	....	2rd	1rd	....	....	8	12	.400	6-6	1-1	1-5	0-0	1-1	7-11
1999	23	15	2	0	8-4	2rd	4rd	2rd	4rd	....	....	26	13	.667	10-3	1-1	14-8	1-1	7-4	19-9
2000	14	20	1	2	11-4	SF	1rd	4rd	4rd	....	....	36	19	.655	0-3	8-3	21-11	7-2	13-5	23-14
2001	2	17	3	5	24-2	W	W	SF	SF	....	....	56	14	.800	16-2	5-1	35-11	0-0	7-4	49-10
2002	3	17	1	3	20-3	W	SF	QF	QF	....	....	48	16	.750	14-4	4-1	29-10	1-1	3-4	45-12
TOTALS		**155**	**13**	**14**	**114-33**	....	....	....	....	**9-3**	....	**348**	**142**	**.710**	**97-40**	**36-12**	**190-73**	**25-17**	**52-35**	**296-107**

Held number one tour ranking 4 times for a total of 18 weeks. Last ranked number one in 2002.

• CARLSSON, Kent   Kent Carlsson

Male. Born: Jan. 3, 1968. Eskilstuna, Sweden. Height: 5' 11". Weight: 160 lbs. Plays: right.
Status: Turned Pro 1983. Earnings: $998,956. Highest Ranking: 6 (Dec. 1988).

Year	Rk	TP	TW	TF	GS	Aus	Fre	Wim	US	DC	Oly	MW	ML	Pct	CL	GR	HD	CP	IN	OD
1983	794	1	0	0	0-0	....	....	....	....	....	....	0	1	.000	0-1	0-0	0-0	0-0	0-0	0-1
1984	139	8	0	0	2-1	....	3rd	....	....	....	....	7	8	.467	7-8	0-0	0-0	0-0	0-0	7-8
1985	50	12	0	1	1-1	....	2rd	....	....	....	....	17	12	.586	17-10	0-0	0-2	0-0	0-2	17-10
1986	13	15	2	2	2-2	....	3rd	....	1rd	1-0	....	44	13	.772	39-10	0-0	5-3	0-0	2-1	42-12
1987	12	10	2	2	3-1	....	4rd	....	....	3-0	....	37	8	.822	35-7	0-0	2-1	0-0	0-0	37-8
1988	6	12	5	2	3-1	....	4rd	....	....	0-1	....	50	7	.877	50-7	0-0	0-0	0-0	0-1	50-6
1989	309	6	0	1	0-0	....	....	....	....	....	....	5	6	.455	5-6	0-0	0-0	0-0	0-0	5-6
TOTALS		**64**	**9**	**8**	**11-6**	....	....	....	....	**4-1**	....	**160**	**55**	**.744**	**153-49**	**0-0**	**7-6**	**0-0**	**2-4**	**158-51**

• CASALS, Rosie   Rosemary Casals

Female. Born: Sept. 16, 1948. San Francisco, CA, United States. Height: 5' 2". Weight: 120 lbs. Plays: right.
Status: Turned Pro 1970. Earnings: $1,364,955. Highest Ranking: 3 (Dec. 1970). HOF: 1996

Year	Rk	TP	TW	TF	GS	Aus	Fre	Wim	US	FC	Oly	MW	ML	Pct	CL	GR	HD	CP	IN	OD
1964	....	1	0	0	....	....	....	....	3rd	....	....	....	....	....	....	....	....	....	....	....
1965	....	1	0	0	....	....	....	....	1rd	....	....	....	....	....	....	....	....	....	....	....
1966	9	2	0	0	....	....	....	4rd	SF	....	....	....	....	....	....	....	....	....	....	....
1967	6	4	0	0	....	SF	4rd	SF	4rd	4-0	....	....	....	....	....	....	....	....	....	....
1968	....	4	1	2	6-3	....	4rd	4rd	3rd	....	....	6	3	.667	1-1	5-2	0-0	0-0	0-0	6-3
1969	6	4	0	3	14-4	QF	QF	SF	SF	....	....	14	4	.778	3-1	11-3	0-0	0-0	0-0	14-4
1970	3	4	1	1	13-3	....	QF	SF	F	....	....	13	3	.813	3-1	10-2	0-0	0-0	0-0	13-3
1971	4	15	2	12	6-2	....	....	2rd	F	....	....	6	2	.750	0-0	6-2	0-0	0-0	0-0	6-2
1972	7	6	3	1	8-3	....	3rd	SF	QF	....	....	8	3	.727	0-1	8-2	0-0	0-0	0-0	8-3
1973	5	5	3	3	7-2	....	....	QF	QF	....	....	8	2	.800	1-1	7-2	0-0	0-0	0-0	8-2

Year	Rk	TP	TW	TF	GS	Aus	Fre	Wim	US	FC	Oly	MW	ML	Pct	CL	GR	HD	CP	IN	OD
1974	6	3	0	2	6-2	....	....	4rd	QF	....	....	10	3	.769	0-0	6-2	1-1	3-1	3-1	7-2
1975	10	3	0	0	3-2	....	....	4rd	1rd	....	....	3	3	.500	0-1	3-1	0-0	0-1	0-1	3-2
1976	6	4	0	1	7-2	....	....	QF	QF	4-1	....	11	3	.786	3-1	4-1	0-0	4-1	4-1	7-2
1977	6	16	0	0	7-2	....	....	QF	4rd	....	....	35	16	.686	7-3	4-1	7-4	17-8	17-8	18-8
1978	22	14	0	0	0-0	....	....	....	....	....	....	21	14	.600	2-1	0-1	1-2	18-10	18-10	3-4
1979	28	23	0	0	2-3	....	1rd	3rd	1rd	....	....	19	23	.452	1-3	3-3	5-7	10-10	10-10	9-13
1980	59	25	0	0	0-3	1rd	....	2rd	2rd	....	....	14	25	.359	0-0	4-6	4-8	6-11	6-12	8-13
1981	55	12	0	0	3-4	1rd	2rd	1rd	4rd	....	....	8	12	.400	0-3	1-4	5-3	2-2	2-2	6-10
1982	98	8	0	0	1-2	....	....	2rd	2rd	....	....	4	8	.333	0-1	2-3	1-3	1-1	1-1	3-7
1983	56	12	0	0	4-2	....	....	3rd	3rd	....	....	9	12	.429	1-1	4-3	4-5	0-3	0-3	9-9
1984	172	4	0	0	1-2	....	....	1rd	2rd	....	....	1	4	.200	0-2	0-1	1-1	0-0	0-0	1-4
1985	183	4	0	0	1-1	....	....	....	2rd	....	....	1	4	.200	0-1	0-0	1-3	0-0	0-0	1-4
1986	....	2	0	0	0-0							0	2	.000	0-1	0-0	0-1	0-0	0-0	0-2
1988	....	2	0	0	0-0							0	2	.000	0-1	0-0	0-1	0-0	0-1	0-1
1989	....	2	0	0	0-0							0	2	.000	0-1	0-0	0-1	0-0	0-0	0-2
1990	....	1	0	0	0-0							0	1	.000	0-1	0-0	0-0	0-0	0-0	0-1
1991	....	1	0	0	0-0							0	1	.000	0-0	0-0	0-1	0-0	0-0	0-1
TOTALS		182	10	25	89-42	....	....	....	....	8-1		191	152	.557	22-26	78-39	30-41	61-48	61-50	130-102

Doubles Titles: Wim (5), US (4)

• CASH, Pat   Patrick Hart Cash

Male. Born: May 27, 1965. Melbourne, Australia. Height: 6'. Weight: 185 lbs. Plays: right.
Status: Turned Pro 1982. Earnings: $1,946,128. Highest Ranking: 7 (Dec. 1987).

Year	Rk	TP	TW	TF	GS	Aus	Fre	Wim	US	DC	Oly	MW	ML	Pct	CL	GR	HD	CP	IN	OD
1981	342	5	0	0	0-1	1rd	....	....	....	....	....	2	5	.286	0-0	1-4	0-0	1-1	1-1	1-4
1982	44	11	1	0	3-2	QF	....	....	1rd	....	....	17	10	.630	0-1	13-4	1-3	3-2	4-3	13-7
1983	38	24	1	0	8-4	4rd	1rd	4rd	3rd	5-3	....	38	23	.623	5-10	25-9	3-4	5-1	5-1	33-22
1984	8	17	0	1	13-4	QF	1rd	SF	SF	3-1	....	29	17	.630	4-4	12-3	7-6	6-4	6-5	23-12
1985	67	9	0	0	1-1	....	....	2rd	....	1-1	....	12	9	.571	1-2	4-2	0-1	7-4	8-5	4-4
1986	24	11	0	0	4-2	....	....	QF	1rd	6-0	....	24	11	.686	2-1	10-1	10-7	2-2	7-4	17-7
1987	7	20	3	2	12-3	F	1rd	W	1rd	4-0	....	46	17	.730	2-4	20-2	14-6	10-5	16-7	30-10
1988	20	9	0	1	13-3	F	4rd	QF	....	2-0	....	25	9	.735	5-1	6-2	12-4	2-2	2-2	23-7
1989	368	4	0	0	3-1	4rd	....	....	....	0-2	....	4	4	.500	0-2	0-0	4-2	0-0	0-2	4-2
1990	80	11	1	1	5-2	....	....	4rd	3rd	2-0	....	20	10	.667	0-0	5-2	13-6	2-2	3-3	17-7
1991	113	11	0	0	4-3	3rd	2rd	2rd	....	....	....	14	11	.560	1-3	4-2	5-2	4-4	4-4	10-7
1992	199	4	0	0	2-2	2rd	....	2rd	....	....	....	5	4	.556	0-0	4-2	1-2	0-0	0-0	5-4
1994	723	2	0	0	0-0	....	....	....	....	....	....	0	2	.000	0-0	0-0	0-2	0-0	0-0	0-2
1995	237	7	0	0	0-2	1rd	....	1rd	....	....	....	5	7	.417	0-1	0-2	2-2	3-2	3-2	2-5
1996	763	3	0	0	0-1	....	....	1rd	....	....	....	0	3	.000	0-0	0-1	0-2	0-0	0-0	0-3
1997	362	7	0	0	0-2	1rd	....	1rd	....	....	....	2	7	.222	0-1	0-1	2-4	0-1	0-2	2-5
TOTALS		155	6	5	68-33	....	....	....	....	23-7	....	243	149	.620	20-30	104-37	74-53	45-30	59-41	184-108

• CAWLEY, Evonne   see GOOLAGONG, Evonne, page 846

• CHANG, Michael   Michael Chang

Male. Born: Feb. 22, 1972. Hoboken, NJ, United States. Height: 5' 9". Weight: 160 lbs. Plays: right.
Status: Turned Pro 1988. Earnings: $19,070,332. Highest Ranking: 2 (Sept. 1996).

Year	Rk	TP	TW	TF	GS	Aus	Fre	Wim	US	DC	Oly	MW	ML	Pct	CL	GR	HD	CP	IN	OD
1987	163	4	0	0	1-1	....	....	....	2rd	....	....	4	4	.500	0-0	0-0	4-4	0-0	0-0	4-4
1988	30	14	1	0	6-3	....	3rd	2rd	4rd	....	....	23	13	.639	4-3	1-2	13-8	5-1	6-1	17-12
1989	5	18	2	1	13-2	....	W	4rd	4rd	2-0	....	47	16	.746	12-1	3-1	22-8	10-6	13-7	34-9
1990	15	22	1	2	9-3	....	QF	4rd	3rd	2-2	....	36	21	.632	6-6	4-2	19-8	7-5	9-8	27-13
1991	15	21	1	1	7-3	....	QF	1rd	4rd	....	....	47	20	.701	6-2	2-2	24-11	15-5	20-7	27-13
1992	6	26	3	2	9-4	3rd	3rd	1rd	SF	....	2rd	57	23	.713	9-6	0-1	39-8	9-8	16-10	41-13
1993	8	26	5	2	8-4	2rd	2rd	3rd	QF	....	....	66	21	.759	9-3	2-2	43-10	12-6	20-7	46-14
1994	6	27	6	3	9-3	....	3rd	QF	4rd	....	....	66	21	.759	9-4	4-1	34-10	19-6	24-8	42-13
1995	5	23	4	5	16-4	SF	F	2rd	QF	....	....	65	19	.774	14-2	1-1	31-10	19-6	25-8	40-11
1996	2	22	3	5	14-4	F	3rd	1rd	F	2-0	....	65	19	.774	5-3	0-1	50-9	10-6	16-8	49-11
1997	3	26	5	0	13-4	SF	4rd	1rd	SF	2-2	....	57	21	.731	10-4	3-3	44-9	0-5	8-8	49-13
1998	29	19	2	2	5-4	2rd	3rd	2rd	2rd	....	....	35	17	.673	10-6	1-1	24-7	0-3	7-5	28-12
1999	50	22	0	0	2-3	2rd	1rd	....	2rd	....	....	27	22	.551	2-4	0-0	21-17	4-1	9-6	18-16
2000	32	27	1	1	4-4	1rd	3rd	2rd	2rd	....	1rd	42	26	.618	6-5	7-3	27-16	2-2	9-5	33-21

Year	Rk	TP	TW	TF	GS	Aus	Fre	Wim	US	DC	Oly	MW	ML	Pct	CL	GR	HD	CP	IN	OD
2001	94	21	0	0	2-4	1rd	2rd	2rd	1rd	....	....	16	21	.432	4-6	1-2	11-13	0-0	3-3	13-18
2002	124	18	0	0	2-4	1rd	1rd	2rd	2rd	....	....	7	18	.280	1-2	1-3	5-13	0-0	0-3	7-15
TOTALS		**336**	**34**	**24**	**120-54**	....	....	....	....	**8-4**	....	**660**	**302**	**.686**	**107-57**	**30-25**	**411-161**	**112-60**	**185-94**	**475-208**

• CLEMENT, Arnaud

Arnaud Clement

Male. Born: Dec. 17, 1977. Aix-en-Provence, France. Height: 5' 8". Weight: 140 lbs. Plays: right.
Status: Turned Pro 1996. Earnings: $2,837,975. Highest Ranking: 10 (Apr. 2001).

Year	Rk	TP	TW	TF	GS	Aus	Fre	Wim	US	DC	Oly	MW	ML	Pct	CL	GR	HD	CP	IN	OD
1997	101	9	0	0	2-2	....	1rd	3rd	....	....	....	10	9	.526	1-2	2-1	2-1	5-5	7-6	3-3
1998	105	25	0	0	0-4	1rd	1rd	1rd	1rd	....	....	13	25	.342	3-6	1-3	4-10	5-6	7-7	6-18
1999	56	25	0	1	6-4	2rd	2rd	2rd	4rd	....	....	22	25	.468	4-6	2-3	15-10	1-6	5-9	17-16
2000	18	28	1	0	9-4	4rd	2rd	2rd	QF	0-1	2rd	36	27	.571	3-6	2-3	23-15	8-3	10-6	26-21
2001	17	28	0	1	12-4	F	1rd	4rd	4rd	4-2	....	37	28	.569	6-7	3-3	24-13	4-5	8-8	29-20
2002	38	26	0	1	9-4	2rd	3rd	4rd	4rd	2-2	....	32	26	.552	8-8	6-2	12-13	6-3	10-7	22-19
TOTALS		**141**	**1**	**3**	**38-22**	....	....	....	....	**6-5**	....	**150**	**140**	**.517**	**25-35**	**16-15**	**80-62**	**29-28**	**47-43**	**103-97**

• CLERC, Jose-Luis

Jose-Luis Clerc

Male. Born: Aug. 16, 1958. Buenos Aires, Argentina. Height: 6' 1". Weight: 175 lbs. Plays: right.
Status: Turned Pro 1978. Earnings: $1,987,036. Highest Ranking: 5 (Dec. 1981).

Year	Rk	TP	TW	TF	GS	Aus	Fre	Wim	US	DC	Oly	MW	ML	Pct	CL	GR	HD	CP	IN	OD
1976	....	0	0	0	....	....	....	....	1-0	....	....	0	0	.000	0-0	0-0	0-0	0-0	0-0	0-0
1978	15	20	3	4	3-4	1rd	2rd	1rd	3rd	3-1	....	45	17	.726	38-12	1-3	2-1	4-1	4-1	41-16
1979	16	22	1	1	7-3	....	2rd	4rd	4rd	1-3	....	52	21	.712	34-14	4-2	11-2	3-3	3-3	49-18
1980	8	28	6	1	4-4	2rd	2rd	3rd	1rd	5-1	....	68	22	.756	50-9	4-3	8-3	6-7	6-7	62-15
1981	5	20	6	1	10-3	....	SF	3rd	4rd	4-3	....	58	14	.806	46-5	2-1	8-2	2-6	6-7	52-7
1982	6	27	5	1	5-2	....	SF	....	1rd	1-0	....	66	22	.750	57-11	0-0	2-2	7-9	7-9	59-13
1983	8	19	4	1	1-3	....	2rd	1rd	1rd	2-2	....	31	15	.674	26-8	0-1	5-1	0-5	0-5	31-10
1984	33	15	0	1	1-1	....	2rd	....	....	2-2	....	19	15	.559	12-10	0-0	5-3	2-2	2-2	17-13
1985	29	15	0	0	2-2	....	3rd	....	1rd	1-2	....	25	15	.625	23-12	0-0	2-3	0-0	0-0	25-15
1989	....	4	0	0	0-1	....	1rd	....	....	....	....	1	4	.200	1-4	0-0	0-0	0-0	0-0	1-4
TOTALS		**170**	**25**	**10**	**33-23**	....	....	....	....	**20-14**	....	**365**	**145**	**.716**	**287-85**	**11-10**	**43-17**	**24-33**	**28-34**	**337-111**

• CLIJSTERS, Kim

Kim Clijsters

Female. Born: June 8, 1983. Bilzen, Belgium. Height: 5' 8". Weight: 150 lbs. Plays: right.
Status: Turned Pro 2000. Earnings: $3,649,280. Highest Ranking: 3 (Mar. 2002).

Year	Rk	TP	TW	TF	GS	Aus	Fre	Wim	US	FC	Oly	MW	ML	Pct	CL	GR	HD	CP	IN	OD
1999	47	8	1	1	5-2	....	....	4rd	3rd	....	....	19	7	.731	2-2	3-1	6-2	8-2	12-3	7-4
2000	18	19	2	1	2-4	1rd	1rd	2rd	2rd	2-2	....	30	17	.638	1-2	2-2	17-9	10-4	15-6	15-11
2001	5	21	3	3	17-4	4rd	F	QF	QF	4-0	....	58	18	.763	15-5	7-2	28-11	8-1	14-2	44-16
2002	4	21	4	2	11-4	SF	3rd	2rd	4rd	1-0	....	51	17	.750	10-3	2-2	33-11	6-1	18-2	33-15
TOTALS		**69**	**10**	**7**	**35-14**	....	....	....	....	**7-2**	....	**158**	**59**	**.728**	**28-12**	**14-7**	**84-33**	**32-8**	**59-13**	**99-46**

• COETZER, Amanda

Amanda Coetzer

Female. Born: Oct. 22, 1971. Hoopstad, South Africa. Height: 5' 2". Weight: 120 lbs. Plays: right.
Status: Turned Pro 1988. Earnings: $5,231,834. Highest Ranking: 3 (Nov. 1997).

Year	Rk	TP	TW	TF	GS	Aus	Fre	Wim	US	FC	Oly	MW	ML	Pct	CL	GR	HD	CP	IN	OD
1988	153	2	0	0	0-0	....	....	....	....	....	....	3	2	.600	2-1	0-0	1-1	0-0	0-0	3-2
1989	63	13	0	0	3-3	....	4rd	1rd	1rd	....	....	16	13	.552	8-6	1-2	7-5	0-0	0-0	16-13
1990	75	19	0	0	1-3	....	1rd	2rd	1rd	....	....	16	19	.457	4-5	1-2	11-11	0-1	0-3	16-16
1991	67	19	0	1	2-3	....	2rd	2rd	1rd	....	....	15	19	.441	5-6	1-2	9-11	0-0	0-1	15-18
1992	17	18	0	0	4-2	....	3rd	....	3rd	7-2	3rd	38	18	.679	17-9	0-0	20-8	1-1	1-1	37-17
1993	15	21	2	1	4-4	1rd	2rd	2rd	3rd	1-1	....	43	19	.694	12-6	2-2	25-8	4-3	4-4	39-15
1994	18	20	1	1	11-4	2rd	4rd	4rd	QF	....	....	38	19	.667	12-4	3-1	21-11	2-3	4-5	34-14
1995	19	22	0	2	4-4	3rd	2rd	2rd	1rd	4-0	....	34	22	.607	11-6	1-1	16-11	6-4	6-6	28-16
1996	17	24	0	1	13-4	SF	4rd	2rd	QF	1-3	2rd	33	24	.579	7-5	1-1	25-14	0-4	5-7	28-17
1997	4	28	2	1	14-4	SF	SF	2rd	4rd	3-1	....	61	26	.701	27-7	1-1	23-14	10-4	15-7	46-19
1998	17	24	1	0	8-4	4rd	1rd	2rd	QF	....	....	32	23	.582	10-5	1-2	16-11	5-5	7-7	25-16
1999	11	25	0	2	5-4	4rd	1rd	3rd	1rd	4-1	....	37	25	.597	6-6	4-2	23-14	4-3	9-7	28-18
2000	11	24	1	1	6-4	2rd	3rd	2rd	3rd	....	QF	46	23	.667	19-5	2-2	21-13	4-3	10-6	36-17
2001	19	22	1	1	8-4	QF	3rd	3rd	1rd	....	....	32	21	.604	16-6	2-2	11-11	3-2	5-6	27-15
2002	21	22	0	0	6-4	4rd	1rd	2rd	3rd	....	....	30	22	.577	5-5	1-2	19-12	5-3	6-6	24-16
TOTALS		**303**	**8**	**11**	**89-51**	....	....	....	....	**20-8**	....	**474**	**295**	**.616**	**161-82**	**21-22**	**248-155**	**44-36**	**72-66**	**402-229**

The Registers

• CONNORS, Jimmy — James Scott Connors

Male. Born: Sept. 2, 1952. Belleville, IL, United States. Height: 5' 10". Weight: 155 lbs. Plays: left.
Status: Turned Pro 1972. Earnings: $8,641,040. Highest Ranking: 1 (July 1974). HOF: 1998

Year	Rk	TP	TW	TF	GS	Aus	Fre	Wim	US	DC	Oly	MW	ML	Pct	CL	GR	HD	CP	IN	OD
1970	....	1	0	0	0-1	....	....	....	1rd	....	....	0	1	.000	0-0	0-1	0-0	0-0	0-0	0-1
1971	....	2	0	2	1-1	....	....	1rd	2rd	....	....	2	2	.500	0-0	1-1	1-1	0-0	0-0	2-2
1972	....	14	6	3	5-3	....	2rd	QF	1rd	....	....	18	8	.692	6-2	4-2	1-2	7-2	7-3	11-5
1973	3	21	11	3	8-3	....	1rd	QF	QF	....	....	27	10	.730	0-2	13-4	12-2	2-2	5-3	22-7
1974	1	17	15	2	20-0	W	....	W	W	....	....	32	2	.941	0-0	23-1	6-1	3-1	3-1	29-1
1975	1	14	9	6	16-3	F	....	F	F	3-1	....	29	5	.853	11-1	13-3	5-1	0-0	5-1	24-4
1976	1	18	12	4	11-1	....	....	QF	W	....	....	82	6	.932	25-0	9-1	20-3	28-2	32-3	50-3
1977	1	13	8	5	12-2	....	....	F	F	....	....	37	5	.881	14-2	7-1	5-1	11-2	11-2	26-3
1978	1	14	10	2	13-1	....	....	F	W	....	....	65	4	.942	12-1	6-1	18-1	29-2	34-2	31-2
1979	2	18	8	4	15-3	....	SF	SF	SF	....	....	68	10	.872	12-1	5-1	27-3	24-5	29-5	39-5
1980	3	19	6	2	15-3	....	SF	SF	SF	....	....	70	13	.843	18-6	5-1	17-3	30-3	30-3	40-10
1981	3	16	4	2	14-3	....	QF	SF	SF	2-0	....	61	12	.836	15-3	5-1	24-4	17-4	26-5	35-7
1982	2	17	7	4	18-1	....	QF	W	W	....	....	78	10	.886	7-2	13-0	36-3	22-5	28-7	50-3
1983	3	15	4	1	14-2	....	QF	4rd	W	....	....	52	11	.825	4-1	9-1	25-5	14-4	16-5	36-6
1984	2	19	5	3	16-3	....	SF	F	SF	5-2	....	74	14	.841	8-3	10-2	30-4	26-5	29-7	45-7
1985	4	14	0	2	15-3	....	SF	SF	SF	....	....	48	14	.774	11-3	5-2	18-6	14-3	14-3	34-11
1986	8	15	0	4	2-2	....	....	1rd	3rd	....	....	45	15	.750	0-0	5-2	25-7	15-6	15-6	30-9
1987	4	19	0	3	14-3	....	QF	SF	SF	....	....	52	19	.732	4-1	10-2	33-10	5-6	9-7	43-12
1988	7	12	2	2	7-2	....	....	4rd	QF	....	....	40	10	.800	0-0	5-2	29-6	6-2	14-3	26-7
1989	14	15	2	0	6-3	....	2rd	2rd	QF	....	....	31	13	.705	5-5	1-1	25-6	0-1	10-3	21-10
1990	936	3	0	0	0-0	....	....	....	....	....	....	0	3	.000	0-0	0-0	0-2	0-1	0-3	0-0
1991	48	14	0	0	9-3	....	3rd	3rd	SF	....	....	19	14	.576	2-2	2-1	13-7	2-4	5-5	14-9
1992	84	15	0	0	1-3	....	1rd	1rd	2rd	....	....	17	15	.531	2-2	0-1	15-10	0-2	4-4	13-11
1993	....	5	0	0	0-0	....	....	....	....	....	....	3	5	.375	0-2	0-0	3-3	0-0	3-1	0-4
1994	....	3	0	0	0-0	....	....	....	....	....	....	1	3	.250	1-1	0-0	0-1	0-1	0-2	1-1
1995	427	2	0	0	0-0	....	....	....	....	....	....	2	2	.500	0-0	2-1	0-1	0-0	0-0	2-2
1996	1298	1	0	0	0-0	....	....	....	....	....	....	0	1	.000	0-1	0-0	0-0	0-0	0-0	0-1
TOTALS		**336**	**109**	**54**	**232-49**	....	....	....	....	**10-3**	....	**953**	**227**	**.808**	**157-41**	**153-33**	**388-93**	**255-63**	**329-84**	**624-143**

Held number one tour ranking 9 times for a total of 268 weeks. Last ranked number one in 1983. Doubles Titles: Wim (1), US (1).

• COOPER, Ashley — Ashley John Cooper

Male. Born: Sept. 15, 1936. Melbourne, Australia. Height: 5' 10". Weight: –. Plays: right.
Status: Amateur. Earnings: –. Highest Ranking: 1 (Dec. 1957). HOF: 1991

Year	Rk	TP	TW	TF	GS	Aus	Fre	Wim	US	DC	Oly	MW	ML	Pct	CL	GR	HD	CP	IN	OD
1954	....	3	0	0	....	QF	2rd	....	2rd	....	....	....	....		....	....	....	....	....	....
1955	....	3	0	0	....	QF	....	1rd	3rd	....	....	....	....		....	....	....	....	....	....
1956	7	3	0	0	....	QF	....	4rd	QF	....	....	....	....		....	....	....	....	....	....
1957	1	4	1	2	....	W	SF	F	F	1-1	....	....	....		....	....	....	....	....	....
1958	1	4	3	0	....	W	SF	W	W	1-1	....	....	....		....	....	....	....	....	....
1968	....	1	0	0	2-1	....	3rd	....	....	0-0	....	2	1	.667	2-1	0-0	0-0	0-0	0-0	2-1
TOTALS		**18**	**4**	**2**	**2-1**	....	....	....	....	**2-2**		**2**	**1**	**.667**	**2-1**	**0-0**	**0-0**	**0-0**	**0-0**	**2-1**

Held number one world ranking 2 times during amateur era. Doubles Titles: Aus (1), Fre (2), US (1).

• CORRETJA, Alex — Alex Corretja Verdegay

Male. Born: Apr. 11, 1974. Barcelona, Spain. Height: 5' 11". Weight: 155 lbs. Plays: right.
Status: Turned Pro 1991. Earnings: $9,828,939. Highest Ranking: 2 (Feb. 1999).

Year	Rk	TP	TW	TF	GS	Aus	Fre	Wim	US	DC	Oly	MW	ML	Pct	CL	GR	HD	CP	IN	OD
1992	86	13	0	1	0-2	....	1rd	....	1rd	....	....	11	13	.458	5-8	0-0	6-5	0-0	0-0	11-13
1993	73	23	0	0	0-2	....	1rd	....	1rd	....	....	24	23	.511	24-20	0-0	0-3	0-0	0-0	24-23
1994	22	23	1	1	3-3	....	3rd	2rd	1rd	....	....	44	22	.667	39-18	1-1	4-3	0-0	0-0	44-22
1995	48	26	0	0	4-2	....	4rd	....	2rd	....	....	25	26	.490	24-18	0-0	1-7	0-1	0-1	25-25
1996	23	25	0	3	7-4	2rd	2rd	2rd	QF	....	....	37	25	.597	23-11	2-2	12-8	0-4	0-4	37-21
1997	12	25	3	2	6-2	2rd	4rd	....	3rd	....	....	49	22	.690	38-9	0-0	10-8	1-5	1-6	48-16
1998	3	26	5	2	11-4	3rd	F	1rd	4rd	4-1	....	57	21	.731	27-8	0-2	24-7	6-4	10-5	47-16
1999	26	23	0	3	5-3	2rd	QF	....	1rd	1-1	....	37	23	.617	24-10	0-0	13-10	0-3	1-4	36-19
2000	8	24	5	0	7-3	2rd	QF	....	3rd	3-0	3rd	54	19	.740	26-5	0-0	26-11	2-3	8-6	46-13
2001	16	21	1	1	8-2	....	F	....	3rd	1-0	....	34	20	.630	25-8	0-1	9-9	0-2	2-5	32-15
2002	19	21	2	0	7-3	1rd	SF	....	3rd	2-1	....	39	19	.672	24-8	1-1	14-10	0-1	3-3	36-16
TOTALS		**250**	**17**	**13**	**58-30**	....	....	....	....	**11-3**		**411**	**233**	**.638**	**279-123**	**4-7**	**119-81**	**9-23**	**25-34**	**386-199**

• COSTA, Albert   Albert Costa Casals

Male. Born: June 25, 1975. Lerida, Spain. Height: 5' 11". Weight: 165 lbs. Plays: right.
Status: Turned Pro 1993. Earnings: $6,367,250. Highest Ranking: 6 (July 2002).

Year	Rk	TP	TW	TF	GS	Aus	Fre	Wim	US	DC	Oly	MW	ML	Pct	CL	GR	HD	CP	IN	OD
1993	221	2	0	0	0-0	....	....	....	....	....	....	2	2	.500	2-2	0-0	0-0	0-0	0-0	2-2
1994	52	18	0	0	0-3	....	1rd	1rd	1rd	....	....	15	18	.455	15-16	0-1	0-1	0-0	0-0	15-18
1995	24	23	1	1	4-1	....	QF	....	....	....	....	33	22	.600	32-19	0-0	1-2	0-1	0-1	33-21
1996	13	32	3	3	3-4	2rd	2rd	2rd	1rd	3-1	2rd	52	29	.642	34-11	1-3	17-11	0-4	0-5	52-24
1997	19	24	2	2	6-3	QF	3rd	....	1rd	2-2	....	44	22	.667	25-7	0-0	19-11	0-4	0-5	44-17
1998	14	27	2	2	5-4	2rd	4rd	2rd	1rd	....	....	47	25	.653	34-8	1-1	12-12	0-4	0-6	47-19
1999	18	25	3	3	2-4	1rd	3rd	1rd	1rd	....	....	40	22	.645	30-9	0-1	8-10	2-2	3-3	37-19
2000	26	26	0	0	5-3	1rd	QF	....	2rd	3-2	1rd	32	26	.552	17-11	0-0	12-13	3-2	4-5	28-21
2001	40	22	0	0	3-2	....	1rd	....	4rd	....	....	26	22	.542	16-12	0-0	8-8	2-2	4-4	22-18
2002	9	23	1	2	11-2	4rd	W	....	2rd	....	....	35	22	.614	28-8	0-0	7-11	0-3	1-6	34-16
TOTALS		**222**	**12**	**13**	**39-26**	....	....	....	....	**8-5**	....	**326**	**210**	**.608**	**233-103**	**2-6**	**84-79**	**7-22**	**12-35**	**314-175**

• COURIER, Jim   James Spencer Courier

Male. Born: Aug. 17, 1970. Sanford, FL, United States. Height: 6' 1". Weight: 180 lbs. Plays: right.
Status: Turned Pro 1988. Earnings: $14,033,132. Highest Ranking: 1 (Feb. 1992).

Year	Rk	TP	TW	TF	GS	Aus	Fre	Wim	US	DC	Oly	MW	ML	Pct	CL	GR	HD	CP	IN	OD
1987	346	2	0	0	0-0	....	....	....	....	....	....	0	2	.000	0-1	0-0	0-1	0-0	0-0	0-2
1988	43	15	0	0	1-1	....	....	....	2rd	....	....	21	15	.583	5-3	0-0	12-10	4-2	8-3	13-12
1989	24	19	1	0	5-3	....	4rd	1rd	3rd	....	....	29	18	.617	8-4	0-1	19-10	2-3	7-4	22-14
1990	25	22	0	0	7-4	2rd	4rd	3rd	2rd	....	....	42	22	.656	16-8	2-1	16-8	8-5	10-7	32-15
1991	2	23	3	2	20-3	4rd	W	QF	F	1-3	....	58	20	.744	10-3	4-1	37-10	7-6	9-8	49-12
1992	1	23	5	4	20-2	W	W	3rd	SF	2-2	3rd	69	18	.793	16-3	2-1	36-7	15-7	23-11	46-7
1993	3	22	5	3	22-3	W	F	4rd	....	....	....	58	17	.773	12-1	6-1	39-9	1-6	9-8	49-9
1994	13	19	0	2	12-4	SF	SF	2rd	2rd	4-0	....	47	19	.712	15-5	5-2	19-8	8-4	10-5	37-14
1995	8	26	4	1	13-4	QF	4rd	2rd	SF	2-2	....	61	22	.735	3-4	1-2	49-12	8-4	22-9	39-13
1996	16	18	1	0	8-3	QF	QF	1rd	....	....	....	28	17	.622	8-4	2-2	10-7	8-4	8-4	20-13
1997	21	22	3	0	3-4	4rd	1rd	1rd	1rd	3-0	....	37	19	.661	6-4	2-3	27-9	2-3	8-4	29-15
1998	77	23	1	0	1-2	....	2rd	1rd	....	2-2	....	21	22	.488	10-9	0-1	8-11	3-1	4-3	17-19
1999	32	21	0	1	6-4	3rd	2rd	4rd	1rd	2-1	....	31	21	.596	6-4	4-2	16-13	5-2	13-5	18-16
2000	290	5	0	0	0-1	1rd	....	....	....	....	....	4	5	.444	0-0	0-0	4-5	0-0	3-2	1-3
TOTALS		**260**	**23**	**13**	**118-38**	....	....	....	....	**16-10**	....	**506**	**237**	**.681**	**115-53**	**28-17**	**292-120**	**71-47**	**134-73**	**372-164**

Held number one tour ranking 4 times for a total of 58 weeks. Last ranked number one in 1993.

• COURT, Margaret   see SMITH COURT, Margaret, page 888

• CREALY, Dick   Dick Crealy

Male. Born: Sept. 18, 1944. Australia. Height: –. Weight: –. Plays: right.
Status: Amateur. Earnings: –. Highest Ranking: –.

Year	Rk	TP	TW	TF	GS	Aus	Fre	Wim	US	DC	Oly	MW	ML	Pct	CL	GR	HD	CP	IN	OD
1963	....	1	0	0	....	3rd	....	....	....	....	....	....	....	....	....	....	....	....	....	....
1964	....	1	0	0	....	3rd	....	....	....	....	....	....	....	....	....	....	....	....	....	....
1966	....	2	0	0	....	2rd	....	1rd	....	....	....	....	....	....	....	....	....	....	....	....
1967	....	3	0	0	....	3rd	1rd	3rd	....	....	....	....	....	....	....	....	....	....	....	....
1968	....	3	0	0	6-3	QF	3rd	2rd	....	....	....	6	3	.667	2-1	4-2	0-0	0-0	0-0	6-3
1969	....	5	0	0	5-4	2rd	2rd	3rd	2rd	....	....	7	5	.583	3-2	4-3	0-0	0-0	0-0	7-5
1970	....	6	1	1	8-4	F	4rd	2rd	1rd	3-2	....	8	5	.615	3-2	5-3	0-0	0-0	0-0	8-5
1971	....	6	0	0	1-3	2rd	2rd	1rd	....	....	....	3	6	.333	2-3	1-2	0-0	0-1	0-1	3-5
1972	....	5	0	1	3-3	QF	1rd	2rd	....	....	....	4	5	.444	1-3	3-2	0-0	0-0	0-0	4-5
1973	....	6	0	0	1-3	1rd	1rd	....	2rd	....	....	4	6	.400	0-1	2-3	2-2	0-0	0-0	4-6
1974	61	8	0	0	5-4	3rd	2rd	3rd	1rd	....	....	8	8	.500	2-2	5-4	0-1	1-1	1-1	7-7
1975	....	12	1	0	4-3	SF	1rd	2rd	....	....	....	12	11	.522	5-5	5-4	2-1	0-1	0-1	12-10
1976	38	25	0	0	3-4	QF	1rd	1rd	1rd	....	....	30	25	.545	23-15	3-3	3-2	1-5	2-6	28-19
1977	....	10	0	0	3-43rd/2rd	1rd	1rd	....	....	....	....	10	10	.500	5-5	5-5	0-0	0-0	0-0	10-10
1978	131	27	0	0	2-4	2rd	1rd	1rd	2rd	....	....	12	27	.308	6-11	2-5	2-5	2-6	2-7	10-20
1979	....	9	0	0	0-1	....	1rd	....	....	....	....	1	9	.100	0-3	1-2	0-2	0-2	0-3	1-6
1980	....	1	0	0	0-0	....	....	....	....	....	....	2	1	.667	0-0	0-0	2-1	0-0	0-0	2-1
1981	....	1	0	0	0-0	....	....	....	....	....	....	1	1	.500	0-0	0-0	1-1	0-0	0-0	1-1
TOTALS		**131**	**2**	**2**	**41-40**	....	....	....	....	**3-2**	....	**108**	**122**	**.470**	**52-53**	**40-38**	**12-15**	**4-16**	**5-19**	**103-103**

Doubles Titles: Aus (1), Fre (1), US (1)

• CURREN, Kevin — Kevin Curren

Male. Born: Mar. 2, 1958. Durban, South Africa. Height: 6' 1". Weight: 170 lbs. Plays: right.
Status: Turned Pro 1979. Earnings: $3,055,510. Highest Ranking: 9 (Dec. 1983).

Year	Rk	TP	TW	TF	GS	Aus	Fre	Wim	US	DC	Oly	MW	ML	Pct	CL	GR	HD	CP	IN	OD
1978	91	2	0	0	1-1	....	....	....	2rd	....	....	1	2	.333	0-0	0-0	1-2	0-0	0-0	1-2
1979	195	12	0	0	1-1	....	....	....	2rd	....	....	5	12	.294	0-2	1-1	4-9	0-0	1-3	4-9
1980	47	13	0	0	5-2	3rd	....	4rd	....	....	....	16	13	.552	0-0	7-4	9-6	0-3	2-5	14-8
1981	57	19	1	0	5-3	2rd	....	2rd	4rd	....	....	23	18	.561	2-2	8-5	13-8	0-3	3-7	20-11
1982	17	18	1	2	2-2	....	....	3rd	1rd	....	....	33	17	.660	0-1	6-2	8-3	19-11	24-11	9-6
1983	9	19	0	1	5-1	....	....	SF	....	....	....	32	19	.627	1-3	9-2	7-4	15-10	16-11	16-8
1984	15	16	0	1	9-2	F	....	4rd	2rd	....	....	32	16	.667	1-1	13-4	5-1	13-10	13-10	19-6
1985	10	13	1	2	6-2	....	....	F	1rd	....	....	25	12	.676	0-0	8-2	3-6	14-4	14-5	11-7
1986	18	20	1	1	1-2	....	....	1rd	2rd	....	....	36	19	.655	2-3	1-2	16-8	17-6	18-7	18-12
1987	37	17	0	0	2-2	3rd	....	2rd	....	....	....	21	17	.553	0-1	4-3	14-9	3-4	5-5	16-12
1988	23	15	0	1	1-2	....	....	1rd	2rd	....	....	30	15	.667	0-0	3-2	20-9	7-4	10-6	20-9
1989	20	17	1	0	2-1	....	....	3rd	....	....	....	33	16	.673	1-1	3-2	19-8	10-5	13-6	20-10
1990	71	19	0	0	7-2	....	....	QF	4rd	....	....	20	19	.513	1-2	5-2	8-8	6-7	7-8	13-11
1991	58	20	0	0	2-2	....	....	2rd	2rd	....	....	18	20	.474	0-1	2-2	7-11	9-6	12-9	6-11
1992	147	16	0	0	1-3	....	2rd	1rd	1rd	....	....	12	16	.429	1-1	1-3	10-11	0-1	1-3	11-13
1993	....	1	0	0	0-0	....	....	....	....	....	....	0	1	.000	0-0	0-0	0-1	0-0	0-0	0-1
TOTALS		**237**	**5**	**8**	**50-28**	....	....	....	....	....	....	**337**	**232**	**.592**	**9-18**	**71-36**	**144-104**	**113-74**	**139-96**	**198-136**

Doubles Titles: US (1)

• DALTON, Judy — Judith Anne Marshall Tegart Dalton

Female. Born: Dec. 12, 1937. Melbourne, Australia. Height: –. Weight: –. Plays: right.
Status: Turned Pro 1970. Earnings: –. Highest Ranking: 7 (Dec. 1968).

Year	Rk	TP	TW	TF	GS	Aus	Fre	Wim	US	FC	Oly	MW	ML	Pct	CL	GR	HD	CP	IN	OD
1957	....	1	0	0	....	3rd	....	....	....	....	....	....	....	....	....	....	....	....	....	....
1958	....	1	0	0	....	3rd	....	....	....	....	....	....	....	....	....	....	....	....	....	....
1959	....	1	0	0	....	3rd	....	....	....	....	....	....	....	....	....	....	....	....	....	....
1961	....	1	0	0	....	4rd	....	....	....	....	....	....	....	....	....	....	....	....	....	....
1962	....	4	0	0	....	QF	3rd	4rd	2rd	....	....	....	....	....	....	....	....	....	....	....
1963	....	4	0	0	....	3rd	2rd	3rd	4rd	....	....	....	....	....	....	....	....	....	....	....
1964	....	4	0	0	....	QF	4rd	4rd	4rd	....	....	....	....	....	....	....	....	....	....	....
1965	....	3	0	0	....	QF	....	3rd	3rd	....	....	....	....	....	....	....	....	....	....	....
1966	....	4	0	0	....	QF	4rd	4rd	3rd	2-1	....	....	....	....	....	....	....	....	....	....
1967	10	4	0	0	....	QF	4rd	QF	4rd	....	....	....	....	....	....	....	....	....	....	....
1968	7	2	0	0	8-2	....	....	F	QF	....	....	8	2	.800	0-0	8-2	0-0	0-0	0-0	8-2
1969	....	2	0	0	3-2	1rd	....	QF	....	....	....	3	2	.600	0-0	3-2	0-0	0-0	0-0	3-2
1970	....	4	0	0	7-4	QF	2rd	4rd	3rd	4-0	....	11	4	.733	5-1	6-3	0-0	0-0	0-0	11-4
1971	9	3	0	1	8-2	....	....	SF	QF	....	....	8	2	.800	0-0	8-2	0-0	0-0	0-0	8-2
1972	....	2	0	0	2-2	....	4rd	3rd	....	....	....	2	2	.500	1-1	1-1	0-0	0-0	0-0	2-2
1974	....	1	0	0	3-1	QF	....	....	....	....	....	3	1	.750	0-0	3-1	0-0	0-0	0-0	3-1
1975	....	1	0	0	1-1	....	....	2rd	....	....	....	1	1	.500	0-0	1-1	0-0	0-0	0-0	1-1
1976	....	1	0	0	0-1	1rd	....	....	....	....	....	0	1	.000	0-0	0-1	0-0	0-0	0-0	0-1
1977	....	2	0	0	2-2	1rd/QF	....	....	....	....	....	2	2	.500	0-0	2-2	0-0	0-0	0-0	2-2
1978	....	1	0	0	0-0	....	....	....	....	....	....	1	1	.500	0-0	1-1	0-0	0-0	0-0	1-1
TOTALS		**46**	**0**	**1**	**34-17**	....	....	....	....	**6-1**	....	**39**	**18**	**.684**	**6-2**	**33-16**	**0-0**	**0-0**	**0-0**	**39-18**

Doubles Titles: Aus (4), Fre (1), Wim (1), US (2)

• DATE, Kimiko — Kimiko Date

Female. Born: Sept. 28, 1970. Kyoto, Japan. Height: 5' 4". Weight: 115 lbs. Plays: right.
Status: Turned Pro 1988. Earnings: $1,974,253. Highest Ranking: 4 (Nov. 1995).

Year	Rk	TP	TW	TF	GS	Aus	Fre	Wim	US	FC	Oly	MW	ML	Pct	CL	GR	HD	CP	IN	OD
1989	120	5	0	0	1-3	....	2rd	1rd	1rd	....	....	6	5	.545	1-1	3-2	2-2	0-0	0-0	6-5
1990	78	8	0	0	5-3	4rd	....	2rd	2rd	1-1	....	11	8	.579	0-0	1-1	10-6	0-1	0-1	11-7
1991	32	11	0	0	2-3	2rd	....	1rd	2rd	1-0	....	13	11	.542	0-0	2-2	10-8	1-1	1-1	12-10
1992	21	15	1	1	6-4	2rd	4rd	2rd	2rd	2-0	2rd	29	14	.674	6-3	2-2	16-7	5-2	5-2	24-12
1993	13	12	1	2	6-3	2rd	2rd	....	QF	....	....	24	11	.686	1-2	1-1	18-6	4-2	4-2	20-9
1994	9	16	2	0	11-4	SF	1rd	3rd	QF	1-2	....	33	14	.702	3-5	2-2	26-5	2-2	2-2	31-12
1995	4	13	1	3	14-4	3rd	SF	QF	4rd	2-0	....	41	12	.774	11-3	6-2	16-6	8-1	8-1	33-11
1996	8	18	2	0	9-4	2rd	4rd	SF	1rd	2-2	QF	36	16	.692	3-2	5-2	27-8	1-4	1-4	35-12
TOTALS		**98**	**7**	**6**	**54-28**	....	....	....	....	**9-5**	....	**193**	**91**	**.680**	**25-16**	**22-14**	**125-48**	**21-13**	**21-13**	**172-78**

• DAVENPORT, Lindsay   Lindsay Davenport

Female. Born: June 8, 1976. Palos Verdes, CA, United States. Height: 6' 2". Weight: 175 lbs. Plays: right.
Status: Turned Pro 1993. Earnings: $14,842,061. Highest Ranking: 1 (Oct. 1998).

Year	Rk	TP	TW	TF	GS	Aus	Fre	Wim	US	FC	Oly	MW	ML	Pct	CL	GR	HD	CP	IN	OD
1991	339	2	0	0	0-1	....	....	....	2rd	....	....	1	2	.333	0-0	0-0	1-2	0-0	0-0	1-2
1992	159	5	0	0	1-1	....	....	....	2rd	....	....	2	5	.286	0-3	0-0	2-2	0-0	0-0	2-5
1993	20	17	1	0	7-4	3rd	1rd	3rd	4rd	2-1	....	33	16	.673	10-4	2-2	18-8	3-2	3-2	30-14
1994	6	18	2	0	12-4	QF	3rd	QF	3rd	4-1	....	49	16	.754	17-6	4-1	21-5	7-4	7-4	42-12
1995	12	14	1	0	11-4	QF	4rd	4rd	2rd	2-0	....	33	13	.717	8-1	3-1	15-8	7-3	7-4	26-9
1996	9	18	3	0	11-4	4rd	QF	2rd	4rd	4-0	W	51	15	.773	9-1	2-2	29-6	11-6	13-7	38-8
1997	3	22	6	0	12-4	4rd	4rd	2rd	SF	2-0	....	59	16	.787	10-4	1-1	38-8	10-3	18-4	41-12
1998	1	21	6	0	21-3	SF	SF	QF	W	2-0	....	69	15	.821	13-4	4-1	42-7	10-3	19-5	50-10
1999	2	17	7	0	21-3	SF	QF	QF	SF	2-0	....	61	10	.859	9-2	7-1	35-6	10-2	11-2	50-8
2000	2	16	4	0	19-3	W	1rd	F	F	3-0	2rd	60	12	.833	1-1	7-2	41-8	11-1	14-2	46-10
2001	1	16	7	0	14-3	SF	....	SF	QF	....	....	62	9	.873	0-0	9-1	45-8	8-1	19-0	43-9
2002	12	9	0	4	5-1	....	....	....	SF	2-0	....	26	9	.743	0-0	0-0	23-8	3-1	7-4	19-5
TOTALS		**175**	**37**	**4**	**134-35**	....	....	....	....	**23-2**	....	**506**	**138**	**.786**	**77-26**	**39-12**	**310-76**	**80-26**	**118-34**	**388-104**

Held number one tour ranking 5 times for a total of 37 weeks. Last ranked number one in 2002. Doubles Titles: Fre (1), Wim (1), US (1).

• DECUGIS, Julie   see **HALARD, Julie,** page 848

• DENT, Phil   Phil Dent

Male. Born: Feb. 14, 1950. Sydney, Australia. Height: 6'. Weight: 175 lbs. Plays: right.
Status: Turned Pro 1969. Earnings: –. Highest Ranking: –.

Year	Rk	TP	TW	TF	GS	Aus	Fre	Wim	US	DC	Oly	MW	ML	Pct	CL	GR	HD	CP	IN	OD
1968	....	2	0	0	3-2	QF	....	1rd	....	....	....	3	2	.600	0-0	3-2	0-0	0-0	0-0	3-2
1969	....	4	0	0	3-4	2rd	2rd	3rd	1rd	....	....	3	4	.429	1-1	2-3	0-0	0-0	0-0	3-4
1970	....	3	0	0	4-3	3rd	3rd	2rd	....	....	....	4	3	.571	1-1	3-2	0-0	0-0	0-0	4-3
1971	....	7	1	0	3-4	2rd	1rd	2rd	2rd	....	....	3	6	.333	0-2	3-3	0-0	0-1	0-1	3-5
1972	....	1	0	0	0-1	....	....	....	1rd	....	....	0	1	.000	0-0	0-1	0-0	0-0	0-0	0-1
1973	49	9	0	0	4-3	1rd	3rd	....	3rd	....	....	9	9	.500	5-3	2-3	2-3	0-0	0-0	9-9
1974	43	3	0	1	6-2	F	....	2rd	....	....	....	7	3	.700	1-1	6-2	0-0	0-0	0-0	7-3
1975	33	9	0	0	4-4	1rd	1rd	4rd	2rd	1-1	....	12	9	.571	3-4	7-3	2-2	0-0	0-0	12-9
1976	37	17	0	3	4-3	2rd	....	4rd	1rd	....	....	17	17	.500	1-2	4-3	4-2	8-10	8-10	9-7
1977	22	16	0	0	14-5	QF/2rd	SF	QF	2rd	2-1	....	36	16	.692	20-7	11-5	3-2	2-2	2-2	34-14
1978	87	25	0	0	3-4	2rd	1rd	3rd	1rd	1-0	....	21	25	.457	8-10	7-5	3-4	3-6	5-7	16-18
1979	46	20	2	0	4-4	QF	1rd	1rd	1rd	....	....	27	18	.600	3-7	19-5	5-4	0-2	2-3	25-15
1980	42	19	0	2	5-2	3rd	....	4rd	....	2-0	....	28	19	.596	8-7	14-6	5-3	1-3	2-4	26-15
1981	62	21	0	0	2-3	3rd	....	1rd	1rd	....	....	26	21	.553	0-0	12-6	9-9	5-6	5-7	21-14
1982	65	19	0	0	3-2	4rd	....	....	1rd	....	....	17	19	.472	5-3	4-2	4-7	4-7	4-8	13-11
1983	....	5	0	0	0-1	2rd	....	....	....	....	....	0	5	.000	0-0	0-1	0-2	0-2	0-2	0-3
TOTALS		**180**	**3**	**6**	**62-47**	....	....	....	....	**6-2**	....	**213**	**177**	**.546**	**56-48**	**97-52**	**37-38**	**23-39**	**28-44**	**185-133**

Doubles Titles: Aus (1)

• DENTON, Steve   Steve Denton

Male. Born: Sept. 5, 1956. Kingsville, TX, United States. Height: 6' 2". Weight: 180 lbs. Plays: right.
Status: Turned Pro 1978. Earnings: $1,084,664. Highest Ranking: –.

Year	Rk	TP	TW	TF	GS	Aus	Fre	Wim	US	DC	Oly	MW	ML	Pct	CL	GR	HD	CP	IN	OD
1978	246	2	0	0	0-0	....	....	....	....	....	....	1	2	.333	1-1	0-0	0-1	0-0	0-0	1-2
1979	229	5	0	0	0-0	....	....	....	....	....	....	1	5	.167	0-1	0-0	1-3	0-1	0-1	1-4
1980	403	3	0	0	0-0	....	....	....	....	....	....	0	3	.000	0-0	0-0	0-0	0-3	0-3	0-0
1981	24	17	0	0	5-3	....	1rd	1rd	....	....	....	19	17	.528	1-3	9-4	8-8	1-2	2-6	17-11
1982	13	24	0	3	12-4	F	1rd	4rd	4rd	....	....	43	24	.642	1-2	9-4	22-8	11-10	18-13	25-11
1983	58	23	0	1	3-3	3rd	....	1rd	3rd	....	....	25	23	.521	2-2	4-4	8-7	11-10	11-13	14-10
1984	149	21	0	1	1-4	1rd	1rd	1rd	2rd	....	....	13	21	.382	3-4	2-5	1-5	7-7	7-9	6-12
1985	241	10	0	0	2-3	2rd	....	2rd	1rd	....	....	3	10	.231	0-0	2-3	0-3	1-4	1-4	2-6
1986	300	7	0	0	0-0	....	....	....	....	....	....	2	7	.222	0-0	0-1	1-4	1-2	1-2	1-5
1987	560	1	0	0	0-1	1rd	....	....	....	....	....	0	1	.000	0-0	0-0	0-1	0-0	0-0	0-1
TOTALS		**113**	**0**	**5**	**23-18**	....	....	....	....	....	....	**107**	**113**	**.486**	**8-13**	**26-22**	**41-39**	**32-39**	**40-51**	**67-62**

Doubles Titles: US (1)

• DIBBS, Eddie   Eddie Dibbs

Male. Born: Feb. 23, 1951. Brooklyn, NY, United States. Height: 5' 7". Weight: 160 lbs. Plays: right.
Status: Turned Pro 1971. Earnings: $2,016,426. Highest Ranking: 6 (Dec. 1977).

Year	Rk	TP	TW	TF	GS	Aus	Fre	Wim	US	DC	Oly	MW	ML	Pct	CL	GR	HD	CP	IN	OD
1971	....	1	0	0	0-0	....	....	....	....	....	....	1	1	.500	0-0	0-0	1-1	0-0	0-0	1-1
1972	....	1	0	0	1-1	....	....	....	2rd	....	....	1	1	.500	0-0	1-1	0-0	0-0	0-0	1-1
1973	28	6	3	0	0-2	....	1rd	....	1rd	....	....	7	3	.700	6-1	1-2	0-0	0-0	0-0	7-3
1974	20	10	1	1	4-2	....	4rd	2rd	....	....	....	19	9	.679	12-3	3-2	2-3	2-1	3-2	16-7
1975	18	9	2	0	9-2	....	SF	....	QF	....	....	15	7	.682	13-4	0-1	2-2	0-0	1-1	14-6
1976	9	27	4	4	9-2	....	SF	....	QF	....	....	58	23	.716	43-11	0-0	1-3	14-9	14-10	44-13
1977	6	17	3	4	3-2	....	2rd	....	3rd	....	....	21	14	.600	11-6	0-0	3-2	7-6	10-8	11-6
1978	6	25	4	4	6-2	....	QF	....	3rd	....	....	58	21	.734	36-8	0-0	3-3	19-10	19-11	39-10
1979	10	22	1	4	8-2	....	QF	....	QF	....	....	56	21	.727	34-11	0-0	12-4	10-6	18-9	38-12
1980	13	20	2	2	3-2	....	3rd	....	2rd	....	....	47	18	.723	34-9	0-0	5-3	8-6	10-7	37-11
1981	27	16	2	0	2-1	....	3rd	....	....	....	....	36	14	.720	32-10	0-0	4-3	0-1	2-2	34-12
1982	56	18	0	1	0-0	....	....	....	....	....	....	26	18	.591	19-10	0-0	5-3	2-5	3-6	23-12
1983	90	10	0	0	0-0	....	....	....	....	....	....	16	10	.615	15-9	0-0	0-0	1-1	1-1	15-9
1984	....	5	0	0	0-0	....	....	....	....	....	....	1	5	.167	1-5	0-0	0-0	0-0	0-0	1-5
TOTALS		**187**	**22**	**20**	**45-18**	....	....	....	....	....	....	**362**	**165**	**.687**	**256-87**	**5-6**	**38-27**	**63-45**	**81-57**	**281-108**

• DOKIC, Jelena   Jelena Dokic

Female. Born: Apr. 12, 1983. Belgrade, . Height: 5' 9". Weight: 130 lbs. Plays: right.
Status: Turned Pro 1998. Earnings: $2,682,428. Highest Ranking: 4 (Aug. 2002).

Year	Rk	TP	TW	TF	GS	Aus	Fre	Wim	US	FC	Oly	MW	ML	Pct	CL	GR	HD	CP	IN	OD
1998	341	1	0	0	0-0	....	....	....	....	2-0	....	0	1	.000	0-0	0-0	0-1	0-0	0-0	0-1
1999	43	13	0	0	6-4	3rd	1rd	QF	....	4-2	....	15	13	.536	4-4	4-2	6-5	1-2	1-2	14-11
2000	26	21	0	0	9-4	1rd	2rd	SF	4rd	3-0	SF	35	21	.625	9-4	6-2	15-13	5-2	6-3	29-18
2001	8	26	3	3	8-4	1rd	3rd	4rd	4rd	....	....	53	23	.697	16-8	6-3	23-10	8-2	12-4	41-19
2002	9	28	2	3	8-3	....	QF	4rd	2rd	....	....	53	26	.671	20-7	8-2	24-13	1-4	6-8	47-18
TOTALS		**89**	**5**	**6**	**31-15**	....	....	....	....	**9-2**	....	**156**	**84**	**.650**	**49-23**	**24-9**	**68-42**	**15-10**	**25-17**	**131-67**

Represented Australia in the Federation Cup (1998-2000)

• DRYSDALE, Cliff   Eric Clifford Drysdale

Male. Born: May 26, 1941. Nelspruit, South Africa. Height: 6' 2". Weight: 170 lbs. Plays: right.
Status: Turned Pro 1968. Earnings: –. Highest Ranking: 4 (Dec. 1965).

Year	Rk	TP	TW	TF	GS	Aus	Fre	Wim	US	DC	Oly	MW	ML	Pct	CL	GR	HD	CP	IN	OD
1962	....	3	0	0	....	....	1rd	1rd	3rd	4-3	....	....	....	....	....	....	....	....	....	....
1963	....	3	0	0	....	....	2rd	1rd	2rd	1-2	....	....	....	....	....	....	....	....	....	....
1964	....	3	0	0	....	....	QF	2rd	3rd	2-0	....	....	....	....	....	....	....	....	....	....
1965	4	3	0	1	....	....	SF	SF	F	6-1	....	....	....	....	....	....	....	....	....	....
1966	9	3	0	0	....	....	SF	SF	3rd	6-2	....	....	....	....	....	....	....	....	....	....
1967	10	3	0	0	....	....	QF	4rd	2rd	8-3	....	....	....	....	....	....	....	....	....	....
1968	9	3	1	1	5-2	....	....	3rd	QF	....	....	5	2	.714	0-0	5-2	0-0	0-0	0-0	5-2
1969	9	4	0	2	4-3	....	1rd	QF	1rd	....	....	7	4	.636	3-2	4-2	0-0	0-0	0-0	7-4
1970	....	2	0	1	3-2	....	....	3rd	2rd	....	....	3	2	.600	0-0	3-2	0-0	0-0	0-0	3-2
1971	9	8	3	2	2-2	QF	....	1rd	....	....	....	7	5	.583	2-1	2-2	0-0	3-2	3-2	4-3
1972	....	4	0	4	3-1	....	....	....	4rd	....	....	9	4	.692	0-0	3-1	6-2	0-1	2-2	7-2
1973	23	7	0	0	3-2	....	2rd	....	3rd	....	....	9	7	.563	2-2	4-3	2-1	1-1	1-1	8-6
1974	19	5	1	0	2-1	....	....	3rd	....	1-1	....	4	4	.500	2-1	2-2	0-1	0-0	0-0	4-4
1975	36	4	0	1	1-1	....	....	....	2rd	....	....	6	4	.600	1-1	0-0	2-2	3-1	3-1	3-3
1976	25	14	0	2	1-1	....	....	2rd	....	....	....	17	14	.548	4-3	1-1	5-4	7-6	7-6	10-8
1977	27	8	0	0	2-2	....	....	3rd	1rd	....	....	11	8	.579	0-1	2-1	1-2	8-4	8-4	3-4
1978	47	10	1	0	0-1	....	....	....	1rd	....	....	6	9	.400	0-0	0-0	1-3	5-6	5-6	1-3
1979	....	12	0	0	0-1	....	....	1rd	....	....	....	5	12	.294	1-1	1-2	3-5	0-4	1-6	4-6
1980	185	2	0	0	1-1	....	....	2rd	....	....	....	1	2	.333	0-0	1-1	0-0	0-1	0-1	1-1
TOTALS		**101**	**6**	**14**	**27-20**	....	....	....	....	**28-12**	....	**90**	**77**	**.539**	**15-12**	**28-19**	**20-20**	**27-26**	**30-29**	**60-48**

Doubles Titles: US (1)

• DURIE, Jo   Jo Durie

Female. Born: July 27, 1960. Bristol, Great Britain. Height: 6'. Weight: 150 lbs. Plays: right.
Status: Turned Pro 1977. Earnings: $1,224,016. Highest Ranking: 5 (Apr. 1984).

Year	Rk	TP	TW	TF	GS	Aus	Fre	Wim	US	FC	Oly	MW	ML	Pct	CL	GR	HD	CP	IN	OD
1977	....	1	0	0	0-1	....	....	1rd	....	....	....	0	1	.000	0-0	0-1	0-0	0-0	0-0	0-1
1978	123	2	0	0	0-1	....	....	1rd	....	....	....	0	2	.000	0-0	0-1	0-0	0-1	0-1	0-1

Year	Rk	TP	TW	TF	GS	Aus	Fre	Wim	US	FC	Oly	MW	ML	Pct	CL	GR	HD	CP	IN	OD
1979	73	3	0	0	0-1	....	....	2rd	....	....	....	2	3	.400	0-0	1-2	0-0	1-1	1-1	1-2
1980	53	9	0	1	0-2	....	1rd	1rd	....	....	....	5	9	.357	2-2	3-3	0-0	0-4	0-4	5-5
1981	31	14	0	0	7-4	3rd	1rd	4rd	4rd	1-0	....	16	14	.533	3-4	6-5	6-3	1-2	3-3	13-11
1982	28	22	0	1	5-4	3rd	2rd	1rd	3rd	1-2	....	26	22	.542	5-3	10-6	7-6	4-7	6-8	20-14
1983	6	22	2	1	15-4	QF	SF	3rd	SF	2-1	....	49	20	.710	11-4	16-4	14-4	8-8	10-9	39-11
1984	24	16	0	0	6-4	2rd	2rd	QF	1rd	1-1	....	16	16	.500	2-5	8-4	2-4	4-3	4-4	12-12
1985	26	20	0	0	5-4	3rd	1rd	4rd	1rd	1-1	....	18	20	.474	1-3	9-6	5-9	3-2	3-3	15-17
1986	23	18	0	0	4-3	....	1rd	3rd	3rd	0-1	....	24	18	.571	3-3	4-3	10-6	7-6	7-7	17-11
1987	73	19	0	0	5-4	4rd	1rd	3rd	2rd	1-2	....	11	19	.367	1-2	5-5	4-8	1-4	1-5	10-14
1988	61	19	0	0	3-4	2rd	2rd	2rd	1rd	....	....	19	19	.500	1-2	7-5	9-10	2-2	2-3	17-16
1989	118	14	0	0	2-3	3rd	1rd	....	1rd	1-1	....	9	14	.391	0-1	2-2	7-10	0-1	0-2	9-12
1990	64	14	0	1	1-3	2rd	....	1rd	1rd	0-1	....	13	14	.481	0-0	7-4	6-7	0-3	0-3	13-11
1991	60	19	0	0	5-4	2rd	1rd	2rd	4rd	0-1	....	14	19	.424	0-3	2-3	7-10	5-3	5-3	9-16
1992	60	18	0	0	3-4	2rd	3rd	1rd	1rd	1-2	....	14	18	.438	4-4	6-3	3-7	1-4	1-4	13-14
1993	191	13	0	0	0-2	....	....	1rd	1rd	0-2	....	4	13	.235	0-4	1-1	2-4	1-4	1-5	3-8
1994	....	4	0	0	0-1	....	....	1rd	....	3-1	....	1	4	.200	0-0	0-3	1-1	0-0	0-0	1-4
1995	....	3	0	0	1-1	....	....	2rd	....	....	....	1	3	.250	0-0	1-3	0-0	0-0	0-0	1-3
TOTALS		**250**	**2**	**4**	**62-54**	....	....	....	....	**12-16**	....	**242**	**248**	**.494**	**33-40**	**88-64**	**83-89**	**38-55**	**44-65**	**198-183**

• DURR, Françoise   Françoise Durr "Frankie" Browning

Female. Born: Dec. 25, 1942. Algiers, Algeria. Height: 5' 4". Weight: 120 lbs. Plays: right.
Status: Turned Pro 1967. Earnings: –. Highest Ranking: 3 (Dec. 1967).

Year	Rk	TP	TW	TF	GS	Aus	Fre	Wim	US	FC	Oly	MW	ML	Pct	CL	GR	HD	CP	IN	OD
1960	....	1	0	0	....	....	2rd	....	....	....	....	....	....	....	....	....	....	....	....	....
1961	....	1	0	0	....	....	3rd	....	....	....	....	....	....	....	....	....	....	....	....	....
1962	....	2	0	0	....	....	4rd	3rd	....	....	....	....	....	....	....	....	....	....	....	....
1963	....	2	0	0	....	....	4rd	2rd	....	0-2	....	....	....	....	....	....	....	....	....	....
1964	....	3	0	0	....	....	2rd	2rd	3rd	3-1	....	....	....	....	....	....	....	....	....	....
1965	10	4	0	0	....	QF	QF	4rd	QF	1-2	....	....	....	....	....	....	....	....	....	....
1966	8	3	0	0	....	....	QF	QF	QF	1-1	....	....	....	....	....	....	....	....	....	....
1967	3	4	1	0	....	QF	W	3rd	SF	1-0	....	....	....	....	....	....	....	....	....	....
1968	....	3	0	0	8-3	....	4rd	QF	3rd	....	....	8	3	.727	2-1	6-2	0-0	0-0	0-0	8-3
1969	....	5	1	0	6-4	2rd	3rd	2rd	3rd	....	....	6	4	.600	2-1	4-3	0-0	0-0	0-0	6-4
1970	10	5	1	4	10-3	....	3rd	SF	QF	2-1	....	12	4	.750	3-1	9-3	0-0	0-0	0-0	12-4
1971	6	10	6	4	8-3	....	QF	QF	3rd	....	....	8	3	.727	3-1	5-2	0-0	0-0	0-0	8-3
1972	9	5	0	4	8-3	....	SF	SF	QF	3-0	....	11	3	.786	3-1	8-2	0-0	0-0	0-0	11-3
1973	....	4	1	0	7-3	....	SF	4rd	1rd	....	....	7	3	.700	4-1	3-2	0-0	0-0	0-0	7-3
1974	10	3	0	0	2-2	....	2rd	2rd	....	....	....	2	3	.400	0-0	2-2	0-0	0-1	0-1	2-2
1975	9	3	0	2	2-2	....	2rd	2rd	....	....	....	2	3	.400	1-1	1-1	0-0	0-1	0-1	2-2
1976	8	4	0	1	4-2	....	4rd	4rd	....	....	....	5	4	.556	2-1	2-1	1-1	0-2	0-2	5-2
1977	32	20	0	1	2-2	....	3rd	1rd	2-1	....	....	15	20	.429	0-3	5-3	1-4	9-10	9-10	6-10
1978	33	11	0	1	2-1	....	3rd	....	2-0	....	....	14	11	.560	2-1	6-2	5-4	1-4	5-5	9-6
1979	86	9	0	0	0-3	....	1rd	2rd	1rd	1-0	....	3	9	.250	1-2	1-2	0-1	1-4	1-4	2-5
TOTALS		**102**	**10**	**17**	**59-31**	....	....	....	....	**16-8**	....	**93**	**70**	**.571**	**23-14**	**52-25**	**7-10**	**11-22**	**15-23**	**78-47**

Represented France in the Federation Cup (1964-1979). Doubles Titles: Fre (5), US (2).

• EDBERG, Stefan   Stefan Edberg

Male. Born: Jan. 19, 1966. Vastervik, Sweden. Height: 6' 2". Weight: 170 lbs. Plays: right.
Status: Turned Pro 1983. Earnings: $20,630,941. Highest Ranking: 1 (Aug. 1990).

Year	Rk	TP	TW	TF	GS	Aus	Fre	Wim	US	DC	Oly	MW	ML	Pct	CL	GR	HD	CP	IN	OD
1982	523	3	0	0	0-0	....	....	....	....	....	....	0	3	.000	0-1	0-0	0-2	0-0	0-2	0-1
1983	53	10	0	0	1-3	2rd	....	2rd	1rd	....	....	12	10	.545	4-2	2-3	6-5	0-0	6-3	6-7
1984	20	18	1	0	6-4	QF	2rd	2rd	2rd	....	....	32	17	.653	5-3	4-3	14-5	9-6	14-9	18-8
1985	5	23	4	2	16-3	W	QF	4rd	4rd	2-2	....	60	19	.759	9-3	9-1	25-7	17-8	25-9	35-10
1986	5	24	3	4	8-3	....	2rd	3rd	SF	4-1	SF	70	21	.769	15-3	7-3	32-5	16-10	26-10	44-11
1987	2	19	7	4	17-3	W	2rd	SF	SF	2-0	....	78	12	.867	8-3	14-2	42-5	14-2	24-2	54-10
1988	5	21	3	4	18-3	SF	4rd	W	4rd	6-1	....	67	18	.788	11-4	12-1	28-9	16-4	23-7	44-11
1989	3	18	2	6	19-3	QF	F	F	4rd	3-1	....	64	16	.800	14-2	6-2	29-6	15-6	21-7	43-9
1990	1	22	7	5	13-3	F	1rd	W	1rd	2-0	....	70	15	.824	3-5	10-1	39-5	18-4	22-6	48-9
1991	1	23	6	2	21-3	SF	QF	SF	W	0-2	....	76	17	.817	9-6	10-1	39-7	18-3	23-5	53-12
1992	2	27	3	3	19-3	F	3rd	QF	W	3-2	1rd	68	24	.739	10-6	7-2	32-6	19-10	23-13	45-11
1993	5	27	1	3	16-4	F	QF	SF	2rd	2-2	....	61	26	.701	17-8	7-2	24-9	13-7	17-10	44-16
1994	7	29	3	1	8-4	SF	1rd	2rd	3rd	6-2	....	60	26	.698	9-7	3-2	33-9	15-8	16-9	44-17

Year	Rk	TP	TW	TF	GS	Aus	Fre	Wim	US	DC	Oly	MW	ML	Pct	CL	GR	HD	CP	IN	OD
1995	9	21	1	1	7-4	4rd	2rd	2rd	3rd	3-1	....	42	20	.677	10-4	2-2	26-11	4-3	8-5	34-15
1996	15	26	0	1	9-4	2rd	4rd	2rd	QF	2-1	....	46	26	.639	14-7	6-2	18-13	8-4	9-7	37-19
TOTALS		311	41	36	178-47	....	....	....	....	35-15	....	806	270	.749	138-64	99-27	387-104	182-75	257-104	549-166

Held number one tour ranking 5 times for a total of 72 weeks. Last ranked number one in 1992. Doubles Titles: Aus (2), US (1).

• EDMONDSON, Mark Mark "Eddo" Edmondson

Male. Born: June 24, 1954. Gosford, Australia. Height: 6' 1". Weight: 190 lbs. Plays: right.
Status: Turned Pro 1975. Earnings: $1,451,680. Highest Ranking: 20 (Dec. 1981).

Year	Rk	TP	TW	TF	GS	Aus	Fre	Wim	US	DC	Oly	MW	ML	Pct	CL	GR	HD	CP	IN	OD
1975	212	3	0	0	1-2	1rd	....	2rd	....	....	....	1	3	.250	0-0	1-3	0-0	0-0	0-0	1-3
1976	35	22	2	0	8-3	W	1rd	3rd	1rd	....	....	26	20	.565	15-15	8-2	2-1	1-2	1-2	25-18
1977	99	14	0	0	7-4	QF/	2rd	2rd	3rd	3-0	....	12	14	.462	5-7	4-4	2-2	1-1	1-1	11-13
1978	79	17	1	0	2-4	2rd	1rd	2rd	1rd	....	....	15	16	.484	5-6	8-3	1-4	1-3	2-4	13-12
1979	72	26	0	2	3-4	QF	1rd	1rd	1rd	1-3	....	26	26	.500	5-9	14-7	4-5	3-5	4-7	22-19
1980	102	23	0	0	2-3	3rd	1rd	1rd	....	2-0	....	18	23	.439	4-8	5-5	4-5	5-5	5-6	13-17
1981	20	31	3	3	7-4	SF	1rd	2rd	3rd	0-2	....	59	28	.678	9-9	25-4	14-8	11-7	16-9	43-19
1982	24	28	0	0	6-3	1rd	....	SF	2rd	3-1	....	31	28	.525	7-6	12-7	4-6	8-9	9-10	22-18
1983	39	21	0	1	4-2	3rd	....	3rd	....	2-0	....	19	21	.475	3-6	6-5	8-6	2-4	3-6	16-15
1984	145	18	0	0	2-3	2rd	....	3rd	1rd	....	....	9	18	.333	2-3	5-4	1-7	1-4	1-5	8-13
1985	115	10	0	0	0-3	1rd	1rd	1rd	....	....	....	9	10	.474	3-2	6-6	0-2	0-0	0-1	9-9
1986	307	9	0	0	0-2	....	1rd	1rd	....	....	....	3	9	.250	0-2	1-2	2-4	0-1	2-3	1-6
1987	523	1	0	0	1-1	3rd	....	....	....	....	....	1	1	.500	0-0	1-1	0-0	0-0	0-0	1-1
TOTALS		223	6	6	43-38	....	....	....	....	11-6	....	229	217	.513	58-73	96-53	42-50	33-41	44-54	185-163

Doubles Titles: Aus (4), Fre (1)

• EMERSON, Roy Roy Stanley Emerson

Male. Born: Nov. 3, 1936. Black Butt, Australia. Height: 6'. Weight: 175 lbs. Plays: right.
Status: Turned Pro 1967. Earnings: $400,000. Highest Ranking: 1 (Dec. 1964). HOF: 1982

Year	Rk	TP	TW	TF	GS	Aus	Fre	Wim	US	DC	Oly	MW	ML	Pct	CL	GR	HD	CP	IN	OD
1954	....	4	0	0	....	3rd	1rd	2rd	3rd	....	....	....	....	....	....	....	....	....	....	....
1955	....	1	0	0	....	3rd	....	....	....	....	....	....	....	....	....	....	....	....	....	....
1956	....	3	0	0	....	4rd	....	3rd	QF	....	....	....	....	....	....	....	....	....	....	....
1957	....	2	0	0	....	....	....	4rd	4rd	....	....	....	....	....	....	....	....	....	....	....
1958	....	1	0	0	....	QF	....	....	....	....	....	....	....	....	....	....	....	....	....	....
1959	7	4	0	0	....	QF	QF	SF	QF	4-1	....	....	....	....	....	....	....	....	....	....
1960	6	4	0	0	....	SF	3rd	QF	3rd	....	....	....	....	....	....	....	....	....	....	....
1961	2	4	1	0	....	W	QF	QF	W	2-0	....	....	....	....	....	....	....	....	....	....
1962	2	4	0	3	....	F	F	4rd	F	....	....	....	....	....	....	....	....	....	....	....
1963	3	4	2	0	....	W	W	QF	4rd	2-0	....	....	....	....	....	....	....	....	....	....
1964	1	4	3	0	....	W	QF	W	W	8-0	....	....	....	....	....	....	....	....	....	....
1965	1	4	2	0	....	W	SF	W	QF	1-1	....	....	....	....	....	....	....	....	....	....
1966	3	4	1	0	....	W	QF	QF	SF	2-0	....	....	....	....	....	....	....	....	....	....
1967	2	4	2	0	....	W	W	4rd	QF	2-0	....	....	....	....	....	....	....	....	....	....
1968	....	4	1	2	9-3	....	QF	4rd	4rd	....	....	9	3	.750	4-1	5-2	0-0	0-0	0-0	9-3
1969	....	7	2	2	11-4	3rd	4rd	4rd	QF	....	....	11	5	.688	3-1	8-3	0-0	0-1	0-1	11-4
1970	....	2	0	4	7-2	....	....	QF	4rd	....	....	7	2	.778	0-0	7-2	0-0	0-0	0-0	7-2
1971	4	4	0	0	5-2	QF	....	4rd	....	....	....	9	4	.692	2-1	5-2	0-0	2-1	2-1	7-3
1972	12	3	0	3	0-1	....	....	....	2rd	....	....	0	3	.000	0-0	0-1	0-2	0-0	0-1	0-2
1973	12	4	1	3	0-0	....	....	....	....	....	....	8	3	.727	0-0	0-0	3-2	5-1	5-1	3-2
1974	82	3	0	0	0-0	....	....	....	....	....	....	3	3	.500	0-0	0-0	2-2	1-1	1-1	2-2
1976	....	2	0	0	0-0	....	....	....	....	....	....	0	2	.000	0-1	0-0	0-1	0-0	0-0	0-2
1977	....	2	0	0	0-0	....	....	....	....	....	....	3	2	.600	0-0	0-0	3-1	0-1	0-1	3-1
1983	....	1	0	0	0-0	....	....	....	....	....	....	0	1	.000	0-1	0-0	0-0	0-0	0-0	0-1
TOTALS		79	15	17	32-12	....	....	....	....	21-2	....	50	28	.641	9-5	25-10	8-8	8-5	8-6	42-22

Held number one world ranking 2 times during amateur era. Doubles Titles: Aus (3), Fre (6), Wim (3), US (4).

• ENQVIST, Thomas Karl John Thomas Enqvist

Male. Born: Mar. 13, 1974. Stockholm, Sweden. Height: 6' 3". Weight: 190 lbs. Plays: right.
Status: Turned Pro 1991. Earnings: $9,784,703. Highest Ranking: 4 (Nov. 1999).

Year	Rk	TP	TW	TF	GS	Aus	Fre	Wim	US	DC	Oly	MW	ML	Pct	CL	GR	HD	CP	IN	OD
1989	1103	1	0	0	0-0	....	....	....	....	....	....	0	1	.000	0-1	0-0	0-0	0-0	0-0	0-1
1990	472	1	0	0	0-0	....	....	....	....	....	....	0	1	.000	0-1	0-0	0-0	0-0	0-0	0-1
1991	229	5	0	0	0-0	....	....	....	....	....	....	1	5	.167	0-1	0-0	1-2	0-2	1-4	0-1

Year	Rk	TP	TW	TF	GS	Aus	Fre	Wim	US	DC	Oly	MW	ML	Pct	CL	GR	HD	CP	IN	OD
1992	63	10	1	0	1-1	2rd	....	....	....	....	....	16	9	.640	2-2	0-0	7-4	7-3	8-4	8-5
1993	87	24	1	0	3-4	1rd	1rd	1rd	4rd	....	....	18	23	.439	1-5	0-2	13-11	4-5	6-8	12-15
1994	60	19	0	0	3-3	2rd	1rd	....	3rd	....	....	23	19	.548	0-2	0-0	21-11	2-6	4-7	19-12
1995	7	28	5	1	3-3	3rd	1rd	1rd	2rd	0-2	....	63	23	.733	8-3	1-2	44-14	10-4	18-6	45-17
1996	9	32	3	0	8-4	QF	1rd	2rd	4rd	6-1	3rd	58	29	.667	3-6	2-2	38-15	15-6	24-8	34-21
1997	28	24	1	1	3-1	4rd	....	....	....	4-2	....	39	23	.629	1-3	0-0	16-11	22-9	25-10	14-13
1998	22	17	2	1	5-3	2rd	3rd	3rd	....	1-0	....	36	15	.706	7-3	4-2	16-7	9-3	15-6	21-9
1999	4	31	3	1	9-4	F	2rd	3rd	1rd	0-2	....	48	28	.632	8-6	2-2	33-12	5-8	16-10	32-18
2000	9	25	2	3	8-4	1rd	3rd	4rd	4rd	....	....	51	23	.689	9-6	3-2	32-11	7-4	11-8	40-15
2001	24	22	0	0	7-3	....	4rd	QF	1rd	....	....	33	22	.600	11-7	4-2	16-11	2-2	11-5	22-17
2002	44	17	1	0	5-4	2rd	2rd	2rd	3rd	2-1	....	28	16	.636	6-6	1-2	19-8	2-1	8-1	20-15
TOTALS		**256**	**19**	**7**	**55-34**	....	....	....	....	**13-8**	....	**414**	**237**	**.636**	**56-52**	**17-16**	**256-117**	**85-53**	**147-77**	**267-160**

• EVERT, Chris   Christine Marie Evert

Female. Born: Dec. 21, 1954. Fort Lauderdale, FL, United States. Height: 5' 6". Weight: 125 lbs. Plays: right.
Status: Turned Pro 1973. Earnings: $8,896,195. Highest Ranking: 1 (Nov. 1975). HOF: 1995

Year	Rk	TP	TW	TF	GS	Aus	Fre	Wim	US	FC	Oly	MW	ML	Pct	CL	GR	HD	CP	IN	OD
1971	10	5	4	0	4-1	....	....	....	SF	....	....	4	1	.800	0-0	4-1	0-0	0-0	0-0	4-1
1972	3	8	4	3	9-2	....	....	SF	SF	....	....	10	2	.833	1-1	9-2	0-0	0-0	0-0	10-2
1973	3	16	12	4	15-3	....	F	F	SF	....	....	18	3	.857	7-1	10-2	0-0	1-1	1-1	17-3
1974	3	20	16	4	20-2	F	W	W	SF	....	....	23	3	.885	8-1	14-2	0-0	1-1	1-1	22-2
1975	1	20	16	2	17-1	....	SF	W	W	....	....	24	3	.889	14-0	5-1	1-1	4-2	4-2	20-1
1976	1	15	12	3	13-0	....	....	W	W	....	....	15	2	.882	7-1	7-1	0-0	1-2	1-2	14-0
1977	1	15	11	3	12-1	....	....	SF	W	5-0	....	62	3	.954	12-1	10-1	11-1	29-2	29-2	33-1
1978	1	11	7	3	11-1	....	....	F	W	5-0	....	53	4	.930	5-1	15-2	15-0	18-2	18-2	35-2
1979	2	21	8	5	18-2	....	W	F	F	4-0	....	84	13	.866	24-1	12-1	21-4	27-7	30-8	54-5
1980	1	15	8	3	18-1	....	W	F	W	4-0	....	68	7	.907	20-0	10-1	17-0	21-6	21-6	47-1
1981	1	15	9	4	21-3	F	SF	W	SF	5-0	....	68	6	.919	30-1	16-1	16-3	6-1	8-2	60-4
1982	2	16	10	3	21-2	W	SF	F	W	5-0	....	69	6	.920	22-2	10-1	29-1	8-2	10-3	59-3
1983	2	15	6	7	15-2	....	W	3rd	F	....	....	56	9	.862	22-0	2-1	19-4	13-4	13-5	43-4
1984	2	14	6	7	24-3	W	F	F	F	....	....	67	8	.893	23-3	16-2	21-1	7-2	12-2	55-6
1985	2	18	10	7	23-3	F	W	F	SF	....	....	79	8	.908	23-1	16-2	21-2	19-3	19-3	60-5
1986	2	13	6	3	17-2	....	W	SF	SF	3-1	....	59	7	.894	23-2	5-1	21-2	10-2	10-2	49-5
1987	3	18	5	4	14-3	....	SF	SF	QF	4-1	....	72	13	.847	23-2	9-2	26-7	14-2	18-3	54-10
1988	3	15	4	4	18-3	F	3rd	SF	SF	....	3rd	61	11	.847	13-1	5-1	37-6	6-3	10-4	51-7
1989	....	9	0	3	9-2	....	....	SF	QF	5-0	....	32	9	.780	5-2	7-1	19-5	1-1	1-1	31-8
TOTALS		**279**	**154**	**72**	**299-37**	....	....	....	....	**40-2**	....	**924**	**118**	**.887**	**282-21**	**182-26**	**274-37**	**186-43**	**206-49**	**718-70**

Held number one tour ranking 8 times for a total of 262 weeks. Last ranked number one in 1985. Competed as Chris Evert Lloyd 1979-1986. Doubles Titles: Fre (2), Wim (1).

• FEDERER, Roger   Roger Federer

Male. Born: Aug. 8, 1981. Basel, Switzerland. Height: 6' 1". Weight: 175 lbs. Plays: right.
Status: Turned Pro 1998. Earnings: $3,737,328. Highest Ranking: 6 (Nov. 2002).

Year	Rk	TP	TW	TF	GS	Aus	Fre	Wim	US	DC	Oly	MW	ML	Pct	CL	GR	HD	CP	IN	OD
1998	302	3	0	0	0-0	....	....	....	....	....	....	2	3	.400	0-1	0-0	2-1	0-1	2-2	0-1
1999	64	17	0	0	0-2	....	1rd	1rd	....	1-3	....	13	17	.433	0-5	0-2	4-5	9-5	12-7	1-10
2000	29	30	0	0	7-4	3rd	4rd	1rd	3rd	2-1	SF	36	30	.545	3-7	2-3	21-15	10-5	20-10	16-20
2001	13	22	1	0	13-4	3rd	QF	QF	4rd	3-1	....	49	21	.700	9-5	9-3	21-9	10-4	21-8	28-13
2002	6	25	3	0	6-4	4rd	1rd	1rd	4rd	4-0	....	58	22	.725	12-4	5-3	30-11	11-4	24-7	34-15
TOTALS		**97**	**4**	**0**	**26-14**	....	....	....	....	**10-5**	....	**158**	**93**	**.629**	**24-22**	**16-11**	**78-41**	**40-19**	**79-34**	**79-59**

• FERNANDEZ, Mary Joe   Mary Joe Fernandez

Female. Born: Aug. 19, 1971. Lugar de Nacimiento, Dominican Republic. Height: 5' 8". Weight: 120 lbs. Plays: right.
Status: Turned Pro 1974. Earnings: $5,258,471. Highest Ranking: 4 (Oct. 1990).

Year	Rk	TP	TW	TF	GS	Aus	Fre	Wim	US	FC	Oly	MW	ML	Pct	CL	GR	HD	CP	IN	OD
1984	....	2	0	0	0-0	....	....	....	....	....	....	0	2	.000	0-0	0-0	0-2	0-0	0-0	0-2
1985	99	6	0	0	1-2	....	1rd	....	2rd	....	....	5	6	.455	0-2	0-0	5-4	0-0	0-0	5-6
1986	27	14	0	0	6-3	....	QF	1rd	3rd	....	....	18	14	.563	10-5	1-2	7-4	0-3	0-3	18-11
1987	20	14	0	0	6-3	....	2rd	4rd	3rd	....	....	24	14	.632	9-5	3-2	11-6	1-1	4-3	20-11
1988	15	10	0	0	5-2	....	4rd	4rd	3rd	....	....	22	10	.688	3-3	7-2	11-4	1-1	2-1	20-9
1989	12	15	0	0	10-4	3rd	SF	4rd	1rd	....	....	32	15	.681	6-2	6-2	15-7	5-4	11-6	21-9
1990	4	12	2	0	15-3	F	QF	....	SF	....	....	40	10	.800	7-3	3-1	22-4	8-2	13-2	27-8
1991	8	19	0	0	16-4	SF	QF	SF	3rd	3-1	....	49	19	.721	10-4	9-2	25-9	5-4	7-5	42-14

Year	Rk	TP	TW	TF	GS	Aus	Fre	Wim	US	FC	Oly	MW	ML	Pct	CL	GR	HD	CP	IN	OD
1992	6	17	0	0	15-4	F	3rd	3rd	SF	....	SF	51	17	.750	12-4	6-2	27-8	6-3	9-4	42-13
1993	7	14	1	0	12-3	QF	F	3rd	....	....	....	34	13	.723	12-3	3-2	16-4	3-4	3-4	31-9
1994	14	12	1	0	9-4	4rd	3rd	3rd	3rd	4-1	....	25	11	.694	10-4	2-1	13-5	0-1	0-1	25-10
1995	8	17	2	0	11-4	4rd	1rd	QF	QF	2-4	....	31	15	.674	4-6	4-1	16-4	7-4	7-4	24-11
1996	14	17	0	0	10-3	4rd	4rd	QF	....	2-0	SF	32	17	.653	10-4	8-2	13-8	1-3	1-4	31-13
1997	9	19	1	0	15-4	SF	QF	4rd	4rd	1-2	....	40	18	.690	13-4	3-2	23-8	1-4	2-6	38-12
1998	4	8	0	0	2-1	....	....	....	3rd	....	....	8	8	.500	1-1	0-0	7-6	0-1	0-1	8-7
1999	17	12	0	0	8-3	3rd	4rd	1rd	4rd	....	....	17	12	.586	7-2	0-1	9-8	1-1	1-2	16-10
2000	....	1	0	0	0-0	....	....	....	....	....	....	0	1	.000	0-0	0-0	0-1	0-0	0-0	0-1
TOTALS		209	7	0	141-47	....	....	....	....	12-8	....	428	202	.679	114-52	55-22	220-92	39-36	60-46	368-156

Represented the United States in the Federation Cup (1991-1997). Doubles Titles: Aus (1), Fre (1).

• FERREIRA, Wayne   Wayne Richard Ferreira

Male. Born: Sept. 15, 1971. Johannesburg, South Africa. Height: 6' 1". Weight: 185 lbs. Plays: right.
Status: Turned Pro 1989. Earnings: $9,227,992. Highest Ranking: 6 (May 1995).

Year	Rk	TP	TW	TF	GS	Aus	Fre	Wim	US	DC	Oly	MW	ML	Pct	CL	GR	HD	CP	IN	OD
1990	173	5	0	0	1-1	....	....	2rd	....	....	....	2	5	.286	0-0	1-2	1-3	0-0	0-0	2-5
1991	50	21	0	0	6-4	4rd	2rd	2rd	2rd	....	....	26	21	.553	4-4	2-2	16-11	4-4	7-6	19-15
1992	12	27	2	2	14-4	SF	3rd	4rd	QF	5-0	2rd	49	25	.662	12-7	9-1	25-11	3-6	9-9	40-16
1993	22	25	0	2	10-4	4rd	2rd	4rd	4rd	6-0	....	38	25	.603	3-4	7-2	24-11	4-8	7-9	31-16
1994	12	31	5	2	9-4	4rd	1rd	QF	3rd	3-1	....	69	26	.726	7-5	11-4	43-10	8-7	15-7	54-19
1995	9	30	4	0	6-4	2rd	3rd	4rd	1rd	3-1	....	58	26	.690	14-3	5-3	21-14	18-6	18-7	40-19
1996	10	30	2	1	6-4	2rd	4rd	3rd	1rd	1-3	QF	49	28	.636	9-6	5-3	32-13	3-6	4-8	45-20
1997	43	22	0	0	10-3	4rd	3rd	3rd	4rd	3-1	....	29	22	.569	7-8	2-1	17-11	3-2	3-2	26-20
1998	26	27	0	0	6-4	2rd	3rd	4rd	1rd	0-3	....	33	27	.550	7-6	3-1	15-12	8-8	9-10	24-17
1999	53	25	0	1	4-4	4rd	1rd	1rd	1rd	2-0	....	29	25	.537	5-4	3-3	17-14	4-4	6-6	23-19
2000	13	23	1	0	9-4	4rd	3rd	4rd	2rd	2-0	1rd	43	22	.662	7-4	5-3	30-12	1-3	12-5	31-17
2001	62	21	0	0	2-4	3rd	1rd	1rd	1rd	2-2	....	16	21	.432	3-5	5-3	7-11	1-2	6-5	10-16
2002	39	18	0	0	9-4	QF	1rd	3rd	4rd	....	....	24	18	.571	3-4	5-2	15-11	1-1	3-2	21-16
TOTALS		305	14	8	92-48	....	....	....	....	27-11	....	465	291	.615	81-60	63-30	263-144	58-57	99-76	366-215

• FERRERO, Juan Carlos   Juan Carlos Ferrero

Male. Born: June 12, 1980. Onteniente, Spain. Height: 6'. Weight: 160 lbs. Plays: right.
Status: Turned Pro 1998. Earnings: $5,969,350. Highest Ranking: 2 (Apr. 2002).

Year	Rk	TP	TW	TF	GS	Aus	Fre	Wim	US	DC	Oly	MW	ML	Pct	CL	GR	HD	CP	IN	OD
1999	43	9	1	0	0-1	....	....	....	1rd	....	....	16	8	.667	15-5	0-0	0-2	1-1	1-2	15-6
2000	12	26	0	2	10-3	3rd	SF	....	4rd	5-0	QF	46	26	.639	23-7	0-1	20-15	3-3	5-7	41-19
2001	5	25	4	2	10-4	2rd	SF	3rd	3rd	1-1	....	57	21	.731	34-5	2-1	18-11	3-4	5-8	52-13
2002	4	27	2	3	9-3	....	F	2rd	3rd	1-1	....	48	25	.658	21-8	1-1	22-13	4-3	13-10	35-15
TOTALS		87	7	7	29-11	....	....	....	....	7-2	....	167	80	.676	93-25	3-3	60-41	11-11	24-27	143-53

• FORGET, Guy   Guy Forget

Male. Born: Jan. 4, 1965. Casablanca, Morocco. Height: 6' 3". Weight: 175 lbs. Plays: left.
Status: Turned Pro 1982. Earnings: $5,666,692. Highest Ranking: 7 (Dec. 1991).

Year	Rk	TP	TW	TF	GS	Aus	Fre	Wim	US	DC	Oly	MW	ML	Pct	CL	GR	HD	CP	IN	OD
1982	70	13	0	0	3-2	3rd	3rd	....	....	....	....	16	13	.552	6-6	1-2	6-4	3-1	5-2	11-11
1983	188	23	0	0	0-3	....	1rd	1rd	1rd	....	....	7	23	.233	4-14	0-1	1-4	2-4	2-5	5-18
1984	36	15	0	0	5-4	4rd	1rd	3rd	1rd	0-2	....	19	15	.559	4-4	8-4	5-3	2-4	5-5	14-10
1985	61	21	0	0	1-4	1rd	1rd	1rd	2rd	....	....	18	21	.462	9-8	2-4	6-7	1-2	6-5	12-16
1986	25	24	1	0	4-3	....	4rd	1rd	2rd	2-0	3rd	32	23	.582	8-7	2-2	14-7	8-7	17-8	15-15
1987	54	20	0	0	5-3	....	1rd	4rd	3rd	2-0	....	22	20	.524	5-6	4-2	8-8	5-4	9-6	13-14
1988	48	19	0	0	4-4	2rd	3rd	1rd	2rd	....	....	24	19	.558	9-7	4-2	8-6	3-4	4-5	20-14
1989	36	11	1	1	0-1	1rd	....	....	....	....	....	15	10	.600	2-2	0-0	6-4	7-4	7-5	8-5
1990	16	24	1	1	6-4	2rd	3rd	4rd	1rd	2-0	....	40	23	.635	20-6	6-2	10-8	4-7	4-7	36-16
1991	7	27	6	1	12-4	QF	4rd	QF	2rd	6-2	....	63	21	.750	9-7	4-2	31-5	19-7	26-7	37-14
1992	11	24	1	3	9-4	2rd	2rd	QF	4rd	2-0	2rd	47	23	.671	9-7	4-2	15-6	19-8	25-9	22-14
1993	152	9	0	0	4-1	QF	....	....	....	1-1	....	9	9	.500	2-3	0-0	6-4	1-2	2-3	7-6
1994	40	17	0	1	5-2	....	....	QF	2rd	....	....	22	17	.564	6-4	4-3	9-6	3-4	8-6	14-11
1995	73	26	0	1	3-4	2rd	2rd	2rd	1rd	0-2	....	19	26	.422	3-6	6-3	5-9	5-8	5-10	14-16
1996	61	24	1	0	5-4	1rd	3rd	1rd	4rd	1-1	....	25	23	.521	3-4	1-3	15-10	6-6	13-8	12-15
1997	1101	5	0	0	0-1	1rd	....	....	....	....	....	0	5	.000	0-0	0-0	0-3	0-2	0-2	0-3
TOTALS		302	11	8	66-48	....	....	....	....	16-8	....	378	291	.565	99-91	46-32	145-94	88-74	138-93	240-198

Represented France in the Davis Cup (1984-1996)

• FRANULOVIC, Zeijko   Zeijko Franulovic

Male. Born: June 13, 1947. . Height: –. Weight: –. Plays: right.
Status: Turned Pro 1968. Earnings: –. Highest Ranking: –.

Year	Rk	TP	TW	TF	GS	Aus	Fre	Wim	US	DC	Oly	MW	ML	Pct	CL	GR	HD	CP	IN	OD
1966	....	1	0	0	....	....	1rd	....	....	....	....	....	....	....	....	....	....	....	....	....
1967	....	1	0	0	....	....	2rd	....	....	1-1	....	....	....	....	....	....	....	....	....	....
1968	....	2	0	0	1-2	....	4rd	1rd	1-2	....	....	1	2	.333	1-1	0-1	0-0	0-0	0-0	1-2
1969	....	5	0	2	5-3	....	QF	2rd	1rd	2-2	....	5	5	.500	4-2	1-2	0-0	0-1	0-1	5-4
1970	....	10	3	1	8-2	....	F	3rd	....	7-1	....	10	7	.588	7-2	2-1	0-0	1-4	1-4	9-3
1971	....	14	4	2	7-3	....	SF	2rd	2rd	3-1	....	11	10	.524	6-2	2-2	2-1	1-5	1-5	10-5
1972	....	1	0	0	0-1	....	1rd	....	....	....	....	0	1	.000	0-1	0-0	0-0	0-0	0-0	0-1
1973	....	1	0	0	1-1	....	2rd	....	....	1-1	....	1	1	.500	1-1	0-0	0-0	0-0	0-0	1-1
1974	70	2	0	0	2-1	....	3rd	....	....	2-2	....	3	2	.600	3-2	0-0	0-0	0-0	0-0	3-2
1975	68	5	0	1	4-2	....	3rd	....	3rd	0-1	....	5	5	.500	5-4	0-0	0-1	0-0	0-1	5-4
1976	44	17	1	0	6-3	....	4rd	2rd	3rd	2-2	....	21	16	.568	20-12	1-2	0-0	0-2	0-2	21-14
1977	42	8	1	0	2-2	....	1rd	....	3rd	2-0	....	7	7	.500	6-6	0-0	0-1	1-1	1-1	6-6
1978	38	21	0	0	1-1	....	2rd	....	....	1-1	....	27	21	.563	22-15	0-0	0-1	5-5	5-5	22-16
1979	102	24	0	0	0-1	....	1rd	....	....	1-0	....	21	24	.467	12-12	0-0	6-4	3-8	9-11	12-13
1980	86	20	0	0	0-1	....	1rd	....	....	0-1	....	20	20	.500	20-16	0-0	0-3	0-1	0-4	20-16
1981	182	9	0	0	0-1	....	1rd	....	....	....	....	7	9	.438	5-6	0-0	2-2	0-1	1-2	6-7
1982	140	6	0	0	0-0	....	....	....	....	....	....	3	6	.333	2-4	0-0	1-1	0-1	1-2	2-4
1983	....	3	0	0	0-1	....	1rd	....	....	....	....	0	3	.000	0-3	0-0	0-0	0-0	0-0	0-3
TOTALS		**150**	**9**	**6**	**37-25**	....	....	....	**23-15**			**142**	**139**	**.505**	**114-89**	**6-8**	**11-13**	**11-29**	**19-38**	**123-101**

• FRASER, Neale   Neale Fraser

Male. Born: Oct. 3, 1933. Melbourne, Australia. Height: 6' 1". Weight: –. Plays: left.
Status: Amateur. Earnings: –. Highest Ranking: 1 (Dec. 1959). HOF: 1984

Year	Rk	TP	TW	TF	GS	Aus	Fre	Wim	US	DC	Oly	MW	ML	Pct	CL	GR	HD	CP	IN	OD
1952	....	1	0	0	....	4rd	....	....	....	....	....	....	....	....	....	....	....	....	....	....
1953	....	1	0	0	....	4rd	....	....	....	....	....	....	....	....	....	....	....	....	....	....
1954	....	4	0	0	....	4rd	3rd	2rd	4rd	....	....	....	....	....	....	....	....	....	....	....
1955	....	3	0	0	....	4rd	....	1rd	4rd	....	....	....	....	....	....	....	....	....	....	....
1956	6	3	0	0	....	SF	....	QF	SF	....	....	....	....	....	....	....	....	....	....	....
1957	5	4	0	1	....	F	QF	SF	3rd	....	....	....	....	....	....	....	....	....	....	....
1958	4	4	0	1	....	SF	QF	F	SF	....	....	....	....	....	....	....	....	....	....	....
1959	1	4	1	1	....	F	SF	QF	W	8-0	....	....	....	....	....	....	....	....	....	....
1960	1	4	2	1	....	F	QF	W	W	1-1	....	....	....	....	....	....	....	....	....	....
1961	8	1	0	0	....	....	....	4rd	....	2-0	....	....	....	....	....	....	....	....	....	....
1962	4	3	0	0	....	SF	SF	SF	....	....	....	....	....	....	....	....	....	....	....	....
1963	....	1	0	0	....	....	2rd	....	....	....	....	....	....	....	....	....	....	....	....	....
1965	....	2	0	0	....	....	2rd	3rd	....	....	....	....	....	....	....	....	....	....	....	....
1968	....	1	0	0	2-1	....	....	....	....	....	....	2	1	.667	0-0	2-1	0-0	0-0	0-0	2-1
1972	....	2	0	0	2-2	3rd	....	1rd	....	....	....	2	2	.500	0-0	2-2	0-0	0-0	0-0	2-2
1973	....	2	0	0	0-2	1rd	....	1rd	....	....	....	0	2	.000	0-0	0-2	0-0	0-0	0-0	0-2
1974	....	2	0	0	1-2	1rd	....	2rd	....	....	....	1	2	.333	0-0	1-2	0-0	0-0	0-0	1-2
1975	....	1	0	0	0-1	1rd	....	....	....	....	....	0	1	.000	0-0	0-1	0-0	0-0	0-0	0-1
TOTALS		**43**	**3**	**4**	**5-8**	....	....	....	**11-1**			**5**	**8**	**.385**	**0-0**	**5-8**	**0-0**	**0-0**	**0-0**	**5-8**

Held number one world ranking 2 times during amateur era. Doubles Titles: Aus (3), Fre (3), Wim (2), US (3).

• FROMHOLTZ, Dianne   Dianne Fromholtz Balestrat

Female. Born: Aug. 10, 1956. Albury, Australia. Height: 5' 4". Weight: 120 lbs. Plays: left.
Status: Turned Pro 1973. Earnings: $1,145,377. Highest Ranking: 4 (Mar. 1979).

Year	Rk	TP	TW	TF	GS	Aus	Fre	Wim	US	FC	Oly	MW	ML	Pct	CL	GR	HD	CP	IN	OD
1971	....	1	0	0	0-1	1rd	....	....	....	....	....	0	1	.000	0-0	0-1	0-0	0-0	0-0	0-1
1973	....	7	5	0	3-2	QF	....	1rd	....	....	....	3	2	.600	0-0	3-2	0-0	0-0	0-0	3-2
1974	....	10	4	1	5-4	2rd	3rd	1rd	3rd	3-1	....	8	5	.615	5-2	3-3	0-0	0-0	0-0	8-5
1975	....	8	0	1	4-4	3rd	3rd	1rd	2rd	....	....	5	7	.417	3-3	1-2	1-1	0-1	0-1	5-6
1976	5	5	1	1	8-2	....	....	4rd	SF	2-0	....	11	3	.786	5-1	3-2	1-1	2-1	2-1	9-3
1977	8	23	2	3	7-2	F/	....	....	4rd	3-2	....	34	18	.654	7-3	12-5	4-3	11-7	11-7	23-11
1978	10	12	2	0	5-2	....	....	4rd	3rd	2-0	....	24	10	.706	0-0	13-2	3-3	8-5	8-5	16-5
1979	6	27	1	0	11-3	....	SF	QF	4rd	4-1	....	60	26	.698	12-4	7-4	13-8	28-10	28-10	32-16
1980	12	23	0	0	10-3	....	SF	4rd	2rd	4-3	....	46	23	.667	6-4	6-2	9-5	25-12	26-13	20-10
1981	38	16	0	0	2-4	1rd	3rd	3rd	1rd	4-0	....	15	16	.484	11-7	1-4	2-4	1-1	1-2	14-14
1982	32	16	0	0	2-2	2rd	....	....	2rd	2-1	....	18	16	.529	3-2	2-2	6-6	7-6	7-6	11-10
1983	75	14	0	0	0-2	....	....	1rd	1rd	2-1	....	9	14	.391	8-6	0-1	0-3	1-4	1-4	8-10

Year	Rk	TP	TW	TF	GS	Aus	Fre	Wim	US	FC	Oly	MW	ML	Pct	CL	GR	HD	CP	IN	OD
1984	101	4	1	0	1-1	2rd	....	....	....	....	....	3	3	.500	0-0	3-3	0-0	0-0	0-0	3-3
1985	30	17	0	0	3-4	3rd	1rd	2rd	1rd	....	....	17	17	.500	0-2	9-6	8-6	0-3	4-5	13-12
1986	21	13	0	0	3-1	....	....	4rd	....	....	....	19	13	.594	0-0	5-3	8-4	6-6	6-6	13-7
1987	21	12	0	0	6-4	3rd	2rd	QF	1rd	....	....	19	12	.613	1-2	9-4	6-3	3-3	3-3	16-9
1988	57	14	0	0	2-3	1rd	....	2rd	2rd	....	....	14	14	.500	0-0	4-3	9-10	1-1	1-3	13-11
1989	112	10	0	0	0-2	1rd	....	1rd	....	....	....	6	10	.375	0-0	1-2	5-8	0-0	3-3	3-7
1990	....	2	0	0	0-1	1rd	....	....	....	....	....	0	2	.000	0-0	0-0	0-2	0-0	0-0	0-2
TOTALS		**234**	**16**	**6**	**72-47**	....	....	....	....	**24-9**	....	**311**	**212**	**.595**	**61-36**	**82-51**	**75-67**	**93-60**	**101-69**	**210-144**

Doubles Titles: Aus (1)

• GADUSEK, Bonnie   Bonnie Gadusek

Female. Born: Sept. 11, 1963. Pittsburgh, PA, United States. Height: 5' 7". Weight: 130 lbs. Plays: right.
Status: Turned Pro 1981. Earnings: $594,189. Highest Ranking: 8 (July 1984).

Year	Rk	TP	TW	TF	GS	Aus	Fre	Wim	US	FC	Oly	MW	ML	Pct	CL	GR	HD	CP	IN	OD
1981	35	9	0	0	1-2	2rd	1rd	....	....	....	....	7	9	.438	2-5	2-3	3-1	0-0	0-0	7-9
1982	18	20	0	1	4-1	....	3rd	....	QF	....	....	24	20	.545	12-7	0-0	5-5	7-8	7-9	17-11
1983	19	13	0	2	2-1	....	....	....	4rd	....	....	14	13	.519	10-5	0-0	4-4	0-4	0-4	14-9
1984	13	12	1	2	1-1	....	....	....	4rd	....	....	18	11	.621	10-4	0-0	3-3	5-4	5-4	13-7
1985	10	14	4	1	5-2	....	4rd	2rd	3rd	....	....	32	10	.762	9-2	0-1	13-4	10-3	11-4	21-6
1986	12	7	0	0	4-1	....	....	....	QF	....	....	19	7	.731	3-1	0-0	10-3	6-3	6-3	13-4
1987	460	2	0	0	0-1	....	....	....	1rd	....	....	1	2	.333	0-0	0-0	1-2	0-0	0-0	1-2
TOTALS		**77**	**5**	**6**	**17-9**	....	....	....	....	....	....	**115**	**72**	**.615**	**46-24**	**2-4**	**39-22**	**28-22**	**29-24**	**86-48**

• GARRISON, Zina   Zina Lynne Garrison Jackson

Female. Born: Nov. 16, 1963. Houston, TX, United States. Height: 5' 4". Weight: 135 lbs. Plays: right.
Status: Turned Pro 1982. Earnings: $4,590,816. Highest Ranking: 4 (Nov. 1989).

Year	Rk	TP	TW	TF	GS	Aus	Fre	Wim	US	FC	Oly	MW	ML	Pct	CL	GR	HD	CP	IN	OD
1980	....	2	0	0	0-1	....	....	....	2rd	....	....	2	2	.500	0-0	0-0	0-1	2-1	2-1	0-1
1981	....	4	0	0	0-1	....	....	....	1rd	....	....	3	4	.429	0-0	0-0	0-1	3-3	3-3	0-1
1982	16	14	0	0	10-4	1rd	QF	4rd	4rd	....	....	22	14	.611	7-3	10-4	5-5	0-2	0-3	22-11
1983	10	18	0	0	8-4	SF	1rd	2rd	4rd	....	....	38	18	.679	11-6	13-5	6-2	8-5	8-5	30-13
1984	9	22	1	0	6-4	1rd	4rd	2rd	3rd	0-1	....	47	21	.691	15-7	6-5	11-3	15-6	20-6	27-15
1985	8	21	2	0	13-4	QF	2rd	SF	QF	2-1	....	53	19	.736	12-4	11-4	16-4	14-7	19-7	34-12
1986	11	23	1	0	6-3	....	3rd	2rd	4rd	1-0	....	49	22	.690	8-5	4-2	23-6	14-9	16-10	33-12
1987	9	19	2	0	6-2	QF	....	4rd	4rd	....	....	44	17	.721	8-4	8-1	17-6	11-6	18-7	26-10
1988	9	21	0	0	13-4	2rd	4rd	QF	SF	....	SF	52	21	.712	13-6	9-3	25-9	5-3	7-4	45-17
1989	4	18	3	0	12-4	QF	3rd	2rd	SF	....	....	59	15	.797	3-2	12-3	27-7	17-3	23-5	36-10
1990	10	21	1	0	14-4	QF	1rd	F	QF	3-2	....	51	20	.718	6-4	12-2	23-9	10-5	12-6	39-14
1991	12	18	0	0	10-4	4rd	1rd	QF	4rd	1-0	....	38	18	.679	2-3	7-2	19-8	10-5	12-6	26-12
1992	18	21	1	0	9-3	4rd	....	4rd	4rd	....	1rd	36	20	.643	5-4	5-3	20-7	6-6	11-6	25-14
1993	14	21	2	0	7-4	3rd	1rd	4rd	3rd	....	....	43	19	.694	0-3	9-3	22-8	12-5	20-6	23-13
1994	24	16	0	0	7-4	1rd	1rd	QF	4rd	....	....	24	16	.600	0-3	8-2	12-7	4-4	7-6	17-10
1995	22	17	1	0	7-4	3rd	1rd	3rd	4rd	....	....	25	16	.610	1-4	9-2	6-5	9-5	9-6	16-10
1996	255	9	0	0	0-1	....	....	....	1rd	....	....	1	9	.100	0-1	0-0	0-5	1-3	1-3	0-6
TOTALS		**285**	**14**	**0**	**128-55**	....	....	....	....	**7-4**	....	**587**	**271**	**.684**	**91-59**	**123-41**	**232-93**	**141-78**	**188-90**	**399-181**

• GERULAITIS, Vitas   Vitas Kevin Gerulaitis

Male. Born: July 26, 1954. Brooklyn, NY, United States. Died: Sept. 17, 1994. Height: 6'. Weight: 155 lbs. Plays: right.
Status: Turned Pro 1971. Earnings: $2,778,748. Highest Ranking: 3 (Feb. 1978).

Year	Rk	TP	TW	TF	GS	Aus	Fre	Wim	US	DC	Oly	MW	ML	Pct	CL	GR	HD	CP	IN	OD
1971	....	1	0	0	0-1	....	....	....	1rd	....	....	0	1	.000	0-0	0-1	0-0	0-0	0-0	0-1
1972	....	1	0	0	1-1	....	....	....	2rd	....	....	1	1	.500	0-0	1-1	0-0	0-0	0-0	1-1
1973	....	2	0	0	0-1	....	....	....	1rd	....	....	1	2	.333	0-0	0-1	1-1	0-0	0-0	1-2
1974	47	5	1	0	1-2	....	....	1rd	2rd	....	....	4	4	.500	0-0	1-2	0-1	3-1	3-2	1-2
1975	15	5	2	5	1-2	....	....	1rd	2rd	....	....	2	3	.400	1-1	0-1	1-1	0-0	1-1	1-2
1976	18	15	1	3	7-2	....	....	QF	4rd	2-0	....	23	14	.622	7-3	4-1	0-2	12-8	12-8	11-6
1977	4	9	5	4	14-2	/W	....	SF	4rd	....	....	22	4	.846	9-1	11-1	0-0	2-2	2-2	20-2
1978	5	13	3	2	10-2	....	....	SF	SF	3-1	....	29	10	.744	3-2	5-1	5-1	16-6	16-6	13-4
1979	4	22	4	4	11-3	....	SF	1rd	F	5-1	....	63	18	.778	24-4	0-2	15-3	24-9	29-9	34-9
1980	9	20	3	3	10-4	1rd	F	4rd	2rd	1-1	....	50	17	.746	24-5	9-4	10-4	7-4	11-5	39-12
1981	9	19	1	2	8-3	....	1rd	4rd	SF	....	....	44	18	.710	7-5	3-1	18-5	16-7	18-8	26-10
1982	5	19	5	2	8-3	....	QF	QF	1rd	....	....	60	14	.811	16-3	4-1	18-4	22-6	27-7	33-7
1983	20	21	1	0	3-4	2rd	1rd	2rd	3rd	....	....	32	20	.615	4-4	2-4	16-6	10-6	18-7	14-13

Year	Rk	TP	TW	TF	GS	Aus	Fre	Wim	US	DC	Oly	MW	ML	Pct	CL	GR	HD	CP	IN	OD
1984	17	21	1	2	7-4	2rd	2rd	4rd	4rd	....	....	34	20	.630	8-3	3-2	11-6	12-9	12-11	22-9
1985	81	15	0	0	4-3	....	1rd	3rd	3rd	....	....	12	15	.444	0-5	2-1	8-5	2-4	2-4	10-11
1986	790	2	0	0	0-0	....	....	....	....	....	....	0	2	.000	0-0	0-0	0-0	0-2	0-2	0-0
TOTALS		**190**	**27**	**28**	**85-37**	....	....	....	....	**11-3**	....	**377**	**163**	**.698**	**103-36**	**45-24**	**103-39**	**126-64**	**151-72**	**226-91**

Doubles Titles: Wim (1)

• GILBERT, Brad   Brad Gilbert

Male. Born: Aug. 9, 1961. Oakland, CA, United States. Height: 6' 1". Weight: 175 lbs. Plays: right.
Status: Turned Pro 1982. Earnings: $5,509,060. Highest Ranking: 6 (Dec. 1989).

Year	Rk	TP	TW	TF	GS	Aus	Fre	Wim	US	DC	Oly	MW	ML	Pct	CL	GR	HD	CP	IN	OD
1981	282	5	0	0	0-0	....	....	....	....	....	....	5	5	.500	2-2	0-0	2-2	1-1	1-1	4-4
1982	54	14	1	0	1-1	....	....	....	2rd	....	....	19	13	.594	3-3	0-0	11-7	5-3	7-4	12-9
1983	62	27	0	0	2-4	1rd	1rd	3rd	1rd	....	....	33	27	.550	6-5	2-2	15-14	10-6	11-8	22-19
1984	23	25	2	1	6-4	4rd	2rd	3rd	2rd	....	....	39	23	.629	3-4	4-2	19-9	13-8	13-8	26-15
1985	18	25	3	2	3-4	3rd	1rd	1rd	3rd	....	....	53	22	.707	7-3	1-2	32-9	13-8	13-8	40-14
1986	11	20	4	0	6-2	....	....	4rd	4rd	2-2	SF	47	16	.746	3-1	4-4	30-7	10-4	18-5	29-11
1987	13	25	1	4	8-4	3rd	2rd	3rd	QF	....	....	57	24	.704	5-4	3-2	40-11	9-7	12-8	45-16
1988	21	16	1	1	1-1	....	....	....	2rd	....	....	30	15	.667	2-2	0-0	20-9	8-4	8-4	22-11
1989	6	22	5	3	0-2	....	....	1rd	1rd	2-0	....	60	17	.779	4-2	0-1	40-8	16-6	21-6	39-11
1990	10	26	3	2	6-2	....	....	QF	3rd	3-1	....	50	23	.685	3-5	4-1	27-10	16-7	21-8	29-15
1991	19	24	0	3	4-4	3rd	1rd	3rd	1rd	3-0	....	37	24	.607	0-5	3-2	23-12	11-5	15-6	25-17
1992	26	26	0	1	5-4	1rd	1rd	3rd	4rd	....	....	39	26	.600	0-2	7-3	25-16	7-5	14-9	25-17
1993	35	28	0	2	6-3	....	3rd	2rd	4rd	0-2	....	31	28	.525	3-2	2-5	23-17	3-4	8-8	23-20
1994	77	20	0	1	2-2	....	2rd	2rd	....	....	....	18	20	.474	1-2	1-1	16-14	0-3	4-5	14-15
1995	....	5	0	0	0-1	1rd	....	....	....	....	....	1	5	.167	0-0	0-0	1-4	0-1	1-3	0-2
TOTALS		**308**	**20**	**20**	**50-38**	....	....	....	....	**10-5**	....	**519**	**288**	**.643**	**42-42**	**31-25**	**324-149**	**122-72**	**167-91**	**352-197**

• GIMENO, Andres   Andres Gimeno

Male. Born: Aug. 3, 1937. Barcelona, Spain. Height: –. Weight: –. Plays: right.
Status: Turned Pro 1961. Earnings: –. Highest Ranking: 10 (Dec. 1969).

Year	Rk	TP	TW	TF	GS	Aus	Fre	Wim	US	DC	Oly	MW	ML	Pct	CL	GR	HD	CP	IN	OD
1956	....	2	0	0	....	....	1rd	3rd	....	....	....	....	....	....	....	....	....	....	....	....
1957	....	2	0	0	....	....	3rd	1rd	....	....	....	....	....	....	....	....	....	....	....	....
1958	....	2	0	0	....	....	3rd	2rd	....	2-2	....	....	....	....	....	....	....	....	....	....
1959	....	2	0	0	....	QF	....	3rd	....	7-2	....	....	....	....	....	....	....	....	....	....
1960	....	2	0	0	....	QF	2rd	....	....	2-0	....	....	....	....	....	....	....	....	....	....
1968	....	3	0	0	5-3	....	SF	3rd	1rd	....	....	5	3	.625	3-1	2-2	0-0	0-0	0-0	5-3
1969	10	6	1	2	13-4	F	QF	4rd	4rd	....	....	15	5	.750	3-1	10-3	0-0	2-1	2-1	13-4
1970	10	3	1	1	5-2	....	....	SF	1rd	....	....	5	2	.714	0-0	5-2	0-0	0-0	0-0	5-2
1971	....	5	1	0	0-2	2rd	....	1rd	....	....	....	2	4	.333	1-1	0-2	0-0	1-1	1-1	1-3
1972	10	10	4	2	10-2	....	W	2rd	4rd	6-1	....	10	6	.625	6-1	4-2	0-1	0-3	0-4	10-2
1973	....	1	0	0	1-1	....	2rd	....	....	1-0	....	1	1	.500	1-1	0-0	0-0	0-0	0-0	1-1
TOTALS		**38**	**7**	**6**	**34-14**	....	....	....	....	**18-5**	....	**38**	**21**	**.644**	**14-5**	**21-11**	**0-1**	**3-5**	**3-6**	**35-15**

• GOMEZ, Andres   Andres "Gogo" Gomez

Male. Born: Feb. 27, 1960. Guayaquil, Ecuador. Height: 6' 4". Weight: 185 lbs. Plays: left.
Status: Turned Pro 1979. Earnings: $4,385,040. Highest Ranking: 4 (June 1990).

Year	Rk	TP	TW	TF	GS	Aus	Fre	Wim	US	DC	Oly	MW	ML	Pct	CL	GR	HD	CP	IN	OD
1978	....	0	0	0	0-0	....	....	....	1-2	....	....	0	0	.000	0-0	0-0	0-0	0-0	0-0	0-0
1979	64	8	0	0	1-1	....	....	....	2rd	1-1	....	11	8	.579	10-7	0-0	1-1	0-0	0-0	11-8
1980	43	23	0	0	2-3	....	2rd	1rd	2rd	....	....	36	23	.610	30-17	2-2	2-2	2-2	3-3	33-20
1981	37	22	1	1	3-2	....	2rd	....	3rd	1-1	....	36	21	.632	32-16	0-0	4-3	0-2	2-4	34-17
1982	15	27	2	1	3-2	....	4rd	1rd	....	3-2	....	50	25	.667	37-16	0-1	3-2	10-6	10-7	40-18
1983	14	21	1	3	6-2	....	4rd	....	4rd	3-3	....	43	20	.683	21-10	0-0	16-6	6-4	12-5	31-15
1984	5	19	5	1	12-3	....	QF	QF	QF	3-1	....	63	14	.818	37-5	4-1	11-3	11-5	11-5	52-9
1985	15	16	1	1	2-1	....	3rd	....	....	2-1	....	28	15	.651	10-7	0-0	11-3	7-5	10-7	18-8
1986	10	26	4	2	5-3	....	QF	1rd	2rd	2-2	....	59	22	.728	36-9	0-1	18-5	5-7	5-7	54-15
1987	11	19	1	1	10-3	....	QF	4rd	4rd	5-1	....	46	18	.719	23-8	3-1	15-6	5-3	5-3	41-15
1988	24	19	0	2	3-2	....	2rd	....	3rd	2-1	....	36	19	.655	17-7	0-0	17-9	2-3	7-5	29-14
1989	17	19	2	0	4-3	....	2rd	2rd	3rd	....	....	32	17	.653	18-8	1-1	12-7	1-1	4-3	28-14
1990	6	30	3	1	9-3	4rd	W	1rd	1rd	....	....	37	27	.578	23-6	0-1	10-10	4-10	4-12	33-15
1991	68	20	1	0	0-1	....	....	1rd	....	....	....	20	19	.513	6-8	0-0	8-10	6-1	6-2	14-17
1992	177	12	0	0	1-2	1rd	2rd	....	....	2-0	....	10	12	.455	8-9	0-0	2-3	0-0	0-0	10-12

Year	Rk	TP	TW	TF	GS	Aus	Fre	Wim	US	DC	Oly	MW	ML	Pct	CL	GR	HD	CP	IN	OD
1993	....	6	0	0	0-0	....	....	....	....	2-0	....	2	6	.250	2-4	0-0	0-2	0-0	0-1	2-5
1995	....	0	0	0	0-0	....	....	....	....	2-0	....	0	0	.000	0-0	0-0	0-0	0-0	0-0	0-0
TOTALS		**287**	**21**	**14**	**61-31**	....	....	....	....	**29-15**	....	**509**	**266**	**.657**	**310-137**	**10-8**	**130-72**	**59-49**	**79-64**	**430-202**

Doubles Titles: Fre (1)

• GONZALEZ, Pancho   Ricardo Alonso "Pancho" Gonzalez

Male. Born: May 9, 1928. Los Angeles, CA, United States. Died: July 3, 1995. Height: 6' 2". Weight: 180 lbs. Plays: right.
Status: Turned Pro 1950. Earnings: $911,078. Highest Ranking: 1 (Dec. 1949). HOF: 1968

Year	Rk	TP	TW	TF	GS	Aus	Fre	Wim	US	DC	Oly	MW	ML	Pct	CL	GR	HD	CP	IN	OD
1947	....	1	0	0	....	....	....	....	1rd	....	....	....	....	....	....	....	....	....	....	....
1948	3	1	1	0	....	....	....	....	W	....	....	....	....	....	....	....	....	....	....	....
1949	1	3	1	0	....	....	SF	4rd	W	2-0	....	....	....	....	....	....	....	....	....	....
1968	....	4	1	0	10-3	....	SF	3rd	QF	0-0	....	10	3	.769	5-1	5-2	0-0	0-0	0-0	10-3
1969	....	6	2	0	8-3	3rd	....	4rd	4rd	0-0	....	10	4	.714	0-0	8-3	0-0	2-1	2-1	8-3
1970	....	2	1	0	2-1	....	....	....	3rd	0-0	....	2	1	.667	0-0	2-1	0-0	0-0	0-0	2-1
1971	....	3	1	0	3-2	....	....	2rd	3rd	0-0	....	3	2	.600	0-0	3-2	0-0	0-0	0-0	3-2
1972	....	4	1	0	1-2	....	....	2rd	2rd	0-0	....	1	3	.250	0-0	1-2	0-1	0-0	0-0	1-3
1973	....	2	0	0	0-1	....	....	....	1rd	0-0	....	3	2	.600	0-0	0-1	3-1	0-0	0-0	3-2
1976	....	1	0	0	0-0	....	....	....	....	0-0	....	0	1	.000	0-0	0-0	0-0	0-1	0-1	0-0
TOTALS		**27**	**8**	**0**	**24-12**	....	....	....	....	**2-0**	....	**29**	**16**	**.644**	**5-1**	**19-11**	**3-2**	**2-2**	**2-2**	**27-14**

Held number one world ranking 1 time during amateur era. Doubles Titles: Fre (1), Wim (1).

• GOOLAGONG, Evonne   Evonne Fay Goolagong Cawley

Female. Born: July 31, 1951. Griffith, Australia. Height: 5' 6". Weight: 130 lbs. Plays: right.
Status: Turned Pro 1969. Earnings: $1,399,431. Highest Ranking: 1 (Dec. 1971). HOF: 1988

Year	Rk	TP	TW	TF	GS	Aus	Fre	Wim	US	FC	Oly	MW	ML	Pct	CL	GR	HD	CP	IN	OD
1967	....	1	0	0	....	3rd	....	....	....	....	....	....	....	....	....	....	....	....	....	....
1968	....	1	0	0	2-1	3rd	....	....	....	0-0	....	2	1	.667	2-1	0-0	0-0	0-0	0-0	2-1
1969	....	1	0	1	1-1	QF	....	....	....	....	....	1	1	.500	0-0	1-1	0-0	0-0	0-0	1-1
1970	....	8	6	0	3-2	3rd	....	2rd	....	....	....	5	2	.714	0-0	5-2	0-0	0-0	0-0	5-2
1971	1	14	11	3	16-1	F	W	W	....	2-0	....	16	1	.941	6-1	10-1	0-0	0-0	0-0	16-1
1972	2	14	9	5	15-4	F	F	F	3rd	3-0	....	18	4	.818	4-1	14-3	0-0	0-0	0-0	18-4
1973	2	19	9	10	18-4	F	SF	SF	F	4-0	....	26	4	.867	10-1	14-3	0-0	2-1	2-1	24-4
1974	2	9	6	3	14-2	W	....	QF	F	4-0	....	19	2	.905	4-1	14-2	0-0	1-1	1-1	18-2
1975	5	10	4	5	15-2	W	....	F	F	3-1	....	19	6	.760	8-3	10-1	0-0	1-2	1-2	18-4
1976	2	12	8	4	16-2	W	....	F	F	4-1	....	25	3	.893	5-1	11-1	0-0	9-1	9-1	16-2
1977	....	4	4	0	5-1	/W	....	4rd	....	....	....	15	0	1.000	0-0	15-0	0-0	0-0	0-0	15-0
1978	3	13	6	3	5-2	....	....	SF	....	....	....	36	7	.837	0-0	10-2	6-1	20-5	20-5	16-2
1979	4	12	4	1	9-2	....	....	SF	QF	....	....	46	8	.852	14-4	11-1	13-2	8-1	8-1	38-7
1980	5	17	1	1	7-1	2rd	....	W	....	....	....	37	16	.698	6-3	11-2	2-1	18-10	18-10	19-6
1981	....	3	0	0	2-1	QF	....	....	....	....	....	5	3	.625	0-0	5-3	0-0	0-0	0-0	5-3
1982	17	7	0	1	1-2	2rd	....	2rd	....	2-1	....	8	7	.533	0-1	6-5	2-1	0-0	0-0	8-7
1983	37	7	0	0	2-1	....	3rd	....	....	....	....	9	7	.563	8-5	1-1	0-0	0-1	0-1	9-6
1985	....	1	0	0	0-0	....	....	....	....	....	....	0	1	.000	0-0	0-0	0-1	0-0	0-1	0-0
TOTALS		**153**	**68**	**37**	**131-29**	....	....	....	....	**22-3**	....	**287**	**73**	**.797**	**67-22**	**138-28**	**23-6**	**59-22**	**59-23**	**228-52**

Competed as Evonne Goolagong until 1977. Doubles Titles: Aus (5), Wim (1).

• GOTTFRIED, Brian   Brian Edward Gottfried

Male. Born: Jan. 27, 1952. Baltimore, MD, United States. Height: 6'. Weight: 165 lbs. Plays: right.
Status: Turned Pro 1970. Earnings: $2,782,514. Highest Ranking: 5 (Dec. 1977).

Year	Rk	TP	TW	TF	GS	Aus	Fre	Wim	US	DC	Oly	MW	ML	Pct	CL	GR	HD	CP	IN	OD
1970	....	1	0	0	0-1	....	....	....	1rd	....	....	0	1	.000	0-0	0-1	0-0	0-0	0-0	0-1
1971	....	2	0	0	0-1	....	....	....	1rd	....	....	1	2	.333	0-0	0-1	1-1	0-0	0-0	1-2
1972	....	3	0	0	2-3	....	2rd	2rd	1rd	....	....	2	3	.400	1-1	1-2	0-0	0-0	0-0	2-3
1973	21	10	2	2	3-2	....	2rd	....	3rd	....	....	9	8	.529	1-2	3-3	5-3	0-0	0-0	9-8
1974	29	11	1	1	3-3	....	2rd	2rd	2rd	....	....	13	10	.565	5-3	2-3	5-3	1-1	3-2	10-8
1975	23	11	3	2	6-3	....	4rd	4rd	2rd	1-1	....	14	8	.636	8-4	4-2	0-1	2-1	2-1	12-7
1976	10	24	1	3	9-3	....	4rd	4rd	4rd	....	....	53	23	.697	18-9	3-2	7-3	25-9	29-10	24-13
1977	5	19	5	10	11-3	....	F	2rd	QF	3-1	....	58	14	.806	16-4	8-3	16-2	18-5	22-7	36-7
1978	7	25	3	1	10-3	....	3rd	QF	QF	2-2	....	60	22	.732	18-6	4-1	17-7	21-8	28-11	32-11
1979	17	25	2	2	7-3	....	3rd	3rd	4rd	....	....	52	23	.693	9-5	7-3	23-6	13-9	26-12	26-11
1980	11	27	4	0	13-4	3rd	4rd	SF	4rd	0-2	....	68	23	.747	16-5	16-4	15-5	21-9	27-9	41-14
1981	19	23	1	3	6-3	....	3rd	2rd	4rd	....	....	47	22	.681	3-3	6-2	27-9	11-8	22-12	25-10

Year	Rk	TP	TW	TF	GS	Aus	Fre	Wim	US	DC	Oly	MW	ML	Pct	CL	GR	HD	CP	IN	OD
1982	21	25	2	2	3-3	....	2rd	2rd	2rd	0-1	....	43	23	.652	1-2	4-2	26-10	12-9	21-11	22-12
1983	21	20	1	0	7-3	....	4rd	4rd	2rd			31	19	.620	7-7	6-2	13-7	5-3	12-4	19-15
1984	91	18	0	0	4-3	....	4rd	1rd	2rd	....	....	13	18	.419	7-6	0-3	4-5	2-4	2-4	11-14
TOTALS		244	25	26	84-41	....	....	....	....	6-7	....	464	219	.679	110-57	64-34	159-62	131-66	194-83	270-136

Doubles Titles: Fre (2), Wim (1)

• GOURLAY, Helen   Helen Gourlay Cawley

Female. Born: Dec. 23, 1946. Australia. Height: –. Weight: –. Plays: –.
Status: Turned Pro 1968. Earnings: –. Highest Ranking: –.

Year	Rk	TP	TW	TF	GS	Aus	Fre	Wim	US	FC	Oly	MW	ML	Pct	CL	GR	HD	CP	IN	OD
1964	....	1	0	0	....	QF	....	....	....			....	....	....	....	....	....	....	....	....
1965	....	1	0	0	....	4rd						....	....	....	....	....	....	....	....	....
1966	....	3	0	0	....	4rd	1rd	2rd				....	....	....	....	....	....	....	....	....
1967	....	3	0	0	....	3rd	3rd	1rd				....	....	....	....	....	....	....	....	....
1968	....	2	0	0	5-2	....	3rd	4rd	....			5	2	.714	2-1	3-1	0-0	0-0	0-0	5-2
1969	....	3	0	0	4-3	QF	2rd	3rd				4	3	.571	1-1	3-2	0-0	0-0	0-0	4-3
1970	....	3	0	0	4-3	....	1rd	2rd	QF			4	3	.571	0-1	4-2	0-0	0-0	0-0	4-3
1971	....	6	0	2	8-4	QF	F	1rd	2rd			8	4	.667	5-1	3-3	0-0	0-0	0-0	8-4
1972	....	5	0	0	6-4	SF	4rd	4rd	1rd	1-1		7	5	.583	1-1	6-4	0-0	0-0	0-0	7-5
1973	....	2	0	0	0-2	....	....	1rd	1rd			0	2	.000	0-0	0-2	0-0	0-0	0-0	0-2
1974	....	4	0	1	4-3	2rd	....	3rd	2rd			4	3	.571	0-0	4-3	0-0	0-0	0-0	4-3
1975	....	7	0	0	2-3	2rd	....	2rd	2rd	2-2		4	7	.364	3-3	1-2	0-1	0-1	0-1	4-6
1976	....	2	0	0	4-2	SF	....	....	3rd			4	2	.667	1-1	3-1	0-0	0-0	0-0	4-2
1977	28	11	0	0	13-5	SF/F	3rd	4rd	2rd			18	11	.621	4-3	13-5	1-2	0-1	0-1	18-10
1978	....	1	0	0	0-0	....	....	....	....			0	1	.000	0-0	0-1	0-0	0-0	0-0	0-1
1980	....	3	0	0	0-1	1rd	....	....	....			1	3	.250	0-0	1-3	0-0	0-0	0-0	1-3
TOTALS		57	0	3	50-32	....	....	....	....	3-3		59	46	.562	17-12	41-29	1-3	0-2	0-2	59-44

Doubles Titles: Aus (4), Wim (1)

• GRAEBNER, Clark   Clark Edward Graebner

Male. Born: Nov. 4, 1943. Cleveland, OH, United States. Height: 6' 2". Weight: 175 lbs. Plays: right.
Status: Turned Pro 1969. Earnings: –. Highest Ranking: 7 (Dec. 1968).

Year	Rk	TP	TW	TF	GS	Aus	Fre	Wim	US	DC	Oly	MW	ML	Pct	CL	GR	HD	CP	IN	OD
1960	....	1	0	0	....	....	....	....	2rd			....	....	....	....	....	....	....	....	....
1961	....	1	0	0	....	....	....	....	2rd			....	....	....	....	....	....	....	....	....
1962	....	1	0	0	....	....	....	....	1rd			....	....	....	....	....	....	....	....	....
1963	....	1	0	0	....	....	....	....	2rd			....	....	....	....	....	....	....	....	....
1964	....	2	0	0	....	....	....	1rd	3rd			....	....	....	....	....	....	....	....	....
1965	....	2	0	0	....	....	....	2rd	3rd			....	....	....	....	....	....	....	....	....
1966	....	3	0	0	....	....	4rd	2rd	QF	2-0		....	....	....	....	....	....	....	....	....
1967	8	2	0	0	....	....	....	4rd	W			....	....	....	....	....	....	....	....	....
1968	7	2	0	0	10-2	....	....	SF	SF	9-2		12	2	.857	0-0	12-2	0-0	0-0	0-0	12-2
1969	....	2	0	0	5-2	....	....	QF	QF			5	2	.714	0-0	5-2	0-0	0-0	0-0	5-2
1970	....	6	3	0	6-2	....	....	QF	4rd			9	3	.750	3-1	6-2	0-0	0-0	0-0	9-3
1971	....	10	3	4	6-2	....	....	3rd	QF			7	7	.500	0-0	6-2	0-0	1-5	1-5	6-2
1972	....	3	0	1	4-3	....	3rd	2rd	2rd			4	3	.571	2-1	2-2	0-0	0-0	0-0	4-3
1973	48	6	1	1	0-1	....	....	....	1rd			3	5	.375	0-0	0-2	3-3	0-0	0-0	3-5
1974	99	2	0	1	2-2	....	....	1rd	3rd			2	2	.500	0-0	2-2	0-0	0-0	0-0	2-2
1975	....	1	0	0	0-1	....	....	....	1rd			0	1	.000	0-1	0-0	0-0	0-0	0-0	0-1
1976	....	3	0	0	0-0	....	....	....	....			0	3	.000	0-0	0-0	0-1	0-2	0-2	0-1
TOTALS		48	7	7	33-15	....	....	....	....	11-2	....	42	28	.600	5-3	33-14	3-4	1-7	1-7	41-21

Doubles Titles: Fre (1)

• GRAF, Steffi   Steffi Maria Graf

Female. Born: June 14, 1969. Mannheim, Germany. Height: 5' 9". Weight: 130 lbs. Plays: right.
Status: Turned Pro 1982. Earnings: $21,895,277. Highest Ranking: 1 (Aug. 1987).

Year	Rk	TP	TW	TF	GS	Aus	Fre	Wim	US	FC	Oly	MW	ML	Pct	CL	GR	HD	CP	IN	OD
1982	214	1	0	0	0-0	....	....	....	....			0	1	.000	0-0	0-0	0-1	0-0	0-1	0-0
1983	98	15	0	0	1-2	1rd	2rd	....	....			21	15	.583	14-7	3-4	2-3	2-1	3-2	18-13
1984	22	14	0	0	7-4	3rd	3rd	4rd	1rd			19	14	.576	7-6	7-4	5-3	0-1	4-2	15-12
1985	6	13	0	0	11-3	....	4rd	4rd	SF			40	13	.755	14-4	3-1	22-7	1-1	4-2	36-11
1986	3	14	8	0	9-2	....	QF	....	SF	2-0		64	6	.914	25-1	0-0	20-3	19-2	19-2	45-4
1987	1	13	11	0	19-2	....	W	F	F	5-0		75	2	.974	32-0	6-1	28-1	9-1	9-1	66-2

Year	Rk	TP	TW	TF	GS	Aus	Fre	Wim	US	FC	Oly	MW	ML	Pct	CL	GR	HD	CP	IN	OD
1988	1	14	11	0	27-0	W	W	W	W	....	W	72	3	.960	20-1	7-1	38-1	7-1	7-1	65-2
1989	1	16	14	0	27-1	W	F	W	W	3-0	....	86	2	.977	23-2	7-1	42-0	14-0	19-0	67-2
1990	1	15	10	0	24-3	W	F	SF	F	....	....	72	5	.935	20-2	5-1	23-1	24-1	24-1	48-4
1991	2	15	7	0	21-3	QF	SF	W	SF	2-0	....	65	8	.890	19-2	7-1	23-4	16-2	16-2	49-6
1992	2	15	8	0	17-2	....	F	W	QF	5-0	F	71	7	.910	30-3	7-1	13-2	21-2	21-2	50-5
1993	1	16	10	0	26-1	F	W	W	W	0-1	....	76	6	.927	21-2	7-1	32-1	16-2	16-2	60-4
1994	1	13	7	0	18-3	W	SF	1rd	F	....	....	58	6	.906	14-2	0-1	38-2	6-1	6-1	52-5
1995	1	11	9	0	21-0	....	W	W	W	....	....	47	2	.959	11-1	7-1	21-1	8-1	12-1	35-1
1996	1	11	7	0	21-0	....	W	W	W	3-1	....	54	4	.931	16-1	7-1	22-2	9-1	9-1	45-3
1997	28	4	1	0	7-2	4rd	QF	....	....	....	....	16	3	.842	10-2	0-0	3-1	3-1	3-1	13-3
1998	9	12	3	0	5-2	....	....	3rd	4rd	....	....	33	9	.786	0-0	6-2	15-6	12-1	13-2	20-7
1999	3	10	1	0	17-2	QF	W	F	....	....	....	33	9	.786	9-1	6-1	16-6	2-1	4-2	29-7
TOTALS		**222**	**107**	**0**	**278-32**	....	....	....	....	**20-2**	....	**902**	**115**	**.887**	**285-37**	**85-22**	**363-46**	**169-20**	**189-26**	**713-91**

Held number one tour ranking 7 times for a total of 378 weeks. Last ranked number one in 1997. Doubles Titles: Wim (1).

• GROSJEAN, Sebastien   Sebastien Grosjean

Male. Born: May 29, 1978. Marseille, France. Height: 5' 9". Weight: 155 lbs. Plays: right.
Status: Turned Pro 1996. Earnings: $4,726,122. Highest Ranking: 4 (Oct. 2002).

Year	Rk	TP	TW	TF	GS	Aus	Fre	Wim	US	DC	Oly	MW	ML	Pct	CL	GR	HD	CP	IN	OD
1997	141	4	0	0	0-1	....	1rd	....	....	....	....	0	4	.000	0-2	0-0	0-0	0-2	0-2	0-2
1998	89	19	0	0	3-3	....	1rd	4rd	1rd	....	....	16	19	.457	7-8	4-2	3-5	2-4	2-5	14-14
1999	27	28	0	2	4-4	1rd	3rd	3rd	1rd	2-3	....	36	28	.563	12-8	3-2	13-10	8-8	10-11	26-17
2000	19	27	1	1	6-4	3rd	3rd	1rd	3rd	2-0	....	44	26	.629	9-7	6-2	25-12	4-5	14-7	30-19
2001	6	27	1	2	12-4	SF	SF	3rd	1rd	1-2	....	51	26	.662	19-8	3-4	23-13	6-1	17-7	34-19
2002	17	23	1	0	6-3	2rd	QF	....	2rd	6-2	....	43	22	.662	16-6	0-0	18-13	9-3	20-7	23-15
TOTALS		**128**	**3**	**5**	**31-19**	....	....	....	....	**11-7**	....	**190**	**125**	**.603**	**63-39**	**16-10**	**82-53**	**29-23**	**63-39**	**127-86**

• HAAS, Tommy   Thomas Mario Haas

Male. Born: Apr. 3, 1978. Hamburg, Germany. Height: 6' 2". Weight: 180 lbs. Plays: right.
Status: Turned Pro 1996. Earnings: $5,621,787. Highest Ranking: 2 (May 2002).

Year	Rk	TP	TW	TF	GS	Aus	Fre	Wim	US	DC	Oly	MW	ML	Pct	CL	GR	HD	CP	IN	OD
1996	196	3	0	0	0-1	....	....	....	1rd	....	....	4	3	.571	0-0	0-0	4-3	0-0	1-1	3-2
1997	41	17	0	1	3-2	....	....	2rd	3rd	....	....	22	17	.564	5-3	2-2	10-8	5-4	7-5	15-12
1998	34	26	0	1	3-4	1rd	1rd	3rd	2rd	4-0	....	41	26	.612	10-6	3-2	19-13	9-5	14-9	27-17
1999	11	27	1	3	12-4	SF	3rd	3rd	4rd	3-1	....	47	26	.644	13-8	7-3	22-11	5-4	12-6	35-20
2000	23	22	0	3	6-4	2rd	3rd	3rd	2rd	2-0	F	36	22	.621	12-8	2-2	14-8	8-4	11-6	25-16
2001	8	25	4	0	5-4	2rd	2rd	1rd	4rd	2-0	....	57	21	.731	7-6	1-2	41-10	8-3	23-5	34-16
2002	11	21	0	1	11-3	SF	4rd	....	4rd	1-0	....	45	21	.682	18-7	0-0	26-13	1-1	5-4	40-17
TOTALS		**141**	**5**	**9**	**40-22**	....	....	....	....	**12-1**	....	**252**	**136**	**.649**	**65-38**	**15-11**	**136-66**	**36-21**	**73-36**	**179-100**

• HALARD, Julie   Julie Halard Decugis

Female. Born: Sept. 10, 1970. Versailles, France. Height: 5' 8". Weight: 128 lbs. Plays: right.
Status: Turned Pro 1986. Earnings: $3,096,734. Highest Ranking: 7 (Feb. 2000).

Year	Rk	TP	TW	TF	GS	Aus	Fre	Wim	US	FC	Oly	MW	ML	Pct	CL	GR	HD	CP	IN	OD
1987	62	5	0	0	3-2	....	2rd	....	3rd	....	....	9	5	.643	6-3	0-0	2-1	1-1	1-1	8-4
1988	75	15	0	0	2-4	2rd	2rd	1rd	1rd	....	....	11	15	.423	6-5	2-4	3-5	0-1	0-2	11-13
1989	119	16	0	0	2-4	1rd	1rd	2rd	2rd	....	....	10	16	.385	5-9	1-1	2-5	2-1	2-2	8-14
1990	41	17	0	0	6-4	3rd	3rd	2rd	2rd	2-1	....	22	17	.564	9-5	1-2	12-8	0-2	0-3	22-14
1991	20	24	1	0	4-4	2rd	2rd	2rd	2rd	....	....	44	23	.657	13-6	3-2	26-13	2-2	2-3	42-20
1992	27	15	1	0	6-4	1rd	3rd	4rd	2rd	....	2rd	23	14	.622	16-5	3-1	4-7	0-1	0-1	23-13
1993	29	19	0	0	7-4	QF	3rd	1rd	2rd	2-2	....	28	19	.596	6-7	0-1	19-10	3-1	7-4	21-15
1994	21	23	1	0	6-4	2rd	QF	1rd	2rd	3-1	....	41	22	.651	17-4	0-1	19-14	5-3	10-6	31-16
1995	51	18	1	0	3-4	1rd	3rd	1rd	2rd	2-2	....	21	17	.553	10-4	0-1	8-8	3-4	5-6	16-11
1996	15	13	2	0	3-2	3rd	2rd	....	....	3-1	....	31	11	.738	8-4	0-0	13-4	10-3	10-3	21-8
1997	15	1	0	0	0-0	....	....	....	....	....	....	0	1	.000	0-0	0-0	0-1	0-0	0-0	0-1
1998	22	25	2	0	3-3	....	2rd	3rd	1rd	0-2	....	34	23	.596	9-8	7-1	18-14	0-0	2-4	32-19
1999	9	22	2	0	9-4	2rd	4rd	3rd	4rd	....	....	47	20	.701	13-3	7-1	24-11	3-5	7-8	40-12
2000	15	25	2	0	4-4	QF	1rd	1rd	1rd	1-1	3rd	32	23	.582	2-4	7-2	20-13	3-4	6-6	26-17
TOTALS		**238**	**12**	**0**	**58-47**	....	....	....	....	**13-10**	....	**353**	**226**	**.610**	**120-67**	**31-17**	**170-114**	**32-28**	**52-49**	**301-177**

Doubles Titles: US (1)

• HANIKA, Sylvia   Sylvia Hanika

Female. Born: Nov. 30, 1959. Munich, Germany. Height: 5' 8". Weight: 135 lbs. Plays: left.
Status: Turned Pro 1977. Earnings: $1,296,560. Highest Ranking: 5 (Sept. 1983).

Year	Rk	TP	TW	TF	GS	Aus	Fre	Wim	US	FC	Oly	MW	ML	Pct	CL	GR	HD	CP	IN	OD
1978	35	10	1	2	0-3	....	1rd	2rd	1rd	2-0	....	16	9	.640	3-2	10-4	0-1	3-2	3-2	13-7
1979	16	15	1	2	6-3	....	1rd	3rd	QF	1-1	....	18	14	.563	8-5	3-2	4-4	3-3	3-4	15-10
1980	14	22	0	1	4-4	3rd	3rd	2rd	2rd	2-2	....	34	22	.607	7-4	5-5	13-5	9-8	17-11	17-11
1981	6	22	1	3	9-3	....	F	1rd	QF	....	....	54	21	.720	14-5	0-1	18-7	22-8	25-9	29-12
1982	10	24	1	0	2-2	....	2rd	4rd	....	....	....	39	23	.629	10-6	2-3	7-5	20-9	23-10	16-13
1983	5	20	0	6	11-4	QF	3rd	3rd	QF	....	....	46	20	.697	8-4	5-2	6-5	27-9	27-10	19-10
1984	17	22	1	0	7-4	2rd	3rd	1rd	QF	2-1	....	31	21	.596	13-8	1-3	10-6	7-4	8-6	23-15
1985	21	15	0	0	6-3	....	4rd	2rd	3rd	....	....	22	15	.595	7-3	1-1	11-7	3-4	3-5	19-10
1986	50	14	1	0	1-3	....	1rd	1rd	2rd	....	....	14	13	.519	8-4	1-2	1-3	4-4	4-5	10-8
1987	14	19	0	2	12-4	4rd	4rd	4rd	4rd	....	....	32	19	.627	4-3	6-4	11-5	11-7	15-9	17-10
1988	17	23	0	2	10-4	4rd	4rd	3rd	3rd	3-1	3rd	47	23	.671	20-8	4-3	20-9	3-3	10-6	37-17
1989	41	14	0	0	5-4	1rd	4rd	1rd	3rd	....	....	18	14	.563	8-4	0-1	9-7	1-2	2-3	16-11
1990	123	10	0	0	2-2	....	2rd	....	2rd	....	....	7	10	.412	3-4	0-0	4-5	0-1	0-1	7-9
TOTALS		**230**	**6**	**18**	**75-43**	....	....	....	....	**10-5**		**378**	**224**	**.628**	**113-60**	**38-31**	**114-69**	**113-64**	**140-81**	**238-143**

• HANTUCHOVA, Daniela   Daniela Hantuchova

Female. Born: Apr. 23, 1983. Poprad, Slovakia (Slovak Republic). Height: 5' 11". Weight: 125 lbs. Plays: right.
Status: Turned Pro 1999. Earnings: $1,506,035. Highest Ranking: 8 (Oct. 2002).

Year	Rk	TP	TW	TF	GS	Aus	Fre	Wim	US	FC	Oly	MW	ML	Pct	CL	GR	HD	CP	IN	OD
1999	201	1	0	0	0-0	....	....	....	....	....	....	0	1	.000	0-0	0-0	0-1	0-0	0-1	0-0
2000	108	15	0	0	0-0	....	....	....	....	....	....	16	15	.516	5-5	1-2	7-6	3-2	8-5	8-10
2001	38	20	0	0	2-4	1rd	2rd	2rd	1rd	4-2	....	38	20	.655	11-6	5-2	16-10	6-2	17-5	21-15
2002	8	27	1	1	13-4	3rd	4rd	QF	QF	6-2	....	57	26	.687	11-7	6-2	34-15	6-2	17-8	40-18
TOTALS		**63**	**1**	**1**	**15-8**	....	....	....	....	**10-4**		**111**	**62**	**.642**	**27-18**	**12-6**	**57-32**	**15-6**	**42-19**	**69-43**

• HANTZE, Karen   see SUSMAN, Karen, page 891

• HARDENNE, Justine   see HENIN, Justine, page 850

• HAYDON, Ann   Adrianne Shirley Haydon Jones

Female. Born: Oct. 17, 1938. Birmingham, Great Britain. Height: 5' 7". Weight: 135 lbs. Plays: left.
Status: Turned Pro 1967. Earnings: –. Highest Ranking: 2 (Dec. 1967). HOF: 1985

Year	Rk	TP	TW	TF	GS	Aus	Fre	Wim	US	FC	Oly	MW	ML	Pct	CL	GR	HD	CP	IN	OD
1956	....	1	0	0	....	....	....	2rd	....	....	....	....	....	....	....	....	....	....	....	....
1957	7	3	0	0	....	....	SF	3rd	QF	....	....	....	....	....	....	....	....	....	....	....
1958	8	3	0	0	....	....	QF	SF	3rd	....	....	....	....	....	....	....	....	....	....	....
1959	7	2	0	0	....	....	....	QF	SF	....	....	....	....	....	....	....	....	....	....	....
1960	6	3	0	0	....	....	3rd	SF	QF	....	....	....	....	....	....	....	....	....	....	....
1961	3	3	1	1	....	....	W	4rd	F	....	....	....	....	....	....	....	....	....	....	....
1962	8	2	0	0	....	....	SF	SF	....	....	....	....	....	....	....	....	....	....	....	....
1963	5	3	0	1	....	....	F	SF	SF	1-1	....	....	....	....	....	....	....	....	....	....
1964	....	2	0	0	....	....	....	QF	QF	1-2	....	....	....	....	....	....	....	....	....	....
1965	5	4	0	0	....	2rd	QF	4rd	QF	0-2	....	....	....	....	....	....	....	....	....	....
1966	4	2	1	0	....	....	W	SF	....	3-0	....	....	....	....	....	....	....	....	....	....
1967	2	3	0	2	....	....	QF	F	F	3-1	....	....	....	....	....	....	....	....	....	....
1968	6	3	0	0	15-3	....	F	SF	SF	....	....	15	3	.833	5-1	10-2	0-0	0-0	0-0	15-3
1969	2	3	1	0	15-2	SF	F	W	....	....	....	15	2	.882	5-1	10-1	0-0	0-0	0-0	15-2
1970	7	1	0	0	0-0	....	....	....	....	2-1	....	2	1	.667	0-0	2-1	0-0	0-0	0-0	2-1
TOTALS		**38**	**3**	**4**	**30-5**	....	....	....	....	**10-7**	....	**32**	**6**	**.842**	**10-2**	**22-4**	**0-0**	**0-0**	**0-0**	**32-6**

Competed as Anne Haydon until 1962. Doubles Titles: Fre (3).

• HELDMAN, Julie   Julie Heldman

Female. Born: Dec. 8, 1945. Berkeley, CA, United States. Height: –. Weight: –. Plays: right.
Status: Turned Pro 1969. Earnings: –. Highest Ranking: 5 (Dec. 1969).

Year	Rk	TP	TW	TF	GS	Aus	Fre	Wim	US	FC	Oly	MW	ML	Pct	CL	GR	HD	CP	IN	OD
1960	....	1	0	0	....	....	....	....	1rd	....	....	....	....	....	....	....	....	....	....	....
1961	....	1	0	0	....	....	....	....	2rd	....	....	....	....	....	....	....	....	....	....	....
1962	....	1	0	0	....	....	....	....	2rd	....	....	....	....	....	....	....	....	....	....	....
1963	....	1	0	0	....	....	....	....	2rd	....	....	....	....	....	....	....	....	....	....	....
1964	....	1	0	0	....	....	....	....	4rd	....	....	....	....	....	....	....	....	....	....	....
1965	....	3	0	0	....	....	2rd	4rd	1rd	....	....	....	....	....	....	....	....	....	....	....

Year	Rk	TP	TW	TF	GS	Aus	Fre	Wim	US	FC	Oly	MW	ML	Pct	CL	GR	HD	CP	IN	OD
1966	....	2	0	0	....	....	QF	3rd	....	4-0	....									
1968	....	3	0	0	5-3	....	3rd	3rd	2rd	....	....	5	3	.625	2-1	3-2	0-0	0-0	0-0	5-3
1969	5	5	1	0	9-3	....	QF	QF	QF	3-1	....	12	4	.750	6-2	6-2	0-0	0-0	0-0	12-4
1970	....	4	1	0	7-2	....	SF	4rd	....	2-1	....	9	3	.750	6-2	3-1	0-0	0-0	0-0	9-3
1971	....	5	1	1	6-3	....	3rd	3rd	3rd	....	....	6	3	.667	2-1	4-2	0-0	0-0	0-0	6-3
1972	....	2	0	0	2-2	....	....	2rd	3rd	....	....	2	2	.500	0-0	2-2	0-0	0-0	0-0	2-2
1973	9	5	2	1	5-2	....	....	3rd	QF	....	....	5	2	.714	0-0	5-2	0-0	0-0	0-0	5-2
1974	5	11	2	2	12-4	SF	QF	2rd	SF	2-2	....	15	7	.682	5-3	9-3	0-0	1-1	1-1	14-6
1975	....	6	0	0	1-2	....	1rd	....	2rd	2-2	....	3	6	.333	3-5	0-0	0-0	0-1	0-1	3-5
TOTALS		**51**	**7**	**4**	**47-21**	....	....	....	....	**13-6**		**57**	**30**	**.655**	**24-14**	**32-14**	**0-0**	**1-2**	**1-2**	**56-28**

• HENIN, Justine Justine Henin Hardenne

Female. Born: June 1, 1982. Marloie, Belgium. Height: 5' 5". Weight: 125 lbs. Plays: right.
Status: Turned Pro 2000. Earnings: $2,425,250. Highest Ranking: 4 (Oct. 2002).

Year	Rk	TP	TW	TF	GS	Aus	Fre	Wim	US	FC	Oly	MW	ML	Pct	CL	GR	HD	CP	IN	OD
1999	69	7	1	0	1-2	....	2rd	....	1rd	2-0	....	13	6	.684	6-2	0-0	2-2	5-2	7-3	6-3
2000	48	14	0	0	4-3	2rd	....	1rd	4rd	0-1	....	28	14	.667	3-2	1-2	23-8	1-2	8-5	20-9
2001	7	21	3	3	17-4	4rd	SF	F	4rd	4-0	....	60	18	.769	18-4	10-1	31-10	1-3	10-5	50-13
2002	5	23	2	4	12-4	QF	1rd	SF	4rd	2-0	....	52	21	.712	16-4	7-2	23-14	6-1	15-6	37-15
TOTALS		**65**	**6**	**7**	**34-13**	....	....	....	....	**8-1**		**153**	**59**	**.722**	**43-12**	**18-5**	**79-34**	**13-8**	**40-19**	**113-40**

• HENMAN, Tim Timothy Henry Henman

Male. Born: Sept. 6, 1974. Oxford, Great Britain. Height: 6' 1". Weight: 170 lbs. Plays: right.
Status: Turned Pro 1993. Earnings: $8,183,078. Highest Ranking: 4 (July 2002).

Year	Rk	TP	TW	TF	GS	Aus	Fre	Wim	US	DC	Oly	MW	ML	Pct	CL	GR	HD	CP	IN	OD
1994	161	5	0	0	0-1	....	....	1rd	....	....	....	3	5	.375	0-0	1-3	2-2	0-0	0-0	3-5
1995	99	7	0	0	2-2	....	....	2rd	2rd	2-2	....	6	7	.462	0-0	3-3	2-2	1-2	1-2	5-5
1996	29	25	0	0	8-4	2rd	1rd	QF	4rd	4-0	2rd	36	25	.590	0-1	7-3	13-12	16-9	17-10	19-15
1997	17	26	2	2	7-4	3rd	1rd	QF	2rd	1-1	....	48	24	.667	2-4	8-3	23-10	15-7	19-9	29-15
1998	7	31	2	2	8-4	1rd	1rd	SF	4rd	4-0	....	59	29	.670	3-5	7-2	36-17	13-5	18-10	41-19
1999	12	29	0	4	9-4	3rd	3rd	SF	1rd	3-1	....	44	29	.603	7-8	9-2	19-14	9-5	14-9	30-20
2000	10	27	2	3	10-4	4rd	3rd	4rd	3rd	3-1	1rd	57	25	.695	9-6	5-3	31-13	12-3	18-6	39-19
2001	9	22	2	1	12-4	4rd	3rd	SF	3rd	2-0	....	51	20	.718	8-5	9-2	28-12	6-1	15-4	36-16
2002	8	20	1	3	11-4	4rd	2rd	SF	3rd	3-1	....	50	19	.725	8-5	9-2	27-9	6-3	10-5	40-14
TOTALS		**192**	**9**	**15**	**67-31**	....	....	....	....	**22-6**		**354**	**183**	**.659**	**37-34**	**58-23**	**181-91**	**78-35**	**112-55**	**242-128**

• HEWITT, Bob Robert Anthony John Hewitt

Male. Born: Jan. 12, 1940. Dubbo, Australia. Height: 6' 3". Weight: 205 lbs. Plays: right.
Status: Turned Pro 1968. Earnings: $1,000,000. Highest Ranking: 6 (Dec. 1967). HOF: 1992

Year	Rk	TP	TW	TF	GS	Aus	Fre	Wim	US	DC	Oly	MW	ML	Pct	CL	GR	HD	CP	IN	OD
1958	....	1	0	0	....	3rd	....	....	....	....	....	....	....	....	....	....	....	....	....	....
1959	....	3	0	0	....	3rd	1rd	3rd	....	....	....	....	....	....	....	....	....	....	....	....
1960	....	4	0	0	....	SF	2rd	3rd	3rd	....	....	....	....	....	....	....	....	....	....	....
1961	....	3	0	0	....	4rd	4rd	4rd	....	....	....	....	....	....	....	....	....	....	....	....
1962	8	3	0	0	....	SF	2rd	QF	....	....	....	....	....	....	....	....	....	....	....	....
1963	....	3	0	0	....	SF	4rd	3rd	....	....	....	....	....	....	....	....	....	....	....	....
1964	....	3	0	0	....	4rd	4rd	QF	....	....	....	....	....	....	....	....	....	....	....	....
1965	....	2	0	0	....	....	4rd	4rd	....	....	....	....	....	....	....	....	....	....	....	....
1966	....	1	0	0	....	....	....	QF	....	....	....	....	....	....	....	....	....	....	....	....
1967	6	2	0	0	....	....	4rd	2rd	....	7-0	....	....	....	....	....	....	....	....	....	....
1968	....	2	0	0	4-2	....	3rd	4rd	....	3-0	....	4	2	.667	1-1	3-1	0-0	0-0	0-0	4-2
1969	....	3	1	1	2-2	....	3rd	1rd	....	4-0	....	2	2	.500	2-1	0-1	0-0	0-0	0-0	2-2
1970	....	5	1	2	4-3	....	2rd	4rd	2rd	....	....	7	4	.636	4-2	3-2	0-0	0-0	0-0	7-4
1971	....	3	1	0	1-2	....	....	1rd	2rd	....	....	1	2	.333	0-0	1-2	0-0	0-0	0-0	1-2
1972	....	12	4	0	3-3	....	1rd	1rd	4rd	....	....	6	8	.429	0-2	3-2	0-0	3-4	3-4	3-4
1974	....	4	0	0	1-1	....	....	2rd	....	5-2	....	2	4	.333	0-1	1-2	1-1	0-0	1-1	1-3
1975	....	4	1	0	3-2	....	....	1rd	4rd	....	....	9	4	.692	7-2	0-1	2-1	0-0	2-1	7-3
1976	....	14	0	0	0-2	....	....	1rd	1rd	....	....	4	14	.222	2-5	0-1	1-2	1-6	2-7	2-7
1977	....	11	0	0	0-4	1rd/	1rd	1rd	1rd	....	....	10	11	.476	7-5	0-3	3-2	0-1	0-1	10-10
1978	....	18	0	0	2-3	....	1rd	3rd	1rd	....	....	4	18	.182	1-9	2-1	0-5	1-3	1-4	3-14

Year	Rk	TP	TW	TF	GS	Aus	Fre	Wim	US	DC	Oly	MW	ML	Pct	CL	GR	HD	CP	IN	OD
1979	....	3	0	0	0-0	....	....	....	....	....	....	0	3	.000	0-1	0-0	0-2	0-0	0-1	0-2
1980	....	1	0	0	0-0	....	....	....	....	....	....	0	1	.000	0-0	0-0	0-1	0-0	0-0	0-1
TOTALS		105	7	5	20-24	....	....	....	....	19-2	....	49	73	.402	24-29	13-16	7-14	5-14	9-19	40-54

Represented South Africa in the Davis Cup (1967-1974). Doubles Titles: Aus (2), Fre (1), Wim (5), US (1).

• HEWITT, Leyton   Lleyton Glynn Hewitt

Male. Born: Feb. 24, 1981. Adelaide, Australia. Height: 5' 11". Weight: 150 lbs. Plays: right.
Status: Turned Pro 1998. Earnings: $10,862,801. Highest Ranking: 1 (Nov. 2001).

Year	Rk	TP	TW	TF	GS	Aus	Fre	Wim	US	DC	Oly	MW	ML	Pct	CL	GR	HD	CP	IN	OD
1997	722	1	0	0	0-1	1rd	....	....	....	....	....	0	1	.000	0-0	0-0	0-1	0-0	0-0	0-1
1998	113	10	1	0	0-1	1rd	....	....	....	....	....	10	9	.526	0-0	1-2	7-6	2-1	2-1	8-8
1999	22	21	1	3	5-4	2rd	1rd	3rd	3rd	4-2	....	44	20	.688	6-5	10-3	22-10	6-2	9-6	35-14
2000	7	23	4	1	11-4	4rd	4rd	1rd	SF	6-2	1rd	61	19	.763	11-5	8-2	37-11	5-1	11-5	50-14
2001	1	24	6	0	16-3	3rd	QF	4rd	W	7-1	....	80	18	.816	14-5	16-2	50-10	0-1	15-3	65-15
2002	1	20	5	2	15-3	1rd	4rd	W	SF	1-0	....	61	15	.803	10-5	14-0	33-9	4-1	13-3	48-12
TOTALS		99	17	6	47-16	....	....	....	....	18-5	....	256	82	.757	41-20	49-9	149-47	17-6	50-18	206-64

Held number one tour ranking 1 time for a total of 59 weeks. Last ranked number one in 2002.

• HIGUERAS, Jose   Jose Higueras

Male. Born: Mar. 1, 1953. Granada, Spain. Height: 5' 10". Weight: 165 lbs. Plays: right.
Status: Turned Pro 1974. Earnings: $1,406,355. Highest Ranking: 7 (Dec. 1983).

Year	Rk	TP	TW	TF	GS	Aus	Fre	Wim	US	DC	Oly	MW	ML	Pct	CL	GR	HD	CP	IN	OD
1973	....	0	0	0	0-0	....	....	....	....	0-2	....	0	0	.000	0-0	0-0	0-0	0-0	0-0	0-0
1974	....	4	0	0	3-2	....	3rd	2rd	....	3-1	....	5	4	.556	3-2	2-2	0-0	0-0	0-0	5-4
1975	46	5	0	1	2-2	....	1rd	....	3rd	3-5	....	5	5	.500	5-5	0-0	0-0	0-0	0-0	5-5
1976	42	11	1	1	3-2	....	3rd	2rd	....	....	....	17	10	.630	17-9	0-0	0-1	0-0	0-1	17-9
1977	30	9	1	1	7-2	....	QF	....	4rd	6-1	....	12	8	.600	9-6	0-0	0-1	3-1	3-1	9-7
1978	14	19	4	1	1-1	....	2rd	....	....	0-2	....	55	15	.786	49-11	0-0	1-1	5-3	5-3	50-12
1979	9	24	3	3	5-2	....	QF	2rd	....	2-2	....	59	21	.738	55-13	1-1	2-1	1-6	1-6	58-15
1980	32	14	0	0	0-1	....	1rd	....	....	1-2	....	16	14	.533	15-13	0-0	0-0	1-1	1-1	15-13
1981	36	22	0	1	0-1	....	1rd	....	....	....	....	35	22	.614	34-21	0-0	1-1	0-0	0-0	35-22
1982	11	24	2	2	5-1	....	SF	....	....	....	....	55	22	.714	50-15	0-0	4-3	1-4	1-4	54-18
1983	7	16	2	2	6-2	....	SF	....	2rd	....	....	49	14	.778	40-11	0-0	8-2	1-1	1-1	48-13
1984	21	16	2	0	3-1	....	4rd	....	....	....	....	26	14	.650	23-11	0-0	3-3	0-0	0-2	26-12
1985	....	13	0	0	1-1	....	2rd	....	....	....	....	7	13	.350	6-11	0-0	1-2	0-0	0-0	7-13
1986	....	1	0	0	0-0	....	....	....	....	....	....	2	1	.667	0-0	0-0	2-1	0-0	0-0	2-1
TOTALS		178	15	12	36-18	....	....	....	....	15-15	....	343	163	.678	306-128	3-3	22-16	12-16	12-19	331-144

• HINGIS, Martina   Martina Hingis

Female. Born: Sept. 30, 1980. Kosice, Slovakia (Slovak Republic). Height: 5' 7". Weight: 130 lbs. Plays: right.
Status: Turned Pro 1994. Earnings: $18,344,660. Highest Ranking: 1 (Mar. 1997).

Year	Rk	TP	TW	TF	GS	Aus	Fre	Wim	US	FC	Oly	MW	ML	Pct	CL	GR	HD	CP	IN	OD
1993	....	1	0	0	0-0	....	....	....	....	....	....	5	1	.833	0-0	0-0	0-0	5-1	5-1	0-0
1994	87	5	0	0	0-0	....	....	....	....	....	....	9	5	.643	0-0	0-0	7-3	2-2	9-5	0-0
1995	16	13	0	0	6-4	2rd	3rd	1rd	4rd	2-1	....	22	13	.629	7-3	0-1	13-7	2-2	8-5	14-8
1996	4	18	2	0	14-4	QF	3rd	4rd	SF	6-1	2rd	51	16	.761	10-5	3-1	24-6	14-4	28-5	23-11
1997	1	17	12	0	27-1	W	F	W	W	4-0	....	75	5	.938	11-1	7-1	43-2	14-2	23-3	52-2
1998	2	18	5	0	23-3	W	SF	SF	F	6-0	....	67	13	.838	18-2	5-1	33-7	11-3	14-4	53-9
1999	1	20	7	0	19-3	W	F	1rd	F	....	....	71	13	.845	19-2	0-1	41-7	11-3	19-5	52-8
2000	1	19	9	0	20-4	F	SF	1rd	SF	....	....	77	10	.885	12-2	7-1	43-6	15-1	23-1	54-9
2001	4	18	3	0	16-4	F	SF	1rd	SF	....	....	60	15	.800	17-5	0-1	39-7	4-2	6-3	54-12
2002	10	12	2	2	9-2	F	....	....	4rd	....	....	34	10	.773	2-1	0-0	28-8	4-1	5-2	29-8
TOTALS		141	40	2	134-25	....	....	....	....	18-2	....	471	101	.823	96-21	22-7	271-53	82-21	140-34	331-67

Held number one tour ranking 5 times for a total of 209 weeks. Last ranked number one in 2001. Represented Switzerland in the Federation Cup (1995-1998). Doubles Titles: Aust (4), Fre (2), Wim (2), US (1).

• HLASEK, Jakob   Jakob Hlasek

Male. Born: Nov. 12, 1964. Prague, Czech Republic. Height: 6' 2". Weight: 170 lbs. Plays: right.
Status: Turned Pro 1983. Earnings: $5,892,962. Highest Ranking: 8 (Dec. 1988).

Year	Rk	TP	TW	TF	GS	Aus	Fre	Wim	US	DC	Oly	MW	ML	Pct	CL	GR	HD	CP	IN	OD
1982	227	2	0	0	0-0	....	....	....	....	0-1	....	1	2	.333	0-0	0-0	1-2	0-0	1-2	0-0
1983	179	7	0	0	2-1	....	....	3rd	....	....	....	5	7	.417	0-2	2-1	1-3	2-1	3-3	2-4

Year	Rk	TP	TW	TF	GS	Aus	Fre	Wim	US	DC	Oly	MW	ML	Pct	CL	GR	HD	CP	IN	OD
1984	88	20	0	0	3-4	3rd	2rd	2rd	1rd	3-1	....	18	20	.474	2-6	6-6	8-6	2-2	6-5	12-15
1985	33	23	0	1	3-4	3rd	2rd	1rd	1rd	2-1	....	29	23	.558	9-7	2-2	9-8	9-6	13-9	16-14
1986	32	28	0	1	3-3	....	2rd	3rd	1rd	3-3	3rd	35	28	.556	18-11	2-1	6-9	9-7	12-10	23-18
1987	23	20	0	0	5-4	2rd	1rd	4rd	3rd	5-1	....	31	20	.608	6-7	3-2	12-5	10-6	13-7	18-13
1988	8	17	2	3	6-4	1rd	3rd	2rd	4rd	....	....	49	15	.766	11-4	1-1	22-7	15-3	22-5	27-10
1989	30	21	1	1	3-3	1rd	4rd	1rd	....	4-0	....	28	20	.583	9-7	0-1	6-6	13-6	14-8	14-12
1990	17	25	1	0	4-4	1rd	2rd	2rd	3rd	1-2	....	42	24	.636	6-6	2-2	17-7	17-9	18-9	24-15
1991	20	28	1	1	7-4	1rd	QF	2rd	3rd	3-1	....	50	27	.649	7-4	4-2	18-10	21-11	27-12	23-15
1992	36	28	0	0	3-4	1rd	1rd	3rd	2rd	6-2	3rd	31	28	.525	6-8	2-2	10-11	13-7	17-12	14-16
1993	68	30	0	0	4-3	....	2rd	3rd	2rd	0-4	....	22	30	.423	3-5	2-5	8-12	9-8	9-10	13-20
1994	71	25	0	0	3-3	2rd	1rd	3rd	....	3-1	....	25	25	.500	3-4	5-3	12-10	5-8	8-12	17-13
1995	36	28	0	2	1-4	1rd	1rd	1rd	2rd	2-1	....	34	28	.548	9-5	0-2	14-13	11-8	12-9	22-19
1996	74	30	0	0	9-4	2rd	3rd	4rd	4rd	2-2	....	25	30	.455	5-7	5-3	10-13	5-7	6-11	19-19
TOTALS		332	5	9	56-49	....	....	....	....	34-20	....	425	327	.565	94-83	36-33	154-122	141-89	181-124	244-203

Represented Switzerland in the Davis Cup (1982-1996). Doubles Titles: Fre (1).

• HOAD, Lew   Lewis Alan Hoad

Male. Born: Nov. 23, 1934. Sydney, Australia. Died: July 3, 1994. Height: 5' 8". Weight: 175 lbs. Plays: right.
Status: Turned Pro 1957. Earnings: –. Highest Ranking: 1 (Dec. 1956). HOF: 1980

Year	Rk	TP	TW	TF	GS	Aus	Fre	Wim	US	DC	Oly	MW	ML	Pct	CL	GR	HD	CP	IN	OD
1951	....	1	0	0	....	4rd	....	....	....	....	....	....	....	....	....	....	....	....	....	....
1952	10	4	0	0	....	4rd	2rd	4rd	QF	....	....	....	....	....	....	....	....	....	....	....
1953	5	4	0	0	....	4rd	QF	QF	SF	2-0	....	....	....	....	....	....	....	....	....	....
1954	7	3	0	0	....	....	4rd	QF	QF	0-1	....	....	....	....	....	....	....	....	....	....
1955	3	3	0	1	....	F	....	QF	SF	6-1	....	....	....	....	....	....	....	....	....	....
1956	1	4	3	1	....	W	W	W	F	2-0	....	....	....	....	....	....	....	....	....	....
1957	....	3	1	0	....	SF	3rd	W	....	....	....	....	....	....	....	....	....	....	....	....
1968	....	1	0	0	2-1	....	2rd	3rd	....	....	....	2	1	.667	0-0	2-1	0-0	0-0	0-0	2-1
1970	....	2	0	0	4-2	....	4rd	2rd	....	....	....	4	2	.667	3-1	1-1	0-0	0-0	0-0	4-2
1972	....	1	0	0	0-1	....	2rd	1rd	....	....	....	0	1	.000	0-0	0-1	0-0	0-0	0-0	0-1
TOTALS		26	4	2	6-4	....	....	....	....	10-2	....	6	4	.600	3-1	3-3	0-0	0-0	0-0	6-4

Held number one world ranking 1 time during amateur era. Doubles Titles: Aus (3), Fre (1), Wim (3), US (1).

• HUBER, Anke   Anke Huber

Female. Born: Dec. 4, 1974. Bruchsal, Germany. Height: 5' 8". Weight: 130 lbs. Plays: right.
Status: Turned Pro 1989. Earnings: $4,768,292. Highest Ranking: 4 (Oct. 1996).

Year	Rk	TP	TW	TF	GS	Aus	Fre	Wim	US	FC	Oly	MW	ML	Pct	CL	GR	HD	CP	IN	OD
1989	203	1	0	0	0-0	....	....	....	....	....	....	1	1	.500	0-0	0-0	1-1	0-0	1-1	0-0
1990	34	11	1	1	3-3	3rd	....	2rd	1rd	1-1	....	15	10	.600	1-2	1-1	9-6	4-1	4-2	11-8
1991	14	15	1	0	10-4	QF	3rd	4rd	2rd	3-1	....	33	14	.702	9-4	3-1	18-7	3-2	8-2	25-12
1992	11	16	0	0	7-4	QF	2rd	3rd	1rd	5-0	QF	36	16	.692	14-5	2-1	12-6	8-4	11-6	25-10
1993	10	16	1	2	13-4	4rd	SF	4rd	3rd	1-0	....	42	15	.737	17-4	3-1	16-7	6-3	7-4	35-11
1994	12	20	3	0	7-4	3rd	4rd	2rd	2rd	3-1	....	41	17	.707	16-5	1-1	11-6	13-5	20-6	21-11
1995	10	18	1	1	12-4	4rd	4rd	4rd	4rd	2-2	....	42	17	.712	9-5	3-1	19-7	11-4	14-5	28-12
1996	6	20	3	3	11-4	F	4rd	3rd	1rd	3-1	3rd	49	17	.742	9-3	7-1	22-9	11-4	17-6	32-11
1997	14	23	0	2	7-4	4rd	1rd	3rd	3rd	2-0	....	36	23	.610	3-5	4-2	20-11	9-5	11-8	25-15
1998	21	20	0	0	5-2	SF	....	....	1rd	0-2	....	24	20	.545	0-1	0-0	20-14	4-5	9-11	15-9
1999	16	26	0	0	5-3	2rd	....	1rd	QF	....	....	31	26	.544	4-3	1-2	19-14	7-7	11-10	20-16
2000	19	18	2	0	10-4	1rd	4rd	4rd	QF	3-0	....	32	16	.667	21-4	3-1	8-11	0-0	1-2	31-14
2001	18	21	0	2	6-3	....	2rd	4rd	3rd	1-1	....	36	21	.632	9-7	3-1	18-9	6-4	12-8	24-13
TOTALS		225	12	11	96-43	....	....	....	....	24-9	....	418	213	.662	112-48	31-13	193-108	82-44	126-71	292-142

• HUNT, Lesley   Lesley Hunt

Female. Born: May 29, 1950. Australia. Height: –. Weight: –. Plays: –.
Status: Turned Pro 1968. Earnings: –. Highest Ranking: 9 (Dec. 1974).

Year	Rk	TP	TW	TF	GS	Aus	Fre	Wim	US	FC	Oly	MW	ML	Pct	CL	GR	HD	CP	IN	OD
1965	....	1	0	0	....	2rd	....	....	....	....	....	....	....	....	....	....	....	....	....	....
1966	....	1	0	0	....	3rd	....	....	....	....	....	....	....	....	....	....	....	....	....	....
1967	....	1	0	0	....	3rd	....	....	....	....	....	....	....	....	....	....	....	....	....	....
1968	....	2	0	0	2-2	....	4rd	2rd	....	....	....	2	2	.500	2-1	0-1	0-0	0-0	0-0	2-2
1969	....	4	0	0	3-4	QF	1rd	1rd	3rd	....	....	3	4	.429	0-1	3-3	0-0	0-0	0-0	3-4
1970	....	4	0	0	8-4	QF	3rd	2rd	QF	....	....	8	4	.667	2-1	6-3	0-0	0-0	0-0	8-4
1971	....	4	0	0	10-4	SF	2rd	4rd	QF	....	....	10	4	.714	1-1	9-3	0-0	0-0	0-0	10-4

Year	Rk	TP	TW	TF	GS	Aus	Fre	Wim	US	FC	Oly	MW	ML	Pct	CL	GR	HD	CP	IN	OD
1972	....	3	0	0	3-3	....	3rd	2rd	3rd	1-0	....	4	3	.571	0-1	4-2	0-0	0-0	0-0	4-3
1973	....	3	0	1	3-2	....	....	4rd	2rd	....	....	3	2	.600	0-0	3-2	0-0	0-0	0-0	3-2
1974	9	3	0	0	6-3	QF	....	2rd	QF	....	....	6	3	.667	0-0	6-3	0-0	0-0	0-0	6-3
1975	....	2	0	0	0-2	....	....	2rd	1rd	....	....	0	2	.000	0-1	0-1	0-0	0-0	0-0	0-2
1976	....	6	0	2	1-3	....	1rd	3rd	2rd	....	....	1	4	.200	0-2	1-1	0-0	0-1	0-1	1-3
1977	....	6	0	0	1-3	....	1rd	2rd	3rd	....	....	2	6	.250	1-2	1-4	0-0	0-0	0-0	2-6
1978	31	26	0	0	6-3	....	3rd	2rd	QF	....	....	26	26	.500	5-5	7-5	8-6	6-10	6-10	20-16
1979	....	7	0	0	0-0	....	....	....	....	....	....	2	7	.222	0-2	0-0	0-1	2-4	2-4	0-3
TOTALS		**73**	**0**	**3**	**43-33**	....	....	....	....	**1-0**	....	**67**	**67**	**.500**	**11-17**	**40-28**	**8-7**	**8-15**	**8-15**	**59-52**

• IVANISEVIC, Goran   Goran Simun Ivanisevic

Male. Born: Sept. 13, 1971. Split, Hrvatska (Croatia). Height: 6' 4". Weight: 180 lbs. Plays: left.
Status: Turned Pro 1988. Earnings: $19,748,638. Highest Ranking: 2 (July 1994).

Year	Rk	TP	TW	TF	GS	Aus	Fre	Wim	US	DC	Oly	MW	ML	Pct	CL	GR	HD	CP	IN	OD
1988	371	4	0	0	0-1	....	....	1rd	....	....	1rd	1	4	.200	0-1	0-1	0-1	1-1	1-1	0-3
1989	40	26	0	1	9-4	QF	4rd	2rd	2rd	2-3	....	31	26	.544	17-13	1-1	11-8	2-4	4-6	27-20
1990	9	24	1	4	11-4	1rd	QF	SF	3rd	2-0	....	50	23	.685	22-6	5-1	14-9	9-7	15-8	35-15
1991	16	24	1	1	7-4	3rd	2rd	2rd	4rd	4-0	....	41	23	.641	13-10	6-1	12-6	10-6	15-7	26-16
1992	4	23	4	2	13-4	2rd	QF	F	3rd	....	SF	61	19	.763	13-6	7-2	16-5	25-6	34-7	27-12
1993	7	24	3	3	5-3	....	3rd	3rd	2rd	4-0	....	54	21	.720	15-5	2-2	14-8	23-6	28-7	26-14
1994	5	29	2	4	14-4	QF	QF	F	1rd	3-1	....	65	27	.707	23-7	7-2	10-8	25-10	26-12	39-15
1995	10	25	1	1	5-4	1rd	1rd	SF	1rd	2-2	....	46	24	.657	18-6	8-3	12-9	8-6	9-7	37-17
1996	4	31	5	5	14-4	3rd	4rd	QF	SF	1-1	1rd	77	26	.748	7-6	5-2	30-10	35-8	35-9	42-17
1997	15	25	3	2	5-4	QF	1rd	2rd	1rd	3-1	....	53	22	.707	7-5	5-2	20-11	21-4	22-5	31-17
1998	12	29	1	4	9-4	1rd	1rd	F	4rd	....	....	44	28	.611	3-5	8-2	25-13	8-8	13-9	31-19
1999	62	26	0	0	5-3	....	1rd	4rd	3rd	....	....	22	26	.458	1-6	5-2	9-12	7-6	7-8	15-18
2000	129	22	0	0	1-4	2rd	1rd	1rd	1rd	3-0	1rd	11	22	.333	0-4	2-2	9-13	0-3	5-8	6-14
2001	12	23	1	0	9-1	....	....	W	3rd	2-1	....	29	22	.569	1-3	8-2	16-14	4-3	9-10	20-12
2002	243	7	0	0	1-1	2rd	....	....	....	2-0	....	6	7	.462	0-0	0-0	4-6	2-1	2-2	4-5
TOTALS		**342**	**22**	**27**	**108-49**	....	....	....	....	**28-9**	....	**591**	**320**	**.649**	**140-83**	**69-25**	**202-133**	**180-79**	**225-106**	**366-214**

Represented Yugoslavia in the Davis Cup (1989-1991)

• JAEGER, Andrea   Andrea Jaeger

Female. Born: June 4, 1965. Chicago, IL, United States. Height: 5' 6". Weight: 135 lbs. Plays: right.
Status: Turned Pro 1980. Earnings: $1,379,066. Highest Ranking: 2 (Aug. 1981).

Year	Rk	TP	TW	TF	GS	Aus	Fre	Wim	US	FC	Oly	MW	ML	Pct	CL	GR	HD	CP	IN	OD
1979	....	2	1	0	0-1	....	....	....	2rd	....	....	0	1	.000	0-0	0-0	0-1	0-0	0-0	0-1
1980	7	20	3	4	8-3	....	1rd	QF	SF	....	....	50	17	.746	8-4	8-3	27-5	7-5	15-6	35-11
1981	4	21	3	6	11-4	QF	SF	4rd	2rd	5-0	....	65	18	.783	20-3	16-5	9-5	20-5	21-7	44-11
1982	3	19	2	5	15-4	SF	F	4rd	SF	....	....	64	17	.790	15-4	11-3	17-6	21-4	21-5	43-12
1983	3	17	1	5	15-3	....	SF	F	QF	3-1	....	54	16	.771	26-6	9-2	9-3	10-5	13-6	41-10
1984	42	6	0	1	0-1	....	1rd	....	....	....	....	9	6	.600	0-1	0-0	4-1	5-4	9-5	0-1
1985	....	5	0	0	2-2	....	2rd	....	2rd	....	....	5	5	.500	1-1	0-0	4-3	0-1	0-1	5-4
1986	....	1	0	0	0-0	....	....	....	....	....	....	0	1	.000	0-0	0-0	0-1	0-0	0-0	0-1
1987	....	1	0	0	0-0	....	....	....	....	....	....	3	1	.750	3-1	0-0	0-0	0-0	0-0	3-1
TOTALS		**92**	**10**	**21**	**51-18**	....	....	....	....	**8-1**	....	**250**	**82**	**.753**	**73-20**	**44-13**	**70-25**	**63-24**	**79-30**	**171-52**

• JARRYD, Anders   Anders Jarryd

Male. Born: July 13, 1961. Lidkoping, Sweden. Height: 5' 11". Weight: 155 lbs. Plays: right.
Status: Turned Pro 1980. Earnings: $5,374,736. Highest Ranking: 6 (Dec. 1984).

Year	Rk	TP	TW	TF	GS	Aus	Fre	Wim	US	DC	Oly	MW	ML	Pct	CL	GR	HD	CP	IN	OD
1980	182	1	0	0	0-0	....	....	....	....	....	....	1	1	.500	1-1	0-0	0-0	0-0	0-0	1-1
1981	100	12	0	1	0-2	....	1rd	1rd	....	....	....	11	12	.478	6-7	1-2	1-2	3-1	4-3	7-9
1982	60	17	2	0	2-2	....	3rd	1rd	....	2-1	....	23	15	.605	13-9	0-1	3-3	7-2	10-4	13-11
1983	19	21	0	2	4-4	4rd	1rd	1rd	3rd	3-1	....	38	21	.644	14-8	5-3	12-6	7-4	11-6	27-15
1984	6	22	2	2	6-3	....	4rd	1rd	4rd	2-1	....	48	20	.706	18-5	0-1	20-5	10-9	21-11	27-9
1985	8	22	1	3	12-3	....	4rd	SF	QF	4-0	....	56	21	.727	11-6	7-1	17-7	21-7	28-10	28-11
1986	19	16	1	1	5-3	....	3rd	2rd	3rd	....	3rd	32	15	.681	6-3	1-2	5-4	20-6	23-7	9-8
1987	15	20	0	1	11-4	QF	2rd	QF	4rd	3-0	....	43	20	.683	9-5	8-3	16-8	10-4	17-8	26-12
1988	32	15	0	0	7-4	QF	1rd	2rd	3rd	2-0	....	29	15	.659	6-5	1-1	17-7	5-2	5-3	24-12
1989	31	15	0	2	3-4	2rd	2rd	1rd	2rd	....	....	23	15	.605	2-1	0-1	7-7	14-6	14-6	9-9
1990	73	13	1	0	3-2	....	2rd	2rd	2rd	....	....	14	12	.538	2-2	1-1	4-6	7-3	7-5	7-7
1991	45	21	0	1	4-4	2rd	1rd	2rd	3rd	....	....	26	21	.553	1-4	4-2	7-7	14-8	14-9	12-12

Year	Rk	TP	TW	TF	GS	Aus	Fre	Wim	US	DC	Oly	MW	ML	Pct	CL	GR	HD	CP	IN	OD
1992	149	17	0	1	1-4	1rd	1rd	2rd	1rd	....	....	11	17	.393	0-3	1-2	2-6	8-6	8-6	3-11
1993	65	19	1	0	1-3	2rd	1rd	1rd	....	....	....	15	18	.455	1-5	1-3	1-4	12-6	12-7	3-11
1994	109	12	0	1	0-1	1rd	....	....	....	....	....	12	12	.500	1-1	0-1	2-5	9-5	10-6	2-6
1995	118	17	0	1	1-2	....	....	2rd	1rd	....	....	13	17	.433	0-2	5-3	4-10	4-2	7-6	6-11
1996	410	8	0	0	0-1	....	....	1rd	....	....	....	1	8	.111	0-1	0-2	0-2	1-3	1-3	0-5
TOTALS		268	8	16	60-46	....	....	....	....	16-3		396	260	.604	91-68	35-29	118-89	152-74	192-100	204-160

Doubles Titles: Aus (1), Fre (3), Wim (2), US (2)

• JAUSOVEC, Mimi   Mimi Jausovec

Female. Born: July 20, 1956. 7/20/1956, Yugoslavia. Height: 5' 3". Weight: 110 lbs. Plays: right.
Status: Turned Pro 1975. Earnings: $933,926. Highest Ranking: 6 (Mar. 1982).

Year	Rk	TP	TW	TF	GS	Aus	Fre	Wim	US	FC	Oly	MW	ML	Pct	CL	GR	HD	CP	IN	OD
1973	....	1	0	0	0-0	....	....	....	....	2-0	....	1	1	.500	1-1	0-0	0-0	0-0	0-0	1-1
1974	....	3	0	0	4-3	....	2rd	3rd	2rd	....	....	4	3	.571	1-1	3-2	0-0	0-0	0-0	4-3
1975	40	4	0	0	3-3	....	2rd	4rd	1rd	0-1	....	3	4	.429	1-3	2-1	0-0	0-0	0-0	3-4
1976	11	8	2	0	8-3	....	2rd	4rd	SF	1-1	....	9	6	.600	6-2	2-1	0-0	1-3	1-3	8-3
1977	11	16	1	1	11-2	....	W	3rd	QF	....	....	23	14	.622	12-3	1-1	2-2	8-8	8-8	15-6
1978	19	20	1	0	9-3	....	F	QF	2rd	1-1	....	30	19	.612	13-4	8-4	2-3	7-8	7-8	23-11
1979	20	27	0	0	3-3	....	2rd	2rd	2rd	1-1	....	31	27	.534	10-7	1-2	8-8	12-10	15-11	16-16
1980	17	23	0	0	10-3	SF	3rd	....	QF	1-1	....	35	23	.603	5-4	6-3	12-5	12-11	18-14	17-9
1981	11	27	0	0	11-4	3rd	QF	QF	2rd	1-0	....	56	27	.675	16-5	10-5	7-6	23-11	26-14	30-13
1982	12	23	1	0	2-4	2rd	4rd	2rd	2rd	....	....	35	22	.614	8-5	2-5	5-5	20-7	23-9	12-13
1983	23	17	0	0	10-3	....	F	3rd	3rd	....	....	23	17	.575	13-6	3-2	6-5	1-4	1-5	22-12
1984	87	19	0	0	4-3	....	3rd	1rd	3rd	2-2	....	14	19	.424	12-9	0-2	2-3	0-5	0-6	14-13
1985	71	13	0	0	2-3	....	2rd	1rd	2rd	1-1	....	10	13	.435	7-5	0-1	3-6	0-1	0-2	10-11
1986	179	4	0	0	2-2	....	3rd	1rd	....	....	....	2	4	.333	2-2	0-1	0-1	0-0	0-0	2-4
1987	....	3	0	0	0-1	1rd	....	....	....	....	....	1	3	.250	1-2	0-0	0-0	0-1	0-1	1-2
1988	....	3	0	0	0-1	1rd	....	....	....	....	....	1	3	.250	1-2	0-0	0-1	0-0	0-0	1-3
TOTALS		211	5	1	79-41	....	....	....	....	10-8	....	278	205	.576	109-61	38-30	47-45	84-69	99-81	179-124

Doubles Titles: Fre (1)

• JOHANSSON, Thomas   Thomas Johansson

Male. Born: Mar. 24, 1975. Linkoping, Sweden. Height: 5' 11". Weight: 165 lbs. Plays: right.
Status: Turned Pro 1994. Earnings: $4,339,844. Highest Ranking: 7 (June 2002).

Year	Rk	TP	TW	TF	GS	Aus	Fre	Wim	US	DC	Oly	MW	ML	Pct	CL	GR	HD	CP	IN	OD
1993	418	1	0	0	0-0	....	....	....	....	....	....	2	1	.667	0-0	0-0	0-0	2-1	2-1	0-0
1994	485	2	0	0	0-1	1rd	....	....	....	....	....	0	2	.000	0-1	0-0	0-1	0-0	0-0	0-2
1995	126	3	0	0	0-1	....	1rd	....	....	....	....	1	3	.250	0-1	0-0	0-1	1-1	1-2	0-1
1996	60	21	0	0	6-4	2rd	2rd	4rd	2rd	....	....	28	21	.571	4-5	4-2	13-10	7-4	11-6	17-15
1997	39	29	2	0	2-4	2rd	1rd	2rd	1rd	....	....	32	27	.542	1-6	1-3	15-13	15-5	20-9	12-18
1998	17	31	0	2	6-4	1rd	1rd	3rd	QF	1-1	....	45	31	.592	2-6	4-3	22-13	17-9	26-13	19-18
1999	40	26	1	0	1-2	1rd	....	2rd	....	1-1	....	22	25	.468	1-7	1-1	16-12	4-5	8-8	14-17
2000	39	27	1	0	9-4	2rd	2rd	4rd	QF	....	1rd	22	26	.458	1-5	3-3	16-14	2-4	9-8	13-18
2001	18	27	2	0	6-4	3rd	1rd	2rd	4rd	4-2	....	46	25	.648	4-5	11-1	26-16	5-3	9-7	37-18
2002	14	25	1	0	8-2	W	2rd	1rd	....	2-1	....	29	24	.547	7-7	2-2	17-12	3-3	6-9	23-15
TOTALS		192	7	2	38-26	....	....	....	....	8-5	....	227	185	.551	20-43	26-15	125-92	56-35	92-63	135-122

• JONES, Anne   see HAYDON, Anne, page 849

• JORDAN, Barbara   Barbara Jordan

Female. Born: Apr. 2, 1957. Milwaukee, WI, United States. Height: 5' 5". Weight: 125 lbs. Plays: right.
Status: Turned Pro 1979. Earnings: $145,534. Highest Ranking: 37 (Dec. 1980).

Year	Rk	TP	TW	TF	GS	Aus	Fre	Wim	US	FC	Oly	MW	ML	Pct	CL	GR	HD	CP	IN	OD
1977	....	1	0	0	1-1	....	....	....	3rd	....	....	1	1	.500	1-1	0-0	0-0	0-0	0-0	1-1
1978	....	4	1	0	1-2	....	....	3rd	1rd	....	....	1	3	.250	0-0	1-1	0-2	0-0	0-0	1-3
1979	55	16	1	0	5-2	W	1rd	2rd	3rd	....	....	6	15	.286	1-3	5-4	0-5	0-3	0-3	6-12
1980	58	8	0	0	0-2	....	1rd	3rd	2rd	....	....	3	8	.273	0-3	0-2	3-1	0-2	0-2	3-6
1981	73	9	0	0	1-2	....	2rd	....	2rd	....	....	3	9	.250	2-4	0-0	1-3	0-2	0-2	3-7
1982	76	12	0	0	0-2	....	1rd	2rd	1rd	....	....	3	12	.200	0-5	2-2	0-1	1-4	1-4	2-8
1983	143	8	0	0	2-3	1rd	1rd	3rd	1rd	....	....	3	8	.273	0-1	3-4	0-3	0-0	0-1	3-7
1984	201	1	0	0	0-1	1rd	....	....	....	....	....	0	1	.000	0-1	0-0	0-0	0-0	0-0	0-1
1985	146	6	0	0	0-2	....	....	1rd	1rd	....	....	1	6	.143	0-0	0-1	1-5	0-0	0-0	1-6
TOTALS		65	2	0	10-17	....	....	....	....	....	....	21	63	.250	4-18	11-14	5-20	1-11	1-12	20-51

• JORDAN, Kathy

Kathy Jordan

Female. Born: Dec. 3, 1959. Bryn Mawr, PA, United States. Height: 5'8". Weight: 130 lbs. Plays: right.
Status: Turned Pro 1979. Earnings: $1,592,111. Highest Ranking: 5 (Mar. 1984).

Year	Rk	TP	TW	TF	GS	Aus	Fre	Wim	US	FC	Oly	MW	ML	Pct	CL	GR	HD	CP	IN	OD
1978	....	2	0	1	1-1	....	....	....	2rd	....	....	2	2	.500	1-1	0-0	1-1	0-0	0-0	2-2
1979	11	15	2	1	5-2	....	....	4rd	4rd	....	....	19	13	.594	0-1	4-2	11-6	4-4	4-4	15-9
1980	13	21	0	0	9-3	....	QF	4rd	4rd	1-0	....	38	21	.644	6-3	3-2	10-4	19-12	21-13	17-8
1981	15	18	0	0	8-4	3rd	3rd	4rd	4rd	....	....	28	18	.609	3-3	8-5	6-3	11-7	11-7	17-11
1982	21	19	1	0	1-2	....	....	3rd	1rd	....	....	21	18	.538	3-2	3-3	6-4	9-9	9-9	12-9
1983	14	22	0	5	15-4	F	4rd	QF	4rd	....	....	44	22	.667	5-3	14-6	15-5	10-8	10-8	34-14
1984	10	12	0	2	7-3	....	2rd	SF	2rd	2-1	....	25	12	.676	5-4	10-2	3-3	7-3	8-4	17-8
1985	19	17	0	1	4-2	....	2rd	4rd	4rd	3-2	....	31	17	.646	0-0	5-4	15-8	11-5	12-6	19-11
1986	15	15	0	1	6-3	....	1rd	4rd	4rd	....	....	25	15	.625	0-2	6-2	13-6	6-5	6-5	19-10
1987	36	10	0	0	0-2	....	....	1rd	1rd	....	....	12	10	.545	0-0	1-3	7-5	4-2	5-3	7-7
1989	....	1	0	0	0-0	....	....	....	....	....	....	0	1	.000	0-0	0-0	0-1	0-0	0-0	0-1
1990	205	6	0	0	0-2	....	....	1rd	1rd	....	....	2	6	.250	0-0	1-2	1-4	0-0	1-1	1-5
TOTALS		**158**	**3**	**11**	**56-28**	....	....	....	....	**6-3**		**247**	**155**	**.614**	**23-19**	**55-31**	**88-50**	**81-55**	**87-60**	**160-95**

Doubles Titles: Aus (1), Fre (1), Wim (2), US (1)

• KAFELNIKOV, Yevgeny

Yevgeny Kafelnikov

Male. Born: Feb. 18, 1974. Sochi, Russian Federation. Height: 6'3". Weight: 185 lbs. Plays: right.
Status: Turned Pro 1992. Earnings: $23,202,345. Highest Ranking: 1 (May 1999).

Year	Rk	TP	TW	TF	GS	Aus	Fre	Wim	US	DC	Oly	MW	ML	Pct	CL	GR	HD	CP	IN	OD
1992	314	4	0	0	0-0	....	....	....	....	....	....	1	4	.200	0-1	0-0	0-2	1-1	1-1	0-3
1993	104	11	0	0	1-1	....	2rd	....	....	2-1	....	12	11	.522	4-4	0-0	3-3	5-4	5-4	7-7
1994	11	31	3	1	8-4	2rd	3rd	3rd	4rd	7-1	....	67	28	.705	17-10	5-2	22-8	23-8	24-9	43-19
1995	6	36	4	1	15-4	QF	SF	QF	3rd	5-3	....	73	32	.695	21-12	6-2	19-7	27-11	31-15	42-17
1996	3	29	4	6	11-2	QF	W	1rd	....	4-0	....	80	25	.762	29-7	4-2	16-5	31-11	34-13	46-12
1997	5	30	3	1	8-3	....	QF	4rd	2rd	1-1	....	55	27	.671	14-11	8-1	17-8	16-7	19-9	36-18
1998	11	32	3	3	4-3	....	2rd	1rd	4rd	3-0	....	57	29	.663	8-9	5-2	22-11	22-7	24-10	33-19
1999	2	35	3	2	15-3	W	2rd	3rd	SF	3-3	....	61	32	.656	10-9	2-4	30-13	19-6	23-11	38-21
2000	5	37	2	3	13-4	F	QF	2rd	3rd	1-2	W	66	35	.653	12-13	4-2	37-16	13-4	25-10	41-25
2001	4	30	2	2	15-4	QF	QF	3rd	SF	2-1	....	69	28	.711	11-8	5-2	38-15	15-3	29-8	40-20
2002	27	31	2	0	5-4	2rd	2rd	3rd	2rd	3-2	....	39	29	.574	4-12	7-1	21-12	7-4	13-9	26-20
TOTALS		**306**	**26**	**19**	**95-32**	....	....	....	....	**31-14**		**580**	**280**	**.674**	**130-96**	**46-18**	**225-100**	**179-66**	**228-99**	**352-181**

Held number one tour ranking 1 time for a total of 6 weeks. Last ranked number one in 1999. Doubles Titles: Fre (3), US (1).

• KIEFER, Nicolas

Nicolas Kiefer

Male. Born: July 5, 1977. Holzminden, Germany. Height: 6'. Weight: 175 lbs. Plays: right.
Status: Turned Pro 1995. Earnings: $4,008,806. Highest Ranking: 4 (Jan. 2000).

Year	Rk	TP	TW	TF	GS	Aus	Fre	Wim	US	DC	Oly	MW	ML	Pct	CL	GR	HD	CP	IN	OD
1994	1212	1	0	0	0-0	....	....	....	....	....	....	0	1	.000	0-0	0-0	0-0	0-1	0-1	0-0
1995	202	3	0	0	0-0	....	....	....	....	....	....	3	3	.500	0-0	0-0	0-0	3-3	3-3	0-0
1996	127	9	0	0	0-1	1rd	....	....	....	....	....	7	9	.438	3-4	1-1	1-2	2-2	2-2	5-7
1997	32	17	1	1	4-2	....	1rd	QF	....	....	....	26	16	.619	3-4	5-2	6-4	12-6	17-7	9-9
1998	35	29	0	0	9-4	QF	2rd	3rd	3rd	1-2	....	34	29	.540	6-6	2-3	21-15	5-5	8-7	26-22
1999	6	28	3	2	5-4	3rd	1rd	2rd	3rd	0-2	....	54	25	.684	3-4	6-1	37-14	8-6	10-9	44-16
2000	20	18	2	0	8-4	QF	1rd	1rd	QF	....	1rd	30	16	.652	1-3	2-2	25-10	2-1	2-2	28-14
2001	42	29	0	1	4-4	2rd	1rd	4rd	1rd	2-2	....	29	29	.500	7-8	4-2	11-13	7-6	9-9	20-20
2002	72	28	0	1	2-4	1rd	1rd	3rd	1rd	1-2	....	21	28	.429	2-7	7-3	9-14	3-4	5-7	16-21
TOTALS		**162**	**6**	**5**	**32-23**	....	....	....	....	**4-8**	....	**204**	**156**	**.567**	**25-36**	**27-14**	**110-72**	**42-34**	**56-47**	**148-109**

• KILSCH, Claudia

see **KOHDE KILSCH, Claudia**, page 856

• KING, Billie Jean

Billie Jean Moffitt King

Female. Born: Nov. 22, 1943. Long Beach, CA, United States. Height: 5'4". Weight: 130 lbs. Plays: right.
Status: Turned Pro 1968. Earnings: $1,966,487. Highest Ranking: 1 (Dec. 1966). HOF: 1987

Year	Rk	TP	TW	TF	GS	Aus	Fre	Wim	US	FC	Oly	MW	ML	Pct	CL	GR	HD	CP	IN	OD
1959	....	1	0	0	....	....	....	....	1rd	....	....	....	....	....	....	....	....	....	....	....
1960	....	1	0	0	....	....	....	....	3rd	....	....	....	....	....	....	....	....	....	....	....
1961	....	2	0	0	....	....	....	2rd	2rd	....	....	....	....	....	....	....	....	....	....	....
1962	....	2	0	0	....	....	....	SF	1rd	....	....	....	....	....	....	....	....	....	....	....
1963	4	2	0	1	....	....	....	F	4rd	4-0	....	....	....	....	....	....	....	....	....	....
1964	7	2	0	0	....	....	....	SF	QF	3-1	....	....	....	....	....	....	....	....	....	....

Year	Rk	TP	TW	TF	GS	Aus	Fre	Wim	US	FC	Oly	MW	ML	Pct	CL	GR	HD	CP	IN	OD
1965	4	3	0	1	....	SF	....	SF	F	2-1	....									
1966	1	2	1	0	....	....	....	W	2rd	3-1	....									
1967	1	3	2	0	....	....	QF	W	W	4-0	....			....		....	....	....	....	....
1968	1	4	2	1	16-2	W	SF	W	F	....	....	16	2	.889	4-1	12-1	0-0	0-0	0-0	16-2
1969	3	9	5	3	14-4	F	QF	F	QF	....	....	14	4	.778	2-1	12-3	0-0	0-0	0-0	14-4
1970	2	7	5	2	8-2	....	....	QF	F	....	....	8	2	.800	3-1	5-1	0-0	0-0	0-0	8-2
1971	3	24	17	6	10-1	....	....	SF	F	....	....	10	1	.909	0-0	10-1	0-0	0-0	0-0	10-1
1972	1	16	10	6	17-0	....	W	W	W	....	....	17	0	1.000	5-1	12-1	0-0	0-0	0-0	17-0
1973	2	11	7	3	8-1	....	....	W	3rd	....	....	8	1	.889	0-0	8-1	0-0	0-0	0-0	8-1
1974	1	9	6	2	9-1	....	....	QF	W	....	....	9	1	.900	0-0	9-1	0-0	0-0	0-0	9-1
1975	4	4	2	2	7-1	....	....	W	....	....	....	7	1	.875	0-0	7-1	0-0	0-0	0-0	7-1
1976	....	1	0	0	0-0	....	....	....	....	5-0	....	5	1	.833	0-0	0-0	0-0	5-1	5-1	0-0
1977	2	10	6	1	6-2	....	....	QF	QF	5-0	....	36	4	.900	12-2	8-1	10-1	6-1	6-1	30-3
1978	5	10	0	0	4-1	....	....	QF	....	....	....	25	10	.714	0-0	8-2	4-1	13-7	13-7	12-3
1979	5	14	2	1	9-2	....	....	QF	SF	....	....	30	12	.714	0-0	12-5	12-4	6-3	7-4	23-8
1980	6	18	3	0	6-2	....	QF	QF	....	....	....	39	15	.722	3-1	3-1	5-2	28-11	28-12	11-3
1981	....	5	0	0	0-0	....	....	....	....	....	....	4	5	.444	0-1	0-1	0-0	4-3	4-3	0-2
1982	14	19	1	0	8-4	QF	3rd	SF	1rd	....	....	26	18	.591	4-4	13-4	0-2	9-8	9-8	17-10
1983	13	6	1	0	6-2	2rd	....	SF	....	....	....	17	5	.773	1-1	11-2	0-0	5-2	5-2	12-3
TOTALS		**185**	**70**	**29**	**128-25**	....	....	....	....	**26-3**		**271**	**82**	**.768**	**34-13**	**130-26**	**31-10**	**76-36**	**77-38**	**194-44**

Held number one world ranking 2 times during amateur era. Competed as Billie Jean Moffitt until 1964. Doubles Titles: Fre (1), Wim (10), US (5).

• KODES, Jan
Jan Kodes

Male. Born: Mar. 1, 1946. Prague, Czech Republic. Height: 5' 9". Weight: –. Plays: right.
Status: Turned Pro 1969. Earnings: $673,197. Highest Ranking: 5 (Dec. 1971). HOF: 1990

Year	Rk	TP	TW	TF	GS	Aus	Fre	Wim	US	DC	Oly	MW	ML	Pct	CL	GR	HD	CP	IN	OD
1966	....	1	0	0	....	....	2rd	....	....	4-2	....									
1967	....	1	0	0	....	....	4rd	....	....	1-1	....			....		....	....	....	....	....
1968	....	1	0	0	0-1	....	1rd	1rd	....	3-1	....	0	1	.000	0-0	0-1	0-0	0-0	0-0	0-1
1969	....	5	0	0	5-3	....	4rd	2rd	2rd	2-0	....	11	5	.688	7-2	2-2	0-0	2-1	2-1	9-4
1970	....	9	2	1	7-1	....	W	1rd	....	3-1	....	11	7	.611	11-1	0-1	0-0	0-5	0-5	11-2
1971	....	10	2	4	13-2	....	W	1rd	F	5-3	....	20	8	.714	11-2	6-2	0-1	3-3	3-3	17-5
1972	....	9	1	2	9-3	....	QF	SF	2rd	5-1	....	18	8	.692	10-3	6-2	1-1	1-2	2-3	16-5
1973	9	8	2	3	17-2	....	QF	W	F	4-3	....	21	6	.778	7-2	13-1	0-1	1-2	1-2	20-4
1974	17	7	0	0	10-3	....	4rd	QF	4rd	3-1	....	17	7	.708	4-2	10-3	2-1	1-1	3-2	14-5
1975	19	8	1	4	7-3	....	4rd	2rd	4rd	7-1	....	14	7	.667	11-3	2-2	0-1	1-1	1-2	13-5
1976	19	17	1	3	6-2	....	3rd	....	QF	0-1	....	32	16	.667	21-8	0-0	4-1	7-8	11-8	21-8
1977	40	9	0	1	5-3	....	4rd	1rd	3rd	1-1	....	11	9	.550	9-4	0-1	2-2	0-2	2-4	9-5
1978	119	16	0	0	2-2	....	3rd	1rd	....	1-2	....	11	16	.407	7-9	0-1	3-3	1-3	4-6	7-10
1979	92	17	0	0	2-3	....	2rd	1rd	2rd	....	....	17	17	.500	10-9	0-1	7-7	0-0	2-4	15-13
1980	....	13	0	0	2-2	....	2rd	2rd	....	....	....	5	13	.278	4-7	1-1	0-3	0-2	0-3	5-10
1981	....	7	0	0	0-2	....	1rd	1rd	....	....	....	1	7	.125	1-5	0-1	0-1	0-0	0-1	1-6
1982	....	5	0	0	0-0	....	....	....	....	....	....	0	5	.000	0-5	0-0	0-0	0-0	0-0	0-5
1983	....	1	0	0	0-0	....	....	....	....	....	....	0	1	.000	0-1	0-0	0-0	0-0	0-0	0-1
TOTALS		**144**	**9**	**18**	**85-32**	....	....	....	....	**39-18**		**189**	**133**	**.587**	**113-63**	**40-19**	**19-22**	**17-30**	**31-44**	**158-89**

• KOHDE KILSCH, Claudia
Claudia Kohde Kilsch

Female. Born: Dec. 11, 1963. Saarbruecken, Germany. Height: 6' 1". Weight: 150 lbs. Plays: right.
Status: Turned Pro 1980. Earnings: $2,227,116. Highest Ranking: 5 (Dec. 1985).

Year	Rk	TP	TW	TF	GS	Aus	Fre	Wim	US	FC	Oly	MW	ML	Pct	CL	GR	HD	CP	IN	OD
1980	78	9	0	0	0-2	1rd	1rd	....	....	....	....	8	9	.471	1-3	5-3	2-2	0-1	2-3	6-6
1981	20	24	3	0	1-4	1rd	1rd	2rd	1rd	....	....	24	21	.533	10-6	5-6	2-4	7-5	7-6	17-15
1982	19	25	1	0	7-4	3rd	2rd	4rd	3rd	4-1	....	34	24	.586	4-6	9-5	13-5	8-8	9-9	25-15
1983	24	21	0	0	8-4	3rd	3rd	4rd	2rd	3-1	....	32	21	.604	13-7	11-5	3-4	5-5	5-6	27-15
1984	8	16	1	0	11-4	3rd	4rd	4rd	4rd	....	....	42	15	.737	15-3	11-4	11-4	5-4	11-6	31-9
1985	5	20	1	0	14-4	SF	SF	QF	QF	....	....	48	19	.716	12-5	11-4	19-5	6-5	12-7	36-12
1986	7	20	0	0	8-3	....	4rd	3rd	4rd	1-3	....	39	20	.661	15-8	6-2	5-2	13-8	13-8	26-12
1987	10	17	0	0	16-4	SF	QF	QF	QF	3-2	....	38	17	.691	14-6	8-3	14-6	2-2	2-2	36-15
1988	12	20	1	0	9-3	SF	3rd	....	3rd	4-0	2rd	43	19	.694	10-6	13-3	15-6	5-4	5-5	38-14
1989	36	14	0	0	6-4	QF	1rd	3rd	1rd	2-1	....	18	14	.563	0-2	6-3	9-6	3-3	3-3	15-11
1990	46	17	1	0	3-3	1rd	2rd	3rd	....	....	....	17	16	.515	8-5	4-3	0-3	5-5	5-6	12-10

Year	Rk	TP	TW	TF	GS	Aus	Fre	Wim	US	FC	Oly	MW	ML	Pct	CL	GR	HD	CP	IN	OD
1991	84	19	0	0	3-4	1rd	2rd	3rd	1rd	....	....	14	19	.424	5-6	3-3	0-5	6-5	6-5	8-14
1992	79	14	0	0	2-3	2rd	1rd	2rd	....	....	....	11	14	.440	2-5	1-2	5-3	3-4	3-4	8-10
TOTALS		236	8	0	88-46	....	....	....	17-8	....		368	228	.617	109-68	93-46	98-55	68-59	83-70	285-158

Doubles Titles: Wim (1), US (1)

• KORDA, Petr   Petr Korda

Male. Born: Jan. 23, 1968. Prague, Czech Republic. Height: 6' 3". Weight: 160 lbs. Plays: left.
Status: Turned Pro 1987. Earnings: $10,448,450. Highest Ranking: 7 (Dec. 1992).

Year	Rk	TP	TW	TF	GS	Aus	Fre	Wim	US	DC	Oly	MW	ML	Pct	CL	GR	HD	CP	IN	OD
1985	794	1	0	0	0-0	....	....	....	....	....	....	0	1	.000	0-0	0-0	0-1	0-0	0-1	0-0
1987	87	1	0	0	0-0	....	....	....	....	....	....	2	1	.667	2-1	0-0	0-0	0-0	0-0	2-1
1988	188	13	0	0	3-3	....	2rd	3rd	1rd	2-0	....	8	13	.381	3-7	2-1	1-3	2-2	3-3	5-10
1989	59	8	0	1	0-0	....	....	....	....	....	....	13	8	.619	6-5	0-0	0-0	7-3	7-3	6-5
1990	38	27	0	0	3-4	2rd	2rd	1rd	2rd	1-1	....	24	27	.471	5-8	0-1	5-10	14-8	17-10	7-17
1991	9	26	2	3	2-4	2rd	2rd	1rd	1rd	1-2	....	45	24	.652	9-5	0-1	20-10	16-8	17-10	28-14
1992	7	33	3	4	7-4	1rd	F	2rd	1rd	3-1	....	62	30	.674	18-8	1-1	27-11	16-10	24-12	38-18
1993	12	24	1	2	8-4	QF	2rd	4rd	1rd	2-1	....	54	23	.701	8-4	7-3	23-10	16-6	20-7	34-16
1994	18	22	0	3	1-3	1rd	1rd	2rd	....	3-1	....	38	22	.633	8-5	1-1	17-8	12-8	12-8	26-14
1995	41	23	0	0	9-4	3rd	1rd	4rd	QF	2-0	....	27	23	.540	3-5	5-2	16-12	3-4	5-5	22-18
1996	34	20	1	1	4-3	1rd	3rd	....	3rd	2-3	....	42	19	.689	10-3	2-1	17-8	13-7	15-8	27-11
1997	13	25	1	3	9-4	1rd	4rd	4rd	QF	2-0	....	55	24	.696	10-5	7-2	14-9	24-8	26-8	29-16
1998	13	23	2	0	11-3	W	1rd	QF	1rd	....	....	34	21	.618	6-5	5-2	21-7	2-7	4-8	30-13
1999	....	12	0	0	3-2	3rd	2rd	....	....	....	....	6	12	.333	1-4	0-1	3-5	2-2	2-2	4-10
TOTALS		258	10	17	60-38	....	....	....	18-9	....		410	248	.623	89-65	30-16	164-94	127-73	152-85	258-163

Doubles Titles: Aus (1)

• KOURNIKOVA, Anna   Anna Kournikova

Female. Born: June 7, 1981. Moscow, Russian Federation. Height: 5' 8". Weight: 125 lbs. Plays: right.
Status: Turned Pro 1995. Earnings: $3,517,390. Highest Ranking: 8 (Nov. 2000).

Year	Rk	TP	TW	TF	GS	Aus	Fre	Wim	US	FC	Oly	MW	ML	Pct	CL	GR	HD	CP	IN	OD
1995	281	1	0	0	0-0	....	....	....	4rd	1-1	1rd	1	1	.500	0-0	0-0	0-0	1-1	1-1	0-0
1996	57	5	0	0	3-1	....	....	....	2rd	1-1	....	5	5	.500	0-0	0-0	4-3	1-2	2-3	3-2
1997	32	10	0	0	8-4	2rd	3rd	SF	2rd	1-1	....	17	10	.630	6-3	5-1	6-6	0-0	1-1	16-9
1998	13	19	0	1	8-3	3rd	4rd	....	4rd	....	....	40	19	.678	12-4	3-1	23-12	2-3	7-7	33-12
1999	12	19	0	1	9-3	4rd	4rd	4rd	....	....	....	35	19	.648	13-5	6-2	11-7	5-5	7-6	28-13
2000	8	29	0	1	7-4	4rd	2rd	2rd	3rd	0-3	....	47	29	.618	6-5	2-2	26-13	13-9	16-12	31-17
2001	74	10	0	0	4-1	QF	....	....	....	....	....	10	10	.500	0-0	0-0	6-6	4-4	5-7	5-3
2002	35	24	0	1	0-4	1rd	1rd	1rd	1rd	....	....	28	24	.538	6-8	0-2	18-13	4-1	6-3	22-21
TOTALS		117	0	4	39-20	....	....	....	2-5	....		183	117	.610	43-25	16-8	94-60	30-25	45-40	138-77

Doubles Titles: Aus (2)

• KRAJICEK, Richard   Richard Peter Stanislav Krajicek

Male. Born: Dec. 6, 1971. Rotterdam, Netherlands. Height: 6' 5". Weight: 195 lbs. Plays: right.
Status: Turned Pro 1989. Earnings: $9,977,484. Highest Ranking: 4 (Mar. 1999).

Year	Rk	TP	TW	TF	GS	Aus	Fre	Wim	US	DC	Oly	MW	ML	Pct	CL	GR	HD	CP	IN	OD
1991	40	21	1	0	6-4	4rd	2rd	3rd	1rd	....	....	26	20	.565	4-4	4-3	17-9	1-4	4-5	22-15
1992	10	25	2	1	12-3	SF	3rd	3rd	4rd	2-0	....	49	23	.681	5-5	4-2	28-9	12-7	15-8	34-15
1993	15	23	1	1	12-4	2rd	SF	4rd	4rd	0-2	....	35	22	.614	11-7	5-2	14-8	5-5	5-6	30-16
1994	17	17	3	0	3-3	....	3rd	1rd	2rd	1-1	....	33	14	.702	13-4	5-1	12-5	3-4	8-4	25-10
1995	11	28	2	1	4-4	2rd	2rd	1rd	3rd	1-3	....	41	26	.612	7-9	2-2	14-11	18-4	20-8	21-18
1996	7	29	1	2	13-3	3rd	QF	W	1rd	0-1	....	46	28	.622	13-7	9-1	15-10	9-10	9-10	37-18
1997	11	22	3	1	8-3	....	3rd	4rd	QF	....	....	49	19	.721	5-4	9-2	20-8	15-5	15-5	34-14
1998	10	17	2	1	9-3	....	3rd	SF	3rd	....	....	45	15	.750	9-4	9-2	10-4	17-5	17-5	28-10
1999	10	23	2	1	9-4	3rd	2rd	3rd	QF	1-1	....	43	21	.672	3-4	4-3	26-10	10-4	15-6	28-15
2000	36	15	0	1	8-4	2rd	3rd	2rd	QF	1-0	....	26	15	.634	7-4	6-3	10-6	3-2	4-3	22-12
2002	112	6	0	0	4-2	....	....	QF	1rd	....	....	7	6	.538	0-0	4-2	3-4	0-0	0-0	7-6
TOTALS		226	17	9	88-37	....	....	....	6-8	....		400	209	.657	77-52	61-23	169-84	93-50	112-60	288-149

• KRICKSTEIN, Aaron   Aaron Krickstein

Male. Born: Aug. 2, 1967. Ann Arbor, MI, United States. Height: 6'. Weight: 160 lbs. Plays: right.
Status: Turned Pro 1983. Earnings: $3,710,447. Highest Ranking: 8 (Dec. 1989).

Year	Rk	TP	TW	TF	GS	Aus	Fre	Wim	US	DC	Oly	MW	ML	Pct	CL	GR	HD	CP	IN	OD
1983	94	6	1	0	3-1	....	....	....	4rd	....	....	8	5	.615	0-3	0-0	8-1	0-1	0-1	8-4
1984	12	20	3	2	3-2	....	2rd	....	3rd	....	....	34	17	.667	24-9	0-0	9-4	1-4	1-4	33-13
1985	29	22	0	1	3-2	....	4rd	1rd	....	2-2	....	26	22	.542	14-13	0-1	9-6	3-2	3-3	23-19
1986	26	22	0	1	4-2	....	2rd	....	4rd	1-1	....	39	22	.639	17-9	0-0	19-9	3-4	5-5	34-17
1987	61	13	0	0	2-1	....	3rd	....	....	1-1	....	15	13	.536	13-9	0-0	2-4	0-0	0-1	15-12
1988	15	24	0	2	4-2	....	1rd	....	QF	....	....	50	24	.676	12-7	0-0	31-13	7-4	11-6	39-18
1989	8	23	3	0	12-4	4rd	2rd	4rd	SF	....	....	50	20	.714	9-7	3-1	28-8	10-4	11-6	39-14
1990	20	25	0	2	9-3	4rd	3rd	....	QF	2-0	....	39	25	.609	6-5	0-1	23-11	10-8	14-10	25-15
1991	34	21	0	1	8-4	4rd	2rd	2rd	4rd	....	....	31	21	.596	7-4	1-1	15-12	8-4	8-5	23-16
1992	28	16	1	1	5-2	4rd	3rd	....	....	....	....	31	15	.674	10-5	0-0	19-9	2-1	4-2	27-13
1993	45	20	1	0	4-3	....	2rd	3rd	2rd	....	....	26	19	.578	5-6	3-2	17-7	1-4	1-4	25-15
1994	36	25	0	0	7-4	3rd	4rd	3rd	1rd	....	....	30	25	.545	4-4	2-2	22-15	2-4	4-6	26-19
1995	72	24	0	0	9-4	SF	1rd	4rd	2rd	....	....	16	24	.400	1-5	3-1	11-11	1-7	2-8	14-16
1996	1165	4	0	0	0-1	1rd	....	....	....	....	....	0	4	.000	0-0	0-0	0-3	0-1	0-1	0-3
TOTALS		**265**	**9**	**10**	**73-35**	....	....	....	....	**6-4**		**395**	**256**	**.607**	**122-86**	**12-9**	**213-113**	**48-48**	**64-62**	**331-194**

• KRIEK, Johan   Johan Christian Kriek

Male. Born: Apr. 5, 1958. Pongola, South Africa. Height: 5'9". Weight: 170 lbs. Plays: right.
Status: Turned Pro 1978. Earnings: $2,383,794. Highest Ranking: –.

Year	Rk	TP	TW	TF	GS	Aus	Fre	Wim	US	DC	Oly	MW	ML	Pct	CL	GR	HD	CP	IN	OD
1978	27	11	0	2	5-2	....	....	2rd	QF	....	....	22	11	.667	2-2	1-1	13-6	6-2	11-5	11-6
1979	35	20	1	0	6-3	....	1rd	3rd	QF	....	....	28	19	.596	2-4	2-2	14-7	10-6	15-9	13-10
1980	18	24	0	2	6-2	....	....	3rd	SF	....	....	38	24	.613	0-1	3-2	15-9	20-12	23-13	15-11
1981	13	18	3	1	12-2	W	....	QF	3rd	....	....	38	15	.717	3-3	20-3	7-6	8-3	10-5	28-10
1982	12	24	3	1	12-2	W	....	QF	3rd	....	....	41	21	.661	1-3	12-4	11-6	17-8	17-8	24-13
1983	15	22	3	1	8-3	QF	....	3rd	4rd	....	....	39	19	.672	5-4	10-2	16-7	8-6	10-7	29-12
1984	13	19	2	1	9-3	SF	....	4rd	3rd	....	....	37	17	.685	2-1	15-3	14-7	6-6	8-7	29-10
1985	14	22	1	2	6-3	QF	....	3rd	2rd	....	....	43	21	.672	1-1	13-5	20-10	9-5	9-5	34-16
1986	23	14	0	0	7-3	....	SF	2rd	3rd	....	....	20	14	.588	4-1	1-1	8-7	7-5	7-5	13-9
1987	48	21	1	0	5-4	2rd	1rd	4rd	3rd	....	....	26	20	.565	2-3	3-2	19-12	2-3	4-4	22-16
1988	39	18	0	2	3-3	2rd	....	1rd	3rd	....	....	25	18	.581	1-2	2-2	17-11	5-3	8-5	17-13
1989	52	10	0	0	2-3	3rd	....	1rd	1rd	....	....	12	10	.545	1-1	2-2	9-7	0-0	4-1	8-9
1990	....	1	0	0	0-0	....	....	....	....	....	....	0	1	.000	0-0	0-0	0-1	0-0	0-0	0-1
1991	....	7	0	0	0-1	....	....	1rd	....	....	....	3	7	.300	0-0	1-3	0-2	2-2	2-2	1-5
1992	....	1	0	0	0-0	....	....	....	....	....	....	0	1	.000	0-0	0-0	0-1	0-0	0-1	0-0
TOTALS		**232**	**14**	**12**	**81-34**	....	....	....	....	....		**372**	**218**	**.631**	**24-26**	**85-32**	**163-99**	**100-61**	**128-77**	**244-141**

• KUCERA, Karol   Karol Kucera

Male. Born: Mar. 4, 1974. Bratislava, Czech Republic. Height: 6'2". Weight: 170 lbs. Plays: right.
Status: Turned Pro 1992. Earnings: $4,354,264. Highest Ranking: 6 (Sept. 1998).

Year	Rk	TP	TW	TF	GS	Aus	Fre	Wim	US	DC	Oly	MW	ML	Pct	CL	GR	HD	CP	IN	OD
1991	351	1	0	0	0-0	....	....	....	....	....	....	1	1	.500	1-1	0-0	0-0	0-0	0-0	1-1
1992	214	1	0	0	0-0	....	....	....	....	....	....	0	1	.000	0-1	0-0	0-0	0-0	0-0	0-1
1993	181	3	0	0	0-1	....	1rd	....	....	....	....	1	3	.250	1-2	0-0	0-0	0-1	0-1	1-2
1994	57	13	0	1	1-3	....	2rd	1rd	1rd	4-0	....	13	13	.500	10-8	0-1	1-2	2-2	2-2	11-11
1995	74	27	1	0	1-4	1rd	1rd	2rd	1rd	3-1	....	21	26	.447	5-12	6-2	3-8	7-4	9-6	12-20
1996	63	25	0	0	6-4	3rd	3rd	3rd	1rd	6-0	2rd	18	25	.419	2-6	2-2	11-12	3-5	3-6	15-19
1997	24	28	1	2	1-4	2rd	1rd	1rd	1rd	4-0	....	37	27	.578	11-10	4-2	6-7	16-8	18-9	19-18
1998	8	31	2	2	9-4	SF	1rd	1rd	QF	2-2	....	53	29	.646	17-10	2-3	24-10	10-6	14-12	39-17
1999	17	23	1	0	7-3	QF	1rd	4rd	....	3-1	....	43	22	.662	8-7	8-3	14-8	13-4	14-6	29-16
2000	73	24	0	0	3-4	1rd	3rd	2rd	1rd	1-2	2rd	28	24	.538	11-7	3-2	12-12	2-3	4-4	24-20
2001	102	15	0	0	0-1	1rd	....	....	....	1-2	....	12	15	.444	3-5	1-1	7-6	1-3	8-6	4-9
2002	83	17	0	0	2-3	2rd	1rd	....	2rd	0-1	....	18	17	.514	1-5	2-1	12-9	3-2	3-2	15-15
TOTALS		**208**	**5**	**5**	**30-31**	....	....	....	....	**24-9**	....	**245**	**203**	**.547**	**70-74**	**28-17**	**90-74**	**57-38**	**75-54**	**170-149**

Represented Slovakia in the Davis Cup (1994-2002)

• KUERTEN, Gustavo   Gustavo Kuerten

Male. Born: Sept. 10, 1976. Florianopolis, Brazil. Height: 6' 3". Weight: 165 lbs. Plays: right.
Status: Turned Pro 1995. Earnings: $13,456,299. Highest Ranking: 1 (Dec. 2000).

Year	Rk	TP	TW	TF	GS	Aus	Fre	Wim	US	DC	Oly	MW	ML	Pct	CL	GR	HD	CP	IN	OD
1996	88	10	0	0	0-1	....	1rd	....	....	3-0	....	12	10	.545	7-7	0-0	1-1	4-2	4-2	8-8
1997	14	26	1	2	10-3	2rd	W	1rd	3rd	2-2	....	36	25	.590	16-10	0-2	17-8	3-5	5-6	31-19
1998	23	27	2	0	3-4	2rd	2rd	1rd	2rd	2-1	....	41	25	.621	26-12	0-2	14-10	1-1	5-3	36-22
1999	5	27	2	0	13-4	2rd	QF	QF	QF	3-1	....	50	25	.667	23-6	4-1	20-13	3-5	5-8	45-17
2000	1	27	5	2	9-3	1rd	W	3rd	1rd	2-3	QF	63	22	.741	28-6	2-2	28-12	5-2	10-4	53-18
2001	2	24	6	2	12-2	2rd	W	....	QF	3-1	....	60	18	.769	36-3	0-0	23-12	1-3	1-7	59-11
2002	37	15	1	1	6-3	1rd	4rd	....	4rd	1-0	....	25	14	.641	11-6	0-0	10-6	4-2	4-3	21-11
TOTALS		**156**	**17**	**7**	**53-20**	....	....	....	....	**16-8**		**287**	**139**	**.674**	**147-50**	**6-7**	**113-62**	**21-20**	**34-33**	**253-106**

Held number one tour ranking 3 times for a total of 43 weeks. Last ranked number one in 2001.

• LAPENTTI, Nicolas   Nicolas Alexander Lapenti

Male. Born: Aug. 13, 1976. Guayaquil, Ecuador. Height: 6' 2". Weight: 185 lbs. Plays: right.
Status: Turned Pro 1995. Earnings: $4,508,139. Highest Ranking: 6 (Nov. 1999).

Year	Rk	TP	TW	TF	GS	Aus	Fre	Wim	US	DC	Oly	MW	ML	Pct	CL	GR	HD	CP	IN	OD
1994	....	0	0	0	0-0	....	....	....	....	1-1	....	0	0	.000	0-0	0-0	0-0	0-0	0-0	0-0
1995	125	2	1	0	0-0	....	....	....	....	4-2	....	5	1	.833	5-1	0-0	0-0	0-0	0-0	5-1
1996	121	19	0	1	1-4	1rd	1rd	2rd	1rd	5-0	1rd	11	19	.367	9-9	1-2	1-7	0-1	0-2	11-17
1997	64	20	0	1	2-3	....	2rd	1rd	2rd	2-2	....	19	20	.487	16-13	0-1	3-6	0-0	0-2	19-18
1998	92	30	0	0	1-4	2rd	1rd	1rd	1rd	3-1	....	19	30	.388	14-16	0-2	5-11	0-1	0-3	19-27
1999	8	26	2	1	8-4	SF	2rd	2rd	2rd	6-0	....	58	24	.707	25-9	1-1	22-10	10-4	13-9	45-15
2000	24	29	0	1	5-4	2rd	4rd	1rd	2rd	4-1	....	43	29	.597	16-9	3-3	22-14	2-3	2-4	41-25
2001	23	26	1	0	4-3	2rd	2rd	....	3rd	0-3	....	30	25	.545	15-9	0-3	12-10	3-3	5-5	25-20
2002	29	28	1	1	7-4	4rd	1rd	QF	1rd	2-0	....	34	27	.557	16-12	4-1	12-12	2-2	4-4	30-23
TOTALS		**180**	**5**	**5**	**28-26**	....	....	....	....	**27-10**		**219**	**175**	**.556**	**116-78**	**9-13**	**77-70**	**17-14**	**24-29**	**195-146**

• LAVER, Rod   Rodney George "Rocket" Laver

Male. Born: Aug. 9, 1938. Rockhampton, Australia. Height: 5' 8". Weight: 145 lbs. Plays: left.
Status: Amateur. Earnings: $1,564,213. Highest Ranking: 1 (Dec. 1961). HOF: 1981

Year	Rk	TP	TW	TF	GS	Aus	Fre	Wim	US	DC	Oly	MW	ML	Pct	CL	GR	HD	CP	IN	OD
1956	....	4	0	0	....	3rd	1rd	1rd	1rd	....	....	....	....	....	....	....	....	....	....	....
1957	....	1	0	0	....	3rd	....	....	....	....	....	....	....	....	....	....	....	....	....	....
1958	....	4	0	0	....	4rd	1rd	3rd	4rd	....	....	....	....	....	....	....	....	....	....	....
1959	5	4	0	1	....	4rd	3rd	F	QF	6-4	....	....	....	....	....	....	....	....	....	....
1960	2	4	1	2	....	W	3rd	F	F	2-0	....	....	....	....	....	....	....	....	....	....
1961	1	4	1	2	....	F	SF	W	F	2-0	....	....	....	....	....	....	....	....	....	....
1962	1	4	4	0	....	W	W	W	W	2-0	....	....	....	....	....	....	....	....	....	....
1968	1	3	1	3	15-2	....	F	W	4rd	....	....	15	2	.882	6-1	9-1	0-0	0-0	0-0	15-2
1969	1	10	10	3	26-0	W	W	W	W	....	....	31	0	1.000	7-1	19-0	0-0	5-1	5-1	26-0
1970	2	15	12	6	5-2	....	....	4rd	4rd	....	....	9	3	.750	0-0	5-2	0-0	4-1	4-1	5-2
1971	4	9	5	5	5-2	3rd	....	QF	....	....	....	16	4	.800	5-1	5-2	0-0	6-2	6-2	10-2
1972	4	8	5	2	3-1	....	....	....	4rd	....	....	7	3	.700	0-0	3-1	2-1	2-1	2-1	5-2
1973	8	8	5	3	2-1	....	....	3rd	4-0	....	....	5	3	.625	0-0	2-1	0-1	3-1	3-1	2-2
1974	4	6	5	0	0-0	....	....	....	....	....	....	10	1	.909	5-1	0-0	5-1	0-1	0-1	10-1
1975	10	9	5	0	3-1	....	....	....	4rd	....	....	7	4	.636	5-2	0-0	1-1	1-1	1-1	6-3
1976	73	11	5	0	0-0	....	....	....	....	....	....	7	6	.538	0-2	0-0	3-1	4-3	4-3	3-3
1977	124	5	0	0	1-1	....	....	2rd	....	....	....	3	5	.375	0-0	1-2	2-2	0-1	0-1	3-4
1979	....	1	0	0	0-0	....	....	....	....	....	....	0	1	.000	0-0	0-0	0-1	0-0	0-0	0-1
TOTALS		**110**	**59**	**27**	**60-10**	....	....	....	**16-4**	....		**110**	**32**	**.775**	**28-8**	**44-9**	**13-8**	**25-12**	**25-12**	**85-22**

Held number one world ranking 2 times during amateur era and 2 times during the open era. Represented the United States in the Davis Cup (1973).
Doubles Titles: Aus (4), Fre (1), Wim (1).

• LECONTE, Henri   Henri Leconte

Male. Born: July 4, 1963. Lillers, France. Height: 6' 1". Weight: 175 lbs. Plays: left.
Status: Turned Pro 1980. Earnings: $3,917,596. Highest Ranking: 6 (Dec. 1986).

Year	Rk	TP	TW	TF	GS	Aus	Fre	Wim	US	DC	Oly	MW	ML	Pct	CL	GR	HD	CP	IN	OD
1980	440	4	0	0	0-1	....	1rd	....	....	....	....	0	4	.000	0-2	0-0	0-1	0-1	0-1	0-3
1981	....	6	0	0	1-2	....	1rd	2rd	....	....	....	3	6	.333	0-2	3-2	0-1	0-1	0-2	3-4
1982	28	24	1	0	0-3	....	1rd	1rd	1rd	0-2	....	30	23	.566	9-12	1-3	18-7	2-1	15-6	15-17
1983	30	26	0	2	2-2	....	2rd	2rd	....	3-3	....	38	26	.594	18-9	1-3	14-8	5-6	11-8	27-18
1984	27	20	1	1	3-2	....	2rd	....	3rd	3-1	....	29	19	.604	11-6	1-2	8-6	9-5	13-7	16-12

The Registers

Year	Rk	TP	TW	TF	GS	Aus	Fre	Wim	US	DC	Oly	MW	ML	Pct	CL	GR	HD	CP	IN	OD
1985	16	27	2	1	13-4	4rd	QF	QF	4rd	0-4	....	47	25	.653	22-7	13-4	10-9	2-5	6-9	41-16
1986	6	16	2	1	14-3	....	SF	SF	QF	4-0	2rd	42	14	.750	23-4	9-2	7-2	3-6	6-7	36-7
1987	21	21	0	0	8-4	3rd	1rd	QF	4rd	0-2	....	23	21	.523	5-10	7-3	5-5	6-3	6-4	17-17
1988	9	25	2	2	13-4	3rd	F	4rd	3rd	3-3	....	51	23	.689	26-9	3-1	8-5	14-8	18-9	33-14
1989	115	13	0	0	0-1	1rd	....	....	....	2-2	....	12	13	.480	5-4	0-0	0-2	7-7	7-7	5-6
1990	30	18	0	0	8-4	3rd	QF	2rd	2rd	3-1	....	28	18	.609	19-8	4-3	4-4	1-3	2-4	26-14
1991	159	12	0	0	3-2	....	2rd	3rd	....	3-0	....	11	12	.478	7-6	2-1	1-3	1-2	3-2	8-10
1992	61	16	0	0	9-4	1rd	SF	3rd	3rd	2-0	2rd	21	16	.568	9-8	2-1	2-3	8-4	9-6	12-10
1993	100	15	1	0	3-3	....	1rd	4rd	1rd	0-1	....	13	14	.481	1-6	8-1	1-4	3-3	3-4	10-10
1994	93	17	0	0	1-3	2rd	1rd	1rd	....	1-1	....	17	17	.500	3-6	5-3	4-4	5-4	6-5	11-12
1995	134	14	0	0	0-1	....	....	1rd	....	....	....	8	14	.364	2-7	1-3	3-2	2-2	2-2	6-12
1996	998	4	0	0	0-1	....	1rd	....	....	....	....	0	4	.000	0-2	0-1	0-1	0-0	0-1	0-3
TOTALS		278	9	7	78-44	....	....	....	....	24-20	....	373	269	.581	160-108	60-33	85-67	68-61	107-84	266-185

Doubles Titles: Fre (1)

• LENDL, Ivan

Ivan Lendl

Male. Born: Mar. 7, 1960. Ostrava, Czech Republic. Height: 6' 2". Weight: 175 lbs. Plays: right.
Status: Turned Pro 1978. Earnings: $21,262,417. Highest Ranking: 1 (Feb. 1983). HOF: 2001

Year	Rk	TP	TW	TF	GS	Aus	Fre	Wim	US	DC	Oly	MW	ML	Pct	CL	GR	HD	CP	IN	OD
1978	74	7	0	0	0-1	....	1rd	....	....	0-2	....	9	7	.563	4-3	0-0	2-3	3-1	5-4	4-3
1979	20	18	0	1	4-3	....	4rd	1rd	2rd	3-3	....	38	18	.679	23-11	0-1	14-5	1-1	10-4	28-14
1980	6	35	7	3	9-4	2rd	3rd	3rd	QF	7-0	....	105	28	.789	42-9	5-3	31-5	27-11	32-11	73-17
1981	2	24	10	5	9-3	....	F	1rd	4rd	2-2	....	96	14	.873	46-7	0-1	41-4	9-2	30-3	66-11
1982	3	24	15	5	9-2	....	4rd	....	F	3-1	....	106	9	.922	45-6	0-0	21-3	40-0	40-0	66-9
1983	2	23	7	6	20-4	F	QF	SF	F	1-0	....	75	16	.824	14-5	14-3	16-3	31-5	33-6	42-10
1984	3	19	3	8	20-3	4rd	W	SF	F	1-3	....	62	16	.795	16-5	7-3	10-3	29-5	33-6	29-10
1985	1	18	11	3	20-3	SF	F	4rd	W	1-0	....	84	7	.923	31-2	7-2	29-3	17-0	22-0	62-7
1986	1	15	9	3	20-1	....	W	F	W	....	....	74	6	.925	17-1	6-1	30-2	21-2	25-3	49-3
1987	1	15	8	4	24-2	SF	W	F	W	....	....	74	7	.914	14-1	10-2	33-2	17-2	21-2	53-5
1988	2	11	3	2	20-4	SF	QF	SF	F	....	....	41	8	.837	15-1	5-1	17-3	4-3	4-3	37-5
1989	1	17	10	2	21-3	W	4rd	SF	F	....	....	79	7	.919	21-2	11-1	38-2	9-2	14-2	65-5
1990	3	17	5	1	16-2	W	....	SF	QF	....	....	54	12	.818	0-0	10-1	21-6	23-5	26-6	28-6
1991	5	21	3	3	13-3	F	....	3rd	SF	....	....	55	18	.753	3-2	2-2	31-8	19-6	25-7	30-11
1992	8	25	1	3	12-4	QF	2rd	4rd	QF	....	....	50	24	.676	8-7	3-2	29-10	10-5	15-7	35-17
1993	19	25	2	2	1-4	1rd	1rd	2rd	1rd	....	....	33	23	.589	15-7	1-2	6-9	11-5	11-7	22-16
1994	54	18	0	1	4-3	4rd	1rd	....	2rd	....	....	28	18	.609	4-4	0-0	23-13	1-1	1-1	27-17
TOTALS		332	94	52	222-49	....	....	....	....	18-11	....	1063	238	.817	318-73	81-25	392-84	272-56	347-72	716-166

Held number one tour ranking 8 times for a total of 270 weeks. Last ranked number one in 1989.

• LEWIS, Chris

Chris Lewis

Male. Born: Mar. 9, 1957. Auckland, New Zealand. Height: 5' 11". Weight: 155 lbs. Plays: right.
Status: Turned Pro 1976. Earnings: –. Highest Ranking: –.

Year	Rk	TP	TW	TF	GS	Aus	Fre	Wim	US	DC	Oly	MW	ML	Pct	CL	GR	HD	CP	IN	OD
1976	127	12	0	0	2-2	2rd	....	2rd	....	....	....	8	12	.400	2-4	2-2	0-2	4-4	4-4	4-8
1977	151	5	0	1	4-41rd/3rd	3rd	1rd	....	....	....	....	5	5	.500	2-1	3-4	0-0	0-0	0-0	5-5
1978	40	25	1	0	1-3	....	2rd	1rd	1rd	....	....	32	24	.571	27-15	2-2	0-2	3-5	3-5	29-19
1979	63	19	0	0	1-3	1rd	2rd	....	1rd	....	....	11	19	.367	10-13	0-2	1-4	0-0	0-0	11-19
1980	66	23	0	0	2-3	1rd	2rd	2rd	....	....	....	24	23	.511	16-10	4-5	0-3	4-7	4-7	20-16
1981	32	27	1	4	5-4	3rd	2rd	2rd	2rd	....	....	43	26	.623	10-6	13-9	14-7	6-4	12-7	31-19
1982	57	20	0	1	6-3	3rd	2rd	3rd	3rd	....	....	33	20	.623	19-9	9-7	5-4	0-0	0-0	33-20
1983	25	25	0	1	8-4	3rd	1rd	F	2rd	....	....	37	25	.597	13-8	15-6	8-6	1-5	3-7	34-18
1984	101	19	0	0	1-4	2rd	1rd	2rd	1rd	....	....	17	19	.472	12-11	2-4	3-3	0-1	0-2	17-17
1985	118	12	1	0	3-3	2rd	2rd	2rd	....	....	....	11	11	.500	3-6	3-3	5-1	0-1	0-1	11-10
1986	....	2	0	0	0-0	....	....	....	....	....	....	0	2	.000	0-0	0-0	0-2	0-0	0-0	0-2
TOTALS		189	3	7	33-33	....	....	....	....	....	....	221	186	.543	114-83	53-44	36-34	18-25	26-33	195-153

• LLOYD, Chris see **EVERT, Chris**, page 841

• LLOYD, John

John Lloyd

Male. Born: Aug. 27, 1954. Leigh-On-Sea, Great Britain. Height: 5' 10". Weight: 165 lbs. Plays: right.
Status: Turned Pro 1973. Earnings: –. Highest Ranking: –.

Year	Rk	TP	TW	TF	GS	Aus	Fre	Wim	US	DC	Oly	MW	ML	Pct	CL	GR	HD	CP	IN	OD
1973	....	7	0	0	4-3	....	2rd	3rd	2rd	....	....	5	7	.417	1-1	4-3	0-2	0-1	0-1	5-6
1974	97	9	1	0	2-4	2rd	1rd	1rd	2rd	2-2	....	4	8	.333	0-2	3-4	1-2	0-0	1-1	3-7
1975	93	10	0	0	2-3	....	2rd	1rd	2rd	....	....	9	10	.474	6-5	2-3	1-2	0-0	1-1	8-9
1976	61	15	0	0	3-4	2rd	1rd	1rd	3rd	1-3	....	11	15	.423	3-6	1-3	3-2	4-4	6-5	5-10
1977	33	14	0	3	7-4	/F	1rd	2rd	2rd	0-1	....	14	14	.500	1-5	6-2	4-4	3-3	7-5	7-9
1978	66	25	0	0	4-3	....	3rd	1rd	3rd	6-4	....	25	25	.500	11-9	3-2	3-7	8-7	8-10	17-15
1979	146	21	0	1	3-2	....	2rd	1rd	3rd	1-3	....	12	21	.364	8-9	0-3	3-5	1-4	2-6	10-15
1980	356	9	0	0	0-1	....	....	1rd	....	....	....	1	9	.100	1-2	0-1	0-3	0-3	0-3	1-6
1981	225	8	0	0	1-2	....	2rd	1rd	....	....	....	6	8	.429	0-0	2-2	4-5	0-1	0-1	6-7
1982	197	15	0	0	2-3	1rd	3rd	1rd	....	....	....	8	15	.348	2-2	3-6	3-5	0-2	1-4	7-11
1983	77	14	0	0	6-4	4rd	1rd	1rd	4rd	1-2	....	11	14	.440	1-3	6-7	4-3	0-1	0-1	11-13
1984	37	19	0	0	7-4	2rd	2rd	3rd	QF	1-3	....	17	19	.472	2-3	2-7	9-5	4-4	4-4	13-15
1985	42	21	0	0	7-4	QF	2rd	3rd	2rd	3-0	....	23	21	.523	2-2	7-4	11-10	3-5	5-6	18-15
1986	210	10	0	0	0-2	....	1rd	1rd	....	1-1	....	6	10	.375	1-3	0-2	2-3	3-2	3-2	3-8
TOTALS		197	1	4	48-43	....	....	....	....	16-19		152	196	.437	39-52	39-49	48-58	26-37	38-50	114-146

• LUTZ, Bob

Bob Lutz

Male. Born: Aug. 29, 1947. Lancaster, PA, United States. Height: 5' 11". Weight: 180 lbs. Plays: right.
Status: Turned Pro 1971. Earnings: $1,165,276. Highest Ranking: 7 (Dec. 1972).

Year	Rk	TP	TW	TF	GS	Aus	Fre	Wim	US	DC	Oly	MW	ML	Pct	CL	GR	HD	CP	IN	OD
1966	....	2	0	0	....	....	....	1rd	1rd	....	....	....	....	.	....	....	....	....	....	....
1967	....	2	0	0	....	....	....	1rd	4rd	....	....	....	....	.	....	....	....	....	....	....
1968	....	2	0	0	2-2	....	....	1rd	3rd	1-0	....	2	2	.500	0-0	2-2	0-0	0-0	0-0	2-2
1969	....	3	0	0	4-2	....	....	QF	1rd	....	....	4	3	.571	0-0	4-2	0-0	0-1	0-1	4-2
1970	....	3	0	1	3-3	3rd	....	3rd	1rd	....	....	3	3	.500	0-0	3-3	0-0	0-0	0-0	3-3
1971	....	9	2	1	12-4	SF	4rd	3rd	4rd	....	....	14	7	.667	4-2	9-3	0-0	1-2	1-2	13-5
1972	....	4	1	2	3-1	....	....	....	4rd	....	....	3	3	.500	0-0	3-1	0-1	0-1	0-1	3-2
1973	35	3	0	1	0-0	....	....	....	....	....	....	0	3	.000	0-1	0-1	0-1	0-0	0-0	0-3
1974	48	9	0	1	1-3	....	1rd	1rd	2rd	....	....	10	9	.526	1-2	1-3	7-3	1-1	1-1	9-8
1975	22	5	1	2	0-2	....	....	1rd	1rd	....	....	5	4	.556	0-1	0-1	2-1	3-1	3-1	2-3
1976	20	18	0	3	4-2	....	....	3rd	3rd	....	....	24	18	.571	7-5	4-2	3-3	10-8	10-9	14-9
1977	34	13	0	2	3-3	....	1rd	3rd	2rd	....	....	22	13	.629	3-3	7-3	6-5	6-2	7-4	15-9
1978	30	17	1	1	3-2	....	....	1rd	4rd	....	....	28	16	.636	4-2	0-1	15-5	9-8	15-9	13-7
1979	36	16	1	0	3-2	....	....	4rd	1rd	....	....	25	15	.625	1-1	8-3	6-6	10-5	10-5	15-10
1980	21	21	3	0	2-3	....	2rd	2rd	1rd	....	....	38	18	.679	1-1	1-3	25-8	11-6	21-8	17-10
1981	101	17	0	0	2-1	....	....	3rd	....	....	....	11	17	.393	0-0	2-1	7-9	2-7	3-10	8-7
1982	122	15	0	0	4-2	....	....	2rd	4rd	....	....	10	15	.400	1-2	1-1	6-7	2-5	3-6	7-9
1983	....	2	0	1	0-1	....	....	....	1rd	....	....	5	2	.714	0-0	0-0	1-1	4-1	4-1	1-1
1984	....	2	0	0	0-0	....	....	....	....	....	....	3	2	.600	0-0	0-0	3-2	0-0	0-0	3-2
1985	....	1	0	0	0-0	....	....	....	....	....	....	1	1	.500	0-0	0-0	1-1	0-0	0-0	1-1
TOTALS		164	9	15	46-33	....	....	....	1-0	....		208	151	.579	22-20	45-30	82-53	59-48	78-58	130-93

Doubles Titles: Aus (1), US (5)

• MAJOLI, Iva

Iva Majoli

Female. Born: Aug. 12, 1977. Zagreb, Hrvatska (Croatia). Height: 5' 9". Weight: 135 lbs. Plays: right.
Status: Turned Pro 1991. Earnings: $4,258,381. Highest Ranking: 4 (Feb. 1996).

Year	Rk	TP	TW	TF	GS	Aus	Fre	Wim	US	FC	Oly	MW	ML	Pct	CL	GR	HD	CP	IN	OD
1992	50	6	0	0	1-1	....	....	....	2rd	....	....	7	6	.538	2-1	0-0	3-4	2-1	4-2	3-4
1993	46	13	0	0	4-2	....	4rd	....	2rd	2-1	....	13	13	.500	4-3	0-0	4-6	5-4	5-6	8-7
1994	13	19	0	3	6-3	....	4rd	1rd	4rd	1-0	....	39	19	.672	14-5	2-2	16-7	7-5	11-6	28-13
1995	9	14	2	1	4-3	....	QF	1rd	1rd	2-1	....	29	12	.707	11-5	0-1	9-3	9-3	16-4	13-8
1996	7	19	2	2	8-3	QF	QF	....	1rd	4-1	QF	41	17	.707	12-5	2-1	10-6	17-5	20-7	21-10
1997	6	26	3	0	12-3	1rd	W	QF	2rd	2-2	....	45	23	.662	19-4	4-2	15-11	7-6	13-9	32-14
1998	25	21	0	0	8-4	3rd	QF	2rd	2rd	3-1	....	26	21	.553	12-7	1-1	7-7	6-6	7-8	19-13
1999	163	13	0	0	0-1	....	....	....	1rd	0-2	....	5	13	.278	4-5	0-0	1-7	0-1	1-3	4-10
2000	73	12	0	1	1-1	....	2rd	....	....	0-1	1rd	14	12	.538	5-5	0-0	8-5	1-2	4-3	10-9
2001	42	24	0	1	4-4	3rd	1rd	1rd	3rd	....	....	23	24	.489	3-6	0-1	17-14	3-3	11-7	12-17
2002	32	26	1	1	6-4	2rd	2rd	3rd	3rd	1-3	....	24	25	.490	15-10	2-1	7-11	0-3	1-5	23-20
TOTALS		193	8	9	54-29	....	....	....	15-12	....		266	185	.590	101-56	11-9	97-81	57-39	93-60	173-125

• MALEEVA, Katerina   Katerina Maleeva

Female. Born: May 7, 1969. Sofia, Bulgaria. Height: 5' 6". Weight: 120 lbs. Plays: right.
Status: Turned Pro 1984. Earnings: $2,220,371. Highest Ranking: 6 (July 1990).

Year	Rk	TP	TW	TF	GS	Aus	Fre	Wim	US	FC	Oly	MW	ML	Pct	CL	GR	HD	CP	IN	OD
1984	93	3	0	0	0-0	....	....	....	....	2-1	....	4	3	.571	2-1	0-0	2-1	0-1	2-2	2-1
1985	28	22	2	1	4-4	3rd	3rd	1rd	1rd	4-0	....	34	20	.630	16-7	3-3	10-7	5-3	5-4	29-16
1986	28	21	0	0	7-3	....	4rd	3rd	3rd	2-1	....	26	21	.553	9-6	2-1	5-4		10-10	16-11
1987	13	18	2	0	5-3	....	4rd	1rd	3rd	3-1	....	38	16	.704	16-5	0-1	16-5	6-5	7-6	31-10
1988	11	18	1	2	7-3	....	1rd	4rd	QF	....	3rd	36	17	.679	9-6	3-1	22-8	2-2	2-3	34-14
1989	15	14	3	1	4-2	....	4rd	....	2rd	3-0	....	34	11	.756	13-6	0-0	21-5	0-0	11-1	23-10
1990	6	16	1	2	15-4	QF	QF	QF	4rd	....	....	47	15	.758	15-4	4-1	22-7	6-3	9-4	38-11
1991	11	18	1	2	11-4	QF	3rd	4rd	3rd	1-2	....	36	17	.679	5-5	3-1	24-7	4-4	4-4	32-13
1992	16	20	0	0	10-4	4rd	2rd	QF	3rd	2-1	2rd	33	20	.623	8-7	4-1	14-6	7-6	10-7	23-13
1993	22	18	0	1	10-4	4rd	4rd	1rd	QF	1-1	....	29	18	.617	10-7	0-1	11-7	8-3	10-4	19-14
1994	36	18	1	0	2-4	1rd	2rd	1rd	2rd	2-1	....	22	17	.564	6-5	0-1	8-7	8-4	11-6	11-11
1995	278	13	0	0	0-3	1rd	1rd	1rd	....	0-2	....	1	13	.071	0-4	0-1	1-4	0-4	0-5	1-8
1996	217	7	0	0	0-0	....	....	....	....	....	....	5	7	.417	1-3	0-0	2-3	2-1	4-3	1-4
TOTALS		**206**	**11**	**9**	**75-38**	....	....	....	....	**20-10**	....	**345**	**195**	**.639**	**110-66**	**19-12**	**158-71**	**58-46**	**85-59**	**260-136**

• MALEEVA, Maggie   Magdalena Maleeva

Female. Born: Apr. 1, 1975. Sofia, Bulgaria. Height: 5' 6". Weight: 125 lbs. Plays: right.
Status: Turned Pro 1989. Earnings: $2,593,327. Highest Ranking: 4 (Jan. 1996).

Year	Rk	TP	TW	TF	GS	Aus	Fre	Wim	US	FC	Oly	MW	ML	Pct	CL	GR	HD	CP	IN	OD
1989	211	3	0	0	0-0	....	....	....	....	....	....	1	3	.250	1-1	0-0	0-2	0-0	0-0	1-3
1990	72	10	0	0	3-3	....	3rd	2rd	1rd	....	....	12	10	.545	4-2	1-1	4-4	3-3	3-3	9-7
1991	38	16	0	1	4-4	4rd	1rd	1rd	1rd	1-1	....	18	16	.529	6-5	0-1	9-8	3-2	3-2	15-14
1992	20	16	1	0	6-4	1rd	3rd	1rd	QF	2-0	3rd	32	15	.681	16-6	0-1	8-3	8-5	8-5	24-10
1993	16	16	0	1	11-4	4rd	4rd	3rd	4rd	2-0	....	38	16	.704	12-4	2-1	16-6	8-5	8-5	30-11
1994	11	14	2	0	7-4	4rd	1rd	2rd	4rd	2-1	....	33	12	.733	9-7	1-1	10-3	13-1	13-1	20-11
1995	6	14	3	3	2-3	1rd	2rd	....	2rd	1-1	....	35	11	.761	13-5	0-0	1-2	21-4	21-4	14-7
1996	18	15	0	1	4-3	....	4rd	2rd	....	....	3rd	20	15	.571	9-5	1-2	4-4	6-4	6-5	14-10
1997	36	21	0	0	4-3	....	1rd	3rd	3rd	....	....	21	21	.500	1-2	5-3	12-12	3-4	8-8	13-13
1998	115	7	0	0	0-1	1rd	....	....	....	0-3	....	5	7	.417	0-0	0-0	3-5	2-2	3-4	2-3
1999	89	10	1	0	0-1	....	1rd	....	....	....	....	19	9	.679	3-4	3-1	9-1	4-3	4-3	15-6
2000	22	25	0	1	4-4	1rd	3rd	2rd	2rd	....	....	33	25	.569	6-8	1-2	15-11	11-4	16-7	17-18
2001	16	25	1	2	4-4	1rd	1rd	4rd	2rd	....	....	35	24	.593	8-5	3-2	9-12	15-5	19-9	16-15
2002	14	25	1	1	8-4	4rd	1rd	4rd	3rd	3-1	....	35	24	.593	7-5	7-3	12-13	9-3	14-9	21-15
TOTALS		**217**	**9**	**10**	**57-42**	....	....	....	....	**11-7**	....	**337**	**208**	**.618**	**95-59**	**24-18**	**112-86**	**106-45**	**126-65**	**211-143**

• MALEEVA, Manuela   Manuela Maleeva Fragniere

Female. Born: Feb. 14, 1967. St. Legier, Sweden. Height: 5' 8". Weight: 125 lbs. Plays: right.
Status: Turned Pro 1982. Earnings: $3,244,811. Highest Ranking: 3 (Feb. 1985).

Year	Rk	TP	TW	TF	GS	Aus	Fre	Wim	US	FC	Oly	MW	ML	Pct	CL	GR	HD	CP	IN	OD
1982	60	8	0	0	4-4	2rd	2rd	2rd	3rd	....	....	11	8	.579	3-2	6-4	2-2	0-0	0-0	11-8
1983	31	17	0	0	5-3	....	3rd	2rd	3rd	2-1	....	21	17	.553	16-11	2-3	3-3	0-0	0-1	21-16
1984	6	21	5	0	7-3	....	4rd	QF	1rd	3-0	....	51	16	.761	30-5	4-1	5-4	12-6	15-8	36-8
1985	7	20	1	0	13-4	QF	QF	4rd	4rd	3-1	....	49	19	.721	16-6	10-3	10-5	13-5	15-6	34-13
1986	8	21	0	0	9-3	....	3rd	4rd	QF	3-0	....	45	21	.682	16-6	7-2	12-4	10-9	10-9	35-12
1987	8	18	2	0	10-4	4rd	QF	2rd	4rd	3-1	....	47	16	.746	19-5	6-3	12-4	10-4	12-5	35-11
1988	6	17	2	0	6-3	....	3rd	1rd	QF	....	SF	45	15	.750	9-4	0-1	23-5	13-5	18-5	27-10
1989	9	16	2	0	8-2	....	QF	....	QF	2-1	....	36	14	.720	11-3	0-0	17-6	8-5	10-6	26-8
1990	9	16	0	0	8-3	....	QF	1rd	QF	....	....	42	16	.724	7-3	0-1	19-6	16-6	19-7	23-9
1991	10	18	3	0	5-3	2rd	2rd	....	4rd	2-1	....	45	15	.750	10-3	0-0	18-8	17-4	17-4	28-11
1992	9	13	1	0	13-3	QF	3rd	3rd	SF	3-0	QF	37	12	.755	16-6	2-1	13-3	6-2	6-2	31-10
1993	11	18	2	0	11-4	4rd	3rd	2rd	SF	....	....	36	16	.692	8-7	1-1	16-5	11-3	13-4	23-12
1994	....	4	1	0	4-1	QF	....	....	....	....	....	12	3	.800	0-1	0-0	4-1	8-1	8-1	4-2
TOTALS		**207**	**19**	**0**	**103-40**	....	....	....	....	**21-5**	....	**477**	**188**	**.717**	**161-62**	**38-20**	**154-56**	**124-50**	**143-58**	**334-130**

Represented Bulgaria in the Federation Cup (1983-1992)

• MANCINI, Alberto

Alberto Mancini

Male. Born: May 20, 1969. Misiones, Argentina. Height: 5' 11". Weight: 175 lbs. Plays: right.
Status: Turned Pro 1987. Earnings: $1,543,120. Highest Ranking: 9 (Dec. 1989).

Year	Rk	TP	TW	TF	GS	Aus	Fre	Wim	US	DC	Oly	MW	ML	Pct	CL	GR	HD	CP	IN	OD
1987	130	5	0	0	0-0	....	....	....	....	....	....	2	5	.286	2-5	0-0	0-0	0-0	0-0	2-5
1988	19	16	1	0	0-1	....	1rd	....	....	....	....	29	15	.659	27-14	0-0	2-1	0-0	0-0	29-15
1989	9	19	2	0	7-2	....	QF	4rd	2-1	....	....	36	17	.679	26-10	1-1	8-4	1-2	1-2	35-15
1990	127	19	0	0	1-2	....	2rd	....	1rd	3-1	....	13	19	.406	13-12	0-1	0-5	0-1	0-1	13-18
1991	22	17	0	3	3-2	....	4rd	....	1rd	....	....	25	17	.595	23-11	0-0	0-3	2-3	2-3	23-14
1992	31	24	0	2	2-2	....	3rd	....	1rd	1-3	1rd	27	24	.529	14-10	0-0	12-13	1-1	1-4	26-20
1993	139	24	0	0	1-3	2rd	1rd	....	1rd	2-2	....	13	24	.351	8-17	0-0	5-7	0-0	0-0	13-24
1994	395	4	0	0	0-0	....	....	....	....	....	....	2	4	.333	1-3	0-0	1-1	0-0	0-0	2-4
TOTALS		**128**	**3**	**5**	**14-12**	....	....	....	....	**8-7**		**147**	**125**	**.540**	**114-82**	**1-2**	**28-34**	**4-7**	**4-10**	**143-115**

• MANDLIKOVA, Hana

Hana Mandlikova

Female. Born: Feb. 19, 1962. Prague, Czech Republic. Height: 5' 8". Weight: 132 lbs. Plays: right.
Status: Turned Pro 1978. Earnings: $3,340,959. Highest Ranking: 3 (Apr. 1984). HOF: 1994

Year	Rk	TP	TW	TF	GS	Aus	Fre	Wim	US	FC	Oly	MW	ML	Pct	CL	GR	HD	CP	IN	OD
1978	45	6	2	0	2-2	....	2rd	....	3rd	....	....	10	4	.714	5-1	4-2	1-1	0-0	0-0	10-4
1979	17	18	5	0	9-4	QF	QF	4rd	2rd	3-1	....	22	13	.629	6-3	13-4	3-3	0-3	1-4	21-9
1980	5	25	6	3	17-3	W	SF	4rd	F	2-2	....	77	19	.802	20-7	18-3	25-5	14-4	24-6	53-13
1981	4	22	3	1	19-3	QF	W	F	QF	4-0	....	55	19	.743	14-3	9-3	11-5	21-8	21-10	34-9
1982	7	18	0	3	10-4	2rd	SF	2rd	F	3-1	....	36	18	.667	12-5	8-5	15-7	1-1	3-3	33-15
1983	12	21	0	1	12-4	2rd	QF	4rd	QF	5-0	....	49	21	.700	21-6	9-5	13-5	6-5	7-6	42-15
1984	13	15	5	1	14-3	....	SF	SF	QF	5-0	....	51	10	.836	14-4	5-1	6-4	26-1	26-2	25-8
1985	3	17	3	2	17-3	SF	QF	3rd	W	5-0	....	59	14	.808	8-3	10-4	27-5	14-2	18-3	41-11
1986	4	15	0	6	14-3	....	SF	F	4rd	4-1	....	48	15	.762	15-3	8-2	7-2	18-8	22-9	26-6
1987	5	16	3	2	10-2	W	2rd	....	4rd	3-1	....	50	13	.794	8-3	12-1	17-6	13-3	16-4	34-9
1988	29	7	0	0	7-3	QF	2rd	3rd	....	....	....	15	7	.682	2-2	2-1	9-3	2-1	5-2	10-5
1989	14	19	0	0	8-4	4rd	1rd	3rd	3rd	....	....	34	19	.642	6-4	3-2	21-10	4-3	10-5	24-14
1990	....	9	0	0	3-2	3rd	....	2rd	....	....	....	8	9	.471	1-2	1-2	6-5	0-0	0-0	8-9
TOTALS		**208**	**27**	**19**	**142-40**	....	....	....	....	**34-6**	....	**514**	**181**	**.740**	**132-46**	**102-35**	**161-61**	**119-39**	**153-54**	**361-127**

Doubles Titles: US (1)

• MARKS, John

John Marks

Male. Born: Dec. 9, 1952. Sydney, Australia. Height: –. Weight: –. Plays: right.
Status: Turned Pro 1975. Earnings: –. Highest Ranking: –.

Year	Rk	TP	TW	TF	GS	Aus	Fre	Wim	US	DC	Oly	MW	ML	Pct	CL	GR	HD	CP	IN	OD
1975	....	1	0	0	0-0	....	....	....	....	....	....	5	1	.833	0-0	5-1	0-0	0-0	0-0	5-1
1976	....	5	0	0	0-2	1rd	....	1rd	....	....	....	1	5	.167	1-2	0-2	0-1	0-0	0-0	1-5
1977	....	6	0	0	0-4	1rd/1rd	....	1rd	1rd	....	....	1	6	.143	1-3	0-3	0-0	0-0	0-0	1-6
1978	....	12	0	2	6-2	F	2rd	....	....	....	....	8	12	.400	2-6	5-4	0-1	1-1	1-2	7-10
1979	....	25	0	0	0-4	1rd	1rd	1rd	1rd	....	....	3	25	.107	1-9	1-7	1-5	0-4	1-6	2-19
1980	....	3	0	0	0-0	....	....	....	....	....	....	2	3	.400	0-0	0-1	2-1	0-1	0-1	2-2
TOTALS		**52**	**0**	**2**	**6-12**	....	....	....	....	....		**20**	**52**	**.278**	**5-20**	**11-18**	**3-8**	**1-6**	**2-9**	**18-43**

• MARTIN, Todd

Todd Christopher Martin

Male. Born: July 8, 1970. Hinsdale, IL, United States. Height: 6' 6". Weight: 205 lbs. Plays: right.
Status: Turned Pro 1990. Earnings: $7,773,050. Highest Ranking: 4 (Sept. 1999).

Year	Rk	TP	TW	TF	GS	Aus	Fre	Wim	US	DC	Oly	MW	ML	Pct	CL	GR	HD	CP	IN	OD
1990	269	3	0	0	0-1	....	....	....	1rd	....	....	3	3	.500	0-0	1-1	2-3	0-0	0-0	3-3
1991	133	8	0	0	5-2	....	4rd	....	3rd	....	....	10	8	.556	3-2	3-1	2-3	2-2	2-2	8-6
1992	87	19	0	0	3-2	....	....	2rd	3rd	....	....	22	19	.537	3-3	4-3	12-10	3-3	5-6	17-13
1993	13	24	1	4	6-4	1rd	1rd	QF	3rd	....	....	45	23	.662	10-4	8-2	21-12	6-5	12-8	33-15
1994	10	22	2	3	18-4	F	3rd	SF	SF	3-1	....	53	20	.726	10-4	12-1	22-8	9-7	14-7	39-13
1995	18	26	1	1	11-4	3rd	4rd	4rd	4rd	2-1	....	47	25	.653	7-7	4-2	26-10	10-6	16-7	31-18
1996	12	22	1	2	11-4	3rd	3rd	SF	3rd	4-0	....	55	21	.724	8-5	7-2	31-10	9-4	17-6	38-15
1997	81	7	0	0	1-1	....	....	....	2rd	....	....	13	7	.650	0-0	0-0	7-3	6-4	12-6	1-1
1998	16	23	2	0	5-4	2rd	1rd	4rd	2rd	1-1	....	44	21	.677	7-3	3-2	25-12	9-4	19-8	25-13
1999	7	21	1	2	14-3	QF	....	QF	F	1-3	....	42	20	.677	7-2	5-2	30-13	0-3	7-8	35-12
2000	55	13	0	0	7-4	2rd	1rd	2rd	SF	0-1	1rd	14	13	.519	1-4	2-2	11-7	0-0	0-0	14-13
2001	57	12	0	0	8-4	QF	1rd	4rd	2rd	1-1	....	13	12	.520	2-4	3-1	8-7	0-0	0-1	13-11
2002	47	16	0	0	4-4	3rd	2rd	2rd	1rd	....	....	24	16	.600	3-3	4-2	17-11	0-0	5-3	19-13
TOTALS		**216**	**8**	**12**	**93-41**	....	....	....	....	**11-8**	....	**385**	**208**	**.649**	**61-41**	**56-21**	**214-109**	**54-38**	**109-62**	**276-146**

• MARTINEZ, Conchita   Conchita Martinez

Female. Born: Apr. 16, 1972. Monzon, Spain. Height: 5' 7". Weight: 130 lbs. Plays: right.
Status: Turned Pro 1988. Earnings: $10,117,481. Highest Ranking: 2 (Oct. 1995).

Year	Rk	TP	TW	TF	GS	Aus	Fre	Wim	US	FC	Oly	MW	ML	Pct	CL	GR	HD	CP	IN	OD
1988	40	8	1	0	3-2	....	4rd	....	1rd	2-1	....	16	7	.696	6-4	0-0	7-2	3-1	3-1	13-6
1989	7	13	3	0	8-3	2rd	QF	....	4rd	4-1	....	38	10	.792	12-3	0-0	24-5	2-2	6-3	32-7
1990	11	13	3	0	6-2	....	QF	....	3rd	4-0	....	42	10	.808	18-5	0-0	21-3	3-2	3-2	39-8
1991	9	16	3	0	8-2	....	QF	....	QF	4-1	....	40	13	.755	24-3	0-0	12-7	4-3	6-6	34-7
1992	8	20	1	0	8-4	4rd	QF	2rd	1rd	3-2	QF	50	19	.725	24-7	3-2	16-6	7-4	7-4	43-15
1993	4	18	5	0	15-4	4rd	QF	SF	4rd	5-0	....	71	13	.845	25-3	5-1	28-6	13-3	22-6	49-7
1994	3	20	4	0	18-3	QF	SF	W	3rd	4-1	....	57	16	.781	27-6	7-1	20-7	3-3	5-5	52-11
1995	2	16	6	0	20-4	SF	SF	SF	SF	6-0	....	63	10	.863	28-1	5-1	25-5	5-3	5-4	58-6
1996	5	20	2	0	17-4	QF	SF	4rd	SF	4-1	QF	51	18	.739	19-5	4-2	19-7	9-4	10-6	41-12
1997	12	19	0	0	10-4	4rd	4rd	3rd	3rd	....	....	37	19	.661	14-6	2-1	17-8	4-4	4-5	33-14
1998	8	23	2	0	14-4	F	4rd	3rd	4rd	2-4	....	40	21	.656	18-5	2-1	19-10	1-5	3-8	37-13
1999	15	23	1	0	11-4	3rd	QF	3rd	4rd	....	....	38	22	.633	20-6	2-1	14-11	2-4	2-5	36-17
2000	5	24	1	0	14-4	SF	F	2rd	3rd	3-3	2rd	51	23	.689	22-6	1-1	24-12	4-4	5-5	46-18
2001	35	16	0	0	7-3	2rd	3rd	QF	....	1-2	....	20	16	.556	11-9	5-2	4-4	0-1	1-3	19-13
2002	34	26	0	1	5-4	2rd	2rd	3rd	2rd	2-2	....	28	26	.519	8-9	2-1	18-15	0-1	5-4	23-22
TOTALS		275	32	1	164-51	....	....	....	....	44-18	....	642	243	.725	276-78	38-14	268-108	60-44	87-67	555-176

• MAURESMO, Amelie   Amelie Mauresmo

Female. Born: July 5, 1979. Saint Germain en Laye, France. Height: 5' 9". Weight: 140 lbs. Plays: right.
Status: Turned Pro 2000. Earnings: $3,164,636. Highest Ranking: 4 (Oct. 2002).

Year	Rk	TP	TW	TF	GS	Aus	Fre	Wim	US	FC	Oly	MW	ML	Pct	CL	GR	HD	CP	IN	OD
1995	290	1	0	0	0-1	....	1rd	....	....	....	....	0	1	.000	0-1	0-0	0-0	0-0	0-0	0-1
1996	159	2	0	0	1-1	....	2rd	....	....	....	....	2	2	.500	1-1	1-1	0-0	0-0	0-0	2-2
1997	109	6	0	0	1-1	....	2rd	....	....	....	....	4	6	.400	3-3	0-0	0-0	1-3	1-3	3-3
1998	29	20	0	0	5-4	3rd	1rd	2rd	3rd	0-2	....	20	20	.500	8-8	1-2	9-7	2-3	4-5	16-15
1999	10	16	1	2	10-3	F	2rd	....	4rd	2-0	....	33	15	.688	7-4	0-0	22-8	4-3	12-4	21-11
2000	16	14	1	2	4-3	2rd	4rd	1rd	....	....	1rd	24	13	.649	13-4	0-1	7-6	4-2	6-4	18-9
2001	9	16	4	1	9-4	4rd	1rd	3rd	QF	4-1	....	46	12	.793	17-4	2-1	22-6	5-1	14-4	32-8
2002	6	17	2	0	17-4	QF	4rd	SF	SF	3-1	....	48	15	.762	9-4	7-2	29-7	3-2	10-5	38-10
TOTALS		92	8	5	47-21	....	....	....	....	9-4	....	177	84	.678	58-29	11-7	89-34	19-14	47-25	130-59

• MAYER, Eugene   Gene Mayer

Male. Born: Apr. 11, 1956. Flushing, NY, United States. Height: 6'. Weight: 150 lbs. Plays: right.
Status: Turned Pro 1973. Earnings: $1,382,422. Highest Ranking: 4 (Dec. 1980).

Year	Rk	TP	TW	TF	GS	Aus	Fre	Wim	US	DC	Oly	MW	ML	Pct	CL	GR	HD	CP	IN	OD
1973	....	1	0	0	0-0	....	....	....	....	....	....	1	1	.500	0-0	0-0	1-1	0-0	0-0	1-1
1975	144	1	0	0	1-1	....	....	....	2rd	....	....	1	1	.500	1-1	0-0	0-0	0-0	0-0	1-1
1976	148	11	0	1	1-2	....	....	1rd	2rd	....	....	6	11	.353	3-6	0-1	0-1	3-3	3-3	3-8
1977	142	11	0	0	2-3	....	1rd	2rd	2rd	....	....	4	11	.267	3-5	1-3	0-2	0-1	0-1	4-10
1978	64	14	1	0	1-3	....	1rd	1rd	2rd	....	....	13	13	.500	6-5	2-2	2-2	3-4	3-4	10-9
1979	12	22	1	2	8-3	....	4rd	4rd	3rd	....	....	52	21	.712	11-4	3-1	26-7	12-9	26-11	26-10
1980	4	20	5	3	4-2	....	....	QF	1rd	....	....	70	15	.824	13-5	4-1	19-4	34-5	39-7	31-8
1981	7	12	4	1	3-1	....	....	....	4rd	....	....	36	8	.818	2-2	0-0	17-3	17-3	26-4	10-4
1982	8	13	1	2	8-2	....	....	QF	QF	3-1	....	40	12	.769	10-2	4-1	17-5	9-4	14-6	26-6
1983	10	13	2	1	2-1	....	....	....	3rd	1-1	....	26	11	.703	1-1	0-0	17-5	8-5	15-7	11-4
1984	18	15	0	2	4-2	....	....	1rd	QF	....	....	24	15	.615	11-4	0-1	5-4	8-6	8-7	16-8
1985	366	1	0	0	0-0	....	....	....	....	....	....	2	1	.667	0-0	0-0	0-0	2-1	2-1	0-0
1986	....	1	0	0	0-0	....	....	....	....	....	....	0	1	.000	0-1	0-0	0-0	0-0	0-0	0-1
TOTALS		135	14	12	34-20	....	....	....	....	4-2	....	275	121	.694	61-36	14-10	104-34	96-41	136-51	139-70

• MAYOTTE, Tim   Tim Mayotte

Male. Born: Aug. 3, 1960. Springfield, MA, United States. Height: 6' 3". Weight: 185 lbs. Plays: right.
Status: Turned Pro 1979. Earnings: $2,663,672. Highest Ranking: 9 (Dec. 1987).

Year	Rk	TP	TW	TF	GS	Aus	Fre	Wim	US	DC	Oly	MW	ML	Pct	CL	GR	HD	CP	IN	OD
1979	422	4	0	0	0-1	....	....	....	1rd	....	....	0	4	.000	0-3	0-0	0-1	0-0	0-0	0-4
1980	171	4	0	0	0-2	1rd	....	....	1rd	....	....	4	4	.500	1-1	0-1	0-1	3-1	3-1	1-3
1981	30	16	0	1	9-3	QF	....	QF	3rd	....	....	32	16	.667	0-0	12-5	15-8	5-3	7-4	25-12
1982	29	22	0	2	8-4	3rd	1rd	SF	2rd	....	....	33	22	.600	0-1	14-5	8-9	11-7	13-8	20-14
1983	16	18	0	0	8-4	SF	1rd	QF	1rd	....	....	23	18	.561	0-2	11-4	5-6	7-6	7-7	16-11
1984	44	20	0	1	6-4	2rd	1rd	4rd	4rd	....	....	23	20	.535	1-2	12-6	6-6	4-6	4-7	19-13
1985	12	20	1	1	8-3	4rd	....	4rd	4rd	....	....	47	19	.712	0-0	13-5	19-5	15-9	15-9	32-10

Year	Rk	TP	TW	TF	GS	Aus	Fre	Wim	US	DC	Oly	MW	ML	Pct	CL	GR	HD	CP	IN	OD
1986	15	17	1	1	4-2	....	....	QF	1rd	1-2	F	27	16	.628	1-1	10-2	7-9	9-4	11-6	16-10
1987	9	20	5	0	3-2	....	....	3rd	2rd	0-2	....	44	15	.746	0-1	6-2	18-8	20-4	29-6	15-9
1988	10	23	4	1	7-3	....	2rd	QF	3rd	....	....	48	19	.716	2-4	4-1	28-8	14-6	22-7	26-12
1989	13	18	1	1	9-3	....	2rd	QF	QF	....	....	30	17	.638	3-4	5-2	15-7	7-4	8-5	22-12
1990	37	19	0	3	0-3	1rd	....	1rd	1rd	....	....	18	19	.486	0-0	1-3	3-9	14-7	14-7	4-12
1991	114	13	0	0	3-2	....	....	4rd	1rd	....	....	12	13	.480	0-0	3-1	7-8	2-4	4-5	8-8
1992	....	1	0	0	0-0	....	....	....	....	....	....	0	1	.000	0-0	0-0	0-0	0-1	0-1	0-0
TOTALS		**215**	**12**	**11**	**65-36**	....	....	....	....	**1-4**	....	**341**	**203**	**.627**	**8-19**	**91-37**	**131-85**	**111-62**	**137-73**	**204-130**

• MCENROE, John   John Patrick McEnroe, Jr.

Male. Born: Feb. 16, 1959. Wiesbaden, Germany. Height: 5' 11". Weight: 170 lbs. Plays: left.
Status: Turned Pro 1977. Earnings: $12,539,622. Highest Ranking: 1 (Mar. 1980). HOF: 1999

Year	Rk	TP	TW	TF	GS	Aus	Fre	Wim	US	DC	Oly	MW	ML	Pct	CL	GR	HD	CP	IN	OD
1977	21	8	0	0	9-3	....	2rd	SF	4rd	....	....	20	8	.714	11-5	5-1	0-0	4-2	4-2	16-6
1978	4	20	5	2	5-2	....	....	1rd	SF	2-0	....	72	15	.828	14-5	5-2	24-5	29-3	42-5	30-10
1979	3	22	10	3	9-1	....	....	4rd	W	8-0	....	87	12	.879	9-1	9-1	21-3	48-7	54-7	33-5
1980	2	24	9	6	15-2	....	3rd	F	W	1-2	....	78	15	.839	12-4	17-1	15-3	34-7	39-7	39-8
1981	1	20	10	1	18-1	....	QF	W	W	7-1	....	74	10	.881	4-2	13-0	28-2	29-6	34-6	40-4
1982	1	14	5	5	11-2	....	....	F	SF	8-0	....	71	9	.888	6-1	11-2	21-3	33-3	41-3	30-6
1983	1	18	7	3	18-3	SF	QF	W	4rd	2-2	....	63	11	.851	8-3	16-2	16-4	23-2	28-2	35-9
1984	1	16	13	1	20-1	....	F	W	W	7-1	....	82	3	.965	12-6	13-0	17-1	36-0	42-1	40-2
1985	2	17	8	2	18-4	QF	SF	QF	F	....	....	71	9	.888	13-3	7-2	25-1	26-3	31-3	40-6
1986	14	8	3	0	0-1	....	....	....	1rd	....	....	22	5	.815	0-0	0-0	15-3	7-2	7-2	15-3
1987	10	12	0	5	4-2	....	1rd	....	QF	1-1	....	34	12	.739	7-3	0-0	12-4	15-5	16-6	18-6
1988	11	12	2	1	5-3	....	4rd	2rd	2rd	1-1	....	30	10	.750	4-3	1-1	15-4	10-2	10-2	20-8
1989	4	14	3	0	10-3	QF	....	SF	2rd	2-0	....	47	11	.810	0-0	5-1	21-5	21-5	25-6	22-5
1990	13	16	1	2	8-3	4rd	....	1rd	SF	....	....	33	15	.688	0-0	3-2	21-7	9-6	14-6	19-9
1991	28	19	1	1	5-3	....	1rd	4rd	3rd	2-0	....	33	18	.647	0-2	5-2	18-10	10-4	16-6	17-12
1992	20	18	0	0	12-4	QF	1rd	SF	4rd	....	....	32	18	.640	2-3	8-2	15-7	7-6	9-7	23-11
1994	....	1	0	0	0-0	....	....	....	....	....	....	0	1	.000	0-0	0-0	0-0	0-1	0-1	0-0
TOTALS		**259**	**77**	**32**	**167-38**	....	....	....	....	**41-8**	....	**849**	**182**	**.823**	**106-37**	**118-19**	**284-62**	**341-64**	**412-72**	**437-110**

Held number one tour ranking 14 times for a total of 170 weeks. Last ranked number one in 1985. Represented the United States in the Davis Cup (1978-1991). Doubles Titles: Wim (5), US (4).

• MCKINLEY, Chuck   Charles Robert McKinley, Jr.

Male. Born: Jan. 5, 1941. St. Louis, MO, United States. Died: Aug. 10, 1986. Height: 5' 8". Weight: 155 lbs. Plays: right.
Status: Amateur. Earnings: –. Highest Ranking: 2 (Dec. 1963). HOF: 1986

Year	Rk	TP	TW	TF	GS	Aus	Fre	Wim	US	DC	Oly	MW	ML	Pct	CL	GR	HD	CP	IN	OD
1957	....	1	0	0	....	....	....	....	2rd	....	....	....	....	....	....	....	....	....	....	....
1958	....	1	0	0	....	....	....	....	2rd	....	....	....	....	....	....	....	....	....	....	....
1960	....	1	0	0	....	....	....	....	QF	1-1	....	....	....	....	....	....	....	....	....	....
1961	5	2	0	1	....	....	....	F	3rd	4-2	....	....	....	....	....	....	....	....	....	....
1962	5	2	0	0	....	....	....	2rd	SF	4-0	....	....	....	....	....	....	....	....	....	....
1963	2	2	1	0	....	....	....	W	SF	6-2	....	....	....	....	....	....	....	....	....	....
1964	5	2	0	0	....	....	....	SF	SF	1-1	....	....	....	....	....	....	....	....	....	....
1965	....	1	0	0	....	....	....	....	4rd	....	....	....	....	....	....	....	....	....	....	....
1966	....	1	0	0	....	....	....	....	4rd	....	....	....	....	....	....	....	....	....	....	....
1967	....	1	0	0	....	....	....	....	1rd	....	....	....	....	....	....	....	....	....	....	....
1968	....	1	0	0	2-1	....	....	....	3rd	....	....	2	1	.667	0-0	2-1	0-0	0-0	0-0	2-1
1969	....	1	0	0	0-1	....	....	....	1rd	....	....	0	1	.000	0-0	0-1	0-0	0-0	0-0	0-1
1973	....	1	0	0	0-0	....	....	....	....	....	....	0	1	.000	0-0	0-0	0-1	0-0	0-0	0-1
TOTALS		**17**	**1**	**1**	**2-2**	....	....	....	**16-6**	....		**2**	**3**	**.400**	**0-0**	**2-2**	**0-1**	**0-0**	**0-0**	**2-3**

Doubles Titles: US (3)

• MCMILLAN, Frew   Frew Donald McMillan

Male. Born: May 20, 1942. Springs, South Africa. Height: 6'. Weight: 155 lbs. Plays: right.
Status: Amateur. Earnings: $609,072. Highest Ranking: –. HOF: 1992

Year	Rk	TP	TW	TF	GS	Aus	Fre	Wim	US	DC	Oly	MW	ML	Pct	CL	GR	HD	CP	IN	OD
1962	....	1	0	0	....	....	....	2rd	....	....	....	....	....	....	....	....	....	....	....	....
1963	....	1	0	0	....	....	....	2rd	....	....	....	....	....	....	....	....	....	....	....	....
1964	....	3	0	0	....	....	1rd	1rd	2rd	....	....	....	....	....	....	....	....	....	....	....
1965	....	2	0	0	....	....	....	2rd	1rd	....	....	....	....	....	....	....	....	....	....	....
1966	....	2	0	0	....	....	....	2rd	2rd	....	....	....	....	....	....	....	....	....	....	....

Year	Rk	TP	TW	TF	GS	Aus	Fre	Wim	US	DC	Oly	MW	ML	Pct	CL	GR	HD	CP	IN	OD
1967	....	2	0	0	....	....	3rd	1rd	....	....	....	....	....	....	....	....	....	....	....	....
1968	....	2	0	0	1-2	....	2rd	1rd	....	1-0	....	1	2	.333	1-1	0-1	0-0	0-0	0-0	1-2
1969	....	2	0	0	1-2	....	2rd	1rd	....	....	....	1	2	.333	1-1	0-1	0-0	0-0	0-0	1-2
1970	....	3	0	1	3-2	....	....	3rd	2rd	....	....	4	3	.571	1-1	3-2	0-0	0-0	0-0	4-3
1971	....	6	0	0	2-4	1rd	3rd	2rd	1rd	....	....	2	6	.250	1-2	1-3	0-0	0-1	0-1	2-5
1972	....	6	0	0	5-3	....	2rd	1rd	QF	....	....	10	6	.625	4-2	4-2	0-1	2-1	2-1	8-5
1973	....	7	0	2	0-3	....	1rd	1rd	1rd	1-0	....	6	7	.462	0-1	4-3	2-2	0-1	1-2	5-5
1974	46	6	1	1	1-2	....	....	1rd	2rd	....	....	3	5	.375	0-1	1-2	2-2	0-0	2-1	1-4
1975	59	4	0	0	1-2	....	....	1rd	2rd	....	....	1	4	.200	1-2	0-1	0-1	0-0	0-1	1-3
1976	86	15	1	1	3-2	....	....	1rd	4rd	....	....	9	14	.391	3-2	0-2	1-3	5-7	6-9	3-5
1977	61	8	0	0	1-2	....	....	2rd	1rd	....	....	5	8	.385	0-1	1-2	4-3	0-2	0-3	5-5
1978	124	14	0	0	2-2	....	....	3rd	1rd	....	....	6	14	.300	0-1	2-1	2-6	2-6	4-9	2-5
1979	....	8	0	0	0-0	....	....	....	....	....	....	4	8	.333	0-0	0-0	4-6	0-2	3-5	1-3
1980	....	4	0	0	0-0	....	....	....	....	....	....	0	4	.000	0-0	0-0	0-3	0-1	0-3	0-1
1981	....	1	0	0	0-0	....	....	....	....	....	....	0	1	.000	0-1	0-0	0-0	0-0	0-0	0-1
TOTALS		**97**	**2**	**5**	**20-26**	....	....	....	....	**2-0**	....	**52**	**84**	**.382**	**12-16**	**16-20**	**15-27**	**9-21**	**18-35**	**34-49**

Doubles Titles: Fre (1), Wim (3), US (1)

• MCNAMARA, Peter

Peter McNamara

Male. Born: July 5, 1955. Melbourne, Australia. Height: 6' 1". Weight: 165 lbs. Plays: right.
Status: Turned Pro 1975. Earnings: $1,046,935. Highest Ranking: 10 (Dec. 1981).

Year	Rk	TP	TW	TF	GS	Aus	Fre	Wim	US	DC	Oly	MW	ML	Pct	CL	GR	HD	CP	IN	OD
1975	205	3	0	0	1-2	2rd	....	1rd	....	....	....	2	3	.400	0-0	2-3	0-0	0-0	0-0	2-3
1976	193	1	0	0	0-1	1rd	....	....	....	....	....	0	1	.000	0-0	0-1	0-0	0-0	0-0	0-1
1977	181	2	0	0	0-21rd/1rd	....	....	....	....	....	....	0	2	.000	0-0	0-2	0-0	0-0	0-0	0-2
1978	65	14	0	0	3-2	3rd	....	2rd	....	....	....	13	14	.481	9-6	3-4	1-3	0-1	1-2	12-12
1979	48	26	1	1	3-3	3rd	1rd	2rd	....	....	....	39	25	.609	30-16	5-4	4-4	0-1	0-2	39-23
1980	29	24	1	1	9-4	SF	4rd	1rd	3rd	3-1	....	38	23	.623	22-11	4-3	5-4	7-5	8-6	30-17
1981	10	17	2	0	12-4	QF	4rd	QF	3rd	3-2	....	46	15	.754	24-6	7-3	6-3	9-3	11-4	35-11
1982	10	24	0	5	4-2	....	QF	1rd	....	1-2	....	42	24	.636	28-14	0-1	2-1	12-8	14-9	28-15
1983	22	5	1	0	0-0	....	....	....	....	....	....	10	4	.714	0-1	0-0	0-1	10-2	10-3	0-1
1984	741	1	0	0	0-1	1rd	....	....	....	....	....	0	1	.000	0-0	0-1	0-0	0-0	0-0	0-1
1985	249	9	0	0	0-3	1rd	1rd	1rd	....	0-2	....	4	9	.308	1-5	1-3	0-0	2-1	2-3	2-6
1986	336	1	0	0	0-0	....	....	....	....	2-0	....	3	1	.750	0-0	0-0	3-1	0-0	1-1	2-1
1987	....	1	0	0	0-1	1rd	....	....	....	....	....	0	1	.000	0-0	0-1	0-0	0-0	0-0	0-1
TOTALS		**128**	**5**	**7**	**32-25**	....	....	....	....	**9-7**	....	**197**	**123**	**.616**	**114-59**	**22-26**	**21-17**	**40-21**	**47-30**	**150-94**

Doubles Titles: Aus (1), Wim (2)

• MECIR, Miroslav

Miroslav "Gattone" Mecir

Male. Born: May 19, 1964. Bojnice, Czech Republic. Height: 6' 3". Weight: 180 lbs. Plays: right.
Status: Turned Pro 1983. Earnings: $2,632,538. Highest Ranking: 6 (Dec. 1987).

Year	Rk	TP	TW	TF	GS	Aus	Fre	Wim	US	DC	Oly	MW	ML	Pct	CL	GR	HD	CP	IN	OD
1983	101	6	0	0	0-1	1rd	....	....	....	1-1	....	12	6	.667	5-2	6-3	0-0	1-1	1-1	11-5
1984	60	19	0	2	1-3	2rd	1rd	2rd	....	....	....	22	19	.537	10-8	4-6	7-4	1-1	8-4	14-15
1985	9	20	2	2	3-3	....	3rd	1rd	2rd	4-2	....	40	18	.690	23-8	0-1	6-4	11-5	13-7	27-11
1986	9	21	1	2	11-3	....	2rd	QF	F	4-2	W	45	20	.692	22-11	6-1	10-2	7-6	11-7	34-13
1987	6	26	6	3	14-4	QF	SF	3rd	QF	3-1	....	74	20	.787	31-7	10-2	19-3	14-8	14-8	60-12
1988	13	15	1	2	7-2	....	....	SF	3rd	3-1	....	38	14	.731	3-2	5-1	20-7	10-4	10-5	28-9
1989	18	18	1	1	10-4	F	1rd	3rd	3rd	1-1	....	20	17	.541	0-8	2-1	14-3	4-5	4-5	16-12
1990	116	8	0	0	4-3	4rd	1rd	2rd	....	2-0	....	11	8	.579	0-1	1-2	3-3	7-2	7-2	4-6
TOTALS		**133**	**11**	**13**	**50-23**	....	....	....	....	**18-8**	....	**262**	**122**	**.682**	**94-47**	**34-17**	**79-26**	**55-32**	**68-39**	**194-83**

• MEDVEDEV, Andrei

Andrei Medvedev

Male. Born: Aug. 31, 1974. Kiev, Ukraine. Height: 6' 4". Weight: 200 lbs. Plays: right.
Status: Turned Pro 1991. Earnings: $6,721,560. Highest Ranking: 6 (Dec. 1993).

Year	Rk	TP	TW	TF	GS	Aus	Fre	Wim	US	DC	Oly	MW	ML	Pct	CL	GR	HD	CP	IN	OD
1990	1007	1	0	0	0-0	....	....	....	....	....	....	0	1	.000	0-0	0-0	0-0	0-1	0-1	0-0
1991	226	7	0	0	0-0	....	....	....	....	....	....	5	7	.417	4-6	0-0	0-0	1-1	1-1	4-6
1992	24	14	3	0	3-1	....	4rd	....	....	....	....	32	11	.744	23-5	0-0	2-1	7-5	9-6	23-5
1993	6	27	3	2	12-4	3rd	SF	2rd	QF	3-0	....	57	24	.704	26-6	6-3	16-6	9-9	10-10	47-14
1994	15	20	2	1	8-3	....	QF	4rd	2rd	....	....	34	18	.654	25-8	3-2	3-4	3-4	3-5	31-13
1995	16	27	1	0	9-4	QF	4rd	2rd	2rd	2-0	....	39	26	.600	17-10	1-2	14-8	7-6	7-6	32-20
1996	36	23	1	1	5-4	2rd	2rd	1rd	4rd	2-0	....	34	22	.607	14-10	0-1	14-7	6-4	6-4	28-18

Year	Rk	TP	TW	TF	GS	Aus	Fre	Wim	US	DC	Oly	MW	ML	Pct	CL	GR	HD	CP	IN	OD
1997	27	25	1	0	8-4	4rd	4rd	3rd	1rd	4-1	....	34	24	.586	19-6	2-2	12-11	1-5	1-6	33-18
1998	62	24	0	1	3-4	2rd	1rd	2rd	2rd	2-2	....	24	24	.500	5-8	2-3	13-9	4-4	6-6	18-18
1999	30	23	0	1	11-4	2rd	F	2rd	4rd	4-0	....	26	23	.531	11-8	1-2	6-7	8-6	9-8	17-15
2000	58	16	0	0	3-3	1rd	4rd	1rd	....	3-0	....	23	16	.590	20-8	1-2	1-5	1-1	1-2	22-14
2001	156	17	0	0	1-3	2rd	1rd	1rd	....	2-1	....	11	17	.393	5-8	0-1	4-6	2-2	2-4	9-13
TOTALS		224	11	6	63-34	....	....	....	....	22-4	....	319	213	.600	169-83	16-18	85-64	49-48	55-59	264-154

• MELVILLE, Kerry see REID, Kerry, page 880

• METREVELI, Alexander Alex Metreveli

Male. Born: Nov. 2, 1944. Tbilisi, Georgia. Height: –. Weight: –. Plays: right.
Status: Amateur. Earnings: –. Highest Ranking: –.

Year	Rk	TP	TW	TF	GS	Aus	Fre	Wim	US	DC	Oly	MW	ML	Pct	CL	GR	HD	CP	IN	OD
1962	....	1	0	0	....	....	....	....	3rd			....	....	....	....	....	....	....	....	....
1963	....	1	0	0	....	....	....	1rd		0-2		....	....	....	....	....	....	....	....	....
1964	....	1	0	0	....	....	....	3rd		1-3		....	....	....	....	....	....	....	....	....
1965	....	2	0	0	....	....	2rd	3rd				....	....	....	....	....	....	....	....	....
1966	....	2	0	0	....	....	QF	2rd				....	....	....	....	....	....	....	....	....
1967	....	1	0	0	....	....	....	1rd		2-3		....	....	....	....	....	....	....	....	....
1968	....	1	0	0	3-1	....	1rd	4rd		6-0	....	3	1	.750	0-0	3-1	0-0	0-0	0-0	3-1
1969	....	3	0	0	1-2	....	1rd	2rd		5-1	....	1	3	.250	0-2	1-1	0-0	0-0	0-0	1-3
1970	....	3	0	0	6-3	....	4rd	2rd	3rd	6-0	....	6	3	.667	3-1	3-2	0-0	0-0	0-0	6-3
1971	....	3	1	0	4-2	....	2rd	4rd		5-1	....	4	2	.667	1-1	3-1	0-0	0-0	0-0	4-2
1972	....	8	4	0	11-3	SF	SF	QF		7-1	....	13	4	.765	6-2	7-2	0-0	0-0	0-0	13-4
1973	34	7	2	1	9-3	QF	F	F		5-1	....	14	5	.737	2-2	12-3	0-0	0-0	0-0	14-5
1974	13	6	1	3	9-3	....	2rd	QF	QF	4-0	....	17	5	.773	4-2	13-3	0-0	0-0	0-0	17-5
1975	47	5	0	0	6-4	QF	2rd	4rd	1rd	1-1	....	8	5	.615	1-2	7-3	0-0	0-0	0-0	8-5
1976	63	13	0	0	3-2	....	....	3rd	2rd	6-0	....	13	13	.500	2-2	3-2	0-1	8-8	8-8	5-5
1977	147	2	0	0	0-0	....	....	....	....		....	1	2	.333	0-0	0-0	1-1	0-1	0-1	1-1
1978	....	1	0	0	0-0	....	....	....	....	2-0	....	1	1	.500	1-1	0-0	0-0	0-0	0-0	1-1
1979	....	0	0	0	0-0	....	....	....	....	2-1	....	0	0	.000	0-0	0-0	0-0	0-0	0-0	0-0
TOTALS		60	8	4	52-23	....	....	....	....	52-14	....	81	44	.648	20-15	52-18	1-2	8-9	8-9	73-35

Represented the USSR in the Davis Cup (1963-1979)

• MIHAI, Florenta Florenta Mihai

Female. Born: Sept. 2, 1955. Romania. Height: –. Weight: –. Plays: –.
Status: Turned Pro 1975. Earnings: –. Highest Ranking: –.

Year	Rk	TP	TW	TF	GS	Aus	Fre	Wim	US	FC	Oly	MW	ML	Pct	CL	GR	HD	CP	IN	OD
1975	....	2	0	0	0-1	....	1rd	....	....	1-1	....	1	2	.333	1-2	0-0	0-0	0-0	0-0	1-2
1976	....	4	0	0	4-3	....	SF	1rd	1rd	2-1	....	4	4	.500	4-2	0-1	0-0	0-1	0-1	4-3
1977	33	9	0	1	7-3	....	F	2rd	3rd	....	....	8	9	.471	7-3	0-1	1-2	0-3	0-3	8-6
1978	....	20	0	0	0-2	....	1rd	1rd	....	0-3	....	6	20	.231	0-4	1-7	1-2	4-7	4-7	2-13
1979	....	4	0	0	1-1	....	....	....	2rd	....	....	1	4	.200	0-0	0-0	1-1	0-3	0-3	1-1
1980	....	5	0	0	0-1	....	....	1rd	....	....	....	1	5	.167	1-1	0-2	0-0	0-2	0-2	1-3
TOTALS		44	0	1	12-11	....	....	....	....	3-5	....	21	44	.323	13-12	1-11	3-5	4-16	4-16	17-28

• MOFFITT, Billie Jean see KING, Billie Jean, page 855

• MOROZOVA, Olga Olga Morozova

Female. Born: Feb. 22, 1949. Moscow, Russian Federation. Height: 5' 7". Weight: 130 lbs. Plays: right.
Status: Amateur. Earnings: –. Highest Ranking: 7 (Nov. 1975).

Year	Rk	TP	TW	TF	GS	Aus	Fre	Wim	US	FC	Oly	MW	ML	Pct	CL	GR	HD	CP	IN	OD
1966	....	1	0	0	....	....	....	1rd	....			....	....	....	....	....	....	....	....	....
1967	....	1	0	0	....	....	1rd	....	....			....	....	....	....	....	....	....	....	....
1968	....	2	0	0	0-2	....	2rd	1rd	....			0	2	.000	0-1	0-1	0-0	0-0	0-0	0-2
1969	....	3	1	0	4-2	....	3rd	4rd	....			4	2	.667	2-1	2-1	0-0	0-0	0-0	4-2
1970	....	9	6	1	4-3	....	2rd	2rd	3rd			4	3	.571	1-1	3-2	0-0	0-0	0-0	4-3
1971	....	6	4	1	3-2	....	2rd	2rd	....			3	2	.600	1-1	2-1	0-0	0-0	0-0	3-2
1972	10	8	4	4	9-4	QF	QF	4rd	QF			9	4	.692	2-1	7-3	0-0	0-0	0-0	9-4
1973	....	5	1	1	6-3	....	2rd	QF	3rd			7	4	.636	2-2	5-2	0-0	0-0	0-0	7-4
1974	8	4	2	2	10-2	....	F	F	....			10	2	.833	5-1	5-1	0-0	0-0	0-0	10-2
1975	7	8	1	0	10-4	QF	SF	QF	2rd			10	7	.588	5-3	5-2	0-1	0-1	0-1	10-6
1976	....	2	0	0	5-2	....	....	QF	3rd			5	2	.714	1-1	4-1	0-0	0-0	0-0	5-2
1977	....	4	0	0	0-0	....	....	....	....			6	4	.600	0-0	0-0	0-0	6-4	6-4	0-0

Year	Rk	TP	TW	TF	GS	Aus	Fre	Wim	US	FC	Oly	MW	ML	Pct	CL	GR	HD	CP	IN	OD
1978	....	1	0	0	0-0	....	....	....	....	4-0	....	4	1	.800	0-0	4-1	0-0	0-0	0-0	4-1
1979	....	2	0	0	0-0	....	....	....	....	2-2	....	2	2	.500	2-2	0-0	0-0	0-0	0-0	2-2
1980	....	1	0	0	0-0	....	....	....	....	2-1	....	2	1	.667	2-1	0-0	0-0	0-0	0-0	2-1
TOTALS		**57**	**19**	**9**	**51-24**	....	....	....	....	**8-3**	....	**66**	**36**	**.647**	**23-15**	**37-15**	**0-1**	**6-5**	**6-5**	**60-31**

Doubles Titles: Fre (1)

• MOYA, Carlos
Carlos Moya Llompart

Male. Born: Aug. 27, 1976. Palma de Mallorca, Spain. Height: 6' 3". Weight: 175 lbs. Plays: right.
Status: Turned Pro 1995. Earnings: $8,376,152. Highest Ranking: 1 (Mar. 1999).

Year	Rk	TP	TW	TF	GS	Aus	Fre	Wim	US	DC	Oly	MW	ML	Pct	CL	GR	HD	CP	IN	OD
1995	63	8	1	0	0-0	....	....	....	....	....	....	11	7	.611	11-7	0-0	0-0	0-0	0-0	11-7
1996	28	29	1	1	2-4	1rd	2rd	1rd	2rd	2-0	....	43	28	.606	36-16	0-2	3-5	4-5	6-7	37-21
1997	7	31	1	5	8-4	F	2rd	2rd	1rd	3-1	....	56	30	.651	27-12	1-2	25-11	3-5	5-8	51-22
1998	5	30	2	2	14-3	2rd	W	2rd	SF	3-3	....	49	28	.636	32-10	2-2	15-11	0-5	3-7	46-21
1999	24	24	0	1	5-4	1rd	4rd	2rd	2rd	1-1	....	38	24	.613	19-10	4-2	15-11	0-1	0-2	38-22
2000	41	21	1	1	3-3	....	1rd	1rd	4rd	....		32	20	.615	16-8	1-2	15-9	0-1	4-3	28-17
2001	19	25	1	1	8-4	QF	2rd	2rd	3rd	1-1	....	35	24	.593	18-8	1-2	12-11	4-3	4-5	31-19
2002	5	25	4	2	4-3	2rd	3rd	....	2rd	....		59	21	.738	34-7	0-1	22-12	3-1	10-4	49-17
TOTALS		**193**	**11**	**14**	**44-25**	....	....	....	....	**10-6**		**323**	**182**	**.640**	**193-78**	**9-13**	**107-70**	**14-21**	**32-36**	**291-146**

Held number one tour ranking 1 time for a total of 2 weeks. Last ranked number one in 1999.

• MUSTER, Thomas
Thomas "Moo Man" Muster

Male. Born: Oct. 2, 1967. Leibnitz, Austria. Height: 5' 11". Weight: 165 lbs. Plays: left.
Status: Turned Pro 1985. Earnings: $12,224,410. Highest Ranking: 1 (Feb. 1996).

Year	Rk	TP	TW	TF	GS	Aus	Fre	Wim	US	DC	Oly	MW	ML	Pct	CL	GR	HD	CP	IN	OD
1984	309	3	0	0	0-0	....	....	....	....	1-0	....	3	3	.500	1-1	0-0	2-2	0-0	1-1	2-2
1985	98	8	0	0	0-1	....	1rd	....	....	3-0	....	9	8	.529	8-7	0-0	1-1	0-0	1-1	8-7
1986	47	17	1	0	1-2	....	2rd	....	1rd	4-2	....	18	16	.529	17-10	0-0	1-5	0-1	1-4	17-12
1987	56	16	0	0	4-3	....	3rd	1rd	3rd	4-2	....	22	16	.579	13-10	0-1	9-5	0-0	3-2	19-14
1988	16	20	4	2	2-3	1rd	3rd	....	1rd	4-0	....	51	16	.761	43-9	0-0	3-5	5-2	6-3	45-13
1989	21	9	0	1	4-1	SF	....	....	....	2-0	....	19	9	.679	4-2	0-0	11-4	4-3	6-3	13-6
1990	7	21	3	2	10-3	3rd	SF	....	4rd	6-0	....	51	18	.739	37-11	0-0	10-2	4-5	6-5	45-13
1991	35	21	2	0	0-1	....	1rd	....	....	0-1	....	30	19	.612	28-13	0-1	2-3	0-2	0-2	30-17
1992	18	26	3	0	3-3	3rd	2rd	1rd	....	....	1rd	39	23	.629	30-13	0-1	7-5	2-4	2-5	37-18
1993	9	28	7	2	8-4	2rd	4rd	1rd	QF	....	....	77	21	.786	55-10	0-1	18-7	4-3	4-3	73-18
1994	16	28	3	0	10-4	QF	3rd	1rd	QF	4-0	....	58	25	.699	37-9	0-1	18-10	3-5	5-5	53-20
1995	3	30	12	2	12-2	3rd	W	....	4rd	2-2	....	86	18	.827	65-2	0-0	11-6	10-10	12-10	74-8
1996	5	27	7	0	10-3	4rd	4rd	....	QF	3-0	....	68	20	.773	46-3	4-2	15-8	3-7	5-7	63-13
1997	9	26	2	1	7-3	SF	3rd	....	1rd	3-1	....	46	24	.657	9-9	2-2	29-8	6-5	10-8	36-16
1998	25	20	0	1	6-3	1rd	QF	....	3rd	....		32	20	.615	20-11	0-1	11-7	1-1	1-1	31-19
1999	189	11	0	0	0-2	1rd	1rd	....	....	....		5	11	.313	1-6	0-0	4-5	0-0	0-0	5-11
TOTALS		**311**	**44**	**11**	**77-38**	....	....	....	....	**36-8**	....	**614**	**267**	**.697**	**414-126**	**6-10**	**152-83**	**42-48**	**63-60**	**551-207**

Held number one tour ranking 2 times for a total of 6 weeks. Last ranked number one in 1996.

• NAGELSEN, Betsy
Betsy Nagelsen

Female. Born: Oct. 23, 1956. St. Petersburg, FL, United States. Height: 5' 9". Weight: 135 lbs. Plays: right.
Status: Turned Pro 1974. Earnings: $1,013,028. Highest Ranking: 17 (Mar. 1982).

Year	Rk	TP	TW	TF	GS	Aus	Fre	Wim	US	FC	Oly	MW	ML	Pct	CL	GR	HD	CP	IN	OD
1974	....	4	0	1	2-3	....	1rd	3rd	3rd	....	....	2	3	.400	0-1	2-2	0-0	0-0	0-0	2-3
1975	51	2	0	0	1-2	....	2rd	2rd	....	....	....	1	2	.333	1-1	0-1	0-0	0-0	0-0	1-2
1976	53	4	1	0	2-2	....	1rd	1rd	3rd	....	....	2	3	.400	2-1	0-2	0-0	0-0	0-0	2-3
1977	30	7	1	0	0-2	....	....	2rd	1rd	....	....	4	6	.400	2-2	1-2	0-0	1-2	1-2	3-4
1978	87	14	0	0	4-4	F	2rd	2rd	1rd	....	....	8	14	.364	2-3	4-4	1-5	1-2	1-2	7-12
1979	54	10	1	0	0-1	....	....	1rd	....	....	....	3	9	.250	0-1	0-2	1-2	2-4	2-4	1-5
1980	34	18	0	0	1-4	3rd	1rd	3rd	3rd	....	....	8	18	.308	0-1	3-5	3-8	2-4	2-6	6-12
1981	23	16	2	0	3-3	2rd	....	4rd	2rd	....	....	8	14	.364	1-1	6-4	1-3	0-6	0-6	8-8
1982	54	12	0	0	0-2	....	1rd	2rd	....	....	....	7	12	.368	1-3	0-3	1-2	5-4	5-4	2-8
1983	61	18	0	0	2-4	2rd	1rd	3rd	1rd	....	....	10	18	.357	1-4	2-5	1-5	6-4	6-4	4-14
1984	77	12	0	0	1-4	1rd	1rd	2rd	1rd	....	....	5	12	.294	0-3	2-4	3-5	0-0	1-1	4-11
1985	45	12	0	0	1-4	2rd	1rd	1rd	1rd	....	....	6	12	.333	0-1	3-5	2-5	1-1	2-3	4-9
1986	47	13	0	0	3-2	....	....	4rd	2rd	....	....	13	13	.500	0-0	6-3	4-7	3-3	3-3	10-10
1987	61	11	0	0	1-2	2rd	....	....	2rd	....	....	12	11	.522	0-0	4-2	8-6	0-3	0-3	12-8
1988	107	15	0	0	2-2	....	....	1rd	3rd	....	....	9	15	.375	0-0	4-5	5-9	0-1	0-2	9-13

Year	Rk	TP	TW	TF	GS	Aus	Fre	Wim	US	FC	Oly	MW	ML	Pct	CL	GR	HD	CP	IN	OD
1989	45	13	0	0	1-2	....	....	1rd	2rd	....	....	17	13	.567	0-0	6-3	11-9	0-1	2-4	15-9
1990	92	9	0	0	2-2	....	1rd	3rd	....	....	....	7	9	.438	0-1	5-3	2-5	0-0	0-1	7-8
1991	....	1	0	0	0-1	....	....	1rd	....	....	....	0	1	.000	0-0	0-1	0-0	0-0	0-0	0-1
1992	....	5	0	0	0-0	....	....	....	....	....	....	1	5	.167	0-0	1-1	0-2	0-2	0-2	1-3
1993	598	4	0	0	0-0	....	....	....	....	....	....	0	4	.000	0-0	0-0	0-2	0-2	0-3	0-1
1994	....	1	0	0	0-0	....	....	....	....	....	....	0	1	.000	0-0	0-0	0-1	0-0	0-0	0-1
TOTALS		201	5	1	26-46	....	....	....	....	....	....	123	195	.387	10-23	49-57	43-76	21-39	25-50	98-145

Doubles Titles: Aus (2)

• NALBANDIAN, David — David Nalbandian

Male. Born: Jan. 1, 1982. Cordoba, Argentina. Height: 5' 11". Weight: 170 lbs. Plays: right.
Status: Turned Pro 2000. Earnings: $1,151,200. Highest Ranking: 12 (Nov. 2002).

Year	Rk	TP	TW	TF	GS	Aus	Fre	Wim	US	DC	Oly	MW	ML	Pct	CL	GR	HD	CP	IN	OD
2000	248	2	0	0	0-0	....	....	....	....	....	....	0	2	.000	0-1	0-0	0-1	0-0	0-0	0-2
2001	47	9	0	0	2-1	....	....	....	3rd	....	....	17	9	.654	14-6	0-0	2-2	1-1	1-1	16-8
2002	12	26	2	1	9-4	2rd	3rd	F	1rd	0-1	....	36	24	.600	15-11	6-1	9-9	6-3	8-5	28-19
TOTALS		37	2	1	11-5	....	....	....	....	0-1	....	53	35	.602	29-18	6-1	11-12	7-4	9-6	44-29

• NASTASE, Ilie — Ilie Nastase

Male. Born: July 19, 1946. Bucharest, Romania. Height: 6'. Weight: 165 lbs. Plays: right.
Status: Turned Pro 1969. Earnings: $2,076,761. Highest Ranking: 1 (Aug. 1973). HOF: 1991

Year	Rk	TP	TW	TF	GS	Aus	Fre	Wim	US	DC	Oly	MW	ML	Pct	CL	GR	HD	CP	IN	OD
1959	....	0	0	0	....	....	....	....	....	0-2	....	....	....	....	....	....	....	....	....	....
1962	....	0	0	0	....	....	....	....	....	1-3	....	....	....	....	....	....	....	....	....	....
1966	....	2	0	0	....	....	3rd	1rd	....	....	....	....	....	....	....	....	....	....	....	....
1967	....	2	0	0	....	....	3rd	1rd	....	....	....	....	....	....	....	....	....	....	....	....
1968	....	2	1	0	1-1	....	2rd	....	....	....	....	1	1	.500	1-1	0-0	0-0	0-0	0-0	1-1
1969	....	7	0	0	5-3	....	1rd	3rd	4rd	....	....	7	7	.500	2-2	5-2	0-2	0-1	0-1	7-6
1970	5	5	2	2	7-2	....	QF	4rd	....	....	....	11	3	.786	8-2	3-1	0-0	0-0	0-0	11-3
1971	7	11	7	5	9-3	....	F	2rd	3rd	....	....	20	4	.833	12-2	3-2	0-0	5-1	5-1	15-4
1972	3	18	11	4	13-2	....	1rd	F	W	....	....	33	7	.825	11-4	13-1	4-2	5-1	8-1	25-6
1973	1	21	15	3	11-2	....	W	4rd	2rd	....	....	37	6	.860	13-0	9-2	11-3	4-1	5-2	32-4
1974	10	14	6	5	9-3	....	QF	4rd	3rd	....	....	23	8	.742	13-3	10-4	0-0	0-1	0-1	23-7
1975	7	13	5	4	7-3	....	3rd	2rd	QF	....	....	25	8	.758	17-5	1-1	7-2	0-0	7-2	18-6
1976	4	18	6	7	10-2	....	....	F	SF	....	....	56	12	.824	8-3	11-1	7-1	30-7	30-7	26-5
1977	9	10	2	2	9-3	....	QF	QF	2rd	....	....	18	8	.692	8-3	6-2	0-0	4-3	4-3	14-5
1978	16	16	2	3	4-1	....	....	QF	....	....	....	27	14	.659	11-3	4-2	5-3	7-6	9-7	18-7
1979	50	20	0	1	1-2	....	1rd	....	2rd	....	....	24	20	.545	6-5	0-0	9-6	9-9	9-9	15-11
1980	79	17	0	0	3-2	....	....	3rd	2rd	....	....	18	17	.514	4-3	2-1	7-6	5-7	5-7	13-10
1981	73	26	0	2	2-4	1rd	3rd	1rd	1rd	....	....	22	26	.458	3-8	1-4	10-8	8-6	12-9	10-17
1982	118	26	0	0	4-3	....	2rd	1rd	4rd	....	....	16	26	.381	7-10	0-2	6-8	3-6	5-10	11-16
1983	169	13	0	0	2-2	....	3rd	....	1rd	....	....	8	13	.381	4-6	1-3	3-4	0-0	2-1	6-13
1984	202	14	0	0	0-2	....	1rd	1rd	1rd	....	....	4	14	.222	0-6	0-0	3-5	1-3	3-6	1-8
1985	430	4	0	0	0-1	....	....	....	1rd	....	....	1	4	.200	0-2	0-0	1-2	0-0	1-1	0-3
TOTALS		259	57	38	97-41	....	....	....	....	1-5	....	351	198	.639	128-68	69-28	73-52	81-52	105-68	246-132

Held number one tour ranking 1 time for a total of 40 weeks. Last ranked number one in 1974. Doubles Titles: Fre (1), Wim (1), US (1).

• NAVRATILOVA, Martina — Martina Navratilova

Female. Born: Oct. 18, 1956. Prague, Czech Republic. Height: 5' 7". Weight: 140 lbs. Plays: left.
Status: Turned Pro 1975. Earnings: $20,527,874. Highest Ranking: 1 (July 1978). HOF: 2000

Year	Rk	TP	TW	TF	GS	Aus	Fre	Wim	US	FC	Oly	MW	ML	Pct	CL	GR	HD	CP	IN	OD
1973	....	16	0	0	5-3	....	QF	3rd	1rd	....	....	23	16	.590	12-7	2-2	2-1	7-6	7-6	16-10
1974	....	19	1	0	5-3	....	QF	1rd	3rd	....	....	32	18	.640	11-3	8-4	1-2	12-9	13-10	19-8
1975	4	24	4	9	17-4	F	F	QF	SF	5-0	....	88	20	.815	25-5	9-3	16-4	38-8	43-8	45-12
1976	4	17	2	1	5-2	....	....	SF	1rd	....	....	41	15	.732	1-3	14-2	4-2	22-8	22-8	19-7
1977	3	22	6	4	9-2	....	....	QF	SF	....	....	68	16	.810	12-2	8-1	10-5	38-8	38-8	30-8
1978	1	20	11	0	11-1	....	....	W	SF	....	....	80	9	.899	2-1	13-0	14-3	51-5	51-5	29-4
1979	1	23	10	0	11-1	....	....	W	SF	....	....	89	13	.873	3-1	13-2	23-4	50-6	53-7	36-6
1980	3	24	11	0	11-3	SF	....	SF	4rd	....	....	87	13	.870	9-1	12-4	23-5	43-4	46-5	41-8
1981	3	23	10	0	19-3	W	QF	SF	F	....	....	89	13	.873	11-2	21-4	21-4	36-3	43-5	46-8
1982	1	18	15	0	20-2	F	W	W	QF	5-0	....	90	3	.968	15-0	21-1	22-1	32-1	40-1	50-2
1983	1	17	16	0	23-1	W	4rd	....	....	....	....	86	1	.989	12-1	19-0	27-0	28-0	33-0	53-1
1984	1	15	13	0	25-1	SF	W	W	W	....	....	78	2	.975	16-0	27-1	17-0	18-1	18-1	60-1

Year	Rk	TP	TW	TF	GS	Aus	Fre	Wim	US	FC	Oly	MW	ML	Pct	CL	GR	HD	CP	IN	OD
1985	1	17	12	0	25-2	W	F	W	F	....	....	84	5	.944	14-1	29-0	24-3	17-1	17-1	67-4
1986	1	17	14	0	20-1	....	F	W	W	5-0	....	89	3	.967	15-2	13-0	17-0	44-1	49-1	40-2
1987	2	12	4	0	25-2	F	F	W	W	....	....	56	8	.875	13-3	17-2	20-2	6-1	11-1	45-7
1988	2	16	9	0	18-4	SF	4rd	F	QF	....	....	70	7	.909	17-2	12-1	26-3	15-1	25-1	45-6
1989	2	15	8	0	16-3	QF	....	F	F	5-0	....	73	7	.913	6-2	17-1	30-2	20-2	25-2	48-5
1990	3	13	6	0	10-1	....	....	W	4rd	....	....	52	7	.881	14-3	13-0	12-2	13-2	13-2	39-5
1991	4	14	5	0	10-2	....	....	QF	F	....	....	53	9	.855	6-3	15-1	15-2	17-3	21-4	32-5
1992	5	12	4	0	6-2	....	....	SF	2rd	....	....	38	8	.826	1-1	6-2	14-1	17-4	22-4	16-4
1993	3	13	5	0	8-2	....	....	SF	4rd	....	....	46	8	.852	2-1	12-2	15-2	17-3	24-4	22-4
1994	8	15	1	0	6-2	....	1rd	F	....	....	....	33	14	.702	7-5	8-2	8-2	10-5	17-6	16-8
2002	....	1	0	0	0-0	....	....	....	....	....	....	1	1	.500	0-0	1-1	0-0	0-0	0-0	1-1
TOTALS		**383**	**167**	**14**	**305-47**	....	....	....	....	**20-0**		**1446**	**216**	**.870**	**224-49**	**310-36**	**361-50**	**551-82**	**631-90**	**815-126**

Held number one tour ranking 9 times for a total of 331 weeks. Last ranked number one in 1987. Represented the United States in the Federation Cup (1982-1989). Doubles Titles: Aus (8), Fre (7), Wim (7), US (9).

• NEWCOMBE, John   John David Newcombe

Male. Born: May 23, 1944. Sydney, Australia. Height: 6'. Weight: 170 lbs. Plays: right.
Status: Turned Pro 1967. Earnings: $1,062,408. Highest Ranking: 1 (Dec. 1967). HOF: 1986

Year	Rk	TP	TW	TF	GS	Aus	Fre	Wim	US	DC	Oly	MW	ML	Pct	CL	GR	HD	CP	IN	OD
1960	....	1	0	0	....	3rd	....	....	....	....	....	....	....	....	....	....	....	....	....	....
1961	....	2	0	0	....	....	3rd	1rd	....	....	....	....	....	....	....	....	....	....	....	....
1962	....	3	0	0	....	QF	4rd	2rd	....	....	....	....	....	....	....	....	....	....	....	....
1963	....	4	0	0	....	QF	2rd	1rd	4rd	0-2	....	....	....	....	....	....	....	....	....	....
1964	....	4	0	0	....	QF	2rd	1rd	3rd	3-0	....	....	....	....	....	....	....	....	....	....
1965	8	3	0	0	....	SF	QF	4rd	....	....	....	....	....	....	....	....	....	....	....	....
1966	6	3	0	1	....	....	3rd	3rd	F	....	....	....	....	....	....	....	....	....	....	....
1967	1	4	1	0	....	SF	4rd	W	1rd	1-1	....	....	....	....	....	....	....	....	....	....
1968	6	3	1	0	7-2	....	....	4rd	QF	....	....	7	2	.778	0-0	7-2	0-0	0-0	0-0	7-2
1969	3	7	2	5	18-4	QF	QF	F	SF	....	....	25	5	.833	10-1	14-3	0-0	1-1	1-1	24-4
1970	1	5	3	6	13-2	QF	....	W	SF	....	....	13	2	.867	0-0	13-2	0-0	0-0	0-0	13-2
1971	1	10	6	1	8-2	3rd	....	W	1rd	....	....	15	4	.789	2-1	8-2	0-0	5-1	5-1	10-3
1972	6	10	7	0	4-2	QF	....	....	3rd	....	....	9	3	.750	0-0	4-2	5-1	0-1	0-1	9-2
1973	2	10	3	5	12-1	W	1rd	....	W	5-2	....	21	7	.750	1-3	15-1	1-1	4-2	4-2	17-5
1974	2	16	9	1	12-3	QF	....	QF	SF	....	....	22	7	.759	0-0	16-6	3-1	3-1	3-1	19-7
1975	20	2	1	0	5-1	W	....	....	....	3-0	....	6	1	.857	0-0	5-1	1-1	0-0	0-0	6-1
1976	21	9	0	1	7-3	F	1rd	3rd	....	4-2	....	18	9	.667	4-2	7-2	4-2	3-3	3-3	15-6
1977	119	2	0	0	3-1	/QF	....	....	....	....	....	3	2	.600	0-0	3-2	0-0	0-0	0-0	3-2
1978	24	17	0	2	3-1	....	....	4rd	....	....	....	20	17	.541	5-7	5-2	5-4	5-4	7-5	13-12
1979	....	3	0	0	0-0	....	....	....	....	....	....	4	3	.571	0-0	0-0	4-3	0-0	2-1	2-2
1980	....	2	0	0	0-0	....	....	....	....	....	....	0	2	.000	0-0	0-0	0-2	0-0	0-1	0-1
1981	....	1	0	0	0-0	....	....	....	....	....	....	0	1	.000	0-0	0-0	0-1	0-0	0-0	0-1
TOTALS		**121**	**33**	**22**	**92-22**	....	....	....	....	**16-7**		**163**	**65**	**.715**	**22-14**	**97-25**	**23-16**	**21-13**	**25-16**	**138-50**

Held number one world ranking 1 time during amateur era and 3 times during open era. Last ranked number one in 1974. Held number one world ranking 1 time during amateur era. Doubles Titles: Aus (5), Fre (3), Wim (6), US (3).

• NIESSEN, Helga   Helga Masthoff-Niessen

Female. Born: Nov. 11, 1941. Germany. Height: –. Weight: –. Plays: –.
Status: Amateur. Earnings: –. Highest Ranking: 5 (Dec. 1970).

Year	Rk	TP	TW	TF	GS	Aus	Fre	Wim	US	FC	Oly	MW	ML	Pct	CL	GR	HD	CP	IN	OD
1963	....	2	0	0	....	....	....	2rd	2rd	....	....	....	....	....	....	....	....	....	....	....
1964	....	1	0	0	....	....	....	3rd	....	....	....	....	....	....	....	....	....	....	....	....
1965	....	3	0	0	....	2rd	1rd	2rd	....	0-1	....	....	....	....	....	....	....	....	....	....
1966	....	1	0	0	....	....	....	1rd	....	3-1	....	....	....	....	....	....	....	....	....	....
1967	....	0	0	0	....	....	....	....	....	2-1	....	....	....	....	....	....	....	....	....	....
1968	....	1	0	0	1-1	....	....	2rd	....	....	....	1	1	.500	0-0	1-1	0-0	0-0	0-0	1-1
1969	....	1	0	0	0-0	....	....	....	....	2-0	....	2	1	.667	2-1	0-0	0-0	0-0	0-0	2-1
1970	....	3	0	0	8-2	....	F	QF	....	3-1	....	11	3	.786	8-2	3-1	0-0	0-0	0-0	11-3
1971	....	2	0	1	1-1	....	1rd	3rd	....	....	....	1	1	.500	0-0	1-1	0-0	0-0	0-0	1-1
1972	....	4	0	1	3-2	....	SF	2rd	....	2-1	....	5	3	.625	3-1	2-2	0-0	0-0	0-0	5-3
1973	....	5	0	1	7-2	....	QF	....	SF	2-1	....	10	4	.714	5-3	4-1	1-1	0-0	0-0	10-4
1974	....	4	1	0	7-2	....	SF	QF	....	4-0	....	12	3	.800	9-2	3-1	0-0	0-0	0-0	12-3
1975	....	3	0	0	1-1	....	2rd	....	....	1-2	....	2	3	.400	2-3	0-0	0-0	0-0	0-0	2-3
1976	....	3	0	0	5-2	QF	QF	....	....	2-1	....	7	3	.700	3-1	2-1	0-0	2-1	2-1	5-2
1977	....	3	0	0	3-2	....	3rd	2rd	....	2-1	....	5	3	.625	2-1	3-2	0-0	0-0	0-0	5-3

Year	Rk	TP	TW	TF	GS	Aus	Fre	Wim	US	FC	Oly	MW	ML	Pct	CL	GR	HD	CP	IN	OD
1978	....	2	0	0	3-1	....	QF	....	....	....	....	4	2	.667	4-2	0-0	0-0	0-0	0-0	4-2
1979	....	1	0	0	0-0	....	....	....	....	....	....	0	1	.000	0-1	0-0	0-0	0-0	0-0	0-1
TOTALS		**39**	**1**	**3**	**39-16**	....	....	....	....	**23-10**	....	**60**	**28**	**.682**	**38-17**	**19-10**	**1-1**	**2-1**	**2-1**	**58-27**

• NOAH, Yannick   Yannick Simone Camille Noah

Male. Born: May 18, 1960. Sedan, France. Height: 6' 4". Weight: 190 lbs. Plays: right.
Status: Turned Pro 1977. Earnings: $3,440,390. Highest Ranking: 3 (July 1986).

Year	Rk	TP	TW	TF	GS	Aus	Fre	Wim	US	DC	Oly	MW	ML	Pct	CL	GR	HD	CP	IN	OD
1977	305	1	0	0	0-1	....	1rd	....	....	....	....	0	1	.000	0-1	0-0	0-0	0-0	0-0	0-1
1978	49	15	2	1	3-4	1rd	3rd	2rd	1rd	1-1	....	21	13	.618	17-6	1-3	0-2	3-2	3-3	18-10
1979	25	17	3	0	6-3	....	2rd	3rd	4rd	5-1	....	34	14	.708	16-4	2-2	13-5	3-3	6-5	28-9
1980	23	16	0	1	6-3	1rd	4rd	....	4rd	1-1	....	29	16	.644	14-5	1-2	11-5	3-4	7-5	22-11
1981	12	21	2	1	7-3	....	QF	1rd	4rd	1-1	....	52	19	.732	22-6	1-2	10-6	19-5	26-8	26-11
1982	9	20	4	1	7-2	....	QF	....	4rd	6-2	....	57	16	.781	36-11	0-0	19-1	2-4	13-5	44-11
1983	5	16	3	1	11-1	....	W	....	QF	3-1	....	39	13	.750	23-5	1-1	9-4	6-3	6-4	33-9
1984	10	10	0	1	4-1	....	QF	....	....	2-0	....	25	10	.714	11-4	2-1	9-3	3-2	5-3	20-7
1985	7	23	3	2	9-3	....	4rd	3rd	QF	1-3	....	51	20	.718	20-4	2-1	21-9	8-6	19-10	32-10
1986	4	15	2	3	5-1	....	4rd	....	3rd	....	....	43	13	.768	17-2	0-0	15-5	11-6	15-7	28-6
1987	8	14	2	1	8-3	QF	QF	2rd	....	....	....	34	12	.739	9-5	4-3	13-2	8-2	13-2	21-10
1988	12	12	1	0	7-3	4rd	4rd	....	2rd	4-1	....	36	11	.766	16-6	0-0	9-3	11-2	13-2	23-9
1989	16	17	0	1	4-3	1rd	1rd	....	QF	1-3	....	22	17	.564	0-2	0-0	16-8	6-7	6-7	16-10
1990	40	23	1	0	8-4	SF	3rd	1rd	2rd	1-1	....	22	22	.500	3-6	1-3	15-7	3-6	6-8	16-14
1991	190	7	0	0	0-0	....	....	....	....	....	....	7	7	.500	6-4	0-0	0-1	1-2	1-3	6-4
1995	557	3	0	0	0-0	....	....	....	....	....	....	1	3	.250	0-1	0-0	1-1	0-1	1-2	0-1
1996	1294	1	0	0	0-0	....	....	....	....	....	....	0	1	.000	0-0	0-0	0-1	0-0	0-1	0-0
TOTALS		**231**	**23**	**13**	**85-35**	....	....	....	....	**26-15**	....	**473**	**208**	**.695**	**210-72**	**15-18**	**161-63**	**87-55**	**140-75**	**333-133**

• NORMAN, Magnus   Magnus Norman

Male. Born: May 30, 1976. Filipstad, Sweden. Height: 6' 2". Weight: 200 lbs. Plays: right.
Status: Turned Pro 1995. Earnings: $4,381,587. Highest Ranking: 2 (June 2000).

Year	Rk	TP	TW	TF	GS	Aus	Fre	Wim	US	DC	Oly	MW	ML	Pct	CL	GR	HD	CP	IN	OD
1992	679	1	0	0	0-0	....	....	....	....	....	....	0	1	.000	0-0	0-0	0-0	0-1	0-1	0-0
1995	174	2	0	0	0-0	....	....	....	....	....	....	3	2	.600	3-2	0-0	0-0	0-0	0-0	3-2
1996	86	10	0	0	1-2	1rd	2rd	....	....	....	....	13	10	.565	7-4	0-0	6-6	0-0	3-1	10-9
1997	22	27	1	1	7-4	1rd	QF	3rd	2rd	....	....	42	26	.618	20-7	2-2	9-10	11-7	14-10	28-16
1998	52	32	1	1	2-4	1rd	2rd	1rd	2rd	2-2	....	28	31	.475	17-13	2-2	5-11	4-5	7-9	21-22
1999	15	27	5	0	6-4	2rd	1rd	3rd	4rd	1-1	....	44	22	.667	20-8	2-3	22-10	0-1	4-4	40-18
2000	4	30	5	1	15-4	SF	F	2rd	4rd	2-0	3rd	67	25	.728	27-7	1-1	37-14	2-3	6-8	61-17
2001	49	22	0	3	3-2	4rd	1rd	....	....	2-2	....	25	22	.532	5-9	0-0	19-12	1-1	3-3	22-19
2002	107	19	0	1	0-2	....	1rd	....	1rd	....	....	12	19	.387	5-9	0-0	7-10	0-0	1-2	11-17
TOTALS		**170**	**12**	**7**	**34-22**	....	....	....	....	**7-5**	....	**234**	**158**	**.597**	**104-59**	**7-8**	**105-73**	**18-18**	**38-38**	**196-120**

• NOVACEK, Karel   Karel Novacek

Male. Born: Mar. 30, 1965. Prostejov, Czech Republic. Height: 6' 3". Weight: 180 lbs. Plays: right.
Status: Turned Pro 1984. Earnings: $3,732,203. Highest Ranking: 8 (Dec. 1991).

Year	Rk	TP	TW	TF	GS	Aus	Fre	Wim	US	DC	Oly	MW	ML	Pct	CL	GR	HD	CP	IN	OD
1984	156	6	0	0	2-1	....	3rd	....	....	....	....	6	6	.500	6-4	0-0	0-2	0-0	0-2	6-4
1985	159	4	0	0	0-1	....	1rd	....	....	....	....	4	4	.500	4-3	0-0	0-1	0-0	0-0	4-4
1986	33	15	1	1	0-3	....	1rd	1rd	1rd	....	....	16	14	.533	7-7	0-1	8-5	1-1	9-5	7-9
1987	76	23	0	1	4-3	....	QF	1rd	1rd	2-1	....	19	23	.452	16-11	0-1	1-6	2-5	2-7	17-16
1988	127	13	0	0	1-2	....	1rd	2rd	....	....	....	13	13	.500	12-8	1-1	0-1	0-3	0-3	13-10
1989	74	16	1	0	3-2	....	3rd	2rd	....	0-2	....	16	15	.516	15-11	1-1	0-0	0-3	0-3	16-12
1990	34	31	1	1	7-4	3rd	4rd	3rd	1rd	0-1	....	31	30	.508	18-11	2-2	8-10	3-7	4-8	27-22
1991	8	35	4	1	5-4	1rd	1rd	4rd	3rd	2-2	....	57	31	.648	33-10	3-1	8-5	13-15	15-16	42-15
1992	23	29	3	0	1-3	2rd	1rd	1rd	....	2-2	....	42	26	.618	30-11	0-1	2-7	10-7	10-8	32-18
1993	17	27	2	3	6-3	....	QF	1rd	3rd	2-2	....	43	25	.632	21-14	0-3	10-2	12-6	12-6	31-19
1994	28	33	1	0	7-4	3rd	1rd	1rd	SF	1-1	....	37	32	.536	18-15	3-2	12-9	4-6	4-6	33-26
1995	125	24	0	0	3-4	4rd	1rd	1rd	1rd	....	....	13	24	.351	7-11	0-1	4-7	2-5	2-5	11-19
1996	409	3	0	0	0-0	....	....	....	....	....	....	1	3	.250	0-1	0-0	1-2	0-0	0-0	1-3
TOTALS		**259**	**13**	**7**	**39-34**	....	....	....	....	**9-11**	....	**298**	**246**	**.548**	**187-117**	**10-14**	**54-57**	**47-58**	**58-69**	**240-177**

• NOVAK, Jiri   Jiri Novak

Male. Born: Mar. 22, 1975. Zlin, Czech Republic. Height: 6' 3". Weight: 190 lbs. Plays: right.
Status: Turned Pro 1993. Earnings: $5,133,004. Highest Ranking: 5 (Oct. 2002).

Year	Rk	TP	TW	TF	GS	Aus	Fre	Wim	US	DC	Oly	MW	ML	Pct	CL	GR	HD	CP	IN	OD
1993	280	1	0	0	0-0	....	....	....	....	....	....	1	1	.500	1-1	0-0	0-0	0-0	0-0	1-1
1994	218	1	0	0	0-0	....	....	....	....	....	....	0	1	.000	0-1	0-0	0-0	0-0	0-0	0-1
1995	55	9	0	0	0-1	....	....	....	1rd	....	....	5	9	.357	4-7	0-0	0-1	1-1	1-1	4-8
1996	52	25	1	1	3-4	1rd	2rd	2rd	2rd	1-0	1rd	31	24	.564	13-10	1-1	13-9	4-4	9-6	22-18
1997	48	20	0	0	2-3	2rd	....	1rd	2rd	1-1	....	21	20	.512	1-4	0-1	16-12	4-3	5-6	16-14
1998	74	22	1	0	0-3	....	1rd	1rd	1rd	....	....	20	21	.488	15-11	0-1	4-7	1-2	3-4	17-17
1999	41	25	0	0	7-4	3rd	2rd	2rd	4rd	1-0	....	29	25	.537	10-9	2-1	15-11	2-4	7-6	22-19
2000	53	26	0	0	3-4	2rd	1rd	1rd	3rd	3-1	1rd	27	26	.509	10-7	0-1	14-12	3-6	5-8	22-18
2001	29	21	2	0	5-3	....	3rd	2rd	3rd	1-2	....	29	19	.604	15-4	1-1	7-9	6-5	9-9	20-10
2002	7	26	0	2	11-4	SF	3rd	2rd	4rd	3-0	....	53	26	.671	15-7	1-2	33-14	4-3	15-8	38-18
TOTALS		**176**	**4**	**3**	**31-26**	....	....	....	....	**10-4**		**216**	**172**	**.557**	**84-61**	**5-8**	**102-75**	**25-28**	**54-48**	**162-124**

• NOVOTNA, Jana   Jana Novotna

Female. Born: Oct. 2, 1968. Brno, Czech Republic. Height: 5' 9". Weight: 140 lbs. Plays: right.
Status: Turned Pro 1987. Earnings: $11,249,134. Highest Ranking: 2 (July 1997).

Year	Rk	TP	TW	TF	GS	Aus	Fre	Wim	US	FC	Oly	MW	ML	Pct	CL	GR	HD	CP	IN	OD
1986	172	4	0	0	0-2	....	1rd	1rd	....	....	....	0	4	.000	0-2	0-1	0-0	0-1	0-1	0-3
1987	49	17	0	0	8-3	....	3rd	4rd	4rd	....	....	21	17	.553	8-6	3-2	7-6	3-3	4-4	17-13
1988	45	20	1	0	1-4	1rd	1rd	2rd	1rd	....	2rd	24	19	.558	4-6	8-3	11-8	1-2	6-5	18-14
1989	11	18	1	0	10-4	3rd	QF	4rd	2rd	3-1	....	48	17	.738	18-3	3-1	20-9	7-4	7-4	41-13
1990	13	17	1	0	15-4	3rd	SF	QF	QF	3-0	....	43	16	.729	6-2	8-2	26-10	3-2	5-3	38-13
1991	7	18	2	0	14-4	F	QF	2rd	4rd	3-1	....	47	16	.746	10-4	4-2	26-6	7-4	14-5	33-11
1992	10	19	0	0	8-4	4rd	4rd	3rd	1rd	2-1	1rd	38	19	.667	11-7	5-2	7-5	15-5	15-5	23-14
1993	6	19	2	0	14-4	2rd	QF	F	4rd	1-2	....	47	17	.734	12-7	6-1	11-5	18-4	21-5	26-12
1994	4	15	3	0	13-4	QF	1rd	QF	SF	....	....	43	12	.782	6-4	4-1	21-5	12-2	17-2	26-10
1995	11	13	1	0	14-4	4rd	3rd	SF	QF	4-1	....	30	12	.714	2-2	5-1	16-5	7-4	9-5	21-7
1996	3	17	4	0	13-3	....	SF	QF	QF	3-0	SFB	54	13	.806	12-2	6-2	20-5	16-4	22-5	32-8
1997	2	19	4	0	12-3	....	3rd	F	QF	2-0	....	54	15	.783	13-4	9-1	16-7	16-3	23-7	31-8
1998	3	20	4	0	16-2	....	QF	W	SF	1-1	....	51	16	.761	16-5	11-1	19-7	5-4	10-7	41-9
1999	....	16	1	0	11-4	3rd	4rd	QF	3rd	....	....	26	15	.634	7-5	4-1	13-7	2-2	6-3	20-12
TOTALS		**232**	**24**	**0**	**149-49**	....	....	....	....	**22-7**		**526**	**208**	**.717**	**125-59**	**76-21**	**213-85**	**112-44**	**159-61**	**367-147**

Doubles Titles: Aus (2), Fre (3), Wim (4), US (3)

• NYSTROM, Joakim   Joakim Nystrom

Male. Born: Feb. 20, 1963. Skelleftea, Sweden. Height: 6' 2". Weight: 155 lbs. Plays: right.
Status: Turned Pro 1980. Earnings: $2,074,947. Highest Ranking: 7 (Dec. 1986).

Year	Rk	TP	TW	TF	GS	Aus	Fre	Wim	US	DC	Oly	MW	ML	Pct	CL	GR	HD	CP	IN	OD
1980	....	1	0	0	0-0	....	....	....	....	....	....	0	1	.000	0-1	0-0	0-0	0-0	0-0	0-1
1981	73	12	0	0	1-3	1rd	1rd	2rd	....	....	....	13	12	.520	10-7	1-3	1-1	1-1	2-2	11-10
1982	167	15	0	0	3-2	....	4rd	1rd	....	0-1	....	10	15	.400	10-8	0-1	0-3	0-3	0-6	10-9
1983	27	17	1	1	8-3	4rd	3rd	....	4rd	0-2	....	27	16	.628	13-9	9-3	5-4	0-0	1-1	26-15
1984	11	24	4	1	7-4	4rd	2rd	2rd	4rd	1-0	....	57	20	.740	30-10	3-2	20-4	4-4	16-5	41-15
1985	11	22	2	1	12-4	4rd	QF	3rd	QF	....	....	50	20	.714	23-6	4-2	14-6	9-6	13-8	37-12
1986	7	22	5	1	6-3	....	1rd	3rd	QF	3-0	....	59	17	.776	22-8	2-1	15-3	20-5	20-5	39-12
1987	16	19	1	0	6-3	....	4rd	3rd	2rd	....	....	34	18	.654	23-10	2-1	4-4	5-3	6-4	28-14
1988	69	15	0	0	4-3	....	3rd	3rd	1rd	....	....	13	15	.464	10-9	2-1	1-4	0-1	0-2	13-13
1989	331	8	0	0	0-1	1rd	....	....	....	....	....	2	8	.200	2-5	0-0	0-2	0-1	0-1	2-7
TOTALS		**155**	**13**	**5**	**47-26**	....	....	....	....	**4-3**		**265**	**142**	**.651**	**143-73**	**23-14**	**60-31**	**39-24**	**58-34**	**207-108**

• OKKER, Tom   Tom Samuel Okker

Male. Born: Feb. 22, 1944. Amsterdam, Netherlands. Height: 5' 9". Weight: 145 lbs. Plays: right.
Status: Amateur. Earnings: $1,257,200. Highest Ranking: 4 (Dec. 1968).

Year	Rk	TP	TW	TF	GS	Aus	Fre	Wim	US	DC	Oly	MW	ML	Pct	CL	GR	HD	CP	IN	OD
1964	....	2	0	0	....	....	....	2rd	1rd	1-3	....	....	....	....	....	....	....	....	....	....
1965	....	3	0	0	....	3rd	2rd	1rd	....	1-1	....	....	....	....	....	....	....	....	....	....
1966	....	3	0	0	....	4rd	4rd	4rd	....	3-1	....	....	....	....	....	....	....	....	....	....
1967	....	2	0	0	....	....	QF	2rd	....	1-1	....	....	....	....	....	....	....	....	....	....
1968	....	4	2	2	9-2	....	....	QF	F	2-0	....	9	2	.818	0-0	9-2	0-0	0-0	0-0	9-2
1969	....	13	8	4	9-3	1rd	SF	QF	1rd	....	....	16	5	.762	9-2	4-2	0-0	3-1	3-1	13-4
1970	....	8	5	1	6-3	QF	....	2rd	4rd	....	....	6	3	.667	0-0	6-3	0-0	0-0	0-0	6-3

Year	Rk	TP	TW	TF	GS	Aus	Fre	Wim	US	DC	Oly	MW	ML	Pct	CL	GR	HD	CP	IN	OD
1971	....	9	2	4	11-3	SF	....	4rd	SF	....	....	21	7	.750	7-2	11-3	0-0	3-2	3-2	18-5
1972	....	6	1	3	2-1	....	....	....	3rd	....	....	11	5	.688	0-0	2-1	9-3	0-1	4-2	7-3
1973	4	14	7	3	7-2	....	QF	....	4rd	1-1	....	24	7	.774	8-2	4-2	8-2	4-1	7-2	17-5
1974	6	7	2	3	6-2	....	....	4rd	4rd	....	....	14	5	.737	0-0	6-2	8-2	0-1	5-2	9-3
1975	11	6	2	3	5-2	....	....	QF	2rd	0-1	....	13	4	.765	1-2	10-1	2-1	0-0	2-1	11-3
1976	23	15	0	0	4-2	....	....	3rd	3rd	....	....	27	15	.643	3-3	5-2	6-3	13-7	17-9	10-6
1977	31	7	1	0	3-1	....	....	4rd	....	....	....	7	6	.538	0-1	3-1	4-2	0-2	4-4	3-2
1978	50	17	0	1	5-3	....	1rd	SF	1rd	1-1	....	20	17	.541	9-8	6-2	3-4	2-3	5-4	15-13
1979	56	19	1	0	4-2	....	....	QF	1rd	1-1	....	20	18	.526	3-5	4-1	11-6	2-6	2-8	18-10
1980	107	13	0	0	2-2	....	....	3rd	1rd	0-2	....	11	13	.458	2-5	2-1	5-4	2-3	5-4	6-9
1981	....	5	0	0	0-1	....	....	1rd	....	....	....	1	5	.167	0-1	0-1	1-3	0-0	1-2	0-3
TOTALS		**153**	**31**	**24**	**73-29**	....	....	....	....	**11-12**	....	**200**	**112**	**.641**	**42-31**	**72-24**	**57-30**	**29-27**	**58-41**	**142-71**

Doubles Titles: Fre (1), US (1)

• OLMEDO, Alex   Alejandro "Chief" Olmedo

Male. Born: Mar. 24, 1936. Arequipa, Peru. Height: 6' 1". Weight: –. Plays: right.
Status: Turned Pro 1960. Earnings: –. Highest Ranking: 2 (Dec. 1959). HOF: 1987

Year	Rk	TP	TW	TF	GS	Aus	Fre	Wim	US	DC	Oly	MW	ML	Pct	CL	GR	HD	CP	IN	OD
1955	....	1	0	0	....	....	....	....	2rd	....	....	....	....	....	....	....	....	....	....	....
1956	....	1	0	0	....	....	....	....	4rd	....	....	....	....	....	....	....	....	....	....	....
1957	....	2	0	0	....	....	....	1rd	1rd	....	....	....	....	....	....	....	....	....	....	....
1958	....	1	0	0	....	....	....	....	QF	4-0	....	....	....	....	....	....	....	....	....	....
1959	2	3	2	1	....	W	....	W	F	1-1	....	....	....	....	....	....	....	....	....	....
1968	....	2	0	0	2-2	....	....	3rd	3rd	....	....	2	2	.500	0-0	2-2	0-0	0-0	0-0	2-2
1969	....	2	0	0	0-2	....	1rd	1rd	....	....	....	0	2	.000	0-1	0-1	0-0	0-0	0-0	0-2
1970	....	1	0	0	1-1	....	....	2rd		....	....	1	1	.500	0-0	1-1	0-0	0-0	0-0	1-1
1971	....	2	0	1	0-1	....	....	1rd		....	....	1	2	.333	0-0	0-1	1-1	0-0	0-0	1-2
1972	....	4	0	1	2-3	....	3rd	2rd	3rd	....	....	3	4	.429	1-2	2-2	0-0	0-0	0-0	3-4
1973	....	1	0	0	0-0	....	....	....	....	....	....	0	1	.000	0-0	0-0	0-1	0-0	0-0	0-1
1974	....	1	0	0	0-0	....	....	....	....	....	....	0	1	.000	0-0	0-0	0-1	0-0	0-0	0-1
1977	....	1	0	0	0-0	....	....	....	....	....	....	1	1	.500	0-0	0-0	0-0	1-1	1-1	0-0
TOTALS		**22**	**2**	**3**	**5-9**	....	....	....	....	**5-1**	....	**8**	**14**	**.364**	**1-3**	**5-7**	**1-3**	**1-1**	**1-1**	**7-13**

Represented the United States in the Davis Cup (1958-1959). Doubles Titles: US (1).

• O'NEIL, Chris   Chris O'Neil

Female. Born: Mar. 19, 1956. Newcastle, Australia. Height: 5' 9". Weight: 135 lbs. Plays: right.
Status: Amateur. Earnings: $56,291. Highest Ranking: 67 (Dec. 1978).

Year	Rk	TP	TW	TF	GS	Aus	Fre	Wim	US	FC	Oly	MW	ML	Pct	CL	GR	HD	CP	IN	OD
1973	....	1	0	0	0-1	1rd	....	....	....	....	....	0	1	.000	0-0	0-1	0-0	0-0	0-0	0-1
1974	....	4	0	0	1-3	1rd	....	3rd	1rd	....	....	1	4	.200	0-0	1-4	0-0	0-0	0-0	1-4
1975	....	2	0	0	1-2	2rd	....	1rd	....	....	....	1	2	.333	0-0	1-2	0-0	0-0	0-0	1-2
1976	....	2	0	0	0-2	1rd	1rd	....	....	....	....	0	2	.000	0-1	0-1	0-0	0-0	0-0	0-2
1977	....	3	0	0	0-3	1rd/	1rd	2rd	....	....	....	0	3	.000	0-1	0-2	0-0	0-0	0-0	0-3
1978	....	7	1	0	5-3	W	1rd	1rd	2rd	....	....	7	6	.538	1-2	6-2	0-2	0-0	0-1	7-5
1979	....	6	0	0	0-3	....	1rd	2rd	2rd	....	....	1	6	.143	0-2	1-3	0-1	0-0	0-0	1-6
1980	....	4	0	0	0-0	....	....	....	....	....	....	2	4	.333	1-1	1-1	0-1	0-1	0-1	2-3
1981	....	5	0	0	0-2	....	2rd	1rd	....	....	....	0	5	.000	0-0	0-3	0-0	0-0	0-0	0-5
1982	....	6	0	0	1-1	2rd	....	....	....	....	....	3	6	.333	1-3	2-2	0-0	0-1	0-1	3-5
1983	....	14	0	0	0-2	....	1rd	1rd	....	....	....	4	14	.222	0-4	2-4	2-6	0-0	0-1	4-13
TOTALS		**54**	**1**	**0**	**8-22**	....	....	....	....	....	....	**19**	**53**	**.264**	**3-16**	**14-25**	**2-10**	**0-2**	**0-4**	**19-49**

• ORANTES, Manolo   Manuel "Manolo" Orantes

Male. Born: Feb. 6, 1949. Granada, Spain. Height: 5' 10". Weight: 165 lbs. Plays: left.
Status: Turned Pro 1969. Earnings: $1,398,303. Highest Ranking: 2 (Aug. 1973).

Year	Rk	TP	TW	TF	GS	Aus	Fre	Wim	US	DC	Oly	MW	ML	Pct	CL	GR	HD	CP	IN	OD
1967	....	0	0	0	....	....	....	....	1-4	....	....	....	....	....	....	....	....	....	....	....
1968	....	2	0	0	3-2	QF	1rd	1rd	....	0-1	....	3	2	.600	0-0	3-2	0-0	0-0	0-0	3-2
1969	....	4	0	0	3-3	....	3rd	1rd	2rd	4-1	....	4	4	.500	3-2	1-2	0-0	0-0	0-0	4-4
1970	....	2	0	2	5-2	....	4rd	3rd	....	7-2	....	5	2	.714	3-1	2-1	0-0	0-0	0-0	5-2
1971	....	4	1	1	3-2	....	1rd	1rd	4rd	5-1	....	4	3	.571	1-1	3-2	0-0	0-0	0-0	4-3
1972	....	11	5	3	11-3	....	SF	SF	3rd	3-1	....	24	6	.800	14-1	7-2	2-1	1-2	1-2	23-4
1973	7	13	4	6	3-2	....	2rd	....	3rd	2-0	....	15	9	.625	7-3	2-1	6-2	0-3	2-4	13-5
1974	11	10	0	5	10-3	....	F	4rd	2rd	3-1	....	18	10	.643	9-4	6-5	3-1	0-0	3-1	15-9

Year	Rk	TP	TW	TF	GS	Aus	Fre	Wim	US	DC	Oly	MW	ML	Pct	CL	GR	HD	CP	IN	OD
1975	5	12	8	5	7-1	....	1rd	....	W	4-2	....	24	4	.857	23-2	0-0	1-2	0-0	1-2	23-2
1976	4	20	7	5	8-2	....	QF	....	QF	0-1	....	56	13	.812	46-9	0-0	5-1	5-3	10-4	46-9
1977	7	12	3	5	4-1	....	....	....	QF	5-3	....	29	9	.763	21-3	0-0	0-0	8-6	8-6	21-3
1978	12	18	3	0	4-2	....	QF	....	1rd	1-1	....	43	15	.741	33-9	0-0	3-2	7-4	7-4	36-11
1979	19	18	1	1	4-2	....	4rd	2rd	....	2-1	....	32	17	.653	28-13	1-1	0-0	3-3	3-3	29-14
1980	58	8	0	1	3-1	....	4rd	....	....	....	....	15	8	.652	15-8	0-0	0-0	0-0	0-0	15-8
1981	45	19	1	0	0-1	....	1rd	....	....	....	....	29	18	.617	29-16	0-0	0-2	0-0	0-1	29-17
1982	41	10	1	0	0-0	....	2rd	....	....	....	....	17	9	.654	17-8	0-0	0-1	0-0	0-1	17-9
1983	74	17	0	1	1-1	....	....	....	....	....	....	17	17	.500	17-16	0-0	0-1	0-0	0-1	17-16
1984	....	5	0	0	0-0	....	....	....	....	....	....	0	5	.000	0-3	0-0	0-0	0-2	0-2	0-3
TOTALS		**185**	**34**	**35**	**69-28**	....	....	....	....	**37-19**	....	**335**	**151**	**.689**	**266-99**	**25-16**	**20-13**	**24-23**	**35-30**	**300-121**

• OSUNA, Rafe   Rafael Herrera Osuna

Male. Born: Sept. 15, 1938. Mexico City, Mexico. Died: June 6, 1969. Height: 5' 10". Weight: –. Plays: right.
Status: Amateur. Earnings: –. Highest Ranking: 1 (Dec. 1963). HOF: 1979

Year	Rk	TP	TW	TF	GS	Aus	Fre	Wim	US	DC	Oly	MW	ML	Pct	CL	GR	HD	CP	IN	OD
1958	....	1	0	0	....	....	1rd	....	....	1-0	....	....	....	....	....	....	....	....	....	....
1960	....	2	0	0	....	....	3rd	3rd	....	1-0	....	....	....	....	....	....	....	....	....	....
1961	....	1	0	0	....	....	....	SF	....	2-2	....	....	....	....	....	....	....	....	....	....
1962	6	2	0	0	....	....	QF	SF	....	5-3	....	....	....	....	....	....	....	....	....	....
1963	1	2	1	0	....	....	3rd	W	....	2-1	....	....	....	....	....	....	....	....	....	....
1964	10	3	0	0	....	....	4rd	QF	SF	2-1	....	....	....	....	....	....	....	....	....	....
1965	....	3	0	0	....	....	3rd	QF	SF	2-2	....	....	....	....	....	....	....	....	....	....
1966	....	1	0	0	....	....	....	....	3rd	2-2	....	....	....	....	....	....	....	....	....	....
1967	....	2	0	0	....	....	....	2rd	4rd	2-2	....	....	....	....	....	....	....	....	....	....
1968	....	0	0	0	0-0	....	....	....	....	2-2	....	0	0	.000	0-0	0-0	0-0	0-0	0-0	0-0
1969	....	0	0	0	0-0	....	....	....	....	4-0	....	0	0	.000	0-0	0-0	0-0	0-0	0-0	0-0
TOTALS		**17**	**1**	**0**	**0-0**	....	....	....	....	**25-15**	....	**0**	**0**	**.000**	**0-0**	**0-0**	**0-0**	**0-0**	**0-0**	**0-0**

Held number one world ranking 1 time during amateur era. Doubles Titles: Wim (2), US (1).

• PANATTA, Adriano   Adriano Panatta

Male. Born: July 9, 1950. Rome, Italy. Height: 6'. Weight: –. Plays: right.
Status: Turned Pro 1969. Earnings: $776,187. Highest Ranking: 4 (Aug. 1976).

Year	Rk	TP	TW	TF	GS	Aus	Fre	Wim	US	DC	Oly	MW	ML	Pct	CL	GR	HD	CP	IN	OD
1969	....	3	0	0	0-2	1rd	1rd	....	....	....	....	0	3	.000	0-2	0-1	0-0	0-0	0-0	0-3
1970	....	2	0	0	3-2	....	4rd	1rd	....	1-1	....	3	2	.600	3-1	0-1	0-0	0-0	0-0	3-2
1971	....	4	1	0	4-2	....	3rd	3rd	....	1-1	....	5	3	.625	3-2	2-1	0-0	0-0	0-0	5-3
1972	....	4	0	2	5-3	....	QF	3rd	1rd	2-2	....	9	4	.692	7-2	2-2	0-0	0-0	0-0	9-4
1973	14	6	1	5	7-2	....	SF	....	3rd	2-0	....	9	5	.643	6-2	2-2	1-1	0-0	0-0	9-5
1974	34	5	1	1	3-2	....	2rd	3rd	....	3-3	....	4	4	.500	1-2	3-2	0-0	0-0	0-0	4-4
1975	14	10	2	3	7-2	....	SF	3rd	....	0-2	....	17	8	.680	9-4	2-1	6-3	0-0	6-3	11-5
1976	7	12	2	1	10-2	....	W	3rd	2rd	10-1	....	35	10	.778	28-6	3-2	2-1	2-1	2-1	33-9
1977	23	13	1	0	7-3	....	QF	2rd	3rd	3-3	....	15	12	.556	10-4	4-4	0-1	1-3	1-3	14-9
1978	23	22	1	2	4-2	....	2rd	....	4rd	0-2	....	41	21	.661	26-12	0-1	5-2	10-6	12-7	29-14
1979	29	18	0	0	6-3	....	3rd	QF	1rd	7-4	....	27	18	.600	16-7	4-2	3-5	4-4	4-4	23-14
1980	34	17	1	2	2-2	....	1rd	3rd	....	4-2	....	29	16	.644	21-7	2-1	0-2	6-6	6-6	23-10
1981	39	14	0	0	3-2	....	2rd	....	3rd	2-1	....	20	14	.588	16-8	0-0	3-3	1-3	1-4	19-10
1982	76	18	0	0	1-1	....	2rd	....	....	1-3	....	12	18	.400	7-12	0-0	5-5	0-1	5-5	7-13
1983	71	7	0	0	0-0	....	....	....	....	0-1	....	2	7	.222	2-5	0-0	0-1	0-1	0-1	2-6
TOTALS		**155**	**10**	**16**	**62-30**	....	....	....	....	**36-26**	....	**228**	**145**	**.611**	**155-76**	**24-20**	**25-24**	**24-25**	**37-34**	**191-111**

• PARKER, Frank   Frank Andrew Parker

Male. Born: Jan. 31, 1916. Milwaukee, WI, United States. Height: 5' 8". Weight: 145 lbs. Plays: right.
Status: Amateur. Earnings: –. Highest Ranking: 1 (Dec. 1948). HOF: 1966

Year	Rk	TP	TW	TF	GS	Aus	Fre	Wim	US	DC	Oly	MW	ML	Pct	CL	GR	HD	CP	IN	OD
1932	....	1	0	0	....	....	....	....	3rd	....	....	....	....	....	....	....	....	....	....	....
1933	....	1	0	0	....	....	....	....	3rd	....	....	....	....	....	....	....	....	....	....	....
1934	....	1	0	0	....	....	....	....	QF	....	....	....	....	....	....	....	....	....	....	....
1935	....	1	0	0	....	....	....	....	4rd	....	....	....	....	....	....	....	....	....	....	....
1936	....	1	0	0	....	....	....	....	SF	....	....	....	....	....	....	....	....	....	....	....
1937	9	2	0	0	....	....	....	SF	SF	3-1	....	....	....	....	....	....	....	....	....	....
1938	....	1	0	0	....	....	....	....	4rd	....	....	....	....	....	....	....	....	....	....	....
1939	5	1	0	0	....	....	....	....	4rd	1-1	....	....	....	....	....	....	....	....	....	....

Year	Rk	TP	TW	TF	GS	Aus	Fre	Wim	US	DC	Oly	MW	ML	Pct	CL	GR	HD	CP	IN	OD
1940	....	1	0	0	....	....	....	....	QF	....	....	....	....	....	....	....	....	....	....	....
1941	....	1	0	0	....	....	....	....	4rd	....	....	....	....	....	....	....	....	....	....	....
1942	....	1	0	1	....	....	....	....	F	....	....	....	....	....	....	....	....	....	....	....
1943	....	1	0	0	....	....	....	....	QF	....	....	....	....	....	....	....	....	....	....	....
1944	....	1	1	0	....	....	....	....	W	....	....	....	....	....	....	....	....	....	....	....
1945	....	1	1	0	....	....	....	....	W	....	....	....	....	....	....	....	....	....	....	....
1946	9	1	0	0	....	....	....	....	QF	6-0	....	....	....	....	....	....	....	....	....	....
1947	3	1	0	1	....	....	....	....	F	....	....	....	....	....	....	....	....	....	....	....
1948	1	3	1	0	....	....	W	4rd	QF	2-0	....	....	....	....	....	....	....	....	....	....
1949	5	3	1	0	....	....	W	QF	SF	....	....	....	....	....	....	....	....	....	....	....
1968	....	1	0	0	0-1	....	....	....	....	....	....	0	1	.000	0-0	0-1	0-0	0-0	0-0	0-1
TOTALS		24	4	2	0-1	....	....	....	....	12-2	....	0	1	.000	0-0	0-1	0-0	0-0	0-0	0-1

Held number one world ranking 1 time during amateur era. Doubles Titles: Fre (1), US (1).

• PARUN, Onny
Onny Parun

Male. Born: Apr. 15, 1947. Wellington, New Zealand. Height: 6' 2". Weight: 170 lbs. Plays: right.
Status: Amateur. Earnings: –. Highest Ranking: –.

Year	Rk	TP	TW	TF	GS	Aus	Fre	Wim	US	DC	Oly	MW	ML	Pct	CL	GR	HD	CP	IN	OD
1967	....	1	0	0	....	....	....	2rd	....	0-2	....	....	....	....	....	....	....	....	....	....
1968	....	2	0	0	2-2	....	1rd	3rd	....	0-2	....	2	2	.500	0-1	2-1	0-0	0-0	0-0	2-2
1969	....	3	0	0	1-3	....	1rd	2rd	1rd	0-2	....	1	3	.250	0-1	1-2	0-0	0-0	0-0	1-3
1970	....	3	0	0	0-2	....	1rd	1rd	2rd	2-2	....	1	3	.250	1-1	0-2	0-0	0-0	0-0	1-3
1971	....	4	0	0	6-3	....	1rd	QF	3rd	4-0	....	6	4	.600	0-1	6-2	0-1	0-0	0-0	6-4
1972	....	8	0	0	6-3	....	2rd	QF	2rd	0-2	....	7	8	.467	1-4	5-2	0-1	1-1	1-2	6-6
1973	40	10	0	2	11-3	F	3rd	....	QF	4-2	....	17	10	.630	3-2	9-3	4-4	1-1	2-2	15-8
1974	21	13	2	2	6-4	3rd	4rd	1rd	2rd	2-0	....	14	11	.560	4-2	6-7	0-1	4-1	4-1	10-10
1975	26	10	0	1	8-3	....	QF	3rd	3rd	2-1	....	20	9	.690	13-5	2-2	2-2	4-1	5-2	15-7
1976	29	19	1	1	3-1	....	....	4rd	1rd	1-2	....	31	18	.633	12-9	3-1	10-1	6-7	6-7	25-11
1977	149	18	0	0	4-4	/1rd	1rd	3rd	3rd	1-2	....	12	18	.400	7-7	3-4	1-2	1-5	1-5	11-13
1978	....	11	0	0	0-2	....	1rd	1rd	....	1-1	....	1	11	.083	0-8	0-1	1-1	0-1	0-1	1-10
1979	....	15	0	0	1-2	....	....	2rd	1rd	3-0	....	3	15	.167	2-6	1-1	0-7	0-1	0-3	3-12
1980	100	19	0	0	3-3	1rd	....	4rd	1rd	2-1	....	15	19	.441	3-7	3-3	8-8	1-1	3-3	12-16
1981	200	13	0	0	0-2	1rd	1rd	....	....	....	....	4	13	.235	0-7	1-4	3-2	0-0	0-1	4-12
1982	....	2	0	0	0-0	....	....	....	....	1-1	....	1	2	.333	0-0	1-1	0-1	0-0	0-0	1-2
TOTALS		151	4	5	51-37	....	....	....	....	23-20	....	135	146	.480	46-61	43-36	31-30	15-19	22-27	113-119

Doubles Titles: Fre (1)

• PAULUS, Barbara
Barbara Paulus

Female. Born: Sept. 1, 1970. Vienna, Austria. Height: 5' 9". Weight: 135 lbs. Plays: right.
Status: Turned Pro 1986. Earnings: $1,294,945. Highest Ranking: 10 (Nov. 1996).

Year	Rk	TP	TW	TF	GS	Aus	Fre	Wim	US	FC	Oly	MW	ML	Pct	CL	GR	HD	CP	IN	OD
1986	187	3	0	0	0-0	....	....	....	....	....	....	4	3	.571	4-3	0-0	0-0	0-0	0-0	4-3
1987	96	10	0	0	2-2	....	3rd	1rd	....	....	....	11	10	.524	11-8	0-1	0-0	0-1	0-1	11-9
1988	25	12	1	0	2-1	....	3rd	....	....	....	3rd	21	11	.656	14-7	0-0	7-3	0-1	1-2	20-9
1989	24	18	0	0	4-2	....	2rd	....	4rd	1-2	....	31	18	.633	19-9	0-0	12-9	0-0	2-2	29-16
1990	15	16	1	0	6-3	4rd	....	1rd	4rd	3-1	....	35	15	.700	9-1	0-2	23-9	3-3	7-4	28-11
1991	25	15	0	0	2-2	2rd	....	....	2rd	1-2	....	17	15	.531	1-1	0-0	10-11	6-3	6-4	11-11
1992	205	8	0	0	0-2	1rd	....	....	1rd	....	2rd	4	8	.333	3-3	0-0	1-5	0-0	0-0	4-8
1994	259	7	0	0	0-0	....	....	....	....	....	....	5	7	.417	0-0	0-0	5-7	0-0	0-0	5-7
1995	108	9	2	0	5-4	4rd	1rd	2rd	2rd	....	....	21	7	.750	9-3	1-1	9-2	2-1	2-1	19-6
1996	23	20	1	0	5-3	2rd	3rd	....	3rd	1-2	....	38	19	.667	23-8	0-0	8-6	7-5	7-6	31-13
1997	24	16	1	0	4-3	....	4rd	2rd	1rd	1-1	....	32	15	.681	18-6	1-1	8-5	5-3	8-4	24-11
1998	45	19	0	0	0-4	1rd	1rd	1rd	1rd	....	....	17	19	.472	10-8	0-1	7-10	0-0	2-2	15-17
TOTALS		153	6	0	30-26	....	....	....	....	7-8	....	236	147	.616	121-57	2-6	90-67	23-17	35-26	201-121

• PECCI, Victor
Victor Pecci

Male. Born: Oct. 15, 1955. Asuncion, Paraguay. Height: 6' 4". Weight: 190 lbs. Plays: right.
Status: Turned Pro 1974. Earnings: $994,408. Highest Ranking: –.

Year	Rk	TP	TW	TF	GS	Aus	Fre	Wim	US	DC	Oly	MW	ML	Pct	CL	GR	HD	CP	IN	OD
1974	55	2	0	0	0-1	....	1rd	....	....	....	....	0	2	.000	0-2	0-0	0-0	0-0	0-0	0-2
1975	55	7	0	0	1-2	....	2rd	1rd	....	....	....	10	7	.588	6-4	1-1	2-1	1-1	3-2	7-5
1976	34	23	2	0	3-3	....	2rd	2rd	2rd	....	....	30	21	.588	19-11	1-1	7-4	3-5	3-6	27-15
1977	39	7	0	1	0-2	....	1rd	....	1rd	....	....	3	7	.300	3-5	0-0	0-1	0-1	0-1	3-6

Year	Rk	TP	TW	TF	GS	Aus	Fre	Wim	US	DC	Oly	MW	ML	Pct	CL	GR	HD	CP	IN	OD
1978	46	22	1	2	4-3	....	4rd	1rd	2rd	....	....	27	21	.563	20-10	1-2	2-4	4-5	5-7	22-14
1979	11	21	3	4	10-3	....	F	3rd	3rd	....	....	53	18	.746	36-9	7-2	8-3	2-4	2-4	51-14
1980	35	21	1	1	5-4	2rd	2rd	3rd	2rd	....	....	37	20	.649	26-13	8-4	1-1	2-2	2-2	35-18
1981	17	21	2	2	5-2	....	SF	1rd	....	....	....	47	19	.712	43-16	0-1	2-1	2-1	4-2	43-17
1982	681	18	0	0	1-1	1rd	2rd	....	....	5-1	....	19	18	.514	15-13	1-2	3-3	0-0	3-2	16-16
1983	55	16	1	0	1-1	....	2rd	....	....	2-1	....	20	15	.571	15-12	0-0	4-3	1-1	4-1	16-14
1984	38	14	0	1	0-1	....	1rd	....	....	1-2	....	18	14	.563	14-10	1-1	2-1	1-2	3-3	15-11
1985	110	21	0	1	0-3	....	1rd	1rd	1rd	3-1	....	15	21	.417	10-12	1-2	2-6	2-1	2-1	13-20
1986	140	8	0	0	0-1	....	1rd	....	....	2-2	....	6	8	.429	6-8	0-0	0-0	0-0	0-0	6-8
1987	....	9	0	0	0-0	....	....	....	....	3-1	....	9	9	.500	6-8	0-0	3-1	0-0	0-0	9-9
1988	....	1	0	0	0-0	....	....	....	....	1-0	....	1	1	.500	1-1	0-0	0-0	0-0	0-0	1-1
1989	....	1	0	0	0-0	....	....	....	....	0-1	....	0	1	.000	0-0	0-0	0-1	0-0	0-0	0-1
1990	....	1	0	0	0-0	....	....	....	....	0-1	....	0	1	.000	0-1	0-0	0-0	0-0	0-0	0-1
TOTALS		213	10	12	30-27	....	....	....	....	17-10	....	295	203	.592	220-135	21-16	36-30	18-23	31-31	264-172

• PERNFORS, Mikael   Mikael Pernfors

Male. Born: July 16, 1963. Malmo, Sweden. Height: 5' 8". Weight: 150 lbs. Plays: right.
Status: Turned Pro 1985. Earnings: $1,363,793. Highest Ranking: 10 (Sept. 1986).

Year	Rk	TP	TW	TF	GS	Aus	Fre	Wim	US	DC	Oly	MW	ML	Pct	CL	GR	HD	CP	IN	OD
1984	434	3	0	0	0-1	....	....	....	1rd	....	....	0	3	.000	0-2	0-0	0-1	0-0	0-0	0-3
1985	165	5	0	0	0-1	....	....	....	1rd	....	....	3	5	.375	3-3	0-0	0-1	0-1	0-1	3-4
1986	12	20	0	1	10-3	....	F	4rd	2rd	2-1	....	37	20	.649	15-9	4-2	10-5	8-4	8-5	29-15
1987	33	17	0	0	3-3	....	1rd	4rd	1rd	0-1	....	21	17	.553	7-7	3-1	8-6	3-3	6-5	15-12
1988	19	14	2	1	2-2	....	1rd	....	3rd	....	....	31	12	.721	3-3	0-0	26-8	2-1	8-4	23-8
1989	48	17	0	0	6-4	3rd	1rd	2rd	4rd	1-1	....	20	17	.541	1-3	1-1	12-8	6-5	7-6	13-11
1990	175	6	0	0	4-2	QF	....	....	1rd	....	....	4	6	.400	0-0	0-0	4-4	0-2	0-3	4-3
1991	239	7	0	0	0-1	....	....	....	1rd	....	....	4	7	.364	3-3	0-0	1-4	0-0	0-0	4-7
1992	237	3	0	0	0-1	....	....	....	1rd	....	....	1	3	.250	0-1	0-0	1-2	0-0	0-0	1-3
1993	32	16	1	0	1-1	....	....	....	2rd	....	....	19	15	.559	5-4	0-0	13-7	1-4	3-5	16-10
1994	....	7	0	0	0-2	1rd	1rd	....	....	....	....	0	7	.000	0-5	0-0	0-2	0-0	0-0	0-7
1995	667	1	0	0	0-0	....	....	....	....	....	....	0	1	.000	0-1	0-0	0-0	0-0	0-0	0-1
1996	1268	1	0	0	0-0	....	....	....	....	....	....	0	1	.000	0-1	0-0	0-0	0-0	0-0	0-1
TOTALS		117	3	2	26-21	....	....	....	....	3-3	....	140	114	.551	37-42	8-4	75-48	20-20	32-29	108-85

• PHILIPPOUSSIS, Mark   Mark Anthony Philippoussis

Male. Born: Nov. 7, 1976. Melbourne, Australia. Height: 6' 4". Weight: 200 lbs. Plays: right.
Status: Turned Pro 1994. Earnings: $5,380,987. Highest Ranking: 8 (Apr. 1999).

Year	Rk	TP	TW	TF	GS	Aus	Fre	Wim	US	DC	Oly	MW	ML	Pct	CL	GR	HD	CP	IN	OD
1994	304	3	0	0	0-1	1rd	....	....	....	....	....	1	3	.250	0-0	0-0	1-3	0-0	0-1	1-2
1995	32	18	0	3	2-2	1rd	....	....	3rd	1-1	....	26	18	.591	4-4	1-2	12-9	9-3	9-3	17-15
1996	30	23	1	0	8-4	4rd	2rd	2rd	4rd	2-0	3rd	34	22	.607	7-5	1-2	25-11	1-4	10-6	24-16
1997	18	24	3	2	5-3	....	4rd	1rd	3rd	2-2	....	48	21	.696	13-4	7-1	20-11	8-5	12-7	36-14
1998	15	21	1	1	12-4	2rd	2rd	QF	F	....	....	33	20	.623	6-5	4-2	18-9	5-4	10-5	23-15
1999	19	19	2	0	7-3	4rd	1rd	QF	....	3-1	....	35	17	.673	7-5	5-2	20-8	3-2	15-7	20-10
2000	23	21	1	2	11-4	4rd	4rd	QF	2rd	1-1	3rd	43	22	.662	4-5	5-2	28-12	6-3	13-4	30-18
2001	106	9	1	0	0-0	....	....	....	....	....	....	10	8	.556	0-0	0-0	9-7	1-1	8-5	2-3
2002	80	14	0	1	5-4	2rd	2rd	4rd	1rd	....	....	14	14	.500	2-5	5-2	7-7	0-0	0-1	14-13
TOTALS		154	9	9	50-25	....	....	....	....	9-5	....	244	145	.627	43-33	28-13	140-77	33-22	77-39	167-106

• PIERCE, Mary   Mary Caroline Pierce

Female. Born: Jan. 15, 1975. Montreal, QUE, Canada. Height: 5' 10". Weight: 150 lbs. Plays: right.
Status: Turned Pro 1989. Earnings: $6,451,861. Highest Ranking: 3 (Jan. 1995).

Year	Rk	TP	TW	TF	GS	Aus	Fre	Wim	US	FC	Oly	MW	ML	Pct	CL	GR	HD	CP	IN	OD
1989	236	3	0	0	0-0	....	....	....	....	....	....	0	3	.000	0-2	0-0	0-1	0-0	0-1	0-2
1990	106	7	0	0	1-1	....	2rd	....	....	....	....	6	7	.462	5-4	0-0	1-1	0-2	0-2	6-5
1991	26	10	1	0	4-2	....	3rd	....	3rd	2-0	....	23	9	.719	7-2	0-0	14-6	2-1	2-1	21-8
1992	13	14	3	0	6-2	....	4rd	....	4rd	2-1	2rd	34	11	.756	13-5	0-0	9-2	12-4	12-4	22-7
1993	12	16	1	1	10-3	QF	4rd	....	4rd	....	....	38	15	.717	13-5	0-0	19-6	6-4	15-6	23-9
1994	5	18	0	5	13-3	4rd	F	....	QF	2-2	....	45	18	.714	18-8	0-0	15-5	12-5	17-7	28-11
1995	5	18	2	2	13-3	W	4rd	2rd	3rd	2-2	....	37	16	.698	9-5	1-1	22-5	5-5	9-7	28-9
1996	20	13	0	1	7-3	2rd	3rd	QF	....	1-1	2rd	19	13	.594	10-5	4-2	4-4	1-2	1-2	18-11
1997	7	17	1	4	15-4	F	4rd	4rd	4rd	2-2	....	46	16	.742	21-4	4-1	16-8	5-3	7-5	39-11
1998	7	16	4	1	8-4	QF	2rd	1rd	4rd	....	....	35	12	.745	7-4	0-1	18-6	10-1	17-3	18-9

Year	Rk	TP	TW	TF	GS	Aus	Fre	Wim	US	FC	Oly	MW	ML	Pct	CL	GR	HD	CP	IN	OD
1999	5	21	1	4	12-4	QF	2rd	4rd	QF	....	....	45	20	.692	11-5	3-1	24-10	7-4	12-6	33-14
2000	7	13	2	0	14-3	4rd	W	2rd	4rd	....	....	29	11	.725	15-3	1-1	13-6	0-1	0-1	29-10
2001	130	8	0	0	2-1	3rd				....	....	6	8	.429	1-3	0-0	5-5	0-0	0-1	6-7
2002	52	13	0	0	6-4	1rd	QF	3rd	1rd	....	....	14	13	.519	11-6	2-2	1-5	0-0	0-0	14-13
TOTALS		**187**	**15**	**18**	**111-37**	....	....	....	....	**11-8**		**377**	**172**	**.687**	**141-61**	**15-9**	**161-70**	**60-32**	**92-46**	**285-126**

Represented France in the Federation Cup (1991-1997). Doubles Titles: Fre (1).

• PIETRANGELI, Nicky   Nicola "Nicky" Pietrangeli

Male. Born: Sept. 11, 1933. Tunis, Italy. Height: 5' 11". Weight: –. Plays: right.
Status: Amateur. Earnings: –. Highest Ranking: 3 (Dec. 1959). HOF: 1986

Year	Rk	TP	TW	TF	GS	Aus	Fre	Wim	US	DC	Oly	MW	ML	Pct	CL	GR	HD	CP	IN	OD
1954	....	2	0	0	....	....	3rd	2rd		1-2	....	....								
1955	....	3	0	0	....	....	3rd	QF	3rd	3-2	....	....								
1956	10	2	0	0	....	....	QF	4rd		8-2	....	....								
1957	9	3	0	0	....	QF	1rd	1rd	....	4-2	....	....								
1958	7	2	0	0	....	....	3rd	4rd	....	7-3	....	....								
1959	3	2	1	0	....	....	W	1rd	....	7-1	....	....								
1960	3	2	1	0	....	....	W	SF		8-3	....	....								
1961	4	2	0	1	....	....	F	3rd	....	7-4	....	....								
1962	....	3	0	0	....	....	QF	3rd	1rd	5-3	....	....								
1963	....	2	0	0	....	....	QF	3rd	....	1-1	....	....								
1964	7	3	0	1	....	....	F	2rd	2rd	4-0	....	....								
1965	....	3	0	0	....	....	4rd	4rd	3rd	6-0	....	....								
1966	....	2	0	0	....	....	3rd	1rd		3-1	....	....								
1967	....	2	0	0	....	....	3rd	2rd		5-1	....	....								
1968	....	1	0	0	0-1	....	2rd	1rd		4-3	....	0	1	.000	0-0	0-1	0-0	0-0	0-0	0-1
1969	....	3	0	0	0-2	....	1rd	1rd		4-2	....	1	3	.250	1-2	0-1	0-0	0-0	0-0	1-3
1970	....	1	0	0	2-1	....	3rd	1rd		....	....	2	1	.667	2-1	0-0	0-0	0-0	0-0	2-1
1971	....	2	0	0	2-1	....	3rd			1-1	....	3	2	.600	3-2	0-0	0-0	0-0	0-0	3-2
1972	....	3	0	0	4-2	....	4rd	3rd		....	....	4	3	.571	2-2	2-1	0-0	0-0	0-0	4-3
1973	....	3	0	0	0-2	....	1rd	1rd		....	....	0	3	.000	0-2	0-1	0-0	0-0	0-0	0-3
TOTALS		**46**	**2**	**2**	**8-9**	....	....	....	....	**78-31**		**10**	**13**	**.435**	**8-9**	**2-4**	**0-0**	**0-0**	**0-0**	**10-13**

Doubles Titles: Fre (1)

• PILIC, Nikki   Nikola Pilic

Male. Born: Aug. 27, 1939. Split, Yugoslavia. Height: 6' 3". Weight: –. Plays: left.
Status: Turned Pro 1967. Earnings: –. Highest Ranking: 7 (Dec. 1967).

Year	Rk	TP	TW	TF	GS	Aus	Fre	Wim	US	DC	Oly	MW	ML	Pct	CL	GR	HD	CP	IN	OD
1960	....	1	0	0	....	....		2rd		....	....	....								
1961	....	2	0	0	....	....	4rd	3rd	....	....	....	....								
1962	....	4	0	0	....	3rd	2rd	2rd	1rd	3-1	....	....								
1963	....	2	0	0	....	....	3rd	1rd	....	2-2	....	....								
1964	....	2	0	0	....	....	4rd	2rd	....	5-0	....	....								
1965	....	2	0	0	....	....	3rd	....	1rd	4-2	....	....								
1966	....	1	0	0	....	....		1rd	....	1-1	....	....								
1967	7	3	0	0	....	....	SF	3rd	3rd	1-0	....	....								
1968	....	2	0	0	3-2	....	....	1rd	4rd		....	3	2	.600	0-0	3-2	0-0	0-0	0-0	3-2
1969	....	6	1	1	3-3	....	2rd	1rd	3rd	....	....	5	5	.500	2-2	2-2	0-0	1-1	1-1	4-4
1970	....	4	1	1	5-3	3rd	....	2rd	4rd	....	....	5	3	.625	0-0	5-3	0-0	0-0	0-0	5-3
1971	....	4	0	1	5-2	2rd	1rd	3rd	4rd	....	....	7	4	.636	1-1	5-2	0-0	1-1	1-1	6-3
1972	....	5	1	1	2-1	....	....	....	3rd	....	....	5	4	.556	0-0	2-1	3-3	0-0	2-1	3-3
1973	15	6	0	1	10-2	....	F	....	QF	....	....	15	6	.714	6-2	4-1	5-3	0-0	2-1	13-5
1974	33	2	0	1	2-1	....	....	3rd	....	4-2	....	2	2	.500	0-1	2-1	0-0	0-0	0-0	2-2
1975	50	5	1	0	2-2	....	3rd	1rd	....	2-1	....	4	4	.500	4-3	0-1	0-0	0-0	0-0	4-4
1976	68	8	0	0	4-2	....	2rd	4rd	....	2-2	....	9	8	.529	4-6	5-2	0-0	0-0	0-0	9-8
1977	91	3	0	0	2-2	....	1rd	3rd	....	3-1	....	3	3	.500	1-2	2-1	0-0	0-0	0-0	3-3
1978	....	7	0	0	1-1	....	2rd	....	....	....	....	2	7	.222	2-7	0-0	0-0	0-0	0-0	2-7
TOTALS		**69**	**4**	**6**	**39-21**	....	....	....	....	**27-12**		**60**	**48**	**.556**	**20-24**	**30-16**	**8-6**	**2-2**	**6-4**	**54-44**

Doubles Titles: US (1)

• PIOLINE, Cedric   Cedric Adrien Pioline

Male. Born: June 15, 1969. Neuilly/Seine, France. Height: 6' 2". Weight: 175 lbs. Plays: right.
Status: Turned Pro 1989. Earnings: $6,921,029. Highest Ranking: 5 (May 2000).

Year	Rk	TP	TW	TF	GS	Aus	Fre	Wim	US	DC	Oly	MW	ML	Pct	CL	GR	HD	CP	IN	OD
1989	202	3	0	0	0-1	....	1rd	....	....	....	....	0	3	.000	0-3	0-0	0-0	0-0	0-0	0-3
1990	118	12	0	0	0-2	1rd	1rd	....	....	....	....	5	12	.294	5-8	0-0	0-1	0-3	0-3	5-9
1991	51	20	0	0	2-4	1rd	2rd	1rd	....	....	....	21	20	.512	11-9	1-1	6-6	3-4	5-5	16-15
1992	33	27	0	1	7-4	2rd	4rd	2rd	3rd	....	....	31	27	.534	9-10	1-2	13-10	8-5	11-7	20-20
1993	10	27	0	5	12-4	2rd	2rd	QF	F	....	....	51	27	.654	11-8	8-3	19-9	13-7	17-8	34-19
1994	51	31	0	1	3-4	1rd	2rd	1rd	3rd	1-1	....	31	31	.500	7-8	1-3	16-12	7-8	10-10	21-21
1995	56	28	0	0	6-4	1rd	2rd	QF	2rd	3-1	....	27	28	.491	8-8	5-3	8-10	6-7	9-9	18-19
1996	21	24	1	2	9-3	....	QF	4rd	3rd	6-2	....	44	23	.657	13-5	3-2	15-8	13-8	24-11	20-12
1997	20	29	1	1	10-3	....	3rd	F	4rd	0-3	....	36	28	.563	13-8	6-5	9-7	8-8	10-10	26-18
1998	18	29	0	2	8-4	4rd	SF	1rd	1rd	2-1	....	41	29	.586	13-8	1-2	16-12	11-7	13-9	28-20
1999	13	33	1	0	9-4	1rd	1rd	QF	SF	6-2	....	43	32	.573	4-9	12-2	20-15	7-6	13-11	30-21
2000	16	22	2	0	6-4	1rd	4rd	2rd	3rd	0-1	....	32	20	.615	13-4	3-3	8-9	8-4	10-5	22-15
2001	83	22	0	0	4-4	3rd	2rd	2rd	1rd	....	....	17	22	.436	7-8	2-2	8-11	0-1	3-4	14-18
2002	119	16	0	0	0-2	....	1rd	1rd	1rd	....	....	10	16	.385	4-6	2-3	4-5	0-2	3-3	7-13
TOTALS		**323**	**5**	**12**	76-47	....	....	....	18-11	....		**389**	**318**	**.550**	**118-102**	**45-31**	**142-115**	**84-70**	**128-95**	**261-223**

• POTTER, Barbara   Barbara Potter

Female. Born: Oct. 22, 1961. Waterbury, CT, United States. Height: 5' 9". Weight: 135 lbs. Plays: left.
Status: Turned Pro 1979. Earnings: $1,376,580. Highest Ranking: 7 (Dec. 1982).

Year	Rk	TP	TW	TF	GS	Aus	Fre	Wim	US	FC	Oly	MW	ML	Pct	CL	GR	HD	CP	IN	OD
1978	62	6	0	0	0-2	....	....	2rd	2rd	....	....	4	6	.400	0-0	2-2	0-2	2-2	2-2	2-4
1979	47	18	0	0	2-2	....	....	1rd	3rd	....	....	7	18	.280	0-3	1-3	3-7	3-6	3-6	4-12
1980	25	21	0	0	2-2	....	....	3rd	3rd	....	....	22	21	.512	0-0	2-3	9-8	11-10	13-13	9-8
1981	10	24	1	0	8-3	2rd	....	4rd	SF	....	....	46	23	.667	0-0	12-6	9-4	25-13	26-14	20-9
1982	8	23	2	0	5-3	3rd	....	QF	2rd	....	....	40	21	.656	1-1	9-6	5-5	25-9	26-10	14-11
1983	25	19	0	0	7-3	3rd	....	QF	2rd	....	....	24	19	.558	2-2	8-6	4-3	10-8	10-8	14-11
1984	12	17	0	0	9-3	QF	....	4rd	4rd	....	....	35	17	.673	0-0	11-4	7-4	17-9	18-10	17-7
1985	17	17	1	0	6-4	2rd	1rd	QF	2rd	....	....	31	16	.660	2-2	8-3	12-4	9-7	11-9	20-7
1986	24	10	0	0	0-0	....	....	....	....	....	....	14	10	.583	0-0	1-1	7-2	6-7	6-7	8-3
1987	12	14	1	0	1-2	....	....	2rd	1rd	....	....	25	13	.658	0-0	1-1	7-5	17-7	17-7	8-6
1988	10	15	1	0	9-3	4rd	....	4rd	4rd	1-0	....	37	14	.725	0-0	9-3	26-9	2-2	5-4	32-10
1989	105	5	0	0	0-1	1rd	....	....	....	....	....	5	5	.500	0-0	0-0	4-3	1-2	5-4	0-1
TOTALS		**189**	**6**	**0**	49-28	....	....	....	1-0	....		**290**	**183**	**.613**	**5-8**	**64-38**	**93-56**	**128-81**	**142-94**	**148-89**

• PROISY, Patrick   Patrick Proisy

Male. Born: Sept. 10, 1949. Eureux, France. Height: 5' 11". Weight: 155 lbs. Plays: right.
Status: Amateur. Earnings: –. Highest Ranking: –.

Year	Rk	TP	TW	TF	GS	Aus	Fre	Wim	US	DC	Oly	MW	ML	Pct	CL	GR	HD	CP	IN	OD
1968	....	1	0	0	0-1	....	2rd	....	....	....	....	0	1	.000	0-1	0-0	0-0	0-0	0-0	0-1
1969	....	3	0	0	0-2	....	1rd	....	1rd	....	....	0	3	.000	0-2	0-1	0-0	0-0	0-0	0-3
1970	....	2	0	0	0-2	....	1rd	1rd	....	....	....	0	2	.000	0-1	0-1	0-0	0-0	0-0	0-2
1971	....	5	0	0	5-3	....	QF	2rd	1rd	3-2	....	11	5	.688	6-2	1-2	4-1	0-0	0-0	11-5
1972	....	6	1	1	7-4	2rd	F	2rd	2rd	3-1	....	8	5	.615	6-2	2-3	0-0	0-0	0-0	8-5
1973	41	5	0	0	4-3	SF	1rd	....	1rd	2-2	....	6	5	.545	0-1	4-2	2-2	0-0	0-0	6-5
1974	74	6	0	0	3-2	....	3rd	2rd	....	....	....	5	6	.455	4-4	1-2	0-0	0-0	0-0	5-6
1975	43	5	0	1	2-3	....	3rd	1rd	1rd	....	....	3	5	.375	3-4	0-1	0-0	0-0	0-0	3-5
1976	....	10	0	1	1-3	....	2rd	1rd	1rd	1-1	....	11	10	.524	10-8	1-2	0-0	0-0	0-0	11-10
1977	44	5	1	0	2-2	....	2rd	....	2rd	1-1	....	8	4	.667	8-4	0-0	0-0	0-0	0-0	8-4
1978	96	10	0	0	1-1	....	2rd	....	....	....	....	12	10	.545	8-7	0-0	2-2	2-1	4-3	8-7
1979	96	13	0	0	0-1	....	1rd	....	....	....	....	14	13	.519	14-10	0-0	0-3	0-0	0-2	14-11
1980	158	15	0	0	0-1	....	1rd	....	....	....	....	11	15	.423	6-12	0-0	4-2	1-1	3-2	8-13
1981	....	6	0	0	1-1	....	2rd	....	....	....	....	3	6	.333	3-5	0-0	0-1	0-0	0-1	3-5
TOTALS		**92**	**2**	**3**	26-29	....	....	....	10-7	....		**92**	**90**	**.505**	**68-63**	**9-14**	**12-11**	**3-2**	**7-8**	**85-82**

• RAFTER, Patrick   Patrick Michael Rafter

Male. Born: Dec. 28, 1972. Mount Isa, Australia. Height: 6' 1". Weight: 190 lbs. Plays: right.
Status: Turned Pro 1991. Earnings: $11,103,311. Highest Ranking: 1 (July 1999).

Year	Rk	TP	TW	TF	GS	Aus	Fre	Wim	US	DC	Oly	MW	ML	Pct	CL	GR	HD	CP	IN	OD
1991	294	1	0	0	0-0	....	....	....	....	....	....	0	1	.000	0-0	0-0	0-1	0-0	0-0	0-1
1992	301	3	0	0	0-1	1rd	....	....	....	....	....	0	3	.000	0-0	0-1	0-2	0-0	0-0	0-3
1993	57	11	0	0	2-3	1rd	....	3rd	1rd	....	....	11	11	.500	0-0	3-2	5-7	3-2	4-3	7-8

Year	Rk	TP	TW	TF	GS	Aus	Fre	Wim	US	DC	Oly	MW	ML	Pct	CL	GR	HD	CP	IN	OD
1994	21	29	1	1	8-4	3rd	4rd	2rd	3rd	2-2	....	45	28	.616	4-4	7-2	27-14	7-8	10-9	35-19
1995	68	25	0	0	4-4	4rd	1rd	1rd	2rd	1-1	....	32	25	.561	3-7	2-3	22-12	5-3	5-3	27-22
1996	62	20	0	0	4-4	2rd	1rd	4rd	1rd	....	....	25	20	.556	4-5	8-4	12-9	1-2	1-2	24-18
1997	2	30	1	6	15-3	1rd	SF	4rd	W	3-3	....	65	29	.691	10-3	9-3	40-19	6-4	16-8	49-21
1998	4	27	6	0	13-3	3rd	2rd	4rd	W	2-1	....	60	21	.741	1-3	8-3	41-8	10-7	15-8	45-13
1999	16	17	1	2	9-4	3rd	3rd	SF	1rd	4-0	....	38	16	.704	10-4	11-2	17-10	0-0	2-1	36-16
2000	15	20	1	2	7-3	....	2rd	F	1rd	2-1	2rd	34	19	.642	2-5	14-2	13-10	5-2	5-4	29-15
2001	7	19	1	3	14-4	SF	1rd	F	4rd	4-2	....	48	18	.727	2-3	12-3	34-12	0-0	0-3	48-15
TOTALS		**202**	**11**	**14**	**76-33**	....	....	....	....	**18-10**	....	**358**	**191**	**.652**	**36-34**	**74-25**	**211-104**	**37-28**	**58-41**	**300-151**

Held number one tour ranking 1 time for a total of 1 week. Last ranked number one in 1999. Doubles Titles: Aus (1).

• RALSTON, Denny
Robert Dennis Ralston

Male. Born: July 27, 1942. Bakersfield, CA, United States. Height: 6' 2". Weight: 170 lbs. Plays: right.
Status: Turned Pro 1968. Earnings: –. Highest Ranking: 5 (Dec. 1966). HOF: 1987

Year	Rk	TP	TW	TF	GS	Aus	Fre	Wim	US	DC	Oly	MW	ML	Pct	CL	GR	HD	CP	IN	OD
1958	....	1	0	0	....	....	....	....	1rd	....	....	....	....	....	....	....	....	....	....	....
1959	....	1	0	0	....	....	....	....	1rd	....	....	....	....	....	....	....	....	....	....	....
1960	10	2	0	0	....	....	....	2rd	3rd	1-0	....	....	....	....	....	....	....	....	....	....
1961	....	1	0	0	....	....	....	3rd	....	1-0	....	....	....	....	....	....	....	....	....	....
1962	....	2	0	0	....	....	....	3rd	1rd	1-0	....	....	....	....	....	....	....	....	....	....
1963	7	2	0	0	....	....	....	2rd	QF	6-1	....	....	....	....	....	....	....	....	....	....
1964	9	2	0	0	....	....	....	1rd	QF	0-2	....	....	....	....	....	....	....	....	....	....
1965	9	2	0	0	....	....	....	SF	QF	3-1	....	....	....	....	....	....	....	....	....	....
1966	5	3	0	1	....	....	4rd	F	4rd	2-1	....	....	....	....	....	....	....	....	....	....
1968	8	2	0	0	8-2	....	....	QF	QF	....	....	8	2	.800	0-0	8-2	0-0	0-0	0-0	8-2
1969	....	4	0	1	8-3	....	3rd	4rd	4rd	....	....	8	4	.667	2-1	6-2	0-0	0-1	0-1	8-3
1970	....	4	1	1	8-3	SF	....	4rd	QF	....	....	8	3	.727	0-0	8-3	0-0	0-0	0-0	8-3
1971	....	5	0	0	4-3	3rd	....	3rd	2rd	....	....	7	5	.583	1-1	4-3	0-0	2-1	2-1	5-4
1973	....	2	0	0	0-0	....	....	....	....	....	....	0	2	.000	0-0	0-0	0-2	0-0	0-0	0-2
1974	....	3	0	0	0-1	....	....	1rd	....	....	....	1	3	.250	0-0	0-1	1-1	0-1	0-1	1-2
1975	....	1	0	0	0-1	....	....	....	1rd	....	....	0	1	.000	0-1	0-0	0-0	0-0	0-0	0-1
1976	....	7	0	0	0-0	....	....	....	....	....	....	1	7	.125	0-0	0-0	1-3	0-4	0-4	1-3
1977	....	2	0	0	1-1	....	....	2rd	....	....	....	1	2	.333	0-0	1-1	0-1	0-0	0-0	1-2
1978	....	1	0	0	0-0	....	....	....	....	....	....	0	1	.000	0-0	0-0	0-0	0-1	0-1	0-1
1980	....	1	0	0	0-0	....	....	....	....	....	....	0	1	.000	0-0	0-0	0-1	0-0	0-0	0-1
TOTALS		**48**	**1**	**3**	**29-14**	....	....	....	....	**14-5**	....	**34**	**31**	**.523**	**3-3**	**27-12**	**2-8**	**2-8**	**2-8**	**32-23**

Doubles Titles: Fre (1), US (3)

• RAMIREZ, Raul
Raul Carlos Ramirez

Male. Born: June 20, 1953. Ensenada, Mexico. Height: 6'. Weight: –. Plays: right.
Status: Turned Pro 1971. Earnings: $2,217,971. Highest Ranking: 5 (Dec. 1976).

Year	Rk	TP	TW	TF	GS	Aus	Fre	Wim	US	DC	Oly	MW	ML	Pct	CL	GR	HD	CP	IN	OD
1971	....	1	0	0	0-1	....	....	....	1rd	....	....	0	1	.000	0-0	0-1	0-0	0-0	0-0	0-1
1972	....	2	0	0	2-1	....	....	....	3rd	1-1	....	2	2	.500	0-0	2-1	0-1	0-0	0-0	2-2
1973	26	7	1	1	3-3	....	2rd	1rd	3rd	6-2	....	8	6	.571	1-1	2-2	4-2	1-1	1-1	7-5
1974	18	13	1	1	8-3	....	QF	2rd	4rd	1-0	....	21	12	.636	6-3	8-5	7-3	0-1	3-2	18-10
1975	13	14	4	1	11-3	....	QF	QF	4rd	4-0	....	18	10	.643	13-2	4-2	0-4	1-2	1-5	17-5
1976	5	27	4	5	11-3	....	SF	SF	2rd	1-1	....	64	23	.736	33-7	9-2	5-2	17-12	20-13	44-10
1977	8	15	2	3	6-3	....	SF	2rd	1rd	....	....	38	13	.745	6-3	10-2	13-5	9-3	14-5	24-8
1978	8	27	2	6	12-3	....	QF	QF	QF	1-1	....	61	25	.709	25-8	4-2	15-5	17-10	17-11	44-14
1979	41	23	1	0	1-3	....	1rd	2rd	1rd	1-0	....	28	22	.560	14-9	1-1	9-7	4-5	10-8	18-14
1980	36	19	1	1	3-3	....	4rd	1rd	1rd	1-1	....	29	18	.617	13-5	3-3	7-6	6-4	6-5	23-13
1981	34	18	0	1	2-3	....	1rd	2rd	2rd	3-1	....	26	18	.591	9-5	1-2	9-6	7-5	9-6	17-12
1982	25	13	0	2	1-1	....	....	....	2rd	3-1	....	31	13	.705	15-7	0-0	15-5	1-1	1-1	30-12
1983	76	6	1	0	0-1	....	....	1rd	....	....	....	11	5	.688	0-0	0-1	10-3	1-1	1-1	10-4
TOTALS		**185**	**17**	**21**	**60-31**	....	....	....	....	**22-8**	....	**337**	**168**	**.667**	**135-50**	**44-24**	**94-49**	**64-45**	**83-58**	**254-110**

Doubles Titles: Fre (2)

• REID, Kerry   Kerry Anne Melville Reid

Female. Born: Aug. 7, 1947. Mosman, Australia. Height: 5' 5". Weight: 130 lbs. Plays: right.
Status: Amateur. Earnings: $750,000. Highest Ranking: 5 (Dec. 1971).

Year	Rk	TP	TW	TF	GS	Aus	Fre	Wim	US	FC	Oly	MW	ML	Pct	CL	GR	HD	CP	IN	OD
1963	....	1	0	0	....	3rd	....	....	....	....	....	....	....	....	....	....	....	....	....	....
1964	....	1	0	0	....	2rd	....	....	....	....	....	....	....	....	....	....	....	....	....	....
1965	....	1	0	0	....	3rd	....	....	....	....	....	....	....	....	....	....	....	....	....	....
1966	10	2	0	0	....	SF	....	3rd	SF	....	....	....	....	....	....	....	....	....	....	....
1967	9	4	0	0	....	SF	SF	3rd	4rd	1-1	....	....	....	....	....	....	....	....	....	....
1968	....	2	0	0	5-2	3rd	4rd	3rd	....	4-0	....	9	2	.818	7-1	2-1	0-0	0-0	0-0	9-2
1969	7	5	0	1	7-4	SF	QF	2rd	1rd	2-1	....	9	5	.643	5-2	4-3	0-0	0-0	0-0	9-5
1970	8	6	3	2	10-3	F	1rd	4rd	QF	....	....	10	3	.769	0-0	10-3	0-0	0-0	0-0	10-3
1971	5	6	2	1	9-3	....	2rd	QF	SF	....	....	9	3	.750	1-1	8-2	0-0	0-0	0-0	9-3
1972	8	9	1	6	8-3	....	4rd	3rd	F	....	....	8	4	.667	1-2	7-2	0-0	0-0	0-0	8-4
1973	7	8	1	4	9-3	SF	....	QF	QF	....	....	9	3	.750	0-0	9-3	0-0	0-0	0-0	9-3
1974	7	8	0	4	12-3	SF	....	SF	QF	....	....	12	4	.750	0-1	12-3	0-0	0-0	0-0	12-4
1975	....	4	0	4	4-2	....	2rd	QF	....	....	....	4	3	.571	3-1	1-1	0-0	0-1	0-1	4-2
1976	....	4	0	1	5-3	1rd	....	QF	2rd	3-0	....	8	4	.667	1-2	4-2	0-0	3-1	3-1	5-4
1977	10	21	2	0	15-3	W/SF	....	QF	4rd	4-1	....	44	19	.698	9-3	22-5	4-3	9-8	9-8	35-11
1978	8	24	1	4	6-2	....	....	4rd	4rd	4-0	....	51	23	.689	4-1	12-3	15-7	20-12	20-12	31-11
1979	9	22	0	0	7-2	....	....	4rd	QF	2-1	....	44	22	.667	11-5	6-3	16-7	11-7	13-7	31-15
1980	....	1	0	0	0-0	....	....	....	....	....	....	0	1	.000	0-0	0-0	0-0	0-1	0-1	0-0
1983	....	1	0	0	0-0	....	....	....	....	....	....	1	1	.500	1-1	0-0	0-0	0-0	0-0	1-1
1984	....	1	0	0	0-0	....	....	....	....	....	....	0	1	.000	0-1	0-0	0-0	0-0	0-0	0-1
1985	....	1	0	0	0-0	....	....	....	....	....	....	1	1	.500	1-1	0-0	0-0	0-0	0-0	1-1
TOTALS		**132**	**10**	**27**	**97-33**					**20-4**		**219**	**99**	**.689**	**44-22**	**97-31**	**35-17**	**43-30**	**45-30**	**174-70**

Doubles Titles: Aus (1), Wim (1)

• RICHEY, Nancy   Nancy Anne Richey Gunter

Female. Born: Aug. 23, 1942. San Angelo, TX, United States. Height: 5' 3". Weight: 120 lbs. Plays: right.
Status: Turned Pro 1968. Earnings: –. Highest Ranking: 1 (Dec. 1968).

Year	Rk	TP	TW	TF	GS	Aus	Fre	Wim	US	FC	Oly	MW	ML	Pct	CL	GR	HD	CP	IN	OD
1959	....	1	0	0	....	....	....	....	3rd	....	....	....	....	....	....	....	....	....	....	....
1960	....	1	0	0	....	....	....	....	QF	....	....	....	....	....	....	....	....	....	....	....
1961	....	1	0	0	....	....	....	2rd	....	....	....	....	....	....	....	....	....	....	....	....
1962	....	2	0	0	....	....	....	3rd	3rd	....	....	....	....	....	....	....	....	....	....	....
1963	9	1	0	0	....	....	....	....	QF	....	....	....	....	....	....	....	....	....	....	....
1964	6	3	0	0	....	....	4rd	QF	SF	3-1	....	....	....	....	....	....	....	....	....	....
1965	8	3	0	0	....	....	SF	QF	SF	....	....	....	....	....	....	....	....	....	....	....
1966	5	4	0	3	....	F	F	QF	F	....	....	....	....	....	....	....	....	....	....	....
1967	4	3	1	0	....	W	....	4rd	2rd	....	....	....	....	....	....	....	....	....	....	....
1968	1	9	8	0	12-1	....	W	SF	....	3-0	....	12	1	.923	7-1	5-1	0-0	0-0	0-0	12-1
1969	1	3	0	2	13-3	....	SF	QF	F	4-0	....	13	3	.813	4-1	9-2	0-0	0-0	0-0	13-3
1970	3	7	6	1	4-1	....	....	....	SF	....	....	4	1	.800	0-0	4-1	0-0	0-0	0-0	4-1
1971	4	5	0	2	11-3	....	....	SF	QF	3rd	....	11	3	.786	5-1	4-1	2-1	0-0	0-0	11-3
1972	2	11	5	2	4-2	....	....	QF	1rd	....	....	21	6	.778	2-1	19-4	0-1	0-0	0-0	21-6
1973	....	2	0	6	0-0	....	3rd	....	2rd	....	....	0	2	.000	0-2	0-0	0-0	0-0	0-0	0-2
1974	....	1	0	1	0-0	....	....	....	QF	....	....	1	1	.500	0-0	0-0	0-0	1-1	1-1	0-0
1975	....	3	1	0	0-0	....	....	2rd	1rd	....	....	5	2	.714	0-1	0-0	5-1	0-1	0-1	5-1
1976	....	1	0	0	0-0	....	....	....	2rd	....	....	0	1	.000	0-0	0-0	0-0	0-1	0-1	0-0
1977	....	7	2	1	5-2	....	3rd	....	4rd	....	....	5	5	.500	5-3	0-0	0-0	0-2	0-2	5-3
1978	....	9	0	0	1-2	....	2rd	....	1rd	....	....	6	9	.400	1-2	0-0	2-2	3-5	3-5	3-4
TOTALS		**77**	**23**	**18**	**50-14**					**10-1**		**78**	**34**	**.696**	**24-12**	**41-9**	**9-5**	**4-10**	**4-10**	**74-24**

Competed as Nancy Gunter 1970-1975. Doubles Titles: Aus (1), Wim (1), US (2).

• RIOS, Marcelo   Marcelo Andres Rios Mayorga

Male. Born: Dec. 26, 1975. Santiago, Chile. Height: 5' 9". Weight: 160 lbs. Plays: left.
Status: Turned Pro 1994. Earnings: $9,404,181. Highest Ranking: 1 (Mar. 1998).

Year	Rk	TP	TW	TF	GS	Aus	Fre	Wim	US	DC	Oly	MW	ML	Pct	CL	GR	HD	CP	IN	OD
1993	549	1	0	0	0-0	....	....	....	....	0-1	....	0	1	.000	0-1	0-0	0-0	0-0	0-0	0-1
1994	107	11	0	0	2-2	....	2rd	....	2rd	....	....	12	11	.522	10-9	0-0	2-2	0-0	0-0	12-11
1995	25	24	3	1	1-3	....	2rd	1rd	1rd	3-1	....	41	21	.661	27-10	1-2	8-8	5-1	6-3	35-18
1996	11	26	1	3	4-3	1rd	4rd	....	2rd	5-0	....	57	25	.695	32-10	0-0	18-10	7-5	11-7	46-18
1997	10	27	1	4	14-4	QF	4rd	4rd	QF	6-0	....	60	26	.698	27-9	5-2	18-9	10-6	10-6	50-20
1998	2	24	7	1	12-4	F	QF	1rd	3rd	3-0	....	68	17	.800	23-5	0-2	28-8	17-2	20-4	48-13

Year	Rk	TP	TW	TF	GS	Aus	Fre	Wim	US	DC	Oly	MW	ML	Pct	CL	GR	HD	CP	IN	OD
1999	9	21	3	2	7-2	....	QF	....	4rd	2-2	....	47	18	.723	27-7	0-0	20-10	0-1	7-4	40-14
2000	37	24	1	0	2-2	....	1rd	....	3rd	1-0	1rd	30	23	.566	14-11	0-0	16-11	0-1	5-2	25-21
2001	39	21	2	0	3-3	1rd	2rd	....	3rd	3-0	....	31	19	.620	5-7	0-0	25-11	1-1	7-5	24-14
2002	24	20	0	1	6-2	QF	....	....	3rd	1-2	....	31	20	.608	6-6	0-0	25-11	0-3	5-5	26-15
TOTALS		**199**	**18**	**12**	**51-25**	....	....	....	....	**24-6**	....	**377**	**181**	**.676**	**171-75**	**6-6**	**160-80**	**40-20**	**71-36**	**306-145**

Held number one tour ranking 2 times for a total of 6 weeks. Last ranked number one in 1998.

• ROCHE, Tony   Anthony Dalton Roche

Male. Born: May 17, 1945. Tarcutta, Australia. Height: 5' 10". Weight: 175 lbs. Plays: left.
Status: Turned Pro 1968. Earnings: $529,199. Highest Ranking: 2 (Dec. 1969). HOF: 1986

Year	Rk	TP	TW	TF	GS	Aus	Fre	Wim	US	DC	Oly	MW	ML	Pct	CL	GR	HD	CP	IN	OD
1963	....	3	0	0	....	....	1rd	1rd	3rd	....	....	....	....		....	....	....	....	....	....
1964	....	4	0	0	....	QF	2rd	2rd	QF	1-0	....	....	....		....	....	....	....	....	....
1965	7	3	0	1	....	SF	F	2rd	....	....	....	....	....		....	....	....	....	....	....
1966	4	4	1	0	....	QF	W	QF	3rd	....	....	....	....		....	....	....	....	....	....
1967	5	3	0	1	....	SF	F	2rd	....	....	....	....	....		....	....	....	....	....	....
1968	4	2	0	1	8-2	....	....	F	4rd	....	....	8	2	.800	0-0	8-2	0-0	0-0	0-0	8-2
1969	2	12	6	5	19-4	SF	SF	SF	F	....	....	28	6	.824	9-2	15-3	0-0	4-1	4-1	24-5
1970	3	5	2	2	12-3	QF	....	QF	F	....	....	12	3	.800	0-0	12-3	0-0	0-0	0-0	12-3
1971	....	4	0	0	1-2	3rd	....	1rd	....	....	....	3	4	.429	1-1	1-2	0-0	1-1	1-1	2-3
1972	....	2	1	0	0-0	2rd	....	....	....	....	....	0	1	.000	0-0	0-0	0-1	0-0	0-0	0-1
1973	....	2	0	1	0-0	....	....	....	....	....	....	0	2	.000	0-0	0-1	0-1	0-0	0-0	0-2
1974	23	5	0	1	5-3	2rd	....	3rd	3rd	1-0	....	6	5	.545	1-1	5-3	0-0	0-1	0-1	6-4
1975	12	5	0	1	9-3	SF	....	SF	2rd	0-2	....	17	5	.773	1-1	16-4	0-0	0-0	0-0	17-5
1976	50	10	1	0	6-2	QF	....	4rd	....	2-0	....	12	9	.571	0-1	6-2	0-1	6-5	6-5	6-4
1977	19	5	1	1	2-23rd/1rd	....	....	....	....	1-0	....	7	4	.636	0-0	3-2	0-0	4-2	4-2	3-2
1978	32	10	1	0	3-2	QF	....	1rd	....	2-1	....	15	9	.625	2-1	11-4	0-1	2-3	2-4	13-5
1979	197	3	0	0	2-1	3rd	....	....	....	....	....	3	3	.500	0-0	3-2	0-0	0-0	0-0	3-3
1980	....	2	0	0	0-0	....	....	....	....	....	....	3	2	.600	0-0	2-1	1-1	0-0	1-1	2-1
TOTALS		**84**	**13**	**14**	**67-24**	....	....	....	....	**7-3**	....	**114**	**55**	**.675**	**14-8**	**82-29**	**1-5**	**17-13**	**18-15**	**96-40**

Doubles Titles: Aus (5), Fre (2), Wim (5), US (1)

• RODDICK, Andy   Andrew Stephen Roddick

Male. Born: Aug. 30, 1982. Omaha, NE, United States. Height: 6' 2". Weight: 190 lbs. Plays: right.
Status: Turned Pro 2000. Earnings: $1,914,649. Highest Ranking: 9 (Aug. 2002).

Year	Rk	TP	TW	TF	GS	Aus	Fre	Wim	US	DC	Oly	MW	ML	Pct	CL	GR	HD	CP	IN	OD
2000	160	5	0	0	0-1	....	....	....	1rd	....	....	4	5	.444	0-0	0-0	4-5	0-0	0-0	4-5
2001	16	19	3	0	8-3	....	3rd	3rd	QF	3-0	....	42	16	.724	12-1	5-3	23-10	2-2	8-5	34-11
2002	10	24	2	2	7-4	2rd	1rd	3rd	QF	4-2	....	56	22	.718	14-7	4-2	34-11	4-2	14-4	42-18
TOTALS		**48**	**5**	**2**	**15-8**	....	....	....	....	**7-2**	....	**102**	**43**	**.703**	**26-8**	**9-5**	**61-26**	**6-4**	**22-9**	**80-34**

• ROSE, Merv   Mervyn Gordon "Rosie" Rose

Male. Born: Jan. 23, 1930. Coffs Harbour, Australia. Height: 6'. Weight: –. Plays: left.
Status: Turned Pro 1958. Earnings: –. Highest Ranking: 3 (Dec. 1958). HOF: 2001

Year	Rk	TP	TW	TF	GS	Aus	Fre	Wim	US	DC	Oly	MW	ML	Pct	CL	GR	HD	CP	IN	OD
1949	....	1	0	0	....	4rd	....	....	....	....	....	....	....		....	....	....	....	....	....
1950	....	3	0	0	....	QF	....	3rd	2rd	....	....	....	....		....	....	....	....	....	....
1951	10	4	0	0	....	QF	QF	1rd	4rd	0-2	....	....	....		....	....	....	....	....	....
1952	4	4	0	0	....	SF	4rd	SF	SF	....	....	....	....		....	....	....	....	....	....
1953	6	4	0	1	....	F	4rd	SF	4rd	....	....	....	....		....	....	....	....	....	....
1954	6	3	1	0	....	W	QF	QF	....	....	....	....	....		....	....	....	....	....	....
1955	10	3	0	0	....	QF	QF	2rd	....	....	....	....	....		....	....	....	....	....	....
1956	....	1	0	0	....	QF	....	....	....	....	....	....	....		....	....	....	....	....	....
1957	6	2	0	0	....	....	SF	QF	....	....	....	....	....		....	....	....	....	....	....
1958	3	3	1	0	....	SF	W	SF	....	....	....	....	....		....	....	....	....	....	....
1971	....	1	0	0	0-1	1rd	....	....	....	....	....	0	1	.000	0-0	0-1	0-0	0-0	0-0	0-1
1972	....	1	0	0	1-1	2rd	....	....	....	....	....	1	1	.500	0-0	1-1	0-0	0-0	0-0	1-1
TOTALS		**30**	**2**	**1**	**1-2**	....	....	....	....	**0-2**	....	**1**	**2**	**.333**	**0-0**	**1-2**	**0-0**	**0-0**	**0-0**	**1-2**

• ROSEWALL, Ken   Kenneth Robert "Muscles" Rosewall

Male. Born: Nov. 2, 1934. Sydney, Australia. Height: 5'7". Weight: 135 lbs. Plays: right.
Status: Turned Pro 1956. Earnings: $1,600,300. Highest Ranking: 2 (Dec. 1953). HOF: 1980

Year	Rk	TP	TW	TF	GS	Aus	Fre	Wim	US	DC	Oly	MW	ML	Pct	CL	GR	HD	CP	IN	OD
1951	....	1	0	0	....	3rd	....	....	....	....	....	....	....	....	....	....	....	....	....	....
1952	10	4	0	0	....	QF	2rd	2rd	QF	....	....	....	....	....	....	....	....	....	....	....
1953	2	4	2	0	....	W	W	QF	SF	1-1	....	....	....	....	....	....	....	....	....	....
1954	3	4	0	1	....	SF	4rd	F	SF	1-1	....	....	....	....	....	....	....	....	....	....
1955	2	3	1	1	....	W	....	SF	F	11-0	....	....	....	....	....	....	....	....	....	....
1956	2	3	1	1	....	F	....	F	W	2-0	....	....	....	....	....	....	....	....	....	....
1968	3	4	2	0	15-2	....	W	4rd	SF	....	....	15	2	.882	7-1	8-2	0-0	0-0	0-0	15-2
1969	4	6	1	3	13-4	3rd	F	3rd	QF	....	....	16	5	.762	6-1	7-3	0-0	3-1	3-1	13-4
1970	2	8	5	4	13-1	....	....	F	W	....	....	22	3	.880	6-1	13-1	0-0	3-2	3-2	19-1
1971	3	9	7	1	10-1	W	....	SF	....	....	....	13	2	.867	0-0	10-1	0-0	3-1	3-1	10-1
1972	2	9	6	4	6-1	W	....	....	3rd	....	....	12	3	.800	0-0	6-1	3-2	3-1	3-1	9-3
1973	6	10	5	0	5-2	2rd	....	....	SF	....	....	10	5	.667	0-0	5-2	4-2	1-1	1-1	9-4
1974	8	2	0	3	12-2	....	....	F	F	....	....	12	2	.857	0-0	12-2	0-0	0-0	0-0	12-2
1975	6	7	3	1	3-1	....	....	4rd	....	2-0	....	12	4	.750	4-1	5-2	3-1	0-0	0-0	12-4
1976	13	11	2	2	4-1	SF	....	....	....	....	....	21	9	.700	6-3	4-1	4-2	7-3	7-3	14-6
1977	12	7	1	2	9-3	SF/QF	....	....	3rd	....	....	12	6	.667	2-2	7-2	1-1	2-1	2-1	10-5
1978	34	13	0	0	2-1	3rd	....	....	....	....	....	17	13	.567	3-5	7-3	6-3	1-2	4-3	13-10
1979	....	5	0	0	0-0							4	5	.444	0-0	3-2	1-3	0-0	0-1	4-4
1980	....	3	0	0	0-0							3	3	.500	0-0	1-1	1-1	1-1	2-2	1-1
TOTALS		**113**	**36**	**23**	**92-19**	....	....	....	....	**17-2**	....	**169**	**62**	**.732**	**34-14**	**88-23**	**23-15**	**24-13**	**28-16**	**141-47**

Doubles Titles: Aus (3), Fre (2), Wim (2), US (2)

• RUSEDSKI, Greg   Greg Rusedski

Male. Born: Sept. 6, 1973. Montreal, QUE, Canada. Height: 6'4". Weight: 190 lbs. Plays: left.
Status: Turned Pro 1991. Earnings: $7,801,603. Highest Ranking: 4 (Oct. 1997).

Year	Rk	TP	TW	TF	GS	Aus	Fre	Wim	US	DC	Oly	MW	ML	Pct	CL	GR	HD	CP	IN	OD
1992	158	2	0	0	0-0	....	....	....	....	....	....	2	2	.500	0-0	0-0	2-2	0-0	0-0	2-2
1993	48	10	1	1	0-1	....	....	1rd	....	....	....	16	9	.640	0-0	5-1	3-6	8-2	8-3	8-6
1994	117	29	0	0	3-4	1rd	3rd	2rd	1rd	....	....	21	29	.420	2-5	6-4	9-15	4-5	4-6	17-23
1995	38	26	1	1	5-3	3rd	....	4rd	1rd	2-0	....	34	25	.576	5-2	3-3	23-15	3-5	11-10	23-15
1996	48	27	1	0	2-4	1rd	2rd	2rd	1rd	4-0	3rd	38	26	.594	4-4	5-3	19-15	10-4	15-7	23-19
1997	6	25	2	4	10-4	1rd	1rd	QF	F	1-1	....	53	23	.697	4-5	13-2	18-11	18-5	24-10	29-13
1998	9	24	2	3	4-4	3rd	1rd	1rd	3rd	3-0	....	53	22	.707	1-5	1-2	36-10	15-5	33-8	20-14
1999	14	28	2	2	10-4	2rd	4rd	4rd	4rd	2-2	....	48	26	.649	5-7	8-3	17-12	18-4	22-7	26-19
2000	69	21	0	0	1-3	....	1rd	1rd	2rd	....	1rd	19	21	.475	1-4	2-3	11-10	5-4	11-8	8-13
2001	31	24	1	0	9-4	4rd	2rd	4rd	3rd	....	....	39	23	.629	3-4	9-3	22-13	5-3	10-6	29-17
2002	31	20	2	0	7-3	3rd	....	4rd	3rd	....	....	33	18	.647	0-1	6-3	24-11	3-3	6-6	27-12
TOTALS		**236**	**12**	**11**	**51-34**	....	....	....	....	**12-3**	....	**356**	**224**	**.614**	**25-37**	**58-27**	**184-120**	**89-40**	**144-71**	**212-153**

Represented Great Britian in the Davis Cup (1995-1999)

• RUZICI, Virginia   Virginia Ruzici

Female. Born: Jan. 31, 1955. Cimpa-Turzil, Romania. Height: 5'8". Weight: –. Plays: right.
Status: Turned Pro 1975. Earnings: $1,183,728. Highest Ranking: 8 (May 1979).

Year	Rk	TP	TW	TF	GS	Aus	Fre	Wim	US	FC	Oly	MW	ML	Pct	CL	GR	HD	CP	IN	OD
1973	....	2	0	0	0-2	....	1rd	2rd	....	3-0	....	3	2	.600	3-1	0-1	0-0	0-0	0-0	3-2
1974	....	6	0	0	1-3	....	2rd	2rd	1rd	0-3	....	1	6	.143	1-4	0-2	0-0	0-0	0-0	1-6
1975	....	3	0	0	1-3	....	2rd	1rd	1rd	0-1	....	1	3	.250	1-2	0-1	0-0	0-0	0-0	1-3
1976	....	4	0	0	8-3	....	SF	1rd	QF	2-1	....	8	4	.667	8-2	0-1	0-0	0-1	0-1	8-3
1977	16	17	1	0	3-2	....	2rd	4rd	....	....	....	16	16	.500	4-3	0-1	4-3	8-9	8-9	8-7
1978	12	31	5	0	14-2	....	W	QF	QF	2-1	....	53	26	.671	15-4	8-3	15-7	15-12	15-12	38-14
1979	13	23	0	0	5-3	1rd	QF	4rd	....	....	....	43	23	.652	13-5	9-5	7-5	14-8	14-9	29-14
1980	11	29	3	0	11-4	QF	F	2rd	4rd	3-0	....	69	26	.726	23-5	8-5	20-7	18-9	25-12	44-14
1981	12	29	0	0	9-4	1rd	QF	QF	3rd	2-1	....	53	29	.646	26-8	7-4	8-8	12-9	15-12	38-17
1982	11	22	3	0	8-3	....	QF	4rd	4rd	....	....	44	19	.698	21-5	2-1	11-6	10-7	11-9	33-10
1983	18	18	1	0	5-3	....	2rd	4rd	1rd	2-0	....	29	17	.630	13-9	3-1	6-4	7-3	10-4	19-13
1984	44	23	0	0	6-3	....	4rd	2rd	3rd	....	....	21	23	.477	13-7	1-1	2-6	5-9	5-12	16-11
1985	41	20	1	0	1-3	....	1rd	2rd	1rd	....	....	27	19	.587	17-6	1-2	7-7	2-4	2-6	25-13

Year	Rk	TP	TW	TF	GS	Aus	Fre	Wim	US	FC	Oly	MW	ML	Pct	CL	GR	HD	CP	IN	OD
1986	....	2	0	0	0-0	....	....	....	....	....	....	0	2	.000	0-0	0-0	0-2	0-0	0-1	0-1
1987	....	7	0	0	1-1	....	2rd	....	....	....	....	5	7	.417	5-5	0-0	0-2	0-0	0-1	5-6
TOTALS		236	14	0	73-39	....	....	....	....	14-7		373	222	.627	163-66	39-28	80-57	91-71	105-88	268-134

Doubles Titles: Fre (1)

• SABATINI, Gabriela   Gabriela Sabatini

Female. Born: May 16, 1970. Buenos Aries, Argentina. Height: 5' 9". Weight: 130 lbs. Plays: right.
Status: Turned Pro 1985. Earnings: $8,785,850. Highest Ranking: 3 (Feb. 1989).

Year	Rk	TP	TW	TF	GS	Aus	Fre	Wim	US	FC	Oly	MW	ML	Pct	CL	GR	HD	CP	IN	OD
1984	74	5	0	0	2-1	....	....	....	3rd	2-0	....	7	5	.583	2-1	0-0	5-4	0-0	0-0	7-5
1985	11	19	1	0	7-3	....	SF	3rd	1rd	3-0	....	51	18	.739	23-7	3-2	22-7	3-2	3-2	48-16
1986	10	23	1	0	11-3	....	4rd	SF	4rd	2-1	....	52	22	.703	22-7	8-2	13-6	9-7	12-8	40-14
1987	6	20	3	0	13-3	....	SF	QF	QF	2-1	....	64	17	.790	22-5	7-2	20-8	15-2	18-4	46-13
1988	4	18	4	0	14-3	....	SF	4rd	F	....	F	65	14	.823	18-3	6-2	30-6	11-3	14-5	51-9
1989	3	16	4	0	14-4	SF	4rd	2rd	SF	....	....	58	12	.829	21-3	1-1	30-5	6-3	11-3	47-9
1990	5	16	2	0	17-3	3rd	4rd	SF	W	....	....	49	14	.778	10-4	5-1	24-6	10-3	13-4	36-10
1991	3	16	5	0	19-4	QF	SF	F	QF	....	....	62	11	.849	21-2	6-1	24-5	11-3	11-3	51-8
1992	3	17	5	0	19-4	SF	SF	SF	QF	....	....	65	12	.844	23-2	5-1	29-7	8-2	12-3	53-9
1993	5	18	0	0	17-4	SF	QF	QF	QF	....	....	51	18	.739	21-6	6-2	22-8	2-2	2-2	49-16
1994	7	18	1	0	13-4	SF	1rd	4rd	SF	....	....	42	17	.712	8-6	3-1	23-8	8-2	8-3	34-14
1995	7	18	1	0	13-4	1rd	QF	QF	SF	3-1	....	44	17	.721	12-5	4-1	24-8	4-3	7-4	37-13
1996	....	10	0	0	5-2	4rd	....	....	....	....	3rd	14	10	.583	0-1	0-0	14-8	0-1	0-3	14-7
TOTALS		214	27	0	164-42	....	....	....	....	13-3		624	187	.769	203-52	54-16	280-86	87-33	111-44	513-143

Doubles Titles: Wim (1)

• SADRI, John   John Sadri

Male. Born: Sept. 19, 1956. Charlotte, NC, United States. Height: 6' 2". Weight: 180 lbs. Plays: right.
Status: Turned Pro 1976. Earnings: $895,455. Highest Ranking: –.

Year	Rk	TP	TW	TF	GS	Aus	Fre	Wim	US	DC	Oly	MW	ML	Pct	CL	GR	HD	CP	IN	OD
1976	360	1	0	0	0-0	....	....	....	....	....	....	0	1	.000	0-1	0-0	0-0	0-0	0-0	0-1
1978	84	7	0	0	4-2	3rd	....	....	3rd	....	....	6	7	.462	0-2	3-2	3-3	0-0	1-2	5-5
1979	30	22	0	1	8-3	F	....	3rd	2rd	....	....	27	22	.551	5-3	8-4	7-6	7-9	8-10	19-12
1980	16	25	1	0	5-4	QF	1rd	2rd	2rd	....	....	44	24	.647	0-2	12-5	14-7	18-10	20-11	24-13
1981	48	21	0	1	2-3	1rd	....	3rd	1rd	....	....	22	21	.512	0-1	8-5	3-5	11-10	11-10	11-11
1982	32	24	1	1	3-3	4rd	....	1rd	1rd	....	....	31	23	.574	3-2	10-6	3-6	15-9	15-10	16-13
1983	120	14	0	0	1-3	2rd	....	1rd	2rd	....	....	10	14	.417	0-0	1-4	3-3	6-7	6-7	4-7
1984	30	16	0	0	7-3	4rd	....	QF	1rd	....	....	25	16	.610	4-2	11-5	9-6	1-3	1-3	24-13
1985	46	25	0	1	2-3	3rd	....	2rd	1rd	....	....	25	25	.500	0-0	6-4	8-10	11-11	11-12	14-13
1986	130	21	0	2	3-2	....	....	3rd	2rd	....	....	12	21	.364	0-1	3-4	4-10	5-6	5-7	7-14
1987	173	11	0	0	1-2	1rd	....	2rd	....	....	....	8	11	.421	1-1	3-6	4-4	0-0	1-1	7-10
TOTALS		187	2	6	36-28	....	....	....	....	....		210	185	.532	13-15	65-45	58-60	74-65	79-73	131-112

• SAFIN, Marat   Marat Safin

Male. Born: Jan. 27, 1980. Moscow, Russian Federation. Height: 6' 4". Weight: 195 lbs. Plays: right.
Status: Turned Pro 1997. Earnings: $8,402,773. Highest Ranking: 1 (Nov. 2000).

Year	Rk	TP	TW	TF	GS	Aus	Fre	Wim	US	DC	Oly	MW	ML	Pct	CL	GR	HD	CP	IN	OD
1997	194	1	0	0	0-0	....	....	....	....	....	....	0	1	.000	0-0	0-0	0-0	0-1	0-1	0-0
1998	48	18	0	0	6-3	....	4rd	1rd	4rd	1-2	....	17	18	.486	6-8	0-1	10-7	1-2	2-3	15-15
1999	25	33	1	1	6-3	3rd	4rd	....	2rd	3-3	....	39	32	.549	11-10	0-2	15-12	13-8	16-11	23-21
2000	2	34	7	2	12-3	1rd	QF	2rd	W	1-2	1rd	73	27	.730	25-9	3-2	31-13	14-3	20-9	53-18
2001	11	29	2	1	14-4	4rd	3rd	QF	SF	0-2	....	45	27	.625	6-7	5-2	22-14	12-4	12-8	33-19
2002	3	27	1	2	13-4	F	SF	2rd	2rd	6-1	....	56	26	.683	22-8	1-1	20-14	13-3	18-9	38-17
TOTALS		142	11	6	51-17	....	....	....	....	11-10		230	131	.637	70-42	9-8	98-60	53-21	68-41	162-100

Held number one tour ranking 3 times for a total of 9 weeks. Last ranked number one in 2001.

• SAMPRAS, Pete   Pete Sampras

Male. Born: Aug. 12, 1971. Washington, DC, United States. Height: 6' 1". Weight: 175 lbs. Plays: right.
Status: Turned Pro 1988. Earnings: $43,280,489. Highest Ranking: 1 (Apr. 1993).

Year	Rk	TP	TW	TF	GS	Aus	Fre	Wim	US	DC	Oly	MW	ML	Pct	CL	GR	HD	CP	IN	OD
1988	97	10	0	0	0-1	....	....	....	1rd	....	....	10	10	.500	0-1	0-0	8-7	2-2	2-2	8-8
1989	81	19	0	0	4-4	1rd	2rd	1rd	4rd	....	....	18	19	.486	2-3	2-2	13-10	1-4	2-5	16-14
1990	5	21	4	0	10-2	4rd	....	1rd	W	....	....	51	17	.750	0-1	6-2	27-8	18-6	18-6	33-11

Year	Rk	TP	TW	TF	GS	Aus	Fre	Wim	US	DC	Oly	MW	ML	Pct	CL	GR	HD	CP	IN	OD
1991	6	23	4	4	6-3	....	2rd	2rd	QF	0-2	....	52	19	.732	3-3	5-3	25-7	19-6	23-8	29-11
1992	3	24	5	2	15-3	....	QF	QF	F	3-1	3rd	72	19	.791	22-8	7-2	25-5	18-4	22-6	50-13
1993	1	24	8	1	23-2	SF	QF	W	W	....	....	85	16	.842	14-4	7-1	43-6	21-5	21-5	64-11
1994	1	22	10	2	21-2	W	QF	W	4rd	2-2	....	77	12	.865	12-2	11-1	37-3	17-6	17-6	60-6
1995	1	21	5	4	20-2	F	1rd	W	W	6-0	....	72	16	.818	7-5	12-1	37-6	16-5	21-6	51-10
1996	1	19	8	1	18-3	3rd	SF	QF	W	....	....	65	11	.855	5-3	4-1	46-4	10-3	25-3	40-8
1997	1	20	8	0	19-2	W	3rd	W	4rd	2-1	....	55	12	.821	2-4	8-1	35-5	10-2	24-3	31-9
1998	1	21	4	3	17-3	QF	2rd	W	SF	....	....	61	17	.782	9-3	8-1	30-10	14-3	26-6	35-11
1999	3	13	5	0	8-1	....	2rd	W	....	....	....	40	8	.833	4-3	12-1	23-5	1-1	8-1	32-7
2000	3	15	2	2	18-3	SF	1rd	W	F	1-1	....	42	13	.764	2-4	11-1	28-7	1-1	3-3	39-10
2001	10	16	0	4	13-4	4rd	2rd	4rd	F	....	....	35	16	.686	3-4	6-2	26-10	0-0	2-2	33-14
2002	13	18	1	1	11-3	4rd	1rd	2rd	W	1-1	....	27	17	.614	5-6	2-3	20-8	0-0	1-1	26-17
TOTALS		286	64	24	203-38	....	....	....	....	15-8	....	762	222	.774	90-54	101-22	423-101	148-48	215-63	547-160

Held number one tour ranking 11 times for a total of 286 weeks. Last ranked number one in 2000.

• SANCHEZ, Arantxa — Arantxa Sanchez Vicario

Female. Born: Dec. 18, 1971. Barcelona, Spain. Height: 5' 7". Weight: 125 lbs. Plays: right.
Status: Turned Pro 1985. Earnings: $16,472,594. Highest Ranking: 1 (Feb. 1995).

Year	Rk	TP	TW	TF	GS	Aus	Fre	Wim	US	FC	Oly	MW	ML	Pct	CL	GR	HD	CP	IN	OD
1986	124	11	0	0	0-0	....	....	....	....	1-1	....	16	11	.593	14-8	0-0	2-2	0-1	1-2	15-9
1987	47	14	0	0	4-3	....	QF	1rd	1rd	1-1	....	13	14	.481	12-7	0-1	1-4	0-2	0-3	13-11
1988	18	17	1	0	7-3	....	QF	1rd	4rd	3-0	1rd	33	16	.673	25-10	0-1	8-5	0-0	0-1	33-15
1989	5	16	2	0	15-2	....	W	QF	QF	4-1	....	51	14	.785	28-5	4-1	16-6	3-2	3-2	48-12
1990	7	17	2	0	6-3	....	2rd	1rd	SF	3-1	....	41	15	.732	21-7	5-1	8-2	7-5	7-5	34-10
1991	5	16	1	0	19-4	SF	F	QF	QF	5-0	....	61	15	.803	22-6	9-2	25-4	5-3	5-3	56-12
1992	4	19	2	0	16-4	SF	SF	2rd	F	4-1	SF	66	17	.795	30-8	1-1	30-5	5-3	8-4	58-13
1993	2	18	4	0	18-4	SF	SF	4rd	SF	5-0	....	77	14	.846	32-3	3-1	39-9	3-1	6-2	71-12
1994	2	18	9	0	23-2	F	W	4rd	W	5-0	....	77	9	.895	32-2	3-1	38-5	4-1	4-1	73-8
1995	3	17	2	0	21-4	F	F	F	4rd	3-3	....	49	15	.766	23-4	6-1	19-8	1-2	1-2	48-13
1996	2	24	2	0	19-4	QF	F	F	4rd	1-5	F	57	22	.722	24-6	6-1	23-8	4-7	5-8	52-14
1997	9	24	0	0	15-4	3rd	QF	SF	QF	2-2	....	47	24	.662	13-7	8-1	21-13	5-3	7-7	40-17
1998	4	22	2	0	19-3	QF	W	QF	QF	2-2	....	48	20	.706	13-5	6-2	29-9	0-4	3-6	45-14
1999	17	19	1	0	9-4	2rd	SF	2rd	4rd	....	....	24	18	.571	14-6	1-2	9-8	0-2	0-3	24-15
2000	9	21	0	0	15-4	QF	SF	4rd	4rd	4-2	QF	45	21	.682	19-6	3-1	22-9	1-5	3-6	42-15
2001	17	25	2	0	4-3	....	2rd	2rd	3rd	2-1	....	36	23	.610	20-7	1-1	14-14	1-1	4-5	32-18
2002	53	26	0	1	0-3	1rd	1rd	....	1rd	5-2	....	26	26	.500	16-11	0-0	10-14	0-1	1-4	25-22
TOTALS		324	30	1	210-54	....	....	....	....	50-22	....	767	294	.723	358-108	56-18	314-125	39-43	58-64	709-230

Held number one tour ranking 3 times for a total of 12 weeks. Last ranked number one in 1995. Doubles Titles: Aus (3), Wim (1), US (2).

• SANCHEZ, Emilio — Emilio Sanchez

Male. Born: May 29, 1965. Madrid, Spain. Height: 5' 11". Weight: 164 lbs. Plays: right.
Status: Turned Pro 1984. Earnings: $5,333,851. Highest Ranking: 8 (Dec. 1990).

Year	Rk	TP	TW	TF	GS	Aus	Fre	Wim	US	DC	Oly	MW	ML	Pct	CL	GR	HD	CP	IN	OD
1984	112	13	0	0	3-2	....	4rd	1rd	....	4-0	....	10	13	.435	9-8	0-2	1-2	0-1	0-2	10-11
1985	64	15	0	0	2-1	....	3rd	....	....	1-0	....	17	15	.531	16-11	0-0	1-4	0-0	1-2	16-13
1986	16	28	3	1	3-3	....	4rd	1rd	1rd	2-2	2rd	54	25	.684	45-12	0-1	4-4	5-8	5-8	49-17
1987	17	32	4	2	8-3	....	4rd	4rd	3rd	3-3	....	60	28	.682	45-14	3-1	8-9	4-4	6-9	54-19
1988	17	25	1	3	9-3	....	QF	2rd	QF	2-4	....	43	24	.642	28-12	1-1	14-7	0-4	2-5	41-19
1989	19	18	1	2	2-1	....	....	....	3rd	1-2	....	38	17	.691	22-9	0-0	16-6	0-2	0-2	38-15
1990	8	27	2	0	3-3	1rd	1rd	....	4rd	3-1	....	50	25	.667	28-13	0-0	15-4	7-8	7-8	43-17
1991	14	28	3	2	4-4	1rd	2rd	1rd	4rd	1-3	....	43	25	.632	26-10	0-3	15-9	2-3	2-3	41-22
1992	21	28	1	1	9-4	4rd	4rd	1rd	4rd	1-1	QF	48	27	.640	26-13	0-1	19-7	3-6	6-7	42-20
1993	41	26	0	1	0-3	1rd	1rd	....	1rd	....	....	28	26	.519	23-16	0-0	5-9	0-1	0-1	28-25
1994	76	26	0	0	1-3	2rd	1rd	1rd	1rd	....	....	17	26	.395	13-18	0-0	4-7	0-1	0-1	17-25
1995	109	22	0	0	2-2	....	2rd	....	2rd	....	....	13	22	.371	12-18	0-0	1-3	0-1	0-1	13-21
1996	202	16	0	0	0-2	1rd	....	1rd	....	....	....	7	16	.304	5-11	0-1	2-4	0-0	0-1	7-15
1997	1040	4	0	0	0-0	....	....	....	....	....	....	0	4	.000	0-4	0-0	0-0	0-0	0-0	0-4
TOTALS		308	15	12	46-34	....	....	....	....	18-14	....	428	293	.594	298-169	4-10	105-75	21-39	29-50	399-243

Doubles Titles: Fre (2), US (1)

• SANTANA, Manolo   Manuel "Manolo" Santana

Male. Born: May 10, 1938. Madrid, Spain. Height: –. Weight: –. Plays: right.
Status: Turned Pro 1974. Earnings: –. Highest Ranking: 1 (Dec. 1966). HOF: 1985

Year	Rk	TP	TW	TF	GS	Aus	Fre	Wim	US	DC	Oly	MW	ML	Pct	CL	GR	HD	CP	IN	OD
1958	....	1	0	0	....	....	....	1rd	....	2-2	....	....	....	....	....	....	....	....	....	....
1959	....	2	0	0	....	....	....	3rd	2rd	4-1	....	....	....	....	....	....	....	....	....	....
1960	....	2	0	0	....	....	QF	3rd	....	0-2	....	....	....	....	....	....	....	....	....	....
1961	3	2	1	0	....	....	W	2rd	....	5-0	....	....	....	....	....	....	....	....	....	....
1962	3	2	0	0	....	....	SF	QF	....	0-2	....	....	....	....	....	....	....	....	....	....
1963	4	2	0	0	....	....	SF	SF	....	6-2	....	....	....	....	....	....	....	....	....	....
1964	6	3	1	0	....	....	W	4rd	2rd	4-0	....	....	....	....	....	....	....	....	....	....
1965	2	2	1	0	....	....	2rd	....	W	11-1	....	....	....	....	....	....	....	....	....	....
1966	1	2	1	0	....	....	....	W	SF	3-1	....	....	....	....	....	....	....	....	....	....
1967	3	1	0	0	....	....	....	1rd	....	11-1	....	....	....	....	....	....	....	....	....	....
1968	....	1	0	0	2-1	....	....	3rd	....	7-2	....	2	1	.667	0-0	2-1	0-0	0-0	0-0	2-1
1969	....	3	0	0	6-2	....	4rd	....	4rd	4-0	....	7	3	.700	4-2	3-1	0-0	0-0	0-0	7-3
1970	....	3	1	1	6-2	....	4rd	....	4rd	9-2	....	6	2	.750	3-1	3-1	0-0	0-0	0-0	6-2
1973	....	1	0	0	0-0	....	....	....	....	1-1	....	0	1	.000	0-0	0-0	0-0	0-1	0-1	0-0
1976	....	6	0	0	0-0	....	....	....	....	....	....	4	6	.400	4-6	0-0	0-0	0-0	0-0	4-6
1977	....	1	0	0	0-1	....	....	....	1rd	....	....	0	1	.000	0-1	0-0	0-0	0-0	0-0	0-1
1978	....	1	0	0	0-0	....	....	....	....	....	....	1	1	.500	0-0	1-1	0-0	0-0	0-0	1-1
TOTALS		**35**	**5**	**1**	**14-6**	....	....	....	....	**67-17**		**20**	**15**	**.571**	**11-10**	**9-4**	**0-0**	**0-1**	**0-1**	**20-14**

Held number one world ranking 1 time during amateur era. Doubles Titles: Fre (1).

• SCHETT, Barbara   Barbara Schett

Female. Born: Mar. 10, 1976. Innsbruck, Austria. Height: 5' 9". Weight: 150 lbs. Plays: right.
Status: Turned Pro 1992. Earnings: $2,597,962. Highest Ranking: 7 (Sept. 1999).

Year	Rk	TP	TW	TF	GS	Aus	Fre	Wim	US	FC	Oly	MW	ML	Pct	CL	GR	HD	CP	IN	OD
1991	753	1	0	0	0-0	....	....	....	....	0-1	....	0	1	.000	0-1	0-0	0-0	0-0	0-0	0-1
1992	299	1	0	0	0-0	....	....	....	....	....	....	0	1	.000	0-1	0-0	0-0	0-0	0-0	0-1
1993	136	5	0	0	0-0	....	....	....	....	0-1	....	4	5	.444	2-3	0-0	0-0	2-2	2-2	2-3
1994	100	14	0	0	0-3	....	1rd	1rd	1rd	2-1	....	9	14	.391	4-4	0-1	2-7	3-2	3-2	6-12
1995	83	12	0	0	0-3	1rd	1rd	....	1rd	0-2	....	8	12	.400	5-5	0-0	2-6	1-1	1-1	7-11
1996	38	20	1	0	5-4	4rd	1rd	2rd	2rd	0-1	....	23	19	.548	11-6	1-1	6-7	5-5	6-6	17-13
1997	38	23	1	0	4-4	3rd	1rd	2rd	2rd	1-3	....	21	22	.488	14-8	1-1	5-12	1-1	1-7	20-15
1998	23	27	0	2	6-4	4rd	1rd	2rd	3rd	3-1	....	35	27	.565	15-9	1-1	15-13	4-4	7-8	28-19
1999	8	25	0	1	12-4	4rd	3rd	4rd	QF	1-1	....	47	25	.653	13-7	3-1	27-13	4-4	9-7	38-18
2000	23	25	1	0	7-4	4rd	4rd	1rd	2rd	2-1	QF	32	24	.571	11-5	0-2	15-14	6-3	11-6	21-18
2001	21	25	0	0	10-4	3rd	4rd	3rd	4rd	2-0	....	31	25	.554	9-7	2-1	18-14	2-3	3-5	28-20
2002	40	23	0	0	5-4	3rd	2rd	2rd	2rd	2-2	....	26	23	.531	10-7	1-1	13-12	2-3	4-6	22-17
TOTALS		**201**	**3**	**3**	**49-34**	....	....	....	....	**13-13**		**236**	**198**	**.544**	**94-63**	**9-9**	**103-98**	**30-28**	**47-50**	**189-148**

• SEDGMAN, Frank   Frank Allan Sedgman

Male. Born: Oct. 29, 1927. Mount Albert, Australia. Height: 5' 11". Weight: 170 lbs. Plays: right.
Status: Turned Pro 1953. Earnings: $250,000. Highest Ranking: 1 (Dec. 1951). HOF: 1979

Year	Rk	TP	TW	TF	GS	Aus	Fre	Wim	US	DC	Oly	MW	ML	Pct	CL	GR	HD	CP	IN	OD
1946	....	1	0	0	....	4rd	....	....	....	....	....	....	....	....	....	....	....	....	....	....
1947	....	1	0	0	....	3rd	....	....	....	....	....	....	....	....	....	....	....	....	....	....
1948	....	4	0	0	....	QF	4rd	4rd	4rd	....	....	....	....	....	....	....	....	....	....	....
1949	4	3	1	0	....	W	....	QF	QF	5-2	....	....	....	....	....	....	....	....	....	....
1950	2	4	1	1	....	W	4rd	F	3rd	7-1	....	....	....	....	....	....	....	....	....	....
1951	1	4	1	0	....	SF	SF	QF	W	2-0	....	....	....	....	....	....	....	....	....	....
1952	1	4	2	1	....	F	F	W	W	2-0	....	....	....	....	....	....	....	....	....	....
1970	....	1	0	0	1-1	2rd	....	....	....	....	....	1	1	.500	0-0	1-1	0-0	0-0	0-0	1-1
1971	....	4	0	0	3-3	2rd	1rd	3rd	....	....	....	3	4	.429	0-1	3-2	0-1	0-0	0-0	3-4
1972	....	1	0	0	2-1	3rd	....	....	....	....	....	2	1	.667	0-0	2-1	0-0	0-0	0-0	2-1
1973	....	2	0	0	0-2	1rd	1rd	....	....	....	....	0	2	.000	0-0	0-2	0-0	0-0	0-0	0-2
1974	....	1	0	0	0-1	1rd	....	....	....	....	....	0	1	.000	0-0	0-1	0-0	0-0	0-0	0-1
1975	....	1	0	0	0-1	2rd	....	....	....	....	....	0	1	.000	0-0	0-1	0-0	0-0	0-0	0-1
1976	....	2	0	0	1-1	2rd	....	....	....	....	....	1	2	.333	0-0	1-1	0-1	0-0	0-0	1-2
TOTALS		**33**	**5**	**2**	**7-10**	....	....	....	....	**16-3**	....	**7**	**12**	**.368**	**0-1**	**7-9**	**0-2**	**0-0**	**0-0**	**7-12**

Held number one world ranking 2 times during amateur era. Doubles Titles: Aus (2), Fre (2), Wim (3), US (2).

• SEGURA, Pancho   Francisco Olegario "Pancho" Segura

Male. Born: June 20, 1921. Guayaquil, Ecuador. Height: 5' 6". Weight: –. Plays: right.
Status: Turned Pro 1947. Earnings: –. Highest Ranking: –. HOF: 1984

Year	Rk	TP	TW	TF	GS	Aus	Fre	Wim	US	DC	Oly	MW	ML	Pct	CL	GR	HD	CP	IN	OD
1941	....	1	0	0	....	....	....	....	2rd	....	....	....	....	....	....	....	....	....	....	....
1942	....	1	0	0	....	....	....	....	QF	....	....	....	....	....	....	....	....	....	....	....
1943	....	1	0	0	....	....	....	....	SF	....	....	....	....	....	....	....	....	....	....	....
1944	....	1	0	0	....	....	....	....	SF	....	....	....	....	....	....	....	....	....	....	....
1945	....	1	0	0	....	....	....	....	SF	....	....	....	....	....	....	....	....	....	....	....
1946	....	3	0	0	....	....	3rd	3rd	QF	....	....	....	....	....	....	....	....	....	....	....
1947	....	2	0	0	....	....	....	1rd	QF	....	....	....	....	....	....	....	....	....	....	....
1968	....	1	0	0	1-1	....	....	....	....	....	....	1	1	.500	0-0	1-1	0-0	0-0	0-0	1-1
1969	....	1	0	0	0-0	....	....	....	....	....	....	0	1	.000	0-0	0-0	0-0	0-1	0-1	0-0
1970	....	1	0	0	1-1	....	....	....	....	....	....	1	1	.500	0-0	1-1	0-0	0-0	0-0	1-1
TOTALS		**13**	**0**	**0**	**2-2**	....	....	....	....	....		**2**	**3**	**.400**	**0-0**	**2-2**	**0-0**	**0-1**	**0-1**	**2-2**

• SEIXAS, Vic   Elias Victor Sexia, Jr.

Male. Born: Aug. 30, 1923. Philaldelphia, PA, United States. Height: 6' 1". Weight: 180 lbs. Plays: right.
Status: Turned Pro 1973. Earnings: –. Highest Ranking: 3 (Dec. 1953). HOF: 1971

Year	Rk	TP	TW	TF	GS	Aus	Fre	Wim	US	DC	Oly	MW	ML	Pct	CL	GR	HD	CP	IN	OD
1940	....	1	0	0	....	....	....	....	3rd	....		....	....	....	....	....	....	....	....	....
1941	....	1	0	0	....	....	....	....	3rd	....		....	....	....	....	....	....	....	....	....
1942	....	1	0	0	....	....	....	....	2rd	....		....	....	....	....	....	....	....	....	....
1944	....	1	0	0	....	....	....	....	2rd	....		....	....	....	....	....	....	....	....	....
1946	....	1	0	0	....	....	....	....	3rd	....		....	....	....	....	....	....	....	....	....
1947	....	1	0	0	....	....	....	....	4rd	....		....	....	....	....	....	....	....	....	....
1948	....	1	0	0	....	....	....	....	4rd	....		....	....	....	....	....	....	....	....	....
1949	....	1	0	0	....	....	....	....	1rd	....		....	....	....	....	....	....	....	....	....
1950	7	3	0	0	....	....	QF	SF	3rd	....		....	....	....	....	....	....	....	....	....
1951	4	1	0	1	....	....	....	....	F	2-1		....	....	....	....	....	....	....	....	....
1952	5	2	0	0	....	....	....	QF	4rd	5-1		....	....	....	....	....	....	....	....	....
1953	3	4	1	1	....	SF	F	W	F	2-4		....	....	....	....	....	....	....	....	....
1954	4	4	1	0	....	QF	QF	QF	W	2-1		....	....	....	....	....	....	....	....	....
1955	4	4	0	0	....	QF	QF	2rd	SF	1-2		....	....	....	....	....	....	....	....	....
1956	4	2	0	0	....	....	....	SF	SF	2-2		....	....	....	....	....	....	....	....	....
1957	7	2	0	0	....	....	....	QF	QF	9-1		....	....	....	....	....	....	....	....	....
1958	....	1	0	0	....	....	....	....	QF	....		....	....	....	....	....	....	....	....	....
1959	....	1	0	0	....	....	....	....	2rd	....		....	....	....	....	....	....	....	....	....
1960	....	1	0	0	....	....	....	....	4rd	....		....	....	....	....	....	....	....	....	....
1961	....	1	0	0	....	....	....	....	3rd	....		....	....	....	....	....	....	....	....	....
1962	....	1	0	0	....	....	....	....	4rd	....		....	....	....	....	....	....	....	....	....
1963	....	1	0	0	....	....	....	....	3rd	....		....	....	....	....	....	....	....	....	....
1964	....	1	0	0	....	....	....	....	4rd	....		....	....	....	....	....	....	....	....	....
1965	....	1	0	0	....	....	....	....	4rd	....		....	....	....	....	....	....	....	....	....
1966	....	1	0	0	....	....	....	....	2rd	....		....	....	....	....	....	....	....	....	....
1967	....	2	0	0	....	....	....	2rd	2rd	....		....	....	....	....	....	....	....	....	....
1968	....	1	0	0	1-1	....	....	....	....	....		1	1	.500	0-0	1-1	0-0	0-0	0-0	1-1
1969	....	2	0	0	0-2	....	....	....	....	....		0	2	.000	0-0	0-2	0-0	0-0	0-0	0-2
TOTALS		**44**	**2**	**2**	**1-3**	....	....	....	**23-12**			**1**	**3**	**.250**	**0-0**	**1-3**	**0-0**	**0-0**	**0-0**	**1-3**

Doubles Titles: Aus (1), Fre (2), US (2)

• SELES, Monica   Monica Seles

Female. Born: Dec. 2, 1973. Novi Sad, Yugoslavia. Height: 5' 10". Weight: 155 lbs. Plays: left.
Status: Turned Pro 1989. Earnings: $14,615,549. Highest Ranking: 1 (Mar. 1991).

Year	Rk	TP	TW	TF	GS	Aus	Fre	Wim	US	FC	Oly	MW	ML	Pct	CL	GR	HD	CP	IN	OD
1988	86	3	0	0	0-0	....	....	....	....	....	....	5	3	.625	0-0	0-0	5-3	0-0	0-0	5-3
1989	6	9	1	0	11-3	....	SF	4rd	4rd	....	....	33	8	.805	10-1	3-1	8-2	12-4	17-5	16-3
1990	2	15	9	0	13-2	....	W	QF	3rd	....	....	54	6	.900	22-0	4-1	18-2	10-3	10-3	44-3
1991	1	16	10	0	21-0	W	W	....	W	....	....	74	6	.925	19-2	0-0	40-3	15-1	15-1	59-5
1992	1	15	10	0	27-1	W	W	F	W	....	....	70	5	.933	19-1	6-1	33-3	12-1	12-1	58-5
1993	8	4	2	0	7-1	W	....	....	....	....	....	17	2	.895	2-1	0-0	11-1	4-1	8-1	9-1
1995	1	2	1	0	6-1	....	....	....	F	....	....	11	1	.917	0-0	0-0	11-1	0-0	0-0	11-1
1996	2	13	5	0	17-3	W	QF	2rd	F	4-0	QF	48	8	.857	5-1	5-1	28-2	10-4	10-4	38-4
1997	5	16	3	0	11-3	....	SF	3rd	QF	....	....	45	13	.776	13-4	3-2	27-4	2-3	2-3	43-10
1998	6	15	2	0	14-3	....	F	QF	QF	4-0	....	46	13	.780	15-4	4-1	20-5	7-3	7-3	39-10

Year	Rk	TP	TW	TF	GS	Aus	Fre	Wim	US	FC	Oly	MW	ML	Pct	CL	GR	HD	CP	IN	OD
1999	6	14	1	0	16-4	SF	SF	3rd	QF	2-1	....	38	13	.745	13-3	2-2	21-7	2-1	2-1	36-12
2000	4	16	3	0	12-3	....	QF	QF	QF	2-0	SFB	58	13	.817	17-2	4-1	32-9	5-1	9-1	49-12
2001	10	14	4	0	7-2	QF	....	....	4rd	....	....	40	10	.800	0-1	0-0	40-9	0-0	4-1	36-10
2002	7	16	2	1	17-4	SF	QF	QF	QF	3-1	....	49	14	.778	10-3	4-1	32-9	3-1	7-3	42-11
TOTALS		**168**	**53**	**1**	**179-30**	....	....	....	....	**15-2**	....	**588**	**115**	**.836**	**145-23**	**35-11**	**326-60**	**82-23**	**103-27**	**485-90**

Held number one tour ranking 5 times for a total of 178 weeks. Last ranked number one in 1996. Represented the United States in the Federation Cup (1996-2002).

• SHRIVER, Pam

Pamela Howard Shriver

Female. Born: July 4, 1962. Baltimore, MD, United States. Height: 6'. Weight: 160 lbs. Plays: right.
Status: Turned Pro 1979. Earnings: $5,460,566. Highest Ranking: 3 (Feb. 1984). HOF: 2002

Year	Rk	TP	TW	TF	GS	Aus	Fre	Wim	US	FC	Oly	MW	ML	Pct	CL	GR	HD	CP	IN	OD
1978	13	8	1	0	8-2	....	....	3rd	F	....	....	14	7	.667	1-1	3-3	6-1	4-2	4-2	10-5
1979	33	13	0	0	1-1	....	....	2rd	1rd	....	....	9	13	.409	1-1	4-3	2-5	2-4	2-4	7-9
1980	9	20	1	0	9-3	QF	....	4rd	QF	....	....	47	19	.712	3-2	13-4	25-7	6-6	6-6	41-13
1981	7	24	1	0	11-3	SF	....	SF	4rd	....	....	53	23	.697	6-2	14-3	17-7	16-11	18-13	35-10
1982	6	18	0	0	10-3	SF	....	4rd	SF	....	....	41	18	.695	3-2	9-4	13-5	16-7	19-9	22-9
1983	4	16	2	0	12-4	SF	3rd	2rd	SF	....	....	47	14	.770	2-1	13-3	16-3	16-7	16-7	31-7
1984	4	15	2	0	10-3	QF	....	QF	QF	....	....	43	13	.768	0-0	15-4	9-3	19-6	19-6	24-7
1985	4	18	4	0	10-3	3rd	....	QF	QF	....	....	54	14	.794	2-3	19-4	19-3	14-4	23-4	31-10
1986	6	17	2	0	4-2	....	....	1rd	QF	....	....	47	15	.758	0-0	10-1	14-5	23-9	26-10	21-5
1987	4	17	4	0	12-3	QF	....	SF	QF	5-0	....	65	13	.833	0-0	30-5	21-4	14-4	17-5	48-8
1988	5	18	4	0	9-3	4rd	....	SF	2rd	....	QF	60	14	.811	0-0	24-3	20-8	16-3	20-4	40-10
1989	17	14	0	0	4-3	3rd	....	3rd	1rd	....	....	24	14	.632	0-0	7-3	12-7	5-4	7-5	17-9
1990	66	5	0	0	2-1	3rd	....	....	....	....	....	8	5	.615	0-0	0-0	3-3	5-2	5-2	3-3
1991	37	18	0	0	6-3	3rd	....	3rd	3rd	....	....	21	18	.538	0-0	7-3	11-11	3-4	3-6	18-12
1992	31	18	0	0	4-3	3rd	....	2rd	2rd	....	....	25	18	.581	0-0	6-3	11-10	8-5	8-6	17-12
1993	38	13	0	0	0-2	1rd	....	....	1rd	....	....	14	13	.519	0-0	3-2	4-6	7-5	7-6	7-7
1994	63	16	0	0	4-4	2rd	1rd	3rd	2rd	....	....	13	16	.448	0-1	4-3	7-7	2-5	5-6	8-10
1995	109	11	0	0	1-3	1rd	....	1rd	2rd	....	....	7	11	.389	0-0	4-3	1-4	2-4	2-4	5-7
1996	177	9	0	0	1-3	1rd	....	2rd	1rd	....	....	4	9	.308	0-0	2-2	1-6	1-1	1-2	3-7
1997	....	1	0	0	0-0	....	....	....	....	....	....	2	1	.667	0-0	0-0	0-1	0-0	2-1	0-0
TOTALS		**289**	**21**	**0**	**118-52**	....	....	....	....	**5-0**	....	**598**	**268**	**.691**	**18-13**	**187-56**	**214-106**	**179-93**	**210-108**	**388-160**

Doubles Titles: Aus (7), Fre (4), Wim (5), US (5)

• SMITH, Stan

Stan Smith

Male. Born: Dec. 14, 1946. Pasadena, CA, United States. Height: 6' 4". Weight: 185 lbs. Plays: right.
Status: Turned Pro 1969. Earnings: $1,774,881. Highest Ranking: 1 (Dec. 1972). HOF: 1987

Year	Rk	TP	TW	TF	GS	Aus	Fre	Wim	US	DC	Oly	MW	ML	Pct	CL	GR	HD	CP	IN	OD
1964	....	1	0	0	....	....	....	....	2rd	....	....	....	....	....	....	....	....	....	....	....
1965	....	1	0	0	....	....	....	2rd	....	....	....	....	....	....	....	....	....	....	....	....
1966	....	2	0	0	....	....	....	4rd	1rd	....	....	....	....	....	....	....	....	....	....	....
1967	....	2	0	0	....	....	....	3rd	3rd	....	....	....	....	....	....	....	....	....	....	....
1968	....	2	0	0	1-2	....	....	2rd	2rd	....	....	1	2	.333	0-0	1-2	0-0	0-0	0-0	1-2
1969	7	5	1	0	7-3	....	4rd	4rd	2rd	2-0	....	9	4	.692	3-1	4-2	2-1	0-1	0-1	9-3
1970	8	10	5	1	8-3	3rd	1rd	4rd	QF	....	....	15	5	.750	3-1	8-3	0-0	4-1	4-1	11-4
1971	2	10	5	3	17-2	....	QF	F	W	2-0	....	31	5	.861	8-2	13-1	6-1	4-2	4-2	27-3
1972	1	13	9	1	14-2	....	QF	W	QF	7-1	....	30	4	.882	5-2	11-1	10-1	4-1	9-1	21-3
1973	5	19	8	2	8-2	....	4rd	....	SF	3-2	....	22	11	.667	6-2	5-1	5-3	6-5	8-6	14-5
1974	9	12	4	1	9-3	....	1rd	SF	QF	....	....	23	8	.742	4-2	15-2	2-2	2-2	2-2	21-6
1975	21	8	1	3	3-3	....	4rd	1rd	1rd	1-1	....	8	7	.533	3-2	1-3	4-2	0-0	0-0	8-7
1976	16	22	0	2	8-3	3rd	....	4rd	4rd	....	....	41	22	.651	13-8	7-3	9-4	12-7	14-8	27-14
1977	24	16	1	2	9-4	/3rd	4rd	4rd	2rd	....	....	29	15	.659	6-3	10-4	9-5	4-3	8-5	21-10
1978	25	19	2	1	4-3	....	3rd	1rd	3rd	....	....	34	17	.667	3-3	0-1	17-4	14-9	22-11	12-6
1979	21	21	2	1	6-3	....	3rd	3rd	3rd	....	....	43	19	.694	5-2	7-3	21-6	10-8	19-10	24-9
1980	30	20	1	1	2-2	....	....	3rd	1rd	....	....	27	19	.587	0-0	5-2	9-8	13-9	14-11	13-8
1981	23	18	0	0	4-2	....	....	4rd	2rd	....	....	28	18	.609	0-2	4-2	19-10	5-4	12-7	16-11
1982	152	11	0	0	2-2	....	....	2rd	2rd	....	....	8	11	.421	0-1	1-2	7-8	0-0	5-3	3-8
1983	227	11	0	0	0-2	....	....	1rd	1rd	....	....	4	11	.267	0-0	0-2	3-8	1-1	1-3	3-8
1984	....	1	0	0	0-0	....	....	....	....	....	....	0	1	.000	0-0	0-0	0-1	0-0	0-0	0-1
1985	....	1	0	0	0-0	....	....	....	....	....	....	0	1	.000	0-0	0-0	0-1	0-0	0-0	0-1
TOTALS		**225**	**39**	**18**	**102-41**	....	....	....	....	**15-4**	....	**353**	**180**	**.662**	**59-31**	**92-34**	**123-65**	**79-53**	**122-71**	**231-109**

Doubles Titles: Aus (1), US (5)

• SMITH COURT, Margaret   Margaret Smith Court

Female. Born: July 16, 1942. Albury, Australia. Height: 5'9". Weight: 150 lbs. Plays: right.
Status: Turned Pro 1968. Earnings: $550,000. Highest Ranking: 1 (Dec. 1962). HOF: 1979

Year	Rk	TP	TW	TF	GS	Aus	Fre	Wim	US	FC	Oly	MW	ML	Pct	CL	GR	HD	CP	IN	OD
1959	....	1	0	0	....	2rd	....	....	....	....	....	....	....	....	....	....	....	....	....	....
1960	....	1	1	0	....	W	....	....	....	....	....	....	....	....	....	....	....	....	....	....
1961	4	4	1	0	....	W	QF	QF	SF	....	....	....	....	....	....	....	....	....	....	....
1962	1	4	3	0	....	W	W	2rd	W	....	....	....	....	....	....	....	....	....	....	....
1963	1	4	2	1	....	W	QF	W	F	4-0	....	....	....	....	....	....	....	....	....	....
1964	1	4	3	0	....	W	W	F	4rd	4-0	....	....	....	....	....	....	....	....	....	....
1965	1	4	3	1	....	W	F	W	W	3-0	....	....	....	....	....	....	....	....	....	....
1966	2	3	1	0	....	W	SF	SF	....	....	....	....	....	....	....	....	....	....	....	....
1968	4	17	14	0	6-3	F	....	QF	QF	4-0	....	10	3	.769	4-1	6-3	0-0	0-0	0-0	10-3
1969	1	19	18	0	21-1	W	W	SF	W	3-0	....	24	1	.960	9-1	15-1	0-0	0-0	0-0	24-1
1970	1	21	21	0	23-0	W	W	W	W	2-0	....	25	0	1.000	6-1	19-0	0-0	0-0	0-0	25-0
1971	3	13	10	1	11-2	W	3rd	F	....	....	....	11	2	.846	2-1	9-1	0-0	0-0	0-0	11-2
1972	2	13	10	2	4-1	....	....	....	SF	....	....	4	1	.800	0-0	4-1	0-0	0-0	0-0	4-1
1973	1	20	18	1	21-1	W	W	SF	W	....	....	21	1	.955	6-1	15-1	0-0	0-0	0-0	21-1
1975	6	8	1	3	10-3	QF	....	SF	QF	....	....	11	4	.733	3-1	7-2	0-0	1-1	1-1	10-3
1976	....	2	0	1	0-0	....	....	....	....	....	....	0	1	.000	0-0	0-1	0-0	0-0	0-0	0-1
1977	....	6	0	1	0-0	....	....	....	....	....	....	16	5	.762	0-0	0-0	4-1	12-4	12-4	4-1
Totals		**144**	**106**	**11**	**96-11**	....	....	....	....	**20-0**	....	**122**	**18**	**.871**	**30-6**	**75-10**	**4-1**	**13-5**	**13-5**	**109-13**

Held number one world ranking 4 times during amateur era and 3 times during the open era. Competed as Margaret Smith until 1967. Doubles Titles: Aus (8), Fre (4), Wim (2), US (7).

• SOLOMON, Harold   Harold Solomon

Male. Born: Sept. 17, 1952. Washington, DC, United States. Height: 5'6". Weight: 130 lbs. Plays: right.
Status: Turned Pro 1971. Earnings: $1,802,769. Highest Ranking: 7 (Dec. 1980).

Year	Rk	TP	TW	TF	GS	Aus	Fre	Wim	US	DC	Oly	MW	ML	Pct	CL	GR	HD	CP	IN	OD
1971	....	1	0	0	0-0	....	....	....	....	....	....	3	1	.750	0-0	0-0	3-1	0-0	0-0	3-1
1972	....	3	0	0	4-3	....	QF	1rd	2rd	4-1	....	4	3	.571	3-1	1-2	0-0	0-0	0-0	4-3
1973	....	5	0	0	2-2	....	3rd	....	1rd	2-0	....	7	5	.583	6-3	1-2	0-0	0-0	0-0	7-5
1974	15	14	1	2	5-2	....	SF	1rd	....	0-2	....	19	13	.594	10-4	0-5	9-3	0-1	2-2	17-11
1975	17	14	4	2	7-2	....	QF	....	4rd	....	....	14	10	.583	12-5	0-0	2-3	0-2	1-4	13-6
1976	8	28	5	3	6-2	....	F	....	1rd	....	....	47	23	.671	26-9	0-0	5-4	16-10	18-11	29-12
1977	14	14	3	0	8-3	....	4rd	1rd	SF	....	....	28	11	.718	17-3	0-2	6-3	5-3	8-5	20-6
1978	9	26	2	3	5-2	....	3rd	....	4rd	3-1	....	54	24	.692	28-9	0-0	18-6	8-9	8-10	46-14
1979	8	23	3	4	6-2	....	4rd	....	4rd	....	....	59	20	.747	27-8	0-0	19-7	13-5	21-6	38-14
1980	7	25	4	1	8-2	....	SF	....	4rd	....	....	63	21	.750	25-8	0-0	22-5	16-8	16-8	47-13
1981	22	22	0	1	2-2	....	1rd	....	3rd	....	....	30	22	.577	13-9	0-0	12-9	5-4	5-7	25-15
1982	66	23	0	0	3-2	....	2rd	....	3rd	....	....	22	23	.489	5-6	0-0	14-9	3-8	7-11	15-12
1983	285	18	0	0	0-1	....	....	....	1rd	....	....	5	18	.217	4-10	0-0	1-6	0-2	0-2	5-16
1984	222	6	0	0	2-1	....	3rd	....	....	....	....	4	6	.400	3-5	0-0	0-0	1-1	1-1	3-5
1985	106	6	0	0	0-0	....	....	....	....	....	....	4	6	.400	3-2	0-0	1-4	0-0	0-0	4-6
1986	240	8	0	0	0-1	....	....	1rd	....	....	....	4	8	.333	2-4	0-1	2-3	0-0	0-0	4-8
1991	....	1	0	0	0-0	....	....	....	....	....	....	0	1	.000	0-0	0-0	0-1	0-0	0-0	0-1
Totals		**237**	**22**	**16**	**58-27**	....	....	....	....	**9-4**	....	**367**	**215**	**.631**	**184-86**	**2-12**	**114-64**	**67-53**	**87-67**	**280-148**

Doubles Titles: US (1)

• SPIRLEA, Irina   Irina Spirlea

Female. Born: Mar. 26, 1974. Bucharest, Romania. Height: 5'9". Weight: 150 lbs. Plays: right.
Status: Turned Pro 1990. Earnings: $2,652,068. Highest Ranking: 7 (Oct. 1997).

Year	Rk	TP	TW	TF	GS	Aus	Fre	Wim	US	FC	Oly	MW	ML	Pct	CL	GR	HD	CP	IN	OD
1991	208	3	0	0	0-0	....	....	....	....	2-2	....	2	3	.400	0-1	0-0	2-2	0-0	0-0	2-3
1992	165	6	0	0	0-1	....	1rd	....	....	0-2	1rd	0	6	.000	0-6	0-0	0-0	0-0	0-0	0-6
1993	63	5	0	1	0-0	....	....	....	....	....	....	10	5	.667	5-2	0-0	0-1	5-2	5-2	5-3
1994	43	18	1	1	4-4	1rd	4rd	2rd	1rd	3-1	....	21	17	.553	17-6	1-2	3-8	0-1	0-3	21-14
1995	21	20	1	1	7-4	4rd	3rd	3rd	1rd	....	....	36	19	.655	20-6	2-2	10-7	4-4	4-4	32-15
1996	11	20	1	0	7-4	2rd	4rd	2rd	3rd	....	....	35	19	.648	15-4	2-2	12-9	6-4	7-5	28-14
1997	8	24	0	1	15-4	QF	4rd	4rd	SF	....	....	47	24	.662	9-6	8-3	23-11	7-4	13-7	34-17
1998	15	26	1	1	6-4	1rd	1rd	4rd	4rd	....	....	36	25	.590	12-5	7-3	9-11	8-6	11-9	25-16
1999	35	25	0	1	4-4	1rd	3rd	1rd	3rd	....	....	20	25	.444	9-6	1-2	8-13	2-4	3-7	17-18
2000	167	12	0	0	0-3	1rd	1rd	1rd	....	....	....	4	12	.250	1-5	0-1	3-6	0-0	2-2	2-10
Totals		**159**	**4**	**6**	**43-28**	....	....	....	....	**5-5**	....	**211**	**155**	**.577**	**88-47**	**21-15**	**70-68**	**32-25**	**45-39**	**166-116**

• STEVENS, Greer   Greer Stevens

Female. Born: Feb. 15, 1957. Russian Federation. Height: –. Weight: –. Plays: –.
Status: Turned Pro 1974. Earnings: –. Highest Ranking: 7 (July 1980).

Year	Rk	TP	TW	TF	GS	Aus	Fre	Wim	US	FC	Oly	MW	ML	Pct	CL	GR	HD	CP	IN	OD
1974	....	1	0	0	2-1	....	....	3rd	....	....	....	2	1	.667	0-0	2-1	0-0	0-0	0-0	2-1
1975	....	2	0	0	4-2	....	....	3rd	3rd	....	....	4	2	.667	2-1	2-1	0-0	0-0	0-0	4-2
1976	....	3	0	0	3-2	....	....	4rd	2rd	....	....	3	3	.500	0-1	3-1	0-0	0-1	0-1	3-2
1977	13	13	0	0	4-2	....	....	4rd	2rd	3-1	....	20	13	.606	1-1	10-4	1-1	8-7	8-7	12-6
1978	17	7	0	0	0-0	....	....	....	....	....	....	8	7	.533	0-1	0-0	0-0	8-6	8-6	0-1
1979	12	18	1	0	4-2	....	....	4rd	4rd	....	....	26	17	.605	0-1	4-2	11-5	11-9	11-9	15-8
1980	10	17	0	0	6-3	QF	....	QF	1rd	....	....	35	17	.673	0-0	12-4	4-3	19-10	19-11	16-6
TOTALS		**61**	**1**	**0**	**23-12**	....	....	....	....	**3-1**		**98**	**60**	**.620**	**3-5**	**33-13**	**16-9**	**46-33**	**46-34**	**52-26**

Represented South Africa in the Federation Cup (1977)

• STICH, Michael   Michael Stich

Male. Born: Oct. 18, 1968. Pinneberg, Germany. Height: 6' 4". Weight: 175 lbs. Plays: right.
Status: Turned Pro 1988. Earnings: $12,628,890. Highest Ranking: 2 (Nov. 1993).

Year	Rk	TP	TW	TF	GS	Aus	Fre	Wim	US	DC	Oly	MW	ML	Pct	CL	GR	HD	CP	IN	OD
1989	100	12	0	0	1-3	....	2rd	1rd	1rd	....	....	11	12	.478	3-4	5-3	0-2	3-3	3-4	8-8
1990	42	26	1	0	6-4	3rd	2rd	3rd	2rd	0-2	....	29	25	.537	3-7	3-2	20-10	3-6	11-8	18-17
1991	4	30	4	3	17-3	3rd	SF	W	QF	4-2	....	73	26	.737	19-7	10-1	30-10	14-8	19-11	54-15
1992	15	23	2	1	11-4	QF	3rd	QF	2rd	2-0	2rd	47	21	.691	14-8	9-1	13-8	11-4	13-6	34-15
1993	2	28	6	3	12-4	SF	4rd	QF	1rd	7-1	....	76	22	.776	23-7	10-2	17-7	26-6	35-6	41-16
1994	9	27	3	2	7-4	1rd	2rd	1rd	F	3-3	....	60	24	.714	20-6	8-2	15-9	17-7	20-9	40-15
1995	12	20	1	3	8-4	3rd	4rd	1rd	4rd	5-1	....	47	19	.712	12-6	4-2	23-8	8-3	13-4	34-15
1996	20	15	1	1	10-3	....	F	4rd	2rd	....	....	25	14	.641	7-2	5-2	2-4	11-6	11-7	14-7
1997	65	13	0	0	6-2	2rd	....	SF	....	....	....	17	13	.567	4-4	7-2	1-2	5-5	5-5	12-8
TOTALS		**194**	**18**	**13**	**78-31**	....	....	....	....	**21-9**		**385**	**176**	**.686**	**105-51**	**61-17**	**121-60**	**98-48**	**130-60**	**255-116**

Doubles Titles: Wim (1)

• STOCKTON, Dick   Dick Stockton

Male. Born: Feb. 18, 1951. New York, NY, United States. Height: 6' 2". Weight: 180 lbs. Plays: right.
Status: Turned Pro 1973. Earnings: $1,063,385. Highest Ranking: 10 (Dec. 1977).

Year	Rk	TP	TW	TF	GS	Aus	Fre	Wim	US	DC	Oly	MW	ML	Pct	CL	GR	HD	CP	IN	OD
1967	....	1	0	0	....	....	....	....	1rd	....	....	....	....	....	....	....	....	....	....	....
1968	....	1	0	0	1-1	....	....	....	2rd	....	....	1	1	.500	0-0	1-1	0-0	0-0	0-0	1-1
1969	....	1	0	0	0-1	....	....	....	1rd	....	....	0	1	.000	0-0	0-1	0-0	0-0	0-0	0-1
1970	....	2	0	0	1-1	....	....	....	2rd	....	....	2	2	.500	1-1	1-1	0-0	0-0	0-0	2-2
1971	....	2	0	1	1-1	....	....	....	2rd	....	....	3	2	.600	0-0	1-1	2-1	0-0	0-0	3-2
1972	....	2	0	0	5-2	....	....	3rd	4rd	....	....	5	2	.714	0-0	5-2	0-0	0-0	0-0	5-2
1973	27	7	0	1	2-2	....	3rd	....	1rd	1-0	....	6	7	.462	2-2	2-3	2-2	0-0	0-0	6-7
1974	16	7	2	1	6-2	....	....	SF	3rd	....	....	10	5	.667	0-0	7-3	0-1	3-1	3-1	7-4
1975	30	5	1	2	2-1	....	....	....	3rd	....	....	7	4	.636	2-1	0-0	2-2	3-1	4-2	3-2
1976	15	19	0	0	5-2	....	....	2rd	QF	1-1	....	45	18	.714	22-6	3-2	5-3	15-7	15-7	30-11
1977	10	14	3	2	9-3	3rd/	....	4rd	QF	0-2	....	36	11	.766	10-3	10-4	1-1	15-3	15-3	21-8
1978	23	18	1	2	7-3	....	SF	1rd	3rd	....	....	23	17	.575	8-4	0-1	2-2	13-10	13-11	10-6
1979	55	20	0	0	3-3	....	1rd	1rd	4rd	2-0	....	20	20	.500	3-4	3-2	6-5	8-9	8-9	12-11
1980	138	15	0	0	1-2	....	....	2rd	1rd	....	....	6	15	.286	1-2	2-2	1-6	2-5	2-6	4-9
1981	98	15	0	1	2-2	....	....	1rd	3rd	....	....	14	15	.483	5-3	1-3	6-7	2-2	2-2	12-13
1982	184	18	0	0	1-2	....	....	2rd	1rd	....	....	7	18	.280	3-5	1-2	0-6	3-5	3-6	4-12
1983	480	2	0	0	0-1	....	....	....	1rd	....	....	1	2	.333	0-0	0-0	1-2	0-0	0-0	1-2
1984	....	3	0	0	0-2	....	....	1rd	1rd	....	....	0	3	.000	0-0	0-1	0-2	0-0	0-0	0-3
TOTALS		**152**	**8**	**10**	**46-31**	....	....	....	....	**4-3**		**186**	**143**	**.565**	**57-31**	**37-29**	**28-40**	**64-43**	**65-47**	**121-96**

• STOLLE, Fred   Frederick Sydney Stolle

Male. Born: Oct. 8, 1938. Hornsby, Australia. Height: 6' 3". Weight: –. Plays: right.
Status: Turned Pro 1967. Earnings: $500,000. Highest Ranking: 2 (Dec. 1964). HOF: 1985

Year	Rk	TP	TW	TF	GS	Aus	Fre	Wim	US	DC	Oly	MW	ML	Pct	CL	GR	HD	CP	IN	OD
1958	....	1	0	0	....	3rd	....	....	....	....	....	....	....	....	....	....	....	....	....	....
1960	....	3	0	0	....	3rd	2rd	1rd	....	....	....	....	....	....	....	....	....	....	....	....
1961	....	3	0	0	....	SF	3rd	2rd	....	....	....	....	....	....	....	....	....	....	....	....
1962	....	4	0	0	....	QF	4rd	3rd	2rd	....	....	....	....	....	....	....	....	....	....	....
1963	5	2	0	1	....	....	2rd	F	....	....	....	....	....	....	....	....	....	....	....	....
1964	2	4	0	3	....	F	4rd	F	F	6-2	....	....	....	....	....	....	....	....	....	....

Year	Rk	TP	TW	TF	GS	Aus	Fre	Wim	US	DC	Oly	MW	ML	Pct	CL	GR	HD	CP	IN	OD
1965	3	4	1	2	....	F	W	F	2rd	2-0	....	....	....	....	....	....	....	....	....	....
1966	2	4	1	0	....	SF	QF	2rd	W	2-0	....	....	....	....	....	....	....	....	....	....
1968	....	4	1	0	4-3	....	2rd	4rd	2rd	....	....	4	3	.571	1-1	3-2	0-0	0-0	0-0	4-3
1969	....	7	2	0	13-4	QF	QF	4rd	QF	....	....	15	5	.750	6-2	9-3	0-0	0-0	0-0	15-5
1970	....	2	0	0	1-2	....	....	1rd	3rd	....	....	1	2	.333	0-0	1-2	0-0	0-0	0-0	1-2
1971	....	4	0	1	4-2	3rd	....	4rd	....	....	....	5	4	.556	1-1	4-2	0-0	0-1	0-1	5-3
1972	....	2	0	1	4-1	....	....	....	QF	....	....	5	2	.714	0-0	4-1	1-1	0-0	0-0	5-2
1973	36	2	1	1	0-0	....	....	....	....	....	....	1	1	.500	0-0	0-0	1-1	0-0	0-0	1-1
1975	....	1	0	0	0-1	....	....	....	1rd	....	....	0	1	.000	0-1	0-0	0-0	0-0	0-0	0-1
1976	....	1	0	0	0-0	....	....	....	....	....	....	0	1	.000	0-0	0-0	0-0	0-1	0-1	0-0
1977	....	1	0	0	1-1	....	....	....	2rd	....	....	1	1	.500	1-1	0-0	0-0	0-0	0-0	1-1
1978	....	1	0	0	0-1	....	....	1rd	....	....	....	0	1	.000	0-0	0-1	0-0	0-0	0-0	0-1
1982	....	1	0	0	0-0	....	....	....	....	....	....	0	1	.000	0-0	0-0	0-0	0-1	0-1	0-0
TOTALS		**51**	**6**	**9**	**27-15**	....	....	....	....	**10-2**	....	**32**	**22**	**.593**	**9-6**	**21-11**	**2-2**	**0-3**	**0-3**	**32-19**

Doubles Titles: Aus (3), Fre (2), Wim (2), US (3)

• STOVE, Betty
Betty Blippina Stove

Female. Born: June 24, 1945. Rotterdam, Netherlands. Height: 5' 11". Weight: 155 lbs. Plays: right.
Status: Turned Pro 1969. Earnings: $1,047,356. Highest Ranking: 5 (July 1977).

Year	Rk	TP	TW	TF	GS	Aus	Fre	Wim	US	FC	Oly	MW	ML	Pct	CL	GR	HD	CP	IN	OD
1964	....	2	0	0	....	....	....	2rd	1rd	1-1	....	....	....	....	....	....	....	....	....	....
1965	....	2	0	0	....	....	1rd	1rd	....	....	....	....	....	....	....	....	....	....	....	....
1966	....	1	0	0	....	....	....	3rd	....	1-0	....	....	....	....	....	....	....	....	....	....
1967	....	3	0	0	....	3rd	2rd	2rd	....	....	....	....	....	....	....	....	....	....	....	....
1969	....	2	0	0	0-1	....	....	2rd	....	3-1	....	3	2	.600	3-1	0-1	0-0	0-0	0-0	3-2
1970	....	2	0	0	0-2	....	1rd	2rd	....	5-0	....	5	2	.714	3-1	2-1	0-0	0-0	0-0	5-2
1971	....	3	0	0	3-3	....	3rd	2rd	1rd	....	....	3	3	.500	2-1	1-2	0-0	0-0	0-0	3-3
1972	....	4	0	1	5-3	....	3rd	4rd	3rd	2-0	....	7	3	.700	0-1	7-2	0-0	0-0	0-0	7-3
1973	....	3	0	0	3-3	....	3rd	1rd	2rd	....	....	3	3	.500	2-1	1-2	0-0	0-0	0-0	3-3
1974	....	2	0	0	1-2	....	....	1rd	2rd	....	....	1	2	.333	0-0	1-2	0-0	0-0	0-0	1-2
1975	22	4	0	0	5-2	....	....	QF	2rd	....	....	5	4	.556	1-2	4-1	0-0	0-1	0-1	5-3
1976	7	6	0	1	3-2	....	....	4rd	1rd	3-1	....	7	5	.583	0-1	3-2	0-0	4-2	4-2	3-3
1977	7	18	0	4	11-2	....	....	F	SF	3-0	....	44	18	.710	10-3	14-3	6-3	14-9	14-9	30-9
1978	8	24	0	4	5-2	....	4rd	4rd		2-1	....	48	24	.667	0-0	7-3	13-8	28-13	28-13	20-11
1979	22	24	0	0	5-3	....	3rd	4rd	2rd	2-1	....	23	24	.489	7-4	5-2	6-7	5-11	5-12	18-12
1980	28	23	0	0	5-4	3rd	2rd	3rd	1rd	....	....	23	23	.500	1-2	15-6	2-7	5-8	6-11	17-12
1981	123	19	0	0	1-4	2rd	1rd	2rd	1rd	....	....	5	19	.208	0-2	2-4	2-5	1-8	1-8	4-11
1982	47	15	0	0	2-3	2rd	2rd	....	1rd	....	....	9	15	.375	2-4	7-5	0-5	0-1	0-2	9-13
1983	....	2	0	0	0-0	....	....	....	....	....	....	0	2	.000	0-0	0-2	0-0	0-0	0-0	0-2
TOTALS		**159**	**0**	**10**	**49-36**	....	....	....	....	**22-5**	....	**186**	**149**	**.555**	**31-23**	**69-38**	**29-35**	**57-53**	**58-58**	**128-91**

Doubles Titles: Fre (2), Wim (1), US (3)

• SUKOVA, Helena
Helena Sukova

Female. Born: Feb. 23, 1965. Prague, Czech Republic. Height: 6' 2". Weight: 150 lbs. Plays: right.
Status: Turned Pro 1983. Earnings: $6,391,245. Highest Ranking: 4 (Mar. 1985).

Year	Rk	TP	TW	TF	GS	Aus	Fre	Wim	US	FC	Oly	MW	ML	Pct	CL	GR	HD	CP	IN	OD
1981	74	1	0	0	2-1	3rd	....	....	....	4-0	....	2	1	.667	0-0	2-1	0-0	0-0	0-0	2-1
1982	25	26	1	0	0-4	1rd	2rd	1rd	1rd	3-1	....	31	25	.554	7-4	4-5	10-7	10-9	12-10	19-15
1983	17	21	0	0	7-4	3rd	4rd	1rd	3rd	3-2	....	37	21	.638	15-9	8-4	10-5	4-3	6-4	31-17
1984	7	25	1	0	12-4	F	1rd	4rd	QF	4-1	....	52	24	.684	6-6	16-4	12-5	18-9	22-11	30-13
1985	9	23	0	0	12-4	QF	2rd	QF	QF	3-2	....	57	23	.713	6-3	18-5	20-9	13-6	16-7	41-16
1986	5	24	2	0	15-3	....	SF	QF	F	4-1	....	73	22	.768	14-5	9-2	21-4	29-11	29-11	44-11
1987	7	22	2	0	14-4	4rd	4rd	QF	SF	2-1	....	61	20	.753	6-3	17-4	20-8	18-5	20-6	41-14
1988	8	20	1	0	15-4	QF	QF	QF	4rd	5-0	2rd	54	20	.730	8-2	9-4	26-9	11-5	13-6	41-14
1989	8	18	1	0	14-4	F	2rd	4rd	QF	2-2	....	41	17	.707	2-3	5-2	28-9	6-3	7-5	34-12
1990	14	17	0	0	11-3	SF	....	4rd	4rd	....	....	41	17	.707	2-1	10-3	19-8	10-5	12-6	29-11
1991	17	19	1	0	5-4	3rd	2rd	1rd	3rd	....	....	34	18	.654	8-5	1-2	16-6	9-5	12-6	22-12
1992	12	18	2	0	7-3	3rd	....	3rd	4rd	2-0	2rd	41	16	.719	6-3	5-2	20-7	10-4	17-5	24-11
1993	17	16	0	0	10-2	....	....	QF	F	2-1	....	26	16	.619	3-2	7-2	15-8	1-4	1-5	25-11
1994	22	15	0	0	7-3	3rd	3rd	4rd	....	....	....	22	15	.595	4-3	4-2	5-5	9-5	9-6	13-9
1995	29	15	0	0	3-4	2rd	1rd	2rd	2rd	6-1	....	18	15	.545	4-3	2-2	5-4	7-6	7-6	11-9
1996	27	16	0	0	5-4	3rd	1rd	2rd	3rd	3-0	1rd	20	16	.556	0-2	5-2	6-8	9-4	9-6	11-10

Year	Rk	TP	TW	TF	GS	Aus	Fre	Wim	US	FC	Oly	MW	ML	Pct	CL	GR	HD	CP	IN	OD
1997	80	21	0	0	4-4	1rd	2rd	4rd	1rd	....	....	8	21	.276	1-3	3-2	2-11	2-5	2-7	6-14
1998	....	2	0	0	0-2	1rd	....	1rd	....	....	....	0	2	.000	0-0	0-1	0-1	0-0	0-0	0-2
TOTALS		319	10	0	143-61	....	....	....	44-12	....		618	309	.667	92-57	125-49	235-114	166-89	194-107	424-202

Doubles Titles: Aus (2), Fre (1), Wim (4), US (2)

• SUNDSTROM, Henrik   Henrik Sundstrom

Male. Born: Feb. 29, 1964. Lund, Sweden. Height: 6' 2". Weight: 160 lbs. Plays: right.
Status: Turned Pro 1981. Earnings: $819,393. Highest Ranking: 7 (Dec. 1984).

Year	Rk	TP	TW	TF	GS	Aus	Fre	Wim	US	DC	Oly	MW	ML	Pct	CL	GR	HD	CP	IN	OD
1981	315	5	0	0	0-0	....	....	....	....	....	....	0	5	.000	0-4	0-0	0-1	0-0	0-1	0-4
1982	82	10	0	1	2-3	2rd	....	1rd	2rd	....	....	14	10	.583	10-4	1-3	3-3	0-0	2-2	12-8
1983	23	21	1	2	5-4	2rd	4rd	3rd	1rd	0-2	....	31	20	.608	25-10	3-5	1-4	2-1	3-2	28-18
1984	7	24	3	3	8-3	....	QF	2rd	4rd	6-0	....	54	21	.720	47-11	1-1	3-2	3-7	5-8	49-13
1985	22	18	0	1	3-4	2rd	4rd	1rd	1rd	2-0	....	29	18	.617	25-9	0-2	4-6	0-1	0-2	29-16
1986	77	20	1	1	1-3	....	2rd	1rd	1rd	....	....	21	19	.525	21-13	0-1	0-3	0-2	0-4	21-15
1987	210	13	0	0	2-3	....	3rd	1rd	1rd	....	....	5	13	.278	5-11	0-1	0-1	0-0	0-0	5-13
1988	....	2	0	0	0-1	1rd	....	....	....	....	....	0	2	.000	0-1	0-0	0-1	0-0	0-0	0-2
1989	....	1	0	0	0-0	....	....	....	....	....	....	0	1	.000	0-1	0-0	0-0	0-0	0-0	0-1
TOTALS		114	5	8	21-21	....	....	....	....	8-2		154	109	.586	133-64	5-13	11-21	5-11	10-19	144-90

• SUSMAN, Karen   Karen Janice Hantze Susman

Female. Born: Dec. 11, 1942. San Diego, CA, United States. Height: 5' 7". Weight: –. Plays: right.
Status: Turned Pro 1969. Earnings: –. Highest Ranking: 4 (Dec. 1962).

Year	Rk	TP	TW	TF	GS	Aus	Fre	Wim	US	FC	Oly	MW	ML	Pct	CL	GR	HD	CP	IN	OD
1958	....	1	0	0		....	....	....	3rd	....	....	....			....	....	....	....	....	....
1959	....	1	0	0		....	....	....	QF	....	....	....			....	....	....	....	....	....
1960	....	2	0	0		....	....	QF	3rd	....	....	....			....	....	....	....	....	....
1961	10	2	0	0		....	....	QF	3rd	....	....	....			....	....	....	....	....	....
1962	4	2	1	0		....	....	W	3rd	....	....	....			....	....	....	....	....	....
1964	8	3	0	0		....	QF	3rd	QF	....	....	....			....	....	....	....	....	....
1969	....	1	0	0	0-1	....	....	....	1rd	....	....	0	1	.000	0-0	0-1	0-0	0-0	0-0	0-1
1977	....	1	0	0	0-1	....	....	2rd	....	....	....	0	1	.000	0-0	0-1	0-0	0-0	0-0	0-1
1978	....	1	0	0	0-0	....	....	....	....	....	....	1	1	.500	0-0	0-0	1-1	0-0	0-0	1-1
1980	....	1	0	0	0-1	....	....	....	3rd	....	....	0	1	.000	0-0	0-0	0-1	0-0	0-0	0-1
TOTALS		15	1	0	0-3	....	....	....	....	....		1	4	.200	0-0	0-2	1-2	0-0	0-0	1-4

Competed as Karen Hantze until 1962. Doubles Titles: Wim (2), US (1).

• TANNER, Roscoe   Roscoe Tanner

Male. Born: Oct. 15, 1951. Chattanooga, TN, United States. Height: 6'. Weight: 170 lbs. Plays: left.
Status: Turned Pro 1969. Earnings: $1,696,108. Highest Ranking: 4 (July 1979).

Year	Rk	TP	TW	TF	GS	Aus	Fre	Wim	US	DC	Oly	MW	ML	Pct	CL	GR	HD	CP	IN	OD
1969	....	1	0	0	0-1	....	....	....	1rd	....	....	0	1	.000	0-0	0-1	0-0	0-0	0-0	0-1
1970	....	2	0	0	0-1	....	....	....	2rd	....	....	0	2	.000	0-1	0-1	0-0	0-0	0-0	0-2
1971	....	2	0	0	2-1	....	....	....	3rd	....	....	3	2	.600	0-0	2-1	1-1	0-0	0-0	3-2
1972	....	5	0	2	6-2	....	....	3rd	QF	....	....	14	5	.737	0-1	6-2	4-1	4-1	4-1	10-4
1973	24	8	0	1	2-1	....	....	....	3rd	....	....	11	8	.579	0-0	3-3	6-4	2-1	2-1	9-7
1974	14	10	2	3	8-3	....	1rd	4rd	SF	....	....	20	8	.714	2-2	12-3	4-2	2-1	2-1	18-7
1975	9	9	2	4	9-3	....	3rd	SF	3rd	3-1	....	21	7	.750	4-2	9-2	8-1	0-2	3-3	18-4
1976	11	25	4	4	8-2	....	....	SF	4rd	2-0	....	50	21	.704	12-5	6-2	16-5	16-9	16-9	34-12
1977	15	17	2	2	9-3	W/1rd	....	1rd	4rd	1-1	....	25	15	.625	6-4	13-4	3-2	3-5	3-5	22-10
1978	11	19	2	1	9-3	....	4rd	4rd	4rd	....	....	46	17	.730	7-4	3-1	18-5	18-7	20-8	26-9
1979	5	21	2	3	11-2	....	....	F	SF	....	....	61	19	.763	5-2	10-2	21-5	25-10	25-10	36-9
1980	14	16	0	1	8-2	....	....	QF	QF	....	....	36	16	.692	0-1	7-2	14-6	15-7	15-7	21-9
1981	11	24	1	3	6-3	2rd	....	2rd	QF	3-2	....	54	23	.701	1-1	10-5	20-8	23-9	28-10	26-13
1982	43	17	0	1	4-2	....	....	4rd	2rd	....	....	20	17	.541	0-0	4-2	10-8	6-7	6-7	14-10
1983	37	13	0	0	8-3	3rd	....	QF	3rd	....	....	16	13	.552	0-1	6-3	7-5	3-4	4-5	12-8
1984	....	11	0	0	0-1	....	....	....	1rd	....	....	3	11	.214	1-1	0-0	1-8	1-2	1-2	2-9
1985	....	1	0	0	0-0	....	....	....	....	....	....	0	1	.000	0-0	0-0	0-0	0-1	0-1	0-0
TOTALS		201	15	25	90-33	....	....	....	9-4	....		380	186	.671	38-25	91-34	133-61	118-66	129-70	251-116

• TAUZIAT, Nathalie   Nathalie Tauziat

Female. Born: Oct. 17, 1967. Bangui, Central African Republic. Height: 5' 5". Weight: 140 lbs. Plays: right.
Status: Turned Pro 1984. Earnings: $6,633,727. Highest Ranking: 3 (May 2000).

Year	Rk	TP	TW	TF	GS	Aus	Fre	Wim	US	FC	Oly	MW	ML	Pct	CL	GR	HD	CP	IN	OD
1984	296	1	0	0	0-1	....	1rd	....	....	....	....	0	1	.000	0-1	0-0	0-0	0-0	0-0	0-1
1985	112	3	0	0	2-1	....	3rd	....	....	2-0	....	4	3	.571	2-2	0-0	2-1	0-0	1-1	3-2
1986	67	18	0	0	2-3	....	2rd	2rd	1rd	0-1	....	12	18	.400	3-5	4-3	3-6	2-4	2-5	10-13
1987	25	21	0	0	5-3	....	4rd	2rd	2rd	1-1	....	32	21	.604	11-5	4-3	14-10	3-3	4-5	28-16
1988	27	20	0	0	5-3	....	4rd	2rd	2rd	....	2rd	31	20	.608	9-6	2-3	18-9	2-2	5-4	26-16
1989	25	20	0	2	2-3	....	1rd	1rd	3rd	0-1	....	31	20	.608	10-5	2-2	15-10	4-3	4-5	27-15
1990	18	22	1	1	9-3	....	4rd	4rd	4rd	2-1	....	48	21	.696	7-4	8-3	20-9	13-5	17-7	31-14
1991	13	20	0	1	7-3	....	QF	4rd	1rd	1-1	....	38	20	.655	9-4	5-3	14-9	10-4	11-5	27-15
1992	14	21	0	2	8-3	....	4rd	QF	2rd	2-1	2rd	41	21	.661	11-6	8-3	16-9	6-3	8-5	33-16
1993	18	20	1	0	11-4	4rd	3rd	4rd	4rd	....	....	44	19	.698	7-4	8-3	20-8	9-4	14-6	30-13
1994	35	21	0	0	4-4	1rd	2rd	3rd	2rd	....	....	29	21	.580	5-4	6-3	10-9	8-5	9-7	20-14
1995	27	20	1	0	6-3	....	3rd	3rd	3rd	....	....	27	19	.587	7-4	9-2	9-8	2-5	4-7	23-12
1996	30	24	0	1	4-3	....	2rd	3rd	2rd	....	1rd	30	24	.556	8-7	9-3	11-9	2-5	2-7	28-17
1997	11	22	1	2	6-3	....	3rd	QF	1rd	....	....	42	21	.667	6-4	11-2	17-11	8-4	17-8	25-13
1998	10	24	0	2	9-3	....	1rd	F	4rd	....	....	42	24	.636	3-5	9-2	19-11	11-6	19-10	23-14
1999	7	27	2	2	7-3	....	2rd	QF	3rd	....	....	37	25	.597	5-5	11-3	8-11	13-6	17-10	20-15
2000	10	27	1	0	7-4	2rd	3rd	1rd	QF	....	....	36	26	.581	5-4	4-3	18-11	9-8	16-11	20-15
2001	13	22	1	1	7-3	....	1rd	QF	4rd	....	....	34	21	.618	2-4	9-2	21-11	2-4	8-8	26-13
TOTALS		**353**	**8**	**14**	**101-53**	....	....	....	....	**8-6**	....	**558**	**345**	**.618**	**110-79**	**109-43**	**235-152**	**104-71**	**158-111**	**400-234**

Represented France in the Federation Cup (1985-1992)

• TEACHER, Brian   Brian David Teacher

Male. Born: Dec. 23, 1954. San Diego, CA, United States. Height: 6' 3". Weight: 175 lbs. Plays: right.
Status: Turned Pro 1973. Earnings: $1,426,514. Highest Ranking: –.

Year	Rk	TP	TW	TF	GS	Aus	Fre	Wim	US	DC	Oly	MW	ML	Pct	CL	GR	HD	CP	IN	OD
1973	....	3	0	0	1-1	....	....	....	2rd	....	....	2	3	.400	0-0	1-1	1-2	0-0	0-0	2-3
1974	121	3	0	0	2-1	....	....	....	3rd	....	....	5	3	.625	0-0	2-1	3-2	0-0	0-0	5-3
1975	109	3	0	0	0-1	....	....	....	1rd	....	....	2	3	.400	0-1	0-0	2-1	0-1	0-1	2-2
1976	81	10	0	1	1-2	....	....	2rd	1rd	....	....	8	10	.444	1-4	1-1	5-2	1-3	1-3	7-7
1977	54	20	1	2	2-51rd/1rd	2rd	1rd	2rd	....	....	....	14	19	.424	5-6	1-5	7-5	1-3	5-5	9-14
1978	81	19	1	1	6-3	....	3rd	2rd	4rd	....	....	30	18	.625	6-5	2-3	7-4	15-6	15-6	15-12
1979	61	18	1	0	4-3	....	2rd	4rd	1rd	....	....	19	17	.528	3-2	10-2	5-7	1-6	3-7	16-10
1980	12	26	1	5	11-2	W	....	3rd	4rd	....	....	59	25	.702	1-1	15-4	24-9	19-11	19-11	40-14
1981	16	15	1	1	2-2	....	....	2rd	2rd	....	....	30	14	.682	1-1	5-3	15-6	9-4	9-4	21-10
1982	18	20	1	1	9-3	QF	....	QF	2rd	....	....	41	19	.683	5-3	10-3	13-7	13-6	15-8	26-11
1983	29	23	2	1	3-3	3rd	....	3rd	1rd	....	....	33	21	.611	4-3	5-4	15-8	9-6	13-7	20-14
1984	51	18	0	2	0-2	....	....	1rd	1rd	....	....	23	18	.561	10-5	6-3	6-6	1-4	1-4	22-14
1985	66	16	0	1	3-3	2rd	....	1rd	3rd	....	....	17	16	.515	2-2	4-4	10-7	1-3	2-4	15-12
1986	104	13	0	0	1-2	....	....	2rd	1rd	....	....	8	13	.381	2-3	1-2	1-5	4-3	4-3	4-10
TOTALS		**207**	**8**	**15**	**45-33**	....	....	....	....	....	....	**291**	**199**	**.594**	**40-36**	**63-36**	**114-71**	**74-56**	**87-63**	**204-136**

• TEGART, Judy   see DALTON, Judy, page 835

• TELTSCHER, Eliot   Eliot Teltscher

Male. Born: Mar. 15, 1959. Palos Verdes, CA, United States. Height: 5' 10". Weight: 150 lbs. Plays: right.
Status: Turned Pro 1976. Earnings: $1,653,997. Highest Ranking: 8 (Dec. 1981).

Year	Rk	TP	TW	TF	GS	Aus	Fre	Wim	US	DC	Oly	MW	ML	Pct	CL	GR	HD	CP	IN	OD
1976	239	1	0	0	0-0	....	....	....	....	....	....	1	1	.500	0-0	0-0	0-0	1-1	1-1	0-0
1977	106	8	0	0	1-3	/1rd	....	3rd	1rd	....	....	6	8	.429	0-2	1-2	2-2	3-2	3-2	3-6
1978	42	15	1	1	2-1	....	....	....	3rd	....	....	21	14	.600	5-3	0-0	15-6	1-5	1-6	20-8
1979	27	25	1	0	3-2	....	4rd	....	1rd	....	....	38	24	.613	16-9	0-0	15-8	7-7	13-11	25-13
1980	10	27	2	5	6-2	....	3rd	....	QF	....	....	69	25	.734	27-10	0-0	17-4	25-11	25-11	44-14
1981	8	20	2	2	4-2	....	1rd	....	QF	....	....	54	18	.750	20-8	0-0	24-5	10-5	13-6	41-12
1982	14	22	0	2	5-2	....	4rd	....	4rd	1-2	....	41	22	.651	20-10	0-0	12-7	9-5	11-6	30-16
1983	13	24	1	1	10-3	QF	4rd	....	QF	1-1	....	44	23	.657	13-9	3-1	17-6	11-7	11-7	33-16
1984	9	21	2	1	2-1	....	....	....	3rd	....	....	42	19	.689	4-5	0-0	19-6	19-8	22-9	20-10
1985	24	13	0	0	2-2	....	2rd	2rd	....	3-1	....	22	13	.629	3-3	1-1	6-3	12-6	12-6	10-7
1986	53	13	0	0	3-3	....	3rd	1rd	2rd	....	....	14	13	.519	7-6	0-1	2-3	5-3	5-3	9-10
1987	20	14	1	1	0-1	....	....	1rd	....	....	....	24	13	.649	5-4	0-0	14-7	5-2	7-3	17-10

Year	Rk	TP	TW	TF	GS	Aus	Fre	Wim	US	DC	Oly	MW	ML	Pct	CL	GR	HD	CP	IN	OD
1988	140	8	0	1	0-0	....	....	....	....	....	....	11	8	.579	1-1	0-0	10-6	0-1	1-1	10-7
1990	....	2	0	0	0-0	....	....	....	....	....	....	1	2	.333	0-0	0-0	1-2	0-0	0-0	1-2
Totals		213	10	14	38-22	....	....	....		5-4		388	203	.657	121-70	5-5	154-65	108-63	125-72	263-131

• TOMANOVA, Renata   Renata Tomanova Roth

Female. Born: Dec. 9, 1954. Czech Republic. Height: –. Weight: –. Plays: –.
Status: Turned Pro 1973. Earnings: –. Highest Ranking: –.

Year	Rk	TP	TW	TF	GS	Aus	Fre	Wim	US	FC	Oly	MW	ML	Pct	CL	GR	HD	CP	IN	OD
1973	....	2	0	0	2-2	....	3rd	1rd	....	....	....	2	2	.500	2-1	0-1	0-0	0-0	0-0	2-2
1974	....	2	0	0	1-2	....	1rd	2rd	....	....	....	1	2	.333	0-1	1-1	0-0	0-0	0-0	1-2
1975	....	4	0	0	3-3	....	3rd	3rd	1rd	4-1	....	7	4	.636	6-3	1-1	0-0	0-0	0-0	7-4
1976	....	8	0	3	11-4	F	F	3rd	3rd	....	....	11	5	.688	6-2	5-2	0-0	0-1	0-1	11-4
1977	....	20	0	1	4-3	....	QF	3rd	2rd	....	....	15	20	.429	6-4	3-3	1-4	5-9	5-9	10-11
1978	....	21	0	0	7-4	QF	2rd	3rd	3rd	3-0	....	24	21	.533	5-4	11-5	5-5	3-7	3-7	21-14
1979	....	21	0	0	6-4	SF	QF	1rd	2rd	....	....	16	21	.432	9-6	4-5	0-5	3-5	3-6	13-15
1980	....	22	0	0	3-4	2rd	1rd	1rd	4rd	3-1	....	21	22	.488	11-7	3-5	7-7	0-3	0-3	21-19
1981	....	15	0	0	4-4	1rd	2rd	3rd	3rd	1-1	....	15	15	.500	9-7	1-3	5-5	0-0	0-1	15-14
1982	....	12	0	0	1-4	2rd	2rd	2rd	1rd	....	....	9	12	.429	7-8	1-2	1-2	0-0	0-0	9-12
1983	....	9	0	0	0-3	....	1rd	1rd	1rd	....	....	1	9	.100	1-7	0-1	0-1	0-0	0-0	1-9
1984	....	1	0	0	0-0	....	....	....	....	....	....	0	1	.000	0-1	0-0	0-0	0-0	0-0	0-1
1985	....	2	0	0	0-0	....	....	....	....	....	....	1	2	.333	1-2	0-0	0-0	0-0	0-0	1-2
1986	....	2	0	0	0-0	....	....	....	....	....	....	0	2	.000	0-2	0-0	0-0	0-0	0-0	0-2
Totals		141	0	4	42-37	....	....	....		11-3		123	138	.471	63-55	30-29	19-29	11-25	11-27	112-111

Doubles Titles: Aus (1)

• TURNBULL, Wendy   Wendy May "Rabbit" Turnbull

Female. Born: Nov. 26, 1952. Brisbane, Australia. Height: 5' 4". Weight: 120 lbs. Plays: right.
Status: Turned Pro 1975. Earnings: $2,769,024. Highest Ranking: 3 (Jan. 1985).

Year	Rk	TP	TW	TF	GS	Aus	Fre	Wim	US	FC	Oly	MW	ML	Pct	CL	GR	HD	CP	IN	OD
1970	....	1	0	0	0-1	2rd	....	....	....	....	....	0	1	.000	0-0	0-1	0-0	0-0	0-0	0-1
1972	....	2	0	0	1-2	2rd	....	1rd	....	....	....	1	2	.333	0-0	1-2	0-0	0-0	0-0	1-2
1973	....	6	2	0	3-3	3rd	1rd	3rd	....	....	....	3	4	.429	0-1	3-2	0-1	0-0	0-0	3-4
1974	....	2	0	0	2-2	2rd	....	2rd	....	....	....	2	2	.500	0-0	2-2	0-0	0-0	0-0	2-2
1975	72	2	0	0	2-2	3rd	....	1rd	....	....	....	2	2	.500	0-0	2-2	0-0	0-0	0-0	2-2
1976	30	7	3	0	4-4	2rd	3rd	3rd	1rd	....	....	4	4	.500	2-2	2-2	0-0	0-0	0-0	4-4
1977	9	17	0	2	7-2	....	....	2rd	F	....	....	29	17	.630	7-3	6-2	7-4	9-8	9-8	20-9
1978	7	23	0	2	7-2	....	....	4rd	SF	2-2	....	48	23	.676	1-1	12-5	15-8	20-9	20-9	28-14
1979	7	27	2	3	10-3	....	F	QF	3rd	2-0	....	61	25	.709	9-4	12-4	20-8	20-9	22-10	39-15
1980	8	26	2	6	11-4	F	QF	QF	3rd	4-1	....	72	24	.750	13-2	18-3	14-6	27-13	29-14	43-10
1981	8	24	1	0	9-3	SF	....	QF	3rd	2-1	....	46	23	.667	8-3	13-4	7-6	18-10	18-10	28-13
1982	5	21	2	4	7-3	QF	....	4rd	4rd	1-0	....	46	19	.708	3-2	9-3	6-4	28-10	29-11	17-8
1983	8	19	1	2	8-3	QF	....	4rd	3rd	2-1	....	46	18	.719	7-4	15-4	7-4	17-6	17-6	29-12
1984	5	17	0	1	12-3	SF	....	4rd	SF	0-1	....	37	17	.685	0-1	15-6	12-3	10-7	10-7	27-10
1985	14	18	0	1	7-3	3rd	....	3rd	4rd	4-0	....	40	18	.690	0-0	15-6	15-6	10-6	10-6	30-12
1986	18	17	0	0	4-2	....	....	1rd	QF	0-2	....	17	17	.500	2-3	1-2	6-5	8-7	8-7	9-10
1987	23	16	0	0	4-3	4rd	....	QF	2rd	....	....	20	16	.556	0-0	8-6	4-5	8-5	10-6	10-10
1988	136	16	0	0	0-2	....	....	1rd	1rd	....	2rd	5	14	.263	0-0	2-4	2-6	1-4	1-5	4-9
1989	264	4	0	0	1-2	1rd	....	2rd	....	....	....	2	4	.333	0-0	1-1	1-3	0-0	0-0	2-4
Totals		263	13	21	99-49	....	....	....		17-8		481	250	.658	52-26	137-61	116-69	176-94	183-99	298-151

Doubles Titles: Fre (1), Wim (1), US (2)

• TURNER, Lesley   Lesley Rosemary Turner Bowrey

Female. Born: Aug. 16, 1942. Sydney, Australia. Height: –. Weight: –. Plays: right.
Status: Amateur. Earnings: –. Highest Ranking: 2 (Dec. 1963). HOF: 1997

Year	Rk	TP	TW	TF	GS	Aus	Fre	Wim	US	FC	Oly	MW	ML	Pct	CL	GR	HD	CP	IN	OD
1959	....	1	0	0	....	QF	....	....	....	....	....	....	....	....	....	....	....	....	....	....
1960	....	1	0	0	....	4rd	....	....	....	....	....	....	....	....	....	....	....	....	....	....
1961	....	4	0	0	....	4rd	3rd	2rd	QF	....	....	....	....	....	....	....	....	....	....	....
1962	7	4	0	1	....	QF	F	QF	4rd	....	....	....	....	....	....	....	....	....	....	....
1963	2	3	1	0	....	SF	W	4rd	....	0-1	....	....	....	....	....	....	....	....	....	....
1964	3	4	0	1	....	F	SF	SF	2rd	4-0	....	....	....	....	....	....	....	....	....	....
1965	3	3	1	0	....	4rd	W	QF	....	3-0	....	....	....	....	....	....	....	....	....	....
1966	....	1	0	0	....	4rd	....	....	....	....	....	....	....	....	....	....	....	....	....	....

Year	Rk	TP	TW	TF	GS	Aus	Fre	Wim	US	FC	Oly	MW	ML	Pct	CL	GR	HD	CP	IN	OD
1967	5	4	0	2	....	F	F	QF	SF	0-2	....	....	....	....	....	....	....	....	....	....
1968	8	1	0	0	3-1	....	....	QF	....	....	....	3	1	.750	0-0	3-1	0-0	0-0	0-0	3-1
1969	10	3	0	0	10-3	2rd	SF	QF	2rd	....	....	10	3	.769	4-1	6-2	0-0	0-0	0-0	10-3
1971	....	4	0	1	6-3	2rd	QF	4rd	....	....	....	6	3	.667	3-1	3-2	0-0	0-0	0-0	6-3
1973	....	2	0	0	2-2	3rd	....	....	2rd	....	....	2	2	.500	0-0	2-2	0-0	0-0	0-0	2-2
1975	....	1	0	0	0-1	1rd	....	....	....	....	....	0	1	.000	0-0	0-1	0-0	0-0	0-0	0-1
1976	....	1	0	0	2-1	QF	....	....	....	....	....	2	1	.667	0-0	2-1	0-0	0-0	0-0	2-1
1977	....	1	0	0	0-1	1rd/	....	....	....	....	....	0	1	.000	0-0	0-1	0-0	0-0	0-0	0-1
1978	....	3	0	0	2-2	....	3rd	2rd	....	....	....	2	3	.400	2-1	0-2	0-0	0-0	0-0	2-3
TOTALS		41	2	5	25-14	....	....	....	....	7-3	....	25	15	.625	9-3	16-12	0-0	0-0	0-0	25-15

Doubles Titles: Aus (3), Fre (2), Wim (1), US (1)

• VILAS, Guillermo   Guillermo Vilas

Male. Born: Aug. 17, 1952. Buenos Aires, Argentina. Height: 5' 11". Weight: 175 lbs. Plays: left.
Status: Turned Pro 1970. Earnings: $4,923,882. Highest Ranking: 2 (Apr. 1975). HOF: 1991

Year	Rk	TP	TW	TF	GS	Aus	Fre	Wim	US	DC	Oly	MW	ML	Pct	CL	GR	HD	CP	IN	OD
1970	....	2	0	0	0-1	....	....	1rd	....	1-1	....	0	2	.000	0-1	0-1	0-0	0-0	0-0	0-2
1972	....	4	0	2	3-3	....	3rd	1rd	2rd	1-0	....	7	4	.636	6-2	1-2	0-0	0-0	0-0	7-4
1973	31	6	1	0	2-2	....	3rd	....	1rd	1-1	....	5	5	.500	3-3	0-1	2-1	0-0	0-0	5-5
1974	5	14	7	1	7-3	....	3rd	3rd	4rd	7-1	....	25	7	.781	9-3	12-3	4-1	0-0	4-1	21-6
1975	2	14	5	3	15-3	....	F	QF	SF	2-0	....	33	9	.786	18-4	7-2	3-2	5-1	8-3	25-6
1976	6	22	6	3	13-3	....	QF	QF	SF	....	....	54	16	.771	27-6	4-1	9-3	14-6	16-7	38-9
1977	2	26	16	6	21-2	F/	W	3rd	W	6-0	....	38	10	.792	20-3	8-4	5-1	5-2	5-2	33-8
1978	5	14	7	1	17-3	W	F	3rd	4rd	1-1	....	58	7	.892	34-4	11-2	8-1	5-1	10-1	48-7
1979	6	25	4	5	14-3	W	QF	2rd	4rd	2-2	....	70	21	.769	30-6	16-2	14-5	10-8	18-10	52-11
1980	5	20	3	4	10-3	SF	QF	....	4rd	5-1	....	66	17	.795	42-5	6-2	13-5	5-5	5-5	61-12
1981	6	20	3	7	8-4	3rd	4rd	1rd	4rd	6-1	....	70	17	.805	59-9	2-2	6-2	3-4		67-13
1982	4	23	7	5	11-2	....	F	....	SF	3-0	....	77	16	.828	49-5	0-0	10-3	18-8	18-8	59-8
1983	11	21	3	4	6-3	....	QF	1rd	3rd	5-1	....	56	18	.757	39-10	0-1	8-3	9-4	13-5	43-13
1984	28	15	0	0	2-2	....	1rd	....	3rd	1-1	....	18	15	.545	12-9	0-0	5-4	1-2	3-3	15-12
1985	39	14	0	0	2-2	....	2rd	....	2rd	....	....	17	14	.548	16-11	0-0	1-3	0-0	0-0	17-14
1986	22	14	0	1	4-3	....	QF	1rd	1rd	....	....	19	14	.576	19-12	0-1	0-1	0-0	0-0	19-14
1987	71	14	0	0	1-1	....	2rd	....	....	....	....	18	14	.563	18-12	0-0	0-2	0-0	0-1	18-13
1988	126	15	0	0	1-1	....	2rd	....	....	....	....	11	15	.423	11-13	0-0	0-2	0-0	0-0	11-15
1989	....	4	0	0	0-1	....	1rd	....	....	....	....	2	4	.333	2-4	0-0	0-0	0-0	0-0	2-4
1992	....	2	0	0	0-0	....	....	....	....	....	....	0	2	.000	0-2	0-0	0-0	0-0	0-0	0-2
TOTALS		289	62	42	137-45	....	....	....	....	41-10	....	644	227	.739	414-124	67-24	88-39	75-41	103-50	541-178

• WADE, Virginia   Sarah Virginia Wade

Female. Born: July 10, 1945. Bournemouth, Great Britain. Height: 5' 7". Weight: 135 lbs. Plays: right.
Status: Turned Pro 1968. Earnings: $1,542,278. Highest Ranking: 2 (Dec. 1968). HOF: 1989

Year	Rk	TP	TW	TF	GS	Aus	Fre	Wim	US	FC	Oly	MW	ML	Pct	CL	GR	HD	CP	IN	OD
1962	....	1	0	0	....	....	....	2rd	....	....	....	....	....	....	....	....	....	....	....	....
1963	....	1	0	0	....	....	....	2rd	....	....	....	....	....	....	....	....	....	....	....	....
1964	....	2	0	0	....	....	....	2rd	4rd	....	....	....	....	....	....	....	....	....	....	....
1965	....	2	0	0	....	....	....	4rd	2rd	....	....	....	....	....	....	....	....	....	....	....
1966	....	2	0	0	....	....	....	2rd	QF	....	....	....	....	....	....	....	....	....	....	....
1967	8	3	0	0	....	....	4rd	QF	4rd	3-1	....	....	....	....	....	....	....	....	....	....
1968	2	8	5	8	6-1	....	....	1rd	W	2-2	....	8	3	.727	2-2	6-1	0-0	0-0	0-0	8-3
1969	9	12	7	0	7-3	....	2rd	3rd	SF	1-2	....	8	5	.615	2-3	6-2	0-0	0-0	0-0	8-5
1970	5	10	5	2	10-3	....	4rd	SF	4rd	4-2	....	14	5	.737	5-2	9-3	0-0	0-0	0-0	14-5
1971	7	11	9	0	3-2	....	1rd	4rd	....	....	....	3	2	.600	0-1	3-1	0-0	0-0	0-0	3-2
1972	5	8	4	3	13-3	W	QF	QF	QF	4-1	....	17	4	.810	2-1	15-3	0-0	0-0	0-0	17-4
1973	6	14	6	4	11-4	QF	3rd	QF	QF	2-0	....	13	4	.765	4-1	9-3	0-0	0-0	0-0	13-4
1974	4	10	5	3	7-3	....	2rd	SF	2rd	3-1	....	12	4	.750	4-2	7-2	0-0	1-1	1-1	11-4
1975	5	15	6	2	7-2	....	....	QF	SF	3-0	....	11	6	.647	7-1	3-1	0-0	1-4	1-4	10-2
1976	3	6	2	4	6-2	....	....	SF	2rd	2-1	....	10	3	.769	2-1	6-1	0-0	2-1	2-1	8-2
1977	4	16	3	1	11-1	....	....	W	QF	3-1	....	43	13	.768	5-2	10-1	5-2	23-8	23-8	20-5
1978	4	26	3	2	6-2	....	....	SF	3rd	2-2	....	67	23	.744	0-0	14-5	27-6	26-12	26-12	41-11
1979	8	24	0	0	9-3	....	2rd	QF	QF	2-1	....	51	24	.680	3-3	9-3	20-8	19-10	19-10	32-14
1980	15	23	0	1	7-3	....	3rd	4rd	3rd	0-2	....	29	23	.558	4-5	4-3	2-4	19-11	19-12	10-11
1981	30	22	0	0	4-3	....	4rd	3rd	....	2-3	....	22	22	.500	6-7	0-3	5-3	11-9	11-9	11-13
1982	59	13	0	0	2-3	....	3rd	2rd	1rd	1-0	....	7	13	.350	2-5	1-2	4-4	0-2	0-2	7-11
1983	40	10	0	0	6-4	2rd	1rd	QF	2rd	2-1	....	12	10	.545	4-5	7-3	1-1	0-1	0-1	12-9

Year	Rk	TP	TW	TF	GS	Aus	Fre	Wim	US	FC	Oly	MW	ML	Pct	CL	GR	HD	CP	IN	OD
1984	61	11	0	0	4-4	2rd	1rd	3rd	2rd	....	....	6	11	.353	0-2	3-4	1-1	2-4	2-4	4-7
1985	89	9	0	0	4-3	2rd	2rd	3rd	....	....	....	7	9	.438	1-2	3-3	3-3	0-1	0-1	7-8
TOTALS		**259**	**55**	**31**	**123-49**	....	....	....	**36-20**		....	**340**	**184**	**.649**	**53-45**	**115-44**	**68-32**	**104-64**	**104-65**	**236-120**

Doubles Titles: Aus (1), Fre (1), US (3)

• WALSH, Sharon

Sharon Walsh Pete

Female. Born: Feb. 24, 1952. San Francisco, CA, United States. Height: 5' 8". Weight: 135 lbs. Plays: right.
Status: Turned Pro 1971. Earnings: $751,138. Highest Ranking: 22 (Feb. 1982).

Year	Rk	TP	TW	TF	GS	Aus	Fre	Wim	US	FC	Oly	MW	ML	Pct	CL	GR	HD	CP	IN	OD
1969	....	1	0	0	0-1	....	....	....	1rd	....	....	0	1	.000	0-0	0-1	0-0	0-0	0-0	0-1
1970	....	4	0	0	4-2	....	....	3rd	3rd	1-2	....	5	4	.556	0-1	5-3	0-0	0-0	0-0	5-4
1971	....	1	0	0	2-1	QF	....	....	....	....	....	2	1	.667	0-0	2-1	0-0	0-0	0-0	2-1
1972	....	3	0	0	2-3	....	1rd	2rd	3rd	....	....	2	3	.400	0-1	2-2	0-0	0-0	0-0	2-3
1973	....	3	0	0	1-3	....	2rd	1rd	1rd	....	....	1	3	.250	1-1	0-2	0-0	0-0	0-0	1-3
1974	....	3	0	1	2-2	....	....	2rd	2rd	....	....	2	2	.500	0-0	2-2	0-0	0-0	0-0	2-2
1975	65	3	0	0	0-3	....	1rd	2rd	1rd	....	....	0	3	.000	0-2	0-1	0-0	0-0	0-0	0-3
1976	41	1	0	0	0-1	....	....	....	2rd	....	....	0	1	.000	0-1	0-0	0-0	0-0	0-0	0-1
1977	41	15	0	0	0-3	....	1rd	1rd	1rd	....	....	9	15	.375	2-3	0-3	1-3	6-6	6-6	3-9
1978	44	24	0	0	0-3	....	1rd	2rd	2rd	....	....	13	24	.351	1-3	6-5	1-6	5-10	5-10	8-14
1979	61	15	0	1	5-4	F	2rd	1rd	1rd	....	....	9	15	.375	1-1	5-5	2-6	1-3	1-4	8-11
1980	39	18	0	0	0-3	1rd	....	1rd	2rd	....	....	14	18	.438	4-2	5-6	4-9	1-1	2-2	12-16
1981	26	17	0	0	6-3	2rd	....	3rd	4rd	....	....	20	17	.541	1-1	9-6	4-4	6-6	6-6	14-11
1982	64	19	0	0	3-4	3rd	2rd	2rd	1rd	....	....	10	19	.345	0-1	5-5	1-4	4-9	4-9	6-10
1983	45	12	0	0	3-3	3rd	....	2rd	1rd	....	....	11	12	.478	0-0	7-5	1-5	3-2	3-2	8-10
1984	38	12	0	0	3-3	QF	....	1rd	1rd	....	....	8	12	.400	0-0	7-5	0-3	1-4	1-4	7-8
1985	130	17	0	0	0-3	1rd	....	1rd	1rd	....	....	8	17	.320	0-0	1-6	3-5	4-6	4-7	4-10
1986	195	4	0	0	0-1	....	....	....	1rd	....	....	2	4	.333	0-0	0-0	2-4	0-0	1-1	1-3
1987	82	15	0	0	2-4	1rd	1rd	3rd	1rd	....	....	11	15	.423	0-1	4-6	6-6	1-2	1-2	10-13
1988	388	6	0	0	0-2	1rd	....	1rd	....	....	....	0	6	.000	0-0	0-4	0-2	0-0	0-0	0-6
TOTALS		**193**	**0**	**2**	**33-52**	....	....	....	**1-2**		....	**127**	**192**	**.398**	**10-18**	**60-68**	**25-57**	**32-49**	**34-53**	**93-139**

• WARWICK, Kim

Kim Warwick

Male. Born: Apr. 8, 1952. Sydney, Australia. Height: 5' 11". Weight: 170 lbs. Plays: right.
Status: Turned Pro 1971. Earnings: $994,045. Highest Ranking: –.

Year	Rk	TP	TW	TF	GS	Aus	Fre	Wim	US	DC	Oly	MW	ML	Pct	CL	GR	HD	CP	IN	OD
1971	....	1	0	0	0-1	....	....	1rd	....	....	....	0	1	.000	0-0	0-1	0-0	0-0	0-0	0-1
1972	....	2	0	1	1-2	2rd	....	1rd	....	....	....	1	2	.333	0-0	1-2	0-0	0-0	0-0	1-2
1973	....	3	0	0	0-2	1rd	1rd	....	....	....	....	0	3	.000	0-1	0-1	0-1	0-0	0-0	0-3
1974	39	4	0	1	3-3	2rd	....	3rd	1rd	....	....	3	4	.429	0-0	3-3	0-0	0-1	0-1	3-3
1975	48	5	0	0	5-3	QF	....	3rd	2rd	....	....	7	5	.583	2-2	4-2	0-0	1-1	1-1	6-4
1976	67	22	1	0	6-4	3rd	1rd	3rd	3rd	....	....	14	21	.400	6-8	4-3	2-2	2-8	2-8	12-13
1977	50	14	0	1	4-5	1rd/1rd	2rd	4rd	1rd	....	....	13	14	.481	7-6	5-5	1-2	0-1	0-1	13-13
1978	41	23	0	2	3-4	3rd	1rd	2rd	1rd	1-0	....	29	23	.558	11-7	8-4	3-4	7-8	7-9	22-14
1979	51	26	0	0	3-4	3rd	2rd	1rd	1rd	....	....	30	26	.536	8-10	9-6	6-5	7-5	10-6	20-20
1980	22	26	1	3	7-3	F	2rd	2rd	....	....	....	39	25	.609	10-10	15-6	9-5	5-4	8-6	31-19
1981	84	14	0	0	3-1	QF	....	....	....	0-2	....	6	14	.300	0-2	3-2	1-6	2-4	2-7	4-7
1982	42	15	0	0	4-2	....	....	1rd	QF	....	....	14	15	.483	2-4	2-3	6-5	4-3	4-3	10-12
1983	259	8	0	0	2-2	1rd	....	....	3rd	....	....	3	8	.273	0-0	0-1	3-5	0-2	0-3	3-5
1984	194	4	0	0	1-1	2rd	....	....	....	....	....	6	4	.600	3-1	2-2	0-0	1-1	1-1	5-3
1985	497	3	0	0	0-0	....	....	....	....	....	....	1	3	.250	0-0	1-1	0-1	0-1	0-1	1-2
1988	600	1	0	0	0-0	....	....	....	....	....	....	1	1	.500	0-0	0-0	1-1	0-0	0-0	1-1
TOTALS		**171**	**2**	**8**	**42-37**	....	....	....	**1-2**		....	**167**	**169**	**.497**	**49-51**	**57-42**	**32-37**	**29-39**	**35-47**	**132-122**

• WASHINGTON, MaliVai

MaliVai Washington

Male. Born: June 20, 1969. Glen Cove, NY, United States. Height: 5' 11". Weight: 175 lbs. Plays: right.
Status: Turned Pro 1989. Earnings: $3,239,865. Highest Ranking: 11 (Oct. 1992).

Year	Rk	TP	TW	TF	GS	Aus	Fre	Wim	US	DC	Oly	MW	ML	Pct	CL	GR	HD	CP	IN	OD
1988	329	3	0	0	0-0	....	....	....	....	....	....	1	3	.250	0-0	0-0	1-2	0-1	0-1	1-2
1989	199	5	0	0	1-1	....	....	....	2rd	....	....	2	5	.286	0-0	0-1	2-3	0-1	0-1	2-4
1990	93	16	0	0	2-3	....	1rd	2rd	2rd	....	....	13	16	.448	3-2	1-3	9-7	0-4	3-5	10-11
1991	49	22	0	0	3-4	1rd	1rd	2rd	3rd	....	....	33	22	.600	5-3	6-3	13-11	9-5	10-6	23-16
1992	13	24	2	4	6-4	3rd	2rd	1rd	4rd	....	....	50	22	.694	11-3	5-3	30-10	4-6	9-6	41-16
1993	23	23	0	2	9-4	4rd	4rd	2rd	3rd	2-0	....	39	23	.629	4-4	4-3	23-10	8-6	8-7	31-16

Year	Rk	TP	TW	TF	GS	Aus	Fre	Wim	US	DC	Oly	MW	ML	Pct	CL	GR	HD	CP	IN	OD
1994	30	24	1	0	5-4	QF	1rd	1rd	2rd	....	....	36	23	.610	5-5	3-3	22-12	6-3	7-4	29-19
1995	26	29	0	2	1-4	1rd	2rd	1rd	1rd	....	....	31	29	.517	6-9	1-2	14-13	10-5	14-8	17-21
1996	23	25	1	1	10-4	4rd	1rd	F	2rd	0-2	QF	33	24	.579	7-5	6-2	17-11	3-6	5-8	28-16
1997	256	6	0	0	3-1	4rd	....	....	....	0-1		6	6	.500	1-1	0-0	5-5	0-0	0-2	6-4
1998	178	10	0	0	1-1	2rd	....	....	1rd			10	10	.500	1-1	0-0	9-9	0-0	2-2	8-8
1999	1231	2	0	0	0-0	....						0	2	.000	0-0	0-1	0-1	0-0	0-0	0-2
TOTALS		**189**	**4**	**9**	**41-30**	....	....	....	....	**2-3**	....	**254**	**185**	**.579**	**43-33**	**26-21**	**145-94**	**40-37**	**58-50**	**196-135**

• WILANDER, Mats   Mats Arne Olof Wilander

Male. Born: Aug. 22, 1964. Vaxjo, Sweden. Height: 6'. Weight: 170 lbs. Plays: right.
Status: Turned Pro 1980. Earnings: $7,976,256. Highest Ranking: 1 (Sept. 1988). HOF: 2002.

Year	Rk	TP	TW	TF	GS	Aus	Fre	Wim	US	DC	Oly	MW	ML	Pct	CL	GR	HD	CP	IN	OD
1980	283	4	0	0	0-0	....	....	....	....	....	....	1	4	.200	1-3	0-0	0-0	0-1	0-1	1-3
1981	69	12	0	1	2-2	1rd	....	3rd	....	0-2	....	13	12	.520	4-6	2-3	3-1	4-2	7-3	6-9
1982	7	22	4	3	13-2	....	W	4rd	4rd	3-1	....	61	18	.772	36-5	3-1	18-6	4-6	17-9	44-9
1983	4	20	9	2	18-3	W	F	3rd	QF	8-0	....	82	11	.882	42-2	12-1	19-3	9-5	14-5	68-6
1984	4	17	3	3	16-3	W	SF	2rd	QF	5-1	....	54	14	.794	24-7	7-1	14-2	9-4	14-6	40-8
1985	3	24	3	7	17-3	F	W	1rd	SF	4-2	....	69	21	.767	40-7	6-3	13-4	10-7	12-8	57-13
1986	3	15	2	3	8-3	....	3rd	4rd	4rd	4-0	....	54	13	.806	19-4	3-1	21-4	11-4	15-5	39-8
1987	3	23	5	4	16-3	....	F	QF	F	6-1	....	71	18	.798	40-4	4-2	15-6	12-6	14-7	57-11
1988	1	17	6	0	25-1	W	W	QF	W	2-3	....	53	11	.828	19-4	4-1	29-2	1-4	2-6	51-5
1989	12	18	0	1	10-4	2rd	QF	QF	2rd	3-3	....	34	18	.654	15-7	7-2	8-5	4-4	4-6	30-12
1990	41	15	1	1	5-2	SF	....	....	1rd	1-1	....	22	14	.611	2-3	0-0	15-8	5-3	6-5	16-9
1991	157	10	0	1	4-2	4rd	2rd	....	....	....	....	9	10	.474	3-6	0-1	5-2	1-1	3-2	6-8
1993	326	7	0	0	2-1	....	....	3rd	....	....	....	3	7	.300	1-2	0-0	2-4	0-1	0-2	3-5
1994	126	20	0	0	3-3	4rd	1rd	....	1rd	....	....	17	20	.459	7-8·	0-0	10-12	0-0	0-0	17-20
1995	46	20	0	0	4-4	1rd	2rd	3rd	2rd	0-2	....	21	20	.512	4-7	2-1	14-11	1-1	1-3	20-17
1996	198	11	0	0	1-1	....	2rd	....	....			7	11	.389	7-5	0-0	0-3	0-3	0-3	7-8
TOTALS		**255**	**33**	**26**	**144-37**	....	....	....	....	**36-16**	....	**571**	**222**	**.720**	**264-80**	**50-17**	**186-73**	**71-52**	**109-71**	**462-151**

Held number one tour ranking 1 time for a total of 20 weeks. Last ranked number one in 1989. Doubles Titles: Wim (1).

• WILLIAMS, Serena   Serena Williams

Female. Born: Sept. 26, 1981. Saginaw, MI, United States. Height: 5' 8". Weight: 130 lbs. Plays: right.
Status: Turned Pro 1995. Earnings: $10,041,992. Highest Ranking: 1 (July 2002).

Year	Rk	TP	TW	TF	GS	Aus	Fre	Wim	US	FC	Oly	MW	ML	Pct	CL	GR	HD	CP	IN	OD
1997	99	2	0	0	0-0	....	....	....	....	....	....	3	2	.600	0-0	0-0	0-0	3-2	3-2	0-0
1998	20	11	0	0	8-4	2rd	4rd	3rd	3rd	....	....	26	11	.703	6-2	4-2	16-7	0-0	4-2	22-9
1999	4	12	5	1	11-2	3rd	3rd	....	W	1-0	....	41	7	.854	7-3	0-0	31-4	3-1	8-1	33-6
2000	4	11	3	2	12-3	4rd	....	SF	QF	....	....	37	8	.822	0-1	5-1	32-6	0-0	7-1	30-7
2001	6	10	3	1	18-4	QF	QF	QF	F	....	....	38	7	.844	4-1	4-1	30-5	0-0	3-1	35-7
2002	1	13	8	2	21-0	....	W	W	W	....	....	56	5	.918	17-2	7-1	28-3	4-1	7-1	49-4
TOTALS		**59**	**19**	**6**	**70-13**	....	....	....	....	**1-0**	....	**201**	**40**	**.834**	**34-9**	**20-5**	**137-25**	**10-4**	**32-8**	**169-33**

Held number one tour ranking 1 time for a total of 28 weeks. Last ranked number one in 2002. Doubles Titles: Aus (2), Fre (1), Wim (2), US (1).

• WILLIAMS, Venus   Venus Starr Williams

Female. Born: June 17, 1980. Lynwood, CA, United States. Height: 6' 1". Weight: 160 lbs. Plays: right.
Status: Turned Pro 1994. Earnings: $11,902,908. Highest Ranking: 1 (Feb. 2002).

Year	Rk	TP	TW	TF	GS	Aus	Fre	Wim	US	FC	Oly	MW	ML	Pct	CL	GR	HD	CP	IN	OD
1994	....	1	0	0	0-0	....	....	....	....	....	....	1	1	.500	0-0	0-0	0-0	1-1	1-1	0-0
1995	204	3	0	0	0-0	....	....	....	....	....	....	2	3	.400	0-0	0-0	0-2	2-1	2-1	0-2
1996	204	5	0	0	0-0	....	....	....	....	....	....	2	5	.286	0-1	0-0	2-3	0-1	0-1	2-4
1997	22	13	0	1	7-3	....	2rd	1rd	F	....	....	19	13	.594	2-2	1-2	14-7	2-2	3-3	16-10
1998	5	16	3	4	17-4	QF	QF	QF	SF	....	....	53	13	.803	9-2	4-2	35-8	5-1	14-3	39-10
1999	3	19	6	4	15-4	QF	4rd	QF	SF	3-1	....	61	13	.824	14-2	4-1	37-7	6-3	17-4	44-9
2000	3	10	6	1	18-1	....	QF	W	W	....	W	41	4	.911	6-3	7-1	25-0	3-1	3-1	38-3
2001	3	11	6	1	19-2	SF	1rd	W	W	....	....	46	5	.902	5-2	7-1	32-2	2-1	2-1	44-4
2002	2	16	7	4	22-4	QF	F	F	F	....	....	62	9	.873	14-2	6-1	42-5	0-1	9-2	53-7
TOTALS		**94**	**28**	**14**	**98-18**	....	....	....	....	**3-1**	....	**287**	**66**	**.813**	**50-14**	**29-8**	**187-34**	**21-12**	**51-17**	**236-49**

Held number one tour ranking 1 time for a total of 11 weeks. Last ranked number one in 2002. Doubles Titles: Aus (2), Fre (1), Wim (2), US (1).

• ZVEREVA, Natalia   Natalia "Natasha" Zvereva

Female. Born: Apr. 16, 1971. Minsk, Russian Federation. Height: 5' 8". Weight: 135 lbs. Plays: right.
Status: Turned Pro 1988. Earnings: $7,792,503. Highest Ranking: 5 (May 1989).

Year	Rk	TP	TW	TF	GS	Aus	Fre	Wim	US	FC	Oly	MW	ML	Pct	CL	GR	HD	CP	IN	OD
1986	92	3	0	1	0-0	....	....	....	....	1-3	....	4	3	.571	0-1	0-0	0-1	4-1	4-1	0-2
1987	19	11	0	2	7-3	....	3rd	4rd	3rd	1-1	....	22	11	.667	3-2	4-2	9-6	6-1	6-2	16-9
1988	7	21	0	4	9-3	....	F	4rd	1rd	2-3	QF	42	21	.667	9-2	8-2	16-12	9-5	11-6	31-15
1989	27	18	0	2	5-3	....	1rd	3rd	4rd	1-1	....	24	18	.571	5-5	2-2	10-6	7-5	10-6	14-12
1990	12	17	2	0	9-4	2rd	4rd	QF	2rd	5-0	....	42	15	.737	12-5	7-2	19-3	4-5	4-5	38-10
1991	21	19	0	1	8-4	4rd	2rd	2rd	4rd	1-1	....	30	19	.612	8-4	5-2	14-9	3-4	4-5	26-14
1992	12	20	0	0	11-4	2rd	QF	QF	3rd	....	3rd	34	20	.630	16-6	5-2	15-6	6-5	13-7	24-12
1993	19	19	0	1	13-4	3rd	4rd	QF	QF	....	....	37	19	.661	8-5	5-2	15-6	9-6	13-7	24-12
1994	10	13	1	3	3-3	1rd	4rd	1rd	....	5-0	....	30	12	.714	8-3	3-2	7-4	12-3	12-4	18-8
1995	14	17	0	1	9-4	QF	1rd	3rd	4rd	4-1	....	31	17	.646	6-3	5-2	17-7	3-5	5-6	26-11
1996	53	13	0	0	5-4	1rd	3rd	2rd	3rd	3-1	3rd	13	13	.500	2-2	3-3	6-6	2-2	2-4	11-9
1997	25	20	0	0	7-4	3rd	4rd	1rd	3rd	4-1	....	25	20	.556	5-4	5-3	15-10	0-3	2-5	23-15
1998	16	21	0	0	9-4	3rd	2rd	SF	2rd	6-1	....	34	21	.618	6-4	8-2	15-10	5-5	6-7	28-14
1999	27	23	1	0	5-4	3rd	2rd	2rd	2rd	2-3	....	26	22	.542	6-8	8-2	10-10	2-2	3-6	23-16
2000	79	13	0	0	5-3	2rd	4rd	2rd	....	....	1rd	11	13	.458	5-5	2-2	3-5	1-1	1-2	10-11
2002	....	1	0	0	0-1	....	....	1rd	....	....	....	0	1	.000	0-0	0-1	0-0	0-0	0-0	0-1
TOTALS		**249**	**4**	**15**	**105-52**	....	....	....	....	**35-16**	....	**405**	**245**	**.623**	**99-59**	**70-31**	**163-102**	**73-53**	**90-72**	**315-173**

Represented Belarus in the Federation Cup (1998-1999). Doubles Titles: Aus (3), Fre (6), Wim (5), US (4).

RECORDS – COMBINED SINGLES / DOUBLES TITLES, SEASON

MEN
27—John McEnroe (10-17), 1979
23—Ilie Nastase, (15-8), 1973
23—Rod Laver (17-6), 1969
21—Guillermo Vilas (17-4), 1977

WOMEN
38—Billie Jean King (17-21), 1971
29—Margaret Smith Court (21-8), 1970
29—Martina Navratilova (15-14), 1982
29—Martina Navratilova (16-13), 1983

Gussy Moran, 1950
The Californian always did have an artistic touch, whether in her attire or simply swinging a racket.

Appendix

RECORDS – MOST ACES, ONE MATCH, SINGLES

MEN

54—Gary Muller (d. Peter
     Lundgren, Wimbledon
     qualifying, Roehampton, 1993)
49—Richard Krajicek (lost to
     Yevgeny Kafelnikov, QF, U.S.
     Open, 1999)
46—Goran Ivanisevic (lost to
     Magnus Norman, 2nd rd.,
     Wimbledon, 1997)
44—Mark Philippoussis (vs. Byron
     Black, Kuala Lumpur, 1995)
44—Goran Ivanisevic (d. Daniel
     Vacek, 3rd rd. Wimbledon, 1998)

WOMEN

22—Brenda Schultz-McCarthy
     (d. Iva Majoli, QF, Birmingham,
     England, 1994)
18—Venus Williams (Stanford, 2000)
17—Schultz-McCarthy (d. Audra
     Keller, 1st rd., U.S. Open, 1995)
17—Schultz-McCarthy (lost to
     Arantxa Sanchez Vicario,
     1st rd., Chase Championships,
     New York, 1996)
17—Alicia Molik (d. Sylvia Talaja,
     1st rd., Australian Open, 2000)

Appendix A

International Tennis Hall of Fame

International Tennis Hall of Fame and Museum
The spectacular building and grounds, built at Newport, Rhode Island, in 1880 and renovated in 1997, have become the game's spiritual home.

James Van Alen was a tennis innovator whose best idea was the tie-breaker and whose second-best idea came from his wife. Candace (Candy) Van Alen had been a columnist, editorial writer and foreign correspondent and was a high-spirited character comfortable about speaking her mind. In 1952, she told her husband that what the sport needed was a national hall of fame.

He agreed and put mementos on display in a single room at the historic Newport Casino in Newport, Rhode Island where he presided. His private enterprise was sanctioned by the U.S. Tennis Association in 1954, and the first class of inductees was enshrined the following year. Until 1975, it was the U.S. Tennis Hall of Fame, limited to American players. Briton Fred Perry was the first inductee as it became the International Hall

in 1975. The International Tennis Federation gave the Hall its official recognition in 1986.

By 2003, the International Tennis Hall of Fame had admitted 183 members comprising outstanding players, administrators, coaches and journalists from 18 nations.

A $7.5-million renovation completed in 1997 restored the Casino to its original splendor from the days when it was a playground for Newport society. The wooden building, a historic landmark renowned for its picturesque architecture, was the first major commission for Stanford White of McKim, Mead and White, the premier architectural firm of The Gilded Age, at the behest of New York publisher James Gordon Bennett, desiring to establish a new club. Completed in 1880, the Newport Casino originally housed ground-floor shops below well-appointed club rooms. (The Casino takes its name from the Italian, a place to play. It was not built as a gambling parlor, although one can safely assume the odd gentlemen's wager has been placed in the clubrooms and on the grounds.) The landscaped grounds include a 5,000-seat lawn tennis stadium, a dozen grass courts and indoor courts.

The inaugural U.S. National Lawn Tennis Championships was held on the Casino's grass courts in 1881, a year after it opened, and continued there until 1915, when the tournament (today known as the U.S. Open) moved to Forest Hills, N.Y. Davis Cup matches were played at the Casino in 1921 (Japan over Australia) and 1991 (U.S. over Spain).

The Hall has three categories of membership: Recent Players, who can still be active but no longer a "significant factor" in competition; Master Players, who have been retired at least 20 years; and, Contributors, including writers, coaches and administrators.

Those elected in the Recent Player category need to receive at least 75 percent of the votes cast by an international panel of tennis reporters.

An induction ceremony is held each year in July during the Jimmy Van Alen Cup Championship, a stopover on the ATP tour, the only pro tournament still played on grass in North America. The Hall's newest members deliver an acceptance speech, some of which have been memorable. The most memorable recently have been those of Martina Navratilova and Jimmy Connors.

The Hall of Fame's museum boasts one of the world's largest collections of tennis memorabilia with more than 7,000 pieces, including a tilthead racquet presented in 1876 to 15-year-old Mary Gray as a prize for winning a ladies' singles tournament at Admiralty House, Bermuda.

The Casino also houses a research center with a vast collection of programs; 100,000 photographs; more than 2,000 books, yearbooks and media guides; plus oral histories of 45 greats from Don Budge to Althea Gibson. The center is open by appointment.

The Hall, a non-profit institution, is open to the public every day except Thanksgiving and Christmas. The historic grass courts are the oldest in the world in continuous use. They are also open to the public, as is the venue for court tennis, also known as real tennis in Britain, the ancient game that gave birth to lawn tennis. The cavern-like 90-by-40-foot court with red concrete floor is one of only 10 of its kind left in the United States

and is the only one open to the public.

Visitors to the cradle of American tennis at 194 Bellevue Ave. in Newport can also make a pilgrimage to the plaque of the man who, through the persuasion of his wife, brought the Hall into being. Van Alen, three-time U.S. champion at court tennis, was inducted in 1965. He died at 88 in 1991; Candy died at 89 in 2002.

HALL OF FAME INDUCTEES

NAME, CITIZENSHIP	YEAR INDUCTED	CATEGORY
George Adee, United States	1964	Administrator
Fred Alexander, United States	1961	Player
Wilmer Allison, United States	1963	Player
Manuel Alonso, Spain	1977	Player
Malcolm Anderson, Australia	2000	Player
Arthur Ashe, United States	1985	Player
Juliette Atkinson, United States	1974	Player
H.W. 'Bunny' Austin, Great Britain	1997	Player
Tracy Austin, United States	1992	Player
Lawrence Sr. Baker, United States	1975	Administrator
Maud Barger-Wallach, United States	1958	Player
Boris Becker, Germany	2003	Player
Karl Behr , United States	1969	Player
Pauline Betz (Addie), United States	1965	Player
Bjorn Borg, Sweden	1987	Player
Jean Borotra, France	1976	Player
Lesley Turner Bowrey, Australia	1997	Player
John Bromwich, Australia	1984	Player
Norman Brookes, Australia	1977	Player
Louise Brough (Clapp), United States	1967	Player
Mary K. Browne, United States	1957	Player
Jacques Brugnon, France	1976	Player
Don Budge, United States	1964	Player
Maria Bueno, Brazil	1964	Player
Mabel Cahill, Ireland	1976	Player
Oliver Campbell, United States	1955	Player
Rosie Casals, United States	1996	Player
Malcolm Chace, United States	1961	Player
Philippe Chatrier, France	1992	Administrator
Clarence Clark, United States	1983	Player
Joseph Clark, United States	1955	Player
William Clothier, United States	1956	Player
Henri Cochet, France	1976	Player
Arthur W. 'Bud' Jr. Collins, United States	1994	Journalist
Maureen Connolly (Brinker), United States	1968	Player
Jimmy Connors, United States	1998	Player
Ashley Cooper, Australia	1991	Player
Jack Crawford, Australia	1979	Player
Joseph F. Cullman 3rd, United States	1990	Administrator
Allison Danzig, United States	1968	Journalist
Herman CBE David, Great Britain	1998	Administrator
Dwight Davis, United States	1956	Player
Lottie Dod, Great Britain	1983	Player
John Doeg, United States	1962	Player
Laurence Doherty, Great Britain	1980	Player
Reggie Doherty, Great Britain	1980	Player
Dorothea Douglass (Chambers), United States	1981	Player
Jaroslav Drobny, Czechoslovakia	1983	Player
Margaret Osborne duPont, United States	1967	Player
Françoise Durr, France	2003	Player
James Dwight, United States	1955	Player
Roy Emerson, Australia	1982	Player
Pierre Etchebaster, France	1978	CourtTennis
Chris Evert, United States	1995	Player
Bob Falkenburg, United States/Brazil	1974	Player

Neale Fraser, Australia	1984	Player	Alex Olmedo, Peru	1987	Player
Shirley Fry-Irvin, United States	1970	Player	Rafael Osuna, Mexico	1979	Player
Charles Garland, United States	1969	Player	Mary Outerbridge, United States	1979	Innovator
Althea Gibson, United States	1971	Player	Sarah Palfrey Fabyan Cooke (Danzig), U.S.	1963	Player
Richard 'Pancho' Gonzalez, United States	1968	Player	Frank Parker, United States	1966	Player
Evonne Goolagong (Cawley), Australia	1988	Player	Gerald Patterson, Australia	1989	Player
Bryan 'Bitsy' Grant, United States	1972	Player	J. Edward 'Budge' Patty, United States	1977	Player
David Gray, Great Britain	1985	Journalist	Theodore Pell, United States	1966	Player
Clarence Griffin, United States	1970	Player	Fred Perry, Great Britain	1975	Player
King of Sweden Gustav V, Sweden	1980	Patron	Tom Pettitt, Great Britain	1982	CourtTennis
Harold Hackett, United States	1961	Player	Nicola Pietrangeli, Italy	1986	Player
Ellen Hansell, United States	1965	Player	Adrian Quist, Australia	1984	Player
Darlene Hard, United States	1973	Player	Dennis Ralston, United States	1987	Player
Doris Hart, United States	1969	Player	Ernest Renshaw, Great Britain	1983	Player
Ann Haydon Jones, Great Britain	1985	Player	William Renshaw, Great Britain	1983	Player
Gladys Heldman, United States	1979	Journalist	Vincent Richards, United States	1961	Player
W.E. 'Slew' Hester, United States	1981	Administrator	Nancy Richey, United States	2003	Player
Bob Hewitt, Australia/South Africa	1992	Player	Bobby Riggs, United States	1967	Player
Lew Hoad, Australia	1980	Player	Tony Roche, Australia	1986	Player
Harry Hopman, Australia	1978	Player	Ellen Roosevelt, United States	1975	Player
Hazel Hotchkiss (Wightman), United States	1957	Player	Mervyn Rose, Australia	2001	Player
Fred Hovey, United States	1974	Player	Ken Rosewall, Australia	1980	Player
Joe Hunt, United States	1966	Player	Dorothy Round (Little), Great Britain	1986	Player
Lamar Hunt, United States	1993	Administrator	Elizabeth Ryan, United States	1972	Player
Frank Hunter, United States	1961	Player	Manuel Santana, Spain	1985	Player
Helen Hull Jacobs, United States	1962	Player	Dick Savitt, United States	1976	Player
Bill Johnston, United States	1958	Player	Ted Schroeder, United States	1966	Player
Perry Jones, United States	1970	Administrator	Eleonora Sears, United States	1968	Player
Robert Kelleher, United States	2000	Administrator	Richard Sears, United States	1955	Player
Billie Jean Moffitt King, United States	1987	Player	Frank Sedgman, Australia	1979	Player
Jan Kodes, Czechoslovakia	1990	Player	Francisco 'Pancho' Segura, Ecuador	1984	Player
Jack Kramer, United States	1968	Player	Vic Seixas, United States	1971	Player
Rene Lacoste, France	1976	Player	Frank Shields, United States	1964	Player
Al Laney, United States	1979	Journalist	Pam Shriver, United States	2002	Player
William Larned, United States	1956	Player	Henry Slocum, United States	1955	Player
Art Larsen, United States	1956	Player	Margaret Smith (Court), Australia	1979	Player
Rod Laver, Australia	1981	Player	Stan Smith, United States	1987	Player
Ivan Lendl, Czechoslovakia	2001	Player	Fred Stolle, Australia	1985	Player
Suzanne Lenglen, France	1978	Player	May Sutton (Bundy), United States	1956	Player
George Lott, United States	1964	Player	Bill Talbert, United States	1967	Player
Gene Mako, United States	1973	Player	Bill Tilden, United States	1959	Player
MollaBjurstedt Mallory, Norway/United States	1958	Player	Lance Tingay, Great Britain	1982	Journalist
Hana Mandlikova, Czechoslovakia/Australia	1994	Player	Ted Tinling, Great Britain	1986	Innovator
Alice Marble, United States	1964	Player	Brian Tobin, Australia	2003	Administrator
Alastair Martin, United States	1973	Administrator	Bertha Townsend (Toulmin), United States	1974	Player
William McChesney Martin, United States	1982	Administrator	Tony Trabert United States	1970	Player
Dan Maskell, Great Britain	1996	Journalist	James Van Alen, United States	1965	Innovator
John McEnroe, United States	1999	Player	John Van Ryn, United States	1963	Player
Ken McGregor, Australia	1999	Player	Guillermo Vilas, Argentina	1991	Player
Kathleen McKane (Godfree), Great Britain	1978	Player	Ellsworth Vines, United States	1962	Player
Chuck McKinley, United States	1986	Player	Gottfried Von Cramm, Germany	1977	Player
Maurice McLoughlin, United States	1957	Player	Virginia Wade, Great Britain	1989	Player
Frew McMillan, South Africa	1992	Player	Marie Wagner, United States	1969	Player
Don McNeill, United States	1965	Player	Holcombe Ward, United States	1956	Player
Elisabeth Moore, United States	1971	Player	Watson Washburn, United States	1965	Player
Angela Mortimer (Barrett), Great Britain	1993	Player	Malcolm Whitman, United States	1955	Player
Gardnar Mulloy, United States	1972	Player	Mats Wilander, Sweden	2002	Player
R.Lindley Murray, United States	1958	Player	Anthony Wilding, Great Britain/New Zealand	1978	Player
Julian Myrick, United States	1963	Administrator	RichardN. Williams 2nd, United States	1957	Player
Ilie Nastase, Romania	1991	Player	Helen Wills (Moody Roark), United States	1959	Player
Martina Navratilova, Czechoslovakia/U.S.	2000	Player	Walter Clopton Wingfield, Great Britain	1997	Innovator
John Newcombe, Australia	1986	Player	Sidney Wood, United States	1964	Player
Arthur Nielsen, United States	1971	Patron	Robert Wrenn, United States	1955	Player
Betty Nuthall (Shoemaker), Great Britain	1977	Player	Beals Wright, United States	1956	Player

HALL OF FAME BIOGRAPHIES

(For player biographies, see Chapter 25. Recent inductees
and non-player biographies appear below.)

2003 INDUCTEES

BORIS BECKER
Germany (1968–)   *See page 641.*

FRANÇOISE DURR
France (1942–)

The Psychedelic Strokeswoman, Françoise Germaine 'Frankie' Durr, astounded and confounded foes over a 19-year career as the finest French woman since Suzanne Lenglen. She may have appeared a pushover, pushing the ball here and there with frequently soft shots made with strange grips and odd swipes, but that was deceptive. She could beat anybody with quickness, accuracy, anticipation, smarts and combativeness. Born Dec. 25, 1942, in Algiers, Algeria, of French parentage, she was her country's brightest tennis figure for years, the lone winner of the French female title (1967 over Lesley Turner, 4-6, 6-3, 6-4) between Simone Mathieu in 1938 and Mary Pierce in 2000. In 1968 she went for dollars as a member of the original female pro troupe.

A splendid volleyer and tactician she won 11 doubles majors with 6 different partners: 5 straight French, 1967-71; 2 U.S., 1969, '72; 3 French mixed, 1968, '71, '73; 1 Wimbledon mixed, 1976.

Durr, a sturdy 5-5, 120 pounds, was an inhabitant of the World Top Ten 8 years, No. 3 in 1967. As a Federation Cup regular for 10 years she had the best French mark in singles, 16-8 (31-17 overall).

Durr won 26 singles, 42 doubles titles. In 1971, 3 of her 5 singles crowns were national titles: Swiss, Canadian, U.S. Clay Court. She is married to American Boyd Browning and lives in the U.S.

NANCY RICHEY
France (1942–)

Nobody had more powerful groundstrokes in the wooden racket era than Nancy Ann Richey, whose flat forehand and backhand, both single-handed, were as big and booming as Texas where she grew up. Born Aug. 23, 1942, at San Angelo, she is the older half (by four years) of the game's most extraordinary sister-brother combo—Nancy and Cliff—schooled in San Angelo by teaching pro father, George Richey. As the only amateur woman

to win a major during the open era (French 1968 over Ann Jones, 5-7, 6-4, 6-1), she had won her first major, the Australian in 1967 over Lesley Turner, 6-1, 6-4. Those were added to 3 doubles majors: Australian, Wimbledon, 1966; U.S., 1965, attesting to volleying skill. But she preferred baselining, winning a female record 6 straight U.S. Clay Court titles (covering a 33 match streak), 1963-68. She won the U.S. Indoor, 1965, and Hard Court, 1961, titles.

Slight at 5-6, 130, but whippy and very well-coordinated, she played for the U.S., helping win 8 Wightman Cups between 1962 and 1970 and the 1969 Federation Cup.

She won 69 singles titles (25 pro) during an 18 year career spanning amateur and open eras. She played as Mrs. Kenneth Gunter 1970-75.

BRIAN TOBIN
Australia (1930–)

Tennis has been a guiding theme for Australian Brian Tobin all his life, from nationally ranked player to the highest administrative position in the game: President of the ITF (International Tennis Federation) for nine years. During his tenure the game made tremendous strides, reaching out to more countries and players throughout the world every year, expanding teaching programs and supervising the expansion of the ITF's crown jewels, Davis and Fed Cups.

A Melburnian, born Dec. 5, 1930, he was in his country's Top Ten as an amateur player, No. 8 between 1956 and 1962, and won the U.S. singles champion in the 35-and-over category at Forest Hills in 1967. That year he captained a traveling squad of world-class Aussies, and joined one of them, Davis Cupper Ray Ruffels, to reach the doubles final at the Newport (R.I.) Invitational, where he returned to be anointed for the Hall of Fame in 2003 as an administrator. Tobin captained the victorious Australian Fed Cup team in 1964.

However, the marks he made with executive skills largely earned him his place in the Hall. A long-time volunteer, he became president of the national association, Tennis Australia, in 1983, serving through 1989, formative years during which the Melbourne Park complex came into being as home of the Australian Open, the most modern of the major venues.

After a stint as executive vice president of the ITF, 1989-91, he was elected as president in 1991, and oversaw world-wide expansion of the game.

HALL OF FAME BIOGRAPHIES NON-PLAYERS

COURT TENNIS

PIERRE ETCHEBASTER

France (1893–1980)
Hall of Fame 1978

A Basque maestro of the racket in the complex game of court tennis, the short, trim, elegant Pierre Etchebaster, a professional, was probably the greatest to roam the arcane concrete cubicle. Migrating to New York from his French homeland, he became the resident paragon at the Racquet & Tennis Club on Park Avenue, as player and instructor. Traveling to London to challenge for the world title in 1927, he lost to the champion G. F. Covey, 7-sets-to-5 in Prince's Club.

However, a year later on the same court he dethroned Covey, 7-5. Thereafter, he repelled seven challenges himself, the first at Prince's, the remainder on his home paving, Racquet & Tennis.

He retired as unbeaten champion in 1954 at age 60. A right-hander, he was born Dec. 8, 1893, in St. Jean de Luz, France, and died there March 24, 1980. He entered the Hall Fame in 1978.

TOM PETTITT

Great Britain (1859–1946)
Hall of Fame 1982

As a youngster, 17, English-born Tom Pettitt emigrated to Boston. He became a wizard at racket sports, and was immensely popular as teaching professional of court tennis at Boston's Tennis & Racquet Club, and that game as well as lawn tennis at the Newport (R.I.) Casino, where he was a familiar walrus-mustachioed figure for 65 years until his death in 1946. He was one of the very first lawn tennis players and instructors, having learned the game in 1876, shortly after its inception. He stopped teaching in 1929, remaining at the Casino as its supervisor. A nimble 5-foot-9, 176 pounder, he could beat any of the members at either lawn or court tennis in his heyday. An old pal, Jimmy Van Alen, liked to tell about Tom using a taped champagne bottle as a bat and winning friendly lawn tennis games. Tom entered the Hall of Fame in 1982 on the basis of his world championship court tennis prowess.

He won the title in a successful 1885 challenge to George Lambert, 7-sets-to-5, at King Henry VIII's old playpen, Hampton Court, outside of London. In an 1890 defense he turned back Charles Saunders, 7-5, at St. Stephens Green, Ireland, resigning the title later unbeaten. Pettitt was born Dec. 19, 1859, in Beckenham, England, and died Oct. 17, 1946, in Newport, R.I.

JOURNALISTS

BUD COLLINS

United States (1929–)
Hall of Fame 1994

Ubiquitous Arthur Worth 'Bud' Collins, Jr. is the most visible and versatile U.S. tennis journalist. An estimable writer, broadcaster, editor, he is a man about the game whose wit, understanding and flamboyance make him more recognizable than many star players. His memory and knowledge of tennis, its history and characters, is encyclopedic.

From printed page to broadcast booth, he is identified with the sport he has done much to popularize, yet to protect for the purists. "He is to tennis what pasta is to Italy," was a line in a *Sports Illustrated* profile. Born June 17, 1929, in Lima, Ohio, he grew up in Berea (outside of Cleveland) about 50 yards from the dirt tennis courts of Baldwin-Wallace College, from which he graduated in 1951, and where his father had been head coach of football, basketball, baseball and track, as well as athletic director. He moved east after U.S. Army service in 1954 to attend Boston University graduate school, then joined the *Boston Herald* as a sportswriter. In 1963, the year he shifted to the *Boston Globe,* Collins first did television commentary (covering the U.S. Doubles at Longwood Cricket Club) for Boston's PBS outlet, WGBH, a station that for the next 20 years, with Greg Harney as producer, would pioneer American coverage of the sport.

He worked the U.S. Open for CBS (1968-72), signed on with NBC in 1972 (thereafter closely identified with that network's presentation of Wimbledon and the French), becoming the point man for all the dualists— print-television journalists—to follow. At the *Globe* his columns on sport, travel, and a variety of other subjects, including coverage of the Vietnam War, are a continuing delight. His prose and commentary style are as multi-hued as Joseph's Amazing Technicolor Dream Coat. Seldom one to take himself or sports too seriously, he brightens reports with nicknames as colorful as his rainbow neckties and trousers, occasionally with flights of fancy. However, he can be absolutely authentic, a meticulous curator of the game's annals, passionate keeper of the flame.

He also writes for magazines and newspapers across the world such as the *Independent* in London, and the *Age* in Melbourne. His books include *The Education of a Tennis Player* (with Rod Laver, 1971), *Evonne! On the Move* (with Evonne Goolagong, 1974), a memoir, *My Life with the Pros* (1989) and three editions of *Bud Collins' Tennis Encyclopedia*. In 1999, he was tapped for the Associated Press' Red Smith Award, the top honor in U.S. sports journalism, and named to the National Sportswriters and Sportscasters Hall of Fame in 2002.

Although he refers to himself—and everyone else who plays below the level of the pros—as a "hacker," Collins is an accomplished now-and-again player, known for his touch, tactical cunning and preference for playing barefoot on grass courts. He won the U.S. Indoor mixed doubles (with Top Tenner Janet Hopps) in 1961, and was a finalist in the French Senior doubles (with Jack Crawford) in 1975. Engaging and irrepressible, he has even coached tennis, the Brandeis University varsity, 1959-63, whose 'name' player was future hippie icon Abbie Hoffman.   *—Barry S. Lorge*

ALLISON DANZIG
United States (1898–1987)
Hall of Fame 1968

The familiar and authoritative identification that topped *New York Times* stories for 45 years—By Allison Danzig—was reassuring to readers until his retirement in 1967. Before that he was a sportswriter for the *Brooklyn Eagle,* developing an incisive, perceptive style that made him the widest regarded literary voice of the game in the U.S. Al Danzig, the first journalist to enter the Hall of Fame (1968), was a thoroughgoing gentleman respected throughout the game and his profession. He covered the game from its first great impact during the Tilden, Wills and Lenglen days of the 1920s to the dawn of the open era, and also was a nationally known chronicler of college football, rowing and the Olympic Games.

He was one of the few who could write knowledgeably about court tennis, ancestor of lawn tennis. Born in Waco, Tex., Feb. 27, 1898, he graduated from Cornell, where he played football despite a diminutive stature, and served in the U.S. Army during World War I. He became a New Yorker following college, but kept Texas in his speech, and in the kitchen. This soft-spoken man was celebrated for his torrid chili. Always immaculately turned out—coat and tie whatever the summer temperature on the Eastern grass circuit—he was generous in helping young reporters and had the respect of generations of players. He wrote books on tennis, football, the Olympics and court tennis. Danzig died Jan. 27, 1987, in Ridgewood, N.J. The Danzig Award, established by Longwood Cricket Club in Boston—he was the first recipient in 1963-honors leading tennis writers, and is presented periodically during the U.S. Pro Championships.

DAVID GRAY
Great Britain (1927–1983)
Hall of Fame 1985

David Gray was such a fine chronicler of the game for two decades with an exceptional English newspaper, *The Guardian,* that many regretted his departure from journalism in 1976 to become an official of the ITF. A well-educated and witty man, he showed his grasp of tennis, its figures, matches, history and politics in his literate daily reports from across the world. But he served the game well, even without byline, as the ITF's diplomatic general secretary from 1976 until his untimely death of cancer in 1983. He was also secretary of the Men's International Professional Tennis Council.

As a journalist he strongly advocated the abolition of phony amateurism and the adoption of open tennis in 1968. Gray was influential in reorganizing the Davis Cup, returning tennis to the Olympics in 1988 and broadening the game's base, especially by encouraging its development on the African continent. Among the large and competitive British press contingent he was a standout, and he brought to the game's administration a keen overall view and perception.

A graduate of Birmingham University, he worked his way up to the *Guardian* through the *Wolverhampton Express and Star,* the *Northern Daily Telegraph* and the *News Chronicle.* He could, and did, write anything and everything well, a political reporter and theater critic before getting the tennis assignment. A collection of his writings, *Shades of Gray,* was published in 1988 by Willow Books (William Collins & Sons).

He was born Dec. 31, 1927, in Kingswinford, England, and died Sept 6, 1983, in London. He was named to the Hall of Fame in 1985.

GLADYS HELDMAN

United States (1922–)
Hall of Fame 1979

For more than two decades, brilliant Gladys Medalie Heldman was the game's anchor, first as founder-owner-publisher-editor-chief-writer of *World Tennis* magazine (launched in 1953), later as the instigator and house-mother of a separate professional circuit for women, begun in 1970. Under her guidance, *WT* became the international literary voice of tennis. A slim, petite dynamo, who often seemed shy, she came to tennis through marriage to a first-flight player, left-handed Julius Heldman, who was the U.S. junior champ in 1936.

She, a previously non-athletic New Yorker, quickly absorbed his enthusiasm for the game, becoming a maven. Their two daughters, Trixie and Julie, held national junior rankings, and Julie went on to win the Italian Open in 1969, and rank No. 5 in the world that year and in 1974. In 1970, Gladys and her magazine became the allies of disgruntled female players—Billie Jean King and Rosie Casals foremost—who felt, justifiably, that they were being demeaned, financially and attitudinally, by the game's male establishment. They believed it was necessary to break away from the traditional dual-sex tournament format and go it alone.

Heldman encouraged them, and urged a friend, Joe Cullman, head of Philip Morris, to provide an initial bankroll. Joined by the 'Houston Nine' (King, Casals, daughter Julie, Peaches Bartkowicz, Kerry Melville, Valerie Ziegenfuss, Nancy Richey, Kristy Pigeon, Judy Tegart Dalton), Heldman staged the first Virginia Slims tournament in that city late in 1970.

They prompted Virginia Slims to underwrite a 1971 tour, and the stunning progress of the 'Long Way Babies' commenced.

Heldman, who became a better-than-average player herself, sold the magazine and withdrew from tennis politics in the mid-1970s, and now lives with her husband in Santa Fe, N.M. She was born May 13, 1922, in New York, and entered the Hall of Fame in 1979.

AL LANEY

United States (1895–1988)
Hall of Fame 1979

A fine writer who made his name covering sports, Albert Gillis Laney was usually associated with tennis and golf, but he covered everything on the menu, from big league baseball to football to championship fights, with his usual understanding of what was at foot, and a keen reportorial touch. Laconic, mustachioed, usually beneath a gray fedora, he settled in Paris for a time after World War I, worked for James Joyce as secretary, and joined the staff of the renowned *Paris Herald* (now the *International Herald Tribune*).

He had an eye for compelling features, and his coverage of the epic 1926 showdown of Suzanne Lenglen and Helen Wills at Cannes graces several anthologies. He spanned the generations, having observed another epic, the Maurice McLoughlin-Norman Brookes Davis Cup duel at Forest Hills in 1914, and worked as a reporter until his last newspaper, the *New York Herald Tribune,* folded in 1966.

His *Courting the Game,* a tennis memoir, remains one of the splendid tennis books. Laney was born Jan. 11, 1895, in Pensacola, Fla., retained a Southern lilt in his speech, and died Jan. 31, 1988, in Spring Valley, N.Y. He entered the Hall of Fame in 1979.

DAN MASKELL

Great Britain (1908–1992)
Hall of Fame 1996

To his legion of admirers Dan Maskell was the voice of Wimbledon from his first broadcast for BBC-TV in 1951 to his last in 1991. Dan's mellow and mellifluous tones, always thoughtful, always reverent, never wasteful, would illuminate the matches he covered with masterly understatement. Dan's reflections—perhaps a subtle change of tactics or a revealing grimace that told a story—added to the enjoyment of his viewers without being intrusive. "Oh, I say!" was a trademark, a meaningful exclamation that told much in three words.

Before his television career began, Dan spent two years with BBC-radio at Wimbledon, working as the summarizer with Max Rolbertson. He didn't miss a single day of play at Wimbledon from 1929 to 1991, and had seen every final from 1924.

Maskell was born April 11, 1908, in the London neighborhood of Fulham, just a pitch-and-putt from Queen's Club. He was the seventh of eight children, the fourth boy. As he grew up Dan was captivated by the glamor of the famous club with its affluent members, many of them prominent in the worlds of entertainment, politics and sport.

First as a ballboy, then as a coach—never having a

chance to play as an amateur—Dan was on the Queen's staff from 1923 to 1929 when he moved to the All England Lawn Tennis and Croquet Club at Wimbledon to become their first-ever teaching professional. For 16 years Maskell, an excellent player, was the professional champion of Britain.

In 1933 Dan was surprised to be selected to accompany the British Davis Cup team to Paris for the semifinal against the U.S. This was unprecedented in those amateur days. Professionals never aided teams, which seems curious today when most leading players have personal coaches. Victories over the U.S. and then Cup-holding France began a four-year British reign, with Maskell a fundamental part of that success.

It was partly this team experience that prepared Dan to make an important contribution to his country during World War II. As the Royal Air Force's first rehabilitation officer, he revealed qualities of devotion and innovation that were recognized by the Crown with the award of an OBE (Order of the British Empire) in 1945.

Following the war Dan resumed his duties at the All England Club for nine years. In 1955 he ended his coaching duties there to become the Lawn Tennis Association's training manager. He was in charge of the training of coaches and promoting the game nationwide. He also coached Prince Charles and Princess Anne. In 1982 he received his second award from the Crown, a CBE (Commander of the British Empire) for services to tennis, including broadcasting, and also an honorary MA degree from Loughborough University, where he was based during the war.

He died Dec. 10, 1992, at 82.   *—John Barrett*

LANCE TINGAY

Great Britain (1915–1990)
Hall of Fame 1982

As the dean of a sizeable platoon of British tennis writers of his time, Lance Tingay, friendly, erudite, helpful to colleagues, covered the game for a half-century, present as it evolved from the amateur into the open and highly professional era. He covered his first Wimbledon in 1932 and was the thorough, informed and informative tennis correspondent for *The Daily Telegraph* of London from 1950 to 1980, writing his dispatches from across the world.

Ever good humored, even while pounding his typewriter on deadline, he was a leading historian of the game, the author of *History of Lawn Tennis in Pictures,*

One Hundred Years of Wimbledon, and *Royalty and Lawn Tennis,* and he wrote for numerous tennis publications and yearbooks. Tingay was born in London July 15, 1915, and died there March 10, 1990. He was named to the Hall of Fame in 1982.

INNOVATORS

HERMAN DAVID

Great Britain (1905–1974)
Hall of Fame 1998

History will view Herman David as the man who, through sheer force, initiated open tennis.

As chairman of the Diamond Development Company, Herman was acknowledged as a world expert on industrial diamonds. Exposing fakes was second nature to him. Born in Birmingham, England, June 26, 1905, Herman had already played county tennis for Warwickshire before going up to New College, Oxford to read history. Having earned his blue, he was selected for Davis Cup duty in Britain's first round tie versus Poland in 1932 and won both his singles.

After serving with the RAF as an operations controller during World War II, Herman had captained British Davis Cup teams in the 1950s and knew, as everyone close to the game did, that the unworkable amateur rules were being openly flouted by leading players in every country.

When he became chairman of the All England Club in 1959, it was inevitable that Herman would work fearlessly to expose the flaws in the game he loved. At an Extraordinary General Meeting of the Club that year the members had carried a motion that called upon the LTA (Lawn Tennis Association of Britain) to stage an open Championship in 1960. At that stage Britain's governing body were not yet ready to take precipitate action that might have resulted in expulsion from the International Tennis Federation.

The narrow failure of a motion to adopt open tennis at the ITF's annual meeting in 1961 persuaded David that he would have to work behind the scenes. By 1967 he was satisfied that the climate was right. The eight-man professional tournament staged on Wimbledon's Centre Court one month after that year's Championships was a shot across the bow of the ITF. When Rod Laver beat Ken Rosewall in a superb final that was broadcast by BBC2 to launch color television in Britain, the world realized what they had been missing.

This was the first time that professionals had been allowed to compete in one of the traditional amateur strongholds. It sent shock waves around the world.

At the All England Club's annual meeting in December 1967, David proposed that the following year's Championships should be open to all players, amateurs and professionals. "Amateur tennis has become a living lie," he said, a phrase which accurately reflected the feelings of the members who carried the motion unanimously. By now opinions at the LTA had altered. At their general meeting a few days later the LTA endorsed the club's stand and gave approval for an open Wimbledon in 1968.

At last Herman David's dream had been realized. Tennis had finally become an honest sport. He died Feb. 25, 1974, at his home in Wimbledon, and was elevated to the Hall in 1998. – *John Barrett*

TED TINLING
Great Britain (1910–1990)
Hall of Fame 1986

The Leaning Tower of Pizzazz, 6-foot-5 Cuthbert Collingwood Tinling entered the Hall of Fame in 1986 as a many-faceted benefactor of the game. Witty and literate, a man who had served as a lieutenant colonel in intelligence for the British army during World War II, Tinling, a right-hander, was a good enough player to compete on the English circuit after the war. But it was as an involved bystander that he served the game well, first as a teenager on the Riviera where he, spending winters for reasons of ill health, umpired matches, including some for the great Suzanne Lenglen.

He was master of ceremonies at Wimbledon until one of his careers, that of designer-dressmaker, made him for a time *persona non grata*. That occurred in 1949 when he scandalously (or so it seemed to the tournament committee) equipped American Gertrude 'Gussy' Moran with lace panties that drew hordes of photographers and spectators. Ted made beautiful as well as avant-garde costumes for many female players, including Maureen Connolly, Maria Bueno, Billie Jean King, Margaret Court and Evonne Goolagong.

He was couturier for the newly formed Virginia Slims circuit, and later the Slimsies' minister of protocol and emcee, a strong advocate of the women's game. An unmistakable bald-headed beacon, he was of immeasurable value late in life as historian and writer who had observed most of the game's luminaries, and as liaison between the players and Wimbledon. Outspoken, generous in informing and counseling newcomers to the game, Ted could make light of his own death, remarking on one of his last days: "Send me a fax to hell to let me know if Jennifer [Capriati] wins Wimbledon." He was born June 23, 1910, in Eastbourne, England, and died May 23, 1990, in Cambridge, England.

MARY OUTERBRIDGE
United States (1852–1986)
Hall of Fame 1981

Celebrated as the 'Mother of Tennis,' Mary Ewing Outerbridge was undoubtedly one of the pioneers, but the claims by her adherents that she introduced the game to the U.S. are undocumented. The story is that she, a New Yorker, saw soldiers of the British garrison playing tennis in Bermuda, where she was vacationing in 1874, the year of the game's patenting and early marketing. Intrigued, she is said to have taken a set home where her brother, Emilius Outerbridge, and friends set up a court at the Staten Island Cricket and Baseball Club.

Tennis was indeed introduced to the U.S. at several locations in 1874, the first documented instance in Arizona. Outerbridge was born March 9, 1852, in Philadelphia, died May 3, 1886 (five years after the first U.S. Championships), on Staten Island, and entered the Hall of Fame in 1981.

JIMMY VAN ALEN
United States (1902–1991)
Hall of Fame 1965

James Henry Van Alen, born Sept. 19, 1902, in his beloved Newport, R.I., was intimately involved with tennis as player, organizer and—best known—innovator whose pet idea, the tie-breaker, radically altered the game, making it more televisable in the U.S. As a U.S. singles champ at court tennis in 1933, 1938 and 1940, he was good enough at that abstruse ancestor of lawn tennis to warrant a Hall of Fame spot as a player. He played tennis well enough to have won his blue at his alma mater, Cambridge, appeared in the Wimbledon, French and U.S. Championships, and played in the Newport Casino Invitational, where he had a win over fellow Hall of Famer George Lott.

He would become director of that tournament, a leader in the preservation of the aging wooden Casino (the cradle of U.S. tennis), and, at the instigation of his wife, Candy, the guiding light in founding the Hall of

Fame to which he was elected in 1965.

Feeling the game's scoring should be simplified and deuce done away with, he lobbied tirelessly on behalf of his creation, VASSS: Van Alen Streamlined Scoring System. Among the elements were single point scoring and 21-point or 31-point matches (à la table tennis), no-ad (games scored 1-2-3-4, maximum 7-points, sudden death at 3-3), medal play (à la golf, based on single point totals for specific numbers of rounds), and, the most celebrated—tie-breakers.

Unveiled in 1965 at the Casino Pro Championships, which he personally sponsored for $10,000 prize money, the seminal tie-breaker needed retooling. That he did with veteran referee Mike Blanchard, and some counseling by historian Frank Phelps. Eventually it became sudden death (best-of-9 points).

Amazingly this breaker was accepted by the USTA, and used in U.S. championship events from 1970 through 1974. Thereafter the USTA embraced the current ITF-approved 'lingering death,' as Van Alen disparagingly called the best-of-12 point version that requires a 2-point margin for victory, thus can extend into double figures.

A man of old family wealth, Jimmy hoped to give the game a common touch, and became an avuncular, almost cherubic figure in planter's straw hat and burgundy blazer at the Casino. His love for tennis was endless, as well as his delight in shaking up the establishment with his brainstorms. He served in the U.S. Navy during World War II, and died July 3, 1991, in Newport. Jimmy would have enjoyed the irony: That semifinal day at Wimbledon Michael Stich deposed champion Stefan Edberg by winning three breakers while Edberg never lost his serve. Such a match could not have been played during nearly a century before Van Alen. A bequest of his wife, Candy, assured that a professional tournament would always continue at the Casino as the Jimmy Van Alen Cup.

MAJ. WALTER CLOMPTON WINGFIELD
Great Britain (1833–1912)
Hall of Fame 1997

Long overdue for admission to the International Tennis Hall of Fame, Major Walter Clopton Wingfield entered in 1997.

This imaginative Englishman, who had the idea for the modern game of tennis, and patented it in 1874, was born into a well-to-do military family Oct. 16, 1833 at the Old Ruabon Vicarage in Wales, the home of his paternal grandparents. His parents were there on extended leave from Canada where his father served as a captain of the Sixty-Sixth, the Berkshire Regiment. At three, Walter's mother died in childbirth, and he and his sister were cared for by the mother's father, Col. Michel, who was transferred home having commanded the Royal Artillery in Canada.

In 1838 his father, now a major, left the service, returned home and, with his brother, Watkin, raised Walter until the young man, after attending Sandhurst, became an officer in the First Dragoon Guards. Uncle Watkin had served in India where he was renowned as a linguist. He later became an artist and playwright. His play, *The Hidden Treasure*, became the longest running play in London for many years.

Walter served in India during the Sepoy Revolt. From India his regiment went to China where Wingfield, now a captain, led a British force through some skirmishes with the Chinese. His trophy was a Pekingese dog, a breed he introduced to England. While in India, Wingfield married and soon thereafter wife and infant son returned to England where he sold his commission. He was 25, had inherited the estate of Rhysnant in Wales, but preferred the more stimulating life in London, associating with intellectuals and artists.

Wingfield joined the Montgomeryshire Yeomanry as a major. He also was made a Gentleman-at-Arms, the royal guards of the Royal Family. Throughout his life he was an active participant in many sports: court/real tennis, rackets, bicycling, and was a champion billiards player. From these interests, he saw the need for healthy exercise, as the 'Industrial Revolution' brought thousands from the farms to cities bereft of open fields and woodlands.

Innumerable croquet courts, well cared for but seldom if ever used, were in existence. In a stroke of genius, Wingfield felt those courts could be used for a new racket, ball and net game, an outdoor version of court tennis. As many others, he played rackets, an energetic racket-and-ball game played against a wall at numerous taverns. He went about designing portable equipment—net posts and net—that could be installed on a lined court, preferably the lawn of an unused croquet court.

Working in confidence, he conducted several weeks of trials at several country estates. Rackets were designed and made in substantial quantity, as were the several other needs, the equipment fitting into an easily-carried box containing everything required for four to play. The most important aspects, which were novel, were written rules of the game, along with helpful instructions. The rules of *The Major's Game of Lawn Tennis* were printed in December 1873, not long after his 40th birthday, and entered at Stationers Hall in February 1874.

Wingfield's gifts to us were not limited to lawn tennis, for with invention of the modern bicycle he designed one called 'The Butterfly' and wrote a book on group riding in formation. He devoted many of his later years to food and its preparation.

Such a good man deserved a better life than he was given. His eldest son, a naval midshipman, was lost at sea attempting the rescue of a shipmate. His second son died of disease contracted in an Assam tea plantation, and his last son was killed by an accidental gun shot while in Paris. His wife, Alice, afflicted with mental illness and declared insane early in life, never recovered.

Wingfield died April 18, 1912, the time of the sinking of the *Titanic*, at age of 79.   — *George Alexander*

ADMINISTRATORS

GEORGE ADEE
United States (1874–1948)
Hall of Fame 1964

George Townsend Adee made his sporting name as an All-American quarterback at Yale in 1894. He was elevated to the Hall of Fame in 1964, for his contributions to tennis on the administrative side. He was president of the USTA four years, 1916-19, and was also a member of the Davis Cup and Amateur Rules committees. A New Yorker, he was an enthusiastic tennis player, good enough to appear six times in the U.S. Championships singles between 1903 and 1909. He served in the U.S. Army in the Spanish-American War and World War I. Born Jan. 4, 1874, in Stonington, Conn., he died July 31, 1948, in New York.

LARRY BAKER
United States (1890–1980)
Hall of Fame 1975

Lawrence Adams Baker, very active in USTA affairs, was an officer beginning in 1932, and president three years, 1948-50. He was a founder of the National Tennis Foundation, and captained the U.S. Davis Cup team for its 1953 win over Canada at Montreal. He sponsored the Baker Cup, a U.S. vs. Canada event for seniors. Baker

was born June 20, 1890, in Lowdensville, S.C., lived in East Hampton, N.Y., and died there Oct. 15, 1980. He entered the Hall of Fame in 1975.

PHILIPPE CHATRIER
France (1926–2000)
Hall of Fame 1992

As player, journalist and administrator, Philippe Chatrier, a Parisian, made a tremendous impact on the game, and was instrumental in its growth and success, particularly during the open era. He was a good enough player to win the French junior titles in singles and doubles in 1945, play internationally for France, and later captained the Davis Cup team.

Serving dual roles as president of the French Federation of Tennis (1972-92) and the ITF (1977-91) he was largely responsible for the renaissance of the French Open, placing it on par with the other three majors and overseeing the splendid updating of Stade Roland Garros. He fought valiantly against over-commercialization of the game, and led a campaign to restore tennis to the Olympic Games, a goal realized in 1988 after a 64-year interval.

Championing the Grand Slam concept, he worked hard to ally the four major championships in staying at the pinnacle. He is a member of the International Olympic Committee. An intelligent chronicler of the game, he was a Paris newspaperman, and founded one of the leading magazines of the sport, *Tennis de France*. The central court at Roland Garros is named for him. He was born Feb. 2, 1926, in Paris, and died there June 23, 2000.

JOE CULLMAN
United States (1912–)
Hall of Fame 1990

A lifelong love of the game led Joseph Frederick Cullman III to become a working angel in tennis, a moonlighter away from his principal position as chairman and CEO of the Philip Morris Co. As such he benefitted tennis extraordinarily in several ways. He was chairman of the U.S. Open at Forest Hills in 1969 and 1970, formative years, and was instrumental in getting the original Open, 1968, televised.

In 1970, at the behest of another Hall of Fame member, Gladys Heldman, he came to the financial and spiritual rescue of the women, up to then second-class citizens of tournament tennis. With the backing of one of his products, Virginia Slims, a separate women's professional circuit was born. It continues as the Corel Tour.

He was president and chairman of the International Tennis Hall of Fame 1982-88, a period during which the Hall's home, the revered and historic Newport Casino, made a recovery from years of decline, and became a sound and viable institution. A Yale alumnus, he built a tennis complex, the Cullman Center, for his alma mater. Joe is a New Yorker, born there April 9, 1912, and entered the Hall of Fame in 1990.

SLEW HESTER
United States (1912–93)
Hall of Fame 1981

A fine athlete, a football player at Millsaps College in his native Mississippi, William Ewing Hester won numerous tennis trophies. Among them were U.S. senior doubles titles such as the Grass Court 45s with Alex Wellford in 1957. But, as one of the most thoughtful and forceful USTA presidents, burly Slew made an indelible mark on the game by determining to expand the scope and potential of the U.S. Open by moving the event from Forest Hills after the 1977 Championships.

He took the Open a few miles away to Flushing Meadow and the swiftly constructed, Hester-inspired-and-overseen U.S. National Tennis Center in time for the 1978 Open. There the event annually set tennis attendance records. A gregarious cigar-smoking oilman from Jackson, Hester earned a bronze star while serving in the U.S. Army in World War II.

He was a USTA officer from 1969-77 when he became president for a two-year term. Born May 8, 1912, in Hazlehurst, Mass., he was inducted into the Hall of Fame in 1981, and died Feb. 8, 1993, in Jackson, Miss.

LAMAR HUNT
United States (1932–)
Hall of Fame 1993

A man about Halls of Fame, Texan Lamar Hunt entered the tennis valhalla in 1993, having been inducted previously into the Professional Football Hall of Fame and the Soccer Hall of Fame.

Although he played football—"I sat on the bench"—at Southern Methodist, Hunt, scion of a prominent Dallas oil industry family, made his mark in American and international sport with his organizational and promotional strengths.

He was a leading founder of the American Football League, which eventually merged with the NFL. And with his daughter, Hunt has been credited with the naming of the Super Bowl. He is owner of the Kansas City Chiefs and for a time owned the Dallas Tornados in the North American Soccer League.

It was as a partner in the establishment of World Championship Tennis (WCT)—and later its guiding light—that he was a strong global influence in transforming and professionalizing the tournament game. In 1967, a New Orleans friend, Dave Dixon, enlisted Hunt's aid in forming WCT. Headquartered in Dallas, WCT hastened the dawn of open tennis with the signing of the elite of the amateurs.

WCT developed a circuit and season of its own, leading the way to increased paydays for the pros that forced the rest of the tennis world to catch up.

Unfortunately (and ungratefully), the Association of Tennis Professionals, in reorganizing the men's tour in 1990, froze WCT out, and Hunt's organization ceased operations after 23 years of raising standards within the professional game. Hunt was born Aug. 2, 1932, in Eldorado, Ark., and lives in Dallas.

PERRY T. JONES
United States (1890–1970)
Hall of Fame 1970

A powerful figure in making Southern California a tennis vineyard of champions, Perry Thomas Jones oversaw the game from his office at the Los Angeles Tennis Club for well over a quarter-century. As president of the Southern California Association and director of the Pacific Southwest Championships, he was active in the game from bottom to top, singling out promising juniors for attention and travel and making his tournament one of the best in the U.S.

In short, Perry T., or Mr. Jones, as he was called, stood imposingly as Mr. Tennis of the West Coast, an exceptional fund-raiser whose judgment and help forwarded the careers of numerous stars, including Jack Kramer, Billie Jean King and Dennis Ralston.

The last was Alex Olmedo, the Peruvian student at the University of Southern California. Maneuvering controversially, Jones got him, the only non-citizen to play for the U.S., approved for the Davis Cup team in 1958, citing the fact that Peru had no team. Jones, the captain that year, was understandably eager to have Olmedo aboard. Olmedo led the U.S. to the Cup over Australia. Jones also captained the losing 1959 team. He was born June 22, 1890, in Etiwanda, Cal., and died Sept. 16, 1970, in Los Angeles. He entered the Hall of Fame in 1970.

BOB KELLEHER
United States (1913–)
Hall of Fame 2000

No one has had a longer or more distinguished career in tennis than Robert Joseph Kelleher, a federal judge in Los Angeles, who marked his 90th birthday March 5, 2003. New York born, raised near the West Side Tennis Club, Forest Hills, he was a junior member and, for several years, during the U.S. Championships, was a ball-boy there. Bob recalls working Bill Tilden's farewell to the Championships he had ruled for so long, a semifinal loss in 1930 to the champ, Johnny Doeg, 10-8, 6-3, 3-6, 12-10, and that the great figure was "haughty and grumpy, stalling to buy time. I remember Doeg [21, Tilden's junior by 16 years] yelling, 'Come on Bill—let's play tennis!'"

That has always been Kelleher's outlook, getting on with things intelligently, in sport, law and life—with firmness, understanding and a well-tuned sense of humor, but ever moving ahead. His nature guided him well as he shepherded an historically recalcitrant U.S. Tennis Association into the uncharted land of 'opens' in 1968. The game was lucky that he was USTA president at the time, willing to buck the "old goats," as he called them, longtime officials who sought to maintain the status-quo of phony amateurism, preferring to keep the game cloistered in small private clubs.

Although the USTA has been blessed with few progressive presidents, Kelleher was one of a handful, the right man at the right time to plant the seeds that would blossom. (Fellow Hall of Famer 'Slew' Hester, who thought big, in lifting the U.S. Open to Flushing Meadow from Forest Hills in 1978, was another.)

Like his co-revolutionary, Herman David, Wimbledon chairman (also a Hall of Famer), Kelleher "refused to be associated with a crooked enterprise," the tarnished system of under-the-table payments to so-called amateurs. He wanted to "start anew, with everything in the open." That's what he orchestrated in the U.S. as David did in Britain, respectful but independent of one another. With the two leading powers supporting open tennis, the ITF, largely anti-open, had no choice but to follow.

A lifelong love of tennis has spurred his urge to pre-serve and promote the game as player, administrator and fan. He was a fine player on the Williams College varsity, graduating in 1935. Finishing Harvard Law in 1938, he moved to Los Angeles to open a highly-regarded law practice before entering the U.S. Navy in World War II (1943-45) for duty as an officer in the Pacific. He was appointed to the federal bench in 1970.

He won the U.S. Hard Court 45s doubles with Elbert Lewis, 1958, 60, 62. His wife, Gracyn Wheeler Kelleher (1918-80), made the U.S. Top Ten five times between 1935 and 1940, No. 4 in 1936.

For two years, 1962-63, he captained the U.S. Davis Cup team, confidently and calmly leading an arduous campaign of six series, covering four continents, to the grand prize at Adelaide in '63. Cracking an Australian stranglehold of four years, Chuck McKinley and Dennis Ralston were his workhorses.

ALASTAIR MARTIN
United States (1915–1978)
Hall of Fame 1973

A mild yet determined man, Alastair Bradley Martin qualified for 1973 induction to the Hall of Fame on two counts: He was a progressive vice president and president of the USTA during the critical transition period between the amateur and open eras. And he was one of the finest of all court tennis players, U.S. amateur champion in singles eight times, doubles 10 times. He also challenged the great pro Pierre Etchebaster (a fellow Hall of Fame member) for Etchebaster's world title, vainly in 1950 and 1952.

Alastair was a good enough lawn tennis player to have competed in the U.S. Championships at Forest Hills several times before and after World War II. As vice president of the USTA in 1967 and 1968, he worked closely with president Bob Kelleher, advocating, with the British, the revolutionary adoption of open tennis.

He was USTA president in the trying days of 1969-70 as the game became professionalized, and the amateur associations maintained their standing. He founded the Eastern Tennis Patrons in 1951 and served as president of the National Tennis Foundation. A New Yorker, he was born there March 11, 1915.

BILL MARTIN
United States (1906–1998)
Hall of Fame 1982

A distinguished figure in finance and government

when Chairman of the Federal Reserve Board for 20 years (1951-70), William McChesney Martin was long devoted to the game, working behind the scenes to improve its condition in such positions as president of the National Tennis Foundation and the International Tennis Hall of Fame.

In 1992 he was elected honorary chairman of the Hall, and worked diligently to make sure that its home, the historic Newport Casino (imperiled by age and apathy), was preserved and put into fine condition.

Martin married into an honored tennis family, wedding Cynthia Davis, daughter of Dwight Davis, donor of the Cup bearing his name. Like the Davises, he was raised in St. Louis, born there Dec. 17, 1906. He entered the Hall of Fame in 1982 and resided and died in Washington, D.C. July 27, 1998.

JULIAN MYRICK

United States (1880–1969)
Hall of Fame 1963

A New Yorker, though born March 1, 1880, in Murfreesboro, N.C., Julian Southall Myrick was inducted into the Hall of Fame in 1963 on the basis of his administrative ability and contributions to the game in the U.S. Known as 'Uncle Mike' to friends and associates—and was an actual uncle of 1931 Wimbledon camp Sidney Wood. He was president of the USTA 1920-22 and an active committeeman. He was a leader in enlarging the U.S. Championships, influential in construction of the Forest Hills Stadium, at a cost of $300,000, in 1923, and launching the Wightman Cup competition between U.S. and British women, the first edition of which inaugurated the stadium. He died in New York, Jan. 4, 1969.

PATRONS

KING GUSTAV V

Sweden (1858–1950)
Hall of Fame 1980

A grand patron of the game and an enthusiastic player into his 90s, King Gustav V of Sweden learned to play during a visit to Britain in 1878, and founded his country's first tennis club on his return home. In 1936 he founded the King's Cup. Eventually disbanded during the open era, it was a men's indoor team competition for European countries. He became king on Dec. 8, 1907, ruled for 43 years and was often seen playing friendly

events on the Riviera.

Entered under the pseudonym, Mr. G., looking like an aged Mr. Chips in spectacles, white mustache, flannels and straw hat, he frequently took part in handicap tourneys, partnered by famous players such as Suzanne Lenglen. During World War II this widely respected ruler interceded to obtain better treatment for the Nazi-imprisoned Davis Cup stars, Jean Borotra of France and Gottfried von Cramm of Germany, and may have saved their lives.

Gustav was born June 16, 1858, in Drottningholm, Sweden and died Oct. 29, 1950. He was elected to the Hall of Fame in 1980.

ARTHUR NIELSEN

United States (1897–1980)
Hall of Fame 1971

Arthur Charles Nielsen's name is synonymous with television—the Nielsen Ratings—but he was long an avid player and a generous patron, contributing much time and money to the construction of tennis courts. One such monument to his memory is the Nielsen Center at his alma mater, the University of Wisconsin, where he was captain of the tennis varsity three years, 1916-18.

He continued playing after graduation, teaming with Arthur Nielsen, Jr., to win the U.S. Father and Son doubles titles of 1946 and 1948, and he was good enough to play singles in the U.S. Championships of 1918. A Chicagoan, he was born there, Sept. 5, 1897, and died there, June 1, 1980. He entered the Hall of Fame in 1971.

Appendix B

World Rankings

Worked rankings are delightfully controversial because there is no official, single source for them. Since 1973, the Association of Tennis Professionals and the Women's Tennis Association have rated their flocks weekly by computer. The ATP and WTA year-end ranking seems to be the most widely accepted standard and, therefore, the one we use here. Prior to the use of the computer, rankings were a matter of judgment, usually made by tennis journalists. Here, we have employed those of the well-traveled authorities of London's *The Daily Telegraph*, with time out for World Wars I and II: Wallis Myers (1913-1938), John Olliff (1939-51) and Lance Tingay (1952-67). Finally, rankings listed for 1968-1972 are those of the editor of *Total Tennis*, Bud Collins.

*Indicates tie

MEN

1913
1. Tony Wilding (NZ)
2. * Norman Brookes (AUS)
   * Maurice McLoughlin (US)
4. Jim Cecil Parke (IRL)
5. Dick Williams (US)
6. Percy Dixon (ENG)
7. Otto Froitzheim (GER)
8. Stanley Doust (AUS)
9. André Gobert (FRA)
10. Max Decugis (FRA)

1914
1. Maurice McLoughlin (US)
2. * Norman Brookes (AUS)
   * Tony Wilding (NZ)
4. Otto Froitzheim (GER)
5. Dick Williams (US)
6. Jim Cecil Parke (IRL)
7. Arthur Lowe (ENG)
8. F. Gordon Lowe (ENG)
9. Heinrich Kleinschroth (GER)
10. Max Decugis (FRA)

1919
1. * Gerald Patterson (AUS)
   * Bill Johnston (US)
3. André Gobert (FRA)
4. Bill Tilden (US)
5. Norman Brookes (AUS)
6. Algernon Kingscote (ENG)
7. Dick Williams (US)
8. Percival Davson (ENG)
9. Willis Davis (US)
10. William Laurentz (FRA)

1920
1. Bill Tilden (US)
2. Bill Johnston (US)
3. Algernon Kingscote (ENG)
4. Jim Cecil Parke (IRL)
5. André Gobert (FRA)
6. Norman Brookes (AUS)
7. Dick Williams (US)
8. William Laurentz (FRA)
9. Zenzo Shimidzu (JPN)
10. Gerald Patterson (AUS)

1921
1. Bill Tilden (US)
2. Bill Johnston (US)
3. Vinnie Richards (US)
4. Zenzo Shimidzu (JPN)
5. Gerald Patterson (AUS)
6. James Anderson (AUS)
7. Brian Norton (RSA)
8. Manuel Alonso (ESP)
9. Dick Williams (US)
10. André Gobert (FRA)

1922
1. Bill Tilden (US)
2. Bill Johnston (US)
3. Gerald Patterson (AUS)
4. Vinnie Richards (US)
5. Jim Anderson (AUS)
6. Henri Cochet (FRA)
7. Pat O'Hara Wood (AUS)
8. Dick Williams (US)
9. Algernon Kingscote (ENG)
10. André Gobert (FRA)

1923
1. Bill Tilden (US)
2. Bill Johnston (US)
3. Jim Anderson (AUS)
4. Dick Williams (US)
5. Frank Hunter (US)
6. Vinnie Richards (US)
7. Brian Norton (RSA)
8. Manuel Alonso (ESP)
9. Jean Washer (BEL)
10. Henri Cochet (FRA)

1924
1. Bill Tilden (US)
2. Vinnie Richards (US)
3. Jim Anderson (AUS)
4. Bill Johnston (US)
5. René Lacoste (FRA)
6. Jean Borotra (FRA)
7. Howard Kinsey (US)
8. Gerald Patterson (AUS)
9. Henri Cochet (FRA)
10. Manuel Alonso (ESP)

1925
1. Bill Tilden (US)
2. Bill Johnston (US)
3. Vinnie Richards (US)
4. René Lacoste (FRA)
5. Dick Williams (US)
6. Jean Borotra (FRA)
7. Gerald Patterson (AUS)
8. Manuel Alonso (ESP)
9. Brian Norton (RSA)
10. Takeichi Harada (JPN)

1926
1. René Lacoste (FRA)
2. Jean Borotra (FRA)
3. Henri Cochet (FRA)
4. Bill Johnston (US)
5. Bill Tilden (US)
6. Vinnie Richards (US)
7. Takeichi Harada (JPN)
8. Manuel Alonso (ESP)
9. Howard Kinsey (US)
10. Jacques Brugnon (FRA)

1927
1. René Lacoste (FRA)
2. Bill Tilden (US)
3. Henri Cochet (FRA)
4. Jean Borotra (FRA)
5. Manuel Alonso (ESP)
6. Frank Hunter (US)
7. George Lott (US)
8. John Hennessey (US)
9. Jacques Brugnon (FRA)
10. Jan Kozeluh (TCH)

1928
1. Henri Cochet (FRA)
2. René Lacoste (FRA)
3. Bill Tilden (US)
4. Frank Hunter (US)
5. Jean Borotra (FRA)
6. George Lott (US)
7. Bunny Austin (ENG)
8. John Hennessey (US)
9. Umberto de Morpurgo (ITA)
10. John Hawkes (AUS)

1929
1. Henri Cochet (FRA)
2. René Lacoste (FRA)
3. Jean Borotra (FRA)
4. Bill Tilden (US)
5. Frank Hunter (US)
6. George Lott (US)
7. John Doeg (US)
8. John Van Ryn (US)
9. Bunny Austin (ENG)
10. Umberto de Morpurgo (ITA)

1930
1. Henri Cochet (FRA)
2. Bill Tilden (US)
3. Jean Borotra (FRA)
4. John Doeg (US)
5. Frank Shields (US)
6. Wilmer Allison (US)
7. George Lott (US)
8. Umberto de Morpurgo (ITA)
9. Christian Boussus (FRA)
10. Bunny Austin (ENG)

1931
1. Henri Cochet (FRA)
2. Bunny Austin (ENG)
3. Ellsworth Vines (US)
4. Fred Perry (ENG)
5. Frank Shields (US)
6. Sidney Wood (US)
7. Jean Borotra (FRA)
8. George Lott (US)
9. Jiro Satoh (JPN)
10. John Van Ryn (US)

1932
1. Ellsworth Vines (US)
2. Henri Cochet (FRA)
3. Jean Borotra (FRA)
4. Wilmer Allison (US)
5. Cliff Sutter (US)
6. Daniel Prenn (GER)
7. Fred Perry (ENG)
8. Gottfried von Cramm (GER)
9. Bunny Austin (ENG)
10. Jack Crawford (AUS)

1933
1. Jack Crawford (AUS)
2. Fred Perry (ENG)
3. Jiro Satoh (JPN)
4. Bunny Austin (ENG)
5. Ellsworth Vines (US)
6. Henri Cochet (FRA)
7. Frank Shields (US)
8. Sidney Wood (US)
9. Gottfried von Cramm (GER)
10. Lester Stoefen (US)

1934
1. Fred Perry (ENG)
2. Jack Crawford (AUS)
3. Gottfried von Cramm (GER)
4. Bunny Austin (ENG)
5. Wilmer Allison (US)
6. Sidney Wood (US)
7. Roderich Menzel (TCH)
8. Frank Shields (US)
9. Giorgio de Stefani (ITA)
10. Christian Boussus (FRA)

1935
1. Fred Perry (ENG)
2. Jack Crawford (AUS)
3. Gottfried von Cramm (GER)
4. Wilmer Allison (US)
5. Bunny Austin (ENG)
6. Don Budge (US)
7. Frank Shields (US)
8. Viv McGrath (AUS)
9. Christian Boussus (FRA)
10. Sidney Wood (US)

1936
1. Fred Perry (ENG)
2. Gottfried von Cramm (GER)
3. Don Budge (US)
4. Adrian Quist (AUS)
5. Bunny Austin (ENG)
6. Jack Crawford (AUS)
7. Wilmer Allison (US)
8. Bryan Grant (US)
9. Henner Henkel (GER)
10. Viv McGrath (AUS)

1937
1. Don Budge (US)
2. Gottfried von Cramm (GER)
3. Henner Henkel (GER)
4. Bunny Austin (ENG)
5. Bobby Riggs (US)
6. Bryan Grant (US)
7. Jack Crawford (AUS)
8. Roderich Menzel (TCH)
9. Frank Parker (US)
10. Charlie Hare (ENG)

1938
1. Don Budge (US)
2. Bunny Austin (ENG)
3. John Bromwich (AUS)
4. Bobby Riggs (US)
5. Sidney Wood (US)
6. Adrian Quist (AUS)
7. Roderich Menzel (TCH)
8. Jiro Yamagishi (JPN)
9. Gene Mako (US)
10. Franjo Puncec (YUG)

1939
1. Bobby Riggs (US)
2. John Bromwich (AUS)
3. Adrian Quist (AUS)
4. Franjo Puncec (YUG)
5. Frank Parker (US)
6. Henner Henkel (GER)
7. Don McNeill (US)
8. Elwood Cooke (US)
9. Welby Van Horn (US)
10. Joe Hunt (US)

1946
1. Jack Kramer (US)
2. Ted Schroeder (US)
3. Jaroslav Drobny (TCH)
4. Yvon Petra (FRA)
5. Marcel Bernard (FRA)
6. John Bromwich (AUS)
7. Tom Brown (US)
8. Gardnar Mulloy (US)
9. Frank Parker (US)
10. Geoff Brown (AUS)

1947
1. Jack Kramer (US)
2. Ted Schroeder (US)
3. Frank Parker (US)
4. John Bromwich (AUS)
5. Jaroslav Drobny (TCH)
6. Dinny Pails (AUS)
7. Tom Brown (US)
8. Budge Patty (US)
9. Joszef Asboth (HUN)
10. Gardnar Mulloy (US)

1948
1. Frank Parker (US)
2. Ted Schroeder (US)
3. Pancho Gonzalez (US)
4. John Bromwich (AUS)
5. Jaroslav Drobny (TCH)
6. Eric Sturgess (RSA)
7. Bob Falkenburg (US)
8. Joszef Asboth (HUN)
9. Lennart Bergelin (SWE)
10. Adrian Quist (AUS)

1949
1. Pancho Gonzalez (US)
2. Ted Schroeder (US)
3. Bill Talbert (US)
4. Frank Sedgman (AUS)
5. Frank Parker (US)
6. Eric Sturgess (RSA)
7. Jaroslav Drobny (TCH)
8. Budge Patty (US)
9. Gardnar Mulloy (US)
10. Billy Sidwell (AUS)

1950
1. Budge Patty (US)
2. Frank Sedgman (AUS)
3. Art Larsen (US)
4. Jaroslav Drobny (EGY)
5. Herbie Flam (US)
6. Ted Schroeder (US)
7. Vic Seixas (US)
8. Ken McGregor (AUS)
9. Bill Talbert (US)
10. Eric Sturgess (RSA)

1951
1. Frank Sedgman (AUS)
2. Dick Savitt (US)
3. Jaroslav Drobny (EGY)
4. Vic Seixas (US)
5. Tony Trabert (US)
6. Ted Schroeder (US)
7. Ken McGregor (AUS)
8. Herbie Flam (US)
9. Art Larsen (US)
10. Mervyn Rose (AUS)

1952
1. Frank Sedgman (AUS)
2. Jaroslav Drobny (EGY)
3. Ken McGregor (AUS)
4. Mervyn Rose (AUS)
5. Vic Seixas (US)
6. Herbie Flam (US)
7. Gardnar Mulloy (US)
8. Eric Sturgess (RSA)
9. Dick Savitt (US)
10. *Ken Rosewall (AUS)
   *Lew Hoad (AUS)

1953
1. Tony Trabert (US)
2. Ken Rosewall (AUS)
3. Vic Seixas (US)
4. Jaroslav Drobny (EGY)
5. Lew Hoad (AUS)
6. Mervyn Rose (AUS)
7. Kurt Nielsen (DEN)
8. Budge Patty (US)
9. Sven Davidson (SWE)
10. Enrique Morea (ARG)

1954
1. Jaroslav Drobny (EGY)
2. Tony Trabert (US)
3. Ken Rosewall (AUS)
4. Vic Seixas (US)
5. Rex Hartwig (AUS)
6. Mervyn Rose (AUS)
7. Lew Hoad (AUS)
8. Budge Patty (US)
9. Art Larsen (US)
10. * Enrique Morea (ARG)
   *Ham Richardson (US)
   *Sven Davidson (SWE)

1955
1. Tony Trabert (US)
2. Ken Rosewall (AUS)
3. Lew Hoad (AUS)
4. Vic Seixas (US)
5. Rex Hartwig (AUS)
6. Budge Patty (US)
7. Ham Richardson (US)
8. Kurt Nielsen (DEN)
9. Jaroslav Drobny (EGY)
10. *Sven Davidson (SWE)
   *Mervyn Rose (AUS)

1956
1. Lew Hoad (AUS)
2. Ken Rosewall (AUS)
3. Ham Richardson (US)
4. Vic Seixas (US)
5. Sven Davidson (SWE)
6. Neale Fraser (AUS)
7. Ashley Cooper (AUS)
8. Dick Savitt (US)
9. Herbie Flam (US)
10. * Budge Patty (US)
   * Nicola Pietrangeli (ITA)

1957
1. Ashley Cooper (AUS)
2. Mal Anderson (AUS)
3. Sven Davidson (SWE)
4. Herbie Flam (US)
5. Neale Fraser (AUS)
6. Mervyn Rose (AUS)
7. Vic Seixas (US)
8. Budge Patty (US)
9. Nicola Pietrangeli (ITA)
10. Dick Savitt (US)

1958
1. Ashley Cooper (AUS)
2. Mal Anderson (AUS)
3. Mervyn Rose (AUS)
4. Neale Fraser (AUS)
5. Luis Ayala (CHI)
6. Ham Richardson (US)
7. Nicola Pietrangeli (ITA)
8. Ulf Schmidt (SWE)
9. Barry MacKay (US)
10. Sven Davidson (SWE)

1959
1. Neale Fraser (AUS)
2. Alex Olmedo (PER)
3. Nicola Pietrangeli (ITA)
4. Barry MacKay (US)
5. Rod Laver (AUS)
6. Luis Ayala (CHI)
7. Roy Emerson (AUS)
8. Bernard Bartzen (US)
9. Ramanathan Krishnan (IND)
10. Ian Vermaak (RSA)

1960
1. Neale Fraser (AUS)
2. Rod Laver (AUS)
3. Nicola Pietrangeli (ITA)
4. Barry MacKay (US)
5. Butch Buchholz, Jr. (US)
6. Roy Emerson (AUS)
7. Luis Ayala (CHI)
8. Ramanathan Krishnan (IND)
9. Jan-Erik Lundquist (SWE)
10. Dennis Ralston (US)

1961
1. Rod Laver (AUS)
2. Roy Emerson (AUS)
3. Manolo Santana (ESP)
4. Nicola Pietrangeli (ITA)
5. Chuck McKinley (US)
6. Ramanathan Krishnan (IND)
7. Luis Ayala (CHI)
8. Neale Fraser (AUS)
9. Jan-Erik Lundquist (SWE)
10. Ulf Schmidt (SWE)

1962
1. Rod Laver (AUS)
2. Roy Emerson (AUS)
3. Manolo Santana (ESP)
4. Neale Fraser (AUS)
5. Chuck McKinley (US)
6. Rafael Osuna (MEX)
7. Marty Mulligan (AUS)
8. Bob Hewitt (AUS)
9. Ramanathan Krishnan (IND)
10. Wilhelm Bungert (GER)

1963
1. Rafael Osuna (MEX)
2. Chuck McKinley (US)
3. Roy Emerson (AUS)
4. Manolo Santana (ESP)
5. Fred Stolle (AUS)
6. Frank Froehling III (US)
7. Dennis Ralston (US)
8. Boro Jovanovic (YUG)
9. Mike Sangster (ENG)
10. Marty Mulligan (AUS)

1964
1. Roy Emerson (AUS)
2. Fred Stolle (AUS)
3. Jan-Erik Lundquist (SWE)
4. Wilhelm Bungert (GER)
5. Chuck McKinley (US)
6. Manolo Santana (ESP)
7. Nicola Pietrangeli (ITA)
8. Christian Kuhnke (GER)
9. Dennis Ralston (US)
10. Rafael Osuna (MEX)

1965
1. Roy Emerson (AUS)
2. Manolo Santana (ESP)
3. Fred Stolle (AUS)
4. Cliff Drysdale (RSA)
5. Marty Mulligan (AUS)
6. Jan-Erik Lundquist (SWE)
7. Tony Roche (AUS)
8. John Newcombe (AUS)
9. Dennis Ralston (US)
10. Arthur Ashe (US)

1966
1. Manolo Santana (ESP)
2. Fred Stolle (AUS)
3. Roy Emerson (AUS)
4. Tony Roche (AUS)
5. Dennis Ralston (US)
6. John Newcombe (AUS)
7. Arthur Ashe (US)
8. Istvan Gulyas (HUN)
9. Cliff Drysdale (RSA)
10. Ken Fletcher (AUS)

1967
1. John Newcombe (AUS)
2. Roy Emerson (AUS)
3. Manolo Santana (ESP)
4. Marty Mulligan (AUS)
5. Tony Roche (AUS)
6. Bob Hewitt (RSA)
7. Nikki Pilic (YUG)
8. Clark Graebner (US)
9. Arthur Ashe (US)
10.* Jan Leschly (DEN)
   * Wilhelm Bungert (GER)
   * Cliff Drysdale (RSA)

1968
1. Rod Laver (AUS)
2. Arthur Ashe (US)
3. Ken Rosewall (AUS)
4. Tony Roche (AUS)
5. Tom Okker (NED)
6. John Newcombe (AUS)
7. Clark Graebner (US)
8. Dennis Ralston (US)
9. Cliff Drysdale (RSA)
10. Pancho Gonzalez (US)

1969
1. Rod Laver (AUS)
2. Tony Roche (AUS)
3. John Newcombe (AUS)
4. Ken Rosewall (AUS)
5. Tom Okker (NED)
6. Pancho Gonzalez (US)
7. Stan Smith (US)
8. Arthur Ashe (US)
9. Cliff Drysdale (RSA)
10. Andres Gimeno (ESP)

1970
1. John Newcombe (AUS)
2. Ken Rosewall (AUS)
3. Tony Roche (AUS)
4. Rod Laver (AUS)
5. Ilie Nastase (ROM)
6. Tom Okker (NED)
7. Cliff Richey (US)
8. Stan Smith (US)
9. Arthur Ashe (US)
10. Andres Gimeno (ESP)

1971
1. John Newcombe (AUS)
2. Stan Smith (US)
3. Ken Rosewall (AUS)
4. Rod Laver (AUS)
5. Jan Kodes (TCH)
6. Arthur Ashe (US)
7. Ilie Nastase (ROM)
8. Tom Okker (NED)
9. Cliff Drysdale (RSA)
10. Marty Riessen (US)

1972
1. Stan Smith (US)
2. Ken Rosewall (AUS)
3. Ilie Nastase (ROM)
4. Rod Laver (AUS)
5. Arthur Ashe (US)
6. John Newcombe (AUS)
7. Bob Lutz (US)
8. Tom Okker (NED)
9. Marty Riessen (US)
10. Andres Gimeno (ESP)

1973 *(Compter rankings begin)*
1. Ilie Nastase (ROM)
2. John Newcombe (AUS)
3. Jimmy Connors (US)
4. Tom Okker (NED)
5. Stan Smith (US)
6. Ken Rosewall (AUS)
7. Manuel Orantes (ESP)
8. Rod Laver (AUS)
9. Jan Kodes (TCH)
10. Arthur Ashe (US)

1974
1. Jimmy Connors (US)
2. John Newcombe (AUS)
3. Bjorn Borg (SWE)
4. Rod Laver (AUS)
5. Guillermo Vilas (ARG)
6. Tom Okker (NED)
7. Arthur Ashe (US)
8. Ken Rosewall (AUS)
9. Stan Smith (US)
10. Ilie Nastase (ROM)

1975
1. Jimmy Connors (US)
2. Guillermo Vilas (ARG)
3. Bjorn Borg (SWE)
4. Arthur Ashe (US)
5. Manuel Orantes (ESP)
6. Ken Rosewall (AUS)
7. Ilie Nastase (ROM)
8. John Alexander (AUS)
9. Roscoe Tanner (US)
10. Rod Laver (AUS)

1976
1. Jimmy Connors (US)
2. Bjorn Borg (SWE)
3. Ilie Nastase (ROM)
4. Manuel Orantes (ESP)
5. Raul Ramirez (MEX)
6. Guillermo Vilas (ARG)
7. Adriano Panatta (ITA)
8. Harold Solomon (US)
9. Eddie Dibbs (US)
10. Brian Gottfried (US)

1977
1. Jimmy Connors (US)
2. Guillermo Vilas (ARG)
3. Bjorn Borg (SWE)
4. Vitas Gerulaitis (US)
5. Brian Gottfried (US)
6. Eddie Dibbs (US)
7. Manuel Orantes (ESP)
8. Raul Ramirez (MEX)
9. Ilie Nastase (ROM)
10. Dick Stockton (US)

1978
1. Jimmy Connors (US)
2. Bjorn Borg (SWE)
3. Guillermo Vilas (ARG)
4. John McEnroe (US)
5. Vitas Gerulaitis (US)
6. Eddie Dibbs (US)
7. Brian Gottfried (US)
8. Raul Ramirez (MEX)
9. Harold Solomon (US)
10. Corrado Barazzutti (ITA)

1979
1. Bjorn Borg (SWE)
2. Jimmy Connors (US)
3. John McEnroe (US)
4. Vitas Gerulaitis (US)
5. Roscoe Tanner (US)
6. Guillermo Vilas (ARG)
7. Arthur Ashe (US)
8. Harold Solomon (US)
9. Jose Higueras (ESP)
10. Eddie Dibbs (US)

1980
1. Bjorn Borg (SWE)
2. John McEnroe (US)
3. Jimmy Connors (US)
4. Gene Mayer (US)
5. Guillermo Vilas (ARG)
6. Ivan Lendl (TCH)
7. Harold Solomon (US)
8. Jose-Luis Clerc (ARG)
9. Vitas Gerulaitis (US)
10. Eliot Teltscher (US)

1981
1. John McEnroe (US)
2. Ivan Lendl (TCH)
3. Jimmy Connors (US)
4. Bjorn Borg (SWE)
5. Jose-Luis Clerc (ARG)
6. Guillermo Vilas (ARG)
7. Gene Mayer (US)
8. Eliot Teltscher (US)
9. Vitas Gerulaitis (US)
10. Peter McNamara (AUS)

1982
1. John McEnroe (US)
2. Jimmy Connors (US)
3. Ivan Lendl (TCH)
4. Guillermo Vilas (ARG)
5. Vitas Gerulaitis (US)
6. Jose-Luis Clerc (ARG)
7. Mats Wilander (SWE)
8. Gene Mayer (US)
9. Yannick Noah (FRA)
10. Peter McNamara (AUS)

1983
1. John McEnroe (US)
2. Ivan Lendl (TCH)
3. Jimmy Connors (US)
4. Mats Wilander (SWE)
5. Yannick Noah (FRA)
6. Jimmy Arias (US)
7. Jose Higueras (ESP)
8. Jose-Luis Clerc (ARG)
9. Kevin Curren (RSA)
10. Gene Mayer (US)

1984
1. John McEnroe (US)
2. Jimmy Connors (US)
3. Ivan Lendl (TCH)
4. Mats Wilander (SWE)
5. Andres Gomez (ECU)
6. Anders Jarryd (SWE)
7. Henrik Sundstrom (SWE)
8. Pat Cash (AUS)
9. Eliot Teltscher (US)
10. Yannick Noah (FRA)

1985
1. Ivan Lendl (TCH)
2. John McEnroe (US)
3. Mats Wilander (SWE)
4. Jimmy Connors (US)
5. Stefan Edberg (SWE)
6. Boris Becker (GER)
7. Yannick Noah (FRA)
8. Anders Jarryd (SWE)
9. Miloslav Mecir (TCH)
10. Kevin Curren (RSA)

1986
1. Ivan Lendl (TCH)
2. Boris Becker (GER)
3. Mats Wilander (SWE)
4. Yannick Noah (FRA)
5. Stefan Edberg (SWE)
6. Henri Leconte (FRA)
7. Joakim Nystrom
8. Jimmy Connors (US)
9. Miloslav Mecir (TCH)
10. Andres Gomez (ECU)

1987
1. Ivan Lendl (TCH)
2. Stefan Edberg (SWE)
3. Mats Wilander (SWE)
4. Jimmy Connors (US)
5. Boris Becker (GER)
6. Miloslav Mecir (TCH)
7. Pat Cash (AUS)
8. Yannick Noah (FRA)
9. Tim Mayotte (US)
10. John McEnroe (US)

1988
1. Mats Wilander (SWE)
2. Ivan Lendl (TCH)
3. Andre Agassi (US)
4. Boris Becker (GER)
5. Stefan Edberg (SWE)
6. Kent Carlsson (SWE)
7. Jimmy Connors (US)
8. Jakob Hlasek (SUI)
9. Henri Leconte (FRA)
10. Tim Mayotte (US)

1989
1. Ivan Lendl (TCH)
2. Boris Becker (GER)
3. Stefan Edberg (SWE)
4. John McEnroe (US)
5. Michael Chang (US)
6. Brad Gilbert (US)
7. Andre Agassi (US)
8. Aaron Krickstein
9. Alberto Mancini (ARG)
10. Jay Berger (US)

1990
1. Stefan Edberg (SWE)
2. Boris Becker (GER)
3. Ivan Lendl (TCH)
4. Andre Agassi (US)
5. Pete Sampras (US)
6. Andres Gomez (ECU)
7. Thomas Muster (AUT)
8. Emilio Sanchez (ESP)
9. Goran Ivanisevic (CRO)
10. Brad Gilbert (US)

1991
1. Stefan Edberg (SWE)
2. Jim Courier (US)
3. Boris Becker (GER)
4. Michael Stich (GER)
5. Ivan Lendl (TCH)
6. Pete Sampras (US)
7. Guy Forget (FRA)
8. Karel Novacek (TCH)
9. Petr Korda (TCH)
10. Andre Agassi (US)

1992
1. Jim Courier (US)
2. Stefan Edberg (SWE)
3. Pete Sampras (US)
4. Goran Ivanisevic (CRO)
5. Boris Becker (GER)
6. Michael Chang (US)
7. Petr Korda (TCH)
8. Ivan Lendl (US)
9. Andre Agassi (US)
10. Richard Krajicek (NED)

1993
1. Pete Sampras (US)
2. Michael Stich (GER)
3. Jim Courier (US)
4. Sergi Bruguera (ESP)
5. Stefan Edberg (SWE)
6. Andrei Medvedev (UKR)
7. Goran Ivanisevic (CRO)
8. Michael Chang (US)
9. Thomas Muster (AUT)
10. Cedric Pioline (FRA)

1994
1. Pete Sampras (US)
2. Andre Agassi (US)
3. Boris Becker (GER)
4. Sergi Bruguera (ESP)
5. Goran Ivanisevic (CRO)
6. Michael Chang (US)
7. Stefan Edberg (SWE)
8. Alberto Berasategui (ESP)
9. Michael Stich (GER)
10. Todd Martin (US)

1995
1. Pete Sampras (US)
2. Andre Agassi (US)
3. Thomas Muster (AUT)
4. Boris Becker (GER)
5. Michael Chang (US)
6. Yevgeny Kafelnikov (RUS)
7. Thomas Enqvist (SWE)
8. Jim Courier (US)
9. Wayne Ferreira (RSA)
10. Goran Ivanisevic (CRO)

1996
1. Pete Sampras (US)
2. Michael Chang (US)
3. Yevgeny Kafelnikov (RUS)
4. Goran Ivanisevic (CRO)
5. Thomas Muster (AUT)
6. Boris Becker (GER)
7. Richard Krajicek (NED)
8. Andre Agassi (US)
9. Thomas Enqvist (SWE)
10. Wayne Ferreira (RSA)

1997
1. Pete Sampras (US)
2. Patrick Rafter (AUS)
3. Michael Chang (US)
4. Jonas Bjorkman (SWE)
5. Yevgeny Kafelnikov (RUS)
6. Greg Rusedski (GBR)
7. Carlos Moya (ESP)
8. Sergi Bruguera (ESP)
9. Thomas Muster (AUT)
10. Marcelo Rios (CHI)

1998
1. Pete Sampras (US)
2. Marcelo Rios (CHI)
3. Alex Corretja (ESP)
4. Patrick Rafter (AUS)
5. Carlos Moya (ESP)
6. Andre Agassi (US)
7. Tim Henman (GBR)
8. Karol Kucera (SVK)
9. Greg Rusedski (GBR)
10. Richard Krajicek (NED)

1999
1. Andre Agassi (US)
2. Yevgeny Kafelnikov (RUS)
3. Pete Sampras (US)
4. Thomas Enqvist (SWE)
5. Gustavo Kuerten (BRA)
6. Nicolas Kiefer (GER)
7. Todd Martin (US)
8. Nicolas Lapentti (ECU)
9. Marcelo Rios (CHI)
10. Richard Krajicek (NED)

2000
1. Gustavo Kuerten (BRA)
2. Marat Safin (RUS)
3. Pete Sampras (US)
4. Magnus Norman (SWE)
5. Yevgeny Kafelnikov (RUS)
6. Andre Agassi (US)
7. Lleyton Hewitt (AUS)
8. Alex Corretja (ESP)
9. Thomas Enqvist (SWE)
10. Tim Henman (GBR)

2001
1. Lleyton Hewitt (AUS)
2. Gustavo Kuerten (BRA)
3. Andre Agassi (US)
4. Yevgeny Kafelnikov (RUS)
5. Juan Carlos Ferrero (ESP)
6. Sebastien Grosjean (FRA)
7. Patrick Rafter (AUS)
8. Tommy Haas (GER)
9. Tim Henman (GBR)
10. Pete Sampras (US)

2002
1. Lleyton Hewitt (AUS)
2. Andre Agassi (US)
3. Marat Safin (RUS)
4. Juan Carlos Ferrero (ESP)
5. Carlos Moya (ESP)
6. Roger Federer (SUI)
7. Jiri Novak (CZE)
8. Tim Henman (GBR)
9. Albert Costa (ESP)
10. Andy Roddick (US)

WOMEN

1921
1. Suzanne Lenglen (FRA)
2. Molla Bjurstedt Mallory (US)
3. Mary K. Browne (US)
4. Elizabeth Ryan (US)
5. Kitty McKane (ENG)
6. May Sutton Bundy (US)
7. Irene Peacock (IND)
8. Geraldine Beamish (ENG)
9. Eleanor Goss (US)
10. Marion Zinderstein Jessup (US)

1922
1. Suzanne Lenglen (FRA)
2. Molla Bjurstedt Mallory (US)
3. Helen Wills (US)
4. Kitty McKane (ENG)
5. Geraldine Beamish (ENG)
6. Irene Peacock (IND)
7. Elizabeth Ryan (US)
8. Marion Zinderstein Jessup (US)
9. May Sutton Bundy (US)
10. Margaret Molesworth (AUS)

1923
1. Suzanne Lenglen (FRA)
2. Kitty McKane (ENG)
3. Helen Wills (US)
4. Geraldine Beamish (ENG)
5. Molla Bjurstedt Mallory (US)
6. Eleanor Goss (US)
7. Elizabeth Ryan (US)
8. Didi Vlasto (FRA)
9. Leslie Bancroft (US)
10. Margaret Molesworth (AUS)

1924
1. Suzanne Lenglen (FRA)
2. Kitty McKane (ENG)
3. Helen Wills (US)
4. Molla Mallory (US)
5. Mary K. Browne (US)
6. Eleanor Goss (US)
7. Elizabeth Ryan (US)
8. Phyllis Satterthwaite (ENG)
9. Marion Zinderstein Jessup (US)
10. Sylvia Lance (AUS)

1925
1. Suzanne Lenglen (FRA)
2. Helen Wills (US)
3. Kitty McKane (ENG)
4. Elizabeth Ryan (US)
5. Molla Bjurstedt Mallory (US)
6. Eleanor Goss (US)
7. D. Douglass Chambers (ENG)
8. Joan Fry (ENG)
9. Marguerite Billout (FRA)
10. Marion Zinderstein Jessup (US)

1926
1. Suzanne Lenglen (FRA)
2. Kitty McKane Godfree (ENG)
3. Lili de Alvarez (ESP)
4. Molla Bjurstedt Mallory (US)
5. Elizabeth Ryan (US)
6. Mary K. Browne (US)
7. Joan Fry (ENG)
8. Phoebe Holcroft Watson (ENG)
10. Marion Zinderstein Jessup (US)
* Didi Vlasto (FRA)

1927
1. Helen Wills (US)
2. Lili de Alvarez (ESP)
3. Elizabeth Ryan (US)
4. Molla Bjurstedt Mallory (US)
5. Kitty McKane Godfree (ENG)
6. Betty Nuthall (ENG)
7. Bobbie Heine (RSA)
8. Joan Fry (ENG)
9. Kea Bouman (NED)
10. Charlotte Hosmer Chapin (US)

1928
1. Helen Wills (US)
2. Lili de Alvarez (ESP)
3. Daphne Akhurst (AUS)
4. Eileen Bennett (ENG)
5. Phoebe Holcroft Watson (ENG)
6. Elizabeth Ryan (US)
7. Cilly Aussem (GER)
8. Kea Bouman (NED)
9. Helen Jacobs (US)
10. Esna Boyd (AUS)

1929
1. Helen Wills Moody (US)
2. Phoebe Holcroft Watson (ENG)
3. Helen Jacobs (US)
4. Betty Nuthall (ENG)
5. Bobbie Heine (RSA)
6. S. Passemard Mathieu (FRA)
7. Eileen Bennett (ENG)
8. Paula von Reznicek (GER)
9. Peggy Saunders Michell (ENG)
10. Elsie Goldsack (ENG)

1930
1. Helen Wills Moody (US)
2. Cilly Aussem (GER)
3. Phoebe Holcroft Watson (ENG)
4. Elizabeth Ryan (US)
5. S. Passemard Mathieu (FRA)
6. Helen Jacobs (US)
7. Phyllis Mudford (ENG)
8. Lili de Alvarez (ESP)
9. Betty Nuthall (ENG)
10. Hilde Krahwinkel (GER)

1931
1. Helen Wills Moody (US)
2. Cilly Aussem (GER)
3. E. Bennett Whittingstall (ENG)
4. Helen Jacobs (US)
5. Betty Nuthall (ENG)
6. Hilde Krahwinkel (GER)
7. S. Passemard Mathieu (FRA)
8. Lili de Alvarez (ESP)
9. Phyllis Mudford (ENG)
10. Elsie Goldsack Pittman (ENG)

1932
1. Helen Wills Moody (US)
2. Helen Jacobs (US)
3. S. Passemard Mathieu (FRA)
4. Lolette Payot (SUI)
5. Hilde Krahwinkel (GER)
6. Mary Heeley (ENG)
7. E. Bennett Whittingstall (ENG)
8. Marie Luise Horn (GER)
9. Kay Stammers (ENG)
10. Josane SigarT (BEL)

1933
1. Helen Wills Moody (US)
2. Helen Jacobs (US)
3. Dorothy Round (ENG)
4. Hilde Krahwinkel (GER)
5. Margaret Scriven (ENG)
6. S. Passemard Mathieu (FRA)
7. Sarah Palfrey (US)
8. Betty Nuthall (ENG)
9. Lolette Payot (SUI)
10. Alice Marble (US)

1934
1. Dorothy Round (ENG)
2. Helen Jacobs (US)
3. Hilde Krahwinkel Sperling (GER)
4. Sarah Palfrey (US)
5. Margaret Scriven (ENG)
6. S. Passemard Mathieu (FRA)
7. Lolette Payot (SUI)
8. Joan Hartigan (AUS)
9. Cilly Aussem (GER)
10. Carolin Babcock (US)

1935
1. Helen Wills Moody (US)
2. Helen Jacobs (US)
3. Kay Stammers (ENG)
4. Hilde Krahwinkel Sperling (GER)
5. Sarah Palfrey Fabyan (US)
6. Dorothy Round (ENG)
7. Mary Arnold (US)
8. S. Passemard Mathieu (FRA)
9. Joan Hartigan (AUS)
10. Peggy Scriven (ENG)

1936
1. Helen Jacobs (US)
2. Hilde Krahwinkel Sperling (GER)
3. Dorothy Round (ENG)
4. Alice Marble (US)
5. S. Passemard Mathieu (FRA)
6. Jadwiga Jedrzejowska (POL)
7. Kay Stammers (ENG)
8. Anita Lizana (CHI)
9. Sarah Palfrey Fabyan (US)
10. Carolin Babcock (US)

1937
1. Anita Lizana (CHI)
2. Dorothy Round Little (ENG)
3. Jadwiga Jedrzejowska (POL)
4. Hilde Krahwinkel Sperling (GER)
5. S. Passemard Mathieu (FRA)
6. Helen Jacobs (US)
7. Alice Marble (US)
8. Marie Luise Horn (GER)
9. Mary Hardwick (ENG)
10. Dorothy Bundy (US)

1938
1. Helen Wills Moody (US)
2. Helen Jacobs (US)
3. Alice Marble (US)
4. Hilde Krahwinkel Sperling (GER)
5. S. Passemard Mathieu (FRA)
6. Jadwiga Jedrzejowska (POL)
7. Sarah Palfrey Fabyan (US)
8. Bobbie Heine Miller (RSA)
9. Kay Stammers (ENG)
10. Nancye Wynne (AUS)

1939
1. Alice Marble (US)
2. Kay Stammers (ENG)
3. Helen Jacobs (US)
4. Hilde Krahwinkel Sperling (GER)
5. S. Passemard Mathieu (FRA)
6. Sarah Palfrey Fabyan (US)
7. Jadwiga Jedrzejowska (POL)
8. Mary Hardwick (ENG)
9. Valerie Scott (ENG)
10. Virginia Wolfenden (US)

1946
1. Pauline Betz (US)
2. Margaret Osborne (US)
3. Louise Brough (US)
4. Doris Hart (US)
5. Pat Canning Todd (US)
6. Dorothy Bundy (US)
7. Nelly Adamson Landry (FRA)
8. Kay Stammers Menzies (ENG)
9. Shirley Fry (US)
10. Virginia Wolfenden Kovacs (US)

1947
1. Margaret Osborne duPont (US)
2. Louise Brough (US)
3. Doris Hart (US)
4. Nancye Wynne Bolton (AUS)
5. Pat Canning Todd (US)
6. Sheila Piercey Summers (RSA)
7. Jean Bostock (ENG)
8. Barbara Krase (US)
9. Betty Hilton (ENG)
10. Magda Rurac (ROM)

1948
1. Margaret Osborne duPont (US)
2. Louise Brough (US)
3. Doris Hart (US)
4. Nancye Wynne Bolton (AUS)
5. Pat Canning Todd (US)
6. Jean Bostock (ENG)
7. Sheila Piercey Summers (RSA)
8. Shirley Fry (US)
9. Magda Rurac (ROM)
10. Nelly Adamson Landry (FRA)

1949
1. Margaret Osborne duPont (US)
2. Louise Brough (US)
3. Doris Hart (US)
4. Nancye Wynne Bolton (AUS)
5. Pat Canning Todd (US)
6. Betty Hilton (ENG)
7. Sheila Piercey Summers (RSA)
8. Annelies Ullstein Bossi (ITA)
9. Joan Curry (ENG)
10. Jean Walker-Smith (ENG)

1950
1. Margaret Osborne duPont (US)
2. Louise Brough (US)
3. Doris Hart (US)
4. Pat Canning Todd (US)
5. Barbara Scofield (US)
6. Nancy Chaffee (US)
7. Beverly Baker (US)
8. Shirley Fry (US)
9. Annelies Ullstein Bossi (ITA)
10. Maria Weiss (ARG)

1951
1. Doris Hart (US)
2. Maureen Connolly (US)
3. Shirley Fry (US)
4. Nancy Chaffee Kiner (US)
5. Jean Walker-Smith (ENG)
6. Jean Quertier (ENG)
7. Louise Brough (US)
8. Beverly Baker Fleitz (US)
9. Pat Canning Todd (US)
10. Kay Tuckey Maule (ENG)

1952
1. Maureen Connolly (US)
2. Doris Hart (US)
3. Louise Brough (US)
4. Shirley Fry (US)
5. Pat Canning Todd (US)
6. Nancy Chaffee Kiner (US)
7. Thelma Coyne Long (AUS)
8. Jean Walker-Smith (ENG)
9. Jean Quertier-Rinkel (ENG)
10. Dorothy Head Knode (US)

1953
1. Maureen Connolly (US)
2. Doris Hart (US)
3. Louise Brough (US)
4. Shirley Fry (US)
5. Margaret Osborne duPont (US)
6. Dorothy Head Knode (US)
7. Suzi Kormoczi (HUN)
8. Angela Mortimer (ENG)
9. Helen Fletcher (ENG)
10. Jean Quertier-Rinkel (ENG)

1954
1. Maureen Connolly (US)
2. Doris Hart (US)
3. Beverly Baker Fleitz (US)
4. Louise Brough (US)
5. Margaret Osborne duPont (US)
6. Shirley Fry (US)
7. Betty Rosenquest Pratt (US)
8. Helen Fletcher (ENG)
9. Angela Mortimer (ENG)
10.* Ginette Bucaille (FRA)
   * Thelma Coyne Long (AUS)

1955
1. Louise Brough (US)
2. Doris Hart (US)
3. Beverly Baker Fleitz (US)
4. Angela Mortimer (ENG)
5. Dorothy Head Knode (US)
6. Barbara Breit (US)
7. Darlene Hard (US)
8. Beryl Penrose (AUS)
9. Pat Ward (ENG)
10.* Suzi Kormoczi (HUN)
   * Shirley Fry (US)

1956
1. Shirley Fry (US)
2. Althea Gibson (US)
3. Louise Brough (US)
4. Angela Mortimer (ENG)
5. Suzi Kormoczi (HUN)
6. Angela Buxton (ENG)
7. Shirley Bloomer (ENG)
8. Pat Ward (ENG)
9. Betty Rosenquest Pratt (JAM)
10.*Darlene Hard (US)
   *Margaret Osborne duPont (US)

1957
1. Althea Gibson (US)
2. Darlene Hard (US)
3. Shirley Bloomer (ENG)
4. Louise Brough (US)
5. Dorothy Head Knode (US)
6. Vera Puzejova (TCH)
7. Ann Haydon (ENG)
8. Yola Ramirez (MEX)
9. Christine Truman (ENG)
10. Margaret Osborne duPont (US)

1958
1. Althea Gibson (US)
2. Suzi Kormoczi (HUN)
3. Beverly Baker Fleitz (US)
4. Darlene Hard (US)
5. Shirley Bloomer (ENG)
6. Christine Truman (ENG)
7. Angela Mortimer (ENG)
8. Ann Haydon (ENG)
9. Maria Bueno (BRA)
10. Dorothy Head Knode (US)

1959
1. Maria Bueno (BRA)
2. Christine Truman (ENG)
3. Darlene Hard (US)
4. Beverly Baker Fleitz (US)
5. Sandra Reynolds (RSA)
6. Angela Mortimer (ENG)
7. Ann Haydon (ENG)
8. Suzi Kormoczi (HUN)
9. Sally Moore (US)
10. Yola Ramirez (MEX)

1960
1. Maria Bueno (BRA)
2. Darlene Hard (US)
3. Sandra Reynolds (RSA)
4. Christine Truman (ENG)
5. Suzi Kormoczi (HUN)
6. Ann Haydon (ENG)
7. Angela Mortimer (ENG)
8. Jan Lehane (AUS)
9. Yola Ramirez (MEX)
10. Renee Schuurman (RSA)

1961
1. Angela Mortimer (ENG)
2. Darlene Hard (US)
3. Ann Haydon (ENG)
4. Margaret Smith (AUS)
5. Sandra Reynolds (RSA)
6. Yola Ramirez (MEX)
7. Christine Truman (ENG)
8. Suzi Kormoczi (HUN)
9. Renee Schuurman (RSA)
10. Karen Hantze (US)

1962
1. Margaret Smith (AUS)
2. Maria Bueno (BRA)
3. Darlene Hard (US)
4. Karen Hantze Susman (US)
5. Vera Puzejova Sukova (TCH)
6. Sandra Reynolds Price (RSA)
7. Lesley Turner (AUS)
8. Ann Haydon (ENG)
9. Renee Schuurman (RSA)
10. Angela Mortimer (ENG)

1963
1. Margaret Smith (AUS)
2. Lesley Turner (AUS)
3. Maria Bueno (BRA)
4. Billie Jean Moffitt (US)
5. Ann Haydon Jones (ENG)
6. Darlene Hard (US)
7. Jan Lehane (AUS)
8. Renee Schuurman (RSA)
9. Nancy Richey (US)
10. Vera Puzejova Sukova (TCH)

1964
1. Margaret Smith (AUS)
2. Maria Bueno (BRA)
3. Lesley Turner (AUS)
4. Carole Caldwell Graebner (US)
5. Helga Schultze (GER)
6. Nancy Richey (US)
7. Billie Jean Moffitt (US)
8. Karen Hantze Susman (US)
9. Robyn Ebbern (AUS)
10. Jan Lehane (AUS)

1965
1. Margaret Smith (AUS)
2. Maria Bueno (BRA)
3. Lesley Turner (AUS)
4. Billie Jean King (US)
5. Ann Haydon Jones (ENG)
6. Annette Van Zyl (RSA)
7. Christine Truman (ENG)
8. Nancy Richey (US)
9. Carole Caldwell Graebner (US)
10. Françoise Durr (FRA)

1966
1. Billie Jean King (US)
2. Margaret Smith (AUS)
3. Maria Bueno (BRA)
4. Ann Haydon Jones (ENG)
5. Nancy Richey (US)
6. Annette Van Zyl (RSA)
7. Norma Baylon (ARG)
8. Françoise Durr (FRA)
9. Rosie Casals (US)
10. Kerry Melville (AUS)

1967
1. Billie Jean King (US)
2. Ann Haydon Jones (ENG)
3. Françoise Durr (FRA)
4. Nancy Richey (US)
5. Lesley Turner (AUS)
6. Rosie Casals (US)
7. Maria Bueno (BRA)
8. Virginia Wade (ENG)
9. Kerry Melville (AUS)
10. Judy Tegart (AUS)

1968
1. Billie Jean King (US)
2. Virginia Wade (ENG)
3. Nancy Richey (US)
4. Margaret Smith Court (AUS)
5. Maria Bueno (BRA)
6. Ann Haydon Jones (ENG)
7. Judy Tegart (AUS)
8. Lesley Turner Bowrey (AUS)
9. Annette Van Zyl duPlooy (RSA)
10. Rosie Casals (US)

1969
1. Margaret Smith Court (AUS)
2. Ann Haydon Jones (ENG)
3. Billie Jean King (US)
4. Nancy Richey (US)
5. Julie Heldman (US)
6. Rosie Casals (US)
7. Kerry Melville (AUS)
8. Mary Ann Eisel (US)
9. Virginia Wade (ENG)
10. Lesley Turner Bowrey (AUS)

1970
1. Margaret Smith Court (AUS)
2. Billie Jean King (US)
3. Rosie Casals (US)
4. Nancy Richey (US)
5. Virginia Wade (ENG)
6. Helga Niessen Masthoff (GER)
7. Ann Haydon Jones (ENG)
8. Kerry Melville (AUS)
9. Karen Krantzcke (AUS)
10. Françoise Durr (FRA)

1971
1. Billie Jean King (US)
2. Evonne Goolagong (AUS)
3. Margaret Smith Court (AUS)
4. Rosie Casals (US)
5. Kerry Melville (AUS)
6. Françoise Durr (FRA)
7. Virginia Wade (ENG)
8. Helga Niessen Masthoff (GER)
9. Judy Tegart (AUS)
10. Chris Evert (US)

1972
1. Billie Jean King (US)
2. Margaret Smith Court (AUS)
3. Nancy Richey Gunter (US)
4. Chris Evert (US)
5. Virginia Wade (ENG)
6. Evonne Goolagong (AUS)
7. Rosie Casals (US)
8. Kerry Melville (AUS)
9. Françoise Durr (FRA)
10. Olga Morozova (US)S.R.

1973 *(Compter rankings begin)*
1. Margaret Smith Court (AUS)
2. Billie Jean King (US)
3. E. Goolagong Cawley (AUS)
4. Chris Evert (US)
5. Rosie Casals (US)
6. Virginia Wade (GBR)
7. Kerry Melville (AUS)
8. Nancy Richey Gunter (US)
9. Julie Heldman (US)
10. Helga Niessen Masthoff (GER)

1974
1. Billie Jean King (US)
2. E. Goolagong Cawley (AUS)
3. Chris Evert (US)
4. Virginia Wade (GBR)
5. Julie Heldman (US)
6. Rosie Casals (US)
7. Kerry Melville (AUS)
8. Olga Morozova (RUS)
9. Lesley Hunt (AUS)
10. Françoise Durr (FRA)

1975
1. Chris Evert (US)
2. Billie Jean King (US)
3. E. Goolagong Cawley (AUS)
4. Martina Navratilova (TCH)
5. Virgina Wade (GBR)
6. Margaret Smith Court (AUS)
7. Olga Morozova (RUS)
8. Nancy Richey Gunter (US)
9. Françoise Durr (FRA)
10. Rosie Casals (US)

1976
1. Chris Evert (US)
2. E. Goolagong Cawley (AUS)
3. Virginia Wade (GBR)
4. Martina Navratilova (TCH)
5. Sue Barker (GBR)
6. Betty Stove (NED)
7. Dianne Fromholtz (AUS)
8. Mima Jausovec (YUG)
9. Rosie Casals (US)
10. Françoise Durr (FRA)

1977
1. Chris Evert (US)
2. Billie Jean King (US)
3. Martina Navratilova (TCH)
4. Virginia Wade (GBR)
5. Sue Barker (GBR)
6. Rosie Casals (US)
7. Betty Stove (NED)
8. Dianne Fromholtz (AUS)
9. Wendy Turnbull (AUS)
10. Kerry Melville Reid (AUS)

1978
1. Martina Navratilova (TCH)
2. Chris Evert (US)
3. E. Goolagong Cawley (AUS)
4. Virgina Wade (GBR)
5. Billie Jean King (US)
6. Tracy Austin (US)
7. Wendy Turnbull (AUS)
8. Kerry Melville Reid (AUS)
9. Betty Stove (NED)
10. Dianne Fromholtz (AUS)

1979
1. Martina Navratilova (TCH)
2. Chris Evert Lloyd (US)
3. Tracy Austin (US)
4. E. Goolagong Cawley (AUS)
5. Billie Jean King (US)
6. Dianne Fromholtz (AUS)
7. Wendy Turnbull (AUS)
8. Virginia Wade (GBR)
9. Kerry Melville Reid (AUS)
10. Sue Barker (GBR)

1980
1. Chris Evert Lloyd (US)
2. Tracy Austin (US)
3. Martina Navratilova (TCH)
4. Hana Mandlikova (TCH)
5. E. Goolagong Cawley (AUS)
6. Billie Jean King (US)
7. Andrea Jaeger (US)
8. Wendy Turnbull (AUS)
9. Pam Shriver (US)
10. Greer Stevens (RSA)

1981
1. Chris Evert Lloyd (US)
2. Tracy Austin (US)
3. Martina Navratilova (US)
4. Andrea Jaeger (US)
5. Hana Mandlikova (TCH)
6. Sylvia Hanika (GER)
7. Pam Shriver (US)
8. Wendy Turnbull (AUS)
9. Bettina Bunge (HUN)
10. Barbara Potter (US)

1982
1. Martina Navratilova (US)
2. Chris Evert Lloyd (US)
3. Andrea Jaeger (US)
4. Tracy Austin (US)
5. Wendy Turnbull (AUS)
6. Pam Shriver (US)
7. Hana Mandlikova (TCH)
8. Barbara Potter (US)
9. Bettina Bunge (HUN)
10. Sylvia Hanika (GER)

1983
1. Martina Navratilova (US)
2. Chris Evert Lloyd (US)
3. Andrea Jaeger (US)
4. Pam Shriver (US)
5. Sylvia Hanika (GER)
6. Jo Durie (GBR)
7. Bettina Bunge (HUN)
8. Wendy Turnbull (AUS)
9. Tracy Austin (US)
10. Zina Garrison (US)

1984
1. Martina Navratilova (US)
2. Chris Evert Lloyd (US)
3. Hana Mandlikova (TCH)
4. Pam Shriver (US)
5. Wendy Turnbull (AUS)
6. Manuela Maleeva (BUL)
7. Helena Sukova (TCH)
8. Claudia Kohde-Kilsch (GER)
9. Zina Garrison (US)
10. Kathy Jordan (US)

1985
1. Martina Navratilova (US)
2. Chris Evert Lloyd (US)
3. Hana Mandlikova (TCH)
4. Pam Shriver (US)
5. Claudia Kohde-Kilsch (GER)
6. Steffi Graf (GER)
7. Manuela Maleeva (BUL)
8. Zina Garrison (US)
9. Helena Sukova (TCH)
10. Bonnie Gadusek (US)

1986
1. Martina Navratilova (US)
2. Chris Evert Lloyd (US)
3. Steffi Graf (GER)
4. Hana Mandlikova (TCH)
5. Helena Sukova (TCH)
6. Pam Shriver (US)
7. Claudia Kohde-Kilsch (GER)
8. Manuela Maleeva (BUL)
9. Kathy Rinaldi (US)
10. Gabriela Sabatini (ARG)

1987
1. Steffi Graf (GER)
2. Martina Navratilova (US)
3. Chris Evert (US)
4. Pam Shriver (US)
5. Hana Mandlikova (TCH)
6. Gabriela Sabatini (ARG)
7. Helena Sukova (TCH)
8. Manuela Maleeva (BUL)
9. Zina Garrison (US)
10. Claudia Kohde-Kilsch (GER)

1988
1. Steffi Graf (GER)
2. Martina Navratilova (US)
3. Chris Evert (US)
4. Gabriela Sabatini (ARG)
5. Pam Shriver (US)
6. M. Maleeva Fragniere (BUL)
7. Natalia Zvereva (RUS)
8. Helena Sukova (TCH)
9. Zina Garrison (US)
10. Barbara Potter (US)

1989
1. Steffi Graf (GER)
2. Martina Navratilova (US)
3. Gabriela Sabatini (ARG)
4. Zina Garrison (US)
5. Arantxa Sanchez (ESP)
6. Monica Seles (YUG)
7. Conchita Martinez (ESP)
8. Helena Sukova (TCH)
9. M. Maleeva Fragniere (BUL)
10. Chris Evert

1990
1. Steffi Graf (GER)
2. Monica Seles (YUG)
3. Martina Navratilova (US)
4. Mary Joe Fernandez (US)
5. Gabriela Sabatini (ARG)
6. Katerina Maleeva
7. Aranxta Sanchez Vicario (ESP)
8. Jennifer Capriati (US)
9. M. Maleeva Fragniere (SUI)
10. Zina Garrison (US)

1991
1. Monica Seles (YUG)
2. Steffi Graf (GER)
3. Gabriela Sabatini (ARG)
4. Martina Navratilova (US)
5. Aranxta Sanchez Vicario (ESP)
6. Jennifer Capriati (US)
7. Jana Novotna (TCH)
8. Mary Joe Fernandez (US)
9. Conchita Martinez (ESP)
10. M. Maleeva Fragniere (SUI)

1992
1. Monica Seles (YUG)
2. Steffi Graf (GER)
3. Gabriela Sabatini (ARG)
4. Arantxa Sanchez Vicario (ESP)
5. Martina Navratilova (US)
6. Mary Joe Fernandez (US)
7. Jennifer Capriati (US)
8. Conchita Martinez (ESP)
9. M. Maleeva Fragniere (SUI)
10. Jana Novotna (TCH)

1993
1. Steffi Graf (GER)
2. Arantxa Sanchez Vicario (ESP)
3. Martina Navratilova (US)
4. Conchita Martinez (ESP)
5. Gabriela Sabatini (ARG)
6. Jana Novotna (TCH)
7. Mary Joe Fernandez (US)
8. Monica Seles (YUG)
9. Jennifer Capriati (US)
10. Anke Huber (GER)

1994
1. Steffi Graf (GER)
2. Arantxa Sanchez Vicario (ESP)
3. Conchita Martinez (ESP)
4. Jana Novotna (TCH)
5. Mary Pierce (FRA)
6. Lindsay Davenport (US)
7. Gabriela Sabatini (ARG)
8. Martina Navratilova (US)
9. Kimiko Date (JPN)
10. Natalia Zvereva (RUS)

1995
1. * Steffi Graf (GER)
   * Monica Seles (US)
2. Conchita Martinez (ESP)
3. Arantxa Sanchez Vicario (ESP)
4. Kimiko Date (JPN)
5. Mary Pierce (FRA)
6. Magdalena Maleeva (BUL)
7. Gabriela Sabatini (ARG)
8. Mary Joe Fernandez (US)
9. Iva Majoli (CRO)
10. Anke Huber (GER)

1996
1. Steffi Graf (GER)
2. *Monica Seles (US)
   *Arantxa Sanchez Vicario (ESP)
3. Jana Novotna (TCH)
4. Martina Hingis (SUI)
5. Conchita Martinez (ESP)
6. Anke Huber (GER)
7. Iva Majoli (CRO)
8. Kimiko Date (JPN)
9. Lindsay Davenport (US)
10. Barbara Paulus (AUT)

1997
1. Martina Hingis (SUI)
2. Jana Novotna (TCH)
3. Lindsay Davenport (US)
4. Amanda Coetzer (RSA)
5. Monica Seles (US)
6. Iva Majoli (CRO)
7. Mary Pierce (FRA)
8. Irina Spirlea (ROM)
9. Arantxa Sanchez Vicario (ESP)
10. Mary Joe Fernandez (US)

1998
1. Lindsay Davenport (US)
2. Martina Hingis (SUI)
3. Jana Novotna (TCH)
4. Arantxa Sanchez Vicario (ESP)
5. Venus Williams (US)
6. Monica Seles (US)
7. Mary Pierce (FRA)
8. Conchita Martinez (ESP)
9. Steffi Graf (GER)
10. Nathalie Tauziat (FRA)

1999
1. Martina Hingis (SUI)
2. Lindsay Davenport (US)
3. Venus Williams (US)
4. Serena Williams (US)
5. Mary Pierce (FRA)
6. Monica Seles (US)
7. Nathalie Tauziat (FRA)
8. Barbara Schett (AUT)
9. Julie Halard-Decugis (FRA)
10. Amelie Mauresmo (FRA)

2000
1. Martina Hingis (SUI)
2. Lindsay Davenport (US)
3. Venus Williams (US)
4. Monica Seles (US)
5. Conchita Martinez (ESP)
6. Serena Williams (US)
7. Mary Pierce (FRA)
8. Anna Kournikova (RUS)
9. Arantxa Sanchez Vicario (ESP)
10. Nathalie Tauziat (FRA)

2001
1. Lindsay Davenport (US)
2. Jennifer Capriati (US)
3. Venus Williams (US)
4. Martina Hingis (SUI)
5. Kim Clijsters (BEL)
6. Serena Williams (US)
7. Justine Henin (BEL)
8. Jelena Dokic (YUG)
9. Amelie Mauresmo (FRA)
10. Monica Seles (US)

2002
1. Serena Williams (US)
2. Venus Williams (US)
3. Jennifer Capriati (US)
4. Kim Clijsters (BEL)
5. Justine Henin (BEL)
6. Amelie Mauresmo (FRA)
7. Monica Seles (US)
8. Daniela Hantuchova (SVK)
9. Jelena Dokic (YUG)
10. Martina Hingis (SUI)

MEN'S DOUBLES

1990
1. Pieter Aldrich & Danie Visser
2. Scott Davis & David Pate
3. Rick Leach & Jim Pugh
4. Grant Connell & Glenn Michibata
5. Guy Forget & Jakob Hlasek
6. Sergio Casal & Emilio Sanchez
7. Neil Broad & Gary Muller
8. Darren Cahill & Mark Kratzmann
9. Jorge Lozano & Todd Witsken
10. Udo Riglewski & Michael Stich

1991
1. John Fitzgerald & Anders Jarryd
2. Ken Flach & Robert Seguso
3. Scott Davis & David Pate
4. Grant Connell & Glenn Michibata
5. Todd Woodbridge & Mark Woodforde
6. Patrick Galbraith & Todd Witsken
7. Luke Jensen & Laurie Warder
8. Tom Nijssen & Cyril Suk
9. Udo Riglewski & Michael Stich
10. Sergio Casal & Emilio Sanchez

1992
1. Todd Woodbridge & Mark Woodforde
2. Jim Grabb & Richey Reneberg
3. Kelly Jones & Rick Leach
4. John Fitzgerald & Anders Jarryd
5. Tom Nijssen & Cyril Suk
6. Sergio Casal & Emilio Sanchez
7. Mark Kratzmann & Wally Masur
8. Steve DeVries & David Macpherson
9. Grant Connell & Glenn Michibata
10. Jakob Hlasek & Marc Rosset

1993
1. Grant Connell & Patrick Galbraith
2. Jacco Eltingh & Paul Haarhuis
3. Todd Woodbridge & Mark Woodforde
4. David Adams & Andrei Olhovskiy
5. Luke Jensen & Murphy Jensen
6. Sergio Casal & Emilio Sanchez
7. Tom Nijssen & Cyril Suk
8. Mark Kratzmann & Wally Masur
9. Ken Flach & Rick Leach
10. Shelby Cannon & Scott Melville

1994
1. Jacco Eltingh & Paul Haarhuis
2. Todd Woodbridge & Mark Woodforde
3. Byron Black & Jonathan Stark
4. Grant Connell & Patrick Galbraith
5. Jan Apell & Jonas Bjorkman
6. David Adams & Andrei Olhovskiy
7. Tom Nijssen & Cyril Suk
8. Sergio Casal & Emilio Sanchez
9. Pat McEnroe & Jared Palmer
10. Henrik Holm & Anders Jarryd

1995
1. Todd Woodbridge & Mark Woodforde
2. Jacco Eltingh & Paul Haarhuis
3. Grant Connell & Patrick Galbraith
4. Cyril Suk & Daniel Nestor
5. Mark Knowles & Daniel Nestor
6. Rick Leach & Scott Melville
7. Tommy Ho & Brett Steven
8. Luis Lobo & Javier Sanchez
9. Jared Palmer & Richey Reneberg
10. Sergio Casal & Emilio Sanchez

1996
1. Todd Woodbridge & Mark Woodforde
2. Byron Black & Grant Connell
3. Mark Knowles & Daniel Nestor
4. Sebastien Lareau & Alex O'Brien
5. Guy Forget & Jakob Hlasek
6. Jacco Eltingh & Paul Haarhuis
7. Yevgeny Kafelnikov & Daniel Vacek
8. Jonas Bjorkman & Nicklas Kulti
9. Libor Pimek & Byron Talbot
10. Ellis Ferreira & Jan Siemerink

1997
1. Todd Woodbridge & Mark Woodforde
2. Jacco Eltingh & Paul Haarhuis
3. Rick Leach & Jonathan Stark
4. Yevgeny Kafelnikov & Daniel Vacek
5. Mahesh Bhupathi & Leander Paes
6. Ellis Ferreira & Patrick Galbraith
7. Sebastien Lareau & Alex O'Brien
8. Mark Knowles & Daniel Nestor
9. Jonas Bjorkman & Nicklas Kulti
10. Luis Lobo & Javier Sanchez

1998
1. Jacco Eltingh & Paul Haarhuis
2. Mahesh Bhupathi & Leander Paes
3. Todd Woodbridge & Mark Woodforde
4. Mark Knowles & Daniel Nestor
5. Ellis Ferreira & Rick Leach
6. Olivier Delaitre & Fabrice Santoro
7. * Sandon Stolle & Cyril Suk
   * Sebastien Lareau & Alex O'Brien
8. Donald Johnson & Montana F
9. Jonas Bjorkman & Patrick Rafter
10. Yevgeny Kafelnikov & Daniel Vacek

1999
1. Mahesh Bhupathi & Leander Paes
2. Sebastien Lareau & Alex O'Brien
3. Todd Woodbridge & Mark Woodforde
4. Ellis Ferreira & Rick Leach
5. Wayne Black & Sandon Stolle
6. David Adams & John-Laffnie de Jager
7. Jonas Bjorkman & Patrick Rafter
8. Paul Haarhuis & Jared Palmer
9. Piet Norval & Kevin Ullyett
10. Jiri Novak & David Rikl

2000
1. Todd Woodbridge & Mark Woodforde
2. Ellis Ferreira & Rick Leach
3. Paul Haarhuis & Sandon Stolle
4. Alex O'Brien & Jared Palmer
5. Jiri Novak & David Rikl
6. Wayne Ferreira & Yevgeny Kafelnikov
7. Donald Johnson & Piet Norval
8. David Adams & John-Laffnie de Jager
9. Joshua Eagle & Andrew Florent
10. Nicklas Kulti & Mikael Tillstrom

2001
1. Bjorkman Jonas & Todd Woodbridge
2. Donald Johnson & Jared Palmer
3. Jiri Novak & David Rikl
4. Mahesh Bhupathi & Leander Paes
5. Wayne Black & Kevin Ullyett
6. Peter Pala & Pavel Vizner
7. Bob Bryan & Mike Bryan
8. Mark Knowles & Brian MacPhie
9. Michael Hill & Jeff Tarango
10. * Joshua Eagle & Andrew Florent
    * Ellis Ferreira & Rick Leach

2002
1. Mark Knowles & Daniel Nestor
2. Jonas Bjorkman & Todd Woodbridge
3. Bob Bryan & Mike Bryan
4. Donald Johnson & Jared Palmer
5. Mahesh Bhupathi & Max Mirnyi
6. Wayne Black & Kevin Ullyett
7. Martin Damm & Cyril Suk
8. Joshua Eagle & Sandon Stolle
9. Paul Haarhuis & Yevgeny Kafelnikov
10. Jiri Novak & Radek Stepanek

Appendix C

ATP and Other Men's Pro Tours

Stan Smith, 1973 Victory over Arthur Ashe in the third WCT final.

Men's professional tournament tennis—with the exception of the four major championships—has been conducted under the jurisdiction of the ATP since 1990. In 2002, the ATP conducted 66 tournaments in 31 countries for total prize money of $61 million.

There are two primary levels of tournaments: The International Series, to which a majority of the tournaments belong, and an elite nine tournaments called the Tennis Masters Series, events that offer larger purses and attract the bigger names. They are spread across the world in this order: Indian Wells, Calif., Key Biscayne, Fla., Monte Carlo, Rome, Hamburg, Montreal/Toronto, Cincinnati, Madrid and Paris (Indoor). Although the top players are expected to participate in the nine Tennis Masters Series tournaments, as well as the four majors (Australian, French, Wimbledon and U.S.), it is a demand never fully met.

Throughout each year, players accumulate points based on their results in the Tennis Masters Series,

International Series events and the major championships. The top eight players qualify for the lucrative, year-end Tennis Masters Cup. The Tennis Masters Cup was created in 1999 when the ATP and ITF agreed to merge their season-ending championships, the ATP World Championship and the ITF's Grand Slam Cup. Prior to that, the year-end finale was called the Masters Championship, launched in 1971 in Tokyo.

The Association of Tennis Professionals (ATP), an organization of male touring pros, was founded in 1972 as a union, but has metamorphosed into a management company with some player input. It has been influential in governing tournament conditions, conduct, prize-money and structure. It operated under the umbrella of the Grand Prix, the worldwide organizer of men's pro tournament tennis, until it broke away in 1989 and took over control of the men's game by launching the ATP Tour. In 2001, for marketing reasons, 'Tour' was dropped from the name.

Leading Money Winners

1968

Rod Laver	$70,359
Tony Roche	63,504
Ken Rosewall	61,307
John Newcombe	57,011
Pancho Gonzalez	38,987
Cliff Drysdale	37,880
Andres Gimeno	36,542
Roy Emerson	35,188
Dennis Ralston	34,626
Fred Stolle	34,335

1969

Rod Laver	$124,000
Tony Roche	75,045
Tom Okker	65,451
Roy Emerson	62,629
John Newcombe	52,610
Ken Rosewall	46,796
Pancho Gonzales	46,288
Marty Riessen	43,441
Fred Stolle	43,160
Arthur Ashe	42,030

1970

Rod Laver	$201,453
Arthur Ashe	141,018
Ken Rosewall	140,455
Cliff Richey	97,000
Roy Emerson	96,485
Stan Smith	95,251
John Newcombe	78,251
Pancho Gonzalez	77,365
Clark Graebner	68,000
Tony Roche	67,232

1971

Rod Laver	$292,717
Ken Rosewall	138,371
Tom Okker	120,465
Ilie Nastase	114,000
Arthur Ashe	104,642
Stan Smith	103,806
John Newcombe	101,514
Marty Riessen	81,310
Clark Graebner	75,400
Cliff Richey	75,000

1972

Ilie Nastase	$176,000
Stan Smith	142,300
Ken Rosewall	132,950
John Newcombe	120,600
Arthur Ashe	119,775
Rod Laver	100,200
Tom Okker	90,004
Jimmy Connors	90,000
Marty Riessen	74,436
Cliff Drysdale	68,433

1973

Ilie Nastase	$228,750
Stan Smith	204,225
Tom Okker	173,500
Jimmy Connors	156,400
John Newcombe	133,050
Arthur Ashe	127,850
Rod Laver	120,125
Ken Rosewall	110,950
Manuel Orantes	97,175
Brian Gottfried	87,850

1974

Jimmy Connors	$285,490
Guillermo Vilas	266,210
John Newcombe	258,230
Bjorn Borg	206,160
Ilie Nastase	172,805
Arthur Ashe	151,760
Stan Smith	138,500
Raul Ramirez	135,185
Rod Laver	117,450
Tom Okker	116,285

1975

Arthur Ashe	$326,750
Manuel Orantes	269,785
Guillermo Vilas	249,287
Bjorn Borg	221,088
Raul Ramirez	211,385
Ilie Nastase	180,536
Brian Gottfried	167,960
Jimmy Connors	163,135
Roscoe Tanner	150,459
John Alexander	138,050

1976

Raul Ramirez	$484,343
Jimmy Connors	315,081
Manuel Orantes	281,880
Guillermo Vilas	238,738
Arthur Ashe	236,933
Harold Solomon	236,690
Eddie Dibbs	233,428
Brian Gottfried	231,075
Wojtek Fibak	219,086
Roscoe Tanner	208,719

1977

Guillermo Vilas	$766,065
Brian Gottfried	458,791
Jimmy Connors	428,919
Bjorn Borg	337,020
Eddie Dibbs	283,555
Dick Stockton	277,626
Vitas Gerulaitis	260,883
Raul Ramirez	244,763
Wojtek Fibak	238,035
Bob Hewitt	219,163

1978

Eddie Dibbs	$575,273
Bjorn Borg	469,441
Raul Ramirez	463,868
John McEnroe	460,285
Jimmy Connors	392,153
Wojtek Fibak	384,665
Vitas Gerulaitis	380,444
Harold Solomon	353,234
Ilie Nastase	351,843
Brian Gottfried	349,771

1979

Bjorn Borg	$1,008,742
John McEnroe	1,001,745
Jimmy Connors	699,605
Vitas Gerulaitis	413,578
Guillermo Vilas	375,966
Peter Fleming	351,778
Roscoe Tanner	255,551
Eddie Dibbs	249,551
Harold Solomon	240,333
Wojtek Fibak	234,694

1980

John McEnroe	$972,369
Bjorn Borg	731,762
Ivan Lendl	583,406
Jimmy Connors	570,060
Gene Mayer	397,156
Guillermo Vilas	378,217
Wojtek Fibak	368,073
Vitas Gerulaitis	340,823
Brian Gottfried	296,800
Jose-Luis Clerc	280,697

1981

John McEnroe	$991,000
Ivan Lendl	846,037
Jimmy Connors	405,872
Guillermo Vilas	402,261
Jose-Luis Clerc	327,375
Vitas Gerulaitis	288,475
Heinz Gunthardt	278,642
Peter McNamara	273,066
Eliot Teltscher	267,630
Roscoe Tanner	245,380

1982

Ivan Lendl	$2,028,850
Jimmy Connors	1,173,850
Guillermo Vilas	932,150
John McEnroe	842,725
Jose-Luis Clerc	635,400
Tomas Smid	582,700
Wojtek Fibak	533,626
Vitas Gerulaitis	450,875
Johan Kriek	449,098
Steve Denton	401,079

1983

Ivan Lendl	$1,747,128
John McEnroe	1,206,844
Mats Wilander	1,119,650
Guillermo Vilas	677,035
Jimmy Connors	598,047
Tomas Smid	457,886
Yannick Noah	378,394
Jimmy Arias	340,033
Brian Teacher	332,948
Kevin Curren	306,852

1984

John McEnroe	$2,026,109
Ivan Lendl	1,060,196
Jimmy Connors	974,400
Mats Wilander	671,256
Tomas Smid	591,037
Andres Gomez	444,143
Jimmy Arias	364,176
Anders Jarryd	359,162
Joakim Nystrom	326,478
Henrik Sundstrom	320,412

1985

Ivan Lendl	$1,971,074
John McEnroe	1,455,611
Mats Wilander	1,081,697
Stefan Edberg	731,152
Boris Becker	625,757
Jimmy Connors	562,336
Anders Jarryd	534,822
Yannick Noah	406,881
Tomas Smid	404,460
Robert Seguso	394,908

1986

Ivan Lendl	$1,987,537
Boris Becker	1,434,324
Stefan Edberg	1,028,906
Joakim Nystrom	841,242
Mats Wilander	653,652
Andres Gomez	610,121
Yannick Noah	575,015
Guy Forget	504,820
Henri Leconte	449,422
Anders Jarryd	442,036

1987

Ivan Lendl	$2,003,656
Stefan Edberg	1,587,467
Miloslav Mecir	1,205,326
Mats Wilander	1,164,674
Pat Cash	565,934
Anders Jarryd	561,977
Boris Becker	558,979
Emilio Sanchez	538,158
Brad Gilbert	507,187
Tim Mayotte	458,821

1988

Mats Wilander	$1,726,731
Boris Becker	1,696,953
Stefan Edberg	1,402,802
Ivan Lendl	983,938
Andre Agassi	822,062
Jakob Hlasek	624,716
Emilio Sanchez	555,146
Henri Leconte	554,491
Kent Carlsson	546,539
Tim Mayotte	505,754

1989

Ivan Lendl	$2,344,367
Boris Becker	2,216,823
Stefan Edberg	1,661,491
John McEnroe	946,023
Brad Gilbert	900,848
Michael Chang	682,130
Aaron Krickstein	582,651
Alberto Mancini	510,430
Anders Jarryd	485,873
Andre Agassi	478,901

1990

Pete Sampras	$2,900,057
Stefan Edberg	2,095,901
Andre Agassi	1,741,382
Boris Becker	1,587,502
Brad Gilbert	1,555,733
Ivan Lendl	1,445,742
Goran Ivanisevic	1,020,945
Andres Gomez	972,613
Michael Chang	866,070
David Wheaton	791,240

1991

David Wheaton	$2,479,239
Stefan Edberg	2,363,575
Pete Sampras	1,908,413
Ivan Lendl	1,888,983
Jim Courier	1,848,171
Michael Stich	1,670,116
Michael Chang	1,461,730
Guy Forget	1,401,772
Boris Becker	1,228,708
Andre Agassi	982,611

1992

Michael Stich	$2,777,411
Stefan Edberg	2,441,804
Boris Becker	2,293,687
Jim Courier	2,253,385
Pete Sampras	1,995,087
Michael Chang	1,924,467
Goran Ivanisevic	1,858,241
Petr Korda	1,350,353
Andre Agassi	1,127,834
Richard Krajicek	1,063,241

1993

Pete Sampras	$4,579,325
Michael Stich	3,749,021
Jim Courier	3,584,321
Petr Korda	3,142,229
Stefan Edberg	2,740,759
Michael Chang	2,006,024
Sergi Bruguera	1,959,984
Boris Becker	1,865,839
Goran Ivanisevic	1,818,897
Andrei Medvedev	1,301,143

1994

Pete Sampras	$4,857,812
Sergi Bruguera	3,531,874
Stefan Edberg	2,589,161
Goran Ivanisevic	2,485,278
Andre Agassi	2,441,667
Boris Becker	2,279,756
Magnus Larsson	2,139,105
Michael Chang	2,039,495
Michael Stich	2,033,623
Jim Courier	1,921,584

1995

Pete Sampras	$5,415,066
Goran Ivanisevic	3,777,862
Boris Becker	3,712,358
Andre Agassi	2,975,738
Thomas Muster	2,887,979
Michael Chang	2,655,870
Sergi Bruguera	2,058,044
Yevgeny Kafelnikov	1,841,561
Todd Martin	1,455,558
Wayne Ferreira	1,276,216

1996

Boris Becker	$4,313,007
Pete Sampras	3,702,919
Yevgeny Kafelnikov	3,363,365
Goran Ivanisevic	3,007,985
Thomas Muster	2,875,496
Michael Chang	2,015,699
Richard Krajicek	1,861,761
Thomas Enqvist	1,668,547
Andre Agassi	1,629,928
Mark Woodforde	1,332,027

1997

Pete Sampras	$6,498,311
Yevgeny Kafelnikov	3,207,757
Patrick Rafter	2,923,519
Michael Chang	2,541,830
Thomas Muster	2,166,590
Jonas Bjorkman	1,950,375
Gustavo Kuerten	1,586,753
Petr Korda	1,515,483
Greg Rusedski	1,515,473
Goran Ivanisevic	1,458,257

1998

Pete Sampras	$3,931,497
Marcelo Rios	3,420,054
Patrick Rafter	2,867,017
Alex Corretja	2,702,569
Carlos Moya	2,572,553
Yevgeny Kafelnikov	2,543,077
Jonas Bjorkman	1,916,237
Greg Rusedski	1,860,437
Andre Agassi	1,836,233
Goran Ivanisevic	1,542,177

1999

Andre Agassi	$4,269,265
Pete Sampras	2,816,406
Yevgeny Kafelnikov	2,360,498
Greg Rusedski	2,122,535
Marcelo Rios	1,794,244
Gustavo Kuerten	1,762,269
Thomas Enqvist	1,729,056
Tim Henman	1,537,594
Tommy Haas	1,447,308
Richard Krajicek	1,348,977

2000

Gustavo Kuerten	$4,701,610
Yevgeny Kafelnikov	3,755,599
Marat Safin	3,524,959
Thomas Enqvist	2,381,060
Pete Sampras	2,254,598
Andre Agassi	1,884,443
Magnus Norman	1,846,269
Lleyton Hewitt	1,642,572
Alex Corretja	1,530,062
Wayne Ferreira	1,237,864

2001

Gustavo Kuerten	$4,091,004
Lleyton Hewitt	4,045,618
Yevgeny Kafelnikov	3,238,889
Andre Agassi	2,341,766
Marat Safin	2,207,702
Juan Ferrero Carlos	2,179,671
Sebastien Grosjean	1,918,584
Patrick Rafter	1,670,592
Tommy Haas	1,544,640
Goran Ivanisevic	1,245,040

2002

Lleyton Hewitt	4,619,386
Juan Carlos Ferrero	2,761,498
Andre Agassi	2,186,006
Roger Federer	1,995,027
Yevgeny Kafelnikov	1,778,810
Carlos Moya	1,772,314
Marat Safin	1,719,408
Jiri Novak	1,454,130
Albert Costa	1,434,439
Sebastien Grosjean	1,331,157

No. 1 Ranking

Since the computer rankings were adopted in 1973, 20 different players have held the top spot, as follows:

*(includes week of December 30, 2002)

WEEKS NO. 1

Pete Sampras (USA)	286
Ivan Lendl (CZE)	270
Jimmy Connors (USA)	268
John McEnroe (USA)	170
Bjorn Borg(SWE)	109
Andre Agassi (USA)	87
Stefan Edberg (SWE)	72
Lleyton Hewitt (AUS)	59
Jim Courier (USA)	58
Gustavo Kuerten (BRA)	43
Ilie Nastase (ROM)	40
Mats Wilander (SWE)	20
Boris Becker (GER)	12
Marat Safin (RUS)	9
John Newcombe (AUS)	8
Yevgeny Kafelnikov (RUS)	6
Thomas Muster (AUT)	6
Marcelo Rios (CHI)	6
Carlos Moya (ESP)	2
Patrick Rafter (AUS)	1

No. 1 History

Since Ilie Nastase first reached No. 1 on the ATP Rankings on August 23, 1973, there have been 79 changes at the top.
*(includes week of December 30, 2002)

PLAYER	WEEKS	DATE
Ilie Nastase (1)	40	Aug. 23, 1973
John Newcombe (2)	8	June 3, 1974
Jimmy Connors (3)	160	July 29, 1974
Bjorn Borg (4)	1	Aug. 23, 1977
Connors	84	Aug. 30, 1977
Borg	6	Apr. 9, 1979
Connors	7	May 21, 1979
Borg	34	July 9, 1979
John McEnroe (5)	3	Mar. 3, 1980
Borg	20	Mar. 24, 1980
McEnroe	1	Aug. 11, 1980
Borg	46	Aug. 18, 1980
McEnroe	2	July 6, 1981
Borg	2	July 20, 1981
McEnroe	58	Aug. 3, 1981
Connors	7	Sept. 13, 1982
McEnroe	1	Nov. 1, 1982
Connors	1	Nov. 8, 1982
McEnroe	11	Nov. 15, 1982
Connors	1	Jan. 31, 1983
McEnroe	1	Feb. 7, 1983
Connors	2	Feb. 14, 1983
Ivan Lendl (6)	11	Feb. 28, 1983
Connors	3	May 16, 1983
McEnroe	1	June 6, 1983
Connors	3	June 13, 1983
McEnroe	17	July 4, 1983
Lendl	6	Oct. 31, 1983
McEnroe	4	Dec. 12, 1983
Lendl	9	Jan. 9, 1984
McEnroe	13	Mar. 12, 1984
Lendl	1	June 11, 1984
McEnroe	3	June 18, 1984
Lendl	5	July 9, 1984
McEnroe	53	Aug. 13, 1984
Lendl	1	Aug. 19, 1985
McEnroe	2	Aug. 26, 1985
Lendl	157	Sept. 9, 1985
Mats Wilander (7)	20	Sept. 12, 1988
Lendl	80	Jan. 30, 1989
Stefan Edberg (8)	24	Aug. 13, 1990
Boris Becker (9)	3	Jan. 28, 1991
Edberg	20	Feb. 18, 1991
Becker	9	July 8, 1991
Edberg	22	Sept. 9, 1991
Jim Courier (10)	6	Feb. 10, 1992
Edberg	3	Mar. 23, 1992
Courier	22	Apr. 13, 1992
Edberg	3	Sept. 14, 1992
Courier	27	Oct. 5, 1992
Pete Sampras (11)	19	Apr. 12, 1993
Courier	3	Aug. 23, 1993
Sampras	82	Sept. 13, 1993
Andre Agassi (12)	30	Apr. 10, 1995
Sampras	12	Nov. 6, 1995
Agassi	2	Jan. 29, 1996
Thomas Muster (13)	1	Feb. 12, 1996
Sampras	3	Feb. 19, 1996
Muster	5	Mar. 11, 1996
Sampras	102	Apr. 15, 1996
Marcelo Rios (14)	4	Mar. 30, 1998
Sampras	15	Apr. 27, 1998
Rios	2	Aug. 10, 1998
Sampras	20	Aug. 24, 1998
Carlos Moya (15)	2	Mar. 15, 1999
Sampras	5	Mar. 29, 1999
Yevgeny Kafelnikov (16)	6	May 3, 1999
Sampras	3	June 14, 1999
Agassi	3	July 5, 1999
Patrick Rafter (17)	1	July 26, 1999
Sampras	6	Aug. 2, 1999
Agassi	52	Sept. 13, 1999
Sampras	10	Sept. 11, 2000
Marat Safin (18)	2	Nov. 20, 2000
Gustavo Kuerten (19)	8	Dec. 4, 2000
Safin	4	Jan. 29, 2001
Kuerten	5	Feb. 26, 2001
Safin	3	Apr. 2, 2001
Kuerten	30	Apr. 22, 2001
Lleyton Hewitt (20)	59	Nov. 19, 2001

ATP Annual Awards

Top Player

2002	Lleyton Hewitt
2001	Lleyton Hewitt
2000	Gustavo Kuerten
1999	Andre Agassi
1998	Pete Sampras
1997	Pete Sampras
1996	Pete Sampras
1995	Pete Sampras
1994	Pete Sampras
1993	Pete Sampras
1992	Jim Courier
1991	Stefan Edberg
1990	Stefan Edberg
1989	Boris Becker
1988	Mats Wilander
1987	Ivan Lendl
1986	Ivan Lendl
1985	Ivan Lendl
1984	John McEnroe
1983	John McEnroe
1982	Jimmy Connors
1981	John McEnroe
1980	Bjorn Borg
1979	Bjorn Borg
1978	Bjorn Borg
1977	Bjorn Borg
1976	Bjorn Borg
1975	Arthur Ashe

Top Doubles Team

2002	Mark Knowles and Daniel Nestor
2001	Jonas Bjorkman and Todd Woodbridge
2000	Todd Woodbridge and Mark Woodforde
1999	Mahesh Bhupathi and Leander Paes
1998	Jacco Eltingh and Paul Haarhuis
1997	Todd Woodbridge and Mark Woodforde
1996	Todd Woodbridge and Mark Woodforde
1995	Todd Woodbridge and Mark Woodforde
1994	Jacco Eltingh and Paul Haarhuis
1993	Grant Connell and Patrick Galbraith
1992	Todd Woodbridge and Mark Woodforde
1991	John Fitzgerald and Anders Jarryd
1990	Pieter Aldrich and Danie Visser
1989	Rich Leach and Jim Pugh
1988	Rich Leach and Jim Pugh
1987	Stefan Edberg and Anders Jarryd
1986	Hans Gildemeister and Andres Gomez
1985	Ken Flach and Robert Seguso
1984	Peter Fleming and John McEnroe
1983	Peter Fleming and John McEnroe
1982	Sherwood Stewart and Ferdi Taygan
1981	Peter Fleming and John McEnroe
1980	Bob Lutz and Stan Smith
1979	Peter Fleming and John McEnroe
1978	Bob Hewitt and Frew McMillan
1977	Bob Hewitt and Frew McMillan
1976	Brian Gottfried and Raul Ramirez
1975	Brian Gottfried and Raul Ramirez

Most Improved Player

2002	Paradorn Srichaphan
2001	Goran Ivanisevic
2000	Marat Safin
1999	Nicolas Lapentti
1998	Andre Agassi
1997	Patrick Rafter
1996	Tim Henman
1995	Thomas Enqvist
1994	Yevengy Kafelnikov
1993	Todd Martin
1992	Henrik Holm
1991	Jim Courier
1990	Peter Sampras
1989	Michael Chang
1988	Andre Agassi
1987	Peter Lundgren
1986	Mikael Pernfors
1985	Boris Becker
1984	not given
1983	Jimmy Arias
1982	Peter McNamara
1981	Ivan Lendl
1980	not given
1979	Victor Pecci
1978	John McEnroe
1977	Brian Gottfried
1976	Wojtek Fibak
1975	Vitas Gerulatis
1974	Guillermo Vilas
1973	Vijay Amritraj

Newcomer

2002	Paul-Henri Mathieu
2001	Andy Roddick
2000	Oliver Rochus
1999	Juan Carlos Ferrero
1998	Marat Safin
1997	Julian Alonso
1996	Dominik Hrbaty
1995	Mark Philippoussis
1994	Albert Costa
1993	Patrick Rafter
1992	Andrei Medvedev
1991	Byron Black
1990	Fabrice Santoro
1989	Sergi Bruguera
1988	Michael Chang
1987	Richey Reneberg
1986	Ulf Stenlund
1985	Jaime Yzaga
1984	Bob Green
1983	Scott Davis
1982	Chip Hooper
1981	Tim Mayotte
1980	Mel Purcell
1979	Vince Van Patten
1978	John McEnroe
1977	Tim Gullikson
1976	Wojtek Fibak
1975	Vitas Gerulatis

Stefan Edberg Sportsmanship

2002	Paradorn Srichaphan
2001	Patrick Rafter
2000	Patrick Rafter
1999	Patrick Rafter
1998	Alex Corretja
1997	Patrick Rafter
1996	Alex Corretja
1995	Stefan Edberg
1994	Todd Martin
1993	Todd Martin
1992	Stefan Edberg
1991	John Fitzgerald

1990	Stefan Edberg
1989	Stefan Edberg
1988	Stefan Edberg
1987	Miloslav Mecir
1986	Yannick Noah
1985	Mats Wilander
1984	Brian Gottfried
1983	Jose Higueras
1982	Steve Denton
1981	Jose-Luis Clerc
1980	Jaime Fillol
1979	Stan Smith
1978	not given
1977	Arthur Ashe

Comeback Player

2002	Richard Krajicek
2001	Guillermo Canas
2000	Sergi Bruguera
1999	Chris woodruff
1998	Younes El Aynaoui
1997	Sergi Bruguera
1996	Stephane Simian
1995	Derrick Rostagno
1994	Guy Forget
1993	Mikael Pernfors
1992	Henri Leconte
1991	Jimmy Connors
1990	Thomas Muster
1989	Goran Prpic

1988	not given
1987	not given
1986	not given
1985	not given
1984	not given
1983	Butch Walts
1982	Jeff Borowiak
1981	Bob Lutz
1980	not given
1979	Arthur Ashe

Grand Prix Masters/ATP World Championship/Tennis Masters Cup

The Grand Prix Masters was a playoff for the top eight players at the end of a year-long series of Grand Prix tournaments. The players earned the right to play the Masters by accumulating points in tournaments throughout the year. It became a prestigious event from the time the first Masters was played under the sponsorship of Pepsi in 1970. Other sponsors included Commercial 1972-76, Colgate, 1977-79, Volvo 1980-1984, and Nabisco 1985-1989. When the MIPTC (Men's International Professional Tennis Council) disbanded at the end of 1989, the ATP (Association of Tennis Professionals) took over their own tour with IBM as the sponsor from 1990 to 1992. When that transition occurred, the ATP moved the eight-player, round-robin event from Madison Square Garden in New York (where it had been since 1977) to the Festhalle in Frankfurt.

Grand Prix Masters
1970 (Tokyo) Stan Smith won a round-robin among six players with 4-1 record ($15,000)
1971 (Paris) Ilie Nastase won a round-robin among seven players with 6-0 record ($15,000)
1972 (Barcelona) Ilie Nastase ($15,000) d. Stan Smith ($10,000) 6-3, 6-2, 3-6, 2-6, 6-3
1973 (Boston) Ilie Nastase ($15,000) d. Tom Okker ($10,000) 6-3, 7-5, 4-6, 6-3
1974 (Melbourne) Guillermo Vilas ($40,000) d. Ilie Nastase ($17,500) 7-6, 6-2, 3-6, 3-6, 6-4
1975 (Stockholm) Ilie Nastase ($40,000) d. Bjorn Borg ($20,000) 6-2, 6-2, 6-1
1976 (Houston) Manuel Orantes ($42,000) d. Wojtek Fibak ($20,000) 5-7, 6-2, 0-6, 7-6 (7-1), 6-1
1977 (New York) Jimmy Connors ($100,000) d. Bjorn Borg ($64,000) 6-4, 1-6, 6-4
1978 (New York) John McEnroe ($100,000) d. Arthur Ashe ($64,000) 6-7, 6-3, 7-5
1979 (New York) Bjorn Borg ($100,000) d. Vitas Gerulaitis ($64,000) 6-2, 6-2

1980 (New York) Bjorn Borg ($100,000) d. Ivan Lendl ($64,000) 6-4, 6-2, 6-2
1981 (New York) Ivan Lendl ($100,000) d. Vitas Gerulaitis ($50,000) 6-7 (5-7), 2-6, 7-6 (8-6), 6-2, 6-4
1982 (New York) Ivan Lendl ($100,000) d. John McEnroe ($60,000) 6-4, 6-4, 6-2
1983 (New York) John McEnroe ($100,000) d. Ivan Lendl ($60,000) 6-3, 6-4, 6-4
1984 (New York) John McEnroe ($100,000) d. Ivan Lendl ($60,000) 7-5, 6-0, 6-4
1985 (New York) Ivan Lendl ($100,000) d. Boris Becker ($70,000) 6-2, 7-6 (7-1), 6-3
1986 (New York) Ivan Lendl ($210,000) d. Boris Becker ($110,000) 6-4, 6-4, 6-4
1987 (New York) Ivan Lendl ($210,000) d. Mats Wila nder ($90,000) 6-2, 6-2, 6-3
1988 (New York) Boris Becker ($285,000) d. Ivan Lendl ($135,000) 5-7, 7-6 (7-5), 3-6, 6-2, 7-6 (7-5)
1989 (New York) Stefan Edberg ($285,000) d. Boris Becker ($165,000) 4-6, 7-6 (8-6), 6-3, 6-1

ATP World Championships
1990 (Frankfurt) Andre Agassi ($950,000) d. Stefan Edberg ($400,000) 5-7, 7-6 (7-5), 7-5, 6-2
1991 (Frankfurt) Pete Sampras ($1,020,000) d. Jim Courier ($395,000) 3-6, 7-6 (7-5), 6-3, 6-4
1992 (Frankfurt) Boris Becker ($1,090,000) d. Jim Courier ($465,000) 6-4, 6-3, 7-5
1993 (Frankfurt) Michael Stich ($1,240,000) d. Pete Sampras ($610,000) 7-6 (7-3), 2-6, 7-6 (9-7), 6-2
1994 (Frankfurt) Pete Sampras ($1,225,000) d. Boris Becker ($665,000) 4-6, 6-3, 7-5, 6-4
1995 (Frankfurt) Boris Becker ($1,225,000) d. Michael Chang ($575,000) 7-6 (7-3), 6-0, 7-6 (7-5)
1996 (Hanover) Pete Sampras ($1,340,000) d. Boris Becker ($640,000) 3-6, 7-6 (7-5), 7-6 (7-4), 6-7 (11-13), 6-4
1997 (Hanover) Pete Sampras ($1,340,000) d. Yevgeny Kafelnikov ($640,000) 6-3, 6-2, 6-2
1998 (Hanover) Alex Corretja ($1,360,000) d. Carlos Moya ($660,000) 3-6, 3-6, 7-5, 6-3, 7-5
1999 (Hanover) Pete Sampras ($1,385,000) d. Andre Agassi ($800,000) 6-1, 7-5, 6-4

Tennis Masters Cup
2000 (Lisbon) Gustavo Kuerten ($1,400,000) d. Andre Agassi ($820,000) 6-4, 6-4, 6-4
2001 (Sydney) Lleyton Hewitt ($1,520,000) d. Sebastien Grosjean ($700,000) 6-3, 6-3, 6-4
2002 (Shanghai) Lleyton Hewitt ($1,400,000) d. Juan Carlos Ferrero ($700,000) 7-5, 7-5, 2-6, 2-6, 6-4

World Championship Tennis

World Championship Tennis (WCT), Dallas-based, was the first solid promoter of the open era. The 1967 brainchild of Dave Dixon of New Orleans soon had to be bailed out and taken over by his partners Lamar Hunt and Al Hill, Jr., in Dallas. Dixon and aide Bob Briner hastened the advent of opens by skimming the cream of amateurism late in 1967, signing John Newcombe, Tony Roche, Cliff Drysdale, Nikki Pilic and Roger Taylor to pro contracts. Adding pros Dennis Ralston, Pierre Barthes, Butch Buchholz to the mix called the 'Handsome Eight,' WCT began as a small circuit in 1968, but expanded under the guidance of Hunt and his director, Mike Davies, to a global operation, attracting TV and substantial sponsorship dollars.

The tour climaxed with the season-ending playoffs for the eight top finishers in Dallas. Starting in 1971 with an astounding first prize of $50,000, by far the richest (won by Ken Rosewall), it became a focal point of the year every May through 1989. WCT alternately battled and integrated with the ITF's Grand Prix circuit until 1990. That year the Grand Prix and WCT were killed by Hamilton Jordan, new chief of the ATP, who rearranged the male tennis in establishing the ATP Tour.

WCT FINALS

1971	Ken Rosewall d. Rod Laver 6-4, 1-6, 7-6, 7-6
1972	Ken Rosewall d. Rod Laver 4-6, 6-0, 6-3, 6-7, 7-6
1973	Stan Smith d. Arthur Ashe 6-3, 6-3, 4-6, 6-4
1974	John Newcombe d. Bjorn Borg 4-6, 6-3, 6-2, 6-3
1975	Arthur Ashe d. Bjorn Borg 3-6, 6-4, 6-4, 6-0
1976	Bjorn Borg d. Guillermo Vilas 1-6, 6-1, 7-5, 6-1
1977	Jimmy Connors d. Dick Stockton 6-7, 6-1, 6-4, 6-3
1978	Vitas Gerulaitis d. Eddie Dibbs 6-3, 6-2, 6-1
1979	John McEnroe d. Bjorn Borg 7-5, 4-6, 6-2, 7-6
1980	Jimmy Connors d. John McEnroe 2-6, 7-6, 6-1, 6-2
1981	John McEnroe d. Johan Kriek 6-1, 6-2, 6-4
1982	Ivan Lendl d. John McEnroe 6-2, 3-6, 6-3, 6-3
1983	John McEnroe d. Ivan Lendl 6-2, 4-6, 6-3, 6-7, 7-6
1984	John McEnroe d. Jimmy Connors 6-1, 6-2, 6-3
1985	Ivan Lendl d. Tim Mayotte 7-6, 6-4, 6-1
1986	Anders Jarryd d. Boris Becker 6-7, 6-1, 6-1, 6-4
1987	Miloslav Mecir d. John McEnroe 6-0, 3-6, 6-2, 6-2
1988	Boris Becker d. Stefan Edberg 6-4, 1-6, 7-5, 6-2
1989	John McEnroe d. Brad Gilbert 6-3, 6-3, 7-6

Grand Slam Cup

The Grand Slam Cup was organized by the ITF in 1990 to compete with the ATP Championship as a year-end attraction, continuing the divisive rivalry of the two bodies. Containing a similar cast of players, it brings together in Munich the top 16 in finishers during the four majors. It offers $6 million in prize money, and the largest first prize (varying according to a bonus scheme). The winners the first three years (Pete Sampras, David Wheaton, Michael Stich) got a flat $2 million each.

1990	Pete Sampras ($2,000,000) d. Brad Gilbert ($1,000,000) 6-3, 6-4, 6-2
1991	David Wheaton ($2,000,000) d. Michael Chang ($1,000,000) 7-5, 6-2, 6-4
1992	Michael Stich ($2,000,000) d. Michael Chang ($1,000,000) 6-2, 6-3, 6-2
1993	Petr Korda ($1,625,000) d. Michael Stich ($812,500) 2-6, 6-4, 7-6 (7-5), 2-6, 11-9
1994	Magnus Larrson ($1,500,000) d. Pete Sampras ($750,000) 7-6 (8-6), 4-6, 7-6 (7-5), 6-4
1995	Goran Ivanisevic ($1,625,000) d. Todd Martin ($812,500) 7-6 (7-4), 6-3, 6-4
1996	Boris Becker ($1,875,000) d. Goran Ivanisevic ($812,500) 6-3, 6-4, 6-4

International Tennis Federation Men's Singles Champions

1978	Bjorn Borg (SWE)
1979	Bjorn Borg (SWE)
1980	Bjorn Borg (SWE)
1981	John McEnroe (USA)
1982	Jimmy Connors (USA)
1983	John McEnroe (USA)
1984	John McEnroe (USA)
1985	Ivan Lendl (TCH)
1986	Ivan Lendl (TCH)
1987	Ivan Lendl (TCH)
1988	Mats Wilander (SWE)
1989	Boris Becker (GER)
1990	Ivan Lendl (TCH)
1991	Stefan Edberg (SWE)
1992	Jim Courier (USA)
1993	Pete Sampras (USA)
1994	Pete Sampras (USA)
1995	Pete Sampras (USA)
1996	Pete Sampras (USA)
1997	Pete Sampras (USA)
1998	Pete Sampras (USA)
1999	Andre Agassi (USA)
2000	Gustavo Kuerten, Brazil
2001	Lleyton Hewitt (AUS)
2002	Lleyton Hewitt (AUS)

ITF Junior Men's World Champions

1978	Ivan Lendl (TCH)
1979	Raul Viver (ECU)
1980	Thierry Tulasne (FRA)
1981	Patrick Cash (AUS)
1982	Guy Forget (FRA)
1983	Stefan Edberg (SWE)
1984	Mark Kratzmann (AUS)
1985	Claudio Pistolesi (ITA)
1986	Javier Sanchez (ESP)
1987	Jason Stoltenberg (AUS)
1988	Nicolas Pereira (VEN)
1989	Nicklas Kulti (SWE)
1990	Andrea Gaudenzi (ITA)
1991	Thomas Enqvist (SWE)
1992	Brian Dunn (USA)
1993	Marcelo Rios (CHI)
1994	Federico Browne (ARG)
1995	Mariano Zabaleta (ARG)
1996	Sebastien Grosjean (FRA)
1997	Arnand Di Pasquale (FRA)
1998	Roger Federer (SUI)
1999	Kristian Pless (DEN)
2000	Andy Roddick (USA)
2001	Gilles Muller (LUX)
2002	Richard Gasquet (FRA)

ITF Men's Doubles Champions

1996	Todd Woodbridge & Mark Woodforde (AUS)
1997	Todd Woodbridge & Mark Woodforde (AUS)
1998	Jacco Eltingh & Paul Haarhuis (NED)
1999	Mahesh Bhupathi & Leander Paes (IND)
2000	Todd Woodbridge & Mark Woodforde (AUS)
2001	Jonas Bjorkman (SWE) & Todd Woodbridge (AUS)
2002	Mark Knowles (BAH) & Daniel Nestor (CAN)

Appendix D

WTA and Other Women's Pro Tours

What began as a one-off, $7,500 invitational event in 1970, is now the WTA Tour, a multi-million-dollar enterprise that in 2003 will see more than 1,000 female players from 76 nations compete at 60 events. Tournaments will be held in 34 countries and total prize money will exceed $50 million.

Women's professional tennis is organized and conducted by the WTA. The tour comprises nine Tier I events (where prize money exceeds $1.2 million), the major championships and the year end Tour Championships, as well as 51 other 'tiered' events.

The richest tournament—indeed, the most lucrative event in women's sports—is the Tour Championships. The top eight ranked singles players and top four doubles

teams will compete in 2003 for a total purse of $3 million, with $1 million going to the singles champion.

The women's game has come a long way from its humble beginnings. Led by Billie Jean King, the women broke away from the men's tour with a single, $7,500 invitational event in 1970. That tournament, unsanctioned by the USTA, spawned a 14-event tour in 1971 called the Virginia Slims Circuit that offered $309,000 in prizes.

Following three years of bickering, the USTA was finally forced to accept an independent women's tour that, from 1974, was organized under the auspices of a new women's guild, the Women's Tennis Association. King was its first president.

Leading Money Winners

1971
Billie Jean King	$117,000
Jo Durie	65,000
Rosie Casals	62,000
Judy Datton	33,867
Kerry Melville-Reid	29,762
Ann Jones	26,148
Margaret Smith Court	26,000
Evonne Goolagong	25,000
Virginia Wade	24,000
Nancy Richey	15,300

1972
Billie Jean King	119,000
Rosie Casals	70,000
Kerry Melville-Reid	55,000
Nancy Richey	50,800
Margaret Smith Court	47,000
Jo Durie	46,000
Evonne Goolagong	42,000
Virginia Wade	32,800
Wendy Overton	20,000
Karen Krantzcke	19,312

1973
Margaret Smith Court	$204,400
Billie Jean King	194,000
Chris Evert	152,002
Evonne Goolagong	108,127
Rosie Casals	104,375
Kerry Melville-Reid	65,650
Virginia Wade	60,100
Nancy Richey	43,112
Betty Stove	33,475
Françoise Durr	33,275

1974
Chris Evert	$261,460
Billie Jean King	173,225
Evonne Goolagong	102,506
Virginia Wade	85,389
Rosie Casals	72,389
Julie Heldman	60,511
Kerry Melville	56,022
Françoise Durr	41,277
Olga Morozova	40,877
Betty Stove	40,249

1975
Chris Evert	$370,227
Martina Navratilova	173,688
Evonne Goolagong	143,985
Virginia Wade	142,483
Margaret Court	114,146
Billie Jean King	105,900
Françoise Durr	62,635
Rosie Casals	62,302
Betty Stove	60,845
Olga Morozova	58,751

1976
Chris Evert	$343,165
E. Goolagong-Cawley	209,952
Virginia Wade	159,213
Rosie Casals	128,685
Martina Navratilova	128,535
Betty Stove	98,358
Sue Barker	92,493
Françoise Durr	70,830
Billie Jean King	70,470
Mona Guerrant	45,910

1977
Chris Evert	$503,134
Martina Navratilova	300,317
Billie Jean King	274,149
Betty Stove	229,162
Virginia Wade	193,476
Sue Barker	180,458
Kerry Melville-Reid	139,567
Rosie Casals	126,139
Wendy Turnbull	98,568
Françoise Durr	92,703

1978
Chris Evert	$454,486
Martina Navratilova	450,757
Virginia Wade	300,027
Kerry Reid	208,766
Wendy Turnbull	189,583
E. Goolagong-Cawley	180,844
Betty Stove	177,243
Virginia Ruzici	151,379
Billie Jean King	149,492
Regina Mariskova	88,894

1979
Martina Navratilova	$618,698
Chris Evert-Lloyd	528,457
Tracy Austin	485,426
Wendy Turnbull	291,945
Dianne Fromholtz	252,745
Sue Barker	177,143
Billie Jean King	169,834
Betty Stove	168,567
E. Goolagong-Cawley	167,132
Virginia Wade	141,478

1980
Martina Navratilova	$749,250
Tracy Austin	645,628
Chris Evert-Lloyd	448,509
Hana Mandlokva	369,767
Wendy Turnbull	308,213
Billie Jean King	298,413
Andrea Jaeger	220,296
E. Goolagong-Cawley	218,505
Virginia Ruzici	190,937
Kathy Jordan	178,804

1981
Martina Navratilova	$865,437
Chris Evert-Lloyd	572,162
Tracy Austin	453,409
Andrea Jaeger	392,115
Pam Shriver	366,530
Hana Mandlikova	339,602
Wendy Turnbull	225,161
Anne Smith	192,311
Sylvia Hanika	190,898
Virginia Ruzici	179,115

1982
Martina Navratilova	$1,475,055
Chris Evert-Lloyd	689,485
Andrea Jaeger	423,315
Wendy Turnbull	371,196
Pam Shriver	354,168
Barbara Potter	270,015
Bettina Bunge	248,598
Hana Mandlikova	231,283
Sylvia Hanika	215,151
Anne Smith	212,754

1983

Martina Navratilova	$1,456,030
Chris Evert-Lloyd	430,436
Pam Shriver	312,216
Andrea Jaeger	261,954
Kathy Jordan	211,786
Jo Durie	211,342
Wendy Turnbull	206,391
Andrea Temesvari	168,301
Sylvia Hanika	154,950
Hana Mandlikova	151,762

1984

Martina Navratilova	$2,173,556
Chris Evert-Lloyd	593,135
Hana Mandlikova	470,580
Pam Shriver	454,080
Manuela Maleeva	326,057
Helena Sukova	282,443
Wendy Turnbull	255,095
Claudia Kohde-Kilsch	213,899
Barbara Potter	162,478
Zina Garrison	179,014

1985

Martina Navratilova	$1,328,829
Chris Evert-Lloyd	972,782
Hana Mandlikova	579,847
Helena Sukova	422,387
Pam Shriver	419,686
Claudia Kohde-Kilsch	398,120
Zina Garrison	274,470
Manuela Maleeva	271,271
Carling Bassett	197,591
Kathy Rinaldi	191,750

1986

Martina Navratilova	$1,905,841
Chris Evert-Lloyd	833,755
Helena Sukova	695,846
Steffi Graf	612,118
Pam Shriver	566,163
Hana Mandlikova	421,145
Claudia Kohde-Kilsch	367,906
Gabriela Sabatini	264,139
Zina Garrison	226,899
Wendy Turnbull	205,243

1987

Steffi Graf	$1,063,785
Martina Navratilova	932,102
Chris Evert	769,943
Pam Shriver	703,030
Helena Sukova	490,792
Gabriela Sabatini	465,933
Lori McNeil	401,524
Hana Mandlikova	340,410
Zina Garrison	328,694
Claudia Kohde-Kilsch	321,773

1988

Steffi Graf	$1,378,128
Martina Navratilova	1,333,782
Gabriela Sabatini	995,399
Chris Evert	698,649
Pam Shriver	621,327
Helena Sukova	388,317
Zina Garrison	381,535
Natalia Zvereva	361,354
Lori McNeil	346,118
Manuela Maleeva	250,174

1989

Steffi Graf	$1,562,905
Martina Navratilova	975,614
Gabriela Sabatini	580,801
Arantxa Sanchez Vicario	504,098
Zina Garrison	490,653
Helena Sukova	381,579
Jana Novotna	360,896
Monica Seles	239,361
Mary Joe Fernandez	236,455
Larisa Savchenko	235,122

1990

Steffi Graf	$1,921,853
Monica Seles	1,637,222
Martina Navratilova	1,330,794
Gabriela Sabatini	975,490
Jana Novotna	645,500
Zina Garrison	602,203
Helena Sukova	562,715
Mary Joe Fernandez	518,366
Arantxa Sanchez Vicario	517,662
Natalia Zvereva	462,770

1991

Monica Seles	$2,457,758
Steffi Graf	1,468,336
Gabriela Sabatini	1,192,971
Martina Navratilova	989,986
Arantxa Sanchez Vicario	799,340
Jana Novotna	766,369
Mary Joe Fernandez	672,035
Natalia Zvereva	558,002
Jennifer Capriati	535,617
Gigi Fernandez	455,228

1992

Monica Seles	$2,622,352
Steffi Graf	1,691,139
A. Sanchez Vicario	1,376,355
Gabriela Sabatini	1,207,565
Martina Navratilova	731,933
Natalia Zvereva	657,694
Mary Joe Fernandez	605,908
Jana Novotna	511,184
Gigi Fernandez	479,187
Helena Sukova	473,112

1993

Steffi Graf	$2,821,337
A. Sanchez Vicario	1,938,239
Conchita Martinez	1,208,795
Martina Navratilova	1,036,119
Gabriela Sabatini	957,680
Jana Novotna	926,646
Natalia Zvereva	857,160
Gigi Fernandez	671,063
Helena Sukova	655,573
Mary Joe Fernandez	611,681

1944

A. Sanchez Vicario	$2,943,665
Conchita Martinez	1,540,167
Steffi Graf	1,487,980
Jana Novotna	876,119
Natalia Zvereva	874,592
Gabriela Sabatini	874,470
Martina Navratilova	851,082
Mary Pierce	768,614
Gigi Fernandez	742,650
Lindsay Davenport	600,745

1995

Steffi Graf	$2,538,620
A. Sanchez Vicario	1,456,516
Conchita Martinez	1,266,558
Natalia Zvereva	867,287
Jana Novotna	787,936
Gabriela Sabatini	718,978
Mary Pierce	698,838
Anke Huber	620,969
Kimiko Date	607,113
Brenda Schultz-McCarthy	577,807

1996

Steffi Graf	$2,664,178
A. Sanchez Vicario	1,858,444
Jana Novotna	1,354,307
Martina Hingis	1,330,996
Monica Seles	1,154,499
Conchita Martinez	1,111,401
Iva Majoli	962,855
Lindsay Davenport	871,393
Anke Huber	691,335
Mary Joe Fernandez	553,771

1997

Martina Hingis	$3,400,196
Jana Novotna	1,685,115
Lindsay Davenport	1,533,101
Iva Majoli	1,227,332
Monica Seles	914,020
A. Sanchez Vicario	890,512
Mary Pierce	881,639
Mary Joe Fernandez	769,132
Natalia Zvereva	746,643
Irina Spirlea	720,758

1998

Martina Hingis	$3,175,631
Lindsay Davenport	2,697,788
Jana Novotna	2,039,192
Venus Williams	1,712,246
A. Sanchez Vicario	1,505,964
Monica Seles	1,003,514
Nathalie Tauziat	990,224
Natalia Zvereva	931,945
Patty Schnyder	901,828
Mary Pierce	895,417

1999

Martina Hingis	$3,291,780
Lindsay Davenport	2,734,205
Serena Williams	2,605,102
Venus Williams	2,316,005
Steffi Graf	1,248,867
Mary Pierce	996,442
Nathalie Tauziat	864,507
Monica Seles	822,218
A. Sanchez Vicario	807,921
Anna Kournikova	748,424

2000

Martina Hingis	$3,457,049
Lindsay Davenport	2,444,734
Venus Williams	2,074,150
Mary Pierce	1,208,018
Monica Seles	1,140,850
Conchita Martinez	1,067,930
Anna Kournikova	984,930
Serena Williams	926,818
Julie Halard-Decugis	879,570
A. Sanchez Vicario	819,689

2001

Venus Williams	$2,662,610
Jennifer Capriati	2,268,624
Serena Williams	2,136,263
Lindsay Davenport	2,102,242
Martina Hingis	1,765,116
Kim Clijsters	1,335,659
Jelena Dokic	1,169,716
Justine Henin	998,704
Lisa Raymond	949,385
Nathalie Tauziat	925,785

2002

Serena Williams	$3,935,668
Venus Willimas	2,583,571
Jennifer Capriati	2,217,939
Kim Clijsters	1,754,376
Martina Hingis	1,467,584
Justine Henin	1,213,093
Daniela Hantuchova	1,188,379
Monica Seles	1,096,630
Amelie Mauresmo	1,073,807
Jelena Dokic	918,633

No. 1 Ranking

Since the computer rankings were adopted in 1975, 11 different players have held the top spot, as follows:
*(includes week of December 30, 2002)

WEEKS NO. 1

Steffi Graf (GER)	378
Martina Navratilova (USA)	331
Chris Evert (USA)	262
Martina Hingis (SUI)	209
Monica Seles (USA)	178
Lindsay Davenport (USA)	37
Serena Williams (USA)	26
Tracy Austin (USA)	22
Jennifer Capriati (USA)	17
A. Sanchez Vicario (ESP)	12
Venus Williams (USA)	11

No. 1 History

Eleven players have held the No. 1 spot since the WTA adopted its computer ranking system in 1975. The top spot has changed 53 times.
*(includes week of December 30, 2002)

PLAYER	WEEKS	DATE
Chris Evert	140	Nov. 3, 1975
Martina Navratilova	26	July 10, 1978
Evert	2	Jan. 14, 1979
Navratilova	4	Jan. 28, 1979
Evert	7	Feb. 25, 1979
Navratilova	10	Apr. 16, 1979
Evert	11	Jun. 25, 1979
Navratilova	31	Sep. 10, 1979
Tracy Austin	2	Apr. 7, 1980
Navratilova	10	Apr. 21, 1980
Austin	20	Jul. 1, 1980
Evert	76	Nov. 18, 1980
Navratilova	2	May 3, 1982
Evert	4	May 17, 1982
Navratilova	156	June 14, 1982
Evert	18	June 10, 1985
Navratilova	2	Oct. 14, 1985
Evert	4	Oct. 28, 1985
Navratilova	90	Nov. 25, 1985
Steffi Graf	186	Aug. 17, 1987
Monica Seles	21	Mar. 11, 1991
Graf	1	Aug. 5, 1991
Seles	1	Aug. 12, 1991
Graf	3	Aug. 19, 1991
Seles	91	Sept. 9, 1991
Graf	87	Jun. 7, 1993
A. Sanchez Vicario	2	Feb. 6, 1995
Graf	1	Feb. 20, 1995
Sanchez Vicario	6	Feb. 27, 1995
Graf	5	Apr. 10, 1995
Sanchez Vicario	4	May 15, 1995
Graf	9	Jun. 12, 1995
Graf & Seles	64	Aug. 15, 1995
Graf	2	Nov. 4, 1996
Graf & Seles	1	Nov. 18, 1996
Graf	17	Nov. 25, 1996
Martina Hingis	80	Mar. 31, 1997
Lindsay Davenport	17	Oct. 12, 1998
Hingis	21	Feb. 8, 1999
Davenport	5	Jul. 5, 1999
Hingis	34	Aug. 9, 1999
Davenport	5	Apr. 3, 2000
Hingis	1	May 8, 2000
Davenport	1	May 15, 2000
Hingis	73	May 22, 2000
Jennifer Capriati	3	Oct. 15, 2001
Davenport	3	Nov. 5, 2001
Capriati	10	Jan. 14, 2002
Venus Williams	6	Feb. 25, 2002
Capriati	3	Mar. 18, 2002
Williams	4	Apr. 22, 2002
Capriati	4	May 20, 2002
Williams	4	Jun. 10, 2002
Serena Williams	3	Jul. 8, 2002

WTA Tour Annual Awards

Top Player

1977 Virginia Wade
1978 Martina Navratilova
1979 Martina Navratilova
1980 Tracy Austin
1981 Chris Evert
1982 Martina Navratilova
1983 Martina Navratilova
1984 Martina Navratilova
1985 Martina Navratilova
1986 Martina Navratilova
1987 Steffi Graf
1988 Steffi Graf
1989 Steffi Graf
1990 Steffi Graf
1991 Monica Seles
1992 Monica Seles
1993 Steffi Graf
1994 Steffi Graf
1995 Steffi Graf
1996 Steffi Graf
1997 Martina Hingis
1998 Lindsay Davenport
1999 Lindsay Davenport
2000 Venus Williams
2001 Jennifer Capriati
2002 Serena Williams

Top Doubles Team

1977 Martina Navratilova and Betty Stove
1978 Billie Jean King and Martina Navratilova
1979 Billie Jean King and Martina Navratilova
1980 Kathy Jordan and Anne Smith
1981 Martina Navratilova and Pam Shriver
1982 Martina Navratilova and Pam Shriver
1983 Martina Navratilova and Pam Shriver
1984 Martina Navratilova and Pam Shriver
1985 Martina Navratilova and Pam Shriver
1986 Martina Navratilova and Pam Shriver
1987 Martina Navratilova and Pam Shriver
1988 Martina Navratilova and Pam Shriver
1989 Jana Novotna and Helena Sukova
1990 Jana Novotna and Helena Sukova
1991 Gigi Fernandez and Jana Novotna
1992 Larisa Neiland and Natalia Zvereva
1993 Gigi Fernandez and Natalia Zvereva
1994 Gigi Fernandez and Natalia Zvereva
1995 Gigi Fernandez and Natalia Zvereva
1996 Jana Novotna and Arantxa Sanchez Vicario
1997 Gigi Fernandez and Natalia Zvereva
1998 Martina Hingis and Jana Novotna
1999 Martina Hingis and Anna Kournikova
2000 Serena Williams and Venus Williams
2001 Lisa Raymond and Rennae Stubbs
2002 Virginia Ruano Pascal and Paola Suarez

Most Improved Player

1977 Wendy Turnbull
1978 Virginia Ruzici
1979 Sylvia Hanika
1980 Hana Mandlikova
1981 Barbara Potter
1982 Sabina Simmonds
1983 Andrea Temesvari
1984 Kathy Jordan
1985 Helena Sukova
1986 Steffi Graf
1987 Lori McNeil
1988 Arantxa Sanchez Vicario
1989 Arantxa Sanchez Vicario
1990 Monica Seles
1991 Garbiela Sabatini
1992 Kimiko Date
1993 Magdalena Maleeva
1994 Mary Pierce
1995 Chanda Rubin
1996 Martina Hingis
1997 Amanda Coetzer
1998 Patty Schynder
1999 Serena Williams
2000 Elena Dementieva
2001 Justine Henin
2002 Daniela Hantuchova

Most Impressive Newcomer

1977 Tracy Austin
1978 Pam Shriver
1979 Kathy Jordan
1980 Andrea Jaeger
1981 Kathy Rinaldi
1982 Zina Garrison
1983 Carling Bassett Seguso
1984 Manuela Maleeva
1985 Gabriela Sabatini
1986 Stephanie Rehe
1987 Arantxa Sanchez Vicario
1988 Natalia Zvereva
1989 Conchita Martinez
1990 Jennifer Capriati
1991 Andrea Strnadova
1992 Debbie Graham
1993 Iva Majoli
1994 Irina Spirlea
1995 Martina Hingis
1996 Anna Kournikova
1997 Venus Williams
1998 Serena Williams
1999 Kim Clijsters
2000 Daja Bedanova
2001 Daniela Hantuchova
2002 Svetlana Kuznetsova

Karen Krantzke Sportsmanship

1978 Evonne Goolagong
1979 Chris Evert
1980 Evonne Goolagong-Cawley
1981 Diane Desfor
1982 Nancy Yeargin
1983 Sharon Walsh-Pete
1984 Marcella Mesker
1985 Peanut Louie-Harper
1986 Peanut Louie-Harper
1987 Anne Minter
1988 Svetlana Parkhomenko
1989 Gretchen Magers
1990 Mercedes Paz
1991 Judith Wiesner
1992 Jill Hetherington
1993 Nicole Arendt
1994 Kimberly Po
1995 Amanda Coetzer
1996 Yayuk Basuki
1997 Amanda Coetzer
1998 Yayuk Basuki
1999 Ai Sugiyama
2000 Kim Clijsters
2001 Kim Clijsters
2002 Kim Clijsters

Comeback Player

1987 Bettina Bunge
1988 Pascale Paradis
1989 Kathy Rinaldi
1990 Elizabeth Smylie
1991 Stephanie Rehe
1992 Jenny Byrne
1993 Elizabeth Smylie
1994 Meredith McGrath
1995 Monica Seles
1996 Jennifer Capriati
1997 Mary Pierce
1998 Monica Seles
1999 Sabine Appelmans
2000 Iva Majoli
2001 Barbara Schwartz
2002 Corina Morariu

WTA Championships

The Women's Tennis Association season-concluding playoffs are best known as the Virginia Slims Championships (the original sponsorship, 1972–78 and 1983–94), but have also operated under other sponsorships, such as Avon, Corel, and Chase.

In the fall of 1970 a breakaway group of nine women, including ringleaders Billie Jean King and Rosie Casals, guided by Gladys Heldman, founder-publisher of *World Tennis* magazine, were determined to establish pro tennis with decent prize money for women. Virginia Slims put up prize money for the first small tournament, Houston ($7,500), and the Houston Nine (Casals, King, Valerie Ziegenfuss, Nancy Richey, Kristy Pigeon, Judy Tegart Dalton, Kerry Melville, Julie Heldman, Peaches Bartkowicz) bucked their national associations by going on their own. Casals won $1,700, over Dalton, 5-7, 6-1, 7-5, and in effect a genuine professional tour for women was launched. A Slims winter circuit followed in 1971, and the playoffs for leaders in a points system was instituted in 1972 on clay at Boca Raton, Fla., with the 32 top players. An amateur, Chris Evert, won, and turned down the $12,000 first prize. After 1973 it became an indoor event, played principally in California until settling into New York's Madison Square Garden in 1979. It has taken various forms—round robin, double-elimination—but since 1983 has been a straight elimination tourney for the top 16 women and 8 doubles teams. In 1984, the singles final became the only best-of-five set test for women.

Virginia Slims Championships
1972	(Boca Raton, Fla.) Chris Evert d. Kerry Melville 7-5, 6-4
1973	(Boca Raton, Fla.) Chris Evert d. Nancy Richey 6-3, 6-3
1974	(Los Angeles) Evonne Goolagong d. Chris Evert 6-3, 6-4
1975	(Los Angeles) Chris Evert d. Martina Navratilova 6-4, 6-2
1976	(Los Angeles) Evonne Goolagong d. Chris Evert 6-3, 5-7, 6-3
1977	(New York) Chris Evert d. Sue Barker 2-6, 6-1, 6-1
1978	(Oakland) Martina Navratilova d. Evonne Goolagong 7-6, 6-4

Avon Championships
1979	(New York) Martina Navratilova d. Tracy Austin 6-3, 3-6, 6-2
1980	(New York) Tracy Austin d. Martina Navratilova 6-2, 2-6, 6-2
1981	(New York) Martina Navratilova d. Andrea Jaeger 6-3, 7-6 (7-3)
1982	(New York) Sylvia Hanika d. Martina Navratilova 1-6, 6-3, 6-4

Virginia Slims Championships
1983	(New York) Martina Navratilova d. Chris Evert 6-2, 6-0
1984	(New York) Martina Navratilova d. Chris Evert Lloyd 6-3, 7-5, 6-1
1985	(New York) Martina Navratilova d. Helena Sukova 6-3, 7-5, 6-4
1986	(spring) (New York) Martina Navratilova d. Hana Mandlikova 6-2, 6-0, 3-6, 6-1
1986	(fall) (New York) Martina Navratilova d. Steffi Graf 7-6 (7-1), 6-3, 6-2
1987	(New York) Steffi Graf d. Gabriela Sabatini 4-6, 6-4, 6-0, 6-4
1988	(New York) Gabriela Sabatini d. Pam Shriver 7-5, 6-2, 6-2
1989	(New York) Steffi Graf d. Martina Navratilova 6-4, 7-5, 2-6, 6-2
1990	(New York) Monica Seles d. Gabriela Sabatini 6-4, 5-7, 3-6, 6-4, 6-2
1991	(New York) Monica Seles d. Martina Navratilova 6-4, 3-6, 7-5, 6-0
1992	(New York) Monica Seles d. Martina Navratilova 7-5, 6-3, 6-1
1993	(New York) Steffi Graf d. Arantxa Sanchez Vicario 6-1, 6-4, 3-6, 6-1
1994	(New York) Gabriela Sabatini d. Lindsay Davenport 6-3, 6-3, 6-4

Corel Championships
1995	(New York) Steffi Graf d. Anke Huber 6-1, 2-6, 6-1, 4-6, 6-3

Chase Championships
1996	(New York) Steffi Graf d. Martina Hingis 6-3, 4-6, 6-0, 4-6, 6-0
1997	(New York) Jana Novotna d. Mary Pierce 7-6, 6-2, 6-3
1998	(New York) Martina Hingis d. Lindsay Davenport 7-5, 6-4, 4-6, 6-2
1999	(New York) Lindsay Davenport d. Martina Hingis 6-4, 6-2
2000	(New York) Martina Hingis d. Monica Seles 6-7 (5), 6-4, 6-4

Sanex Championships
2001	(Munich) Serena Williams d. Lindsay Davenport, walkover

Home Depot Championships
2002	(Los Angeles) Kim Clijsters d. Serena Williams 7-5, 6-3

Colgate Series/Toyota Series Champions (Women)

In the early years of the Virginia Slims Tour, another compatible tour sprang up: the Colgate Series (1976) followed by the Toyota Series (1979), also with season ending playoffs for leading tour players. This tour stopped operating after 1982.

1976	(Palm Springs, Cal.) Chris Evert d. Françoise Durr 6-1, 6-2
1977	(Palm Springs, Cal.) Chris Evert d. Billie Jean King 6-2, 6-2
1978	(Palm Springs, Cal.) Chris Evert d. Martina Navratilova 6-3, 6-3
1979	(Landover, Md.) Martina Navratilova d. Tracy Austin 6-2, 6-1
1980	(Landover, Md.) Tracy Austin d. Andrea Jaeger 6-2, 6-2
1981	(East Rutherford, N.J.) Tracy Austin d. Martina Navratilova 2-6, 6-4, 6-2
1982	(East Rutherford, N.J.) Martina Navratilova d. Chris Evert Lloyd 4-6, 6-1, 6

International Tennis Federation Women's Singles Champions

1978 Chris Evert Lloyd (USA)
1979 Martina Navratilova (TCH)
1980 Chris Evert Lloyd (USA)
1981 Chris Evert Lloyd (USA)
1982 Martina Navratilova (USA)
1983 Martina Navratilova (USA)
1984 Martina Navratilova (USA)
1985 Martina Navratilova (USA)
1986 Martina Navratilova (USA)
1987 Steffi Graf (GER)
1988 Steffi Graf (GER)
1989 Steffi Graf (GER)
1990 Steffi Graf (GER)
1991 Monica Seles, Yugoslavia
1992 Monica Seles, Yugoslavia
1993 Steffi Graf (GER)
1994 Arantxa Sanchez Vicario (ESP)
1995 Steffi Graf (GER)
1996 Steffi Graf, Germany
1997 Martina Hingis, Switzerland
1998 Lindsay Davenport (USA)
1999 Martina Hingis, Switzerland
2000 Martina Hingis, Switzerland
2001 Jennifer Capriati (USA)
2002 Serena Williams (USA)

ITF Women's Doubles Champions

1996 Lindsay Davenport & Mary Joe Fernandez (USA)
1997 Lindsay Davenport (USA) & Jana Novotna (CZE)
1998 Lindsay Davenport (USA) & Natalia Zvereva (BLR)
1999 Martina Hingis (SUI) & Anna Kournikova (RUS)
2000 Julie Halard-Decugis (FRA) & Ai Sugiyama (JPN)
2001 Lisa Raymond (USA) & Rennae Stubbs (AUS)
2002 Paola Suarez (ARG) & Virginia Ruano Pascual (ESP)

ITF Junior Women's World Champions

1978 Hana Mandlikova (TCH)
1979 Mary-Lou Piatek (USA)
1980 Susan Mascarin (USA)
1981 Zina Garrison (USA)
1982 Gretchen Rush (USA)
1983 Pascale Paradis (FRA)
1984 Gabriela Sabatini (ARG)
1985 Laura Garrone (ITA)
1986 Patricia Tarabini (ARG)
1987 Natalia Zvereva (URS)
1988 Cristina Tessi (ARG)
1989 Florencia Labat (ARG)
1990 Karina Habsudova (TCH)
1991 Zdenka Malkova (TCH)
1992 Rossana De Los Rios (PAR)
1993 Nino Louarssabichvili (GEO)
1994 Martina Hingis (SUI)
1995 Anna Kournikova (RUS)
1996 Amelie Mauresmo (FRA)
1997 Cara Black (ZIM)
1998 Jelena Dokic (AUS)
1999 Lina Krasnoroutskaia (RUS)
2000 Maria Emilia Salerni (ARG)
2001 Svetlana Kuznetsova (RUS)
2002 Barbora Strycova (CZE)

The growth of prize money on the women's tours

	(In U.S. Dollars)	Tour sponsor
1971	$309,100	Virginia Slims
1972	$501,275	Virginia Slims
1973	$775,000	Virginia Slims
1974	$1 million	Virginia Slims
1975	$1.5 million	Virginia Slims
1976	$2.2 million	Virginia Slims
1977	$4.2 million	Virginia Slims, Colgate
1978	$4.5 million	Virginia Slims, Colgate
1979	$6.2 million	Avon, Colgate
1980	$7.2 million	Avon, Colgate
1981	$7.4 million	Avon, Toyota
1982	$8.9 million	Avon, Toyota
1983	$10.2 million	Virginia Slims
1984	$11 million	Virginia Slims
1985	$12.5 million	Virginia Slims
1986	$14.2 million	Virginia Slims
1987	$15 million	Virginia Slims
1988	$16.7 million	Virginia Slims
1989	$17.9 million	Virginia Slims
1990	$23 million	Kraft General Foods
1991	$24.6 million	Kraft General Foods
1992	$25.5 million	Kraft General Foods
1993	$33 million	Kraft General Foods
1994	$35 million	WTA TOUR
1995	$35 million	WTA TOUR
1996	$36 million	Corel
1997	$38 million	Corel
1998	$40 million	Corel
1999	$45 million	WTA TOUR
2000	$47 million	Sanex
2001	$50 million	Sanex
2002	$51.7 million	Sanex

Appendix E

U.S. Pro Championships

Although there were earlier instances of professional tournaments offering prize money, particularly in France and Britain, with teaching professionals/coaches as entries, the U.S. Pro Championships stands as the oldest continous such event. It began in 1927 on courts of the small, since vanished, Notlek Tennis Club on the West Side of Manhattan, starring the newly avowed touring pros, Vinnie Richards and Howard Kinsey, from the Pyle troupe, and was played for a $2,000 purse. Richards won

first prize, $1,000. The tournament, never very healthy financially, somehow kept going, often changing surfaces and locations, surviving indoors (1955–62) in Cleveland as the 'World Pro Championships.'

In 1963 at Forest Hills it went bankrupt (only Pancho Gonzalez, who negotiated a prior guarantee, got paid), and seemed finished at last. The tournament was revived at Boston's Longwood Cricket Club in 1964 and continued there until its demise following the 1999 event.

YEAR	WINNER	RUNNER-UP	SCORE
1927	Vinnie Richards	Howard Kinsey	11-9, 6-4, 6-3
1928	Vinnie Richards	Karel Kozeluh	8-6, 6-3, 0-6, 6-2
1929	Karel Kozeluh	Vinnie Richards	6-4, 6-4, 4-6, 4-6, 7-5
1930	Vinnie Richards	Karel Kozeluh	2-6, 10-8, 6-3, 6-4
1931	Bill Tilden	Vinnie Richards	7-5, 6-2, 6-1
1932	Karel Kozeluh	Hans Nusslein	6-2, 6-2, 7-5
1933	Vinnie Richards	Frank Hunter	6-3, 6-0, 6-2
1934	Hans Nusslein	Karel Kozeluh	6-4, 6-2, 1-6, 7-5
1935	Bill Tilden	Karel Kozeluh	0-6, 6-1, 6-4, 0-6, 6-4
1936	Joseph Whalen	Charles Wood	4-6, 4-6, 6-3, 6-2, 6-3
1937	Karel Kozeluh	Bruce Barnes	6-2, 6-3, 4-6, 4-6, 6-1
1938	Fred Perry	Bruce Barnes	6-3, 6-2, 6-4
1939	Ellsworth Vines	Fred Perry	8-6, 6-8, 6-1, 20-18
1940	Don Budge	Fred Perry	6-3, 5-7, 6-4, 6-3
1941	Fred Perry	Dick Skeen	6-4, 6-8, 6-2, 6-3
1942	Don Budge	Bobby Riggs	6-2, 6-2, 6-2
1943	Lt. Bruce Barnes	John Nogrady	6-1, 7-9, 7-5, 4-6, 6-3
1944	Not Held		
1945	Welby Van Horn	John Nogrady	6-4, 6-2, 6-2
1946	Bobby Riggs	Don Budge	6-3, 6-1, 6-1
1947	Bobby Riggs	Don Budge	3-6, 6-3, 10-8, 4-6,6-3
1948	Jack Kramer	Bobby Riggs	14-12, 6-2, 3-6, 7-5
1949	Bobby Riggs	Don Budge	9-7, 3-6, 6-3, 6-3
1950	Pancho Segura	Frank Kovacs	6-4, 1-6, 8-6, 4-4, retired
1951	Pancho Segura	Pancho Gonzalez	6-3, 6-4, 6-2
1952	Pancho Segura	Pancho Gonzalez	3-6, 6-4, 3-6, 6-4, 6-0
1953	Pancho Gonzalez	Don Budge	4-6, 6-4, 7-5, 6-2
1954	Pancho Gonzalez	Frank Sedgman	6-3, 9-7, 3-6, 6-2
1955	Pancho Gonzalez	Pancho Segura	21-16, 19-21, 21-8, 20-22, 21-19*
1956	Pancho Gonzalez	Pancho Segura	21-15, 13-21, 21-14, 22-20*
1957	Pancho Gonzalez	Pancho Segura	6-3, 3-6, 7-5, 6-1
1958	Pancho Gonzalez	Lew Hoad	3-6, 4-6, 14-12, 6-1, 6-4
1959	Pancho Gonzalez	Lew Hoad	6-4, 6-2, 6-4
1960	Alex Olmedo	Tony Trabert	7-5, 6-4
1961	Pancho Gonzalez	Frank Sedgman	6-3, 7-5
1962	Butch Buchholz	Pancho Segura	6-4, 6-3, 6-4

YEAR	WINNER	RUNNER-UP	SCORE
1963	Ken Rosewall	Rod Laver	6-4, 6-2, 6-2
1964	Rod Laver	Pancho Gonzalez	4-6, 6-3, 7-5, 6-4
1965	Ken Rosewall	Rod Laver	6-4, 6-3, 6-3
1966	Rod Laver	Ken Rosewall	6-4, 4-6, 6-2, 8-10, 6-3
1967	Rod Laver	Andres Gimeno	4-6, 6-4, 6-3, 7-5
1968	Rod Laver	John Newcombe	6-4, 6-4, 9-7
1969	Rod Laver	John Newcombe	7-5, 6-2, 4-6, 6-1
1970	Tony Roche	Rod Laver	3-6, 6-4, 1-6, 6-2, 6-2
1971	Ken Rosewall	Cliff Drysdale	6-4, 6-3, 6-0
1972	Bob Lutz	Tom Okker	6-4, 2-6, 6-1, 6-4
1973	Jimmy Connors	Arthur Ashe	6-3, 4-6, 6-4, 3-6, 6-2
1974	Bjorn Borg	Tom Okker	7-6 (7-3), 6-1, 6-1
1975	Bjorn Borg	Guillermo Vilas	6-3, 6-4, 6-2
1976	Bjorn Borg	Harold Solomon	6-7 (3-7), 6-4, 6-1, 6-2
1977	Manuel Orantes	Eddie Dibbs	7-6 (7-3), 7-5, 6-4
1978	Manuel Orantes	Harold Solomon	6-4, 6-3
1979	Jose Higueras	Hans Gildemeister	6-3, 6-1
1980	Eddie Dibbs	Gene Mayer	6-2, 6-1
1981	Jose-Luis Clerc	Hans Gildemeister	0-6, 6-3, 6-2
1982	Guillermo Vilas	Mel Purcell	6-4, 6-0
1983	Jose-Luis Clerc	Jimmy Arias	6-3, 6-1
1984	Aaron Krickstein	Jose-Luis Clerc	7-6 (7-2), 3-6, 6-4
1985	Mats Wilander	Martin Jaite	6-2, 6-4
1986	Andres Gomez	Martin Jaite	7-5, 6-4
1987	Mats Wilander	Kent Carlsson	7-6 (7-5), 6-1
1988	Thomas Muster	Lawson Duncan	6-2, 6-2
1989	Andres Gomez	Mats Wilander	6-1, 6-4
1990	Martin Jaite	Libor Nemecek	7-5, 6-3
1991	Andres Gomez	Andrei Cherkasov	7-5, 6-3
1992	Ivan Lendl	Richey Reneberg	6-3, 6-3
1993	Ivan Lendl	Todd Martin	5-7, 6-3, 7-6 (7-4)
1994	Ivan Lendl	MaliVai Washington	7-5, 7-6 (7-5)
1995	not completed, rain		
1996	not played		
1997	Sjeng Schalken	Marcelo Rios	7-5, 6-3
1998	Michael Chang	Paul Haarhuis	6-3, 6-4
1999	Marat Safin	Greg Rusedski	6-4, 7-6

VASSS Scoring

Appendix F

London Pro and French Pro Championships

Besides the U.S. Pro, the highest regarded tournaments among the pros during the years prior to open tennis were the London Indoor Pro and the French Pro Championships. The French was held in Paris, mostly at Stade Roland Garros, but 1963-67 indoors at Stade Coubertin. The London event, usually known as Wembley, was played at the Empire Pool.

LONDON INDOOR PRO

YEAR	WINNER	RUNNER-UP	SCORE
1934	Ellsworth Vines	Hans Nusslein	round robin
1935	Ellsworth Vines	Bill Tilden	6-1, 6-3, 5-7, 3-6, 6-3
1936	Ellsworth Vines	Hans Nusslein	6-4, 6-4, 6-2
1937	Hans Nusslein	Bill Tilden	6-4, 3-6, 6-3, 2-6, 6-2
1938	Hans Nusslein	Bill Tilden	7-5, 3-6, 6-3, 3-6, 6-2
1939	Don Budge	Hans Nusslein	round robin
1940-48		not held	
1949	Jack Kramer	Bobby Riggs	6-4, 6-2, 6-3
1950	Pancho Gonzalez	Welby Van Horn	6-3, 6-2, 6-4
1951	Pancho Gonzalez	Pancho Segura	6-2, 6-2, 2-6, 6-4
1952	Pancho Gonzalez	Jack Krame	3-6, 3-6, 6-2, 6-4, 7-5
1953	Frank Sedgman	Pancho Gonzalez	6-1, 6-2, 6-2
1954-55		not held	
1956	Pancho Gonzalez	Frank Sedgman	4-6, 11-9, 11-9, 9-7
1957	Ken Rosewall	Pancho Segura	1-6, 6-3, 6-4, 3-6, 6-4
1958	Frank Sedgman	Tony Trabert	6-4, 6-3, 6-4
1959	Mal Anderson	Pancho Segura	4-6, 6-4, 3-6, 6-3, 8-6
1960	Ken Rosewall	Pancho Segura	5-7, 8-6, 6-1, 6-3
1961	Ken Rosewall	Lew Hoad	6-3, 3-6, 6-2, 6-3
1962	Ken Rosewall	:Lew Hoad	6-4, 5-7, 15-13, 7-5
1963	Ken Rosewall	Lew Hoad	6-4, 6-2, 4-6, 6-3
1964	Rod Laver	Ken Rosewall	7-5, 4-6, 5-7, 8-6, 8-6
1965	Rod Laver	Andres Gimeno	6-2, 6-3, 6-4
1966	Rod Laver	Ken Rosewall	6-2, 6-2, 6-3
1967	Rod Laver	Ken Rosewall	2-6, 6-1, 1-6, 8-6, 6-2
1968	Ken Rosewall	John Newcombe	6-4, 4-6, 7-5, 6-4

FRENCH PRO CHAMPIONSHIPS

YEAR	WINNER	RUNNER-UP	SCORE
1930	Karel Kozeluh	Albert Burke	6-1, 6-2, 6-1
1931	Martin Plaa	Robert Ramillon	6-3, 6-1, 3-6, 6-2
1932	Robert Ramillon	Martin Plaa	6-4, 3-6, 8-6, 6-4
1933	Bill Tilden	Henri Cochet	6-2, 6-4, 6-2
1934	Bill Tilden	Martin Plaa	6-2, 6-4, 7-5
1935	Ellsworth Vines	Hans Nusslein	10-8, 6-4, 3-6, 6-1
1938	Henri Cochet	Robert Ramillon	6-3, 6-1, 6-1
1939	Don Budge	Ellsworth Vines	6-2, 7-5, 6-3
1940-1952		not held	
1953	Frank Sedgman	Pancho Gonzalez	6-1, 6-3
1954-55		not held	
1956	Tony Trabert	Pancho Gonzalez	6-3, 4-6, 5-7, 8-6, 6-2
1957		not held	
1958	Ken Rosewall	Lew Hoad	3-6, 6-2, 6-4, 6-0
1959	Tony Trabert	Frank Sedgman	6-4, 6-4, 6-4
1960	Ken Rosewall	Lew Hoad	6-2, 2-6, 6-2, 6-1
1961	Ken Rosewall	Pancho Gonzalez	2-6, 6-4, 6-3, 8-6
1962	Ken Rosewall	Andres Gimeno	3-6, 6-2, 7-5, 6-2
1963	Ken Rosewall	Rod Laver	6-8, 6-4, 5-7, 6-3, 6-4
1964	Ken Rosewall	Rod Laver	6-3, 7-5, 3-6, 6-3
1965	Ken Rosewall	Rod Laver	6-3, 6-2, 6-4
1966	Ken Rosewall	Rod Laver	6-3, 6-2, 14-12
1967	Rod Laver	Andres Gimeno	6-4, 8-6, 4-6, 6-2
1968	Rod Laver	John Newcombe	6-2, 6-2, 6-3

Appendix G

One-Night Stands of the Bygone Pros

Until the dawn of open tennis in 1968, the usual format for the handful of playing pros—outlaws beyond the boundaries of traditional amateur tourneys—was a tour of one-night stands, indoors on a portable canvas court, across the U.S., and sometimes other countries as well. The champion of the previous tour went head-to-head against a challenger, most often the leading amateur who had turned pro, as during the winter of 1934, when rookie Ellsworth Vines, 23, brought down the biggest name, Bill Tilden, 41, by 47 matches to 26.

After resisting promoters for several years, Tilden finally turned pro in 1931, having failed to extricate the Davis Cup from France or win a long-desired eighth U.S. title. He then toured victoriously against the Czech master, Karel Kozeluh, and repeated the next winter against German Hans Nusslein. Nusslein had the edge in 1933, but since Tilden had the drawing power he was the rookie Vines' opponent. Vines' triumphant campaign over Tilden, his senior by 18 years, left him in charge to fend off Fred Perry, 1937. Tilden stuck around, as did a few others, to play secondary roles.

Whoever the promoter, he lured the leading amateur with a guarantee against a percentage of gate receipts, making a similar type of deal with the champion, and generally paying the others' salaries. It all began in November 1926 as promoter Charles C. Pyle transformed the first troupe—Suzanne Lenglen, Mary K. Browne, Vinnie Richards, Howard Kinsey, Harvey Snodgrass, Paul Feret—from amateurs to pros en masse, principally to capitalize on Lenglen's gate appeal on a North American tour. The last challenge tour, 1963, was Australian-dominated as pros Ken Rosewall and Lew Hoad personally guaranteed 1962 Grand Slammer Rod Laver $125,000 over three years to give up his amateur status, and put them back in business.

Although the pros grew slightly in numbers and began leaning toward tournament formats in 1964, hastening the day of opens, tours continued into 1968,

but merely as exhibitions, lacking the king-of-the-hill aspect. Pancho Gonzalez, the losing challenger in his first tour against player-promoter Jack Kramer, 1949–50, later became the most successful king-of-the-canvas.

Here are the best-documented tours:

1926–27—Suzanne Lenglen d. Mary K. Browne, 38-0
1928—Karel Kozeluh d. Vinnie Richards, 13-7
1931—Bill Tilden d. Karel Kozeluh, 63-13; Tilden d. Vinnie Richards, 4-0
1932—Bill Tilden d. Hans Nusslein and Vinnie Richards
1933—Hans Nusslein d. Bill Tilden
1934—Ellsworth Vines d. Bill Tilden, 47-26
1935—Ellsworth Vines d. Lester Stoefen, Bruce Barnes, Bill Tilden, others
1935—Bill Tilden d. George Lott, 73-27; Ellsworth Vines d. Tilden, Lester Stoefen, Bruce Barnes and others
1936—Bill Tilden d. Bruce Barnes and others; Ellsworth Vines d. Lester Stoefen, Bill Tilden and others; Ethel Burkhardt Arnold d. Jane Sharp
1937—Ellsworth Vines d. Fred Perry, 32-29; Perry d. Bill Tilden, 4-3
1938—Ellsworth Vines d. Fred Perry, 49-35
1939—Don Budge d. Ellsworth Vines, 21-18; Don Budge d. Fred Perry, 18-11
1941—Don Budge d. Bill Tilden, 51-7; Alice Marble d. Mary Hardwick, 17-3
1942—Don Budge won a round-robin tour with a 54-18 record, 15-10 over Bobby Riggs. Others: Bobby Riggs, 36-36; Frank Kovacs, 25-26; Fred Perry, 23-30
1946–47—Bobby Riggs d. Don Budge, 23-21
1947—Pauline Betz d. Sarah Palfrey Fabyan Cooke
1947–48—Jack Kramer d. Bobby Riggs, 69-20
1949–50—Jack Kramer d. Pancho Gonzalez, 96-27
1950–51—Jack Kramer d. Pancho Segura, 64-28; Pauline Betz d. Gussy Moran
1953—Jack Kramer d. Frank Sedgman, 54-41; Pancho Segura d. Ken McGregor
1954—Pancho Gonzalez d. Frank Sedgman and Pancho Segura, round-robin, both, 30-21; Segura d. Sedgman, 23-22
1955–56—Pancho Gonzalez d. Tony Trabert, 74-27
1957—Pancho Gonzalez d. Ken Rosewall, 50-26
1958—Pancho Gonzalez d. Lew Hoad, 51-36
1959—Pancho Gonzalez d. Lew Hoad, Mal Anderson and Ashley Cooper, round-robin
1959–60—Althea Gibson d. Karol Fageros, 114-4
1959–60—Pancho Gonzalez d. Alex Olmedo, Ken Rosewall and Pancho Segura, round-robin
1961—Pancho Gonzalez leading winner in tour involving Butch Buchholz, Barry MacKay, Andres Gimeno, Lew Hoad, Alex Olmedo, Frank Sedgman, Tony Trabert, Ashley Cooper
1963—Ken Rosewall, Rod Laver finished 1-2 on tour also including Luis Ayala, Butch Buchholz, Andres Gimeno, Barry MacKay

Appendix H

World Team Tennis

Sacramento Capitals, 2002
World Team Tennis champions, left to right, Brian MacPhie, Ashley Harkleroad, Mark Knowles, Coach Wayne Bryan, Elena Likhovtseva.

World Team Tennis Champions

1974	Denver d. Philadelphia, 27-21, 28-24
1975	Pittsburgh d. Oakland-San Francisco, 25-26, 28-25, 21-14
1976	New York d. Oakland-San Francisco, 31-23, 29-21, 31-13
1977	New York d. Phoenix, 27-22, 28-17
1978	Los Angeles d. Boston, 24-21, 30-20, 26-27, 28-25
1981	Los Angeles finished first
1982	Dallas finished first
1983	Chicago d. Los Angeles, 26-20
1984	San Diego d. Long Beach, 30-13
1985	San Diego d. St. Louis, 25-24
1986	San Antonio d. Sacramento, 25-23
1987	Charlotte d. San Antonio, 25-20
1988	Charlotte d. New Jersey, 27-22
1989	San Antonio d. Sacramento, 27-25
1990	Los Angeles d. Raleigh, 27-16
1991	Atlanta d. Los Angeles, 27-16
1992	Atlanta d. Newport Beach, 30-17
1993	Wichita d. Newport Beach, 26-23
1994	New Jersey d. Idaho, 28-25
1995	New Jersey d. Atlanta, 28-20
1996	St. Louis d. Delaware, 27-16
1997	Sacramento finished first
1998	Sacramento d. New York, 30-13
1999	Sacramento d. Springfield, 23-15
2000	Sacramento d. Delaware, 21-20
2001	Philadelphia d. Springfield, 20-18
2002	Sacramento d. New York, 21-13

City team franchises, the foundation of major pro sports in the U.S., came to tennis with the establishment of World Team Tennis in 1973. The original league lasted five years, folding because of large financial losses after the 1978 season. Founded by Dennis Murphy, Jordan Kaiser and Larry King (then husband of Billie Jean King), the WTT operated with 16 cities between Boston and Honolulu in 1974, a high point, and involved most of the game's leading players during its lifespan. They were well paid to ignore the summer season and play team tennis, a new concept in which teams had both male and female players. It was single-set tennis, five sets (men's and women's singles and doubles plus mixed doubles) constituting a match, the score based on total games won. Fearing the summer competition, the International Tennis Federation railed against WTT, and the French Open barred players from the league in 1974, a move which deprived Jimmy Connors, who won the other three majors, a shot at a Grand Slam.

A feature of the first season was the unprecedented appearance of women coaching professional teams containing men. Billie Jean King led the Philadelphia Freedoms, Rosie Casals the Detroit Loves.

Billie Jean King revived the concept modestly under the masthead of Team Tennis in 1981, with a shorter season, and few big-name players, although Connors and Martina Navratilova came aboard in 1991 with Los Angeles and Atlanta respectively. In 1992, Team Tennis resumed using the old name, World Team Tennis.

A number of big names have participated in WTT over the past few years including, Andre Agassi, Lindsay Davenport, Monica Seles, Andy Roddick, Martina Navratilova and Jim Courier. The championship trophy is called the King Trophy in honor of founder Billie Jean King.

The league fielded 10 teams in 2003.

Credits
Photographs and Illustrations

Adams, Russ: pp. 312, 318, 324, 330, 336, 342, 348, 354, 370, 376, 382, 389, 394, 621; Insert pp. 3 (lower left), 4 (top right).

Bucher, Siggi: Front cover; pp. x, 398, 402, 433, 614, 631; Insert pp. 11 (top left), 14-15, 16 (top left; top right; lower left).

Collection of Bud Collins: pp. 1, 52, 90

Collection of International Tennis Hall of Fame: pp. 3, 20, 25, 29, 31, 33, 35, 39, 42, 44, 49, 55, 62, 65, 68, 75, 78, 80, 82, 88, 115, 138, 211, 229, 253, 272, 415, 441, 477, 529, 599, 621, 625, 633, 901, 923

Mullane, Fred & Susan/Camerawork USA: pp. 365, 385

Ruthling Klaussen, Anita: p. xxi

The SPORT Collection: pp. 19, 23, 27, 46, 59, 72, 84, 86, 106, 113, 116, 120, 123 (Lawrence Schiller), 126, 129, 132, 135, 141, 144, 147 (S. Haas), 150, 153, 156 (M. Blumenthal), 159 (M. Blumenthal), 162, 166, 169 (T. Tomsic), 173, 176 (T. Tomsic), 180, 184, 189 (C. Gunther), 194 (D. Sutton), 199, 204 (N. Leifer), 213 (K. Fitzgerald), 214 (K. Fitzgerald), 220 (D. Norenberg), 231, 237 (B. Silverman), 242, 248 (K. Fitzgerald), 259 (K. Fitzgerald), 265 (K. Fitzgerald), 278, 283, 288 (K. Fitzgerald), 294 (D. Wolberg), 300 (A. Seitz), 306 (J. McDonough), 407 (B. Peterson), 411 (M. Blumenthal), 413 (M. Blumenthal), 418 (K. Fitzgerald), 426 (P. Travers), 443, 503, 563 (M. Blumenthal), 763, 791; 899 (Dr. H.E. Edgerton), Insert pp. 1, 2, 3 (M. Blumenthal, top left; M. Blumenthal, lower right), 4 (T. Tomsic, top left; M. Blumenthal, lower left; K. Fitzgerald, lower right), 5 (A. Freni, lower left), 6 (B. Peterson, top left; L. Schiller, top right; lower left), 7 (M. Blumenthal), 8, 9 (top right, lower right), 10 (top left; top right; lower left), 11 (M. Blumenthal), 12 (K. Fitzgerald), 13 (D. Affa, top left; M. Blumenthal, lower left; R. Colby, lower right); Back cover (N. Leifer).

World Team Tennis, p. 937

Zimmer, Paul/Bettman/CORBIS/MAGMA: p. 360

Contributors

Total Tennis: The Ultimate Tennis Encyclopedia is the work of many, many hands over many, many years. The contributions of a great many of these are eloquently noted by Bud Collins in his Acknowledgements at the front of the book. An emphatic second nod here, however, to those no longer with us whose vivid words live on: Allison Danzig, the former great of *The New York Times*, who wrote several of the biographies and whose prose is widely quoted elsewhere, and Lance Tingay, the sage of *The Daily Telegraph*, who combined with George Alexander on the early history of the game in Chapter 1, as well as four writers whose profile pieces first appeared in *SPORT* magazine—Al Stump, Will Grimsley, John M. Ross and Dick Schaap.

Significant contributions to the 1919-1945 seasonal reviews came from Stan Isaacs, while Barry Lorge toiled on 1946-1967 and combined with Steve Flink and Joe Gergen on the 1968-2002 renditions. Other articles originally written for *SPORT* magazine and re-printed here by permission were the work of Ed Fitzgerald, Dave Anderson, Tony Kornheiser, Marty Bell and Richard O'Connor. Joel Drucker supplied the insight on the Williams sisters while Tom Hawthorn contributed to The Major Championships and International Play sections. Yeoman service to compile the statistics was performed by Sean Lahman, with input from Frank Phelps, the dean of tennis researchers; Mark Young, archivist at the International Tennis Hall of Fame; John Partington, who provided source material for tennis in Great Britain and Australia; and Randy Bonferraro, whose film and video archive was a substantial benefit.

Peter Grucza and John Pasternak diligently massaged the database to produce the material for the exhaustive record sections as well as the Player Registers. Bob Dunn was tireless in his editing work. Paul Hodgson, with input from Pasternak, oversaw all aspects of the book's design, Grucza was a demon working with the myriad photographs and Julie Leahey was invaluable on several fronts. Jim O'Leary was the glue that held the entire project together while Greg Oliver was the man who actually made it all happen in something reasonably close to the prescribed time frame. To all of them and others we've surely missed, our heartfelt thanks.

www.sportclassicbooks.com